The Official Gun Digest® Book of

GUNS & PRICES

10th EDITION

Edited by
JERRY LEE

Published by

Gun Digest® Books, an imprint of F+W,
A Content + eCommerce Company
Krause Publications • 700 East State Street
• Iola, WI 54990-0001
715-445-2214 • 888-457-2873
www.krausebooks.com

To order books or other products call toll-free 1-800-258-0929
or visit us online at www.gundigeststore.com

ISSN: 1936-7783

ISBN-13: 978-1-4402-4429-2
ISBN-10: 1-4402-4429-4

Cover and design by Tom Nelsen
Edited by Jerry Lee and Chris Berens

Printed in the United States of America

CONTENTS

LISTINGS:

A

S

ACKNOWLEDGMENTS

The editor wishes to acknowledge the following individuals for their input, advice, information and support for this and previous editions of *The Official Gun Digest Book of Guns & Prices*:

Jim Supica, Director and Phil Schreier, Senior Curator of the National Firearms Museum at the NRA complex in Fairfax, Virginia; authors Tom Turpin, Terry Wieland, Garry James, Don Findley, Steve Ash, John Taffin, Jim Wilson, Rich Grassi, Gary Paul Johnston, Kevin Muramatsu, Patrick Sweeney, Charlie Petty, Rick Hacker, Max Prasac, Holt Bodinson, Jim Foral, Frank James, Bill Hamm, Stan Trzoniec and Jon Sundra; and auction executives/collectors/retailers Wes Dillon, Patrick Hogan, David Moore, Dave LaRue, Jim Ciolli, Jr., Marc Murphy, John R. Hansen, Rick Verzal, Jay Schachter, Roy Marcot, Mike Clark, Alan Heldreth, John Powell, Dave Sanders and John Puglisi.

Many executives and representatives of the firearms industry have been very helpful in providing information on their products and organizations including specifications and company history. These include industry professionals like Ken Jorgensen (Sturm, Ruger & Co.), Paul Thompson (Browning), Scott Grange (Winchester), Paul Pluff (Smith & Wesson), Dwight van Brunt (Kimber), Jessica Kallam (Remington/Para USA/Marlin/Bushmaster), Linda Powell (Mossberg), Bud Fini (SIG-Sauer), Mike Nischalke and Karen Lutto (Steyr), Barbara Fausti (Fausti), Keith Bernkrant (European American Armory), Jamie Harvey (Cimarron), Wes Lang (Caesar Guerini), and Val Forgett (Navy Arms/Gibbs Rifle Co.).

I also would like to express my appreciation to the production staff who so ably assisted me in gathering and submitting all of the information necessary to produce this publication: Chris Berens, Managing Editor; Delores May, proofreader and data input specialist; and Tom Nelsen, art designer. Their long hours, professionalism and support are greatly appreciated.

CONTRIBUTING EDITORS

J.B. Barnes
Stevens single-shot rifles and pistols
29 Ridgeview Dr.
Dry Ridge, KY 41035
859-824-5086

Bailey Brower, Jr.
Remington and Savage pistols
P.O. Box 111
Madison, NJ 07940
baileybrower@yahoo.com

Bud Bugni
Winchester Model 42s
P.O. Box 762
Sutter Creek, CA 95685
209-267-5402

Tom Caceci
Blackpowder revolvers
1405 Westover Drive
Blacksburg, VA 24060

Jim Cate
J.P. Sauer Pistols
406 Pine Bluff Dr.
Chattanooga, TN 37412
423-892-6320

Kevin Cherry
Winchester and Colt Commemoratives
3402 West Wendover Ave.
Greensboro, NC 27407
336-854-4182

Joseph Cornell
Browning, Colt, pre-64 Winchesters
2655 West 39th Ave.
Denver, CO 80211
303-455-1717
worthologist@aol.com

Jason Devine
Winchester lever action rifles
250 Commercial Street
Unit 3011
Manchester, NH 03101
Jason@amoskeag.com

Richard Freer
*Belgian Browning and pre-64
Winchester shotguns*
8928 Spring Branch Drive
Houston, TX 77080
713-467-3016

Rick Hacker
Colt SAA and 1911s
12400 Ventura Blvd., Ste. 705
Studio City, CA 91604

Dr. Daniel Menser
Winchester Model 21 shotguns
320-522-0859
papa_menser@yahoo.com

Gale Morgan
Luger and Mauser pistols
Pre-WWI pistols
P.O. Box 72
Lincoln, CA 95648

Jim Rankin
Walther pistols
3615 Coral Gables, FL 33134
305-446-1792

Bob Rayburn
Colt Woodsman
P.O. Box 97104
Lakewood, WA 98497
rayburn@colt22.com

Dean Rinehart
Pre-64 Winchester Rifles, Colt Woodsman
P.O. Box 5
Gallipolis, OH 45631

John Dougan
Ruger and Great Western Single Actions
102 ½ E. Rogers Blvd.
Skiatook, OK 74070

Don Findley
Ruger Standard Auto Pistols
5312 84th St.
Lubbock, Texas 79424
donfindley@door.net

Lee Newton
Ruger No. 1s
www.classicsportingarms.com

Rick Verzal
Ruger firearms and memorabilia
www.rugercollectorsassocation.com

Terry Wieland
English and European Shotguns
terrywieland@mac.com

AUCTION HOUSES

Among the many resources used by the editors to determine trends in firearms values are the prices realized at recent auctions. These resources include the following auction houses, which are the largest and best in the field of modern and antique firearms.

Amoskeag Auctions
250 Commercial Street, Suite 3011, Manchester, NH 03101
www.amoskeag-auction.com

Bonhams & Butterfields
220 San Bruno Ave., San Francisco, CA 94103
www.bonhams.com

Heritage Auctions
3500 Maple Ave., 17th Floor, Dallas, TX 75219
www.ha.com

James D. Julia, Inc.
203 Skowhegan Rd., Fairfield, ME 04937
www.juliaauctions.com

Little John's Auctions
1740 W. La Veta Ave., Orange, CA 92868
www.littlejohnsauctions.com

Poulin Antiques and Auctions
199 Skowhegan Road, Fairfield, ME 04937
www.poulinantiques.com

Rock Island Auction Co
7819 42nd Street West, Rock Island, IL 61201
www.rockislanduaction.com

GRADING SYSTEM

In the opinion of the editor, all grading systems are subjective. It is our task to offer the collector and dealer a measurement that most closely reflects a general consensus on condition. The system we present seems to come closest to describing a firearm in universal terms. We strongly recommend that the reader acquaint himself with this grading system before attempting to determine the correct price for a particular firearm's condition. Remember, in most cases condition determines price.

NIB—New in Box

This category can sometimes be misleading. It means that the firearm is in its original factory carton with all of the appropriate papers. It also means the firearm is new; that it has not been fired and has no wear. This classification brings a substantial premium for both the collector and shooter.

Excellent

Collector quality firearms in this condition are highly desirable. The firearm must be in at least 98 percent condition with respect to blue wear, stock or grip finish, and bore. The firearm must also be in 100 percent original factory condition without refinishing, repair, alterations or additions of any kind. Sights must be factory original as well. This grading classification includes both modern and antique (manufactured prior to 1898) firearms.

Very Good

Firearms in this category are also sought after both by the collector and shooter. Modern firearms must be in working order and retain approximately 92 percent original metal and wood finish. It must be 100 percent factory original, but may have some small repairs, alterations, or non-factory additions. No refinishing is permitted in this category. Antique firearms must have 80 percent original finish with no repairs.

Good

Modern firearms in this category may not be considered to be as collectable as the previous grades, but antique firearms are considered desirable. Modern firearms must retain at least 80 percent metal and wood finish, but may display evidence of old refinishing. Small repairs, alterations, or non-factory additions are sometimes encountered in this class. Factory replacement parts are permitted. The overall working condition of the firearm must be good as well as safe. The bore may exhibit wear or some corrosion, especially in antique arms. Antique firearms may be included in this category if their metal and wood finish is at least 50 percent original factory finish.

Fair

Firearms in this category should be in satisfactory working order and safe to shoot. The overall metal and wood finish on the modern firearm must be at least 30 percent and antique firearms must have at least some original finish or old re-finish remaining. Repairs, alterations, non factory additions, and recent refinishing would all place a firearm in this classification. However, the modern firearm must be in working condition, while the antique firearm may not function. In either case the firearm must be considered safe to fire if in a working state.

Poor

Neither collectors nor shooters are likely to exhibit much interest in firearms in this condition. Modern firearms are likely to retain little metal or wood finish. Pitting and rust will be seen in firearms in this category. Modern firearms may not be in working order and may not be safe to shoot. Repairs and refinishing would be necessary to restore the firearm to safe working order. Antique firearms will have no finish and will not function. In the case of modern firearms their principal value lies in spare parts. On the other hand, antique firearms in this condition may be used as "wall hangers" or as an example of an extremely rare variation or have some kind of historical significance.

Pricing Sample Format:

	NIB	EXC.	V.G.	GOOD	FAIR	POOR
Model 2000						
	1250	950	775	500	350	150

PRICING

The prices given in this book reflect RETAIL values. This is important. You will generally not realize full retail value if you trade a gun in on another or sell it to a dealer. In this situation, your trade-in gun will be valued at wholesale, which is generally substantially below retail value.

Unfortunately for shooters and collectors, there is no central clearinghouse for firearms prices. The prices given in this book are designed as a guide, not as a quote. This is an important distinction because prices for firearms vary with the time of the year, with geographical location, and sometimes for no apparent reason. For example, interest in firearms is at its lowest point in the summer. People are not as interested in shooting and collecting at this time of the year as they are in playing golf or taking a vacation. Therefore, prices are depressed slightly and guns that may sell quickly during the hunting season or the winter months may not sell well at all during this time of year. Geographical location also plays an important part in pricing. Political pundits are often heard to say that all politics is local. Well, the same can be said, in many ways, for the price of firearms. For instance, a Winchester Model 70 in a .264 caliber will bring a higher price in the Western states than along the Eastern seaboard. Smaller gauges and calibers seem to be more popular along both coasts and mid-sections of the United States than in the more open western sections of the country.

It is not practical to list prices in this book with regard to time of year or location. What is given is a reasonable price based on sales at gun shows, auction houses, *Gun Digest the Magazine* prices, and information obtained from knowledgeable collectors and dealers. In certain cases there will be no price indicated under a particular condition but rather the notation "N/A" or the symbol "—." This indicates that there is no known price available for that gun in that condition or the sales for that particular model are so few that a reliable price cannot be given. This will usually be encountered only with very rare guns, with newly introduced firearms, or more likely with antique firearms in those conditions most likely to be encountered. Most antique firearms will be seen in the good, fair and poor categories.

Note that the prices in this book are a GENERAL GUIDE as to what a willing buyer and willing seller might agree on. So how is the reader to use this book? *Guns & Prices* can be used as an identification guide and as a source of starting prices for a planned firearms transaction. If you start by valuing a given firearm according to the values listed in this book, you will not be too far off the mark.

In the final analysis, a firearm is worth only what someone is willing to pay for it. New trends arise quickly, and there are many excellent bargains to be found in today's market. With patience and good judgment – and with this book under your arm – you, too, can find them.

ADDITIONAL CONSIDERATIONS

As stated in the pricing section, this publication offers a general guide to prices. There are many factors that may affect the value of a firearm. We have attempted to be as comprehensive as possible, but we cannot cover all possible factors that may influence the worth of any given firearm. Some of these circumstances will be discussed so that the shooter and collector will have a better idea of how certain factors may affect prices.

Firearms have been admired and coveted, not only for their usefulness, but also for their grace and beauty. Since the beginning of the 19th century, firearms makers have adorned their guns with engraving, fine woods, or special order features that set their products apart from the rest. There is no feasible way to give the collector every possible variation of the firearms presented in this book. However, in a general way, certain special factors will significantly influence the price of a firearm.

Perhaps the most recognizable special feature collectors agree affects the price of a firearm is engraving. The artistry, beauty, and intricate nature of engraving draw all collectors toward it. But, firearms engraving is a field unto itself requiring years of experience to determine proper chronological methods and the ability to identify the engraver in question. Factory engraving generally brings more of a premium than after-market engraving. To be able to determine factory work is a difficult task, full of pitfalls. In some cases, factories like Colt and Winchester may have records to verify original factory engraving work. Whereas other manufacturers such as Parker, Remington, or Savage may not have these records. Whenever a firearm purchase is to be made with respect to an engraved gun, it is in the collector's best interest to secure an expert opinion and/or a factory letter prior to the purchase. Engraved firearms are expensive. A mistake could cost the collector thousands of dollars; proceed with caution.

The 18th century was also a time when pistols and rifles were purchased by or given to historically important individuals. Firearms have also been an important part of significant historical events such as the Battle of the Little Bighorn or the Battle of Bull Run or some other meaningful event in our nation's history. Many of these firearms are in museums where the public can enjoy, see and appreciate them. Others are in private collections that seldom, if ever, are offered for sale. If the collector should ever encounter one of these historically important firearms, it cannot be stressed strongly enough to secure an expert determination as to authenticity. Museum curators are perhaps the best source of information for these types of firearms. As with engraved guns, historical firearms are usually expensive, and without documentation their value is questionable.

Special features and variations are also a desirable part of firearms collecting. As with engraving, special order guns can bring a considerable premium. The Colt factory has excellent records regarding its firearms and will provide the collector with a letter of authenticity. Winchester records are not as comprehensive, but rifles made prior to 1908 may have documentation. Other firearm manufacturers either do not have records or do not provide the collector with documentation. This leaves the collector in a difficult position. Special order sights, stocks, barrel lengths, calibers, and so forth must be judged on their own merits. As with other factors, an expert should be consulted prior to purchase. Sometimes this can be difficult. Experienced collectors, researchers, and museums will generally provide the kind of information a collector needs before purchasing a special order or unique firearm.

Perhaps the best advice is for the collector to take his time. Do not be in a hurry, and do not allow yourself to be rushed into making a decision. Learn as much as possible about the firearms you are interested in collecting or shooting. Try to keep current with prices through *Gun Digest The Magazine* and this publication. Go to gun shows, not just to buy or sell, but to observe and learn. It is also helpful to join a firearms club or association. These groups have older, experienced collectors who are glad to help the beginner or veteran. Firearms collecting is a rewarding hobby. Firearms are part of our nation's history and represent an opportunity to learn more about their role in that American experience. If done skillfully, firearms collecting can be a profitable hobby as well.

ABOUT
THE EDITOR

Jerry Lee has been the editor of numerous gun related books and magazines. These include *Gun Digest*, which is the annual flagship of Gun Digest Books, the firearms division of Krause Publications and publisher of *Standard Catalog of Firearms*. He is also the author and editor of the recently published *Standard Catalog of Ruger Firearms*, a hardcover book dedicated to the guns of Bill Ruger. Previously Jerry was the editor of several popular firearms magazines including *Guns*, *Rifle Shooter*, *Handguns*, and dozens of Special Interest editions of *Guns & Ammo* and *Shooting Times*. He was also editor of a group of custom newsstand magazines published for *Smith & Wesson, Remington, Ruger, Mossberg* and several other manufacturers in the industry. Jerry is an NRA Life Member and a frequent contributor to the NRA's online editions. Born and raised on a farm in West Texas, he now resides in the hills of West Virginia with his wife, Susan.

INTRODUCTION

Welcome to **Guns & Prices 2015, 10th Edition**! As in all of the previous editions, many of the firearm values are have been updated, and those updates are based on a variety of factors including supply and demand, overall economic conditions and recent selling prices. Other revisions are made to many of the gun descriptions of current production firearms to reflect changes in specifications, caliber choices and other features. Each year as new gun models are introduced to the market, their information and prices are added to this continually expanding volume.

Inside these pages you will find detailed descriptions, historical information and estimated values for more than 15,000 different firearm models and variations. Almost every make and model of guns made in or imported into the United States since the early part of the 19th century can be found in this book.

For those interested in a more in-depth look at specific categories of firearms, Krause Publications offers these excellent titles: *Flayderman's Guide to Antique American Firearms*, *Gun Digest Book of Modern Gun Values*, *Gun Digest Illustrated Guide to Modern Firearms*, *Standard Catalog of Military Firearms* and *Gun Digest Buyer's Guide to Tactical Rifles*. The company also has published several titles that focus on the guns of specific manufacturers, such as *Standard Catalog of Ruger Firearms*, *Standard Catalog of Colt Firearms*, *Standard Catalog of Browning Firearms* and similar books covering the guns of Winchester, Smith & Wesson and others. And we mustn't forget the title that is the flagship of the Krause group of gun books, *Gun Digest*, complete with its many technical articles, historical profiles, test reports and hunting stories, plus a catalog of current production firearms.

—Jerry Lee

A

	NIB	EXC.	V.G.	GOOD	FAIR	POOR

A.A.
Azanza & Arrizabalaga
Eibar, Spain

A.A.

—	300	175	150	100	50

Reims

6.35mm or 7.65mm caliber semi-automatic pistol, with 6- or 8-round magazine capacity. Most pistols have their slides marked: 1914 Model Automatic Pistol "Reims" Patent.

—	200	175	150	100	50

A.A.A.
Aldazabal
Eibar, Spain

Modelo 1919

7.65mm semi-automatic pistol, with 9-round magazine capacity. Trademark of knight's head over three As is on side of slide and grips.

—	200	175	150	100	50

A. J. ORDNANCE

Delayed blowback action that is unique, in every shot was double-action. Pistol was chambered for .45 ACP cartridge and had a 3.5" stainless steel barrel, with fixed sights and plastic grips. Detachable magazine held 6 shots. Standard finish was matte blue. Chrome plating was available and would add approximately 15 percent to values listed.

1950	1300	800	400	250	175

A-SQUARE
Bedford, Kentucky/Chamberlain, South Dakota

Hannibal Grade

Using P-17 Enfield action, with 22" to 26" barrel. Rifle chambered for 32 calibers from 7mm Rem. Magnum up to and including .500 A-Square Magnum and .577 Tyrannosaur. Blued, with checkered walnut pistol-grip stock. Introduced in 1986. Weights range from 9 lbs. to 13.25 lbs., depending on caliber. **NOTE:** Add 5 percent for Kentucky-built rifles.

3200	2700	1800	1000	600	350

Caesar Grade

Utilizing Remington Model 700 action. Chambered for same cartridges as above, with exception that A-Square proprietary cartridges are not available. Also made in left-hand version. Introduced in 1986. Weighs 8.5 to 11 lb. range.

3200	2700	1800	1000	600	350

Hamilcar Grade

Smaller and lighter version of Hannibal Grade. Designed to be chambered for .30-06 cartridges. Weighs 8 to 8.5 lbs. Introduced in 1994.

3200	2700	1800	1000	600	350

Genghis Khan Model

Designed for varmint shooting. Fitted with heavyweight barrel. Offered in .22-250, .243 Win., 6mm Rem., .25-06, .257 Wby. and .264 Win. Barrel length and pull are to customer's specifications. No iron sights fitted to this model. Weight about 11 lbs.

3200	2700	1800	1000	600	350

A & R SALES SOUTH
El Monte, California

A&R Sales South also made frames for custom 1911 builds.

45 Auto

Alloy-frame version of Colt Model 1911 semi-automatic pistol.

475	325	200	150	125	100

	NIB	EXC.	V.G.	GOOD	FAIR	POOR

Mark IV Sporter

Semi-automatic copy of M-14 military rifle. Manufactured in .308-caliber (7.65mm NATO) only.

NIB	EXC.	V.G.	GOOD	FAIR	POOR
950	650	500	375	195	100

ABADIE
Liege, Belgium

System Abadie Model 1878

9mm double-action revolver, with 6-shot cylinder, octagonal barrel and integral ejector rod.

NIB	EXC.	V.G.	GOOD	FAIR	POOR
—	550	350	175	125	90

System Abadie Model 1886

Heavier version of above.

NIB	EXC.	V.G.	GOOD	FAIR	POOR
—	575	400	200	125	90

ABBEY, F.J. & CO.
Chicago, Illinois

Abbey Brothers produced a variety of percussion rifles and shotguns, which are all individual design. Prices listed represent what a plain F.J. Abbey & Company firearm might realize.

Rifle

NIB	EXC.	V.G.	GOOD	FAIR	POOR
—	—	1750	800	450	200

Shotgun

NIB	EXC.	V.G.	GOOD	FAIR	POOR
—	—	2500	1750	575	150

ABBEY, GEORGE T.
Utica, New York, and Chicago, Illinois

George T. Abbey originally worked in Utica, New York, from 1845 to 1852. He moved to Chicago in 1852 and was in business until 1874. He manufactured a wide variety of percussion and cartridge firearms. Values listed represent those of his most common products.

Single-Barrel Shotgun

NIB	EXC.	V.G.	GOOD	FAIR	POOR
—	—	1750	850	550	200

Side-by-Side Shotgun

NIB	EXC.	V.G.	GOOD	FAIR	POOR
—	—	2550	1200	675	250

Over/Under Shotgun

NIB	EXC.	V.G.	GOOD	FAIR	POOR
—	—	2750	1300	975	250

ABESSER & MERKEL
Suhl, Germany

Crown Grade

Model is a single-barrel Trap gun, with Greener cross bolt-action and two underbolt locks. Offered in 12-gauge, with barrel lengths from 28" to 34". Ventilated rib standard. Skip line checkering. Pistol- or straight-grip stock. Weight between 7 and 7.5 lbs. Engraved receiver with game scenes.

NIB	EXC.	V.G.	GOOD	FAIR	POOR
—	6000	4925	3825	1000	—

Diamond Grade

Side-by-side shotgun offered in 12-, 16-, 20-, 28-gauge and .410 bore. Auto ejectors, double triggers and full coverage engraving. Artistic stock carving behind frame. Skip line checkering. Many extras offered on this grade will affect price. Barrel lengths from 25" to 32". Weight from 6.5 lbs. to 7 lbs. Prices are for standard gun with no extras. **NOTE:** Add 50 percent for 20-gauge; 100 percent for 28-gauge or .410 bore.

NIB	EXC.	V.G.	GOOD	FAIR	POOR
—	12000	9200	8050	3000	700

Empire Grade

Side-by-side shotgun, with Anson-Deeley action. Receiver is fully engraved, with game birds and fine scroll. Stock is carved behind action. Checkering is fine skip line-style. Auto ejectors. Pistol- or straight-grip stock, with or without Monte Carlo and cheekpiece. Prices listed are for pre-war guns, with fluid steel barrels. **NOTE:** Add 50 percent for 20-gauge; 100 percent for 28-gauge or .410 bore.

NIB	EXC.	V.G.	GOOD	FAIR	POOR
—	13500	11150	9200	2500	700

NIB	EXC.	V.G.	GOOD	FAIR	POOR

Excelsior Grade

Side-by-side shotgun fitted with engraved side plates. Anson-Deeley action with double triggers. Fine line checkering. Figured walnut stock. All gauges offered from 12- to .410 bore. Barrel lengths from 25" to 32". Many extra cost options available. **NOTE:** Add 50 percent for 20-gauge; 100 percent for 28-gauge or .410 bore.

—	9000	7500	6500	3100	700

Diana Grade

Over/under combination gun, with Greener cross bolt-action. Safety located on side of pistol grip. Iron sights. Set trigger for rifle barrel. Wide variety of centerfire calibers offered, with barrel lengths from 26" to 30".

—	9500	8250	6250	3200	700

Vandalia Grade

Over/under gun chambered for 2.75" 12-gauge shells. Barrel lengths from 28" to 32". Walnut stock, with pistol- or straight-grip. Skip line checkering. Double triggers with extractors. Premium for factory multi-barrel combinations.

—	7250	6000	4500	3300	700

Nimrod

This is a drilling, with Greener cross bolt-action and double under bolt. Safety located on side of grip. Top two barrels may be 12-, 16- or 20-gauge. Bottom barrel offered in a variety of centerfire calibers. Iron sights. Pistol- or straight-grip stock. Receiver engraved with game scenes. **NOTE:** Add 50 percent for 20-gauge.

—	13000	9950	6000	4995	700

Magazine Rifle

Bolt-action rifle offered in a wide variety of calibers. Barrel lengths from 24" to 30". Calibers from 6.5mm to .404 Rimless. This model may have Zeiss scope or other special order features that will affect price. **NOTE:** Add $2000 for Magnum actions.

—	4900	3950	3350	1100	700

ACCU-MATCH
Mesa, Arizona

Accu-Match Custom Pistol

Competition pistol built on Colt 1911 design. Chambered for .45 ACP. Fitted with 5.5" match grade stainless steel barrel slide and frame, with extended slide release and safety. Fitted with beavertail grip safety and wraparound finger groove rubber grips. Pistol has threaded three port compensator and dual action recoil spring system, with three-dot sight system.

1050	750	550	400	300	175

ACCU-TEK
Chino, California

AT-380SS

Introduced in 1991. Semi-automatic pistol chambered for .380 ACP cartridge. Fitted with 2.75" barrel, with adjustable rear sight for windage. Black composition grips. Stainless steel construction. Furnished with 5-round magazine. Weight about 20 oz.

245	165	100	75	50	25

AT-380 II

Introduced in 2004. Pistol chambered for .380 ACP cartridge. Fitted with 2.8" barrel. Magazine capacity 6 rounds. Stainless steel. Magazine release on bottom of grip. Weight about 23 oz.

255	175	125	100	75	35

CP-9SS

Semi-automatic double-action-only stainless steel pistol. Chambered for 9mm cartridge. Fitted with 3.2" barrel, with adjustable rear sight for windage. Magazine capacity 8 rounds. Grips black checkered nylon. Weight about 28 oz. Introduced in 1992.

295	225	150	100	75	50

CP-45SS

Similar to Model CP-9SS. Chambered for .45 ACP cartridge. Furnished with 6-round magazine. Introduced in 1996.

300	245	195	150	125	75

	NIB	EXC.	V.G.	GOOD	FAIR	POOR

CP-40SS
Introduced in 1992. Similar to CP-9SS. Chambered for .40 S&W cartridge. Furnished with 7-round magazine.

	300	245	195	150	125	75

BL-9
Semi-automatic double-action-only pistol. Chambered for 9mm cartridge. Furnished with 5-round magazine. Barrel length 3". Grips black composition. Finish black. Weight about 22 oz. Introduced in 1997.

	295	225	150	100	75	50

BL-380
Similar to Model BL-9. Chambered for .380 ACP cartridge. Introduced in 1997.

	255	175	125	100	75	35

HC-380SS
.380 ACP semi-automatic pistol. Has 2.75" barrel. Stainless steel finish. Weight about 28 oz. Furnished with 10-round magazine. Introduced in 1993.

	255	175	125	100	75	35

AT-32SS
Similar to Model AT-380SS. Chambered for .32 ACP cartridge. Introduced in 1991.

	225	175	110	75	50	40

LT-380
Single-action semi-automatic pistol in .380 ACP, with 6-shot magazine and 2.8" barrel. Blued or two-tone stainless slide, with aluminum frame. Black, pink, purple or OD green grips. Introduced in 2012.

	250	225	190	150	125	90

ACHA
Domingo Acha
Vizcaya, Spain

Atlas
6.35mm semi-automatic pistol, manufactured during 1920s, in Model 1906 Browning style. Grips are plain checkered hard rubber. Some grips had ACHA trademark of Count's head. Name "Atlas" appears on slide. Later models incorporated a grip safety.

	—	250	175	100	75	50

Looking Glass (Ruby-Style)
7.65mm semi-automatic pistol in Ruby-style. Pistols furnished with 7-, 9- or 12-round magazine.

	—	265	195	100	75	50

Looking Glass
6.35mm or 7.65mm caliber semi-automatic pistol. Various markings seen on these pistols and their grips. They were sold in both France and Spain by different distributors. Pistol pictured has two trademarks: "Domingo Acha" on grips and "Fabrique D'Arms de Guerre De Grande Presision" on slide.

	—	295	175	110	75	50

ACME
See—Davenport Arms Co., Maltby Henley & Co., and Merwin & Hulbert & Co.

ACME ARMS
New York, New York

A trade name found on .22-, .32-caliber revolvers and 12-gauge shotguns. Marketed by Cornwall Hardware Company.

.22 Revolver
7-shot single-action revolver.

	—	375	275	175	125	75

.32 Revolver
5-shot single-action revolver.

	—	400	300	200	150	100

NIB	EXC.	V.G.	GOOD	FAIR	POOR

Shotgun

12-gauge double-barrel shotgun, with external hammers.

—	400	275	175	125	75

ACME HAMMERLESS
Made by Hopkins & Allen
Norwich, Connecticut

Acme Hammerless

.32- or .38-caliber, 5-shot revolver. Either exposed or enclosed hammer. Sometimes known as "Forehand 1891".

—	295	225	175	50	25

ACTION ARMS LTD.
Philadelphia, Pennsylvania

AT-84, AT-88

Pistol is Swiss version of CZ-75. Built at ITM, Solothurn, Switzerland. AT-84 chambered for 9mm cartridge; AT-88 for .41 Action Express. Both have 4.75" barrel. 9mm has magazine capacity of 15 rounds; .41 AE has 10 rounds. Finish either blue or chrome. Walnut grips.

750	550	450	375	300	150

AT-84P, AT-88P

As above, with 3.7" barrel and smaller frame.

750	550	450	375	300	150

AT-84H, AT-88H

As above, with 3.4" barrel and smaller frame.

750	550	450	375	300	150

Timber Wolf Carbine

Introduced in 1989. Slide-action carbine features 18.5" barrel. Adjustable rear sight and blade front sight. Chambered for .357 Magnum or .38 Special cartridges. Offered in blue or hard chrome finish. Weight about 5.5 lbs. Built in Israel by Israel Military Industries.

850	595	395	300	200	125

Action Arms/IMI Uzi Carbine Models A and B

16" barreled semi-automatic version of Uzi sub-machine gun. Chambered in 9mm Parabellum, .41 AE, .45 ACP. Built by IMI (Israeli Military Industries). **NOTE:** Add 10 percent for nylon Uzi case and accessories.

1700	1450	1150	850	600	250

ADAMS / DEANE, ADAMS & DEANE
London, England
London Armoury Co. (After 1856)

Revolvers based upon Robert Adams' patents, were manufactured by firm of Deane, Adams & Deane. Although more technically advanced than pistols produced by Samuel Colt, Adams' revolvers were popular primarily in England and British Empire.

Adams Model 1851 Self-Cocking Revolver

.44-caliber double-action percussion revolver, with 7.5" octagonal barrel and 5-shot cylinder. Barrel and frame blued. Cylinder case hardened. Grips walnut. Top strap marked "Deane, Adams and Deane 30 King William St. London Bridge". Revolver does not have hammer spur and functions only as double-action.

—	4000	2975	1475	775	400

Adams Pocket Revolver

As above in .31-caliber, with 4.5" barrel.

—	3750	2875	1375	750	400

Beaumont-Adams Revolver

As above, with Tranter Patent loading lever. Hammer made with a spur.

—	2500	1950	950	695	300

NIB	EXC.	V.G.	GOOD	FAIR	POOR

ADAMY GEBRUDER
Suhl, Germany

Over/Under Shotgun

12- or 16-gauge double-barrel over/under shotgun, with 26" to 30" barrels. Double triggers. Walnut stock.

—	2100	1700	1250	750	400

ADIRONDACK ARMS CO. / A.S. BABBITT CO.
Plattsburgh, New York

Orvil M. Robinson Patent Rifle

Robinson tube-fed repeating rifle was made in New York, between 1870 and 1874. Early models 1870-1872 marked "A.S. Babbitt"; later models 1872-1874 "Adirondack Arms Co." Company was sold to Winchester in 1874, but they never produced Robinson after that date. Rifle has been found in two styles: first with small fingers on hammer to cock and operate mechanism; second with buttons on receiver to retract bolt and cock hammer. Rifle made in .44-caliber, with octagonal barrel usually found in 26" or 28" length. Frames predominantly brass. Some iron frames have been noted and will bring a premium of approximately 25 percent. Barrel and magazine tube have blued finish.

First Model

—	6500	5200	2700	1300	500

Second Model

—	6500	5200	2700	1300	500

ADLER
Engelbrecht & Wolff
Blasii, Germany

Extremely rare and unusually designed semi-automatic pistol. Adapted for 7.25mm Adler cartridge. Striker-fired blowback pistol, with 3.4" barrel. Single-column magazine has 8-round capacity. Weight about 24 oz. Produced in a very limited number. Probably only a few hundred between 1906 and 1907.

—	—	10000	8750	2750	1250

ADVANCED SMALL ARMS INDUSTRIES
Solothurn, Switzerland

One Pro .45

Introduced in 1997. Built in Switzerland by ASAI. Pistol features 3" barrel chambered for .45 ACP cartridge. Based on short-recoil operation. Available in double-action or double-action-only. Also available is a kit (purchased separately) to convert pistol to .400 CorBon caliber. Pistol weighs about 24 oz. empty.

1000	725	595	425	195	100

ADVANTAGE ARMS U.S.A., INC.
Distributed by Wildfire Sports
St. Paul, Minnesota

Model 422

.22- or .22 Magnum caliber four-barrel derringer, with 2.5" barrels. Entirely made of aluminum alloy. Finished in blue or nickel-plate. Manufactured in 1986 and 1987.

225	125	100	85	65	45

AERO
Manufactura De Armas De Fuego
Guernica, Spain

Model 1914 (Aero)

7.65mm caliber semi-automatic pistol, with 3.25" barrel in Ruby design. "Aero" name on slide along with an airplane. Magazine capacity 7 rounds. Weight about 23 oz.

—	350	250	200	125	95

AETNA ARMS CO.
New York

.22-caliber spur trigger revolver, with octagonal barrel and 7-shot cylinder. Barrel marked "Aetna Arms Co. New York". Manufactured approximately 1870 to 1880. Copy of S&W No. 1.

—	—	550	375	150	100

	NIB	EXC.	V.G.	GOOD	FAIR	POOR

AFC
Auguste Francotte
Liege, Belgium

One of the most prolific makers of revolvers, in Liege, during the last half of the 19th century. Estimated over 150 different revolvers made and marketed by them, before they were forced out of business by German occupation of 1914. Francotte produced many variations from Tranter copies to pinfires, early Smith & Wesson designs to 11mm M1871 Swedish troopers revolver. They made break-open revolvers and produced only one semi-automatic, a 6.35mm blowback design. A good portion of their pistols were produced for the wholesale market and sold under other names. These particular revolvers will bear letters "AF" stamped somewhere on frame. Because of the vast number and variety of pistols produced by this company, cataloging and pricing is beyond the scope of this or any general reference book. Suggested that any examples encountered, be researched on an individual basis. More information on Francotte, see information under that listing.

Model 1895

One of earliest Francotte pistols. Chambered for 8mm cartridge. Lever-operated repeater. Marked "A. Francotte & Co. Makers" on top of slide.

—	7000	5500	4150	2300	1500

Trainer

Single-shot target pistol. Made for competition in .22-caliber short. "AFC" trademark on left side of frame. Model probably not made by Francotte, but sold by that firm and others.

—	3800	3150	2700	2175	1500

Semi-Auto

6.35mm, 6-shot detachable magazine pocket pistol, with blue finish. Model marked "A. Francotte A Liege" on frame.

—	425	300	195	125	90

AFFERBACH, W. A.
Philadelphia, Pennsylvania

Maker known to have produced copies of Henry Derringer's percussion pocket pistols. Though uncommon, their values would be approximately as listed.

—	—	2750	2200	995	300

AGNER (SAXHOJ PRODUCTS, INC.)
Copenhagen, Denmark

Model M 80

.22-caliber single-shot stainless steel target pistol, with 5.9" barrel, adjustable sights and walnut grips. Pistol fitted with dry fire mechanism. Also available in left-hand version. Imported from 1981 to 1986.

—	1250	875	600	450	200

AGUIRRE
Eibar, Spain

Spanish manufacturer of pistols prior to World War II.

Basculant

6.35mm semi-automatic pistol. Marked on slide "Cal. 6.35 Automatic Pistol Basculant".

—	275	150	125	75	50

LeDragon

As above, with slide marked "Cal. 6.35 Automatic Pistol LeDragon". Patterned after Browning Model 1906. Stylized dragon molded into grips.

—	275	150	125	75	50

AGUIRRE Y ARANZABAL (AYA)
Eibar, Spain

SIDE-BY-SIDES

Matador

12-, 16-, 20-, 28-gauge or .410 bore boxlock double-barrel shotgun, with 26", 28" or 30" barrels. Single-selective trigger and automatic ejectors. Blued, with walnut stock. Manufactured from

	NIB	EXC.	V.G.	GOOD	FAIR	POOR

1955 to 1963. **NOTE:** 28-gauge and .410 bore add 100 percent.

	—	550	415	350	300	200

Matador II

As above in 12- or 20-gauge, with ventilated rib.

	—	575	425	375	300	200

Matador III

As above, with 3" chambers.

	—	600	450	395	325	200

Bolero

As above, with non-selective single trigger and extractors. Manufactured until 1984.

	—	500	375	325	295	200

Iberia

12- or 20-gauge Magnum boxlock double-barrel shotgun, with 26", 28" or 30" barrels. Double triggers and extractors. Blued, with walnut stock.

	—	600	450	395	325	200

Iberia II

Similar to above in 12- or 16-gauge, with 28" barrels and 2.75" chambers.

	—	625	500	425	325	250

Model 106

12-, 16- or 20-gauge boxlock double-barrel shotgun, with 28" barrels. Double triggers and extractors. Blued, with walnut stock. Manufactured until 1985.

	—	600	500	400	300	250

Model 107-LI

As above, with receiver lightly engraved and English-style stock. In 12- or 16-gauge only.

	—	675	575	495	325	275

Model 116

12-, 16- or 20-gauge sidelock double-barrel shotgun, with 27" to 30" barrels. Double triggers and ejectors. Engraved, blued, with walnut stock. Manufactured until 1985.

	—	1095	975	800	500	350

Model 117

As above, with 3" chambers.

	—	1150	1000	850	600	400

Model 117 "Quail Unlimited

As above in 12-gauge only, with 26" barrels. Receiver engraved "Quail Unlimited of North America". Forty-two were manufactured.

	—	1500	1200	875	650	425

Model 210

Exposed hammer 12- or 16-gauge boxlock shotgun, with 26" to 28" barrels. Double triggers. Blued, with walnut stock. Manufactured until 1985.

	—	800	675	550	400	325

Model 711 Boxlock

12-gauge boxlock double-barrel shotgun, with 28" or 30" barrels. Ventilated ribs. Single-selective trigger and automatic ejectors. Manufactured until 1984.

	—	900	800	700	500	350

Model 711 Sidelock

As above, with sidelocks. Manufactured in 1985 only.

	—	1200	1000	750	500	400

Senior

Custom order 12-gauge double-barrel sidelock shotgun. Gold inlaid and engraved. Made strictly to individual customer's specifications.

	17000	13750	9750	7000	4500	2250

	NIB	EXC.	V.G.	GOOD	FAIR	POOR

OVER/UNDERS

Model 79 "A"

12-gauge boxlock over/under double-barrel shotgun, with 26", 28" or 30" barrels. Single-selective trigger and automatic ejectors. Blued, with walnut stock. Manufactured until 1985.

	—	1250	1050	925	750	500

Model 79 "B"

As above, with moderate amount of engraving.

	—	1350	1150	950	800	575

Model 79 "C"

As above, with extensive engraving.

	—	2000	1800	1500	1150	675

Model 77

As above, patterned after Merkel shotgun.

	—	3000	2700	2000	1500	1000

Coral "A"

12- or 16-gauge over/under boxlock double-barrel shotgun, with 26" or 28" barrels. Ventilated ribs, double triggers and automatic ejectors. Fitted with Kersten cross bolt. Manufactured until 1985.

	—	1250	900	700	500	300

Coral "B

As above, with engraved French case hardened receiver.

	—	1400	1100	750	600	350

RECENTLY IMPORTED SHOTGUNS

SIDELOCK SIDE-BY-SIDES

AyA sidelock shotguns use Holland & Holland system. Feature double triggers, articulated front trigger, cocking indicators, bushed firing pins, replaceable firing pins, replaceable hinge pins and chopper lump barrels. Frame and sidelocks case-colored. Weight between 5 and 7 lbs., depending on gauge and barrel length. Barrel lengths offered in 26", 27", 28" and 29" depending on gauge. All stocks are figured walnut, with hand checkering and oil finish. Available with several extra cost options that may affect price. Also influencing price of new guns is fluctuating dollar in relation to Spanish currency.

Model No. 1

Offered in 12-, 16-, 20- and 28-gauge, or .410 bore, with special English scroll engraving. Fitted with automatic ejectors and straight grip stock. Exhibition quality wood.

	—	10500	8000	4750	2300	700

Model No. 1 Round Body

As above, with round body action.

	—	11500	9000	5250	—	—

Model No. 1 Deluxe

Deluxe version of No. 1, with finer wood and engraving. **NOTE:** Round body add $350.

	—	11500	9000	5250	2400	700

Model No. 2

Offered in 12-, 16-, 20-, 28-gauge and .410 bore. Has automatic ejectors, straight-grip and select walnut stock.

	—	5000	4000	2500	1850	700

Model No. 2 Round Body

As above, with round body action.

	—	5200	4250	2750	1950	700

Model No. 53

Chambered for 12-, 16- and 20-gauge. Features three locking lugs, side clips, automatic ejectors and straight-grip stock.

	6900	5500	4000	2750	1000	700

	NIB	EXC.	V.G.	GOOD	FAIR	POOR

Model No. 56

Available in 12-gauge only. Features three locking lugs, side clips, special wide action body and raised matted rib. Select walnut straight-grip stock.

	10500	8700	6750	5400	2000	1000

Model XXV Sidelock

Offered in all gauges. Fitted with Churchill-type rib. Automatic ejectors, select straight-grip and walnut stock standard.

	5900	5250	4250	3200	1750	1000

BOXLOCK SIDE-BY-SIDES

These AyA guns utilize Anson & Deeley system. Double locking lugs, detachable cross pin and separate trigger plate that gives access to firing mechanism. Frame case-colored. Barrels are chopper lump. Firing pins bushed. Automatic safety and ejectors standard. Barrels offered in 26", 27" and 28", depending on gauge. Weight between 5 and 7 lbs., depending on gauge.

Adarra

This model is offered in all major gauges, with the option of double non-selective or selective single triggers. Grade 2 walnut stock has a hand rubbed oil finish, cut checkering, straight-grip and a splinter fore-end. Receiver has a bold foliate engraving pattern, with choice of color case-hardened, old silver or white finish. Introduced in 2013.

	4250	3800	3000	2450	1500	500

Model XXV Boxlock

Available in 12- and 20-gauge only. Hand checkered select walnut stock, with straight-grip stock.

	—	3500	2250	800	600	350

Model No. 4

Available in 12-, 16-, 20-, 28-gauge and .410 bore. Hand checkered select walnut stock, with straight-grip. Light scroll engraving. **NOTE:** Add 75 percent for 28-gauge and .410 bore.

	—	3000	2650	1250	—	—

Model No. 4 Deluxe

Same as above, with select walnut stock and slightly more engraving coverage. **NOTE:** Add 75 percent for 28-gauge and .410 bore.

	—	5000	3995	1500	1000	550

OVER/UNDERS

These AyA shotguns are similar in design and appearance to Gebruder Merkel over/under sidelocks, with three-part fore-end, Kersten cross bolt and double under locking lugs.

Model No. 37 Super

Available in 12-, 16- or 20-gauge. Ventilated rib, automatic ejectors, internally gold-plated sidelocks. Offered with three different types of engraving patterns; ducks, scroll or deep cut engraving. Very few of this model imported into U.S.

	—	12000	9500	5000	3500	2000

Model Augusta

Top-of-the-line AyA model offered in 12-gauge only. Features presentation wood and deep cut scroll engraving. Very few imported into U.S.

	—	18000	8000	4500	3500	1500

AIR MATCH
Paris, Kentucky

Air Match 500

.22-caliber single-shot target pistol, with 10.5" barrel, adjustable sights and adjustable front-mounted counterweights. Blued, with walnut grips. Imported from 1984 to 1986.

	775	595	425	300	250	125

AJAX ARMY

Single-Action

Spur-trigger single-action solid-frame revolver. Chambered for .44 rimfire cartridge. Had 7" barrel. Blued, with walnut grips. Manufactured in 1880s.

	—	750	450	365	275	200

NIB	EXC.	V.G.	GOOD	FAIR	POOR

AKDAL
Istanbul, Turkey

This company manufactures several firearms that have recently been imported into the United States, including the Ghost pistol series and several AR-style semi-auto shotguns.

Ghost

A 9mm striker-fired polymer-frame pistol, with features similar to the Glock. It has a 15-round magazine and interchangeable grip backstraps of different sizes.

NIB	EXC.	V.G.	GOOD	FAIR	POOR
400	325	275	200	150	100

MKA 1919

A 12-gauge shotgun built on an AR-15 type frame. Features include a detachable 5-round magazine and three interchangeable choke tubes.

NIB	EXC.	V.G.	GOOD	FAIR	POOR
550	450	350	285	225	150

ALAMO RANGER
Spain

Double-action Spanish copy of Colt SAA. Chambered for .38 Long Colt or .38 Special. Cylinder held 6 shots. Finish blued; grips checkered hard rubber. Maker of this pistol unknown.

NIB	EXC.	V.G.	GOOD	FAIR	POOR
—	350	225	115	75	45

ALASKA
Norwich, Connecticut
See—Hood Firearms Co.

ALDAZABAL
Eibar, Spain
Aldazabal, Leturiondo & CIA

Model 1919

Vest pocket semi-automatic pistol. Copied from FN Browning Model 1906. Caliber 6.35mm.

NIB	EXC.	V.G.	GOOD	FAIR	POOR
—	295	175	125	75	50

Military Model

Semi-automatic pistol in Ruby-style. Caliber 7.65mm, with 9-round magazine.

NIB	EXC.	V.G.	GOOD	FAIR	POOR
—	375	275	195	125	75

Aldazabal

Another typical low-quality "Eibar" -type semi-automatic. Browning blowback copy. Chambered for 7.65mm cartridge. Had 7-shot detachable magazine, blued finish, with checkered wood grips. Company ceased production before Spanish Civil War.

NIB	EXC.	V.G.	GOOD	FAIR	POOR
—	295	165	115	65	40

ALERT
Norwich, Connecticut
See—Hood Firearms Co.

ALEXIA
Norwich, Connecticut
See—Hopkins & Allen

ALFA
Eibar, Spain
See—Armero Especialistas Reunides

ALKARTASUNA FABRICA DE ARMAS
Guernica, Spain

Company began production during World War I, to help Gabilondo y Urresti supply sidearms to the French. After hostilities ceased, they continued to produce firearms under their own name. They produced a number of variations in both 6.35mm and 7.65mm marked "Alkar". Collector interest is very thin. Factory burned down in 1920 and by 1922 business had totally ceased.

	NIB	EXC.	V.G.	GOOD	FAIR	POOR

Alkar

6.35mm semi-automatic pistol, with cartridge counter in grip plates. One variation of many. Built in 6.35mm or 7.65mm.

	NIB	EXC.	V.G.	GOOD	FAIR	POOR
	—	295	250	195	125	100

Alkar (Ruby-Style)

7.65mm semi-automatic pistol built in Ruby-style. Pistol supplied to French government during World War I.

	NIB	EXC.	V.G.	GOOD	FAIR	POOR
	—	295	225	165	100	90

ALL RIGHT FIREARMS CO.
Lawrence, Massachusetts

Little All Right Palm Pistol

Squeezer-type pocket pistol, invented by E. Boardman and A. Peavy in 1876. Made in .22-caliber. Had 5-shot cylinder, with 1-5/8" or 2-3/8" barrel. Barrel octagonal, with tube on top which houses sliding trigger. Finish nickel. Black hard rubber grips have "Little All Right" & "All Right Firearms Co., Manufacturers Lawrence, Mass. U.S.A." molded into them. Several hundred produced in late 1870s.

	NIB	EXC.	V.G.	GOOD	FAIR	POOR
	—	4000	3250	2950	1050	300

ALLEN, ETHAN
Grafton, Massachusetts

Founded by Ethan Allen in early 1800s. It became a prolific gun-making firm, that evolved from Ethan Allen to Allen & Thurber, as well as Allen & Wheelock Company. It was located in Norwich, Connecticut and Worchester, Massachusetts, as well as Grafton. Eventually it became Forehand & Wadsworth Company in 1871, after the death of Ethan Allen. There were many and varied firearms produced under all headings described above. If one desires to collect Ethan Allen firearms, it would be advisable to educate oneself, as there are a number of fine publications available on the subject. Basic models and their values are listed.

First Model Pocket Rifle

Manufactured by Ethan Allen in Grafton, Massachusetts. Bootleg-type under-hammer single-shot pistol, chambered for .31 percussion. Larger-caliber versions have also been noted. Barrel lengths from 5" to 9" that were part-octagon in configuration. Iron mountings. Blued, with walnut grips. Barrel marked, "E. Allen/ Grafton/Mass." as well as "Pocket Rifle/Cast Steel/Warranted". Approximately 2,000 manufactured from 1831 to 1842.

	NIB	EXC.	V.G.	GOOD	FAIR	POOR
	—	—	—	1650	750	200

Second Model Pocket Rifle

Rounded-frame round-grip version of First Model.

	NIB	EXC.	V.G.	GOOD	FAIR	POOR
	—	—	—	1550	650	200

Bar Hammer Pistol

Double-action pistol, with top-mounted bar hammer. Chambered for .28- to .36-caliber percussion. Half-octagon barrels were from 2" to 10" in length. They screwed out of the frame so it was possible to breech load them. Finish blued. Rounded walnut grips. They were marked, "Allen & Thurber/Grafton Mass." Approximately 2,000 manufactured between early 1830s and 1860.

	NIB	EXC.	V.G.	GOOD	FAIR	POOR
	—	—	—	1650	725	200

Tube Hammer Pistol

Version similar to Bar Hammer. Curved hammer without spur. Few hundred manufactured between early 1830s and 1840s.

	NIB	EXC.	V.G.	GOOD	FAIR	POOR
	—	—	—	2900	1300	400

Side Hammer Pistol

Single-shot target-type pistol. Chambered for .34-, .41- and .45-caliber percussion. Part-octagon barrel from 6" to 10" in length. Wooden ramrod mounted under barrel. Hood quality rear sight that was adjustable. Ornate trigger guard had a graceful spur at its rear. Finish blued. Rounded walnut grip. Barrel marked, "Allen & Thurber, Worchester". Approximately 300 manufactured in late 1840s and early 1850s.

	NIB	EXC.	V.G.	GOOD	FAIR	POOR
	—	—	—	1400	650	200

Center Hammer Pistol

Single-action chambered for .34-, .36- or .44-caliber percussion. Half-octagon barrel from 4" to 12" in length. Centrally mounted hammer that was offset to right side to allow for sighting the pistol. Finish blued, with walnut grips. Marked, "Allen & Thurber, Allen Thurber & Company". Some specimens marked, "Allen & Wheelock". Several thousand manufactured between late 1840s and 1860.

	NIB	EXC.	V.G.	GOOD	FAIR	POOR
	—	—	—	1400	650	200

	NIB	EXC.	V.G.	GOOD	FAIR	POOR

Double-Barrel Pistol

Side-by-side double-barrel pistol, with single trigger. Chambered for .36-caliber percussion, with 3" to 6" round barrels. Finish blued, with walnut grips. Examples with ramrod mounted under barrel have been noted. Flute between barrels was marked, "Allen & Thurber", "Allen Thurber & Company" or "Allen & Wheelock". Approximately 1,000 manufactured in 1850s.

	NIB	EXC.	V.G.	GOOD	FAIR	POOR
	—	—	—	1250	600	150

Allen & Wheelock Center Hammer Pistol

Single-action pocket pistol, chambered for .31- to .38-caliber percussion. Octagon barrels from 3" to 6" in length. Finish blued. Square butt walnut grips. Barrel marked, "Allen & Wheelock". Approximately 500 manufactured between 1858 and 1865.

	NIB	EXC.	V.G.	GOOD	FAIR	POOR
	—	—	—	1100	550	100

Allen Thurber & Company Target Pistol

Deluxe single-action target pistol. Chambered for .31- or .36-caliber percussion. Had heavy octagon barrel from 11" to 16" in length. Wooden ramrod mounted underneath barrel. Mountings were German silver. Detachable walnut stock. Deluxe engraved patchbox. Weapon was engraved and barrel marked, "Allen Thurber & Co./Worchester/Cast Steel". Firearm furnished in fitted case, with stock, false muzzle and various accessories. Considered to be very high grade target pistol in its era. Values listed are for complete-cased outfit. Very few manufactured in 1850s. **NOTE:** Pistols without attachable stock deduct 75 percent.

	NIB	EXC.	V.G.	GOOD	FAIR	POOR
	—	—	—	9000	4000	1000

Ethan Allen Pepperboxes

During the period from early 1830s to 1860s, company manufactured over 50 different variations of revolving pepperbox-type pistol. They were commercially quite successful and actually competed successfully with Colt revolving handguns for more than a decade. Widely used throughout United States, as well as Mexico and during our Civil War. They are widely collectible, because of the number of variations that exist. Potential collector should avail himself of information available on the subject. These pepperboxes can be divided into three categories.

No. 1: Manufactured from 1830s until 1842, at Grafton, Massachusetts.

No. 2: Manufactured from 1842 to 1847, at Norwich, Connecticut.

No. 3: Manufactured from 1847 to 1865, at Worchester, Massachusetts.

There are a number of subdivisions among these three basic groups, that would pertain to trigger type, size, barrel length, etc. It would be impossible to cover all 50 of these variations in a text of this type. We strongly suggest a qualified individual appraisal be secured, if contemplating a transaction. Values of these pepperbox pistols in excellent condition would be between $1,500 and $5,000. Most examples will be seen in fair to good condition and will bring $1,000 to $2,000 depending on variation.

Large Frame Pocket Revolver

Double-action pocket revolver chambered for .34-caliber percussion. Octagon barrel from 3" to 5" in length. No sights. The 5-shot unfluted cylinder was game scene engraved. Finish blued. Rounded walnut grips. Bar-type hammer. First conventional revolver manufactured by this company. Directly influenced by pepperbox pistol, for which Ethan Allen had become famous. Marked, "Allen & Wheelock" as well as "Patented April 16, 1845". Approximately 1,500 manufactured between 1857 and 1860.

	NIB	EXC.	V.G.	GOOD	FAIR	POOR
	—	—	—	1400	700	350

Small Frame Pocket Revolver

Version similar to Large Frame Pocket Revolver, except chambered for .31-caliber percussion. Octagon barrel length 2" to 3.5". Slightly smaller in size, but finished and marked the same. Approximately 1,000 made between 1858 and 1860.

	NIB	EXC.	V.G.	GOOD	FAIR	POOR
	—	—	—	1400	700	350

Side Hammer Belt Revolver

Single-action revolver, chambered for .34-caliber percussion. Octagon barrel from 3" to 7.5" in length. Featured a hammer mounted on right side of frame and 5-shot engraved unfluted cylinder. Cylinder access pin is inserted from rear of weapon. Finish blued. Case-colored hammer and trigger guard. Flared butt walnut grips. Marked, "Allen & Wheelock". Two basic types. Values for early model, of which 100 manufactured between 1858 and 1861.

	NIB	EXC.	V.G.	GOOD	FAIR	POOR
	—	—	—	1500	750	300

Standard Model

Second type was Standard Model. Spring-loaded catch on trigger guard, as opposed to friction catch on early model. Approximately 1,000 manufactured between 1858 and 1861.

	NIB	EXC.	V.G.	GOOD	FAIR	POOR
	—	—	—	1200	595	200

	NIB	EXC.	V.G.	GOOD	FAIR	POOR

Side Hammer Pocket Revolver

Version chambered for .28-caliber percussion. Had 2" to 5" octagon barrel. Frame slightly smaller than belt model.

Early Production
100 manufactured.

—	—	—	1300	725	250

Standard Production
1,000 manufactured.

—	—	2100	975	400	225

Side Hammer Navy Revolver

Large-frame military-type revolver. Similar to Side Hammer Belt Model. Chambered for .36-caliber percussion. Features octagon 5.5" to 8" barrel, with 6-shot engraved cylinder. Early production guns have friction style catch to secure trigger guard/loading lever on the left sideplate. Approximately 100 manufactured between 1858 and 1861.

Early Production

—	—	—	4300	1975	575

Standard Model
Has a spring-loaded catch on the rear of the trigger guard. 1,000 manufactured.

—	—	—	3700	1700	475

Center Hammer Army Revolver

Large military-type single-action revolver chambered for .44-caliber percussion. Had 7.5" half-octagon barrel and 6-shot unfluted cylinder. Hammer mounted in center of frame. Finish blued. Case-colored hammer and trigger guard. Walnut grips. Barrel marked, "Allen & Wheelock. Worchester, Mass. U.S./Allen's Pt's. Jan. 13, 1857. Dec. 15, 1857, Sept. 7, 1858". Approximately 700 manufactured between 1861 and 1862.

—	—	7500	4500	1875	500

Center Hammer Navy Revolver

Similar to Army Revolver. Chambered for .36-caliber percussion, with 7.5" full-octagon barrel. Examples have been noted with 5", 6" or 8" barrels.

—	—	—	4300	1975	475

Center Hammer Percussion Revolver

Single-action revolver chambered for .36-caliber percussion. Octagonal 3" or 4" barrel, with 6-shot unfluted cylinder. Finish blued, with walnut grips. Model supposedly was made for Providence, Rhode Island, Police Department and has become commonly referred to as "Providence Police Model". Approximately 700 manufactured between 1858 and 1862.

—	—	2500	1750	750	200

Lipfire Army Revolver

Large military-type single-action revolver. Chambered for .44 lipfire cartridge. Had 7.5" half-octagon barrel, with 6-shot unfluted cylinder that had notches at its rear for cartridge lips. Finish blued. Case-colored hammer and trigger guard. Square butt walnut grips. Barrel marked, "Allen & Wheelock, Worchester, Mass." Resembled Center Hammer Percussion Army Revolver. Two basic variations. Total of 250 Lipfire Army Revolvers manufactured in early 1860s.

Early Model
Top hinged loading gate.

—	—	—	4500	2200	600

Late Model
Bottom hinged loading gate.

—	—	—	4000	1700	400

Lipfire Navy Revolver

Similar to Army model. Chambered for .36 lipfire cartridge, with octagonal 4", 5", 6", 7.5" or 8" barrel. Approximately 500 manufactured in 1860s.

—	—	—	3300	1300	400

Lipfire Pocket Revolver

Smaller version chambered for .32 lipfire cartridge, with octagonal 4", 5" or 6" barrel. Approximately 200 manufactured in early 1860s.

—	—	—	2200	950	250

NIB	EXC.	V.G.	GOOD	FAIR	POOR

.32 Side Hammer Rimfire Revolver

Single-action spur-trigger pocket revolver chambered for .32-caliber rimfire cartridge. Octagonal barrels from 3" to 5" in length. Finish blued. Flared-butt and walnut grips. Marked, "Allen & Wheelock Worchester, Mass." Three variations, with a total of approximately 1,000 manufactured between 1859 and 1862.

First Model
Rounded top strap.

NIB	EXC.	V.G.	GOOD	FAIR	POOR
—	—	1125	800	450	150

Second Model
Marked on frame July 3, 1860

NIB	EXC.	V.G.	GOOD	FAIR	POOR
—	—	1100	795	425	150

Third Model
Patent dates 1858 and 1861.

NIB	EXC.	V.G.	GOOD	FAIR	POOR
—	—	1050	775	400	125

.22 Side Hammer Rimfire Revolver

Smaller version of .32 revolver chambered for .22 rimfire cartridge. Octagonal barrels from 2.25" to 4" in length. Has 7-shot unfluted cylinder. Many variations. Approximately 1,500 manufactured between 1858 and 1862.

Early Model First Issue
Access pin enters from rear.

NIB	EXC.	V.G.	GOOD	FAIR	POOR
—	—	1300	850	475	100

Second Issue
Access pin enters from front.

NIB	EXC.	V.G.	GOOD	FAIR	POOR
—	—	1300	850	475	100

Third Issue
Separate rear sight.

NIB	EXC.	V.G.	GOOD	FAIR	POOR
—	—	1425	1250	600	150

Fourth to Eighth Issue
Very similar, values the same.

NIB	EXC.	V.G.	GOOD	FAIR	POOR
—	—	900	750	300	100

Single-Shot Center Hammer

Single-shot derringer-type pistol. Chambered for .22-caliber rimfire cartridge. Had part-octagon barrels from 2" to 5.5" in length that swung to right side for loading. Some had automatic ejectors, others did not. Frame either brass or iron, with bird's-head or squared butt walnut grips. Marked, "Allen & Wheelock" or "E. Allen & Co." Very few manufactured in early 1860s.

Early Issue
Full-length octagon barrel. Round iron frame. Rarely encountered.

NIB	EXC.	V.G.	GOOD	FAIR	POOR
—	—	1275	1150	400	100

Standard Issue
Squared butt or bird's-head.

NIB	EXC.	V.G.	GOOD	FAIR	POOR
—	—	1175	1050	300	100

.32 Single-Shot Center Hammer

Larger-frame pocket pistol chambered for .32 rimfire cartridge. Has part- or full-octagon barrel 4" or 5" in length. Swung to right side for loading. Otherwise similar to .22-caliber version.

NIB	EXC.	V.G.	GOOD	FAIR	POOR
—	—	1175	1050	300	100

Vest Pocket Derringer

Small pocket pistol chambered for .22 rimfire cartridge. Had 2" part-octagon barrel that swung to right-hand side for loading. Cartridges were manually extracted. Featured brass frame. Blued or plated barrel and walnut bird's-head grips. Barrel marked, "Allen & Co. Makers". Extremely small firearm. Approximately 200 manufactured between 1869 and 1871.

NIB	EXC.	V.G.	GOOD	FAIR	POOR
—	—	1595	975	425	100

.32 Derringer

Similar to Vest Pocket version. Larger in size and chambered for .32 rimfire cartridge. Had part-octagon barrel from 2" to 4" in length that swung to right for loading. Version featured automatic extractor. Barrel marked, "E. Allen & Co. Worchester, Mass." Very rare firearm. Made between 1865 and 1871.

NIB	EXC.	V.G.	GOOD	FAIR	POOR
—	—	1495	875	395	100

	NIB	EXC.	V.G.	GOOD	FAIR	POOR

.41 Derringer

Same size and configuration as .32-caliber model, except chambered for .41 rimfire cartridge. Barrel lengths of 2.5" to 2.75". Markings the same. Approximately 100 manufactured, between 1865 and 1871.

	NIB	EXC.	V.G.	GOOD	FAIR	POOR
	—	—	2200	950	350	100

Center Hammer Muzzleloading Rifle

Single-shot rifle chambered for .44-caliber percussion. Had 36" round barrel, with octagonal breech. Center-mounted hammer offset to right for sighting. Iron mountings. Finish browned. Case-colored lock. Ramrod mounted under barrel. Walnut buttstock, with crescent buttplate and no forearm. Approximately 100 manufactured in 1850s.

	NIB	EXC.	V.G.	GOOD	FAIR	POOR
	—	—	1850	600	250	125

Side Hammer Muzzleloading Rifle

Similar to Center Hammer model, with hammer mounted on right side of lock. Chambered for .38-caliber percussion, with octagon barrel from 28" to 32" in length. Occasionally found with a patchbox. Barrel browned. Case-colored lock, walnut stock with crescent butt-plate. Several hundred manufactured from early 1840s to 1860s.

	NIB	EXC.	V.G.	GOOD	FAIR	POOR
	—	—	2750	900	350	150

Combination Gun

Either over/under or side-by-side rifle. Chambered for 12-gauge and .38-caliber percussion. Barrels from 28" to 34" in length. Two hammers and double triggers. Ramrod mounted either beneath or on right side of barrels. Finish browned, with walnut stock. Examples with patchbox have been noted. Production was very limited. Over/under versions worth approximately 20 percent more than side-by-side values given. Manufactured between 1840s and 1860s.

	NIB	EXC.	V.G.	GOOD	FAIR	POOR
	—	—	6000	4350	1750	600

Side Hammer Breechloading Rifle

Unique rifle chambered for .36- to .50-caliber percussion. Offered with various-lengths and part-octagon barrels. Unusual breech mechanism that was activated by a rotating lever, which resembled a water faucet. Barrel browned. Case-colored lock and walnut stock. Marked, "Allen & Wheelock/ Allen's Patent July 3, 1855". Approximately 500 manufactured between 1855 and 1860.

	NIB	EXC.	V.G.	GOOD	FAIR	POOR
	—	—	3550	1600	500	350

Drop Breech Rifle

Single-shot rifle chambered for .22- through .44 rimfire cartridges. Part-octagon barrel from 23" to 28" in length. Breech activated by combination trigger guard action lever. Opening breech automatically ejected empty cartridge. External hammer manually cocked. Featured an adjustable sight. Barrel blued. Case-colored frame and walnut stock. Marked, "Allen & Wheelock/ Allen's Pat. Sept. 18, 1860". Approximately 2,000 manufactured between 1860 and 1871.

	NIB	EXC.	V.G.	GOOD	FAIR	POOR
	—	—	1550	600	200	100

Lipfire Revolving Rifle

A 6-shot cylinder-type rifle chambered for .44-caliber lipfire cartridge. Unfluted cylinder, with slots at its rear to allow for cartridge lips. Round barrels were 26" to 28" in length, with octagon breech. Finish blued. Case-colored frame and walnut buttstock. Not marked with maker's name. Approximately 100 manufactured between 1861 and 1863.

	NIB	EXC.	V.G.	GOOD	FAIR	POOR
	—	—	18500	7000	2000	775

Double-Barrel Shotgun

Side-by-side shotgun chambered for 10- or 12-gauge. Barrel length 28". Loaded by means of trapdoor-type breech that had a lever handle. Finish blued, with checkered walnut stock. Few hundred manufactured between 1865 and 1871.

	NIB	EXC.	V.G.	GOOD	FAIR	POOR
	—	—	1800	800	250	125

ALLEN & THURBER

See—Ethan Allen

ALLEN & WHEELOCK

See—Ethan Allen

ALLEN FIREARMS

Santa Fe, New Mexico

See—Aldo Uberti

NIB	EXC.	V.G.	GOOD	FAIR	POOR

ALPHA ARMS CO.
Flower Mound, Texas

Alpha Arms Co. produced high-grade bolt-action rifles, on a semi-custom basis. Manufactured a number of standard models, but offered many options at additional cost. Some of these options were custom sights, finishes and octagonal barrels. These extra features would add to value of models listed. Company operated from 1983 until 1987.

Jaguar Grade I

Built on Mauser-type action, with barrel lengths from 20" to 24". Chambered for most calibers between .222 Rem. and .338 Win. Magnum. Stock made from a synthetic laminated material the company called "Alphawood". Introduced in 1987 and only produced that year.

1700	1100	750	500	300	200

Jaguar Grade II

Similar to Grade I, with Douglas Premium barrel.

1825	1275	800	500	400	250

Jaguar Grade III

Has Douglas barrel plus hand-honed trigger and action. Three-position safety like Winchester Model 70.

1950	1500	1050	700	400	200

Jaguar Grade IV

Has all features of Grade III, with specially lightened action and sling-swivel studs.

2000	1750	1200	900	500	250

Alpha Big-Five

Similar to Jaguar Grade IV. Chambered for .300 Win. Magnum, .375 H&H Magnum and .458 Win. Magnum. Reinforced through-bolt stock to accommodate recoil of larger caliber cartridges for which it was chambered. Had Decelerator recoil pad. Manufactured in 1987 only. **NOTE:** Add 20 percent for .458.

2200	1850	1500	950	600	300

Alpha Grand Slam

Features same high quality as Jaguar models. Available in left-hand model. Has fluted bolt, laminated stock and matte blue finish. **NOTE:** Deduct 10 percent for left-hand version.

1700	1500	1250	700	450	250

Alpha Custom

Similar to Grand Slam, with select grade stock.

1700	1500	1250	750	500	250

Alpha Alaskan

Similar to Grand Slam. Chambered for .308 Win., .350 Rem. Magnum, .358 Win. and .458 Win. Magnum. Features all stainless steel construction. **NOTE:** Add 20 percent for .458.

2000	1750	1450	850	500	250

ALSOP, C.R.
Middletown, Connecticut

This firearms manufacturer made revolvers during 1862 and 1863. They made two basic models: Navy; and Pocket. Some collectors consider Alsop to be a secondary U.S. martial handgun, but no verifying government contracts are known to exist.

First Model Navy Revolver

.36-caliber revolver, with 3.5", 4.5", 5.5" or 6.5" barrel length and 5-shot cylinder. Has blued finish, wood grips and peculiar hump in its backstrap. First model has a safety device, which blocks the spur trigger. This device is found on serial numbers 1-100. Markings are: "C.R. Alsop Middletown, Conn. 1860 & 1861" on barrel; cylinder, "C.R. Alsop" & "Nov. 26th, 1861"; side plate, "Patented Jan. 21st, 1862".

—	—	3850	1300	500	350

Standard Model Navy Revolver

Exactly the same as First Model, without safety device. Serial numbered 101 to 300.

—	—	3350	900	300	225

NIB	EXC.	V.G.	GOOD	FAIR	POOR

Pocket Model Revolver

.31-caliber 5-shot revolver, with spur trigger, 4" round barrel, blued finish and wood grips. Very similar in appearance to Navy model, but smaller in size. Marked: "C.R. Alsop Middletown, Conn. 1860 & 1861" on barrel; cylinder, "C.R. Alsop Nov. 26th, 1861". Serial numbered 1-300.

—	—	1700	700	200	125

AMAC
American Military Arms Corporation
(formerly Iver Johnson)
Jacksonville, Arkansas

Iver Johnson Arms Co. was founded in 1871 in Fitchburg, Massachusetts. One of the oldest and most successful of old-line arms companies, on which our modern era has taken its toll. In 1984 company moved to Jacksonville, Arkansas; in 1987 it was purchased by American Military Arms Corporation. This company has released some of the older designs as well as some new models. In 1993, company went out of business. Original Iver Johnson line is listed under its own heading.

U.S. Carbine .22

Semi-automatic military-style carbine, patterned after M1 of WWII fame. Chambered for .22 LR cartridge. Has 18.5" barrel. Features military-style peep sights and 15-shot detachable magazine.

325	250	175	100	75	50

Wagonmaster Lever-Action Rifle

Chambered for .22 rimfire cartridge. Has 18.5" barrel. Styled after Win. 94. Stock has straight-grip; fore-end a barrel band. Adjustable sights. Tube magazine that holds 15 LR cartridges.

295	225	150	100	75	50

Wagonmaster .22 Magnum

Same as Wagonmaster. Chambered for .22 rimfire Magnum.

325	250	175	125	95	50

Targetmaster Pump-Action Rifle

Model is a slide- or pump-action chambered for .22 rimfire cartridge. Has 18.5" barrel, with adjustable sights and straight-grip stock. Holds 12 LR cartridges.

325	175	145	115	75	50

Li'L Champ Bolt-Action Rifle

Model is a scaled-down single-shot chambered for .22 rimfire cartridge. Has 16.25" barrel, adjustable sights, molded stock and nickel-plated bolt. Overall length 33". Designed to be an ideal first rifle for a young shooter.

175	125	75	45	35	20

M .30 Cal. Carbine

Military-style carbine styled after M1 of WWII fame. Chambered for .30 Carbine cartridge. Has 18" barrel, with military-style sights and hardwood stock. Detachable 5-, 15- and 30-round magazines available.

425	300	225	175	125	90

Paratrooper .30 Carbine

Similar to M1 model, with folding stock.

495	395	325	250	160	100

Enforcer .30 Carbine

A 9.5" pistol version of M1 Carbine. No buttstock.

625	500	395	300	150	100

Long Range Rifle System/AMAC Model 5100

Specialized long-range bolt-action rifle. Chambered for .50-caliber Browning Machine gun cartridge. Has 33" barrel and special muzzle-brake system. Custom order version in .338- or .416-caliber also available.

4100	3550	2900	2000	900	450

TP-22 and TP-25

Compact double-action pocket automatic styled after Walther TP series. Chambered for .22 rimfire or .25 centerfire cartridges. Has 2.75" barrel, fixed sights and black plastic grips. Detachable magazine holds 7 shots. Finish blue or nickel-plated. **NOTE:** Nickel-plated version worth 10 percent more than blue.

265	195	150	100	75	50

NIB	EXC.	V.G.	GOOD	FAIR	POOR

AMAC 22 Compact or 25 Compact

Compact single-action semi-automatic pocket pistol. Chambered for .22 rimfire or .25 ACP cartridge. Has 2" barrel, 5-shot magazine, plastic grips and blue or nickel finish. **NOTE:** Add 10 percent for nickel.

265	195	150	100	75	50

AMERICAN ARMS, INC.
North Kansas City, Missouri

SIDE-BY-SIDE SHOTGUNS

York/Gentry

These two designations cover the same model. Prior to 1988, this model was called York. In 1988, receiver was case-colored and designation changed to Gentry. Model chambered for 12-, 20-, 28-gauge and .410 bore.. Had chrome-lined barrels from 26" to 30" in length, double triggers, 3" chambers and automatic ejectors. Boxlock action featured scroll engraving. Walnut stock was hand checkered. Introduced in 1986.

750	625	450	300	200	150

10 Gauge Magnum Shotgun

10-gauge, with 3.5" chambers and 32" barrels. Featured scroll-engraved chromed boxlock action and double triggers. Imported from Spain in 1986 only.

850	750	550	350	250	150

12 Gauge Magnum Shotgun

As above, chambered for 12-gauge 3.5" Magnum shell.

800	700	500	300	200	150

Brittany

Chambered for 12- and 20-gauge, with 25" or 27" barrels and screw-in choke tubes. Had solid matted rib and case-colored engraved boxlock action. Automatic ejectors, single-selective trigger, hand checkered walnut straight-grip stock, with semi-beavertail fore-end, were standard on this model. Introduced in 1989.

850	750	600	450	375	200

Turkey Special

Utilitarian model designed to be an effective turkey hunting tool. Chambered for Magnum 10- and 12-gauges. Has 26" barrels. Finish Parkerized. Stock finished in non-glare matte. Sling-swivel studs and recoil pad are standard. Introduced in 1987.

800	700	450	350	250	150

Waterfowl Special

Similar to Turkey Special. Chambered for 10-gauge only. Furnished with camouflaged sling. Introduced in 1987.

950	850	550	350	250	150

Specialty Model

Similar to Turkey Special. Offered in 12-gauge 3.5" Magnum.

875	750	500	300	200	150

Derby

Chambered for 12-, 20-, 28-gauge and .410 bore. Has 26" or 28" barrels, with 3" chambers and automatic ejectors. Either double- or single-selective triggers offered. Sidelock action is scroll engraved and chromed. Checkered straight-grip stock and forearm are oil-finished. Introduced in 1986. No longer imported. **NOTE:** Add 10 percent for 28 gauge or .410 bore; 50 percent for two-gauge sets.

1150	975	850	650	450	300

Grulla #2

Top-of-the-line model. Chambered for 12-, 20-, 28-gauge and .410 bore. Barrels are 26" or 28", with concave rib. Hand-fitted full sidelock action is extensively engraved and case-colored. Various chokes, double triggers and automatic ejectors. Select walnut straight-grip stock. Splinter fore-end is hand checkered and has a hand-rubbed oil finish. Introduced in 1989. No longer imported.

2500	1750	1250	900	500	250

	NIB	EXC.	V.G.	GOOD	FAIR	POOR

OVER/UNDER SHOTGUNS

F.S. 200

Trap or skeet model chambered for 12-gauge only. Had 26" Skeet & Skeet barrels or 32" Full choke barrels on trap model. Barrels were separated and had a vent rib. Boxlock action had Greener crossbolt and was black or matte chrome-plated. Featured single-selective trigger, automatic ejectors and checkered walnut pistol-grip stock. F.S. 200 imported in 1986 and 1987 only.

—	675	575	465	350	150	

F.S. 300

Similar to F.S. 200, with lightly engraved side plates and 30" barrel. Offered in trap grade. Imported in 1986 only.

—	800	675	565	450	250	

F.S. 400

Similar to F.S. 300, with engraved matte chrome-plated receiver. Imported in 1986 only.

—	1100	950	800	650	350	

F.S. 500

Similar to F.S. 400, with same general specifications. Not imported after 1985.

—	1150	1000	850	700	350	

Waterfowl Special

Chambered for 12-gauge Magnum, with 3.5" chambers. Has 28" barrels, with screw-in choke tubes. Automatic ejectors and single-selective trigger. Finish Parkerized, with matte finished stock, sling swivels and camouflaged sling and recoil pad. Introduced in 1987.

875	700	500	350	300	150	

Waterfowl 10 Gauge

Same as Waterfowl Special. Chambered for 10-gauge Magnum, with double triggers.

975	850	600	400	300	200	

Turkey Special

Similar to Waterfowl Special in 10-gauge, with 26" barrel and screw-in choke tubes.

975	850	600	350	300	200	

Lince

Chambered for 12- and 20-gauge. Has 26" or 28" barrels, with 3" chambers and various chokes. Boxlock action has Greener crossbolt, either blued or polished and chrome-plated. Barrels blued, with ventilated rib. Single-selective trigger and automatic ejectors. Imported in 1986 only.

—	500	425	350	300	200	

Silver Model

Similar to Lince. Plain un-engraved brushed-chrome-finished receiver. Imported in 1986 and 1987.

—	500	425	350	300	200	

Silver I

Similar to Silver. Available in 12-, 20-, 28-gauge and .410 bore. Has single-selective trigger, fixed chokes, extractors and recoil pad. Introduced in 1987. **NOTE:** Add $25 for 28-gauge and .410 bore guns.

650	550	325	275	200	175	

Silver II

Similar to Silver I, with screw-in choke tubes, automatic ejectors and select walnut. Introduced in 1987. **NOTE:** Add $25 for 28-gauge and .410 bore guns.

750	650	450	350	300	150	

Silver II Lite

Introduced in 1994. Designed as an upland game gun. Offered in 12-, 20- and 28-gauge, with 26" barrels. Chambered for both 2.75" and 3" shells. Frame made from a lightweight steel alloy. No longer imported.

875	775	550	400	300	150	

Silver Competition/Sporting

Offered in 12-gauge, with choice of 28" or 30" barrels which are made from chrome moly. Barrels have elongated forcing cones, chromed bores and are ported to help reduce recoil.

	NIB	EXC.	V.G.	GOOD	FAIR	POOR

Comes with interchangeable choke tubes. Single-selective trigger is mechanical. Weighs about 7.5 lbs. In 1996 a 20-gauge model was added, with 28" barrel and 3" chambers.

	950	800	600	400	300	150

Silver Hunter

Introduced in 1999. Offered in 12- and 20-gauge, with 26" and 28" barrels. Single-selective trigger with extractors. Choke tubes standard. Weight about 7 lbs.

	625	500	400	300	200	100

Bristol/Sterling

Chambered for 12- and 20-gauge. Various barrel lengths, with vent rib and screw-in choke tubes. Chambers are 3". Chrome-finished action is boxlock, with Greener crossbolt and game scene engraved on side plates. Automatic ejectors and single-selective trigger. Introduced in 1986. In 1989, designation was changed to Sterling. No longer imported.

	825	750	675	500	400	200

Sir

Chambered for 12- and 20-gauge, with 3" chambers, various barrel lengths, chokes and ventilated rib. Chrome-finished sidelock action has Greener crossbolt and engraved with a game scene. Automatic ejectors and single-selective trigger. Imported in 1986. No longer imported.

	—	875	750	625	500	250

Royal

Chambered for 12- and 20-gauge. Manufactured in various barrel lengths and chokes, with vent rib and 3" chambers. Chrome-finished sidelock action has Greener crossbolt and profusely scroll-engraved. Automatic ejectors and single-selective trigger. Select pistol-grip walnut stock is hand checkered and oil-finished. Imported in 1986 and 1987. No longer imported.

	—	1500	1275	1000	800	400

Excelsior

Similar to Royal, with extensive deep relief engraving and gold inlays. Imported in 1986 and 1987. No longer imported.

	—	1750	1500	1200	875	450

SINGLE-BARREL SHOTGUNS

AASB

Standard single-barrel break-open hammerless shotgun. Chambered for 12-, 20-gauge and .410 bore. Has 26" barrel, with various chokes and 3" chambers. Pistol-grip stock and matte finish. Introduced in 1988. No longer imported.

	100	85	75	60	45	25

Campers Special

Similar to standard model, with 21" barrel and folding stock. Introduced in 1988. No longer imported.

	110	95	85	70	50	35

Youth Model

Chambered for 20-gauge and .410 bore. Has 12.5" stock, with recoil pad. Introduced in 1989. No longer imported.

	115	100	80	65	50	35

Slugger

Version has 24" barrel, with rifle sights. Chambered for 12- and 20-gauge, with recoil pad. No longer imported.

	115	100	80	65	50	35

10 Gauge Model

Chambered for 10-gauge 3.5" Magnum. Has 32" full choke barrel and recoil pad. Introduced in 1988. No longer imported.

	175	145	100	85	60	45

Combo Model

Similar in appearance to other single-barrel models. Offered in interchangeable-barreled rifle/shotgun combination—28" barreled .22 Hornet and 12-gauge; or 26" barreled .22 LR and 20-gauge. Furnished with fitted hard case to hold interchangeable barrels. Introduced in 1989. No longer imported.

	250	200	175	145	110	75

	NIB	EXC.	V.G.	GOOD	FAIR	POOR

SEMI-AUTO SHOTGUNS

Phantom Field

Chambered for 12-gauge and fitted with choice of 24", 26" or 28" barrels. Fitted with 3" chamber. Gas operated action. Choke tubes standard. Five-round magazine. Checkered walnut stock. Weight about 7 lbs. Introduced in 1999.

400	350	300	225	125	75

Phantom Synthetic

Same as above. Furnished with checkered synthetic stock. Weight about 6.75 lbs. Introduced in 1999.

400	350	300	225	125	75

Phantom HP

Features 19" threaded barrel for external choke tubes. Five-round magazine. Weight about 6.75 lbs. Introduced in 1999.

400	375	325	300	150	95

RIFLES

ZCY.308

An AK-47 type design and chambered in .308 Winchester. Imported in 1988 only.

700	600	475	375	300	200

AKY39

Semi-automatic version of Soviet AK-47. Manufactured by Yugoslavia. Offered with folding tritium night sights and wooden fixed stock. Imported in 1988.

—	600	475	390	300	200

AKF39

Same rifle as AKY39, with metal folding stock.

—	625	550	475	300	200

AKC47

Basically same rifle as AKY39, without tritium night sights.

—	575	450	375	300	200

AKF47

Same rifle as AKC47, with metal folding stock.

—	625	550	475	300	200

EXP-64 Survival Rifle

.22-caliber semi-automatic take-down rifle. Self-storing in a floating oversized plastic stock. Rifle has 21" barrel, with open sights and crossbolt safety. A 10-shot detachable magazine. Importation by American Arms began in 1989.

165	150	125	95	75	50

SM-64 TD Sporter

.22 LR semi-automatic, with take-down 21" barrel. Adjustable sights, checkered hardwood stock and fore-end. Importation began in 1989.

195	155	110	85	65	45

1860 Henry

Replica of lever action Henry rifle. Brass frame. Steel half-octagon barrel, with tube magazine. Chambered for .44-40 or .45 Long Colt. Offered in 18.5" or 24" barrels. Weight with 24" barrel about 9.25 lbs. Built by Uberti.

950	800	650	400	300	200

1866 Winchester

Replica of Winchester 1866. Offered in .44-40 or .45 Long Colt. Barrel lengths in 19" or 24". Brass frame. Weight about 8.25 lbs. for 24" barrel model. Built by Uberti.

825	700	495	300	200	100

1873 Winchester

Replica of Winchester Model 1873. Offered with choice of 24" or 30" barrels. Chambered for .44-40 or .45 Long Colt. Case hardened steel frame. Weight about 8.25 lbs. for 24" model. Built by

	NIB	EXC.	V.G.	GOOD	FAIR	POOR

Uberti. **NOTE:** Add $80 for 30" barrel.

| | 850 | 725 | 550 | 325 | 225 | 125 |

1885 Single-Shot High Wall

Chambered for .45-70 cartridge. Winchester replica fitted with 28" round barrel. Weight about 8.75 lbs. Built by Uberti.

| | 850 | 695 | 550 | 350 | 200 | 100 |

Sharps Cavalry Carbine

Sharps replica fitted with 22" round barrel. Chambered for .45-70 cartridge. Adjustable rear sight. Weight about 8 lbs.

| | 700 | 600 | 425 | 350 | 200 | 100 |

Sharps Frontier Carbine

Similar to Cavalry carbine, with 22" octagonal barrel and double set triggers. Weight about 7.75 lbs.

| | 775 | 625 | 475 | 375 | 225 | 125 |

Sharps Sporting Rifle

Features 28" octagonal barrel. Chambered for .45-70 or .45-120 cartridge. Double set triggers. Adjustable rear sight. Checkered walnut stock. Weight about 9 lbs.

| | 775 | 625 | 475 | 375 | 225 | 125 |

Sharps 1874 Deluxe Sporting Rifle

Similar to above, with browned barrels.

| | 800 | 650 | 500 | 395 | 250 | 150 |

HANDGUNS

Model EP-.380

High-quality stainless steel pocket pistol. Chambered for .380 ACP cartridge. Double-action semi-automatic that holds 7 shots and has 3.5" barrel. Grips are checkered walnut. Imported from West Germany beginning in 1988.

| | 425 | 365 | 325 | 275 | 225 | 100 |

Model PK-22

Domestic semi-automatic chambered for .22 LR. Double-action with 3.5" barrel and 8-shot finger extension magazine. Made of stainless steel and has black plastic grips. Manufactured in U.S.A. by American Arms.

| | 245 | 200 | 150 | 125 | 100 | 75 |

Model CX-22

Compact version of PK-22, with 2.75" barrel and 7-shot magazine. Manufacture began in 1989.

| | 225 | 200 | 165 | 125 | 100 | 75 |

Model TT Tokarev

Yugoslavian version of Soviet Tokarev. Chambered for 9mm Parabellum, with safety added to make importation legal. Has 4.5" barrel, 9-shot magazine and blued finish. Checkered plastic grips. Importation began in 1988.

| | 350 | 225 | 175 | 150 | 125 | 100 |

Model ZC-.380

Scaled-down version of Tokarev. Chambered for .380 ACP. Has 3.5" barrel and holds 8 shots. Finish and grips are same as on full-sized version. Importation from Yugoslavia began in 1988.

| | 295 | 225 | 175 | 150 | 125 | 100 |

Aussie Model

Introduced in 1996. Australian-designed semi-automatic pistol made in Spain. Chambered for 9mm or .40 S&W cartridge. Polymer frame, with nickeled steel slide. Sold with 10-shot magazine. Barrel length 4.75"; weight 23 oz.

| | 400 | 350 | 300 | 250 | 200 | 100 |

Regulator

Built by Uberti. Single-action revolver has case hardened frame, polished brass trigger guard and backstrap. Barrel and cylinder are blued. One piece walnut grips. Choice of chambers in .44-40, .45 LC or .357 Magnum. Barrel lengths 4.75", 5.5" to 7.5". Weight about 34 oz., with 5.75" barrel.

| | 395 | 325 | 275 | 175 | — | — |

	NIB	EXC.	V.G.	GOOD	FAIR	POOR

Regulator Deluxe

Same as above, with steel trigger guard and backstrap. Chambered in .45 Long Colt only.

	375	300	250	150	—	—

AMERICAN ARMS
Garden Grove, California

Eagle .380

Pistol was a stainless steel copy of Walther PPKS. Semi-automatic blowback chambered for .380 ACP. Double-action, 3.25" barrel and 6-shot detachable magazine. Optional feature a black Teflon finish, that would increase value by 10 percent. Company ceased production in 1985.

	—	325	250	195	150	100

AMERICAN ARMS CO.
Boston, Massachusetts

History of American Arms is rather sketchy. It appears the company was formed in 1853 as G. H. Fox Co., then became American Tool & Machine Co. in 1865. In 1870, they formed a new corporation called American Arms Company, with George Fox as principle stockholder. This corporation was dissolved in 1873; a second American Arms Co. was incorporated in 1877 and a third in 1890. It is unclear if these corporations had essentially the same owners, but George H. Fox appears as a principle owner in two of the three. One could assume that financial problems forced them to bankrupt one corporation and reorganize under another. American Arms manufactured firearms in Boston, Massachusetts, from 1866 until 1893. In 1893 they moved to Bluffton, Alabama and manufactured guns until 1901.

Fox Model "Swing Out" Hammer Double

Manufactured from 1870 to 1884. Designed by George H. Fox, not to be confused with A.H. Fox. Model unusual, in that barrel swings to right for loading and barrel release is located on tang. Comes in 10- and 12-gauge, 26", 28", 30" and 32" with twist Damascus or laminated barrels. Early production models have conventional soldered together barrels. Later variations after 1878, feature a unique design in that barrels are dovetailed together. Guns could be ordered with several options and choices of finish. These would add premium value to a particular gun.

	—	—	2000	950	400	150

Semi-Hammerless Double

Manufactured from 1892 to 1901. Features cocking lever that cocks an internal firing pin. Comes in 12-gauge, with 30" twist barrels.

	—	—	1500	750	350	150

Whitmore Model Hammerless Double

Manufactured from 1890 to 1901. Comes in 10-, 12- and 16-gauge, with 28", 30" or 32" twist laminated or Damascus barrels. Marked "Whitmore's Patent".

	—	—	1500	775	375	150

Semi-Hammerless Single-Barrel

Manufactured from 1882 to 1901. Comes in 10-, 12- and 16-gauge, with 28", 30" or 32" twist or Damascus barrel.

	—	—	1500	750	300	100

TOP-BREAK REVOLVERS

Spur Trigger Single-Action Five-Shot Revolver

Revolvers made between 1883 and 1887 in .38 S&W only. Feature an unusual manual ring extractor and double-fluted cylinder. Nickel plated, with hard rubber grips. Marked "American Arms Company Boston Mass.

	—	550	300	100	75	25

Standard Trigger Double-Action Model 1886 Revolver

Standard trigger and trigger guard. Comes in .32 short and .38 S&W, with 3.5" barrel. Blue or nickel finish. Early models equipped with ring extractor and double fluted cylinder. Later variations have standard star extractor and single fluted cylinder.

	—	750	300	100	75	25

Hammerless Model 1890 Double-Action

Manufactured from 1890 to 1901. Has adjustable single- or double-stage trigger pull and several unusual safety devices. Comes in .32 and .38 S&W, with 3.25" ribbed barrel, fluted cylinder, nickel

	NIB	EXC.	V.G.	GOOD	FAIR	POOR

finish, hard rubber grips with logo and ivory or mother of pearl grips. Marked "American Arms Co. Boston/Pat. May 25, 1886". Top strap marked "Pat. Pending" on early models and "Pat's May 25'86/Mar 11'89/June 17'90" on later models.

	NIB	EXC.	V.G.	GOOD	FAIR	POOR
	—	750	300	100	75	25

DOUBLE-BARREL DERRINGERS

American Arms Co. manufactured a two-barrel derringer-style pocket pistol. Barrels were manually rotated to load and fire the weapon. Pistol had nickel-plated brass frame, blued barrels and walnut grips. Markings were: "American Arms Co. Boston, Mass." on one barrel and "Pat. Oct. 31, 1865" on other barrel. Approximately 2,000-3,000 produced between 1866 and 1878. Beware of fakes!

Combination .22 caliber R.F. and .32 caliber R.F.

Two-caliber combination, with 3" barrel and square butt only. Most common variation.

	NIB	EXC.	V.G.	GOOD	FAIR	POOR
	—	—	850	350	150	100

.32 caliber R.F., Both Barrels

3" barrel, with square butt.

	NIB	EXC.	V.G.	GOOD	FAIR	POOR
	—	—	1050	500	195	125

.38 caliber R.F., Both Barrels

2-5/8" barrel, with bird's-head grips.

	NIB	EXC.	V.G.	GOOD	FAIR	POOR
	—	—	1100	550	225	150

.38 caliber R.F., Both Barrels

2-5/8" barrel, with bird's-head grip. Rare variation.

	NIB	EXC.	V.G.	GOOD	FAIR	POOR
	—	—	2500	1075	350	200

.41 caliber R.F., Both Barrels

2-5/8" barrel, with square butt only.

	NIB	EXC.	V.G.	GOOD	FAIR	POOR
	—	—	1850	900	200	100

AMERICAN BARLOCK WONDER

See—Crescent Arms Co.

AMERICAN CLASSIC

(Eagle Imports)
Wanamassa, NJ

American Classic 1911-A1

Full-size 1911-A1-style semi-automatic chambered in .45 ACP. Series 70 lockwork, 8-round magazine with bumper pad, lowered ejection port, throated barrel, checkered wood grips, military-style sights, matte blue or hard chrome finish and 5" barrel. Weight 39 oz. American Classic II has additional features including Novak-style sights, combat trigger and hammer, extended safety and slide stop, front slide serrations, deep blue or hard chrome finish. **NOTE:** Add $35 for Classic II; $50 for hard chrome finish.

	NIB	EXC.	V.G.	GOOD	FAIR	POOR
	435	400	350	325	250	200

American Classic Commander/Amigo

Same features as American Classic II, except 4.25" barrel, weight 35 oz. Amigo model is Officer's Model style, with 3.5" barrel, 7-round magazine. **NOTE:** Add $50 for hard chrome finish; $35 for Amigo model.

	NIB	EXC.	V.G.	GOOD	FAIR	POOR
	460	425	360	335	260	200

American Classic Trophy Model

Same features as American Classic II, except 5.5" barrel, dovetail front fiber optic sight, Novak-style rear, ambidextrous safety, reverse plug recoil system with full-length guide rod, beveled mag well, checkered mainspring housing and hard chrome finish.

	NIB	EXC.	V.G.	GOOD	FAIR	POOR
	650	600	550	500	400	300

American Classic .22 Model

Full-size alloy-frame 1911-style pistol. Chambered for .22 LR. Same dimensions as American Classic, with military-type sights, checkered wood grips, matte blue finish and two 10-round magazines.

	NIB	EXC.	V.G.	GOOD	FAIR	POOR
	300	275	230	200	160	100

NIB	EXC.	V.G.	GOOD	FAIR	POOR

AMERICAN DERRINGER CORP.
Waco, Texas

Model 1 Derringer

Fashioned after Remington over/under derringer. High quality rugged pistol. Built from high tensile strength stainless steel. Over 60 different rifle and pistol calibers to choose from, on special order. Upper barrel can be chambered different from lower barrel, on request. Available in high polish finish or satin finish. Offered with rosewood, bacote, walnut or blackwood grips. Ivory, bonded ivory, stag or pearl are available at extra cost. Overall length 4.8"; barrel length 3"; width across frame .9"; width across grip 1.2". Typical weight 15 oz. in .45 caliber. All guns furnished with French fitted leatherette case. Prices determined by caliber. **NOTE:** Premium for rifle cartridges.

Caliber: .22 Long Rifle through .357 Magnum and .45 ACP

550	450	350	285	225	150

Calibers: .41 Mag., .44-40, .44 Special, .44 Mag., .45 Long Colt, .410 Bore, .22 Hornet, .223 Rem., 30-30, and .45-70 Gov't.

600	525	450	350	250	150

Model 1 Lady Derringer

Similar to Model 1. Chambered for .38 Special, .32 Magnum, .45 Colt or .357 Magnum. Offered in two grades. **NOTE:** Add $75 for .45 Colt and .45/.410; $50 for .357 Magnum.

Deluxe

High polished stainless steel. Scrimshawed ivory grips, with cameo or rose design.

700	600	500	300	225	150

Deluxe Engraved

Same as above. Hand engraved in 1880s style.

750	600	500	400	250	150

Model 1 NRA 500 Series

Limited edition of 500. Available in gold and blue finishes over stainless steel.

600	450	300	150	125	100

Model 1 Texas Commemorative

Built with solid brass frame and stainless steel barrel. Dimensions same as Model 1. Grips are stag or rosewood and offered in .45 Colt, .44-40 or .38 Special. Barrels marked "Made in the 150th Year of Texas Freedom". Limited to 500 pistols in each caliber.

Caliber: .38 Special

425	350	250	150	100	75

Calibers: .45 Colt and .44-40

600	450	300	200	125	100

Deluxe Engraved

Special serial number engraved on backstrap.

700	550	395	350	175	125

Model 1 125th Anniversary Commemorative

Built to commemorate 125th anniversary of derringer, 1866 to 1991. Similar to Model 1. Marked with patent date "December 12, 1865". Brass frame and stainless steel barrel. Chambered for .44-40, .45 Colt or .38 Special.

425	350	250	150	100	65

Deluxe Engraved

650	475	375	250	175	100

Model 2 Pen Pistol

Introduced in 1993. Legal pistol that cannot be fired from its pen position. Requires it be pulled apart and bent 80 degrees to fire. Made from stainless steel. Offered in .22 LR, .25 ACP and .32 ACP. Length in pen form 5.6"; pistol form 4.2". Barrel length 2". Diameter varies from 1/2" to 5/8". Weight 5 oz. No longer in production.

600	395	300	225	100	85

Model 3

Single-barrel derringer. Barrel length 2.5" and swings down to load. Frame and barrel stainless steel. Offered in .38 Special or .32 Magnum. Weighs about 8 oz. Discontinued.

200	175	115	75	65	50

	NIB	EXC.	V.G.	GOOD	FAIR	POOR

Model 4

Similar in appearance to Model 3. Fitted with 4.1" barrel. Overall length 6"; weight about 16.5 oz. Chambered for 3" .410 bore, .45 Long Colt, .44 Magnum or .357 Magnum. **NOTE:** Add $150 for .45-70; $100 for .44 Magnum.

	NIB	EXC.	V.G.	GOOD	FAIR	POOR
	500	425	350	250	100	75

Engraved

	NIB	EXC.	V.G.	GOOD	FAIR	POOR
	1000	900	600	400	275	150

Alaskan Survival Model

Similar to Model 4, with upper barrel chambered for .45-70 and lower barrel for .45 LC or .410. Both barrels can also be chambered for .44 Magnum or .45-70. Comes with over-sized rosewood grips.

	NIB	EXC.	V.G.	GOOD	FAIR	POOR
	700	625	395	250	175	100

Model 6

Double-barrel derringer fitted with 6" barrel chambered for .45 LC or .410 bore. Weighs about 21 oz. Rosewood grips are standard. Optional calibers .357 Magnum or .45 ACP. **NOTE:** Oversize grips optional and add about $35 to value.

	NIB	EXC.	V.G.	GOOD	FAIR	POOR
	750	600	450	300	150	100

Engraved

	NIB	EXC.	V.G.	GOOD	FAIR	POOR
	1000	900	700	450	275	150

Double-Action Derringer

High Standard-type double-barrel double-action derringer. Chambered for .22 LR or .22 Magnum. Barrel length 3.5"; overall length 5.125". Weighs about 11 oz. Finish blue with black grips.

NIB	EXC.	V.G.	GOOD	FAIR	POOR
295	245	175	100	85	75

DA 38 Double-Action Derringer

Similar to above. Chambered for .38 Special, .357 Magnum, 9mm Luger and .40 S&W. Finish satin stainless. Grip made from aluminum. Grips are rosewood or walnut. **NOTE:** For .40 S&W add $40.

	NIB	EXC.	V.G.	GOOD	FAIR	POOR
	500	400	300	200	150	100

Mini Cop 4-Shot

Four-barrel derringer chambered for .22 Magnum Rimfire cartridge.

	NIB	EXC.	V.G.	GOOD	FAIR	POOR
	600	395	300	225	100	85

Cop 4-Shot

Same as above. Chambered for .357 Magnum cartridge.

	NIB	EXC.	V.G.	GOOD	FAIR	POOR
	1000	900	500	325	175	100

Model 7 Derringer—Lightweight

Manufactured as a backup gun for police officers. Frame and barrels made of aircraft aluminum alloy; other parts are stainless steel. Weighs 7.5 oz. Appearance and function are similar to Model 1. Finish is a gray matte, with thin matte-finished grips of rosewood or bacote. Chambered for and priced as listed.

.32 S&W Long / .32 Magnum

	NIB	EXC.	V.G.	GOOD	FAIR	POOR
	500	400	250	125	100	75

.38 S&W and .380 ACP

	NIB	EXC.	V.G.	GOOD	FAIR	POOR
	500	400	250	125	100	75

.22 LR and .38 Special

	NIB	EXC.	V.G.	GOOD	FAIR	POOR
	500	400	250	125	100	75

.44 Special

	NIB	EXC.	V.G.	GOOD	FAIR	POOR
	650	525	400	300	250	150

Model 8

Single-action two-shot target pistol, with manually operated hammer block safety. Safety automatically disengages when hammer is cocked. Barrel length 8". Chambered for .45 Colt and .410 shotshell. Weight 24 oz.

	NIB	EXC.	V.G.	GOOD	FAIR	POOR
	700	600	475	350	175	100

Engraved

	NIB	EXC.	V.G.	GOOD	FAIR	POOR
	1500	1000	675	450	300	125

NIB	EXC.	V.G.	GOOD	FAIR	POOR

Model 10 Derringer

Similar to Model 1, with frame of aluminum alloy. All other parts including barrels, stainless steel. Has a gray matte finish and thin grips of rosewood or bacote. Weighs 10 oz. Chambered for .38 Special, .45 ACP or .45 Colt. **NOTE:** For .45 Colt add $75.

500	375	250	125	100	75

Model 11 Derringer

Stainless steel barrel and all other parts aluminum. Weighs 11 oz. Chambered for .38 Special, .380 Auto, .32 Magnum, .22 LR and .22 Magnum. Grips and finish are the same as on Model 10.

500	375	250	125	100	75

Semmerling LM-4

LM-4 was designed as ultimate police backup/defense weapon. Manually operated 5-shot repeater only 5.2" long, 3.7" high and 1" wide. Chambered for .45 ACP. Undoubtedly smallest 5-shot .45 ever produced. LM-4 made of a special tool steel. Either blued or at extra cost hard chrome-plated. Stainless steel version also available. LM-4 is not a semi-automatic, although it physically resembles one. Slide is flicked forward and back after each double-action squeeze of the trigger. This weapon is virtually hand-built. Features high visibility sights and smooth trigger. **NOTE:** Hard chrome add $200; stainless steel add 35 percent.

3500	3000	2000	1500	600	200

LM-5

Built of stainless steel. Semi-automatic chambered for .32 or .25 Auto. Barrel length 2.25"; overall length 4"; height 3". Wooden grips standard. Offered in limited quantities. Weight about 15 oz. Discontinued.

550	450	295	150	100	50

Millennium Series 2000

Chambered for .38 Special, .45 Colt or .44-40. Single-action. Fitted with scrimshaw grips, with yellow rose of Texas on left side and Lone Star flag on right side. Weight about 15 oz. Supplied with red velvet box with silver inlay. Introduced in 1999.

500	325	200	150	100	75

Gambler Millennium 2000

Similar to Millennium Series. Fitted with rosewood grips, with etched Lone Star of Texas. Supplied with brown leatherette box, with copper logo inlay.

700	600	500	350	200	100

Women of Texas Series

Same features as Millennium Series 2000. Stamped "Women of Texas Series 2000".

700	600	500	350	200	100

Cowboy Series 2000

Same features as Gambler Millennium 2000. Stamped on barrel "Cowboy Series 2000" .

700	600	500	350	200	100

AMERICAN FIRE ARMS MFG. CO., INC.
San Antonio, Texas

Company operated between 1972 and 1974, producing .25 ACP pocket pistol and stainless steel .38 Special derringer. A .380 Auto was produced on an extremely limited basis.

American .38 Special Derringer

Well-made stainless steel over/under derringer. Similar in appearance and function to old Remington over/under. Had 3" barrels that pivoted upward for loading. Single-action that had an automatic selector and spur trigger. Smooth grips were of walnut. Approximately 3,500 manufactured between 1972 and 1974.

—	300	225	150	125	90

American .25 Automatic

Small blowback semi-automatic pocket pistol. Chambered for .25 ACP cartridge. Had 2" barrel. Made of stainless steel or blued carbon steel. Grips were plain uncheckered walnut. Detachable magazine held 7 shots. Manufactured until 1974. **NOTE:** Stainless steel add 20 percent.

—	275	200	125	100	75

American .380 Automatic

Similar to .25 except larger. Barrel was 3.5". Made in stainless steel only. Grips were smooth walnut and held 8 shots. Only 10 of these .380s manufactured between 1972 and 1974. Extremely rare,

NIB	EXC.	V.G.	GOOD	FAIR	POOR

but there is little collector base for this company's products. Value is difficult to estimate.

	600	550	475	375	200

AMERICAN FRONTIER FIREARMS
Aguanga, California

1871, 72 Open Top Standard Model

Offered in .38- or .44-caliber, with non-rebated cylinder. Barrel lengths 7.5" or 8" in round. Blued finish except silver backstrap and trigger guard. Walnut grips.

795	625	500	400	225	100

Richards & Mason Conversion 1851 Navy Standard Model

Offered in .38- and .44-calibers, with Mason ejector assembly and non-rebated cylinder. Choice of octagon barrels in 4.75", 5.5" or 7.5". Blued finish, with blued backstrap and trigger guard. Walnut grips.

795	625	500	400	225	100

1860 Richards Army Model

Chambered for .44 Colt and .38-caliber. Rebated cylinder with or without ejector assembly. Barrel length 7.5". High polish blue finish, with silver trigger guard and case hardened frame. **NOTE:** Guns shipped without ejector assembly will be supplied with a ramrod and plunger, typical of the period.

795	625	500	400	225	100

AMERICAN GUN CO., NEW YORK
Norwich, Connecticut
Maker—Crescent Firearms Co.

Side-by-Side Shotgun

Typical trade gun made around turn of the century, by Crescent Firearms Co., to be distributed by H. & D. Folsom. These are sometimes known as "Hardware Store Guns", as that is where many were sold. This particular gun chambered for 12-, 16- or 20-gauge and produced with or without external hammers. Length of barrels varied as did chokes. Some produced with Damascus barrels; some with fluid steel. Latter are worth approximately 25 percent more. **NOTE:** Full listing of most variations of Crescent Arms Co. and shotguns marked with American Gun Co., see "Crescent F.A. Co.

Knickerbocker Pistol—See Knickerbocker

AMERICAN HISTORICAL FOUNDATION
Ashland, Virginia

American Historical Foundation, is a private organization that commissions historical commemorative's. Secondary market sales are infrequent and difficult to confirm. American Historical Foundation sells only direct and not through dealers or distributors. For information on past and current issues, contact American Historical Foundation at 10195 Maple Leaf Court, Ashland, VA 23005.

AMERICAN INDUSTRIES
Cleveland, Ohio
aka CALICO LIGHT WEAPONS SYSTEMS
Sparks, Nevada

Calico M-100

Semi-automatic carbine. Has 16.1" barrel, with flash suppressor. Chambered for .22 LR. Features folding stock, full shrouding hand guards, 100-round capacity, helical feed, detachable magazine, ambidextrous safety, pistol-grip storage compartment, black finished alloy frame and adjustable sights. Introduced in 1986.

500	400	350	250	200	100

Calico M-100P/M-110

Similar to M-100. .22 rimfire, with 6" barrel, muzzle-brake and no shoulder stock.

500	400	350	250	200	75

Calico M-100S Sporter/M-105

Similar to Model 100, with futuristically styled walnut buttstock and forearm.

500	400	350	250	200	75

Calico M-101 Solid Stock Carbine

Introduced in 1994. Features 100-round magazine and composite buttstock that is removable.

550	450	400	300	200	75

	NIB	EXC.	V.G.	GOOD	FAIR	POOR

Calico M-900

Black polymer-stocked rifle similar to M-100S. Chambered for 9mm Parabellum. Has delayed blowback action. Features stainless steel bolt and alloy receiver. Cocking handle is non-reciprocating. Rear sight is fixed, with adjustable front. A 50-round magazine standard; 100-round model optional. Introduced in 1989.

750	575	425	350	275	100

Calico M-950 Pistol

Similar to Model 900 rifle, with 6" barrel. No shoulder stock.

750	575	425	350	275	100

Calico M-951

M-951 is a tactical carbine, with sliding buttstock. Barrel 6" in length; weighs about 7 lbs.

750	575	425	350	275	100

Calico M-951S

Same as above. Furnished with more conventional buttstock. Referred to as light tactical carbine. Weighs about 7.25 lbs.

750	575	425	350	275	100

AMERICAN INTERNATIONAL
Salt Lake City, Utah
aka American Research & Development

180 Carbine (SAM-180)

Firearm imported from Austria. Semi-automatic 16.5" barreled carbine. Chambered for .22 LR. Sights are adjustable and stock made of high-impact plastic. Unique drum magazine holds 177 rounds and affixed to top of receiver. A select-fire version available for law enforcement agencies, only, and optional laser lock sight system. Later manufactured by Feather Industries in Boulder, Colorado. Now known as SAM-180.

1400	1200	650	400	200	100

AMERICAN TACTICAL IMPORTS
Summerville, So. Carolina

AT CS/FS Series

These SA/DA pistols in 9mm, .40 S&W and .45 ACP, were made in Turkey and imported into the U.S. in 2010 and 2011. Model designations were CS9, CS40, C45; and FS9, FS40. Features include a high-capacity magazine, ported slide and polymer frame.

350	300	250	200	150	100

AT MS380

Similar to Beretta Cheetah design. This .380 model was imported from Turkey in 2010.

325	285	225	185	135	100

GSG-522

Semi-automatic tactical rifle chambered in .22 LR. Features include 16.25" barrel; black finish overall; polymer fore-end and buttstock; backup iron sights; receiver-mounted Picatinny rail; 10-round magazine. Several other rifle and carbine versions available. This model is part of ATI's German Sporting Gun Series.

425	365	325	250	200	100

GSG-AK

Part of the German Sporting Gun Series, this model is patterned after the AK-47. Offered in several variations and stock designs. **NOTE:** Add 25 percent for hardwood stock and gold receiver; 20 percent for adjustable polymer stock.

325	285	225	185	135	100

FX Series

Series of 1911-style .45 ACP pistols imported from Philippines. Available in single- or double-stack magazines. Offered in various barrel lengths, with diamond-checkered wood grips, low-profile sights, blue or stainless finishes. FX Thunderbolt model has adjustable sights, Picatinny rail, competition or bull barrel. Other variations include FX Fat Boy, a high-capacity, double-stack model with 3.2" barrel; FX 45K with threaded barrel and bobbed hammer; mid-size Commander style FX GI; and Officer-size Titan model. **NOTE:** Add $200 for Thunderbolt model (shown); $100 for 45K or Fat Boy.

500	465	425	375	250	150

	NIB	EXC.	V.G.	GOOD	FAIR	POOR

SX Cavalry Shotgun

This over/under series of shotguns is made in Turkey. Offered in 12-, 20-, 28-gauges and .410 bore. Features include Turkish walnut stock, five choke tubes, single selective trigger, extractors and alloy receiver with light engraving.

425	375	325	275	225	200

TAC-P, TAC-S Shotgun Series

This duo of tactical shotguns consists of a slide-action (TAC-P) and semi-auto model (TAC-S) with similar features. In 12-gauge only. Barrel length is 18.5", with a cylinder bore and synthetic stock has a pistol-grip. Both models are also available with an interchangeable 28" barrel, with three choke tubes. **NOTE:** Add $100 for this option.

TAC-P

225	200	165	125	100	75

TAC-S

325	285	225	185	135	100

AMERICAN WESTERN ARMS INC. (AWA)
Delray Beach, Florida

Lightning Rifle LE

Copy of Colt Lightning slide-action rifle. Chambered for .32-20, .38 Special, .38-40, .44-40 or .45 Colt cartridge. Choice of round barrel lengths in 20" or 24". Engraved AWA logo and stag scene on receiver. Limited edition to 500 guns.

1200	950	775	500	300	175

Lightning Rifle

Slide-action rifle chambered for those cartridges above. Choice of 24" round or octagon barrel. Blued finish. **NOTE:** Add $40 for octagon barrel.

800	675	500	400	300	175

Lightning Carbine

As above, with 20" round or octagon barrel. **NOTE:** Add $40 for octagon barrel.

800	675	500	400	300	175

Lightningbolt

Handgun version of Lightning rifle, with 12" barrel and variety of finishes. Chambered in .45 Colt. Values shown are for blued version.

1000	800	675	500	400	200

AMES, N.P. PISTOLS
Springfield, Massachusetts

Overall length-11-5/8"; barrel length-6"; caliber-.54. Markings: on lockplate forward of hammer "N.P. AMES/SPRINGFIELD/MASS", on tail either "USN" or "USR" over date; on barrel standard U.S. Navy inspection marks. N. P. Ames of Springfield, Massachusetts received a contract from U.S. Navy, in September 1842, for delivery of 2,000 single-shot muzzle-loading percussion pistols. All are distinguished by having a lock mechanism that lies flush with right side of stock. On first 300 Ames pistols, this lock terminates in a point; balance produced made with locks with a rounded tail. This "boxlock" had been devised by Henry Nock in England and was adapted to U.S. Navy for percussion pistols they ordered from Ames and Derringer. In addition to the 2,000 pistols for Navy, U.S. Revenue Cutter Service purchased 144 (distinguished by "U S R" marks) for the forerunner of U.S. Coast Guard. Latter commands triple price over "U S N" marked pistols, while Navy pistols with pointed tails quadruple value.

—	—	2700	1100	650	400

AMES SWORD CO.
Chicopee Falls, Massachusetts

Turbiaux Le Protector

Ames Sword Co., became one of three U.S. companies that produced this unique, French palm-squeezer pistol. Design consists of a round disk, with protruding barrel on one side and lever on the other. Disk contains a cylinder that holds either seven 8mm rimfire or ten 6mm rimfire cartridges. Barrel protrudes between fingers and lever trigger is squeezed to fire the weapon. Design was patented in 1883 and sold successfully in France into 1890s. In 1892, Peter Finnegan bought the patents and brought them to Ames Sword. He contracted with them to produce 25,000 pistols for Minneapolis Firearms Company. After approximately 1,500 were delivered, Finnegan declared insolvency and after litigation, Ames secured full patent rights. Ames Company produced Protector Revolvers until at least 1917. (See Chicago Firearms Co.

	NIB	EXC.	V.G.	GOOD	FAIR	POOR

and Minneapolis Firearms Co.)

	—	—	3500	1800	900	550

AMT
formerly Arcadia Machine and Tool
Irwindale, California
See also—Galena Industries Inc.

AMT is one of several companies that succeeded Auto Mag Corp., original manufacturer of Auto Mag pistols, operated from approximately 1984 to 1998. Prices in this section are for these earlier AMT-built guns, only. In 1998, Galena Ind., of Sturgis, South Dakota, purchased the rights to produce most of the AMT-developed firearms and manufactured several models from 1999 to 2001. In 2005, the rights to several AMT models were acquired by Crusader Gun Co. of Houston, parent company of High Standard Mfg. Co. Also see listing for Auto Mag.

HANDGUNS

Lightning

Single-action semi-automatic .22-caliber pistol. Available with barrel lengths of 5" (Bull only), 6.5", 8.5", 10.5" and 12.5" (either Bull or tapered). Adjustable sights as well as trigger. Grips are checkered black rubber. Manufactured between 1984 and 1987.

—	450	350	215	125	85

Bull's Eye Regulation Target

As above, with 6.5" vent rib bull barrel, wooden target grips and extended rear sight. Manufactured in 1986 only.

—	475	375	250	200	100

Baby Automag

Similar to above, with 8.5" ventilated rib barrel and Millett adjustable sights. Approximately 1,000 manufactured.

—	600	450	375	225	150

Automag II

Stainless steel semi-automatic .22 Magnum pistol. Available with 3-3/8", 4.5 and 6" barrel lengths, Millett adjustable sights and grips of black grooved plastic. First manufactured in 1987.

700	600	500	400	200	100

Automag III

Semi-automatic pistol chambered for .30 Carbine and 9mm Win. Magnum cartridge. Barrel length 6.37"; overall length 10.5". Magazine capacity 8 rounds. Fitted with Millett adjustable rear sight and carbon fiber grips. Stainless steel finish. Pistol weighs 43 oz.

600	500	400	250	100	80

Automag IV

Similar in appearance to Automag III. Chambered for .45 Win. Magnum. Magazine capacity 7 rounds. Weight 46 oz.

700	600	500	400	225	100

Automag V

Introduced in 1993. Similar in appearance to Automag models. Chambered for .50-caliber cartridge. Limited production run of 3,000 pistols, with special serial number from "1 of 3000" to "3000 of 3000". Barrel length 6.5". Magazine capacity 5 rounds. Weighs 46 oz. Production stopped in 1995. **NOTE:** Add $300 each for extra conversion barrels in .45 WM or 10mm.

800	700	600	500	400	150

Javelina

Produced in 1992. Chambered for 10mm cartridge. Fitted with 7" barrel, with adjustable sights. Rubber wrap-around grips. Adjustable trigger. Magazine is 8 rounds. Weight about 47 oz.

1000	900	750	600	400	200

Back Up Pistol

Small semi-automatic pocket pistol. Chambered for .22 LR or .380 ACP cartridges. Fitted with 2.5" barrel. Offered with black plastic or walnut grips. Weighs 18 oz. Magazine capacity 5 rounds. Originally manufactured by TDE, then Irwindale Arms Inc. and then by AMT.

450	325	175	125	100	85

	NIB	EXC.	V.G.	GOOD	FAIR	POOR

.45 ACP, .40 S&W, 9mm

	NIB	EXC.	V.G.	GOOD	FAIR	POOR
	465	350	200	150	100	85

.38 Super, .357 SIG, .400 CorBon
NOTE: Prices for current production by High Standard Mfg. Co.

	NIB	EXC.	V.G.	GOOD	FAIR	POOR
	475	360	250	200	150	100

9mm, .38 Super, .40 S&W, .45 ACP

	NIB	EXC.	V.G.	GOOD	FAIR	POOR
	475	425	375	325	200	100

.380 Back Up II

Introduced in 1993. Similar to Back Up model. Addition of double safety extended finger grip on magazine and single-action-only. Special order pistol only.

	NIB	EXC.	V.G.	GOOD	FAIR	POOR
	425	300	250	200	150	100

Hardballer/Government Model

Similar to Colt Gold Cup .45 ACP. Offered in two versions: first has fixed sights and rounded slide top; second has adjustable Millett sights and matte rib. Magazine capacity 7 rounds. Wraparound rubber grips are standard. Long grip safety, beveled magazine well and adjustable trigger common to both variations. Weight 38 oz.

Hardballer
Adjustable sights.

	NIB	EXC.	V.G.	GOOD	FAIR	POOR
	600	500	350	275	200	125

Government Model
Fixed sights.

	NIB	EXC.	V.G.	GOOD	FAIR	POOR
	575	475	300	250	150	100

Longslide
Similar to Hardballer Model. Fitted with 7" barrel. Magazine capacity 7 rounds. Weighs 46 oz.

	NIB	EXC.	V.G.	GOOD	FAIR	POOR
	750	550	395	275	200	125

.400 Accelerator

Similar to models above. Chambered for .400 CorBon cartridge. Fitted with 7" barrel. Fully adjustable sights. Introduced in 1997.

	NIB	EXC.	V.G.	GOOD	FAIR	POOR
	600	500	350	275	200	125

Commando

Built on Government model-type action. Chambered for .40 S&W cartridge. Fitted with 5" barrel and fully adjustable sights. Introduced in 1997.

	NIB	EXC.	V.G.	GOOD	FAIR	POOR
	550	425	300	200	125	75

On Duty

Semi-automatic pistol. Features double-action-only trigger action or double-action with decocker. Chambered for 9mm, .40 S&W or .45 ACP calibers. Barrel length 4.5"; overall length 7.75". Finish is a black anodized matte. Carbon fiber grips are standard. Furnished with 3-dot sights. Weighs 32 oz.

	NIB	EXC.	V.G.	GOOD	FAIR	POOR
	450	350	250	200	150	100

Skipper

Identical to Hardballer, with 1" shorter barrel and slide. Discontinued in 1984.

	NIB	EXC.	V.G.	GOOD	FAIR	POOR
	—	450	325	275	200	125

Combat Skipper

Similar to Colt Commander. Discontinued in 1984.

	NIB	EXC.	V.G.	GOOD	FAIR	POOR
	—	425	300	250	200	125

RIFLES

Lightning

Patterned after Ruger 10/22. Said to have been discontinued for that reason. Rifle has 22" barrel and 25-round detachable magazine, with folding stock. Introduced in 1986.

	NIB	EXC.	V.G.	GOOD	FAIR	POOR
	375	250	175	125	75	50

Small Game Hunter

As above, with full stock and 10-round magazine. Introduced in 1986.

	NIB	EXC.	V.G.	GOOD	FAIR	POOR
	350	225	175	150	125	100

	NIB	EXC.	V.G.	GOOD	FAIR	POOR

Small Game Hunter II

Semi-automatic rifle chambered for .22 LR cartridge. Stock is checkered black matte nylon. Fitted with removable recoil pad for ammo, cleaning rod and knife. Rotary magazine holds 10 rounds. Stainless steel barrel and action. Barrel is a heavy weight target type, 22" long. Weight 6 lbs.

350	225	175	150	125	100

Hunter

Semi-automatic rifle chambered for .22 Rimfire Magnum cartridge. Stock is checkered black matte nylon. Other features similar to Small Game Hunter II, including weight.

375	250	200	150	125	100

Magnum Hunter

Similar to above. Chambered for .22 Rimfire Magnum cartridge. Fitted with 22" accurized barrel. Barrel and action are stainless steel. Comes standard with 5-round magazine and composite stock. Laminated stock was available at an extra cost, as is a 10-round magazine.

525	400	350	250	200	150

Target Model

Semi-automatic rifle chambered for .22 LR cartridge. Fitted with 20" target barrel. Weight about 7.5 lbs. Choice of Fajen or Hogue stock. **NOTE:** Hogue stock deduct $50.

600	500	450	300	200	—

Challenge Edition

Custom ordered .22-caliber semi-automatic rifle. Built on Ruger 10/22-like receiver. Offered in 18" or 22" barrel lengths, with all stainless steel construction. McMillan fiberglass stock. Weaver-style scope mounts.

1050	800	550	400	300	175

Single-Shot Standard

Custom-built rifle, with choice of barrel length, composite stock, adjustable trigger, post '64 Winchester action, all in stainless and chrome moly steel. Chambered for all standard calibers. First offered in 1996.

875	675	500	350	200	175

Single-Shot Deluxe

Custom-built rifle on Mauser-type action, with choice of match grade barrel lengths and custom Kevlar stock. Built from stainless and chrome moly steel. Chambered for all standard calibers. First offered in 1996.

1800	1400	950	650	400	225

Bolt-Action Repeating—Standard

Similar in construction and features to Standard Single-Shot rifle.

840	675	500	350	200	175

Bolt-Action Repeating—Deluxe

Similar in construction and features to Deluxe Single-Shot rifle.

1800	1400	950	650	400	225

ANCION MARX
Liege, Belgium

Company began production in 1860s, with a variety of cheaply made pinfire revolvers. They later switched to solid-frame, centerfire, "Velo-Dog"-type revolvers, chambered for 5.5mm or 6.35mm. They were marketed in various countries under many different trade names. Some of the names they will be found under are Cobalt, Extracteur, LeNovo, Lincoln and Milady. Quality of these revolvers is quite poor and collector interest, almost non-existent. Values do not usually vary because of trade names.

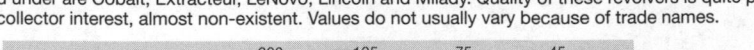

—	—	200	135	75	45

ANDERSON
Anderson, Texas

Under Hammer Pistol

Unmarked under hammer percussion pistol. Chambered for .45-caliber. Had 5" half-round/half-octagonal barrel, with all steel saw handle-shaped frame, flared butt with walnut grips. Finish blued. Little information on this pistol.

—	—	900	400	150	100

NIB	EXC.	V.G.	GOOD	FAIR	POOR

ANDRUS & OSBORN
Canton, Connecticut

Under Hammer Pistol

Pistol of percussion type. Chambered for .25-caliber. Part-round/part-octagonal barrel is 6" long. Features small silver star inlays along its length. Barrel marked "Andrus & Osborn/Canton Conn.", with an eagle stamped beside it. Marked "Cast Steel" near breech. Grips walnut. Finish browned. Active 1863 to 1867.

—	—	1550	625	200	100

ANSCHÜTZ, J.G. GMBH
Ulm, Germany

Originally founded in 1856, by Julius and Lusie Anschutz. Company was originally called J.G. Anschutz and manufactured a wide variety of firearms. In 1950 in Ulm, the new company was founded: J.G. Anschutz GmbH. Values for new guns fluctuate according to currency variations.

Mark 10 Target

Single-shot bolt-action rifle. Chambered for .22 LR cartridge. Has 26" heavy barrel, with adjustable target-type sights. Finish blued. Walnut target stock had an adjustable palm rest. Manufactured between 1963 and 1981.

500	425	350	210	150	100

Model 1403D

Single-shot target rifle chambered for .22 LR cartridge. Has 26" barrel. Furnished without sights. Has fully adjustable trigger. Blued finish, with walnut target-type stock.

850	775	675	500	375	250

Model 1407

Similar to Mark 10. Furnished without sights. Known as "I.S.U." model. Discontinued in 1981.

525	450	375	235	175	100

Model 1408

Heavier-barreled version of Model 1407.

525	450	375	240	180	105

Model 1411

Designed specifically to be fired from prone position.

750	650	450	210	150	100

Model 1413 Match

High-grade competition version, with heavy target barrel. Furnished without sights; optional sights extra. Walnut stock has adjustable cheekpiece.

775	675	550	400	275	150

Model 1416D HB Classic

Chambered for .22 LR cartridge. Magazine capacity 5 rounds. Fitted with match grade trigger and target grade barrel. Checkered walnut stock. Built on the 64 action.

900	725	595	400	225	125

Model 1416D KL Classic

Sporting rifle chambered for .22 LR cartridge. Fitted with American-style stock of European walnut or hardwood. Built on Anschutz Match 64 action. Left-handed model also offered.

900	725	595	300	200	100

Model 1416D Custom

Chambered for .22 LR cartridge. Features European-style stock, with Monte Carlo cheekpiece and schnabel fore-end.

875	650	550	300	200	100

Model 1418D KL Mannlicher

Hunting rifle, with full-length Mannlicher-type stock. Made with hand-checkered walnut. Chambered for .22 LR, with 5-round magazine. Open iron sights. Weight about 5.5 lbs.

1200	950	700	450	200	150

Model 1418/19

Lower-priced sporter model. Formerly imported by Savage Arms.

700	650	425	200	125	85

	NIB	EXC.	V.G.	GOOD	FAIR	POOR

Model 1433D

Centerfire version of Model 54 target rifle. Chambered for .22 Hornet. Special-order item. Features set trigger and 4-round detachable magazine. Finish blued, with full length Mannlicher stock. Discontinued in 1986.

	1500	950	700	400	200	100

Model 1533

Similar to Model 1433D, except chambered for .222 Remington cartridge. This model has a Mannlicher-style stock. Discontinued in mid 1990s.

	1200	1050	900	750	600	300

Model 1449D Youth

Bolt-action rifle chambered for .22 LR cartridge. Fitted with 16" barrel and adjustable rear sight. Stock is European hardwood, with 12.25" length of pull. Magazine capacity 5 rounds. No longer imported.

	450	300	250	100	75	60

Model Woodchucker

Sold by distributor RSR. Bolt-action .22-caliber. Similar to Model 1449D Youth.

	450	300	250	100	75	60

Model 1451E Target

Single-shot .22-caliber target rifle. Fitted with 22" barrel. Can be fitted with micrometer iron sights or telescope sights. Checkered pistol-grip and adjustable buttplate. Weight about 6.25 lbs.

	625	500	400	200	125	75

Model 1451R Sporter Target

Bolt-action target rifle chambered for .22 LR cartridge. Fitted with target-style stock and 22" heavy barrel. Furnished with no open sights. Two-stage target trigger is standard. Weight about 6.5 lbs.

	650	525	425	225	175	100

Model 1451D Custom

Similar to above. Fitted with checkered walnut sporting stock, with Monte Carlo comb and cheekpiece. Barrel length 22.75", with open sights. Weight about 5 lbs.

	675	550	450	250	150	100

Model 1451D Classic

Similar to Model 1451 Custom, with straight walnut stock. Weight about 5 lbs.

	700	600	500	300	150	100

Model 1516D KL Classic

Same as above. Chambered for .22 Magnum cartridge.

	775	600	500	300	200	100

Model 1516D KL Custom

Same as above. Chambered for .22 Magnum cartridge.

	850	650	550	450	250	100

Model 1517D Classic

Based on the 64 action. Bolt-action rifle chambered for .17 HMR cartridge. Fitted with 23" barrel. Checkered walnut stock. Magazine capacity 4 rounds. Weight about 5.5 lbs. Introduced in 2003.

	975	800	700	550	400	300

Model 1517D HB Classic

Similar to Model 1516D. Fitted with heavy barrel without sights. Weight about 6.2 lbs. Introduced in 2003.

	1050	850	750	550	400	300

Model 1517D Monte Carlo

Chambered for .17 HMR cartridge. Fitted with 23" barrel. Checkered walnut stock, with schnabel fore-end and Monte Carlo comb. Weight about 5.5 lbs. Introduced in 2003.

	1000	825	725	550	400	300

Model 1517MPR Multi-Purpose Rifle

Introduced in 2003. Features 25.5" heavy barrel without sights, two-stage trigger, hardwood stock with beavertail fore-end. Chambered for .17 HMR cartridge. Weight about 9 lbs. **NOTE:**

NIB	EXC.	V.G.	GOOD	FAIR	POOR

Available with a number of extra cost options.

NIB	EXC.	V.G.	GOOD	FAIR	POOR
1100	925	800	600	450	350

Model 1518D Mannlicher

Same as above. Chambered for .22 Magnum.

1200	950	700	350	225	125

Model 184

High-grade bolt-action sporting rifle chambered for .22 LR cartridge. Has 21.5" barrel, with folding-leaf sight. Finish blued, with checkered walnut Monte Carlo stock and schnabel fore-end. Manufactured between 1963 and 1981.

575	425	315	225	150	100

Model 54 Sporter

High-grade bolt-action sporting rifle chambered for .22 LR cartridge. Has 24" tapered round barrel and 5-shot detachable magazine. Features folding leaf-type rear sight. Finish blued, with checkered walnut Monte Carlo stock. Manufactured between 1963 and 1981.

750	675	600	350	250	125

Model 54M

Version chambered for .22 Rimfire Magnum cartridge.

800	700	625	375	275	125

Model 141

Bolt-action sporter chambered for .22 LR cartridge. Has 23" round barrel, with blued finish and walnut Monte Carlo stock. Manufactured between 1963 and 1981.

800	650	450	200	150	100

Model 141M

Chambered for .22 Rimfire Magnum cartridge.

825	675	475	225	175	100

Model 164

Bolt-action rifle. Fitted with 23" round barrel. Chambered for .22 LR cartridge. Has Monte Carlo stock with open sights. Magazine holds 5 rounds.

700	625	475	325	175	100

Model 164M

Same as above. Chambered for .22 Win. Magnum cartridge.

725	650	500	225	175	100

Model 153

Bolt-action sporting rifle chambered for .222 Remington cartridge. Has 24" barrel, with folding-leaf rear sight. Finish blued, with checkered French walnut stock. Featuring rosewood fore-end tip and pistol-grip cap. Manufactured between 1963 and 1981.

900	750	575	300	225	150

Model 153-S

Version offered with double-set triggers.

950	775	615	350	275	150

Model 64

Single-shot bolt-action rifle. Chambered for .22 LR cartridge. Has 26" round barrel. Furnished without sights. Finish blued. Walnut target-type stock featured beavertail forearm and adjustable buttplate. Manufactured between 1963 and 1981.

600	450	350	200	150	100

Model 64MS

Version designed for silhouette shooting. Has 21.25" barrel, blued finish and target-type walnut stock with stippled pistol-grip.

950	850	625	400	300	200

Model 64 MPR

Multi-purpose target repeater. Chambered for .22 LR cartridge. Fitted with 25.5" heavy barrel. Offered with optional sights. Choice of stainless steel barrel, with beavertail or beavertail with swivel rail. Weight about 9 lbs.

1100	850	700	400	300	200

	NIB	EXC.	V.G.	GOOD	FAIR	POOR

Model 64P

Bolt-action pistol, with adjustable trigger. Action is grooved for scope mounts and stock is synthetic. Barrel length 10". Chambered for .22 LR cartridge. Weight about 3 lb. 8 oz. Introduced in 1998.

	595	500	450	250	175	75

Model 64P Mag

Same as above. Chambered for .22 WMR cartridge.

	650	525	475	275	175	75

Model 54.18MS

High-grade silhouette rifle chambered for .22 LR cartridge. Has 22" barrel. Match-grade action, with fully adjustable trigger. Furnished without sights. Finish blued, with target-type walnut stock.

	2150	1500	995	500	300	200

Model 54.MS REP

Repeating rifle, with five-shot detachable magazine. Thumbhole stock, with vented forearm.

	2100	1600	1050	500	300	200

Model 2000 MK

Single-shot rifle chambered for .22 LR cartridge. Has 26" round barrel, with target-type sights. Finish blued, with walnut stock. Not imported after 1988.

	650	600	450	200	150	100

Model 2007 Supermatch

Introduced in 1993. Target rifle chambered for .22 LR cartridge. Has 19.75" barrel fitted to Match 54 action. Trigger is a two-stage. Stock is standard ISU configuration, with adjustable cheekpiece. Weighs about 10.8 lbs. Offered in left-hand model.

	2350	1850	1350	750	350	200

Model 2013 Supermatch

Similar to above. Fitted with International stock, with palm rest and buttstock hook. Weighs about 12.5 lbs.

	3200	2600	1850	1250	600	300

Model 1903D

Designed for advanced junior shooter. Target rifle has 25.5" barrel on Match 64 action, with single stage trigger. Walnut stock is fully adjustable. Weighs about 9.5 lbs. Offered in left-hand model.

	950	800	700	400	300	200

Model 1803D

High-grade target rifle chambered for .22 LR cartridge. Has 25.5" heavy barrel, with adjustable target sights. Features adjustable trigger. Finish blued, with light-colored wood stock. Dark stippling on pistol-grip and forearm. Stock features adjustable cheekpiece and buttplate. Introduced in 1987.

	1200	1000	775	600	450	200

Model 1808D RT Super

Single-shot running-boar type rifle. Chambered for .22 LR cartridge. Has 32.5" barrel furnished without sights. Finish blued, with heavy target-type walnut stock with thumbhole. Furnished with barrel weights. Weighs about 9.4 lbs. Available in left-hand version.

	1500	1300	1150	750	450	250

Model 1907ISU Standard Match

Chambered for .22 LR cartridge. Designed for both prone and position shooting. Weight 11.2 lbs. Built on a Match 54 action. Fitted with 26" barrel. Two-stage trigger. Removable cheekpiece and adjustable buttstock.

	1600	1350	1000	450	300	200

Model 1910 Super Match II

High-grade single-shot target rifle chambered for .22 LR cartridge. Has 27.25" barrel. Furnished with diopter-type target sights. Finish blued, with adjustable cheekpiece and buttplate. Walnut thumbhole stock. Hand and palm rest are not included.

	2300	1850	1400	900	500	250

Model 1911 Prone Match

Version has stock designed specifically for firing from prone position.

	1850	1550	1050	650	400	250

NIB	EXC.	V.G.	GOOD	FAIR	POOR

Model 1913 Super Match

Virtually hand-built match target rifle. Chambered for .22 LR cartridge. Features single-shot action. Has adjustable diopter-type sights on 27.25" heavy barrel. Custom-made gun. Features every target option conceivable. Finish blued, with fully adjustable walnut stock.

NIB	EXC.	V.G.	GOOD	FAIR	POOR
2700	2100	1600	1000	500	250

Model 1827B Biathlon

Repeating bolt-action target rifle chambered for .22 LR cartridge. Specially designed for biathlon competition. Production is quite limited and on a custom basis.

NIB	EXC.	V.G.	GOOD	FAIR	POOR
1850	1500	1150	800	400	250

Model 1827BT Biathlon

Similar to above. Features straight-pull Fortner bolt system. Available in left-hand model.

NIB	EXC.	V.G.	GOOD	FAIR	POOR
2900	2350	1750	1000	500	250

Achiever

Introduced in 1993. Target rifle chambered for .22 LR cartridge. Designed for beginner shooter. Furnished with 5-shot clip, but can be converted to single-shot with an adapter. Barrel length 19.5". Action is Mark 2000, with two-stage trigger. Stock pull is adjustable from 12" to 13". Weighs about 5 lbs.

NIB	EXC.	V.G.	GOOD	FAIR	POOR
525	400	295	150	125	100

Achiever Super Target

Designed for advanced junior shooter. Has 22" barrel. Weighs about 6.5 lbs.

NIB	EXC.	V.G.	GOOD	FAIR	POOR
575	450	325	175	125	100

Bavarian 1700

Classic-style sporting rifle chambered for .22 LR, .22 Rimfire Magnum, .22 Hornet and .222 Remington cartridges. Features 24" barrel, with adjustable sights. Has detachable magazine. Blued finish. Checkered walnut European-style Monte Carlo stock, with cheekpiece. Introduced in 1988. Values shown are for centerfire.

NIB	EXC.	V.G.	GOOD	FAIR	POOR
1300	950	600	400	300	200

Classic 1700

Similar in appearance to Bavarian. Furnished with American-style stock, with fluted comb. Same calibers as Bavarian. Weighs 6.75 lbs. **NOTE:** "Meister Grade" fancy wood stocks add $175.

NIB	EXC.	V.G.	GOOD	FAIR	POOR
1300	950	600	400	300	200

Custom 1700

Similar to Bavarian and Classic in caliber offerings, but offered with fancy European walnut stock, with roll-over cheekpiece with Monte Carlo. Pistol-grip has palm swell. Fitted with a white lined rosewood grip cap, with white diamond insert. Fore-end is schnabel type and stock checkered in ship line pattern. **NOTE:** "Meister Grade" fancy wood stocks add $175.

NIB	EXC.	V.G.	GOOD	FAIR	POOR
1650	1275	750	400	300	200

Model 1700 Mannlicher

Similar to 1700 Classic. Fitted with full-length stock. **NOTE:** "Meister Grade" fancy wood stocks add $175.

NIB	EXC.	V.G.	GOOD	FAIR	POOR
1550	1200	850	550	350	200

Model 1700 FWT

Model has same specifications as 1700 Custom. Fitted with McMillan laminated fiberglass stock. Weighs about 6.25 lbs.

NIB	EXC.	V.G.	GOOD	FAIR	POOR
1225	900	700	500	300	200

Model 1700 FWT Deluxe

Same as above. Fitted with laminated wood grain stock.

NIB	EXC.	V.G.	GOOD	FAIR	POOR
1125	900	800	550	300	200

Model 1710 D Classic

Bolt-action .22-caliber rifle, with 23.6" barrel and no sights. Walnut stock checkered. Magazine capacity 5 rounds. Weight about 7.3 lbs.

NIB	EXC.	V.G.	GOOD	FAIR	POOR
1300	1050	800	—	—	—

Model 1710 D HB Classic

Same as above, with heavy barrel. Weight about 8 lbs.

NIB	EXC.	V.G.	GOOD	FAIR	POOR
1350	1050	750	475	300	150

	NIB	EXC.	V.G.	GOOD	FAIR	POOR

Model 1710 D KL Monte Carlo

Same as Classic, with Monte Carlo stock. Folding leaf rear sight, with hooded front sight. Weight about 7.5 lbs.

	NIB	EXC.	V.G.	GOOD	FAIR	POOR
	1300	1000	775	425	325	175

Model 1710 D HB Classic 150 Years Anniversary Version

Similar to Model 1710 D HB Classic, with heavy stainless barrel. Stock laser-engraved, with 150th anniversary and 1901 "Germania" logos. Introduced in 2007. Only 150 units were produced.

	NIB	EXC.	V.G.	GOOD	FAIR	POOR
	2100	1700	1200	700	400	200

Model 1712 Silhouette Sporter

Chambered in .22 LR. Features include two-stage trigger, deluxe walnut stock, 21.6" blued sightless barrel and 5-shot magazine.

	NIB	EXC.	V.G.	GOOD	FAIR	POOR
	1150	925	675	425	200	100

Model 1702 D HB Classic

Chambered in .17 Mach 2. Features include finely-tuned double-stage trigger, walnut stock, 23" blued heavy sightless barrel and 5-shot magazine.

	NIB	EXC.	V.G.	GOOD	FAIR	POOR
	1300	1150	700	450	250	125

Model 1502 D HB Classic

Similar to Model 1702 D HB, with single-stage trigger and fewer refinements. **NOTE:** Add 10 percent for beavertail fore-end.

	NIB	EXC.	V.G.	GOOD	FAIR	POOR
	600	400	300	200	100	50

Model 1907 Club

Single-shot economy target rifle chambered in .22 LR. Features include target trigger, short lock time, 26" blued barrel, micrometer rear peep and hood front sights. Ambidextrous removable cheekpiece and walnut buttstock, with rubber buttplate and stock spacers. Weighs 9.7 lbs.

	NIB	EXC.	V.G.	GOOD	FAIR	POOR
	1800	1500	1200	900	—	—

Model 1717 D Classic

Bolt-action model chambered for .17 HMR cartridge. Fitted with 23.6" barrel, with no sights. Checkered walnut stock. Weight about 7.3 lbs.

	NIB	EXC.	V.G.	GOOD	FAIR	POOR
	1375	1000	675	475	300	150

Model 1717 D HB Classic

Same as above, with heavy barrel. Weight about 8 lbs.

	NIB	EXC.	V.G.	GOOD	FAIR	POOR
	1475	1200	700	495	325	175

Model 1727

Straight-pull action repeater based on Biathlon type action, with very fast lock time. Chambered for .22 Hornady Magnum Rimfire cartridge. German walnut stock, with cheekpiece and schnabel fore-end. Match-grade 22" barrel. Inatroduced in 2014.

	NIB	EXC.	V.G.	GOOD	FAIR	POOR
	3000	2650	2100	1450	800	350

Model 1730 D Classic

Bolt-action rifle chambered for .22 Hornet cartridge. Fitted with 23.6" barrel. Magazine capacity 5 rounds. Checkered walnut stock. No sights. Weight about 7.3 lbs.

	NIB	EXC.	V.G.	GOOD	FAIR	POOR
	1625	1325	750	525	350	225

Model 1730 D HB Classic

Same as above, with heavy barrel. Weight about 8 lbs.

	NIB	EXC.	V.G.	GOOD	FAIR	POOR
	1550	1250	700	495	325	175

Model 1730 D KL Monte Carlo

Model has Monte Carlo stock and folding leaf rear sight, with hooded front sight. Weight about 7.5 lbs.

	NIB	EXC.	V.G.	GOOD	FAIR	POOR
	1625	1325	750	525	350	225

Model 1733D KL Mannlicher

Introduced in 1993. Features Mannlicher stock built on a Match 54 action. Stock has rosewood schnabel tip. Checkering is done in a skip-line pattern. Chambered for .22 Hornet. Weighs about 6.25 lbs.

	NIB	EXC.	V.G.	GOOD	FAIR	POOR
	1450	1150	675	475	300	175

	NIB	EXC.	V.G.	GOOD	FAIR	POOR

Model 1740 D Classic

Bolt-action model chambered for .222 Remington cartridge. Checkered walnut stock, with no sights. Magazine capacity 3 rounds. Weight about 7.3 lbs.

	NIB	EXC.	V.G.	GOOD	FAIR	POOR
	1625	1325	750	525	350	225

Model 1743D

Chambered for classic .222 Remington cartridge. Model features a full-length Mannliche stock. Other features similar to 1740D series.

	NIB	EXC.	V.G.	GOOD	FAIR	POOR
	1350	1150	900	700	500	250

Model 1740 D HB Classic

Same as above, with heavy barrel. Weight about 7.3 lbs.

	NIB	EXC.	V.G.	GOOD	FAIR	POOR
	1550	1250	700	495	325	175

Model 1740 D KL Monte Carlo

Model fitted with Monte Carlo stock. Folding leaf rear sight and hooded front sight. Weight about 7.3 lbs.

	NIB	EXC.	V.G.	GOOD	FAIR	POOR
	1625	1325	750	525	350	225

Model 1770D

Built on an action designed specifically for centerfire cartridges. Chambered for .223 Remington round. Model has a medium weight 22" barrel, detachable 3-round magazine and large bolt handle. Choice of classic Monte Carlo or German-style walnut stock. Introduced in 2009.

	NIB	EXC.	V.G.	GOOD	FAIR	POOR
	2100	1700	1200	900	650	300

Model 1780D

A centerfire rifle chambered for .30-06 or .308 Winchester. Features include a 21" barrel, five-round detachable magazine and choice of a classic sporter walnut, thumbhole or camo finished stock.

	NIB	EXC.	V.G.	GOOD	FAIR	POOR
	1200	1050	900	750	600	300

Model 520/61

Blowback-operated semi-automatic rifle. Chambered for .22 LR cartridge. Has 24" barrel and 10-round detachable magazine. Finish blued, with checkered walnut stock. Discontinued in 1983.

	NIB	EXC.	V.G.	GOOD	FAIR	POOR
	675	550	300	200	100	85

Model 525 Sporter

Semi-automatic rifle chambered for .22 LR cartridge. Has 24" barrel, with adjustable sights and 10-round detachable magazine. Finish blued, with checkered Monte Carlo-type stock. Introduced in 1984. Carbine version with 20" barrel was originally offered, but discontinued in 1986.

	NIB	EXC.	V.G.	GOOD	FAIR	POOR
	725	600	450	250	175	100

Model RX22

An AR-style semi-automatic rifle chambered for .22LR cartridge. Features are similar to most AR-type rimfire rifles, including 16.5" barrel, Picatinny accessory rail, 10-shot magazine, folding iron backup sights, fixed or folding adjustable stock with pistol-grip and choice of black or desert tan finish. Also available with skeletonized wood stock. Made in Germany and imported by Steyr.

	NIB	EXC.	V.G.	GOOD	FAIR	POOR
	850	720	600	450	300	150

Exemplar

Bolt-action pistol built on Model 64 Match Action. Chambered for .22 LR cartridge. Has 10" barrel, with adjustable sights and 5-shot detachable magazine. Features adjustable two-stage trigger, with receiver grooved for attaching a scope. Walnut stock and fore-end are stippled. Introduced in 1987, discontinued in 1997.

	NIB	EXC.	V.G.	GOOD	FAIR	POOR
	500	400	300	225	175	100

Exemplar XIV

Similar to standard Exemplar, with 14" barrel. Introduced in 1988.

	NIB	EXC.	V.G.	GOOD	FAIR	POOR
	600	500	400	250	200	100

Exemplar Hornet

Chambered for .22 Hornet cartridge. Introduced in 1988.

	NIB	EXC.	V.G.	GOOD	FAIR	POOR
	800	650	575	300	200	100

	NIB	EXC.	V.G.	GOOD	FAIR	POOR

ANTI GARROTTER
England

Percussion belt pistol marked "Balls Pat. Steel". Oval is 7" long and barrel protrudes 1.5"; approximately .45-caliber. A cord runs from lock up and through sleeve and is fired by pulling the cord. Beware of modern fakes.

NIB	EXC.	V.G.	GOOD	FAIR	POOR
—	—	7500	3000	800	400

APACHE
Eibar, Spain
See—Ojanguren Y Vidosa

APALOZO HERMANOS
Zumorraga, Spain

Spanish manufacturer from approximately 1920 to 1936. Trademark, dove-like bird normally found impressed into grips.

Apaloza
Copy of Colt Police Positive revolver.

NIB	EXC.	V.G.	GOOD	FAIR	POOR
—	275	150	100	65	45

Paramount
Copy of Model 1906 Browning. Chambered for 6.35mm. "Paramount" stamped on slide and top of each grip plate.

NIB	EXC.	V.G.	GOOD	FAIR	POOR
—	275	175	100	50	30

Triomphe
Copy of Browning Model 1906 in caliber 6.35mm. Slide inscribed "Pistolet Automatique Triomphe Acier Comprime". "Cal. 6.35mm" stamped on each grip plate along with dove logo.

NIB	EXC.	V.G.	GOOD	FAIR	POOR
	275	175	100	50	30

AR-7 INDUSTRIES
Meriden, Connecticut

AR-7 Explorer
Semi-automatic .22-caliber takedown rifle. Fitted with 16" barrel and 8-round magazine. Adjustable rear peep sight. Weight 2.5 lbs.

NIB	EXC.	V.G.	GOOD	FAIR	POOR
200	150	90	65	50	25

AR-7C Explorer
Same as above, with camo stock.

NIB	EXC.	V.G.	GOOD	FAIR	POOR
225	175	100	65	50	25

AR-7 Sporter
Similar to standard AR-7, with metal skeleton stock. Aluminum ventilated shrouded barrel. Weight about 3.8 lbs.

NIB	EXC.	V.G.	GOOD	FAIR	POOR
250	150	120	75	65	35

AR-7 Target
Features tubular stock, with cantilever 3-9x40mm scope. Fitted with 16" bull barrel. Weight about 5.7 lbs.

NIB	EXC.	V.G.	GOOD	FAIR	POOR
300	200	150	75	65	35

AR-7 Bolt-Action
Model similar in all respects to standard semi-automatic AR-7, with bolt-action.

NIB	EXC.	V.G.	GOOD	FAIR	POOR
225	120	90	65	50	25

ARCUS
Bulgaria

Arcus-94
Introduced in 1998. Semi-automatic pistol chambered for 9mm cartridge. Fitted with ambidextrous safety and 10-round magazine. Imported from Bulgaria.

NIB	EXC.	V.G.	GOOD	FAIR	POOR
425	325	275	200	150	100

ARIZAGA, G.
Eibar, Spain

Spanish manufacturer prior to World War II.

	NIB	EXC.	V.G.	GOOD	FAIR	POOR

Arizaga (Model 1915)

7.65mm semi-automatic pistol. Patterned after Ruby-style military pistols. Magazine capacity 9 or 12 rounds. Wood grips.

	NIB	EXC.	V.G.	GOOD	FAIR	POOR
	—	275	195	100	75	45

Mondial

Similar design to Astra pistol in 100 series. Chambered for 6.35mm cartridge. Has Owl and Mondial on each grip plate.

	—	300	190	145	75	45

Pinkerton

Arizaga's standard model known to exist, with cartridge counter. Slide marked "Pinkerton Automatic 6.35".

	—	295	175	100	75	45

Warwick

Same design as Mondial in caliber 7.65mm. "Warwick" appears on each grip plate.

	—	300	190	145	75	45

ARIZMENDI, FRANCISCO
Eibar, Spain

Originally founded in 1890s, company was reformed in 1914 and manufactured semi-automatic pistols.

Singer

Singer was manufactured in a number of different variations and in calibers 6.35mm and 7.65mm. Earlier called Victor. 6.35mm model resembled Browning 1906; 7.65mm model Browning Model 1910.

6.35mm

	—	225	195	100	50	35

7.65mm

	—	175	125	75	50	35

Teuf Teuf

Teuf Teuf was chambered in calibers 6.35mm and 7.65mm. The 7.65mm was only slightly larger than 6.35mm model. Pistol copied its name from Browning Model 1906 and from Belgium Teuf Teuf. Pistol shown is a cartridge indicator model.

6.35mm

	—	225	195	100	50	35

7.65mm

	—	225	195	100	50	35

Walman

Walman was manufactured in a number of variations. In calibers 6.35mm, 7.65mm and .380-caliber. Earliest semi-automatic production was in 1908 through 1926. Certain variations were called American Model. Model in .380-caliber had a squeeze grip safety.

6.35mm

	—	225	195	100	50	35

7.65mm

	—	250	200	125	60	35

.380

	—	260	225	145	60	35

Arizmendi

Solid-frame folding-trigger revolver chambered for 7.65mm or .32-caliber. Normal markings are trademark "FA" and a circled five-pointed star.

		200	150	80	50	25

Boltun—1st Variation

Bolton semi-automatic pistol was made in both calibers 6.35mm and 7.65mm. Almost an exact copy of Belgian Pieper. 7.65mm model was only slightly larger than 6.35mm model.

6.35mm

	—	250	195	125	60	35

	NIB	EXC.	V.G.	GOOD	FAIR	POOR

7.65mm

	—	250	195	125	60	35

Boltun—2nd Variation

Boltun 2nd variation chambered for 7.65mm cartridge. Almost an exact copy of Browning Model 1910. Made into 1930s.

	—	250	195	125	60	35

Roland

Chambered for 6.35 and 7.65mm cartridges. Manufactured during 1920s. The 7.65mm was only slightly larger than 6.35mm model.

6.35mm

	—	250	150	90	60	35

7.65mm

	—	250	150	90	60	35

Puppy

Variation of "Velo-Dog" revolver. Barrel stamped "Puppy". Frame bearing "FA" trademark.

	—	250	195	125	60	35

Pistolet Automatique

Normal markings include "FA" trademark.

	—	250	195	125	60	35

Kaba Spezial

6.35mm semi-automatic pistol. Patterned after Browning Model 1906. Kaba Spezial was originally made by August Menz of Suhl, Germany and sold by Karl Bauer of Berlin, Germany. Name "Kaba" was derived from first two initials of Karl Bauer. These two pistols do not look alike.

	—	275	150	100	50	35

Ydeal

The model Ydeal was made in four variations and three: 6.35mm, 7.65mm and .380-calibers. All four variations resemble Browning Model 1906, with 7.65mm and .380-caliber being slightly larger.

6.35mm

	—	225	175	100	60	35

7.65mm

	—	225	175	100	60	35

.380

	—	225	175	100	60	35

ARIZMENDI, ZULAICA
Eibar, Spain

Cebra Pistol

Semi-automatic 7.65mm pistol. Patterned after Ruby-style of Spanish automatics. Slide marked "Pistolet Automatique Cebra Zulaica Eibar", together with letters "A.Z." in an oval. Generally found with checkered wood grips.

	—	250	150	100	50	35

Cebra Revolver

Copy of a Colt Police Positive revolver marked "Made in Spain". Word "Cebra" cast in grips.

	—	250	150	125	75	50

ARMALITE, INC.
Costa Mesa, California
Geneseo, Illinois (current production)

In 1995, Eagle Arms purchased Armalite trademark and certain other assets. New companies are organized under Armalite name. Original company formed in mid 1950s, developed AR-10, which in turn led to development of M-16 series of service rifles, still in use today. All current models are produced at Geneseo, Illinois, facility.

AR-24 Pistol

15-shot, 9mm, double-action, semi-automatic pistol. Steel frame, fixed or adjustable sights. Compact version available. Introduced 2006. Pricing is for full-size pistol, with adjustable sights.

	NIB	EXC.	V.G.	GOOD	FAIR	POOR

NOTE: Deduct 15 percent for fixed sight versions.

	NIB	EXC.	V.G.	GOOD	FAIR	POOR
	595	450	325	275	200	125

AR-24 Tactical Custom

Similar to above, with tactical refinements including stippled front and back straps, 3-dot luminous sights, etc. Also available in compact version (shown).

NIB	EXC.	V.G.	GOOD	FAIR	POOR
630	475	350	300	225	150

AR-17 Shotgun

Gas-operated semi-automatic 12-gauge shotgun, with 24" barrel and interchangeable choke tubes. Receiver and barrel are made of an aluminum alloy, with an anodized black or gold finish. Stock and forearm are of plastic. Approximately 2,000 manufactured during 1964 and 1965. **NOTE:** Add 10 percent for gold finish.

NIB	EXC.	V.G.	GOOD	FAIR	POOR
750	625	400	300	225	100

AR-7 Explorer Rifle

.22 LR semi-automatic carbine, with 16" barrel. Receiver and barrel partially made of an alloy. Most noteworthy feature of this model, is that it can be disassembled and component parts stored in plastic stock. Manufactured between 1959 and 1973. Reintroduced in 1999.

NIB	EXC.	V.G.	GOOD	FAIR	POOR
375	300	200	150	100	85

AR-7 Custom

As above, with walnut cheekpiece stock. Manufactured between 1964 and 1970.

NIB	EXC.	V.G.	GOOD	FAIR	POOR
475	400	300	250	200	185

AR-180

Gas-operated semi-automatic rifle chambered for .223 or 5.56mm cartridge. AR-180 is civilian version of AR18, which is fully automatic. Simple and efficient rifle that was tested by various governments and found to have potential. Rifle was also manufactured by Howa Machinery Ltd. and Sterling Armament Co. of England. Most common version is manufactured by Sterling. Those built by Armalite and Howa bring a small premium.

Howa

NIB	EXC.	V.G.	GOOD	FAIR	POOR
1500	1250	900	700	450	200

Sterling

NIB	EXC.	V.G.	GOOD	FAIR	POOR
1150	900	700	500	350	175

AR-180B

Similar to original AR-180. Chambered for .223 cartridge. Fitted with 19.8" barrel and integral muzzle-brake. Lower receiver is polymer while upper receiver is sheet steel. Trigger group is standard M15. Accepts standard M15 magazines. Weight about 6 lbs.

NIB	EXC.	V.G.	GOOD	FAIR	POOR
750	625	500	400	300	125

AR-10A4 Rifle

Introduced in 1995. Features 20" stainless steel heavy barrel. Chambered for .308 Win. or .243 Win. cartridge. Has a flattop receiver, optional two-stage trigger, detachable carry handle and scope mount. Equipped with two 10-round magazines. Weight about 9.6 lbs. **NOTE:** Stainless steel barrel add $100.

NIB	EXC.	V.G.	GOOD	FAIR	POOR
1500	1250	900	700	500	200

AR-10A4 Carbine

Similar to above. Chambered for .308 Win. cartridge. Fitted with 16" barrel. Flattop receiver. Sold with two 10-round magazines. Weight about 9 lbs. **NOTE:** Stainless steel barrel add $100.

NIB	EXC.	V.G.	GOOD	FAIR	POOR
1500	1250	900	700	500	200

AR-10A2 Rifle

Model has 20" heavy barrel. Chambered for .308 cartridge, without removable carry handle. Weight about 9.8 lbs. **NOTE:** Stainless steel barrel add $100.

NIB	EXC.	V.G.	GOOD	FAIR	POOR
1500	1250	900	700	500	200

AR-10A2 Carbine

Similar to above, with 16" barrel. Weight about 9 lbs. **NOTE:** Stainless steel barrel add $100.

NIB	EXC.	V.G.	GOOD	FAIR	POOR
1500	1250	900	700	500	200

AR-10B

Chambered for .308 cartridge. Fitted with 20" barrel. Trigger is single-stage or optional two-stage match type. Model has several early M16 features such as tapered handguard, pistol-grips and short buttstock in original brown color. Fitted with early charging handle. Limited production.

	NIB	EXC.	V.G.	GOOD	FAIR	POOR

Weight about 9.5 lbs. Introduced in 1999.

	1600	1250	900	700	500	200

AR-10(T) Rifle

Model features 24" heavy barrel, with two-stage trigger. Front sight and carry handle are removable. Handguard is fiberglass. Weight about 10.4 lbs.

	1850	1400	875	600	450	225

AR-10(T) Carbine

Similar to AR-10T, with 16.25" target weight barrel. Weight about 8.5 lbs.

	1850	1400	875	600	450	225

AR-10(T) Ultra

Chambered for .300 Remington Ultra Short Action Magnum cartridge. Barrel length 24". Two-stage National Match trigger. Offered in choice of green or black stock. Sold with 5-round magazine.

	1850	1400	875	600	450	225

AR-10 SOF

Introduced in 2003. Features M4-style fixed stock. Flattop receiver. Chambered for .308 cartridge. Offered in both A2 and A4 configurations.

	1850	1400	875	600	450	225

AR-10 .338 Federal

Similar to AR-10. Chambered in .338 Federal.

	1650	1400	1250	900	500	250

M15 SOF

Model chambered for .223 cartridge. Fitted with flattop receiver and M4-style fixed stock. Introduced in 2003. Offered in both A2 and A4 configurations.

	1150	925	675	475	300	150

M15A2 HBAR

Model introduced in 1995. Features 20" heavy barrel chambered for .223 cartridge. A2-style forward assist, recoil check brake. Formerly sold with 10-round magazine. Weight about 8.2 lbs.

	1100	850	600	500	375	125

M15A2 National Match

Chambered for .223 cartridge. Variation features 20" stainless steel match barrel, with two-stage trigger, A2-style forward assist and hard coated anodized receiver. Equipped with 10-round magazine. Weight about 9 lbs.

	1475	1200	850	600	375	200

M15A2-M4A1C Carbine

Similar to M15A2 heavy barrel, with 16" heavy barrel. Flattop receiver, with detachable carry handle. Introduced in 1995. **NOTE:** Add $100 for Match trigger.

	1100	900	700	500	300	125

M15A2-M4C Carbine

Similar to M4A1C Carbine, with flattop receiver and detachable carry handle.

	1000	850	600	500	300	125

M15A4(T) Eagle Eye

Chambered for .223 cartridge. Fitted with 24" stainless steel heavy weight barrel. Has National Match two-stage trigger, Picatinny rail and NM fiberglass handguard tube. Sold with 7-round magazine and 4-section cleaning rod with brass tip, sling, owner's manual and lifetime warranty.

	1500	1100	800	600	350	150

M15A4 Special Purpose Rifle (SPR)

Model fitted with 20" heavy barrel, detachable front sight and carry handle, NM sights and Picatinny rail. Weight about 7.8 lbs.

	1200	900	750	600	375	175

M15A4 Action Master

Variation features 20" stainless steel heavy barrel, with two-stage trigger, Picatinny rail and fiberglass handguard tube. Weight about 9 lbs.

	1450	1000	850	600	375	175

NIB	EXC.	V.G.	GOOD	FAIR	POOR

M15A4 Eagle Spirit

Similar to Action Master above, with 16" stainless steel barrel. Weight about 7.6 lbs.

NIB	EXC.	V.G.	GOOD	FAIR	POOR
1450	1000	850	600	375	175

M15A4 Carbine 6.8 & 7.62x39

Shorty carbine version of AR-15. Chambered in 6.8 Remington and 7.62x39. 16" chrome-lined barrel with flash suppressor, front and rear Picatinny rails for mounting optics and two-stage tactical trigger. Ten-round magazine. Anodized aluminum/phosphate finish. Overall length 36.6"; weight: 7 lbs.

NIB	EXC.	V.G.	GOOD	FAIR	POOR
950	800	650	500	350	200

M15-22

This model was made in 2011 in .22 Long Rifle caliber on a .223 lower receiver, with most standard AR-style features.

NIB	EXC.	V.G.	GOOD	FAIR	POOR
600	500	400	350	250	150

AR-30M

Chambered for .338 Lapua, .300 Win. Magnum or .308 Winchester cartridges. Barrel length 26" with muzzle-brake. Adjustable buttstock. Weight about 12 lbs. Reduced version of AR-50. **NOTE:** Add $150 for .338 Lapua.

NIB	EXC.	V.G.	GOOD	FAIR	POOR
1600	1400	1250	1000	500	195

AR-30A1 Standard

Introduced in 2013. This is an upgraded version of the bolt-action AR-30M. Improvements include better ergonomics and versatility. Chambered in .300 Win. Magnum or .338 Lapua. **NOTE:** Add $125 to these values for .338 Lapua caliber. A target version with an adjustable fixed stock is available, add $200 for this model.

NIB	EXC.	V.G.	GOOD	FAIR	POOR
2600	2250	1900	1250	700	350

AR-31

This target model in .308 Winchester, has an 18" or 24" barrel, stock that's adjustable for length-of-pull and comb height, bipod, muzzle-brake and single-stage trigger. It accepts Armalite AR-10B double-stack magazines up to 25-round capacity.

NIB	EXC.	V.G.	GOOD	FAIR	POOR
3000	2600	2200	1500	800	400

AR-50

Introduced in 2000. Chambered for .50 BMG or .416 Barrett. Fitted with 31" tapered barrel threaded for recoil check (muzzle-brake). Trigger is single-stage. Stock is 3-section type with extruded fore-end. Adjustable Pachmayr buttplate. Picatinny rail. Finish is magnesium phosphated steel and hard anodized aluminum. Bipod. Single shot. Weight about 33 lbs. **NOTE:** Add $400 for National Match Model.

NIB	EXC.	V.G.	GOOD	FAIR	POOR
3400	2650	2000	1500	750	300

PRE-BAN MODELS

Golden Eagle

Fitted with 20" stainless extra-heavy barrel, with NM two-stage trigger and NM sights. Sold with 30-round magazine. Weight about 9.4 lbs.

NIB	EXC.	V.G.	GOOD	FAIR	POOR
1500	1200	950	800	400	200

HBAR

Pre-ban rifle has 20" heavy barrel, 30-round magazine and sling. Weight about 8 lbs.

NIB	EXC.	V.G.	GOOD	FAIR	POOR
1300	1000	850	700	350	175

M4C Carbine

Pre-ban variation fitted with 16" heavy barrel, collapsible stock and fixed flash suppressor. Weight about 6.2 lbs.

NIB	EXC.	V.G.	GOOD	FAIR	POOR
1300	1000	850	700	350	175

ARMAS DE FUEGO
Guernica, Spain
See—Alkartasuna Fabrica de Armas

ARMERO ESPECIALISTAS
Eibar, Spain

	NIB	EXC.	V.G.	GOOD	FAIR	POOR

Alfa

Alfa" was a trademark given a number of revolvers based upon both Colt and Smith & Wesson designs. In calibers ranging from .22- to .44-calibers. **NOTE:** Add 50 percent for S&W N-frame copies.

—	250	200	100	75	50	

Omega

Semi-automatic 6.35 or 7.65mm pistol marked "Omega" on slide and grips.

—	225	175	100	75	50	

ARMES DE CHASSE
Chadds Ford, Pennsylvania

Importer of firearms manufactured by Franchi, P. Beretta and other arms manufactured in Germany.

Model EJ

Over/under Anson & Deeley action 12-gauge shotgun, with double triggers as well as automatic ejectors. Blued barrels, silver finished receiver and checkered walnut stock. Manufactured in Germany. Introduced in 1989.

1500	1250	900	650	500	250	

Model EU

As above, with ventilated rib barrel. Nonselective single trigger. Introduced in 1989.

1600	1300	850	650	500	250	

Highlander

Side-by-side double-barrel 20-gauge shotgun, with boxlock action. Available in various barrel lengths and choke combinations, with double triggers and manual extractors. Blued, with checkered walnut stock. Manufactured in Italy. Introduced in 1989.

1350	800	650	350	250	125	

Chesapeake

As above chambered for 3.5" 12-gauge shell. Bores are chrome-lined and suitable for steel shot. Fitted with automatic ejectors and double triggers. Manufactured in Italy. Introduced in 1989.

1450	995	700	475	400	200	

Balmoral

English-style straight grip 12-, 16- or 20-gauge boxlock shotgun. Fitted with false side plates. Receiver and side plates case hardened. Barrels blued. Fitted with single trigger and automatic ejectors. Manufactured in Italy. Introduced in 1989.

1200	925	725	500	400	200	

Model 70E

A 12-, 16- or 20-gauge side-by-side shotgun. Fitted with 27" or 28" barrels. Action based upon Anson & Deeley design, with Greener crossbolt. Receiver case hardened. Barrels blued. Walnut stock checkered. Manufactured in Germany. Introduced in 1989.

1225	925	725	500	400	200	

Model 74E

As above, with game scene engraving. More fully figured walnut stock. Introduced in 1989.

1475	1050	900	650	500	250	

Model 76E

As above, with engraved false side plates. Fully figured walnut stock. Introduced in 1989.

2000	1500	1100	750	600	300	

ARMINEX LTD.
Scottsdale, Arizona

Tri-Fire

Semi-automatic pistol chambered for 9mm, .38 Super or .45 ACP cartridges. Fitted with 5", 6" or 7" stainless steel barrels. Presentation cases were available at an extra cost of $48. Approximately 250 manufactured from 1981 to 1985. **NOTE:** Available with conversion units that add approximately $130 if in excellent condition.

950	800	600	300	175	100	

NIB	EXC.	V.G.	GOOD	FAIR	POOR

Target Model

As above, with 6" or 7" barrel.

1000	850	650	350	225	100

ARMINUS

See—Freidrich Pickert

See—Hermann Weirauch

See—F. I. E.

ARMITAGE INTERNATIONAL, LTD.

Seneca, South Carolina

Scarab Skorpion

Blowback-operated semi-automatic pistol. Patterned after Czechoslovakian Scorpion sub-machine gun. Chambered for 9mm cartridge, with 4.6" barrel having military-type sights. Fitted with 32-round detachable box magazine. Standard finish is matte black. Grips are plastic.

650	550	400	300	175	100

ARMSCO FIREARMS CORP.

Ankara, Turkey
U.S.A.—Des Plaines, Illinois

Built by Huglu Hunting Firearms Corporation in Turkey, which was established in 1927. Armsco is U.S. representative. First year of business in U.S. was 2002.

SINGLE-SHOT

Model 301A

Single-shot model offered in 12-, 16-, 20-, 28-gauge and .410 bore. Barrel lengths from 22" to 32" depending on gauge. Checkered walnut stock. Weight varies from 5- to 5.5 lbs. depending on gauge.

200	150	75	50	35	25

SIDE-BY-SIDES

Model 202B

Boxlock shotgun offered in 12-, 16-, 20-, 28-gauge and .410 bore. Barrel lengths from 22" to 32" depending on gauge. Double triggers. Hand engraved about 50 percent coverage. Fixed chokes or choke tubes. Checkered walnut stock with cheekpiece. Weight about 6.4- to 7.3 lbs. depending on gauge.

550	425	325	200	125	50

Model 202A

Same as above. Offered with standard buttstock.

775	625	450	300	175	75

Model 201A

Offered in gauges from 12- to .410. Sideplates with 50 percent hand engraving. Choice of single or double triggers.

695	525	450	300	175	75

Model 200A

Boxlock in gauges 12- to .410, with single trigger. Hand engraved 50 percent coverage.

750	575	450	300	175	75

Model 205A

Offered in gauges 12- to .410, with barrel lengths 22" to 32" depending on gauge. Boxlock frame with 60 percent hand engraved coverage. Single trigger. Checkered walnut stock. Weights are 6.1- to 6.8 lbs. depending on gauge.

990	750	600	425	200	100

	NIB	EXC.	V.G.	GOOD	FAIR	POOR

Model 210AE

Offered in 12-, 16- and 20-gauge, with single trigger and automatic ejectors. Boxlock frame is 60 percent hand engraved. Optional fixed or choke tubes.

NIB	EXC.	V.G.	GOOD	FAIR	POOR
1250	950	700	450	300	200

Model 210BE

Same as above, with double triggers.

NIB	EXC.	V.G.	GOOD	FAIR	POOR
1150	850	675	450	300	200

OVER/UNDERS

Model 104A

Chambered for 12- through .410 bores, with double triggers. Barrel lengths from 22" to 32" depending on gauge. Ventilated rib. Checkered walnut stock. Fixed or choke tubes. Weight from 6.6- to 7.3 lbs. depending on gauge. Receiver is 15 percent hand engraved.

NIB	EXC.	V.G.	GOOD	FAIR	POOR
425	300	250	200	125	75

Model 103D

Same as above, with single trigger and schnabel forearm.

NIB	EXC.	V.G.	GOOD	FAIR	POOR
595	475	375	325	175	75

Model 103DE

Same as above, with automatic ejectors.

NIB	EXC.	V.G.	GOOD	FAIR	POOR
750	575	525	425	200	75

Model 103C

Similar to Model 103D, with blued receiver, gold inlaid birds and 40 percent engraving coverage.

NIB	EXC.	V.G.	GOOD	FAIR	POOR
720	550	525	425	200	75

Model 103CE

Same as above, with automatic ejectors.

NIB	EXC.	V.G.	GOOD	FAIR	POOR
870	650	575	475	225	100

Model 103F

Similar to Model 103D, with 80 to 100 percent hand engraved side plates.

NIB	EXC.	V.G.	GOOD	FAIR	POOR
850	625	550	450	225	100

Model 103FE

Same as above, with automatic ejectors.

NIB	EXC.	V.G.	GOOD	FAIR	POOR
970	750	600	475	250	125

Model 101SE

Offered in 12-gauge only. Barrel lengths 28", 30" or 32" with ventilated rib. Single trigger and automatic ejectors. Hand engraved receiver. Checkered walnut stock. Weight from 6.6- to 7.3 lbs. depending on barrel length.

NIB	EXC.	V.G.	GOOD	FAIR	POOR
1325	975	750	450	275	125

Model 101BE

Same as above, with adjustable comb.

NIB	EXC.	V.G.	GOOD	FAIR	POOR
1325	975	750	450	275	125

SEMI-AUTOS

Model 401A

Semi-automatic shotgun. Uses short-recoil inertia-operated system. Chambered for 12-gauge shell up to 3". Barrel lengths from 22" to 32". Ventilated rib. Plastic or walnut stock. Fixed or choke tubes. Fully engraved receiver. Weight from 6.9- to 7.2 lbs. depending on barrel length. Magazine capacity 6 rounds.

NIB	EXC.	V.G.	GOOD	FAIR	POOR
425	350	275	225	125	75

Model 401B

Same as above, with 4-round magazine capacity.

NIB	EXC.	V.G.	GOOD	FAIR	POOR
425	350	275	225	125	75

	NIB	EXC.	V.G.	GOOD	FAIR	POOR

Model 501GA

Gas-operated shotgun chambered for 3" 12-gauge shell. Barrel lengths from 22" to 32". Black receiver with 15 percent hand engraved coverage. Magazine capacity 7 rounds. Walnut or plastic stock. Weight from 6.8- to 7.3 lbs. depending on barrel length.

425	350	275	225	125	75

Model 501GB

Same as above, with 4-round magazine.

425	350	275	225	125	75

Model 601GB

Same as Model 501GB, with full coverage engraved silver receiver.

450	375	300	250	125	75

Model 601GA

Same as Model 501GA, with 7-round magazine capacity.

450	375	300	250	125	75

Model 701GA

Model chambered for 20-gauge 3" shell. Fitted with barrel lengths from 22" to 32". Ventilated rib. Walnut stock. Fixed or choke tubes. Magazine capacity 7 rounds. Weight 6- to 6.4 lbs. depending on barrel length.

450	375	300	225	125	75

Model 701GB

Same as above, with 4-round magazine.

450	375	300	225	125	75

PUMP-ACTIONS

Model 801A

Slide-action 12-gauge shotgun, with plastic stock. Barrel length from 22" to 32". Fixed or choke tubes. Magazine capacity 7 rounds. Weight about 7 lbs.

300	275	250	175	100	50

Model 801B

Same as above, with 4-round magazine.

300	275	250	175	100	50

ARMSCOR PRECISION INTERNATIONAL
Pahrump, Nevada

Armscor Precision International imports firearms made by Arms Corporation of the Philippines.

RIFLES

M14R

Civilian version of U.S. M14 rifle. Manufactured from new and surplus parts. Introduced in 1986.

1350	900	500	300	200	100

M14 National Match

As above. Built to A.M.T.U. MIL specifications. Introduced in 1987.

1650	1250	800	500	400	200

FAL

Civilian version of FN FAL rifle. Assembled from new and Argentine surplus parts. Introduced in 1987.

1600	1250	800	400	300	150

M36 Israeli Sniper Rifle

Specialized weapon built upon Armscorp M14 receiver in Bullpup style. Barrel length 22" of free floating design for accuracy. Chambered for .308 cartridge. There is an integral flash suppressor and a bipod. Furnished with 20-shot detachable magazine. This civilian version first offered for sale in 1989.

3200	2650	2000	1500	850	400

	NIB	EXC.	V.G.	GOOD	FAIR	POOR

Expert Model

.22-caliber semi-automatic rifle, with 21" barrel, open sights and 10-shot magazine. Introduced in 1989.

NIB	EXC.	V.G.	GOOD	FAIR	POOR
225	200	175	145	100	80

Model M14P

.22-caliber bolt-action rifle. Fitted with 23" barrel, open sights and 5-shot detachable magazine. Mahogany stock.

NIB	EXC.	V.G.	GOOD	FAIR	POOR
150	90	75	50	35	25

Model M14D

As above, with adjustable rear sight and checkered stock. Manufactured in 1987 only.

NIB	EXC.	V.G.	GOOD	FAIR	POOR
165	100	85	60	40	25

Model 14Y

Bolt-action rifle chambered for .22 LR cartridge. Fitted with 18" barrel and 10-round magazine. Weight about 5.2 lbs.

NIB	EXC.	V.G.	GOOD	FAIR	POOR
150	125	100	75	50	25

Model 12Y

Bolt-action rifle is a single-shot. Chambered for .22 LR. Fitted with 18" barrel. Weight about 5 lbs.

NIB	EXC.	V.G.	GOOD	FAIR	POOR
125	100	75	50	35	25

Model 1400

Bolt-action rifle chambered for .22 LR cartridge. Fitted with 22.5" barrel and 10-round magazine. Weight about 6.5 lbs.

NIB	EXC.	V.G.	GOOD	FAIR	POOR
225	200	150	125	100	75

Model M1500

.22 Magnum bolt-action rifle. Fitted with 22.5" barrel, open sights, 5-shot magazine and checkered mahogany stock. Weight about 6.5 lbs.

NIB	EXC.	V.G.	GOOD	FAIR	POOR
250	200	150	125	100	75

Model M1600

.22-caliber copy of U.S. M16 rifle, with 18" barrel and detachable 15-round magazine. Weight about 6.2 lbs.

NIB	EXC.	V.G.	GOOD	FAIR	POOR
300	200	125	100	75	50

Model M1600R

As above, with stainless steel collapsible stock and shrouded barrel. No longer in production.

NIB	EXC.	V.G.	GOOD	FAIR	POOR
325	225	150	125	100	75

Model M1600C

As above, with 20" barrel and fiberglass stock. No longer in production.

NIB	EXC.	V.G.	GOOD	FAIR	POOR
300	200	125	100	75	50

Model M1600W

As above, with mahogany stock. No longer in production.

NIB	EXC.	V.G.	GOOD	FAIR	POOR
300	200	125	100	75	50

Model M1800

.22 Hornet bolt-action rifle. Fitted with 22.5" barrel, 5-shot magazine and mahogany Monte Carlo-style stock. Weight about 6.6 lbs.

NIB	EXC.	V.G.	GOOD	FAIR	POOR
250	200	150	75	50	35

Model 20C

Chambered for .22 LR, with 15-round magazine and 18.25" barrel. Weight about 6.2 lbs.

NIB	EXC.	V.G.	GOOD	FAIR	POOR
175	150	90	70	50	40

Model M20P

.22-caliber 15-shot semi-automatic rifle. Fitted with 20.75" barrel, open sights and plain mahogany stock. Weight about 6.3 lbs.

NIB	EXC.	V.G.	GOOD	FAIR	POOR
175	150	90	70	50	40

Model M2000

As above, with adjustable sights and checkered stock. Weight about 6.4 lbs.

NIB	EXC.	V.G.	GOOD	FAIR	POOR
175	150	90	70	50	40

	NIB	EXC.	V.G.	GOOD	FAIR	POOR

Model AK22S

.22-caliber semi-automatic rifle resembling Russian AKA47. Barrel length 18.5", 15-round magazine and mahogany stock. Weight about 7.5 lbs.

	NIB	EXC.	V.G.	GOOD	FAIR	POOR
	275	225	195	125	75	50

Model AK22F

As above, with folding stock. No longer in production.

	NIB	EXC.	V.G.	GOOD	FAIR	POOR
	275	225	195	125	75	50

HANDGUNS

Hi-Power

Argentine-made version of Browning semi-automatic pistol. Chambered for 9mm, with 4.75" barrel. Matte finish, with checkered synthetic grips. Introduced in 1989.

	NIB	EXC.	V.G.	GOOD	FAIR	POOR
	450	350	300	250	200	100

Detective HP—Compact

As above, with 3.5" barrel.

	NIB	EXC.	V.G.	GOOD	FAIR	POOR
	475	375	350	275	200	100

P22

Copy of Colt Woodsman .22-caliber semi-automatic pistol. Available with 4" or 6" barrels and 10-shot magazine. Finish blued, grips of checkered hardwood. Introduced in 1989.

	NIB	EXC.	V.G.	GOOD	FAIR	POOR
	250	150	125	100	75	50

SD9

Israeli-made 9mm double-action semi-automatic pistol, with 3" barrel. Assembled extensively from sheet metal stampings. Loaded chamber indicator and 6-round magazine. This model also known as Sirkus SD9. Manufactured by Sirkus Industries in Israel. Introduced in 1989.

	NIB	EXC.	V.G.	GOOD	FAIR	POOR
	300	250	200	150	100	75

Armscor 1911A1-45 FS GI

1911-style semi-automatic pistol. Chambered in .45 ACP (8 rounds) , 9mm Parabellum, .38 Super (9 rounds). Features include checkered plastic or hardwood grips, 5" barrel, Parkerized steel frame and slide, drift adjustable sights. **NOTE:** Add $50 for Commander or Officer's model.

	NIB	EXC.	V.G.	GOOD	FAIR	POOR
	400	350	300	250	200	100

Model M100

Double-action swing-out cylinder revolver. Chambered for .22, .22 Magnum and .38 Special cartridges. Has 4" ventilated rib barrel. Six-shot cylinder and adjustable sights. Blued, with checkered mahogany grips. No longer in production.

	NIB	EXC.	V.G.	GOOD	FAIR	POOR
	200	175	150	110	80	50

Model 200P

Introduced in 1990. This 6-shot revolver chambered for .38 Special cartridge. Fitted with 4" barrel, fixed sights and wood or rubber grips. Weighs about 26 oz.

	NIB	EXC.	V.G.	GOOD	FAIR	POOR
	180	150	125	100	85	60

Model 200TC

Introduced in 1990. Similar to above. Fitted with adjustable sights and checkered wood grips. Weight about 28 oz.

	NIB	EXC.	V.G.	GOOD	FAIR	POOR
	200	175	150	125	100	75

Model 200DC

Similar to Model 200P, with 2.5" barrel. Weight about 22 oz.

	NIB	EXC.	V.G.	GOOD	FAIR	POOR
	175	150	125	100	85	60

Model 201S

Similar to Model 200P in stainless steel.

	NIB	EXC.	V.G.	GOOD	FAIR	POOR
	200	175	150	125	100	75

Model 202

Chambered for 38 Special cartridge. This 6-shot revolver fitted with 4" barrel and fixed sights. Blued finish. Weight about 27 oz.

	NIB	EXC.	V.G.	GOOD	FAIR	POOR
	150	120	95	75	50	25

	NIB	EXC.	V.G.	GOOD	FAIR	POOR

Model 206

Similar to Model 202, with 2.88" barrel. Weight about 25 oz.

NIB	EXC.	V.G.	GOOD	FAIR	POOR
180	140	110	75	50	25

Model 210

Same as Model 202, with adjustable sights. Weight about 27 oz.

NIB	EXC.	V.G.	GOOD	FAIR	POOR
200	150	125	75	50	25

MAP1 FS

Single-/double-action 9mm semi-automatic, with 16+1 capacity. Fixed sights, 4.45" barrel, weight 40.5 oz. Nickel alloy steel frame and slide. (Shorter, lighter MS model has 3.66" barrel.) Introduced 2006.

NIB	EXC.	V.G.	GOOD	FAIR	POOR
—	350	300	200	125	75

MAPP1 FS

Single-/double-action 9mm semi-automatic, with 16+1 capacity. Fixed sights, 4.45" barrel, weight 40.5 oz. Polymer frame with integrated accessory rail and nickel alloy steel slide. (Shorter, lighter MS model has 3.66" barrel.) Introduced 2006.

NIB	EXC.	V.G.	GOOD	FAIR	POOR
—	350	300	200	175	75

Model 1911-A1

Semi-automatic pistol similar in design to Colt Model 1911 pistol. Chambered for .45 ACP cartridge. Fitted with 5" barrel. Blued finish. Magazine capacity 8 rounds. Weight about 39 oz. Also sold under Charles Daly name.

NIB	EXC.	V.G.	GOOD	FAIR	POOR
500	400	300	200	150	75

Model 1911-A2

Same as above, with double column magazine and 13 round capacity. Weight about 43 oz.
NOTE: Add $100 for two-tone finish; $130 for chrome finish.

NIB	EXC.	V.G.	GOOD	FAIR	POOR
600	500	375	250	195	110

SHOTGUNS

Model 30D

Slide-action 12-gauge shotgun. Fitted with 28" or 30" barrels and various chokes. Magazine holds 6 cartridges. Weight about 7.6 lbs.

NIB	EXC.	V.G.	GOOD	FAIR	POOR
200	175	150	125	100	75

Model 30DG

As above, with 20" barrel, fitted rifle sights and 7-shot magazine. Weight about 7.2 lbs.

NIB	EXC.	V.G.	GOOD	FAIR	POOR
175	150	125	100	80	70

Model 30R

As above, with shotgun bead sights, 18.5" or 20" barrel. Weight between 7- and 7.2 lbs. depending on barrel length.

NIB	EXC.	V.G.	GOOD	FAIR	POOR
175	150	125	100	80	70

Model 30RP

As above, with auxiliary black composition pistol-grip and 18.5" barrel.

NIB	EXC.	V.G.	GOOD	FAIR	POOR
175	150	125	100	80	70

Model 30 SAS1

Slide-action 12-gauge, with 20" barrel and heat shield. Chambered for 3" shell. Open cylinder choke. Parkerized finish. Weight about 8 lbs.

NIB	EXC.	V.G.	GOOD	FAIR	POOR
200	150	100	75	50	25

ARNOLD ARMS

Arlington, Washington

Company offered a wide range of rifles and calibers, including its own proprietary cartridges, from 6mm Arnold to .458 Arnold. Rifles were built on choice of actions, including Apollo, Remington, Sako and Winchester. These action choices affect base price of rifle. Out of business in 2002. Values vary with geography. **NOTE:** Add $1100 for Apollo actions to all applicable models, unless otherwise noted.

Varminter I

Model features heavy match grade barrel, with straight taper. Lengths from 24" to 26". Calibers from .222 Rem. to .257 Arnold Magnum. Choice of McMillian Varmint stock in various finishes.

NIB	EXC.	V.G.	GOOD	FAIR	POOR

Pacific Research Varmint stock in flat black. Weight from 9- to 11 lbs. depending on caliber and configuration.

NIB	EXC.	V.G.	GOOD	FAIR	POOR
2600	2000	1450	1050	700	200

Varminter II

Variation features 24" to 26" medium weight match barrel, with choice of McMillan or Pacific Research sporter stocks. Choice of triggers. Weight 7.5- to 9 lbs. depending on configuration. Calibers from .223 Rem. to .257 Arnold Magnum.

NIB	EXC.	V.G.	GOOD	FAIR	POOR
2600	2000	1450	1050	700	200

Alaskan

Bolt-action rifle chambered for calibers .223 to .338 Win. Magnum. Barrel lengths 22" to 26" depending on caliber. Stocks are synthetic in black woodland or arctic camo. Sights optional. Rifle drilled and tapped for scope mounts. Trigger fully adjustable. Choice of chrome moly steel or stainless steel. Introduced in 1996.

NIB	EXC.	V.G.	GOOD	FAIR	POOR
2600	2000	1450	1050	700	200

Alaskan Trophy

Similar to Alaskan Rifle. Chambered for .300 Magnums to .458 Win. Magnum. Barrel lengths 24" to 26" depending on caliber. Choice of walnut, synthetic or fibergrain stock. Fitted with iron sights. Choice of stainless or chrome moly steel. Introduced in 1996.

NIB	EXC.	V.G.	GOOD	FAIR	POOR
3100	2500	1450	1050	700	200

Alaskan Guide

Model offered in choice of calibers .257 to .338 Magnum. Barrel lengths 22" to 26" depending on caliber. Buyer has choice of "A" English walnut stock or deluxe synthetic stock. No open sights.

Synthetic Stock

NIB	EXC.	V.G.	GOOD	FAIR	POOR
3700	2900	2200	1400	650	300

Walnut Stock

NIB	EXC.	V.G.	GOOD	FAIR	POOR
4300	3400	2500	1475	700	325

Grand Alaskan

Version fitted with AAA fancy select or exhibition wood. Built in calibers .300 Magnum to .458 Win. Magnum.

AAA" English Walnut

NIB	EXC.	V.G.	GOOD	FAIR	POOR
6000	5000	3750	2500	1500	450

Exhibition" Grade Walnut

NIB	EXC.	V.G.	GOOD	FAIR	POOR
7400	6000	5000	3900	1650	325

Safari

Introduced in 1996. Features calibers .223 to .458 Win. Magnum. Barrel lengths 22" to 26" depending on caliber. Apollo is a controlled or push feed type, with one-piece cone-head bolt. Fully adjustable trigger, with chrome moly or stainless steel construction. Sights are optional. Rifle drilled and tapped for scope mounts. Choice of A fancy English or AA fancy English walnut.

A" Fancy English Walnut

NIB	EXC.	V.G.	GOOD	FAIR	POOR
4300	3500	2700	1650	800	300

AA" Fancy English Walnut

NIB	EXC.	V.G.	GOOD	FAIR	POOR
4400	3500	2700	1650	800	300

African Trophy

Similar to Safari Rifle. Stocked in AAA fancy walnut, with wraparound checkering.

NIB	EXC.	V.G.	GOOD	FAIR	POOR
6300	5000	3250	2500	1750	300

Grand African

Similar to Safari rifle, with addition of Exhibition Grade wood. Calibers .338 to .458 Magnum.

NIB	EXC.	V.G.	GOOD	FAIR	POOR
7600	6100	5000	3900	1650	325

Serengeti Synthetic

Similar to Safari rifle, with fibergrain stock in classic or Monte Carlo style. Checkering or stipple finish. Calibers .243 to .300 Magnum. Introduced in 1996.

NIB	EXC.	V.G.	GOOD	FAIR	POOR
2600	2100	1600	1150	700	225

	NIB	EXC.	V.G.	GOOD	FAIR	POOR

African Synthetic

Similar to Safari rifle, with fibergrain stock, checkering or stipple finish. Calibers .338 to .458 Magnum.

	NIB	EXC.	V.G.	GOOD	FAIR	POOR
	3300	2600	1800	1400	750	250

Neutralizer Mark I

Built on Remington 700 or Winchester action. Bolt-action rifle chambered in choice of calibers from .223 to .300 Win. Magnum. Barrel length 24" to 26" depending on caliber, with Magnum barrels up to 28". A fiberglass tactical stock, with adjustable cheekpiece and buttplate is standard in various finishes. **NOTE:** Winchester action $400 less.

	NIB	EXC.	V.G.	GOOD	FAIR	POOR
	2900	2300	1700	1300	700	275

Neutralizer Mark II

Same as above, with Apollo action.

	NIB	EXC.	V.G.	GOOD	FAIR	POOR
	4000	3200	2250	1700	900	325

Benchrest Rifles

Custom built. Unable to price individual rifles.

Prone Rifles

Custom built. Unable to price individual rifles.

X-Course Rifles

Custom built. Unable to price individual rifles.

1,000 Yard Match Rifles

Custom built. Unable to price individual rifles.

Fully Accurized Production Rifles

Rifles offered in standard blue or stainless steel, with walnut or synthetic stock. Chambered from .223 to .338 Win. Magnum. Built on Remington, Ruger or Winchester actions.

	NIB	EXC.	V.G.	GOOD	FAIR	POOR
	1250	1100	750	600	400	200

AROSTEGUI, EULOGIO
Eibar, Spain

Azul Royal (Model 31)

Semi-automatic or fully automatic pistol in calibers 7.63 Mauser, 9mm Bergmann or .38 ACP. Manufactured between 1935 and 1940. Fitted with 10-round integral magazine. **NOTE:** Add 300 percent for fully automatic machine pistol version. NFA/BATFE regulations apply.

	NIB	EXC.	V.G.	GOOD	FAIR	POOR
	—	3000	2500	1000	500	300

Super Azul (M-34)

Semi-automatic or fully automatic pistol in 7.63mm Mauser, 9mm Bergmann and .38 ACP. Manufactured between 1935 and 1940. Has removable box magazine with capacity of 10, 20 or 30 rounds. Also known as the War Model or Standard Model. **NOTE:** Add 300 percent for fully automatic machine pistol version. NFA/BATFE regulations apply.

	NIB	EXC.	V.G.	GOOD	FAIR	POOR
	—	3000	2500	1000	500	300

Azul 6.35mm

6.35mm semi-automatic pistol. Copied after Model 1906 Browning. Frame marked with letters "EA" in a circle. A retriever is molded in the grips. Magazine capacity 6 or 9 rounds.

	NIB	EXC.	V.G.	GOOD	FAIR	POOR
	—	250	200	150	100	75

Azul 7.65mm

7.65mm semi-automatic pistol. Copied after Model 1910 FN. Magazine capacity 7 or 9 rounds.

	NIB	EXC.	V.G.	GOOD	FAIR	POOR
	—	250	200	150	100	75

Velo-Dog

Folding trigger 5.5mm or 6.35mm revolver bearing trademark "EA" on grips.

	NIB	EXC.	V.G.	GOOD	FAIR	POOR
	—	175	100	75	50	30

ARRIETA S.L.
Elgoibar, Spain

Company produces a wide variety of double-barrel shotguns. Price range from $450 to more than $30,000. It is recommended that highly engraved examples, as well as small bore arms, be individually appraised. **NOTE:** For 20- or 28-gauge and .410 bore, add 10 percent to values shown.

	NIB	EXC.	V.G.	GOOD	FAIR	POOR

490 Eder

Double-barrel boxlock shotgun, with double triggers and extractors. Discontinued in 1986.

	NIB	EXC.	V.G.	GOOD	FAIR	POOR
	—	550	425	325	250	100

500 Titan

Holland & Holland-style sidelock double-barrel shotgun, with French case hardened and engraved locks. Double triggers on extractors. No longer imported after 1986.

	NIB	EXC.	V.G.	GOOD	FAIR	POOR
	—	675	500	400	300	150

501 Palomara

As above, but more finely finished. Discontinued in 1986.

	NIB	EXC.	V.G.	GOOD	FAIR	POOR
	—	800	600	500	400	200

505 Alaska

As above, but more intricately engraved. Discontinued in 1986.

	NIB	EXC.	V.G.	GOOD	FAIR	POOR
	—	900	750	600	500	250

510 Montana

Holland & Holland-style sidelock double-barrel shotgun, with internal parts gold-plated.

	NIB	EXC.	V.G.	GOOD	FAIR	POOR
	3200	2750	1250	850	500	250

550 Field

As above, without internal parts gold-plated.

	NIB	EXC.	V.G.	GOOD	FAIR	POOR
	3200	2750	1250	850	500	250

557 Standard

As above, but more finely finished.

	NIB	EXC.	V.G.	GOOD	FAIR	POOR
	4000	3200	2200	1500	750	500

558 Patria

As above, but more finely finished.

	NIB	EXC.	V.G.	GOOD	FAIR	POOR
	3650	3150	1750	1250	800	400

560 Cumbre

As above, but featuring intricate engraving.

	NIB	EXC.	V.G.	GOOD	FAIR	POOR
	3800	3200	1800	1200	800	400

570 Lieja

	NIB	EXC.	V.G.	GOOD	FAIR	POOR
	4500	3750	2600	1800	900	550

575 Sport

	NIB	EXC.	V.G.	GOOD	FAIR	POOR
	4750	3750	2250	1700	1200	750

578 Victoria

Engraved in the English manner, with floral bouquets.

	NIB	EXC.	V.G.	GOOD	FAIR	POOR
	6000	5000	3750	2250	1000	750

585 Liria

As above, but more finely finished.

	NIB	EXC.	V.G.	GOOD	FAIR	POOR
	6500	5500	4250	3000	2000	1000

588 Cima

	NIB	EXC.	V.G.	GOOD	FAIR	POOR
	4800	4000	2250	1500	900	400

590 Regina

	NIB	EXC.	V.G.	GOOD	FAIR	POOR
	4250	3500	2700	1750	1000	500

595 Principe

As above, but engraved with relief-cut hunting scenes.

	NIB	EXC.	V.G.	GOOD	FAIR	POOR
	7500	6000	4000	3000	2000	1000

600 Imperial

Double-barrel shotgun has a self-opening action.

	NIB	EXC.	V.G.	GOOD	FAIR	POOR
	8500	7000	6000	4500	3000	2000

	NIB	EXC.	V.G.	GOOD	FAIR	POOR

601 Imperial Tiro

As above, but nickel-plated. Fitted with self-opening action.

	9000	7500	6500	4000	2500	1500

801

Detachable sidelock self-opening action double-barrel shotgun. Engraved in manner of Churchill.

	10000	8500	7500	5000	3000	2000

802

As above, with Holland & Holland-style engraving.

	11000	9000	8000	6000	4000	2000

803

As above, with Purdey-style engraving.

	9500	7500	6000	4000	3000	2000

871

Model features hand detachable sidelocks, with Holland ejectors. Scroll engraving.

	5300	4400	2500	1500	1000	750

872

Same features as Model 871, with addition of more engraving coverage using a tighter scroll.

	12500	10500	9000	7000	5000	2000

873

Features hand detachable sidelocks and game scene engraving.

	13000	11000	9000	7000	5000	2000

874

Same features as above, with addition of blued frame and gold line outlines.

	11000	9000	8000	6000	4000	2000

875

Custom manufactured sidelock double-barrel shotgun. Built solely to customer's specifications.

	15000	11500	9000	7000	5000	2000

R-1 Double Rifle

	15000	12500	10500	6000	3000	1000

R-2 Double Rifle

	18000	16000	14000	11000	5000	2000

ARRIZABALAGA, HIJOS DE C.
Eibar, Spain

Arrizabalaga

7.65mm semi-automatic pistol, with 9-shot magazine. Lanyard ring fitted to butt. Checkered wood grips. "ARRIZABALAGA" on slide.

	—	275	175	125	75	50

Campeon

Model 1919 6.35mm, 7.65mm or 9mm Kurtz semi-automatic pistol. Slide marked "Campeon Patent 1919"; plastic grips "Campeon". Supplied with 6- or 8-round magazines. **NOTE:** Add 25 percent for 9mm Kurtz.

	—	325	275	195	75	50

Jo Lo Ar

Model 1924 semi-automatic pistol, with tip-up barrel, cocking lever and no trigger guard. Jo Lo Ar was built in five calibers: 6.35mm, 7.65mm, 9mm Kurtz, 9mm Largo and .45 ACP. "Jo-Lo-Ar" appears on slide and grips. Premium for larger calibers. **NOTE:** Add 400 percent for .45.

	—	1100	925	800	450	200

Sharpshooter

6.35mm, 7.65mm or 9mm Corto (short) semi-automatic pistol. Fitted with a cocking lever. Barrel tips up for cleaning or when using as a single-shot. "SHARPSHOOTER" appears on slide.

	—	400	300	225	150	100

ARSENAL, INC.
Las Vegas, Nevada

SA M-7

Semi-automatic rifles manufactured in U.S. Similar to AK-47 in appearance. Chambered for 7.62x39 cartridge. Fitted with 16" barrel. Black polymer stock.

| 1000 | 800 | 550 | 325 | 200 | 125 |

SA M-7 Classic

As above, with blonde wood stock.

| 1050 | 850 | 600 | 325 | 200 | 125 |

SA M-7S

Similar to SA M-7, with scope rail added.

| 1025 | 875 | 575 | 325 | 200 | 125 |

SA RPK-5

Similar to SA M-7. Chambered for 5.56 NATO. Has 23.5" heavy barrel, with folding tripod and muzzle threads.

| 1600 | 1350 | 1000 | 750 | 600 | 400 |

SA RPK-7

Chambered for 7.62x39 cartridge. Rifle similar to RPK. Fitted with 23" barrel with bipod. Solid blonde wood stock, with trap in stock for cleaning kit.

| 975 | 800 | 595 | 325 | 200 | 125 |

SAS M-7

Based on the Bulgarian ARM1F, with under-folding stock. Chambered for 7.62x39mm. Made from 2004 to 2007.

| 1000 | 850 | 650 | 500 | 300 | 150 |

SAS M-7 Classic

Based on the Russian AKS-47, with heavy barrel, blonde wood and under-folding stock. Introduced in 2007.

| 1650 | 1400 | 1100 | 825 | 500 | 200 |

SLR-104

Chambered for 5.45x39.5 cartridge, with Bulgarian-made receiver and barrel. Other parts made in U.S.A. Mil-spec polymer stock, with folding buttstock. Introduced in 2003.

| 950 | 800 | 600 | 450 | 300 | 150 |

SLR-106

Chambered for 5.56 NATO/.223 round, with Bulgarian stamped receiver, original Bulgarian chrome lined, hamer-forged barrel. U.S. made polmer stock, with left-side folding buttstock. Other features include pistol-grip, removable muzzle-brake, black or desert sand color and Picatinny rails.

| 950 | 800 | 600 | 450 | 300 | 150 |

SLR-107

Chambered for 7.62x39 caliber. General features are similar to SLR-106 model.

| 950 | 800 | 600 | 450 | 300 | 150 |

ASCASO
Cataluna, Spain

Spanish Rebublican Government

Copy of Astra Model 400. Chambered for 9mm Largo cartridge. Barrel marked "F. Ascaso Tarrassa" in an oval. Built by the Spanish government during Spanish Civil War. Very few were made.

| — | 850 | 750 | 550 | 300 | 200 |

ASHEVILLE ARMORY
Asheville, North Carolina

Enfield-Type Rifle

.58-caliber percussion rifle, with 32.5" barrel and full stock secured by two iron barrel bands. Finished in white brass trigger guard and buttplate on walnut stock. Lockplate marked "Asheville,

	NIB	EXC.	V.G.	GOOD	FAIR	POOR

N.C." Approximately 300 made in 1862 and 1863.

	—	—	42000	19200	5000	3250

ASHTON, PETER & WILLIAM
Middletown, Connecticut

Under Hammer Pistol

.28- to .38-caliber single-shot percussion revolver, with 4" or 5" half-octagonal barrels marked "P.H. Ashton" or "W. Ashton". Blued or browned, with walnut grips. Active 1850s.

	—	—	1100	500	200	100

ASTON, H./H. ASTON & CO. PISTOLS
Middleton, Connecticut

Overall length 14"; barrel length 8.5"; caliber .54. Markings: on lockplate forward of hammer "U S/H. ASTON" or "U S/H. ASTON & CO.", on tail "MIDDTN/CONN/(date)"; on barrel, standard government inspection marks. Henry Aston of Middleton, Connecticut received a contract from U.S. War Department in February 1845, for 30,000 single-shot percussion pistols. These were delivered between 1846 and 1852, after which Ira N. Johnston continued production under a separate contract. Three thousand of these pistols were purchased for Navy usage. Many of these were subsequently marked with a small anchor on barrel near breech. These Navy purchases will command a slight premium.

	—	—	4700	4500	1750	500

ASTRA-UNCETA SA
Guernica, Spain

Astra is a brand name placed on guns built by Esperanza y Unceta and then Unceta y Cia. This Spanish company has now incorporated its trade name into its corporate name and is now know as Astra-Unceta SA. Firm under direction of Don Pedron Unceta and Don Juan Esperanza began business in Eibar on July 17, 1908 and moved to Guernica in 1913. Astra trademark was adopted on November 25, 1914. Esperanza began production of the Spanish Army's Campo Giro pistol in 1913. Model 1921 was marketed commercially as Astra 400. After Spanish Civil War, Unceta was one of only four handgun companies permitted to resume manufacturing operations. An interesting and informative side note is that pistols with 1000 to 5000 model numbers were made after 1945. Astra merged with Star before going out of business in 2006.

Victoria

6.35mm semi-automatic pistol, with 2.5" barrel. Blued, with black plastic grips. Manufactured prior to 1913.

	—	300	250	200	150	100

Astra 1911

6.35mm and 7.65mm semi-automatic pistol. External hammer. Checkered hard rubber grips. 7.65mm model was manufactured before 6.35mm model.

	—	375	275	175	100	75

Astra 1924

6.35mm semi-automatic pistol, with 2.5" barrel. Slide marked "Esperanza y Unceta Guernica Spain Astra Cal 6.35 .25". Blued, with black plastic grips.

	—	300	200	125	100	75

Astra 100 (Old Model)

Semi-automatic pistol in caliber 7.65mm. Checkered hard rubber grips. Magazine capacity 12 rounds. Introduced after WWII.

	—	550	400	300	200	100

Astra 200

6.35mm semi-automatic pistol, with 2.5" barrel and 6-shot magazine. Fitted with grip safety. Also known as "Firecat" in United States. Manufactured from 1920 to 1966. **NOTE:** Add 25 percent for factory engraving.

	—	300	200	125	100	75

Astra 400 or Model 1921

9x23 Bergman (9mm Largo) caliber semi-automatic pistol, with 6" barrel. Blued, with black plastic grips. Adopted for use by the Spanish Army. Approximately 106,000 made prior to 1946. Recent importation has depressed the price of these guns. **NOTE:** Any with Nazi proofs marks are worth a 100 percent premium, but caution is advised.

	—	475	400	250	75	40

	NIB	EXC.	V.G.	GOOD	FAIR	POOR

Astra 300

As above in 7.65mm or 9mm short. Those used during WWII by German forces bear Waffenamt marks. Approximately 171,000 manufactured prior to 1947. **NOTE:** Nazi-proofed add 25 percent.

	NIB	EXC.	V.G.	GOOD	FAIR	POOR
	—	650	475	250	150	100

Astra 600

Similar to Model 400 in 9mm Parabellum. In 1943 and 1944 approximately 10,500 manufactured. Some of these WWII guns will have Nazi proof stamp and bring a premium. A further 49,000 were made in 1946 and commercially sold.

	—	575	375	275	175	100

Astra 700

Single-action semi-automatic pistol in caliber 7.65mm. Magazine capacity 9 rounds. Introduced in 1926.

	—	500	400	300	150	100

Astra 800

Similar to Model 600, with external hammer and loaded chamber indicator. Blued, with plastic grips having trade name "Condor" cast in them. Approximately 11,400 made from 1958 to 1969.

	—	1500	1200	850	500	300

Astra 900

Modified copy of Mauser Model C96 semi-automatic pistol. Blued, with walnut grips. **NOTE:** Early examples with small Bolo grip marked "Hope" on chamber will bring a 20 percent premium. Serial numbers 32,788 through 33,774 were used by German Army in WWII and bring a 50 percent premium. Add 50 percent for matching Astra-made stock.

	—	3000	2250	1500	600	300

Astra 1000

Single-action semi-automatic pistol in caliber 7.65mm. Magazine capacity 12 rounds. Introduced after WWII.

	—	750	600	450	200	100

Astra 2000

Single-action semi-automatic pistol in .22- or 6.35mm caliber. No grip safety. With external hammer. Blued, with plastic grips.

	—	225	200	175	150	90

Astra 3000

Model 300 in 7.65mm or 9mm short, with 6- or 7-shot magazine. Loaded chamber indicator. Manufactured from 1948 to 1956.

	—	600	500	325	200	100

Astra 4000 Falcon

Semi-automatic pistol known later as "Falcon". Calibers were .22 LR, 7.65mm and 9mmK. Magazine capacity 7, 8 and 10 rounds. Manufactured beginning 1955.

	—	575	475	325	200	100

Astra 5000 Constable

.22, 7.65mm or 9mm short semi-automatic pistol (resembling Walther PP pistol), with 3.5" barrel. Blued, chrome-plated or stainless steel, with plastic grips. Also available with 6" barrel as a sport model. Introduced in 1965. **NOTE:** Add 15 percent for Constable Sport version with 6" barrel and adjustable sight.

	—	395	300	250	200	100

Astra 7000

Enlarged version of Model 2000 in .22-caliber.

	—	575	475	325	200	100

Astra A-80

.38 Super, 9mm or .45-caliber double-action semi-automatic pistol, with 3.75" barrel. Magazine capacity 9- or 15-shot, depending on caliber. Blued or chrome-plated, with plastic grips. Introduced in 1982.

	450	350	300	250	200	100

Astra A-90

As above in 9mm or .45-caliber only. Introduced in 1986.

	400	350	300	250	200	100

	NIB	EXC.	V.G.	GOOD	FAIR	POOR

Constable A-60

.380-caliber double-action semi-automatic pistol, with 3.5" barrel, adjustable sights and 13-shot magazine. Blued, with plastic grips. Introduced in 1986.

400	300	200	150	100	75

Astra Cadix

.22- or .38 Special double-action revolver, with 4" or 6" barrel. Swing-out cylinder holds 5- or 9-shots. Blued, with plastic grips. Manufactured from 1960 to 1968.

—	225	175	125	90	70

.357 Double-Action Revolver

Similar to Cadix in .357 Magnum caliber, with 3", 4", 6" or 8.5" barrel. Adjustable sights and 6-shot cylinder. Blued or stainless steel, with walnut grips. Manufactured from 1972 to 1988. **NOTE:** Stainless steel add 10 percent.

295	250	175	125	100	75

.44/.45 Double-Action Revolver

As above in .41-, .44 Magnum or .45 ACP caliber, with 6" or 8.5" barrels and 6-shot cylinder. Blued or stainless steel, with walnut grips. Manufactured from 1980 to 1987. **NOTE:** Stainless steel add 25 percent.

—	375	325	250	200	100

Terminator

As above in .44 Special or .44 Magnum, with 2.75" barrel. Adjustable sights and 6-shot cylinder. Blued or stainless steel, with rubber grips. **NOTE:** Stainless steel add 10 percent.

—	380	330	255	200	100

Convertible Revolver

Similar to .357 D/A revolver. Accompanied by a cylinder chambered for 9mm Parabellum. Barrel length 3". Blued, with walnut grips. Introduced in 1986.

—	395	325	275	150	100

RECENTLY IMPORTED PISTOLS

Model A-70

Lightweight semi-automatic pistol chambered for 9mm or .40 S&W cartridge. Fitted with 3-dot combat sights. Barrel 3.5" long. Magazine capacity 8 rounds for 9mm; 7 rounds for .40 S&W. Black plastic grips. Blue finish standard. Weight 29 oz. **NOTE:** Add $35 for nickel finish.

350	275	225	175	150	100

Model A-75

Introduced in 1993. All standard features of Model 70 plus selective double-/single trigger action and decocking lever. Chambered for 9mm, .40 S&W or .45 ACP. Offered in blue or nickel finish, with steel or alloy frame in 9mm only. Weight: steel frame in 9mm and .40 S&W is 31 oz.; .45 ACP is 34.4 oz.; featherweight 9mm is 23.5 oz. **NOTE:** Add $35 for nickel finish.

375	325	250	200	150	100

Model A-100

Semi-automatic service pistol. Chambered for 9mm Parabellum, .40 S&W or .45 ACP cartridges. Trigger is double-action for first shot, single-action for follow-up shots. Equipped with decocking lever. Barrel 3.8" long; overall length 7.5". Magazine capacity: 9mm is 17 rounds; .40 S&W is 13 rounds; .45 is 9 rounds. Blue or nickel finish standard. Weight about 34 oz. Also available in featherweight model 9mm at 26.5 oz. **NOTE:** Add $35 for nickel finish.

400	350	300	250	200	100

Model A-100 Carry Comp

Similar to Model A-100, with 4.25" barrel and 1" compensator. Blue finish only. Weight about 38 oz. Magazine capacity: 9mm is 17 rounds; .40 S&W and .45 ACP is 10 rounds.

475	375	300	250	200	100

ATCSA
Armas de Tiro y Casa
Eibar, Spain

Colt Police Positive Copy

.38-caliber 6-shot revolver resembling Colt Police Positive.

—	250	125	100	60	40

	NIB	EXC.	V.G.	GOOD	FAIR	POOR

Target Pistol

.22-caliber single-shot target pistol utilizing a revolver frame.

	NIB	EXC.	V.G.	GOOD	FAIR	POOR
	—	300	175	125	100	55

AUBREY, A.J.
Meriden, Connecticut

Double-Barrel Shotguns

Good quality doubles made for Sears. Value depends on condition, grade and model. Prices range between $100 and $1,500.

AUER, B.
Louisville, Kentucky

Pocket Pistol

.60-caliber percussion pocket pistol, with 4" octagonal barrel. Long tang extending well back along grip. Browned silver furniture. Checkered walnut stock. Lock marked "B. Auer". Produced during 1850s.

	NIB	EXC.	V.G.	GOOD	FAIR	POOR
	—	—	1700	700	250	100

AUGUSTA MACHINE WORKS
Augusta, Georgia

1851 Colt Navy Copy

.36-caliber percussion revolver, with 8" barrel and 6-shot cylinder. Unmarked except for serial numbers. Stop cylinder slots 6 or 12. Blued, with walnut grips. Very rare revolver.

	NIB	EXC.	V.G.	GOOD	FAIR	POOR
	—	—	62500	40000	17500	5000

AUSTIN & HALLECK, INC.
Weston, Missouri; later Provo, Utah

Model 320 LR BLU

In-line percussion bolt-action rifle. Fitted with 26" half octagon-half round barrel in .50-caliber. Receiver and barrel blue. Adjustable trigger. Receiver drilled and tapped for scope mount. Stock is black synthetic, with checkering. Weight about 7.87 lbs.

	NIB	EXC.	V.G.	GOOD	FAIR	POOR
	450	375	300	250	200	100

Model 320 S/S

Similar to above, with stainless steel barrel and action.

	NIB	EXC.	V.G.	GOOD	FAIR	POOR
	500	400	300	250	200	100

Model 420 LR Classic

Similar to Model 320 series. Standard lightly figured Maple stock in classic configuration. Available in blue or stainless steel. Premium for fancy wood.

	NIB	EXC.	V.G.	GOOD	FAIR	POOR
	500	425	300	250	200	100

Model 420 LR Monte Carlo

Same as classic series, with Monte Carlo stock and cheekpiece. Premium for fancy wood.

	NIB	EXC.	V.G.	GOOD	FAIR	POOR
	500	425	300	250	200	100

Mountain Rifle

.50-caliber percussion or flintlock rifle, with double-set triggers, 32" octagonal barrel, buckhorn sights, curly Maple stock and crescent steel buttplate. Weight about 7.5 lbs. Premium for fancy wood.

	NIB	EXC.	V.G.	GOOD	FAIR	POOR
	500	400	300	250	200	100

AUSTRALIAN AUTOMATIC ARMS LTD.
Tasmania, Australia

SAR

5.56mm semi-automatic rifle, with 16.25" or 20" barrel, 5- or 20-shot magazine, black plastic stock and fore-end. Imported from 1986 to 1989.

	NIB	EXC.	V.G.	GOOD	FAIR	POOR
	1200	950	650	350	250	125

SAP

10.5" barreled pistol version of above. Imported from 1986 to 1989.

	NIB	EXC.	V.G.	GOOD	FAIR	POOR
	1150	900	600	325	250	125

	NIB	EXC.	V.G.	GOOD	FAIR	POOR

SP

Sporting rifle version of SAR, with wood stock and 5-shot magazine. Introduced in 1989.

	975	850	575	300	250	125

AUTAUGA ARMS INC.
Prattville, Alabama

MK II

.32 ACP semi-automatic blowback pistol, with double-action trigger. Barrel length 2.25". Fixed sights. Overall length 4.25". Weight about 13.5 oz. Magazine capacity 6 rounds. Introduced in 1999.

	325	275	225	195	150	100

AUTO MAG
Various Manufacturers

Popular stainless steel semi-automatic pistol. Developed by Sanford Arms Company of Pasadena, California, in 1960s. Chambered for a special cartridge known as .44 AMP, which had a 240-grain .44-caliber bullet. Production of this arm has been carried out by a number of companies over the past 40-plus years, beginning in 1971. Believed that fewer than 10,000 have been produced by eight manufacturers involved.

AMT "C" SERIES

There were 100 guns produced in this series. First 50 were serial numbered with a "C" prefix. Second 50 were serial numbered "LAST 1" through "LAST 50". Available with 6.5" ventilated rib or 10" tapered barrel.

AUTO MAG, INC.
Irwindale, California

In 1998, this company was formed to produce 1,000 Harry Sanford Commemorative pistols. Chambered for .44 AMP cartridge. Each pistol comes in a walnut display case, special serial number, Harry Sanford's signature and name Auto Mag on receiver. Last retail price for Auto Mag is $2,750.

AUTO MAG CORP.
Pasadena, California

Serial number range A0000 through A3300. Made with 6.5" ventilated rib barrel. Chambered in .44 AMP only.

.44 AMP

	2700	1850	1475	995	600	300

HIGH STANDARD (2)
Hamden, Connecticut

High Standard was national distributor for Auto Mag in 1974 and 1975. These guns chambered for .44 AMP and .357 AMP. HS Cat. #9346 for .44 AMP, #9347 for .357 AMP.

High Standard sold 134 Auto Mags with "H" prefix. Serial numbers are between H1 and H198, one at H1566 and three between H17219 and H17222. Of these 108 were .44 AMP and 26 were .357 AMP.

High Standard also sold 911 Auto Mags between serial numbers A05278 and A07637. Of these, 777 were .44 AMP and 108 were .357 AMP.

	2200	1900	1350	900	600	300

KENT LOMONT

Pistols made by this maker are essentially proto-types, it is advised that potential purchasers secure a qualified appraisal.

L. E. JURRAS CUSTOM

Custom maker produced a limited number of Auto Mag pistols in 1977. These arms are worth approximately 35-50 percent more than standard production models.

TDE CORP.
El Monte, California

Serial number range A05016 through A08300. Standard 6.5" vent rib barrel. Also available in 8" and 10" barrel lengths. Chambered for .44 AMP and .357 AMP.

.357 AMP

	1750	1300	900	700	500	300

NIB	EXC.	V.G.	GOOD	FAIR	POOR

.44 AMP

| 1950 | 1550 | 1000 | 800 | 600 | 300 |

TDE CORP.
North Hollywood, California

Serial number range A3400 through A05015. Made with 6.5" vent rib barrel. Chambered in .44 AMP and .357 AMP.

.357 AMP

| 2300 | 1850 | 1325 | 900 | 600 | 300 |

.44 AMP

| 2150 | 1700 | 1250 | 850 | 600 | 300 |

TDE-OMC

Known as solid-bolt or "B" series. Serial number range is B00001 through B00370. Either 6.5" vent rib or 10" tapered barrels are available.

| 2550 | 2100 | 1600 | 1000 | 600 | 300 |

AUTO ORDNANCE CORP.

Auto Ordnance makes reproductions of 1911 Government Model pistol, Thompson sub-machine gun (semi-auto only) and M-1 Carbine. Variations of 1911 are marketed under both Auto Ordnance and Thompson brand names. In 1999, the company was bought by Kahr Arms and moved from West Hurley, New York to Worcester, Massachusetts.

Auto Ordnance 1911A1

Standard model in .45 ACP with 5"barrel, Parkerized finish, fixed sights, plastic or checkered walnut grips. Also offered in 9mm, .38 Super, 10mm (all discontinued in 1996) and .40 S&W (disc. 1993). Blue, satin nickel and two-tone finish were optional until 2005. In 2011 a 100th Anniversary Model was introduced, with appropriate rollmarks. **NOTE:** Add $35 for nickel, two-tone finish or 100th Anniversary Model.

| 565 | 525 | 475 | 400 | 300 | 200 |

Thompson Model 1911TC

.45 ACP semi-automatic, with fixed sights and 7+1 capacity. Stainless frame and slide. 5" barrel, weight 39 oz. Laminate grips.

| 650 | 525 | 395 | 300 | 200 | 100 |

Thompson Model 1911CAF

.45 ACP semi-automatic, with fixed sights and 7+1 capacity. Aluminum frame and stainless slide. 5" barrel, weight 31.5 oz. Laminate grips.

| 650 | 525 | 395 | 300 | 200 | 100 |

Thompson 1911 A1—Standard

9mm, .38 Super or .45-caliber copy of Colt Model 1911 A1. Weighs 39 oz. **NOTE:** 9mm and .38 Super add $20. 9mm and .38 Super discontinued in 1997.

| 475 | 325 | 275 | 200 | 150 | 100 |

Thompson 1911 A1—Parkerized

| 475 | 325 | 275 | 200 | 150 | 100 |

Thompson 1911 A1—Deluxe

Same as above in Hi-profile white 3-dot sight system. Black textured rubber wraparound grips.

| 800 | 650 | 500 | 300 | 150 | 100 |

Thompson 1911 A1—Custom High Polish

Introduced in 1997. Features special high polish blued finish, with numerous special options. Stocks rosewood, with medallion. Fitted with 5" barrel. Chambered for .45 ACP. Weight about 39 oz.

| 575 | 475 | — | — | — | — |

Thompson 1911 A1—10mm

Same as above. Chambered for 10mm cartridge. Magazine capacity 8 rounds. Discontinued in 1997.

| 700 | 550 | 400 | 250 | 175 | 100 |

Thompson 1911 A1—Duo Tone

Chambered for .45 ACP. Slide blued. Frame satin nickel. Discontinued in 1997.

| 500 | 425 | 350 | 225 | 150 | 100 |

	NIB	EXC.	V.G.	GOOD	FAIR	POOR

Thompson 1911 A1—Satin Nickel

Chambered for .45 ACP or .38 Super. Finish satin nickel on both frame and slide. Blade front sight. Black checkered plastic grips. Discontinued in 1997.

	500	425	350	225	150	100

Thompson 1911 A1—Competition

Chambered for .45 ACP or .38 Super. Fitted with 5" barrel, compensator and other competition features. Such as, custom Commander hammer, flat mainspring housing, beavertail grip safety, full-length recoil guide rod, extended ejector, slide stop and thumb safety. Weighs 42 oz.; 10" overall. Discontinued in 1997. **NOTE:** .38 Super add $10.

	700	625	500	350	300	150

Thompson 1911 A1—Pit Bull

Chambered for .45 ACP. Fitted with 3.5" barrel. High profile sights. Black textured rubber wraparound grips. Magazine capacity 7 rounds. Weighs 36 oz.

	500	425	350	225	150	100

Thompson 1911 A1—General

Commander-size pistol, with 4.5" barrel. High profile sights. Chambered for .45 ACP or .38 Super. Weighs 37 oz. Discontinued in 1997.

	500	425	350	225	150	100

ZG-51 "Pit Bull

Same as above, with 3.5" barrel in .45-caliber. Introduced in 1988. In 1994 renamed "PIT BULL". Discontinued.

	500	425	350	225	150	100

Thompson 1927 A1 Standard (New York Production)

Semi-automatic version of Thompson sub-machine gun. Chambered for .45 ACP cartridge, with 16.5" barrel. Is 18" with compensator. Blued, with walnut stock. Weight 13 lbs.

	1250	850	650	400	300	150

1927 A1 Deluxe/Model T1

As above, with finned barrel, adjustable sights, pistol-grip forearm and 50-round drum magazine (costing an additional $250). Violin-shaped carrying case adds approximately $150 to values listed.

	1350	950	695	400	300	150

1927 A1C/Model T5

As above, with aluminum alloy receiver. Introduced in 1984.

	1175	825	625	400	300	150

1927 A1 Commando/Model T1-C

Introduced in 1998. Features 16.5" finned barrel with compensator. Finish Parkerized, with black wood finish. Furnished with 30-round magazine and black nylon sling. Weight about 13 lbs.

	1250	850	650	400	300	150

1927 A5 Pistol/TA5

Pistol version of Model 1927 A1, with 13" finned barrel, aluminum alloy receiver and no shoulder stock. Reintroduced in 2008 with 10" barrel as Model TA5. Value of original model is debatable, with advertised prices higher than those shown here, but few apparent sales. TA5 version is expected to depress value of original 1927 A5s.

	2200	1300	1000	800	500	150

1927 A3

.22-caliber variation of Model 1927 A1, with 16" barrel and aluminum alloy receiver. No longer in production. **NOTE:** Add $500 for drum magazine.

	1350	900	675	550	425	150

T1SB

Short-barreled (10.5" finned and compensated) variant of semi-automatic M1. Accepts drum magazines. Requires Form 3. Introduced 2005.

	1500	1150	695	400	300	150

M1SB

Short-barreled (10.5" finned and compensated) variant of semi-automatic M1. Does not accept drum magazines. Requires Form 3.

	1500	1150	695	400	300	150

NIB	EXC.	V.G.	GOOD	FAIR	POOR

M1 Carbine

Newly manufactured replica of military M1 carbine. Chambered in .30 Carbine. Introduced 2005. Birch stock, Parkerized finish. **NOTE:** Add 5 percent for walnut stock.

950	800	650	500	300	125

AUTO POINTER
Yamamoto Co.
Tokyo, Japan

Auto Pointer Shotgun

12- or 20-gauge semi-automatic shotgun, with 26", 28" or 30" barrels. Aluminum alloy frame. Blued, with checkered walnut stock. Originally imported by Sloan's, no longer available. Clone of Browning A-5.

—	475	350	250	175	100

AXTELL RIFLE CO.
Riflesmith, Inc.
Sheridan, Montana

#1 Long Range Creedmore

Single-shot rifle. Chambered for .40-50BN, .40-70SS, .40-70BN, .40-90, .45-70, .45-90 and .45-100. Weight about 10 lbs. Numerous options will affect price.

4700	3750	3000	2200	1400	300

New Model Sharps 1877

Chambered for .45-90, .45-100 and .45-70 cartridges. Fitted with choice of 30" to 34" half round-half octagon barrel, with double-set triggers.

5200	4000	3250	2500	1500	250

#2 Long Range

Long Range #2 rifle. Chambered for all same calibers as #1 Long Range Creedmore. Weight about 10 lbs.

3900	3000	1900	900	550	300

Lower Sporting Rifle

Chambered for same calibers as above. Weight between 9 and 12 lbs. depending on barrel options.

2600	2000	1375	700	400	200

Business Rifle

Same calibers as above. Weight about 8.5 lbs.

2400	1800	1275	700	400	200

Overbaugh Schuetzen

Chambered for .40-50BN and .40-50 straight. Weight 11 to 14 lbs. depending on barrel options.

4400	3500	3000	2200	1400	300

AYA

For AyA shotguns, see entry under Aguirre y Aranzabal.

AZPIRI
Eibar, Spain

Spanish manufacturer of pistols prior to World War II.

Avion

6.35mm semi-automatic pistol. Copied after Model 1906 Browning. Marked "Pistolet Automatique Avion Brevete" on slide as well as on each side of grip plate along with an airplane logo. Manufactured from 1914 to 1918.

—	250	175	100	75	45

Colon

As above in 6.35mm caliber. Marked "Automatic Pistol Colon".

—	250	175	100	75	45

B

	NIB	EXC.	V.G.	GOOD	FAIR	POOR

B.R.F.
South Africa

B.R.F.

.25-caliber semi-automatic pistol. Similar to P.A.F., with 2" barrel and 6-shot magazine. "U-SA" means Union of South Africa. Little is known about manufacturer of this pistol, its origin or dates of manufacture.

—	295	195	125	100	70

BABBIT, A. S.
Plattsburgh, New York
See—Adirondack Arms

BABCOCK, MOSES
Charlestown, Massachusetts

Babcock Under Hammer Cane Gun

.52-caliber percussion cane gun, with 27" barrel. Overall length about 33". Folding trigger under hammer, with wood handle. Hammer marked "Moses Babcock/Charlestown". Active 1850s and 1860s.

—	—	2950	950	350	200

BACON ARMS CO.
Norwich, Connecticut

Bacon Arms operated from 1862 until 1891. They have become known primarily for production of cheaply made, solid-frame, rimfire revolvers known as "Suicide Specials". Bacon manufactured and sold under a number of different trademarks. They were: Bacon, Bonanza, Conqueror, Express, Gem, Governor, Guardian and Little Giant. Collector interest is low and values for all trademarks are quite similar.

—	295	225	100	75	50

BAER CUSTOM, LES
Hillsdale, Illinois

Long-standing 1911 pistolsmith is now producing custom quality 1911 pistols on a semi-production basis. Each pistol features a large number of custom characteristics such as forged steel frame, full slide recoil rod, double-serrated slide, beveled magazine well, checkered front strap, beavertail safety, extended magazine release button, Bo-Mar sights and many others, depending on specific model. Representative sampling of these fine Baer pistols appears below.

COMPETITION PISTOLS

Baer 1911 Ultimate Master Combat Pistol-Compensated

Chambered for .45 ACP. Fitted with triple-port tapered cone compensator.

2660	1850	1000	750	600	300

Baer 1911 Ultimate Master Steel Special

Designed for steel targets and Bianchi-style competition. Similar to above, but designed for light loads. Chambered for .38 Super. Hard chrome finish.

2900	2250	1500	950	750	350

Baer 1911 Ultimate Master Combat Pistol

Similar to other Baer Master series pistols. Offered in .45 ACP, .400 CorBon and .38 Super. Fitted with a large number of special features. Offered in 5" or 6" version. The 5" version also offered in 9x23 caliber.

6" Model

2600	1950	1350	850	650	350

5" Model

2670	1920	1425	800	600	350

Baer 1911 Ultimate Master Para

Designed for IPSC competition. Offered in Unlimited version, with compensator and scope or Limited version, with iron sights and no compensator.

	NIB	EXC.	V.G.	GOOD	FAIR	POOR

Unlimited Model
.45 ACP, .38 Super, 9x23.

	NIB	EXC.	V.G.	GOOD	FAIR	POOR
	3400	2700	1750	1200	850	400

Limited Model

	NIB	EXC.	V.G.	GOOD	FAIR	POOR
	2900	2000	1500	900	650	300

Baer 1911 Bullseye Wadcutter Pistol
Designed for use with wadcutter loads only. Chambered for .45 ACP. **NOTE:** Version also offered with Baer Optical mount add $125; 6" slide with LoMount BoMar sight add $200.

	NIB	EXC.	V.G.	GOOD	FAIR	POOR
	1650	1250	800	600	500	250

Baer 1911 National Match Hardball Pistol
Designed for DCM matches. Chambered for .45 ACP.

	NIB	EXC.	V.G.	GOOD	FAIR	POOR
	1425	1050	700	500	400	200

Baer 1911 Target Master
Designed for NRA centerfire matches. Chambered for .45 ACP.

	NIB	EXC.	V.G.	GOOD	FAIR	POOR
	1450	1150	750	550	450	250

Baer 1911 IPSC Action Pistol
Chambered for .45 ACP, with blued slide and frame.

	NIB	EXC.	V.G.	GOOD	FAIR	POOR
	1700	1350	850	600	450	300

Baer 1911 P.P.C. Distinguished Match
Introduced in 1999. Features 5" barrel, with adjustable Aristrocrat rear sight. Many, many special features such as double serrated slide, lowered and flared ejection port, extended ambi safety, checkered front strap, etc. Offered in .45 ACP and 9mm, with supported chamber. Blued finish and one magazine. **NOTE:** Add approximately $400 for 9mm model.

	NIB	EXC.	V.G.	GOOD	FAIR	POOR
	1950	1450	900	650	475	300

Baer 1911 P.P.C. Open Class
Similar to above. Fitted with 6" barrel and slide. Chambered for .45 ACP and 9mm, with supported chamber. Blued finish. Introduced in 1999. **NOTE:** Add approximately $400 for 9mm model.

	NIB	EXC.	V.G.	GOOD	FAIR	POOR
	2150	1550	950	700	500	350

DUTY & DEFENSE PISTOLS

Baer 1911 Premier II
Designed as a duty or defense pistol. Chambered for .45 ACP, .400 CorBon and 9x23 cartridges. Fitted with 5" slide. **NOTE:** Add $150 for stainless steel version; $100 for .400 CorBon; $250 for 9x23.

	NIB	EXC.	V.G.	GOOD	FAIR	POOR
	1790	1350	900	600	450	250

Baer 1911 Premier II—6" barrel
Same as above. Fitted with 6" match grade barrel. **NOTE:** Add $100 for .400 CorBon; $300 for .38 Super. 9x23 not offered with 6" slide.

	NIB	EXC.	V.G.	GOOD	FAIR	POOR
	1990	1600	1100	900	700	350

Baer 1911 Premier II—Light Weight (LW1)
Same features as standard Premier II, with reduced weight aluminum frame. Furnished with low mount LCB adjustable rear sight. Offered in .45 ACP only.

	NIB	EXC.	V.G.	GOOD	FAIR	POOR
	1900	1550	1100	900	700	350

Baer 1911 Premier II—Light Weight (LW2)
Same as above, with fixed combat-style rear sight.

	NIB	EXC.	V.G.	GOOD	FAIR	POOR
	1900	1550	1100	900	700	350

Baer 1911 Premier II—Super-Tac
Similar to standard Premier II models, with low mount adjustable rear night sight and front sight. Special BEAR COAT finish. Offered in .45 ACP, .40 S&W, .400 CorBon. **NOTE:** Dual caliber .45 ACP/.400 CorBon combo add $200.

	NIB	EXC.	V.G.	GOOD	FAIR	POOR
	2280	1700	900	900	700	350

Baer 1911 Prowler III
Similar to Premier II, with tapered cone stub weight, full-length guide rod and reverse plug. Special order only.

	NIB	EXC.	V.G.	GOOD	FAIR	POOR
	2580	1700	1200	950	700	350

NIB	EXC.	V.G.	GOOD	FAIR	POOR

Baer 1911 Prowler IV

Chambered for .45 ACP or .38 Super. Built on Para-Ordnance oversize frame. Fitted with 5" slide. Special order only. **NOTE:** Optional 6" barrel and slide add $300.

2580	1900	1250	900	650	300

Baer 1911 Custom Carry—Commanche Length

Chambered for .45 ACP. Has several options including 4.5" barrel, stainless steel slide and frame, lightweight aluminum frame with blued steel slide. As of 2000, furnished with night sights. **NOTE:** Stainless steel add $40; lightweight frame add $130.

1850	1400	950	600	450	250

Baer 1911 Custom Carry—5

Same as above. Offered with 5" slide. Not offered in aluminum frame. **NOTE:** Add $40 for stainless steel.

2120	1700	950	600	450	250

Baer 1911 Thunder Ranch Special

Features steel frame and slide, with front and rear serrations. Deluxe fixed rear sight, with tritium insert. Checkered front strap. Numerous special features. Slim line grips, with Thunder Ranch logo. Seven-round magazine standard. Special serial numbers with "TR" prefix. Offered in .45 ACP. **NOTE:** Add 10 percent for Comanche length; 5 percent for home defense model.

1990	1500	950	600	450	250

Baer 1911 Thunder Ranch Special Engraved Model

As above, with engraved frame and slide.

6600	4750	2500	1500	1150	650

Baer S.R.P. (Swift Response Pistol)

Chambered for .45 ACP. Built on Para-Ordnance frame. This unit similar to one supplied to FBI. Supplied with wooden presentation box. **NOTE:** S.R.P. models built on Baer frame or shorter 4.5" frame subtract $300 from NIB through Fair prices.

2590	2250	1750	1200	850	400

Baer 1911 Monolith

Introduced in 1999. Features 5" barrel and slide with extra long dust cover. Chambered in .45 ACP, .400 CorBon, .40 S&W, 9x23, 9mm, or .38 Super all with supported chamber. Many special features such as BoMar sights, Commander-style hammer, speed trigger, etc. Blued finish with one magazine. Weight about 37 oz. **NOTE:** All other supported calibers add $250.

1850	1500	950	675	500	325

Baer 1911 Monolith Heavyweight

Introduced in 1999. Similar to Monolith, with addition of heavier frame that adds 3.5 oz. Same calibers as available on Monolith. Weight about 40 oz. **NOTE:** All other supported calibers add $200.

1930	1700	1100	775	425	250

Baer 1911 Monolith Tactical Illuminator

Introduced in 1999. Same features as Monolith Heavyweight, with addition of light mounted under dust cover. Offered in .45 ACP and .40 S&W with supported chamber. Weight with light about 44 oz. **NOTE:** All other supported calibers add $275.

1850	1500	1050	795	425	250

Baer 1911 Monolith Commanche

Fitted with 4.25" slide and dust cover covering length of slide. Has all features of standard Monolith. Comes with night sights and deluxe fixed rear sight. Edges rounded for tactical carry. Chambered in .45 ACP only. Introduced in 2001.

1990	1750	1100	650	400	225

Baer 1911 Monolith Commanche Heavyweight

Exactly as above, with thicker dust cover to add an additional 2 oz. of weight. Introduced in 2001.

2150	1800	1000	600	375	200

Baer 1911 Stinger

Features shorter Officer's grip frame and Commanche slide and barrel. Many special features. Offered in .45 ACP. Choice of aluminum frame with blued slide; aluminum frame with stainless steel slide; stainless steel frame and slide. Weight in aluminum about 28 oz.; stainless steel about 34 oz. Introduced in 1999. **NOTE:** Aluminum frame and blued slide with supported calibers add

	NIB	EXC.	V.G.	GOOD	FAIR	POOR

$300; aluminum frame with stainless slide and supported chamber add $340; stainless frame and slide with supported chamber add $140.

	1890	1600	1050	750	400	225

Baer 1911 Stinger Stainless

Same as above, with stainless steel frame and slide. Introduced in 2001.

	1970	1670	1100	775	425	250

NEW CONCEPT PISTOLS

Line of 1911 pistols offers custom features at slightly lower cost. Each succeeding grade offers a few more features.

Baer 1911 Concept I

Chambered for .45 ACP. Fitted with BoMar sights.

	1690	1450	975	750	550	300

Baer 1911 Concept II

Same as above. Fitted with Baer adjustable sights.

	1690	1450	975	750	550	300

Baer 1911 Concept III

Same as above, with stainless steel frame. Blued steel slide. BoMar sights.

	1840	1550	975	800	550	300

Baer 1911 Concept IV

Same as above, with Baer adjustable sights.

	1840	1550	975	800	550	300

Baer 1911 Concept V

Model has both stainless steel slide and frame. BoMar sights.

	1950	1890	975	800	550	300

Baer 1911 Concept V 6"

Identical to Concept V, with addition of 6" barrel and slide. Introduced in 1999.

	2050	1990	1075	900	650	350

Baer 1911 Concept VI

Same as above. Fitted with Baer adjustable sights.

	2050	1990	1075	900	650	350

Baer 1911 Concept VI L.W.

Same as above. Built on aluminum frame, with supported chamber. National Match barrel.

	2050	1990	1075	900	650	350

Baer 1911 Concept VII

Features all blued 4.5" steel frame and slide. Baer fixed night sights.

	2050	1990	1075	900	650	350

Baer 1911 Concept VIII

Same as above, with stainless steel slide and frame. Fixed combat night sights standard.

	2100	1850	1500	1250	700	300

Baer 1911 Concept IX

Version has lightweight aluminum frame, with 4.5" steel slide.

	2100	1850	1500	1250	700	300

Baer 1911 Concept X

Features 4.5" stainless steel slide. Lightweight aluminum frame.

	2100	1850	1500	1250	700	300

Baer Lightweight .22 caliber 1911 Models

4.5" Model with fixed sights

	1525	1400	950	800	550	300

5" Model with fixed sights

	1625	1400	950	800	550	300

	NIB	EXC.	V.G.	GOOD	FAIR	POOR

5" Model with Bo-Mar sights

	NIB	EXC.	V.G.	GOOD	FAIR	POOR
	1700	1475	1000	850	600	300

Baer Limited Edition Presentation Grade 1911

Fully hand engraved Baer 1911, with special bluing in presentation wooden box.

	NIB	EXC.	V.G.	GOOD	FAIR	POOR
	6590	3995	2500	1750	1150	500

Model 1911 Twenty-Fifth Anniversary

Custom-engraved limited collector edition .45 ACP semi-automatic. Built on fully functional equipped Baer Premier II. Hand engraved both sides of slide and frame. Les Baer signature. Inlaid with white gold. Ivory grips. Deep blue finish. Presentation box. Introduced 2006.

	NIB	EXC.	V.G.	GOOD	FAIR	POOR
	6590	3995	2500	1750	1150	500

Ultimate Recon

Semi-automatic with integral Picatinny rail, 5" barrel, .45 ACP. Blue or chrome. Comes with SureFire X-200 light. Fixed sights. 4-pound trigger. Two 8-round magazines. Cocobolo grips. Add $500 for hard chrome.

	NIB	EXC.	V.G.	GOOD	FAIR	POOR
	3070	2590	1650	1100	775	450

RIFLES

AR .223 Ultimate Super Varmint

Fitted with choice of 18", 20" or 24" heavy barrels, with 1-in-12 twist. Flat top rail. Choice of single or two-stage trigger. Aluminum free-floating handguard. Bear Coat finish. Introduced in 2000.

	NIB	EXC.	V.G.	GOOD	FAIR	POOR
	1975	1600	1300	900	600	300

AR .223 Ultimate Super Match

Introduced in 2002. Wide number of custom features, with barrel lengths from 18" to 24". Special match carrier with integral rail system.

	NIB	EXC.	V.G.	GOOD	FAIR	POOR
	2125	1700	1400	1000	750	500

AR .223 M4-A2 Flattop

Features flat top rail and match bolt and carrier. 16" barrel has integral compensator. Single-stage trigger. Knights Armament Systems rail adapter. Bear Coat finish. Introduced in 2000.

	NIB	EXC.	V.G.	GOOD	FAIR	POOR
	2175	1725	1425	1025	675	400

AR .223 IPSC Action Model

Similar to above, with 18" Super Match heavy barrel. Integral compensator. Introduced in 2000.

	NIB	EXC.	V.G.	GOOD	FAIR	POOR
	2300	1875	1550	1100	700	450

AR .223 Ultimate NRA Match

Numerous custom features. Fitted with 30" barrel. Special front and rear sights. **NOTE:** Add $750 for special sight package.

	NIB	EXC.	V.G.	GOOD	FAIR	POOR
	2500	2000	1350	900	600	375

Bullpup Muzzleloader

.50-caliber muzzleloader. Fitted with 28" stainless steel barrel, Williams front sight and M16 National Match rear sight. Maple or synthetic stock. Internal ignition system. Discontinued. **NOTE:** Add $30 for maple stock and stainless steel.

	NIB	EXC.	V.G.	GOOD	FAIR	POOR
	750	575	395	300	225	165

Thunder Ranch Rifle

.223 model fitted with bench-rest 16" barrel. Upper receiver has carry handle and top rail. Free-floating handguard, jewel two-stage trigger, floating front sight and many other custom features. "Thunder Ranch" logo stamped on lower receiver. Weight about 7.5 lbs. Introduced in 2004.

	NIB	EXC.	V.G.	GOOD	FAIR	POOR
	2500	2000	1350	900	600	375

Monolith .308 S.W.A.T.

Military type match sniper rifle. Chambered in .308 Winchester. Solid full-length Picatinny rail for scope mounting. DuPont-S coating on barrel, two-stage trigger group with choice of 18", 20" (standard) or 24" barrel. Two magazines and soft case included. Introduced in 2011.

	NIB	EXC.	V.G.	GOOD	FAIR	POOR
	3500	3000	2600	2000	1000	500

NIB	EXC.	V.G.	GOOD	FAIR	POOR

BAFORD ARMS, INC.
Bristol, Tennessee

Thunder Derringer

.410 bore or .44 Special single-shot pistol, with 3" interchangeable barrels and spur trigger. Additional interchangeable barrels are chambered in calibers from .22 to 9mm. Also available with scope. Blued, with walnut grip. Introduced in 1988. **NOTE:** Add $50 for interchangeable barrel.

175	110	85	70	55	35

Fire Power Model 35

9mm semi-automatic pistol, with 4.75" barrel, Millett adjustable sights and 14-shot magazine. Fitted with combat safety hammer and Pachmayr grips. Stainless steel. Introduced in 1988.

550	450	365	300	250	125

BAIKAL
Izhevsk, Russia

Baikal is a Russian firearms manufacturer, with a history that goes back to World War II when it made military weapons like Tokarev pistols for the old Soviet Union. After the war, company expanded into sporting firearms, mainly shotguns.

Baikal IJ-27E1C

12- or 20-gauge Magnum over/under shotgun, with 26" Skeet-Skeet or 28" Modified-Full ventilated rib barrels, single-selective trigger and extractors. Blued, with walnut stock.

375	275	200	150	100	75

Baikal TOZ - 34

12- or 28-gauge double-barrel shotgun, with 26" or 28" barrels, double triggers, cocking indicators and extractors. Blued, with checkered walnut stock. Also available with silver-plated receiver.

400	300	250	200	100	75

Model MC-8-0

12-gauge double-barrel shotgun, with 26" Skeet-Skeet or 28" Full-Modified barrels, hand fitted action and engraved receiver.

2000	1250	950	700	500	250

Model MC-5-105

Model TOZ-34, with engraved receiver.

1200	850	700	500	300	150

Model MC-7

As above, with relief engraved receiver.

2250	1750	1200	800	550	250

IZH18/MP18

Single-barrel shotgun chambered for 12- and 20-gauge or .410 bore. Choice of 26.5" or 29.5" barrels. Hardwood stock and ejectors. Introduced in 1999.

95	75	50	35	25	10

IZK18MAX

Similar to above, with polished nickel receiver, vent rib, walnut stock, screw-in chokes and ejectors. Offered in 12- and 20-gauge and .410 bore.

170	125	100	75	50	25

IZH43

Side-by-side available in 12-, 16-, 20-, 28-gauge or .410 bore. Barrel lengths 20" to 28" depending on gauge. Internal hammers. Single-selective trigger, ejectors. Walnut stock. **NOTE:** Add $80 for 28-gauge and .410 bore.

350	275	200	150	100	75

IZH43K

Introduced in 1999. A 12- or 20-gauge, 3" side-by-side external hammer shotgun. Barrel lengths 18.5", 20", 24", 26" and 28". Single-selective or double trigger. Engraved side plates. Walnut stock with pistol-grip. Weight about 7.3 lbs. **NOTE:** Deduct $40 for double triggers.

375	300	250	175	125	100

	NIB	EXC.	V.G.	GOOD	FAIR	POOR

MP213 Coach Gun

Similar to above, with internal hammers. Single or double triggers. Weight about 7 lbs. Barrel inserts for .45-70 were offered. **NOTE:** Add 25 percent for .45-70 inserts.

NIB	EXC.	V.G.	GOOD	FAIR	POOR
650	500	400	350	100	75

IZH27

Over/under gun chambered for 12-, 20-, 28-gauge and .410 bore. Choice of 26.5" or 28.5" barrels. Walnut stock. Single trigger with ejectors. Fixed chokes. **NOTE:** Add $35 for screw-in chokes; $85 for 28-gauge and .410 bore.

NIB	EXC.	V.G.	GOOD	FAIR	POOR
350	275	200	150	100	75

MP233

Over/under gun chambered for 12-gauge 3" shell, with choice of 26", 28" or 30" barrels. Walnut checkered stock. Single or double triggers. Screw-in chokes. Removable trigger assembly. Weight about 7.3 lbs. Introduced in 1999.

NIB	EXC.	V.G.	GOOD	FAIR	POOR
700	600	500	400	175	100

IZH94/MP94

Over/under combination gun, with 12-gauge upper barrel and centerfire rifle lower barrel. Barrel lengths 24" or 26". Model offered as an over/under rifle in calibers .222, .223, 6.5x55, .308, .30-06 or 7.62x39. A .410/.22LR or .410/.22 WMR model is available. Walnut stock single or double trigger. Weight about 8 - 10 lbs. Open sights. **NOTE:** Deduct 40 percent for .410.

NIB	EXC.	V.G.	GOOD	FAIR	POOR
525	475	425	350	300	175

IZH81

Pump-action shotgun chambered for 12-gauge 3" shells. Barrel lengths 20", 26" or 28". Five-round detachable magazine. Walnut stock. **NOTE:** Add $60 for vent rib.

NIB	EXC.	V.G.	GOOD	FAIR	POOR
300	225	165	125	97	50

MP131K

Pump-action shotgun, with choice of two different feeding sources: tubular magazine or detachable 3- or 5-round box magazine.

NIB	EXC.	V.G.	GOOD	FAIR	POOR
300	225	165	125	97	50

MP133

Slide-action shotgun chambered for 12-gauge 3.5" shell. Available barrel lengths 20", 24", 26" or 28". Vent rib on all barrel lengths except 20". Walnut stock. Choke tubes for all barrel lengths except 20" (Cylinder choke). Introduced in 2001.

NIB	EXC.	V.G.	GOOD	FAIR	POOR
300	225	165	125	95	50

MP153

Semi-automatic shotgun chambered for 12-gauge 3" shell. Barrels 26" or 28". Walnut or black synthetic stock. Weight about 7.8 lbs. Screw-in chokes. Introduced in 1999.

NIB	EXC.	V.G.	GOOD	FAIR	POOR
400	325	250	200	100	65

IZH35

Semi-automatic pistol chambered for .22 LR cartridge. Fully adjustable target-grip, adjustable trigger assembly, cocking indicator, detachable scope. Fitted with 6" barrel. Introduced in 2000.

NIB	EXC.	V.G.	GOOD	FAIR	POOR
500	400	350	200	165	95

MP310

Originally imported as Model IZH2. Over/under now marketed as MP310. Offered in 12- and 20-gauge or .410 bore, with 26" or 28" barrels. Hammer forged barrels, machined steel receiver. Monoblock checkered walnut two-piece stock. Hard chrome-lined barrels, ventilated rib, ejectors, auto safety and single selective trigger.

NIB	EXC.	V.G.	GOOD	FAIR	POOR
475	425	350	300	250	200

MP220

Side-by-side field gun has single selective trigger, ejectors, machined steel boxlock receiver, checkered walnut stock with recoil pad, splinter fore-end, automatic tang safety and screw-in chokes. In 12-, 16-, 20-, 28-gauge and .410 bore. Weight is 8 to 10 lbs.

NIB	EXC.	V.G.	GOOD	FAIR	POOR
300	250	200	175	150	100

CURRENTLY IMPORTED BAIKAL SHOTGUNS
Importer—European American Armory

A custom-made O/U shotgun with detachable sidelocks. Produced in limited quantities and most often to the purchaser's specifications.

BAILONS GUNMAKERS, LTD.
Birmingham, England

Most products of this company **were** produced strictly on custom order. No longer in business.

Hunting Rifle

Bolt-action sporting rifle. Produced in a variety of calibers with 24" barrel, open sights, double-set triggers and 3- or 4-shot magazine. Blued, with well-figured walnut stock. Values listed for standard grade rifle.

| 3500 | 2950 | 2450 | 1900 | 675 | 325 |

BAKER, M.A.
Fayetteville, North Carolina

In business from 1857 through 1862. Baker produced sporting arms prior to Civil War. During Civil War, Baker altered muskets and "common rifles". In addition, it is thought Baker made rifles for State of North Carolina with lockplates stamped "M.A. Baker/Fayetteville/N.C.". These rifles resembled U.S. Model 1841 Rifle and had these characteristics: overall length 51.5"; barrel length 35.125"; caliber .50.

| — | — | 26000 | 13500 | 3200 | 1500 |

BAKER, THOMAS

Baker shotguns and rifles were extensively imported into United States during nineteenth and early twentieth centuries. His premises were as follows:

1 Stonecutter Street	1838-1844
Bury Street, St. James	1844-1850
34 St. James Street	1850
88 Fleet Street	1851-1881
88 Fleet Street & 21 Cockspur Street	1882-1898
88 Fleet Street & 29 Glasshouse Street	1899-1905
29 Glasshouse Street	1905-1915
64 Haymarket	1915

BAKER, WILLIAM
Marathon, Syracuse and Ithaca, New York

William Baker designed and built double barrel shotguns from approximately 1869 until his death in 1889. His hammerless designs were used by Baker Gun & Forging Company of Batavia, New York, which was established by his brother Elias in early 1890.

BAKER GAS SEAL
London, England

.577-caliber percussion revolver, with 6.5" octagonal barrel and 6-shot cylinder. When hammer is cocked, cylinder is forced forward tightly against barrel breech, thus creating a gas seal. Blued case hardened, with walnut grips.

| — | 2500 | 1900 | 1500 | 875 | 350 |

BAKER GUN & FORGING CO.
Batavia, New York

Baker Gun & Forging Company founded in early 1890, by Elias Baker, brother of William Baker. Made from drop forged parts, Baker single-/double barrel shotguns quickly gained a reputation for strength and reliability among shooters of the period. Offered in a wide variety of grades, from plain utilitarian to heavily embellished models. Baker shotguns have in recent years become highly collectible. Company was sold on December 24, 1919, to H. & D. Folsom Arms Company of Norwich, Connecticut. Folsom Company had, for almost 20 years, been Baker Company's sole New York City agent and had marketed at least one Baker model that was only made for them. From 1919 to approximately 1923, Folsom continued to assemble and make Baker shotguns. Late model Bakers were made by Crescent Firearms Company and have serial numbers with an "F" suffix.

Baker Gun & Forging Company was first the American arms manufacturer to:

1. Make a single barrel trap shotgun.
2. Make a single barrel trap shotgun with ventilated rib.
3. Make arms with an intercepting firing pin block safety.
4. Make a double barrel shotgun, with hammers directly behind the firing pins.
5. Use a long swinging sear, that once adjusted, gave consistent trigger pull throughout the working life of an arm. Baker shotguns manufactured between 1913 and 1923, that were engraved by Rudolph J. Kornbrath, command substantial price premiums over values listed.

	NIB	EXC.	V.G.	GOOD	FAIR	POOR

Baker Trap Gun

12-gauge single barrel boxlock shotgun, with 30" or 32" barrel. Blued case hardened, with walnut stock.

	NIB	EXC.	V.G.	GOOD	FAIR	POOR
	—	1800	1450	1050	500	250

Elite Grade

Standard scrollwork. Simple game scenes engraved on receiver.

	—	2800	2400	1500	1000	600

Superba

Heavily engraved on receiver and sides of barrel breech.

	—	4500	3300	1800	1200	1000

Expert Grade Double Shotgun

Highest grade shotgun manufactured by Baker Gun & Forging Company. General specifications as above. Stock of imported English or French walnut. Engraving full coverage type and partially chiselled. Automatic ejectors and single trigger, if requested. Built on special order only.

	—	7000	5500	4000	1800	750

Deluxe Grade Double Shotgun

Designation given those Expert Grade shotguns produced by H. & D. Folsom from 1919 to 1923. Characteristics identical to those listed for Baker Expert Grade Double Shotgun. **NOTE:** Add 80 percent for this model. Very rare.

Black Beauty Double Shotgun

Made solely for H. & D. Folsom Arms Company. A 12- or 16-gauge double barrel shotgun, with sidelocks; 26", 28", 30" or 32" barrels in 12-gauge; 26", 28" or 30" barrels in 16-gauge. Barrels blued, receiver case hardened, sideplates finished with black oxide, stock is walnut. Automatic ejectors and single trigger are extra cost options.

	—	1150	1000	850	700	250

Grade S Double Shotgun

As above, with simple engraving.

	—	1550	1250	950	500	250

Grade R Double Shotgun

As above, with case hardened sideplates. Engraved with simple scrollwork and game scenes.

	—	1950	1500	1100	600	300

Paragon Grade Shotgun

As above, with finely cut scrollwork and detailed game scenes engraved on sideplates. Stock of finely figured walnut.

	—	4000	3000	2200	1000	500

Paragon Grade—Model NN

As above, but more finely engraved. Built on special order only. Automatic ejectors.

	—	4500	3500	2700	2000	800

Batavia Special

12- or 16-gauge double barrel shotgun, with sidelocks; 28", 30" or 32" barrels in 12-gauge; 28" or 30" barrels in 16-gauge. Blued case hardened, with walnut stock. Double triggers.

	—	850	550	450	225	175

Batavia Brush Gun

12- or 16-gauge double barrel shotgun, with sidelocks and 26" barrels. Blued case hardened, with walnut stock. Sling rings and swivels optional.

	—	750	600	550	225	175

Batavia Leader

12- or 16-gauge double barrel shotgun, with sidelocks; 26", 28", 30" or 32" barrels in 12-gauge; 26", 28" or 30" barrels in 16-gauge. Blued case hardened, with walnut stock. Double triggers.

	—	1500	1000	600	400	200

Batavia Damascus

As above, with Damascus barrels.

	—	1750	1200	600	225	175

	NIB	EXC.	V.G.	GOOD	FAIR	POOR

Baker Hammer Gun

10-, 12- or 16-gauge double barrel shotgun, with sidehammers. 30" and 32" barrels in 10-gauge; 26" to 32" barrels in 12-gauge; 26" to 30" barrels in 16-gauge. Browned case hardened, with walnut stock. Double triggers.

—	450	350	275	195	100	

Batavia Automatic Rifle

.22-caliber semi-automatic rifle, with 24" round barrel. Detachable 7-shot magazine. Blued, with walnut stock.

—	625	550	300	160	70	

BALL REPEATING CARBINE
Lamson & Co.
Windsor, Vermont

Ball Repeating Carbine

.50-caliber lever-action repeating carbine, with 20.5" round barrel and 7-shot magazine. Receiver marked "E.G. Lamson & Co./Windsor, Vt./U.S./Ball's Patent/June 23, 1863/Mar. 15, 1864". Blued case hardened, with walnut stock. Late production examples of this carbine have been noted with browned or bright barrels. In excess of 1,500 made between 1864 and 1867.

—	—	5500	3000	1100	500	

BALLARD, C. H.
Worcester, Massachusetts

Single-Shot Derringer

.41-caliber rimfire spur trigger single-shot pistol, with 2.75" barrel marked "Ballard's". Blued, with silver-plated frame. Walnut grips. Manufactured during 1870s. **NOTE:** Iron frame model add 20 percent.

—	—	1775	1450	550	225	

BALLARD PATENT ARMS
(until 1873; after 1875, see MARLIN)

On Nov. 5, 1861 C.H. Ballard, of Worcester, Massachusetts, received a patent for a breechloading mechanism that would remain in production for nearly thirty years. Ballard patented a breechblock that tilted down at its front to expose breech by activating lever/triggerguard. During the twelve years that followed, Ballard rifles, carbines and shotguns were produced by five interrelated companies. Four of these were successive: Ball & Williams, R. Ball & Co. (both of Worcester, Massachusetts), Merrimack Arms & Manufacturing Co. and Brown Manufacturing Company (both of Newburyport, Massachusetts). These four companies produced Ballard arms in a successive serial range (1 through approximately 22,000), all marked on top of frame and barrel where it joins the frame. In 1863 another company, Dwight, Chapin & Company of Bridgeport, Connecticut, also produced Ballard rifles and carbines in a larger frame size, but in a different serial range (1 through about 1,900), usually marked on left side of frame below agents' mark. Large frame carbines and rifles were produced to fulfill a U.S. War Department contract initially for 10,000 of each, subsequently reduced to 1,000 of each, issued to Merwin & Bray sole agents for Ballard Patent Arms between 1862 and 1866. Most production during this period concentrated on military contracts, either for U.S. War Department or state of Kentucky, although state of New York also purchased 500 for its state militia.

Ballard (Ball & Williams) Sporting Rifles, First Type (Serial numbers 1-100)

Barrel length 24"; caliber .38 rimfire. Markings: "BALL & WILLIAMS/Worcester, Mass." and "BALLARD'S PATENT/Nov. 5, 1861" on octagonal barrel. Distinctive feature of earliest production of Ballard rifles is presence of internal extractor conforming to patent specifications. After approximately 100 rifles, this feature was dropped in favor of a manual extractor located under the barrel.

—	—	5000	3000	1250	500	

Ballard (Ball & Williams) Sporting Rifles, Second Type (Serial numbers 200-1600, and 1600-14,000, interspersed with martial production)

Barrel length 24", 28" or 30" usually octagonal, but part round/part octagonal as well; calibers .32, .38 and .44 rimfire. Markings: "BALL & WILLIAMS/Worcester, Mass.", "BALLARD'S PATENT/ Nov. 5, 1861" and "MERWIN & BRAY, AGT'S/ NEW YORK", on facets of barrel until about serial no. 9000. Thereafter, patent name and date on right side of frame and manufacturer and agents on left side of frame. On early production (200 to 1500), extractor knob is smaller and crescent shaped. Early production (prior to about serial no. 10,000) have solid breechblocks; after that

NIB	EXC.	V.G.	GOOD	FAIR	POOR

number breechblocks are made in two halves. A few of these arms were made with bronze frames to facilitate engraving and plating. These should command a higher premium.

NIB	EXC.	V.G.	GOOD	FAIR	POOR
—	—	2000	1650	730	280

Ballard (Ball & Williams) Sporting Rifles, Third Type
(Serial numbers 14,000-15,000)

These arms essentially the same as second type in characteristics, but have Merwin & Bray's alternate percussion mechanism built into breechblock. Hammer is accordingly marked on left side "PATENTED JAN. 5, 1864".

NIB	EXC.	V.G.	GOOD	FAIR	POOR
—	—	1400	1100	550	225

Ballard (Ball & Williams) Military Carbines
(Serial numbers 1500-7500, and 8500-10500)

Overall length 37.25"; barrel (bore) length 22"; caliber .44 rimfire. Markings: same as Ballard/Ball & Williams sporting rifles second type. Additional marks on U.S. War Department purchases include inspector's initials "MM" or "GH" on left side of frame and "MM" on barrel, breechblock, buttplate and on left side of buttstock in script within an oval cartouche. Three thousand of earlier production (serial numbers 1700 through about 5000) of these carbines were sold to state of Kentucky under an August 1862 contract, extended in April 1863. In November 1863, Kentucky contracted for an additional 1,000 carbines. In the interim, state of New York purchased 500 for distribution to its militia. U.S. War Department ordered 5,000 under a contract signed in January of 1864, but Ball & Williams delivered only 1,500 (serial numbers noted in range of 9800 through 10600) while concentrating production on their more lucrative Kentucky contract. Another 600 of the federal contract were partially inspected (serial numbers about 6500 to 7100-MM in cartouche in stock only), but were rejected because barrels had been rifled prior to proofing; these were sold to Kentucky in September 1864 on an open market purchase. Carbines marked with federal inspection marks usually bring a premium.

NIB	EXC.	V.G.	GOOD	FAIR	POOR
—	—	5775	4150	1750	675

Ballard (Ball & Williams) "Kentucky" Half-Stock Rifles

Overall length 45.375"; barrel (bore) length 30"; caliber .44 rimfire. These half-stock rifles bear standard Ball & Williams markings upon their barrels. In addition they have state ownership mark "KENTUCKY" on barrel forward of rear sights. Total of 1,000 (serial numbers about 7100 through 8550) were contracted by Kentucky in November 1863 and delivered between January and April 1864.

NIB	EXC.	V.G.	GOOD	FAIR	POOR
—	—	2300	1900	800	350

Ballard (Ball & Williams) "Kentucky"Full-Stock Rifles

Overall length 45.25"; barrel (bore) length 30"; caliber .46 rimfire. Marked on frame with standard Ball & Williams manufacturer (left), agent (left) and patent (right) markings. Rifles are additionally distinguished by state ownership mark "KENTUCKY" stamped into top of frame near breech. Kentucky contracted for 3,000 of these arms in November 1863, initially in .56-caliber. However, by mutual consent of state and contractors, in February 1864 caliber of arms was changed to .46. All deliveries were made in this caliber, beginning in July 1864 and continuing until March 1865 (serial numbers 10,400 to 14,500).

NIB	EXC.	V.G.	GOOD	FAIR	POOR
—	—	2100	1750	620	295

Ballard (Dwight, Chapin & Co.) Carbines

Overall length 37.75"; barrel (bore) length 22"; caliber .56 rimfire. Markings: on left side of round-topped frame "BALLARD'S PATENT/NOV. 5 1861"; on right side of frame "DWIGHT, CHAPIN & CO./BRIDGEPORT CONN." (through serial no. about 125, deleted after that number) over "MERWIN & BRAY/AGT'S N.Y." over serial no. Inspection letters "D" frequently appear on carbines with Dwight, Chapin, & Co. markings, indicative of preliminary inspection by E. M. Dustin, of U.S. Ordnance Department. Often mistaken as early Ballard production from a fictitious Fall River, Massachusetts, factory, these carbines and their complementing rifles were in fact not placed into production until 1863, as evident by split, two-piece breechblocks. Both carbines and rifles originated from a contract entered into between U.S. War Department and Merwin & Bray in October 1862 for 10,000 of each arm, subsequently reduced to 1,000 of each by Commission on Ordnance and Ordnance Stores. Because Ball & Williams facilities were tied up with Kentucky contracts, Merwin & Bray turned to small parts maker of Dwight, Chapin & Co. in Bridgeport, Connecticut. Although they tooled for production, they fell short of scheduled delivery dates and although about 100 carbines had been inspected, no deliveries were accepted (due to caliber problems) by U.S. government, effectively bankrupting Dwight, Chapin & Co. Completed carbines and unfinished parts were sent to Worcester and assembled by Ball & Williams. Merwin & Bray sold all 1,000 carbines in Kentucky in April 1864 on an open market purchase.

NIB	EXC.	V.G.	GOOD	FAIR	POOR
—	—	2450	2000	825	350

Ballard (Dwight, Chapin & Co.) Full-Stock Rifles

Overall length 53"; barrel (bore) length 30"; caliber .56 rimfire. Markings: same as Dwight, Chapin & Co. carbines, but none found with "DWIGHT, CHAPIN & CO./BRIDGEPORT, CONN." stamping

	NIB	EXC.	V.G.	GOOD	FAIR	POOR

above agents marks. History of these rifles same as .56-caliber carbines, with serial numbers interspersed in production of carbines (1 through 1850). Evidently only about 650 rifles were completed of the 1,000 set up. Of these, 35 were sold to a U.S. agent in Florida in February 1864 and 600 to Kentucky in April 1864 with the 1,000 carbines.

		2450	2000	825	350

Ballard (R. Ball & Co.) Sporting Rifles

Overall length varies according to barrel length; barrel (bore) length usually 24", 28" and 30"; calibers .32, .38, .44 and .46 rimfire. Markings: frame markings of R. Ball & Co. rifles are similar to Ball & Williams production, only eliminating Ball & Williams marking on left side. Cartridge size, e.g. "No. 44", usually also stamped on top of barrel or frame. Merwin & Bray's patented alternate ignition device usually present with left side of hammer usually marked "PATENTED JAN. 5, 1864". Serial numbers (which follow in sequence with Ball & Williams production. i.e. after no. about 15,800) appear on top of barrel and frame. After William Williams withdrew from Ball & Williams partnership in mid-1865, business continued under name of R. Ball & Co., with Richard Ball's son-in-law, E.J. Halstead, in charge after the former's paralytic stroke in the fall of 1865.

		2650	2200	975	400

Ballard (R. Ball & Co.) Carbines

Overall length 37.25"; barrel (bore) length 22"; caliber .44 rimfire. Markings: same as R. Ball & Co. sporting rifles; "No. 44" on top of frame near breech. Although firm evidence is elusive, approximately 1,000 of these carbines were manufactured in anticipation of a Canadian contract, which never came to fruition. Serial numbers are interspersed with sporting rifles, in 16,400 through 17,700 range. All are equipped with Merwin & Bray dual ignition block.

		1825	1500	580	225

Ballard (Merrimack Arms & Manufacturing Co.) Sporting Rifles

Overall length varies with barrel length; usual barrel lengths 24", 28", 30"; calibers .22, .32, .44, .46, .50 rimfire. Markings: left side of frame marked with both manufacturing and patent marks, "MERRIMACK ARMS & MFG. CO./NEWBURYPORT, MASS." over "BALLARD'S PATENT/ NOV. 5, 1861". Caliber usually marked on top of barrel or frame, e.g. "No. 38" together with serial no. Left side of hammer marked "PATENTED JAN. 5, 1864" if breech fitted with Merwin & Bray's alternate ignition device. In spring of 1866 Edward Bray of Brooklyn, New York, former partner of Joseph Merwin, purchased Ballard machinery from R. Ball & Co. and set up a new plant in Newburyport, Massachusetts, primarily for production of sporting rifles. Glut of surplus arms on the market following American Civil War, however, forced him into bankruptcy in early 1869, after producing only about 2,000 Ballard rifles, carbines and a limited number of 20-gauge shotguns. Serial numbers continue in sequence of Ball & Williams/R. Ball & Co. production (serial numbers about 18,000 through 20,300). Prices of these rifles will vary considerably depending on degree of finish and engraving.

		2200	1900	775	350

Ballard (Merrimack Arms & Manufacturing Co.) Carbines

Overall length 37.25"; barrel (bore) length 22"; caliber .44 rimfire. Markings: same as Merrimack Arms & Mfg. Co. sporting rifles. In March 1866, state of New York purchased 100 Ballard carbines (serial numbers about 18,500 to 18,600) for use by its prison guards. In January 1870, an additional 70 (serial numbers 19,400 to 19,500) were purchased from New York City arms merchants Merwin, Hulbert & Co. to arm guards at Sing Sing Prison. Between these two purchases Merrimack Arms & Mfg. Co. had shortened its new "tangless" frames by .125", prime distinction between the two purchases. Despite rarity of both types of carbines, they do not command high prices.

		1750	1400	550	300

Ballard (Brown Mfg. Co.) Sporting Rifles

Dimensions: same as Merrimack Arms & Mfg. Co. sporting rifles. Markings: left side of frame marked with manufacturer, "BROWN MFG. CO. NEWBURYPORT, MASS.". Over patent, "BALLARD'S PATENT/ NOV. 5, 1861". Serial no. on top of barrel and frame. Upon the failure of Merrimack Arms & Manufacturing Company in early 1869, plant was purchased by John Hamilton Brown, who continued producing Ballard patent rifles until 1873 in a serial range consecutive with that of its three predecessors (Ball & Williams, R. Ball & Co. and Merrimack Arms & Mfg. Co.). Approximately 2,000 Ballard arms were produced during period of Brown's manufacture of Ballard (serial numbers about 20,325 through 22,100). Brown-made Ballards' tend to exhibit finer finishing than earlier produced rifles, accounting for their average higher value. Special features, such as breakdown facility and side extractors (on .22 cal. rifles) will also positively affect prices.

		2200	1825	675	350

Ballard (Brown Mfg. Co.) Full-Stock Military Rifles

Overall length 52.5"; barrel (bore) length 30"; caliber .46 rimfire. Markings: same as Brown Mfg. Co. sporting rifles, with addition of caliber marking, "No. 46", on top of barrel forward of rear sight. Cause for production of Ballard/Brown military rifle has yet to be determined, but it

NIB	EXC.	V.G.	GOOD	FAIR	POOR

has been speculated that they were possibly manufactured in anticipation of a sale to France during Franco-Prussian War. In any event, sale was not culminated and many, if not most, of estimated 1,000 produced were "sporterized" by shortening fore-stock and sold by commercial dealers in United States. Serial numbers concentrate in 20,500 through 21,600 range, with sporting rifles interspersed in the sequence. Rifles that have not been sporterized command a premium.

—	—	2350	1950	800	350

BALLARD RIFLE AND CARTRIDGE CO.
Onsted, Michigan

All models feature American black walnut stocks, case hardening and rust blued barrels. There are a number of special order features that are available with these rifles.

No. 1-1/2 Hunter's Rifle

Features 30" round barrel, single trigger, S lever, plain fore-end and rifle buttstock. Blade front sight and Rocky Mountain rear sight are standard. Calibers from .32-40 to .50-70. Weight about 10.5 lbs.

3000	2350	1950	1200	700	300

No. 1-3/4 Far West Rifle

Offered with 30" round barrel in standard or heavy weight. Single-/double-set triggers, S lever, ring-style lever, blade front sight and Rocky Mountain rear sight. Offered in calibers from .32-40 to .50-90. Weight with standard 30" barrel about 10.5 lbs.; heavyweight barrel 11.75 lbs.

2900	2400	1900	1200	700	300

No. 2 Sporting Model

Stocked in plain walnut, with crescent butt. Offered in 24", 26", 28" or 30" octagon barrel, with blade front and Rocky Mountain rear sights. Straight-grip action with S lever, in calibers .38-40, .44-40 and .45 Colt. Discontinued.

2050	1650	1300	1225	700	300

No. 3 Gallery Rifle

Chambered for .22-caliber rimfire cartridge. Features 24", 26" or 30" lightweight octagon barrel. Rifle-style buttstock, with steel crescent buttplate, S lever, blade and Rocky Mountain sights. Weight with standard 26" barrel about 7.5 lbs.

3000	2650	2300	1200	700	300

No. 3F Fine Gallery Rifle

Same as above, with fancy checkered walnut stock, pistol-grip, single-/double-set triggers, full-loop lever, light Schuetzen buttstock, globe front and tang rear sight. Weight with standard 26" barrel about 7.75 lbs.

3500	3000	2400	1500	750	300

No. 4 Perfection Model

Features plain walnut stock, with rifle or shotgun butt. Offered in 28", 30" or 32" octagon barrel, with blade front sight and Rocky Mountain rear sight. Straight-grip action, with single-/double-set triggers. S lever or ring lever. Calibers from .32-40 to .50-90.

3400	2900	2300	1200	700	300

No. 4-1/2 Mid-Range Model

Features checkered fancy walnut stock. Standard or heavy weight half octagon barrel 30" or 32", with single-/double-set triggers. Pistol-grip hard rubber or steel shotgun butt, horn fore-end cap, full-loop lever and globe front sight. Offered in calibers from .32-40 to .40-70. Weight with standard barrel 10.75 lbs.; heavy barrel 11.5 lbs.

3200	2650	2100	1100	600	250

No. 5 Pacific Model

Features 30" or 32" octagon barrel in standard or heavy weight. Stocks in rifle or shotgun configuration, double-set triggers, ring lever, blade front sight and Rocky Mountain rear sight. Calibers from .38-55 to .50-90. Weight with standard 30" barrel 10.75 lbs.; heavyweight barrel 12 lbs.

3350	2600	2250	1200	700	300

No. 5-1/2 Montana Model

Model has fancy walnut stock, double-set triggers and ring lever. Shotgun steel butt. Barrels 28", 30" or 32" extra heavy octagon, in calibers .45-70, .45-110 and .50-90. Under barrel wiping rod. Weight about 14.5 lbs.

3300	2600	2000	110	600	225

	NIB	EXC.	V.G.	GOOD	FAIR	POOR

No. 6 Off-Hand Rifle Model (Schuetzen)

Features fancy walnut checkered stock, with hand rubbed finish. Heavy Schuetzen buttplate. Horn insert on fore-end. Choice of 30", 32" or 34" half-octagon barrel, with globe front sight. Straight-grip action with double-set triggers, Schuetzen ball, spur lever and deluxe rust bluing. Offered in .22 LR, .32-40, .38-55, .40-65 and .40-70 calibers.

NIB	EXC.	V.G.	GOOD	FAIR	POOR
3300	2700	2100	1100	600	250

No. 7 Long Range Model

Features fancy walnut checkered stock, with 32" or 34" standard or heavy weight half octagon barrel. Pistol-grip stock, with rubber or steel shotgun butt, single-/double-set triggers, full-loop lever, horn fore-end cap and globe front sight. Calibers from .32-40 to .45-110. Weight with standard 32" barrel 11.75 lbs.; heavyweight barrel 12.25 lbs.

NIB	EXC.	V.G.	GOOD	FAIR	POOR
3100	2550	2200	1100	600	250

No. 8 Union Hill Model

Features 30" or 32" half-octagon standard or heavy barrel, single-/double-set triggers, pistol-grip stock with cheekpiece, full-loop lever, hook Schuetzen buttplate and fancy walnut checkered stock. Offered in calibers from .22 LR to .40-70. Weight with standard barrel in .32-caliber 10.5 lbs.; heavyweight barrel in .40-caliber 11.5 lbs. Not furnished with sights.

NIB	EXC.	V.G.	GOOD	FAIR	POOR
3600	2000	1700	900	450	200

Model 1885 High Wall

Single-shot rifle. Chambered for a wide variety of calibers from .18 Bee to .577 Express. Barrel lengths to 34". American walnut stock. Many options to choose from that will affect price. Introduced in 2000.

NIB	EXC.	V.G.	GOOD	FAIR	POOR
3050	2500	2000	1175	650	275

BALLESTER—MOLINA

See—Hafdasa

BAR-STO PRECISION MACHINE

Burbank, California

Bar-Sto 25

.25-caliber semi-automatic pistol, with brushed stainless steel receiver and slide. Walnut grips. Produced in 1974.

NIB	EXC.	V.G.	GOOD	FAIR	POOR
—	325	275	175	125	100

BARRETT, F.A. MFG. CO.

Murfreesboro, Tennessee

Barrett MRAD

Chambered in .338 Lapua Magnum, with user-changeable barrel system. Match-grade trigger. Thumb-operated safety can be configured to right or left. Folding stock has adjustable cheekpiece and length of pull. Finished in Barrett's Multi-Role Brown. Introduced in 2011.

NIB	EXC.	V.G.	GOOD	FAIR	POOR
5500	4675	3950	2500	1000	500

Model 82 Rifle

.50-caliber BMG semi-automatic rifle, with 37" barrel and 11-shot magazine. Barrel fitted with muzzle-brake. Receiver with telescope. Approximate weight 35 lbs. Parkerized. Manufactured from 1985 to 1987.

NIB	EXC.	V.G.	GOOD	FAIR	POOR
6000	5500	4750	2250	1500	400

Model 82A1

As above, with 29" barrel without sights. 10-round magazine. 10X telescope and iron sights optional. Comes with hard carrying case. Weight 28.5 lbs.

NIB	EXC.	V.G.	GOOD	FAIR	POOR
8000	7000	4000	2750	1600	400

Model 95M

Introduced in 1995. .50-caliber BMG bolt-action rifle. Features 29" barrel and 5-round magazine. Scope optional. Weight 22 lbs.

NIB	EXC.	V.G.	GOOD	FAIR	POOR
6000	4000	3200	2000	1400	300

Model 99

Single-shot bolt-action rifle. Chambered for .50 BMG or .416 Barrett. Standard barrel length 32". Optional barrel lengths 25" or 29". Weight about 25 lbs. with 32" barrel. **NOTE:** Add $200 for fluted barrel.

NIB	EXC.	V.G.	GOOD	FAIR	POOR
4300	3450	1700	1200	600	175

	NIB	EXC.	V.G.	GOOD	FAIR	POOR

Model 107

Chambered for .50-caliber cartridge. Semi-automatic rifle fitted with 29" barrel and muzzle-brake. Bipod detachable and adjustable. M1913 accessory rail. Supplied with two 10-round magazines. Weight about 32 lbs.

	NIB	EXC.	V.G.	GOOD	FAIR	POOR
	9650	8000	7000	6000	4000	1000

Model 468

Built on semi-automatic AR-15-style lower receiver. Features 16" barrel, with muzzle-brake. Chambered for 6.8 SPC cartridge. Folding front and rear sight. Integrated Rail system. Weight about 7.3 lbs.

	2800	2100	1450	975	650	225

REC7 Gen II

This piston-driven AR-style model was introduced in 2008. Chambered in 5.56 NATO or 6.8 SPC. Mag-pull MOE pistol-grip stock, 16" barrel, Barrett handguard with KeyMod rail attachment. Other features are flash suppressor, flip-up iron sights and 30-shot magazine. Offered in black, gray, Flat Dark Earth or OD green finish. **NOTE:** Deduct $400 for 2008-2013 first generation production.

	2250	1800	1200	850	500	200

BARRETT, J. B. AND A.B. & CO.
Wytheville, Virginia
Barrett Muskets and Rifled Muskets

Overall length 57.75"; barrel length 41.5" to 42"; caliber .69. Markings: although Barretts placed no marks of their own on their alterations, most were effected on Virginia Manufactory muskets, whose lockplates are marked "VIRGINIA/Manufactory" forward of hammer and "RICHMOND/(date)" on tail. For many years collectors considered adaptations of Hall rifles and carbines from breech-loaders to muzzle-loaders to be the product of J.B. Barrett & Co. of Wytheville. Recent evidence, however, confirms that those adaptations were actually effected in Danville, Virginia, by another firm (see READ & WATSON). Nevertheless, Barretts of Wytheville did adapt arms during early years of American Civil War. Adaptation effected almost exclusively upon Virginia Manufactory flintlock muskets, consisted of percussioning by means of cone-in-barrel and rifling of barrels with seven narrow grooves. In 1861 and 1862, Barretts percussioned a total of 1250 muskets, of which 744 were rifled.

	—	—	—	16500	6750	2200

BASCARAN, MARTIN A.
Eibar, Spain

Spanish manufacturer of pistols prior to World War II.

Martian 6.35mm

6.35mm semi-automatic pistol. Slide marked "Automatic Pistol Martian". Blued, with black plastic grips having monogram "MAB" cast in them.

	—	275	195	135	100	75

Martian 7.65mm

Semi-automatic pistol patterned after Ruby military pistols. "Martian" stamped on slide. Wood grips and lanyard loop.

	—	275	195	135	100	75

Thunder

Semi-automatic pistol in caliber 6.35mm. Almost a duplicate of Martian. "Thunder" stamped on slide and each grip plate.

	—	275	195	135	100	75

BAUER, F. A. CORP.
Fraser, Michigan
The Rabbit

.22-caliber-by-.410 bore combination rifle/shotgun, with tubular metal stock. Manufactured between 1982 and 1984. Similar to Garcia Bronco.

	—	325	300	225	125	75

Bauer 25 Automatic

.25-caliber semi-automatic pistol. Made of stainless steel, with 2.5" barrel and 6-shot magazine. Walnut or imitation pearl grips. Manufactured from 1972 to 1984. After 1984, this pistol was produced under the name of Fraser for a few years. **NOTE:** Add 15 percent for NIB.

	—	250	200	165	125	80

	NIB	EXC.	V.G.	GOOD	FAIR	POOR

BAYARD
Herstal, Belgium
See—Pieper, H. & N. and Bergmann

BAYONNE, MANUFACTURE D'ARMES
aka MAB
Bayonne, France

Model A

Manufactured in 1921. Chambered for 6.35mm cartridge. Patterned after Browning Model 1906. Squeeze grip safety, with 6-round magazine.

—	295	175	115	75	50

Model B

Manufactured in 1932. Chambered for 6.35mm cartridge. Exposed hammer, no grip safety and 6-round magazine.

—	275	165	90	75	50

Model C

Manufactured in 1933. Chambered for 7.65mm and .380 cartridge. Patterned after Browning Model 1910. Seven-round magazine.

—	325	225	200	125	90

Model D

Manufactured in 1933. Chambered for 7.65mm and .380 cartridge. Basically a Model C, with longer barrel and 9-round magazine. **NOTE:** Add 100 percent for Nazi-marked pistols.

—	400	300	250	125	100

Model E

Manufactured in 1949. Chambered for 6.35mm cartridge. Patterned after Model D, with streamlined grips and 10-round magazine.

—	425	325	300	150	125

Model F

Manufactured in 1950. Chambered for .22 LR cartridge. Interchangeable barrel lengths, target grips and 10-round magazine.

—	425	325	200	150	125

Model G

Manufactured in 1951. Chambered for .22 LR and 7.65mm cartridge. Some with Dural frames. Magazine capacity: 10 rounds .22 LR; 8 rounds 7.65mm.

—	450	350	225	150	125

Model GZ

Manufactured in calibers .22 LR, 6.35mm, 7.65mm and .380. Almost identical to Model G. Dural frames and two-tone finishes on some variations.

—	450	350	275	150	125

Model P-8 & P-15

In 1966 MAB manufactured Model P-8 and Model P-15 in 9mm Parabellum, with 8- and 15-round magazines. Basically the same gun, with different magazine capacities. Model P-15 went to French military as well as some commercial sales.

—	475	350	300	250	175

Model P-15 M1 Target

MAB Model P-15 was manufactured for target shooting using 9mm Parabellum cartridge. Most M1 Target MABs were purchased by French military for their target teams.

—	875	750	500	350	175

Model R

Manufactured in caliber 7.65mm Long in 1951. Model R similar to Model D. Model R's later produced in several calibers: .22 LR furnished with 10-round magazine and two different barrel lengths; 7.65mm had 9-round magazine; .380 and 9mm Parabellum fitted with 8-round magazines. **NOTE:** Deduct 15 percent for 7.65 Long.

.22 Long Rifle

—	350	250	225	150	125

	NIB	EXC.	V.G.	GOOD	FAIR	POOR
7.65mm & 7.65mm Long & .380						
	—	350	250	225	150	125
9mm Parabellum						
	—	400	300	250	150	125

Model R PARA Experimental

In late 1950's, MAB began experimenting with Model R in caliber 9mm Parabellum. There were many of these experimental-type pistols. The 8-round, rotating barrel Model R shown, led directly to Model P-15 series.

	—	1500	1250	1000	500	250

Model "Le Chasseur

Manufactured in 1953. "Le Chasseur" was a target model in .22 LR. Had 9-round magazine, external hammer, target sights and grips. **NOTE:** MAB pistols sold in U.S.A. were retailed by Winfield Arms Company of Los Angeles, California. Marked "Made in France for WAC". This does not affect value.

	—	300	200	150	125	90

BEATTIE, J.
London, England

Beattie produced a variety of revolvers during percussion period, some of which were imported into United States. During the period this firm was in business, it was located at these London addresses:

43 Upper Marylebone Street	1835-1838
52 Upper Marylebone Street	1838-1842
52 Upper Marylebone Street & 223 Regent Street	1842-1846
205 Regent Street	1851-1882
104 Queen Victoria Street	1882-1894

Beattie Gas Seal Revolver

.42-caliber single-action percussion revolver, with 6.25" octagonal barrel. When hammer is cocked, cylinder is forced forward against barrel breech, thus effecting a gas seal. Blued case hardened, with walnut grips.

	—	—	5100	3500	2200	1100

BEAUMONT, ADAMS
See—Adams

BEAUMONT
Maastrict, Netherlands

1873 Dutch Service Revolver, Old Model

9.4mm double-action 6-shot revolver. Weight 2 lbs. 12 oz.

	—	—	695	400	200	100

1873 Dutch Service Revolver, New Model

As above, with 6-shot cylinder.

	—	—	695	400	200	100

1873 KIM, Small Model

As above, with octagonal barrel. 5-shot cylinder.

	—	—	775	500	250	125

BECKER AND HOLLANDER
Suhl, Germany

Beholla

Semi-automatic pistol in caliber 7.65mm. Introduced in 1908 in Germany. Manufactured by Becker & Hollander until 1920. After that date three different companies produced Beholla under names of Stenda, Menta and Leonhardt.

	—	500	350	225	175	100

BEEMAN PRECISION ARMS, INC.
Santa Rosa, California

Although primarily known as an importer and retailer of airguns, Beeman Precision Arms, Inc., has marketed several firearms.

	NIB	EXC.	V.G.	GOOD	FAIR	POOR

MP-08

.380-caliber semi-automatic pistol, with 3.5" barrel and 6-shot magazine. Resembling German Luger. Blued. Introduced in 1968.

	475	375	275	225	200	125

P-08

As above in .22-caliber, with 8-shot magazine. Walnut grips. Introduced in 1969.

	475	375	275	225	200	125

SP Standard

.22-caliber single-shot target pistol, with 8" to 15" barrels. Fitted with adjustable sights and walnut grips. Imported in 1985 and 1986.

	325	225	200	175	150	100

SP Deluxe

As above, with walnut fore-end.

	350	250	225	200	150	100

BEERSTECHER, FREDERICK
Philadelphia, Pennsylvania (1846-1856)
Lewisburg, Pennsylvania (1857-1868)

Superposed Load Pocket Pistol

.41-caliber superposed load percussion pistol, with an average barrel length of 3". German silver mounts. Walnut stock. Hammer fitted with movable twin striker head so the first charge in barrel can be fired and then second fired. Lock normally marked "F. Beerstecher's/Patent 1855". Prospective purchasers are advised to secure a qualified appraisal prior to acquisition.

	—	—	6400	4800	3500	1050

BEHOLLA
See—Becker and Hollander

BEISTEGUI, HERMANOS
Eibar, Spain
See—Grand Precision

BENELLI
Italy

SHOTGUNS

SL SERIES

Model SL-121 V

Semi-automatic 12-gauge, with 3" chambers and various barrel lengths and chokes. Black anodized alloy receiver. Discontinued in 1985.

	650	500	400	350	300	150

Model SL-121 Slug

Similar to SL-121 V, with 21" cylinder-bore barrel. Rifle sights. Discontinued in 1985.

	700	550	400	350	300	150

Model SL-123 V

Model has improved fast third-generation action. Otherwise resembles earlier SL-121.

	750	600	500	400	350	200

Model SL-201

20-gauge, with 26" Improved Cylinder barrel. Similar in appearance to SL-123.

	500	475	425	350	300	150

M SERIES

M3 Super 90

Improved version of Benelli pump-action and semi-automatic inertia recoil system. Shotgun can be converted from pump to semi-automatic, by turning a spring-loaded ring located at end of forearm. Has rotating bolt system. Chambered for 12-gauge, with 3" chamber. Has 19.75" barrel with cylinder bore and rifle sights, with 7-round tubular magazine. Matte black finish,

	NIB	EXC.	V.G.	GOOD	FAIR	POOR

black fiberglass pistol-grip stock and forearm. Introduced in 1986. **NOTE:** Add $50 for open rifle sights.

| | 1300 | 1100 | 900 | 700 | 450 | 300 |

M3 Super 90 Folding Stock

Same as above. Furnished with folding tubular steel stock.

| | 1500 | 1350 | 1150 | 850 | 600 | 300 |

M4

Adopted by U.S. Marine Corps, this 12-gauge shotgun features a choice of three modular buttstock and two barrel configurations. Top-mounted Picatinny rail. Barrel length 18.5". Magazine capacity 6 rounds. Ghost ring sights. Weight about 8.4 lbs. Matte black finish. Introduced in 2003. Civilian version does not have collapsible buttstock.

| | 1550 | 1150 | 875 | 725 | 500 | 200 |

M1014 Limited Edition

Introduced in 2003. Version of M4. Fitted with skeleton buttstock. Special U.S. flag engraving on receiver. Fitted with 18.5" barrel and Picatinny rail, with ghost ring sights. Limited to 2,500 shotguns.

| | 1600 | 1200 | 900 | 750 | 550 | 250 |

M1 Practical

Designed for IPSC events. Features over sized safety, speed loader, larger bolt handle, muzzle-brake, adjustable ghost ring sight and optics rail. Offered with extended magazine tube and 26" barrel. Weighs about 7.6 lbs.

| | 1150 | 900 | 750 | 500 | 275 | 125 |

M1 Super 90 Tactical

Semi-automatic 12-gauge shotgun, with inertia recoil system. Features 18.5" plain barrel. Three screw-in choke tubes. Available in standard polymer or pistol-grip stock. Ghost ring sights standard. Gun weighs 6.5 lbs. Introduced in 1993.

| | 900 | 700 | 600 | 500 | 450 | 250 |

M1 Super 90 Slug Gun

Equipped with standard black polymer stock and 19.75" plain barrel. Fitted with 7-shot magazine. Ghost ring sights are an option. Weighs 6.7 lbs. Camo model introduced in 2000. **NOTE:** Add $100 for Camo model.

| | 1000 | 750 | 550 | 450 | 350 | 250 |

M1 Super 90 Entry Gun

Fitted with black polymer pistol-grip stock and 14" plain barrel. Magazine holds 5 shells. Plain or ghost ring sights available. CAUTION: NFA Weapon, Restricted sale, Class III Transfer required.

M1 Super 90 Defense Gun

Comes standard with polymer pistol-grip stock, 19.75" barrel, plain or ghost ring sights. Offered in 12-gauge only. Weighs 7.1 lbs.

| | 900 | 700 | 600 | 500 | 450 | 250 |

M1 Super 90 Field

Similar to other Super 90 series guns, with 21", 24", 26" or 28" vent rib barrel and screw-in choke tubes. In 1998 this model was available with 24" rifled bore and matte rib. Add $80 for this barrel. Left-hand model added in 2000. In 2001 this model was offered in 20-gauge as well.

| | 900 | 650 | 600 | 550 | 450 | 200 |

M1 Super 90 Camo Field

Same as above, with camouflage receiver barrel, buttstock and forearm. Offered in 24", 26" and 28" vent rib barrels. Introduced in 1997. In 1998 this model also offered with 21" vent rib barrel. Left-hand model added in 2000. In 2001 this model offered in 20-gauge as well.

M1 Field Steady Grip

Introduced in 2003. Features vertical pistol-grip, drilled and tapped receiver. Extra Full choke tube. Barrel length 24". Weight about 7.3 lbs.

| | 1175 | 900 | 600 | 325 | 175 | 100 |

M1 Super 90 Sporting Special

Introduced in 1993. This 12-gauge shotgun similar to Super 90, with addition of non-reflective surfaces, 18.5" plain barrel and 3 choke tubes (IC, Mod, Full). Gun fitted with ghost ring sights.

| | 725 | 600 | 500 | 400 | 350 | 200 |

M2 Practical with ComforTech

Introduced in 2005. Chambered for 12-gauge 3" shell. Fitted with 25" plain barrel, with compensator and ghost ring rear sight. Receiver fitted with Picatinny rail. Magazine capacity 8 rounds. Weight about 7.6 lbs.

NIB	EXC.	V.G.	GOOD	FAIR	POOR
1200	1000	750	595	400	275

M2 Tactical

12-gauge 3" gun fitted with 18.5" barrel, with choke tubes and choice of rifle or ghost ring sights. Pistol-grip or extended pistol-grip. Black synthetic stock. Magazine capacity 5 rounds. Weight about 7 lbs. **NOTE:** Add $70 for ComforTech version; $65 for ghost ring sights.

NIB	EXC.	V.G.	GOOD	FAIR	POOR
1250	1050	850	600	400	275

M2 Field with ComforTech

12-gauge model offered with 21", 24", 26" or 28" barrel. Black matte synthetic finish or Max-4, Timber or APG camo. 20-gauge has 24" or 26" barrel in black, Timber or APG. Average 12-gauge weight 7 lbs.; 20-gauge 5.8 lbs. Add $75 for camo.

NIB	EXC.	V.G.	GOOD	FAIR	POOR
1000	750	500	525	300	200

M2 Field without ComforTech

Same features as above, without ComforTech features. Available only in satin walnut, with 26" or 28" barrel.

NIB	EXC.	V.G.	GOOD	FAIR	POOR
1075	825	550	525	300	200

MONTEFELTRO SERIES

Montefeltro Super 90

Introduced in 1987. Similar to Super 90 Field. Checkered walnut stock and forearm, with gloss finish. Offered with 21", 24", 26" or 28" vent rib barrel. Available in 12-gauge only, with 3" chambers. Offered in left-hand model also.

NIB	EXC.	V.G.	GOOD	FAIR	POOR
900	700	600	500	450	350

Montefeltro 20 Gauge

Introduced in 1993. Features walnut checkered stock, with 26" vent rib barrel. In 1995 a 24" vent rib barrel offered. Weighs 5.75 lbs. **NOTE:** Add $75 for short stock model.

NIB	EXC.	V.G.	GOOD	FAIR	POOR
900	700	600	500	450	350

Montefeltro 20 Gauge Camo

Same as above, with Realtree Camo finish. Offered with 26" vent rib barrel. Introduced in 1998.

NIB	EXC.	V.G.	GOOD	FAIR	POOR
950	750	700	600	500	400

Montefeltro 20 Gauge Limited

Introduced in 1995. Features finely etched nickel plate receiver, with scroll and game scenes highlighted in gold. Stock is select grade walnut. Fitted with 26" vent rib barrel.

NIB	EXC.	V.G.	GOOD	FAIR	POOR
1750	1250	800	500	400	350

Montefeltro Silver

Same features as the standard Montefeltro model, but with bright blue nickel receiver and AA-grade walnut stock.

NIB	EXC.	V.G.	GOOD	FAIR	POOR
1500	1250	950	700	350	200

Montefeltro (2005)

Updated version of Montefeltro series. Slight change in receiver, different trigger, upgraded wood and name "Montefeltro" in gold on receiver. Offered in 12- or 20-gauge, with 3" chambers. Checkered select walnut stock, with pistol-grip. Choice of 24", 26" or 28" vent rib barrel, with choke tubes. Red bar front sight. Weight for 12-gauge about 6.9 lbs.; 20-gauge about 5.6 lbs.

NIB	EXC.	V.G.	GOOD	FAIR	POOR
1300	1000	950	700	500	350

Montefeltro Compact

In 20-gauge only. This model has a 24" or 26" barrel, shorter length-of-pull and satin finish stock. Introduced in 2012.

NIB	EXC.	V.G.	GOOD	FAIR	POOR
1000	850	600	450	300	200

Montefeltro Synthetic

Model was introduced in 2013 in 12-gauge only, with a black synthetic stock and 26" or 28" barrel.

NIB	EXC.	V.G.	GOOD	FAIR	POOR
1000	850	600	450	300	200

	NIB	EXC.	V.G.	GOOD	FAIR	POOR

BLACK EAGLE SERIES

Black Eagle Competition Gun

Offered in 12-gauge only. Fitted with etched receiver, mid rib bead, competition stock and 5 screw-in choke tubes. Available in 26" or 28" vent rib barrel. Upper receiver steel while lower receiver is lightweight alloy. Weighs 7.3 lbs.

NIB	EXC.	V.G.	GOOD	FAIR	POOR
1300	800	750	700	400	275

Black Eagle

Similar to Black Eagle Competition Model, with standard grade wood. Matte black finish on receiver. Introduced in 1997.

NIB	EXC.	V.G.	GOOD	FAIR	POOR
900	600	475	325	225	150

Black Eagle Executive Series

Offered in 12-gauge only. Special order only shotgun. Offered with 21", 24", 26", 28" vent rib barrels. Each grade or level of gun engraved with increasing levels of coverage. Stock is fancy walnut.

Grade I

NIB	EXC.	V.G.	GOOD	FAIR	POOR
6200	5000	3500	2500	1500	700

Grade II

NIB	EXC.	V.G.	GOOD	FAIR	POOR
7000	5500	4000	3000	1600	800

Grade III

NIB	EXC.	V.G.	GOOD	FAIR	POOR
8500	6500	4750	3200	1800	900

SUPER BLACK EAGLE SERIES

Super Black Eagle

Similar to Montefeltro Super 90 Hunter, with polymer or walnut stock and forearm. Offered with 24", 26" or 28" vent rib barrel and 5 screw-in choke tubes. Chambered for 12-gauge from 2.75" to 3.5". Introduced in 1989. The 24" barrel introduced in 1993.

NIB	EXC.	V.G.	GOOD	FAIR	POOR
1200	950	650	500	300	200

Super Black Eagle Left-Hand

Introduced in 1999. Same as Black Eagle in left-hand version. Camo version also available.

NIB	EXC.	V.G.	GOOD	FAIR	POOR
1200	950	650	500	300	200

Super Black Eagle Custom Slug Gun

12-gauge model has 24" rifled barrel, with 3" chamber. Comes standard with matte metal finish. Weighs 7.6 lbs.

NIB	EXC.	V.G.	GOOD	FAIR	POOR
1100	800	750	600	500	350

Super Black Eagle Camo Gun

Introduced in 1997. Features 24", 26" or 28' vent rib barrels chambered for 12-gauge shells. Has Realtree Xtra Brown Camo finish. Stock is camo polymer as is forearm.

NIB	EXC.	V.G.	GOOD	FAIR	POOR
1300	1000	750	600	500	400

Super Black Eagle Steady Grip

Similar to above. Equipped with vertical pistol-grip. Drilled and tapped receiver. Extra Full choke tube. Barrel length 24". Weight about 7.3 lbs. Introduced in 2003.

NIB	EXC.	V.G.	GOOD	FAIR	POOR
1465	1100	650	575	325	225

Super Black Eagle Limited Edition

Introduced in 1997. Features 26" vent rib barrel, matte metal finish and satin select grade wood stock. Nickel plated receiver is finely etched with scroll and game scenes. Limited to 1,000 guns.

NIB	EXC.	V.G.	GOOD	FAIR	POOR
2000	1500	1050	750	525	375

SUPER BLACK EAGLE II SERIES

Series of guns introduced in 2005. Major features are new butt pad, grip and cryogenically treated barrels for which specially designed longer choke tubes are required. Benelli offers this series with or without "ComforTech" features. This system reduces recoil up to 48 percent and muzzle climb by 15 percent.

Super Black Eagle II with ComforTech

Offered in 12-gauge, with 3.5" chambers. Barrel lengths 24", 26" or 28", with choke tubes and red bar front sight. Available in synthetic or various camo finishes. Magazine capacity 3 rounds. Weight about 7.2 lbs. with 26" barrel.

NIB	EXC.	V.G.	GOOD	FAIR	POOR
1465	1100	700	600	365	250

	NIB	EXC.	V.G.	GOOD	FAIR	POOR

Super Black Eagle II without ComforTech

Model without ComforTech. Same options as above, with addition of walnut stock. **NOTE:** Add $60 for walnut stock; $110 for camo models.

NIB	EXC.	V.G.	GOOD	FAIR	POOR
1355	1000	650	575	325	225

Super Black Eagle II Rifled Slug with ComforTech

12-gauge 3" chamber gun, with 24" rifled barrel and adjustable sights. Available with synthetic stock or Timber HD camo stock. Weight about 7.4 lbs. **NOTE:** Add $120 for Camo version.

NIB	EXC.	V.G.	GOOD	FAIR	POOR
1535	1150	650	575	325	225

Super Black Eagle II Turkey Gun

12-gauge 3" chamber shotgun (3.5" chambers on non-ComforTech guns). Fitted with 24" smooth bore barrels and choke tubes. Red bar front sight. Weight about 7.1 lbs. Available with Timber HD camo stock, with or without ComforTech. **NOTE:** Add $130 for ComforTech version.

NIB	EXC.	V.G.	GOOD	FAIR	POOR
1455	1050	700	600	365	250

Super Black Eagle II Steady Grip

12-gauge 3.5" chamber gun. Fitted with 24" barrel and red bar front sight. Choke tubes. Stock is camo, with steady grip pistol-grip. Weight about 7.3 lbs. Model comes without ComforTech.

NIB	EXC.	V.G.	GOOD	FAIR	POOR
1200	950	650	500	300	200

LEGACY SERIES

Legacy

Features coin finished alloy receiver. Introduced in 1998. Chambered for 12-gauge 2.75" or 3" shell. Fitted with 26" or 28" vent rib barrel. Mid and front sights. Weight about 7.5 lbs. Buttstock and forearm are select walnut. 20-gauge added in 1990 with 24" or 26" vent rib barrels. Weight 6 lbs.

NIB	EXC.	V.G.	GOOD	FAIR	POOR
1300	800	750	700	400	275

Legacy Limited Edition

Offered in both 12- and 20-gauge. Features select walnut stock and etched game scenes with gold filled accents. 12-gauge features waterfowl scenes; 20-gauge has upland game scenes. 12-gauge fitted with 28" barrel; 20-gauge has 26" barrel. Introduced in 2000. Limited to 250 guns in each gauge.

NIB	EXC.	V.G.	GOOD	FAIR	POOR
1600	1200	900	550	375	295

Legacy (2005)

Updated version of Legacy. Changes are in engraving pattern, upgraded wood, improved trigger and slightly different receiver style. Offered in 12- and 20-gauge, with 3" chambers. Choice of 26" or 28" vent rib barrel, with choke tubes. Red bar front sight. Checkered select walnut stock, with pistol-grip. Magazine capacity 4 rounds. Weight for 12-gauge about 7.4 lbs.; 20-gauge about 5.8 lbs. **NOTE:** Add $30 for 20-gauge.

NIB	EXC.	V.G.	GOOD	FAIR	POOR
1435	1050	900	575	325	225

NOVA SERIES

Nova

"Slide-action series" introduced in 1999. Features polymer molded frame, with steel cage chambered for 3.5" shells. Choice of 24", 26" or 28" vent rib barrels. A 18.5" slug barrel also offered. Two- or four-shot magazine extensions offered as well. Weight with 28" barrel 8 lbs. Choice of camo or black synthetic pistol-grip stock. In 2001 offered in 20-gauge.

NIB	EXC.	V.G.	GOOD	FAIR	POOR
350	275	225	175	150	75

Nova Slug

12-gauge shotgun has 18.5" cylinder bored barrel, with open rifle or ghost ring sights. Black synthetic stock. Chambered for 2.75" or 3" shells. Magazine capacity 4 rounds. Weight about 7.2 lbs. Introduced in 2000. **NOTE:** Add $40 for ghost ring sights.

NIB	EXC.	V.G.	GOOD	FAIR	POOR
350	275	225	200	150	95

Nova Rifled Slug

Introduced in 2000. This 12-gauge features 24" rifled barrel, with open rifle sights. Black synthetic or Timber HD camo stock. Chambered for 2.75" or 3" shells. Magazine capacity 4 rounds. Weight about 8 lbs. **NOTE:** Add $75 for Camo version.

NIB	EXC.	V.G.	GOOD	FAIR	POOR
525	425	350	250	175	125

	NIB	EXC.	V.G.	GOOD	FAIR	POOR

Nova Field Slug Combo

12-gauge 3" gun equipped with 24" and 26" barrel. 26" barrel fitted with vent rib and choke tube; 24" barrel is rifled and fitted with cantilever scope mount. Black synthetic stock.

NIB	EXC.	V.G.	GOOD	FAIR	POOR
545	425	325	250	175	125

Nova H2O Pump

Introduced in 2003. Features a largely polymer exterior, with corrosion-resistant finish. Barrel, magazine tube, magazine cap, trigger group and other internal parts are nickel plated. Chambered for 12-gauge. Fitted with 18.5" barrel. Black synthetic stock. Magazine capacity 4 rounds. Open rifle sights. Weight about 7.2 lbs.

NIB	EXC.	V.G.	GOOD	FAIR	POOR
600	500	400	250	150	100

Supernova

Introduced in 2006. Supernova incorporates Benelli's ComforTech stock system into Nova pump shotgun. Available in 24", 26" and 28" barrel lengths in matte black synthetic; 24" and 26" barrel lengths in Advantage Timber camo; 26" and 28" barrel lengths in Max-4 camo. Weight about 8 lbs. with 28" barrel. All versions chambered for 3.5" shells. Three choke tubes. Add 15 percent for camo versions.

NIB	EXC.	V.G.	GOOD	FAIR	POOR
475	375	250	175	150	75

Supernova SteadyGrip

As above, with extended pistol-grip in 24" barrel only. Matte black synthetic or Advantage Timber stock. Add 15 percent for camo model.

NIB	EXC.	V.G.	GOOD	FAIR	POOR
455	375	250	175	150	75

Supernova Tactical

Matte black synthetic stock, with 18" barrel. Available with ComforTech or pistol-grip stock. Fixed cylinder bore. Open rifle sights. Ghost ring sights optional.

NIB	EXC.	V.G.	GOOD	FAIR	POOR
400	325	225	150	125	75

SPORT SERIES

Sport Model

Introduced in 1997. First shotgun with removable interchangeable carbon fiber vent ribs. Offered in 12-gauge only with choice of 26" or 28" barrels; 20-gauge with 28" barrel. Butt pad adjustable. Weight: 7 lbs. for 26" models; 7.3 lbs. for 28" models.

NIB	EXC.	V.G.	GOOD	FAIR	POOR
1300	1000	650	400	250	100

SuperSport with ComforTech

Introduced in 2005. Offered in 12-gauge, with 3" chamber or 20-gauge with 28" barrel. Choice of 28" or 30" carbon fiber barrel, with choke tubes and red bar front sight. Weight about 7.25 lbs.

NIB	EXC.	V.G.	GOOD	FAIR	POOR
1670	1250	800	575	395	200

Sport II Model

Introduced in 2003. Features cryogenically treated barrels and extra-long choke tubes. Chambered for 12-gauge shell in 2.75" or 3", with 28" or 30" barrel; 20-gauge with 28" barrel. Vent rib and choke tubes. Magazine capacity 4 rounds. Red bar front sight. Weight about 7.9 lbs.

NIB	EXC.	V.G.	GOOD	FAIR	POOR
1470	1100	700	475	325	150

Cordoba

Introduced in 2005. Chambered for 12-gauge 3" shell. Fitted with cryogencially treated ported barrels in 28" or 30" lengths, with extended choke tubes. Vent rib is 10mm width. Synthetic stock, with adjustable length butt pads. Red bar front sight. Weight about 7.25 lbs.

NIB	EXC.	V.G.	GOOD	FAIR	POOR
1800	1530	1200	850	375	295

Vinci

Gas-operated 12-gauge semi-automatic shotgun chambered for 2.75" and 3". Features include modular disassembly; interchangeable choke tubes; 24" to 28" ribbed barrel; black, MAX-4HD or APG HD finish; synthetic contoured stocks; optional Steady-Grip model. Weight 6.7 to 6.9 lbs.

NIB	EXC.	V.G.	GOOD	FAIR	POOR
1200	1000	850	600	400	300

Super Vinci

Unlike Vinci, Super Vinci fires 12-gauge 2.75", 3" and 3.5" magnum ammunition interchangeably. Barrel lengths: 26" or 28". Features Crio chokes, red bar front sight, metal bead mid sight. Receiver drilled and tapped for scope mounting. Weight about 7 lbs. Available in black synthetic, Realtree MAX-4 or Realtree APG camo finish. New in 2011. **NOTE:** Add $100 for camo finish.

NIB	EXC.	V.G.	GOOD	FAIR	POOR
1400	1150	900	650	450	350

NIB	EXC.	V.G.	GOOD	FAIR	POOR

Ultra Light

Inertia-driven 12-gauge semi-automatic. Features alloy receiver, carbon fiber rib and small proportions to bring weight down to about 6 lbs. Walnut stock, with Weathercoat finish. Chambered for 3" shells. Offered in 24" or 26" barrel only, with 5 Crio chokes. Introduced 2006.

| 1435 | 1050 | 900 | 575 | 325 | 225 |

Executive Series

Limited edition 12-gauge semi-automatic, with engraved grey lower receiver, highly polished blue barrel and upper receiver. Extra select grade walnut stock. Made in three grades, Type 1, Type 2 and Type 3, with increasing levels of engraving and wood. Limited importation.

Type 1

| 6250 | 5000 | 4000 | 3000 | — | — |

Type 2

| 7250 | 6000 | 5000 | 4000 | — | — |

Type 3

| 8500 | 7200 | 6200 | 5000 | — | — |

Raffaello Series

Limited production 12-gauge semi-automatic, available only through Benelli World Class dealers. Offered in three grades, Standard, Deluxe and Deluxe Legacy. Deluxe grade has scroll engraving and coin finished receiver. Deluxe Legacy has gold inlaid wildlife, high-grade walnut stock and also made in 20-gauge. **NOTE:** Add 25 percent for Deluxe grade; 50 percent for Deluxe Legacy.

| 1600 | 1450 | 1150 | 800 | 600 | 400 |

Ethos

Ethos features a recoil reduction system advertised as reducing felt recoil by 42 percent. The Benelli intertia-driven operating system cycles all loads. Other features include a totally new receiver design, a two-part carrier latch for easy loading, AA-grade checkered walnut stock, and choice of engraved nickel-plated or anodized receiver. **NOTE:** Add $200 for engraved/nickel receiver.

| 1800 | 1550 | 1200 | 850 | 400 | 200 |

RIFLES

Model R1 Rifle

Introduced in 2003. Chambered for .30-06 or .300 Win. Magnum cartridge. Barrels cryogenically treated. Action is gas operated. Interchangeable barrel offered in 20" and 22" in .30-06 and 20" and 24" in .300 Win. Magnum. Walnut stock. Detachable magazine has 4-round capacity. Weight about 7 to 7.2 lbs. depending on caliber and barrel length. In 2005 .270 WSM and .300 WSM calibers were added.

| 1080 | 850 | 675 | 500 | 350 | 225 |

Model R1 Carbine

As above, with 20" barrel chambered for .30-06 or .300 Win. Magnum calibers. Weight about 7 lbs.

| 1080 | 850 | 675 | 500 | 350 | 225 |

Model R1 ComforTech Rifle

Similar to Model R1, with ComforTech recoil-absorbing stock. Additional chamberings .270 and .300 WSM. Introduced 2006. Add 10 percent for RealTree camo and adjustable comb.

| 1350 | 1100 | 700 | 475 | 325 | 150 |

Model MR1 Rifle

Gas-operated semi-automatic rifle chambered in 5.56 NATO. Features include 16" 1:9 hard chrome-lined barrel, synthetic stock with pistol-grip, rotating bolt, military-style aperture sights with picatinny rail. Comes equipped with 5-round detachable magazine but accepts M16 magazines.

| 1135 | 965 | 800 | 550 | 350 | 250 |

HANDGUNS

Model B-76

All-steel double-action semi-automatic chambered for 9mm Parabellum. Has 4.25" barrel, fixed sights and 8-round detachable magazine.

| 675 | 500 | 400 | 300 | 200 | 100 |

	NIB	EXC.	V.G.	GOOD	FAIR	POOR

Model B-76S

Target version of B-76. Has 5.5" barrel, adjustable sights and target-grips.

875	700	550	300	200	100

Model B-77

Similar to B-76 except chambered for .32 ACP.

425	300	250	200	150	100

Model B-80

Similar to B-76 except chambered for .30 Luger cartridge.

525	395	300	200	150	100

Model B-80S

Target version of B-80, with 5.5" barrel and adjustable sights. Features target-grips.

575	475	400	300	200	100

Model MP90S Match (World Cup)

Semi-automatic single-action pistol. Chambered for .22 Short, .22 LR or .32 S&W wadcutter. Fitted with 4.375" barrel, with walnut match style fully adjustable grips, blade front sight and fully adjustable rear sight. Barrel has adjustable weights below. Magazine capacity 5 rounds. Weight about 39 oz. Previously imported by European American Armory, now imported by Benelli USA. **NOTE:** Add 10 percent for .32 S&W.

1450	1250	950	700	400	200

Model MP95E Match (Atlanta)

Similar to above, with anatomically shaped grips. Choice of blue or chrome finish. Previously imported by European American Armory, now imported by Benelli U.S.A. **NOTE:** Add $60 for chrome finish.

750	600	450	350	225	125

BENTLEY, DAVID
Birmingham, England

Bentley was a prolific maker of both percussion and cartridge arms between 1845 and 1883. Those arms in cases can be dated by addresses listed.

New Church Street	1845-1849
55 Hockley Street	1849-1854
5 Lower Loveday Street	1855-1860
61 & 62 Lower Loveday Street	1860-1863
44 Shadwell Street	1863-1871
Tower Works, Aston	1871-1883

BENTLEY, JOSEPH
Birmingham and Liverpool, England

Best known for his transitional and later patented percussion revolvers, Bentley worked at these addresses:

Birmingham11 Steelhouse Lane	1829-1837
14 St. Mary's Row	1840-1864
Liverpool143 Dale Street	1840-1842
12 South Castle Street	1842-1851
40 Lime Street & 65 Castle	1852-1857
65 Castle & 37 Russell Street	1857-1862

Bentley Revolver

.44-caliber double-action percussion revolver, with 7" barrel and 5-shot cylinder. Blued case hardened, with walnut grips.

—	—	4500	2750	2000	750

BERETTA, DR. FRANCO
Brescia, Italy

This series of shotguns made by Beretta company in Brescia, Italy and imported under Dr. Franco Beretta name in 1980s.

Black Diamond Field Model

Over/under series offered in all standard gauges. Walnut stock, coin-finished receiver, fixed chokes, SST and auto ejectors. **NOTE:** Four embellished grades were offered, Grades One through Four, with increasing levels of scrollwork, engraving and higher grades of French walnut stocks.

800	650	500	400	300	200

	NIB	EXC.	V.G.	GOOD	FAIR	POOR

Grade One

| | 1400 | 1200 | 1000 | 850 | 400 | 200 |

Grade Two

| | 1600 | 1400 | 1200 | 1000 | 500 | 300 |

Grade Three

| | 2200 | 1900 | 1650 | 1400 | 600 | 300 |

Grade Four

| | 3500 | 2800 | 2250 | 1750 | 700 | 350 |

Gamma Standard

12-, 16- or 20-gauge boxlock over/under shotgun, with 26" or 28" barrels, single trigger and automatic ejectors. Blued French case hardened, with walnut stock. Imported from 1984 to 1988.

| | 900 | 775 | 600 | 425 | 250 | 100 |

Gamma Deluxe

As above, but more finely finished.

| | 1200 | 975 | 800 | 600 | 350 | 125 |

Gamma Target

As above in trap or skeet version. Imported from 1986 to 1988.

| | 1200 | 975 | 800 | 600 | 350 | 125 |

America Standard

.410 bore boxlock over/under shotgun, with 26" or 28" barrels. Blued French case hardened, with walnut stock. Imported from 1984 to 1988.

| | 650 | 475 | 325 | 275 | 200 | 100 |

America Deluxe

As above, but more finely finished.

| | 695 | 525 | 375 | 300 | 225 | 100 |

Europa

As above, with 26" barrel and engraved action. Imported from 1984 to 1988.

| | 800 | 725 | 575 | 425 | 275 | 100 |

Europa Deluxe

As above, but more finely finished.

| | 850 | 775 | 625 | 475 | 300 | 1005 |

Francia Standard

.410 bore boxlock double-barrel shotgun, with varying barrel lengths, double triggers and manual extractors. Blued, with walnut stock. Imported from 1986 to 1988.

| | 600 | 500 | 375 | 250 | 125 | 100 |

Alpha Three

12-, 16- or 20-gauge boxlock double-barrel shotgun, with 26" or 28" barrels, single triggers and automatic ejectors. Blued French case hardened, with walnut stock. Imported from 1984 to 1988.

| | 750 | 650 | 500 | 325 | 150 | 100 |

Beta Three

Single-barrel break-open field-grade gun. Chambered for all gauges and offered with ventilated rib barrel from 24" to 32" in length. Receiver is chrome-plated and stock of walnut. Imported from 1985 to 1988.

| | 325 | 225 | 200 | 175 | 125 | 40 |

BERETTA, PIETRO
Brescia, Italy

PISTOLS

Model 1915

7.65mm and 9mm Glisenti caliber semi-automatic pistol, with 3.5" barrel, fixed sights and 8-shot magazine. Blued, with walnut grips. The 7.65mm pistol has single-line inscription while 9mm Glisenti has double line. Various styles of wood grips on this model. Manufactured between 1915 and 1922. Replaced by Model 1915/19.

| | — | 1300 | 1000 | 800 | 500 | 250 |

	NIB	EXC.	V.G.	GOOD	FAIR	POOR

Model 1915/1917

Improved version of above pistol. Chambered for 7.65mm cartridge. Also incorporates a new barrel-mounting method and longer cutout in top of slide. **NOTE:** Add 100 percent for Navy Model.

	—	500	350	275	200	100

Model 1919

Similar to Model 1915 in 6.35mm caliber. Manufactured with minor variations. Different names between 1919 and 1940s.

	—	550	450	350	300	150

Model 1923

9mm Glisenti caliber semi-automatic pistol, with 4" barrel and 8-shot magazine. Blued with steel grips. Slide marked, "Brev 1915-1919 Mlo 1923". Manufactured from 1923 to 1935.

	—	1600	1200	600	265	175

Model 1931

7.65mm caliber semi-automatic pistol, with 3.5" barrel and open-top slide. Blued, with walnut grips. Marked "RM" separated by an anchor.

	—	495	425	325	250	180

Model 1934

As above with 9mm short (.380 ACP) caliber. Slide marked "P. Beretta Cal. 9 Corto-Mo 1934 Brevet Gardone VT." This inscription is followed by date of manufacture that was given numerically, followed by a Roman numeral that denoted year of manufacture on Fascist calendar, which began in 1922. Examples are marked "RM" (Navy), "RE" (Army), "RA" (Air Force) and "PS" (Police). Manufactured between 1934 and 1959.

	—	400	365	250	175	100

Air Force "RA" marked

	—	575	500	375	250	175

Navy "RM" marked

	—	650	575	400	275	200

Model 1934 Romanian Contract

Identical to Model 1934, except slide marked "9mm Scurt" instead of 9mm Corto.

	—	500	450	375	275	175

Model 1935

As above in 7.65mm caliber. Post-war versions are known. Manufactured from 1935 to 1959.

	—	400	375	250	175	125

Model 318

Improved version of old Model 1919, with butt reshaped to afford a better grip. Chambered for .25 ACP cartridge. Has 2.5" barrel. Variety of finishes with plastic grips. In U.S. known as "Panthe". Manufactured between 1935 and 1946.

	—	350	275	250	175	125

Model 418

As above, with rounded grip and cocking indicator. Known as "Bantam" in U.S. Introduced in 1947.

	—	275	225	175	125	90

Model 420

Engraved and chrome-plated Model 418.

	—	350	300	275	200	150

Model 421

Engraved gold-plated Model 418, with tortoise-shell grips.

	—	475	425	325	250	150

Model 948

.22 LR version of Model 1934. Either 3.5" or 6" barrel.

	—	350	300	200	125	90

Model 949 Olympic Target

.22-caliber semi-automatic pistol, with 8.75" barrel, adjustable sights and muzzle-brake. Blued, with checkered walnut grips. Manufactured from 1959 to 1964.

	—	750	600	500	400	200

NIB	EXC.	V.G.	GOOD	FAIR	POOR

U22 Neos 4.5/6.0

Semi-automatic .22-caliber pistol. Introduced in 2002. Chambered for .22 LR cartridge. Fitted with 4.5" or 6" barrel, with integral scope rail. Magazine capacity 10 rounds. Weight about 32- to 36 oz. depending on barrel length.

250	200	165	125	100	75

U22 Neos 4.5 Inox/6.0 Inox

Same as above, with special two-tone finish.

300	250	195	150	100	75

U22 Neos 6.0/7.5 DLX

Introduced in 2003. Features 6" or 7.5" barrel, with target sights and polymer grips with inlays. Adjustable trigger and interchangeable sights. Laser-engraved slide. Weight about 36 oz.

335	275	200	150	100	75

U22 Neos 6.0/7.5 Inox DLX

As above, with Inox finish.

385	300	215	165	115	90

BERETTA 70 SERIES

These pistols began production in 1958 replacing Models 1934, 1935, 948 and 949. During late 1960s, several of these models briefly utilized a 100 series designation for U.S. market. During latter part of 1970s, a magazine safety was added to 70 series and pistols became known as Model 70S. The 70S designation replaced model designations 70 through 75 making these older model numbers obsolete. Only Model 76 designation continued.

The 70 Series design included a cross bolt safety, sear block safety, slide hold-open device and push-button magazine release. Shortly after its introduction, cross bolt safety pushbutton was replaced with lever-type sear block safety located in the same place.

NOTE: Above information was supplied by contributing editor John Stimson, Jr.

Model 70 (Model 100)

Model 948 with cross bolt safety, hold-open device and push-button magazine release. Fixed sights. There are a number of sub-variations available chambered for .22 LR, .32 ACP and .380 ACP cartridges. Available with 3.5" or 5.9" barrel. Has a detachable magazine. Also known as "Puma" when marketed in U.S. by J.L. Galef & Sons. Introduced in 1958. Discontinued in 1985.

525	450	350	275	125	85

Model 70S

Improved Model 70. Chambered for 7.65 (.32 ACP), 9mm Corto (.380 ACP) and .22 LR cartridge. Magazine capacity 7, 8 and 9 rounds respectively.

550	475	375	295	125	85

Model 71/Jaguar (Model 101)

Similar to above. Chambered for .22 LR cartridge. Magazine capacity 10 rounds. Frame is alloy. Fitted with 5.9" barrel. Models imported into U.S. prior to 1968 were fitted with 3.5" barrels.

425	375	300	225	125	85

Model 72

Essentially a Model 71. Sold with two sets of barrels; 3.5" and 5.9". Fixed sights.

450	400	325	250	150	125

Model 76 (102)

A .22 LR target pistol. Barrel shrouded with an aluminum sleeve. Rear part of sleeve extended above slide to hold an adjustable rear sight. Marketed in U.S. as "Sable". Magazine capacity 10 rounds. Briefly after 1968, imported into U.S. as Model 102 "New Sable".

450	400	300	200	125	75

Model 950/Minx

.22-caliber semi-automatic pistol, with 2.25" barrel hinged at front. This could be pivoted forward for cleaning or loading, making this either a semi-automatic or single-shot pistol. Blued, with plastic grips. Introduced in 1955. A 4" barrel version also available. Known as "Minx" in U.S.

325	250	215	145	95	50

Model 950B/Jetfire

As above in .25-caliber. Known as "Jetfire" in U.S.

325	250	215	145	95	50

	NIB	EXC.	V.G.	GOOD	FAIR	POOR

Model 950 Jetfire Inox

Same as Model 950 Jetfire, with stainless steel finish. Introduced in 2000.

	335	250	175	135	85	50

Model 3032 Tomcat

Double-action semi-automatic pistol. Similar in appearance to Model 950. Chambered for .32 ACP cartridge. Barrel length 2.45"; overall length 5". Fixed blade front sight and drift adjustable rear sight. Plastic grips. Seven-round magazine. Blued or matte black finish. Weight 14.5 oz. **NOTE:** Blued finish add $30.

	375	325	250	200	1350	75

Model 3032 Tomcat Inox

Same as above, with stainless steel finish. Introduced in 2000.

	400	325	250	195	125	75

Model 3032 Tomcat Titanium

Same as above, with titanium finish and plastic grips. Weight about 16 oz. Introduced in 2001.

	575	450	350	290	210	150

Alley Cat

Introduced in 2001. Special limited run promotion pistol. Chambered for .32 ACP cartridge. Model is a Tomcat, with special features such as AO Big Dot night sights. Supplied with an Alcantara inside-the-pants holster.

	575	450	350	290	210	150

Model 951

9mm caliber semi-automatic pistol, with 4.5" barrel and fixed sights. Blued, with plastic grips. Known as "Brigadier" at one time. Introduced 1952.

	—	450	375	275	150	100

Model 20

.25 ACP double-action pistol, with 2.5" barrel and 9-shot magazine. Blued, with walnut or plastic grips. Discontinued in 1985.

	300	250	195	150	90	75

Model 21 Bobcat

Small frame semi-automatic pistol. Chambered for .22 LR or .25 ACP cartridge. Features 2.4" tip-up barrel with fixed sights. Magazine capacity of 8 rounds (.25 ACP) or 7 rounds (.22 LR). Comes with plastic or walnut grips. Deluxe version with gold line engraving. Pistol weighs about 11 to 11.8 oz. depending on caliber.

Standard Model

	325	275	250	225	175	95

Model 21EL

Gold engraved model.

	395	350	325	280	195	110

Model 21 Inox

Stainless steel.

	325	250	200	140	95	75

Model 90

Double-action semi-automatic .32 auto pocket pistol, with 3.5" barrel and 8-round magazine. Manufactured from 1969 to 1983.

	—	395	350	295	200	125

Model 92

9mm caliber double-action semi-automatic pistol, with 5" barrel, fixed sights and 16-round double-stack magazine. Blued, with plastic grips. Introduced in 1976. Now discontinued.

	800	600	500	400	250	200

Model 92SB-P

As above, with polished finish. Manufactured from 1980 to 1985.

	625	475	400	325	250	200

Model 92SB Compact

As above, with 4.3" barrel and shortened grip frame that holds a 14-shot magazine. Blued or nickel-plated, with wood or plastic grips. Nickel version worth additional 15 percent. Wood grips

	NIB	EXC.	V.G.	GOOD	FAIR	POOR

add $20 to value. Introduced in 1980. Discontinued in 1985.

	500	425	375	325	250	200

Model 92FS

Current production Model 92 chambered for 9mm Parabellum cartridge. Barrel length 4.9". Rear sight is 3-dot combat drift adjustable. Magazine capacity 15 rounds. Semi-automatic pistol features double-/single-action operation. Safety is manual type. Frame is light alloy sandblasted and anodized black. Barrel slide is steel. Grips are plastic checkered, with black matte finish. Equipped with spare magazine cleaning rod and hard carrying case. Pistol weighs 34.4 oz. empty.

	550	450	350	300	200	150

Model 92FS Inox

Introduced in 2001. Chambered for 9mm cartridge. Fitted with 4.9" barrel. Slide is black stainless steel, with lightweight frame and combat-style trigger guard, reversible magazine release and ambidextrous safety. Gray wrap-around grips. Weight about 34 oz.

	695	575	425	350	225	175

Model 96

Identical to Model 92FS. Fitted with 10-round magazine. Chambered for .40 S&W. Introduced in 1992.

	550	450	350	300	200	150

Model 96 Combat

Introduced in 1997. Single-action-only, with competition tuned trigger. Developed for practical shooting competition. Barrel length 5.9". Supplied with weight as standard. Rear sight is adjustable target type. Tool kit included as standard. Weight 40 oz.

	1700	1300	950	575	350	175

Model 96 Stock

Similar to Model 96 in double-/single-action, with half-cock notch for cocked and locked carry. Fitted with 4.9" barrel with fixed sights. Three interchangeable front sights are supplied as standard. Weight 35 oz. Introduced in 1997. No longer in U.S. product line.

	1350	950	775	500	325	150

Model 96A1

An evolution of the M9 service pistol for military and law enforcement. Chambered in .40 S&W, this model comes with three 12-round magazines. Features include an integral Picatinny accessory rail, improved recoil buffer and Bruniton finish.

	700	600	475	375	250	150

Model 92/96FS Inox

Same as above except barrel, slide, trigger, extractor and other components are made of stainless steel. Frame made of lightweight anodized aluminum alloy. Model 96FS discontinued in 1993.

	650	550	450	350	300	200

Model 92/96FS Centurion

Chambered for 9mm or .40 S&W (Model 96). Features 4.3" barrel, but retains full grip to accommodate 15-round magazine (9mm); 10 rounds (.40 S&W). Weighs about 33.2 oz. Introduced in 1993. Black sandblasted finish.

	550	450	400	300	200	150

Model 92FS/96 Brigadier

Same as 92FS and 96, with heavier slide to reduce felt recoil. Removable front sight. Weight about 35 oz.

	700	550	400	300	150	75

Model 92FS/96 Brigadier Inox

Same as above, with stainless steel finish. Introduced in 2000.

	750	600	475	325	175	100

Model 92G-SD/96G-SD

Introduced in 2003. Features a decock mechanism built around single-/double-action trigger system. In addition, pistol has an integral accessory rail on frame. Fitted with 9mm or .40 S&W, 4.9" barrel, with heavy slide and 3-dot tritium sights. Weight about 35 oz.

	1000	750	500	350	195	125

NIB	EXC.	V.G.	GOOD	FAIR	POOR

Model 92F

9mm Parabellum caliber double-action semi-automatic pistol, with 4.9" barrel, fixed sights and 15-shot double-stack magazine and an extended base. Matte blued finish, with walnut or plastic grips. Introduced in 1984. No longer in production.

500	400	350	300	200	150

Model 92F U.S. Marked Slide

A special limited edition of 100 pistols made for the Armed Forces Reserves, with BER prefix serial numbers and U.S. M9 markings on frame and slide.

1700	1500	1250	900	—	—

Model 92F Compact

As above, with 4.3" barrel and 13-shot magazine. No longer in production.

500	400	350	300	200	150

Model 92/96 Compact "Type M

Essentially same as Model 92FS Compact, with exception of single column magazine that holds 8 rounds and reduces grip thickness of pistol. Weighs 30.9 oz. Discontinued in 1993, reintroduced in 1998. Model 96 version (.40 S&W) introduced in 2000. **NOTE:** Add $90 for Tritium night sights.

700	550	350	300	200	150

Model 92/96M Compact Inox

Same as above, with stainless steel slide and frame. Introduced in 2000.

700	550	450	350	300	200

Model 92D Compact "Type M

Same as above, with double-action-only trigger function. **NOTE:** Add $90 for Tritium night sights.

550	450	350	300	200	150

Model 92FS Deluxe

Identical dimensions to full size Model 92FS. Addition of gold-plated engraved frame and gold-plated extra magazine. In fitted leather presentation hard case. Grips walnut briar, with gold initial plate. Introduced in 1993.

5500	4500	3000	2000	1500	1000

Model 92FS "470th Anniversary" Limited Edition

Limited to only 470 pistols worldwide. Features high polish finish, with stainless steel gold-filled engravings, walnut grips, Anniversary logo on top of slide and on back of chrome plated magazine. Supplied with walnut case.

2075	1300	800	600	375	200

Model 92/96D

Same specifications as standard Model 92 and Model 96. Variation has no visible hammer. Double-action-only. No manual safety. Weighs 33.8 oz.

425	375	325	275	200	150

Model 92/96DS

Same as above, with same manual safety as found on 92FS pistol. Introduced in 1994.

425	375	325	275	200	150

Model 92G/96G

Designed for French Gendarmerie. This model has now been adopted for French Air Force as well as other government agencies. Features hammer drop lever that does not function as safety when lever is released, but lowers hammer and returns to ready to fire position automatically. Offered to law enforcement agencies only.

650	550	475	400	250	100

Model 92/96 Vertec

Introduced in 2002. Chambered for 9mm or .40 S&W cartridges. Fitted with 4.7" barrel. Double-/single-action trigger. Features a new vertical grip design, with shorter trigger reach and thin grip panels. Removable front sight and integral accessory rail on frame. Magazine capacity 10 rounds. Weight about 32 oz.

700	575	425	300	225	165

Model 92 Competition Conversion Kit

Kit includes 7.3" barrel, with counterweight and elevated front sight, semi-automatic, walnut grips and fully adjustable rear sight. Comes in special carrying case, with basic pistol. **NOTE:** Kit Price Only.

500	350	300	200	150	100

	NIB	EXC.	V.G.	GOOD	FAIR	POOR

Model 92/96 Combo

Features specially designed Model 96 pistol, with extra 92FS slide and barrel assembly. Barrel lengths are 4.66". Sold with one 10-round magazine in both 9mm and .40 S&W.

NIB	EXC.	V.G.	GOOD	FAIR	POOR
850	725	600	425	275	200

Model M9 Limited Edition

Introduced in 1995 to commemorate 10th Anniversary of U.S. military's official sidearm. This 9mm pistol limited to 10,000 units. Special engraving on slide with special serial numbers. Slide stamped "U.S. 9mm M9-BERETTA U.S.A.-65490".

Standard Model

NIB	EXC.	V.G.	GOOD	FAIR	POOR
825	700	450	300	200	100

Deluxe Model

Walnut grips, with gold plated hammer and grip screws.

NIB	EXC.	V.G.	GOOD	FAIR	POOR
875	750	500	350	200	100

Model 92 Billennium

Introduced in 2001. Limited production pistol of 2,000 units world wide. Chambered for 9mm cartridge. Steel frame, with checkered front and backstrap. Nickel alloy finish, with unique engraving. Carbon fiber grips. Interchangeable sights, with adjustable rear sight. Carry case standard. Single action.

NIB	EXC.	V.G.	GOOD	FAIR	POOR
1200	1000	800	600	475	325

92 Steel-I

Steel-frame semi-automatic in 9mm or .40 S&W. Single- or single-/double-action. 15+1 capacity, 4.7" barrel, weight 42.3 oz. IDPA certified. Fixed 3-dot sights. Introduced 2006.

NIB	EXC.	V.G.	GOOD	FAIR	POOR
1075	850	600	475	300	150

M9A1

Semi-automatic single-/double-action in 9mm developed for U.S. Marine Corps. Capacity 10+1 or 15+1. Fixed sights. Introduced 2006.

NIB	EXC.	V.G.	GOOD	FAIR	POOR
825	650	450	300	195	125

ELITE TEAM SERIES

In 1999, Beretta introduced a new series of pistols based on company's M92/96 pistol. Each of these pistols has specific features for specific shooting requirements.

Model 92/96 Custom Carry

Fitted with 4.3" barrel, shortened grip and low profile control levers. Safety lever is left side only. Magazine capacity 10 rounds. "CUSTOM CARRY" engraved on slide. Chambered for 9mm or .40 S&W calibers.

NIB	EXC.	V.G.	GOOD	FAIR	POOR
625	500	400	300	200	100

Model 92/96 Border Marshall

Commercial version of pistol built for Immigration and Naturalization Service. Fitted with heavy-duty steel slide and short 4.7" I.N.S. style barrel. Rubber grips and night sights are standard. "BORDER MARSHALL" engraved on slide. Offered in 9mm or .40 S&W calibers.

NIB	EXC.	V.G.	GOOD	FAIR	POOR
750	600	475	350	225	150

Model 92G/96G Elite

Chambered for 9mm or .40 S&W calibers. Fitted with 4.7" stainless steel barrel and heavy-duty Brigadier-style slide. Action is decock only. Slide has both front and rear serrations. Hammer is skeletonized. Beveled magazine well. Special "ELITE" engraving on slide. Weight about 35 oz.

NIB	EXC.	V.G.	GOOD	FAIR	POOR
825	650	450	375	250	165

Model 92G Elite II

Version of Elite was developed for competition shooter. Fitted with 4.7" barrel and heavy slide. Has skeletonized hammer. Beveled magazine well and extended release. Checkered front and backstrap grip. Weight about 35 oz.

NIB	EXC.	V.G.	GOOD	FAIR	POOR
925	725	550	395	275	150

Model 92FS Inox Tactical

Model has satin matte finish on its stainless steel slide. Frame is anodized aluminum. Black rubber grips and night sights are standard. Offered in 9mm only.

NIB	EXC.	V.G.	GOOD	FAIR	POOR
775	625	500	350	225	100

	NIB	EXC.	V.G.	GOOD	FAIR	POOR

COUGAR SERIES

Model 8000/8040/8045 Cougar

Compact size pistol using a short recoil rotating barrel. Features a firing pin lock, chrome lined barrel, anodized aluminum alloy frame, with Bruniton finish. Overall length 7"; barrel length 3.6"; overall height 5.5"; unloaded weight 33.5 oz. Offered in double-/single-action as well as double-action-only. Magazine holds 10 rounds. Available in 9mm or .40 S&W. In 1998 Beretta added .45 ACP caliber. **NOTE:** Add $50 for .45 ACP models

625	525	400	350	250	150

Model 8000/8040/8045 Mini Cougar

Introduced in 1997. Similar in design to full size model. Offered in 9mm, .40 S&W or .45 ACP. Fitted with 3.6" barrel (3.7" on .45 ACP). Empty weight 27 oz. Offered in double-/single-action or double-action-only. Magazine capacity: 10 rounds for 9mm; 8 rounds for .40 S&W. Weight between 27 oz. and 30 oz. depending on caliber. **NOTE:** Add $50 for .45 ACP models.

500	450	350	225	125	75

Model 8000F—Cougar L

Similar to above. Fitted with a shortened grip frame. Chambered for 9mm cartridge. Fitted with a 3.6" barrel. Overall height as been reduced by .4". Weight about 28 oz. Introduced in 2003.

600	500	400	300	175	95

Model 9000F

Introduced in 2000. Chambered for 9mm or .40 S&W cartridge. Fitted with 3.4" barrel. Has polymer frame. "F" type has single-/double-action trigger. Fixed sights. Magazine capacity 10 rounds. Weight about 27 oz.; overall length 6.6"; overall height 4.8". External hammer and black finish.

550	450	350	200	125	75

Model 9000D

Same as above, with double-action-only trigger.

550	450	350	275	150	100

Model 9000S

Chambered for 9mm or .40 S&W cartridges. Magazine capacity 10 rounds. Optional spacer Model 92/96 magazines can also be used. Three-dot sight system. Accessory magazine bottom that extends when griped, but retracts when holstered is standard. Steel alloy frame and slide. Weight about 27 oz. Introduced in 2001.

550	450	350	200	125	75

CHEETAH SERIES

Model 84/Cheetah

Small semi-automatic pistol chambered for .380 cartridge. Double-column magazine that holds 13 rounds. Offered in blue or nickel finish. Grips are checkered black plastic or checkered wood.

450	375	325	275	200	150

Model 84BB

Similar to Model 84, but incorporates different features such as a firing pin blocking device and loaded chamber indicator. Single-column magazine holds 8 rounds of .380 shells. Discontinued in 1993.

425	375	325	275	200	150

Model 85/Cheetah

Similar in appearance to Model 84. Features single-column magazine, with capacity of 8 rounds. Available in blue or nickel finish. Grips are checkered black plastic. Pistol weighs 22 oz.

600	475	325	275	200	150

Model 86/Cheetah

.380 ACP semi-automatic pistol has 4.4" tip-up barrel. Magazine capacity 8 rounds. Furnished with checkered wood grips. Pistol weighs 23 oz.

675	500	300	250	200	150

Model 87/Cheetah

.22-caliber double-action semi-automatic target pistol, with 3.8" or 6" barrel, adjustable sights and 7-shot magazine. Blued, with checkered walnut grips. Introduced in 1986.

650	525	375	250	200	150

	NIB	EXC.	V.G.	GOOD	FAIR	POOR

Model 87 Target

.22-caliber single-action target pistol. Features adjustable rear sight, integral scope base and external hammer. Anodized aluminum frame. Weight about 41 oz. Introduced in 2000.

	NIB	EXC.	V.G.	GOOD	FAIR	POOR
	700	600	395	250	200	150

Model 89/Gold Standard

.22-caliber semi-automatic target pistol, with adjustable sights and 10-shot detachable magazine. Matte finish, with hand-fitting walnut grips. Introduced in 1988.

	NIB	EXC.	V.G.	GOOD	FAIR	POOR
	900	725	550	400	300	150

Model PX4 Storm Pistol

Introduced in 2005. Features single-/double action trigger, with decocker and chambered for 9mm, .45 ACP or .40 S&W cartridges. Fitted with 4" barrel. Interchangeable grip backstraps. Reversible magazine release button. Picatinny rail. Fixed sights. Magazine capacity: 14 rounds .40 S&W; 17 rounds 9mm. Weight about 27.5 lbs. Compact model has 3.2" barrel and smaller grip frame. Magazine capacity reduced by two rounds.

	NIB	EXC.	V.G.	GOOD	FAIR	POOR
	500	450	375	250	195	125

Model PX4 Storm Subcompact

Similar to above, with smaller dimensions and chambered in 9mm and .40 S&W only. Round capacity: 10- (.40) or 13- (9mm). Overall length 6.2". Weight: 26.1 oz.

	NIB	EXC.	V.G.	GOOD	FAIR	POOR
	500	450	375	250	195	125

Model PX4 Storm SD (Special Duty)

Similar to PX4 Storm in .45 ACP only. Matte black slide and OD polymer frame, 9- or 10-round magazine. Overall length 8.2". Weight 28.6 oz.

	NIB	EXC.	V.G.	GOOD	FAIR	POOR
	900	750	575	450	300	150

90-Two

Wrap-around polymer grip standard or slim. Single-/double-action semi-automatic in 9mm (10+1, 15+1 or 17+1 capacity) or .40 S&W (10+1 or 12+1 capacity). Types D, F or G. Fixed sights. 4.9" barrel, 32.5 oz. Introduced 2006. **NOTE:** Add 10 percent for luminous sights.

	NIB	EXC.	V.G.	GOOD	FAIR	POOR
	600	475	350	290	210	150

BU9 Nano

Micro-compact DA-only 9mm, with 6+1 round capacity, 3" barrel, polymer frame, adjustable sights. Weight 17 oz. Introduced 2011.

	NIB	EXC.	V.G.	GOOD	FAIR	POOR
	425	375	300	225	150	100

Pico

Similar to the Nano, except chambered in .380 ACP with a more compact design. Double-action-only firing system, with a 2.7" barrel. Width .725", weight 11.5 oz. Adjustable sights, ambidextrous slide release and comes with two 6+1 magazines. Introduced in 2013.

	NIB	EXC.	V.G.	GOOD	FAIR	POOR
	350	320	250	200	150	100

Stampede

Introduced in 2003. Single-action revolver chambered for .45 Colt, .44-40 or .357 Magnum cartridge. Choice of 4.75", 5.5" or 7.5" barrel. Blued, with Beretta case color and black polymer grips. Weight about 2.3 lbs. depending on barrel length. Discountinued in 2013.

	NIB	EXC.	V.G.	GOOD	FAIR	POOR
	525	400	275	195	125	75

Stampede Buntline

.45 Colt with 18" barrel, satin-finish grips and gold Beretta medallion. Other features similar to Stampede Blue model.

	NIB	EXC.	V.G.	GOOD	FAIR	POOR
	800	700	550	475	350	250

Stampede Nickel

Similar to Stampede Blue, with brushed nickel finish and walnut grips.

	NIB	EXC.	V.G.	GOOD	FAIR	POOR
	500	400	295	195	125	75

Stampede Deluxe

As above, with charcoal blue finish and Beretta case color. Select walnut grips.

	NIB	EXC.	V.G.	GOOD	FAIR	POOR
	620	500	375	250	195	125

Stampede Patton Model

Similar to Deluxe model, with light engraving on case color frame, light gold inlays and faux ivory grips.

	NIB	EXC.	V.G.	GOOD	FAIR	POOR
	900	800	700	600	450	350

	NIB	EXC.	V.G.	GOOD	FAIR	POOR

Stampede Bisley

Single-action 6-shot Bisley. Replica revolver in .45 Colt or .357 Magnum. Blued, with 4.75", 5.5" or 7.5" barrel. Introduced 2006. **NOTE:** Add 10 percent for nickel.

	620	500	375	250	195	125

Laramie

Break-open single-action revolver. Reminiscent of S&W #3. Chambered for.45 LC or .38 Special. Six-shot cylinder. Adjustable rear sight. 5" or 6.5" barrels. Introduced 2006. Discontinued 2008. Made by Beretta subsidiary Uberti. **NOTE:** Add 10 percent for nickel finish.

	1000	875	595	375	225	145

RIFLES

1873 Renegade Short Lever-Action Rifle

Lever-action rifle chambered in .45 Colt, .357 Magnum. Patterned after 1873 Winchester. Features include 20" round barrel, blued finish, checkered walnut buttstock and fore-end, adjustable rear sight and fixed blade front. Ten-round tubular magazine.

	1400	1050	875	595	375	225

Gold Rush Slide-Action Rifle and Carbine

External replica of old Colt Lightning Magazine Rifle. Chambered in .357 Magnum and .45 Colt. Features include 20" round or 24.5" octagonal barrel, case-hardened receiver, walnut buttstock and fore-end, crescent buttplate, 13-round (rifle) or 10-round (carbine) magazine. Available as Standard Carbine, Standard Rifle or Deluxe Rifle.

	1200	1050	875	595	375	225

Cx4 Storm

Introduced in 2003. Semi-automatic carbine has 16.6" barrel. Chambered for 9mm, .40 S&W or .45 ACP cartridge. Synthetic stock, with rubber recoil pad that has adjustable stock spacers. Ghost ring rear sight, with adjustable post front sight. Forward accessory rail. Magazine capacity: 10 rounds .40 S&W or 9mm; 8 rounds .45 ACP. Weight about 5.75 lbs.

	800	650	500	350	200	100

AR-70

.223-caliber semi-automatic rifle, with 17.7" barrel, adjustable diopter sights and 8- or 30-shot magazine. Black epoxy finish, with synthetic stock. Weight about 8.3 lbs. No longer imported into U.S.

	2100	1900	1500	1000	750	400

ARX 100

A tactical semi-automatic rifle that is a civilian version of ARX-160 select-fire military rifle developed for the Italian Armed Forces. (This is not to be confused with ARX-160 .22 rimfire rifle.) Modular design allows easy maintenance. Standard configuration is with four Picatinny rails. All controls are ambidextrous. Chambered for 5.56 NATO. Introduced in 2013.

	1750	1400	1050	800	550	250

ARX 160

Similar in appearance and operation to ARX 100 design, but chambered in .22 Long Rifle.

	500	425	350	250	150	100

BM-59 Standard Grade

Gas-operated semi-automatic rifle, with detachable box magazine. Chambered for .308 cartridge. Walnut stock. Barrel length 19.3" with muzzle-brake. Magazine capacity 5, 10 or 20 rounds. Weight about 9.5 lbs.

	3000	2700	2100	1500	400	200

Model 500 Custom

Bolt-action rifle in three action lengths, 24" barrel, open sights. Chambered in .222 Rem., .223 Rem., .243 Win., .270 Win., .308 Win., .30-06. Blued finish and checkered walnut stock. Offered in several grades.

	—	600	525	400	325	275

Model 500S

	—	625	550	425	350	300

Model 500DL

	—	1400	1250	1000	775	650

	NIB	EXC.	V.G.	GOOD	FAIR	POOR

Model 500DEELL

	—	1600	1450	1200	975	800

Model 500DEELLS

	—	1625	1475	1225	1000	825

Model 501

.243- or .308-caliber bolt-action rifle, with 23" barrel, furnished without sights and 6-shot magazine. Blued, with checkered walnut stock. Discontinued in 1986. Offered in same variations as Model 500 series-501S, 501DL, 501DLS, 501EELL and 501EELLS. Values for this series are same as for 500 series rifles.

Model 502

.270, 7mm Rem. Magnum and .30-06 caliber bolt-action rifle, with 24" barrel (without sights) and 5-shot magazine. Blued, with checkered walnut stock. Discontinued in 1986. Available in same variations as Model 500 and Model 501. Valued approximately 10 percent higher in each variation.

Mato Standard

Bolt-action rifles built on Mauser 98 type action, with controlled-round feed, three-position safety, adjustable trigger. Chambered in .270 Win., .280 Rem., .30-06, .300 Win. Magnum, .338 Win. Magnum. Composite stock.

1200	1000	800	600	300	175

Mato Deluxe

Bolt-action rifle introduced into Beretta product line in 1997. Stock is XXX Claro walnut, with hand-rubbed oil finish and black fore-end tip. Chambered for .270 Win., .280, .30-06, 7mm Magnum, .300 Magnum, .338 Magnum and .375 H&H. Weight about 8 lbs.

2000	1500	1000	750	350	200

PREMIUM RIFLES

Model S689 Sable

9.3x74R or .30-06 caliber over/under rifle, with boxlock action, 23" ribbed barrels and express-type sights. Blued case hardened or nickel-plated, with checkered walnut stock. Double triggers and automatic ejectors. Offered in three grades. **NOTE:** Add $1,200 extra 20-gauge barrel with forearm; $2,000 scope with claw mounts.

Silver Sable

3850	3000	2500	1750	1200	300

Gold Sable

6500	5500	4500	3000	1500	350

Diamond Sable

12750	10000	7500	5500	2000	1000

SSO Express

.375 H&H and .458 Win. Magnum caliber over/under double barrel rifle, with 23" barrels, folding express sights, double triggers and automatic ejectors. Furnished with fitted case. Available on custom order basis. Should be individually appraised.

18000	13000	9500	6000	3500	2500

SSO5 Express

More finely finished version of above.

20000	15000	11000	8000	5000	3000

SSO6

Premium grade sidelock over/under express rifle. Equipped with double triggers. Offered in 9.3x74R, .375 H&H Magnum and .458 Win. Magnum. Fitted with 24" barrel, with express sights. Claw mounts for Zeiss scopes are available from factory. Receiver is case-colored, with light scroll engraving. Special select walnut used in stock and forearm, with fine line checkering. Stock comes with cheekpiece and rubber recoil pad. Furnished with leather case. Weighs about 11 lbs.

62000	52000	34000	24000	10000	3000

SSO6 EELL

Offered in same calibers as above. Furnished with hand engraved game scenes, with gold inlays. Walnut stock is special select briar, with fine diamond line checkering.

110000	90000	70000	40000	18000	10000

	NIB	EXC.	V.G.	GOOD	FAIR	POOR

Model 455

Premium grade side-by-side express rifle, with slide locks. Available in these calibers: .375 H&H Magnum, .458 Win. Magnum, .470 Nitro Express, .500 Nitro Express and .416 Rigby. Receiver is case-colored, without engraving. Walnut stock highly figured, with fine line checkering. Comes supplied with express sights. Claw mounts and Zeiss scope offered at customer's request only on .375, .458 and .416. Weighs about 11 lbs.

	80000	70000	55000	40000	20000	5000

Model 455 EELL

Same as above. Furnished with case-colored game scene engraving, with gold inlays. Walnut briar stock, with fine diamond line checkering. Supplied with leather case and accessories.

	110000	85000	60000	45000	25000	10000

SHOTGUNS

Beretta shotguns are marked with a symbol or "0" stamping to indicate type of fixed choke in barrel or barrels. Usually this stamping is on side of barrel in rear, near receiver on semi-automatics and near ejectors on double barrel shotguns. Beretta shotguns with screw-in Mobilchoke tubes will have notches cut in them to indicate amount of choke placed in tube.

BL SERIES

BL series of over/under shotguns were manufactured between 1968 and 1973. Chambered for 12-, 20- or 28-gauge. Offered with 26", 28" or 30" vent ribbed barrels, with various choke combinations. They feature boxlock actions and offered with single-/double triggers and manual extractors or automatic ejectors. Finish blued, with checkered walnut stocks. Configurations differ basically in quality of materials, workmanship and degree of ornamentation. **NOTE:** Add 50 percent for 20-gauge; 75 percent for 28-gauge.

BL-1

	—	500	450	350	225	150

BL-2

	—	425	375	300	250	200

BL-2/S (Speed Trigger)

	—	450	400	325	275	225

BL-2 Stakeout
18" barrel.

	—	400	350	275	225	175

BL-3

	—	600	550	475	425	350

BL-3 Competition

	—	650	600	525	475	400

BL-4

	—	800	750	650	525	425

BL-4 Competition

	—	850	800	700	575	450

BL-5

	—	900	850	725	575	450

BL-5 Competition

	—	950	900	775	600	475

BL-6
Sidelock.

	—	1250	1150	1000	850	675

BL-6 Competition

	—	1300	1200	1050	900	725

Model S55 B

12- or 20-gauge over/under shotgun, with 26", 28" or 30" ventilated rib barrels, various choke combinations and boxlock action with single-selective trigger and extractors. Blued, with

	NIB	EXC.	V.G.	GOOD	FAIR	POOR

checkered walnut stock.

	—	550	500	400	325	275

Model S56 E

As above more finely finished.

	—	600	550	450	375	325

Model S58 Competition

As above, with 26" or 30" barrels, wide vent ribs. Competition-type stocks.

	—	700	650	550	475	400

Silver Snipe

12- or 20-gauge over/under shotgun, with 26", 28" or 30" barrels. Boxlock action, with double trigger and extractors. Blued, with checkered walnut stock. Manufactured from 1955 through 1967. Single-selective trigger version, with ventilated rib and automatic ejectors would be worth approx. an additional 50 percent.

	—	600	475	325	275	200

Golden Snipe

As above, with ventilated rib and automatic ejectors. Single-selective trigger add 10 percent.

	—	800	675	500	350	200

Model 57 E

As above more finely finished. Manufactured between 1955 and 1967.

	—	825	775	600	475	250

ASEL Model

12- or 20-gauge over/under shotgun, with 26", 28" or 30" ventilated rib barrel and various choke combinations. Single-selective trigger and automatic ejectors. Blued, with checkered pistol-grip stock. Manufactured between 1947 and 1964. Prices listed for 20-gauge. **NOTE:** 12-gauge deduct $1000 from Exc. condition price; EELL grade add 30 percent.

	—	4250	2500	1200	750	400

Model 409 PB

12-, 16-, 20- and 28-gauge boxlock double-barrel shotgun, with 27", 28" or 30" barrels, double triggers and extractors. Various choke combinations. Blued, with checkered walnut stock. Manufactured between 1934 and 1964. **NOTE:** Add 50 percent for 20-gauge; 100 percent for 28-gauge.

	—	1100	850	625	500	250

Model 410

As above, with 32" Full-choke barrel. Blued, with checkered walnut stock. Introduced in 1934, 10-gauge only.

	—	1500	1250	850	600	300

Model 410 E

More finely finished version of 409PB.

	—	900	825	650	500	275

Model 411 E

Model 410, with false sideplates and more heavily engraved. Manufactured between 1934 and 1964.

	—	2100	1750	1250	800	425

Model 424

12- and 20-gauge boxlock shotgun, with 26" or 28" barrels, double triggers, various choke combinations and extractors. Blued, with checkered walnut stock. In 20-gauge designated Model 426 and worth an additional 50 percent.

		950	875	675	500	225

Model 426 E

As above, with silver inlays and heavier engraving, single-selective trigger and automatic ejectors. Not imported after 1983.

	—	1150	1075	875	700	350

Model 625

12- or 20-gauge boxlock double-barrel shotgun, with 26", 28" or 30" barrels, various choke combinations, double triggers and extractors. Moderately engraved. Blued, with checkered

	NIB	EXC.	V.G.	GOOD	FAIR	POOR

walnut grip. Imported between 1984 and 1986. **NOTE:** Add 50 percent for 20-gauge.

| | 1200 | 900 | 750 | 600 | 500 | 250 |

Model 626 Field Grade

12- or 20-gauge boxlock double barrel shotgun, with 26" or 28" barrel, various choke combinations, single trigger and automatic ejectors. Engraved, blued with checkered walnut stock. Imported between 1984 and 1988.

| | 1400 | 1000 | 825 | 700 | 575 | 475 |

Model 626 Onyx

Boxlock side-by-side shotgun offered in 12- and 20-gauge. Choice of 26" or 28" solid rib barrels, with screw-in chokes. Double triggers are standard, but single trigger available on request. Receiver anti-glare black matte finish. Stock walnut, with hand checkering and pistol-grip. Weight: 12-gauge 6 lbs. 13 oz.; 20-gauge 6 lbs. 13 oz.

| | 1600 | 1250 | 850 | 750 | 500 | 400 |

Model 627 EL

Offered in 12-gauge only, with choice of 26" or 28" solid rib barrels. Walnut is highly figured and fine cut checkered. Receiver silver, with side plates engraved with scroll. Comes with hard case.

| | 2600 | 2000 | 1750 | 1500 | 1250 | 650 |

Model 627 EELL

Same as above. Fitted with scroll engraved side plates and game scenes. Walnut highly figured, with fine line checkering. Straight-grip stock also offered. Comes with hard case.

| | 3850 | 3500 | 3000 | 2500 | 1500 | 1000 |

GR Series

Moderately priced series of side-by-side boxlock double shotguns. Imported from 1968 to about 1976. Offered in 12- or 20-gauge, with fixed chokes. GR-2 has double triggers with folding front trigger, extractors. GR-3 has single selective trigger, better wood. GR-4 has automatic ejectors, higher grade wood. Prices shown are for 12-gauge models. **NOTE:** Add 50 percent for 20-gauge.

GR-1

| | 1000 | 850 | 700 | 600 | 500 | 350 |

GR-2

| | 1150 | 950 | 800 | 700 | 600 | 400 |

GR-3

| | 1250 | 1050 | 900 | 800 | 700 | 500 |

Silver Hawk

10- or 12-gauge boxlock double-barrel shotgun, with 30" barrels, double triggers and extractors. Blued, with silver-finished receiver and checkered walnut stock. 10-gauge version worth an additional 20 percent. Discontinued in 1967.

| | — | 700 | 500 | 375 | 250 | 150 |

Silver Hawk Featherweight

Similar to above. Made in 12-, 16-, 20- and 28-gauge, with 26", 28", 30" or 32" barrels. Standard choices of fixed chokes. Single-/double triggers. Automatic ejectors. **NOTE:** Add 10 percent for single trigger; 50 percent for 20-gauge; 80 percent for 28-gauge.

| | 1000 | 875 | 750 | 600 | 450 | 300 |

Model 470 Silver Hawk

Introduced in 1997 to commemorate Beretta's 470 years in the gunmaking business. Offered in 12- or 20-gauge configurations. Receiver silver chrome with engraving. Top lever checkered, with gold inlaid hawk's head. Fitted with straight-grip stock, splinter forearm of select walnut with oil finish. Choice of 26" or 28" barrels, with auto ejection or manual extraction. Weight: 12-gauge about 6.5 lbs.; 20-gauge about 6 lbs.

| | 2400 | 2000 | 1500 | — | — | — |

Model 470 Silver Hawk EL

Introduced in 2002. Features color case hardened frame and side plates, with gold filled game scene engraving. Offered in 12- or 20-gauge, with choice of 26" or 28" barrels. Weight: 5.9 lbs. for 20-gauge; 6.5 lbs. for 12-gauge.

| | 4800 | 4000 | 3000 | — | — | — |

Model 471 Silver Hawk

Introduced in 2003. Side-by-side shotgun has boxlock receiver. Offered in 12- and 20-gauge. Choice of 26" or 28" barrels, pistol-grip with beavertail fore-end or straight-grip stock with

NIB	EXC.	V.G.	GOOD	FAIR	POOR

splinter fore-end. Straight-grip stock, with case color receiver is available at a premium. Select walnut stock with oil finish. Single-selective trigger. Weight: about 6.5 lbs. in 12-gauge; 5.9 lbs. in 20-gauge. **NOTE:** Add $350 for straight-grip stock, with case color receiver.

NIB	EXC.	V.G.	GOOD	FAIR	POOR
2875	2250	1300	800	450	300

Model 486 Parallelo

Side-by-side model introduced in 2014. Chambered in 12-gauge only, with a round action decorated with English style scroll engraving and scalloped coin-finish. Checkered walnut stock has a straight-grip, with splinter fore-end. Other features include single selective trigger, choice of automatic ejectors or manual extractors and choke tubes or fixed chokes.

NIB	EXC.	V.G.	GOOD	FAIR	POOR
4600	3700	2900	2200	1200	500

BERETTA "SO" SERIES & OTHER PREMIUM SHOTGUNS

Over/under shotguns fitted with side-locks, automatic ejectors, single-/double triggers. Barrel lengths from 26" to 30", with a wide variety of choke combinations. Introduced 1948 in 12-gauge only. No longer imported as production gun in 1986. Many of these SO guns were sold through firm of Garcia, a sporting goods firm and distributor. Various grades are priced according to quality of wood, finish engraving coverage and the like. Do not confuse these earlier Beretta shotguns with present line of premium grade Berettas now being imported into U.S.

SO-1

NIB	EXC.	V.G.	GOOD	FAIR	POOR
—	3000	2400	1500	800	400

SO-2

NIB	EXC.	V.G.	GOOD	FAIR	POOR
—	4000	2700	2000	900	500

SO-3

NIB	EXC.	V.G.	GOOD	FAIR	POOR
—	5000	4400	3500	1500	1000

SO-4 (Garcia SO3EL)

NOTE: Fully engraved Garcia Model SO3-EL add 80 percent.

NIB	EXC.	V.G.	GOOD	FAIR	POOR
—	7900	6900	3500	2000	1500

SO-5 (Garcia SO-3 EELL)

NIB	EXC.	V.G.	GOOD	FAIR	POOR
—	—	7900	5900	3500	2500

SO-6 (450 or 451 EL) Side-by-Side

Fitted with Holland & Holland-style sidelocks and third fastener.

NIB	EXC.	V.G.	GOOD	FAIR	POOR
—	7500	6500	5500	3500	2500

SO-7 (451 EELL) Side-by-Side

NIB	EXC.	V.G.	GOOD	FAIR	POOR
—	8900	7900	5900	4000	3000

SO-5 Trap

Premium grade Beretta over/under shotgun. Built for competition trap shooting. Available in 12-gauge, with 30" vent rib barrels standard. Barrels in 28" and 32" may be special ordered. Receiver silver with light scroll engraving. Stock is select highly figured walnut, with pistol-grip. Offered in International or Monte Carlo dimensions. Special trap rubber recoil pad is furnished. Weighs 8 lbs. 2 oz. Furnished with leather case and tools.

NIB	EXC.	V.G.	GOOD	FAIR	POOR
20500	16000	12000	6500	3000	600

SO-5 Trap 2 Barrel Set

NIB	EXC.	V.G.	GOOD	FAIR	POOR
23500	18500	13000	6500	3000	600

SO-5 Sporting Clays

Offered in 12-gauge only, with 28", 30" or 32" barrels; 26" on special order. Sporting clay dimension walnut stock, with pistol-grip and rubber recoil pad. Weighs 7 lbs. 8 oz.

NIB	EXC.	V.G.	GOOD	FAIR	POOR
20500	10000	7500	5000	2750	500

SO-5 Skeet

Same general specifications as SO-5 Trap. Furnished to skeet dimensions. Offered in 12-gauge only, with 26" or 28" vent rib barrels choked skeet. Weighs 7 lbs. 8 oz.

NIB	EXC.	V.G.	GOOD	FAIR	POOR
20500	16000	7500	5000	2750	500

SO-6 EL

Premium grade Beretta available in several different configurations. Similar to SO-5. Available in 12-gauge only. Features true side-lock action, single-selective or non-selective trigger, fixed or screw-in choke tubes. Receiver offered in silver finish or case hardened, without engraving. Highly select walnut, with fine line checkering. Choice of pistol- or

	NIB	EXC.	V.G.	GOOD	FAIR	POOR

straight-grip. Supplied with leather fitted hard case. Weighs about 7 lbs. 4 oz. depending on barrel length.

SO-6 Trap

	NIB	EXC.	V.G.	GOOD	FAIR	POOR
	26500	13000	8500	5000	1700	500

SO-6 Skeet

	NIB	EXC.	V.G.	GOOD	FAIR	POOR
	26500	13000	8500	5000	1700	500

SO-6 Sporting Clays

	NIB	EXC.	V.G.	GOOD	FAIR	POOR
	26500	13000	8500	5000	1700	500

SO-6 EELL

Higher grade in SO-6 series. Features silver receiver, custom engraving with scroll or game scenes. Gold inlays are available on request. Choice of barrel lengths from 26" to 30". Choice of pistol- or straight-grip. All the same features of SO-6, with higher fit and finish. Offered in 12-gauge only.

	NIB	EXC.	V.G.	GOOD	FAIR	POOR
	43750	33500	27000	20000	12000	600

SO-6 EESS

Same specifications as SO-6 EELL grade. Ruby, sapphire or emerald side plates, with diamond brilliants.

	NIB	EXC.	V.G.	GOOD	FAIR	POOR
	88500	75000	55000	30000	—	—

SO-7

One of Beretta's best-grade sidelock double-barrel shotgun. Elaborately engraved. Has highest grade walnut in the stock. No longer in production.

	NIB	EXC.	V.G.	GOOD	FAIR	POOR
	—	10500	8850	7250	5500	4500

SO-9

Model over/under is Beretta's highest grade. Offered in 12-, 20-, 28-gauge and .410 bore. True side lock (removable) receiver is highly engraved, with scroll or game scenes by Italy's finest craftsmen. Barrel lengths 26" to 30", with solid hand filed rib. Walnut stock is finest available. Either pistol- or straight-grip. Stock dimensions to customers request. A custom fitted leather case, with accessories is supplied with gun. Custom order gun. Independent appraisal is strongly suggested prior to sale.

	NIB	EXC.	V.G.	GOOD	FAIR	POOR
	38000	30000	22000	15000	7500	2000

SO-10

Beretta's custom-made highest grade over/under sidelock. In 12-, 20-, 28-gauge or .410 bore. Receiver machined from a solid block of tri-alloy steel. Polishing of surfaces all done by hand. Highest grade walnut stock made to owner's specifications. Numerous engraving patterns. Introduced in 2003

	NIB	EXC.	V.G.	GOOD	FAIR	POOR
	85000	78000	65000	50000	—	—

Jubilee Field Grade (Giubileo)

Introduced in 1998. Beretta's finest boxlock over/under shotgun. Fitted with sideplates without screws. Offered in 12-, 20-, 28-gauge and .410 bore, with 26" to 30" barrel depending on gauge. Each gun richly engraved with fine scroll and signed by master engravers. Highly figured walnut, with pistol- or straight-grip. Weights range from about 7 lbs. in 12-gauge to 5.5 lbs. in .410 bore.

Single Gun

	NIB	EXC.	V.G.	GOOD	FAIR	POOR
	14750	12000	825	4500	2200	600

Matched Pair

	NIB	EXC.	V.G.	GOOD	FAIR	POOR
	32650	—	—	—	—	—

Jubilee Sporting Grade

Similar to above model in terms of finish. Offered in 12-gauge only. Choice of 30" or 32" barrels. Pistol-grip standard. **NOTE:** Two barrel combination, with 20-gauge barrel and extended chokes add $1,500.

	NIB	EXC.	V.G.	GOOD	FAIR	POOR
	14750	12000	8250	4500	2200	600

Jubilee II (Giublio)

Side-by-side model offered in 12- or 20-gauge only, with straight-grip stocks. Choice of 26" or 28" barrels. Full coverage scroll engraving and highly figured walnut. Double triggers by special order only. Weight about: 12-gauge 6.5 lbs.; 20-gauge 6 lbs.

Single Gun

	NIB	EXC.	V.G.	GOOD	FAIR	POOR
	14750	12000	8250	4500	2200	600

	NIB	EXC.	V.G.	GOOD	FAIR	POOR

Matched Pair

	32650	2600	17000	9200	4000	900

ASE Deluxe Sporting

Boxlock over/under gun offered in 12-gauge only, with choice of 28" or 30" barrels. Classic European scroll engraving. Offered in both field and competition configuration. Weighs about 7.5 lbs. for 12-gauge.

	25000	18500	12000	900	700	400

Model 687 EELL Gallery Special

Special version of this model. Especially engraved guns, with upgraded wood that are only made for Beretta Galleries. Offered in 12-, 20-, 28-gauge and .410 bore.

Single Gun

	8500	7300	5900	4500	3300	500

Special Combo—20/28 Gauge

	9500	8600	6700	5800	4000	600

Matched Pair

	17100	15500	11500	8000	4750	700

Imperiale Montecarlo

Side-by-side gun chambered for 12-, 20-, 28-gauge shell. True sidelock action. Choice of 26", 27" or 28" barrels, with fixed chokes. Other lengths by special request. Weight about: 7.3 lbs. for 12-gauge; 6.5 lbs. for 20-gauge; 6.2 lbs. for 28-gauge. Master engraved and signed. **NOTE:** Too scarce to value. Seek qualified appraisal.

Diana

Side-by-side gun chambered for 12- or 20-gauge, with choice of barrel lengths. Action is true sidelock, with exposed hammers. Weight about: 12-gauge 7.2 lbs.; 20-gauge 6.4 lbs. Master engraved and signed. **NOTE:** Too scarce to value. Seek qualified appraisal.

Model 451 Series

Custom order sidelock shotgun. Prospective purchasers are advised to secure a qualified appraisal prior to acquisition.

	8000	6900	5000	4000	2000	700

Model 450 Series

Model same as 451 series, with exception of being a Holland & Holland sidelock design. Prospective purchasers are advised to secure a qualified appraisal prior to acquisition.

	9000	7500	5800	4500	2500	1000

Model 452

Premium grade side-by-side shotgun fitted with sidelocks (removable). Offered in 12-gauge only. 26", 28" or 30" solid rib barrels. Receiver highly polished silver finish, without engraving. Triggers may be double-/single-selective or single non-selective. Stock and forearm special select walnut, with fine line checkering. Choice of pistol- or straight-grip. Comes with leather hard case. Weighs about 6 lbs. 13 oz.

	24000	19000	14500	8500	4500	2500

Model 452 EELL

Same as above. Furnished with fine scroll or game scene engraving. Highest grade walnut furnished for stock and forearm. Leather case with accessories furnished.

	31000	27500	19500	11000	7000	600

BERETTA ONYX SERIES

Series designation first used in 2003 to simplify product line. Instead of using numeric model references, company now refers to these guns and others by series name.

Onyx

Over/under gun offered in 12-, 20- and 28-gauge. Choice of 26" or 28" barrels. Features boxlock action, with select checkered walnut stock, single-selective trigger, schnabel fore-end and auto safety. Black rubber recoil pad. Blued barrels and action. Weight about 6.8 lbs. for 12-gauge.

	1675	1350	950	650	475	200

Onyx Waterfowler 3.5

As above in 12-gauge, with 3.5" chamber. Matte black finish.

	1750	1400	1050	700	500	250

NIB	EXC.	V.G.	GOOD	FAIR	POOR

White Onyx

Introduced in 2003. Features receiver machined in a jeweled pattern, with satin nickel alloy. Offered in 12-, 20- and 28-gauge, with choice of 26" or 28" barrels. Select checkered walnut stock, with schnabel fore-end. Weight about 6.8 lbs. for 12-gauge.

| 1775 | 1425 | 1250 | 700 | 500 | 250 |

Onyx Pro

Introduced in 2003. Over/under shotgun offered in 12-, 20- and 28-gauge. Choice of 26" or 28" vent rib barrels, with choke tubes. Single-selective trigger. Checkered X-Tra wood stock. Gel-Tek recoil pad. Supplied with plastic carry case. Weight about 6.8 lbs.

| 1700 | 1300 | 1000 | 600 | 400 | 200 |

Onyx Pro 3.5

As above in 12-gauge, with 3.5" chamber. Weight about 6.9 lbs. Introduced in 2003.

| 1700 | 1300 | 1000 | 600 | 400 | 200 |

BERETTA 682 SERIES

682/682 Gold

High-grade quality-built over/under shotgun. Offered in 12- and 20-gauge. Also available in some configurations in 28-gauge and .410 bore, with barrel lengths from 26" to 34" depending on type of shooting required. Fitted with single-selective trigger and automatic ejectors. Barrels fitted with ventilated rib and various fixed or screw-in choke combinations. Stock is high-grade walnut, with fine checkering in stock dimensions to fit function of gun. Frame is silver, with light scroll borders on most models. This model covers a wide variety of applications. These are listed by grade and/or function:

NOTE: Beretta Competition Series shotguns are also referred to as 682 Gold Competition Series guns, such as Model 682 Gold Trap or Model 682 Gold X Trap Combo and so forth.

682 Super Skeet

Model offered in 12-gauge only, with 28" vent rib barrels choked skeet and skeet. Single-selective trigger and auto ejectors standard. This Super Skeet features ported barrels and adjustable length of pull and drop. Fitted hard case standard. Weighs 7 lbs. 8 oz.

| 1800 | 1400 | 1100 | 850 | 650 | 300 |

682 Gold Skeet

Standard 12-gauge skeet. Features choice of 26" or 28" vent rib barrels, choked skeet and skeet. Walnut stock of International dimensions, with special skeet rubber recoil pad. Gun supplied with hard case. Weighs 7 lbs. 8 oz.

| 1700 | 1300 | 1000 | 800 | 650 | 300 |

682 4 Barrel Set

Skeet gun fitted with 4 barrels in 12-, 20-, 28-gauge and .410 bore. Each barrel is 28", choked skeet and skeet. Fitted with vent rib.

| 4000 | 3500 | 3000 | 2500 | 2000 | 650 |

682 Super Sporting/682 Gold Sporting Ported

Built for sporting clays. This 12- or 20-gauge model features ported barrel, adjustable length of pull and drop. Fitted with 28" or 30" vent barrel, with screw-in chokes; fixed chokes on special order. Checkered walnut stock, with pistol-grip and recoil pad. Supplied with case. Introduced in 1993. Weight: 12-gauge 7 lbs. 8 oz.; 20-gauge 6 lbs. 3 oz.

| 2400 | 2000 | 1600 | 1100 | 700 | 350 |

682 Gold Sporting

Standard version of 12- or 20-gauge Super Sporting. Choice of 28" or 30" vent rib barrel, with screw-in chokes. Checkered walnut stock, with recoil pad. Introduced in 1993.

| 2000 | 1650 | 1400 | 1250 | 950 | 350 |

682 Sporting Combo

Similar to 682 Sporting, with addition of two 12-gauge 28" and 30" barrels, fitted with screw-in chokes. Supplied with hard case.

| 3200 | 2700 | 2250 | 1750 | 1250 | 650 |

682 Super Trap

12-gauge trap model (20-gauge set of barrels is available on special order) features ported 30" or 32" ventilated rib barrels, with fixed or screw-in chokes. Automatic ejectors, single non-selective trigger, standard. Checkered walnut stock can be adjusted for length of pull and drop of comb. Offered in Monte Carlo or International dimensions. Weight about 8 lbs. 6 oz.

| 2300 | 2000 | 1700 | 1250 | 950 | 500 |

NIB	EXC.	V.G.	GOOD	FAIR	POOR

682 Top Single Super Trap

Same as Super Trap. Available in single barrel configuration of 32" or 34".

NIB	EXC.	V.G.	GOOD	FAIR	POOR
2600	2150	1700	1350	950	500

682 Top Combo Super Trap

This configuration features single barrel and over/under barrel, both interchangeable. Combinations are: 30"/32" and 30"/34".

NIB	EXC.	V.G.	GOOD	FAIR	POOR
3300	2975	2350	1750	1250	650

682 Trap

Standard variation of Beretta trap gun. This 12-gauge comes standard with 30" vent rib barrels. However, 28" and 32" barrels can be special ordered. Fixed or screw-in chokes available. Three-position sliding trigger allows for adjustable length of pull. Checkered walnut stock, with recoil pad standard. Stock available in Monte Carlo or International dimensions. Customer has choice of silver or black receiver. Comes cased.

NIB	EXC.	V.G.	GOOD	FAIR	POOR
2300	1950	1700	1250	900	450

682 Top Single Trap

12-gauge single barrel trap gun available in 32" or 34" vent rib barrel.

NIB	EXC.	V.G.	GOOD	FAIR	POOR
2000	1600	1200	1000	600	450

682 Mono Combo Trap

Special configuration features single barrel, with vent rib set to place single barrel in bottom position of what would normally be an over/under setup. Second barrel is an over/under also provided as part of the set. Single barrel is 34" and over/under set is 32" in length.

NIB	EXC.	V.G.	GOOD	FAIR	POOR
2500	2100	1500	1200	750	500

682 Top Combo

Trap combination features standard placement single barrel, with interchangeable over/under barrel. Barrel sets available in 30"/32", 30"/34" and 32"/34". Barrels fitted with ventilated rib.

NIB	EXC.	V.G.	GOOD	FAIR	POOR
2500	2000	1500	1000	950	500

682 Gold Trap with Adjustable Stock

Introduced in 1998. Over/under features choice of 30" or 32" barrels, with Monte Carlo stock and adjustable drop, cast and comb. Trigger adjustable for length of pull. Selected walnut stock, with oil finish. Black rubber recoil pad standard. Weight about 8.8 lbs. **NOTE:** Add $800 for Top Combo set.

NIB	EXC.	V.G.	GOOD	FAIR	POOR
2200	1800	1500	—	—	—

682 Gold Skeet with Adjustable Stock

Introduced in 1999. This 12-gauge features skeet stock with adjustable comb. Stock drop and cast may also be adjusted. Graystone receiver. Comes with case. Offered in choice of 28" or 30" barrels. Single-selective trigger adjustable for length of pull. Black rubber recoil pad standard. Weight about 7.5 lbs.

NIB	EXC.	V.G.	GOOD	FAIR	POOR
2000	1700	1500	1200	900	600

682 Gold "Live Bird

Introduced in 1995. Has gray receiver, with select walnut stock. Single-selective trigger is adjustable for length of pull. Offered in 12-gauge only, with 30" barrels. Average weight 8.8 lbs.

NIB	EXC.	V.G.	GOOD	FAIR	POOR
2550	1950	1595	1150	850	400

S682 Gold E Trap

Chambered for 12-gauge 3", with choice of 30" or 32" barrels overbored and choke tubes. Highly select walnut stock, with black rubber pad. Single-selective trigger, with adjustable length of pull. Beavertail fore-end. Adjustable Monte Carlo stock. Front white bead with mid bead sight. Carry case standard. Weight about 8.8 lbs. Introduced in 2001.

NIB	EXC.	V.G.	GOOD	FAIR	POOR
3900	3300	2750	1800	900	450

S682 Gold E Trap Combo

Offers same features as Trap model, with interchangeable over/under barrels. Top single barrel with under rib. Introduced in 2001.

NIB	EXC.	V.G.	GOOD	FAIR	POOR
5600	4400	3100	1700	800	350

S682 Gold E Skeet

12-gauge skeet gun features special skeet-style stock, with beavertail fore-end. Adjustable stock. Barrel lengths 28" or 30". Single-selective trigger. Weight about 7.5 lbs. Introduced in 2001.

NIB	EXC.	V.G.	GOOD	FAIR	POOR
4000	3600	2750	1500	625	350

	NIB	EXC.	V.G.	GOOD	FAIR	POOR

S682 Gold E Sporting

12-gauge model. Choice of 28", 30" or 32" barrels, with extended choke tubes and tapered top rib. White front sight and mid bead. Sporting clay-style stock of select walnut. Weight about 7.6 lbs. Introduced in 2001.

NIB	EXC.	V.G.	GOOD	FAIR	POOR
4150	3200	2350	1200	475	300

Model 685

Lower priced over/under chambered for 12- or 20-gauge, with 3" chambers. Satin-chromed boxlock action, with single trigger and extractors. Not imported after 1986.

NIB	EXC.	V.G.	GOOD	FAIR	POOR
—	750	675	550	375	200

BERETTA 686 SERIES

686/686 Silver Perdiz Sporting

Beretta over/under shotgun available in a number of different configurations. This basic model features ventilated rib barrels from 24" to 30"; 30" is a special order. Screw-in chokes or fixed chokes are available. All configurations offered in 12- and 20-gauge, with 28-gauge and .410 bore available in special order only. Fitted with checkered American walnut stock, with black rubber recoil pad and special grip cap. Some models have silver receiver, with scroll engraving and others have black receivers with gold-filled contours. This 686 series was renamed in 1994.

686 Essential/Silver Essential

Introduced in 1994. This 686 model designed to be an entry level 686. Offers all mechanical features of 686 series, without any frills. Offered in 12-gauge only, with 26" or 28" barrels with open-side rib. Plain walnut stock, with checkering and plain blue receiver. Weighs about 6.7 lbs. Renamed Silver Essential in 1997.

NIB	EXC.	V.G.	GOOD	FAIR	POOR
900	750	600	450	350	200

686 Ultra Light Onyx

Features black anodized light alloy receiver accented with an engraved gold-filled "P. Beretta" signature. Available in 12-gauge only, with 26" or 28" vent rib barrels. Chokes fixed or screw-in type. Weighs 5 lbs. 1 oz.

NIB	EXC.	V.G.	GOOD	FAIR	POOR
1050	850	750	600	500	400

686 Onyx

Similar in appearance to Ultra Light Onyx. Available in 12- or 20-gauge, with vent rib barrel lengths from 26" to 28". Chambers are 3" or 3.5". Checkered walnut stock offered in pistol- or straight-grip. Choice of choke types. Weight: 12-gauge 6 lbs.13 oz.; 20-gauge 6 lbs. 3 oz. A 12-gauge version with 3.5" chambers and 28" barrel offered (new in 1999) with matte wood finish, matte black receiver, beavertail fore-end, with fingerwells and silver finish trigger.

NIB	EXC.	V.G.	GOOD	FAIR	POOR
1800	1350	950	650	500	400

686 Onyx 2 Barrel Set

Same as above. Supplied with 20-gauge 28" vent rib barrel; 28-gauge 26" vent rib barrel.

NIB	EXC.	V.G.	GOOD	FAIR	POOR
2100	1650	1500	800	650	500

686 Silver Receiver

Model is basic 686. Features plain semi-matte silver receiver. Available in 12- or 20-gauge; 28-gauge available on special order. Vent rib barrels offered in lengths from 24" to 30", with fixed chokes or choke tubes.

NIB	EXC.	V.G.	GOOD	FAIR	POOR
1200	895	775	650	500	400

686 L/686 Silver Perdiz

Same as above. Furnished with scroll engraved silver receiver. Offered in 28-gauge, with 26" or 28" vent rib barrels. Weighs 5 lbs. 5 oz.

NIB	EXC.	V.G.	GOOD	FAIR	POOR
1200	950	750	650	500	400

686 Silver Pigeon

Introduced in 1996. Replaces Silver Perdiz. Has electroless nickel finish on scroll engraved receiver. Offered in 12-, 20- and 28-gauge, with 26" or 28" barrels. Average weight 6.8 lbs. New variation introduced in 1999. Features 20-gauge gun with 28" barrels, straight-grip stock and matte nickel receiver.

NIB	EXC.	V.G.	GOOD	FAIR	POOR
1800	1450	950	600	400	200

Sporting

NIB	EXC.	V.G.	GOOD	FAIR	POOR
1500	1050	750	600	400	200

	NIB	EXC.	V.G.	GOOD	FAIR	POOR

Trap (30")

	1400	1000	700	500	400	300

Trap Top Mono (32" or 34")

	1300	900	600	500	400	300

686 Silver Pigeon S

Essentially same as Silver Pigeon models. Packaged with carrying case that includes five choke tubes, accessory recoil pad and sling swivels. A .410-bore offering on a proportionally smaller receiver was added in 2006. **NOTE:** Add $700 for two barrel 20/28 gauge set.

2000	1600	1275	825	575	350

686E Sporting

Offered in 12- or 20-gauge, with choice of 28" or 30" barrels. Five Beretta screw-in chokes. Modern ellipsis receiver engraving. Special carrying case. Introduced with new styling in 2001.

2100	1700	1350	825	575	350

686 EL/Gold Perdiz

Model available in 12- or 20-gauge, with 26" or 28" vent rib barrels. Receiver silver, with scroll engraving fitted with side plates. Fitted hard case comes with gun.

1900	1350	1100	800	700	350

686 Hunter Sport

Sporting clay 12- or 20-gauge shotgun. Features silver receiver, with scroll engraving. Wide 12.5mm target rib. Radius recoil pad. Offered in 26" or 28" vent rib barrels, with screw-in chokes. Offered first time in 1993.

1200	950	750	600	500	250

686 Onyx Hunter Sport

Same as above. Offered in 12-gauge only, with matte black finish on receiver and barrels. Weighs 6 lbs.13 oz. Introduced in 1993.

1100	850	650	600	500	250

BERETTA WING SERIES

686 Whitewing

Introduced in fall of 1998. Over/under shotgun chambered for 12-gauge shell. Fitted with 26" or 28" barrels, with Beretta's choke system. Receiver polished nickel, with engraved game scenes and gold-plated trigger. Walnut pistol-grip stock, with gloss finish.

1350	1025	800	550	375	250

686 Blackwing

Introduced in 2002. Similar to Whitewing, with exception of blued receiver and schnabel fore-end.

1450	1100	900	600	425	300

686 Sporting Combo

Same specifications as Hunter Sport, with addition of interchangeable 30" 12-gauge barrel.

1900	1600	1250	1000	700	325

686 Collection Trap

Introduced in 1996. Features special multi-colored stock and fore-end. Offered in 12-gauge only, with 30" barrels. Factory recoil pad standard. Average weight 7.7 lbs.

1500	1000	750	500	400	300

686 Collection Sport

Similar to above. Offered with 28" barrels.

1500	975	750	500	400	300

686 Quail Unlimited 2002 Covey Limited Edition

Offered in 20- or 28-gauge, with 26" or 28" vent rib barrels. Choke tubes. Engraved receiver with gold quail inlays. Weight about 6.8 lbs.

1950	1550	1250	1000	700	325

686 Ringneck Pheasants Forever

Introduced in 2003. Chambered for 12- or 20-gauge. Fitted with 26" or 28" vent rib barrels. Checkered walnut stock, with pistol-grip. Single-selective trigger. Gel-Tek recoil pad. Schnabel

	NIB	EXC.	V.G.	GOOD	FAIR	POOR

fore-end. Weight about 6.8 lbs. on 12-gauge.

	2025	1550	1100	750	450	275

BERETTA ULTRALIGHT SERIES

Ultralight

Over/under chambered for 12-gauge 2.75" shells. Fitted with choice of 26" or 28" barrels. Receiver is light aluminum alloy nickel finish, with game scene engraving. Black rubber recoil pad standard. Single-selective trigger, pistol-grip and schnabel forearm. Weight about 5.75 lbs.

	1900	1500	900	600	375	175

Ultralight Deluxe

Similar to above. Offered only with 28" barrels. Nickel receiver is gold game scene engraved. First offered in 1998.

	2400	2000	1600	1100	700	350

BERETTA 687/PIGEON SERIES

687/687 Silver Pigeon Sporting

Similar to Model 686. Slightly more ornate version. This series renamed in 1994.

687 L/Silver Pigeon

Offered in 12- or 20-gauge, with 26" or 28" vent rib barrels. Boxlock receiver scroll engraved with game scenes. Auto ejectors and double-/single triggers offered.

	1800	1100	950	800	650	300

687 Silver Pigeon II

Introduced in 1999. Features deep relief game scene engraving on silver receiver. Select walnut stock, with oil finish. Available in 12-gauge only. Choice of 26" or 28" vent rib barrels. Single-selective trigger. Weight about 6.8 lbs.

	2500	1900	1250	700	425	300

687 Silver Pigeon Sporting

Sporting clays version available in 12- or 20-gauge, with 28" or 30" barrels.

	1900	1400	1000	700	425	300

687 Silver Pigeon II Sporting

Introduced in 1999. Features deep relief engraving, with oil finished select walnut stock. Schnabel fore-end. Single-selective trigger. Offered in 12-gauge only. Choice of 28" or 30" barrels. Black rubber recoil pad. Weight about 7.7 lbs.

	2500	1900	1250	800	475	325

Silver Pigeon S

New in 2007. Silver Pigeon S Series features scroll and floral engraving on satin nickel-alloy finished receiver. Available in 12-, 20- and 28-gauge, with 26" or 28" barrels. .410 bore with 28" barrels. All come with five chokes. Weight about 6.8 lbs.

	1800	1475	900	600	375	275

Silver Pigeon S Combo

Combo model comes with 26" 20-gauge barrels; 28" 28-gauge barrels.

	2200	1875	100	900	600	300

687 Sporting Combo

Offered in 12-gauge only, with two sets of 12-gauge interchangeable vent rib barrels in 28" and 30".

	2500	2100	1850	1500	750	400

687 Silver Pigeon IV

Introduced in 2003 for U.S. market. Features black finish receiver full scroll engraving, with gold-filled game birds. Select oil-finished walnut stock, with Gel-Tek recoil pad. Offered in 12-, 20- or 28-gauge, with 26" or 28" barrels. Single-selective trigger, with fluted beavertail fore-end. Weight about 6.8 lbs. in 12-gauge.

	2665	1950	1850	1500	750	400

687 Silver Pigeon V

Top-of-the-line model in Silver Pigeon Series. Available in 12-, 20- and 28-gauge, with 26" and 28" barrels and .410 bore (added in 2006). Pistol-grip stock of richly figured walnut, with oil finish. Color case-hardened receiver, with gold-filled game bird inlays. English stocked versions of 20-, 28-gauge and .410 bore added in 2006.

	3595	2400	1700	1250	750	375

687 EL/687 Gold Pigeon

Model offered with scroll engraved gold inlaid game animals. Fitted with side plates. Stock highly figured walnut, with fine line checkering. Available in 12-, 20-, 28-gauge or .410 bore in 26" or 28" vent rib barrels, with screw-in chokes. Comes with fitted hard case. Weight: 12-gauge 6 lbs. 13 oz.; 20-gauge 6 lbs. 3 oz.; 28-gauge/.410 bore 5 lbs. 5 oz. Series renamed in 1994. In 2001 Beretta enhanced the engraving on the Model 687EL Gold Pigeon.

12 and 20 gauge

NIB	EXC.	V.G.	GOOD	FAIR	POOR
3400	2450	1800	1200	750	350

28 gauge and .410 bore

NIB	EXC.	V.G.	GOOD	FAIR	POOR
3450	2500	1850	1250	800	400

687 EL Gold Pigeon Sporting

Sporting clays model chambered for 12-gauge. Fitted with 28" or 30" vent rib barrels. Offered new in 1993. Comes with fitted hard case.

NIB	EXC.	V.G.	GOOD	FAIR	POOR
3400	2450	1750	1250	900	450

687 EELL/Diamond Pigeon

Same as above including gauge and barrel offerings. Furnished with more fully figured walnut and finer checkering. Fitted with side plates that are scroll engraved with fine cut game scenes. This grade also available in straight-grip English stock version in 20-gauge as well as combo set of 20-gauge and 28-gauge interchangeable 26" barrels. All 687 EELL Models fitted with hard case. Series renamed in 1994.

12 and 20 gauge

NIB	EXC.	V.G.	GOOD	FAIR	POOR
6500	5200	4500	3000	1500	700

28 gauge and .410 bore

NIB	EXC.	V.G.	GOOD	FAIR	POOR
7000	5500	4500	3000	1500	700

Combo

NIB	EXC.	V.G.	GOOD	FAIR	POOR
8000	6800	5000	3500	1300	500

687 EELL Diamond Pigeon Skeet

Same as above. Addition of skeet configuration. A 12-gauge version offered with 28" vent rib barrels choked Skeet and Skeet. Weighs about 7 lbs. 8 oz. A 4 barrel set also offered with interchangeable 12-, 20-, 28-gauge and .410 bore barrels choked Skeet and Skeet.

12 gauge

NIB	EXC.	V.G.	GOOD	FAIR	POOR
3500	3000	2500	1750	1450	475

4 Barrel Set

NIB	EXC.	V.G.	GOOD	FAIR	POOR
6400	5000	4500	3750	2500	1500

With Adjustable Stock

Same as Skeet version above, with adjustable comb, drop and cast. Introduced in 1999.

NIB	EXC.	V.G.	GOOD	FAIR	POOR
5000	4000	3200	2500	1500	500

687 EELL Diamond Pigeon Sporting

Sporting clays version of 687 EELL. In 12-gauge only, with 28" vent rib barrels fitted with screw-in chokes.

NIB	EXC.	V.G.	GOOD	FAIR	POOR
6000	4750	3500	2500	1750	1200

687 EELL Trap

Fitted with International or Monte Carlo trap stock dimensions. Offered in 12-gauge, with 30" vent rib barrels fixed or screw-in choke tubes. Weighs about 8 lbs. 6 oz.

NIB	EXC.	V.G.	GOOD	FAIR	POOR
4000	3000	2500	2000	1500	1000

687 EELL Top Combo

Single barrel trap gun. Choice of one single barrel set and one over/under steel rod barrel. In 30"/32" or 32"/34".

NIB	EXC.	V.G.	GOOD	FAIR	POOR
4700	3500	3000	2250	2000	1000

687 EELL King Ranch

Similar to Silver Pigeon Grade IV, with special cowboy and western engraving. In 20- or 28-gauge only. Introduced 2006. Discontinued in 2009.

NIB	EXC.	V.G.	GOOD	FAIR	POOR
3300	2750	2200	1700	1250	800

Model 692

Introduced in 2014, this model replaces the 682 series with some features from that series and others from the high-grade DT10 Trident. It has a 1.6" wide receiver for improved balance and

	NIB	EXC.	V.G.	GOOD	FAIR	POOR

weight distribution. In 12-gauge only. Features include 30" or 32" barrels, extra long forcing cones, adjustable trigger and ejectors/extractors, and an optional adjustable comb that can be set to the shooter's drop and cast needs. Gun's balance can also be adjusted by way of weights in the buttstock. This competition-level gun is offered in Sporting, Trap and Skeet configurations. **NOTE:** Add $500 for adjustable stock.

692 Sporting

NIB	EXC.	V.G.	GOOD	FAIR	POOR
4000	3500	3000	2500	—	—

692 Trap

NIB	EXC.	V.G.	GOOD	FAIR	POOR
3800	3300	2800	2200	—	—

692 Skeet

NIB	EXC.	V.G.	GOOD	FAIR	POOR
4400	3700	3200	2800	—	—

Model FS-1

Single-barrel boxlock shotgun in all gauges. A 26" or 28" full choke barrel. Blued, with checkered walnut stock. Also known as "Companion". **NOTE:** Deduct 25 percent for 12-gauge.

NIB	EXC.	V.G.	GOOD	FAIR	POOR
—	300	225	175	125	90

TR-1 Trap

12-gauge single-barrel boxlock trap gun, with 32" ventilated rib full choke barrel. Blued, with checkered Monte Carlo stock. Manufactured between 1968 and 1971.

NIB	EXC.	V.G.	GOOD	FAIR	POOR
—	375	250	200	150	100

TR-2 Trap

As above, with high competition-type vent rib. Manufactured between 1969 and 1973.

NIB	EXC.	V.G.	GOOD	FAIR	POOR
—	400	275	225	175	125

Mark II Trap

12-gauge boxlock single-barrel trap shotgun, with 32" or 34" full-choke barrel, competition-type rib and automatic ejector. Blued, with checkered Monte Carlo type walnut stock. Manufactured between 1972 and 1976.

NIB	EXC.	V.G.	GOOD	FAIR	POOR
—	800	625	525	450	275

MODEL ASE 90/GOLD SERIES

Competition trap model over/under shotgun. Features trigger lock assembly that is removable in the field so a spare can be used in event of failure. Single non-selective trigger has three-way adjustment. Ventilated rib is wide and side ribs are also ventilated. Walnut stock and forearms are interchangeable. Special trap recoil pad standard. Receiver silver, with gold inlays or blued on special order. ASE 90 weighs about 8 lbs. 6 oz.

ASE 90 Pigeon

Equipped with 28" barrels choked Improved-Modified and Full.

NIB	EXC.	V.G.	GOOD	FAIR	POOR
6750	5250	3750	2750	1200	500

ASE 90 Trap

Comes standard with 30" vent rib barrels.

NIB	EXC.	V.G.	GOOD	FAIR	POOR
5950	5250	3750	2750	1200	500

ASE 90 Gold X Trap Combo

Introduced in 1993. Set features single barrel and interchangeable over/under barrels in 30"/32" and 30"/34" combinations.

NIB	EXC.	V.G.	GOOD	FAIR	POOR
6950	2500	1750	1200	700	350

ASE 90 Skeet

Skeet version of ASE 90 series. Features same basic specifications as trap model. Configured for competition skeet. Offered in 12-gauge only, with 28" Skeet and Skeet chokes. Weighs about 7 lbs. 11 oz.

NIB	EXC.	V.G.	GOOD	FAIR	POOR
5950	2500	1750	1200	700	350

ASE 90 Sporting Clay

Configured for sporting clays competition. Offered in 12-gauge only, with 28" or 30" vent rib barrels.

NIB	EXC.	V.G.	GOOD	FAIR	POOR
6950	5200	4000	3000	1500	1000

Model SL-2

12-gauge slide-action shotgun, with 26", 28" or 30" ventilated rib barrels. Various chokes. Blued, with checkered walnut stock. Manufactured between 1968 and 1971.

NIB	EXC.	V.G.	GOOD	FAIR	POOR
—	350	300	250	200	150

	NIB	EXC.	V.G.	GOOD	FAIR	POOR

Pigeon Series

As above in three grades.

Silver Pigeon

	—	300	250	200	150	110

Gold Pigeon

	—	450	400	300	250	200

Ruby Pigeon

	—	600	550	450	375	275

DT 10 TRIDENT SERIES

These shotguns feature removable trigger mechanism, overbored barrels and special choke tubes.

DT 10 Trident Trap

12-gauge over/under, with a number of options. Barrel is 30" or 32". Highly select walnut stock fitted with Monte Carlo comb. Stock also adjustable. Rib type is 3/8" with progressive step. Full black rubber recoil pad. Weight about 8.8 lbs. Top single model also offered with 34" barrel. Introduced in 2000.

	8000	6000	5000	2750	1600	500

DT 10 Trident Trap Combo Top

Same as above, with both over/under barrels and single barrel combo.

	10000	8000	6500	4700	3000	500

DT 10 Trident Trap Bottom Single

Introduced in 2001. Features choice of 30"/34"- or 32"/34" barrel combo. Select walnut stock. Fitted with adjustable point-of-impact rib. Weight about 8.8 lbs.

	13250	10500	7500	4700	3000	500

DT 10 Trident Skeet

12-gauge skeet model. Fitted with 28" or 30" barrel. Walnut stock is adjustable. Weight about 8 lbs. Introduced in 2000.

	8000	7000	5000	2850	1875	400

DT 10 Trident Sporting

12-gauge over/under. Fitted with 28", 30" or 32" barrels. Highly figured walnut stock, with schnabel fore-end. Weight about 8 lbs. Introduced in 2000.

	12000	10000	6000	2850	1875	400

DT 11

Top of the line Beretta competition over/under model. Upgraded from DT10 series, with an even wider frame, high-grade hand-checkered walnut stock made to customer's specifications, redesigned top lever and safety selector. In 12-gauge only. Barrel choices are 29.5", 30" or 32", with choke tubes or fixed modified and full chokes, and 2.750" chambers. Variations include Sporting, Skeet, Trap and International Trap, and several sub-categories. Values shown are for the base models in each category.

Sporting

	7900	6700	5400	4400	—	—

Skeet

	7400	6400	5300	4300	—	—

Trap

	8000	6800	5500	4500	—	—

International Trap

	7400	6400	5300	4300	—	—

SV10 Perennia

New in 2008. Perennia over/under is a 3" 12-gauge shotgun. Featuring oil-finished select walnut stock and laser-engraved nickel high-phosphorous-based finish on receiver. Barrels are 26" or 28". Features Optimachoke HP system introduced in 2008. User-selectable automatic or mechanical shell extraction. Beretta's Kick-Off recoil reduction system available on 28" Perennia. Includes five choke tubes and plastic carrying case. Add $400 for Kick-Off version.

	3250	2000	1450	800	600	300

	NIB	EXC.	V.G.	GOOD	FAIR	POOR

SEMI-AUTOMATIC SHOTGUNS

AL SERIES

A 12- or 20-gauge semi-automatic shotgun, with 26", 28" or 30" barrels. Various choke combinations. Blued, with checkered walnut stock. Manufactured between 1969 and 1976.

AL-1

—	400	375	300	225	150	

AL-2

—	350	300	250	175	125	

AL-2 Competition

—	400	350	300	225	175	

AL-2 Magnum

—	425	375	325	250	200	

AL-3

—	400	350	300	225	175	

AL-3 Deluxe Trap

—	775	700	600	500	425	

Model 301

Improved version of AL Series. Manufactured between 1977 and 1982. Also available as slug gun, with 22" barrel and rifle sights.

—	400	350	300	225	175	

Model 1200 Field Grade

12-gauge semi-automatic shotgun, with 28" ventilated rib barrel, screw-in choke tubes and 4-round tubular magazine. Matte blued, with checkered walnut or black synthetic stock. Introduced in 1984.

450	400	300	250	200	150	

Model 1200 Magnum

3" chamber.

585	525	425	325	250	200	

Model 1200 Riot

20" cyl. bore barrel.

585	525	425	325	250	200	

Model 1201

This 12-gauge semi-automatic shotgun, has a short recoil system. Features synthetic stock, with matte black finish and lightweight alloy receiver. Available in two basic configurations: Field Grade choice of 24", 26" and 28" vent rib barrel with screw-in chokes; Riot Model with 18" plain cylinder choked barrel and full or pistol-grip-only stock (introduced in 1993). Weight: Field Grade about 6 lbs. 12 oz.; Riot Model about 6 lbs. 5 oz. **NOTE:** Riot Model with pistol-grip add $40; Riot Model with Tritium sights add $75.; ghost ring sights add $100.

Field Grade

450	400	350	300	200	150	

Riot Model

650	500	400	350	250	175	

Model 302

12- or 20-gauge semi-automatic shotgun. Using 2.75" or 3" shells interchangeably, various barrel lengths and screw-in choke tubes. Blued, with checkered walnut stock. Manufactured between 1982 and 1987.

—	400	350	275	200	150	

Model 302 Super Lusso

As above, with heavily engraved receiver and gold-plated contrasting parts. Presentation grade walnut used for hand checkered stock. Discontinued in 1986.

—	2150	2000	1600	1050	850	

	NIB	EXC.	V.G.	GOOD	FAIR	POOR

Model Vittoria/Pintail

Semi-automatic 12-gauge shotgun. Introduced to Beretta product line in 1993. Has short recoil operation. Offered with 24" or 26" vent rib barrel, with screw-in chokes. A 24" rifled choke tube version for slugs is also available. Non-reflective matte finish is put on all wood and metal surfaces. Equipped with sling swivels and walnut stock. Weighs about 7 lbs. Renamed in 1994.

600	500	420	350	250	200

ES100 Pintail Synthetic

Introduced in 1999. Essentially same as Pintail above. Addition of black synthetic stock and choice of 24", 26" or 28" vent rib barrels, with screw-in chokes. Weight about 7 lbs.

550	450	385	325	250	200

ES100 Pintail Rifled Slug

Introduced in 1997. Features 24" fully rifled barrel, with adjustable rear sight and removable blade front sight. Receiver is drilled and tapped for scope mount. Hardwood stock with matte finish. Anodized aluminum alloy receiver. Weight about 7 lbs. Fitted with 3" chambers.

650	550	450	400	250	200

ES100 Rifled Slug

Variation same as Pintail Rifled Slug. Addition of black synthetic stock. Introduced in 1999.

600	500	425	350	250	200

ES100 Rifled Slug Combo

Same as above, with addition of 28" smooth bored barrel.

700	600	525	450	350	250

ES100 NWTF Special Camo

12-gauge fitted with 24" barrel and 3" chambers. Stock Mossy Oak camo. Metal black matte finish. Weight about 7.3 lbs. Introduced in 1999.

975	750	550	375	210	150

A-303 SERIES

12- or 20-gauge semi-automatic shotgun, with 26", 28", 30" or 32" ventilated rib barrels and screw-in choke tubes. Blued, with checkered walnut stock. Introduced in 1987. Various models differ slightly in configuration and/or quality of materials.

Model A-303

650	600	475	375	300	250

Model A-303 Upland

24" barrel.

680	650	525	425	350	300

Model A-303 Sporting Clay

735	700	575	475	400	350

Model A-303 Competition (Trap or Skeet)

675	650	530	425	350	300

Model A-303 Slug Gun

22" barrel with sights.

680	650	525	425	350	300

Model A-303 Youth Gun

Version of Model 303. Available in 20-gauge, with shorter length of pull 13.5", than standard. Fitted with rubber recoil pad, screw-in choke tubes and checkered walnut stock.

500	450	400	300	250	200

Model A-303 Ducks Unlimited

Commemorative version of Model 303. Chambered for 12- or 20-gauge. Manufactured: 5,500 in 12-gauge (1986 and 1987); 3,500 in 20-gauge (1987 and 1988). Commemorative firearms are collectible when NIB, with all furnished materials.

12 Gauge

575	500	425	325	275	225

20 Gauge

675	600	525	425	375	325

	NIB	EXC.	V.G.	GOOD	FAIR	POOR

MODEL AL390/MALLARD SERIES

Series of 12-gauge semi-automatic shotguns. Features self-compensating gas-operating recoil system. All loads from target to 3" Magnums can be used in same gun. Field Model features anodized light alloy receiver, with scroll engraving and matte black receiver top. Magazine capacity 3 rounds. Checkered walnut stock, with recoil pad. Available in vent rib barrel lengths from 24" to 30", with 32" on special request. A 22" or 24" slug plain barrel also available. Chokes are fixed or screw-in at customer's option. Shotgun weighs about 7 lbs. Beginning in 1996 Beretta offered Silver Mallard shotguns chambered for 20-gauge shell and available with 24", 26 or 28" barrels. Average weight for these 20-gauge guns is 6.4 lbs.

Field Grade

NIB	EXC.	V.G.	GOOD	FAIR	POOR
800	600	450	350	300	200

Slug Gun

NIB	EXC.	V.G.	GOOD	FAIR	POOR
800	600	450	350	300	200

Synthetic Stock

NIB	EXC.	V.G.	GOOD	FAIR	POOR
800	600	450	350	300	200

Camouflage

NIB	EXC.	V.G.	GOOD	FAIR	POOR
800	600	450	350	300	200

Deluxe Grade/Gold Mallard

Gold-filled game animals and select walnut stock.

NIB	EXC.	V.G.	GOOD	FAIR	POOR
700	650	500	350	300	200

AL390 Trap

NIB	EXC.	V.G.	GOOD	FAIR	POOR
675	600	500	400	300	200

AL390 Super Trap

Features ported barrels in 30" or 32", adjustable length of pull and comb.

NIB	EXC.	V.G.	GOOD	FAIR	POOR
800	700	600	500	300	200

AL390 Skeet

NIB	EXC.	V.G.	GOOD	FAIR	POOR
625	550	450	350	250	200

AL390 Super Skeet

Features ported barrel, adjustable cast and length of pull, with adjustable drop. 12-gauge only.

NIB	EXC.	V.G.	GOOD	FAIR	POOR
1000	800	600	500	300	200

AL390 Sporting

NIB	EXC.	V.G.	GOOD	FAIR	POOR
700	550	450	350	250	200

20 gauge

Same as above in 20-gauge. Introduced in 1997. Weight about 6.8 lbs.

NIB	EXC.	V.G.	GOOD	FAIR	POOR
800	600	450	350	250	200

Ported

NIB	EXC.	V.G.	GOOD	FAIR	POOR
725	650	550	400	300	200

AL390 Sport Gold Sporting

Introduced in 1997. Similar to above models, with silver sided receiver and gold engraving. Select walnut stock. 12-gauge only, with choice of 28" or 30" vent rib barrels. Weight about 7.6 lbs.

NIB	EXC.	V.G.	GOOD	FAIR	POOR
1100	900	700	450	300	175

AL390 Sport Sporting Youth

Semi-automatic shotgun. Offered in 20-gauge only, with 26" vent rib barrel. Length of pull 13.5", with adjustable drop and cast on buttstock. Introduced in 1997. Weight about 6.7 lbs.

NIB	EXC.	V.G.	GOOD	FAIR	POOR
825	675	500	350	200	175

AL390 NWTF Special Youth

Introduced in 1999. Features shortened walnut stock, with 24" 20-gauge vent rib barrel. Black matte finish. Weight about 6.4 lbs.

NIB	EXC.	V.G.	GOOD	FAIR	POOR
900	700	525	375	225	175

AL390 Sport Sporting Youth Collection

Same as above, with multi-colored stock and forearm. Introduced in 1997.

NIB	EXC.	V.G.	GOOD	FAIR	POOR
900	750	525	375	225	175

	NIB	EXC.	V.G.	GOOD	FAIR	POOR

AL390 Sport Diamond Sporting
Introduced in 1998. Features silver sided receiver, with gold engraving. Select walnut stock, with oil finish and adjustable for drop and cast. Available in 12-gauge, with 28" or 30" barrels. Sold with spare trigger group and orange front sight beads. Weight about 7.6 lbs.

3000	2600	1950	1300	600	300

AL390 Camo
12-gauge shotgun offered with 24" or 28" vent rib barrel. Barrel, receiver, stock and forearm have woodland camo finish. Weight about 7.5 lbs. Offered first time in 1997.

995	775	595	450	300	150

AL390 Waterfowl/Turkey Model
Matte finish.

550	500	450	350	300	250

AL390 NWTF Special Camo

1100	875	625	500	325	150

AL390 NWTF Special Synthetic

925	750	595	450	300	150

Super Trap
Ported barrels, adjustable comb and length of pull.

975	800	650	500	325	175

Super Skeet
Ported barrels, adjustable comb and length of pull.

950	800	650	500	325	175

3901 SERIES
Series introduced in 2005. Built around A390 shotgun. The 3901 guns feature gas operating system, choke tubes and removable trigger group.

Model 3901
Introduced in 2003. Semi-automatic shotgun offered in 12-gauge, with 26" or 28" barrel. Charcoal gray synthetic stock. Black rubber recoil pad. Non-reflective black finish. Weight about 7.5 lbs.

730	575	450	300	225	175

Model 3901 RL
As above in 20-gauge, with reduced-length buttstock. Introduced in 2003.

730	575	450	300	225	175

Model 3901 Camo
12-gauge offered in Mossy Oak Shadowgrass camo stock. Choice of 24" or 26" barrel. Introduced in 2003.

840	650	475	350	250	175

Model 3901 Citizen
Offered in 12- or 20-gauge, with 26" or 28" vent rib barrels and choke tubes. Black synthetic stock. Rubber recoil pad. Weight about: 7.6 lbs. 12-gauge; 7 lbs. 20-gauge.

750	600	450	300	225	175

Model 3901 Statesman
As above, with checkered walnut stock.

850	675	475	325	250	175

Model 3901 Ambassador
Model has all features of Statesman. Fitted with select checkered X-tra wood stock, with Gel-Tek recoil pad. Weight about: 7.2 lbs. 12-gauge; 6.6 lbs. 20-gauge.

950	750	525	450	350	200

Model 3901 Target RL
Gas-operated semi-automatic chambered in 3" 12-gauge. Specifically designed for smaller-stature shooters, with adjustable length of pull from 12" to 13". Stock adjustable for cast on or cast off. Adjustable comb and Sporting style flat rib. Available in 12-gauge only, with 26" or 28" barrel.

895	700	550	400	295	175

NIB	EXC.	V.G.	GOOD	FAIR	POOR

AL 391 URIKA SERIES

Urika

Introduced in 2000. Semi-automatic shotgun offered in 12- and 20-gauge. Choice of barrels from 24" to 30" depending on gauge. Stock walnut, with checkered grip and fore-end. Rubber recoil pad. Gold trigger. Choke tubes. Weight about: 7.3 lbs. 12-gauge; 6 lbs. 20-gauge.

850	750	600	450	300	175

Urika Synthetic

Same as above. Fitted with black synthetic stock and gripping inserts. Offered in 12-gauge only. Introduced in 2000.

950	750	625	525	325	200

Urika Camo

12-gauge offered with Realtree Hardwoods camo or Advantage Wetlands camo. In 24" or 26" barrels. Weight about 7.3 lbs. First introduced in 2000.

1050	800	650	550	300	175

Urika Gold

Features 26" or 28" barrel, with choke tubes. Black receiver model offered in both 12- and 20-gauge. Weight about 7.3 lbs. Silver receiver model (lightweight) available in 12- gauge only. Weight about 6.6 lbs. Both configurations fitted with highly figured walnut stock. Gold trigger. Introduced in 2000.

900	825	750	675	325	200

Urika Youth

20-gauge features walnut stock, with shorter length of pull than standard and 24" barrel. Weight about 6 lbs. Introduced in 2000.

900	800	600	450	275	195

Urika Sporting

Offered in 12- and 20-gauge. Fitted with 28" or 30" barrels. Select walnut checkered stock. Gold trigger. Chambered for 3" shells. Weight about: 7.3 lbs. 12-gauge; 6 lbs. 20-gauge. Introduced in 2000.

1100	750	600	500	350	175

Urika Gold Sporting

Offered in 12-gauge, with black or silver receiver. The 20-gauge offered with black receiver only. Fitted with 28" or 30" barrels. Highly select checkered walnut stock. Chambered for 3" shells. Introduced in 2000. **NOTE:** Add $30 for 12-gauge silver receiver.

1295	950	700	600	450	175

Urika Trap

12-gauge fitted with 30" or 32" barrels. Select checkered walnut stock, with Monte Carlo comb. Chambered for 3" shells. Weight about 7.2 lbs. Introduced in 2000.

1000	750	600	500	350	175

Urika Gold Trap

Similar to standard Urika Trap, with highly selected checkered walnut stock and black receiver.

1295	950	700	600	450	175

Urika Parallel Target RL/SL

This is a 12-gauge competition model, fitted with 28" or 30" barrels and select walnut Monte Carlo stock. The "RL" has standard stock configurations, while the "SL" has a shorter length of pull.

1100	750	600	500	350	200

URIKA OPTIMA MODELS

First offered in 2003, these shotguns are similar to standard Urika model. Feature Beretta's Optima-Bore overbored barrels, with flush Optima-Choke Plus tubes.

Urika Optima

Offered in 12-gauge, with 26" or 28" vent rib barrel. Checkered select walnut stock. Gold trigger. Chamber is 3". Weight about 7.3 lbs.

1500	1175	825	650	450	300

Urika Synthetic Optima

As above, with synthetic stock and rubber inserts. Weight about 7.4 lbs.

1300	1105	750	575	400	325

	NIB	EXC.	V.G.	GOOD	FAIR	POOR

Urika Optima Camo

As above, with camo stock.

NIB	EXC.	V.G.	GOOD	FAIR	POOR
1350	1195	950	625	450	250

URIKA 2 SERIES

Introduced in 2007. Urika 2 is an enhanced version of original AL391 Urika. Improvements include addition of spinning self-cleaning action for faster cycling and longer functioning periods between cleanings.

Urika 2 X-Tra Grain

Series features Beretta's wood-enhancement treatment to highlight color contrast of wood. Offered in 3", 12- and 20-gauge, with 26" and 28" barrels. A 20-gauge youth model, with shorter stock and 24" barrel also offered.

NIB	EXC.	V.G.	GOOD	FAIR	POOR
1000	900	725	575	400	250

Urika 2 Gold

Select oil-finished wood stock and fore-end, with gold-filled game bird inlays on receiver. 12-gauge 28" barrel; 20-gauge 26" barrel.

NIB	EXC.	V.G.	GOOD	FAIR	POOR
1350	1075	725	500	375	250

Urika 2 Kick-Off

Waterfowl models feature Beretta's Kick-Off recoil reduction system. Matte black synthetic, Max-4 or Realtree AP finish, with 26" or 28" barrel. Deduct 30 percent for models without Kick-Off. Add 10 percent for camo finish.

NIB	EXC.	V.G.	GOOD	FAIR	POOR
1200	950	700	475	350	225

Urika 2 Sporting X-Tra Grain

Sporting clay model in 12- and 20-gauge, with 28" or 30" barrel.

NIB	EXC.	V.G.	GOOD	FAIR	POOR
1200	950	700	475	350	225

Urika 2 Gold Sporting

Enhanced wood, with gold inlays and floral motif engraving on receiver. In 12-gauge, with 28" or 30" barrel.

NIB	EXC.	V.G.	GOOD	FAIR	POOR
1300	1025	775	525	375	275

Urika 2 Parallel Target X-Tra Grain

Target model in 12-gauge, with 28", 30" or 32" barrel.

NIB	EXC.	V.G.	GOOD	FAIR	POOR
1250	975	750	525	375	295

Urika 2 Gold Parallel Target

Enhanced wood, with gold inlays and floral motif engraving on receiver. In 12-gauge, with 30" or 32" barrel.

NIB	EXC.	V.G.	GOOD	FAIR	POOR
1400	1075	750	525	395	265

AL391 Covey

Introduced in 2003. Offered in 20-gauge, with 26" or 28" vent rib barrel. Select walnut stock. Gold-filled game scenes. Weight about 5.9 lbs. Limited to 1,000 guns.

NIB	EXC.	V.G.	GOOD	FAIR	POOR
1350	1075	725	500	375	250

AL391 Ringneck

As above, with gold-filled pheasants. In 12-gauge only. Weight about 7.3 lbs. Limited to 1,000 guns. Introduced in 2003.

NIB	EXC.	V.G.	GOOD	FAIR	POOR
1360	1075	800	550	400	300

AL391 Teknys

Features nickel receiver, with polished sides and anti-glare top. Offered in 12- or 20-gauge, with 26" or 28" vent rib barrel. Xtra-wood stock with Gel-Tek recoil. Weight about: 7.2 lbs. 12-gauge; 5.9 lbs. 20-gauge. Introduced in 2003.

NIB	EXC.	V.G.	GOOD	FAIR	POOR
1150	900	750	500	350	250

AL391 Teknys Gold

As above, with engraved hunting scene on receiver, gold plated trigger, jeweled breech bolt and carrier. Select walnut checkered stock with oil finish. Introduced in 2003.

NIB	EXC.	V.G.	GOOD	FAIR	POOR
1465	1100	850	575	425	325

AL391 Teknys Gold Target

Similar to AL391 Teknys Gold, with adjustable comb, 8.5 oz. recoil reducer and additional stepped rib for trap shooting. 30" barrel.

NIB	EXC.	V.G.	GOOD	FAIR	POOR
1665	1300	975	600	450	350

	NIB	EXC.	V.G.	GOOD	FAIR	POOR

AL391 Teknys King Ranch

Introduced in 2005.

	NIB	EXC.	V.G.	GOOD	FAIR	POOR
	1650	1300	1000	725	625	375

AL391 XTREMA SERIES

AL391 Xtrema 3.5

Introduced in 2002. This model is a Urika overbuilt to handle 12-gauge 3.5" super magnum loads. Offered with choice of 24", 26" or 28" vent rib barrels, with black synthetic stock or choice of various camo stocks. Weight about 7.8 lbs. **NOTE:** Add $100 for camo finish.

	NIB	EXC.	V.G.	GOOD	FAIR	POOR
	1150	900	750	500	350	250

AL391 Xtrema2

Upgraded version of Xtrema. Additional recoil-reducing features introduced in 2005. Available with 24", 26" or 28" barrels, with black Max-4 HD or Hardwoods HD synthetic stock. Optima-Bore five choke system. Optional Kick Off recoil reduction feature available. **NOTE:** Add 10 percent for camo finish; 30 percent for Kick Off option.

	NIB	EXC.	V.G.	GOOD	FAIR	POOR
	1300	950	800	650	400	300

AL391 Xtrema2 Slug Gun

24" rifled barrel version of Xtrema2. Introduced in 2006. Black synthetic only. **NOTE:** Add 10 percent for Kick Off option.

	NIB	EXC.	V.G.	GOOD	FAIR	POOR
	1200	925	800	650	400	300

UGB25 XCEL

Introduced in 2005. Semi-automatic break-open competition trap gun. Chambered for 12-gauge 2.75" shell. Gun is fed from side with bottom ejection. Choice of 30" or 32" barrel, with high trap-style interchangeable rib. Choke tubes. Checkered walnut stock has adjustable comb and length of pull. Weight about 7.7 to 9 lbs. depending on barrel length and rib.

	NIB	EXC.	V.G.	GOOD	FAIR	POOR
	3595	2800	2150	1675	850	450

A400 Xplor Unico

Self-regulation gas-operated shotgun. Chambered to shoot all 12-gauge loads from 2.75" to 3.5". Features include Kick-Off hydraulic damper; 26" or 28" "Steelium" barrel, with interchangeable choke tubes; anodized aluminum receiver; sculpted, checkered walnut buttstock and fore-end. **NOTE:** Add $100 for Kick-Off Recoil reduction system.

	NIB	EXC.	V.G.	GOOD	FAIR	POOR
	1500	1250	1050	800	550	300

A400 Xcel Sporting

Similar to Xplor Unico, except designed for Sporting Clays competition. 12-gauge, 3" chambers, with 28" 30" and 32" barrels. Blue aluminum receiver, optional Kick-Off recoil reduction system. Gun Pod optional system available, with digital readout of temperature, ammo pressure and other information. **NOTE:** Add $100 for Kick-Off Recoil reduction system or Gun Pod.

	NIB	EXC.	V.G.	GOOD	FAIR	POOR
	1600	1300	1050	800	550	300

A400 Extreme KO

Uses Beretta's Blink gas-operating system. Said to be able to handle all 12-gauge loads from 2.750" to 3.500". Includes Kick-Off recoil reduction system. Synthetic stock offered in black or camo, with non-slip rubber gripping sections.

	NIB	EXC.	V.G.	GOOD	FAIR	POOR
	1500	1250	1000	800	600	350

TX4 Storm

Gas-operated semi-automatic shotgun. Chambered for 3" 12-gauge shells. Features include 18" barrel, with interchangeable choke tubes; adjustable ghost ring rear sight, with military-style front sight; adjustable length of pull; integral Picatinny rail on receiver; 5+1 capacity; soft rubber grip inlays in buttstock and fore-end.

	NIB	EXC.	V.G.	GOOD	FAIR	POOR
	1200	1000	750	500	350	250

BERGER, JEAN MARIUS
St. Etienne, France

Berger

Berger was a magazine-fed repeating pistol in 7.65mm. Self loader and cocker. Had all characteristics of semi-automatic except for recoil operating system.

	NIB	EXC.	V.G.	GOOD	FAIR	POOR
	—	5900	4750	3750	3000	2000

BERGMANN, EINHAND
See—Lignose

BERGMANN, THEODOR
Gaggenau, Germany

Theodor Bergmann was a successful industrialist, designer and sometimes inventor, with a deep interest in firearms based in Gaggenau, Germany. His first automatic pistol patent dates from 1892. By 1894 he had prototype pistols, refined with the help of Louis Schmeisser, being evaluated by various governments. When his designs went into commercial production in 1896, however, they were actually manufactured by firm of V. Charles Schilling in Suhl, the heart of German arms manufacture. Later he licensed manufacture of his "Mars" pistol to Anciens Establishment Pieper ("Bayard") and after WWI affiliated with Lignose firm, producing a line of .25 caliber pocket pistols, first under Bergmann name but later marketed as Lignose. Still later several pistol designs from August Menz firm were marketed under "Bergmann Erben" trademark, though it's doubtful if Bergmann firm actually had much part in their production or sale.

Model 1894 Bergmann Schmeisser

Model 1894 was made in prototype form only. Few examples surviving. Known serial numbers no higher than mid teens. Most are large framed. Chambered for 8mm Bergmann-Schmeisser cartridge. At least one was made in 7.5mm Swiss revolver for Swiss army testing. A few very compact versions, with a unique folding trigger for 5mm Bergmann. Early Bergmann pistols had no extractor, counting on gas pressure to blow the fired (rimless-groove-less) cartridge from chamber. Too rare to price.

Model 1896 Number 2

1896 Number 2 pistols were quite compact. Chambered for 5mm Bergmann cartridge. Early Number 2s also featured a folding trigger and no extractor. After serial 500 or so reverted to a more conventional in-the-frame trigger and an extractor was added. About 2000 of later model were produced. Cased sets are known. Add about 50 percent to value.

Folding Trigger

| — | 8000 | 5000 | 3250 | 1500 | 800 |

Conventional

| — | 5000 | 3500 | 2250 | 1000 | 600 |

Model 1896 Number 3

Number 3 was a larger version of Number 2. Chambered for 6.5mm Bergmann cartridge. Early examples had a slim grip frame. Up to about serial 800 were made without extractors like early Number 2s. These bring about 20 percent premium over later examples. Number 3 serials range to a little over 4000. Add about 20 percent for dealer markings (usually English) and 50 percent for cased sets. A few target models, with long barrel, adjustable sights and set triggers are known. Will bring about three times the price of a standard Number 3.

First Variation

| — | 4050 | 3500 | 2750 | 1650 | 800 |

Second Variation

| — | 3500 | 3200 | 2500 | 1650 | 800 |

Third Variation

| — | 3700 | 3200 | 2500 | 1650 | 800 |

Holster and Stock Model

| — | 6300 | 5700 | 4950 | 3250 | 2750 |

Model 1896 Number 4

Number 4 is identical to Number 3. Chambered for a unique 8mm Bergmann cartridge. Serialed in same series with Number 3. Both Number 4 and its cartridge are rare; probably fewer than 200 were ever made.

| — | 8000 | 6500 | 5000 | 3700 | 2900 |

Model 1897 Number 5

Bergmann's first attempt at a more powerful arm for military market. A unique side-moving locking system and 10-shot removable box magazine. 7.8mm cartridge resembled 7.63mm Mauser, with a longer neck. Add 60 percent for original metal framed leather holster-stock.

| — | 8550 | 6900 | 4950 | 3000 | 2250 |

Model 1897 Number 5 Carbine

Limited number of approximately 1000 Bergmann Model 5s were made, with 12" barrel. Solid wood detachable buttstock and marked "Karabiner Bergmann" on action cover. Very few were made with full-length Mannlicher-type stock and sold as Bergmann Model 1897/07 Sporting Carbine; these are worth about 50 percent more than long barreled pistol, with detachable stock.

| — | 12500 | 10000 | 6000 | 3000 | 2000 |

	NIB	EXC.	V.G.	GOOD	FAIR	POOR

Bergmann Simplex

Simplex combined some features of 1896 pistols. Improvements developed from "Mars", resulting in a reasonable compact pocket pistol that came on the market in early 1900s. Chambered for unique Bergmann-Simplex 8mm cartridge, however, competition from better Browning and other designs doomed it to a short production life. Very early examples had checkered wood grips and bring a premium, as do very late examples (above serial 3000) that have magazine release behind magazine instead of on front of frame.

—	3450	2950	2000	900	600	

Bergmann Mars

Mars was Bergmann's first really successful pistol aimed at military market. Early examples, about 100 of total 1000 or so Mars pistols made, were chambered for 7.63mm Mauser cartridge. Later Mars pistols identified by a large "9mm" on chamber, were chambered for special 9mm cartridge that later became known as 9mm Bergmann-Bayard. Mars was adopted by Spanish government in 1905 as their first military automatic pistol, but none were ever delivered by Bergmann. At least two Mars pistols were also made in .45 caliber for U.S. Army trials in 1906, but did not perform well and were dropped from the trials; these are too rare to price. **NOTE:** Add 25 percent for low serial number guns chambered for 7.63mm Mauser; add 50 percent for original Bergmann Mars holster stock.

—	7000	5300	3850	2500	1650	

Bergmann Bayard Model 1908

Shortly after receiving Spanish contract for Mars pistol, Bergmann's arrangement with Schilling to produce Bergmann pistols ended. However, he negotiated an arrangement with Anciens Establishment Pieper (Bayard) to produce Mars and after some minor modifications, AEP filled the Spanish contract. They also marketed the gun commercially and later secured a production contract from Danish army as Model 1910. Spanish contract (proofed with a small circle divided into three segments) and very early commercial pistols have hard rubber grips that proved very fragile in service; these bring a premium as do original unmodified Danish contract guns (with a contract number and Danish letter D proof). A few Model 1908 Bergmann Bayards were equipped with leather and wood holster stocks; a complete rig is worth at least twice the price of an unslotted pistol.

—	3500	2700	1600	775	550	

Bergmann Post War Pistols

Shortly after WWI ended, Bergmann came on the market with a line of .25-caliber pocket pistols; the 2 and 3 were conventional vest pocket designs with a short and long grip frame respectively; the 2a and 3a were identical except for an "Einhand" (one-hand) feature that enabled user to cycle slide by pulling front of trigger guard with his trigger finger. Soon into production (at about serial 8000) Bergmann affiliated with Lignose firm and later Model 2 and 3 pistols were marketed under Lignose name.

Model 2 and 3

—	325	275	200	150	100	

Model 2a and 3a

—	400	375	325	275	150	

Bergmann Erben Pistols

Bergmann Erben pistols appear to be an attempt by Bergmann family to keep Bergmann name associated with firearms, without actually investing any design or production effort. Bergmann Erben pistols were all August Menz designs and were undoubtedly made by Menz as well. Most noteworthy was "Spezial" model, a very sophisticated double-action .32 pocket pistol that could be cocked for single-action fire by pulling and then releasing trigger. Also noteworthy were several compact vest pocket .25s that also bore Bergmann Erben name.

Bergmann Erben Spezial

—	1650	1350	900	650	400	

Bergmann Erben Model II Pistol

—	550	495	330	225	125	

BERNARDELLI, VINCENZO
Brescia, Italy

Established in 1721, this company originally manufactured military arms. Entered commercial sporting arms market in 1928.

HANDGUNS

Vest Pocket Model

Similar to Walther Model 9. In 6.35mm caliber semi-automatic pistol, with 2.25" barrel and 5-shot magazine. An extended 8-shot version also available. Blued, with plastic grips. Manufactured

	NIB	EXC.	V.G.	GOOD	FAIR	POOR

between 1945 and 1948.

	—	350	250	180	125	100

Pocket Model

As above in 7.65mm caliber. Also offered with extended barrels that protruded beyond end of slide. Introduced in 1947.

	—	300	225	200	150	100

Baby Model

As above in .22 short or LR. Manufactured between 1949 and 1968.

	—	300	225	175	125	95

Sporter Model

.22-caliber semi-automatic pistol, with 6", 8" or 10" barrels and adjustable sights. Blued, with walnut grips. Manufactured between 1949 and 1968.

	—	325	250	200	150	125

Revolvers

.22 rimfire and .32-caliber double-action revolver, with 1.5", 2" or 5" barrels. A .22-caliber 7" barrel version, with adjustable sights also available. Manufactured between 1950 and 1962.

	—	250	175	150	125	100

Model 60

.22, .32 ACP or .380 ACP caliber semi-automatic pistol, with 3.5" barrel and fixed sights. Blued, with plastic grips. Manufactured since 1959.

	—	275	200	175	150	115

Model 68

.22 rimfire caliber or .25 ACP semi-automatic pistol, with 2" barrel and 5-shot magazine. Blued, with plastic grips. No longer imported into U.S.

	—	200	175	150	100	75

Model 80

.22 or .380 ACP caliber semi-automatic pistol, with 3.5" barrel and adjustable sights. Blued, with plastic grips. Imported between 1968 and 1988.

	—	250	200	150	125	95

Model AMR

As above, with 6" barrel.

	450	350	200	150	100	90

Model 69

.22-caliber semi-automatic target pistol, with 6" heavy barrel and 10-shot magazine. Blued, with checkered walnut grips.

	450	375	300	225	150	100

Model PO10

.22-caliber single-action semi-automatic target pistol, with 6" barrel, adjustable target sights, barrel weights and adjustable trigger. Matte-black finish, with stippled walnut grips. Introduced in 1989. Weight 40 oz. Sold with special hard case.

	800	700	500	300	200	100

Model PO18

7.65mm or 9mm Parabellum caliber double-action semi-automatic pistol, with 4.75" barrel and 16-shot double stack detachable magazine. All-steel construction. Blued, with plastic grips. Walnut grips available for an additional $40. Introduced in 1985.

	550	450	300	275	200	100

Model PO18 Compact

As above, with 4" barrel and shorter grip frame. 14-shot double-column magazine. Introduced in 1989.

	550	450	300	275	200	100

Model P. One

Full-size semi-automatic pistol. Chambered for 9mm or .40 S&W calibers. Fitted with 4.8" barrel. Can be fired double-/single-action. Ten-shot magazine. Weight 2.14 lbs. Available in black or chrome finish. Add $50 for chrome finish.

	625	525	400	275	200	100

	NIB	EXC.	V.G.	GOOD	FAIR	POOR

Model P. One-Compact

Same as above, with 4" barrel. Offered in .380 caliber, 9mm and .40 S&W. Weight 1.96 lbs.

	650	550	400	275	200	100

Practical VB Target

Designed for Practical shooting. This 9mm pistol has 6" barrel, with choice of 2 or 4 port compensator. Fitted with numerous extra features. Weighs 2.2 lbs.

	1500	1200	850	600	400	200

Practical VB Custom

As above, but designed for IPSC rules.

	2250	1900	1400	900	600	300

Model USA

.22, .32 ACP or .380 ACP caliber semi-automatic pistol, with 3.5" barrel, adjustable sights, steel frame and loaded chamber indicator. Blued, with plastic grips.

	450	350	200	150	100	90

SHOTGUNS

MODEL 115 SERIES

12-gauge over/under boxlock double-barrel shotgun, with various barrel lengths and choke combinations. Single triggers and automatic ejectors.

Model 115

	1525	1250	900	700	550	300

Model 115S

	2000	1750	1200	800	600	300

Model 115L

	2500	2000	1500	900	650	300

Model 115E

	5200	4800	4200	3500	2500	1850

Model 115 Trap

	2200	1950	1400	950	750	600

Model 115S Trap

	2700	2450	1900	1450	1150	900

Model 115E Trap

	5250	4800	4200	3500	2500	1850

MODEL 190 SERIES

12-gauge over/under shotgun, with various barrel lengths and choke combinations. Single-selective trigger and automatic ejectors. Engraved and silver-finished, with checkered walnut stock. Introduced in 1986. Various versions differ in degree of ornamentation and quality of materials utilized in construction.

Model 190

	1050	950	750	600	475	400

Model 190MC

	1150	1050	850	700	575	500

Model 190 Special

	1350	1150	950	800	675	600

Model 190 Combo Gun

.243, .308 or .30-06 caliber and 12-, 16- or 20-gauge combination over/under rifle shotgun, with boxlock action, double triggers and automatic ejectors. Blued, with checkered walnut stock. Introduced in 1989.

	1625	1425	925	775	650	575

	NIB	EXC.	V.G.	GOOD	FAIR	POOR

ORIONE SERIES

12-gauge boxlock over/under shotgun, with various barrel lengths and choke combinations. Finishes and triggers optional, as were extractors or automatic ejectors.

Orione

	NIB	EXC.	V.G.	GOOD	FAIR	POOR
	1150	900	700	500	400	200

Orione S

	NIB	EXC.	V.G.	GOOD	FAIR	POOR
	1150	900	700	500	400	200

Orione L

	NIB	EXC.	V.G.	GOOD	FAIR	POOR
	1250	1000	800	600	500	250

Orione E

	NIB	EXC.	V.G.	GOOD	FAIR	POOR
	1350	1150	850	600	500	250

S. Uberto I Gamecock

12-, 16-, 20- or 28-gauge boxlock side-by-side shotgun, with 25.75" or 27.5" barrels, various chokes, double triggers and extractors. Automatic ejectors were available and would be worth a 20 percent premium. Blued, with checkered stock.

	NIB	EXC.	V.G.	GOOD	FAIR	POOR
	—	950	700	500	350	250

Brescia

12-, 16- or 20-gauge sidelock double-barrel shotgun, with exposed hammers, various barrel lengths, choke combinations, sidelock action, double triggers and manual extractors. Blued, with English-style checkered walnut stock.

	NIB	EXC.	V.G.	GOOD	FAIR	POOR
	1850	900	700	450	350	225

Italia

Higher grade version of Brescia.

	NIB	EXC.	V.G.	GOOD	FAIR	POOR
	2250	1250	750	600	400	250

Italia Extra

Highest grade hammer gun Bernardelli produces.

	NIB	EXC.	V.G.	GOOD	FAIR	POOR
	5900	2750	1500	1000	750	300

UBERTO SERIES

12-, 16-, 20- or 28-gauge Anson & Deeley boxlock double barrel shotgun, with various barrel lengths and choke combinations. Increased value of various models depends on degree of engraving options and quality of materials and workmanship utilized in their construction.

S. Uberto 1

	NIB	EXC.	V.G.	GOOD	FAIR	POOR
	1000	800	650	475	350	250

S. Uberto 1E

	NIB	EXC.	V.G.	GOOD	FAIR	POOR
	1100	900	700	500	350	250

S. Uberto 2

	NIB	EXC.	V.G.	GOOD	FAIR	POOR
	1500	1100	800	500	350	250

S. Uberto 2E

	NIB	EXC.	V.G.	GOOD	FAIR	POOR
	1750	1350	950	600	400	250

S. Uberto F.S.

	NIB	EXC.	V.G.	GOOD	FAIR	POOR
	2000	1500	1100	800	400	250

S. Uberto F.S.E.

	NIB	EXC.	V.G.	GOOD	FAIR	POOR
	2250	1750	1200	800	400	250

ROMA SERIES

Similar to S. Uberto Series, with false sideplates. Values of respective variations result from degree of ornamentation and quality of materials and workmanship utilized in construction.

Roma 3

	NIB	EXC.	V.G.	GOOD	FAIR	POOR
	1550	1200	800	600	300	200

Roma 3E

	NIB	EXC.	V.G.	GOOD	FAIR	POOR
	1750	1300	900	650	300	200

	NIB	EXC.	V.G.	GOOD	FAIR	POOR

Roma 4

	NIB	EXC.	V.G.	GOOD	FAIR	POOR
	1950	1400	1100	750	400	250

Roma 4E

	NIB	EXC.	V.G.	GOOD	FAIR	POOR
	2000	1500	1200	750	400	250

Roma 6

	NIB	EXC.	V.G.	GOOD	FAIR	POOR
	2100	1750	1400	850	500	250

Roma 6E

	NIB	EXC.	V.G.	GOOD	FAIR	POOR
	2200	1800	1400	850	500	250

Roma 7

	NIB	EXC.	V.G.	GOOD	FAIR	POOR
	2900	2500	1800	1200	700	350

Roma 8

	NIB	EXC.	V.G.	GOOD	FAIR	POOR
	3500	3000	2250	1550	850	400

Roma 9

	NIB	EXC.	V.G.	GOOD	FAIR	POOR
	4000	3500	2750	1700	950	450

Elio

12-gauge boxlock double-barrel shotgun, with various barrel lengths and choke combinations, lightweight frame, double triggers and extractors. Scroll-engraved, silver-finished receiver, blued barrels and select checkered walnut stock.

	NIB	EXC.	V.G.	GOOD	FAIR	POOR
	1000	800	600	500	350	250

Elio E

As above, with automatic ejectors.

	NIB	EXC.	V.G.	GOOD	FAIR	POOR
	1100	900	700	550	350	250

Hemingway

As above, with coin finished receiver engraved with hunting scenes, 23.5" barrels, double-/single trigger and select checkered walnut stock. Available in 12-, 20- and 28-gauge.

	NIB	EXC.	V.G.	GOOD	FAIR	POOR
	1750	1350	900	700	400	250

Hemingway Deluxe

Same as above fitted with full side plates.

	NIB	EXC.	V.G.	GOOD	FAIR	POOR
	2250	1750	1200	800	400	250

Las Palomas Pigeon Model

Live pigeon gun in 12-gauge, with single trigger.

	NIB	EXC.	V.G.	GOOD	FAIR	POOR
	3800	3250	2500	2000	1500	750

HOLLAND V.B. SERIES

12- or 20-gauge sidelock shotgun, with various barrel lengths, detachable Holland & Holland-type locks, single triggers and automatic ejectors. Models listed vary in amount of engraving and quality of their wood. Prospective purchasers are advised to secure a qualified appraisal prior to acquisition.

Holland V.B. Liscio

	NIB	EXC.	V.G.	GOOD	FAIR	POOR
	8000	5500	4000	3000	2000	1000

Holland V.B. Inciso

	NIB	EXC.	V.G.	GOOD	FAIR	POOR
	10250	7500	5250	4000	2500	1250

Holland V.B. Lusso

	NIB	EXC.	V.G.	GOOD	FAIR	POOR
	11000	8000	6000	4500	2500	1250

Holland V.B. Extra

	NIB	EXC.	V.G.	GOOD	FAIR	POOR
	13000	10000	7500	5500	3000	1500

Holland V.B. Gold

	NIB	EXC.	V.G.	GOOD	FAIR	POOR
	45000	30000	22500	15000	7500	3000

Luck

Over/under shotgun, with single-selective trigger or double triggers and automatic ejectors. Choice of fixed chokes or choke tubes. Available in 12-gauge. Blued or coin finish receiver.

	NIB	EXC.	V.G.	GOOD	FAIR	POOR
	1400	1100	850	600	400	200

	NIB	EXC.	V.G.	GOOD	FAIR	POOR

Giardino/Garden Gun (9mm Rimfire)

Semi-automatic shotgun chambered for 9mm shot cartridge. Fitted with 4-round magazine. Weight 5 lbs.

NIB	EXC.	V.G.	GOOD	FAIR	POOR
850	595	425	300	250	100

RIFLES

Carbina VB Target

Semi-automatic carbine chambered for .22 LR cartridge. Barrel is 20.8". Magazine capacity 10 rounds.

650	550	400	300	200	100

Comb 2000

Rifle-shotgun combination in 12- or 16-gauge, with variety of centerfire calibers to choose from. Barrels are 23.5" long. Set trigger, special rib for scope mount and cheekpiece stock, with pistol-grip. Weight 6.75 lbs.

2900	2100	1200	800	400	250

Express 2000

Over/under double rifle chambered for variety of European calibers. Fitted with automatic ejectors, double-set triggers or single trigger, muzzle adjustment device. Barrel length 23.5".

3350	2550	1700	1200	600	300

Express VB

Side-by-side double rifle, chambered for variety of European calibers up to .375 H&H. Double-/single trigger, auto ejectors and finely engraved receiver with beavertail forearm. Cheekpiece stock with pistol-grip.

5900	4900	3750	2000	1000	750

Express VB Deluxe

Same as above, with side plates and select walnut stock finely checkered.

6300	5200	4000	2000	1000	750

Minerva

Side-by-side double rifle, with exposed hammers chambered for 9.3x74R cartridge. Fitted with fancy walnut stock, double triggers, hand-cut rib and other high-quality features.

6700	5900	4550	2500	1200	750

BERNARDON MARTIN
St. Etienne, France

Small firm active between 1906 and 1912. Gun designer was Martin and money man was Bernadon.

1907/8 Model

7.65mm caliber semi-automatic pistol. Left side of slide marked "Cal. 7.65mm St. Etienne". Trademark "BM" molded into grips. Sometimes found with 32-round horseshoe magazine. Occasionally Bernardon Martin pistol will be noted with word "Hermetic" stamped on slide in letters that do not match other markings on weapon. This was but another name for Model 1907/8. Guns with this stamping were most likely assembled after company ceased operations. **NOTE:** Add 50 percent for horseshoe magazine.

—	1100	875	700	450	275

1908/9 Model

Introduced late in 1908. Similar to Model 1907/8, with addition of grip safety.

—	925	775	600	375	225

BERNEDO, VINCENZO
Eibar, Spain

B C

B C in caliber 6.35mm and most of barrel exposed. Recoil spring is housed in rear of receiver. B C closely resembles Tanque pistol.

—	325	225	200	175	150

Bernado

Model 7.65mm is in Spanish style of Ruby automatic pistols.

—	225	150	125	75	50

	NIB	EXC.	V.G.	GOOD	FAIR	POOR

BERSA
Ramos Mejia, Argentina

Model 644

A blowback pocket pistol chambered for .22 LR. Trigger system single-action. Barrel length 3.5"; overall length 6.57"; weight empty about 28 oz. This is basic Bersa model from which its other models derive their design and function.

NIB	EXC.	V.G.	GOOD	FAIR	POOR
275	175	150	125	100	75

Model 622

Similar to Model 644, with slightly longer barrel.

NIB	EXC.	V.G.	GOOD	FAIR	POOR
275	175	150	125	100	75

Model 97

Slightly larger version of Model 644. Chambered for 9mm Short.

NIB	EXC.	V.G.	GOOD	FAIR	POOR
275	175	150	125	100	75

Model 23

.22 rimfire caliber double-action semi-automatic pistol, with 3.5" barrel and 10-shot detachable magazine. Blued or satin nickel-plated, with checkered walnut grips.

NIB	EXC.	V.G.	GOOD	FAIR	POOR
300	200	150	125	100	75

Model 223

As above, with squared trigger guard and nylon grips. Imported after 1988.

NIB	EXC.	V.G.	GOOD	FAIR	POOR
—	275	175	125	100	75

Model 224

As above, with 4" barrel. Imported after 1988.

NIB	EXC.	V.G.	GOOD	FAIR	POOR
—	275	175	125	100	75

Model 225

As above, with 5" barrel. Discontinued in 1986.

NIB	EXC.	V.G.	GOOD	FAIR	POOR
—	275	175	125	100	75

Model 226

As above, with 6" barrel. Discontinued in 1988.

NIB	EXC.	V.G.	GOOD	FAIR	POOR
—	275	175	125	100	75

Model 323

.32 ACP caliber single-action semi-automatic pistol, with 3.5" barrel, fixed sights and 7-shot detachable magazine. Blued, with molded plastic grips. Not imported after 1986.

NIB	EXC.	V.G.	GOOD	FAIR	POOR
—	225	125	100	75	50

Model 383

As above in .380 caliber. Discontinued in 1988.

NIB	EXC.	V.G.	GOOD	FAIR	POOR
—	250	150	125	90	75

Model 383A

.380 ACP caliber double-action semi-automatic pistol, with 3.5" barrel, fixed sights and 7-shot magazine. Blued, with checkered walnut grips. Overall length 6.6"; weight about 24 oz. Available in blue or nickel finish.

NIB	EXC.	V.G.	GOOD	FAIR	POOR
300	200	150	125	100	75

Model 83

Similar to above model, with double-action operating system. Weighs about 26 oz. Introduced in 1988.

NIB	EXC.	V.G.	GOOD	FAIR	POOR
300	200	150	125	100	75

Model 85

As above, with double-column magazine. Introduced in 1988.

NIB	EXC.	V.G.	GOOD	FAIR	POOR
350	250	200	150	100	75

Model 86

Similar to Model 85 in .380-caliber. Features matte blue or satin nickel finish, wrap around rubber grips and three-dot sight. Magazine capacity 13 rounds

NIB	EXC.	V.G.	GOOD	FAIR	POOR
350	250	225	200	150	100

	NIB	EXC.	V.G.	GOOD	FAIR	POOR

Thunder 9

Introduced in 1993. A double-action 9mm pistol that features ambidextrous safety, reversible extended magazine release, ambidextrous slide release, adjustable trigger stop, combat-style hammer, three-dot sights and matte blue finish. Magazine capacity 15 rounds.

	NIB	EXC.	V.G.	GOOD	FAIR	POOR
	350	275	250	200	150	100

Series 95/Thunder 380

Semi-automatic double-action pistol chambered for .380 cartridge. Choice of matte blue or nickel finish. Barrel length 3.5". Fixed sights. Magazine capacity 7 rounds. Weight about 23 oz. **NOTE:** Add $50 for nickel.

	NIB	EXC.	V.G.	GOOD	FAIR	POOR
	260	200	150	100	75	50

Thunder 380 Matte Plus

Semi-automatic double-action blued pistol in .380, with 15-round magazine. Fixed sights and polymer grips. Introduced 2006.

	NIB	EXC.	V.G.	GOOD	FAIR	POOR
	350	275	250	200	150	100

Thunder 9 Ultra Compact

Available blued or stainless, with 10- or 13-round capacity. Double-action chambered for 9mm. Barrel length 3.5". Weight 25 oz. Fixed sights and polymer grips. Introduced 2006. **NOTE:** Add $50 for stainless.

	NIB	EXC.	V.G.	GOOD	FAIR	POOR
	395	300	250	200	150	100

Thunder 9/40 High Capacity Series

Double-action semi-automatic available chambered for 9mm or .40 S&W. Matte blued or satin nickel-plate. Fixed sights and polymer grips. LOA 7.5", Barrel length 4.25". Weight 26 oz. Introduced 2006.

	NIB	EXC.	V.G.	GOOD	FAIR	POOR
	395	300	250	200	150	100

Thunder Deluxe

Semi-automatic double-action pistol. Chambered for .380 cartridge. Blued finish. Fixed sights. Barrel length 3.5". Weight about 23 oz. Magazine capacity 9 rounds.

	NIB	EXC.	V.G.	GOOD	FAIR	POOR
	325	225	175	100	75	50

BERTRAND, JULES
Liege, Belgium

Le Novo

6.35mm caliber double-action revolver. Manufactured in 1890s. Only identifying markings are "JB" trademark on grips.

	NIB	EXC.	V.G.	GOOD	FAIR	POOR
	—	300	225	175	100	50

Lincoln

As above in 7.65mm caliber.

	NIB	EXC.	V.G.	GOOD	FAIR	POOR
	—	300	225	175	100	50

Le Rapide

6.35mm caliber semi-automatic pistol. Jules Bertrand logo on slide as well as Le Rapide. Both are on each side of grip plates.

	NIB	EXC.	V.G.	GOOD	FAIR	POOR
	—	350	275	200	125	50

BERTUZZI
Brescia, Italy

OVER/UNDER SHOTGUNS

Zeus

12-, 16-, 20- or 28-gauge sidelock shotgun, with automatic ejectors, single-selective trigger and deluxe checkered walnut stock. Custom order in various barrel lengths and chokes. Engraved. Rarely seen on used gun market.

18000 - 39000

Zeus Extra Lusso

As above, with best wood and engraving. Cased.

35000 - 79000

	NIB	EXC.	V.G.	GOOD	FAIR	POOR

Zeus Boss System

Chambered for 12-, 16-, 20- or 28-gauge. Fitted with Boss locking system and ejectors. One-of-a-kind gun with best quality wood and engraving.

65000 - 134000

Gull Wing

Burtuzzi's best gun, with unique sidelock design mounted on a center plate. Release located on top of safety to allow sidelock access. These shotguns usually take about three years to build. Consult distributor about options and availability.

125000 +

Ariete Extra Lusso

Best quality hammer gun in all gauges from 12 to 28. Limited quantities.

65000 +

SIDE-BY-SIDE SHOTGUNS

Orione

12-, 16-, 20- or 28-gauge boxlock shotgun, with Anson & Deeley through bolt. In various barrel lengths and chokes, single-selective trigger and automatic ejectors. Hand checkered walnut stock, with semi-beavertail forearm. Engraving.

25500 - 39950

Venere

Best quality sidelock gun, with traditional or round frame. Special order to customer specifications. Engraved guns bring a premium.

29000 - 69000

Ariete

Best quality hammer gun, with or without self cocking hammers and ejectors. Offered in 12-gauge through .410 bore. Many options.

25000 - 55000

Gull Wing

One-of-a-kind custom built gun, with quick release sidelocks. Delivery time about three years. Contact distributor for more information.

85000 +

BIG HORN ARMORY
Cody, Wyoming

Big Horn Armory Model 89 Rifle and Carbine

Lever-action rifle or carbine chambered for .500 S&W Magnum. Features include 18" or 22" barrel; walnut or maple stocks with pistol-grip; aperture rear and blade front sights; recoil pad; sling swivels; enlarged lever loop; magazine capacity 5 (rifle) or 7 (carbine) rounds.

NIB	EXC.	V.G.	GOOD	FAIR	POOR
1800	1500	1100	750	600	300

BIGHORN ARMS CO.
Watertown, South Dakota

Target Pistol

.22-caliber single-shot pistol resembling semi-automatic. Ventilated rib barrel 6" in length. Stock of molded plastic.

NIB	EXC.	V.G.	GOOD	FAIR	POOR
—	275	175	100	85	65

Shotgun

Single-shot 12-gauge shotgun, with 26" barrel blued. Plastic stock.

NIB	EXC.	V.G.	GOOD	FAIR	POOR
—	195	115	65	50	30

BIGHORN RIFLE CO.
Orem, Utah

Bighorn Rifle

A formr custom rifle manufacturer located in Orem, Utah. These made-to-order rifles were available in any caliber, with various options. Values are speculative.

NIB	EXC.	V.G.	GOOD	FAIR	POOR
2000	1650	1200	850	650	300

NIB	EXC.	V.G.	GOOD	FAIR	POOR

BILHARZ, HALL & CO.
Location Unknown

CONFEDERATE CARBINES

Breechloading ("Rising Breech") Carbine

Overall length 40"; barrel length 21"; caliber 54. Markings: either "P" or "P/CS" on upper left side of barrel and top of rising breech. Peculiar feature of this carbine is manner in which breechblock exposes chamber. A box-like chamber at rear of barrel rises vertically to expose chamber for a paper cartridge by activating lever/trigger-guard mechanism. Only 100 of this type were delivered to Confederacy in September 1862. Two types of front sight blades are known, but neither affects value.

—	—	50000	22500	5000	2100

Muzzleloading Carbine

Overall length 37.5"; barrel length 22"; caliber .58. Markings: "P/CS" on upper left of barrel near breech; "CSA" on top near breech. Modeled after Springfield U.S. M1855 rifle carbine, Bilharz, Hall & Co. muzzleloading carbine has often been mistakenly identified as a product of D.C. Hodgkins & Sons of Macon, Georgia. Serial numbers (found internally) belie that identification. Instead these arms are part of deliveries made to Richmond from middle of 1863 until March 1864. Serial numbers, noted in excess of 700, suggest that about 1,000 were produced. Two basic types, earlier (through serial number 300) were made with brass nosecaps; later type (about serial number 310 through at least 710) have pewter nosecaps on short fore-stock; neither type affects value.

—	—	25000	10000	3000	1650

BILLINGHURST, WILLIAM
Rochester, New York

Billinghurst originally worked for James and John Miller of Rochester. After James Miller's death in 1837, Billinghurst established his own shop where he produced revolving rifles based upon Miller's 1829 patent. While these arms were originally made with percussion ignition systems (either pill or percussion cap), later examples using self-contained metallic cartridges are sometimes encountered. Billinghurst also established a well-deserved reputation for making extremely accurate percussion target pistols and rifles.

Under Hammer Pistol

Pistol is somewhat different than most under hammers encountered. Barrels are 12" to 18" in length. Heavy octagonal construction. Chambered from .30- to .38-caliber and utilize percussion ignition system. Higher grade versions feature a part-round barrel. Important to note that no two pistols are alike. These pistols were furnished with detachable shoulder stocks and a good many were cased with telescopic sights and false muzzles. This is a high quality weapon; if encountered with optional accessories, it would definitely warrant an individual appraisal. This firearm was manufactured in 1850s and 1860s. **NOTE:** Shoulder stock add 50 percent.

—	—	4750	2150	800	400

Revolving Rifle

Calibers vary from .40 to .50 with barrels from 24" to 29"; walnut stocks. Barrels marked: "W. Billinghurst, Rochester, N.Y.", or "W. Billinghurst".

—	—	7900	3700	950	400

BILLINGS
Location Unknown

Pocket Pistol

.32 rimfire caliber single-shot spur trigger pistol, with 2.5" round barrel. An unusually large grip. Barrel stamped "Billings Vest Pocket Pistol Pat. April 24, 1866". Blued, with walnut grips. Manufactured between 1865 and 1868.

—	—	3500	1500	550	195

BINGHAM LTD.
Norcross, Georgia

PPS 50

.22 rimfire caliber semi-automatic rifle. Patterned after Soviet PPSH sub-machine gun, with 16" barrel and 50-round drum magazine. Blued, walnut or beech stock with vented hand guard. Manufactured between 1976 and 1985.

—	575	400	275	225	100

	NIB	EXC.	V.G.	GOOD	FAIR	POOR

AK-22

.22 rimfire caliber semi-automatic rifle. Patterned after Soviet AK-47, with 15- or 29-shot magazine. Walnut or beech stock. Manufactured between 1976 and 1985.

	NIB	EXC.	V.G.	GOOD	FAIR	POOR
	—	365	225	150	100	75

Bantam

.22 rimfire or .22 rimfire magnum caliber bolt-action rifle, with 18.5" barrel. Manufactured between 1976 and 1985.

	NIB	EXC.	V.G.	GOOD	FAIR	POOR
	—	200	85	70	50	35

BISMARCK
Location Unknown

Pocket Revolver

.22-caliber spur trigger revolver, with 3" round ribbed barrel and 7-shot unfluted cylinder. Brass frame. Remainder plated with rosewood grips. Barrel marked "Bismarck". Manufactured in 1870s.

	NIB	EXC.	V.G.	GOOD	FAIR	POOR
	—	—	550	225	90	50

BITTERLICH, FRANK J.
Nashville, Tennessee

A .41-caliber single-shot percussion pistol in a variety of octagonal barrel lengths, German silver mounts, walnut stock. Barrel and locks marked "Fr.J. Bitterlich/Nashville, Tenn." Produced between 1861 and 1867.

	NIB	EXC.	V.G.	GOOD	FAIR	POOR
	—	—	5500	4900	1900	850

BITTNER, GUSTAV
Wieport, Bohemia

Bittner

7.7mm Bittner caliber repeating pistol, with 4.5" barrel. Bolt containing firing pin rotates to lock breech. Operated by finger lever that encloses trigger. Manufactured in mid-1890s. Fewer than 500 made.

	NIB	EXC.	V.G.	GOOD	FAIR	POOR
	—	15000	10500	8000	4000	2000

BLAKE, J. H.
New York, New York

Blake Bolt-Action Rifle

.30-40 Krag caliber bolt-action rifle, with 30" barrel and 7-shot magazine. Stock secured by three barrel bands. Blued, with walnut stock. Manufactured between 1892 and 1910.

	NIB	EXC.	V.G.	GOOD	FAIR	POOR
	—	—	3500	1700	675	200

BLANCH, JOHN
London, England

Blanch Percussion Pistol

.69-caliber single-shot percussion pistol, with 5" Damascus barrel. Engraved frame and hammer, with walnut grip. Manufactured in 1830s.

	NIB	EXC.	V.G.	GOOD	FAIR	POOR
	—	—	6750	2950	1450	875

BLAND, THOMAS & SONS
London, England

Established in 1840, this firm has produced or marketed a wide variety of percussion and cartridge arms. Over the years, firm has occupied a variety of premises in London, some of them concurrently.

41 Whittall Street	1840-1867
41, 42, 43 Whittall Street	1867-1886
106 Strand	1872-1900
430 Strand	1886-1900
2 William IV Street	1900-1919
4-5 William IV Street	1919-1973
New Row, St. Martin's Lane	1973-

BLASER JAGDWAFFEN
Germany

RIFLES

Model K77

Single-shot rifle chambered in a variety of calibers. A 24" barrel and silver-plated engraved receiver. Walnut stock. Introduced in 1988. Discontinued in 1990. **NOTE:** Extra barrels add $750 per barrel.

NIB	EXC.	V.G.	GOOD	FAIR	POOR
2400	1850	1200	850	650	300

Model R-84

Bolt-action sporting rifle. Chambered in a variety of calibers, with 23" or 24" barrel. Interchangeable barrels available for this model. Walnut stock. Imported beginning in 1988.

NIB	EXC.	V.G.	GOOD	FAIR	POOR
2500	2000	1400	950	700	300

Model R-93 LX

A straight-pull-back bolt-action rifle, with interchangeable barrels. In calibers from .22-250 to .416 Rem. Magnum. Barrel length for standard calibers is 22" and Magnum calibers 26". Magazine capacity 3 rounds. Receiver is drilled and tapped for Blaser scope mounts. Weight about 7 lbs. Two-piece walnut stock. Introduced by SIGARMS into U.S. in 1998. **NOTE:** Add $200 for left-hand rifles; $800 for .416 Rem. Magnum.

NIB	EXC.	V.G.	GOOD	FAIR	POOR
1700	1400	1100	800	600	300

Model R-93 Prestige

Updated and upgraded standard model, with all features of R-93 LX. Light scroll engraving on receiver.

NIB	EXC.	V.G.	GOOD	FAIR	POOR
3275	2750	1800	1300	700	350

Model R-93 Classic

Similar to above. Choice of calibers and barrel lengths. Addition of highly figured walnut stock and game scene engraved receiver. **NOTE:** Add $200 for left-hand rifles; $800 for .416 Rem. Magnum.

NIB	EXC.	V.G.	GOOD	FAIR	POOR
2900	2400	1750	1250	900	300

Model R-93 Luxus

Updated and upgraded model of R-93 Classic. Features high grade Turkish walnut stock, with ebony fore-end. Side plates engraved with game scenes.

NIB	EXC.	V.G.	GOOD	FAIR	POOR
5000	4000	3000	2000	1000	500

Model R-93 Synthetic

Also available in same wide range of interchangeable barrels and calibers. Features one-piece black synthetic stock. **NOTE:** Add $200 for left-hand rifles; $800 for .416 Rem. Magnum.

NIB	EXC.	V.G.	GOOD	FAIR	POOR
1800	1500	1000	850	600	400

Model R-93 Attache

Features custom made stock of highly figured walnut, with cheekpiece, leather covered buttplate, silver pistol-grip cap, ebony fore-end tip and custom checkering. Sold with leather carrying case. **NOTE:** Add $200 for left-hand rifles.

NIB	EXC.	V.G.	GOOD	FAIR	POOR
5500	4650	3300	2450	1650	500

Model R-93 Safari Synthetic

Chambered for .416 Rem. Magnum cartridge. Fitted with 24" heavy barrel, with open sights. Weight 9.5 lbs. Black synthetic stock. Other Blaser barrels will interchange on this model.

NIB	EXC.	V.G.	GOOD	FAIR	POOR
2100	1700	1250	875	500	275

Model R-93 Safari LX

Same as R-93 Safari Synthetic, with exception of two-piece walnut stock.

NIB	EXC.	V.G.	GOOD	FAIR	POOR
2500	2000	1550	1000	750	350

Model R-93 Safari Classic

Features engraved receiver and fancy walnut stock.

NIB	EXC.	V.G.	GOOD	FAIR	POOR
2500	2000	1550	1000	750	350

Model R-93 Safari Attache

Top-of-the-line version of R-93 series. Features engraved receiver, fancy walnut stock and other custom options found on R-93 Attache model.

NIB	EXC.	V.G.	GOOD	FAIR	POOR
6000	5000	3950	2900	1500	400

	NIB	EXC.	V.G.	GOOD	FAIR	POOR

Model R-93 Grand Luxe

Offered in same wide range of calibers as other Blaser models. Addition of high grade walnut stock, fully hand engraved receiver and matching scroll sideplates. Introduced in 1999. **NOTE:** Add $200 for left-hand rifles.

6000	5000	4000	2000	1000	395

Model R-8 Professional

Improved variation of R-93 action, with detachable magazine. Offered in many calibers from .222 Rem. to 10.3x60R. Offered in several high grade models similar to those in R-93 series. Prices shown are for basic model, with synthetic stock. **NOTE:** Add 15 to 300 percent for high grade versions.

3000	2300	1700	1200	750	300

Model R-8 Professional Success

Similar to R-8 Professional model, except with synthetic thumbhole stock in Dark Brown or Dark Green color. Leather inlays are optional. Introduced in 2013.

3600	3000	2300	1850	900	400

Model R-8 Professional Hunter

Chambered in most popular dangerous-game calibers. This model has high-grade wood, all steel receiver, with several stock and finish options.

6500	5400	4300	2900	1850	900

Model K-95 Standard

Single-shot model, with break-open action. Receiver is aluminum, with engraving on side plates. Barrel length 23.6" for standard calibers and 25.6" for magnum calibers. Oil finish Turkish walnut stock. Interchangeable barrels in calibers from .243 to .300 Wby. Magnum. Weight about 5.5 lbs. Introduced in 2001.

3500	2500	1500	1150	700	325

Model K-95 Luxus

Same as above, with fancy Turkish walnut stock. Hand engraving on receiver and side plates.

4300	3750	2500	1900	900	400

Model K-95 Stutzen

Introduced in 2003. Break-action single-shot rifle offered in 23 calibers. Fancy walnut Mannlicher-style two-piece stock. Interchangeable barrels.

5400	4650	3200	2250	1000	450

Ultimate Bolt-Action

Unique bolt-action design imported into U.S. in 1980s. Chambered in most popular calibers from .22-250 to .375 H&H. Features include interchangeable barrels and bolt heads, single set trigger, exposed hammer. Left-hand models at no additional cost. Available in several high-grade models. Prices shown are for standard model. **NOTE:** Add premium of 15 to 200 percent for higher grade engraving and wood.

1500	1200	1000	800	550	300

Model R-93 Long Range Sporter

Introduced in 1998. Bolt-action rifle chambered for .308 Win. cartridge. Barrel length 24" without muzzle-brake. Removable box magazine holds 10 rounds. Stock is aluminum and fully adjustable. Weight about 10.4 lbs. No longer in production.

2200	1775	1250	875	500	275

Model R-93 (LRS2)

Introduced in 2000. A second generation version of Long Range Sporter model above. Chambered for .300 Win. Magnum and .308, both of which are interchangeable. Also chambered for .338 Lapua cartridge which does not interchange with other calibers. Cheekpiece improved. New front rail has been added to this model. Barrel length 24" without muzzle-brake. Weight about 10.4 lbs. **NOTE:** .338 Lapua add $350.

3475	2700	1900	1275	800	375

Blaser S2 Double Rifle

Series of side-by-side double rifles offered in two different models, Standard and Safari. Standard calibers range from .22 Hornet to 9.3x74R, including several European rimmed cartridges. Safari model chamberings for .375 H&H, .470 NE, .500/416 NE and 500 NE. Both series available in standard or five higher grades offering increasing levels of wood and engraving. Higher grade models are in order, Luxus, Super Luxus, Exclusive, Super Exclusive and Imperial. Prices shown are for basic standard models. Extra sets of barrels in different calibers offered, including shotgun barrels. Barrel sets are not interchangeable between Standard and Safari models. **NOTE:** Add 15

	NIB	EXC.	V.G.	GOOD	FAIR	POOR

to 200 percent or more for higher grades.

Standard

NIB	EXC.	V.G.	GOOD	FAIR	POOR
6800	6000	5200	4200	2500	1000

Safari

NIB	EXC.	V.G.	GOOD	FAIR	POOR
9500	8500	7000	5800	3500	1500

SHOTGUNS

F3 Series

Over/under series of shotguns. Offered in standard, sporting, skeet and trap models in 12- or 20-gauge. Available with various barrel lengths and options, including extra barrel sets. Add 40 percent for additional set of barrels. Offered in several higher grades, each with increasing levels of engraving and wood upgrades. For higher grades, add the following to prices shown below: Luxus Grade 20 percent; Grand Lux Grade 60 percent; Super Lux Grade 80 percent; Baroness Grade 100 percent; Exclusive Grade 115 percent; Super Exclusive Grade 200 percent; Imperial Grade 300 percent.

—

Game Standard

NIB	EXC.	V.G.	GOOD	FAIR	POOR
5500	4700	3900	3000	2000	1000

Sporting Standard and Skeet

NIB	EXC.	V.G.	GOOD	FAIR	POOR
6500	5500	4600	3750	2500	1000

Super Trap and Super Sport

NIB	EXC.	V.G.	GOOD	FAIR	POOR
7500	6750	5900	4500	3000	1000

HANDGUNS

Blaser HHS

Single-shot pistol has R93 receiver. Fitted with 14" barrel and pistol-grip fancy Turkish walnut stock. All R93 calibers are offered in both right-/left-hand models. Introduced in 2003. **NOTE:** Add $100 for left-hand models.

NIB	EXC.	V.G.	GOOD	FAIR	POOR
4250	3250	2000	1300	70	400

BLISS, F. D.
New Haven, Connecticut

Bliss Pocket Revolver

.25-caliber spur trigger revolver, with 3.25" octagon barrel, 6-shot magazine and square butt. Blued, with hard rubber or walnut grips. Barrel stamped "F.D. Bliss New Haven, Ct." There was an all-brass framed version made early in production. This model would be worth approximately 50 percent more than values listed here for standard model. Approximately 3,000 manufactured circa 1860 to 1863.

NIB	EXC.	V.G.	GOOD	FAIR	POOR
—	—	975	525	125	75

BLISS & GOODYEAR
New Haven, Connecticut

Pocket Model Revolver

.28-caliber percussion revolver, with 3" octagonal barrel, 6-shot magazine, unfluted cylinder. Solid frame, with removable side plate. Blued, with brass frame and walnut grips. Approximately 3,000 manufactured in 1860.

NIB	EXC.	V.G.	GOOD	FAIR	POOR
—	—	1800	550	225	150

BLUNT & SYMS
New York, New York

Under Hammer Pepperbox

Pepperboxes produced by Blunt & Syms are noteworthy for the fact they incorporate a ring trigger cocking/revolving mechanism and a concealed under hammer. They were produced in a variety of calibers and standard finish was blued. Normally these pistols are found marked simply "A-C" on face of barrel group. Some examples though are marked "Blunt & Syms New York". This firm was in business from approximately 1837 to 1855.

Small Frame Round Handle .25-.28 Caliber

NIB	EXC.	V.G.	GOOD	FAIR	POOR
—	—	1800	1300	675	175

Medium Frame Round Handle .31 Caliber

NIB	EXC.	V.G.	GOOD	FAIR	POOR
—	—	1850	1450	725	195

	NIB	EXC.	V.G.	GOOD	FAIR	POOR

Round Handle Dragoon .36 Caliber

—	—	2900	1050	900	295

Medium Frame Saw Handle .31 Caliber

—	—	2000	750	375	175

Saw Handle Dragoon .36 Caliber

—	—	2800	1350	750	225

Dueling Pistol

.52-caliber percussion single-shot pistol, with octagonal barrel normally of 9" length. Steel furniture, with walnut stock. Barrel marked "B&S New York/Cast Steel".

—	—	—	1750	725	325

Single-Shot Bar Hammer

.36-caliber single-shot percussion pistol, with 6" half-octagonal barrel and bar hammer. Blued or browned, with walnut grips. Marked as above.

—	—	1200	700	450	200

Side Hammer Pocket Pistol

.31- or .35-caliber single-shot percussion pistol, with 2.5" to 6" octagonal barrel. Blued, with walnut grips.

—	—	1250	650	425	195

Side Hammer Belt Pistol

As above in calibers ranging from .36 to .44, with barrel lengths of 4" or 6".

—	—	1400	750	375	150

Ring Trigger Pistol

.36-caliber percussion single-shot pistol, with 3" to 5" half-octagonal barrel and ring trigger. Blued, with walnut grips.

—	—	1025	650	375	150

Double Barrel Pistol

.36- to .44-caliber percussion double barrel pistol, with 7.5" barrels and walnut grips. Ring trigger variation of this model isknown.

—	—	1350	650	275	125

Double Barrel Under Hammer Pistol

As above, with two under hammers in .34-caliber and 4" barrels.

—	—	1750	875	425	200

Derringer Style Pistol

.50-caliber single-shot percussion pistol, with 3" barrel, German silver mounts and walnut stock. Lock marked "Blunt & Syms/New York".

—	—	1800	675	395	200

BOBERG ARMS CORP.
White Bear Lake, Minnesota

XR9

Semi-automatic chambered in 9mm, with 3.35 (XR9-S) or 4.2" (XR9-L) barrel. Striker-fired with locked-breech action, rotating barrel, stainless steel slide, aluminum frame. Magazine capacity 7-rounds. Fixed low-profile 3-dot sights. Patented new design lifts cartridges straight into chamber, eliminating need for feed ramp and allowing for a longer barrel than other subcompact pistols. Introduced in 2013. **NOTE:** Add $350 for platinum or onyx finish.

900	800	700	—	—	—

BODEO
Location Unknown

Italian Service Revolver

System Bodeo Modello 1889 (Enlisted Model)

—	750	550	400	250	100

Modello 1889 (Officer's Model)

—	750	550	400	250	100

NIB	EXC.	V.G.	GOOD	FAIR	POOR

BOLUMBURO, G.
Eibar, Spain

Bristol

Semi-automatic pistol in caliber 7.65mm. Made in style of Ruby military pistols. "Bristol" stamped on slide. Wood grips.

—	295	185	150	90	40

Marina 6.35mm

Semi-automatic pistol in caliber 6.35mm. "Marina" stamped on each grip's plate.

—	295	195	150	90	40

Marina 7.65mm

As above in 7.65mm, with "Marina" stamped on slide. Wood grips and lanyard loop.

—	275	195	150	90	40

Rex

Semi-automatic pistol in caliber 7.65mm. "Rex" stamped on slide. Wood grips and lanyard loop.

—	275	195	150	90	40

BOND ARMS INC.
Grandbury, Texas

Texas Defender

Stainless steel over/under derringer. Chambered for a variety of calibers such as .45 Colt/.410, .357 Magnum, 9mm, .45 ACP and .44 Magnum. Barrels are interchangeable. Grips are laminated black ash or rosewood. Barrel length 3", with blade front sight and fixed rear sight. Weight about 21 oz. Introduced in 1997. Add 300 percent for full factory engraved model.

—	400	300	200	150	100

Snake Slayer IV

Modern variation of Remington over/under derringer. Interchangeable 4.5" barrel assemblies, rosewood grip panels, stainless finish, fixed sights. Chambered for .410-bore shotshell/.45 LC, 9mm, 10mm, .40 S&W, .45 ACP.

—	400	300	200	150	100

Snake Slayer

3.5" barrels; weighs 22 oz. Interchangeable barrel assemblies, rosewood grip panels, stainless fixed sights. Chambered for .410-bore shotshell/.45 LC, 9mm, 10mm, .40 S&W, .45 ACP.

—	400	300	200	150	100

Cowboy Defender

Derringer with 3" barrels. Weighs 19 oz. Interchangeable barrels, rosewood grip panels, stainless fixed sights. Variety of chambering options such as .410-bore, .45 LC, .357 Magnum, .38 Special, .45 ACP, .44 Special, .44-40 Win, .40 S&W, 10mm, etc. No trigger guard. Automatic extractor (except for 9mm, 10mm, .40 S&W, .45 ACP).

395	350	300	225	150	75

Century 2000

Similar to Cowboy Defender, with 3.5" barrels to allow use of .410 Magnum shotshells, .357/.38 Special, .45 ACP, .44 Special, .44-40 Win, .40 S&W, 10mm, etc. Automatic extractor (except for 9mm, 10mm, .40 S&W, .45 ACP).

425	375	300	225	150	75

BOOM
Hatfield, Massachusetts
See—Shattuck, C.S.

BORCHARDT
Berlin, Germany
Waffenfabrik Lowe

Borchardt

Forerunner of German Luger. Borchardt was a semi-automatic pistol. Chambered for 7.65mm Borchardt cartridge. Fitted with 6.5" barrel. Magazine held 8 rounds. Pistol was designed by Hugo Borchardt and manufactured by Ludwig Lowe of Berlin. Later models manufactured by DWM, Deutsch Waffen Und Munitionsfabriken, Berlin. Many Borchardts come with a case which

	NIB	EXC.	V.G.	GOOD	FAIR	POOR

holds shoulder stock, holster, extra magazines and numerous other accessories.

Pistol Only

	NIB	EXC.	V.G.	GOOD	FAIR	POOR
	—	23000	15000	8000	4000	2000

Pistol with Case and Accessories

	NIB	EXC.	V.G.	GOOD	FAIR	POOR
	—	35000	20000	12000	7500	4000

BORSIG
East Germany

Borsig is East German version of Soviet Makarov pistol. A double-action chambered for Soviet 9x18mm cartridge. Its appearance is nearly identical to Makarov.

	NIB	EXC.	V.G.	GOOD	FAIR	POOR
	—	300	225	150	100	75

BOSIS, LUCIANO
Brescia, Italy

Bosis is a maker of high-grade sidelock over/under and side-by-side guns in gauges 12, 20, 28 and .410. These guns are made on custom-order basis.

Over/Under

Values for used guns in excellent condition begin at $30,000. Secure an expert appraisal prior to sale.

Side-by-Side

Values for used guns in excellent condition begin at $20,000. Secure an expert appraisal prior to sale. **NOTE:** Small gauge guns will bring a premium of 20 percent.

BOSS & CO.
London, England

Thomas Boss worked for great British gunmaker Joseph Manton before becoming a pieceworker to the London trade. In 1891 John Robertson was taken in as a partner and under his control the firm was established as one of London's best gunmakers, rivaled only by James Purdey. Current Boss shotgun prices begin at around £60,000 ($96,000 U.S.) and double rifles about £85,000 ($136,000 U.S.). Many of the older models are encountered on used gun market. A professional appraisal is strongly advised before establishing a buying or selling price.

BOSWELL, CHARLES
London, England

One of England's more established makers of best-quality rifles and shotguns. In 1988 company was purchased by an American consortium and Cape Horn Outfitters of Charlotte, North Carolina was appointed their sole agent.

Double Rifle, Boxlock

.300 Holland & Holland, .375 Holland & Holland or .458 Winchester Magnum double-barrel boxlock rifle, with double triggers and walnut stock. Other features were made to customer's specifications. A .600 Nitro Express version was also available. **NOTE:** .600 Nitro Express add 25 percent.

	NIB	EXC.	V.G.	GOOD	FAIR	POOR
	—	47000	39500	29500	19950	600

Double Rifle, Sidelock

As above, with Holland & Holland-style sidelocks. **NOTE:** .600 Nitro Express add 25 percent.

	NIB	EXC.	V.G.	GOOD	FAIR	POOR
	—	63000	47500	35000	22000	600

BOSWORTH, B. M.
Warren, Pennsylvania

Under Hammer Pistol

.38-caliber single-shot percussion pistol, with under hammer and 6" half-octagonal barrel. Frame marked "BM Bosworth". Browned, with brass grips forming part of frame. Made circa 1850 to 1860.

	NIB	EXC.	V.G.	GOOD	FAIR	POOR
	—	—	1850	800	295	125

BRAENDLIN ARMOURY
London, England

.450-caliber 8-barrel pistol, with hinged barrels, rotating firing pin and double-action lock. Manufactured during 1880s.

	NIB	EXC.	V.G.	GOOD	FAIR	POOR
	—	—	8550	5500	3500	1850

| NIB | EXC. | V.G. | GOOD | FAIR | POOR |

BRAND
New York
Maker—E. Robinson

Brand Breech Loading Carbine
.50 rimfire caliber carbine, with 22" barrel secured by one barrel band. Frame marked "Brand's Patent July 29,1862/E. Robinson Manfr/New York". Carbine was produced in limited numbers, primarily for trial purposes.

NIB	EXC.	V.G.	GOOD	FAIR	POOR
—	—	6800	2950	1250	550

BREDA, ERNESTO
Milan, Italy

Andromeda Special
12-gauge boxlock shotgun, with various barrel lengths and chokes, single-selective triggers and automatic ejectors. Engraved satin-finished, with checkered walnut stock.

—	1150	775	595	425	300

Vega Special
12-gauge boxlock over/under shotgun, with 26" or 28" barrels, various choke combinations, single-selective trigger and automatic ejectors. Engraved and blued, with checkered walnut stock.

—	850	700	600	375	275

Vega Special Trap
As above, with competition-styled stock, 30" or 32" barrels and full chokes.

—	1350	1050	850	500	350

Sirio Standard
Similar to Vega, with extensive engraving and higher degree of finishing. There is a 28" barreled skeet version available in this model.

—	2750	2000	1950	1350	650

Standard Semi-Automatic
12-gauge semi-automatic shotgun, with 25" or 27" ventilated rib barrels, screw-in choke tubes, engraved receiver and checkered walnut stock.

—	375	275	225	175	125

Grade I
As above, with more engraving and finer wood.

—	650	475	325	225	175

Grade II
A more elaborately engraved version of the Grade I.

—	850	600	450	375	250

Grade III
The most deluxe version in this line, with select walnut and extensive engraving.

—	1050	800	650	575	250

Magnum Model
Same as standard in 12-gauge Magnum.

—	435	325	250	175	75

Gold Series Antares Standard
12-gauge semi-automatic shotgun, with 25" or 27" ventilated rib barrel and screw-in choke tubes. Blued, with checkered walnut stock.

—	650	425	350	275	225

Gold Series Argus
As above, with alloy frame.

—	650	475	375	300	250

Gold Series Aries
As above in 12-gauge Magnum.

—	700	495	400	325	275

	NIB	EXC.	V.G.	GOOD	FAIR	POOR

M1 Garand

Virtual duplicate of US M1 Garand. Chambered in .30-06. Made in mid-1950s by Breda under contract for Denmark. Values shown are for correct, non-import marked specimens. Deduct up to 50 percent for built-up parts guns or non-matching guns.

—	2200	1595	800	400	250	

BREN 10
Huntington Beach, California
See—Dornaus & Dixon Inc.

Manufactured from 1983 until 1986. Deduct 15 percent for aftermarket magazines.

Standard Bren 10

10mm caliber double-action semi-automatic pistol, with 5" barrel and 10-shot magazine. Stainless frame and satin-blued slide. Manufactured between 1983 and 1986. Value includes original factory magazine.

2625	1925	1400	850	550	325	

M & P Model

As above, with matte black finish.

2700	2100	1550	925	595	385	

Special Forces Model

Chambered for 10mm cartridge. Similar to M&P model. Offered in two models: Model D has a dark finish; Model L has a light finish. Prices listed are for Model D. Add 25 percent for Model L.

2800	2200	1750	1000	800	500	

Dual-Master Presentation Model

As above, with .45-caliber extra barrel slide. Fitted walnut case.

6125	4375	2190	1225	875	500	

Marksman Model

Similar to Standard Model in .45 caliber. There were 250 manufactured for "Marksman Shop" in Chicago, Illinois.

2450	1750	1325	700	300	275	

Jeff Cooper Commemorative

Suppose to be 2,000 manufactured in 1986, but no one knows how many were actually produced. Some estimates are less than 10. Chambered for 10mm. High-gloss blue finish, with 22 kt. gold-plated details. Grips are laser engraved. Whole affair furnished in a walnut display case.

6125	4375	—	—	—	—	

Bren 10 (2010 Series)

Several Bren 10 models were manufactured by Vltor in Tucson, Arizona from 2010 to 2011. Limited production of approximately 2000 guns. Specifications similar to original Standard and Marksman models with choice of 4" or 5" barrels, 10mm or .45 ACP chambering, stainless or two-tone finish.

1100	1000	850	700	500	300	

BRETTON
Ste. Etienne, France

Baby Standard

12- or 20-gauge over/under shotgun, with various barrel lengths, choke combinations and double triggers. Blued, checkered walnut stock.

1350	975	725	550	400	325	

Deluxe Grade

12-, 16- and 20-gauge over/under shotgun. Engraved coin-finished receiver, with walnut stock.

2150	1875	1400	800	500	325	

BRIGGS, H. A.
Norwich, Connecticut

Briggs Single-Shot Pistol

.22-caliber single-shot spur trigger pistol, with 4" part-round/part-octagonal barrel and downward rotating breechblock. Blued, with walnut grips. Frame marked "H.A. Briggs/Norwich, Ct." Manufactured in 1850s and 1860s.

—	—	2950	1250	450	200	

BRILEY MANUFACTURING INC.
Houston, Texas

El Presidente Model—Unlimited

1911-style pistol can be built on a Caspian Arms STI or SVI frame. Includes scope mount, compensator, match barrel, cocking sight, lowered and flared ejection port, front and rear serrations, aluminum guide rod and numerous other custom features. Offered in most calibers. Blued finish.

NIB	EXC.	V.G.	GOOD	FAIR	POOR
2400	2000	1450	1000	700	350

Versatility Plus Model—Limited

Built on a 1911 frame, with BoMar sight, checkered mainspring housing and checkered front strap. Many other custom features. Available in .45 ACP, .40 S&W and 9mm.

NIB	EXC.	V.G.	GOOD	FAIR	POOR
1950	1650	1200	800	400	225

Versatility Model—Limited

Similar to above model, without several features such as checkered front strap. Available in .45 ACP, .40 S&W, 9mm.

NIB	EXC.	V.G.	GOOD	FAIR	POOR
1475	1150	800	575	265	195

Lightning Model—Action Pistol

Built on a 1911 frame. Features many custom components including titanium compensator. Weight no more than 40 oz. Available in 9mm and .38 Super only.

NIB	EXC.	V.G.	GOOD	FAIR	POOR
2450	1950	1300	850	425	200

Carry Comp Model—Defense

Built on a 1911 frame. Features dual port cone compensator, with many custom features. Barrel length about 5". Offered in .45 ACP only.

NIB	EXC.	V.G.	GOOD	FAIR	POOR
2450	2000	1550	1000	500	250

BRIXIA
Brescia, Italy

Model 12

Commercial version of Model 1910 Glisenti in 9mm Glisenti caliber. Brixia was a simplified Glisenti and was made to replace Glisenti for military market. Italian military did not accept them and only a few were made for commercial market. Only markings are monogram eagle holding a shield cast in grips.

NIB	EXC.	V.G.	GOOD	FAIR	POOR
—	1300	950	7850	450	325

BRNO ARMS
Uhersky Brod, Czech Republic

Brno firearms have been manufactured since 1918 in what was once known as Czechosolvakia, now the Czech Republic. Various Brno rifles, pistols, shotguns and combination guns have been brought into U.S. since late 1940s by several importers including Continental Arms, Magnum Research, Bohemia Arms, EAA and others. There has been a close association between Brno and CZ (Ceska Zbrojovka) for many years. CZ-USA of Kansas City, Kansas, is current importer of both brands. Only Brno models currently being imported are single-shot and over/under rifles and over/under combination rifle/shotguns.

ZG-47

Bolt-action rifle based on Mauser system. Chambered for .270, 7x57, 7x64, .30-06, 8x57, 8x60, 8x64S, 9.3x62 and on special order 10.75x68. Barrel length 23.6". Adjustable trigger. Hinged floorplate. Weight about 7.7 lbs.

Standard

NIB	EXC.	V.G.	GOOD	FAIR	POOR
—	1000	900	800	650	400

Deluxe

NIB	EXC.	V.G.	GOOD	FAIR	POOR
—	1100	950	850	600	450

ZH-SERIES

Double barrel over/under boxlock series of shotguns. Interchangeable barrels in shotgun and rifle configurations, of various lengths, double triggers and automatic ejectors. Models listed represent different gauges and/or calibers offered. **NOTE:** ZH models with set triggers and cheekpiece add $75; interchangeable barrels add between $300 and $400 depending on gauge and caliber.

ZH-300

NIB	EXC.	V.G.	GOOD	FAIR	POOR
—	675	575	400	325	250

	NIB	EXC.	V.G.	GOOD	FAIR	POOR

ZH-301
12-gauge/12-gauge.

	—	600	500	400	350	200

ZH-302
12-gauge/12-gauge Skeet.

	—	600	550	450	400	250

ZH-303 12
12-gauge/12-gauge Trap.

	—	600	550	450	400	250

ZH-304
12-gauge/7x57R.

	—	1000	800	500	400	250

ZH-305
12-gauge/6x52R.

	—	900	700	500	400	225

ZH-306
12-gauge/6x50R Magnum.

	—	850	650	450	350	200

ZH-308
12-gauge/7x65R.

	—	850	700	500	400	225

ZH-309
12-gauge/8x57 JRS.

	—	850	700	500	400	225

ZH-321
16-gauge/16-gauge.

	—	750	625	450	400	225

ZH-324
16-gauge/7x57R.

	—	875	700	500	400	225

ZH-328
16-gauge/7x65R.

	—	850	700	500	400	225

Model 300 Combo
Model ZH-300, with 8 interchangeable barrels in a fitted case. Introduced in 1986.

5000	4000	3000	2750	2000	1500

Model 500
Model ZH-300, with acid-etched decoration, automatic ejectors and 12-gauge.

	—	800	600	425	350	275

ZP-49
12-gauge sidelock double-barrel shotgun, with double triggers and automatic ejectors. Blued, with walnut stock. Imported in 1986 only.

	—	1050	800	650	450	325

ZP-149
As above, without engraving.

	—	600	500	400	300	200

ZP-349
As above, with buttstock having cheekpiece and beavertail forearm.

	—	800	650	500	350	250

	NIB	EXC.	V.G.	GOOD	FAIR	POOR

ZBK-100

Single barrel shotgun in 12- or 20-gauge, with 27" barrel and walnut stock. Weight about 5.5 lbs.

	NIB	EXC.	V.G.	GOOD	FAIR	POOR
	250	200	150	125	100	75

RIFLES

ZKW-465 (Hornet Sporter)

.22 Hornet caliber bolt-action rifle, with 23" barrel, express sights and double-set triggers. Blued, with walnut stock.

	NIB	EXC.	V.G.	GOOD	FAIR	POOR
	—	1500	1100	950	800	550

Model 21H

6.5x57mm, 7x57mm or 8x57mm caliber bolt-action sporting rifle, with 23.625" barrel, express sights and double-set triggers. Blued, with walnut stock.

	—	1250	1050	900	750	600

Model 22F

As above, with Mannlicher-style stock. Barrel length 20.5".

	—	1295	1100	900	650	500

Model I

.22-caliber bolt-action rifle, with 22.75" barrel having folding leaf rear sights. Blued, with walnut stock.

	—	550	400	300	250	200

Model II

As above, with a more finely figured walnut stock.

		595	450	350	300	225

ZKM 611

Semi-automatic rifle chambered for .17 HMR or .22 WRM cartridge. Fitted with 20" barrel. Magazine capacity 6 rounds. Weight about 6.2 lbs.

	700	625	525	300	175	125

ZKM 451

Semi-automatic rifle chambered for .22 LR cartridge. Fitted with 22" barrel. Magazine capacity 7 rounds. Weight about 5.25 lbs.

	450	300	250	125	100	75

ZKM 451 LUX

Same as above, with select walnut stock.

	500	350	250	150	125	100

ZBK 680

.22 Hornet or .222-caliber bolt-action rifle, with 23.5" barrel, double set triggers and 5-shot magazine. Blued, with walnut stock.

	925	750	550	400	325	225

Super Express Rifle

Over/under sidelock double-barrel rifle, with 23.5" barrels, double triggers and automatic ejectors. Engraved, blued with walnut stock. Available in 6 grades:

Standard Model

5500	4150	3000	2500	1750	1250

Grade I

7500	5900	4750	4500	3600	3250

Grade II

6500	5150	4000	3500	2750	2250

Grade III

6250	4900	3950	3250	2750	2250

Grade IV

6000	4700	3500	3000	2500	2250

Grade V

5750	3950	3250	2750	2250	1750

	NIB	EXC.	V.G.	GOOD	FAIR	POOR

Grade VI

	NIB	EXC.	V.G.	GOOD	FAIR	POOR
	4900	4250	3100	2600	1950	1500

ZH-344/348/349

Over/under rifle chambered for 7x57R, 7x65R, or 8x57JRS.

NIB	EXC.	V.G.	GOOD	FAIR	POOR
1500	975	700	550	400	275

Model 98 Standard

Bolt-action rifle chambered for a variety of calibers from 7x64 to 9.3x62. Fitted with 23" barrel, figured walnut stock, buttplate and open sights. Weight about 7.25 lbs. **NOTE:** Set trigger add $100.

NIB	EXC.	V.G.	GOOD	FAIR	POOR
800	650	400	300	200	150

Model 98 Full Stock

Same as above, with full one-piece stock and set trigger.

NIB	EXC.	V.G.	GOOD	FAIR	POOR
1000	700	500	400	350	200

ZK 99

Tip-up centerfire rifle chambered for a wide variety of calibers from 6.5x57R to .30-06. Barrel length 23". Weight about 5.75 lbs.

NIB	EXC.	V.G.	GOOD	FAIR	POOR
995	750	550	395	200	150

ZBK 110

Single-shot tip-open rifle chambered for .22 Hornet, .222 Rem., 5.6x50R Magnum and 5.6x52R. Barrel length 23.5". Open sights. Walnut stock without checkering. Weight about 6 lbs.

NIB	EXC.	V.G.	GOOD	FAIR	POOR
450	350	250	200	150	75

ZBK 110 LUX

Same as above, with select walnut stock and checkering. Open sights.

NIB	EXC.	V.G.	GOOD	FAIR	POOR
440	350	250	200	150	75

ZBK 110 Super Lux

Same as above, with fancy walnut stock and checkering. Open sights.

NIB	EXC.	V.G.	GOOD	FAIR	POOR
650	525	400	300	150	75

HANDGUNS

ZKR 551

Double-/single-action revolver, with 6-round cylinder. Adjustable rear sight. Walnut grips. Fitted with 6" barrel. Chambered for .38, .32 S&W Long and .22 LR. Weight about 35 oz.

NIB	EXC.	V.G.	GOOD	FAIR	POOR
1800	1350	900	700	500	275

BROLIN ARMS
La Verne, California

Brolin Arms was in business from approximately 1995 to 2000. Imported handguns from Hungary, Mauser military rifles from Europe and shotguns from China. Company also manufactured a series of 1911-pattern pistols

LEGEND SERIES—1911 AUTO PISTOL

L45—Standard Auto Pistol

Standard model, with 5" barrel chambered for .45 ACP. Fitted with throated match barrel, polished feed ramp, lowered ejection port, beveled magazine well and fixed sights. Other custom features as well. Finish matte blue, with 7-round magazine. Weight about 36 oz.

NIB	EXC.	V.G.	GOOD	FAIR	POOR
550	400	295	200	125	75

L45C—Compact Auto Pistol

Similar to standard model, with 4.5" barrel. Weight about 32 oz.

NIB	EXC.	V.G.	GOOD	FAIR	POOR
595	550	325	225	150	100

L45T

Version of L45 series. Introduced in 1997. Fitted with compact slide on full-size frame. Weight 36 oz. **NOTE:** Novak sights add $50.

NIB	EXC.	V.G.	GOOD	FAIR	POOR
595	550	325	200	125	75

	NIB	EXC.	V.G.	GOOD	FAIR	POOR

PATRIOT SERIES—DPC CARRY-COMP PISTOLS

P45 Comp—Standard Carry Comp

Features 4" barrel, with integral compensator cut into slide. Other features are custom beavertail grip safety, adjustable aluminum trigger, flat-top slide and checkered wood grips. Weight about 37 oz.

NIB	EXC.	V.G.	GOOD	FAIR	POOR
600	550	375	225	110	95

P45C Comp—Compact Carry Comp

Similar to above. Fitted with 3.25" barrel. Weight about 33 oz. **NOTE:** Two-tone finish add $20.

NIB	EXC.	V.G.	GOOD	FAIR	POOR
600	550	375	225	110	95

P45T

Addition to Patriot Series introduced in 1997. Has all features of Patriot pistols. Fitted with compact slide and full size frame. Weight about 35 oz. Available in two-tone finish for additional $20. **NOTE:** Novak sights add $50.

NIB	EXC.	V.G.	GOOD	FAIR	POOR
600	550	375	225	110	95

TAC SERIES—TACTICAL 1911 PISTOLS

TAC-11

Series and model introduced in 1997. Has all features of L45 series. Additions of special 5" conical match barrel, Novak Low Profile sights, black rubber contour grips, "iron claw" extractor and optional night sights. Chambered for .45 ACP. Supplied with 8-round magazine. Weight about 37 oz. **NOTE:** Tritium night sights add $90.

NIB	EXC.	V.G.	GOOD	FAIR	POOR
650	575	395	250	150	100

TAC SERIES—DOUBLE-ACTION PISTOLS

MS45

Full-size double-action pistol chambered for .45 ACP cartridge. Fitted with 8-round magazine and low- profile 3-dot sights. Standard finish matte blue. **NOTE:** Add $20 for royal blue finish.

NIB	EXC.	V.G.	GOOD	FAIR	POOR
650	575	395	250	150	100

M45

Similar to above, with longer barrel. Chambered for .45 ACP and 8-round magazine. **NOTE:** Add $20 for royal blue finish.

NIB	EXC.	V.G.	GOOD	FAIR	POOR
550	475	300	250	150	100

M40

Same as M45. Chambered for .40 S&W cartridge. Magazine capacity 10 rounds. **NOTE:** Novak sights add $50.

NIB	EXC.	V.G.	GOOD	FAIR	POOR
500	400	275	250	150	100

M90

Same as M45. Chambered for 9mm cartridge. Magazine capacity 10 rounds. **NOTE:** Add $20 for royal blue finish.

NIB	EXC.	V.G.	GOOD	FAIR	POOR
500	400	300	250	150	100

MC40

Compact version of full-size double-action models. Fitted with full-size frame, but shorter slide. Chambered for .40 S&W cartridge. Magazine capacity 10 rounds. **NOTE:** Add $20 for royal blue finish.

NIB	EXC.	V.G.	GOOD	FAIR	POOR
600	500	300	250	150	100

MC90

Same as above chambered for 9mm cartridge.

NIB	EXC.	V.G.	GOOD	FAIR	POOR
500	400	275	250	150	100

MB40

Super-compact double-action pistol. Features concealed hammer. Chambered for .40 S&W cartridge. Magazine capacity 6 rounds. **NOTE:** Add $20 for royal blue finish.

NIB	EXC.	V.G.	GOOD	FAIR	POOR
550	450	300	250	150	100

MB90

Same as above chambered for 9mm cartridge.

NIB	EXC.	V.G.	GOOD	FAIR	POOR
550	450	300	250	150	100

	NIB	EXC.	V.G.	GOOD	FAIR	POOR

PRO SERIES—COMPETITION PISTOL

Pro-Stock—Competition Pistol

Chambered for .45 ACP. Designed for competition shooter. Many special features standard such as full-length recoil guide, front strap high relief cut, serrated flat mainspring housing, ambidextrous thumb safety and fully adjustable rear sight. Barrel length 5". Weight about 37 oz. **NOTE:** Two-tone finish add $20.

NIB	EXC.	V.G.	GOOD	FAIR	POOR
700	600	500	350	175	100

Pro-Comp—Competition Pistol

Similar to competition model above. Fitted with integral compensator and 4" barrel. Weight about 37 oz. **NOTE:** Two-tone finish add $20.

NIB	EXC.	V.G.	GOOD	FAIR	POOR
750	650	500	375	200	100

SHOTGUNS

LAWMAN SERIES—PERSONAL SECURITY SHOTGUN

HL18SB

Pump-action 12-gauge shotgun, with 18.5" barrel, black synthetic stock and bead sights. Weight about 7 lbs. Introduced in 1997. Copy of Remington Model 870.

NIB	EXC.	V.G.	GOOD	FAIR	POOR
295	250	195	150	95	50

HL18SR

Same as above. Fitted with rifle sights.

NIB	EXC.	V.G.	GOOD	FAIR	POOR
325	275	225	175	125	65

HL18SBN

Same as above, with nickel finish.

NIB	EXC.	V.G.	GOOD	FAIR	POOR
270	200	150	100	75	50

HL18WB

This version has wood stock and bead sights.

NIB	EXC.	V.G.	GOOD	FAIR	POOR
295	250	195	150	95	50

HL18WR

Same as above. Fitted with rifle sights.

NIB	EXC.	V.G.	GOOD	FAIR	POOR
270	200	150	100	75	50

FIELD SERIES—PUMP ACTION FIELD GUN

HF24SB

12-gauge pump action shotgun, with 24" barrel, matte finish, black synthetic stock and bead sights. Weight about 7.3 lbs. Introduced in 1997.

NIB	EXC.	V.G.	GOOD	FAIR	POOR
270	200	150	100	75	50

HF28SB

Same as above. Fitted with 28" barrel. Weight 7.4 lbs.

NIB	EXC.	V.G.	GOOD	FAIR	POOR
270	200	150	100	75	50

HF24WB

Features 24" barrel, with wood stock.

NIB	EXC.	V.G.	GOOD	FAIR	POOR
270	200	150	100	75	50

HF28WB

Same as above, with 24" barrel.

NIB	EXC.	V.G.	GOOD	FAIR	POOR
270	200	150	100	75	50

Slug Special

Slide-action shotgun chambered for 3" 12-gauge shells. Available with choice of 18.5" or 22" barrels. Rifle or ghost ring sights. Available with fixed improved cylinder choke, 4" extended rifled choke, or fully rifled barrel. Choice of wood or synthetic stocks.

NIB	EXC.	V.G.	GOOD	FAIR	POOR
270	200	150	100	75	50

Turkey Special

12-gauge 3" model. Fitted with 22" extra full choke vent rib barrel. Choice of wood or synthetic stock.

NIB	EXC.	V.G.	GOOD	FAIR	POOR
270	200	150	100	75	50

	NIB	EXC.	V.G.	GOOD	FAIR	POOR

FIELD COMBO—TWO BARREL COMBO SET
HC28SB
Set consists of 18.5" and 28" barrel, synthetic stock, pistol-grip, bead sight.

	300	250	200	125	75	50

HC28SR
Same as above, with rifle and bead sight.

	320	250	200	125	75	50

HC28WB
Features wood stock, pistol-grip and bead sight.

	300	250	200	125	75	50

HC28WR
Same as above, with wood stock. Rifle and bead sight.

	320	250	200	125	75	50

SEMI-AUTOMATIC SHOTGUNS

BL-12 Security
12-gauge shotgun has 3" chamber and 5-round magazine. Fitted with 18.5" vent rib barrel. Synthetic stock standard.

	350	325	295	200	150	75

BL-12 Field
Similar to above, with 28" vent rib barrel. Choice of wood or synthetic stock.

	350	325	295	200	150	75

SAS-12 Security
12-gauge shotgun chambered for 2.75" 12-gauge shells. Fitted with 24" vent rib or rifle sight barrel. Detachable box magazine; 3 round standard, 5 round optional. Synthetic stock.

	350	325	295	200	150	75

RIFLES

Legacy
.50-caliber muzzleloader, with in-line ignition system. Walnut stain hardwood stock and recoil pad. Finish blue or chrome. **NOTE:** Add $20 for chrome finish.

	180	150	100	75	50	15

Mitchell PPS-50
Semi-automatic rifle chambered for .22 LR cartridge. Detachable 10-round magazine. Copy of Russian PPSh machine gun used in WWII.

	400	325	275	225	175	100

MAUSER RIFLES
All of these Mauser rifles introduced in 1998, to Brolin product line.
Lightning Model
Features sliding bolt that locks directly into barrel. Chambered for 7.62x39mm cartridge and .308 Win. Blue finish. Choice of colored synthetic stocks. Open sights standard.

	550	450	350	325	200	100

Lightning Hunter Model
Features detachable magazine, recoil pad, blued finish, checkered wood stock and choice of open or no sights, with scope mounts included. Calibers from .243 to .300 Win. Magnum. **NOTE:** Add $50 for open sights; $50 for stainless steel.

	650	500	350	325	200	100

Lightning Hunter All Weather Model
Same as above, with black synthetic stock.

	700	550	350	325	200	100

Lightning Varmint Model
Features of this model same as Lightning Hunter Model. Addition of heavy fluted barrel, with special varmint wood or synthetic stock. Chambered for .22-250 and .243 cartridges.

	900	700	550	450	300	125

	NIB	EXC.	V.G.	GOOD	FAIR	POOR

Lightning Sniper

Features heavy fluted barrel, with detachable magazine. Choice of special wood or synthetic stock. Built-in bi-pod rail. Offered in .308 or 300 Win. Magnum calibers.

| 1000 | 800 | 600 | 450 | 300 | 125 |

Lightning Professional

Model has heavy fluted barrel, no sights and recoil compensator. Tuned trigger system standard. All-weather adjustable stock, with pistol-grip. Available in .308 or .300 Win. Magnum calibers.

| 900 | 700 | 550 | 395 | 300 | 125 |

2000 Classic

2000 Classic features interchangeable caliber system for cartridges in same action length. Detachable magazine. High-grade walnut stock, with cut checkering and rosewood fore-end. Single set trigger standard. Offered in .270, .308, .30-06, 7mm Rem. Magnum and .300 Win. Magnum.

| 1500 | 1250 | 800 | 495 | 300 | 125 |

2000 Varmint

Features heavy fluted barrel, with special varmint wood stock and accessory rail. Offered in .22-250 and .243 calibers. Standard without sights.

| 2200 | 1700 | 1200 | 800 | 400 | 200 |

2000 Sniper

Features interchangeable caliber system, heavy fluted barrel, no sights, single set trigger, all-weather stock, with built-in bi-pod rail. Offered in .308 and .300 Win. Magnum calibers.

| 2200 | 1750 | 1250 | 800 | 400 | 200 |

2000 Professional

Has all features of Sniper rifle. Addition of recoil compensator and special all-weather pistol-grip stock. Each rifle custom built.

| 3500 | 2750 | 1700 | 90 | 550 | 250 |

20/22

High-quality .22 bolt-action rifle. Chambered for .22 LR or .22 Magnum cartridge. Available in both standard and deluxe configuration. Add $100 for deluxe version.

| 750 | 575 | 475 | 395 | 300 | 125 |

1898 Commemorative

Celebrates 100 year anniversary of '98 Mauser. Chambered for 8mm Mauser cartridge. Limited edition rifle.

| 2300 | 1750 | 1400 | 1000 | 675 | 300 |

98

Original Mauser action built to Safari calibers. Chambered for .375 H&H or .416 Rigby.

| 10000 | 8000 | 6250 | 5000 | 1500 | 400 |

CUSTOM SHOP

Formula One RZ

High-performance competition race gun. Many special features such as supported barrel chamber, 6-port compensator, tuned trigger, extended magazine release and many other options as standard. Chambered for .38 Super, .40 S&W cartridges. Blue finish. Add $400 for double-action.

| 2500 | 2000 | 1400 | 1050 | 700 | 350 |

Formula One RS

Designed as Limited Class competition gun, with 5" barrel. Chambered for .38 Super, .40 S&W or .45 ACP calibers. Features adjustable rear sight, tuned trigger, checkered front strap, mainspring housing and other special features. Add $300 for double-action.

| 2000 | 1600 | 1250 | 875 | 500 | 350 |

Formula Z

Custom-built combat pistol. Chambered for .40 S&W, .400 CorBon or .45 ACP calibers. Fitted with 4" or 5" barrel. Features many extra-cost features as standard.

| 1300 | 1000 | 650 | 425 | 300 | 150 |

NIB	EXC.	V.G.	GOOD	FAIR	POOR

MITCHELL SINGLE-ACTION REVOLVERS

Single-Action Army Model

Offered in 4.75", 5.5" or 7.5" barrel lengths. Chambered for .45 Long Colt, .357 Magnum or .44-40 calibers. Offered in blue finish, with case hardened frame or nickel finish. Available with dual cylinders, i.e. .45 LC/.45 ACP. Add $50 for nickel finish; $150 for dual cylinder models.

NIB	EXC.	V.G.	GOOD	FAIR	POOR
395	350	275	175	125	75

BRONCO
Eibar, Spain

See— Echave & Arizmendi
(Firearms International & Garcia)

BROOKLYN F. A. CO.
Brooklyn, New York

Slocum Pocket Revolver

.32-caliber spur-trigger revolver, with 3" round barrel. Frame silver-plated brass and scroll engraved; remainder blued or plated with walnut grips. Barrel marked "B.A. Co. Patented April 14, 1863". Approximately 10,000 manufactured in 1863 and 1864. Cylinder has five individual tubes that slide forward to open for loading and then ejecting spent cartridges.

NIB	EXC.	V.G.	GOOD	FAIR	POOR
—	—	975	325	120	75

Slocum Unfluted Cylinder Pocket Revolver

As above in .22- or .32-caliber, with 5- or 7-shot cylinder. Approximately 250 manufactured in .32 rimfire and 100 in .22 rimfire. **NOTE:** .22-caliber add 25 percent.

NIB	EXC.	V.G.	GOOD	FAIR	POOR
—	—	1300	450	225	125

BROWN, E.A. MANUFACTURING CO.
Alexandria, Minnesota

Brown Classic Single-Shot Pistol

Falling block single-shot pistol, with 15" match grade barrel. Chambered for calibers from .17 Ackley to .45-70 Government. Walnut thumbrest grips. Handfitted. Introduced in 1998.

NIB	EXC.	V.G.	GOOD	FAIR	POOR
1200	1000	750	600	400	200

Brown Model 97D Single-Shot Rifle

Single-shot falling block rifle. Chambered for calibers from .17 Ackley to .45-70 Government. Barrel lengths up to 26". Sporter-style stock with pistol-grip, cheekpiece and schnabel fore-end. Blue/black finish. Weight about 6 lbs. No sights.

NIB	EXC.	V.G.	GOOD	FAIR	POOR
1200	1000	750	600	400	200

BROWN, ED PRODUCTS
Perry, Missouri

There are a number of extra options available on Ed Brown handguns and rifles that may affect values. In August of 2010, Ed Brown announced he would no longer be accepting orders for new rifles and, for an indefinite period of time, would be focusing on his core business of handguns. Rifle parts and limited services remain available.

Commander Bobtail

Features 4.25" barrel. Chambered for .45 ACP, .400 CorBon, .40 S&W, .38 Super, 9x23 or 9mm Luger cartridge. Modified Hogue grips from exotic wood standard. Completely handmade and built to customer's specifications. Many available options.

NIB	EXC.	V.G.	GOOD	FAIR	POOR
2200	1700	1200	700	500	300

RIFLES

NOTE: There are a number of extra-cost options that are offered by this company on its rifles that may affect value. Consult the company or an export prior to a purchase.

Classic Custom

Chambered for .45 ACP cartridge. Custom built pistol, with many extra features such as Videki trigger, Ed Brown wide thumb safety, stainless steel thumb safety, extended safety, adjustable rear sight, etc. All hand-fitted parts.

NIB	EXC.	V.G.	GOOD	FAIR	POOR
3100	2400	1700	950	450	300

	NIB	EXC.	V.G.	GOOD	FAIR	POOR

Class A Limited

Custom-built pistol offered in a number of different calibers from .45 ACP to 9mm Luger. Fitted with 4.25" Commander length slide. Many special features. Price listed for basic pistol.

	2450	1750	1300	800	500	325

Kobra Custom .45

Introduced in 2002. Features a snakeskin treatment on fore-strap, mainspring housing and slide. Novak night sights and Hogue checkered wood grips standard. Many other custom features.

	1995	1400	1150	675	400	250

Kobra Carry .45

Same as above, with shorter grip frame and barrel.

	2195	1500	1200	700	425	275

Executive Target

1911 Executive Elite modified for target/range, with adjustable BoMar rear sight, ambidextrous safety. Weight 38 oz. Barrel 5". Chambered for .45 ACP. Magazine 7-rounds.

	2550	2000	1500	950	450	300

Executive Elite

Government model 5" barrel, weight 38 oz., chambered for .45 ACP, 7-round magazine. Fixed sights. Blue/blue, stainless/blue or all-stainless.

	2300	1800	1350	900	400	275

Executive Carry

4.25" commander model .45 ACP, with Ed Brown Bobtail. Weight 38 oz., 7-round magazine, fixed sights. Blue/blue, stainless/blue or all-stainless.

	2400	1900	1500	950	450	300

Special Forces

Blue/blue 1911 semi-automatic, with 5" barrel and fixed 3-dot night sights. Chambered for .45 ACP. Weight 38 oz., 7-round magazine. Cocobolo grips.

	2195	1600	1150	800	550	275

RIFLES

Savanna

Fitted with long action. Chambered for calibers from .257 Ackley to .338 Win. Magnum. Barrel lightweight 24" for standard calibers; 24" medium weight for magnum calibers. Talley scope mounts included. Fiberglass stock, recoil pad, steel trigger guard and floorplate standard.

	3800	3000	1995	1500	900	400

Damara

Similar to Savanna in lightweight configuration, with natural-finish stainless barrel.

	3200	2650	2000	1300	650	400

Varmint

Custom-made rifle, with short single-shot action, 26" medium weight barrel or 24" heavyweight barrel. H-S Precision stock. Available in calibers from .222 to 6.5/.284.

	3500	2800	2000	1300	750	400

Bushveld

Model based on a Dakota controlled feed action. Fitted with 24" medium or heavyweight barrel. Calibers from .330 Dakota to .458 Win. Magnum. Detachable box magazine. Monte Carlo fiberglass stock, recoil pad, steel trigger and floorplate standard, as is Talley scope mounts. Weight about 8.5 lbs.

	4400	3250	2000	1500	900	400

Express

Centerfire bolt-action rifle. Chambered for a wide variety of large Africa-class calibers. Dropped box magazine, fully controlled feed, fluted bolt, McMillan stock, iron sights.

	3600	2900	2350	1600	800	400

Marine Sniper

Duplicate of Vietnam-era McMillan sniper rifle. Controlled feed, fluted bolt, hinged floorplate, woodland camo stock, blackened stainless steel barrel and receiver. Offered in .308 and .300

	NIB	EXC.	V.G.	GOOD	FAIR	POOR

Win. Magnum calibers. Weight about 9.25 lbs.

	3700	2950	2350	1600	900	400

Light Tactical

Short-action rifle, with lightweight floorplate and trigger guard. Fitted with 21" medium-weight barrel. Black fiberglass stock, with aluminum bedding block. Available in calibers from .22-250 to .308.

	4100	2950	2000	1500	900	400

Tactical

Similar to above. Built on long action, with heavy weight 26" blued barrel. McMillan A-3 black tactical stock. Available in .308 and .300 Win. Magnum.

	3900	3350	2500	1600	950	400

Ozark

Rifle built on short action, with blind magazine. A 21" lightweight barrel fitted for standard calibers; medium weight 21" barrel for magnum calibers. Chambered for calibers from .22-250 to .308. Talley scope mounts included as is fiberglass stock, recoil pad, steel trigger guard and floorplate.

	3800	3000	1995	1500	900	400

Denali

Lighter-weight version of Ozark, with 22" super light weight barrel. Chambered for calibers .25-06 to .300 WSM. Weight about 6.75 lbs.

	3800	3000	1995	1500	900	400

Peacekeeper

Single-shot long-action rifle. Chambered for .30-378 Wby., .338-378 Wby. or .338 Lapua caliber. Fitted with heavy 26" barrel with muzzle-brake. Fiberglass tactical stock with recoil pad. Leupold Mark 4 scope mounts standard. Weight about 13 lbs.

	4500	3250	2100	1300	800	400

BROWN MANUFACTURING CO.

Newburyport, Massachusetts
Also See—Ballard Patent Arms

Southerner Derringer

.41-caliber spur-trigger single-shot pocket pistol, with pivoted 2.5" or 4" octagonal barrel marked "Southerner". Silver-plated or blued, with walnut grips. Manufactured by Merrimack Arms Co. from 1867 to 1869; Brown Manufacturing Co. from 1869 to 1873.

Brass Framed
2.5" barrel.

	—	—	875	600	325	125

Iron Frame
2.5" barrel (Brown Mfg. only).

	—	—	1025	800	500	200

Brass Frame 4" Barrel

	—	—	3700	2000	1500	500

Brown Mfg. Co./Merrill Patent Breechloading Rifles

Overall length 54.75"; barrel (bore) length 35"; caliber .577. Markings: On breechblock-bolt mechanism, "BROWN MFG. CO. NEWBURYPORT, MASS./PATANTED OCT. 17, 1871". Patent issued to George Merrill in 1871, permitted Brown Manufacturing Co. to alter probably up to 1,000 English P1853 rifle-muskets to single-shot breechloading system. Large bolt handle projecting upward at end of breech readily distinguishes these arms.

	—	—	2500	1250	800	300

BROWN PRECISION, INC.

Los Molinos, California

This company pioneered manufacture of fiberglass gunstocks in 1960s. Since 1975 has been making custom rifles on various Winchester, Remington and Ruger actions. Calibers available include virtually any popular chambering available in original action. Company offers many optional features, which will affect values. Values shown are for base models of current and recent production. Deduct $1,000 for rifles made on customer-supplied action.

	NIB	EXC.	V.G.	GOOD	FAIR	POOR

Custom High Country

NOTE: Add $900 for take down model.

	NIB	EXC.	V.G.	GOOD	FAIR	POOR
	4250	3500	2750	1800	1000	600

Pro Hunter

	NIB	EXC.	V.G.	GOOD	FAIR	POOR
	4800	4000	3000	2000	1400	1000

Pro Hunter Elite

NOTE: Add $900 for takedown model.

	NIB	EXC.	V.G.	GOOD	FAIR	POOR
	6000	5200	4200	3000	2000	1200

Pro Varminter/Light Varminter

	NIB	EXC.	V.G.	GOOD	FAIR	POOR
	3500	2750	2000	1200	800	500

Tactical Elite

	NIB	EXC.	V.G.	GOOD	FAIR	POOR
	4250	3500	2750	1800	1000	600

EARLY PRODUCTION

Open Country Varmint Rifle (disc. 1992)

	NIB	EXC.	V.G.	GOOD	FAIR	POOR
	1200	900	700	600	400	250

Law Enforcement Model (disc. 1992)

	NIB	EXC.	V.G.	GOOD	FAIR	POOR
	1200	900	700	600	400	250

Blaser Action Model (disc. 1989)

	NIB	EXC.	V.G.	GOOD	FAIR	POOR
	1600	1200	800	650	500	350

BROWNING ARMS CO.
Morgan, Utah

Early Semi-Automatic Pistols

In the period between 1900 and the development of Model 1935 Hi-Power Pistol, Browning had a number of semi-automatic pistols manufactured by Fabrique Nationale of Herstal, Belgium. They were Models 1900, 1903, 1905, 1910, 1922, Baby and 1935 Model Hi-Power. These firearms will be listed in more detail, with their respective values in Fabrique Nationale section of this text.

Hi-Power Modern Production

This version of FN Model 1935 is quite similar in appearance to original described in FN section. Chambered for 9mm Parabellum cartridge. Has 4.75" barrel. Models built before passage of crime bill have double column, 13-round detachable box magazine, blued, with checkered walnut grips. Has fixed sights and been produced in its present configuration since 1954. Add 10 percent premium for adjustable sights. Matte-nickel version offered between 1980 and 1984 was also available and would be worth approximately 15 percent additional. From 1994 to 2010 available in .40 S&W. **NOTE:** Add $60 for adjustable sights; 35 percent for internal extractor.

Spur Hammer Version

	NIB	EXC.	V.G.	GOOD	FAIR	POOR
	875	750	600	500	300	150

Round Hammer Version

	NIB	EXC.	V.G.	GOOD	FAIR	POOR
	1050	900	725	600	450	200

Hi-Power—.30 Luger

Version similar to standard Hi-Power, except chambered for .30 Luger cartridge. Approximately 1,500 imported between 1986 and 1989. Slide marked "FN". Browning-marked versions are quite rare and worth approximately 30 percent additional.

	NIB	EXC.	V.G.	GOOD	FAIR	POOR
	1000	900	725	450	300	200

Tangent Sight Model

Version similar to standard Hi-Power, with addition of adjustable rear sight calibrated to 500 meters. Approximately 7,000 imported between 1965 and 1978. **NOTE:** If grip frame is slotted to accept a detachable shoulder stock add approximately 20 percent to value; but be wary of fakes. Add an additional 10 percent for "T" series serial numbers.

	NIB	EXC.	V.G.	GOOD	FAIR	POOR
	1200	1050	900	650	450	200

Renaissance Hi-Power

Heavily engraved version, with matte-silver finish. Features synthetic-pearl grips and gold-plated trigger. Import ended in 1979.

Spur Hammer Model

	NIB	EXC.	V.G.	GOOD	FAIR	POOR
	2950	2600	2100	1750	1000	600

	NIB	EXC.	V.G.	GOOD	FAIR	POOR

Ring Hammer Model

NIB	EXC.	V.G.	GOOD	FAIR	POOR
3100	2850	2400	2000	1500	900

Adjustable Sight Spur Hammer Model

NIB	EXC.	V.G.	GOOD	FAIR	POOR
3000	2650	2100	1750	1000	600

Renaissance .25 Caliber

NIB	EXC.	V.G.	GOOD	FAIR	POOR
2400	2100	1700	1500	1000	600

Renaissance .380 Caliber

With pearl grips.

NIB	EXC.	V.G.	GOOD	FAIR	POOR
2700	2400	2000	1600	1000	600

Renaissance .380 Caliber (Model 1971)

With wood grips and adjustable sights.

NIB	EXC.	V.G.	GOOD	FAIR	POOR
2300	2000	1700	1500	900	500

Cased Renaissance Set

Features one example of fully engraved and silver-finished .25 ACP "Baby", .380 ACP pistol and Hi-Power. Set furnished in a fitted walnut case or black leatherette. Imported between 1955 and 1969. **NOTE:** Early coin finish sets add 30 percent.

NIB	EXC.	V.G.	GOOD	FAIR	POOR
9500	8000	6000	3000	—	—

Louis XVI Model

Heavily engraved Hi-Power pistol. Features leaf-and-scroll pattern, satin-finished, checkered walnut grips. Furnished in fitted walnut case. To realize its true potential, this pistol must be NIB. Imported between 1980 and 1984.

Diamond Grip Model

NIB	EXC.	V.G.	GOOD	FAIR	POOR
3150	2500	2000	800	400	300

Medallion Grip Model

NIB	EXC.	V.G.	GOOD	FAIR	POOR
1950	1750	1600	800	400	300

Hi-Power Centennial Model

Version similar to standard fixed-sight Hi-Power. Chrome-plated, with inscription "Browning Centennial/1878-1978" engraved on slide. Furnished with fitted case. There were 3,500 manufactured in 1978. As with all commemorative pistols, in order to realize its collector potential, this model should be NIB with all supplied material. Prices for pistols built in Belgium

NIB	EXC.	V.G.	GOOD	FAIR	POOR
1075	875	700	450	300	200

Hi-Power Capitan

New version of Hi-Power model. Fitted with tangent sights. Introduced in 1993. Furnished with walnut grips. Weighs about 32 oz. Assembled in Portugal.

NIB	EXC.	V.G.	GOOD	FAIR	POOR
900	750	600	400	250	200

Hi-Power Practical

First introduced in 1993. Furnished with blued slide and chrome frame. Has Pachmayr wraparound rubber grips, round-style serrated hammer and removable front sight. Available with adjustable sights. Weighs 36 oz. Assembled in Portugal.

NIB	EXC.	V.G.	GOOD	FAIR	POOR
845	625	500	300	200	175

Hi-Power Silver Chrome Model

Furnished in hard chrome. Fitted with wraparound Pachmayr rubber grips. Weighs 36 oz. Assembled in Portugal. Add 10 percent for models with all Belgian markings. Introduced in 1981. Dropped from Browning product line in 1984. Reintroduced in 1991.

NIB	EXC.	V.G.	GOOD	FAIR	POOR
750	575	500	425	225	200

Hi-Power .40 S&W

Introduced in 1994. New version of Hi-Power furnished with adjustable sights, molded grips, 5" barrel and 10-round magazine. Weighs about 35 oz. Discontinued 2010.

NIB	EXC.	V.G.	GOOD	FAIR	POOR
800	600	450	300	200	150

Hi-Power Mark III

Introduced in 1991. Matte blued or green finish, low-profile fixed sights and two-piece molded grips, with thumb rest. Weighs 32 oz.

NIB	EXC.	V.G.	GOOD	FAIR	POOR
900	700	500	300	200	175

	NIB	EXC.	V.G.	GOOD	FAIR	POOR

Hi-Power Gold Classic

A limited edition model introduced in 1984. A planned production of 500, but less than 350 were made. Elaborate engraving with five gold inlays, silver/gray finish, carved and checkered wood grips.

NIB	EXC.	V.G.	GOOD	FAIR	POOR
4500	3850	3000	2000	—	—

Hi-Power Classic

As above, except with less engraving and no gold inlays.

NIB	EXC.	V.G.	GOOD	FAIR	POOR
2200	1650	1100	800	600	400

Baby Browning

.25-caliber semi-automatic is same as FN Baby Model. Made by Fabrique Nationale in Belgium from 1931 until 1983. Many were imported into U.S., with Browning rollmark from 1954 to 1968. See "Baby" Model under Fabrique Nationale section for more details. Prices shown for Browning-marked model.

NIB	EXC.	V.G.	GOOD	FAIR	POOR
750	600	500	450	350	200

Browning Model 1955

Semi-automatic pistol same as FN Model 1910. From 1912 to 1983 in .32 ACP and .380 ACP. See Fabrique Nationale section for more information. Imported into U.S. by Browning from 1954 to 1968. Prices shown for Browning-marked pistols. **NOTE:** Add $200 for .32 ACP

NIB	EXC.	V.G.	GOOD	FAIR	POOR
800	700	550	450	350	200

Pro-9/Pro-40

9mm or .40 S&W double-action pistol fitted with 4" barrel. Stainless steel slide. Grips are composite, with interchangeable backstrap inserts. Magazine capacity 16 rounds 9mm; 14 rounds .40 S&W. Weight about 30 oz.

NIB	EXC.	V.G.	GOOD	FAIR	POOR
600	500	375	—	—	—

BDA-380

Double-action semi-automatic pistol. Chambered for .380 ACP cartridge. Features 3.75" barrel, with 14-round double-stack detachable magazine. Finish blued or nickel-plated, with smooth walnut grips. Manufactured in Italy by Beretta. Introduced in 1977. **NOTE:** Add 10 percent for nickel finish.

NIB	EXC.	V.G.	GOOD	FAIR	POOR
625	400	325	275	200	150

BDA

Double-action semi-automatic pistol. Manufactured between 1977 and 1980 for Browning by SIG-Sauer of Germany. Identical to SIG-Sauer Model 220. Chambered for 9mm Parabellum, .38 Super and .45 ACP cartridges. **NOTE:** .38 Super would be worth approximately 30 percent additional.

NIB	EXC.	V.G.	GOOD	FAIR	POOR
—	525	425	375	300	235

BDM Pistol

Double-action semi-automatic pistol. Chambered for 9mm cartridge. Fitted with selector switch that allows shooter to choose between single-/double-action model. Features 4.75" barrel, with adjustable rear sight. Magazine capacity 15 rounds. Weighs 31 oz. First introduced in 1991.

NIB	EXC.	V.G.	GOOD	FAIR	POOR
560	450	350	250	200	150

BDM Silver Chrome

Variation of BDM introduced in 1997. Features silver chrome finish on slide and frame, balance in contrasting matte blue finish.

NIB	EXC.	V.G.	GOOD	FAIR	POOR
560	450	350	250	200	150

BDM Practical

Introduced in 1997. Same as above, with silver chrome on frame only.

NIB	EXC.	V.G.	GOOD	FAIR	POOR
560	450	350	250	200	150

BPM-D

Introduced in 1997. New version of BDM (Browning Pistol Model Decocker) features double-action pistol, with first shot fired double-action and subsequent shots fired single-action. No manual safety. Decock lever also releases slide.

NIB	EXC.	V.G.	GOOD	FAIR	POOR
525	400	300	250	200	150

BRM-DAO

9mm pistol is a redesigned version of Model BDM. Initials stand for "Browning Revolver Model Double-Action-Only". Has finger support trigger guard for two-handed control. All other features same as BPM-D pistol. Weight about 31 oz.

NIB	EXC.	V.G.	GOOD	FAIR	POOR
525	400	300	250	200	150

	NIB	EXC.	V.G.	GOOD	FAIR	POOR

Nomad
Blowback-operated semi-automatic pistol. Chambered for .22 LR cartridge. Offered with 4.5" or 6.75" barrel. Has 10-round detachable magazine, with adjustable sights and all-steel construction. Finish blued, with black plastic grips. Manufactured between 1962 and 1974 by FN.

500	360	275	150	75	50

Challenger
More deluxe target pistol. Chambered for .22 LR cartridge. Offered with 4.5" or 6.75" barrel. Has 10-round magazine. Constructed entirely of steel. Adjustable sights. Finish blued, with gold-plated trigger. Checkered wraparound walnut grips. Manufactured between 1962 and 1974 by FN.

600	475	300	250	200	140

Renaissance Challenger
Version fully engraved, satin-nickel finish. Furnished with fleece-lined pouch.

2600	2300	1600	750	500	350

Gold Line Challenger
Version blued and has gold-inlaid line around outer edges of pistol. It was cased in fleece-lined pouch. Built in Belgium.

2600	2300	1600	750	500	350

Challenger II
Blowback-operated semi-automatic pistol. Chambered for .22 LR cartridge. Has 6.75" barrel, with alloy frame. Finish blued, with phenolic impregnated hardwood grips. Manufactured between 1976 and 1982 in Salt Lake City, Utah.

—	450	325	175	140	100

Challenger III
Version features 5.5" bull barrel, with adjustable sights. Manufactured between 1982 and 1984 in Salt Lake City, Utah. A 6.75" tapered-barrel version was available and known as Sporter.

—	400	300	150	125	90

Browning Collector's Association Edition
Fully engraved. 100 manufactured. Fitted with two-piece grip.

2950	2250	1650	1200	800	400

Medalist
High-grade semi-automatic target pistol. Chambered for .22 LR cartridge. Has 6.75" vent rib barrel, with adjustable target sights. Supplied with three barrel weights and dry-fire-practice mechanism. Finish blued, with target type thumbrest walnut grips. Manufactured between 1962 and 1974 by FN. Four additional high-grade versions of this pistol that differed in degree of ornamentation.

1350	1000	800	675	375	250

International Medalist
About 700 sold in U.S. from 1977 to 1980. Barrels were 5.875" long. Built in Belgium.

1200	900	600	450	300	150

Second Model International Medalist
Same as above, with flat-sided barrel, dull finish and adjustable palm rest. Built in Belgium.

875	725	450	300	200	150

Gold Line Medalist
Introduced in 1962. Discontinued in 1974. Estimated 400 guns produced.

3350	2750	2250	1000	750	500

Renaissance Medalist
Model built entirely in Belgium from 1970 to 1974, with one-piece grip.

3750	3000	2500	1200	900	700

BUCK MARK SERIES

Buck Mark
Blowback-operated semi-automatic pistol. Chambered for .22 LR cartridge. Has 5.5" bull barrel, with adjustable sights; 11-round detachable magazine; matte blued, with skip-line checkered synthetic grips. Introduced in 1985. Produced in U.S. **NOTE:** Add $25 for stainless steel version,

	NIB	EXC.	V.G.	GOOD	FAIR	POOR

introduced in 2005.

	350	250	175	135	110	85

Buck Mark Plus

Version similar to standard, with plain wood grips. Introduced in 1987. Produced in U.S.

	395	300	200	150	100	75

Nickel

Introduced in 1991. **NOTE:** Add $35 to above prices.

Buck Mark Varmint

Version has 9.75" bull barrel, with full-length ramp to allow scope mounting. No sights. Introduced in 1987. Produced in U.S.

	395	300	250	200	175	125

Buck Mark Silhouette

Version features 9.75" bull barrel, with adjustable sights. Introduced in 1987.

	450	350	285	220	185	140

Buck Mark 22 Micro

Version of Buck Mark 22. Fitted with 4" bull barrel. Available in blue, matte blue or nickel finish. Also in Micro Plus variation, with walnut grips. Weighs 32 oz. Introduced in 1992. **NOTE:** Add $25 for stainless steel version. Introduced in 2005.

	350	275	175	135	110	85

Plus

	350	275	175	150	125	90

Plus Nickel

Introduced in 1996. **NOTE:** Add $75 to above price.

Buck Mark 5.5

.22 caliber pistol has 5.5" heavy bull barrel fitted with target sights. Offered in three separate models:

Blued Target

Version has blued finish, contoured walnut grips, target sights. Weighs 35.5 oz. Introduced in 1990.

	475	395	250	150	100	100

Blued Target (2005)

Introduced in 2005. Features new target-style Cocabolo grips, full length scope mount. Hooded target sights. Weighs 35 oz.

	525	425	300	200	150	100

Gold Target

Same as above. Has gold anodized frame and top rib. Slide blue. Walnut grips. Introduced in 1991.

	550	425	300	200	150	125

Field

Same action and barrel as Target Model, with adjustable field sights. Sights are hoodless. Slide and barrel blued; rib and frame anodized blue. Grips are walnut. Introduced in 1991.

	450	345	225	150	100	100

Field (2005)

Features new target style grips and full-length scope rail. Weight about 35 oz.

	525	425	295	225	165	100

Buck Field Plus

.22-caliber pistol has 5.5" barrel, with Truglo/Marbles' front sight. Grips laminated rosewood. Barrel polished blue. Weight about 24 oz.

	425	325	225	200	150	75

Buck Mark Bullseye

Introduced in 1996. Designed for metallic silhouette competition. Fluted barrel 7.25" long. Adjustable trigger pull, adjustable rear sight, removable barrel are some of the features. Weight about 36 oz. Choice of laminated wood grips or rubber grips. **NOTE:** Add $90 for rosewood target grips; $150 for stainless.

	550	425	275	175	125	75

NIB	EXC.	V.G.	GOOD	FAIR	POOR

Buck Mark Unlimited Match

Fitted with 14" barrel and top rib. Front sight hood slightly rearward of muzzle for maximum sight radius of 15". All other features same as Silhouette model. Weighs 64 oz.

NIB	EXC.	V.G.	GOOD	FAIR	POOR
700	525	375	225	175	125

Buck Mark Challenge

Introduced in 1999. Features lightweight 5.5" barrel, with adjustable rear sight. Smaller grip diameter. Matte blue finish. Magazine capacity 10-rounds. Weight about 25 oz.

NIB	EXC.	V.G.	GOOD	FAIR	POOR
350	250	200	175	125	100

Buck Mark Camper

Fitted with heavy 5.5" barrel. Matte blue finish. Magazine capacity 10-rounds. Weight about 34 oz. Introduced in 1999. **NOTE:** Add $60 for stainless steel version.

NIB	EXC.	V.G.	GOOD	FAIR	POOR
300	225	150	125	100	75

Buck Mark Camper Cocobola UDX

Similar to above, with cocobolo Ultra DX grips and TruGlo front sight. Introduced 2008.

NIB	EXC.	V.G.	GOOD	FAIR	POOR
375	295	245	150	100	75

Buck Mark Camper Stainless UFX

This model features a tapered bull 5.5" barrel, overmolded FX ambidextrous grips, with checkered panels, Pro-Target adjustable sights and a gold-plated trigger.

NIB	EXC.	V.G.	GOOD	FAIR	POOR
330	285	215	175	125	100

Buck Mark Practical URX Fiber Optic

Matte grey finish, 5.5" tapered bull barrel, Ultragrip RX ambi-grips, adjustable ProTarget rear sight, with TruGlo fiber optic front sight. Introduced 2008.

NIB	EXC.	V.G.	GOOD	FAIR	POOR
350	300	20	150	100	75

Buck Mark Hunter

.22 LR pistol features 7.25" heavy round barrel, with Tru-glo/Marbles front sights, adjustable rear sight and integrated scope base. Grips Cocabolo target-style. Weight about 38 oz. Introduced in 2005.

NIB	EXC.	V.G.	GOOD	FAIR	POOR
375	275	225	175	125	100

Buck Mark Limited Edition 25th Anniversary

Limited to 1,000 pistols. Features 6.75" barrel, with matte blued finish and scrimshaw etched ivory grips. Pistol rug furnished as standard equipment.

NIB	EXC.	V.G.	GOOD	FAIR	POOR
495	350	300	225	150	125

Buck Mark Bullseye Target

Blowback single action .22 LR semi-automatic. Matte blued, heavy 7.25" round and fluted stainless bull barrel. Laminated rosewood grip, adjustable sights. Introduced 2006.

NIB	EXC.	V.G.	GOOD	FAIR	POOR
695	450	300	225	150	175

Buck Mark Bullseye Target URX

Blowback single-action semi-automatic in .22 LR. Matte blued, heavy 7.25" round and fluted bull barrel. Grooved, rubberized grip. Weight 39 oz. Adjustable sights. Introduced 2006.

NIB	EXC.	V.G.	GOOD	FAIR	POOR
475	400	325	225	150	175

Buck Mark Contour 5.5 URX

Blowback single-action .22 semi-automatic. Matte blued, contoured 5.5" barrel. Full-length scope base. Weight 36 oz. Adjustable sights. Multiple barrel lengths and options. Introduced 2006.

NIB	EXC.	V.G.	GOOD	FAIR	POOR
425	365	300	250	200	100

Buck Mark Contour Lite 5.5 URX

.22 LR blowback single-action semi-automatic. Matte blued, contoured 5.5" barrel. Full-length scope base. Weight 28 oz. Adjustable sights. Multiple barrel lengths and options. Introduced 2006.

NIB	EXC.	V.G.	GOOD	FAIR	POOR
475	395	325	275	225	150

Buck Mark FLD Plus Rosewood UDX

22 LR blowback single-action semi-automatic. "FLD" sculpted grip, with rosewood panels. Blued, contoured 5.5" barrel. Weight 34 oz. Adjustable rear sight, fiber optic front sight. Multiple barrel lengths and options. Introduced 2006.

NIB	EXC.	V.G.	GOOD	FAIR	POOR
475	395	325	275	225	150

NIB	EXC.	V.G.	GOOD	FAIR	POOR

Buck Mark Lite Splash 5.5 URX

Blowback single-action semi-automatic. Matte blued finish, gold splash anodizing. Chambered for .22 LR, 5.5" barrel. Rubberized ambidextrous grip. Adjustable sights; fiber optic front sight. Weight 28 oz. Available with 7.5" barrel. Introduced 2006.

450	375	325	275	225	150

Buck Mark Micro Standard Stainless URX

With 4" stainless barrel in .22 LR. Weighs 32 oz. Ambidextrous rubberized grip. Adjustable sights. Available in alloy steel. Introduced 2006.

395	350	325	275	225	150

Buck Mark Micro Bull

4" stainless bull barrel; .22 LR; weight 33 oz. Plastic grip panels. Adjustable sights. Introduced 2006.

350	275	225	175	125	100

Buck Mark Plus Stainless Black Laminated UDX

Similar to Buck Mark Standard. Stainless UDX, with ambidextrous grips. Introduced 2007.

495	375	300	225	150	125

Buck Mark Plus UDX

Similar to Buck Mark FLD Plus, with ambidextrous walnut grips. Introduced 2007.

425	350	300	225	150	125

Full Line Dealer Buck Mark Plus Rosewood UDX

Similar to Buck Mark Plus UDX, with ambidextrous rosewood grips. Available only to full-line and Medallion-level Browning dealers. Introduced 2007.

425	350	300	225	150	125

Buck Mark Plus Stainless UDX

.22 LR semi-automatic, with finger-grooved wood grips. Barrel 5.5". Weight 34 oz. Adjustable sights, fiber optic front sight. Available blued alloy steel. Introduced 2006.

450	350	300	225	150	125

Buck Mark Standard Stainless URX

.22 LR semi-automatic. Stainless bull barrel 5.5". Weight 34 oz. Ambidextrous rubberized grip. Adjustable sights. Available in alloy steel. Introduced 2006.

400	325	275	200	125	100

Browning 1911-22

Scaled-down version of 1911A1. Chambered in .22 LR. Aluminum slide, alloy frame, blowback operated, with single-action trigger. Controls are standard 1911 including thumb and grip safeties. Other features include 10-round magazine, brown composite grips, matte blue finish. Weight 16 oz. Barrel length 4.25". Compact model has 3.625" barrel. Introduced in 2011. **NOTE:** Add $400 for Anniversary Edition.

500	450	400	350	300	200

Browning 1911-22 A1 Polymer Frame w/Rail

Polymer frame variation with 4.25" or 3.625" barrel. Extended grip safety, stipled black laminate grip, accessory rail, skelton trigger and hammer. Weight from 13 to 14 oz. Other features are similar to standard 1911-22.

575	500	450	400	300	200

Browning 1911-22 Polymer Desert Tan

This polymer variation has a two-tone Desert Tan/Black finish. Also offered with bright pink composite grips. Other features are similar to standard 1911-22.

500	425	385	350	325	180

SHOTGUNS

SUPERPOSED SHOTGUNS

Series of over/under double-barrel shotguns. Chambered for 12-, 20-, 28-gauge and .410 bore. Offered with vent rib barrels from 26.5" to 32" in length. Features various choke combinations. Shotgun built on boxlock action. Features double-/single-selective triggers. Automatic ejectors. A number of versions offered that differ in amount of ornamentation and quality of materials and workmanship utilized in manufacture. Values for small-bore models are generally higher. Series introduced in 1930. Manufactured by Fabrique Nationale in Belgium. Factory restored guns or

NIB	EXC.	V.G.	GOOD	FAIR	POOR

very fine non-factory restorations Superposed guns will bring close to factory original prices. **NOTE:** Extra factory installed barrels add $1000 to $2500 depending on grade of gun.

PRE-WAR SUPERPOSED, 1930-1940

Browning Superposed shotgun prices are divided into three different categories. First category for pre-war guns built from 1930 to 1940. These pre-war Superposed guns manufactured in 12-gauge only from serial number 1 to around 17,000. These shotguns were offered in four different grades: Grade I, Pigeon, Diana and Midas. **NOTE:** Add 15 percent for twin-single triggers; 10 percent for vent rib. Deduct 25 percent for recoil pads or shorter than standard stocks.

Grade I

NIB	EXC.	V.G.	GOOD	FAIR	POOR
—	2500	1950	1200	450	300

Pigeon

NIB	EXC.	V.G.	GOOD	FAIR	POOR
—	5500	4200	3000	1500	800

Diana

NIB	EXC.	V.G.	GOOD	FAIR	POOR
—	7500	6000	4750	2000	900

Midas

NIB	EXC.	V.G.	GOOD	FAIR	POOR
—	12500	9500	5000	2500	1000

SUPERPOSED FROM 1947-1959

Second category of Superposed produced and sold from 1947 to 1959. Built in 12- and 20-gauge; as well as 28-gauge and .410 bore which were introduced in 1959. These shotguns were graded using a Roman numeral system instead of names. They are: Grade I, Grade II, Grade III, Grade IV, Grade V and Grade VI. Values listed are for 12-gauge. Add premium or deductions as listed. Number of 28-gauge and .410 bore guns sold in late 1959 number less than 100; Grade VI sold in North America unknown, but most likely very small. This is a very rare grade. Proceed with caution. **NOTE:** Add 60 percent for 20-gauge; 100 percent for 28-gauge and .410 (1959 only). Deduct 40 percent for trap; 10 percent for standard weight 12-gauge Grade I.

Grade I

NIB	EXC.	V.G.	GOOD	FAIR	POOR
3700	2500	1400	900	300	250

Grade II

NIB	EXC.	V.G.	GOOD	FAIR	POOR
6500	4500	2500	1200	600	375

Grade III

NIB	EXC.	V.G.	GOOD	FAIR	POOR
7000	6000	3900	2200	750	450

Grade IV

NIB	EXC.	V.G.	GOOD	FAIR	POOR
10000	8500	4500	2400	1200	550

Grade V

NIB	EXC.	V.G.	GOOD	FAIR	POOR
10000	7500	4000	2400	1200	650

Grade VI

NIB	EXC.	V.G.	GOOD	FAIR	POOR
17000	15000	8500	4000	2200	850

SUPERPOSED FROM 1960-1976

Browning Superposed shotguns built from 1960 to 1976 revert back to older grade names. They are Grade I, Pigeon, Pointer, Diana and Midas. These shotguns were available in 12-, 20-, 28-gauge and .410 bore. This last production period is a little more complicated due to manufacturing changes that some collectors consider important, such as round knobs and long tangs.

Prices listed reflect Superposed field guns produced from 1960 to 1965 in round pistol-grip knob, with long trigger guard tang in 12-gauge. All other variations during this period one should consider:

Salt wood damage deduct a minimum of 60 percent; round knob short tang (circa 1966-1969) deduct 50 percent; flat knob short tang (circa 1969-1971) deduct 50 percent; flat knob long tang (circa 1971-1976) deduct 25 percent; New Style Skeet and Lightning Trap (recoil pad, flat knob, full beavertail forearm) with long trigger guard tang (1971-1976) deduct 35 percent; with short trigger guard tang deduct 40 percent; Broadway rib deduct an additional 10 percent; skeet chokes on field guns deduct 5 percent; recoil pads on 2.75" chambered field guns deduct 20 percent; Master engraver signed guns (Funken, Watrin, Vrancken) add 10 percent; shorter than standard stock length deduct 25 percent; barrel lengths of 32" add 10 percent; 20-gauge add 50 percent; 28-gauge add 100 percent; .410 bore add 60 percent. **NOTE:** These premiums could double for higher grade models in NIB or Excellent condition.

Grade I Standard Weight

NIB	EXC.	V.G.	GOOD	FAIR	POOR
3000	2000	1500	700	500	250

Grade I Lightweight

NIB	EXC.	V.G.	GOOD	FAIR	POOR
3200	2200	1600	800	600	300

	NIB	EXC.	V.G.	GOOD	FAIR	POOR

Pigeon Grade

	6500	5500	3800	2000	1000	600

Pointer Grade—(Rare)

	10500	8050	5600	3000	2000	1000

Diana Grade

	11000	8250	5700	3000	2000	1000

Midas Grade

FN also built Exhibition Grades that were sold in this country under Browning name. Collectors consider a true Exhibition Grade as one not having a "C" prefix in serial number. These particular guns are considered quite desirable and should be appraised on an individual basis. Superposed in this category can range in price from $10,000 to $20,000 depending on gauge, engraving coverage and options.

Second type of Exhibition Grade known as "C" type that was first sold in U.S. from about 1973 to 1977 and is so called because of "C" prefix in serial number. There were about 225 of these guns sold in U.S. They came in quite a few grades and some were specially ordered. Although lower grades are not considered by some to be true exhibitions (pre-C series) highest "C" series grades are a match to the best of older exhibitions. In 2000, an all option Superlight 2 barrel set with sideplates engraved by Vranken sold for $22,000. Generally depending on gun, prices will range between $6,000 and $25,000. These "C" grade guns should also be appraised individually.

	15000	12000	9000	7000	5000	4000

Superposed Superlight

First introduced in 1967 in 12-gauge; 1969 in 20-gauge. Special order 28-gauge and .410 bore are also seen. Offered in 26.5" barrel lengths, with 27.5" barrels in 12-gauge and 28" barrels in smaller bores available on special order. Features rounded frame and straight-grip stock, with tapered solid or vent rib barrels. Regular production on Superlight ended in 1976 for grades listed. Production did continue for Superlight in P series beginning in 1977. **NOTE:** Add 50 percent premium for 20-gauge; 100 percent premium for 28-gauge; 30 percent premium for .410 bore.

Grade I

	4500	3750	1800	700	500	250

Pigeon Grade

	7000	5900	4000	2500	1000	800

Pointer Grade—(Rare)

	11000	9000	6000	3500	2000	1000

Diana Grade

	11000	8500	6500	3500	2000	1000

Midas Grade

	15500	12000	9000	7000	5000	4000

SUPERPOSED PRESENTATION GRADE SERIES

Superposed shotguns listed were manufactured between 1977 and 1984 by FN in Belgium. Models listed differ in amount of ornamentation and quality of materials and workmanship utilized in construction. This series was also available in a Superlight configuration.

NOTE: Due to the tremendous variation of P-Series guns, prices here reflect Superlight configuration. An all option Superlight with checkered butt, oil finish and three-piece fore-end will bring 25-30 percent more. For all other variations one should consider:

Trap guns deduct 35 percent; new style skeet deduct 30 percent; skeet choked field guns deduct 5 percent; recoil pads on field guns deduct 30 percent; flat knob long tang hunting guns with no options deduct 35 percent; flat knob long tang hunting guns with all options add 25 percent; guns signed by J. Baerten add 5 percent; P-4V guns with no gold deduct 20 percent; hand filed vent rib add 5 percent; Presentation Grade guns with extra sets of barrels add approximately $1,500 to $2,500 depending on gauge and combination.

P1, P2, and P3 grades add premium listed:
   20-gauge guns—55 percent.
   28-gauge guns—100 percent.
   .410 bore—30 percent.
P4 grade add premium listed:
   20-gauge guns—55 percent.
   28-gauge guns—100 percent.
   .410 bore—40 percent.

Presentation 1 (without gold inlays)

	4500	3700	1900	1000	600	500

	NIB	EXC.	V.G.	GOOD	FAIR	POOR

Presentation 1 Gold-inlaid

	7500	6000	3250	1400	700	500

Presentation 2 (without gold inlays)

	6250	5250	3700	1800	1000	600

Presentation 2 Gold-inlaid

	10000	8500	4950	2500	1500	1000

Presentation 3 Gold-inlaid

NOTE: Early hand-engraved P3 models (approximately 25 produced) add 40 percent. These early guns are rare, proceed with caution.

	12000	9500	5500	4000	2000	1300

Presentation 4 Gold-inlaid

NOTE: P4 Grade guns with no gold, deduct approximately 20 percent.

	17500	15000	9800	6750	5000	3500

SUPERPOSED WATERFOWL LIMITED EDITION SERIES

Model issued in three different versions: Mallard, Pintail and Black Duck. Each edition was limited to 500 guns, all in 12-gauge.

1981 Mallard Issue

	9500	7000	4900	3300	1900	1100

1982 Pintail Issue

	9500	7000	4900	3300	1900	1100

1983 Black Duck Issue

	10000	7000	4900	3300	1900	1100

Bicentennial Model

Produced in 1976 to commemorate 200 year anniversary of America. Total of 53 guns built in this special edition. All of these Superposed were 12-gauge, with 28" barrels. Each was numbered for one of fifty states plus District of Columbia. Two additional guns were built for Smithsonian Institution and Liege Firearms Museum. All were fitted with side plates, with gold inlays. To reflect their true value, guns must be in unfired condition, in their original case and with all papers.

	15000	9000	5950	2750	1500	1000

FN/BROWNING SUPERPOSED

Number of FN Browning Superposed B-25 shotguns were imported into this country by Browning in various grades. These Superposed were intended originally for FN's European market. There are a large number of variations and grades. It is strongly suggested that an expert appraisal be sought prior to sale. These guns are marked with both Browning and FN barrel address.

Classic

Produced about 2,500 guns in 1986. Offered in 20-gauge, with 26" barrels. Silver gray receiver, with engraving.

	4000	3200	2650	2000	800	300

Gold Classic

Similar to above. More finely finished. Engraved with gold inlays. About 350 built in 1986.

	9000	7500	5000	2450	1750	400

Custom Shop B25 & B125 Superposed

These special order Superposed models were available from the Browning Custom Shop from mid 1980s through 1990s for Model B25 and until 2004 for B125. Several grades were offered with different levels of engraving and wood quality, all in 12- or 20-gauge. B125 models were assembled in Belgium, with components manufactured in other countries to hold down costs. B25s were made entirely in Belgium. Values shown here are for these discontinued models. For information on current Superposed high-grade models, contact the Browning Custom Shop at 801-876-2711 or on line at www.browning.com.

B-125 Hunting or Sporting Clays Model

A-Style Engraving

	3800	3200	2700	2000	1500	700

B-Style Engraving

	4100	3500	3000	2450	1800	800

	NIB	EXC.	V.G.	GOOD	FAIR	POOR

B125 Hunting or Sporting Clays Model

C-Style Engraving

	NIB	EXC.	V.G.	GOOD	FAIR	POOR
	4500	3800	3300	2750	2000	900

B-125 Trap Model

C-Style Engraving

	NIB	EXC.	V.G.	GOOD	FAIR	POOR
	4800	4000	3500	2950	2000	900

B-25

Grade 1

	NIB	EXC.	V.G.	GOOD	FAIR	POOR
	10000	8000	6200	4500	2500	—

FN/BROWNING SUPRPOSED

Pigeon Grade

	NIB	EXC.	V.G.	GOOD	FAIR	POOR
	14000	11800	8500	6700	2500	—

FN/BROWNING SUPERPOSED

Pointer Grade

	NIB	EXC.	V.G.	GOOD	FAIR	POOR
	15500	12000	9800	7500	3000	—

Diana Grade

	NIB	EXC.	V.G.	GOOD	FAIR	POOR
	16500	13000	10800	8400	3500	—

Midas Grade

	NIB	EXC.	V.G.	GOOD	FAIR	POOR
	17500	13800	11300	9000	3500	—

Custom Shop BSL

Side-by-side equipped with Browning sidelock barrel, Holland & Holland-type locks, with double trigger and auto ejectors. Assembled and finished by Labeau-Courally. Offered in 12- and 20-gauge. Engraved grayed or case colored receiver. Introduced into Browning product line in 2001.

Case Colored Receiver (BSL Grade LC1)

	NIB	EXC.	V.G.	GOOD	FAIR	POOR
	15000	12500	9000	—	—	—

Engraved Gray Receiver (BSL Grade LC2)

	NIB	EXC.	V.G.	GOOD	FAIR	POOR
	18000	16000	12500	—	—	—

Liege

Over/under shotgun chambered for 12-gauge. Offered with 26.5", 28" or 30" vent rib barrels and various choke combinations. Features boxlock action, with non-selective single trigger and automatic ejectors. Finish blued, with checkered walnut stock. Approximately 10,000 manufactured between 1973 and 1975. U.S. versions marked Browning Arms Company on barrel.

	NIB	EXC.	V.G.	GOOD	FAIR	POOR
	1500	850	650	450	300	200

B27

Improved version of Liege. Was imported into U.S., some without Browning Arms Company markings and only FN barrel address. Others may have both barrel addresses. Offered in a number of variations that differed in amount of ornamentation and quality of materials and workmanship utilized. Features same action as Liege over/under gun.

Standard

	NIB	EXC.	V.G.	GOOD	FAIR	POOR
	1200	950	650	350	250	200

Deluxe

	NIB	EXC.	V.G.	GOOD	FAIR	POOR
	1600	1200	850	500	350	250

Deluxe Trap

	NIB	EXC.	V.G.	GOOD	FAIR	POOR
	1600	1200	850	450	300	250

Deluxe Skeet

	NIB	EXC.	V.G.	GOOD	FAIR	POOR
	1600	1200	850	450	300	250

Grand Deluxe

	NIB	EXC.	V.G.	GOOD	FAIR	POOR
	2000	1500	1000	650	500	400

City of Liege Commemorative
250 manufactured.

	NIB	EXC.	V.G.	GOOD	FAIR	POOR
	2500	1650	1000	600	450	300

	NIB	EXC.	V.G.	GOOD	FAIR	POOR

ST-100

Over/under trap gun. Features separated barrels, with adjustable point of impact. Chambered for 12-gauge. Has 30" or 32" barrel, with full choke and floating ventilated rib. Features single trigger and automatic ejectors. Finish blued, with checkered walnut stock. Manufactured by FN between 1979 and 1981.

3750	2700	1800	1000	700	400

CITORI SERIES

Over/under double-barrel shotgun chambered for all gauges. Offered with vent rib barrels of 26" through 30" in length. Has boxlock action, with single-selective trigger and automatic ejectors. Various grades differ in amount of ornamentation and quality of materials and workmanship utilized in construction. Series is manufactured in Japan by B.C. Miroku. Introduced in 1973. **NOTE:** All Citori models, add 15-20 percent premium for 28-gauge and .410; 30 percent for 16-gauge.

Grade I

1200	900	725	550	425	300

Upland Special—Grade I

Offered with straight-grip stock and 24" rib barrels. Available in 12- or 20-gauge. Weighs 6 lbs. 11 oz. in 12-gauge; 6 lbs. in 20-gauge. Introduced in 1984.

1350	950	700	600	400	300

Grade II—1978 to 1983

—	1500	1300	1000	650	400

Grade II—Choke Tubes

1600	1400	1000	775	650	400

Grade V—1978 to 1984

2900	2300	1600	950	750	400

Grade V with sideplates—1981 to 1984

2950	2500	2100	1500	800	400

Grade VI—Choke Tubes

1950	1650	1200	1000	750	500

Citori Hunter

Features full pistol-grip stock, with beavertail forearm and high-gloss walnut. Chambered for 12-gauge with 2.75", 3" or 3.5" chambers. Choice of 26", 28" or 30" barrels. The 20-gauge choice of 26" or 28" barrels. Weight: 12-gauge from 7 lbs. 13 oz. to 8 lbs. 9 oz. depending on barrel length; 20-gauge about 6.75 lbs. **NOTE:** Add $75 for 3.5" models.

1500	1100	850	650	550	450

Citori Sporting Hunter

Same features as Hunter, with exception of stock configuration. Sporting Hunter has Sporting model buttstock and Superposed-style forearm. Fitted with contoured sporting recoil pad. Introduced in 1998. **NOTE:** Add $75 for 3.5" models.

1550	1400	1050	750	550	450

Citori Satin Hunter

Chambered for 12-gauge shells. Hunting-style stock. Choice of 26" or 28" barrels. Special satin wood finish, with matte black receiver and barrels. Offered in Grade I only. Weight about 8 lbs. Introduced in 1999. **NOTE:** Add $100 for 3.5" chamber.

1250	1000	825	700	500	375

Citori Satin Hunter Micro Midas

Budget-priced Citori, with same features and handling qualities that have made other Citoris so popular. Available in 12- or 20-gauge, with 24" or 26" barrels. Satin-finished walnut stock, with 13" length of pull. Vector-Pro lengthened forcing cones. Weight: 6 lbs. 3 oz. to 6 lbs. 10 oz. New in 2011.

1300	1050	900	800	500	300

Citori Lightning

Lightweight version that features a slimmer profile. Has checkered round-knob pistol-grip stock. Offered in all gauges. Same barrel lengths as standard Citori. Features screw-in choke tubes known as Invectors. Introduced in 1988. Offered in 12-, 16-, 20-, 28-gauge and .410 bore. Weights are 6.5 lbs. to 8 lbs. depending on gauge and barrel length. Models differ in amount of ornamentation and quality of materials and workmanship utilized. **NOTE:** Add $300 for 28-gauge and .410 bore models; $150 for 16-gauge.

Grade I

1650	1200	900	600	450	375

	NIB	EXC.	V.G.	GOOD	FAIR	POOR
Grade III	2450	1900	1400	975	600	450
Grade IV	2610	1950	1450	1025	650	500
Grade VI	3800	3000	2250	1500	700	550
Grade VII	4800	4000	3000	2300	1900	1500

Citori Lightning Feather

Introduced in 1999. Features a lightweight alloy receiver. Offered in 12-gauge Grade I only, with choice of 26" or 28" barrels. Weight with 28" barrels about 7 lbs. 11 oz. In 2000, this model offered in 20-gauge, with 26" or 28" barrels and 3" chambers. Weight of 20-gauge about 6.5 lbs.

1870	1400	975	595	400	300

Citori Lightning Feather Combo

Features 20- and 28-gauge barrel, both 27" long. The 20-gauge with 3" chambers; 28-gauge with 2.75" chambers. Pistol-grip stock. Weight about 6.25 lbs. Supplied with Browning luggage case. Introduced in 2000.

3200	2400	2000	1500	1000	500

Citori Feather XS

Offered in 12-, 20-, 28-gauge and .410 bore. Has lightweight alloy receiver. Fitted with walnut stock, pistol-grip, black recoil pad and schnabel forearm. Triple trigger system. Hi-Viz Comp sight system standard. Weight about 7 lbs. 12-gauge; 6.5 lbs. 20-gauge; 6 lbs. 28-gauge; 6 lbs. .410 bore. Introduced in 2000.

2000	1500	1200	900	600	400

Citori Superlight Feather

Chambered for 12- or 20-gauge, with straight-grip stock and schnabel forearm. Has alloy receiver. Checkered walnut stock. Offered with 26" barrels. Weight about 6 lbs. Introduced in 2002.

1940	1450	1100	800	550	350

Citori Super Lightning Grade I

Introduced in 2005. This 12- or 20-gauge features blued receiver, with gold line border. Checkered satin finished select walnut stock, with pistol-grip and schnabel forearm. Barrels are 26" or 28", with choke tubes. Recoil pad on 12-gauge. Weight about 8 lbs. 12-gauge; 6.75 lbs. 20-gauge.

1865	1400	1050	750	500	300

Citori Classic Lightning Grade I

Offered in 12- or 20-gauge, with choice of 26" or 28" vent rib barrels and choke tubes. Receiver scroll engraved on silver nitride finish. Checkered select walnut stock, with oil finish. Forearm is Lightning style. Recoil pad on 12-gauge. Weight about 8 lbs. 12-gauge; 6.75 lbs. 20-gauge. Introduced in 2005.

1890	1425	1075	775	525	325

Citori Classic Lightning Feather Grade I

Introduced in 2005. Features high relief engraved alloy receiver. Chambered for 12- or 20-gauge. Fitted with 26" or 28" vent rib barrels and choke tubes. Checkered select stock, with schnabel forearm. Recoil pad on 12-gauge. Weight about 7 lbs. 12-gauge; 6.25 lbs. 20-gauge.

1950	1450	1100	775	525	325

Citori 525 Sporting

Introduced in 2002. Chambered for 12- or 20-gauge. Fitted with choice of 28" or 30" vent rib ported barrels. Stock redesigned with Euro checkering pattern and more pronounced palm swell. Weight about 8 lbs. 12-gauge; 7 lbs. 20-gauge. In 2003 offered in both 28-gauge and .410 bore. **NOTE:** Add $275 for adjustable comb.

2320	1750	1250	800	550	350

Citori 525 Field

As above, with choice of 26" or 28" barrels. Barrels are unported. Ventilated recoil pad. Introduced in 2002. In 2003 offered in both 28-gauge and .410 bore.

1980	1475	950	700	500	325

	NIB	EXC.	V.G.	GOOD	FAIR	POOR

Citori 525 Golden Clays Sporting

Same features as 525 Sporting, with oil-finished high stock, engraved receiver and gold inlays. In 2003 offered in both 28-gauge and .410 bore.

	NIB	EXC.	V.G.	GOOD	FAIR	POOR
	4450	3250	2600	1950	1200	550

Citori 525 Feather

Lightweight Citori features alloy receiver, with steel breech face and high-relief engraving. Stock and schnabel fore-end Grade II/III oil finished walnut. Available in 12-, 20-, 28-gauge and .410 bore, with 26" or 28" barrels. All but 28-gauge have 3" chambers. Weight about 6.9 lbs. 12-gauge; 5.5 to 5.7 lbs. in others. Three choke tubes.

	NIB	EXC.	V.G.	GOOD	FAIR	POOR
	2300	1750	1250	800	550	350

Citori 625 Sporting

Introduced in 2008. This 2.75" 12-gauge has 28", 30" or 32" ported barrels. Browning's Vector Pro lengthened forcing cones system. Stock and schnabel fore-end Grade III/IV walnut. Steel receiver has silver nitride finish, with high-relief engraving and gold embellishment. Five choke tubes included. Weight 7.9 to 8.2 lbs. Add 5 percent for adjustable comb stock.

	NIB	EXC.	V.G.	GOOD	FAIR	POOR
	3500	2700	1975	1200	850	550

Citori 625 Sporting Left-Hand

As above, but configured for left-hand shooters.

	NIB	EXC.	V.G.	GOOD	FAIR	POOR
	3500	2700	1975	1200	850	550

Citori 625 Field

26" or 28" barrels, gloss oil finish Grade II/III walnut stock and schnabel fore-end. Steel receiver, with silver nitride finish and high-relief engraving. Three choke tubes. Chambered for 12-, 20-, 28-gauge and .410. Weight: 7 lbs. 14 oz. to 6 lbs. 12 oz.

	NIB	EXC.	V.G.	GOOD	FAIR	POOR
	2400	1900	1400	975	600	450

Citori Model 725

Over/under 12-gauge only, with 26" or 28" barrels, Invector DS choke tubes. New action design has lower profile than other Citori models. Single selective mechanical trigger, automatic ejectors, checkered Grade II/III walnut stock, with gloss finish and recoil pad. Silver nitride finish, with high relief engraving. Introduced in 2012. Higher grade models available with more engraving and higher grade wood.

	NIB	EXC.	V.G.	GOOD	FAIR	POOR
	2100	1700	1250	1000	—	—

Grade III

	NIB	EXC.	V.G.	GOOD	FAIR	POOR
	3300	2750	—	—	—	—

Grade V

	NIB	EXC.	V.G.	GOOD	FAIR	POOR
	5200	4400	—	—	—	—

Citori Esprit

Introduced in 2002. Features removable decorative sideplates, schnabel forearm and high-grade walnut stock. Offered in 12-gauge only, with 28" vent rib barrels. Weight about 8.25 lbs.

	NIB	EXC.	V.G.	GOOD	FAIR	POOR
	2450	1975	1400	975	600	450

Citori Sporting Clays

Specifically designed for sporting clay shooting. Offered in 12-gauge only. Each model is back-bored, ported and fitted with Invector-Plus choke tubes. Barrels are chrome-plated. Receiver blued, with gold inscription. Pigeon Grade has gold detailing and high grade gloss walnut stock. Signature Grade features red and black print on stock, with gold decals. Trigger is adjustable to three length of pull positions. Comes with three interchangeable trigger shoes. Each model fitted with rubber recoil pad.

	NIB	EXC.	V.G.	GOOD	FAIR	POOR
	2450	1975	1400	975	600	450

Citori Lightning Sporting

Features rounded pistol-grip and Lightning forearm, with choice of high or low vent rib. Chambered for 3" shells. Offered in 28" or 30" barrels. Weighs about 8.5 lbs. Introduced in 1989.

	NIB	EXC.	V.G.	GOOD	FAIR	POOR
	1400	1000	800	600	450	300

Pigeon Grade

	NIB	EXC.	V.G.	GOOD	FAIR	POOR
	1450	1100	900	650	450	300

Golden Clays

First introduced in 1994.

	NIB	EXC.	V.G.	GOOD	FAIR	POOR
	2800	2250	1650	900	450	300

	NIB	EXC.	V.G.	GOOD	FAIR	POOR

Citori Privilege

High-grade model features game scene engraved sideplates, unique checkering pattern oil finish high-grade walnut stock, with pistol-grip. Offered in 12-gauge only. Choice of 26" or 28" barrels. Weight about 8 lbs. Introduced in 2000. In 2001 a 20-gauge version, with 26" or 28" barrels was introduced. Discontinued in 2003.

| 4600 | 4000 | 3000 | 2500 | 1500 | 1000 |

Citori XS Sporting Clays

Introduced in 1999. Features silver nitride receiver, gold accents and European-style stock, with schnabel fore-end. Available in 12- or 20-gauge. Choice of 28", 30" or 32" barrels. Weight varies: 8 lbs. 12-gauge to 7 lbs. 20-gauge.

| 2600 | 2050 | 1450 | 1000 | 625 | 475 |

Citori Ultra XS Skeet

Model offered in 12=gauge only. Choice of 28" or 30" ported barrels. Chambered for 2.75" shells. Semi-beavertail forearm. Triple trigger system standard. Adjustable comb optional. Walnut stock, with pistol-grip. Black recoil pad. Weight about 7.75 lbs. Introduced in 2000. In 2001 a 20-gauge version with 28" or 30" barrels was introduced. **NOTE:** Add $275 for adjustable comb.

| 2535 | 1900 | 1375 | 950 | 600 | 450 |

Citori XS Special

12-gauge 2.75" chamber gun. Choice of 30" or 32" vent rib barrels, porting and extended choke tubes. Checkered walnut stock, with adjustable comb and pistol-grip. Semi-beavertail forearm. Silver engraved receiver. Weight about 8.7 lbs.

| 2825 | 2100 | 1550 | 1100 | 675 | 475 |

Citori Plus

Features adjustable point of impact from 3" to 12" above point of aim. Receiver on Grade I blued, with scroll engraving. Walnut stock is adjustable. Forearm is a modified beavertail style. Available in 30" or 32" barrels that are backbored and ported. Non-ported barrels are optional. Weighs about 9 lbs. 6 oz. Introduced in 1989.

Grade I

| 1300 | 1075 | 750 | 500 | 400 | 300 |

Pigeon Grade

| 1850 | 1500 | 950 | 700 | 500 | 300 |

Signature Grade

| 1750 | 1450 | 950 | 700 | 500 | 300 |

Golden Clays

| 2850 | 2295 | 1500 | 900 | 450 | 300 |

Citori Trap Combination Set

Version offered in Grade I only. Features 34" single barrel and 32" set of over/under barrels. Furnished in fitted case. Has been discontinued.

| — | 1950 | 1350 | 950 | 800 | 700 |

GTI Model

Features 13mm wide rib ventilated side ribs, pistol-grip stock, semi-beavertail forearm. Offered in 28" or 30" barrel. Weighs about 8 lbs. Not offered in Pigeon Grade. Introduced in 1989.

Grade I

| 1200 | 975 | 750 | 600 | 450 | 300 |

Signature Grade

| 1200 | 975 | 750 | 600 | 450 | 300 |

Golden Clays

| 2575 | 1975 | 1250 | 900 | 450 | 300 |

Ultra Sporter - (Sporting Clays)

Introduced in 1995. Replaces GTI model. Features 10mm to 13mm tapered rib. Offered with blued or gray receiver. Walnut stock, with pistol-grip and semi-beavertail forearm. Fitted with adjustable comb and length of pull. Offered in 12-gauge only, with 28" or 30" barrels. Average weight 8 lbs. **NOTE:** Ultra Sporters with adjustable comb add $200 to NIB price.

| 1550 | 1200 | 800 | 550 | 400 | 300 |

Golden Clays

| 2900 | 2300 | 1600 | 1100 | 750 | 400 |

	NIB	EXC.	V.G.	GOOD	FAIR	POOR

Citori Superlight

Lighter-weight version of Citori. Chambered for all gauges. Offered with same features as Lightning Series. Grades differ in amount of ornamentation, quality of materials and workmanship utilized. Series introduced in 1983.

Citori Superlight Feather

Introduced in 1999. Features straight-grip stock, with schnabel fore-end. Lightweight alloy receiver. Offered in 12-gauge Grade I only. Choice of 26" or 28" barrels. Weight with 28" barrels about 6 lbs. 6 oz.

1700	1250	895	600	475	350

Micro Lightning

Offered in 20-gauge only. Has reduced dimensions for smaller shooters. Available with 24" vent rib barrels. Weighs 6 lbs. 3 oz. Introduced in 1991.

1100	895	700	600	400	300

Gran Lightning

Essentially a Grade I Lightning, with high grade select walnut stock and satin finish. Receiver and barrels blued. Offered in 12- and 20-gauge. Choice of 26" or 28" vent rib barrels. Choke tubes standard. Weighs about 8 lbs. 12-gauge; 6 lbs. 11 oz. 20-gauge. Introduced in 1990. In 2004, 28-gauge and .410 bore were added.

2550	1900	1300	975	650	350

Grade I

1300	975	750	500	425	350

Grade III

1625	1375	1050	750	550	450

Grade V

Discontinued 1984.

—	1800	1350	950	750	500

Grade VI

2000	1750	1300	1000	800	500

Citori White Lightning

Introduced in 1998. Features silver nitride scroll engraved receiver. Offered in 3" 12- and 20-gauge. Choice of 26" or 28" barrels. In 2004 available in 28-gauge and .410 bore. Weight about 8 lbs. 12-gauge; 6.8 lbs. 20-gauge. Invector-Plus chokes standard. Lightning-style stock. **NOTE:** Add $75 for 28-gauge and .410 models.

1500	1200	950	700	600	375

Citori White Upland Special

Introduced in 2000. Features shortened straight-grip stock, schnabel forearm and 24" barrel. Fitted with 2.75" barrel. Chambered for 12- and 20-gauge only. Weight about 6.75 lbs.

1650	1200	975	725	625	395

Citori Skeet

Series of guns chambered for all gauges. Designed for competition skeet shooting. Similar to standard Citori, with high-post target rib and 26" or 28" barrels. Versions differ in amount of engraving, quality of materials and workmanship utilized.

Grade I

1000	925	750	550	425	350

Grade II

Discontinued 1983.

—	1000	900	750	450	300

Grade III

1500	1200	900	750	450	300

Grade V

Discontinued 1984.

1600	1200	900	750	450	300

Grade VI

2000	1750	1200	900	450	300

	NIB	EXC.	V.G.	GOOD	FAIR	POOR

Golden Clays
First introduced in 1994.

	NIB	EXC.	V.G.	GOOD	FAIR	POOR
	2400	2000	1500	900	450	300

3 Gauge Sets
Consists of 20-, 28-gauge and .410 bore. Interchangeable 28" vent rib barrels. Introduced in 1987.

Grade I

	NIB	EXC.	V.G.	GOOD	FAIR	POOR
	2600	2100	1500	1250	1000	800

Grade III

	NIB	EXC.	V.G.	GOOD	FAIR	POOR
	3400	2900	2300	1750	1300	1000

Grade VI

	NIB	EXC.	V.G.	GOOD	FAIR	POOR
	3500	3000	2500	2000	1500	1100

4 Gauge Sets
Set has 12-, 20-, 28-gauge and .410 bore. Interchangeable vent rib barrels in 26" or 28" lengths. Introduced in 1981.

Grade I

	NIB	EXC.	V.G.	GOOD	FAIR	POOR
	3400	2750	2250	1700	1250	900

Grade III

	NIB	EXC.	V.G.	GOOD	FAIR	POOR
	3500	2900	2500	1900	1350	900

Grade VI

	NIB	EXC.	V.G.	GOOD	FAIR	POOR
	3900	3300	2900	2250	1400	950

Citori Trap
Version similar to standard Citori. Offered in 12-gauge only, with 30" or 32" barrels. Features high rib, Monte Carlo-type stock, with recoil pad. Versions differ in amount of ornamentation, quality of materials and workmanship utilized.

Grade I

	NIB	EXC.	V.G.	GOOD	FAIR	POOR
	1200	975	750	550	425	350

Plus Trap
Adjustable rib and stock. Introduced in 1989.

	NIB	EXC.	V.G.	GOOD	FAIR	POOR
	1700	1450	1000	750	600	500

Grade II
Discontinued 1983.

	NIB	EXC.	V.G.	GOOD	FAIR	POOR
	—	1200	1000	675	450	350

Grade III

	NIB	EXC.	V.G.	GOOD	FAIR	POOR
	1600	1450	1000	750	600	500

Grade V
Discontinued 1984.

	NIB	EXC.	V.G.	GOOD	FAIR	POOR
	—	1500	1350	900	650	450

Grade VI

	NIB	EXC.	V.G.	GOOD	FAIR	POOR
	2200	1900	1550	1250	1000	800

Citori XT Trap
Introduced in 1999. Fitted with contoured beavertail Monte Carlo stock, with or without adjustable comb. Grayed receiver highlighted in gold, with light scroll work. Choice of 30" or 32" barrels. Weight about 8 lbs. 11 oz. **NOTE:** Add $275 for adjustable comb.

	NIB	EXC.	V.G.	GOOD	FAIR	POOR
	2500	1700	1200	900	650	395

Golden Clays
First introduced in 1994.

	NIB	EXC.	V.G.	GOOD	FAIR	POOR
	2950	2250	1500	900	450	300

Signature Grade

	NIB	EXC.	V.G.	GOOD	FAIR	POOR
	2150	1750	900	600	450	300

Citori XT Trap Gold
Introduced in 2005. Features gold game scene engraving pattern on silver receiver. Choice of 30" or 32" vent rib ported barrels, with choke tubes. Checkered select walnut stock, with adjustable

	NIB	EXC.	V.G.	GOOD	FAIR	POOR

comb and semi-beavertail forearm. Stock also has adjustable length of pull and recoil reduction system. Weight about 9 lbs.

	4520	3300	2900	2250	1400	650

Model 325 Sporting Clays

Introduced in 1993. Has European design featuring scroll-engraved grayed receiver, schnabel forearm, 10mm wide vent rib, three interchangeable and adjustable trigger shoes. Back-bore barrels are ported. Fitted with choke tubes. Available in 12- and 20-gauge. 12-gauge offered with 28", 30" or 32" barrels; 20-gauge 28" or 30" barrels fitted with conventional chokes. Weight about: 12-gauge 7 lbs. 14 oz.; 20-gauge 6 lbs. 12 oz.

	1550	1200	900	700	450	300

Special Sporting

Similar to Sporting model. Fitted with 2.75" chamber. Choice of 28", 30" or 32" ported barrels. Fitted with high post rib. Stock has full pistol-grip. Optional adjustable comb. Weighs about 8.3 lbs. depending on barrel length.

Grade I

	1350	975	750	600	450	300

Signature Grade

	1350	1000	750	600	450	300

Pigeon Grade

	1500	1300	850	600	450	300

Golden Clays

	2600	1975	1250	900	450	300

Model 425 Sporting Clays

Citori over/under gun offered in 12- and 20-gauge. Choice of 28" and 30" barrels. On 12-gauge 32" barrels available. Barrels fitted with 10mm wide rib. Invector chokes are standard. Average weight 7 lbs. 14 oz. Introduced in 1995.

	1650	1200	850	600	450	300

Model 425 Golden Clays

Same as above, with high-grade wood. Engraved receiver. **NOTE:** Model 425 with adjustable comb add $200 to NIB price.

	3000	2450	1650	1100	600	300

Light Sporting 802ES (Extended Swing)

Introduced in 1996. Features 28" vent rib barrel, with 2" stainless steel extension tubes for extended swing of 30". Additional 4" extension also included. Thus barrel can be 28", 30" or 32" according to needs. Chambered for 12-gauge, with adjustable length of pull. Walnut stock, pistol-grip and schnabel forearm. Weight about 7.5 lbs.

	—	1500	900	700	500	250

Citori Plus Combo

Features single-barrel trap and interchangeable over/under set of barrels. Other features similar to Citori Plus Grade 1. Barrel combinations: 32" over/under with 34" single barrel; 30" over/under barrel with 32" or 34" single barrel. Introduced in 1989.

	2500	2100	1750	1100	700	450

Citori Ultra XS Prestige

New in 2008. This 12-gauge sporting clays model features adjustable comb. Grade III/IV walnut stock, with right hand palm swell. Ported barrels are 28", 30" or 32". Gold accented high relief Ultra XS Special engraving on steel/silver nitride finish receiver. Weight about 8 lbs.

	4500	3300	2900	2250	1400	600

BT-99 SERIES

BT-99

Break-open single-barrel trap gun. Chambered for 12-gauge only. Offered with 32" or 34" vent rib barrel, with screw-in choke tubes. Features boxlock action, with automatic ejectors. Finish blued, with checkered walnut stock and beavertail forearm. Introduced in 1968 by B.C. Miroku.

	1000	850	750	500	400	350

BT-99 Stainless

First introduced in 1993.

	1675	1250	900	700	550	350

	NIB	EXC.	V.G.	GOOD	FAIR	POOR

BT-99 Signature Grade I

First introduced in 1993.

	1300	1050	700	600	500	300

BT-99 Pigeon Grade

First introduced in 1993.

	1600	1250	800	650	500	300

BT-99 Golden Clays

First introduced in 1994. In 2003 offered with adjustable comb. Weight about 9 lbs. Available with 32" or 34" barrel.

	3700	2500	1750	1100	500	300

BT-99 Plus

Version features adjustable vent rib and recoil reduction system. Has adjustable stock, recoil pad and back-bored barrel. Introduced in 1989.

	1350	1200	900	700	500	300

BT-99 Plus—Pigeon Grade

	1700	1300	900	800	550	350

BT-99 Plus—Signature Grade

	1600	1200	850	700	500	300

BT-99 Plus Stainless—Grade I

Same as standard version. Offered in stainless steel. First introduced in 1993. Available in 32" and 34" barrels. Weighs about 8 lbs. 11 oz.

	1700	1350	900	700	500	350

BT-99 Plus—Golden Clays

First introduced in 1994.

	2700	2250	1750	900	450	300

BT-99 Plus Micro

Slightly reduced dimensions. Offered in barrel lengths from 28" to 34". Weighs about 8 lbs. 6 oz. Introduced in 1991.

	1350	1100	900	700	500	300

BT-99 Grade III

New in 2008. BT-99 features gloss finish Monte Carlo Grade III/IV walnut stock. Gold accented high relief engraving on receiver. Add 10 percent for adjustable comb stock.

	2400	1950	1250	750	550	350

BT-100 SERIES

BT-100

First introduced in 1995. Single-barrel trap features adjustable trigger pull and length of pull. Stock Monte Carlo or adjustable comb. Barrel 32" or 34". Choice blue or stainless finish. Weight about 8.9 lbs.

	2500	1900	1200	700	500	300

BT-100 Satin

Introduced in 1999. Features matte black receiver. Available in 32" or 34" barrels without ejector selector. Grade I only.

	1950	1300	1050	600	400	200

BT-100 Thumbhole

Same as standard BT-100, with additional feature of thumbhole stock. Offered in blue and stainless.

	2575	2000	1350	1000	600	400

Recoilless Trap

First introduced in 1993. Features advanced design that eliminates recoil up to 72 percent. Receiver a special bolt-action single-shot and black anodized. Fitted with adjustable ventilated rib so point of impact can be moved. Adjustable length of pull. Standard Model a 12-gauge with 30" barrel. Micro Model fitted with 27" barrels. Choke tubes supplied. Standard Model weighs 9 lbs. 1 oz.; Micro Model 8 lbs. 10 oz.

	1250	1100	900	700	500	350

BSS SERIES
BSS
Side-by-side double-barrel shotgun. Chambered for 12- or 20-gauge. Offered with 26", 28" or 30" barrel. Various choke combinations. Features boxlock action. Automatic ejectors. Early guns had nonselective single trigger; late production selective trigger. Finish blued, with checkered walnut stock and beavertail forearm. Manufactured between 1978 and 1987 by B.C. Miroku. **NOTE:** Add 20 percent single-selective trigger; 50 percent 20-gauge.

| 1200 | 1000 | 850 | 750 | 550 | 400 |

BSS Grade II
Version features game scene engraving and satin coin finished receiver. Discontinued in 1984. **NOTE:** Add 50 percent for 20-gauge.

| 3000 | 2500 | 1850 | 1400 | 1100 | 800 |

BSS Sporter
Version features English-style straight-grip stock and splinter forearm. Stock was oil-finished. Offered with 26" or 28" barrel. **NOTE:** 20-gauge add 25 percent.

| 2400 | 2000 | 1550 | 975 | 650 | 400 |

BSS Sidelock
Version features engraved sidelock action. Offered in 12- or 20-gauge, with 26" or 28" barrel. Has straight-grip stock and splintered forearm. Manufactured in Korea between 1983 and 1987. Last few dozen 12-gauge sidelocks produced were an uncatalogued version of earlier guns. These guns had very finely engraved game scenes, with English scroll. Add 30 percent premium for this variation. **NOTE:** Add 30 percent to these prices for 20-gauge guns.

| 4000 | 3500 | 2200 | 1750 | 800 | 500 |

CYNERGY SERIES
Series introduced in 2004. Browning calls it third generation over/under gun. Cynergy has a number of new design features such as monolock hinge system for lower profile, inflex recoil pad, new mechanical trigger system, adjustable comb, back-bored barrels and impact ejectors.

Cynergy Field
12-gauge 3" model features checkered walnut stock and forearm. Silver nitrate receiver with engraving. Choice of 26" or 28" vent rib barrels, with choke tubes. Weight about 7.75 lbs. Synthetic stock with adjustable comb offered. **NOTE:** Synthetic stock deduct $40.

| 2050 | 1800 | 1400 | 1000 | 575 | 325 |

Cynergy Classic Field
More traditionally styled 12-gauge was added to Cynergy line in 2006. Features steel receiver, with silver nitride finish and game bird scenes on each side. Satin finish walnut stock and schnabel style fore-end. Three choke tubes. Available in barrel lengths of 26" and 28". Average weight 7.75 lbs.

| 2150 | 1850 | 1400 | 1000 | 575 | 325 |

Cynergy Field Small Gauge
Introduced in 2005. Chambered for 20-, 28-gauge and .410 bore. Choice of 26" or 28" vent rib barrels. Weight about 6.25 lbs.

| 2100 | 1850 | 1450 | 1050 | 575 | 325 |

Cynergy Sporting
As above, with higher grade walnut stock. Choice of 28", 30" or 32" vent rib barrels, with choke tubes. Ported barrels. Hi-Viz front sight. Weight about 8 lbs. Synthetic stock with adjustable comb offered. **NOTE:** Synthetic stock deduct $40.

| 2000 | 1600 | 1200 | 900 | 500 | 300 |

Cynergy Classic Sporting
New for 2006. Traditionally styled version of Cynergy Sporting. Available in 12-gauge, with 28", 30" or 32" ported barrels. Oil finish walnut stock, with schnabel fore-end. Browning logo on steel receiver, with silver nitride finish. Three Invector-Plus Midas Grade choke tubes. Average weight 7.75 lbs.

| 2750 | 2200 | 1800 | 900 | 500 | 300 |

Cynergy Classic Field Grade III
Similar to Classic Cynergy Field, with full coverage high-relief engraving on receiver and top lever. Gloss finish Grade III/IV walnut.

| 3400 | 2600 | 2000 | 1650 | 950 | 550 |

NIB	EXC.	V.G.	GOOD	FAIR	POOR

Cynergy Classic Field Grade VI
Similar to Cynergy Classic Field Grade III, with more extensive gold-highlighted engraving.

5100	4200	3450	2300	1400	600

Cynergy Sporting Adjustable Comb
Similar to Cynergy Sporting, with comb adjustable for cast and drop. Average weight 8.2 lbs. Introduced 2006.

2900	2000	1475	1050	750	450

Cynergy Sporting Small Gauge
As above in 20- or 28-gauge. Choice of 28", 30" or 32" ported barrels in 20-gauge; 28" or 30" ported barrels in 28-gauge. Weight about 6.25 to 6.5 lbs. depending on barrel length. Introduced in 2005.

2300	1750	1200	850	625	400

Cynergy Feather
Lightweight Cynergy 12-gauge introduced in 2006; followed by 20-, 28-gauge and .410 bore versions in 2008. Satin finish walnut stock. Weight about 6.5 lbs. 12-gauge; 5 lbs. in others.

2400	1800	1300	950	675	450

Cynergy Feather Composite
As above, with synthetic stock and fore-end. 12-gauge only.

2300	1700	1200	950	675	450

Cynergy Euro Sporting
Sporting clays and skeet versions come in 2.75" 12- and 20-gauge, with 28", 30" or 32" barrels. Stock oil finish Grade III/IV walnut. Three choke tubes. Weight about 8 lbs. 12-gauge; 6.5 lbs. 20-gauge.

3500	2800	2200	1650	950	550

Cynergy Euro Field
Similar to Cynergy Euro Sporting. Has Invenctor Plus tubes in 12- and 20-gauge. Standard Invector tubes on 28-gauge and .410 bore.

2500	1900	1200	700	500	300

Cynergy Euro Sporting Composite with Adjustable Comb
Similar to Euro Sporting Composite, with adjustable comb.

3800	3000	2000	1650	950	550

Cynergy Classic Trap Unsingle Combo
Trap shotgun in 12-gauge. Comes with double barrel set in 32/34", 32/32", 30/34" or 30/32". Gloss finish Monte Carlo Grade III/IV walnut stock, with right hand palm swell. Adjustable comb. Weight about 8.9 lbs. Four choke tubes. Aluminum fitted carrying case.

4800	3800	2900	2250	1400	600

EARLY PRODUCTION AUTO-5
Series of recoil-operated semi-automatic shotguns. Designed by John M. Browning. Offered in 12- or 16-gauge. Barrel lengths 26", 28", 30" or 32", with various chokes and ribs. Has unique square-back action that has become instantly recognizable. Finish blued, with checkered walnut round-knob stock. Various versions differ in amount of ornamentation, type of rib, quality of materials and workmanship utilized in construction. Series manufactured in Belgium by FN between 1903 and 1939. First example appeared in U.S. in 1923. Pre-WWI 16-gauge guns introduced in 1936, had 2.5625" chambers; early models should be inspected by qualified gunsmith before firing.

NOTE: 16-gauge not converted to 2.75" chamber deduct 30 percent. Grade III or Grade IV prices are not nearly as affected by chamber length because of their rarity. Original pre-war barrels were serial numbered to gun. Extra barrels serial numbered to gun add $100 for plain barrels, $200 for matte rib barrels, $275 for vent rib barrels. Extra barrels on Grade IV guns add an additional 30 percent to these barrel prices. Prices given are for guns with original barrels serial numbered to gun. Remember safety is located in front of trigger guard. Deduct 10 to 25 percent for "suicide safety" in trigger guard.

Grade I—Plain Barrel

—	850	750	600	400	275

Grade I—Matte Rib

—	1100	975	800	550	350

	NIB	EXC.	V.G.	GOOD	FAIR	POOR	

Grade I—Vent Rib

	—	1000	900	725	525	325	

Grade II—Plain Barrel

	—	1500	1200	1000	600	350	

Grade II—Matte Rib

	—	2000	1500	1150	700	350	

Grade II—Vent Rib

	—	1900	1400	1050	500	350	

Grade III—Plain Barrel

	—	2800	1900	1350	775	385	

Grade III—Matte Rib

	—	3600	3000	2000	900	450	

Grade III—Vent Rib

	—	3500	2900	1850	800	400	

Grade IV—Plain Barrel

	—	4000	3500	2500	1000	500	

Grade IV—Matte Rib

	—	4500	3800	2850	1200	700	

Grade IV—Vent Rib

	—	4400	3700	2750	1100	600	

American Browning Auto-5

Recoil-operated semi-automatic shotgun was another variation of early-production Auto-5. Chambered for 12-, 16- or 20-gauge. Manufactured by Remington Company for Browning. Quite similar to Remington's Model 11 shotgun. Features Browning logo and different type of engraving. Approximately 45,000 manufactured between 1940 and 1942. **NOTE:** Add 20 percent for vent rib; 10 percent for 20-gauge.

	—	675	575	450	375	200	

MID-PRODUCTION AUTO-5—FN MANUFACTURE STANDARD WEIGHT

Version of recoil-operated semi-automatic Auto-5 shotguns. Manufactured by FN in Belgium between 1952 and 1976. Offered in 12- or 16-gauge, with 26" through 32" barrels. Various chokes. Finish blued, with checkered walnut stock. Black buttplate marked "Browning Automatic" with "FN" in center oval. Guns made prior to 1967 will be found with round knob pistol-grips. Flatbottom variation introduced in 1967. **NOTE:** Add 25 percent for guns with round-knob pistol-grip; 35 percent for straight-grip stock; 20 percent for 16-gauge guns NIB or excellent condition.

Plain Barrel

1100	900	800	650	400	300	

Matte Rib

1400	1100	900	700	500	350	

Vent Rib

1300	1000	850	650	450	325	

Auto-5 Lightweight

Version chambered for 12- or 20-gauge. Featured lighter-weight scroll-engraved receiver. Manufactured between 1952 and 1976 by FN. 20-gauge introduced in 1958. **NOTE:** Add 15 percent for vent rib; 50 percent for 20-gauge.

1200	900	650	550	450	350	

Auto-5 Magnum

Version featured 3" chambers. Offered with 26" through 32" full-choke barrels. Manufactured between 1958 and 1976 by FN. 12-gauge introduced in 1958; 20-gauge in 1967. **NOTE:** Add 20 percent for vent rib; 50 percent for 20-gauge.

1100	850	600	500	400	300	

Auto-5 Skeet

Version similar to Lightweight Model. Chambered for 12- or 20-gauge, with 26" or 28" vent rib skeet-choked barrel. **NOTE:** Add 50 percent for 20-gauge.

1250	1000	700	600	450	350	

	NIB	EXC.	V.G.	GOOD	FAIR	POOR

Auto-5 Trap Model

Version similar to standard-weight model, except chambered for 12-gauge only, with 30" vent rib full-choke barrel. Manufactured by FN until 1971.

	1200	900	650	550	450	350

Sweet Sixteen

Version similar to standard-weight. Chambered for 16-gauge only. Has gold-plated trigger. Manufactured by FN between 1936 and 1976. Not all A-5 16-gauges are Sweet Sixteens. Look for gold-plated trigger "Sweet Sixteen" script and lack of a suicide safety. **NOTE:** Add 50 percent for matte or ventilated rib in NIB or excellent condition; 25 percent for others.

	1650	1500	1100	900	550	400

Buck Special

Version features 24" cylinder-bore barrel, with adjustable rifle sights. Produced in 12- and 20-gauge 2.75" and 3" Magnum chambers; 16-gauge with 2.75" chambers. Manufactured by FN between 1963 and 1976. Prices for 12-gauge guns. **NOTE:** Add 50 percent for 16- or 20-gauge.

	1250	1000	800	650	450	350

Two Millionth Commemorative

Version commemorated two millionth Auto-5 shotgun produced by FN. Engraved with special high-polish blue finish. High-grade checkered walnut stock. Furnished in a black fitted case along with a book on Browning Company. There were 2,500 manufactured between 1971 and 1974. As with all commemoratives, it must be NIB to realize its top potential.

	3200	1850	950	625	475	300

LATE PRODUCTION AUTO-5—B.C. MIROKU MANUFACTURE

In 1976 production of Auto-5 shotgun was begun by B.C. Miroku in Japan. This move was accomplished after approximately 2,750,000 Auto-5 shotguns were manufactured by FN in Belgium between 1903 and 1976. Japanese-manufactured guns, in the opinion of many knowledgeable people, show no less quality or functionality but are simply not as desirable from a collector's standpoint. In 1999 Browning discontinued production of Auto-5 shotgun.

NOTE: Since discontinuance of Auto-5, values for Japanese examples have risen, approaching those of Belgian guns.

Auto-5 Light 12

Version chambered for 12-gauge 2.75" chamber only. Offered with lightweight receiver. Barrel has vent rib and choke tubes. Introduced in 1975.

	950	800	675	500	400	350

Auto-5 Light 20

Version similar to Light 12. Chambered for 20-gauge only.

	1200	1000	850	700	500	400

Auto-5 Magnum

Version features 3" chambers. Offered with 26", 28", 30" or 32" barrels. Introduced in 1976 by Miroku. Discontinued in 1996.

	1000	800	600	450	350	300

Auto-5 Buck Special

Version has 24" barrel cylinder-bored with adjustable sights. Introduced by Miroku in 1976.

	1000	800	600	450	350	300

Auto-5 Skeet

Competition model features 26" or 28" skeet-bored barrels, with vent rib. Manufactured between 1976 and 1983 by Miroku.

	825	550	450	350	—	200

Sweet Sixteen

Version similar to Belgian-produced Sweet Sixteen. Offered standard with vent rib and screw-in Invector choke tubes. Introduced in 1988 by Miroku. Discontinued in 1992.

	1350	1100	750	550	375	225

A-5 DU 50th Anniversary

High-grade version of Auto-5. Produced to commemorate 50th Anniversary of Ducks Unlimited. Highly engraved. Features high-gloss bluing and fancy checkered walnut stock. Approximately 5,500 manufactured by Miroku in 1987. Auctioned by Ducks Unlimited chapters to raise money for their organization. Because of this fact, it is difficult to furnish an accurate

	NIB	EXC.	V.G.	GOOD	FAIR	POOR

value. Commemorative firearms and, as such, must be NIB with all furnished materials to command premium collector value. We furnish what we feel is a general value.

	NIB	EXC.	V.G.	GOOD	FAIR	POOR
	3000	2000	800	600	450	300

A-5 DU Sweet Sixteen

Special version of Miroku-manufactured Sweet Sixteen. Auctioned by Ducks Unlimited chapters in 1988. There were 5,500 produced. All specifications and cautions that were furnished for 50th Anniversary gun also apply here.

	NIB	EXC.	V.G.	GOOD	FAIR	POOR
	2500	1500	850	600	400	300

Auto-5 Classic

Special limited edition series of A-5 shotguns built in 12-gauge only. Classic is photo-etched with game scenes on silver gray receiver. 5,000 of these guns were manufactured in 1984. Gold Classic similar in appearance, but features gold inlays and limited to 500 guns.

Classic

	NIB	EXC.	V.G.	GOOD	FAIR	POOR
	2000	1675	1200	750	525	300

Gold Classic

Produced by FN.

	NIB	EXC.	V.G.	GOOD	FAIR	POOR
	8500	7000	5000	3000	—	—

Auto-5 Light Buck Special

Lightweight version of Buck Special. Chambered for 2.75" shell. Fitted with 24" vent rib barrel. Conventional choked for slug or buckshot. Barrel has adjustable rear sight and ramp front sight. Weighs 8 lbs.

	NIB	EXC.	V.G.	GOOD	FAIR	POOR
	850	650	550	450	375	225

Auto-5 Stalker

New for 1992. Available in lightweight or magnum version. Light Stalker available in 12-gauge, with 26" or 28" barrel and choke tubes. Magnum Stalker offered in 12-gauge (3" chamber), with 28" or 30" barrel and choke tubes. Weight: Light Stalker 8 lbs. 4 oz.; Magnum Stalker 8 lbs. 11 oz.

Light Stalker

	NIB	EXC.	V.G.	GOOD	FAIR	POOR
	775	600	550	400	300	225

Magnum Stalker

	NIB	EXC.	V.G.	GOOD	FAIR	POOR
	800	650	600	375	275	250

Auto-5 Final Tribute Limited Edition

Introduced in 1999. Commemorative A-5 limited to 1,000 shotguns. Represents final production of this model. Chambered for 12-gauge shell. Fitted with 28" vent rib barrel. Has special engraved receiver.

	NIB	EXC.	V.G.	GOOD	FAIR	POOR
	5000	3750	2500	2000	1300	500

Browning A5

With squared "hump-back" receiver, A5 similar in appearance to Classic Auto-5. Totally different semi-automatic shotgun. Operates with Browning's new short-recoil Kinematic action. In 12-gauge only, with 3" chamber. A5 designed to function with a wide range of 2.75" and 3" loads. Barrel length 26", 28" or 30", with ventilated rib. Brass bead front, ivory bead middle sights and three Invector DS choke tubes. A5 Hunter model has checkered walnut stock. Also offered with black composite stock (A5 Stalker) or Mossy Oak Duck Blind or Break-Up Infinity camo finish or with black composite stock. All are shim adjustable for cast and drop. Introduced in 2012. **NOTE:** Deduct $100 for Stalker model.

	NIB	EXC.	V.G.	GOOD	FAIR	POOR
	1400	1200	950	700	—	—

Browning A5 Ultimate

Higher-trade variation with brushed satin finish and engraved receiver with intricate scroll, pheasants and mallards. Other features include: oil-finished Grade III walnut stock, ivory middle bead, fiber optic front sight and Vector Pro lengthened forcing cone.

	NIB	EXC.	V.G.	GOOD	FAIR	POOR
	1600	1350	1000	750	400	250

Double Automatic Shotgun

Short recoil-operated semi-automatic shotgun. Chambered for 12-gauge only. Offered with 26", 28" or 30" barrels plain or vent ribbed. Has various chokes. Receiver steel. Finish blued or silver, with checkered walnut stock. Tubular magazine holds only two shots—hence its name. Manufactured between 1954 and 1972. **NOTE:** Vent rib add 25 percent.

	NIB	EXC.	V.G.	GOOD	FAIR	POOR
	—	800	650	550	400	250

NIB	EXC.	V.G.	GOOD	FAIR	POOR

Twelvette Double Auto

Version similar to Double Automatic. Except, has aircraft aluminum alloy frame color-anodized in blue, silver, green, brown or black. Red-, gold- or royal blue-colored receivers were rarest colors and would command approximately 50 to 75 percent premium. Offered with plain or vent rib barrel. Approximately 65,000 produced between 1954 and 1972. **NOTE:** Vent rib add 25 percent.

—	850	725	600	450	300

Twentyweight Double Auto

Version similar in all respects to Twelvette, except .75 lb. lighter. Offered with 26.5" barrel. Manufactured between 1952 and 1971. **NOTE:** Vent rib add 25 percent.

—	900	800	700	500	350

2000 SERIES

B-2000

Gas-operated semi-automatic shotgun. Chambered for 12- or 20-gauge. Offered with 26", 28" or 30" vent rib barrel and various chokes. Finish blued, with checkered walnut stock. Assembled in Portugal from parts manufactured by FN in Belgium. Approximately 115,000 imported between 1974 and 1981.

625	550	475	300	225	175

B-2000 Magnum

Version features barrel with 3" chambers. Offered standard with recoil pad.

775	575	500	300	225	175

B-2000 Buck Special

Version has 24" cylinder-bored barrel, with rifle sights.

625	475	425	275	225	175

B-2000 Trap

Version has 30" full-choke barrel, with floating rib. Monte Carlo-type trap stock.

600	475	425	275	225	175

B-2000 Skeet

Version features 26" skeet-bored barrel, with floating vent rib. Skeet-type stock. **NOTE:** Add 20 percent for 20-gauge gun.

—	595	450	375	275	200

80 SERIES

B-80

Gas-operated semi-automatic shotgun. Chambered for 12- or 20-gauge. Features 3" magnum potential by simply exchanging barrel. Features various-length barrels. Offered with screw-in Invector chokes as of 1985. Receiver steel or lightweight aluminum alloy. Finish blued, with checkered walnut stock. Assembled in Portugal from parts manufactured by Beretta in Italy. Manufactured between 1981 and 1988. **NOTE:** Add 20 percent for 20-gauge gun.

—	550	450	375	325	225

B-80 Buck Special

Version features 24" cylinder-bored barrel, with rifle sights. Discontinued in 1984.

—	495	400	350	300	200

B-80 DU Commemorative

Version was produced to be auctioned by American Ducks Unlimited chapters. In order to realize collector potential, it must be NIB with all supplied materials. Values supplied are general.

950	650	550	425	325	275

GOLD SERIES

Gold 10

First introduced in 1993. Gas-operated 5-shot semi-automatic shotgun. Chambered for 10-gauge shell. Offered with 26", 28" or 30" vent rib barrel. Standard model has walnut stock, blued receiver and barrel. Stalker Model fitted with graphite composite stock, non-glare finish on receiver and barrel. Both models fitted with choke tubes. Weighs about 10 lbs. 10 oz.

950	700	550	450	300	150

Gold Evolve

Introduced in 2004. Updated version of original Gold gun. Features newly designed receiver, magazine cap, ventilated rib design, checkering pattern and Hi-Viz sights. Offered in 12-gauge

	NIB	EXC.	V.G.	GOOD	FAIR	POOR

3" chamber. Choice of 26", 28" or 30" barrel, with choke tubes. Weight about 7 lbs. for 28" model.

	1195	875	700	525	400	225

Gold Light 10 Gauge Camo

10-gauge offered with 26" or 28" barrels and Mossy Oak or Shadow Grass camo. Lightweight alloy receiver reduces weight to 9 lb. 10 oz. Introduced in 2001.

	1275	975	775	595	450	250

Gold 10 Gauge Combo

10-gauge has choice of two vent rib barrels in lengths of 24"/26" or 24"/28". Walnut stock, with black ventilated recoil pad. Weight with 28" barrels about 10 lbs. 10 oz.

	1150	800	675	500	375	250

Gold Stalker

	1025	725	550	450	300	150

Gold Classic Stalker

Introduced in 1999. Features classic Browning squared receiver and shim-adjustable stock. Chambered for 12-gauge shells. Choice of 26" or 28" vent rib barrels. Has 3" chambers. Black synthetic stock. Weight about 7 lbs. 3 oz.

	850	675	550	400	275	125

Gold 3-1/2" 12 Gauge

Introduced in 1997. Features 3.5" chamber. Can operate 2.75" or 3" shells as well. Choice of barrel lengths from 26" to 30". Invector-Plus chokes. Magazine capacity: 4/2.75" shells; 3/3" shells; or 3/3.5" shells. Weight about 7 lbs. 10 oz.

	1000	795	595	450	200	150

Gold 12 Gauge Hunter

Introduced in 1994. Semi-automatic shotgun built on same gas operating system as Gold 10. Offered with 26", 28" or 30" barrel. Magazine capacity: 4/3" shells. Walnut stock has full checkered pistol-grip, with black rubber recoil pad. Invector-Plus choke tubes supplied. Weighs about 7.5 lbs. Available (1998) in Stalker version, with non-glare matte metal parts and stocks.

	750	525	400	300	200	150

Gold Classic Hunter

Introduced in 1999. Features squared receiver, fully adjustable selected walnut stock and deep blued barrels. Choice of 26", 28" or 30" vent rib barrel. Offered with 3" chamber 12-gauge only.

	850	600	500	400	275	225

Gold Classic 20 Gauge

Offered with 26" or 28" vent rib barrels and select walnut stock. Shim-adjustable. Squared receiver. Weight about 6 lbs. 12 oz. Introduced in 1999.

	795	600	500	400	275	225

Gold Classic High Grade

Introduced in 1999. Features traditional square receiver, with engraved silver gray finish. Offered in 12-gauge only, with 3" chambers and 28" vent rib barrel. Select walnut stock. Weight about 7 lbs. 6 oz.

	1500	1200	775	500	225	165

Gold Deer Hunter

Introduced in 1997. Features choice of fully rifled or smooth bore barrel and Invector choke system. Both versions come with cantilever scope mount. Stock and forearm select walnut. Receiver has non-glare black finish. Barrel satin finish. Barrel length 22" on both barrels. Weight about 7 lbs. 12 oz. Price listed for smoothbore barrel. **NOTE:** Fully rifled version add $40.

	875	650	500	400	200	150

Gold Deer Hunter 20 Gauge

Same as above. Chambered for 20-gauge 3" shell. Furnished with fully rifled 22" barrel. Cantilever scope mount. Introduced in 2001.

	1025	900	625	495	300	200

Gold Deer Stalker

Introduced in 1999. Same as above. Fitted with black synthetic stock.

	950	700	600	500	300	150

	NIB	EXC.	V.G.	GOOD	FAIR	POOR

Gold Deer Mossy Oak
Introduced in 1999. Camo finish.

	825	675	575	450	200	125

Gold Waterfowl Mossy Oak Shadow Grass
Introduced in 1999. Camo finish.

	950	700	600	500	200	125

Gold Waterfowl Mossy Oak Breakup
Introduced in 2000. Camo finish.

	950	700	575	450	200	125

Gold Turkey/Waterfowl Mossy Oak
Introduced in 1999. Camo finish.

	950	700	575	450	200	125

Gold Turkey/Waterfowl Stalker
Introduced in 1999. Features black synthetic stock, 24" barrel, Hi-Viz sight and 3" or 3.5" chambers. Weight about 7 lbs. 4 oz.

	900	650	575	450	200	125

Gold Turkey/Waterfowl Hunter
12-gauge 3" or 3.5" chambered gun. Offered with 24" vent rib barrel. Select walnut stock, with black ventilated recoil pad. Weight about 7 lbs. Introduced in 1999.

	875	625	550	450	200	125

Gold NWTF Series
Model finished in Mossy Oak Breakup pattern. Bears "NWTF" logo on buttstock. Fitted with 24" barrel, Hi-Viz front sight, X-full extended Turkey choke. Offered in configurations listed.

Gold Light 10 Gauge

	1350	950	775	600	425	175

Gold 12 Gauge

3.5" Chamber, Shadow Grass

	1275	900	725	550	375	150

3" Chamber

	1100	775	650	575	375	150

3.5" Chamber Ultimate Turkey Gun

	1280	1000	900	725	375	200

Gold Hunter
Chambered for 12- and 20-gauge. Offered in 26" or 28" barrel lengths. Weighs about 6.8 lbs.

	750	625	400	300	200	150

Gold Sporting Clays
Introduced in 1996. Features ported barrel in 28" or 30" lengths. Recoil pad standard. Weight about 7.5 lbs.

	800	675	475	375	200	150

Gold Ladies/Youth Sporting Clays
Offered in 12-gauge only, with 2.75" chambers. Features 28" vent rib barrel. Overall dimensions have been adjusted to fit women. Black solid recoil pad. Weight about 7 lbs. 6 oz. Introduced in 1999.

	1200	895	625	450	300	125

Gold "Golden Clays" Ladies Sporting Clays
Introduced in 2005. 12-gauge 2.75" chambered gun. Fitted with 28" vent rib ported barrel, with 4 choke tubes. Silver receiver engraved with gold enhancements. Weight about 7.75 lbs.

	1500	1375	1050	800	575	300

Gold "Golden Clays" Sporting Clays
As above, with standard stock dimensions. Choice of 28" or 30" barrels. Introduced in 2005.

	1800	1300	1050	800	575	300

	NIB	EXC.	V.G.	GOOD	FAIR	POOR

Gold Micro

Introduced in 2001. Features 20-gauge gun, with 26" barrel, smaller pistol-grip, shorter length of pull. Back-bored barrel, with choke tubes. Weight about 6 lb. 10 oz.

	925	650	575	475	300	125

Gold Upland

Offered in 12- or 20-gauge. Barrel lengths: 12-gauge 24"; 20-gauge 26". Straight-grip stock with 3" chamber. Weight: 12-gauge 7 lbs.; 20-gauge 6.75 lbs. Introduced in 2001.

	950	700	600	475	300	125

Gold Fusion

Features a new style vent rib, adjustable comb pro-comp sight and five choke tubes. Offered in 12-gauge, 3" chambers with 26" or 28" barrels. Introduced in 2001. In 2002 offered in 20-gauge as well as 12-gauge, with choice of 26" or 28" vent rib barrel. Weight about: 12-gauge 7 lbs.; 20-gauge 6.5 lbs.

	900	725	650	495	300	125

Gold Fusion High Grade

Similar to Gold Fusion. Addition of high grade Turkish walnut stock, silver nitride receiver with game scene in gold. Five choke tubes and hard case standard. Introduced in 2005.

	1600	1250	900	625	450	300

Golden Clays

Introduced in 1999. Chambered for 12-gauge shell with 2.74" chamber. Choice of 28" or 30" vent rib ported barrels. Engraved silver gray receiver. Select walnut stock. Weight about 7 lbs. 3 oz.

	1250	1000	825	675	425	300

Gold Superlite Hunter

Introduced in 2006. Uses an aluminum alloy receiver and alloy magazine tube to reduce weight to about 7 lbs. in 12-gauge. Gloss finish walnut stock. Available with 3" or 3.5" chamber and 26" or 28" barrel. Magazine cut-off feature on 3.5" model. A 6.5 lb. 20-gauge with 3" chamber and 26" or 28" barrel also offered. Three choke tubes. Add 15 percent for 3.5" chamber.

	900	650	575	475	300	125

Gold Superlite FLD Hunter

Similar to Gold Superlite Hunter, with semi-humpback style receiver, satin finish walnut stock and 3" chamber only. Magazine cut-off on 12-gauge models. Adjustable shim system and three choke tubes.

	925	650	575	475	300	125

Gold Superlite Micro

Similar to Gold Superlite Hunter, with compact dimensions for smaller shooters. Only in 20-gauge, with 26" barrel. Weighs about 6.25 lbs. Three choke tubes.

	925	650	575	475	300	125

500 SERIES

A-500G/A-500R

Self-adjusting gas-operated semi-automatic shotgun. Chambered for 12-gauge only. Offered with 26", 28" or 30" barrels, with vent rib and screw-in Invector choke tubes. Has 3" chambers. Can fire any load interchangeably. Finish blued, with checkered walnut stock and recoil pad. Features light engraving. Introduced in 1987. The 2008 recoil version (A-500R) has a slightly better reputation for functioning than gas-operated A-500G. Values are roughly similar.

	575	490	425	350	275	225

A-500G Sporting Clays

Gas-operated version designed for sporting clays. Features choice of 28" or 30" vent rib barrel, with semi-gloss finish and gold lettering "Sporting Clays". Ventilated recoil pad standard. Weighs about 8 lbs.

	550	425	350	300	200	150

A-500R Hunting Model

Similar in appearance to A-500G. Except, this model operates on a short recoil design. Buttstock features full pistol-grip. Available with 26", 28" or 30" vent rib barrels. Choke tubes standard. Weighs about 7 lbs. 13 oz.

	475	385	300	250	200	150

	NIB	EXC.	V.G.	GOOD	FAIR	POOR

A-500R Buck Special

Same as Hunting Model, with addition of adjustable rear sight, contoured front ramp sight and gold bead. Choke tubes standard, as is 24" barrel. Weighs 7 lbs. 11 oz.

500	425	350	300	225	150

SILVER SERIES

Value-priced series of gas-operated autoloaders. Introduced in 2006. All models feature semi-humpback design and aluminum alloy receiver. Weights vary from 7.25 to 7.5 lbs. depending on barrel length and stock material. Three choke tubes provided with all models.

Silver Hunter

Features satin finish walnut stock and fore-end. Available with 3" chambers in 26", 28" and 30" barrel lengths or 3.5" chamber in 26" or 28" barrel lengths. Add 15 percent for 3.5" chamber. A 20-gauge version with 26" or 28" barrels became available in 2008.

1000	850	700	500	400	250

Silver Stalker

Similar to Silver Hunter, with matte black composite stock and fore-end. Sling swivel studs. 3.5" chamber only.

825	675	550	375	275	175

Silver Micro

20-gauge, with 26" barrel. Shorter stock dimensions for smaller shooters.

825	695	550	375	275	175

Silver Sporting Micro

This 2.75" 12-gauge includes adjustment spacers for changing stock length. Barrel is 28". Three choke tubes included. Weight about 7 lbs.

1150	900	725	600	375	250

Silver NWTF

New in 2008. This 3" 12-gauge turkey gun is fully camouflaged with Mossy Oak's New Break-Up pattern. Barrel 24" outfitted with fiber-optic rifle sights. Weight about 7 lbs. Add 10 percent for 3.5" chamber.

1100	900	725	600	375	250

Silver Rifled Deer

New in 2008. This 3" 12-gauge slug gun features rifled barrel, with cantilever scope mount. Finishes include satin walnut, black composite and Mossy Oak New Break-Up camo. Add 10 percent for camo finish.

1100	900	725	600	375	250

Silver–Mossy Oak

Similar to Silver Stalker. Choice of Mossy Oak New Break-Up with 26" barrel or Mossy Oak New Shadow Grass with 26" or 28" barrel.

925	650	575	475	300	125

MAXUS SERIES

Introduced in 2009. Replacement for Gold line.

Maxus

Autoloading shotgun chambered for 3" or 3.5" shells. Aluminum receiver, lightweight profile 26" or 28" barrel with vent rib, composite stock, Vector Pro lengthened forcing cone, DuraTouch Armor Coating overall. Weight 6-7/8 lbs.

Maxus Stalker

Matte black finish overall. Add $150 for 3.5".

1200	975	800	625	475	300

Maxus Mossy Oak Duck Blind

Mossy Oak Duck Blind finish overall. Add $150 for 3.5".

1300	975	800	625	475	300

Maxus Hunter

Gas-operated auto-loader available with 3" or 3.5" magnum chambers. Barrel lengths: 26", 28", 30" (22" for rifled version). Lengthened forcing cone. Stock is shim-adjustable for length of pull, cast and drop. Glossy-finished walnut stock, with 22 lpi checkering. Also offered in Mossy Oak Break-Up Infinity camo and Rifled Deer version with Mossy Oak Break-up Infinity camo. Weight about 7 lbs. Introduced in 2011.

NIB	EXC.	V.G.	GOOD	FAIR	POOR
1200	1000	850	650	400	300

Maxus Sporting Carbon

Gas-operated 12-gauge auto-loader, with 3" chamber. Aluminum alloy receiver has satin nickel finish, laser engraving. Barrel lengths 28" or 30". Gloss-finished high-grade walnut stock. Available with carbon fiber stock and Rifled Deer Stalker version with cantilevered scope base and 22" barrel. New 2011. **NOTE:** Deduct 15 percent for Deer Stalker/Carbon

NIB	EXC.	V.G.	GOOD	FAIR	POOR
1390	1200	950	700	450	350

Maxus Sporting Golden Clays

Top of the Maxus line, with satin nickel finished receiver, gold enhanced engraving, grade III walnut stock and fore-end. Features include a High Viz fiber optic front sight, extra fast trigger lock time, stock adjustable for length of pull, cast and comb height.

NIB	EXC.	V.G.	GOOD	FAIR	POOR
1700	1500	1150	850	400	250

BPS SERIES

Slide-action shotgun chambered for 10-, 12- or 20-gauge. Offered with various length vent rib barrels, with screw-in Invector chokes. Features 3" magnum chambers, bottom-ejection system that effectively makes it ambidextrous. Has double slide bars and 5-shot tubular magazine. Constructed of all steel. Introduced by B.C. Miroku in 1977.

BPS Field Grade

NIB	EXC.	V.G.	GOOD	FAIR	POOR
350	300	275	200	200	150

28 Gauge

Introduced in 1994. Weight approximately 7 lbs.

NIB	EXC.	V.G.	GOOD	FAIR	POOR
425	325	295	225	210	150

BPS Magnum

10- or 12-gauge, 3.5" chambers.

NIB	EXC.	V.G.	GOOD	FAIR	POOR
510	400	350	300	250	150

BPS Waterfowl 12 Gauge Camo

Introduced in 1999.

NIB	EXC.	V.G.	GOOD	FAIR	POOR
525	425	350	300	250	150

BPS Waterfowl 12 Gauge Mossy Oak Break-Up

NIB	EXC.	V.G.	GOOD	FAIR	POOR
575	475	375	325	250	150

BPS Mossy Oak New Break-up

Similar to BPS Hunter, with Mossy Oak New Break-up camo finish overall; chambers 3" and 3.5"; 12-gauge only.

NIB	EXC.	V.G.	GOOD	FAIR	POOR
750	625	400	300	200	150

BPS Mossy Oak Duck Blind

Similar to above, with Mossy Oak Duck Blind finish overall.

NIB	EXC.	V.G.	GOOD	FAIR	POOR
750	625	400	300	200	150

BPS Rifled Deer Mossy Oak New Break-up

Similar to BPS Rifled Deer Hunter, with Mossy Oak New Break-up camo finish overall.

NIB	EXC.	V.G.	GOOD	FAIR	POOR
750	625	400	300	200	150

BPS NWTF Series

Model finished in Mossy Oak Breakup pattern. Bears NWTF logo on buttstock. Fitted with 24" barrel, Hi-Viz front sight, Extra Full extended turkey choke. Introduced in 2001. Offered in configurations listed.

10 Gauge

NIB	EXC.	V.G.	GOOD	FAIR	POOR
625	475	400	325	200	125

12 Gauge 3.5" Chamber

NIB	EXC.	V.G.	GOOD	FAIR	POOR
625	475	400	325	200	125

12 Gauge 3" Chamber

NIB	EXC.	V.G.	GOOD	FAIR	POOR
550	450	375	325	200	125

	NIB	EXC.	V.G.	GOOD	FAIR	POOR

BPS Stalker

Matte finish black stock.

	NIB	EXC.	V.G.	GOOD	FAIR	POOR
	435	390	325	275	200	150

BPS Stalker—Combo

Combination of 28" vent rib barrel and choice of 22" fully rifle barrel or 20.5" Invector barre, with Extra Full turkey choke. Introduced in 2000.

	NIB	EXC.	V.G.	GOOD	FAIR	POOR
	650	525	475	325	200	125

BPS Game Gun

These models are designed for turkey and deer hunting. Introduced in 1992 in 12-gauge only, with 20.5" barrel. Turkey Special has fixed extra-full-choke barrel, while Deer Special originally came with 5" rifled tube. In 1998, a fully rifled barrel became an option for Deer Special. In 2007, a 20-gauge version was introduced. Turkey Special is drilled and tapped for scope mounts. Deer Special has cantilever mounting system plus iron sights. Deduct 15 percent for Deer Special without a fully rifled barrel.

Game Gun Deer Special (shown above)

	NIB	EXC.	V.G.	GOOD	FAIR	POOR
	600	500	425	375	325	250

Game Gun Turkey Special

	NIB	EXC.	V.G.	GOOD	FAIR	POOR
	400	375	350	325	300	250

BPS 10 Gauge Mossy Oak Shadow Grass Camo

Introduced in 1999.

	NIB	EXC.	V.G.	GOOD	FAIR	POOR
	575	475	375	325	175	125

BPS 10 Gauge Turkey

Fitted with 24" vent rib barrel, black synthetic stock and black solid recoil pad. Introduced in 1999. Weight about 9 lbs. 2 oz.

	NIB	EXC.	V.G.	GOOD	FAIR	POOR
	525	425	375	325	200	125

BPS Micro 20 Gauge

Features 22" vent rib barrel, shorter pistol-grip stock and lighterweight. Weight about 6.75 lbs. Introduced in 2001.

	NIB	EXC.	V.G.	GOOD	FAIR	POOR
	450	350	300	250	200	125

BPS Upland Special

Chambered for 20-gauge shell. Fitted with 22" vent rib barrel. Walnut stock is straight-grip. Weight about 6.5 lbs. Available in 12- or 20-gauge, with 22" barrel. A 16-gauge version, with 24" or 26" barrel introduced in 2008. A very beautiful little pump.

	NIB	EXC.	V.G.	GOOD	FAIR	POOR
	550	375	300	275	200	125

BPS Small Gauge

Introduced in 2000. Chambered for 28-gauge and .410 bore. The 28-gauge offered with choice of 26" or 28" vent rib barrel and Invector chokes. The .410 available with 26" vent rib barrel and Invector chokes. Both 28-gauge and .410 bore weigh about 6.75 lbs.

	NIB	EXC.	V.G.	GOOD	FAIR	POOR
	525	450	325	275	200	125

BPS Pigeon Grade

Furnished in 12-gauge only, with high grade walnut stock and gold trimmed receiver.

	NIB	EXC.	V.G.	GOOD	FAIR	POOR
	500	400	300	225	175	125

BPS Buck Special

24" barrel with sights.

	NIB	EXC.	V.G.	GOOD	FAIR	POOR
	450	400	350	300	225	175

BPS Trap Model

	NIB	EXC.	V.G.	GOOD	FAIR	POOR
	—	375	325	275	200	150

BPS Micro Trap

Similar to BPS Trap Model, with compact dimensions (13.75" length of pull, 48.25" overall length). 12-gauge only. CAUTION: Do not interchange Invector choke tubes with Invector-Plus choke tubes. May cause personal injury.

	NIB	EXC.	V.G.	GOOD	FAIR	POOR
	700	—	—	—	—	—

BPS Youth Model

Short stock, 22" barrel.

	NIB	EXC.	V.G.	GOOD	FAIR	POOR
	435	390	325	275	200	150

	NIB	EXC.	V.G.	GOOD	FAIR	POOR

BPS Waterfowl Deluxe

Version chambered for 12-gauge 3" chamber. Features etched receiver, with gold-plated trigger. Otherwise, similar to standard BPS.

NIB	EXC.	V.G.	GOOD	FAIR	POOR
—	600	525	425	325	250

BPS Ducks Unlimited Versions

Limited-edition guns produced to be auctioned by Ducks Unlimited. Furnished with a case. Must be NIB with furnished materials to realize their collector potential.

NIB	EXC.	V.G.	GOOD	FAIR	POOR
650	525	425	325	250	175

MODEL 12

Grade I

Slide-action shotgun chambered for 20- and 28-gauge, with 26" modified choke and vent rib barrel. Reproduction of Winchester Model 12 shotgun. Has 5-round tubular magazine, with floating high-post rib and takedown feature. Blued, with walnut stock. Introduced in 1991. Total production limited to 7,000 guns.

NIB	EXC.	V.G.	GOOD	FAIR	POOR
825	625	425	300	250	200

Grade V

Extensively engraved version of Grade I Model 12. Features select walnut stock, with deluxe checkering and high-gloss finish. Gold inlays. Introduced in 1991. Production limited to 5,000 guns. Discontinued 1992. **NOTE:** 28-gauge add 30 percent.

NIB	EXC.	V.G.	GOOD	FAIR	POOR
1300	950	700	450	—	—

LIMITED EDITION MODEL 42

New version of .410 bore pump shotgun. Last produced by Winchester in 1963. Available in two grades, both fitted with 26" vent rib barrels. Grade I features plain blued receiver, with walnut stock. Grade V features blued receiver, with scroll engraving and gold inlays. Both models choked Full. Weight 6 lbs. 4 oz.

Grade I

NIB	EXC.	V.G.	GOOD	FAIR	POOR
900	600	500	400	—	—

Grade V

NIB	EXC.	V.G.	GOOD	FAIR	POOR
1450	1000	700	500	—	—

A-BOLT SHOTGUN

Introduced in 1995. Bolt-action shotgun offered in 12-gauge, with 3" chamber. Rifled barrel version 22" long, while Invector barrel version 23" long, with 5" rifle tube installed. Has 2-shot detachable magazine. Average weight about 7 lbs. Considered "Rolls Royce" of bolt shotguns and becoming quite desirable. Manufacture ceased in 1998. **NOTE:** Invector rifled choke tube model deduct $50.

Hunter Version

NIB	EXC.	V.G.	GOOD	FAIR	POOR
1000	850	750	500	300	100

Stalker Version

NIB	EXC.	V.G.	GOOD	FAIR	POOR
900	750	650	400	200	100

RIFLES

High-Power Bolt-Action Rifle

High-grade bolt-action sporting rifle manufactured by FN in Belgium (from 1959 to 1975) or Sako of Finland (from 1961 to 1975). Built on either Mauser or Sako action. Chambered for a number of popular calibers from .222 Remington up to .458 Winchester Magnum. Three basic grades that differed in amount of ornamentation, quality of materials and workmanship utilized. Certain calibers are considered to be rare and will bring a premium from collectors of this firearm. We recommend securing a qualified appraisal on these rifles if a transaction is contemplated. We furnish general values only.

NOTE: From 1959 through 1966, FN Mauser actions with long extractors were featured. These Mauser actions will bring a premium depending on caliber. From 1967 on, FN Supreme actions with short extractors were used. Only .30-06 and .270 calibers continued with long extractor Mauser actions.

CAUTION: Buyer and seller alike, some rare calibers may be worth as much as 100 percent or more over prices listed for rare calibers such as .284 Win., .257 Roberts, 300 H&H, and .308 Norma Magnum. High-Power bolt-action rifles seemed to be particularly hard hit by salt wood.

That is why short extractor rifles bring less than long extractor guns. No factory replacement stocks are known to still be available. Deduct 20-25 percent for short extractor rifles. Proceed with caution.

Safari Grade
Standard model and calibers.

NIB	EXC.	V.G.	GOOD	FAIR	POOR
1600	1350	1100	850	400	300

Medallion Grade
Scroll engraved, standard calibers.

NIB	EXC.	V.G.	GOOD	FAIR	POOR
3200	2500	1900	1400	750	400

Olympian Grade
Extensive game scene engraving, standard calibers.

NIB	EXC.	V.G.	GOOD	FAIR	POOR
8500	6300	5250	4250	2500	1500

Model BBR
Bolt-action sporting rifle chambered for various popular calibers. Has 24" barrel, with adjustable trigger and fluted bolt. Features detachable magazine under floorplate, furnished without sights. Finish blued, with checkered walnut Monte Carlo stock. Manufactured between 1978 and 1984 by Miroku.

NIB	EXC.	V.G.	GOOD	FAIR	POOR
675	575	400	350	275	200

BOSS™ SYSTEM
Introduced by Browning in 1994. New accuracy system allows shooter to fine-tune his Browning rifle to particular load he is using. Consists of a tube on end of rifle muzzle that allows shooter to select best setting for ammunition type. System also reduces recoil. BOSS stands for "Ballistic Optimizing Shooting System". This option will add approximately $80 to value of particular Browning rifle on which it is fitted.

X-BOLT SERIES
Introduced in 2008. X-Bolt series of rifle features adjustable three-position Feather Trigger system, newly-designed bolt release, improved scope mounting system, tang safety. Generally slimmer sleeker profile.

X-Bolt Composite Stalker
Features include steel receiver, matte blue finish, free-floating crowned barrel, matte black composite stock with palm swell, Inflex recoil pad. Various barrel lengths depending on chambering, which include both medium and long cartridges ranging from .243 Winchester to .338 Winchester Magnum. Introduced in 2008.

NIB	EXC.	V.G.	GOOD	FAIR	POOR
850	700	600	500	350	200

X-Bolt Stainless Stalker
Similar to above, with stainless steel receiver and barrel. Various barrel lengths depending on chambering, which include both medium and long cartridges ranging from .243 Winchester to .375 H&H Magnum. Introduced in 2008.

NIB	EXC.	V.G.	GOOD	FAIR	POOR
850	700	600	500	350	200

X-Bolt Hunter
Similar to above, with sculpted satin-finished walnut stock and cut checkering. Low-luster blued barrel and receiver. Various barrel lengths depending on chambering, which include both medium and long cartridges ranging from .243 Winchester to .338 Winchester Magnum. Left-hand model available.

NIB	EXC.	V.G.	GOOD	FAIR	POOR
850	700	600	500	350	200

X-Bolt Medallion
Similar to above, with high-gloss finish and engraved blued barrel and receiver. Various barrel lengths depending on chambering, which include both medium and long cartridges ranging from .243 Winchester to .375 H&H Magnum. Introduced in 2008. Available in left-hand version.

NIB	EXC.	V.G.	GOOD	FAIR	POOR
1000	850	700	600	500	350

X-Bolt Micro Hunter
Similar to Browning X-Bolt Hunter, with compact dimensions (13.3125" length of pull, 41.25" overall length). Left-hand available.

NIB	EXC.	V.G.	GOOD	FAIR	POOR
800	700	600	500	350	200

X-Bolt Varmint Stalker
Similar to X-Bolt Stalker, with medium-heavy free-floated barrel, target crown, composite stock. Cartridges .223, .22-250, .243 Winchester and .308 Winchester only.

NIB	EXC.	V.G.	GOOD	FAIR	POOR
1000	850	700	600	500	350

	NIB	EXC.	V.G.	GOOD	FAIR	POOR

X-Bolt RMEF White Gold

Similar to X-Bolt Medallion, with gold-engraved matte stainless finish. Rocky Mountain Elk Foundation grip cap. Chambered in .325 WSM only.

NIB	EXC.	V.G.	GOOD	FAIR	POOR
1300	1000	850	650	550	375

X-Bolt RMEF Special Hunter

Similar to above. Matte blued finish, without gold highlights.

NIB	EXC.	V.G.	GOOD	FAIR	POOR
900	700	600	500	350	200

A-BOLT SERIES

NOTE: In 2004, new calibers were offered for A-Bolt series depending on model. They are .25 WSSM and .223 Rem. All A-Bolt II Descriptions: "II" designation dropped from A-Bolt name in 2006.

A-Bolt Hunter

Current bolt-action rifle manufactured by B.C. Miroku. Chambered for various popular calibers. Offered with 22", 24" or 26" barrel. Has short or long action. Adjustable trigger. Detachable box magazine mounted under floorplate. Furnished without sights. Blued, with checkered walnut stock. Introduced in 1985.

NIB	EXC.	V.G.	GOOD	FAIR	POOR
575	400	350	300	250	200

A-Bolt II Hunter

Introduced in 1994. New model features newly designed anti-bind bolt and improved trigger system. In 2001, .300 Winchester Short Magnum cartridge offered for this model. In 2003, a left-hand model introduced.

NIB	EXC.	V.G.	GOOD	FAIR	POOR
795	575	400	300	250	200

A-Bolt II Hunter WSSM

Similar to A-Bolt Hunter. Chambered for .223 WSSM and .243 WSSM cartridges. Stock design different, with addition of longer pistol-grip and thicker forearm. Weight about 6.25 lbs. Introduced in 2003.

NIB	EXC.	V.G.	GOOD	FAIR	POOR
795	575	400	300	250	200

A-Bolt II Micro Hunter

Introduced in 1999. Features shorter length of pull and shorter barrel length than Hunter model. Offered in .22 Hornet, .22-250, 7mm-08, .308, .243 and .260 calibers. Weight about 6 lbs. In 2003, .270 WSM, 7mm WSM and .300 WSM calibers were added for this model as well as left-hand version. **NOTE:** Add $30 for left-hand; $30 for WSM calibers.

NIB	EXC.	V.G.	GOOD	FAIR	POOR
650	525	350	250	200	150

A-Bolt II Classic Hunter

Features Monte Carlo stock, low luster bluing, select walnut and double bordered checkering. Offered in .30-06, .270, 7mm Rem. Magnum and .300 Win. Magnum. No sights. Weight about 7 lbs. Introduced in 1999.

NIB	EXC.	V.G.	GOOD	FAIR	POOR
675	500	395	250	200	150

A-Bolt Stainless Hunter

Features black composite stock, stainless steel receiver and barrel, no sights. Chamberings range from .243 Winchester to .300 WSM. Weight about 6.5 lbs. Introduced in 2008.

NIB	EXC.	V.G.	GOOD	FAIR	POOR
800	650	450	300	250	200

A-Bolt Classic Hunter WSSM

As above, but chambered for .223 WSSM and .243 WSSM cartridges. Weight about 6.25 lbs. Introduced in 2003.

NIB	EXC.	V.G.	GOOD	FAIR	POOR
800	650	450	300	250	200

A-Bolt Mountain Ti

Features lightweight stainless steel 23" barrel, titanium receiver and lightweight fiberglass stock. Chambered for .270 WSM, 7mm WSM and .300 WSM cartridges. Weight about 5.5 lbs. Calibers: .243, 7mm-08, .308, .325 WSM. Introduced in 2004.

NIB	EXC.	V.G.	GOOD	FAIR	POOR
1695	1300	1050	800	575	350

A-Bolt Composite Stalker

Supplied with composite stock and matte finish bluing. Offered in .338 Win. Magnum, .300 Win. Magnum, 7mm Rem. Magnum, .25-06, .270, .280, .30-06. Introduced in 1988. In 2001, .300 Winchester Short Magnum cartridge was offered for this model. Calibers: .223 WSSM, .243 WSSM, .25 WSSM, .223, .243, .7mm-08, .270 WSM, 7mm WSM, .300 WSM, .325 WSM, .25-06, .270, .280, .30-06, 7mm RM, .300 WM, .338 WM. Add 10 percent for BOSS or left-hand version.

NIB	EXC.	V.G.	GOOD	FAIR	POOR
550	350	300	250	200	150

	NIB	EXC.	V.G.	GOOD	FAIR	POOR

A-Bolt II Composite Stalker

Same as above, with 1994 improvements. **NOTE:** Add $80 for BOSS system.

NIB	EXC.	V.G.	GOOD	FAIR	POOR
670	525	400	300	250	200

A-Bolt Composite Stalker WSSM

As above, but chambered for .223 WSSM or .243 WSSM cartridge. Weight about 6 lbs. Introduced in 2003.

NIB	EXC.	V.G.	GOOD	FAIR	POOR
700	550	400	300	250	200

A-Bolt Stainless Stalker

Bolt-action rifle. Calibers: .223 WSSM, .243 WSSM, .25 WSSM, .223, .243, .7mm-08, .270 WSM, 7mm WSM, .300 WSM, .325 WSM, .25-06, .270, .280, .30-06, 7mm RM, .300 WM, .338 WM, .375 H&H. Barrel: 22", 23", 24", 26" stainless steel, sightless (except for .375 H&H). Magazine: Detachable box. Stock: Black composite. Add 10 percent for BOSS system and left-hand version. **NOTE:** .300 and .338 calibers add $30.

NIB	EXC.	V.G.	GOOD	FAIR	POOR
600	450	400	350	300	250

A-Bolt II Composite Stainless Stalker

Same as above, with 1994 improvements. **NOTE:** Magnum calibers add $30; BOSS system add $110.

NIB	EXC.	V.G.	GOOD	FAIR	POOR
850	650	550	400	300	250

A-Bolt Stainless Stalker WSSM

As above, but chambered for .223 WSSM and .243 WSSM calibers. Stock design slightly different from standard A-Bolt Stalker. Weight about 6 lbs. Introduced in 2003.

NIB	EXC.	V.G.	GOOD	FAIR	POOR
880	675	550	400	300	250

A-Bolt Carbon Fiber Stainless Stalker

Features a Christensen Arms patent carbon barrel. Chambered for .22-250 or .300 Win. Magnum. Weight about: 6.25 lbs. short action; 7 lbs. long action. Introduced in 2000. In 2001, .300 Winchester Short Magnum cartridge offered for this model.

NIB	EXC.	V.G.	GOOD	FAIR	POOR
1400	1200	1000	900	700	350

A-Bolt II Heavy Barrel Varmint

Introduced in 1994. Features all A-Bolt II improvements in a heavy barrel varmint rifle. Offered in .22-250 and .223 Rem. calibers, with 22" barrel. Equipped with black laminated wood stock.

NIB	EXC.	V.G.	GOOD	FAIR	POOR
685	600	525	425	325	250

A-Bolt Varmint Stalker

Introduced in 2002. Features new armor coated synthetic stock. Matte blue metal finish. Chambered for .223 Rem. and .22-250 Rem. cartridges. Fitted with 24" barrel on .223 and 26" barrel on .22-250. Weight about 8 lbs.

NIB	EXC.	V.G.	GOOD	FAIR	POOR
790	650	525	425	325	250

A-Bolt Varmint Stalker WSSM

As above, but chambered for .223 WSSM and .243 WSSM cartridges. Weight about 7.75 lbs. Introduced in 2003.

NIB	EXC.	V.G.	GOOD	FAIR	POOR
815	650	525	425	325	250

A-Bolt Eclipse M-1000

Thumbhole stock. Calibers: .270, .30-06, 7mm RM, .22-250, .308, .270 WSM, .7mm WSM, .300 WSM. Add 10 percent for BOSS. Fitted with 26" barrel with BOSS system. Stock laminated hardwood, with gray/black finish. Forearm benchrest style. Weight about 9 lbs. 13 oz.

NIB	EXC.	V.G.	GOOD	FAIR	POOR
1135	700	625	450	350	250

A-Bolt Eclipse M-1000 WSM & Stainless

Introduced in 2004. Offered in all WSM calibers. M-1000 blued with heavy barrel; stainless fitted with heavy bull barrel. Barrel length 26". Weight 9.85 lbs. No sights. **NOTE:** Add $200 for stainless model.

NIB	EXC.	V.G.	GOOD	FAIR	POOR
1050	825	675	500	350	200

A-Bolt Eclipse Varmint

Introduced in 1996. Features thumbhole stock made from gray/black laminated hardwood. Offered in two versions: short-action, heavy-barrel; long and short action, with standard-weight barrel. Weighs about: 9 lbs.; standard-barrel 7.5 lbs. depending on caliber.

NIB	EXC.	V.G.	GOOD	FAIR	POOR
950	800	600	500	400	250

NIB	EXC.	V.G.	GOOD	FAIR	POOR

Euro-Bolt

First introduced in 1993. A-Bolt variation features rounded bolt shroud, Mannlicher-style bolt handle, continental-style stock. Cheekpiece and schnabel-style forearm. Finish is low-luster blue. Offered in .270, .30-06 and 7mm Rem. Magnum calibers. Weighs about 7 lbs.

NIB	EXC.	V.G.	GOOD	FAIR	POOR
650	500	450	350	250	150

A-Bolt II Euro Bolt

Same as above, with 1994 improvements.

NIB	EXC.	V.G.	GOOD	FAIR	POOR
850	500	450	350	250	150

NRA A-Bolt Wildlife Conservation Collection

Commemorates NRA's Environment Conservation and Hunting Outreach Program. Caliber: .243 Win. Barrel: 22" blued sightless. Stock satin-finish walnut. NRA Heritage logo lasered on buttstock. MSRP: $797.

A-Bolt Medallion Model

Calibers: .223 WSSM, .243 WSSM, .25 WSSM, .223, .243, .7mm-08, .270 WSM, 7mm WSM, .300 WSM, .325 WSM, .25-06, .270, .280, .30-06, 7mm RM, .300 WM, .338 WM. Add 10 percent for BOSS or left-hand version. **NOTE:** Add $35 for .300 and .338 calibers.

NIB	EXC.	V.G.	GOOD	FAIR	POOR
800	600	500	400	300	250

A-Bolt II Medallion

Same as above, with 1994 improvements. In 2003, offered in left-hand version.

NIB	EXC.	V.G.	GOOD	FAIR	POOR
765	600	450	350	300	250

A-Bolt II Medallion WSSM

As above chambered for .223 WSSM or .243 WSSM cartridge. Weight about 6.25 lbs. Introduced in 2003.

NIB	EXC.	V.G.	GOOD	FAIR	POOR
795	650	525	450	400	325

A-Bolt Gold Medallion

Version has fancy grade walnut stock with cheekpiece. Lightly engraved. Gold-inlaid letters. Introduced in 1988.

NIB	EXC.	V.G.	GOOD	FAIR	POOR
690	625	550	450	400	325

A-Bolt II Gold Medallion

Same as above, with 1994 improvements.

NIB	EXC.	V.G.	GOOD	FAIR	POOR
690	625	550	450	400	325

A-Bolt II White Gold Medallion

Features gold engraved stainless receiver and barrel, select walnut stock, with brass spacers and rosewood caps. European-style cheekpiece. No sights. Introduced in 1999. Offered in .30-06, .270, 7mm Rem. Magnum and .300 Win. Magnum. Weight about 7 lbs. 8 oz.

NIB	EXC.	V.G.	GOOD	FAIR	POOR
1100	800	650	500	425	350

A-Bolt White Gold Medallion RMEF

Introduced in 2003. Special edition for Rocky Mountain Elk Foundation. Chambered for 7mm Rem. Magnum. Fitted with 26" barrel. Both action and barrel stainless steel. Special RMEF logo on grip cap. Weight about 7.75 lbs. Add 5 percent for WSM calibers.

NIB	EXC.	V.G.	GOOD	FAIR	POOR
1200	950	750	600	450	325

A-Bolt Custom Trophy

Introduced in 1998. Features gold highlights on barrel and receiver, select walnut stock, with shadowline cheekpiece and skeleton pistol-grip. Barrel octagonal. Chambered for .270 and .30-06 with 24" barrel and 7mm Rem. Magnum and .300 Win. Magnum with 26" barrel. Weight varies from 7 lbs. 11 oz. to 7 lbs. 3 oz. depending on caliber.

NIB	EXC.	V.G.	GOOD	FAIR	POOR
1300	1000	800	650	425	300

A-Bolt Big Horn Sheep Issue

High-grade version of A-Bolt. Chambered for .270 cartridge. Features deluxe skipline checkered walnut stock, with heavily engraved receiver and floorplate. Two gold sheep inlays. There were 600 manufactured in 1986 and 1987.

NIB	EXC.	V.G.	GOOD	FAIR	POOR
1050	800	600	450	400	325

A-Bolt Micro-Medallion

Smaller version of A-Bolt Hunter. Chambered for popular cartridges that fit short action. Has 20" barrel without sights and 3-round magazine. Introduced in 1988.

NIB	EXC.	V.G.	GOOD	FAIR	POOR
525	475	400	350	300	250

	NIB	EXC.	V.G.	GOOD	FAIR	POOR

A-Bolt II Micro-Medallion

Same as above, with 1994 improvements.

	525	475	400	350	300	250

A-Bolt Pronghorn Issue

Deluxe version of A-Bolt. Chambered for .243 cartridge. Heavily engraved and gold inlaid. Features presentation-grade walnut stock, with skipline checkering and pearl-inlaid borders. There were 500 manufactured in 1987.

	1300	1000	750	500	400	325

A-Bolt Special Hunter RMEF

Similar to A-Bolt Hunter. Honors Rocky Mountain Elk Foundation. Chambered in .325 WSM. Satin finish. Introduced 2007.

	800	600	500	400	300	250

A-Bolt White Gold RMEF

Similar to A-Bolt Special Hunter RMEF, with stainless barrel, receiver and glossy finish. Introduced 2007.

	1100	775	600	475	325	200

A-Bolt Target

Similar to A-Bolt, with 28" heavy bull blued barrel and receiver. Satin finish gray laminated stock, with adjustable comb and semi-beavertail fore-end. Chambered in .223, .308 Winchester and .300 WSM.

	1275	1000	800	650	425	300

A-Bolt Target Stainless

Similar to above, with stainless receiver and barrel.

	1500	1275	1000	800	650	425

A-Bolt .22 Grade I

Bolt-action sporting rifle. Chambered for .22 LR or .22 Magnum cartridges. Features 60-degree bolt and 22" barrel. Available with or without open sights. Has 5-round detachable magazine. Adjustable trigger. Finish blued, with checkered walnut stock. Introduced in 1986. **NOTE:** .22 Magnum add 15 percent.

	340	275	210	150	125	100

A-Bolt .22 Gold Medallion

Deluxe high-grade version features select stock, with rosewood pistol-grip cap and fore-end tip. Lightly engraved. Gold-filled letters. Introduced in 1988.

	450	400	350	300	225	175

AB3 Composite Stalker

Made on an A-Bolt action, with synthetic stock, matte blue finish and free-floating barrel. Stock has textured grip panels and polymer recoil pad. Picatinny rail scope mount included. The 3-round magazine is detachable. Offered in: .270 Win., 7mm Rem. Magnum, .30-06, .300 Win. Magnum, .300 WSM.

	525	450	400	350	300	200

T-BOLT SERIES

T-Bolt Model T-1

Unique straight-pull bolt-action sporting rifle. Chambered for .22 caliber cartridges. Has 22" barrel, with open sights and 5-round magazine. Finish blued, with plain walnut stock. Manufactured between 1965 and 1974 by FN. Many T-Bolt rifles affected by salt wood. Proceed with caution. Reintroduced in 2006 with rotary magazine.

	—	550	395	350	150	100

T-Bolt Model T-2

Version similar to T-1, with select checkered walnut stock and 24" barrel.

	800	600	450	375	250	200

T-Bolt (2006)

Reintroduction of classic and collectible T-bolt straight-pull .22 rifle. Introduced in 2006. Chambered for .17 HMR, .22 WMR or .22 LR.

	600	475	450	375	250	200

	NIB	EXC.	V.G.	GOOD	FAIR	POOR

T-Bolt Target/Varmint

Similar to reintroduced T-Bolt, with floating heavy target barrel and other accurizing refinements. Introduced 2007.

NIB	EXC.	V.G.	GOOD	FAIR	POOR
650	525	500	425	300	250

T-Bolt Target/Varmint Stainless

Similar to above, with stainless steel receiver and barrel. Introduced 2008.

NIB	EXC.	V.G.	GOOD	FAIR	POOR
850	725	650	525	350	325

T-Bolt Composite Hunter

Sporter version of new T-Bolt, with black composite Monte Carlo stock and glossy blue barrel and receiver. Chambered in .17 HMR, .22 WMR or .22 LR. Scope not included. Introduced 2008.

NIB	EXC.	V.G.	GOOD	FAIR	POOR
675	525	500	425	300	250

T-Bolt Composite Target/Varmint

Sporter version of new T-Bolt Target/Varmint, with black composite Monte Carlo stock and glossy blue barrel and receiver. Chambered in .17 HMR, .22 WMR or .22 LR. Scope not included. Introduced 2008.

NIB	EXC.	V.G.	GOOD	FAIR	POOR
700	550	525	450	325	275

T-Bolt Composite Target/Varmint Left-Hand

Similar to T-Bolt Composite Target/Varmint in left-hand version.

NIB	EXC.	V.G.	GOOD	FAIR	POOR
725	550	525	450	325	275

T-Bolt Sporter

Sporter version of new T-Bolt, with satin walnut stock and bright blue barrel and receiver. Scope not included. Introduced 2008.

NIB	EXC.	V.G.	GOOD	FAIR	POOR
700	550	525	450	325	275

T-Bolt Sporter Left-Hand

Similar to Browning T-Bolt Sporter in left-hand version.

NIB	EXC.	V.G.	GOOD	FAIR	POOR
700	550	525	450	325	275

T-Bolt Composite Sporter Left-Hand

Similar to Browning T-Bolt Sporter Left-Hand, with composite stock.

NIB	EXC.	V.G.	GOOD	FAIR	POOR
700	550	525	450	325	275

Acera Straight Pull Rifle

Introduced in 1999. Features straight-action bolt system. Chambered for .30-06 with 22" barrel; .300 Win. Magnum with 24" barrel. Open sights optional as is BOSS system. Detachable box magazine. Checkered walnut stock. Prices listed for .30-06, with no sights and no BOSS. **NOTE:** Add $100 for .300 Win. Magnum with no sights and no BOSS.

NIB	EXC.	V.G.	GOOD	FAIR	POOR
1100	775	600	475	325	200

Model 52 Limited Edition

Based on design of original Winchester Model 52 .22-caliber bolt-action rifle. Fitted with 24" barrel and oil finished walnut stock. Metal pistol-grip cap and rosewood fore-end tip. Drilled and tapped for scope. Five-round detachable magazine. Blued finish. Weight about 7 lbs. From 1991 to 1992, 5,000 Model 52s were built.

NIB	EXC.	V.G.	GOOD	FAIR	POOR
1000	875	700	600	—	—

BPR-22

Short-stroke slide action rifle. Chambered for .22 LR and Magnum cartridges. Has 20.25" barrel, with open sights and 11-round tubular magazine. Finish blued, with checkered walnut stock. Manufactured between 1977 and 1982. **NOTE:** Add $100 for models chambered for .22 Magnum.

NIB	EXC.	V.G.	GOOD	FAIR	POOR
—	500	350	215	125	95

BPR-22 Grade II

Version engraved. Select walnut stock. **NOTE:** Add 20 percent for models chambered for .22 Magnum.

NIB	EXC.	V.G.	GOOD	FAIR	POOR
—	600	400	275	225	150

Trombone Model

Slide-action rifle chambered for .22 LR cartridge. Has 24" barrel, with open sights and takedown design. Tubular magazine and hammerless action. Approximately 150,000 manufactured by FN between 1922 and 1974. Approximately 3,200 were imported by Browning

NIB	EXC.	V.G.	GOOD	FAIR	POOR

in 1960s. Marked with FN barrel address or Browning Arms address. Browning-marked guns worth approximately 40 percent additional. Values given for FN-marked guns.

| 1300 | 1000 | 800 | 700 | 450 | 325 |

Semi-Automatic .22 (SA-22)

Blowback-operated semi-automatic rifle. Chambered for .22 Long Rifle or Short cartridge. Features take-down barrel design, with 19.25" barrel and 11-round tubular magazine inside buttstock. Loaded through a hole in middle of buttstock. Finish blued, with checkered walnut stock and beavertail forearm. Lightweight compact firearm manufactured by FN between 1956 and 1974 for U.S. marked guns. A number of versions that differ in amount of ornamentation, quality of materials and workmanship.

Grade I

NOTE: Grade I .22 Short add 50 percent; Early Wheel Sight manufactured 1959-1960 add 20 percent.

| 850 | 700 | 600 | 500 | 400 | 350 |

Grade II

French grayed receiver. **NOTE:** Grade II short add 300 percent.

| 1600 | 1200 | 900 | 700 | 300 | 200 |

Grade III

French grayed receiver. **NOTE:** Premium engravers add 40 percent to Grade III; Grade III short add 800 percent; unsigned Grade III, 1956-1960 deduct 20 percent.

| 3250 | 2700 | 1900 | 1200 | 700 | 400 |

Semi-Auto .22 (SA-22, Miroku Mfg.)

Similar to Belgian FN, except produced as of 1976 by B.C. Miroku in Japan. Collector interest not as high as in FN version.

Grade I

| 600 | 500 | 400 | 275 | 125 | 100 |

Grade II

Discontinued 1984.

| 900 | 700 | 525 | 375 | 225 | 150 |

Grade III

Discontinued 1983.

| 1300 | 1000 | 750 | 500 | 300 | 200 |

Grade VI

Gold plated animals.

| 1200 | 950 | 750 | 525 | 325 | 275 |

Semi-Auto .22 High Grade 100th Anniversary

A limited production model, with octagon barrel, high relief engraving, highly polished blueing, gold bead front sight and grade III/IV walnut stock. Engraving features John M. Browning's likeness on top of receiver, 100th Anniversary logo and small game animals. Made in Japan by Miroku during 2014, with production limited to 100 rifles. MSRP $2000.

| 1800 | 1650 | — | — | — | — |

BAR-22

Blowback-operated semi-automatic rifle. Chambered for .22 LR cartridge. Has 20.25" barrel, with open sights and 15-round tubular magazine. Features polished lightweight alloy receiver. Finished blue, with checkered walnut stock. Manufactured between 1977 and 1985 by Miroku.

| — | 600 | 525 | 290 | 160 | 125 |

BAR-22 Grade II

Deluxe version, with engraved silver-finished receiver. Select walnut stock. Discontinued in 1985.

| — | 695 | 575 | 375 | 175 | 150 |

Buck Mark Rifle

Model uses same design as Buck Mark pistol. Fitted with 18" barrel (heavy on target model) and thumbhole pistol-grip. Magazine capacity 10 rounds. Integral rail scope mount. Introduced in 2001. Weight about: 4.25 lbs. Sporter; 5.5 lbs. Target model.

Target Model

| 595 | 460 | 325 | 250 | 195 | 125 |

	NIB	EXC.	V.G.	GOOD	FAIR	POOR

Sporter Model

	NIB	EXC.	V.G.	GOOD	FAIR	POOR
	590	450	325	250	195	125

Buck Mark Field Target Gray Laminate

Introduced in 2003. Features lightweight carbon composite barrel, gray laminate stock and integral scope rail. Chambered for .22 cartridge. Fitted with 18" barrel. Weight: 5.5 lbs. standard; 3.75 lbs. Lite model.

	NIB	EXC.	V.G.	GOOD	FAIR	POOR
	650	525	400	325	250	175

Patent 1900 High Power

Semi-automatic sporting rifle. Chambered for .35 Remington cartridge. Similar in configuration to Remington Model 8 rifle. Has 22" barrel, with open sights and 5-round integral magazine. Finish blued, with plain walnut stock. Approximately 5,000 manufactured between 1910 and 1931. Deluxe model, with ribbed barrel and checkered walnut stock available. Worth approximately 15 percent additional. Very rare in USA.

	NIB	EXC.	V.G.	GOOD	FAIR	POOR
	—	1500	1000	700	475	300

BAR SERIES

Bar High Power Rifle

Gas-operated semi-automatic sporting rifle. Chambered for various popular calibers from .243 up to .338 Magnum cartridges. Offered with 22" or 24" barrel, with folding leaf sight until 1980. Finish blued, with checkered walnut stock. Various grades offered, differed in amount of ornamentation, quality of materials and workmanship utilized. Earlier models manufactured in Belgium by FN; these guns would be worth approximately 15 percent additional over guns assembled in Portugal from parts manufactured by FN. Early .338 Magnum model rarely encountered and would be worth approximately 25 percent additional. Grade I values furnished are for Portuguese-assembled guns from 1977 until introduction of BAR Mark II in 1993. This model introduced in 1967; discontinued in 1977.

Grade I

	NIB	EXC.	V.G.	GOOD	FAIR	POOR
	1000	725	650	475	225	100

Grade I Magnum

	NIB	EXC.	V.G.	GOOD	FAIR	POOR
	1150	750	675	400	250	125

Grade II Deluxe

1967-1974.

	NIB	EXC.	V.G.	GOOD	FAIR	POOR
	1200	900	825	475	300	175

Grade II Deluxe Magnum

1968-1974.

	NIB	EXC.	V.G.	GOOD	FAIR	POOR
	1275	950	850	500	325	200

Grade III

Discontinued 1984. **NOTE:** Grade III offered in two variations. First was hand-engraved and produced in Belgium. Second was photo-etched and built in Belgium and assembled in Portugal. Second variation will not be as valuable as first.

	NIB	EXC.	V.G.	GOOD	FAIR	POOR
	1700	1450	1100	800	400	250

Grade III Magnum

Discontinued 1984. **NOTE:** Prices indicated are for 1970 through 1974 production. Guns assembled in Portugal deduct 30 percent. .338 Win. Magnum caliber rare in Grade III add 75 percent premium.

	NIB	EXC.	V.G.	GOOD	FAIR	POOR
	1800	1550	1150	850	400	250

Grade IV

Game scene engraved. Hand-engraved from 1970 through 1976, then etched thereafter. Grade IV rifles discontinued in 1984. **NOTE:** Pre-1977 rifles add 40 percent; premium engraving add 10 percent.

	NIB	EXC.	V.G.	GOOD	FAIR	POOR
	2600	2200	1500	1000	500	400

Grade IV Magnum

	NIB	EXC.	V.G.	GOOD	FAIR	POOR
	2800	2400	1600	1100	500	450

Grade V

Gold Inlaid: 1971-1974.

	NIB	EXC.	V.G.	GOOD	FAIR	POOR
	6500	5800	4500	3200	1400	700

Grade V Magnum

1971-1974. **NOTE:** Special order variations on Grade V rifles, add up to 100 percent.

	NIB	EXC.	V.G.	GOOD	FAIR	POOR
	6750	6000	4600	3300	1500	750

NIB	EXC.	V.G.	GOOD	FAIR	POOR

North American Deer Rifle Issue

Deluxe version of BAR. Chambered for .30-06 only. Features photo etched silver-finished receiver and deluxe checkered walnut stock. Produced and furnished 600 with walnut case and accessories. Discontinued in 1983. As with all commemorative's, it must be NIB to command premium values.

NIB	EXC.	V.G.	GOOD	FAIR	POOR
4000	3600	2400	1800	450	250

BAR Mark II Safari Rifle

Improved version of BAR. First introduced by Browning in 1967. Announced in 1993, this Mark II design uses a new gas system, with newly designed buffering system to improve reliability. Has new bolt release lever, new easily removable trigger assembly. Available with- or with-out sights. Walnut stock, with full pistol-grip and recoil pad on magnum gun are standard. Receiver blued, with scroll engraving. Rifles with magnum calibers have 24" barrel; standard calibers fitted with 22" barrel. Available in .243, .308, .270, .30-06, 7mm Rem. Magnum, .300 Win. Magnum, .338 Win. Magnum. Standard calibers weigh about 7 lbs. 9 oz.; magnum calibers 8 lbs. 6 oz. **NOTE:** Add 30 percent for .270 Wby. Magnum, which was made for one year only.

NIB	EXC.	V.G.	GOOD	FAIR	POOR
825	750	600	450	250	150

BAR Mark II Lightweight

Version of Mark II. Introduced in 1997. Features lightweight alloy receiver and shortened 20" barrel. Offered in .30-06, .270 Win., .308 Win. and .243 Win. calibers. Not offered with BOSS system. Weight about 7 lbs. 2 oz.

NIB	EXC.	V.G.	GOOD	FAIR	POOR
750	600	500	425	175	125

BAR Composite Stalker

Introduced in 2001. Features composite buttstock and fore-end, with removable magazine. Offered in short action (.243 and .308) with sights; standard action (.270 and .30-06) with no sights; magnum calibers (7mm, .330 Win., and .338) with no sights and with BOSS system. **NOTE:** Magnum calibers add $75; BOSS add $140.

NIB	EXC.	V.G.	GOOD	FAIR	POOR
900	725	550	425	175	125

BAR High Grade Models

Models will feature high grade walnut stock, with highly polished blued barrel. Receivers will be grayed with game animals: mule deer and whitetail on standard calibers (.270 and .30-06); elk and moose on magnum calibers (7mm magnum and .300 Win. Magnum).

NIB	EXC.	V.G.	GOOD	FAIR	POOR
1825	1450	1100	800	550	400

BAR ShortTrac

Introduced in 2004. Features ability to chamber magnum cartridges. Offered in .270 WSM, 7mm WSM, .325 WSM, .300 WSM, .243 and .308. Fitted with 23" barrel in magnum calibers; 22" barrel in non-magnum. Receiver alloy steel. Redesigned stock adjustable for length of pull. Weight about: 7.25 lbs. magnum calibers; 6.75 lbs. others. Add 10 percent for camo finish.

NIB	EXC.	V.G.	GOOD	FAIR	POOR
950	650	450	350	250	200

BAR ShortTrac Stalker

Similar to BAR ShortTrac, with matte blue barrel. Composite stock. Introduced 2006.

NIB	EXC.	V.G.	GOOD	FAIR	POOR
850	670	550	450	350	250

BAR ShortTrac Left-Hand

Similar to BAR ShortTrac in left-hand. Introduced 2007.

NIB	EXC.	V.G.	GOOD	FAIR	POOR
950	650	450	350	250	200

BAR ShortTrac Mossy Oak New Break-up

Similar to BAR ShortTrac, with Mossy Oak Break-up finish overall.

NIB	EXC.	V.G.	GOOD	FAIR	POOR
1275	1000	750	600	475	350

BAR ShortTrac Digital Green

Similar to above, with Digital Green camo finish overall.

NIB	EXC.	V.G.	GOOD	FAIR	POOR
1275	1000	750	600	475	350

BAR LongTrac

Similar to above. Made for long action calibers such as .270, .30-06, 7mm Rem. Magnum and .300 Win. Magnum. Barrel length 22" for .270 and .30-06; 24" for other two calibers. Weight about: 7 lbs. .270 and .30-06; 7.5 lbs. 7mm and .300. Introduced in 2004. Add 10 percent for camo finish. **NOTE:** Add $75 for magnum calibers.

NIB	EXC.	V.G.	GOOD	FAIR	POOR
950	650	450	350	250	200

BAR LongTrac Stalker

Long-action version of BAR ShortTrac Stalker.

NIB	EXC.	V.G.	GOOD	FAIR	POOR
850	670	550	450	350	250

	NIB	EXC.	V.G.	GOOD	FAIR	POOR

BAR LongTrac Left-Hand

Similar to BAR Long-Trac in left hand. Introduced 2007.

	NIB	EXC.	V.G.	GOOD	FAIR	POOR
	950	1000	750	600	475	350

BAR LongTrac Mossy Oak New Break-up

Similar to BAR LongTrac, with Mossy Oak Break-up finish overall.

	1275	1000	750	600	475	350

Model BPR

Initials "BPR" stands for Browning Pump Rifle. Introduced in 1997. Similar in appearance to BAR. Offered in both long-/short-action calibers, with barrel lengths from 22" to 24". Short action calibers: .243 Win. and .308 Win. Long action calibers: .270 Win., .30-06, 7mm Rem. Magnum and .300 Win. Magnum. Weight about 7 lbs. 3 oz. Discontinued 2003.

	800	675	525	400	300	200

BL SERIES

BL-22 Grade I

Lever-action rifle chambered for .22 rimfire cartridge. Has 18" barrel, with tubular magazine and folding leaf rear sight. Western-style firearm that features an exposed hammer. Finish blued, with walnut stock. Introduced in 1970 by Miroku.

	450	350	200	150	125	100

BL-22 Grade II

Similar to above, with scroll-engraved receiver. Checkered select walnut stock.

	475	350	225	175	150	125

BL-22 Field Series Grade I

Introduced in 2005. Features satin nickel receiver, walnut stock with no checkering. Blued trigger. Magazine capacity 16 rounds. Weight about 5 lbs.

	495	375	350	200	150	100

BL-17 Field Series Grade I

As above chambered for .17 Mach 2 cartridge. Weight about 5.2 lbs.

	650	575	400	200	150	100

BL-22 Field Series Grade II

As above, with checkered stock, gold trigger. Scroll engraving on receiver.

	555	425	350	200	150	125

BL-17 Field Series Grade II

As above chambered for .17 Mach 2 cartridge.

	700	600	450	250	150	125

BL-22 Grade II Octagon

Introduced in 2005. Has 24" octagon barrel chambered for .22 Long and Long Rifle cartridges. Receiver silver nitride, with scroll engraving and gold trigger. Magazine capacity 16 rounds. Gold bead front sight. Weight about 5.25 lbs.

	725	550	375	275	200	150

BL-17 Grade II Octagon

As above, but chambered for the .17 Mach 2 cartridge. Magazine capacity 16 rounds. Weight about 5.35 lbs. Introduced in 2005.

	750	575	375	275	200	150

BL-22 Classic

Introduced in 1999. Same features as BL-22 Grade I.

	425	375	275	200	175	125

BL-22 NRA Grade 1

Similar to BL-22 Grade 1, with "NRA" logo lasered on buttstock.

	500	450	350	300	—	—

BL-22 Gray Laminate Stainless

Similar to BL-22, with gray laminated stock, nickeled receiver and stainless steel barrel. Introduced 2006.

	725	550	375	275	200	150

	NIB	EXC.	V.G.	GOOD	FAIR	POOR

BL-22 Micro Midas

Chambered for .22 LR. Designed for younger shooter, with 12" length of pull. Lever action, with short 33-degree throw. Full-length tubular magazine, American walnut stock, gloss finish, straight-grip. Receiver steel, with blued finish. Grooved for scope mounts. New 2011.

400	350	300	250	200	150

Model 81 BLR

Contemporarily designed lever-action sporting rifle. Chambered for various popular calibers from .22-250 up to .358 Winchester. Has 20" barrel, with adjustable sights. Features 4-round detachable magazine and rotary locking bolt. Finish blued, with checkered walnut stock and recoil pad. Introduced in 1971. Manufactured that year in Belgium. In 1972, manufacture moved to Miroku in Japan. In 2003, straight-grip stock introduced and WSM calibers added from .270 to .300. Weight about 6.5 lbs. **NOTE:** Belgian-manufactured version add 20 percent.

895	675	500	300	200	150

BLR Lightning (Lightweight)

Introduced in 1996. Features lightweight aluminum receiver, with walnut stock and checkered pistol-grip. Offered in both long and short action calibers from .223 Rem. to 7mm Rem. Magnum. Barrel length 20" for short action calibers; 22" to 24" for long action calibers. Open sights standard. Weight about 7 lbs. depending on caliber. In 2003 a straight-grip stock introduced.

740	600	450	300	200	150

BLR Lightweight '81

Features straight-grip checkered walnut stock. Fitted with 20" or 22" barrel; magazine capacity 4 or 5 rounds, both depending on caliber. Chambered for calibers .22-25-, .243, 7mm-08, .308, .358, .450 Marlin, .270 WSM, .300 WSM and .325 WSM. Offered in long action chambered for .270, .30-06, 7mm Rem. Magnum and .300 Win. Magnum. Weight from 6.5 lbs. to 7.75 lbs. depending on caliber. **NOTE:** Add 20 percent for long action; $70 for WSM calibers.

730	550	425	325	225	125

BLR Lightweight Takedown

Similar to BLR Lightweight, with takedown feature. Introduced 2007.

775	650	575	375	200	150

BLR Lightweight '81 Stainless Takedown

Similar to above, with stainless steel barrel and receiver. Introduced 2008.

975	850	695	475	350	225

Model B-78

Introduced in 1973. Single-shot lever-action falling block. Offered in several calibers from .22-250 to .45-70. Barrel lengths from 24" to 26" in round or octagonal shape. No sights except .45-70. Checkered walnut stock. First built in 1973. Discontinued in 1983. **NOTE:** Add 15 percent for .45-70 caliber.

1400	1100	850	600	350	250

Model 53

Offered in 1990. Reproduction of Winchester Model 53. Like original, chambered for .32-20 cartridge. Limited edition offering confined to 5,000 rifles. Features hand-cut checkering, high-grade walnut stock, full pistol-grip and semi-beavertail fore-end. Pistol-grip fitted with metal grip cap. Barrel length 22". Finish blue.

900	800	650	500	325	200

Model 65 Grade I

Limited-edition lever-action rifle. Chambered for .218 Bee cartridge. Has tapered round 24" barrel, with open sights. Patterned after Winchester Model 65. Has 7-round tubular magazine. Finish blued, with plain walnut stock. Metal buttplate. Manufactured 3,500 in 1989.

850	675	500	300	—	150

Model 65 High Grade

Deluxe version features silver-finished scroll engraved receiver, with gold animal inlays and gold-plated trigger. Features select checkered walnut stock. Manufactured 1,500 in 1989.

1650	1200	825	500	—	—

Model 71 Grade I

Reproduction of Winchester Model 71. Chambered for .348 cartridge. Has 20" or 24" barrel, with open sights and 4-round tubular magazine. Finish blued, with plain walnut stock. Manufactured 4,000 20" carbines; 3,000 24" rifles, in 1986 and 1987.

—	950	750	595	400	250

	NIB	EXC.	V.G.	GOOD	FAIR	POOR	

Model 71 High Grade

Version similar to Grade I. Scroll engraved grayed receiver, with gold-plated trigger and gold inlays. Manufactured 3,000 each of carbines and rifles in 1986 and 1987.

NIB	EXC.	V.G.	GOOD	FAIR	POOR
—	1400	950	750	500	325

Jonathan Browning Centennial Mountain Rifle

Limited edition blackpowder rifle. Chambered for .50 ball. Fitted with 30" octagon barrel and single set trigger. Figured walnut stock and engraved lock plate. Cased, with powder horn. Limited to 1,000 rifles in 1978.

NIB	EXC.	V.G.	GOOD	FAIR	POOR
1250	750	600	450	—	250

Jonathan Browning Mountain Rifle

Same as above, without fancy wood case or engraving. Chambered for .45 or .54 caliber.

NIB	EXC.	V.G.	GOOD	FAIR	POOR
800	500	400	300	—	175

Model 1878 (Original)

Based on John M. Browning's first patent. Single-shot rifle only firearm manufactured by Browning brothers. Offered in several calibers. Only a few hundred probably exist with Ogden, Utah barrel address. Design later sold to Winchester. Sold under Winchester name as Model 1885 High Wall.

NIB	EXC.	V.G.	GOOD	FAIR	POOR
—	50000	40000	30000	15000	5000

Model 1885 High Wall

Single-shot rifle, with falling block action and octagonal free-floating barrel. Similar to Model 78. Introduced in 1985. Stock is high grade walnut, with straight-grip and recoil pad. Furnished with 28" barrel. Offered in these calibers: .223, .22-250, .270, .30-06, 7mm Rem. Magnum, .45-70 Gov't. Weighs about 8 lbs. 12 oz.

NIB	EXC.	V.G.	GOOD	FAIR	POOR
1275	950	650	500	200	100

Model 1885 Low Wall

Introduced in 1995. Similar to above in a more accurate version of original Low Wall. Thin octagon barrel 24" in length. Trigger pull adjustable. Walnut stock fitted with pistol-grip and schnabel forearm. Offered in .22 Hornet, .223 Rem. and .243 Win. calibers. Weight about 6.4 lbs.

NIB	EXC.	V.G.	GOOD	FAIR	POOR
1150	850	550	400	300	150

Model 1885 Low Wall Traditional Hunter

Introduced in 1998. Similar to Low Wall, with half-octagon half-round 24" barrel. Chambered for .357 Magnum, .44 Magnum and .45 Colt cartridges. Case colored receiver and crescent butt, with tang sight also featured. Weight about 6.5 lbs.

NIB	EXC.	V.G.	GOOD	FAIR	POOR
1150	850	550	400	300	150

Model 1885 BPCR (Black Powder Cartridge Rifle)

Introduced in 1996 for BPCR metallic silhouette shoots. Chambered for .45-70 or .40-60 caliber. Receiver case colored, 28" round barrel fitted with vernier sight with level. Walnut stock has checkered pistol-grip. Fitted with tang sight. Weight about 11 lbs.

NIB	EXC.	V.G.	GOOD	FAIR	POOR
1600	1300	800	400	300	150

Model 1885 BPCR Creedmoor Type

Introduced in 1998. Chambered for .45-90 cartridge. Features 34" heavy half-round barrel, with long range tang sight and wind gauge front sight. Weight about 11 lbs. 13 oz.

NIB	EXC.	V.G.	GOOD	FAIR	POOR
1800	1500	1150	900	500	300

Model 1885 High Wall Traditional Hunter

Variation of Model 1885 series. Introduced in 1997. Fitted with an oil finish walnut stock and crescent buttplate. Barrel octagonal and 28" in length. Rear sight buckhorn. Fitted with tang-mounted peep sight. Front sight gold bead classic style. Chambered for .30-30, .38-55 and .45-70 cartridges. Weight about 9 lbs. In 1998, .454 Casull caliber added.

NIB	EXC.	V.G.	GOOD	FAIR	POOR
1200	950	700	575	400	275

Model 1886 Grade I

Lever action sporting rifle. Patterned after Model 1886 Winchester. Chambered for .45-70 cartridge. Has 26" octagonal barrel, with full-length tubular magazine. Finish blued, with walnut stock. Crescent buttplate. Manufactured 7,000 in 1986.

NIB	EXC.	V.G.	GOOD	FAIR	POOR
1350	950	725	600	450	300

Carbine

NIB	EXC.	V.G.	GOOD	FAIR	POOR
950	650	550	400	325	250

	NIB	EXC.	V.G.	GOOD	FAIR	POOR

Model 1886 High Grade

Deluxe version of Model 1886. Features game scene engraving, with gold accents and checkered select walnut stock. "1 of 3,000" engraved on top of barrel. Manufactured 3,000 in 1986.

	1900	1600	1000	700	—	—

Carbine

	1600	1100	900	600	—	—

Model 1886 Montana Centennial

Similar to High Grade, with different engraving pattern. Designed to commemorate Centennial of State of Montana. There were 2,000 manufactured in 1986. All commemorative's must be NIB with all supplied materials to command collector interest.

	2000	1600	1200	—	—	—

B-92 Carbine

Lever-action sporting rifle. Patterned after Winchester Model 92. Chambered for .357 Magnum and .44 Magnum cartridges. Has 20" barrel, with 11-round tubular magazine. Finish blued, with walnut stock. Discontinued in 1986. **NOTE:** Add 10 percent for Centennial Model; 30 percent for .357 Magnum.

	—	700	625	400	250	120

Model 1895 Grade I

Lever-action sporting rifle. Chambered in .30-40 Krag and .30-06 cartridge. Patterned after Model 1895 Winchester. Has 24" barrel and 4-round integral box magazine. Buckhorn rear sight and blade front. Finish blued, with walnut stock. Manufactured 6,000 in .30-06 and 2,000 chambered for .30-40 Krag, in 1984.

	—	950	675	475	375	275

Model 1895 High Grade

Deluxe engraved version of Model 1895. Has gold-inlaid game scenes and gold-plated trigger. Features checkered select walnut stock. Produced 2,000 in 1984 — 1,000 in each caliber.

	—	1500	1250	900	700	400

Express Rifle

Over/under superposed rifle. Chambered for .270 Winchester or .30-06 cartridges. Has 24" barrels, with folding express sights and automatic ejectors. Features a single trigger. Receiver engraved. Finished blue, with deluxe checkered walnut stock. Introduced in 1980. Discontinued in 1986.

	—	6500	3950	2000	1100	800

Custom Shop Express Rifles

Produced in two different models, Herstall and CCS 375. Both are custom-built, with choice of engraving patterns.

	N/A	23000	17500	12000	5500	700

Continental Set

Consists of Express Rifle chambered for .30-06 cartridge. Furnished with an extra set of 20-gauge over/under barrels. Shotgun barrels are 26.5" in length. Single trigger, automatic ejectors and heavily engraved receiver. Select walnut stock hand checkered and oil-finished. Furnished with a fitted case. Manufactured 500 between 1978 and 1986.

	10000	9250	8000	4500	2000	1000

BRUCE & DAVIS
Webster, Massachusetts

Double-Barreled Pistol

.36-caliber double-barrel percussion pistol, with 3" to 6" round barrels. Barrel rib marked "Bruce & Davis". Blued, with walnut grips. Manufactured during 1840s.

	—	—	925	400	175	100

BRUCHET
Ste. Etienne, France

Model A Shotgun

12-gauge or .410 bore side-by-side shotgun, with double triggers and automatic ejectors. Barrel lengths and chokes to customer specifications. Produced on limited basis (50 per year) since 1982. Base price listed.

	3600	2750	1900	1450	1000	500

	NIB	EXC.	V.G.	GOOD	FAIR	POOR

Model B

As above, with finer finish and spring-assisted action opener. Imported since 1982.

NIB	EXC.	V.G.	GOOD	FAIR	POOR
6950	5250	4000	3000	2250	1250

BRUFF, R.P.
New York, New York

Pocket Pistol

.41-caliber single-shot percussion pistol, with 2.5" to 3" barrels. Marked "R.P. Bruff NY" in an arch and "Cast Steel". German silver, with checkered walnut stock. Manufactured between 1861 and 1870.

NIB	EXC.	V.G.	GOOD	FAIR	POOR
—	—	1900	825	225	100

BRYCO ARMS
Carson City, Nevada
See—Jennings

BSA GUNS LTD.
Birmingham, England

Established in 1861, this firm has produced a wide variety of firearms over the years. Most common of these arms that are currently available in United States are listed.

SINGLE-SHOT

No. 12 Cadet Martini

.310-caliber single-shot Martini action rifle, with 29" barrel, adjustable sights and straight-grip walnut stock. Manufactured approximately 80,000 from 1911 to 1913. Many of those imported into U.S. were altered to .22-caliber.

NIB	EXC.	V.G.	GOOD	FAIR	POOR
—	750	500	300	150	100

Centurian Match Rifle

As above in .22-caliber, with 24" barrel, adjustable sights. Pistol-grip walnut stock.

NIB	EXC.	V.G.	GOOD	FAIR	POOR
—	600	450	300	200	100

Model 13 Sporter

As above in .22 Hornet, with hunting sights.

NIB	EXC.	V.G.	GOOD	FAIR	POOR
—	650	425	300	225	100

Martini International Match

As above, with heavy match barrel, ISU-style sights and match stock. Manufactured from 1950 to 1953.

NIB	EXC.	V.G.	GOOD	FAIR	POOR
—	750	575	325	250	125

Martini International Light

As above, with 26" lighter weight barrel.

NIB	EXC.	V.G.	GOOD	FAIR	POOR
—	750	575	325	250	125

Martini International ISU

As above meeting ISU specifications, with 28" barrel. Manufactured from 1968 to 1976.

NIB	EXC.	V.G.	GOOD	FAIR	POOR
—	850	675	400	325	200

BOLT-ACTIONS

Royal

Bolt-action sporting rifle. Manufactured in a variety of calibers. 24" barrel, with checkered French walnut stock.

NIB	EXC.	V.G.	GOOD	FAIR	POOR
—	550	500	250	200	100

Majestic Deluxe

.22 Hornet, .222, .243, 7x57mm, .308 or .30-06 bolt-action sporting rifle, with 22" barrel. Folding rear sight, checkered walnut stock, with schnabel fore-end tip. Imported from 1959 to 1965. **NOTE:** Add 60 percent for .22 Hornet.

NIB	EXC.	V.G.	GOOD	FAIR	POOR
—	550	350	250	200	100

Majestic Deluxe Featherweight

As above in .270 or .458 Magnum, with thinner barrel. **NOTE:** Add 25 percent for .458; 75 percent for .458.

NIB	EXC.	V.G.	GOOD	FAIR	POOR
—	550	350	250	200	100

	NIB	EXC.	V.G.	GOOD	FAIR	POOR

Monarch Deluxe

As above drilled and tapped for telescopic sight. Available in heavy barreled varmint version in .222- or .243-caliber. Imported from 1966 to 1974.

	NIB	EXC.	V.G.	GOOD	FAIR	POOR
	—	550	375	275	225	100

HERTERS U9

Firm of Herters, Inc. of Waseca, Minnesota, imported BSA rifle actions beginning in 1965 that were used for custom-made rifles. Commencing in 1986, BSA began production of a new line of bolt-action sporting rifles on Model CF-2 action. Standard production models listed.

Sporter/Classic

Hunting rifle available in a variety of calibers, with checkered walnut stock. Introduced in 1986.

	NIB	EXC.	V.G.	GOOD	FAIR	POOR
	—	450	325	275	200	100

Varminter

As above, with matte-finished heavy barrel in .222-, .22-250- or .243-caliber. Introduced in 1986.

	NIB	EXC.	V.G.	GOOD	FAIR	POOR
	—	350	275	225	175	100

Stutzen Rifle

As above, with 20.5" barrel. Mannlicher-style stock.

	NIB	EXC.	V.G.	GOOD	FAIR	POOR
	—	475	350	275	225	100

Regal Custom

As above, with engraved receiver, checkered walnut stock and ebony fore-end. Imported only in 1986.

	NIB	EXC.	V.G.	GOOD	FAIR	POOR
	—	925	750	600	500	250

CFT Target Rifle

.308-caliber single-shot version of above, with 26.5" barrel and adjustable sights. Imported only in 1987.

	NIB	EXC.	V.G.	GOOD	FAIR	POOR
	—	750	600	550	400	200

SHOTGUNS

Royal

Side-by-side chambered for 12- or 20-gauge 3" shells. Choice of 26" or 28" barrels, with multi-chokes. Checkered select walnut stock, with straight-grip. Splinter forearm. Case colored receiver, with side plates. Single selective trigger. Recoil pad standard. Weight about: 7.25 lbs. 12-gauge; 6.75 lbs. 20-gauge.

	NIB	EXC.	V.G.	GOOD	FAIR	POOR
	1500	1150	900	675	—	—

Classic

Side-by-side offered in 12-, 16-, 20-, 28-gauge and .410 bore. Choice of 26" or 28" barrels, except for 28-gauge and .410 bore where 26" barrels are only length offered. Checkered walnut stock, with pistol-grip. Case colored box lock receiver, with scroll engraving. Semi-beavertail forearm. Recoil pad and choke tubes standard. Weight about: 7.25 lbs. 12-gauge; 6.75 lbs. 16-gauge; 6.6 lbs. 20-gauge; 6.25 lbs. 28-gauge; 6.5 lbs. .410 bore.

	NIB	EXC.	V.G.	GOOD	FAIR	POOR
	1300	975	800	600	400	200

Falcon

Over/under in 12- or 20-gauge with 3" chambers. Choice of 26" or 28" barrels, with ventilated rib and choke tubes. Checkered walnut stock, with pistol-grip. Case colored scroll engraved receiver. Single selective trigger. Automatic ejectors. Recoil pad standard. Weight about: 7.25 lbs. 12-gauge; 7 lbs. 20-gauge.

	NIB	EXC.	V.G.	GOOD	FAIR	POOR
	1200	900	875	500	300	150

Falcon Sporting

Similar to Falcon. Offered only in 12-gauge, with 2.75" chambers. Choice of 28" or 30" ventilated rib barrels, with 5 chokes tubes. Barrels ported. Checkered walnut stock, with schnabel forearm. Weight about 7.7 lbs.

	NIB	EXC.	V.G.	GOOD	FAIR	POOR
	1250	950	775	475	275	125

Silver Eagle

Over/under chambered for 12- or 20-gauge 3" shell. Fitted with 26" or 28" vent rib barrels, with choke tubes. Checkered walnut stock, with pistol-grip. Single selective trigger. Blued box lock receiver. Recoil pad standard. Weight about: 7.2 lbs. 12-gauge; 6.75 lbs. 20-gauge.

	NIB	EXC.	V.G.	GOOD	FAIR	POOR
	490	375	300	250	200	125

NIB	EXC.	V.G.	GOOD	FAIR	POOR

Silver Eagle II

Similar to Silver Eagle above. Addition of automatic ejectors.

590	425	275	225	175	100

200 Series

Series of semi-automatic shotguns. Chambered for 12-, 16-, 20-, 28-gauge and .410 bore. Offered with 26" or 28" vent rib barrels, with choke tubes in 12-, 16- and 20-gauge; 28-gauge and .410 bore in 26" barrels only.. All gauges offered with walnut or synthetic stocks. 20-gauge offered in a youth model, with shortened stock. All gauges have 3" chambers except for 28-gauge, with 2.75" chambers. Weights range from 7.4 lbs. to 6.5 lbs. **NOTE:** Add $70 for walnut stock.

390	290	225	200	100	75

300 SM Series

Semi-automatic series offered in 12-gauge only, with 3.5" chambers. Choice of 24", 26" or 28" vent rib barrels, with choke tubes. Synthetic stock. Weighs about 7.3 lbs.

420	315	250	225	175	100

BUCO
Germany

Buco Gas Pistol

Odd firearm looks more like a telescope than pistol. Chambered for 10.55mm gas cartridge. Single-shot. Overall approximately 5.5" long in its open or cocked position. Barrel is smooth bore and 3.75" in length. No sights and no safety—one simply pulls inner tube back much like extending a telescope, unscrews end cap, inserts round and screws cap back into place. When needed, a thumbnail is used to depress sear and fire pistol. Marked on end cap "Buco DRGM". No more information available as to quantity or year of manufacture.

—	—	650	500	350	150

BUDISCHOWSKY
Norton Armament Corp.
Mt. Clemens, Michigan

TP-70

.22 or .25 ACP caliber semi-automatic pistol, with 2.5" barrel, fixed sights and 6-shot magazine. Stainless steel, with plastic grips. Manufactured between 1973 and 1977.

NOTE: German-designed Budischowsky was originally made in Michigan by Norton Armament Corp. Michigan-made Budischowsky's are considered better quality than later examples made in Florida and Utah. Deduct 15% for non-Michigan manufacture.

.22 Rimfire Caliber

550	425	350	300	225	150

.25 ACP Caliber

525	400	325	275	175	125

BUL TRANSMARK LTD.
Tel-Aviv, Israel

Model M5

This model was brought into the USA from 1996 to 2010 by several importers, including ISA, KBI, EAA and others. Semi-automatic bears a resemblance to Model 1911. Frame polymer, slide stainless steel. Available in 9mm, .38 Super, .40 S&W and .45 ACP. Magazine limited to 10 rounds. **NOTE:** Add 40 to 60 percent for IPSC competition models.

750	600	450	350	200	100

BULLARD REPEATING ARMS CO.
Springfield, Massachusetts

Designed by James H. Bullard. Rifles listed were manufactured in competition with those produced by Whitney Arms Company and Winchester Repeating Arms Company. Approximately 12,000 made between 1886 and 1890.

Small Frame

.32-40 and .38-45 caliber lever action rifle, with 26" octagonal barrel. Half or full length magazine tube. Blued or case hardened, with walnut stock. Receiver stamped "Bullard Repeating Arms Company/Springfield, Mass., U.S.A. Pat. Aug. 16, 1881". Caliber marked on top of frame.

—	—	4000	2050	675	300

	NIB	EXC.	V.G.	GOOD	FAIR	POOR

Large Frame

.40-75 through .45-85 caliber lever action rifle, with 28" octagonal barrel. Other features and markings as above. Can be custom ordered in .50-95 and .50-115.

	NIB	EXC.	V.G.	GOOD	FAIR	POOR
	—	—	5150	2500	875	400

Carbine

.45-70 caliber lever action rifle, with 22" round barrel. Sliding dust cover on receiver. Marking and finish as above.

	NIB	EXC.	V.G.	GOOD	FAIR	POOR
	—	—	7950	3800	1500	500

Musket

.45-70 caliber lever action rifle, with 30" round barrel. Full-length stock secured by two barrel bands. Rod under barrel, military sights and same sliding cover on receiver as found on Carbine. Examples noted without manufacturer's markings.

	NIB	EXC.	V.G.	GOOD	FAIR	POOR
	—	—	7500	3500	1500	500

BULLDOG SINGLE-SHOT PISTOL
Connecticut Arms & Manufacturing Co.
Naubuc, Connecticut

Bulldog

.44- or .50-caliber single-shot spur trigger pistol, with 4" or 6" barrels. Pivoting breechblock that moves to left for loading. Blued, case hardened and stamped "Connecticut Arms & Manf. Co. Naubuc Conn. Patented Oct. 25, 1864". Only a few hundred manufactured. .50-caliber 6" barreled versions would be worth an additional 40 percent. Produced between 1866 and 1868.

	NIB	EXC.	V.G.	GOOD	FAIR	POOR
	—	—	1650	675	275	150

BURGESS GUN CO.
Buffalo, New York
Also See—Colt and Whitney

One of the most prolific 19th century designers was Andrew Burgess, who established his own company in 1892. Burgess Gun Company manufactured slide action shotguns and rifles, operated by a unique pistol-grip prior to their being purchased by Winchester Repeating Arms Company in 1899. Arms based on Burgess' patents were manufactured by a variety of American gun makers. Serial numbers for all Burgess shotguns begin at 1000.

12 Gauge Slide Action Shotgun

12-gauge slide-action shotgun, with 28" or 30" barrel. Blued, with walnut stock. Available with 6 grades of engraving. Values listed are for standard plain model.

Burgess engraving grades (1-4)

	NIB	EXC.	V.G.	GOOD	FAIR	POOR
	—	—	1700	700	250	125

Folding Shotgun

As above, with 19.5" barrel. Hinged so it may be folded back against buttstock.

	NIB	EXC.	V.G.	GOOD	FAIR	POOR
	—	—	4550	1750	650	300

Slide Action Rifle

Extremely rare rifle based upon shotgun design described above. Manufactured in at least three calibers, with varying barrel lengths. Blued, with walnut stock.

	NIB	EXC.	V.G.	GOOD	FAIR	POOR
	—	—	3950	1500	500	250

BURGSMULLER, K.
Krelensen, Germany

Burgo

Rohm RG10 under another name. It is a poor quality inexpensive .38-caliber revolver. Examples marketed by Burgsmuller are so marked. Virtually worthless.

Regent

Regent is a .22-caliber revolver that resembles Colt Police Positive in appearance. Higher quality than Burgo. Manufacturer not known.

	NIB	EXC.	V.G.	GOOD	FAIR	POOR
	—	165	125	75	50	5

BURNSIDE RIFLE CO.
Bristol Firearms Co.
Bristol & Providence, Rhode Island

	NIB	EXC.	V.G.	GOOD	FAIR	POOR

Bristol, Rhode Island

Historically desirable firearm for Civil War collectors. Designer, Ambrose E. Burnside, was to become a well- known Union general. Rifle, of which there were four distinct models, was used quite extensively in Civil War. This carbine was manufactured first by Bristol Firearms Co., which made entire production of first model and also some of second model. In 1862 Burnside Firearms Co. was formed. They produced remainder of second models and all third and fourth models. Production ceased entirely in 1865.

Burnside Carbine 1st Model

Produced by Bristol. Chambered for .54-caliber. Breechloader that uses percussion ignition system, but features a cartridge of sorts made of copper and a tape priming device that was located inside frame. Has 22" round barrel, with no fore-end, walnut stock and inspector's cartouche. Finish blued and case-colored. Frame stamped "Burnside's /Patent/March 25th/1856". Approximately 250 1st Models manufactured.

—	—	15000	6000	1500	500

2nd Model

2nd Model features an improved breechblock opening mechanism located inside trigger guard. Barrel is 21" long. Other features similar to 1st Model. Marked either "Bristol Firearm Co." or "Burnside Rifle Co./Providence-R.I.". Barrel marked "Cast Steel 1861" and some breechblock devices marked "G.P. Foster Pat./April 10th 1860". Approximately 1,500 2nd Models manufactured in 1861 and 1862.

—	—	5500	2500	750	300

3rd Model

Differs from 2nd Model in it has a fore-end, with a barrel band and slightly modified hammer. Markings same as Burnside-manufactured 2nd Models. Approximately 2,000 produced in 1862.

—	—	3500	1250	500	250

4th Model

Differs from others in it features a hinged breech that permits simpler loading of odd-shaped Burnside percussion cartridge. Frame marked "Burnside's Patent/Model of 1864". Other features similar to 3rd Model. Approximately 50,000 manufactured between 1862 and 1865.

—	—	4000	2000	800	400

BUSHMASTER FIREARMS INTERNATIONAL
Ilion, New York

In 2006, Bushmaster was purchased by Freedom Group, parent company of Remington, Marlin/H&R, DPMS, Para USA and Dakota Arms. In 2011, Bushmaster plant in Maine was closed and production moved to Remington facility in Ilion, New York.

ACR Enhanced

Semi-automatic Adaptive Combat Rifle chambered in 5.56 NATO. Barrel is quickly interchangeable and available in 10.5", 14.5", 16.5" and 18.5". AAC Blackout 51T flash hider, 3-rail enhanced hand guard, with 7-position folding/telescoping stock. A-TACs model has fixed A-frame composite camo stock, with rubber butt pad and sling mounts. Introduced in 2013.

2450	2200	1900	—	—	—

XM15-E2S Target Model

Furnished with 20" heavy barrel and A-2 stock. Weight 8.35 lbs. **NOTE:** Add $10 for 24" barrel; $20 for 26" barrel; $75 for A3 carry handle.

800	675	550	400	300	200

XM15-E2S V-Match Competition Rifle

Model specially designed competition rifle, with 20", 24" or 26" barrel lengths. Fitted with black anodized aluminum handguard. Weight about 8.1 lbs. **NOTE:** Add $75 for A3 carry handle.

950	800	700	450	350	250

XM15-E2S V-Match Carbine

As above, with 16" barrel. Weight about 6.9 lbs. **NOTE:** Add $75 for A3 carry handle.

900	700	575	450	350	250

XM15 3-Gun Enhanced Carbine

Designed for 3-Gun competition, with crimson anodized upper and lower receiver, 16" mid-length stainless barrel, 15" carbon fiber free-float tube, Rolling Thunder compensator and Timney trigger. Other features include Boron nitride bolt carrier group, Bravo Company charging handle, ambidextrous selector switch, Magpul MIAD grip and MOE stock. Introduced in 2014.

1485	1225	1000	750	500	250

	NIB	EXC.	V.G.	GOOD	FAIR	POOR

XM15-E2S Shorty Carbine

This "post-ban" model M16 is a gas-operated semi-automatic rifle. Chambered for .223 Remington cartridge. Fitted with heavy 16" barrel and 30-round magazine. Overall length 35"; empty weight 6.72 lbs. **NOTE:** Add $50 for fluted barrel; $75 for A3-type carry handle.

	NIB	EXC.	V.G.	GOOD	FAIR	POOR
	—	675	550	450	300	200

XM15-E2S Dissipator

Similar to above model, with 16" barrel. Fitted with longer plastic handguard to give a longer sight radius. Weight 7.2 lbs. **NOTE:** Add $75 for A3 carry handle.

	NIB	EXC.	V.G.	GOOD	FAIR	POOR
	950	775	600	450	300	200

M4 Post-Ban Carbine

Introduced in 2001. Features 14.5" barrel, with permanently attached Mini Y Comp muzzle-brake (total length 16") and pinned fixed-length Tele-style stock. Chambered for .223-caliber. M16A2 rear sight. Supplied with 10-round magazine. Weight about 6.6 lbs.

	NIB	EXC.	V.G.	GOOD	FAIR	POOR
	1050	900	750	450	300	200

M4A3 Post-Ban Carbine

Same as above, with removable carry handle. Introduced in 2001.

	NIB	EXC.	V.G.	GOOD	FAIR	POOR
	1125	975	825	500	400	300

DCM Competition Rifle

Features 20" extra heavy barrel, with free floating fore-end. Competition sights and trigger. Supplied with buttstock weight and hard carrying case, 10-round magazine.

	NIB	EXC.	V.G.	GOOD	FAIR	POOR
	1350	1075	800	600	500	350

11.5" Barrel Carbine

AR-style carbine chambered in 5.56/.223. Features include 11.5" chrome-lined barrel, with permanently attached BATF-approved 5.5" flash suppressor, fixed or removable carry handle, optional optics rail, 30-round magazine. Overall length 31.625". Weight 6.46 or 6.81 lbs.

	NIB	EXC.	V.G.	GOOD	FAIR	POOR
	900	775	600	450	300	200

Heavy-Barreled Carbine

AR-style semi-automatic carbine chambered in 5.56/.223. Features include chrome-lined heavy profile 16" vanadium steel barrel, fixed or removable carry handle, six-position telestock. Overall length 32.5". Weight 6.93 lbs. to 7.28 lbs.

	NIB	EXC.	V.G.	GOOD	FAIR	POOR
	1000	850	700	550	300	200

Modular Carbine

AR-style carbine chambered in 5.56/.223. Features include 16" chrome-lined chrome-moly vanadium steel barrel, skeleton stock or six-position telestock, clamp-on front sight and detachable flip-up dual aperture rear 30-round magazine. Overall length 36.25". Weight 7.3 lbs.

	NIB	EXC.	V.G.	GOOD	FAIR	POOR
	1450	1200	1000	750	400	250

M17S Bullpup

Gas-operated semi-automatic rifle in bull-pup design. Chambered for .223 cartridge. Fitted with 21.5" barrel. Weight 8.2 lbs.

	NIB	EXC.	V.G.	GOOD	FAIR	POOR
	800	675	500	400	300	200

Gas Piston Rifle

Semi-automatic AR-style rifle chambered in .223. Features include 16" barrel, telescoping stock, carry handle, 30-round magazine and piston assembly rather than direct gas impingement. Overall length 32.5". Weight 7.46 lbs.

	NIB	EXC.	V.G.	GOOD	FAIR	POOR
	1750	1375	1050	800	650	300

6.8 SPC Carbine

AR-style semi-automatic rifle chambered in 6.8 SPC. Features include 16" M4 profile barrel, with Izzy muzzle-brake, 26-round magazine, six-position telestock. Available in A2 (fixed carry handle) or A3 (removable carry handle) configuration. Overall length 32.75". Weight 6.57 lbs. Also chambered in 7.62x39mm.

	NIB	EXC.	V.G.	GOOD	FAIR	POOR
	1200	1150	950	800	650	300

Carbon 15 9mm Carbine

Semi-automatic carbine chambered in 9mm Parabellum. Carbon fiber frame, 16" steel barrel, six-position telescoping stock, 30- round detachable magazine. Introduced 2006.

	NIB	EXC.	V.G.	GOOD	FAIR	POOR
	1000	850	700	550	475	300

NIB	EXC.	V.G.	GOOD	FAIR	POOR

Carbon 15 Top Loading Rifle
Semi-automatic rifle chambered in .223. Carbon fiber frame, 16" steel barrel, retractable stock, Picatinny rail, 10-round fixed magazine. Based on AR-15. Introduced 2006.

1000	850	700	550	475	300

Carbon 15 Quad Rail Flattop
Semi-automatic AR-style in 5.56 NATO. M4 contour 16.5" barrel, with A2 flash hider, fixed front sight bases and bayonet lug. Flat top upper receiver, with Mission First tactical pomer quad rail and four rail covers. Six-position adjustable stock. New in 2013.

800	700	600	—	—	—

Predator
Semi-automatic rifle chambered in .223. 20" DCM-type barrel, fixed composite buttstock, 2-stage competition trigger, Picatinny rail, .500" scope risers. Based on AR-15. Introduced 2006.

1100	900	750	600	525	325

Carbon 15 .22 Rimfire Rifle
Similar to Shorty carbine. Chambered in .22 LR. Blowback, with 10-round magazine.

625	495	350	275	200	150

.308 Hunter
Designed for the hunter. Chambered in .308 Winchester, with 20" heavy-fluted barrel. Chrome lined bore and chamber. Features include 5-round magazine, mid-length gas system, two .75" mini risers for optics mounting, Hogue rubberized pistol-grip, standard A2 stock. Vista Hunter has A2 grip. Weight about 8.5 lbs. **NOTE:** Add $100 for Vista Hunter if NIB.

1400	1100	925	775	500	300

ORC Series
Optics Ready Carbine series for shooters who wish to add various optical holograph, red dot or scope sights. Chambered in .223/5.56, with magazine capacity of 30 rounds or .308 with 20-round magazine. Gas piston system taps gas from barrel much like AK and FAL designs. Provides a cleaner operation with less recoil. Detented plug in gas block allows for easy cleaning. Barrel length 16"; weight 6.6 lbs. (.223) to 7.75 lbs. (.308). **NOTE:** Add $60 for .308 chambering.

1125	965	825	700	500	300

.450 Carbine
Chambered for .450 Bushmaster cartridge providing big-bore power in AR platform. Developed with Hornady Mfg., cartridge propels a 250-grain bullet at 2200 fps, ideal for most North American big game. Barrel length 16" or 20", A3 flattop receiver with Picatinny rail. Weight about 8.5 lbs.

1200	1025	900	750	550	350

Bushmaster AK Carbine
AR-type rifle, with AK-type muzzle-brake and permanently pinned suppressor. 5.56 NATO caliber.

1100	950	800	650	300	200

Bushmaster .300 AAC Blackout
AR-type rifle chambered for .300 AAC cartridge. Developed by Advanced Armament Corporation, which is now part of Freedom Group that owns Bushmaster. Round's ballistics are similar to 7.62x39 and .300 Whisper wildcat. .300 AAC is factory loaded by Remington, including a sub-sonic load. Compatible with AR-15 magazines.

1300	1050	875	700	300	200

BA50 .50 BMG Rifle and Carbine
Bolt-action 10-round repeater intended for long-range target shooting. 30" barrel, muzzle-brake. Carbine has 20" barrel.

5000	4200	3700	3000	—	—

Carbon 15 .223 Pistol
AR-style semi-automatic pistol chambered in 5.56/.223. Features include 7.5" stainless steel barrel, carbon composite receiver, shortened handguard, full-length optics rail, A2-type front sight with dual-aperture flip-up rear. 30-round magazine. Overall length 20". Weight 2.88 lbs.

800	700	550	400	300	200

Carbon-15 9mm Pistol
Operating controls similar to AR-type rifles, 30 round capacity. Weight with loaded magazine 5.5 lbs. Carbon fiber receiver, fore-end and grip, with Chrome Moly steel barrel. Full length Picatinny

	NIB	EXC.	V.G.	GOOD	FAIR	POOR

rail.

	800	700	550	400	300	200

Type 97 Pistol

Similar to above, without handguard.

	750	650	500	400	300	200

XM15 Patrolman's Pistol

This law-enforcement-only model has a 7" or 10.5" barrel, with flash hider, A2 pistol-grip and knurled free-float handguard. Enhanced model has Barnes Precision free-float lightweight quad rail, Magpul MOE pistol-grip and trigger guard. **NOTE:** Add $200 for enhanced model.

	825	750	600	500	400	250

BUTLER, WM. S.
Rocky Hill, Connecticut

Butler Single-Shot Pistol

.36-caliber single-shot percussion pocket pistol, with 2.5" barrel. Frame and grip made in one piece. Frame marked "Wm. S. Butler's Patent/Patented Feb.3, 1857".

	—	—	975	385	150	50

BUTTERFIELD, JESSE
Philadelphia, Pennsylvania

Butterfield Army Revolver

.41-caliber revolver, with 7" octagonal barrel and unfluted 5-shot cylinder. Features a special priming device, disk that was loaded in front of trigger guard. Brass frame, blued with walnut grips. Frame stamped "Butterfield's Patent Dec. 11, 1855/Phila.". Approximately 650 manufactured in 1861 and 1862.

	—	—	6000	2250	875	450

Butterfield Pocket Pistol

.41-caliber single-shot percussion pistol, with 2" to 3.5" barrel. German silver, with walnut stocks. Lock marked "Butterfield's/Patent Dec 11, 1855". Extremely rare. Manufactured in 1850s.

	—	—	9000	4250	1650	1000

C

	NIB	EXC.	V.G.	GOOD	FAIR	POOR

CABANAS, INDUSTRIAS S.A.
Aguilas, Mexico

This company manufactures a variety of bolt-action single-shot rifles that utilize .22-caliber blanks to propel a .177-caliber pellet. Scarce, but not especially valuable.

Mini-82 Youth

NIB	EXC.	V.G.	GOOD	FAIR	POOR
75	65	50	40	30	20

R-83 Larger Youth

NIB	EXC.	V.G.	GOOD	FAIR	POOR
85	75	60	50	40	30

Safari A

NIB	EXC.	V.G.	GOOD	FAIR	POOR
100	90	75	50	40	30

Varmint

NIB	EXC.	V.G.	GOOD	FAIR	POOR
125	110	90	75	—	35

Espronceda IV

NIB	EXC.	V.G.	GOOD	FAIR	POOR
125	110	90	75	50	35

Leyre

NIB	EXC.	V.G.	GOOD	FAIR	POOR
140	125	100	85	65	50

Master

NIB	EXC.	V.G.	GOOD	FAIR	POOR
150	130	110	100	75	60

CALICO
Cleveland, Ohio
See—American Industries, Inc.

CAMEX-BLASER USA, INC.
Ft. Worth, Texas
See—Blaser Jagdwaffen

CAMPO GIRO
Eibar, Spain

Esperanza y Unceta Model 1904

Designed by Lt. Col. Venancio Aguirre. This pistol was produced in limited numbers.

NIB	EXC.	V.G.	GOOD	FAIR	POOR
—	3000	2000	1500	1000	800

Model 1910

Similar to the above, in 9mm Largo. Tested, but not adopted by the Spanish army.

NIB	EXC.	V.G.	GOOD	FAIR	POOR
—	2000	1500	1000	800	600

Model 1913

An improved version of the above. About 1,300 made.

NIB	EXC.	V.G.	GOOD	FAIR	POOR
—	1500	1250	850	600	500

Model 1913/16

An improved version of the above. About 13,000 built.

NIB	EXC.	V.G.	GOOD	FAIR	POOR
—	2000	1550	1000	600	350

CARACAL

Caracal-F

Chambered for the 9mm Parabellum, the Caracal has a DAO trigger and is striker-fired. Features include a polymer frame, steel slide, ambidextrous magazine releases and an 18-round magazine. Weight 26.5 ounces. Barrel length is 4.1". Finish is matte blue. Caracal-C is compact variation with 3.5" barrel. Weighs 24.7 oz. Made in the United Arab Emirates. Introduced in 2011.

NIB	EXC.	V.G.	GOOD	FAIR	POOR
535	465	400	300	200	100

	NIB	EXC.	V.G.	GOOD	FAIR	POOR

CARD, S. W.
Location Unknown

Under Hammer Pistol

A .34-caliber single-shot percussion pocket pistol, with a 7.75" half octagonal barrel marked "S.W. Card" and "Cast Steel". Blued with walnut grips.

—	—	1500	450	150	50

CARLTON, M.
Haverhill, New Hampshire

Under Hammer Pistol

A .34-caliber percussion under hammer single-shot pistol, with a 3.5" to 7.75" half-octagonal barrel marked "M. Carleton & Co.". Browned with walnut grips. Active 1830s and 1840s.

—	—	1800	600	200	100

CASARTELLI, CARLO
Brescia, Italy

Sidelock Shotgun

Custom order sidelock shotgun. Available in any gauge, barrel length, choke, automatic ejectors, single-selective trigger and choice of engraving style.

16000	14500	10500	8250	6000	4000

Kenya Double Rifle

Custom order full sidelock rifle that is available in all standard and magnum calibers.

33000	29000	24000	18900	13000	9000

Africa Model

A bolt-action rifle built on a square-bridge magnum Mauser action. Chambered for the heavy magnum calibers and can be taken down for transport. Other features are on a custom order basis.

9750	8800	7500	5750	4750	3750

Safari Model

Built on a standard Mauser bolt-action and is chambered for the non-magnum calibers.

8000	7200	5800	4500	3250	2500

CASE WILLARD & CO.
New Hartford, Connecticut

Under Hammer Pistol

A .31-caliber single-shot percussion pistol, with a 3" half-octagonal barrel marked "Case Willard & Co./New Hartford Conn." Blued brass frame with walnut grips.

—	—	1400	550	200	100

CASPIAN ARMS, LTD.
Hardwick, Vermont

This company is primarily a 1911 component manufacturer.

Vietnam Commemorative

Government Model engraved by J.J. Adams and nickel-plated. Walnut grips have a branch service medallion inlaid and gold plating was available for an additional $350. There were 1,000 manufactured in 1986.

1800	1350	950	650	475	300

CASULL ARMS, INC.
Afton, Wyoming

CA 2000

Chambered for the .22 LR cartridge, this stainless steel revolver has a 5-round cylinder with a fold-up trigger. Double-action-only. Palm sized. Most recently produced "Velo-Dog". Discontinued.

550	425	350	250	200	175

CA 3800

Chambered for the .38 Casull cartridge (124 gr. 1800+fps), this pistol is fitted with a 6" match barrel and has a magazine capacity of 8 rounds. Full-length two-piece guide rod. Checkering on

NIB	EXC.	V.G.	GOOD	FAIR	POOR

front strap and mainspring housing is 20 lpi. Match trigger and numerous other special features. Weight about 40 oz. Introduced in 2000. Discontinued. **NOTE:** Add $300 for extra .45 ACP barrel.

2600	2050	1700	1200	650	300

CENTURY GUN COMPANY
Evansville, Knightstown & Greenfield, Indiana

Former manufacturer of large-caliber revolvers made in Evansville or Knightstown, Indiana between 1973 and 2001 or Greenfield, Indiana between 2002 and 2004.

Model 100

Single-action revolver, with six-round capacity. Chambered originally for .45-70 Government and later for .30-30 Win., .375 Win., .444 Marlin, .50-70 and .50-110. Barrel lengths from 6.5" to 12", weight from 5.5- to 6 lbs. Adjustable sights, crossbolt safety. Prices shown are for .45-70 caliber. **NOTE:** Add 100 percent for .50-110 caliber, 20 percent for others. For early production .45-70 guns marked Evansville, Indiana, add 100 to 200 percent if in excellent condition.

1200	1100	900	750	400	200

CENTURY INTERNATIONAL ARMS CO.
Delray Beach, Florida

Century International Arms is a leading importer of military firearms. It was founded in 1961 in Albans, Vermont, moved to Boca Raton, Florida in 1997 and to Delray Beach in 2004. Many models are original military surplus, others have been re-stocked or re-barreled to make satisfactory hunting rifles. Inventory changes frequently and some models are imported in limited quantities. The company also imports new handguns, rifles and shotguns from various manufacturers and countries. The listed firearms represent only a few of the many models imported recently or in the past.

Centurion 39 AK Pistol

This current production AK-47 style pistol has a 11.4" barrel, black polymer stock and pistol-grip. Other features include four Picatinny rails and M-16 type birdcage muzzle-brake.

825	700	550	400	300	200

Centurion UC-9 Carbine

Based on the UZI submachine gun in semi-automatic and chambered in 9mm. Comes with folding stock, 16" barrel and two 32-round magazines.

900	750	600	500	400	250

Centurion Over/Under Shotgun

This is a new shotgun in 12-, 20-, 28-gauge and.410 bore, with 2.75" chambers. Walnut stock is checkered. Receiver is blue. Offered in 28" vent rib barrels in full and modified chokes. Weight about 7.35 lbs. for the 12-gauge; 5.3 lbs. for the .410 bore.

—	375	325	225	175	125

Centurion 98 Sporter

This is refinished and rebuilt on a surplus German Mauser 98 action, with new commercial 22" barrel. No sights. Synthetic stock, with recoil pad is standard. Chambered for .270 or .30-06. Weighs about 7 lbs. 13 oz.

—	300	250	175	150	100

Century Centurion 14

This bolt-action rifle uses an Enfield Pattern 14 action. Drilled and tapped for scope mount. Barrel is 24" and chambered for 7mm Rem. Magnum. Walnut stock is checkered, with pistol-grip and Monte Carlo comb. No sights.

350	300	250	175	150	100

C93 Pistol

Based on Hecker & Koch MP-5 in semi-automatic. Chambered in 5.56 NATO or 7.63x39mm, with 8.5" barrel with flash suppressor and two 40-round magazines.

900	750	600	500	400	250

CZ 999 / CZ 40

Based on CZ 9 and CZ 40 pistols in 9mm or 40 S&W, with 3.5" or 4.24" barrels. 15-round double-stack magazines. Current model made by Zastava in Serbia.

450	400	350	300	200	150

Enfield Sporter No. I Mark III

This refinished rifle has a cut down Sporter-style stock. Action and sights are original. Caliber is .303.

—	250	200	150	100	50

	NIB	EXC.	V.G.	GOOD	FAIR	POOR

Enfield Sporter No. 4 Mark I
With new walnut stock.

	NIB	EXC.	V.G.	GOOD	FAIR	POOR
	—	260	210	150	100	50

TOZ-17
An original Russian rifle chambered for the .22 LR. Has a 21" barrel and 5-round magazine. Checkered stock and iron sights. Weighs about 5.4 lbs.

	—	175	135	110	50	40

TOZ-17-1
Same as above, with hooded front sight and tangent rear sight. Receiver is grooved for scope mount.

	—	185	145	120	60	50

Mexican Mauser Model 1910 Sporter
This rifle has been converted from a military rifle to a sporter by cutting down the stock. The metal is refinished and the barrel has been re-bored and re-chambered for the .30-06 cartridge. Box magazine holds 5 rounds. Barrel is 23" and rifle weighs about 8 lbs.

	—	185	145	120	60	50

FAL Sporter
This is a refinished FAL receiver and barrel installed in a synthetic thumbhole stock. The flash suppressor and bayonet lug have been removed. Barrel is 20.75" and weight approximately 10 lbs.

1000	850	650	450	350	150

M-14 Rifle
Imported from China by Century International, this rifle features a 22" barrel chambered for the .308 Win. cartridge. Stock is walnut with rubber pad. Parkerized finish. Weight approximately 8.25 lbs.

750	650	550	300	150	100

M85 Mini Mauser
Bolt action rifle in .22 Hornet, .223 Rem., or 7.62x39mm. Offered with standard Monte Carlo or full-length Mannlicher-style stock. Barrel lengths are 18", 20" or 22". Current production model made in Serbia by Zastava.

500	400	325	250	200	150

Tiger Dragunov Rifle
This is a shortened version of the Russian SVD sniper rifle. Fitted with a 20.8" barrel and chambered for the 7.62x54R cartridge. Rifle is sold with a 5-round magazine and a 4x range finding scope. Imported from Russia. Weight about 8.5 lbs.

1000	850	700	500	350	150

GP WASR 10 Rifle
AK-47 design in 7.62x39mm caliber. Comes with two double-stack 30-round magazines. Available with 5- or 10-round fixed magazine. New, made by Romarm in Romania.

500	400	325	275	200	100

Pietta SAA Millenium
Patterned after the Colt Single Action Army Model of 1873. Chambered in .22 LR, .357 Magnum, .44-40 Win. or .45 Colt, with 4.75", 5.5" or 7.5" barrel, hardwood walnut-stained grips and case-colored frame. Made in Italy by Pietta

400	350	300	250	200	150

Pietta Semi-Auto Shotgun
Made in 20-gauge only, with 28" vent rib barrel and four choke tubes. Stock is black polymer, metal finish is matte black, dark nickel or bright nickel. Inertia operating system is similar to that of the Benelli line.

750	675	600	500	350	200

PW 87
A lever-action shotgun patterned after the Winchester Model 1887. Made in 12-gauge only, with 19" barrel, modified choke and hardwood stock. New production model imported from China.

350	300	250	200	150	100

Shooter's Arms 1911 Pistol
Standard 1911-A .45 ACP design in full-size version, with 5" barrel or Commodore model with 4.25" barrel. Magazine capacity is 8 shots. New, manufactured in the Philippines.

450	375	325	275	200	100

	NIB	EXC.	V.G.	GOOD	FAIR	POOR

Saiga Semi-auto Shotgun

A 12-gauge shotgun based on AK-47 design. Five-round capacity. Weight 7.9 lbs. Has a 19" barrel, black synthetic stock, sight rail. Made in Russia.

600	500	425	375	200	100

S.A.R. Series

AK-47 style semi-automatic rifle, with wood stock and forearm. Capacity 10 or 30 rounds. Chambered for 7.62x39mm, 5.45x39mm or .223. Made in Romania by Romarm.

800	650	500	350	200	100

CETME
Madrid, Spain

Cetme Autoloading Rifle

A .308-caliber semi-automatic rifle, with a fluted chamber, 17.74" barrel, aperture rear sight and 20-round detachable magazine. Black with a military-style wood stock. Identical in appearance to the H&K 91 assault rifle.

1500	1100	800	600	350	200

CHAMPLIN FIREARMS
Enid, Oklahoma

Champlin Firearms Company manufactures custom order rifles built to customer's specifications. Prospective purchasers are advised to secure a qualified appraisal prior to purchase.

Bolt-Action Rifle

These arms featured round or octagonal barrels, set triggers, a variety of sights and well figured walnut stocks.

5500	4500	3500	2900	2200	1500

CHAPMAN, CHARLES
Chattanooga, Tennessee

Chapman produced a limited number of percussion carbines and rifles during the Civil War. Carbines had an overall length of 39.5" and .54-caliber barrels 24" in length. Their furniture was of brass. Chapman rifles resembled the U.S. Model 1841 rifle, but did not have patch boxes. Overall length 48.5", barrel length 33", caliber .58. Chapman rifles and carbines are marked "C. CHAPMAN" on the lockplates. Prospective purchasers are strongly advised to secure an expert appraisal prior to acquisition.

—	—	38000	17500	3000	1000

CHAPMAN, G. & J.
Philadelphia, Pennsylvania

Chapman Pocket Revolver

A .32-caliber revolver with a 4" round barrel and 7-shot cylinder. The frame is made of brass while the barrel and cylinder are of steel. The barrel is marked "G.& J. Chapman/Philada/Patent Applied For/1861". Manufactured during the1860s.

—	—	2550	1050	550	275

CHAPUIS ARMES
France

RGP Shotgun

A 16- or 20-gauge boxlock shotgun. Most options are available on order.

3000	2500	2000	1800	1250	900

RG Express Model 89 Rifle

A 7x65R, 8x57 JRS, 9.3x74R and .375 Holland & Holland caliber sidelock double-barreled rifle. The other features are at the customer's order.

6500	5750	4800	4000	3000	1500

Utility Grade Express Model Rifle

A side-by-side boxlock-action double rifle, with case colored or coin finish receiver. Offered in a variety of calibers: 9.3x74R, 8x57JRS, 7x65R, 8x75RS and .30-06. Checkered walnut stock with pistol-grip.

6000	4800	4000	3000	1500	750

	NIB	EXC.	V.G.	GOOD	FAIR	POOR

St. Bonnet Model Shotgun

This model is a side-by-side shotgun, with sideplates on a boxlock-action. Scroll engraved case colored receiver. Straight-grip stock and double triggers. Offered in 12-, 16- or 20- gauge.

NIB	EXC.	V.G.	GOOD	FAIR	POOR
4000	3250	2000	1250	800	500

Super Orion Rifle Series

This series of over/under rifles was offered in a wide range of European calibers plus, .30-06 and .300 Win. Magnum. Several grades were available. Prices shown are for C-15 model, which was imported in the 1990s. These rifles also were offered with a set of shotgun barrels. Currently imported by William Larkin Moore in Scottsdale, Arizona.

NIB	EXC.	V.G.	GOOD	FAIR	POOR
8000	7000	5200	4000	2000	1000

African PH Model Grade I Rifle

A boxlock-action double rifle offered in a wide variety of calibers. Caliber determines retail price. Hand engraved case colored receiver. Pistol-grip stock, with European-style cheekpiece.

.470 Nitro & .416 Rigby

NIB	EXC.	V.G.	GOOD	FAIR	POOR
12500	9500	8500	6000	3750	700

.375 H&H

NIB	EXC.	V.G.	GOOD	FAIR	POOR
9500	7500	6250	4000	2500	600

.300 Win. Magnum

NIB	EXC.	V.G.	GOOD	FAIR	POOR
8500	6500	5250	3000	1750	500

.30-06, 9.3x74R

NIB	EXC.	V.G.	GOOD	FAIR	POOR
8000	6000	5000	3000	1750	500

African PH Model Grade II

Same as above, with master engraving and game scenes. Add 20 to 25 percent to above NIB prices.

CHARTER ARMS
Shelton, Connecticut

Founded in 1962, Charter Arms has had several name and location changes. Original production was in Stratford, Connecticut until 1991 and in Ansonia, Connecticut from 1992 to 1996. From 1998 to 2005 the company name was Charter 2000. It was located in Shelton, Connecticut, where the current company, again known as Charter Arms is headquartered.

Bulldog

Chambered for the .44 Special cartridge and fitted with a 2.5" barrel. Stainless steel or blued frame, with 5-round cylinder. Round butt and fixed sights. Weight is 21 oz. **NOTE:** For stainless steel add $20.

NIB	EXC.	V.G.	GOOD	FAIR	POOR
320	250	175	125	75	50

Police Bulldog

This model is chambered for the .38 Special cartridge and fitted with a 4" bull or tapered barrel. Full rubber grips. Blued finish. Weight about 24 oz. Introduced in 2002.

NIB	EXC.	V.G.	GOOD	FAIR	POOR
320	250	175	125	75	50

Undercover

Chambered for the .38 Special cartridge and fitted with a 2" barrel. Stainless steel or blued frame, with 5-round cylinder. Round butt. Weight about 20 oz. **NOTE:** For stainless steel add $20.

NIB	EXC.	V.G.	GOOD	FAIR	POOR
280	225	175	150	100	75

Off Duty

This .38 Special revolver has an aluminum frame and 2" barrel. Combat grips. Double-action-only. Weight about 12 oz. Introduced in 2002.

NIB	EXC.	V.G.	GOOD	FAIR	POOR
350	250	200	150	100	75

Pathfinder

This is a stainless steel revolver chambered for the .22-caliber cartridge. Fitted with a 2" barrel and wood grips. Weight about 17 oz. Introduced in 2002.

NIB	EXC.	V.G.	GOOD	FAIR	POOR
265	200	165	125	75	50

Mag Pug

Chambered for the .357 Magnum cartridge and fitted with a 2.2" ported barrel. Stainless steel or blued frame. Weight about 24 oz.

NIB	EXC.	V.G.	GOOD	FAIR	POOR
320	250	175	125	75	50

	NIB	EXC.	V.G.	GOOD	FAIR	POOR

Dixie Derringer

Stainless steel with 1.125" barrels. Chambered for the .22 LR or .22 Magnum cartridges. Weight about 8 oz. Introduced in 2002. **NOTE:** For .22 Magnum model add $10.

	NIB	EXC.	V.G.	GOOD	FAIR	POOR
	190	150	125	100	50	25

Field King Rifle

Available with blue or stainless steel finish. Chambered for .25-06, .270, .30-06 or .308, with 22" barrel. Magazine capacity 4 rounds. Checkered fiberglass stock with cheekpiece. Weight about 8 lbs.

	NIB	EXC.	V.G.	GOOD	FAIR	POOR
	300	225	175	125	75	50

Field King Carbine

Same as above, with 18" barrel compensator (20" total). Chambered for .308.

	NIB	EXC.	V.G.	GOOD	FAIR	POOR
	350	250	200	150	75	50

CHARTER ARMS CORP.
Ansonia, Connecticut/Shelton, Connecticut

Police Undercover

This model is chambered for the .38 Special or the .32 Magnum. Fitted with a 2" barrel in blue or stainless steel finish. Offered with walnut or rubber grips. The overall length is 6.25" and weight between 16 oz. and 19 oz. depending on grips and finish.

	NIB	EXC.	V.G.	GOOD	FAIR	POOR
	350	300	175	150	100	75

Undercover Stainless Steel

As above in stainless steel.

	NIB	EXC.	V.G.	GOOD	FAIR	POOR
	390	325	225	175	125	100

Undercover Lite

Similar to Undercover, with lightweight aluminum alloy frame. Frame finishes: black/stainless, red/stainless and red/black.

	NIB	EXC.	V.G.	GOOD	FAIR	POOR
	390	325	225	175	125	100

Undercoverette

As above, with a thinner grip and in .32 S&W.

	NIB	EXC.	V.G.	GOOD	FAIR	POOR
	350	300	250	125	100	75

Bulldog

Similar to the Undercover model in .44 Special caliber, with a 2.5" or 3" barrel and 5-shot cylinder. Discontinued; replaced by Target and Pug models.

	NIB	EXC.	V.G.	GOOD	FAIR	POOR
	325	275	225	175	125	100

Stainless Steel Bulldog

As above in stainless steel.

	NIB	EXC.	V.G.	GOOD	FAIR	POOR
	350	300	250	200	150	125

Heller Commemorative Bulldog

Fully engraved model in .44 Special, with wood presentation case and engraved knife. Commemorating the U.S. Supreme Court Heller case of 2011, affirming Second Amendment rights. Only 250 made.

	NIB	EXC.	V.G.	GOOD	FAIR	POOR
	1400	1200	1000	—	—	—

Target Bulldog

As above in .357 Magnum or .44 Special, with a 4" barrel. Fitted with adjustable rear sights. Blued, with walnut grips. Manufactured from 1986 to 1988, later reintroduced.

	NIB	EXC.	V.G.	GOOD	FAIR	POOR
	350	300	250	200	150	125

Pathfinder

Similar to the above in .22 LR or .22 Magnum caliber, with a 2", 3" or 6" barrel. Adjustable sights.

	NIB	EXC.	V.G.	GOOD	FAIR	POOR
	350	300	250	200	150	125

Pathfinder Stainless Steel

As above in stainless steel.

	NIB	EXC.	V.G.	GOOD	FAIR	POOR
	360	310	260	210	160	135

Bulldog Pug

Chambered for the .44 Special cartridge. Fitted with a 2.5" barrel. Available with walnut or neoprene grips in blue or stainless steel finish. Choice of spur or pocket hammer. Cylinder

	NIB	EXC.	V.G.	GOOD	FAIR	POOR

holds 5 rounds. Overall length is 7"; weight between 20 oz. and 25 oz. depending on grip and finish.

	350	300	250	200	150	125

Stainless Steel Bulldog

As above in stainless steel.

	375	325	275	225	175	125

Bulldog Tracker

As above, with a 2.5", 4" or 6" barrel. In .357 Magnum only.

	375	325	275	225	175	125

Police Bulldog

As above in .32 H&R Magnum, .38 Special or .44 Special, with 3.5" or 4" barrel.

	350	300	250	200	150	125

Stainless Steel Police Bulldog

As above in stainless steel and available in .357 Magnum.

	350	300	250	200	150	125

Off Duty

Chambered for the .38 Special or .22 LR, this revolver is fitted with a 2" barrel. Offered with either walnut or rubber grips, blue or stainless steel finish and choice of spur or pocket hammer. Weight of the .38 special version is between 17 oz. and 23 oz., depending on grip and finish. The .22 LR version weighs between 19 oz. and 22 oz. The overall length is 4.75". A nickel finish with rubber grips is also offered.

	325	275	225	175	125	100

Pit Bull

9mm Federal, .38 Special or .357 Magnum caliber double-action revolver, with 2.5", 3.5" or 4" barrel. Blued, with rubber grips.

	400	350	250	175	125	90

Pitbull Rimless

Improved version of above, with dual coil-spring extractor system. Design does not require use of moon clips. Chambered in 9mm (6-round capacity) or .40 S&W (5 rounds). Barrel is 2.2", stainless glass beaded finish. Black rubber grips and fixed sights.

	400	350	300	275	225	175

The Mag Pug

A 5-shot revolver chambered for .357 Magnum. Stainless or blue. Ported 2.2" barrel. 23 oz. Fixed sights, rubber grips.

	350	300	250	200	150	125

Charter Arms Southpaw

Five-shot snubnose revolver chambered in .38 Special +P. Five-shot cylinder, 2" barrel, matte black aluminum alloy frame, with stainless steel cylinder. Cylinder latch and crane assembly are on right side of frame for convenience of left-hand shooters. Rubber Pachmayr-style grips. Weight: 12 oz.

	400	350	250	175	125	90

Pink Lady

Similar to Undercover Lite, with pink anodized frame. .38 Special only. Available as Chic Lady, with high polish pink finish and pink faux alligator case. DAO version is also available. **NOTE:** Add $50 for Chic Lady model.

	375	325	275	225	175	125

Goldfinger

Similar to Undercover Lite, with gold anodized frame. .38 Special only.

	375	325	275	225	175	125

Patriot

Built on Bulldog frame but chambered in .327 Federal Magnum (six-shot). Rubber grips, 2.2" or 4" barrel. Comes with Kershaw "327" knife.

	425	300	225	175	150	100

Dixie Derringer, Current Production

Stainless mini-revolver chambered for .22 LR (5 oz.) or .22 Magnum (6 oz.). 5-shot, 1.175" barrel.

	175	140	100	75	50	25

	NIB	EXC.	V.G.	GOOD	FAIR	POOR

Explorer II Pistol

A .22-caliber semi-automatic pistol, with 6", 8" or 10" barrels. Available with a camo, black, silver or gold finish and plastic grips. Discontinued in 1986.

NIB	EXC.	V.G.	GOOD	FAIR	POOR
225	175	125	65	45	25

Model 40

A .22-caliber double-action semi-automatic pistol, with a 3.5" barrel and 8-shot magazine. Stainless steel with plastic grips. Manufactured from 1984 to 1986.

NIB	EXC.	V.G.	GOOD	FAIR	POOR
—	275	225	200	150	100

Model 79K

A .32- or .380-caliber double-action semi-automatic pistol, with a 3.5" barrel and 7-shot magazine. Stainless steel with plastic grips. Manufactured from 1986 to 1988.

NIB	EXC.	V.G.	GOOD	FAIR	POOR
—	350	300	250	180	125

Model 42T

A .22-caliber semi-automatic pistol, with a 6" barrel and adjustable sights. Blued with walnut grips. Manufactured in 1984 and 1985.

NIB	EXC.	V.G.	GOOD	FAIR	POOR
500	450	400	325	265	200

AR-7 Explorer Rifle

A .22-caliber semi-automatic rifle, with a 16" barrel, 8-shot magazine and hollow plastic stock which can house the barrel when detached.

NIB	EXC.	V.G.	GOOD	FAIR	POOR
175	125	80	60	40	25

CHEYTAC
Arco, Idaho

M-200

This bolt-action rifle is chambered for the .408 CheyTac cartridge. Detachable barrel length is 30" with muzzle-brake. Magazine capacity 7 rounds. Integral bipod. No sights, but receiver has attachable Picatinny rail. Weight about 27 lbs.

NIB	EXC.	V.G.	GOOD	FAIR	POOR
10995	8250	6900	5400	3000	700

M-310

This is a single-shot bolt-action rifle chambered for the .408 CheyTac cartridge. Fitted with a 25" barrel with muzzle-brake. McMillian A-5 stock with adjustable cheekpiece. Match grade trigger. Picatinny rail. Weight about 16.5 lbs.

NIB	EXC.	V.G.	GOOD	FAIR	POOR
4395	3250	2750	1875	1300	500

CHIAPPA ARMS
Dayton, Ohio

1911-22

1911-style semi-automatic pistol chambered in .22 LR. Features include alloy frame; steel barrel; matte blue-black or bright nickel finish, walnut-like grips, two 10-round magazines, fixed sights. Straight blowback action. **NOTE:** Add $25 for target model with adjustable sights, $25 for OD or tan finish.

NIB	EXC.	V.G.	GOOD	FAIR	POOR
260	225	200	150	100	75

M9-22

Replica of Beretta M9 9mm military pistol. Chambered for .22 Long Rifle, with checkered black plastic or checkered wooden grips. Operating features are identical to the 9mm version. Tactical model has threaded barrel. **NOTE:** Add $25 for this variation.

NIB	EXC.	V.G.	GOOD	FAIR	POOR
325	275	225	200	150	100

Rhino

Unique revolver chambered in 9x19, 9x21, .357 Magnum and .40 S&W. Features include 2", 4", 5" or 6" barrel; fixed or adjustable sights; visible hammer or hammerless design. Weight 24 to 33 oz. Walnut or synthetic grips with black frame; hexagonal-shaped cylinder. Unique design fires from bottom chamber of cylinder. **NOTE:** Add $75 for wood grips; $100 for brushed nickel finish (White Rhino model); $300 for gold finish (Rhino 60DS). Deduct $200 for polymer frame model.

NIB	EXC.	V.G.	GOOD	FAIR	POOR
800	700	600	500	400	300

1873-22

Replica of Colt Single Action Army revolver. Chambered in .22 Long Rifle, with 6-round cylinder. Introduced in 2011 and discontinued in 2012. Available with extra cylinder in .22 WMR. **NOTE:**

	NIB	EXC.	V.G.	GOOD	FAIR	POOR

Add $50 for extra cylinder; $40 for target model.

| | 175 | 150 | 125 | 100 | 85 | 60 |

1873-22-10

Same features as above, with 10-round cylinder. Available with extra cylinder in .22 WMR. Also offered in .17 HMR caliber, with adjustable sights. **NOTE:** Add $50 for .22 WMR extra cylinder; $30 for .17 HMR model.

| | 200 | 175 | 150 | 115 | 90 | 75 |

Model 1886 Kodiak Rifle

Lever-action rifle chambered for .45-70 Government cartridge. Replica of Winchester 1886, with 18.5" half-octagon barrel, express sights, black synthetic stock and hard-chrome matte gray finish. Standard model has four-round half-length tubular magazine. Trapper model has 6-shot magazine, blue finish and walnut stock. **NOTE:** Deduct $150 for Trapper model.

| | 1200 | 1050 | 900 | 700 | 500 | 400 |

Model 1892 Rifle

Replica of Winchester model 1892 lever-action rifle. Chambered for .38 Special, .357 Magnum, .38-40 WCF, .44-40 WCF, .44 Magnum, .45 Colt. Offered in several variations, with barrel lengths from 16" to 24" with different sighting options. Take-down model with octagonal barrel available. **NOTE:** Add $200 for take-down model; $100 for buckhorn rear/interchangeable blade front sights.

| | 900 | 750 | 600 | 500 | 400 | 250 |

Model 1887 Shotgun

Lever-action limited edition replica of Model 1887 Winchester 12-gauge, with 5-shot magazine, 22" or 28" barrel and choke tubes.

| | 1000 | 900 | 750 | 600 | 400 | 250 |

CHICAGO, F. A. CO.
Chicago, Illinois

Protector Palm Pistol—Standard Model

Nickel-Plated/Black Grips

A .32-caliber radial cylinder revolver designed to fit in the palm of the hand and to be operated by a hinged lever mounted to the rear of the circular frame. The sideplates are marked "Chicago Firearms Co., Chicago, Ill." and "The Protector". Blued with hard rubber grip panels or nickel-plated with pearl grip panels. Manufactured by the Ames Manufacturing Company. **NOTE:** Add 25 percent for pearl grip panels without cracks or chips. Add 50 percent for blued finish.

| | — | — | 3000 | 2000 | 1000 | 750 |

CHIPMUNK RIFLES/ROGUE RIFLE CO.
Lewiston, Idaho

Chipmunk Single-Shot Standard Rifle

A .22 or .22 rimfire Magnum caliber bolt-action rifle, with 16.25" barrel and open sights. Weight approximately 3.5 lbs.

| | 185 | 150 | 125 | 100 | 80 | 60 |

Deluxe Chipmunk

As above, with a hand-checkered walnut stock.

| | 230 | 180 | 135 | 100 | 80 | 60 |

Chipmunk .17 HMR

Similar to the Standard Model, but chambered for the .17 HMR cartridge. Introduced in 2002.

| | 200 | 160 | 125 | 100 | 75 | 45 |

Chipmunk TM

Introduced in 2002, this model features a micrometer rear sight. Stock has accessory rail installed and is adjustable for length of pull. Barrel: 18" heavy type. Weight about 5 lbs.

| | 325 | 250 | 150 | 125 | 100 | 75 |

Silhouette Pistol

A .22-caliber bolt-action pistol, with a 14.5" barrel, open sights and pistol-grip walnut stock.

| | 150 | 125 | 100 | 80 | 60 | 40 |

CHRISTENSEN ARMS
Gunnison, Utah

There are a number of custom options offered by this company for its rifles. Many of these options may affect price. Prices listed are for standard models with standard features.

Carbon One
This is a bolt-action rifle, with Remington 700 action chambered for .17- through .243-caliber. Fitted with a custom trigger, match-grade stainless steel barrel and black synthetic stock. Weight about 6 lbs.

| 3900 | 2750 | 1900 | 1200 | 700 | 500 |

Carbon Lite
This model is similar to above, but weighs about 5 lbs.

| 3900 | 2750 | 1900 | 1200 | 700 | 500 |

Carbon King
This model utilizes a Remington 700 BDL long action and is chambered for .25-caliber through .30-06. Stainless steel barrel, custom trigger and black synthetic stock are standard. Weight approximately 6.5 lbs.

| 3900 | 2750 | 1900 | 1200 | 700 | 500 |

Carbon Cannon
Similar to above model and chambered for belted magnum calibers. Weight about 7 lbs.

| 3900 | 2750 | 1900 | 1200 | 700 | 500 |

Carbon Challenge I
This rifle is built on a Ruger 10/22 action. Fitted with a Volquartsen trigger, stainless steel bull barrel and black synthetic stock. Weight approximately 3.5 lbs. Add 20 percent for .17-caliber.

| 1800 | 1300 | 875 | 600 | 400 | 175 |

Carbon Challenge II
Similar to above model. Fitted with an AMT action and trigger. Weight about 4.5 lbs. Discontinued.

| 1295 | 995 | 700 | 550 | 325 | 125 |

Carbon Tactical
This bolt-action model uses a Remington 700 BDL action and is available in most any caliber. Fitted with a custom trigger, match-grade stainless steel barrel and black synthetic stock. Weight about 7 lbs.

| 3900 | 2750 | 1900 | 1200 | 700 | 500 |

Carbon Conquest
Chambered for the .50-caliber BMG cartridge, this rifle is built on a McMillan stainless steel bolt action. Magazine capacity of 5 rounds. Barrel length is 32" with muzzle-brake. Composite stock. Weight about 20 lbs. **NOTE:** For single-shot model deduct $1,000.

| 6250 | 4000 | 3250 | 1700 | 875 | 400 |

Carbon One Hunter
Semi-custom bolt-action rifle built around choice of receivers; steel barrel encased in carbon alloy shroud; synthetic stock. All popular calibers. Weight: 6.5-7 lbs.

| 1500 | 1300 | 875 | 550 | 375 | 125 |

Carbon Ranger Repeater
Semi-custom bolt-action rifle chambered in .50 BMG. Five-shot magazine; steel Pac-Nor barrel encased in carbon alloy. Muzzle- brake. Weight: 20 lbs.

| 8000 | 7000 | 5500 | 4000 | 2000 | 1000 |

Carbon Ranger Single Shot
Similar to Repeater but single shot.

| 6500 | 5000 | 3000 | 2000 | 1100 | 500 |

1911 Officers Model
Christensen makes a series of 1911-type pistols in .45 ACP caliber. These ar offered in full-size, Commander and Officers sizes (shown) in both standard and lightweight variants. Features include stainless steel slide, aerospace aluminum mainspring housing, adjustable trigger, tritium night sights, Cerakote finish, carbon-fiber grips and ambidextrous safety. **NOTE:** Add 50 percent for Damascus model, with damascus-pattern finish, Novak Trijicon sights, skeletonized hammer and trigger.

| 2800 | 2350 | 1850 | 1200 | 750 | 400 |

	NIB	EXC.	V.G.	GOOD	FAIR	POOR

CHURCHILL
Various European Manufacturers and Importers

SIDE-BY-SIDE SHOTGUNS

Windsor I

A 10-, 12-, 16-, 20-, 28-gauge and .410 bore Anson & Deeley double-barrel boxlock shotgun. Barrel lengths from 23" through 32", various choke combinations, double triggers and extractors. Scroll-engraved silver-finished, with checkered walnut pistol-grip and fore-end.

NIB	EXC.	V.G.	GOOD	FAIR	POOR
800	600	500	400	300	200

Windsor II

As above in 10-, 12- and 20-gauge only, with automatic ejectors. Not imported after 1987.

NIB	EXC.	V.G.	GOOD	FAIR	POOR
800	600	550	450	350	250

Windsor VI

As above with sidelocks. Chambered for 12- and 20-gauge only, with automatic ejectors. Not imported after 1987.

NIB	EXC.	V.G.	GOOD	FAIR	POOR
1100	800	750	650	500	350

Royal

A 12-, 20-, 28-gauge and .410 bore boxlock double-barrel shotgun, with various barrel lengths and chokes, double triggers and extractors. Case hardened, with checkered walnut stock. Introduced in 1988.

NIB	EXC.	V.G.	GOOD	FAIR	POOR
650	500	425	350	275	125

OVER/UNDER SHOTGUNS

Monarch

A 12-, 20-, 28-gauge or .410 bore over/under shotgun, with a boxlock-action, 25", 26" or 28" ventilated rib barrels. Either double- or a single-selective trigger extractors and a checkered walnut stock.

NIB	EXC.	V.G.	GOOD	FAIR	POOR
600	475	425	375	300	150

Windsor III

A 12-, 20-gauge and .410 bore boxlock double-barrel shotgun, with 27" or 30" ventilated rib barrels, extractors, single-selective trigger, scroll-engraved, silver finished and checkered walnut stock.

NIB	EXC.	V.G.	GOOD	FAIR	POOR
700	575	525	475	400	200

Windsor IV

As above, with screw-in choke tubes standard. Introduced in 1989.

NIB	EXC.	V.G.	GOOD	FAIR	POOR
975	775	650	500	425	200

Regent

As above in 12- and 20-gauge, with 27" ventilated rib barrels, screw-in choke tubes, scroll-engraved false sideplates, automatic ejectors, single-selective trigger and checkered walnut stock. Not imported after 1986.

NIB	EXC.	V.G.	GOOD	FAIR	POOR
950	750	650	550	450	250

Regent II

As above, with finer overall finishing.

NIB	EXC.	V.G.	GOOD	FAIR	POOR
1250	1000	850	750	500	250

Regent Shotgun/Rifle Combination

A .222, .223, .243, .270, .308 or .30-06 caliber/12-gauge over/under rifle/shotgun, with a 25" ventilated rib, automatic ejectors and single-selective trigger. Silver finished, scroll engraved and checkered walnut stock.

NIB	EXC.	V.G.	GOOD	FAIR	POOR
1050	825	725	600	450	250

Windsor Grade Semi-Automatic

A 12-gauge semi-automatic shotgun, with 26", 28" or 30" ventilated rib barrels and screw-in choke tubes. An etched and anodized alloy receiver, with checkered walnut stock.

NIB	EXC.	V.G.	GOOD	FAIR	POOR
500	375	325	275	225	175

NIB	EXC.	V.G.	GOOD	FAIR	POOR

Regent Grade Semi-Automatic

Chambered for 12-gauge, with choice of 26", 28" or 30" barrels. Standard chokes or choke tubes. Walnut stock with pistol-grip. Introduced in 1984 and discontinued in 1986. Weight about 7.5 lbs.

500	375	325	275	225	175

Windsor Grade Slide-Action

A 12-gauge slide-action shotgun, with a 26" through 30" ventilated rib barrel, various chokes, double slide rails and an anodized alloy receiver. Checkered walnut stock. Discontinued in 1986.

—	500	375	300	250	175

RIFLES

Highlander

A .25-06 through .300 Winchester Magnum caliber bolt-action rifle, with a 22" barrel, with or without sights, a 3-shot magazine and a checkered walnut stock.

575	425	375	300	250	200

Regent

As above, with a Monte Carlo-style comb and cheekpiece. Discontinued in 1988.

—	650	500	425	350	275

CHURCHILL, E. J. LTD.
London, England

One of One Thousand Rifle

A .270 to .458 Magnum caliber bolt-action rifle, with 24" barrel and a select French walnut stock, trap pistol-grip cap and recoil pad. Only 100 actually produced for the 20th anniversary of Interarms in 1973.

—	1750	1050	850	700	550

Premier Over/Under

This is a sidelock ejector gun available in 12-, 20- or 28-gauge. Single- or double-trigger with choice of finish. Barrel lengths built to order. Deluxe Turkish walnut with choice of grip. Fine scroll engraving. Weight for 12-gauge about 7 lbs.; 20-gauge about 6.75 lbs. Many extra cost options available. **NOTE:** Add $3,000 for 28-gauge guns.

47000	36500	26000	20000	10000	800

Premier Side-by-Side

Similar to the over/under gun, with side-by-side barrels. Also offered in 16-gauge as well as 12-, 20- and 28-gauge. Weights about 6.5 lbs. for 12-gauge; 6 lbs. for 16-gauge; 5.8 lbs. for 20-gauge. Many extra options are available. **NOTE:** Add $3,000 for 28-gauge guns.

38000	30000	20000	16500	7000	600

Premier Double Rifle

Similar in construction to the side-by-side shotgun, this rifle is chambered for the .300 H&H, .375 H&H or .500 Nitro Express. Weight 9.5 lbs. for the .300; 9.75 lbs. for the 375; 12.5 lbs. for the .500. Many extra-cost options. **NOTE:** Add $3,000 for .500 N.E. guns.

55000	45000	35000	20000	13000	800

Baronet Magazine Rifle

This rifle uses the standard Mauser 98 action, with fully adjustable trigger, 3 position safety and box release floor plate. Barrel length is custom to order. Border engraving. Chambered for the .30-06 or .375 H&H. Weight for .30-06 about 8.5 lbs.; .375 about 9 lbs. Many extra-cost options offered. Seek an expert opinion prior to a sale.

13000	9750	7000	45000	2750	575

CHYLEWSKI, WITOLD
Switzerland

A 6.35mm caliber semi-automatic pistol, with a 6-round magazine marked "Brevete Chylewski" and bears the name "Neuhausen" on the left side of the pistol. Approximately 1,000 were made between 1910 and 1918. This pistol was designed to be cocked with one hand.

—	—	1250	850	550	275

NIB	EXC.	V.G.	GOOD	FAIR	POOR

CIMARRON, F. A. CO.
Fredericksburg, Texas

In business since 1984, this company imports quality firearms from Uberti, Armi San Marco, Pedersoli and others. Cimarron also sells Uberti-manufactured blackpowder Colt reproductions, from Patterson to Model 1862 Pocket. For prices and specifications on these models see Uberti section.

Model No. 3 Schofield

This version of the Schofield is manufactured for Cimarron by Armi San Marco in Italy. Its parts are interchangeable with the original. It is offered in several variations and calibers. Discontinued. Beware of latch locking problems. **NOTE:** Add $100 for standard nickel finish; $150 for custom nickel finish.

Civilian Model

Fitted with 7" barrel and offered in .38 Special, .44 Russian/.44 Special, .44 WCF, .45 Schofield, .45 Long Colt.

NIB	EXC.	V.G.	GOOD	FAIR	POOR
875	600	525	425	300	125

Military Model

Essentially the same as the Civilian Model except for its markings.

NIB	EXC.	V.G.	GOOD	FAIR	POOR
875	600	525	425	300	125

Wells Fargo

Similar to the Military and Civilian Model. Fitted with a 5" barrel. Calibers are the same.

NIB	EXC.	V.G.	GOOD	FAIR	POOR
875	600	525	425	300	125

Model 1872 Open Top

This revolver is offered in a number of different calibers and configurations. It is chambered for the .44 SP, .44 Colt, .44 Russian, .45 Schofield, .38 Colt, .38 Special. It can be fitted with Army or Navy grips. Barrel lengths are 4.75", 5.5" or 7.5". Offered in regular blued finish, charcoal blue finish or original finish. **NOTE:** Add $40 for charcoal finish; $50 for original finish; $25 for silver-plated back strap and trigger guard.

NIB	EXC.	V.G.	GOOD	FAIR	POOR
450	400	350	300	200	100

COLT SINGLE-ACTION ARMY CONFIGURATIONS

Cimarron Arms reproduction of the 1873 Colt Single-Action Army revolver comes in two basic configurations. First is the "Old Model", with black powder frame screw-in cylinder pin retainer and circular bull's eye ejector head. Second is the "pre-war Model" style frame, with spring loaded cross-pin cylinder retainer and half moon ejector head. Old Model revolvers are available in authentic old style charcoal blue finish at an extra charge. Unless otherwise stated all of these Colt reproductions are produced by Uberti of Italy. Plain walnut grips are standard unless noted. **NOTE:** Relic finish offered by Cimarron as an extra cost item on its revolvers. This finish duplicates the old worn antique finish seen on many used historical Colts. Add $40 to the NIB price for any Cimarron revolver with this finish.

General Custer 7th Cavalry Model

Has U.S. military markings and fitted with 7.5" barrel on an Old Model frame. Offered in .45 LC only.

NIB	EXC.	V.G.	GOOD	FAIR	POOR
525	450	350	300	200	100

Rough Rider U.S. Artillery Model

This version of the Old Model fitted with a 5.5" barrel and chambered for .45 LC.

NIB	EXC.	V.G.	GOOD	FAIR	POOR
550	450	350	300	200	100

Frontier Six Shooter

This revolver is offered with a choice of 4.75", 5.5" or 7.5" barrel. Chambered for .38 WCF, .357 Magnum, .44 WCF, .45 LC or .45 LC with extra .45 ACP cylinder. **NOTE:** Add $40 to NIB price for charcoal blue finish; $30 for extra .45 ACP cylinder; $50 for stainless steel.

NIB	EXC.	V.G.	GOOD	FAIR	POOR
450	350	300	275	175	75

Sheriff's Model no ejector

Fitted with a 3" barrel and chambered in .44 WCF or .45 LC. Built on an Old Model frame.

NIB	EXC.	V.G.	GOOD	FAIR	POOR
450	350	300	275	175	75

New Sheriff's Model w/ejector

This variation is fitted with a 3.5" barrel with ejector and available in .357 Magnum, .44 WCF, .44 Special and .45 LC. For checkered walnut grips add $35.

NIB	EXC.	V.G.	GOOD	FAIR	POOR
500	400	325	275	175	75

NIB	EXC.	V.G.	GOOD	FAIR	POOR

Wyatt Earp Buntline

This is a limited edition model fitted with a 10" barrel. Chambered for the .45 LC cartridge. Model P frame. Silver shield inlaid in grip.

775	600	500	425	300	125

New Thunderer

The frame is based on the Old Model fitted with a bird's-head grip. Choice of plain or checkered walnut grips. Originally offered in 3.5" or 4.75" barrel lengths; in 1997 5.5" barrels were offered. Chambered for .357 Magnum, .44 WCF, .44 Special or .45 LC/.45 ACP. Add $35 for checkered grips.

575	450	325	275	175	75

Thunderer Long Tom

Same as the New Thunderer except for a barrel length of 7.5".

550	425	350	275	175	75

Thunderstorm

Single-action revolver in blue or stainless finish, with checkered wood grips. Chambered in .357 Magnum or .45 Colt, with 3.5" or 4.75" barrel. Wide target sights with action smoothed for competition. Add $100 for stainless finish.

875	775	700	500	400	300

Lightning

Similar to the Thunderer, with a smaller grip frame. Chambered for the .38 Special cartridge or .22 LR and fitted with 3.5", 4.75" or 5.5" barrel. Finish is blue, with case hardened frame.

475	375	315	250	150	65

Lightning .32s

This model features two cylinders chambered for the .32-20 and the .32 H&R cartridges. Choice of 3.5", 4.75" or 5.5" barrel. Introduced in 2004.

550	400	350	275	175	75

New Model P

Offered in either Old Model or Pre-War styles. Choice of 4.75", 5.5" or 7.5" barrel. Chambered for .32 WCF, .38 WCF, .44 WCF, .44 Special or .45 LC.

475	400	325	275	175	75

Stainless Frontier Model P

This model is a Model P in stainless steel. Chambered for the .357 Magnum or .45 LC cartridge. Barrels are 4.75", 5.5" or 7.5". Introduced in 2004.

550	450	400	300	200	100

A.P. Casey Model P U.S. Cavalry

Fitted with a 7.5" barrel and chambered for .45 LC, this revolver has U.S. markings (APC) on an Old Model frame.

550	375	325	250	150	75

Rinaldo A. Carr Model P U.S. Artillery

This is a Model P built on an Old Model frame. Chambered for .45 LC and fitted with a 5.5" barrel. U.S. markings (RAC).

550	425	375	275	175	100

Evil Roy Model

This model features a Model P frame, with wide square-notch rear sight and wide-width front sight. Slim grips checkered or smooth. Tuned action with lightened trigger. Chambered for the .357 Magnum, .45 LC or .44-40 cartridge. Barrel lengths 4.75" or 5.5". Introduced in 2004.

625	550	475	375	250	125

Model P Jr.

Similar to the Model P, but sized 20 percent smaller. Chambered for the .38 Special cartridge and fitted with 3.5" or 4.75" barrels. Blue, with case hardened frame.

475	400	325	250	150	75

Model P Jr. .32s

This model introduced in 2004, features two cylinders chambered for the .32-20 and the .32 H&R cartridges. Choice of 3.5", 4.75" or 5.5" barrel.

550	400	350	250	150	75

NIB	EXC.	V.G.	GOOD	FAIR	POOR

Cimarron 1880 Frontier Flat Top

Introduced in 1998, this model is a target version of the Colt Single-Action Army. Rear sight is adjustable for windage and front adjustable for elevation. Offered with choice of 4.75", 5.5" or 7.5" barrels and chambered for .45 LC, .45 Schofield, .44 WCF and .357 Magnum. Choice of Model P frame or Pre-War frame.

550	450	325	225	150	100

Cimarron Bisley

Exact copy of the Colt Bisley, with case hardened frame. Choice of 4.75", 5.5" or 7.5" barrels and calibers from .45 LC, .45 Schofield, .44 WCF to .357 Magnum. Introduced in 1998.

550	450	325	225	150	100

Cimarron Bisley Flat Top

Offered in the same barrel lengths and calibers as the standard Bisley, with the addition of a windage adjustable rear sight and elevation adjustable front sight. Introduced in 1998.

550	450	325	225	150	100

El Pistolero

This budget-priced revolver was introduced in 1997. Features a brass backstrap and trigger guard, with plain walnut grips. Offered in 4.75", 5.5" and 7.5" barrel lengths. Chambered for .45 LC or .357 Magnum.

350	250	200	125	75	50

Doc Holliday Thunderer

This nickel-plated SAA in .45 LC has a 3.5" barrel and Cimarron Tru Ivory grips. Comes with a matching numbered dagger and a shoulder holster designed to carry both items.

1300	1000	800	650	450	300

Rooster Shooter SAA

Replica of SAA used by John Wayne in many movies. Chambered in .357 Magnum, .44-40 or .45 LC. Antique grey finish and artificial ivory grips. Introduced in 2010.

800	700	525	400	300	250

Man With No Name SAA

Replica of gun used by Clint Eastwood in several "spaghetti westerns". In .45 LC, with 4.75" or 5.5" barrel, cased-colored finish, wood grips and rattlesnake inlay. Introduced in 2010.

750	650	550	425	300	250

RICHARDS CONVERSIONS

NOTE: Relic finish offered by Cimarron as an extra cost item on its revolvers. This finish duplicates the old worn antique finish seen on many used historical Colts. Add $40 to the NIB price for any Cimarron revolver with this finish.

Model 1851

Chambered for .38 Special, .38 Colt and .44 Colt. Fitted with 5" or 7" barrels.

550	450	325	225	150	100

Model 1861

Chambered for .38 Special, .38 Colt and .44 Colt. Fitted with 5" or 7" barrels.

550	450	325	225	150	100

Model 1860

Chambered for .38 Special, .38 Colt and .44 Colt. Fitted with 5" or 7.5" barrels.

550	450	325	225	150	100

Model 1911A1

Manufactured by Chiappa, standard full-size replica of Colt .45 ACP Government Model in blue, polished blue or nickel finish. **NOTE:** Add 40 percent for nickel finish; 30 percent for polished blue finish.

525	450	400	325	250	200

RIFLES

Model 1865 Spencer

Chambered for the .56-50 centerfire cartridge.

1350	975	775	650	375	250

	NIB	EXC.	V.G.	GOOD	FAIR	POOR

Henry Civil War Model
Offered in .44 WCF or .45 LC with 24.25" barrel. **NOTE:** For charcoal blue or white finish add $80.

	1400	1200	1000	625	350	200

Henry Civilian Model
Same as above, without military markings.

	1200	925	750	625	350	200

Model 1866 Yellowboy Carbine
Reproduction of the Winchester model 1866. Fitted with a 19" barrel and chambered for .38 Special, .44 WCF or .45 LC. **NOTE:** For charcoal blue add $40.

	1000	850	600	525	300	150

Model 1866 Yellowboy Rifle
Same as above, fitted with a 24.25" barrel. **NOTE:** For charcoal blue add $40.

	1100	900	600	525	300	150

Model 1866 Yellowboy Trapper
As above, with a 16" barrel.

	950	725	600	525	300	150

Model 1873 Winchester Rifle
This lever-action rifle is offered in .357 Magnum, .44 WCF or .45 LC. Fitted with a 24.25" barrel. **NOTE:** Add $40 for charcoal blue; $140 for pistol-grip option.

	1150	925	750	675	400	200

Model 1873 Long Range Rifle
Similar to Model 1873, but fitted with a 30" barrel. **NOTE:** Add $140 for pistol-grip option; $1,250 for 1 of 1000 engraving option.

	1175	950	775	675	400	200

Model 1873 Carbine
Same as the standard Model 1873, but fitted with a 19" barrel. **NOTE:** For charcoal blue add $40.

	1150	925	750	675	400	200

Model 1873 Short Rifle
This model is fitted with a 20" barrel. Production ceased in 1998. **NOTE:** For charcoal blue add $40.

	1150	925	750	675	400	200

Model 1873 Trapper
As above, with 16" barrel.

	1150	925	750	675	400	200

Model 1873 Deluxe Sporting Rifle
This model is fitted with a 24" barrel, checkered walnut stock and pistol-grip.

	1220	925	850	725	400	200

Model 1873 Evil Roy Rifle
This model is chambered for the .357 or .45 Colt cartridge and fitted with a 20" barrel.

	1450	1200	950	700	400	200

Model 1873 Larry Crow Signature Series Rifle
Chambered for the .357 Magnum or .45 Colt cartridge and fitted with a 20" barrel.

	1550	1300	1050	800	400	200

Model 1892 Solid Frame Rifle
Offered with either 20" or 24" octagon barrels and chambered for the .357 Magnum, .44WCF or .45 Colt cartridges.

	850	675	575	450	300	150

Model 1892 Takedown Rifle
As above, with takedown feature.

	975	775	675	525	375	200

	NIB	EXC.	V.G.	GOOD	FAIR	POOR

Model 1886

Replica of Winchester 1886. Caliber .45-70 Government.

	1400	1250	900	750	400	250

Billy Dixon Model 1874 Sharps

A reproduction of Model 1874 Sharps rifle chambered for the .45-70 cartridge. Fitted with a 32" tapered octagon barrel. Stock is hand checkered, with oil finish walnut. Double set triggers standard.

	1650	1225	1100	700	500	250

Remington Rolling Block

This Remington reproduction was introduced to Cimarron in 1997 and represents the Rolling Block Sporting rifle, with 30" tapered octagon barrel and chambered for .45-70 cartridge. Hand-checkered satin-finished walnut stock.

	1300	1000	900	550	300	175

Adobe Walls Rolling Block

This model is chambered for the .45-70 cartridge and is fitted with a 30" octagon barrel. Hand-checkered walnut stock, with hand finishing. Case colored receiver and German silver nose cap. Weight about 10.13 lbs. Introduced in 2004.

	1425	1050	950	600	350	225

Model 1885 High Wall

Reproduction of the Winchester Model 1885. Chambered for .45-70, .45-90, .45-120, .40-65, .348 Win., .30-40 Krag or .38-55 cartridges. Fitted with a 30" barrel. Walnut stock and case colored receiver.

	995	800	650	500	300	125

Model 1885 Deluxe High Wall

As above, with checkered walnut stock and pistol-grip.

	1175	875	700	550	300	125

Model 1885 Low Wall

Introduced in 2004, this model is chambered for the .22 LR, .22 Hornet, .30-30, .32-20, .38-40, .357 Magnum, .44-40 and .44 Magnum cartridges. Hand checkered walnut stock, with pistol-grip. Octagon barrel is 30" long. Single- or double-set trigger.

	1175	850	700	550	300	125

Texas Ranger Carbine

This model is a copy of the Sharps Model 1859 Military Carbine. Round barrel is 22" long. Receiver is case colored. Stock is American black walnut. Chambered for the .45-70 cartridge. Marked "T*S" on the barrel. Introduced in 2004.

	1200	900	725	600	350	150

Sharps Silhouette

Offered in .45-70 or .40-65 calibers, with 32" octagon barrel. Introduced in 1998.

	1095	850	700	600	350	150

Quigley Sharps Sporting Rifle

This rifle is chambered for the .45-70 or .45-120 caliber and fitted with a heavy 34" octagon barrel. Introduced in 1998.

	1725	1350	1175	700	450	275

Sharp's No. 1 Sporting Rifle

Plain walnut stock with pistol-grip. Fitted with a 32" barrel. Chambered for the .45-70 cartridge.

	1350	1050	900	500	300	150

Pride of the Plains Model

Based on the Sharps Model 1874 Sporting Rifle, this model chambered for the .45-70 cartridge. Features a 32" octagon barrel, hand-checkered walnut stock with pistol-grip, coin nickel receiver, Creedmore tang sight and target front sight with inserts. Introduced in 2004.

	1620	1200	925	500	300	150

Professional Hunter Model

This model is the basic Sharps Model 1874 chambered for the .45-70 cartridge. Fitted with a 32" barrel, case colored receiver, walnut stock with shotgun butt and double-set triggers. Introduced in 2004.

	1160	850	725	500	300	150

	NIB	EXC.	V.G.	GOOD	FAIR	POOR

Big Fifty Model

Chambered for the .50-90 cartridge and fitted with a 34" half-octagon barrel. Fancy walnut stock with hand checkering and pistol-grip. Case colored receiver, German silver nose cap and Hartford-style Soule Creedmore sights, with spirit level and globe front sight. Weight about 11 lbs. Introduced in 2004.

1890	1400	1150	700	450	275

Springfield Trapdoor Carbine

Based on the famous Springfield design. Chambered for the .45-70.

1250	1000	800	500	300	150

Springfield Trapdoor Officer's Model

This is the Officer's version of the Springfield Trapdoor model. Chambered for .45-70.

1150	900	775	500	275	150

U.S. Shooting Team Creedmoor Sharps

Chambered in .45-70, with 34" round barrel, hand-checkered European walnut stock with hand-rubbed oil finish and color case-hardened frame. The sales of this model a percentage, was used to win the first organized shooting event in the United States, will be donated by Cimarron to the USA Shooting Team in support of their efforts in international shooting sports. Made in Italy by Chiappa and imported by Cimarron.

1400	1150	900	700	400	200

SHOTGUNS

1878 Coach Gun

Side-by-side double-barrel 12-gauge, with hammers, double triggers, 22" or 26" barrels. Standard or polished blue "U.S.A." finish. **NOTE:** Add $100 for U.S.A. finish.

500	425	375	300	250	200

1881 Coach Gun

Side-by-side double barrel in 12- or 20-gauge, with 22", 26", 28" or 30" barrels. Hammerless design. Interchangeable choke tubes. Walnut stock with straight- or pistol-grip.

600	500	400	325	275	225

Model 1887 Shotgun

Lever-action limited edition replica of Model 1887 Winchester 12-gauge, with 5-shot magazine, 20", 22", 24" or 28" barrel. Color case-hardened frame.

1150	975	750	600	400	250

Model 1897 Shotgun

Replica of Winchester 12-gauge pump-action model. Exposed hammer, semi-pistol-grip walnut stock, choke tubes.

500	400	350	300	200	150

CLAPP, HOFFMAN & CO. CLAPP, GATES & CO. RIFLES
Alamance, North Carolina

Maker of Confederate Civil War rifles, 1862 - 1864. Overall length: Types I, II, & III 51.25" to 52", Type IV varies between 46.5" and 51"; barrel length: Types I, II, & III 35.25" to 36", Type IV varies between 31.25" and 35.875"; caliber: Types I, II, & III .50, Type IV .577; markings: none. Despite the absence of makers marks, the Clapp, Gates & Co. products are readily distinguished by their part-round, part-octagonal (octagonal section on Types I to III, about 4" long, 4.75" to 5.5" on Type IV rifles) barrels having only a slightly raised bolster projecting from the upper right quarter. This small bolster accommodates the boxlock that distinguished the first 100 rifles produced. This gave way to a standard percussion lock on subsequent production, which required that the hammer bend sharply to the left to strike the cone. Type I and Type II rifles were adapted to a "footprint" saber bayonet lug on the right side of the barrel; Types III and IV also had a saber bayonet lug on the right side of the barrel but of the standard pattern. Types III and IV are distinguished by their caliber, the former being .50, the latter .577. Prices reflect Type II through IV production; Type I (while extant) has never been offered for sale and would presumably bring a significantly higher premium.

—	—	39500	19500	3900	1200

	NIB	EXC.	V.G.	GOOD	FAIR	POOR

CLARK, F. H.
Memphis, Tennessee

Pocket Pistol

A .41-caliber single-shot percussion pistol, with a 3.5" to 5" barrel, German silver mounts and end cap. The barrel is stamped "F.H. Clark & Co./Memphis". Manufactured in the 1850s and 1860s.

—	—	5350	1900	550	200

CLASSIC DOUBLES
Tochigi City, Japan

Importer of Japanese shotguns, formerly imported by Winchester as the Model 101 and Model 23. These models were discontinued by Winchester in 1987 and imported by Classic Doubles until 1990.

Model 201 Classic

A 12- or 20-gauge boxlock side-by-side double-barrel shotgun, with 26" ventilated rib barrels, screw-in choke tubes single-selective trigger and automatic ejectors. Blued, with checkered walnut stock and beavertail forearm.

2400	1950	1700	1500	1250	900

Model 201 Small Bore Set

As above, with a smaller receiver and two sets of barrels. Chambered for 28-gauge and .410 bore. Barrels are 28" in length.

4100	3500	2950	2250	1750	1250

Model 101 Classic Field Grade I

A 12- or 20-gauge over/under shotgun, with 25.5" or 28" ventilated rib barrels, screw-in choke tubes, automatic ejectors and a single-selective trigger. Engraved, blued with checkered walnut stock.

2000	1750	1500	1250	1000	700

Classic Field Grade II

As above, in 28-gauge and .410 bore. Highly engraved, with a coin-finished receiver and a deluxe walnut stock. A round knob pistol-grip and fleur-de-lis checkering.

2500	2000	1750	1500	1250	900

Classic Sporter

As above in 12-gauge only, with 28" or 30" barrels, ventilated rib and screw-in choke tubes. The frame is coin-finished, with light engraving and a matted upper surface to reduce glare. The stock is select walnut. This model was designed for sporting clays.

2250	1800	1500	1250	1000	700

Waterfowl Model

As above with 30" barrels, 3" chambers, vent rib and screw-in choke tubes. The overall finish is a subdued matte with light engraving.

1650	1350	1000	850	650	500

Classic Trap Over/Under

Designed for competition trap shooting, with 30" or 32" barrels, a ventilated center and top rib, automatic ejectors, screw-in choke tubes and a single trigger. Blued, with light engraving and a walnut stock in straight or Monte Carlo style.

2250	1750	1500	1250	1000	700

Classic Trap Single

As above, with a single 32" or 34" barrel.

2250	1800	1500	1250	1000	700

Classic Trap Combo

As above, with a single barrel and a set of over/under barrels.

3000	2500	2000	1750	1250	1000

Classic Skeet

As above, with 27.5" barrels.

2250	1750	1500	1250	1000	700

Classic Skeet 4 Gauge Set

As above, furnished with four sets of barrels chambered for 12-, 20-, 28-gauge, and .410 bore.

4150	3750	3000	2500	1850	1500

CLEMENT, CHAS.
Liege, Belgium

Model 1903

A 5.5mm Glisenti caliber semi-automatic pistol. Barrel raises at the muzzle to begin the loading procedure.

NIB	EXC.	V.G.	GOOD	FAIR	POOR
—	575	475	350	220	110

Model 1907

As above, in 6.35mm and 7.65mm caliber.

NIB	EXC.	V.G.	GOOD	FAIR	POOR
—	475	395	325	200	100

Model 1908

Similar to the Model 1907, with the magazine release at the bottom of the frame. Fitted with a larger grip.

NIB	EXC.	V.G.	GOOD	FAIR	POOR
—	575	450	295	200	125

Model 1909

A semi-automatic pistol in 6.35mm and 7.65mm calibers. Similar to the Model 1908, with barrel and chamber housing in one piece.

NIB	EXC.	V.G.	GOOD	FAIR	POOR
—	575	450	300	225	100

Model 1910

Redesigned version of the above, with the barrel and housing all one piece. This unit is held in position by the trigger guard.

NIB	EXC.	V.G.	GOOD	FAIR	POOR
—	575	475	395	350	275

Model 1912

A 6.35mm caliber semi-automatic pistol marked "Clement's Patent"; others, "Model 1912 Brevet 243839". This model is quite different from earlier Clement models.

NIB	EXC.	V.G.	GOOD	FAIR	POOR
—	425	295	250	195	100

American Model

Revolver copy of the Colt Police Positive. Chambered for .38-caliber.

NIB	EXC.	V.G.	GOOD	FAIR	POOR
—	425	295	250	150	90

CLERKE PRODUCTS
Santa Monica, California

Hi-Wall

A copy of the Winchester Model 1885 High Wall rifle, with the action activated by a lever and the receiver is case colored. This rifle is chambered for almost all of the modern calibers. Features a 26" barrel, walnut stock with a pistol-grip and schnabel fore-end. Manufactured between 1972 and 1974.

NIB	EXC.	V.G.	GOOD	FAIR	POOR
975	850	650	425	300	200

Deluxe Hi-Wall

As above, with a half-round/half-octagonal barrel, select walnut stock and a recoil pad. Manufactured between 1972 and 1974.

NIB	EXC.	V.G.	GOOD	FAIR	POOR
1100	975	750	525	400	250

COBRA ENTERPRISES, INC.
Salt Lake City, Utah

DERRINGERS

Standard Series

Offered chambered in .22 LR, .22 WMR, .25 ACP and .32 ACP. Over/under barrels are 2.4". Pearl or laminate wood grips. Weight about 9.5 oz. Introduced in 2002.

NIB	EXC.	V.G.	GOOD	FAIR	POOR
250	200	160	125	100	75

Long Bore Series

This series is chambered for the .22 WMR, .38 Special or the 9mm cartridge. Fitted with a 3.5" barrel. Black synthetic, laminate oak or laminate rosewood grips. Chrome or black finish. Weight about 16 oz.

NIB	EXC.	V.G.	GOOD	FAIR	POOR
250	200	160	125	100	75

	NIB	EXC.	V.G.	GOOD	FAIR	POOR

Big Bore Series

Chambered for the .22 WMR, .32 H&R Magnum and the .38 Special. Barrel length is 2.75". Choice of black synthetic, laminate oak or laminate rosewood grips. Chrome or black finish. Weight about 14 oz.

250	200	160	125	100	75

SEMI-AUTOMATIC PISTOLS

C-32/C-380

Chambered for the .32 ACP or .380 cartridges. Fitted with a 2.8" barrel. Chrome or black finish. Magazine capacity 5 rounds for the .380 and 6 rounds for the .32 ACP. Weight about 22 oz.

175	125	80	60	40	25

C-9mm

This is a double-action-only pistol chambered for the 9mm cartridge. Fitted with a 3.3" barrel. Magazine capacity 10 rounds. Load indicator. Polymer grips. Weight about 21 oz.

275	215	150	115	75	45

Patriot .45

This is double-action-only pistol chambered for the .45 ACP cartridge. Barrel length is 3". Frame is black polymer. Slide is stainless steel. Magazine capacity 6 rounds. Weight about 20 oz.

350	225	150	115	75	45

COBRAY INDUSTRIES
S.W.D., Inc.
Atlanta, Georgia

M-11 Pistol

A 9mm caliber semi-automatic pistol. It fires from the closed bolt and made of steel stampings, with a parkerized finish. Patterned after, though a good deal smaller than, the Ingram Mac 10. **NOTE:** Add $70 for stainless steel; $150 for pre-ban models.

—	375	295	150	100	75

M-12

Same as above, but chambered for the .380 ACP cartridge. **NOTE:** Add $150 for pre-ban models.

—	375	295	150	100	75

TM-11 Carbine

As above in 9mm caliber, with a 16.25" shrouded barrel and a telescoping metal shoulder stock.

—	450	350	225	150	100

TM-12 Carbine

As above, but chambered for the .380 ACP cartridge.

—	450	350	225	150	100

Terminator Shotgun

A single-shot 12- or 20-gauge shotgun that fires from an open bolt position. The cocked bolt is released to slam home on the shell when the trigger is pulled. The 18" barrel is cylinder bored. There is a telescoping wire stock and the finish is Parkerized. We have seen many of these advertised at sky-high prices, but junk is junk.

—	175	125	80	60	40

COCHRAN TURRET
C. B. Allen
Springfield, Massachusetts

Under Hammer Turret Rifle

A .36- or .40-caliber percussion radial cylinder rifle, with 31" or 32" octagonal barrels and walnut stocks. The barrel marked "Cochrans/Many/Chambered/&/Non Recoil/Rifle" and the top strap "C.B. Allen / Springfield". These rifles were produced in the variations listed. Manufactured during the late 1830s and 1840s.

1st Type

Fitted with a circular top strap secured by two screws. Serial numbered from 1 to approximately 30.

—	—	—	18000	6500	2150

	NIB	EXC.	V.G.	GOOD	FAIR	POOR

2nd Type

Fitted with a rectangular hinged top strap, the locking catch of which serves as the rear sight. Serial numbered from approximately 31 to 155.

NIB	EXC.	V.G.	GOOD	FAIR	POOR
—	—	29500	15000	5100	1800

3rd Type

As above, with a smaller hammer and a plain trigger guard.

NIB	EXC.	V.G.	GOOD	FAIR	POOR
—	—	18000	15000	5100	1800

Pistol

Action similar to above with 4" to 7" barrels.

NIB	EXC.	V.G.	GOOD	FAIR	POOR
—	—	26500	21000	9700	3000

CODY, MICHAEL & SONS
Nashville, Tennessee

Received a contract with the State of Tennessee for "Mississippi" rifles with brass patchboxes in late 1861. Barrel length 36"; caliber .54. Cody often used reworked Model 1817 rifle barrels and sporting pattern single screw lockplates. Rifles are unmarked except for large engraved serial number on top of breech plug tang.

NIB	EXC.	V.G.	GOOD	FAIR	POOR
—	—	29500	13000	2150	775

COFER, T. W.
Portsmouth, Virginia

Cofer Navy Revolver

A .36-caliber spur trigger percussion revolver, with a 7.5" octagonal barrel and 6-shot cylinder. The top strap is marked "T.W. Cofer's/Patent" and the barrel "Portsmouth, Va." This revolver was manufactured in limited quantities during the Civil War.

NIB	EXC.	V.G.	GOOD	FAIR	POOR
—	—	120000	43500	6500	1500

COGSWELL
London, England

Cogswell Pepperbox Pistol

A .47-caliber 6-shot percussion pepperbox, with case hardened barrels, German silver frame and walnut grips. Normally marked "B. Cogswell, 224 Strand, London" and "Improved Revolving Pistol".

NIB	EXC.	V.G.	GOOD	FAIR	POOR
—	—	4400	1950	975	550

COLTON MANUFACTURING CO.
Toledo, Ohio

The Colton Manufacturing Co. provided Sears with its first American-made hammerless house brand double. Sears advertised their sidelock hammerless gun as "the equal of any gun made, regardless of price" in their 1900 Fall catalog No. 110. There were four models: three sideplated boxlock-types and a unique unitized coil spring driven striker assembly version. All these, especially the latter, were designed to be mass produced. Many of the distinctive sidelock-within-a-sideplated model were produced but they are seldom seen today either because they were used-up or did not hold up well and were scrapped. Sears replaced Colton with the more traditional design Fryberg gun in 1902. Values depend on grade. There appears to be at least two levels of quality and condition ranging from $300 to $1,500. Colton-marked guns are scarce.

COLT'S PATENT FIRE ARMS MANUFACTURING COMPANY
Hartford, Connecticut

COLT PATERSON MODELS

Pocket or Baby Paterson Model No. 1

The Paterson was the first production revolver manufactured by Colt. First made in 1837. The Model 1 or Pocket Model is the most diminutive of the Paterson line. The revolver is serial numbered in its own range, #1 through #500. The numbers are not visible without dismantling the revolver. The barrel lengths run from 1.75" to 4.75". The standard model has no attached loading lever. The chambering is .28-caliber percussion and holds five shots. Finish is all blued and the grips are varnished walnut. It has a roll-engraved cylinder scene and the barrel is stamped "Patent Arms Mfg. Co. Paterson N.J. Colt's Pt." Cased examples in Very Good or better condition can bring upwards of $200,000.

NIB	EXC.	V.G.	GOOD	FAIR	POOR
—	—	125000	50000	19500	5000

	NIB	EXC.	V.G.	GOOD	FAIR	POOR

Belt Model Paterson No. 2

The Belt Model Paterson is a larger revolver, with a straight-grip and an octagonal barrel that is 2.5" to 5.5" in length. Chambered for .31-caliber percussion and holds five shots. The finish is all blued, with varnished walnut grips and no attached loading lever. It has a roll-engraved cylinder scene and the barrel is stamped "Patent Arms Mfg. Co. Paterson N.J. Colt's Pt." The serial number range is #1-#850 and shared with the #3 Belt Model. Made from 1837-1840. An excellent cased example was auctioned by Rock Island Auction in 2007 for $414,000.

—	—	225000	75000	28500	7500

Belt Model Paterson No. 3

This revolver is quite similar to the Model #2, except that the grips are curved outward at the bottom to form a more hand-filling configuration. They are serial numbered in the same #1-#850 range. Some attached loading levers have been noted on this model, but they are extremely rare and would add approximately 35 percent to the value.

—	—	250000	95000	40000	10000

Ehlers Model Pocket Paterson

John Ehlers was a major stockholder and treasurer of the Patent Arms Mfg. Co. when it went bankrupt. He seized the assets and inventory. These revolvers were Pocket Model Patersons that were not finished at the time. Ehlers had them finished and marketed them. They had an attached loading lever and the abbreviation "Mfg Co." was deleted from the barrel stamping. There were 500 revolvers involved in the Ehlers variation totally. They were produced from 1840-1843.

—	—	—	75000	30000	8300

Ehlers Belt Model Paterson

The same specifications apply to this larger revolver as they do to the Ehlers Pocket Model. It falls within the same 500 revolver involvement and is rare.

—	—	—	75000	30000	8000

Texas Paterson Model No. 5

This is the largest and most sought after of the Paterson models, also known as the Holster Model. It has been verified as actually seeing use by both the military and civilians on the American frontier. It is chambered for .36-caliber percussion, holds five shots and has an octagonal barrel that ranges from 4" to 12" in length. It has been observed with and without the attached loading lever, but those with it are rare. Finish is blued, with a case-colored hammer. The grips are varnished walnut. The cylinder is roll-engraved; barrel is stamped "Patent Arms Mfg. Co. Paterson, N.J. Colts Pt." Most Texas Patersons are well used and have a worn appearance. One in excellent or V.G. condition would be highly prized. A verified military model would be worth a great deal more than standard, so a qualified appraisal would be essential. The serial number range is #1-#1000. Manufactured from 1838-1840. The attached loading lever brings approximately a 25 percent premium.

An 1836 Colt Paterson Revolver sold in September, 2011, for $977,500 at a Heritage Auction in Dallas, Texas. (The price includes a 15% buyer's premium.) This is believed to be a world record for the sale of a single American firearm. The very rare No. 5 Holster Model with a 9" barrel, ivory grips, attached loading lever and accessories in a box, is the finest known surviving example of Samuel Colt's first revolver. Two other Colt percussion revolvers were sold at the same auction for more than $800,000. (See Third Model Dragoon and Model 1861 Navy listings.) Such prices are extreme exceptions to the values of typical models.

—	—	300000	150000	60000	17500

Colt Model 1860 Army

Fluted Cylinder

675	575	400	300	200	125

COLT REVOLVING LONG GUNS 1837-1847

First Model Ring Lever Rifle

This was actually the first firearm manufactured by Colt; the first revolver appeared a short time later. There were 200 of the First Models made in 1837 and 1838. Octagonal barrel of the First Model is 32" long and browned, while the rest of the finish is blued. Stock is varnished walnut with a cheekpiece inlaid with Colt's trademark. The ring lever located in front of the frame is pulled to rotate the 8-shot cylinder and cock the hammer. The rifle is chambered for .34-, .36-, .38-, .40- and .44-caliber percussion. The cylinder is roll-engraved and the barrel is stamped "Colt's Patent/Patent Arms Mfg. Co., Paterson, N. Jersey". This model has a top strap over the cylinder. They were made both with and without an attached loading lever. The latter is worth approximately 10 percent more.

—	—	—	90000	40000	9750

	NIB	EXC.	V.G.	GOOD	FAIR	POOR

Second Model Ring Lever Rifle

This model is quite similar in appearance to the First Model. Its function is identical. The major difference is the absence of the top strap over the cylinder. It had no trademark stamped on the cheekpiece. The Second Model is offered with a 28" and a 32" octagonal barrel and is chambered for .44-caliber percussion, holding 8 shots. There were approximately 500 produced from 1838-1841. The presence of an attached cheekpiece would add approximately 10 percent to the value.

	NIB	EXC.	V.G.	GOOD	FAIR	POOR
—	—	—	80000	19500	8000	

Model 1839 Shotgun

This model is quite similar in appearance to the 1839 Carbine. Chambered for 16-gauge and holds six shots. It has a Damascus pattern barrel. The most notable difference is a 3.5" (instead of a 2.5") long cylinder. There were only 225 of these made from 1839-1841. Markings are the same as on the Carbine.

	NIB	EXC.	V.G.	GOOD	FAIR	POOR
—	—	37500	29500	11000	6000	

Model 1839 Carbine

This model has no ring, but features an exposed hammer for cocking and rotating the 6-shot cylinder. Chambered for .525 smoothbore and comes standard with a 24" round barrel. Other barrel lengths have been noted. Finish is blued, with a browned barrel and a varnished walnut stock. Cylinder is roll-engraved and the barrel is stamped "Patent Arms Mfg. Co. Paterson, N.J.-Colt's Pt." There were 950 manufactured from 1838-1841. Later variations of this model are found with the attached loading lever standard. Earlier models without one would bring approximately 25 percent additional. There were 360 purchased by the military and stamped "WAT" on the stock. These would be worth twice what a standard model would bring.

	NIB	EXC.	V.G.	GOOD	FAIR	POOR
—	—	36000	25000	13500	7900	

Model 1839/1848 Carbine

In 1848, Colt acquired a number of Model 1839 Carbines (approximately 40) from the state of Rhode Island. In an effort to make them marketable they were refinished and the majority fitted with plain cylinders (brightly polished) having integral ratchets around the arbor hole. Barrel length 24"; caliber .525; barrel browned; cylinder polished; frame blued; furniture case hardened; walnut stock varnished.

	NIB	EXC.	V.G.	GOOD	FAIR	POOR
—	—	70000	55000	18500	6500	

Model 1854 Russian Contract Musket

In 1854, Colt purchased a large number of U.S. Model 1822 flintlock muskets that the company altered to percussion cap ignition and rifled. The reworked muskets are dated 1854 on the barrel tang and at the rear of the lockplate. In most instances the original manufactory marks, such as Springfield or Harpers Ferry at the rear of the lockplate, have been removed, while the U.S. and eagle between the hammer and bolster remain. The percussion nipple bolster is marked COLT'S PATENT. Some examples have been noted with the date 1858. Barrel length 42"; caliber .69; lock and furniture burnished bright; walnut stock oil finished.

	NIB	EXC.	V.G.	GOOD	FAIR	POOR
—	15000	10000	5000	1500	750	

COLT WALKER-DRAGOON MODELS

Walker Model Revolver

The Walker is a massive revolver. Weighs 4 lbs., 9 oz. and has a 9" part-round/part-octagonal barrel. The cylinder holds six shots and chambered for .44-caliber percussion. There were 1,000 Walker Colts manufactured in 1847 and nearly all of them saw extremely hard use. Originally this model had a roll-engraved cylinder, military inspection marks and barrel stamping that read "Address Saml. Colt-New York City". Practically all examples noted have had these markings worn or rusted beyond recognition. Because the Walker is perhaps the most desirable and sought-after Colt from a collector's standpoint and because of the extremely high value of a Walker in any condition, qualified appraisal is definitely recommended. These revolvers were serial numbered A, B, C, D Company 1-220 and E Company 1-120. An Excellent example was auctioned by James D. Julia in 2008 for $920,000.

	NIB	EXC.	V.G.	GOOD	FAIR	POOR
—	900000	675000	400000	200000	59500	

Civilian Walker Revolver

This model is identical to the military model, but has no martial markings. They are found serial numbered 1001 through 1100.

	NIB	EXC.	V.G.	GOOD	FAIR	POOR
—	—	500000	395000	195000	58000	

Whitneyville Hartford Dragoon

This is a large 6-shot, .44-caliber percussion revolver. It has a 7.5" part-round/part-octagonal barrel. Frame, hammer and loading lever are case colored. Remainder is blued, with a brass trigger guard and varnished walnut grips. There were only 240 made in late 1847. Serial numbers run from 1100-1340. Model is often referred to as a Transitional Walker. Some of the parts used

	NIB	EXC.	V.G.	GOOD	FAIR	POOR

in its manufacture were left over from the Walker production run. This model has a roll-engraved cylinder scene and barrel is stamped "Address Saml. Colt New York-City". An extremely rare model.

		—	—	140000	100000	55000	28500

Walker Replacement Dragoon

This extremely rare Colt (300 produced) is sometimes referred to as the "Fluck", in memory of the gentleman who first identified it as a distinct and separate model. Produced by Colt as replacements to the military for Walkers that were no longer fit for service due to mechanical failures. They were large 6-shot .44-caliber percussion revolvers, with 7.5" part-round/part-octagonal barrels. Serial numbers ran from 2216 to 2515. The frame, hammer and loading lever are case-colored; the remainder blued. Grips, which are longer than other Dragoons and similar to the Walkers, are of varnished walnut and bear the inspectors mark "WAT" inside an oval cartouche on one side and the letters "JH" on the other. Frame is stamped "Colt's/ Patent/U.S." The letter "P" appears on various parts of the gun.

		—	—	75000	55000	25000	6000

First Model Dragoon

Another large 6-shot .44-caliber percussion revolver. It has a 7.5" part-round/part-octagonal barrel. Frame, hammer and loading lever are case colored; the remainder blued, with a brass grip frame and square backed trigger guard. Trigger guard is silver-plated on the Civilian Model only. Another distinguishing feature on the First Model is the oval cylinder stop notches. The serial number range is 1341-8000. There were approximately 7,000 made. The cylinder is roll-engraved; barrel stampings read "Address Saml. Colt, New York City." "Colt's Patent" appears on the frame. Military Models the letters "U.S." also appear on the frame.

Military Model

	—	110000	75000	40000	20000	3500

Civilian Model

	—	90000	55000	35000	18000	3000

Second Model Dragoon

Most of the improvements that distinguish this model from the First Model are internal and not readily apparent. The most obvious external change is the rectangular cylinder-stop notches. This model is serial numbered from 8000-10700. Total production of approximately 2,700 revolvers manufactured in 1850 and 1851. There is a Civilian Model, Military Model and an extremely rare variation that was issued to the militias of New Hampshire and Massachusetts (marked "MS.").

Civilian Model

	—	75000	55000	35000	25000	3500

Military Model

	—	85000	62500	40000	30000	3000

Militia Model

	—	90000	75000	45000	30000	3000

Third Model Dragoon

This is the most common of all large Colt percussion revolvers. Approximately 10,500 were manufactured from 1851 through 1861. Quite similar in appearance to the Second Model and the most obvious external difference is the round trigger guard. Third Model Dragoon was the first Colt revolver available with a detachable shoulder stock. There are three basic types of stocks and all are quite rare as only 1,250 were produced. There are two other major variations we will note—the "C.L." Dragoon, which was a militia-issued model and is rare and the late-issue model with an 8" barrel. These are found over serial number 18000 and only 50 were produced.

A historic cased Gustave Young-engraved ivory-gripped Colt Third Model Dragoon was sold for $805,000 at a Texas auction in 2011. The revolver was inscribed "Colonel P.M. Milliken". Milliken was an officer of the 1st Ohio volunteer calvary and was killed leading a charge against the Confederate Army at Stone River, Tennessee in 1862. Two other Colt percussion revolvers were sold at the same auction for more than $800,000. (See Texas Paterson No. 5 and Model 1861 Navy listings.) Such prices are extreme exceptions to the values of typical models.

Civilian Model

	—	50000	35000	15000	2500	1000

Military Model

	—	65000	47000	30000	17500	3000

Shoulder Stock Cut Revolvers

	—	70000	51000	35000	20000	3000

	NIB	EXC.	V.G.	GOOD	FAIR	POOR

Shoulder Stocks

	—	—	15000	8000	4000	2000

C.L. Dragoon

Hand engraved, not stamped.

	—	80000	60000	57500	17500	3000

8" Barrel Late Issue

	—	67000	55000	42500	25000	3000

Hartford English Dragoon

This is a variation of the Third Model Dragoon. The only notable differences are the British proof-marks and the distinct #1-#700 serial number range. Other than these two features, the description given for the Third Model would apply. These revolvers were manufactured in Hartford, but were finished at Colt's London factory from 1853-1857. Some bear the hand-engraved barrel marking "Col. Colt London". Many of the English Dragoons were elaborately engraved and individual appraisal would be a must. Two hundred revolvers came back to America in 1861 to be used in the Civil War.

	—	50000	35000	25000	12000	3000

Model 1848 Baby Dragoon

This is a small 5-shot .31-caliber percussion revolver. An octagonal barrel in lengths of 3", 4", 5" and 6". Most were made without an attached loading lever, although some with loading levers have been noted. Frame, hammer and loading lever (when present) are case colored; barrel and cylinder blued. Grip frame and trigger guard are silver-plated brass. Approximately 15,500 manufactured between 1847 and 1850. Serial range is between 1-5500. Barrels are stamped "Address Saml. Colt/ New York City". Some have been noted with the barrel address inside brackets. Frame is marked "Colt's/Patent". The first 10,000 revolvers have the Texas Ranger/Indian roll-engraved cylinder scene; later guns the stagecoach holdup scene. This is a popular model and many fakes have been noted. **NOTE:** Attached loading lever add 15 percent.

Texas Ranger/Indian Scene

	—	—	19500	12000	6500	2000

Stagecoach Holdup Scene

	—	—	20500	13000	7000	2000

Model 1849 Pocket Revolver

This is a small either 5- or 6-shot .31-caliber percussion revolver. An octagonal barrel of 3", 4", 5" or 6" in length. Most had loading gates, but some did not. Frame, hammer and loading lever are case colored; cylinder and barrel are blued. Grip frame and round trigger guard are made of brass and are silver plated. Both large and small trigger guard variations noted. Most plentiful of all the Colt percussion revolvers, with approximately 325,000 manufactured over a 23-year period, 1850-1873. There are over 200 variations of this model and one should consult an expert for individual appraisals. There are many fine publications specializing in the field of Colt percussion revolvers that would be helpful in the identification of the variations. Values represented here are for the standard model.

	—	4000	3400	2950	1200	300

London Model 1849 Pocket Revolver

Identical in configuration to the standard 1849 Pocket Revolver. London-made models have a higher quality finish and their own serial number range, 1-11000. Manufactured from 1853 through 1857. Feature a roll-engraved cylinder scene and the barrels are stamped "Address Col. Colt/London". The first 265 revolvers, known as early models, have brass grip frames and small round trigger guards. They are quite rare and worth approximately 50 percent more than the standard model that has a steel grip frame and large oval trigger guard.

	—	6000	5000	3500	1200	300

Model 1851 Navy Revolver

This is, undoubtedly, the most popular revolver Colt produced in the medium size and power range. It is a 6-shot .36-caliber percussion revolver, with a 7.5" octagonal barrel. It has an attached loading lever. Basic model has a case colored frame hammer and loading lever, with silver-plated brass grip frame and trigger guard. Grips are varnished walnut. Colt manufactured approximately 215,000 of these fine revolvers between 1850 and 1873. Basic Navy features a roll-engraved cylinder scene of a battle between the navies of Texas and Mexico. There are three distinct barrel stampings—serial number 1-74000, "Address Saml. Colt New York City"; serial number 74001-101000 "Address Saml. Colt. Hartford, Ct."; and serial number 101001-215000 "Address Saml. Colt New York U.S. America". The left side of the frame is stamped "Colt's/ Patent" on all variations. This model is also available with a detached shoulder stock. Values for the stocks today are nearly as high as for the revolver itself. Careful appraisal should be secured

	NIB	EXC.	V.G.	GOOD	FAIR	POOR

before purchase. The number of variations within the 1851 Navy model designation makes it necessary to read specialized text available on the subject.

Square Back Trigger Guard, 1st Model, Serial #1-1000

	NIB	EXC.	V.G.	GOOD	FAIR	POOR
	—	—	50000	42500	27000	5500

Square Back Trigger Guard, 2nd Model, Serial #1001-4200

	—	—	37500	30000	10000	2500

Small Round Trigger Guard, 3rd Model, Serial #4201-85000

	—	—	9500	8000	2500	500

Large Round Trigger Guard, 4th Model, Serial #85001-215000

	—	—	9500	8000	2500	500

Martial Model

U.S." stamped on the left side of frame; inspector's marks and cartouche on the grips.

	—	—	42000	20000	7000	1000

Shoulder Stock Variations

1st and 2nd Model Revolver cut for stock only. Expert appraisal recommended prior to purchase of these very rare variations.

Stock Only

	—	—	22000	17000	7000	1250

3rd Model Cut For Stock

Revolver only.

	—	—	17500	11500	4000	1250

Stock

	—	—	12500	9000	3750	1000

London Model 1851 Navy Revolver

These revolvers are physically similar to the U.S.-made model, with the exception of the barrel address which reads "Address Col. Colt. London". Also, British proof-marks stamped on the barrel and cylinder. There were 42,000 made between 1853 and 1857. They have their own serial number range #1-#42,000. There are two major variations of the London Navy. Again, a serious purchaser would be well advised to seek qualified appraisal as fakes have been noted.

1st Model

Serial #1-#2,000, with a small round brass trigger guard and grip frame. Squareback guard worth a 40 percent premium.

	—	—	16500	8000	2150	700

2nd Model

Serial #2,001-#42,000, steel grip frame and large round trigger guard.

	—	—	15000	7500	1800	600

Hartford Manufactured Variation

Serial numbers in the 42,000 range.

	—	—	15000	7500	1800	600

COLT SIDE HAMMER MODELS

Model 1855 Side Hammer "Root" Pocket Revolver

The "Root", as it's popularly known, was the only solid-frame revolver Colt ever made. It has a spur trigger, walnut grips and hammer mounted on the right side of the frame. Standard finish is a case colored frame, hammer and loading lever, with the barrel and cylinder blued. Chambered for both .28-caliber and .31-caliber percussion. Each caliber has its own serial number range—1-30000 for the .28-caliber; 1-14000 for the .31-caliber. Model consists of seven basic variations. The serious student should avail himself of the fine publications dealing with this model in depth. Colt produced the Side Hammer Root from 1855-1870.

Model 1 and 1A Serial #1-384

3.5" octagonal barrel, .28-caliber roll-engraved cylinder. Hartford barrel address without pointing hand.

	—	—	12000	6000	3500	1200

Model 2 Serial #476-25000

Same as Model 1, with pointing hand barrel address.

	NIB	EXC.	V.G.	GOOD	FAIR	POOR
	—	—	7500	3500	1900	500

Model 3 Serial #25001-30000
Same as the Model 2, with a full fluted cylinder.

NIB	EXC.	V.G.	GOOD	FAIR	POOR
—	—	7500	3500	1900	500

Model 3A and 4 Serial #1-2400
.31-caliber, 3.5" barrel, Hartford address, full fluted cylinder.

NIB	EXC.	V.G.	GOOD	FAIR	POOR
—	—	7250	3250	1800	500

Model 5 Serial #2401-8000
.31-caliber, 3.5" round barrel, address "Col. Colt New York".

NIB	EXC.	V.G.	GOOD	FAIR	POOR
—	—	6500	2900	1300	300

Model 5A Serial #2401-8000
Same as Model 5, with a 4.5" barrel.

NIB	EXC.	V.G.	GOOD	FAIR	POOR
—	—	6500	2900	1300	300

Models 6 and 6A Serial #8001-11074
Same as Model 5 and 5A, with roll-engraved cylinder scene.

NIB	EXC.	V.G.	GOOD	FAIR	POOR
—	—	6750	2995	1350	300

Models 7 and 7A Serial #11075-14000
Same as Models 6 and 6A, with a screw holding in the cylinder pin.

NIB	EXC.	V.G.	GOOD	FAIR	POOR
—	—	6750	2995	1350	300

COLT SIDE HAMMER LONG GUNS

Model 1855 Sporting Rifle, 1st Model

This is a 6-shot revolving rifle, chambered for .36-caliber percussion. Comes with a 21", 24", 27" or 30" round barrel that is part octagonal where it joins the frame. Stock is walnut, with either an oil or a varnish finish. Frame, hammer and loading lever are case colored; rest of the metal blued. Hammer is on the right side of the frame. The 1st Model has no fore-end and an oiling device is attached to the barrel underlug. Trigger guard has two spur-like projections in front and in back of the bow. Roll-engraved cylinder scene depicts a hunter shooting at five deer and is found only on this model. Standard stampings are "Colt's Pt./1856" and "Address S. Colt Hartford, Ct. U.S.A."

Early Model

Low serial numbers, with a hand-engraved barrel marking "Address S. Colt Hartford, U.S.A."

NIB	EXC.	V.G.	GOOD	FAIR	POOR
—	—	16500	15000	5500	1500

Production Model

NIB	EXC.	V.G.	GOOD	FAIR	POOR
—	—	15000	12000	3000	1000

Model 1855 1st Model Carbine

Identical to the 1st Model Rifle, but offered with a 15" and 18" barrel.

NIB	EXC.	V.G.	GOOD	FAIR	POOR
—	—	12500	9500	3000	1000

Model 1855 Half Stock Sporting Rifle

Although this rifle is quite similar in appearance and finish to the 1st Model, there are some notable differences. Features a walnut fore-end that protrudes halfway down the barrel. Two types of trigger guards—a short projectionless one or a long model, with a graceful scroll. There is a 6-shot model chambered for .36- or .44-caliber or a 5-shot model chambered for .56-caliber. Cylinder is fully fluted. Markings are "Colt's Pt/1856" and "Address Col. Colt/Hartford Ct. U.S.A." Approximately 1,500 manufactured between 1857 and 1864.

NIB	EXC.	V.G.	GOOD	FAIR	POOR
—	—	12500	9500	3500	1000

Model 1855 Full Stock Military Rifle

This model holds 6-shots in its .44-caliber chambering and 5-shots when chambered for .56-caliber. Another side hammer revolving rifle that resembles the Half Stock model. Barrels are round and part-octagonal where they join the frame. Come in lengths of 21", 24", 27", 31" and 37". Hammer and loading lever are case colored; rest of the metal parts blued. Walnut buttstock and full length fore-end are oil finished and sling swivels. Cylinder is fully fluted. Military models have provisions for affixing a bayonet, military-style sights and bear the "U.S." martial mark on examples that were actually issued to the military. Standard stampings found on this model are "Colt's Pt/1856" and "Address Col. Colt Hartford, Ct. U.S.A." An estimated 9,300 manufactured between 1856 and 1864.

Martially Marked Models

NIB	EXC.	V.G.	GOOD	FAIR	POOR
—	—	42500	25000	9500	2000

	NIB	EXC.	V.G.	GOOD	FAIR	POOR

Without Martial Markings

| | | | 13500 | 9750 | 3500 | 1000 |

Model 1855 Full Stock Sporting Rifle

This model is similar in appearance to the Military model, with these notable exceptions. No provision for attaching a bayonet, sling swivels and it has sporting-style sights. Buttplate is crescent shaped. This model has been noted chambered for .56-caliber in a 5-shot version and chambered for .36-, .40-, .44- and .50-caliber in 6-shot variation. Quite scarce in .40- and .50-caliber and will bring a 10 percent premium. Standard markings are "Colt's Pt/1856" and "Address Col. Colt/Hartford Ct. U.S.A." Production on this model was quite limited (several hundred at most) between 1856 and 1864.

| | — | — | 20000 | 13500 | 4000 | 1000 |

Model 1855 Revolving Carbine

This model is similar in appearance to the 1855 Military Rifle. Barrel lengths of 15", 18" and 21", plus the absence of a fore-end make the standard Carbine Model readily identifiable. Markings are the same. Approximately 4,400 manufactured between 1856 and 1864.

| | | | 13500 | 9500 | 4000 | 1000 |

Model 1855 Artillery Carbine

Identical to the standard carbine, but chambered for .56-caliber only. It has a 24" barrel, full-length walnut fore-end and a bayonet lug.

| | — | — | 23500 | 17000 | 5500 | 1500 |

Model 1855 British Carbine

This is a British-proofed version, with barrel lengths up to 30". Has a brass trigger guard, buttplate and chambered for .56-caliber only. This variation usually found in the 10000-12000 serial number range.

| | | | 18500 | 13000 | 3750 | 1000 |

Model 1855 Revolving Shotgun

This model very much resembles the Half Stock Sporting Rifle. Made with a 27", 30", 33" and 36" smoothbore barrel. Has a 5-shot cylinder chambered for .60- or .75-caliber (20- or 10-gauge). Model has a case-colored hammer and loading lever; rest of the metal blued, with an occasional browned barrel noted. Buttstock and fore-end are of walnut, either oil or varnish-finished. Model has no rear sight and a small trigger guard, with the caliber stamped on it. Some have been noted with the large scroll trigger guard; these would add 10 percent to the value. Rarest shotgun variation would be a full stocked version in either gauge. Qualified appraisal would be highly recommended. Model is serial numbered in its own range #1-#1100. Manufactured from 1860-1863.

.60 Caliber (20 gauge)

| | — | — | 22500 | 10000 | 3500 | 1000 |

.75 Caliber (10 gauge)

| | — | — | 22500 | 10000 | 3500 | 1000 |

Model 1861 Single-Shot Rifled Musket

With the advent of the Civil War, the Union army seriously needed military arms. Colt was given a contract to supply 112,500 1861-pattern percussion single-shot muskets. Between 1861 and 1865, 75,000 were delivered. They have 40" rifled barrels chambered for .58-caliber. Musket is equipped with military sights, sling swivels and a bayonet lug. Metal finish is bright steel and stock is oil-finished walnut. Military inspector's marks are found on all major parts. "VP" over an eagle is stamped on the breech along with a date. Colt address and a date are stamped on the lockplate. A large number of these rifles were altered to the Snyder breech loading system for the Bey of Egypt.

Production Model

| | — | — | 5500 | 2000 | 750 | 450 |

COLT PERCUSSION REVOLVERS

Model 1860 Army Revolver

This model was the third most produced of the Colt percussion handguns. It was the primary revolver used by the Union Army during the Civil War. Colt delivered 127,156 of these revolvers to be used during those hostilities. It is a 6-shot .44-caliber percussion revolver. Either a 7.5" or 8" round barrel, with an attached loading lever. Frame, hammer and loading lever are case colored; barrel and cylinder are blued. Trigger guard and front strap are brass and back-strap is blued steel. Grips are one-piece walnut. Early models have barrels stamped "Address Saml. Colt Hartford Ct.". Later models stamped "Address Col. Saml. Colt New-York U.S. America". "Colt's/Patent" is stamped on the left side of the frame; ".44 Cal." on the trigger guard. Cylinder is roll

NIB	EXC.	V.G.	GOOD	FAIR	POOR

engraved with naval battle scene. Between 1860 and 1873, Colt manufactured 200,500 of these 1860 Army Revolvers.

Martial Marked Model

NIB	EXC.	V.G.	GOOD	FAIR	POOR
—	14000	8500	7500	3500	900

Civilian Model

This model found in either 3- or 4-screw variations and may or may not be cut for a shoulder stock. Civilian models are usually better finished.

NIB	EXC.	V.G.	GOOD	FAIR	POOR
—	10000	7500	6000	3000	800

Full Fluted Cylinder Model

Approximately 4,000 Army's were made, with full fluted cylinders. They appear in the first 8,000 serial numbers.

NIB	EXC.	V.G.	GOOD	FAIR	POOR
—	20000	16500	15000	7000	2000

Model 1861 Navy Revolver

This model is a 6-shot 7.5" round-barreled .36-caliber percussion revolver. Frame, hammer and attached loading lever are case colored. Barrel and cylinder are blued. Grip frame and trigger guard are silver-plated brass. Grips are of one-piece walnut. Cylinder has the roll-engraved naval battle scene and the barrel stamping is "Address Col. Saml. Colt New-York U.S. America". The frame is stamped "Colts/Patent" with "36 Cal." on the trigger guard. Not many variations within the 1861 Navy model designation. Less than 39,000 were made between 1861 and 1873.

A very exceptional cased and engraved presentation-grade Model 1861 Navy was sold at auction in 2011 for $805,000. Three Colt percussion revolvers sold for over $800,000 at the auction. (See Texas Paterson No. 5 and Third Model Dragoon listings.) Such prices are extreme exceptions to the values of typical models.

Fluted Cylinder Model

Approximately first 100 were made with full fluted cylinders.

NIB	EXC.	V.G.	GOOD	FAIR	POOR
—	35000	25000	15000	6000	3000

Military Model

Marked "U.S." on frame, inspector's cartouche on grip. 650 were marked "U.S.N." on the butt.

NIB	EXC.	V.G.	GOOD	FAIR	POOR
—	30000	22000	14000	5500	2500

Shoulder Stock Model

Only 100 3rd-type stocks made. Appear between serial #11000-#14000. These are very rare revolvers.

Revolver

NIB	EXC.	V.G.	GOOD	FAIR	POOR
—	—	—	—	5000	1500

Stock

NIB	EXC.	V.G.	GOOD	FAIR	POOR
—	—	—	10000	4250	1000

Civilian Model

NIB	EXC.	V.G.	GOOD	FAIR	POOR
—	18000	9000	6000	4000	2000

Model 1862 Pocket Navy Revolver

This is a smaller 5-shot .36-caliber percussion revolver. Resembles the configuration of the 1851 Navy. Has a 4.5", 5.5" or 6.5" octagonal barrel, with an attached loading lever. Frame, hammer and loading lever are case colored; barrel and cylinder blued. Grip frame and trigger guard are silver-plated brass; one-piece grips of varnished walnut. The stagecoach holdup scene is roll-engraved on the cylinder. Frame is stamped "Colt's/Patent"; the barrel "Address Col. Saml. Colt New-York U.S. America". Approximately 19,000 manufactured between 1861 and 1873. Serial numbered in the same range as the Model 1862 Police. Because a great many were used for metallic cartridge conversions, they are quite scarce today.

NOTE: The London Address Model with blued steel grip frame would be worth more than the standard model. Add 50 percent. Longer barrels will bring a premium over the 4.5" length.

Standard Production Model

NIB	EXC.	V.G.	GOOD	FAIR	POOR
—	—	6000	3750	1200	500

Model 1862 Police Revolver

This is a slim attractively designed revolver. Some consider it the most aesthetically pleasing of all Colt percussion designs. It has a 5-shot half-fluted cylinder chambered for .36-caliber. Offered with a 3.5", 4.5", 5.5" or 6.5" round barrel. Frame, hammer and loading lever are case colored; barrel and cylinder blued. Grip frame is silver-plated brass; one-piece grips varnished walnut. Barrel stamped "Address Col. Saml Colt New-York U.S. America"; frame has "Colt's/Patent" on the left side. One of the cylinder flutes marked "Pat Sept. 10th 1850". Approximately 28,000

NIB	EXC.	V.G.	GOOD	FAIR	POOR

manufactured between 1861 and 1873. Many were converted to metallic cartridge use, so they are quite scarce on today's market.

NOTE: The London Address Model would be worth approximately twice the value of the standard model. Longer barrels will bring a premium over the 3.5" or 4.5" length.

Standard Production Model

NIB	EXC.	V.G.	GOOD	FAIR	POOR
—	—	6000	2950	1000	400

COLT METALLIC CARTRIDGE CONVERSIONS

Thuer Conversion Revolver

Although quite simplistic and not commercially successful, the Thuer Conversion was the first attempt by Colt to convert the percussion revolvers to the new metallic cartridge system. This conversion was designed around the tapered Thuer cartridge and consists of a ring that replaced the back part of the cylinder, which had been milled off. This ring is stamped "Pat. Sep./15, 1868". The ejection position is marked with the letter "E". These conversions have rebounding firing pins and are milled to allow loading from the front of the revolver. This conversion was undertaken on the six different models listed; all other specifications, finishes, markings, etc., not directly affected by the conversion would be the same as previously described. From a collectible and investment standpoint, the Thuer Conversion is very desirable. Competent appraisal should be secured if acquisition is contemplated. **NOTE:** Blued models will bring higher prices than nickel models in the same condition.

Model 1849 Pocket

NIB	EXC.	V.G.	GOOD	FAIR	POOR
—	60000	35000	15500	4000	2000

Model 1851

NIB	EXC.	V.G.	GOOD	FAIR	POOR
—	—	28000	18000	5000	2000

Model 1860 Army

NIB	EXC.	V.G.	GOOD	FAIR	POOR
—	—	30000	19500	6000	2000

Model 1861 Navy

NIB	EXC.	V.G.	GOOD	FAIR	POOR
—	—	30000	19500	6000	2000

Model 1862 Police

NIB	EXC.	V.G.	GOOD	FAIR	POOR
—	—	20000	13500	3500	1500

Model 1862 Pocket Navy

NIB	EXC.	V.G.	GOOD	FAIR	POOR
—	—	25000	16000	3500	1500

Richards Conversion, 1860 Army Revolver

This was Colt's second attempt at metallic cartridge conversion. It met with quite a bit more success than the first. Richards Conversion was designed for the .44 Colt cartridge. It has a 6-shot cylinder and an integral ejector rod to replace the loading lever that had been removed. Other specifications pertaining to the 1860 Army Revolver remain as previously described, if they are not directly altered by the conversion. Richards Conversion adds a breechplate, with a firing pin and its own rear sight. Approximately 9,000 of these Conversions manufactured between 1873 and 1878. **NOTE:** Blued models will bring higher prices than nickel models in the same condition.

Civilian Model

NIB	EXC.	V.G.	GOOD	FAIR	POOR
—	20000	10000	3950	2000	600

Martially Marked

This variation is found with mixed serial numbers and a second set of conversion serial numbers. The "U.S." is stamped on left side of barrel lug and inspector's cartouche appears on the grip. A very rare Colt revolver.

NIB	EXC.	V.G.	GOOD	FAIR	POOR
—	30000	18000	15000	8000	2000

Transition Richards Model

Variation is marked by the presence of a firing pin hammer.

NIB	EXC.	V.G.	GOOD	FAIR	POOR
—	15000	9500	7000	3000	1200

Richards-Mason Conversion, 1860 Army Revolver

This conversion is different from the Richards Conversion, in a number of readily apparent aspects. Barrel was manufactured with a small lug much different in appearance than seen on the standard 1860 Army. Breechplate does not have its own rear sight and there is a milled area to allow the hammer to contact the base of the cartridge. These Conversions were also chambered for the .44 Colt cartridge and the cylinder holds 6 shots. There is an integral ejector rod in place of the loading lever. Barrels on some are stamped either "Address Col. Saml. Colt New-York U.S. America" or "Colt's Pt. F.A. Mfg. Co. Hartford, Ct." Patent dates 1871 and 1872 are stamped on the left side of the frame. Finish of these revolvers, as well as grips, were for the most part the same as on the

	NIB	EXC.	V.G.	GOOD	FAIR	POOR

unconverted Armies; for the first time, nickel-plated guns are found. Approximately 2,100 of these Conversions produced in 1877 and 1878. **NOTE:** Blued models will bring higher prices than nickel models in the same condition.

	NIB	EXC.	V.G.	GOOD	FAIR	POOR
	—	22000	13500	7000	2500	800

Richards-Mason Conversions 1851 Navy Revolver

These revolvers were converted in the same way as the 1860 Army previously described. Major difference being the caliber .38 either rimfire or centerfire. Finishes are mostly the same as on unconverted revolvers, but nickel-plated guns are not rare. **NOTE:** Blued models will bring higher prices than nickel models in the same condition.

Production Model Serial #1-3800

	NIB	EXC.	V.G.	GOOD	FAIR	POOR
	—	15000	11000	5500	2000	800

U.S. Navy Model Serial #41000-91000

USN" stamped on butt; steel grip frame.

	NIB	EXC.	V.G.	GOOD	FAIR	POOR
	—	20000	16000	9500	3000	1000

Richards-Mason Conversion 1861 Navy Revolver

Specifications for this model are the same as for the 1851 Navy Conversion described above, with the base revolver being different. There were 2,200 manufactured in the 1870s. **NOTE:** Blued models will bring higher prices than nickel models in the same condition.

Standard Production Model Serial #100-3300

	NIB	EXC.	V.G.	GOOD	FAIR	POOR
	—	20000	11500	6250	1500	500

U.S. Navy Model Serial #1000-9999

	NIB	EXC.	V.G.	GOOD	FAIR	POOR
	—	24000	15000	7500	3500	1000

Model 1862 Police and Pocket Navy Conversions

Conversion of these two revolver models is the most difficult to catalog of all the Colt variations. Approximately 24,000 of these produced between 1873 and 1880. There are five basic variations, with a number of sub-variations. Confusion is usually caused by different ways in which these were marked. Depending upon what parts were utilized, caliber markings could be particularly confusing. One must also consider the fact that many of these conversion revolvers found their way into secondary markets, such as Mexico, Central and South America. They were either destroyed or received sufficient abuse to obliterate most identifying markings. Five basic variations are all chambered for either the .38 rimfire or the .38 centerfire cartridge. All held 5 shots and most were found with the round roll-engraved stagecoach holdup scene. Half-fluted cylinder from the 1862 Police is quite rare on the conversion revolver and not found at all on some of the variations. Finishes on these guns were pretty much the same as they were before conversion, but not unusual to find nickel-plated specimens. Basic variations are listed. **NOTE:** Blued models will bring higher prices than nickel models in the same condition. Half-fluted cylinder add 20 percent.

Round Barrel Pocket Navy with Ejector

	NIB	EXC.	V.G.	GOOD	FAIR	POOR
	—	—	7500	3500	1600	800

3.5" Round Barrel Without Ejector

	NIB	EXC.	V.G.	GOOD	FAIR	POOR
	—	—	5500	2500	1000	300

4.5" Octagonal Barrel Without Ejector

	NIB	EXC.	V.G.	GOOD	FAIR	POOR
	—	—	6500	3500	1200	400

Model 1862 Pocket Navy Octagon Barrel with Ejector

	NIB	EXC.	V.G.	GOOD	FAIR	POOR
	—	—	7500	3850	1500	600

Model 1862 Police Round Barrel with Ejector

	NIB	EXC.	V.G.	GOOD	FAIR	POOR
	—	—	7500	3850	1500	600

Model 1871-1872 Open Top Revolver

This model was the first revolver Colt manufactured especially for a metallic cartridge. It was not a conversion. Frame, 7.5" or 8" round barrel and 6-shot cylinder were produced for the .44 rimfire metallic cartridge. Grip frame and some internal parts were taken from the 1860 Army and the 1851 Navy. Although this model was not commercially successful and not accepted by the U.S. Ordinance Department, it did pave the way for the Single-Action Army that came out shortly, thereafter, and was an immediate success. Model is all blued, with a case colored hammer. There are some with silver-plated brass grip frames, but most are blued steel. One-piece grips are of varnished walnut. Cylinder is roll-engraved with the naval battle scene. Barrel stamped "Address Col. Saml. Colt New-York U.S. America". Later production revolvers are barrel stamped "Colt's Pt. F.A. Mfg. Co. Hartford, Ct. U.S.A." First 1,000 revolvers were stamped "Colt's/Patent". After that, 1871 and 1872 patent dates

	NIB	EXC.	V.G.	GOOD	FAIR	POOR

appeared on the frame. There were 7,000 revolvers manufactured in 1872 and 1873.

1860 Army Grip Frame

—	—	27500	15000	4500	800

1851 Navy Grip Frame

—	—	29000	17500	4000	1200

COLT DERRINGERS AND POCKET REVOLVER

First Model Derringer

This is a small all-metal single-shot. Chambered for the .41 rimfire cartridge. The 2.5" barrel pivots to the left and downward for loading. Model engraved with a scroll pattern and has been noted blued, silver or nickel-plated. Barrel is stamped "Colt's Pt. F.A. Mfg. Co./Hartford Ct. U.S.A/ No.1." ".41 Cal." stamped on frame under the release catch. Approximately 6,500 of this model manufactured from 1870-1890. The first single-shot pistol Colt produced.

—	3500	2500	1200	800	400

Second Model Derringer

Although this model has the same odd shape as the First Model, it is readily identifiable by the checkered varnished walnut grips and the "No 2" on the barrel after the address. It is also .41 rimfire and has a 2.5" barrel that pivots in the same manner as the First Model. Approximately 9,000 of these manufactured between 1870 and 1890. **NOTE:** Add 100 percent for .41 Centerfire model.

—	1800	1300	800	400	250

Third Model Derringer

This model was designed by Alexander Thuer, who was also responsible for Colt's first metallic cartridge conversion. Often referred to as the "Thuer Model" for this reason. Chambered for the .41 rimfire cartridge and has a 2.5" barrel that pivots to the right (but not down) for loading. Third Model has a more balanced appearance than its predecessors and its commercial success (45,000 produced between 1875 and 1910) reflects this. Barrel on this model stamped "Colt" in small block letters on the first 2,000 guns. Remainder of production features the "COLT"in large italicized print. The ".41 Cal." stamped on the left side of the frame. Model will be found with the barrel blued or plated in either silver or nickel and the bronze frame plated. Grips are varnished walnut. **NOTE:** Blued models will bring a premium over nickel in the same condition. Add 25 percent for .41 Centerfire model.

First Variation, Early Production

Has a raised area ("pregnant frame") on the underside of the frame through which the barrel screw passes. Spur is not angled. Small block "Colt" lettering on barrel.

—	3500	2500	2000	1200	600

First Variation, Late Production

Similar to early production, but has large italicized "COLT" on barrel.

—	3000	2000	1200	800	400

Production Model

—	1800	1300	800	400	250

House Model Revolver

There are two basic versions of this model. Both chambered for the .41 rimfire cartridge. The 4-shot version is known as the "Cloverleaf" due to the shape of the cylinder when viewed from the front. Approximately 7,500 of nearly 10,000 House revolvers were this 4-shot configuration. Offered with a 1.5" or 3" barrel. The 1.5" length is quite rare and some octagonal barrels in this length have been noted. The 5-shot round-cylinder version accounts for the rest of the production. Found with serial numbers over 6100 and offered with a 2.875" length barrel only. Model stamped on the top strap "Pat. Sept. 19, 1871". Model has brass frames that were sometimes nickel-plated. Barrels are found either blued or plated. Grips are varnished walnut or rosewood. Slightly fewer than 10,000 of both variations manufactured from 1871-1876. **NOTE:** Blued models will bring a premium over nickel in the same condition.

Cloverleaf with 1.5" Round Barrel

—	3750	3000	2000	1250	400

Cloverleaf with 3" Barrel

—	—	1750	1500	500	200

House Pistol with 5-Shot Round Cylinder

—	—	1550	1300	500	200

Open Top Pocket Revolver

This is a .22-caliber rimfire 7-shot revolver, that was offered with either a 2.375" or 2.875" barrel. Model was a commercial success, with over 114,000 manufactured between 1871 and 1877. Would undoubtedly been a great deal more sold had not the cheap copies begun to flood the market at that time, forcing Colt to drop this model from the line. Revolver has a silver or nickel-plated brass frame and a nickel-plated or blued barrel and cylinder. Grips are varnished walnut. Cylinder bolt slots are found toward the front on this model. "Colt's Pt. F.A. Mfg. Co./Hartford, Ct. U.S.A." stamped on the barrel and ".22 Cal." on left side of frame. **NOTE:** Blued models will bring a premium over nickel in the same condition.

Early Model with Ejector Rod

—	—	2000	1750	800	400

Production Model without Ejector Rod

—	—	1250	600	300	150

New Line Revolver .22

This was the smallest framed version of the five distinct New Line Revolvers. Has a 7-shot cylinder and a 2.25" octagonal barrel. Frame is nickel-plated and balance of revolver is either nickel-plated or blued. Grips are of rosewood. Approximately 55,000 of these made from 1873-1877. Colt also stopped production of the New Lines rather than try to compete with the "Suicide Specials". "Colt New .22" is found on the barrel; ".22 Cal." on the frame. The barrel is also stamped "Colt's Pt. F.A. Mfg.Co./Hartford, Ct. U.S.A." **NOTE:** Blued models will bring higher prices than nickel models in the same condition.

1st Model

Short cylinder flutes.

—	—	1300	600	300	150

2nd Model

Long cylinder flutes.

—	—	750	500	250	125

New Line Revolver .30

This is a larger version of the .22 New Line. Basic difference is size, caliber, caliber markings and offering of a blued version with case colored frame. Approximately 11,000 manufactured from 1874-1876. **NOTE:** Prices are for nickel finish. Blued models will bring a premium of 100 percent.

—	—	1000	750	300	150

New Line Revolver .32

Same basic revolver as the .30-caliber, except it is chambered for the .32-caliber rimfire and .32-caliber centerfire and is so marked. There were 22,000 of this model manufactured from 1873-1884. Model was offered with the rare 4" barrel and this variation would be worth nearly twice the value of a standard model. **NOTE:** Prices are for nickel finish. Blued models will bring a premium of 100 percent.

—	—	1550	850	300	150

New Line Revolver .38

Approximately 5,500 of this model manufactured between 1874 and 1880. Chambered for either the .38 rimfire or .38 centerfire caliber and is so marked. This model in a 4" barrel would also bring twice the value. **NOTE:** Prices are for nickel finish. Blued models will bring a premium of 100 percent.

—	—	1500	800	400	200

New Line Revolver .41

This is the "Big Colt", as it was sometimes known in advertising of its era. Chambered for the .41 rimfire and the .41 centerfire and is so marked. The large caliber of this variation makes this the most desirable of the New Lines to collectors. Approximately 7,000 of this model manufactured from 1874-1879. A 4"-barreled version would again be worth a 100 percent premium. **NOTE:** Prices are for nickel finish. Blued models will bring a premium of 100 percent.

—	—	2000	1375	650	300

New House Model Revolver

This revolver is similar to the other New Lines, except it features a square-butt instead of the bird's-head configuration, a 2.25" round barrel without ejector rod and a thin loading gate. Chambered for the .32 (rare), .38 and the .41 centerfire cartridges. Finish was either full nickel-plated or blued, with a case colored frame. Grips are walnut, rosewood or (for the first time on a Colt revolver) checkered hard rubber, with an oval around the word "Colt". Barrel address is the same as on the other New Lines. Frame is marked "New House" with the caliber. Approximately 4,000 manufactured between 1880-1886. .32-caliber model would bring a 10

NIB	EXC.	V.G.	GOOD	FAIR	POOR

percent premium. **NOTE:** Prices are for nickel finish. Blued models will bring a premium of 100 percent.

		V.G.	GOOD	FAIR	POOR
—	—	1495	1000	450	250

New Police Revolver

This was the final revolver in the New Line series. Chambered for .32, .38 and .41 centerfire caliber. The .32 and .41 are quite rare. Offered in barrel lengths of 2.25", 4.5", 5.5" and 6.5". An ejector rod is found on all but the 2.5" barrel. Finish is either nickel or blued and case colored. Grips are hard rubber, with a scene of a policeman arresting a criminal embossed on them; thusly the model became known to collectors as the "Cop and Thug" model. Barrel stamping is as the other New Lines; frame stamped "New Police .38". Approximately 4,000 of these manufactured between 1882-1886. **NOTE:** The .32- and .41-caliber versions of this model will bring a 40-50 percent premium. Blued models and models with 5.5" or 6.5" barrels will bring a premium. Short barrel model will bring about 50 percent of the listed prices.

Long Barrel Model with Ejector

			GOOD	FAIR	POOR
—	—	—	3250	1400	700

COLT SINGLE ACTION ARMY REVOLVER

The Colt Single Action Army or Peacemaker, as it is sometimes referred to, is one of the most widely collected and recognized firearms in the world. Few interruptions or changes in design, it has been manufactured from 1873 until the present. The variations in this model are myriad. Produced in 30 different calibers and barrel lengths from 2.5" to 16", with 4.75", 5.5" and 7.5" standard. The standard finish is blued, with a case colored frame. Many are nickel-plated. Examples have been found silver-/gold-plated, with combinations thereof. Finest engravers in the world have used the SAA as a canvas to display their artistry. Standard grips from 1873-1883 were walnut, either oil-stained or varnished. From 1883 to approximately 1897 the standard grips were hard rubber, with eagle and shield. After this date, at serial number 165000, the hard rubber grips featured the Rampant Colt. Many special-order grips were available, notably pearl and ivory, which were often checkered or carved in ornate fashion. Variables involved in establishing values on this model are extreme. Added to this, one must also consider historical significance, since the SAA played a big part in the formative years of the American West. Fortunately for those among us interested in the SAA, there are a number of fine publications available dealing exclusively with this model. It is my strongest recommendation that it be acquired and studied thoroughly to prevent extremely expensive mistakes. The Colt factory records are nearly complete for this model and research should be done before acquisition of rare or valuable specimens. The Colt factory will provide a letter documenting the history of a particular model for a fee of $100, as of 2014. For historically significant, factory engraved or celebrity owned guns, fees may be higher. The Archive department's address is: Colt Archive Properties, P. O. Box 1868, Hartford, CT 06144. Some research data can be obtained by telephone: 800-962-2658 ext. 1343.

For our purposes we will break down the Single-Action Army production as follows:

Antique or Black Powder, 1873-1898, serial number 1-175000

The cylinder axis pin is retained by a screw in the front of the frame.

Pre-war, 1899-1940, serial number 175001-357859

The cylinder axis pin is retained by a spring-loaded button through the side of the frame. This method is utilized on the following models, as well.

Post-war 2nd Generation, 1956-1978, serial number 0001SA-99999SA

3rd Generation, 1978-Present, serial #SA1001. A breakdown of production by caliber will follow the chapter. It is important to note that the rarer calibers and the larger calibers bring higher values in this variation.

NOTE: As a rule of thumb, nickel guns will bring a deduction of 20-30 percent. For revolvers with 4.75" barrels add 10-15 percent. For checkered grips add 20 percent.

COLT ANTIQUE SINGLE-ACTION ARMY REVOLVER

1st Year Production "Pinched Frame" 1873 Only

It is necessary to categorize this variation on its own. This is one of the rarest and most interesting of all the SAAs—not to mention that it is the first. On this model the top strap is pinched or constricted approximately .5" up from the hammer to form the rear sight. Highest surviving serial number having this feature is #156, lowest #1. From these numbers it is safe to assume that the first run of SAAs were all pinched-frame models; but there is no way to tell how many there were, since Colt did not serial number the frames in the order that they were manufactured. An educated guess would be there were between 50 and 150 pinched frame guns in all and that they were all made before mid-July 1873. The reason for the change came about on the recommendation of Capt. J.R. Edie, a government inspector who thought that the full fluted top strap would be a big improvement in the sighting capabilities of the weapon. Barrel length of the first model is 7.5"; standard caliber .45 Colt; proper grips were of walnut. Front sight blade is German silver. Needless to say, this model will rarely be encountered, and if it is, it should never be purchased without competent appraisal.

—	—	275000	250000	125000	90000

Early Military Model 1873-1877

Serial number range on this first run of military contract revolvers extends to #24000. Barrel address is in the early script style with the # symbol preceding and following. Frame bears the martial marking "US" and the walnut grips have the inspector's cartouche stamped on them. Front sight is steel as on all military models; barrel length, 7.5". Caliber is .45 Colt and the ejector rod head is the bull's-eye or donut style, with a hole in the center of it. Finish features the military polish and case colored frame, with the remainder blued. Authenticate any potential purchase; many spurious examples have been noted.

—	115000	75000	40000	30000	15000

Early Civilian Model 1873-1877

This model is identical to the Early Military Model, but has no military acceptance markings or cartouches. Some could have the German silver front sight blade. The early bull's-eye ejector rod head is used on this model. The Civilian Model has a higher degree of polish than is found on the military models. Finish on these early models could be plated or blued, with a case colored frame. Model also has a script barrel address. Grips are standard one-piece walnut. Ivory-grip models are worth a premium.

—	75000	60000	45000	25000	12500

.44 Rimfire Model 1875-1880

This model was made to fire the .44 Henry Rimfire cartridge. It was to be used as a compatible companion sidearm to the Henry and Winchester 1866 rifles, that were used extensively during this era. However, this was not the case; and the .44 Rimfire was doomed to economic failure as soon as it appeared on the market. By that time, it had already been established that large-caliber centerfire cartridges were a good deal more efficient than their rimfire counterparts. The large-caliber rimfires were deemed obsolete before this Colt ever hit the market. The result of this was that Colt's sales representatives sold most of the production to obscure banana republics in South and Central America, where this model received much abuse. Most had the original 7.5" barrels cut down; nearly all were denied even the most basic maintenance, making the survival rate of this model quite low. All this adds to its desirability as a collector's item and makes the risk of acquiring a fake that much greater. This model is unique in that it was the only SAA variation to have its own serial number range, starting with #1 and continuing to #1892, the latest known surviving specimen. The block style barrel markings were introduced during this production run. At least 90 of these revolvers were converted by the factory to .22 rimfire and one was shipped chambered for .32 rimfire.

—	—	75000	50000	30000	15000

Late Military Model 1878-1891

The later Military Models are serial numbered to approximately #136000. They bear the block-style barrel address without the # prefix and suffix. Frames are marked "US" and grips have the inspector's cartouche. Finish is the military-style polish, case colored frame and remainder blued. Grips are oil-stained walnut. On the military marked Colts, it is imperative that potential purchases be authenticated as many fakes have been noted. **NOTE:** Revolvers produced from 1878 to 1885 will command a premium. Seek an expert appraisal prior to sale.

—	68000	39500	14000	10000	6000

Artillery Model 1895-1903

A number of "US" marked SAAs were returned either to the Colt factory or to the Springfield Armory, where they were altered and refinished. These revolvers have 5.5" barrels and any combination of mixed serial numbers. They were remarked by the inspectors of the era. They have a case colored frame, blued cylinder and barrel. Some have been noted all blued within this variation. This model, as with the other military marked Colts, should definitely be authenticated before purchase. Some of these revolvers fall outside the 1898 antique cutoff date that has been established by the government. In our experience are not quite as desirable to investors. They are generally worth approximately 20 percent less. Add a 50 percent premium for specimens marked "New York State Militia". These have 7.5" barrels and only 800 are documented in Colt records. Be sure to obtain documentation from the factory for these models.

—	18000	12500	8000	4000	3000

London Model

These SAAs were manufactured to be sold through Colt's London Agency. Barrel is stamped "Colt's Pt. F.A. Mfg. Co. Hartford, Ct. U.S.A. Depot 14 Pall Mall London". This model is available in various barrel lengths. They are generally chambered for .45 Colt, .450 Boxer, .450 Eley, .455

	NIB	EXC.	V.G.	GOOD	FAIR	POOR

Eley and rarely .476 Eley, the largest of the SAA chamberings. A good many of these London Models were cased and embellished and should be individually appraised. This model should be authenticated as many spurious examples have been noted.

	—	22000	15000	10000	4500	2000

Frontier Six-Shooter 1878-1882

Several thousand SAAs were made with the legend "Colt's Frontier Six Shooter" acid-etched into the left side of the barrel instead of being stamped. This etching is not deep and today collectors will become ecstatic if they discover a specimen with mere vestiges of the etched panel remaining. These acid-etched SAAs are serial numbered #45000-#65000. They have various barrel lengths and finishes, but all are chambered for the .44-40 caliber.

	—	40000	20000	14000	7000	5000

Sheriff's or Storekeeper's Model 1882-1898

This model was made in several barrel lengths: 2.5", 3", 3.5", 4", 4.75" and 7.5". The 2.5" and 7.5" guns are very rare and can bring premiums of 25 to 50 percent, depending on condition. Most have 4" barrels. It features no ejector rod or housing and the frame is made without the hole in the right forward section to accommodate the ejector assembly. The Sheriff's or Storekeeper's Model is numbered above serial #73000. Manufactured with various finishes and chambered for numerous calibers. This model continued after 1898 into the smokeless or modern era. Examples with smokeless-powder frame made after 1898 are worth approximately 20 percent less. Although faking this model is quite difficult, it has been successfully attempted. **NOTE:** Nickel models will command a premium.

75000	65000	50000	38000	22000	8000

Flattop Target Model 1888-1896

This model is highly regarded and sought after by collectors. It is not only rare (only 925 manufactured), but is an extremely attractive and well-finished variation. Chambered for 22 different calibers from .22 rimfire to .476 Eley. The .22 rimfire, .38 Colt, .41 and .45 Colt are the most predominant chamberings. The 7.5" barrel length is the most commonly encountered. Serial number range is between #127000-#162000. Some have been noted in higher ranges. Finish is all blued, with a case colored hammer. Checkered grips are either hard rubber or walnut. The most readily identifying feature of the flattop is the lack of a groove in the top strap and the sight blade dovetailed into the flattop. Front sight has a removable blade insert. Values given are for a standard production model chambered for the calibers previously mentioned as being the most common. It is important to have other calibers individually appraised, as variance in values can be quite extreme.

	—	35000	25000	15000	8000	4000

Bisley Model 1894-1915

This model was named for the target range in Great Britain where their National Target Matches were held, since the nineteenth century. Model was designed as a target revolver, with an odd humped-back grip that was supposed to better fill the hand while target shooting. Also easily identified by the wide low profile hammer spur, wide trigger and the name "Bisley" stamped on the barrel. Bisley production fell within the serial number range #165000-#331916. There were 44,350 made. Offered in 16 different chamberings from .32 Colt to .455 Eley. The most common calibers were .32-20, .38-40, .41, .44-40 and .45 Colt. Barrel lengths are 4.75", 5.5" and 7.5". Frame and hammer are case-colored; remainder blued. Smokeless powder models produced after 1899 utilized the push-button cylinder pin retainer. Grips are checkered hard rubber. This model was actually designed with English sales in mind; though it did sell well over there, American sales accounted for most of the Bisley production. Values we provide here cover the standard calibers and barrel lengths. Rare calibers and/or other notable variations can bring greatly fluctuating values.

	—	9000	6500	4500	2500	1200

Bisley Model Flattop Target 1894-1913

This model is quite similar to the Standard Bisley Model, with the flattop frame and dovetailed rear sight feature. Also has the removable front sight insert. Has an all-blued finish with case-colored hammer only and available with a 7.5" barrel. Smokeless powder models produced after 1899 utilized the push-button cylinder pin retainer. Calibers are the same as the standard Bisley. Colt manufactured 976 of these revolvers. Advice regarding appraisal would also apply.

	—	25000	16000	9500	3500	1800

Standard Civilian Production Models 1876-1898

This final designated category for the black powder or antique SAAs includes all the revolvers not previously categorized. Barrel lengths from 4.75", 5.5" and 7.5" and are chambered for any one of 30 different calibers. Finishes could be blued, blued and case colored or plated in nickel, silver, gold or combinations thereof. Grips could be walnut, hard rubber, ivory, pearl, stag or bone. The possibilities are endless. Values given here are for the basic model and we

NIB	EXC.	V.G.	GOOD	FAIR	POOR

again strongly advise securing qualified appraisal when not completely sure of any model variation.

NOTE: Add a 20 percent premium for serial numbers between 54000 and 130000, 40 percent for serial numbers between 22000 and 54000. Add 20 to 30 percent for original box, depending on condition. Add 10 percent for 4.75" barrel.

—	35000	24000	12000	8000	3000

COLT PRE-WAR SINGLE ACTION ARMY REVOLVER 1899-1940

Standard Production Pre-war Models (1899-1940)

The 1899 cutoff has been thoroughly discussed, but it is interesting to note that the actual beginning production date for smokeless models was 1900. The pre-war Colts are, all in all, quite similar to the antiques—the finishes, barrel lengths, grips, etc. Calibers are also similar, with the exception of the obsolete ones being dropped and new discoveries added. Most apparent physical difference between the smokeless powder and black powder models is the previously discussed method of retaining the cylinder axis pin. Pre-war Colts utilized the spring-loaded button through the side of the frame. Black powder models utilized a screw in the front of the frame. Values we furnish for this model designation are for these standard models only. Serial number range on the pre-war SAAs is 175001-357859. Any variation can have marked effects on value fluctuations. Qualified appraisal should be secured. **NOTE:** Scarce chamberings command 30 percent to 100 percent premium. Early production guns can also bring a premium. Add 30 percent for serial numbers in the 300,000 to 328,000 range and 50 percent for those between 175,000 and 328,000.

—	15000	10000	6000	4000	2000

Long Fluted Cylinder Model (1913-1915)

Strange as it may seem, the Colt Company has an apparent credo they followed to never throw anything away. That credo was never more evident than with this model. These Long Flute Cylinders were actually left over from the model 1878 Double-Action Army Revolvers. Someone in the hierarchy at Colt had an inspiration that drove the gunsmiths on the payroll slightly mad: to make these cylinders fit the SAA frames. There were 1,478 of these Long Flutes manufactured. Chambered for the .45 Colt, .38-40, .32-20, .41 Colt and the .44 Smith & Wesson Special. Offered in the three standard barrel lengths and were especially well-polished, having what has been described as Colt's "Fire Blue" on the barrel and cylinder. Frame and hammer are case colored. Fitted with checkered hard rubber grips and are particularly fine examples of Colt's craft. Rare.

—	17500	10000	6000	3250	2000

COLT POST-WAR SINGLE ACTION ARMY REVOLVER (AKA SECOND GENERATION)

Standard Post-war Model (1956-1975)

In 1956 the shooting and gun-collecting fraternity succeeded in convincing Colt there was a market for a re-introduced SAA. The revolver was brought back in the same external configuration. Only changes were internal. Basic specifications as to barrel length and finish availability were the same. Calibers available were .38 Special, .357 Magnum, .44 Special and .45 Colt. Serial number range of the re-introduced 2nd Generation Colt is #000ISA-73000SA. Values are established by four basic factors: caliber (popularity and scarcity), barrel length, finish and condition. The .38 Special is the rarest caliber, but the .45 Colt and .44 Special are more sought after than the .357 Magnum. Special feature revolvers such as the 350 factory-engraved guns produced during this period, must be individually appraised. The ivory situation in the world today has become quite a factor, as ivory grips are found on many SAAs. Remember as always, when in doubt secure a qualified appraisal. **NOTE:** Values shown are for 5.5" barrel models. Add 15 percent for 4.75"; 10 percent for 7.5"; 20 percent for nickel finish; $250 for ivory grips.

.38 Special

3000	2500	1700	1100	800	600

.357 Magnum

2500	2000	1200	900	700	600

.44 Special

3250	2600	1800	1100	1000	750

.45 Colt

3400	2900	2000	1500	1000	750

	NIB	EXC.	V.G.	GOOD	FAIR	POOR

Sheriff's Model (1960-1975)

Between 1960 and 1975, there were approximately 500 Sheriff's Models manufactured. The first of these were marketed by Centennial Arms. They have 3" barrels and no ejector rod assemblies. Frames were made without the hole for the ejector rod to pass through. They were blued, with case colored frames; 25 revolvers were nickel-plated and would bring a sizable premium if authenticated. Barrels are marked "Colt Sheriff's Model". Serial number has an "SM" suffix. Chambered for the .45 Colt cartridge. **NOTE:** Nickel finish add 100 percent.

3000	2200	1800	1200	850	600

Buntline Special (1957-1975)

The "Buntline Special" was named after a dime novelist named Ned Buntline, who supposedly gave this special long barrel revolver to Wyatt Earp. The story is suspected to be purely legend as no Colt records exist to lend it credence. Be that as it may, the Colt factory decided to take advantage of the market and produced the 12" barreled SAA from 1957-1974. Approximately 3,900 were manufactured. Chambered for the .45 Colt cartridge. Offered in the blued and case colored finish. Only 65 Buntlines are nickel-plated, making this an extremely rare variation that definitely should be authenticated before purchase. Walnut grips are the most commonly noted, but they are also offered with the checkered hard rubber grips. Barrels are marked on the left side "Colt Buntline Special .45". **NOTE:** Nickel finish add 100 percent.

2400	1600	1250	850	600	500

New Frontier (1961-1975)

The New Frontier is readily identified by its flattop frame and adjustable sight. It also has a high front sight. Colt manufactured approximately 4,200 of them. Chambered for the .357 Magnum, .45 Colt, .44 Special (255 produced) and rarely (only 49 produced) in .38 Special. A few were chambered for the .44-40 cartridge. The 7.5" barrel length is by far the most common, but the 4.75" and 5.5" barrels are also offered. Standard finish is case colored and blued. Nickel-plating and full blue are offered but are rarely encountered. Standard grips are walnut. Barrel is stamped on the left side "Colt New Frontier S.A.A." The serial has the "NF" suffix. **NOTE:** 4.75" barrel add 25 percent. 5.5" barrel add 20 percent. Full Blue add 50 percent. .38 Special add 50 percent. .44 Special add 30 percent. .44-40 add 30 percent.

2500	1850	1200	800	600	500

New Frontier Buntline Special (1962-1967)

This model is rare, as Colt only manufactured 70 during this five-year period. Similar to the standard Buntline, with a 12" barrel. Chambered for .45 Colt only.

3500	2750	2000	1500	1000	700

COLT THIRD GENERATION
SINGLE ACTION ARMY 1976-1981

In 1976 Colt made some internal changes in the SAA. External configuration was not altered. Serial number range began in 1976 with #80000SA and in 1978 #99999SA was reached. At this time the suffix became a prefix. The new serial range began with #SA01001. This model's value is determined in much the same manner as was described in the section on 2nd Generation SAAs. Caliber, barrel length, finish and condition are once again the four main determining factors. Prevalence of special-order guns was greater during this period and many more factory-engraved SAAs were produced. Colt's Custom Shop was quite active during this period. Custom guns are valued according to the prevailing market. **NOTE:** 4.75" barrel add 10 percent, nickel plated add 10 percent, ivory grips add $250.

.357 Magnum

1200	950	800	700	600	500

.44-40

1300	1100	900	750	600	500

.44-40 Black Powder Frame
(Screw Retaining Cylinder Pin)

1425	1200	1000	800	650	550

.44 Special

1500	1300	1100	900	700	600

.45 Colt

1450	1250	1050	850	650	550

Sheriff's Model 3rd Generation

This model is similar to the 2nd Generation Sheriff's Model. Serial number and the fact this model is also chambered for the .44-40 are the only external differences. Colt offered this model with interchangeable cylinders—.45 Colt/.45 ACP or .44-40/.44 Special—available in 3" barrel, blued

	NIB	EXC.	V.G.	GOOD	FAIR	POOR

and case colored finish standard. **NOTE:** Interchangeable cylinders add 30 percent, nickel finish add 10 percent, ivory grips add $250.

NIB	EXC.	V.G.	GOOD	FAIR	POOR
1300	1075	900	750	600	500

Buntline Special 3rd Generation

Same basic configuration as the 2nd Generation, with the 12" barrel. Standard finish blued and case-colored, chambered for .45 Colt and has checkered hard rubber grips. **NOTE:** Nickel finish add 20 percent.

NIB	EXC.	V.G.	GOOD	FAIR	POOR
1500	1275	1000	900	700	600

New Frontier 3rd Generation

This model similar in appearance to the 2nd Generation guns. The 3rd Generation New Frontiers have five-digit serial numbers; 2nd Generation guns four-digit numbers. That and the calibers offered are basically the only differences. The 3rd Generations are chambered for the .44 Special and .45 Colt and are rarely found in .44-40. Barrel lengths are 7.5" standard, with the 4.75" and 5.5" rarely encountered. **NOTE:** .44-40 add 20 percent, 4.75" barrel add 35 percent, 5.5" barrel add 25 percent.

NIB	EXC.	V.G.	GOOD	FAIR	POOR
1650	1225	750	550	500	400

COLT RECENT PRODUCTION
SINGLE ACTION ARMY 1982-PRESENT

Standard Single Action Army Optional Features:

Nickel finish add $125. Royal blue finish add $200. Mirror brite finish add $225. Gold plate add $365. Silver plate add $365. Class A engraving add $875. Class B engraving add $1,200. Class C engraving add $1,500. Class D engraving add $1,750. Buntline engraving add 15 percent.

NIB	EXC.	V.G.	GOOD	FAIR	POOR
1050	950	850	650	500	300

Colt Cowboy (CB1850)

Introduced in 1998, this model is a replica of the Single Action Army. Features a modern transfer bar safety system. Made in USA using some Canadian-built parts. Offered with 5.5" barrel and chambered for .45 Colt. Sights are fixed, with walnut grips. Blued barrel with case colored frame. Discontinued in 2003.

NIB	EXC.	V.G.	GOOD	FAIR	POOR
850	650	500	400	300	200

Colt Single Action Army "Legend Rodeo

A limited-edition revolver built to commemorate Colt's official PRCA sponsorship. Limited to 1,000. Chambered for .45 LC fitted with a 5.5" barrel. Nickel finish Buffalo horn grips, with gold medallions. Machine engraved and washed in gold. Discontinued 1998.

NIB	EXC.	V.G.	GOOD	FAIR	POOR
2750	2250	—	—	—	—

Frontier Six Shooter (2008)

New reintroduction of classic .44-40 Peacemaker. Black powder-style frame and 4.75", 5.5" and 7.5" barrel lengths. Blued finish, with color casehardened frame or nickel. Discontinued 2010.

NIB	EXC.	V.G.	GOOD	FAIR	POOR
1550	1100	750	600	400	200

Sheriff's and Storekeeper's Model (2008)

New reintroduction of classic Sheriff's (4" barrel) and Storekeeper's Model (3" barrel), without ejector assembly. Black powder-style frame. Blued finish, with color casehardened frame or nickel. .45 Colt or .44-40. Discontinued 2010.

NIB	EXC.	V.G.	GOOD	FAIR	POOR
1550	1100	750	600	400	200

175th Anniversary SAA Limited Edition

From the Colt Custom Shop to celebrate the 175th anniversary of the Colt Company. This model was introduced in 2011, with production limited to 175 units in each of the three standard barrel lengths; 4.75", 5.5" and 7.5". In .45 Colt only features include a black powder frame, Royal Blue finish, 24 karat Gold plated scroll on the frame, cylinder and barrel depicting the Rampant Colt icon, Colt Dome, Serpentine Colt, Sam Colt signature and a banner with the text "1836 — 175th Anniversary — 2011".

NIB	EXC.	V.G.	GOOD	FAIR	POOR
1425	1350	1000	—	—	—

New Frontier Third Generation, Current Production

Reintroduction of the adjustable-sighted, flattop-frame version of the Single Action Army, last made in 1983. Chambered in .357 Magnum, .44 Special or .45 Colt and in all three standard barrel lengths. Rear sight is adjustable for windage and elevation. There is a ramp style front sight. Finish is Colt's Royal Blue on both the barrel and cylinder, with a color case hardened frame. Two-piece walnut grips are decorated with a gold medallion. Introduced in 2011.

NIB	EXC.	V.G.	GOOD	FAIR	POOR
1300	1225	900	700	600	500

NIB	EXC.	V.G.	GOOD	FAIR	POOR

COLT SCOUT MODEL

A surprising number of Colt pistols are still found in their original boxes, even older models. This can add 100 percent to the value of the pistol. My thanks to Bruce Buckner, Jr., for his suggestions for and corrections to this section. Anyone wishing to procure a factory letter authenticating a Single Action Army should do so by writing to: COLT HISTORIAN, P.O. BOX 1868, HARTFORD, CT 06144. There is a charge of $75 per serial number for this service. If Colt cannot provide the desired information, $10 will be refunded. Enclose the Colt model name, serial number and your name and address, along with the check.

Frontier Scout (1957-1971)

This is a scaled-down version of the SAA. Chambered for the .22 LR with an interchangeable .22 Magnum cylinder. Offered with a 4.75" or a 9.5" barrel. Frame is alloy. First year production frame were duotone, with frame left in the white and the balance of the revolver blued. All blue models and wood grips became available in 1958. In 1961 the duotone model was dropped from production. All the Q series guns were offered in duotone finish; F series guns were made in duotone and full blue. A .22 Magnum model was first offered in 1959. In 1964 dual cylinders were introduced. These revolvers have "Q" or "F" serial number suffixes. In 1960 the "K" series Scout was introduced and featured a heavier frame, nickel plating and wood grips. The majority of commemorative revolvers are of this type. This series was discontinued in 1970. Prices are about 15 percent higher than for the "Q" and "F" series guns. **NOTE:** 9.5" Buntline add 50 percent, extra cylinder add 10 percent.

450	325	200	175	125	90

Peacemaker & New Frontier .22

This model is similar to the Frontier Scout, with a steel case-colored or blued frame. Fitted with old style black plastic eagle grips. Peacemaker 22 and New Frontier 22 revolvers were initially offered with 4.75", 6" and 7.5" barrels (Buntline). After about one year of production the 4.75" barrel was discontinued and a 4.4" barrel was offered in each model. Also has an interchangeable .22 Magnum cylinder.

The Peacemaker 22 was only available with a steel receiver and a color-casehardened finish. Grip frames were alloy. Same is true of the New Frontier 22 revolvers except that (as noted in the book), the New Frontier 22 GS series was available with color-casehardened or blue receivers. Both Peacemaker 22 and New Frontier 22 revolvers were available in single caliber (.22 LR only) and dual caliber (.22 LR and .22 Magnum) models. The factory had separate model numbers for these variations. Also, the factory offered "P" series or "62" model Frontier Scouts and Buntline Scouts. This was a significant model variation. Most of these revolvers had a "G" suffix although some built in 1974 had a "L" suffix. In 1982 through 1986 a New Frontier model with cross-bolt safety was offered. This model is often referred to as the "GS" series. This revolver was offered with adjustable sights only. No Peacemakers were offered in this series.

550	475	300	200	150	100

Scout Model SAA (1962-1971)

This is basically a scaled-down version of the SAA chambered for the .22 LR cartridge. This model is offered with a 4.75", 6" or 7" barrel. Earlier production has case-colored frames with the remainder blued; later production is all blued. Grips are checkered hard rubber. This model was discontinued in 1986.

400	275	200	150	100	75

COLT ANTIQUE LONG ARMS

Berdan Single-Shot Rifle

This is a scarce rifle on today's market. Approximately 30,200 manufactured, but nearly 30,000 of them were sent to Russia. This rifle was produced from 1866-1870. A trapdoor-type action chambered for .42 centerfire. Standard model has a 32.5" barrel; carbine 18.25". Finish is blued, with a walnut stock. Rifle was designed and patent held by Hiram Berdan, Commander of the Civil War "Sharpshooters" Regiment. This was actually Colt's first cartridge arm. The 30,000 rifles and 25 half-stocked carbines that were sent to Russia were in Russian Cyrillic letters. Few examples made for American sales have Colt's name and Hartford address on the barrel.

Russian Order
30,000 manufactured.

—	15000	10000	5000	1500	750

Carbine Russian Order
25 manufactured.

—	18000	12500	6500	1800	750

U.S. Sales
100 manufactured.

—	15000	10000	5000	1500	750

NIB	EXC.	V.G.	GOOD	FAIR	POOR

Carbine U.S. Sales
25 manufactured.

NIB	EXC.	V.G.	GOOD	FAIR	POOR
—	18000	12500	6500	1800	750

Colt-Franklin Military Rifle

This rifle was not a successful venture for Colt. Patents were held by William B. Franklin, a vice-president of the company. This was a bolt-action rifle, with a primitive gravity-fed box magazine. Chambered for the .45-70 government cartridge, has a 32.5" barrel and is blued, with a walnut stock. Rifle has the Colt Hartford barrel address and is stamped with an eagle's head and U.S. inspectors marks. There were only 50 of these rifles produced and it is believed they were prototypes intended for government sales. This was not to be and production ceased after approximately 50 were manufactured in 1887 and 1888.

NIB	EXC.	V.G.	GOOD	FAIR	POOR
—	—	9500	5000	2000	1100

Colt-Burgess Lever-Action Rifle

This represented Colt's only attempt to compete, with Winchester for the lever-action rifle market. It is said when Winchester started to produce revolving handguns for prospective marketing, Colt dropped the Burgess from its line. This rifle is chambered for .44-40, has a 25.5" barrel and a 15-shot tubular magazine. Carbine version has a 20.5" barrel and 12-shot magazine. Finish is blued, with a case-colored hammer and lever. Stock is walnut, with an oil finish. Colt Hartford address is on the barrel and "Burgess Patents" stamped on bottom of lever. There were 3,775 rifles manufactured—1,219 with round barrels and 2,556 with octagonal barrels. There were also 2,593 Carbines. The Burgess was produced from 1883-1885.

Rifle - Octagonal Barrel

NIB	EXC.	V.G.	GOOD	FAIR	POOR
—	—	10000	8000	4000	1500

Rifle - Round Barrel

NIB	EXC.	V.G.	GOOD	FAIR	POOR
—	—	9800	7800	3800	1200

Carbine

NIB	EXC.	V.G.	GOOD	FAIR	POOR
—	—	15000	10000	5000	2000

Baby Carbine
Lighter frame and barrel (RARE).

NIB	EXC.	V.G.	GOOD	FAIR	POOR
—	—	18000	13000	7000	3000

Lightning Slide-Action, Medium-Frame

This was the first slide-action rifle Colt produced. Chambered for .32-20, .38-40 and .44-40. Intended to be a companion piece to the SAAs in the same calibers. Rifle has a 26" barrel with 15-shot tube magazine; carbine a 20" barrel with 12-shot magazine. Finish is blued, with case-colored hammer; walnut stock is oil-finished; fore-end usually checkered. Colt name and Hartford address are stamped on the barrel along with the patent dates. Approximately 89,777 manufactured between 1884 and 1902.

Rifle

NIB	EXC.	V.G.	GOOD	FAIR	POOR
—	—	5500	3500	2000	1000

Carbine

NIB	EXC.	V.G.	GOOD	FAIR	POOR
—	—	7500	4000	2500	1500

Military Rifle or Carbine
.44-40 caliber, short magazine tube, bayonet lug, and sling swivels.

NIB	EXC.	V.G.	GOOD	FAIR	POOR
—	—	7000	4000	2000	1500

Baby Carbine
1 lb., lighter version of standard carbine.

NIB	EXC.	V.G.	GOOD	FAIR	POOR
—	—	8750	5500	3000	2000

San Francisco Police Rifle
.44-40 caliber, #SFP 1-SFP401 on bottom tang.

NIB	EXC.	V.G.	GOOD	FAIR	POOR
—	—	9000	6000	3000	2000

Lightning Slide-Action Small-Frame

This is a well-made rifle and first of its type Colt manufactured. Chambered for the .22 Short and Long. Standard barrel length is 24"; finish blued with a case-colored hammer. Stock is walnut; some checkered, some not. Barrel is stamped with the Colt name, Hartford address and patent dates. There were 89,912 manufactured between 1887 and 1904.

NIB	EXC.	V.G.	GOOD	FAIR	POOR
—	6000	4800	2500	1500	1000

	NIB	EXC.	V.G.	GOOD	FAIR	POOR

Lightning Slide-Action, Large-Frame (Express)

This rifle is similar in appearance to the medium-frame Lightning, though larger in size. Chambered in larger rifle calibers of the era, from .38-56 up to .50-95 Express. Larger calibers are more desirable from a collector's standpoint. The rifle has a 28" barrel; carbine a 22" barrel. Finish is blued, with a case-colored hammer. Stock is oiled walnut; fore-end checkered. Colt name and Hartford address are stamped on the barrel along with patent dates. Rifle is quite large and has come to be known as the "Express model". Colt manufactured 6,496 between 1887 and 1894.

Rifle - Octagonal Barrel

	NIB	EXC.	V.G.	GOOD	FAIR	POOR
	—	—	10500	5500	2000	1000

Rifle - Round Barrel

	NIB	EXC.	V.G.	GOOD	FAIR	POOR
	—	—	10500	5500	2000	1000

Carbine
22" barrel.

	NIB	EXC.	V.G.	GOOD	FAIR	POOR
	—	—	12500	6500	2500	1000

Baby Carbine
22" barrel 1 lb. lighter.

	NIB	EXC.	V.G.	GOOD	FAIR	POOR
	—	—	12500	6500	2500	950

Model 1878 Double-Barrel Shotgun

This model is chambered in 10- or 12-gauge and has 28", 30" or 32" barrels. It is a sidelock double-trigger hammer gun, with case-colored locks and breech. Barrels are browned Damacus-patterned. Checkered walnut stock is varnished or oil-finished. Colt's Hartford address is stamped on the barrel rib; Colt's name on the lock. This has been regarded as one of the finest shotguns made in America, although Colt had difficulty competing with the less expensive European imports of the day. Production ceased after only 22,690 were manufactured between 1878 and 1889. **NOTE:** Fully engraved model add 300 percent.

	NIB	EXC.	V.G.	GOOD	FAIR	POOR
	—	—	4500	2250	750	300

Model 1883 Double-Barrel Shotgun

This model is a hammerless boxlock, chambered for 8-, 10- or 12-gauge. Barrels are 28", 30" or 32"; features double triggers. Frame and furniture are case-colored; barrels browned with Damascus pattern. Checkered walnut stock is varnished or oil-finished. Colt's Hartford address is stamped on the barrel rib. "Colt" is stamped on each side of the frame. Again, as in the Model 1878, this is rated as one of the finest of all American-made shotguns. There were many special orders and they require individual appraisal. Colt manufactured 7,366 of these guns between 1883 and 1895. **NOTE:** Fully engraved model add 300 percent. For 8-gauge add 200 percent.

	NIB	EXC.	V.G.	GOOD	FAIR	POOR
	—	3000	2000	1400	775	400

Double-Barrel Rifle

This is one of the rarest of all Colt firearms and a prize for the Colt collector. Only 35 of these guns manufactured. They were said to be the special interest of Caldwell Hart Colt, Samuel Colt's son, who was an avid arms collector. It is said that most of the 35 guns produced wound up in his collection or those of his friends. Gun is chambered for .45-70 or one of the larger variations thereof. It is an exposed hammer sidelock with double triggers. The locks, breech and furniture are case-colored; barrels browned or blued. Barrels are 28" in length and checkered stock was oil-finished or varnished walnut. Barrel rib stamped with the Colt name and Hartford address. Locks are also stamped "Colt". One must exercise extreme caution in dealing with this model as there have been Model 1878 shotguns converted into double rifles. Colt manufactured the 35 guns over the period 1879-1885.

	NIB	EXC.	V.G.	GOOD	FAIR	POOR
	—	95000	75000	35500	—	—

COLT DOUBLE-ACTION REVOLVERS

Model 1877 "Lightning" and "Thunderer"

The Model 1877 was Colt's first attempt at manufacturing a double-action revolver. Shows a striking resemblance to the Single Action Army. Sales on this model were brisk, with over 166,000 produced between 1877 and 1909. Chambered for two different cartridges. The .38 Colt known as "Lightning" and .41 Colt as "Thunderer". Standard finishes are blued, with case-colored frame and nickel plate. Bird's-head grips are of checkered rosewood on early guns and hard rubber on majority of the production run. Barrel lengths most often encountered are 2.5" and 3.5" without an ejector rod and 4.5" and 6" with the rod. Other barrel lengths from 1.5" through 10" were offered. Model 1877 holds 6 shots in either caliber. There were quite a few different variations found within this model designation. Values furnished are for standard variations. Antiques made before 1898 would be more desirable from an investment standpoint. These revolvers have a reputation as "watchmaker's nightmares" and non-functioning examples command substantially reduced prices. **NOTE:** Premium for blued guns

NIB	EXC.	V.G.	GOOD	FAIR	POOR

add 25 percent. Premium for shorter than 2.5" add 50 percent. .41-caliber "Thunderer" add 10 percent. Over 6" barrel add 50 percent. London barrel address add 20 percent. .32-caliber add 50 percent. Rosewood grips add 10 percent.

Model 1877 "Lightning" and "Thunderer"

Without Ejector, 2.5" and 3.5" Barrel

NIB	EXC.	V.G.	GOOD	FAIR	POOR
—	3000	2000	800	500	350

With Ejector, 4.5" and 6" Barrel

NIB	EXC.	V.G.	GOOD	FAIR	POOR
—	3000	1800	800	750	450

Model 1878 "Frontier

This model is a large and somewhat ungainly looking revolver. Has a solid frame with a removable trigger guard. Cylinder does not swing out and there is a thin loading gate. Bird's-head grips made of checkered hard rubber; walnut would be found on the early models. Finish either blued and case-colored or nickel-plated. Model 1878 holds 6 shots and standard barrel lengths are 4.75", 5.5" and 7.5", with an ejector assembly and 3", 3.5" and 4" without. Standard chamberings for the Model 1878 are .32-20, .38-40, .41 Colt, .44-40 and .45 Colt. This model was fairly well received because it is chambered for the large calibers that were popular in that era. Colt manufactured 51,210 between 1878 and 1905. Antique models made before 1898 would be more desirable from an investment standpoint. **NOTE:** Add a 15 percent premium for blued revolvers. Add 10-50 percent premium for calibers other than .44-40 or .45.

Standard

NIB	EXC.	V.G.	GOOD	FAIR	POOR
—	5000	3200	1600	800	400

Omnipotent

Special order version of model above, with the name "Omnipotent" stamped on barrel.

NIB	EXC.	V.G.	GOOD	FAIR	POOR
—	8000	7000	6000	3000	1000

Sheriff's Model

Chambered for .44-40 or .45 Colt. Barrel lengths of 3.5" or 4".

NIB	EXC.	V.G.	GOOD	FAIR	POOR
—	6000	4000	2000	1000	800

Model 1902 (Philippine or Alaskan Model)

This is a U.S. Ordnance contract Model 1878. It has a 6" barrel and chambered for .45 Colt. Finish blued and there is a lanyard swivel on the butt. Model bears the U.S. inspector's marks. It is sometimes referred to as the Philippine or the Alaskan model. Trigger guard is quite a bit larger than standard.

NIB	EXC.	V.G.	GOOD	FAIR	POOR
—	5500	3500	1800	1000	600

Model 1889 Navy—Civilian Model

The 1889 Navy is an important model from a historical standpoint. It was the first double-action revolver Colt manufactured, with a swing-out cylinder. They produced 31,000 of them between 1889 and 1894. Model 1889 is chambered for the .38 Colt and the .41 Colt cartridges. Cylinder holds 6 shots. Offered with a 3", 4.5" or 6" barrel; finish was either blued or nickel-plated. Grips are checkered hard rubber, with the "Rampant Colt" in an oval molded into them. Patent dates 1884 and 1888 appear in the barrel marking and serial numbers stamped on the butt. **NOTE:** Add premium for blued models. For 3" barrel add 20 percent.

NIB	EXC.	V.G.	GOOD	FAIR	POOR
—	2250	1500	1000	600	300

Model 1889 U.S. Navy—Martial Model

This variation has a 6" barrel, chambered for .38 Colt and offered in blued finish only. "U.S.N." stamped on the butt. Most Navy models were altered at the Colt factory to add Model 1895 improvements. Original unaltered specimen would be worth as much as 50 percent premium over altered values listed.

NIB	EXC.	V.G.	GOOD	FAIR	POOR
—	6000	5000	2500	1000	500

Model 1892 "New Army and Navy" —Civilian Model

This model similar in appearance to the 1889 Navy. Main differences are improvements to the lock-work function. It has double bolt stop notches, double cylinder locking bolt and shorter flutes on the cylinder. The .38 Smith & Wesson and .32-20 were added to the .38 Colt and .41 Colt chamberings. Checkered hard rubber grips are standard, with plain walnut grips found on some contract series guns. Barrel lengths and finishes are the same as described for the Model 1889. Patent dates 1895 and 1901 appear stamped on later models. Colt manufactured 291,000 of these revolvers between 1892 and 1907. Antiques before 1898 are more desirable from an investment standpoint. **NOTE:** For 3" barrel add 20 percent.

NIB	EXC.	V.G.	GOOD	FAIR	POOR
—	1500	800	500	200	100

Model 1892 U.S. Navy—Martial Model

NIB	EXC.	V.G.	GOOD	FAIR	POOR
—	2500	2000	800	600	400

	NIB	EXC.	V.G.	GOOD	FAIR	POOR

Model 1892 U.S. Army—Martial Model

	NIB	EXC.	V.G.	GOOD	FAIR	POOR
	—	2500	2000	800	600	400

Model 1894/1896 Army

	NIB	EXC.	V.G.	GOOD	FAIR	POOR
	—	2200	2000	800	600	400

Model 1905 Marine Corps

This model is a variation of New Army and Navy Model. Derived from the late production, with its own serial range #10001-10926. Only 926 produced between 1905 and 1909. Quite rare on today's market and is eagerly sought after by Colt Double-Action collectors. Model is chambered for the .38 Colt and .38 Smith & Wesson Special cartridges. Holds 6 shots, has a 6" barrel and offered in a blued finish only. Grips are checkered walnut and quite different than those found on previous models. "U.S.M.C." stamped on the butt; patent dates of 1884, 1888 and 1895 stamped on the barrel. Of these revolvers 125 were earmarked for civilian sales and do not have the Marine Corps markings; these will generally be found in better condition. Values are similar.

	NIB	EXC.	V.G.	GOOD	FAIR	POOR
	—	3000	2500	2000	1500	750

New Service Model

This model was in continual production from 1898 through 1944. Chambered for 11 different calibers: .38 Special, .357 Magnum, .38-40, .44 Russian, .44 Special, .44-40, .45 ACP, .45 Colt, .450 Eley, .455 Eley and .476 Eley. Offered in barrel lengths from 2" to 7.5", either blued or nickel-plated. Checkered hard rubber grips were standard until 1928. Then checkered walnut grips were used, with an inset Colt medallion. This was the largest swing-out cylinder double-action revolver that Colt ever produced. Approximately 356,000 were manufactured over the 46 years they were made. There are many different variations of this revolver and one should consult a book dealing strictly with Colt for a thorough breakdown and description. **NOTE:** Add 30 percent for nickel finish; 40 percent for factory ivory or pearl grips.

Early Model, #1-21000

	NIB	EXC.	V.G.	GOOD	FAIR	POOR
	—	2250	1800	1200	600	300

Early Model Target, #6000-15000

Checkered walnut grips, flattop frame, 7.5" barrel.

	NIB	EXC.	V.G.	GOOD	FAIR	POOR
	—	3000	1500	550	300	200

Improved Model, #21000-325000

Has internal locking improvements.

	NIB	EXC.	V.G.	GOOD	FAIR	POOR
	—	1850	1500	800	400	200

Improved Target Model, #21000-325000

	NIB	EXC.	V.G.	GOOD	FAIR	POOR
	—	2250	1500	550	300	200

U.S. Army Model 1909, #30000-50000

5.5" barrel, .45 Colt, walnut grips, "U.S. Army Model 1909" on butt.

	NIB	EXC.	V.G.	GOOD	FAIR	POOR
	—	2350	1900	1400	700	350

U.S. Navy Model 1909, #50000-52000

Same as above with "U.S.N." on butt.

	NIB	EXC.	V.G.	GOOD	FAIR	POOR
	—	3000	2400	1700	1000	500

U.S. Marine Corps Model 1909, #21000-23000

Checkered walnut grips, "U.S.M.C." on butt.

	NIB	EXC.	V.G.	GOOD	FAIR	POOR
	—	3500	2900	2200	1500	700

U.S. Army Model 1917, #150000-301000

Smooth walnut grips, 5.5" barrel, .45 ACP. Model designation stamped on butt.

	NIB	EXC.	V.G.	GOOD	FAIR	POOR
	—	1300	900	600	300	225

Model 1917 Civilian, #335000-336000

Approximately 1,000 made in .45 ACP only, from Army parts overrun. No military markings.

	NIB	EXC.	V.G.	GOOD	FAIR	POOR
	—	1500	950	600	250	200

Late Model New Service, #325000-356000

Checkered walnut grips and internal improvements.

	NIB	EXC.	V.G.	GOOD	FAIR	POOR
	—	1550	975	650	300	225

Shooting Master, #333000-350000

Round-butt, checkered walnut grips with Colt medallion, 6" barrel, "Colt Shooting Master" on barrel, flattop frame with target sights. Chambered for .38 Special cartridge. **NOTE:** Add 100

NIB	EXC.	V.G.	GOOD	FAIR	POOR

percent premium for .44 Special, .45 ACP and .45 Colt.

—	1950	1200	850	400	300

Magnum Model New Service, Over #340000
Chambered for .357 Magnum, .38 Special.

—	2400	2000	1000	500	200

New Pocket Model

This was the first swing-out cylinder, double-action pocket revolver made by Colt. Chambered for .32 Colt and .32 Smith & Wesson. Holds 6 shots and offered with barrel lengths of 2.5", 3.5", 5" and 6". Finish is blued or nickel-plated. Grips are checkered hard rubber, with the oval Colt molded into them. "Colt's New Pocket" stamped on the frame. Patent dates 1884 and 1888 are stamped on the barrel of later-production guns. Approximately 30,000 of these manufactured between 1893 and 1905. Antiques made before 1898 are more desirable. **NOTE:** Early production without patent dates add 25 percent; 5" barrel add 10 percent.

1200	1000	750	600	400	200

Pocket Positive

Externally, this is the same revolver as the New Pocket, but has positive lock feature. Manufactured between 1905 and 1940.

1100	900	700	550	350	200

Army Special Model

This is a heavier-framed improved version of the New Army and Navy revolver. Chambered for the .32-20, .38 Colt, .38 Smith & Wesson and .41 Colt. Offered with a 4", 4.5", 5" and 6" barrel. Finish is blued or nickel-plated and grips are checkered hard rubber. Serial number range is #291000-#540000 and manufactured between 1908-1927.

1000	850	650	500	350	200

New Police Model

This model appears similar to the New Pocket Model. Frame is stamped "New Police". Chambered for the .32 Colt, .32 Colt New Police and .32 Smith & Wesson cartridges. Barrel lengths are 2.5", 4" and 6". Finishes are blued or nickel-plated. Colt manufactured 49,500 of this model from 1896-1907. New York City Police Department purchased 4,500 of these revolvers and the backstraps are so marked. Also a target model of this revolver, which 5,000 were produced, features a 6" barrel, with a flattop frame and target sights. **NOTE:** New York Police marked add 30 percent. Target model add 20 percent.

1050	900	700	550	350	200

Police Positive

Externally the same as the New Police. Additions of the positive lock feature and two new chamberings—.38 New Police and .38 Smith & Wesson. Manufactured from 1905-1947.

—	700	475	250	200	150

Police Positive Target

Basically the same as the New Police Target, with positive lock feature. Chambered in .22 LR, .22 WRF as well as other cartridges offered in earlier model. Deduct 20 percent for WRF. **NOTE:** A .22-caliber Police Positive chambered for .22 Short and Long cartridge may be seen with British proofs. Several such revolvers were sold to London Armory in this configuration during the late 1920s. A NIB example recently sold for $1,200.

—	800	600	300	175	100

Police Positive Special

Model is similar to the Police Positive. Has a slightly larger frame to accept the longer cylinder needed to chamber more powerful cartridges such as the .38 Special, in addition to the original chamberings. Manufactured from 1907-1973.

—	600	450	250	150	100

Police Positive Special Mark V

Introduced in 1994, this is an updated version of the Police Positive Special. Model features an underlug 4" barrel, with rubber grips and fixed sights. Butt is rounded. Revolver is rated to fire .38-caliber +P rounds. Overall length 9" and weighs approximately 30 oz.

550	400	300	150	100	85

Officer's Model Target 1st Issue

This revolver is chambered for the .38 Special cartridge. Has a blued 6" barrel. Flattop frame with adjustable target sights. Colt manufactured this model from 1904-1908.

1800	1450	1000	800	500	250

NIB	EXC.	V.G.	GOOD	FAIR	POOR

Officer's Model Target 2nd Issue

Model similar to the 1st Issue, but offered in .22 LR, .32 Police Positive caliber and .38 Special. Furnished with a 4", 4.5", 5", 6" and 7.5" barrel in .38 Special only. Checkered walnut grips. Colt manufactured this model between 1908 and 1940.

1700	1350	950	700	400	225

Camp Perry Single-Shot

This model was created by modifying an Officer's Model frame to accept a special flat single-shot "cylinder". This flat chamber pivots to the left side and downward for loading. Pistol is chambered for .22 LR and offered with an 8" (early production) or 10" (late production) barrel. Finish is blued, with checkered walnut grips. The name "Camp Perry Model" is stamped on the left side of the chamber; caliber is on the barrel. Colt named this model after the site of the U.S. Target Competition held annually at Camp Perry, Ohio. Colt manufactured 2,525 of these between 1920 and 1941. **NOTE:** This gun serial numbered 101-2525 with 2488 produced from 1926-1941. In 1934 standard barrel length was reduced from 10" to 8" at approximately serial number 2150. Add 100 percent premium for 10" barrel. Add 50 percent premium for original box.

—	2500	1750	950	600	400

Officer's Model Match

Introduced in 1953, this model is similar to the Officer's Model Target. Chambered for either the .22-caliber cartridge or .38 Special, with 6" barrel. Revolver is fitted with a heavy tapered barrel, wide hammer spur, with adjustable rear sight and ramp front sight. Sold with checkered walnut target grips. Blued finish is standard. Discontinued in 1970. Standard of long action could be fired both double- or single-action. The .22-caliber version prices are listed. Officer's Model Match in .38-caliber will bring approximately 20 percent less. **NOTE:** This model also produced in .22 Magnum. Rather a rare gun in this caliber, with approximately 800 produced.

—	750	600	450	350	250

.22 Caliber in Short Action—Single-Action-Only

—	1000	750	600	500	350

Official Police

This was a popular revolver in the Colt line for many years. Manufactured from 1927 to 1969. Chambered for .32-20 and .41 Colt. These calibers were discontinued in 1942 and 1930, respectively. The .38 Special was chambered throughout the entire production run and .22 LR was added in 1930. This model holds 6 shots, has a square-butt and is offered with 2", 4", 5" and 6" barrel lengths. Grips are checkered walnut. Finish is either blued or nickel-plated. **NOTE:** Add 10 percent nickel-plated; 20 percent .22 LR; 80 to 100 percent rare round-butt model; deduct 10 percent for 1947-1969 production. These barrels have no patent dates.

1000	850	600	400	300	200

Commando Model

This model, for all intents and purposes, is an Official Police. Chambered for .38 Special, with a 2", 4" or 6" barrel. Model is Parkerized and stamped "Colt Commando" on the barrel. Approximately 50,000 manufactured between 1942-1945 for use in World War II. **NOTE:** Add 30 percent for 2" barrel.

2000	1600	1000	750	500	300

Marshal Model

This is an Official Police marked "Colt Marshal" on the barrel and an "M" suffix in the serial number. Has a 2" or 4" barrel and round butt. Finish is blued. Approximately 2,500 manufactured between 1954 and 1956.

1950	1500	1000	800	500	250

Colt .38 SF-VI

Introduced in 1995, this model is essentially a Detective Special in stainless steel, with a new internal mechanism. Has a transfer bar safety mechanism. Fitted with a 2" barrel and cylinder holds 6 rounds of .38 Special. A 4" barrel in bright stainless steel also available. Weight 21 oz. and overall length 7".

650	475	350	225	150	100

Colt .38 SF-VI Special Lady

Introduced in 1996, this 2" barrel version is similar to above model. Addition of a bright finish and bobbed hammer. Weight 21 oz.

650	450	300	200	150	100

Detective Special 1st Issue / 2nd Issue

This model is actually a Police Positive Special, with a 2" barrel. Originally chambered for .32 New Police, .38 New Police (which were discontinued) and .38 Special, which continued until end of production run. Finish is blued or nickel and offered with wood or plastic grips. Over 400,000

NIB	EXC.	V.G.	GOOD	FAIR	POOR

manufactured between 1926 and 1972. A few 2nd issue (post WWII) units came with 3" barrels. **NOTE:** For pre-war 1st issue (serial number 331000 - 490000) add 50 percent. For nickel finish add 25 percent. For 3" barrel add 30 percent.

1250	1100	800	700	450	225

Detective Special 3rd Issue

Basically a modernized, streamlined version. Features a 2" or 3" barrel, shrouded ejector rod, wraparound checkered walnut grips and chambered for .38 Special. Finished in blue or nickel plate. Made from 1973 to 1986 and 1993 to 1995. **NOTE:** Add $50 for nickel finish.

950	800	700	600	500	250

Detective Special II (DS-II)

Introduced in 1997, this version of the Detective special, features new internal lock work and a transfer bar safety mechanism. Fitted with a 2" barrel, capacity of 6 rounds and chambered for .38 Special. In 1998 this model was offered chambered for .357 Magnum cartridge as well. Rubber combat style grips are standard. Weight approximately 21 oz. Stainless steel finish.

650	475	300	225	—	—

Colt Magnum Carry

Introduced in 1999, this model is essentially a renamed Detective Special II. Stainless steel finish. Weight 21 oz.

650	475	300	250	—	—

Banker's Special

Bankers Special is a 2" barreled, easily concealed revolver. Designed with bank employees in mind. Chambered for .38 Special and offered in blued finish. Also offered in .22-caliber. Grips are rounded but full-sized. Colt utilized this feature in advertising this model. U.S. Postal Service equipped its railway mail clerks with this model. Approximately 35,000 manufactured between 1926 and 1943. **NOTE:** Nickel models will command a premium. .22-caliber will command a premium of up to 50 percent.

—	1500	975	500	250	150

Cobra 1st Issue

Cobra 1st Issue is simply an alloy-framed lightweight version of the Detective Special. Weighs only 15 oz. Cobra is chambered for .32, .38 Special and .22 LR. Model available in either round- or square-butt version, with a 4" barrel only. Manufactured between 1950 and 1973.

—	850	650	525	200	100

Cobra 2nd Issue

Same as the Cobra 1st Issue in .38 Special only. Streamlined with wraparound walnut grips and shrouded ejector rod. **NOTE:** For nickel add 30 percent.

—	525	375	250	150	100

Agent 1st Issue

Basically the same as the Cobra 1st Issue, with a shortened grip frame. This was done to make the Agent more concealable. Colt manufactured the Agent 1st Issue from 1955-1973.

—	650	400	225	150	100

Border Patrol

Model is quite rare, as Colt manufactured only 400 of them in 1952. Basically a Police Special, with a heavy 4" barrel. Chambered for the .38 Special and built to be strong. Finish is blued. Serial numbered in the 610000 range.

—	5000	3000	2000	1000	500

Agent L.W. 2nd Issue

A streamlined version, with the shrouded ejector rod. Last four years of its production was matte finished. Colt manufactured this model between 1973 and 1986.

—	550	400	275	175	150

Aircrewman Special

This model especially fabricated for the Air Force, to be carried by their pilots for protection. Extremely lightweight at 11 oz. Frame and cylinder are made of aluminum alloy. Has a 2" barrel and chambered for the .38 Special. Finish was blued, with checkered walnut grips. Approximately 1,200 manufactured in 1951 and marked "U.S." or "A.F.

—	4500	2500	1500	800	250

Courier

Another version of the Cobra. Features a shorter grip frame and a 3" barrel. Chambered for .32 and .22 rimfire. Approximately 3,000 manufactured in 1955 and 1956. **NOTE:** .22 Rimfire add

	NIB	EXC.	V.G.	GOOD	FAIR	POOR

20 percent.

	1300	750	600	500	350	150

Trooper

Designed specifically by Colt to fill the need for a large, heavy-duty, powerful revolver, that was accurate. Trooper filled that need. Offered with a 4" or 6" barrel, blued or nickel finishes and checkered walnut grips. Trooper chambered for .38 Special, .357 Magnum and there is a .22 rimfire version for the target shooters. Manufactured between 1953 and 1969. **NOTE:** Add 10 percent for .357 or .22.

	—	600	475	300	150	100

Colt .357 Magnum

Deluxe version of Trooper. Offered with a special target, wide hammer and large target-type grips. Sights are the same as Accro target model. Features a 4" or 6" barrel, blued finish and manufactured between 1953 and 1961. Fewer than 15,000 produced.

	—	675	495	300	200	150

Diamondback

This model is a medium-frame, duty-type weapon suitable for target work. Has short frame of the Detective Special, with the ventilated rib 2.5", 4" or 6" barrel. Chambered for .38 Special and .22 rimfire for the target shooters. Finish is blued or nickel-plated, with checkered walnut grips. Diamondback features adjustable target sights, wide target hammer and a steel frame. Manufactured between 1966 and 1986. Very few Diamondbacks were chambered for the .22 WMR. Another premium should be added for these models. Since fakes exist, a factory letter documenting this chambering is strongly advised. **NOTE:** Premium of 100 percent for 2.5" barrel or nickel finish in .22 LR caliber; 20 percent in .38 Special.

.38 Special

	1200	1000	650	550	400	250

.22 Long Rifle

	1800	1500	1000	750	500	300

Viper

Alloy-framed revolver chambered for the .38 Special. It has a 4" barrel. Manufactured between 1977 and 1984. Viper is essentially a lightweight version of the Police Positive.

	1000	750	500	200	125	100

Python

Python was often described as the Cadillac of the Colt double-action revolver line. Originally designed to be a large-frame .38 Special target revolver, but shortly before Python was introduced in 1955, Colt management decided to chamber it for the .357 Magnum. (A .38 Special 8" barrel variation was made in the early 1980s. See separate listing.) Python was offered in barrel lengths of 2.5", 3" (very rare), 4", 6" and 8". Features included a ventilated rib, full lug barrel and adjustable rear sight. Finish choices were Royal Blue, nickel plated, matte stainless and high polished "Ultimate" stainless. Python remained in the catalog as a regular production item until 1996. The following year Colt Custom Shop started making Python on a special-order-only basis. Known as Python Elite, it was produced by the Custom Shop until 2006.

Blue or Royal Blue Finish

	2200	1900	1500	1100	750	500

NOTE: For early production from 1955 to 1969 with checkered wood grips (serial number 1 — 99999) add 50 percent. Also add 50 percent for 2.5" or 3" barrel. A Colt Archive Letter is recommended for the 3" barrel model.

Nickel Finish

	2150	1800	1400	950	500	350

NOTE: Add 60 to 75 percent for 2.5" barrel, depending on condition level. Add 300 to 500 percent for 3" barrel and a Colt Archive Letter is recommended.

Matte Stainless Steel

	2400	2000	1650	1250	800	600

Ultimate Bright Stainless

	2300	1900	1550	1200	750	500

Python Elite

This Custom Shop model features a stainless steel satin finish or blued finish. Adjustable red ramp front sight. Custom wood grips and choice of 4" or 6" barrel. **NOTE:** Value estimates shown are for Royal Blue finish. Deduct 20 percent for the more common stainless Elite model.

	2800	2500	2000	1500	850	600

NIB	EXC.	V.G.	GOOD	FAIR	POOR

Python .38 Special

An 8" barreled Python chambered for .38 Special only. Limited-production venture was not a success. Offered in blue only. **NOTE:** Add 40 to 50 percent for nickel finish.

2000	1900	1500	1100	650	400

Python Hunter

Hunter was a special 8" .357 Magnum Python, with an extended eye relief Leupold 2X scope. Grips are neoprene, with gold Colt medallions. Revolver with mounted scope and accessories. Fitted into a Halliburton extruded aluminum case. Hunter was manufactured in 1981 only.

3900	3200	2600	2000	1350	700

Python Silhouette

In .357-caliber, with 8" barrel. This model is similar to Python Hunter, except for Silhouette barrel markings. As with the Hunter, Leupold 2x scope is included.

4000	3300	2700	2050	1400	750

Python Ten Pointer

Similar to Hunter model, except it came from the factory with a 3x Burris scope and two sets of grips, wood and composite.

3300	3000	2350	1650	1000	600

Python Grizzly

This hybrid limited edition was from the Colt Custom Shop in the mid '90s. Only 999 were made. It featured a Python Magna-Ported barrel and Colt King Cobra frame.

4350	4000	3300	2400	1500	800

Metropolitan MK III

This revolver is basically a heavier-duty version of the Official Police. Chambered for .38 Special and fitted with a 4" heavy barrel. Finished in blue only and manufactured from 1969-1972.

750	525	350	250	100	75

Lawman MK III

This model offered chambered for the .357 Magnum, with a 2" or 4" barrel. Checkered walnut grips and either blued or nickel-plated. Colt manufactured the Lawman between 1969 and 1983.

—	550	400	300	200	100

Lawman MK V

An improved version of the MK III. Entailed a redesigned grip, shorter lock time and improved double-action. Manufactured 1982-1985.

525	375	300	200	150	100

Trooper MK III

This revolver was intended to be the target-grade version of MK III series. Offered with a 4", 6" or 8" vent-rib barrel, with a shrouded ejector rod similar in appearance to the Python. Chambered for the .22 LR, .22 Magnum and .357 Magnum. Features adjustable target sights, checkered walnut target grips and either blued or nickel-plated. Manufactured between 1969 and 1983.

750	400	325	200	150	100

Trooper MK V

Improved version of the MK III. Manufactured between 1982 - 1985.

825	550	375	200	150	100

Boa

Basically a deluxe version of the Trooper MK V. Has all the same features plus high polished blue found on the Python. Colt manufactured 1,200 of these revolvers in 1985. Entire production was purchased and marketed by Lew Horton Distributing Company in Southboro, Massachusetts.

1200	850	475	325	250	150

Peacekeeper

Designed as a duty-type weapon, with target capabilities. Offered with a 4" or 6" barrel chambered for .357 Magnum. Features adjustable sights and neoprene combat-style grips. Matte blued finish. Manufactured between 1985 - 1987.

650	475	375	200	150	100

King Cobra

King Cobra has a forged steel frame, barrel and a full length ejector rod housing. Barrel is fitted with a solid rib. Model equipped with an adjustable white outline rear sight and a red insert front

NIB	EXC.	V.G.	GOOD	FAIR	POOR

sight. Colt black neoprene combat style grips are standard. Discontinued. **NOTE:** In 1998 all King Cobras were drilled and tapped for scope mounts.

Blued

875	650	375	250	200	100

Stainless Steel

Offered in 4" or 6" barrel lengths. In 1997 this model was introduced with optional barrel porting. No longer in production.

975	725	400	275	200	125

High Polish Stainless Steel

975	725	400	275	200	125

Anaconda

This double-action .44 Magnum revolver was introduced in 1990. Offered with 4", 6" or 8" barrel lengths. The 4" model weighs 47 oz., 6" model weighs 63 oz. and 8" model weighs 59 oz. Anaconda holds 6 rounds and available with a matte stainless steel finish. For 1993 a new chambering in .45 Colt was offered. This model offered with a 6" or 8" barrel in a matte stainless steel finish. Revolver chambered for the .44 Remington Magnum cartridge. Currently offered with a 6" or 8" barrel and adjustable red-insert front and white-outline rear sights. Constructed of matte-finished stainless steel and has black neoprene finger groove grips, with gold Colt medallions. In 1996 the Realtree model was offered with 8" barrel. Chambered for the .44 Magnum cartridge. Furnished with either adjustable rear sight and ramp front sights or special scope mount. No longer in production. Reintroduced in 2001 in .44 Magnum with 4", 6" or 8" barrel. Once again, discontinued. **NOTE:** In 1998, Anaconda was drilled and tapped for scope mounts and buyers had the option of barrel porting.

.44 Magnum

1300	950	650	495	300	200

.45 Colt

1200	850	600	450	300	200

Realtree Camo Model—Adjustable Sights

1600	1100	750	575	350	250

Realtree Camo Model—Scope Mounts

1600	1100	750	575	350	250

COLT SEMI-AUTOMATIC PISTOLS

The Colt Firearms Co. was the first of the American gun manufacturers to take the advent of the semi-automatic pistol seriously. This pistol design was becoming popular among European gun makers in the late 1880s and early 1900s. In the United States, however, the revolver was firmly ensconced as the accepted design. Colt realized that if the semi-automatic could be made to function reliably, it would soon catch on. Powers that be at Colt were able to negotiate with some of the noted inventors of the day, including Browning, to secure or lease the rights to manufacture their designs. Colt also encouraged the creativity of their employees, with bonuses and incentives. Through this innovative thinking, Colt soon became the leader in semi-automatic pistol sales—a position that they have never really relinquished to any other American gun maker. Colt semi-automatic pistols represent an interesting field for the collector of Colt handguns. There were many variations with high enough production to make it worthwhile to seek them out. There are a number of fine books on the Colt semi-automatics and anyone wishing to do so will be able to learn a great deal about them. Collector interest is high in this field and values are definitely on the rise.

Model 1900

This was the first of Colt automatic pistols. Actually a developmental model, with only 3,500 being produced. Model 1900 was not really a successful design. Quite clumsy and out of balance in the hand, however, it was reliable in function during Army trials. This model chambered for the .38 Rimless smokeless cartridge. A detachable magazine that holds seven cartridges. Barrel is 6" in length. Finish is blued, with a case-colored hammer and safety/sight combination. Grips are either plain walnut, checkered walnut or hard rubber. Pistol is a Browning design and the left side of slide is stamped "Browning's Patent" with the 1897 patent date. Colt sold 200 pistols to the Navy and 200 to the Army for field trials and evaluation. The remaining 3,300 were sold on the civilian market. Manufactured from 1900-1903. **NOTE:** Many of the original 1900 pistols had the original sight/safety converted to Model 1902 configuration. These are worth about 50 percent less than unconverted pistols.

Standard Civilian Production

—	10000	7500	3500	1250	750

U.S. Navy Military Model

—	17500	12000	7500	2500	1000

NIB	EXC.	V.G.	GOOD	FAIR	POOR

U.S. Army Military Model—1st Contract

NIB	EXC.	V.G.	GOOD	FAIR	POOR
—	20000	15000	10000	4000	2000

U.S. Army Military Model—2nd Contract

NIB	EXC.	V.G.	GOOD	FAIR	POOR
—	16000	10000	6300	2000	1500

Model 1902 Sporting Pistol

This model chambered for the .38 ACP cartridge. Has a 7-round detachable magazine, 6" barrel and is blued. Checkered hard rubber grips featuring the "Rampant Colt" molded into them. Most notable features of the 1902 Sporting Model are the rounded butt, rounded hammer spur, dovetailed rear sight and 1897-1902 patent dates. Colt manufactured approximately 7,500 of these pistols between 1903 and 1908.

NIB	EXC.	V.G.	GOOD	FAIR	POOR
—	4000	3000	2000	750	450

Model 1902 Military Pistol

Early Model with Front of Slide Serrated

NIB	EXC.	V.G.	GOOD	FAIR	POOR
—	6000	5000	4000	1500	750

Standard Model with Rear of Slide Serrated

NIB	EXC.	V.G.	GOOD	FAIR	POOR
—	5000	4000	3000	1000	400

U.S. Army Marked, #15001-15200 with Front Serrations

NIB	EXC.	V.G.	GOOD	FAIR	POOR
—	12000	10000	7500	2000	1000

Model 1903 Pocket Hammer Pistol

First automatic pocket pistol Colt produced. Essentially identical to the 1902 Sporting Model, with a shorter slide. Barrel length 4.5" and chambered for the .38 ACP cartridge. Blued, with a case-colored hammer. Checkered hard rubber grips that have "Rampant Colt" molded into them. Detachable magazine holds 7 rounds. Approximately 26,000 manufactured between 1903 - 1929.

NIB	EXC.	V.G.	GOOD	FAIR	POOR
—	4000	3000	1200	800	400

Model 1903 Hammerless, .32 Pocket Pistol (Model M)

Second pocket automatic Colt manufactured. Another of John Browning's designs, it developed into one of Colt's most successful pistols. Chambered for the .32 ACP cartridge. Initially the barrel length was 4", then shortened to 3.75". Detachable magazine holds 8 rounds. Standard finish is blue, with quite a few nickel plated. Early model grips are checkered hard rubber, with the "Rampant Colt" molded into them. Many of the nickel plated pistols had pearl grips. In 1924 the grips were changed to checkered walnut, with Colt medallions. Name of this model can be misleading as it is not a true hammerless, but a concealed hammer design. Features a slide stop and grip safety. Colt manufactured 572,215 civilian versions of this pistol and approximately 200,000 more for military contracts. Manufactured between 1903 and 1945. **NOTE:** Early Model 1897 patent date add 40 percent. Nickel-plated with pearl grips add $100. 4" barrel to #72,000 add 20 percent.

NIB	EXC.	V.G.	GOOD	FAIR	POOR
1200	1000	500	450	300	200

U.S. Military Model

Serial prefix M, marked "U.S. Property" on frame, Parkerized finish. **NOTE:** Pistols issued to General Officers will command a premium of 50 percent.

NIB	EXC.	V.G.	GOOD	FAIR	POOR
2000	1500	1000	800	600	500

Model 1908 Hammerless .380 Pocket Pistol

Essentially the same as the .32 Pocket Pistol, chambered for the more potent .380 ACP, also known as the 9mm Browning short. Other specifications are the same. Colt manufactured approximately 138,000 in this caliber for civilian sales. An unknown number were sold to the military. **NOTE:** Nickel with pearl grips add $100.

Standard Civilian Model

NIB	EXC.	V.G.	GOOD	FAIR	POOR
1600	1300	1000	700	500	350

Military Model

Serial prefix M, marked "U.S. Property" on frame, blue finish. General Officer's pistol add 50 percent.

NIB	EXC.	V.G.	GOOD	FAIR	POOR
—	2800	2000	1300	800	500

Model 1908 Hammerless .25 Vest Pocket Model

This was the smallest automatic Colt made. Chambered for the .25 ACP cartridge. Has a 2" barrel and is 4.5" long overall. Weighs a mere 13 oz. A true pocket pistol. Detachable magazine holds 6 shots. Offered in blue or nickel-plate, with grips of checkered hard rubber and checkered walnut on later versions. Has a grip safety, slide lock and a magazine disconnect safety. Another Browning design and Fabrique Nationale manufactured this pistol in Belgium before Colt picked up the rights to make it in the U.S. A commercial success by Colt's standards, with

NIB	EXC.	V.G.	GOOD	FAIR	POOR

approximately 409,000 manufactured between 1908 and 1941. **NOTE:** Add 30 percent for nickel finish, 50 percent for factory pearl grips.

Civilian Model

—	750	500	300	200	100

Military Model

U.S. Property" marked on right frame. Very rare.

—	3500	2500	1350	450	300

Model 1905 .45 Automatic Pistol

Spanish American War and experiences with the Moros in the Philippine campaign, taught a lesson about stopping power or the lack of it. United States Army was convinced they needed a more powerful handgun cartridge. This led Colt to the development of a .45 caliber cartridge suitable for the semi-automatic pistol. Model 1905 and the .45 rimless round were the result. In actuality, this cartridge was not nearly powerful enough to satisfy the need, but it led to the development of the .45 ACP. Colt believed this pistol/cartridge combination would be a success and was geared up for mass production. The Army actually bought only 200 of them and total production was approximately 6,300 from 1905 to 1911. Pistol has a 5" barrel and detachable 7-shot magazine. Blued, with a case-colored hammer. Grips are checkered walnut. Hammer was rounded on first 3,600 pistols and changed to a spur hammer on later models. Right side of slide stamped "Automatic Colt / Caliber 45 Rimless Smokeless". This model was not a commercial success for Colt—possibly because it has no safety, whatsoever, except for the floating inertia firing pin. The 200 military models have grip safeties only. A small number (believed to be less than 500) of these pistols were grooved to accept a shoulder stock. Stocks were made of leather and steel, and double as a holster. These pistols have been classified "Curios and Relics" under the provisions of the Gun Control Act of 1968.

Civilian Model

—	7000	5000	3000	1500	800

Military Model, Serial #1-201

—	15000	12000	8000	4000	1000

COLT 1911/1911A1

Early Colt "1911 Commercial Government Model

Serial numbers through about C4500, high polish on all parts and fire-blue finish on trigger, slide stop, thumb safety, hammer pins, ejector and stock screws. Pistols in the latter part of the serial range did not have fire blued stock screws. Pistols through about serial C350 had the dimpled magazine catch. Main spring housing pin was rounded on both ends in the pistols through about serial C2000. Keyhole (punch and sawcut) magazines were shipped on pistols through serial C3500. **NOTE:** Three-digit serial number add 20 percent. Two-digit serial number add 40 percent. For finish 99-100 percent add 30-50 percent.

—	15000	10000	7500	3500	2000

Standard Colt "1911 Commercial Model" with Un-numbered Slide

Above, about serial # C4500 with un-numbered slide to about serial #C127300. No fire blue. Polished finished but not mirror finish. Loop magazine until about C90000. A number of variations exist within this wide serial range such as slide nomenclature and position of the "Rampant Colt", but none currently receives any particular premium. **NOTE:** Finish 99-100 percent add 20-50 percent.

—	3750	2400	1600	1000	800

Standard Colt "1911 Commercial Government Model" with Numbered Slide

Colt started to number the slide, with the receiver's serial number at about serial #C127300. This practice continued for commercial production through WWII and all 1911 commercial pistols after about serial C127300 to about serial C136000 (when 1911A1 production had taken over). The first numbered slide pistols (in the C127xxx range) had the slide numbered on the bottom of the slide rail. This only lasted a short time and the numbering was moved to behind the firing pin stop plate by serial C128000. Subtract 20 percent for a mismatched slide number. Changes between the 1911 Commercial Government Model and the 1911A1 Commercial Government were phased in during this period. **NOTE:** Finish 99-100 percent add 20-50 percent.

—	3500	2100	1400	900	650

FOREIGN CONTRACTS

Colt "1911 Commercial Government Model" Argentine Contracts

Multiple contracts were awarded by Argentina between 1914 and 1948 to supply .45-caliber pistols to their armed forces, police and government agencies. These contracts totaled 21,616

NIB	EXC.	V.G.	GOOD	FAIR	POOR

pistols of which 2,151 were the 1911 model. Pistols differ from the Standard Government Model in that they are usually marked with an Argentine crest as well as the normal Colt commercial markings including the C prefix serial number. Colt also supplied Argentina the 1911A1 model "modelo 1927" that had its own serial number range of #1 to #10000 with no C prefix. Most of these pistols are well used, reblued, had mixed parts and have import markings. Prices listed are for completely original pistols. Reblue=Fair/Poor. **NOTE:** Finish 99-100 percent add 20-100 percent.

—	1500	1100	750	500	400

Colt "1911 Commercial Government Model" Russian Order

This variation chambered for .45 ACP and has Russian version of "Anglo Zakazivat" stamped on the frame. About 51,000 of these blued pistols manufactured in 1915-1916. Found between serial numbers C21000 and C89000. This variation is rarely encountered today, but a few have recently been imported and advertised. One should be extremely cautious and verify the authenticity if contemplating a purchase, as fakes have been noted. Despite market uncertainties demand for original pistols is high. (Reblue=Fair/Poor)

—	8500	4000	3000	2000	600

Colt "1911 Commercial Government Model" Canadian Contract

This group of 5099 pistols, serial numbered between about C3077 and C13500, were purchased by the Canadian Government in 1914. Most observed pistols appear to be unmarked and can be identified only by a Colt factory letter. Others have been observed with the Canadian Broad Arrow property mark, as well as unit markings. Often these unit markings are applied in a very rudimentary manner that detracts considerably from the appearance. (Any applied markings done crudely, deduct 10-50 percent.) Due to the nature of these markings, a Colt factory letter is probably a requirement to authenticate these pistols. Refinish=Fair/Poor. **NOTE:** Finish. 99-100 percent add 20-50 percent.

—	3100	2200	1450	950	650

Colt "1911 Commercial Government Model" British Contract

This series is chambered for the British .455 cartridge and marked on the right side of the slide. The British "Broad Arrow" proofmark will often be found. These pistols were made in 1915-1919 and follow the same numeric serial number sequence as the normal Government models, except that the "C" prefix was replaced with a "W". They are commercial series pistols. Magazine well of these .455 pistols is slightly larger than a standard Cal. .45 Auto pistol and will accept a Cal.45 magazine, but a standard Cal. 45 will not accept a Cal. .455 magazine. All pistols in the W19001 to W19200 range, as well as some in the W29000 range, are believed to be JJ marked above the left trigger guard bow. Add 25 percent for JJ marked. Some pistols in the C101000 to about C109000 range have RAF marks as well as a welded ring in the lanyard loop. Most RAF pistols have been refinished and many have been converted to .45 cal. by changing the barrels. Refinish=Fair/Poor. **NOTE:** Finish. 99-100 percent add 20-50 percent. Add 25 percent for RAF. Wrong barrel less 35 percent.

—	3200	2000	1250	850	650

Norwegian Kongsberg Vapenfabrikk Pistol Model 1912 (Extremely Rare)

Serial number 1-96. **NOTE:** Pistols are so rare that almost any price would not be out of order for an original pistol. Finish 99-100 percent add 20-30 percent.

—	5000	3200	2200	1600	1200

Norwegian Kongsberg Vapenfabrikk Pistol Model 1914

Serial number 97-32854. **NOTE:** Finish 99-100 percent add 20-50 percent.

—	1350	1050	900	770	600

Norwegian Kongsberg Vapenfabrikk Model 1914 (Copy)

Serial number 29615 to 30535. Waffenamt marked on slide and barrel. CAUTION: Fakes have been reported. Any Waffenamt-marked pistol outside this serial range is probably counterfeit. **NOTE:** Finish 99-100 percent add 20-30 percent.

—	4500	2700	2000	1200	900

MODEL 1911 U.S. MILITARY SERIES

For a complete look at the many variations of the Colt Model 1911 that were made for U.S. Military forces, see Standard Catalog of Military Firearms, 7th Edition. This publication covers history, technical data, photos and values of the world's military arms and accessories. The following is a brief summary of estimated values for Model 1911 pistols manufactured for U.S. forces between 1912 and 1919.

Colt 1912

Serial number range 1-17250.

—	10000	7000	5000	2500	800

NIB	EXC.	V.G.	GOOD	FAIR	POOR

Colt 1913-1915

Serial number ranges 17251-72570, 83856-102596, 107597-113496, 120567-125566, 133187-137400.

	EXC.	V.G.	GOOD	FAIR	POOR
—	5800	4500	3000	1500	500

Colt 1917-1918

Serial number range 137401-594000.

	EXC.	V.G.	GOOD	FAIR	POOR
—	4500	3000	2000	1000	500

Springfield Armory 1914-1916

Serial number ranges 72751-83855, 102597-107596, 113497-120566, 125567-133186.

	EXC.	V.G.	GOOD	FAIR	POOR
—	6000	4750	3500	2000	800

Remington-UMC 1918-1919

Serial number range 1-21676.

	EXC.	V.G.	GOOD	FAIR	POOR
—	6000	4750	3500	2000	800

North American Arms 1918

Less than 100 manufactured in Canada, but none delivered to U.S. government. One of the most rare 1911 models, so beware of fakes. Get an expert appraisal before buying or selling.

	EXC.	V.G.	GOOD	FAIR	POOR
—	—	30000	20000	10000	—

PRE-WWII COLT "1911A1 COMMERCIAL GOVERNMENT MODEL

The commercial "Government Models" made by Colt between the wars may be the best pistols that Colt ever produced. Civilian configurations of the 1911 and 1911A1 were known as "Government Models". Identical to the military models, with the exception of fit, finish and markings. However, commercial production of the 1911A1 pistols stopped when WWII started. Therefore, production changes of the 1911A1 pistols were not carried over to the contemporary commercial pistols, because there was no contemporary commercial production. The "C" serial number prefix designated the commercial series until 1950, when it was changed to a "C" suffix. "Government Model" pistols were polished and blued until about serial number C230,000, when the top, bottom and rear were matte finished. Words "Government Model" as well as "Verified Proof" mark were stamped on all but about the first 500 pistols, when post-war production commenced at C220,000. Some of these first 500 also lacked the verified proof mark. First post-war pistols used some leftover military parts such as triggers and stocks. Pre-war pistols all had checkered walnut grips. Post-war pistols generally had plastic grips until the "midrange" serial when the wood grips returned. There were a number of different commercial models manufactured. They are individually listed.

Manufactured by Colt from 1925-1942 from about serial number C136000 to about serial number C215000. Only a few pistols from serial #C202000 to C215000 were shipped domestically, as most were shipped to Brazil or renumbered into military models. See Model 1911A1 commercial to military conversions.

Standard Colt "1911A1 Commercial Government Model" Domestic Sales

These pistols have numbered slides. NO foreign markings, Swartz safeties and additions whatsoever. **NOTE:** Finish 99-100 percent add 30-60 percent.

	EXC.	V.G.	GOOD	FAIR	POOR
—	4500	3500	2500	1000	500

Standard Colt "1911A1 Commercial Government Model" Export Sales

Usually with foreign crest or foreign inscription of a county such as Argentina or Brazil. Pistol has a numbered slide. Some variations with foreign markings are more rare than standard domestic pistols, and have a developed local following who have raised their prices considerably. Argentine pistols do not have the collector interest that the others or the "Standard" domestic pistols have. Four factors have reduced collector interest in the Argentine Colt pistols compared to the rest:

1. Most of the Argentine-marked pistols have been recently imported and have the legally required important markings.

2. Many of the Argentine-marked pistols have been advertised and sold in the wholesale trade publications at utility prices.

3. Most of the recent import pistols from Argentina have been refinished or are in "well used" condition.

4. Most of the recent import pistols from Argentina have had some parts changed or swapped with other pistols and are not in original condition. The few Argentine pistols that remain in original and excellent or better condition usually sell for less than their "plain Jane" counterparts, and they sell for much less than the rarer Brazilian and Mexican pistols.

NIB	EXC.	V.G.	GOOD	FAIR	POOR

Argentine Colt-made 1911A1 model pistols without Swartz safeties

NOTE: Finish 99-100 percent add 20-30 percent.

NIB	EXC.	V.G.	GOOD	FAIR	POOR
—	1500	1000	650	550	450

Brazilian, Mexican, and other South American (except Argentina)

Colt-made "1911A1 Commercial Government Model" pistols.
NOTE: Finish 99-100 percent add 20-100 percent.

NIB	EXC.	V.G.	GOOD	FAIR	POOR
—	6500	4500	2800	1700	1000

Colt National Match Caliber .45, Pre-WWII, .45 (without Swartz safeties)

National Match Commercial pistol, was introduced by Colt at the 1930 National Matches at Camp Perry. Production began in 1932. Right side of the slide marked "NATIONAL MATCH" and the mainspring housing had no lanyard loop. National Match modifications to the standard pistol, as described in Colt literature included: A tighter barrel, better sights and a hand polished action. The tighter barrel probably amounted to a tighter fit between the barrel bushing and barrel. Hand polishing of the action probably produced a greatly improved trigger pull, but overall, the barrel slide lockup was probably only superficially improved. Colt also advertised a "Selected Match Grade" barrel. Colt advertising indicated that scores using National Match pistols improved greatly and probably did to a degree, but most of the improvement was probably due to the improved (wider) sights and improved trigger pull. Very first pistols had fixed sights, but by about SN C177,000 the "Stevens Adjustable Rear Target Sight" was available. Both fixed and adjustable sights were available thereafter throughout production. Total number of National Match pistols, with each type of sight is not known, but one author (Kevin Williams, Collecting Colt's National Match Pistols) estimates that the percentage of adjustable sight equipped National Match pistols may have been only 20 percent. Note that the Colt National Match pistol is not referred to here as a "1911A1", because this pistol lacks the military lanyard loop that is present in all Standard Government Models. This is simply a matter of personal preference. Also note that "Colt National Match" Pre-war pistols are also "Government Models" as the receiver was marked as such throughout production. **NOTE:** Finish 99-100 percent add 30-60 percent.

With Adjustable Sights

NIB	EXC.	V.G.	GOOD	FAIR	POOR
—	9000	6500	4500	2500	900

Fixed Sights

NIB	EXC.	V.G.	GOOD	FAIR	POOR
—	7500	5000	3000	1750	750

Swartz Safeties, Pre-WWII, Firing Pin and Hammer/Sear

The "Swartz Safeties" are a pair of devices that Colt installed in 1911A1 commercial "Government Models" and 1911A1 Commercial National Match pistols in the late 1930s and early 1940s. First device, a firing pin block that was actuated by the grip safety, prevented the firing pin from moving forward unless the grip safety was squeezed. Second, Swartz Safety Device the Hammer/Sear safety prevented a possible unsafe half cock position. Swartz firing pin block safety can be observed by pulling the slide back all the way and looking at the top of the frame. A Swartz-safety-equipped 1911A1 pistol will have a second pin protruding up next to the conventional disconnect pin. This second pin pushes a spring loaded piston in the rear part of the slide that is visible when the slide is pulled back and the slide is viewed from underneath. This piston, in turn, blocks the firing pin when relaxed. A second Swartz safety (the Swartz Sear Safety), is usually built into pistols equipped with the Swartz firing pin block safety. The sear safety can sometimes be detected by the drag marks of the notched sear on the round portion of the hammer that the sear rides on. Pulling the hammer all the way back will expose these drag marks if they are visible. Presence of the drag marks, however, does not ensure that the Swartz-modified sear safety parts are all present. Disassembly may be required to verify the correct parts are all present.

The Swartz Safeties are referred to in Colt Factory letters as the "NSD" (New Safety Device). (From SN C162,000 to C215,000 about 3,000 total National Match pistols were made with and without Swartz safeties.) The number of National Match pistols having the Swartz safeties is unknown. However, only a few pistols below serial C190000 had the safeties installed and of the pistols made after C190000, most were Standard Models shipped to Brazil and Argentina. Brazilian pistols were without the safeties or the cutouts. Argentine pistols were shipped in two batches of 250 pistols each. Both of these Argentine batches appear to have had the safeties installed as a number of them have recently been imported into the U.S.A. Probably much less than half of the total Colt made National Match pistols had the Swartz safeties. Total number of pistols (both Standard Government Model and National Match) shipped with Swartz safeties is probably much less than 3,000. And, probably much less than half of the total Colt made National Match pistols had the Swartz safeties. Swartz safeties were also installed in late Super .38 and Super Match .38 pistols.

NIB	EXC.	V.G.	GOOD	FAIR	POOR

Standard Colt 1911A1 Commercial "GOVERNMENT MODEL" Marked Pistol with Numbered Slide

Swartz safeties", no foreign markings. Fixed sights only, no additions whatsoever. Rare, seldom seen. **NOTE:** Finish 99-100 percent add 20-50 percent.

NIB	EXC.	V.G.	GOOD	FAIR	POOR
—	5500	4200	3000	1500	850

Colt National Match Caliber Pre-WWII, .45. Pre-WWII (with "Swartz Safeties")

Serial number C186,000-C215,000 probably less than 1,500 pistols. Colt would rework fixed sights equipped pistols on a repair order, with Stevens adjustable sight. Therefore, a Colt letter showing that the pistol was originally shipped with adjustable sights is in order for any adjustable sight-equipped pistol. **NOTE:** Finish 99-100 percent add 30-60 percent.

Stevens Adjustable Sights

NIB	EXC.	V.G.	GOOD	FAIR	POOR
—	10000	7500	5000	3000	1500

Fixed Sights

NIB	EXC.	V.G.	GOOD	FAIR	POOR
—	8500	6000	4000	2500	1200

Standard 1911A1 Pre-WWII, "GOVERNMENT MODEL" Export Sales

With "Swartz Safeties" and usually a foreign crest or foreign inscription mainly from Argentina. Vast majority of Swartz equipped foreign contract pistols were shipped to Argentina, but Argentine pistols do not have the collector interest that others or the plain domestic pistols have. Four factors reduce collector interest in the Colt made Argentine pistols compared to the rest:

1. Most of the Argentine-marked pistols have been recently imported and have the legally required Import Markings.

2. Many of the Argentine-marked pistols have been advertised and sold in the wholesale trade publications at utility prices.

3. Most of the recent import Argentine pistols have been refinished or are in "well used" condition.

4. Most of the recent import pistols from Argentina have had some parts changed or swapped with other pistols and are not in original condition.

Few of these Argentine Swartz equipped pistols that remain in original and excellent or better condition, usually sell for less than their "plain Jane" domestic counterparts and sell for much less than much rarer Brazilian and Mexican pistols. Perhaps these depressed prices represent a bargain for collectors, with an eye to the future when the supply of these extremely rare pistols dries up. 100 percent reblue = Fair/Poor. **NOTE:** Finish 99-100 percent add 20-30 percent.

NIB	EXC.	V.G.	GOOD	FAIR	POOR
—	1400	1050	900	650	550

Normal Brazilian and Mexican Pistols (w/Swartz Safeties)

These pistols do not normally have Swartz safeties, but if any were found, they would be expected to sell for at least the amount listed. **NOTE:** Finish 99-100 percent add 20-30 percent.

NIB	EXC.	V.G.	GOOD	FAIR	POOR
—	9500	7000	4000	2500	1200

Argentine Contract Pistols "Modelo Argentino 1927, Calibre .45

These pistols delivered to Argentina in 1927. Right side of slide marked with the two-line inscription "Ejercito Argentino Colt Cal .45 Mod. 1927". Also the Argentine National Seal and "Rampant Colt". SN 1-10,000. Verified proof, Assembler's mark and Final inspectors mark under left stock by upper bushing. None had Swartz Safeties. Most of these pistols were reblued. Reblued = Fair/Poor. **NOTE:** Abundance of these and other refinished Argentine pistols has depressed the prices of all original finish Argentine pistols. Finish 99-100 percent add 20-50 percent

NIB	EXC.	V.G.	GOOD	FAIR	POOR
—	1400	1050	850	600	400

Military to Commercial Conversions

Some 1911 Military pistols that were brought home by GIs, were subsequently returned to the Colt factory by their owners for repair or refinishing. If the repair included a new barrel, the pistol would have been proof fired and a normal Verified proof mark affixed to the trigger guard bow in the normal commercial practice. If the pistol was refinished between about 1920 and 1942, the slide would probably be numbered to the frame again in the normal commercial practice. These pistols are really remanufactured Colt pistols of limited production and should be valued at least that of a contemporary 1911A1 commercial pistol. Only pistols marked with identifiable Colt markings should be included in this category. Very seldom seen. Since Colt rework records are lost, reworked and refinished pistols without identifiable Colt applied markings are probably not verifiable as Colt reworks and should be considered refinished pistols of unknown pedigree. **NOTE:** Finish 99-100 percent add 30 percent.

NIB	EXC.	V.G.	GOOD	FAIR	POOR
—	1900	1300	975	550	425

NIB	EXC.	V.G.	GOOD	FAIR	POOR

Super .38 1929 Model, Pre-WWII

Pistol is identical in outward physical configuration to the .45 ACP Colt Commercial. Chambered for the .38 Super cartridge and magazine holds 9 rounds. Right side of slide marked "Colt Super .38 Automatic" in two lines, followed by the "Rampant Colt". Last few thousand pre-war Super .38 pistols made, had Swartz Safety parts installed. Some pistols were assembled post-war, with leftover parts. Post-war-assembled pistols did not have Swartz safeties installed but most (possibly all) had the cutouts. In 1945, 400 pistols were purchased by the U.S. Government. These 400 pistols bear the G.H.D. acceptance mark as well as the Ordnance crossed cannons. (G.H.D. and Ordnance marked add 30-50 percent. A factory letter is probably necessary here.) Some collectors feel that post-war assembly and post-war chemical tank bluing adds a premium, others feel that it requires a deduction. Post-war assembly may add 15 percent or it may deduct 15 percent. **NOTE:** Finish 99-100 percent add 33 percent. Swartz Safeties add 20 percent. For nickel finish add 50 percent.

	5000	4000	3000	2000	1000

Super Match .38 1935 Model, Pre-WWII

Only 5,000 of these specially fit and finished target-grade pistols were manufactured. Have fixed sights or the Stevens adjustable sights and top surfaces are matte-finished to reduce glare. Twelve hundred pistols were purchased and sent to Britain in 1939, at the then-costly rate of $50 per unit. Last few thousand pre-war Super .38 pistols made had the Swartz safety parts installed, but some pistols were assembled post-war with leftover parts. Post-war-assembled pistols did not have the Swartz safeties installed, but most (possibly all) had the cutouts. In 1945, 400 pistols were purchased by the U.S. Government. These 400 pistols bear the G.H.D. acceptance mark as well as the Ordnance crossed cannons. G.H.D. and Ordnance marked add 30-50 percent. A factory letter is probably necessary here. Swartz Safeties add 20 percent. Some collectors feel that post-war assembly and post-war chemical tank bluing adds a premium, others feel that it requires a deduction. Post-war assembly may add 15 percent or it may deduct 15 percent. **NOTE:** Finish 99-100 percent add 20-75 percent for both models.

Adjustable Sights

	11500	8000	5000	3000	2000

Fixed Sights

	10000	6500	4000	2000	1250

MODEL 1911A1 U.S. MILITARY SERIES

A complete look at the many variations of the Colt Model 1911A1 that were made for U.S. Military forces, see Standard Catalog of Military Firearms, 7th Edition. This publication covers history, technical data, photos and values of the world's military arms and accessories. Following is a summary of estimated values for Model 1911A1 pistols manufactured for U.S. forces between 1924 and the end of WWII in 1945.

Colt

NOTE: For Army or Navy variations, with blue finish made between 1937 and 1939 add 100 to 200 percent. Serial number range 710000-717281.

	3500	3200	2500	1000	500

Ithaca

	2000	1650	1200	900	600

Remington Rand

	2000	1650	1200	900	600

Union Switch & Signal

	5000	4200	3200	2400	1200

Singer Mfg. Co.

NOTE: Highly collectible model and fakes are known to exist. 500 these guns were made, with serial numbers from S800001 to S800500. An appraisal from a recognized Colt expert is strongly suggested, whether buying or selling.

	48000	40000	28000	18000	6000

COLT 1911A1 POST WWII COMMERCIAL PRODUCED, DOMESTIC SALES, 1946-1969

SN C220,000 to about C220,500

No "GOVERNMENT MODEL" marking. Few have no verified proof. Many parts are leftover military. **NOTE:** Finish 99-100 percent add 20-50 percent.

	2300	1650	1150	950	750

	NIB	EXC.	V.G.	GOOD	FAIR	POOR

SN C220,500 to about C249,000 verified proof and "GOVERNMENT MODEL" marking

Many parts are leftover military in first few thousand pistols. No foreign markings. **NOTE:** Finish 99-100 percent add 20-30 percent. Less 30 percent for foreign markings.

	—	1600	1100	750	500	400

SN 255,000-C to about 258,000-C Slide Factory Roll Marked "PROPERTY OF THE STATE OF NEW YORK", verified proof, and "GOVERNMENT MODEL" marking (250 pistols total)

Few leftover military parts are still used. Few pairs of pistols remain as consecutive pairs. **NOTE:** Finish 99-100 percent add 20-50 percent. Add 10 percent for consecutive pairs.

	—	1700	1200	800	550	450

SN 249,500-C to about 335,000-C, verified proof and "GOVERNMENT MODEL" marking

No foreign markings. **NOTE:** Finish 99-100 percent add 20-30 percent. Less 30 percent for foreign markings.

	—	1600	1100	750	500	400

SN 334,500-C to about 336,169-C, BB (Barrel Bushing) marked

About 1000 pistols. Verified proof and "GOVERNMENT MODEL" marking. **NOTE:** Finish 99-100 percent add 20-50 percent.

	—	1500	1000	700	575	450

ACE AND SERVICE MODEL ACE

Rebuilt from service pistols at Springfield Armory, between 1955 and about 1967 and Rock Island in 1968. These pistols were built and rebuilt each year, with a portion being sold to competitors by the NRA. Each year improvements were added to the rebuild program. Four articles in the "National Rifleman" document these pistols well: August 1959, April 1963, June 1966 and July 1966. Many parts for these pistols have been available and many "Look Alike" pistols have been built by basement armorers. Pistols generally came with a numbered box and shipping papers. Prices listed are for pistols with numbered box or papers. Less box and papers deduct 30 percent. When well-worn, these pistols will offer little over a standard pistol. Early pistols are much less commonly seen, but seem to be less sought after since they look largely like normal issue pistols.

Ace Model .22 Pistol

Starting on June 21, 1913, the U.S. Military along with "Springfield Armory" and "Colt Patented Firearms Manufacturing Co." attempted to develop a .22 cal. rimfire pistol that could be used for training purposes. By 1927, the military became convinced that a pistol identical to the standard "Service Pistol", but in .22 cal. rimfire was impractical and dropped the idea. In 1930 Colt purchased advertising that, in effect, requested the shooting public to let the company know if they would be interested in a .22 rimfire pistol built similar to the "Government Model". The response must have been positive because in 1931 the Colt Ace appeared on the market. Ace uses the same frame as the "Government Model", with a highly modified slide and a heavy barrel. Chambered for .22 LR cartridge only. Size is the same as the larger-caliber version and weight is 36 oz. Operation is straight blowback. Ace has a 10-round detachable magazine and features "Improved Ace Adjustable Target Sight". Markings on left side of slide are the same as on the "Government Model"; right side reads "Colt Ace 22 Long Rifle". First the Army purchased a few pistols (totaling 206) through 1936. The Army concluded that the function of Ace was less than perfect, as they concluded the .22 rimfire lacked the power to consistently and reliably operate the slide. Approximately 11,000 Ace pistols were manufactured and in 1941 they were discontinued. Many owners today find that although ACE is somewhat selective to ammunition, with full power loads it is a highly reliable pistol when properly cleaned and maintained. **NOTE:** Finish 99-100 percent add 33 percent.

	—	4500	3000	1800	950	700

Pre-1945 Service Model Ace .22 R. F. Pistol

In 1937 Colt introduced this improved version of the Ace Pistol. It utilizes a floating chamber, invented by David "Carbine" Williams the firearm's designer who invented the "Short Stroke Gas Piston", that is the basis of the MI carbine, while serving time on a Southern chain gang. Colt advertised that this pistol, with its floating chamber would give the Service Model Ace the reliability and "feel" of a .45 Auto. Today, owners of the Service Model ACE pistols find they require regular maintenance and cleaning in order to keep the close-fitting floating chamber from binding. Furthermore, fouling appears to be much worse with some brands and types of ammunition. Most owners feel that although the perceived recoil of the Service Model ACE is noticeably greater than that of the ACE, it falls far short of a .45 Auto's recoil. Serial number is prefixed by the letters "SM". External configuration is the same as Ace. Slide is marked "Colt Service Model Ace .22 Long Rifle". Most were sold to the Army and some on a commercial basis. There were a total of 13,803 manufactured before production ceased in 1945. **NOTE:** Finish 99-100 percent add 20-30 percent for both models. Add 20 percent for "US Property" marking.

	NIB	EXC.	V.G.	GOOD	FAIR	POOR

Blued pistols (before about SN SM 3840)

	NIB	EXC.	V.G.	GOOD	FAIR	POOR
	—	7000	5000	3000	1150	1000

Parkerized pistols (after about SN SM 3840)

	—	5000	3000	1800	950	700

Service Model Ace-Post-War

Introduced in 1978, this model is similar to pre-war model. Production ceased in 1982. **NOTE:** Finish 99-100 percent add 20-30 percent.

	—	1100	950	875	800	600

Conversion Units .22-.45, .45-.22

In 1938 Colt released a .22-caliber conversion unit. With this kit, one who already owned a "Government Model" could simply switch the top half and fire inexpensive .22 rimfire ammunition. Unit consists of a slide marked "Service Model Ace" barrel, with floating chamber, ejector, slide lock, bushing, recoil spring, 10-shot magazine and box. Conversion Units feature the Stevens adjustable rear sight. Later that same year a kit to convert the Service Model Ace to .45 ACP was offered. In 1942 production of these units ceased. The .22 kit was reintroduced in 1947; .45 kit was not brought back. (Finish 99-100 percent add 20-30 percent.) Subtract 20 percent if box is missing. Be alert, as sometimes a conversion unit is found on a Service Model ACE receiver and a Service model Ace upper is sold as a "Conversion Unit". Conversion Units are ALWAYS marked "Conversion Unit". "Service Model ACE" pistols lack the "Conversion Unit" marking. **NOTE:** Finish 99-100 percent add 20-30 percent.

Pre-war and Post-war "U" numbered Service Model Ace Conversion Unit, .22-.45 (to convert .45 cal. to .22 cal.)

The pre-war conversion units were serial numbered U1-U2000.

	—	1200	950	550	500	450

Post-war Conversion Units

These were serial numbered U2001-U2670.

	—	650	550	500	450	425

Pre-war Service Model Ace (Re-) Conversion Unit, .45-22

To convert Convert SMA .22 Cal. to .45 Cal. SN 1-SN 112. Watch out for fakes.

	5000	3500	2500	1500	750	550

Post-war .22 Conversion Unit Unnumbered

30 percent premium for Stevens adjustable sights, 1946 only.

	600	400	350	250	225	175

Military National Match .45 Pistols

Rebuilt from service pistols at Springfield Armory, between 1955 and about 1967 and Rock Island in 1968. Pistols were built and rebuilt each year, with a portion being sold to competitors by the NRA. Each year improvements were added to the rebuild program. Four articles in the "National Rifleman" document these pistols well: August 1959, April 1963, June 1966 and July 1966. Many parts for these pistols have been available and many "Look Alike" pistols have been built by basement armorers. Pistols generally came with a numbered box and shipping papers. Prices listed are for pistols with numbered box or papers. Less box and papers deduct 30 percent. When well-worn, these pistols will offer little over a standard pistol. Early pistols are much less commonly seen, but seem to be less sought after since they look largely like normal issue pistols. **NOTE:** Finish 99-100 percent add 20-30 percent.

	—	1500	1075	775	600	475

Military National Match Pistols (Drake Slide)

In 1964, Springfield Armory used some of these specially machined and hardened slides to build the Military National Match pistols that year. This year's pistol is perhaps the most identifiable NM pistol due to the unique slide marking. However, Drake was only the supplier of the slides that year. Colt supplied the slides in the following year (1965). **NOTE:** Finish 99-100 percent add 20-30 percent.

	—	1550	1100	790	610	485

Gold Cup National Match (pre-Series 70)

Model is chambered for the .45 ACP. Features the flat mainspring housing of the 1911 and has a match-grade barrel and bushing. Parts were hand fitted and slide has an enlarged ejection port. Trigger is the long version, with an adjustable trigger stop and sights are adjustable target type. Finish is blued, with checkered walnut grips and gold medallions. Slide is marked "Gold Cup

NIB	EXC.	V.G.	GOOD	FAIR	POOR

National Match". Serial number is prefixed by the letters "NM". Pistol was manufactured from 1957 to 1970. **NOTE:** Finish 99-100 percent add 20-30 percent.

NIB	EXC.	V.G.	GOOD	FAIR	POOR
—	1100	850	625	500	400

Gold Cup MKIII National Match

This pistol is identical to the Gold Cup .45, except chambered for the .38 Mid-Range Wad Cutter round. Manufactured from 1961 until 1974. **NOTE:** Finish 99-100 percent add 20-30 percent.

NIB	EXC.	V.G.	GOOD	FAIR	POOR
1800	1500	1000	600	450	350

Colt 1911A1 AMU (Army Marksmanship Unit)

NOTE: For Army modified pistols deduct 70 percent.

NIB	EXC.	V.G.	GOOD	FAIR	POOR
—	2700	2250	1450	900	400

COLT LICENSED AND UNLICENSED FOREIGN-MADE 1911A1 AND VARIATIONS

Argentine D.G.F.M.

Direccion General de Fabricaciones Militares made at the F.M.A.P. (Fabrica Militar de Arms Portatiles [Military Factory of Small Arms]). Licensed copies SN 24,000 to 112,494. Parts are generally interchangeable with Colt-made 1911A1 type pistols. Most pistols were marked "D.G.F.M. - (F.M.A.P.)". Late pistols marked FM within a cartouche on right side of slide. Pistols are found both with and without import markings, often in excellent condition, currently more often in refinished condition and with a seemingly endless variety of slide markings. None of these variations have yet achieved any particular collector status or distinction, unless new in box. In fact, many of these fine pistols have and continue to be used as the platforms for the highly customized competition and target pistols that are currently popular. Refinished=Fair/Poor. **NOTE:** Finish 99-100 percent-NIB add 10-30 percent)

NIB	EXC.	V.G.	GOOD	FAIR	POOR
1500	1000	700	400	350	300

Argentine-Made Ballester Molina

Un-licensed Argentine redesigned versions. (Parts are NOT interchangeable with Colt except for the barrel and magazine.) These pistols are found both with and without import markings. Pistols without import markings usually have a B prefix number stamped on the left rear part of the mainspring housing and are often in excellent to new original condition. Vast majority of currently available pistols are found in excellent but refinished condition. Only the pistols with no import markings that are in excellent-to-new original condition have achieved any particular collector status. Most of these pistols that are being sold today are being carried and shot rather than being collected. Refinished = Fair/Poor. **NOTE:** Finish 99-100 percent-NIB add 10-30 percent.

NIB	EXC.	V.G.	GOOD	FAIR	POOR
	600	375	300	215	190

Brazilian Models 1911A1

Made by "Fabrica de Itajuba" in Itajuba, Brazil. The Imbel Model 973, made by "Industriade Material Belico do Brazil" in Sao Paulo, Brazil. The Itajuba is a true copy of the Colt 1911A1 and the Imbel is also believed to be a true copy. However, an Imbel has yet to be examined by the author. Too rarely seen in the U.S.A. to establish a meaningful price.

COLT MODEL 1911A1
1970 - CURRENT

Model 1911A1 was manufactured by Colt until 1971, when the Series 70 Government Model superseded it. Modifications in the new model were slightly heavier slide and slotted collet barrel bushing. In 1983, Colt introduced the Series 80 models, which had an additional passive firing pin safety lock. Half-cock notch was also redesigned. Beginning of 1992 another change was made to Model 1911A1 in the form of an enhanced pistol. Included were the Government models, Commander, Officer's, Gold Cup and Combat Elite. These modifications are the result of Colt's desire to meet the shooters demand for a more "customized" pistol. Colt chose some of the most popular modifications to perform on their new enhanced models. They include beavertail safety grip, slotted Commander-style hammer, relief cut under the trigger guard, beveled magazine well, slightly longer trigger, flat top rib and angled slide serrations. Model 1911A1 may be the most modified handgun in the world.

MKIV Series 70 Government Model

Model is essentially a newer version of the 1911A1. Has the prefix "70G" from 1970-1976, "G70" from 1976-1980 and "70B" from 1980-1983, when production ceased. This model is offered in blue or nickel plate. Checkered walnut grips, with the Colt medallion. Chambered for .45 ACP, .38 Super, 9mm and 9mm Steyr (foreign export only). **NOTE:** Add 25 percent for nickel finish, 15 percent for .38 Super.

NIB	EXC.	V.G.	GOOD	FAIR	POOR
950	775	600	400	250	200

MKIV Series 70 Gold Cup National Match

Newer version of the 1957 National Match. Features a slightly heavier slide and Colt Elliason sights. Chambering is .45 ACP only. Accurizer barrel and bushing was introduced on this model.

NIB	EXC.	V.G.	GOOD	FAIR	POOR

Manufactured from 1970-1983.

NIB	EXC.	V.G.	GOOD	FAIR	POOR
1500	1200	1000	650	500	400

Series 70 Gunsite Pistol

Model features a 5" barrel, thin rosewood grips, Gold Cup serrations, Heinie front sight and Novak rear sight, plus several other special features. Available in blue or stainless steel. Introduced in 2004.

NIB	EXC.	V.G.	GOOD	FAIR	POOR
1200	1050	825	600	400	200

Series 70 Gunsite Pistol Commander

As above, with 4.25" barrel.

NIB	EXC.	V.G.	GOOD	FAIR	POOR
1200	1050	825	600	400	200

COLT ENHANCED GOVERNMENT MODELS

In 1992, Colt introduced a new set of features for its Model 1911A1 series pistols. New features include: a flattop slide, angled rear slide serrations, scalloped ejection port, combat style hammer, beavertail grip safety, relief cut-under trigger guard and long trigger. Models that are affected by this new upgrade are: Delta Elite, Combat Elite, Government Model, Combat Commander, Lightweight Commander, Officer's ACP, Officer's ACP Lightweight.

COMMANDER SERIES

This is a Shortened version of the Government model. Has a 4.25" barrel, a lightweight alloy frame and a rounded spur hammer. Total weight of the Commander is 27.5 oz. Serial number has the suffix "LW". Commander is chambered for the .45 ACP, 9mm and .38 Super. Some were chambered for 7.65 Parabellum for export only. Commander was introduced in 1949.

Pre-70 Series (1949-1969)
NOTE: Deduct 20 percent for 9mm.

NIB	EXC.	V.G.	GOOD	FAIR	POOR
1500	1250	1000	800	600	400

Series 70 (1970-1983)

NIB	EXC.	V.G.	GOOD	FAIR	POOR
1200	1000	850	700	600	300

Series 80 (1983-1996)

NIB	EXC.	V.G.	GOOD	FAIR	POOR
900	750	600	500	400	300

Combat Commander

Combat Commander was produced in response to complaints from some quarters about the excessive recoil and rapid wear of the alloy-framed Commander. This model is simply a Commander, with a steel frame. Combat Commander weighs 32 oz. and offered in blue or satin nickel, with walnut grips. No longer in production. **NOTE:** Add 40 percent for Series 70 model

NIB	EXC.	V.G.	GOOD	FAIR	POOR
850	550	475	375	300	200

MK IV Series 80 Government Model

This model introduced in 1983. It is, for all purposes, externally the same as the Series 70. Basic difference is the addition of the new firing pin safety on this model. No longer in production.

Blued

NIB	EXC.	V.G.	GOOD	FAIR	POOR
850	725	600	500	400	250

Nickel Plated

NIB	EXC.	V.G.	GOOD	FAIR	POOR
1000	800	650	500	400	250

Stainless Steel

NIB	EXC.	V.G.	GOOD	FAIR	POOR
950	800	650	500	400	250

Polished Stainless Steel

NIB	EXC.	V.G.	GOOD	FAIR	POOR
1000	800	700	500	400	250

Colt 1991A1

The 1991 Series is a direct descendant of the original Model 1911. The long trigger, flat mainspring housing and recoil spring system are like the original design. Upgrades include high profile white dot sights and lowered ejection port. Based on the Series 80 MKIV Colt design, it was introduced In 1992. Early models were offered in 9mm. The standard model is in .45 ACP, with a 7+1 capacity. A .38 Super version is available. See separate listing.

NIB	EXC.	V.G.	GOOD	FAIR	POOR
850	750	500	350	150	125

M1991A1 Commander

Chambered for the .45 ACP, this model has all the same features as standard M1991A1, with a slightly shorter 4.25" barrel. Reintroduced in 2004. **NOTE:** In 1997, Colt offered this model in

	NIB	EXC.	V.G.	GOOD	FAIR	POOR

stainless steel, with fixed white dot sights. Add $100 to NIB price.

| | 800 | 550 | 400 | 300 | 225 | 125 |

M1991A1 Compact

Chambered for the .45 ACP, this model has a 3.25" barrel. It is 1.5" shorter than standard M1991A1 model and .375" shorter in height. Magazine holds 6 rounds. No longer in production. **NOTE:** In 1997, Colt offered this model in stainless steel, with fixed white dot sights. Add $50 to NIB price.

| | 850 | 600 | 425 | 300 | 150 | 125 |

M1991A1 .38 Super

Has the same features as .45 ACP M1991A1 Government Model, except chambered for .38 Super cartridge. Magazine capacity is 9 + 1. Available only with bright stainless steel finish.

| | 1100 | 875 | 650 | 500 | 375 | 300 |

MK IV Series 80 Gold Cup National Match

Externally the same as Series 70 Gold Cup, with new firing pin safety.

Blued

| | 1200 | 900 | 675 | 500 | 350 | 250 |

Stainless Steel

| | 1200 | 900 | 675 | 500 | 350 | 250 |

Polished Stainless Steel

| | 1200 | 900 | 675 | 500 | 350 | 250 |

Officer's ACP

Shortened version of Government Model. Has a 3.5" barrel and weighs 37 oz. Chambered for the .45 ACP only and has checkered walnut grips. Officer's ACP introduced in 1985. No longer in production.

Blued

| | 1000 | 700 | 525 | 325 | 250 | 200 |

Matte Blued

| | 1000 | 700 | 525 | 325 | 250 | 200 |

Satin Nickel

Discontinued 1985.

| | 1050 | 750 | 575 | 375 | 295 | 200 |

Stainless Steel

| | 1100 | 800 | 625 | 425 | 345 | 200 |

Lightweight Officer's ACP

An alloy-framed version that weighs 24 oz. Introduced in 1986. No longer in production.

| | 1000 | 700 | 525 | 325 | 250 | 200 |

Concealed Carry Officer's Model

Model features a lightweight aluminum frame, with stainless steel Commander slide. Barrel length 4.25" and chambered for .45 ACP cartridge. Fitted with lightweight trigger, combat style hammer and Hogue grips. Weight approximately 34 oz. Introduced in 1998. No longer in production.

| | 1000 | 700 | 525 | 325 | 250 | 200 |

Delta Gold Cup

Introduced in 1992, Delta Gold Cup is chambered for the 10mm. Features a 5" barrel, stainless steel finish, adjustable Accro sights, special trigger and black rubber wraparound grips. Features all of the new "Enhanced" model features. No longer in production.

| | 1050 | 875 | 700 | 600 | 400 | 200 |

Delta Elite

Model is chambered for the 10mm Norma cartridge. Offered in blue or stainless steel. Grips are black neoprene, with the Delta medallion. Features a high-profile three-dot combat sight system. Delta Elite introduced in 1987. No longer in production.

Blued

| | 1200 | 925 | 650 | 425 | 300 | 250 |

Stainless Steel

| | 1250 | 950 | 675 | 400 | 300 | 250 |

	NIB	EXC.	V.G.	GOOD	FAIR	POOR

Polished Stainless Steel

	NIB	EXC.	V.G.	GOOD	FAIR	POOR
	1250	950	675	400	300	250

Combat Elite

Specialized Government model that has a 5" barrel and adjustable Accro sights. Chambered either in .45 ACP or .38 Super. Weighs 38 oz., has an 8-round magazine for the .45 ACP and a 9-round magazine for the .38 Super. Finish either blue or matte stainless steel. No longer in production. (Colt issued a recall notice for the safety on this model in June 2009. Pistols with serial numbers from CG10000E to CG11293E should be sent to the factory for parts replacement.)

1050	875	700	600	400	200

Combat Target Model

Introduced in 1996, this 5" barrel 1911 model features a fitted barrel, Gold Cup-style trigger, tuned action, flat top slide, relieved ejection port, skeletonized hammer, wide grip safety, high cut trigger guard, beveled magazine well, and adjustable sights. Weight 39 oz. Offered in both blue and stainless steel. Chambered for the new 9x23 cartridge as well as the .45 ACP and the .38 Super. No longer in production. In 1997, Colt expanded Target Model to include a number of different variations. They are listed. **NOTE:** Add $50 for stainless steel version.

1050	875	700	600	400	200

Combat Target Commander

Barrel length is 4.25". Chambered for .45 ACP. Stainless steel finish. Weight is 36 oz. Has all other Combat Target features. No longer in production.

1050	875	700	600	400	200

Combat Target Officer's ACP

Fitted with a 3.5" barrel and chambered for .45 ACP. Stainless steel finish. Weight about 34 oz. Has all other Combat Target features. No longer in production.

1050	875	700	600	400	200

Special Combat Government

Pistol features a 5" barrel, double diamond rosewood grips, extended ambidextrous thumb safety. Steel checkered mainspring housing, with extended magazine well. Chambered for the .45 ACP or .38 Super cartridges. Adjustable Bomar rear sight. Magazine capacity 8 rounds. Choice of hard chrome or blue/satin nickel finish.

2000	1700	1500	1200	800	400

Special Combat Government Carry Model

1911-style semi-automatic pistol, chambered in .45 ACP (8+1) or .38 Super (9+1). Semi-custom features include Novak front and rear night sights, skeletonized three-hole trigger, slotted hammer, black/silver synthetic grips, Smith & Alexander upswept beavertail grip, palm swell safety and extended magazine well. Wilson tactical ambidextrous safety. 5" barrel. Available blued, hard chrome, or blue/satin nickel finish depending on chambering.

1450	1100	900	650	400	300

Close Quarters Battle (CQB) Pistol

From the Colt Custom Shop, this .45 ACP model was designed for and is primarily manufactured for the U.S. Marine Corps. It features a Desert Tan Cerakoted receiver and slide, 5" National Match barrel with accessory rail and a flat, serrated mainspring housing with extended grip safety and lanyard loop. Grips are G-10 composite and sights are Novak 3-Dot Night Sights.

1850	1700	1500	1200	800	400

XSE SERIES MODEL O PISTOLS

Introduced in 1999, these models are an enhanced version of Colt 1911. Features front slide serrations, checkered, double diamond rosewood grips, adjustable McCormick trigger, three-dot dovetail rear sights, ambidextrous safety, enhanced tolerances, aluminum frame and stainless steel slide. Chambered for .45 ACP cartridge.

XSE Model O Government (01070XS)

Fitted with a 5" barrel and 8-round magazine.

950	800	595	475	350	200

XSE Model O Concealed Carry Officer's (09850XS)

Fitted with a 4.25" barrel and 7-round magazine.

1000	850	625	475	350	200

	NIB	EXC.	V.G.	GOOD	FAIR	POOR

XSE Model O Commander (04012XS)

Fitted with a 4.25" barrel and 8-round magazine.

NIB	EXC.	V.G.	GOOD	FAIR	POOR
950	800	595	475	350	200

XSE Model O Lightweight Commander (04860XS)

Fitted with a 4.25" barrel and 8-round magazine. Weight about 26 oz.

NIB	EXC.	V.G.	GOOD	FAIR	POOR
950	800	595	475	350	200

1991 SERIES MODEL O PISTOLS

This series pistol introduced in 1991 and replaces the standard Colt 1911 series. Features checkered rubber composite grips, smooth trigger, fixed sights, beveled magazine well, standard thumb safety and service style grip safety. Chambered for .45 ACP cartridge and 7-round magazine.

1991 Model O Government Matte (01991)

Fitted with a 5" barrel, black matte finish, carbon steel frame and slide.

NIB	EXC.	V.G.	GOOD	FAIR	POOR
800	650	495	350	295	200

1991 Model O Government Stainless (01091)

Fitted with a 5" barrel, mattel stainless finish on stainless steel frame and slide.

NIB	EXC.	V.G.	GOOD	FAIR	POOR
920	700	550	400	300	200

1991 Model O Commander Stainless (04091U)

Fitted with a 4.25" barrel and matte stainless finish. Stainless steel frame and slide.

NIB	EXC.	V.G.	GOOD	FAIR	POOR
920	700	550	400	300	200

1991 Model O Commander (04691)

Fitted with a 4.25" barrel and black matte finish. Carbon steel frame and slide.

NIB	EXC.	V.G.	GOOD	FAIR	POOR
870	650	—	—	—	—

Colt Defender

Single-action pistol introduced in 1998. Features a lightweight aluminum alloy frame and stainless steel slide. Chambered for the .45 ACP or .40 S&W cartridge and fitted with a 3" barrel. Magazine capacity 7 rounds. Rubber wraparound grips. Weight approximately 23 oz.; overall length 6.75".

NIB	EXC.	V.G.	GOOD	FAIR	POOR
850	650	475	300	250	200

Colt Defender Model O (07000D)

Model takes the place of Defender and introduced in 2000. Brushed stainless finish, with a 3" barrel. Skeletonized composite trigger, beveled magazine well, extended thumb safety and upswept beavertail, with palm swell. Chambered for .45 ACP only. (Colt issued a recall notice for the guide pad on this model in June 2009. Pistols with serial numbers from DR33036 to DR35948 should be sent to the factory for parts replacement.)

NIB	EXC.	V.G.	GOOD	FAIR	POOR
950	700	525	350	200	145

1911 – WWI Replica

Single-action semi-automatic, chambered in .45 ACP. Faithful external reproduction of the WWI-era service pistol, with original-style rollmarks grips, sights, carbonia blue finish, etc. Series 70 lockwork. Made from 2003 - 2009.

NIB	EXC.	V.G.	GOOD	FAIR	POOR
1025	850	625	575	400	200

1911 - WWI 1918 Replica

Based on military model made in 1918. Black finish and World War I rollmarks. Offered in a Presentation Grade, with blue or nickel finish and Colt Custom Shop "A" engraving. Excellent or new condition could add a premium of 100 percent. Made in 2008 and 2009. (Colt issued a recall notice for the safety on this model in June of 2009. Pistols with serial numbers from 1001WWI to 3431WWI should be sent to the factory for parts replacement.)

NIB	EXC.	V.G.	GOOD	FAIR	POOR
900	800	600	500	400	200

1911A1 - WWII Replica

Replica of U.S. Military sidearm of World War II. Parkerized finish, WWII-ear rollmarks, lanyard loop, original style composite grips and packaging. Made in .45 ACP only, by the Colt Custom Shop from 2001 to 2004. Series 70 lockwork. (Colt issued a recall notice for the safety on this model in June 2009. Pistols with serial numbers from 4597WMK to 5414WMK should be sent to the factory for parts replacement.)

NIB	EXC.	V.G.	GOOD	FAIR	POOR
1075	950	700	575	400	200

NIB	EXC.	V.G.	GOOD	FAIR	POOR

Colt New Agent Double Action Only

Similar to New Agent single action, except has double-action-only operating system. Spurless hammer design, with second-strike capability and no manual safety. Double-diamond slim fit grips, snag free trench sighting system, 7-shot magazine. In .45 ACP only. (Colt issued a recall notice for the safety and guide pad on this model in June of 2009. Pistols with serial numbers from GT01001 to GT04505 should be sent to the factory for parts replacement.)

850	750	600	500	400	200

Colt Model 1991 DAO

Double-action-only version of the Lightweight Government Model. Spur-less hammer design, with second-strike capability and no manual safety. Double-diamond slim fit grips, 7-shot magazine. In .45 ACP only. Introduced in 2011.

950	800	700	550	400	250

Colt Model 1911 100th Anniversary Series

These two limited edition Model 1911s, were introduced in 2011 to commemorate the 100th anniversary of the legendary pistol. Model 1911ANVIII is based on the 1918 configuration, with custom rollmarks on the receiver relating to the 100th anniversary. Higher grade version, Model 1911ANVII, features scroll engraving and historic Colt symbols highlighted in 24 karat gold. Comes in a glass-topped walnut display case. Production was limited to 750 units. Higher grade variants limited to 100 units, with A, B, C or D levels of engraving scheduled at prices ranging from $2640 to $6528.

1911ANVII

2150	1800	1500	—	—	—

1911ANVIII

1075	900	750	—	—	—

Gunsite Model 1911

Made from 2003 to 2005 to commemorate the Gunsite Shooting Academy. Special features include: Heinie front and Novak rear sights, Chip McCormick hammer and sear, checkered rosewood grips and flat serrated mainspring housing. Chambered in .45 ACP, with two 8-shot magazines.

1350	1050	900	800	650	350

Colt Government Model 1911 .22 LR Series

Licensed reproduction of the 1911A1 in .22 LR, manufactured by Umarex USA. Blow-back action, with 12-shot magazine. Other standard 1911 specifications including 5" barrel, thumb and grip safeties, diamond checkered wood grips, blue finish and drift-adjustable rear sight. (Gold Cup has fully adjustable sight.) Weight approximately 33 ounces. Offered in three variants: standard model, Rail Gun and Gold Cup. Introduced in 2011. Prices below are for standard model.

350	300	275	225	175	100

Colt Concealed Carry

Chopped lightweight 1911-style semi-automatic, chambered in .45 ACP. Weighs 25 oz. unloaded; overall length 6.75"; 7+1 capacity; Series 80 lockwork; black anodized aluminum frame, with double-diamond wood grips. Introduced 2007.

950	700	525	350	200	150

New Agent

7+1 .45 ACP semi-automatic, with aluminum frame, fixed sights, Series 80 action, slim-fit grips and 6.75" overall length. Introduced 2007.

950	700	525	350	200	150

Colt Rail Gun

1911-style semi-automatic pistol, chambered in .45 ACP. Stainless steel frame and slide, front and rear slide serrations, skeletonized trigger, integral accessory rail, Smith & Alexander upswept beavertail grip, palm swell safety, white dot front sight and Novak rear. Rosewood double diamond grips, tactical thumb safety, National Match barrel. Capacity 8+1.

950	700	525	350	200	150

Double Eagle

Chambered for 9mm, .38 Super, 10mm Auto and .45 ACP cartridges. Has a 5" barrel and 8-round detachable box magazine. Constructed of stainless steel and checkered black synthetic grips. Sights are fixed and utilize the three-dot system. Manufactured from 1990 to 1996. Add 20 percent for 9mm, .38 Super or 10mm.

1000	800	650	500	400	300

NIB	EXC.	V.G.	GOOD	FAIR	POOR

Double Eagle Officer's Model

Compact version of the double-action Double Eagle pistol, chambered for .45 ACP only. No longer in production.

1025	850	625	575	400	200

Double Eagle Combat Commander

Based on the standard Double Eagle design, with a slightly shorter 4.25" barrel. Double Eagle Combat Commander fits between the standard model and the smaller Officer's Model. Available in .45 ACP and .40 S&W (1993). Weighs 36 oz., holds 8 rounds, has white dot sights and checkered Xenoy grips. Finish is matte stainless steel. No longer in production.

1025	850	625	575	350	200

Double Eagle First Edition

This version of double-action Double Eagle pistol is chambered for the 10mm Auto. Furnished with a Cordura holster, double-magazine pouch, three magazines and a zippered black Cordura case.

1100	875	650	500	375	300

Pocket Nine

Double-action semi-automatic pistol, chambered for the 9mm cartridge. Frame is aluminum alloy and slide is stainless steel. Barrel length 2.75". Magazine capacity 6 rounds. Wraparound rubber grips standard. Overall length 5.5". Weight approximately 17 oz. No longer in production.

950	700	525	350	250	175

Tac Nine

Introduced in 1999, this double-action-only semi-automatic pistol is chambered for the 9mm cartridge. Has a 2.75" barrel, with an aluminum alloy frame and stainless steel slide. Tritium night sights. Wraparound rubber grips are standard. Finish is black oxide. Enhanced tolerances. Weight about 17 oz. No longer in production.

975	725	550	375	250	175

Mustang

More compact version of the .380 Government Model. Has a 2.75" barrel and 5-round detachable magazine. No longer in production. **NOTE:** Nickel finish add 10 percent. Stainless steel add 10 percent.

850	650	475	300	250	200

Mustang PocketLite

Lightweight version of Mustang. Features an aluminum alloy receiver. Finish is blued only and has synthetic grips. Introduced in 1987. Discontinued 1999. Reintroduced 2012. **NOTE:** Deduct 20 percent for 2012 model.

800	600	475	300	250	200

Government Pocketlite LW

Similar to Mustang, but fitted with a 3.25" barrel and 7-round magazine. Has an aluminum frame and stainless steel slide. Fixed sights. Black composition grips. Weight approximately 15 oz. No longer in production.

850	650	475	300	250	200

Mustang Pocketlite XSP

Similar in design and operation to standard Mustang Pocketlite model, except it has a polymer receiver, black finish and squared trigger guard. Introduced in 2013.

550	500	400	300	250	200

Mustang Plus II

This version of Mustang pistol, features 2.75" barrel with longer grip frame that accommodates a 7-round magazine. Introduced in 1988. Offered in blue and stainless steel. No longer in production. **NOTE:** Stainless steel add 10 percent.

850	650	475	300	250	200

Colt Pony

Introduced in 1997, this semi-automatic pistol is chambered for the .380 ACP. Fitted with a 2.75" barrel and bobbed hammer. Double-action-only. Grips are black composition. Sights are ramp front with fixed rear. Finish is Teflon and stainless steel. Magazine capacity 6 rounds. Overall length 5.5". Weight 19 oz. No longer in production.

850	650	475	300	250	200

NIB	EXC.	V.G.	GOOD	FAIR	POOR

Colt Pony PocketLite

Same as above, with aluminum and stainless steel frame. Weight approximately 13 oz. No longer in production.

NIB	EXC.	V.G.	GOOD	FAIR	POOR
850	650	475	300	250	200

.380 Series 80 Government Model

Single-action blowback-operated semi-automatic pistol, chambered for the .380 ACP cartridge. Has a 3.25" barrel and 7-round magazine. Sights are fixed. Available either blued, nickel plated or stainless steel. Synthetic grips. Introduced in 1985. No longer in production. **NOTE:** Nickel finish and stainless steel add 10 percent.

NIB	EXC.	V.G.	GOOD	FAIR	POOR
875	675	500	325	275	200

Colt CZ40

Introduced in 1998, this double-action .40 S&W pistol, was built for Colt by CZ in the Czech Republic. Fitted with a 4" barrel and black polymer grips. Frame is alloy, with a carbon steel slide and blue finish. Magazine capacity 10 rounds. Weight approximately 34 oz. No longer in production.

NIB	EXC.	V.G.	GOOD	FAIR	POOR
900	750	600	500	400	225

Colt Model 2000

Introduced in 1992, Model 2000 was a new departure for Colt from its traditional service style semi-automatic pistols. Chambered for the 9mm, Model 2000 is a double-action-only pistol, with a 4.5" barrel and choice between polymer or aluminum alloy frame. Polymer frame model weighs 29 oz. Aluminum alloy frame weighs 33 oz. Grips are black composition and sights are white dot. Pistol dropped from the Colt line in 1994.

NIB	EXC.	V.G.	GOOD	FAIR	POOR
700	595	400	300	250	200

COLT .22 RIMFIRE
SEMI-AUTOMATIC PISTOLS

For the Colt Ace, see Model 1911 section.

COLT WOODSMAN

The original Colt .22 Target Model was designed by John Moses Browning and improved by engineers at Colt Firearms prior to the start of production in 1915, and major design updates were made in 1947 and again in 1955. Those three designs constitute what collectors call the three series of Woodsman pistols. First Series refers to all those built on the frame used prior to and during World War II. Second Series includes all versions built on the second frame design from 1947 until 1955, and Third Series means the third frame design as used from 1955 to the end of production in 1977.

Each series had a Target Model, a Sport Model, and a Match Target Model. All models are very similar: the Sport Model, for example, is merely the Target Model with a short barrel, and in some cases different sights or grips. The Match Target is nearly the same as the Sport or Target Model, but with a heavier, slab-sided barrel, a squared-off frame at the front of the receiver to mate with the heavy barrel, and improved sights. In the post-war years only there were also three very similar economy models: First the Challenger, then the Huntsman, and finally the Targetsman. The actions of the economy models are identical to the higher-end models of the same period internally; they lack only some of the refinements.

These guns were not assembled in strict numerical sequence. Furthermore, even when changes were made, old parts were used up at the same time new parts were being introduced. As a result, there is no hard and fast serial number dividing line for any particular feature, and serial number overlaps of several thousand are common.

All models of the Woodsman line, in all three series, are discussed here, but there are numerous variations in details that are primarily of interest to specialized collectors. For more details see Bob Rayburn's Colt Woodsman Pocket Guide, a 96-page pocket-sized guide to the Colt Woodsman line, available for $10 (including shipping) from:

Bob Rayburn
PO Box 97104
Lakewood, WA 98497 or online at www.colt22.com or
www.coltwoodsman.com

Values listed here are for the pistol only, without extras, for guns in the middle of each condition range. These are guidelines to the prevailing retail values for the collector or shooter who is buying it as the end user, not what one might expect to receive from a gun dealer who is buying it to resell. Furthermore, within the Excellent and Very Good condition categories, there is a considerable spread in value, especially for the older and more collectible versions. Excellent, for example, means 98 percent or more original blue, but a very nice pre-Woodsman with 100 percent of the original blue would likely be worth twice as much to a serious collector as one with only 98 percent. At the other end of the condition scale, in the Fair and Poor categories, the individual values of component parts become significant, and effectively set a floor value. A poor condition, rusty, pitted pre-Woodsman

NIB	EXC.	V.G.	GOOD	FAIR	POOR

or First Series Match Target would still have good value if it included the original magazine and grips in nice condition, for example. In addition, there are sometimes rare variations within the broad categories that can significantly enhance the value. Include the original crisp condition box, instructions, and tools, and the value goes up more, especially for high condition early guns. On the other hand, rust, pitting (even very minor), rebluing, or other non-factory modifications will significantly reduce the values from those listed in the Very Good category or better.

FIRST SERIES

In 1915, intended market was the target shooter and there was only one model: Colt .22 LR Automatic Target Pistol. That model, however, proved to be very popular not only with target shooters, but also with hunters, trappers, campers and other outdoorsmen. Management at Colt noticed this, of course, and decided to give the pistol a new name that more closely reflected its widespread use. THE WOODSMAN, was the name chosen and that roll mark was added to the side of receiver in 1927, at approximately serial number 54000. To further satisfy the broader market, Colt introduced the Sport Model in 1933 and the Match Target Model in 1938. Compact and beautifully balanced Sport Model was a near perfect "kit gun" for the outdoorsman. Match Target was designed for the special needs of the serious target shooters. Approximately 54,000 pre-Woodsmans (all with 6.625" barrels) and a combined total of approximately 110,000 Woodsman marked Sport and Target Models were produced in the first series. Sport Model and Target Model were serial numbered together after the Sport Model was added to the line in 1933. It was not possible to easily determine how many of each were manufactured. Safe to say Target Model far outnumbered the Sport Model. During the war years of 1942-45, Match Target was the only Woodsman model built. Virtually the entire production was for the US military.

Pre-Woodsman

Model made from 1915-1927. Has a 10-round magazine, blue finish, checkered walnut grips and 6.625" barrel. Designed for .22 LR standard velocity ammunition. Rear sight adjustable for windage, front sight for elevation. Up until approximately serial number 31000 the barrel was a very thin, so-called "pencil barrel". Barrel weight and diameter were increased slightly in 1922, to what collectors now call the "medium weight barrel". Also numerous small changes in grips, magazines and markings over the years. Approximately 54,000 were made in all variations.

—	2000	1300	850	350	200

Woodsman Target

Initially, this was exactly the same as the late pre-Woodsman, with the exception of THE WOODSMAN marking on side of receiver. Later there were small changes in sights, trigger and markings. In 1934, the barrel profile was again modified to a larger diameter, heavier barrel. This third and final pre-WWII barrel profile lacked the fillet or step-down, as was present on the earlier pencil barrel and medium barrel, therefore commonly called the "straight taper" barrel. A significant modification occurred in 1932, when a new heat-treated mainspring housing and stiffer recoil spring were phased in to allow use of increasingly popular high velocity .22 LR ammunition. While this change had widely reported to have taken place at serial number 83790, it was actually phased in over a period of time and a range of serial numbers, spanning at least 81000-86000, within which range both standard and high speed versions can be found. Fortunately, Colt changed marking on the back of mainspring housing (see photo) to allow visual differentiation. Colt also sold a conversion kit to modify the older guns for use with high velocity ammunition. Kit consisted of a new style mainspring housing, stiffer recoil spring and coil type magazine spring for use in the very early guns that had a Z type magazine spring.

1800	1600	1000	500	250	200

Woodsman Sport

THE WOODSMAN, proving to be increasingly popular with outdoorsmen of all types, Colt decided to market a Woodsman better suited for "take along" gun for hiking, camping, etc. This was accomplished in 1933, by merely shortening the barrel from 6.625" to 4.5" and announcing the new Sport Model. Other than barrel length, the only difference between the Target Model and Sport Model was an adjustable front sight on Target Model and fixed front sight on Sport Model. Later, a front sight adjustable for elevation would be an available option for Sport Model. Colt called this arrangement "Target Sights". Indeed, it was the same front sight used on Target Model. First Series Sport Model, with adjustable front sight will command a premium of approximately 25 percent over the values listed.

2000	1700	1200	600	250	200

Woodsman Match Target

Colt introduced Match Target Woodsman in 1938, with its own serial number series beginning at MT1 and continuing until 1944 with serial number MT16611. New features included larger grips, heavier barrel (6.625") and rear sight fully adjustable for both windage and elevation. To signify its intended market, a Bullseye Target pattern was placed on side of barrel. That led to its nickname "Bullseye Match Target". Elongated one-piece wraparound walnut grips also picked up a nickname due to their unusual shape. Unfortunately, the so-called "Elephant Ear" grips are

NIB	EXC.	V.G.	GOOD	FAIR	POOR

somewhat fragile and often broken. In addition, many serious target shooters of the day replaced them with custom grips with thumb rest and palm swell. Original grips were set aside and eventually lost or discarded. For those reasons, original grips are often missing and that severely affects value. Values listed assume original one-piece walnut wraparound Elephant Ear grips, no cracks, repairs or modifications and a correct Match Target marked magazine. Values listed for Fair and Poor condition are primarily salvage value and reflect the high value of original "Elephant Ear" grips and Match Target marked magazines for spare parts. Approximately 11,000 produced for civilian market from 1938-1942.

NIB	EXC.	V.G.	GOOD	FAIR	POOR
3600	3400	2200	1500	700	600

Military Woodsman Match Target

After the United States entered World War II at the end of 1941, civilian production at Colt stopped and total effort devoted to U.S. military. Slightly more than 4000 First Series Match Target Woodsman's were delivered on U.S. Government contract from 1942-1944. Most of them, but not all, had serial numbers above MT12000. With possible rare exceptions, they all had U.S. Property or U.S. military markings, standard blue finish, 6.625" barrel and extended length plastic stocks. Plastic stocks are sometimes erroneously called elephant ear stocks. Military plastic stocks are still relatively easy to find and inexpensive. Since they will fit any First Series Colt Woodsman, they are often used as replacement grips on non-military guns. Since military guns had plastic grips, rather than the costly and desirable "Elephant Ear" grips, salvage value in Fair and Poor condition range is less than that for civilian model.

NIB	EXC.	V.G.	GOOD	FAIR	POOR
—	3400	1900	950	550	350

SECOND SERIES

After World War II, Colt entered a lengthy period of clearing up government contracts and retooling for the civilian market. Woodsman line was extensively revised and modernized. Second Series guns began appearing near the end of 1947, although no appreciable numbers were shipped until 1948. Second Series Woodsman had essentially the same action and many of the same internals as First Series guns, but larger, heavier and a longer grip frame. New features included a magazine safety, automatic slide stop when magazine was emptied, fully adjustable rear sight, heavier barrels and a 6" barrel length on Target and Match Target Models, rather than 6.625" as on First Series. Other new features included a push button magazine release just aft of trigger guard like that on large frame Government Model semi-automatics, lanyard ring concealed in butt and provision for attaching a plastic grip adapter to the backstrap, thereby accommodating different sized hands. Elevation adjustment was incorporated into rear sight of all Woodsman models and adjustable front sight replaced with a fixed blade. Serial numbers restarted at 1-S and are intermixed for all three models. Approximately 146,000 of the three models were produced.

In 1950, Colt added Challenger to Second Series pistols, first of the economy models. Internally, Challenger is nearly identical to Woodsman pistols of same era, but externally lacks most of the refinements introduced with Second Series Woodsman. Has no magazine safety, automatic slide stop, adjustable sights, push button magazine release, lanyard ring or grip adapters. Available with either a 4.5" or 6" barrel and had its own serial number series beginning with 1-C. Approximately 77,000 were produced.

Woodsman Target 6" barrel

NIB	EXC.	V.G.	GOOD	FAIR	POOR
2500	1700	1400	800	350	200

Woodsman Sport 4.5" barrel

NIB	EXC.	V.G.	GOOD	FAIR	POOR
1800	1500	1000	800	500	250

Woodsman Match Target 6" barrel

NIB	EXC.	V.G.	GOOD	FAIR	POOR
2500	1450	1250	950	600	350

Woodsman Match Target 4.5" barrel

Introduced in 1950.

NIB	EXC.	V.G.	GOOD	FAIR	POOR
2500	1800	1500	1100	650	400

Challenger 4.5" barrel

NIB	EXC.	V.G.	GOOD	FAIR	POOR
1000	900	600	450	300	200

Challenger 6" barrel

NIB	EXC.	V.G.	GOOD	FAIR	POOR
800	700	475	400	250	200

THIRD SERIES

In 1955, Colt again redesigned the Woodsman line. Most obvious change was in location of magazine release, which was again placed at heel of butt, just like First Series guns. Other changes made over time in markings, grips, sights, and trigger. Sport, Target and Match Target models continued. Challenger was replaced by very similar Huntsman, with either a 4.5" or 6" barrel. In

	NIB	EXC.	V.G.	GOOD	FAIR	POOR

1959, Targetsman was added to line. Targetsman differs from the Huntsman only in having an adjustable rear sight and thumbrest on left grip panel. Available with a 6" barrel only. All Third Series models had black plastic grips until 1960 and checkered walnut grips thereafter. Huntsman has no thumbrest on grips. All other Third Series models have a thumbrest on left grip panel.

It is difficult to impossible to determine how many of each model was produced in Third Series, due to a very complex serial numbering scheme. Approximately 1000 Third Series Sport, Target and Match Target Models were numbered at the end of Second Series serial number range, from 146138-S to 147138-S. Numbers were then restarted at 160001-S, so there are no post-WWII Woodsmans with numbers in the 148xxx-S to 159xxx-S range. Challenger serial numbers, meanwhile, had reached approximately 77143-C prior to Challenger being replaced by Huntsman (note the C suffix, for Challenger). Huntsman initially continued in Challenger serial number series, although numbers skipped forward to 90000-C before restarting. Targetsman, when added to the line early in 1959, joined the Huntsman in using the -C suffix serial numbers, which were by then up to 129300-C. Then in 1969, when Woodsman serial numbers had reached 241811-S and the -C numbers had reached 194040-C, Colt decided to integrate the serial numbers for all versions of the Woodsman, Huntsman and Targetsman and restart numbering again. This time they started with 001001S. That worked fine until numbers reached 099999S and rolled over to 100000S. Numbers used in 1951-52 were then being inadvertently duplicated, with one small exception: earlier guns had a -S suffix while the later ones had only an S (no hyphen before the S). Apparently that was not enough of a distinction to satisfy federal regulations, so when Colt discovered the error after approximately 1,330 had already been numbered, the existing "double headers" were hand stamped with an S prefix, in addition to the S suffix, in order to salvage them. Serial numbers were then restarted yet again, this time at 300000S, and continued to 317736S, when production ended.

Woodsman Target 6" barrel

1050	925	600	450	275	175

Woodsman Sport 4.5" barrel

1100	1000	700	500	300	200

Woodsman Match Target 6" barrel

1250	1150	900	725	500	300

Woodsman Match Target 4.5" barrel

Added to line in 1950.

1600	1400	1050	800	550	350

Huntsman 6.5" barrel

825	700	500	365	225	175

Targetsman 6" barrel, 4.5" (rare)

900	750	525	400	250	200

Colt Junior Pocket Model

This diminutive unit is only 4.5" long overall and weighs 12 oz. Colt did not manufacture this pistol, but rather had it made for them by Astra in Spain. Pistol introduced in 1958 and chambered for .25 ACP. One year later a .22 Short version appeared. Both had external hammers and detachable 6-round magazines. Passage of the 1968 Gun Control Act, made import of a weapon this size illegal, so Colt discontinued its relationship with Astra. Pistol was re-introduced in 1970 as an American-made product and produced for two more years. Production ceased in 1972. Astra also made this pistol and called it the Cub. **NOTE:** .22 Short add 25 percent.

525	375	250	175	125	75

Cadet / Colt .22

Introduced in 1994, this .22-caliber semi-automatic pistol offered with a 4.5" barrel and stainless steel finish. Model was renamed Colt .22 in 1995. Sights are fixed and magazine capacity 11 rounds. Overall length 8.625" and weight approximately 33 oz.

350	300	265	225	125	50

Colt .22 Target

Introduced in 1995, this model features a 6" bull barrel, removable front sight and adjustable rear sight. Black composite monogrip stock. Stainless steel finish. Weight 40.5 oz.

475	325	300	250	150	75

COLT MODERN LONG ARMS

Colteer I-22

Single-shot bolt-action rifle, chambered for .22 LR or .22 Magnum. Plain uncheckered walnut stock, 20" barrel and adjustable sights. Approximately 50,000 manufactured between 1957 and 1966.

350	300	175	125	90	25

NIB	EXC.	V.G.	GOOD	FAIR	POOR

Stagecoach

Semi-automatic saddle ring carbine. Chambered for .22 LR, 16.5" barrel and a 13-shot tubular magazine. Stock is fancy walnut and receiver has stagecoach holdup scene roll-engraved on it. Approximately 25,000 manufactured between 1965 and 1975.

450	400	350	200	150	100

Courier

Model similar to Stagecoach, with pistol-grip stock and beavertail forearm. Manufactured between 1970 and 1975.

425	400	300	200	125	90

Colteer

Less-expensive version of Stagecoach. Features a 19.5" barrel, 15-shot tubular magazine and stock in a plainer grade walnut. No roll engraving. Approximately 25,000 manufactured between 1965 and 1975. Add 50 percent for .22 rimfire magnum.

425	400	300	175	100	90

Colt "57" Bolt-Action Rifle

Rifle manufactured for Colt by Jefferson Mfg. Co of New Haven, Connecticut. Utilizes a Fabrique Nationale Mauser action and checkered American walnut stock, with a Monte Carlo comb. Rifle offered with adjustable sights. Chambered for .243 or .30-06. Also a deluxe version features higher-grade wood. Approximately 5,000 manufactured in 1957. **NOTE:** Deluxe version add 20 percent.

675	550	450	350	300	225

Coltsman Bolt-Action Rifle

Coltsman was manufactured for Colt by Kodiak Arms. Utilizes either a Mauser or Sako action. Rifle offered in .243, .308, .30-06 and .300 Winchester Magnum. Barrel length of 22", 24" in Magnum chambering. Stock is checkered American walnut. Approximately 10,000 manufactured between 1958 and 1966. Deluxe version features a higher-grade skipline-checkered walnut stock and rosewood fore-end tip; called "The Coltsman Custom". **NOTE:** Coltsman Custom add 50 percent.

700	650	550	450	350	250

Coltsman Pump Shotgun

Model manufactured by Jefferson Arms, utilizing an aluminum alloy frame made by Franchi. Chambered for 12-, 16- and 20-gauge. Has a 26" or 28" plain barrel. Approximately 2,000 manufactured between 1961 and 1965.

375	350	300	275	200	150

Semi-Automatic Shotgun

Shotgun manufactured for Colt by the firm of Luigi Franchi in Italy. Features an aluminum alloy receiver and chambered for 12- or 20-gauge. Barrel length is 26", 28", 30" or 32"—either vent rib or plain. Deluxe version "The Custom Auto", features a fancy walnut stock and a hand engraved receiver. Approximately 5,300 manufactured between 1962 and 1966. **NOTE:** Custom Auto add 25 percent.

400	375	325	300	225	175

Double-Barrel Shotgun

During 1961 and 1962, Colt had approximately 50 side-by-side shotguns made for them by a French gun manufacturer. They have the Colt name on breech area of barrels and are in 467000-469000 serial range. There is little information available on this gun and Colt never went past the test-market stage.

—	1200	950	650	500	400

Colt Light Rifle

Introduced in 1999, this bolt-action rifle offered in both long and short action calibers from .243 to .300 Win. Magnum. Fitted with a 24" barrel and adjustable trigger. Stock is black synthetic. Action and barrel are matte black. Long action calibers. Weight about 6 lbs., with short action rifle about 5.4 lbs. Adjustable trigger. No sights.

	700	600	500	400	200

Colt Sauer Bolt-Action Rifle

High quality and unique rifle, manufactured for Colt by J.P. Sauer & Son of Germany. Rifle features a non-rotating bolt that makes Colt Sauer action smoother functioning than most. Has a 24" barrel, skipline-checkered walnut stock, rosewood fore-end tip, pistol-grip cap and recoil pad. There are five basic configurations: Standard Action chambered for .25-06, .270 Winchester and .30-06; Short Action chambered for .22-250, .243 Winchester and .308 Winchester; Magnum Action chambered for .7mm Remington Magnum, .300 Winchester Magnum and .300 Weatherby Magnum; "Grand Alaskan" and "Grand African" heavier versions chambered for .375 Holland &

NIB	EXC.	V.G.	GOOD	FAIR	POOR

Holland Magnum and .458 Winchester Magnum, respectively. Rifles were all discontinued by Colt in 1985.

Colt Sauer Short Action

NOTE: Standard Action add $50. Magnum Action add 20 percent. "Grand Alaskan" add 50 percent. "Grand African" add 75 percent.

2000	1950	1850	1500	800	500

Colt Model 2012 SA308

This precision rifle series is offered in several configurations. The 2012 SA308 is a tactical model in .308 Winchester, with 22" spiral fluted heavy stainless steel match-grade barrel with muzzle-brake. Other fetures are an aluminum stock with pistol-grip, aluminum handguard with 2/3-length Picatinny rail and an ajustable Timney single stage trigger. Weight approximately 13 lbs. The 2012 MT308T model has similar features, with a custom Manners composite stock in Coyote Tan finish and weight of 10.25 lbs. The 2012 LT is available in .308 or 260 Remington, with gray laminate stock, medium heavy 22" barrel and weight of 8.5 lbs. These rifles are a joint effort, with Colt Custom Shop and Cooper Firearms of Montana.

SA308

3250	2750	2200	1750	900	400

MT308T

2800	2350	1850	1400	600	300

LT

2400	1950	1450	1000	500	250

Colt Sauer Drilling

A rather unique firearm. One which many American enthusiasts are not familiar—a 3-barreled gun. Features a side-by-side shotgun in 12-gauge, over a .30-06 or .243 rifle barrel. Name based on German word for three, as this is where the concept was developed. Quite popular in Europe where game preserve style of hunting is prevalent, but has little use in America where our hunting seasons don't often overlap. Drilling has 25" barrels and pop-up sights for rifle barrel and nicely engraved. Discontinued by Colt in 1985.

4500	4000	3000	2000	1500	1100

Colt-Sharps Rifle

Introduced in 1970 as the last word in sporting rifles. Colt-Sharps is a falling-block action that was advertised as a modern Sharps-Borchardt. Undertaking was first-class all the way. Finish is high polish blue, with a deluxe-grade hand-checkered walnut stock and fore-end. Rifle chambered for .17 Remington, .22-250, .243, .25-06, 7mm Remington Magnum, .30-06 and .375 Holland & Holland Magnum; offered cased with accessories. Manufactured between 1970 and 1977. Add 25 percent for .375.

6000	4900	3200	1550	800	500

COLT AR-15 & SPORTER RIFLES

PRICING NOTICE: It is estimated the value of pre-ban AR-15s declined 10-15 percent, since the 1994-2004 Assault Weapons ban has lapsed, but market has once again spiked due to demand. Pricing status of the AR-15 is still volatile.

AR-15 Sporter (Model #6000)

Semi-automatic rifle firing from a closed bolt. Introduced into Colt product line in 1964. Similar in appearance and function to military version, the M-16. Chambered for .223 cartridge. Fitted with a standard 20" barrel, no forward assist, no case deflector, but with a bayonet lug. Weighs about 7.5 lbs. Dropped from production in 1985.

2150	1800	1600	1500	600	400

AR-15 Sporter w/Collapsible Stock (Model #6001)

Same as above, fitted with a 16" barrel and folding stock. Weighs approximately 5.8 lbs. Introduced in 1978 and discontinued in 1985.

2750	2450	2100	1800	600	400

AR-15 Carbine (Model #6420)

Introduced in 1985, model has a 16" standard weight barrel. All other features are same as previous discontinued AR-15 models. Version dropped from Colt product line in 1987.

2200	1900	1700	1600	600	400

AR-15 9mm Carbine (Model #6450)

Same as above, chambered for 9mm cartridge. Weighs 6.3 lbs.

2250	1950	1750	1650	700	400

NIB	EXC.	V.G.	GOOD	FAIR	POOR

AR-15A2 Sporter II (Model #6500)

Introduced in 1984, this was an updated version, with a heavier barrel and forward assist. AR sight still utilized. Weighs approximately 7.8 lbs.

NIB	EXC.	V.G.	GOOD	FAIR	POOR
1850	1500	1300	1050	550	400

AR-15A2 Government Model Carbine (Model #6520)

Added to Colt line in 1988, this 16" standard barrel carbine featured for the first time a case deflector and improved A2 rear sight. Model fitted with a 4-position telescoping buttstock. Weighs about 5.8 lbs.

NIB	EXC.	V.G.	GOOD	FAIR	POOR
2300	2000	1750	1650	700	400

AR-15A2 Government Model (Model #6550)

Model introduced in 1988 is the rifle equivalent to the Carbine. Features a 20" A2 barrel, forward assist, case deflector, but still retains the bayonet lug. Weighs about 7.5 lbs. Discontinued in 1990. USMC model.

NIB	EXC.	V.G.	GOOD	FAIR	POOR
2300	2000	1750	1650	700	400

AR-15A2 H-Bar (Model #6600)

Introduced in 1986, this version features a special 20" heavy barrel. All other features are the same as A2 series of AR15s. Discontinued in 1991. Weighs about 8 lbs.

NIB	EXC.	V.G.	GOOD	FAIR	POOR
1950	1750	1500	950	700	500

AR-15A2 Delta H-Bar (Model #6600DH)

Same as above, fitted with a 3x9 scope and detachable cheekpiece. Dropped from the Colt line in 1990. Weighs about 10 lbs.

NIB	EXC.	V.G.	GOOD	FAIR	POOR
2350	2100	1800	1650	850	600

Sporter Lightweight Rifle

Lightweight model has a 16" barrel and finished in matte black. Available in either .223 Rem. caliber (Model #6530) that weighs 6.7 lbs., (Model #6430) 9mm caliber weighing 7.1 lbs. or (Model #6830) 7.65x39mm that weighs 7.3 lbs. The .223 furnished with two five-round box magazines as is the 9mm and 7.65x39mm. Cleaning kit and sling are also supplied with each new rifle. Buttstock and pistol-grip are made of durable nylon and handguard is reinforced fiberglass and aluminum lined. Rear sight is adjustable for windage and elevation. Newer models are referred to simply as Sporters. Not fitted with a bayonet lug and receiver block. Has different size pins. **NOTE:** Model 6830 will bring about $25 less than these prices.

NIB	EXC.	V.G.	GOOD	FAIR	POOR
1500	1300	1000	600	400	300

Sporter Target Model Rifle (Model #6551)

This 1991 model is a full size version of the Lightweight Rifle. Target Rifle weighs 7.5 lbs. and has a 20" barrel. Offered in .223 Rem. caliber only, with target sights adjustable to 800 meters. New rifles are furnished with two 5-round box magazines, sling and cleaning kit. **NOTE:** For post-9/94 guns deduct 30 percent.

NIB	EXC.	V.G.	GOOD	FAIR	POOR
1700	1400	1100	650	400	300

Sporter Match H-Bar (Model #6601)

This 1991 variation of the AR-15 is similar to the Target Model, but has a 20" heavy barrel chambered for the .223-caliber. Model weighs 8 lbs. and has target type sights adjustable out to 800 meters. Supplied with two 5-round box magazines, sling and cleaning kit.

NIB	EXC.	V.G.	GOOD	FAIR	POOR
1700	1400	1100	650	400	300

AR-15 (XM16E1)

Rifle made upon request for foreign contracts. Very rare. Proceed with caution. Variation will command a premium price over standard AR-15 rifle. Secure an appraisal before purchase.

Sporter Match Delta H-Bar (Model #6601 DH)

Same as above, but supplied with a 3x9 scope. Weighs about 10 lbs. Discontinued in 1992.

NIB	EXC.	V.G.	GOOD	FAIR	POOR
2300	1900	1600	1300	600	400

Match Target H-BAR Compensated (Model #6601C)

Same as regular Sporter H-BAR, with addition of a compensator.

NIB	EXC.	V.G.	GOOD	FAIR	POOR
2200	1900	1600	1300	600	400

Colt Match Target M4

Similar to above, with carbine-length barrel.

NIB	EXC.	V.G.	GOOD	FAIR	POOR
2200	1900	1600	1300	600	400

	NIB	EXC.	V.G.	GOOD	FAIR	POOR

Sporter Competition H-Bar (Model #6700)

Introduced in 1992, Competition H-Bar is available in .223-caliber, with a 20" heavy barrel counterbored for accuracy. Carry handle is detachable, with target sights. With the carry handle removed the upper receiver is dovetailed and grooved for Weaver-style scope rings. Model weighs approximately 8.5 lbs. New rifles are furnished with two 5-round box magazines, sling and cleaning kit. **NOTE:** For post-9/94 guns deduct 35 percent.

1800	1500	1300	1000	500	350

Sporter Competition H-Bar Select w/scope (Model #6700CH)

This variation is identical to Sporter Competition, with the addition of factory mounted scope. Rifle has also been selected for accuracy. Comes complete with a 3-9X rubber armored variable scope, scope mount, carry handle with iron sights and nylon carrying case.

2000	1800	1400	1000	600	400

Match Target Competition H-BAR Compensated (Model #6700C)

Same as Match Target, with compensator.

2000	1800	1400	1000	600	400

AR-15 Carbine Flat-top Heavyweight/Match Target Competition (Model #6731)

This variation in Sporter series features a heavyweight 16" barrel, with flat-top receiver chambered for the .223 cartridge. Equipped with a fixed buttstock. Weight about 7.1 lbs.

1200	1000	800	600	400	300

AR-15 Tactical Carbine (Model #6721)

Version similar to above model, with exception of buttstock which is telescoping and adjusts to 4 positions. Chambered for the .223 cartridge. Weight about 7 lbs. Majority of these guns were for law enforcement only. Only 134 rifles are pre-ban. **NOTE:** 100 percent premium if serial number is below BD000135.

1400	1200	1000	800	600	400

Sporter H-Bar Elite/Accurized Rifle (Model #6724)

Variation introduced in 1996. Features a free floating 24" stainless steel match barrel, with an 11 degree target crown and special Teflon coated trigger group. Handguard is all-aluminum, with twin swivel studs. Weight approximately 9.26 lbs.

1500	1250	900	550	400	300

Colt SP901

New hunting type modular rifle, chambered in .308 Winchester. Interchangeable upper receiver in .223 Remington. Fully floating 16" chrome lined barrel. One-piece monolithic receiver ready for optical sights. Adjustable front and rear sights. Ambidextrous magazine release, bolt catch and safety.

1700	1600	—	—	—	—

Colt SP6920

Sporter version of classic Colt M4 carbine. Chambered for .223 Remington. Chrome-lined bore with 6 grooves, 1" to 7" right hand twist. Four-position collapsible stock. Flattop receiver with removable carry handle. Matte black finish. Introduced in 2011.

975	850	725	600	400	200

Colt SP6940

Same gun as SP6920, with one-piece upper receiver. Fully floated barrel, which allows easier mounting of optical, laser or light accessories. No carry handle. Matte black finish. Introduced in 2011.

1275	1075	900	700	500	300

COLT CUSTOM SHOP

Colt Custom Shop offers various customizing, upgrading and engraving services on current catalog models For information, contact Colt at www.colt.com or 800-962-2658. Shown here is a sampling of previously customized models.

Special Combat Government Model (Competition)

Competition ready model. Chambered for the .45 ACP. Fitted with a skeletonized trigger, upswept grip safety, custom tuned action, polished feed ramp, throated barrel, flared ejection port, cutout commander hammer, two 8-round magazines, hard chromed slide and receiver, extended thumb safety, Bomar rear sight, Clark dovetail front sight and flared magazine funnel. Pistol has been accurized and shipped with a certified target.

1750	1200	800	500	300	200

	NIB	EXC.	V.G.	GOOD	FAIR	POOR

Special Combat Government Model (Carry)

Model has all the same features as competition model, except it has a royal blue finish, special bar-dot night sights, ambidextrous safety. Also been accurized and shipped with a certified target.

	1550	1000	700	400	300	200

Gold Cup Commander

Chambered for .45 ACP. Features: heavy-duty adjustable target sights, beveled magazine well, serrated front strap, checkered mainspring housing, wide grip safety, Palo Alto wood grips and stainless steel or royal blue finish.

	1400	875	650	600	500	375

U.S. Shooting Team Gold Cup

Limited edition Gold Cup .45 ACP, with special blue, sights, grips. U.S. Shooting Team logo rolled on the slide. Limited to 500 pistols and built for Lew Horton..

	1400	875	650	600	500	375

Gold Cup Trophy

Introduced in 1997, model features .45 ACP 5" barrel 1911, with choice of stainless steel or blue finish. Several custom features such as skeletonized hammer and trigger. Adjustable rear sight and wraparound rubber grips are standard. Pistol has been accurized and shipped with a target. Magazine capacity 7 or 8 rounds. Weight approximately 39 oz.

	1000	900	675	625	525	400

McCormick Commander

Limited edition pistol made for Lew Horton in 1995. Limited to 100 pistols. Has many special features. Slide is engraved and there is a gold rampant colt on the slide.

	1600	1000	750	600	500	375

McCormick Officer

Lew Horton exclusive pistol, has factory installed McCormick parts and hard chrome finish. Total of 500 guns built in 1995.

	1500	875	650	600	500	375

McCormick Factory Racer

Limited edition pistol from Lew Horton. Full size government model, with hard chrome finish, special barrel, trigger safety and other custom features. Each gun rollmarked "McCormick Factory Racer" on the slide. Special serial numbers from MFR001 to MFR500.

	1300	775	650	600	500	375

Colt Classic .45 Special Edition

Lew Horton model limited to 400 pistols. Features a royal blue polish with special "Classic .45" gold etched on the slide. Pearlite grips.

	1300	775	650	600	500	375

125th Anniversary Edition Peacemaker

Introduced in 1998, model features a V-shaped rear sight, with two-line patent date. Barrel is 4.75" and chambered for .45 Colt cartridge. Cylinder is second generation type and hammer is knurled. Frame and hammer are case colored, with blue barrel. Grips are two piece walnut, with oil finish. Special serial number range SA74000 to SA75999.

	1950	1350	950	600	500	375

Custom Anaconda

Custom-tuned action, Magnaported barrel, with Elliason rear sight. Contoured trigger is polished smooth. Comes with Pachmayr grips and brushed stainless steel finish.

	1950	1275	800	600	300	200

Ultimate Python

Custom tuned action, with both Elliason and Accro sighting systems. Both rubber and walnut grips are included. Bright stainless steel or royal blue finish. Available only with 6" barrel.

	1800	1275	800	600	300	200

Anaconda Hunter

Comes with a Leupold 2X scope, heavy-duty mounts, cleaning accessories, both walnut and rubber grips, in a hard case. Furnished only with an 8" barrel.

	1800	1275	800	600	300	200

	NIB	EXC.	V.G.	GOOD	FAIR	POOR

Bobbed Detective Special

First offered in 1994, this model features bobbed hammer, front sight with night sight and honed action. Available in either chrome or blue finish.

	775	600	450	300	150	100

Limited Class .45 ACP

1911 auto. Designed for tactical competition. Supplied with a parkerized matte finish, lightweight composite trigger, extended ambidextrous safety, upswept grip safety, beveled magazine well. Accurized and shipped with a signed target. Introduced in 1993.

	1450	1050	650	450	300	200

Compensated Model .45 ACP

Competition pistol has a hard chrome receiver, bumper on magazine, extended ambidextrous safety, blue slide with full profile BAT compensator, Bomar rear sight and flared funnel magazine well. Introduced in 1993.

	1450	1050	650	450	300	200

Compensated .45 ACP Commander

Introduced in 1998 and limited to 500 pistols. Model fitted with a full-length guide rod, extended beavertail safety, skeletonized hammer, Novak-style sights and checkered walnut double-diamond grips.

	1350	975	575	400	300	200

Nite Lite .380

Supplied with a bar-dot night sight, special foil mark on barrel slide, Teflon-coated alloy receiver, stainless slide, high-capacity grip-extension magazine and standard magazine. Shipped with a soft carrying case. Introduced in 1993.

	1350	975	575	400	300	200

Standard Tactical Model

Built for 20th Anniversary of IPSC competition shooting in 1996. Built on Colt Government model, with round top slide and chambered for .45 ACP. Many special features and serial numbers. Limited to 1,500 pistols.

	1450	875	600	450	300	200

Superior Tactical Model

Same as above. Built on an enhanced frame, with many custom features. Special serial numbers limited to 500 pistols.

	1550	975	700	550	400	200

Deluxe Tactical Model

Same as above, with added features. Limited to 250 pistols.

	1650	1075	800	650	500	300

COLT REPRODUCTION PERCUSSION REVOLVERS

Revolvers listed were manufactured in a variety of styles (cylinder form, stainless steel, etc.) that affect prices. Factory engraved examples command a considerable premium over the prices listed. Imported from Italy.

Walker

Made from 1979 to 1981; serial numbers 1200-4120 and 32256 to 32500.

	950	750	500	—	—	—

Walker Heritage Model

	1000	—	—	—	—	—

First Model Dragoon

Made from 1980 to 1982; serial numbers 24100-34500.

	595	400	300	—	—	—

Second Model Dragoon

Made from 1980 to 1982; serial numbers as above.

	595	400	300	—	—	—

Third Model Dragoon

Made from 1980 to 1982; serial numbers as above.

	595	400	300	—	—	—

	NIB	EXC.	V.G.	GOOD	FAIR	POOR

Model 1848 Pocket Pistol
Made in 1981; serial numbers 16000-17851.

NIB	EXC.	V.G.	GOOD	FAIR	POOR
600	425	325	—	—	—

Model 1851 Navy Revolver
Made from 1971 to 1978; serial numbers 4201-25100 and 24900-29150.

NIB	EXC.	V.G.	GOOD	FAIR	POOR
595	400	300	—	—	—

Model 1860 Army Revolver
Made from 1978 to 1982; serial numbers 201000-212835.

NIB	EXC.	V.G.	GOOD	FAIR	POOR
595	400	300	—	—	—

Model 1861 Navy Revolver
Made during 1980 and 1981; serial numbers 40000-43165.

NIB	EXC.	V.G.	GOOD	FAIR	POOR
595	400	300	—	—	—

Model 1862 Pocket Pistol
Made from 1979 to 1984; serial numbers 8000-58850.

NIB	EXC.	V.G.	GOOD	FAIR	POOR
595	400	300	—	—	—

Model 1862 Police Revolver
Made from 1979 to 1984; serial numbers in above range.

NIB	EXC.	V.G.	GOOD	FAIR	POOR
595	400	300	—	—	—

COLT BLACKPOWDER ARMS
Brooklyn, New York

These blackpowder revolvers and rifles were made under license from Colt. Imported from Italy. No longer in business.

1842 Paterson Colt No. 5 Holster Model
Model is a copy of No. 5 Holster model and chambered for the .36-caliber ball. Fitted with a 7.5" octagon barrel. Hand engraved. Special order revolver.

NIB	EXC.	V.G.	GOOD	FAIR	POOR
1900	1200	900	600	450	200

Walker
This .44-caliber large-frame revolver is fitted with a 9" barrel.

NIB	EXC.	V.G.	GOOD	FAIR	POOR
975	600	350	300	200	150

Walker 150th Anniversary Model
Marked "A Company No. 1" in gold. Introduced 1997.

NIB	EXC.	V.G.	GOOD	FAIR	POOR
975	600	350	300	200	150

Whitneyville Hartford Dragoon
Similar in appearance to Walker colt. Revolver fitted with a 7.5" barrel and silver plated iron backstrap and trigger guard. Limited edition, with a total of 2,400 guns built. Serial numbers between 1100 through 1340.

NIB	EXC.	V.G.	GOOD	FAIR	POOR
1075	700	450	32	225	200

Marine Dragoon
Special limited edition presentation grade in honor of U.S. Marine Corps.

NIB	EXC.	V.G.	GOOD	FAIR	POOR
1100	725	450	32	225	200

3rd Model Dragoon
Another large-frame revolver, with 7.5" barrel, brass backstrap, 3-screw frame and unfluted cylinder.

NIB	EXC.	V.G.	GOOD	FAIR	POOR
675	500	350	300	200	150

Steel Backstrap

NIB	EXC.	V.G.	GOOD	FAIR	POOR
600	425	375	325	200	150

Fluted Cylinder

NIB	EXC.	V.G.	GOOD	FAIR	POOR
610	435	375	325	200	150

Cochise Dragoon
Commemorative issue Third Model, with gold inlay frame and barrel with special grips.

NIB	EXC.	V.G.	GOOD	FAIR	POOR
975	600	350	300	200	150

	NIB	EXC.	V.G.	GOOD	FAIR	POOR

Colt 1849 Model Pocket

Small-frame revolver chambered in .31-caliber, with 4" barrel. Fitted with one-piece walnut grips.

	575	475	325	275	200	150

Colt 1851 Model Navy

Medium-frame revolver chambered in .36-caliber, with 7.5" barrel. Walnut grips and case color frame.

	635	575	400	300	200	125

Dual Cylinder

	675	595	400	300	200	125

Colt Model 1860 Army

Model chambered in .44-caliber, with roll engraved cylinder and one piece walnut grips. Barrel length is 8".

	675	575	400	300	200	125

Dual Cylinder

	700	600	450	350	225	150

Colt 1860 Officer's Model

Deluxe version of standard 1860. Special blued finish and gold crossed sabres. This is a 4-screw frame, with 8" barrel and 6-shot rebated cylinder.

	675	575	450	375	250	150

Colt Model 1860 Army Gold U.S. Cavalry

Features a gold engraved cylinder and gold barrel bands.

	650	575	450	375	250	150

Stainless Steel

	575	400	350	300	200	150

Colt 1860 Heirloom Edition

Elaborately engraved revolver done in Tiffany-style. Fitted with Tiffany-style grips.

	4100	3000	2175	1400	850	450

Colt Model 1861 Navy

This .36-caliber revolver features a 7.5" barrel, with engraved cylinder, case colored frame and one piece walnut grips.

	700	550	350	300	200	150

General Custer

Same as above, with engraved frame and cylinder.

	975	850	700	500	300	200

Colt Model 1862 Pocket Navy

Small-frame revolver. Fitted with a round engraved cylinder, 5" octagon barrel and hinged loading lever. Chambered for .36-caliber.

	550	475	325	275	200	150

Colt Model 1862 Trapper-Pocket Police

Small-frame revolver. Fitted with a 3.5" barrel, silver backstrap and trigger guard. Cylinder is semi-fluted and chambered in .36-caliber.

	600	475	325	275	200	150

Colt 1861 Musket

Civil War musket chambered in .58-caliber. Lockplate, hammer, buttplate, three barrel bands and 40" barrel are finished bright. Stock is a one-piece oil-finish affair. Bayonet and accessories are extra.

	800	650	500	325	275	150

Artillery Model

Same as above, fitted with a 31.5" barrel.

	800	650	500	325	275	150

Presentation 1 of 1000

Limited to 1,000 guns. Special finished with a high polish and Colt's signature in gold on trigger guard. Sold with special custom wooden case.

	1650	1300	750	600	450	300

	NIB	EXC.	V.G.	GOOD	FAIR	POOR

Presentation 1 of 1000 - Artillery Model

Same as above, with 31.5" barrel.

	1650	1300	750	600	450	300

Colt Gamemaster .50

Introduced in 1997, this rifle is similar to above in general outline and in .50-caliber. Fitted with a 31.5" barrel and weighs about 13 lbs.

	800	650	475	300	225	125

COLUMBIA ARMORY

Columbia, Tennessee

A trade name applied to a variety of solid frame cartridge revolvers made by John T. Smith Company of Rock Falls, Connecticut. They were marked "SAFETY HAMMERLESS REVOLVER". This model was made under several trade names.

	—	—	225	110	75	50

COLUMBUS F. A. MFG. CO.

Columbus, Georgia

Columbus Revolver

A .36-caliber double-action percussion revolver, with a 6-shot unfluted cylinder and a 7.5" octagonal barrel. Similar in appearance to the 1851 Colt Navy. The pistol is browned steel, with brass gripstraps and walnut grips. Barrel is marked "Columbus Fire Arms Manuf. Co/Columbus Ga.". 100 revolvers were manufactured in 1863 and 1864.

	—	—	115000	55000	35000	12500

COMANCHE

Buenos Aires, Argentina
See—Firestorm

Comanche I

Single-/double-action revolver chambered in .22 LR. Nine-shot cylinder, 6" barrel, adjustable sights, blued or stainless steel construction with rubber grips.

	225	150	100	65	35	15

Comanche II

Similar to above in .38 Special, with 2", 3" or 4" barrel.

	225	150	100	65	35	15

Comanche III

Similar to above in .357 Magnum and additional 6" barrel option.

	250	150	100	65	35	15

Super Comanche

Single-shot break-action pistol chambered in .410/.45 Colt. Matte black finish, rubber grips.

	195	150	125	85	50	25

COMMANDO ARMS

Knoxville, Tennessee

Formerly known as Volunteer Enterprises. The name change took place in 1978.

Mark III Carbine

A .45 ACP caliber semi-automatic rifle, with a 16.5" barrel, peep rear sight and vertical fore-grip. Manufactured between 1969 and 1976.

	675	550	375	300	225	150

Mark 9 Carbine

As above in 9mm caliber.

	675	550	375	300	225	150

Mark .45

The new designation for the Mark III after the company changed its name.

	675	550	375	300	225	150

	NIB	EXC.	V.G.	GOOD	FAIR	POOR

COMPETITOR CORP.
New Ipswich, New Hampshire

Competitor Single-Shot

This single-shot pistol is chambered for calibers from .22 LR to .50 Action Express. Choice of barrels lengths from 10.5", 14" and 16". Ramp front sight. Adjustable single stage trigger. Interchangeable barrels. Matte blue finish. Weight approximately 59 oz. depending on barrel length. Introduced in 1988.

NIB	EXC.	V.G.	GOOD	FAIR	POOR
465	325	275	225	175	125

CONNECTICUT ARMS CO.
Norfolk, Connecticut

Pocket Revolver

A .28-caliber spur trigger revolver, with 3" octagonal barrel, 6-shot unfluted cylinder, using a cup-primed cartridge and loads from the front of the cylinder. There is a hinged hook on the side of the frame under the cylinder that acts as the extractor. Silver-plated brass blued, with walnut grips. The barrel is marked "Conn. Arms Co. Norfolk, Conn." Approximately 2,700 manufactured in the 1860s.

NIB	EXC.	V.G.	GOOD	FAIR	POOR
—	—	950	750	300	100

CONNECTICUT SHOTGUN MANUFACTURING COMPANY
New Britain, Connecticut

RBL Side-By-Side Shotgun

Round-action SXS shotguns made in the USA. Chambered in 12-, 16-, 20-, 28-gauge and .410 bore with scaled frames. Barrel lengths 26", 28", 30" and 32", with five TruLock choke tubes. Deluxe fancy-grade walnut buttstock and fore-end, Quick Change recoil pad in two lengths. Various dimensions and options available depending on gauge. Values shown are for 12-gauge. **NOTE:** Add 20 percent for 20-gauge; 30 percent for 28-gauge; 75 percent for .410 bore.

NIB	EXC.	V.G.	GOOD	FAIR	POOR
4000	2950	2000	1275	800	400

A-10 American

Sidelock design in 12-, 20- or 28-gauge with XX grade walnut stock and light scroll engraving. Offered in standard barrel lengths from 26" to 32". Options include higher-grade wood and engraving. Prices shown are for standard model. Introduced in 2010

NIB	EXC.	V.G.	GOOD	FAIR	POOR
7500	6000	4500	3500	—	

Model 21

This is a faithful rendition of the famous Winchester side-by-side shotgun that was in production from 1931 to 1959. On custom-order from 1960 to 1993. Made in all gauges and standard barrel lengths, with many options. Each gun is custom made to order. Introduced in 2002. Prices are for standard 12-, 16- and 20-gauge models. **NOTE:** Add $3000 for 28-gauge or .410 bore, plus $10,000 if made on optional small frame.

NIB	EXC.	V.G.	GOOD	FAIR	POOR
15000	12000	9500	7000	3500	—

Model 21 Grand American

As above with high-grade gold-inlayed engraving, AAA-grade walnut stock, with elaborate checkering and carving patterns. Comes with two sets of barrels. **NOTE:** Add $3000 for 28-gauge or .410 bore, plus $10,000 if made on optional small frame.

NIB	EXC.	V.G.	GOOD	FAIR	POOR
25000	20000	17500	15000	8000	—

Model 21 Over/Under

An over/under model patterned after classic Winchester side-by-side. Made on the same machining and tooling, and with the same manufacturing techniques as the SxS model, resulting in virtually the same balance, feel and appearance. Features include automatic ejectors, single-selective trigger, American walnut stock with straight- or pistol-grip. Made only in 20-gauge, with 26", 28", 30" or 32" barrels that are steel-shot compatible and comes with five choke tubes. Wood upgrades are available at prices up to $900.

NIB	EXC.	V.G.	GOOD	FAIR	POOR
3400	2900	2450	1900	1350	750

Model 21 Side-By-Side Rifle

In .22 Long Rifle caliber, this very unique double rifle is built on a frame even smaller than the .410 frame. Each gun is custom made, with many upgrades and engraving options available. The higher grades have a MRSP from $30,000 to $34,000. **NOTE:** A few custom made-to-order models in various centerfire calibers have been built in the past, with very limited production. Values are estimated to be approximately 50 percent higher than the rimfire model.

NIB	EXC.	V.G.	GOOD	FAIR	POOR
22500	18000	14000	—	—	—

NIB	EXC.	V.G.	GOOD	FAIR	POOR

A.H. Fox

Conn. Shotgun Co. also makes high-grade side-by-side shotguns, based on the classic A.H. Fox models of the early 20th century. These are CE and DE grades, with many available options and upgrades. Prices shown are for the base CE model.

| 16500 | 12000 | 9500 | — | — | — |

CONNECTICUT VALLEY ARMS CO.
Norcross, Georgia

RIFLES

Express Rifle

A .50-caliber double-barrel percussion rifle, with 28" barrels. Blued, with a walnut stock. **NOTE:** Deluxe version add 25 percent.

| 625 | 475 | 425 | 375 | 325 | 200 |

Over/Under Rifle

A .50-caliber double-barrel over/under rifle, with 26" barrels. Blued, with a walnut stock.

| 600 | 475 | 425 | 375 | 325 | 200 |

Hawken Rifle

A .50-caliber with a 28" octagonal barrel, double set triggers and a walnut stock.

| 450 | 325 | 275 | 225 | 150 | 100 |

Presentation Grade Hawken

As above, with an engraved lock, patchbox and finely figured stock.

| 550 | 425 | 375 | 325 | 275 | 200 |

Pennsylvania Long Rifle

A .50-caliber flintlock rifle, with a 40" octagonal barrel, double set triggers and a walnut stock.

| 475 | 400 | 350 | 300 | 250 | 175 |

Kentucky Rifle

A .45-caliber percussion rifle, with a 33.5" octagonal barrel and walnut stock.

| 275 | 225 | 175 | 150 | 100 | 75 |

Mountain Rifle

A .50- or .54-caliber percussion half-stock rifle.

| 300 | 225 | 175 | 125 | 100 | 75 |

Blazer Rifle

A .50-caliber percussion rifle, with a 28" octagonal barrel and walnut stock.

| 150 | 125 | 100 | 85 | 65 | 45 |

Apollo Shadow SS

Introduced in 1993, this rifle features an in-line stainless steel bolt spring-action. A 24" blued round barrel with octagonal one piece receiver drilled and tapped. Stock is black hardwood-textured with Dura Grip. Pistol-grip and recoil pad. Offered in either .50- or .54-caliber. Weighs about 9 lbs.

| 175 | 150 | 125 | 100 | 75 | 50 |

Apollo Classic

Similar to the above Apollo Model, with dark brown stained laminated hardwood stock. Pistol-grip, raised comb and recoil pad. Weighs about 8.5 lbs.

| 215 | 175 | 150 | 125 | 100 | 75 |

Apollo Carbelite

Offered in .50-caliber, with percussion bolt and 27" blued round taper barrel. Octagonal receiver drilled and tapped. Fitted with Carbelite composite stock with Monte Carlo and cheekpiece with pistol-grip. Weighs approximately 7.5 lbs.

| 280 | 225 | 175 | 150 | 100 | 75 |

Apollo Starfire

Chambered for the .50-caliber bullet, this rifle is an in-line type, with 24" stainless steel barrel. Synthetic stock, checkered pistol-grip, raised comb and cheekpiece. Weight about 6.5 lbs.

| 225 | 175 | 150 | 125 | 100 | 75 |

	NIB	EXC.	V.G.	GOOD	FAIR	POOR

Apollo Eclipse Rifle

Offered in either .50- or .54-caliber, with 24" round barrel and blued steel receiver. Synthetic stock, with checkered pistol, raised comb and cheekpiece. Approximate weight 6.5 lbs.

	NIB	EXC.	V.G.	GOOD	FAIR	POOR
	175	150	125	100	85	65

Apollo Dominator

Fitted with a synthetic thumbhole stock and a 24" round barrel, this rifle is chambered for the .50-caliber bullet. Introduced in 1996. Weight approximately 8.5 lbs.

	NIB	EXC.	V.G.	GOOD	FAIR	POOR
	300	225	175	150	100	75

Apollo Brown Bear

This .50-caliber rifle is fitted with a hardwood stock, pistol-grip, raised comb and cheekpiece. Barrel is round and 24". Introduced in 1996. Weight about 6.5 lbs.

	NIB	EXC.	V.G.	GOOD	FAIR	POOR
	200	175	150	125	100	75

Frontier Carbine

Fitted with a 24" blued barrel, this rifle is offered in .50-caliber percussion or flintlock. Case hardened lock, with hardwood stock. Weighs about 6.75 lbs.

	NIB	EXC.	V.G.	GOOD	FAIR	POOR
	150	125	100	85	75	50

Plainsman Rifle

This .50-caliber percussion rifle has a 26" octagonal barrel, with case hardened lock and hardwood stock. Weight about 6.5 lbs.

	NIB	EXC.	V.G.	GOOD	FAIR	POOR
	130	115	100	85	75	50

Panther Carbine

This percussion rifle is available in either .50- or .54-caliber. Fitted with a 24" blued octagonal barrel and Hawken-style case hardened lock. Stock is textured black Dura Grip over hardwood, with Monte Carlo comb, cheekpiece and pistol-grip. Weight approximately 7.5 lbs.

	NIB	EXC.	V.G.	GOOD	FAIR	POOR
	150	125	100	85	75	50

Bushwacker Rifle

This .50-caliber percussion rifle is fitted with a 26" octagonal barrel. Case hardened engraved lock, brown stained hardwood stock and rounded nose. Weight about 7.5 lbs.

	NIB	EXC.	V.G.	GOOD	FAIR	POOR
	135	115	100	85	75	50

Trophy Carbine

This carbine is fitted with a 24" half-round/half-octagon barrel and Hawken-style lock. Stock is walnut with Monte Carlo comb, cheekpiece and pistol-grip. Offered in .50- or .54-caliber percussion and weighs about 6.75 lbs.

	NIB	EXC.	V.G.	GOOD	FAIR	POOR
	215	175	150	125	100	75

Varmint Rifle

This is a lightweight percussion rifle in .32-caliber, with 24" octagon barrel and case-colored lock. Stock is hardwood. Weighs about 6.75 lbs.

	NIB	EXC.	V.G.	GOOD	FAIR	POOR
	175	150	125	100	85	75

Woodsman Rifle LS

Introduced in 1994, this rifle features a 26" blued octagon barrel, with dark brown stained laminated hardwood stock. Offered in .50- or .54-caliber percussion. Weighs about 6.5 lbs.

	NIB	EXC.	V.G.	GOOD	FAIR	POOR
	135	115	100	85	75	50

Frontier Hunter Carbine

Offered in either .50- or .54-caliber, this percussion rifle is fitted with a 24" blued octagon barrel. Case hardened 45° offset hammer. Stock is dark stained laminated hardwood. Weighs about 7.5 lbs.

	NIB	EXC.	V.G.	GOOD	FAIR	POOR
	170	150	125	100	75	50

Grey Wolf Rifle

Offered in either .50- or .54-caliber percussion, this rifle is fitted with a 26" matte blue octagon barrel. Case hardened engraved lock. Stock is matte gray composite, with raised comb, checkered pistol-grip and buttplate. Weighs about 6.5 lbs.

	NIB	EXC.	V.G.	GOOD	FAIR	POOR
	160	125	100	85	75	50

Lone Grey Wolf Rifle

Introduced in 1994, this .50-caliber percussion rifle features a 26" matte blued octagon barrel. The trigger guard is oversized. The composite stock is black and has a raised comb, checkered

	NIB	EXC.	V.G.	GOOD	FAIR	POOR

pistol-grip and recoil pad. Weighs about 6.5 lbs.

	185	150	125	100	75	50

Timber Wolf Rifle

Introduced in 1994, this model is similar to the above model, but furnished with Realtree composite stock. Raised comb, checkered pistol-grip and buttplate. Weighs about 6.5 lbs.

	185	165	140	100	75	50

Tracker Carbine LS

Introduced in 1994, this carbine is fitted with a 21" blued half-round/half-octagon barrel. A Hawken-style lock. Stock is laminated dark brown with matte finish and straight-grip. Chambered for .50-caliber percussion. Weighs about 6.5 lbs.

	185	165	140	100	75	50

Stag Horn

Introduced in 1996, this in-line rifle is chambered for the .50- or .54-caliber bullet. The round barrel is 24" with blued finish. Stock is synthetic, with checkered pistol-grip, raised comb and cheekpiece. Weight about 6.5 lbs.

	175	150	125	100	85	65

Electra

A .50-caliber inline muzzleloader that uses electronic-arc ignition rather than caps or primers. Powered by common 9v battery. Finishes include stainless/camo, stainless/black composite and blued/black composite. Introduced in 2007. Price given is for stainless/camo version.

	600	500	400	300	200	100

Accura MR

Break-action .50-caliber in-line ignition muzzleloading rifle, with weather guard finish, adjustable trigger, quick release breech plug, 416 stainless steel barrel and camo polymer stock. Barrel length is 25", weight 6.2 lbs. Introduced 2012.

	525	450	400	350	300	250

Optima V2

Break-action .50-caliber in-line ignition muzzleloading rifle, with black or Realtree camo finish, quick release breech plug, 416 stainless steel barrel and polymer standard or thumb-hole stock. Barrel length is 26", weight 6.7 lbs. **NOTE:** Add $25.00 for thumbhole stock.

	360	300	275	235	200	185

SHOTGUNS

Brittany 11 Shotgun

A .410 bore double-barrel percussion shotgun, with 24" barrels, double triggers and walnut stock.

	425	350	250	150	125	75

Trapper Shotgun - #1

A 12-gauge percussion single-barrel shotgun, with 28" barrel threaded for choke tubes and walnut stock.

	275	250	225	175	150	100

Classic Turkey Double-Barrel Shotgun

A 12-gauge percussion breech-loading shotgun, with 28" barrel. Checkered stock is European walnut with straight-grip. Weighs about 9 lbs.

	495	375	275	200	175	100

Trapper Shotgun #2

A single-barrel 12-gauge shotgun, with 28" barrel. Stock is straight-grip hardwood with checkering. Supplied with three interchangeable chokes. Weighs about 6 lbs.

	295	250	200	150	100	75

PISTOLS

Made by Pedersoli, Uberti and other Italian makers.

Siber

A .45-caliber percussion pistol patterned after the Swiss Siber.

	450	325	275	225	150	100

	NIB	EXC.	V.G.	GOOD	FAIR	POOR

Kentucky

A .45-caliber single-shot percussion pistol, with 10" barrel and walnut stock.

NIB	EXC.	V.G.	GOOD	FAIR	POOR
140	125	100	80	60	40

Philadelphia Derringer

A .45-caliber single-shot percussion pistol, with 3.25" barrel and walnut stock.

NIB	EXC.	V.G.	GOOD	FAIR	POOR
125	95	50	40	30	20

Sheriff's Model

A .36-caliber percussion revolver, nickel-plated with walnut grips.

NIB	EXC.	V.G.	GOOD	FAIR	POOR
225	200	175	150	125	100

3rd Model Dragoon

NIB	EXC.	V.G.	GOOD	FAIR	POOR
225	200	175	150	125	100

Colt Walker Replica

NIB	EXC.	V.G.	GOOD	FAIR	POOR
425	295	225	200	175	150

Remington Bison

NIB	EXC.	V.G.	GOOD	FAIR	POOR
250	225	200	175	150	125

Pocket Police

NIB	EXC.	V.G.	GOOD	FAIR	POOR
135	110	100	85	65	45

Pocket Revolver

Chambered for .31-caliber. Fitted with 4" octagon barrel. Cylinder holds five bullets. Solid brass frame. Weighs about 15 oz.

NIB	EXC.	V.G.	GOOD	FAIR	POOR
225	150	85	75	60	50

Wells Fargo

NIB	EXC.	V.G.	GOOD	FAIR	POOR
225	150	85	75	60	50

1851 Navy

NIB	EXC.	V.G.	GOOD	FAIR	POOR
250	225	200	175	150	125

1861 Navy

NIB	EXC.	V.G.	GOOD	FAIR	POOR
250	225	200	175	150	125

1860 Army

NIB	EXC.	V.G.	GOOD	FAIR	POOR
250	225	200	175	150	125

1858 Remington

NIB	EXC.	V.G.	GOOD	FAIR	POOR
275	225	125	100	75	50

1858 Remington Target

As above, but fitted with adjustable sights.

NIB	EXC.	V.G.	GOOD	FAIR	POOR
275	225	125	100	75	50

Bison

A 6-shot .44-caliber revolver, with 10.25" octagonal barrel. Solid brass frame. Weighs about 48 oz.

NIB	EXC.	V.G.	GOOD	FAIR	POOR
275	225	125	100	75	50

Hawken Pistol

A .50-caliber percussion pistol, with 9.75" octagon barrel. Stock is hardwood. Weighs about 50 oz.

NIB	EXC.	V.G.	GOOD	FAIR	POOR
250	180	115	75	65	50

CONSTABLE, R.
Philadelphia, Pennsylvania

Pocket Pistol

A single-shot percussion pistol, with a 3" round or octagonal barrel. German-silver mounts and walnut stock. These pistols are marked "R. Constable Philadelphia" and were manufactured during the late 1840s and 1850s.

NIB	EXC.	V.G.	GOOD	FAIR	POOR
—	—	2200	1100	550	200

	NIB	EXC.	V.G.	GOOD	FAIR	POOR

CONTENTO/VENTUR

SIDE-BY-SIDES

Model 51

A 12-, 16-, 20-, 28-gauge and .410 bore boxlock double-barrel shotgun, with 26", 28", 30" and 32" barrels. Various chokes, extractors and double triggers. Checkered walnut stock. Introduced in 1980 and discontinued in 1985.

	—	500	350	300	225	150

Model 52

As above in 10-gauge.

	—	500	350	300	225	150

Model 53

As above, with scalloped receiver, automatic ejectors and available with a single-selective trigger. Discontinued in 1985. **NOTE:** Single-selective trigger add 25 percent.

	—	550	400	350	250	200

Model 62

A 12-, 20- or 28-gauge Holland & Holland sidelock shotgun, with various barrel lengths and chokes, automatic ejectors, cocking indicators, floral engraved receiver and checkered walnut stock. Discontinued in 1982.

	—	1150	800	750	600	450

Model 64

As above, but more finely finished. No longer in production.

	—	1250	900	850	700	550

OVER/UNDERS

Over/Under

A 12-gauge over/under shotgun, with 32" barrels, screw-in choke tubes, a high ventilated rib, automatic ejectors and standard single-selective trigger. Checkered with Monte Carlo walnut stock.

	—	1250	900	750	600	500

Mark 2

As above, with an extra single-barrel and fitted in a leather case.

	—	1500	1200	1050	900	800

Mark 3

As above, but engraved with a finely figured walnut stock.

	—	1850	1500	1250	1100	950

Mark 3 Combo

As above, with an extra single-barrel and fitted in a leather case.

	—	3200	2600	2250	1750	1300

CONTINENTAL
RWM
Cologne, Germany

Continental Pocket Pistol (6.35mm)

A 6.35mm caliber semi-automatic pistol, with 2" barrel, internal hammer and 7-shot detachable magazine. Blued, with plastic grips and slide marked "Continental Kal. 6.35". Produced during the 1920s.

NOTE: This pistol may have been manufactured in Spain and carried German proof marks, because it was sold by RWM in Germany.

	—	300	150	125	100	75

Continental Pocket Pistol (7.65mm)

A German-made pistol chambered for the 7.65mm cartridge. Fitted with 3.9" barrel. Rear sight is a U-notch in the slide. Magazine capacity 8 rounds. Weight about 20 oz. Made prior to 1914.

	—	500	300	225	150	100

	NIB	EXC.	V.G.	GOOD	FAIR	POOR

CONTINENTAL ARMS CO.
Norwich, Connecticut

Pepperbox

A .22-caliber 5-barrel pepperbox, with a spur trigger and 2.5" barrels marked "Continental Arms Co. Norwich Ct. Patented Aug. 28, 1866". Some examples of this pistol are to be found marked "Ladies Companion".

—	—	2250	1000	350	250	

CONTINENTAL ARMS CO.
Leige, Belgium

Double Rifle

A .270, .303, .30-40, .30-06, .348, 375 H&H, .400 Jeffreys, .465, .475, .500 and .600 Nitro Express caliber Anson & Deeley boxlock double-barreled rifle, with 24" or 26" barrels. Double triggers and checkered walnut stock.

—	6500	4500	3750	3000	2250	

COOK & BROTHER RIFLES AND CARBINES
New Orleans, Louisiana

In early 1861, Ferdinand W.C. Cook and his brother Francis L. Cook, both English emigres, joined to form Cook & Brother in New Orleans to manufacture rifles and carbines following the English P1853 series for the newly seceded state of Louisiana and its neighbors. Between June 1861 and the federal occupation of New Orleans in April 1862, this firm produced about 200 cavalry and artillery carbines and about 1000 rifles. Having successfully moved the armory's machinery before federal occupation, the firm continued manufacture of rifles in Selma, Alabama during 1862, probably completing another 1,000 rifles with the New Orleans lock markings from the parts brought with them. Re-established in Athens, Georgia in early 1863, the firm continued to build both carbines and rifles, manufacturing more than 5,500 above the New Orleans production through 1864. The firm's products were clearly among the best small arms made within the Confederacy.

Cook & Brother Rifles (New Orleans & Selma production)

Overall length 48.75"; barrel length 33"; caliber .58. Markings: representation of a Confederate flag ("Stars & Bars") and "COOK & BROTHER/N.O./1861 (or) 1862" on lock; same usually on barrel together with serial number and "PROVED" near breech. Rifles in the early production have long range rear sights and unusual two piece block and blade front sights as well as an integral bayonet lug with guide on right side of barrel. Later production utilizes a brass clamping ring for the bayonet, a block open rear sight and a simple block and blade front sight. Earlier production will claim a premium if in good condition.

—	—	35000	15500	3000	1650	

Cook & Brother Carbines (New Orleans production)

Overall length 40" (artillery), 37" (cavalry); barrel length 24" (artillery), 21" to 21.5" (cavalry); caliber .58. Markings: As on Cook & Brother rifles (New Orleans production) artillery and cavalry carbines were produced in New Orleans in a separate serial range from the rifles. Total production is thought not to have exceeded 225, divided evenly between 1861 and 1862 dates. In addition to the overall and barrel lengths, the main difference between the artillery and cavalry carbines is the manner in which they were carried. The former bears standard sling rings on the upper band and the trigger guard strap, the latter has a bar with a ring on the left side of the stock. Both are exceedingly rare.

—	—	20000	8500	5000	1500	

Cook & Brother Rifles (Athens production)

Overall length 49"; barrel length 33"; caliber .58. Markings: representation of a Confederate flag ("Stars & Bars") and "COOK & BROTHER/ATHENS GA./date (1863 or 1864) and serial number on lock; "PROVED" on barrel near breech; serial number on various metal parts. After re-establishing their plant at Athens, Georgia, in the spring of 1863, Cook & Brother continued to manufacture rifles in a consecutive serial range after their New Orleans/Selma production (beginning about serial number 2000) and continued to make arms well into 1864 (through at least serial number 7650) until Sherman's army threatened the plant and necessitated the employment of its workforce in a military capacity as the 23rd Battalion Georgia State Guard.

—	—	21000	9300	3000	900	

Cook & Brother Carbines (Athens production)

Overall length 40" (artillery) or 37" (cavalry); barrel lengths 24" (artillery) or 21" to 21.5" (cavalry); caliber .58. Markings: same as on Athens production rifles. Artillery and cavalry carbines were manufactured in the same serial range as the Athens production rifles (about 2000 through 7650). As in New Orleans production, the artillery and cavalry carbines are

	NIB	EXC.	V.G.	GOOD	FAIR	POOR

distinguished from one another by their respective lengths. Unlike New Orleans/Selma production, however, some of the cavalry carbines are mounted with sling swivels of the artillery style, while others bear the sling ring on the left side and additionally have a swivel ring to secure the ramrod.

—	—	27500	9800	3900	1250

COONAN ARMS/COONAN INC.
Blaine, Minnesota

The original Coonan Arms was based in St. Paul, Minnesota from 1983 to 1994 and in Maplewood, Minnesota from 1994 to 1998. That company ceased operations in 1998. The current manufacturer was established as Coonan Inc. in 2009 and is located in Blaine, Minnesota. **NOTE:** For 6" barrel add $40; Bomar adjustable sights add $130; .38 Special conversion add $40; checkered walnut grips add $40; with Teflon slide add $100; with Teflon frame add $100.

Model A

A .357 Magnum semi-automatic pistol, with 5" barrel, 7-shot detachable magazine and fixed sights. Stainless steel with walnut grips. Introduced in 1981 and discontinued in 1984.

1200	1000	875	500	350	275

Model B

An improved version of the above, with a linkless barrel system, extended grip safety, enclosed trigger bar and a more contoured grip. A 6" barrel is available, as are adjustable sights, as extra cost options. A .38 Special conversion is also available. Introduced in 1985. A number of other options are also available that will affect value.

1300	1175	925	675	500	300

Comp I

As above, with 6" barrel, attached compensator and a stippled front grip strap. Introduced in 1989.

1600	1250	1000	700	550	350

Comp I Deluxe

As above, with a blued stainless steel slide, checkered grip straps and a finer finishing.

1650	1300	1050	750	600	400

Classic (Current Production)

This model features an integrated compensator, with 5" barrel. Pistol is supplied with checkered walnut grips, Millett adjustable rear sight and two-tone Teflon finish. Magazine capacity 7 rounds; weight 42 oz.; overall length 8.3".

1000	900	700	600	—	—

Cadet

Chambered for the .357 magnum cartridge, this model has 3.9" barrel, with smooth walnut grips and fixed rear sight. Magazine capacity 6 rounds; weight about 39 oz.; overall length 7.8". Height of pistol is 5.3". Coonan Arms refers to this model as the "Short Grip".

1150	875	675	500	400	400

Cadet II

Same as above, with a standard grip. Magazine capacity of this model 7 rounds.

1150	875	675	500	400	200

.41 Magnum Model

Introduced in 1997, this model is chambered for the .41 Magnum cartridge and fitted with a 5" barrel. Smooth walnut grips and fixed sights.

1700	1250	975	800	550	350

COOPER, J. M. & CO.
Philadelphia, Pennsylvania

Pocket Revolver

A .31-caliber percussion double-action revolver, with 4", 5" or 6" octagonal barrel and 6-shot unfluted cylinder. Blued, with walnut grips. During the first two years of production they were made in Pittsburgh, Pennsylvania and were so marked. Approximately 15,000 were manufactured between 1864 and 1869. **NOTE:** Pittsburgh-marked models add 20 percent.

—	—	1850	775	200	100

	NIB	EXC.	V.G.	GOOD	FAIR	POOR

COOPER ARMS
Stevensville, Montana

Model 36 Marksman

This is a premium bolt-action repeating rifle chambered for the .22 LR cartridge. In centerfire calibers of .17 CCM and .22 Hornet. The 23" Shilen barrel is mated to a solid bar stock receiver. High grade walnut is used in stocks that are fine-lined checkered. Manufactured from 1992 to 1999.

Standard

NIB	EXC.	V.G.	GOOD	FAIR	POOR
1100	900	700	500	300	200

Classic

NIB	EXC.	V.G.	GOOD	FAIR	POOR
1800	1200	800	600	400	200

Custom Classic

NIB	EXC.	V.G.	GOOD	FAIR	POOR
2000	1650	1150	850	600	300

Western Classic

Octagon barrel and case color metal.

NIB	EXC.	V.G.	GOOD	FAIR	POOR
2800	2200	1500	850	600	300

BR-50 w/Jewell Trigger

NIB	EXC.	V.G.	GOOD	FAIR	POOR
1800	1450	1100	800	600	300

IR-50-50 w/Jewell Trigger

NIB	EXC.	V.G.	GOOD	FAIR	POOR
1800	1450	1100	800	600	300

Featherweight w/Jewell Trigger

NIB	EXC.	V.G.	GOOD	FAIR	POOR
1800	1450	1100	800	600	300

Model 38/40

This bolt-action rifle is chambered for the .17 AK Hornet, .22 K Hornet or .22 Hornet. Made as a repeater in the early '90s, as a single-shot from 1997 to the present. Model 40 has a 3-lug bolt and some Anschutz parts.

Classic

NIB	EXC.	V.G.	GOOD	FAIR	POOR
1800	1500	1100	800	600	300

Custom Classic

NIB	EXC.	V.G.	GOOD	FAIR	POOR
2000	1750	1250	850	600	300

Western Classic (octagon barrel)

NIB	EXC.	V.G.	GOOD	FAIR	POOR
2900	2300	1750	1300	700	350

Mannlicher Model

NIB	EXC.	V.G.	GOOD	FAIR	POOR
3650	3000	2450	1850	800	450

Model 21

This bolt-action single-shot rifle is chambered for these cartridges: .221 Fireball, .222, .223, 6x45, 6x47, .17 Mach IV and the .17 Rem. A 24" stainless steel Shilen match grade barrel is fitted. AAA claro walnut is used. Oval forearm, ambidextrous palm swell, 22 lpi checkering, oil finish and Pachmayr buttpad are all standard features. Weighs approximately 8 lbs.

Varmint Extreme

NIB	EXC.	V.G.	GOOD	FAIR	POOR
1600	1250	900	700	500	250

Classic

NIB	EXC.	V.G.	GOOD	FAIR	POOR
1600	1250	900	700	500	250

Custom Classic

NIB	EXC.	V.G.	GOOD	FAIR	POOR
1900	1700	1300	850	600	300

Western Classic

NIB	EXC.	V.G.	GOOD	FAIR	POOR
2800	2200	1500	850	600	300

Benchrest w/Jewell Trigger

NIB	EXC.	V.G.	GOOD	FAIR	POOR
2100	1800	1250	850	600	300

Model 22

This is a bolt-action single-shot rifle chambered for a variety of calibers: 6mm PPC, .22-250, .220 Swift, .243, .25-06, .308, .22 BR, 7.62x39, 6.5x55. A Pachmayr decelerator pad is standard. Weight approximately 8.5 lbs.

Pro Varmint Extreme

NIB	EXC.	V.G.	GOOD	FAIR	POOR
1750	1500	1200	800	600	300

	NIB	EXC.	V.G.	GOOD	FAIR	POOR

Benchrest w/Jewell Trigger

	2100	1800	1300	900	650	300

Model 22 Repeater

Same as above, with magazine and chambered for .22-25, .308, 7mm-08 and .243.

Classic

	2400	2000	1750	1250	800	325

Custom Classic

	2650	2200	1850	1400	900	400

Western Classic

	3000	2350	1950	1500	900	400

Model 52 Classic

Long-action repeater offered virtually any centerfire caliber from .22-250 to .340 Weatherby. Model 52 Classic has oil-finished AA Claro walnut stock, hand checkering, matte finish. Also offered with synthetic stock as Excalibur. Custom Classic has more extensive checkering, ebony fore-end cap. Western Classic available in any caliber, has octagon barrel, case-hardened action, engraving. Introduced in 2007. **NOTE:** Add $150 for Excalibur, $1200 for Custom Classic, $2000 for Western Classic.

	1500	1300	1000	800	500	300

Model 54

Similar to above except with short action and in these calibers: .22-250, .243 Win., .250 Savage, .260 Rem., 7mm-08 Rem., .308 Win. Optional models same as Model 52 plus three varmint variants. **NOTE:** Add $150 for Excalibur, $400 for Varmint Extreme, $1200 for Custom Classic, $2000 for Western Classic.

	1500	1300	1000	800	500	300

Model 57

Bolt-action repeater chambered for the following rimfire calibers: .17 Mach II, .17 HMR, .22 LR or .22 Win. Magnum. Offered in several versions including standard model, with checkered walnut stock, matte finish, steel grip cap. **NOTE:** Add $500 for Custom Classic, $1200 for Western Classic

	1400	1200	950	750	500	300

COOPERATIVA OBRERA
Eibar, Spain

Longines

A 7.65mm caliber semi-automatic pistol. The slide is marked "Cal. 7.65 Automatic Pistol Longines".

	—	275	175	150	110	85

COPELAND, FRANK
Worcester, Massachusetts

Copeland Pocket Revolver .22

A .22 cartridge spur trigger revolver, with a 2.5" barrel, 7-shot magazine, unfluted cylinder and lock notches on the front. Frame is brass blued walnut or rosewood grips. The barrel marked "F. Copeland, Worcester, Mass." Manufactured in the 1860s.

	—	—	700	300	125	100

Copeland .32 Revolver

A .32-caliber spur trigger revolver, with a 5-shot fluted cylinder and an iron frame. Nickel-plated. The barrel marked "F. Copeland, Sterling, Mass." Manufactured in the 1860s.

	—	—	700	300	150	75

COSMI, A. & F.
Torrette, Italy

Semi-Automatic

A 12- and 20-gauge top-break semi-automatic shotgun, with various barrel lengths and chokes. An 8-shot magazine and ventilated rib. This is basically a custom-built made-to-order gun. There is a standard and deluxe model, with differences in the degree of embellishment.

Standard Model

	14000	8500	4750	3250	2200	1500

	NIB	EXC.	V.G.	GOOD	FAIR	POOR

Deluxe Model

	NIB	EXC.	V.G.	GOOD	FAIR	POOR
	15500	9500	6000	4250	3250	1750

COSMOPOLITAN ARMS CO.
Hamilton, Ohio

Breech Loading Rifle

A .52-caliber single-shot percussion rifle, with a 31" round barrel. The frame marked "Cosmopolitan Arms Co. Hamilton O. U.S./Gross Patent". Blued with a walnut buttstock. Approximately 100 were made between 1859 and 1862.

—	—	7000	2750	775	450

COWLES & SON
Chicopee, Massachusetts

Single-Shot

A .22- or .30-caliber single-shot spur trigger pistol, with 3.25" round barrel. Silver-plated brass frame blued, with walnut grip. Approximately 200 manufactured in 1865.

—	—	1500	775	250	100

CPA RIFLES
Dingman's Ferry, Pennsylvania

This company builds rifles based on the Stevens Model 44-1/2. Several different configurations are offered, which are listed. **NOTE:** There are a number of special order options and custom features available at extra charge that will affect value.

Schuetzen Rifle

This model is usually built to order as to stock style, caliber, barrel size, shape and length. Many calibers are available from .22 Short to .40-65 Winchester. Sights are extra.

2900	2250	1600	975	600	300

Silhouette Rifle

This model as produced is approved for BPCR competition by the NRA. This model has either a sporting-style stock with low comb or the Model 52 style with more drop. Calibers are from .38-55 to .45-110, with other calibers available. Standard barrel is #4 part octagon 30" in length. Sights are extra.

2550	1900	1350	700	550	250

Sporting Rifle

This model uses a sporting-style stock, with standard forearm and schnabel tip. Rifles are offered in rimmed calibers including .222, .225, .22 Hornet and others. Standard barrels are round or part octagon, with weights from #1 to #5 and up to 28" in length. Sights are extra.

2475	1900	1350	700	550	250

Varmint Rifle

As above, with a semi-beavertail forearm.

2475	1900	1350	700	550	250

CRAUSE, CARL PHILLIP MUSKETS AND RIFLES
Herzberg, Germany

Carl Phillip Crause (who signed his products only with his last name) operated a gun manufactory in Herzberg on the Harz in the northwestern German kingdom of Hannover from the close of the Napoleonic Wars until 1857. The main production of his factory was devoted to military arms for Hannover and the surrounding principalities. Weapons of his manufacture included the Brunswick M1835 and M1848 rifles, the Hannovarian M1850 and M1854 rifle-muskets and yager rifles, and the M1840 and M1849 rifle-muskets of the Hanseatic League (a coalition of the north German states of Oldenberg, Hamburg, Bremen, and Lubeck). The latter two arms were subsequently altered to accept the elongated projectiles popular during the 1850s. A few thousand evidently were imported into the United States and saw service during the American Civil War.

Hanseatic League M1840 Rifled Musket

Overall length 55.5"; barrel length 40.25"; caliber .70. Markings: on lockplate forward of hammer, "Crause in Herzberg" in script, the "s" in the archaic form, appearing as an "f". Of the 6,000 muskets of this type made, approximately half were sent to the United States in 1861 during the arms crisis that accompanied the outbreak of the American Civil War. A total of 2,680 of these were issued to Ohio and at least one regiment (the 56th Ohio) was armed with these rifled muskets. These arms were mistakenly identified during the period as being Saxon due to the similarity of the large squared off foresection of the lockplate.

—	—	1700	800	375	200

	NIB	EXC.	V.G.	GOOD	FAIR	POOR

Oldenberg M1849 Rifled Musket

Overall lengths 55.5" to 56.625" (long version), 49.5" (short version); barrel lengths 39" to 39.125" (long version), 33" (short version); caliber .69-.72 (rifled). Markings: "Crause in Herzberg" inscribed in script on the backstrap of the hammer housing, the "s" in archaic form, appearing as an "f". Nicknamed the "Cyclops" because its large center-hung hammer is pierced with a large window that served as its rear sight. A few hundred of these clumsy rifled muskets may have been intermixed with the shipments of "Saxon" muskets imported in 1861 or 1862 into the United States during the American Civil War.

—	—	1975	850	400	250	

CRESCENT F. A. CO.
Norwich, Connecticut

The company made good quality inexpensive single- and double-barrel shotguns at its Norwich works, beginning about 1892. It was bought by H&D Folsom of New York City, large importers and distributors of firearms and sporting goods, so they could add an American-made sidelock hammer side-by-side to their extensive range of imported guns. The Crescent guns were offered in 12-, 16-, 20- and 28-gauges and later, 44XL shot caliber with Damascus twist laminated or Armory steel barrels depending on the shooter's wants. In 1898 VL&D said these were the best American hammer guns in the market for the money.

Huge quantities of these "Hardware Guns" were produced in a profusion of private brands as well as in Folsom's house brand "American Gun Co. of NY". In 1922 the Crescent brand replaced the "American Gun Co. of NY". and can be found on many thousands of doubles. In 1905 Crescent's first hammerless sidelock was introduced as the American Gun Co. "Knickerbocker" Model No. 6. This very popular model became the Crescent "Peerless" No. 6 in 1922. In 1928 it became the Crescent "Empire" No. 60 and in 1931 the Crescent-Davis "New Empire" No. 88, "New Empire" No. 9 and "Empire" No. 9.

Crescent was bought by J. Stevens Arms Co., Division of Savage Arms Corp. about 1930. It was merged with Davis-Warner Arms Corp. successors to N.R. Davis & Sons Co. and became Crescent-Davis Arms Corp. In 1932 the operation was moved to the Stevens plant at Springfield, Mass. where some sidelock doubles were assembled. Crescent-Davis brand guns remained in Steven's full line catalog until 1941, but from 1937 to 1941 the doubles sold in the C-D brand were on either Stevens or Davis boxlock frames.

DOUBLES

Triumph—Hammerless Boxlock

—	800	650	425	300	200	

Model 2655—Laminated Barrels Hammer Sidelock

—	575	450	325	200	150	

Model 2665—Damascus Barrels Hammer Sidelock

—	575	450	325	200	150	

Crescent American Hammer Gun No. 0—Hammer Sidelock

—	400	325	250	200	100	

American Machine Made 2641—Hammer Sidelock

—	450	350	300	250	200	

American Machine Made 2650—Hammer Sidelock

—	575	450	325	200	150	

American Machine Made 2660—Damascus Barrels Hammer Sidelock

—	700	550	400	275	175	

American Gun Co. NY No. 1 Armory—Hammerless Sidelock

—	450	325	250	200	100	

American Gun Co. NY No. 2—Hammerless Sidelock

—	575	450	300	250	200	

American Gun Co. No. 3—Damascus Barrels Hammer Sidelock

—	700	550	425	300	250	

American Gun Co. No. 4—Hammer Sidelock

—	800	650	525	400	300	

	NIB	EXC.	V.G.	GOOD	FAIR	POOR

American Gun Co. No. 5—Damascus Barrels Hammer Sidelock

	—	925	800	650	450	350

Folsom Arms Co. No. 0 Armory—Hammer Sidelock

	—	450	325	250	200	100

Folsom Arms Co. No. 2—Hammer Sidelock

	—	575	450	300	200	150

Folsom Arms Co. No. 3—Damascus Barrel

	—	700	550	425	300	200

Knickerbocker No. 6 Armory—Hammerless Sidelock

	—	450	325	250	200	100

Knickerbocker No. 7—Hammerless Sidelock

	—	450	325	250	200	100

Knickerbocker No. 8—Damascus Barrels Hammerless Sidelock

	—	575	450	300	250	200

New Knickerbocker Armory—Hammerless Sidelock

	—	450	325	250	200	100

New Knickerbocker WT—Hammerless Sidelock

	—	500	375	250	200	150

New Knickerbocker Damascus Barrels—Hammerless Sidelock

	—	575	450	300	250	200

American Gun Co. Small Bore No. 28—Straight Stock Hammer Sidelock

	—	925	775	650	400	300

American Gun Co. Small Bore No. 44—Straight Stock Hammer Sidelock

	—	1025	825	700	475	350

American Gun Co. No. 0—Armory Straight Stock— Hammer Sidelock

	—	400	300	250	200	100

American Gun Co. No. 28—Nitro Straight Stock—Hammer Sidelock

	—	925	775	650	400	300

American Gun Co. No. 44—Nitro Straight Stock—Hammer Sidelock

	—	1025	825	700	475	350

American Gun Co. Midget Field No. 28—Hammer Sidelock

	—	925	775	650	400	300

American Gun Co. Midget Field No. 44—Hammer Sidelock

	—	1025	825	700	500	350

Crescent 1922 Model No. 66—Quail—Hammerless Sidelock

	—	700	550	400	275	175

Crescent Firearms Co. No. 0—Hammer Sidelock

	—	450	350	250	200	150

Crescent Firearms Co. No. 0—Nickel—Hammer Sidelock

	—	600	450	350	250	200

Crescent Firearms Co. No. 6—Peerless—Hammerless Sidelock

	—	450	350	250	200	150

Crescent Firearms Co. No. 6E—Peerless Engraved—Hammerless Sidelock

	—	700	550	400	275	175

Crescent Firearms Co. No. 66—Quail—Hammerless Sidelock

	—	750	550	425	300	200

	NIB	EXC.	V.G.	GOOD	FAIR	POOR

Crescent Firearms Co. No. 60—Empire—Hammerless Sidelock

	—	500	400	350	300	200

Crescent Firearms Co. No. 6—Peerless—Hammerless Sidelock

	—	450	350	300	200	150

Crescent Firearms Co. No. 44—Improved—Hammer Sidelock

	—	800	600	500	400	300

Crescent Empire No. 60—Hammerless Sidelock

	—	400	300	250	200	100

New Crescent Empire Red Butt—Hammerless Sidelock

	—	450	350	250	200	150

Crescent New Empire No. 88—Hammerless Sidelock

	—	450	350	250	200	150

Crescent New Empire No. 9—Hammerless Sidelock

	—	400	300	250	200	100

Crescent Certified Empire No. 60—Hammerless Sidelock

	—	450	300	250	200	150

Crescent Certified Empire No. 9—Hammerless Sidelock

	—	500	375	300	250	200

Crescent Certified Empire No. 88—Hammerless Sidelock

	—	575	450	400	350	300

Crescent Davis No. 600—Hammerless Boxlock

	—	450	350	300	250	200

Crescent Davis No. 900—Hammerless Boxlock

	—	575	450	400	350	300

Single-Shot

Made in 12-, 16-, 20-, 28-gauge and .410. Barrel lengths were 26", 28", 30" and 32", with various chokes. It had an exposed hammer, fluid steel barrel and walnut pistol-grip stock.

	—	200	125	100	75	50

Revolver

A typical S&W copy made by Crescent in Norwich, Connecticut. It was a top-break double-action, that was found either blued or nickel-plated, with checkered black hard rubber grips. The cylinder held 5 shots and was chambered for the .32 S&W cartridge.

	—	250	150	125	85	40

Crescent Certified Shotgun NFA, Curio or Relic

The Crescent Certified Shotgun is a .410 smooth bore pistol with a 12.25" barrel. Manufactured from approximately 1930 to 1932 by the Crescent-Davis Arms Corp., Norwich, Connecticut, and possibly thereafter until 1934 by the J. Stevens Arms Co., which purchased the company. In various distributor catalogs, it is termed the "Ever-Ready" Model 200 and advertised with a blued frame. Specimens have been observed with "tiger-stripe" (like an H&R Handy-Gun) or Colt SAA or Winchester-type case hardening. Total production is unknown but serial numbers ranging from 1305 to 3262 have been observed, suggesting it may have been fewer than 4,000. The Treasury Department ruled the .410 Crescent to be a "firearm" in the "any other weapon" category under the NFA in 1934, when its retail price was about $11.

The barrel is marked proof tested 410 gauge on top and 2-1/2 IN SHELLS on the middle left side. The receiver's left side is stamped crescent certified shotgun/crescent-davis arms corporation/ norwich, conn., u.s.a. The earliest guns also have .410 stamped at the top of the left side of the receiver near the breech, but this marking does not appear on later guns. It is a rather heavy (57 oz. unloaded) handgun. **NOTE:** Add $100 to $300 for original cardboard box.

	—	975	725	550	350	250

Brand Names Used by Crescent Arms

American Bar Lock Wonder made for Sears, Roebuck & Co.
American Boy made for Townley Metal & Hardware Co.
American Gun Co. (H & D Folsom house brand)
American Gun Company of New York

	NIB	EXC.	V.G.	GOOD	FAIR	POOR

American Nitro

Armory Gun Co.Baker Gun Co. (if no foreign proof marks)

T. Barker New York-if a sidelock hammerless double without proofs.

Bellmore Gun Co.Berkshire No. 3000 made for Shapleigh Hardware Co. of St. Louis, MO

Black Beauty-hammerless doubles

Bluefield Clipper

Bluegrass Arms Co. made for Belknap Hardware Co. of Louisville, KY

Blue Whistler

Bridge Black PrinceBridge Gun Co.

Bridge Gun Works

Bridgeport Arms Co. (if no foreign proof marks)

Bright Arms Co.

Canadian Belle

Carolina Arms Co. made for Smith Wadsworth Hardware Co. of Charlotte, NC

Caroline Arms

Central Arm Co. made for Shapleigh Hardware Co. of St. Louis, MO

Chatham Arms Co.

Cherokee Arms Co. made for C. M. McClung Co. of Knoxville, TN

Chesapeake Gun Co.

Chicago Long Range Wonder 1908-1918 made for Sears, Roebuck & Co. of Chicago, IL

Colonial

Columbian New York Arms Co.

Compeer made for Van Camp Hardware & Iron Co. of Indianapolis, IN

Connecticut Arms Co.

Cumberland Arms Co.

Crescent Fire Arms Co.

Creve Cour (if no foreign proof marks) made for Isaac Walker Hardware Co. of Peoria, IL

CrusoDaniel Boone Gun Co. made for Belknap Hardware Co. of Louisville, KY

Delphian Arms Co. (some models without foreign proof marks) made for Supplee-Biddle
    Hardware Co. of Philadelphia, PA

Delphian Manufacturing Co. (some models)

Diamond Arms Co. (some models) made for Shapleigh Hardware Co. of St. Louis, MO

Dunlap Special made for Dunlap Hardware Co. of Macon, GAE.C. Mac made for E.C.
    Meacham Arms Co. of St. Louis, MO

Elgin Arms Co. made for Strauss & Schram and Fred Biffar & Co. both of Chicago, IL

Elmira Arms Co.

Empire Arms Co. made for Sears, Roebuck & Co. of Chicago, IL

Empire State Arms Co.

Enders Oakleaf made for Shapleigh Hardware Co. of St. Louis, MO

Enders Special Service made for Shapleigh Hardware Co.

Enders Royal Service made for Shapleigh Hardware Co.

Essex made for Belknap Hardware Co. of Louisville, KY

Excel made for Montgomery Ward & Co. of Chicago, IL

Farwell Arms Co. made for Farwell, Ozmun & Kirk of St. Paul, MN

Faultless made for John M. Smythe Co. of Chicago, IL

Faultless Goose Gun made for John M. Smyth Co. of Chicago, IL

The Field after 1894

Folsom Arms Co. (also used by H & D Folsom on Belgian imports)

F.F. Forbes (H & D Folsom house brand)

Fort Pitt Arms Co.

Fremont Arms Co. (also used on Belgian imports)

Gold Medal Wonder

Greenfield (some models) made for Hibbard, Spencer, Bartlett & Co. of Chicago, ILH.B.C.
    (some models) made for Hudson's Bay Co. of Canada

H.S.B. & Co. (some models) made for Hibbard, Spencer,Bartlett & Co. of Chicago, IL

Hanover Arms Co. (if no foreign proof marks)

NIB	EXC.	V.G.	GOOD	FAIR	POOR

S.H. Harrington (if no foreign proof marks)

Hartford Arms Co. made for both Simmons Hardware and Shapleigh Hardware Co. of St. Louis, MO

Harvard (H & D Folsom house brand)

Hermitage (some models) made for Grey-Dusley Hardware Co. of Nashville, TN

Hip Spe Bar (some models) made for Hibbard, Spencer, Bartlett & Co. of Chicago, IL

Hibbard (some models) made for Hibbard, Spencer, Bartlett & Co. of Chicago, IL

Howard Arms Co. made for Fred Biffar & Co. of Chicago, IL

Hudson (some models) made for Hibbard, Spencer, Bartlett & Co. of Chicago, IL

Hunter made for Belknap Hardware Co. Louisville, KY

Interstate Arms Co. made for Townley Metal & Hardware Co. of Kansas City, MO

Jackson Arms Co. made for C.M. McClung & Co. of Knoxville, TN

Joseph Arms Co. Norwich, Conn.

K K and Keen Kufter (some models) made for Shapleigh

Hardware Co. of St. Louis, MO

Kingsland Special and Kingsland 10 Star made for Geller, Ward & Hasner of St. Louis, MO

Kirk Gun Co. made for Farwell, Ozmun & Kirk of St. Paul, MN

Knickerbocker (up to 1915, H & D Folsom house brand)

Knockabout (before 1925) made for Montgomery Ward & Co. of Chicago, IL

Knoxall (only hammerless doubles)

Laclede Gun Co.

Lakeside made for Montgomery Ward & Co. of Chicago, IL

Leader Gun Co. made for Charles Williams Stores of New York, NY

Lee's Special and Lee's Munner Special made for Lee Hardware Co. of Salina, KS

Long Range Marvel, Long Range Winner, and Long Range Wonder made between 1893 to 1909 for Sears, Roebuck & Co. of Chicago, IL

F.A. LoomisMarshwoodMassachusetts Arms Co. made before 1920 for Blish, Mizet and Silliman Hardware Co. of Atchison, KS

Mears (if no foreign proof marks)

Metropolitan made for Siegal-Cooper Co. of New York, NY

Minnesota Arms Co. made for Farwell, Ozmun, Kirk & Co. of St. Paul, MN

Mississippi Arms Co. St. Louis (some models) made for Shepleigh Hardware Co. of St. Louis, MO

Mississippi Valley Arms Co. (some models) made for Shapleigh Hardware Co. of St. Louis, MO

Mohawk made for Glish, Mizet and Lilliman Hardware Co. of Atchinson, KS

Monitor

R. Murdock, National Firearms Co. (some models)

National Arms Co. hammer doubles (without foreign proof marks) and hammerless doubles made for May Hardware Co. of Washington, D.C. and Moskowitz and Herbach Co. of Philadelphia, PA

New Britain Arms Co.'s Monarch

New Elgin Arms Co.

New EmpireNew England (some models after 1914) made for Sears, Roebuck & Co.

New England Arms Co. (some models)

Newport Model CN made for Hibbard, Spencer, Bartlett and Co. of Chicago

Newport Model WN (some models) made for Hibbard, Spencer, Bartlett and Co. of Chicago

New Rival made for Van Camp Hardware and Iron Co. of Indianapolis, IN

New York Arms Co. made for Garnet Carter Co. of Chattanooga, TN

	NIB	EXC.	V.G.	GOOD	FAIR	POOR

New York Machine Made (some models)

New York Match Gun (some models)

New York Nitro Hammerless

Nitro Bird made for Conover Hardware Co. of Kansas City, MO

Nitro Hunter made for Belknap Hardware Co. of Louisville, KY

Nitro King 1908 to 1917 made for Sears, Roebuck & Co. of Chicago, IL

Norwich Arms Co.

Not-Noc Manufacturing Co. made for Belknap Hardware Co. of Louisville, KY and
    Canton Hardware Co. of Canton, OH

Osprey made for Lou J. Eppinger, Detroit, MI

Oxford made for Belknap Hardware Co. of Louisville, KY

Peerless (H & D Folsom house brand)

Perfection made for H. G. Lipscomb & Co. of Nashville, TN

Piedmont made for Piedmont Hardware Co. of Danville, PA

Piedmont Arms Co.

Pioneer Arms (if no foreign proof marks) made for Kruse and Baklmann Hardware Co. of
    Cincinnati, OH

Quail (H & D Folsom house brand)

Queen City made for Elmira Arms Co. of Elmira, NY

Red Chieftan (model 60) made for Supplee Biddle Hardware Co. of Philadelphia, PARev-
    O-Noc (some models) made for Hibbard, Spencer, Bartlett & Co. of Chicago, IL

Rich-Con made for Richardson & Conover Hardware Co.Charles Richter (some models)
    made for New York Sporting Goods Co. of New York, NY

Rickard Arms Co. made for J. A. Rickard Co. of Schenectady, NYRival (some models)
    made for Van Camp Hardware and Iron Co. of Indianapolis, IN

Rocket SpecialRoyal Service made for Shapleigh Hardware Co. of St. Louis, MO

Rummel Arms Co. made for A. J. Rummel Arms Co. of Toledo, OH

Ruso (if no foreign proof marks)St. Louis Arms Co. (sidelock hammerless doubles) made
    for Shapleigh Hardware Co. of St. Louis, MO

Seminole (hammerless) unknown

Shue's Special made for Ira M. Shue of Hanover, PA

Smithsonian (some models)

John M. Smythe & Co. made for John M. Smythe Hardware Co. of Chicago, IL

Southern Arms Co. (some models)

Special Service made for Shapleigh Hardware Co. of St. Louis, MO

Spencer Gun Co. made for Hibbard, Spencer, Bartlett & Co. of Chicago, IL

Sportsman (some models) made for W. Bingham & Co. of Cleveland, OH

Springfield Arms Co. used until 1930. (H & D Folsom house brand). This brand was also
    used by Stevens and James Warner guns.Square Deal made for Stratton, Warren
    Hardware Co. of Memphis, TN

Star Leader (some models)

State Arms Co. made for J.H. Lau & Co. of New York, NY

Sterling Arms Co.

Sullivan Arms Co. made for Sullivan Hardware Co. of Anderson, SC

Superior (some models) made for Paxton & Gallagher Co. of Omaha, NE

Syco (some models) made for Wyeth Hardware Co. of St. Joseph, MO

Ten Star & Ten Star Heavy Duty (if no foreign proof marks) made for Geller, Ward &
    Hasner Co. of St. Louis, MO

Tiger (if no foreign proof marks) made for J.H. Hall & Co. of Nashville, TN

Townley's Pal and Townley's American Boy made for Townley Metal & Hardware Co. of

	NIB	EXC.	V.G.	GOOD	FAIR	POOR

Kansas City, MO

Trap's Best made for Watkins, Cottrell Co. of Richmond, VA

Triumph (some models) made for Sears, Roebuck & Co. of Chicago, IL

Tryon Special (some models) made for Edward K. Tryon Co. of Philadelphia, PA

U.S. Arms Co. (if no foreign proof marks) made for Supplee-Biddle Hardware Co. of Philadelphia, PA

U.S. FieldUtica Firearms Co. (some models) made for Simmons Hardware Co. of St. Louis, MO

Victor & Victor Special made for Hibbard, Spencer, Bartlett & Co. of Chicago, IL

Virginia Arms Co. made for Virginia-Carolina Co. of Richmond, VA

Volunteer (some models) made for Belknap Hardware Co. of Louisville, KY

Vulcan Arms Co. made for Edward K. Tryon Co. of Philadelphia, PA

Warren Arms Co. (if no foreign proof marks)

Washington Arms Co. (some models)

Wauregan (some models)

Wautauga (some models) made for Wallace Hardware Co. Morristown, TN

Wildwood made for Sears, Roebuck & Co. of Chicago, IL

Wilkinson Arms Co. (if no foreign proof marks) made for Richmond Hardware Co. of Richmond, VA

Wilshire Arms Co. made for Stauffer, Eshleman & Co. of New Orleans, LA

Winfield Arms Co. (H & D Folsom house brand)

Winoca Arms Co. made for Jacobi Hardware Co. of Philadelphia, PA

Witte Hardware Co. (some models) made for Witte Hardware Co. of St. Louis, MO

Wolverine Arms Co. made for Fletcher Hardware Co. of Wilmington, NC

Worthington Arms Co. made for George Worthington Co. of Cleveland, OH

CRISPIN, SILAS
New York, New York

Crispin Revolver

A .32 Crispin caliber 5- or 6-shot revolver produced in limited quantities. Some are marked "Smith Arms Co., New York City. Crispin's Pat. Oct. 3, 1865". The most noteworthy feature of these revolvers is that the cylinder is constructed in two pieces so that the belted Crispin cartridge can be used. It is believed that these revolvers were only made on an experimental basis, between 1865 and 1867.

NIB	EXC.	V.G.	GOOD	FAIR	POOR
—	—	19000	7500	2500	1000

CROSSFIRE
LaGrange, Georgia

This combination rifle/shotgun is manufactured by Saco Defense, Inc. for Crossfire. It is the first production firearm to combine the shotgun and rifle into a pump action multi-shot weapon.

MK-1

This model is designed to fire both a .223 Rem. cartridge and a 12-gauge 3" shotgun shell from two different barrels. It is a dual action long gun operated with a pump action. Overall length of the gun is 38". The shotgun has a 4-round detachable magazine, while the rifle has an AR-15 type 5-round magazine. Shotgun barrel is furnished with choke tubes. Offered in black oxide finish or camo finish. Weight approximately 8.6 lbs. Introduced in 1999. **NOTE:** Add $100 for camo finish.

NIB	EXC.	V.G.	GOOD	FAIR	POOR
2200	1700	1350	775	500	250

CRUCELEGUI, HERMANOS
Eibar, Spain

A 5mm, 6.35mm, 7.65mm and 8mm caliber double-action revolver. The trade names used were; Puppy, Velo-Mith, Le-Brong, Bron-Sport, C.H. and Brong-Petit.

NIB	EXC.	V.G.	GOOD	FAIR	POOR
—	250	150	80	60	35

	NIB	EXC.	V.G.	GOOD	FAIR	POOR

CUMMINGS, O. S.
Lowell, Massachusetts

Cummings Pocket Revolver

A .22-caliber spur trigger revolver, with 3.5" ribbed round barrel and 7-shot fluted cylinder. Nickel-plated with rosewood grip. The barrel is stamped "O.S. Cummings Lowell, Mass." Approximately 1,000 manufactured in the 1870s.

—	—	675	300	150	100	

CUMMINGS & WHEELER
Lowell, Massachusetts

Pocket Revolver

Similar to the Cummings Pocket Revolver, with subtle differences: such as length of flutes on cylinder; size and shape of grip. Barrel is slightly longer and is marked "Cummings & Wheeler, Lowell, Mass.

—	—	750	350	150	100	

CUSTOM GUN GUILD
Doraville, Georgia

Wood Model IV

A falling block single-shot rifle produced in a number of popular calibers. Barrel lengths from 22" to 28". Stock of select checkered walnut. This is a lightweight rifle, at approximately 5.5 lbs. Manufactured for one year only, 1984. Not often encountered on today's market.

—	3750	2750	2500	1750	1000	

CZ - STRAKONICE
Strakonice, Czech Republic

This firm is a separate company from the one located in Uhershy Brod. Prior to the collapse of the Soviet Union both companies were owned and operated by the state.

Model TT 40/45/9

This is a semi-automatic pistol chambered for the .40 S&W, .45 ACP or 9mm cartridges. Fitted with a 3.8" barrel. Trigger is single-/double-action or double-action-only. Magazine capacity 10 rounds. Weight about 26 oz.

575	425	300	200	125	100	

CZ
(Ceska Zbrojovka)
Uhersky Brod, Czech Republic

Established by Karel Bubla and Alois Tomiska in 1919. This company later merged with Hubertus Engineering Company. In 1949 the company was nationalized. CZ regularly exports 90 percent of its production to over 80 countries.

NOTE: As of 1998, CZ firearms have been imported exclusively by CZ-USA, a wholly-owned distribution subsidiary of Ceska Zbrojovka a.s. Uhersky Brod, (CZUB) of the Czech Republic.

Fox

A 6.35mm caliber semi-automatic pistol, with a 2.125" barrel, tubular slide, a folding trigger and no trigger guard. Fox and CZ are inscribed on the slide. The CZ logo is on each grip plate. Blued with plastic grips. Manufactured between 1919 and 1936.

—	900	750	600	400	200	

CZ 1921 Praga

A semi-automatic pistol in 7.65mm caliber. The first service pistol manufactured in Czechoslovakia. Production began in 1920. Praga is stamped on the slide and on each grip plate for commercial models. The service models were fitted with wood grips.

—	650	550	475	350	200	

Army Pistol 1922 (Nickl-Pistole)

Designed by Josef Nickl of Mauser. First approved by the Army in 1921, this pistol was chambered for the .380 ACP (9mmKurtz/9x17mm) cartridge. Plagued by design problems, it was produced only in 1922 and 1923. Fewer than 22,000 were built.

—	650	500	350	200	150	

	NIB	EXC.	V.G.	GOOD	FAIR	POOR

CZ 1922

A semi-automatic pistol in caliber 6.35mm. Very similar to the Fox above. It has no sights but is fitted with a conventional trigger guard. CZ is stamped on the slide and the CZ logo on each grip plate. Grips are plastic or wood. Manufactured between 1922 and 1936.

—	550	450	350	300	200

CZ 1924

The first large-production military pistol produced by CZ. Chambered for the 9mmK cartridge. It is the first of the CZ models with wraparound grips of both wood and plastic. CZ logo is seen on plastic grips. A lanyard loop is attached to the base of the butt. Manufactured from 1925 to 1932.

—	650	500	400	300	200

CZ 1927

A semi-automatic pistol chambered for the 7.65mm cartridge, marked the same as the CZ 1924, but the cocking grooves on the slide are cut vertically instead of sloped as on the earlier model. This model was blued, with checkered wrap-around, plastic grips. These early guns were beautifully made and marked, "Ceska Zbrojovka AS v Praze". After the war these pistols continued in production until 1951. There were more than 500,000 manufactured.

NOTE: Some of these pistols were made with an extended barrel for the use of a silencer. This variation brings a large premium. Fewer than 10 CZ27s were made in .22-caliber. An expert opinion is suggested if a sale is contemplated. **NOTE:** Nazi-proofed add 50 percent.

—	650	475	300	200	165

CZ 1936

A 6.35mm caliber semi-automatic pistol, with 2.5" barrel and double-action-only lockwork. It has plastic wrap-around grips, with the CZ logo on each side. It replaced the Model 1922 in 1936. Discontinued in 1940 because of wartime production.

—	450	350	300	200	100

CZ 1938

A semi-automatic double-action pistol in caliber 9mmK. Manufactured for the Czechoslovakian military from 1938 to 1940. Barrel length is 4.7". Weight about 32 oz. Magazine capacity 8 rounds. Wrap-around plastic grips with the CZ logo on each side.

—	550	500	400	300	200

CZ 1945

This model is a small .25-caliber (6.35mm) pocket pistol that is double-action-only. It was produced and sold after World War II. It is a modified version of the CZ 1936. Approximately 60,000 were built between 1945 and 1949.

—	350	300	250	175	125

CZ 1950

This is a blowback-operated semi-automatic double-action pistol chambered for the 7.65mm cartridge. It is patterned after the Walther Model PP, with a few differences. The safety catch is located on the frame instead of the slide; the trigger guard is not hinged as on the Walther. It is dismantled by means of a catch on the side of the frame. Although intended to be a military pistol designed by the Kratochvil brothers, it proved to be underpowered and was adopted by the police. There were few released on the commercial market.

—	250	150	125	100	50

CZ 1952

This Czech army sidearm is a semi-automatic pistol chambered for the 7.62mm cartridge and fitted with a 4.7" barrel. It has a very complex locking system using two rollers inside the frame. Magazine capacity 8 rounds. Weight about 34 oz. Production ended in 1956.

—	300	275	225	125	75

Model 1970

This model was an attempt to correct dependability problems with the Model 50. There is little difference to see externally between the two except for markings and the grip pattern. Production began during the 1960s and ended in 1983.

—	250	200	150	100	75

RIFLES

Model 52 (7.62 x 45) Carbine

—	450	300	250	200	125

	NIB	EXC.	V.G.	GOOD	FAIR	POOR

Model 52/57 (7.62 x 39)

	NIB	EXC.	V.G.	GOOD	FAIR	POOR
	—	525	325	275	225	150

CZ-USA
Kansas City, Kansas

CZ first entered the U.S. market in 1990 through various distributors. In January 1998 CZ-USA opened its office in Kansas City, Kansas. This office includes full sales and warranty service as well as an on-site gunsmith.

RIFLES

CURRENTLY IMPORTED CZ RIFLES— CZ-USA

CZ Model 3

This bolt-action rifle introduced in 2004, is produced in the U.S.A. Offered in both right- and left-hand configurations. Chambered for the Winchester Short Magnums: .270, 7mm and .300. Walnut stock with choice of stainless steel or blue finish. Fitted with a 24" barrel. No sights. Magazine is 3 rounds. Weight about 7.5 lbs. **NOTE:** Add $30 for stainless steel.

970	675	575	400	200	100

CZ 452-2E LUX

This bolt-action rifle is chambered for the .22 LR or .22 Win. Magnum cartridge. It is fitted with a 24.8" barrel, with hooded front and adjustable rear sight. Trigger is adjustable for pull. The pistol-grip stock is a European-style Turkish walnut. Supplied with a 5-round magazine. Blued finish. Weight approximately 6.6 lbs. **NOTE:** Add $40 for .22 WMR.

490	350	225	150	125	100

CZ ZKM-452D

As above, with a walnut Monte Carlo-style stock.

—	425	300	225	150	100

CZ 452-2E ZKM Style

Similar to the above model, but chambered for .22 LR only and fitted with a black synthetic stock and matte nickel finish. Fitted with a 22.5" barrel. Weight about 6 lbs.

475	325	225	175	125	100

CZ 452 Training Rifle

Chambered for the .22 LR cartridge and fitted with a 24.8" barrel. Detachable magazine has 5-round capacity. Beechwood stock. Adjustable sights. Weight about 5.4 lbs.

375	275	175	150	125	100

CZ 452 American Classic

This model is chambered for the .22 LR and .22 Win. Magnum cartridge. Features an American-style Circassian walnut stock with 18 lpi checkering. Fitted with a 21" barrel, with recessed target crown. Supplied with a 5-round magazine. Blued finish. Weight about 6.5 lbs. Introduced in 1999. In 2005 the .17 Mach 2 caliber was offered. **NOTE:** Add $40 for .22 WMR. or .17 HMR.

465	350	250	150	12	100

CZ 452 Varmint

This bolt-action rifle is chambered for the .22 LR cartridge and fitted with a 20" barrel. American-style Turkish walnut stock. Blued finish. Weight about 7.5 lbs. In 2005 the .17 Mach 2 was offered. **NOTE:** Add $20 for .17 Mach 2 caliber.

420	300	250	200	150	125

CZ 452 Scout

This model is designed for the younger shooter and features a shortened buttstock, 16.2" barrel and reduced weight receiver. Chambered for the .22 LR cartridge. Open adjustable sights. Weight is 3.9 lbs. Introduced in 2000.

275	200	150	125	100	75

CZ 452 Style

Chambered for the .22 LR cartridge and fitted with a 22.5" barrel. This model features a synthetic stock with matte nickel finish. Magazine capacity is 5 or 10 rounds. Weight about 5.3 lbs.

400	300	250	225	125	75

	NIB	EXC.	V.G.	GOOD	FAIR	POOR

CZ 452 Silhouette

Designed for small silhouette competition shooting, this .22-caliber rifle has a synthetic stock and blued finish. Barrel length 22.5". Weight about 5.3 lbs.

	NIB	EXC.	V.G.	GOOD	FAIR	POOR
	400	300	250	225	125	75

CZ 452 FS

This model introduced in 2004, is chambered for the .22 LR or .22 WMR cartridge. Fitted with a full-length Turkish walnut stock. Barrel length 20.5". Adjustable sights. Weight about 6.5 lbs.

	NIB	EXC.	V.G.	GOOD	FAIR	POOR
	475	350	265	200	150	100

CZ 513 Basic

This model is a simplified version of the CZ 452. It features a plain beechwood stock, with no checkering. Iron sights. Chambered for the .22 LR cartridge. Barrel length 21". Weight about 5.4 lbs. Introduced in 2004.

	NIB	EXC.	V.G.	GOOD	FAIR	POOR
	275	200	170	125	100	75

CZ 511

This is a semi-automatic rifle chambered for the .22 LR cartridge. Fitted with a 22" barrel. Two-position rear sight. Supplied with an 8-round magazine. Cross bolt safety. Turkish walnut stock. Blued finish. Weight approximately 5.4 lbs.

	NIB	EXC.	V.G.	GOOD	FAIR	POOR
	400	335	250	175	125	75

CZ Model 527

This bolt-action model is chambered for the .22 Hornet, .222 Rem. and the .223 Rem. Rear sight is adjustable and checkered stock is walnut. Barrel length 23.6" and magazine capacity is 5 rounds. Weight approximately 6.2 lbs.

	NIB	EXC.	V.G.	GOOD	FAIR	POOR
	600	500	400	300	225	125

CZ 527 American Classic

Introduced in 1999, this model features a 20.5" barrel with American-style Turkish walnut stock. Weight approximately 7.6 lbs. Blued finish. In 2005 this model was chambered for the .204 Ruger cartridge with 22" barrel. **NOTE:** Add $170 for English walnut stock; $200 for fancy American walnut; $30 for maple; $30 for laminate stock.

	NIB	EXC.	V.G.	GOOD	FAIR	POOR
	600	500	400	300	200	100

CZ 527 Lux

This is a bolt-action center fire rifle, chambered for .22 Hornet, .222 Rem. or .223 Rem. cartridge. Fitted with 23.6" barrel, with a hooded front sight and fixed rear sight. Trigger is an adjustable single-set type. Turkish walnut stock is in the Bavarian style. Blued finish. Supplied with a 5-round magazine. Weight approximately 6.6 lbs.

	NIB	EXC.	V.G.	GOOD	FAIR	POOR
	600	475	350	250	150	100

CZ 527 Premium (Lux)

Introduced in 2000, this model features hand fitted actions, fancy walnut stock, 18 lpi checkering and satin finish. Offered in .22 Hornet and .223 Rem. Barrel length 22". Magazine capacity 5 rounds. Weight about 6.2 lbs.

	NIB	EXC.	V.G.	GOOD	FAIR	POOR
	650	525	400	300	175	125

CZ 527 FS

Similar to the above model, but fitted with a 20.5" barrel and Mannlicher-style stock. Blued finish. Weight about 6 lbs.

	NIB	EXC.	V.G.	GOOD	FAIR	POOR
	690	525	400	300	175	125

CZ 527 Varmint

Chambered for the .17 Hornet, .17 Remington, .204 Ruger, .222 Remington and .223 Remington cartridges. Fitted with a 24" heavy barrel. Checkered Turkish walnut, gray laminate or black H-S Precision Kevlar stock. No sights. Detachable magazine. Weight about 7.2 lbs. **NOTE:** Add $50 for laminate; $150 for Kevlar stock.

	NIB	EXC.	V.G.	GOOD	FAIR	POOR
	600	475	350	175	125	100

CZ 527 Carbine

This model introduced in 2000, is chambered for the 7.62x39 cartridge and fitted with a 18.5" barrel. Detachable magazine capacity is 5 rounds. Open sights. Weight about 6 lbs.

	NIB	EXC.	V.G.	GOOD	FAIR	POOR
	600	475	350	225	175	100

CZ 527 Prestige

An upgraded CZ 527 American, with jeweled bolt, semi-fancy Turkish walnut with hand rubbed finish. Chambered for the .22 Hornet or .223 Remington cartridges. Barrel length 21.9". Weight

	NIB	EXC.	V.G.	GOOD	FAIR	POOR

about 6.2 lbs. Introduced in 2001.

	NIB	EXC.	V.G.	GOOD	FAIR	POOR
	880	675	600	475	275	150

CZ Model 537

This bolt-action rifle is chambered for the .270, .308 and .30-06 cartridges. The rear sight is adjustable and stock checkered walnut. Barrel length 23.6". Magazine capacity 5 rounds. Weight approximately 7.9 lbs. Discontinued.

600	475	375	250	200	100

CZ 550 American Classic

Similar to the Model CZ 550, this rifle is chambered for the .243, .308, .270 and .30-06 cartridges. Fitted with a 20.5" barrel and American-style Turkish walnut stock. No sights. Supplied with 5-round internal magazine. Blued finish. Weight about 7.6 lbs. Introduced in 1999.

620	500	400	300	200	100

CZ Model 550

Chambered for the .243, .270, .30 and .30-06 cartridges, this bolt-action rifle features a 24" barrel and high comb walnut stock. No open sights. Weight about 7.25 lbs.

700	525	400	300	200	100

CZ Model 550 Battue Lux

Chambered for the .30-06 cartridge. Ramp rear sight. Barrel length 20.25". Weight approximately 7.25 lbs. Checkered walnut stock.

700	525	400	300	200	100

CZ Model 550 FS Battue

Same as above, with full-length stock.

750	600	500	375	200	100

CZ Model 550 Minnesota

This model is chambered for the .270 Win. and .30-06 calibers. Barrel length 23.5". Weight approximately 7.25 lbs. No sights. Supplied with recoil pad.

650	550	450	325	225	125

CZ Model 550 Minnesota DM

Same as above, with detachable magazine. Calibers are .270 Win. and .308.

725	575	475	350	225	125

CZ 550 Prestige

This model is similar to the CZ 550 American, with the added features of jeweled bolt, semi-fancy walnut and hand rubbed finish. Chambered for the .270 or .30-06 cartridges, with 23.6" barrel. Weight approximately 7.3 lbs. Introduced in 2001.

700	625	550	425	300	175

CZ 550 Lux

This rifle is chambered for the 7x57, 6.5x55 SE and the 9.3x62 cartridges. Barrel length 23.6". Fixed magazine capacity 5 rounds. Bavarian-style stock with Turkish walnut. Open sights. Weight about 7.3 lbs.

575	450	375	200	150	75

CZ 550 Varmint

This model is chambered for the .308 Win. cartridge and is fitted with a 25.6" heavy barrel. No sights. Checkered walnut varmint-style stock. Ventilated recoil pad. Single set trigger. Detachable magazine holds 4 rounds. Weight about 9.3 lbs. In 2004 an HS Precision Kevlar stock was also offered on this model. **NOTE:** Add $200 for Kevlar stock.

650	500	400	300	200	100

CZ 550 Varmint Laminate

As above, with a gray laminate stock and offered in .22-250. Introduced in 2002.

750	600	450	350	200	125

CZ 550 Safari Magnum

Chambered for the .300 Win. Magnum, .375 H&H, .458 Win. Magnum and the .416 Rigby cartridges, this bolt-action rifle is fitted with a 25" barrel and 5-round internal magazine. Sights are one standing and two folding express rear with a hooded front sight. Blued finish. Bavarian-style Turkish walnut stock. Weight about 9.2 lbs.

925	750	500	400	300	200

CZ 550 American Safari Magnum

Introduced in 2004, this model is similar to the Safari Magnum above, with an American pattern stock. Offered with American walnut, brown laminate or camo laminate stock. Also offered with fancy American walnut stock. **NOTE:** Add $200 for laminate stock; $600 for fancy wood stock.

925	750	500	400	300	200

CZ 550 Ultimate Hunting Rifle

Similar to CZ550 Safari Magnum, but chambered for .300 Win. Magnum only. Custom select wood and 23.6" barrel. Accuracy guaranteed at one MOA to 1000 yards. Introduced 2006.

3600	3000	2450	1500	675	300

CZ 550 Premium

Introduced in 2000, this model features a hand fitted action, fancy walnut stock and 18 lpi checkering. Chambered for .30-06 and .270 Win. cartridges. Barrel length 23.6". Weight about 7.3 lbs.

925	750	500	400	300	200

CZ 550 Medium Magnum

This model is designed around a mid-sized magnum action. Fitted with a 23.6" barrel and has a fixed magazine capacity of 5 rounds. Chambered for the .300 Win. Magnum or the 7mm Rem. Magnum. Single-set trigger and adjustable rear sight. Weight about 7.3 lbs. Introduced in 2001.

700	575	425	300	200	100

CZ 550 Safari Classic Custom

Chambered for the .404 Jeffery, .450 Rigby or .505 Gibbs. Fancy grade checkered walnut stock. Single-set trigger. Express sights. **NOTE:** Add $100 for .505 Gibbs.

2400	2000	1400	750	400	300

CZ 584

A combination 12-gauge/7x57Rmm, .222- or .308-caliber over/under combination rifle/shotgun. Automatic ejectors, 24.5" ventilated rib barrels and single triggers. Blued with a walnut stock.

1000	775	600	500	400	200

CZ ZKK 600

Offered in 7x57mm, 7x64mm, .270 or .30-06. Features a Mauser-type bolt-action, with controlled feed, non-rotating extractor and dovetailed receiver in three action lengths. **NOTE:** Add $100 to prices for pop-up receiver sight that was discontinued in 1977.

750	625	500	425	325	175

CZ ZKK 601

As above, in .243- or .308-caliber.

700	600	500	425	325	175

CZ ZKK 602

As above, in .300 Holland & Holland, .375 Holland & Holland or .458 Winchester Magnum.

800	700	600	500	400	200

CZ 700 Sniper M1

Introduced in 2001, this rifle is chambered for the .308 Winchester cartridge and fitted with a 25.6" heavy barrel. Receiver has permanently attached Weaver rail. Laminated stock has adjustable cheekpiece and buttplate, with adjustable trigger. Magazine capacity 10 rounds. Weighs approximately 12 lbs.

2350	1800	1300	700	400	200

CZ 750 Sniper

Bolt-action rifle; .308 Win. 10-shot detachable magazine, 26" blued barrel, two scope mount systems, polymer stock, weighs 12 lbs. Introduced 2006.

2000	1750	1550	1050	600	325

CZ 455 American

Updated version of popular CZ 452. Action forged from steel billets. Walnut stock, cut checkering, oil finish. No sights furnished, 20.5" barrel. Trigger adjustable for weight and pull. Detachable magazine. Available with CZ Switch Barrel Set in .22 LR and .17 HMR. Single barrel guns chambered for .22LR, .22 WMR or .17 HMR. Thumb-hole Varmint Model available, with thumb-hole camo stock, single-set trigger, fluted barrel. **NOTE:** Add $150 Thumb-hole Varmint Model; $100 Switch Barrel set.

350	300	250	220	170	100

	NIB	EXC.	V.G.	GOOD	FAIR	POOR

CZ 512

Rimfire semi-automatic rifle. Dual guide rods for smooth operation. Hammer forged barrel, adjustable sights. Receiver is machined for 11mm dovetail mounts. Field stripping via a coin modular design for simple takedown. Aluminum upper receiver with polymer lower. Beechwood stock. Chambered for the .22LR and .22 WMR.

400	350	295	220	185	125

CZ 550 Urban Sniper

Compact profile in a modern sniper rifle. Free floating 16" barrel, with target crown. Surefire muzzle brake, with suppressor compatibility. Bell & Carlson fiberglass stock, aluminum bedding block, oversized bolt handle and single stage trigger. Available with a 5- or 10-round magazine. Chambered for the .308 Winchester, with other calibers on request.

2000	1725	1400	950	500	300

SHOTGUNS

CZ 581

A 12-gauge over/under double-barrel boxlock shotgun, with 28" ventilated rib barrels, single trigger and automatic ejectors. Blued, with a walnut stock.

875	700	600	450	400	200

CZ 712

This is a gas-operated semi-automatic 12-gauge 3" chamber shotgun, built on a lightweight alloy receiver. Offered with a choice of 26" or 28" vent rib barrels. Magazine is 4 rounds. Checkered walnut stock, with blued finish. Weight about 7 lbs. Introduced in 2004.

425	325	275	200	150	100

CZ 720

This model is similar to the above, but chambered for the 20-gauge 3" shell. Offered with a choice of 26" or 28" vent rib barrels. Walnut stock. Weight about 6 lbs. Introduced in 2004.

425	325	275	200	150	100

Redhead

This over/under is available in 12-, 20- or 28-gauge, with choke tubes and .410 bore with fixed chokes. Barrel lengths are 26" or 28". Single-selective trigger with extractors on 28-gauge and .410 bore models. Checkered walnut stock with pistol-grip. Receiver finish is silver. Weight from 6 lbs. to 8 lbs. depending on gauge.

795	625	500	350	200	150

Canvasback

This over/under gun is offered in 12- or 20-gauge. Fitted with 26" or 28" barrels, with choke tubes. Single-selective trigger with extractors. Black receiver finish. Weight about 7.5 lbs.

695	550	450	350	200	150

Woodcock

Available in 12-, 20-, 28-gauge and .410 bore, with 26" or 28" barrel, choke tubes except for fixed chokes on the .410 bore. Single-selective trigger with ejectors except for 12- and 20-gauge. Receiver is case colored with sideplate. Checkered walnut stock with pistol-grip. **NOTE:** Add $75 for 28-gauge and .410 bore models.

1055	825	625	450	300	225

Woodcock Custom Grade

Similar to the Woodcock model, but stocked with Grade IV walnut. Offered only in 20-gauge with 28" barrels.

1500	1250	975	600	400	200

Mallard

This 12- or 20-gauge over/under gun is fitted with double triggers and extractors. Barrel length 28". Checkered walnut stock with pistol-grip. Coin finish receiver.

695	550	450	350	200	150

Durango

This side-by-side gun is offered in 12- or 20-gauge, with 20" barrels and choke tubes. Extractors. Case colored receiver. Single trigger. Checkered walnut with pistol-grip.

795	625	550	400	300	200

Amarillo

As above, with double triggers.

700	550	425	350	250	150

	NIB	EXC.	V.G.	GOOD	FAIR	POOR

Ringneck

This side-by-side gun is chambered for the 12-, 16-, 20-, 28-gauge and .410 bore, with 26" or 28" barrels and choke tubes. Case colored receiver with side plates. Single-selective trigger with extractors. Checkered walnut stock with pistol-grip. **NOTE:** Add $100 for 16-gauge; $175 for 28-gauge and .410 bore models.

NIB	EXC.	V.G.	GOOD	FAIR	POOR
870	675	575	400	300	200

Ringneck Custom Grade

Select Grade IV walnut is used in the manufacture of this 20-gauge, with 28" barrels.

NIB	EXC.	V.G.	GOOD	FAIR	POOR
1200	1000	700	450	300	200

Bobwhite

As above, with straight-grip stock and double triggers.

NIB	EXC.	V.G.	GOOD	FAIR	POOR
795	625	550	400	300	200

Partridge

New in 2008, this side-by-side is available in 12-, 20-, 28-gauge and .410 bore, with 3" chambers (2.75" in 28-gauge), each with a frame scaled to its bore size. White chrome-plated receiver with scroll engraving. Boxlock action and double triggers. Straight-grip stock and splinter fore-end. Barrels are 28" in 12- and 20-gauge; 26" in 28-gauge and .410 bore. Includes five choke tubes (.410 bore is choked IC/MOD). **NOTE:** Add 20 percent for 28-gauge and .410 bore.

NIB	EXC.	V.G.	GOOD	FAIR	POOR
795	625	550	400	300	200

Grouse

New in 2008, the Grouse is a single trigger side-by-side in 12-, 20-, 28-gauge and .410 bore, with 3" chambers (2.75" in 28-gauge). White chrome-plated receiver with scroll engraving. Prince of Wales grip and semi-beavertail schnabel fore-end. Barrels are 28" in 12- and 20-gauge and 26" in 28-gauge and .410 bore. Includes five choke tubes (.410 is choked IC/MOD). Add 20 percent for 28-gauge and .410 bore.

NIB	EXC.	V.G.	GOOD	FAIR	POOR
995	800	700	550	450	300

CZ Sporting

This dedicated sporting clays over/under is a 12-gauge, with an adjustable comb stock and fore-end of #3 Circassian walnut. It features chrome-lined barrels back-bored to .736 and automatic ejectors. Barrels are 30" or 32". Five choke tubes included. Weight about 9 lbs.

NIB	EXC.	V.G.	GOOD	FAIR	POOR
2400	1800	1300	700	400	200

Hammer Coach

12-gauge cowboy gun, with double triggers, color case hardened receiver, external hammers and Turkish walnut pistol-grip stock and fore-end. Fixed IC and modified chokes. Introduced 2006.

NIB	EXC.	V.G.	GOOD	FAIR	POOR
795	625	550	400	300	200

PISTOLS

All currently imported CZ pistols can be ordered with tritium night sights with the exception of models CZ 97B and CZ 100. Add $80 for this option. **NOTE:** Substantial premium for factory-engraved examples.

CZ 75

Designed by the Koucky brothers in 1975, this model bears little resemblance to previous CZ pistols. Considered by many, including the late Jeff Cooper, to be the best pistol ever to come from the Czech Republic and one of the finest semi-automatics in the world. Chambered for the 9mm Parabellum cartridge, it is copied in many countries. This pistol has a breechlock system utilizing a Browning-style cam. The slide rides on the inside of the slide rails. Magazine capacity 15 rounds, barrel length 4.72", overall length 8" and the empty pistol weighs 34.5 oz. Offered in black paint, matte or polished blue finish.

NIB	EXC.	V.G.	GOOD	FAIR	POOR
500	450	425	400	325	250

CZ 75 B

Introduced in 1994, this CZ model is an updated version of the original CZ 75. Features a pinned front sight, a commander hammer, non-glare ribbed barrel and a squared trigger guard. Also offered in .40 S&W chamber. **NOTE:** Add $30 for .40 S&W; $20 for glossy blue; $25 for dual tone finish; $25 for nickel; $80 for tritium night sights.

NIB	EXC.	V.G.	GOOD	FAIR	POOR
510	400	300	250	175	125

CZ 75 30th Anniversary

Introduced in 2005, this model features special 30th anniversary engraving, gold inlays, gold plated controls, high gloss blue finish, engraved blonde finished birch grips. Magazine capacity 15 rounds. Limited to 1,000 pistols.

NIB	EXC.	V.G.	GOOD	FAIR	POOR
850	675	500	400	300	200

	NIB	EXC.	V.G.	GOOD	FAIR	POOR

CZ 75 Compact

Introduced in 1992, this is a compact version of the CZ 75. Barrel length 3.9", overall length 7.3" and weight about 32 oz. Offered in black paint, matte or polished blue finish. Traditional single-/double-action. In 2005 this model was offered with accessory rail and ambidextrous manual safety. Add $50 to prices. **NOTE:** Add $30 for .40 S&W; $20 for glossy blue; $25 for dual tone finish; $25 for nickel; $80 for tritium night sights.

475	425	300	250	175	125

CZ 75 Compact D

Essentially the same as the CZ 75 Compact, with a decocking double-action system and lightweight alloy frame. Weight approximately 25 oz. **NOTE:** Only 20 of these pistols were imported into the U.S. No longer in production. Expert appraisal suggested prior to sale.

555	450	300	225	150	100

CZ 75 B Tactical

Chambered for the 9mm Luger cartridge and fitted with a 4.7" barrel. This pistol has a single-/double-action trigger. Fixed sights. Rubber grips. Slide is black polycoat and the frame is a military green finish. Weight about 35 oz. Add 10 percent for night sights.

475	400	325	250	175	125

CZ 75 BD

Has all the same features as the Model 75 B, with the addition of a decocking double-action. Black polycoat finish.

450	400	300	225	150	100

CZ BD Compact

Introduced in 2001, this model features a 3.9" barrel, with decocking lever. Chambered for the .40 S&W cartridge. Blued finish. Magazine capacity 10 rounds. Weight about 32 oz. All other features same as CZ 75 B Compact.

400	350	300	225	150	100

CZ BD Compact Carry

Same as the model above, with rounded edges including trigger guard.

425	375	300	225	150	100

CZ 75 B SA

This model was introduced in 2000. Features a single-action trigger designed for competitive shooting that can be carried in condition one. Fitted with a straight trigger, manual safety and chambered for the 9mm cartridge. Weight about 35 oz.

520	400	325	225	150	100

CZ 75 Semi-Compact

This model was introduced in 1994. It has the same barrel length as the Compact (3.9"), but has the same full-size grip as the CZ 75. Magazine capacity 15 rounds of 9mm. Overall length is 7.3".

495	350	300	250	175	100

CZ 75 D PCR Compact

Introduced in 2000, this pistol is chambered for the 9mm cartridge. Features a light alloy frame and 3.9" barrel. Trigger is both single-/double-action with decocking lever. Low profile sights. Serrated front and rear backstrap. Designed for the Czech national police force. Magazine capacity 10 rounds. Weight about 27 oz.

525	425	350	225	150	100

CZ 75 Champion

This model is chambered for the .40 S&W, 9mm and 9x21 cartridges. Single-action-only trigger with straight trigger. Fitted with a 4.5" barrel, low profile adjustable sights and three port compensator. Furnished with blue slide and nickel frame. Hand fitted. Weight about 36 oz.

1475	1150	975	675	500	300

CZ 75 DAO

This model is similar to the CZ 75, with a double-action-only trigger, no safety lever and a spurless hammer. Offered in 9mm and .40 S&W. Barrel length 4.7". Weight about 35 oz. Introduced in 2000.

695	525	450	350	250	175

CZ P-01

Introduced in 2002, this pistol replaced the CZ 75 with the Czech National Police. It features a forged aluminum alloy frame and 3.8" barrel. Decocker single-/double-action. Fixed sights. Fitted with M3 accessory rail. Rubber grips and 14-round magazine. Black polycoat finish. Weight about 29 oz.

NIB	EXC.	V.G.	GOOD	FAIR	POOR
525	475	400	335	300	275

CZ P-06

This is the .40 S&W version of the P-01. Magazine capacity 10 rounds.

NIB	EXC.	V.G.	GOOD	FAIR	POOR
585	525	450	400	350	300

CZ P-09 Duty

Full-size high-capacity variation of P-01/P-06 series. Chambered in 9mm (19 round magazine) or .40 S&W (15 rounds). Low-profile sights, Picatinny rail, black polymer frame and black steel slide. P-07 model is single-stack variation

NIB	EXC.	V.G.	GOOD	FAIR	POOR
475	425	385	325	300	260

CZ 75 Standard IPSC (ST)

Designed and built for IPSC competition. Chambered for .40 S&W and fitted with a 5.4" barrel. Single-action-only trigger. Special high-profile sights. Weight about 45 oz.

NIB	EXC.	V.G.	GOOD	FAIR	POOR
1000	850	775	625	500	300

CZ 75 M IPSC

Similar to the CZ 75 Standard IPSC, with the addition of a two-port compensator and blast shield to protect frame-mounted optics. Slide racker standard. Red Dot optics. Barrel length 3.9". Weight about 45 oz. Introduced in 2001.

NIB	EXC.	V.G.	GOOD	FAIR	POOR
1350	1200	1050	675	550	325

CZ 75 Silver Anniversary Model

This model commemorates the 25th anniversary of the CZ Model 75 pistol. Features a high polish nickel finish, with walnut grips. The number "25" is inlaid in the grips. A total of 1000 pistols will be produced, with about 500 allocated for the U.S. market.

NIB	EXC.	V.G.	GOOD	FAIR	POOR
850	700	600	500	400	225

CZ 75 Stainless

All steel construction, double-stack magazines, 3-dot fixed sights and chambered for 9mm., 16+1 or 10+1 capacity and 4.72" barrel. The first stainless from CZ. Introduced 2006.

NIB	EXC.	V.G.	GOOD	FAIR	POOR
675	550	425	350	275	150

CZ 75 SP-01 Shadow

Chambered 9mm for IPSC "Production" Division competition. 19+1 capacity, 4.72" barrel., 41 oz., wood grip. Introduced 2006.

NIB	EXC.	V.G.	GOOD	FAIR	POOR
650	600	500	400	300	175

CZ 75 SP-01 Shadow Custom

Chambered in 9mm Parabellum. Steel slide and frame, CZ Custom Shop trigger job. Cold hammer-forged barrel, fiber-optic front sight, aluminum grips and 19-round magazine. Weight 36 ounces, 4.7" barrel and dual-tone finish. Customized for IPSC Production division. Introduced in 2011.

NIB	EXC.	V.G.	GOOD	FAIR	POOR
585	525	450	400	350	300

CZ 75 TS Czechmate

Comes with all parts necessary to compete in IPSC Open or Limited divisions. Chambered in 9mm Parabellum. Steel slide and frame, single-action grips. Comes with compensator and C-More red dot sight installed and ambidextrous slide racker. Includes front-sight adapter that replaces compensator, rear sight, ambidextrous safeties, aluminum grips, magazine well, one 26- and three 20-round magazines. Weight 48 ounces, 5.4" barrel, matte blue finish. Introduced in 2011.

NIB	EXC.	V.G.	GOOD	FAIR	POOR
2900	2500	2000	1500	800	350

CZ 75 Tactical Sport

Single-action for IPSC competition. Chambered in 9mm and .40 S&W. Dual tone (nickel/blued). Capacity 20+1 (9mm) or 16+1 (.40 S&W). 5.4" barrel; 45 oz. Introduced 2006.

NIB	EXC.	V.G.	GOOD	FAIR	POOR
1100	900	675	500	400	200

CZ 85 B

This model is similar in appearance to the CZ 75, but offers some new features such as ambidextrous safety and slide stop levers, squared trigger guard, adjustable sight and ribbed slide. Caliber, magazine capacity and weight are same as CZ 75. **NOTE:** Add $30 for .40 S&W $20 for glossy blue; $25 for dual tone finish; $25 for nickel finish.

NIB	EXC.	V.G.	GOOD	FAIR	POOR
525	475	425	300	250	175

	NIB	EXC.	V.G.	GOOD	FAIR	POOR

CZ 85 Combat

Similar to the CZ 85, with the addition of adjustable sights, walnut grips, round hammer and free dropping magazine. **NOTE:** Add $30 for .40 S&W $20 for glossy blue; $25 for dual tone finish; $25 for nickel finish.

NIB	EXC.	V.G.	GOOD	FAIR	POOR
500	450	325	250	175	125

CZ 40B

Introduced in 2002, this model is similar to the CZ 75. Features an alloy frame similar in shape to the Colt Model 1911. It is a single-/double-action design. Barrel length is 4.7". Magazine capacity 10 rounds. Chambered for the .40 S&W cartridge. Weight about 35 oz.

NIB	EXC.	V.G.	GOOD	FAIR	POOR
625	500	400	300	200	125

CZ Kadet

Chambered for the .22 LR cartridge and fitted with a 4.7" barrel. This model is a fixed barrel blowback semi-automatic pistol. Adjustable sights and blue finish. Weight about 36 oz.

NIB	EXC.	V.G.	GOOD	FAIR	POOR
510	400	300	225	175	100

CZ 75 Kadet Conversion

This is a separate conversion kit for the CZ 75/85 series. It converts these pistols to .22 LR. Adjustable rear sight. Supplied with 10-round magazine.

NIB	EXC.	V.G.	GOOD	FAIR	POOR
300	225	200	150	100	50

CZ 2075 RAMI

Introduced in 2004, this 9mm or .40 S&W pistol is fitted with a 3" barrel. It has a single-/double-action trigger. The design based on the CZ Model 75. Magazine capacity 10 rounds for the 9mm and 8 rounds for the .40 S&W. Weight about 25 oz.

NIB	EXC.	V.G.	GOOD	FAIR	POOR
450	400	350	300	250	175

CZ 83

This is a fixed-barrel .380-caliber pistol. Features an ambidextrous safety and magazine catch behind the trigger guard. The pistol is stripped by means of a hinged trigger guard. Barrel length 3.8", overall length 6.8" and weight about 23 oz. **NOTE:** For nickel finish add $5. In 1993 Special Editions of this pistol were introduced. These Special Editions consist of special finishes for the then-currently imported CZ pistols. They are high polish blue, nickel, chrome, gold and a combination of these finishes. These Special Edition finishes may affect price; they add between $100 and $250 to the cost of the pistol when new.

NIB	EXC.	V.G.	GOOD	FAIR	POOR
475	325	200	175	150	125

CZ 97 B

This pistol was planned for production in the summer of 1997. Chambered for the .45 ACP cartridge. Fitted with a 4.8" barrel and has a single-/double-action mode. Magazine capacity 10 rounds. Wood grips with blue finish. Weight approximately 40 oz.

NIB	EXC.	V.G.	GOOD	FAIR	POOR
665	525	400	300	175	100

CZ 100

This is a semi-automatic pistol introduced in 1996. Chambered for the 9mm or .40 S&W cartridge. It has a plastic frame and steel slide. Barrel length 3.75". Weight approximately 24 oz. U.S. magazine capacity 10 rounds.

NIB	EXC.	V.G.	GOOD	FAIR	POOR
525	450	325	2000	150	100

D

	NIB	EXC.	V.G.	GOOD	FAIR	POOR

D. W. M.
Berlin, Germany
See—Luger & Borchardt

Model 22

A 7.65mm caliber semi-automatic pistol, with 3.5" barrel. Blued with walnut grips; later changed to plastic grips. Approximately 40,000 manufactured between 1921 and 1931.

—	950	775	500	400	250

DAEWOO
Pusan, Korea

DH-40

Semi-automatic pistol chambered for .40 S&W cartridge. Has a 4.13" barrel and magazine capacity of 11 rounds. Weight approximately 32 oz.

495	375	300	250	175	100

DP-51B

Semi-automatic pistol chambered for the 9mm cartridge. Fitted with a 4.13" barrel. Magazine capacity 13 rounds. Overall length is 7.5"; weight approximately 28 oz.

400	325	275	225	175	100

DP-51SB

More compact design, with 3.6" barrel and 10-round magazine. Weight 27 oz. Stainless steel finish.

450	395	275	225	175	100

DP-51CB

Same as above, fitted with a 3.6" barrel. Magazine capacity 10 rounds. Weight about 26 oz.

450	375	300	250	175	100

DP-52

Semi-automatic pistol chambered for .22 LR cartridge. Has 3.82" barrel length and magazine capacity 10 rounds. Operates in double/single-action modes. Overall length 6.7"; weight approximately 23 oz.

395	325	250	200	150	100

DH380

Introduced in 1996, this semi-automatic pistol is chambered for the .380 ACP cartridge. Fitted with a 3.8" barrel and magazine capacity of 8 rounds. Firing model is double/single-action. Weight approximately 24 oz.

425	375	275	225	150	100

DR200

Introduced in 1996, this post-ban semi-automatic rifle is chambered for the .223 Rem. cartridge. Features a black matte finish, with a synthetic thumbhole stock. Barrel length 18.3". Uses AR-15 magazines, not included with rifle. Weight about 9 lbs.

975	875	500	400	300	150

K-2/AR-100 (Max I)

A 5.56mm caliber pre-ban semi-automatic rifle, with an 18" barrel. Gas-operated rotary bolt-action, magazines interchangeable with those from the M-16. Black. Introduced in 1985. No longer imported.

1450	1200	950	700	500	400

K1A1 (Max II)

Rifle is quite similar to K-2/AR-100, with a folding composite stock.

1450	1200	950	700	500	400

DAEWOO PRECISION IND., LTD.
South Korea

USAS 12

12-gauge semi-automatic shotgun, with 18.25" cylinder-bored barrel. Either 10-shot box magazine or 20-shot drum magazine. Parkerized with composition stock. Model no longer imported.

	NIB	EXC.	V.G.	GOOD	FAIR	POOR

WARNING: As of May 1, 2001, this firearm must be registered with ATF and transfer tax of $200 paid. This firearm classified as a destructive device. Unregistered guns will be considered contraband after this date. Persons in possession will be in violation of federal law. Value speculative.

DAISY
Rogers, Arkansas

VL Rifle

A .22 combustible cartridge single-shot rifle, with an 18" barrel and plastic stock. Cartridge is ignited by compressed air. Manufactured during 1968 and 1969. Believed that fewer than 20,000 were made. Add considerable premium if large quantity of VL ammunition is present.

275	100	85	75	50	25

VL Presentation Model

As above, with a walnut stock. Approximately 4,000 made in 1968 and 1969.

275	150	125	100	75	50

VL Cased Presentation Model

As above, with gold plaque inlaid in the stock. Fitted case containing 300 VL cartridges.

325	200	175	125	100	75

Model 2201/2211

Bolt-action single-shot rifle chambered for .22 LR cartridge. Fitted with a 19" barrel and octagon shroud. Ramp blade front sight, with adjustable notch rear sight. Synthetic stock Model 2211 and walnut stock Model 2201. Trigger is adjustable. Weight about 6.5 lbs.

200	150	100	60	50	25

Model 2202/2212

Similar to above model in appearance, but fitted with a 10-round rotary magazine. Synthetic stock Model 2212 and walnut stock Model 2202. Weight about 6.5 lbs.

200	150	100	60	50	25

Model 2203/2213

Semi-automatic rifle chambered for .22 LR cartridge. Has 7-round magazine and 19" barrel. Synthetic stock Model 2213 and walnut stock Model 2203. Weight approximately 6.5 lbs.

225	175	125	75	75	50

DAKIN GUN CO.
San Francisco, California

Model 100

A 12- and 20-gauge boxlock double-barrel shotgun, with 26" or 28" barrels, various chokes, extractors and double triggers. Engraved, blued, with a checkered walnut stock. Manufactured in the 1960s.

—	475	325	275	200	100

Model 147

As above, with ventilated rib barrels.

—	450	375	250	200	100

Model 160

As above, with single-selective trigger.

—	700	600	450	250	150

Model 215

As above, but more finely finished.

—	1800	1600	1100	500	250

Model 170

A 12-, 16- and 20-gauge over/under shotgun, with 26" or 28" ventilated rib barrels, various chokes and double triggers. Blued and lightly engraved. Discontinued in the 1960s.

—	500	425	350	275	150

DAKOTA ARMS, INC.
Sturgis, South Dakota

This company was formed by Don Allen. He was a fine craftsman in the field of custom rifles. The company offers four basic models, with a number of options to fit the customers' needs or wants.

	NIB	EXC.	V.G.	GOOD	FAIR	POOR

Workmanship and materials are of the highest quality. In business since 1987, the company was purchased by Remington Arms Co. in 2009. **NOTE:** All prices are base prices. Dakota offers a number of extra cost options that can greatly affect the value of its rifles and shotguns.

RIFLES

Dakota 76 Classic
A .257 Roberts, .270 Winchester, .280 Remington, .30-06, 7mm Remington Magnum, .338, .300 Winchester Magnum and the .458 Winchester Magnum bolt-action rifle, with a 23" barrel and Mauser-type extractor. Checkered walnut stock. Manufactured in 1987.

5000	4250	3000	1650	800	400

Dakota 76 Varmint Grade
Introduced in 1996, this rifle chambered for a variety of cartridges from the .17 Rem. to the 6mm PPC. Single-shot bolt-action design available in right-/left-hand versions. Barrel length 24". Varmint-style stock is semi-fancy walnut, with oil finish and no checkering. Many extra cost options offered for this model.

2500	2000	1500	1100	800	400

Varmint Hunter
Model built on Model 97 action. Standard features are fiberglass stock, round-action single-shot, adjustable trigger and black recoil pad. Barrel length 24". Offered in calibers from .220 Swift to .308 Winchester. Weight about 8 lbs. Introduced in 1999.

2195	1750	1000	750	600	300

Safari Grade
Chambered in .375 H&H, .458 Winchester Magnum and other short Magnum calibers. Features an ebony fore-end tip, one-piece magazine assembly and open sights. Weighs approximately 8.5 lbs.

6500	5250	2000	1350	700	350

Alpine Grade
As above, but lighter in weight. Chambered for .22-250, .243, 6mm, .250-3000, 7mm/08, .308 and .358. Introduced in 1989.

5400	3950	3000	2000	700	350

African Grade
As above in .416 Rigby, .416 Dakota, .404 Jeffery and .450 Dakota. Walnut especially selected for strength, with crossbolts through the stock. Weighs between 9 and 10 lbs.

7300	5750	4500	2200	1075	400

Model 10 Single-Shot
Built on a single-shot falling action, this rifle features a 23" barrel and choice of XX grade wood with oil finish. Fine line checkering, steel grip cap and .5" recoil pad are also standard. Weighs about 5.5 lbs.

4500	4000	2750	1550	900	400

Model 10 Single-Shot Magnum
Same as above, in calibers .338 Win. Magnum to .416 Dakota. Weight about 6.5 lbs.

5895	4600	3200	1900	1000	450

Dakota .22 Long Rifle Sporter
Fitted with a 22" barrel. X grade oil finish walnut, with fine line checkering and steel grip cap. A .5" black recoil pad standard. Weighs about 6.5 lbs. Model ceased production in 1998.

1750	1300	800	650	500	275

Dakota .22 Long Rifle Sporter (New Model)
This is a reintroduction (2003) of Dakota .22 rifle.

2800	2500	2000	1350	700	350

Model 97 Long Range Hunter
Introduced in 1997, this bolt-action rifle offered in 13 calibers: .250-6, .257 Roberts, .270 Win., .280 Rem., 7mm Rem. Magnum, 7mm Dakota Magnum, .30-06, .300 Win. Magnum, .300 Dakota Magnum, .338 Win. Magnum, .330 Dakota Magnum, .375 H&H and .375 Dakota Magnum. Barrel length depends on caliber, but are either 24" or 26". Trigger is fully adjustable. Many other special features. Stock is black synthetic, with one-piece bedding. Black recoil pad standard. Weight approximately 7.7 lbs.

2800	2400	2200	1500	800	375

	NIB	EXC.	V.G.	GOOD	FAIR	POOR

Model 97 Lightweight Hunter

Introduced in 1998, this rifle features barrel lengths from 22" to 24" in both short-/long-actions. Special lightweight composite stock is used. Calibers offered range from .22-250 to .330 Dakota Magnum. Weights are between 6.15 to 6.5 lbs., depending on caliber and barrel length. **NOTE:** Add 50 to 70 percent for Deluxe with AAA grade wood.

2000	1500	1100	800	500	375

Model T-76 Longbow Tactical Rifle

Long range tactical bolt-action rifle available in 3 calibers: .338 Lapua, .300 Dakota Magnum and .330 Dakota Magnum. Fiberglass stock is an A-2 McMillan in black or olive green. Adjustable length of pull, with bipod spike in forearm. The 28" stainless steel is .950 diameter at the muzzle, with muzzle-brake. Rifle sold with a number of accessories; case with bipod, tool kit and tool box. Weight about 13.7 lbs.

4600	4250	3000	1650	800	400

Model 76 Traveler

Model introduced in 1999 and built on a modified Model 76 design. Stock is wood. Disassembly is threadless. Offered in standard length action, short magnum-action and long-action in both left-/right hand. Offered in three grades.

Classic

6200	5500	4000	2700	1800	900

Safari

6900	5900	4200	3000	2000	1200

African

7600	6500	5000	3200	2000	1200

Classic Predator

Bolt-action rifle is chambered for the .17 VarTarg, .17 Rem., .17 Tactical, .20 VarTarg, .20 Tactical, .20 PPC, .204 Ruger, .221 Rem. Fireball, .222 Rem., .222 Rem. Magnum, .223 Rem., .22 BR, 6 PPC and the 6 BR. Fitted with a 22" stainless steel barrel, checkered special select Claro walnut stock, with cheekpiece.

3800	3000	2200	1700	800	375

Serious Predator

As above, with AAA Claro walnut stock.

3000	2250	2000	1650	800	400

All-Weather Predator

As above, with varmint style composite stock.

2500	2000	1600	1000	500	300

Double Rifle

Available in most common calibers. Fitted with exhibition walnut, with pistol-grip. Barrel is 25". Round-action with selective ejectors, recoil pad and hard case. Prices listed for guns without engraving.

30000	24000	18000	10000	3500	800

Little Sharps Rifle

Introduced in 2003, a smaller version (20 percent) of full size Sharps rifle. Standard rifle has 26" octagon barrel, straight-grip stock with XX walnut, steel buttplate and blade front sight. Offered in calibers from .17 HMR to .30-40 Krag. Weight around 8 lbs.

5500	3950	2750	2000	1500	400

Limited Edition .30-06 Model 76

Ultra-decked-out version of Model 76; commemorates 100th anniversary of .30-06 cartridge; production limited to 101 units. Introduced 2006.

8000	5500	4000	2650	1700	500

Limited Edition .30-06 Model 10

Ultra-decked-out version of Model 10; commemorates 100th anniversary of .30-06 cartridge; production limited to 101 units. Introduced 2006.

8000	5500	4000	2650	1700	500

	NIB	EXC.	V.G.	GOOD	FAIR	POOR

SHOTGUNS

Classic Grade
Grade features case colored round-action, with straight-grip and fancy walnut oil finish stock. Forearm is splinter type. Double trigger standard, with choice of chokes. No longer in production.

| 7950 | 5200 | 4400 | 3000 | 2000 | 600 |

Premier Grade
Grade features case colored round-action, with 50 percent engraving coverage. Exhibition grade English walnut stock, with straight-grip and splinter forearm. Oil rubbed finish. Double triggers are standard, with choice of chokes. **NOTE:** Add 10 percent for 28-gauge and .410 bore.

| 13950 | 9500 | 7000 | 4750 | 2900 | 500 |

Dakota American Legend
Introduced in 1996, this side-by-side shotgun offered in 12-, 20- and 28-gauge and .410 bore. Concave rib, splinter forearm, double triggers, straight-grip stock, 27" barrels and full scroll engraving on frame. Many additional extra cost options are offered that can greatly affect price. Base price listed.

| 18000 | 14000 | 11500 | 7900 | 5000 | 600 |

Dakota Shotgun
Similar to American Legend. Offered in two grades of finish. New grades first offered in 1997.

DAKOTA ARMS INC.—FERLIB SHOTGUNS

In 2000, Dakota Arms Inc. became the exclusive importer of Ferlib shotguns in the U.S. Models listed are imported and sold by Dakota Arms Inc.

Model 7
| 10950 | 8000 | 6500 | 5000 | 4000 | 700 |

Prince Model
| 11950 | 9000 | 7500 | 6000 | 4500 | 700 |

Prince Model Side-Lever
| 14500 | 10500 | 8500 | 7000 | 5500 | 700 |

Rex
| 14950 | 11000 | 8500 | 7000 | 5500 | 700 |

Premier
| 16950 | 12500 | 10000 | 7200 | 5500 | 600 |

Sideplate Model
| 14400 | 10500 | 8500 | 7000 | 5500 | 700 |

Sideplate Model with Gold
| 15100 | 11250 | 10000 | 7200 | 5500 | 600 |

Sideplate with Scroll
| 14000 | 10500 | 8500 | 7000 | 5500 | 700 |

Hammer Gun
| 19000 | 14000 | 12000 | 10000 | 5000 | 700 |

H.H. Model—no engraving
| 20000 | 15000 | 13000 | 11000 | 570 | 675 |

Esposizione
| 25500 | 18000 | 13000 | 10000 | 7000 | 700 |

L'Inglesina
| 25500 | 18000 | 13000 | 10000 | 7000 | 700 |

Model E "Fantasy
| 39500 | 27500 | 22000 | 15500 | 11000 | 700 |

Boss—no engraving
| 29500 | 20000 | 15000 | 10000 | 7000 | 750 |

	NIB	EXC.	V.G.	GOOD	FAIR	POOR

DAKOTA ARMS INC.—SIACE SHOTGUNS

Imported from Italy in 2004 and called Dakota SuperLight. Shotguns are side-by-sides, with boxlock actions.

Field

Available in 12-, 16-, 20-, 24-, 28- and 32-gauge as well as .410 bore. Case colored receiver with select Turkish walnut. Checkering is 24 lpi. Double triggers. Border engraving. Weight about 5.5 lbs. for 20-gauge. **NOTE:** Add $600 for 16-, 32-gauge and .410 bore.

4500	3500	2400	1775	1100	500

Grade II

As above, with 65 percent coverage of English scroll. **NOTE:** Add $700 for 16-, 32-gauge and .410 bore.

5500	4250	3200	1600	800	400

Grade III

As above, with deeply cut vine and leaf scroll. Deluxe Turkish walnut and 65 percent coverage of English scroll. **NOTE:** Add $800 for 16-, 32-gauge and .410 bore.

6500	5000	4000	3000	1650	400

DALY, CHARLES

Charles Daly was co-founder of Schoverling & Daly sporting goods company in New York City in 1865. The company imported some of the better-made shotguns from Europe and Charles Daly was used as the brand name. Daly trademark was sold several times over the years, with various owners importing guns from Belgium, Germany, Japan, Italy and other countries.

EARLY PRUSSIAN GUNS

Commander Over/Under Model 100

Boxlock over/under Anson & Deeley action shotgun chambered for all gauges. Choice of barrel length and chokes, double triggers (standard) or single-selective trigger. Blued, with a checkered walnut stock. Manufactured in Belgium in late 1930s.

—	1000	750	475	275	200

Commander Over/Under Model 200

As above, with a better-grade walnut stock.

—	1100	850	550	300	200

Superior Side-by-Side

As above, with an Anson & Deeley boxlock action and double triggers. Blued, with a walnut stock. Not manufactured after 1933. **NOTE:** Add $600 for 20-gauge, $1000 for 10-gauge.

—	1400	950	650	450	250

Empire Side-by-Side

As above, but engraved with a better grade of walnut.

—	3750	3000	2250	1250	600

NOTE: Prices shown for Empire and Diamond grade models are for those manufactured by Sauer. Add 20 to 30 percent for Linder manufacture.

Diamond Grade Side-by-Side

A deluxe version of above.

—	5750	4500	3750	3000	1200

Regent Diamond Grade Side-by-Side

Custom order version of above.

—	11500	8500	7000	5500	2500

Empire Over/Under

A 12-, 16- and 20-gauge Anson & Deeley boxlock shotgun. Choice of barrel length and choke, double triggers and automatic ejectors. Engraved with fine quality scrollwork and walnut stock. Discontinued in 1933.

—	3500	2750	2000	1150	500

Diamond Grade Over/Under

As above, but more finely finished.

—	5500	3750	3250	2500	1250

	NIB	EXC.	V.G.	GOOD	FAIR	POOR

SEXTUPLE SINGLE-BARREL TRAP

Empire Grade
A 12-gauge boxlock single-barrel shotgun, with 30"-34" Full choke barrels, ventilated rib and automatic ejectors. Strong action features six locking lugs. Engraved with a walnut stock. Manufactured after 1933.

	NIB	EXC.	V.G.	GOOD	FAIR	POOR
	—	2950	2450	1850	1500	750

Regent Diamond Grade
As above, with more engraving and better grade walnut stock.

	—	7500	6300	5500	4500	2000

DRILLINGS

Superior Grade
A 12-, 16- and 20-gauge over/under rifle/shotgun, with a rifle barrel in .25-20, .25-35 or .30-30. Engraved with a walnut stock. Not manufactured after 1933.

	—	3700	2450	1800	1450	800

Diamond Grade
As above, with more engraving and better grade of walnut in the stock.

	—	5250	4500	3750	3000	1500

Regent Diamond Grade
As above, with elaborate engraving and highest quality walnut stock.

	—	12500	9500	7200	5800	3000

B.C. MIROKU GUNS

Empire Grade Side-by-Side
A 12-, 16- and 20-gauge Anson and Deeley boxlock shotgun, with 26", 28" and 30" barrels, various chokes, extractors and a single trigger. Blued, with a checkered walnut stock. Manufactured between 1968 and 1971. **NOTE:** Add 10 percent for ventilated rib barrels and/or 20-gauge.

	—	750	550	375	200	100

Superior Grade Single Barrel Trap
A 12-gauge boxlock shotgun, with 32" or 34" ventilated rib barrels, Full choke and automatic ejector. Blued, with Monte Carlo walnut stock. Manufactured between 1968 and 1976.

	—	675	525	450	350	200

Over/Unders
A 12-, 20- and 28-gauge and .410 bore boxlock shotgun, with 26", 28" and 30" barrels and ventilated ribs. Various choke combinations were offered, with single-selective triggers and automatic ejectors. Blued, with checkered walnut stocks. Differences between grades are degree and quality of engraving and grade of walnut used for stock. Smaller-bore guns bring a premium as listed. Manufactured between 1963 and 1976 by B.C. Miroku. **NOTE:** Add 10 percent 20-gauge; 20 percent 28-gauge; 30 percent .410.

Venture Grade

	—	900	675	500	375	200

Venture Grade Skeet or Trap
Offered with either 26" Skeet & Skeet or 30" Full choke.

	—	800	550	475	375	200

Field Grade
Chambered for 12- and 20-gauge only.

	—	900	700	500	425	200

Superior Grade

	—	1200	900	600	525	200

Superior Grade Trap

	—	800	600	525	425	200

Diamond Grade

	—	1800	1400	975	650	300

	NIB	EXC.	V.G.	GOOD	FAIR	POOR

Diamond Grade Trap or Skeet

With either 26" Skeet & Skeet or 30" Full choke barrels and Monte Carlo stocks. **NOTE:** Wide rib add 5 percent.

	NIB	EXC.	V.G.	GOOD	FAIR	POOR
	—	1500	1100	800	650	350

ITALIAN MANUFACTURE
SEMI-AUTOMATIC SHOTGUNS

Manufactured by the firm Breda in Milan, Italy. Semi-automatic "Novamatic" produced in 1968. All other models began Italian production in 1976. Imported by KBI, Inc. until 2010.

Novamatic Lightweight

A 12-gauge semi-automatic shotgun, with 26" or 28" ventilated rib barrel and screw-in choke tubes. Receiver is alloy, with checkered walnut stock. Imported under the Daly name in 1968 only.

	—	400	325	275	175	125

Novamatic Trap

As above, with Monte Carlo stock and 30" full choke barrel.

	—	415	340	290	200	150

Charles Daly Automatic

A 12-gauge Magnum semi-automatic shotgun, with 26" or 28" ventilated rib barrels, screw-in choke tubes and 5-shot magazine. A slug gun is available, with rifle sights. Checkered walnut grip in two versions—pistol-grip and English-style straight-grip. **NOTE:** Choke-tube model would be worth a 10 percent premium.

	—	475	395	300	225	150

Field Grade

Introduced in 1999, this model has several variations all in 12-gauge. Standard gun choice of 24", 26", 28" or 30" barrels, with screw-in chokes and synthetic stocks. Slug gun offered with 22" barrel in blue or nickel finish. A full coverage camo model offered in same configurations as field grade. **NOTE:** Add $30 for nickel slug gun; $100 for camo gun.

	425	365	255	200	150	100

Superior Grade Hunter

Offered in 12-gauge, with choice of 26", 28" or 30" ventilated rib barrels. Walnut stock, with hand checkering. Gold trigger and highlights. Introduced in 1999.

	550	425	365	245	160	100

Superior Grade Sporting

Same as above, with 28" or 30" ported barrel and select walnut stock.

	570	450	365	245	160	100

Superior Grade Trap

This 12-gauge model offered with a choice of 30" or 32" ventilated rib barrel. Walnut stock with hand checkering. Introduced in 1999.

	625	475	390	270	185	100

Field Hunter VR-MC

This series of 3" semi-automatic 12-gauges is finished in one of four Realtree/Advantage camo patterns or matte black. Barrels are 24", 26" or 28". Advantage Timber model available in 20-gauge and black matte available in 20- and 28-gauge. **NOTE:** Add 15 percent for camo.

	425	365	255	200	150	100

Field Hunter VR-MC Youth

As above, with 1.6" shorter stock and 22" barrel. 20-gauge only.

	400	345	230	165	125	100

Superior II

New in 2007, Superior II line of semi-automatics features oil-finished Turkish walnut stocks and three chokes.

	600	525	395	275	200	100

Hunter

Available in 12- and 20-gauge, with 26" or 28" barrel. 28-gauge with 26" barrel.

	600	525	395	275	200	100

	NIB	EXC.	V.G.	GOOD	FAIR	POOR

Sport
In 12-gauge only, with 28" or 30" ported barrel and wide rib.

NIB	EXC.	V.G.	GOOD	FAIR	POOR
600	525	395	275	200	100

Trap
In 12-gauge 30" ported barrel only, with Monte Carlo comb and wide rib.

NIB	EXC.	V.G.	GOOD	FAIR	POOR
650	550	425	275	200	100

Field Hunter Maxi-Mag VR-MC Semi-Auto
This 3.5" 12-gauge comes in one of three Realtree/Advantage camos and matte black, with 24", 26" or 28" ported barrel. **NOTE:** Add 15 percent for camo.

NIB	EXC.	V.G.	GOOD	FAIR	POOR
425	365	255	200	150	100

TURKISH SHOTGUNS

Model 105
This 3" 12-gauge over/under features an engraved nickel-plated steel receiver, double triggers and extractors. Chokes are fixed Modified and Full with 28" barrels; or Modified and Improved Cylinder with 26" barrels.

NIB	EXC.	V.G.	GOOD	FAIR	POOR
600	450	395	300	175	100

Model 106/206
Similar to Model 105, but in 12-, 20- and 28-gauge and .410 bore. Model 106 has a blued receiver, with raised gold ducks and rounded pistol-grip. All but the .410 include three screw-in chokes. Barrels are 26" or 28" in 12- and 20-gauge and 26" in 28-gauge and .410. Frames are scaled to gauge. **NOTE:** Add $50 for 28-gauge and .410 bore; $50 for model 206 with SST, ejectors.

NIB	EXC.	V.G.	GOOD	FAIR	POOR
650	495	395	300	175	100

Model 306
This 3" side-by-side is offered in 12- and 20-gauge, with 26" or 28" barrels. Turkish walnut stock, gold-plated single selective trigger and extractors. Three choke tubes.

NIB	EXC.	V.G.	GOOD	FAIR	POOR
400	350	295	175	115	75

PUMP SHOTGUNS

Field Grade
This 12-gauge pump gun offered with 24", 26", 28" or 30" barrels. Fixed chokes. A slug gun offered with 18.5" barrels, with blue or nickel finish. Camo version also offered. First introduced in 1999. Model also offered in 20-gauge in both full size and youth. **NOTE:** Add $10 for nickel gun; $80 for full camo gun.

NIB	EXC.	V.G.	GOOD	FAIR	POOR
300	225	165	125	100	65

Field Tactical
This pump gun chambered for the 12-gauge shell. Fitted with an 18.5" barrel and fixed blade front sight . An 18.5" slug barrel with adjustable sights is also offered. Black synthetic stock. Blued or nickel finish. **NOTE:** Add $30 for nickel finish.

NIB	EXC.	V.G.	GOOD	FAIR	POOR
350	275	190	150	125	75

Field Hunter MM (Maxi-Mag)
This is a 12-gauge pump gun chambered for the 3.5" Magnum shell. Offered with choice of 24", 26" or 28" vent rib ported barrels. Black synthetic stock, with camo stock also available. Weight about 6.75 lbs. **NOTE:** Add $50 for camo finish.

NIB	EXC.	V.G.	GOOD	FAIR	POOR
275	225	150	125	100	65

Field Hunter Maxi-Mag VR-MC Pump
Newer versions of Maxi-Mag are recognized by an updated fore-end and availability in Timber or Hardwoods camo or matte black. All are 3.5" 12-gauge, with a 24", 26" or 28" ported barrel. **NOTE:** Add 15 percent for camo.

NIB	EXC.	V.G.	GOOD	FAIR	POOR
350	300	255	200	150	100

OVER/UNDER GUNS

Country Squire Over/Under Folding
Model features a folding stock ,with over/under ventilated rib barrels 25.5" in length. Gold double triggers and walnut stock. Chokes are Full and Full.

NIB	EXC.	V.G.	GOOD	FAIR	POOR
550	450	325	250	175	125

NIB	EXC.	V.G.	GOOD	FAIR	POOR

Field II Hunter

A 12-, 20-, 28-gauge and .410 bore over/under shotgun, with 26" or 28" chrome-lined ventilated rib barrels. Crossbolt boxlock-action, single-selective trigger and extractors. Blued, with a stamped checkered walnut stock. Introduced in 1989. Weight for 12-gauge guns about 7 lbs.; 28-gauge and .410 bore guns about 6.75 lbs. **NOTE:** Add $150 for ejectors.

900	775	575	400	250	200

Field Ultra Light

Introduced in 1999, model offered in either 12- or 20-gauge, with 26" barrel choked Improved Cylinder/Modified. Receiver is aluminum alloy. Walnut stock, with pistol-grip and slim fore-end. Weight approximately 5.5 lbs.

950	850	650	450	—	—

Field III

An economy level model in 12- or 20-gauge, imported from Turkey in the 1980s.

400	350	300	250	200	150

Empire

Similar to Field II Hunter, with automatic ejectors, screw-in choke tubes and a silver-finished receiver. Walnut stock is hand-checkered. Introduced in 1989.

1150	1000	750	500	400	200

Empire II EDL Hunter

Offered in 12-, 20-, 28-gauge and .410 bore. Features 26" or 28" vent rib barrels (26" only on 28-gauge or .410), choke tubes on the 12- and 20-gauge and fixed chokes on 28-gauge and .410 guns. Receiver has game scene engraving, with nine gold inlays. Weight 6.25 to 7.25 lbs. depending on gauge.

2000	1500	1100	700	375	200

Empire Sporting

Model offered in 12-gauge, with choice of 28" or 30" barrels. Fitted with a Monte Carlo stock and automatic ejectors.

1850	1425	1000	600	375	200

Empire Grade Combination

An over/under, with a 12-gauge top barrel and rifle lower barrel. Rifle calibers are .22 Hornet, .223 Rem., .22-250, .243, .270, .308 and .30-06. Barrel length 23.5". Weight about 7.25 lbs.

2190	1600	1150	800	375	200

Empire Trap

This 12-gauge model features a Monte Carlo stock with 30" barrels.

2250	1650	1200	750	325	150

Empire Grade Trap Combo

Model features a 30" over/under barrel, with an additional 32" single barrel. Buttstock has fully adjustable comb. Introduced in 1999. **NOTE:** Deduct $600 for non-adjustable stock.

4000	3000	2000	1450	675	375

Diamond GTX DL Hunter

As above in 12- and 20-gauge Magnum. Various barrel lengths and screw-in choke tubes, single trigger, automatic ejectors and select walnut stock. Extra fancy walnut stock and hand engraved frame.

9000	8000	6000	5000	2000	1000

Diamond GTX Sporting

This 12-gauge model features a choice of 28" or 30" barrels, with automatic ejectors and Monte Carlo stock.

5900	4500	2750	1250	900	450

Diamond GTX Trap or Skeet

As above, with 26" or 30" barrels. Available in 1989. **NOTE:** Wide rib add 5 percent.

5900	4500	2750	1250	900	400

Diamond GTX Trap Combo

This model has a fully adjustable stock. Choice of 30" over/under barrels and 32" single barrel.

7500	5700	4250	2650	1000	450

	NIB	EXC.	V.G.	GOOD	FAIR	POOR

Presentation Grade

As above, with a Purdey-type boxlock action and engraved false sideplates. Stock of deluxe French walnut. Discontinued in 1986.

	—	5500	3750	1650	900	450

Superior II

A 12-, 20-, 28-gauge and .410 bore over/under shotgun, with 26" or 28" ventilated rib barrels. Various chokes, single trigger and automatic ejectors. Engraved, blued with a walnut stock. Weight: 12- and 20-gauge about 7 lbs.; 28-gauge and .410 about 6.75 lbs.

	625	550	350	300	200	150

Superior II Sporting

This 12-gauge model fitted with choice of 28" or 30" barrels, Monte Carlo stock and automatic ejectors.

	650	575	375	325	225	165

Superior Grade Trap

This 12-gauge gun fitted with 30" barrels, Monte Carlo stock and automatic ejectors.

	1700	1250	900	625	425	200

Superior Grade Combination

This is an over/under, with 12-gauge top barrel and rifle lower barrel. Rifle calibers are .22 Hornet, .223 Rem. and .30-06. Barrel length 23.5". Weight about 7.25 lbs.

	1480	1100	800	550	350	175

SINGLE-BARREL SHOTGUNS

Empire Trap Mono

Single barrel trap gun, with choice of 30" or 32" barrels. Automatic ejectors and Monte Carlo fully adjustable stock. **NOTE:** Deduct $600 for non-adjustable stock.

	2450	1800	1250	900	375	175

Diamond GTX Mono

Model has fully adjustable stock. Barrel choice 30". Automatic ejectors are standard.

	6500	5250	3750	1750	900	400

SIDE-BY-SIDE GUNS

Field Hunter

A side-by-side boxlock gun chambered for 10-, 12-, 20-, 28-gauge and .410 bore. Barrel length from 26" to 32" depending on gauge. Extractors are standard. Weight from 8.75 lbs. to 6.75 lbs. depending on gauge. Nickel receiver, with game scene engraving. **NOTE:** Add $40 for 28-gauge and .410 guns; $100 for automatic ejectors.

	1190	850	600	400	250	100

Superior Hunter

A 12-, 20- and 28 gauge as well as .410 bore boxlock double-barrel shotgun, with 26" or 28" barrels, various chokes, boxlock action and single trigger. Blued, with a walnut stock. In 2002, this model was offered in 10-gauge with 28" barrels. **NOTE:** Add $50 for 28-gauge and .410 guns.

	1660	1200	850	600	350	150

Empire Hunter

Offered in 12- and 20-gauge, with 26" or 28" barrels. Chokes are fixed. Weight about 7 lbs. Silver receiver with game scene engraving, straight stock, splinter forearm, automatic ejectors.

	2120	1500	1100	700	400	200

Diamond DL

Offered in 12-, 20-, 28-gauge and .410 bore, with 26" or 28" barrels and fixed chokes. Fancy walnut straight-grip stock, hand detachable sidelocks, 100 percent hand engraving coverage. Hand fit and finished. Weight: 12- and 20-gauge about 6.75 lbs.; 28-gauge and .410 about 5.75 lbs. Model generally made on special order only. **NOTE:** Add $450 for 28-gauge and .410 bore.

	6700	5000	3500	1500	750	350

	NIB	EXC.	V.G.	GOOD	FAIR	POOR

Diamond Regent DL

High grade model of above, with best quality engraving, hand-checkered AAA-grade walnut stock, fixed chokes. Limited importation in 1997.

	NIB	EXC.	V.G.	GOOD	FAIR	POOR
	18000	16000	12500	—	—	—

Country Squire Side-by-Side Folding

Model features a folding stock, with 25.5" barrels, gold double triggers and walnut stock. Chokes are Full and Full.

	475	375	275	200	145	100

Model 306

In 12- or 20-gauge, with 26" or 28" barrels, choke tubes, single trigger and extractors. Imported from Turkey from 2006 to 2008.

	600	525	450	300	200	150

Classic Coach

Same features as Model 306 above, except with 20" barrels and 12-gauge only.

	650	575	500	350	200	150

RIFLES

Field Grade Mauser 98

Bolt-action rifle offered in a wide variety of calibers from .243 Win. to .458 Win. Magnum. Barrel length 23" for all calibers. Stock is black synthetic. Open sights. **NOTE:** Add $175 for .375 H&H and .458 Win. Magnum; $50 for stainless steel.

	460	350	300	225	150	100

Field Grade Mini-Mauser 98

Version chambered for short cartridges such as .22 Hornet, .223, .22-250 and 7.62x39mm. Barrel length 19.25". Magazine capacity 5 rounds.

	600	475	350	250	175	125

Superior Grade Mauser 98

Model similar to Field Grade Mauser, with addition of hand-checkered walnut stock.

	600	425	325	225	165	100

Superior Grade Mini-Mauser 98

Same as Field Grade Mini-Mauser, with addition of hand-checkered walnut stock.

	600	450	325	250	150	100

Field Grade Rimfires

Chambered for .22 LR cartridge and fitted with a 22" barrel. Bolt-action version, 20" barrel in semi-automatic version or 17.5" barrel in bolt-action. Youth model 16.25" barrel in bolt-action single-shot True Youth model. **NOTE:** Add $25 for True Youth model.

	120	100	75	50	25	10

Superior Grade Rimfires

Chambered for .22, .22 Magnum or .22 Hornet in bolt-action or .22 LR semi-automatic. Walnut stock with checkering. Open sights. **NOTE:** Add $20 for .22 Magnum model; $170 for .22 Hornet model.

	175	125	100	75	50	25

Superior II Grade Rimfire

Version introduced in 2005 and chambered for .22 LR, .22 WMR or .17 HMR cartridges. Fitted with a 22" barrel. Open sights on the .22 LR and drilled and tapped for scope mounts on the .22 WMR and .17 HMR models. Oiled walnut stocks with checkering. **NOTE:** Add $40 for .22 Magnum model; $75 for .17 HMR.

	260	200	175	150	125	100

Empire Grade Rimfires

Empire Grade has select walnut stock, with 24 lpi hand-cut checkering. Grip and forearm caps highly polished and blued metal finish. Same configurations as Superior Grade rifles. **NOTE:** Add $20 for .22 Magnum model; $100 for .22 Hornet model.

	335	275	225	175	125	100

Superior Grade Express

Chambered for .30-06 cartridge and fitted with 23.5" barrel. Open sights, with dovetail receiver for scope mounting. Silver receiver with game scene engraving. Checkered walnut stock with

	NIB	EXC.	V.G.	GOOD	FAIR	POOR

sling swivels. Weight about 7.75 lbs.

	3250	2700	1800	1475	1000	500

Empire Express

Chambered for .30-06, .375 H&H or .416 Rigby cartridge, with open sights and dovetail receiver for scope mounting. Barrel length 23.5". Checkered walnut stock, with Bavarian-style cheekpiece. Silver game scene engraved receiver. Weight about 8 lbs. **NOTE:** Add $700 for .375 H&H and .416 Rigby models.

	3600	3000	2300	1775	1250	600

DM-4 Series

This series of rifles and carbines were manufactured in 2008 and 2009, with forged aluminum alloy receivers, manganese phosphate or stainless barrels, forward assist and other features typically found on quality made AR-type models. All were chambered in 5.56 NATO. Many of the popular AR configurations were offered with 16" or 20" barrels, sighting and grip options, mounting rails, finishes and other regular features found in the AR family. Prices shown are for standard DM-4 Carbine. Many available options can double these values.

	950	825	700	500	—	—

SHOTGUNS - 2013 AND CURRENT

Model 600

In 2013, Samco Global Arms of Miami, FL. purchased the Charles Daly trademark from the previous importer K.B.I. of Harrisburg, PA. and began importing a series of shotguns. Among these are the Model 600 semi-automatic, offered in several variations including field and sporting clays, with synthetic, camo or wood stocks, in 12-, 20- and 28-gauges. These are gas-operated guns, with standard barrel lengths with choke tubes that are cmpatible with Remington's REM-choke series. Values shown are for field model. **NOTE:** Add $50 for camo; $100 for sporting model.

	525	450	400	350	300	250

Model 300

Pump-action series, with features similar to Model 600.

	400	375	300	250	200	150

HANDGUNS

Daly ZDA

Introduced in 2005, pistol chambered for the 9mm or .40 S&W cartridge. Fitted with a 4.5" ramped barrel. Ambidextrous slide release/dececker/lock as well as magazine release. Loaded chamber indicator. Magazine capacity 15 rounds for 9mm and 12 rounds for .40 S&W.

	590	450	375	300	175	100

Field 1911-A1 FS/MS/CS

Chambered for .45 ACP, with choice of 5" (FS), 4" (MS) or 3.5" (CS) barrel. Various special features such as front and rear slide serrations, extended beavertail safety and lightweight trigger. Magazine capacity 8 rounds. Overall length 8.75".

	575	400	300	200	175	115

Superior 1911-A1 EFS/EMS/ECS

Same as Field Grade described above, with blued frame and stainless steel slide. Introduced in 1999.

	550	450	350	200	175	115

Empire 1911-A1 EFS

Same as Field Grade. Full stainless, with both stainless steel slide and frame. Introduced in 1999.

	630	475	350	225	195	125

Field 1911-A2P

Same as above, with 10-round magazine.

	570	450	350	225	195	125

.22 Caliber Conversion Kit

Offered with adjustable sights for models with 5" barrel only. First offered in 1999.

	200	150	100	65	45	25

	NIB	EXC.	V.G.	GOOD	FAIR	POOR

Field 1911-A1 PC

Model fitted with a 4" barrel and slide. Has a polymer frame. Produced under license from STI. Introduced in 1999.

	575	400	300	200	175	115

Superior 1911-A1 PC

Same as model above, with stainless steel slide and black polymer frame. Introduced in 1999.

	595	425	325	225	195	125

Field 1911 Target EFST

Fitted with a 5" barrel and chambered for the .45 ACP cartridge. Eight-round magazine. Blued finish. Fully adjustable rear sight, with dovetail front sight. Weight about 40 oz.

	620	475	350	240	195	125

Empire 1911 Target EFST

As above, with stainless steel finish.

	790	600	475	350	240	125

Empire Custom Match Target

Same as Empire Target, with hand polished stainless steel finish and 20 lpi checkered front strap.

	800	600	500	375	255	135

Daly HP

Introduced in 2003, this U.S.-made 9mm pistol is similar to the famous Browning Hi-Power. Fitted with a 5" barrel. XS sighting system. Weight about 35 oz.

	550	400	350	225	195	125

Daly M-5 Government

A polymer frame pistol chambered for the 9mm, .40 S&W or the .45 ACP cartridge. Fitted with a 5" barrel, high rise beavertail and ambidextrous safety. Low profile sights. Weight around 34 oz. Made in Israel by BUL. Introduced in 2003.

	720	575	400	275	225	100

Daly M-5 Commander

Same as above. Fitted with a 4.375" barrel. Weight about 30 oz.

	720	575	400	275	225	100

Daly M-5 Ultra-X

An ultra compact model.

	720	575	400	275	225	100

Daly M-5 IPSC

Model has a 5" barrel. Fitted with a stainless steel slide and adjustable sights. Flared and lowered ejection port. Extended magazine release. Weight about 34 oz.

	1500	1150	725	600	325	125

Daly Classic 1873 Single-Action Revolver

Chambered for .45 Colt or .357 Magnum. Revolver offered with 4.75", 5.5" or 7.5" barrel. Choice of walnut or simulated ivory grips. Stainless steel, blue or case colored finish. Introduced in 2005. Imported from Italy. **NOTE:** Add $30 for steel backstrap and trigger guard; $200 for stainless steel.

	450	350	285	250	195	150

DAN ARMS OF AMERICA
Allentown, Pennsylvania

These are Italian-made shotguns. Manufactured by Silmer and imported by Dan Arms of America. Production ceased in 1988.

SIDE-BY-SIDES

Field Grade

Boxlock shotgun chambered for all gauges, with 26" or 28" barrels. Various choke combinations, double triggers and extractors. Blued, with walnut stock.

	—	325	265	225	150	125

Deluxe Field Grade

As above, with single trigger and automatic ejectors.

	—	465	400	325	250	200

	NIB	EXC.	V.G.	GOOD	FAIR	POOR

OVER/UNDERS

Lux Grade I
A 12- and 20-gauge over/under shotgun, with a 26", 28" or 30" ventilated rib barrels, double triggers and extractors. Blued finish, with walnut stock.

—	325	265	200	150	100	

Lux Grade II
As above in 12-gauge only, with single trigger.

—	350	300	250	200	150	

Lux Grade III
As above in 20-gauge only, with automatic ejectors.

—	400	325	275	225	175	

Lux Grade IV
As above in 12-gauge only, with screw-in choke tubes.

—	450	375	325	275	200	

Silver Snipe
A 12- or 20-gauge shotgun. Manufactured to custom order, with engraved false sideplates and select walnut stock.

—	1250	1000	800	600	350	

DANCE & BROTHERS CONFEDERATE REVOLVERS
Columbia, Texas

J.H., G.P. and D.E. Dance began production of percussion revolvers for the Confederate States of America in Columbia, Texas, in mid-1862, moving to Anderson, Texas in early 1864. Based on surviving serial numbers, combined output at both places did not exceed 350 pistols. Most of these were in the "Army" (.44-caliber) size but a limited number of "Navy" (.36-caliber) were also manufactured. Nearly all are distinguished by the absence of a "recoil shield" on the frame behind the cylinders. As Colt M1851 "Navy" revolvers closely resemble the Dance Navy revolvers, great care must be exercised in examining revolvers purported to be Dance Navies.

.36 Caliber

—	—	85000	67500	20000	7000	

.44 Caliber

—	—	90000	68000	20000	5500	

DANIEL DEFENSE
Savannah, Georgia

DDM4
This series of AR-type carbines comes in six variations. Different receiver and stock configurations, and rail/sight systems. All have 16" barrels and available in 5.56 NATO, with some offered in 6.8 SPC or .300 Blackout calibers.

1450	1250	1000	800	500	300	

MK 12
New in 2014, this model is in 5.56 NATO caliber, with 20-round Magpul magazine, 18" barrel, glass-filled polymer stock, with Soft Touch overmolding and pistol-grip.

1875	1600	1300	500	400	250	

DANSK REKYLRIFFEL SYNDIKAT
Copenhagen, Denmark

This firm was founded in 1896. In 1936 it became known as Madsen, makers of the famous Madsen light machine gun. Schouboe pistols were designed by Jens Schouboe, chief engineer for Dansk. They were developed in 1900-1902. First year of manufacture was in 1902.

Schouboe Model 1902
A 7.65mm caliber semi-automatic pistol, with conventional blowback design. Production began in 1903 and ended in 1908, with fewer than 1,000 manufactured.

—	15500	12000	8200	5000	3000	

Schouboe Model 1904
A semi-automatic pistol in caliber 11.35mm. Model 1904 was an enlarged Model 1902. Name Dansk Rekylriffel is stamped on the slide.

—	24500	20500	16500	11000	5000	

NIB	EXC.	V.G.	GOOD	FAIR	POOR

Schouboe Model 1907

An 11.35mm caliber semi-automatic pistol. Designed to fire a 55-grain, copper-aluminum-and-wood projectile at a velocity of 1625 fps. Pistol has the name Dansk Rekylriffel and Schouboe stamped on slide. Some of these pistols had grip frames slotted for stocks. Five hundred were manufactured before production stopped in 1917. **NOTE:** Combination holster/shoulder stocks were made for this model, but are extremely rare. If present with a pistol, they would add approximately $5,000 to the value.

—	24000	20000	16000	10500	5000

Schouboe Model 1907 9mm

As above, but chambered for 9mm cartridge. Very few of these pistols were built.

—	14000	11000	8250	5500	3000

Schouboe Model 1910/12

Model chambered for 11.35mm cartridge. Involved in U.S. military tests in 1912.

—	24500	21500	16500	11000	5000

Schouboe Model 1916

Model also chambered for 11.35mm cartridge. Fitted with a very large slide release and safety lever on left side of pistol. Name of manufacturer is stamped on slide.

—	24000	21050	16500	11000	5000

DARDICK CORP.
Hamden, Connecticut

Perhaps one of the most unusual firearms to have been designed and marketed in the United States during the 20th century. It utilizes a "tround" which is a triangular plastic case enclosing a cartridge. Action of these arms consists of a revolving carrier that brings the trounds from the magazine into line with the barrel. Discontinued in 1962. Values below are for boxed examples, with a supply of tround ammunition. Deduct 50 to 75 percent for un-boxed loose examples, without ammunition.

Series 110

3" barrel. Chambered in .38 Dardick only.

—	2500	1650	1500	1100	500

Series 1500

6" barrel. Chambered for .22, .30 and .38 Dardick. **NOTE:** Carbine conversion kit consisting of a long barrel and shoulder stock was available and would bring a premium of $750 to $1400 depending on the condition.

—	5000	3000	1750	1500	900

DARLING, B. & B. M.
Belingham, Massachusetts

Pepperbox Pistol

A .30-caliber percussion 6-shot pepperbox, with 3.25" length barrels. Blued, with walnut grips. One of the rarest American pepperboxes and copies are known to have been made. Consequently, prospective purchasers are advised to secure a qualified appraisal prior to acquisition. Manufactured during the late 1830s.

—	—	4950	1950	600	600

DARNE, S. A.
St. Etienne, France

SIDE-BY-SIDE SHOTGUNS

A 12-, 16-, 20- or 28-gauge sliding breech double-barrel shotgun. Manufactured in a variety of barrel lengths and numerous optional features. Manufactured from 1881 to 1979. **NOTE:** Darnes have been undergoing a surge in popularity the last few years, because of their unique design. Depending on circumstances and amount of factory engraving and ornamentation present, individual examples may bring considerably in excess of values listed below. Deduct 25 percent for 2.5" chambers.

Model R11

—	2500	2000	1200	800	550

Model R13

—	3000	2600	2250	1100	750

	NIB	EXC.	V.G.	GOOD	FAIR	POOR

Model R15

	—	4000	3000	2450	1500	750

Model V19

	—	4500	3600	2950	2050	1250

Model V22

	—	5000	4100	3500	2500	1700

Model V Hors Series No. I

	—	7500	5500	4050	3250	1500

DAVENPORT FIREARMS CO.
Providence, Rhode Island
Norwich, Connecticut

Double-Barrel Shotguns

Text and prices by Nick Niles. William Hastings Davenport's company, also made and marked double-barrel, visible hammer guns in Providence, R.I. on Orange St., 1880-1882 and in Norwich, Conn. ca. 1890-1909. All are monbloc designs of which there were four models. 1st model, made at Providence, ca. 1881, had hammers rising out of the boxlock frame. 2nd model, made in Norwich, Conn. about 1898, is a typical boxlock. 3rd model, made in Norwich, Conn., ca. 1909, has small sidelocks set in larger boxlock frames. Its barrels have un-notched extensions and notched underlugs. 4th model, also from Norwich, possibly made after the 1901 takeover by Hopkins & Allen, also has sidelocks set in boxlock frames, but the barrels have half moon lugs and notched barrel extensions. Few Davenport doubles are seen, although single barrel guns are often found.

1st Model

	—	1200	875	500	400	300

2nd Model

	—	700	450	300	200	150

3rd Model

	—	1200	875	500	400	300

4th Model

	—	900	450	300	250	200

Single-Barrel Shotgun

A 10-, 12-, 16- or 20-gauge side-hammer single-barrel shotgun, with 26" to 36" barrels and extractors. Blued, case hardened, with walnut stock. Manufactured from approximately 1880 to 1915.

	—	—	450	300	150	75

8 Gauge Goose Gun

As above in 8-gauge.

	—	—	550	250	175	100

Falling Block Single-Shot Rifle

A .22, .25 or .32 rimfire single-shot rifle, with 24" round barrel and exposed hammer. Blued, with walnut stock. Barrel marked "The W.H. Davenport Fire Arms Co. Norwich, Conn. U.S.A. Patented Dec. 15, 1891". Manufactured between 1891 and 1910.

			675	425	325	200

DAVIDSON, F.A.
Eibar, Spain

Arms bearing this name were manufactured in Spain by Fabrica De Armas.

Model 63B

A 12-, 16-, 20-, 28-gauge or .410 bore double-barrel boxlock shotgun, with 25" to 30" barrels. Engraved, nickel-plated with a walnut stock. Made from 1963 to 1976.

	—	350	225	200	150	100

Model 69 SL

A 12- or 20-gauge sidelock double-barrel shotgun, with 26" or 28" barrels and finished as above.

	—	425	350	300	225	125

	NIB	EXC.	V.G.	GOOD	FAIR	POOR

Stagecoach Model 73

A 12- or 20-gauge Magnum sidelock double-barrel shotgun, with 20" barrels and exposed hammers.

	NIB	EXC.	V.G.	GOOD	FAIR	POOR
	—	300	250	175	150	100

DAVIS, A. JR.
Stafford, Connecticut

Under Hammer Pistol

A .31-caliber single-shot under hammer percussion pistol, with a 7.5" half octagonal barrel and brass frame. Grips are maple and formed with a bottom tip. Top strap marked "A. Davis Jr./ Stafford Conn.

	NIB	EXC.	V.G.	GOOD	FAIR	POOR
	—	—	1250	775	350	100

DAVIS, N.R. & CO./DAVIS, N.R. & SONS
(See also Davis-Warner Arms Corporation)

Manufacturer of percussion and later cartridge shotguns, from 1853 to 1919. Cartridge shotguns embodied Nathan R. Davis' patented improvements of 1879, 1884 and 1886. Though only made in plain serviceable grades, Davis shotguns were extremely well made and lived up to the company's motto "As Good as the Best".

Grade A and B Hammerless Shotguns

Made in 12- or 16-gauge, with 28", 30" or 32" barrels.

	NIB	EXC.	V.G.	GOOD	FAIR	POOR
	—	900	675	400	200	100

Grade C Hammerless Shotgun

Made in 10-gauge, with 30" or 32" barrels.

	NIB	EXC.	V.G.	GOOD	FAIR	POOR
	—	900	675	400	200	100

Grade D and DS Hammer Shotguns

Made in 12- or 16-gauge, with 28", 30" or 32" barrels.

	NIB	EXC.	V.G.	GOOD	FAIR	POOR
	—	875	675	425	200	100

Grade E and F Single-Barrel Shotguns

Made in 12- or 16-gauge, with 30" or 32" barrels.

	NIB	EXC.	V.G.	GOOD	FAIR	POOR
	—	350	250	125	75	50

N.R. DAVIS BRANDS

1st Button Opener—Hammer Boxlock

	NIB	EXC.	V.G.	GOOD	FAIR	POOR
	—	475	325	250	150	100

1st Sidelever—Hammer Boxlock

	NIB	EXC.	V.G.	GOOD	FAIR	POOR
	—	475	325	250	150	100

2nd Sidelever—Hammer Boxlock

	NIB	EXC.	V.G.	GOOD	FAIR	POOR
	—	475	325	250	150	100

1st Toplever—Hammer Boxlock

	NIB	EXC.	V.G.	GOOD	FAIR	POOR
	—	475	325	250	150	100

2nd Toplever—Hammer Boxlock

	NIB	EXC.	V.G.	GOOD	FAIR	POOR
	—	475	325	250	150	100

3rd Toplever—Hammer Boxlock

	NIB	EXC.	V.G.	GOOD	FAIR	POOR
	—	475	325	250	150	100

1879 1st Model—Hammer Boxlock

	NIB	EXC.	V.G.	GOOD	FAIR	POOR
	—	475	325	250	150	100

1879 2nd Model—Damascus Barrel—Hammer Boxlock

	NIB	EXC.	V.G.	GOOD	FAIR	POOR
	—	475	325	250	150	100

1885—Hammerless Boxlock

	NIB	EXC.	V.G.	GOOD	FAIR	POOR
	—	475	325	250	150	100

1886 Rival—Hammerless Boxlock

	NIB	EXC.	V.G.	GOOD	FAIR	POOR
	—	350	275	200	150	100

	NIB	EXC.	V.G.	GOOD	FAIR	POOR

1886 Rival Improved—Hammerless Boxlock

	NIB	EXC.	V.G.	GOOD	FAIR	POOR
	—	350	275	200	150	100

1897 "G" —Hammer Sidelock

	—	350	275	200	150	100

N.R. DAVIS & SONS BRAND

Hammerless 1900—Boxlock

	—	350	275	200	150	100

Hammerless A—Damascus Barrel—Boxlock

	—	350	275	200	150	100

Hammerless B—Boxlock

	—	350	275	200	150	100

Hammerless C—Engraved Damascus Barrel—Boxlock

	—	400	325	250	150	100

Hammerless D—Engraved—Boxlock

	—	475	375	300	250	200

New Model—Hammerless Boxlock

	—	350	275	200	150	100

"D.S." Straight Stock—Engraved—Hammerless Boxlock

	—	350	275	200	150	100

Davis Special—Hammerless Boxlock

	—	925	650	500	400	250

Davis "B" Manga Steel—Hammerless Boxlock

	—	925	650	500	400	250

CRESCENT-DAVIS BRANDS

Model No. 600—Hammerless Boxlock

	—	700	550	300	200	100

Model No. 900—Hammerless Boxlock

	—	700	550	300	200	100

DAVIS-WARNER ARMS CORPORATION
Norwich, Connecticut

Established in 1917, when N.R. Davis & Sons purchased the Warner Arms Company. Manufactured shotguns, as well as revolvers and semi-automatic pistols. Ceased operations in 1930. Crescent Arms Company purchased the proprietary rights to the name and briefly assembled shotguns under the name (probably from parts acquired in the purchase), until Crescent was in turn purchased by J.C. Stevens. Initially, Davis-Warner shotguns were identical to those made by Davis, but they subsequently made a Davis Grade B.S. Hammerless, Davis-Warner Expert and Davis Grade D.S. Pistols made by the company included .32-caliber revolvers and two Browning Patent semi-automatics made in Belgium for the company.

Davis Grade B.S. Hammerless Shotgun

Made in 12-, 16- or 20-gauge, with 28", 30" or 32" barrels.

	—	875	650	400	200	100

Davis-Warner Expert Hammerless

Made in 12-, 16- or 20-gauge, with 26", 28", 30" or 32" barrels.

	—	875	650	400	200	100

"BS"—Hammerless Boxlock

	—	350	275	200	150	100

"Maximin"—Hammerless Boxlock

	—	475	325	250	200	150

"DS"—Hammerless Boxlock

	—	350	275	200	150	100

	NIB	EXC.	V.G.	GOOD	FAIR	POOR

Deluxe—Hammerless Boxlock

	—	350	275	200	150	100

Premier—Hammerless Boxlock

	—	350	275	200	150	100

Peerless Ejector—Hammerless Boxlock

	—	475	325	250	200	150

Hypower—Hammerless Boxlock

	—	475	325	250	200	150

Ajax (Model 800)

	—	475	325	250	150	100

Ajax—Hammerless Boxlock

	—	350	275	200	150	100

Certified (Savage)

	—	475	325	250	150	100

Deluxe Special (Model 805)

Automatic ejectors.

	—	575	450	300	200	150

Premier Special (Model 802)

	—	575	450	300	200	150

Premier (Model 801)

	—	475	325	250	150	100

Warner Infallible Semi-Automatic Pistol

Fyrberg Patent .32 ACP. Not a particularly robust design.

	—	350	275	175	125	75

Davis-Warner Swing-Out Revolver

Double-action .32-caliber revolver, with 5" or 6" barrel.

	—	200	150	120	75	50

Davis-Warner Semi-Automatic Pistols

Browning Patent .25 ACP, .32 ACP or .380 caliber pistols.

	—	350	275	175	125	75

DAVIS & BOZEMAN
Central, Alabama

Pattern 1841 Rifle

A .58-caliber single-shot percussion rifle, with a 33" round barrel, full walnut stock, two barrel bands, brass furniture and an iron ramrod. Lock marked "D. & B. Ala." as well as the serial number and date of manufacture.

	—	—	40000	16500	3500	1750

DAVIS INDUSTRIES
Mira Loma, California

This company was founded in 1987 by Jim Davis in Chino, California. Company ceased operations in 2001. Remaining stocks and production machinery purchased by Cobra Enterprises, 1960 S. Milestone Drive, Suite F, Salt Lake City, UT 84104.

D-Series Deringer

A .22 LR, .22 WMR, .25 ACP and .32 ACP caliber double-barrel over/under derringer, with 2.4" barrels. Black Teflon or chrome-plated finish, with laminated wood grips. Weighs approximately 9.5 oz.

150	75	40	30	25	20

Big Bore D-Series

Similar to above model, but chambered for .38 Special and .32 H&R Magnum. Barrel length 2.75". Weighs about 11.5 oz.

150	75	40	30	25	20

	NIB	EXC.	V.G.	GOOD	FAIR	POOR

Long Bore D-Series

Introduced in 1994, this two-shot pistol is chambered for .22 LR , .22 WMR, .32 ACP, .32 H&R Magnum, .380 ACP, 9mm and .38 Special cartridges. Barrel length 3.75"; overall length 5.65"; weight approximately 13 oz.

NIB	EXC.	V.G.	GOOD	FAIR	POOR
150	75	40	30	25	20

P-32

A .32-caliber semi-automatic pistol, with a 2.8" barrel and 6-shot magazine. Black Teflon or chrome-plated finish, with laminated wood grips. Overall length 5.4". Weighs approximately 22 oz.

NIB	EXC.	V.G.	GOOD	FAIR	POOR
150	75	40	30	25	20

P-380

As above, in .380-caliber.

NIB	EXC.	V.G.	GOOD	FAIR	POOR
175	85	65	50	40	30

DAW, G. H.
London, England

Daw Revolver

A .38-caliber double-action percussion revolver, with 5.5" barrel marked "George H. Daw, 57 Threadneedle St. London, Patent No. 112". Blued, with walnut grips. Manufactured in the 1860s.

NIB	EXC.	V.G.	GOOD	FAIR	POOR
—		5750	3500	1975	1000

DEANE-HARDING
London, England

Revolver

A .44-caliber percussion revolver, with 5.25" barrel and 5-shot cylinder. Blued, case hardened with walnut grips. Manufactured during the late 1850s.

NIB	EXC.	V.G.	GOOD	FAIR	POOR
—	—	8500	2750	1475	850

DECKER, WILHELM
Zella St. Blasii, Germany

A 6.35mm double-action revolver, with 6-shot cylinder and concealed hammer. Unusual bar-type trigger design. Blued, with plastic grips. Manufactured prior to 1914. Very few of these revolvers were produced.

Revolver

NIB	EXC.	V.G.	GOOD	FAIR	POOR
—	2100	1500	750	325	100

DEMIRETT, J.
Montpelier, Vermont

Under-Hammer Pistol

A .27-caliber single-shot percussion pistol, with 3" to 8" barrels and an under hammer. The barrel marked "J. Demerrit / Montpelier / Vermont". Blued, with maple, walnut or stag horn grips. Active from 1866 to the mid-1880s.

NIB	EXC.	V.G.	GOOD	FAIR	POOR
—	—	2700	825	350	200

DEMRO
Manchester, Connecticut

XF-7 Wasp Carbine

A 9mm or .45-caliber semi-automatic carbine, with 16.5" barrel and folding stock. Fires from open bolt.

NIB	EXC.	V.G.	GOOD	FAIR	POOR
—	750	600	450	300	150

T.A.C. Model 1

As above, with fixed stock.

NIB	EXC.	V.G.	GOOD	FAIR	POOR
—	750	600	450	300	150

DERINGER REVOLVER AND PISTOL CO.
Philadelphia, Pennsylvania

After Henry Deringer's death, his name was used by I.J. Clark, who manufactured rimfire revolvers on Charles Foehl's patents between 1870 and 1879.

	NIB	EXC.	V.G.	GOOD	FAIR	POOR

Deringer Model I

A .22-caliber spur trigger revolver, with hinged octagonal barrel and 7-shot cylinder. Manufactured circa 1873.

	NIB	EXC.	V.G.	GOOD	FAIR	POOR
	—	—	—	650	275	150

Deringer Model II

As above, with round barrel and also available in .32-caliber.

	—	—	—	425	200	100

Centennial 1876

A .22-, .32- or .38-caliber solid frame revolver.

	—	—	—	900	450	200

DERINGER RIFLES AND PISTOLS, HENRY
Philadelphia, Pennsylvania

Henry Deringer Sr. and his son, Henry Jr., were well established in Philadelphia by the close of the War of 1812, having made both sporting and military rifles at that place since the turn of the century. Henry Jr. continued in the gun trade until the outbreak of the American Civil War, primarily producing flintlock and percussion military rifles. At least 2,500 "Northwest guns" and 1,200 rifles for the Indian trade, a few percussion martial pistols, but most importantly the percussion pocket pistols that became so popular they took on his misspelled name as a generic term, the "derringers".

Deringer U.S. M1814 Military Rifle

Overall length 48.5"; barrel length 32.75"; caliber .54. Markings: on lockplate, "US/H. DERINGER/PHILADA", on top flat of barrel, "H. DERINGER/PHILADA" and standard U.S. proofmarks. U.S. M1814 rifle is distinguished by its part octagonal barrel, whose bands were secured by wedge-shaped spring bands and distinctive finger ridges on the triggerguard strap. Henry Deringer Sr. received a contract for 2,000 of these rifles in 1814, but delivered only 50 that year, devoting his resources instead to a more lucrative Pennsylvania state contract for rifles.

	—	—	9000	2950	1500	850

Deringer U.S. M1817 Military Rifle (Types I & II)

Overall length 51.25"; barrel length 36"; caliber .54. Markings: on lockplate, "US/H. DERINGER/PHILADA" forward of cock, date on tail; standard U.S. proofmarks on barrel. U.S. M1817 "common" rifle followed much the same design elements as its predecessor, U.S. M1814 rifle; however, barrel is fully round, with its bands secured by full band springs and on earlier production, finger ridges on the triggerguard strap were eliminated in favor of a plain strap formed into a handgrip. On the 6,000 rifles manufactured under his 1840 contract, Deringer eliminated the "pistol-grip" in favor of a plain strap, distinguishing Type 11 production from Type 1. As one of four major contractors for the U.S. M1817 rifle, Deringer produced a total of 111,000 rifles for the U.S. War Department. Many of the rifles from the first two contracts (2,000 in 1821, 3,000 in 1823) were distributed to Southern states under the 1808 Militia Act. Accordingly, Deringer M1817 rifles altered to percussion by traditional Southern methods may generate a premium.

In Flintlock

	—	—	8000	3500	1750	800

Altered to Percussion

	—	—	4000	1250	600	400

Deringer Original Percussion Martial Rifles (Types I & II)

Overall length 51.25"; barrel length 36"; caliber .54. Markings: Type I-on lockplate forward of hammer "DERINGER/PHILA"; also known to exist with standard U.S. M1817 lock markings and barrel marks; Type II-on lockplate forward of hammer "US/DERINGER/PHILADELA" or "DERINGER/PHILADELA" and same on top of barrel. Although Type I rifle of this series appears at first glance to be a late contract rifle altered to percussion by means of the cone-in barrel method, in fact it is an original percussion rifle made by Deringer from modified spare parts that remained after the completion of his 1840 contract. Type 11 rifle also evidences having been made from modified parts; however, its cone is set in an elongated bolster brazed to the right side of the barrel. Speculation concerning these rifles is rampant; however, available evidence indicates that Deringer produced about 600 of these, most likely produced at the beginning of the American Civil War.

	—	—	4750	1550	800	450

Deringer Original Percussion Rifle-Muskets

Overall length 57.75"; barrel length 42"; caliber .69. Markings: on lock forward of hammer, "US/ DERINGER/PHILADELA". Just as original percussion rifle appears to be an altered arm, the rare

	NIB	EXC.	V.G.	GOOD	FAIR	POOR

Deringer rifle muskets at first appear to have been flintlocks. However, these arms are original percussion, having been made from spare or rejected parts from the U.S. M1816 muskets. Brazed bolsters are identical in style to that of Type 11 original percussion rifles made by Deringer. Barrels are rifled with seven grooves and barrels accordingly bear a rear sight. Deringer probably assembled a hundred of these rifles in 1861 to arm some company of Pennsylvania's early war regiments.

	NIB	EXC.	V.G.	GOOD	FAIR	POOR
	—	—	4000	1300	725	450

Deringer U.S. Navy Contract "Boxlock" Pistols

Overall length 11.625"; barrel length 6"; caliber .54. Markings: on lockplate, "US/DERINGER/ PHILADELIA" or merely "DERINGER/PHILADEL\" in center, the tail either plain or marked "U.S.N./(date)"; barrels sometimes marked with U.S. Navy inspection marks. Deringer was granted a contract with the U.S. Navy in 1845 for 1,200 of the new "boxlock" percussion pistols also made by Ames. All of these appear to have been delivered. From the extra parts, Deringer is thought to have assembled several hundred extra pistols, some of which he rifled. The latter bring a premium, even though quantities remain enigmatic.

	NIB	EXC.	V.G.	GOOD	FAIR	POOR
	—	—	4050	1550	1225	750

Deringer Percussion Pocket Pistols

The most famous of Henry Deringer's products, an estimated 15,000 were produced between the Mexican War through the Civil War, usually in pairs. Popularity of the pistol is attested in large number of imitations and nickname "Derringer" applied to them, even when clearly not Deringer's products. Prices can fluctuate widely based on agent marks occasionally found on barrel. Care is advised in purchasing purported "true" derringers. Beware of fakes!

	NIB	EXC.	V.G.	GOOD	FAIR	POOR
	—	—	7000	2250	1600	800

Principal Makers of Deringer-Style Pocket Pistols

William AFFLERBACH, Philadelphia, PA

Balthaser AUER, Louisville, KY

Frederick BEERSTECHER, Philadelphia and Lewisburg, PA

Franz J. BITTERLICH, Nashville, TN

BLUNT & SYMS, New York, NY

Richard P. BRUFF, New York, NY

Jesse S. BUTTERFIELD, Philadelphia, PA

Daniel CLARK, Philadelphia, PA

Richard CONSTABLE, Philadelphia, PA

DELONG & SON, Chattanooga, TN

MOSES DICKSON, Louisville, KY

Horace E. DIMICK, St. Louis, MO

Gustau ERICHSON, Houston, TX

B.J. EUSTACE & Company, St. Louis, MO

James E. EVANS, Philadelphia, PA

W.S. EVANS, Philadelphia, PA

FIELD, LANGSTROTH & Company, Philadelphia, PA

Daniel FISH, New York, NY

FOLSOM BROTHERS & Company, New Orleans, LA

August G. GENEZ, New York, NY

George D. H. GILLESPIE, New York, NY

Frederick G. GLASSICK, Memphis, TN

James GOLCHER, Philadelphia, PA

Joseph GRUBB & Company, Philadelphia, PA

John H. HAPPOLDT, Charlestown, SC

John M. HAPPOLDT, Columbus, GA & Charlestown, SC

HAWS & WAGGONER, Columbia, SC

HODGKINS & SONS, Macon, GA

Louis HOFFMAN, Vicksburg, MS

HYDE & GOODRICH, New Orleans, LA

Joseph JACOB, Philadelphia, PA

	NIB	EXC.	V.G.	GOOD	FAIR	POOR

William W. KAYE, Philadelphia, PA

Benjamin KITTERIDGE, Cincinnati, OH

Peter W. KRAFT, Columbia, SC

John KRIDER, Philadelphia, PA

Jacob KUNTZ, Philadelphia, PA

Martille La FITTE, Natchitoches, LA

A. Frederich LINS, Philadelphia, PA

C. LOHNER, Philadelphia, PA

John P. LOWER, Denver, CO

A.R. MENDENHALL, Des Arc, AK

John MEUNIER, Milwaukee, WI

William D. MILLER, New York, NY

MURPHY & O'CONNELL, New York, NY

— — NEWCOMB, Natchez, MS

Charles A. OBERTEUFFER, Philadelphia, PA

Stephen O'DELL, Natchez, MS

Henry C. PALMER, St. Louis, MO

R. PATRICK, New York, NY

REID & TRACY, New York, NY

William ROBERTSON, Philadelphia, PA

ROBINSON & KRIDER, Philadelphia, PA

Ernst SCHMIDT & Company, Houston, TX

SCHNEIDER & GLASSICK, Memphis, TN

W.A. SEAVER, New York, NY

Paul J. SIMPSON, New York, NY

SLOTTER & Company, Philadelphia, PA

Patrick SMITH, Buffalo, NY

SPRANG & WALLACE, Philadelphia, PA

Adam W. SPIES, New York, NY

Casper SUTER, Selma, AL

Jacob F. TRUMPLER, Little Rock, AK

Edward TRYON, Jr., Philadelphia, PA

George K. TRYON, Philadelphia, PA

TUFTS & COLLEY, New York, NY

WOLF, DASH & FISHER, New York, NY

Alfred WOODHAM, New York, NY

Andrew WURFFLEIN, Philadelphia, PA

John WURFFLEIN, Philadelphia, PA

Agent Names Found On Deringer Pocket Pistols

W.C. ALLEN, San Francisco, CA

W.H. CALHOUN, Nashville, TN

CANFIELD & BROTHERS, Baltimore, MD

F. H. CLARK & CO., Memphis, TN

COLEMAN & DUKE, Cahaba, AL

M.W. GALT & BROTHER, Washington, DC

J.B. GILMORE, Shreveport, LA

A.B. GRISWOLD & CO., New Orleans, LA

HYDE & GOODRICH, New Orleans, LA

LULLMAN & VIENNA, Memphis, TN

A.J. MILLSPAUGH, Shreveport, LA

NIB	EXC.	V.G.	GOOD	FAIR	POOR

H.G. NEWCOMB, Natchez, MS

A.J. PLATE, San Francisco, CA

J.A. SCHAFER, Vicksburg, MS

S.L. SWETT, Vicksburg, MS

A.J. TAYLOR, San Francisco, CA

WOLF & DURRINGER, Louisville, KY

DESENZANI, LABORATORIES ARMI
Brescia, Italy

Over/Under

These custom made guns are all unique. Used guns in excellent condition will bring $35,000. Values increase depending on the small gauges, amount and coverage of engraving.

Side-By-Side

These custom made guns are all unique. Used guns in excellent condition will bring $25,000. Values increase depending on the small gauges, amount and coverage of engraving.

DESERT EAGLE

Desert Eagle is a semi-automatic gas-operated pistol chambered for the .357 Magnum, .41 Magnum, .44 Magnum and .50 Action Express. Produced by Israel Military Industries until 2009 and now made in U.S. Pistols furnished with a standard 6" barrel, but 10" and 14" interchangeable barrels are offered as options. Also available are these interchangeable barrels that are Mag-Na-Ported. Standard material used for frame is steel, but stainless and aluminum are also available. Standard finish for these pistols is black oxide, but custom finishes are available on special order. These special finishes are: gold, stainless steel, satin nickel, bright nickel, polished blue, camo, matte chrome, polished chrome, brushed chrome and matte chrome with gold. All of these special order finishes, as well as the optional barrels, will affect the price of these pistols. Prices listed here will reflect standard pistols only.

Desert Eagle .357 Magnum

Standard with 6" barrel and black oxide finish. Magazine capacity 9 rounds. Standard weight 58 oz.

1250	900	700	500	400	250

Desert Eagle .41 Magnum/.44 Magnum

Standard barrel length 6", with black oxide finish. Magazine capacity 8 rounds. Weight for standard 63 oz. **NOTE:** Add 10 percent for .41.

1350	900	700	500	400	250

Desert Eagle .50 Action Express

Standard barrel length 10", with black oxide finish. Magazine capacity 7 rounds. Standard weight 72 oz.

1450	900	700	500	400	250

Desert Eagle Mark XIX

Introduced in 1996, this new design is manufactured in the U.S. and allows interchangeability of barrels to switch calibers between the same receiver. Single receiver can be turned into six different pistols in three Magnum calibers. Available are .50 A.E., .44 Magnum and .357 Magnum in barrel lengths of 6" or 10". Separate magazines are also required. Eight different finishes offered as well. Separate bolt assembly is necessary to convert the .44/.50 calibers to the .357. There are so many different possibilities with this design that only basic pistol prices are given. Extra barrel assemblies are an additional cost. Prices range from $160 to $280 depending on caliber and length. **NOTE:** These custom shop finishes for Desert Eagle pistols are available in: Satin nickel, bright nickel, polished and deep blued, matte hard chrome, polished hard chrome, brushed hard chrome, 24K gold. All finishes except gold add $195 to price of pistol. For gold finish add $500. For gold appointments add $195.

.50A.E. w/6" Barrel

1450	900	700	500	300	200

.50A.E. w/10" Barrel

1350	1000	750	500	300	200

.44 Mag. w/6" Barrel

1250	900	700	450	300	200

.44 Mag. w/10" Barrel

1350	1000	750	500	300	200

	NIB	EXC.	V.G.	GOOD	FAIR	POOR

.357 Mag. w/6" Barrel

| | 1250 | 900 | 700 | 450 | 300 | 200 |

.357 Mag. w/10" Barrel

| | 1350 | 1000 | 750 | 500 | 300 | 200 |

.440 CorBon w/6" Barrel (1999)

| | 1200 | 950 | 700 | 600 | 500 | 300 |

.440 CorBon w/10" Barrel (1999)

| | 1300 | 1000 | 750 | 650 | 550 | 325 |

Bolt Assembly—.44/.50 or .357

| | 220 | 175 | 150 | 100 | 75 | 50 |

Mark XIX Component System

Introduced in 2000, this system features a Mark XIX frame with a .44 Magnum 6" and 10" barrels; .50AE with 6" and 10" barrel; .357 Magnum with 6" and 10" barrel. Supplied with ICC aluminum case. Also offered with 6" only barrel components or 10" only barrel components.

6" & 10" Component System

| | 3990 | 2990 | 2500 | 1875 | 1150 | 500 |

6" Component System

| | 2575 | 1900 | 1500 | 1200 | 700 | 350 |

10" Component System

| | 2815 | 2100 | 1600 | 1325 | 725 | 400 |

Baby Eagle

Baby Eagle is a smaller version of the Desert Eagle. All-steel construction, extra long slide rail, nylon grips, combat style trigger guard, ambidextrous thumb safety and decocking safety. Double-action design and available in 9mm, .40 S&W, .41 Action Express. Standard finish is black oxide, but matte chrome and brushed are offered as optional finishes. Fixed sights are standard. Fixed night sights and adjustable night sights are options.

.40 S&W (Standard)

Supplied with 4.5" barrel and black oxide finish. Magazine capacity 10 rounds. Empty weight 38 oz.

| | 500 | 400 | 350 | 300 | 250 | 200 |

9mm (Standard)

Fitted with a 4.5" barrel and black oxide finish. Magazine capacity 16 rounds. Empty weight 38 oz.

| | 500 | 400 | 350 | 300 | 250 | 200 |

Baby Eagle

.41 Action Express

Model has a 4.7" barrel and black oxide finish. Magazine capacity 11 rounds. Empty weight 38 oz.

| | 500 | 400 | 350 | 300 | 250 | 200 |

Short Barrel (Semi-Compact)

This 9mm, 40 S&W or .45 ACP model features a 3.6" barrel, with frame-mounted safety. Weight about 36 oz. Magazine holds 10 rounds.

| | 500 | 400 | 350 | 300 | 250 | 200 |

Short Barrel/Short Grip (Compact)

This 9mm or .40 S&W version has a 3.6" barrel and shorter grip (3.25") than standard. Magazine capacity still 10 rounds. Weight about 38 oz. Frame-mounted safety.

| | 500 | 400 | 350 | 300 | 250 | 200 |

Semi-Compact Polymer

Pistol has a polymer frame and 3.9" barrel chambered for 9mm or .40 S&W cartridge. Weight about 29 oz.

| | 500 | 400 | 325 | 285 | 225 | 175 |

Compact Polymer

As above, with 3.6" barrel and short grip. Weight about 27 oz.

| | 500 | 400 | 325 | 285 | 225 | 175 |

	NIB	EXC.	V.G.	GOOD	FAIR	POOR

Mountain Eagle

Semi-automatic pistol chambered for .22 LR cartridge. Features a 6.5" barrel, with adjustable rear sight. Grip is a one-piece molded plastic checkered, with raised side panels. Magazine capacity 15 rounds, with 20-round magazine available as an option. Black oxide finish is standard. Pistol weighs 21 oz.

	275	175	150	125	100	75

Mountain Eagle Target Edition

Similar to the standard Mountain Eagle. Fitted with an 8" accurized barrel, two-stage target trigger, jeweled bolt, adjustable sights with three interchangeable blades and range case.

	295	225	195	150	125	85

Mountain Eagle Compact Edition

Similar to above, with a 4.5" barrel and short grip.

	295	225	195	150	125	85

Lone Eagle

Single-shot rotating breech pistol designed to fire centerfire cartridges. Standard finish is a black oxide blue luster. Barrel is drilled and tapped for scope mounts. Standard barrel length 14". Fixed, adjustable, or silhouette sights are offered as options. Stock assembly made from Lexan. Handgun offered in these calibers: .22-250, .223, .22 Hornet, .243, .30-30, .30-06, .308, .357 Magnum, .358 Win., .35 Rem., .44 Magnum, .444 Marlin, 7mm-08, 7mm Bench Rest. Weighs between 4 lbs. 3 oz. to 4 lbs. 7 oz. depending on caliber.

	400	300	275	250	200	125

Lone Eagle (New Model)

Introduced in 1996, this improved Lone Eagle model features 15 interchangeable barreled actions from .22 Hornet to .444 Marlin. Available in both black and chrome actions, with or without muzzle-brake. The 7.62x39 action introduced in 1996 also. Sights can be fixed, adjustable or silhouette type. Weight from 4 lbs. 3 oz. to 4 lbs. 7 oz. depending on caliber. Prices listed reflect black action and fixed sights. **NOTE:** Add $100 for muzzle-brake; $30 for chrome action; $35 for adjustable sights; $130 for silhouette sights.

	425	325	175	150	125	100

Micro Desert Eagle Pistol

Small-frame DAO pocket pistol chambered in .380 ACP. Features include a 2.22" barrel, fixed low-profile sights, steel slide, aluminum alloy frame, nickel-teflon finish, six-round capacity. Overall length 4.52". Weight: 14 oz.

	450	350	250	200	150	100

Model 1911 Desert Eagle

Based on the classic 1911 design, this model comes in two sizes: 1911 G, full-size (5") or 1911 C, mid-size (4.33"), with custom-type features like extended beavertail grip safety, extended thumb safety and mag release, enlarged ejection port, beveled mag well and double-diamond wood grips. Comes with black finish, fixed sights and two 8-shot mags. A 3" barrel model (Undercover) is also available, with aluminum frame, 6-shot magazine and ajustable sights. **NOTE:** Add $50 for Undercover model.

	1450	1250	1000	800	500	300

MR9 / MR40

This family of pistols has a Walther polymer frame, with a Magnum Research stainless slide and barrel made in U.S.A. Striker-fired operation, with internal safeties. Offered in 9mm or .40 S&W, with 4", 4.15" or 4.5" barrels. The integral polymer grips have interchangeable palm swells of different sizes.

	500	400	325	250	200	125

Mountain Eagle Rifle

Limited edition rifle (1,000), with Sako action and composite stock. Chambered for the .270, .280, .30-06, .300 Win., .338 Win, 7mm Magnum. Introduced in 1994. Additional calibers are .300 Weatherby, .375 H&H, .416 Rem., and 7mm STW. Barrel length 24". Average weight about 7.74 lbs. **NOTE:** Add $150 for muzzle-brake; $300 for .375 H&H and .416 Rem.; $100 for left-hand actions.

	2295	1700	1150	800	400	175

Mountain Eagle Varmint Edition

Chambered for .222 Rem. and .223 Rem. cartridges. Fitted with a 26" stainless Krieger barrel. Kevlar-graphite stock. Weight approximately 9 lbs. 13 oz.

	2295	1750	1150	800	400	175

	NIB	EXC.	V.G.	GOOD	FAIR	POOR

Magnum Lite Rimfire Rifles

These rifles are built with Ruger 10/22 actions and graphite barrels. There are several variations depending on stock configuration. **NOTE:** For Clark Custom Upgrades add $130 to price of each Magnum Lite rifle.

Hogue and Fajen Scope-Hi Stock

NIB	EXC.	V.G.	GOOD	FAIR	POOR
650	495	400	300	200	125

Fajen Thumbhole Sporter

NIB	EXC.	V.G.	GOOD	FAIR	POOR
700	550	450	300	200	125

Fajen Thumbhole Silhouette

NIB	EXC.	V.G.	GOOD	FAIR	POOR
800	650	500	300	200	125

Turner Barracuda

NIB	EXC.	V.G.	GOOD	FAIR	POOR
800	650	500	300	200	125

Magnum Lite Centerfire Rifles

These rifles are built on Sako actions and fitted with graphite barrels. Introduced in 1999. Offered in two configurations, both with synthetic stock.

Heavy Barrel

Fitted with a 26", 1.2" diameter barrel, with a 1-in-14 twist. Chambered for .223 cartridge. Weight approximately 7.8 lbs

NIB	EXC.	V.G.	GOOD	FAIR	POOR
2295	1700	1150	800	400	295

Sport Taper Barrel

Fitted with a 24" tapered barrel and chambered for the .280 Rem., 7mm Magnum, .30-06, .300 Win. Magnum. Weight about 6.4 lbs.

NIB	EXC.	V.G.	GOOD	FAIR	POOR
2295	1700	1150	800	400	295

Tactical Rifle

Introduced in 2000, rifle features a 26" match grade barrel chambered for the .223, .22-250, .308, or .300 Win. Magnum cartridges. Barrel is made from carbon fiber. Action is a Remington Model 700. H-S Precision tactical stock, with adjustable comb. Adjustable trigger. Weight approximately 8.3 lbs.

NIB	EXC.	V.G.	GOOD	FAIR	POOR
2400	1800	1250	850	400	295

DESERT INDUSTRIES
Las Vegas, Nevada
See—Steel City Arms

DESTROYER CARBINE
Spain

Destroyer Carbine

A 9mm Bayard/Large caliber bolt-action rifle, with 20" barrel and 7-shot magazine. Full length stock, with two barrel bands.

NIB	EXC.	V.G.	GOOD	FAIR	POOR
—	500	395	200	100	35

DETONICS
Middlestadt, Illinois

Current manufacturer of Detonics 1911-style pistols.

Combat Master

Latest version of the very first compact 1911 developed in the 1970s by the original Detonics company. In .45 ACP, with 3.5" octagonal barrel, two-tone finish, aluminum/Dymondwood grips, 6+1 capacity, stainless steel frame and slide. Weight 30 oz. Introduced in 2010.

NIB	EXC.	V.G.	GOOD	FAIR	POOR
850	775	700	550	—	—

Fitted with a 3.5" barrel chambered for the .45 ACP, .40 S&W, .357 SIG, .38 Super, or the 9mm Para cartridges. Checkered rosewood grips. Low profile fixed sights. Magazine capacity is 6 rounds. Height of pistol is 4.75". Overall length is 7". Weight is about 34 oz. All stainless steel including springs. Introduced in 2005.

NIB	EXC.	V.G.	GOOD	FAIR	POOR
1300	1050	650	425	300	175

Nemesis HT

Full-size with 5" barrel, chambered in .40 S&W. Weight 38 oz., capacity 9+1. Other features same as above. Introduced in 2011.

NIB	EXC.	V.G.	GOOD	FAIR	POOR
1950	1800	1500	1100	—	—

	NIB	EXC.	V.G.	GOOD	FAIR	POOR

Street Master

Chambered for the .45 ACP cartridge and fitted with a 5" barrel. Checkered rosewood grips. All stainless steel including springs. Height is 4.75". Overall length is 8.5". Weight is about 39 oz. Magazine capacity is 6 rounds. Fixed sights. Introduced in 2005.

1200	950	675	450	325	195

DTX

Polymer-frame double-action-only pistol, chambered in 9mm or .40 S&W. Barrel 4.25". Weight 25 oz., capacity 16+1 (9mm), 14+1 (.40). Introduced in 2011.

975	900	775	625	450	250

Model 9-11-01

This model, introduced in 2005, is chambered for the .45 ACP cartridge and fitted with a 5" barrel. All stainlees steel construction. Checkered rosewood grips. Height is about 5.5". Overall length is 8.625". Weight is about 43 oz. Magazine capacity is 7 rounds. Fixed sights.

1200	950	675	450	325	195

DETONICS FIREARMS
INDUSTRIES / NEW DETONICS / DECTONICS USA LLC
Bellevue, Washington / Phoenix, Arizona / Pendergrass, Georgia

This series of compact 1911-type pistols, was first manufactured by Detonics Firearms Industries in Bellvue, WA from 1976 to 1988. That firm was sold to New Detonics Mfg. Corp. of Phoenix, AZ, which operated from 1989 to 1992. In 2004 the brand was resurrected and returned to production by Detonics USA in Pendergrass, GA. Then in 2007 Detonics USA and all if its predecessors was sold to a group of investors who established the current company, known only as Detonics, in Middlestadt, IL.

Mark I

A .45-caliber semi-automatic pistol, with 3.25" barrel and 6-shot magazine. Matte blued with walnut grips. Discontinued in 1981.

—	550	450	400	300	200

Mark II

As above, with satin nickel-plated finish. Discontinued in 1979.

—	550	450	400	300	200

Mark III

As above, with hard chrome plating. Discontinued in 1979.

—	600	500	450	350	250

Mark IV

As above, with polished blue finish. Discontinued in 1981.

—	550	450	400	300	200

Combat Master

The Mark I in 9mm, .38 Super or .45-caliber.

975	800	600	500	400	250

Combat Master Mark V

As above, in stainless steel with a matte finish. Discontinued in 1985.

975	800	600	500	400	250

Combat Master Mark VI

As above, with adjustable sights and sides of slide polished. 1,000 were made in .451 Detonics Magnum caliber. **NOTE:** .451 Detonics Magnum add 40 percent.

900	750	600	500	400	250

Combat Master Mark VII

As above, without sights. **NOTE:** .451 Detonics Magnum add 40 percent.

900	750	600	500	400	250

Military Combat MC2

As above, in 9mm, .38 Super or .45-caliber. Fixed sights, dull finish and Pachmayr grips. Discontinued in 1984.

675	600	500	425	300	200

	NIB	EXC.	V.G.	GOOD	FAIR	POOR

Scoremaster

As above, in .45- or .451 Detonics Magnum, with 5" or 6" barrel, Millet sights and grip safety.

NIB	EXC.	V.G.	GOOD	FAIR	POOR
1250	1000	800	600	400	250

Janus Competition Scoremaster

As above, in .45-caliber with compensated barrel. Introduced in 1988.

NIB	EXC.	V.G.	GOOD	FAIR	POOR
1750	1450	1250	850	650	300

Servicemaster

As above, with a 4.25" barrel, interchangeable sights and matte finish. Discontinued in 1986.

NIB	EXC.	V.G.	GOOD	FAIR	POOR
—	1000	800	600	400	200

Pocket 9

A 9mm double-action semi-automatic pistol, with 3" barrel and 6-shot magazine. Matte finish stainless steel. Discontinued in 1986.

NIB	EXC.	V.G.	GOOD	FAIR	POOR
—	400	350	275	225	175

Combat Master

Fitted with a 3.5" barrel chambered for the .45 ACP, .40 S&W, .357 SIG, .38 Super or the 9mm Para cartridges. Checkered rosewood grips. Low profile fixed sights. Magazine capacity 6 rounds. Height of pistol 4.75". Overall length 7". Weight about 34 oz. All stainless steel including springs. Introduced in 2005, by Detonics USA.

NIB	EXC.	V.G.	GOOD	FAIR	POOR
1300	1050	650	425	300	175

Street Master

Chambered for .45 ACP cartridge and fitted with a 5" barrel. Checkered rosewood grips. All stainless steel including springs. Height 4.75". Overall length 8.5". Weight about 39 oz. Magazine capacity 6 rounds. Fixed sights. Introduced in 2005, by Detonics USA.

NIB	EXC.	V.G.	GOOD	FAIR	POOR
1200	950	675	450	325	195

Model 9-11-01

Introduced in 2005, by Detonics USA. Chambered for .45 ACP cartridge and fitted with a 5" barrel. All stainless steel construction. Checkered rosewood grips. Height about 5.5". Overall length 8.625". Weight about 43 oz. Magazine capacity 7 rounds. Fixed sights.

NIB	EXC.	V.G.	GOOD	FAIR	POOR
1200	950	675	450	325	195

DEUTSCHE WERKE
Erfurt, Germany

Ortgies

Semi-automatic pistol in 6.35mm and 7.65mm. The 6.35mm pistol manufactured in 1921 and 7.65mm model in 1922 by Ortgies Company. Pistols had "HO" logo for Heinrich Ortgies on each grip. Later, Ortgies Company was bought by Deutsche Werke. Grip logo was "D". Over the period Ortgies were manufactured with four different slide legends.

NIB	EXC.	V.G.	GOOD	FAIR	POOR
—	450	325	275	200	100

Ortgies 9mm

As above, with addition of a hold-open button on left side of slide. Caliber is 9mmk, aka .380 ACP.

NIB	EXC.	V.G.	GOOD	FAIR	POOR
—	450	375	250	175	100

DEVISME, F. P.
Paris, France

One of the more popular French gunsmiths of the mid-19th century. F.P. Devisme manufactured a wide variety of firearms. Including single-shot percussion pistols, double-barrel percussion rifles and shotguns, percussion revolvers and cane guns. After 1858, this maker manufactured cartridge weapons of the same style as his percussion arms. Quality of all his products is uniformly high and impossible to provide a generalized price guide.

DIAMOND
Turkey

Gold Series Semi-Automatic Shotgun

Chambered for 12-gauge shell, with 3" chamber. Barrel length 28". Turkish walnut stock or synthetic stock. Black receiver, with gold-filled engraving. Also available with 24" slug barrel with sights. **NOTE:** Add $50 for walnut stock.

NIB	EXC.	V.G.	GOOD	FAIR	POOR
350	300	200	150	100	75

NIB	EXC.	V.G.	GOOD	FAIR	POOR

Gold Series Pump-Action Shotgun

Offered with same features as semi-automatic Gold gun, with slide-action. **NOTE:** Add $25 for walnut stock.

| 300 | 250 | 175 | 125 | 100 | 75 |

Silver Series Mariner Semi-Automatic Shotgun

A 12-gauge stainless steel and anodized alloy semi-automatic gun, with 3" chambers. Fitted with 22" ventilated rib barrel and synthetic stock.

| 425 | 350 | 275 | 200 | 150 | 100 |

Silver Series Mariner Pump-Action Shotgun

A 12-gauge pump gun, with 20" slug barrel and synthetic stock. Stainless steel and alloy.

| 350 | 275 | 200 | 150 | 100 | 75 |

Diamond Elite Semi-Automatic Shotgun

A 12-gauge 3" chamber shotgun. Offered with 22" to 28" barrels, with 3 choke tubes. Engraved receiver.

| 325 | 275 | 200 | 150 | 100 | 75 |

Diamond Panther Pump-Action Shotgun

As above, in a slide-action configuration.

| 250 | 200 | 200 | 150 | 100 | 75 |

Diamond Panther Semi-Automatic Shotgun

A 12-gauge gun, with 3" chambers and 20" or 28" ventilated rib barrel. Furnished with 3 choke tubes. Synthetic stock.

| 325 | 275 | 200 | 150 | 100 | 75 |

Diamond Elite Pump-Action Shotgun

As above, with slide-action. Offered with 18.5" slug barrel.

| 300 | 250 | 175 | 125 | 100 | 75 |

Diamondback DB9 Semi-Automatic Pistol

Polymer-frame striker-fired mimi-compact 9mm, with 6+1 capacity and weight of 11 oz. Very compact design, with a 3" barrel, overall length 5.6", height 4" and width .80". Available in several finishes including black, stainless, pink, orange and teal. Introduced in 2011. **NOTE:** Add $200 for Crimson Trace laser grip.

| 435 | 385 | 325 | 300 | — | — |

Diamondback DB380 Semi-Automatic Pistol

Small variation of DB9. Chambered for .380. Barrel length 2.8"; weight 8.8 oz. Introduced in 2011. **NOTE:** Add $200 for Crimson Trace laser grip.

| 385 | 325 | 285 | 250 | — | — |

DICKINSON, E. L. & J.
Springfield, Massachusetts

Ranger

A .32-caliber spur trigger revolver, with 6-shot cylinder.

| — | — | 525 | 450 | 200 | 100 |

Single-Shot

A .32-caliber single-shot pistol, with 3.75" hinged barrel, silver plated brass frame, blued barrel and walnut grips.

| — | — | 775 | 650 | 250 | 100 |

DICKSON, NELSON & CO.
Dawson, Georgia

Rifle

A .58-caliber single-shot percussion rifle, with 34" barrel, full stock secured by two barrel bands, brass furniture and iron loading rod. Lock marked "Dickson/Nelson & Co./C.S." as well as "Ala." and date of manufacture. Prospective purchasers are advised to secure a qualified appraisal prior to acquisition. Carbine version of this arm known and has a 24" barrel.

| — | — | 39500 | 14000 | 3000 | 2000 |

	NIB	EXC.	V.G.	GOOD	FAIR	POOR

DIMICK, H.E.
St. Louis, Missouri

Percussion Pistol

This maker primarily known for half stock Plains Rifles, he also manufactured a limited number of percussion pistols. These vary in length, caliber, stock form and type of furniture. Values listed should only be used as a rough guide. Prospective purchasers should secure a qualified appraisal prior to acquisition. Active 1849 to 1873.

—	—	—	7500	2750	900

DOMINGO ACHA
See—Acha

DOMINO
Brescia, Italy

Model OP 601 Match Pistol

A .22-caliber short semi-automatic pistol, with 5.6" vented barrel, target sights, adjustable and removable trigger. Blued, with adjustable walnut grips.

1700	1200	800	550	300	175

Model SP 602 Match Pistol

As above, in .22 LR caliber.

1700	1200	800	550	300	175

DORNAUS & DIXON ENTERPRISES, INC.
Huntington Beach, California
See—Bren 10

DORNHEIM, G.C.
Suhl, Germany

Gecado Model 11

A 6.35mm semi-automatic pistol, bearing the name "Gecado" on the slide. Fitted with a 2.2" barrel. Magazine capacity 6 rounds. Weight about 15 oz. Marketed by G.C. Dornheim. Copy of FN Browning Model 1906.

—	300	225	125	75	50

Gecado 7.65mm

A 7.65mm semi-automatic pisto, bearing the name "Gecado" on the slide. Fitted with 2.6" barrel. Magazine capacity 7 rounds. Weight about 21 oz. Marketed by G.C. Dornheim.

—	275	150	125	75	50

DOUBLESTAR CORP.
Winchester, Kentucky

Star EM-4

Chambered for .223 cartridge and fitted with a 16" barrel. Rifle supplied with A-2 or flat top upper and Colt M-4 handguard.

915	750	600	500	275	125

Star-15

Model has 20" barrel, A-2 buttstock and handguard. Supplied with A-2 or flat top upper. In .223 or 7.62x39 calibers.

775	625	575	450	225	100

Star Lightweight Tactical Rifle

Fitted with a 15" fluted barrel, permanently attached muzzle-brake and short tactical buttstock. Supplied with A-2 or flat top upper.

880	700	575	450	225	100

Star Carbine

Model has 16" match grade barrel. Supplied with either A-2 or non-collapsing CAR buttstock. Upper receiver A-2 style or flat top. In .223 or 7.62x39 calibers.

775	625	575	450	225	100

	NIB	EXC.	V.G.	GOOD	FAIR	POOR

Star DS-4 Carbine

Model features 16" M-4 barrel, with 6 position buttstock, oval handguard and A-2 flash hider. Weight about 6.75 lbs. Choice of A-2 or flattop upper receiver.

875	700	575	450	225	100

Star Super Match Rifle

Choice of match grade barrel lengths; 16", 20", 22" or 24". Rifle supplied with flat top upper or tactical Hi-Rise upper. **NOTE:** Add $50 for .204 Ruger or 6.8 SPC; $100 for 6.5 Grendel, all discontinued.

950	800	675	450	225	100

Star Critterslayer

Model fitted with 24" fluted super match barrel, with flat top upper and free floating handguard. Match 2 stage trigger. Fitted with Harris LMS swivel bipod and Ergo grip, with palm swell.

1300	1000	750	600	395	175

DSC Expedition Rifle

Offered with 16" or 20" lightweight barrel and integral muzzle-brake. Stock sights and receiver are A-2 configuration.

825	650	575	450	225	100

DSC Star-15 CMP Service Rifle

Fitted with 20" chrome lined heavy match barrel. National Match front and rear sights. CMP free float handguard. National Match trigger. A-2 upper receiver.

1000	750	650	575	450	225

DSC Star CMP Improved Service Rifle

Similar to above model, with 20" Wilson Arms premium grade heavy match barrel. McCormick single- or two-stage Match trigger and Tippie Competition rear sight.

1299	975	825	650	575	300

DSC Star 15 Lightweight Tactical

Model fitted with 16" fluted heavy barrel and tactical "shorty" A-2 buttstock.

880	700	575	450	225	100

DSC Star Dissipator

Model features 16" barrel, with full length handguard. Available with A-2 or flattop upper receiver.

875	700	575	450	225	100

DSC Star 15 9mm Carbine

Chambered for 9mm cartridge and fitted with a 16" heavy barrel. A-2 or flattop upper receiver. Available with A-2 or CAR buttstock.

995	750	650	575	450	225

1911 Combat Pistol

Full-size Government Model .45 ACP, with 5" barrel, stainless slide, forged frame, black finish. Novak white-dot LoMount sights, Picatinny rail, 8-shot magazine, checkered wood grips. Introduced 2010.

1150	1000	800	700	400	300

DOUG TURNBULL MANUFACTURING CO.
Bloomfield, New York

Company began operation in 1983 as a one-man shop. Today the company numbers 14 people and does finish work for most major firearms manufacturers. Company also installs Miller single triggers. Models listed are a series of special run firearms produced by Turnbull.

DT COLT

This model is a current Colt SAA reworked to look like the pre-1920 SAA. Assigned serial numbers beginning with 001DT. Revolvers are offered in .45 Colt, .44-40 and .38-40 calibers. Barrel lengths 4.75", 5.5" and 7.5". Standard DT has color case hardened frame and rest of the gun charcoal blue. Cylinder flutes are enlarged and front of the cylinder is beveled. Many special options offered which will affect cost. Prices listed are for standard revolvers. Values for these very special guns is strictly what the market will bear.

Year Offered—1998

1795	—	—	—	—	—

	NIB	EXC.	V.G.	GOOD	FAIR	POOR

Year Offered—1999

2250	—	—	—	—	—

Year Offered—2000

2500	—	—	—	—	—

EHBM Colt

A Colt SAA current production revolver, limited to 50 guns. Chambered of .45 Colt and fitted with a 5.5" barrel. Special features. Serial numbers EHBM01 to EHBM50. First offered in 2000.

2650	2300	1600	1250	700	500

Smith & Wesson No. 3 Schofield

Introduced in 2002, a special new production S&W Schofield. Special serial numbers with "DTR" prefix starting with serial number 0001. Frame, barrel and cylinder are charcoal blued. Trigger, trigger guard and barrel latch are bone color case hardened. Factory wood grips are standard. Engraving is optional.

2300	2450	1900	1550	875	500

Colt/Winchester Cased Set

Cased set, with Colt Model 1873 engraved revolver and Winchester Model 1894. Colt chambered for .45 Colt cartridge and fitted with a 7.5" barrel. Engraving is "B" coverage. Model 1894 chambered for .45 Colt cartridge and in the saddle ring configuration. Engraving pattern #9 with deer. Checkered walnut stock. Limited to five sets total. Serial numbers 160DT to 164DT.

5750	4300	3750	2500	1500	600

General Patton Colt

Limited run of engraved Colt Model 1873 Single Action Army revolvers. Fitted with ivory grips and full-coverage engraving. Chambered for .45 Colt cartridge and fitted with 4.75" barrel. Helfricht-style engraving. Silver-plated finish. Limited to 10 revolvers total. Serial numbers GP01 to GP10.

5250	4000	3250	2000	1000	400

Theodore Roosevelt Colt

Colt SAA revolver features carved ivory grips, full coverage engraving, with gold cylinder, hammer and ejector rod. Chambered for .44-40 cartridge and fitted with 7.5" barrel. Nimschke-style engraving. Balance of gun silver plated. Supplied with fitted case. Limited to 25 revolvers total. Serial numbers TR01 to TR25.

7750	6000	5000	4000	3000	600

Theodore Roosevelt Winchester Model 1876

Custom rifle limited to 25 pieces. Serial numbered from TR01 to TR-25. Each rifle engraved and checkered in style of original. Chambered for .45-70 cartridge. Fitted with 28" half round barrel. Gold inlaid stock oval. Portion of the proceeds of each rifle goes to benefit the Doug Turnbull Conservation Laboratory at the National Firearms Museum.

29000	—	—	—	—	—

Cowboy Classic

Custom-tuned and authentically finished USFA 1873-style single-action revolver. Chambered in virtually all historically-correct centerfire cartridges. Barrel: 4.75", 5.5" and 7.5". Black hard rubber grips standard. Bone charcoal case-hardened and charcoal blue finish. Introduced 2006.

1650	1300	950	675	400	300

Model 1911 Heritage

This made-to-order reproduction of the original design in the year 1911, is made to have the look and feel of pistols made during WWI. Chambered in .45 ACP, features include hand-checkered American black walnut double-diamond grips, color case hardened frame and hammer, a short and wide checkered spur hammer and two two-tone magazines. Several other variants are offered including Commander size and engraved models

2075	1750	1200	700	400	250

DOWNSIZER CORPORATION
Santee, California

Model WSP

Introduced in 1999 and billed as world's smallest pistol by manufacturer. Single-/double-action-only pistol, with tip-up barrel. Chambered for .22 Magnum, .32 Magnum, .357 Magnum, 9mm, .40 S&W and .45 ACP cartridges. Barrel length 2.1". Overall length 3.25". Height 2.25", thickness .9". Weight approximately 11 oz. Built from stainless steel.

400	325	275	225	175	125

NIB	EXC.	V.G.	GOOD	FAIR	POOR

DPMS
St. Cloud, Minnesota

Panther Bull A-15
AR-15 type rifle chambered for the .223 cartridge. Fitted with 20" stainless steel bull barrel. A-2 style buttstock. No sights. Barrel has 1:9 twist. Flat top receiver. Handguard is aluminum free float tube. Upper and lower receivers are hard coated black. Weight about 9.5 lbs. Each rifle comes standard with two 7-round magazines, sling and cleaning kit.

900	700	550	400	275	125

Panther Bull 24
Similar to model above. Fitted with a 24" bull barrel. Flat top receiver. Weight about 10 lbs.

950	750	600	400	275	125

Panther Deluxe Bull 24 Special
Model fitted with 24" stainless steel fluted bull barrel. Adjustable A-2 style buttstock. Flat top receiver. Adjustable sniper pistol-grip. Weight about 10 lbs.

1150	900	750	400	275	125

Panther Extreme Super Bull 24
Model fitted with 24" stainless steel extra heavy bull barrel (1.150" dia.). Skeletonized stock. Flat top receiver. Weight about 11.75 lbs.

1200	800	650	400	275	125

Panther Bulldog
Fitted with 20" stainless steel fluted bull barrel. Black synthetic A-2-style buttstock. Flat top receiver. Adjustable trigger. Weight about 10 lbs.

1200	975	800	400	275	125

Panther Bull Sweet 16
Model fitted with 16" stainless steel bull barrel. Flat top receiver. Weight about 7.75 lbs.

1100	900	550	400	275	125

Panther Bull SST 16
Similar to model above, with stainless steel lower receiver. Weight about 9 lbs.

1300	975	650	400	275	125

Panther Bull Classic
Model fitted with 20" 4150 steel bull barrel. Square front post sight, adjustable A-2 rear sight. Weight about 9.75 lbs.

1200	800	650	400	275	125

Panther Arctic
Model similar to above, with 20" fluted bull barrel and flat top receiver. Black A-2 style buttstock, with white coat finish on receiver and handguard. Black Teflon finish on barrel. Weight about 8.25 lbs.

1075	850	700	400	275	125

Panther Classic
Fitted with 20" 4150 steel heavy barrel. Square front post sight and A-2 rear sight. A-2 round handguard. Weight about 9.5 lbs.

800	600	500	400	275	125

Panther DCM
Model similar to above, with 20" stainless steel heavy barrel and NM rear sight. DCM free-float handguard. Adjustable trigger. Weight about 9.5 lbs.

950	750	600	400	275	125

Panther Classic 16 Post Ban
Model fitted with 1" 4150 steel heavy barrel. A-2 style sights. Round handguard. Weight about 7.25 lbs.

775	600	500	400	275	125

Panther Free Float 16 Post Ban
Similar to model above, with 16" barrel. Fitted with vented free-floated barrel and tube handguard. Weight approximately 7.25 lbs.

825	650	550	400	275	125

	NIB	EXC.	V.G.	GOOD	FAIR	POOR

Panther Southpaw Post Ban

Model fitted with 20" 4150 steel heavy barrel. A-2 style sights. Upper receiver modified for left-hand ejection. Weight about 9.5 lbs.

	875	700	600	400	275	125

Panther Race Gun

Similar to Panther Bull, with 24" fluted bull barrel. Sights: JP Micro adjustable rear, JP front sight adjustable for height. Includes Lyman globe and Shaver inserts.

	1875	1500	800	500	275	125

Panther Tuber

Similar to Panther Bull 24, with 16" barrel and cylindrical aluminum shroud.

	700	600	500	400	275	125

Single Shot Rifle

AR-15 style single-shot rifle, with manually-operated bolt. No magazine.

	775	500	400	275	125	100

Panther Pardus

Similar to Panther Post Ban, with 16" bull barrel, telescoping buttstock and tan Teflon finish. Introduced 2006.

	1200	850	700	400	275	200

Panther 20th Anniversary Rifle

Similar to Panther Post-ban, with 20" bull barrel and engraved, chrome-plated lower receiver. Introduced 2006.

	2500	2000	1550	800	500	300

Panther 6.8 Rifle

Similar to Panther DCM, with 20" chrome-moly barrel and chambered for 6.8x43 Remington SPC. Introduced 2006.

	1000	850	700	400	275	125

Panther Mark 12

Similar to other Panthers, with flash hider and other refinements. Introduced 2007.

	1300	850	700	400	275	125

Panther SDM-R

Similar to other Panthers, with stainless steel barrel and Harris bipod. Introduced 2007.

	1200	850	700	400	275	125

LRT-SASS

Semi-automatic rifle based on AR-15 design. Chambered in .308 Win., 18" stainless steel barrel with flash hider. Collapsible Vitor Clubfoot carbine stock and 19-round detachable magazine. Introduced 2006.

	1900	1600	1475	1000	600	350

LR-260

Similar to LRT-SASS, with 24" stainless steel barrel and chambered in .260 Remington. Also available with 20" chrome-moly barrel as LR-260H. Introduced 2006.

	1300	1000	900	800	500	300

LR-243

Similar to LR-260, with 20" chrome-moly barrel and chambered in .243 Win. Introduced 2006.

	1150	950	800	650	500	300

LR-204

Similar to LRT-260. Chambered in .204 Ruger. Introduced 2006.

	1000	800	650	500	400	300

Panther Arms 5.56 Oracle

Semi-automatic AR-style rifle chambered in 5.56 NATO. Features include 16" 4140 chrome-moly 1:9 barrel; phosphated steel bolt; oval Glacier Guard hand guard; flattop upper with Picatinny rail; aluminum lower; two 30-round magazines; Pardus 6-position telescoping stock. Also available on larger platform in .308 Winchester/7.62 NATO.

	700	575	500	400	300	200

	NIB	EXC.	V.G.	GOOD	FAIR	POOR

Panther 3G1

Semi-automatic AR-style rifle chambered in 5.56 NATO. Features include 18" 416 stainless 1:9 barrel; phosphated steel bolt; VTAC modular hand guard; flattop upper with Picatinny rail; aluminum lower; two 30-round magazines; Magpul CTR adjustable stock.

1000	850	700	600	400	300

Prairie Panther

Semi-automatic AR-style rifle chambered in 5.56 NATO. Features include 20" 416 stainless fluted heavy 1:8 barrel; phosphated steel bolt; free-floated carbon fiber hand guard; flattop upper with Picatinny rail; aluminum lower; two 30-round magazines; skeletonized Zytel stock; finished in King Desert Shadow camo overall.

1150	1000	850	700	450	300

Panther RAPTR

Semi-automatic AR-style rifle chambered in 5.56 NATO. Features include 16" 4140 chrome-moly 1:9 barrel; phosphated steel bolt; ERGO Z-Rail 4-rail hand guard; front vertical grip; standard A-2 sights; aluminum lower; four 30-round magazines. Discontinued 2012.

1350	1025	800	625	350	250

Panther REPR

Semi-automatic AR-style rifle chambered in .308 Win./7.62 NATO. Features include 18" 416 stainless steel 1:10 barrel; phosphated steel bolt; 4-rail free-floated hand guard; no sights; aluminum lower; two 19-round magazines; Coyote Brown camo finish overall.

2100	1850	1400	1000	650	350

Panther 308 Mk12

Semi-automatic AR-style rifle chambered in .308 Win./7.62 NATO. Features include 16" 4140 chrome-moly heavy 1:10 barrel; phosphated steel bolt; 4-rail free-floated hand guard; flip-up front and rear sights; aluminum lower; two 19-round magazines; matte black finish overall; Magpul CTR adjustable stock.

1500	1100	850	700	450	300

Panther A-15 Pump Rifle

Model has 20" 4150 steel heavy barrel, with A-2 style sights. Fitted with A-2 compensator and modified to slide-action. Weight about 8.5 lbs.

1400	1050	700	600	500	300

Panther A-15 Pump Pistol

Same as above. Fitted with 10.5" barrel. Weight about 5 lbs.

1450	1100	750	575	450	300

Panther DCM .22 LR

Rimfire version of Panther series, with 20" fluted stainless H-Bar barrel, A-2 upper receiver, National Match sights. Also available with 16" barrel (Panther AP4) and flat-top receiver. **NOTE:** Deduct $75 for AP4 model

850	750	600	450	300	150

Panther Lite 308/338

Chambered for .308 Win. or .338 Federal. A-3 Flattop design, with 20" free-floated barrel and handguard. Various options offered.

1350	1200	900	650	400	200

Panther 6.5

Basic Panther model chambered for 6.5 Creedmoor. Stainless steel free-floated 24" barrel, A-3 Flattop upper, mil-spec stock.

1100	975	750	550	350	200

6.8 SPCII Hunter

Chambered for Remington 6.8 SPC cartridge, with 18" barrel and Miculek compensator. A-3 Flattop design with forward assist. Skeletonized stock.

1150	1025	800	600	400	250

300 AAC Blackout

Chambered for .300 AAC cartridge. Chrome-lined 16" heavy barrel comes with Blackout suppressor adapter. AP4 stock, free-float handguard.

1100	975	750	550	350	200

	NIB	EXC.	V.G.	GOOD	FAIR	POOR

308 Recon

Similar to 300 AAC Blackout model, except chambered for .308 Winchester. Standard weight, 16" barrel with Blackout suppressor adapter. A-3 Flattop upper receiver, Magpul MOE stock with 4-Rail handguard.

1350	1200	1000	750	500	250

DREYSE

See—Rheinmetall

DRISCOLL, J.B.

Springfield, Massachusetts

Single-Shot Pocket Pistol

Small pistol chambered for .22 rimfire. Has a 3.5" octagonal barrel that pivots downward for loading after trigger-like hook under the breech is pulled. Spur trigger, silver-plated brass frame and blued barrel. Square butt is flared at bottom and grips are walnut. Approximately 200 manufactured in late 1860s.

—	—	1000	375	100	50

DRULOV

Czech Republic

This Company was part of the national co-operative under communist rule when Czech Republic was part of Czechoslovakia. The company was formed in 1948. Company specialized in low-cost but well made rimfire target pistols.

Model 70 Standard

Model a bolt-action single-shot pistol chambered for the .22 LR. Knob at rear of frame opened the bolt. When bolt is closed firing pin is cocked. Barrel is 9.75" long, with an adjustable front sight for windage. Rear sight is adjustable for elevation. Wooden wraparound grips, with thumb rest are standard. Weighs about 44 oz.

—	300	200	175	100	75

Model 70 Special

Same as above, with addition of set trigger.

—	350	250	200	150	100

Model 75

Model features set trigger, better sights and grip. Rear sight is fully adjustable.

—	400	300	250	200	150

Pav

Target pistol introduced between WWI and WW II. Inexpensive pistol with fixed front sight and notch for rear sight. Like other models above, also a single-shot chambered for .22 LR cartridge. Barrel is 10.25" and weighs about 35 oz.

—	175	150	100	75	50

DSA, INC.

Barrington, Illinois

DSA, Inc. began selling its rifles to the public in 1996. Based on actual blueprints of the famous FN/FAL rifle, SA58 rifles are made in the U.S. All SA58 rifles are fitted with fully adjustable gas system, Type I, II or III forged receiver, hand-lapped barrel, muzzle-brake, elevation adjustable post front sight, windage adjustable rear peep sight with 5 settings from 200 to 600 meters, detachable metric magazine, adjustable sling and hard case. DSA also manufactures a series of AR-15 type rifles and carbines. Virtually all parts are made by DSA.

SA58

SA58 24" Bull

Fitted with a 24" stainless steel barrel and .308 match chamber. Overall length 44.5". Weight approximately 11.5 lbs.

1750	1500	1150	800	500	300

SA58 21" Bull

Same as above. Fitted with 21" stainless steel barrel. Weight about 11.1 lbs.

1750	1500	1150	800	500	300

	NIB	EXC.	V.G.	GOOD	FAIR	POOR

SA58 Medium Contour

Model offered with 21" barrel. Either stainless steel or blued steel. Weight about 10.5 lbs. **NOTE:** Add $250 for stainless steel.

NIB	EXC.	V.G.	GOOD	FAIR	POOR
1550	1300	1150	800	500	300

SA58 Carbine

Model fitted with 16.25" barrel. Barrel cut for factory light bipod. Blued finish. Stainless steel version also available. Overall length 37.5". Weight about 8.35 lbs. **NOTE:** Add $250 for stainless steel.

NIB	EXC.	V.G.	GOOD	FAIR	POOR
1600	1400	1150	800	500	300

SA58 Standard

Model has 21" barrel cut for factory light bipod. Weight about 8.75 lbs. Blued finish.

NIB	EXC.	V.G.	GOOD	FAIR	POOR
1600	1400	1150	800	500	300

SA58 Tactical

Fitted with 16.25" fluted barrel, black synthetic stock, Type I receiver, adjustable sights and detachable magazine. Blued finish. Weight about 8.25 lbs.

NIB	EXC.	V.G.	GOOD	FAIR	POOR
1600	1400	1150	800	500	300

SA58 Congo

This .308 model features 18" bipod-cut barrel, with short Belgian-style flash hider. Type I receiver with carry handle. Synthetic buttstock and pistol-grip. Aluminum lower. Detachable magazine. Adjustable sights. Weight about 8.6 lbs.

NIB	EXC.	V.G.	GOOD	FAIR	POOR
1800	1550	1250	800	500	300

SA58 Para Congo

Model fitted with Type II receiver, carry handle and 18" bipod-cut barrel. Short Belgian-style flash hider. Steel lower. Folding steel Para stock. Adjustable sights. Weight about 9.85 lbs.

NIB	EXC.	V.G.	GOOD	FAIR	POOR
1800	1550	1250	800	500	300

SA58 Predator

Offered in .308, .260 Rem. or .243. Rifle has Type I receiver, 16" medium carbine barrel with target crown or 19" medium barrel with target crown. Green furniture. Aluminum lower. Picatinny rail. Weight about 9 lbs. with 16" barrel.

NIB	EXC.	V.G.	GOOD	FAIR	POOR
1600	1450	1100	800	475	200

SA58 Graywolf

This .308 model fitted with 21" match grade barrel and target crown. Type I receiver. Aluminum lower. Extended safety. Picatinny rail. Target pistol-grip with standard or X-series buttstock. Versa-pod bipod. Weight about 13 lbs.

NIB	EXC.	V.G.	GOOD	FAIR	POOR
2100	1600	1250	800	500	300

SA58 T48 Replica

Chambered for .308 cartridge and fitted with 21" barrel. Replica Browning flash hider. Supplied with 10- or 20-round fixed magazine and stripper clip top cover. Wooden stock. Weight about 9.7 lbs.

NIB	EXC.	V.G.	GOOD	FAIR	POOR
1600	1400	1250	800	475	200

DS-AR

S1 Rifle

Introduced in 2004, this 5.56-caliber rifle features 20" or 24" bull barrel. Picatinny gas black sight base. Flattop receiver. Free floating aluminum handguard. A-2 stock. Ten-round magazine. Discontinued.

NIB	EXC.	V.G.	GOOD	FAIR	POOR
950	750	600	425	225	150

CVI Carbine

Similar to model above, with 16" barrel, forged front sight base and integral muzzle-brake. D-4 handguard. Fixed CAR buttstock. Ten-round magazine. Discontinued.

NIB	EXC.	V.G.	GOOD	FAIR	POOR
900	700	600	425	225	150

LE4 Carbine

As above, with pre-ban features. For law enforcement only. Discontinued.

NIB	EXC.	V.G.	GOOD	FAIR	POOR
1150	850	600	425	225	150

	NIB	EXC.	V.G.	GOOD	FAIR	POOR

DS-AR S Series Rifle

Introduced in 2005, this rifle chambered for .223 cartridge. Fitted with choice of 16", 20" or 24" stainless steel match grade bull barrel. A-2 stock with free floating handguard. Flattop receiver, National Match 2 stage trigger. Magazine capacity 10, 20 or 30 rounds.

1350	1050	800	525	225	150

DS-AR Carbine

Chambered for .223 cartridge and fitted with 16" D4 barrel and flash hider. Choice of: fixed or collapsible stock; forged flattop or A-2 upper receiver. Magazine capacity 10, 20 or 30 rounds. Introduced in 2005.

1350	1050	800	525	225	150

DS-AR Rifle

As above, with 20" heavy barrel, flash hider and fixed stock. Introduced in 2005.

1350	1050	800	525	225	150

DS-AR DCM Rifle

Chambered for .223 cartridge with Wylde chamber. Fitted with 20" match grade Badger barrel. DCM free float handguard system. National Match two-stage trigger. National Match rear sight. A-2 upper receiver. Introduced in 2005.

1595	1250	950	625	425	225

DS-AR CQB MRP

Introduced in 2005, this model features 16" chrome lined barrel and A-2 flash hider. Collapsible stock with MRP quad rail. Monolithic rail platform upper. Flattop or A-2 upper receiver. Supplied with 30-round magazine.

2595	1850	1400	1025	600	300

DSA Z4 Gas Trap Carbine (GTC)

Model introduced in 2005. Fitted with 16" chrome lined barrel, M4 profile fluted and Vortec flash hider. Collapsible 6-position stock, with free float tactical rail. Gas trap system. Flattop upper receiver. Magazine capacity 10, 20 or 30 rounds.

1675	1250	950	625	425	225

ZM-4 Series

Series of AR-15 type models. Features forged upper and lower receivers, flattop upper, fixed or collapsible stocks, 16" or 20" barrels, black finish or OD Green. **NOTE:** Add $200 for Spartan model with Robar bolt, Magpul trigger guard, Phantom Flashider, 30-round magazine.

750	650	600	500	300	150

BOLT-ACTION RIFLES

DS-MP1

Bolt-action rifle chambered for .308 cartridge. Built on custom Remington 700 action and fitted with 21" Badger barrel, with target crown. Black McMillan A5 stock. Matte black finish. Introduced in 2004.

2800	2100	1675	1050	650	425

HANDGUNS

B&T TP9 Tactical Pistol

Swiss made recoil-operated rotating-bolt semi-automatic, chambered in 9mm Parabellum. Semi-automatic civilian-legal version of B&T TP9SF select-fire sub-machine gun. Imported from Switzerland by DSA from 2008 to 2011.

1100	950	775	600	475	350

DUBIEL ARMS CO.
Sherman, Texas

Dubiel Arms was a manufacturer of custom bolt-action rifles in Sherman, Texas from 1975 to about 1987. Joseph Dubiel and Dr. John Tyson were founders and co-owners of the company. Dubiel's father was John Dubiel, a well-known gunsmith in Oklahoma in the 1920s and '30s. It is believed that Texas rifles were based on his original designs. Actions featured a bolt with five locking lugs and a short 36-degree bolt rotation. Rifles were available with many options, stock designs and custom features. Made in most popular centerfire calibers. Several Dubiel rifles are on display at the Buffalo Bill Historical Center in Cody, Wyoming. In May of 2012, co-founder Dr. John Tyson made a presentation of nine rifles to the NRA National Firearms Museum in Fairfax, Virginia. Prices shown are estimated values of basic models. Various options would increase these values significantly.

5000	3500	2800	2000	—	—

DUMOULIN
Herstal, Belgium

Guns produced by Ernest Dumoulin are essentially handmade to customer's order. They are of highest quality, both in materials and workmanship. There are many options available that have a tremendous impact on value fluctuations. Models and values listed here are base prices.

SHOTGUNS

Europa Model

Side-by-side double-barrel chambered for 12-, 20-, 28-gauge and .410 bore. Available in any length barrel and choke combination. Anson & Deeley boxlock action and automatic ejectors. One has the option of double- or single-selective triggers and choice of six different moderate engraving patterns. Select walnut stock is oil-finished. Introduced in 1989. Basic values are listed.

| 3500 | 2750 | 1950 | 1250 | 800 | 400 |

Leige Model

Side-by-side double-barrel chambered for 12-, 16-, 20- and 28-gauge. Similar to Europa, with greater degree of finish and more engraving. Walnut is of a higher grade. Introduced in 1986.

| 5750 | 4200 | 2750 | 1500 | 950 | 425 |

Continental Model

Side-by-side chambered for 12-, 20-, 28-gauge and .410 bore. Barrel lengths and chokes are on custom-order basis. A true sidelock action, with automatic ejectors and choice of triggers. Six different engraving patterns and stock is made of high grade, hand-checkered, oil-finished walnut. Introduced in 1989.

| 7500 | 6000 | 4500 | 3000 | 1500 | 400 |

Etendart Model

Side-by-side chambered for 12-, 20- and 28-gauge. Best grade side-by-side built on purely made-to-order basis. Profusely engraved and uses exhibition grade walnut in its stock. There are 12 different engraving patterns from which to choose. Cost is according to embellishments chosen. Values given here are for basic model.

| 14500 | 11000 | 8500 | 4000 | 3000 | 700 |

Superposed Express International

An over/under chambered for 20-gauge. Furnished with a set of rifle barrels. Customer's choice of seven calibers. Walnut is a deluxe grade and engraving available at extra cost. Made-to-order gun. Value here for the most basic model. Discontinued in 1985

| — | 2500 | 2000 | 1250 | 750 | 400 |

Boss Royal Model

Best grade over/under chambered for 12-, 20- and 28-gauge. Full sidelock gun made to customer's specifications, using finest materials and workmanship available. Introduced in 1987.

| 18500 | 15000 | 12000 | 8000 | 4500 | 700 |

Eagle Model Combination Gun

Model has a rifle barrel or shotgun barrel that is chambered for 12- or 20-gauge. Rifle calibers available are .22 Hornet, .222 Remington, .222 Remington Magnum, 6mm, .243, .25-06, .30-06, 6.5 x 57R, 7 x 57R, 8 x 57JRS and 9.3 x 74R. Action is boxlock, with automatic ejectors. Other specifications are on custom-order basis. Introduced in 1989.

| 2750 | 2250 | 1500 | 950 | 750 | 400 |

DOUBLE RIFLES

Europa I

Made-to-order over/under double-barreled rifle. Available in same calibers as Eagle Combination gun. Has Anson & Deeley boxlock. All other options to customer's specifications.

| 6000 | 4700 | 3500 | 4000 | 1250 | 500 |

Continental I Model

More deluxe over/under rifle, with true sidelock-action. Calibers the same as Europa. Specifications are to customer's order, with 12 engraving patterns to choose from at extra cost. Introduced in 1989.

| 9000 | 7150 | 5500 | 4000 | 2000 | 600 |

	NIB	EXC.	V.G.	GOOD	FAIR	POOR

Pionnier Express Rifle

Side-by-side double rifle, chambered for .22 Hornet through .600 Nitro Express. Anson & Deeley boxlock-action and quite deluxe throughout. Specifications are to customer's order. There are basically 12 models available (P-1 through P-XII). Differences among these models are in degree of ornamentation and quality of walnut used for the stock. Values range from approximately $10,000 to $15,000 for basic models.

Aristocrat Model

Low-profile single-shot chambered for all calibers up to .375 H&H. Deluxe made-to-order rifle, with exhibition-grade walnut and 12 engraving patterns available.

	NIB	EXC.	V.G.	GOOD	FAIR	POOR
	—	9500	7500	5800	3000	700

BOLT-ACTION RIFLES

Centurion Model

Custom-order rifle built on Mauser or Sako action. Chambered for all calibers from .270 to .458 Winchester Magnum. Barrel lengths available were 21.5", 24" and 25.5"; many engraving options from which to choose. Stock of deluxe French walnut, with rosewood fore-end tip and pistol-grip cap. Discontinued in 1986.

	NIB	EXC.	V.G.	GOOD	FAIR	POOR
	7500	6000	5000	4000	—	—

Centurion Classic

Similar to Mauser-actioned Centurion. Chambered for non-Magnum calibers only. Walnut used for stock is a better grade.

	NIB	EXC.	V.G.	GOOD	FAIR	POOR
	1275	950	750	600	500	400

Diane

More deluxe version of Centurion Classic.

	NIB	EXC.	V.G.	GOOD	FAIR	POOR
	1800	1550	1250	900	650	500

Amazone

A 20" barreled full-length stocked upgraded version of Diane.

	NIB	EXC.	V.G.	GOOD	FAIR	POOR
	2100	1750	1400	950	700	500

Bavaria Deluxe

Similar to Centurion, with same barrel lengths and calibers available. Engraving styles available are more deluxe. Discontinued in 1985.

	NIB	EXC.	V.G.	GOOD	FAIR	POOR
	2350	1800	1400	950	700	500

Safari Model

Similar to Bavaria Deluxe. Chambered for heavy Magnum calibers only.

	NIB	EXC.	V.G.	GOOD	FAIR	POOR
	3275	2700	1900	1450	900	500

Safari Sportsman

Built on a Magnum Mauser action. Chambered for .375 H&H, .404 Jeffreys, .416 Rigby and .505 Gibbs. A true big game rifle. Made available in 1986.

	NIB	EXC.	V.G.	GOOD	FAIR	POOR
	4500	3650	2400	1550	1100	—

African Pro

More deluxe version of Safari Sportsman. Folding leaf rear sight, hooded front sight and ebony or buffalo horn fore-end tip.

	NIB	EXC.	V.G.	GOOD	FAIR	POOR
	5200	3950	2700	1700	1300	750

DUSEK, F.
Opocno, Czech Republic

Dusek commenced business in mid-1920s and continued to make firearms through WWII. They manufactured pistols for Nazi Germany under the contract code "aek". After the war, the communists took over and Dusek's designs were relegated to the CZ factory.

Perla

This 6.35mm pistol has a fixed barrel and open-topped slide. Resembles a Walther design and is striker-fired. Slide is marked "Automat Pistole Perla 6.35mm"; grips, "Perla 6.35". Dusek made this model from early 1930s until WWII.

	NIB	EXC.	V.G.	GOOD	FAIR	POOR
	—	335	225	165	100	80

Duo

DAK-5 Replace with DAK-6-7. **NOTE:** Nazi-marked examples will bring a 25 percent premium.

	NIB	EXC.	V.G.	GOOD	FAIR	POOR
	—	375	250	195	100	80

84 GUN CO.
Eighty Four, Pennsylvania

In business for a brief time in early 1970s. Company produced three basic bolt-action rifles—each in four grades that differ in amounts of embellishment and grades of wood. There is little known about this company and its products. Basic models are listed and values are approximate.

Classic Rifle
Grade 1 - Grade 4 available. $650—$1800

Lobo Rifle
Grade 1 - Grade 4 available. $625—$2700

Pennsylvania Rifle
Grade 1 - Grade 4 available. $625—$2800

E.M.F. CO., INC.
Santa Ana, California
See—Uberti, Aldo

An importer and a distributor of quality Italian-made reproduction firearms. Most of its offerings are listed in the section dealing with Aldo Uberti firearms. E.M.F. also markets a line of 1911 pistols made in the Philippines.

Hartford Bisley
Single-action revolver fitted with Colt Bisley grip. Chambered for .45 Long Colt as well as .32-20, .357 Magnum, .38-40 and .44-40 calibers. Barrel lengths 4.75", 5.5 and 7.5". Plain walnut grips.

NIB	EXC.	V.G.	GOOD	FAIR	POOR
525	425	300	225	145	105

Hartford Express
Single-action Colt SAA frame and barrel, with Colt Lightning-style grip. Chambered for .45 Long Colt in 4.75", 5.5" or 7.5" barrel lengths.

NIB	EXC.	V.G.	GOOD	FAIR	POOR
525	425	300	225	145	105

Hartford Pinkerton
Model features 4" barrel, with ejector and bird's-head grip. Chambered for 45 Long Colt, .32-20, .357 Magnum, .38-40, .44-40 and .44 Special.

NIB	EXC.	V.G.	GOOD	FAIR	POOR
525	425	300	225	145	105

Citadel 1911
Full-size 1911A1-type pistol In .45 ACP, with skeletonized trigger and hammer. Extended ambidextrous thumb safety and slide stop, front and rear slide grooves and flared ejection port. Built by Armscor in the Philippines.

NIB	EXC.	V.G.	GOOD	FAIR	POOR
500	425	350	300	250	200

EAGLE ARMS, DIVISION OF ARMALITE
Geneseo, Illinois

Previous manufacturer of AR-15 type rifles from 1990 to 2005. From 1995 to 2002, a division of ArmaLite, Inc.

PRE-BAN MODELS

Golden Eagle
Model identical in design to AR-15. Fitted with 20" stainless steel extra-heavy barrel. National Match sights and two-stage trigger. Weight about 9.4 lbs.

NIB	EXC.	V.G.	GOOD	FAIR	POOR
1050	950	750	575	400	225

HBAR
Similar to above, with heavy 20" barrel. Weight about 8 lbs.

NIB	EXC.	V.G.	GOOD	FAIR	POOR
1250	950	750	575	400	225

SPR
Similar to above, with exception of detachable carry handle. Weight about 7.6 lbs.

NIB	EXC.	V.G.	GOOD	FAIR	POOR
1250	950	750	575	400	225

	NIB	EXC.	V.G.	GOOD	FAIR	POOR

M4C Carbine

Model features 16" barrel, with 4.33" flash suppressor. Retractable stock. Weight approximately 6.2 lbs.

	1250	950	750	575	400	225

M4A1C Carbine

Similar to above, with detachable carry handle. Weight about 6 lbs.

	1250	950	750	575	400	225

POST-BAN MODELS

Golden Eagle

Reintroduction of earlier model. Limited production in 2002.

	1050	850	750	575	400	225

AR-10 Match Rifle

Chambered for .308 Win., with 20" or 24" chrome-moly barrel. Features include flattop upper receiver, black stock and forearm, 10-round magazine.

	1000	900	750	500	400	200

Model M15 Series

Chambered for .223 or .308 in various AR-15 type configurations. Manufactured from 2002 to 2005. **NOTE:** Add $200 for .308-caliber; $150 for Eagle Spirit model with National Match accessories.

ECHAVE & ARIZMENDI
Eibar, Spain

Basque, Echasa, Dickson, or Dickson Special Agent

These four pistols are the same semi-automatic pistols. Chambered in .22 LR, 6.35mm, 7.65mm and 9mmK respectively. Magazine capacities are 10, 9, 7 and 6 rounds. Manufactured with alloy frames and various finish combinations. Specific model names are stamped on slides and grip plates.

	—	295	185	125	90	50

Bronco Model 1913

Semi-automatic pistol in caliber 6.35mm. Patterned after Browning Model 1906, with squeeze grip safety. "Bronco" stamped on slide and each side of grip plate.

	—	295	185	125	90	50

Bronco Model 1918

Semi-automatic pistol chambered for both 6.35mm or 7.65mm. Both are patterned after Browning Model 1906, with squeeze grip safety. The 7.65mm pistol approximately .5" longer and higher than the 6.35mm. Magazine capacity of 7 rounds. The 6.35mm pistol has a magazine capacity of 6 rounds.

	—	295	185	125	90	50

Echasa

Similar to 6.35mm Bronco, without grip safety. Marked "Model 1916".

	—	295	185	125	90	50

Lightning

Renamed version of Bronco in 6.35mm.

	—	295	185	125	90	50

Lur Panzer

Copy of Luger toggle-lock-action chambered for .22 rimfire. Almost an exact copy, except for different trigger assembly and less robust mainspring. Marked "Lur Cal.22 LR Made in Spain". Plastic grips have "Panzer" molded into them.

	—	265	225	150	125	100

Pathfinder

Semi-automatic pistol similar to above Bronco. In calibers 6.35mm and 7.65mm. Sold in U.S. by Stoeger. The 7.65mm Pathfinder holds 12 rounds. Values listed are for both pistol models.

	—	295	185	125	90	50

Protector Model 1915 and 1918

Semi-automatic pistol in caliber 6.35mm. Similar to Echasa model. "Protector" stamped on slide while grip plates have various logos of firms that marketed the pistol.

	—	275	185	100	70	40

	NIB	EXC.	V.G.	GOOD	FAIR	POOR

Selecta Model 1918

Semi-automatic pistol chambered for 7.65mm cartridge. Patterned after Protector, but chambered for 7.65mm. "Selecta" stamped on slide and Echave Arizmendi logo on each of grip plates.

	—	295	185	125	90	50

ECHEVERRIA, STAR-BONIFACIO SA (STAR)
Eibar, Spain

An old-line Spanish company that survived the Spanish Civil War. Founded in 1908 by Jean Echeverria, but early records of the company were lost during the civil war. Early pistols the company produced were patterned after the Mannlicher designs and trade name Star was the closest thing to Steyr that could be used. After the close of WWI, the company began production of the open-topped slide Star for which they have become known. They also produced a large 1911-type pistol that was successful. During the civil war, the plant was damaged and company records destroyed; but after the cessation of hostilities, they were one of only three gun companies that were allowed to remain in business. Company is now defunct.

Star Model 1908

First pistol produced under Star banner. A Mannlicher copy chambered for 6.35mm. A 3" fixed barrel and open-topped slide. Detachable magazine holds 8 shots. Finish blued and grips are checkered plastic. Slide marked "Automatic Pistol Star Patent".

	—	350	275	200	150	100

Star Model 1914

Similar to Model 1908, with 5" barrel and larger grips that have Star name molded into them. Model was first to have six-pointed star surrounded by rays of light (that became Star trademark) stamped on its slide.

	—	350	275	200	150	100

Star Model 1919

A copy of Mannlicher design. Differs from its predecessors chiefly in the way pistol is disassembled. Model has a spring catch at top of trigger guard, a small spur on hammer and magazine release was relocated to a button behind the trigger guard instead of a catch at bottom of butt. Chambered for 6.35mm, 7.65mm and 9mm short, with various barrel lengths offered. Maker's name, as well as Star trademark stamped into slide. Produced until 1929.

	—	350	275	200	150	100

Star Model 1919 New Variation

Same as above, with full spur hammer.

	—	350	275	200	150	100

Modelo Militar

Represents the first pistol Star produced that was not a Mannlicher design copy. Model copied from Colt 1911. Chambered initially for 9mm Largo in hopes of securing a military contract. When this contract was awarded to Astra, Star chambered Model 1919 for .38 Super, .45 ACP and put it on the commercial market. Model like Colt 1911—has a Browning-type swinging link and same type of lock up. However, there is no grip safety and thumb safety functions differently. **NOTE:** Add 30 percent for guns marked .38 Super.

	—	425	325	245	175	125

Star Model A

Modification of Model 1919. Chambered for 7.65mm, 7.63mm Mauser, 9mm Largo and .45 ACP cartridge. Slide similar in appearance to 1911 Colt. Spur hammer has a small hole in it. Early models had no grip safety, but later production added this feature. Some models slotted for addition of shoulder stock.

	—	425	325	245	175	125

Star Model B

Similar to Model A, except almost an exact copy of Colt 1911. Chambered for 9mm Parabellum and has a spur hammer with no hole. Introduced in 1928.

	—	425	325	245	175	125

Star Model C

Model B chambered for 9mm Browning Long cartridge. Manufactured in 1920s.

	—	350	265	175	125	90

Star Model CO

Pocket pistol similar to early open-topped Star pistols. Chambered for 6.35mm cartridge and finish blued, with checkered plastic grips that bear Star name and logo. Manufactured between 1930 and 1957.

	—	275	195	125	100	75

	NIB	EXC.	V.G.	GOOD	FAIR	POOR

Star Model D

Medium-sized pistol similar in appearance to smaller Model A. Chambered for 9mm Short cartridge and called "Police and Pocket Model" after it was adopted by the Spanish police. Manufactured between 1930 and 1941.

	NIB	EXC.	V.G.	GOOD	FAIR	POOR
	—	500	400	300	200	100

Star Model DK Starfire

Single-action .380, with 3-1/8" barrel, fixed sights, brown plastic grips. Imported from 1957 until 1968. Alloy frame available in blue finish or various colors. **NOTE:** Add $100 for colored frame.

NIB	EXC.	V.G.	GOOD	FAIR	POOR
550	425	400	350	300	150

Star Model E

Pocket pistol chambered for 6.35mm cartridge. A 2.5" barrel and external hammer. Detachable magazine holds 5 rounds. Finish blued, with checkered plastic grips. Manufactured between 1932 and 1941.

	EXC.	V.G.	GOOD	FAIR	POOR
—	250	195	165	110	80

Star Model F

First of .22-caliber Star pistols. Has a 4" barrel, 10-shot magazine and fixed sights. Finish blued and plastic grips checkered. Manufactured between 1942 and 1967.

	EXC.	V.G.	GOOD	FAIR	POOR
—	300	265	200	110	75

Star Model F Target

Similar to Model F, with 6" barrel.

	EXC.	V.G.	GOOD	FAIR	POOR
—	325	275	210	125	100

Star Model F Sport

Has a 5" barrel. Manufactured between 1962 and 1967.

	EXC.	V.G.	GOOD	FAIR	POOR
—	325	275	210	125	100

Star Model F Olympic

Has a 6" barrel and adjustable sights. Furnished with muzzle-brake and barrel weights. Manufactured between 1942 and 1967.

	EXC.	V.G.	GOOD	FAIR	POOR
—	350	265	175	125	90

Star Model F Olympic Rapid Fire

Similar to Olympic. Chambered for .22 Short only.

	EXC.	V.G.	GOOD	FAIR	POOR
—	375	295	185	150	125

Star Model FR

Has an adjustable sight and a slide stop. The 4" barrel is heavier with flattened sides. Manufactured between 1967 and 1972.

	EXC.	V.G.	GOOD	FAIR	POOR
—	325	275	210	125	100

Star Model FRS

Similar to Model FR, with 6" barrel. Also available chrome-plated, with white checkered plastic grips. Introduced in 1967.

	EXC.	V.G.	GOOD	FAIR	POOR
—	295	225	175	125	100

Star Model FM

Heavier-framed version of Model FRS. Has a 4.5" barrel and available in blue or chrome-plated. Introduced in 1972.

	EXC.	V.G.	GOOD	FAIR	POOR
—	325	275	210	125	100

Star Model H

Similar to old Model CO—only larger in size. Chambered for 7.65mm cartridge. Manufactured between 1932 and 1941.

	EXC.	V.G.	GOOD	FAIR	POOR
—	250	195	150	125	100

Star Model HK

Pocket-sized version of Model F. Chambered for .22 Short. Has a 2.5" barrel and quite scarce on today's market.

	EXC.	V.G.	GOOD	FAIR	POOR
—	325	275	210	125	100

Star Model HN

Simply Model H chambered for 9mm Short cartridge. Manufactured and discontinued same time as Model H was.

	EXC.	V.G.	GOOD	FAIR	POOR
—	275	202	165	125	100

	NIB	EXC.	V.G.	GOOD	FAIR	POOR

Star Model I

Improved version of Model H, with 4" barrel and re-contoured grip. Chambered for 7.65mm and produced until 1941. After the war it was resumed and survived until mid-1950s. Replaced by modernized Model IR that would be valued approximately the same.

	NIB	EXC.	V.G.	GOOD	FAIR	POOR
	—	250	195	150	125	100

Star Model M

Similar to Model B. Chambered for .38 Auto (NOT .38 Super) cartridge.

	—	375	295	185	150	125

Star Model P

Post-war version of Model B. Fitted with 5" barrel and chambered for .45 ACP cartridge. Checkered walnut grips and blued finish.

	—	400	350	265	195	125

Star Model CU "Starlet

Similar to Model CO, with an alloy frame that was anodized in black, blue, gray, green or gold. A steel slide that is blued or chrome-plated. Checkered white plastic grips and chambered for .25 ACP cartridge. Has a 2.5" barrel, fixed sights and 5-shot magazine. Introduced in 1975 and not imported after 1986.

	—	250	175	145	100	75

Star Model 1941 S

Add 100 percent to prices listed for pistols issued to Spanish Air Force, with box cleaning rod, instruction sheet and two numbered magazines.

	—	250	210	175	125	75

Star Model BKS "Starlight

Smallest locked-breech automatic chambered for the 9mm cartridge at the time. Has an alloy frame and 4.25" barrel. Similar in appearance to scaled-down Colt 1911, without grip safety. Has an 8-shot magazine. Either blued or chrome-plated, with checkered plastic grips. Manufactured between 1970 and 1981.

	—	325	275	210	125	100

Star Model PD

Chambered for .45 ACP cartridge. Has a 4" barrel, alloy frame, 6-shot magazine, adjustable sights. Blued, with checkered walnut grips. Introduced in 1975.

	400	325	275	225	175	125

Star Model BM

Steel-framed 9mm styled after Colt 1911. Has an 8-shot magazine and 4" barrel. Available either blued or chrome-plated.

	350	300	250	200	150	125

Star Model BKM

Similar to Model BM, with alloy frame.

	375	325	275	225	175	125

Star Model 28

First of Star's Super 9s. Double-action semi-automatic chambered for 9mm Parabellum cartridge. Has a 4.25" barrel and steel frame. Magazine holds 15 shots. Construction of this pistol was totally modular and has no screws in its design. Blued, with checkered synthetic grips. Manufactured in 1983 and 1984.

	425	365	295	200	150	100

Star Model 30M

Improved version of Model 28, that is quite similar in appearance. Introduced in 1985.

	450	350	300	250	200	125

Star Model 30/PK

Similar to Models 28 and 30M, with lightweight alloy frame.

	450	350	300	250	200	125

Megastar

Double-action semi-automatic pistol chambered for 10mm or .45 ACP cartridge. Features a three-position ambidextrous selective decocking lever, rubber grips, combat-style trigger guard,

	NIB	EXC.	V.G.	GOOD	FAIR	POOR

slotted hammer and checkered mainspring housing. Barrel length 4.6"; magazine capacity 12 rounds. Available in blue or Starvel (brushed chrome). Weighs 47.6 oz.

	500	450	350	250	200	100

Firestar M43, M40, and M45

Compact large caliber semi-automatic pistol offered in: M43, 9mm; M40, .40 S M45, .45 ACP. Features an ambidextrous safety, steel frame and slide, checkered rubber grips. Barrel is 3.4" on M43 and M40 and 3.6" on M45. Choice of finish blue or Starvel (brushed chrome). Finger rest magazine optional. Weight for M43 and M40 30 oz.; M45 weighs 35 oz. Introduced in 1990.

	400	300	250	200	150	100

Starfire Model 31P

Model evolved from Models 28 and 30. Chambered for either 9mm Parabellum or .40 S&W. Trigger action is double-/single-action. Barrel length 3.9". Fitted with two-position safety/decocking lever. Magazine capacity for 9mm is 15 rounds; .40 S&W holds 11 rounds. Weighs 39 oz.

	425	350	300	250	200	100

Starfire Model 31PK

Similar to Model 31P. Built on an alloy frame. Chambered for 9mm only, with 15-round magazine capacity. Weight 30 oz.

	400	325	275	225	200	100

Ultrastar

Introduced in 1994. Compact 9mm or .40 S&W semi-automatic pistol. Polymer frame features 3.57" barrel, 9-round magazine, blued finish and overall length of 7". Weighs about 26 oz. Has a double-action operating system, windage adjustable rear sight and ambidextrous two-position safety.

	400	365	305	275	200	100

ECLIPSE
Enterprise Gun Works
Pittsburgh, Pennsylvania

Single-Shot Derringer

Pocket pistol was made by the firm of James Bown & Son, doing business as Enterprise Gun Works. Chambered for .22 or .32-caliber rimfire cartridges. A few in .25 rimfire have been noted and would add approximately 25 percent to values listed. Barrel 2.5" in length and part-round/part-octagonal. Pivots sideways for loading. A spur trigger and bird's-head grip. Barrel stamped "Eclipse". Made of nickel-plated iron, with walnut grips. Approximately 10,000 manufactured between 1870 and 1890.

	—	—	650	250	100	75

EL DORADO ARMS
See—United Sporting Arms, Inc.

ELGIN CUTLASS
(C.B. Allen / Merrill, Mossman and Blair)
Springfield and Amherst, Massachusetts

Manufactured by two companies—C.B. Allen of Springfield, Massachusetts and Morill, Mosman and Blair of Amherst, Massachusetts. A unique pistol that has an integral knife attachment affixed to the gun barrel. Designed and patented by George Elgin and simultaneously produced by the two companies. Inspiration for this weapon was supposedly Jim Bowie, who at that time had made a name as a knife fighter with his large "Bowie" knife. Blades for these pistols were supplied by N.P. Ames of the famed Ames Sword Co. These pistols are much sought after and one must exercise caution as fraudulent examples have been noted.

C. B. ALLEN-MADE PISTOLS

U.S. Navy Elgin Cutlass Pistol

Chambered for .54-caliber percussion and has a 5" octagonal smooth-bore barrel. Bowie-style blade is 11" long by 2" wide. Forged together with the trigger guard and knuckle guard that protects the grip. Handle is walnut. Pistol was issued to U.S. Navy's Wilkes-South Sea Exploration Expedition and markings are "C.B. Allen / Springfield / Mass." "Elgin's Patent" and letters "CB", "CBA" along with date 1837. If the sheath that was issued with this knife pistol is included and in sound condition, it would add approximately $700 to value. There were 150 manufactured for U.S. Navy in 1838.

	—	—	35500	14000	7500	4750

	NIB	EXC.	V.G.	GOOD	FAIR	POOR

Civilian Model

Chambered for .35- or .41-caliber percussion. Has a 4" octagonal barrel, with 7.5"-10" knife blade, round trigger guard, but does not have knuckle bow across the grip, as found on military model. Marked "C.B. Allen Springfield, Mass." Blades marked "N.P. Ames" have been noted. Approximately 100 manufactured in 1837.

—	—	33500	13000	6250	3250	

MORILL, MOSMAN AND BLAIR-MADE PISTOLS

Small Model

Main difference in the pistols of the two makers is; this model has a round barrel and square-back trigger guard, that comes to a point at the rear. This version chambered for .32-caliber percussion and has 2.75" barrel. Knife blade is 7.5" in length and screwed to frame. Model is unmarked except for a serial number. Number produced is unknown. Manufactured in 1837.

—	—	33500	13000	6250	3250	

Large Model

Chambered for .36-caliber percussion and has a 4" round barrel and 9" knife blade. Pistol usually marked "Cast Steel" and serial numbered. Blade etched with an American eagle, stars and urn with flowers. "Elgin Patent" etched in center. Manufactured in 1837.

—	—	37000	14500	7000	3900	

ELLS, JOSIAH
Pittsburgh, Pennsylvania

POCKET REVOLVER

Three distinct variations of this percussion revolver. Chambered for .28- and .31-caliber and have 6-shot unfluted cylinders. They have been noted with 2.5", 3" and 3.75" octagonal barrels.

Model 1

First model has an open-topped frame and chambered for .28 caliber. Cylinder holds 5- or 6-shots and hammer is of the bar type. Offered with 2.5" or 3" barrel. Markings are "J. Ells; Patent; 1854". Approximately 625 manufactured between 1857 and 1859.

—	—	1700	875	375	200	

Model 2

Second model similar to first, with solid-topped frame. They have 5-shot cylinders and 3.75" long barrels. Approximately 550 manufactured.

—	—	1750	750	365	200	

Model 3

Third model radically different from its forerunners. Closed-top frame and conventional spur-type hammer that strikes from right side. Functions either as a double-/single-action. Chambered for .28-caliber, 5-shot cylinder and 3.75" barrel. About 200 manufactured between 1857 and 1859.

—	—	1850	995	425	200	

ENDERS, CARL
Suhl, Germany

Side-by-Side Shotgun

Percussion damascus double-barrel side-by-side in 12-gauge. Ornate checkering, with cheekpiece and engraved metal work. This firm made high-quality firearms, mostly side-by-side guns. Gun pictured was made circa 1850-1860. Firm in business about 1835 to approximately 1890.

—		1250	550	300	150	

ENFIELD AMERICAN, INC.
Atlanta, Georgia

MP-45

Blowback-operated semi-automatic assault pistol, chambered for .45 ACP cartridge. Offered with barrel lengths 4.5" through 18.5". Long barrel features a shroud. Finish is Parkerized. Four different magazines available in 10, 20, 30 and 50 round capacities. Manufactured in 1985 only.

—	575	475	295	175	125	

NIB	EXC.	V.G.	GOOD	FAIR	POOR

ENTREPRISE ARMS, INC.
Irwindale, California

ELITE SERIES

Basic model with stainless steel barrels, fixed sights, squared trigger guard, adjustable match trigger, checkered slide release, high ride grip safety, flat mainspring housing and a number of other special features. Magazine capacity 10 rounds.

Elite P500

Chambered for .45 ACP. Fitted with 5" barrel. Weight about 40 oz.

600	500	400	350	200	100

Elite P425

Model has 4.25" barrel. Weight approximately 38 oz.

600	500	400	350	200	100

Elite P325

Model has 3.25" barrel. Weight of 36 oz.

600	500	400	350	200	100

TACTICAL SERIES

Model has ambidextrous thumb lock, lightweight match hammer and matching sear. National match barrel with match extractor, full length one-piece guide rod, Novak sights, dovetail front sight, matte black finish and host of other features. Magazine capacity 10 rounds.

Tactical P500

Model chambered for .45 ACP cartridge and 5" barrel. Weight approximately 40 oz.

900	795	600	495	350	100

Tactical P425

Model fitted with 4.25" barrel. Weighs about 38 oz.

900	795	600	495	350	100

Tactical P325

Model fitted with 3.25" barrel. Weight of 36 oz.

900	795	600	495	350	100

Tactical P325 Plus

Model features 3.25" barrel and fitted to full size Government model frame. Weight about 37 oz.

950	800	615	500	365	105

TITLEIST NATIONAL MATCH SERIES

Model chambered for either .45 ACP or .40 S&W cartridge. Has all features of Elite Series. Adjustable rear sight and dovetail Patridge front sight. Many other special features.

Titleist P500

Model fitted with 5" barrel. Weight about 40 oz. **NOTE:** Add $20 for .40 S&W chambering.

900	795	600	495	350	100

Boxer Model

Chambered for .45 ACP cartridge and fitted with 5" barrel. Features a ramped bull barrel, wide ambi safety and high-mass chiseled slide. Weight approximately 44 oz.

1200	975	750	600	375	125

TOURNAMENT SERIES

These are top-of-the-line models that have all the features of Elite Series, plus over-sized magazine release button, checkered front strap and flared extended magazine well.

TSM I

Limited class competition pistol. All models are hand crafted. Fitted with 5" barrel and choice of calibers. Weight about 40 oz.

1900	1750	1375	900	675	300

TSM II

Long slide model, with cocking serrations on front and rear of slide. Barrel is 6". Weight about 44 oz.

2300	1750	1375	900	675	300

	NIB	EXC.	V.G.	GOOD	FAIR	POOR

TSM III

Open class pistol designed for scope mount. Barrel is 5.5" long. Fitted with 7-port compensator. Many other custom features. Weight about 44 oz.

	2500	2000	1525	1050	700	310

ERA
Brazil

ERA Side-by-Side Shotgun

Inexpensive shotgun chambered for 12-, 20-gauge and .410 bore. Offered with 26", 28" or 30" barrels and various choke combinations. Double triggers and extractors, with checkered hardwood pistol-grip stock. Gun also available as: Quail model, with 20" barrel; Riot model with 18" barrel. These two models not offered in .410 bore.

—	200	150	125	100	75

ERA Over/Under Shotgun

Chambered for 12- or 20-gauge, with 28" ventilated rib barrels that were choked full and modified. Boxlock with double triggers, extractors and hardwood stock. Also offered in trap and skeet model, chambered for 12-gauge only and appropriately choked. **NOTE:** Latter two models would be worth 10 percent premium over values listed.

—	325	275	250	200	150

ERICHSON, G.
Houston, Texas

Pocket Pistol

Close copy of Philadelphia-style Henry Deringer. Chambered for .45-caliber percussion and has 3.25" barrel. Mountings are German silver and not engraved; stock is walnut. Hammer is deeply fluted and fore-end carved. Barrel marked "G. Erichson / Houston, Texas". Number produced unknown, but examples are scarce. Manufactured in the 1850s and 1860s.

—	—	6500	3000	1000	400

ERMA WERKE WAFFENFABRIK
Erfurt, Germany
Post-war Dachau, Germany

Known primarily as a manufacturer of sub-machine guns, they are also in the handgun and rifle business. In 1933 they answered the German army's need for an inexpensive practice weapon by producing a .22 rimfire conversion unit for the Luger pistol. This was marketed commercially and available for many years. Success of this unit led the company to produce other inexpensive target and plinking pistols. After the war, they were reorganized in the western sector and resumed sub-machine gun production. In 1964 they returned to the sporting firearms business, with the introduction of their .22 rimfire Luger-lookalike pistol. Since then, they have produced many like-quality firearms. They were imported by Excam of Hialeah, Florida. This association is now terminated and they are currently imported by Beeman Precision in Santa Rosa, California and Mandell Shooting Supplies in Scottsdale, Arizona.

PISTOLS

Erma .22 Luger Conversion Unit

Produced for the German army in 1933 and then became a successful commercial item. It would turn a standard 9mm or 7.65mm Luger into an inexpensive-to-shoot .22 rimfire. Unit consists of barrel insert, breech block and toggle unit, with its own lightened recoil spring and .22 magazine. Unit was furnished with a wooden box. There were many different sized units to fit various caliber and barrel-length Lugers, but all used the same parts and concept. These units have become desirable to Luger collectors.

—	500	425	350	275	200

.22 Target Pistol (Old Model)

Semi-automatic target pistol in caliber .22 LR. Offered with 4", 6" or 8" barrels. Frame made from cast zinc alloy and there is an external hammer. Adjustable sights and balance weights were available. Magazine capacity 10 rounds. Weight about 35 oz. Manufactured in 1936 and 1937.

—	800	725	500	350	100

.22 Target Pistol (New Model) Master Model

Improved version of old model. Features new grip angle and magazine and takedown device like that of the Luger. There were interchangeable barrels and three basic models — "Sport", "Hunter" and "Master". Difference was length of barrels — 4", 8" and 12" respectively. Magazine

	NIB	EXC.	V.G.	GOOD	FAIR	POOR

capacity 10 rounds. Weight about 39 oz. Manufactured between 1937 and 1940. Discontinued due to Erma's involvement in the war effort.

	—	850	700	500	400	125

KGP SERIES

Made to resemble the Luger quite closely. They utilized mechanical features of the .22 conversion unit and developed a pistol around it. Many different versions of this pistol chambered for .22 rimfire, .32 ACP and .380 ACP. Original designation was KGP-68; but the Gun Control Act of 1968 required that a magazine safety be added and model was re-designated KGP-68A. Last designations for the three calibers are KGP-22, KGP-32 and KGP-38. Manufactured between 1964 - 1986 and their values listed.

KGP-68

A 4" barrel and chambered for .32 ACP and .380 ACP cartridges. Has a 6-shot magazine and anodized alloy receiver. Weight about 23 oz. Model also known as Beeman MP-08.

	—	450	400	300	200	100

KGP-69

A .22 rimfire version of this series, with 8-shot magazine capacity. Weight about 30 oz. Also known as Beeman P-08.

	—	300	200	150	100	75

KGP-22

Later version of KGP-69 chambered for .22 rimfire.

	—	350	300	250	200	125

KGP-32 & KGP-38

Two designations are later versions of KGP-68 and 68A.

	—	350	300	250	200	125

ET-22 "Navy Luger" Long-Barreled Pistol

A rare firearm. According to some estimates only 375 were produced. Features a 11.75" barrel and chambered for .22 rimfire cartridge. Artillery Luger-type rear sight and checkered walnut grips, with a smooth walnut fore-end. Pistol furnished with a red-felt-lined black leatherette case.

	—	900	675	400	250	150

ESP 85A

High-quality target pistol imported by Mandall Shooting Supply. Features an interchangeable barrel system that converts chambering from .22 rimfire to .32 S&W long wad cutter. Barrels are both 6" in length. Adjustable and interchangeable sights and 5- or 8-shot detachable magazine. Weight about 41 oz. Finish blued and grips are stippled target types. Gun furnished in padded hard case, with two extra magazines and takedown tools. Introduced in 1989.

1100	1000	850	700	550	450

EP-25

Semi-automatic pistol in caliber 6.35mm. Fitted with 2.75" barrel. Weight about 18 oz. Mostly marketed outside of Germany. Polished blue finish and wood grips. Erma stamped on slide and on each grip plate.

	—	275	195	150	100	75

RX-22 and PX-22

Semi-automatic .22 rimfire copy of Walther PPK. Has a 7-round magazine. Assembled in U.S., with parts from Germany by various companies that marketed the pistol in U.S. Black plastic wraparound grips, with Erma logo on each side.

	—	240	175	150	100	75

REVOLVERS

ER-772 Match

Target revolver chambered for .22 rimfire. Has 6" shrouded barrel with solid rib. Swing-out cylinder holds 6-shots and sights are adjustable. Finish blued, with stippled target grips. Introduced in 1989.

1000	800	600	350	250	200

ER-773 Match

Similar to ER-772, except chambered for .32 S&W long cartridge.

900	750	500	375	250	200

NIB	EXC.	V.G.	GOOD	FAIR	POOR

ER-777

Basically similar revolver to ER-773, except it has 4.5" or 5" barrel and chambered for .357 Magnum cartridge. Revolver is larger and has standard sport grips. Introduced in 1989.

NIB	EXC.	V.G.	GOOD	FAIR	POOR
800	600	450	350	250	200

RIFLES

EM1.22

Semi-automatic .22 rimfire version of M1 Carbine. Has an 18" barrel and 15-round magazine. Manufactured between 1966 and 1976.

—	350	225	150	125	100

EG-72, EG-722

A 15-shot slide-action carbine chambered for .22 rimfire. A 18.5" barrel and open sights. Finish is blued. Manufactured between 1970 and 1985.

—	250	165	100	75	50

EG-712, EG-73

Lever copy of Winchester 94 Carbine. Chambered for .22 rimfire or .22 rimfire Magnum (EG-73). Has an 18.5" barrel and holds 15-shots in a tubular magazine. Manufactured between 1973 and 1985.

—	250	175	150	125	100

SR-100

Long-range precision bolt-action rifle, chambered for .308 Win., .300 Win. Magnum or .338 Lapua calibers. Barrel length on .308 Win. is 25.25", other calibers 29.25". All barrels fitted with muzzle-brake. Trigger is adjustable. Stock laminated, with thumbhole and adjustable recoil pad and cheekpiece. Weight about 15 lbs.

8800	7000	5000	2750	1300	600

ERQUIAGA
Eibar, Spain

Another Spanish company that commenced business during WWI, as a subcontractor on the French "Ruby" contract. They manufactured the usual poor quality, 7.65mm Eibar-type pistol.

Fiel

Trade name found on Ruby subcontract pistol described above. Marked "Erquiaga y Cia Eibar Cal. 7.65 Fiel".

—	200	150	125	100	75

Fiel 6.35

After the end of WWI, a 1906 Browning copy was made. Chambered for 6.35mm cartridge. Markings are "Automatic Pistol 6.35 Fiel No. 1". Later models had "EMC" molded into grip.

—	195	135	100	75	50

Marte

Another poor-quality "Eibar" -type pistol. Chambered for 6.35mm. Made in early 1920s.

—	195	135	100	75	50

ERRASTI, A.
Eibar, Spain

Errasti manufactured a variety of inexpensive yet serviceable pistols, from early 1900s until the Spanish Civil War.

Velo Dog

Usual cheap solid-frame folding-trigger revolvers one associates with model designation. Chambered in 5.5mm and 6.35mm. Made in early 1900s.

—	195	135	100	75	50

M1889

In 1915-1916 Errasti produced the 10.4mm Italian army service revolver. Quality was reasonably good. Marked "Errasti Eiber" on the right side of frame.

—	400	295	200	125	75

Errasti

Two "Eibar"-type Browning copies were made under this trade name. One chambered for 6.35mm the other 7.65mm. Both marked "Automatic Pistol Errasti".

—	195	135	110	75	50

	NIB	EXC.	V.G.	GOOD	FAIR	POOR

Errasti Oscillante

Manufactured in the 1920s, these revolvers were copied from Smith & Wesson Military & Police design. Chambered for .32-, .38- and .44-calibers, with .38 being most frequently encountered. **NOTE:** Add 30 percent for .44-caliber.

—	250	195	125	95	50

Dreadnaught, Goliath and Smith Americano

These three trade names found on a group of poor quality nickel-plated revolvers. Made from 1905 through 1920. Obvious copies of Iver Johnson design. They had break-open actions, ribbed barrel and chambered for .32-, .38- and .44-calibers. They are scarce today, as most have long since fallen apart. **NOTE:** Add 30 percent for .44-caliber.

—	225	175	100	75	50

ESCODIN, M.
Eibar, Spain

This company made a Smith & Wesson revolver copy from 1924 through 1931. Chambered for .32 and .38 Special. Only marking is a coat of arms stamped on left side of frame.

—	175	125	100	75	50

ESCORT
Turkey

SEMI-AUTOMATIC SHOTGUNS

Model AS

This 12-gauge 3" model is fitted with 28" vent rib barrel and choke tubes. Walnut stock. Black finish. Magazine capacity 4 rounds. Weight about 7 lbs.

450	365	245	200	150	100

Model PS

This 12-gauge 3" model similar to above, with black polymer stock and finish. Also offered in Shadow Grass camo or Mossy Oak Break-Up camo. Choice of Spark or TriViz front sights. Barrel length 28" except for TriViz variation with 24" barrel. Weight about 7 lbs. **NOTE:** Add $100 for camo coverage; add $45 for TriViz model.

500	400	300	200	150	100

Model PS AimGuard

This 12-gauge 3" model is fitted with 20" fixed choke barrel in Cylinder bore. Black polymer stock and finish. Magazine capacity 5 rounds. Weight about 6.4 lbs.

400	295	200	125	100	75

Combo Model

This 12-gauge 3" model is offered with two sets of barrels: one 28" with Full choke tube; the other 24" with Turkey choke tube. Polymer stock with Mossy Oak Break-Up. Receiver is fitted with a dovetail mount. Weight about 7 lbs.

575	425	365	295	200	100

Escort Semi-Auto Slug Gun

Slug gun available in 12- or 20-gauge. Rifled barrel 22" long with 1:26 twist. Self-regulating gas piston. Has Hi-Viz sights and equipped with a cantilevered scope base. Black synthetic stock. Overall length, 42". Weight: 6.3 lbs. (20-gauge), 7 lbs. (12-gauge).

530	475	375	300	250	200

Escort Extreme Series

Available for either 12-gauge 3" or 3.5" Magnum, with 28" barrel, Hi-Viz sights and choke tubes. Several camo patterns for turkey or waterfowl hunting. Extreme Waterfowl Youth model available in 20-gauge with 22" barrel.

Extreme 3.5

800	675	500	400	300	200

Extreme 3

700	600	450	400	300	150

Extreme Waterfowl Youth

600	525	400	350	300	150

NIB	EXC.	V.G.	GOOD	FAIR	POOR

PUMP-ACTION SHOTGUNS

Field Hunter

This 12-gauge 3" model fitted with 28" vent rib barrel and choke tubes. Offered with black polymer stock of Mossy Oak Break-Up or Shadow Grass camo pattern. A 24" barrel with TriViz also offered. Magazine capacity 4 rounds. Weight about 7 lbs. **NOTE:** Add $50 for camo finish; $100 for TriViz sights.

325	225	165	135	100	75

AimGuard

This 12-gauge 3" model fitted with 20" barrel and fixed Cylinder bore choke. Black polymer stock. Magazine capacity 5 rounds. Weight about 6.4 lbs. **NOTE:** Add 10 percent for 18" barrel and nickel finish.

325	225	165	135	100	75

Escort Pump Slug Gun

Same specifications as semi-automatic except slide-action. Weight: 6 lbs. (20-gauge), 6.7 lbs. (12-gauge).

430	385	290	250	200	150

ESPIRIN, HERMANOS
Eibar, Spain

Euskaro

Poor-quality often unsafe revolver. Manufactured from 1906 until WWI. They are copies of Iver Johnson design break-open actions. Chambered for .32-, .38- and .44-calibers. Product epitomizes the worst Eibar had to offer during pre-Civil War era. **NOTE:** Add 30 percent for .44-caliber.

—	200	125	75	50	25

EUROARMS OF AMERICA
Winchester, Virginia

An importer of blackpowder muzzle-loading firearms, primarily replicas of early American weapons.

REVOLVERS

1851 Navy

Replica of Colt revolver chambered for .36- or .44-caliber percussion. Has a squareback silver-plated trigger guard and 7.5" barrel.

275	225	170	110	75	45

1851 Navy Police Model

Chambered for .36-caliber, with 5-shot fluted cylinder and 5.5" barrel.

275	225	170	110	75	45

1851 Navy Sheriff's Model

A 5" barreled version of Navy Model.

275	225	170	110	75	45

1851 "Schneider & Glassick" Navy

Replica of Confederate revolver chambered for .36- or .44-caliber percussion.

150	100	80	60	50	35

1851 "Griswold & Gunnison" Navy

Replica of Confederate revolver chambered for .36- or .44-caliber percussion.

285	235	170	110	75	45

1862 Police

Replica of Colt Model 1862 chambered for .36-caliber percussion, with 7.5" barrel and steel frame.

275	225	170	110	75	45

1860 Army

Replica of Colt revolver chambered for .44-caliber percussion. Offered with 5" or 8" barrel.

275	225	170	110	75	45

	NIB	EXC.	V.G.	GOOD	FAIR	POOR

1861 Navy
Replica of Colt revolver chambered for .36-caliber percussion.

	275	225	170	110	75	45

1858 Remington Army or Navy
Replicas of Remington percussion revolvers chambered for .36- or .44-caliber.

	275	225	170	110	75	45

RIFLES

Rifles listed are modern replicas of early American and British firearms. They are good quality and quite serviceable.

Cook & Brother Carbine

	595	500	375	250	195	100

1863 J.P. Murray

	595	500	375	250	195	100

1853 Enfield Rifled Musket

	610	525	375	250	195	100

1858 Enfield Rifled Musket

	610	525	375	250	195	100

1861 Enfield Musketoon

	500	375	250	195	100	65

1803 Harper's Ferry

	595	500	375	250	195	100

1841 Mississippi Rifle

	595	500	375	250	195	100

Pennsylvania Rifle

	400	350	275	225	150	100

Hawken Rifle

	400	350	275	225	150	100

Cape Gun

	450	395	325	275	200	150

Buffalo Carbine

	450	395	325	275	200	150

1862 Remington Rifle

	450	395	325	275	200	150

Zouave Rifle

	450	395	325	275	200	150

SHOTGUNS

Duck Gun
Single-barreled percussion fowling piece chambered for 8-, 10- or 12-gauge. Has a 33" smoothbore barrel and case-colored hammer and lock. Stock is walnut with brass mountings. Introduced in 1989. **NOTE:** Add 20 percent for 8-gauge.

	450	395	325	275	200	150

Standard Side-by-Side
Side-by-side chambered for 12-gauge percussion. Has 28" barrels, with engraved locks and walnut stock.

	475	400	350	295	200	125

NIB	EXC.	V.G.	GOOD	FAIR	POOR

EUROPEAN AMERICAN ARMORY CORP./U.S. SPORTING GOODS, INC.
Rockledge, Florida

EAA WITNESS PISTOLS

EAA Witness P-Series Full Size

Introduced in 1998, this is a full size polymer frame pistol. Chambered for 9mm, .40 S&W, .45 ACP, .38 Super and 10mm cartridges. Barrel length 4.55". Overall length 8.5" with an empty weight of 31 oz. Rear sight adjustable for windage. Magazine capacity: 9mm is 28 rounds; .40 S&W is 15 rounds; .45 ACP is 10 rounds; 10mm is 15 rounds. **NOTE:** Add $30 for ported barrel.

525	425	325	225	180	100

EAA Witness P-Series Carry-Comp

Model is fitted with 4.25" ported barrel. Chambered for .45 ACP.

470	375	275	200	150	100

EAA Witness P-Series Compact

Similar to above, with barrel length of 3.55". Weight about 26 oz. **NOTE:** Add $30 for ported barrel.

450	350	250	200	150	100

EAA Witness P-S Series

Built on a different frame size from P-Series pistols. Chambered for .22 LR, 9mm or .40 S&W cartridges. Barrel length 4.55". Weight about 31 oz.

400	325	275	200	150	100

EAA Witness Carry Comp

Model offered in 9mm, .41 AE, .40 S&W and .45 ACP. Features a 1" steel compensator. Barrel is 4.1" long. Overall length the same as standard model as is magazine capacity. Offered in blue or blue chrome finish. Weighs 34 oz. **NOTE:** For .45 ACP add 15 percent.

Old Configuration

425	350	300	250	200	175

New Configuration

500	450	375	325	250	175

EAA Witness Standard

Available in 9mm, .41 AE, .40 S&W and .45 ACP, with 4.5" barrel. Magazine capacity: 9mm-16 rounds; .41 AE-11 rounds; .40 S&W-12 rounds; .45 ACP-10 rounds. Offered in blue, chrome, two-tone and stainless steel. Weighs approximately 33 oz. **NOTE:** For chrome, two-tone and stainless steel add 5 percent.

Old Configuration

385	325	275	225	175	125

New Configuration

500	375	295	225	175	125

EAA Witness Subcompact

Offered in same calibers as standard model, but fitted with 3.66" barrel and shorter grip. Magazine capacity: 9mm-13 rounds; .41 AE-9 rounds; .40 S&W-9 rounds; .45 ACP-8 rounds. Weighs about 30 oz. Offered in blue, chrome, two-tone and stainless steel. **NOTE:** For chrome, two-tone and stainless steel add 5 percent.

Old Configuration

425	350	295	235	175	125

New Configuration

460	350	275	225	175	125

EAA Witness Sport L/S

Model features longer slide for its 4.75" barrel. Offered in 9mm, .41 AE, .40 S&W and .45 ACP. Magazine capacity: 9mm-19 rounds; .41 AE-13 rounds; .40 S&W-14 rounds; .45 ACP-11 rounds. Also fitted with adjustable rear sight and extended safety. Available in two-tone finish. Weighs about 34.5 oz. A ported barrel offered as an option. **NOTE:** For .45 ACP add 10 percent to prices.

Old Configuration

625	550	500	400	300	200

New Configuration

625	550	500	400	300	200

NIB	EXC.	V.G.	GOOD	FAIR	POOR

EAA Witness Combo 9/40

Model offers a 9mm conversion kit and .40 S&W conversion kit. Kits consist of a slide, barrel, recoil spring, guide and magazine. Available in standard or subcompact size in blue, chrome, or two-tone finish. **NOTE:** For chrome or two-tone finish add 5 percent.

595	495	425	350	275	175

EAA Witness Silver Team Match

Designed as a competition pistol. Fitted with 5.25" barrel. Features: dual chamber compensator, single-action trigger, extended safety, competition hammer, paddle magazine release, checkered walnut grips and adjustable rear sight or drilled and tapped for scope mount. Offered in: 9mm-19 rounds; .40 S&W-14 rounds; .41 AE-13 rounds; .45 ACP-11 rounds; and 9 x 21. Finish is blue and weight approximately 34 oz.

900	800	700	600	450	300

EAA Witness Sport

Model built on standard Witness frame. Addition of an adjustable rear sight and extended safety. Offered in 9mm, .41 AE, .40 S&W, .45 ACP in standard model magazine capacity. Weighs 33 oz. Available in two-tone finish. **NOTE:** For .45 ACP add 10 percent.

Old Configuration

550	475	400	300	200	150

New Configuration

550	475	400	300	200	150

EAA Witness Hunter

Model features camo finish with 6" barrel. Chambered for .45 ACP or 10mm cartridge. Drilled and tapped for scope mount and adjustable sights. Magazine capacity 10 rounds. Weight about 41 oz. Also available with blued finish.

975	800	575	395	250	150

EAA Witness Gold Team Match

This is a full race competition pistol. Features triple chamber compensator, beaver tail grip safety, beveled magazine well, adjustable rear sight or drilled and tapped for scope mount, extended safety and magazine release, competition hammer, square trigger guard, checkered front and backstrap, competition grips and hard chrome finish. Same barrel length, magazine capacity and calibers as Silver Team Match. Weighs 38 oz.

1700	1250	900	750	600	400

EAA Witness Limited Class Pistol

Model built on Witness Match frame. Features competition grips, high-capacity magazine, extended safety and magazine release, single-action trigger, long slide with adjustable rear sight and match grade barrel. Offered in 9mm, .40 S&W, .38 Super and .45 ACP, with blue finish.

1200	975	725	550	400	300

EAA Witness Stock

Introduced in 2005, this pistol features a 4.5" tapered cone barrel chambered for 9mm, .40S&W, .45ACP or .10mm cartridge. Hard chrome finish, extended safety, wood checkered grips and fully adjustable sights. Weight about 33 oz.

825	695	595	400	200	100

EAA Witness Multi Class Pistol Package

This package consists of one Witness Limited Class pistol, with a complete unlimited class top half. Top half is made up of standard length slide with super sight, recoil guide and spring, match grade competition barrel (threaded for compensator) and a dual chamber compensator. Available in 9mm, .40 S&W, 9 x 21, .45 ACP, 9 x 23 and .38 Super. Finish is blue.

1700	1350	850	600	300	200

EAA Witness Elite Match

Single-action semi-automatic featuring 4.5" polygonal rifled steel barrel, adjustable rear sights, rubber grips. Two-tone finish. Chambered for 9 mm (18+1), 10 mm (15+1), 38 Super (15+1), .40 S&W (15+1) and .45 ACP (10+1). Weight 33 oz. Introduced 2006.

725	600	450	300	200	100

EAA Witness 1911

Made by Tanfoglio in Italy. This is a standard size 1911 in .45 ACP. Made in two variations, one with a steel frame (shown) and the other is polymer. Operating controls are standard 1911, with added features like an accessory rail, flat mainspring housing, skeleton hammer and trigger, extended grip

NIB	EXC.	V.G.	GOOD	FAIR	POOR

safety and ambidextrous manual safety. Introduced in 2014. Values shown are for polymer model. **NOTE:** Add $250 for steel frame.

NIB	EXC.	V.G.	GOOD	FAIR	POOR
525	435	350	275	200	150

Zastava EZ Pistol

CZ75 clone. Single-/double-action pistol, with 4" (Full Size) or 3.5" (Compact) barrel and polymer frame. Chambered in 9mm, .40 S&W or .45 ACP. Magazine capacity varies from 7 rounds (.45 ACP) to 15 (9mm).

NIB	EXC.	V.G.	GOOD	FAIR	POOR
375	300	265	225	165	100

Thor

Single-shot pistol chambered for .223 Rem., .270 Win., .30-06, .300 Win., .308, .375 Win., .44 Magnum, .45-70, .50 S&W, .7mm-08 or .7mm Rem. Magnum. Fitted with 14" barrel. Receiver has an integral top rail for scope mount. Weight about 5 lbs.

NIB	EXC.	V.G.	GOOD	FAIR	POOR
1150	850	675	500	355	145

OTHER EAA IMPORTED FIREARMS

BUL 1911 SERIES

BUL Government

Chambered for .45 ACP cartridge and fitted with 4.8" barrel. Polymer frame. Tactical rear sight, with dovetail front sight. Fully checkered grip. Black or stainless steel slide. Weight about 24 oz. Magazine capacity 10 rounds. Introduced in 2002. **NOTE:** Add $50 for stainless steel slide.

NIB	EXC.	V.G.	GOOD	FAIR	POOR
550	450	300	200	125	75

Commander

Same as above. Fitted with 3.8" barrel.

NIB	EXC.	V.G.	GOOD	FAIR	POOR
550	450	300	200	125	75

Stinger

This model has a 3" barrel.

NIB	EXC.	V.G.	GOOD	FAIR	POOR
550	450	300	200	125	75

EAA Big Bore Bounty Hunter

Model is a single-action revolver made in Germany. Features three-position hammer, forged barrel and walnut grips. Offered in .357 Magnum, .45 Long Colt and .44 Magnum. Barrel lengths 4.5", 5.5" or 7.5". Choice of finish includes blue or case-colored frame, chrome, gold or blue and gold. **NOTE:** For chrome, gold or blue and gold finish add 20 percent.

NIB	EXC.	V.G.	GOOD	FAIR	POOR
400	300	225	175	150	125

EAA Small Bore Bounty Hunter

Single-action .22-caliber revolver. Wood grips and available in blue or blue and brass finish. Barrel lengths 4.75", 6" and 9". Chambered for .22 LR or .22 Winchester Rimfire Magnum.

NIB	EXC.	V.G.	GOOD	FAIR	POOR
275	200	145	125	75	60

EAA Bounty Hunter Shotgun—External Hammers

Side-by-side shotgun with external hammers. Chambered for 10-, 12-, 16-, 20-, 28-gauge and .410 bore. Offered in barrel lengths of 20", 24" and 26".

NIB	EXC.	V.G.	GOOD	FAIR	POOR
375	300	250	175	150	125

EAA Bounty Hunter Shotgun—Traditional

Same as above, with internal hammers. Offered in 12- or 20-gauge.

NIB	EXC.	V.G.	GOOD	FAIR	POOR
300	250	200	150	100	75

EAA F.A.B. 92 Pistol

Model is a semi-automatic pistol similar to Witness. Fitted with hammer drop safety and slide mounted safety, that is both a double-/single-action. Available in either full size (33 oz.) or compact size (30 oz.). Full size version has 4.5" barrel while compact is fitted with 3.66" barrel. Offered in 9mm or .40 S&W in blue, two-tone or chrome finish.

NIB	EXC.	V.G.	GOOD	FAIR	POOR
395	300	225	175	125	100

EAA European Standard Pistol

Single-action semi-automatic pistol, with external hammer, slide grip serrations, wood grips and single column magazine. Barrel length 3.2" and overall length 6.5". Chambered for .22 LR, 380 ACP and .32 ACP. Magazine capacity 10 rounds for .22 LR, 7 rounds for .380 and .32. Offered in blue, blue/chrome, chrome, blue/gold. Weighs 26 oz.

NIB	EXC.	V.G.	GOOD	FAIR	POOR
195	155	110	95	75	50

NIB	EXC.	V.G.	GOOD	FAIR	POOR

EAA European Target Pistol

Model features adjustable rear sight, external hammer, single-action trigger, walnut target grips and adjustable weight system. Chambered for .22 LR. Offered in blue finish and weighs 40 oz.

NIB	EXC.	V.G.	GOOD	FAIR	POOR
355	295	225	175	150	100

EAA Windicator Standard Grade

German-built model is a double-action revolver chambered for .22 LR, .22 Winchester Rimfire Magnum, .32 H&R and .38 Special. Offered in 2", 4" and 6" barrel lengths. Cylinder capacity for .22 LR/.22 WRM is 8 rounds, .32 H&R is 7 rounds and .38 Special is 6 rounds. Cylinder is unfluted. Finish is blue.

NIB	EXC.	V.G.	GOOD	FAIR	POOR
275	165	135	110	75	60

EAA Windicator Basic Grade

Model chambered for .38 Special or .357 Magnum, with 2" barrel. Fluted cylinder holds 6 rounds. Finish is blue.

NIB	EXC.	V.G.	GOOD	FAIR	POOR
275	165	135	110	75	60

EAA Windicator Tactical Grade

Model similar in appearance to standard grade. Chambered for .38 Special, with 2" or 4" barrel. The 4" barrel has an integral compensator. Finish is blue.

2" Barrel

NIB	EXC.	V.G.	GOOD	FAIR	POOR
190	150	125	100	80	60

4" Barrel

NIB	EXC.	V.G.	GOOD	FAIR	POOR
250	200	150	125	100	75

EAA Windicator Target Grade

Model has these special features: adjustable trigger pull, walnut grips, adjustable rear sight, drilled and tapped for scope mount, target hammer, adjustable trigger stop. Fitted with 6" target barrel. Chambered for .22 LR, .38 Special, .357 Magnum. Blue finish.

NIB	EXC.	V.G.	GOOD	FAIR	POOR
350	275	225	200	150	100

EAA PM2 Shotgun

Pump-action 12-gauge shotgun, with 6-round box magazine. Barrel length 20" and finish is either blue or chrome. Stock is black composite. Weight 6.8 lbs. Discontinued in 1993. **NOTE:** Add $100 for optional night sights.

NIB	EXC.	V.G.	GOOD	FAIR	POOR
450	350	300	250	200	150

EAA HW 60 Rifle

German-made target rifle chambered for .22 LR. Features an adjustable trigger and other target and match grade components. Barrel length 26.8", stock is stippled walnut and finish is blue. Weighs approximately 10.8 lbs.

Target Grade

NIB	EXC.	V.G.	GOOD	FAIR	POOR
700	595	500	400	300	200

Match Grade

NIB	EXC.	V.G.	GOOD	FAIR	POOR
795	675	550	450	350	250

EAA SABATTI

These firearms are made by Sabatti firm in Gardone, Italy. It is an old line company, having been in the firearms business since 1674. Company also produces and supplies component parts to many of Italy's premier gun makers. These shotguns and rifles are manufactured for the cost-conscious buyer.

EAA Sabatti Falcon

Field grade over/under shotgun, with checkered walnut stock and pistol-grip, boxlock action, double triggers and extractors. Offered in 12- or 20-gauge with 3" chambers. Also available in 28-gauge and .410 bore with 26" or 28" barrels. Barrel lengths are available in 26", 28" or 30". Chokes are fixed.

12/20 Gauge

NIB	EXC.	V.G.	GOOD	FAIR	POOR
575	425	400	350	300	250

28/.410

NIB	EXC.	V.G.	GOOD	FAIR	POOR
625	480	425	375	325	275

EAA SP 1822

Sabatti rifle chambered for .22 LR. Semi-automatic carbine, with two-piece adjustable stock.

NIB	EXC.	V.G.	GOOD	FAIR	POOR
225	175	125	100	85	60

NIB	EXC.	V.G.	GOOD	FAIR	POOR

EAA SP 1822H

Heavy barrel version of above model without sights. Receiver fitted with scope mount base.

| 225 | 175 | 125 | 100 | 85 | 60 |

EAA SP 1822TH

This variation also has a heavy barrel without sights, with base mounts. One-piece Bell and Carlson thumb hole stock is feature of this model.

| 350 | 260 | 225 | 175 | 125 | 90 |

EAA Sporting Clay Basic

Model features single-selective trigger, extractors, checkered walnut stock and pistol-grip, extra wide rib. Flued receiver with scroll engraving. Offered in 12-gauge only, with 28" fixed choke barrel.

| 350 | 275 | 250 | 200 | 150 | 100 |

EAA Sporting Clay Pro

Model similar to basic sporting clay. Addition of a select walnut stock, screw-in choke tubes, automatic ejectors, recoil pad. Comes with hard shell case.

| 950 | 720 | 650 | 550 | 450 | 300 |

EAA Sporting Clay Pro Gold

Same as above, with gold inlay receiver.

| 1000 | 750 | 650 | 550 | 450 | 300 |

EAA Saba

Model is a side-by-side shotgun. Features an engraved silver boxlock receiver, double-/single triggers, selective ejectors, solid raised matted rib and select European walnut checkered stock. Offered in 12-, 20-, 28-gauge and .410 bore. Barrel length 26" or 28" with fixed chokes.

| 775 | 600 | 500 | 400 | 300 | 250 |

EAA/Saiga Shotgun

Semi-automatic shotgun based on AK-47 design. Chambered for 12-, 20-gauge and .410 bore. Barrel lengths 20", 24", 26" or 28". Blued finish with optional camo finish. Detachable 5-round box magazine. Introduced in 1999. **NOTE:** Deduct $175 for .410 variation.

| 600 | 525 | 450 | 350 | 200 | 125 |

EAA/Saiga Rifle

Same as above, but chambered for 7.62x39 or .308 cartridge. Fitted with 20" barrel. Choice of wood or synthetic stock. Introduced in 1999. **NOTE:** Add $100 for .308 caliber.

| 550 | 450 | 300 | 200 | 125 | 75 |

EAA Rover 870

High-quality bolt-action rifle. Walnut stock is checkered, with rubber recoil pad. Adjustable rear sight and receiver is drilled and tapped for scope mount. Barrel length 22". Chambered for these cartridges: .22-250, .243, .25-06, .270, .308, .30-06, 7mm Rem. Magnum, .300 and .338 Win. Magnum.

| 585 | 445 | 375 | 300 | 200 | 125 |

EAA Benelli Silhouette Pistol

Specialized competition pistol, with a semi-automatic action. Stocks are match type walnut with stippling. Palm shelf is adjustable. Barrel 4.3" long. Fully adjustable sights. Chambered for .22 LR, .22 Short and .32 WC. Supplied with loading tool and cleaning rod. The .22 Caliber version weighs 38.5 oz. Overall length 11.7".

| 2000 | 1350 | 995 | 750 | 600 | 400 |

MP94 Combo Gun

An over/under combination model, with a 12-gauge shotgun barrel atop a rifle barrel. Chambered for either .223 or .308. A .410/22 LR version is also available. Barrels are 20". Stock is checkered walnut. Sights are an adjustable rear and ramp front with bead. Other features include double triggers, Picatinny scope rail and four choke tubes for the shotgun barrel.

| 675 | 525 | 400 | 300 | 250 | 125 |

Model .410/22 LR

| 485 | 400 | 325 | 250 | 200 | 125 |

Model 221 Double Rifle

An affordable side-by-side double rifle in .30-06 or .45-70, with 23.5" barrels, checkered walnut stock, double triggers and extractors. Sights are an adjustable rear and ramp front with bead,

	NIB	EXC.	V.G.	GOOD	FAIR	POOR

plus a Picatinny or 11mm scope rail.

	NIB	EXC.	V.G.	GOOD	FAIR	POOR
	1000	850	650	500	400	350

EVANS, J. E.
Philadelphia, Pennsylvania

Pocket Pistol

Copy of Philadelphia-made Henry Deringer pistol and chambered for .41-caliber. Utilizes the percussion ignition system and has barrels from 2.5" to 3" in length. Stock is walnut, with checkered grip and mountings are scroll engraved German silver. Barrel marked "J.E. Evans Philada." Manufactured in the 1850s.

—	—	1250	1850	775	350

EVANS REPEATING RIFLE CO.
Mechanic Falls, Maine

Incorporated in 1873, this firm produced repeating rifles based upon patents issued to Warren R. Evans (1868-1871) and later George F. Evans (1877, 1878 and 1879). Most distinctive feature of these arms is they used a butt magazine operating on the principle of an Archimedean screw. Distributed by Merwin, Hulbert & Company, as well as Schuyler, Hartley & Graham, Evans rifles met with some success. One of their earliest advocates was William F. Cody (Buffalo Bill). Company ceased operations in 1879, after approximately 15,000 arms had been made.

LEVER-ACTION RIFLES

Rifle is totally unique for a number of reasons. Holds the most rounds of any repeating rifle that did not have a detachable magazine, with capacities up to 38 rounds on some models. Rifle was chambered for its own cartridge—the .44 Evans of which there were two versions: a 1" cartridge in the "Old Model" and "Transition Model" and a 1.5" cartridge in "New Model". Finish on these rifles is blued, with nickel-plated levers and buttplates noted on some examples. Stocks are walnut. Approximately 12,250 models manufactured between 1873 and 1879.

Old Model

This variation chambered for 1" .44 Evans cartridge. Has a butt stock that covers only the top half of revolving 34-shot magazine located in butt of rifle. Buttplate appears as if it is reversed and markings on the "Old Model" are "Evans Repeating Rifle/Pat. Dec. 8, 1868 & Sept. 16, 1871". There are three versions of Old Model listed. Manufactured between 1874 and 1876 and serial numbered 1-500.

Military Musket

This version has 30" barrel, with two barrel bands and provisions for a bayonet. Only 50 estimated manufactured.

—	—	3750	1700	500	200

Sporting Rifle

Approximately 300 of this model produced, with 26", 28" or 30" octagonal barrel.

—	—	1950	900	500	200

Carbine

This variation has 22" barrel, with one barrel band and sling swivel. There were 150 produced.

—	—	3500	1450	500	200

Transitional Model

Has a buttstock that covers both top and bottom of rotary magazine, with an exposed portion in middle of the butt. Buttplate does not have backward appearance and barrel marked "Evans Repeating Rifle Mechanic Falls Me./Pat Dec. 8, 1868 & Sept. 16, 1871". This version manufactured in 1876 and 1877. Serial numbered between 500-2185, for a total of approximately 1,650 manufactured.

Military Musket

Has a 30" barrel and two barrel bands. 150 were produced.

—	—	3000	1750	650	200

Carbine

Four hundred-fifty were produced, with 22" barrel and one barrel band.

—	—	2950	1700	600	200

Sporting Rifle

Has 26", 28" or 30" barrel. There were 1,050 produced.

—	—	2250	1000	300	150

	NIB	EXC.	V.G.	GOOD	FAIR	POOR

Montreal Carbine

Special issue marked "Montreal", sold by R.H. Kilby, Evans' Canadian sales agent. Between 50 and 100 produced.

	NIB	EXC.	V.G.	GOOD	FAIR	POOR
	—	—	3250	1150	450	250

New Model

Approximately 10,000 New Model were produced. Chambered for 1.5" .44 Evans cartridge, with magazine capacity reduced to 28. Frame was redesigned and rounded at top and fore-end fit flush to receiver. Lever and hammer are streamlined and a dust cover over loading gate. Markings are same as on Transitional Model, with "U.S.A." added to last line. This version was not serial numbered and any numbers found are assembly numbers only

Military Musket

3,000 produced, with 30" barrel and two barrel bands.

	NIB	EXC.	V.G.	GOOD	FAIR	POOR
	—	—	3950	1750	450	275

Carbine

4,000 produced, with 22" barrel, one barrel band and sling swivel.

	NIB	EXC.	V.G.	GOOD	FAIR	POOR
	—	—	2150	950	500	250

Sporting Rifle

3,000 produced, with 26", 28" or 30" octagonal barrels.

	NIB	EXC.	V.G.	GOOD	FAIR	POOR
	—	—	2500	2000	800	300

EXCAM
Hialeah, Florida

An importer of firearms, not a manufacturer. Erma and Uberti products imported by this company are under their own heading in this book. Other products that they imported are listed here. No longer in business.

TA 76

Patterned after Colt Single Action Army and chambered for .22 rimfire cartridge. Has a 4.75", 6" or 9" barrel and blue finish, with wood grips. Offered with brass trigger guard and backstrap. Also offered chrome-plated. A combo model with an extra .22 Magnum cylinder is available and would add 10 percent to listed values.

	NIB	EXC.	V.G.	GOOD	FAIR	POOR
	—	100	75	65	40	25

TA 38 Over/Under Derringer

Two-shot derringer patterned after Remington derringer. Chambered for .38 Special cartridge. Has 3" barrels that pivot upward for loading. Blued, with checkered nylon grips. Discontinued in 1985.

	NIB	EXC.	V.G.	GOOD	FAIR	POOR
	—	100	75	65	40	25

TA 90

Double-action semi-automatic copy of CZ-75, that some experts rate as the finest combat handgun in the world. Chambered for 9mm Parabellum and has a 4.75" barrel. Constructed of steel and finished with matte blue or chrome. Checkered wood or rubber grips. Detachable magazine holds 15 rounds.

	NIB	EXC.	V.G.	GOOD	FAIR	POOR
	425	375	325	275	200	150

BTA-90B

Compact version of TA 90. Has a 3.5" barrel and 12-round detachable magazine. Similar in all other respects to standard model. Rubber grips only.

	NIB	EXC.	V.G.	GOOD	FAIR	POOR
	425	375	325	275	200	150

TA 90 SS

Competition version of TA 90. Similar to standard model, except it is compensated and features adjustable sights. Offered either blued or chrome-plated. Introduced in 1989.

	NIB	EXC.	V.G.	GOOD	FAIR	POOR
	650	575	500	400	325	225

TA 41, 41C, and 41 SS

Series of pistols identical to TA 90 series, except they are chambered for .41 Action Express cartridge. Values are about 10 percent higher than 9mm versions. Introduced in 1989.

Warrior Model W 722

Double-action revolver chambered for .22 rimfire and .22 rimfire Magnum, with an interchangeable cylinder. Has a 6" barrel, adjustable sights and 8-shot cylinder capacity. Blued, with checkered plastic grips. Model not imported after 1986.

	NIB	EXC.	V.G.	GOOD	FAIR	POOR
	—	100	75	50	35	20

	NIB	EXC.	V.G.	GOOD	FAIR	POOR

Model W384

Double-action revolver chambered for .38 Special cartridge, with 4" or 6" vent rib barrel. Blued finish and plastic grips. Discontinued in 1986.

	NIB	EXC.	V.G.	GOOD	FAIR	POOR
	—	175	125	100	75	50

Model W357

Similar to W384, except chambered for .357 Magnum cartridge. Discontinued in 1986.

	—	200	150	125	100	75

Targa GT 26

A blowback-operated semi-automatic pistol, chambered for .25 ACP cartridge. Has a 2.5" barrel and 6-shot detachable magazine. Finished in blue or matte chrome, with choice of alloy or steel frame. Grips are wood.

Steel Frame Version

125	90	75	50	40	30

Alloy Frame Version

100	75	50	35	30	25

GT 22

Semi-automatic pistol, chambered for .22 LR cartridge. Has a 4" barrel, fixed sights and 10-round magazine. Available either blued or matte chrome-plated, with wooden grips.

200	175	150	125	90	70

GT 22T

Similar to GT 22, with 6" barrel and adjustable target-type sights.

225	200	175	150	100	75

GT 32

Blowback-operated semi-automatic pistol, chambered for .32 ACP cartridge. Has a 7-round magazine and either blued or matte chrome-plated, with wood grips.

200	175	150	125	90	75

GT 380

Similar to GT 32, except chambered for .380 ACP cartridge.

225	175	150	125	100	75

GT 380XE

Similar to GT 380, with 11-shot high-capacity detachable magazine.

225	200	175	150	125	100

EXCEL INDUSTRIES
Ontario, California

Accelerator Pistol

Semi-automatic pistol currently available in .22 WMR or 5.7x28mm. Previously chambered for .22 LR, .17 HMR and .17 Mach 2. Barrel length 6.5" or 8.5" and diameter .875". Stainless steel with polymer grip. Barrel fitted with an aluminum rib, target sights and Weaver base. Magazine capacity 9 rounds. Weight about 54 oz. Introduced in 2004. **NOTE:** Add $50 to $75 for red dot optical sight or factory-mounted scope; $100 for 5.7x28mm chambering.

425	320	250	165	125	75

Accelerator Rifle

As above, with 18" fluted stainless steel barrel and black polymer pistol-grip stock. Fully adjustable removable sights on a Weaver rail. Weight about 8 lbs. Introduced in 2004.

465	350	275	195	150	100

X-22

Blow-back semi-automatic in .22 LR, with 10- or 25-round magazine. Barrel is 4.375", overall length 12". Sights are fully adjustable. Frame is CNC-machined aluminum, with accessory rail. Rifle variation with 18" barrel is also available, with comparable values.

385	300	250	200	150	100

X-57 / X-30

Centerfire series of AR-type pistols, chambered in 5.7x28mm or .30 Carbine. Magazine capacity: 25-rounds 5.7; 20-rounds .30 Carbine; 10-rounds where required by law. Features are similar to X-22 model, except barrel length is 8.5", overall length 16". Rifle variation with 18" barrel is also available, with comparable values.

600	515	425	350	250	150

F

NIB	EXC.	V.G.	GOOD	FAIR	POOR

F.A.S.
Italy

Model 601

A high-grade competition target pistol, chambered for .22 Short cartridge. Semi-automatic, with 5.5" barrel and adjustable target sights. Detachable magazine holds 5 rounds. Finish is blued, with wrap-around target grips. Discontinued in 1988.

NIB	EXC.	V.G.	GOOD	FAIR	POOR
—	1450	1150	775	550	300

Model 602

Similar to Model 601, except chambered for .22 LR. Discontinued in 1987.

NIB	EXC.	V.G.	GOOD	FAIR	POOR
—	1250	975	725	500	250

Model 603

Chambered for .32 S&W wadcutter cartridge and features adjustable grips. Discontinued in 1987.

NIB	EXC.	V.G.	GOOD	FAIR	POOR
—	1350	1075	775	500	250

F.I.E.
Hialeah, Florida

Firearms Import and Export engaged in the business of importing Franchi shotgun (which is listed under its own heading) and Arminius revolver (which is made in Germany). They were also distributors for Titan semi-automatic pistols, which are manufactured in U.S.A. They were also importing a series of 9mm pistols from Italy, that are produced by Tanfoglio and known as TZ series. F.I.E. no longer in business as of 1990.

HANDGUNS

TZ 75

Copy of CZ 75 Czechoslovakian combat pistol, produced by Tanfoglio in Italy. A 9mm double-action semi-automatic, with a 4.75" barrel, all-steel construction, fixed sights and 15-shot magazine. Offered either blued or matte chrome plated, with wood or rubber grips.

NIB	EXC.	V.G.	GOOD	FAIR	POOR
450	350	300	250	200	150

TZ 75 Series 88

Improved version that is also chambered for .41 Action Express cartridge. Has a firing pin safety and can be carried cocked and locked. Few other minor changes. Introduced in 1988.

NIB	EXC.	V.G.	GOOD	FAIR	POOR
500	375	325	250	200	150

KG-99

Blowback-operated semi-automatic assault pistol, chambered for 9mm Parabellum cartridge. Has a 36-round magazine. Discontinued in 1984.

NIB	EXC.	V.G.	GOOD	FAIR	POOR
550	450	350	250	200	150

Spectre Assault Pistol

Assault-type semi-automatic pistol, chambered for 9mm Parabellum. Has a 30- or 50-round magazine available. Introduced in 1989.

NIB	EXC.	V.G.	GOOD	FAIR	POOR
800	675	575	400	300	200

Titan II .22

Semi-automatic pistol chambered for .22 LR. Has a 10-shot magazine and blued finish, with walnut grips. Made in the U.S.A.

NIB	EXC.	V.G.	GOOD	FAIR	POOR
275	150	100	75	50	25

Titan E32

Single-action blowback-operated semi-automatic pistol, that was chambered for .32 ACP and now chambered for .380 ACP cartridge. Finish is blue or chrome-plated. Grips are walnut.

NIB	EXC.	V.G.	GOOD	FAIR	POOR
300	175	150	125	100	75

Super Titan 11

Similar to Titan, except it has a 12-round high-capacity magazine.

NIB	EXC.	V.G.	GOOD	FAIR	POOR
325	200	175	150	100	75

Titan 25

Smaller version of Titan Series, chambered for .25 ACP cartridge. Blued or chrome-plated.

NIB	EXC.	V.G.	GOOD	FAIR	POOR
200	75	50	40	30	20

	NIB	EXC.	V.G.	GOOD	FAIR	POOR

Titan Tigress
Similar to Titan 25, except gold-plated and cased.

	NIB	EXC.	V.G.	GOOD	FAIR	POOR
	225	115	90	75	50	30

D38 Derringer
Two-shot over/under Remington-style derringer. Chambered for .38 Special cartridge and chrome-plated. Dropped from line in 1985.

	NIB	EXC.	V.G.	GOOD	FAIR	POOR
	145	75	45	35	25	20

D86 Derringer
Single-shot derringer with 3" barrel. Chambered for .38 Special cartridge and chrome-plated. An ammunition storage compartment in butt and transfer bar safety makes it safer to carry. Introduced in 1986.

	NIB	EXC.	V.G.	GOOD	FAIR	POOR
	150	80	65	50	35	20

SINGLE ACTION ARMY REPLICA REVOLVERS
There is a series of single-action .22-caliber revolvers, that were patterned after Colt Single Action Army. Manufactured in U.S.A. or Brescia, Italy. They are inexpensive and of fair quality. Differences between these models are basically barrel lengths, type of sights and finish. All are chambered for .22 LR and have interchangeable .22 Magnum cylinders. We list them for reference purposes.

Cowboy

	NIB	EXC.	V.G.	GOOD	FAIR	POOR
	250	125	100	80	75	50

Gold Rush

	NIB	EXC.	V.G.	GOOD	FAIR	POOR
	250	125	100	80	75	50

Texas Ranger

	NIB	EXC.	V.G.	GOOD	FAIR	POOR
	200	85	75	50	35	20

Buffalo Scout
NOTE: Add 50 percent for faux "gold" -plated Yellow Rose of Texas variant.

	NIB	EXC.	V.G.	GOOD	FAIR	POOR
	175	80	70	50	35	20

Legend S.A.A.

	NIB	EXC.	V.G.	GOOD	FAIR	POOR
	250	125	100	80	75	50

ARMINIUS REVOLVERS

Hombre
Single-action made in Germany by Arminius. Patterned after Colt Single Action Army revolver. Hombre chambered for .357 Magnum, .44 Magnum and .45 Colt cartridges. Offered with 5.5", 6" or 7.5" barrel. Case-colored frame, blued barrel and cylinder, with smooth walnut grips. Backstrap and trigger guard offered in brass. Will bring a 10 percent premium.

	NIB	EXC.	V.G.	GOOD	FAIR	POOR
	325	225	175	125	100	75

Model 522TB
Swing-out cylinder double-action revolver, chambered for .22 rimfire cartridge. Has a 4" barrel and blued, with wood grips.

	NIB	EXC.	V.G.	GOOD	FAIR	POOR
	250	125	100	75	50	30

722
Similar to 522, with an 8-shot cylinder and 6" barrel. Available with chrome finish.

	NIB	EXC.	V.G.	GOOD	FAIR	POOR
	250	125	100	75	50	30

532TB
A 7-shot double-action revolver, chambered for .32 S&W cartridge. Has a 4" barrel, adjustable sights and finished in either blue or chrome.

	NIB	EXC.	V.G.	GOOD	FAIR	POOR
	250	130	110	80	60	40

732B
Similar to 532TB, with 6" barrel and fixed sights. Discontinued in 1988.

	NIB	EXC.	V.G.	GOOD	FAIR	POOR
	225	100	80	65	50	35

Standard Revolver
Double-action swing-out cylinder revolver, chambered for .32 Magnum or .38 Special. Has a 4" or 6" barrel. Fixed sights and blued, with wood grips. Model made in U.S.A. Introduced in 1989.

	NIB	EXC.	V.G.	GOOD	FAIR	POOR
	225	100	75	50	35	20

NIB	EXC.	V.G.	GOOD	FAIR	POOR

Models 384TB and 386TB

These two models are double-action. Chambered for .38 Special cartridge. The 384 has a 4" barrel; 386 has a 6" barrel. Available in blue or chrome plate. Both discontinued in 1985.

250	125	100	85	65	50

Model 357TB

Similar to 384TB, except chambered for .357 Magnum cartridge. Offered with 3", 4" or 6" barrel.

250	125	100	85	65	50

222, 232, and 382TB

These models are double-action swing-out cylinder revolvers. Chambered for .22 rimfire, .32 S&W and .38 Special. They are 2"-barreled snub-nosed revolvers, with either blued or chrome-plated finishes. Discontinued in 1985.

200	100	75	50	40	25

Model 3572

Similar revolver to 382TB, except chambered for .357 Magnum cartridge. Discontinued in 1984.

250	125	100	85	65	50

SHOTGUNS AND RIFLES

Model 122

Bolt-action rifle, chambered for .22 rimfire, with 21" barrel and adjustable sights. Has a 10-shot magazine and walnut Monte Carlo stock. Introduced in 1986.

200	100	75	50	35	25

Single-Shot

Brazilian made chambered for 12- or 20-gauge and .410 bore. Single-barrel break-open, with 25" through 30" barrel lengths. Various chokes. Blued, with a wood stock. Introduced in 1985.

150	100	60	45	35	25

S.O.B.

Similar to single-shot, with 18.5" barrel and pistol-grip instead of standard stock. Discontinued in 1984.

165	110	60	45	35	25

Sturdy Over/Under

Chambered for 12- and 20-gauge. Has 3" chambers and 28" vent rib barrels, with various chokes. An over/under with double triggers and extractors. Frame is engraved and silver finished. Manufactured in Italy by Maroccini and imported between 1985 and 1988.

400	300	225	175	150	100

Brute

Side-by-side chambered for 12- or 20-gauge and .410 bore. Has 19" barrels, double triggers and extractors, with a wood stock. Dropped from line in 1984.

300	200	125	100	75	50

SPAS-12

A unique shotgun in that it can function as a pump or automatic, with the touch of a button. A paramilitary-type shotgun. Chambered for 12-gauge, with 21.5" barrel and 9-shot tube magazine. Has an alloy receiver and optional folding stock. Finish is all black. Manufactured by Franchi in Italy. **NOTE:** Some early models had detachable wood stocks. These are rarely encountered. Seek a qualified appraiser for evaluations.

1500	1100	900	700	400	300

LAW-12

A paramilitary-type 12-gauge semi-automatic shotgun, that is gas-operated. Has a 9-shot tube magazine. Barrel is 21.5" in length and choked cylinder bore. Has a military special black finish and black synthetic stock.

850	650	400	300	200	100

SAS-12

A paramilitary-type slide-action shotgun, chambered for 12-gauge. Has a 21.5" barrel and choked cylinder bore. Finish is similar to LAW-12. Manufactured by Franchi in Italy.

850	650	500	400	300	200

	NIB	EXC.	V.G.	GOOD	FAIR	POOR

FABARM
Brescia, Italy

In 1998, H&K took over importation of Fabarm shotgun line in U.S. Imported by Tristar and Sig Arms from 2005 - 2009. Currently imported by Fabarm USA.

SEMI-AUTOMATIC SHOTGUNS

Ellegi Standard

Gas-operated semi-automatic shotgun, chambered for 12-gauge. Has a 28" vent rib barrel, with choice of choke. Receiver is blue anodized alloy, with a photo-etched game scene. Stock and forearm are checkered walnut. Introduced in 1989. Ellegi Model available in six other configurations. Differences are in barrel length and choke, type of choke tubes and finish. Basically the guns are quite similar to standard model. These variations are listed.

700	625	525	450	350	250

Ellegi Multichoke

700	625	525	450	350	250

Ellegi Innerchoke

725	650	550	475	375	275

Ellegi Magnum

725	650	550	475	375	275

Ellegi Super Goose

800	725	625	550	450	350

Ellegi Slug

775	700	600	525	425	325

Ellegi Police

575	500	450	400	300	225

XLR5 Velocity

Semi-automatic 12-gauge shotgun, designed for clay target shooting. With 2.75" chamber, Turkish walnut stock, adjustable comb and rib, 30" or 32" barrel and five choke tubes. Also available in left-hand configuration. Velocity Silver model has titanium receiver. **NOTE:** Add $150 for left-hand model; $300 for Velocity Silver.

2300	2000	1650	1350	—	—

SLIDE-ACTION SHOTGUNS

Model S.D.A.S.S.

Chambered for 12-gauge with 3" chamber. Offered with 20" or 24.5" barrel, threaded for external choke tubes. Model has 8-shot tube magazine, twin action bars, alloy receiver and matte black finish. Defensive-type shotgun and imported since 1989. Special Police and Martial Model are variations of basic slide-action. Differ in barrel length and choke. Police Model has a shrouded barrel.

350	275	200	150	100	75

Special Police

525	475	425	350	275	200

Martial Model

475	425	375	300	225	175

SINGLE-SHOT SHOTGUNS

Omega Standard

Has an alloy receiver chambered for 12- or 20-gauge and .410 bore. Has 26" or 28" barrels, with various chokes. Finish is black, with a beech stock. Introduced in 1989.

150	125	100	75	50	40

Omega Goose Gun

Chambered for 12-gauge only, with 35.5" full-choke barrel.

195	140	125	100	75	50

	NIB	EXC.	V.G.	GOOD	FAIR	POOR

SIDE-BY-SIDE SHOTGUNS

Beta Model

Double-barrel is chambered for 12-gauge only, with choice of barrel length and choke. Boxlock action, with false side plates, single trigger and automatic ejectors. Finish is blued, with checkered select walnut stock. Introduced in 1989.

NIB	EXC.	V.G.	GOOD	FAIR	POOR
925	850	750	600	450	300

Beta Europe

Deluxe version features single-selective triggers. A game scene engraved coin-finished receiver. Stock is straight English style, with a splinter fore-end. Introduced in 1989.

NIB	EXC.	V.G.	GOOD	FAIR	POOR
1750	1500	1250	1000	750	500

OVER/UNDER SHOTGUNS

Field Model

Chambered for 12-gauge. Has 29" vent rib barrels, with various chokes. Receiver is coin-finished and stock checkered walnut. Discontinued in 1985.

NIB	EXC.	V.G.	GOOD	FAIR	POOR
900	700	600	500	400	300

Gamma Field

Chambered for 12- or 20-gauge. Offered with 26", 28" or 29" vent rib barrels and various choke combinations. Screw-in choke tubes are available and would be worth a 10 percent premium. Has a boxlock coin-finished receiver that is moderately engraved and checkered walnut stock.

NIB	EXC.	V.G.	GOOD	FAIR	POOR
925	850	775	650	500	350

Gamma Paradox Gun

Chambered for 12-gauge only. Top barrel is rifled for accurate placement of slugs. Barrels are 25" long, with vented rib. Bottom barrel has three screw-in choke tubes. Has a single-selective trigger and automatic ejectors. Finish is similar to Field Model. Introduced in 1989.

NIB	EXC.	V.G.	GOOD	FAIR	POOR
1000	900	825	750	600	450

Gamma Trap or Skeet

Competition-grade guns. Either with 27.5" barrel and five screw-in choke tubes on skeet model, or 29" barrel with screw-in trap chokes. Both models feature single-selective triggers and automatic ejectors; trap model has Monte Carlo stock. Moderately engraved and coin-finished boxlock actions. Introduced in 1989.

NIB	EXC.	V.G.	GOOD	FAIR	POOR
1000	900	825	750	600	450

Gamma Sporting Competition Model

Designed for Sporting Clays and chambered for 12-gauge only. The 29" barrel has a wide rib and furnished with five screw-in choke tubes. It has single-selective trigger, automatic ejectors and checkered walnut stock, with a competition recoil pad. Finished like skeet and trap models. Introduced in 1989.

NIB	EXC.	V.G.	GOOD	FAIR	POOR
1000	900	825	750	600	450

Elos

Over/under offered only in 20- or 28-gauge, with round action, 28" barrels, 5 choke tubes, steel or aluminum alloy frame, with case colored or titanium finish. Stock and fore-end are checkered Turkish walnut, with hand-rubbed oil finish. Deluxe model features game scene engraving and premium grade Turkish walnut. Values shown are for standard 20-gauge. New in 2013. **NOTE:** Add $150 for 28-gauge; $500 for Deluxe model.

NIB	EXC.	V.G.	GOOD	FAIR	POOR
2050	1750	1425	1100	850	450

Axis Competition

Competition-grade over/under in 12-gauge only. Two variants are offered: Sporting and Trap. Both feature Turkish walnut stocks, with adjustable comb. Sporting model has 30" or 32" barrels; Trap barrels are 32" or 34", with high-profile adjustable rib and Fabarm's removable Kinetik recoil reduction system. New in 2013.

Sporting

NIB	EXC.	V.G.	GOOD	FAIR	POOR
2600	2200	1800	1250	900	450

Trap

NIB	EXC.	V.G.	GOOD	FAIR	POOR
3700	3000	2500	1850	1100	550

	NIB	EXC.	V.G.	GOOD	FAIR	POOR

H&K 1997-2004 IMPORTED SHOTGUNS

Camo Lion

Introduced in 1999, this 12-gauge model features a ported barrel system in 24", 26" or 28" lengths. Wetlands camo finish. Five choke tubes and hard plastic case included. Weight about 7 lbs.

800	650	450	300	175	100

Red Lion

A 12-gauge semi-automatic, with 3" chambers. Has a three-shot magazine, matte finish and walnut stock. Rubber vented recoil pad, with leather cover and set of five choke tubes. Available with 24", 26" or 28" vent rib barrel. Weight about 7 lbs.

800	650	450	300	175	100

Red Lion Ducks Unlimited 2001

Model offered only through Ducks Unlimited banquet program. This is a 12-gauge, 28" barrel, with select walnut stock. Oil finish. Unique serial numbers from 0001DU2001 to 3600DU2001. Receiver engraved with waterfowl scene and DU logo. Comes with lockable case. Limited to 3,600 shotguns.

975	775	625	500	325	200

Gold Lion

Has many features of Red Lion model, with addition of high-grade oil-finished walnut stock and olive wood pistol-grip cap. Trigger is gold plated.

800	650	450	300	175	100

Gold Lion Mark III

Semi-automatic model is an improved version of Gold Lion. Addition of enhanced walnut stock, lightweight receiver with scroll engraving and gold inlays. Fitted with 28" TriBore barrel and chambered for 3", 12-gauge shell. Supplied with five choke tubes. Weight about 7.2 lbs.

975	775	625	500	325	200

Sporting Clays Lion

Model introduced in 1999, features a ported barrel and special "TriBore" system. Offered in 12-gauge with 28" barrel. Walnut stock with rubber recoil pad, gold-plated trigger, matte blue finish, red front sight bar, 10mm channeled rib, two extra front sights (green and white) and set of five choke tubes. Weight about 7.2 lbs.

975	775	625	500	325	200

Rex Lion

Introduced in 2002, model features 12-gauge gun, with 3" chambers and 26" or 28" vent rib barrel. Choke tubes. High-grade walnut stock, with Olive wood grip cap. Silver and black frame, with scroll engraving and gold inlay. Weight about 7 lbs. Limited edition.

1050	800	650	450	300	175

Sporting Clays Extra

Introduced in 2000, model features 28" or 30" vent rib barrel, with carbon fiber finish on both barrel and receiver. Also supplied with eight competition choke tubes and fitted luggage case. Stock is adjustable. Weight about 7.3 lbs.

850	675	450	300	175	100

Tactical Semi-Auto

A 12-gauge semi-automatic shotgun, fitted with 20" barrel threaded for chokes. Receiver-mounted Picatinny rail. Flip-up front sight. Optional magazine extension has 7-round capacity. Optional pistol-grip. Weight about 6.6 lbs. Introduced in 2001.

650	550	400	265	150	100

Home Security HD

Semi-automatic shotgun chambered for 12-gauge 3" shell. Fitted with 20" plain barrel, with cylinder screw-in choke. Matte black finish. Black polymer stock. Magazine capacity 5 rounds. Weight about 7.5 lbs.

600	475	300	225	150	100

H368

This 12-gauge 3" model, features 28" tri-bore vent rib barrel, matte black synthetic stock or Realtree camo stock. Lightweight alloy matte black receiver. Magazine capacity 2 rounds. Weight about 7.2 lbs. Introduced in 2003. Available in a left-hand model. **NOTE:** Add $60 for camo stock; $90 for left-hand model.

650	550	400	265	150	100

	NIB	EXC.	V.G.	GOOD	FAIR	POOR

FP6 Field Pump

Introduced in 2001, model features black alloy receiver with screw-in chokes. Chambered for 12-gauge with 28" barrel. Black synthetic stock. Optional 24" rifled barrel. Weight about 7 lbs. Available in Mossy Oak Break-up Camo.

NIB	EXC.	V.G.	GOOD	FAIR	POOR
375	350	275	225	175	100

FP6

A 12-gauge slide-action shotgun, with 3" chamber, 20" barrel, heat shield black polymer stock and threaded barrel for exterior chokes. Weight about 6.6 lbs. Available with carbon fiber finish.

NIB	EXC.	V.G.	GOOD	FAIR	POOR
500	400	300	200	125	100

FP6 with Rail

Introduced in 1999, this model similar to standard FP6, with addition of Picatinny rail mounted on top of receiver. Also fitted with flip-up front sight. In 2003 this model offered with 20" TriBore barrel, with barrel threaded choke, new style front sight and ghost ring rear sight. **NOTE:** Available with 14" barrel. Requires BATF tax and all NFA rules apply to purchase and sale of this restricted shotgun. Accessory wire stock and pistol-grip available for an additional $150.

NIB	EXC.	V.G.	GOOD	FAIR	POOR
510	410	300	200	125	100

Max Lion

This over/under gun chambered for 12- or 20-gauge, 3" shell. Fitted with single-selective trigger, auto ejectors, high grade walnut stock, leather covered recoil pad, set of five choke tubes and fitted luggage-style case. Choice of 26", 28" or 30" barrels on 12-gauge guns and 26" or 28" on 20-gauge guns. Weight about 7.5 lbs. for 12-gauge and 7 lbs. for 20-gauge. **NOTE:** In 1999 Max Lion was offered with TriBore barrel system. Models with this system add $70 to NIB price.

NIB	EXC.	V.G.	GOOD	FAIR	POOR
1200	900	700	550	300	175

Max Lion Light

Introduced in 2000, model features 24" barrels in both 12- and 20-gauge. Receiver has gold game bird inlay. Single trigger, automatic ejectors and select walnut stock. Weight about 7 lbs.

NIB	EXC.	V.G.	GOOD	FAIR	POOR
1200	900	700	550	300	175

Max Lion Paradox

Introduced in 2002, model features 12-gauge 3" gun, with 24" barrels. Bottom barrel is rifled. Case hardened receiver, with checkered walnut stock. Weight about 7.6 lbs.

NIB	EXC.	V.G.	GOOD	FAIR	POOR
1425	1175	900	700	550	300

Sporting Clays Competition Lion

Model available in 12- or 20-gauge, with 28" 10mm channeled rib barrels. Single-selective trigger and automatic ejectors. Recoil reducer installed in buttstock. Ported barrels. Set of 5 choke tubes standard. Leather covered recoil pad. High grade walnut stock. Introduced in 1999.

NIB	EXC.	V.G.	GOOD	FAIR	POOR
925	825	600	500	300	150

Sporting Clays Max Lion

Chambered for 12-gauge 3" shell and fitted with 32" TriBore vent rib barrel. Select walnut stock with hand checkering, adjustable trigger and leather covered recoil pad. Engraved gold inlay receiver is case colored. Supplied with eight choke tubes. Weight approximately 7.9 lbs. Introduced in 2003.

NIB	EXC.	V.G.	GOOD	FAIR	POOR
925	825	600	500	300	150

Sporting Clays Competition Extra

This 12-gauge model features a choice of 28" or 30" barrels. Walnut stock adjustable. Finish carbon fiber. Gun supplied with set of eight choke tubes. Introduced in 2000. Weight about 7.8 lbs.

NIB	EXC.	V.G.	GOOD	FAIR	POOR
1000	775	625	500	400	150

Black Lion Competition

Similar to Max Lion. Choice of gauges, barrel lengths and features. Less figured walnut stock and black receiver finish.

NIB	EXC.	V.G.	GOOD	FAIR	POOR
1050	795	650	525	425	175

Monotrap

Single barrel trap gun, with 30" vent rib barrel. Forearm has built-in recoil reduction system. Single-selective trigger and automatic ejectors. Adjustable comb. Shotgun is 12-gauge built on 20-gauge receiver. Weight about 6 lbs. Introduced in 2000.

NIB	EXC.	V.G.	GOOD	FAIR	POOR
1800	1350	1100	750	600	500

NIB	EXC.	V.G.	GOOD	FAIR	POOR

Silver Lion

Model available in both 12- and 20-gauge, with 26" or 28" barrel. 30" barrels in 12-gauge. Silver finish receiver etched and stock high quality walnut, with leather covered pad. Scalable forearm standard. Single-selective trigger and auto ejectors. Five chokes tubes are included. Weight about 7.5 lbs. for 12-gauge; 7 lbs. for 20-gauge.

925	825	600	500	300	150

Silver Lion Youth

This 20-gauge over/under features shortened buttstock and 24" ported barrels. Single-selective trigger and automatic ejectors standard. Walnut stock. Rubber recoil pad. Silver steel receiver. Weight approximately 6 lbs. Introduced in 1999.

800	775	675	500	325	150

Super Light Lion Youth

Similar to Silver Lion Youth model, but chambered for 12-gauge shells. Aluminum receiver and 24" ported barrels. Introduced in 1999. Weight about 6.5 lbs.

800	775	675	500	325	150

Ultra Mag Lion

This model is a 12-gauge, with 3.5" chambers, black receiver, single-selective trigger, auto ejectors, blackened walnut stock, leather covered recoil pad and set of five choke tubes. Barrel length 28". Weight 7.9 lbs.

800	775	675	500	325	150

Super Light Lion

Model features lightweight alloy receiver, with 12 gauge 24" barrels, single-selective trigger, non-auto ejectors, walnut stock, five choke tubes and leather covered recoil pad. Weight about 6.5 lbs. **NOTE:** For TriBore system add $125.

800	775	675	500	325	150

Camo Turkey Mag

Introduced in 1999, model features unported TriBore 20" barrel. Receiver has Picatinny rail on top. Full extra brown camo finish. Chambered for 12-gauge with 3.5" chambers. Weight about 7.5 lbs.

925	825	600	500	300	150

Ultra Camo Mag Lion

This 12-gauge 3.5" model fitted with 28" barrels. Wetlands camo pattern finish. Non-automatic ejectors. Weight about 8 lbs. Introduced in 1999. Standard with steel screw-in chokes and regular screw-in chokes.

925	825	600	500	300	150

Classic Lion Grade I

Offered in 12-gauge with 3" chambers. Single-selective trigger, auto-ejectors, walnut stock and buttplate. Fitted with 26" barrels. Weight about 7 lbs.

1200	925	825	600	500	300

Classic Lion Grade II

Similar to Grade I, with addition of oil finished stock and removable sideplates. Game scene engraving. Weight 7.2 lbs.

1200	925	825	600	500	300

Classic Lion Elite

Introduced in 2002, this 12-gauge model features 26" or 28" barrels. Case colored receiver and straight-grip stock. Fixed chokes. Weight about 7 lbs.

1300	1025	850	650	525	315

FABBRI, ARMI
Gardone V.T., Italy

Fabbri Armi currently manufactures one of the best shotguns in the world. Available as a custom made-to-order item and are not often seen in the used gun market. Values for guns of this nature and quality are impossible to accurately establish in a book of this nature. There are so many options and conditions that make prices fluctuate greatly. We give an estimated figure, as a base starting point. See Karl Lippard's book *Fabbri Shotguns*, Colorado Springs, Colorado, VM Publications 1998, for more value details.

Side-by-Side Shotgun

Chambered for 12- or 20-gauge, with all other features on custom-order basis. Model no longer in production. **NOTE:** Deduct $10,000 for Type One Model.

39500	27000	18500	15000	10000	8000

NIB	EXC.	V.G.	GOOD	FAIR	POOR

Over/Under Shotgun

Chambered for 12- or 20-gauge, with all other features on custom-order basis. Prices listed are for Boehler barrels. **NOTE:** Add 50 percent for vacuum arc remelted steel barrels. Deduct 50 percent for Phoenix barrels.

NIB	EXC.	V.G.	GOOD	FAIR	POOR
41500	26000	18500	15000	10000	8000

FABRIQUE NATIONALE
Herstal, Belgium

In 1889, Fabrique Nationale (or FN) was founded by a group of Belgian investors for the purpose of manufacturing Mauser rifles for the Belgian army. This was to be accomplished under the license from Mauser, with the technical assistance of Ludwig Loewe of Berlin. A few years later, in the late 1890s, John Browning arrived in Europe seeking a manufacturer for his semi-automatic shotgun. He had severed his ties with Winchester, after a disagreement. This led to a long association that worked out extremely well for both parties. Later Browning became associated with Colt and the world market was divided—with the Eastern Hemisphere going to FN and the Western Hemisphere to Colt. In this section, we list arms that bear the FN banner. The FN-manufactured firearms produced under the Browning banner, are listed in the Browning section of this book.

PISTOLS

Model 1900

Blowback-operated semi-automatic pistol, chambered for 7.65mm cartridge. Has a 4" barrel and fixed sights. Blued, with molded plastic grips. Manufactured between 1899 and 1910. Model referred to as "Old Model".

NIB	EXC.	V.G.	GOOD	FAIR	POOR
—	750	525	350	200	150

Model 1903

Considerable improvement over Model 1900. Also a blowback-operated semi-automatic; recoil spring located under barrel and firing pin travels through slide after being struck by a hidden hammer. Barrel is held in place by five locking lugs that fit into five grooves in frame. Pistol chambered for 9mm Browning long cartridge and has a 5" barrel. Finish is blued, with molded plastic grips. Detachable magazine holds 7 rounds. There is a detachable shoulder stock/holster along with a 10-round magazine that was available for this model. Accessories are extremely rare and if present, would make the package worth approximately five times that of the pistol alone. Approximately 58,000 manufactured between 1903 and 1939.

NIB	EXC.	V.G.	GOOD	FAIR	POOR
—	1000	750	500	275	175

Model 1905/1906

A smaller version of Model 1903, designed to be a pocket pistol and chambered for 6.35mm cartridge. Became known as "Vest Pocket" model and was also basis for many Eibar copies. Has a 2.5" barrel and produced in two distinct variations. First variation had no safety lever or slide lock and relied on grip safety. Second variation, that occurred at approximately serial number 100000, added this safety lever and slide lock, which helped simplify dismantling of pistol. Available either blued or nickel-plated. Plated models would bring a 10 percent premium. Approximately 1,086,100 manufactured between 1906 and 1959. Known in U.S. as Model 1905 and in Europe as Model 1906.

1st Variation, Under Serial Number 100000

NIB	EXC.	V.G.	GOOD	FAIR	POOR
—	500	395	275	200	125

2nd Variation, Over Serial Number 100000

NIB	EXC.	V.G.	GOOD	FAIR	POOR
—	475	350	250	175	100

Model 1910

Chambered for 7.65mm and 9mm short. Has a 3.5" barrel, blued and molded plastic grips. Principal difference between this model and its predecessors, is the recoil spring on Model 1910 is wrapped around the barrel. This gives the slide a more graceful tubular appearance, instead of old slab-sided look. This model has triple safety features of 1906 Model, 2nd variation. This model adopted by police forces around the world. Manufactured between 1912 and 1954. **NOTE:** Add $100 for .380 (9mm Short) chambering.

NIB	EXC.	V.G.	GOOD	FAIR	POOR
675	600	500	400	300	175

Model 1922

Variation of Model 1910. Made for military and police use in several European countries, between 1922 and 1944. **NOTE:** Add 75 percent if Nazi marked with original magazine; 100 percent for "WaA613" marking.

NIB	EXC.	V.G.	GOOD	FAIR	POOR
—	350	225	175	125	100

	NIB	EXC.	V.G.	GOOD	FAIR	POOR

"Baby" Model

A smaller and lighter version of Model 1906. Chambered for 6.35mm cartridge and has a 2" barrel. No grip safety or slide lock on this model. Appears to be more square in shape than Model 1906. Offered in blue, with molded plastic grips. Early models have word "Baby" molded into grips; post-1945 versions do not. Also a nickel-plated version with pearl grips. Over 500,000 of these manufactured between 1931 and 1983. Late-production specimens command a slight premium.

800	650	500	300	225	150

MODEL 1935/HI-POWER/GP

Last design from John Browning developed between 1925 and 1935. Pistol known as Model 1935, P-35, Hi-Power or HP and also GP (which stood for "Grand Puissance") and referred to by all those names at one time or another. HP is essentially an improved version of Colt 1911 design. Swinging link replaced with fixed cam, which was less prone to wear. Chambered for 9mm Parabellum and has a 13-round detachable magazine. Only drawback to the design, that the trigger pull is not as fine as that of the 1911, as there is a transfer bar instead of stirrup arrangement. This is necessary, due to increased magazine capacity resulting in thicker grip. Barrel is 4.75" in length. External hammer with manual and magazine safety. Available with various finishes and sight options. Furnished with shoulder stock. Model 1935 used by many countries as their service pistol, as there are many variations. We list these versions and their approximate values.

Pre-War Commercial Model

Found with sliding tangent rear sight and slotted for detachable shoulder stock. Manufactured from 1935 until 1940.

Tangent Sight Version

NOTE: Wood holster stock add 50 percent.

—	2000	1800	1500	1000	400

Pre-War Military Contract

Model 1935 adopted by many countries as a service pistol. Following, is a list:

Belgium

—	3000	2600	2000	600	375

Canada and China

—	2500	2000	950	650	400

Great Britain

—	2500	1700	1000	550	325

Estonia

—	3000	2600	2000	600	375

Holland

—	3000	2600	2000	650	400

Latvia

—	3000	2600	2000	775	500

Lithuania

—	2800	2000	1200	650	400

Romania

—	3000	2600	2000	775	500

German Military Pistole Model 640(b)

In 1940, Germany occupied Belgium and took over the FN plant. Production of Model 1935 continued, with Germany taking the output. FN plant was assigned production code "ch" and many thousands were produced. Finish on these Nazi guns runs from as fine as Pre-war Commercial series to downright crude. Possible to see how war was progressing for Germany by finish on their weapons. One must be cautious with some of these guns as there have been fakes noted, with their backstraps cut for shoulder stocks, producing what would appear to be a more expensive variation. Individual appraisal should be secured if any doubt exists.

Fixed Sight Model

—	1000	750	400	300	250

Tangent Sight Model

50,000 manufactured.

—	1500	1000	700	550	400

	NIB	EXC.	V.G.	GOOD	FAIR	POOR

Captured Pre-war Commercial Model

These pistols were taken over when plant was occupied. Slotted for stocks and have tangent sights. Few produced between serial number 48,000 and 52,000. All noted have WA613 Nazi proof mark. Beware of fakes!

	—	1700	1400	1150	750	500

Post-War Military Contract

Manufactured from 1946, they embody some design changes—such as improved heat treating and barrel locking. Pistols produced after 1950, do not have barrels that can interchange with earlier model pistols. Earliest models have an "A" prefix on serial number and do not have the magazine safety. Pistols were produced for many countries and there were many thousands manufactured.

Fixed Sight

	—	750	425	375	300	250

Tangent Sight

	—	1000	675	575	400	300

Slotted and Tangent Sight

	—	1500	1050	750	500	400

Post-War Commercial Model

Introduced in 1950 and 1954. Those imported into U.S.A. are marked Browning Arms Co. These pistols have commercial polished finish.

Fixed Sight

	—	850	500	350	300	250

Tangent Sight

	—	1000	650	500	400	350

Slotted and Tangent Sight

	—	1500	1100	800	550	450

RIFLES

Model 1889

	—	350	250	200	125	100

Model 1949 or SAFN 49

	—	600	500	300	225	150

Model 30-11 Sniper Rifle

	—	5000	4500	3500	2750	2000

FN-FAL

50.00—21" Rifle Model

	3000	2750	2250	2000	1850	1000

50.63—18" Paratrooper Model

	3800	3350	2950	2750	2450	1100

50.64—21" Paratrooper Model

	3300	3000	2700	2200	1900	1000

50.41—Synthetic Butt H-Bar

	2800	2400	2000	1800	1200	1000

50.42—Wood Butt H-Bar

	2800	2400	2000	1800	1200	1000

FN-FAL "G" Series (Type I Receiver)

Standard

	6500	5000	4000	3000	2000	1000

Lightweight

	6500	5000	4000	3000	2000	1000

FN CAL

	7000	6500	5000	3000	1500	1000

	NIB	EXC.	V.G.	GOOD	FAIR	POOR

FNC

NOTE: Prices are for Belgian-made guns only.

Standard

Fixed stock, 16" or 18" barrel.

NIB	EXC.	V.G.	GOOD	FAIR	POOR
3000	2800	2500	2000	1500	1000

Paratrooper Model

Folding stock, 16" or 18" barrel.

NIB	EXC.	V.G.	GOOD	FAIR	POOR
3000	2800	2500	2000	1500	1000

Musketeer Sporting Rifles

Bolt-action rifle built on Mauser-action. Chambered for various popular cartridges. Has a 24" barrel and blued, with checkered walnut stock. Manufactured between 1947 and 1963.

NIB	EXC.	V.G.	GOOD	FAIR	POOR
—	450	350	300	250	200

Deluxe Sporter

Higher-grade version of Musketeer, with same general specifications. Manufactured between 1947 and 1963.

NIB	EXC.	V.G.	GOOD	FAIR	POOR
—	550	450	400	275	200

FN Supreme

Chambered for popular standard calibers. Has a 24" barrel, with an aperture sight and checkered walnut stock. Manufactured between 1957 and 1975.

NIB	EXC.	V.G.	GOOD	FAIR	POOR
—	800	650	500	450	400

Supreme Magnum Model

Similar to standard Supreme, except chambered for .264 Win. Magnum, 7mm Rem. Magnum and .300 Win. Magnum. Furnished with recoil pad. Manufactured between same years as standard model.

NIB	EXC.	V.G.	GOOD	FAIR	POOR
—	800	650	500	400	400

FAIRBANKS, A. B.
Boston, Massachusetts

Fairbanks All Metal Pistol

Odd pistol was produced of all metal. A one-piece cast brass frame, handle, an iron barrel and lock system. Chambered for .33-caliber and utilizes percussion ignition system. Barrel lengths noted are 3" to 10". Barrels are marked "Fairbanks Boston. Cast Steel". Manufactured between 1838 and 1841.

NIB	EXC.	V.G.	GOOD	FAIR	POOR
—	—	1050	350	150	75

FALCON FIREARMS
Northridge, California

Portsider

Copy of Colt 1911. Built for left-handed individual. Constructed of stainless steel and similar in all other respects to Colt. Introduced in 1986. A scarce 1911.

NIB	EXC.	V.G.	GOOD	FAIR	POOR
700	575	450	375	300	225

Portsider Set

Matching serial numbered pair. Consisting of a left- and right-handed version of this model. It was cased. Only 100 manufactured in 1986 and 1987.

NIB	EXC.	V.G.	GOOD	FAIR	POOR
1400	1250	1000	750	600	475

Gold Falcon

Frame machined from solid 17-karat gold. Slide is stainless steel and sights have diamond inlays. Engraved to customer's order. Only 50 manufactured.

NIB	EXC.	V.G.	GOOD	FAIR	POOR
50000	30000	25000	15000	7500	700

FAMARS, A. & S.
Brescia, Italy

A.Famars shotgun is one of the world's finest and was available on a custom order basis. This makes it quite difficult to accurately establish values in a book of this nature. We list them and give an estimated value in their basic form only. The company ceased production in 2012.

	NIB	EXC.	V.G.	GOOD	FAIR	POOR

Engraving Pattern Descriptions (Older Discontinued Patterns)

S2—Traditional fully engraved fine English scroll, with coverage highlighting selected areas of the receiver and fore-end metal. Wood grade is AA.

S3—Traditional hand-engraved scroll, with some open areas around the scroll coverage on the receiver and fore-end metal. Wood grade is AAA.

S4—Traditional full coverage, intricate and high in detail. Patterns may be English, German or game scene. Wood grade is AAAA.

S5—Grade S4 patterns with animals inlaid in 24k gold. Wood grade is AAAA.

S4E—Extremely high detail scenes and elaborate ornamental work, where the subject matter is selected by the customer. Wood grade is AAAAA.

S5E—Similar to the S4E level, but with raised or flush gold inlay work. Wood grade is AAAAA.

SXO—The best work by the world's best engravers. Museum quality. Wood grade is AAAAAA.

Zeus

Engraved side-by-side boxlock in 12-, 20-, 28-gauge and .410 bore. **NOTE:** Add 10 percent for smaller gauges.

In the white

NIB	EXC.	V.G.	GOOD	FAIR	POOR
19000	12000	9000	6500	4750	750

D2 pattern

NIB	EXC.	V.G.	GOOD	FAIR	POOR
20000	12000	9000	6500	4750	750

S3 pattern

NIB	EXC.	V.G.	GOOD	FAIR	POOR
22000	20000	12000	9000	6500	900

Tribute

Engraved side-by-side droplock, offered in 12- or 20-gauge.

In the white

NIB	EXC.	V.G.	GOOD	FAIR	POOR
21400	20800	12000	9000	6500	900

D2 pattern

NIB	EXC.	V.G.	GOOD	FAIR	POOR
22600	20500	12000	9000	6500	900

S3 pattern

NIB	EXC.	V.G.	GOOD	FAIR	POOR
24300	22000	12000	9000	6500	900

Venus

Side-by-side sidelock shotgun, with choice of engraving patterns and coverage. Offered in 12-, 20-, 28-gauge or .410 bore.

In the white

NIB	EXC.	V.G.	GOOD	FAIR	POOR
32700	30500	20000	12000	9000	900

D2 pattern

NIB	EXC.	V.G.	GOOD	FAIR	POOR
33900	31500	—	—	—	—

D3 pattern

NIB	EXC.	V.G.	GOOD	FAIR	POOR
37000	10500	—	—	—	—

D4 pattern

NIB	EXC.	V.G.	GOOD	FAIR	POOR
42800	39000	—	—	—	—

D5 pattern

NIB	EXC.	V.G.	GOOD	FAIR	POOR
48200	42000	—	—	—	—

D4E pattern

NIB	EXC.	V.G.	GOOD	FAIR	POOR
53500	47500	—	—	—	—

D5E pattern

NIB	EXC.	V.G.	GOOD	FAIR	POOR
58500	51500	—	—	—	—

DXO pattern

NIB	EXC.	V.G.	GOOD	FAIR	POOR
85000	55000	—	—	—	—

Veneri

Side-by-side sidelock shotgun.

NIB	EXC.	V.G.	GOOD	FAIR	POOR
32000	30000	—	—	—	—

D2 pattern

NIB	EXC.	V.G.	GOOD	FAIR	POOR
32700	30500	—	—	—	—

	NIB	EXC.	V.G.	GOOD	FAIR	POOR

Jorema Royal

An over/under shotgun with sidelocks. Offered in 12-, 20-, 28-gauge and .410 bore. **NOTE:** Add 15 percent for smaller gauges.

In the white

	32700	26000	—	—	—	—

S2 pattern

	33900	20000	—	—	—	—

S3 pattern

	37300	29500	—	—	—	—

S4 pattern

	42900	33500	—	—	—	—

S5 pattern

	48200	29500	—	—	—	—

S4E pattern

	53500	42500	—	—	—	—

S5E pattern

	53500	42500	—	—	—	—

SXO pattern

	85000	66500	—	—	—	—

Excaliber BL

An over/under shotgun, with single trigger and removable trigger group. Offered in 12-, 20-, 28-gauge and .410 bore.

	11800	6500	—	—	—	—

Excalibur BL Extra

Finer engraving than standard.

	15455	8900	—	—	—	—

Excalibur BL Prestige

Finer engraving than BL Extra.

	17820	10750	—	—	—	—

Excalibur BLX

Over/under shotgun with sideplates.

	11150	9000	—	—	—	—

Excalibur BLX Extra

Same as above, with finer engraving.

	16759	14000	—	—	—	—

Excalibur BLX Prestige

Finer engraving than BLX Extra.

	16900	13750	—	—	—	—

Excalibur SL

Over/under shotgun with sidelocks.

	26125	14800	—	—	—	—

Excalibur SL Extra

Same as above, with finer engraving.

	30000	16000	—	—	—	—

Excalibur SL Prestige

Finer engraving than SL Extra.

	33000	18000	—	—	—	—

Excalibur Express

An over/under double rifle in calibers from 7x65R to .375 H&H.

	20196	11500	—	—	—	—

	NIB	EXC.	V.G.	GOOD	FAIR	POOR

Excalibur Express Extra

Same as above, with finer engraving.

	27060	12000	—	—	—	—

Excalibur Express Prestige

Finer engraving than Express Extra.

	32065	15250	—	—	—	—

African Express

Side-by-side boxlock double rifle. Calibers from .22 Long Rifle to .600 NE.

	34000	17500	—	—	—	—

Venus Express Professional

Side-by-side double rifle with sidelocks.

	45000	34500	—	—	—	—

Venus Express Extra

Side-by-side double rifle with sidelocks. Calibers from .375 H&H to .500 NE.

	95750	50000	—	—	—	—

FARROW ARMS CO.
Holyoke, Massachusetts
Mason, Tennessee

Farrow Falling Block Rifle

Designed by W.M. Farrow, a target shooter, who had worked on Ballard rifles for the Marlin company. Farrow rifles are chambered for various calibers and have barrel lengths from 28"- 36" of octagonal configuration. Feature tang sights and are either all blued or have a nickel-plated receiver. Stocks are walnut. Two grades offered, that varied according to grade of wood used. Rifles are quite scarce on today's market. Number manufactured between 1885 and 1900 is unknown.

No. 1 Model

Fancy walnut with checkering and Schutzen buttplate.

	—	—	13500	4500	1950	750

No. 2 Model

Plainer wood and no checkering.

	—	—	11000	3300	1600	500

FAUSTI, STEFANO
Italy

Fausti has been manufacturing quality over/under and side-by-side shotguns in Italy, for the European market since 1948. In 2009, the company established an office in Fredericksburg, Virginia and now imports a wide range of models

OVER/UNDER SHOTGUNS

Low-profile boxlock design scaled to various gauges. All standard barrel lengths with five choke tubes (.410 has fixed M/F). Offered in 12-, 16-, 20-, 28-gauges and .410 bore in four grades: Caledon (shown), Caledon SL, Class and Class SL, each with increased level of walnut laser engraving and inlays. Features include automatic ejectors, single selective trigger, rounded pistol-grip. SL models have false side plates. Prices shown are for 12- and 20-gauge models. **NOTE:** Add $500 for 16-, 28-gauge or .410 bore.

Caledon

	1800	1450	1200	950	600	400

Caledon SL

	2500	2000	1600	1350	900	500

Class

	2200	1750	1400	1100	750	500

Class SL

	2900	2250	1700	1450	1000	500

NIB	EXC.	V.G.	GOOD	FAIR	POOR

Round Body

Similar to other over/under models, except built on Fausti-designed rounded receiver. AAA grade oil finished walnut stock. Not available in 12-gauge. Prices shown are for 20-gauge. **NOTE:** Add $500 for 16-, 28-gauge or .410 bore.

NIB	EXC.	V.G.	GOOD	FAIR	POOR
3750	3200	2600	2000	1200	500

MAGNIFICENT SERIES

Higher grade series with AAA+ walnut stock and deep-sculpted engraving. Offered in a field version and sporting clays model (shown). Prices shown are for 12- or 20-gauge. **NOTE:** Add $500 for 16-, 28-gauge or .410 bore.

Magnificent Field

NIB	EXC.	V.G.	GOOD	FAIR	POOR
4500	3600	3000	2400	1600	700

Magnificent Sporting

NIB	EXC.	V.G.	GOOD	FAIR	POOR
5400	4500	3750	3000	2000	900

SIDE-BY-SIDE SHOTGUNS

Model DEA

Built on a low boxlock action, with modified Anson & Deeley mechanism. Straight-grip AAA-grade oil-finished walnut stock. Automatic ejectors, non-selective single trigger. Made in 12-, 16-, 20-, 28-gauges and .410 bore. Also offered as Duetto model, with interchangeable 28-gauge and .410 bore barrel sets. Prices shown are for 12- or 20-gauge. **NOTE:** Add $500 for other gauges; $1800 for Duetto model.

NIB	EXC.	V.G.	GOOD	FAIR	POOR
3000	2500	2000	1600	1000	500

RIFLES

Classic Express Rifle

Over/under design, with oil finished walnut stock, automatic ejectors and choice of double or single trigger. Calibers are .30-06, .444 Marlin, .45-70, 30R Blaser, 8x57 JRS and 9.3x74R. Barrels are 24" with adjustable fiber optic sight.

NIB	EXC.	V.G.	GOOD	FAIR	POOR
4500	3600	3000	2400	1600	700

FAYETTEVILLE ARMORY PISTOLS AND RIFLES
Fayetteville, North Carolina

In 1861, the U.S. Arsenal at Fayetteville, North Carolina, was seized by officials of that state and later turned over to the government of Confederate States of America. While still controlled by the state of North Carolina, a number of inferior flintlock arms were altered at the arsenal from flint to percussion, including a number of U.S. M1836 pistols and U.S. M1819 Hall rifles (the latter also shortened and remodeled into cavalry carbines). In accordance with an agreement between the governors of Virginia and North Carolina, rifle machinery seized at the former U.S. Armory at Harpers Ferry, Virginia, was also sent to Fayetteville, where in 1862 the Confederacy began construction of rifles modeled after U.S. M1855 rifle. Production continued until 1865, when the advance of Sherman's armies necessitated evacuation of the armory.

Fayetteville Armory Percussion Pistols (U.S. M1836 Pistols, Altered)

Overall length 13.25"; barrel length 8.5"; caliber .54. Markings: same as U.S. M1836 contact pistols, i.e. the locks either marked with eagle head over "A. WATERS/MILBURY MS./(date)" or "US/R. JOHNSON/MIDDN CONN./(date)" and various barrel proofmarks; also occasionally marked "N. CAROLINA".

Fayetteville Armory altered approximately 900 U.S. M1836 pistols from flintlock to percussion. These arms were altered by enlarging the flint touchhole and screwing in a cylindrical drum in place of the pan and frizzen. Distinguishing feature of Fayetteville alteration is the clean-out screw at face of cylinder and "S" shaped hammer, not unlike that used on post-1862 dated rifles.

NIB	EXC.	V.G.	GOOD	FAIR	POOR
—	—	3250	1350	950	400

Fayetteville Armory Rifles (Types I through IV)

Overall length 49.125"; barrel length 33"; caliber .58. Markings: on barrel, an eagle over "C.S.A./ FAYETTEVILLE" forward of the hammer and date on rounded tail. "CSA" also found on buttplates; date on top of barrel; proofmarks (eagle head, "V" and "P") on left quarter of barrel near breech.

From 1862 to early 1865, Fayetteville Armory produced four variants of old U.S. M1855 rifle on machinery that had been lent to North Carolina by Virginia, after its capture in April 1861. Earliest 1862 production (Type I) utilized unmilled lockplates captured at Harpers Ferry

NIB	EXC.	V.G.	GOOD	FAIR	POOR

and distinguished by having a "hump" (where the Maynard primer would have been milled) that extends to arc of hammer. Type II production utilized newly made locks received from Richmond during balance of 1862; they had a relatively low "hump" whose upper surface matched contour of stock. By end of 1862, Fayetteville was producing its own lock, the plate of which resembled U.S. M1861 rifle musket, but with a distinctive "S" shaped hammer. This lock distinguishes both type III and type IV production. All rifles made through 1863 continued to bear a saber bayonet lug on right side of barrel. In 1864, however, this was eliminated in favor of a triangular socket bayonet. Absence of the saber bayonet lug and remodeled front sight distinguishes type IV production. Because the barrel machinery went to Richmond, production at Fayetteville was continually hindered, seldom reaching more than 300 per month in three years that Fayetteville rifle was manufactured. (Note: Rarity of Type I production will usually generate a premium for that variant.)

NIB	EXC.	V.G.	GOOD	FAIR	POOR
—	—	27500	10500	4000	800

FEATHER INDUSTRIES, INC.
Trinidad, Colorado

AT-22
Blowback-operated semi-automatic chambered for .22 LR cartridge. Removable shrouded 17" barrel and folding metal stock. Adjustable sights and finish is black. Detachable 20-round magazine. Introduced in 1986.

NIB	EXC.	V.G.	GOOD	FAIR	POOR
450	200	175	150	110	75

AT-9
Similar to AT-22, except chambered for 9mm Parabellum cartridge. Has a 16" barrel and 32-round magazine. Introduced in 1988.

NIB	EXC.	V.G.	GOOD	FAIR	POOR
800	675	300	250	175	125

KG-9
A 9mm semi-automatic assault rifle. Introduced in 1989.

NIB	EXC.	V.G.	GOOD	FAIR	POOR
725	500	425	375	300	250

KG-22
Similar in appearance to KG-9, except chambered for .22 LR. Has a 20-round detachable magazine. Introduced in 1989.

NIB	EXC.	V.G.	GOOD	FAIR	POOR
400	275	225	175	125	100

SAR-180
Current incarnation of old American 180, which was manufactured in Austria a number of years ago. Chambered for .22 LR and has a 17.5" barrel. Blowback-operated semi-automatic, that has a 165-round drum magazine that sits on top of the action on flat side. Rear sight is adjustable. Finish is blued, with walnut stock, pistol-grip and fore-end. Model revived by Feather Industries in 1989.

NIB	EXC.	V.G.	GOOD	FAIR	POOR
750	675	600	475	300	200

Mini-AT
Blowback-operated semi-automatic pistol, chambered for .22 LR cartridge. A 5.5"-barreled version of AT-22 rifle and has a 20-round magazine. Manufactured between 1986 and 1989.

NIB	EXC.	V.G.	GOOD	FAIR	POOR
375	250	175	150	125	100

Guardian Angel
Two-shot over/under derringer-style pistol. Chambered for 9mm Parabellum. Can be converted to fire .38 Super cartridge. Constructed of stainless steel and has an internal hammer and fully enclosed trigger. Introduced in 1988.

NIB	EXC.	V.G.	GOOD	FAIR	POOR
225	125	100	75	50	40

FEDERAL ENGINEERING CORP.
Chicago, Illinois

XC-220
Blowback-operated semi-automatic rifle, chambered for .22 LR cartridge. Has a 16.5" barrel and steel receiver that is blued. Stock is black synthetic. Introduced in 1984.

NIB	EXC.	V.G.	GOOD	FAIR	POOR
650	450	375	225	175	125

XC-450
Similar in appearance to XC-220, except chambered for .45 ACP cartridge. Has a 30-round detachable magazine.

NIB	EXC.	V.G.	GOOD	FAIR	POOR
750	525	450	400	300	250

	NIB	EXC.	V.G.	GOOD	FAIR	POOR

XC-900

A 9mm Parabellum version of same basic firearm. Has a 32-round magazine. Introduced in 1984.

	750	525	450	400	300	250

FEDERAL ORDNANCE, INC.
South El Monte, California

An importer, as well as a manufacturer, that basically fabricates new and custom firearms out of existing older military parts. Firearms they import are military surplus weapons. Firearms covered here are of Federal Ordnance manufacture.

M-14 Semi-Automatic

Semi-automatic version of M-14 service rifle. Constructed of a newly manufactured receiver, that has no selector and select surplus G.I. parts. Rifle is refinished to original specifications and furnished with a 20-round magazine. Has either a wood or fiberglass stock. Introduced in 1986. Although this model is a battle rifle and falls into the category affected by, wild price fluctuations, we have been experiencing prices for this gun staying fairly stable due to a fairly constant supply. Manufactured since 1986.

—	750	600	550	450	375

Model 714 Broomhandle Mauser

Remanufactured C96-type pistol, chambered for 7.63mm or 9mm Parabellum. Utilizes a new manufactured frame and surplus parts. Features a 10-round detachable magazine, adjustable sights and walnut grips. Manufactured 1986 to 1991. Bolo Model, with a smaller grip, produced in 1988 only.

650	500	400	300	250	100

Model 713 Mauser Carbine

A 16"-barreled version of Mauser, with fixed walnut stock. Standard magazine and chambered for 7.63mm or 9mm Parabellum. Refinished and introduced in 1987.

—	1250	1000	900	700	575

Model 713 Deluxe

Chambered for 7.63mm. Has a 16" barrel, with detachable shoulder stock made of deluxe walnut. Modified to accept detachable magazines and furnished with two 20-shot units. Has a 1000-meter adjustable sight and furnished in a fitted leather case. Only 1,500 manufactured in 1986.

2000	1750	1500	1250	1000	800

Standard Broomhandle

Refurbished surplus C-96 Mauser pistol, with new 7.63mm or 9mm barrel. All springs are replaced and entire gun refinished. Furnished with shoulder stock/holster of Chinese manufacture.

800	650	525	450	350	275

Ranger 1911A1

Federal Ordnance's version of 1911A1 Colt service pistol. Made of all steel, chambered for .45 ACP, has checkered walnut grips and phiosphate-style finish. Introduced in 1988.

500	375	325	275	225	150

FEG (FEGYVER ES GAZKESZULEKGYAR)
Budapest, Hungary

Rudolf Frommer, was a first-class engineer, who became associated with Fegyvergyar in 1896. In 1900, he became manager and held that position until his retirement in 1935. He died one year later in 1936. His designs were successful and prolific. They were used militarily and sold on the commercial market as well.

PISTOLS

Model 1901

An odd pistol that was not successful at all. Chambered for an 8mm cartridge, that was the forerunner of 8mm Roth Steyr. Has a long slender barrel, which was actually a collar with the barrel within. A rotary bolt, external hammer and is recoil-operated. There is a 10-round integral magazine and is loaded from top via a stripper clip. Manufactured from 1903 to 1905.

—	2450	1795	1000	700	350

NIB	EXC.	V.G.	GOOD	FAIR	POOR

Model 1906

Improved version of 1901, chambered for 7.65mm Roth-Sauer cartridge. For all intents and purposes, the same action; on later models a detachable 10-round magazine was adopted. Manufactured between 1906 and 1910 in small quantities.

NIB	EXC.	V.G.	GOOD	FAIR	POOR
—	2300	1750	1000	700	350

Model 1910

Final version in this series of pistols, with the addition of grip safety. Chambered for 7.65mm Browning.

NIB	EXC.	V.G.	GOOD	FAIR	POOR
—	2600	1950	1100	700	350

Frommer Stop Model 1912

Semi-automatic pistol in caliber 7.65mm or 9mmK. Unusual, in that it operates on a long recoil system. Frommer is stamped on the slide, as well as Frommer Stop logo on each side of wood or plastic grip plates.

NIB	EXC.	V.G.	GOOD	FAIR	POOR
—	450	300	225	150	50

Frommer Baby Model

Smaller version of Stop Model 1912,. Designed as a pocket pistol, with 2" barrel and chambered for same calibers. Manufactured at the same time as Stop Model.

NIB	EXC.	V.G.	GOOD	FAIR	POOR
—	375	250	200	125	75

Frommer Lilliput

Pocket pistol chambered for 6.35mm and outwardly resembles Baby. Actually a simple blowback-operated semi-automatic pistol. A good deal less complex to produce. Introduced in 1921.

NIB	EXC.	V.G.	GOOD	FAIR	POOR
—	350	225	175	125	75

Model 1929

Semi-automatic pistol in 9mmK. Based on Browning designed blowback-action. Pistol replaced earlier models. A few of these pistols made in .22 LR.

NIB	EXC.	V.G.	GOOD	FAIR	POOR
—	450	350	225	175	100

.22 Caliber

NIB	EXC.	V.G.	GOOD	FAIR	POOR
—	975	825	725	450	250

Model 1937

Semi-automatic pistol in caliber 7.65mm or 9mmK. Pistol was designed by Frommer and manufactured by Femaru. Also known as Model 1937.

Nazi Proofed 7.65mm Version

NIB	EXC.	V.G.	GOOD	FAIR	POOR
—	450	350	225	175	100

9mm Short Hungarian Military Version

NIB	EXC.	V.G.	GOOD	FAIR	POOR
—	425	325	200	175	100

Model R-9

Copy of Browning Hi-Power semi-automatic pistol. Chambered for 9mm Parabellum and has a 4.75" barrel. Frame is steel and finish is blued, with checkered wood grips. Detachable magazine holds 13 shots and sights are fixed. Imported in 1986 and 1987 only.

NIB	EXC.	V.G.	GOOD	FAIR	POOR
—	375	250	225	175	100

Model AP-9

Pistol has been manufactured in Hungary, under a number of different names. Known as AP-9, Walam 48, AP-66 and Attila. Semi-automatic pistol in calibers 7.65mm and 9mmK. Similar to Walther Model PP. Has a 7-round magazine and alloy frame. Various styles of grip plates.

NIB	EXC.	V.G.	GOOD	FAIR	POOR
—	325	200	150	100	50

Model PPH

Copy of Walther PP, chambered for .380 ACP cartridge. Double-action semi-automatic, with 3" barrel. Alloy frame, blued finish, with thumb rest checkered plastic grips. Imported in 1986 and 1987 only.

NIB	EXC.	V.G.	GOOD	FAIR	POOR
—	350	200	175	100	75

Model B9R

Semi-automatic pistol, chambered for .380 ACP cartridge. Fitted with a 4" barrel. Features double-/single-action trigger operation. Frame is alloy and weighs about 25 oz. Magazine capacity 15 rounds.

NIB	EXC.	V.G.	GOOD	FAIR	POOR
	375	225	200	175	125	75

	NIB	EXC.	V.G.	GOOD	FAIR	POOR

Model PA-63

Same as above, but chambered for 9mm Makarov (9x18mm) cartridge.

	NIB	EXC.	V.G.	GOOD	FAIR	POOR
	—	275	175	125	100	50

Model FP-9

Copy of Browning Hi-Power pistol. Chambered for 9mm Luger cartridge. Features walnut checkered grip, with blue finish. Barrel 5" and overall length 8". Top of slide features full-length ventilated rib, with fixed sights. Weighs 35 oz. Magazine capacity 14 rounds.

	NIB	EXC.	V.G.	GOOD	FAIR	POOR
	300	175	150	125	90	70

Model P9R

Similar to model above and follows Browning Hi-Power lines, with exception of ventilated rib. Barrel length 4.66". Pistol offered in blue or chrome finish. Magazine capacity 15 rounds.

Blue

	NIB	EXC.	V.G.	GOOD	FAIR	POOR
	450	400	325	250	200	150

Chrome

	NIB	EXC.	V.G.	GOOD	FAIR	POOR
	475	425	350	285	235	160

Model P9RK

Similar to model above. Fitted with 4.12" barrel and 7.5" overall length. Finger grooves on front strap and backstrap is serrated. Weighs about 34 oz.

	NIB	EXC.	V.G.	GOOD	FAIR	POOR
	300	200	150	125	90	70

RIFLES

SA-2000-M

Introduced in 1999. Model is a semi-automatic rifle, chambered for 7.62x39mm or .223 cartridge. Fitted with detachable 10-round magazine, synthetic stock and muzzle-brake.

	NIB	EXC.	V.G.	GOOD	FAIR	POOR
	575	450	350	250	150	95

AMD-65 AK47

Hungarian AK-47 clone, chambered in 7.62xc39. Fixed or folding-stock versions are available.

	NIB	EXC.	V.G.	GOOD	FAIR	POOR
	650	495	375	275	175	125

FEINWERKBAU
Oberndorf, Germany

Known predominately for production of high quality, extremely accurate air rifles and pistols. They also produce some of the most accurate target .22-caliber firearms in the world today. These firearms are listed:

Model 2000 Universal

Single-shot bolt-action target rifle, chambered for .22 rimfire cartridge. Has a 26.5" barrel, with adjustable aperture sights and fully adjustable trigger. There were four different stock configurations offered, with stippled pistol grips and forearms. An electronic trigger was available as a $450 option. Discontinued in 1988.

	NIB	EXC.	V.G.	GOOD	FAIR	POOR
	—	1800	1250	950	650	550

Mini 2000

Has a 22" barrel. Electronic trigger available at additional cost.

	NIB	EXC.	V.G.	GOOD	FAIR	POOR
	—	1550	1050	850	550	450

Running Boar Rifle

Has a thumbhole stock, with an adjustable cheekpiece. Furnished without sights. Specially designed for offhand Running Boar Competitions.

	NIB	EXC.	V.G.	GOOD	FAIR	POOR
	—	1800	1250	950	650	550

Match Rifle

Has 26.75" barrel and adjustable cheekpiece stock.

	NIB	EXC.	V.G.	GOOD	FAIR	POOR
	—	1650	1095	850	550	450

Model 2600 Ultra Match Free Rifle

Similar to Model 2000, with laminated thumbhole stock. Heavy 26" barrel, fully adjustable sights and trigger. Offered with electronic trigger for an additional $400. Introduced in 1986.

	NIB	EXC.	V.G.	GOOD	FAIR	POOR
	1950	1400	1150	850	650	550

	NIB	EXC.	V.G.	GOOD	FAIR	POOR

FEMARU
Budapest, Hungary

Hungary became a communist satellite in the mid-1950s. At this time, Femaru company was designated to replace the firm of Fegyvergyar, as the official Hungarian arms manufacturer. The products are of good quality.

Model 37

Semi-automatic pistol built in both 7.65mm and 9mm Short calibers. Well designed pistol of quality construction. Fitted with a grip safety and exposed hammer. Hungarian military adopted the pistol in 1937. Produced until late 1940s. Early guns were marked "Femaru Fegyver es Gepgyar RT Budapest". During the war, Nazi code for these guns was "jhv". The 9mm models have a 7-round magazine; 7.65 models an 8-round magazine. During World War II the Germans designed this pistol the "Pistol Mod 37 Kal 7.65 (Ung)". **NOTE:** Add 75 percent for Nazi proofed examples.

—	350	275	225	150	100

Hege

Complete copy of Walther PP. Chambered for 7.65mm. Manufactured to be sold by Hegewaffen of Germany. Slide is so marked along with Pegasus in a circle. Designation "AP 66 Cal.7.65" also appears. Pistol intended for export sales in U.S. and other western countries.

—	350	225	175	125	100

Tokagypt

15,000 of these pistols built in 1958, under contract for the Egyptian army. Modified version of Soviet TT-33 Tokarev, chambered for 9mm Parabellum, with a safety added. Balance were sold commercially, some under trademark "Firebird".

—	475	350	275	200	125

Walam

Another Walther PP copy of excellent quality. Chambered for 9mm short or .380 ACP. Pistols sold on commercial market—some designated Model 48.

—	350	225	175	125	100

FERLIB
Gardone V.T., Italy

Model F.VI

High-grade side-by-side shotgun. Chambered for all gauges and essentially custom-ordered. Available in various barrel lengths and chokes. Anson and Deeley boxlock-action, double triggers and automatic ejectors. Action is case-colored and stock is hand-checkered select walnut. Single-selective triggers are available for an additional $375. **NOTE:** 28-gauge and .410 bore add 10 percent.

4750	3600	—	—	—	—

Model F.VII

Has scroll-engraved coin-finished frame, but otherwise similar to Model F.VI. Single trigger option and small gauge premium are same.

12000	8500	—	—	—	—

Model F.VII/SC

More deluxe version, with gold inlays and game scene-engraved receiver. Options and premium are same.

13000	9500	—	—	—	—

Model F.VII Sideplate

Features false sideplates that are completely covered with game scene engraving. Model is standard, with single-selective trigger. Small gauge premium is applicable.

15000	10500	—	—	—	—

Model F.VII/SC Sideplate

False sideplate model, with gold inlays accenting the full coverage engraving. **NOTE:** 28-gauge and .410 add 10 percent.

16000	11500	—	—	—	—

Hammer Gun

Features boxlock action with external hammers. Other features are custom ordered to purchaser's specifications.

20000	14500	—	—	—	—

NIB	EXC.	V.G.	GOOD	FAIR	POOR

FERRY, ANDREWS & CO.
Stafford, Connecticut

Under Hammer Pistol

Boot pistol chambered for .36-caliber percussion. Has a 3" part-round, part-octagonal barrel. Similar to other under hammer pistols that were produced in Connecticut and Massachusetts. Top strap marked "Andrews Ferry & Co." Number manufactured unknown. Produced in the 1850s.

—	—	1550	700	395	125

FIALA ARMS COMPANY
New Haven, Connecticut

Fiala Repeating Target Pistol

Different type of pistol than what is commonly encountered. Outwardly it resembles a semi-automatic Colt Woodsman; in actuality it is a manually operated firearm that must be cycled by hand after every shot. Chambered for .22 rimfire and offered with interchangeable barrels in lengths of 3", 7.5" and 20". Also offered a detachable buttstock. Finish is blued and grips are found in both smooth and ribbed walnut. Rear sight is a square-notched blade that tips up into an elevation-adjustable peep sight. Marked "Fiala Arms and Equipment Co. Inc. / New Haven Conn. / Patents Pending" on right side of frame behind grip and Model 1920/Made in U.S.A. on right side of frame above trigger guard. Left side of frame marked "FIALA ARMS" above image of polar bear with "TRADE MARK" below polar bear in area above trigger guard. Pistol furnished in one of three variations of cases that were optionally available: canvas case, black leatherette case velvet-lined and fitted with a lock and key, and tan leather version of leatherette case. A fixed 7.5" barrel variation was also produced. A 7.5" smoothbore barrel was cataloged as a silencer. Some 20" smoothbore barrels were produced. Some pistols bear the names "Columbia Arms Company" and "Botwinik Brothers". Government has classified this pistol with its stock as a "Curio or Relic" and in its complete state a very desirable collectible. **NOTE:** See also Schall & Co.

Complete, Three Barrels, Stock, Tools, and Case

—	2500	2100	1250	675	550

Gun Only

—	800	700	450	275	175

FINNISH LION
Valmet, Sweden

ISU Target Rifle

Single-shot bolt-action rifle, chambered for .22 rimfire cartridge. Has a 27" heavy barrel and target stock with accessories. Features target adjustable sights. Manufactured between 1966 and 1977.

—	475	325	275	200	125

Champion Free Rifle

Has a 29" heavy barrel and double-set triggers. Otherwise similar to ISU model. Manufactured between 1965 and 1972.

—	900	750	600	375	275

Match Rifle

Similar to Champion rifle, with thumbhole stock and adjustable buttplate. Manufactured between 1937 and 1972.

—	900	750	600	375	275

FIOCCHI OF AMERICA, INC.
Ozark, Missouri
See—Pardini and A. Zoli

Imports above firearms. They are listed in their own respective sections.

FIREARMS INTERNATIONAL
Washington, D.C.
See—Star and Garcia

Once importer of Star Model D, as it was sold in U.S.A. They also imported various other .25-caliber Colt copies, that are not considered collectible and would be valued in the $150-and-under range. For the .22/.410 Bronco, see "Garcia".

	NIB	EXC.	V.G.	GOOD	FAIR	POOR

FIRESTORM
Argentina

Firestorm .22 LR

Semi-automatic pistol, chambered for .22 LR cartridge. Ten-round magazine capacity. Matte blue finish or duotone.

NIB	EXC.	V.G.	GOOD	FAIR	POOR
250	185	135	100	75	45

Firestorm .32

Double-action semi-automatic chambered for .32 with 10+1 capacity. Blued, 3.5" barrel, weight 23 oz. Fixed sights and rubber grips. Introduced 2006.

NIB	EXC.	V.G.	GOOD	FAIR	POOR
275	215	155	125	95	50

Firestorm .380

Semi-automatic double-action pistol. Chambered for .380 ACP cartridge and fitted with 3.5" barrel. Fixed three-dot combat sights. Matte blue or duotone finish. Magazine capacity 7 rounds. Weight about 23 oz.

NIB	EXC.	V.G.	GOOD	FAIR	POOR
295	225	195	150	95	50

Mini Firestorm 9mm

This 9mm semi-automatic double-action pistol, fitted with 3.5" barrel. White outline drift adjustable target sights. Matte blue finish. Polymer grips. Magazine capacity 10 rounds. Weight about 25 oz.

NIB	EXC.	V.G.	GOOD	FAIR	POOR
350	275	215	165	115	75

Mini Firestorm .40 S&W

As above, but chambered for .40 S&W cartridge.

NIB	EXC.	V.G.	GOOD	FAIR	POOR
350	275	215	165	115	75

Firestorm .45 Government

Single-action semi-automatic pistol, chambered for .45 ACP cartridge. Fitted with 5.125" barrel and 3 dot fixed combat sights. Magazine capacity 7 rounds. Black rubber grips. Matte blue, nickel or duotone finish. Weight about 36 oz.

NIB	EXC.	V.G.	GOOD	FAIR	POOR
350	275	215	165	115	75

Compact Firestorm .45 Government

As above, with 4.25" barrel. Weight about 34 oz.

NIB	EXC.	V.G.	GOOD	FAIR	POOR
350	275	215	165	115	75

Mini Firestorm .45 Government

As above, with 3.14" barrel. Black polymer grips. Magazine capacity 10 rounds. Weight about 31 oz.

NIB	EXC.	V.G.	GOOD	FAIR	POOR
350	275	215	165	115	75

1911 Mil-Spec Standard Government

1911A1-style single-action semi-automatic. Chambered in .45 ACP; 5.125" barrel, steel frame, 7- or 8-round magazine. Plastic or wood grips, matte blue or deluxe polished blue finish.

NIB	EXC.	V.G.	GOOD	FAIR	POOR
350	275	215	165	115	75

FLETCHER BIDWELL, LLC
Viroqua, Wisconsin

Spencer 1860 Military Carbine

Introduced in 2001, this is a faithful reproduction of original Spencer Carbine. Chambered for .56-50 black powder cartridge but in centerfire. Fitted with blued, 22" round barrel. Magazine capacity 7 rounds in butt tube. Bone charcoal case hardened receiver. Walnut stock. Blade front sight with ladder rear sight, adjustable to 800 yards. Weight about 9 lbs. Built in U.S.

NIB	EXC.	V.G.	GOOD	FAIR	POOR
2750	1950	1500	900	625	400

FLORENCE ARMORY
Florence, Guilford County, North Carolina

Founded in 1862, as a repair facility to alter sporting arms for military use. Majority of work done by H.C. Lamb & Company. In 1862, Captain Z. Coffin ordered stocks, barrels and locks to assemble newly made rifles. Furniture of these arms varied, either being supplied by Glaze & Company or being remainders from Searcy & Moore's production. Number made estimated to be in excess of 300 rifles in both .50- and .54-calibers. These arms (particularly the barrels) exhibit characteristics of North Carolina contract pieces.

NIB	EXC.	V.G.	GOOD	FAIR	POOR
—	—	29500	12500	4000	1450

| NIB | EXC. | V.G. | GOOD | FAIR | POOR |

FNH USA, INC.
McLean, Virginia

Company is a subsidiary of FN Herstal in Belgium. Essentially the sales and marketing arm for FN in U.S. market.

PISTOLS

Model Forty-Nine

Pistol built by FN Manufacturing, Inc. in Columbia, S.C. Has a polymer frame and stainless steel slide. Chambered for 9mm or .40 S&W cartridge. Barrel length 4.25". Magazine capacity 16 rounds for law enforcement and 10 rounds for commercial sales. Features a repeatable secure striker trigger system. Offered in stainless steel or black coated slide. Weight about 26 oz. Offered primarily for sale to law enforcement agencies. Introduced in 2000.

| 470 | 375 | 300 | 250 | 225 | 135 |

Model FNP-9/FNP-40

Introduced in 2003, this pistol chambered for 9mm or .40 S&W cartridge. Fitted with 4" barrel and featuring a polymer frame. Action is double-/single-action design, with ambidextrous manual decocking lever. Fixed sights. Ten-round magazine capacity. Weight about 33 oz.

| 550 | 425 | 375 | 300 | 250 | 125 |

FNP-45

Longer-frame version of FNP-9, chambered for .45 ACP. Barrel length 4.5" and weight 33.3 oz. Ambidextrous mag release and decocker/safety, forward slide serrations. Magazine capacity: 10 or 15 rounds. Black or Flat Dark Earth finish. Interchangeable backstrap inserts.

| 700 | 625 | 500 | 375 | 250 | 150 |

FNP-45 Tactical

Developed for U.S. Joint Combat Pistol Program, this .45 ACP tactical model has 5.3" threaded barrel for a suppressor or other accessories. High-profile combat sights, two mounting bases for optional red dot sights, MIL-STD 1913 rail. Black or Flat Dark Earth finish. Weight: 33.6 oz.

| 1250 | 1050 | 850 | 625 | 350 | 250 |

FNP-45 Competition

Designed as a major caliber competition pistol. Same overall features as FNP-45, plus fiber optic front sight and Picatinny rail. Introduced in 2011.

| 1050 | 850 | 700 | 500 | 300 | 250 |

FNX-9, FNX-40

Chambered in 9mm or .40 S&W. Magazine capacity: 17 (9mm), 14 (.40). Weight 22 to 24 oz. Stainless steel slide has front and rear cocking serrations. Other features include ambidextrous operating controls. Four interchangeable back-strap inserts.

| 600 | 535 | 450 | 325 | 250 | 150 |

FNX-45

.45 ACP variation of FNX series. Magazine capacity 15-rounds. **NOTE:** Add $100 for night sights; $300 Competition model; $400 Tactical model.

| 700 | 625 | 550 | 500 | 450 | 350 |

FNS-9

Striker-fired polymer-frame full-size pistol. Chambered in 9mm or .40 S&W (FNS-40). Capacity: 18 rounds (9mm), 15 (.40). Black or matte silver slide, black polymer frame, ambidextrous safety, magazine release and slide lock. Fixed 3-dot sights. Night sights optional.

| 600 | 525 | 450 | 400 | 350 | 300 |

FNH Five-seveN

Single-action design chambered for 5.7x28mm round. Magazine capacity 10 or 20 rounds. Matte black, olive drab green or Flat Dark Earth finish. Ambidextrous safety and accessory mounting rail. Barrel length 4", weight 21 oz. Three-dot combat sights, adjustable rear.

| 1100 | 975 | 800 | 575 | 250 | 150 |

Model HP-SA

Famous John Browning design Hi-Power pistol. Chambered for 9mm or .40 S&W cartridge. Barrel length 4.6". Magazine capacity 10 rounds. Weight around 32 oz. Blued finish.

| 900 | 750 | 595 | 400 | 200 | 125 |

	NIB	EXC.	V.G.	GOOD	FAIR	POOR

Model HP-SA-SFS

Introduced in 2003, this variant of Hi-Power pistol. Features single-/double-action mechanism, that allows cocked-and-locked carry, with hammer and slide locked. When safety is pushed off hammer is set in cocked position and fired single action.

NIB	EXC.	V.G.	GOOD	FAIR	POOR
900	750	595	400	200	125

Model HP-DA/HP-DAO

Model offered in two different configurations. First with double-/single-action trigger; second is double-action-only. Chambered for 9mm cartridge. Fitted with fixed sights. Magazine capacity 15 rounds for law enforcement and 10 rounds for commercial sales. Weight about 31 oz. Intended primarily for law enforcement sales. Introduced in 2000.

NIB	EXC.	V.G.	GOOD	FAIR	POOR
900	750	595	400	200	125

Model HP-DA/HP-DAO Compact

As above in smaller and lighter package.

NIB	EXC.	V.G.	GOOD	FAIR	POOR
900	750	595	400	200	125

Model BDA/BDAO Compact

Short recoil compact pistol, chambered for 9mm Parabellum cartridge. Fitted with double-/single-action trigger or double-action-only trigger. Each configuration has 10-round magazine capacity. Weight about 28 oz. Corrosion-resistant finish. Fixed sights.

NIB	EXC.	V.G.	GOOD	FAIR	POOR
800	650	500	395	200	125

RIFLES

Rifles produced at FN manufacturing in U.S.

SPECIAL POLICE RIFLES (FN SPR)

FNAR

Semi-automatic chambered in .308 Winchester. Cold hammer-forged, 16" standard or 20" heavy barrel. Magazine capacity 5 or 10 rounds. Weight: 8.5 to 10 lbs. Receiver-mounted optical rail, with additional rails on fore-end. Matte black synthetic stock, with fully adjustable comb and length of pull via interchangeable inserts. Match-grade model available.

NIB	EXC.	V.G.	GOOD	FAIR	POOR
1600	1350	1050	800	450	300

FN A1 SPR

Chambered for .308 and 7.62x51mm cartridge. Bolt-action. Fitted with 24" heavy barrel and no sights. Choice of hinged floorplate or detachable box magazine. Stock is McMillan A3 tactical. Weight about 10.75 lbs.

NIB	EXC.	V.G.	GOOD	FAIR	POOR
1600	1350	1175	900	725	375

FN A1a SPR

Similar to above model. Fitted with 20" heavy fluted barrel. McMillan A3 tactical stock. Weight about 9.75 lbs.

NIB	EXC.	V.G.	GOOD	FAIR	POOR
1600	1350	1175	900	725	375

FN A2 SPR

Fitted with 24" heavy barrel. McMillan A4 tactical stock. Badger Ordinance scope base. Weight about 10.75 lbs.

NIB	EXC.	V.G.	GOOD	FAIR	POOR
2190	1750	1550	1275	900	400

FN A3 SPR

Model has 24" heavy barrel, with McMillan A4 adjustable stock. Badger Ordinance scope base and Badger Ordinance or FN scope rings. Supplied with FNH Parker-Hale type or Harris bipod. Weight about 10.75 lbs.

NIB	EXC.	V.G.	GOOD	FAIR	POOR
2450	1950	1650	1375	950	450

FN A4 SPR

Fitted with 24" heavy barrel. McMillan A4 adjustable tactical stock. Scope base and rings standard. Choice of several tactical scopes. Bipod, sling, drag bag, kill flash, tool kit, cleaning kit, hard case. Weight about 10.75 lbs.

NIB	EXC.	V.G.	GOOD	FAIR	POOR
5000	4250	3500	2800	2200	1700

FN A5 SPR

Model has 20" heavy fluted barrel threaded for a suppressor. Special McMillan tactical stock. Rest of features same as FN A4 model.

NIB	EXC.	V.G.	GOOD	FAIR	POOR
6500	5750	4500	3700	2900	2000

	NIB	EXC.	V.G.	GOOD	FAIR	POOR

FN A5M

Similar to FN A5 SPR, with McMillan fiberglass tactical stock, standard optics rail. Chambered in .300 WSM or .308 Win. Barrel length 20" to 24", standard or fluted.

	NIB	EXC.	V.G.	GOOD	FAIR	POOR
	3000	2600	2200	1800	1400	1000

FN PS90

Semi-automatic bullpup model chambered for 5.7x28mm caliber, with 10- or 30-round magazine. Barrel is 16", with integrated muzzle-brake. Design features downward ejection, three M1913 accessory rails.

	NIB	EXC.	V.G.	GOOD	FAIR	POOR
	2000	1500	1200	1000	800	500

FNH-USA Ballista

Modular multi-caliber bolt-action tactical rifle. Chambered for .308 Win., .300 Win. Magnum or .338 Lapua. Accessory conversion kits available for each caliber. Aluminum alloy receiver, adjustable trigger, fluted 24" or 25" barrel. Ambidextrous folding stock adjustable for length of pull, comb height, buttplate height, cast-on and cast-off. New in 2012.

	NIB	EXC.	V.G.	GOOD	FAIR	POOR
	6250	5700	5000	4000	—	—

FNH-USA SCAR 16S/17S

Semi-automatic tactical rifle chambered for .223 (16S) or .308 Win. (17S), with 10- or 30-round magazines. Black or FDE finish, hard anodize aluminum receiver, telescoping side-folding polymer stock, integrated optics rail. Barrel length 16.25".

	NIB	EXC.	V.G.	GOOD	FAIR	POOR
	3000	2400	2000	1500	1100	700

FN A5a SPR

Model has 20" heavy fluted barrel threaded for a suppressor. Special SPR McMillan adjustable tactical stock. Weight about 9.75 lbs.

	NIB	EXC.	V.G.	GOOD	FAIR	POOR
	2460	1975	1650	1375	950	450

FN PBR (Patrol Bolt Rifle)

Introduced in 2004. Rifle chambered for .308 or .300 WSM. Offered with four different barrel lengths: 18", 20", 22" or 24". Fitted with two-piece MIL spec M1913 rail. Black Hogue stock. Magazine capacity 4 rounds. Weight about 9 lbs.

	NIB	EXC.	V.G.	GOOD	FAIR	POOR
	1000	950	900	800	700	400

PGM PRECISION RIFLES

Rifles made by PGM Precision, a subsidary of FN, in Poisy Cedex, France.

Ultima Ratio Intervention

Bolt-action rifle, chambered for .308 and 7.62x51mm cartridge. Fitted with 23.6" ribbed barrel and integral muzzle-brake. Folding bipod. Stock trigger group and action are fixed to a rigid metal girder. Stock is adjustable. No sights. Magazine capacity 5 or 10 rounds. Weight about 13.25 lbs., depending on configuration.

	NIB	EXC.	V.G.	GOOD	FAIR	POOR
	9000	7995	6000	3250	1795	700

Ultima Ratio Commando I

Similar to above model, with 18.5" fluted barrel and muzzle-brake. Weight about 12 lbs.

	NIB	EXC.	V.G.	GOOD	FAIR	POOR
	9100	8050	6100	3250	1795	700

Ultima Ratio Commando II

Similar to Commando I, with folding stock.

	NIB	EXC.	V.G.	GOOD	FAIR	POOR
	8320	—	—	—	—	—

FN-Mini-Hecate

Chambered for .308 cartridge. Bolt-action rifle features free-loading interchangeable 18.5", 19.7", 21.7" or 23.6" match-grade barrel. Collapsible buttstock. Magazine capacity 10 rounds. Weight about 14 lbs. Introduced in 2001.

	NIB	EXC.	V.G.	GOOD	FAIR	POOR
	9100	8050	6100	3250	1795	700

.338 Lapua

Similar to Mini-Hecate, but chambered for .33 Lapua cartridge. Fitted with 27.2" barrel and integral muzzle-brake. Collapsible buttstock. Weight about 15 lbs. Magazine capacity 10 rounds.

	NIB	EXC.	V.G.	GOOD	FAIR	POOR
	10500	9000	7750	6000	3750	1475

SHOTGUNS

FNH-USA SC1

Over/under shotgun designed for competition. 12-gauge only, with 28" or 30" ported and back-bored barrels, Invector-Plus choke tubes, ventilated rib and mid-bead. Checkered wood, laminate

	NIB	EXC.	V.G.	GOOD	FAIR	POOR

wood or blue stock adjustable for comb height, cast and length of pull. Weight 8 to 8.2 lbs.

	2000	1700	1450	1100	900	500

FN Police Shotgun

Slide-action 12-gauge shotgun, chambered for 3" 12-gauge shell. Barrel length 18". Magazine capacity 7 rounds. Black synthetic stock. Corrosion-resistant finish. Weight about 6.5 lbs.

	350	275	200	150	125	100

FN Tactical Police

Similar to standard model, with ported barrel, collapsible stock and pistol-grip. Weight about 6.5 lbs.

	550	475	400	300	200	100

FN Self-Loading Police

Gas-operated semi-automatic shotgun. Fitted with Picatinny rail and short stock. Chambered for 12-gauge shell. Magazine capacity 6 rounds. Weight about 7.75 lbs.

	1000	800	600	400	300	200

FOEHL, C.
Philadelphia, Pennsylvania

Derringer

A .41-caliber percussion single-shot pistol, with 2" barrel, German silver mounts and walnut stock. Lock marked "C. Foehl".

	—	—	1950	750	300	110

FOEHL & WEEKS
Philadelphia, Pennsylvania

Columbian

A .32- or .38-caliber revolver, marked with patent date "20 January 1891".

	—	—	350	150	75	50

Columbian Automatic

A .38-caliber revolver, with hinged barrel and cylinder assembly.

	—	—	400	200	100	75

Perfect

As above, with concealed hammer. Also in .32-caliber.

	—	—	400	200	100	75

FOGARTY
American Repeating Rifle Co.
Boston, Massachusetts

Fogarty Repeating Rifle and Carbine

Limited number of repeating rifles and carbines, based upon Valentine Fogarty's patents. Produced between 1866 and 1867. Calibers of these arms varies. Normal barrel lengths are 20" and 28". Blued, casehardened, with walnut stocks. American Repeating Rifle Company purchased by Winchester Repeating Arms Company in 1869.

Rifle

	—	—	9500	4050	1250	450

Carbine

	—	—	9500	4050	1250	450

FOLSOM, H&D ARMS CO.

Large distributor of double-/single barrel shotguns, produced by Crescent Firearms Co., Norwich, Connecticut. Folsom owned and later sold to Savage Arms Co. the Crescent Firearms Co., Davis Warner Co. and Baker Gun Co. around 1930. For more information see Crescent Firearms Co.

FOLSOM, H.
St. Louis, Missouri

Derringer

A .41-caliber single-shot percussion pocket pistol, with 2.5" barrel. German silver mounts and walnut stock. Barrel marked "H. Folsom".

	—	—	1150	800	350	275

NIB	EXC.	V.G.	GOOD	FAIR	POOR

FORBES RIFLES, LLC
Westbrook, Maine

Model 24B

A production version of Model 24 made by New Ultra Light Arms Co. Chambered in .25-06, .270, 7mm Rem. Magnum, .30-06 and .300 Win. Magnum. Barrel length 24", black composite stock, no sights. Introduced 2011. Add $100 for stainless and/or left-hand version.

1300	1200	1100	900	700	350

FOREHAND & WADSWORTH
Worcester, Massachusetts

Established in 1871 and operated under the above name until 1890, when it became Forehand Arms Company. Hopkins & Allen purchased the company in 1902.

Single-Shot Derringer

A .22-caliber single-shot pocket pistol, with 2" half-octagonal pivoted barrel. Spur trigger and nickel- or silver-plated frame. Walnut grips. Barrel marked "Forehand & Wadsworth Worcester".

—	—	1450	600	250	100

Single-Shot .41 Derringer

As above in .41-caliber, with 2.5" round barrel.

—	—	1000	850	450	200

Side-Hammer .22

A .22-caliber spur trigger revolver, with 2.25" to 4" octagonal barrel. 7-shot cylinder. Blued or nickel-plated, with walnut grips.

—	—	675	475	200	100

Center Hammer

A .32-caliber spur trigger revolver, with 3.5" octagonal barrel and 6-shot cylinder. Blued or nickel-plated, with rosewood or walnut grips. Top strap commonly found marked "Terror".

—	—	400	300	200	100

Old Model Army Single-Action Revolver

A .44 Russian caliber revolver, with 7.5" round barrel and 6-shot cylinder. Barrel marked "Forehand & Wadsworth, Worcester, Mass. U.S. Patd. Oct. 22, '61, June 27, '71 Oct. 28, '73". Blued with walnut grips. Approximately 250 manufactured between 1872 and 1878.

—	—	4000	3250	2000	500

New Model Army Single-Action Revolver

Similar to above, with 6.5" barrel and half-cock notch on hammer. Approximately 250 made between 1878 and 1882. Interesting Note: In 2008, United States Fire Arms announced plans to remanufacture this model.

—	—	3750	3000	2250	500

Double-Action Revolver

A .32 or .38 centerfire or rimfire caliber double-action revolver, with 3.5" barrel and 6- or 7-shot cylinder. The .32-caliber version marked "Forehand & Wadsworth Double-Action" and .38-caliber "American Bulldog". Manufactured from 1871 to 1890.

—	400	300	200	100	35

British Bulldog

A .32 or .38 centerfire solid frame double-action revolver, resembling Webley Bulldog.

—	—	395	300	150	75

British Bulldog .44

As above in .44 Webley caliber, with 5" barrel and 5-shot cylinder.

—	—	450	325	175	100

Swamp Angel

A .41-caliber single-action revolver, with 3" barrel and 5-shot cylinder. Top strap marked "Swamp Angel".

—	—	425	275	100	50

	NIB	EXC.	V.G.	GOOD	FAIR	POOR

FOREHAND ARMS CO. 1898-1902

Perfection Automatic

A .32- or .38-caliber double-action revolver, with hinged barrel and cylinder assembly. Varying barrel lengths. Blued or nickel-plated, with hard rubber grips.

	NIB	EXC.	V.G.	GOOD	FAIR	POOR
	—	275	250	100	75	50

Double-Barrel Shotguns

Good quality hammer and hammerless doubles, but few produced until taken over by Hopkins and Allen Firearms Co. Values from $100 to $1,000 depending on grade and condition.

FOWLER, B. JR.
Hartford, Connecticut

Percussion Pistol

A .38-caliber single-shot percussion pistol, with 4" half octagonal barrel, iron frame and maple grips. Barrel marked "B. Fowler, Jr." Manufactured between 1835 and 1838.

	NIB	EXC.	V.G.	GOOD	FAIR	POOR
	—	—	995	550	325	150

FOX, A. H.
Philadelphia, Pennsylvania

Ansley H. Fox established Fox Gun Company, in Baltimore, Maryland, in 1896. Subsequently, he made arms under the name Philadelphia Gun Company. As of 1905, he operated under the name A.H. Fox. In 1930, this company was purchased by Savage Arms Company, who continued manufacturing all grades of Fox shotguns. As of 1942, Savage Company only made plainer grades.

NOTE: Fox Model B double shotguns see Savage Arms Co.

Sterlingworth

A 12-, 16- or 20-gauge boxlock double-barrel shotgun, with 26", 28" or 30" barrels. Double triggers and extractors. Automatic ejectors were also available and would add approximately 30 percent to values listed. Blued, casehardened, with walnut stock. Manufactured from 1911 to 1946. **NOTE:** Add 50 percent for 20-gauge; 25 percent for 16-gauge.

	NIB	EXC.	V.G.	GOOD	FAIR	POOR
	—	2000	1600	1000	500	275

Sterlingworth Deluxe

As above, with an ivory bead recoil pad and optional 32" barrel. **NOTE:** Add 50 percent for 20 gauge; 25 percent for 16-gauge.

	NIB	EXC.	V.G.	GOOD	FAIR	POOR
	—	2500	1900	1250	700	400

SP Grade

A 12-, 16- or 20-gauge boxlock double-barrel shotgun, with varying length barrels. Double triggers and extractors. **NOTE:** Add 35 percent for 20-gauge; 15 percent for Automatic ejectors; 25 percent for 16-gauge.

	NIB	EXC.	V.G.	GOOD	FAIR	POOR
	—	1600	1325	1050	450	225

HE Grade

Similar to early A Grade and offered in 12- and 20-gauge. Chambers were 2.25" standard, with 3" chambers available on request. Marked on the barrel "Not Warranted". This referred to pattern density, not barrel quality. Only sixty 20-gauge HE Grades appear in factory records. Manufactured from 1923 to 1942. **NOTE:** Add 20 percent for single-selective trigger; 100 percent premium for 20-gauge.

	NIB	EXC.	V.G.	GOOD	FAIR	POOR
	—	5000	4200	3200	2000	1000

High Grade Guns A-FE

Fox Company as well as Savage Arms Company, produced a variety of shotguns decorated in varying grades. Available in 12-, 16- and 20-gauge. Value for these arms depends on particular features of these arms. Prospective purchasers are advised to secure a qualified appraisal prior to acquisition. **NOTE:** A 25 percent premium should be added to grades below, for small gauge and guns with single selective trigger.

A Grade

Built from 1905 to 1942.

	NIB	EXC.	V.G.	GOOD	FAIR	POOR
	—	2100	1700	1225	600	400

AE Grade (Automatic Ejectors)

Built from 1905 to 1946.

	NIB	EXC.	V.G.	GOOD	FAIR	POOR
	—	2400	2000	1600	900	700

	NIB	EXC.	V.G.	GOOD	FAIR	POOR

B Grade
Built from 1905 to 1918.

	NIB	EXC.	V.G.	GOOD	FAIR	POOR
	—	3100	2700	1950	1100	500

BE Grade
Built from 1905 to 1918.

	NIB	EXC.	V.G.	GOOD	FAIR	POOR
	—	4500	3600	3000	2000	1000

C Grade
Built from 1905 to 1913.

	NIB	EXC.	V.G.	GOOD	FAIR	POOR
	—	3300	2700	2150	1100	550

CE Grade
Built from 1905 to 1946.

	NIB	EXC.	V.G.	GOOD	FAIR	POOR
	—	5500	4500	3750	2500	1200

XE Grade
Built from 1914 to 1945.

	NIB	EXC.	V.G.	GOOD	FAIR	POOR
	—	7500	6700	5000	3000	1500

D Grade
Built from 1906 to 1913.

	NIB	EXC.	V.G.	GOOD	FAIR	POOR
	—	9300	8000	5150	2750	1000

DE Grade
Built from 1906 to 1945.

	NIB	EXC.	V.G.	GOOD	FAIR	POOR
	—	12500	11000	8000	3750	1800

F Grade
Built from 1906 to 1913.

	NIB	EXC.	V.G.	GOOD	FAIR	POOR
	—	25000	16800	9000	5700	3000

FE Grade
Built from 1906 to 1940.

	NIB	EXC.	V.G.	GOOD	FAIR	POOR
	—	28000	21000	11500	7700	5000

Single Barrel Trap Guns

A 12-gauge single barrel boxlock shotgun, with 30" or 32" ventilated rib barrels and automatic ejector. Approximately 571 single-barrel trap guns manufactured. Produced in four grades as listed:

J Grade
Built from 1919 to 1936.

	NIB	EXC.	V.G.	GOOD	FAIR	POOR
	—	3100	2400	1750	1050	600

K Grade
Built from 1919 to 1931. Approximately 75 built.

	NIB	EXC.	V.G.	GOOD	FAIR	POOR
	—	4350	3300	2450	1650	950

L Grade
Built from 1919 to 1931. Approximately 25 built.

	NIB	EXC.	V.G.	GOOD	FAIR	POOR
	—	5750	3900	3150	2150	1200

M Grade
Built from 1919 to 1932. A total of 9 guns built.

	NIB	EXC.	V.G.	GOOD	FAIR	POOR
	—	15000	10000	6500	4700	2500

RECENTLY MANUFACTURED A.H. FOX SHOTGUNS

In 1993, Connecticut Shotgun Manufacturing Company of New Britain, Connecticut, announced production of A.H. Fox shotgun in 20-gauge exclusively. Gun is hand-built and constructed to same dimensions and standards as original Fox. Gun offered in five grades, with many standard features and several optional ones as well. Each shotgun built to order. Because these guns are newly built and have no pricing history, only manufacturer's retail price for base gun will be given. Extra sets of barrels, single triggers and other extra costs options will greatly affect price.

NIB	EXC.	V.G.	GOOD	FAIR	POOR

CE Grade
Retail price: $19,500

XE Grade
Retail price: $22,000

DE Grade
Retail price: $25,000

FE Grade
Retail price: $30,000

Exhibition Grade
This is the company's highest grade. Features any optional detail the customer desires, including custom engraving and exhibition quality wood. Retail price: On request from CSMC.

FRANCHI, L.
Brescia, Italy

BOXLOCK SIDE-BY-SIDE-SHOTGUNS

Astore
A 12-gauge boxlock shotgun. Manufactured in a variety of barrel lengths, with double triggers and automatic ejectors. Blued, with straight walnut stock. Manufactured from 1937 to 1960.

NIB	EXC.	V.G.	GOOD	FAIR	POOR
2900	1600	750	500	350	200

Astore II
As above, but more finely finished.

NIB	EXC.	V.G.	GOOD	FAIR	POOR
3150	1850	900	700	450	250

Astore 5
As above, but more finely finished.

NIB	EXC.	V.G.	GOOD	FAIR	POOR
3350	2150	1250	950	600	300

Airone
Similar to Astore. Manufactured during 1940s.

NIB	EXC.	V.G.	GOOD	FAIR	POOR
2900	1600	750	500	350	200

SIDELOCK SIDE-BY-SIDE SHOTGUNS
A 12- 16- or 20-gauge sidelock double-barrel shotgun. Manufactured in a variety of barrel lengths, with single-selective trigger and automatic ejectors. Produced in the following grades, they differ as to engraving, coverage and quality of wood:

Condor

NIB	EXC.	V.G.	GOOD	FAIR	POOR
7500	6500	4500	3500	2500	1250

Imperial

NIB	EXC.	V.G.	GOOD	FAIR	POOR
10000	8500	6000	4500	3250	1500

Imperiales

NIB	EXC.	V.G.	GOOD	FAIR	POOR
10500	9000	6500	5000	3500	1500

No. 5 Imperial Monte Carlo

NIB	EXC.	V.G.	GOOD	FAIR	POOR
15000	12500	9000	7500	5000	2000

No. 11 Imperial Monte Carlo

NIB	EXC.	V.G.	GOOD	FAIR	POOR
16000	13500	10000	8000	5500	2000

Imperial Monte Carlo Extra

NIB	EXC.	V.G.	GOOD	FAIR	POOR
20000	17500	12500	9500	7500	3500

Highlander
Introduced in 2003, this model features either 12-, 20- or 28-gauge gun, fitted with 26" barrels and fixed chokes. Select walnut straight-grip stock, with splinter fore-end. Coin finished steel receiver. Single trigger. Weight: 6.4 lbs. 12-gauge; 5.8 lbs. 20-gauge; 5.7 lbs. 28-gauge. **NOTE:** Add $150 for 28-gauge.

NIB	EXC.	V.G.	GOOD	FAIR	POOR
1800	1600	1200	850	475	300

	NIB	EXC.	V.G.	GOOD	FAIR	POOR

OVER/UNDER SHOTGUNS

Priti Deluxe Model

A 12- or 20-gauge over/under boxlock double-barrel shotgun, with 26" or 28" ventilated rib barrels. Single trigger and automatic ejectors. Introduced in 1988.

NIB	EXC.	V.G.	GOOD	FAIR	POOR
400	350	300	250	200	150

Falconet

A 12-, 16-, 20-, 28-gauge and .410 bore boxlock double-barrel shotgun, with single-selective trigger and automatic ejectors. Receiver was anodized in tan, ebony or silver finishes. Manufactured from 1968 to 1975. **NOTE:** Add 10 percent for silver receiver; 25 percent 28-gauge and .410 bore.

NIB	EXC.	V.G.	GOOD	FAIR	POOR
650	550	425	350	250	200

Falconet Skeet

As above, with 26" skeet barrel. Wide rib and receiver casehardened. Manufactured from 1970 to 1974.

NIB	EXC.	V.G.	GOOD	FAIR	POOR
950	850	700	550	450	250

Falconet International Skeet

As above, but more finely finished.

NIB	EXC.	V.G.	GOOD	FAIR	POOR
1050	950	750	600	475	250

Falconet Trap

As above, with 30" Modified Full choke barrel and trap stock. Manufactured from 1970 to 1974.

NIB	EXC.	V.G.	GOOD	FAIR	POOR
1000	900	700	550	450	250

Falconet International Trap

As above, but more finely finished.

NIB	EXC.	V.G.	GOOD	FAIR	POOR
1050	950	750	600	475	250

Peregrine Model 451

A 12-gauge boxlock double-barrel shotgun, with 26" or 28" ventilated rib barrels. Alloy receiver, single-selective trigger and automatic ejectors. Manufactured in 1975.

NIB	EXC.	V.G.	GOOD	FAIR	POOR
800	675	495	375	275	200

Peregrine Model 400

As above, with steel frame.

NIB	EXC.	V.G.	GOOD	FAIR	POOR
850	775	600	400	300	200

Aristocrat

Similar to above, with 26", 28" or 30" ventilated rib barrels. Manufactured from 1960 to 1969.

NIB	EXC.	V.G.	GOOD	FAIR	POOR
850	725	600	400	300	200

Aristocrat Magnum

As above, with 3" chambers and 32" Full choke barrels.

NIB	EXC.	V.G.	GOOD	FAIR	POOR
895	775	675	450	300	200

Aristocrat Silver King

As above, with French case hardened receiver. Available in four grades of decoration.

NIB	EXC.	V.G.	GOOD	FAIR	POOR
950	875	775	475	350	200

Aristocrat Deluxe

NIB	EXC.	V.G.	GOOD	FAIR	POOR
1250	1000	875	575	400	200

Aristocrat Supreme

NIB	EXC.	V.G.	GOOD	FAIR	POOR
1650	1400	950	700	575	250

Aristocrat Imperial

NIB	EXC.	V.G.	GOOD	FAIR	POOR
2950	2450	1950	1250	950	450

Aristocrat Monte Carlo

NIB	EXC.	V.G.	GOOD	FAIR	POOR
3750	3200	2950	2000	1500	750

Model 2003 Trap

A 12-gauge boxlock double-barrel shotgun, with 30" or 32" ventilated rib barrels. Single-selective trigger and automatic ejectors. Manufactured in 1976.

NIB	EXC.	V.G.	GOOD	FAIR	POOR
1450	1300	900	650	500	250

	NIB	EXC.	V.G.	GOOD	FAIR	POOR

Model 2004 Trap

A single-barreled version of Model 2003.

	1450	1300	900	650	500	250

Model 2005 Combination Trap

Model 2003, with both single and set of over/under barrels.

	2800	2400	1950	1200	950	450

Model 3000 "Undergun"

As above, with single barrel fitted with high ventilated rib so it fires from lower barrel position.

	3050	2850	2200	1500	1200	600

Alcione Classic

Introduced in 2004, this 12-gauge 3" model features 26" or 28" ventilated rib barrels. Side rib ventilated. Walnut stock with schnabel fore-end. Optional 20-gauge barrels. Weight about 7.5 lbs.

	1300	975	800	600	500	250

Alcione T (Titanium)

Introduced in 2002, this model is similar to Alcione Field. Has an aluminum alloy frame, with titanium inserts. Available in 12- and 20-gauge with 3" chambers. Choice of 26" or 28" vent rib barrels, with choke tubes. Weight about 6.8 lbs. for 12- and 20-gauge.

	1400	1150	950	700	600	300

Alcione T Two-Barrel Set

As above, with two-barrel set: One 12-gauge 28"; other 20-gauge 26". Introduced in 2004.

	1600	1275	1100	800	650	350

Alcione Field Model

A 12-gauge boxlock double-barrel shotgun, with 26" or 28" ventilated rib barrels. Single-selective trigger and automatic ejectors. Engraved silver receiver. Weight about 7.5 lbs.

	1200	995	800	525	300	150

Alcione Sporting

This over/under gun designed for sporting clays competition. Fitted with mechanical triggers and ported barrels. Offered in 12-gauge only, with 30" barrels. Select walnut stock. Removable sideplates. Weight about 7.5 lbs.

	1550	1250	995	775	400	200

Alcione LF

This 12- or 20-gauge model, features barrels of 26" in 20-gauge and 28" in 12 gauge. Both gauges are chambered for 3" shells. Walnut stock. Receiver is aluminum alloy, with etched games scenes and gold fill. Weight about 6.8 lbs.

	1300	1050	700	450	300	200

Alcione SL Sport

As above, but more finely finished. French casehardened receiver.

	1375	1125	775	525	375	275

Alcione SP

Chambered for 12-gauge shell and fitted with 28" vent rib barrels and choke tubes. Full slide lock-style side plates, with engraving of gold pheasants and mallards. Weight about 7.5 lbs. Introduced in 2003.

	1700	1450	975	700	575	345

ALCIONE SIDEPLATES

Alcione Classic SX

This 12-gauge 3" model similar to Alcione Field SX above, with blued receiver. Available with choice of 26" or 28" vent rib barrels. An extra 12-gauge 30" ported barrel and 20-gauge barrels are also optional. Weight about 7.5 lbs. Introduced in 2004.

	1400	1150	950	700	600	300

Alcione Field SX

Model fitted with high grade walnut stock, fine checkering and engraved receivers. Gold filled etched side plates. Offered with 26" or 28" barrels. Weight about 7.3 lbs.

	1600	1250	995	775	400	200

	NIB	EXC.	V.G.	GOOD	FAIR	POOR

Veloce

Introduced in 2001, this model chambered for 20- or 28-gauge only. Barrels: 20-gauge 28";
28-gauge 26". Aluminum alloy receiver. Engraved side plates, with gold filled game scenes.
Mechanical trigger. Select walnut stock. Approximate weight: 20-gauge 5.8 lbs.; 28-gauge 5.5
lbs.

	NIB	EXC.	V.G.	GOOD	FAIR	POOR
	1375	1125	775	525	375	275

Veloce English Stock

Introduced in 2002. Model similar to Veloce, with straight-grip stock. Offered in 20- and
28-gauge, with 26" vent rib barrels. Choke tubes. Approximate weight: 20-gauge 5.7 lbs.;
28-gauge 5.5 lbs.

	NIB	EXC.	V.G.	GOOD	FAIR	POOR
	1400	1150	950	700	600	300

Veloce Grade II

This 20- or 28-gauge model, features extra-select-grade walnut stock, with gold-filled birds and
scroll engraving. The 20-gauge offered with either 26" or 28" vent rib barrel, while 28-gauge fitted
with 26" vent rib barrel. Approximate weight: 20-gauge 5.75 lbs.; 28-gauge 5.5 lbs.

	NIB	EXC.	V.G.	GOOD	FAIR	POOR
	1600	1275	1100	800	650	350

Veloce Squire Set

Model features a two-barrel set in 20- and 28-gauge. Each barrel set fitted with 26" vent rib
barrels. Select walnut stock, gold-emblished game scenes, jeweled monoblocs and filigreed top
lever. Weight about 5.5 lbs. Introduced in 2003.

	NIB	EXC.	V.G.	GOOD	FAIR	POOR
	2100	1775	1600	1200	800	400

Renaissance

Renaissance Series introduced in 2006. These over/unders feature ultra-light alloy receivers,
oil-finished walnut stocks, Prince of Wales pistol-grips, cut checkering and Twin Shock Absorber
recoil pads with gel insert. The 3" 12- and 20-gauges have 26" or 28" barrels; 28-gauge has
26" barrel. Weights average 6.2 lbs. in 12-gauge, 5.8 lbs. in 20-gauge and 5.5 lbs. in 28-gauge.
NOTE: Add 5 percent to values shown for 28-gauge.

Field

Walnut stock, with engraved receiver.

	NIB	EXC.	V.G.	GOOD	FAIR	POOR
	1600	1250	995	775	400	200

Classic

A-Grade walnut, with gold inlaid receiver.

	NIB	EXC.	V.G.	GOOD	FAIR	POOR
	1650	1300	1050	825	450	250

Elite

AA-Grade Walnut, with gold inlaid receiver.

	NIB	EXC.	V.G.	GOOD	FAIR	POOR
	1900	1550	1295	1050	650	275

Sporting

This 3" 12-gauge model introduced in 2007. Features 30" barrel, A-Grade walnut stock,
engraved receiver with gold inlay and adjustable comb. Weight about 7.9 lbs.

	NIB	EXC.	V.G.	GOOD	FAIR	POOR
	1975	1625	1350	1300	825	325

Aspire

This diminutive over/under is made only in 28-gauge and .410 bore, for the discerning small-bore
shooter. Features include round-action receiver and standard items expected for a quality over/
under, such as single-selective trigger, automatic ejectors, AA-grade oil-finished walnut stock,
ventilated rib and choke tubes. Barrels are 28" and weight just under 6 lbs.

	NIB	EXC.	V.G.	GOOD	FAIR	POOR
	1950	1675	1425	1200	950	450

SEMI-AUTOMATIC SHOTGUNS

AL48

A 12- or 20-gauge semi-automatic shotgun, with 24" to 30" ventilated rib barrels (those made
after 1989, threaded for choke tubes) and an alloy receiver. Walnut stock. Manufactured since
1950. Values shown are for current production. **NOTE:** Add 10 percent for Magnum Model; $75
for 28-gauge model.

	NIB	EXC.	V.G.	GOOD	FAIR	POOR
	725	550	300	250	150	100

AL 48 Short Stock (Modern)

Same as above in 20-gauge, with shorter length of pull. First imported in 2000.

	NIB	EXC.	V.G.	GOOD	FAIR	POOR
	700	525	275	250	150	100

	NIB	EXC.	V.G.	GOOD	FAIR	POOR

AL 48 Deluxe English Stock (Modern)

Similar to standard AL 48, with straight-grip stock. Offered in 20- and 28-gauge, with 26" vent rib barrel and choke tubes. Weight about 5.5 lbs. Introduced in 2002.

NIB	EXC.	V.G.	GOOD	FAIR	POOR
800	625	375	275	175	100

Hunter Model AL48 (1950-1970)

As above, with an etched receiver and more finely figured wood. **NOTE:** Magnum Model add 10 percent.

NIB	EXC.	V.G.	GOOD	FAIR	POOR
550	350	300	250	200	150

Eldorado AL48 (1954-1975)

As above, but more finely finished. Manufactured from 1954 to 1975.

NIB	EXC.	V.G.	GOOD	FAIR	POOR
600	425	325	250	200	150

Crown Grade

As above, with hand-done engraving and finely figured walnut stocks.

NIB	EXC.	V.G.	GOOD	FAIR	POOR
1800	1450	1200	800	475	250

Diamond Grade

As above, with hand-done engraving and finely figured walnut stocks.

NIB	EXC.	V.G.	GOOD	FAIR	POOR
2300	1850	1375	900	575	300

Imperial Grade

As above, with hand-done engraving and finely figured walnut stocks.

NIB	EXC.	V.G.	GOOD	FAIR	POOR
2800	2450	1850	1250	950	450

Model 500

A 12-gauge semi-automatic shotgun, with 28" ventilated rib barrel and walnut stock. Introduced in 1976. **NOTE:** Deluxe version add 10 percent.

NIB	EXC.	V.G.	GOOD	FAIR	POOR
500	425	375	295	150	100

Model 520 "Eldorado Gold"

An engraved and gold-inlaid version of above.

NIB	EXC.	V.G.	GOOD	FAIR	POOR
1250	1050	850	550	300	150

Model 530 Trap

Model 500, with 30" or 32" ventilated rib barrel and trap stock.

NIB	EXC.	V.G.	GOOD	FAIR	POOR
675	600	500	400	300	150

Prestige Model

A 12-gauge semi-automatic shotgun, manufactured in a variety of barrel lengths. After 1989 barrels threaded for choke tubes. Alloy receiver and walnut stock.

NIB	EXC.	V.G.	GOOD	FAIR	POOR
675	550	475	350	250	150

Elite Model

As above, with etched receiver and more finely figured stock.

NIB	EXC.	V.G.	GOOD	FAIR	POOR
700	600	525	350	250	150

SPAS12

A 12-gauge slide-action/semi-automatic shotgun, with 21.5" barrel and 9-shot magazine. Anodized, black finish, with composition folding or fixed stock.

NIB	EXC.	V.G.	GOOD	FAIR	POOR
1450	1000	800	600	475	300

Black Magic Game Model

A 12-gauge Magnum semi-automatic shotgun, with 24" to 28" ventilated rib barrels. Threaded for choke tubes, gold anodized alloy receiver, blackened barrel and walnut stock. Also available in trap or skeet configuration. **NOTE:** Add 10 percent for Skeet Model; 15 percent for Trap Model.

NIB	EXC.	V.G.	GOOD	FAIR	POOR
750	600	525	300	250	100

Black Magic Hunter

A 12- or 20-gauge Magnum double-barrel shotgun, with 28" ventilated rib barrels. Threaded for choke tubes, single-selective triggers and automatic ejectors. Blued, with a walnut stock. Introduced in 1989.

NIB	EXC.	V.G.	GOOD	FAIR	POOR
700	550	475	300	250	100

	NIB	EXC.	V.G.	GOOD	FAIR	POOR

Black Magic Lightweight Hunter

As above, with 26" barrels and 2.75" chambers.

NIB	EXC.	V.G.	GOOD	FAIR	POOR
975	850	650	400	300	150

Variomax 912

Introduced in 2001, this model chambered for 12-gauge 3.5" shell. Offered with choice of 24", 26", 28" or 30" barrels with vent rib. Black synthetic stock. Weight about 7.6 lbs. Choke tubes. In 2002 a walnut stock added as an option. **NOTE:** Add $50 for walnut stock.

NIB	EXC.	V.G.	GOOD	FAIR	POOR
700	550	475	300	250	100

Variomax 912 Camo

Same as above, with Advantage Timber camo finish.

NIB	EXC.	V.G.	GOOD	FAIR	POOR
750	600	525	300	250	100

Variomax 912 SteadyGrip

Introduced in 2005, model features extended pistol-grip. Advantage H-D camo stock, with 24" vent rib barrel and choke tubes. Weight about 8 lbs.

NIB	EXC.	V.G.	GOOD	FAIR	POOR
775	625	550	325	265	100

Variopress 612 Sporting

A 12-gauge semi-automatic gas-operated shotgun, with 30" ported barrel. Extended choke tubes. Select walnut stock, with stock drop kit. Magazine capacity 5 rounds. Weight about 7 lbs. First imported in 2000.

NIB	EXC.	V.G.	GOOD	FAIR	POOR
700	550	475	300	250	100

Variopress 612 Field

This 12-gauge model offered with barrel lengths from 24" to 28". Stock configurations are walnut, synthetic or camo. Magazine capacity 5 rounds. Weight about 7 lbs., depending on barrel length.

NIB	EXC.	V.G.	GOOD	FAIR	POOR
700	550	475	300	250	100

Variopress 612 Defense

This 12-gauge gun fitted with 18.5" barrel and black synthetic stock. Matte black finish. Choke is cylinder. Weight about 6.5 lbs. Magazine capacity 5 rounds. First imported in 2000.

NIB	EXC.	V.G.	GOOD	FAIR	POOR
600	500	425	350	250	150

Variopress 620 Field

Model offered in 20-gauge, with choice of walnut or camo stock. Barrel lengths from 24" to 28". Magazine capacity 5 rounds. Weight about 6 lbs. **NOTE:** Add $50 for camo stock.

NIB	EXC.	V.G.	GOOD	FAIR	POOR
700	550	475	300	250	100

Variopress 620 Short Stock

Same as above, with 12.5" length of pull and walnut stock. First imported in 2000.

NIB	EXC.	V.G.	GOOD	FAIR	POOR
700	550	475	300	250	100

Model 712

Semi-automatic shotgun, chambered for 12-gauge 3" shell. Choice of 24", 26" or 28" vent rib barrels with choke tubes. Offered in several different finishes: Weathercoat (synthetic wood), Max-4 camo and Timber HD. Choice of synthetic wood, black synthetic or camo stock. Weight about 6.8 lbs. to 7 lbs., depending on stock and barrel length. Introduced in 2004.

Weathercoat

NIB	EXC.	V.G.	GOOD	FAIR	POOR
700	600	500	375	200	100

Camo

NIB	EXC.	V.G.	GOOD	FAIR	POOR
725	625	525	400	225	125

Synthetic

NIB	EXC.	V.G.	GOOD	FAIR	POOR
775	650	550	425	250	150

Model 720

Similar to Model 712, but chambered for 20-gauge 3" shell. Offered with 24", 26" or 28" vent rib barrels. Choice of Max-4, Timber HD finish or walnut stock, with 12.5" lop. Introduced in 2004.

Camo

NIB	EXC.	V.G.	GOOD	FAIR	POOR
750	650	550	425	250	150

Walnut Short Stock

NIB	EXC.	V.G.	GOOD	FAIR	POOR
725	625	525	400	225	125

	NIB	EXC.	V.G.	GOOD	FAIR	POOR

Weathercoat

Introduced in 2005, with 28" ventilated rib barrel. Weight about 6.2 lbs.

	NIB	EXC.	V.G.	GOOD	FAIR	POOR
	775	650	550	425	250	150

I-12

Introduced in 2005, this 12-gauge model offered with 3" chambers and choice of 24", 26" or 28" vent rib barrels. Available with synthetic, walnut, Max-4 or Timber H-D stock. Choke tubes. Weight about 7.5 lbs., depending on barrel length.

	NIB	EXC.	V.G.	GOOD	FAIR	POOR
	1200	900	600	500	350	200

I-12 White Gold

Similar to Inertia I-12, with highly figured walnut stock. White gold game bird scene on a satin nickel receiver. Introduced in 2006. Available only with 28" barrel. Weight about 7.7 lbs.

	NIB	EXC.	V.G.	GOOD	FAIR	POOR
	1400	1050	750	600	425	250

Fenice

This small-frame semi-automatic is built on Franchi's classic recoil-operated AL-48 design. No recoil problem, however, as the Fenice is only in 28-gauge and .410 bore. Among the quality features are a AA-grade European walnut stock, 26" or 28" barrel with ventilated rib and nickel-plated receiver with scroll engraving and inlayed game bird scene. Weight: 20-gauge 5.75 lbs.; 28-gauge 5.4 lbs.

	NIB	EXC.	V.G.	GOOD	FAIR	POOR
	1150	1000	850	620	450	300

Intensity

This semi-automatic operates on the Inertia Driven system, which is designed to operate with 2.75", 3" and 3.5" 12-gauge shells. Barrel lengths are 26", 28" or 30" and weight of all three length models is between 6.7 and 6.9 lbs. Synthetic stock makes it ideal for all weather conditions. Several Realtree and Mossy Oak camo designs are available. **NOTE:** Add $100 for camo models if in good or better condition.

	NIB	EXC.	V.G.	GOOD	FAIR	POOR
	975	800	675	500	375	300

RIFLES

Centennial Semi-Automatic

A .22-caliber semi-automatic rifle, with 21" barrel, adjustable sights, Alloy receiver and walnut stock. Manufactured in 1968 only. **NOTE:** Deluxe Engraved Model add 20 percent.

	NIB	EXC.	V.G.	GOOD	FAIR	POOR
	550	375	325	250	175	125

FRANCOTTE, A.
Liege, Belgium

For pistols and revolvers See—AFC.

Jubilee

A 12-, 16-, 20- and 28-gauge Anson & Deeley boxlock double-barrel shotgun, with various barrel lengths and chokes. Automatic ejectors, double triggers and walnut stock.

	NIB	EXC.	V.G.	GOOD	FAIR	POOR
	—	2000	1350	1100	850	450

No. 14

	NIB	EXC.	V.G.	GOOD	FAIR	POOR
	—	3000	2050	1700	1300	650

No. 18

	NIB	EXC.	V.G.	GOOD	FAIR	POOR
	—	3500	3000	2200	1500	750

No. 20

	NIB	EXC.	V.G.	GOOD	FAIR	POOR
	—	4000	3600	2250	1750	900

No. 25

	NIB	EXC.	V.G.	GOOD	FAIR	POOR
	—	5000	3900	2750	2000	1000

No. 30

	NIB	EXC.	V.G.	GOOD	FAIR	POOR
	—	6000	4200	3500	3000	1500

Eagle Grade No. 45

	NIB	EXC.	V.G.	GOOD	FAIR	POOR
	—	9000	7000	3500	2000	1000

Knockabout

Plain version of Jubilee Model, in 12-, 16-, 20-, 28-gauge and .410 bore. **NOTE:** Add 20 percent for 20-gauge; 30 percent for 28-gauge; 40 percent for .410 bore.

	NIB	EXC.	V.G.	GOOD	FAIR	POOR
	—	2700	2000	1000	650	500

	NIB	EXC.	V.G.	GOOD	FAIR	POOR

Sidelock Side-by-Side

A 12-, 16-, 20-, 28-gauge and .410 bore sidelock shotgun, ordered per customer's specifications. Extensive scroll engraving, deluxe walnut stock and finely checkered. **NOTE:** The .410 will bring a premium from $1,200 - $1,500.

NIB	EXC.	V.G.	GOOD	FAIR	POOR
25000	20000	12000	6500	5000	3500

Deluxe Sidelock Side-by-Side

As above, with gold-inlaid hunting scenes.

NIB	EXC.	V.G.	GOOD	FAIR	POOR
30000	24000	16000	8000	5750	4800

CUSTOM MADE SHOTGUNS & RIFLES

These shotguns and rifles were all custom built to customer's specifications. Gauge (including 24- and 32-gauge), caliber, barrel length, engraving, wood type and style are all individually produced. No two are alike. These shotguns and rifles should be individually appraised before sale. Prices listed are subject to fluctuations in international currency.

Custom Side-by-Side Shotguns

Available in 12-, 16-, 20-, 28-gauge and .410 bore, in either boxlock or sidelock actions. Barrel length, engraving, wood type and style are at customer's discretion. Retail prices range from:
Basic Boxlock with 27.5" barrels and walnut stock with double triggers in 12-, 16- and 20-gauge without engraving—$18,000

Basic Boxlock in 28-gauge or .410 bore without engraving—$14,000

Basic Boxlock with 26.5" or 28" barrels and deluxe walnut stock, with scroll engraving and double triggers in 12-, 16- and 20-gauge—$23,000

Basic Boxlock in 28-gauge or .410 bore—$28,000

Prices for 24- and 32-gauge are extra. These prices do not include engraving.

Custom Double Rifles

These custom built double rifles were offered, in calibers from 9.3x74R to .470 Nitro Express, in boxlock or sidelock actions. Barrel length, engraving, wood type and style are at customer's discretion. Retail prices range from:
Prices for 24- and 32-gauge are extra. These prices do not include engraving.

Boxlock in 9.3x74R, 8x57JRS and other European calibers-$14,000

Boxlock in.375 H&H and.470 NE—$19,000

Sidelock in 9.3x74R, etc.—$23,700

Sidelock in large calibers—$32,000

Custom Single-Shot Mountain Rifles

These single-shot rifles were offered in rimmed cartridges, but rimless cartridge rifles can be built on special request. Barrel length, engraving, wood type and style are at customer's discretion. Retail prices range from:
Boxlock in rimmed calibers—Prices start at $13,000

Sidelock in 7x65R and 7mm Rem. Magnum—Prices start at $24,000

Custom Bolt-Action Rifles

These bolt-action rifles utilize a Mauser 98 type action, with adjustable trigger. Offered in calibers from .17 Bee to .505 Gibbs. Barrel lengths are 21" to 24.5". Engraving, wood type and style are at customers' discretion. Retail prices range from:

Standard bolt-action calibers: .270, .30-06, 7x64, 8x60S and 9.3x62—Prices start at $7,650

Short-action calibers: .222, .223—Prices start at $9,100

Magnum-action calibers: 7mm Rem. Magnum, .300 Win. Magnum, .338 Win. Magnum, .375 H&H

and .458 Win. Magnum—Prices start at $8,400

African calibers: .416 Rigby, .460 Wby., .505 Gibbs—Prices start at $12,250

Please Note: Prices listed are for basic models. They do not reflect the extensive list of options available on these custom firearms.

FRANKLIN, C. W.
Liege, Belgium

Manufacturer of utilitarian shotguns, with either exposed or enclosed hammers. Circa 1900.

Single-Barrel

—	150	75	50	35	20

Damascus Barrel Double

—	250	150	125	100	65

Steel Barrel Double

—	300	175	150	125	90

FRANKONIA JAGD
Favorit, Germany

Seldom seen in U.S.A. Values extremely variable, based on local market, chambering and other factors.

Favorit Standard

Chambered for various European calibers, this bolt-action rifle has 24" barrel and set triggers. Blued, with checkered walnut stock.

—	450	295	260	175	125

Favorit Deluxe

As above, with more finely figured stock.

—	475	325	275	200	150

Safari Model

As above, in Magnum calibers.

—	1400	950	675	275	200

Heeren Rifle

Best quality single-shot rifle, with 26" octagonal barrel, double-set triggers and adjustable sights. Engraved with hand checkered high-grade walnut. Blued. Produced in a variety of calibers.

—	5000	3050	2500	1700	1250

FRASER F. A. CORP.
Fraser, Michigan

Fraser .25 cal.

A .25 ACP caliber semi-automatic pistol, with 2.25" barrel and 6-round magazine. Stainless steel with black nylon grips. There is a 24 kt. gold-plated model, that is worth approximately $100 additional. Later made under Fraser name, by a different company in 1990.

250	175	125	100	50	35

FREEDOM ARMS
Freedom, Wyoming

"Percussion" Mini-Revolver

A .22-caliber spur trigger revolver, with 1", 1.75" or 3" barrel lengths, 5-shot cylinder and bird's-head grip. Stainless steel. Belt buckle available that houses the pistol for an additional $40.

300	250	195	125	100	75

Bostonian (aka Boot Gun)

As above, with 3" barrel in .22 Magnum. Discontinued 1992.

375	300	225	150	80	60

Patriot (aka Boot Gun)

As above, in .22 LR caliber. Discontinued 1992.

375	300	225	150	80	60

NIB	EXC.	V.G.	GOOD	FAIR	POOR

Minuteman
As above, with 3" barrel. Discontinued in 1988.

375	300	225	150	80	60

Ironsides
As above in .22 Magnum, with 1" or 1.75" barrel.

375	300	225	150	80	60

Celebrity
As above, with belt buckle mount for either .22 or .22 Magnum revolvers. **NOTE:** .22 Magnum Model add $25.

400	325	275	225	150	100

PREMIER AND FIELD GRADE REVOLVERS

Both grades use the same materials and machining tolerances. Difference is in finish, standard components and warranty.

Premier Grade has a bright brushed finish, screw adjustable rear sight, laminated hardwood grips and limited lifetime warranty.

Field Grade has matte finish, adjustable rear sight for elevation only, Pachmayr rubber grips and one year warranty.

Casull Field Grade Model 83
A .454 Casull Magnum revolver, with 4.75", 6", 7.5" and 10" barrel. Standard fixed sights. Fires a 225-grain bullet. Also offered in .50 AE, .475 Linebaugh, .44 Rem. Magnum, .41 Magnum and .357 Magnum. Adjustable sights available as a $75 option. Matte stainless steel with black rubber Pachmayr grips. Introduced in 1988. **NOTE:** Add $75 for .454 Casull, .475 Linebaugh or .50 AE calibers.

1825	1400	800	550	—	—

Casull Premier Grade Model 83
A .454 Magnum, .44 Rem. Magnum, .45 Win. Magnum, .475 Linebaugh and .50 AE, with replaceable forcing and walnut grips. Finish is brush stainless steel. Adjustable sights are an extra cost option on this model as well. Offered in barrel lengths of 4.75", 6", 7.5" and 10" except for .475 Casull. .55 Wyoming Express added in 2006. **NOTE:** Extra cylinders are available for these models in .45 Colt, .45 Win. Magnum and .45 ACP. Add $250 to price of gun for each cylinder. Add $75 for .454 Casull, .475 Linebaugh or .50 AE calibers.

2150	1800	1250	850	500	350

Model 97
Revolver chambered for either .357 Magnum, .45 Colt, .44 Special and .22 LR cartridges. Available in Field or Premier grades, with choice of 4.25", 5.5" or 7.5" barrel. Optional .45 ACP cylinder of .45 Colt and .38 Special cylinder for .357 Magnum model. In 2004 this model was also offered in .17 HMR and .32 H&R Magnum calibers. **NOTE:** There are a number of extra-cost options that will affect price. Some of these options are sights, grips, Mag-Na-Port barrels, slings and trigger over-travel screws. Add $265 for extra .38 Special, .45 ACP cylinder or .22 WMR cylinder. Add $475 for extra fitted .22 LR match grade cylinder. Add $215 for match grade chambered, instead of .22 LR sport chamber.

1800	1350	1000	600	400	300

Model 353
Chambered for .357 Magnum cartridge, with choice of 4.75", 6", 7.5" or 9" barrel length. Adjustable sights. Model designation no longer used; see Model 97.

Field Grade

1650	1300	950	550	350	250

Premier Grade

2150	1800	1250	700	500	300

Signature Edition
As above, with highly polished finish, rosewood grips, 7.5" barrel only and fitted case. Serial numbers are DC1-DC2000. (DC represents Dick Casull, designer of firearm.) Total of 2,000 were made.

2500	1950	1300	750	550	350

	NIB	EXC.	V.G.	GOOD	FAIR	POOR

Model 252

Stainless steel version of large frame revolver, chambered for .22 LR cartridge. Available in 5.12", 7.5" or 10" barrel lengths. Matte finish. Designation no longer used; see Model 97. **NOTE:** Optional .22 Magnum cylinder available for $250.

Silhouette Class
10" barrel.

1700	1150	850	600	450	250

Varmint Class
5.12" or 7.5" barrel.

1700	1150	850	600	450	250

Model 757

Introduced in 1999, this 5-shot revolver chambered for .475 Linebaugh cartridge. Fitted with adjustable sights. Offered in both Field and Premier grades. Choice of 4.75", 6" or 7.5" barrel lengths. Designation no longer used; see Model 83.

Field Grade

1400	1100	750	500	400	300

Premier Grade

1800	1450	1100	750	500	400

Model 654

This 5-shot revolver chambered for .41 Magnum cartridge. Adjustable sights. Introduced in 1999. Designation no longer used; see Model 97.

Field Grade

1325	1050	750	500	400	300

Premier Grade

1750	1400	1100	750	500	400

Model 83 .500 Wyoming Express

Similar to Model 83, but chambered in .500 Wyoming Express. Introduced 2007.

2150	1800	1250	700	500	300

FREEMAN, AUSTIN T.
Hoard's Armory
Watertown, New York

Freeman Army Model Revolver

A .44-caliber percussion revolver, with 7.5" round barrel, 6-shot unfluted cylinder with recessed nipples. Blued, walnut grips, casehardened rammer and hammer. Frame marked "Freeman's Pat. Dec. 9, 1862/Hoard's Armory, Watertown, N.Y." Several thousand manufactured in 1863 and 1864.

—	—	5800	2200	550	200

FRIGON
Clay Center, Kansas

An importer of guns manufactured by Marocchi of Italy.

FT I

A 12-gauge boxlock single-barrel shotgun, with 32" or 34" ventilated rib barrel. Full choke, automatic ejector and interchangeable stock. Blued. Introduced in 1986.

950	750	650	550	450	300

FTC

As above, with two sets of barrels (a single ventilated rib trap barrel and a set of over/under ventilated rib barrels). In a fitted case. Introduced in 1986.

1750	1400	1150	800	650	500

FS-4

A four gauge set (12-, 20-, 28-gauge and .410 bore). Introduced in 1986.

2500	2100	1750	1500	1100	750

FROMMER
See—FEG (Fegyver Es Gazkeszulekgyar)

FRUHWIRTH
Austria

M1872 Fruhwirth System Rifle

An 11mm bolt-action rifle, with 25" barrel and 6-shot magazine. Blued, with full-length walnut stock.

—	650	425	300	195	100

FUNK, CHRISTOPH
Suhl, Germany

Christoph Funk began his gun business before 1900. The vast majority of long guns were the best quality. Some collectors believe that J.P. Sauer built receivers for Funk, but this is not known for certain. Funk produced shotguns, shotgun-rifle combinations and double rifles. Some were exported to England and U.S. Most of U.S. imports are in the more common North American calibers, such as .300 Savage, 30-30, 32-20 Winchester and 12- or 16-gauge. Most are found with only a right-hand extension arm, which locks into the receiver, but some higher grades have both extension arms. Quality of these guns is extremely high. Guns were probably not made after 1940. Quality of engraving and caliber determines value. American calibers will command a higher price. Prices listed are for American calibers.

Double Rifles

—	2950	2250	1450	600	400

Prewar Drilling in 16 or 12 gauge

—	4500	3750	2500	1200	—

FURR ARMS
J. & G. Sale, Inc.
Prescott, Arizona

In addition to producing reproductions of various cannon, this company also manufactured one-tenth to three-quarter scale reproductions of Gatling guns. Furr products are highly desirable in some circles, with the Gatling .22 reproductions typically commanding prices in excess of $18,000 in mint, unfired condition.

FYRBERG, ANDREW
Worcester and Hopkinton, Massachusetts

Double-Barrel Shotguns

Fyrberg did work for Iver Johnson and C.S. Shattuck Co. of Hatfield, Mass. He began producing a hammerless double about 1902, a well designed boxlock with coil mainsprings. An estimated 2,000 were produced at Hopkinton and Worcester, Mass. Some have been made at Meriden, Conn. Sears cataloged the Fyrberg guns in 1902 to about 1908.

—	525	425	300	200	150

Revolvers

A 3"-barreled .32-caliber and 3.5" .38-caliber revolver, with round ribbed barrels and round butts. Grips bear the trademark "AFCo". Model most likely made by Iver Johnson for Andrew Fyrberg.

—	250	145	100	75	50

G

	NIB	EXC.	V.G.	GOOD	FAIR	POOR

GABBET-FAIRFAX, H.
Birmingham, England

Mars

Designed by Hugh Gabbet-Fairfax, this semi-automatic pistol first produced on an experimental basis by Webley & Scott Revolvers in the 1890s. After Webley gave up on the idea an extremely limited number were built by Mars Automatic Pistol Syndicate, Ltd., 1897 to 1905. Pistol produced in four calibers; 8.5mm Mars, 9mm Mars, .45 Mars Short Case, and .45 Mars Long Case. Most powerful handgun cartridge of its time and remained so until well after World War II. It is estimated that only about 80 of these pistols were ever produced. **NOTE:** Webley examples are worth a premium.

—	45000	30500	19500	9200	6000

GABILONDO Y CIA
See—Llama

GABILONDO Y URRESTI
Guernica, Spain
Elgoibar, Spain
See—Llama

Spanish firm founded in 1904 to produce inexpensive revolvers of Velo-Dog type. Sometime around 1909 the firm began to manufacture Radium revolver. In 1914 the company produced a semi-automatic pistol distributed as Ruby. This pistol soon became the mainstay of the company, with orders of 30,000 pistols a month for the French army. End of WWI Gabilondo Y Urresti moved to Elgoeibar, Spain. Company produced a Browning 1910 replica pistol until early 1930s. It was at this point that Gabilondo began to manufacture a Colt Model 1911 copy that became known as Llama. For information of specific Llama models see Llama section. Pistols listed reflect pre-Llama period and are so marked, with the trade name of that particular model. Monogram "GC" frequently appears on grips but not on slide.

Velo-Dog Revolver

A 6.35mm double-action revolver with 1.5" barrel, folding trigger and concealed hammer. Blued, with walnut grips. Manufactured from 1904 to 1914.

—	295	195	125	75	50

Radium

Semi-automatic pistol in caliber 7.65mm. Produced both for commercial and military market in Ruby style. "Radium" stamped on slide as well as top of each grip plate.

—	295	195	125	100	70

Ruby

A 7.65mm caliber semi-automatic pistol. Discontinued in 1930.

—	250	175	150	100	75

Bufalo 6.35mm

Semi-automatic pistol in caliber 6.35mm. Copy of Browning Model 1906, with squeeze grip safety. Has "Bufalo" stamped on slide and Gabilondo logo along with a buffalo's head on each side of grip plates. Manufactured between 1918 and 1925. **NOTE:** Spelling of "Bufalo" as it appears on pistol.

—	275	175	150	100	75

Bufalo 7.65mm

Semi-automatic pistol in caliber 7.65mm. Patterned after Browning Model 1910, with squeeze grip safety. There were two models, with either 7- or 9-round magazine. Model with 9-round magazine usually fitted with wood grips and lanyard ring. Buffalo's head is inset in each grip plate. Manufactured between 1918 and 1925.

—	275	175	125	100	75

Bufalo 9mmK

Semi-automatic pistol in caliber 9mmK. Nearly same pistol as 7.65mm model, but fitted with grip safety. "Bufalo" stamped on slide and Gabilondo logo and buffalo's head are on each grip plate. Manufactured between 1918 and 1925.

—	295	205	145	105	70

	NIB	EXC.	V.G.	GOOD	FAIR	POOR

Danton 6.35mm

Semi-automatic pistol in caliber 6.35mm. Patterned after Browning Model 1906, with grip safety. "Danton" appears on slide as well as grips. Gabilondo logo on each grip plate. Manufactured between 1925 and 1931.

	—	275	175	125	100	75

Danton War Model

Semi-automatic pistol in caliber 7.65mm. Similar to Bufalo above and made with-/without grip safety. Came in two models, with 9- and 20-round magazines. Fitted with lanyard ring. "Danton" stamped on slide and grips. Gabilondo logo on each side of grip plate. Manufactured between 1925 and 1931.

Nine-Round Magazine

	—	275	175	125	100	75

Twenty-Round Magazine

	—	550	325	250	200	100

Perfect

Semi-automatic pistol chambered for 6.35mm and 7.65mm cartridges. Cheap low-priced pistol marketed by Mugica. Pistols usually have the word "Perfect" on grips. Slide may be stamped with the name MUGICA, but many are not.

	—	275	175	125	100	75

Plus Ultra

Pistol chambered for 7.65mm cartridge and built from 1925 to 1933. Had a 20-round magazine that gave the pistol an unusual appearance. "Plus Ultra" appears on slide and grips. Gabilondo logo on each grip plate. Equipped with lanyard ring.

	—	1200	875	650	425	250

GALAND, C.F.
Liege, Belgium

Galand, Galand & Sommerville, Galand Perrin (Galand M1872)

A 7mm, 9mm and 12mm caliber double-action revolver, with 6-shot cylinder and open frame. A unique ejection system that by means of rotating a lever downward from the trigger guard, causes barrel and cylinder to slide forward leaving ejector and spent cases behind. Circa 1872.

	—	—	1350	875	550	150

Velo-Dog

A 5.5mm Velo-Dog caliber fixed trigger and guard double-action revolver, with open-top design. Later models (.22 and 6.35mm caliber) feature folding triggers and no trigger guards.

	—	250	165	125	75	50

Le Novo

As above, with concealed hammer and in 6.35mm caliber.

	—	250	165	125	75	50

Tue-Tue

A .22 short 5.5mm Velo-Dog and 6.35mm caliber double-action revolver. Concealed hammer, folding trigger and swing-out cylinder, with central extractor. Introduced in 1894.

	—	250	165	125	75	50

GALAND & SOMMERVILLE
Liege, Belgium
See—Galand

GALEF (ZABALA)
Zabala Hermanos & Antonio Zoli
Spain

Zabala Double

A 10-, 12-, 16- and 20-gauge boxlock shotgun, with 22" to 30" barrel and various chokes. Hardwood stock. **NOTE:** Add 50 percent for 10-gauge.

	—	450	300	175	100	75

NIB	EXC.	V.G.	GOOD	FAIR	POOR

Companion

Folding 12-gauge to .410 bore single-shot underlever shotgun, with 28" or 30" barrel.

—	200	145	105	50	25

Monte Carlo Trap

A 12-gauge underlever single-shot shotgun, with 32" ventilated rib barrel.

—	325	275	150	100	75

Silver Snipe, Golden Snipe, and Silver Hawk

See—Antonio Zoli

GALENA INDUSTRIES INC.
Sturgis, South Dakota

In 1998, Galena Industries purchased the rights to use AMT trademark and manufacturing rights to many, but not all, AMT designs. For AMT models made by AMT see that section. This company's designs have been acquired by Crusader/High Standard of Houston, Texas.

AMT Backup

Model features double-action-only trigger system and offered in both stainless steel and matte black finish. Small frame .380 Backup weighs 18 oz. with its 2.5" barrel. Large frame Backups are fitted with 3" barrel and offered in 9mm, .38 Super, .357 Sig., .40 S&W, .400 CorBon and .45 ACP. Weights are approximately 23 oz. and magazine capacity 5 to 6 rounds, depending on caliber. **NOTE:** Add $50 for .38 Super, .357 Sig, and .400 CorBon.

525	375	275	200	125	100

Automag II

Semi-automatic pistol chambered for .22 WMR cartridge. Offered in 3.38", 4.5" or 6" barrel lengths. Magazine capacity 9 rounds, except for 3.38" model where capacity is 7 rounds. Weight about 32 oz.

695	550	325	225	125	100

Automag III

Pistol chambered for .30 Carbine cartridge. Barrel length 6.38". Weight about 43 oz. Stainless steel finish.

800	675	375	250	150	100

Automag IV

Model chambered for .45 Winchester Magnum cartridge. Fitted with 6.5" barrel. Magazine capacity 7 rounds. Weight approximately 46 oz.

800	675	375	250	150	100

Automag .440 CorBon

Semi-automatic pistol chambered for .440 CorBon cartridge and fitted with 7.5" barrel. Magazine capacity 5 rounds. Finish matte black. Weight about 46 oz. Checkered walnut grips. Introduced in 2000. Special order only.

1000	900	750	575	400	175

Galena Accelerator

Model has 7" barrel built on 1911 frame. Chambered for .400 CorBon. Magazine capacity 7 rounds. Weight about 46 oz. Finish stainless steel.

850	725	550	400	300	100

Galena Hardballer

Pistol based on Colt Model 1911 design. Chambered for .45 ACP cartridge. Fitted with 5" barrel. Magazine capacity 7 rounds. Finish stainless steel. Adjustable trigger and beveled magazine well. Offered chambered for .40 S&W and .400 CorBon cartridges. Weight about 38 oz.

1000	900	750	575	400	175

Galena Longslide

Model chambered for .45 ACP cartridge and fitted with 7" barrel. Magazine capacity 7 rounds. Weight about 46 oz. Finish stainless steel.

850	725	550	400	300	10

Galena Commando

Commando chambered for .40 S&W cartridge. Fitted with 4" barrel. Magazine capacity 8 rounds. Weight about 38 oz. Finish stainless steel.

550	400	295	225	175	100

GALESI, INDUSTRIA ARMI
Brescia, Italy

Rino Galesi Armi, Collebeato, Italy, manufactured shotguns, revolvers and automatic pistols. Firm's name changed from Rino Galesi Armi to Industria Armi Galesi to Rigarmi di Rino Galesi. Their semi-automatic pistols were designated by model year, model number and a 500 Series. Most models named in the 500 Series came after the firm changed its name to Industria Armi Galesi.

Model 1923

A 6.35mm and 7.65mm caliber semi-automatic pistol. Has a squeeze grip safety and wood grip plates with crest. Model 1923 stamped on slide.

NIB	EXC.	V.G.	GOOD	FAIR	POOR
—	275	195	145	75	50

Model 1930

A 6.35mm and 7.65mm caliber semi-automatic pistol. Very few were made in 1946 in 9mm Parabellum. Based on 1910 Browning design. Blued, with plastic grips. Slide marked "Brevetto Mod. 1930".

NIB	EXC.	V.G.	GOOD	FAIR	POOR
—	275	195	145	75	50

9mm Parabellum

NIB	EXC.	V.G.	GOOD	FAIR	POOR
—	600	500	400	300	100

Model 6

Updated Model 1930. Manufactured approximately 1938 to 1948 in calibers; 22 Short, .22 Long, .22 LR, 6.35mm, 7.65mm and 9mm Short.

NIB	EXC.	V.G.	GOOD	FAIR	POOR
—	350	175	100	75	50

Model 9

Manufactured from approximately 1947 to 1956 in calibers .22 Short, .22 Long, .22 LR, 6.35mm, 7.65mm and 9mm Short. Also listed under 500 Series. The .22 versions were marketed as "the smallest .22 pistols ever built".

NIB	EXC.	V.G.	GOOD	FAIR	POOR
—	295	175	100	75	50

GALIL
Israel Military Industries
Israel

Model AR (.223)

NOTE: Add $600 for .308-caliber.

NIB	EXC.	V.G.	GOOD	FAIR	POOR
3000	2400	2000	1500	900	700

Model ARM

NIB	EXC.	V.G.	GOOD	FAIR	POOR
3400	2700	2000	1500	900	700

Sniper Rifle

NIB	EXC.	V.G.	GOOD	FAIR	POOR
8500	7500	6000	4000	3000	2000

Hadar II

NIB	EXC.	V.G.	GOOD	FAIR	POOR
1300	1100	800	650	500	400

GALLAGER
Richardson & Overman
Philadelphia, Pennsylvania

Gallager Carbine

A .50-caliber single-shot percussion carbine, with 22.25" barrel, saddle ring and walnut stock. Blued and case hardened. Approximately 23,000 were made during the Civil War.

Percussion Model

As above, in .56-62 rimfire caliber. Approximately 5,000 of this model made.

NIB	EXC.	V.G.	GOOD	FAIR	POOR
—	—	3900	2450	1500	500

Spencer Cartridge Model

NIB	EXC.	V.G.	GOOD	FAIR	POOR
—	—	3425	1950	1350	400

NIB	EXC.	V.G.	GOOD	FAIR	POOR

GAMBA, RENATO
Gardone V. T., Italy

SIDE-BY-SIDE SHOTGUNS

Hunter Super
A 12-gauge Anson & Deeley boxlock double-barrel shotgun. Variety of barrel lengths and chokes, double triggers and extractors. Engraved and silver-plated.

NIB	EXC.	V.G.	GOOD	FAIR	POOR
1250	900	700	550	450	250

Principessa
A 12-, 20- or 28-gauge boxlock shotgun. Engraved checkered stock.

NIB	EXC.	V.G.	GOOD	FAIR	POOR
1850	1250	900	700	500	250

Oxford 90
A 12- or 20-gauge sidelock shotgun, with various barrel lengths and chokes. Purdey locking system, double triggers and automatic ejectors. Walnut stock.

NIB	EXC.	V.G.	GOOD	FAIR	POOR
4250	3250	1700	900	600	300

Oxford Extra
Same as above, with fine engraving.

NIB	EXC.	V.G.	GOOD	FAIR	POOR
5200	4000	2250	1500	900	450

Gamba 624 Prince
Fitted with Wesley Richards-type frame, select walnut stock and fine hand engraving. Offered in 12-gauge with 28" barrels.

NIB	EXC.	V.G.	GOOD	FAIR	POOR
4800	3900	2500	1500	850	400

Gamba 624 Extra
Same as above, with deep floral engraving.

NIB	EXC.	V.G.	GOOD	FAIR	POOR
8000	5000	4500	2500	1250	600

London
A 12- or 20-gauge Holland & Holland sidelock shotgun, with various barrel lengths and chokes. Double- or single-selective trigger, automatic ejectors. Walnut stock.

NIB	EXC.	V.G.	GOOD	FAIR	POOR
7000	5500	4500	2500	1250	700

London Royal
As above, with engraved hunting scenes.

NIB	EXC.	V.G.	GOOD	FAIR	POOR
8000	6500	5000	3750	2000	950

Ambassador Gold and Black
A 12- and 20-gauge Holland & Holland sidelock shotgun, with various barrel lengths and choke combinations. Single-selective trigger, automatic ejectors and a single gold line engraved on barrels and frame. Walnut stocks.

NIB	EXC.	V.G.	GOOD	FAIR	POOR
25000	19000	13500	9500	5000	2500

Ambassador Executive
Gamba's best quality shotgun produced in 12- or 20-gauge to customer's specifications.

NIB	EXC.	V.G.	GOOD	FAIR	POOR
28000	20000	15000	10000	5000	2500

OVER/UNDER SHOTGUNS

Country Model
A 12- and 20-gauge over/under shotgun, with 28" or 30" ventilated rib barrels, double triggers, extractors. Walnut stock.

NIB	EXC.	V.G.	GOOD	FAIR	POOR
650	550	400	300	275	200

Grifone Model
A 12- and 20-gauge over/under shotgun, with 26", 28" or 30" ventilated rib barrels, single-selective trigger and automatic ejectors. Boxlock action silver-plated, with walnut stock. Available with screw-in chokes. This would add 10 percent to values.

NIB	EXC.	V.G.	GOOD	FAIR	POOR
800	650	550	350	250	200

Europa 2000
A 12-gauge over/under shotgun in various barrel lengths and choke combinations. Single-selective trigger and automatic ejectors. Engraved silver-plated boxlock action, with false

	NIB	EXC.	V.G.	GOOD	FAIR	POOR

sideplates and walnut stock.

	1250	900	700	550	350	250

Grinta Trap and Skeet

A 12-gauge over/under shotgun, with 26" Skeet or 30" Full choke barrels, single-selective trigger, automatic ejectors and some engraving. Walnut stock.

	1350	900	700	550	350	250

Victory Trap and Skeet

As above, but more finely finished.

	1650	1150	850	600	400	250

Edinburg Match

As above, with slightly different engraving patterns.

	1250	1000	800	600	400	250

Boyern 88 Combination Gun

A 12-gauge combination over/under rifle/shotgun, with double triggers and extractors. Engraved game scenes and coin-finished, with walnut stock.

	1250	900	700	500	400	250

DAYTONA SERIES

Competition shotgun first introduced into U.S. in 1986 as Type I. Type I available in different configurations, with base model selling for about $4,000 until 1991. In 1994 Gamba introduced Daytona in a wide variety of configurations and grades under a new designation called Type II. Primary difference was in location of stock bolt. Only about 80 Daytona Type II shotguns are allocated to U.S. per year. High quality shotgun with an excellent reputation. Prices listed are for 12-gauge. 20-gauge guns available on special request.

Daytona Trap

Offered in 12-gauge with 30" or 32" barrels. Select walnut stock with hand checkering. Removable trigger group, improved Boss lock-up and boxlock receiver.

	5900	4750	3000	2250	1200	600

Daytona Sporting

Available in 12-gauge, with 30" barrel, screw-in chokes and single-selective trigger.

	4000	3250	2500	1900	1200	700

Daytona Skeet

Offered in 12-gauge, with 29" barrels and single-selective trigger.

	4000	3250	2500	1900	1200	700

Daytona America Trap

Offered in 12-gauge, with 30" or 32" barrels, high adjustable rib, adjustable stock and single trigger.

	4000	3250	2500	1900	1200	700

Daytona Game

Offered in 12-gauge, with 28" barrels and single trigger. **NOTE:** Add $300 for black frame with gold inlaid names and logo.

	3900	3500	3000	2250	1200	700

Daytona Grade 6 Engraving

Fine English scroll hand engraving, edged with gold line work.

Daytona Trap and Skeet Models

	13000	5000	4000	3000	1500	700

Daytona Sporting Model

	13500	5000	4000	3000	1500	700

Daytona Grade 5 Engraving

Deep relief floral engraving, with gold inlaid griffons.

Daytona Trap and Skeet Models

	14000	9000	6500	5000	2500	1200

Daytona Sporting Model

	14500	9000	6500	5000	2500	1200

	NIB	EXC.	V.G.	GOOD	FAIR	POOR

Daytona Grade 4 Engraving

Flying eagle in a landscape and very fine English scroll by master engravers.

Daytona Trap and Skeet Models

NIB	EXC.	V.G.	GOOD	FAIR	POOR
16250	10000	7500	5500	3000	1500

Daytona Sporting Model

NIB	EXC.	V.G.	GOOD	FAIR	POOR
16750	10000	7500	5500	3000	1500

Daytona SL Grade 3 Engraving

Fitted with engraved game scene sideplates and fine English scroll by master engravers.

Daytona Trap and Skeet Models

NIB	EXC.	V.G.	GOOD	FAIR	POOR
18750	15000	11000	7500	3500	1750

Daytona Sporting Model

NIB	EXC.	V.G.	GOOD	FAIR	POOR
19250	11000	9000	6500	3500	1750

Daytona Game

NIB	EXC.	V.G.	GOOD	FAIR	POOR
18750	11000	9000	6500	3500	1750

Daytona SLHH Grade 2 Engraving

Fitted with sideplates and Boss lock-up system, automatic ejectors, figured walnut stock. Fine game scene engraving signed by a master. Offered in 12-gauge with 28" barrels.

NIB	EXC.	V.G.	GOOD	FAIR	POOR
36250	16000	12500	9500	6000	3000

Daytona SLHH Grade 1 Gold Engraving

Same as above, with gold inlaid game scenes and floral-style engraving signed by master engraver. Offered in 12-gauge with 28" barrels.

NIB	EXC.	V.G.	GOOD	FAIR	POOR
43500	17000	13000	9500	5500	2500

Daytona SLHH "One of Thousand"

Same as above, but game scene is executed at customers direction. A totally custom ordered gun. Available in all configurations.

NIB	EXC.	V.G.	GOOD	FAIR	POOR
125000	70000	35000	15500	7500	600

CONCORDE GAME SHOTGUNS

This over/under model offered as a slightly less expensive alternative to Daytona Series guns. Base gun available with blued or chromed action. Extra barrel are interchangeable in both 12- and 20-gauge, with 28" barrels and single triggers.

NIB	EXC.	V.G.	GOOD	FAIR	POOR
6000	4250	3000	1500	750	450

Concorde Trap

Available in 12 gauge, with 30" or 32" barrels, single trigger.

NIB	EXC.	V.G.	GOOD	FAIR	POOR
—	2000	1500	1000	600	450

Concorde Skeet

Available in 12-gauge, with 29" barrels and single trigger.

NIB	EXC.	V.G.	GOOD	FAIR	POOR
6000	4250	3000	1500	750	450

Concorde Sporting

Offered in 12-gauge, with 30" barrels, screw-in chokes and single-selective trigger.

NIB	EXC.	V.G.	GOOD	FAIR	POOR
6100	2900	2000	1500	900	500

Concorde Game Grade 7 Engraving

Game scene engraving, with fine English scroll.

NIB	EXC.	V.G.	GOOD	FAIR	POOR
8700	4000	3250	2250	1200	600

Concorde Game Grade 8 Engraving

English scroll engraving.

NIB	EXC.	V.G.	GOOD	FAIR	POOR
6250	3000	2500	1750	1000	500

Concorde 2nd Generation

Similar to Concorde series, with fixed trigger group. Black or chrome frame. Automatic ejectors. Select walnut stock. Choice of 12- or 20-gauge, with 28" or 30" barrels and single trigger. Introduced in 2002.

NIB	EXC.	V.G.	GOOD	FAIR	POOR
6100	4850	3200	1950	750	300

	NIB	EXC.	V.G.	GOOD	FAIR	POOR

Le Mans

Model chambered for 12-gauge shell and fitted with choice of 28" or 30" barrels. Automatic ejectors. Single-selective trigger. Five choke tubes. Introduced in 2002.

	1750	1200	850	625	475	200

Hunter II

This 12-gauge model has an alloy frame, with reinforced barrel and automatic ejectors. Five choke tubes. Single-selective trigger. Barrel lengths of 26" to 27.5". Introduced in 2002.

	1600	1100	750	525	375	150

RIFLES

Safari Express

A 7x65R, 9.3x74R or .375 H&H caliber boxlock double-barrel rifle, with 25" barrels, open sights, double triggers, automatic ejectors and coin-finished scroll engraved receiver. Walnut stock.

	8500	6500	4500	1750	750	350

Mustang

A 5.6x50, 6.5x57R, 7x65R, .222 Rem., .270 Win. or .30-06 caliber sidelock single barrel rifle, with double-set triggers, engraved sidelock action and walnut stock.

	8500	6500	4500	1750	750	350

RGZ 1000

7x64, .270 Win., 7mm Rem. Magnum and .300 Win. Magnum caliber Mauser 98 bolt-action, with 20.5" barrel. Walnut pistol-grip stock and cheekpiece.

	1100	900	750	550	400	200

RGX 1000 Express

As above, with double-set triggers and 23.75" barrel.

	1250	950	750	550	400	200

PISTOLS

SAB G90

A 7.65 Parabellum or 9mm caliber double-action semi-automatic pistol, with 4.75" barrel and 15-shot magazine. Blued or chrome-plated, with walnut grips.

	575	450	350	300	250	175

SAB G91 Compact

As above, with 3.5" barrel and 12-shot magazine.

	550	400	325	275	225	150

Trident Fast Action

A .32 S&W or .38 Special caliber double-action revolver, with 2.5" or 3" barrel and 6-shot cylinder. Blued, with walnut grips.

	500	400	300	250	200	150

Trident Super

As above, with 4" ventilated rib barrel.

	550	400	325	275	225	150

Trident Match 900

As above, with 6" heavy barrel, adjustable sights. Target type walnut grips.

	850	700	550	400	350	200

GARAND
(U.S. M-1 Rifle)

This was the standard issue rifle for U.S. military services from 1936 to 1957. In .30-06 caliber, it is a gas-operated semi-automatic, fed by an 8-round clip that is inserted in the open action from above. Garand series was made in several variants and manufactured by many different companies over its 20 years of service. A complete history of John Garand's great rifle, see Standard Catalog of Military Firearms, published by Gun Digest Books/Krause Publications. Prices shown below are for rifles in original, unaltered condition. Many rifles seen on today's market have been restored or refinished and values should be reduced from 30 to 50 percent.

	NIB	EXC.	V.G.	GOOD	FAIR	POOR

Rebuilt Rifle, any manufacture

	1200	1000	800	600	—	—

DCM Rifles

	—	850	575	450	—	—

Navy Trophy Rifles U.S.N. Crane Depot Rebuild

	—	1800	1000	900	—	—

AMF Rebuild

	—	1000	900	750	—	—

H&R Rebuild

NOTE: These rifles MUST be original and validated by experts.

	—	900	800	700	—	—

SPRINGFIELD ARMORY PRODUCTION

Gas trap sn: ca 81-52,000

	—	40000	35000	25000	—	—

Gas trap/modified to gas port

	—	5000	3500	2500	—	—

Pre-Dec. 7, 1941 gas port production sn: ca 410,000

	—	4000	2200	1300	900	400

WWII Production sn: ca 410,000-3,880,000

	—	1400	1100	900	750	500

Post-WWII Production sn: ca 4,200,000-6,099,361

	—	1100	850	650	500	450

Winchester Educational Contract sn: 100,000-100,500

	—	10000	6000	4500	2000	700

Winchester sn: 100,501-165,000

	—	6500	4500	3000	1100	550

Winchester sn: 1,200,00-1,380,000

	—	5500	4500	2500	750	400

Winchester sn: 2,305,850-2,536,493

	—	3500	2800	1500	500	300

Winchester sn: 1,601,150-1,640,000 "win-13

	—	3500	2200	1800	1500	850

Harrington & Richardson Production

	—	1800	1200	900	600	300

International Harvester Production

	—	2200	1500	800	500	250

International Harvester/with Springfield Receiver (postage stamp)

	—	2800	1500	1000	—	—

International Harvester/with Springfield Receiver (arrow head)

	—	2800	1500	1000	—	—

International Harvester/with Springfield Receiver (Gap letter)

	—	2800	1500	1000	—	—

International Harvester/with Harrington & Richardson Receiver

	—	1900	1200	900	—	—

British Garands (Lend Lease)

	—	1300	1200	875	500	275

	NIB	EXC.	V.G.	GOOD	FAIR	POOR

M1 Garand Cutaway

NOTE: For examples with documentation add 300 percent.

	NIB	EXC.	V.G.	GOOD	FAIR	POOR
	—	3000	2500	1000	600	500

SCOPED VARIANTS (SNIPER RIFLES)

NOTE: Sniper rifles must have sales or verification papers.

M1C

	—	10000	8000	5000	—	—

M1D (USMC Issue) MC 1952

	—	3800	3000	2000	—	—

National Match

Type I

	—	4500	2500	1800	—	—

Type II

	—	3200	2200	1500	—	—

GARATE, ANITUA/G.A.C.
Eibar, Spain

Charola

A 5.5mm Clement semi-automatic pistol, with magazine located in front of trigger and exposed hammer.

	—	1500	1200	750	500	400

Cosmopolite

A .38-caliber copy of Colt Police Positive. Manufactured from 1920 to 1930.

	—	275	165	125	100	75

El Lunar

Resembling Colt Police Positive in 8mm Lebel caliber. Revolver made for French government in 1915 and 1916.

	—	300	175	150	125	100

G.A.C.

Copy of Smith & Wesson Military & Police revolver. Manufactured between 1930 and 1936 in .32-20 caliber. Marked "G.A.C. Firearms Mfg. Co.

	—	250	150	125	100	75

Modelo Militar

Close copy of Smith & Wesson Triple Lock/New Century N-frame revolver. Chambered in .44 Special. Marked "G.A.C.

	—	325	250	200	175	75

Express or Danton

A 7.65mm caliber "Eibar" semi-automatic pistol, with 9-shot magazine.

	—	275	150	100	75	50

British Service Old Pattern No.2 Mk. I Trocaola Aranzabal Military Revolver

A .455 caliber double-action break-open revolver, with 5" barrel. Adopted by Royal Army in November of 1915 and known as "Pistol OP No. 1 Mark 1".

	—	450	250	200	150	100

L'Eclair

A 5.5mm Velo-Dog caliber folding-trigger double-action revolver, with 6-shot cylinder. Manufactured from 1900 to 1914. Not to be confused with the chocolate confectionary.

	—	250	145	100	75	50

Sprinter

A 6.35mm caliber semi-automatic pistol marked "The Best Automatique Pistol Sprinter Patent 6.35mm Cartridge.". Manufactured before WWI.

	—	250	145	125	75	50

	NIB	EXC.	V.G.	GOOD	FAIR	POOR

La Lira

Copy of Mannlicher Model 1901 in .32 ACP caliber, with removable magazine marked "System La Lira" on breech; "Para Cartoucho Browning 7.65mm" on barrel; "G.A.C." on grips. Produced prior to WWI.

	NIB	EXC.	V.G.	GOOD	FAIR	POOR
	—	1200	1000	700	400	300

Triumph

Identical to La Lira model marked "Triumph Automatic Pistol".

	NIB	EXC.	V.G.	GOOD	FAIR	POOR
	—	1200	1000	700	400	300

GARATE, HERMANOS
Ermua, Spain

Cantabria

A 6.35mm caliber folding-trigger double-action revolver, with concealed hammer, cocking spur and short barrel resembling slide on a semi-automatic. Name "Cantabria" stamped on left side.

	NIB	EXC.	V.G.	GOOD	FAIR	POOR
	—	300	175	125	100	75

Velo-Stark

Double-action folding-trigger revolver, with concealed hammer.

	NIB	EXC.	V.G.	GOOD	FAIR	POOR
	—	250	150	100	75	50

GARBI
Eibar, Spain

Model 51-B

A 12-gauge boxlock shotgun. Also available in 16- and 20-gauge, with double triggers, automatic ejectors, case hardened or coin-finished receiver and walnut stock.

	NIB	EXC.	V.G.	GOOD	FAIR	POOR
	1750	1200	850	600	—	—

Model 62-B

A 12-gauge sidelock shotgun. Also chambered for 16- and 20-gauge, with double triggers, extractors and cocking indicators. Engraved case hardened or coin-finished receiver and walnut stock.

	NIB	EXC.	V.G.	GOOD	FAIR	POOR
	1500	1050	850	650	325	175

Model 71

A 12-, 16- or 20-gauge Holland & Holland sidelock shotgun, with various barrel lengths and choke combinations. Automatic ejectors and single-selective trigger. Engraved with fine English-style scrollwork and walnut stock. Discontinued in 1988.

	NIB	EXC.	V.G.	GOOD	FAIR	POOR
	2500	2000	1800	1500	700	225

Model 100

A 12-, 16- or 20-gauge Holland & Holland sidelock shotgun, with chopper-lump barrels, automatic ejectors and single trigger. Engraved in Purdey style, with walnut stock.

	NIB	EXC.	V.G.	GOOD	FAIR	POOR
	3500	3000	2500	2000	900	250

Model 101

As above, with floral engraving. Discontinued in 1988 in this form, then furnished with hand-engraved Continental scroll and round body action.

	NIB	EXC.	V.G.	GOOD	FAIR	POOR
	6100	5250	3250	2500	1000	350

Model 102

As above, with Holland & Holland style engraving. Also in 28-gauge. Discontinued in 1988.

	NIB	EXC.	V.G.	GOOD	FAIR	POOR
	4500	3750	3200	1600	600	250

Model 103A

Model has Purdey-style engraving, with high grade wood and checkering.

	NIB	EXC.	V.G.	GOOD	FAIR	POOR
	14100	10000	7500	5500	2750	1000

Model 103A Royal

Same as above, with special high quality engraving, very fancy wood, hand matted rib.

	NIB	EXC.	V.G.	GOOD	FAIR	POOR
	16000	12500	8500	6500	3750	1200

Model 103B

In 12-, 16-, 20- or 28-gauge Holland & Holland sidelock shotgun. Various barrel lengths and choke combinations. Chopper-lump barrels, Holland & Holland easy-opening mechanism,

	NIB	EXC.	V.G.	GOOD	FAIR	POOR

automatic ejectors, single-selective trigger and Purdey-type scroll engraving.

	NIB	EXC.	V.G.	GOOD	FAIR	POOR
	21600	16750	10500	7750	6000	1500

Model 103B Royal

Same as above, with high quality engraving, very fancy wood, hand matted rib.

	22500	18000	13000	8500	4200	1600

Model 120

As above, with engraved hunting scenes. Discontinued in 1988.

	21600	16750	10500	7750	6000	1500

Model 200

As above, Magnum proofed double locking screws and 100 percent floral scroll engraving.

	17100	13500	9500	6500	300	1250

Model Special

A special order gun. Too rare to price.

Express Rifle

Best-quality sidelock side-by-side double rifle. Stock has pistol-grip and cheekpiece. Choice of English scroll or floral engraving. Calibers are 7x65R, 9.3x74R or .375 H&H.

	21000	15000	12000	7750	6000	1500

GARCIA
(formerly Firearms International of Wash., D.C.)

Garcia Bronco

Single-shot .410 bore shotgun or .22 LR or .22 Magnum rifle, with swing out action. Modeled somewhat after old Hamilton No. 7. Barrel length 18.5". Stock is one-piece metal skeletonized affair. Weight approximately 3.5 lbs. Introduced in 1968. Discontinued in 1978. Built in U.S.A.

	350	250	225	125	90	50

Garcia Bronco .22/.410

Over/under shotgun/rifle combination. Over barrel .22 LR and under barrel chambered for .410 bore. Barrel length 18.5". One-piece metal skeletonized stock. Introduced in 1976. Discontinued in 1978. Weight about 4 lbs.

	500	375	295	200	115	75

Garcia Musketeer

Model is a bolt-action rifle chambered for .243, .264, .270, .30-06, .307 Win. Magnum, .308 Norma, 7mm Rem. Magnum and .300 Win. Magnum. Fitted with checkered walnut stock, open sights, pistol-grip, hinged floorplate and adjustable trigger. Introduced in 1970. Discontinued in 1972.

	600	500	350	250	200	150

GARRET, J. & F. CO.
Greensboro, North Carolina

Garrett Single-Shot Pistol

A .54-caliber single-shot percussion pistol, with 8.5" round barrel, swivel ramrod, walnut stock and brass mounts. Marked on barrel breech "G.W." or "S.R." Approximately 500 made in 1862 and 1863.

	—	—	4550	165	1000	500

GASSER, LEOPOLD
Ottakring, Austria

M1870

An 11mm caliber double-action revolver, with 9.3" or 14.75" barrel and 6-shot cylinder. Marked "Gasser Patent, Guss Stahl". Bears an Austrian eagle and apple pierced by an arrow, with words "Schutz Mark".

	—	650	425	230	175	125

M1870/74

As above, with steel frame.

	—	650	425	350	175	125

	NIB	EXC.	V.G.	GOOD	FAIR	POOR

Gasser-Kropatschek M1876

A 9mm caliber M1870/74. Weight 1 lb. 11 oz.

	NIB	EXC.	V.G.	GOOD	FAIR	POOR
	—	600	400	300	150	100

Montenegrin Gasser

A 10.7mm caliber double-action revolver, with 5" or 6" barrel and 5-shot cylinder. Engraved silver and gold inlay. Ivory or bone grips. Values given are for plain, unadorned model. Embellished models will need individual appraisal.

	—	650	425	350	200	150

Rast & Gasser M1898

A 8mm caliber double-action revolver, with 4.75" barrel, 8-shot cylinder, solid-frame with loading gate and integral ejector rod.

	—	650	425	350	175	125

GATLING ARMS CO.
Birmingham, England

Established in 1888, this company remained in operation until approximately 1890. Although primarily involved with marketing of Gatling Guns, it did market one revolver listed.

Kynoch-Dimancea

A .38- or .45-caliber double-action hammerless revolver, with 6-shot cylinder. Loading system rather unusual—a spur that resembles a hammer is pulled down allowing barrel and cylinder to pivot and to be pulled forward. During this motion empty cases are ejected and new ones could be inserted. Marked "The Gatling Arms and Ammunition Co. Birmingham"; also marked "Dimancea Patent".

	—	—	2400	1275	750	350

GAUCHER
France

GN 1

Single-shot bolt-action pistol chambered for .22 LR. Fitted with 10" barrel, blade front sight and adjustable rear sight. Adjustable trigger. Hardwood target grips. Weight approximately 38 oz. Introduced in 1990.

	525	425	350	225	145	100

GAULOIS
St. Etienne, France
See—Le Francais

GAVAGE, A.
Liege, Belgium

A 7.65mm caliber semi-automatic pistol, with fixed barrel and concealed hammer. Similar in appearance to Clement. Markings with "AG" molded into grips. Some have been found bearing German Waffenamts. Manufactured from 1930s to 1940s.

	—	450	325	250	150	100

GAZANAGA, ISIDRO
Eibar, Spain

Destroyer M1913

A 6.35mm or 7.65mm caliber semi-automatic pistol. The 6.35mm model copied after 1906 Browning. "Destroyer" stamped on slide and Isidro logo on each side of grip plate. Produced through WWI.

	—	295	195	145	75	50

Destroyer M1916

A 7.65mm caliber semi-automatic pistol, with 7- or 9-shot magazine. Ruby style pistol manufactured by the Spanish during WWI. "Destroyer" stamped on slide. Wood grips.

	—	325	225	125	75	50

Destroyer Revolver

A good quality .38-caliber copy of Colt Police Positive.

	—	295	165	155	100	75

	NIB	EXC.	V.G.	GOOD	FAIR	POOR

Super Destroyer

A 7.65mm caliber copy of Walther PP. Slide stamped "Pistola Automatica 7.65 Super Destroyer".

	NIB	EXC.	V.G.	GOOD	FAIR	POOR
	—	325	195	175	100	75

Surete

As above in 7.65mm caliber. Marked "Cal. 7.65 Pistolet Automatique Surete", with "IG" stamped on frame.

	NIB	EXC.	V.G.	GOOD	FAIR	POOR
	—	295	165	155	100	75

GECO
See—Genschow, G.

GEHA
Germany

An altered Mauser 98 rifle re-barreled for use with 12-gauge shotgun shells. Barrel length 26.5", military stock shortened to half length and butt inlaid with a brass medallion marked "Geha". Manufactured from approximately 1919 to 1929.

	NIB	EXC.	V.G.	GOOD	FAIR	POOR
	—	375	225	150	100	75

GEM
Bacon Arms Company
Norwich, Connecticut
See—Bacon Arms Company

Gem Pocket Revolver

A .22-caliber spur trigger revolver, with 1.25" octagonal barrel. Frame is iron, engraved nickel-plated, with walnut or ivory grips. Barrel marked "Gem". Manufactured between 1878 and 1883.

	NIB	EXC.	V.G.	GOOD	FAIR	POOR
	—	—	1950	700	300	145

GENEZ, A. G.
New York, New York

Located at 9 Chambers Street, Genez made a wide variety of firearms during his working life (ca. 1850 to 1875). Most commonly encountered of his arms today are single-shot percussion pistols and percussion double-barrel shotguns. More rarely seen are single-shot percussion target rifles. A number of arms he made were decorated by Louis D. Nimschke. Genez products signed by Nimschke command considerable premiums over values for standard firearms listed.

Double-Barrel Shotgun

Most often encountered in 12-gauge. Varying barrel lengths, blued steel furniture and walnut stock.

	NIB	EXC.	V.G.	GOOD	FAIR	POOR
	—	—	2800	1950	500	250

Pocket Pistol

A .41-caliber single-shot percussion pistol, with 3" barrel, German silver mountings and walnut stock. Manufactured in 1850s and 1860s.

	NIB	EXC.	V.G.	GOOD	FAIR	POOR
	—	—	3950	1850	500	175

GENSCHOW, G.
Hamburg, Germany

Geco

A 6.35mm, 7.65mm, .32 Long and 8mm Lebel caliber folding trigger double-action revolver.

	NIB	EXC.	V.G.	GOOD	FAIR	POOR
		275	175	100	75	50

German Bulldog

A .32-, .38- and .45-caliber folding trigger double-action revolver, with solid frames, integral ejector rods and loading gates. Proofmarks indicate Belgian manufacture.

	NIB	EXC.	V.G.	GOOD	FAIR	POOR
	—	275	175	110	75	50

GEORGIA ARMORY
Milledgeville, George

Established in 1862, this concern produced a rifle based upon U.S. Model 1855 Harper's Ferry Rifle. Nearly identical in all respects to Harpers Ferry, Georgia Armory rifle had a lockplate patterned

	NIB	EXC.	V.G.	GOOD	FAIR	POOR

after U.S. Model 1841 Rifle. Lock marked "G.A. ARMORY" over date (1862 or 1863). Buttplate tangs marked with serial numbers. Highest known serial number is 309. Rifles were fitted with saber bayonets.

	NIB	EXC.	V.G.	GOOD	FAIR	POOR
	—	—	65000	22000	10500	3000

GERING, H. M. & CO.
Arnstadt, Germany

Leonhardt

Semi-automatic pistol in caliber 7.65mm. Almost identical to Beholla pistol made by Becker. Leonhardt stamped on slide. These pistols were made for the German Army during WWI.

	—	425	325	250	200	100

GERSTENBERGER & EBERWEIN
Gussenstadt, Germany

Em-Ge, G.& E., Omega & Pic

Series of poor-quality revolvers sold in U.S.A. before 1968. .22- and .32-calibers, with 2.25" barrels and 6-shot cylinder. Editor does not consider these safe to shoot, even if new in box.

	—	Worthless.	—	—	—	—

GEVARM
St. Etienne, France

Model A-6

This .22-caliber semi-automatic rifle fires from an open bolt. Fitted with a one-piece stock. Furnished with 8-round magazine. The E-1 20-magazine will not fit A-6 without hand fitting. Add 15 percent for higher-end A7 model. These rifles are increasingly popular on the secondary market because of their open-bolt design.

	—	800	695	475	275	165

E-1 Autoloading Rifle

A .22-caliber semi-automatic rifle, with 19" barrel, 8-shot magazine, blued with walnut grips. Two-piece stock. A 20-round magazine is an option.

	—	550	450	295	200	150

GIB
Eibar, Spain

10 Gauge Shotgun

A 10-gauge Magnum boxlock double-barrel shotgun, with 32" matte-ribbed barrels. Case hardened, blued with walnut grips.

	—	700	495	275	150	100

GIBBS, J. & G. / GIBBS, GEORGE
Bristol, England

Established in 1835, this concern continues in business to this day. J. & G. Gibbs 4 Redcliffe Street 1835-1842; George Gibbs 142 Thomas Street; Clare Street; 39 Corn Street. While initially known for exceptionally accurate single-shot rifles, the firm subsequently established a reputation for first quality bolt-action magazine rifles in a variety of large bore calibers. Bolt rifles by Gibbs, Rigby and others have become extremely desirable, especially in the African chamberings.

GIBBS
New York, New York

Gibbs Carbine

A .52-caliber single-shot percussion carbine, with sliding 22" round barrel. Blued case hardened with walnut stock. Lock marked with American eagle and "Wm. F. Brooks/Manf New York/1863". Breech marked "L.H. Gibbs/Patd/Jany 8, 1856". Only 1,050 produced.

	—	—	5950	2200	900	350

Gibbs Pistol

A caliber percussion pistol made by Hull & Thomas of Ilion, New York, in 1855 or 1856.

	—	—	3600	2750	1250	400

	NIB	EXC.	V.G.	GOOD	FAIR	POOR

GIBBS GUNS, INC.
Greenback, Tennessee

Mark 45 Carbine

A .45 ACP caliber semi-automatic rifle, with 16.5" barrel, 5-, 15-, 30- or 90-shot magazine. Blued, with walnut buttstock and fore-end. Nickel-plated model available as an option. Would bring approximately $25 additional. Discontinued in 1988.

650	475	275	200	125	100

GIBBS RIFLE COMPANY
Martinsburg, West Virginia

Gibbs Rifle Company was founded in 1991, by Val Forgett III, originally to refurbish and distribute various older military firearms. The company over the years has imported numerous black powder replicas from Europe and has also produced historical remakes and specialty rifles.

Enfield No. 5 Jungle Carbine

Remake of original British rifle. Chambered for .303 cartridge and fitted with 20" barrel and flash hider. Magazine capacity 10 rounds. Weight about 7.75 lbs. New stock.

350	295	200	150	100	50

Enfield No. 7 Jungle Carbine

Model chambered for .308 Winchester cartridge. Fitted with 20" barrel and flash hider. Magazine capacity 12 rounds. Adjustable rear sight. Original wood. Weight about 8 lbs.

650	575	475	350	250	200

Quest Extreme Carbine

An updated design of No. 5 Jungle Carbine. Chambered for .303 cartridge with 20" barrel. Nickel finish and new hardwood stock. Brass butt trap. Weight about 7.75 lbs.

350	295	200	150	100	50

Quest II Extreme Carbine

Updated version of No. 7 Jungle Carbine, with nickel finish, see-through scope mount and hardwood stock. Chambered for .308 cartridge. Magazine capacity 12 rounds. Barrel length 20". Weight about 8 lbs.

350	295	200	150	100	50

Quest III Extreme Carbine

Similar to Quest II, with synthetic stock.

400	325	200	150	100	50

Summit 45-70 Carbine

Bolt-action built on Enfield No. 4 action. Re-barreled to .45-70 caliber. Fitted to 21" barrel. MIL SPEC peep sight and checkered walnut stock. Weight about 8.5 lbs.

400	325	225	175	125	75

Mauser M71/84

Chambered for 11mm Mauser cartridge and fitted with 31.5" barrel. Model has been arsenal reconditioned, but otherwise original. Weight about 10 lbs.

300	250	175	150	100	50

Mauser M88 Commission Rifle

Fitted with 30" barrel and chambered for 8mm cartridge. Model has been arsenal reconditioned, but otherwise original. Weight about 10 lbs.

200	175	120	100	65	50

M98K Israeli Mauser

Re-barreled to .308 Win. by Israeli Arsenal. Made in three grades; Standard, Grade 2 and Grade 1 (best grade). **NOTE:** Add $50 for Grade 2, $100 for Grade 1.

350	300	250	200	150	100

NIB	EXC.	V.G.	GOOD	FAIR	POOR

M1903-A4 Springfield Sniper Model

Replica of 1903-A3, with original Remington action, new barrels in .30-06, C model stock. New copy of M73B1 scope with Redfield-type rings and mounts. Parkerized finish.

900	800	650	500	300	150

GIBBS TIFFANY & CO.
Sturbridge, Massachusetts

Under Hammer Pistol

A .28-caliber single-shot percussion pistol, with 3" to 8" barrels. Browned iron frame, walnut or maple pointed handle trimmed with brass. Top strap marked "Gibbs Tiffany & Co." Active 1820 to 1838.

—	—	1250	650	250	100

GILLESPIE
New York, New York

Derringer Type Pocket Pistol

A .41-caliber single-shot percussion pistol, with 2.5" barrel and walnut stock. Manufactured from 1848 to 1870.

—	—	2950	1350	500	200

GLAZE, W. & CO.
Columbia, South Carolina
See—B. & B. M. Darling

GLOCK
Deutsch-Wagram, Austria
Smyrna, Georgia

First imported into U.S.A. in 1985. Completely manufactured in Austria until 2004 when Glock opened its plant in Georgia to produce polymer frames. Offered in many models, but main differences are caliber, sighting systems, barrel, slide and grip length, and magazine capacity. In 2010 Gen4 (fourth generation) of Glock pistols was introduced. Gen4 features include three interchangeable back-straps, reversible magazine release button, improved recoil spring assembly and rough-textured frame (RTF) to enhance grip traction. As of 2013, all new-production units of the following models had Gen4 features: M17, M19, M20, M21, M22, M23, M26, M27, M29, M30, M31, M32, M33, M34, M35, M37. **NOTE:** Add $70 if equipped with Meprolight night sights; $90 if equipped with Trijicon night sights; $30 if equipped with adjustable sights; 10 percent for Gen4 if NIB.

Glock 17

Model chambered for 9mm Parabellum cartridge. Double-action-only semi-automatic that has a 4.49" barrel and 17-shot detachable magazine. Empty weight 21.91 oz.

520	425	325	300	275	175

Glock 17C

Similar to Model 17, with additional feature of an integral ported barrel. Specifications are same except for weight: 17C weighs 21.9 oz. Available with OD green frame.

525	475	350	300	275	175

Glock 17CC

Introduced in 1998, this is a compensated competition version of C variation. Fitted with extended slide stop lever, extended magazine release, adjustable sights and target trigger pull. This is a special order item only.

650	600	500	400	300	200

Glock 17L Competition Model

Version features 6" compensated barrel and adjustable sights. Trigger is fine-tuned to provide between 5- to 8-lbs. trigger pull. Introduced in 1988. In 1990 this pistol won I.P.S.C. World Stock Gun Championship. Pistol has limited availability in U.S. Available with OD green frame.

700	600	475	350	300	225

Glock 19

Similar in appearance to Model 17. Compact version, with 4" barrel and smaller grip that will accept either 15-round or standard 17-round magazine that protrudes a bit. Weight 20.99 oz. empty. Grip straps on this model are serrated as they are on other Glock models. Introduced in 1988 and currently in production. Available with OD green frame.

525	475	350	300	275	175

	NIB	EXC.	V.G.	GOOD	FAIR	POOR

Glock 19C

Same as above, with integral ported barrel. Weight 20.7 oz. Available with OD green frame.

	550	475	350	300	275	175

Glock 19CC

Introduced in 1998, this is a compensated competition version of C variation. Fitted with extended slide stop lever, extended magazine release, adjustable sights and target trigger pull. This is special order item only.

	700	600	500	350	300	275

Glock 22

Almost identical in appearance to Model 17. Model 22 chambered for .40 S&W cartridge. Standard with 15-round clip. Slightly larger and heavier slide. Weight 22.36 oz. Available with OD green frame.

	525	475	350	300	275	175

Glock 22C

Same as Glock 22 model, with addition of integral ported barrel. Weight 22.5 oz. Available with OD green frame.

	550	475	350	300	275	175

Glock 22CC

Introduced in 1998, this is a compensated competition version of C variation. Fitted with extended slide stop lever, extended magazine release, adjustable sights and target trigger pull. This is special order item only.

	700	600	500	350	300	275

Glock 23

Model 23 chambered for .40 S&W cartridge. Slide is slightly heavier and larger than Model 19. Weight 21.67 oz. Glock 23 magazine holds 13 rounds. Available with OD green frame.

	525	475	350	300	275	175

Glock 23C

Same as above, with integral ported barrel. Weight 20.9 oz. Available with OD green frame.

	550	475	350	300	275	175

Glock 23CC

Introduced in 1998, this is a compensated competition version of C variation. Fitted with extended slide stop lever, extended magazine release, adjustable sights and target trigger pull. This is special order item only.

	700	600	500	350	300	275

Glock 24

Chambered for .40 S&W cartridge. Fitted with 6" barrel. Weight 26.5 oz.

	675	550	400	350	300	175

Glock 24C

Same as above, with ported barrel.

	700	525	400	300	250	200

Glock 24CC

Introduced in 1998, this is a compensated competition version of C variation. Fitted with extended slide stop lever, extended magazine release, adjustable sights and target trigger pull. This is special order item only.

	700	600	500	350	300	275

Glock 20 and Glock 21

Both of these models are identical in physical appearance except for caliber: Model 20 chambered for 10mm cartridge; Model 21 chambered for .45 ACP. Barrel length on both is 4.60". Model 20 has 15-round clip and weighs 26.35 oz.; Model 21 has 13-round magazine and weighs 25.22 oz. Available with OD green frame.

	550	425	350	300	250	200

Glock 20 SF Short Frame Pistol

DAO semi-automatic similar to Glock Model 20, with short-frame design. Chambered in 10mm Auto. Features include 4.61" barrel, with hexagonal rifling, fixed sights, extended sight radius. Overall length 8.07". Weight 27.51 oz.

	550	475	350	300	275	175

	NIB	EXC.	V.G.	GOOD	FAIR	POOR

Glock 21 SF

Slenderized version of Model 21, with slimmer frame and ambidextrous magazine catch. Introduced 2007.

	550	475	350	300	275	175

Glock 20C and 21C

Same as Models 20 and 21, with integral ported barrel. Available with OD green frame.

	600	475	400	325	250	200

Glock 20CC/21CC

Introduced in 1998, this is a compensated competition version of C variation. Fitted with extended slide stop lever, extended magazine release, adjustable sights and target trigger pull. This is special order item only.

	700	600	500	350	300	275

Glock 26 and Model 27

Both of these models are identical except for caliber. Introduced in 1995, these are subcompact versions of the full-size Glocks. Model 26 chambered for 9mm cartridge; Model 27 chambered for .40 S&W cartridge. Magazine capacity; 9mm is 10 rounds and .40-caliber version holds 9 rounds. Overall length 6.25". Barrel length of 3.5". Height is 4.1875" and width is 1.25". Weight for both models about 20 oz. Standard are a dot front sight and white outline rear adjustable sight. Available with OD green frame.

	550	475	350	300	275	175

Glock 29 and Glock 30

These two pistols were introduced in 1997. Model 29 chambered for 10mm cartridge; Model 30 chambered for .45 ACP cartridge. Barrel length 3.78". Weight about 24 oz. Overall length 6.77". Model 29 magazine capacity 10 rounds; Model 30 has standard capacity of 10 rounds, with optional capacity of 9 rounds. Model 30 with 10-round magazine in place protrudes slightly below grip. With 9-round magazine in place fits flush with bottom of grip. Available with OD green frame.

	550	475	350	300	275	175

Glock 29 SF Short Frame Pistol

DAO semi-automatic similar to Glock Model 29, with short-frame design. Chambered in 10mm Auto. Features include 3.78" barrel with hexagonal rifling, fixed sights, extended sight radius. Overall length 6.97" . Weight 24.52 oz.

	575	495	350	300	275	175

Glock 31

Chambered for .357 SIG cartridge, this pistol fitted with 4.5" barrel and magazine capacity of 10 rounds (15 rounds law enforcement). Overall length 7.3", height 5.4", weight about 23.3 oz. Introduced in 1998. Available with OD green frame.

	550	475	350	300	275	175

Glock 31C

Same as Model 31, with integral compensator. Available with OD green frame.

	575	495	350	300	275	175

Glock 31CC

Introduced in 1998, this is a compensated competition version of C variation. Fitted with extended slide stop lever, extended magazine release, adjustable sights and target trigger pull. This is special order item only.

	700	600	500	350	300	275

Glock 32

Similar to the Glock 31 except fitted with a 4" barrel. Overall length is 6.85" and height is 5". Magazine capacity is 10 rounds (13 rounds law enforcement). Weight is approximately 21.5 oz. Introduced in 1998. Also available with OD green frame.

	575	495	350	300	275	175

Glock 32C

Same as above, with integral ported barrel and slide. Available with OD green frame.

	700	600	500	350	300	275

Glock 32CC

Introduced in 1998, this is a compensated competition version of C variation. Fitted with extended slide stop lever, extended magazine release, adjustable sights and target trigger pull.

	NIB	EXC.	V.G.	GOOD	FAIR	POOR

This is special order item only.

| | 700 | 600 | 500 | 350 | 300 | 275 |

Glock 33

This .357 SIG model has 3.5" barrel. Overall length 6.3". Height 4.2". Weight about 17.7 oz. Introduced in 1998. Available with OD green frame.

| 575 | 495 | 350 | 300 | 275 | 175 |

Glock 34

Model chambered for 9x19 cartridge and has 5.3" barrel. Overall length of 8.2". Magazine capacity 10 rounds. Empty weight approximately 23 oz. Available with OD green frame.

| 575 | 495 | 350 | 300 | 275 | 175 |

Glock 35

Glock 35 chambered for .40 S&W cartridge. Same dimensions as Glock 34 except for weight is 24.5 oz. Available with OD green frame.

| 700 | 600 | 500 | 350 | 300 | 275 |

Glock 36

Introduced in 1999, this model similar to Model 30. Fitted with single-column magazine capacity of 6 rounds. Width of pistol is .14" less than Model 30. Barrel length 3.78". Weight 20 oz. Available with OD green frame.

| 575 | 495 | 350 | 300 | 275 | 175 |

Glock 37

Semi-automatic pistol chambered for .45 G.A.P. cartridge, which is slightly shorter than .45 ACP cartridge. Cartridge has a muzzle speed of 951 fps and muzzle energy of 405 ft. lbs. Fitted with 4.49" barrel. Height 5.5". Overall length 7.3". Weight about 26 oz. Available with OD green frame.

| 575 | 495 | 350 | 300 | 275 | 175 |

Glock 38

This .45 G.A.P. pistol is fitted with 4" barrel. Height 5" and overall length 6.85". Magazine capacity 8 rounds. Weight about 24 oz. Introduced in 2005. Available with OD green frame.

| 575 | 495 | 350 | 300 | 275 | 175 |

Glock 39

Introduced in 2005, this sub-compact .45 G.A.P. pistol has 3.46" barrel. Height 4.17" and overall length 6.3". Magazine capacity 8 rounds. Weight about 19.3 oz. Available with OD green frame.

| 575 | 495 | 350 | 300 | 275 | 175 |

Glock 41 Sport/Service Competition

Much like the Gen 4 Model 21, with 5.3" barrel, RTF frame, octagonal rifling, interchangeable backstraps, dual recoil spring and new trigger system. Introduced in 2014.

| 650 | 550 | 425 | 325 | — | — |

Glock 42

Sub-compact model chambered in .380 ACP. Barrel is 3.5" with hexagonal rifling. Has a new trigger system, dual spring operating assembly and slimmest frame of any Glock, less than 1" in diameter. New in 2014.

| 575 | 475 | 400 | 300 | — | — |

GODDARD

See—B. & B. M. Darling

GOLDEN EAGLE
Nikko Limited
Tochigi, Japan

SHOTGUNS

Golden Eagle Model 5000 Grade I

A 12- or 20-gauge over/under shotgun, with 26", 28" and 30" barrels, ventilated ribs and various choke combinations. Single-selective trigger and automatic ejectors. Blued, with walnut stock that has an eagle's head inlaid into pistol-grip cap. Manufactured between 1976 and early 1980s.

| 1000 | 900 | 750 | 600 | 475 | 250 |

	NIB	EXC.	V.G.	GOOD	FAIR	POOR

Grade I Skeet
As above, with 26" or 28" barrel and wide competition rib.

NIB	EXC.	V.G.	GOOD	FAIR	POOR
1100	900	750	600	475	250

Grade I Trap
Similar to skeet model, with 30" or 32" barrel.

NIB	EXC.	V.G.	GOOD	FAIR	POOR
1200	900	750	600	475	250

Model 5000 Grade II
As above, but more finely finished with a gold eagle's head inlaid in receiver.

NIB	EXC.	V.G.	GOOD	FAIR	POOR
1100	1000	800	600	475	250

Grandee Grade III
As above, but more elaborately engraved.

NIB	EXC.	V.G.	GOOD	FAIR	POOR
2500	2000	1750	1400	850	500

RIFLES

Model 7000 Grade I
Mauser bolt-action rifle. Chambered for all popular American calibers, with 24" or 26" barrel, walnut stock and rosewood pistol-grip cap and fore-end tip.

NIB	EXC.	V.G.	GOOD	FAIR	POOR
700	600	500	375	300	200

Model 7000 African
As above in .375 H&H and .458 Win. Magnum caliber. Open sights.

NIB	EXC.	V.G.	GOOD	FAIR	POOR
800	650	550	400	325	250

Model 7000 Grade II
As above, but engraved.

NIB	EXC.	V.G.	GOOD	FAIR	POOR
900	750	625	450	350	275

GONCZ CO.
Hollywood, California

GC Carbine
A 7.63mm Mauser, 9mm Parabellum, .38 Super and .45 ACP caliber semi-automatic rifle, with 16.1" barrel. Black with walnut stock. Later production models were stainless steel.

NIB	EXC.	V.G.	GOOD	FAIR	POOR
650	500	395	275	200	125

GC Stainless
As above in stainless steel. Introduced in 1987.

NIB	EXC.	V.G.	GOOD	FAIR	POOR
800	550	425	325	250	175

GC Collector's Edition
Limited edition with hand-polished finish.

NIB	EXC.	V.G.	GOOD	FAIR	POOR
875	600	500	425	350	225

Halogen Carbine
GC Carbine, with powerful light source mounted under barrel. Chambered for 9mm and .45 ACP only.

NIB	EXC.	V.G.	GOOD	FAIR	POOR
750	500	395	275	200	125

Laser Carbine
As above, with laser sighting system effective to 400 yards.

NIB	EXC.	V.G.	GOOD	FAIR	POOR
1500	1250	1000	750	650	500

GA Pistol
GC Carbine, with 9.5" shrouded barrel and 16- or 18-shot magazine. Black with one-piece grip. Manufactured between 1985 and 1987.

NIB	EXC.	V.G.	GOOD	FAIR	POOR
525	400	295	200	150	100

GAT-9 Pistol
As above, in 9mm caliber with adjustable trigger and hand-honed action.

NIB	EXC.	V.G.	GOOD	FAIR	POOR
600	475	375	300	225	150

	NIB	EXC.	V.G.	GOOD	FAIR	POOR

GA Collector's Edition

Hand-polished stainless steel limited production of above.

	825	675	600	500	400	300

GS Pistol

Model GA with plain 5" barrel. Pistols were made in stainless steel in 1987.

	350	275	225	175	125	75

GS Collector's Edition

Hand-polished limited-production stainless steel version of GS.

	775	625	550	475	350	250

GOUDRY, J.F.
Paris, France

Double-action 10-shot turret pistol. Marked on barrel rib J.F. Goudry Paris and Systeme A. Norl. By raising the gate on left side the turret can be removed and reloaded or another preloaded turret inserted.

	—	—	6500	2000	1000	500

GOVERNOR
Norwich, Connecticut

Governor Pocket Revolver

A .22-caliber spur trigger revolver, with 3" barrel and 7-shot cylinder. Revolvers were made from modified Bacon pepperboxes. Top strap marked "Governor". Manufactured from approximately 1868 to 1874.

	—	—	725	650	250	100

GRABNER G.
Kolibri Rehberg, Austria
See—Kolibri

GRAND PRECISION, FABRIQUE D'ARMES DE
Eibar, Spain

Bulwark Model 1913

Model chambered for 6.35mm cartridge and is an exact copy of Browning Model 1906. Complete with squeeze grip safety. Marketed by Beistegui Hermanos. Bulwark stamped on slide and B.H. stamped on grip plate.

	—	295	195	150	75	40

Bulwark Model 1914

Chambered for 7.65mm cartridge. Style of Ruby military pistols of WWI. Magazine capacity 9 rounds.

	—	275	225	150	75	40

Bulwark 6.35mm

Semi-automatic pistol in caliber 6.35mm. Patterned after Browning Model 1906. Marketed by Beistegue Hermanos.

	—	250	175	115	75	40

Libia 6.35mm

Model also patterned after Browning Model 1906, with squeeze safety. Libia stamped on slide and each grip plate. Marketed by Beistegui Hermanos.

	—	275	225	150	750	40

Libia 7.65mm

Similar to model above. Chambered for 7.65mm cartridge.

	—	275	225	150	75	40

GRANGER, G.
St. Etienne, France

Side-by-Side Shotgun

Custom-order 12-, 16- and 20-gauge boxlock double-barrel shotgun. Manufactured since 1902. Because the gun is imported, value of the dollar frequently determines price movement.

	—	16500	13000	8500	4250	1500

	NIB	EXC.	V.G.	GOOD	FAIR	POOR

GRAS
France

Model 1874

An 11mm caliber bolt-action rifle, with 32" barrel, walnut stock, barrel band and metal tip. Bayonet is a spike blade, with wood handle and brass butt cap.

—	500	375	225	150	75

GREAT WESTERN ARMS COMPANY
Los Angeles, California

The popularity of western television programs in the early 1950s, spawned a renewed interest in guns that were seen in almost every episode, primarily the Single Action Army revolver. At about the same time that Bill Ruger was designing his company's first single-action, the Single Six, a group of investors in the Los Angeles area, were preparing to launch Great Western Arms Company. Among this group was Dan Reeves, owner of the Los Angeles Rams professional football team, and several other prominent area businessmen.

Ruger's .22 LR Single Six hit the market in 1953 and by spring of 1954, Great Western unveiled a faithful copy of the Colt Single Action Army, chambered in several centerfire calibers, including .38 Special, .357 Magnum, .357 Atomic, .44 special, .44-40, .44 Magnum, .45 Colt and .22 Long Rifle. This was the first of many Colt SAA clones. (The .357 Atomic was a propriety cartridge that never got off the ground, a .357 with a slightly lengthened case. It apparently was never commercially loaded.) The standard single-action was known as the Frontier Model and was made in the same barrel lengths as the original: 4.750", 5.500" and 7.500", plus a 12" Buntline Model. Grips were faux stag, walnut, with optional real stag, walnut, ivory and other materials on the handful of presentation grade engraved models. Some of the high-grade models were made for prominent political leaders and celebrities, including President Dwight D. Eisenhower, John Wayne and Elvis Presley. In addition to the Frontier Model, Great Western offered several other single-action variations that are listed below, as well as a copy of the Remington Double Derringer in either .38 S&W or .38 Special.

The company went through several ownership changes and had a tough time competing with Ruger and later Colt, which resurrected the original SAA in 1956. In 1959, the name and assets of the company were purchased by EMF (Early and Modern Firearms Co.) and in 1964 Great Western products were discontinued. The name was resurrected in 2003, when EMF imported a series of single-action revolvers, known as Great Western II 1873 SA, until about 2009. See separate listing below for these firearms.

Centerfire Single-Action

800	725	500	350	250	200

.22 Long Rifle Single-Action

600	525	450	375	300	200

Fast Draw Model

Brass backstrap and trigger guard.

700	550	475	400	300	225

Deputy Model

4"barrel with full length sight rib. **NOTE:** Calibers other than standard such as .22 Hornet, .32-20, .45 ACP, .22 Magnum, .30 Carbine or .357 Atomic add 10 percent premium. Factory plated pistols add 10 percent. Factory cased pistols add 20 percent. Sheriff's Model or Buntline Special add 15 percent. Factory ivory grips add $175; stag grips add $95 and pearl grips add $150. Factory-engraved guns will add $750 to $3,500 to prices depending on coverage.

1000	850	600	425	250	—

Derringer Models

These two-shot over/unders were based on Remington Derringer of late 19th Century. Chambered for either .38 S&W or .38 Special. Some models were factory engraved and presented to Hollywood celebrities.

Engraved Model

—	1100	900	700	400	150

Standard Model

—	625	475	275	175	100

	NIB	EXC.	V.G.	GOOD	FAIR	POOR

GREAT WESTERN II
Santa Ana, California

These single-action revolvers were made by Pietta in Italy. EMF, owner of the Great Western name, began importing these guns in 2003.

Custom 1873 SA

Chambered in .357, .44-40 and .45 Colt in standard SAA barrel lengths. Offered in blue, blue with color case hardening, satin nickel or bright nickel finish. Ivory or stag grips. Engraved models were available. Imported from 2003 to 2010. **NOTE:** Add a premium of up to $100 for stag grips.

NIB	EXC.	V.G.	GOOD	FAIR	POOR
750	625	500	400	300	200

Stainless 1873 SA

NIB	EXC.	V.G.	GOOD	FAIR	POOR
800	650	550	450	300	200

Paladin Model

In .45 Colt, with 3.5", 5.5" or 7.5" barrel, ivory grips, blue finish. Introduced in 2013.

NIB	EXC.	V.G.	GOOD	FAIR	POOR
480	400	325	275	200	175

Liberty Model

Similar to Paladin Model, except with laser engraving. Made in .357 Magnum and .45 Coalt.

NIB	EXC.	V.G.	GOOD	FAIR	POOR
550	475	400	350	300	200

GREEN, E.
Cheltenham, England

Green

A .450- and .455-caliber double-action revolver. Popular with its military users in late 1800s.

NIB	EXC.	V.G.	GOOD	FAIR	POOR
—	—	2000	875	550	300

GREENE
Milbury, Massachusetts

Greene Breechloading Rifle

A .53-caliber single-shot bolt-action percussion rifle, with 35" barrel, under hammer and full length walnut stock secured by three barrel bands. Marked "Greene's Patent/Nov. 17, 1857". Approximately 4,000 made by A.H. Waters Armory between 1859 and 1862.

NIB	EXC.	V.G.	GOOD	FAIR	POOR
—	—	3250	1050	400	200

GREENER, W. W. LTD.
Birmingham, England

Perhaps the best known manufacturer of double-barrel shotguns in England during the 19th Century. Greener was also a prolific author. His name will forever be associated with "Greener Crossbolt". Greener hammer-model shotguns were quite popular in United States during last half of 19th century. Company is still in business in Birmingham and makes a limited number of custom guns. Current prices on used gun market range for basic boxlock non-ejector models in the $1,500 to $2,000 range. Top of the line models from first half of 20th century can bring $100,000 or more. Because of the wide range of models and grades, a professional appraisal would be necessary before any transaction.

GREIFELT & CO.
Suhl, Germany

OVER/UNDER SHOTGUNS

Grade No. 1

NOTE: Add 25 percent for 28-gauge and .410 bore.

NIB	EXC.	V.G.	GOOD	FAIR	POOR
—	3750	3250	2950	1750	1000

Grade No. 3

Similar to No. 1, with less engraving. Manufactured prior to WWII. **NOTE:** Add 25 percent for 28-gauge and .410 bore.

NIB	EXC.	V.G.	GOOD	FAIR	POOR
—	3250	2700	1850	1250	750

Model 143E

Post-war version of No. 1. Not made in 28-gauge or .410 bore.

NIB	EXC.	V.G.	GOOD	FAIR	POOR
—	2750	2300	1650	1200	750

	NIB	EXC.	V.G.	GOOD	FAIR	POOR

Combination Gun

Combination over/under rifle/shotgun. Manufactured in all bores and variety of rifle calibers, with 24" or 26" barrels. Made prior to 1939. **NOTE:** Deduct 40 percent if rifle caliber is obsolete. Add 25 percent for 28-gauge and .410 bore; 10 percent for automatic ejectors.

—	5800	4750	3950	2500	1250	

SIDE-BY-SIDE SHOTGUNS

Model 22

A 12- or 20-gauge boxlock double-barrel shotgun, with 28" or 30" barrels, sideplates, double triggers and extractors. Blued, case hardened with walnut stock. Manufactured after 1945.

—	2500	1950	1500	500	200	

Model 22E

As above, with automatic ejectors.

—	2750	2300	1650	550	225	

Model 103

A 12- and 16-gauge boxlock shotgun, with 28" or 30" barrel, double triggers and extractors. Walnut stock, with pistol-, straight- or English-style-grip. Post-war model.

—	2250	1800	1350	400	175	

Model 103E

As above, with automatic ejectors.

—	2500	1950	1500	500	200	

Drilling

A 12-, 16- or 20-gauge double-barrel shotgun. Fitted with a rifle barrel. Chambered for variety of cartridges. Barrel length 26", boxlock-action, double triggers, extractors and folding rear sight. Manufactured prior to 1939. **NOTE:** Deduct 40 percent if rifle caliber is obsolete. Add 10 percent for 20-gauge.

—	3750	3200	2950	900	300	

GRENDEL, INC.
Rockledge, Florida

P-10 Pistol

A .380-caliber semi-automatic pistol, with 3" barrel, 11-shot magazine, matte black finish and black plastic grips. Pistol has plastic frame and magazine. Offered in electroless nickel-plate, as well as a green Teflon finish for slightly higher price. **NOTE:** Add $5 for green finish; $15 for electroless nickel.

295	250	195	150	125	75	

P-12

Semi-automatic double-action pistol, chambered for .380 ACP cartridge. Fitted with 3" barrel, checkered polymer grips, and blued finish. Magazine capacity 10 rounds. Weight about 13 oz. Introduced in 1992.

295	250	195	150	125	75	

P-30

Introduced in 1990, this double-action semi-automatic pistol chambered for .22 WMR cartridge. Fitted with 5" or 8" barrel. Fixed sights. Magazine capacity 30 rounds. Weight about 21 oz. Discontinued in 1994.

450	350	275	125	85	75	

P-30L

Same as above, in 8" barrel only. Discontinued in 1994.

450	350	275	125	85	75	

P-30M

Similar to P-30. Fitted with removable muzzle-brake.

450	350	275	125	85	75	

P-31

Semi-automatic pistol chambered for .22 WMR cartridge. Fitted with 11" barrel, muzzle-brake. Black matte finish. Weight approximately 48 oz. Introduced in 1991. No longer in production.

450	350	275	125	85	75	

	NIB	EXC.	V.G.	GOOD	FAIR	POOR

RIFLES

SRT-20F Compact Rifle

A .308-caliber bolt-action rifle, with 20" finned match grade barrel, 9-shot magazine, folding synthetic stock, integral bipod and no sights.

NIB	EXC.	V.G.	GOOD	FAIR	POOR
575	500	425	325	250	100

SRT-24

As above, with 24" barrel. Discontinued in 1988.

NIB	EXC.	V.G.	GOOD	FAIR	POOR
600	525	450	350	275	100

R-31 Carbine

Semi-automatic carbine introduced in 1991. Chambered for .22 WMR cartridge. Fitted with 16" barrel. Muzzle-brake and telescoping tubular stock. Magazine capacity 30 rounds. Weight about 4 lbs. Discontinued in 1994.

NIB	EXC.	V.G.	GOOD	FAIR	POOR
300	250	200	150	125	100

GRIFFIN & HOWE
Bernardsville, New Jersey

Established in 1923, this firm manufactures on custom order a variety of bolt-action sporting rifles. These rifles have an excellent reputation and are quite desirable. Starting prices for currently manufactured rifles is around $15,000. Values of older models in excellent condition range from $4,000 to $10,000 and much higher for engraved rifles. Griffin & Howe also are agents for various European shotgun makers.

GRIFFON
South Africa

Griffon 1911 A1 Combat

Semi-automatic single-action pistol, chambered for .45 ACP cartridge. Fitted with 4" ported barrel. Aluminum trigger and high-profile sights are standard. Frame is chrome and slide blued. Magazine capacity 7 rounds.

NIB	EXC.	V.G.	GOOD	FAIR	POOR
600	500	400	295	200	125

GRISWOLD & GRIER
See—Griswold & Gunnison

GRISWOLD & GUNNISON
Griswoldville, Georgia

1851 Navy Type

A .36-caliber percussion revolver, with 7.5" barrel and 6-shot cylinder. Frame and grip straps made of brass. Barrel and cylinder made of iron. Approximately 3,700 made between 1862 and 1864 for Confederate government. **NOTE:** This revolver sometimes referred to as Griswold and Grier.

NIB	EXC.	V.G.	GOOD	FAIR	POOR
—	—	38500	14000	2750	1350

GROSS ARMS CO.
Tiffin, Ohio

Pocket Revolver

A .25- and .30-caliber spur trigger revolver, with 6" octagonal barrel, 7-shot cylinder and marked "Gross Arms Co., Tiffin, Ohio". Blued, with walnut grips. Only a few hundred manufactured between 1864 and 1866.

NIB	EXC.	V.G.	GOOD	FAIR	POOR
—	—	1700	600	300	150

GRUBB, J. C. & CO.
Philadelphia, Pennsylvania

Pocket Pistol

A .41-caliber single-shot percussion pistol, with various barrel lengths. German silver, walnut stock and engraved lock and trigger guard. Lock marked "J.C. Grubb". Several hundred manufactured between 1860 and 1870.

NIB	EXC.	V.G.	GOOD	FAIR	POOR
—	—	1550	800	650	170

NIB	EXC.	V.G.	GOOD	FAIR	POOR

GRULLA
Eibar, Spain

Model 216RL

Side-by-side shotgun offered in 12-, 16-, 20-, 28-gauge and .410 bore. Barrel length 28". Articulated double triggers. Action body is H&H side locks. Select walnut, with straight-grip and splinter fore-end. Fixed chokes. Choice of different styles of engraving. Weight range from 7.1 lbs. for 12-gauge to 6 lbs. for .410 bore. **NOTE:** Add $300 for 28-gauge and .410 bore.

NIB	EXC.	V.G.	GOOD	FAIR	POOR
9000	5750	3500	2000	1350	500

Royal

High-grade side-by-side series offered in all standard gauges. Featuring Holland & Holland seven-pin style sidelock and H&H, Purdey or Churchill style engraving. Custom made to buyer's specifications, with select exhibition grade walnut stock and forearm. Choice of several metal finishes. **NOTE:** Add $1000 for Purdey-style engravine; $2000 for Churchill.

NIB	EXC.	V.G.	GOOD	FAIR	POOR
22750	19500	16000	10000	—	—

Consort

Side-by-side model, with double triggers, H&H style assisted-opening action, drop forged demi-block chopper lump barrels with concave rib and choice of old silver or case-hardened finish. This is a true sidelock action, with five pins, double safety sears and extensive engraving. Stock and forearm are hand checkered, with hand rubbed oil finish. Chamberings are available in all standard guages.

NIB	EXC.	V.G.	GOOD	FAIR	POOR
11500	9800	8000	5500	—	—

GUERINI, CAESAR
Italy

This line of Italian over/under guns was introduced into U.S.A. in 2004.

Flyway

Over/under 12-gauge 3" gun offered with either 28" or 30" vent rib barrels, with choke tubes. Checkered walnut stock with pistol-grip. Trap-style forearm with finger grooves. Single-selective trigger and ejectors. Weight about 8 lbs. depending on barrel length.

NIB	EXC.	V.G.	GOOD	FAIR	POOR
2795	2300	1750	1300	900	500

Woodlander

Model offered in 12-, 20- and 28-gauge, with choice of 26" or 28" vent rib barrels and choke tubes. Frame is case hardened, with gold ruffed grouse on bottom of receiver. Checkered Circassian walnut stock, with straight-grip and oil finished. Single-selective trigger and ejectors. Weight about: 6.25 lbs. 20-gauge; 6.15 lbs. 28-gauge.

NIB	EXC.	V.G.	GOOD	FAIR	POOR
2795	2300	1750	1300	900	500

Magnus Light

Model offered in 12-, 20- or 28-gauge, with choice of 26" or 28" vent rib barrels and choke tubes. Alloy frame with Tinaloy finish and side plates. Scroll engraved with gold game birds. Checkered walnut stock with Prince of Wales-style pistol-grip. Weight about: 6 lbs. 12-gauge; 5.4 lbs. 20-gauge; 5.25 lbs. 28-gauge.

NIB	EXC.	V.G.	GOOD	FAIR	POOR
3500	2995	2000	1500	1000	500

Magnus

Similar to Magnus Light, with case hardened steel receiver. Weight about: 6.75 lbs. 12-gauge; 6.5 lbs. 20-gauge; 6.25 lbs. 28-gauge.

NIB	EXC.	V.G.	GOOD	FAIR	POOR
3500	2995	2000	1500	1000	500

Tempio

Over/under gun offered in 12-, 20- and 28-gauge, with choice of 26" or 28" barrels and choke tubes. Checkered Circassian walnut stock, with Prince of Wales-style pistol-grip. Alloy receiver is a gray finish of Tinaloy. Engraved with scroll and gold game birds. Single-selective trigger with ejectors. Weight about: 6.8 lbs. 12-gauge; 6.4 lbs. 20-gauge; 6.25 lbs. 28-gauge.

NIB	EXC.	V.G.	GOOD	FAIR	POOR
2450	2000	1500	1050	600	250

Forum/Forum Sporting

Model offered in 12-, 20- and 28-gauge, with choice of 26" or 28" barrels on Forum. Forum Sporting has 30", 32" or 34" barrels. Gun has silver receiver, with scroll and game scene engraving and side plates. **NOTE:** Add $300 for Forum Sporting.

NIB	EXC.	V.G.	GOOD	FAIR	POOR
7250	6000	4750	3250	1600	700

	NIB	EXC.	V.G.	GOOD	FAIR	POOR

Summit Sporting/Summit Limited

Offered in 12-, 20- or 28-gauge, with choice of 30" or 32" vent rib barrels and extended choke tubes. Alloy receiver with engraving. Single-selective trigger adjustable for length of pull. Ejectors. Checkered walnut stock, with pistol-grip. Weight about: 8 lbs. 12-gauge; 7.5 lbs. 20-gauge; 7.45 lbs. 28-gauge. **NOTE:** Summit Limited add $300.

2950	2300	1650	1200	750	300

Magnus Sporting

Model similar to Summit, with upgraded wood and sidelock-style receiver. Scroll engraving and gold game birds.

3500	2900	2300	1650	1000	500

Essex

Over/under with oil-finished stock and coin finished receiver. Scroll engraving. Available in 12-, 20-, 28-gauge and .410 bore all with 3" chambers. New in 2006.

4250	3500	2300	1650	1000	500

Ellipse Evo

Rounded action in 12-, 20- or 28-gauge, with coin-finished receiver, hand-rubbed oil-finished stock with rounded grip, choke tubes and 28" barrels. Choice of selective or non-selective trigger, manual or automatic safety. Also offered in 12-gauge sporting (Evolution) and Limited versions. **NOTE:** Add $1800 for Evolution model, deduct $1500 for Limited.

5000	4000	2800	2000	1500	700

Apex

This over/under series is offered in 12-, 20-, 28-gauge and .410 bore versions, with coin-finished scroll-engraved receiver and hand-rubbed oil-finished walnut stock. Barrels are currently only 28", but early models were made with 26" and 30". Five choke tubes are included. A Sporting Clays model is available, with 32" barrels in 12-gauge only, with high-grade walnut stock. **NOTE:** Add $500 for Sporting Clays model if excellent or better condition.

6900	5800	4900	3500	2250	900

GUION, T. F.
New Orleans, Louisiana

Pocket Pistol

A .41-caliber single-shot percussion pistol, with 2.5" barrel, German silver mountings and walnut stock. Manufactured in 1850s.

—	—	2150	1850	550	275

GUNCRAFTER INDUSTRIES
Huntsville, Arkansas

This manufacturer of 1911-style pistols offers several different models, with typical 1911 features.

CCO

Chambered in 9mm, .45 ACP and manufacturer's own proprietary .50 GI caliber. Barrel lengths include standard 5" plus 4.25" and 6". All guns are made-to-order. **NOTE:** Add 50 percent for 6" model.

2500	1800	1350	1000	450	300

GUNWORKS LTD.
Buffalo, New York

Model 9 Derringer

Over/under derringer chambered in 9mm, .38 Special, .38 Super and .357 Magnum caliber. Barrels 2.5", with a spur trigger and Millet sights. Nickel-plate with walnut grips. Manufacturing ceased in 1986.

—	175	125	90	75	50

GUSTAF, CARL
Eskilstuna, Sweden

Bolt-Action Rifle

A 6.5x55, 7x64, .270, 7mm Magnum, .308, .30-06 and 9.3x62 caliber bolt-action rifle, with 24" barrel. Blued, with walnut stock in either classic style or with Monte Carlo cheekpiece. Manufactured between 1970 and 1977.

—	700	600	450	325	150

Grade II

As above, with better walnut and rosewood pistol-grip cap and fore-end tip.

NIB	EXC.	V.G.	GOOD	FAIR	POOR
—	850	650	475	375	175

Grade III

As above, with high-gloss finish and finely figured walnut stock.

NIB	EXC.	V.G.	GOOD	FAIR	POOR
—	950	700	550	475	275

Deluxe Bolt-Action

As above, with engraved floorplate and trigger guard, Damascened bolt and high-grade French walnut stock. Manufactured between 1970 and 1977.

NIB	EXC.	V.G.	GOOD	FAIR	POOR
—	1250	900	650	450	300

Varmint Model

A .222, .22-250, .243 and 6.5x55 caliber bolt-action rifle, with 27" barrel and large bolt knob made of Bakelite. Furnished without open sights and has a heavy target-type stock. Manufactured in 1970 only.

NIB	EXC.	V.G.	GOOD	FAIR	POOR
—	700	600	450	325	150

Grand Prix Target

A .22-caliber single-shot bolt-action rifle, with 27" barrel and adjustable weights. Furnished without sights and with adjustable butt target stock. Only manufactured in 1970.

NIB	EXC.	V.G.	GOOD	FAIR	POOR
—	700	600	450	325	150

Model 2000

A 6.5x55, .243, .270, .308 and .30-06 caliber bolt-action rifle, with 60 percent bolt lift and cold swagged barrel and action. Furnished with open sights. Blued, walnut stock with Monte Carlo cheekpiece. Manufactured until 1985.

NIB	EXC.	V.G.	GOOD	FAIR	POOR
—	675	575	400	300	150

GWYN & CAMPBELL
Hamilton, Ohio

Union Carbine

A .52-caliber single-shot breech loading percussion carbine, with round/octagonal 20" barrel marked "Gwyn & Campbell/ Patent/1862/ Hamilton,O". Blued, case hardened with walnut stock. Approximately 8,500 made between 1862 and 1865.

NIB	EXC.	V.G.	GOOD	FAIR	POOR
—	—	4000	1975	500	300

H&R 1871, LLC
Gardner, Massachusetts
See—Harrington & Richardson

H.J.S. INDUSTRIES, INC.
Brownsville, Texas

Frontier Four Derringer

A .22-caliber four-barreled pocket pistol, with 2.5" sliding barrels, stainless steel frame, barrel grip and walnut grips. Recalled due to risk of unintentional discharge.

NIB	EXC.	V.G.	GOOD	FAIR	POOR
—	450	400	275	150	50

Lone Star Derringer

A .38 Special caliber single-shot spur trigger pistol, with 2.5" barrel. Stainless steel with wood grips.

NIB	EXC.	V.G.	GOOD	FAIR	POOR
—	300	250	175	125	50

H-S PRECISION, INC.
Rapid City, South Dakota

SPR Sporter Rifle

Bolt-action rifle offered in long and short actions, with any standard SAAMI caliber. Match grade stainless steel barrel lengths are 22", 24" or 26", with optional muzzle-brake available. Synthetic stock offered in various colors. Weight between 7.5 and 7.75 lbs. depending on barrel length. Magazine capacity 4 rounds for standard calibers and 3 rounds for magnum calibers.

NIB	EXC.	V.G.	GOOD	FAIR	POOR
2375	1800	1400	900	500	250

SPL Lightweight Sporter

Introduced in 2005, this model features 22", 24" or 26" fluted barrel, with choice of short or long action calibers. Detachable magazine. No sights. Pro-series synthetic stock. Weight under 7 lbs.

NIB	EXC.	V.G.	GOOD	FAIR	POOR
2400	1825	1425	925	525	275

PHR Professional Hunter Rifle

Bolt-action rifle chambered for magnum calibers only and fitted with 24" or 26" stainless steel match grade fluted barrel (except .416 Rigby). Built in recoil reduced in synthetic stock with choice of colors. Matte black finish. Weight between 7.75 lbs. and 8.25 depending on barrel length and caliber. Offered in any standard SAAMI caliber. Magazine capacity 3 rounds.

NIB	EXC.	V.G.	GOOD	FAIR	POOR
3000	2400	1650	1050	575	300

BHR Big Game Professional Hunter Rifle

Introduced in 2005, this model has same features as PHR series, with addition of adjustable iron sights and specially designed stock. Weight about 7.75 to 8.25 lbs. depending on caliber and barrel length.

NIB	EXC.	V.G.	GOOD	FAIR	POOR
3100	2500	1850	1175	625	350

PHL Professional Hunter Lightweight Rifle

Model features weight of 5.75 lbs. Fitted with Pro-Series stock and choice of 20" or 22" contoured fluted stock. Matte black teflon finish. Detachable magazine. Chambered for short action calibers. Introduced in 2005.

NIB	EXC.	V.G.	GOOD	FAIR	POOR
3100	2500	1850	1175	625	350

VAR Varmint Rifle

Offered in long or short action, with .17 Rem., 6mm PPC and .223 Rem. in single-shot. Fitted with match grade stainless steel fluted barrel in 24" or 26" lengths. Available in a lightweight 20" barrel. Synthetic stock in choice of colors, with 20" barrel guns offered with thumbhole stocks. Black matte finish. Weight between 8 and 8.25 lbs. for standard rifles and 7.5 and 7.75 lbs. for 20" barrel guns. Available in any standard SAAMI caliber.

NIB	EXC.	V.G.	GOOD	FAIR	POOR
2600	2050	1650	1050	575	300

Varmint Take-Down Rifle

Take-down bolt-action rifle offered in stainless steel long or short action, with 24" stainless steel match grade fluted barrel. Matte black finish. Weight between 8.5 and 9 lbs. **NOTE:** Add $1,000 for extra barrel with same head size caliber; $1,200 for extra barrel with different head size caliber.

NIB	EXC.	V.G.	GOOD	FAIR	POOR
3700	2900	2050	1450	600	400

	NIB	EXC.	V.G.	GOOD	FAIR	POOR

Professional Hunter Take-Down Rifle

Take-down rifle offered in magnum and super magnum calibers, with 24" fluted stainless steel barrel. Built in recoil reducer. Matte black finish. Weight between 8.25 and 8.75 lbs.

NIB	EXC.	V.G.	GOOD	FAIR	POOR
4500	3200	2400	1650	750	450

Varmint Pistol

Bolt-action single-shot pistol chambered for a wide variety of calibers from .17 Rem. to 7mm BR. Fitted with heavy contour fluted stainless steel match barrel. Synthetic stock with center grip. Matte black finish. Weight about 5.25 to 5.5 lbs.

NIB	EXC.	V.G.	GOOD	FAIR	POOR
2200	1500	950	600	400	225

Silhouette Pistol

Same as above, with sporter contoured barrel. Weight about 4.5 lbs.

NIB	EXC.	V.G.	GOOD	FAIR	POOR
2100	1400	950	600	400	225

HTR Heavy Tactical Rifle

Bolt-action model features stainless steel long or short action, with fluted stainless steel 24" heavy barrel. Stock is synthetic, with adjustable cheekpiece and length of pull. Any standard SAAMI caliber available. Weight about 10.75 to 11.25 lbs. Matte black finish.

NIB	EXC.	V.G.	GOOD	FAIR	POOR
2750	2250	1850	1175	625	350

Short Tactical

Chambered for .308 cartridge and fitted with 20" fluted barrel. Matte teflon finish. Pro-Series tactical stock.

NIB	EXC.	V.G.	GOOD	FAIR	POOR
2750	2250	1850	1175	625	350

RDR Rapid Deployment Rifle

Similar to model above, with 20" stainless steel fluted barrel and smaller stock. Thumbhole stock on request. Magazine is 4 rounds. Matte black finish. Offered in any short action SAAMI calibers. Weight between 7.5 and 7.75 lbs.

NIB	EXC.	V.G.	GOOD	FAIR	POOR
2750	2250	1850	1175	625	350

TTD Tactical Take-Down System

Take-down rifle chambered for any standard SAAMI caliber and fitted with 24" fluted heavy stainless steel barrel. Magazine capacity 4 rounds for standard calibers and 3 rounds for magnum calibers. Synthetic stock adjustable for length of pull and cheekpiece. Matte black finish. Weight between 11.25 and 11.75 lbs.

NIB	EXC.	V.G.	GOOD	FAIR	POOR
4600	3800	2400	1650	750	450

HAENEL, C. G.
Suhl, Germany

Established in 1840, this company began to manufacture semi-automatic pistols after Hugo Schmeisser joined the firm in 1921 as its chief engineer.

Model 1

A 6.35mm caliber semi-automatic pistol, with 2.48" barrel, striker-fired, 6-shot magazine. Weight approximately 13.5 oz. Left side of the slide stamped "C.G. Haenel Suhl-Schmeisser Patent". Each grip panel marked "HS" in an oval.

NIB	EXC.	V.G.	GOOD	FAIR	POOR
—	500	400	295	200	125

Model 2

As above, but shorter (2" barrel) and lighter in weight (12 oz.). "Schmeisser" molded into grips.

NIB	EXC.	V.G.	GOOD	FAIR	POOR
—	550	425	350	225	150

HAFDASA
Buenos Aires, Argentina

Ballester-Molina

Copy of Colt Model 1911 semi-automatic pistol, differing only in absence of grip safety, smaller grip and finger grooves on slide. Slide stamped "Pistola Automatica Cal. .45 Fabricado por HAFDASA Patentes Internacional Ballester Molina Industria Argentina". Introduced in 1941.

NIB	EXC.	V.G.	GOOD	FAIR	POOR
—	475	400	300	225	100

Criolla

A .22-caliber automatic pistol similar to Ballester-Molina. Some were sold commercially under trademark "La Criolla".

NIB	EXC.	V.G.	GOOD	FAIR	POOR
—	1000	800	650	500	250

	NIB	EXC.	V.G.	GOOD	FAIR	POOR

Hafdasa

A .22-caliber semi-automatic pistol with tubular receiver. A true hammerless striker-fired, with angled grip. Markings are "HA" on butt.

	—	400	325	275	200	100

Zonda

As above marked "Zonda".

	—	400	325	275	200	100

Rigaud

A semi-automatic copy of Colt Model 1911, with no grip safety. Caliber is .45 ACP and later .22 LR. Barrel length 5". Magazine capacity 7 rounds. The .22-caliber introduced in 1940.

	—	475	400	300	225	100

Campeon

Same as Ballester-Molina, with floating chamber to accommodate .22 LR cartridge. Three variations of target model: sights, trigger and barrel lengths. Pistol first introduced in 1941 and produced until 1953.

	—	750	550	400	300	200

HAHN, WILLIAM
New York, New York

Pocket Pistol

A .41-caliber single-shot percussion pistol, with 2.5" round barrel, German silver mountings and walnut stock. Manufactured in 1860s and 1870s.

	—	—	1950	1050	475	250

HALE, H. J.
Bristol, Connecticut

Under Hammer Pistol

A .31-caliber single-shot under hammer percussion pistol, with 5" or 6" part-round, part-octagonal barrel. Iron frame, with either pointed or round walnut butt. Markings read "H.J.Hale/ Warranted/Cast Steel". Manufactured during 1850s.

	—	—	995	375	245	125

HALE & TULLER
Hartford, Connecticut

Under Hammer Pistol

A .44-caliber single-shot under hammer percussion pistol, with 6" tapered round barrel and pointed walnut grip. Manufactured at Connecticut State Prison between 1837 and 1840.

	—	—	975	450	200	125

HALL, ALEXANDER
New York, New York

Revolving Rifle

A .58-caliber percussion revolving rifle, with 15-shot open centered cylinder. Frame was made of brass. Barrel and cylinder of iron. Stock of walnut. Manufactured during 1850s in limited quantities. Very rare firearm.

	—	—	27500	12500	3750	1300

HALL-NORTH
Middletown, Connecticut

MODEL 1840 CARBINE

Carbine manufactured by Simeon North and chambered for .52-caliber percussion. Single-shot breech-loading smoothbore, with 21" round barrel. Full-length stock held on by two barrel bands. Ramrod mounted under barrel and mountings are of iron. Lock is case hardened and barrel brown. Stock is walnut. Markings are "US/S. North/Midltn/ Conn." Two distinct variations, both produced under military contract.

Type 1 Carbine

Model has squared right-angled breech lever mounted on trigger plate. There were 500 manufactured in 1840.

	—	—	9000	4000	1750	1000

	NIB	EXC.	V.G.	GOOD	FAIR	POOR

Type 2 Carbine

Variation features curved breech-operating lever known as fishtail. Approximately 6,000 manufactured from 1840 to 1843. Some have an 8" bar and ring.

—	—	7500	2500	1100	550	

HAMBUSH, JOSEPH
Ferlach, Austria

Boxlock Side-by-Side Shotgun

Custom-order boxlock double-barrel shotgun chambered for all gauges. Single-selective or double trigger and automatic ejectors. Features workmanship of high order and all specifications could vary with customer's wishes. Engraved with hunting scenes. Rare gun and not often encountered on today's market. **NOTE:** Pricing only estimated as not enough are traded to provide accurate values.

—	1950	1100	950	575	375	

Sidelock Side-by-Side Shotgun

Similar to above. Features full sidelock-action.

—	3800	2500	1750	1600	1350	

HAMILTON RIFLE COMPANY
Plymouth, Michigan

Manufacturer of inexpensive .22-caliber rifles established by Clarence J. Hamilton and his son Coello. Company was established in 1898 in Plymouth, Michigan. Company ceased production in 1945. Over 1 million rifles were produced between 1900 and 1911.

NOTE: Despite the fact there were many Hamilton rifles sold, most of these little guns were used hard and many did not survive. Hamilton rifles in excellent condition are hardly ever encountered. No prices are quoted for rifles in this condition as few exist. Further information about these rifles is gratefully accepted by the editor.

Model 7

First rifle produced by this company. Made entirely of castings and stampings. Nickel plated. Chambered for .22 Short cartridge, with 8" brass-lined barrel that pivots for loading. Stock was metal skeleton. Production ceased in 1901. Total of 44,000 rifles produced.

—	750	500	450	300	195	

Model 11

Similar to Model 7. Fitted with board-like walnut stock. Markings stamped into buttstock: "Hamilton Rifles Co., Plymouth, Mich., Pat. Pending No. 11". Model 11 produced from 1900 to 1902. Approximately 22,000 were sold.

—	700	475	300	200	150	

Model 15

Produced from 1901 to 1910, Model 15 was chambered for .22 Short with 8" brass lined barrel. Walnut stock. Design was an under lever single-shot, with loading port under barrel. Cocking knob located at rear of frame. Blued finish. Approximately 234,000 were sold.

—	675	400	200	150	100	

Model 19

Similar to Model 15, with modified loading port and 12" barrel. Few Model 19s have been seen with 13" barrels. These will bring a premium. Produced from 1903 to 1910. About 59,000 were sold.

—	700	475	300	200	150	

Model 23

First bolt-action rifle made by this company. Receiver is steel tube with loading port in top where barrel joins receiver. Bolt handle located at extreme rear of bolt. Cocking knob must be operated manually. Walnut stock either rounded or flat. Chamberd for .22 Short and .22 Long cartridges. 15" brass lined barrel. Blued finish. Weighs about 3 lbs. Produced from 1905 to 1909. About 25,000 were sold.

—	700	475	300	200	150	

Model 27

Single-shot tip-up .22-caliber rifle, with stamped steel receiver. Barrel length 16" brass lined or 14.875"; overall length 30". First produced in 1906.

—	475	300	200	150	100	

	NIB	EXC.	V.G.	GOOD	FAIR	POOR

Model 027

As above with walnut stock. First produced in 1908.

	NIB	EXC.	V.G.	GOOD	FAIR	POOR
	—	495	300	200	150	100

Model 31

Introduced in 1910, this single-shot rifle is chambered for .22 Short and Long cartridge. Fitted with 15.75" barrel with brass liner. A tip-up design. Blued finish. Weighs about 2.25 lbs.

	NIB	EXC.	V.G.	GOOD	FAIR	POOR
	—	725	575	400	250	200

Model 35 or Boys' Military Rifle

Single-shot .22-caliber rifle, with full-length oval walnut straight-grip stock and 15.75" brass lined barrel. Produced from 1915 to 1918. Sold with stamped steel bayonet. Few bayonets survive. **NOTE:** Add $150 for bayonet to prices.

	NIB	EXC.	V.G.	GOOD	FAIR	POOR
	—	950	700	450	250	125

Model 39

Only repeating rifle built by this company. Hammerless slide-action design, with tubular magazine. Magazine capacity 15 rounds of .22 Short. Barrel length 16" with brass liner. Walnut stock with blade front sight. Produced from 1922 to 1930. Weighs about 4 lbs.

	NIB	EXC.	V.G.	GOOD	FAIR	POOR
	—	575	300	200	150	100

Model 43

Bolt-action design with loading port on top of barrel. No external cocking knob, but bolt is pulled to rear when in locked position. Chambered for .22 Short and .22 Long cartridges. 15.75" brass lined barrel. Fitted with an oval walnut stock, with blade front sight and open non-adjustable rear sight. Weighs about 3 lbs. Built from 1924 to 1932.

	NIB	EXC.	V.G.	GOOD	FAIR	POOR
	—	575	300	200	150	100

Model 47

Bolt-action single-shot rifle, with loading port located on top of barrel. Chambered for .22 Short and Long cartridges. Cocking knob located at rear of bolt handle. Early Model 47 were built with 16" brass lined barrels. Later examples were fitted with 18.25" steel lined barrels. Early guns had an oval buttstock while later guns had a pistol-grip stock. Very late guns had an all-steel barrel. Produced from 1927 to 1932.

	NIB	EXC.	V.G.	GOOD	FAIR	POOR
	—	575	475	300	200	150

Model 51

Conventional type bolt-action rifle, with cocking knob located at rear of bolt. Two styles of buttstocks were used: flat style and later an oval shape. First Hamilton rifle chambered for .22 LR cartridge. Barrel was 20" steel. Finish was blue. Weight approximately 3.5 lbs. Produced from 1935 to 1941.

	NIB	EXC.	V.G.	GOOD	FAIR	POOR
	—	550	400	250	200	150

Model 55

Bolt-action rifle chambered for .22 Short, Long and LR cartridges. Fitted with 20" steel barrel, with bead front sight and open adjustable rear sight. Walnut stock. Rarest Hamilton rifle. Only one example is known. Produced from late 1941 to early 1942.

	NIB	EXC.	V.G.	GOOD	FAIR	POOR
	—	1000	—	—	—	—

HAMMERLI, SA
Lenzburg, Switzerland

RIFLES

Model 45 Smallbore Rifle

A .22-caliber bolt-action single-shot, with 27.5" heavy barrel, aperture rear and globe target front sight. Match rifle-type thumbhole stock. Manufactured between 1945 and 1957.

	NIB	EXC.	V.G.	GOOD	FAIR	POOR
	—	825	700	595	450	250

Model 54 Smallbore Rifle

As above, with adjustable buttplate. Manufactured between 1954 and 1957.

	NIB	EXC.	V.G.	GOOD	FAIR	POOR
	—	850	725	625	475	275

	NIB	EXC.	V.G.	GOOD	FAIR	POOR

Model 503 Smallbore Free Rifle

Similar to Model 54, with free rifle-style stock.

	NIB	EXC.	V.G.	GOOD	FAIR	POOR
	—	800	675	575	450	225

Model 506 Smallbore Match Rifle

Later version of Smallbore target series. Manufactured between 1963 and 1966.

	NIB	EXC.	V.G.	GOOD	FAIR	POOR
	—	850	725	625	475	275

Olympic 300 Meter

A 7x57, .30-06 or .300 H&H Magnum caliber bolt-action single-shot rifle, with 20.5" heavy barrel. Aperture rear globe target front sight, double-set triggers and free rifle-type adjustable thumbhole stock. Wide beavertail forearm and schuetzen-style buttplate. Manufactured between 1945 and 1959.

	NIB	EXC.	V.G.	GOOD	FAIR	POOR
	—	1050	900	725	550	325

Sporting Rifle

Bolt-action single-shot rifle chambered for many popular calibers (American and European). Double-set triggers and classic-style stock.

	NIB	EXC.	V.G.	GOOD	FAIR	POOR
	—	800	675	575	450	225

PISTOLS

Model 100 Free Pistol

A .22-caliber single-shot Martini-action target pistol, with 11.5" octagonal barrel, adjustable sights, single set trigger and walnut stocks. Manufactured from 1933 to 1949.

	NIB	EXC.	V.G.	GOOD	FAIR	POOR
	—	1000	825	700	550	325

Model 101

As above, with heavy round barrel and more sophisticated target sights. Matte-blued finish. Manufactured between 1956 and 1960.

	NIB	EXC.	V.G.	GOOD	FAIR	POOR
	—	1000	825	700	550	325

Model 102

As above, with highly polished blue finish. Manufactured between 1956 and 1960.

	NIB	EXC.	V.G.	GOOD	FAIR	POOR
	—	1000	825	700	550	325

Model 103

Similar to Model 101, with lighter-weight octagonal barrel, high-polished blued finish. Manufactured between 1956 and 1960.

	NIB	EXC.	V.G.	GOOD	FAIR	POOR
	—	1100	925	825	650	425

Model 104

As above, with lightweight round barrel. Manufactured between 1961 and 1965.

	NIB	EXC.	V.G.	GOOD	FAIR	POOR
	—	950	625	550	450	300

Model 105

As above, with redesigned stock and improved action. Manufactured between 1962 and 1965.

	NIB	EXC.	V.G.	GOOD	FAIR	POOR
	—	950	625	550	450	300

Model 106

As above, with improved trigger.

	NIB	EXC.	V.G.	GOOD	FAIR	POOR
	—	950	625	550	450	300

Model 107

Variation fitted with five-level set trigger. Introduced in 1965. Discontinued in 1971.

	NIB	EXC.	V.G.	GOOD	FAIR	POOR
	—	950	625	550	450	300

Model 107 Deluxe

As above, but engraved with carved stock.

	NIB	EXC.	V.G.	GOOD	FAIR	POOR
	—	1500	1250	900	800	500

Model 120-1 Free Pistol

Bolt-action single-shot pistol in .22 LR caliber, with 9.9" barrel, adjustable target sights activated for loading and cocking by an alloy lever on side of bolt. Blued, with checkered walnut grips

	NIB	EXC.	V.G.	GOOD	FAIR	POOR
	—	1200	975	600	425	250

	NIB	EXC.	V.G.	GOOD	FAIR	POOR

Model 120-2

As above, with contoured grips.

	—	1200	975	600	425	250

Model 120 Heavy Barrel

As above, with 5.7" heavy barrel.

	—	1200	975	600	425	250

Model 150

Single-shot Martini-action .22-caliber pistol, with 11.25" barrel, adjustable sights, contoured grips and single-set trigger. Blued with walnut stocks.

	—	1500	1100	775	500	350

Model 152

As above, with 11.25" barrel and electronic release trigger.

	—	1800	1300	1050	600	450

International Model 206

A .22-caliber semi-automatic pistol, with 7.5" barrel, integral muzzle-brake, adjustable sights and walnut grips. Manufactured between 1962 and 1969.

	—	825	700	575	425	300

International Model 207

As above, with adjustable grips.

	—	850	725	600	450	325

International Model 208

A .22-caliber semi-automatic pistol, with 6" barrel, adjustable sights and 8-shot magazine. Adjustable trigger and target grips. Barrel drilled and tapped for addition of barrel weights. Manufactured between 1966 and 1988.

	—	1850	1550	1250	1000	750

International Model 208 Deluxe

As above, with engraved receiver and carved grips. Discontinued in 1988.

	—	3250	2750	2500	2000	1500

International Model 209

A .22 Short caliber semi-automatic pistol, with 4.75" barrel, muzzle-brake, adjustable target sights and 5-shot magazine. Blued, with walnut grips. Manufactured between 1966 and 1970.

	—	1200	975	600	425	250

International Model 210

As above, with adjustable grips.

	—	1225	1000	625	450	275

International Model 211

As above, with non-adjustable thumb rest grips.

	—	1300	1075	700	475	300

Model 212

A .22-caliber semi-automatic pistol, with 5" barrel and adjustable sights. Blued with walnut grips.

	—	1300	1075	700	475	300

Model 230

A .22 Short caliber semi-automatic pistol, with 6.3" barrel, 5-shot magazine, adjustable sights and walnut grip. Manufactured between 1970 and 1983.

	—	1350	1125	750	525	325

Model 232

A .22 Short caliber semi-automatic pistol, with 5" barrel, adjustable sights and 6-shot magazine. Contoured walnut grips. Introduced in 1984.

	—	1300	1075	700	475	300

Model 280

New state-of-the-art target pistol from Hammerli. Features a modular design and frame of carbon fiber material. Has 4.6" barrel, with adjustable sights, trigger and grips. Chambered for .22 LR or

	NIB	EXC.	V.G.	GOOD	FAIR	POOR

.32 wadcutter. Magazine holds 5 rounds. Introduced in 1988.

	NIB	EXC.	V.G.	GOOD	FAIR	POOR
	—	1800	1500	1350	1000	600

Model SP 20

Introduced in 1998, this pistol has a very low sight line. Features a wide variety of special items such as adjustable buffer system, anatomically shaped trigger in various sizes, various receiver colors, change over caliber system from .22 LR to .32 S&W.

NIB	EXC.	V.G.	GOOD	FAIR	POOR
1750	1325	900	800	500	—

HAMMERLI-WALTHER
Lenzburg, Switzerland

These target pistols were produced by Hammerli under license from Walther after WWII. This project continued until approximately 1963, when production ceased.

Olympia Model 200 Type 1952

A .22-caliber semi-automatic pistol, with 7.5" barrel, 10-shot magazine, adjustable target sights. Blued, with walnut grips. Manufactured between 1952 and 1958.

	EXC.	V.G.	GOOD	FAIR	POOR
—	900	775	575	475	350

Model 200 Type 1958

As above, with integral muzzle-brake. Manufactured between 1958 and 1963.

	EXC.	V.G.	GOOD	FAIR	POOR
—	950	725	625	495	350

Model 201

Model 200 Type 1952, with 9.5" barrel. Manufactured between 1955 and 1957.

	EXC.	V.G.	GOOD	FAIR	POOR
—	950	725	625	495	350

Model 202

Similar to Model 201, with adjustable walnut grips. Manufactured between 1955 and 1957.

	EXC.	V.G.	GOOD	FAIR	POOR
—	950	725	625	495	350

Model 203

Similar to Model 200, with adjustable grips. Available with or without muzzle-brake.

	EXC.	V.G.	GOOD	FAIR	POOR
—	950	725	625	495	350

Model 204

A .22-caliber semi-automatic pistol, with 7.5" barrel, muzzle-brake and barrel weights. Manufactured between 1956 and 1963.

	EXC.	V.G.	GOOD	FAIR	POOR
—	975	750	650	525	375

Model 205

As above, with adjustable target grips. Manufactured between 1956 and 1963.

	EXC.	V.G.	GOOD	FAIR	POOR
—	1000	775	675	575	450

HAMMOND BULLDOG
Connecticut Arms & Mfg. Co.
Naubuc, Connecticut

Hammond Bulldog

A .44 rimfire single-shot spur trigger pistol, with 4" octagonal barrel that pivots to open. Blued, with checkered walnut grips. Manufactured from 1864 to approximately 1867.

	EXC.	V.G.	GOOD	FAIR	POOR
—	775	550	375	250	100

HAMMOND MFG. CO., GRANT
New Haven, Connecticut

Military Automatic Pistol

A .45 ACP caliber semi-automatic pistol, with 6.75" barrel and 8-shot magazine. Blued, with checkered walnut grips. Marked on right of slide "Grant Hammond Mfg. Corp. New Haven, Conn." Left side shows patent dates. Manufactured in 1917. As all known specimens of this pistol exhibit differences, it is believed they were only made as prototypes. Highest serial number known is under 20. TOO RARE TO PRICE.

	NIB	EXC.	V.G.	GOOD	FAIR	POOR

Grant Hammond 7.65mm Pistol

A semi-automatic pistol in 7.65mm caliber. Has a blow-forward action and spur hammer. TOO RARE TO PRICE.

HANKINS, WILLIAM
Philadelphia, Pennsylvania

Pocket Revolver

A .26-caliber spur trigger percussion revolver, with 3" octagonal barrel and 5-shot unfluted cylinder. Blued, with walnut grips. Approximately 650 manufactured in 1860 and 1861.

—	—	3250	1700	600	200	

HANUS, BILL
Newport, Oregon

Bill Hanus Classic

The late Bill Hanus was a dealer and importer of various European shotguns, until his passing in 2012. In the 1980s and 1990s he imported his own private brand of side-by-side doubles from Ignacio Ugartechea and several other manufacturers in Italy, in 16-, 20-, 28-gauge and .410 bore. These guns had double trigger ejectors and English-style stocks.

2500	2000	1350	900	625	350	

HARRINGTON & RICHARDSON, INC.
Madison, North Carolina

One of the oldest manufacturers of firearms in the United States. Original Harrington and Richardson started in 1871 and was in existence until 1986. For all those years, the company was located in Worcester, Massachusetts. After the original company closed, in 1991 a new company, H&R 1871 was formed in Gardner, Massachusetts. In 2000, H&R 1871 was purchased by Marlin Firearms. The assets of Marlin, including H&R 1871 and its subsidiary, New England Firearms (NEF), were bought by Remington in 2007. H&R's corporate office is now located with Remington and Marlin in Madison, North Carolina, while the production facilities are at the former Remington plant in Ilion, New York. The New England Firearms brand has been used for the marketing of some H&R products in recent years. See separate listing under New England Firearms (NEF).

Model No. 1

A .32- or .38-caliber spur-trigger single-action revolver, with 3" octagonal barrel, solid frame, 7-shot or 5-shot cylinder depending on caliber. Nickel-plated, with checkered rubber bird's-head grips. Barrel marked "Harrington & Richardson Worcester, Mass." Approximately 3,000 manufactured in 1877 and 1878.

—	300	250	200	125	75	

Model No. 1-1/2

A .32-caliber spur-trigger single-action revolver, with 2.5" octagonal barrel and 5-shot cylinder. Nickel-plated, round-butt rubber grips with an "H&R" emblem molded in. Approximately 10,000 manufactured between 1878 and 1883.

—	300	150	125	75	50	

Model No. 2-1/2

As above, with 3.25" barrel and 7-shot cylinder. Approximately 5,000 manufactured between 1878 and 1883.

—	300	150	125	75	50	

Model No. 3-1/2

Similar to Model 2-1/2 except in .38 rimfire caliber, with 3.5" barrel and 5-shot cylinder. Approximately 2,500 manufactured.

—	300	175	150	100	75	

Model No. 4-1/2

A .41 rimfire caliber spur trigger revolver, with 2.5" barrel and 5-shot cylinder. Approximately 1,000 manufactured.

—	600	400	200	125	90	

Model 1880

A .32 or .38 S&W centerfire caliber double-action revolver, with 3" round barrel, solid frame and 5- or 6-shot cylinder depending on caliber. Nickel-plated, with hard rubber grips. Marked "Harrington & Richardson Worcester, Mass." Approximately 4,000 manufactured between 1880 and 1883.

—	250	200	175	125	90	

	NIB	EXC.	V.G.	GOOD	FAIR	POOR

The American Double-Action

A .32, .28 or .44 centerfire caliber double-action revolver, with 2.5", 4.5" or 6" round or octagonal barrel, 5- or 6-shot fluted cylinder depending on caliber. Solid frame nickel-plated, with some blue models noted. Grips are hard rubber. Marked "The American Double Action." Some noted are marked "H&R Bulldog". Approximately 850,000 manufactured between 1883 and 1940. **NOTE:** Add 150 percent for .44.

	—	250	125	100	85	65

The Young America Double-Action

A .22 rimfire or .32 S&W centerfire caliber double-action revolver, with 2", 4.5" or 6" round or octagonal barrels. Solid frame and 5- or 7-shot cylinder depending on caliber. Blued or nickel-plated, with hard rubber grips. Marked "Young America Double Action" or "Young America Bulldog". Approximately 1,500,000 manufactured between 1884 and 1941.

	—	200	125	100	85	65

Hunter

A .22-caliber double-action revolver, with 10" octagonal barrel and 9-shot fluted cylinder. Blued, with checkered walnut grips.

	—	400	300	200	150	100

Trapper

As above, with 6" octagonal barrel and 7-shot cylinder. Otherwise similar to Hunter.

	—	300	200	125	100	75

Self-Loader

A 6.35mm or 7.65mm semi-automatic pistol, with 2" or 3.5" barrel, 6- or 8-shot magazine. Similar in outline to Webley. Larger 7.65 model has a grip safety. Blued or nickel-plated, with checkered hard rubber grips that bear the H&R monogram. Slide marked "H&R Self-Loading", with 1907 or 1909 patent dates. Approximately 16,500 manufactured in 6.35mm between 1912 and 1916 and 34,500 in 7.65mm manufactured between 1916 and 1924. **NOTE:** Add 10 percent for .32.

	—	500	400	275	200	125

First Model Hand Ejector

A .32 or .38 centerfire caliber double-action revolver, with 3.25" ribbed round barrel. Version does not feature automatic ejection found on later models. Nickel-plated, with hard rubber grips. Company name marked on barrel. Approximately 6,000 manufactured between 1886 and 1888.

	—	200	150	125	90	65

Model 1 Double-Action Revolver

A .32, .32 Long and .38 S&W caliber double-action revolver, with 3.25" ribbed round barrel and 5- or 6-shot cylinder depending on caliber. Nickel-plated, with hard rubber grips. Approximately 5,000 manufactured between 1887 and 1889.

	—	175	145	110	80	50

Model 2

Similar to Model 1, with 2.5", 3.25", 4", 5" or 6" barrels. Grips feature H&R target logo. Approximately 1,300,000 manufactured between 1889 and 1940.

	—	125	100	80	65	40

Knife Model

Model 2, with 4" ribbed round barrel having a folding 2.25" double-edged knife mounted under barrel. Blued or nickel-plated. Approximately 2,000 manufactured between 1901 and 1917.

	—	1500	1000	700	500	150

Model 922 First Issue

A .22-caliber double-action revolver, with 2.5", 4" or 6" barrel. Blued, with checkered walnut grips.

	—	150	125	100	75	50

Target Model

A .22 LR or .22 WRF caliber double-action revolver, with 7-shot cylinder, break-open frame and 6" barrel. Fixed sights. Blued, with checkered walnut grips.

	—	150	125	100	75	50

.22 Special

A .22 LR or .22 WRF double-action break-open revolver, with 6" barrel and 7-shot cylinder. Blued, with checkered walnut grips.

	—	300	200	125	90	65

	NIB	EXC.	V.G.	GOOD	FAIR	POOR

Expert
As above, with 10" barrel.

	NIB	EXC.	V.G.	GOOD	FAIR	POOR
	—	400	300	200	100	50

No. 199 Sportsman
A .22-caliber single-action break-open revolver, with 6" barrel, adjustable target sights and 9-shot cylinder. Blued, with checkered walnut grips.

	—	275	200	150	100	75

Ultra Sportsman
As above, but more finely finished. Special wide target hammer and improved action.

	—	325	215	175	125	90

Defender
A .38 S&W caliber double-action break-open revolver, with 4" or 6" barrel and fixed sights. Blued, with plastic grips.

	—	275	200	145	75	50

New Defender
A .22-caliber double-action break-open revolver, with 2" barrel and 9-shot cylinder. Blued, with checkered walnut round-butt grips.

	—	225	200	175	125	90

.22 U.S.R.A./Model 195 Single-Shot Match Target Pistol
Also called the Model 195, this pistol underwent nearly constant modifications from its inception in 1928 until production ceased in 1941. Its development was greatly influenced by the United States Revolver Association (USRA), which established certain rules for target pistol shooting. Lack of any H&R-published model chronology for the estimated 3,500 guns manufactured, makes model determination by examination complicated; further difficulty is that H&R supplied newly designed parts to owners of older variations, who would then retrofit their pistols with newer triggers, hammers, sights and trigger guards. Extracted from available literature, the parts represent approximately: 14 different stocks and virtually endless custom variations by Walter F. Roper; 5 different trigger guards; 3 different triggers; 2 different hammers; 2 different extractors; 3 barrel lengths (7", 8", 10"); and 3 barrel rib styles. From this array of potential characteristics, at least four distinct variations can be identified.

.22 U.S.R.A./Model 195 Pistol, Variations 1 to 3

	—	2500	1800	1000	600	200

.22 U.S.R.A./Model 195 Pistol, Variation 4

	—	2200	1500	800	325	250

VARIATION 1, PRE-U.S.R.A., 1928-30: Not marked U.S.R.A., and known as "H&R Single-Shot Pistol." There is no finger rest between trigger guard and front grip strap; it was advertised with "sawhandle" shape grip copied from Model 1 or 2 smooth bore H&R Handy-Gun, manufactured with 10" "hourglass" barrel with a deeply undercut rib. These are the first 500 pistols.

VARIATION 2, U.S.R.A. KEYHOLE BARREL, 1930-31: This is standard "early" model marked U.S.R.A., has a finger rest and non-sawhandle grips; however, several grip shapes were offered as options. Grip screw goes from rear of grip into threaded hold in back grip strap.

VARIATION 3, MODIFIED KEYHOLE BARREL, 1931: Modification of Variation 2 to improve rear sight, barrel catch changed, reduced spent cartridge force by replacing cylindrical extractor with less powerful hinged type and hammer cocking spur and finger rest were made wider. The 8" barrel was offered as an option to standard 10" length and number of different grip shapes was increased. This is a transition model between "early" Variation 2 and "final" Variation 4 designs.

VARIATION 4, TAPERED SLABSIDE BARREL, 1931-41: New "truncated teardrop" barrel cross section shape; new standard barrel length of 7", with 10" optional; adjustable trigger; new sear; grip screw location was changed to front of grip; and front sight was adjustable for elevation. Trigger design was changed from curved to straight beveled type with relocated cocking surfaces and number of grip shapes increased further to 13 types. A front sight protector was supplied as standard equipment and luggage style case offered as an option. It appears that Variation 4 was introduced around 1931; 1932 advertisements describe the fully redesigned gun, but picture Variation 2, indicating H&R probably did not re-photograph the new design. Final variation has a special, tight bore .217" in diameter, with bullet seating .03125" (1/32") into rifling and is among the most accurate of single-shot .22 caliber pistols. Model 195/U.S.R.A. was relatively expensive, costing approximately $30 in 1932 and increased to slightly more than $36 by the time production ended in 1941, yet was the least expensive of all single-shot .22 target pistols of quality.

	NIB	EXC.	V.G.	GOOD	FAIR	POOR

Model 504

A .32 H&R Magnum caliber double-action swing-out cylinder revolver, with 4" or 6" heavy barrel, adjustable sights and 5-shot cylinder. Blued, with either black plastic or walnut grips. Smaller version manufactured with 3" or 4" barrel and round butt.

	—	350	275	150	90	65

Model 532

As above, with a cylinder that has to be removed for loading. Manufactured in 1984 and 1985.

	—	275	175	125	75	50

Model 586

A .32 H&R Magnum caliber double-action revolver, with 4.5", 5.5", 7.5" or 10" barrel, adjustable sights and 5-shot cylinder. Blued, with either black plastic or walnut grips.

	—	325	275	175	150	100

Model 603

A .22 rimfire Magnum caliber double-action revolver, with 6" flat-sided barrel and swing-out 6-shot cylinder. Blued, with smooth walnut grips.

	—	225	165	140	110	85

Model 604

As above, with 6" ribbed heavy barrel.

	—	295	215	175	125	100

Model 622

A .22-caliber solid-frame double-action revolver, with 2.5" or 4" barrel. Blued, with round-butt plastic grips.

	—	150	100	65	50	25

Model 623

As above, but nickel-plated.

	—	165	110	80	60	40

Model 632

As above, in .32 centerfire.

	—	150	90	75	60	30

Model 642

As above, in .22 rimfire Magnum.

	—	150	80	65	50	25

Model 649

Model 622, with 5.5" or 7.5" barrel.

	—	150	125	100	75	50

Model 650

As above, but nickel-plated.

	—	175	150	125	75	50

Model 660

A .22-caliber solid-frame Western-style revolver, with 5.5" barrel and double-action. Blued, with walnut grips. Also known as "Gunfighter".

	—	150	125	100	50	25

Model 666

A .22 or .22 rimfire Magnum caliber double-action revolver, with 6" barrel and 6-shot cylinder. Blued, with plastic grips. Manufactured between 1976 and 1982.

	—	150	125	100	50	25

Model 676

Similar to Model 660. Blued, with case colored frame and walnut grips. Manufactured between 1976 and 1982.

	—	175	150	100	75	50

Model 686

Similar to Model 660 "Gunfighter", with 4.5", 5.5", 7.5", 10" or 12" barrel.

	—	175	150	125	100	75

	NIB	EXC.	V.G.	GOOD	FAIR	POOR

Model 732

A .32-caliber double-action solid-frame revolver, with swingout cylinder, 2.5" or 4" barrel and 6-shot cylinder. Blued, with black plastic grips. Also known as "Guardsman".

		EXC.	V.G.	GOOD	FAIR	POOR
	—	150	125	90	65	45

Model 733

As above, but nickel-plated and 2.5" barrel.

	—	175	150	100	75	50

Model 900

A .22-caliber solid-frame revolver, with removable cylinder, 2.5", 4" or 6" barrel and 9-shot cylinder. Blued, with black plastic grips. Manufactured between 1962 and 1973.

	—	150	125	90	60	40

Model 901

As above, but chrome-plated with white plastic grips. Manufactured in 1962 and 1963 only.

	—	150	125	90	60	40

Model 903

As above, with swing-out cylinder, flat-sided, 6" barrel and 9-shot cylinder. Blued, with walnut grips.

	—	150	125	90	75	50

Model 904

As above, with ribbed heavy barrel.

	—	175	150	125	100	50

Model 905

As above, but nickel-plated.

	—	200	175	150	80	65

Model 922 Second Issue

A .22 rimfire caliber solid-frame revolver, with 2.5", 4" or 6" barrel. Blued, with black plastic grips. Manufactured between 1950 and 1982.

	—	150	90	80	60	40

Model 923

As above, but nickel-plated.

	—	160	90	80	60	40

Model 925

A .38 S&W caliber double-action break-open hand ejector revolver, with 2.5" barrel, adjustable sights and 5-shot cylinder. Blued, with one-piece wraparound grip. Manufactured between 1964 and 1984.

	—	250	175	125	75	50

Model 935

As above, but nickel-plated.

	—	260	200	150	100	50

Model 929

A .22 rimfire solid-frame swing-out revolver, with 2.5", 4" or 6" barrel and 9-shot cylinder. Blued, with plastic grips. Also known as "Sidekick". Manufactured between 1956 and 1985.

	—	225	150	125	65	45

Model 929 Sidekick—New Model

Reintroduced in 1996, this single-/double-action revolver chambered for .22 short, long or LR cartridges. Cylinder holds 9 rounds. Sold with lockable storage case, nylon holster, gun oil and grease samples. Weighs about 30 oz. Made from 1996 - 1999. Discontinued.

	250	175	150	100	75	50

	NIB	EXC.	V.G.	GOOD	FAIR	POOR

Model 929 Sidekick Trapper Edition

As above, with grey laminate grips and special "NTA" Trapper Edition roll stamp on barrel. Made in 1996.

NIB	EXC.	V.G.	GOOD	FAIR	POOR
275	175	150	100	75	50

Model 930

As above, but nickel-plated. Not available with 6" barrel.

NIB	EXC.	V.G.	GOOD	FAIR	POOR
—	250	150	125	65	45

Model 939 Ultra Sidekick

As above, with ventilated rib, flat sided 6" barrel, adjustable sights, thumb rest grips. Features a safety device whereby pistol could not be fired unless it was unlocked by a furnished key. Manufactured between 1958 and 1982.

NIB	EXC.	V.G.	GOOD	FAIR	POOR
—	225	200	150	75	50

Model 939 Premier

Similar to above models, but fitted with 6" barrel, sighting rib, adjustable rear sight, hard wood grips, high polished blued finish. Weighs about 36 oz. Made from 1995 - 1999.

NIB	EXC.	V.G.	GOOD	FAIR	POOR
250	225	200	125	75	50

Model 940

Round-barreled version of above.

NIB	EXC.	V.G.	GOOD	FAIR	POOR
—	225	200	125	75	50

Model 949

A .22-caliber double-action Western-type revolver, with 5.5" barrel, ejector rod, 9-shot gate-loaded cylinder and adjustable sights. Blued, with walnut grips. Manufactured between 1960 and 1985.

NIB	EXC.	V.G.	GOOD	FAIR	POOR
—	200	175	150	75	50

Model 949 Western

Similar to above model, this revolver is offered with choice of 5.5" or 7.5" barrel, adjustable rear sight, walnut grips. Case colored frame and backstrap, with blued cylinder and barrel. Weight about 36 oz.

NIB	EXC.	V.G.	GOOD	FAIR	POOR
250	200	150	100	75	50

Model 950

As above, but nickel-plated.

NIB	EXC.	V.G.	GOOD	FAIR	POOR
—	250	175	125	75	50

Model 976

As above, with case-hardened frame.

NIB	EXC.	V.G.	GOOD	FAIR	POOR
—	200	150	100	75	50

Model 999 Sportsman

A .22 rimfire caliber double-action break-open self ejecting revolver, with 4" or 6" barrel ventilated rib barrel and windage adjustable sights. Blued, with walnut grips. Weighs about 30 oz. with 4" barrel; 34 oz. with 6" barrel.

NIB	EXC.	V.G.	GOOD	FAIR	POOR
500	425	350	295	175	100

Model 999 Engraved

As above, but engraved.

NIB	EXC.	V.G.	GOOD	FAIR	POOR
550	450	375	300	200	125

Amtec 2000

German-designed (Erma) and American-built double-action revolver, introduced in 1996. Offered in 2" or 3" barrel and chambered for .38 Special cartridge. Pachmayr composition grips. Cylinder holds 5 rounds. Weight approximately 25 oz. Discontinued.

NIB	EXC.	V.G.	GOOD	FAIR	POOR
250	200	200	150	75	50

	NIB	EXC.	V.G.	GOOD	FAIR	POOR

SHOTGUNS

Hammerless Double

A 10- or 12-gauge Anson & Deeley hammerless boxlock double-barrel shotgun, with 28", 30" or 32" Damascus barrels in various choke combinations, double triggers and extractors. Engraved, case hardened and walnut stock. Four grades were available. They differ in amount of engraving and quality of materials and workmanship utilized. Approximately 3,500 manufactured between 1882 and 1885.

D Grade

	NIB	EXC.	V.G.	GOOD	FAIR	POOR
	—	650	550	425	300	175

C Grade

	NIB	EXC.	V.G.	GOOD	FAIR	POOR
	—	750	650	500	400	275

B Grade

	NIB	EXC.	V.G.	GOOD	FAIR	POOR
	—	900	750	600	500	350

A Grade

	NIB	EXC.	V.G.	GOOD	FAIR	POOR
	—	2000	1750	1500	1000	550

Harrich No. 1

A 12-gauge boxlock single barrel shotgun, with 32" or 34" ventilated rib, full-choke barrel and automatic ejector. Engraved, blued with checkered walnut stock. Imported between 1971 and 1975.

	NIB	EXC.	V.G.	GOOD	FAIR	POOR
	—	1750	1500	1150	850	650

Single-Barrel Shotguns

Harrington & Richardson manufactured a series of single-barrel break-open shotguns, between 1908 and 1942. Chambered for various gauges, barrel lengths and chokes. Finishes were blued with walnut stocks. Little collector interest in these guns. If in sound condition are desirable as shooters only. They are Models 3, 5, 6, 7, 8, 9, as well as hinged-frame folding design.

	NIB	EXC.	V.G.	GOOD	FAIR	POOR
	—	125	100	85	65	40

Turkey Mag

Single-shot break-open side release gun chambered for 12-gauge 3.5" shell, with screw-in Full choke. Hardwood stock has Mossy Oak finish. Barrel length 24", with bead front sight. Weight about 6 lbs.

	NIB	EXC.	V.G.	GOOD	FAIR	POOR
	175	150	125	100	75	50

Youth Turkey Gun

Similar in appearance to Turkey Mag, but on a smaller scale. Chambered for 20-gauge 3" shell, with 22" barrel. Weighs about 5.5 lbs.

	NIB	EXC.	V.G.	GOOD	FAIR	POOR
	165	140	115	90	60	40

Topper (New Production)

Break-open side release single-shot, available in 12-, 20-gauge and .410 bore. The 12-gauge offered with 28" barrel while others are fitted with 26" barrel. Blued finish, with hardwood stock in black finish and semi-pistol grip. Weight approximately 6 lbs.

	NIB	EXC.	V.G.	GOOD	FAIR	POOR
	150	100	80	60	45	30

Topper Deluxe

	NIB	EXC.	V.G.	GOOD	FAIR	POOR
	170	125	90	70	50	40

Topper Jr. in 20 Gauge and .410 Bore Only

	NIB	EXC.	V.G.	GOOD	FAIR	POOR
	150	100	80	60	45	30

Topper Jr. Classic

Similar to Topper Jr. Features black walnut stock, with butt checkering, white line spacer and black recoil pad. Weighs about 7.5 lbs.

	NIB	EXC.	V.G.	GOOD	FAIR	POOR
	150	100	80	60	45	30

Topper Deluxe Slug

This 12-gauge single-shot has 24" fully rifled barrel, with built-in compensator.

	NIB	EXC.	V.G.	GOOD	FAIR	POOR
	150	115	90	70	50	40

Topper Deluxe Classic

Introduced in 2004, this 12-gauge 3" single shot gun fitted with 28" vent rib barrel and screw-in modified choke. American black walnut stock, with pistol-grip and ventilated recoil pad. Barrel

NIB	EXC.	V.G.	GOOD	FAIR	POOR

has black finish while receiver nickel finish. Weight about 5.5 lbs. In 2005 this model offered in 20-gauge.

NIB	EXC.	V.G.	GOOD	FAIR	POOR
245	200	150	100	75	50

Topper Trap Gun

Similar to above, with select checkered walnut stock, fore-end with fluted comb and full pistol-grip; 30" barrel with two white beads and screw-in chokes (Improved Modified Extended included); deluxe Pachmayr trap recoil pad.

350	275	200	165	145	75

Tamer

Single-shot gun chambered for .410 shell with 3" chamber. Fitted with 19.5" barrel and matte nickel finish. Stock is matte black polymer. Weighs about 6 lbs.

160	125	90	60	45	30

Ultra Slug Hunter

Introduced in 1995, model uses heavy 10-gauge action fitted with 24" 12-gauge barrel. Weight about 8 lbs.

150	115	90	70	50	40

Ultra Slug Hunter Deluxe 20 Gauge

Introduced in 1997, this model chambered for 20-gauge shells and features hand checkered camo laminated wood stock. Fitted with fully rifled heavy slug barrel 24" long.

315	250	200	150	100	75

Ultra Slug Hunter Deluxe 12 Gauge

As above, in 12-gauge with 3" chamber.

315	250	200	150	100	75

Ultra Slug Youth Model

As above chambered for 20-gauge shell. Weight approximately 7 lbs.

260	200	150	100	60	45

Ultra Slug Hunter Bull Barrel

As above chambered for 20-gauge.

150	100	80	60	45	30

Ultra Slug Hunter Thumbhole Stock

Similar to above, with laminated thumbhole stock and blued or stainless steel finish. Weight: 8.5 lbs. **NOTE:** Add 10 percent for stainless.

350	275	—	—	—	—

Ultra Slug Youth Bull Barrel

Same as above, with 22" barrel.

150	100	80	60	45	30

Ultra Lite Slug Hunter

Single-shot break-open shotgun. 12- or 20-gauge with 3" chamber; fully rifled 24" barrel; hardwood stock with walnut finish, full pistol-grip, recoil pad and sling swivels. No iron sights; scope base included. Overall length 40" , weight 5.25 lbs. 20-ga. Youth Model has 20" rifled barrel. Deluxe Model has checkered laminated stock and fore-end.

275	225	150	100	75	50

Camo Laminate Turkey NWTF Edition

Introduced in 1999, this single barrel model features a 12-gauge 3.5" chamber, 22" barrel choked Turkey full. Polished receiver has laser engraved NWTF logo. Stock hand checkered and hardwood laminate, with green, brown and black pattern. Ventilated recoil pad and sling swivels. Camo sling are standard.

250	200	150	100	75	50

Camo Laminate Turkey Youth NWTF Edition

Similar to Camo Turkey above, but chambered for 20-gauge with 3" chambers. Stock laminated hardwood, with special shorter dimensions.

250	200	150	100	75	50

H&R Handy-Gun (rifled barrel) Curio or Relic

Rifled-barrel H&R Handy-Guns were manufactured about 1930-34, but details of their production are not well documented. In H&R catalog #19 (copyright 1931) and #20, .22 and .32-20 are listed as available with blued frame only, 12.25" barrel, with optional ($1.50)

NIB	EXC.	V.G.	GOOD	FAIR	POOR

detachable shoulder stock. Whether .22 W.R.F. version listed on page 83 of the 1932 Stoeger's Bible was manufactured is unknown. Guns that were originally factory fitted for shoulder stock (all are extremely rare) have H.&R. ARMS COMPANY/WORCESTER, MASS.U.S.A./PAT.PENDING stamped on bottom of grip in .125" letters. Production of rifled-barrel H&R Handy-Gun was halted in 1934 when the Treasury Department classified it as a "firearm" under NFA, because it was available with a shoulder stock. Any rifled-barrel H&R Handy-Gun is (and always was) exempt from NFA, if not accompanied by a shoulder stock.

.32-20 W.C.F. serial range mostly from 43851 (?) to 43937 (?)

NIB	EXC.	V.G.	GOOD	FAIR	POOR
—	1600	1100	950	700	600

.22 rimfire serial range from 1 (?) to 223 (?)

NIB	EXC.	V.G.	GOOD	FAIR	POOR
—	1400	1000	750	650	500

H&R Handy-Gun (smooth bore) NFA, Curio or Relic

The .410 bore or 28-gauge H&R Handy-Gun is a single-shot pistol, with 8" or 12.25" smooth bore barrel, made from 1921 to 1934 by Harrington & Richardson Arms Co., Worcester, Massachusetts. Shares internal parts with H&R Model 1915 (No. 5) shotgun, but Handy-Gun's shorter receiver is designed for a pistol-grip, its barrels won't fit No. 5 and these firearms are serial numbered separately. About 54,000 H&R Handy-Guns were manufactured, nearly all for 2.5" shells. Production halted after government ruled H&R Handy-Gun to be a "firearm" in the "any other weapon" category under NFA, when its retail price was about $16. An H&R Handy-Gun with an 18" smooth bore barrel is subject to NFA, but exempt if accompanied by an original (detachable) wire shoulder stock. **NOTE:** Rare variations command premiums: 8" barrel, 25 to 50 percent; 18" barrel (rarest), 200 to 300 percent; unchoked .410, 20 to 30 percent; 28-gauge or Model 3 (only) with factory-equipped original detachable shoulder stock, 150 percent or more; holster, $75 to $200; serial matching box, $100 to $200 or more (i.e., a box for an 8" barrel 28-gauge could be quite expensive).

.410 bore, Model 2, Types II and III

NIB	EXC.	V.G.	GOOD	FAIR	POOR
—	2000	1200	500	250	175

28 gauge, Model 2, Type I

NIB	EXC.	V.G.	GOOD	FAIR	POOR
—	1500	1100	850	695	525

H&R manufactured "private-branded" or "trade-branded" H&R Handy-Guns for other distributors. One variation has ESSEX GUN WORKS on left side of receiver. Another has HIBBARD stamped on left side and MODEL W.H. stamped on right; holster with identical stampings was also available. Most have nickel-plated receivers and are serial numbered within the same ranges as, and have other characteristics identical to, regular-production H&R Handy-Guns, by variation. None of those inspected during this research had any markings identifying H&R as original manufacturer. Anecdotal evidence suggests H&R manufactured a Handy-Gun for an independent telephone company in Colorado; none were located during this research. These materials are copyright 1998 by Eric M. Larson.

Topper (Old Production)

Single-shot break-open shotgun, chambered for various gauges, barrel lengths, chokes. Blued, with hardwood stock. Introduced in 1946.

NIB	EXC.	V.G.	GOOD	FAIR	POOR
—	145	95	75	60	40

Model 088

An external hammer single-shot break-open shotgun chambered for all gauges. Various barrel lengths, chokes and an automatic ejector. Blued, with case colored frame and hardwood stock.

NIB	EXC.	V.G.	GOOD	FAIR	POOR
—	80	65	50	40	30

Model 099

As above, but matte, electroless, nickel-plated.

NIB	EXC.	V.G.	GOOD	FAIR	POOR
—	110	95	75	60	40

Model 162

A 12- or 20-gauge boxlock single-shotgun, with 24" barrel and rifle sights.

NIB	EXC.	V.G.	GOOD	FAIR	POOR
—	125	100	80	65	45

Model 176

A 10-gauge 3.5" Magnum caliber boxlock single barrel shotgun, with heavyweight 36" barrel and Full choke. Manufactured between 1977 and 1985.

NIB	EXC.	V.G.	GOOD	FAIR	POOR
—	225	175	115	75	45

Model 400

A 12-, 16- or 20-gauge slide-action shotgun, with 28" Full choke barrel. Blued, with hardwood stock. Manufactured between 1955 and 1967.

NIB	EXC.	V.G.	GOOD	FAIR	POOR
—	150	125	100	75	50

	NIB	EXC.	V.G.	GOOD	FAIR	POOR

Model 401

As above, with variable choke device. Manufactured between 1956 and 1963.

NIB	EXC.	V.G.	GOOD	FAIR	POOR
—	175	150	125	90	65

Model 402

As above, in a .410 bore. Manufactured between 1959 and 1967.

NIB	EXC.	V.G.	GOOD	FAIR	POOR
—	175	150	125	90	65

Model 440

A 12-, 16- or 20-gauge slide-action shotgun, with 26", 28" or 30" barrel in various chokes. Blued, with hardwood stock. Manufactured between 1968 and 1973.

NIB	EXC.	V.G.	GOOD	FAIR	POOR
—	150	125	100	75	50

Model 442

As above, with ventilated rib barrel and checkered stock. Manufactured between 1969 and 1973.

NIB	EXC.	V.G.	GOOD	FAIR	POOR
—	175	150	125	90	65

Model 403

A .410 bore semi-automatic shotgun, with 26" Full choke barrel. Blued, with hardwood stock. Manufactured in 1964.

NIB	EXC.	V.G.	GOOD	FAIR	POOR
—	300	250	175	100	75

Model 404

A 12-, 20-gauge or .410 bore boxlock double-barrel shotgun, with 26" or 28" barrels, double triggers and extractors. Blued, with walnut stock. Manufactured by Rossi in Brazil and imported between 1969 and 1972.

NIB	EXC.	V.G.	GOOD	FAIR	POOR
—	175	150	125	90	65

Pardner Pump Field Gun Full-Dip Camo

Pump-action shotgun, with steel receiver, double action bars, cross-bolt safety, easy take-down. 28" barrel with 3" chamber and ventilated rib, screw-in Modified choke tube. Synthetic stock, with ventilated recoil pad and grooved fore-end. Realtree APG-HDTM full camo dip finish. Overall length 48.125"; weight 7.5 lbs. Also available in several variations, with hardwood or black synthetic stock. Suggested retail for full camo version $278.

Excell

Introduced in 2005, this semi-automatic shotgun chambered for 12-gauge 3" shell. Fitted with 28" vent rib barrel and choke tubes. Checkered black synthetic stock. Magazine capacity 5 rounds. Weight about 7 lbs.

NIB	EXC.	V.G.	GOOD	FAIR	POOR
400	365	295	200	150	100

Excell Waterfowl

As above, with Real Tree Advantage Wetlands camo finish. Introduced in 2005.

NIB	EXC.	V.G.	GOOD	FAIR	POOR
425	375	325	225	175	125

Excell Turkey

Model fitted with 22" barrel, choke tubes and fiber optic front sight. Real Tree Advantage Hardwoods camo finish. Weight is 7 lbs. Introduced in 2005.

NIB	EXC.	V.G.	GOOD	FAIR	POOR
425	375	325	225	175	125

Excell Combo

Model has black synthetic stock and two barrels: 28" vent rib with choke tubes and 24" rifled barrel. Weight about 7 lbs. depending on barrel length. Introduced in 2005.

NIB	EXC.	V.G.	GOOD	FAIR	POOR
450	395	350	250	195	145

Pinnacle

Over/under gun chambered for 12- or 20-gauge with 3" chambers. Barrel length for 12-gauge 28"; 20-gauge 26"; both with vent ribs and choke tubes. Checkered walnut stock, with recoil pad and pistol-grip. Weight about: 6.75 lbs. 12-gauge; 6.25 lbs. 20-gauge. Introduced in 2005.

NIB	EXC.	V.G.	GOOD	FAIR	POOR
700	600	500	325	175	125

Model 1212

A 12-gauge over/under boxlock shotgun, with 28" ventilated rib barrels. Blued, with walnut stock. Also available with 30" barrels having 3" chambers. Manufactured by Lanber Arms of Spain and imported after 1976.

NIB	EXC.	V.G.	GOOD	FAIR	POOR
—	450	375	325	200	125

	NIB	EXC.	V.G.	GOOD	FAIR	POOR

Long Tom Classic

Introduced in 1996, this limited edition single-barrel shotgun features case hardened frame, with 32" Full choked barrel. Stock hand-checkered black walnut, with crescent buttplate. Chambered for 12-gauge. Weight about 7.5 lbs.

NIB	EXC.	V.G.	GOOD	FAIR	POOR
425	395	325	250	175	125

H&R/NEF Handi-Rifle/Slug Gun Combo

Single-shot break-open rifle/shotgun combos (one rifle barrel, one shotgun barrel per combo) chambered in .44 Magnum/12-gauge rifled slug and .357 Magnum/20-gauge rifled slug. Rifle barrels are not interchangeable; shotgun barrels are interchangeable. Stock black matte high-density polymer, with sling swivel studs, molded checkering and recoil pad. Rifle barrel 22" for both calibers; shotgun barrels 28" (12-gauge) and 24" (20-gauge) fully rifled. No iron sights; scope rail included. Overall length 38" (both rifle chamberings); 42" (12-gauge); 40" (20-gauge). Weight 7 - 8 lbs.

NIB	EXC.	V.G.	GOOD	FAIR	POOR
—	300	250	175	100	75

RIFLES

Model 058

A 20-gauge .22 Hornet, .30-30, .357 Magnum or .44 Magnum caliber rifle/shotgun outfit, with interchangeable barrels. Blued, with hardwood stock.

NIB	EXC.	V.G.	GOOD	FAIR	POOR
—	200	150	100	75	50

Model 258

As above, with matte, electroless nickel-plate finish.

NIB	EXC.	V.G.	GOOD	FAIR	POOR
—	225	175	125	100	75

Reising Model 60

A .45 ACP caliber semi-automatic rifle, with 18.25" barrel and 12- or 20-round detachable magazine. Blued, with walnut stock. Operates on retarded blowback system and developed to be used as police weapon. Manufactured between 1944 and 1946.

NIB	EXC.	V.G.	GOOD	FAIR	POOR
—	2000	1600	1000	450	250

Model 65 Military (Model 58C)

A .22 LR caliber semi-automatic rifle, with 23" barrel and Redfield peep sights. Blued, with walnut stock. Manufactured between 1944 and 1956. **NOTE:** Add 100 percent if USMC marked.

NIB	EXC.	V.G.	GOOD	FAIR	POOR
—	500	300	200	125	90

Model 150

A .22 LR caliber semi-automatic rifle, with 20" barrel and 5-shot magazine. Blued, with walnut stock. Manufactured between 1949 and 1953.

NIB	EXC.	V.G.	GOOD	FAIR	POOR
—	100	80	60	45	30

Model 155 (Shikari)

Single-shot break-open rifle chambered for .44 Magnum or .45-70 cartridge. Has 20" barrel with fixed sights. Finish blued, with full-length walnut stock. Introduced in 1972.

NIB	EXC.	V.G.	GOOD	FAIR	POOR
—	375	300	225	150	100

Model 157

As above in .22 Magnum, .22 Hornet and .30-30 caliber.

NIB	EXC.	V.G.	GOOD	FAIR	POOR
—	350	275	200	125	75

Model 158

A .357 or .44 Magnum single-shot side lever rifle, with 22" barrel. Blued, case hardened, with walnut stock. Available with interchangeable 26" 20-gauge barrel. Manufactured prior to 1986.

NIB	EXC.	V.G.	GOOD	FAIR	POOR
—	350	275	200	125	75

Model 300 Ultra

A .22-250 up to .300 Winchester Magnum caliber bolt-action rifle, with 22" or 24" barrel without sights. High polished blue and checkered walnut stock. Manufactured between 1965 and 1978.

NIB	EXC.	V.G.	GOOD	FAIR	POOR
—	450	400	350	275	175

Model 301 Carbine

As above, with 18" barrel and full-length Mannlicher-style stock.

NIB	EXC.	V.G.	GOOD	FAIR	POOR
—	450	400	350	275	175

NIB	EXC.	V.G.	GOOD	FAIR	POOR

Model 317 Ultra Wildcat

A .17 Rem., .17-223, .222 Rem. and .223 Rem. caliber short Sako bolt-action rifle, with 20" barrel furnished without sights. Blued, with checkered walnut stock. Manufactured between 1968 and 1976.

NIB	EXC.	V.G.	GOOD	FAIR	POOR
—	550	400	350	275	175

HANDI-RIFLE SERIES

Break-action single-shot rifle, that's been around in one form or another since the 1960s. Side lever release, automatic ejection, hardwood stock, transfer bar passive safety. Available in nearly every conceivable rimfire and centerfire chambering (except the biggest centerfires) and now made under auspices of Marlin. Rifle is as good a bargain today as it ever was. Some newer models feature factory scopes, bull barrels, thumbhole stocks and other niceties, but are still Handi-Rifles. Value generally under $300 even in New or Excellent condition, sometimes remarkably under.

H&R Handi-Rifle (current production)

Single-shot rifle offered in a wide range of calibers from .204 Ruger to .500 S&W. Barrel lengths from 20" to 26", with walnut-finished hardwood or synthetic stock and fore-end. **NOTE:** Add $25 for thumbhole stock.

NIB	EXC.	V.G.	GOOD	FAIR	POOR
265	225	175	150	125	75

H&R Survivor

Variation of Handi-Rifle in .223 Rem., .308 Win., or .45 Colt/.410 shotshell combo. Black polymer thumb-hole stock, with pistol-grip, accessory rail, sling and swivels. Storage compartment in buttstock and fore-end.

NIB	EXC.	V.G.	GOOD	FAIR	POOR
290	250	200	175	150	100

Synthetic

Basic Handi-Rifle design, with synthetic buttstock and fore-end (either grooved or beavertail). Available with iron sights or picatinny rail for mounting optics.

NIB	EXC.	V.G.	GOOD	FAIR	POOR
275	200	175	150	100	50

Stainless

Similar to above, with stainless barrel. Chambered in .223, .270 or .30-06.

NIB	EXC.	V.G.	GOOD	FAIR	POOR
295	225	200	175	115	75

Synthetic Handi-Rifle/Slug Gun Combo

Similar to above, with extra slug barrel. Available in .44 Magnum/12-gauge and .357 Magnum/20-gauge. Introduced in 2008.

NIB	EXC.	V.G.	GOOD	FAIR	POOR
—	325	300	225	175	100

Superlite Compact

Similar to Synthetic Handi-Rifle. Weighs only 5.5 lbs. Chambered in .223 and .243. Available with optional scope.

NIB	EXC.	V.G.	GOOD	FAIR	POOR
295	225	200	175	115	75

Ultra Varmint Rifle

Single-shot rifle chambered for .223 Rem. or .22-250 cartridge. Fitted with 22" heavy barrel. Stock hand checkered curly maple (older models) or laminated (newer models), with Monte Carlo cheekpiece. Comes with Picatinny rail for mounting optics. Weighs about 7.5 lbs.

NIB	EXC.	V.G.	GOOD	FAIR	POOR
350	295	175	125	75	50

Ultra Varmint Thumbhole

Similar to above, with laminated thumbhole stock.

NIB	EXC.	V.G.	GOOD	FAIR	POOR
375	325	200	150	100	75

Stainless Steel Ultra Varmint Thumbhole

Similar to above, with stainless steel barrel and matte nickel receiver.

NIB	EXC.	V.G.	GOOD	FAIR	POOR
375	325	200	150	100	75

Ultra Varmint Fluted

Introduced in 2005, model chambered for .204 Ruger, .22-250 or .223 Rem. cartridge. Fitted with 24" fluted barrel with no sights. Stock is black synthetic, with vertical adjustable adjustment knob, recoil pad and adjustable bipod mount. Weight about 7 lbs.

NIB	EXC.	V.G.	GOOD	FAIR	POOR
350	295	175	125	75	50

Model 317P

As above, but more finely finished. Manufactured between 1968 and 1976.

NIB	EXC.	V.G.	GOOD	FAIR	POOR
—	500	475	425	375	250

	NIB	EXC.	V.G.	GOOD	FAIR	POOR

Ultra Rifle—Hunting

Single-shot rifle chambered for .25-06, .308 Win. and .357 Rem. Max. The .25-06 has 26" barrel; other two fitted with 22" barrels. Cinnamon laminated stock standard. Weight about 7 lbs. In 2001 .450 Marlin cartridge was added.

	NIB	EXC.	V.G.	GOOD	FAIR	POOR
	275	200	175	150	100	50

Harrington & Richardson/New England Firearms Stainless Ultra Hunter with Thumbhole Stock

Single-shot break-open rifle chambered in .45-70 Government. 24" stainless steel barrel and receiver with scope mount rail; hammer extension; cinnamon laminate thumbhole stock. Overall length 40" ; weight 8 lbs.

NIB	EXC.	V.G.	GOOD	FAIR	POOR
375	325	200	150	100	75

Ultra Rifle—Varmint

Same as above, chambered for .223 Rem. with 22" barrel. Laminated stock, with checkered pistol-grip.

NIB	EXC.	V.G.	GOOD	FAIR	POOR
375	325	200	150	100	75

Ultra .22 Magnum Rifle

Same as above, chambered for .22 Winchester Magnum. Introduced in 2001.

NIB	EXC.	V.G.	GOOD	FAIR	POOR
295	225	200	175	115	75

Ultra Rifle—Comp

Introduced in 1997, this single-shot rifle features an integral muzzle-brake on barrel end. Available in .270 Win. and .30-06 calibers, with 24" barrels. Camo laminated stock.

NIB	EXC.	V.G.	GOOD	FAIR	POOR
295	225	200	175	115	75

Ultra Rifle Rocky Mountain Elk Foundation Commemorative

Limited edition single rifle chambered for .35 Whelen cartridge. Selected laminated stock with Monte Carlo. Barrel length 26".

NIB	EXC.	V.G.	GOOD	FAIR	POOR
—	450	400	350	275	175

Sportster .17 HMR

A .17 HMR version of Handi-Rifle, with black polymer Monte Carlo stock and Picatinny rail for moutning optics. Overall length 38.25".

NIB	EXC.	V.G.	GOOD	FAIR	POOR
—	250	200	150	100	50

Sportster

A .22 LR or .22 WMR version of Handi-Rifle, with black polymer stock, fluted fore-end and iron sights. Overall length 36.25".

NIB	EXC.	V.G.	GOOD	FAIR	POOR
—	175	150	100	75	50

Sportster Compact

Similar to above, in .22 LR only and 2" shorter length of pull.

NIB	EXC.	V.G.	GOOD	FAIR	POOR
—	150	125	100	75	50

Buffalo Classic

Rifle first produced in 1995. Chambered for .45-70 and .38-55 cartridges. Barrel length 32" with no sights, but dovetail front, drilled and tapped rear. Hand checkered walnut stock, with case colored crescent steel buttplate. Weight about 8 lbs. Since its introduction in 1995, about 2,000 guns produced. Factory anticipates about 1,000 rifles being built each year.

NIB	EXC.	V.G.	GOOD	FAIR	POOR
375	315	225	175	125	50

Wesson & Harrington Brand 125th Anniversary Rifle

Introduced in 1996, rifle commemorates 125th anniversary of the partnership. Special rifle chambered for .45-70 Government cartridge. Receiver hand engraved. Barrel length 32". Stock is American black walnut, with crescent steel butt.

NIB	EXC.	V.G.	GOOD	FAIR	POOR
395	325	250	200	150	75

Ultra Rifle Whitetails Unlimited 1997 Commemorative Edition

Introduced in 1997. Chambered for .45-70 Govt. cartridge. Features hand checkered black walnut stock. Special laser engraving on action and pewter finished medallion in-letted into

	NIB	EXC.	V.G.	GOOD	FAIR	POOR

stock. Barrel length 22".

	325	275	225	175	125	75

CR Carbine

Single-shot rifle based on Handi-Rifle design. Two-piece checkered walnut stock, with schnabel fore-end. Marble front and rear sights, Crescent steel buttplate. Chambered in .45 Colt. Introduced in 2007.

	375	315	225	150	100	50

Model 333

Model 300 in 7mm Magnum caliber. Manufactured in 1974.

	—	250	200	175	125	100

Model 340

A .243 to .308 Winchester caliber bolt-action rifle, with 22" barrel and 5-shot magazine. Blued, with checkered walnut stock.

	—	400	350	300	225	150

Model 360 Ultra Automatic

A .243 Win. and .308 Win. caliber semi-automatic rifle, with 22" barrel, adjustable sights and 3-shot detachable magazine. Blued, with checkered walnut stock. Manufactured between 1965 and 1978.

	—	425	375	275	195	100

Model 451 Medalist

A .22 LR caliber bolt-action rifle, with 26" barrel, open sights and 5-shot detachable magazine. Blued, with walnut stock. Manufactured between 1948 and 1961.

	—	175	150	125	100	75

Model 700

A .22 rimfire Magnum caliber semi-automatic rifle, with 22" barrel, adjustable sights and 5-round detachable magazine. Blued, with checkered walnut stock. Manufactured between 1977 and 1985.

	—	225	200	150	125	85

Model 700 DL

As above, with checkered walnut stock and 4X scope. Manufactured until 1985.

	—	300	250	200	150	100

Model 750

A .22 LR bolt-action single-shot rifle, with 22" barrel, sights and short stock. Blued, with hardwood stock.

	—	100	80	60	45	25

Model 865

A .22 LR caliber bolt-action rifle, with 22" barrel, open sights and 5-shot magazine. Blued, with hardwood stock.

	—	100	80	60	45	25

Model 5200

A .22 LR caliber bolt-action single-shot rifle, with 28" heavy barrel without sights and adjustable trigger. Blued, with target-type walnut stock.

	—	400	350	300	225	125

Model 5200 Sporter

A .22 LR caliber bolt-action rifle, with 24" barrel, adjustable sights and 5-shot magazine. Blued, with walnut stock. Not manufactured after 1983.

	—	400	350	300	225	125

100th Anniversary Officer's Model

Commemorative replica of Officer's Model 1873 Trapdoor Springfield Rifle, with 26" barrel. Engraved and anniversary plaque mounted on stock. Blued, with case colored receiver and

NIB	EXC.	V.G.	GOOD	FAIR	POOR

pewter fore-end tip. There were 10,000 manufactured in 1971. As with all commemorative's, this model most desirable when NIB with all supplied material.

NIB	EXC.	V.G.	GOOD	FAIR	POOR
850	695	500	375	250	175

Custer Memorial Issue

Limited production issue commemorating George Armstrong Custer's Battle of Little Bighorn. Heavily engraved and gold inlaid, with high-grade checkered walnut stock. Furnished in mahogany display case, that included two books dealing with the subject. Two versions produced: Officer's Model, of which 25 were issued commemorating 25 officers that fell with Custer; another version commemorating 243 enlisted men who lost their lives at Little Bighorn. As with all commemorative's to be collectible, they must be NIB with all furnished material.

Officer's Model
25 manufactured.

NIB	EXC.	V.G.	GOOD	FAIR	POOR
3000	2000	1600	1200	500	200

Enlisted Men's Model
243 manufactured.

NIB	EXC.	V.G.	GOOD	FAIR	POOR
1500	1000	600	400	250	150

Model 171

Reproduction of Model 1873 Trapdoor Springfield Carbine, with 22" barrel. Blued, with case colored receiver and walnut stock.

NIB	EXC.	V.G.	GOOD	FAIR	POOR
—	500	450	300	200	125

Model 171-DL

As above, but more finely finished.

NIB	EXC.	V.G.	GOOD	FAIR	POOR
—	550	500	325	250	175

Model 174

Plain copy of Springfield Model 1873 Carbine in .45-70 caliber, with 22" barrel. Manufactured in 1972.

NIB	EXC.	V.G.	GOOD	FAIR	POOR
—	525	400	325	250	175

Model 178

Copy of Springfield Model 1873 rifle, with 32" barrel. Manufactured from 1973 to 1984.

NIB	EXC.	V.G.	GOOD	FAIR	POOR
—	525	400	325	250	175

HARRIS GUNWORKS
Phoenix, Arizona

There are a wide range of extra costs options for all Harris Gunworks models, that in many cases will dramatically affect price.

National Match Rifle

Introduced in 1989, model features bolt-action rifle chambered for 7mm-08 or .308, with 5-round magazine. Fitted with 24" stainless steel match grade barrel, with Canjar trigger. Stock is fiberglass, with adjustable buttplate. Weight about 11 lbs.

NIB	EXC.	V.G.	GOOD	FAIR	POOR
3500	2750	1750	950	600	300

Model 86 Sniper Rifle

Chambered for .308, .30-06, .300 Win. Magnum, with 24" heavy match grade barrel. Stock is a special design McHale fiberglass, with textured grip and forearm. Fitted with recoil pad. Supplied with bipod. Weight about 11.25 lbs. **NOTE:** Add $100 for take-down model.

NIB	EXC.	V.G.	GOOD	FAIR	POOR
2700	2100	1600	1000	600	350

Model 87 Series

Single-shot rifles chambered for .50 BMG. Fitted with 29" barrel and muzzle-brake. Fiberglass stock. Introduced in 1987. Weight approximately 21.5 lbs. **NOTE:** Add $600 for Model 87R 5-shot repeater; $400 for Model 87 5-shot repeater; $300 for Model 92 Bullpup.

NIB	EXC.	V.G.	GOOD	FAIR	POOR
6000	4750	3000	2000	1000	500

Model 88

Bolt-action .50 BMG rifles offered in two different configurations. First variation: fitted with 20" carbon graphite barrel, with add-on recoil arrestor and black teflon finish; second variation: fitted with 16.5" stainless steel barrel, with integral recoil arrestor. Both rifles weigh about 14 lbs. Titanium action available for further weight reduction.

NIB	EXC.	V.G.	GOOD	FAIR	POOR
6000	4750	3000	2000	1000	500

	NIB	EXC.	V.G.	GOOD	FAIR	POOR

Model 89 Sniper Rifle

Bolt-action rifle chambered for .308 cartridge. Fitted with 28" barrel. Supplied with bipod. Stock is fiberglass, with adjustable length of pull and fitted with recoil pad. Weight about 15.25 lbs.

2700	2100	1600	1000	600	350

Model 93

Bolt-action .50 BMG rifle, with folding hinge stock assembly. Furnished with 10- or 20-round magazine. Barrel length 29". Weight approximately 21 lbs.

6000	4750	3000	2000	1000	500

Model 95

Lightweight variation of .50 BMG models featuring Titanium and graphite. Supplied with bipod. Barrel length 29". Weight approximately 18 lbs.

6000	4750	3000	2000	1000	500

Model 96

Gas-operated semi-automatic .50 BMG sniper rifle. Barrel length 29". Detachable 5-round magazine. Weight approximately 25 lbs.

7500	6500	4000	2500	1500	750

Long Range Rifle

Chambered for a variety of cartridges such as .300 Win. Magnum, 7mm Rem. Magnum, .300 Phoenix, .338 Lapua. Single-shot rifle fitted with 26" match grade stainless steel barrel. Fiberglass stock, with adjustable buttplate and cheekpiece. Weight about 14 lbs.

3900	2850	1500	1000	700	350

Target/Benchrest Rifle

Offered in .243, .308, 6mm BR, 6mm PPC and 6mm Rem. Model custom built for customer. Available in both left- and right-hand. Weight about 11 lbs.

3500	2750	1750	950	600	300

Antietam Sharps Rifle

Replica of Sharps Model 1874 sidehammer, introduced in 1994. Chambered for .40-65 or .45-70. Choice of 30" or 32" octagon or round barrel. Stock is fancy walnut. Either straight-, pistol-grip or Creedmoor, with schnabel forearm. Many optional sights offered. Weight about 11.25 lbs.

2600	1950	1200	800	450	200

Signature Classic Sporter

Left- or right-handed bolt-action model, introduced in 1987. Choice of calibers from .22-250 to .375 H&H. Barrel lengths 22", 24" or 26" depending on caliber. Choice of fiberglass stocks in green, beige, brown or black. Wood stock is optional. Weight about 7 lbs. for short action calibers.

3150	2550	1500	1150	500	250

Signature Classic Stainless Sporter

Same as above, with barrel and action made from stainless steel. A .416 Rem. Magnum available in this variation. Model available with interchangeable barrels. **NOTE:** Add $600 for interchangeable barrels.

3200	2650	1600	1250	600	300

Signature Super Varminter

Similar to Classic Sporter, except fitted with a heavy contoured barrel, adjustable trigger and special hand-bedded fiberglass stock. Chambered for .223, .22-250, .220 Swift, .243, 6mm Rem., .25-06, 7mm-08, 7mm BR, .308, .350 Rem. Introduced in 1989.

2900	2250	1600	1050	700	350

Signature Alaskan

Similar to Classic Sporter, except fitted with match grade barrel and single leaf rear sight. Nickel finish. Walnut Monte Carlo stock, with cheekpiece and palm swell grip. Chambered for .270 to .375 H&H. Introduced in 1989.

3950	3200	2200	1500	700	350

Signature Titanium Mountain Rifle

Similar to Classic Sporter, except action is made of titanium alloy and barrel of chrome-moly steel. Stock is graphite reinforced fiberglass. Chambered for .270 to .300 Win. Magnum. Weight about 5.5 lbs. Introduced in 1989. **NOTE:** Add $400 for graphite steel barrel.

3500	2750	1750	950	600	300

	NIB	EXC.	V.G.	GOOD	FAIR	POOR

Sportsman 97

Bolt-action rifle chambered for a variety of calibers from .270 Win. to .338 Win. Stock is fancy grade walnut, Bastogne or English. Talon action is fitted.

NIB	EXC.	V.G.	GOOD	FAIR	POOR
2900	2250	1600	1050	700	350

Talon Safari Rifle

Bolt-action rifle chambered for 16 different calibers from .300 Win. Magnum to .460 Weatherby Magnum. Finish is matte black, with fiberglass Safari stock. Weight between 9 and 10 lbs. depending on caliber.

NIB	EXC.	V.G.	GOOD	FAIR	POOR
4200	3350	2200	1600	1200	600

Talon Sporter Rifle

Bolt-action rifle, introduced in 1991. Uses a pre-64 Model 70 type action, with cone breech. Barrel and action are stainless steel. Chambered for a wide variety of calibers from .22-250 to .416 Rem. Magnum. Choice of walnut or fiberglass stock. Most barrel lengths are 24". Weight about 7.5 lbs. depending on caliber.

NIB	EXC.	V.G.	GOOD	FAIR	POOR
3150	2550	1500	1150	500	250

Double Rifle/Shotgun

Side-by-side gun offered in .470 NE or .500 NE, as well as 12- and 20-gauge guns. Engraved receiver, AAA fancy walnut stocks and 3-leaf express sights are standard. Offered in boxlock and sidelock models.

Boxlock

NIB	EXC.	V.G.	GOOD	FAIR	POOR
15000	12500	9000	5000	2750	1500

Side Lock

NIB	EXC.	V.G.	GOOD	FAIR	POOR
21000	16500	12000	7500	3100	1750

HARTFORD ARMS & EQUIPMENT CO.
Hartford, Connecticut

Established in 1925, this firm was purchased by High Standard Company in 1932.

Single-Shot Target

A .22-caliber single-shot pistol, with 6.75" round barrel, fixed sights and either walnut or composition grips. Frame marked "Manfd. by the/ Hartford Arms and Equip. Co./ Hartford, Conn./ Patented .22 cal./ l.r." on left side in front of their breech. Although this pistol resembles a semi-automatic, it is in fact a single-shot manually operated pistol. **NOTE:** Add $150 premium for guns in original Hartford Arms box numbered to the gun; $250 premium for guns in original High Standard box numbered to the gun.

NIB	EXC.	V.G.	GOOD	FAIR	POOR
—	595	450	325	250	150

Model 1925

Semi-automatic pistol chambered for .22-caliber, with 6.75" round barrel, checkered hard black rubber grips or ribbed walnut grips. Magazine capacity 10 rounds. Frame marked, "manfd. by/ the hartford arms and equip. co./ hartford, conn./ patented/ .22 cal/long rifle" on left side in front of breech. Approximately 5,000 produced from 1925 to 1932. **NOTE:** Add $150 premium for guns in original Hartford Arms box numbered to the gun.

NIB	EXC.	V.G.	GOOD	FAIR	POOR
—	600	475	365	225	175

HATFIELD RIFLE COMPANY
St. Joseph, Missouri

Squirrel Rifle

Flintlock or percussion rifle in .32- to .50-caliber, with 39" barrel, double set triggers, adjustable sights, brass mounts and maple stocks. Available in a wide variety of forms, which affect values. Values listed are for plain standard models.

NIB	EXC.	V.G.	GOOD	FAIR	POOR
550	400	350	300	225	150

SHOTGUNS

Uplander Grade I

A 20-gauge boxlock double-barrel shotgun, with 26" improved cylinder and modified barrel. Matte raised rib, single-selective trigger and automatic ejectors. Case hardened, blued, with deluxe-grade hand-checkered walnut stock. Introduced in 1987.

NIB	EXC.	V.G.	GOOD	FAIR	POOR
1250	1050	750	600	475	200

	NIB	EXC.	V.G.	GOOD	FAIR	POOR	

Uplander Pigeon Grade II

As above, with scroll engraving. Fitted leather case.

NIB	EXC.	V.G.	GOOD	FAIR	POOR
2250	1750	1275	900	650	500

Uplander Super Pigeon Grade III

As above, with deep-relief cut engraving and leather case.

NIB	EXC.	V.G.	GOOD	FAIR	POOR
2500	2200	1700	1400	1000	700

Uplander Golden Quail Grade IV

Gold-inlaid version of above.

NIB	EXC.	V.G.	GOOD	FAIR	POOR
4000	3500	2750	2000	1700	1300

Uplander Woodcock Grade V

As above, with seven 24 kt. gold inlays and best quality engraving. Furnished with leather case.

NIB	EXC.	V.G.	GOOD	FAIR	POOR
5600	5000	4250	3500	2750	2000

HAVILAND & GUNN
Ilion, New York

Gallery Pistol

A .17-caliber rimfire single-shot pistol, with 5" barrel. Barrel and frame made of one piece iron and nickel plated. No markings on these pistols whatsoever. Believed to have been made during 1870s.

NIB	EXC.	V.G.	GOOD	FAIR	POOR
—	—	1150	550	175	100

HAWES & WAGGONER
Philadelphia, Pennsylvania

Pocket Pistol

A .41-caliber single-shot percussion pistol, with 3" barrel, German silver mountings and walnut stock. Manufactured in 1850s.

NIB	EXC.	V.G.	GOOD	FAIR	POOR
—	—	2250	925	475	275

HAWES
Los Angeles, California

Importer of handguns primarily made in Europe.

Courier

A .25-caliber blowback semi-automatic pocket pistol. Manufactured by Galesi.

NIB	EXC.	V.G.	GOOD	FAIR	POOR
—	125	100	75	50	25

Diplomat

A .380 ACP pistol, with external hammer.

NIB	EXC.	V.G.	GOOD	FAIR	POOR
—	150	125	100	75	50

Trophy

J.P. Sauer & Sohn manufactured revolver, with swing-out cylinder and 6" barrel. Chambered for .22 LR and .38 Special. Adjustable sights.

NIB	EXC.	V.G.	GOOD	FAIR	POOR
—	250	200	175	125	90

Medalion

As above, with 3", 4" or 6" barrel and fixed sights.

NIB	EXC.	V.G.	GOOD	FAIR	POOR
—	200	175	125	100	75

Tip-Up Target Pistol

Replica of Stevens Model 35 .22 LR single-shot. Globe front sight, adjustable rear.

NIB	EXC.	V.G.	GOOD	FAIR	POOR
—	275	200	135	75	35

MARSHAL SINGLE-ACTION ARMY REVOLVERS

J. P. Sauer made a Western-styled series for Hawes. Based in appearance on Colt Single-Action Army.

Silver City

A .22 LR or .22 rimfire Magnum caliber single-action revolver, with 5.5" barrel, 6-shot cylinder and fixed sights.

NIB	EXC.	V.G.	GOOD	FAIR	POOR
—	150	125	95	50	25

	NIB	EXC.	V.G.	GOOD	FAIR	POOR

Western

A .357 Magnum, .44 Magnum, .45 Colt, .45 ACP, .44-40, 9mm, .22 LR and .22 rimfire Magnum single-action revolver, with fixed sights. Blued.

	—	350	275	195	100	75

Texas

As above, but nickel-plated.

	—	350	275	195	100	75

Montana

Western Marshal, with brass backstrap and trigger guard.

	—	350	275	195	100	75

Deputy

A .22 LR and .22 rimfire Magnum single-action revolver, with 5.5" barrel and 6-shot cylinder.

	—	150	125	95	50	25

Chief

A .357 Magnum, .44 Magnum and .45 Colt caliber revolver, with 6.5" barrel, 6-shot cylinder and adjustable sights. Blued.

	—	350	275	195	100	75

Federal

A 6-shot single-action revolver in .357 Magnum, .44 Magnum and .45 Colt caliber.

	—	350	275	195	100	75

HAWKEN
St. Louis, Missouri

During early part of the 19th century, Jacob and Samuel Hawken manufactured a variety of flintlock, percussion and cartridge rifles, shotguns and pistols. They are best known, however, for half stock Plains Rifles. Though of a plain nature, these arms were recognized for their accuracy and dependability. Early Hawken rifles will be worth a substantial premium over later examples. Some examples in very good condition may be worth as much as $50,000. Proceed with caution.

HDH, SA.
Henrion, Dassy & Heuschen
Liege, Belgium

Cobold

A 9.4mm Dutch, 10.6mm German, .38- and .45-caliber double-action five-shot revolver, with solid frame, octagonal barrel and an odd safety catch that locks the cylinder.

	—	500	325	275	150	100

Puppy

A 5.5mm to 7.65mm caliber folding trigger double-action revolver. Most are "Velo-Dogs".

	—	200	150	100	75	50

Lincoln

A .22-caliber folding trigger double-action revolver, with solid frame, imitation pearl or ivory grips and engraving.

	—	200	150	100	75	50

Lincoln-Bossu

A 5.5mm or 6.35mm caliber folding trigger double-action revolver ("Velo-Dog" type), with solid-frame and hammerless.

	—	200	150	100	75	50

Left Wheeler

A Colt Police Positive copy in .32- or .38-caliber. Last revolver HDH manufactured.

	—	200	150	125	100	75

HEAVY EXPRESS INC.
Colorado Springs, Colorado

This company built custom-built rifles, using its proprietary nonbelted cartridges from .260 Heavy Express Magnum to .416 Heavy Express Magnum. Company's rifles were built on Ruger Model 77 Mark II and Winchester Model 70 Classic actions. Barrels are 4140 chrome-moly blue and 416R stainless steel.

	NIB	EXC.	V.G.	GOOD	FAIR	POOR

Stocks include factory walnut, laminated or composite designs. Prices listed are for basic guns. Options are not included and will affect price.

Heavy Express Premier—Ruger M77 Mk II

Rifle chambered for .260 HE Magnum, .284 HE Magnum or .300 HE Magnum. Choice of walnut, laminated or composite stocks. **NOTE:** Add $200 for stainless steel.

1500	1150	800	600	350	175

Heavy Express Monarch—Winchester M70 Classic

Same as above. Built on Winchester M70 Classic action. Choice of stocks. **NOTE:** Add $200 for stainless steel.

1775	1400	1000	750	500	250

Heavy Express Monarch—Ruger 77 MK II

Rifle built on Ruger M77 action. Chambered for .338, .350, .375, .416 and .460 HE Magnum cartridges. Choice of stocks. **NOTE:** Add $200 for stainless steel.

1775	1400	1000	750	500	250

Heavy Express Single-Shot—Ruger #1

Rifle chambered in .300, .338, .350 and .416 HE Magnum cartridges. Choice of stocks. **NOTE:** Add $200 for stainless steel.

1775	1400	1000	750	500	250

Heavy Express Premier—Ruger M77 Mk II

Rifle built on Ruger M77 Mk II action in .260 HE Magnum, .284 HE Magnum or .300 HE Magnum. Choice of stocks. **NOTE:** Add $200 for stainless steel.

1500	1150	800	500	400	200

HECKLER & KOCH
Oberndorf/Neckar, Germany

At the end of WWII, the French dismantled Mauser factory as part of their reparations; buildings remained idle until 1949, when firearms production was again allowed in Germany. Heckler & Koch was formed as a machine tool enterprise and occupied vacant Mauser plant. In early 1950s, Edmund Heckler and Theodor Koch began to produce G3 automatic rifle based on Spanish CETME design and progressed to machine guns and sub-machine guns, eventually to production of commercial civilian rifles and pistols. In 1990, company got into financial difficulties because of a failed contract bid. In December 1990, French state consortium GIAT announced the purchase of Heckler and Koch, but a little more than a year later contract was canceled. Later in 1991, company was purchased by Royal Ordnance of Britain. In 2002 the company was sold to a combined group of European investors and long-time company managers.

Model 91 A2

Rifle is recoil-operated, with delayed-roller lock bolt. Chambered for .308 Winchester cartridge. Has a 17.7" barrel, with military style aperture sights. Furnished with 20-round detachable magazine and finished in matte black, with black plastic stock. Some areas of the country have made its ownership illegal.

2800	2400	2000	1500	1150	800

Model 91 A3

Simply Model 91, with retractable metal stock.

3100	2700	2250	1700	1350	900

Model 93 A2

Similar to Model 91 except chambered for .223 cartridge, with 16.4" barrel. Magazine holds 25 rounds. Specifications same as for Model 91.

3000	2500	2000	1500	1150	800

Model 93 A3

Model 93 with retractable metal stock.

3250	2650	2250	1700	1350	900

Model 94 A2

Carbine version chambered for 9mm Parabellum cartridge, with 16.5" barrel. Smaller-scaled weapon, with 15-shot magazine.

4000	3750	3500	3100	2500	1250

	NIB	EXC.	V.G.	GOOD	FAIR	POOR

Model 94 A3

Variation of Model 94, with addition of retractable metal stock.

NIB	EXC.	V.G.	GOOD	FAIR	POOR
4200	3950	3750	3300	2700	1000

Model 270

Model chambered for .22 LR cartridge. Sporting-styled rifle, with 16.5" barrel. Furnished with either 5- or 20-round magazine. Blued, with checkered walnut stock. Discontinued in 1985.

NIB	EXC.	V.G.	GOOD	FAIR	POOR
800	675	500	350	250	150

Model 300

Similar to Model 270 except chambered for .22 rimfire Magnum cartridge. Not imported after 1988.

NIB	EXC.	V.G.	GOOD	FAIR	POOR
1000	800	500	350	250	150

Model 630

Model chambered for .223. Features same roller-delayed semi-automatic action as found on paramilitary-type weapons. Sporting-style rifle with polished blue finish and checkered walnut stock. Barrel is 17.7" long. Magazines offered hold either 4- or 10-rounds. Importation discontinued in 1986.

NIB	EXC.	V.G.	GOOD	FAIR	POOR
1795	1350	900	650	450	300

Model 770

Similar to Model 630 except chambered for .308 Winchester cartridge and 19.7" barrel. Not imported after 1986.

NIB	EXC.	V.G.	GOOD	FAIR	POOR
1795	1350	900	650	450	300

Model 940

Essentially same as Model 770 except chambered for .30-06 cartridge, with 21" barrel. Not imported after 1986.

NIB	EXC.	V.G.	GOOD	FAIR	POOR
2000	1600	1000	600	400	300

Model SL6

Heckler & Koch's current sporting rifle chambered for .223 cartridge, with 17.7" barrel. Features same basic action as military versions. Matte black finish, walnut stock, with vented walnut hand guard. Magazine holds 4 rounds.

NIB	EXC.	V.G.	GOOD	FAIR	POOR
1600	1300	950	650	350	300

Model SL7

Similar to SL6 except chambered for .308 Winchester cartridge and 3-round magazine.

NIB	EXC.	V.G.	GOOD	FAIR	POOR
1600	1300	950	650	350	300

Model SR9

Model introduced into U.S. market after the federal government prohibited importation of H&K's other semi-automatic rifles. SR9 similar to HK91, but certified by BATF as a sporting rifle. Model features special thumbhole stock made of Kevlar reinforced fiberglass. Action is a delayed-roller locked bolt semi-automatic design chambered for .308 Winchester cartridge. Barrel is 19.7" in length and features adjustable rear sight, with hooded front sight. Weighs 10.9 lbs.

NIB	EXC.	V.G.	GOOD	FAIR	POOR
2900	2400	2000	1400	700	500

Model SR9 (T) Target

Similar to standard model SR9, with addition of special MSG90 adjustable buttstock, PSG-1 trigger group and PSG-1 contoured hand grip. Weighs 10.6 lbs.

NIB	EXC.	V.G.	GOOD	FAIR	POOR
3000	2500	2200	1650	950	600

Model SR9 (TC) Target Competition

Similar to Model SR9 (T), with addition of PSG-1 adjustable buttstock. Weighs 10.9 lbs.

NIB	EXC.	V.G.	GOOD	FAIR	POOR
3300	3000	2300	1950	1100	700

BASR Model

Bolt-action rifle chambered for various popular calibers. Stainless steel barrel. Essentially custom built to customer's specifications. Stock is of Kevlar. Quite rare. Only 100 manufactured in 1968.

NIB	EXC.	V.G.	GOOD	FAIR	POOR
—	4000	3600	2750	1300	800

PSG-1

Rifle is a high precision sniping rifle. Features delayed-roller semi-automatic action. Chambered for .308 Winchester cartridge and 5-shot magazine. Barrel length 25.6". Furnished with complete array of accessories including 6x42-power illuminated Hensoldt scope. Weighs 17.8 lbs.

NIB	EXC.	V.G.	GOOD	FAIR	POOR
14500	12500	9000	7500	6000	4000

	NIB	EXC.	V.G.	GOOD	FAIR	POOR

Model SL8-1

New generation .223 rifle modeled after military Model G36. Introduced in 2000. Built of carbon fiber polymer and gas operated. Thumbhole stock with cheekpiece. Barrel length 20.8". Magazine capacity 10 rounds. Adjustable sights. Weight approximately 8.6 lbs.

NIB	EXC.	V.G.	GOOD	FAIR	POOR
1800	1625	1050	700	500	325

SLB 2000

Introduced in 2001. Gas-operated semi-automatic rifle chambered for .30-06 cartridge. Receiver built of lightweight alloy. Barrel is 16.7" in length and will accept interchangeable barrels, at some future date. Oil finished walnut stock. Open sights, with both barrel and receiver drilled and tapped for scope mounts. Magazine capacity 2, 5 or 10 rounds. Weight about 7.25 lbs.

NIB	EXC.	V.G.	GOOD	FAIR	POOR
1200	1000	800	600	400	225

Model USC

Introduced in 2000. Semi-automatic blowback carbine derived from H&K's UMP sub-machine gun. Chambered for .45 ACP cartridge. Fitted with 16" barrel. Skeletonized stock. Accessory rail on top of receiver. Adjustable sights. Magazine capacity 10 rounds. Weight approximately 6 lbs.

NIB	EXC.	V.G.	GOOD	FAIR	POOR
1700	1275	1000	750	400	200

Model MR556A1

Direct descendant of HK416. Semi-automatic gas-piston operating system. Free floating rail hand-guard system, with four Picatinny rails for mounting of optical or lighting accessories. Two-stage trigger. Retractable butt-stock can be locked in any position to suit individual requirements. Chambered for 5.56x45mm NATO round. Magazine capacities: 10, 20 or 30 rounds.

NIB	EXC.	V.G.	GOOD	FAIR	POOR
2900	2475	2100	1300	650	300

PISTOLS

HK4

Blowback-operated semi-automatic pistol based on Mauser HSc design. Chambered for .22 LR, .25 ACP, .32 ACP and .380. These calibers easily converted by switching barrels, recoil springs and magazines. Rimfire model could be changed by rotating breechface. Conversion kits available for all calibers. Barrel is 3" long; finish is blued, with molded plastic thumb rest grips. Pistol sold from 1968-1973 as Harrington & Richardson HK4 and so marked. Discontinued in 1984.

.22 Caliber or .380 Caliber

NIB	EXC.	V.G.	GOOD	FAIR	POOR
—	475	350	250	200	100

.25 Caliber or .32 Caliber

NIB	EXC.	V.G.	GOOD	FAIR	POOR
—	350	300	250	200	100

Conversion Units

NIB	EXC.	V.G.	GOOD	FAIR	POOR
—	150	125	90	60	30

P9

Single-action delayed-blowback semi-automatic pistol chambered for 9mm or 7.65mm Parabellum. Action based on G-3 rifle mechanism. Barrel length 4". Pistol has internal hammer, thumb-operated hammer drop and decocking lever. Also a manual safety and loaded-chamber indicator. Finish is Parkerized. Grips are molded plastic and well contoured. Fixed sights. Manufactured between 1977 and 1984. Model rarer than P9S model.

NIB	EXC.	V.G.	GOOD	FAIR	POOR
800	650	500	400	300	200

P9S

Similar to Model P9 except action features double-action capability. Chambered for .45 ACP and 9mm Parabellum, with 5.5" barrel. Manufactured between 1977 and 1984.

NIB	EXC.	V.G.	GOOD	FAIR	POOR
800	650	500	400	300	200

P9S Target Model

Similar to model P9S. Chambered for 9mm or .45 ACP cartridges. Adjustable sights and trigger. Discontinued in 1984.

NIB	EXC.	V.G.	GOOD	FAIR	POOR
1400	1100	900	600	500	300

P9S Competition

Similar to P9S target, with addition of barrel weights and special competition grips.

NIB	EXC.	V.G.	GOOD	FAIR	POOR
3000	2000	1200	750	500	275

	NIB	EXC.	V.G.	GOOD	FAIR	POOR

VP 70Z

Blowback-operated semi-automatic chambered for 9mm Parabellum cartridge. Striker-fired and double-action-only. Barrel 4.5" long. Double-column magazine holds 18 rounds. Finish blued. Receiver and grip molded from plastic. Discontinued in 1984.

NIB	EXC.	V.G.	GOOD	FAIR	POOR
700	500	350	300	250	200

P7 PSP

First of squeeze-cocked H&K pistols. Single-action semi-automatic placed in firing position by pressure on front of grip strap. This moves striker into battery; firing is then accomplished by single action pressure on trigger, releasing grip strap cocking device and decocking mechanism. This particular model does not have extended finger guard on trigger. Does not have ambidextrous safety. Discontinued in 1984.

NIB	EXC.	V.G.	GOOD	FAIR	POOR
1100	900	700	600	500	400

P7 K3

This is "Squeeze Cocker" chambered for either .380 or .22 LR caliber. Has a recoil buffer that is oil-filled and 3.8" barrel. Magazine holds 8 rounds. Introduced in 1988.

NIB	EXC.	V.G.	GOOD	FAIR	POOR
1800	1600	1350	900	500	300

.22 Caliber Conversion Kit

This unit will convert P7 K3 to fire .22 LR cartridge.

NIB	EXC.	V.G.	GOOD	FAIR	POOR
1500	1200	650	300	150	75

.32 ACP Caliber Conversion Kit

NIB	EXC.	V.G.	GOOD	FAIR	POOR
1000	900	400	100	75	50

P7 M8

This is 8-shot newer version of "squeeze cocker". Has heat-shield finger guard, ambidextrous safety, 4" barrel and 3-dot sight system. Finish is matte blue or nickel, with stippled black plastic grips. No longer in production. **NOTE:** Night sights introduced in 1993 add $100.

NIB	EXC.	V.G.	GOOD	FAIR	POOR
1500	1200	900	700	500	300

P7 M10

New addition to P7 series in 1993. Variation chambered for .40 S&W cartridge. Magazine holds 10 rounds. Finish available either blue or nickel. Pistol weighs 2.69 lbs. **NOTE:** Night sights add $100.

NIB	EXC.	V.G.	GOOD	FAIR	POOR
2750	2250	1600	1100	500	300

P7 M13

Version similar to P7 M8 except it has a double column 13-shot magazine. **NOTE:** Night sights add $100.

NIB	EXC.	V.G.	GOOD	FAIR	POOR
2200	1750	1200	650	500	300

SP89

Introduced in early 1990s. Large frame semi-automatic pistol chambered for 9mm cartridge. Features 15-round magazine and square notch rear sight ,with hooded front sight. Pistol has 4.5" barrel and 13" overall. Weighs 4.4 lbs. In August 1993 no longer imported due to ban on assault pistols.

NIB	EXC.	V.G.	GOOD	FAIR	POOR
4000	3600	3200	2500	1800	1000

USP SERIES

Late in 1999, H&K began shipping its USPs and Mark 23s with an internal locking system. This lock-out is installed in the grip and blocks movement of hammer, trigger and slide. Operated with two pronged key supplied with pistol. This system is in addition to traditional trigger lock that is sold with each H&K firearm. In 2001 stainless steel version of these pistols was discontinued.

In 2005 H&K offered a limited edition run of color frame variations for USP line. These colors are Desert tan, green and gray.

Gray: USP 45 and USP 40 Compact

Green: USP 45, USP 40, USP 40 Compact and USP 45

Tactical Desert Tan: USP 45, USP 40, USP 40 Compact and USP 45 Tactical and Mark 23
Retail prices are same for these color variations as standard black frame pistols

USP 40

Introduced in 1993, this new semi-automatic H&K pistol features a new design that incorporates a short recoil modified Browning action. Chambered for .40 S&W cartridge, this model has 4.13" barrel and magazine capacity of 13 rounds. Stainless steel model introduced in 1996. Weighs 1.74 lbs. Available in seven different variations from traditional double-action to double-action-only and various safety locations and styles. Variants numbered by H&K are listed.

1. DA/SA with safe position and control lever on left side of frame.
2. DA/SA with safe position and control lever on right side of frame.
3. DA/SA without safe position and decocking lever on left side of frame.
4. DA/SA without safe position and decocking lever on left side of frame.
5. DA only with safe position and safety lever on left side of frame.
6. DA only with safe position and safety lever on right side of frame.
7. DA only without control lever.
9. DA/SA with safe position and safety lever on left side of frame.
10. DA/SA with safety lever on the right side of frame.

NOTE: For stainless steel model add $45.

900	800	650	300	250	125

USP 9

Same as USP 40, but chambered for 9mm cartridge. Magazine holds 16 rounds and pistol weighs 1.66 lbs. Choice of seven variations as listed above for USP 40. New for 1993. **NOTE:** Stainless steel add $45.

900	800	650	300	250	125

USP 9SD

Variation of USP 9 fitted with target sights to see over an optional sound suppressor. Barrel threaded left-hand. Does not have O-ring and does not require thread cap. Introduced in 2004.

975	825	675	325	275	150

USP 40 Compact

Same as 9mm Compact model. Chambered for .40 S&W cartridge. Weight about 27 oz. All other dimensions are the same.

900	800	650	300	250	125

USP 45

Introduced in 1995. Slightly larger than the 9mm and .40 S&W models. Barrel length 4.41" and overall length 7.87". Weight is 1.9 lbs. USP 45 available in same variants as other USP models. Magazine capacity 12 rounds. **NOTE:** Stainless steel model add $45.

1100	950	775	500	350	200

USP 9 Compact

Introduced in 1997, this 9mm model is smaller version of full size USP 9. Internal differences due to size. Barrel length .58". Overall length 6.81". Magazine capacity 10 rounds. Weight approximately 26 oz. Available with stainless steel slide. **NOTE:** Add $45 to NIB price.

800	600	450	300	200	150

USP Compact LEM (Law Enforcement Modification)

Introduced in 2002. Identical to USP Compact .40 S&W Variant 7, with double-action-only trigger and special trigger mechanism. Mechanism improves double-action trigger performance and reduces weight of pull to between 7.5 and 8.5 lbs. Offered in blued finish.

1150	1000	750	500	300	150

USP 45 Match

Introduced in 1997, model is match grade variation of USP. Chambered for .45 ACP cartridge. Fitted with 6.02" barrel, with barrel weight assembly. Adjustable rear sight and target front sight. Adjustable trigger stop. Blued finish. Weight approximately 38 oz. Available in stainless steel version. **NOTE:** Add $60 for stainless steel.

1500	1300	1050	800	475	275

USP 45 Compact

Introduced in 1997. Pistol chambered for .45 ACP cartridge. Has 3.8" barrel and overall length of 7.1". Weighs approximately 28 oz. Magazine capacity 8 rounds.

1100	950	775	500	350	200

USP 45 Compact Tactical

Blued semi-automatic .45 ACP. Double-action with 4.46" barrel, 8 round capacity. 27.5 oz. Polymer grip.

1100	950	775	500	350	200

NIB	EXC.	V.G.	GOOD	FAIR	POOR

USP .357 Compact

Introduced in mid-1998. Pistol built on same frame as .40 S&W Compact. Chambered for .357 SIG cartridge. Magazine capacity 10 rounds. Weight about 28 oz.

1000	850	4675	375	250	150

USP 45 Expert

Introduced in fall of 1998. This .45 ACP pistol fitted with 5.2" barrel and slide with 10-round magazine. Overall length 8.7"; height 1.87". Weight approximately 30 oz. Adjustable low-profile sights. Limited availability between 1,000 and 2,500 pistols. In 2003 offered chambered for 9mm and .40 S&W cartridge. **NOTE:** H&K price reduction in 2005.

1355	1200	900	600	300	150

USP 45 Tactical

Pistol introduced in 1998. Enhanced version of USP 45. Fitted with 4.9" threaded barrel, with adjustable high profile target sights. Overall length 8.6"; weight approximately 36 oz. Magazine capacity 10 rounds. Availability limited to 1,000 and 2,500 pistols.

1100	850	625	425	300	175

USP Elite

Introduced in 2003, model features 6.2" barrel chambered for 9mm or .45 ACP cartridge. Fitted with match trigger, adjustable trigger stop, adjustable micrometer rear target sights, extended floorplate and loaded chamber indicator. Weight about 30 oz. empty. Magazine capacity 10 rounds. **NOTE:** H&K price reduction in 2005.

1400	1150	800	575	250	135

USP 45 50th Anniversary Commemorative

Limited to 1,000 pistols. Features high polish blue with 50th anniversary logo engraved in gold and silver. Supplied with custom-made wooden box and commemorative coin. Introduced in 2000.

1100	850	625	425	300	175

P2000 GPM

Introduced in 2003, model similar to USP compact LEM pistol. Several modular features, such as interchangeable back straps, ambidextrous slide release and short trigger reset distance. Chambered for 9mm or .40 S&W cartridge. Fitted with 3.62" barrel. Fixed sights. Magazine capacity 12 rounds for .40 S&W and .357 SIG; 13 rounds for 9mm. Weight about 22 oz. **NOTE:** Add $30 for magazine disconnect.

875	700	500	350	250	125

P2000 SK

Semi-automatic double-action pistol is a subcompact version of P2000. Chambered for 9mm or .40 S&W cartridge as well as .357 SIG. Has 2.5" barrel, with overall length of 6.4". Magazine capacity 10 rounds for 9mm; 12 rounds for .357 SIG; 9 rounds for .40 S&W. Weight about 21 oz. Introduced in 2004.

1100	850	625	425	300	175

Mark 23

Very similar to H&K's US government contract pistol. Developed for special Operation Units. Chambered for .45 ACP. Fitted with 5.87" barrel. Pistol has polymer frame, with steel slide. Magazine capacity 10 rounds on civilian models and 12 rounds on law enforcement models. Barrel threaded for noise suppressor. Weight about 42 oz.

2200	1850	1200	875	500	250

HK45

Full-size autoloader chambered in .45 ACP. Features include polygonal bore, front and rear slide serrations, integrated Picatinny rail, ambi mag release levers, interchangeable backstrap panels, polymer frame, modular action design allowing for double/single-action or double-action-only operation. Measures 7.52" overall length. 10+1 capacity.

1100	850	625	425	300	175

HK45 Compact

Similar to above, with 8 round capacity; overall length 7.2".

1100	850	625	425	300	175

	NIB	EXC.	V.G.	GOOD	FAIR	POOR

P30

Polymer-frame 9mm autoloader. Features include loaded chamber indicator, integral Picatinny rail, oversized trigger guard, double/single-action firing mode with decocker, "Hostile Environment" black finish, ambidextrous, oversized controls. Add 10 percent for longslide variant.

	NIB	EXC.	V.G.	GOOD	FAIR	POOR
	850	675	575	450	250	150

VP9

This 9mm model is the first HK striker-fired pistol since P7 series of 1980s. Similar in appearance and operation as P30, the VP9 trigger has a short light take-up, with solid single-action break. It uses HK ergonomic grip design that comes with three interchangeable backstraps and six side panels to accommodate all hand sizes. Other features include an extended Picatinny accessory rail, machined steel slide and HK's hostile environment finish. Magazine has 15-round capacity. Introduced in 2014.

	NIB	EXC.	V.G.	GOOD	FAIR	POOR
	600	525	450	375	—	—

HEINZELMANN, C.E.
Plochipnam Neckar, Germany

Heim

A 6.35mm semi-automatic pistol, with 2" barrel. Detachable magazine holds 6 rounds. Weight approximately 11 oz. Manufactured during 1930s. Marked on frame "C.E. Heinzelmann Plochingen A.N. Patent Heim-6.35".

	NIB	EXC.	V.G.	GOOD	FAIR	POOR
	—	800	675	550	400	200

HELFRICHT
Zella-Mehlis, Germany

Model 3 Pocket Pistol

A 6.35mm semi-automatic pistol, with 2" barrel and 6-shot magazine. Weight about 11 oz. Blued, with checkered black plastic grips having monogram "KH" cast in them. Pistols have no external sights.

	NIB	EXC.	V.G.	GOOD	FAIR	POOR
	—	500	400	300	200	100

Model 4 Pocket Pistol

Semi-automatic pistol in caliber 6.35mm. Checkered black plastic grips, with "KH" logo on each grip.

	NIB	EXC.	V.G.	GOOD	FAIR	POOR
	—	400	300	200	150	100

HENRION & DASSY
Liege, Belgium

Semi-Automatic

A 6.35mm semi-automatic pistol, with 2.5" barrel and 5-shot magazine. Blued, with black plastic grips marked "H&D".

	NIB	EXC.	V.G.	GOOD	FAIR	POOR
	—	600	500	450	375	275

HENRY, ALEXANDER
Edinburgh, Scotland

Noted for both the rifling system he developed and falling block single-shot rifles he made, Alexander Henry conducted business at these locations:

Single-Shot Rifle

High-grade single-shot features true falling-block action that is activated by a side lever on action. Available in popular European cartridges of the era. Barrel length varies from 22" to 28" in length. Rifle exhibits fine quality materials and workmanship. Select-grade walnut stock and schnabel fore-end are hand checkered. Finish is scroll-engraved and blued. Company manufactured firearms from 1869 until 1895.

	NIB	EXC.	V.G.	GOOD	FAIR	POOR
	—	—	3800	1500	700	400

Double Rifle

Side-by-side double-barreled Express Rifle chambered for .500/450 Black Powder Express cartridge. Damascus barrels and double triggers. Gun is hammerless and features ornate scroll engraving as well as a high-grade hand checkered walnut stock and fore-end. Furnished with fitted leather case and accessories. Manufactured in the 1890s.

	NIB	EXC.	V.G.	GOOD	FAIR	POOR
	—	—	9000	5000	1750	800

	NIB	EXC.	V.G.	GOOD	FAIR	POOR

HENRY
See—Winchester

HENRY REPEATING ARMS COMPANY
Bayonne, New Jersey

Lever-Action
Chambered for .22 LR, Long and Short cartridges. Fitted with 18.25" barrel and weighs 5.5 lbs. Magazine capacity 15 rounds for .22 LR cartridge. Rear sight adjustable and front sight is hooded.

NIB	EXC.	V.G.	GOOD	FAIR	POOR
280	200	155	125	75	50

Carbine
Similar to above, with overall length of 34". Features large loop lever.

NIB	EXC.	V.G.	GOOD	FAIR	POOR
280	200	155	125	75	50

Youth Model
Similar to carbine above, with overall length of 33".

NIB	EXC.	V.G.	GOOD	FAIR	POOR
280	200	155	125	75	50

Lever-Action .22 Magnum
Fitted with 19.5" barrel. Tubular magazine capacity 11 rounds. Checkered deluxe walnut stock. Weight about 5.5 lbs.

NIB	EXC.	V.G.	GOOD	FAIR	POOR
350	300	250	195	125	75

Lever-Action Frontier Model
Similar to Lever Action, with 20" octagon barrel. Chambered in .22 WMR and .17HMR. Introduced 2006.

NIB	EXC.	V.G.	GOOD	FAIR	POOR
375	300	250	175	115	85

Golden Boy
Lever-action rifle chambered for .22 LR, Short or Long cartridges as well as .22 WRM cartridge, in a separate model. Fitted with brass receiver and 20" octagon barrel. Walnut stock. Weight about 6.75 lbs. **NOTE:** Add $70 for .22 WRM model or .17 HMR; $20 for large loop lever; $600 for hand-engraved model.

NIB	EXC.	V.G.	GOOD	FAIR	POOR
550	400	295	200	125	85

Golden Boy Deluxe
Chambered for .22 Long Rifle cartridge and fitted with 20" octagon barrel. Fancy walnut stock. Deeply engraved receiver.

NIB	EXC.	V.G.	GOOD	FAIR	POOR
1250	995	650	400	200	125

Deluxe Engraved Golden Boy Magnum
Similar to Golden Boy Deluxe, but chambered in .22 WMR. Features deluxe deep-cut German-style engraving on receiver. Introduced 2006.

NIB	EXC.	V.G.	GOOD	FAIR	POOR
1275	1000	675	425	225	150

Varmint Express
Lever-action rifle chambered for .17 HMR cartridge and fitted with 20" round barrel. Checkered American walnut stock. Scope mount included. Magazine capacity 11 rounds. Weight about 5.75 lbs.

NIB	EXC.	V.G.	GOOD	FAIR	POOR
45	350	225	175	100	75

Big Boy
Lever-action model chambered for .44 Magnum or .45 Colt cartridge. Octagonal barrel is 20". Magazine capacity 10 rounds. American walnut stock, with straight-grip. Weight about 8.7 lbs. .357 Magnum added 2006.

NIB	EXC.	V.G.	GOOD	FAIR	POOR
725	595	400	300	200	150

Big Boy Deluxe Engraved .44 Magnum
Similar to Big Boy, with deluxe deep-cut German-style engraving on receiver. Introduced 2006.

NIB	EXC.	V.G.	GOOD	FAIR	POOR
1350	1100	850	550	275	175

Big Boy .44 Magnum "Wildlife Edition
Similar to Big Boy .44 Magnum. Fore-end and buttstock laser-engraved, with whitetail deer scenes. Introduced in 2007.

NIB	EXC.	V.G.	GOOD	FAIR	POOR
875	750	625	500	250	125

NIB	EXC.	V.G.	GOOD	FAIR	POOR

Big Boy .45 Colt "Cowboy Edition"

Similar to Big Boy .45 Colt. Fore-end and buttstock laser-engraved, with Old West scenes. Introduced in 2007.

1350	1100	850	550	275	175

.30-30

.30-30 caliber Winchester. Features 20" barrel, straight-grip American walnut stock with rubber butt-pad, XS ghost ring sights, blue finish, weight of 7 lbs. Also available with brass receiver, octagon barrel and adjustable Marble's buck-horn rear sight, bead front. **NOTE:** Add 30 percent for brass receiver/octagon barrel.

650	575	500	400	300	200

Mare's Leg

Caliber: .45 Colt or .22 S/L/LR. Has large-loop lever based on rifle seen in classic Steve McQueen western TV series "Wanted: Dead or Alive". Barrel length 12.9", overall length 25". Weight: 5.8 lbs. (.45 Colt), 4.5 lbs. (.22). Lanyard ring, blue finish, straight-grip walnut stock. Sights are Marble's adjustable semi-buckhorn rear and brass bead front (.45 Colt): adjustable rear and hooded front (.22).

.45 Colt

800	675	500	400	300	200

0.22

315	275	220	175	110	85

Original Henry Rifle

This rifle is virtually identical to the original 1860 version, except for caliber. Chambered for .44-40 (.44 WCF) cartridge, it has a 13 round magazine, hardened brass receiver, with blued steel 24" barrel, folding ladder rear and blade front sights. Buttstock is high grade American walnut. Serial number prefix "BTH" honors Benjamin Tyler Henry, inventor of the rifle that went on to become one of the most legendary firearms in history. Introduced in 2014, original Henry is made in America for the first time since 1864. **NOTE:** Add $1,000 for limited edition model, with deluxe scroll engraving. Limited to 1,000 rifles.

2000	1700	1400	1000	—	—

Pump-Action Rifle

Introduced in 1999. .22-caliber fitted with 18.25" barrel and chambered for .22 LR cartridge. Walnut stock and adjustable rear sight. Weight approximately 5.5 lbs.

350	250	185	135	100	75

U.S. Survival Rifle

Improved version of AR-7 .22-caliber survival rifle issued to Air Force. Breakdown design and features waterproof stock, steel-lined barrel and adjustable sights. Furnished with two 8-round magazines. Overall length when broken down is 16.5".

250	175	115	85	65	40

Pump-Action .22 Octagon Rifle

Similar to Pump-Action Rifle, with 20" octagon barrel. Introduced 2006. **NOTE:** Add 10 percent for .22 WMR.

495	350	225	150	125	75

Mini Bolt

Single-shot bolt-action .22-caliber rifle designed for young shooters. Barrel length 16.25". Overall length 30.25" Stainless steel barrel and receiver. Colored stocks available. Adjustable sights. Weight about 3.25 lbs.

210	165	100	75	50	25

Acu-Bolt

Chambered for .22 LR, .22 WMR or .17 HMR cartridges. Fitted with 20" barrel. Fiberglass stock. Scope mounts. Weight about 4.25 lbs. **NOTE:** Add 10 percent for factory scope.

315	275	200	150	100	75

HERITAGE MANUFACTURING, INC.

Opa Locka, Florida

Stealth

A 9mm semi-automatic pistol. Black polymer frame, with stainless steel slide. Barrel length 3.9", overall length 6.3". Magazine capacity 10 rounds. Weight approximately 20 oz. A .40 S&W version scheduled to be introduced in summer of 1996. Offered with black finish, two-tone black

	NIB	EXC.	V.G.	GOOD	FAIR	POOR

chrome, with stainless steel side panels or black chrome.

| | 275 | 225 | 175 | 150 | 125 | 100 |

Model H25S

Semi-automatic pistol chambered for .25 ACP cartridge. Barrel length 2.25", overall length 4.58". Weight about 13.5 oz. Frame mounted safety. Single-action-only. Available in blue or nickel.

| | 150 | 125 | 100 | 85 | 65 | 50 |

Sentry

Double-action revolver chambered for .38 Special. Cylinder holds 6 rounds. Barrel length 2". Weight about 23 oz. Blue or nickel finish.

| | 130 | 100 | 85 | 65 | 50 | 30 |

Rough Rider

Single-action revolver chambered for .22-caliber cartridges. Barrel lengths 4.75", 6.5" and 9". Cylinder holds 6 rounds. Weight about 34 oz. Available in blue or nickel finish.

| | 165 | 125 | 100 | 75 | 50 | 30 |

With Combination Cylinder—.22 Magnum

| | 190 | 150 | 120 | 75 | 50 | 30 |

With Bird's-Head Grip & Combo Cylinder

| | 190 | 150 | 120 | 75 | 50 | 30 |

Rough Rider .17 HMR
Introduced in 2004.

| | 190 | 150 | 120 | 75 | 50 | 30 |

Rough Rider .32

Six-shot revolver chambered for .32 H&R Magnum centerfire (interchangeably .32 S&W, .32 S&W Long). Black satin finish. Offered with 3.5", 4.75" or 6.5" barrels. 35 oz. (6.5" bbl.). 11.785" LOA.) Fixed sights. Bird's-head grip available.

| | 240 | 190 | 140 | 95 | 75 | 50 |

Rough Rider Big-Bore Series

Six-shot steel-frame revolver chambered for .357, .44-40 or .45 Long Colt. Barrel lengths 4.75", 5.5" or 7.5". 36 oz. Fixed sights. **NOTE:** Add 10 percent for chrome finish.

| | 350 | 275 | 200 | 150 | 100 | 50 |

HEROLD
Franz Jaeger
Suhl, Germany

Bolt-Action Rifle

A .22 Hornet bolt-action sporting rifle, with 24" ribbed barrel, adjustable sights, double set triggers and walnut stock. Imported by Charles Daly and Stoeger Arms prior to WWII.

| | — | 1500 | 850 | 600 | 400 | 250 |

HERTER'S
Waseca, Minnesota

An importer and retailer of European-made firearms. Active until approximately 1980.

REVOLVERS

Guide

A .22-caliber double-action swing-out cylinder revolver, with 6" barrel and 6-shot cylinder. Blued, with walnut grips.

| | — | 125 | 95 | 70 | 45 | 30 |

Power-Mag Revolver

A .357 Magnum, .401 Herter Power Magnum and .44 Magnum caliber single-action revolver, with 4" or 6" barrel and 6-shot cylinder. Blued, with walnut grips. **NOTE:** Add 10 percent for .401.

| | — | 400 | 325 | 200 | 125 | 75 |

Western

As above, in .22-caliber.

| | — | 200 | 150 | 125 | 75 | 50 |

	NIB	EXC.	V.G.	GOOD	FAIR	POOR

RIFLES

J-9 or U-9 Hunter

Mauser-action sporting rifles manufactured in England (J-9) and Yugoslavia (U-9), with 24" barrels and Monte Carlo-style walnut stocks.

	NIB	EXC.	V.G.	GOOD	FAIR	POOR
	—	475	200	155	100	75

J-9 or U-9 Presentation or Supreme

As above, with checkering and sling swivels.

	NIB	EXC.	V.G.	GOOD	FAIR	POOR
	—	550	325	200	150	100

HESSE ARMS
Inver Grove Heights, Minnesota

This previous manufacturer of military style firearms was succeeded by Vulcan Armament, which is no longer in business. Values of Hesse Arms products can vary widely.

HEYM, F. W.
Gleichamberg, Germany

Established 1865 in Suhl, Germany, this company was re-established after WWII in Munnerstadt. Company remained there until 1996 when it moved back to a suburb of Suhl. Post-war arms were originally imported by Paul Jaeger of Grand Junction, Tennessee. Double Gun Imports in Dallas, Texas, is the current importer of Heym firearms.

SINGLE-SHOT RIFLES

Model HR-30

Built on Ruger No. 1 falling-block-action. Chambered for most calibers, with 24" round barrel or 26" barrel in magnum calibers. There is a quarter rib with express sights. Single-set trigger made by Canjar. Rifle engraved with game scene motif. Stock is deluxe hand checkered French walnut, with classic European-style cheekpiece. French case hardened and blued.

	NIB	EXC.	V.G.	GOOD	FAIR	POOR
	4000	3500	3000	2500	2000	1000

Model HR-38

As above, with octagonal barrel.

	NIB	EXC.	V.G.	GOOD	FAIR	POOR
	4600	4200	3600	3000	2300	1200

DOUBLE RIFLES

Model 22 Safety

Over/under combination rifle/shotgun chambered for 16- or 20-gauge over .22 Hornet, .22 WMR, .222 Remington, .222 Remington Magnum, .223, 5.6x50Rmm, 6.5x57Rmm and 7x57Rmm, with 24" barrels. Boxlock action with single trigger, automatic ejectors and automatic decocking mechanism. French case hardening, blued, with walnut stock.

	NIB	EXC.	V.G.	GOOD	FAIR	POOR
	—	3500	3000	2750	1200	900

Model 77B/55B Over/Under Rifle

Over/under rifle manufactured in a variety of calibers, with 25" barrels having open sights and boxlock-action with Kersten double cross bolts. Action is heavily engraved, with game scene motif and silver plated. Model has double triggers, cocking indicators, automatic ejectors and select walnut stock. Barrels machined to accept Zeiss scope, with claw mounts.

	NIB	EXC.	V.G.	GOOD	FAIR	POOR
	—	6000	5500	4000	3250	2500

Model 55BSS

As above with sidelocks.

	NIB	EXC.	V.G.	GOOD	FAIR	POOR
	—	10500	9500	8500	5000	3500

Model 55BF/77BF

Similar to Model 55B, except one barrel rifled and other smooth in 12-, 16- or 20-gauge.

	NIB	EXC.	V.G.	GOOD	FAIR	POOR
	—	6000	5500	5000	3250	2500

Model 55BFSS

As above, with sidelocks.

	NIB	EXC.	V.G.	GOOD	FAIR	POOR
	—	10500	9500	8500	5000	3500

	NIB	EXC.	V.G.	GOOD	FAIR	POOR

Model 88 B

Large bore double-barrel boxlock rifle, with 24" barrels, automatic ejectors, double triggers and select walnut stock.

	—	12500	9750	8750	5500	4000

Model 88 BSS

As above with sidelocks.

	20000	18000	15000	10500	6500	5250

Model 88 Safari

As above, but chambered for .375 Holland & Holland, .458 Winchester Magnum, .470 or .500 Nitro Express calibers, with 25" barrels.

	20000	18000	15000	10000	7000	4750

DRILLINGS

Model 33

Boxlock drilling manufactured in a variety of American and European calibers and gauges. 25" barrels, double triggers and extractors. Case hardened, blued, with walnut stock.

	—	7000	6000	5250	3750	2000

Model 33 Deluxe

Same as above, with game scene engraving.

	—	8500	7000	5750	4500	2500

Model 37

Similar to Model 33 Standard, with full sidelocks.

	—	17500	13000	9500	6000	2500

Model 37 Deluxe

Similar to Model 37, with hand engraved scroll work and fancy walnut stock.

	—	20000	16500	12000	6000	3000

BOLT-ACTION RIFLES

Model SR-20

Mauser-action sporting rifle manufactured in a variety of calibers, with 21", 24" or 26" barrels, open sights, adjustable trigger or set trigger. Blued, with walnut stock.

	2450	2250	1650	750	600	450

Model SR-20 Alpine

As above, with 20" barrel and Mannlicher stock. Introduced in 1989.

	—	2500	2000	1250	850	600

SR-20 Classic Safari

As above, but chambered for .404 Jeffries, .425 Express and .458 Winchester Magnum, with 24" barrel having express sights. Introduced in 1989.

	—	3000	2500	2000	1250	750

SR-20 Classic Sportsman

Model features round barrel without sights. Chambered for many calibers from .243 to .375 H&H. Introduced in 1988. **NOTE:** Add $100 for Magnum calibers.

	2650	2250	1900	900	500	300

SR-20 Trophy

Similar to above Classic Sportsman model, with German bead ramp sight and open quarter rib rear sight. Select walnut stock, with oil finish. Octagonal barrel and rosewood grip cap.

	3000	2500	2250	1800	900	300

Heym Magnum Express

Bolt-action rifle chambered for .338 Lapua, .375 H&H, .416 Rigby, .500 Nitro Express, .500 A-Square and few were built in .600 Nitro Express. Fitted with 24" barrel. Adjustable front sight, three leaf rear express sight. Select hand checkered European walnut stock and many other special features. Introduced in 1989. **NOTE:** Add $4,000 for .600 N.E.

	10000	8000	5000	2500	1750	500

HI-POINT FIREARMS
MKS Supply
Dayton, Ohio

Model C

A 9mm single-action compact semi-automatic pistol, with 3.5" barrel. Magazine capacity 8 rounds. Black or chrome finish. Weight is 32 oz.

125	100	85	75	65	50

Model C Polymer

Same as above, with polymer frame. Weight is 28 oz.

140	110	85	75	65	50

Model C Comp

Introduced in 1998, this 9mm model features 4" barrel with compensator, adjustable sights and 10 round magazine.

170	130	100	90	75	50

Model JH

All steel construction chambered for .45 ACP, with 4.5" barrel. Magazine capacity 7 rounds. Weight is 39 oz.

180	135	100	85	75	50

Model 40SW

Same as above. Chambered for .40 S&W cartridge, 8 round magazine capacity. Weight 39 oz.

180	135	100	85	75	50

Model 9mm Polymer (Model 916)

A polymer-frame 9mm, similar to .40- and .45-caliber models.

160	140	120	100	80	60

Model .45 Polymer

Model has polymer frame and 4.5" barrel. Chambered for .45 ACP cartridge. Magazine capacity 9 rounds. Weight about 32 oz.

180	135	100	85	75	50

Model .40 Polymer

As above, but chambered for .40 S&W cartridge, with magazine capacity of 10 rounds. Weight about 32 oz.

180	135	100	85	75	50

Model CF

Pistol chambered for .380 ACP cartridge and fitted with polymer frame. Magazine capacity 8 rounds. Barrel length 3.5". Weight 29 oz. **NOTE:** Add $25 for compensator model.

120	95	65	40	30	25

.380 ACP Compensated

Semi-automatic with fully-adjustable 3-dot sights, muzzle compensator, 4" barrel, 31 oz. polymer frame. Two magazines: one 10 round, one 8 round. **NOTE:** Add 50 percent for laser sight.

150	125	100	85	75	50

Model 4095 Carbine

.40 S&W semi-automatic carbine. Features include all-weather black, polymer stock, 10 shot magazine, 17.5" barrel, sling swivels, grip mounted clip release, quick on & off thumb safety, rear peep sight, 32.5" OAL and scope mount. **NOTE:** Add $85 for red dot sight.

275	200	150	100	75	50

Model 995 Carbine

Similar to .40 S&W Carbine. Chambered for 9mm Parabellum.

250	190	150	100	75	50

	NIB	EXC.	V.G.	GOOD	FAIR	POOR

Model 4595 Carbine

Similar to 995 and 4095 models. Chambered in .45 ACP.

	300	265	200	150	125	100

HIGGINS, J. C.
Chicago, Illinois

Sears, Roebuck & Company of Chicago used trade name J.C. Higgins on firearms and other sporting goods it sold between 1946 and 1962. Arms bearing this trade name were manufactured by a variety of American gun makers. See High Standard, Mossberg, etc.

HIGH STANDARD
New Haven, Connecticut 1932-1945
Hamden, Connecticut 1946-1977
East Hartford, Connecticut 1977-1984

See High Standard Manufacturing Co., Houston, TX at the end of this section.

LETTER MODELS

Model B

A .22 LR caliber semi-automatic pistol, with either 4.5" or 6.75" round barrel and 10 shot magazine. Blued; came with checkered hard rubber grips (later production versions have checkered grips impressed with High Standard monogram). Introduced 1932, with serial numbers beginning at 5000. Early production utilized Hartford parts. Approximately 65,000 made. Add $75 premium for Type-I-B takedown. Add a $75 premium for early models with Hartford Arms front sight, safety and takedown levers. Box with papers add premium of 15 percent.C&R eligible. Most guns are found in serial number ranges from 5,000 to about 95,894 and 148198 to about 151021.

	—	600	475	215	125	90

Model B-US

Version of Model B, with slight contour modifications to back of frame. Approximately 14,000 made for U.S. government in 1942-1943. Most are marked "PROPERTY OF U.S." on top of barrel and on right side of frame. Monogrammed hard rubber grips. Most guns found in serial number range 92344 to about 111631. **NOTE:** Box with papers add premium of 20 percent.

	—	800	520	375	175	125

Model C

Like Model B except in .22 Short. Introduced 1936; approximately 4,700 made. Both plain and monogrammed hard rubber grips. Available with either 4.5" or 6.75" round barrel. **NOTE:** Add $75 premium for I-A takedown. Add $175 premuim for I-B takedown. Box with papers add premium of 15 percent.

	—	725	450	300	225	150

Model A

Similar to Model B, with checkered walnut grips over an extended grip and adjustable sight. Introduced 1938; approximately 7,300 made. Available with either 4.5" or 6.75" round barrel. Same light barrel as Model B. **NOTE:** Add $175 premium for I-B takedown. Box with papers add premium of 15 percent.

	—	750	500	400	175	125

Model D

Similar to Model A, with heavier weight barrel. (The middle weight barrel.) Available with either 4.5" or 6.75" barrel and optional checkered walnut grips. Introduced 1938; approximately 2,500 made. **NOTE:** Add $175 premium for I-B takedown. Box with papers add premium of 15 percent.

	—	835	490	310	200	130

Model E

Like Model D, with still heavier weight barrel (the heavy weight barrel). Available with either 4.5" or 6.75" barrel. Checkered walnut grips, with thumb rest. Introduced 1938; approximately 2,600 made. **NOTE:** Add $175 for I-B takedown. Box with papers add premium of 18 percent.

	—	1300	925	650	250	140

Model S

Not a production model. Like Model B, with a smooth bore. Nine registered as Model S. Additional five with Model C slides are registered, Model C/S. Note ivory bead front sight. Others may exist but only 14 are registered with BATF. Manufactured in 1939 and 1940. Values for both variations are equal. 6.75" barrels. **NOTE:** Serial numbers for registered samples. Model S:

	NIB	EXC.	V.G.	GOOD	FAIR	POOR

48142; 48143; 48144; 48145; 48146; 59458; 59459; 59474 Model C/S: 59279; 59460; 59469; 59473; 59478

	—	5250	3950	3000	—	—

HAMMER LETTER MODELS

Second models made. Like letter models, with external hammers.

Model H-B, Type 1 Pre-War

Like Model B, with exposed hammer. Introduced 1940; approximately 2,100 made. **NOTE:** Box with papers add premium of 15 percent.

	—	725	425	275	175	125

Model H-B, Type 2 Post-War

Post-war variation has external safety. Approximately 25,000 made. **NOTE:** Box with papers add premium of 15 percent.

	—	550	375	225	150	100

Model H-A

Like Model A, with exposed hammer. Introduced 1940; approximately 1,040 made. **NOTE:** Box with papers add premium of 15 percent.

	—	1600	1100	750	500	300

Model H-D

Like Model D, with exposed hammer. Introduced 1940; approximately 6,900 made. **NOTE:** Box with papers add premium of 15 percent.

	—	1500	1000	650	400	250

Model H-E

Like Model E, with exposed hammer. Introduced 1940; approximately 2,100 made. **NOTE:** Box with papers add premium of 15 percent.

	—	1800	950	700	275	150

Model USA—Model HD

Similar to Model HD, with 4.5" barrel only. Had fixed sights, checkered black hard rubber grips and external safety. Early models blued; later model Parkerized. Introduced 1943; approximately 44,000 produced for U.S. government. **NOTE:** Box with papers add premium of 20 percent.

	—	800	625	450	225	125

Model USA—Model HD-MS

Silenced variation of USA Model HD. Approximately 2,000 produced for OSS during 1944 and 1945. 6.75" shrouded barrel. Early models blued; later model Parkerized. Only a few registered with BATFE or civilian ownership.

	—	6600	5500	—	—	—

Model H-D Military

Similar to HD, with external safety. Early production had checkered plastic grips; later production changed to checkered walnut. Introduced 1945; approximately 150,000 produced. **NOTE:** Box with papers add premium of 15 percent.

	—	600	450	275	200	125

LEVER LETTER MODELS

Third design models incorporate interchangeable barrels, with lever takedown.

G-.380

A .380-caliber semi-automatic pistol, with 5" barrel and 6-shot magazine. Blued, with checkered plastic grips. Fixed sights. Introduced 1947, discontinued 1950; approximately 7,400 made. High Standard's only production centerfire pistol. **NOTE:** Box with papers add premium of 10 percent.

	—	750	550	375	150	115

G-B

Similar characteristics like Model B. with interchangeable 4.5" or 6.75" barrels. Sold with either barrel or as combination with both barrels. Fixed sights. Blued, with monogrammed plastic grips. Last short frame model produced. Introduced 1949, discontinued 1950; approximately 4,900 produced. **NOTE:** Box with papers add premium of 15 percent. Add $225 premium for factory combination.

	—	575	350	250	135	100

	NIB	EXC.	V.G.	GOOD	FAIR	POOR

G-D

Similar characteristics like Model D, with interchangeable 4.5" or 6.75" barrels. Sold with either barrel or as combination with both barrels. Adjustable sights. Blued with checkered walnut grips. Optional checkered thumb rest walnut grips. Introduced 1949, discontinued 1950; approximately 3,300 produced. **NOTE:** Add $325 premium for factory combination, $50 premium for factory target grips. Box with papers add premium of 15 percent.

—	975	750	450	195	125

G-E

Similar characteristics like Model E, with interchangeable 4.5" or 6.75" barrels. Sold with either barrel or as combination with both barrels. Adjustable sights. Blued with checkered thumb rest walnut grips. Introduced 1949, discontinued 1950; approximately 2,900 produced. **NOTE:** Add $375 premium for factory combination. Box with papers add premium of 15 percent.

—	1275	800	450	225	135

Olympic (commonly called "G-O")

New gun design for competitive shooting in .22 Short caliber. 4.5" or 6.75" barrels. Sold with either barrel or as combination with both barrels. Grooved front and back straps on frame. Adjustable sights. Blued, with checkered thumb rest walnut grips. Introduced 1949, discontinued 1950; approximately 1,200 produced. Model uses a special curved magazine. Few guns will utilize a straight-back magazine. Majority of these Olympics use curved magazine, with a humped back. **NOTE:** Add $375 premium for factory combination. Box with papers add premium of 15 percent. Add $300 for the straight magazine variation.

—	1500	875	550	225	125

LEVER NAME MODELS

Fourth design models evolving from lever letter series, with slight changes.

Supermatic

.22 LR caliber pistol, with 10-shot magazine. Heavy round barrel, blued finish; adjustable sights and brown plastic thumb rest grips. Grooved front and back straps on frame. Available with 4.5" or 6.75" barrels or combination with both barrels. Ribbed barrels and provisions for weights. A 2 oz. and 3 oz. weight were provided with this model, as was a filler strip for when weights were not used. **NOTE:** Add $250 for factory combination. Box with papers add premium of 15 percent.

—	750	550	400	275	135

Olympic

.22 Short caliber pistol, with 10-shot magazine. Heavy round barrel, blued finish, adjustable sights and brown plastic thumb rest grips. Grooved front and back straps on frame. Available with 4.5" or 6.75" barrels or combination with both barrels. Ribbed barrels and provisions for weights. Weights of 2 oz. and 3 oz. were provided with this model, as was a filler strip for when weights were not used. **NOTE:** Add $250 for factory combination. Box with papers add premium of 15 percent.

—	1000	750	575	275	150

Field King

.22 LR caliber pistol, with 10-shot magazine. Heavy round barrel, blued finish, adjustable sights and brown plastic thumb rest grips. Available with 4.5" or 6.75" barrels or combination with both barrels. No rib on barrels or provisions for weights. **NOTE:** Add $225 premium for factory combination. Box with papers add premium of 15 percent.

—	575	380	250	150	125

Sport King

.22-caliber pistol, with 10-shot magazine. Lightweight round barrel, blued finish, fixed sights and brown plastic thumb rest grips. Available with 4.5" or 6.75" barrels or combination with both barrels. Early models did not have slide holdback when magazine was empty. Early variation without holdback was produced in about twice the quantity as later models incorporating this feature. **NOTE:** Add $200 premium for factory combination. Box with papers add premium of 15 percent. Add a $25 premium for guns with holdback feature.

425	300	225	155	110

100 SERIES MODELS

Fifth design models evolving from lever name series. Series introduced small pushbutton barrel release takedown and deletes shrouded breech.

Supermatic S-100

Like lever takedown Supermatic, with new takedown. Available with 4.5" or 6.75" barrels or combination with both barrel lengths. Grooved front and back straps on frame. Model produced briefly in 1954. Weights of 2 oz. and 3 oz. were provided with this model, as was filler strip for

	NIB	EXC.	V.G.	GOOD	FAIR	POOR

when weights were not used. **NOTE:** Add $250 for factory combination. Box with papers add premium of 15 percent.

| | — | 825 | 600 | 400 | 175 | 125 |

Olympic O-100

Like lever takedown Olympic, with new takedown. Available with 4.5" or 6.75" barrels or combination with both barrel lengths. Grooved front and back straps on frame. Model produced briefly in 1954. Weights of 2 oz. and 3 oz. were provided with this model, as was filler strip for when weights were not used. **NOTE:** Add $250 for factory combination. Box with papers add premium of 15 percent.

| | — | 1250 | 700 | 475 | 250 | 135 |

Field King FK-100

Like lever takedown Field King, with new takedown. Available with 4.5" or 6.75" barrels or combination with both barrel lengths. Model produced briefly in 1954. **NOTE:** Add $225 premium for factory combination. Box with papers add premium of 15 percent.

| | — | 750 | 495 | 385 | 175 | 125 |

Sport King SK-100

Like lever takedown Sport King, with new takedown. Available with 4.5" or 6.75" barrels or combination with both barrel lengths. Model produced 1954 to 1957. In late 1958 Col. Rex Applegate imported about 300 of these pistols into Mexico. Guns are marked with his company's name "ARMAMEX". Marked "ARMAMEX, MEXICO" on right side of barrel and "SPORT KING/CAL .22 L.R." on left side of barrel. Serial numbers around 870,084-870,383. Note that Applegate guns were made after 102 series was in production. Armamex catalog number 1910. **NOTE:** Add $200 premium for factory combination. Add $250 premium for Armamex version. Box with papers add premium of 10 percent.

| | — | 425 | 250 | 200 | 135 | 100 |

Sport King Lightweight SK-100

Aluminum frame like Flite King LW-100 in .22 LR caliber. Produced 1956 to 1964. Also available nickel plated 1957 to 1960. **NOTE:** Add $150 premium for nickel finish, $200 premium for factory combination. Box with papers add premium of 12 percent.

| | — | 525 | 325 | 200 | 140 | 100 |

Flite King LW-100

.22 Short caliber semi-automatic pistol, with 10-shot magazine. Blued finish with black anodized aluminum frame and slide. Brown plastic checkered thumb rest grips. Fixed sights. Available with 4.5" or 6.75" barrels or combination with both barrel lengths. Model produced 1954 to 1957. **NOTE:** Add $200 for factory combination. Box with papers add premium of 12 percent.

| | — | 550 | 400 | 285 | 145 | 100 |

Dura-Matic M-100

.22 LR caliber semi-automatic pistol, with 10-shot magazine. Striker-fired, fixed sights, blued finish, brown checkered plastic one-piece grip. Takedown by thumb nut. Available with 4.5" or 6.5" barrls or combination with both barrel lengths. Model produced briefly in 1954. **NOTE:** Add $150 premium for factory combination. Box with papers add premium of 12 percent.

| | — | 350 | 225 | 165 | 150 | 95 |

101 SERIES MODELS

Sixth design models evolving from 100 series. Series continued small pushbutton barrel release takedown.

Olympic O-101

.22 Short caliber semi-automatic pistol, with 10-shot magazine. Heavy round barrel, blued finish, adjustable sights and brown plastic thumb rest grips. Grooved front and back straps on frame. Available with 4.5" or 6.75" barrels or combination with both barrel lengths. The 6.75" barrel incorporates a muzzle-brake with one slot on either side of front sight. **NOTE:** Add $250 premium for factory combination. Box with papers add premium of 13 percent.

| | — | 950 | 600 | 450 | 200 | 175 |

Supermatic S-101

.22 LR caliber semi-automatic pistol, with 10-shot magazine. Heavy round barrel, blued finish, adjustable sights and brown plastic thumb rest grips. Grooved front and back straps on frame. Available with 4.5" or 6.75" barrels or combination with both barrel lengths. The 6.75" barrel incorporates a muzzle-brake with one slot on either side of front sight. Produced with U.S. marking for military. **NOTE:** Add $250 premium for factory combination. Box with papers add premium of 13 percent.

| | — | 775 | 475 | 360 | 190 | 130 |

	NIB	EXC.	V.G.	GOOD	FAIR	POOR

Field King FK-101

.22 LR caliber semi-automatic pistol, with 10-shot magazine. Heavy round barrel, blued finish, adjustable sights and brown plastic thumb rest grips. Available with 4.5" or 6.75" barrels or combination with both barrel lengths. **NOTE:** Add $225 premium for factory combination. Box with papers add premium of 15 percent.

	NIB	EXC.	V.G.	GOOD	FAIR	POOR
	—	625	475	360	175	125

Dura-Matic M-101

Like Dura-matic M-100, with slightly different locking method for thumb nut takedown. Produced 1954 to 1970. Later appeared renamed "Plinker" M-101 in 1971 to 1973. Plinker not available with both barrel combinations. Slightly modified version was sold by Sears Roebuck & Co. as J. C. Higgins M-80. **NOTE:** Add $150 premium for factory combination. Box with papers add premium of 10 percent.

	NIB	EXC.	V.G.	GOOD	FAIR	POOR
	—	350	225	140	110	80

Conversion Kits

Kits convert .22 LR to .22 Short and include barrel, aluminum slide and magazine for .22 Short to .22 LR, in which case slide is steel. Prices for kit in original factory boxes. **NOTE:** First advertised for 101 Series guns. Later versions were produced for lever takedown guns. Catalog numbers are unknown for conversion kits for lever takedown guns.

	NIB	EXC.	V.G.	GOOD	FAIR	POOR
	—	600	475	—	—	—

102 & 103 SERIES MODELS

The 102 Series was a major design change incorporating a new frame, with large pushbutton takedown release. Also new was a superb adjustable sight. Little difference between the two series.

Supermatic Trophy

.22 LR caliber semi-automatic pistol, with 10-shot magazine. Tapered barrel with enlarged register at muzzle end to hold a removable muzzle-brake. Super polished blue finish; adjustable sights; 2 and 3 oz. adjustable weights and checkered walnut thumb rest grips. Grooved front and back straps on frame. Available with 6.75", 8" or 10" barrels. Occasionally sold as combination including two barrels. Premiums for 10" barrels and combinations in original boxes. 5.5" bull barrel available in 103s after April 1962, 7.25" fluted barrels available in 103s after April 1963. **NOTE:** Add $125 premium for 8" barrel and $225 premium for 10" barrel. Box with papers add premium of 12 percent. Occasionally found with optional light oak case, which will command a premium of about 14 percent.

	NIB	EXC.	V.G.	GOOD	FAIR	POOR
	—	1100	775	525	200	120

Supermatic Citation

Like Supermatic Trophy, with checkered plastic grips. Blued finish without trophy's super polished finish. Grooved front and back straps on frame. 5.5" bull barrel available in 103s after April 1962. Also produced with U.S. marking for military. **NOTE:** Add $100 premium for 8" barrel and $200 premium for 10" barrel. Box with papers add premium of 12 percent. Occasionally found with optional light oak case, which will command a premium of about 18 percent.

	NIB	EXC.	V.G.	GOOD	FAIR	POOR
	—	725	495	375	165	120

Supermatic Tournament

.22 LR caliber semi-automatic pistol, with 10-shot magazine. Barrels are round and tapered. Blued finish, adjustable sights and checkered plastic grips. Available with 4.5", 6.75" or combination with both barrels. Combinations available in 102 Series only. 5.5" bull barrel replaced the 4.5" barrel in early 1962. Also produced with U.S. marking for military. **NOTE:** Add $200 premium for factory combination. Box with papers add premium of 12 percent.

	NIB	EXC.	V.G.	GOOD	FAIR	POOR
	—	640	475	275	155	110

Olympic

.22 Short caliber version of Supermatic Citation. Early models marked "Olympic Citation", changed to "Olympic" only in 1960. Grooved front and back straps on frame. 6.75", 8" and 10" barrels produced. 5.5" bull barrel available on later 103 production. **NOTE:** Add $125 premium for 8" barrel and $225 premium for 10" barrel and $150 premium for "Olympic Citation" marked guns. Box with papers add premium of 12 percent.

	NIB	EXC.	V.G.	GOOD	FAIR	POOR
	—	1150	600	375	175	120

Olympic ISU

Like an Olympic only available with 6.75" barrel and integral muzzle-brake. Grooved front and back straps on frame. **NOTE:** Box with papers add premium of 12 percent.

	NIB	EXC.	V.G.	GOOD	FAIR	POOR
	—	1150	675	360	165	120

NIB	EXC.	V.G.	GOOD	FAIR	POOR

Olympic Trophy ISU

Olympic ISU with Supermatic Trophy finish. Grooved front and back straps on frame. Produced in 103 Series only. Fewer than 500 produced. **NOTE:** Box with papers add premium of 10 percent.

—	2400	775	375	165	135

Sport King

.22 LR caliber semi-automatic pistol, with 10-shot magazine. Barrels are lightweight, round and tapered. Blued finish; fixed sights and checkered plastic grips. Available with 4.5", 6.75" or combination with both barrel lengths. Produced 1957 to 1970 and 1974 to 1977. Also available 1974 to 1977 with nickel finish. $100 premium for nickel finish and $200 premium for factory combination. **NOTE:** Box with papers add premium of 20 percent.

—	350	300	250	150	100

Flite King

.22 Short caliber version of Sport King Models 102 and 103. Models have steel frames. **NOTE:** Add $200 premium for factory combination. Box with papers add premium of 12 percent.

—	475	360	265	150	100

Sharpshooter

.22 LR caliber semi-automatic pistol, with 10-shot magazine. 5.5" bull barrel, blued finish, adjustable sights, checkered plastic grips. Some produced with Model 103-marked slides. Although the 103-marked guns have 1969 and later serial numbers they were shipped after introduction of Sharpshooter in 1971 and were probably converted from unsold Sport Kings. No premium for 103-marked. Variation without series marked on slide is most plentiful. Produced 1971 to 1977. **NOTE:** Box with papers add premium of 15 percent.

—	500	325	265	154	110

Conversion Kits

Kits convert .22 LR to .22 Short and include barrel, aluminum slide and magazine. Prices for kits in original boxes.

900	700	575	—	—	—

104 SERIES MODELS

Last of slant grip gun designs. Early production marked "Model 104". Later production unmarked.

Supermatic Trophy

.22 LR caliber semi-automatic pistol, with 10-shot magazine. Super polished blue finish; adjustable sights; 2 and 3 oz. adjustable weights, checkered walnut thumb rest grips. Grooved front and back straps on frame. Available with 5.5" bull or 7.25" fluted barrels. Both barrels accept removable muzzle-brake. **NOTE:** Add $150 premium for high polish blue finish. Box with papers add premium of 12 percent.

—	1050	625	425	175	110

Supermatic Citation

.22 LR caliber semi-automatic pistol, with 10-shot magazine. Blue finish, adjustable sights, 2 and 3 oz. adjustable weights, checkered walnut thumb rest grips. Grooved front and back straps on frame. **NOTE:** Box with papers add premium of 12 percent.

—	725	500	325	125	110

Olympic

Like 103 Series 8" barrel models. **NOTE:** Box with papers add premium of 12 percent.

—	1200	650	375	175	110

Olympic ISU

Like 103 model. 6.75" barrel with integral brake. 5.5" version introduced in 1964. Catalogs and price list refer to 9295 as both Olympic and Olympic ISU. Met ISU regulations and included removable muzzle-brake and weights. **NOTE:** Box with papers add premium of 12 percent.

—	1100	625	360	175	110

Victor

.22 LR caliber semi-automatic pistol, with 10-shot magazine. 4.5" and 5.5" slab-sided barrels with either ventilated or solid ribs. Adjustable sights are integral with the rib. Blue finish, barrel tapped for weight, checkered walnut thumb rest grips. Grooved front and back straps on frame. Probably fewer than 600 of these slant grip Victors in all configurations. Probably fewer than 40 each of 4.5" guns. Trigger adjustable for both pull and over-travel. Most guns in serial number range above 2401xxx with few in ML serial number series. Note early

	NIB	EXC.	V.G.	GOOD	FAIR	POOR

vent rib barrels were steel and later ones aluminum, without a change in catalog numbers. BEWARE—fakes exist. **NOTE:** Add $75 premium for steel rib, $200 premium for solid rib and $200 premium for 4.5" barrel. Box with papers add premium of 15 percent.

	—	2750	1500	600	425	250

106 SERIES MODELS

Referred to as military models, this series was designed to provide same grip angles and feel of Colt military model 1911. Design introduced in 1965 and continued through most of 1968.

Supermatic Trophy

Like 104 Series Supermatic Trophy, with new military frame. Stippled front and back straps on frame. **NOTE:** Add $100 premium for high polish blue finish, $200 premium for guns with boxes and accessories if factory records verify model numbers. Box with papers add premium of 12 percent.

	—	1000	600	425	190	120

Supermatic Citation

Like 104 Series Supermatic Citation, with new military frame. Stippled front and back straps on frame. **NOTE:** Add $150 premium for guns with boxes and accessories if factory records verify model numbers. Box with papers add premium of 12 percent.

	—	675	475	300	200	120

Supermatic Tournament

Like 104 Series Supermatic Tournament, with new military frame. Stippled front and back straps on frame. **NOTE:** Add $125 premium for guns with boxes and accessories if factory records verify model numbers. Box with papers add premium of 12 percent.

	—	600	375	250	165	120

Olympic

Listed in catalog not in shipping records. Catalog number 9235 for 5.5" barrel. WARNING: There is no evidence this model was actually produced.

Olympic ISU

Like 104 Series Olympic ISU, with new military frame. Stippled front and back straps on frame. **NOTE:** Add $200 premium for guns with boxes and accessories if factory records verify model numbers. Box with papers add premium of 12 percent.

	—	1050	650	385	200	120

107 SERIES MODELS

Evolutionary successor to 106 Series. Series had frame redesigned to eliminate plugging of spring hole produced with old tooling. During time of this series production, MILITARY marking on frame was removed and then later reappeared near the end of traditional serial number series. MILITARY marking is absent from guns with ML prefixed serial numbers. No premium associated with these variations.

Olympic ISU

Like 106 Series Olympic ISU. **NOTE:** Box with papers add premium of 12 percent.

	—	1100	675	525	225	110

Olympic ISU 1980 Commemorative

Limited edition of 107 Olympic ISU, with 1,000 produced. "USA" prefix on serial numbers from 0001 to 1000. Engraved right side of slide has five gold ring Olympic logo. Offered with lined presentation case. **NOTE:** Prices are for guns with box, papers and presentation case; otherwise deduct $250 for guns in excellent condition.

	—	1500	850	525	300	175

Supermatic Trophy

Like 106 Series Supermatic Trophy. **NOTE:** Box with papers add premium of 12 percent.

	—	925	550	360	200	120

Supermatic Trophy 1972 Commemorative

Limited edition of 107 Supermatic Trophy, with 1000 planned. "T" prefix on serial numbers from 0000 to 999. Engraved right side of slide has five gold ring Olympic logo. Offered with lined presentation case. Only 107 guns listed in shipping records, plus one frame. Couple of proto-

	NIB	EXC.	V.G.	GOOD	FAIR	POOR

types believed to exist in regular serial number series. Prices are for guns in original presentation cases. **NOTE:** One fully engraved gun is known.

	6250	4500	—	—	—	—

Supermatic Citation

Like 106 Series Supermatic Citation. **NOTE:** Box with papers add premium of 12 percent.

	—	625	425	300	225	110

Supermatic Tournament

Like 106 Series Supermatic Tournament. Smooth front and back straps on frame. **NOTE:** Box with papers add premium of 12 percent.

	—	550	360	300	175	110

Sport King

Like 103 Series Sport King, with military frame. **NOTE:** Box with papers add premium of 12 percent.

	—	345	225	195	155	100

Sharpshooter

Like 103 Series Sharpshooter, with military frame. **NOTE:** Box with papers add premium of 12 percent.

	—	450	300	225	175	110

Survival Kit

An electroless nickel Sharpshooter, with 5.5" barrel in canvas carrying case and extra electroless nickel magazine. **NOTE:** Deduct $100 for guns without case and $65 for guns without extra magazine, for guns in excellent condition.

	—	750	500	300	175	110

Victor

.22 LR caliber semi-automatic pistol, with 10-shot magazine. 4.5" and 5.5" slab-sided barrels with either ventilated or solid ribs. Adjustable sights are integral with the rib. Blue finish, barrel tapped for weight, checkered walnut thumb rest grips. Stippled front and back straps on frame. Early ventilated ribs were steel; aluminum replaced steel on later ventilated ribs. Still later a clearance groove was added for spent shell ejection behind barrel. Early models marked THE VICTOR on left side of barrel; later guns marked simply VICTOR on left side of frame. Few transition guns marked in both locations. **NOTE:** Add $125 premium for steel ribs, $125 premium for solid rib guns, premium for 4.5" barreled guns, $140 premium for Hamden guns (7-digit serial numbers and ML prefix serial numbers below ML 25,000). Box with papers add premium of 12 percent.

	—	775	500	350	200	120

10-X

.22 LR caliber semi-automatic pistol, with 10-shot magazine. Matte blue finish, adjustable sights, checkered walnut thumb rest grips painted black. Stippled front and back straps on frame. Available with 5.5" bull barrel. Assembled by a master gunsmith. Gunsmith's initials stamped in frame under left grip panel. Produced in 1981. **NOTE:** Prices are for guns with box and papers including test target. Otherwise deduct $175.

	—	2750	1550	900	350	125

SH SERIES MODELS

Final design produced by High Standard. Change in takedown from large pushbutton introduced with 102 Series and continuing through 107 Series, to hex socket head cap screw takedown.

Supermatic Trophy

Like 107 Supermatic Trophy, with new takedown. **NOTE:** Box with papers add premium of 10 percent.

	—	600	375	275	165	120

Supermatic Citation

Like 107 Supermatic Citation, with new takedown. **NOTE:** Box with papers add premium of 10 percent.

	—	525	350	250	175	120

	NIB	EXC.	V.G.	GOOD	FAIR	POOR

Citation II

New gun like Supermatic Citation, with barrel slabbed on sides like Victor and smooth front and back straps on frame. 5.5" and 7.25" barrels available. Blued finish, adjustable sights. Electroless nickel version utilized in some survival kits. **NOTE:** Box with papers add premium of 10 percent.

	—	475	350	250	155	110

Sport King

Like 107 Sport King, with new takedown. Electroless nickel finish also available. **NOTE:** Box with papers add premium of 10 percent.

	—	300	225	165	140	90

Victor

Like 107 Victor, with new takedown. Only available with 5.5" barrel. **NOTE:** Box with papers add premium of 10 percent.

	—	550	330	250	175	110

Sharpshooter

Like 107 Sharpshooter, with new takedown. Electroless nickel version utilized in some survival kits. **NOTE:** Box with papers add premium of 10 percent.

	—	375	250	200	155	110

10-X

Like 107 10-X, with new takedown. Also available with 7.25" fluted barrel and 5.5" ribbed barrel like Victor. **NOTE:** Prices are for guns with box and papers including test target. Otherwise deduct $150. Add $500 premium for 7.25" barrel, $1,000 for ribbed barrel like Victor.

	—	2350	1450	825	350	125

Survival Kit

Either electroless nickel Sharpshooter or electroless nickel Citation II, with 5.5" barrel in canvas carrying case, with an extra electroless nickel magazine. Two different fabrics utilized during production. **NOTE:** Deduct $100 for guns without case and $65 for guns without extra magazine, for guns in excellent condition.

	—	700	475	275	200	110

Conversion Kits for Military Frame Guns

Kits convert .22 LR to .22 Short and include barrel, aluminum slide and 2 magazines. **NOTE:** Prices are for kits in original boxes.

	—	625	390	—	—	—

DERRINGERS

A .22-caliber or .22 Magnum caliber over/under double-action-only derringer, with 3.50" barrels. Found with three different types of markings.

Type 1 Markings

Type 1 Markings are found on early models which are marked "HI-STANDARD" / "DERRINGER" and have EAGLE logo on left side of barrel. Models marked "D-100" for .22-caliber and "DM-101" for .22 Magnum on left side of barrel. Date range 1962 to about 1967.

Type 2 Markings

Type 2 Markings are found on later models marked "HI- STANDARD" / "DERRINGER" and had TRIGGER logo. Early .22-caliber models marked "D-100" and later .22-caliber models beginning about 1969 were marked "D-101" on left side of barrel. .22 Magnum models marked "DM-101" on left side of barrel. Date range 1967 to about 1970.

Type 3 Markings

Type 3 Markings are found on latest models marked simply "DERRINGER" without HI STANDARD or either logo. These models also marked "D-101" for .22-caliber and "DM-101" for .22 Magnum on left side of barrel.

Blued finish, white or black grips, 1962-1984

	—	250	185	140	80	65

Nickel Finish black grips, introduced 1970

	—	250	185	140	80	65

Electroless Nickel Finish with checkered walnut grips

	—	275	190	145	80	65

	NIB	EXC.	V.G.	GOOD	FAIR	POOR

Silver-Plated Derringer

A .22 Magnum derringer, with presentation case. Faux black mother of pearl grips. 501 made. Serial numbers SP 0 through SP 500. Produced in 1981.

	NIB	EXC.	V.G.	GOOD	FAIR	POOR
	—	500	275	175	90	75

Gold-Plated Derringers

NOTE: Prices for GP serial number guns with presentation case. $100 premium for DM prefix guns in Exc. condition with presentation case. $150 premium for 1960s gold guns in Exc. condition with presentation cases.

	NIB	EXC.	V.G.	GOOD	FAIR	POOR
	—	450	300	200	100	80

REVOLVERS

POLICE-STYLE REVOLVERS

Revolvers begin with R-100 design series and continue through R-109 design series. Later steel-framed Sentinels carry no design series markings. Changes of design series designations indicate design changes to guns. Only R-105 known to date is a private label gun made for Sears. Design series designations and associated catalog numbers listed are best estimates at time of publication.

Earliest Sentinels in 1955 were in separate serial number series from 1 through approximately 45000. They were included in serial number series common to all handguns. In 1974 they were again put in separate serial number series with S prefix: S101 through S79946. Many later guns had V suffix which indicated gun was visually imperfect, but guaranteed to work properly.

Sentinel Aluminum Frames

A 9-shot single-/double-action revolver, with swing-out cylinder for .22 Short, Long or LR cartridges. Fixed sights. Sentinel snub 2.375" barrel model had bobbed hammer from its introduction until 1960. Beginning in 1961 this changed to standard spur hammer with no change in catalog number. Beginning with R-102 series ejector had a spring return. Available in configurations listed.

High Standard private-labeled aluminum-framed Sentinels for both Sears and Western Auto. From 1957 through 1962 High Standard offered 2.375" snub-barreled Sentinel in three different color anodized frames. These guns had nickel-plated cylinders, triggers and hammers. Grips were round-butt ivory-colored plastic. **NOTE:** Add $20 premium for nickel. Deduct $15 for early models without spring return ejector. Add $20 for R-102 marked guns.

	NIB	EXC.	V.G.	GOOD	FAIR	POOR
	—	300	200	125	95	

Gold

	NIB	EXC.	V.G.	GOOD	FAIR	POOR
	—	500	275	185	80	55

Turquoise

	NIB	EXC.	V.G.	GOOD	FAIR	POOR
	—	575	300	185	80	55

Pink

	NIB	EXC.	V.G.	GOOD	FAIR	POOR
	—	575	270	185	80	55

Sentinel Imperial

Has two-piece walnut square-butt grips, ramp front and adjustable rear sights. **NOTE:** Add $15 premium for nickel.

	NIB	EXC.	V.G.	GOOD	FAIR	POOR
	—	300	200	125	95	70

Sentinel Deluxe

Has two-piece walnut square-butt grips and fixed sights. **NOTE:** Add $20 premium for nickel.

	NIB	EXC.	V.G.	GOOD	FAIR	POOR
	—	300	200	125	95	70

Sentinel Snub

Has 2.375" barrel, with round-butt grips. **NOTE:** Add $20 premium for nickel.

	NIB	EXC.	V.G.	GOOD	FAIR	POOR
	—	300	200	125	95	70

Sentinel Steel Frames

Model like Mark I sentinels without Mark I markings. Offered as a combination with cylinders for .22 LR and .22 Win. Magnum. Prices for guns with both cylinders. **NOTE:** Add $25 premium for adjustable sights. Deduct $50 for guns with only one cylinder.

	NIB	EXC.	V.G.	GOOD	FAIR	POOR
	—	350	295	250	115	55

	NIB	EXC.	V.G.	GOOD	FAIR	POOR

Kit Gun

A 9-shot single-/double-action revolver, with swing-out cylinder for .22 Short, Long or LR cartridges. Blue finish, aluminum frame, 4.0" barrel and adjustable sights. Wood round-butt grips.

	—	275	195	125	80	55

Camp Gun

A 9-shot single-/double-action revolver, with swing-out cylinder for .22 Short, Long, LR cartridges or .22 magnum. Available as combination with both cylinders. Blue finished steel frame, adjustable sights. **NOTE:** Add $50 premium for combination with both cylinders.

	—	275	195	120	80	55

Sentinel Mark I

A 9-shot single-/double-action revolver, with swing-out cylinder for .22 Short, Long or LR cartridges. Steel frame and fixed sights. Available with blue and nickel finishes in 2", 3" and 4" barrels. Adjustable sights available on 3" and 4" barreled guns only. Wood square-butt grips. **NOTE:** Add $25 premium for adjustable sights. Add $25 for nickel.

	—	255	180	135	80	55

Sentinel Mark IV

Like Mark I above except in .22 Magnum. **NOTE:** Add $25 premium for nickel. $25 premium for adjustable sights.

	—	275	200	145	80	55

Sentinel Mark II

A .357 Magnum single-/double-action 6-shot revolver, with swing-out cylinder. Blue finish, steel frame, fixed sights. Produced by Dan Wesson for High Standard. Sold 1974 through 1975.

	—	325	265	175	90	60

Sentinel Mark III

Like Mark II above except with adjustable sights. Sold 1974 through 1975.

	—	350	290	200	90	60

Power Plus

A 5-shot single-/double-action revolver, with swing-out cylinder for .38 Special cartridges. Blue finished steel frame. Only 177 guns produced. Serial numbers between PG 1010 and PG 1273.

	—	575	400	275	110	70

Crusader

A .44 Magnum or .45 Colt caliber double-action swing-out cylinder revolver, with unique geared action. Adjustable sights. 6-shot cylinder. First 51 guns had long barrels, special engraving, gold crusader figure on side plate and anniversary rollmark to commemorate High Standard's 50th anniversary.

.45 Colt

NOTE: Prices for serial numbers 0 through 50 with 8.375" barrels.

	—	1000	750	500	350	200

.44 Magnum

NOTE: Prices for serial numbers 51 through 500 with 6.5" barrels.

	—	1200	800	550	375	225

WESTERN-STYLE REVOLVERS

Western-style revolvers begin with W-100 design series and continue through W-106 design series. Later steel-framed Sentinels carry no design series markings. Changes of design series designations indicate design changes to guns. Design series designations and associated catalog numbers listed are best estimates at time of publication.

High Standard private labeled aluminum-framed Western-style revolvers for Sears and Western Auto.

Double Nine with Aluminum Frame

A 9-shot single-/double-action revolver for .22 Short, Long, LR cartridges and all aluminum frame guns. One model has grip straps and trigger guard, with gold plating contrasting with blue frame. **NOTE:** Add $25 premium for nickel.

	—	325	250	195	100	55

	NIB	EXC.	V.G.	GOOD	FAIR	POOR

Double Nine with Steel Frame

Available as .22 Short/Long/LR, .22 magnum or combination with both cylinders. **NOTE:** Add $45 premium for combination models, $20 premium for nickel.

	—	325	250	195	100	55

Longhorn

A 9-shot single-/double-action revolver for .22 Short, Long, LR cartridges and all aluminum frame guns. Blue finish, fixed sights and square-butt grips. One model has grip straps and trigger guard, with gold plating contrasting with blue frame. Sears version exists.

	—	375	300	250	200	100

Longhorns with Steel Frame

Guns available as .22 Short/Long/LR, .22 magnum or combination with both cylinders. **NOTE:** Add $45 premium for combination models and $25 premium for adjustable sights.

	—	375	300	250	200	100

Marshall

A 9-shot single-/double-action revolver for .22 Short, Long or LR cartridges. Blue finish. Aluminum frame, 5.5" barrel, fixed sights and square-butt stag style plastic grips. Offered in special promotion package, with holster, trigger lock and spray can of G-96 gun scrubber. Price for gun only. **NOTE:** Add $40 premium if box, papers and accessories are present and in excellent condition.

	—	350	250	125	80	55

Posse

A 9-shot single-/double-action revolver for .22 Short, Long or LR cartridges. Blue finish, with brass colored grip straps and trigger guard. Aluminum frame, 3.5" barrel, fixed sights and square-butt walnut grips.

	—	400	275	135	90	55

Natchez

A 9-shot single-/double-action revolver for .22 Short, Long or LR cartridges. Aluminum frame, 4.5" barrel, fixed sights and bird's-head-style ivory-colored plastic grips.

	—	450	325	225	125	60

Hombre

A 9-shot single-/double-action revolver for .22 Short/Long/LR cartridges. Blue or nickel finish. Aluminum frame, 4" barrel, fixed sights and square-butt walnut grips. **NOTE:** Add $20 premium for nickel.

	—	375	300	250	200	100

Durango

A 9-shot single-/double-action revolver for .22 Short/Long/LR cartridges. Blue or nickel finish. Aluminum or steel frame, 4.5" or 5.5" barrel, fixed or adjustable sights and square-butt walnut grips. Two models have their grip straps and trigger guard with contrasting plating to blue frame. **NOTE:** Add $20 premium for nickel. Add $25 premium for steel frame and $25 premium for adjustable sights.

	—	375	300	250	200	100

The Gun/High Sierra

A 9-shot single-/double-action revolver for .22 Short, Long or LR cartridges. Available as combination model, with second cylinder in .22 Magnum. Blued finish, with gold plated grip straps and trigger guard. Steel frame, 7" octagonal barrel, fixed or adjustable sights and square-butt walnut grips. Revolver introduced as "The Gun" in February 1973 price list and name changed to "High Sierra" by November 1973 price list. Note that early "The Gun" had neither "High Sierra" markings nor any other name. **NOTE:** Add $60 premium for presentation case, $55 premium for combination models, $25 for adjustable sights.

	—	375	300	250	200	100

BLACKPOWDER REVOLVERS

Guns were series of .36-caliber cap-and-ball revolvers that began production in 1974 and ran through 1976. These are reproductions of Confederate copies of Colt Model 1851 Navy. **NOTE:** Most Confederate copies of Colt had round barrels not octagonal as found on Colts. Frames were made by High Standard and balance of parts by Uberti. Guns were assembled and finished by High Standard.

	NIB	EXC.	V.G.	GOOD	FAIR	POOR

Griswold & Gunnison

Blued finish with brass frame. Six-shot single-action. Commemorative gun came with pine presentation case and brass belt plate depicting Georgia state seal. **NOTE:** Price is for gun in case with accessories. Deduct $100 for gun only in Exc. condition.

—	325	—	175	—	—	

Leech & Rigdon

Blued finish with steel frame. Six-shot single-action. Commemorative gun came with presentation case and reproduction of Civil War belt buckle. **NOTE:** Price is for gun in case with accessories. Deduct $100 for gun only in Exc. condition.

—	325	235	175	—	—	

Schneider & Glassick

Blued finish, with steel frame. Six-shot single-action. Commemorative gun came with presentation case and modern version of Confederate "D" guard Bowie knife.

—	450	235	175	—	—	

Bicentennial 1776-1976

Blued finish, with steel frame. Six-shot single-action. Guns came with two versions of presentation case. One case is pine marked "High Standard" and trigger logo on the lid, with powder flask and silver dollar-sized medallion inside. The other is a brown leatherette covered case with "American Bicentennial 1776-1976" and contains a pewter Bicentennial belt buckle.

—	450	235	175	—	—	

Special Presentation Bicentennial

100 guns were available in presentation cases, with "US" serial number prefixes. Serial numbers US 11 through US 50 are in walnut presentation cases, with purple fitted lining and pewter Bicentennial belt buckle. Top of case marked "Limited Edition / American Bicentennial / 1776 – 1976". Guns are engraved on frame, cylinder barrel, loading lever, and hammer. Catalog number 9339 has a steel frame, with round barrel; catalog number 9340 has a brass frame, with octagonal barrel.

—	675	500	350	—	—	

SHOTGUNS

SEMI-AUTOMATIC SHOTGUNS

Supermatic Field

Gas-operated semi-automatic shotgun. Blued finish, plain pistol-grip walnut stock and forearm, 4 round magazine capacity. Supermatic Field models were superseded by models in Supermatic Deluxe group beginning in 1966. 12-gauge guns have 2.75" chambers; 20-gauge 3" chambers. **NOTE:** Slight premium for 20-gauge.

—	300	250	195	100	75	

Supermatic Special

Like Supermatic Field except with 27" barrel and 6-position click-stop adjustable choke. Supermatic Special models were superseded by models in Supermatic Deluxe group beginning in 1966. 12-gauge guns have 2.75" chambers.

—	300	250	195	100	75	

Supermatic Deluxe

Gas-operated semi-automatic shotgun. Blued finish, Checkered pistol-grip walnut stock and forearm. Four-round magazine capacity. Adjustable choke had 6-click-stop positions. Recoil pad beginning 1966. 12-gauge guns have 2.75" chambers; 20-gauge 3" chambers. **NOTE:** Add $20 premium for vent rib versions.

—	325	275	210	125	95	

Supermatic Citation

Same as Trophy except without ventilated rib. Six click-stop adjustable choke. Catalog number 8220 has a compensator integral with the adjustable choke. 12-gauge guns have 2.75" chambers.

—	300	250	195	100	75	

Supermatic Trophy

Gas-operated semi-automatic shotgun. Blued finish, checkered walnut stock and fore-end. 4 round magazine capacity. Six click-stop adjustable choke. Catalog number 8230 has a compensator integral with the adjustable choke. 12-gauge guns have 2.75" chambers; 20-gauge 3" chambers.

—	300	250	195	100	75	

	NIB	EXC.	V.G.	GOOD	FAIR	POOR

Supermatic Duck

Gas-operated semi-automatic shotgun chambered for 3" magnum and suitable for all 2.75" shells. Blued finish. Checkered pistol-grip walnut stock and forearm. Magazine capacity: five 2.75" shells; four 3" shells. Recoil pad. **NOTE:** Add $20 premium for vent rib versions.

	—	325	275	210	125	95

Supermatic Deer Gun

Like Supermatic Deluxe, with rifle sight. Recoil pad. Receiver tapped for peep sight on catalog number 8246. 12-gauge guns have 2.75" chambers.

	—	300	250	195	100	75

Supermatic Skeet

Same features as Supermatic Deluxe except select American walnut stock and forearm. No recoil pad. 12-gauge 2.75" chambers; 20-gauge 3" chambers.

	—	325	275	210	125	95

Supermatic Trap

Same features as Supermatic Deluxe except select American walnut stock and forearm. Recoil pad. Catalog number 8266 is Executive Trap model, with Fajen Monte Carlo stock. 12-gauge guns have 2.75" chambers.

	—	325	275	210	125	95

PUMP SHOTGUNS

Model 200

Economy 12-gauge pump shotgun, sold as part of promotional package beginning in 1971. Package included Model 200, zippered gun case, plastic trigger lock and G-96 gun lubricant. Prices are for gun alone. **NOTE:** Add $30 for gun with complete promotional package.

	—	175	130	105	90	65

Flite King Field

Slide-action shotgun. Blued finish, plain pistol-grip walnut stock and forearm. Catalog number 8450, magazine capacity: five 2.5" shells; four 3" shells. 12-gauge guns have 2.75" chambers; 20 gauge 3" chambers. **NOTE:** Add 50 percent for .410 bore.

	—	250	195	150	100	65

Flite King Brush

Like Flite King Field except has adjustable rifle sights. Receiver tapped for Williams sight and provision exist for sling swivels. Deluxe models have Williams receiver sight, leather sling with swivels and recoil pad. 12-gauge guns have 2.75" chambers. **NOTE:** Add $10 premium for deluxe model.

	—	265	205	160	100	75

Flite King Special

Like Flite King Field except a 27" barrel, with 6-click-stop adjustable choke. 12-gauge guns have 2.75" chambers; 20-gauge 3" chambers.

	—	250	195	150	100	65

Flite King Deluxe

Slide-action shotgun. Blued finish, checkered pistol-grip walnut stock and forearm. Five-round magazine capacity. Available with-/without vent rib. 8411 and 6411 were boys "Converta Pump" sold with two stocks: one youth size and one full size. Adjustable choke had 6-click-stop positions. Recoil pad beginning 1966 except .410 models. 12-gauge guns have 2.75" chambers; 16- gauge 2.75" chambers; 20-gauge 3" chambers; 28-gauge 2.75" chambers; .410 bore 3" chambers. **NOTE:** Add $20 for vent rib.

	—	265	205	160	100	75

Flite King Citation

Like Flite King Trophy without vent rib. Catalog number 8130 has compensator integral, with 6-click-stop position adjustable choke. 12- and 16-gauge guns have 2.75" chambers.

	—	250	195	150	100	65

Flite King Trophy

Slide-action shotgun. Blued finish, checkered pistol-grip walnut stock and forearm. Five-round magazine capacity. Ventilated rib. Catalog number 8140 has compensator integral, with

	NIB	EXC.	V.G.	GOOD	FAIR	POOR

adjustable choke. 12-gauge guns have 2.75" chambers; 20-gauge 3" chambers.

	—	250	195	150	100	65

Flite King Skeet

Same features as Flite King Deluxe except select American walnut stock and forearm. No recoil pad. 12-gauge guns have 2.75" chambers; 20-gauge 3" chambers; 28-gauge 2.75" chambers; .410 bore 3" chambers.

	—	290	200	150	100	75

Flite King Trap

Same features as Flite King Deluxe except select American walnut stock and forearm. Recoil pad. 8166 is Executive Trap model, with Fajen Monte Carlo stock. Catalog number 6165 is a model with provisions for interchangeable barrels. 12-gauge guns have 2.75" chambers. **NOTE:** Add $25 for Fajen Monte Carlo stock.

	—	275	185	150	100	75

BOLT-ACTION SHOTGUNS
Model 514

Sears version of this shotgun was recalled for safety considerations in late 1990s. Catalog numbers listed are from parts book, which does not provide production dates.

	—	135	85	60	45	25

POLICE SHOTGUNS
Semi-Automatic

Gas-operated semi-automatic 12-gauge shotgun. Plain oiled pistol-grip walnut stock and forearm. Magazine capacity 4 rounds. Recoil pad.

	—	265	205	160	100	75

Model 10-A

Gas-operated semi-automatic 12-gauge shotgun. Bullpup configuration with pistol-grip. Integral carrying handle. Integral flashlight on top of gun. Magazine capacity 4 rounds.

	—	900	725	575	325	225

Model 10-B

Gas-operated semi-automatic 12-gauge shotgun. Bullpup configuration with pistol-grip. Fitted with integral folding carrying handle and mounting provisions for flashlight. Magazine capacity 4 rounds. Carrying case catalog number 50284 and attachable flashlight catalog number 50285, sold optionally. **NOTE:** Values for gun with flashlight.

	—	900	725	575	325	225

Pump

Slide-action 12-gauge shotgun. Plain pistol-grip oiled walnut stock and forearm—changed from walnut to stained and lacquered birch in mid 1970s. 8111/8113 magazine capacity 6 rounds. 8104/8129 magazine capacity 5 rounds. A 1963 flyer mentions #8105 Flite King Brush 20" and #8107 Flite King Deluxe 20" as riot guns. Data on #8105 and #8107 listed under Flite King Brush.

	—	230	160	125	100	75

IMPORTED SHOTGUNS
Supermatic Shadow Automatic

Gas-operated semi-automatic shotgun in 12- and 20-gauge. Interchangeable barrels. Checkered walnut stock and forearm. Special "airflow" rib. Imported from Nikko in Japan.

	—	395	280	200	130	100

Supermatic Shadow Indy Over/Under

Boxlock over/under 12-gauge shotgun, with selective auto ejectors and single trigger. Receiver fully engraved. Skipline checkered walnut stock, with pistol-grip. Ventilated forearm. Recoil pad. Special "airflow" rib. Imported from Nikko in Japan.

	—	860	730	625	475	350

Supermatic Shadow Seven Over/Under

Like Shadow Indy, with standard size vent rib, conventional forearm, no recoil pad, standard checkering and less engraving. Imported from Nikko in Japan.

	—	695	585	480	350	300

	NIB	EXC.	V.G.	GOOD	FAIR	POOR

RIFLES

Sport King/Flite King

.22-caliber slide-action rifle capable of using Short/Long/LR ammunition interchangeably. 24" barrel, open sights and tubular magazine. Magazine capacity 21 Short, 17 Long or 15 LR.

—	175	110	80	65	45

Sport King Field

.22-caliber semi-automatic rifle capable of using Short/Long/LR ammunition interchangeably. 22.25" barrel, open sights and tubular magazine. Magazine capacity 21 Short, 17 Long, 15 LR. Walnut stock.

—	165	95	70	60	40

Sport King Special

Like Sport King Field except Monte Carlo walnut stock, with pistol-grip.

—	185	130	100	60	40

Sport King Deluxe/Sport King

Sport King Special with a new name. Catalog number 6005 is the same gun but called just Sport King. Promotional package offered that included Sport King rifle, zippered gun case, plastic trigger lock and G-96 gun lubricant. This package was catalog number 8007. **NOTE:** Add a 10 percent premium for complete 8007 package in original box.

—	215	145	110	80	50

Sport King Carbine

.22 carbine semi-automatic rifle capable of using Short/Long/LR ammunition interchangeably. 18.25" barrel, open sights and tubular magazine. Magazine capacity 17 Short, 14 Long, 12 LR. Straight-grip walnut stock, with barrel band and sling.

—	195	145	110	80	50

Hi-Power Field Grade

A .270 or .30-06 caliber bolt-action rifle, with 22" barrel, open sights and 4-shot magazine. Blued, with walnut stock.

—	350	265	225	150	100

Hi-Power Deluxe

Like Field Grade except has Monte Carlo-style stock.

—	400	330	275	175	130

HIGH STANDARD MANUFACTURING CO.
Houston, Texas

Company established in 1993. Among its employees are several who worked for High Standard Company that closed its doors in Connecticut in 1984. Remaining semi-automatic pistols in this section were made in Houston. This firm expanded in 2004 by purchasing the assets of AMT-Auto Mag and Interarms.

Supermatic Citation

Chambered for .22 LR. Fitted with 5.5" barrel. Matte blue or Parkerized finish. Weight about 44 oz. Discontinued.

425	325	275	225	175	100

Supermatic Citation MS

Designed for metallic silhouette shooting. Introduced in 1996. Fitted with 10" barrel. Weight approximately 49 oz. Discontinued.

800	650	500	400	325	200

Supermatic Tournament

Chambered for .22 LR and fitted with 5.5" barrel. Matte blue finish. Weight approximately 44 oz.

850	700	550	450	325	200

Supermatic Trophy

Offered with 5.5" or 7.25" barrels and chambered for .22 LR. Adjustable trigger, barrel weights, gold-plated trigger safety, slide stop and magazine catch. Matte blue or Parkerized finish. Weight about 45 oz. **NOTE:** Add 10 percent for 7.25 barrel.

800	650	500	400	325	200

	NIB	EXC.	V.G.	GOOD	FAIR	POOR

Olympic Model

Chambered for .22 Short and fitted with 5.5" bull barrel. Blued finish. Weight approximately 44 oz.

	625	425	300	250	200	100

Olympic ISU

Similar to previous model. Fitted with 6.75" barrel with internal stabilizer. Magazine capacity 5 rounds. Checkered walnut grips. Weight approximately 45 oz. Discontinued in 1995.

	600	500	350	300	200	150

Olympic Rapid Fire

Introduced in 1996. Chambered for .22 Short cartridge, with 4" barrel, integral muzzle-brake and forward mounted compensator. Special grips. Weight is about 46 oz. Discontinued.

	1000	850	700	500	425	300

Sport King

Chambered for .22 LR and fitted with 4.5" or 6.75" barrel. Adjustable rear sight. Weight about 44 oz. Limited edition.

	650	400	225	150	100	80

Victor

With 4.5" barrel and blue or Parkerized finish.

	800	650	500	400	325	200

10-X

Fitted with 5.5" barrel. Weight about 44 oz. From HS Custom Shop.

	1100	950	800	600	425	300

10-X—Shea Model

Fitted with 4.5" or 5.5" barrel. Limited to 150 pistols per year. **NOTE:** Add 10 percent for 5.5 barrel.

	1400	1200	850	750	500	350

Olympic Trophy Space Gun

Semi-automatic pistol chambered in .22 LR. Recreation of famed competition "Space Gun" from 1960s. Features include 8- or 10" barrel; 10 round magazine; adjustable sights; barrel weight; adjustable muzzle-brake; blue-black finish with gold highlights.

	1200	900	800	650	500	200

HAS-15

An A2 configuration AR-15 style rifle, with 16" or 20" barrel with muzzle-brake, 30 shot magazine, fixed or folding stock (carbine). Chambered in .223/5.56 NATO. Previously chambered in 6x45mm.

	800	700	575	425	325	225

HAS-15 Enforcer

M4-style carbine, with 16" barrel. Chambered for 5.56 NATO or .300 Blackout. Features include A2 flash hider, forged aluminum upper and lower receiver, six-position adjustable stock, Picatinny rail.

	1000	850	700	500	400	250

HILL, W.J.
Birmingham, England

Hill's Self-Extracting Revolver

.32-caliber double-action folding trigger revolver, with 3.75" barrel and 6-shot cylinder. Marked "Hill's Patent Self Extractor". Blued, with walnut grips.

	—	—	1025	495	295	150

HILLIARD, D. H.
Cornish, New Hampshire

Under Hammer Pistol

.34-caliber under hammer percussion pisto,l with varying barrel lengths. Blued, with walnut grips. Active 1842 to 1877.

	—	—	950	475	200	100

	NIB	EXC.	V.G.	GOOD	FAIR	POOR

HINO-KOMURA
Tokyo, Japan

7.65mm or 8mm Nambu semi-automatic pistol manufactured in limited quantities between 1905 and 1912. Operation of this pistol involves pulling muzzle forward until slide engages a catch on trigger assembly. Pulling trigger at this point allows barrel to move back and engage cartridge nose into chamber. Squeezing grip safety then allows barrel to slam back into fixed firing pin on breechblock. Prospective purchasers are advised to secure a qualified appraisal prior to acquisition.

NIB	EXC.	V.G.	GOOD	FAIR	POOR
—	3850	3600	3000	2250	1000

HODGKINS, D. C. & SONS
Macon, Georgia
See—Bilharz, Hall & Co.

HOFER, P.
Feriach, Austria

Gunmaker specializing in double-barrel rifles made strictly to custom order. Value depends on local demand, chamberings, and other factors.

HOFFMAN, LOUIS
Vicksburg, Mississippi

Pocket Pistol
.41-caliber percussion pocket pistol, with 3" barrel, German silver mounts and walnut stock. Active 1857 to 1886.

NIB	EXC.	V.G.	GOOD	FAIR	POOR
—	—	900	525	200	100

HOLDEN, C. B.
Worcester, Massachusetts

Open Frame Rifle
.44 rimfire single-shot rifle, with 28" barrel, open sights, silver plated bronze frame and walnut stock. Barrel marked "C.B. Holden Worcester-Mass.". Produced in limited quantities during mid-1860s.

NIB	EXC.	V.G.	GOOD	FAIR	POOR
—	—	2600	1850	675	300

HOLECK, EMANUEL
Czechoslovakia

Holeck Rifle
Chambered for .276 cartridge. Semi-automatic rifle submitted for testing for U.S. military trials in 1920s. Barrel length 21.5", with upper portion slotted for operating handle. Rotating dial at barrel band. Rarely encountered. **NOTE:** Thanks to Jim Supica for research found in his Old Town Station Dispatch, in which one of these rifles was offered for sale.

NIB	EXC.	V.G.	GOOD	FAIR	POOR
—	4250	—	—	—	—

HOLLAND & HOLLAND, LTD.
London, England

Established in 1835, Holland & Holland has manufactured a wide variety of shotguns and rifles during its existence. Greater part of these arms are made to custom order.

DOUBLE RIFLES

No. 2 Grade Double Rifle
Sidelock double-barrel rifle produced in a variety of calibers, with 24" barrels, double triggers, automatic ejectors and express sights. Obsolete cartridges could be worth less. **NOTE:** Add 50 percent for calibers from .400 to .500; 100 percent for over .500.

NIB	EXC.	V.G.	GOOD	FAIR	POOR
20000	17000	12500	10000	—	—

Royal Side-by-Side Rifle
Higher grade version of No. 2, with more elaborate engraving. Values shown are for .300 H&H. **NOTE:** Add 25 percent for larger calibers; 50 to 100 percent for Nitro Express calibers.

NIB	EXC.	V.G.	GOOD	FAIR	POOR
29500	25000	18000	13500	—	—

	NIB	EXC.	V.G.	GOOD	FAIR	POOR

H&H .700 Bore Side-by-Side Rifle

.700 Holland & Holland double-barrel rifle. Weight approximately 18 lbs. Currently manufactured. Because of its uniqueness, buyers should seek a qualified appraisal. Current base price for this model approximately $200,000.

BOLT-ACTION RIFLES

Best Quality Rifle

Price depends on caliber and extra cost options. Retail prices for magazine rifles begin around $41,500, depending on value of the dollar. Due to uniqueness of each rifle an independent appraisal is a must prior to sale.

SHOTGUNS

Holland & Holland has been one of Britain's most prestigious makers of custom-made shotguns, all the way back to mid-19th Century. Currently the company makes several side-by-side and over/under models, with prices starting at approximately $75,000. Values of older models range from $8,000 to $10,000 for boxlock designs; $25,000 to $100,000 for sidelocks.

HOLLOWAY ARMS CO.
Ft. Worth, Texas

HAC Model 7

7.62x54mm semi-automatic rifle, with 20" barrel, adjustable sights, integral telescope mount and 20-shot magazine. Black anodized finish, with folding stock. No longer in production.

2500	2000	1750	1200	600	500

HAC Model 7C

As above, with 16" barrel.

2750	2500	2000	1400	700	500

HAC Model 7S

As above, with heavy barrel.

2850	2650	2100	1500	700	500

HOLMES FIREARMS
Wheeler, Arkansas

MP-22

.22-caliber semi-automatic pistol, with 6" barrel and alloy receiver. Anodized black finish, with walnut grip. Manufactured in 1985.

425	325	250	200	150	100

MP-83

Similar to above in 9mm or .45-caliber. Manufactured in 1985. **NOTE:** Several of Holmes pistols have been declared machine guns by BATFE, because of their easy conversion to full automatics. Make sure before purchase that a Class III license is not required.

550	425	325	250	200	125

HOOD F. A. CO.
Norwich, Connecticut

Manufacturer of spur trigger .22- or .32-caliber revolvers, with varying length barrels and finishes. Many of these revolvers are found stamped only with trade names. This type of handgun is often referred to as a suicide special to denote its poor quality and lack of reliability.

—	—	250	145	75	50

HOPKINS & ALLEN
Norwich, Connecticut
See—Bacon Arms Co. & Merwin Hulbert & Co.

Established in 1868, this company produced a variety of spur trigger revolvers in .22-, .32-, .38- or .41-caliber. Often marked with trade names such as: Acme, Blue Jacket, Captain Jack, Chichester, Defender, Dictator, Hopkins & Allen, Imperial Arms Co., Monarch, Mountain Eagle, Ranger, Tower's Police Safety, Universal and XL.

Some of these revolvers are hinged-frame double-action break-opens, with round-ribbed barrels of various lengths. Blued or nickel-plated, with checkered plastic grips.

—	—	550	275	125	75

	NIB	EXC.	V.G.	GOOD	FAIR	POOR

Dictator

.36-caliber percussion or .38 rimfire single-action revolver, with 4" barrel and 5-shot cylinder. Blued, with walnut grips. Barrel marked "Dictator". Approximately 6,000 percussion revolvers were made and 5,000 rimfire.

	NIB	EXC.	V.G.	GOOD	FAIR	POOR
	—	—	1000	725	400	125

Falling Block Rifle

.22 to .38-55 caliber single-shot rifle, with 24", 26" or 28" octagonal barrel. Blued, with walnut stock. Manufactured between 1888 and 1892.

	NIB	EXC.	V.G.	GOOD	FAIR	POOR
	—	—	1250	650	325	175

Schuetzen Rifle

.22 or .25-20 caliber single-shot rifle, with 26" octagonal barrel, double-set trigger and Schuetzen-type buttplate. Blued, with walnut stock.

	NIB	EXC.	V.G.	GOOD	FAIR	POOR
	—	—	2750	1025	550	200

Navy Revolver

.38-caliber rimfire single-action revolver, with 6.5" barrel marked "Hopkins & Allen Mfg. Co., Pat. Mar. 28, 71, Apr. 27, 75" and 6-shot cylinder. Top strap marked "XL Navy". Blued or nickel-plated, with walnut grips. Several hundred made between 1878 and 1882.

	NIB	EXC.	V.G.	GOOD	FAIR	POOR
	—	—	1950	1650	675	175

Army Revolver

As above in .44 rimfire, with 4.5", 6" or 7.5" barrel. Top strap marked "XL No. 8". Several hundred manufactured between 1878 and 1882.

	NIB	EXC.	V.G.	GOOD	FAIR	POOR
	—	—	2800	2500	925	350

Derringer

.22-caliber single-shot pistol, with hinged 1.75" barrel that pivots downwards for loading. Blued or nickel-plated, with walnut, ivory or pearl grips. Frame marked "Hopkins & Allen Arms Co., Norwich, Conn. U.S.A." Several hundred manufactured in 1880s and 1890s.

	NIB	EXC.	V.G.	GOOD	FAIR	POOR
	—	—	2750	950	330	150

Double-Barrel Shotguns

Hopkins & Allen also made good quality single-/double-barrel shotguns in large numbers. Many sold under private brand names such as Seminole and King Nitro. Both hammer and hammerless versions were offered. Values vary from $100 to $1,000 depending on model and condition.

HOWA MACHINE COMPANY
Japan

Company manufactured bolt-action rifles for Smith & Wesson until 1985 and then for Mossberg in 1986 and 1987. From 1988 to 2000 Howa firearms were imported by Interarms of Alexandria, Virginia. These rifles are now imported by Legacy Sports of Alexandria, Virginia.

Model 1500 Hunter

.22-250, .223, .243, .270, 7mm Remington Magnum .308, .30-06, .300 Win. Magnum and .338 Winchester Magnum caliber bolt-action sporting rifle, with 22" or 24" barrel and 3- or 5-shot magazine. Blued or stainless steel, with checkered walnut stock. In 2002 this rifle offered with black polymer stock. Weight approximately 7.6 lbs. **NOTE:** Add $70 for stainless steel.

NIB	EXC.	V.G.	GOOD	FAIR	POOR
600	500	450	325	225	175

Model 1500 JRS Classic

Offered in blue or stainless steel, with laminated stock. These rifles chambered for .223 through .338 Win. Magnum calibers. Barrel length 22" or 24" depending on caliber. Weight about 8 lbs. **NOTE:** Add $70 for stainless steel.

NIB	EXC.	V.G.	GOOD	FAIR	POOR
650	575	500	375	250	195

Model 1500 Mountain

Introduced in 2004, this bolt-action model chambered for .243, .308 or 7mm-08 cartridges. Fitted with 20" contoured barrel. No sights. Blued finish. Black hardwood stock. Stainless steel offered in .308 only. Magazine capacity 5 rounds. Weight about 6.4 lbs. **NOTE:** Add $115 for stainless steel.

NIB	EXC.	V.G.	GOOD	FAIR	POOR
600	500	450	325	225	175

Model 1500 Trophy

As above, with more finely figured walnut stocks and checkering. Introduced in 1988. No longer imported.

NIB	EXC.	V.G.	GOOD	FAIR	POOR
650	525	450	375	250	195

	NIB	EXC.	V.G.	GOOD	FAIR	POOR

Model 1500 Varmint

As above in .22-250 or .223 caliber, with 24" heavy barrel. Choice of walnut or synthetic stock in blue or stainless. Weight about 9.3 lbs. Introduced in 1988. **NOTE:** Add $70 for stainless steel; $20 for walnut stock.

650	600	500	375	250	195

Model 1500 Varmint Supreme

Model features stainless steel barrel. Chambered for .223, .22-250, .308 and .243. No sights. Choice of black synthetic or laminated stock, with Monte Carlo comb. **NOTE:** Add $110 for thumbhole stock.

650	525	450	375	250	195

Model 1500 Lightning Rifle

Introduced in 1993, this model has black composite checkered stock, with schnabel fore-end. Buttstock is Monte Carlo. Choice of blue or stainless steel. Offered in .223, .22-250, .243, .270, .308, .30-06, 7mm Rem. Magnum, .300 and .338 Win. Magnum/ Weighs about 7.5 lbs. **NOTE:** Add $70 for stainless steel.

600	525	450	325	225	175

Model 1500 Youth

Model chambered for .243, .308 or 7mm-08 cartridge. Barrel length 20". Black hardwood stock, with 1" shorter length of pull than standard. Weight about 6.3 lbs. Introduced in 2004. **NOTE:** Add $115 for stainless steel .308 version.

600	500	400	275	175	125

Model 1500 Thumbhole Sporter

As above, with thumbhole stock. Weight about 8.25 lbs. **NOTE:** Add $70 for stainless steel.

750	625	500	400	275	150

Model 1500 Custom

Chambered for .300 WSM or .300 Win. Magnum cartridge. Fitted with 22" or 24" barrel, depending on caliber. Polymer or laminated stock. Weight around 8 lbs. Blued or stainless steel. **NOTE:** Add $70 for stainless steel.

950	800	700	495	325	175

Realtree Camo Rifle

Introduced in 1993, this bolt-action model features composite stock and 22" barrel. Both metal and stock finish are brown leaf pattern. Receiver is mono-block system; drilled and tapped for scope mounts. Floorplate is hinged and magazine holds 5 rounds. Fitted with sling swivel and recoil pad. Offered in .30-06 and .270 calibers. Weighs 8 lbs.

650	525	400	275	175	125

Texas Safari Rifle

Chambered for .270 Win. or .300 Win. Magnum cartridge. Rifle is modified by gunsmith Bill Wiseman. Blue Teflon finish and 22" or 24" barrel depending on caliber. Laminated stock. Weight about 7.8 lbs.

1200	800	650	525	400	150

Model 1500 PCS (Police Counter Sniper)

Bolt-action offered in .308 Winchester and fitted with 24" heavy barrel. Magazine capacity 5 rounds. Available in blue or stainless steel. Walnut or synthetic stock. Weight approximately 9.3 lbs.

1200	800	650	525	400	150

HOWARD-WHITNEY
New Haven, Connecticut
See—Whitney Arms Co.

HUGLU
Turkey
SIDE-BY-SIDES

Bobwhite

Offered in 12-, 20-, 28-gauge and .410 bore, with 26" or 28" barrels with choke tubes. The .410 bore has fixed chokes. Double triggers with no auto ejectors. Manual safety. Box lock receiver, with silver finish. Walnut stock, with round knob pistol-grip and splinter schnabel fore-end. **NOTE:** Add $200 for 28-gauge or .410 models.

700	550	400	275	175	125

	NIB	EXC.	V.G.	GOOD	FAIR	POOR

Ringneck

Similar to Bobwhite, with single trigger, case colored frame and side plates. Choice of round knob pistol- or straight-grip. Fore-end is beavertail schnabel. **NOTE:** Add $200 for 28-gauge or .410 models.

| 1000 | 750 | 600 | 495 | 300 | 150 |

OVER/UNDERS

Woodcock

Gun available in 12-, 20-, 28-gauge and .410 bore. Choice of 26" or 28" vent rib barrels, with choke tubes. Fixed chokes on .410. Single trigger. No auto ejectors. Manual safety. Receiver finish is case colored. Checkered walnut stock, with round knob pistol-grip and schnabel fore-end. **NOTE:** Add $150 for 28-gauge or .410 models.

| 1050 | 825 | 600 | 495 | 300 | 150 |

Woodcock Deluxe

As above in 12-gauge, with auto ejectors and side plates.

| 1200 | 900 | 750 | 550 | 350 | 185 |

Redhead

Available in 12-, 20-, 28-gauge and .410 bore. Choice of 26" or 28" vent rib barrels, with choke tubes. Fixed chokes on .410. The 20-gauge offered with 24" barrels. Single trigger, no auto ejectors and manual safety. Boxlock receiver with silver finish. Checkered walnut stock, with round knob pistol-grip and schnabel forearm. **NOTE:** Add $150 for 28-gauge or .410 models.

| 800 | 625 | 500 | 400 | 275 | 150 |

Redhead Deluxe

As above in 12- and 20-gauge only, with 26" or 28" barrels. Auto ejectors.

| 900 | 750 | 675 | 395 | 200 | 100 |

Mallard

12- or 20-gauge gun fitted with 28" vent rib barrels and choke tubes. Double triggers and no auto ejectors. Silver receiver. Checkered walnut stock, with round knob pistol-grip and schnabel fore-end.

| 550 | 425 | 300 | 200 | 150 | 75 |

Canvasback

Gun available in 12-, 20-, 28-gauge and .410 bore. Choice of 26" or 28" vent rib barrels, with choke tubes. Fixed chokes on .410. Single trigger, no auto ejectors and manual safety. Black boxlock receiver. Checkered walnut stock, with round knob pistol-grip and schnabel fore-end. **NOTE:** Add $150 for 28-gauge or .410 models.

| 800 | 625 | 500 | 400 | 275 | 150 |

Canvasback Deluxe

As above in 12- and 20-gauge only, with auto ejectors.

| 900 | 750 | 675 | 395 | 200 | 100 |

COWBOY & SINGLE-SHOTS

Cottontail

Single-barrel shotgun in 12- or 20-gauge and .410 bore. Choice of 24" or 28" barrels. Modified choke. No auto ejectors. Silver receiver, with blued barrel. Checkered walnut stock, with pistol-grip.

| 200 | 150 | 100 | 75 | 50 | 25 |

Durango

Side-by-side shotgun chambered for 12- or 20-gauge, with single trigger and choke tubes. Barrel lengths 20". No auto ejectors. Boxlock receiver is case colored. Checkered walnut grips, with round knob pistol-grip and schnabel fore-end.

| 850 | 650 | 500 | 400 | 275 | 150 |

Amarillo

Similar to Durango, with flat-side receiver.

| 700 | 525 | 400 | 300 | 195 | 125 |

SEMI-AUTOMATICS

Sharptail

This 12-gauge 3" gun fitted with choice of 26" or 28" vent rib barrels and choke tubes. Black receiver. Checkered walnut stock, with pistol-grip. Weight about 7.3 lbs.

| 550 | 425 | 300 | 200 | 150 | 95 |

	NIB	EXC.	V.G.	GOOD	FAIR	POOR

Canadian

As above, with alloy frame and matte black finish. Weight about 7 lbs.

NIB	EXC.	V.G.	GOOD	FAIR	POOR
650	525	400	275	165	115

Teal

Model is 20-gauge, with 3" chambers. Choice of 26" or 28" vent rib barrels, with choke tubes. Black alloy receiver. Checkered walnut stock, with pistol-grip.

NIB	EXC.	V.G.	GOOD	FAIR	POOR
550	425	300	200	150	95

COMPETITION GUNS

Vandalia Trap

This 12-gauge trap gun offered with either single-/double-barrel combo: single barrel only; double barrel only. Five choke tubes. Engraved silver receiver. Checkered walnut stock, with pistol-grip and adjustable comb. **NOTE:** For Combo model add $300.

NIB	EXC.	V.G.	GOOD	FAIR	POOR
1900	1400	995	650	395	200

English Sporter

Sporting clays model chambered for 12-gauge shell. Fitted with 30" barrel. Ten choke tubes. Black receiver. Adjustable comb. Checkered walnut stock, with pistol-grip.

NIB	EXC.	V.G.	GOOD	FAIR	POOR
1900	1400	995	650	395	200

CUSTOM GRADES

Custom Grade II

Custom-built side-by-side gun in customer's choice of gauge. Engraved case colored receiver, with side plates. Choice of barrel lengths. Select walnut stock, with hand checkering and round knob pistol-grip.

NIB	EXC.	V.G.	GOOD	FAIR	POOR
2200	1600	1200	950	500	300

Custom Grade IV

Custom-built side-by-side features silver scroll engraved receiver, with side plates. Straight-grip stock. Choice of bore and barrel lengths.

NIB	EXC.	V.G.	GOOD	FAIR	POOR
2800	1900	1400	650	600	350

Custom Grade IV with Upgrade

This is an over/under gun, with extra fancy walnut stock and elaborately engraved silver receiver. Choice of gauge and barrel lengths.

NIB	EXC.	V.G.	GOOD	FAIR	POOR
3150	2200	1600	750	650	350

Custom Grade VI

Highest grade offered, with finest walnut stock and engraving.

NIB	EXC.	V.G.	GOOD	FAIR	POOR
3500	26500	1900	950	775	475

HUNGARY

SA-85M

Pre-ban semi-automatic copy of AKM rifle. Chambered for 7.62x39mm cartridge. Fixed or folding stock.

NIB	EXC.	V.G.	GOOD	FAIR	POOR
1800	1600	1200	850	600	500

HUNT

New Haven, Connecticut
See—Winchester Repeating Arms Co.

HUNTER ARMS CO.

Fulton, New York
See—L. C. Smith

HUSQVARNA

Husqvarna, Sweden

PISTOLS

Model 1907

Pistol is a copy of FN Browning Model 1903 made for Swedish Army. Identical in every way to FN model. Many converted to .380-caliber and imported into U.S. **NOTE:** If converted to .380-caliber

	NIB	EXC.	V.G.	GOOD	FAIR	POOR

reduce values by 50 percent.

	—	400	325	225	150	100

Lahti

9mm caliber semi-automatic pistol, with 5.5" barrel and 8-shot magazine. Designed by Aino Lahti and adopted as standard Swedish sidearm in 1940. Add 75 percent for complete military rig, with holsters and magazines.

	—	800	675	475	225	150

BOLT-ACTION RIFLES

Hi-Power

Bolt-action sporting rifle manufactured in a variety of calibers, with 24" barrel, open sights and beechwood stock. Manufactured between 1946 and 1951.

	—	500	375	275	200	150

Model 1100 Deluxe

As above, with walnut stock. Manufactured between 1952 and 1956.

	—	550	400	325	250	200

Model 1000 Super Grade

As above, with Monte Carlo-style stock. Manufactured between 1952 and 1956.

	—	575	475	350	250	200

Model 3100 Crown Grade

Bolt-action sporting rifle manufactured in a variety of calibers, with 24" barrel. Walnut stock, with black composition fore-end tip and pistol-grip cap. Manufactured between 1954 and 1972.

	—	575	475	350	300	200

Model 4100 Lightweight

As above, with schnabel fore-end tip. Manufactured between 1954 and 1972.

	—	575	475	350	300	200

Model 456

As above, with full length Mannlicher-style stock. Manufactured between 1959 and 1970.

	—	600	500	375	325	200

Model 6000

Model 4100, with express folding sights and finely figured walnut stock. Manufactured between 1968 and 1970.

	—	600	500	400	300	200

Model 9000 Crown Grade

Bolt-action sporting rifle manufactured in a variety of calibers, with 23.5" barrel, open sights, adjustable trigger and walnut stock. Manufactured in 1971 and 1972.

	—	500	425	350	300	250

Model 8000 Imperial Grade

As above, with engraved magazine floor plate, machine jeweled bolt. Finely figured walnut stock. Manufactured in 1971 and 1972.

	—	675	550	475	400	300

DOUBLE SHOTGUNS

Number of pre-war Husqvarna side-by-side shotguns have been imported over the years. While sturdy excellent shotguns, their collector value is rather limited. Those following values apply only to modern fluid-steel (nitro proofed) guns.

	—	500	425	350	300	250

HY-HUNTER, INC.
Burbank, California

Chicago Cub

.22-caliber folding trigger double-action revolver, with 2" barrel and 6-shot cylinder.

	—	50	40	30	25	20

	NIB	EXC.	V.G.	GOOD	FAIR	POOR

Detective
.22 or .22 WMR caliber double-action revolver, with 2.5" barrel and 6-shot cylinder. Blued, with plastic grips.

	—	65	50	40	30	25

Frontier Six Shooter (rimfire)
.22 or .22 WMR caliber single-action revolver, with 6-shot cylinder.

	—	125	95	50	40	30

Frontier Six Shooter(centerfire)
As above in .357 Magnum, .44 Magnum or .45 Colt.

	—	225	195	175	100	50

Maxim
.25-caliber semi-automatic pistol, with 2" barrel and 5-shot magazine.

	—	75	65	50	40	30

Military
.22-, .32- or .380-caliber double-action semi-automatic pistol, with 4" barrel and 6-shot magazine.

	100	80	60	50	40	

Stingray
.25-caliber semi-automatic pistol, with 2.5" barrel and 5-shot magazine.

	—	75	65	50	40	30

Panzer
.22-caliber semi-automatic pistol, with 4" barrel and 7-shot magazine.

	—	75	65	50	40	30

Stuka
Similar to above.

	—	75	65	50	40	30

Automatic Derringer
.22-caliber over/under pocket pistol patterned after Remington Double Derringer.

	—	50	40	30	25	20

Accurate Ace
.22-caliber Flobert-action pistol.

	—	50	40	30	25	20

Favorite
.22 or .22 WMR caliber copy of Steven's single-shot pistol, with 6" barrel and nickel-plated frame.

	—	100	80	70	50	25

Gold Rush Derringer
.22-caliber spur trigger single-shot pistol, with 2.5" barrel.

	—	100	80	70	50	25

Target Model
.22 or .22 WMR bolt-action single-shot pistol, with 10" barrel, adjustable sights and walnut grip.

	—	50	40	30	25	20

HYDE & SHATTUCK
Hatfield, Massachusetts

Queen Derringer
.22-caliber spur trigger single-shot pistol, with 2.5" half octagonal barrel. Blued or nickel-plated, with walnut grips. Barrel normally marked "Queen" sometimes "Hyde & Shattuck". Manufactured between 1876 and 1879.

	—	—	650	400	300	150

HYPER
Jenks, Oklahoma

Single-Shot Rifle
Custom made falling block-action single-shot rifle. Manufactured in a variety of calibers, barrel lengths, barrel types, and stock styles. Manufactured until 1984.

	—	2750	2000	1750	1450	800

	NIB	EXC.	V.G.	GOOD	FAIR	POOR

I.G.I.
Itaiguns International
Zingone de Tressano, Italy

Domino SP602

.22-caliber semi-automatic target pistol, with 6" barrel and 5-shot magazine (inserted into action from top), adjustable trigger and customized grips.

	—	950	725	625	450	250

Domino OP601

As above in .22 short caliber.

	—	950	725	625	450	250

IAB
Industria Armi Bresciane
Brescia, Italy

S-300

12-gauge boxlock single-barrel trap gun, with 30" or 32" barrels having wide ventilated rib. Walnut trap-style stock.

	—	1600	1325	1050	850	450

C-300 Combo

12-gauge over/under boxlock double-barrel shotgun, with 30" or 32" barrels. Single-selective trigger, automatic ejectors, trap-style walnut stock, accompanied by two extra single barrels.

	—	2850	2300	1875	1500	800

C-300 Super Combo

As above, but more finely finished.

	—	3600	2800	2275	1750	900

IAI-AMERICAN LEGENDS
Houston, Texas
RIFLES

M-888 M1 Carbine

Re-creation of U.S. M1 Carbine in .30-caliber. Barrel length 18". Weight about 5.5 lbs. Uses surplus magazines of 15 to 30 rounds. Comes with 10-round magazine. Options of wooden or metal handguard and walnut or birchwood stock.

675	575	400	325	200	100

M-333 M1 Garand

Re-manufactured to GI specifications. Fitted with 24" barrel and GI wood stock. Eight-round capacity. Parkerized finish. Weight about 9.5 lbs.

900	800	625	495	350	150

PISTOLS

M-2000

Government model .45 ACP pistol, fitted with 5" barrel and 7-round magazine. Fixed sights, wood grips and Parkerized finish. Weight about 38 oz.

475	375	325	250	175	100

M-999

Similar to above model, with rubber-style combat grips, extended slide stop, safety and magazine release. Fixed sights. Offered with stainless steel slide and blued frame or all stainless steel. Supplied with 7-round magazine. Weight about 38 oz. **NOTE:** Add $25 for stainless steel frame.

475	350	275	200	125	75

M-777

Same as M-999, fitted with 4.25" barrel. Weight about 36 oz. **NOTE:** Add $25 for stainless steel frame.

475	350	275	200	125	75

	NIB	EXC.	V.G.	GOOD	FAIR	POOR

M-6000

This .45 ACP pistol, fitted with 5" barrel, plastic grips, extended slide stop safety and magazine release. Safety is ambidextrous. Magazine capacity 8 rounds. Fixed sights. Weight about 38 oz.

NIB	EXC.	V.G.	GOOD	FAIR	POOR
475	375	325	250	175	100

M-5000

Model similar to M-6000. Fitted with 4.25" barrel. Weight about 36 oz.

NIB	EXC.	V.G.	GOOD	FAIR	POOR
475	375	325	250	175	100

IGA
Veranopolis, Brazil

Single-Barrel Shotgun

A 12-, 20-gauge or .410 bore single barrel shotgun, with exposed hammer, 28" barrel and hardwood stock.

NIB	EXC.	V.G.	GOOD	FAIR	POOR
150	90	75	50	40	30

Single-Barrel Shotgun Youth Model

Offered in 20-gauge and .410 bore. Model features 22" barrel and shorter than standard buttstock. Weighs 5 lbs.

NIB	EXC.	V.G.	GOOD	FAIR	POOR
150	100	80	60	50	35

Coach Gun

A 12- or 20-gauge and .410 bore boxlock double-barrel shotgun, with 20" barrels, double triggers and extractors. Blued, with hardwood stock. **NOTE:** Add $50 for nickel finish; $60 for engraved butt stock.

NIB	EXC.	V.G.	GOOD	FAIR	POOR
425	325	250	150	100	75

Standard Side-by-Side Uplander

Offered in 12-, 20-, 28-gauge and .410 bore, with 26" and 28" barrels. Checkered hardwood stock, with pistol- or straight-grip, in 20-gauge only. Weighs 6.75 lbs. **NOTE:** Add $40 for choke tubes.

NIB	EXC.	V.G.	GOOD	FAIR	POOR
425	325	250	150	100	75

Uplander Youth

Same as above. Offered in 20-gauge with 24" barrels; .410 bore with 24" barrel. Shorter length of pull. Recoil pad standard.

NIB	EXC.	V.G.	GOOD	FAIR	POOR
450	325	250	150	100	75

Uplander Supreme

Introduced in 2000, this model features high grade walnut stock with checkering, single-selective trigger, choke tubes, and automatic ejectors. Offered in 12- and 20-gauge, with 26" or 28" barrels. Chambered for 3" shells. Soft rubber recoil pad standard.

NIB	EXC.	V.G.	GOOD	FAIR	POOR
600	450	375	300	200	100

Standard Over/Under Condor I

Model offered in 12- or 20-gauge, with 26" or 28" barrels. Fitted with extractors and single trigger. Choke tubes are standard. Checkered hardwood stock, with pistol-grip and recoil pad. Weighs 8 lbs.

NIB	EXC.	V.G.	GOOD	FAIR	POOR
425	300	225	200	150	100

Condor II

Same as above, with double triggers and plastic buttplate.

NIB	EXC.	V.G.	GOOD	FAIR	POOR
400	250	200	150	100	75

Condor Supreme Deluxe

Similar to standard Condor model, but has high grade walnut stock, hand checkering, recoil pad, single-selective trigger and automatic ejectors. Offered in 12- and 20-gauge, with 26" or 28" vent rib barrels. Chambered for 3" shells. Choke tubes standard. First offered in 2000.

NIB	EXC.	V.G.	GOOD	FAIR	POOR
550	400	325	200	150	100

Deluxe Over/Under ERA 2000

Offered in 12-gauge only, with 26" or 28" barrels. Fitted with single trigger and extractors. Choke tubes are standard. Barrels are chrome lined and stock is hand checkered.

NIB	EXC.	V.G.	GOOD	FAIR	POOR
450	325	250	150	100	75

	NIB	EXC.	V.G.	GOOD	FAIR	POOR

INDIAN ARMS CORP.
Detroit, Michigan

Indian Arms .380

.380-caliber semi-automatic pistol, with 3.25" barrel and 6-shot magazine. Made of stainless steel. Finished either in white or blued, with walnut grips. Manufactured from 1975 to 1977.

—	350	250	200	150	100

INDUSTRIA ARMI GALESI
Brescia, Italy
See—Galesi

INGRAM
Military Armament Corp.
Atlanta, Georgia

MAC 10

9mm or .45-caliber open-bolt semi-automatic pistol, with 5.75" barrel and 32-shot magazine. Anodized, with plastic grips. Discontinued. **NOTE:** Accessory kit (barrel extension and extra magazine) add 20 percent.

750	500	375	250	175	100

MAC 10AI

As above, but firing from closed bolt. **NOTE:** Add 300 percent for earlier open-bolt model. Accessory kit add 20 percent.

750	600	250	200	150	100

MAC 11

As above in smaller version and chambered for 9mm cartridge. **NOTE:** Add 300 percent for earlier open-bolt model. Accessory kit add 20 percent.

800	650	350	150	100	50

INTERARMS
Alexandria, Virginia

Importer of arms made by Howa Machine, Star and Walther. This firm no longer in business.

RIFLES

Mark X Viscount

Bolt-action sporting rifle made in a variety of calibers, with 24" barrel, open sights and adjustable trigger. Magazine holds either 3 or 5 cartridges. Manufactured in Yugoslavia. Blued, with walnut stock.

450	300	250	200	175	125

Mark X Lightweight

As above, with 20" barrel and composition stock. Introduced in 1988.

450	300	250	200	175	125

Mini Mark X

As above, with short action in .223-caliber only, 20" barrel, open sights and adjustable trigger. Five-shot magazine. Introduced in 1987.

450	300	250	200	175	125

Mark X American Field

As above, with finely figured walnut stock, ebony fore-end tip, pistol-grip cap, sling swivels and recoil pad. Introduced in 1984.

525	400	350	300	250	175

Whitworth Express Rifle

.375 H&H or .458 Winchester Magnum bolt-action sporting rifle, with 24" barrel, express sights and 3-shot magazine. Blued, with walnut stock. Introduced in 1974.

950	750	550	350	250	200

Whitworth Mannlicher Carbine

.243, .270, 7x57mm, .308 and .30-06 caliber bolt-action rifle, with 20" barrel, open sights, sling swivels and full length stock. Manufactured between 1984 and 1987.

—	725	550	375	250	200

	NIB	EXC.	V.G.	GOOD	FAIR	POOR

Cavalier

Bolt-action sporting rifle. Made in a variety of calibers, with modern style stock having rollover cheekpiece. Discontinued.

	NIB	EXC.	V.G.	GOOD	FAIR	POOR
	—	500	400	350	200	150

Mannlicher Carbine

As above, with 20" barrel and full length stock. Discontinued.

	—	600	500	425	275	195

Continental Carbine

As above, with double set triggers. Discontinued.

	—	625	525	450	300	225

Alaskan Model

Similar to Mark X in .375 H&H or .458 Winchester Magnum, with 24" barrel. Discontinued in 1985.

	—	950	750	550	350	200

22-ATD

.22-caliber semi-automatic rifle, with 19.4" barrel, open sights and 11-shot magazine. Blued, with hardwood stock. Manufactured by Norinco. Introduced in 1987.

	195	125	95	65	50	40

HANDGUNS

Helwan Brigadier

9mm semi-automatic pistol, with 4.5" barrel, fixed sights and 8-shot magazine. Blued, with plastic grips. Introduced in 1988.

	375	275	200	175	125	100

FEG R-9

9mm semi-automatic pistol patterned after Browning 35, with 13-shot magazine. Blued, with walnut grips. Manufactured in 1986 and 1987.

	—	350	250	185	145	100

FEG PPH

.380-caliber double-action semi-automatic pistol, with 3.5" barrel and 6-shot magazine. Blued, with plastic grips.

	—	300	175	150	125	100

Mark II AP

Copy of Walther PP. Chambered for .380 ACP or .22 LR cartridge.

	300	175	125	100	75	50

Mark II APK

Copy of Walther PPK. Chambered for .380 ACP cartridge only.

	300	175	125	100	75	50

Mauser Parabellum Karabiner

9mm caliber semi-automatic carbine, with 11.75" barrel and detachable shoulder stock. Fitted in leather case. **NOTE:** Only 100 imported into U.S. This arm subject to BATFE registration.

	6500	5750	5000	4000	3000	2250

Mauser Parabellum Cartridge Counter

Reproduction of cartridge counter Luger. Fitted in leather case, with only 100 units imported into U.S.

	4000	3000	2500	2000	1500	1000

Virginian Dragoon

Single-action revolver in .357 Magnum, .41 Magnum, .44 Magnum or .45 Colt, with 5", 6", 7.5", 8.75" or 12" barrel, fixed or adjustable sights and 6-shot cylinder. Originally made in Switzerland, then in U.S.A. Discontinued in 1984. **NOTE:** Add 20 percent for Swiss manufacture; 15 percent for 12" barrel.

	—	325	275	200	150	100

Stainless Dragoon

As above in stainless steel.

	—	375	300	245	175	105

	NIB	EXC.	V.G.	GOOD	FAIR	POOR

Virginian Dragoon Silhouette

Similar to stainless Virginia Dragoon, except in .357 or .44 Magnum, with 7.5", 8.375" or 10.5" barrel. Adjustable sights, target grips.

	NIB	EXC.	V.G.	GOOD	FAIR	POOR
	500	425	350	300	250	150

Dragoon Deputy

Similar to Virginia Dragoon except in .357 or .44 Magnum. Blue finish, with case-hardened frame or stainless and 5" barrel.

	NIB	EXC.	V.G.	GOOD	FAIR	POOR
	450	375	300	250	200	125

Virginian .22 Convertible

As above in .22-caliber, with 5.5" barrel.

	NIB	EXC.	V.G.	GOOD	FAIR	POOR
	—	275	200	125	100	75

Virginian Stainless .22 Convertible

As above in stainless steel.

	NIB	EXC.	V.G.	GOOD	FAIR	POOR
	—	295	225	165	100	80

INTERARMS/HIGH STANDARD
Houston, Texas

In 2000, High Standard Manufacturing Company of Houston, Texas resurrected the Interarms name. They began making several AK-style semi-automatic rifles in U.S.A. Following is a sampling of these models.

AK-47 (7.62x39mm)

	NIB	EXC.	V.G.	GOOD	FAIR	POOR
	1000	850	700	500	400	250

AKM Series (7.62x39mm)

	NIB	EXC.	V.G.	GOOD	FAIR	POOR
	550	450	375	300	225	150

AK-74 (5.45x39mm)

	NIB	EXC.	V.G.	GOOD	FAIR	POOR
	600	500	400	325	275	200

INTERDYNAMICS OF AMERICA
Miami, Florida

KG-9

9mm caliber semi-automatic pistol, with 3" barrel and 36-shot magazine. Manufactured from 1981 to 1983. **NOTE:** Earliest models fire from open bolt. Valued at approximately 150 percent of values shown here.

	NIB	EXC.	V.G.	GOOD	FAIR	POOR
	—	800	650	575	500	300

KG-99

As above, with barrel shroud. Manufactured from 1981 to 1984.

	NIB	EXC.	V.G.	GOOD	FAIR	POOR
	—	800	650	575	500	300

KG-99 Stainless

As above in stainless steel. Manufactured in 1984.

	NIB	EXC.	V.G.	GOOD	FAIR	POOR
	—	800	650	575	500	300

KG-99M

More compact version of above. Manufactured in 1984.

	NIB	EXC.	V.G.	GOOD	FAIR	POOR
	—	800	650	575	500	300

INTRATEC USA, INC.
Miami, Florida

This manufacturer was in business from 1985 to 2000, under the names Intratec, and Intratec USA, Inc.

TEC-9

9mm caliber semi-automatic pistol, with 5" shrouded barrel and 36-shot magazine. Introduced in 1985.

	NIB	EXC.	V.G.	GOOD	FAIR	POOR
	450	350	295	200	150	100

TEC-9C

As above, with 16" barrel and folding stock. Manufactured in 1987.

	NIB	EXC.	V.G.	GOOD	FAIR	POOR
	—	450	350	295	200	100

	NIB	EXC.	V.G.	GOOD	FAIR	POOR

TEC-9M

As above, with 3" barrel and 20-shot magazine. Also made in stainless steel.

	450	350	295	200	150	100

TEC-22 "Scorpion"

Similar to above in .22-caliber, with 4" barrel and 30-shot magazine.

	325	225	175	100	75	50

TEC-38

.38-caliber over/under double-action derringer, with 3" barrels. Manufactured between 1986 and 1988.

	—	195	125	90	65	45

IRVING, W.
New York, New York

Single-Shot Derringer

.22-caliber spur trigger single-shot pistol, with 2.75" half octagonal barrel. Silver plated brass frame, blued barrel and rosewood grips. Barrel marked "W. Irving". Manufactured in 1860s. **NOTE:** .32-caliber variation has 3" barrel and worth approximately 40 percent more than values listed.

	—	—	1050	475	195	125

Pocket Revolver 1st Model

.31-caliber spur trigger percussion revolver, with 3" octagonal barrel, 6-shot cylinder and brass frame. Barrel marked "W. Irving". Approximately 50 made between 1858 and 1862.

	—	—	2500	925	275	175

Pocket Revolver 2nd Model

.31-caliber percussion revolver, with 4.5" round barrel, loading lever and either brass or iron frame. Barrel marked "Address W. Irving. 20 Cliff St. N.Y.". Approximately 600 manufactured with brass frame, 1,500 with iron frame. **NOTE:** Brass-frame version will bring a premium of about 35 percent.

	—	—	1450	495	200	100

IRWINDALE ARMS, INC.
Irwindale, California
See—AMT

ISRAELI MILITARY INDUSTRIES
Israel

Civilian firearms manufactured by this firm have been and are being retailed by Action Arms Limited, Magnum Research and Mossberg.

ITHACA GUN CO.
Ithaca, New York

Material was supplied by Walter C. Snyder and is copyrighted in his name. Used with author's permission.

Ithaca Gun Company was founded by William Henry Baker, John VanNatta and Dwight McIntyre. Gun production started during latter half of 1883, at an industrial site located on Fall Creek, Ithaca, New York. Leroy Smith joined the company by 1885 and George Livermore joined the firm in 1887. By 1894 the company was under the exclusive control of Leroy Smith and George Livermore. Many of the company's assets were purchased by Ithaca Acquisition Corporation in 1987 and moved to King Ferry, New York, where it operated until May, 1996. Now, dba, Ithaca Gun Company of Upper Sandusky, Ohio.

HAMMER MODELS

Ithaca Baker Model

First model produced by the company was designed by W.H. Baker and manufactured from 1883 through 1887. Offered in six grades; Quality A ($35) through Quality F ($200), in either 10- or 12-gauge. All Ithaca-produced Baker models had exposed hammers. Grades above Quality B are seldom encountered and an expert appraisal is recommended.

Quality A

	—	900	500	300	200	100

Quality B

	—	1850	1350	750	300	100

	NIB	EXC.	V.G.	GOOD	FAIR	POOR

New Ithaca Gun

New Ithaca Gun introduced in 1888 and discontinued during 1915. Like its predecessor, introduced in same seven grades, Quality A through Quality F. Later Quality F was discontinued. By 1900 a "condensed steel" barreled model named Quality X was introduced. New Ithaca Gun was produced in gauges 10-, 12-, 16- and very rarely 20-gauge. Lower grade models carried logo "New Ithaca Gun" usually within a banner on each side of frame. Like its predecessor, grades above Quality B are seldom encountered and an expert appraisal is recommended. 16-gauge guns command a 30 percent price premium. Extremely rare 20-gauge model requires an expert appraisal.

Quality A

	NIB	EXC.	V.G.	GOOD	FAIR	POOR
	—	1100	775	295	175	100

Quality AA

	NIB	EXC.	V.G.	GOOD	FAIR	POOR
	—	1100	775	295	175	100

Quality B

	NIB	EXC.	V.G.	GOOD	FAIR	POOR
	—	1300	875	450	225	100

Quality X

	NIB	EXC.	V.G.	GOOD	FAIR	POOR
	—	1300	875	450	225	100

The "New Double Bolted Hammer Gun

During 1915, Ithaca Gun Company replaced New Ithaca Gun, with model it referred to as "our new model two bolt hammer gun". New hammer gun had coil springs powering external hammers. The "two bolt" lock up was accomplished by a bottom bolt and top lever engagement, with rear nub of rib extension. Lower grade models were marked on both sides of frame, with a setter dog and logo "Ithaca Gun Co.". The 1915 catalog is last year hammer guns were advertised, but old records indicate a few were sold as late as 1919.

Grades offered were X, A, AA, B, C, D and E. The 1915 catalog advertised a price of $29 for a Quality A model and $150 for elaborately engraved Quality E. All grades were available in 10-, 12- and 16-gauge. Like the New Ithaca Gun grades above Quality B are seldom encountered and an expert appraisal is recommended. 16-gauge guns command a 30 percent price premium. Extremely rare 20-gauge model requires an expert appraisal.

Quality A

	NIB	EXC.	V.G.	GOOD	FAIR	POOR
	—	1300	875	350	225	100

Quality AA

	NIB	EXC.	V.G.	GOOD	FAIR	POOR
	—	1600	1075	450	250	100

Quality B

	NIB	EXC.	V.G.	GOOD	FAIR	POOR
	—	1600	1075	450	250	100

Quality X

	NIB	EXC.	V.G.	GOOD	FAIR	POOR
	—	1600	1075	450	250	100

HAMMERLESS MODELS

First hammerless Ithaca gun was introduced in 1888. All Ithaca double guns were discontinued in 1948. Gauge and grade can usually be found on left front corner of water table of frame. Serial number usually found on right side of same water table on barrel flats and fore-end iron.

Crass Model

Crass Model, named after Ithaca's Frederick Crass who designed it, was introduced in 1888. Offered in Quality 1 through Quality 7. Quality 1P model with no engraving introduced in 1898. Crass Model underwent three major frame redesigns, before it was discontinued during 1901. Gun was available in 10-, 12- and 16-gauge. Automatic ejectors introduced in 1893 and available in any Quality gun at extra cost.

NOTE: 16-gauge guns will command a 20 percent price premium. Guns above Quality 4 are seldom encountered and an expert appraisal is necessary. Automatic ejectors add $250. Serial number range for Crass Model approximately 7000 to 50000.

Quality 1

	NIB	EXC.	V.G.	GOOD	FAIR	POOR
	—	900	575	400	225	100

Quality 1-1/2

	NIB	EXC.	V.G.	GOOD	FAIR	POOR
	—	900	575	400	225	100

Quality 1P

	NIB	EXC.	V.G.	GOOD	FAIR	POOR
	—	900	575	400	225	100

	NIB	EXC.	V.G.	GOOD	FAIR	POOR
Quality 2						
	—	1300	875	600	250	100
Quality 3						
	—	1800	1300	775	325	100
Quality 4						
	—	2250	1850	1075	325	100

Lewis Model

Chester Lewis, an Ithaca Gun employee, was credited with design of this gun that now bears his name. Gun was bolted through rib extension in addition to traditional under bolt. Model was available from 1901 through 1906 and offered in Qualities 1 through 7. Made in 10-, 12- and 16-gauge, after 1906, 20-gauge. Automatic ejectors were offered at an added cost. **NOTE:** Automatic ejectors add about $250 to grades below Quality 4. Serial number range for Lewis Model approximately 55000 to 123600.

	NIB	EXC.	V.G.	GOOD	FAIR	POOR
Quality 1						
	—	900	575	325	175	100
Quality 1 Special						
	—	900	575	325	175	100
Quality 1-1/2						
	—	950	600	350	200	100
Quality 2						
	—	1150	725	500	225	100
Quality 3						
	—	1850	1500	850	425	100
Quality 4						
	—	2700	2350	1900	475	100
Quality 5						
	—	3700	3150	2100	725	300
Quality 6						
	—	6300	4750	3200	775	300
Quality 7						
	—	6300	4750	3200	775	300

Minier Model

Minier Model, named after Ithaca's David Minier, was introduced in 1906 and available through 1908. Offered in Qualities Field through 7 and any grade could be ordered with ejectors. Minier Model was first Ithaca gun to use coil springs to power internal hammers. Model was triple bolted, e.g., two fastenings at rib extension and under bolt. Offered in 10-, 12-, 16- and 20-gauge. **NOTE:** Automatic ejectors add $250 to guns below Quality 4. Serial number range for Minier Model approximately 130000 to 151000.

	NIB	EXC.	V.G.	GOOD	FAIR	POOR
Field Grade						
	—	1150	725	500	225	100
Quality 1						
	—	1150	725	500	225	100
Quality 1 Special						
	—	1150	725	500	225	100
Quality 1-1/2						
	—	1150	725	500	225	100
Quality 2						
	—	1350	700	475	225	100
Quality 3						
	—	2250	1200	575	450	100
Quality 4						
	—	2700	1325	875	450	100

	NIB	EXC.	V.G.	GOOD	FAIR	POOR
Quality 5						
	—	3700	3150	2100	725	300
Quality 6						
	—	5250	4100	1550	725	300
Quality 7						
	—	6800	4300	1700	800	300

Flues Model

Flues Model Ithaca gun, built on three-piece lock mechanism invented and patented by Emil Flues. Introduced in 1908, remained in production through 1926 when it was replaced by Ithaca New Double. Offered in 10-, 12-, 16-, 20- and 28-gauge. Enjoyed longest production life of any Ithaca double gun. Several grades offered beginning with Field Grade and ending with Sousa Special. Flues Model had same bolting system as used on Minier Model. Any grade could have been ordered, with automatic ejectors at an extra cost. Single-selective trigger made by Infallible Trigger Company, offered after 1914 and was first single trigger offered from this company. **NOTE:** Add $200 for factory-ordered single trigger; $200 for automatic ejectors on grades lower than Grade 4. Small gauges command a price premium. 20-gauge gun may command up to 50 percent price premium; 28-gauge Field Grade, perhaps as much as 200 percent. Serial number range for Flues approximately 175000 to 399000. Expert appraisals are recommended on higher-grade, small-gauge models, as they are seldom encountered.

	NIB	EXC.	V.G.	GOOD	FAIR	POOR
Field Grade						
	—	1100	700	375	250	100
Grade 1						
	—	1100	700	375	250	100
Grade 1 Special						
		1100	700	375	250	100
Grade 1-1/2						
		1250	850	500	350	100
Grade 2						
		1350	900	575	400	100
Grade 3						
		2300	1600	800	500	100
Grade 4						
	—	2300	1600	800	500	100
Grade 5						
	—	2800	2200	1650	600	200
Grade 6						
	—	11000	6000	2750	1100	300
Grade 7						
	—	11500	7000	3000	1250	300
Sousa						
	—	17000	12000	7500	3750	N/A

The New Ithaca Double

New Ithaca Double commonly referred to as NID, manufactured from 1926 to 1948. Has the distinction of being last double gun manufactured by factory. NID was bolted by a single rotary top bolt. External cocking indicators were standard on all NID models until about 1934, when they were eliminated from the design. Selective and non-selective single triggers and automatic ejectors, were optional at additional costs. Special variation of NID was introduced in 1932 to accommodate 10-gauge 3.5" magnum ammunition and named appropriately, Magnum 10. All NID guns were available in grades Field, 1, 2, 3, 4, 5, 7 and Sousa (renamed the $1,000 grade after 1936). Magnum 10-gauge and standard 10-, 12-, 16-, 20-, 28-gauge and .410 bore were offered. **NOTE:** Like most collectible double guns, smaller gauges command a price premium over 12-gauge model. 16-gauge Field Grade may command a 25 percent price premium; 20-gauge Field Grade may command up to a 50 percent price premium; 28-gauge and .410 caliber Field Grade models, perhaps as much as 250-300 percent. It is recommended that an expert opinion be sought for valuation of high-grade small-gauge models. Of late, Magnum 10-gauge model also commands a price premium. Few of these guns trade and advice of an expert appraiser is suggested. Add $150 for non-selective single trigger; $250 for single-selective trigger; $300 for ventilated rib; $300 for automatic ejectors for grades below Grade 4; $200 for beavertail forearm; $300 for Monte Carlo buttstock.

	NIB	EXC.	V.G.	GOOD	FAIR	POOR
Field Grade						
	—	1100	700	375	250	100
Grade 1						
	—	1350	850	475	250	100
Grade 2						
	—	1650	900	725	350	100
Grade 3						
	—	2600	1600	1075	425	100
Grade 4						
	—	3250	2700	1600	475	100
Grade 5						
	—	4300	3400	2200	775	200
Grade 7						
	—	12000	7500	4250	1100	300
Sousa Grade						
	—	28000	15000	8000	4000	800

ITHACA CLASSIC DOUBLES (1998-2003)

Special Field Grade

Side-by-side double offered in 16-, 20-, 28-gauge and .410 bore. Choice of matted rib barrel lengths of 26", 28" or 30". Ivory bead front sight. Action is case colored, with light line border engraving. Stock is feather crotch black walnut, with 22 lpi checkering. Choice of pistol- or straight-grip. Double trigger standard. Weight in 20-gauge about 5 lbs. 14 oz.; 28-gauge 5 lbs. 8 oz.; .410 bore 5 lbs. 5 oz.

6200	4750	4000	1700	800	300

Grade 4E

Model available in 16-, 20-, 28-gauge and .410 bore, with 26", 28" and 30" barrels. Has gold plated triggers, jeweled barrel flats and hand tuned locks. Black walnut stock has 28 lpi checkering, with fleur-de-lis pattern. Pistol- or straight-grip stock. Action is hand engraved, with three game scenes and bank note scroll. Case colored frame.

8000	6000	3000	1750	775	300

Grade 7E

Model has all gauges and barrel lengths of above gun. Action is hand engraved, with gold two tone inlays. Exhibition grade black walnut stock, with elaborate patterns. Custom built dimensions.

11000	8750	7500	4250	1100	300

Sousa Grade

Model available in same gauges and barrel lengths as above guns. Stocks with presentation grade black walnut and hand carved with 32 lpi checkering. Action hand engraved, with bank note scroll and gold inlays. Entire gun hand fitted and polished. Extremely limited availability. Special order only. In production from 1998 to 2003.

30000	20000	15000	—	—	—

LEFEVER ARMS COMPANY, INC.

During 1921, Ithaca Gun under the name "The Lefever Arms Company, Inc." introduced a line of lower-cost boxlock guns. See Lefever Arms Company section of this book for prices concerning those guns.

WESTERN ARMS CORPORATION

During 1929, Ithaca Gun Company created Western Arms Corporation, which introduced a new low-cost double gun. That new double gun was named, The Long Range Double. Produced in 12-, 16-, 20-gauge and .410 bore. 20-gauge guns often command a 20 percent premium; .410 bore can command up to 250 percent premium. Model last made at start of World War II.

The Long Range Double

The Long Range Double had walnut stocks that were not checkered. **NOTE:** Add $100 for single trigger guns; $200 for automatic ejectors.

—	550	450	200	150	N/A

NIB	EXC.	V.G.	GOOD	FAIR	POOR

The Long Range Double Deluxe

Usually made exclusively for Montgomery Ward Company. Sold by them under the name Western Field Deluxe. Model had line checkering pattern at grip and on splinter fore-end. Many of Ithaca produced Western Field Deluxe guns had automatic ejectors and that fact was stamped into right barrel. **NOTE:** Add $100 for single triggers; $200 for automatic ejectors.

NIB	EXC.	V.G.	GOOD	FAIR	POOR
—	575	475	300	150	N/A

ITHACA SINGLE-BARREL TRAP GUNS

Ithaca Gun Company introduced a single-barrel trap gun in 1914. Gun was based upon Emil Flues three piece lock design used for double gun, which become known as Flues Model Single-Barrel Trap. Flues Model was discontinued during 1922 and replaced that year by model designed by Ithaca's, Frank Knickerbocker, commonly referred to as "Knick". Knick Model discontinued in 1988, shortly after Ithaca Acquisition Corp. purchased assets of Ithaca Gun Company. For many years, Ithaca Single-Barrel Trap Gun was the gun of choice for many champion shooters.

Flues Model Single-Barrel Trap Gun (1914 to 1922)

Flues Model trap gun was introduced in 1914. Offered in Grades 4, 5, 6 and 7. Lower cost Victory grade introduced in 1919. Highest cost variety Sousa Special introduced in 1918. All Flues model trap guns were made within same serial number sequence as double guns, but do have letter "T" for Trap following serial number. All Flues Models, with exception of Victory Grade, were produced with an automatic ejector. Rubber anti-recoil pad was an option. Guns having a pre-1916 engraving pattern will command highest prices.

Victory Grade

NIB	EXC.	V.G.	GOOD	FAIR	POOR
—	1300	900	700	300	N/A

Grade 4E

NIB	EXC.	V.G.	GOOD	FAIR	POOR
—	2350	1900	1300	400	N/A

Grade 5E

NIB	EXC.	V.G.	GOOD	FAIR	POOR
—	4200	3100	2550	600	N/A

Grade 6E

NIB	EXC.	V.G.	GOOD	FAIR	POOR
—	6300	5250	3200	900	N/A

Grade 7E

NIB	EXC.	V.G.	GOOD	FAIR	POOR
—	8350	6200	4100	1050	N/A

Sousa Grade

NIB	EXC.	V.G.	GOOD	FAIR	POOR
—	16500	11000	9000	2500	N/A

Knick Model Single-Barrel Trap

Knick Model trap gun was introduced during 1922. Based on design credited to Frank Knickerbocker. Design was simple and very serviceable. Had been in continuous production until 1988, when it was discontinued. Model available in Victory, 4, 5, 7 and Sousa Special Grades. Sousa was replaced by: $1,000 Grade in about 1936; which was replaced by $2,000 Grade by 1952; $2,500 Grade by 1960; $3,000 Grade by 1965; $5,000 Grade by 1974; finally, Dollar Grade in early 1980s, as cost of production increased. All Knick models were produced with automatic ejector and rubber anti-recoil pad.

Victory Grade

NIB	EXC.	V.G.	GOOD	FAIR	POOR
2500	1350	900	700	300	N/A

Grade 4E

NIB	EXC.	V.G.	GOOD	FAIR	POOR
3300	2450	1950	1100	500	N/A

Grade 5E

NIB	EXC.	V.G.	GOOD	FAIR	POOR
5500	4400	3300	2750	875	N/A

Grade 7E

NIB	EXC.	V.G.	GOOD	FAIR	POOR
8800	5500	4450	3300	1100	N/A

Sousa Grade

NIB	EXC.	V.G.	GOOD	FAIR	POOR
19000	11000	6600	4400	N/A	N/A

$1,000 to $2,500 Grades

NIB	EXC.	V.G.	GOOD	FAIR	POOR
16500	13500	8800	6500	2200	N/A

$3,000 through the Dollar Grade

NIB	EXC.	V.G.	GOOD	FAIR	POOR
13500	11000	6500	5500	2200	N/A

	NIB	EXC.	V.G.	GOOD	FAIR	POOR

Century Grade Trap (SKB)

12-gauge boxlock single-barrel shotgun, with 32" or 34" ventilated rib barrel. Automatic ejector. Blued, with walnut stock. Manufactured by SKB during 1970s.

	NIB	EXC.	V.G.	GOOD	FAIR	POOR
	—	900	700	550	350	300

Century II (SKB)

An improved version of above model.

	NIB	EXC.	V.G.	GOOD	FAIR	POOR
	—	950	700	600	450	350

ITHACA MODEL 66

Model 66 Supersingle—1963-1978

12-, 20-gauge or .410 bore lever action single-shot shotgun, with 24" barrel. Blued, with walnut stock. **NOTE:** 20-gauge and .410 bore command 50 percent premium.

NIB	EXC.	V.G.	GOOD	FAIR	POOR
300	180	150	125	100	50

Model 66 Youth Grade

Special gun offered for youth market in 20-gauge and .410 bore.

NIB	EXC.	V.G.	GOOD	FAIR	POOR
300	180	150	125	100	50

Model 66 Buck Buster (RS Barrel)

As above in 20-gauge, with Deerslayer 22" barrel fitted with rifle sights.

NIB	EXC.	V.G.	GOOD	FAIR	POOR
325	250	200	150	125	75

Model 66 Vent Rib

NIB	EXC.	V.G.	GOOD	FAIR	POOR
325	250	200	150	125	75

ITHACA AUTO & BURGLAR GUN/NFA, CURIO OR RELIC

Ithaca Auto & Burglar Gun, is a double-barreled 20-gauge smooth bore pistol. Manufactured by Ithaca Gun Company, Ithaca, New York, from 1922 to 1934. Total production approximately 4,500. Made by modifying Ithaca's standard field grade double-barrel shotgun, by shortening barrels and fitting receiver with a pistol-grip. Standard factory guns had blued 10" barrels, case hardened receivers, with legend "Auto & Burglar Gun/ Ithaca Gun Co./Ithaca, New York" and figure of a pointing dog stamped on each side. Barrel length on 21 guns inspected varied to 10.25" (typically in increments divisible by .125"), apparently from inexact factory quality control. Ithaca set a $37.50 retail price when gun was in production, but some dealers sold it for $40 or more. Production halted when government ruled Ithaca Auto & Burglar Gun to be a "firearm" in "any other weapon" category under National Firearms Act (NFA) of 1934.

There are two variations, termed Model A and Model B. Model A utilizes so-called Flues frame (named after Emil Flues who designed it in 1908). Its distinctive grip has a curving butt and large spur. Model A designed for 2.5" shells and is not considered safe to fire using modern ammunition. Approximately 2,500 Model A Auto & Burglar Guns were manufactured from 1922 to 1925, when Flues model was discontinued.

Model B utilizes so-called NID frame (short for New Ithaca Double). Introduced in 1926 and discontinued in 1948. NID is designed for modern ammunition and 2.75" shells. Has cocking indicators and different pistol-grip that is perpendicular to barrel, which lacks distinctive spur. Some Model Bs have been observed with rosettes or "stars" engraved in each side of receiver. Their significance is unknown at this time, but they probably are decorations. Approximately 2,000 Model B Auto & Burglar Guns were manufactured from 1926 to 1934.

Model A

Serial numbered from 343336 to 398365

	NIB	EXC.	V.G.	GOOD	FAIR	POOR
	—	2500	2000	1750	900	500

Model B

Serial numbered from 425000 to 464699

NOTE: Non-standard or special order guns command premiums of 100 percent or more. Original holsters (marked Auto and Burglar Gun/made by/ITHACA GUN CO./ithaca, n.y.) are extremely rare and worth $300 to $500 or more.

	NIB	EXC.	V.G.	GOOD	FAIR	POOR
	—	2750	2200	2000	950	550

ITHACA MODEL 37 REPEATER

Ithaca Model 37 Repeater was introduced in 1937 in 12-gauge, 1938 in 16-gauge and 1939 in 20-gauge. It underwent very few design changes throughout its long life, which ended in 1987. Ithaca Acquisition Corp. acquired assets of Ithaca Gun Company during 1987, renaming the

NIB	EXC.	V.G.	GOOD	FAIR	POOR

gun Model 87. Name has recently been changed again to M37, after assets of Ithaca Acquisition Corp. were purchased in May of 1996 by Ithaca Gun Company, LLC. All Model 37 guns were chambered only for 2.75 ammunition until 1983, when Magnum with 3" chamber was introduced to some configurations. Most Model 37 guns had blued metal and walnut stocks, with exception of Model 37 Field Grade series, which had matte finished metal and Birch stocks. 16-gauge guns were discontinued in 1973. Ithaca Gun closed in April, 2005, but reopened in 2006 as Ithaca Guns USA of Upper Sandusky, Ohio.

NOTE: 20-gauge guns made before 1968 will generally command a price premium.

Model 37/Standard Grade—1937-1983
Guns made before 1968 will enjoy 15 percent price premium; those made before World War II 30 percent price premium.

—	350	200	175	125	75

Model 37S/Skeet Grade—1937-1953
Guns made before World War II will enjoy 50 percent price premium.

—	600	400	350	250	100

Model 37T/Trap—1937-1953
Guns made before World War II will enjoy 50 percent price premium.

—	600	400	350	250	100

Model 37T/Target—1954-1961

—	600	400	350	250	100

Model 37R/Solid Rib—1940-1967
Guns made before World War II will enjoy 50 percent price premium.

—	400	275	225	200	75

Model 37 Military Marked (WWII)
One of the scarcest military shotguns. Built in three different configurations; 30" barrel, 20" barrel and 20" barrel with handguard and bayonet lug (Trench Gun). Rare shotgun, proceed with caution. **NOTE:** Add $200 for government release papers; 150 percent for Trench Gun configuration.

—	2000	1800	1500	—	—

Model 37RD/Deluxe Solid Rib—1954-1962

—	500	375	300	200	100

Model 37 Deerslayer—1959-1987
All Deerslayer models made before 1968 will enjoy 10 to 20 percent price premium.

—	300	250	200	125	75

Model 37 Deluxe Deerslayer—1959-1971

—	300	250	225	125	75

Model 37 Super Deluxe Deerslayer—1959-1987

—	450	325	275	200	100

Model 37 Supreme Grade—1967-1987

—	700	450	350	200	100

Model 37 Field Grade Standard—1983-1985

—	350	200	150	125	75

Model 37 Field Grade Vent Rib—1983-1986

—	350	250	200	125	75

Model 37 Basic Featherlight—1979-1983
Manufactured in 12-gauge only.

—	300	250	200	125	75

Model 37V/Vent Rib—1961-1983
Guns made before 1968 will enjoy 10 to 20 percent price premium.

—	350	300	175	150	75

Model 37RV/Deluxe Vent Rib—1961-1966

—	750	500	300	200	75

	NIB	EXC.	V.G.	GOOD	FAIR	POOR

Model 37D/Deluxe—1955-1977

Guns made before 1968 will enjoy 10 to 20 percent price premium.

	NIB	EXC.	V.G.	GOOD	FAIR	POOR
	—	400	250	175	125	75

Model 37DV/Deluxe Vent Rib—1961-1987

Guns made before 1968 will enjoy 10 to 20 percent price premium.

	NIB	EXC.	V.G.	GOOD	FAIR	POOR
	—	450	300	200	150	100

Model 37 Magnum 3" Chamber—1978-1987

	NIB	EXC.	V.G.	GOOD	FAIR	POOR
	—	400	300	225	125	75

Model 37 Field Grade Magnum—1984-1987

	NIB	EXC.	V.G.	GOOD	FAIR	POOR
	—	300	225	175	125	75

Model 37 UltraLight—1978 to 1987

UltraLight had aluminum alloy frame and trigger plate. Barrels marked Ultra Featherlight. Serial number prefaced with the mark "ULT". Both 12- and 20-gauges offered.

	NIB	EXC.	V.G.	GOOD	FAIR	POOR
	—	475	400	300	150	100

Model 37 English UltraLight—1982-1987

Same as Model 37 UltraLight, with English-style straight-grip stock.

	NIB	EXC.	V.G.	GOOD	FAIR	POOR
	—	500	450	350	150	100

Model 37 Camo

Introduced in 1985, with either green or brown camouflage finish. Offered only in 12-gauge.

	NIB	EXC.	V.G.	GOOD	FAIR	POOR
	—	350	300	200	150	100

Model 37 Bicentennial

Special model produced during 1976 to commemorate the 200th year anniversary of United States. Gun came with full-length trunk-style hard case and pewter belt buckle numbered to gun. Serial number was prefaced with "U.S.A." **NOTE:** Subtract 35 percent if original case and belt buckle are missing.

	NIB	EXC.	V.G.	GOOD	FAIR	POOR
	650	500	300	200	125	75

Model 37 Ducks Unlimited Commemorative, Auction Grade

Special edition made during 1977. Serial number sequence 40-DU0001 to 40-DU1125.

	NIB	EXC.	V.G.	GOOD	FAIR	POOR
	650	400	300	150	100	75

Model 37 Ducks Unlimited Commemorative, Trade Grade

Special edition made during 1977. Lower grade version of Auction Grade. Serial number preceded with the mark DU37040.

	NIB	EXC.	V.G.	GOOD	FAIR	POOR
	450	400	350	200	N/A	N/A

Model 37 2500 Series Centennial

Commemorative Model 37 12-gauge shotgun, with silver-plated receiver and press checkered stocks. Manufactured in 1984.

	NIB	EXC.	V.G.	GOOD	FAIR	POOR
	800	500	300	150	100	75

Model 37 Presentation Series Centennial

Commemorative Model 37 12-gauge shotgun. Gold-plated receiver and high grade hand checkered stocks. Manufactured from 1981 to 1986 and later on special order only.

	NIB	EXC.	V.G.	GOOD	FAIR	POOR
	1500	800	500	150	100	—

Hi-Grade Ithaca Model 37 Guns

Ithaca Gun company offered custom engraving services. Either, from its in-house engraver one of which was retained until about 1972, or through an outside contract engraver, who was usually William Mains. Many customers requested some degree of custom work and guns with various patterns turn up from time to time. Four standard engraving patterns offered to customers, Grade 1, Grade 2, Grade 3 and very elaborate $1,000 Grade pattern. Increasing production costs forced $1,000 Grade to become $2,000 Grade, $2,500 and finally $3,000 Grade over the years. **NOTE:** All factory engraved Model 37 guns are rare and require an expert appraiser to determine an accurate value.

$1,000 Grade

Model 37, with engraved receiver, gold inlays and well-figured walnut stock. Manufactured between 1940 and 1942.

	NIB	EXC.	V.G.	GOOD	FAIR	POOR
	10000	5000	3000	2000	N/A	N/A

	NIB	EXC.	V.G.	GOOD	FAIR	POOR

$2,000 Grade

Manufactured from 1946 to 1957.

	NIB	EXC.	V.G.	GOOD	FAIR	POOR
	10000	5000	3000	2000	N/A	N/A

$3,000 Grade

As above. Manufactured from 1958 to 1967.

	NIB	EXC.	V.G.	GOOD	FAIR	POOR
	8000	4000	2500	1500	N/A	N/A

Model 37 Law Enforcement Weapons

Ithaca Gun Company entered the law enforcement market in 1962. Introduced Model 37 Military and Police (M&P) and Model 37DS Police special (DSPS). M&P Model styled after riot guns, made for various military contracts. DSPS styled after Ithaca Deerslayer. Both models offered with 8-shot capacity after 1968. Chrome finish was an available option after 1976. Both models usually had ring turned slide handles. Only those models available to general public, i.e. barrel lengths of 18" or longer, are listed. **NOTE:** Add 25 percent if marked with police department; 20 percent for 8-shot model in NIB or EXC. condition; additional 15 percent for chrome plated models in similar condition.

Military and Police (M&P)—1962-1986

	550	450	250	200	125	75

DS Police Special—1962-1986

	575	450	250	200	125	75

ITHACA MODEL 87 REPEATER

During 1987, many assets of bankrupt Ithaca Gun Company were purchased by Ithaca Acquisition Corporation. Manufacture of Model 37 resumed that summer, after the gun was renamed Model 87. Many models offered by the old company were continued. All Model 87 field guns were produced with ventilated ribs. All Deerslayer models continued rifle sights, used on Model 37 guns.

Model 87 Basic—1989-1994

Early models had birchwood stocks, later production had walnut. All had ring turned slide handles.

	350	300	250	175	125	75

Model 87 Magnum

12- or 20-gauge magnum slide action shotgun, with 25" barrel. Fitted with screw-in choke tubes and ventilated rib, that is similar to Model 37. Blued, with walnut stock.

	400	350	300	225	150	100

Model 87 Field Grade—1987-1990

Stocks were walnut, with pressed checkering.

	325	250	200	175	125	75

Model 87 Camo—1987-1994

	300	250	200	175	125	75

Model 87 Turkey Gun—1987-1996

	325	250	200	175	125	75

Model 87 Deluxe—1987-1996

Buttstocks and slide handle were walnut, with machine cut checkered pattern.

	375	300	250	200	125	75

Model 87 Ultralite—1987-1990

All IAC manufactured Ultralite guns carry old Model 37 serial number.

	500	350	250	175	125	75

Model 87 English—1993-1996

Hand-checkered walnut stocks. Slide handle styled after pre-war Model 37 slide handle.

	400	350	250	175	125	75

Model 87 Ultralite Deluxe

	400	350	300	250	125	75

Model 87 Supreme Grade—1987-1996

High grade walnut stocks, with hand checkering. Metal had extra fine polish and finish.

	1000	700	500	300	250	100

	NIB	EXC.	V.G.	GOOD	FAIR	POOR

Model 87 Deerslayer Basic—1989-1996

Walnut oil finish butt and slide handle stocks. Slide handle was classic ring turned style.

	300	275	250	200	125	75

Model 87 Deerslayer—1989-1996

Sometimes advertised as Model 87 Deerslayer Field. Buttstock and slide handle were walnut. Usually had pressed checkered pattern. Slide handle was beavertail style.

	350	300	250	200	125	75

Model 87 Deluxe Deerslayer—1989-1996

Buttstock and slide handle were walnut, with machine-cut checkering pattern. Slide handle was beavertail.

	400	350	250	200	125	75

Model 87 Deerslayer II—1988-1996

Model had fixed rifle barrel and Monte Carlo buttstock. Small number of guns specially made with fast twist barrel to handle Brenneke ammunition. Marked "BRENNEKE" on receiver. **NOTE:** Brenneke-marked guns will command a 30 percent price premium.

	550	450	350	200	125	75

Model 87 Home Protection and Law Enforcement

Ithaca Acquisition Corporation continued production of many law enforcement firearms produced by Ithaca Gun Company. Only those models available to general public are listed.

Military & Police—1987-1996

Generally produced with non-checkered walnut buttstock and ring turned slide handle, both of which were oil finished. **NOTE:** Add 20 percent for 8-shot model in NIB or excellent condition; additional 15 percent for chrome plated models in similar condition.

	450	395	275	200	125	75

DS Police Special—1987-1996

Produced with either pressed checkered or non-checkered walnut buttstock and ring-turned slide handle, both lacquer finished. Metal usually finished with a commercial polished blue, but chrome-plated finish also available. **NOTE:** Add 20 percent for 8-shot model in NIB or excellent condition; add an additional 15 percent for chrome plated models in similar condition.

	450	395	275	200	125	75

NEW MODEL 37

During 1996, assets of bankrupt Ithaca Acquisition Corporation were purchased by a new company named Ithaca Gun Company, LLC. One of the first public actions of the new firm was to rename Model 87, Model 37. Before resuming production later that year, serial number of new Model 37 is prefaced with letter "M".

Model 37 Deerslayer II

Model offered in 12- and 20-gauge. Fitted with either 20" or 25" barrels, with rifled bores. Barrels are fixed to receiver. Magazine capacity 5 rounds. Walnut stock. Weight approximately 7 lbs. In 2001 a 16-gauge version, with fixed rifled barrel was offered.

	950	800	650	475	300	200

Smooth Bore Deluxe

Offered in 12-, 16- or 20-gauge, with interchangeable barrels in 20" or 25" and smoothbore for deer. Walnut stock. Magazine capacity 5 rounds. Weight approximately 6.75 lbs. Discontinued.

	675	400	350	275	200	100

Rifled Deluxe

Same as above in 12- and 20-gauge only, with rifled barrels. Discontinued.

	675	400	350	275	200	100

Deerslayer III

Updated slug-only version of classic Model 37 pump-action shotgun, in 12- or 20-gauge. Fully rifled heavy fluted 26" barrel, with 1:28 twist. Bottom ejection. Fancy black walnut stock and fore-end. Blued barrel and receiver.

	1100	950	800	600	400	200

Model 37 28 Gauge

28-gauge pump action shotgun. Scaled down receiver, with traditional Model 37 bottom ejection and easy takedown. 26" or 28" barrel, black walnut stock and fore-end. Available in Fancy

NIB	EXC.	V.G.	GOOD	FAIR	POOR

"A", Fancy "AA" and Fancy "AAA" grades, with increasingly elaborate receiver engraving and decoration. Special order only. Values shown are for "Fancy A" grade.

| 1000 | 850 | 525 | 400 | 350 | 200 |

Model 37 Deluxe Field

Model offered in 12-, 16- and 20-gauge, with interchangeable vent rib barrels of 26", 28" or 30" (12-gauge only). Walnut stock. Magazine capacity 5 rounds. Weight about 7 lbs. Discontinued.

| 625 | 475 | 375 | 250 | 150 | 100 |

Model 37 Deluxe Field English Style

Model offered in 20-gauge only, with 24", 26" or 28" vent rib barrels. Walnut stock. Weight about 7 lbs. Magazine capacity 5 rounds. Discontinued.

| 650 | 475 | 375 | 250 | 150 | 100 |

Model 37 Ultra Featherlight Grouse Special

Based on Classic Model 37, with bottom ejection. Features aluminum receiver and 24" vent rib barrel, with choke tubes. Straight grip stock of American black walnut. Discontinued.

| 650 | 525 | 395 | 275 | 150 | 100 |

Model 37 Ultra Featherlight Youth

Similar to above, with 22" barrel and 12.75" length of pull. Buttstock with ventilated recoil pad. Discontinued.

| 600 | 475 | 375 | 250 | 150 | 100 |

Model 37 Sporting Clays

Model features choice of 24", 26" or 28" wide vent rib barrels, with Briley choke tubes. Receiver has antiqued finish, with scroll engraving and high grade American black walnut. Discontinued.

| 1350 | 1000 | 750 | 575 | 300 | 150 |

Model 37 Trap

Model has similar features as sporting clays, with 30" wide vent rib barrel.

| 900 | 750 | 650 | 475 | 300 | 200 |

Model 37 Women's Endowment Shotgun

Offered in 16- or 20-gauge, with straight-grip stock. Length of pull designed for woman's height of 5'5". American walnut stock, with cut checkering. Discontinued.

| 635 | 500 | 375 | 250 | 150 | 100 |

Model 37 Waterfowler

Available in 12-gauge only, with 28" steel shot barrel. Camo pattern stock. Weight about 7 lbs. Magazine capacity 5 rounds.

| 850 | 700 | 600 | 500 | 275 | 200 |

Model 37 New Classic

Available in 12-, 16- or 20- gauge, with hand checkered walnut stock. Choice of pistol- or straight-grip. High polish bolt and other component parts. Sunburst recoil pad. Interchangeable vent rib barrels in either 26" or 28". Weight about 7 lbs. Discontinued.

| 810 | 625 | 475 | 375 | 250 | 150 |

Model 37 Turkeyslayer

First version of this model made from 1996 to 2004, with 22" barrel and camo stock. Offered in 12- or 20-gauge. Later model introduced in 2010, in 12-gauge only, with 24" fixed barrel, synthetic stock with matte black or camo finish. Available with laminated thumb-hole stock. Other features include Briley extended and ported extra-full turkey choke, lengthened forcing cone, Pachmayr Decelerator recoil pad, Tru-Glo fiber optic front sight. Weight: 7.6 lbs. with standard stock, 8.2 lbs with thumb-hole.

| 800 | 650 | 550 | 400 | 275 | 200 |

Model 37 Home Defense

In 12- or 20-gauge, with 18.5" or 20" barrel, rifle sights and matte blue finish. Black synthetic or wood stock, 20" fixed barrel rifle sights. Magazine holds 8 rounds (12-gauge only); 5 rounds (12- or 20-gauge).

| 700 | 600 | 500 | 400 | 275 | 200 |

Model 37 Hogslayer

In 12-gauge, with 20" rifled barrel and sights. Tubular magazine holds 8 rounds. Matte blued barrel, action and finish. Synthetic stock. Discontinued.

| 450 | 400 | 355 | 300 | 250 | 200 |

	NIB	EXC.	V.G.	GOOD	FAIR	POOR

MODEL 51

A 12- or 20-gauge semi-automatic shotgun, with 26", 28" or 30" ventilated rib barrels. Blued, with walnut stock. Manufactured from 1970 to 1985 as listed.

Model 51A Standard
Plain barrel. **NOTE:** Ventilated rib add $100.

	NIB	EXC.	V.G.	GOOD	FAIR	POOR
	—	400	325	250	150	75

Model 51A Magnum
3" chamber. **NOTE:** Ventilated rib add $100.

	NIB	EXC.	V.G.	GOOD	FAIR	POOR
	—	425	350	275	175	75

Model 51A Waterfowler
Matte finished.

	NIB	EXC.	V.G.	GOOD	FAIR	POOR
	—	425	350	275	175	75

Model 51A Deerslayer

	NIB	EXC.	V.G.	GOOD	FAIR	POOR
	—	325	275	225	150	75

Model 51A Turkey Gun

	NIB	EXC.	V.G.	GOOD	FAIR	POOR
	—	425	350	275	175	75

Model 51 Supreme Trap

	NIB	EXC.	V.G.	GOOD	FAIR	POOR
	—	425	375	325	250	75

Model 51 Supreme Skeet

	NIB	EXC.	V.G.	GOOD	FAIR	POOR
	—	450	400	350	275	200

Model 51 Ducks Unlimited Commemorative

	NIB	EXC.	V.G.	GOOD	FAIR	POOR
	600	500	375	325	275	200

Model 51 Presentation
Engraved receiver.

	NIB	EXC.	V.G.	GOOD	FAIR	POOR
	1500	1250	1000	750	500	300

MAG-10

A 10-gauge magnum semi-automatic shotgun, manufactured in a variety of barrel lengths, styles and finishes. Manufactured from 1975 to 1986 as listed. **NOTE:** Market for Ithaca Mag-10s has declined somewhat, with success of 3.5" 12-gauge load. Apparently because most owners consider their Mag-10s as hunting weapons, not collectors' pieces. Nevertheless, NIB or Excellent+ examples still command fairly high prices, if right buyer can be found.

Standard Grade

	NIB	EXC.	V.G.	GOOD	FAIR	POOR
	—	750	650	600	300	250

Standard Vent Rib Grade

	NIB	EXC.	V.G.	GOOD	FAIR	POOR
	—	850	700	675	550	250

Deluxe Vent Rib Grade

	NIB	EXC.	V.G.	GOOD	FAIR	POOR
	—	1000	775	750	600	250

Supreme Grade

	NIB	EXC.	V.G.	GOOD	FAIR	POOR
	—	1100	850	800	700	250

Roadblocker—Military and Police Model

	NIB	EXC.	V.G.	GOOD	FAIR	POOR
	—	750	650	600	300	250

Presentation Grade
Engraved, gold-inlaid, 200 made.

	NIB	EXC.	V.G.	GOOD	FAIR	POOR
	1875	1500	1100	900	750	300

National Wild Turkey Federation
1985 manufacture.

	NIB	EXC.	V.G.	GOOD	FAIR	POOR
	850	700	600	550	450	350

	NIB	EXC.	V.G.	GOOD	FAIR	POOR

RIFLES

Model X5-C

.22-caliber semi-automatic rifle, with 7-shot magazine. 10-shot magazine available as an extra cost option. Blued, with walnut stock. Manufactured between 1958 and 1964.

NIB	EXC.	V.G.	GOOD	FAIR	POOR
400	200	150	100	75	50

Model X5T Lightning

.22-caliber tubular feed auto-loading rifle, produced between 1959 and 1963. Some models stocked with curly maple stocks. **NOTE:** These guns will command a 25 percent price premium.

NIB	EXC.	V.G.	GOOD	FAIR	POOR
450	175	150	100	75	50

Model X-15 Lightning

Similar to above. Manufactured between 1964 and 1966.

NIB	EXC.	V.G.	GOOD	FAIR	POOR
450	175	150	100	75	50

Model 49 Saddlegun—1961-1979

.22-caliber lever action single-shot rifle, with 18.5" barrel, fixed sights, alloy receiver and hardwood stock. Offered chambered for .22 Magnum in 1962. **NOTE:** Deduct 20 percent for .22 LR.

NIB	EXC.	V.G.	GOOD	FAIR	POOR
350	220	175	100	50	25

Deluxe Grade

Fitted with gold plated trigger and hammer. Equipped with sling and sling swivels.

NIB	EXC.	V.G.	GOOD	FAIR	POOR
400	250	200	125	50	25

Presentation Grade

High grade wood and engraved frame.

NIB	EXC.	V.G.	GOOD	FAIR	POOR
425	300	250	200	50	25

Model 49R—1968-1971

Lever action .22-caliber tubular feed repeater. Magazine capacity 15 LR cartridges.

NIB	EXC.	V.G.	GOOD	FAIR	POOR
350	250	200	150	50	25

Model 72 Saddlegun—1973-1979

.22- or .22 Magnum caliber lever action rifle, with 18.5" barrel. Tubular magazine, open sights and walnut stock. Made by Erma in Germany.

NIB	EXC.	V.G.	GOOD	FAIR	POOR
300	250	225	200	100	25

LSA-55 or 65

Bolt-action sporting rifle, manufactured in a variety of calibers and barrel lengths, by Tikka of Finland. Imported between 1969 and 1977 in models listed.

LSA-55 Standard

NIB	EXC.	V.G.	GOOD	FAIR	POOR
—	500	350	300	250	175

LSA-55 Deluxe

NIB	EXC.	V.G.	GOOD	FAIR	POOR
—	600	375	325	275	200

LSA-55 Varmint Heavy Barrel

NIB	EXC.	V.G.	GOOD	FAIR	POOR
—	600	400	350	300	225

LSA-55 Turkey Gun

12-gauge by .222 Remington caliber over/under combination rifle/shotgun, with 24.5" barrels, single trigger, exposed hammer and walnut stock. Manufactured in Finland by Tikka between 1970 and 1981.

NIB	EXC.	V.G.	GOOD	FAIR	POOR
—	900	700	450	350	275

LSA-65 Long Action

NIB	EXC.	V.G.	GOOD	FAIR	POOR
—	500	350	300	250	175

LSA-65 Deluxe

NIB	EXC.	V.G.	GOOD	FAIR	POOR
—	600	375	325	275	200

HANDGUNS

Model 1911

First 1911 made by Ithaca since WWII. Chambered in .45 ACP, with hand-lapped carbon steel frame and slide. Checkered front strap, skeletonized hammer and trigger, checkered cocobolo grips and choice of adjustable Novak Combat or Bomar Target sights. Other features include stainless steel Match grade barrel bushing and full-length two-piece guide rod. Optional lockable

NIB	EXC.	V.G.	GOOD	FAIR	POOR	

canvas case. Introduced in 2011. **NOTE:** Add $100 for case.

1440	1225	1000	750	—	—

X-Caliber

.22- to .44 Magnum caliber single-shot pistol, with 10" or 15" barrels. Featuring dual firing pin system so that interchangeable barrels could be used. Model 20 is blued; Model 30 Teflon coated. Introduced in 1988. Made by Sterling Arms. **NOTE:** Add 20 percent premium for .44.

600	475	300	225	175	125

IVER JOHNSON ARMS, INC.
Rockledge, Florida

This brand was resurrected in 2006 by Iver Johnson Arms, Inc., a new company based in Rockledge, Florida. This company manufactures several 1911-pattern pistols and imports a series of self-defense pump-action shotguns from Turkey. From 2006 to 2009, a four-barreled derringer, the Frontier Four and two 1911-type pistols under the Raven brand were manufactured.

Frontier Four Derringer

Four-barrel, stainless .22 LR single-action derringer, with unique rotating firing pin. Based on old Sharps derringer. Weight 5.5 oz. Introduced 2006. Discontinued.

195	150	100	75	50	—

Eagle Target Series 1911 .45

All-steel 7+1 capacity 1911 .45 ACP, with 5" Government or 4.5" Commander barrel. Adjustable white outline rear sight and trigger. Polished blue. Introduced 2006. **NOTE:** Add $150 for LR model with accessory rail.

650	550	425	315	250	150

Eagle Target Series 1911 .22 LR

Aluminum slide and frame, 15+1 capacity 1911 .22 LR, with 5" Government or 4.5" Commander barrel. Weight 19 oz. Adjustable white outline rear sight and trigger. Blued or stainless. Introduced 2006.

600	500	400	300	200	100

Raven Series 1911 .45

All-steel 7+1 capacity 1911 .45 ACP, with 5" Government or 4.5" Commander barrel. Fixed sights. Matte blue, Parkerized or two-tone. Introduced 2006. Discontinued.

550	425	315	250	150	100

Raven Series 1911 .22 LR

Aluminum slide and frame, 15+1 capacity 1911 in .22 LR, with 5" Government or 4.5" Commander barrel. Weight 19 oz. Fixed sights. Matte blued or stainless two-tone finish. Introduced 2006. Discontinued.

550	425	315	250	150	100

1911A1

Several variations of the Series 70 type 1911A1 are offered in .45 ACP and 9mm chamberings, in full-size, Commander-size and Officers models. These are available in a wide variety of finishes, including matte blue, polished blue, O.D. Green, Coyote Tan, Pink, Zombie and others. Values are for standard blue finish. **NOTE:** Add 10 to 15 percent for special finishes.

500	450	400	300	250	200

PAS Shotgun

A series of pump-action shotguns designed primarily for self-defense use. All are 12-gauge models, with lightweight alloy black receivers, black polymer stocks with straight- or pistol-grip and choice of sighting systems and accessory rails. **NOTE:** Add 10 to 15 percent for pistol-grip stock and fiber-optic sights.

260	220	180	150	120	90

IVER JOHNSON ARMS & CYCLE WORKS
Middlesex, New Jersey
See — AMAC

Established in 1883 in Fitchburg, Massachusetts. Company has produced a wide variety of firearms during its existence.

HANDGUNS

Trade Name Revolvers

Series of spur trigger revolvers made by Iver Johnson. Bearing only trade names such as Encore, Eclipse, Favorite, Tycoon and Eagle. In general value for these revolvers are listed.

—	250	170	120	95	65

	NIB	EXC.	V.G.	GOOD	FAIR	POOR

Safety Automatic Double-Action

.22, .32 CF or .38 CF caliber double-action revolver. Produced in a variety of barrel lengths with-/without exposed hammers. Manufactured between 1893 and 1950.

	NIB	EXC.	V.G.	GOOD	FAIR	POOR
	—	250	170	120	95	65

Model 1900

.22- to .38-caliber double-action revolver, with 2.5", 4.5" or 6" barrel. Blued or nickel-plated. Rubber grips and no cartridge ejecting system. Manufactured between 1900 and 1947.

	—	250	170	120	95	65

Safety Cycle Automatic

Similar to Safety Automatic, with 2" barrel.

	—	250	170	120	95	65

Petite

.22 Short caliber double-action folding trigger revolver, with 1" barrel and 7-shot cylinder. Nickel-plated, with rubber grips. Introduced in 1909.

	—	350	250	200	150	100

Supershot Sealed 8

.22-caliber double-action revolver, with 6" barrel. Counterbored 8-shot cylinder. Blued, with rubber grips. Manufactured from 1919 to 1957.

	—	250	170	120	95	65

Protector Sealed 8

As above, with 2.5" barrel.

	—	250	170	120	95	65

Supershot 9

Similar to Supershot Sealed 8, with 9-shot un-counterbored cylinder. Manufactured between 1929 and 1949.

	—	250	170	120	95	65

Trigger Cocker Single-Action

.22-caliber single-action revolver, with 6" barrel and 8-shot counterbored cylinder. Blued, with walnut grips. Manufactured between 1940 and 1947.

	—	200	125	100	50	25

.22 Target Single-Action

As above, with adjustable sights and grips. Manufactured between 1938 and 1948.

	—	250	190	150	125	65

Model 844

.22-caliber double-action revolver, with 4.5" or 6" barrel. Adjustable sights and 8-shot cylinder. Manufactured in 1950s.

	—	225	140	100	80	40

Model 855

As above, with single-action and 6" barrel. Manufactured in 1950s.

	—	225	140	100	80	40

Model 55A Sportsmen Target

.22-caliber single-action revolver, with 4.75" or 6" barrel. Fixed sights and 8-shot cylinder. Blued, with walnut grips.

	—	200	125	100	75	35

Model 55S-A Cadet

.22- to .38-caliber single-action revolver, with 2.5" barrel and fixed sights. Blued, with plastic grips. Introduced in 1955.

	—	250	170	120	95	65

Model 57A Target

As above, with 4.5" or 6" barrel and adjustable sights. Manufactured between 1955 and 1975.

	—	175	110	85	60	35

	NIB	EXC.	V.G.	GOOD	FAIR	POOR

Model 66 Trailsman

.22-caliber double-action revolver, with 6" barrel. Adjustable sights and 8-shot cylinder. Blued, with walnut grips. Manufactured between 1958 and 1975.

	NIB	EXC.	V.G.	GOOD	FAIR	POOR
	—	125	75	65	50	25

Model 67 Viking

As above, with safety hammer.

	—	125	75	65	50	25

Model 67S Viking Snub

Same as above. Fitted with 2" barrel.

	—	125	75	65	50	25

Model 50

.22- or .22 Magnum single-action revolver, with 4.75" or 6" barrel and 8-shot cylinder. Either fixed or adjustable sights. Also known as Sidewinder. Manufactured between 1961 and 1975.

	—	125	75	65	50	25

American Bulldog

.22- to .38-caliber double-action revolver, with 2.5" or 4" barrel. Adjustable sights. Blued or nickel-plated, with plastic grips. Manufactured between 1974 and 1976.

	—	175	100	75	50	25

Rookie

.38-caliber revolver, with 4" barrel and 5-shot cylinder. Blued or nickel-plated, with plastic grips.

	—	175	100	75	50	25

Cattleman Series

Manufactured by Aldo Uberti. Listed under that name in this book.

Model X300 Pony

.380 semi-automatic pistol, with 3" barrel and 6-shot magazine. Blued, with plastic grips. Introduced in 1975.

	—	275	195	165	135	85

Trailsman

.22-caliber semi-automatic pistol, with 4.5" or 6" barrel and 10-shot magazine. Blued, with plastic or walnut grips.

	—	275	195	165	135	85

TP22/TP25 Pistol

.22 or .25 ACP caliber double-action semi-automatic pistol, with 2.8" barrel and 7-shot magazine. Blued or nickel-plated, with plastic grips.

	—	275	195	165	135	85

RIFLES

Model X

Bolt action .22-caliber single-shot rifle. Fitted with 22" barrel, open sights and pistol-grip. Manufactured between 1927 and 1932.

	—	175	110	90	70	40

Model XA

As above, with Lyman receiver sight swivels, leather strap and ivory bead. Manufactured between 1927 and 1932.

	—	325	225	175	130	80

Model 2X

Fitted with 24" heavy barrel and adjustable sights. Manufactured between 1932 and 1955.

	—	400	300	250	150	100

Li'L Champ

Chambered for .22 LR cartridge. Bolt-action single-shot rifle. Weighs about 3 lbs.

	—	125	85	70	50	30

	NIB	EXC.	V.G.	GOOD	FAIR	POOR

Long Range Rifle

Single-shot bolt-action rifle, chambered for .50-caliber Browning cartridge. Fitted with 29" fluted barrel and adjustable trigger. Bipod. Comes supplied with 20 power Leupold scope. Limited production. Weight about 36 lbs. Manufactured between 1988 and 1993.

	NIB	EXC.	V.G.	GOOD	FAIR	POOR
	—	4600	4000	3000	2500	1000

JJ 9mm Carbine

Copy of U.S. military M1. Blued finish and hardwood stock. Magazine is 20 rounds. Chambered for 9mm cartridge. Built between 1985 and 1986. **NOTE:** Add 10 percent for folding stock. Deduct 5 percent for plastic stock.

	—	500	400	250	175	100

Delta-786 Carbine

Similar to M1 carbine in 9mm only. Matte finish. Manufactured in 1989.

	—	500	400	250	175	100

Carbine .30 Caliber

Similar to M1 carbine and chambered for .30 carbine cartridge. Offered in various stock configurations. Built from 1985 to 1986; again in 1988 to 1993. **NOTE:** Paratrooper model add $50; Johnson 5.7mm caliber deduct $75. No premium for stainless steel.

	—	600	485	315	250	150

U.S. Carbine .22 Caliber

Same as above. Chambered for .22 LR or .22 Magnum cartridge. Built in 1985 and 1986; again in 1988. Fitted with 15-round magazine.

	—	350	295	225	150	75

Slide Action Targetmaster

Chambered for .22 LR or .22 Magnum cartridge. Rifle has 15-round tubular magazine. Manufactured between 1985 and 1988; again in 1990.

	—	250	170	125	100	50

Wagonmaster Model EW .22 HBL Lever Action

Chambered for .22 LR or .22 Magnum cartridge. Fitted with hardwood stock. Blued finish. Grooved scope mounts. Built in 1985 and 1986; again between 1988 and 1990.

	—	250	175	130	100	50

Model IJ .22 HB Semi-Automatic (Trail Blazer)

Chambered for .22 LR only, with 10-round magazine. Manufactured only in 1985.

	—	225	130	100	60	40

SHOTGUNS

Champion

Single-barrel shotgun, manufactured in a variety of gauges, as well as .44- or .45-caliber, with 26" to 32" barrels. External hammers and automatic ejectors. Blued, with walnut stock. Manufactured between 1909 and 1956.

	—	250	200	150	75	25

Matted Rib Grade

As above in 12-, 16- or 20-gauge, with matte rib barrel. Manufactured between 1909 and 1948.

	—	275	225	175	95	50

Trap Grade

As above in 12-gauge, with 32" ventilated rib barrel. Manufactured between 1909 and 1942.

	—	525	350	275	175	100

Hercules Grade

Boxlock double-barrel shotgun, manufactured in a variety of gauges, with 26" to 32" barrels. Double triggers and extractors. Blued, with walnut stock.

	—	1350	1050	775	550	350

	NIB	EXC.	V.G.	GOOD	FAIR	POOR

NOTE: Add premium for these features:

Single trigger—25 percent
28-gauge—100 percent
20-gauge—50 percent
Engraving—100 percent

Ejectors—25 percent
.410 bore—100 percent
16-gauge—20 percent
Vent rib—25 percent

Skeeter Model

As above, but more finely finished. Discontinued in 1946.

	NIB	EXC.	V.G.	GOOD	FAIR	POOR
	—	2250	1600	1050	750	300

NOTE: Add premium for these features:

Single trigger—25 percent
28-gauge—100 percent
20-gauge—50 percent
Engraving—100 percent

Ejectors—25 percent
.410 bore—100 percent
16-gauge—20 percent
Vent rib—25 percent

Super Trap

12-gauge boxlock double barrel shotgun, with 32" full choked barrels and extractors. Discontinued in 1942. **NOTE:** Add 50 percent for Miller single selective trigger; 35 percent for non-selective single trigger.

	NIB	EXC.	V.G.	GOOD	FAIR	POOR
	—	2650	2000	1350	850	350

Silver Shadow

12-gauge boxlock over/under shotgun, with 26" or 28" ventilated rib barrels. Double triggers and extractors. Blued, with walnut stock. Manufactured in Italy and imported by Iver Johnson. **NOTE:** Available with single trigger, which would increase values listed by approximately 25 percent.

	NIB	EXC.	V.G.	GOOD	FAIR	POOR
	—	550	400	350	300	200

IXL
New York, New York

Pocket Revolver

.31-caliber double-action percussion revolver, with 4" octagonal barrel and 6-shot cylinder. Blued, with walnut grips. Barrel marked "IXL N.York". Approximately 750 made without hammer spurs and 150 with side mounted hammers during 1850s.

	NIB	EXC.	V.G.	GOOD	FAIR	POOR
	—	—	—	1250	600	300

Navy Revolver

As above in .36-caliber. Approximately 100 made, with both center and side mounted hammers during 1850s.

	NIB	EXC.	V.G.	GOOD	FAIR	POOR
	—	—	—	3250	1400	500

J

NIB	EXC.	V.G.	GOOD	FAIR	POOR

JACQUESMART, JULES
Liege, Belgium

Le Monobloc

6.35mm semi-automatic pistol, with 2" barrel and 6-shot magazine. Slide marked "Le Monobloc/ Pistolet Automatique/Brevefte". Blued, with composition grips. Production ceased in 1914.

	550	450	350	200	100
—	550	450	350	200	100

JACQUITH, ELIJAH
Brattleboro, Vermont

Revolving Under Hammer Rifle

Extremely rare .40 caliber percussion revolving rifle, with 34" round-octagonal barrel and 8-shot cylinder. Believed that approximately 25 of these rifles were made in 1838 and 1839. Barrel marked "E. Jaquith Brattleboro. Vt." Prospective purchasers should secure a qualified appraisal prior to acquisition.

		V.G.	GOOD	FAIR	POOR
—	—	18000	7250	2200	2200

JAGER WAFFENFABIK
Suhl, Germany

Jager Semi-Automatic Pistol

7.65mm caliber semi-automatic pistol, with 3" barrel and 7-shot magazine. Largely made from steel stampings. Weight approximately 23 oz. Blued, with plastic grips. Slide marked "Jager-Pistole DRP Angem". Approximately 5,500 were made prior to 1914. **NOTE:** Add 50 percent for Imperial proofed examples.

	EXC.	V.G.	GOOD	FAIR	POOR
—	500	375	325	175	100

JEFFERY, W. J. & CO. LTD.
London, England

Company produced high quality shotguns and rifles. Their products have been used by wealthy sportsmen for many years. They produced guns under their own banner and also as contractors for other distributors. They made guns sold by Army & Navy Department Store in London. Guns of this type were basically custom-ordered and as such are extremely hard to evaluate on a general basis. We supply estimated values for standard rifle models.

Single-Shot

Built on Farquharson Falling Block action. Chambered for many calibers up to .600 Nitro Express. Also a custom-order gun and barrel length was optional. Usually finish is blued with folding express sights. Select hand-checkered walnut stock. These were high quality firearms and values would be determined, for the most part, by options and embellishments on particular specimens. Individual appraisal is definitely advised. Caliber in which rifle is chambered will also have an effect on value. Obsolete calibers bring less and larger express calibers bring more.

	EXC.	V.G.	GOOD	FAIR	POOR
—	9000	6750	3750	21700	900

Boxlock Double Rifle

Boxlock chambered for many different calibers. Found with either top or underlever action and has folding express sights. Stock and forearm are select hand-checkered walnut and finish is usually blue. This was a custom-order proposition and values can be affected by many variables such as caliber options and embellishment. Damascus barreled hammer guns are worth approximately 50 percent less.

	EXC.	V.G.	GOOD	FAIR	POOR
—	22000	15250	10950	3850	2500

Sidelock Double Rifle

Has detachable sidelocks. Otherwise comparable to boxlock version.

	EXC.	V.G.	GOOD	FAIR	POOR
—	35000	22500	12250	7000	4000

JENISON, J. & CO.
Southbridge, Connecticut

Under Hammer Pistol

.28 caliber single-shot under hammer percussion pistol, with 4" half-octagonal barrel marked "J.Jenison & Co./Southbridge, Mass.". Blued, with maple or oak grip. Manufactured during 1850s.

		V.G.	GOOD	FAIR	POOR
—	—	1550	850	400	200

JENKS-HERKIMER
New York
Manufacturer—E. Remington & Son

Jenks Carbine
Identical to Jenks "Mule Ear Carbine" listed in previous entry, except barrel length is 24.25" and lock fitted with Maynard tape primer. Lock marked "Remington's/Herkimer/N.Y." Barrel marked "W. Jenks/USN/RC/P/Cast Steel". Approximately 1,000 carbines manufactured circa 1846.

—	—	5000	4250	1750	750

JENKS-MERRILL
Baltimore, Maryland

An alteration of Jenks Carbine listed previously to a breech loading system developed by J.H. Merrill. Conventional sidelock marked "J. H. Merrill Balto./Pat. July 1858". Breech retains mark "Wm. Jenks/USN". Approximately 300 altered between 1858 and 1860.

—	—	9750	8500	3500	950

JENKS CARBINE
Springfield, Massachusetts
Manufacturer—N. P. Ames

Jenks "Mule Ear Carbine"
.54 caliber percussion side hammer carbine, with 24.5" round barrel and full length stock secured by two barrel bands. Lock case hardened, barrel browned and furniture of brass. Lock marked "N.P.Ames/Springfield/Mass.". Barrel stamped "Wm.Jenks/USN" followed by inspector's initials. Buttstock carries an inspector's cartouche. Approximately 4,250 made between 1841 and 1846. Some marked "USR" for "U.S. Revenue Cutter Service". These would bring approximately 80 percent premium over values listed. However, prospective purchasers should secure a qualified appraisal prior to acquisition.

—	—	4500	3750	1500	600

Jenks Navy Rifle
As above, with 30" round barrel and full-length stock secured by three barrel bands. Approximately 1,000 made for U.S. Navy in 1841.

—	—	5000	4250	1750	750

JENNINGS
Windsor, Vermont
Manufacturer—Robbins & Lawrence
See—Winchester Repeating Arms

JENNINGS F. A., INC.
Carson City, Nevada

Distributor of arms manufactured by Calwestco in Chino, California and Bryco Firearms in Carson City, Nevada.

J-22
.22-caliber semi-automatic pistol, with 2.5" barrel and 6-shot magazine. Aluminum, finished in bright chrome, Teflon or satin nickel. Plastic or wood grips.

150	90	75	65	50	35

Bryco Model 25
.25 caliber semi-automatic pistol, with 2.5" barrel and 6-shot magazine. Constructed and finished as above.

150	90	75	65	50	35

Bryco Model 38
.22, .32 or .380 semi-automatic pistol, with 2.8" barrel and 6-shot magazine. Constructed and finished as above.

150	90	75	65	50	35

Bryco Model 48
Similar to above, with redesigned trigger guard. Squared forward section. Introduced in 1988.

150	90	75	65	50	35

NIB	EXC.	V.G.	GOOD	FAIR	POOR

JERICHO
Israeli Military Industries, Israel

Jericho
9mm or .41 Action Express double-action semi-automatic pistol, with 4.72" barrel, polygonal rifling, ambidextrous safety and fixed sights. Blued, with plastic grips.

575	500	400	350	300	200

JIEFFCO
Liege, Belgium
See—Robar et Cie

JOHNSON, STAN, BYE & CO.
Worcester, Massachusetts

Established in 1871 by Martin Bye and Iver Johnson. Company primarily manufactured inexpensive pistols. In 1883 Johnson assumed full control of the company and renamed it Iver Johnson Arms Company.

Defender, Eagle, Encore, Eureka, Favorite, Lion, Smoker, and Tycoon
.22, .32, .38 or .44 caliber spur trigger revolver. Manufactured with various barrel lengths and normally nickel-plated. Barrel marked with one of the above trade names.

—	—	500	200	75	25

Eclipse
.22 caliber spur trigger single-shot pistol, with 1.5" barrel. Blued, with walnut grips.

—	—	250	100	50	25

American Bulldog
.22, .32, or .38 caliber double-action revolver, with 3" barrel. Blued or nickel-plated. Walnut or composition grips.

—	—	250	100	50	25

JOSLYN
Springfield, Massachusetts
Manufacturer—Springfield Armory

Joslyn Breechloading Rifle
First mass-produced true breechloading cartridge firearm. Manufactured in a national armory. Actions were supplied by Joslyn Firearms Company and rifles chambered for .56-50 rimfire cartridge. Rifle has 35.5" round barrel and full-length stock that is held on by three barrel bands. Lock marked "U.S./Springfield" with "1864" at back. Barrel marked "B. F. Joslyn's Patent/ Oct. 8th, 1861 / June 24th, 1862". Approximately 3,000 manufactured circa 1865. Probably issued to Union forces, but unknown if they saw action before end of Civil War.

—	—	5500	3495	1950	500

Model 1855 Carbine
.54 caliber breech loading single-shot percussion carbine, with 22.5" barrel secured to fore-end by one barrel band. Blued case hardened, with brass mounts. Lock marked "A.H.Waters & Co./ Milbury, Mass." and patent dates stamped on breech lever. Approximately 1,000 manufactured in 1855 and 1856.

—	—	2750	2000	950	300

.50-70 Alteration
Approximately 1,600 Joslyn rifles re-chambered to fire .50-70 centerfire cartridge. Conversion consisted of rechambering and drilling a new firing pin hole after rimfire pin was sealed. No specific serial number range in which these conversions were done. Most of these weapons were eventually converted to smoothbores and sold in Africa. Original military specimens are extremely scarce.

—	—	6000	4200	2500	750

Model 1855 Rifle
Similar to above in .58 caliber, with 38" barrel secured by three barrel bands. Several hundred made in 1856.

—	—	4500	3250	1100	400

JOSLYN
Milbury, Massachusetts
Manufacturer—A. H. Waters

	NIB	EXC.	V.G.	GOOD	FAIR	POOR

JOSLYN FIREARMS COMPANY
Stonington, Connecticut

Model 1862 Carbine

.52 rimfire breech-loading single-shot carbine, with 22" round barrel secured by one barrel band. Blued case hardened, with brass mounts. Lock marked "Joslyn Firearms Co./Stonington/ Conn.", and patent date marked on barrel. Trigger plate is 8" long and upper tang measures 4.5". Approximately 4,000 manufactured in 1862.

—	—	4500	3700	1500	400	

Model 1864 Carbine

As above, with case hardened iron mounts, 7" trigger plate and 2" upper tang. Approximately 12,000 made in 1864 and 1865.

—	—	4200	3300	1100	400	

Army Model Revolver

.44 caliber side hammer percussion revolver, with 8" octagonal barrel and 5-shot cylinder. Blued case hardened, with walnut grips. Barrel marked "B. F. Joslyn/Patd. May 4, 1858". Martially marked examples are worth a premium of approximately 25 percent over values listed.

First Model

With brass trigger guard and iron butt cap. Approximately 500 made in 1861.

—	—	6000	4750	2000	650	

Second Model

Fitted with iron trigger guard. Without butt cap. Approximately 2,500 made in 1861 and 1862.

—	—	5500	4250	1600	500	

JURRAS, LEE
Prescott, Arizona
See—Auto Mag

While Jurras is best known for manufacturing last model of Auto Mag, he also produced the pistol listed sold by J. & G. Sales in Prescott, Arizona.

Howdah Pistol

.375, .416, .460, .475, .500 and .577 caliber single-shot pistol, with 12" barrel, adjustable sights and Nitex finish. Built on Thompson/Center Contender frame. Supposedly, approximately 100 produced.

—	1750	1100	800	650	500	

JUSTICE, P. S.
Philadelphia, Pennsylvania

Percussion Rifle

.58 caliber percussion rifle, with 35" round barrel secured by two barrel bands, browned barrel, polished lock and brass furniture. Lock marked "P.S. Justice/Philada.". Approximately 2,500 manufactured in 1861.

—	—	2300	1900	875	450	

K

K.F.C. (KAWAGUCHIYA FIREARMS CO.)
Japan

E-1 Trap or Skeet Over/Under

12-gauge boxlock double-barrel shotgun, with 26" or 30" barrels, competition rib, single-selective trigger and automatic ejectors. Engraved, blued with walnut stock. Manufactured until 1986.

—	950	800	700	500	300

E-2 Trap or Skeet Over/Under

As above, but more finely finished.

—	1400	1250	1000	750	350

Field Grade Over/Under

As above, with narrow rib and 26" or 28" barrels. Discontinued in 1986.

—	650	575	500	400	275

Model 250

12-gauge semi-automatic shotgun, with 26", 28" or 30" barrels fitted for choke tubes. Matte blued, with walnut stock. Manufactured from 1980 to 1986.

—	350	300	275	200	100

KAHR ARMS
Blauvelt, New York

K9

Semi-automatic pistol chambered for 9mm cartridge. Ultra-compact size. Barrel length 3.5"; overall length 6". Width at slide .9". Magazine capacity 7 rounds. Available in blue or electroless nickel finish. Weight 25 oz. **NOTE:** Add $30 for blackened stainless steel slide; $130 for night sights.

550	425	325	250	150	75

Lady K9

Same as above, with lightened recoil spring.

500	375	300	225	125	50

K9 Elite

Introduced in 2003, this 9mm model features 3.5" barrel and polished stainless steel slide. Magazine capacity 7 rounds. Weight about 25 oz. **NOTE:** Add $110 for night sights.

575	425	350	275	150	100

MK9 Elite

Introduced in 2003, this 9mm model features 3" barrel and polished stainless steel slide. Magazine capacity 7 rounds. Weight about 24 oz. **NOTE:** Add 15 percent for laser grips or night sights.

725	595	450	300	175	100

P9 Compact Polymer

Introduced in 1999, this 9mm model features 3.5" barrel, with double-action-only trigger. Black polymer frame, with stainless steel slide. Overall length 6"; height 4.5"; weight about 18 oz. Magazine capacity 7 rounds.

625	550	475	325	250	100

K9 Compact Polymer Covert

Same as above, with .5" shorter grip frame. Weight about 17 oz. Magazine capacity 6 rounds. Introduced in 1999.

625	550	475	325	250	100

TP9

Introduced in 2004, this 9mm model features black polymer frame, with matte stainless steel slide. Fitted with 4" barrel. Weight about 20 oz. **NOTE:** Add 15 percent for Novak night sights.

625	550	475	325	250	100

	NIB	EXC.	V.G.	GOOD	FAIR	POOR

TP40

Double-action-only semi-automatic pistol chambered in .40 S&W. Black polymer frame, matte stainless slide, 4" barrel, textured polymer grips, 6- or 7-round capacity depending on magazine. Drift-adjustable white bar-dot sights or Novak two-dot tritium sights. Introduced 2006.

	625	550	475	325	250	100

PM9

9mm model fitted with 3" barrel, blackened stainless steel slide and black polymer frame. Magazine capacity 6 rounds. Weight about 16 oz. Introduced in 2004. **NOTE:** Add 15 percent for night sights.

	700	600	475	325	250	100

PM9 Micro

Fitted with 3" barrel and chambered for 9mm cartridge. Weighs about 16 oz. Polymer frame and stainless steel slide. Introduced in 2002.

	700	600	400	300	200	100

CM Series

Chambered for 9mm, .40 S&W or .45 ACP. Similar to PM Series, with standard rifled barrel instead of polygonal. Fewer machined parts. Shipped with one magazine.

	465	425	375	325	300	250

CW380

Striker-fired .380 ACP micro-compact, with DA-only trigger, black polymer frame, matte stainless slide and fixed bar-dot sights. Introduced in 2013.

	385	345	300	275	—	—

K40

Similar to K9, but chambered for .40 S&W cartridge. Magazine capacity 6 rounds. Weight is 26 oz. **NOTE:** Add 15 percent for night sights.

	750	650	450	350	250	150

K40 Elite

Introduced in 2003, this .40 S&W model features 3.5" barrel and polished stainless steel slide. Magazine capacity 6 rounds, with beveled magazine well. Weight about 26 oz. **NOTE:** Add 15 percent for night sights; 10 percent nickel finish; 15 percent black titanium finish; 5 percent K40 stainless steel version.

	800	700	575	400	300	175

K40 Covert

Similar to K40, with .5" shorter grip frame and flush fitting 5-round magazine. Barrel length 3.5". Weight about 25 oz. Finish matte stainless steel.

	575	425	350	275	150	100

MK40

.40 S&W model fitted with 3" barrel. Overall length 5.4" and height 4". Finish matte stainless steel. Magazine capacity 5 rounds. Uses same magazines as K40 Covert. Introduced in 1999.

	700	600	400	300	200	100

MK40 Elite

Introduced in 2003, this .40 S&W model features 3" barrel and polished stainless steel slide. Magazine capacity 5 rounds, with beveled magazine well. Weight about 25 oz. **NOTE:** Add 10 percent for night sights.

	750	625	525	425	225	150

P40

Similar to P9, but chambered for .40 S&W cartridge. Fitted with 3.5" match grade barrel. Matte stainless steel slide and black polymer frame. Supplied with two 6-round stainless steel magazines. Weight approximately 19 oz. Introduced in 2001. **NOTE:** Add $30 for blackened stainless steel slide; $130 for night sights.

	550	425	325	250	150	75

P45

Introduced in 2005, with polymer frame stainless steel slide and chambered for .45 ACP cartridge. Barrel length 3.5". Fixed sights. Magazine capacity 6 rounds. Height 4.8"; overall length 6.3"; slide width 1"; weight about 18.5 oz. **NOTE:** Add 15 percent for night sights.

	675	550	375	275	170	125

	NIB	EXC.	V.G.	GOOD	FAIR	POOR

MK9

9mm model with double-action-only trigger. Barrel length 3"; overall length 5.5"; height 4"; weight approximately 22 oz. One 6-round and 7-round magazine, with grip extension standard. Model fitted with specially designed trigger for shorter trigger stroke. **NOTE:** Add 15 percent for night sights or laser grips.

700	600	400	300	200	100

CW9

9mm model introduced in 2005. Features 3.5" barrel, polymer frame and stainless steel slide. Magazine capacity 7 rounds. Height 4.5"; overall length 6"; slide width .9".

475	375	250	200	150	100

CW40

Semi-automatic with textured polymer grip. Chambered for .40 S&W and 6+1 capacity. Double-action, with 3.6" barrel. Adjustable rear sights. Weight 16.8 oz. Introduced 2006.

500	375	300	225	125	50

Wilson Combat Kahr Pistols

Offered in both K9 and K40 models. Customized pistol by Wilson's Gun Shop. Features hard chrome frame, black slide, 30 lpi checkering on front strap, beveled magazine well and several other special features. Initial production for K40 is 50 pistols; K9 25 pistols.

1300	1050	800	550	325	200

Model 1911PKZ

Model uses Auto-Ordnance 1911 pistols, re-engineered by Kahr Arms. Includes Parkerized finish, lanyard loop and U.S. Army roll mark on slide. Seven-round magazine standard. Introduced in 2001.

475	375	250	—	—	—

Model 1911 Standard

Model features blued finish plastic grips, with Thompson medallion and bullet logo on slide. Seven-round magazine. Introduced in 2001.

450	325	250	200	150	100

Model 1911C

Similar to Standard Model, with 4.25" barrel.

500	400	250	200	150	100

Model 1911WGS Deluxe

Model has blued finish rubber wrap-around grips, with Thompson medallion high profile white dot sights and Thompson bullet logo on slide. Seven-round magazine. Introduced in 2001.

575	475	425	300	225	125

P380 .380 ACP Pistol

DAO semi-automatic pocket pistol chambered in .380 ACP. Features include 2.5" Lothar Walther barrel, black polymer frame and grips, stainless steel slide 6+1 capacity. Overall length 4.9"; weight 11.3 oz. **NOTE:** Add 15 percent for night sights.

625	500	400	295	175	75

CT45

Chambered for .45 ACP and listed by manufacturer as part of its Value Series. Features include black polymer frame, matte stainless slide, 4" barrel and textured polymer grips. It is a double-action-only trigger-cocking system, with locked breech. Browning-type recoil lug, with no magazine disconnect. Overall length 6.6"; weight 24 oz. Similar models with virtually identical features include CT40 in .40 S&W (22 oz.) and CT9 in 9mm (18.5 oz.). Introduced in 2014.

400	365	325	285	250	200

KASSNAR IMPORTS, INC.
Harrisburg, Pennsylvania

Standard Over/Under

12-, 20- or 28-gauge and .410 bore boxlock double-barrel shotgun, with 26" or 28" barrels. Ventilated ribs, single trigger and extractors. Blued, with walnut stock.

350	275	225	200	150	100

Deluxe Over/Under

As above, with more finely figured stock.

400	325	250	225	175	100

	NIB	EXC.	V.G.	GOOD	FAIR	POOR

Standard Side-by-Side

20- or 28-gauge and .410 bore boxlock folding double-barrel shotgun, with 26" barrels. Double triggers and extractors. Blued, with walnut stock.

250	200	175	150	100	75

Deluxe Side-by-Side

As above in .410 bore only, with more finely figured wood.

300	250	200	175	125	75

KBI, INC.
Harrisburg, Pennsylvania

Company previously imported firearms from several manufacturers. These brands included Charles Daly handguns, shotguns and rifles, which are listed in the "D" section under Daly, Charles.

Kassnar PSP-25

.25-caliber semi-automatic pistol, with 2" barrel. Manufactured in Charlottesville, Virginia under license from Fabrique Nationale. Introduced in 1989.

275	200	175	150	100	—

KEBERST INTERNATIONAL
Kendall International
Paris, Kentucky

Model 1A

.338 Lapua Magnum, .338-416 Rigby or .338-06 caliber bolt-action rifle, with 24" barrel having integral muzzle-brake. Fitted with 3-9 power Leupold telescope. Matte blued, with camouflaged composition stock. Manufactured in 1987 and 1988.

—	3750	3000	2500	1800	900

KEL-TEC CNC INDUSTRIES
Cocoa, Florida

Kel-Tec PMR-30

Caliber: .22 WMR, steel barrel and slide, glass reinforced Zytel grip frame. Slide cover, 30-round magazine, single-action trigger, ambidextrous manual safety, fiber optic sights and accessory rail. Fluted 4.3" barrel, with matte black finish. Weight 13.6 oz. New 2011.

360	310	250	200	150	75

P-11

Semi-automatic pistol chambered for 9mm cartridge. Double-action-only. Barrel length 3.1"; overall length 5.6"; weight 14 oz. Magazine capacity 10 rounds. Standard model has blued slide, with black grip. Stainless steel and Parkerized finish are offered as well. **NOTE:** Add $100 for stainless steel; $40 for Parkerized finish; $60 for hard chrome.

320	225	175	125	100	100

P-32

.32-caliber semi-automatic pistol fitted with 2.68" barrel. Double-action-only. Blued slide and frame. Magazine capacity 7 rounds. Overall length 5"; height 3.5"; weight about 6.6 oz. **NOTE:** Add $40 for Parkerized finish; $60 for hard chrome.

305	225	175	125	100	100

P-3AT

Model chambered for .380 cartridge and fitted with 2.75" barrel. Blued finish. Magazine capacity 6 rounds. Weight about 7.3 oz. **NOTE:** Add $40 for Parkerized finish; $60 for hard chrome.

310	225	175	125	100	50

P-40

Model similar to P-11, but chambered for .40 S&W cartridge. Barrel length 3.3". Magazine capacity 9 rounds. Blued finish. Weight approximately 16 oz. **NOTE:** Add $40 for Parkerized finish; $60 for hard chrome.

320	225	175	125	100	100

SUB-2000 Rifle

Introduced in 1996, this semi-automatic rifle chambered for 9mm or .40 S&W cartridge. Barrel length 16.1". Rifle can be folded closed, with overall length of 16". Different grip assembly can be fitted to this rifle allowing for use of different magazines. Weight approximately 4.6 lbs.

375	295	175	125	75	50

	NIB	EXC.	V.G.	GOOD	FAIR	POOR

SU-16

Semi-automatic gas operated rifle chambered for .223 cartridge. Fitted with 18" barrel. Rifle has several unique features: fore-end folds down to form a bipod; stock can store spare magazines; rifle folds into two parts for carry. Weight about 5 lbs. SU-16A, 18.5" barrel; SU-16B, 16" lightweight barrel; SU-16C, 16" barrel folding stock; SU-16CA, 16" standard barrel and stock.

	NIB	EXC.	V.G.	GOOD	FAIR	POOR
	625	525	400	295	200	125

PLR-16

5.56mm NATO gas-operated semi-automatic AR-15-style long-range pistol. Windage-adjustable rear sight. Picatinny rail. Muzzle threaded for muzzle-brake. 9.2" barrel, 51 oz. 10-round or M-16 magazine. Blued finish, polymer construction. Introduced 2006.

	NIB	EXC.	V.G.	GOOD	FAIR	POOR
	650	550	425	325	200	100

RFB Rifle

Bullpup semi-automatic rifle, with 18", 24" or 32" barrel, black laminated stock, third swivel for bipod. Forward ejection; takes FAL-type magazines. Chambered in .308 Winchester. Announced in 2007. Price shown for sporter.

	NIB	EXC.	V.G.	GOOD	FAIR	POOR
	1850	1600	—	—	—	—

KEMPER, SHRIVER & COMPANY
Nashville, Tennessee

Delivered rifles made from sporting arm parts to Ordnance Department at Nashville, from December 1861 to March 1862. In all, 150 arms were assembled. Overall length 48.5"; octagonal barrels shortened 33" and bored to .48-caliber; some fitted with saber bayonet lugs; stocks of military with brass furniture.

	NIB	EXC.	V.G.	GOOD	FAIR	POOR
	—	—	4750	2000	1500	700

KENDALL, INTERNATIONAL
Paris, Kentucky
See—Keberst International

KENDALL, NICANOR
Windsor, Vermont

Under Hammer Pistol

.31- to .41-caliber under hammer percussion pistol, with 4" to 10" octagonal/round barrels marked "N.Kendall/Windsor,Vt." Browned or blued, with brass mounts and maple grips. Manufactured in 1850s.

	NIB	EXC.	V.G.	GOOD	FAIR	POOR
	—	—	1950	600	200	125

KENO
Unknown

Derringer

.22-caliber single-shot spur trigger pistol, with 2.5" barrel, brass frame and walnut grips. Barrel blued or nickel-plated and marked "Keno".

	NIB	EXC.	V.G.	GOOD	FAIR	POOR
	—	—	750	500	175	100

KERR
London, England

Kerr Revolver

.44-caliber double-action percussion revolver, with 5.5" barrel and 6-shot cylinder. Blued, with walnut grips. Frame marked "Kerr's Patent 648" and "London Armoury Bermondsey".

	NIB	EXC.	V.G.	GOOD	FAIR	POOR
	—	—	4250	2000	800	300

KESSLER ARMS CORPORATION
Silver Creek, New York

Bolt-Action Shotgun

12-, 16- or 20-gauge shotgun, with 26" or 28" barrels. Blued, with walnut stock. Manufactured between 1951 and 1953.

	NIB	EXC.	V.G.	GOOD	FAIR	POOR
	—	125	75	50	30	20

Levermatic Shotgun

12-, 16- or 20-gauge lever-action shotgun, with 26" or 28" barrel. Blued, with walnut stock. Manufactured between 1951 and 1953. A nice low-end collectible.

	NIB	EXC.	V.G.	GOOD	FAIR	POOR
	—	300	275	200	150	75

	NIB	EXC.	V.G.	GOOD	FAIR	POOR

KETTNER, EDWARD
Suhl, Germany

Drilling

High-quality three-barreled firearm chambered for 12x12- or 16x16-gauge, over various metric rifle cartridges. Barrels are 25" in length. Features are ejectors, selective triggers and pop-up rifle sights that appear when rifle barrel is selected. Gun is deep-relief engraved in German style and has a high-grade checkered walnut stock. Manufactured between 1922 and 1939.

—	—	3200	1700	900	500

KIMBALL ARMS COMPANY
Detroit, Michigan

Semi-Automatic Pistol

.30-caliber carbine semi-automatic pistol, with 3.5" or 5" barrel. Blued, with plastic grips. Also believed to have been made in .22 Hornet and .357 Magnum, though few legitimate examples have been seen. Manufactured from 1955 to 1958. Approximately 238 made.

—	3000	2000	1500	1000	450

KIMBER MFG., INC.
Yonkers, New York

Kimber of Oregon was established in April 1979 by Greg and Jack Warne. Company produced high quality rimfire and centerfire rifles until going out of business in early 1991. Kimber produced approximately 60,000 rifles during its operation. In April 1993, Greg Warne opened Kimber of America in Clackamas, Oregon. This new company presently manufactures the same high-quality rifles built on an improved Model 82 Sporter action and stock, but in rimfire only. In 1995, company expanded its product line to include centerfire rifles as well as a 1911 .45 ACP semi-automatic pistol line. In 1997, manufacturing operations were consolidated in the New York pistol factory and two factories in Oregon were closed. Guns may be found stamped "Kimber of America", "Kimber, Yonkers, NY" or "Kimber, Clackamas, Oregon".

DISCONTINUED MODELS

Model 82 Classic

.22 LR, .22 Magnum or .22 Hornet bolt-action rifle, with 22" barrel furnished without sights and 4- or 5-shot magazine. Blued, with walnut stock. Discontinued in 1988. **NOTE:** Add 10 percent for Model 82 Series rifles in .22 Magnum caliber; 15 percent for rifles chambered in .22 Hornet.

—	700	600	550	450	350

Cascade

As above, with Monte Carlo-style stock.

—	750	650	600	500	400

Custom Classic

As above in .218 Bee or .25-20.

—	800	725	650	400	300

Mini Classic

Model 82 with 18" barrel. Manufactured in 1988.

—	600	550	475	400	300

Deluxe Grade

Similar to Custom Classic. Introduced in 1989.

1000	850	650	550	450	350

Model 82A Government

.22-caliber bolt-action rifle, with 25" heavy barrel fitted with telescope mounts. Matte blued, with walnut stock. Introduced in 1987.

675	550	450	375	300	200

Continental

Similar to Custom Classic, with 20" barrel, open sights and full length Mannlicher-style stock. Introduced in 1987.

1200	1000	750	500	400	300

	NIB	EXC.	V.G.	GOOD	FAIR	POOR

Super Continental

As above, but more finely finished. Discontinued in 1988.

NIB	EXC.	V.G.	GOOD	FAIR	POOR
1600	1300	1000	750	600	300

Super America

Model 82 but more finely finished. Discontinued in 1988.

NIB	EXC.	V.G.	GOOD	FAIR	POOR
1600	1300	950	850	650	500

Super Grade

As above. Introduced in 1989.

NIB	EXC.	V.G.	GOOD	FAIR	POOR
1600	1300	900	750	600	475

Centennial

Commemorative rifle moderately engraved. Including special match barrel, skeleton buttplate, hand-selected walnut stock and light engraving. Issued to commemorate 100th anniversary of .22 LR cartridge. One hundred manufactured in 1987.

NIB	EXC.	V.G.	GOOD	FAIR	POOR
2500	2250	2000	1750	1500	1150

Brownell

In 1986, 500 commemorative rifles were produced in honor of Leonard Brownell. Featuring a high-grade, Mannlicher-style, full-length walnut stock.

NIB	EXC.	V.G.	GOOD	FAIR	POOR
2000	1500	1000	800	600	500

MODEL 84 SERIES—DISCONTINUED MODELS

Bolt-action rifle manufactured in a variety of smallbore centerfire calibers, with 22" or 24" barrel and 5-shot magazine. Blued, with walnut stock. Variations are listed.

Classic

NIB	EXC.	V.G.	GOOD	FAIR	POOR
1000	900	600	400	250	200

Custom Classic

NIB	EXC.	V.G.	GOOD	FAIR	POOR
1300	1000	700	500	350	200

Deluxe Grade Sporter

NIB	EXC.	V.G.	GOOD	FAIR	POOR
1200	1000	850	750	500	250

Continental

NIB	EXC.	V.G.	GOOD	FAIR	POOR
1800	1300	900	700	500	250

Super Continental

NIB	EXC.	V.G.	GOOD	FAIR	POOR
2000	1700	1100	700	575	250

Super America

NIB	EXC.	V.G.	GOOD	FAIR	POOR
2000	1700	1100	825	600	300

Super Grade

NIB	EXC.	V.G.	GOOD	FAIR	POOR
2100	1800	1200	850	650	300

Ultra Varmint

As above, with 24" stainless steel barrel and laminated birch wood stock. Introduced in 1989.

NIB	EXC.	V.G.	GOOD	FAIR	POOR
1500	1100	900	750	550	250

Super Varmint

As above, with walnut stock. Introduced in 1989.

NIB	EXC.	V.G.	GOOD	FAIR	POOR
1750	1250	1000	850	650	300

Predator

.221 Fireball, .223 Rem., 6mm TCU, 7mm TCU or 6x45mm caliber single-shot bolt-action pistol. Based upon Model 84 action, with 14.75" barrel adopted for telescope. Blued, with walnut stock. Available in two grades as listed. Manufactured in 1987 and 1988 only.

Hunter Grade

NIB	EXC.	V.G.	GOOD	FAIR	POOR
1800	1350	950	600	400	300

Super Grade

NIB	EXC.	V.G.	GOOD	FAIR	POOR
2500	2000	1500	1000	500	400

	NIB	EXC.	V.G.	GOOD	FAIR	POOR

MODEL 89 SERIES/BGR (BIG GAME RIFLES)

Bolt-action sporting rifle, produced in .270 Winchester to .505 Gibbs caliber, with 22" or 24" barrel. Blued, with walnut stock. Variations of this model are listed.

Classic

NIB	EXC.	V.G.	GOOD	FAIR	POOR
800	650	550	400	300	200

Custom Classic

NIB	EXC.	V.G.	GOOD	FAIR	POOR
1000	850	650	450	350	250

Deluxe Grade

NIB	EXC.	V.G.	GOOD	FAIR	POOR
1400	1150	900	650	450	250

Super America

NIB	EXC.	V.G.	GOOD	FAIR	POOR
1800	1250	900	700	500	250

Super Grade

NIB	EXC.	V.G.	GOOD	FAIR	POOR
1800	1250	900	700	500	250

African Grade

NOTE: Add 10 percent for .375 H&H or .505 Gibbs.

NIB	EXC.	V.G.	GOOD	FAIR	POOR
5500	4250	3200	2400	1200	500

MODEL 82C SERIES—DISCONTINUED MODELS

In 1998 Model 82C series rifles went out of production.

Classic

Bolt-action rifle chambered for .22 LR cartridge. Receiver drilled and tapped for sights. Fitted with 22" barrel. Detachable magazine holds 4 rounds. Stock is plain, with standard grade Claro Walnut. Checkering is 18 lpi, with 4 point side panel pattern. Red rubber butt pad and polished steel pistol-grip cap are standard. Weight approximately 6.5 lbs. Reintroduced in 1989.

NIB	EXC.	V.G.	GOOD	FAIR	POOR
900	650	500	400	—	—

Super America

Same as above. Fitted with AAA fancy grade Claro Walnut, with ebony tip and beaded cheekpiece. Hand checkering is 22 lpi in a full-coverage pattern. Steel buttplate and pistol-grip cap are standard.

NIB	EXC.	V.G.	GOOD	FAIR	POOR
2200	1500	1100	750	300	300

Custom Match

Bolt-action .22-caliber has 22" barrel. Stock is AA French walnut, with full coverage checkering. Finish is rust blued. Weight about 6.75 lbs.

NIB	EXC.	V.G.	GOOD	FAIR	POOR
2000	1600	950	700	400	200

Custom Shop Super America (Basic)

Same as above. Furnished with a number of special order options that greatly affect value. Seek an independent appraisal before sale.

Stainless Classic Limited Edition

Introduced in 1996, this limited edition Model 82C is chambered for .22 LR cartridge. Stainless steel barrel is 22" long. A 4-shot magazine is included. Production limited to about 600 rifles.

NIB	EXC.	V.G.	GOOD	FAIR	POOR
1900	1750	1100	800	500	300

SVT (Short Varmint/Target)

First introduced in 1996, this .22-caliber rifle is a single-shot. Fitted with 18" stainless steel fluted barrel. Walnut stock is target style, with no checkering. Weight about 7.5 lbs.

NIB	EXC.	V.G.	GOOD	FAIR	POOR
1350	1050	700	500	400	175

HS (Hunter Silhouette)

Introduced in 1997, this model features 24" half-fluted barrel. Chambered for .22 LR cartridge. Stock is American walnut, with high comb. Trigger fully adjustable. Four-round magazine standard. Weight about 7 lbs.

NIB	EXC.	V.G.	GOOD	FAIR	POOR
1350	1050	700	500	400	175

Single-Shot Varmint

Chambered for .17 Rem. or .223 Rem. cartridge. Fitted with 25" stainless steel fluted barrel. Claro walnut stock, with varmint-style forearm. Weight approximately 7.5 lbs. In 1998, Model 84C series rifle went out of production.

NIB	EXC.	V.G.	GOOD	FAIR	POOR
1500	1175	900	600	400	200

NIB	EXC.	V.G.	GOOD	FAIR	POOR

Sporterized Model 98 Swedish Mausers

These are reconditioned and reworked Mausers. Fitted with new match grade stainless steel fluted barrels in 24" or 26" depending on caliber. Stock is new synthetic checkered. Chambered in .257 Roberts, .270 Win., .280 Rem., .30-06, 7mm Rem. Magnum, .300 Win. Magnum, .338 Win. Magnum and .220 Swift with 25" barrel. **NOTE:** Suggested retail price: $535 for standard calibers; $560 for Magnum.

Sporterized Model 96 Swedish Mausers

Similar to above in terms of reworking and reconditioning. Chambered for these calibers:

.22-250 w/stainless steel heavy barrel fluted—Retail $500.

.243 Win.—$400 to $465 depending on finish.

6.5x55mm—$340 to $370 depending on finish.

7mm-08 Rem.—$415 to $465 depending on finish.

.308 Win.—$415 to $520 depending on finish and barrel configuration.

RECENT PRODUCTION MODELS

17 SERIES

Series of .17 Mach 2 rifles. Introduced in 2005. Features are similar to 22 Series.

Hunter

Fitted with 22" light sporter barrel. No sights. Checkered walnut stock, with black pad and clear stock finish. Magazine capacity 5 rounds. Weight about 6.5 lbs.

NIB	EXC.	V.G.	GOOD	FAIR	POOR
900	700	500	375	250	125

SVT (Short Varmint/Target) (Centerfire)

Model fitted with 18.25" stainless steel bull fluted barrel, with no sights. Checkered walnut stock, with black pad and oil finish. Magazine capacity 5 rounds. Weight about 7.9 lbs.

NIB	EXC.	V.G.	GOOD	FAIR	POOR
1200	950	775	575	350	150

Pro Varmint

Model features 20" stainless steel heavy sporter fluted barrel, with no sights. Stock is gray laminate, with oil finish and no checkering. Magazine capacity 5 rounds. Weight about 6.75 lbs.

NIB	EXC.	V.G.	GOOD	FAIR	POOR
1150	875	675	500	325	150

Classic Varmint

Fitted with 20" heavy sporter fluted barrel, with no sights. Checkered walnut stock, with oil finish. Magazine capacity 5 rounds. Weight about 6.5 lbs.

NIB	EXC.	V.G.	GOOD	FAIR	POOR
1200	950	775	575	350	150

22 SERIES

In 1999, Kimber introduced a new line of bolt-action .22-caliber rimfire rifles. First deliveries were made early in 2000. Series is built on a totally new design from bolt, to magazine, to barrel. All rifles in this series have 5-round magazine capacity. Line replaces Model 82-C series of rifles.

Classic

.22-caliber rifle fitted with 22" barrel. Fully adjustable trigger. Stock is A grade Claro walnut, with 18 lpi checkering. Fitted with Model 70 style safety. Blued finish. Weight about 6.5 lbs.

NIB	EXC.	V.G.	GOOD	FAIR	POOR
1200	950	775	575	350	150

Custom Classic

Fitted with 22" barrel, ebony fore-end tip, hand-rubbed oil finish and 24 lpi checkering. Introduced in 2003. Weight about 6.5 lbs.

NIB	EXC.	V.G.	GOOD	FAIR	POOR
1425	1100	850	675	450	150

Super America

Model features 22" barrel, with fully adjustable trigger. Stock is AAA grade Claro walnut, with 22 lpi wrap-around checkering and ebony fore-end tip. Black recoil pad. Weight about 6.5 lbs.

NIB	EXC.	V.G.	GOOD	FAIR	POOR
1900	1400	1075	775	500	200

SVT (Short Varmint/Target)

Fitted with 18" fluted stainless steel barrel and gray laminated wood stock. High target comb. Weighs about 7.5 lbs. In 2004 this model was offered in Mach 2 .17-caliber.

NIB	EXC.	V.G.	GOOD	FAIR	POOR
1150	875	675	500	325	150

	NIB	EXC.	V.G.	GOOD	FAIR	POOR

Classic Varmint

Introduced in 2003, this model features 20" barrel, with hand-rubbed oil finish and 20 lpi checkering. Weight about 6.5 lbs. In 2004 this model available in Mach 2 .17-caliber.

NIB	EXC.	V.G.	GOOD	FAIR	POOR
1150	875	675	500	325	150

Pro Varmint

Model features heavy fluted 20" stainless steel barrel and gray laminated stock. No sights. Magazine capacity 5 rounds. Weight about 6.75 lbs. Introduced in 2004. Model available in Mach 2 .17-caliber.

NIB	EXC.	V.G.	GOOD	FAIR	POOR
1200	950	775	575	350	150

HS (Hunter Silhouette)

Model fitted with 24" medium sporter match grade barrel, with match chambered and half fluting. Walnut stock, with 18 lpi checkering and Monte Carlo comb. Weight about 7 lbs.

NIB	EXC.	V.G.	GOOD	FAIR	POOR
900	700	500	375	250	125

Youth

Introduced in 2002, this .22-caliber rifle is fitted with 18.5" barrel. Checkered Claro walnut stock, with 12.25" length of pull. Weight about 5.25 lbs.

NIB	EXC.	V.G.	GOOD	FAIR	POOR
850	675	495	300	200	100

Hunter

Lower-priced version of Classic.

NIB	EXC.	V.G.	GOOD	FAIR	POOR
800	650	550	400	300	200

Custom Match Limited Edition

Introduced in 2004, this is a limited edition of 300 rifles. Features checkered French walnut stock of AAA wood and several custom features. Serial numbered from KAN25001-KAN25300.

NIB	EXC.	V.G.	GOOD	FAIR	POOR
2850	2300	—	—	—	—

MODEL 84M SERIES

Classic

Introduced in 2001, this centerfire bolt-action rifle is chambered for .243 Win., .260 Rem., 7mm-08 Rem. and .308 Win. In 2005, this model was offered chambered for .22-250 cartridge. Fitted with 22" light sporter match grade barrel, Claro walnut stock with 20 lpi checkering and satin wood finish. Matted blue finish. Fitted with 1" Pachmayr Decelerator recoil pad. Weight about 5.75 lbs.

NIB	EXC.	V.G.	GOOD	FAIR	POOR
1100	895	700	475	300	150

Montana

Model is essentially a stainless steel version of Model 84M Classic, with black synthetic stock. Weight about 5.25 lbs. Introduced in 2003.

NIB	EXC.	V.G.	GOOD	FAIR	POOR
1200	950	775	575	350	150

Super America

Model first offered in 2003 and available in .243, .260 Rem., 7mm-08 Rem. and .308 Win. Fitted with 22" barrel. In 2005, this model was offered chambered for .223 cartridge. Stock is select walnut, with 24 lpi checkering and fitted with an ebony fore-end tip, cheekpiece and hand-rubbed oil finish. Weight approximately 5.75 lbs., depending on caliber. Magazine capacity 5 rounds.

NIB	EXC.	V.G.	GOOD	FAIR	POOR
1800	1350	1000	650	325	175

Pro Varmint

Rifle chambered for .22-250 Win. cartridge and fitted with 24" stainless steel fluted barrel, with no sights. In 2005, offered in .204 Ruger and .223 calibers. Gray laminated stock. Magazine capacity 5 rounds. Weight is 7.25 lbs. Introduced in 2004.

NIB	EXC.	V.G.	GOOD	FAIR	POOR
1075	800	575	400	300	150

Varmint

Similar to Classic, fitted with stainless steel 26" match grade barrel. Chambered for .22-250 Rem. cartridge. In 2005, offered in .204 Ruger caliber. Fitted with .5" solid recoil pad. Weight approximately 7.4 lbs.

NIB	EXC.	V.G.	GOOD	FAIR	POOR
1000	750	500	375	300	150

	NIB	EXC.	V.G.	GOOD	FAIR	POOR

SVT

Stock in gray laminate, with Monte Carlo comb. Barrel length 18.25" in stainless steel and fluted. Chambered for .223 cartridge. Magazine capacity 5 rounds. Weight about 8.3 lbs.

NIB	EXC.	V.G.	GOOD	FAIR	POOR
1200	950	775	575	350	150

LongMaster VT

Bolt-action rifle chambered for .22-250 cartridge. Fitted with 26" fluted stainless steel match grade barrel. Special laminated target stock. Weight about 10 lbs. No sights. Introduced in 2002.

1200	950	775	575	350	150

LongMaster Classic

Same features as Model 84M Classic, with 24" fluted stainless steel barrel. Chambered for .308 Win. cartridge. In 2005, offered in .223-caliber. Checkered walnut stock. Weight about 7.25 lbs. Introduced in 2002.

1200	950	775	575	350	150

LongMaster Pro

Model introduced in 2003. Single-shot bolt-action rifle fitted with 24" fluted heavy barrel. Chambered for .308 Win. or .22-250 cartridge. Fitted with synthetic benchrest stock. Weight about 7.25 lbs.

1350	1050	700	500	400	175

Tactical

Based on Model 84 action, with 24" medium weight fluted match barrel. Black laminated stock and third swivel for bipod. Chambered in .308 Winchester. Introduced in 2007.

1075	800	575	400	300	150

Model 84L Classic Rifle

Bolt-action rifle chambered in .270 Win. and .30-06. Features include 24" sightless matte blue sporter barrel; hand-rubbed A-grade walnut stock, with 20 lpi panel checkering; pillar and glass bedding; Mauser claw extractor; 3-position M70-style safety; 5-round magazine; adjustable trigger.

1000	850	720	400	300	200

Model 84L Montana

Long-action variation of Model 84 action. Chambered in .25-06 Remington, .270 Winchester, .280 Ackley Improved and .30-06 Springfield. Capacity is 4-rounds in blind magazine. Kevlar-reinforced carbon fiber stock. Match-grade barrel, chamber and trigger. Free-floating 24" barrel is both pillar and glass bedded. Model 70-type 3-position safety. Weight under 6 pounds. Introduced in 2011.

1150	1000	850	600	300	200

MODEL 8400 SERIES

Series introduced in 2003. Features smallest action size compatible with WSM family of cartridges.

Classic

Model fitted with select walnut stock with 20 lpi checkering. Chambered for WSM calibers: .270, 7mm, .300 and .325. Barrel length 24" with no sights. Magazine capacity 3 rounds. Weight about 6.6 lbs. **NOTE:** Add $140 for French walnut.

1000	795	600	475	300	150

Montana

Model features 24" stainless steel barrel, with no sights. Stock is black synthetic, with no checkering. Same calibers as Classic. Weight about 6.25 lbs.

1350	1050	700	500	400	175

Super America

Model fitted with AAA walnut stock, with 24 lpi checkering. Cheekpiece and ebony fore-end tip are standard. Barrel length 24", with no sights. Chambered for the same calibers as Classic. Weight about 6.6 lbs.

1875	1350	1000	650	325	175

Classic Select Grade

Similar to 8400 Classic, with hand-rubbed oil-finished select stock of Claro or French walnut. Introduced 2006.

1100	895	700	475	300	150

	NIB	EXC.	V.G.	GOOD	FAIR	POOR

Tactical

24" heavyweight match barrel, stippled black McMillan stock, third swivel for bipod. Chambered in .308 Winchester. Introduced in 2007.

	1650	1200	800	550	300	150

Advanced Tactical

Similar to Model 8400 Tactical, with KimPro II Dark Earth finish, fully-adjustable stock and hard case. Introduced in 2007.

	1800	1350	1000	650	325	175

Patrol Rifle

Bolt-action tactical rifle chambered in .308 Win. Features include 20" 1:12 fluted sightless matte blue heavy barrel; black epoxy-coated laminated wood stock, with 20 lpi panel checkering; pillar and glass bedding; Mauser claw extractor; 3-position M70-style safety; 5-round magazine; adjustable trigger.

	1300	1100	850	500	350	200

AUGUSTA SHOTGUNS

Shotguns made in Italy for Kimber. Based on Boss-type action, each model fitted with H-Viz sights and Pachmayr Decelerator recoil pads. Back bored. Single-selective trigger and automatic ejectors. Introduced in 2002.

Sporting

Chambered for 12-gauge shell and fitted with choice of barrel lengths from 28.5" to 32". Checkered walnut stock, with pistol grip and schnabel forearm. Blued finish, with silver frame. Weight about 7.75 lbs.

	5000	4500	3000	1750	600	300

Field

Chambered for 12-gauge shell and choice of barrel lengths from 26" to 27.5". Checkered with pistol-grip and beavertail forearm. Weight about 7 lbs.

	4750	3900	2650	1500	475	225

Trap

12-gauge model offered in barrel lengths from 30" to 34". Beavertail forearm. Wide ramped ventilated rib. Weight about 7.75 lbs.

	5200	4700	3000	1750	600	300

Skeet

12-gauge gun has choice of 26" or 27.5" barrels. Barrels fitted with 11mm flat rib. Checkered walnut stock, with beavertail forearm. Weight about 7.5 lbs.

	5200	4700	3000	1750	600	300

VALIER SHOTGUNS

Side-by-side guns introduced into Kimber line in 2005.

Grade I

Lightweight properly-scaled side-by-side in 16- and 20-gauge. Double triggers and extractors. Choked IC and Mod. Color case-hardened receiver, straight stock and splinter fore-end. Hand checkered wood at 24 lpi. Chambered for: 2.75" shells in 16-gauge; 3" shells in 20-gauge.

	3300	2900	2300	1250	600	300

Grade II

Similar to Valier Grade I, with higher grade wood. Choice of color case blued or bone charcoal receiver in 20-gauge; bone charcoal only in 16-gauge. Automatic ejectors.

	4900	3500	2700	1500	700	300

MARIAS SHOTGUNS

Grade I

Single-trigger sidelock over/under, features scroll hand engraving and bone charcoal case colors, with 24 lpi checkered wood. Grade I available with 28" barrels and Prince of Wales stock in 12- and 20-gauge. Chambered for 3" shells. Automatic ejectors. Comes with 5 choke tubes.

	4600	3300	2300	1200	600	300

NIB	EXC.	V.G.	GOOD	FAIR	POOR

Grade II

Similar to Marias Grade I, with higher grade wood. Available in 12-gauge with PW stock or 20-gauge with PW or straight stock in 26", 28" or 30" barrels.

4900	3500	2700	1500	700	300

CLASSIC .45 PISTOLS

CUSTOM SERIES

First introduced in 1996, this is a quality built American-made 1911 designed by Chip McCormick for Kimber. **NOTE:** In 2001 Kimber phased in a new safety system on its pistols: Kimber firing pin safety. Models with this new firing pin safety will bear designation "II" as part of their model name.

Custom

Barrel length 5", with black oxide finish fixed sights. Black synthetic grips. Magazine capacity 8 rounds. Weight about 38 oz. **NOTE:** Night sights add $100.

850	750	650	475	300	150

Custom II

NOTE: Add $10 for Walnut grips; $100 for night sights.

825	675	500	375	250	125

Custom Heritage Edition

Chambered for .45 ACP cartridge and fitted with 5" barrel. Magazine capacity 7 rounds. Checkered front strap, ambidextrous thumb safety, aluminum trigger, hand checkered rosewood grips, special edition markings on slide. Sights are low-profile fixed. Weight about 38 oz. Introduced in 2000.

1150	950	700	495	300	150

Custom Stainless

Similar to Custom in stainless steel. **NOTE:** Night sights add $100.

1000	800	650	475	300	150

Stainless Limited Edition

Similar to Custom Stainless, except for black thumb release, black grip safety, black magazine release button and black barrel bushing. Limited to approximately 1,200 pistols.

1200	950	775	575	350	150

Custom Target

Custom Target has same features as Custom, with addition of adjustable rear sight.

825	675	500	375	250	125

Custom TLE II (Tactical Law Enforcement)

Introduced in 2003, this model features Meprolight three-dot night sights and 30 lpi checkering on front strap. Magazine capacity 7 rounds. Weight about 38 oz. **NOTE:** In 2004 stainless steel version offered. Add $135 for this model.

900	700	500	375	250	125

Custom TLE/RL II

Model similar to TLE, with addition of an integral tactical rail. Weight about 39 oz. Introduced in 2004.

1050	825	675	450	295	150

Stainless II

Chambered for .45 ACP or .40 S&W cartridge. Fitted with 5" barrel and fixed low profile sights. Both frame and slide are satin stainless steel. Magazine capacity for .45 ACP is 7 rounds; 8 rounds for .40 S&W. Weight about 38 oz.

865	650	450	275	150	100

Stainless II (polished)

As above, chambered for .38 Super cartridge. Frame and slide are polished stainless steel. Magazine capacity 9 rounds. Weight about 38 oz. Introduced in 2005.

1150	950	700	495	300	150

Stainless Ultra TLE II

1911-style semi-automatic pistol chambered in .45 ACP. Features include 7-round magazine; full length guide rod; aluminum frame with stainless slide; satin silver finish; checkered frontstrap; 3"

	NIB	EXC.	V.G.	GOOD	FAIR	POOR

barrel; tactical gray double diamond grips; tritium 3-dot night sights.

	1000	900	750	650	500	400

Stainless Target II

Chambered for .45 ACP or .38 Super cartridge, with slide and frame machined from stainless steel. Weight is 38 oz.

	980	750	600	400	250	125

Stainless Target II 9mm/10mm

As above, chambered for 9mm or 10mm cartridge. 9mm pistol has a magazine capacity of 9 rounds; 10mm capacity of 8 rounds. Both pistols are produced on a one-run basis only, with production in low hundreds. Introduced in 2003.

	1150	950	700	495	300	150

Stainless Target II (polished)

As above, chambered for .38 Super cartridge. Frame and slide are polished stainless steel. Magazine capacity 9 rounds. Weight about 38 oz. Introduced in 2005.

	1200	950	775	575	350	150

Stainless Target Limited Edition

Similar to Stainless Target, with black thumb safety, black grip safety, black slide release and black barrel bushing. Model limited to approximately 700 pistols. Introduced in 1998.

	900	700	500	375	250	125

Custom Royal

Model has all features of Custom, plus high polish blue finish, hand checkered walnut grips and long guide rod.

	900	700	500	375	250	125

Custom Royal II

	1500	1100	750	400	250	125

Custom TLE/RL II Special Edition

.45 ACP pistol fitted with 5" barrel and fixed night sights. Steel frame and slide, with tactical accessory rail on frame. Black rubber grips. Black matte finish. Magazine capacity 7 rounds. Weight about 38 oz. Introduced in 2003.

	1150	950	700	495	300	150

Warrior

Introduced in 2005. Chambered for .45 ACP cartridge. Fitted with 5" barrel with night sights. Grips are Kimber G-10 Tactical, with lanyard loop. Accessory rail on frame. KimPro finish. Magazine capacity 7 rounds. Weight about 39 oz.

	1200	950	775	575	350	150

Desert Warrior

Similar to Warrior, with desert tan finish and lighter tan G10 tactical grips.

	1200	950	775	575	350	150

25th ANNIVERSARY LIMITED EDITIONS

Anniversary Custom

Introduced in 2004, this was a limited edition of 1,911 pistols. Chambered for .45 ACP cartridge. Select walnut grips. Serial numbered: KAPC0001-KAPC1911.

	850	650	450	275	150	100

Anniversary Gold Match

.45 ACP pistol limited to 500 pistols. Serial numbered KAPG0001-KAPG0500.

	1200	950	775	575	350	150

Anniversary Match Pair Custom

Matched pair of Custom pistols in .45 ACP. Matching serial numbers and presentation case. Limited to 250 pairs.

	2500	2100	—	—	—	—

	NIB	EXC.	V.G.	GOOD	FAIR	POOR

GOLD MATCH SERIES

Gold Match

All features of Custom Royal, plus BoMar adjustable sights and fancy checkered diamond grips.

NIB	EXC.	V.G.	GOOD	FAIR	POOR
1200	950	775	575	350	150

Gold Match II

NIB	EXC.	V.G.	GOOD	FAIR	POOR
1200	950	775	575	400	150

Stainless Gold Match

Similar to Gold Match, except slide and frame are stainless steel. Introduced in 1998.

NIB	EXC.	V.G.	GOOD	FAIR	POOR
1200	950	775	575	350	150

Gold Team Match II

Introduced in 2003, this .45 ACP 5" barrel model features stainless steel slide and frame along with Kimber Tactical Extractor with loaded chamber indicator. Front strap checkered 30 lpi and grips are red, white and blue. USA Shooting Team logo. Weight about 38 oz.

NIB	EXC.	V.G.	GOOD	FAIR	POOR
1350	1225	950	575	400	150

Team Match II .38 Super

As above, without external extractor. Limited production run. Introduced in 2003.

NIB	EXC.	V.G.	GOOD	FAIR	POOR
1600	1300	1000	575	400	150

TEN II SERIES

In 2002, Polymer series pistols were upgraded to Ten II series. Added features: firing pin block safety, Kimber-made frame of improved dimensions and external extractor. Original Polymer pistol magazines of 10 and 14 rounds will interchange with newer Ten II Series pistols.

Polymer

Model features polymer frame with matte black oxide slide. Sights are McCormick low profile. Barrel length 5"; overall length 8.75"; weight about 34 oz. Magazine is 14 rounds. One 14-round magazine supplied with gun when new.

NIB	EXC.	V.G.	GOOD	FAIR	POOR
700	600	550	395	200	100

Polymer Stainless

Similar to Polymer model, with stainless steel slide. Weight about 34 oz.

NIB	EXC.	V.G.	GOOD	FAIR	POOR
750	650	550	425	225	125

Polymer Target

Introduced in 1998, this pistol has matte black oxide slide, with adjustable sights. Magazine is 14 rounds. Weight about 34 oz.

NIB	EXC.	V.G.	GOOD	FAIR	POOR
950	775	625	450	245	150

Polymer Stainless Target

Same as above, with stainless steel slide. Introduced in 1998.

NIB	EXC.	V.G.	GOOD	FAIR	POOR
950	775	625	450	245	150

Polymer Pro Carry Stainless

Chambered for .45 ACP cartridge, with 4" barrel. McCormick Low Profile sights. Stainless steel slide, with black polymer frame. Weight about 32 oz. Magazine capacity 14 rounds. Introduced in 1999.

NIB	EXC.	V.G.	GOOD	FAIR	POOR
750	675	550	395	200	100

Polymer Stainless Gold Match

Similar to Polymer Gold Match, with addition of stainless steel slide. Chambered for several calibers: .45 ACP, .40 S&W, 9mm and .38 Super. Weight about 34 oz.

NIB	EXC.	V.G.	GOOD	FAIR	POOR
1000	850	775	575	350	150

Pro Carry Ten II

.45 ACP model features 4" bull barrel, with no barrel bushing. Stainless steel slide. Weight about 28 oz.

NIB	EXC.	V.G.	GOOD	FAIR	POOR
850	675	550	395	200	100

Ultra Ten CDP II

Introduced in 2003, model features night sights and rounded edges. Fitted with 3" bull barrel. Chambered for .45 ACP. Weight about 24 oz.

NIB	EXC.	V.G.	GOOD	FAIR	POOR
900	800	700	575	350	150

	NIB	EXC.	V.G.	GOOD	FAIR	POOR

Gold Match Ten II

.45 ACP 5" barrel model has all standard features of Gold Match. Black Polymer frame and blued steel slide. Magazine capacity 14 rounds. Weight approximately 34 oz.

NIB	EXC.	V.G.	GOOD	FAIR	POOR
1200	950	775	575	350	150

BP Ten II

.45 ACP pistol has 5" barrel and 10-round magazine capacity. Steel slide with polymer frame. Fixed sights. Black matte finish. Weight about 30 oz. Introduced in 2003.

NIB	EXC.	V.G.	GOOD	FAIR	POOR
750	675	550	395	200	100

Pro BP Ten II

As above, with 4" barrel. Weight about 31 oz. Introduced in 2003.

NIB	EXC.	V.G.	GOOD	FAIR	POOR
750	675	550	395	200	100

COMPACT SERIES

Compact

Steel frame and slide pistols are fitted with 4" bull barrel and shortened grip (.4" shorter than full size). Offered in .45 ACP. Finish is matte black oxide. Grips are black synthetic. Overall length 7.7"; weight about 43 oz. Introduced in 1998.

NIB	EXC.	V.G.	GOOD	FAIR	POOR
675	550	400	300	200	100

Compact Aluminum

Model has same appearance as Compact, with aluminum frame. Matte black finish. Weight approximately 28 oz. Introduced in 1998.

NIB	EXC.	V.G.	GOOD	FAIR	POOR
675	550	400	300	200	100

Compact Stainless

Same as Compact model, with stainless steel slide and frame. Offered in both .45 ACP and .40 S&W. Introduced in 1998.

NIB	EXC.	V.G.	GOOD	FAIR	POOR
850	675	550	395	200	100

Compact Stainless II

NIB	EXC.	V.G.	GOOD	FAIR	POOR
900	675	500	375	250	125

Compact Stainless Aluminum

Offered in both .45 ACP and .40 S&W. Model features 4" barrel, with stainless steel slide and aluminum frame. Weight about 28 oz. **NOTE:** Add $25 for .40 S&W models.

NIB	EXC.	V.G.	GOOD	FAIR	POOR
750	600	475	300	200	100

PRO CARRY

Pro Carry II

Introduced in 1998, this .45 ACP or .40 S&W model features full-size aluminum frame and 4" slide and bull barrel. Other features are match grade trigger, beveled magazine well, full-length guide rod, low-profile combat sights and 7-round magazine. Finish is matte black oxide. Weight approximately 28 oz. In 2005 model was offered in 9mm.

NIB	EXC.	V.G.	GOOD	FAIR	POOR
850	675	550	395	200	100

Pro Carry II Night Sights

As above fitted with night sights.

NIB	EXC.	V.G.	GOOD	FAIR	POOR
750	675	600	425	250	150

Pro Carry Stainless

Same as Pro Carry, with stainless steel slide. **NOTE:** Add $50 for .38 Super

NIB	EXC.	V.G.	GOOD	FAIR	POOR
850	700	550	395	200	100

Pro Carry Stainless Night Sights

As above fitted with night sights.

NIB	EXC.	V.G.	GOOD	FAIR	POOR
950	750	625	450	275	175

Pro TLE/RL II

Introduced in 2005, this model features .45 ACP, with 4" barrel and night sights. Slide and frame are steel, with steel finish. Accessory rail on frame. Magazine capacity 7 rounds. Weight about 36 oz.

NIB	EXC.	V.G.	GOOD	FAIR	POOR
1150	950	700	495	300	150

	NIB	EXC.	V.G.	GOOD	FAIR	POOR

Stainless Pro TLE/RL II

As above, with stainless steel frame and slide. Introduced in 2005.

	NIB	EXC.	V.G.	GOOD	FAIR	POOR
	1250	925	750	525	350	175

Super Carry Pro

1911-style semi-automatic pistol, chambered in .45 ACP. Features include 8-round magazine; ambidextrous thumb safety; carry melt profiling; full length guide rod; aluminum frame with stainless slide; satin silver finish; super carry serrations; 4" barrel; micarta laminated grips; tritium night sights.

	NIB	EXC.	V.G.	GOOD	FAIR	POOR
	1300	1125	950	500	300	200

SUPER CARRY SERIES

Super Carry Custom HD

.45 Carry Pro pistols, feature stainless steel slide and frame, match-grade barrel and bushing, ambidextrous thumb safety, beaver-tail tang, directional serrations on slide, mainspring housing and front strap. Other features include night sights, 8-round magazine, rounded heel and "melt" treatment for easy carrying. Weight: 38 oz., 5" barrel and Kim-Pro finish. Super Carry Pro has 4" barrel, Ultra has 3" and 6-round magazine. Introduced in 2011.

	NIB	EXC.	V.G.	GOOD	FAIR	POOR
	1400	1200	1000	750	300	200

Super Carry Ultra Plus

Combines full-size round-heel frame of Carry Pro with short slide and 3" barrel of Carry Ultra. Lightweight alloy frame reduces weight to 25 oz., with 8-round magazine. Introduced in 2011.

	NIB	EXC.	V.G.	GOOD	FAIR	POOR
	1350	1150	965	725	300	200

Solo Carry STS

Micro compact pistol, designed for concealed carry. Single-action striker-fired 9mm, with stainless steel slide, alloy frame, 6-round magazine, ambidextrous thumb safety and magazine release. Weight 17 oz.; barrel length 2.7"; width 1.2"; overall length 5.5". Finish is Kim Pro or bright stainless. Introduced in 2011.

	NIB	EXC.	V.G.	GOOD	FAIR	POOR
	650	535	450	400	300	200

ULTRA CARRY II SERIES

Ultra Carry

Chambered for .45 ACP or .40 S&W cartridge. Fitted with 3" barrel and McCormick low profile sights. Grips are black synthetic. Magazine capacity 7 rounds. Weight about 25 oz. Black oxide finish. Introduced in 1999. **NOTE:** Add $100 for night sights.

	NIB	EXC.	V.G.	GOOD	FAIR	POOR
	765	600	475	350	200	100

Ultra Carry II

	NIB	EXC.	V.G.	GOOD	FAIR	POOR
	800	625	500	375	225	125

Ultra Carry Stainless

Same as above, with stainless steel slide. **NOTE:** Add $25 for .40 S&W model; $100 for night sights.

	NIB	EXC.	V.G.	GOOD	FAIR	POOR
	850	650	525	395	245	135

Ultra Carry Stainless II

	NIB	EXC.	V.G.	GOOD	FAIR	POOR
	875	675	550	425	260	150

Micro Carry

Semi-automatic single-action in .380 ACP. Stainless steel slide with aluminum frame, 1911-style controls with ambidextrous thumb safety. Capacity: 6+1. Low-profile, 3-dot night sights. Crimson Trace laser grips available (CDP model). Introduced in 2013. Add $200 for CT grips

	NIB	EXC.	V.G.	GOOD	FAIR	POOR
	600	500	450	400	375	—

Warrior SOC

Full-size 1911-style semi-automatic in .45 ACP. Stainless steel frame, slide, barrel and bushing. Tactical Wedge night sights, Crimson Trace Rail Master laser sights included. Tan/green Kim Pro finish, textured G10 grips, lanyard ring.

	NIB	EXC.	V.G.	GOOD	FAIR	POOR
	1400	1200	1050	850	600	—

Master Carry Series

Semi-automatic 1911-style pistol in .45 ACP. Offered in three sizes: Custom (5" barrel); Pro (4"); Carry (3"). Stainless frame on Custom model, aluminum on Pro and Carry. Crimson Trace laser grips included. Other features include 3-dot Tactical Wedge night sights, Kim Pro II finish,

	NIB	EXC.	V.G.	GOOD	FAIR	POOR

rounded heel grip. Introduced in 2013

	NIB	EXC.	V.G.	GOOD	FAIR	POOR
	1425	1225	1100	900	650	—

CUSTOM SHOP PISTOLS

Centennial Edition 1911

Highly artistic 1911-style semi-automatic pistol, chambered in .45 ACP. Features include color case-hardened steel frame; extended thumb safety; charcoal-blue finished steel slide; 5" match grade barrel; special serial number; solid smooth ivory grips; nitre blue pins; adjustable sights; presentation case. Edition limited to 250 units. Finished by Doug Turnbull Restoration.

NIB	EXC.	V.G.	GOOD	FAIR	POOR
4000	3600	3200	—	—	—

Royal Carry

Limited edition of 600 pistols. Chambered for .45 ACP. Fitted with 4" barrel with night sights. Hand checkered rosewood grips. Steel slide and aluminum frame. High polish blue finish. Magazine capacity 7 rounds. Weight approximately 28 oz. Introduced in 1998.

NIB	EXC.	V.G.	GOOD	FAIR	POOR
1000	800	650	475	300	150

Elite Carry

Introduced in 1998, this custom shop pistol limited to 1,200 pistols. Chambered for .45 ACP with 4" barrel and night sights. Frame is aluminum, with black oxide finish. Slide is steel, with stainless steel finish. Ambidextrous extended thumb safety, checkered front strap, match trigger and hand checkered rosewood grips. Magazine capacity 7 rounds. Weight about 28 oz.

NIB	EXC.	V.G.	GOOD	FAIR	POOR
1000	800	650	475	300	150

Gold Guardian

Limited edition custom shop pistol is limited to 300 pistols. Chambered for .45 ACP. Fitted with 5" barrel with fixed night sights. Stainless steel slide and frame. Ambidextrous extended thumb safety, match grade barrel, extended magazine well, match trigger, special markings and serial number. Magazine capacity 8 rounds; weight about 38 oz. Introduced in 1998.

NIB	EXC.	V.G.	GOOD	FAIR	POOR
1500	1200	950	575	400	150

Combat Carry

Pistol chambered for .45 ACP or .40 S&W cartridge, with 4" barrel. Many custom features and special markings. Stainless steel slide and blued frame. Night sights standard. Weight approximately 28 oz. Introduced in 1999.

NIB	EXC.	V.G.	GOOD	FAIR	POOR
1050	850	675	500	325	165

Gold Combat

Full-size pistol chambered for .45 ACP cartridge. Many custom features. Night sights standard. Special markings. Weight about 38 oz. Blued slide and frame. Introduced in 1999.

NIB	EXC.	V.G.	GOOD	FAIR	POOR
1680	1250	925	700	350	175

Gold Combat II

NIB	EXC.	V.G.	GOOD	FAIR	POOR
1730	1300	925	750	425	200

Gold Combat Stainless

Same as above, with stainless steel slide.

NIB	EXC.	V.G.	GOOD	FAIR	POOR
1725	1300	925	750	425	200

Gold Combat Stainless II

NIB	EXC.	V.G.	GOOD	FAIR	POOR
1680	1250	925	700	350	175

Super Match

Kimber's most accurate .45 ACP pistol. Fitted with 5" barrel and many special features. Adjustable sights. Weight about 38 oz. Stainless steel slide and frame, with two-tone finish. Introduced in 1999.

NIB	EXC.	V.G.	GOOD	FAIR	POOR
1925	1500	900	600	350	175

Super Match II

NIB	EXC.	V.G.	GOOD	FAIR	POOR
1985	1550	900	600	350	175

LTP II

Designed for limited pistol competition. Fitted with external extractor, flat top serrated slide with adjustable sights and extended and beveled magazine well. Fitted with 5" barrel, with tungsten guide rod. Ten-round magazine. Front strap has 20 lpi checkering. Weight about 38 oz.

NIB	EXC.	V.G.	GOOD	FAIR	POOR
2100	1575	925	625	375	200

	NIB	EXC.	V.G.	GOOD	FAIR	POOR

Raptor II

Introduced in 2005, this .45 ACP model features 5" barrel, with night sights. Blued finished. Scale serrations on front strap and slide, along with scaled zebra wood grips. Magazine capacity 8 rounds. Weight about 38 oz.

1215	925	750	525	350	175

Pro Raptor II

Similar to Raptor II, except a 4" barrel. Weight about 35 oz. Introduced in 2005.

1100	825	700	500	300	125

Grand Raptor II

.45 ACP pistol, with 5" match grade stainless steel barrel and adjustable night sights. Black aluminum trigger and rosewood grips. Slide serrations are lizard scale. Stainless steel frame. Slide is matte black and engraved with Custom Shop logo.

1500	1200	950	575	400	150

Ultra Raptor II

.45 ACP model features 3" ramped match grade bushing-less bull barrel. Fixed night sights. Ambidextrous thumb safety. Lizard scale slide serrations. Introduced in 2005.

1250	925	750	525	350	175

Ultra RCP II

Introduced in 2003, this pistol features 3" barrel, aluminum frame and sight rail. Chambered for .45 ACP cartridge. Magazine capacity 7 rounds. Weight 26 oz. No longer in production.

1300	975	795	550	370	195

Gold Combat RL II

Similar to above model, with premium trigger, KimPro finish and rosewood grips. Magazine capacity 8 rounds. Weight about 38 oz. Introduced in 2003.

1775	1325	1100	700	425	245

Target Match

Limited edition of 1,000 pistols. Chambered for .45 ACP cartridge. Matte black frame, with adjustable sights. Match grade barrel and chamber. Solid aluminum trigger. Checkered front strap and underside of trigger guard. Special serial numbers: KTM0001-KTM1000. Introduced in 2005.

1400	1050	875	650	395	175

Super America

Billed as Kimber's ultimate top-of-the-line custom 1911. Polished matte blue finish, scroll engraving, mammoth ivory grips, presentation case with matching sheath knife. Introduced 2007.

3000	2250	1700	1000	600	225

CDP SERIES (Custom Defense Package)

Ultra CDP

Custom shop model, features 3" barrel, night sights, hand checkered rosewood grips and numerous custom features. Finish is stainless steel slide and matte black frame. Chambered for .45 ACP cartridge. Magazine capacity 6 rounds. Weight about 25 oz. Introduced in 2000.

1100	825	700	500	300	125

Ultra CDP II

Compact 1911-style semi-automatic pistol, chambered in .45 ACP. Features include 7-round magazine; ambidextrous thumb safety; carry "melt" profiling; full length guide rod; aluminum frame with stainless slide; satin silver finish; checkered front strap; 3" barrel; rosewood double diamond Crimson Trace laser grips; tritium 3-dot night sights.

1550	1350	850	525	350	175

Compact CDP

Introduced in 2000, features 4" bull barrel, night sights, hand checkered rosewood grips and other custom features. Stainless steel slide and matte black frame. Chambered for .45 ACP cartridge. Magazine capacity 6 rounds. Weight about 28 oz.

1200	950	775	575	350	150

Compact CDP II

1250	995	795	595	350	150

	NIB	EXC.	V.G.	GOOD	FAIR	POOR

Pro CDP

Similar to Compact CDP, with full length grip. Magazine capacity 7 rounds. Weight about 28 oz. Introduced in 2000.

	1100	825	700	500	300	125

Pro CDP II

	1175	900	775	550	350	150

Custom CDP

.45 ACP full-size pistol, fitted with 5" match grade barrel. Stainless steel slide, with front and rear beveled serrations. Matte black steel frame, with checkered rosewood grips. Night sights standard. Introduced in 2001.

	1200	950	775	575	350	150

Custom CDP II

	1250	1000	800	600	375	165

ECLIPSE II SERIES

Eclipse Custom II

Chambered for .45 ACP cartridge and fitted with 5" barrel and match-grade bushing. Fixed night sights. Magazine capacity 8 rounds. Weight about 38 oz. Introduced in 2002. In 2005 model offered in 10mm. **NOTE:** Add $110 for 10mm model.

	1175	900	775	550	350	150

Eclipse Target II

Similar to Eclipse Custom II, with addition of adjustable night sights. Introduced in 2002.

	1200	950	775	575	350	150

Eclipse Ultra II

.45 ACP pistol with 3" barrel. Slide machined from stainless steel forging. Front strap checkering. Fixed night sights. Magazine capacity 7 rounds. Weight about 34 oz. Introduced in 2002.

	1100	825	700	500	300	125

Eclipse Pro II

Similar to Eclipse Ultra II. Features full-length grip frame and 4" barrel. Fixed night sights. Introduced in 2002.

	1100	825	700	500	300	125

Eclipse Pro Target II

Similar to Eclipse Pro, with adjustable night sights. Introduced in 2002.

	1190	950	725	525	325	150

TACTICAL SERIES

Series of pistols introduced in 2003. Each pistol has 30 lpi checkering on front strap and under trigger guard, Meprolight three-dot night sights, extended and beveled magazine well, magazines with extended bumper pads, laminated grips and match grade barrel and chamber.

Tactical Custom II

Chambered for .45 ACP cartridge and fitted with 5" barrel. Magazine capacity 7 rounds. Weight about 31 oz.

	1250	1000	800	600	375	165

Tactical Pro II

Fitted with 4" barrel. Weight about 28 oz.

	1250	1000	800	600	375	165

Tactical Ultra II

Fitted with 3" barrel. Weight about 25 oz.

	1250	1000	800	600	375	165

COVERT SERIES

Custom Covert II

1911-style semi-automatic carry gun, chambered in .45 ACP. Aluminum frame and steel slide. Frame finished in Desert Tan; slide finished in matte black. 5" barrel with 3-dot sights. Introduced in 2007.

	1500	1200	950	575	400	150

	NIB	EXC.	V.G.	GOOD	FAIR	POOR

Pro Covert II

Similar to Custom Covert II, with 4" barrel. Introduced in 2007.

NIB	EXC.	V.G.	GOOD	FAIR	POOR
1500	1200	950	575	400	150

Ultra Covert II

Similar to Pro Covert II, with 3" barrel. Introduced 2007.

NIB	EXC.	V.G.	GOOD	FAIR	POOR
1300	975	795	550	370	195

AEGIS SERIES

Pro Aegis II

1911-style semi-automatic carry gun, chambered in 9mm Parabellum. Aluminum frame and steel slide. Frame finished in matte aluminum; slide finished in matte black. 4" bull barrel with 3-dot sights. Introduced in 2007.

NIB	EXC.	V.G.	GOOD	FAIR	POOR
1000	800	650	475	300	150

Custom Aegis II

Full-size 1911-style semi-automatic carry gun, chambered in 9mm Parabellum. Aluminum frame and steel slide. Frame finished in matte aluminum; slide finished in matte black. 5" bull barrel with 3-dot sights. Introduced in 2007.

NIB	EXC.	V.G.	GOOD	FAIR	POOR
1100	825	700	500	300	125

Ultra Aegis II

Similar to Pro Aegis II, with 4" barrel. Introduced in 2007.

NIB	EXC.	V.G.	GOOD	FAIR	POOR
1100	825	700	500	300	125

RIMFIRE SERIES

Rimfire Custom

Introduced in 2003, this .22-caliber pistol features 5" barrel, with fixed sights and 10-round magazine. Matte black or silver anodized finish. Weight about 23 oz.

NIB	EXC.	V.G.	GOOD	FAIR	POOR
750	525	365	225	150	100

Rimfire Target

As above, with adjustable sights. In 2004 model available in .17-caliber Mach 2.

NIB	EXC.	V.G.	GOOD	FAIR	POOR
800	575	400	275	200	125

Rimfire Super

Introduced in 2004. Features serrated flat top slide, with flutes in upper corners, ambidextrous thumb safety, aluminum trigger and two-tone finish. Weight about 23 oz.

NIB	EXC.	V.G.	GOOD	FAIR	POOR
1100	825	700	500	300	125

.22 LR Conversion Kit

Introduced in 1998, Kimber kit features a complete upper assembly: slide, barrel, guide rod, shock buffer and 10-round magazine. Finish is satin silver or satin blue. Will fit all Kimber 1911 .45 ACP models. In 2005 kit was also offered for .17 Mach 2 cartridge conversion.

NIB	EXC.	V.G.	GOOD	FAIR	POOR
300	250	200	125	75	25

KING PIN
Unknown

Derringer

.22-caliber spur trigger brass constructed single-shot pistol, with 2.5" barrel and walnut grips. Believed to have been made during 1880s.

NIB	EXC.	V.G.	GOOD	FAIR	POOR
—	—	675	200	100	50

KIRRIKALE, ENDUSTRISI
Ankara, Turkey

Kirrikale Pistol

7.65 or 9mm short caliber semi-automatic pistol, with 3.5" barrel and 6-shot magazine. Blued, with plastic grips. Slide marked "MKE"; and "Kirrikale Tufek Fb Cal.—". Imported by Firearms Center in Victoria, Texas and also by Mandall Shooting Supplies. An unauthorized copy of Walther PP, that was imported into U.S. briefly.

NIB	EXC.	V.G.	GOOD	FAIR	POOR
450	350	275	225	150	100

	NIB	EXC.	V.G.	GOOD	FAIR	POOR

KLEINGUENTHER/KDF, INC.
Kleinguenther Distinctive Firearms
Seguin, Texas

Condor

12-gauge boxlock over/under shotgun, with 28" barrels, ventilated ribs, single-selective trigger and automatic ejectors. Blued, with walnut stock. Manufactured in Italy.

	—	700	600	525	375	275

Brescia

A 12-gauge boxlock double-barrel shotgun, with 28" barrels, double triggers and extractors. Blued, with walnut stock. Manufactured in Italy.

	—	400	325	300	200	125

K-14 Insta Fire Rifle

Bolt-action sporting rifle, manufactured in a variety of calibers, with 24" or 26" barrels furnished without sights. Blued, with Monte Carlo-style walnut stock.

	—	1750	1350	1100	500	250

K-15

Similar to above, with 60-degree bolt angle and accurized barrel, guaranteed to fire .5" group at 100 yards. Manufactured with a variety of optional features.

	—	1750	1350	1100	500	250

K-15 Pro-Hunter

As above, with matte blued or electroless nickel-plated and fiberglass stock.

	—	1750	1350	1100	500	250

K-15 Swat Rifle

7.62x54mm caliber bolt-action rifle, with 24" or 26" barrel. Furnished without sights. Parkerized finish and 4-shot magazine. Walnut stock.

	—	1800	1400	1150	700	350

K-15 Dangerous Game

As above in .411 KDF caliber.

	—	2500	2000	1300	1000	700

K-16

Bolt-action sporting rifle, manufactured in a variety of calibers, with 24" or 26" barrel. Furnished without sights, single stage adjustable trigger, accurized barrel and Dupont Rynite stock. Produced with a variety of optional features.

	—	1750	1350	1100	500	250

Titan Menor

.222- or .223-caliber bolt-action rifle, with 24" or 26" barrel. Furnished without sights. Monte Carlo-style or standard schnabel tipped walnut stock. Blued.

	—	1200	900	550	400	200

Titan II Standard

As above, with mid-sized action.

	—	1200	900	550	400	200

Titan II Magnum

As above, with long action. Discontinued in 1988.

	—	1350	1100	675	450	200

Titan .411 KDF Mag.

As above in .411 KDF, with 26" barrel having integral muzzle-brake. Blued or electroless nickel-plated, with walnut stock. Discontinued in 1988.

	—	2500	2000	1300	1000	700

K-22

.22-caliber bolt-action rifle, with 21" free floating barrel. Furnished without sights, adjustable trigger and 5-shot magazine. Also known as Mauser 201.

	—	500	400	300	175	100

Deluxe

	525	425	325	200	125

	NIB	EXC.	V.G.	GOOD	FAIR	POOR

Deluxe Custom

	—	650	550	450	375	225

Deluxe Special Select

	—	1150	850	750	650	325

Model 2005

.22-caliber semi-automatic rifle, with 19.5" barrel, open sights and 5-shot magazine. Blued, with walnut stock. Also, available in deluxe model. Imported in 1986.

250	175	150	100	75	50

Model 2107

.22- or .22-caliber Magnum bolt-action rifle, with 19.5" barrel, open sights and 5-shot magazine. Blued, with walnut stock.

—	375	325	250	150	100

Model 2112

Deluxe version of Model 2107.

—	400	325	275	175	125

KLIPZIG & COMPANY
San Francisco, California

Pocket Pistol

.41-caliber single-shot percussion pistol, with 2.5" barrel, German silver mounts and walnut stocks. Manufactured during 1850s and early 1860s.

—	—	1950	975	400	200

KNICKERBOCKER
Made by Crescent Fire Arms Co.

Knickerbocker Pistol NFA

Knickerbocker is a 14" double-barreled 20-gauge smooth bore pistol, manufactured by Crescent Fire Arms Co. of Norwich, Connecticut. On the basis of its hammerless design and dates of production of similarly designed firearms by Crescent, the Knickerbocker was probably manufactured sometime during early 1900s. Receiver is case hardened and barrels are nickel-plated. Right side of receiver stamped "AMERICAN GUN CO./ NEW YORK U S A"; left side stamped "KNICKERBOCKER". Probably was intended for law enforcement and/or defensive purposes and manufactured using the same techniques used to produce Ithaca Auto & Burglar Gun. Receiver fitted with checkered pistol-grip, resembling that of Model 1 and Model 2 smooth bore H&R Handy-Gun. Only known specimen of Knickerbocker bears serial number 200114. Knickerbocker was classified as "any other weapon" under NFA in 1934, because it was originally designed as "a so-called shotgun with a pistol grip"; because it is concealable (see Treasury Department ruling S.T. 772, dated August 6, 1934). Its rarity precludes being able to reliably estimate its value at this time.

Double-Barrel Shotgun

Knickerbocker was a popular Dutch name for a New Yorker. It was used as a brand on many hammerless sidelock doubles made by Crescent Firearms Co. Valued from $100 to $700 depending on model and condition.

KNIGHT RIFLES
Centerville, Iowa

Company was started in 1985, by Tony Knight. Company produces in-line blackpowder muzzle-loading rifles and a complete line of accessories.

Disc Magnum

Available in .50-caliber, with choice of blued or stainless steel 24" or 26" barrel. Adjustable rear sight. Checkered stock, with palm swell and rubber recoil pad. Stock also offered in black or camo. Adjustable trigger. Weight approximately 8 lbs. **NOTE:** Add $50 for camo finish; $70 for stainless steel.

450	350	300	250	200	150

Bighorn Magnum

Available in .50-caliber, with choice of 22" or 26" blued or stainless steel barrel. Adjustable rear sight. Checkered stock, with rubber recoil pad. Stock also offered in black or camo. Adjustable trigger. Weight about 7.7 lbs. **NOTE:** Add $50 for camo finish; $70 for stainless steel.

325	250	200	175	150	100

	NIB	EXC.	V.G.	GOOD	FAIR	POOR

T-Bolt Magnum

Available in .50-caliber, with choice of blue or stainless steel 22" or 26" barrel. Adjustable rear sight. Composite stock, with rubber recoil pad. Stock also available in camo. Adjustable trigger. Weight about 8 lbs. **NOTE:** Add $50 for camo finish; $70 for stainless steel.

400	325	275	225	150	100

LK-93 Wolverine

Available in .50- or .54-caliber, with choice of 22" blued or stainless steel barrel. Adjustable rear sight. Composite skeleton or thumbhole stock. Stock also available in black or camo. Adjustable trigger. Weight about 6.5 lbs. **NOTE:** Add $50 for camo finish; $70 for stainless steel; $40 for thumbhole stock.

265	200	150	100	75	25

LK-93 Wolverine Youth

Same as above, with shorter length of pull. Offered in black stock only.

275	225	175	125	100	75

American Knight

Available in .50-caliber, with 22" blued barrel. Adjustable rear sight. Black composite stock. Non-adjustable trigger. Weight approximately 6.3 lbs.

200	150	100	75	50	25

MK-85 Hunter

Model offered in .50- or .54-caliber, with blued finish and walnut stock.

550	450	375	325	250	200

MK-85 Predator

Stainless steel version of Hunter model. Offered with composite stock or various camo finishes. **NOTE:** Add $50 for camo finish.

650	525	450	300	250	200

MK-85 Stalker

Model offered in .50- or .54-caliber, with a variety of stock options. Standard stock is composite. Blued finish. **NOTE:** Add $50 for camo finish.

565	450	375	325	250	200

MK-85 Knight Hawk

Model offered in .50- or .54-caliber, with black composite stock and stainless steel.

750	600	500	400	300	200

MK-86 Shotgun

Available in 12-gauge, with 24" extra full choked barrel. Black composite stock, with blued finish.

600	475	375	250	200	150

HK-94 Hawkeye Pistol

.50-caliber pistol, fitted with 12" barrel. Overall length 20"; weight 52 oz. Offered in stainless steel or blued finish. First offered in 1993. Discontinued in 1998. **NOTE:** Add $70 for stainless steel.

400	300	250	200	150	100

Rolling Block Rifle

Rolling-block black powder rifle, similar in design to old Remington rolling block design. 209 primer ignition, .50-caliber barrel rifled for sabots. Finishes include blued/composite, stainless/camo and all-camo. Introduced in 2007. Values shown are for stainless.

375	300	200	125	100	50

Long Range Hunter

.45-, .50- or .52-caliber bolt-action muzzle-loader, with 27" fluted stainless barrel. Said to shoot 4" 3-shot groups at 200 yards. Laminated stock. Introduced in 2007.

525	400	300	200	100	50

KNIGHT'S MANUFACTURING CO.
Vero Beach, Florida

STONER SR-15 RIFLES

SR-15 Match

Chambered for .223 Win. and fitted with target contour 20" free floating barrel. Two-stage match trigger. Flat top receiver. No sights. Weight approximately 7.9 lbs.

1850	1400	1050	750	500	200

	NIB	EXC.	V.G.	GOOD	FAIR	POOR

SR-15 M-5 Rifle

.223 fitted with 20" standard weight barrel, with two-stage target trigger. Hand guard employs RAS accessory system. Fitted with flip-up low profile rear sight. Weight about 7.6 lbs.

	NIB	EXC.	V.G.	GOOD	FAIR	POOR
	1700	1250	950	700	400	200

SR-15 E3 URX Carbine

Similar to SR-15 M-5, with 16" barrel, telescoping buttstock and vertical fore-end grip. Introduced 2006.

	NIB	EXC.	V.G.	GOOD	FAIR	POOR
	2100	1700	1250	950	500	200

SR-15 M-4 Carbine

Model includes RAS system and flip-up rear sight. Two-stage target trigger and 16" lightweight barrel. Weight about 6.8 lbs.

	NIB	EXC.	V.G.	GOOD	FAIR	POOR
	1700	1250	950	700	400	200

STONER SR-25 RIFLES

SR-25 Match

Rifle chambered for .308-caliber and fitted with 24" target contour free floating barrel. Special rifling and twist rate. No sights. Weight about 10.75 lbs.

	NIB	EXC.	V.G.	GOOD	FAIR	POOR
	3495	2600	1850	950	600	400

SR-25 Lightweight Match

.308 rifle fitted with 20" free floating barrel. No sights. Weight about 9.5 lbs.

	NIB	EXC.	V.G.	GOOD	FAIR	POOR
	2995	2250	1500	900	550	350

SR-25 Stoner Carbine

Fitted with 16" free floating barrel and special short non-slip hand guard. Weight about 7.75 lbs.

	NIB	EXC.	V.G.	GOOD	FAIR	POOR
	2995	2250	1500	900	—	—

SR-25 Competition Match

Rifle chambered for either .308 or .260 cartridge and has 26" match barrel. Fitted with special forearm, which rotates in 15 degree increments. Trigger is adjustable two-stage, with extended trigger guard. Special bolt stop and charging handle. Adjustable buttstock. Model may be fitted with several extra cost options that will affect price.

	NIB	EXC.	V.G.	GOOD	FAIR	POOR
	6000	4750	3000	1750	1000	600

SR-25 Mk11 Mod 0 Match Rifle

Introduced in 2004, this rifle features heavy 20" free floating target grade barrel.

	NIB	EXC.	V.G.	GOOD	FAIR	POOR
	5295	3900	2500	1650	100	475

SR-50 Rifle

Semi-automatic rifle chambered for .50 BMG cartridge. Magazine feed. Weight approximately 31 lbs.

	NIB	EXC.	V.G.	GOOD	FAIR	POOR
	7000	5500	4000	3000	2000	750

KOHOUT & SPOLECNOST
Kdyne, Czechoslovakia

Mars

6.35 or 7.65mm caliber semi-automatic pistol. Larger caliber having grip safety. Blued, with plastic grips impressed with word "Mars". Slide marked "Mars 7.65 (or 6.35) Kohout & Spol. Kdyne". Manufactured between 1928 and 1945.

	NIB	EXC.	V.G.	GOOD	FAIR	POOR
	—	350	250	200	150	100

Niva, PZK

Similar to above in 6.35mm caliber.

	NIB	EXC.	V.G.	GOOD	FAIR	POOR
	—	350	250	200	150	100

KOLB, HENRY M.
Philadelphia, Pennsylvania

Revolvers listed were manufactured by Henry Kolb and Charles Foehl until 1912, when R.F. Sedgely replaced Foehl. Manufacture continued until approximately 1938.

Baby Hammerless

.22-caliber folding-trigger double-action revolver, with enclosed hammer and 5-shot cylinder.

	NIB	EXC.	V.G.	GOOD	FAIR	POOR
	—	300	200	150	100	50

	NIB	EXC.	V.G.	GOOD	FAIR	POOR

New Baby Hammerless

Similar to above, with hinged barrel to facilitate loading.

—	300	200	150	100	50

KOLIBRI/FREDERICH PFANNL
Rehberg, Austria

2.7mm

2.7mm semi-automatic pistol, with 7-round magazine. F.P. trademark on grips as well as Kolibri name at bottom of grips. Single cartridge may be worth as much as $75!

—	2500	1550	850	600	400

3mm

3mm semi-automatic pistol, with 6-round magazine. The 3mm version rarer of the two Kolibri pistols. F.P. trademark is on grips.

—	2800	2000	1500	1000	600

KOMMER, THEODOR WAFFENFABRIK
Zella Mehlis, Germany

Model 1

6.35mm semi-automatic pistol, with 8-shot magazine. Blued, with plastic grips. Kommer name on both slide and frame, with T.K. trademark on grips. Manufactured during 1920s.

—	300	250	200	150	90

Model 2

6.35mm semi-automatic pistol, with 6-round magazine. Similar to Model 1906 Browning. Barrel length 2"; weight about 13 oz. Kommer name on slide. Late TH.K. trademark on grips. Manufactured in 1930s.

—	300	250	200	150	90

Model 3

6.35mm semi-automatic pistol, with 9-round magazine. Kommer name on slide. TH.K. trademark on grips. Same as Model 2, with extended grips straps for longer magazine.

—	300	250	200	150	90

Model 4

7.65mm caliber semi-automatic pistol, with 7-shot magazine. Without a grip safety. Similar to FN Model 1901. Barrel length 3"; weight about 20 oz. Slide marked "Waffenfabrik Kommer Zella Mehlis Kal. 7.65". Manufactured between 1936 and 1940.

—	375	325	275	175	100

KONGSBERG
Norway

Thumbhole Sporter

Introduced in 1993, this bolt-action rifle chambered for .22-250 and .308 Win. cartridges. Fitted with 23" heavy barrel. Stock is American walnut, with stippled thumbhole grip and wide fore-end. Cheekpiece is adjustable for height. Weight about 8.5 lbs. Available in both right-/left-hand configurations. **NOTE:** Add 10 percent for left-hand model.

1575	1250	900	550	350	200

Classic Rifle

Model also introduced in 1993. Chambered for a wide variety of calibers from .22-250 to .338 Win. Magnum. Fitted with 23" barrel for standard calibers and 26" barrel for magnum calibers. European walnut stock, with straight comb. Hand checkered. Open sights. Weight about 7.5 lbs., depending on caliber. Offered in both left-/right-hand configurations. **NOTE:** Add 10 percent for left-hand models; 10 percent for magnum calibers.

995	800	650	375	225	125

KORRIPHILA
Germany

HSP

7.65mm Luger, .38 Special, 9mm Police, 9mm Luger, 9mm Steyr, 10mm ACP and .45 ACP caliber. Double-action semi-automatic pistol, with 4" barrel made of stainless steel.

7500	6000	5000	2500	1250	550

	NIB	EXC.	V.G.	GOOD	FAIR	POOR

HSP—Single-Action Only

NIB	EXC.	V.G.	GOOD	FAIR	POOR
7500	6000	5000	2500	1250	550

Odin's Eye

Essentially same model as above. Same calibers, with choice of barrel lengths of 4" or 5". Frame and slide are made of Damascus steel.

NIB	EXC.	V.G.	GOOD	FAIR	POOR
14000	10000	7500	4000	1500	500

KORTH
Germany

Korth started business in Ratzegurg, Germany, in 1954.

Semi-Automatic Pistol

9mm caliber double-action semi-automatic pistol, with 4" barrel, adjustable sights and 13-shot magazine. Other calibers offered; .40 S&W, .357 SIG and 9x21. Optional 5" barrel also offered. Weight about 44 oz. Matte or polished blue, with walnut grips. Introduced in 1985.

NIB	EXC.	V.G.	GOOD	FAIR	POOR
7000	5000	3750	2750	1300	650

Combat Revolver

.22 LR, .22 Magnum, .357 Magnum and 9mm caliber revolver, with 3", 4", 5.25" or 6" barrel and 6-shot cylinder. Barrels and cylinders are interchangeable. Matte or polished blue, with walnut grips.

NIB	EXC.	V.G.	GOOD	FAIR	POOR
5000	3900	3000	1750	1150	700

Match Revolver

Built in same calibers as Combat revolver, with choice of 5.25" or 6" barrel. Adjustable rear sight, with adjustable sight notch widths. Machined trigger shoe. Grips are adjustable match grips, with oiled walnut and matte finish.

NIB	EXC.	V.G.	GOOD	FAIR	POOR
6250	5000	4000	2250	1500	1000

KRAG-JORGENSEN

This was the first bolt-action repeating rifle that used smokeless powder to be adopted by the U.S. government as a service rifle. Adopted as Model 1892, it was similar to the Denmark military rifle, which had been designed by Norwegians Ole Krag and Erik Jorgensen. Most unique part of this design was the side-mounted hinged magazine. With the exception of Model 1898 Practice Rifle, which was chambered for .22 rimfire — all Krag rifles were chambered for .30-40 Government cartridge. From 1892 to 1899, more than a dozen variations were made. Over the years many have been altered or "customized". Values shown here are for unmodified, original rifles. For more on Krag-Jorgensen, see Standard Catalog of Military Firearms 7th Edition (2013) by Phillip Petersen.

Model of 1892

1st Type, Serial number 1 — 1500

NIB	EXC.	V.G.	GOOD	FAIR	POOR
—	20000	12500	6500	3000	900

2nd Type, Serial number 1501 — 24562

NIB	EXC.	V.G.	GOOD	FAIR	POOR
—	10000	7500	4000	2000	600

Model 1892, altered to 1896

NIB	EXC.	V.G.	GOOD	FAIR	POOR
—	1800	950	750	450	200

Model 1896

NOTE: Add 10 percent for carbine variation.

NIB	EXC.	V.G.	GOOD	FAIR	POOR
—	2750	2000	1600	750	300

Model 1898

NOTE: Add a premium of 100 to 120 percent for carbine variation.

NIB	EXC.	V.G.	GOOD	FAIR	POOR
—	1250	900	650	450	200

Model 1898 Practice Rifle (.22 rimfire)

NIB	EXC.	V.G.	GOOD	FAIR	POOR
—	—	4500	2000	850	300

Model 1899 Carbine

NIB	EXC.	V.G.	GOOD	FAIR	POOR
—	1850	1400	900	750	300

	NIB	EXC.	V.G.	GOOD	FAIR	POOR

KRAUSER, ALFRED
Zella Mehlis, Germany

Helfricht or Helkra

6.35mm semi-automatic pistol, with 2" barrel. Produced in four models: fourth, with enclosed barrel. Blued, with composition grips. Manufactured from 1921 to 1929.

	—	475	400	350	250	150

KRICO
Stuttgart, West Germany

Sporting Rifle

.22 Hornet or .222-caliber bolt-action rifle, with 22", 24" or 26" barrels. Single or double set trigger, adjustable sights and 4-shot magazine. Blued, with walnut stock. Manufactured between 1956 and 1962.

	—	650	550	475	375	275

Sporting Carbine

As above, with 20" barrel and full length stock.

	—	675	575	500	400	300

Varmint Special Rifle

Sporting Rifle, with heavier barrel.

	—	650	550	475	375	275

Model 300

.22-caliber bolt-action rifle, with 23.5" barrel, 5-shot magazine and grooved receiver. Blued, with walnut stock. Imported prior to 1989.

	—	700	600	550	400	300

Model 302 and 304

Variations of above. Discontinued in 1986.

	—	700	600	550	400	300

Model 311 Smallbore

.22-caliber bolt-action rifle, with 22" barrel. Double set triggers, adjustable sights and 5- or 10-shot magazine. Blued, with walnut stock. Not imported after 1988.

	—	325	275	225	150	100

Model 320

As above, with 19.5" barrel and full length stock. Discontinued in 1988.

	—	700	600	550	400	300

Model 340

.22-caliber bolt-action rifle, with 21" heavy barrel. Furnished without sights, adjustable trigger and 5-shot magazine. Blued, with walnut stock. Not imported after 1988.

	—	750	625	575	425	325

Model 340 Mini-Sniper

As above, with matte finish. Barrel fitted with muzzle-brake. Stock with raised cheekpiece, as well as ventilated hand guard.

	—	1000	850	750	500	400

Model 340 Kricotronic

Model 340 fitted with electronic trigger. Not imported after 1988.

	—	1450	1000	850	600	500

Model 360S Biathlon Rifle

Introduced in 1991, model features .22 LR straight pull bolt-action, with 5-round magazine. Fitted with 21.25" barrel. Walnut stock, with high comb and adjustable buttplate. Fully adjustable match peep sight. Fitted with 17 oz. match trigger. Weight approximately 9.25 lbs.

	1950	1350	850	500	300	150

Model 360S2 Biathlon Rifle

Same as above, with black epoxy finished walnut stock, with pistol-grip. Weight is 9 lbs.

	1500	1250	800	400	200	100

	NIB	EXC.	V.G.	GOOD	FAIR	POOR

Model 400 Match

Chambered for .22 LR or .22 Hornet. Bolt-action rifle fitted with heavy match 23" barrel and 5-round magazine. Match-style stock of European walnut. Fitted with double set of match triggers. Weight about 8.8 lbs.

	NIB	EXC.	V.G.	GOOD	FAIR	POOR
	900	775	650	500	300	150

Model 400 Sporter

.22 Hornet caliber bolt-action rifle, with 23.5" barrel, open sights and 5-shot magazine. Blued, with walnut stock. Not imported after 1988.

	NIB	EXC.	V.G.	GOOD	FAIR	POOR
	—	750	625	550	425	325

Model 420

As above, with 19.5" barrel, double set triggers and full-length stock. Discontinued in 1988.

	NIB	EXC.	V.G.	GOOD	FAIR	POOR
	—	900	750	675	500	400

Model 440

Similar to Model 340. Not imported after 1988.

	NIB	EXC.	V.G.	GOOD	FAIR	POOR
	—	950	800	700	500	375

Model 500 Kricotronic Match Rifle

Chambered for .22 LR, this bolt-action rifle fitted with 23.6" barrel and tapered bore. Walnut stock, with match-type adjustable buttplate. Electronic ignition system gives fastest lock time. Weight approximately 9.4 lbs.

	NIB	EXC.	V.G.	GOOD	FAIR	POOR
	3900	3000	2400	1650	1000	400

Model 600 Sporter

.17 Remington to .308 Winchester caliber bolt-action rifle, with 23.5" barrel. Open sights and 3-shot magazine. Blued, with walnut stock. Not imported after 1988.

	NIB	EXC.	V.G.	GOOD	FAIR	POOR
	—	1150	950	875	700	575

Model 600 Sniper Rifle

Bolt-action rifle chambered for .222, .223, .22-250, .243 and 308. Fitted with 25.6" heavy barrel, with flack hider. Stock is walnut, with adjustable rubber buttplate. Magazine holds 4 rounds. Weight about 9.2 lbs.

	NIB	EXC.	V.G.	GOOD	FAIR	POOR
	2900	2100	1500	1100	600	300

Model 600 Match Rifle

Chambered for same calibers as 600 Sniper, with addition of 5.6x50 Magnum. Fitted with 23.6" barrel. Match stock is vented in forearm for cooling. Wood is walnut, with cheekpiece. Weight approximately 8.8 lbs.

	NIB	EXC.	V.G.	GOOD	FAIR	POOR
	1500	1100	750	600	300	150

Model 620

As above, with 20.5" barrel, double set triggers and full-length stock.

	NIB	EXC.	V.G.	GOOD	FAIR	POOR
	1500	1100	750	600	300	150

Model 640 Varmint Rifle

Similar to above in .22-250, .222- or .223-caliber, with 23.5" heavy barrel. Not imported after 1988.

	NIB	EXC.	V.G.	GOOD	FAIR	POOR
	—	1250	1025	925	775	625

Model 640 Sniper Rifle

As above, with matte finish. Discontinued in 1988.

	NIB	EXC.	V.G.	GOOD	FAIR	POOR
	1500	1100	750	600	300	150

Model 640 Deluxe Sniper Rifle

As above in .223- or .308-caliber, with 23" barrel, stippled stock and adjustable trigger. Not imported after 1988.

	NIB	EXC.	V.G.	GOOD	FAIR	POOR
	—	1700	1250	1000	750	650

Model 700 Sporter

.270- or .30-06 caliber bolt-action rifle, with 23.5" barrel, open sights, single set trigger and 3-shot magazine. Blued, with walnut stock. Discontinued in 1988.

	NIB	EXC.	V.G.	GOOD	FAIR	POOR
	—	1050	850	750	600	500

Model 720

As above, with 20.5" barrel, double set triggers and full-length stock. Discontinued in 1988.

	NIB	EXC.	V.G.	GOOD	FAIR	POOR
	—	1200	900	750	600	500

	NIB	EXC.	V.G.	GOOD	FAIR	POOR

Model 720 Limited Edition

As above in .270-caliber only, with gold-plated furniture and gold highlighted engraving. Not imported after 1988.

	NIB	EXC.	V.G.	GOOD	FAIR	POOR
	—	2500	2000	1750	1400	900

KRIDER, J. H.
Philadelphia, Pennsylvania

Pocket Pistol

.41-caliber percussion pocket pistol, with 3" barrel, German silver furniture and walnut stock. Barrel marked "Krider Phila." Manufactured during 1850s and 1860s.

	NIB	EXC.	V.G.	GOOD	FAIR	POOR
	—	—	1750	700	300	150

Militia Rifle

.58-caliber percussion rifle, with 39" barrel and full length stock secured by two barrel bands. Barrel is browned and lock marked "Krider". Case hardened and furniture of brass. Several hundred manufactured in 1861.

	NIB	EXC.	V.G.	GOOD	FAIR	POOR
	—	—	4550	2000	750	225

KRIEGHOFF, HEINRICH, GUN CO.
Ulm, Germany

Krieghoff-manufactured Lugers are listed in Luger section.

DRILLINGS AND COMBINATION GUNS

Plus Model

Three-barrel combination rifle/shotgun, produced in a variety of gauges and calibers, with 25" barrels. Double triggers and automatic ejectors. Blued, with walnut stock. Introduced in 1988.

NIB	EXC.	V.G.	GOOD	FAIR	POOR
6600	5250	4100	3500	2000	750

Trumpf Model

Combination rifle/shotgun, produced in a variety of calibers and gauges, with 25" barrels and double triggers. Blued, with walnut stock.

NIB	EXC.	V.G.	GOOD	FAIR	POOR
11000	7700	5100	3500	2000	750

Trumpf Dural

As above lightweight boxlock, with Duraluminum frame. **NOTE:** Add $1,850 for single trigger; $450 for free-floating barrel.

NIB	EXC.	V.G.	GOOD	FAIR	POOR
11000	7700	5100	3500	2000	750

Neptun

Combination over/under rifle/shotgun, with sidelocks. Produced in a variety of gauges and calibers. Engraved, blued with walnut stock.

NIB	EXC.	V.G.	GOOD	FAIR	POOR
15000	12000	10500	5000	2500	1500

Neptun Dural

As above lightweight boxlock, with Duraluminum frame.

NIB	EXC.	V.G.	GOOD	FAIR	POOR
15000	12000	10500	5000	2500	1500

Neptun Primus

Neptun, with relief engraving and detachable sidelocks.

NIB	EXC.	V.G.	GOOD	FAIR	POOR
20000	17000	14000	7500	3500	2000

Neptun Primus Dural

As above lightweight sidelock, with Duraluminum frame.

NIB	EXC.	V.G.	GOOD	FAIR	POOR
20000	18000	14000	7500	3500	2000

Optima

Classic drilling combination of side-by-side shotgun barrels over a rifle barrel. Shotgun offered in 12- or 20-gauge, with rifle barrel in .308 Winchester, .30-06, or a choice of several popular European cartridges. Features include twin-hammer action, with Universal trigger system and combination cocking device and a set trigger integrated in the front trigger. Values shown are for base model. Many options are available.

NIB	EXC.	V.G.	GOOD	FAIR	POOR
10000	8500	6500	5000	3000	900

	NIB	EXC.	V.G.	GOOD	FAIR	POOR

DOUBLE RIFLES

Many optional engraving patterns available for these double rifles that may affect price. Consult an expert prior to sale.

Teck Over/Under

Boxlock over/under rifle, manufactured in a variety of calibers, with 25" barrels. Double triggers, extractors and express sights. Blued, with walnut stock. **NOTE:** .458 Win. Magnum add $1,500.

NIB	EXC.	V.G.	GOOD	FAIR	POOR
9000	8250	6600	5000	2250	1500

Ulm Model

As above, with sidelocks.

NIB	EXC.	V.G.	GOOD	FAIR	POOR
15000	12000	10500	7500	3000	2000

Ulm Primus

As above, with detachable sidelocks.

NIB	EXC.	V.G.	GOOD	FAIR	POOR
23500	19500	16500	11500	7000	3000

Ultra

Boxlock over/under rifle, offered with several different options. Same caliber rifle barrels; different caliber rifle barrels. Built on 20-gauge frame, with game scene engraving. Weights depend on calibers and combinations of calibers, but are between 6.5 lbs. and 8 lbs.

NIB	EXC.	V.G.	GOOD	FAIR	POOR
7500	6100	4400	3000	1500	800

Classic

Side-by-side rifle with side plates. Offered in 7x65R to 9.3x74R calibers, with optional interchangeable 20-gauge shotgun barrel. Single trigger. Choice of standard stock with cheekpiece or classic Bavaria style. Weight approximately 7.25 to 8 lbs., depending on calibers.

NIB	EXC.	V.G.	GOOD	FAIR	POOR
8800	6900	5000	3500	2000	800

Classic Big Five

Similar to Classic, but chambered for .375 H&H, .375 NE, .458 Win. Magnum, .416 Rigby, .470 NE and .500 NE 3". Double trigger, with hinged front trigger. Weighs approximately 9.25 to 10 lbs., depending on caliber. Interchangeable barrels are optional.

NIB	EXC.	V.G.	GOOD	FAIR	POOR
10900	82500	5100	3500	2000	750

SHOTGUNS

Model 32 Standard

12-, 20-, 28-gauge or .410 bore boxlock over/under shotgun, with 26.5" to 32" barrels. Single-selective trigger and automatic ejectors. Blued, with walnut stock. Discontinued in 1980. **NOTE:** 28-gauge or .410 two barrel set add 50 percent. Four-barrel Skeet set add 100 percent.

NIB	EXC.	V.G.	GOOD	FAIR	POOR
—	3000	2500	2000	1100	750

San Remo Grade

NIB	EXC.	V.G.	GOOD	FAIR	POOR
—	5000	3750	1900	1400	1000

Monte Carlo Grade

NIB	EXC.	V.G.	GOOD	FAIR	POOR
—	6250	4850	2750	1650	1250

Crown Grade

NIB	EXC.	V.G.	GOOD	FAIR	POOR
—	8700	6500	4300	2200	1500

Super Crown Grade

NIB	EXC.	V.G.	GOOD	FAIR	POOR
18000	14700	10500	6850	3750	2000

Single Barrel Trap Gun

Model 32, with single 32" to 34" barrel.

NIB	EXC.	V.G.	GOOD	FAIR	POOR
—	3950	3250	1700	1075	600

Teck Over/Under

Similar to Teck double rifle, but offered in 12- and 16-gauge.

NIB	EXC.	V.G.	GOOD	FAIR	POOR
12000	10000	7500	4550	3000	1750

Teck Dural

Same as above, with lightweight aluminum frame.

NIB	EXC.	V.G.	GOOD	FAIR	POOR
12000	10000	7500	4550	3000	1750

	NIB	EXC.	V.G.	GOOD	FAIR	POOR

Ulm

Sidelock over/under offered in both 12- and 16-gauge.

	20000	16500	13000	8000	4500	3000

Ulm Dural

Lightweight version of above model.

	20000	16500	13000	8000	4500	3000

Ulm Primus

Deluxe version of Ulm series, with sidelocks and extensive engraving.

	30000	22250	16500	12000	7000	3500

Ulm Primus Dural

Lightweight version of above model.

	30000	22250	16500	12000	7000	3500

Ultra

Lightweight over/under gun offered in 12- or 20-gauge.

	—	6250	4850	2750	1650	1250

KS-5 Single Barrel Trap

Boxlock 12-gauge only trap gun, with 32" or 34" ventilated tapered rib barrel. Case hardened frame, with satin gray finish. Barrel features adjustable point of impact and offered with screw-in choke tubes. Weight approximately 8.6 lbs.

	8000	7500	5900	3650	1250	800

KS-5 Special

Same as above, with adjustable rib and comb.

	8250	7750	6100	3900	1500	1000

K-80 Trap

Boxlock 12-gauge shotgun, built to trap dimensions. Offered in many variations. Available in over/under trap, with choice of 30" or 32" vent tapered step rib barrels. Single barrel offered in 32" or 34" tapered step rib lengths. Single barrels are adjustable for point of impact. Top single barrel available as well in 34" length. Trap combos are also offered. All barrels offered with or without choke tubes. Checkered walnut stock offered in Monte Carlo or straight trap dimensions. Trap guns weigh approximately 8.75 lbs. Prices listed for Standard Grade. **NOTE:** Bavaria Grade add 70 percent; Danube Grade add 100 percent; Gold Target Grade add 200 percent.

Over/Under Trap

	9800	8000	6000	4200	2500	1000

Unsingle Trap

	11000	9000	7200	5500	3000	1500

Top Single Trap

	11500	10000	8000	6000	3700	1850

Trap Combos

	13000	10700	9600	7400	4300	1900

K-20 Sporting and Field

Compact frame variation of K-80, chambered in 20- or 28-gauge and .410 bore. Barrels are 30" or 32", with five choke tubes and tapered flat rib. Checkered walnut stock, auto ejectors and single selective trigger. Weight approx. 7.25 lbs. Available with extra sets of barrels in other two gauges.

	9000	8000	7000	4000	2200	1000

K-80 Sporting Clays

Frame is the same as trap model, with addition of lightweight alloy model and available in 12-gauge only. Barrel lengths for standard weight model are 28", 30" or 32", with tapered flat rib. Lightweight model offered with 28" or 30" flat rib barrels. Select European walnut stock, with hand checkering and supplied with #3 Sporting stock, with schnabel forearm. Standard weight model weighs about 8.25 lbs.; lightweight model weighs 7.75 lbs. Prices listed are for Standard Grade. **NOTE:** Bavaria Grade add 70 percent; Danube Grade add 100 percent; Gold Target Grade add 200 percent.

	9500	8000	7000	4000	2200	1000

	NIB	EXC.	V.G.	GOOD	FAIR	POOR

K-80 Skeet

Model offered in a number of variations. Standard and Lightweight weight skeet, with 28" or 30" tapered or parallel ribs; International skeet, with 28" parallel broadway rib; 4-barrel skeet set in 12-, 20-, 28-gauge and .410 bore, with 8mm rib. Stock is hand-checkered select European walnut, with choice of several skeet dimensions. Values listed are for Standard Grade. **NOTE:** Bavaria Grade add 70 percent; Danube Grade add 100 percent; Gold Target Grade add 200 percent. Optional Engravings available by special order on NIB or Exc. conditions guns: Add $1500 Parcours; $2800 Parcours Special; $1100 Super Scroll; $2900 Gold Super Scroll; $4700 Custom Bavaria over Bavaria Grade price.

Standard Weight Skeet

7500	6250	4950	3300	2200	1000

Lightweight Skeet

7500	6250	4950	3300	2200	1000

International Skeet

7500	6250	4950	3300	2200	1000

4 Barrel Set

17000	10000	7600	4400	3300	2200

SIDE-BY-SIDE DOUBLES

Essencia Boxlock

High-grade model introduced in 2003. Has round-body receiver, with English-style scroll engraving and gold highlights. Offered in 12-, 16-, 20- and 28-gauges, with 28" or 30" barrels and fixed IC/M chokes. Straight-grip Turkish walnut checkered stock, single (non-selective) or double triggers and automatic ejectors. **NOTE:** Add $1000 for 28-gauge; $1000 for single trigger.

22000	17500	15000	10000	3000	800

Essencia Sidelock

Model also introduced in 2003. Back-action sidelock on three frame sizes, designed for different gauges. Offered in 12-, 16-, 20- and 28-gauges. Barrel lengths 18", 26.5" or 30", with fixed chokes or Briley choke tubes. Receiver is color case hardened, with gold-inlayed engraving. Straight- or pistol-grip Turkish walnut checkered stock, single (non-selective) or double triggers and automatic ejectors. **NOTE:** Add $1000 for 28-gauge; $1000 for single trigger; $1500 for Briley choke tubes.

27000	22500	18000	12000	4000	800

KRNKA, KAREL
Vienna, Austria

Karel Krnka was a talented firearms inventor, born in 1858. He began his career in firearms design as a member of the Austro-Hungarian army. He made many improvements to their service rifle design. After he left the military, he took the job of head engineer, with ill-fated and short-lived "Gatling Gun Company". This company ceased operations in 1890. Krnka then went to work for the patent office and remained there for a few years. In 1898 he became foreman of Roth Cartridge Company and worked with Roth on firearms designs until the death of Roth in 1909. After this, he became associated with Hertenberger Cartridge Company; and finally in 1922 he moved to Czechoslovakia, where he became a firearms designer for the firm of C.Z. He remained at this post until his death in 1926. He recorded his first firearm patent in 1888 for a mechanical repeater with a ring trigger. His best known innovations are the internal butt magazine, that is loaded by means of a stripper clip and rotating locked bolt, with internal firing pin. These designs were never actually turned into a mass-marketed pistol, but were major contributions in the development of a practical semi-automatic pistol design.

Model 1892

—	—	8200	5500	2200	1050

KSN INDUSTRIES
Israel

Golan

Semi-automatic pistol introduced in 1996. Chambered for 9mm or .40 S&W cartridge. Double-action trigger, with ambidextrous controls. Barrel length 3.9" and magazine capacity 10 rounds, in U.S. In the rest of the world 15 rounds for 9mm and 11 rounds for .40 S&W. Weight is 29 oz.

650	525	400	325	200	100

	NIB	EXC.	V.G.	GOOD	FAIR	POOR

Kareen MK II

Single-action semi-automatic pistol, chambered for 9mm cartridge. Barrel length 4.5". Ambidextrous safety and rubber grips. Steel slide and frame. Weight about 34 oz.

NIB	EXC.	V.G.	GOOD	FAIR	POOR
500	395	250	200	150	100

Kareen MK II—Compact

Same as above, with 3.9" barrel. Weight about 32 oz.

NIB	EXC.	V.G.	GOOD	FAIR	POOR
575	425	325	250	200	150

GAL

Same as full size Kareen. Chambered for .45 ACP cartridge.

NIB	EXC.	V.G.	GOOD	FAIR	POOR
575	425	325	250	200	150

KUFAHL, G. L.
Sommerda, Germany

Kufahl Needle-Fire Revolver

Designed and patented in Britain in 1852 by G.L. Kufahl, who tried unsuccessfully to interest a British company in producing it. He then went to the firm of Rheinmettal Dreyse, where a needle-fire gun was produced in 1838. This company manufactured his design. This revolver was chambered for a unique, totally consumed .30-caliber "cartridge". A lead projectile had the ignition percussion cap affixed to its base, with propellant powder in rear. Firing pin had to be long enough to penetrate the powder charge and hit the percussion cap. This does not sound efficient, but realize that these were the days before cartridges. This revolver has a 3.2" barrel and an unfluted cylinder that holds six shots. It is not bored all the way through, but is loaded from the front. Finish is blued, with a modicum of simple engraving and checkered wood grips that protrude all the way over the trigger. Markings are "Fv.V. Dreyse Sommerda".

NIB	EXC.	V.G.	GOOD	FAIR	POOR
—	—	2950	1600	650	400

KYNOCH GUN FACTORY
Birmingham, England

Established by George Kynoch in approximately 1886. Company ceased operation in 1890.

Early Double Trigger Revolver

.45-caliber double trigger revolver, with 6" barrel, 6-shot cylinder and enclosed hammer. Blued, with walnut grips. Manufactured in 1885.

NIB	EXC.	V.G.	GOOD	FAIR	POOR
—	—	1600	950	575	350

Late Double Trigger Revolver

Similar to above in .32-, .38- or .45-caliber. Cocking trigger enclosed within the trigger guard. Approximately 600 revolvers made between 1890 and 1896.

NIB	EXC.	V.G.	GOOD	FAIR	POOR
—	—	2100	1575	900	575

L

NIB	EXC.	V.G.	GOOD	FAIR	POOR

LAGRESE
Paris, France

Lagrese Revolver

Large ornate revolver chambered for .43 rimfire cartridge. Has 6.25" barrel and 6-shot fluted cylinder. Revolver has no top strap; and frame, as well as grip straps are cast in one piece, with barrel screwed into frame. It is loaded through a gate and has double-action lock work. Outstanding feature about this well-made revolver is its extremely ornate appearance. There are more sweeps and curves than could be imagined and in general outline somewhat resembles the leMat, though with a single barrel. Engraved and blued, with well-figured curved walnut grips. Marked "Lagrese Bte a Paris" and manufactured in late 1860s.

—	—	3500	2750	1300	875

LAHTI
Finland
See—Husqvarna

Lahti

Commercial version of Finnish L-35 9mm pistol. Pistols have barrel and trigger guard design of L-35, but barrel extension of Swedish M40. Produced in late 1950s.

—	1250	1000	800	550	300

LAKELANDER
Gulfport, Mississippi

Model 389 Premium

Bolt-action rifle chambered for .270 Win., .308 Win. and .30-06 calibers. Fitted with 22" lightweight barrel. Stock is oil finished walnut, with diamond checkering. Rosewood fore-end cap, black recoil pad and Monte Carlo buttstock. Weight approximately 7.6 lbs. Introduced in 1997.

1750	1350	950	700	375	200

Model 389 Classic

Similar to Premium grade rifle above. Offered with traditional stock, checkering and less fancy walnut stock. Weight approximately 7.3 lbs. Introduced in 1997.

1725	1325	925	675	350	150

Model 389 Match-Maker

Bolt-action chambered for .308 cartridge. Fitted with 21.7" barrel. Stock is target style, with adjustable chin support with benchrest-style buttpad. Weight approximately 8.4 lbs. Introduced in 1997. **NOTE:** Add $50 for magnum calibers.

2250	1850	1350	850	575	250

LAMB, H. C. & CO.
Jamestown, North Carolina

Muzzleloading Rifle

Chambered for .58-caliber and utilizes percussion ignition system. Has 33" barrel and full-length oak stock held on by two barrel bands. Ramrod mounted under barrel made of iron. All other trim is brass. A bayonet lug at muzzle. Rifle was made for Confederacy and workmanship was crude, as it was on most CSA weapons. Stock marked "H.C.Lamb & Co., N.C." Supposedly 10,000 rifles ordered, but approximately 250 manufactured between 1861 and 1863. Rarity of guns of Confederacy gives them a great deal of collector appeal.

—	—	35000	15000	2750	500

LAMES
Chiavari, Italy

Skeet or Trap Grade

Over/under shotgun chambered for 12-gauge, with 26" skeet-and-skeet barrels or 30" or 32" full-choked barrels. Has a competition-style wide vent rib and automatic ejectors. Trigger is single-selective and finish is blued. Trap gun has Monte Carlo stock of checkered walnut. Both models feature recoil pads.

	700	575	475	375	200

	NIB	EXC.	V.G.	GOOD	FAIR	POOR

California Trap Grade

Over/under similar to standard trap model, with separated barrels. All other features the same.

	NIB	EXC.	V.G.	GOOD	FAIR	POOR
	—	775	650	575	475	225

Field Grade

Similar in design to standard trap model, with 3" chambers and barrel lengths of 26", 28" or 30". Field dimensioned stock. Features various choke combinations. Also available with separated barrels of California Trap for an additional 20 percent cost.

	—	475	450	350	250	150

LANBER ARMAS S.A.
Vizcaya, Spain

Model 2072 Slug

Fixed choke double barrel slug gun, with 3" chambers and 20" barrel. Fiber-optic rifle sights. Weight about 6 lbs. Hard-to-find gun.

900	800	650	475	300	200

Model 844 ST

12-gauge over/under shotgun, with 26" or 28" vent rib barrels. Chokes vary and gun features single-selective trigger, extractors and engraved receiver, with blued finish and walnut stock. Gun manufactured until 1986.

—	425	350	300	250	175

Model 844 MST

Similar to Model 844 ST except chambered for 3" Magnum. Has 30" Full and Modified choked barrels.

—	525	450	300	250	175

Model 844 EST

Similar to others, but features automatic ejectors.

—	575	425	350	300	200

Model 844 EST CHR

Has automatic ejectors and double triggers. All other features are same as EST.

—	550	400	325	275	175

Model 2004 LCH

Over/under chambered for 12-gauge and features 28" vent rib barrels, with screw-in choke tubes. Has single-selective trigger, automatic ejectors. Engraved boxlock action that is matte finished, with hand-checkered walnut stock. Discontinued in 1986.

—	775	650	550	475	375

Model 2008 LCH and Model 2009 LCH

Trap and skeet versions of series. Basic differences in barrel lengths and stock dimensions.

—	900	750	650	575	475

Model 2067

20-gauge over/under, with 3" chambers. Has 28" barrels, auto ejectors and oil-finished walnut stock. Weight about 6.6 lbs.

775	650	550	450	375	200

Model 2077 Hunter Light

A 2.75" 12-gauge, with 26" barrels and lightweight alloy receiver. Weight about 6.2 lbs.

850	725	575	475	400	200

Model 2087 Hunter

12-gauge comes with 3" chambers, auto ejectors, oil-finished walnut stock and 28" or 30" barrel. Weight about 7 lbs.

775	650	550	450	375	200

Model 2097 Sporting

Sporting clays model in 12-gauge, with 3" chambers and 28" or 30" barrels. Weight about 7.7 lbs. **NOTE:** Add $50 for Sporting LUX model.

850	725	575	475	400	200

	NIB	EXC.	V.G.	GOOD	FAIR	POOR

Model 2088 Rival I

Sporting clays model is 2.75" 12-gauge, with 28" barrels and case-hardened receiver. Weight about 7.6 lbs.

	NIB	EXC.	V.G.	GOOD	FAIR	POOR
	1600	1300	850	600	400	200

Model 2089 Rival II

This 2.75" 12-gauge sporting clays gun has 30" barrels, one fixed and other threaded for choke tubes. Blued receiver. Weight about 7.9 lbs.

1600	1300	850	600	400	200

Model 2070 Becada

This 3" 12-gauge gun developed for woodcock hunting. Features one fixed choke barrel and one barrel threaded for chokes. Barrel length 23"; weight about 6 lbs.

850	725	575	475	400	200

Model 2531 Victoria I

12-gauge semi-automatic has 3" chamber and 28" barrel, with internal choke tube system. Stock is oil finished walnut and receiver is blued. Weight about 6.8 lbs.

600	500	400	300	200	100

Model 2532 Victoria II

Similar to above. Available with 26" or 28" barrel.

625	525	425	325	225	100

Model 2532 Victoria II EXT

Similar to above, with 24.5" barrel and external choke tube system.

625	525	425	325	225	100

Model 2534

Lighter version of 2532. Weighs about 6.4 lbs., with 26" barrel.

625	525	425	325	225	100

Model 2533 Victoria LUX

Semi-automatic 3" 12-gauge. Features brushed silver finish scrollwork and gold mallard on receiver. Barrel is 26" or 28". Weight about 6.8 lbs.

650	550	450	350	250	100

Model 2533 Victoria LUX EXT

As above, with 24.5" barrel and external choke tube system.

650	550	450	350	250	100

Model 2535 Victoria Slug

Dedicated slug gun has fiber-optic rifle sights atop 24" fixed cylinder barrel.

650	550	450	350	250	100

LANCASTER, CHARLES
London, England

4-Barreled Pistol

Unique pistol for several reasons. Chambered for .476 rimfire cartridge and has four 6.25" barrels. Bore has slightly twisted oval pattern that imparts a spin to bullet. Barrels are hinged at bottom and break downward for loading. Double-action type lockwork, with long difficult trigger pull. Pistol is well made and caliber suitably heavy to insure stopping power. Primary goal was military; successful seeing action in Sudan campaigns of 1882 and 1885. This powerful weapon was also popular with big game hunters as a backup sidearm. Finish is blued, with checkered walnut grips. Marked "Charles Lancaster (Patent) 151 New Bond St. London". Model introduced in 1881. There are smaller-caliber versions of this pistol, with shorter barrels. They are not as well known as large-caliber version and values would be similar as their rarity would be balanced by desirability of large bore models.

—	—	8000	5750	2500	1500

2-Barreled Pistol

Similar to 4 barreled version, with only two superposed barrels. Chambered for a variety of calibers from .320 to .577. Also chambered for 20-gauge and .410 bore shot shell. Advantage to 2 barreled pistol it is lighter and better balanced. The 2 barrel is less common than 4 barrel version.

—	—	6000	3750	1750	1000

	NIB	EXC.	V.G.	GOOD	FAIR	POOR

4-Barreled Shotgun

Company also produced a shotgun in 4 barrel configuration. Chambered for 12- or 16-gauge and has 28" barrels. Gun is as one would imagine, quite heavy and poorly balanced; not a great success.

	NIB	EXC.	V.G.	GOOD	FAIR	POOR
	—	—	6250	4000	2000	1000

Bolt-Action Rifle

High-grade sporting rifle chambered for various different calibers. Barrel is 24" in length; finish blued with classic-styled hand-checkered walnut stock. Discontinued in 1936.

	NIB	EXC.	V.G.	GOOD	FAIR	POOR
	—	3500	1900	1250	800	600

LANG, J.
London, England

Percussion Pistol

Chambered for .60-caliber percussion. Single-barreled muzzle-loading pistol, with 3.25" barrel. Essentially a defensive weapon that was well made. Damascus barrels and ornate engraved hammer and frame.

	NIB	EXC.	V.G.	GOOD	FAIR	POOR
	—	—	4510	3000	1100	600

Gas Seal Revolver

Chambered for .42-caliber percussion and has 4.75" barrel. Unfluted cylinder holds 6 shots and spring-loaded to be forced into barrel when cocked, in order to obtain "Gas Seal" feature desired. Revolver was well made and finished. Lightly engraved, with case-colored cylinder and blued barrel and frame. Grips are finely checkered walnut and markings are "J.Lang 22 Cockspur St. London". This type of firearm was forerunner of later designs such as Russian Nagant. Manufactured in 1850s.

	NIB	EXC.	V.G.	GOOD	FAIR	POOR
	—	—	3000	1500	1000	550

LANGENHAN, FRIEDRICH
Zella Mehlis, Germany

F.L. Selbstlader is not a manufacturer, but the German designation for self-loader used on pistols made by Friedrich Langenhan.

Langenhan Army Model

Blowback-operated semi-automatic pistol chambered for 7.65mm Auto Pistol cartridge. Has 4" barrel and detachable magazine that holds 8 rounds. Weight about 24 oz. Pistol made with separate breechblock that is held into slide by a screw. This feature doomed pistol to eventual failure, when this screw became worn it could loosen when firing and allow breechblock to pivot upwards—and slide would then be propelled rearward and into the face of shooter. Pistol produced with wood grips.

	NIB	EXC.	V.G.	GOOD	FAIR	POOR
	—	375	300	250	175	100

Langenhan Open Model

Semi-automatic pistol similar to Army Model, with some minor variations. Open window in frame. Checkered hard rubber grips, with "FL" logo on each side.

	NIB	EXC.	V.G.	GOOD	FAIR	POOR
	—	400	325	275	200	100

Langenhan Closed Model

Similar to Open Model, with closed frame and other minor variations.

	NIB	EXC.	V.G.	GOOD	FAIR	POOR
	—	400	325	275	200	100

Model 2

Blowback-operated semi-automatic pistol chambered for 6.35mm cartridge. Has 3" barrel and 8-round detachable magazine. Weight about 18 oz. Pistol fires by means of concealed hammer and breechblock separate from rest of slide and held in place by a heavy crossbolt. Finish is blued and grips are molded checkered black plastic, with monogram "F.L." at top. Slide marked "Langenhan 6.35". Manufactured between 1921 and 1936.

	NIB	EXC.	V.G.	GOOD	FAIR	POOR
	—	375	300	250	200	100

Model 3

Similar to Model 2 except somewhat smaller. Barrel is 2.25" in length and butt only large enough to house a 5-round detachable magazine. Weight about 17 oz. Markings are the same with addition of "Model 111" on slide. Manufactured until 1936.

	NIB	EXC.	V.G.	GOOD	FAIR	POOR
	—	325	275	250	200	150

	NIB	EXC.	V.G.	GOOD	FAIR	POOR

LAR MFG. CO.
West Jordan, Utah

Grizzly Mark I

.357 Magnum, .45 ACP, 10mm or .45 Winchester Magnum semi-automatic pistol, with 5.4", 6.5", 8" or 10" barrel. Millett sights, ambidextrous safety and 7-shot magazine. Parkerized, blued or hard-chrome plated, with rubber grips. Available with cartridge conversion units, telescope mounts or compensator. Weight approximately 48 oz. Introduced in 1984.

1400	150	950	700	400	200

Grizzly Mark II

As above, with fixed sights. Without ambidextrous safety. Manufactured in 1986.

—	1300	1050	775	475	300

Grizzly Mark IV

Similar to Mark I, but chambered for .44 Magnum cartridge. Barrel lengths 5.4" or 6.5". Choice of blue or Parkerized finish.

1500	1100	775	500	400	200

Grizzly Mark V

Same as above, but chambered for .50 AE cartridge. Empty weight 56 oz. **NOTE:** Add $200 for nickel finish.

1950	1350	1000	650	425	200

Grizzly State Pistol

Limited edition of 50 Grizzly pistols. Serial numbers match the order in which each state was admitted into the union. Each pistol features state outline, state seal and name of state engraved in gold. Supplied with cherry wood fitted case, with glass top. Chambered for .45 Win. Magnum cartridge.

3000	—	—	—	—	—

Grizzly 50 Big Boar

Single-shot breech loading rifle chambered for .50-caliber BMG cartridge. Barrel is 36" in length. Weighs approximately 30 lbs. **NOTE:** Add $100 for Parkerized finish; $250 for nickel frame; $350 for full nickel finish.

2350	2000	1550	1100	550	300

LARUE TACTICAL
Leander, Texas

OBR (Optimized Battle Rifle)

AR-style series available in 5.56 NATO (.223 Rem.) or 7.62 NATO (.308 Win.) and in several variations and barrel lengths. Hand guard does not touch barrel at any point, resulting in a weapon that remains cool, even after high rates of fire. There is a continuous upper rail for day/night accessories, plus three 3" Picatinny rail sections to be attached anywhere on the hand guard. A two-point adjustable gas selector allows optimum function between suppressed and unsuppressed operation. Barrel lengths available are 12" (Class III model for LE/Military), 16.1", 18" and 20". Values shown are for 5.56 NATO models.

1900	1600	1350	975	550	250

OBR (Optimized Battle Rifle) 7.62 NATO/.308 Win.

Same basic features as 5.56 version, with heavier frame for larger calibers. Barrel lengths are 16", 18" or 20". Has proprietary XTRAXTN chamber for enhanced extraction, with wide range of loads and temperatures.

2800	2400	1900	1400	750	300

LASALLE
France

Slide-Action Shotgun

Chambered for 12- or 20-gauge. Offered with 26", 28" or 30" barrel, with Improved-Cylinder, Modified or Full chokes. Receiver is alloy anodized blue and vent rib barrel is blued. Stock is checkered walnut.

—	275	225	200	150	100

	NIB	EXC.	V.G.	GOOD	FAIR	POOR

Semi-Automatic Shotgun

Gas-operated semi-automatic shotgun chambered for 12-gauge only. Same barrel length and choke combinations as are available on slide-action model. Receiver is also alloy and stock is checkered walnut.

	NIB	EXC.	V.G.	GOOD	FAIR	POOR
	—	325	250	200	175	100

LASERAIM ARMS
Little Rock, Arkansas

Series I

Offered in 10mm or .45 ACP. Single-action semi-automatic pistol. Fitted with 6" barrel with compensator. Adjustable rear sight. Stainless steel frame and barrel, with matte black Teflon finish. Introduced in 1993. Magazine capacity for 10mm is 8 rounds; 7 rounds for .45 ACP. Weight about 46 oz.

NIB	EXC.	V.G.	GOOD	FAIR	POOR
650	550	400	300	200	100

Series II

Similar to Series I except this model has no compensator. Fitted with 5" barrel and stainless steel finish. Compact version has 3-3/8" barrel. Introduced in 1993. Weight 43 oz. for 5" barrel; 37 oz. for compact version.

NIB	EXC.	V.G.	GOOD	FAIR	POOR
625	525	375	275	175	100

Series III

Similar to Series II except offered with 5" barrel only. Dual port compensator. Introduced in 1994. Weight about 43 oz.

NIB	EXC.	V.G.	GOOD	FAIR	POOR
650	550	400	300	200	100

LAURONA
Eibar, Spain

Company has manufactured quality shotguns in Spain since 1941, but there has not been a U.S. importer for many years. Last importer was Galaxy Imports of Victoria, Texas, which brought several models of over/under and side-by-side shotguns into the country from about 1967 to early 1990s. One of the unique features of standard Laurona over/under series was a double trigger system, with each trigger acting as a non-selective single trigger. One trigger fired bottom barrel first, then top barrel; other trigger fired top barrel first then bottom barrel. We thank Thomas Barker of Galaxy Imports for information and specifications in these listings.

Model 67

First over/under Laurona chambered for 12-gauge only. Double triggers and 28" ventilated rib barrels, with extractors. Boxlock action. Barrels are blued and stock is checkered walnut in 20 lpi skip line checkering.

	NIB	EXC.	V.G.	GOOD	FAIR	POOR
	—	400	250	150	75	50

Model 71

Similar to Model 67, with minor cosmetic changes and improvements to facilitate ease of manufacturing. Receiver is bright chromed, with roll engraving depicting dogs on right side and birds on left. Imported and sold by Sears & Roebuck about 1973 and 1974. Earlier models had traditional solid center ribbed blued barrels. Later models had black chrome finished solid ribbed barrels.

	NIB	EXC.	V.G.	GOOD	FAIR	POOR
	—	450	300	200	100	75

MODEL 82

Similar to Model 71, with auto-ejectors. Chambered for 12-gauge only. All barrels separated without center rib. Black Chrome finish and hard chrome bores, with long forcing cones in chambers. Firing pins changed to traditional round type. Many internal parts improved for reliability. Checkering changed from skip diamond to standard 20 lpi. In most respects 82 Models are representative of present-day Laurona over/under shotguns and will share most internal parts. **NOTE:** Super Models listed have nickel-finish receivers featuring delicate fine scroll engraving, with black chrome relief. All barrels have very durable rust-resistant black chrome finish.

Model 82 Game

Barrels are 28" with 2.75" or 3" chambers, long forcing cones, hard chrome bores, 5mm rib and chokes. Finish on barrels is black chrome, with nickel receiver with Louis XVI style engraving. Tulip fore-end, field-style stock, with plastic buttplate. Weighs approximately 7 lbs.

	NIB	EXC.	V.G.	GOOD	FAIR	POOR
	—	550	400	250	125	100

	NIB	EXC.	V.G.	GOOD	FAIR	POOR

Model 82 Super Game
Similar to Model 82 Game except more elaborate and very delicate engraving

	—	600	500	300	125	100

Model 82 Trap Combi
Similar to Model 82 Game except for 28" or 29" barrels. Rib is 8mm. Trap stock fitted with rubber recoil pad. Weight about 7.4 lbs.

	—	700	500	350	300	200

Model 82 Trap Competition
Similar to Model 82 Trap Combi except for 13mm aluminum rib, with long white sight. Engraving consist of motifs on sides of receiver. Beavertail fluted fore-end and Monte Carlo Trap stock, with black rubber special Trap recoil pad. Weight approximately 8 lbs.

	—	700	500	300	250	200

Model 82 Super Trap (U only)
Similar to Model 82 Trap Competition except for special trap Pachmayr recoil pad, with imitation leather face. Engraving very delicate fine scroll. Weight 7 lbs., 12 oz.

	—	650	500	350	300	250

Model 82 Super Skeet
Similar to Model 82 Super Trap except fitted with 28" barrels, choked sheet with field-style buttstock and plastic buttplate. Weight approximately 7 lbs.

	—	650	500	300	250	200

Model 82 Pigeon Competition
Similar to Model 82 Trap Competition except fitted with 28" barrels. Recoil pad is special competition-style Pachmayr, with imitation leather face. Weight about 7 lbs., 13 oz.

	—	650	500	350	300	250

Model 82 Super Pigeon
Similar to Model 82 Super Trap except fitted with 28" barrels. Weight approximately 7 lbs., 9 oz.

	—	675	575	450	300	250

MODEL 83/84/85
NOTE: Super Game models listed were available with an extra set of 20-gauge multi-choke barrels in 26" or 28". Add $400 to Exc. value for these barrels. Models with cast-on stocks for left-hand shooters add $50 to Exc. value.

Model 84S Super Game
Similar to Model 82 Super Game except for new single-selective trigger which is designated by "S" in model number. Chambered for 12-gauge 3" magnum, with 28" barrels and 8mm rib. Weight approximately 7 lbs.

	—	500	400	350	200	100

Model 83MG Super Game
Similar to Model 82 Super Game except this model was the advent of Laurona's new multi-choke. CAUTION! Laurona multi-choke is not compatible with any other brand of screw-in chokes because of black chrome plating on metric threads. Do not attempt to interchange with other guns. Barrel for this model in 12-gauge are 28" in length; 20-gauge 26" or 28". Both are chambered for 3" shell. Rib is 8mm. Weight about 7 lbs.

	—	700	450	350	200	100

Model 85MS Super Game
Similar to Model 83MG Super Game except for single-selective trigger. Chambered for 12- or 20-gauge 3" Magnum. Weight about 7 lbs.

	—	750	650	450	250	200

Model 84S Super Trap
Single-selective trigger with 29" barrels. Chambered for 2.75" shells, with long forcing cones. Aluminum rib is 13mm wide. Auto ejectors. Receiver nickel plated, with fine scroll engraving and black chrome relief. Beavertail forearm and choice of Monte Carlo or standard Trap stock. Weight about 7 lbs., 12 oz.

		1000	750	550	350	250

Model 85MS Super Trap
Similar to Model 82S Super Trap except multi-choke in bottom barrel with fixed choke on top barrel. Weight about 7 lbs., 12 oz.

	—	1100	900	700	500	300

	NIB	EXC.	V.G.	GOOD	FAIR	POOR

Model 85MS Super Pigeon

Similar to Model 85MS Super Trap except with 28" barrels, fixed IM choke on top barrel and multi-choke on bottom barrel. Intended for live bird competition. Weight about 7 lbs., 4 oz.

	—	1100	900	800	600	300

Model 85MS Special Sporting

Similar to Model 85MS Super Pigeon except for field-style buttstock, with plastic buttplate. Intended for upland game. Weight approximately 7 lbs., 4 oz.

	—	1100	900	800	600	300

Model 84S Super Skeet

Similar to Model 85MS Special Sporting except choked skeet and skeet. Weight approximately 7 lbs.

	—	950	900	800	600	300

OVER/UNDER MODELS SILHOUETTE 300

Guns are basically the same as Super series above with these exceptions: Readily identified by white and black chrome stripped receiver, with model engraved on side of receiver. Barrels are multi-choked on both bores and have 11mm steel ribs. **NOTE:** Two types of chokes were used. Some guns came with knurl head-type as in Super models and others were made with flush invector style. Later option for ease of changing chokes is knurl long choke, which is a flush-type with a knurl head added. Both later type chokes, flush and knurl long-type, can be used in early multi-choke models, with some extension showing.

Silhouette 300 Trap

Model has barrels 29" with 2.75" chambers. Long forcing cones, with hard chrome bores and 11mm rib. Beavertail forearm and straight comb trap stock fitted with ventilated black rubber recoil pad are standard. Weight approximately 8 lbs.

	—	1100	800	500	200	100

Silhouette 300 Sporting Clays

Similar to Model 300 Trap except with 28" barrels. Some guns came with 3" chambers. Buttstock is field style, with plastic buttplate or hard rubber sporting clay pad. Weight about 8 lbs.

	—	950	700	600	200	100

Silhouette 300 Ultra Magnum

Similar to Model 300 Sporting Clays except with 3.5" chamber in 12-gauge for waterfowl hunting. Weight about 7 lbs., 8 oz.

	—	1000	800	500	275	150

SIDE-BY-SIDE SHOTGUNS

Models with "X" after model number were made after 1975 and finished with non-rusting black chrome on barrels and action with hard chrome bores. Guns made in 12-, 16- and 20-gauge. Smaller gauges made on special order. Side-by-side shotguns were discontinued by Laurona after 1978 to concentrate on the over/under market.

Model 11

Boxlock action, with triple Greener-type round crossbolt. Independent firing pins bushed into face of the action. Barrels of "Bellota" steel. Made in 12-, 16- and 20-gauge.

	—	400	350	300	200	150

Model 13

Similar to Model 11, with Purdey-type bolting system. Extractor of double radius.

	—	400	350	300	200	150

Model 13X

Barrels and action finished in black chrome, with hard chrome bores.

	—	500	400	300	250	200

Model 13E

Similar to Model 13, with automatic ejectors.

	—	500	400	300	250	200

Model 13XE

Similar to Model 13E except black chrome finish and hard chrome bores.

	—	600	500	400	350	300

	NIB	EXC.	V.G.	GOOD	FAIR	POOR

Model 15 Economic Pluma

Similar to Model 13 except first model has hard chrome bores.

	—	450	400	300	250	200

Model 15X

Similar to Model 15 except black chrome finish and hard chrome bores.

	—	500	400	300	250	200

Model 15E Economic Pluma

Similar to Model 15, with automatic ejectors.

	—	550	450	350	300	250

Model 15XE

Similar to Model 15E except black chrome finish and hard chrome bores.

	—	600	500	400	350	300

Model 52 Pluma

Boxlock action, with back of action scalloped and artistically engraved in fine English-style scroll. Churchill rib and double radius extractor. Hard chrome bores. Weight about 6 lbs.

	—	750	650	500	400	350

Model 52E Pluma

Similar to Model 52, with automatic ejectors. Weight approximately 6 lbs., 2 oz.

	—	850	750	600	500	450

SIDE-BY-SIDE SIDELOCKS

Model 103

Blued sidelock, with some light border engraving. Triple Purdey-type bolting system. Extractor of double radius. Barrels of special "Bellota" steel, with hard chrome bores. Made in 12-, 16- and 20-gauge.

	—	900	800	700	500	400

Model 103E

Similar to Model 103, with automatic ejectors.

	—	1000	800	700	600	500

Model 104X

Case-colored sidelocks, with Purdey-type bolting system. Extractor with double radius. Fine double safety sidelocks. Gas relief vents. Articulated trigger. Hard chrome bores. Demi-block barrels of special "Bellota" steel. Black chrome barrels. Produced in 12-, 16- and 20-gauge, with smaller bores available on special order.

	—	1200	1000	800	700	600

Model 104XE

Same as Model 104X, with Holland automatic selective ejectors.

	—	1350	1100	900	800	700

Model 105X Feather

Same as Model 104X, with concave rib. Weight in 12-gauge approximately 6 lbs., 2 oz.

	—	1250	1000	800	700	600

Model 105XE Feather

Same as Model 105X, with Holland automatic selective ejectors.

	—	1400	1250	1000	800	750

Model 502 Feather

Fine sidelock, with Purdey-type bolting system. Very fine double safety sidelocks hand detachable. Gas relief vents. Holland automatic selective ejectors. Articulated trigger. Inside hard chromed Demi-block barrels of special "Bellota" steel. Outside Black Chrome finish. Fine English-style scroll engraving. Marble gray or Laurona Imperial finish. Churchill or concave type rib. Weight: 12-gauge approximately 6.25 lbs. Offered in 12-, 16- and 20-gauge.

	—	2200	1800	1600	1500	1400

Model 801 Deluxe

Same as Model 502 Feather, but engraving is true deluxe Renaissance style. Fully handmade with Imperial finish. First grade walnut stock and forearm.

	—	4400	4000	3750	2750	2250

	NIB	EXC.	V.G.	GOOD	FAIR	POOR

Model 802 Eagle

Same as Model 801 Deluxe, except highly artistic base relief hand engraving of hunting scenes.

	NIB	EXC.	V.G.	GOOD	FAIR	POOR
	—	5000	4500	4000	3500	3250

LAW ENFORCEMENT ORDNANCE CORP.
Ridgeway, Pennsylvania

Striker 12

Semi-automatic shotgun designed for self-defense. Chambered for 12-gauge and has 18.25" cylinder bored barrel. Unique feature about this gun is its 12-round drum magazine. Barrel is shrouded and stock folds. Fixed-stock model also available. Gun introduced primarily as a law enforcement tool and original models had 12" barrels and were legal for law enforcement agencies and Class 3 licensed individuals only. Shotgun no longer imported into U.S. Shotgun now classified as a Class III weapon and subject to restrictions of BATFE. Be certain that the particular shotgun is transferable before purchase. If there are any questions contact BATFE before purchase. Striker 12 shotguns in excellent condition may sell for as much as $1500.

LAZZERONI ARMS COMPANY
Tucson, Arizona

Model 2000ST-F

This model, as with all Lazzeroni models, is chambered for company's own proprietary calibers. The 6.17 (.243) Spitfire, 6.53 (.257) Scramjet, 6.71 (.264) Phantom, 7.21 (.284) Tomahawk, 7.82 (.308) Patriot and 8.59 (.338) Galaxy. Fitted with 27" match grade barrel, with fully adjustable trigger and removable muzzle-brake. Conventional fiberglass stock.

	NIB	EXC.	V.G.	GOOD	FAIR	POOR
	3700	3000	2200	1500	800	300

Model 2000ST-W

As above, fitted with conventional black wood laminate stock. No longer offered.

	NIB	EXC.	V.G.	GOOD	FAIR	POOR
	4800	3900	2700	1750	1000	350

Model 2000ST-FW

As above, fitted with conventional fiberglass stock and additional black wood laminate stock. No longer offered.

	NIB	EXC.	V.G.	GOOD	FAIR	POOR
	5300	4250	3000	2000	1200	500

Model 2000ST-28

Model is 28" barrel variation of Model 2000 ST. Chambered for 7.82 Warbird cartridge. Introduced in 1999.

	NIB	EXC.	V.G.	GOOD	FAIR	POOR
	5300	4250	3000	2000	1200	500

Model 2000SLR

Model has 28" extra-heavy fluted barrel, with conventional fiberglass stock. Chambered for 6.53 Scramjet, 7.21 Firehawk and 7.82 Warbird.

	NIB	EXC.	V.G.	GOOD	FAIR	POOR
	3900	3100	2300	1600	900	400

Model 2000SP-F

Model fitted with 23" match grade barrel and Lazzeroni thumbhole fiberglass stock. Chambered for all Lazzeroni calibers.

	NIB	EXC.	V.G.	GOOD	FAIR	POOR
	3700	3000	2200	1500	800	300

Model 2000SP-W

Same as above, with black wood laminate thumbhole stock. No longer offered.

	NIB	EXC.	V.G.	GOOD	FAIR	POOR
	4800	3900	2700	1750	1000	350

Model 2000SP-FW

Same as above, but supplied with two stocks: thumbhole fiberglass stock and black wood laminate stock. No longer offered.

	NIB	EXC.	V.G.	GOOD	FAIR	POOR
	5300	4250	3000	2000	1200	500

Model 2000SA

Designed as a lightweight mountain rifle. Chambered for .308, .284 or .338 propriety calibers. Barrel length 24" and fluted except for .338-caliber. Offered in both right-/left-hand models. Stock has Monte Carlo cheekpiece. Weight approximately 6.8 lbs.

	NIB	EXC.	V.G.	GOOD	FAIR	POOR
	4000	3100	2300	1600	900	400

	NIB	EXC.	V.G.	GOOD	FAIR	POOR

Model 2000DG

Offered in Saturn and Meteor calibers only. Fitted with 24" barrel. Rifle weighs about 10 lbs. Fibergrain stock finish, removable muzzle-brake and threaded muzzle protector are standard.

4400	3500	2700	1850	1050	450

Model 700ST

Rifle built around a modified Remington 700 action. Fitted with 26" barrel. Chambered for all Lazzeroni long-action calibers except Saturn and Meteor. Weight about 8 lbs. Synthetic stock.

2400	1850	1550	1200	900	200

Swarovski P.H. 3-12x50 Rifle

1400	1150	925	600	400	150

Savage 16 LZ

Introduced in 2001, model features 24" stainless steel barrel, synthetic stock. Chambered for 7.82 Patriot and 7.21 Tomahawk cartridges. Weight approximately 6.8 lbs. Base price listed.

900	775	500	375	200	100

Sako TRG-S

Model fitted with 26" stainless steel barrel and synthetic stock. Chambered for 7.82 Warbird and 7.21 Firebird cartridges. Weight about 7.9 lbs. Base price listed.

1400	1150	925	600	400	150

Model 2005 Global Hunter

Features include precision CNC-machined 17R stainless steel receiver; stainless steel match-grade button-barrel; Jewel competition trigger; titanium firing pin; slim line graphite/composite stock; precision-machined aluminum-alloy floorplate/trigger guard assembly; Vais muzzle-brake; and Limbsaver recoil pad. Base price listed.

6900	5900	4700	3250	1500	500

LE FORGERON
Liege, Belgium

Model 6020 Double Rifle

Boxlock-actioned side-by-side rifle. Chambered for 9.3x74R cartridge. Has 25" barrels, with double triggers and automatic ejectors. Finish is blued and pistol-grip stock is checkered walnut.

—	6100	4950	4400	3300	1250

Model 6040

Simply Model 6020, with false sideplates. All other specifications the same.

—	6900	5750	4950	3850	1500

Model 6030

Double rifle that has true sidelock action and is engraved. Deluxe French walnut stock.

—	11000	8800	8000	6100	2000

Boxlock Shotgun

Side-by-side double-barreled shotgun chambered for 20- or 28-gauge. Barrel lengths are optional as are choke combinations. Gun has single-selective trigger and automatic ejectors. Engraved and blued, with deluxe French walnut stock. **NOTE:** False sideplates add 20 percent.

—	5500	4400	3600	2500	1000

Sidelock Shotgun

Similar specifications to boxlock, except it has true sidelock action. Generally more deluxe in materials and workmanship.

—	13000	12000	9350	7250	2500

LE FRANCAIS
Francais D'Armes et Cycles de St. Etienne
St. Etienne, France
See—Manufrance

Gaulois

8mm palm pistol designed by Brun-Latrige and manufactured by Le Francais. Furnished with 5-round magazine.

—	—	950	550	400	300

	NIB	EXC.	V.G.	GOOD	FAIR	POOR

Le Francais Model 28 (Type Armee)

Unique pistol chambered for 9mm Browning cartridge. A large pistol, with 5" barrel hinged with a tip-up breech. Blowback-operated semi-automatic pistol that has no extractor. Empty cases are blown out of breech by gas pressure. One feature about this pistol that is desirable, it's possible to tip barrel breech forward like a shotgun and load cartridges singly, while holding contents of magazine in reserve. Weapon has fixed sights and blued finish, with checkered walnut grips. Manufactured in 1928.

—	1250	950	750	500	200	

Police Model (Type Policeman)

Blowback-operated double-action semi-automatic chambered for .25 ACP cartridge. Has 3.5" barrel and 7-round magazine. Same hinged barrel feature of Model 28. Blued, with fixed sights and Ebonite grips. Manufactured 1913 to 1914.

—	800	650	450	300	150	

Officer's Model (Pocket Model)

Also referred to a "Staff Model". Blowback-operated semi-automatic chambered for .25 ACP cartridge. Has 2.5" barrel and concealed hammer. Fixed sights and finish is blued. Grips are Ebonite. Manufactured between 1914 and 1938 in two variations: early and second type.

—	300	250	200	150	100	

Target Model (Type Champion)

Chambered for 6.35mm cartridge and fitted with 6" barrel. Extended magazine base is for grip purchase, not additional cartridges.

—	900	700	550	400	275	

LE MAT
Paris, France

LeMat

Somewhat unique background that makes it a bit controversial among collectors. Foreign-made firearm manufactured in Paris, France, as well as Birmingham, England. Designed and patented by an American, Jean Alexander Le Mat of New Orleans, Louisiana; purchased for use by Confederate States of America and used in Civil War. Curious firearm, as it is a huge weapon that has two barrels. Top 6.5" barrel chambered for .42-caliber percussion and supplied by 9-shot unfluted cylinder that revolves on a 5", .63-caliber smoothbore barrel that doubles as cylinder axis pin. These two barrels are held together by a front and rear ring. Rear sight is a notch in nose of hammer. Attached ramrod on side of top barrel. Weapon marked "Lemat and Girards Patent, London". Finish blued, with checkered walnut grips. Fewer than 3,000 manufactured. Approximately one-half were purchased by Confederate States of America. Made between 1856 and 1865.

—	—	30000	25000	7500	1750	

Baby LeMat

Similar in appearance (though a good deal smaller in size) to standard model pistol. Chambered for .32-caliber percussion. Has 4.25" top barrel and .41-caliber smoothbore lower barrel. Cylinder is unfluted and holds 9 shots. Barrel marked "Systeme Le Mat Bte s.g.d.g. Paris". Has British proofmarks. Blued, with checkered walnut grips. Scarcest model Le Mat. Only an estimated 100 manufactured. Used by Confederate States of America in Civil War.

—	—	28500	22000	1100	3300	

LeMat Revolving Carbine

Chambered for centerfire, rimfire cartridges or percussion. Barrels are half round half octagon and 20" in length. Chambered for a variety of calibers, but usually in percussion .42-caliber, with .62-caliber smoothbore lower barrel.

—	—	31500	25000	11000	3000	

LE PAGE SA.
Liege, Belgium

Pinfire Revolver

Company was in business of revolver manufacture in 1850s. Produced a .40-caliber pinfire revolver, similar to Lefauchaux and other pinfires of the day. Barrel lengths vary and unfluted cylinder holds 6 shots. Pistols are double-action and sometimes found with ornate, but somewhat crude engraving. Finish is blued, with wood grips. Quality of these weapons is fair. They were serviceable, but ammunition created somewhat of a problem. Rather fragile and difficult to handle, with protruding primer pin to contend with.

—	—	775	325	200	125	

	NIB	EXC.	V.G.	GOOD	FAIR	POOR

Semi-Automatic Pistol

Semi-automatic pistol, with open top slide and exposed hammer. Chambered for 6.35mm, 7.65mm, 9mm Short and 9mm Long cartridges. Large grip with finger grooves.

	NIB	EXC.	V.G.	GOOD	FAIR	POOR
	—	875	675	525	300	200

Pocket Pistol

Semi-automatic pistol in caliber 6.35mm. Checkered hard rubber grips, with crossed sword and pistol logo of Le Page on each side of grip.

	NIB	EXC.	V.G.	GOOD	FAIR	POOR
	—	325	275	225	175	75

LEBEAU COURALLY
Liege, Belgium

Company has been in business since 1865. Made more guns for royalty than any other gun company in the world. Prices listed are for guns without engraving. Other extra-cost options will affect price. All guns are built to order. Virtually no upper end for values to these infrequently-encountered guns. Values are certainly well in excess of $30,000 for any model in Very Good or better condition.

LEE FIREARMS CO.
Milwaukee, Wisconsin

Lee Single-Shot Carbine

Rare single-shot break-open carbine that pivots to right side for loading. Chambered for .44 rimfire cartridge. Has 21.5" barrel, with hammer mounted in center of frame. Carbine has walnut buttstock, but no forearm and marked "Lee's Firearms Co. Milwaukee, Wisc.". Approximately 450 manufactured between 1863 and 1865. Few surviving examples and one should be wary of fakes.

	NIB	EXC.	V.G.	GOOD	FAIR	POOR
	—	—	6500	2200	900	400

Lee Sporting Rifle

Similar to military carbine except it has a longer octagonal barrel. Barrel length varied and there were more of these manufactured. Survival rate appears to have been better than for carbine model.

	NIB	EXC.	V.G.	GOOD	FAIR	POOR
	—	—	1750	700	300	150

LEECH & RIGDON
Greensboro, Georgia

Leech & Rigdon Revolver

Confederate revolver patterned after 1851 Colt Navy. Chambered for .36-caliber percussion and has 6-shot unfluted cylinder. The 7.5" barrel is part-octagonal and has a loading lever beneath it. Frame is open-topped; finish is blued, with brass grip straps and walnut one-piece grips. Barrel marked "Leech & Rigdon CSA." Approximately 1,500 revolvers manufactured in 1863 and 1864. All contracted for/by Confederacy and considered to be prime acquisition for collectors. Beware of fakes!

	NIB	EXC.	V.G.	GOOD	FAIR	POOR
	—	—	42000	27500	11000	2750

LEFAUCHAUX, CASIMER & EUGENE
Paris, France

Pinfire Revolver

Pinfire ignition system was invented by Casimir Lefauchaux in 1828, but not widely used until 1850s. Consists of smooth rimless case that contains powder charge and percussion cap. Pin protrudes from side of this case at rear and when struck by hammer is driven into cap, thereby igniting charge and firing weapon. Pistols for this cartridge are slotted at end of cylinder to allow pins to protrude and be struck by downward blow of hammer. This particular revolver chambered for .43-caliber and has 5.25" barrel. Cylinder holds 6 shots; finish is blued, with checkered walnut grips. Manufactured after 1865. Selected for service by French military.

	NIB	EXC.	V.G.	GOOD	FAIR	POOR
	—	—	—	575	250	125

LEFEVER, D. M., SONS & COMPANY
Syracuse, New York

In 1901, when Dan Lefever was forced out of Lefever Arms the company he had founded in 1884, he organized another company to produce a line of high-grade boxlock side-by-side doubles. He operated Lefever, D.M. & sons until his death in 1906, at which time the firm closed its doors. During this five-year period, approximately 1,200 shotguns were made in several grades. This makes them quite rare and difficult to evaluate. It is important to get an appraisal from a trusted source before buying or selling. Prices shown are average values.

	NIB	EXC.	V.G.	GOOD	FAIR	POOR

Lefever Double-Barrel Shotgun

A side-by-side, double-barrel shotgun chambered for 12-, 16- or 20-gauge. It was offered with various barrel lengths and choke combinations that were made to order. It features double triggers and automatic ejectors. A single-selective trigger was available as an option. The finish is blued, with a checkered walnut stock. The individual grades differ in the amount of ornamentation and the general quality of the materials and workmanship utilized in their construction. This model was discontinued in 1906. There are an "Optimus" and an "Uncle Dan" grade, which are top-of-the-line models, that features extremely high quality in materials and workmanship and a great deal of ornamentation. This firearm is extremely rare and seldom found in today's market. It is impossible to evaluate it on a general basis. **NOTE:** For all models listed: 20-gauge add 50 percent. Single-selective trigger add 25 percent.

O Excelsior Grade—Extractors

—	2750	2200	1750	950	700	

Excelsior Grade—Auto Ejectors

—	3250	2700	2100	1250	900	

F Grade, No. 9

—	3700	2950	2350	1500	1100	

E Grade, No. 8

—	4750	4200	3200	2400	1700	

D Grade, No. 7

—	5800	5000	4000	2750	2000	

C Grade, No. 6

—	8000	7000	6000	3000	2500	

B Grade, No. 5

—	8700	8000	7000	3500	3000	

AA Grade, No. 4

—	11500	10500	9000	4200	2750	

LEFEVER ARMS CO.
Syracuse, New York

Founded by Dan Lefever who was a pioneer in the field of breech-loading firearms. Company was founded in 1884, with Lefever as president. He was referred to as "Uncle Dan" within the firearms industry. He was responsible for many improvements in double-barrel shotgun design. He developed the automatic hammerless system in late 1880s. He also developed a compensating action that allowed simple adjustments to compensate for action wear. In 1901 he was forced out of the company and organized another company—D.M. Lefever, Sons & Company—also in Syracuse. Dan Lefever died in 1906 and his new company went out of business. The original company was acquired by Ithaca in 1916. They continued to produce Lefever guns until 1948.

Sideplated Shotgun

Double-barrel side-by-side shotgun chambered for 10-, 12-, 16- or 20-gauge. Offered with 26", 28", 30" or 32" barrels, with various choke combinations. Barrels are either Damascus or fluid steel. Damascus guns have become collectible and in better condition—very good to excellent—can bring nearly the same price as fluid-steel guns. Features a fractional sidelock, because hammers were mounted in frame and sears and cocking indicators were mounted on sideplates. After serial number 25,000, entire locking mechanism was frame mounted and only cocking indicators remained on sideplates. Double triggers are standard. Finish is blued, with checkered walnut stock. A number of variations that differ in amount of ornamentation and quality of materials and workmanship utilized in their construction. Automatic ejectors are represented by the letter "E" after respective grade designation. Shotgun manufactured between 1885 and 1919. We strongly recommend that a qualified appraisal be secured if a transaction is contemplated. Also an Optimus Grade and Thousand Dollar Grade offered. These are extremely high-grade, heavily ornamented firearms inlaid with precious metals. Extremely rare and evaluating them on a general basis is impossible. **NOTE:** All models listed: 20-gauge add 25 percent; single-selective trigger add 10 percent.

H Grade

—	1600	1250	950	550	350	

HE Grade

—	2400	1900	1550	900	650	

G Grade

—	1900	1500	1200	700	425	

	NIB	EXC.	V.G.	GOOD	FAIR	POOR
GE Grade						
	—	2800	2150	1800	1000	650
F Grade						
	—	2400	1900	1550	900	650
FE Grade						
	—	3400	2650	2200	1300	800
E Grade						
	—	3700	2950	2400	1400	900
EE Grade						
	—	7500	6500	3100	1850	1150
D Grade						
	—	4700	3650	3000	1800	1100
DS Grade						
	—	1450	1150	900	500	300
DE Grade						
	—	7250	5750	4600	2800	1750
DSE Grade						
	—	1750	1400	1150	700	500
C Grade						
	—	8500	5700	4200	2400	1500
CE Grade						
	—	9500	6950	5650	3400	2100
B Grade						
	—	10500	7700	5300	3200	2000
BE Grade						
	—	15000	10000	6600	4000	2500
A Grade						
	—	24000	18000	10100	6000	3700
AA Grade						
	—	38000	22000	13200	8000	5000

LEFEVER ARMS COMPANY, INC. (ITHACA)
Syracuse, New York

During 1916, Ithaca Gun company purchased the gun making assets of Syracuse, New York based Lefever Arms Company. Between then and World War I, they continued to manufacture the same sideplate gun that had been made in Syracuse until about 1919, when they were discontinued. Prices for those guns are listed in Sideplated Shotgun section. During 1921, Ithaca Gun Company, under the name Lefever Arms Company, Inc., introduced a line of lower cost boxlock guns. Eventually, six different models were produced. Ithaca's Lefever guns were produced in 12-, 16- and 20-gauge and .410 bore. **NOTE:** 20-gauge guns often command a price premium of 50 percent; .410 bore gun may command up to 200 percent premium.

Nitro Special

Side-by-side double-barrel shotgun chambered for 12-, 16- or 20-gauge and .410 bore. Barrels were offered in lengths of 26" to 32", with various choke combinations. Features boxlock action, with double triggers and extractors standard. Finish is blued, with case-colored receiver and checkered walnut stock. Manufactured between 1921 and 1948. Incredible as it may seem, its price at introduction was $29. **NOTE:** Add 100+ percent for .410; single-selective trigger add $100; automatic ejectors add $200.

—	600	400	250	200	100

Long Range Single-Barrel Trap and Field (Model 2)

Manufactured from 1927 to 1947. Model 2 was a single-barrel gun, with no rib. Like Nitro Special it had walnut stocks. Line cut checkered at grip area of buttstock and on fore-end.

—	500	300	200	150	100

	NIB	EXC.	V.G.	GOOD	FAIR	POOR

Single-Barrel Trap Ventilated Rib (Model 3)

Manufactured from 1927 to 1942. Model 3 was a single-barrel gun, with same ventilated rib used on "Knick" trap gun. Walnut stocks had line cut checkering at grip area of buttstock and on fore-end.

	—	1200	500	250	150	100

Double-Barrel Ventilated Rib Trap (Model 4)

Manufactured during 1929, but cataloged until 1939. Model 4 was a double-barrel gun, with ventilated rib barrel. Walnut stocks had line cut checkering at grip area of buttstock and on beavertail fore-end. Only about 200 units produced.

	—	2000	1200	1000	700	300

A Grade (Model 5)

Manufactured from 1936 to 1939. A Grade was a double-barreled gun. Walnut stocks had pointed checkering cut at grip area of buttstock and on splinter fore-end. Line engraving outlined its nicely sculptured frame. **NOTE:** Single trigger add $200; automatic ejectors add $200; beavertail fore-end add $300.

	—	900	600	400	300	100

Skeet Special (Model 6)

Manufactured from 1936 to 1939. A Grade was a double-barreled gun. Walnut stocks had pointed checkering cut at grip area of buttstock and on beavertail fore-end. Beavertail fore-end, single trigger, automatic ejectors, recoil pad and ivory center and front sight were standard. Frame was sculptured and line engraved like Model 5.

	—	1500	1200	1000	400	100

LEMAN, H. E.
Lancaster, Pennsylvania

Leman Militia Rifle

.58-caliber percussion muzzle-loader has 33" round barrel. Stock is full-length and held on by two barrel bands. Ramrod mounted under barrel. Trim is brass and barrel browned, with case-colored lock. Lock marked "H.E.Leman/Lancaster, Pa." Approximately 500 manufactured between 1860 and 1864. Believed used by Pennsylvania State Militia in Civil War.

	—	—	4750	2000	750	300

LEONARD, G.
Charlestown, Massachusetts

Pepperbox

.31-caliber four-barreled pepperbox, with concealed hammer. Barrels are 3.25" in length. Ring trigger used to cock weapon, while smaller trigger located outside ring is used to fire weapon. Barrels on this pistol do not revolve. Revolving striker inside frame that turns to fire each chamber. Barrels must be removed for loading and capping purposes. Frame is iron and blued, with engraving. Rounded grips are walnut. Barrel stamped "G. Leonard Jr. Charlestown". Fewer than 200 manufactured in 1849 and 1850.

	—	—	1850	725	300	150

LES, INC.
Skokie, Illinois

Rogak P-18

9mm caliber double-action semi-automatic pistol, with 5.5" barrel and 18-shot magazine. Stainless steel. Discontinued.

	—	380	350	295	200	150

LEW HORTON
Westborough, Massachusetts

This company is a full-line distributor of several major firearm manufacturers. They specialize in exclusive special editions of various models.

LEWIS MACHINE & TOOL COMPANY (LMT)
Milan, Illinois

Company founded in 1980 and manufactures a wide range of military-type rifles. Originally, the firm made weapons for law enforcement and government agencies in U.S., but now makes products for civilian community and foreign armed forces.

	NIB	EXC.	V.G.	GOOD	FAIR	POOR

.308 Modular Weapon System (MWSE)

Gas piston operating system, with monolithic rail system with one-piece upper receiver, free floated cryogenically treated barrel which can quickly be changed to another size, two-stage trigger, 20-shot magazine.

NIB	EXC.	V.G.	GOOD	FAIR	POOR
2500	2000	1550	1200	750	400

Defender Standard Model 16

Standard flattop upper receiver, with 16" chrome-lined 1:7"-twist barrel, standard semi-automatic bolt carrier group, tactical charging handle, Generation 1 collapsible buttstock.

NIB	EXC.	V.G.	GOOD	FAIR	POOR
1200	1000	750	500	350	200

CQB Series

Piston operated with CQB/MRP (Close Quarter Battle/Monolithic Rail Platform) upper receiver, 16" chrome lined 5.56" barrel with SOPMOD buttstock and standard trigger group. Also offered in 6.8 SPC. **NOTE:** Add $200 for 6.8 SPC.

NIB	EXC.	V.G.	GOOD	FAIR	POOR
1900	1650	1250	750	450	250

LIDDLE & KAEDING
San Francisco, California

Pocket Revolver

Manufactured by Forehand and Wadsworth, but stamped with above name. Company was a dealer in California and had nothing whatsoever to do with production of this revolver. Chambered for .32 rimfire cartridge. Has 3.25" octagonal barrel and 5-shot fluted cylinder. Frame is iron and finish is blued, with walnut grips. Few hundred manufactured between 1880 and 1886. Dealer's name marked on top strap.

NIB	EXC.	V.G.	GOOD	FAIR	POOR
—	—	575	450	200	75

LIEGEOISE D ARMES
Liege, Belgium

Side-by-Side Boxlock Shotgun

Double-barreled gun chambered for 12- and 20-gauge. Barrels are 28" or 30" in length and choke combinations are varied. Single trigger and automatic ejectors. Action is moderately engraved. Finish is blued, with checkered walnut stock.

NIB	EXC.	V.G.	GOOD	FAIR	POOR
—	900	700	500	400	200

Liegeoise Pistol

Semi-automatic pistol in 6.35mm caliber.

NIB	EXC.	V.G.	GOOD	FAIR	POOR
—	250	200	175	125	75

LIGNOSE
Suhl, Germany

In 1921, Bergmann Industriewerke was incorporated into Aktiengesellschaft Lignose, Berlin, with a manufacturing division in Suhl.

Liliput Model I

Manufactured in caliber 6.35mm during 1920s.

NIB	EXC.	V.G.	GOOD	FAIR	POOR
—	400	300	200	150	100

Lignose Model 2

Pocket Model in 6.35mm caliber.

NIB	EXC.	V.G.	GOOD	FAIR	POOR
—	450	400	350	250	150

Lignose Model 3

Same as Model 2, with 9-round magazine capacity.

NIB	EXC.	V.G.	GOOD	FAIR	POOR
—	750	650	500	400	250

Einhand Model 2A

Unique design resembled Swiss Chylewski. Allows shooter to cock and fire this blowback-operated semi-automatic pistol with one hand (Einhand). Chambered for 6.35mm cartridge and has 2" barrel. Magazine holds 6 shots and finish is blued, with molded horn grips marked "Lignose". Trigger guard on this pistol has a reverse curve that fits finger and moves backward to cock slide. Short-grip model without Einhard feature was Model 2; long grip model without Einhand was Model 3. First 9,000 to 10,000 examples (all four variations serial numbered in same series) were marketed under Bergmann name; only later Lignose. Manufactured in early 1920s by Bergman Company. Firm merged with Lignose under whose name it was produced.

NIB	EXC.	V.G.	GOOD	FAIR	POOR
—	750	650	500	400	250

	NIB	EXC.	V.G.	GOOD	FAIR	POOR

Einhand Model 3A

Similar to Model 2A, with longer grip that houses 9-shot magazine. All other specifications same as Model 2A.

	NIB	EXC.	V.G.	GOOD	FAIR	POOR
	—	850	700	650	500	300

LILLIPUT

See—Menz

LINDE A.

Memphis, Tennessee

Pocket Pistol

Company manufactured a small concealable firearm, patterned after Henry Deringer Philadelphia-type pistol. Chambered for .41-caliber percussion. Has 2.5" barrel, German silver mountings and walnut stock. Manufactured in 1850s.

	NIB	EXC.	V.G.	GOOD	FAIR	POOR
	—	—	2150	875	300	150

LINDSAY, JOHN P.

Union Knife Company
Naugatuck, Connecticut

Union Knife Company manufactured Lindsay 2-shot pistols for inventor John P. Lindsay. There are three separate and distinct models listed.

2 Shot Belt Pistol

An oddity. Single-barreled .41-caliber percussion pistol, with double chamber that contains two powder charges and projectiles that are simultaneously fired by two separate hammers. Hammers are released by a single trigger that allows them to fall in proper sequence. 5.5" octagonal barrel contoured into a radical stepped-down shape and spur trigger. Frame is brass, with scroll engraving. Barrel is blued and marked "Lindsay's Young America". Estimated to be fewer than 100 manufactured between 1860 and 1862.

	NIB	EXC.	V.G.	GOOD	FAIR	POOR
	—	—	4400	1500	700	300

2 Shot Pocket Pistol

Smaller version of Belt Pistol. Chambered for same caliber, but has 4" barrel. Approximately 200 manufactured between 1860 and 1862.

	NIB	EXC.	V.G.	GOOD	FAIR	POOR
	—	—	3500	3000	1100	400

2 Shot Martial Pistol

Large version of Lindsay design. Chambered for .45-caliber smoothbore. Has 8.5" part-round part-octagonal barrel. Other respects similar to smaller models. Inventor tried to sell this pistol to the government, but was unsuccessful. Estimated 100 manufactured between 1860 and 1862.

	NIB	EXC.	V.G.	GOOD	FAIR	POOR
	—	—	—	5400	2200	700

LINS, A. F.

Philadelphia, Pennsylvania

Pocket Pistol

Chambered for .41-caliber percussion. Copy of Henry Deringer pistol. Has 3" barrel, walnut stock and marked "A. Fred. Lins. Philada." Manufactured between 1855 and 1860.

	NIB	EXC.	V.G.	GOOD	FAIR	POOR
	—	—	2100	1075	350	200

Rifled Musket

Single-shot muzzle-loading percussion rifle, chambered for .58-caliber. Has 39" barrel and full-length walnut stock held on by three barrel bands. Iron ramrod mounted under barrel. Mountings are iron. A bayonet lug combined with front sight. Lock marked "A. Fred. Lins/Philada." Rare weapon used by Union forces in Civil War. Approximately 200 manufactured in 1861 and 1862.

	NIB	EXC.	V.G.	GOOD	FAIR	POOR
	—	—	5500	2000	825	300

LITTLE SHARPS RIFLE MFG. CO.

Big Sandy, Montana

Little Sharps Rifle

Hand-built reproduction of single-shot Sharps rifle is 20 percent smaller than original. Chambered for a wide variety of calibers from .22 LR to .375 LSR. A number of extra cost options are available for this rifle. Price listed for basic model.

	NIB	EXC.	V.G.	GOOD	FAIR	POOR
	3250	2750	2000	1500	900	500

LJUTIC INDUSTRIES
Yakima, Washington

Bi-Matic Semi-Automatic

Custom-built gas-operated semi-automatic shotgun, known for its low level of felt recoil. Chambered for 12-gauge. Has 26" to 32" barrels choked for either skeet or trap. Stock specifications are to customer's order. **NOTE:** Add 15 percent for interchangeable chokes.

NIB	EXC.	V.G.	GOOD	FAIR	POOR
2750	2100	1300	800	400	200

Dynatrap Single-Barrel

Single-shot trap gun chambered for 12-gauge. Has 33" vent rib full-choke barrel. Features push-button opener and manual extractor. Stock made to trap specifications. Many options affect value.

NIB	EXC.	V.G.	GOOD	FAIR	POOR
2500	1500	1000	800	400	200

Model X-73 Single-Barrel

Similar features to Dynatrap, with high competition rib. Appraisal is recommended. **NOTE:** Add 15 percent for interchangeable chokes.

NIB	EXC.	V.G.	GOOD	FAIR	POOR
2750	2100	1300	800	400	200

Mono Gun Single-Barrel

Chambered for 12-gauge and has 34" vent rib barrel. Essentially a custom-order proposition that is available with standard, as well as release trigger. Many value-affecting options available. **NOTE:** Add 15 percent for interchangeable chokes.

NIB	EXC.	V.G.	GOOD	FAIR	POOR
6500	5700	4200	3000	1000	—

LTX Model

Deluxe version of Mono Gun, with 33" medium-height vent rib. High-grade walnut stock, with fine hand checkering. Options raise values drastically.

NIB	EXC.	V.G.	GOOD	FAIR	POOR
7500	6200	5000	3500	1500	—

Space Gun

Unique single-barrel gun chambered for 12-gauge, with trap choking. Stock and forearm reminds one of a crutch in appearance, but allows shooter to have in-line control, with little felt recoil. Barrel, forearm and stock are all on one line. There is a recoil pad and high ventilated rib.

NIB	EXC.	V.G.	GOOD	FAIR	POOR
3750	3000	2250	1500	900	200

Bi-Gun Over/Under

Over/under double chambered for 12-gauge. Has 30" or 32" vent ribbed barrels that are separated. Choking is to trap specifications. Stock is deluxe hand-checkered walnut.

NIB	EXC.	V.G.	GOOD	FAIR	POOR
7250	6000	4000	1000	600	200

Bi-Gun Combo

Over/under Bi-Gun supplied with high ribbed single-barrel, in addition to separated over/under barrels.

NIB	EXC.	V.G.	GOOD	FAIR	POOR
10000	7000	4000	2000	1000	200

LM-6 Super Deluxe

Over/under gun made to customer's specifications. Available in 12-gauge, with barrel lengths from 28" to 34". All other specifications are custom. **NOTE:** Extra single-barrel add $7,000.

NIB	EXC.	V.G.	GOOD	FAIR	POOR
15000	11500	7500	5000	2500	1000

LLAMA
Manufactured by Gabilondo y Cia
Vitoria, Spain

Same firm that was founded in 1904 and produced several inexpensive revolvers and pistols prior to 1931. In 1931, company began to produce a semi-automatic pistol based on Colt Model 1911. They were of high quality and have been sold around the world. After Spanish civil war, company moved its facilities to Vitoria, Spain, where it continued to build handguns under Llama trade name. In 1980s, firm introduced a new line of pistols that were more modern in design and function. Llama pistol is still produced today. For Llama pistols built prior to 1936 slide marking reads: "GABILONDO Y CIA ELOEIBAR (ESPANA) CAL 9MM/.380IN LLAMA". For pistols built after 1936 slide marking reads: "LLAMA GABILONDO Y CIA ELOEIBAR (ESPANA) CAL 9MM .380". Current production Llama pistols will show a slide marking with either "LLAMA CAL..." or "GABILONDO Y CIA VITORIA (ESPANA)" and Llama logo. "Llama" is now a trade name for handguns manufactured by Bersa of Argentina.

	NIB	EXC.	V.G.	GOOD	FAIR	POOR

SEMI-AUTOMATICS

Model I-A

7.65mm blowback design introduced in 1933. Magazine capacity 7 rounds. Barrel 3.62"; overall length 6.3"; weight about 19 oz.

	—	275	225	125	100	75

Model II

Chambered for 9mm Short and introduced in 1933. Identical to Model I. Discontinued in 1936.

	—	265	200	150	125	100

Model III

Improved version of Model II. Introduced in 1936. Discontinued in 1954.

	—	275	225	175	125	100

Model III-A

Similar to Model III except chambered for .380 ACP. Addition of Colt-type grip safety. Introduced in 1955. Weight about 23 oz.

	—	300	250	195	125	100

Model IV

Chambered for 9mm Largo or .380 ACP. Not fitted with grip safety. Introduced in 1931. First of Llama designs.

	—	275	225	175	125	100

Model V

Same as Model IV, but intended for export to United States. Stamped "made in Spain" on slide.

	—	275	225	175	125	100

Model VI

Chambered for 9mm Short, without a grip safety.

	—	275	225	175	125	100

Model VII

Introduced in 1932 and manufactured until 1954. Chambered for .38 Auto cartridge. No grip safety.

	—	400	300	225	150	100

Model VIII

Model introduced in 1955. Chambered for .45 ACP, .38 Auto or 9mm Largo. Fitted with a grip safety. Barrel length 5"; overall length 8.5"; weight about 38 oz. Magazine capacity 7 rounds. **NOTE:** Many of these pistols marked ".38". Unclear whether these pistols were intended for use with .38 Super cartridge or with milder .38 Automatic. We do not recommend full-house Super loadings in these pistols.

	—	400	300	225	150	100

Model IX

Chambered for 7.65mm Para, 9mm Largo or .45 ACP. Model has locked breech, with no grip safety. Built from 1936 to 1954.

	—	400	300	200	150	100

Model IX-A

Version of Model IX. Fitted with a grip safety. Current production models chambered for .45 ACP only. Weighs about 30 oz., with 5" barrel.

	—	400	300	200	150	100

Model IX-B

Version of Model IX series. Chambered in .45 ACP. Fitted with extended slide release, black plastic grips and target-type hammer. Offered in blue or satin chrome finish.

	400	300	250	175	125	100

Model IX-C

Last large-frame version of Model IX. Chambered for .45 ACP and fitted with 5.125" barrel. Blade front sight with adjustable rear sight. Magazine capacity 10 rounds. Weight approximately 41 oz.

	400	300	250	200	150	100

	NIB	EXC.	V.G.	GOOD	FAIR	POOR

Model IX-D

Compact frame version with 4.25" barrel and chambered for .45 ACP cartridge. Stocks are black rubber. Fixed front sight with adjustable rear. Introduced in 1995. Magazine capacity 10 rounds. Weight about 39 oz.

450	350	250	200	150	100

Model X

First produced in 1935, this model chambered for 7.65mm cartridge. No grip safety.

—	295	225	150	100	75

Model X-A

Version similar to Model X, with a grip safety. Produced from 1954 to present.

—	300	225	150	100	75

Model XI

Chambered for 9mm Parabellum cartridge. Different from previous models with longer curved butt, ring hammer and vertically grooved walnut grips. Magazine capacity 9 rounds. Barrel length 5". Discontinued in 1954.

—	350	300	250	175	125

Model XI-B

Similar to Model XI, with spur hammer and shorter barrel.

400	375	275	150	100	75

Model XII-B

Chambered for .40 S&W cartridge. Has compact frame.

400	375	275	150	100	75

Model XV

Chambered for .22 LR, this model marked "Especial". Fitted with grip safety. Comes in several finishes and different grip styles. Barrel length 3.6"; overall length 6.5"; weight about 17 oz.

—	325	275	195	125	100

Model XVI

Deluxe version of Model XV, with engraving, ventilated rib and adjustable sights.

—	350	275	200	150	100

Model XVII "Especial

Vest pocket-sized model chambered for .22 Short. Small version of Model XV, with finger-contoured grip.

—	275	225	175	125	100

Model XVIII

Introduced in 1998, this model chambered for .25 ACP cartridge. Offered with gold or chrome finish and stag grips.

—	300	225	175	150	125

Model Omni

Pistol chambered for .45 ACP or 9mm cartridge. Fitted with 4.25" barrel. Blued finish. Adjustable rear sight. Magazine capacity: 7 rounds for .45 ACP; 13 rounds for 9mm. Weight approximately 40 oz. Produced between 1984 and 1986.

475	350	250	150	125	100

Model Max-I

Introduced in 1995, this 1911 design single-action model features choice of 9mm or .45 ACP chambers, with 4.25" barrel or 5.125" barrel. Black rubber grips, with blade front sight and adjustable rear sight. Weight 34 oz. for compact model; 36 oz. for Government model. **NOTE:** Compact model add $25; duo-tone model add $25.

400	350	250	175	150	100

Model Mini-Max

Version chambered for 9mm, .40 S&W or .45 ACP. Furnished with 6-round magazine. Barrel length 3.5". Checkered rubber grips. Introduced in 1996. Weight about 35 oz. Choice of blue, duo-tone, satin chrome or stainless steel. **NOTE:** Add $40 for satin chrome finish; $60 for stainless; $20 for duo-tone finish.

400	375	275	150	100	75

	NIB	EXC.	V.G.	GOOD	FAIR	POOR

Mini-Max Sub Compact

Semi-automatic chambered for 9mm, .40 S&W or .45 ACP cartridge. Fitted with 3.14" barrel. Overall length 6.5"; height 4.5". Skeletonized combat-style hammer. Grips are black polymer. Weight about 31 oz. Introduced in 1999. **NOTE:** Add $40 for satin chrome finish; $60 for stainless; $20 for duo-tone finish.

400	375	275	150	100	75

Model Max-I with Compensator

Similar to Max-I, with addition of compensator. Introduced in 1996. Weight about 42 oz.

450	400	300	175	125	95

Micro-Max

Pistol chambered for .32 ACP or .380 cartridge. Operates on a straight blowback system, with single-action trigger. Black polymer grips. Barrel length 3.6"; overall length 6.5"; height 4.37"; weight approximately 23 oz. Introduced in 1999. **NOTE:** Add $20 for satin chrome finish.

400	375	275	150	100	75

Model 82

Large-frame double-action semi-automatic pistol. Features plastic grips, ambidextrous safety, 3-dot sights. Barrel length 4.25"; overall length 8"; weight approximately 39 oz. Choice of blue or satin chrome finish.

650	500	350	250	150	100

Model 87 Competition

Chambered for 9mm cartridge and fitted with integral muzzle compensator. Has a number of competition features such as beveled magazine well, oversize safety and magazine release. Magazine capacity 14 rounds. Offered between 1989 and 1993.

1200	925	650	525	300	150

Llama Compact Frame Semi-Automatic

9mm or .45 ACP caliber semi-automatic pistol, with 4.25" barrel. Either 7- or 9-shot detachable magazine. Blued. Introduced in 1986.

350	300	225	150	100	75

Llama Small Frame Semi-Automatic

.22, .32 ACP and .380 ACP caliber semi-automatic pistol, with 3.6875" barrel and 7-shot detachable magazine. Either blued or satin chrome finished. **NOTE:** Add $75 for satin chrome finish.

350	300	225	150	100	75

Llama Large Frame Semi-Automatic

9mm, .38 Super or .45 ACP caliber semi-automatic pistol, with 5.25" barrel. Either 7- or 9-shot detachable magazine, depending on caliber. Blued or satin chrome. **NOTE:** Add $125 for satin chrome finish.

450	400	300	175	125	100

Mugica

Eibar gun dealer, Jose Mugica, sold Llama pistols under his private trade name. They are marked "mugica-ebir-spain" on slide. These pistols do not seem to have any additional value over and above their respective Llama models. For the sake of clarification, Mugica models are listed with their Llama counterparts:

Mugica Model 101	Llama Model X
Mugica Model 101-G	Llama Model X-A
Mugica Model 105	Llama Model III
Mugica Model 105-G	Llama Model III-A
Mugica Model 110	Llama Model VII
Mugica Model 110-G	Llama Model VIII
Mugica Model 120	Llama Model XI

Tauler

In an arrangement similar to Mugica, a gun dealer in Madrid sold Llama pistols under his own brand name. Most of these pistols were sold in early 1930s to police and other government officials. Most common Llama models were Models I to VIII. Slide inscriptions were in English and had name Tauler in them. No additional value is attached to this private trademark.

	NIB	EXC.	V.G.	GOOD	FAIR	POOR

REVOLVERS

RUBY EXTRA MODELS

Revolvers produced in 1950s and were copies of Smith & Wessons. Marked "RUBY EXTRA" on left side of frame. Top of grips was a Ruby medallion. Barrel address stamped: gabilondo y cia elgoeibar espana. Ruby Extra Models represent company's attempts to produce and sell a low-cost revolver.

Model XII

Model chambered for .38 Long cartridge. Fitted with 5" barrel and squared butt.

—	200	150	125	100	75	

Model XIII

Chambered for .38 Special, this revolver has a round butt with 4" or 6" ventilated rib barrel. 6" barreled gun fitted with adjustable sights and target grips.

—	225	175	150	125	100	

Model XIV

Offered in .22 LR or .32-caliber. Available in a wide choice of barrel lengths and sights.

—	200	150	125	100	75	

Model XXII Olimpico

Model designed as .38 Special target revolver. Features adjustable anatomic grip, adjustable rear sight, ventilated rib barrel and a web that joins barrel to ejector shroud.

—	275	225	150	125	100	

Model XXIX Olimpico

Model XXII chambered for .22 LR.

—	250	200	150	125	100	

Model XXVI

Chambered for .22 LR, it features traditional grips and shrouded ejector rod.

—	175	150	125	100	75	

Model XXVII

Similar to above, with 2" barrel and chambered for .32 Long cartridge.

—	175	150	125	100	75	

Model XXVIII

Model chambered for .22 LR and fitted with 6" barrel. Has ramp front sight and adjustable rear sight.

—	200	175	150	100	75	

Model XXXII Olimpico

Model is a .32 target revolver, with unusual cylinder and frame design.

—	400	300	250	200	150	

Llama Martial

.22 or .38 Special caliber double-action revolver, with 6-round swingout cylinder, 4" or 6" barrel and adjustable sights. Blued, with checkered hardwood grips. Manufactured between 1969 and 1976. **NOTE:** Add $500 for engraved chrome; $600 for engraved blue; $1,000 to $3,000 for gold model.

—	275	225	200	150	125	

Llama Comanche I

.22-caliber revolver fitted with 6" barrel and 9-shot cylinder. Rubber grips with adjustable sights. Choice of blue or stainless steel. Weight about 39 oz.

240	175	125	100	75	50	

Llama Comanche II

As above in .38 Special caliber, with 6-shot cylinder. Choice of 3" or 4" barrel. Rubber grips and adjustable sights. Blue or stainless steel. Weight about 30 oz.

225	175	125	100	75	50	

Llama Comanche III

As above in .357 Magnum, with 3", 4" or 6" barrel and adjustable sights. Rubber grips. Blue or stainless steel. Weight about 30 oz. for 3" or 4" barrel guns; 39 oz. for 6" barrel gun. Introduced in 1975. **NOTE:** Add 20 percent for satin chrome finish.

275	225	175	125	100	75	

	NIB	EXC.	V.G.	GOOD	FAIR	POOR

Llama Super Comanche

As above in .357 or .44 Magnum, with 10" ventilated rib barrel and adjustable sights. Blued, with walnut grips. Weight about 47 oz.

	NIB	EXC.	V.G.	GOOD	FAIR	POOR
	325	250	200	150	100	75

LOEWE, LUDWIG & CO.
Berlin, Germany
See—Borchardt

During 1870s and 1880s, this firm manufactured a close copy of Smith & Wesson Russian Model for the Russian government. They are marked "Ludwig Loewe Berlin" on top of barrel.

Loewe Smith & Wesson Russian Revolver

	NIB	EXC.	V.G.	GOOD	FAIR	POOR
	—	—	1250	600	325	125

LOHNER, C.
Philadelphia, Pennsylvania

Pocket Pistol

.44-caliber single-shot percussion pistol, with 5" barrel, German silver mounts and walnut grip. Barrel marked "C. Lohner". Manufactured during 1850s.

	NIB	EXC.	V.G.	GOOD	FAIR	POOR
	—	—	1600	675	250	125

LOMBARD, H. C. & CO.
Springfield, Massachusetts

Pocket Pistol

.22-caliber single-shot spur trigger pistol, with 3.5" octagonal barrel. Frame is silver plated, barrel blued and grips are of walnut. Barrel marked "H.C. Lombard & Co. Springfield, Mass.

	NIB	EXC.	V.G.	GOOD	FAIR	POOR
	—	—	500	225	150	100

LONE STAR RIFLE COMPANY
Conroe, Texas

Company builds custom blackpowder rifles. They are built on rolling block design and offered in two basic configurations. There are a wide number of options that will affect the price of these rifles.

Sporting Rifle

Basic configuration that features straight-grip stock, with semi-crescent butt. Offered in a wide variety of calibers from .32-40 to .50-90. Barrel lengths, barrel configurations, wood, triggers, sights, engraving, finishes, hammers and accessories will greatly affect the final price. Basic retail price: $2195.

Target Rifle

Basic configuration that features straight-grip stock, with semi-crescent butt. Offered in a wide variety of calibers from .32-40 to .50-90. Barrel lengths, barrel configurations, wood, triggers, sights, engraving, finishes, hammers and accessories will greatly affect the final price. Basic retail price: $2195.

LORCIN ENGINEERING CO., INC.
Mira Loma, California

Company in business from 1989 to 1999.

Model L-25

.25-caliber semi-automatic pistol, with 2.5" barrel and 7-shot magazine. Weight 14.5 oz.; overall length 4.8". Introduced in 1989.

	NIB	EXC.	V.G.	GOOD	FAIR	POOR
	125	100	75	40	30	20

Model LT-25

Same as above, with aluminum alloy frame. Introduced in 1989.

	NIB	EXC.	V.G.	GOOD	FAIR	POOR
	125	100	75	40	30	20

Model L-22

Chambered for .22 LR cartridge, with 2.5" barrel. Magazine capacity 9 rounds. Introduced in 1989. Weight 16 oz.

	NIB	EXC.	V.G.	GOOD	FAIR	POOR
	125	100	75	40	30	20

	NIB	EXC.	V.G.	GOOD	FAIR	POOR

Model L-380

Semi-automatic pistol chambered for .380 ACP cartridge. Barrel length 3.5", with magazine capacity of 7 rounds. Introduced in 1992. Weight about 23 oz.

	125	100	75	40	30	20

Model L-380 10th Anniversary

Same as above, but frame and slide are plated in 24 karat gold. Limited edition model.

	125	100	75	40	30	20

Model L-32

Same as above, but chambered for .32 ACP cartridge. Introduced in 1992

	125	100	75	40	30	20

Model LH-380

Semi-automatic pistol chambered for .380 ACP cartridge. Barrel length 4.5" and magazine capacity 10 rounds. Offered in black, satin or bright chrome finishes.

	150	125	100	75	60	50

Model L-9mm

Same as above, but chambered for 9mm cartridge. Weight 36 oz.

	150	125	100	75	60	50

Derringer

Over/under pistol chambered for .38 Special, .357 Magnum and .45 ACP. Barrel length 3.5"; overall length 6.5".

	140	120	95	65	50	40

LOWELL ARMS CO.

See—Rollin White Arms Co.

LOWER, J. P.

See—Slotter & Co.

LUGERS

Various Manufacturers

Just before turn of 20th century, Georg Luger redesigned Borchardt semi-automatic pistol so that its mainspring was housed in rear of grip. Resulting pistol was to prove extremely successful and his name has become synonymous with the pistol despite the fact his name never appeared on it.

These companies manufactured Luger pattern pistols at various times.

1. DWM - Deutsch Waffen und Munitions - Karlsruhe, Germany

2. The Royal Arsenal of Erfurt Germany

3. Simson & Company - Suhl, Germany

4. Mauser - Oberndorf, Germany

5. Vickers Ltd. - England

6. Waffenfabrik Bern - Bern, Switzerland

7. Heinrich Krieghoff - Suhl, Germany

DEUTSCH WAFFEN UND MUNITIONS

1899/1900 Swiss Test Model

4.75" barrel, 7.65mm caliber. Swiss Cross in Sunburst stamped over chamber. Serial range runs to three digits. With fewer than 100 manufactured and only one known to exist, it is one of the rarest Lugers and first true Luger that was produced. Model is far too rare to estimate an accurate value.

1900 Swiss Contract

4.75" barrel, 7.65mm caliber. Swiss Cross in Sunburst stamped over chamber. Military serial number range is 2001-5000; commercial range 01-21250. Approximately 2,000 commercial and 3,000 military models manufactured. **NOTE:** Wide trigger add 20 percent.

	—	8000	6750	4000	1500	1000

	NIB	EXC.	V.G.	GOOD	FAIR	POOR

1900 Commercial

4.75" barrel, 7.65mm caliber. Area above chamber is blank. Serial range is 01-19000. Approximately 5,500 manufactured for commercial sale in Germany or other countries. Some have "Germany" stamped on frame. Pistols imported into the U.S. and some were even stamped after bluing.

		EXC.	V.G.	GOOD	FAIR	POOR
	—	8500	6000	3000	1000	650

1900 American Eagle

4.75" barrel, 7.65mm caliber. American Eagle crest stamped over chamber. Serial range between 2000-200000. Approximately 11,000-12,000 commercial models marked "Germany" and 1,000 military test models, without commercial import stamp. Serial numbers of military lots are between 6100-7100. **NOTE:** For these models add a premium of 40 to 50 percent, depending on condition.

			V.G.	GOOD	FAIR	POOR
	—	5500	4000	2000	850	600

1900 Test Eagle

			V.G.	GOOD	FAIR	POOR
	—	7500	5000	3000	2000	1500

1900 Bulgarian Contract

Old model 1900 Type, with no stock lug. Has 4.75" barrel and chambered for 7.65mm cartridge. Bulgarian crest stamped over chamber and safety marked in Bulgarian letters. Serial range 20000-21000, with 1,000 manufactured. Military test model and quite rare, as most were re-barreled to 9mm during the time they were used. Even with 9mm versions, approximately 10 are known to exist. Only variation to feature a marked safety before 1904.

			V.G.	GOOD	FAIR	POOR
	12500	8500	4000	2500	1800	

1900 Carbine

11.75" barrel, 7.65mm caliber. Carbines have a gracefully contoured and finely checkered walnut forearm and detachable shoulder stock. Rear sight on this extremely rare variation is a five-position sliding model located on rear link. Area above chamber is blank. Serial range is three digits or under. This may have been a prototype, as less than 100 were produced. Model far too rare to estimate an accurate value.

1902 Prototype

6" barrel, 7.65mm caliber. Serial numbers are in 10000 range, with capital B and chamber is blank. 6" barrel is of a heavy contour. Less than 10 manufactured. Rarity of this variation precludes estimating value.

1902 Commercial—"Fat Barrel"

Thick 4" barrel, 9mm caliber. Area above chamber is blank. Chambered for 9mm cartridge. Serial numbers fall within 22300-22400 and 22900-23500 range. Approximately 600 manufactured. Greater part of those noted were marked "Germany" for export purposes.

		EXC.	V.G.	GOOD	FAIR	POOR
	—	13500	10500	6000	4000	1500

1902 American Eagle

As above, with an American Eagle stamped over chamber. Chambered for 9mm cartridge. Serial numbers fall within 22100-22300 and 22450-22900 range. Solely intended for export sales in U.S.A. and all are marked "Germany" on frame. Approximately 700 manufactured.

		EXC.	V.G.	GOOD	FAIR	POOR
	—	16000	12000	7000	3750	1300

1902 American Eagle Cartridge Counter

As above, with "Powell Indicating Device" added to left grip. Slotted left grip, with a numbered window that allows visual access to number or rounds remaining in special "indicator magazines". There were 50 Lugers altered in this way at the request of U.S. Board of Ordinance, for U.S. Army evaluation. Serial numbers are 22401-22450. Be especially wary of fakes!

		EXC.	V.G.	GOOD	FAIR	POOR
	—	40000	29000	16000	6000	3500

1902 Carbine

11.75" barrel, 7.65mm caliber. Sight has four positions and is silver-soldered to barrel. Stock and forearm were sold with this weapon. Serial range was 21000-22100, 23500-24900 and 50000 to 50100. Approximately 2,500 manufactured for commercial sale in and out of Germany. Many were imported into United States, but none here have been noted with "Germany" export stamp. **NOTE:** Prices include matching stock. Add 15 percent for 50000 to 50100 serial numbers.

		EXC.	V.G.	GOOD	FAIR	POOR
	22500	17000	10000	3500	2500	

1902 Presentation Carbine

11.75" barrel, 7.65mm caliber. Carbines have initials of owner gold-inlaid above chamber. Furnished with checkered walnut stock and forearm. Only four have been noted in 9000C serial number range. They have initials "GL" for Georg Luger on back of rear toggle. Too rare to estimate value.

1902/06 Carbine (Transitional)

11.75" barrel, 7.65mm caliber. Assembled from Model 1902 parts with new toggle assembly. Four-position sliding sight silver-soldered to barrel and checkered walnut stock and forearm. Approximately 100 manufactured in 23600 serial number range. **NOTE:** Prices include matching stock.

NIB	EXC.	V.G.	GOOD	FAIR	POOR
—	17000	14500	8000	5000	3000

1903 Commercial

4" barrel, 7.65mm caliber. Chamber area is blank. Approximately 50 manufactured for export to France. Serial numbered 25000-25050. Extractor on this model marked "CHARGE".

NIB	EXC.	V.G.	GOOD	FAIR	POOR
—	17000	13000	5000	3200	2500

1904 Navy

6" thick barrel, 9mm caliber. Chamber area is blank and extractor marked "Geladen". Safety marked "Gesichert". Approximately 1,500 manufactured in one- to four-digit serial range, for military issue to German Navy. Toggle has a "lock" similar to 1900 types. **NOTE:** Advised that a professional appraisal be obtained before purchase.

NIB	EXC.	V.G.	GOOD	FAIR	POOR
—	63000	42000	16000	6000	4500

1906 Navy Commercial

New model 1906 Type, with stock lug. Has 6" barrel and chambered for 9mm cartridge. Chamber is blank and extractor marked "Geladen". Safety marked "Gesichert" and some have "Germany" export stamp. Proper magazine has a wood bottom, with concentric circles on sides. Approximately 2,500 manufactured in 25050-65000 serial range. Produced for commercial sales in and outside of Germany.

NIB	EXC.	V.G.	GOOD	FAIR	POOR
—	8000	5800	2700	1500	1000

1906 Commercial

4" barrel, 9mm caliber. Extractor marked "Geladen" and area of frame under safety in its lower position is polished and not blued. Chamber is blank. Approximately 4,000 manufactured for commercial sales. Some have "Germany" export stamp. Serial range is 26500-68000.

NIB	EXC.	V.G.	GOOD	FAIR	POOR
—	5000	4000	1600	800	600

1906 Commercial (Marked Safety)

As above, with area of frame under safety in its lowest position marked "Gesichert". Barrel is 4.75" in length and chambered for 7.65mm cartridge. Approximately 750 manufactured, serial numbered 25050-26800.

NIB	EXC.	V.G.	GOOD	FAIR	POOR
—	6500	5000	2000	800	600

1906 American Eagle

4" barrel, 9mm caliber. Chamber area has the American Eagle stamped upon it. Extractor marked "Loaded". Frame under safety at its lowest point is polished and not blued. Model has no stock lug. Approximately 3,000 manufactured for commercial sale in U.S.A., in serial range 25800-69000. They were supplied with "caliber 9mm Magazines".

NIB	EXC.	V.G.	GOOD	FAIR	POOR
—	6500	4000	1200	700	500

1906 American Eagle (Marked Safety)

4.75" barrel, 7.65mm caliber. Frame under safety at its lowest point marked "Gesichert". Approximately 750 manufactured in 25100-26500 serial number range.

NIB	EXC.	V.G.	GOOD	FAIR	POOR
—	7500	5500	2000	1200	800

1906 American Eagle 4.75" Barrel

As above, with polished bright safety area. Approximately 8,000 manufactured in 26500-69000 serial range.

NIB	EXC.	V.G.	GOOD	FAIR	POOR
—	5000	3000	1100	700	450

1906 U.S. Army Test Luger .45 Caliber

5" barrel, .45 ACP caliber. Sent to United States for testing in 1907. Chamber is blank; extractor marked "Loaded". Frame is polished under safety lever. Trigger on this model has an odd hook at the bottom. Only five of these pistols were manufactured. Buyer Caution: Perfect copies of this pistol are currently being produced.

1906 Swiss Commercial

4.75" barrel, 7.65mm caliber. Swiss Cross in Sunburst appears over chamber. Extractor marked "Geladen". Frame under safety is polished. No stock lug and proofmarks are commercial. Approximately 1,000 manufactured in 35000-55000 serial number range.

NIB	EXC.	V.G.	GOOD	FAIR	POOR
—	5800	4700	2500	1400	800

	NIB	EXC.	V.G.	GOOD	FAIR	POOR

1906 Swiss Military

Swiss Commercial except with military proofmarks.

	—	5500	3800	2200	900	700

1906 Swiss Police Cross in Shield

As above, with shield replacing sunburst on chamber marking. There were 10,215 of both models combined. In 5000-15215 serial number range.

	—	5200	4200	2000	1000	700

1906 Dutch Contract

4" barrel, 9mm caliber. No stock lug and chamber is blank. Extractor marked "Geleden" on both sides and safety marked "RUST", with a curved upward pointing arrow. Pistol manufactured for military sales to Netherlands. Date will be found on barrel of most examples encountered. Dutch refinished their pistols on a regular basis and marked date on barrels. Approximately 4,000 manufactured, serial numbered between 1 and 4000.

	—	5000	3500	1500	800	600

1906 Royal Portuguese Navy

4" barrel, 9mm caliber and no stock lug. Royal Portuguese Naval crest, an anchor under a crown, stamped above chamber. Extractor marked "CARREGADA" on left side. Frame under safety is polished. Approximately 1,000 manufactured with one- to four-digit serial numbers.

	—	11000	8000	6500	4000	2500

1906 Royal Portuguese Army (M2)

4.75" barrel, 7.65mm caliber. No stock lug. Chamber area has Royal Portuguese crest of Mannuel II stamped upon it. Extractor marked "CARREGADA". Approximately 5,000 manufactured, with one- to four-digit serial numbers.

	—	4000	3200	1200	600	500

1906 Republic of Portugal Navy

4" barrel, 9mm caliber. No stock lug and extractor marked "CARREGADA". Model made after 1910, when Portugal had become a republic. Anchor on chamber is under letters "R.P." Approximately 1,000 manufactured, with one- to four-digit serial numbers.

	—	10500	8000	5500	2500	1500

1906 Brazilian Contract

4.75" barrel, 7.65mm caliber. No stock lug and chamber area is blank. Extractor marked "CARREGADA" and frame under safety is polished. Approximately 5,000 manufactured for military sales to Brazil.

	—	3750	2900	1100	750	450

1906 Bulgarian Contract

4.75" barrel, 7.65mm caliber. No stock lug and extractor and safety are marked in cyrillic letters. Bulgarian crest stamped above chamber. Nearly all of the examples located have barrels replaced with 4", 9mm units. This was done after later 1908 model was adopted. Some were refurbished during Nazi era and these pistols bear Waffenamts and usually mismatched parts. Approximately 1,500 manufactured, with serial numbers of one- to four-digits.

	—	10000	7500	5000	3500	1500

1906 Russian Contract

4" barrel, 9mm caliber. No stock lug. Extractor and safety are marked with cyrillic letters. Crossed Nagant rifles are stamped over chamber. Approximately 1,000 manufactured, with one- to four-digit serial numbers; but few survive. An extremely rare variation and caution should be exercised if purchase is contemplated.

	—	16000	12500	6500	4000	2500

1906 Navy 1st Issue

6" barrel, 9mm caliber. Safety and extractor are both marked in German and chamber area is blank. There is a stock lug and unique two-position sliding Navy sight is mounted on rear toggle link. Approximately 12,000 manufactured for German Navy, with serial numbers of one- to five-digits. Wooden magazine bottom features concentric rings. **NOTE:** Many of these pistols had their safety changed so they were "safe" in lower position. Known as "1st issue altered". Value at approximately 20 percent less.

	—	12500	7500	3000	1500	950

	NIB	EXC.	V.G.	GOOD	FAIR	POOR

1906 Navy 2nd Issue

As above, but manufactured to be safe in lower position. Approximately 11,000, 2nd Issue Navies, manufactured with one- to five-digit serial numbers—some with an "a" or "b" suffix. Produced for sale to German Navy.

	NIB	EXC.	V.G.	GOOD	FAIR	POOR
	—	7000	4500	2500	1200	700

1908 Commercial

4" barrel, 9mm caliber. No stock lug and chamber area is blank. Extractor and safety are both marked in German and many examples are marked with "Germany" export stamp. Approximately 9,000 manufactured in 39000-71500 serial number range.

	—	5000	3500	750	600	450

1908 Bulgarian

Considered by many to be the most unique Luger manufactured. It has a 4" barrel, "DWM" logo over the chamber, no stock lug, Cyrillic lettered safety and extractor, Bulgarian crest on middle link and no lanyard loop at rear of frame, but rather at lower end of rear grip strap. Nealy 10,000 manufactured, but few survived the heavy wartime use. Extremely rare in V.G. to Exc. condition.

	—	7500	5500	1500	1000	600

1908 Navy Commercial

6" barrel, 9mm caliber. Has a stock lug, no grip safety and characteristic two-position sliding sight mounted on rear toggle link. Chamber area is blank and safety and extractor are both marked. The "Germany" export stamp appears on some examples. Approximately 1,500 manufactured in 44000-50000 serial number range.

	—	6500	5000	2500	1750	1250

1908 Navy

As above, with "Crown M" military proof. May or may not have concentric rings on magazine bottom. Approximately 40,000 manufactured, with one- to five-digit serial numbers and "a" or "b" suffix. These Lugers are quite scarce, as many were destroyed during and after WWI.

	—	7000	5000	2000	1100	800

1914 Navy

Stamped with dates from 1914-1918 above chamber. Approximately 30,000 manufactured, with one- to five-digit serial numbers with an "a" or "b" suffix. They are scarce, as many were destroyed as a result of WWI. **WARNING:** Many counterfeit pistols reported. **NOTE:** Add 10 percent for 1916 date.

	—	6700	4700	2500	950	700

1908 Military 1st Issue

4" barrel, 9mm caliber. No stock lug and extractor and safety are both marked in German. Chamber is blank. Approximately 20,000 manufactured, with one- to five-digit serial numbers— some with an "a" suffix.

	—	3500	2000	1000	500	350

1908 Military Dated Chamber (1910-1913)

As above, with date of manufacture stamped on chamber.

	—	2500	1700	800	500	350

1913 Commercial

As above, with grip safety. Approximately 1,000 manufactured, with serial numbers 71000-72000; but few have been noted and are considered to be quite rare.

	—	3200	2200	1300	850	600

1914 Military

As above, with stock lug. Chamber dated 1914 - 1918.

	—	2500	1700	600	500	350

1914 Artillery

8" barrel, 9mm caliber. Features a nine-position adjustable sight, which has a base that is an integral part of barrel. Model has stock lug and furnished with military-style flat board stock and holster rig (see Accessories). Chamber dated from 1914-1918 and safety and extractor are both marked. Model was developed for artillery and machine gun crews; many thousands were manufactured, with one- to five-digit serial numbers—some have letter suffixes. Model is quite desirable from a collector's standpoint and is rarer than its production figures would indicate. After the war many were destroyed as the allies deemed them more insidious than other models, for some reason. **NOTE:** Add 100 percent to Models stamped with 1914 date. Complete matching rig adds considerably to value.

	—	5000	3500	1700	1500	900

	NIB	EXC.	V.G.	GOOD	FAIR	POOR

DWM Double Dated

4" barrel, 9mm cartridge. Date 1920 or 1921 stamped over original chamber date of 1910-1918, creating double-date nomenclature. These are arsenal-reworked WWI military pistols and were then issued to German military and/or police units within provisions of Treaty of Versailles. Many thousands of these Lugers were produced.

	—	2000	1000	550	400	300

1920 Police Rework

As above, except the original manufacture date was removed before rework date was stamped. There were many thousands of these produced. **NOTE:** It is not unusual to find with one or two "Police Matched" magazines.

	—	1800	1200	500	350	300

1920 Commercial

Similar to above, with 3.5" to 6" barrels in 7.65mm or 9mm calibers and marked "Germany" or "Made in Germany" for export. Others are unmarked and were produced for commercial sale inside Germany. Some of these pistols are military reworks, with markings and proofmarks removed; others were newly manufactured. Extractors and safety are both marked and chamber is blank. Serial number range is one- to five-digits and letter suffixes often appear. **NOTE:** Add 15 percent for 9mm.

	—	2300	1300	950	450	350

1920 Commercial Navy

6" barrel, 9mm caliber. Some have a stock lug; others have been noted without. Chamber area is generally blank, but some have been found with 1914-1918 dates stamped upon them. These were reworked by DWM from Military Navy Lugers after WWI for commercial sales. They are marked "Germany" or "Made in Germany" and were sold by Stoeger Arms, among others. Extractor and safety are both marked and unique Navy sight is on rear toggle link. No one knows exactly how many were produced, but they are quite scarce.

	—	9000	5000	2100	1100	850

1920 Commercial Artillery

8" barrel, 9mm caliber. Erfurt-manufactured pistols, as well as DWM-manufactured pistols, were reworked in this manner. Export markings "Germany" or "Made in Germany" are found on most examples. Number produced is not known, but examples are quite scarce.

	—	4500	3000	1100	700	450

1920 Long Barrel Commercial

10" to 24" barrels, 7.65mm or 9mm caliber. Extractor and safety are both marked and an artillery model rear sight is used. Model often built to customer's specifications. They are rare and number manufactured is not known.

	—	5000	3450	1500	1000	800

1920 Carbine

11.75" barrel, 7.65mm caliber. Chamber is blank and extractor marked either "Geleden" or "Loaded". Safety is not-marked. Carbine has checkered walnut forearm and stock. Most have "Germany" or "Made in Germany" export stamp. There were few of these carbines manufactured for commercial sales in and outside of Germany. Only two-digit serial numbers observed. **NOTE:** Prices include stock.

	—	14000	10500	5000	2500	1500

1920 Navy Carbine

Assembled from surplus Navy parts, with distinctive two position sliding navy sight on rear toggle link. Most are marked with export stamp and have naval military proofmarks still in evidence. Safety and extractor are marked and rarely one is found chambered for 9mm cartridge. Few were manufactured.

	—	19500	11000	5250	3000	1700

1920 Swiss Commercial

3.5" or 6" barrels, 7.65mm or 9mm caliber. Swiss Cross in Sunburst stamped over chamber and extractor marked "Geladen". Frame under safety is polished. There were a few thousand produced, with serial numbers in one- to five-digit range, sometimes with a letter suffix.

	—	4000	1800	1200	800	600

1923 Stoeger Commercial

3.5" to 24" barrels, 7.65mm or 9mm caliber. There is a stock lug. Chamber area is either blank or has the American Eagle stamped on it. Export stamp and "A.F.Stoeger Inc. New York" is found on right side of receiver. Extractor and safety are marked in German or English. This was model Stoeger registered with U.S. Patent office to secure Luger name and some examples will be so marked. There were less than 1,000 manufactured, with one- to five-digit serial numbers without a

	NIB	EXC.	V.G.	GOOD	FAIR	POOR

letter suffix. Individual appraisal must be secured on barrel lengths above 6". Be wary as fakes have been noted. Values given here are for shorter barreled models. **NOTE:** Add 25 percent for barrel lengths over 8"; 15 percent for three-line model.

	—	6000	4500	1800	1000	700

Abercrombie & Fitch Commercial 100

Swiss Lugers were made for commercial sale in United States by "Abercrombie & Fitch Co. New York. Made in Switzerland". —in either one or two lines—is stamped on top of barrel. Barrel is 4.75" in length and there were 49 chambered for 9mm and 51 chambered for 7.65mm cartridge. Pistol has a grip safety and no stock lug. Swiss Cross in Sunburst stamped over chamber. Extractor is marked, but safety area is polished. Serial range is four digits—some with a letter suffix. This is a rare and desirable Luger. Be careful of fakes on models of this type and rarity.

	—	11000	8000	4500	3000	2000

1923 Commercial

7.5" barrel, 7.65mm caliber. Has a stock lug and chamber area is blank. Extractor and safety are both marked in German. Manufactured for commercial sales in and outside of Germany. Approximately 18,000 produced, with serial numbers in 73500-96000 range.

	—	2500	1800	800	600	450

1923 Commercial Safe & Loaded

As above, except extractor and safety are marked in English "Safe" & "Loaded". Approximately 7,000 manufactured in 73500-96000 serial number range.

	—	3500	2200	1000	800	500

1923 Dutch Commercial & Military

4" barrel, 9mm caliber. Has a stock lug and chamber area is blank. Extractor marked in German and safety marked "RUST", with a downward pointing arrow. Model sold commercially and to military in Netherlands. Approximately 1,000 manufactured in one- to three-digit serial range, with no letter suffix.

	—	4000	2800	1000	850	550

Royal Dutch Air Force

4" barrel, 9mm caliber. Marked with Mauser Oberndorf proofmark. Serial numbered in 10000 to 14000 range. Safety marked "RUST".

	—	5000	2900	1000	800	550

VICKERS LTD.

Vickers was not a manufacturer but an intermediary marketer.

1906 Vickers Dutch

4" barrel, 9mm caliber. No stock lug and uses a grip safety. Chamber is blank and extractor marked "Geleden". "Vickers Ltd." stamped on front toggle link. Safety marked "RUST", with an upward pointing arrow. Examples have been found with an additional date as late as 1933 stamped on barrel. Dates indicate arsenal refinishing and in no way detract from value of this variation. Arsenal reworks are matte-finished and originals are a higher-polished rust blue. Approximately 10,000 manufactured in 1-10100 serial-number range.

	—	3800	3000	1800	1200	750

ERFURT ROYAL ARSENAL

1908 Erfurt

4" barrel, 9mm caliber. No stock lug; year of manufacture from 1910-1913 stamped above chamber. Extractor and safety are both marked in German. "ERFURT" under a crown stamped on front toggle link. Many thousands produced as Germany was involved in WWI. Found in one- to five-digit serial range, sometimes with a letter suffix.

	—	2100	1350	600	400	350

1914 Erfurt Military

4" barrel, 9mm caliber. Has a stock lug and date of manufacture over chamber 1914-1918. Extractor and safety are both marked in German and front link marked "ERFURT" under a crown. Finish on this model is rough; as war progressed in 1917 and 1918 finish got worse. Many thousands produced with one- to five-digit serial numbers, some with letter suffixes.

	—	2000	1100	600	400	350

1914 Erfurt Artillery

8" barrel, 9mm caliber. Has a stock lug. Issued with a flat board-type stock and other accessories which will be covered in the section of this book dealing with same. Sight is a nine-position adjustable model. Chamber is dated 1914 and extractor and safety are both

NIB	EXC.	V.G.	GOOD	FAIR	POOR

marked in German. "ERFURT" under a crown is stamped on front toggle link. A great many manufactured with one- to five-digit serial numbers, some with a letter suffix. Model similar to DWM Artillery, except finish is not as fine.

	EXC.	V.G.	GOOD	FAIR	POOR
—	3750	2200	1100	800	600

Double Date Erfurt

4" barrel, 9mm caliber. Area above chamber has two dates: original 1910-1918 and date of rework, 1920 or 1921. Extractor and safety are both marked in German. Model can be found with or without stock lug. "ERFURT" under a crown is stamped on front toggle link. Police or military unit markings are found on front of grip straps, more often than not. Thousands produced by DWM as well as Erfurt.

	EXC.	V.G.	GOOD	FAIR	POOR
—	1200	700	500	400	350

SIMSON & CO. SUHL, GERMANY

Simson was official rework firm for German army. Thanks to Edward Tinker for his contributions to this section.

Simson & Co. Rework

4" barrels, 9mm caliber. Chamber is blank, but some examples are dated 1917 or 1918. Forward toggle link stamped "SIMSON & CO. Suhl". Extractor and safety are marked in German. Most examples have stock lugs; some have been noted without them. Only difference between military and commercial models is proofmarks.

	EXC.	V.G.	GOOD	FAIR	POOR
—	2750	1650	900	600	500

Simson Grip Safety Rework

4" barrel, 9mm caliber. Grip safety was added. There is a stock lug. Chamber area is blank; extractor is marked but safety is not. Only a few of these commercial reworks manufactured. Caution should be taken to avoid fakes.

	EXC.	V.G.	GOOD	FAIR	POOR
—	3860	2600	1500	850	550

Simson Dated Military

4" barrel, 9mm caliber. There is a stock lug and year of manufacture from 1925-1926 stamped above chamber (below serial number 700). Extractor and safety both marked in German. Checkered walnut grips of Simson-made Lugers are noticeably thicker than others. This is an extremely rare variation. Few seem to have survived.

	EXC.	V.G.	GOOD	FAIR	POOR
—	5300	2600	1800	900	650

Simson S Code

4" barrel, 9mm caliber. Forward toggle link stamped with Gothic S, possibly for "Simson". It has a stock lug and area above chamber is blank. Extractor and safety are both marked. Grips are also thicker. Fewer than 12,000 manufactured, with one- to five-digit serial numbers—some with letter "a" suffix. Pistol quite rare on today's market.

	EXC.	V.G.	GOOD	FAIR	POOR
—	6000	3250	1500	1000	750

EARLY NAZI ERA REWORKS MAUSER

Produced between 1930 and 1933. Normally marked with Waffenamt markings.

Deaths Head Rework

4" barrel, 9mm caliber. Has a stock lug; skull and crossbones are stamped, in addition to date of manufacture, on chamber area. Date was from 1914-1918. Extractor and safety are both marked. Waffenamt proof is present. Thought that this variation was produced for 1930-1933 era "SS" division of Nazi Party. Mixed serial numbers are encountered on this model and do not lower value. A rare Luger on today's market.

	EXC.	V.G.	GOOD	FAIR	POOR
—	3500	1900	950	600	450

Kadetten Institute Rework

4" barrel, 9mm caliber. Has a stock lug and chamber area stamped "K.I." above date 1933. This stood for Cadets Institute, an early "SA" and "SS" officers' training school. Extractor and safety are both marked and Waffenamt is present. Only a few hundred reworked and variation is quite scarce. Be wary of fakes.

	EXC.	V.G.	GOOD	FAIR	POOR
—	4500	2900	1100	800	600

Mauser Unmarked Rework

4" barrel, 9mm caliber. Entire weapon is void of identifying markings. Extensive refurbishing, removal of all markings, re-barreling, etc. Stock lug is present and extractor and safety are marked. Waffenamt proofmark is on right side of receiver. Number manufactured is not known.

	EXC.	V.G.	GOOD	FAIR	POOR
—	2500	1350	850	600	450

	NIB	EXC.	V.G.	GOOD	FAIR	POOR

MAUSER MANUFACTURED LUGERS 1930-1942 DWM

Mauser Oberndorf

4" barrel, 9mm caliber. Has a stock lug, blank chamber area and marked extractor and safety. Early example of Mauser Luger. Front toggle link is still marked DWM. Leftover parts were intermixed with new Mauser parts in production of this pistol. One of the first Lugers to be finished with "Salt" blue process. Approximately 500 manufactured with one- to four-digit serial numbers, with letter "v" suffix. A rare variation.

	8000	6100	2000	1500	900

1934/06 Swiss Commercial Mauser

4.75" barrel, 7.65mm caliber. No stock lug, but has a grip safety. Swiss Cross in Sunburst stamped above chamber. Extractor and safety marked in German. Front toggle link marked with Mauser banner. Approximately 200 manufactured for commercial sale in Switzerland. Variation is very well finished. Serial numbers are all four-digits with a "v" suffix.

—	8000	6000	4000	1800	1000

1935/06 Portuguese "GNR

4.75" barrel, 7.65mm caliber. No stock lug, but has a grip safety. Chamber marked "GNR", representing Republic National Guard. Extractor marked "Carregada"; safety "Seguranca". Mauser banner stamped on front toggle link. Exactly 564 manufactured according to original contract records that Portuguese government made public. All have four-digit serial numbers with a "v" suffix.

	4500	3300	1800	900	750

1934 Mauser Commercial

4" barrel, 7.65mm or 9mm caliber. Has a stock lug and chamber area is blank. Extractor and safety are marked. Mauser banner stamped on front toggle link. Finish on this pistol was very good and grips are either checkered walnut or black plastic, on later models. Few thousand manufactured for commercial sales in and outside of Germany.

—	5500	3500	1650	1100	700

S/42 K Date

4" barrel, 9mm caliber. Has a stock lug and extractor and safety are marked. First Luger that utilized codes to represent maker and date of manufacture. Front toggle link marked S/42 in either Gothic or script; this was code for Mauser. Chamber area stamped with letter "K" code for 1934 year of manufacture. Approximately 10,500 manufactured, with one- to five-digit serial numbers—some with letter suffixes.

	9500	7500	3000	1200	1000

S/42 G Date

As above, with chamber stamped "G" code for year 1935. Gothic lettering was eliminated. Many thousands of this model produced.

	4000	2500	1200	650	450

Dated Chamber S/42

4" barrel, 9mm caliber. Chamber area dated 1936-1940. There is a stock lug. Extractor and safety marked. In 1937, rust blue process was eliminated entirely and all subsequent pistols were salt blued. Many thousands manufactured with one- to five-digit serial numbers—some with letter suffix. **NOTE:** Rarest variation is early 1937, with rust blued and strawed parts, add 20 percent.

—	3000	2100	1100	500	400

S/42 Commercial Contract

4" barrel, 9mm caliber. Has a stock lug, chamber area is dated and marked extractor and safety. Unusual feature, although this was a commercial pistol, front toggle link is stamped S/42, which was military code for Mauser. Only a few hundred manufactured, so perhaps toggles were left over from previous military production runs. Serial number range is four-digits, with letter "v".

	3750	2500	1200	750	450

Code 42 Dated Chamber

4" barrel, 9mm caliber. New German code for Mauser, number 42, stamped on front toggle link. There is a stock lug. Chamber area dated 1939 or 1940. At least 50,000 manufactured, with one- to five-digit serial numbers; some have letter suffixes.

—	2500	1400	1000	600	350

41/42 Code

As above, except date of manufacture is represented by final two digits (e.g. 41 for 1941). Approximately 20,000 manufactured, with one- to five-digit serial number range.

—	4000	2100	1200	800	500

	NIB	EXC.	V.G.	GOOD	FAIR	POOR

byf Code

As above, with "byf" code stamped on toggle link. Year of manufacture, either 41 or 42, stamped on chamber. Model also made with black plastic and walnut grips. Many thousands produced, with one- to five-digit serial numbers—some with a letter suffix.

—	3000	1800	950	450	350	

Persian Contract 4

4" barrel, 9mm caliber. Has a stock lug and Persian crest stamped over chamber. All identifying markings on this variation—including extractor, safety and toggle—are marked in Farsi, Persian alphabet. There were 1,000 manufactured. Serial numbers are also in Farsi.

—	7000	5500	3500	2500	2000	

Persian Contract Artillery

As above, with 8" barrel and nine-position adjustable sight on barrel. Model supplied with flat board stock. There were 1,000 manufactured and sold to Persia.

—	8500	5500	3500	1750	1000	

1934/06 Dated Commercial

4.75" barrel, 7.65mm caliber. Has a grip safety, but no stock lug. Year of manufacture, from 1937-1942, stamped above chamber. Mauser banner stamped on front link. Extractor marked, but safety is not. Approximately 1,000 manufactured, with one- to three-digit serial numbers—some with letter suffix.

—	4500	3100	1400	900	500	

1934 Mauser Dutch Contract

4" barrel, 9mm caliber. Year of manufacture, 1936-1940, stamped above chamber. Extractor marked "Geladen" and safety is marked "RUST", with a downward pointing arrow. Mauser banner stamped on front toggle link. This was a military contract sale. Approximately 1,000 were manufactured, with four-digit serial numbers and letter "v" suffix.

—	4750	3650	2000	1100	850	

1934 Mauser Swedish Contract

4.75" barrel, 9mm or 7.65mm caliber. Chamber dated 1938 or 1939. Extractor and safety are both marked in German. There is a stock lug. Front toggle link stamped with Mauser banner. Only 275 dated 1938; 25 dated 1939 in 9mm; 30 dated 1939 in 7.65mm. Serial number range is four-digits with letter "v" suffix.

—	6000	3800	2000	1500	700	

1934 Mauser Swedish Commercial

4" barrel, 7.65mm caliber. 1940 stamped over chamber; "Kal. 7.65" stamped on left side of barrel. Extractor and safety are both marked and Mauser banner stamped on front toggle link. There is a stock lug. Model is rare. Only a few hundred manufactured, with four-digit serial numbers with letter "w" suffix.

—	4500	2950	1200	850	600	

1934 Mauser German Contract

4" barrel, 9mm caliber. Chamber dated 1939-1942. Front toggle link stamped with Mauser banner. There is a stock lug and extractor and safety are both marked. Grips are either walnut or black plastic. Several thousand manufactured, with one- to five-digit serial numbers—some with letter suffixes. Purchased for issue to police or paramilitary units.

—	4500	3200	1500	800	550	

Austrian Bundes Heer (Federal Army)

4" barrel, 9mm caliber. Chamber is blank and there is a stock lug. Extractor and safety marked in German. Austrian Federal Army Proof stamped on left side of frame above trigger guard. Approximately 200 manufactured, with four-digit serial numbers and no letter suffix.

—	4000	2350	1200	700	500	

Mauser 2 Digit Date

4" barrel, 9mm caliber. Last two digits of year of manufacture—41 or 42—stamped over chamber. There is a stock lug and Mauser banner on front toggle link. Extractor and safety both marked. Proofmarks were commercial. Grips are either walnut or black plastic. Approximately 2,000 manufactured for sale to Nazi political groups. They have one- to five-digit serial numbers; some have letter suffix.

—	3500	2600	1500	900	650	

	NIB	EXC.	V.G.	GOOD	FAIR	POOR

Ku Luger (Prefix or suffix)

4" barrel, 9mm Luger. Probably manufactured by Mauser for German Luftwaffe in early 1940s. Serial number (on left side receiver area) has "Ku" prefix or suffix. Total production estimated at 5000 pieces.

	NIB	EXC.	V.G.	GOOD	FAIR	POOR
	—	4750	3000	1200	900	550

KRIEGHOFF MANUFACTURED LUGERS

1923 DWM/Krieghoff Commercial

4" barrel, 7.65mm or 9mm caliber. Chamber dated 1921 or left blank. There is a stock lug. Front toggle marked DWM, as they manufactured this Luger to be sold by Krieghoff. "Krieghoff Suhl" stamped on back above lanyard loop. Second "F" in Krieghoff was defective and all specimens have this distinctive die strike. Safety and extractor are marked in German. Only a few hundred manufactured, with four-digit serial numbers with letter "i" suffix.

	NIB	EXC.	V.G.	GOOD	FAIR	POOR
	—	5000	3500	1700	900	500

DWM/Krieghoff Commercial

As above, but marked "Heinrich Krieghoff Waffenfabrik Suhl" on right side of frame. Some examples have "Germany" export stamp. Several hundred manufactured, with four-digit serial numbers with a letter suffix.

	NIB	EXC.	V.G.	GOOD	FAIR	POOR
	—	4800	3650	2000	950	800

Krieghoff Commercial Inscribed Side Frame

4" or 6" barrel, 7.65mm or 9mm caliber. 1,000 were marked "Heinrich Krieghoff Waffenfabrik Suhl" on left side of frame and 500 were devoid of this marking. All have dagger and anchor trademark over "H.K. Krieghoff Suhl" on front toggle link. Extractor and safety are both marked. There is a stock lug and grips are of brown checkered plastic. Approximately 1,500 manufactured, with one- to four-digit serial numbers with "P" prefix.

	NIB	EXC.	V.G.	GOOD	FAIR	POOR
	—	8500	6400	3000	2000	1000

S Code Krieghoff

4" barrel, 9mm caliber. Krieghoff trademark stamped on front toggle link and letter "S" stamped over chamber. There is a stock lug. Extractor and safety are both marked. Grips are wood on early manufactured pistols and brown checkered plastic on later examples. Approximately 4,500 manufactured for Luftwaffe, with one- to four-digit serial numbers.

	NIB	EXC.	V.G.	GOOD	FAIR	POOR
	—	8500	5500	2000	950	750

Grip Safety Krieghoff

4" barrel, 9mm caliber. Chamber area is blank and front toggle link stamped with Krieghoff trademark. There is a stock lug and grip safety. Extractor marked "Geleden" and safety marked "FEUER" (fire) in the lower position. Grips are checkered brown plastic. Rare Luger and number produced is not known.

	NIB	EXC.	V.G.	GOOD	FAIR	POOR
	—	9500	5900	3400	1700	900

36 Date Krieghoff

4" barrel, 9mm caliber. It has a stock lug and Krieghoff trademark on front toggle link. Safety and extractor are marked. Grips are brown plastic. Two-digit year of manufacture, 36, stamped over chamber. Approximately 700 produced in 3800-4500 serial number range.

	NIB	EXC.	V.G.	GOOD	FAIR	POOR
	—	9000	6000	2600	1200	950

4 Digit Dated Krieghoff

As above, with date of production, 1936-1945, stamped above chamber. Approximately 9,000 manufactured within 4500-14000 serial number range.

	NIB	EXC.	V.G.	GOOD	FAIR	POOR
	—	7500	6000	3000	1500	750

2nd Series Krieghoff Commercial

4" barrel, 9mm caliber. There is a stock lug and Krieghoff trademark stamped on front link. Chamber area is blank. Extractor and safety are marked. Approximately 500 manufactured for commercial sales inside Germany. Date of manufacture is estimated at 1939-1940. This variation has dark finish that results from bluing without polishing surface, which was done during these years. Grips are coarsely checkered black plastic. Serial number range is one- to three-digits, with a "P" prefix.

	NIB	EXC.	V.G.	GOOD	FAIR	POOR
	—	6500	4200	2200	1300	800

	NIB	EXC.	V.G.	GOOD	FAIR	POOR

Post-War Krieghoff

4" barrel, 9mm caliber. There is a stock lug and chamber area is blank. Extractor and safety are marked. Serial numbers in one- to three-digit range are unusually large—about 3/16ths of an inch. There were 300 post-war Lugers produced for occupation forces. They were assembled from leftover parts and only 150 have Krieghoff trademark on front toggle link—second 150 have blank links.

—	6000	3500	2000	750	650	

Krieghoff Post-War Commercial

As above in 7.65mm caliber. Extractor not marked. Approximately 200 manufactured, with standard-sized two- or three-digit serial numbers. They were supposedly sold to occupation forces in PX stores.

—	6500	3500	2200	700	550	

LUGER ACCESSORIES

Detachable Carbine Stocks

Approximately 13" in length, with sling swivel and horn buttplate.

—	6500	4500	3000	1000	700	

Artillery Stock with Holster

Artillery stock is a flat board style, approximately 13.75" in length. There is a holster and magazine pouches, with straps attached. A desirable addition to Artillery Luger.

—	3500	2500	1000	800	600	

Navy Stock without Holster

As above, but 12.75" in length with metal disc inlaid on left side.

—	4500	3000	1500	800	400	

Ideal Stock/Holster with Grips

Telescoping metal tube stock, with attached leather holster. Used in conjunction with metal-backed set of plain grips that correspond to metal hooks on stock and allow attachment. This Ideal Stock is U.S. patented and is so marked.

—	3500	2000	1500	700	450	

Drum Magazine 1st Issue

A 32-round snail-like affair that is used with Artillery Luger. Also used with adapter in German 9mm sub-machine gun. 1st Issue has a telescoping tube that is used to wind the spring. There is a dust cover that protects interior from dirt.

—	2500	2000	1500	550	300	

Drum Magazine 2nd Issue

As above, with folding spring winding lever.

—	2000	1700	1000	550	300	

Drum Magazine Loading Tool

Tool slipped over magazine and allows spring to be compressed so cartridges could be inserted.

—	1500	800	500	300	200	

Drum Carrying Case

—	500	350	125	100	50	

LATE PRODUCTION MAUSER LUGERS

MANUFACTURED DURING THE 1970S

P.08 Interarms

4" or 6" barrel, 7.65mm or 9mm caliber.

1750	1250	550	400	350	300	

Swiss Eagle Interarms

Swiss-style straight front grip strap and American Eagle crest over chamber. Chambered for 7.65mm or 9mm and offered with 4" or 6" barrel.

1800	950	650	350	325	300	

Cartridge Counter

Chambered for 9mm cartridge. Fitted with slotted grip to show cartridge count in magazine.

2500	1600	1100	750	500	350	

	NIB	EXC.	V.G.	GOOD	FAIR	POOR

Commemorative Bulgarian

Bulgarian crest stamped over chamber. Only 100 produced.

	2200	1600	1100	750	500	350

Commemorative Russian

Crossed Nagant rifles stamped over chamber. Only 100 produced.

	2750	1600	1100	750	500	350

Modern Production Carbine

Splendid reproduction produced on limited basis. Workmanship is excellent. Carbine and stock furnished in case.

	6000	4500	4000	3200	2500	2000

JOHN MARTZ CUSTOM LUGERS

Martz Luger Carbine

16" barrel. Fewer than 100 manufactured.

	—	9000	7000	4500	2500	1000

.45 ACP or .357 SIG

6" barrel, .45 ACP caliber. Assembled from two Luger pistols that were split and welded together. Fewer than 100 manufactured.

	—	5500	4000	3000	—	—

Baby Luger 9mm & 7.65mm

Compact Luger pistol. Fewer than 300 produced.

	—	4000	2500	1500	—	—

Baby Luger .380 ACP

As above in .380 caliber. Seven were manufactured.

	—	8000	6000	4000	—	—

LUNA
Zella-Mehlis, Germany

Model 200 Free Pistol

.22-caliber Martini action single-shot pistol, with 11" barrel, adjustable sights and walnut grips. Manufactured prior to WWII.

	—	1850	1250	800	500	300

Model 300 Free Pistol

Single-shot target pistol chambered for .22 Short cartridge. Fitted with 11" barrel, set trigger, walnut stocks and forearm, with adjustable palm rest. Built about 1929 to 1939.

	—	1950	1250	800	500	300

Target Rifle

.22 or .22 Hornet caliber Martini action single-shot rifle, with 20" barrel, adjustable sights and walnut stock. Manufactured prior to WWII.

	—	1800	1350	850	500	250

LWRC INTERNATIONAL
Cambridge, Maryland

A manufacturer of AR-type rifles for military, law enforcement and civilian markets. All models a proprietary short-stroke, self-regulating, gas piston operating system that prevents the gases from contacting the bolt carrier or receiver. LWRC is acronym for Land Warfare Resources Corporation and previously stood for Leitner-Wise Rifle Company, Inc.

M6-A2

This standard carbine is available in 5.56 NATO/.223 Rem., with 16.1" barrel (10.5" or 14.7" lengths for LE/Military) and in several AR configurations.

	2000	1700	1350	950	550	250

PSD-Pistol

Similar features as M6-A2, with 8" barrel and Magpul MIAD pistol-grip.

	1900	1600	1250	900	500	250

	NIB	EXC.	V.G.	GOOD	FAIR	POOR

SIX8

Similar features to M6-A2, except this model is chambered for 6.8 SPC II cartridge (6.8x43mm), a high-performance version of 6.8 Rem. SPC.

	NIB	EXC.	V.G.	GOOD	FAIR	POOR
	2250	2000	1650	1200	600	300

REPR

Rapid Engagement Precision Rifle is chambered for 7.62 NATO/.308 Win., with 16.1" or 20" barrel. Custom packages including one lower receiver, with two or more barreled uppers are available. Finish colors are black, Flat Dark Earth, Patriot Brown or O.D. Green.

	NIB	EXC.	V.G.	GOOD	FAIR	POOR
	3100	2750	2150	1500	750	350

LYMAN
Middletown, Connecticut

Lyman In-Line

Introduced in 1998. In-line muzzle-loader offered in either .50- or .54-caliber. Fitted with 22" barrel. Hardwood stock. **NOTE:** Add $80 for stainless steel version.

	NIB	EXC.	V.G.	GOOD	FAIR	POOR
	300	250	200	125	75	50

Deerstalker Rifle

Available in either .50- or .54-caliber percussion or flintlock. Fitted with 24" barrel and hardwood stock. **NOTE:** Stainless steel version offered for an additional $80.

	NIB	EXC.	V.G.	GOOD	FAIR	POOR
	375	250	200	150	100	50

Deerstalker Carbine

Same as above, with 21" barrel. Offered in .50-caliber only.

	NIB	EXC.	V.G.	GOOD	FAIR	POOR
	375	250	200	150	100	50

Great Plains Rifle

Rifle offered in .50- or .54-caliber flint or percussion. Barrel length 32". Hardwood stock. **NOTE:** Add $25 for flintlock version; $10 for left-hand rifles. Early models in Excellent condition are showing significant collector potential.

	NIB	EXC.	V.G.	GOOD	FAIR	POOR
	525	400	300	175	125	100

Trade Rifle

Rifle offered in either .50- or .54-caliber, with 28" octagonal barrel and hardwood stock. Polished brass furniture. **NOTE:** Add $25 for flintlock rifle.

	NIB	EXC.	V.G.	GOOD	FAIR	POOR
	300	250	200	125	75	50

Plains Pistol

Available in .50- or .54-caliber percussion.

	NIB	EXC.	V.G.	GOOD	FAIR	POOR
	375	250	200	125	75	50

Model 1878 Sharps

Replica of the famous single shot is in .45-70. Features tang-mounted aperture sight, globe front sight, checkered stock with a comfortable shotgun-style buttplate, laser-engraved sideplate and 30" barrel. Made in Italy by Pedersoli. Imported by Lyman beginning in 2014.

	NIB	EXC.	V.G.	GOOD	FAIR	POOR
	1750	1450	1200	900	—	—

Little Sharps

Also known as Ideal Model, this smaller variation of original Sharps was chambered in a wide range of both rimfire and centerfire calibers. Made in Italy by Armi-Sport. Discontinued.

	NIB	EXC.	V.G.	GOOD	FAIR	POOR
	1500	1200	850	650	500	350

	NIB	EXC.	V.G.	GOOD	FAIR	POOR

M. B. ASSOCIATES-GYROJET
San Ramon, California

Established in 1960 by R. Maynard and Art Biehl. M. B. Associates produced Gyrojet pistols and carbines from 1962 to 1970. Basically a hand held rocket launcher, shooting a 12mm or 13mm spin stablized rocket cartridge, composed of four-part solid rocket fuel. Nose of the round was forced rearward onto a stationary firing pin, igniting fuel, expelling round and recocking for next shot. These were not very accurate and led to MBA's demise. Ammunition typically sells for $35 per round or more. By Dave Rachwal.

Mark I Model A Commemorative
13mm pistol cased with Goddard commemorative medal and 10 dummy rounds. Black anodized finish, with walnut grips.

—	2195	1500	1200	900	500	

Mark I Model B Commemorative
13mm pistol cased with commemorative Goddard medal and 10 dummy rounds. Black with walnut grips or antique nickel with pearlite grips.

—	1895	1695	1000	600	300	

Mark I Model B
13mm pistol cardboard box. Black anodized, with walnut grips usually. Produced in many variations and finishes.

—	995	800	650	400	200	

Mark II Model C
12mm pistol. Black anodized, with walnut grips. Manufactured for 12mm round to conform with 1968 gun control act, because 13mm is 51-caliber and 12mm is 49-caliber.

—	995	800	650	400	200	

Mark I Model A Carbine
13mm black anodized finish, with walnut stock and carrying handle.

—	2495	2195	1700	1000	600	

Mark I Model B Carbine
13mm antique nickel finish, with walnut stock. Sporter carbine and had flared muzzle and sleek lines.

—	1495	800	900	400	200	

M.O.A. CORP.
Dayton, Ohio

Maximum
Single-shot pistol. Manufactured in a variety of calibers from .22 rimfire to .454 Casull, with 8.5", 10" or 14" barrel, adjustable sights, stainless steel receiver, blued barrel and walnut grip. Introduced in 1986. **NOTE:** Add 100 percent for stainless steel barrel.

800	600	475	325	250	125

Carbine
As above, with 18" barrel. Discontinued.

1000	675	525	350	275	150

MAC
See—Ingram

MADSEN
Copenhagen, Denmark

Model 47

—	700	525	400	275	125

	NIB	EXC.	V.G.	GOOD	FAIR	POOR

MAGNUM RESEARCH, INC.
Minneapolis, Minnesota
See Also—Desert Eagle

BFR (Long Cylinder)

Single-action revolver, with long cylinder. Chambered for .22 Hornet, .30-30, .475/.480, .444, .45-70, .460 S&W and .45 LC/.410 with 7.5" or 10" barrel and .444 Marlin with 10" barrel. Also chambered for .500 S&W Magnum. Fitted with adjustable sights and stainless steel finish. Weight about 4 lbs. with 7.5" barrel. Introduced in 1998.

900	775	500	350	200	100

BFR Little Max (Short Cylinder)

Single-action revolver has a standard cylinder chambered for .454 Casull (6.5", 7.5", or 10" barrel), .45 Long Colt (6.5" or 7.5" barrel), .22 Hornet (7.5" barrel) or .50 A.E (7.5" barrel). Weight about 3.5 lbs. with 7.5" barrel. Introduced in 1998. Discontinued.

800	675	500	350	200	100

IMI SP-21

Semi-automatic double-action pistol. Chambered for 9mm, .40 S&W or .45 ACP cartridge. Barrel length 3.9". Magazine capacity 10 rounds for all calibers. Polymer frame, with steel slide and barrel. Weight about 26 oz. Made in Israel by Israel Military Industries. Discontinued.

550	400	300	200	150	100

MALIN, F. E.
London, England

Boxlock and sidelock shotguns made by Malin were imported into United States for a number of years. As these arms were all essentially built to specific customer's requirements, values listed are rough estimates only.

Boxlock Basic Model

Features an Anson & Deeley action and high-grade walnut. All other specification were on custom-order basis. This gun should definitely be individually appraised as values will fluctuate greatly with options.

4800	4000	3500	2500	1850	1000

Sidelock Basic Model

Features a Holland & Holland-type detachable sidelock action. All other features (as on boxlock) were on a custom-order basis. This model should also be appraised individually.

7000	6000	4750	3000	2500	1250

MALTBY, HENLEY AND CO.
New York, New York

Spencer Safety Hammerless Revolver

.32-caliber double-action revolver, with 3" barrel and 5-shot cylinder. Frame and barrel made of brass. Cylinder of steel. Barrel marked "Spencer Safety Hammerless Pat. Jan. 24, 1888 & Oct. 29, 1889". Several thousand manufactured during 1890s.

—	—	325	225	125	75

MANHATTAN FIREARMS COMPANY
Norwich, Connecticut
Newark, New Jersey

Bar Hammer Pistol

.31-, .34- or .36-caliber single-shot percussion pistol, with 2" or 4" barrel. Hammer marked "Manhattan F.A. Mfg. Co. New York". Blued, with walnut grips. Approximately 1,500 made during 1850s.

—	—	1050	750	300	150

Shotgun Hammer Pistol

.36-caliber bar hammer single-shot percussion pistol, with 5.5" half octagonal barrel marked as above. Blued, with walnut grips. Approximately 500 made.

—	—	1050	750	300	150

	NIB	EXC.	V.G.	GOOD	FAIR	POOR

Pepperbox

.28- or .31-caliber double-action percussion pepperbox, with 3", 4" or 5" barrels and 5- or 6-shot barrel groups. Blued, case hardened with walnut grips. Marked as above and also "Cast Steel". Major variations of this pistol are as follows:

Three-shot with 3" Barrel
Manually rotated barrels.

	NIB	EXC.	V.G.	GOOD	FAIR	POOR
	—	—	950	550	250	125

Five-shot with 3", 4", 5" Barrel
Automatically rotated barrels.

	NIB	EXC.	V.G.	GOOD	FAIR	POOR
	—	—	1100	650	450	250

Six-shot with 3" or 4" Barrel
Automatic rotation.

	NIB	EXC.	V.G.	GOOD	FAIR	POOR
	—	—	1100	650	450	250

Six-shot with 5" Barrel
Automatic rotation.

	NIB	EXC.	V.G.	GOOD	FAIR	POOR
	—	—	1600	1200	550	350

Pocket Revolver

.31-caliber percussion revolver, with 4", 5" or 6" barrel and 5- or 6-shot cylinder. Blued, case hardened with walnut grips. Barrel marked "Manhattan Firearms/Manufg. Co. New York" on 5-shot model, serial numbers from 1 to approximately 1,000; "Manhattan Firearms Mfg. Co. New York" on 6-shot model, frame marked "December 27, 1859".

First Model—Five-Shot

	NIB	EXC.	V.G.	GOOD	FAIR	POOR
	—	—	1200	600	450	150

Second Model—Six-Shot

	NIB	EXC.	V.G.	GOOD	FAIR	POOR
	—	—	1200	600	450	150

London Pistol Company

As above marked "London Pistol Company". Approximately 200 manufactured between 1859 and 1861.

	NIB	EXC.	V.G.	GOOD	FAIR	POOR
	—	—	1400	750	450	150

.36 Caliber Percussion Revolver

.36-caliber percussion revolver, with 4", 5" or 6.5" octagonal barrel and 5- or 6-shot cylinder. Blued, case hardened with walnut grips. Approximately 78,000 made between 1859 and 1868. There were five variations.

Model I

A 5-shot cylinder marked "Manhattan Firearms Mfg. Co. New York". Serial numbers from 1 through 4200. **NOTE:** 6" barreled version would be worth a 15 percent premium.

	NIB	EXC.	V.G.	GOOD	FAIR	POOR
	—	—	1500	1050	550	150

Model II

As above, with 1859 patent date marked on barrel. Serial range 4200 to 14500.

	NIB	EXC.	V.G.	GOOD	FAIR	POOR
	—	—	1650	1350	550	150

Model III

A 5-shot cylinder marked "Manhattan Firearms Co. Newark NJ", together with 1859 patent date. Serial numbers from 14500 to 45200.

	NIB	EXC.	V.G.	GOOD	FAIR	POOR
	—	—	1575	1200	500	150

Model IV

As above, with modified recoil shield. Patent date March 8, 1864 added to barrel inscription. Serial numbers from 45200 to 69200.

	NIB	EXC.	V.G.	GOOD	FAIR	POOR
	—	—	1600	1250	450	150

Model V

	NIB	EXC.	V.G.	GOOD	FAIR	POOR
	—	—	1700	1350	550	200

.22 Caliber Pocket Revolver

.22-caliber spur trigger revolver, with 3" barrel and 7-shot cylinder. Blued, silver plated with walnut or rosewood grips. Approximately 17,000 made during 1860s. Fairly close copy of S&W No. 1.

	NIB	EXC.	V.G.	GOOD	FAIR	POOR
	—	—	550	300	250	100

	NIB	EXC.	V.G.	GOOD	FAIR	POOR

Manhattan-American Standard Hero

.34-caliber single-shot percussion pistol, with 2" or 3" round barrel that unscrews for loading. Blued, brass frame with walnut grips. Marked "A.S.T. Co./HERO". Made by American Standard Tool Company, Manhattan's successor. Approximately 30,000 manufactured between 1868 and 1873.

Manhattan Manufactured

Marked "HERO/M.F.A.Co.". Approximately 5,000 produced.

—	—	625	550	250	100

American Standard Manufactured

Approximately 25,000 produced.

—	—	625	500	225	100

MANN, FRITZ
Suhl, Germany

6.35mm Pocket Pistol

6.35mm caliber semi-automatic pistol, with 1.65" barrel and 5-shot magazine. Blued, with plastic grips having name "Mann" cast in them. This pistol, which weighs only 9 oz., is one of the smallest semi-automatic pistols ever manufactured. Made between 1920 and 1922.

—	395	295	200	150	100

7.65mm Pocket Pistol

7.65mm or 9mm short semi-automatic pistol, with 2.35" barrel and 5-shot magazine. Blued, with plastic grips that have name "Mann" cast in them. Manufactured between 1924 and 1929.

—	375	275	200	150	100

MANNLICHER PISTOL
Steyr, Austria
See—Steyr

MANNLICHER SCHOENAUER
Steyr, Austria

Military models and their history, technical data, descriptions and prices see under "Austria-Hungary". Currently imported Mannlicher models, see Steyr.

Model 1903 Carbine

6.5x54mm caliber bolt-action rifle, with 17.7" barrel. Rotary magazine capacity 5 rounds. Folding rear leaf sight, double set triggers and full-length walnut stock. Discontinued prior to WWII.

—	2200	1650	1300	1000	550

Model 1905 Carbine

As above chambered for 9x56mm cartridge. Discontinued prior to WWII.

—	1850	1500	1000	750	550

Model 1908 Carbine

As above chambered for 7x57mm or 8x56mm cartridge. Discontinued prior to WWII.

—	1950	1600	1000	750	550

Model 1910 Carbine

As above chambered for 9.5x57mm cartridge. Discontinued prior to WWII.

—	1850	1500	1000	750	550

Model 1924 Carbine

As above chambered for .30-06 cartridge. Discontinued prior to WWII.

—	2750	2250	1750	1000	550

High Velocity Rifle

As above in 7x64mm Brenneke, .30-06, 8x60Smm Magnum, 9.3x62mm and 10.75x68mm caliber, with 23.5" barrel and folding leaf sight. Half-length walnut stock. Discontinued prior to WWII.
NOTE: Takedown Model add 75 percent.

—	2750	2250	1750	1000	550

Model 1950

.257 Roberts, .270 Winchester and .30-06 caliber bolt-action rifle, with 24" barrel and 5-shot rotary magazine. Blued, with half length walnut stock. Manufactured between 1950 and 1952.

2000	1600	1250	800	650	450

	NIB	EXC.	V.G.	GOOD	FAIR	POOR

Model 1950 Carbine

As above, with 20" barrel and full-length stock.

NIB	EXC.	V.G.	GOOD	FAIR	POOR
2200	1750	1250	800	650	450

Model 1950 6.5 Carbine

As above in 6.5x54mm Mannlicher Schoenauer caliber, with 18.5" barrel and full-length stock.

NIB	EXC.	V.G.	GOOD	FAIR	POOR
2300	1900	1400	1000	650	300

Model 1952

Similar to above, with turned back bolt handle. Manufactured between 1952 and 1956.

NIB	EXC.	V.G.	GOOD	FAIR	POOR
2400	2100	1850	1300	650	300

Model 1952 Carbine

Similar to Model 1950 carbine. Additionally in 7x57mm caliber. Manufactured between 1952 and 1956.

NIB	EXC.	V.G.	GOOD	FAIR	POOR
2450	2100	1850	1300	650	300

Model 1952 6.5mm Carbine

As above in 6.5x54mm Mannlicher Schoenauer caliber, with 18.5" barrel. Manufactured between 1952 and 1956.

NIB	EXC.	V.G.	GOOD	FAIR	POOR
2400	2000	1500	850	650	300

Model 1956 Rifle

.243 or .30-06 caliber bolt-action rifle, with 22" barrel and Monte Carlo-style stock. Manufactured between 1956 and 1960.

NIB	EXC.	V.G.	GOOD	FAIR	POOR
2100	1900	1700	950	650	300

Model 1956 Carbine

As above, with 20" barrel and full-length stock. Manufactured between 1956 and 1960.

NIB	EXC.	V.G.	GOOD	FAIR	POOR
2100	1900	1700	950	650	300

Model 1961 MCA Rifle

As above modified for easier use with telescopic sight.

NIB	EXC.	V.G.	GOOD	FAIR	POOR
1750	1550	1250	1000	800	650

Model 1961 MCA Carbine

As above, with 20" barrel and half-length stock.

NIB	EXC.	V.G.	GOOD	FAIR	POOR
1950	1650	1250	1100	700	600

Model M72 LM Rifle

Fitted with 23" fluted barrel, double set or single trigger and full-length stock. Manufactured between 1972 and 1980.

NIB	EXC.	V.G.	GOOD	FAIR	POOR
—	1300	1050	700	550	450

MANUFRANCE
St. Etienne, France
See—Le Francais

Auto Stand

.22-caliber semi-automatic pistol. Manufactured by Pyrenees and sold by Manufrance under trade name Auto Stand.

NIB	EXC.	V.G.	GOOD	FAIR	POOR
—	250	225	200	150	100

Buffalo Stand

.22-caliber bolt-action pistol, with 12" barrel and adjustable sights. Blued, with walnut stock. Manufactured prior to 1914.

NIB	EXC.	V.G.	GOOD	FAIR	POOR
—	250	225	200	150	100

Le Agent

8mm caliber double-action revolver, with 5" barrel. Blued, with walnut grips.

NIB	EXC.	V.G.	GOOD	FAIR	POOR
—	200	100	175	150	75

	NIB	EXC.	V.G.	GOOD	FAIR	POOR

Le Colonial
As above, with enclosed hammer.

	—	200	175	150	100	75

LeFrancais
Semi-automatic pistol chambered for 7.65mm cartridge. Built on blowback design. 7.65mm pistols were first built in 1950. Production stopped in 1959. Very few of these pistols are in U.S.

	—	525	425	300	200	100

MANURHIN
Saint-Bonnet-le-Chateau, France

Company manufactured Walther PP and PPK models under license. These are marked "Manufacture de Machines du Haut-Rhin" on left front of slide and "Lic Excl. Walther" on left rear. These arms were imported into U.S.A. in early 1950s by Thalson Import Company of San Francisco, California and later by Interarms. Latter are marked "Mark 11" and "Made in France". Manurhin is now owned by Chapuis Armes. **NOTE:** All models add 15 percent for police markings.

Model PP
Similar to Walther Model PP, with revised safety. Discontinued.

	—	400	350	300	225	150

Model PPK/S
Similar to Walther Model PPK/S, with revised safety. Discontinued.

	—	400	350	300	225	150

Model PP Sports
Target version of PP. Chambered for .22-caliber shell. Available in various barrel lengths. Discontinued.

	—	400	350	300	225	150

Model 73 Defense Revolver
.38 Special or .357 Magnum caliber double-action swing-out cylinder revolver, with 2.5", 3" or 4" barrel having fixed sights. Blued, with walnut grips.

	1150	1000	850	750	500	350

Model 73 Gendarmerie
As above, with 5.5", 6" or 8" long barrel and adjustable sights.

	1250	1100	900	800	550	400

Model 73 Sport
Similar to above, with shortened lock time and target-style adjustable sights.

	1250	1100	900	800	550	400

Model 73 Convertible
As above, with interchangeable .22-, .32- or .38-caliber barrels and cylinders.

	2250	1850	1600	1400	950	750

Model 73 Silhouette
Similar to Model 73 Sport in .22 to .357 Magnum caliber, with 10" or 10.75" shrouded barrel. Form fitting walnut grips.

	1200	1050	850	750	500	350

MARATHON PRODUCTS, INC.
Santa Barbara, California

.22 First Shot
.22-caliber single-shot bolt-action rifle, with 16.5" barrel. Overall length 31". Blued, with walnut stock. Manufactured between 1985 and 1987.

	—	75	55	45	30	25

.22 Super Shot
As above, with 24" barrel. Manufactured between 1985 and 1987.

	—	75	55	45	30	25

NIB	EXC.	V.G.	GOOD	FAIR	POOR

.22 Hot Shot Pistol

.22-caliber bolt-action pistol, with 14.5" barrel. Blued, with walnut stock. Manufactured in 1986 and 1987.

—	100	55	45	30	25

Centerfire Rifle

Bolt-action sporting rifle. Manufactured in a variety of calibers, with 24" barrel, open sights, adjustable trigger and 5-shot magazine. Blued, with walnut stock. Manufactured in 1985 and 1986.

—	325	250	200	150	125

MARBLE'S ARMS & MFG. CO.
Gladstone, Michigan

Marble's Game Getter Gun—NFA, curio or relic

Marble's suspended sales of Game Getter in United States after Treasury Department ruled it was a "firearm" under NFA, but continued sales abroad. Retail price in 1934 was about $24 (12" or 15" barrels) to $26 (18" barrels). Bureau of Internal Revenue removed 18" barrel variation from NFA in a Letter Ruling dated March 1, 1939. Today, 12" and 15" barrel variations are controlled under NFA in "any other weapon" category. If shoulder stock is removed from a 12", 15" or 18" barreled Game Getter, however, ATF has ruled it to be a NFA "firearm" subject to a $200 transfer tax.

Model 1908

Serial numbered from A to M; then 001 to 10000.

2750	2200	1600	1150	750	350

Model 1908 was available in two variations. Model 1908A has a flexible rear tang sight and Model 1908B has a filler block. Some confusion about serial numbering exists, because some Marble's factory representatives gave out incorrect information during 1960s and 1970s. According to some letters from this period, on Marble's factory letterhead, serial numbers began with number 700 and ended with 9999. Original factory records, however, disclose that Model 1908 was first shipped from factory in 1909, serial numbered with letters A through M, before beginning numerically with serial number 001 through 10000, when production ended in May, 1914. Serial number 001 was shipped from factory on March 3, 1909 and last Model 1908 was shipped on May 22, 1918.

The markings on the Model 1908 are:

Type I (serial 1 to about 4000)

Type II (about serial 4000 to 9999)

LEFT SIDE:

MANUFACTURED BY THE
MARBLE SAFETY AXE CO.
GLADSTONE, MICH. U.S.A.
Marble Arms & Mfg. Co.

MANUFACTURED BY THE
MARBLE SAFETY AXE CO.
GLADSTONE, MICH. U.S.A.
SUCCESSOR

RIGHT SIDE:

Calibers 22 & 44
Patent Allowed

Calibers 22 & 44
Patent Allowed

Each of the markings on the right side is enclosed within an elongated circle.

OTHER CHARACTERISTICS: Separate flat buttplate attached with two screws up to approximately serial number 1200; afterwards, a flattened buttplate was integrally formed from same round steel used to form skeleton stock. Early stocks have drop adjustment with a knurled collar .375" diameter by .1875" long; at approximately serial number 2500, collar was changed to .500" by .625" long. Hammer spur is curved down up to approximately serial number 2,000, then curve at hammer is up.

Model 1908 was originally designed for .22 short, long or LR and .44 shot and ball ammunition, but the most satisfactory load was long-cased .44-40 that held shot in place with a disk and mouth crimp. The 1915 Marble's catalog stated Model 1908 was available for use with 2" .410 shotgun shell; chambering is slightly different from that of .44-40, but is seldom encountered. Production of Model 1908 was not resumed because of WWI.

Model 1921

2100	1750	1250	900	500	250

To meet continuing demand for the extremely popular 1908, Marble's produced an entirely new gun in 1921. Grip, folding stock (made from cold-rolled sheet metal and nickel-plated) and other features were redesigned. Serial number range for Model 1921 is 10001 (shipped in October 1921) to 20076. Most production of Model 1921 apparently ended around the time of WWII; however, factory records disclose Marble's was exporting 15" barrel Model 1921s into

Canada in 1955, where their registration was not required at that time. Marble's also assembled approximately 200 Model 1921s from parts circa 1960-61 and sold them (without holster) for $200 each.

Model 1921 was originally designed for 2" .410 shotgun shell, but Marble's changed the extractor marking on some guns to 2" or 2-1/2" to indicate factory rechambering for 2.5" shell, which has been reported to have started in 1924. However, change to a 2-1/2" chamber may not have been uniform, because both 2" and 2-1/2" marked guns have been observed in low (14000) and high (19000) serial number ranges. Lowest serial number with 2-1/2" marking observed so far is 14601. Range from approximately 14500 to 17000 have plastic rather than walnut grips, single-bladed rear sight rather than multiple-blade and blued rather than case-hardened hammer. Outside this range, only 19288 has 2" marking; and number 19692 is marked 2-1/2". No Model 1921 Game Getters are known to have been factory chambered for 3" .410 shell.

The markings on the Model 1921 are:

LEFT SIDE:

Marble's
Game Getter Gun
Marble Arms & Mfg.Co.
Gladstone, Mich.U.S.A.

RIGHT SIDE:

UPPER BARREL 22 S.L. LR.&N.R.A
LOWER BARREL .44GG & .410 2"

OTHER CHARACTERISTICS: Other barrel markings for Model 1921 in .410 are .410 2" and .410 2-1/2"; latter appears in serial number range from approximately 15000 to 16600 and in the low 19000 range.

NOTE: Boxed guns (wooden box, Model 1908; cardboard box, Model 1921) with accessories, or 18" barrel variations, nonstandard calibers (.25-20, .32-20, .38-40, etc.) command premiums of 50 to 200 percent or more; an original holster is $75 to $150. Two (2) new-in-box Model 1908 with 15" and 18" barrels sold for $2,700 and $3,600, respectively, in 1994. An original wooden Model 1908 box alone may sell for $500 to $900. All 18" barrel variations are rare.

Marble's Game Getter Pistol and other special-order or experimental Game Getters —NFA, curio or relic

Contemporary articles and advertisements in Hunter-Trader-Trapper and some early Marble's catalogs, state that a small number of Model 1908 Game Getters were originally manufactured (with rifled barrels) for .25-20, .32-20 and .38-40 cartridges. An illustrated advertisement in a 1910 issue of Hunter-Trapper-Trader states that 12", 15" and 18" barrel Game Getters were available for delivery in .25-20, .32-20 and .38-40 and that these firearms were designed as over/under rifles with rifled barrels. An article in October 1913 issue of Outdoor Life states that Marble's was manufacturing a Game Getter pistol, with 10" barrels and that any barrel length could be ordered.

Original factory records have confirmed the manufacture of foregoing Game Getters and clarified their designs. All original guns are thus correctly classified as experimental or special-order guns and all are extremely rare. Factory records disclose that about 20 each of Model 1908 were manufactured with .22/25-20 and .22/.32-20 over/under rifled barrels, but barrel lengths are not specified. No .22/.38-40 Model 1908 Game Getters are listed in factory records, but that may not have precluded a later factory alteration to that configuration. It is important to note that any Model 1908 Game Getter with over/under rifled barrels less than 18" in length is currently subject to registration under NFA as a short barreled rifle, with a $200 transfer tax. Under current law, if these firearms are not registered they are contraband and cannot be legally owned unless ATF administratively removes them from NFA as collector's items.

Factory records disclose that eight Model 1908 Game Getter pistols were manufactured and all were shipped to a Minneapolis hardware store. Two specimens have been located: serial number 3810, with a 8" .22/.44 smooth bore barrel, and serial number 3837, with a 10" .22/.44 smooth bore barrel. Inspection of serial numbers 3810 and 3837 (including removal of grips) reveal they were never fitted with shoulder stocks, because the portion of frame which would have accommodated the stock was never machined out to receive one. Under current law, an original Marble's Game Getter pistol is subject to registration under NFA as an "Any Other Weapon" with a $5 transfer tax. According to very incomplete factory records, a relatively small number—about a dozen—Model 1921 Game Getters were manufactured with

	NIB	EXC.	V.G.	GOOD	FAIR	POOR

.22/.38-40 rifled barrels, but barrel lengths are not specified. It is possible that other factory-original configurations exist, such as .22/.25-20 and others.

MARGOLIN
Tula, Soviet State Arsenal

Model MT Sports

Semi-automatic .22-caliber pistol, with no barrel weights. Not threaded for a compensator. Barrel length 7.5". Furnished with a black plastic case with spare magazine and repair parts. Discontinued.

	NIB	EXC.	V.G.	GOOD	FAIR	POOR
	—	600	500	400	300	200

Model MTS-1

.22 short semi-automatic pistol, with 5.9" barrel having an integral muzzle-brake (7.4" overall), adjustable walnut grips and 6-shot magazine. Normally accompanied by a wooden case with cleaning accessories. Discontinued.

	NIB	EXC.	V.G.	GOOD	FAIR	POOR
	—	1300	1025	800	450	350

Model MTS-2

As above in .22 LR, with 5.9" barrel. Discontinued.

	NIB	EXC.	V.G.	GOOD	FAIR	POOR
	—	1200	900	600	400	350

MARIETTE BREVETTE
Liege, Belgium

A number of European manufacturers produced percussion pepperbox pistols based upon a patent issued to Mariette during 1840s and 1850s. These pistols have detachable barrels that are loaded at breech, double-action ring triggers and internally mounted hammers. Normally blued and foliate engraved.

4" Barrel Pepperbox

	NIB	EXC.	V.G.	GOOD	FAIR	POOR
	—	—	2250	900	400	—

6" Barrel Pepperbox

	NIB	EXC.	V.G.	GOOD	FAIR	POOR
	—	—	2250	900	400	—

MARLIN FIREARMS CO.
Madison, North Carolina

Marlin, along with its subsidiaries Harrington & Richardson/NEF, are now owned by Freedom Group Family of Companies.

BALLARD RIFLES

Established by John Mahlon Marlin in 1863. Marlin manufactured pistols until 1875 when he began production of Ballard rifles. In 1881 he made his first lever-action repeating rifle for which his company became famous.

BALL & WILLIAMS BALLARDS
First Model

This model was the first Ballard produced. Introduced in 1861. Offered with 24" or 28" octagonal barrel. Frame is case colored and barrel is blued. Walnut stock is varnished. Major identifying feature of this model is inside extractor. This was the only Ballard that had this feature before Marlin began to manufacture the rifle in 1875. Barrel stamped "Ball & Williams/Worchester, Mass." and "Ballards Patent/Nov. 5, 1861". Approximately 100 manufactured. Serial numbered from 1-100.

	NIB	EXC.	V.G.	GOOD	FAIR	POOR
	—	—	3000	2500	900	400

Military Rifle

There is not enough known about these rifles and probably never will be. They were chambered most frequently for .44 and .54 rimfire cartridges and feature outside tangs and extractors. Offered with a 30" round barrel and full-length forearm. There are three barrel bands and sling swivels. Government ordered only 35 of these for use in Civil War; if one was to be definitely authenticated as a genuine martial specimen, it would be quite valuable. Many of these rifles were marked "Kentucky" on top of receiver, because militia of that state armed its men with Ballard rifles and carbines. This marking was a sales aid used by the company and does not indicate militia ownership. Number manufactured is not known. Barrel markings are as on First Model.

	NIB	EXC.	V.G.	GOOD	FAIR	POOR
	—	—	5000	2850	1250	300

	NIB	EXC.	V.G.	GOOD	FAIR	POOR

Civil War Military Carbine

This model has a 22" part-round, part-octagonal barrel. Chambered for .44 rimfire cartridge. Has outside tang and extractor. Stock and forearm are walnut, with a barrel band sling swivel. Buttstock bears an oval cartouche surrounding inspector's marks "MM". These letters also appear stamped on major metal parts. Government ordered 1,509 for use in Civil War. Barrel was marked same as rifle.

	NIB	EXC.	V.G.	GOOD	FAIR	POOR
	—	—	5500	3750	1500	500

Sporting Rifle

Chambered for .32, .38 and .44 rimfire cartridges. Octagonal barrel 24", 26" or 28" in length and blued. Frame is case colored. Stock and forearm are varnished walnut. A knob protrudes in front of frame to operate outside manual extractor. Crescent buttplate standard. Approximately 6,500 manufactured. Barrel markings same as on First Model.

	NIB	EXC.	V.G.	GOOD	FAIR	POOR
	—	—	2000	1550	500	200

Sporting Carbine

Similar in appearance to Sporting Rifle, with 22" part-round part-octagonal barrel. Chambered for .44- and .54-caliber cartridge. Sling swivel is found on a barrel band in front. Knob on bottom activates outside extractor. Some encountered with "Kentucky" stamped on top, but this does not affect value. Markings are same as on previous models. There are no production figures available, but some estimate approximately 2,000 were manufactured.

	NIB	EXC.	V.G.	GOOD	FAIR	POOR
	—	—	2200	1750	600	250

Dual Ignition System

This system allows use of rimfire cartridge or percussion method by simply turning striker on hammer from one position to the other. Features a percussion nipple mounted on breechblock and hammer marked "Patented Jan. 5, 1864". Patent was held by Merwin and Bray. This swivel system is usually found on sporting models and would increase value of weapon by 20 percent.

MERRIMACK ARMS CO. AND BROWN

MANUFACTURING CO. (BALLARDS)

Values for Ballard rifles manufactured by these two firms are the same and specifications are similar. Identifying difference is markings "Merrimack Arms & Mfg. Co./Newburyport Mass." or "Brown Mfg. Co. Newburyport, Mass.". Merrimack produced approximately 3,000 of these rifles between 1867 and 1869 serial numbered in 18000-20000 range. Brown produced approximately 1,800 between 1869 and 1873 in 20000-22000 serial number range.

Sporting Rifle

Produced in .22- (rare), .32-, .38-, .44-, .46- and .52-caliber rimfire or percussion. Most encountered feature the dual ignition system and had nipple in breechblock. Round or octagonal barrel in 24", 26" or 28" lengths. Appearance and finish similar to Ball & Williams rifles; major difference is inside tang. Extractor was still outside mounted and manually activated. Exact production breakdown is unknown. There is no premium for dual ignition system on these later guns.

	NIB	EXC.	V.G.	GOOD	FAIR	POOR
	—	—	1700	1250	450	200

Sporting Carbine

Quite similar in appearance to Sporting Rifle, with 22" part-round part-octagonal barrel.

	NIB	EXC.	V.G.	GOOD	FAIR	POOR
	—	—	1800	1350	550	300

Military Rifle

Military Rifle similar to sporting version. Except, has a 30" round barrel and full-length forearm, with three barrel bands. Chambered for .44- and .52-caliber rimfire or percussion, with dual ignition system.

	NIB	EXC.	V.G.	GOOD	FAIR	POOR
	—	—	2000	1500	650	300

Shotgun

Similar to Sporting Rifle in appearance. Chambered for 24-gauge, with a 30" round barrel. A groove milled in top of frame to use as a sight. Butt-plate is shotgun-style instead of usual crescent shape.

	NIB	EXC.	V.G.	GOOD	FAIR	POOR
	—	—	1200	800	350	200

MARLIN-BALLARD RIFLES

Commencing in 1875, Ballard single-shot rifle was made by John Marlin for Schoverling and Daly. In 1881, business was incorporated and became Marlin Firearms Co. All Ballards made from then until 1891, when they were discontinued, were produced under this banner. Only real difference in rifles manufactured during these periods was in markings. Earlier rifles stamped "J.M. Marlin New

	NIB	EXC.	V.G.	GOOD	FAIR	POOR

Haven. Conn. U.S.A./Ballards Patent. Nov. 5, 1861"; post-1881 models stamped "Marlin Firearms Co. New Haven Ct. U.S.A./Patented Feb. 9, 1875/Ballards Patent Nov. 5, 1861".

Ballard Hunters Rifle

Resembles earlier Brown Manufacturing Company rifles. Utilizes many leftover parts acquired by Marlin. Chambered for .32, .38 and .44 rimfire and centerfire. Features John Marlin's unique reversible firing pin that allows same gun to use both rimfire and centerfire ammunition simply by rotating firing pin in breechblock. Model still had external ejector and bears J.M. Marlin markings. Approximately 500 manufactured in 1 to 500 serial range. Produced in 1875 and 1876.

—	—	3700	2750	950	400

Ballard No. 1 Hunters Rifle

Model bears early J.M. Marlin marking only. Manufactured from 1876 until 1880. Discontinued before incorporation. Has 26", 28" and 30" barrel. Chambered for .44 rimfire or centerfire cartridge. Has reversible firing pin and new internal extractor. Production figures are not available. Serial number range between 500 and 4000.

—	—	4500	3000	1000	400

Ballard No. 1-1/2 Hunters Rifle

Similar to No. 1. Chambered for .45-70, .40-63 and .40-65 cartridges. Does not have reversible firing pin. Barrel length 30" and 32". Manufactured between 1879 and 1883. Found with both early and later markings.

—	—	5200	3750	1500	500

Ballard No. 1-3/4 "Far West" Hunters Rifle

Model made by J. M. Marlin only. Similar to No. 1-1/2. Difference being addition of double-set triggers and a ring on opening lever. Manufactured in 1880 and 1881.

—	—	6300	4750	2000	600

Ballard No. 2 Sporting Rifle

Chambered for .32, .38 rimfire or centerfire cartridges and .44 centerfire. Has reversible firing pin. Offered in 26", 28" and 30" barrel lengths. Features "Rocky Mountain" sights. Manufactured between 1876 and 1891. Found with both early and late markings.

—	—	3200	2000	650	200

Ballard No. 3 Gallery Rifle

Similar to No. 2 rifle. Chambered for .22 rimfire cartridge. Has a manually operated external extractor. Sights are same and a 24" barrel was offered in addition to 26", 28" and 30". Manufactured between 1876 and 1891.

—	—	3200	2000	650	200

Ballard No. 3F Gallery Rifle

Deluxe version of No. 3. Has a pistol-grip stock, nickel-plated Schutzen-style buttplate and an opening lever like a repeating rifle. Features a 26" octagonal barrel and oil-finished stock. Manufactured in late 1880s. Quite scarce in today's market.

—	—	6500	4250	1750	500

Ballard No. 4 Perfection Rifle

Chambered for a number of centerfire calibers from .32-40 to .50-70. Barrel lengths from 26" to 30". Sights are "Rocky Mountain" type. Manufactured between 1876 and 1891.

—	—	6500	4250	1750	500

Ballard No. 3-1/2 Target Rifle

Similar to No. 4 Perfection Rifle. Has a checkered stock, with shotgun-style buttplate, 30" barrel and tang peep sight with globe front sight. Chambered for .40-65 cartridge. Manufactured from 1880-1882.

—	—	6500	4250	1750	500

Ballard No. 4-1/2 Mid Range Rifle

Model also a variation of No. 4 Perfection model. Has a higher-grade checkered stock, with shotgun buttplate, 30" part-round part-octagonal barrel. Chambered for .38-40, .40-65 and .45-70 cartridges. Features a Vernier tang peep sight and globe front sight. Manufactured between 1878 and 1882.

—	—	6750	4500	2000	500

	NIB	EXC.	V.G.	GOOD	FAIR	POOR

Ballard No. 4-1/2 A-1 Mid Range Target Rifle

Deluxe version of No. 4-1/2" rifle. Features scroll engraving on frame, with "Ballard A-1" on left and "Mid-Range" on right. Chambered for .38-50 and .40-65 cartridge. Has a high-grade checkered stock, with horn fore-end tip. Sights are highest-grade Vernier tang sight and a spirit lever front sight. Shotgun or rifle-style butt was optional. Manufactured between 1878 and 1880.

		9000	7250	3500	750
—	—	9000	7250	3500	750

Ballard No. 5 Pacific Rifle

Model has a 30" or 32" medium to heavyweight barrel, with a ramrod mounted underneath. Chambered for many different calibers from .38-50 to .50-70. Features "Rocky Mountain" sights, crescent butt, double-set triggers and a ring-style opening lever. Manufactured between 1876 and 1891.

—	—	5500	4750	2000	500

Ballard No. 5-1/2 Montana Rifle

Similar to Pacific Rifle, with an extra heavyweight barrel. Chambered for .45 Sharps cartridge only. Features checkered steel shotgun-style buttplate. Manufactured from 1882-1884. Has late markings only.

—	—	15000	10000	5500	1250

Ballard No. 6 Schuetzen Off Hand Rifle

Model has a 30" or 32" octagonal barrel. Chambered for .40-65, .44-75 and .38-50 cartridges. Stock is of select walnut in high-combed Schuetzen style. Buttplate is nickel-plated. Receiver is not engraved. Sights are Vernier tang type on rear and a spirit lever front. Triggers are double set. Opening lever has a ring and spur. Marked J.M. Marlin only. Manufactured between 1876 and 1880.

—	—	—	6500	2500	500

Ballard No. 6 Schuetzen Rifle

Similar to Off Hand. Produced by later Marlin Firearms Company and was so marked. More deluxe version, with checkered stock, horn fore-end tip and a fully engraved receiver. Chambered for .32-40 and .38-55 cartridges. Manufactured between 1881 and 1891.

—	—	13000	8500	4500	1250

Ballard No. 6-1/2 Off Hand Mid Range Rifle

Chambered for .40-54 Everlasting cartridge only. Has 28" or 30" part-round part-octagonal barrel, Schuetzen-style stock, and plain non-engraved receiver. Manufactured between 1880 and 1882.

—	20000	9500	5500	2500	500

Ballard No. 6-1/2 Rigby Off Hand Mid Range Rifle

Chambered for .38-50 and .40-65 cartridges. Features Rigby ribbed-style barrel in 26" and 28" lengths, with Vernier rear and globe front sights. High grade checkered walnut Schuetzen-style stock, with horn fore-end tip and pistol-grip cap. Buttplate nickel-plated. Opening lever of ring type, with single trigger. Extensively engraved receiver. Manufactured from 1880 to 1882.

—	—	14500	9000	5500	1250

Ballard No. 6-1/2 Off Hand Rifle

Chambered for .32-40 and .38-55 cartridges. Features barrel lengths 28" and 30". Checkered high-grade walnut Schuetzen-style stock, with nickel-plated buttplate. Fore-end tip and pistol-grip cap are of horn. Receiver engraved. Has single trigger, full-ring opening lever, Vernier tang rear sight and spirit lever front sight. Made by Marlin Firearms Company between 1883 and 1891. Found with later markings only.

—	—	14000	9000	5500	1250

Ballard No. 7 "Creedmore A-1" Long Range Rifle

Model is commonly chambered for .44-100 or .45-100 cartridges. Has 34" part-round part-octagonal barrel. High grade checkered pistol-grip stock, with a horn fore-end tip and shotgun-style butt. Sights are a special 1,300-yard Vernier tang rear and a spirit level front. Another sight base on heel of stock for mounting rear sight for ultra long-range shooting. Opening lever is similar to a repeating rifle. Single trigger featured. Receiver engraved and marked "Ballard A-1" on left and "Long Range" on right. Manufactured between 1876 and 1886. Found with both early and late markings.

—	—	15000	9700	5500	1250

	NIB	EXC.	V.G.	GOOD	FAIR	POOR

Ballard No. 7 Long Range Rifle

Similar to "Creedmore A-1". Slightly less deluxe. Engraving less elaborate. Lettering on receiver is absent. Manufactured between 1883 and 1890. Found with later markings only.

	—	—	13500	8000	4500	850

Ballard No. 7A-1 Long Range Rifle

Higher grade version of "Creedmore A-I", with fancier walnut and checkered straight stock. Better sights and deluxe engraving also featured. Manufactured between 1879 and 1883. Found with both markings.

	—	—	16000	1000	5500	1250

Ballard No. 7A-1 Extra Grade Long Range Rifle

Highest grade version of No. 7 rifles. Features 34" "Rigby" -type ribbed round barrel. Usually a special-order rifle, with most features to customer specifications. Manufactured in limited numbers between 1879 and 1883. Found with both markings.

	—	—	19500	11500	6500	1500

Ballard No. 8 Union Hill Rifle

Model has 28" and 30" part-round part-octagonal barrel. Chambered for .32-40 and .38-55 cartridges. Checkered pistol-grip stock, with nickel-plated buttplate; opening lever is fully enclosed ring as on repeaters. Double-set trigger and a tang peep, with globe front sight. Receiver not engraved. Manufactured between 1884 and 1890. Found only with late markings. This was one of the most popular rifles in Ballard line.

			7000	4250	1750	500

Ballard No. 9 Union Hill Rifle

Similar to No. 8. Features a single trigger and better sights. Manufactured between 1884 and 1891. Has later markings only.

			7000	4250	1750	500

Ballard No. 10 Schuetzen Junior Rifle

Model is simply a heavier barreled version of No. 9. Barrel is 32" long. Checkered pistol-grip stock is of off-hand style. Rear sight is a Vernier Mid Range. Front sight is a spirit-level type. Popular model. Manufactured between 1885 and 1891. Found with later markings only.

			7000	4750	2000	650

MARLIN HANDGUNS

1st Model Derringer

First handgun produced by Marlin. Barrel is 2.0625" long and pivots to side for loading. There is a plunger under the frame that is depressed to free barrel. This device is a Ballard patent. Chambered for .22 rimfire cartridge. No extractor. Frame is brass and usually nickel-plated. Has two grooves milled beneath blued barrel. Grips are rosewood. Barrel stamped "J.M. Marlin, New Haven, Ct.". Approximately 2,000 manufactured between 1863 and 1867. Quite scarce on today's market.

	—	—	1350	750	300	100

O.K. Model Derringer

O.K. Model chambered for .22, .30 and .32 rimfire cartridges. Barrel is 2.125" or 3.125" on .32 rimfire. No extractor. Functions as 1st Model. Frame is plated brass, with flat sides. Barrel found blued or nickel-plated. Grips are rosewood. Markings are same as on 1st Model, but located on right side of barrel. Top of barrel marked "O.K." Approximately 5,000 manufactured between 1863 and 1870.

	—	—	1350	750	300	100

Victor Model Derringer

Similar in appearance to "O.K.". Larger in size and chambered for .38-caliber rimfire cartridge. Barrel is 2.6875" long; there was, for the first time, an extractor. Finish and function unchanged. Right side of barrel is stamped "J.M. Marlin/New Haven, Ct./Pat. April 5.1870". "Victor" is stamped on top of barrel. Approximately 4,000 manufactured between 1870 and 1881.

	—	—	1600	1250	500	150

	NIB	EXC.	V.G.	GOOD	FAIR	POOR

Nevermiss Model Derringer

Model was made in three different sizes. Chambered for .22, .32 and .41 rimfire cartridges. Barrel is 2.5" long and swings sideways for loading. Frame is plated brass. Barrels blued or nickel-plated. Grips are rosewood. Frame is grooved under barrels as on 1st model. There is an extractor. Barrel markings are same as on "Victor", with top of barrel marked "Nevermiss". Approximately 5,000 manufactured between 1870 and 1881.

.22 Caliber Model

—	—	1500	1150	500	100

.32 Caliber Model

—	—	1200	750	350	100

.41 Caliber Model

—	—	3750	2500	1000	400

Stonewall Model Derringer

Model is identical to .41-caliber "Nevermiss". Top of barrel is marked "Stonewall". Rarely encountered.

—	—	6000	4250	2000	750

O.K. Pocket Revolver

Solid-frame spur-trigger single-action revolver. Chambered for .22 rimfire short. Round barrel 2.25" and 7-shot cylinder is unfluted. Frame nickel-plated brass, with blue or nickel-plated barrel. Bird's-head grips are rosewood. Cylinder pin is removable and is used to knock empty cases out of cylinder. Top of barrel marked "O.K." and "J.M. Marlin. New Haven, Conn. U.S.A.". Approximately 1,500 manufactured between 1870 and 1875.

—	—	700	500	200	75

Little Joker Revolver

Similar in appearance to "O.K." revolver. Some are reported to have engraving and ivory or pearl grips. Approximately 500 manufactured between 1871 and 1873.

—	—	500	500	350	125

J.M. MARLIN STANDARD POCKET REVOLVERS

In 1872, Marlin began production of its Smith & Wesson look-alike. Manhattan Firearms Company had developed a copy of Model 1 S&W .22 cartridge revolver. In 1868, company ceased business and revolvers were produced by American Standard Tool Company until their dissolution in 1873. In 1872, Marlin had entered into an agreement with this company to manufacture these revolvers, which were no longer protected by Rollin White patent after 1869. Marlin revolvers are similar to those made by American Standard. Only real difference being that Marlin grips are of bird's-head round configuration. A contoured grip frame and a patented pawl spring mechanism is utilized on Marlin revolvers.

Marlin XXX Standard 1872 Pocket Revolver

This is the first in a series of four Standard model revolvers. Chambered for .30-caliber rimfire. Earlier model has an octagonal 3.125" barrel; later, a round 3" barrel. There are round and octagonal barrel variations (with unfluted cylinders) and round barrel variations (with short and long fluted cylinders). All barrels are ribbed and tip up for loading. They have plated brass frames and barrels are nickel-plated. Bird's-head grips are of rosewood or hard rubber, bearing the monogram "M.F.A. Co." inside a star. There is a spur trigger. Markings "J.M. Marlin-New Haven Ct." appear on earlier octagonal barreled models. "U.S.A. Pat. July 1. 1873" was added to later round barreled models. All barrels are marked "XXX Standard 1872". Approximately 5,000 of all types manufactured between 1872 and 1887.

Octagon Barrel—Early Variation

—	—	900	500	300	75

Round Barrel—Non-Fluted Cylinder

—	—	800	400	275	75

Round Barrel—Short Fluted Cylinder

—	—	750	350	200	75

Round Barrel—Long Fluted Cylinder

—	—	750	450	150	75

	NIB	EXC.	V.G.	GOOD	FAIR	POOR

Marlin XX Standard 1873 Pocket Revolver

Model similar in appearance to XXX Standard 1872. Chambered for .22 long rimfire and marked "XX Standard 1873". There are three basic variations: early octagonal barrel with non-fluted cylinder; round barrel with non-fluted cylinder; round barrel with fluted cylinder. Function and features are the same as described for "XXX Standard 1872". Approximately 5,000 manufactured between 1873 and 1887.

Early Octagon Barrel Model

NIB	EXC.	V.G.	GOOD	FAIR	POOR
—	—	900	600	200	100

Round Barrel—Fluted Cylinder

NIB	EXC.	V.G.	GOOD	FAIR	POOR
—	—	750	500	200	75

Round Barrel—Non-Fluted Cylinder

NIB	EXC.	V.G.	GOOD	FAIR	POOR
—	—	875	650	400	100

Marlin No. 32 Standard 1875 Pocket Revolver

Model also similar in appearance to "XXX Standard 1872". Chambered for .32 rimfire cartridge. 3" barrel is round with a rib. 5-shot cylinder is fluted and in two different lengths to accommodate .32 Short or Long cartridge. Finish, function and most markings are same as on previous models, with exception of barrel top marking "No. 32 Standard 1875". Approximately 8,000 manufactured between 1875 and 1887.

NIB	EXC.	V.G.	GOOD	FAIR	POOR
		675	450	200	75

Marlin 38 Standard 1878 Pocket Revolver

Different than its predecessors. Features a steel frame and flat bottom butt, with hard rubber monogram grips. Still a spur trigger and 3.25" ribbed round barrel that tipped up for loading. Chambered for .38 centerfire cartridge. Finish is full nickel plate. Top of barrel marked "38 Standard 1878". Approximately 9,000 manufactured between 1878 and 1887.

NIB	EXC.	V.G.	GOOD	FAIR	POOR
—	—	900	600	250	75

Marlin 1887 Double-Action Revolver

Last handgun Marlin produced and the only double-action. Chambered for .32- or .38-caliber centerfire cartridges. Break-open auto-ejector type. Fluted cylinder holds 6 shots in .32-caliber; 5 shots in .38-caliber. Round ribbed 3.25" barrel. Frame made of steel. Standard finish nickel-plated, with blued trigger guard. Many full-blued examples have been noted. Round butt grips are hard rubber. Top of barrel marked "Marlin Firearms Co. New Haven Conn. U.S.A./Patented Aug. 9 1887". Approximately 15,000 manufactured between 1887 and 1899.

NIB	EXC.	V.G.	GOOD	FAIR	POOR
—	—	800	500	200	75

EARLY PRODUCTION MARLIN RIFLES

Model 1881 Lever-Action Rifle

First Marlin lever-action rifle. Always been regarded as a high quality rifle. Capable of handling large calibers and well received by the shooting public. Chambered for .32-40, .38-55, .40-60, .45-70 and .45-85. The 24", 28" or 30" octagonal barrel is standard. Round barrels were offered and are scarce today. There is a tubular magazine beneath the barrel. Rear sight is buckhorn type, with a blade on front. Ejects its empty cartridges from top. Finish blued, with case colored hammer, lever and buttplate. Walnut stock is varnished. Approximately 20,000 manufactured between 1881 and 1892, but this is not easy to ascertain, as factory records on Marlin rifles are quite incomplete. **NOTE:** Add 200-300 percent premium for 1st Models prior to serial number 600; 15 percent premium for .45-70 caliber.

NIB	EXC.	V.G.	GOOD	FAIR	POOR
—	4000	3000	2000	750	300

Lightweight Model

Thinner frame, lever and barrel. Caliber .32-40 and .38-55. Barrels 24" and 28" only.

NIB	EXC.	V.G.	GOOD	FAIR	POOR
—	3500	2600	1750	600	300

Model 1888 Lever-Action Rifle

Model chambered for .32-20, .38-40 and .44-40 cartridges. Shorter action was designed (chiefly by Lewis Hepburn) to handle pistol cartridges for which it was chambered. Standard barrel was octagonal, but round barrels were available as special-order items. Top ejecting action. Has buckhorn rear and blade front sight. Finish blued, with case colored hammer, lever and buttplate. Walnut stock varnished. Approximately 4,800 manufactured in 1888 and 1889. As with most of these fine old rifles, many special-order options were available that affect today's market value. Individual appraisal would be necessary for these special models, to ascertain both value and authenticity. **NOTE:** Add 40 percent premium for half octagon barrel; 20 percent premium for round barrel.

NIB	EXC.	V.G.	GOOD	FAIR	POOR
—	3500	3000	2500	600	350

	NIB	EXC.	V.G.	GOOD	FAIR	POOR

Model 1889 Lever-Action Rifle

Marlin's first side-eject solid-top rifle. Chambered for .25-20, .32-20, .38-40 and .44-40 cartridges. Features octagonal or round barrels in lengths from 24" to 32", lever latch and buckhorn rear and blade front sights. Finish blued, with case colored hammer, lever and buttplate. Plain walnut stock is varnished. Barrel stamped "Marlin Fire-Arms Co. New Haven Ct. U.S.A./Patented Oct.11 1887 April 2.1889". Many options were offered. Again one must urge individual appraisal on such variations. Values fluctuate greatly due to some seemingly insignificant variation. Approximately 55,000 manufactured between 1889 and 1899.

Production Model
24" barrel.

	NIB	EXC.	V.G.	GOOD	FAIR	POOR
	—	1850	1700	1000	450	150

Short Carbine
15" barrel. 327 produced.

	NIB	EXC.	V.G.	GOOD	FAIR	POOR
	—	—	5000	2250	1000	500

Carbine 20" Barrel and Saddle Ring on Left Side of Receiver

	NIB	EXC.	V.G.	GOOD	FAIR	POOR
	—	—	2250	1250	500	250

Musket
30" barrel, with full-length stock. 68 made in .44-40.

	NIB	EXC.	V.G.	GOOD	FAIR	POOR
	—	—	6500	3000	1250	650

Model 1891 Lever-Action Rifle

Marlin's first rifle designed to fire .22 rimfire; first repeating rifle to accept .22 Short, Long and LR cartridges interchangeably. Chambered for .32 rimfire and centerfire. The 24" octagonal barrel is standard, with buckhorn rear and blade front sights. Finish blued, with case colored hammer, lever and buttplate. Stock is plain walnut. First variation marked "Marlin Fire-Arms Co. New Haven, Ct. U.S.A./Pat'd Nov.19.1878. April 2.1889. Aug.12 1890" on barrel, with solid-topped frame marked "Marlin Safety". Second variation marked the same with "March 1,1892" added. Approximately 18,650 manufactured between 1891 and 1897.

1st Variation
.22 rimfire only. Side loading. Approximately 5,000 made.

	NIB	EXC.	V.G.	GOOD	FAIR	POOR
	—	—	2500	1000	550	300

2nd Variation
.22 and .32 rimfire. .32 centerfire. Tube loading Model 1891. Later model tangs (3rd variation).
NOTE: Add 20 percent for .22 rifle with "1891" stamped on tang. Deduct 50 percent for .32-caliber.

	NIB	EXC.	V.G.	GOOD	FAIR	POOR
	—	—	1500	500	300	150

Model 1892 Lever-Action Rifle

Basically an improved version of Model 1891. Similar to second variation of 1891. Only notable exceptions were tang marking "Model 1892" and "Model 92" on later models. .22 rimfire was scarce in Model 1892. Approximately 45,000 manufactured between 1895 and 1916. There were many options. These special-order guns must be individually appraised to ascertain value and authenticity.

.22 Rimfire
NOTE: Antique (pre-1898) add 20 percent.

	NIB	EXC.	V.G.	GOOD	FAIR	POOR
	—	—	1350	400	250	150

.32 Rimfire and Centerfire

	NIB	EXC.	V.G.	GOOD	FAIR	POOR
	—	—	950	350	150	100

Model 1893 Lever-Action Rifle

Model was first rifle Marlin designed for, then new, smokeless powder cartridges. Chambered for .25-36, .30-30, .32 Special, .32-40 and .38-55. Offered standard: round or octagonal barrel in lengths of 24" to 32"; buckhorn rear and blade front sights. Receiver, lever, hammer and buttplate are case colored. Rest is blued. Stock varnished walnut.

As with all early Marlins, many options were offered and when encountered, will drastically alter value of particular rifle. For this reason, we supply values for basic model and urge securing competent appraisal on non-standard specimens. Barrel on earlier guns marked "Marlin FireArms Co. New Haven, Ct.U.S.A./ Patented Oct.11. 1887.April 2.1889. Aug.1.1893". In 1919, markings were changed to "The Marlin Firearms Corporation/ New Haven, Conn.U.S.A.Patented". Rifles manufactured after 1904 are marked "Special Smokeless Steel" on left side of barrel. Upper tang marked "Model 1893" on early guns;

NIB	EXC.	V.G.	GOOD	FAIR	POOR

"Model 93" on later specimens. Approximately 900,000 manufactured between 1893 and 1935. Factory records are incomplete on Model 1893.

Antique Production (Pre-1898)

NIB	EXC.	V.G.	GOOD	FAIR	POOR
—	3000	2000	650	450	275

Modern Production 1899-1935

NOTE: Add 100 percent premium for musket. Deduct 50 percent for B model with blued receiver.

NIB	EXC.	V.G.	GOOD	FAIR	POOR
—	2000	1100	550	350	225

Model 1894 Lever-Action Rifle

Similar to Model 1893, with a shorter action. Chambered for .25-20, .32-20, .38-40 and .44-40. Offered standard: 24" to 32" round or octagonal barrels with full-length magazine tubes; buckhorn rear and blade front sights. Finish is case colored receiver, lever, hammer and buttplate. Rest is blued. Walnut stock varnished. First versions marked "Marlin Fire-Arms Co., New Haven, Ct.U.S.A./Patented Oct.11, 1887. April 2,1889". Top of frame marked "Marlin Safety" and model designation is not stamped on tang. These early rifles were chambered for .38-40 and .44-40 only. Later rifles added patent date "Aug. 1, 1893"; "Model 1894" was stamped on tang. On latest versions this was shortened to "Model 94". Approximately 250,000 manufactured between 1894 and 1935. This model was produced with a great many options. Individual appraisal should be secured when confronted with these features.

Antique Production (Pre-1898)

NIB	EXC.	V.G.	GOOD	FAIR	POOR
—	2800	2200	1500	750	350

Modern Production (1899-1935)

NOTE: Add 100 percent premium for musket; 25 percent premium saddle ring carbine; 30 percent premium "Baby" carbine.

NIB	EXC.	V.G.	GOOD	FAIR	POOR
—	2500	2000	1200	600	250

Model 1895 Lever-Action Rifle

A large rifle designed to fire larger hunting cartridges. Chambered for .33 W.C.F., .38-56, .40-65, .40-70, .40-83, .45-70 and .45-90. Came standard with: round or octagonal barrels from 26" to 32" in length; bull-length magazine tube; buckhorn rear and blade front sights. Finish is case colored receiver, lever and hammer. Rest is blued. Varnished walnut stock. Barrel markings are same as Model 1894. Top tang marked "Model 1895". After 1896 "Special Smokeless Steel" was stamped on barrel. There were many options available and they have a big effect on value. Approximately 18,000 manufactured between 1895 and 1917.

Antique Production (Pre-1898)

NIB	EXC.	V.G.	GOOD	FAIR	POOR
—	3500	2850	1900	1250	400

Modern Production (1899-1917)

NIB	EXC.	V.G.	GOOD	FAIR	POOR
—	3200	2500	1500	800	300

Model 1897 Lever-Action Rifle

Improved version of Model 1892. Chambered for .22 rimfire only. Came standard with: 24", 26" or 28" round, octagonal or part-round, part-octagonal barrel; buckhorn rear and blade front sights; all were manufactured as takedown rifles. Case colored receiver, lever and hammer. Rest is blued. Walnut stock varnished. Approximately 125,000 manufactured between 1897 and 1917. In 1922, production began with designation changed to "Model 39" which is produced to this day. There were options offered with this rifle that have great effect on value. Take this into consideration and seek qualified appraisal.

Standard Production Rifle

NOTE: First year production antique add 40 percent.

NIB	EXC.	V.G.	GOOD	FAIR	POOR
—	2200	1500	1100	650	200

Deluxe Rifle

Checkering and fancy pistol-grip stock.

NIB	EXC.	V.G.	GOOD	FAIR	POOR
—	3000	2000	1500	850	300

MODERN PRODUCTION MARLIN RIFLES

Model 18

Slide-action model chambered for .22 rimfire cartridges. Offered standard with 20" round or octagonal barrel, open sights and straight walnut stock. Has an exposed hammer. Blued finish, with blued steel buttplate. There is a half-length tubular magazine. Stock features a quick takedown screw on top tang which was marked "Model 18". Manufactured between 1906 and 1909.

NIB	EXC.	V.G.	GOOD	FAIR	POOR
—	1000	800	600	300	150

	NIB	EXC.	V.G.	GOOD	FAIR	POOR

Model 20

Model 20 slide-action chambered for .22 rimfire cartridges. Offered standard with 24" octagonal barrel and open sight, with an exposed hammer. Only made as a "Takedown" receiver model. Blued, with straight walnut stock. Manufactured between 1907 and 1922.

	NIB	EXC.	V.G.	GOOD	FAIR	POOR
	—	1000	800	600	300	150

Model 25

Slide-action model chambered for .22 Short only. Not a commercial success. Standard: 23" round or octagonal barrel; open sights. Called a takedown model, but only stock is removable—receiver does not separate. Has an exposed hammer, tubular magazine and straight walnut stock. Finish is blued. Manufactured in 1909 and 1910.

	NIB	EXC.	V.G.	GOOD	FAIR	POOR
	—	1200	1000	750	450	150

Model 27

Centerfire slide-action rifle. Chambered for .25-20 and .32-20 cartridges, also .25-caliber rimfire cartridge. Features 24" octagonal barrel, with two-thirds-length magazine tube that holds 7 shots. Has open sights, blued finish and straight walnut stock with crescent buttplate. Manufactured from 1910 to 1916. **NOTE:** Deduct 20 percent chambered for .25 rimfire.

NIB	EXC.	V.G.	GOOD	FAIR	POOR
1500	1200	850	500	350	200

Model 27S

Model 27S similar to Model 27, with a sliding button on right side of receiver that permitted gun to be opened while a cartridge was in the chamber. Offered with a round (1913) or octagonal 24" barrel. The .25 rimfire cartridge was added in 1913 to those already available. This model introduced in 1910 and manufactured until 1932. **NOTE:** Deduct 20 percent chambered for .25 rimfire.

NIB	EXC.	V.G.	GOOD	FAIR	POOR
1500	1200	850	500	350	200

Model 29

Slide action model identical to Model 20, with 23" round barrel and smooth walnut fore-end instead of a grooved one as found on Model 20. Manufactured between 1913 and 1916. **NOTE:** Deduct 20 percent chambered for .25 rimfire.

	NIB	EXC.	V.G.	GOOD	FAIR	POOR
	—	1000	800	600	300	150

Model 32

First of hammerless slide-action rifles. Chambered for .22 rimfire. Has 24" octagonal barrel and half-length magazine tube. Model 32 is a takedown rifle, with adjustable sights and features "Ballard" rifling. Blued, with a pistol-grip walnut stock. Advent of WWI and need for Marlin to produce military arms, cut short production of this model. Manufactured in 1914 and 1915 only.

NIB	EXC.	V.G.	GOOD	FAIR	POOR
1500	1200	850	500	350	200

Model 37

Slide-action model same as Model 29, with 24" round barrel and full-length magazine tube. Manufactured between 1913 and 1916.

NIB	EXC.	V.G.	GOOD	FAIR	POOR
900	600	400	250	150	100

Model 38

Hammerless slide-action introduced after end of WWI to replace Model 32. Similar in appearance. Features Rocky Mountain adjustable rear and ivory bead front sight instead of distinctive round Swebilius sight on Model 32. Manufactured between 1920 and 1930.

NIB	EXC.	V.G.	GOOD	FAIR	POOR
900	600	400	250	150	100

Model 40

Slide-action identical to Model 27S centerfire. Barrel marked "Marlin-Rockwell". Top tang stamped "Marlin/Mod. 40". Rare, not many marked in this manner have been noted.

NIB	EXC.	V.G.	GOOD	FAIR	POOR
1600	1300	850	500	350	200

Model 47

Similar to Model 20, with 23" round barrel and improved magazine tube. Has case colored receiver and checkered buttstock. Not offered for sale nor was it listed in Marlin's catalog, but offered free of charge to anyone purchasing four shares of Marlin stock for $100. One other fact about this model it was the first Marlin to be case colored with new cyanide method; this created a tiger-striped pattern that is peculiar to Model 47.

	NIB	EXC.	V.G.	GOOD	FAIR	POOR
	—	1000	800	600	300	150

Model 1936, Rifle or Carbine

Lever-action model is a direct descendant of Model 1893. Chambered for .30-30 and .32 Special cartridge. Stock is streamlined with a pistol-grip added and 20" round barrel. A barrel band and improved sights are utilized. Has a 7-shot tube magazine and semi-beavertail forearm. Receiver,

	NIB	EXC.	V.G.	GOOD	FAIR	POOR

lever and hammer are case colored. Rest is blued. Manufactured between 1936 and 1948. Designated Model 36 in 1937.

1st Variation (early 1936)

Variation has a slight "fish-belly" forearm, long tang, case colored receiver, lever and hammer, with no serial number prefix. These are rare.

NIB	EXC.	V.G.	GOOD	FAIR	POOR
—	1200	850	400	175	125

2nd Variation (late 1936-1947)

Variation has thicker forearm, short tang and "B" serial number prefix.

NIB	EXC.	V.G.	GOOD	FAIR	POOR
—	1000	650	300	150	100

Model 36 Rifle or Carbine (1937-1948)

First and Second variations of this lever-action both have case colored receiver and "C" serial number prefix. Second variation tapped for receiver sight.

NIB	EXC.	V.G.	GOOD	FAIR	POOR
—	800	600	400	195	125

1st & 2nd Variations

NIB	EXC.	V.G.	GOOD	FAIR	POOR
—	800	600	400	195	125

3rd Variation—Blued Receiver

NIB	EXC.	V.G.	GOOD	FAIR	POOR
—	600	400	300	175	100

Model 36 Sporting Carbine

Similar to 1936 Carbine, with 20" barrel. Features two-thirds-length magazine tube and holds 6 shots instead of 7. Front sight is a ramp sight with hood.

NIB	EXC.	V.G.	GOOD	FAIR	POOR
—	800	600	400	195	125

Model 36A-DL Rifle

Lever-action model similar to Model 36A, with deluxe checkered stock. Features sight swivels. Furnished with leather sling.

NIB	EXC.	V.G.	GOOD	FAIR	POOR
1000	800	650	400	225	150

MODEL 336

Information on Model 336 provided by Doug Murray, author and publisher of The 336 (1983). **NOTE:** Beginning in 1980s, Marlin used "S" suffix on its model numbers (e.g., 336CS, 1895S, etc.) to designate models with new crossbolt safety. This suffix has now been dropped in most cases, even though safety remains.

Model 336 Carbine (R.C. Regular Carbine)

Introduced in 1948. Improved version of Model 36. Features a new-type round bolt chrome-plated, with improved extractor and redesigned cartridge carrier that improved feeding. Chambered for .30-30 and .32 Special cartridges. Has 20" tapered round barrel, with Ballard-type rifling. Finish blued, with receiver top matted to reduce reflections. Pistol-grip stock and semi-beavertail fore-end are of American walnut. Features Rocky Mountain-style rear and bead front sights. Hammer is lowered to facilitate scope mounting.

NIB	EXC.	V.G.	GOOD	FAIR	POOR
—	475	325	175	125	100

Model 336C

Same as Model 336 Carbine. In 1951, catalog model designation was changed. In 1952, .35 Remington cartridge was added. In 1963, .32 Special was discontinued.

NIB	EXC.	V.G.	GOOD	FAIR	POOR
—	475	325	175	125	100

Model 336A

Similar to 336C, with 24" barrel and steel fore-end tip instead of a barrel band. Magazine tube is two-thirds-length and holds 6 shots. Introduced in 1948 and built until 1962. Reintroduced in 1973. Discontinued in 1980. In 1950, .35 Rem. was added. In 1960, .32 Special was discontinued.

NIB	EXC.	V.G.	GOOD	FAIR	POOR
—	475	325	175	125	100

Model 336ADL

Differs from Model 336A. Has deluxe wood checkered stock and fore-end, quick detachable swivels, better grade finish and a sling.

NIB	EXC.	V.G.	GOOD	FAIR	POOR
—	650	500	300	150	125

Model 336SC (Sporting Carbine)

Basically a 336A, with fore-end tip. Two-thirds magazine has 20" barrel instead of 24" found on 336A.

NIB	EXC.	V.G.	GOOD	FAIR	POOR
—	400	300	200	150	100

	NIB	EXC.	V.G.	GOOD	FAIR	POOR

Model 336SD (Sporting Deluxe Carbine)

336 SC in a deluxe checkered stock version, with quick detachable swivels. Supplied with a sling. **NOTE:** Scarce model as only 4,392 were built.

—	1000	750	400	200	125

Model 336 MicroGroove Zipper

Advertised as a fast-handling lever-action carbine. Chambered for .219 Zipper cartridges flat trajectory, varmint-type round. Has 20" heavy barrel, which was the feature that doomed it to failure as this was too short to coax maximum performance and accuracy from cartridge. "MicroGroove" rifling that was used did not yield long barrel life; model survived from 1955 through 1959, when it was discontinued. Externally similar to 336 SC. **NOTE:** First few thousand Zippers were made in standard weight barrels, not heavy weight. These are scarce and found in "M" prefix code number. Add 100 percent.

1600	1000	800	600	300	150

Model 336T (Texan)

Straight-stock version of 336C. Chambered for .30-30 cartridge, with 20" barrel. Produced in .35 Rem. from 1953 to 1964; .44 Magnum from 1965 to 1967. Manufactured from 1953-1983.

—	650	475	395	250	175

Model 336DT

Deluxe-stock version of "Texan", with map of Texas and a longhorn carved on butt. Manufactured between 1962 and 1964. Calibers: .30-30 and .35 Rem.

—	700	550	425	275	175

Model 336 "Marauder"

Simply a 336T, with 16.25" barrel and slimmer fore-end. Chambered for .30-30 or .35 Rem. cartridges. Has a gold trigger. Drilled and tapped for both scope mounts and receiver sights. Manufactured in 1963 and 1964.

—	750	675	550	300	150

Model 336 .44 Magnum

This is the 336 "Marauder", with 20" MicroGroove barrel chambered for .44 Magnum cartridge. Holds 10 shots. Introduced in 1963. Not very successful, because of feeding difficulties.

—	600	450	295	150	100

Model 336 "Centennial"

In 1970, a 100th year medallion was embedded into the buttstock of 336 Carbines, 336 Texan and 444 Rifle.

—	625	500	375	250	150

1970 100th Year Commemorative Matched Pair

Deluxe octagonal barreled .30-30, with engraved receiver and deluxe wood with an inlaid medallion, accompanied by a matching Model 339 .22 rimfire rifle. They are numbered the same and furnished in a deluxe luggage case. There were 1,000 sets manufactured in 1970. These are commemoratives. It should be noted that collectors usually will only show interest if they are new and unfired in original packaging. All accessories and brochures should be included for them to be worth top dollar. Once a commemorative has been used, it has no more value than as a shooter.

2250	1750	1200	750	500	400

Model 336 "Zane Grey Century"

Introduced in 1972, 100th year anniversary birth of Zane Grey, famous Western author. Has 22" octagonal barrel chambered for .30-30. Stock is high grade walnut. Features brass buttplate and pistol-grip cap. Zane Grey medallion inlaid into receiver. Manufactured 10,000 in 1972. This is a commemorative rifle and must be new in box to generate top collector appeal.

600	425	275	200	150	100

Model 336 Octagon

Introduced to utilize octagonal barrel making equipment that was on hand from manufacture of commemorative's. Essentially a 336T, with 22" tapered octagonal barrel chambered for .30-30 only. Features full-length magazine tube, slim fore-end with steel cap and classic-style hard rubber buttplate. Walnut stock is straight and lever square. Finish, including trigger, blued. Made in 1973 only.

725	600	500	325	175	150

Model 336ER (Extra Range)

Introduced in 1983. Advertised as being chambered for .307 and .356 Winchester cartridges. .307 was never produced. .356 Winchester was supposed to add new capabilities to this

	NIB	EXC.	V.G.	GOOD	FAIR	POOR

classic rifle, but it never caught on with the shooting public. Discontinued in 1986 after only 2,441 Model ERs were manufactured. Has 20" barrel and 5-shot tube magazine.

	NIB	EXC.	V.G.	GOOD	FAIR	POOR
	—	825	550	300	250	150

Model 336C

Current carbine model of this line. Has a hammer-block safety. Chambered for .30-30, .35 Remington and until 1988, .375 Winchester. Barrel 20" and magazine tube holds 6 shots. Pistol-grip stock and semi-beavertail forearm are American walnut. Has been manufactured since 1984. The 1983 model was known as 336C. Had no hammer-block safety. Weight about 7 lbs.

NIB	EXC.	V.G.	GOOD	FAIR	POOR
475	350	225	200	175	150

Model 336SS

Similar to Model 336C in .30-30 only. Stainless steel barrel and receiver.

NIB	EXC.	V.G.	GOOD	FAIR	POOR
525	400	250	200	150	100

Model 336LTS

Latest version of old "Marauder" carbine. Dubbed LTS or "Lightweight" instead of Marauder, as it was feared the latter designation would be inappropriate in today's society. Features 16.5" barrel, with full-length tube magazine that holds 5 shots. Walnut stock has straight-grip. Barrel band on forearm. Butt has rubber rifle pad. Introduced in 1988. Discontinued.

NIB	EXC.	V.G.	GOOD	FAIR	POOR
675	450	300	250	200	150

Model 336 Cowboy

Similar to Model 336 CS. Available in both .30-30 and .38-55 calibers. Fitted with 24" tapered octagon barrel. Rear sight is Marble buckhorn. Tubular magazine holds 6 rounds. Straight-grip walnut stock has hard rubber buttplate. Weight about 7.5 lbs. First introduced in 1999.

NIB	EXC.	V.G.	GOOD	FAIR	POOR
875	650	525	325	175	150

Model 336M

Introduced in 2000. Chambered for .30-30 cartridge. Features stainless steel receiver and barrel; all other parts are nickel plated. Barrel length 20". Magazine capacity 6 rounds. Checkered walnut stock has Mar-Shield finish. Rubber buttpad. Weight about 7 lbs. Marlin's first stainless steel rifle.

NIB	EXC.	V.G.	GOOD	FAIR	POOR
675	550	425	275	175	125

Model 336CC

Chambered for .30-30 cartridge. Fitted with 20" barrel. Features Mossy Oak Break-Up camo finish. Adjustable rear sight. Weight about 7 lbs. Introduced in 2001.

NIB	EXC.	V.G.	GOOD	FAIR	POOR
500	390	325	250	200	100

Model 336W

Similar to Model 336C in .30-30 only. Gold-plated trigger and hardwood stock. Available with factory-mounted 3x9 scope. **NOTE:** Add 10 percent for scope package.

NIB	EXC.	V.G.	GOOD	FAIR	POOR
450	395	325	250	200	100

Model 336Y "Spike Horn"

Chambered for .30-30 cartridge. Fitted with 16.5" barrel. Features checkered walnut stock with pistol-grip. Magazine capacity 5 rounds. Adjustable rear sight. Weight about 6.5 lbs. Introduced in 2003.

NIB	EXC.	V.G.	GOOD	FAIR	POOR
575	425	300	200	150	100

Model 336XLR

Lever-action chambered in .30-30 or .35 Remington, with 5-shot tubular magazine, 24" stainless steel barrel, along with stainless steel receiver, trigger, trigger guard plate, magazine tube, loading gate and lever. Full pistol-grip, swivel studs and Ballard-type rifling precision fluted bolt. Features solid top receiver with side-ejection, adjustable folding semi-buckhorn rear sight, ramp front sight, tapped for scope mount. Designed for Hornady LEVERevolution cartridges. Introduced 2006.

NIB	EXC.	V.G.	GOOD	FAIR	POOR
625	500	375	250	175	100

Model 336BL

Lever-action chambered for .30-30. Features include 6-shot full length tubular magazine; 18" blued barrel with Micro-Groove rifling (12 grooves); big-loop finger lever; side ejection; blued steel receiver; hammer block safety; brown laminated hardwood pistol-grip stock with fluted comb; cut checkering; deluxe recoil pad; blued swivel studs.

NIB	EXC.	V.G.	GOOD	FAIR	POOR
525	400	250	200	150	100

	NIB	EXC.	V.G.	GOOD	FAIR	POOR

Model 30AS

Similar to 336 CS. Stock made of walnut-finished hardwood instead of genuine American walnut. Chambered for .30-30 only.

	NIB	EXC.	V.G.	GOOD	FAIR	POOR
	395	285	200	175	125	100

Model 375

Introduced in 1980. Has 20" MicroGroove barrel. Chambered for .375 Winchester cartridge. Its appearance much the same as Model 336, with walnut pistol stock and steel fore-end tip. Discontinued in 1983 after 16,315 manufactured.

	NIB	EXC.	V.G.	GOOD	FAIR	POOR
	625	500	375	250	175	100

Model 444

Introduced in 1965. Chambered for .444 Marlin. Essentially a Model 336 action modified to accept larger cartridge. Has 24" round barrel that was cut back to 22" in 1971. Holds 5 shots total. When introduced, featured straight-grip Monte Carlo stock and semi-beavertail fore-end with barrel band. Another band holds the two-thirds-length magazine tube in place. In 1971 stock was changed to pistol-grip, without Monte Carlo comb.

	NIB	EXC.	V.G.	GOOD	FAIR	POOR
	—	600	450	300	175	125

Model 444S

Introduced in 1972. Essentially, later 444 with steel fore-end tip instead of barrel bands.

	NIB	EXC.	V.G.	GOOD	FAIR	POOR
	—	500	350	175	150	125

Model 444SS

In 1984, company added a crossbolt hammer-block safety to 444 S and re-designated it 444 SS. Model currently in production as Model 444, "S" suffix having been dropped.

	NIB	EXC.	V.G.	GOOD	FAIR	POOR
	550	395	300	225	150	125

Model 444P Outfitter

Introduced in 1999. Chambered for .444 Marlin cartridge. Fitted with 18.5" ported barrel. Tubular magazine capacity 5 rounds. Walnut stock, with straight-grip. Ventilated recoil pad standard. Weight about 6.75 lbs. Discontinued 2002.

	NIB	EXC.	V.G.	GOOD	FAIR	POOR
	725	600	425	335	275	200

Model 444XLR

Similar to Model 1895XLR. Chambered in .444 Marlin. Introduced 2006.

	NIB	EXC.	V.G.	GOOD	FAIR	POOR
	625	500	375	250	175	100

Model 1894

Production of Model 336 in .44 Magnum was a frustrating experience. Action was simply too long for a short pistol case. In 1969, Marlin reintroduced Model 1894 chambered for .44 Magnum cartridge. Barrel 20". Full-length magazine tube holds 10 rounds. Features adjustable rear and ramp-type front sight. Finish blued, with matted receiver top. Walnut stock has straight-grip; fore-end a barrel band. From 1969 to 1971 there was a brass saddle ring.

	NIB	EXC.	V.G.	GOOD	FAIR	POOR
	525	375	300	200	150	100

Model 1894 Octagon Barrel

Basically same as Model 1894, with 20" octagonal barrel. Steel fore-end tip instead of barrel band. Manufactured 2,957 in 1973 only.

	NIB	EXC.	V.G.	GOOD	FAIR	POOR
	—	650	525	350	225	100

Model 1894 Sporter

Variation has 20" round barrel, half-length magazine tube that holds 6 shots. Hard rubber classic-style buttplate. Manufactured 1,398 in 1973 only.

	NIB	EXC.	V.G.	GOOD	FAIR	POOR
	625	475	325	250	175	125

Model 1894P

Introduced in 2000. Chambered for .44 Magnum or .44 Special cartridges. Barrel length 16.25". Magazine capacity 8 rounds. Adjustable rear sight. Blued finish, with bead blasted receiver top. Drilled and tapped for scope mount. Weight about 5.75 lbs.

	NIB	EXC.	V.G.	GOOD	FAIR	POOR
	600	450	375	300	150	100

Model 1894CS

Chambered for .38 Special and .357 Magnum cartridges. Features 18.5" round barrel, with full-length magazine tube and two barrel bands. Holds 9 shots. Walnut straight-grip stock.

NIB	EXC.	V.G.	GOOD	FAIR	POOR

Manufactured between 1969 and 1984. In 1984, hammer-block crossbolt safety was added and model number was changed to 1894 CS. All other specifications remained the same. Model is now known, again, as Model 1894C.

NIB	EXC.	V.G.	GOOD	FAIR	POOR
—	525	375	275	125	100

Model 1894M

Similar to other 1894 rifles. Chambered for .22 Magnum cartridge. Features an outside loading tube magazine that holds 11 shots. Barrel 20". Steel fore-end tip instead of barrel band. Manufactured between 1983 and 1988. Only produced with crossbolt safety.

NIB	EXC.	V.G.	GOOD	FAIR	POOR
—	550	450	325	275	150

Model 1894S

Introduced in 1984. Chambered for .41 Magnum and .44 Special/.44 Magnum cartridges. In 1988, .45 Colt chambering offered. Barrel 20". Straight-grip stock. Fore-end has steel cap. Currently produced as Model 1894. Features hammer-block safety.

NIB	EXC.	V.G.	GOOD	FAIR	POOR
550	450	375	275	175	125

Model 1894CL (Classic)

Introduced in 1988. Same basic rifle chambered for old .25-20 and .32-20 cartridges. Also chambered for .218 Bee cartridge. Barrel 22". Half-length magazine tube holds 6 shots. Walnut stock has no white spacers. Has black buttplate. Discontinued in 1993. **NOTE:** Collector interest has been growing since it was discontinued in 1993.

NIB	EXC.	V.G.	GOOD	FAIR	POOR
750	450	350	300	250	150

Model 1894CL (Classic) New

Reintroduced in 2005. Chambered for .32-20 cartridge. Barrel 22", with open sights. Tubular magazine capacity 6 rounds. Checkered straight-grip walnut stock. Weight about 6 lbs. Discontinued.

NIB	EXC.	V.G.	GOOD	FAIR	POOR
700	600	475	395	300	125

Model 1894 Century Limited

Anniversary edition of Marlin Model 1894. Limited to 2,500 rifles. Chambered in .44-40 caliber. Frame engraved and case colored. Fitted with 24" octagon barrel with 10-round magazine tube. Stock semi-fancy walnut with straight-grip and cut checkering, with brass crescent buttplate.

NIB	EXC.	V.G.	GOOD	FAIR	POOR
1500	1200	800	600	400	300

Model 1894 Century Limited Employee Edition

Same as above. Limited to 100 rifles. Has finer grade wood. The Marlin man on horse logo inlaid in gold on right side of receiver.

NIB	EXC.	V.G.	GOOD	FAIR	POOR
3500	3000	2500	—	—	—

Model 1894 Cowboy

Introduced in 1996. Lever-action features 24" tapered octagon barrel, with 10-round tubular magazine. Chambered for .45 Long Colt, a popular cartridge for "Cowboy Action Shooting". Straight-grip checkered stock. Flued steel forearm cap. Weight about 7.5 lbs.

NIB	EXC.	V.G.	GOOD	FAIR	POOR
750	600	450	300	225	150

Model 1894 Cowboy 32

As above chambered for .32 H&R Magnum cartridge. Introduced in 2004.

NIB	EXC.	V.G.	GOOD	FAIR	POOR
750	600	450	300	225	150

Model 1894 Cowboy II

Introduced in 1997. Same as Model 1894 Cowboy chambered for several cartridges. Available in .44-40, .357 Magnum .38 Special and .44 Magnum/.44 Special.

NIB	EXC.	V.G.	GOOD	FAIR	POOR
650	525	300	225	150	100

Model 1894CP

Chambered for .375 Magnum cartridge. Fitted with 16.25" ported barrel. Tubular magazine holds 8 rounds. Checkered American black walnut stock. Adjustable semi-buckhorn rear sight. Receiver drilled and tapped for scope mount. Weight about 5.75 lbs. Introduced in 2001.

NIB	EXC.	V.G.	GOOD	FAIR	POOR
626	575	450	300	225	100

Model 1894SS

Lever-action chambered for .44 Magnum and .44 Special cartridges. Barrel 20", with 10-round magazine. Stainless steel barrel and receiver. Checkered walnut stock, with straight-grip. Rubber buttpad. Weight about 6 lbs. Introduced in 2002.

NIB	EXC.	V.G.	GOOD	FAIR	POOR
650	500	400	300	200	100

	NIB	EXC.	V.G.	GOOD	FAIR	POOR

Model 1894PG

Introduced in 2003. Lever-action chambered for .44 Rem. Magnum cartridge. Fitted with 20" barrel. Checkered walnut stock, with pistol-grip. Magazine capacity 10 rounds. Adjustable rear sight. Blued finish. Weight about 6.5 lbs.

NIB	EXC.	V.G.	GOOD	FAIR	POOR
575	450	300	225	150	100

Model 1894FG

Lever-action chambered for .41 Rem. Magnum cartridge. Fitted with 20" barrel. Checkered walnut stock, with pistol-grip. Magazine capacity 10 rounds. Weight about 6.5 lbs. Introduced in 2003.

NIB	EXC.	V.G.	GOOD	FAIR	POOR
600	450	300	225	150	100

Model 1894 Cowboy

Fitted with 20" barrel. Chambered for .38 Special cartridge. Designed for Cowboy Action Shooting. Special hand-tuned parts. Magazine capacity 10 rounds. Walnut stock, with straight-grip. Case colored receiver, bolt, trigger plate and lever. Weight about 6 lbs. Introduced in 2002. In 2003, offered chambered for .45 Colt cartridge.

NIB	EXC.	V.G.	GOOD	FAIR	POOR
825	750	600	500	300	150

Marlin 1894 Deluxe

Lever-action chambered in .44 Magnum/.44 Special. Features include 10-shot tubular magazine; squared finger lever; side ejection; richly polished deep blued metal surfaces; solid top receiver; hammer block safety; #1 grade fancy American black walnut straight-grip stock and fore-end; cut checkering; rubber rifle butt pad; Mar-Shield finish; blued steel fore-end cap; swivel studs; deep-cut Ballard-type rifling (6 grooves).

NIB	EXC.	V.G.	GOOD	FAIR	POOR
600	500	400	325	250	150

Marlin 1894CSS

Lever-action chambered in .357 Magnum/.38 Special. Features include 9-shot tubular magazine; stainless steel receiver, barrel, lever, trigger and hammer; squared finger lever; side ejection; solid top receiver; hammer block safety; American black walnut straight-grip stock and fore-end; cut checkering; rubber rifle butt pad; Mar-Shield finish.

NIB	EXC.	V.G.	GOOD	FAIR	POOR
725	600	450	350	300	200

Marlin 1894 CSBL

Chambered in .357/.38 Special, with 7-round capacity. Barrel 16.25", stock gray/black laminated. Other features include Marlin's Big Loop lever; stainless steel barrel, receiver, trigger guard plate and loading gate. Ghost ring sighting system, with mounting rail for optical sights. Introduced in 2011.

NIB	EXC.	V.G.	GOOD	FAIR	POOR
800	725	600	500	400	300

Model 1895 and 1895SS

Model 1895 was reintroduced on Model 336 action, that had been modified to handle .45-70 cartridge. This was done to capitalize on nostalgia wave that descended on the country in early 1970s. Features 22" round barrel, with two-thirds-length magazine tube that holds 4 shots. Walnut stock had straight-grip until Model 1895 S was released in 1980, when pistol-grip stock was used. In 1983, Model 1895 SS with crossbolt hammer-block safety was added; currently produced in this configuration. **NOTE:** Early "B" prefix guns below serial number 12000 add 25 percent.

NIB	EXC.	V.G.	GOOD	FAIR	POOR
600	500	325	200	150	100

Model 1895M

Similar to Model 1895. Chambered in .450 Marlin.

NIB	EXC.	V.G.	GOOD	FAIR	POOR
600	500	325	200	150	100

Model 1895 Century Limited

Chambered for .45-70 cartridge. Features: 4-shot tubular magazine; 24" half round/half octagon barrel; semi-fancy walnut stock, with pistol-grip. Receiver French grayed and engraved with the Marlin man on one side and two bears on other. Weight about 7.5 lbs. Discontinued. 299 produced.

NIB	EXC.	V.G.	GOOD	FAIR	POOR
1200	1050	700	500	300	150

Model 1895 Century Limited Employee Edition

Similar to above. Limited to 100 rifles. Company logo inlaid in gold on right side; left side has two cow elk and bull elk.

NIB	EXC.	V.G.	GOOD	FAIR	POOR
2750	2400	1800	1000	—	—

NIB	EXC.	V.G.	GOOD	FAIR	POOR

Model 1895G Guide Gun

Chambered for .45-70 Government cartridge. Has 18.5" ported barrel. Straight-grip walnut stock, with cut checkering and ventilated recoil pad. Adjustable rear sight. Weight about 6.75 lbs. Introduced in 1998.

NIB	EXC.	V.G.	GOOD	FAIR	POOR
650	550	450	350	250	150

Model 1895GS Guide Gun

Introduced in 2001. This .45-70 rifle fitted with 18.5" ported barrel, with 4-round magazine. Stainless steel receiver and barrel. American black walnut stock, with cut checkering and ventilated recoil pad. Adjustable rear semi-buckhorn sight. Weight about 7 lbs. Early models had ported barrel, now discontinued.

NIB	EXC.	V.G.	GOOD	FAIR	POOR
750	650	550	450	350	100

Model 1895 Cowboy

Chambered for .45-70 cartridge. Fitted with 26" tapered octagon barrel. Tubular magazine has 9-round capacity. Adjustable semi-buckhorn rear sight. American black stock, with cut checkering. Hard rubber butt. Weight about 8 lbs. Introduced in 2001.

NIB	EXC.	V.G.	GOOD	FAIR	POOR
650	550	450	350	200	100

Model 1895XLR

Lever-action chambered in .45-70 Government or .450 Marlin; 4-shot tubular magazine; 24" stainless steel barrel; stainless steel receiver, trigger, trigger guard plate, magazine tube, loading gate and lever. Full pistol-grip, swivel studs and Ballard-type rifling precision fluted bolt. Features solid top receiver with side-ejection, adjustable folding semi-buckhorn rear sight, ramp front sight, tapped for scope mount. Designed for Hornady LEVERevolution cartridges. Introduced 2006.

NIB	EXC.	V.G.	GOOD	FAIR	POOR
700	600	525	400	300	150

Model 1895MXLR

Similar to Model 1895XLR. Chambered in .450 Marlin. Introduced 2006.

NIB	EXC.	V.G.	GOOD	FAIR	POOR
700	600	525	400	300	150

Model 1895 SBLR

Similar to Model 1895GS Guide Gun, with stainless steel barrel (18.5"), receiver, large loop lever and magazine tube. Black/gray laminated buttstock and fore-end, XS ghost ring rear sight, hooded ramp front sight, receiver/barrel-mounted top rail for mounting accessory optics. Chambered in .45-70 Government. Overall length 42.5"; weight 7.5 lbs.

NIB	EXC.	V.G.	GOOD	FAIR	POOR
875	700	600	525	400	150

Model 1895GBL

Lever-action chambered in .45-70 Government. Features include 6-shot full-length tubular magazine; 18.5" barrel, with deep-cut Ballard-type rifling (6 grooves); big-loop finger lever; side ejection; solid-top receiver; deeply blued metal surfaces; hammer block safety; pistol-grip two tone brown laminate stock, with cut checkering; ventilated recoil pad; Mar-Shield finish, swivel studs. Introduced 2010.

NIB	EXC.	V.G.	GOOD	FAIR	POOR
550	500	425	350	250	150

Model 308MXLR

Similar to Model 1895MXLR. Chambered in proprietary .308 Marlin Express cartridge.

NIB	EXC.	V.G.	GOOD	FAIR	POOR
700	600	525	400	300	150

Model 308MX

Similar to the Model 308MXLR, with blued receiver and barrel.

NIB	EXC.	V.G.	GOOD	FAIR	POOR
550	450	350	250	150	100

Model 338MXLR

Lever-action chambered for .338 Marlin Express. Features 24" stainless steel barrel; stainless steel receiver, lever and magazine tube; black/gray laminated checkered stock and fore-end; hooded ramp front sight and adjustable semi-buckhorn rear; drilled and tapped for scope mounts; receiver-mounted crossbolt safety. Overall length 42.5"; weight 7.5 lbs.

NIB	EXC.	V.G.	GOOD	FAIR	POOR
700	600	525	400	300	150

Model 338MX

Similar to Model 338MXLR, with blued metal. Walnut stock and fore-end.

NIB	EXC.	V.G.	GOOD	FAIR	POOR
550	450	350	250	150	100

	NIB	EXC.	V.G.	GOOD	FAIR	POOR

Model 1897 Century Limited

Introduced in 1997. Chambered for .22-caliber cartridge. Commemorates 100th anniversary of Model 1897. Fitted with 24" half round/half octagon barrel, with adjustable Marble rear sight and Marble front sight with brass bead. Blued receiver engraved and gold inlaid. Semi-fancy walnut stock. Hard rubber buttplate. Weight about 6.5 lbs.

900	700	575	475	300	200

Model 1897 Century Limited Employee Edition

Similar to above, with additional gold engraving on lever. Limited to 100 rifles.

1800	1400	1000	—	—	—

Model 1897 Cowboy

.22-caliber lever-action rifle. Fitted with 24" tapered octagon barrel, with adjustable Marble buckhorn sight and Marble front sight with brass bead. Full-length tubular magazine holds 26 Shorts, 21 Longs and 19 LR cartridges. Walnut straight-grip stock, with hard rubber buttplate. Weight 7.5 lbs. Introduced in 1999.

700	550	450	350	200	100

Model 1897 Annie Oakley

Introduced in 1998. This .22-caliber features 18.5" tapered octagon barrel, adjustable Marble rear sight and Marble front sight. Blued receiver roll engraved, with gold signature. Stock straight-grip, with blued end cap. Hard rubber buttplate. Weight about 5.5 lbs.

700	600	400	300	200	125

Model 1897 Texan

Chambered for .22-caliber cartridge. Fitted with 20" octagon barrel; walnut stock with straight-grip. Magazine capacity 14 to 21 cartridges depending on type. Weight about 6 lbs. Introduced in 2002.

700	600	400	300	200	125

Glenfield Lever-Action Rifles

Glenfield line of rifles were designed to be sold in large outlet chain stores. Simply cheaper versions that were to be sold for less money. Rifles functioned fine, but birch was used instead of walnut and pressed checkering instead of handcut. Manufactured under Glenfield name between 1964 and 1983. There are five models of Lever-Action Glenfields: 30, 30A, 30AS, 30GT and 36G. Chambered for .30-30 cartridge. Basic differences are slight and in most cases, merely cosmetic. They are good serviceable rifles, but have little or no collector interest or investment potential.

295	250	200	150	125	100

Model 30AW

Lever-action chambered for .30-30 cartridge. Has 20" barrel and 6-round magazine tube. Stock walnut finished birch, with pistol-grip cap. Hard rubber buttplate. Introduced in 1998.

300	250	200	150	125	100

MODEL 39

Model originally evolved from Model 1891, invented by L.L. Hepburn. Model 1891 became Model 1892 and eventually developed into takedown Model 1897. Latter two were produced until 1915, when discontinued in favor of machine gun production for WWI. In 1922, when the company was sold to John Moran and became Marlin Firearms Corp., .22 rimfire lever-action was reintroduced as Model 39. Has been in production in one form or another ever since.

Model 39

Introduced in 1922. Model 39 was chambered for .22 rimfire, had 24" octagonal barrel and takedown receiver. Has full-length magazine tube which holds 25 Shorts, 20 Longs or 18 LR cartridges. Most Model 39s had a spring-loaded button outer magazine tube release. Very early variations had Model '97 type knurled latch release. As Model 39As were being phased in around 1939, many have more modern removable inner magazine tube. Has solid top frame and side ejection, Rocky Mountain rear and ivory bead front sight. Receiver, lever and hammer are case colored; barrel blued. Pistol-grip stock and steel-capped forearm are varnished walnut. Manufactured in this form between 1922 and 1938, with a number of options that could affect value and would warrant an individual appraisal. Model 39s with a "star" stamped on tang, were considered high grade guns by factory inspector and will command a premium in better condition examples. **NOTE:** Model 39s made prior to 1932 that have either no prefix or prefix S on serial number, should not be used with high-speed ammunition. Prefix HS indicates an improved bolt that is safe for this ammunition.

Standard Rifle

—	4000	3000	2000	1000	750

	NIB	EXC.	V.G.	GOOD	FAIR	POOR

Deluxe Rifle

Factory checkering, fancy wood and "star" stamp on tang.

	NIB	EXC.	V.G.	GOOD	FAIR	POOR
	—	4500	3500	2200	1000	750

Model 39A

Improved version of Model 39. Has a heavier tapered round barrel, semi-beavertail forearm and redesigned pistol-grip stock. Rubber buttplate was replaced by one of a synthetic fiber; otherwise, specifications were similar to Model 39. Manufactured from 1939 to 1960. Several variations are listed.

Pre-war Variations (1939-1941)

Case colored receiver, no serial number prefix (1939) or "B" prefix (1940-1941).

	—	2000	1200	800	500	400

Post-war Variations (1945-1953)

Serial number prefixes up to letter "K". Ballard-type deep rifling. **NOTE:** Add 20 percent premium for C prefix 1st post-war variation, with figured wood.

	—	700	575	425	250	200

Post-war Variations (1954-1956)

Serial number prefixes L, M, N, with MicroGroove barrel.

	—	600	495	395	225	125

Golden 39A's" (1954-1963)

Gold trigger, MicroGroove rifling. Serial number prefixes L through W.

	—	550	450	325	195	125

Model 39A Mountie

Basically a carbine version of Model 39A. Features 20" tapered round barrel, straight-grip walnut stock and slimmed-down forearm. Manufactured between 1953 and 1960.

1st Variation

K prefix and 24" barrel, fat forearm. **NOTE:** Add 20 percent for slim forearm.

	—	600	450	300	200	100

Standard

	—	450	325	175	125	100

Model 39A 1960 Presentation Model

Released in 1960. Marlin's 90th Anniversary model. Similar to 39A. Has chrome-plated barrel and receiver, with high grade checkered walnut stock and fore-end. There is a squirrel carved on right side of buttstock. Produced 500 in 1960. This is a commemorative. Desirable to collectors only if NIB with all boxes and papers with which it was originally sold.

	1200	900	500	300	175	125

Model 39M Mountie 1960 Presentation Model

Carbine version of 90th Anniversary model. Same as 39A, with 20" barrel and straight-grip stock. Manufactured 500 in 1960.

	1200	900	500	300	175	125

Model 39ADL

Same as 90th Anniversary issue except blued instead of chrome-plated. Manufactured 3,306 between 1960 and 1963.

	1000	850	500	300	175	125

Model Golden 39A

Similar to 39A, with gold-plated trigger and sling swivels. Manufactured between 1960 and 1983.

	—	650	550	400	250	125

Model 39 Carbine

Slimmer lighter version of Model 39A. Features slimmer fore-end and thinner barrel. Manufactured 12,140 between 1963 and 1967.

	—	550	400	250	175	100

Model 39 Century Limited

Introduction of this model marked 100th Anniversary of the Marlin Company. Features 20" octagonal barrel, with semi-buckhorn rear and brass blade front sight. Stock is fancy walnut, with straight-grip, brass fore-end tip and buttplate. A medallion inlaid into right side of receiver. Brass plate on stock. Manufactured 34,197 in 1970. As a commemorative, needs to be as it came from the factory to command collector interest.

	950	550	300	150	125	100

	NIB	EXC.	V.G.	GOOD	FAIR	POOR

Model 39A Article II

Commemorated National Rifle Association's 100th Anniversary in 1971. Has 24" octagonal barrel, high grade walnut pistol-grip stock, brass fore-end tip and buttplate. Right side of receiver has NRA's Second Amendment "Right to Keep and Bear Arms" medallion inlaid. Manufactured in 1971.

NIB	EXC.	V.G.	GOOD	FAIR	POOR
750	450	300	150	125	100

Model 39M Article II

Same as Model 39A Article II, except a carbine version with 20" octagonal barrel and straight-grip stock. Manufactured 3,824 in 1971. As commemorative, NIB condition is essential to collector interest.

NIB	EXC.	V.G.	GOOD	FAIR	POOR
775	475	325	175	150	100

Model 39A Octagon

Produced because the company had machinery and some leftover barrels from two commemorative models produced in 1970 and 1971. A regular production run that was meant to be used and was not a special issue. Has 24" tapered octagonal barrel. Chambered for .22 rimfire cartridges. Pistol-grip walnut stock, with steel fore-end tip. Manufactured 2,551 in 1972 and 1973. This was not a commercially successful model and discontinued for that reason.

NIB	EXC.	V.G.	GOOD	FAIR	POOR
800	600	400	250	200	175

Model 39M Octagon

This is the 20" octagonal barreled carbine version, with straight-grip stock. Manufactured 2,140 in 1973.

NIB	EXC.	V.G.	GOOD	FAIR	POOR
750	600	400	250	200	175

Model 39D

Essentially Model 39M carbine 20" barrel version, with pistol-grip stock. Manufactured in 1971; reintroduced in 1973. The 1971 version has white line spacers and pistol-grip caps; 1973 version has neither of these features.

NIB	EXC.	V.G.	GOOD	FAIR	POOR
—	625	475	325	195	125

Golden 39A

Current production model of this extremely popular .22 rifle. Features hammer-block crossbolt safety and sling swivel studs. Similar in appearance to its predecessors. Takedown style.

NIB	EXC.	V.G.	GOOD	FAIR	POOR
650	550	425	325	225	200

Model 39TDS

Similar to Model 39AS, with 20" carbine barrel and straight-grip stock. Replaced Model 39M. Introduced in 1988. Superseded by current Golden 39A, which is a takedown design.

NIB	EXC.	V.G.	GOOD	FAIR	POOR
600	475	300	200	150	100

Model 39AWL

Limited edition of 2,000 rifles distributed solely through Wal-Mart. Fitted with 24.5" octagon barrel, select checkered walnut stock, gold filled engraving and stamped "Wildlife For Tomorrow".

NIB	EXC.	V.G.	GOOD	FAIR	POOR
750	600	400	300	200	125

Model 56 Levermatic

Streamlined version of lever-action. Features short lever throw and one-piece walnut stock. Round 22" barrel. Chambered for .22 rimfire cartridges, with 7-shot detachable magazine. Open sights. Gold-plated trigger. Receiver made of aluminum after 1956. Manufactured 31,523 between 1955 and 1964.

NIB	EXC.	V.G.	GOOD	FAIR	POOR
—	325	225	150	75	50

Model 56 "Clipper King" Levermatic

Same as Model 56, except specially packaged. Comes with 4X .22 scope. Name "Clipper King" stamped on barrel. Buttplate red hard rubber. Manufactured only 152 in 1959.

NIB	EXC.	V.G.	GOOD	FAIR	POOR
—	350	250	175	100	75

Model 57 Levermatic

Similar to Model 56, with tube magazine and Monte Carlo stock. In 1960, Marlin went back to a steel receiver on this model. Manufactured 34,628 from 1959 to 1965.

NIB	EXC.	V.G.	GOOD	FAIR	POOR
—	325	225	150	75	50

Model 57M Levermatic

This is the Model 57 chambered for .22 Magnum cartridge. Manufactured 66,889 between 1959 and 1969.

NIB	EXC.	V.G.	GOOD	FAIR	POOR
—	450	350	250	175	100

NIB	EXC.	V.G.	GOOD	FAIR	POOR

Model 62 Levermatic

Similar in appearance to Model 57, except chambered for centerfire .256 Magnum cartridge, with 4-shot magazine. In 1966, .30 carbine cartridge was added. This model has a 23" "MicroGroove" barrel, with open sights and walnut one-piece stock. First 4,000 Model 62s were shipped without serial numbers in violation of federal law. Company recalled rifles for numbering; and to this day, owner of a centerfire Model 62 can return rifle for numbering. Manufactured 15,714 between 1963 and 1969. Add 15 percent for .256. **NOTE:** From 1969 to 1972, first digit of serial number indicates year of manufacture. In 1973, system was changed by having first two digits subtracted from 100 to find year of production. For example: 2717793=100-27=1973.

—	600	475	375	225	100

MISCELLANEOUS RIMFIRE RIFLES

Marlin Firearms Company produced a great many bolt-action rifles, both single-shot and repeaters, starting in 1930 and continuing today. These rifles were low-priced and designed primarily as utility rifles. They also manufactured many auto-loaders of the same type during these years. Glenfield name will also be found on these models, as many were produced to be marketed by large chain outlets. These rifles have limited value as collectibles at the present time, but no one can deny that they're durable accurate good-natured little rifles.

Model 70P "Papoose"

Semi-automatic takedown carbine. Chambered for .22 rimfire family of cartridges. Has 16.25" barrel and 7-shot detachable magazine. Supplied with 4X scope. Bright red case that will float if dropped overboard. Stock walnut-finished birch, with pistol-grip. Rubber buttplate. Introduced in 1986.

275	200	150	100	75	50

Model 70PSS

Same as Model 70P above. Furnished with 10-round magazine. Finished in stainless steel, with synthetic stock. Automatic last shot bolt hold-open.

245	175	125	100	85	60

Model 70HC

This is the Model 70 .22 rimfire semi-automatic that has been produced since 1983, with high-capacity 25-round "Banana" magazine.

200	160	140	110	85	75

Model 9 Camp Carbine

Model has 16.5" barrel. Chambered for 9mm Parabellum pistol cartridge. Has 12- or 20-shot detachable magazine, walnut-finished hardwood pistol-grip stock and sandblasted matte-blued finish. Open sights. Receiver drilled and tapped for scope mounting. Introduced in 1985.

625	500	395	250	175	125

Model 9N

Similar to Model 9mm Carbine. Furnished with nickel-plated metal parts.

650	525	425	275	195	125

Model 45 Camp Carbine

Same as 9mm version. Chambered for .45 ACP cartridge. Has 7-shot detachable magazine. Very hot collectible.

675	600	425	300	225	175

Model 922M

First offered in 1993. A semi-automatic .22 Win. Magnum Rimfire rifle. Features 7-shot clip; 20.5" MicroGrove barrel; receiver sandblasted, drilled and tapped for scope mounting; Monte Carlo black walnut stock, with rubber rifle buff pad; adjustable rear sight and ramp front sight with hood. Weighs 6.5 lbs.

550	450	375	225	150	125

Model 995

Semi-automatic .22 LR only rifle features 7-shot clip, 18" MicroGroove barrel. Receiver grooved for scope mount and has a serrated non-glare top. Adjustable sights. Monte Carlo American black walnut stock, with checkered pistol-grip and forearm. White buttplate spacer standard. Weighs 5 lbs. Introduced in 1979.

175	110	80	70	60	40

Model 995SS

Same as above, with stainless steel finish. Black fiberglass stock. Introduced in 1995.

195	125	100	85	60	50

NIB	EXC.	V.G.	GOOD	FAIR	POOR

Model 990L

Semi-automatic .22 LR Marlin features tubular 14-round magazine, with 22" MicroGrove barrel. Trigger gold plated. Receiver grooved for scope mount. Stock a two-tone brown birch Monte Carlo. Rubber rifle buttpad standard. Weighs 5.75 lbs.

150	120	100	80	65	50

Model 7000

First offered in 1997. A semi-automatic .22 caliber rifle, with 18" heavy barrel. Magazine holds 10 rounds. Black synthetic stock, with Monte Carlo comb and molded checkering. Receiver grooved for scope mount. No sights included. Weight about 6 lbs.

200	150	125	100	75	50

Model 7000T

Target rifle fitted with an 18" barrel with recessed muzzle. No sights. Stock laminated red, white and blue with pistol-grip. Serrated rubber buttplate adjustable for length of pull, height and angle. Weight about 7.5 lbs. Introduced in 1999.

425	375	325	275	150	100

Model 795

Similar to Model 7000 above, with 18" standard weight barrel. Weight about 5 lbs. Available with 4X scope. **NOTE:** Add $5 for scope.

150	115	—	—	—	—

Model 795SS

As above, with stainless steel action and barrel. Black fiberglass stock. Weight about 4.5 lbs. Introduced in 2002.

200	150	125	100	75	50

Model 60

Semi-automatic 14-shot .22-caliber LR. Features 22" MicroGroove barrel, with adjustable rear sight. Receiver grooved for scope mount. Stock birch, with Monte Carlo comb. Weighs 5.5 lbs. Introduced in 1960.

175	125	90	60	50	40

Model 60SS

Introduced in 1993. Similar to Model 60. Features stainless barrel, bolt and magazine tube. All other metal parts are nickel plated. Stock is two-tone black/gray laminated birch Monte Carlo.

275	225	150	125	75	50

Model 60SN

Similar to Model 60SS, with black synthetic stock, molded checkering and swivel studs. Blued metal. Introduced in 2007. Available with factory-mounted 3x9 scope. **NOTE:** Add 10 percent for scope package.

200	150	125	100	75	50

Model 60S-CF

Similar to Model 60SN, with carbon fiber-dipped black synthetic stock, giving it a – quote – "racy, high tech look". Woo-hoo!

250	225	175	125	100	75

Model 60SB

Introduced in 1998. Features stainless steel 22" barrel, bolt and magazine tube. Stock birch, with Monte Carlo. Hard rubber buttplate.

175	125	90	60	50	40

Model 60SSK

Similar to Model 60SB. Addition of black synthetic Monte Carlo stock, with checkering.

195	195	150	125	100	75

Model 60C

Similar to Model 60, with Realtree camo finish. Introduced in 2000.

195	195	150	125	100	75

Model 60DL

Introduced in 2004. Features Monte Carlo hardwood stock, with Walnutone walnut pattern finish. Full pistol-grip. Weight about 5.5 lbs.

175	125	90	60	50	40

	NIB	EXC.	V.G.	GOOD	FAIR	POOR

Model 60DLX

Semi-automatic rifle chambered for .22 LR. Features include 14-shot tubular magazine; side ejection; manual and automatic last-shot bolt hold-opens; receiver top with serrated non-glare finish; cross-bolt safety; steel charging handle; Monte Carlo American walnut-finished hardwood; full pistol-grip; tough Mar-Shield finish; 19" barrel with Micro-Groove rifling. Limited availability.

225	175	125	100	75	50

Model 2000

Bolt-action single-shot target rifle. Chambered for .22 LR. Barrel 22" long MicroGroove design, with match chamber and recessed muzzle. Rear sight fully adjustable target peep sight, with hooded front sight supplied with 10 aperture inserts. Stock Marlin blue fiberglass/Kevlar material, with adjustable buttplate. Aluminum forearm rail, with forearm stop and quick detachable swivel. Weighs 8 lbs. Discontinued.

650	500	400	325	250	200

Model 2000A

A 1996 version of Model 2000. Introduced in 1994. Features adjustable comb and ambidextrous pistol-grip. Marlin logo molded into side of buttstock. Weighs about 8.5 lbs. Discontinued.

750	600	500	375	300	250

Model 2000L

Introduced in 1996. Version of Model 2000. Features black/gray laminated stock. Fitted with heavy 22" barrel and match chamber; two-stage target trigger; rubber buttplate adjustable for length of pull, height and angle. Weight about 8 lbs. Discontinued.

800	650	550	400	325	250

Model 880

Bolt-action clip-fed rifle. Chambered for .22 LR caliber. Clip is a 7-shot magazine. MicroGroove barrel is 22". Has adjustable folding rear sight and ramp front sight with hood. Weighs 5.5 lbs. Introduced in 1988. Discontinued in 2004.

160	135	110	90	75	50

Model 880SS

Introduced in 1994. This .22-caliber rifle features synthetic stock; stainless steel receiver and 22" barrel; 7-shot magazine standard. Discontinued in 2004.

250	175	150	125	75	60

Model 880SQ

Similar to Model 880. Fitted with 22" heavy barrel and no sights. Introduced in 1996. Weight about 7 lbs. Discontinued in 2004.

285	225	200	150	100	75

Model 881

Bolt-action .22-caliber rifle has tubular magazine that holds 25 Shorts, 19 longs and 17 LR. A 22" MicroGroove barrel has adjustable folding rear sight and ramp front sight with hood. Stock black walnut, with Monte Carlo. Rubber rifle buttpad, with sling swivels. Weighs 6 lbs. First offered in 1988. Discontinued in 2004.

175	150	125	100	80	60

Model 882SS

Bolt-action magazine rifle chambered for .22 Magnum cartridge. Stainless steel barrel and action, with black synthetic stock. Marlin "Fire Sights" installed. Introduced in 1998. Discontinued in 2004.

225	175	150	100	75	50

Model 25N

Marlin promotional model. Bolt-action rifle chambered for .22 LR only. Seven-shot clip magazine, with 22" MicroGroove barrel. Receiver grooved for scope mount. Walnut finished birch stock. Weighs 5.5 lbs.

125	90	80	70	50	40

Model 25NC

Similar to above, with Mossy Oak Break-Up camo finish. Introduced in 2000.

125	100	80	70	50	40

Model 25MN

Same as above chambered for .22 Win. Magnum Rimfire cartridge. Weighs 6 lbs.

175	150	125	100	80	60

	NIB	EXC.	V.G.	GOOD	FAIR	POOR

Model 25MNC

Similar to above, with Mossy Oak Break-Up camo finish. Weight about 6 lbs. Introduced in 2001.

	NIB	EXC.	V.G.	GOOD	FAIR	POOR
	195	160	125	100	80	60

Model 17V

Introduced in 2002. Bolt-action rifle chambered for .17 Hornady Magnum Rimfire cartridge. Fitted with 22" heavy barrel. Hardwood stock. No sights. Magazine capacity 7-round detachable magazine. Weight about 6 lbs.

	NIB	EXC.	V.G.	GOOD	FAIR	POOR
	225	200	150	115	90	50

Model 17VS

As above, with stainless steel heavy barrel and action. Laminated stock. Weight about 7 lbs. Discontinued.

	NIB	EXC.	V.G.	GOOD	FAIR	POOR
	285	225	200	150	100	75

Model 15YN "Little Buckaroo"

Marlin promotional model referred to as "Little Buckaroo". Bolt-action .22-caliber single-shot rifle for the beginner. Features MicroGroove 16.25" barrel, adjustable rear sight and receiver grooved for scope mount. Birch stock. Weighs 4.25 lbs.

	NIB	EXC.	V.G.	GOOD	FAIR	POOR
	125	100	75	60	50	40

Model 15N

Bolt-action rifle chambered for .22 Short, Long and LR. Fitted with adjustable rear sight. Full size birch stock interchangeable with Model 15YN. Weight about 4.25 lbs. Introduced in 1998.

	NIB	EXC.	V.G.	GOOD	FAIR	POOR
	185	145	100	75	60	40

Model 15YS (Youth)

Single-shot bolt-action rifle, with shorter-than-standard length of pull. Barrel length 16.25". Hardwood stock. Weight about 4.25 lbs. Introduced in 2002.

	NIB	EXC.	V.G.	GOOD	FAIR	POOR
	175	140	110	65	50	35

Model 81TS

Bolt-action rifle chambered for .22 Short, Long and LR cartridges. Fitted with 22" barrel and tubular magazine. Comes with black Monte Carlo synthetic stock. Adjustable rear sight. Weight about 6 lbs. Introduced in 1998. Discontinued in 2004.

	NIB	EXC.	V.G.	GOOD	FAIR	POOR
	175	140	110	65	50	35

Model 882

Bolt-action rifle chambered for .22 Win. Magnum Rimfire cartridge. A 7-shot clip standard. MicroGroove 22" barrel, with adjustable rear sight and ramp front sight with hood. Receiver grooved for scope mount. Black walnut stock, with Monte Carlo. Rubber rifle butt. Weighs 6 lbs. Introduced in 1988. Discontinued in 2004.

	NIB	EXC.	V.G.	GOOD	FAIR	POOR
	285	225	200	150	100	75

Model 882L

Same as above. Furnished with two-tone brown hardwood Monte Carlo stock. Weighs 6.25 lbs. Discontinued in 2004.

	NIB	EXC.	V.G.	GOOD	FAIR	POOR
	275	215	190	145	90	60

Model 882SS

Same as above. Furnished in stainless steel. Black fiberglass stock. Introduced in 1995. Discontinued in 2004.

	NIB	EXC.	V.G.	GOOD	FAIR	POOR
	285	225	200	150	100	75

Model 882SSV

Variation of Model 882. Introduced in 1997. All in stainless steel. Chambered for .22 WMR cartridge. Fitted with nickel plated 7-round magazine and 22" barrel. Stock black synthetic, with molded checkering. Receiver grooved for scope mount. 1" brushed aluminum scope ring mounts included. Weighs about 7 lbs. Discontinued in 2004.

	NIB	EXC.	V.G.	GOOD	FAIR	POOR
	285	225	200	150	100	75

Model 83TS

Chambered for .22 Win. Magnum cartridge. Fitted with 22" barrel and 12-round tubular magazine. Adjustable rear sight. Bolt-action, with synthetic stock. Weight about 6 lbs. Introduced in 2001. Discontinued in 2004.

	NIB	EXC.	V.G.	GOOD	FAIR	POOR
	250	200	165	145	100	75

NIB	EXC.	V.G.	GOOD	FAIR	POOR	

Model 883

Bolt-action rifle. Chambered for .22 Win. Magnum cartridge, with 12-shot tubular magazine. Furnished with 22" MicroGroove barrel; adjustable rear sight, ramp front sight with hood; checkered American black walnut stock, with Monte Carlo. Weighs 6 lbs. Introduced in 1988. Discontinued in 2004.

285	225	200	150	100	75

Model 883N

Same as above. Furnished with stainless steel barrel, receiver, front breech bolt and striker. All other metal parts, except for sights, are nickel plated. Discontinued in 2004.

285	225	200	150	100	75

Model 883SS

Introduced in 1993. Similar to Model 883, with all metal parts in stainless steel or nickel. Stock is two-tone brown birch Monte Carlo that is not checkered. Discontinued in 2004.

275	215	190	145	90	60

Model 717M2

Introduced in 2005. Semi-automatic chambered for .17 Mach 2 cartridge. Laminated hardwood stock, with Monte Carlo comb. Fitted with 18" barrel and iron sights. Magazine capacity 7 rounds. Weight about 5 lbs.

300	250	200	175	150	125

MODEL 900 SERIES

Bolt action rimfire series was introduced into Marlin line in 2004. Features T-900 fire control system. This is a trigger and safety system that features a wide serrated trigger and improved trigger pull. Safety activation also improved. The 900 series also features drilled and tapped receivers on all models.

Model 983T

Chambered for .22 WMR cartridge. Fitted with 22" barrel. Monte Carlo black fiberglass stock, with checkering. Adjustable sights. Tubular 12-round magazine. Weight about 6 lbs.

285	225	200	150	100	75

Model 983S

As above, with laminated two-tone stock.

285	225	200	150	100	75

Model 983

.22 WMR model features Monte Carlo stock of American black walnut, with full pistol-grip and checkering.

285	225	200	150	100	75

Model 917

Bolt-action rifle chambered in .17 Hornady Magnum Rimfire; 7-shot clip magazine; fiberglass-filled synthetic stock with full pistol-grip; swivel studs and molded-in checkering. Adjustable open rear sight, ramp front. 22" barrel. Introduced 2006.

285	225	200	150	100	75

Model 917V

Chambered for .17 HMR cartridge. Fitted with 22" heavy barrel. Hardwood Monte Carlo stock, with full pistol-grip. No sights. Detachable magazine with 7-round capacity. Weight about 6 lbs.

285	225	200	150	100	75

Model 917VR

Similar to Model 917, with fiberglass-filled synthetic stock. Introduced 2006.

285	225	200	150	100	75

Model 917VS

As above, with gray/black laminated hardwood stock. No sights. Magazine nickel plated. Weight about 7 lbs. Scope bases included.

285	225	200	150	100	75

Model 917VS-CF

Similar to Model 917VS, with carbon fiber-patterned stock.

285	225	200	150	100	75

	NIB	EXC.	V.G.	GOOD	FAIR	POOR

Model 917VSF

Chambered for .17 HMR cartridge. Fitted with 22" heavy stainless steel fluted barrel. No sights. Nickel magazine capacity 7 rounds. Laminated gray stock, with Monte Carlo comb. Weight about 6.75 lbs. Introduced in 2005.

	300	250	200	175	150	125

Model 917VT

Similar to above, with laminated brown thumbhole stock. Introduced 2008.

	350	300	250	175	145	110

Model 917VST

Similar to above, with laminated gray/black thumbhole stock. Introduced 2008.

	400	350	295	245	125	100

Model 917M2

Chambered for .17 Mach 2 cartridge. Fitted with 22" heavy barrel. Monte Carlo hardwood stock, with full pistol-grip. No sights. Scope bases included. Magazine capacity 7 rounds. Weight about 5.5 lbs.

	300	250	200	175	150	125

Model 917M2S

As above, with Monte Carlo gray/black laminated stock. Full pistol-grip. Stainless steel barrel and receiver. Nickel plated magazine.

	325	275	225	200	175	125

Model 982S

Chambered for .22 WMR cartridge. Fitted with 22" stainless steel barrel. Adjustable sights. Black fiberglass stock, with Monte Carlo. Full pistol-grip. Detachable 7-round nickel magazine. Weight about 6 lbs.

	285	225	200	150	100	75

Model 982L

As above, with gray/black laminated stock. Weight about 6.25 lbs.

	300	250	200	175	150	125

Model 982

Similar to 982S, with American black walnut checkered stock, with Monte Carlo. Full pistol-grip. Adjustable sights. Weight about 6 lbs.

	285	225	200	150	100	75

Model 982VS

As above, with black fiberglass Monte Carlo stock. Heavy 22" stainless steel barrel. Nickel plated 7-round magazine. No sights. Weight about 7 lbs.

	325	275	225	200	175	125

Model 982VS-CF

As above, with synthetic stock. Dipped carbon-fiber textured finish.

	325	275	225	200	175	125

Model 925M

As above, with hardwood stock. Full pistol-grip. Fitted with 22" standard weight barrel. Adjustable sights. Weight about 6 lbs.

	250	200	165	145	100	75

Model 925RM

Similar to Model 925M, with black fiberglass-filled synthetic stock.

	250	200	165	145	100	75

Model 925MC

As above, with Monte Carlo Mossy Oak Break-up camo stock. Weight about 6 lbs.

	285	225	200	150	100	75

Model 980V

Chambered for .22 LR cartridge. Fitted with 22" heavy barrel. Black fiberglass stock, with Monte Carlo. Full pistol-grip. No sights. Magazine capacity 7 rounds. Weight about 7 lbs.

	285	225	200	150	100	75

	NIB	EXC.	V.G.	GOOD	FAIR	POOR

Model 980S

As above, with standard weight 22" barrel and 7-round nickel plated magazine. Stainless steel barrel and receiver. Adjustable sights. Weight about 6 lbs.

NIB	EXC.	V.G.	GOOD	FAIR	POOR
285	225	200	150	100	75

Model 980S-CF

As above, with carbon fiber stock. Introduced in 2007.

NIB	EXC.	V.G.	GOOD	FAIR	POOR
285	225	200	150	100	75

Model 981T

Chambered to handle interchangeably .22 Short, Long or LR cartridges in a tubular magazine. Black Monte Carlo fiberglass stock, with full pistol-grip. Adjustable sights. Fitted with standard weight 22" barrel. Weight about 6 lbs.

NIB	EXC.	V.G.	GOOD	FAIR	POOR
285	225	200	150	100	75

Model 981TS

Bolt-action rifle chambered in .22 S/L/LR. Features include tubular magazine (holds 25 Short, 19 Long or 17 Long Rifle) cartridges; thumb safety; red cocking indicator; black fiberglass-filled synthetic stock, with full pistol-grip; molded-in checkering and swivel studs; 22" stainless steel barrel, with Micro-Groove rifling (16 grooves). Adjustable semi-buckhorn folding rear sight, ramp front with high visibility orange front sight post; cutaway Wide-Scan hood. Receiver grooved for scope mount; drilled and tapped for scope bases.

NIB	EXC.	V.G.	GOOD	FAIR	POOR
300	250	225	150	100	75

Model 925

Chambered for .22 LR cartridge. Fitted with 22" standard weight barrel. Adjustable sights. Monte Carlo hardwood stock. Full pistol-grip. Seven-round magazine. Weight about 5.5 lbs.

NIB	EXC.	V.G.	GOOD	FAIR	POOR
225	175	150	125	95	75

Model 925R

As above, with factory-mounted 3x9 scope.

NIB	EXC.	V.G.	GOOD	FAIR	POOR
250	200	165	145	100	75

Model 925C

As above, with Monte Carlo hardwood stock in Mossy Oak Break-up camo pattern. Adjustable sights.

NIB	EXC.	V.G.	GOOD	FAIR	POOR
250	200	165	145	100	75

Model 915Y Compact

Single-shot .22 rimfire rifle, with 16.25" barrel. Hardwood stock, with impressed checkering. Iron sights.

NIB	EXC.	V.G.	GOOD	FAIR	POOR
200	150	125	100	75	50

Model 915YS Compact

Similar to above, with stainless steel receiver and barrel. No checkering. Fiber optic sights.

NIB	EXC.	V.G.	GOOD	FAIR	POOR
225	175	150	125	95	75

Model 322

Model chambered for .222 cartridge. Has 24" medium-weight barrel, with MicroGroove rifling. Checkered walnut pistol-grip stock. Magazine holds 4 shots. Adjustable trigger. Sights are Sako products. Sako receiver fitted for Sako scope mounting bases. Non-Sako receivers were apparently also used. MicroGroove rifling in barrel was not successful for this caliber and accuracy fell off after as few as 500 shots—so this model was dropped and replaced. Serial numbers were Sako. Manufactured 5,859 between 1954 and 1959.

NIB	EXC.	V.G.	GOOD	FAIR	POOR
600	550	450	350	300	200

Model 422

Successor to Model 322. Simply same rifle fitted with 24" featherweight stainless steel barrel. Named "Varmint King". Features Monte Carlo stock, with cheekpiece. Manufactured only 354 between 1956 and 1958.

NIB	EXC.	V.G.	GOOD	FAIR	POOR
950	600	500	400	300	200

Model 455

Built on Fabrique Nationale Belgian Mauser action. Chambered for .308 and .30-06 cartridges. Stainless steel barrel made by Marlin, with 5-shot magazine. Bishop checkered

NIB	EXC.	V.G.	GOOD	FAIR	POOR

walnut stock, with detachable sling swivels and leather sling. Rear sight Lyman 48; front ramp type, with detachable hood. Receiver drilled and tapped for scope mounts. Trigger adjustable Sako unit. Manufactured 1,079 in .30-06; only 59 in .308 between 1955 and 1959.

NIB	EXC.	V.G.	GOOD	FAIR	POOR
—	700	595	425	300	200

Model MR-7

Introduced in 1996. American-made bolt-action centerfire rifle of a totally new design. Chambered for .25-06 (first offered in 1997), .243, .270 Win. .280, .308 or .30-06 cartridges. Fitted with 22" barrel. Has American black walnut stock; 4-shot detachable box magazine. Offered with or without sights. Weight about 7.5 lbs. Discontinued 1999.

NIB	EXC.	V.G.	GOOD	FAIR	POOR
450	350	300	250	175	150

Model MR-7B

Similar to MR-7. Fitted with 4-round blind magazine; birch stock. Offered in .30-06 or .270; with or without sights. Introduced in 1998. Discontinued.

NIB	EXC.	V.G.	GOOD	FAIR	POOR
375	300	250	175	150	100

Model XL7

Introduced in 2008. Centerfire bolt-action rifle, with adjustable Pro-Fire trigger system. 4+1 capacity. Chambered in .25-06, .270 and .30-06. Crowned precision-rifled 22" barrel that is joined to receiver with a pressure nut. Black synthetic stock, with raised cheekpiece. Soft-Tech recoil pad. No sights; drilled and tapped for mounts. **NOTE:** Add $50 for factory scope package.

NIB	EXC.	V.G.	GOOD	FAIR	POOR
325	275	225	200	175	125

Model XL7C

Similar to above, with Realtree APG HD camo finish.

NIB	EXC.	V.G.	GOOD	FAIR	POOR
350	300	250	175	145	110

Model XS7 Short-Action

Similar to Model XL7. Chambered in 7mm-08, .243 Winchester and .308 Winchester. **NOTE:** Add $50 for factory scope package.

NIB	EXC.	V.G.	GOOD	FAIR	POOR
325	275	225	200	175	125

Model XS7Y Youth Rifle

Similar to above, with smaller dimensions.

NIB	EXC.	V.G.	GOOD	FAIR	POOR
325	275	225	200	175	125

Model XS7C Camo

Similar to above, with Realtree APG HD camo stock.

NIB	EXC.	V.G.	GOOD	FAIR	POOR
350	300	250	175	145	110

Model XS7S

Bolt-action rifle similar to Model XS7, with stainless steel barrel, receiver and trigger group. Short action.

NIB	EXC.	V.G.	GOOD	FAIR	POOR
375	325	275	175	150	100

Model XL7

Entry-level bolt action rifle chambered in .25-06 Rem., .270 Win., .30-06 Spr. Features include 4+1 magazine capacity; pillar bedded 22" barrel; Pro-Fire adjustable trigger system; 2-position safety; red cocking indicator; swivel studs; matte blue/black finish; black synthetic stock, with molded in checkering and Soft-Tech recoil pad. No sights.

NIB	EXC.	V.G.	GOOD	FAIR	POOR
325	285	235	200	150	75

MARLIN PUMP SHOTGUNS

Model 1898

Model made in 12-gauge, with exposed hammer. Has takedown receiver. Walnut pistol-grip stock and fore-end. 5-shot tube magazine. Barrel lengths from 26" to 32". Manufactured between 1898 and 1905.

Grade A

Variation has 30", 32" or 38" barrel. Full choke. Plainest grade.

NIB	EXC.	V.G.	GOOD	FAIR	POOR
—	475	425	325	125	75

Grade A Brush or Riot

Same shotgun, with 26" cylinder-bore barrel.

NIB	EXC.	V.G.	GOOD	FAIR	POOR
—	425	375	250	150	100

	NIB	EXC.	V.G.	GOOD	FAIR	POOR

Grade B
Same as Grade A, with special smokeless steel barrel. Checkered stock.

	NIB	EXC.	V.G.	GOOD	FAIR	POOR
	—	675	550	350	150	100

Grade C
More deluxe version, with engraving. Fancier wood.

	NIB	EXC.	V.G.	GOOD	FAIR	POOR
	—	1150	850	550	275	125

Grade D
Variation has Damascus barrel. Greatest amount of engraving.

	NIB	EXC.	V.G.	GOOD	FAIR	POOR
	—	2100	1400	900	450	250

Model 16
Exactly the same as Model 1898, except chambered for 16-gauge only. Four grades are the same. Manufactured between 1903 and 1910.

Grade A

	NIB	EXC.	V.G.	GOOD	FAIR	POOR
	—	500	450	400	250	150

Grade B

	NIB	EXC.	V.G.	GOOD	FAIR	POOR
	—	650	550	400	200	100

Grade C

	NIB	EXC.	V.G.	GOOD	FAIR	POOR
	—	1100	850	500	300	150

Grade D

	NIB	EXC.	V.G.	GOOD	FAIR	POOR
	—	2000	1400	950	425	250

Model 17
An exposed-hammer gun, with a solid frame and straight-grip stock. Chambered for 12-gauge, with 30" or 32" barrel. Manufactured between 1906 and 1908.

	NIB	EXC.	V.G.	GOOD	FAIR	POOR
	—	525	450	275	150	75

Model 17 Brush Gun
Variation similar to standard Model 17, with 26" cylinder-bore barrel.

	NIB	EXC.	V.G.	GOOD	FAIR	POOR
	—	550	475	325	200	100

Model 17 Riot Gun
Variation has 20" cylinder-bore barrel.

	NIB	EXC.	V.G.	GOOD	FAIR	POOR
	—	600	525	325	150	125

Model 19
A takedown gun chambered for 12-gauge. Basically an improved and lightened version of Model 1898. Available in same four grades. Manufactured in 1906 and 1907.

Grade A

	NIB	EXC.	V.G.	GOOD	FAIR	POOR
	—	500	450	250	150	100

Grade B

	NIB	EXC.	V.G.	GOOD	FAIR	POOR
	—	600	550	500	350	225

Grade C

	NIB	EXC.	V.G.	GOOD	FAIR	POOR
	—	750	675	5550	425	300

Grade D

	NIB	EXC.	V.G.	GOOD	FAIR	POOR
	—	1850	1500	1050	400	200

Model 21 "Trap"
Basically same as Model 19, with straight-grip stock. 1907 catalog listed it as a Trap model. Manufactured in 1907 and 1908. Four grades similar to previous models.

Grade A

	NIB	EXC.	V.G.	GOOD	FAIR	POOR
	—	450	450	300	200	100

Grade B

	NIB	EXC.	V.G.	GOOD	FAIR	POOR
	—	600	550	350	200	100

Grade C

	NIB	EXC.	V.G.	GOOD	FAIR	POOR
	—	750	675	500	350	200

Grade D

	NIB	EXC.	V.G.	GOOD	FAIR	POOR
	—	1600	1300	1050	700	550

	NIB	EXC.	V.G.	GOOD	FAIR	POOR

Model 24

Actually an improved version of Model 21. Has pistol-grip stock and exposed hammer. Features automatic recoil lock on slide; matte rib barrel. Otherwise, quite similar to its predecessor. Manufactured between 1908 and 1917.

Grade A

	NIB	EXC.	V.G.	GOOD	FAIR	POOR
—	475	400	350	150	100	

Grade B

—	600	550	450	350	225	

Grade C

—	750	675	550	425	300	

Grade D

—	1600	1300	900	600	400	

Marlin "Trap Gun"

Unique in it has no numerical designation and simply known as "Trap Gun". A takedown gun, with interchangeable barrels from 16" to 32". Straight-grip buttstock, Quite similar in appearance to Model 24. Manufactured between 1909 and 1912.

—	1000	700	525	350	200	

Model 26

Similar to Model 24 Grade A, with solid frame. 30" or 32" barrels.

—	525	450	325	125	100	

Model 26 Brush Gun

Model has 26" cylinder-bored barrel.

—	550	475	325	200	100	

Model 26 Riot Gun

Variation has 20" cylinder-bored barrel.

—	600	525	325	150	125	

Model 28 Hammerless

Model was first of the Marlin hammerless shotguns. A takedown 12-gauge, with barrels from 26" to 32" in length. Stock has pistol-grip. Comes in four grades like its predecessors. Manufactured between 1913 and 1922.

Grade A

—	400	335	200	100	70	

Grade B

—	600	550	350	350	225	

Grade C

—	750	625	550	425	300	

Grade D

—	1700	1200	800	600	300	

Model 28TS Trap Gun

Variation same as Model 28, with 30" Full choke barrel. Matte rib and high-comb straight-grip stock. Manufactured in 1915.

—	725	600	525	425	300	

Model 28T Trap Gun

Variation is deluxe model similar to Model 28TS, with engraving, high-grade walnut and hand checkering. Manufactured in 1915.

—	750	625	550	425	300	

Model 30

Improved version of Model 16, 16-gauge shotgun. Features similar, with addition of improved takedown system and automatic recoil lock on slide. Manufactured between 1910 and 1914.

Grade A

—	550	475	350	200	100	

Grade B

—	600	550	450	200	100	

	NIB	EXC.	V.G.	GOOD	FAIR	POOR

Grade C

	—	750	675	550	250	150

Grade D

	—	1400	1200	1000	700	550

Model 30 Field Grade

Similar to Model 30 Grade B, with 25" modified-choke barrel. Straight-grip stock. Manufactured in 1913 and 1914.

	—	450	375	250	150	100

Model 31

Smaller version of Model 28 Hammerless takedown. Chambered for 16- and 20-gauge. Barrel lengths 26" and 28". Available in usual four grades. Various different chokes. Manufactured between 1915 and 1922.

Grade A

	—	500	450	350	150	100

Grade B

	—	600	550	450	250	150

Grade C

	—	750	675	550	300	150

Grade D

	—	1400	1200	1000	600	300

Model 42/42A

Originally listed as Model 42, but in the second year of production, designation was changed to /42A for no apparent reason than standardization of models. Similar to Model 24, except barrel markings are different. Still an exposed hammer takedown gun chambered for 12-gauge. Manufactured between 1922 and 1933.

	—	375	325	200	150	100

Model 43A

Hammerless model quite similar to Model 28, with different markings and less attention to finishing detail. Manufactured between 1923 and 1930.

	—	400	350	250	150	75

Model 43T

Same as Model 43A takedown hammerless, with 30" or 32" matte rib barrel. Straight-grip stock is of high grade walnut, with non-gloss oil finish. Fitted recoil paid. Manufactured between 1922 and 1930.

	—	500	450	350	200	100

Model 43TS

Custom-order version of Model 43T. Same in all respects, except stock could be ordered to any specifications shooter desired. Manufactured between 1922 and 1930.

	—	700	625	550	250	150

Model 44A

Similar to Model 31. Advertised as its successor. Hammerless takedown chambered for 20-gauge. Features improved bolt opening device located in trigger guard area instead of at the top of receiver. Shorter 4-shot magazine tube. Manufactured from 1922 until 1933.

	—	475	400	275	150	100

Model 44S

Similar to Model 44A, with higher grade walnut stock. Featured hand-cut checkering.

	—	500	425	300	200	100

Model 49

12-gauge exposed-hammer takedown. Combines features of Model 42 and Model 24. Basically a lower-priced model that was never listed in Marlin catalog. Model was part of Frank Kenna's money-raising program—anyone who purchased four shares of stock for $25 per share was given one, free of charge. Manufactured between 1925 and 1928.

	—	700	625	550	250	150

	NIB	EXC.	V.G.	GOOD	FAIR	POOR

Model 53

Hammerless takedown 12-gauge that was not in production for long. Theorized that Model 53 was produced to use up old parts on hand when Model 43 was introduced. Manufactured in 1929 and 1980.

	NIB	EXC.	V.G.	GOOD	FAIR	POOR
	—	450	400	275	175	125

Model 63

Last of the slide-action shotguns produced by Marlin until Model 120 in 1971. Hammerless takedown 12-gauge. Replaced Model 43A in Marlin catalog. Had improvements over earlier guns, but its introduction during Depression did little to bolster sales. Model offered free of charge to anyone purchasing four shares of Marlin stock at $25 per share. Manufactured between 1931 and 1933.

	NIB	EXC.	V.G.	GOOD	FAIR	POOR
	—	500	450	350	200	100

Model 63T

Trap-grade version of Model 63. Has better grade hand-checkered stock. Fitted recoil pad and oil finish. Manufactured between 1931 and 1933.

	NIB	EXC.	V.G.	GOOD	FAIR	POOR
	—	600	525	450	200	125

Model 63TS

Variation same as Model 63T, except stock dimensions were custom-made to customer's specifications. Manufactured between 1931 and 1933.

	NIB	EXC.	V.G.	GOOD	FAIR	POOR
	—	700	625	550	250	150

Premier Mark I

Made by Manufrance and called LaSalle. Marlin was able to purchase them without barrels at a good enough price for them to barrel and market them under their own name. This model is 12-gauge only. Alloy receiver and seven interchangeable barrels in 26" to 30" lengths. Various chokes. Plain stock is French walnut. Biggest problem with this gun is that the light weight (6 lbs.) produced severe recoil and less than enjoyable to shoot. In production from 1959 through 1963, with approximately 13,700 sold.

	NIB	EXC.	V.G.	GOOD	FAIR	POOR
	—	325	225	175	150	100

Premier Mark II

Similar to Mark I, with light engraving. Checkered stock.

	NIB	EXC.	V.G.	GOOD	FAIR	POOR
	—	325	225	175	150	100

Premier Mark IV

Similar to Mark II, with more engraving on receiver. **NOTE:** Add 10 percent for vent rib.

	NIB	EXC.	V.G.	GOOD	FAIR	POOR
	—	325	225	175	150	100

Model 120

Model styled to resemble Winchester Model 12. Advertised as an all steel and walnut shotgun. Offered with interchangeable barrels from 26" to 40". Various chokes were available. Checkered stock walnut, with fitted recoil pad. Tube magazine holds 5 shots, 4 in 3". Trap Model available (1973-1975); slug gun (1974-1984). Manufactured between 1971 and 1985. A really nice gun, if a bit heavy. **NOTE:** Add 10 percent for 36" "Long Tom" barrel.

	NIB	EXC.	V.G.	GOOD	FAIR	POOR
	—	350	300	250	150	125

Model 778 (Glenfield)

Similar to Model 120, with walnut finished hardwood stock instead of walnut. Glenfield name stamped on it. Manufactured between 1979 and 1984.

	NIB	EXC.	V.G.	GOOD	FAIR	POOR
	—	275	225	175	125	100

MARLIN OVER/UNDER & TOP-BREAK SHOTGUNS

Model 60 Single-Barrel Shotgun

Break-open exposed-hammer top lever-opening 12-gauge, with 30" or 32" full-choke barrel. Pistol-grip stock. Approximately 60 manufactured in 1923.

	NIB	EXC.	V.G.	GOOD	FAIR	POOR
		400	350	250	150	75

Model 90 Over/Under Shotgun

Produced in response to a request from Sears Roebuck, that Marlin should manufacture an over/under shotgun for Sears to market in their stores. Guns produced for Sears have prefix 103 in their serial numbers and marked "Ranger" before WWII and "J.C. Higgins" after the war. Prior to 1945, they were not marked Marlin; after that date Sears requested that the company stamp their name on the guns. They were also produced as Marlin Model 90 during the same period. Chambered for 12-, 16- and 20-gauge, as well as .410 bore. The 16- and 20-gauge guns first offered in 1937, with 26" or

28" barrels. In 1939, .410 bore was first offered with 26" barrel and 3" chambers. Barrels are 26", 28" or 30", with various chokes. Action is boxlock with extractors. Guns made prior to 1950 were solid between the barrels; after that date there was a space between barrels. Can be found with double-/ single triggers and checkered walnut stock. Ventilated rib offered as an option beginning in 1949. Be aware that this model was also available as a combination gun in .22 LR/.410, .22 Hornet/.410 and .218 Bee/.410. Approximately 34,000 Model 90s manufactured between 1937 and 1963. **NOTE:** Add 33 percent Single trigger; 25 percent 20-gauge; 300 percent .410 bores; 300 percent premium combination guns. There are other rare gauge and barrel combinations that may affect value.

—	550	425	350	275	200

MARLIN LEVER-ACTION SHOTGUNS

Model .410 Lever-Action Shotgun (Original)

Unique venture for Marlin Company—a lever-action shotgun based on Model 1893 action. Longer loading port, modified tube magazine that held 5 shots and smoothbore barrel chambered for .410 shot shell. Finish blued, with walnut pistol-grip stock and grooved beavertail fore-end. Hard rubber rifle-type buttplate. Available with 22" or 26" full-choke barrel. This gun was also part of the stock purchase plan and was given free of charge to anyone purchasing four shares at $25 per share. Also cataloged for sale. Manufactured between 1929 and 1932.

—	1600	1000	650	500	200

Model .410 Deluxe (Original)

Variation was never cataloged. Essentially same as standard version, with hand-checkered stock. Fore-end does not have grooves as found on standard model. Be wary of fakes!

—	2200	1200	800	400	200

Model .410 (New)

Lever-action shotgun chambered for 2.5" .410 shot shell. Checkered walnut stock, fluorescent front sight. Based on Model 336 action. Discontinued.

700	625	550	450	300	—

Model 410XLR 410 XLR

New in 2009. Latest Marlin .410 shotgun. Built on M1895 chassis. Chambered for 2.5" .410 shot shells. Receiver and barrel stainless. Stock laminated wood.

750	675	575	450	300	—

MARLIN BOLT-ACTION SHOTGUNS

Model 50DL

Bolt-action 12-gauge shotgun. Available with 28" modified barrel, black synthetic stock. Ventilated recoil pad standard. Brass bead front sight. Weight about 7.5 lbs.

300	275	225	150	125	100

Model 55

Chambered for 12-, 16- and 20-gauge, with full or adjustable choke. Barrels 26" or 28". Bolt-action, with 2-shot box magazine. Pistol-grip stock is plain. Manufactured between 1950 and 1965.

—	225	175	100	50	25

Model 55 Swamp Gun

Simply Model 55, with 3" Magnum, 20" barrel. Adjustable choke. Manufactured between 1963 and 1965.

—	300	250	175	75	50

Model 55 Goose Gun

Model 55, with 3" chamber, 36" Full choke 12-gauge barrel. Recoil pad and sling. Introduced in 1962.

375	250	175	150	75	50

Model 55S Slug Gun

Model 55, with 24" cylinder-bore barrel. Rifle sights. Manufactured between 1974 and 1983.

—	250	200	150	100	50

Model 5510 Goose Gun

Chambered for 3.5" 10-gauge. Has 34" Full choke barrel. Recoil pad and sling. Manufactured between 1976 and 1985.

—	400	300	250	175	100

	NIB	EXC.	V.G.	GOOD	FAIR	POOR

Model 55GDL

Bolt-action shotgun fitted with 36" full choke barrel. Reinforced black synthetic stock. Magazine holds two rounds. Ventilated recoil pad standard. First introduced in 1997. Weight about 8 lbs. Discontinued.

| 350 | 325 | 275 | 200 | 150 | 100 |

Model 512 Slugmaster

Introduced in 1994. Bolt-action shotgun features rifled 21" barrel. Equipped with two-shot detachable magazine. Ventilated recoil pad. Special scope also provided. Weight about 8 lbs. Discontinued.

| 350 | 325 | 275 | 200 | 150 | 100 |

Model 512DL Slugmaster

Introduced in 1997. Bolt-action features black synthetic stock, with fully rifled 21" barrel. Chambered for 12-gauge shell. A two-round magazine is standard. Adjustable rear sight, with ramp front sight. In 1998, furnished with "Fire Sights". Receiver drilled and tapped for scope mount. Weight about 8 lbs. Discontinued.

| 395 | 250 | 200 | 150 | 125 | 100 |

Model 512P

Introduced in 1999. Similar to Model 512 DL, with addition of 21" fully rifled and ported barrel. Fire sights standard. Weight about 8 lbs. Discontinued.

| 395 | 250 | 200 | 150 | 125 | 100 |

Model 25MG

Bolt-action .22 Win. Magnum shot shell only. Fitted with 22" smoothbore barrel. Has 7-round magazine. Hardwood stock. Weight about 6 lbs. First introduced in 1999.

| 225 | 175 | 145 | 125 | 100 | 75 |

MODERN L.C. SMITH SHOTGUNS

Modern line of L.C. Smith shotguns made in Europe. Imported into USA under Marlin name from 2005 to 2009.

Model LC410-DB

Side-by-side .410 bore, with fleur-de-lis checkered walnut stock, single selective trigger, selective automatic ejectors, three choke tubes (IC, M, F) and 26" chrome-lined barrels, with solid rib and bead front sight. Case-colored receiver has gold game bird embossed on side and bottom.

| 1800 | 1750 | 1400 | 900 | 600 | 300 |

Model LC28-DB

Similar to above in 28-gauge.

| 1900 | 1850 | 1500 | 1000 | 750 | 300 |

Model LC12-DB

12-gauge double barrel features 3" chambers, single trigger, selective automatic ejectors, three choke tubes (IC, M, F), 28" barrels, with solid rib and bead front sight. Walnut stock checkered. Has fluted comb, beavertail forearm and recoil pad. Case-coloring on receiver and side plates.

| 1400 | 1275 | 875 | 700 | 350 | 200 |

Model LC20-DB

Similar to above in 20-gauge.

| 1600 | 1500 | 1100 | 800 | 400 | 200 |

Model LC12-OU

Over/under features 3" chambers, single selective trigger, selective automatic ejectors, automatic safety, three choke tubes (IC, M, F), 28" barrels, with ventilated rib and bead front sight. Checkered walnut stock, with fluted comb. Recoil pad. Case-coloring on receiver and sideplates.

| 950 | 825 | 600 | 450 | 300 | 200 |

Model LC20-OU

Similar to above in 20-gauge.

| 950 | 825 | 600 | 450 | 300 | 200 |

MARLIN MODERN MUZZLE-LOADERS

Model MLS-50/54

Marlin in-line muzzle-loaders were introduced in 1997. They are stainless steel. Available in .50- or .54-caliber. Barrel 22" long. Adjustable Marble rear sight, ramp front sight with brass bead.

	NIB	EXC.	V.G.	GOOD	FAIR	POOR

Drilled and tapped for scope mount. Black synthetic stock, with molded checkering. Weight about 7 lbs. Discontinued. Not particularly easy to take down for cleaning.

NIB	EXC.	V.G.	GOOD	FAIR	POOR
300	225	200	150	75	50

MAROCCHI ARMI
Brescia, Italy

Model 2000

12-gauge Magnum single-shot, with 28" barrel, exposed hammer and automatic ejector. Blued, with walnut stock.

NIB	EXC.	V.G.	GOOD	FAIR	POOR
—	100	80	65	50	35

Field Master I

12-gauge over/under, with 26" or 28" ventilated rib barrels fitted for choke tubes, single trigger and automatic ejectors. Blued, French case hardened, with walnut stock.

NIB	EXC.	V.G.	GOOD	FAIR	POOR
—	500	395	300	200	150

Field Master II

As above, with single-selective trigger.

NIB	EXC.	V.G.	GOOD	FAIR	POOR
—	525	450	350	225	175

CONQUISTA SERIES

Grade I is standard grade, with special polished steel finish and machined engraved. Stock and forearm are select walnut, with hand checkered 20 lpi. Grade II has roll engraved game scenes. Stock is select figured walnut. Grade III is hand engraved by a master engraver featuring game scenes. Finely figured walnut stock.

Sporting Clays Model

Offered in 12-gauge, with 28", 30" or 32" ventilated rib barrels. Screw in chokes are standard. Adjustable trigger. Weight about 8 lbs.

Grade I

NIB	EXC.	V.G.	GOOD	FAIR	POOR
1950	1700	1175	850	600	300

Grade II

NIB	EXC.	V.G.	GOOD	FAIR	POOR
2350	1900	1475	950	700	350

Grade III

NIB	EXC.	V.G.	GOOD	FAIR	POOR
3350	2850	1825	1150	800	400

Sporting Light—Grade I

Same as above, but slightly smaller dimensions. Available in 28" or 30" barrel length. Weight about 7.5 lbs.

NIB	EXC.	V.G.	GOOD	FAIR	POOR
2050	1700	1175	850	600	300

Sporting Clays Left-Hand Model—Grade I

Same as Sporting Clays Model. Designed for left-handed shooter.

NIB	EXC.	V.G.	GOOD	FAIR	POOR
2150	1700	1175	850	600	300

Lady Sport Model

Offered in 12-gauge only, with 28" or 30" vent rib barrels. Slightly smaller dimensions for women. Weight 7.75 lbs.

Grade I

NIB	EXC.	V.G.	GOOD	FAIR	POOR
2150	1700	1175	850	600	300

Spectrum Grade—Colored Frame

NIB	EXC.	V.G.	GOOD	FAIR	POOR
2100	1750	1200	850	600	300

Lady Sport Left-Handed

Same as above for left-handed shooters.

Grade I

NIB	EXC.	V.G.	GOOD	FAIR	POOR
2100	1750	1200	850	600	300

Spectrum Grade

NIB	EXC.	V.G.	GOOD	FAIR	POOR
2175	1800	1225	850	600	300

	NIB	EXC.	V.G.	GOOD	FAIR	POOR

Trap Model

Built for competition shooter. Features 30" or 32" vent rib barrels. Trap dimension stock. Weight about 8.25 lbs.

Grade I

NIB	EXC.	V.G.	GOOD	FAIR	POOR
2025	1750	1200	850	600	300

Grade II

NIB	EXC.	V.G.	GOOD	FAIR	POOR
2400	1950	1500	1000	750	350

Grade III

NIB	EXC.	V.G.	GOOD	FAIR	POOR
3400	2700	18900	1500	800	400

Skeet Model

Designed for competition shooter. Only 28" vent rib barrel offered as standard. Skeet dimension stock. Skeet chokes. Weight about 7.75 lbs.

Grade I

NIB	EXC.	V.G.	GOOD	FAIR	POOR
2025	1750	1200	850	600	300

Grade II

NIB	EXC.	V.G.	GOOD	FAIR	POOR
2425	1950	1525	1000	750	350

Grade III

NIB	EXC.	V.G.	GOOD	FAIR	POOR
3400	2700	1900	1500	800	400

Classic Doubles Model 92

Offered in 12-gauge only, with 30" vent rib barrels. Adjustable trigger. Walnut stock, with 18 lpi checkering. Weight about 8.12 lbs.

NIB	EXC.	V.G.	GOOD	FAIR	POOR
1650	1350	875	600	500	250

Model 99—Grade I

Over/under gun. Features silver-grayed receiver; boxlock action, with single-selective trigger; pistol-grip stock; schnabel forearm. Sporting models offered with 28", 30" or 32" barrels; trap with 30" or 32" barrels; skeet with 28" or 30" barrels. All barrels supplied with five extended choke tubes.

NIB	EXC.	V.G.	GOOD	FAIR	POOR
3125	2350	1800	750	700	300

Model 99—Grade III

Model has all above features in addition to five flush-mounted choke tubes. Silver game scene engraved receiver.

NIB	EXC.	V.G.	GOOD	FAIR	POOR
5200	3400	2200	950	800	300

MARS

See—Gabbet-Fairfax or Bergmann

MARSTON, S.W.

New York, New York

Double-Action Pepperbox

.31-caliber double-action percussion pepperbox, with 5" barrel group and ring trigger. Blued, with walnut grips. Manufactured between 1850 and 1855.

NIB	EXC.	V.G.	GOOD	FAIR	POOR
—	—	2000	1125	600	250

2-Barrel Pistol

.31- or .36-caliber revolving barrel 2-shot pistol, with ring trigger. Barrel marked "J.Cohn & S.W.Marston-New York". Blued brass frame, with walnut grips. Manufactured during 1850s.

NIB	EXC.	V.G.	GOOD	FAIR	POOR
—	—	2700	1250	450	200

MARSTON, W. W. & CO.

New York, New York

W.W. Marston & Company manufactured a variety of firearms, some of which are marked only with trade names: Union Arms Company, Phoenix Armory, Western Arms Company, Washington Arms Company, Sprague and Marston and Marston and Knox.

Double-Action Single-Shot Pistol

.31- or .36-caliber bar hammer percussion pistol, with 2.5" or 5" half octagonal barrel. Blued, with walnut grips. Manufactured during 1850s.

NIB	EXC.	V.G.	GOOD	FAIR	POOR
—	—	650	325	150	100

	NIB	EXC.	V.G.	GOOD	FAIR	POOR

Pocket Revolver

.31-caliber percussion revolver, with 3.25" to 7.5" barrel and 6-shot cylinder. Blued, with walnut grips. Approximately 13,000 manufactured between 1857 and 1862.

	NIB	EXC.	V.G.	GOOD	FAIR	POOR
	—	—	1250	550	200	125

Navy Revolver

.36-caliber percussion revolver, with 7.5" or 8.5" octagonal barrel and 6-shot cylinder. Blued, with walnut grips. Manufactured between 1857 and 1862.

	NIB	EXC.	V.G.	GOOD	FAIR	POOR
	—	—	3100	1400	600	200

Single-Action Pistol

.31- or .36-caliber percussion pistol, with 4" or 6" barrel. Blued, with walnut grips. Manufactured during 1860s.

	NIB	EXC.	V.G.	GOOD	FAIR	POOR
	—	—	675	580	250	100

Breech-Loading Pistol

.36-caliber breech loading percussion pistol, with 4" to 8.5" half octagonal barrel. Brass or iron frame. Blued case hardened, with walnut grips. Approximately 1,000 manufactured in 1850s.

Brass Frame

	NIB	EXC.	V.G.	GOOD	FAIR	POOR
	—	—	4400	3600	1650	500

Iron Frame

	NIB	EXC.	V.G.	GOOD	FAIR	POOR
	—	—	3900	3000	1100	300

Double-Action Pepperbox

.31-caliber double-action 6-shot percussion pepperbox, with 4" or 5" barrel groups. Bar hammer. Blued case hardened, with walnut grips. Manufactured during 1850s.

	NIB	EXC.	V.G.	GOOD	FAIR	POOR
	—	—	3200	2500	1150	300

3-Barrel Derringer

.22-caliber 3-barreled spur-trigger pocket pistol, with sliding knife blade mounted on left side of 3" barrel group. Blued silver-plated, with walnut grips. Barrel marked "Wm. W. Marston/New York City". Approximately 1,500 manufactured between 1858 and 1864.

Knife Blade Model

	NIB	EXC.	V.G.	GOOD	FAIR	POOR
	—	—	5575	4100	1650	400

Without Knife

	NIB	EXC.	V.G.	GOOD	FAIR	POOR
	—	—	2550	2000	775	200

3-Barrel Derringer .32 Caliber

Similar to above in .32-caliber, with 3" or 4" barrels. Not fitted with knife blade. Approximately 3,000 manufactured between 1864 and 1872.

	NIB	EXC.	V.G.	GOOD	FAIR	POOR
	—	—	3750	3000	825	200

MASQUELIER, S. A.
Liege, Belgium

Carpathe

.243, .270, .7x57mm, 7x65Rmm or .30-06 caliber single-shot rifle, with 24" barrel, adjustable trigger and sights. Blued, with engraved receiver. Walnut stock. Imported until 1986.

	NIB	EXC.	V.G.	GOOD	FAIR	POOR
	—	3750	2950	1950	1250	750

Express

.270, .30-06, 8x57JRSmm or 9.3x74Rmm caliber over/under double-barrel rifle, with 24" barrels, single-selective trigger and automatic ejectors. Blued engraved, with walnut stock. Not imported after 1986.

	NIB	EXC.	V.G.	GOOD	FAIR	POOR
	—	3800	2950	1950	1250	750

Ardennes

As above, but made on custom order only. Discontinued in 1986.

	NIB	EXC.	V.G.	GOOD	FAIR	POOR
	—	8000	6000	3750	2500	1000

Boxlock Side-by-Side Shotgun

12-gauge boxlock double-barrel shotgun. Manufactured in a variety of barrel lengths, with single-selective trigger and automatic ejectors. Blued, with walnut stock. Imported prior to 1987.

	NIB	EXC.	V.G.	GOOD	FAIR	POOR
	—	4750	3500	2500	1500	850

	NIB	EXC.	V.G.	GOOD	FAIR	POOR

Sidelock Side-by-Side Shotgun

Similar to above, with detachable sidelocks. Finely engraved. Imported prior to 1987.

	NIB	EXC.	V.G.	GOOD	FAIR	POOR
	—	14500	11750	7000	5000	1750

MASSACHUSETTS ARMS CO.
Chicopee Falls, Massachusetts

Wesson & Leavitt Dragoon

.40-caliber percussion revolver, with 7" round barrel, 6-shot cylinder and side-mounted hammer. Blued case hardened, with walnut grips. Approximately 800 manufactured in 1850 and 1851.

Early Model with 6" Barrel

Approximately 30 made.

	NIB	EXC.	V.G.	GOOD	FAIR	POOR
	—	—	8500	6600	275	750

Fully Marked 7" Barrel Standard Model

	NIB	EXC.	V.G.	GOOD	FAIR	POOR
	—	—	8000	6050	2200	650

Wesson & Leavitt Belt Revolver

.31-caliber percussion revolver, with 3" to 7" round barrel and 6-shot cylinder. Similar in appearance to above. Approximately 1,000 manufactured in 1850 and 1851.

	NIB	EXC.	V.G.	GOOD	FAIR	POOR
	—	—	3000	1900	775	250

Maynard Primed Belt Revolver

Similar to above, with Maynard tape primer. Approximately 1,000 manufactured between 1851 and 1857.

	NIB	EXC.	V.G.	GOOD	FAIR	POOR
	—	—	3700	2750	880	250

Maynard Primed Pocket Revolver

Similar to above in .28- or .30-caliber, with 2.5" to 3.5" octagonal or round barrels. Approximately 3,000 made between 1851 and 1860.

	NIB	EXC.	V.G.	GOOD	FAIR	POOR
	—	—	1950	1400	625	200

Adams Patent Navy Revolver

As above in .36-caliber, with 6" octagonal barrel. Approximately 600 of the 1,000 made were purchased by U.S. government. **NOTE:** Those bearing inspection marks will bring approximately a 20 percent premium over values listed.

	NIB	EXC.	V.G.	GOOD	FAIR	POOR
	—	—	3750	2500	825	300

Single-Shot Pocket Pistol

.31-caliber single-shot percussion pistol, with 2.5" to 3.5" half octagonal barrel. Maynard tape primer. Barrel marked "Mass. Arms Co/Chicopee Falls" and primer door "Maynard's Patent Sept. 22, 1845". Blued case hardened, with walnut grips. Manufactured in 1850s.

	NIB	EXC.	V.G.	GOOD	FAIR	POOR
	—	—	4000	2750	925	300

MAYNARD CARBINE

Single-shot breechloader chambered for .35- or .50-caliber percussion. Barrel round and 20" in length. Trigger guard is a lever that pivots barrel in break-open fashion when lowered. Finish blued, with case colored frame. Buttstock is walnut and there is no fore-end. This carbine was designed by same Maynard who invented the tape primer system. There are two models—a 1st and 2nd. They were made for both sporting use and as a U.S. Martial carbine. 2nd Model was used considerably during Civil War.

1st Model

Model marked "Maynard Patentee/May 27, 1851/June 17, 1856". Has iron patchbox; curved buttplate; Maynard tape primer system; tang sight. Later production fitted with a sling swivel. Approximately 400 of these carbines are U.S. marked. Total manufactured in late 1850s is unknown.

U.S. Martially Marked

	NIB	EXC.	V.G.	GOOD	FAIR	POOR
	—	—	6500	4050	2000	700

Commercial Model

	NIB	EXC.	V.G.	GOOD	FAIR	POOR
	—	—	4000	3000	1250	400

2nd Model

Chambered for .50-caliber only. Does not have tape primer system or tang sight. There is no patchbox. Buttplate is not as curved as on 1st Model. Marked "Manufactured By/Mass. Arms Co./Chicopee Falls". Approximately 20,000 manufactured between 1860 and 1865. Used by

	NIB	EXC.	V.G.	GOOD	FAIR	POOR

Union forces during Civil War.

	—	—	2500	2050	700	500

Maynard Patent Sporting Rifle

Sporting rifles bearing designations Model 1865, 1873 and 1882 were manufactured in a wide variety of calibers, gauges, stock styles, finishes and options.

—	—	2500	1650	660	200

MATEBA ARMS
Italy

AutoRevolver

Introduced in 2000. Chambered for .357 Magnum or .44 Magnum, with 4", 6" or 8" barrel. Features single-action trigger that has a reciprocating cylinder that fires from bottom chamber rather than top. Firing of the gun cocks hammer and cycles action for next round. Available with or without compensator. Offered in blue or nickel finish. Extra barrels available. Distributed in USA by American Western Arms (AWA). **NOTE:** Guns without compensator deduct $80. Nickel finish add $50. Extra barrel add $140.

1600	1100	900	600	400	200

AutoRevolver Carbine

Similar in principle to a handgun, with 16" or 18" barrel. Walnut buttstock, pistol-grip and fore-end.

1800	1300	1000	700	500	300

MATRA MANURHIN DEFENSE
Mulhouse, France
See—Manurhin

MAUNZ MFG., INC.
Maumee, Ohio

Manufacturer (1970s-1980s) of high-end law enforcement and competition rifles based primarily on M14 military rifle.

Model 77 Service Match Rifle

Semi-automatic rifle chambered in .308 Winchester. Other chamberings on custom order. 22" barrel standard; medium and heavy barrels available. Charcoal gray parkerized finish. Custom rifles had heavyweight Kevlar or graphite/fiberglass stocks covered in black gelcoat. Red/white/blue stocks were also produced. 300 produced.

—	2500	2250	2000	1850	1500

Model 87 Maunz Match Rifle

Semi-automatic rifle chambered in .308 Winchester and 6.30 Maunz; Limited .338 and .45 Maunz chamberings on custom order. Sold only to Master competitors and American Shooters Union members.

—	2500	2200	2000	1500	1200

Model 57 M1A

Semi-automatic rifle chambered in .30-06, .276 and .308 Winchester. Also .45 Maunz (rare). M1 Garand receiver, with M14 parts and National Match barrels. Custom-built glass-bedded stock. Approximately 200 made.

—	1500	1250	1000	800	600

Model 67 Match Grade for Practice

Semi-automatic rifle chambered in .308 Winchester, 6.30 Maunz and .45 Maunz. Camp Perry stamped. Not allowed for Service Rifle competition. Combination of M1 Garand and M14 parts. Approximately 250 made.

—	2000	1800	1500	1200	1500

MAUSER WERKE

Established in 1869 by Peter and Wilhelm Mauser, this company came under effective control of Ludwig Loewe and Company of Berlin in 1887. In 1896, latter company was reorganized under name Deutsches Waffen und Munitionor as it is better known, DWM. **NOTE:** Historical information, technical details, photos and prices see EARLY MODEL 98 SPORTING RIFLES

Wide variety of commercial Model 98 Sporting Rifles were made. Most of which had 23.5" ribbed barrels, open sights, 5-shot magazines, single-/double set triggers and full or semi-pistol grip

	NIB	EXC.	V.G.	GOOD	FAIR	POOR

stocks. **NOTE:** Values listed are representative.

Type A—Short Action

	—	6000	5200	3300	1850	700

Type A—Medium Action

	—	5000	4000	3000	1600	700

Type A—Long Action

	—	6000	5200	3300	1850	700

Type B

	—	4800	3500	2300	1400	500

Type K

	—	7500	6500	4000	2000	700

Type M

	—	4500	3900	3300	1850	700

Type S

	—	4500	3900	3300	1850	700

MODEL 1896 BROOMHANDLE MAUSER PISTOL

Manufactured from 1896 to 1939. Model 1896 Pistol was produced in a wide variety of styles as listed. It is recommended that those considering purchase of any models listed should consult Breathed & Schroeders's System Mauser (Chicago 1967) as it provides detailed descriptions and photographs of various models. **NOTE:** Prices listed are for pistol only. A correct matching stock/holster will add approximately 40 percent to value of each category. Non-matching stock/holster will add $350 and $600 to prices.

"BUYER BEWARE" ALERT by Gale Morgan: I have personally seen English Crest, U.S. Great Seal, unheard-of European dealers, aristocratic Coats-of-Arms and Middle East Medallions beautifully photo-etched into magazine wells and rear panels of some really common wartime commercials, with price tags that have been elevated to $2,500 plus. They are quite eye-catching and if they are sold as customized/modified Mausers, seller can price the piece at whatever the market will bear. However, if sold as a factory original—BUYER BEWARE.

Six-Shot Step-Barrel Cone Hammer

7.63mm semi-automatic pistol, with 5.5" barrel, fixed rear sight and checkered walnut grips. Marked "Ruecklauf Pistole System Mauser, Oberndorf am/Neckar 1896". Very few were manufactured. Too rare to price.

Twenty-Shot Step-Barrel Cone Hammer

As above, with 20-shot extended magazine and tangent rear sight. Engraved "system mauser" on top of chamber. Too rare to price.

System Mauser 10-Shot Cone Hammer

As above, with fixed or tangent rear sight. Step barrel (pictured) is very rare as is tapered barrel. Magazine capacity 10 rounds.

	—	25000	17000	12000	8000	7000

Six-Shot Standard Cone Hammer

Similar to above, with no step in barrel, 6-shot magazine and marked "Waffenfabrik Mauser, Oberndorf A/N" over the chamber. May have fixed or, rarely, tangent rear sight.

	—	15000	12000	6750	4500	3000

Twenty-Shot Cone Hammer

As above, with extended magazine holding 20 cartridges. May have panels or flat sides.

	—	40000	35000	20000	10000	7000

Standard Cone Hammer

As above, with 10-shot magazine and 23-groove grips. Price includes matching stocks.

	—	8000	5000	2000	1400	800

Fixed Sight Cone Hammer

Similar to standard Cone Hammer, except fixed integral sight is machined into barrel extension.

	—	8000	5500	3500	2000	1000

	NIB	EXC.	V.G.	GOOD	FAIR	POOR

Turkish Contract Cone Hammer

As above, but sight marked in Farsi and bearing crest of Sultan Abdul-Hamid II on frame. Approximately 1,000 were made.

	—	15000	12000	8500	5000	2000

Early Transitional Large Ring Hammer

Variation has same characteristics of "Standard Cone Hammer", except hammer has larger open ring.

	—	5500	4000	2500	1150	800

Model 1899 Flat Side—Italian Contract

Similar to above, with 5.5" barrel, adjustable rear sight and frame sides milled flat. Left flat of chamber marked with "DV" proof. Approximately 5,000 manufactured in 1899.

	—	6000	4000	2000	1200	900

Early Flat Side

Similar to above, except with "pinned" rear sight. Without Italian markings.

	—	5000	3500	2800	1000	750

Late Flat Side

Similar to above, with an integral pin mounted adjustable rear sight. Often marked with dealer's names such as "Von Lengerke & Detmold, New York".

	—	4000	3200	2000	1000	750

Flat Side Bolo

Similar to above, with 3.9" barrel, fixed sights. Checkered walnut grips. Very rare.

	—	7500	6000	4000	3000	2000

Early Large Ring Hammer Bolo

As above, with milled frame, adjustable rear sight. Grooved wood or hard rubber grips cast with a floral pattern. 10-shot magazine.

	—	4700	3700	2000	1500	1000

Shallow-Milled Panel Model

Full size. Similar to above, with 5.5" barrel. Either 23-groove walnut or checkered hard rubber grips. Shallow frame panels.

	—	3800	2700	1000	750	500

Deep-Milled Panel Model

As above, with deeper milled panels on sides of receiver.

	—	4500	3000	2000	1000	750

Late Large Ring Hammer Bolo

Similar to Early Large Ring Hammer Bolo, with late style adjustable rear sight.

	—	4000	3000	2000	1000	750

Six-Shot Large Ring Bolo

Similar to above Large Ring Bolo, with six-shot magazine. May be equipped with fixed or tangent sights.

	—	8900	6500	5000	3000	1800

Early Small Ring Hammer Model, Transitional

Model 96, with early long extractor, hammer with small-diameter hole and 5.5" barrel. Grips have 34 grooves.

	—	3200	2000	1500	1000	500

Early Small Ring Hammer Bolo Model

As above, with 3.9" barrel. Wood or hard rubber grips cast with a floral pattern. Serial numbers in 40,000 range.

	—	4500	3000	2000	1500	600

	NIB	EXC.	V.G.	GOOD	FAIR	POOR

Six-Shot Small Ring Hammer Model

As above, with 27-groove walnut grips.

	NIB	EXC.	V.G.	GOOD	FAIR	POOR
	—	8500	6500	3000	1800	1000

Standard Pre-war Commercial

Model 96, with 5.5" barrel, late-style adjustable rear sight and 34-groove walnut grips or checkered hard rubber grips. Often found with dealers markings such as "Von Lengerke & Detmold".

	NIB	EXC.	V.G.	GOOD	FAIR	POOR
	—	3500	2500	1200	650	300

9mm Export Model

As above in 9mm Mauser, with 34-groove walnut grips.

	NIB	EXC.	V.G.	GOOD	FAIR	POOR
	—	3750	2250	1500	1000	700

Mauser Banner Model

Standard pre-war features, except chamber stamped with Mauser Banner trademark and 32-groove walnut grips. Approximately 10,000 were manufactured.

	NIB	EXC.	V.G.	GOOD	FAIR	POOR
	—	4500	3200	2300	1100	600

Persian Contract

Persian rampant lion on left rear panel. Prospective purchasers should secure a qualified appraisal prior to acquisition. Serial numbers in 154000 range.

	NIB	EXC.	V.G.	GOOD	FAIR	POOR
	—	4700	4000	2700	1400	1000

Standard Wartime Commercial

Identical to pre-war Commercial Model 96, except it has 30-groove walnut grips. Rear of hammer stamped "NS" for new safety. Many also bear German or Austrian military acceptance proofs.

	NIB	EXC.	V.G.	GOOD	FAIR	POOR
	—	2500	1750	1000	500	350

9mm Parabellum Military Contract

As above in 9mm Parabellum caliber, with 24-groove grips. Stamped with large "9" filled with red paint. **NOTE:** Add 20 percent to full rig.

	NIB	EXC.	V.G.	GOOD	FAIR	POOR
	—	3500	2500	1000	700	450

1920 Rework

Model 96 modified to barrel length of 3.9" and in 7.63mm Mauser or 9mm Parabellum caliber. Often encountered with police markings.

	NIB	EXC.	V.G.	GOOD	FAIR	POOR
	—	1750	1000	500	400	350

Luger Barreled 1920 Rework

Similar to above. Fitted with Luger 4" barrel or a sighted Luger barrel-band, 12- or 23-groove walnut grips and 9mm caliber.

	NIB	EXC.	V.G.	GOOD	FAIR	POOR
	—	2500	1200	700	500	450

Early Post-war Bolo Model

Model 96 in 7.63mm caliber, with 3.9" barrel, adjustable rear sight and 22-groove walnut grips.

	NIB	EXC.	V.G.	GOOD	FAIR	POOR
	—	3000	2100	1000	400	200

Late Post-war Bolo Model

As above, with Mauser Banner trademark stamped on left rear panel.

	NIB	EXC.	V.G.	GOOD	FAIR	POOR
	—	3000	2000	1000	400	200

French Gendarme Model

Standard Model 96 fitted with 3.9" barrel. Checkered hard rubber grips. Although reputed to have been made under a French contract, no record of that has been found to date.

	NIB	EXC.	V.G.	GOOD	FAIR	POOR
	—	4500	3000	1000	600	350

Early Model 1930

7.63mm caliber Model 96, with 5.2" barrel, grooved side rails, 12-groove walnut grips and late-style safety. **NOTE:** Add 25 percent with correct stocks.

	NIB	EXC.	V.G.	GOOD	FAIR	POOR
	—	3000	2000	1700	800	500

	NIB	EXC.	V.G.	GOOD	FAIR	POOR

Late Model 1930

Similar to above, except for solid receiver rails.

	—	3500	2200	1700	800	400

Model 1930 Removable Magazine

Similar to above, with detachable magazine. Prospective purchasers should secure a qualified appraisal prior to acquisition. Too rare to price.

CARBINE MODELS

Cone Hammer Flat Side Carbine

7.63mm caliber carbine, with 11.75" barrel, early adjustable sight, flat frame and detachable buttstock. Barrel has a full length "rib". Prospective purchasers should secure a qualified appraisal prior to acquisition. Too rare to price. **NOTE:** Watch for fakes.

Large Ring Hammer Transitional Carbine

Similar to above, with milled frame panels. Prospective purchasers should secure a qualified appraisal prior to acquisition.

	—	25000	18000	11000	5000	3000

Large Ring Hammer Flatside Carbine

Similar to above, with 14.5" barrel. Prospective purchasers should secure a qualified appraisal prior to acquisition.

	—	23000	17000	10000	5000	3000

Small Ring Hammer Carbine

Similar to above, with hammer having a smaller diameter hole at its tip. Prospective purchasers should secure a qualified appraisal prior to acquisition. Some late carbines were chambered for 9mm export.

	—	21000	18000	15000	6000	4000

CHINESE COPIES

Chinese Marked, Handmade Copies

Crude copies of Model 96 and unsafe to fire.

	—	500	400	350	250	175

Taku-Naval Dockyard Model

Approximately 6,000 very good quality copies of Model 96 were made at Taku-Naval Dockyard. In several variations, both flat and paneled sides.

	—	3500	2000	1000	600	400

Shansei Arsenal Model

Approximately 8,000 Model 96 pistols were manufactured in .45 ACP caliber. Copies of Model 96 were made by Unceta (Astra) and Zulaica y Cia (Royal) and marketed by the firm of Beistegui Hermanos. These copies are covered in their own sections of this text. **NOTE:** Within past several years, a large quantity of Model 96 pistols exported to or made in China have been imported into United States. It has been reported that some newly made copies of Shansei .45 were recently exported from China. Proceed with caution.

	—	5000	3500	2250	1500	1300

MAUSER POCKET PISTOLS

Model 1910

6.35mm (.25 ACP) caliber pistol, with 3" barrel, 9-shot magazine. Checkered walnut or (scarce) hard rubber wraparound grip. Early examples (below serial 60,000 or so) have a pivoting takedown latch above trigger guard and are identified as "Sidelatch" models by collectors. Later production Models 1910s are often identified as Model 1910/14. Manufactured from 1910 to 1934.

Sidelatch Model

	—	1200	900	600	300	300

Later Production (Model 1910/14)

	—	550	300	200	150	100

Model 1914

Larger version of Model 1910. Chambered for 7.65mm Browning (.32 ACP), with 3.5" or (rarely) 4.5" barrel. Very early examples up to serial 2500 or so had a contoured hump on slide and are

	NIB	EXC.	V.G.	GOOD	FAIR	POOR

called "Humpbacks" by collectors; these bring a considerable premium. Model 1914s with police or military markings bring a small premium. Manufactured between 1914 and 1934.

Model 1914 "Humpback"

	NIB	EXC.	V.G.	GOOD	FAIR	POOR
	—	4000	3000	1750	800	400

Model 1914 (later)

	NIB	EXC.	V.G.	GOOD	FAIR	POOR
	—	475	300	200	150	100

Model 1912/14

While Mauser's pocket pistols were very successful on the commercial market, Mauser was also trying to develop a larger caliber pistol for military use. Most successful of these was Model 1912/14, though only about 200 were ever made. A few of these did reach commercial market and it's likely the pistol would have continued in production had WWI not broken out. Higher serial numbered guns were slotted for Model 1896-style holster stock. Few of these also had tangent sights. **NOTE:** Add 50 percent for shoulder stock.

	NIB	EXC.	V.G.	GOOD	FAIR	POOR
	—	31000	20000	11000	8000	4000

Model WTP I

Mauser's first post-WWI new design. First vest pocket pistol, with 2.5" barrel and 6-shot magazine. Grips were plastic wraparound, with one, two or three grip screws depending on production period. Production ended in late 1930s, when WTP II was introduced.

	NIB	EXC.	V.G.	GOOD	FAIR	POOR
	—	600	300	250	175	125

Model WTP II

WTP II was a much more compact design than its predecessor, with 2" barrel and separate grip panels instead of Mauser's usual wraparound grip. Production was limited by the outbreak of WWII, so WTP II is much scarcer than WTP I. Under French occupation, at least several hundred WTP II's were assembled and sold; these can be identified by their very low electric penciled serial numbers and lack of German proofing. Brings a slight premium over pre-war German manufactured pistols.

	NIB	EXC.	V.G.	GOOD	FAIR	POOR
	—	650	450	325	250	175

Model 1934

In response to competition from Walther and others, in 1934 Mauser spruced up its aging 1910/14 and 1914 pistols with a new high-polish finish and form-fitting swept back grips. Nickel finish was offered, but is very rare (50 percent premium, but beware of re-nickeled blued guns). The 7.65mm pistols became popular with both military and police, but those so marked can bring a considerable premium.

6.35mm

	NIB	EXC.	V.G.	GOOD	FAIR	POOR
	—	525	325	250	200	125

7.65mm Commercial

	NIB	EXC.	V.G.	GOOD	FAIR	POOR
	—	450	325	250	200	125

7.65mm Eagle L proofed

	NIB	EXC.	V.G.	GOOD	FAIR	POOR
	—	675	450	300	250	150

7.56mm Large Eagle over M (Navy)

	NIB	EXC.	V.G.	GOOD	FAIR	POOR
	—	1200	750	450	300	200

MODEL HSC

HSc was a totally new design. Chambered for 7.65mm Browning. Featuring double-action lockwork and partially concealed external hammer. Introduced just as WWII broke out. HSc was produced through the war for both commercial sale and military use. Serials started at 700,000 and first 1500 or so had grip screws located near bottom of grip and bring a large premium. Finish deteriorated as war progressed. Some HSc pistols were even produced under French occupation after the war ended. **NOTE:** Add 20 percent for Waffenamt markings; 50 percent for Navy marked front straps.

Low Grip Screw Model

As above, with screws that attach grip located near bottom of grip. Highly-polished blue checkered walnut grips. Early address without lines and has Eagle N proof. Some have been observed with Nazi Kreigsmarine markings. Approximately 2,000 were manufactured.

	NIB	EXC.	V.G.	GOOD	FAIR	POOR
	—	8000	5000	1800	750	650

Early Commercial Model

Highly polished blued finish, checkered walnut grips, standard Mauser address on slide and Eagle N proofmark. Floorplate of magazine stamped with Mauser Banner.

	NIB	EXC.	V.G.	GOOD	FAIR	POOR
	—	750	500	350	175	125

	NIB	EXC.	V.G.	GOOD	FAIR	POOR

Transition Model
As above, but not as highly finished.

	NIB	EXC.	V.G.	GOOD	FAIR	POOR
	—	525	400	300	150	100

Early Nazi Army Model

	NIB	EXC.	V.G.	GOOD	FAIR	POOR
	—	650	550	400	200	125

Late Nazi Army Model

	NIB	EXC.	V.G.	GOOD	FAIR	POOR
	—	450	375	250	150	100

Early Nazi Navy Model

	NIB	EXC.	V.G.	GOOD	FAIR	POOR
	—	1000	800	550	400	300

Wartime Nazi Navy Model

	NIB	EXC.	V.G.	GOOD	FAIR	POOR
	—	800	600	500	400	200

Early Nazi Police Model

	NIB	EXC.	V.G.	GOOD	FAIR	POOR
	—	600	500	425	250	175

Wartime Nazi Police Model

	NIB	EXC.	V.G.	GOOD	FAIR	POOR
	—	500	400	350	250	175

Wartime Commercial Model
As above, without acceptance markings on trigger guard.

	NIB	EXC.	V.G.	GOOD	FAIR	POOR
	—	425	350	300	200	125

French Manufactured Model
Blued or Parkerized, with walnut or plastic grips. Trigger guard marked on left side with monogram "MR".

	NIB	EXC.	V.G.	GOOD	FAIR	POOR
	—	375	275	225	150	100

Model HSc Post-war Production
In late 1960s, Mauser resumed production of HSc in both 7.65mm and 9mm Browning short (.380). Five thousand post-war HSc pistols were specially marked with an American eagle and bring a slight premium over standard marked pistols. In 1980s, Mauser licensed HSc production to Gamba in Italy, which produced an enlarged frame version of HSc, with a double-column magazine. In both German and Italian production, .380s bring about a 20 percent premium over .32s.

Mauser Production (.32)

	NIB	EXC.	V.G.	GOOD	FAIR	POOR
	—	525	450	300	175	125

Gamba Production
In recent years Mauser has licensed several firms other than Gamba to produce pistols bearing Mauser trademark, such as Browning Hi Power knockoff made in Hungary. In 1999, Mauser was bought by SIG-Sauer and a new large caliber Mauser pistol was announced.

	NIB	EXC.	V.G.	GOOD	FAIR	POOR
	—	600	475	325	200	100

MAUSER RIFLES—RECENT PRODUCTION

In February 1999, SIGARMS announced acquisition of Mauser line of small arms. Current production is in Isny, Germany. Some Mauser rifles were imported and distributed by SIGARMS and later Briley Manufacturing, located in Houston, Texas. Beginning in 2009, Mauser rifles are imported by Mauser USA, San Antonio, Texas.

Model 2000
.270, .308 or .30-06 caliber bolt-action rifle, with 24" barrel, open sights and 5-shot magazine. Blued, with checkered walnut stock. Manufactured between 1969 and 1971 by Heym.

	NIB	EXC.	V.G.	GOOD	FAIR	POOR
	—	600	450	300	200	150

Model 3000
As above, with 22" barrel, no sights and Monte Carlo-style stock. Manufactured from 1971 to 1974 by Heym.

	NIB	EXC.	V.G.	GOOD	FAIR	POOR
	—	600	450	300	200	150

Model 3000 Magnum
As above in 7mm Rem. Magnum, .300 Win. Magnum and .375 H&H Magnum caliber, with 26" barrel and 3-shot integral magazine. Blued, with checkered walnut stock. Produced by Heym.

	NIB	EXC.	V.G.	GOOD	FAIR	POOR
	—	675	525	375	250	200

	NIB	EXC.	V.G.	GOOD	FAIR	POOR

Model 4000

Similar to Model 3000 in .222- or .223-caliber, with folding open sights. Produced by Heym.

	NIB	EXC.	V.G.	GOOD	FAIR	POOR
	—	550	400	250	200	150

Model 225

.243 to. 300 Weatherby Magnum caliber bolt-action rifle, with 24" or 26" barrel, no sights, adjustable trigger and 3- or 5-shot magazine. Blued, with walnut stock.

	NIB	EXC.	V.G.	GOOD	FAIR	POOR
	1400	1250	1000	750	600	500

Model ES340

.22-caliber single-shot bolt-action rifle, with 25.5" barrel, open sights and walnut stock. Manufactured before WWII.

	NIB	EXC.	V.G.	GOOD	FAIR	POOR
	—	300	250	225	175	125

Model DSM34

Similar to above, with 25" barrel and full-length walnut stock. Manufactured prior to WWII.

	NIB	EXC.	V.G.	GOOD	FAIR	POOR
	—	325	275	250	200	150

Model MS420B

Similar to above, with 25" barrel and 5-shot magazine. Manufactured before WWII.

	NIB	EXC.	V.G.	GOOD	FAIR	POOR
	—	375	325	300	275	200

Model ES350

.22-caliber single-shot bolt-action rifle, with 27.5" barrel. Checkered pistol-grip walnut stock. Manufactured before WWII.

	NIB	EXC.	V.G.	GOOD	FAIR	POOR
	—	450	400	375	350	275

Model M410

Similar to above, with 23.5" barrel and 5-shot magazine. Manufactured before WWII.

	NIB	EXC.	V.G.	GOOD	FAIR	POOR
	—	375	325	300	275	200

Model M420

As above, with 25.5" barrel.

	NIB	EXC.	V.G.	GOOD	FAIR	POOR
	375	325	300	275	200	

Model EN310

.22-caliber single-shot bolt-action rifle, with 19.75" barrel, open sights and plain walnut stock. Manufactured before WWII.

	NIB	EXC.	V.G.	GOOD	FAIR	POOR
	—	250	225	200	150	100

Model EL320

As above, with 23.5" barrel. Checkered walnut stock.

	NIB	EXC.	V.G.	GOOD	FAIR	POOR
	—	275	250	225	175	125

Model KKW

.22-caliber single-shot bolt-action rifle, with 26" barrel, ladder rear sight and full-length walnut stock. Manufactured prior to WWII.

	NIB	EXC.	V.G.	GOOD	FAIR	POOR
	—	400	350	300	225	150

Model MS350B

.22-caliber bolt-action rifle, with 26.75" barrel, adjustable rear sight and 5-shot magazine. Blued, with walnut stock.

	NIB	EXC.	V.G.	GOOD	FAIR	POOR
	—	475	400	350	275	200

Model ES340B

Similar to above in single-shot form.

	NIB	EXC.	V.G.	GOOD	FAIR	POOR
	—	375	300	250	175	100

Model MM41OBN

.22-caliber bolt-action rifle, with 23.5" barrel, adjustable sights and 5-shot magazine. Blued, with walnut stock.

	NIB	EXC.	V.G.	GOOD	FAIR	POOR
	—	400	350	300	200	125

Model MS420B

As above, with 26.75" barrel and target-style stock.

	NIB	EXC.	V.G.	GOOD	FAIR	POOR
	—	400	350	300	200	125

Model 107

Bolt-action rifle chambered for .22 LR. Barrel length 21.6". Box magazine has 5-shot capacity. Beechwood checkered Monte Carlo stock is full size, with pistol-grip plastic buttplate. Rear sight adjustable. Metal finish blue. Weighs about 5 lbs.

NIB	EXC.	V.G.	GOOD	FAIR	POOR
265	225	180	150	125	100

Model 201 Standard

Model features 21" medium heavy free-floating barrel. Receiver accepts all rail mounts. Drilled and tapped for scope mount. Magazine capacity 5-shot. Chambered for.22 LR or .22 WMR cartridge. Beechwood stock is hand checkered, with plastic buttplate. Monte Carlo stock fitted with cheekpiece. Weighs about 6.5 lbs.

NIB	EXC.	V.G.	GOOD	FAIR	POOR
600	500	350	200	150	100

Model 66 Standard

Centerfire bolt-action rifle fitted with European Walnut hand-checkered oil finish stock. Stock is half stock design. Rosewood fore-ends and pistol-grip caps are standard. Fitted with rubber recoil pad and 1" quick disconnect sling swivels. Barrels are interchangeable on this model. Barrels with standard calibers is 24". Weighs about 7.5 lbs. Standard calibers are: .243 Win., .270, .308, .30-06, 5.6x57, 6.5x57, 7.64 and 9.3x62.

NIB	EXC.	V.G.	GOOD	FAIR	POOR
1700	1450	1100	700	550	350

Model 66 Magnum

Same as above. Chambered for 7mm Rem. Magnum, .300 and .338 Win. Magnum, 6.5x68, 8x86S, 9.3x64. Fitted with 26" barrel. Weighs about 7.9 lbs.

NIB	EXC.	V.G.	GOOD	FAIR	POOR
1800	1550	1200	800	600	400

Model 66 Safari

Same as above. Chambered for .375 H&H and .458 Win. Magnum. Fitted with 26" barrel. Weighs about 9.3 lbs.

NIB	EXC.	V.G.	GOOD	FAIR	POOR
2600	2000	1250	850	650	400

Model 66 Stuzen

Same as Standard Model 66. Fitted with a full stock. Barrel length 21". Calibers same as Standard. Weighs about 7.5 lbs.

NIB	EXC.	V.G.	GOOD	FAIR	POOR
2500	2100	1500	800	600	400

IDF Mauser Rifle Model 66SP

Bolt-action rifle chambered for .308 Win. cartridge. Adjustable trigger for pull and travel. Barrel length 27". Specially designed stock has broad fore-end and thumbhole pistol-grip. Cheekpiece adjustable as is recoil pad. Supplied with case. This rifle is military issue. Fewer than 100 imported into U.S. by Springfield Armory.

NIB	EXC.	V.G.	GOOD	FAIR	POOR
2250	1575	1100	850	650	400

Model 77

Fitted with a 24" barrel. Bolt-action rifle chambered for .243, .270, 6.5x57, 7x64, .308 and .30-06 calibers. Detachable box magazine. Set trigger. Walnut stock, with cheekpiece. Hand checkering. Weight about 7.25 lbs.

NIB	EXC.	V.G.	GOOD	FAIR	POOR
1250	950	800	650	450	200

Model 77 Ultra

Fitted with a 20" barrel. Chambered for 6.5x57, 7x64 and .30-06 calibers. Weight about 7.5 lbs.

NIB	EXC.	V.G.	GOOD	FAIR	POOR
1250	950	800	650	450	200

Model 77 Mannlicher

Similar to Ultra Model, with full-length Mannlicher stock. Set trigger. Weight about 7.5 lbs.

NIB	EXC.	V.G.	GOOD	FAIR	POOR
1250	950	800	650	450	200

Model 77 Big Game

Chambered for .375 H&H Magnum cartridge. Fitted with a 26" barrel. Weight about 8.5 lbs.

NIB	EXC.	V.G.	GOOD	FAIR	POOR
1100	900	750	600	500	200

Model 86-SR

Introduced in 1993. Bolt-action .308 is sometimes referred to as Specialty Rifle. Fitted with a laminated wood and special match thumbhole stock or fiberglass stock, with adjustable cheekpiece. Stock has rail in forearm and an adjustable recoil pad. Magazine capacity 9 rounds. Finish is a non-glare blue. Barrel length with muzzle-brake is 28.8". Many special features are found on this rifle from adjustable trigger weight to silent safety. Mauser offers many options on

	NIB	EXC.	V.G.	GOOD	FAIR	POOR

this rifle that will affect price. Weight about 11 lbs.

	NIB	EXC.	V.G.	GOOD	FAIR	POOR
	9500	7500	5000	3500	1800	1000

Model 93 SR

Introduced in 1996. A tactical semi-automatic rifle chambered for .300 Win. Magnum or .338 Lapua cartridge. Barrel length 25.5"; overall length 48.4". Barrel fitted with a muzzle-brake. Magazine capacity: 6 rounds .300; 5 rounds .338-caliber. Weight about 13 lbs.

10000	9000	7500	5000	3500	1500

Model 96

Bolt-action rifle chambered for .25-06, .270 Win., 7x64, .308 or .30-06 cartridge. Fitted with a 22" barrel (24" Magnum calibers) and has a 5-round top loading magazine. Receiver drilled and tapped. Checkered walnut stock. No sights. Weight about 6.25 lbs.

700	600	500	300	125	100

Model 98 Standard

Built on classic Mauser square-bridge action, this model has been offered in most popular calibers, including most big magnums for dangerous game. Features include an extra-select hand-checkered walnut stock. This is a custom rifle, with limited production. Values shown are for standard calibers.

8000	6500	5000	3500	2500	700

Model 99 Standard

Bolt-action centerfire sporting rifle. Offered with two stock designs: classic with straight oil finish stock or high luster with cheekpiece and schnabel fore-end and Monte Carlo with rosewood fore-end tip and pistol-grip cap. Chambered for standard calibers: .243, .25-06, .270, .308, .30-06, 5.6x57, 6.5x57, 7x57, 7x64. Barrel length 24"; weight about 8 lbs.

900	700	600	500	400	300

Model 99 Magnum

Same as above. Chambered for magnum calibers: 7mm Rem. Magnum, .257 Wby., .270 Wby., .300 Wby., .300 and .338 Win. Magnum, 8x68S and 9.3x64. Fitted with 26" barrel. Weighs about 8 lbs.

950	750	650	550	400	300

M03

Offered in several variants and grades. Chambered in a wide range of popular calibers from .222 Remington to .375 H&H Magnum. Built on traditional Mauser square-bridge action. Features include barrel interchangeability and manual cocking system, with safety/cocking lever at rear of bolt. Made by Blaser. Values shown are for basic model, with synthetic stock. Higher grade wood and various levels of engraving are available. **NOTE:** Add $500 for checkered walnut stock.

4000	3400	2800	2000	1000	400

M12

Modern Mauser design, with solid steel construction, checkered walnut or synthetic stock with Prince of Wales pistol-grip, three-position safety, detachable magazine and short 60-degree bolt lift. Offered in .22-250, .243, .270, 6.5x55, 7x64, 7mm Rem. Magnum, .308, .30-06, .300 Win. Magnum, 8x57JS, 9.3x62, .338 Win. Magnum. Several variations are available, with barrel lengths of 19", 22" or 24.5" with or without sights. Introduced in 2013. **NOTE:** Add $300 for walnut stock.

1375	1150	900	750	500	300

CURRENT MAUSER PRODUCTION PISTOLS

Model 80 SA

Single-action semi-automatic pistol. Based on Browning Hi-Power design. Chambered for 9mm Parabellum cartridge. Barrel length 4.66"; magazine capacity 14 rounds; weight about 35 oz.

550	475	295	175	125	100

Model Compact DA

Same as above, with double-action trigger. Shorter barrel 4.13". Weighs about 33 oz.

340	320	250	175	125	100

Model 90 DA

Similar to Model 80, with double-action trigger.

550	475	295	175	125	100

	NIB	EXC.	V.G.	GOOD	FAIR	POOR

Model M2 (Imported by SIG ARMS)

Introduced in 2000. Chambered for .45 ACP, .40 S&W or .357 SIG cartridges. Has an aluminum alloy frame and steel slide. Action is an enclosed hammerless striker-fired design. Barrel length 3.5". Fixed sights. Weight about 29 oz. Magazine capacity: 8 rounds .45 ACP; 10 rounds .40 S&W and .357 SIG.

475	400	300	200	150	100

MAVERICK ARMS, INC.
Subsidiary of O. F. Mossberg & Sons, Inc.
Eagle Pass, Texas

Model 88

12-gauge Magnum slide-action shotgun, with 28" or 30" barrels, anodized receiver, composition stock. Introduced in 1989.

250	150	125	100	75	50

Model 88 Slug Pump Shotgun

12-gauge Magnum pump-action shotgun, with interchangeable Cylinder-bore barrel. Black synthetic stock; forearm blued metal finish; 6-shot magazine. **NOTE:** Add $20 for rifled 24" barrel, with adjustable rifle sights.

295	200	100	75	60	50

Model 88 Six-Shot Security Model

12-gauge Magnum pump-action shotgun, with 6-shot magazine. Interchangeable 18.5" Cylinder-bore fixed choke barrel; rugged black synthetic stock and forearm; blued metal finish; brass front sight bead, are also included. **NOTE:** Add 5 percent for Eight-Shot Security Model, with 20" Cylinder-bore fixed choke barrel; 10 percent for heat shield.

295	200	100	75	60	50

Model HS-12

A 12-gauge over/under shotgun offered in several variations. Field model has 28" barrels, with improved-cylinder and modified choke tubes, selective single trigger, extractors and synthetic stock. A tactical model has an 18.5" barrel and Picatinny rails. **NOTE:** Add $50 for this model.

400	375	325	250	200	100

MAYNARD/PERRY
Keen, Walker & Co.
Danville, Virginia

Brass Framed Carbine

Overall length 40"; barrel length 22.5"; caliber .54. Browned blued barrel, brass frame and walnut stock. Manufactured in 1861 and 1862. Fewer than 300 produced.

—	—	33000	14000	8000	1500

MCMILLAN & CO. INC., G.
(Later: Harris/McMillan Gunworks, Harris Gunworks)
Phoenix, Arizona

Competition Model

Custom order bolt-action rifle in .308, 7mm-08 and .300 Winchester Magnum caliber. Barrel length, stock type and dimensions to customer's specifications. Introduced in 1988.

1700	1500	1150	800	600	300

Model 86 Sniper's Rifle

Custom order rifle in .308 Winchester or .300 Winchester Magnum calibers, with synthetic stock. Choice of scope systems. Introduced in 1988.

3250	2700	1900	1100	600	300

Model 86 System

As above, with Ultra scope mounting system, bipod and fitted case. Introduced in 1988.

3700	3250	2300	1800	850	550

Model 87 Long Range Sniper's Rifle

Large stainless steel, single-shot bolt-action rifle in .50 BMG caliber. Featuring a 29" barrel, with an integral muzzle-brake. Camouflaged synthetic stock. Weight 21 lbs. Accurate to 1,500 meters. Introduced in 1988.

6000	5200	4000	2750	1000	500

	NIB	EXC.	V.G.	GOOD	FAIR	POOR

Model 87 System

As above, with bipod and 20X Ultra scope mounting system. Fitted case. Introduced in 1988.

	6500	5700	4400	3150	1200	600

Signature Model

Bolt-action sporting rifle. Manufactured in a variety of calibers up to .375 Holland & Holland, with 22" or 24" stainless barrel, composition stock and either 3- or 4-shot magazine. Introduced in 1988.

	2200	1750	1250	800	600	300

Signature Stainless

Same as above, with barrel and action made of stainless steel. Fiberglass stock. Left- or right-hand model. .416 Rigby also offered in this configuration. Introduced in 1990.

	2500	2050	1650	1000	750	400

Signature Alaskan

Introduced in 1989. Offered in .270, .280 Rem., .30-06, 7mm Rem. Magnum, .300 Win. Magnum, .300 Wby. Magnum, .358 Win. Magnum, .340 Wby. Magnum, .375 H&H. Match grade barrel from 22" to 26" in length. Single leaf rear sight, barrel band front sight.

	3000	2700	2000	1500	950	500

Signature Titanium Mountain

Offered in calibers from .270 Win. to 7mm Rem. Magnum. Match grade barrel produced from titanium. Stock is graphite. Weight about 6.5 lbs.

	3500	3000	2500	1800	950	500

Signature Varminter

Available in calibers .223, .22-250, .220 Swift, .243, 6mm Rem., .25-06, 7mm-08, .308. Barrel lengths from 22" to 26". Heavy barrel configuration, with hand bedded fiberglass stock. Field bipod is standard. Introduced in 1989.

	2500	2000	1500	900	600	400

Talon Safari

Bolt-action rifle offered in various calibers from .300 Win. Magnum to .458 Win. Magnum. Stainless steel barrel is 24". Four-round magazine. Fiberglass stock. Introduced in 1989. Weight about 10 lbs.

	3750	3250	2200	6500	950	500

Talon Sporter

Offered in calibers from .25-06 to .416 Rem. Magnum. 24" barrel with no sights. Built on pre-1964 Winchester Model 70 action. Choice of walnut or fiberglass stock. Weight about 7.5 lbs.

	2500	2000	1750	1250	600	250

Model 300 Phoenix Long Range Rifle

Introduced in 1992. Chambered for .300 Phoenix cartridge. Fitted with 28" barrel. No sights. Fiberglass stock. Weight about 12.5 lbs.

	3000	2500	2050	1450	600	350

Model 40 Sniper

Bolt-action rifle chambered for .308 cartridge. Introduced in 1990. Fitted with 24" match grade heavy weight barrel. No sights. Weight about 9 lbs.

	2500	2000	1500	1150	500	300

Model 92 Bullpup

Single-shot rifle chambered for .50-caliber BMG. Fitted with 26" barrel. No sights. Fiberglass bullpup stock. First introduced in 1995.

	4500	3750	2800	2200	1000	500

Model 93 SN

Bolt-action rifle chambered for .50 BMG. Fitted with 29" barrel with muzzle-brake. Magazine holds 10 rounds. No sights. Weight about 21.5 lbs. Folding fiberglass stock. Introduced in 1995.

	4750	4250	3500	2450	1450	750

McMillan LRHR

Long Range Hunting Rifle, designed for precision shooting. Custom made benchrest tolerances in a long or short action. Chambered in .243 Winchester, .308 Winchester, 7mm Remington, .300 Winchester and .338 Lapua Magnum. Action is pillar bedded. Barrel lengths: 24", 26" or 27", depending on caliber. McMillan A-3 fiberglass stock is standard.

	4750	4000	3000	2500	—	—

MEAD & ADRIANCE
St. Louis, Missouri

Company retailed a variety of single-shot percussion pistols, most of which were manufactured by Ethan Allen of Grafton, Massachusetts. In general, value for pistols marked "Mead & Adriance" are listed.

Single-Shot Pistols

—	—	2500	1650	550	250

MENDENHALL, JONES & GARDNER
Greensboro, North Carolina

Muzzle Loading Rifle

.58-caliber percussion rifle, with 33" barrel. Full-length walnut stock secured by two barrel bands. Finished in white, with lock marked "M.J.&G.,N.C."

—	—	39000	33000	14000	5000

MENZ, AUGUST
Suhl, Germany

Established prior to WWI to manufacture Beholla pistols. Company was purchased by Lignose in 1937.

Menta

Identical to Beholla, which is listed separately.

—	350	250	200	150	100

Liliput

4.25mm caliber semi-automatic pistol, with 2" barrel and 6-shot magazine. Overall length 3.5"; weight 10 oz. Slide marked "Liliput Kal. 4.25". Also manufactured in 6.35mm caliber; overall length 4". Blued, with composition grips.

—	800	600	450	300	200

Menz Model II

As above in 7.65mm caliber.

—	400	300	250	200	125

Menz VP Model

Similar to Model II in 6.35mm caliber, with 2.35" barrel, 6-shot magazine. Fitted with a cocking indicator.

—	400	300	250	200	125

Model III

A total redesign. Quality is much better than previous Menz pistols. Has a closed-top slide, fixed barrel, exposed hammer. Similar to Model 1910 Browning. Produced until 1937.

—	450	350	300	250	150

MERCURY
Liege, Belgium

Model 622 VP

.22-caliber semi-automatic rifle, with 20" barrel, open sights and 7-shot magazine. Blued, with walnut stock. Manufactured by Robar & Son.

—	325	275	250	200	125

MERCURY
Eibar, Spain

Double-Barreled Shotgun

10-, 12- or 20-gauge Magnum boxlock double-barrel shotgun, with 28" or 32" barrels, double triggers and extractors. Blued, with walnut stock. **NOTE:** Add 75 percent for 10-gauge.

—	325	250	225	175	125

MERIDEN FIREARMS CO.
Meriden, Connecticut

Pocket Pistol

.32- or .38-caliber double-action revolver. Manufactured in a variety of barrel lengths, with exposed or enclosed hammer. Nickel-plated with rubber grips. Barrel marked "Meriden Firearms

	NIB	EXC.	V.G.	GOOD	FAIR	POOR

Co. Meriden, Conn. USA." Manufactured between 1895 and 1915.

	—	—	375	200	75	50

Double-Barrel Shotguns

From 1905-1918 Meriden Fire Arms Co., successor to A.J. Aubrey, made 12-, 16- and 20-gauge sidelock double-barrel shotguns. These were better quality hammer and hammerless side-by-sides fitted with twist, laminated, Damascus and steel barrels in grades A to G. Some of these guns were beautifully engraved by same artisans who worked for Parker Bros. and other Connecticut gunmakers. Prices in 1910 ranged from $40 to $250, but they represented great value for the money, as they were superior to the popular Crescent guns which they closely resembled. Current values depend on model, grade, gauge and condition. Difficult to find examples in excellent condition as these were sold by Sears to customers who put them to hard use. In good condition their current values range from $250 for plain Janes to $3,500 or more for top grades, of which few specimens are known.

Single-Barrel Shotguns and Rifles

Meriden Fire Arms Co. also made many single-barrel shotguns and rifles. Current values are determined by growing collector interest and condition.

MERKEL, GEBRUDER
Suhl, Germany

Merkel brothers began manufacturing rifles and shotguns in Suhl, Germany in 1898. Company is best known for its over/under and side-by-side shotguns, but has also produced double-barreled express rifles, drillings with various rifle/shotgun combinations, falling block single-shot rifles and bolt-action rifles. Many experts consider Merkels to be equal in quality to some of the better Italian and English guns. Because of the company's long and complex history, including years during which it operated behind the Iron Curtain, there are many un-catalogued models that may be encountered. Merkel firearms are imported by Merkel USA, a subsidiary of Steyr Arms in Trussville, Alabama.

SIDE-BY-SIDE SHOTGUNS

Model 8

Self-cocking Deeley boxlock action, with cocking indicators. Locking mechanism is a Greener cross-bolt, with double-barrel locking lug. Triggers are single-selective or double. Safety is automatic and tang mounted. Has an extractor. Offered in 12- and 16-gauge with 28" solid rib barrels; 20-gauge with 26.75" barrels. Available with straight- or pistol-grip oil-finished walnut stock. Receiver case colored, with light scroll engraving. Weight about: 12- and 16-gauge 6.8 lbs.; 20-gauge 6 lbs.

1500	1150	900	600	500	400

Model 117/117E

Offered in 12- and 16-gauge, with various barrel lengths. Featured a boxlock action, with double triggers and extractors. Ejectors were available under "E" designation. Boxlock action body was scrupled at rear with fine line scroll engraving.

—	6000	4350	1950	1000	500

Model 118/118E

Offered in 12- and 16-gauge. Similar to above model, with slightly more engraving and better wood. Some engraving coverage on breech end of barrels.

—	7100	4900	2800	1200	650

Model 124/125

Similar to above models, but supplied with extractors for Model 124 and ejectors for Model 125. Both models have more engraving coverage with game scenes. Finer checkering and fancy wood is seen on this model.

Model 124

—	5400	4350	2500	1500	700

Model 125

—	6000	4600	3500	2000	1000

Model 130

One of Merkel's highest grade side-by-side shotguns. Featured sidelock action, extra fancy wood, fine line checkering and full coverage game scene engraving.

—	25500	17500	10000	3200	300

Model 126

Similar to Model 130. Fitted with removable sidelocks.

—	18500	15500	82700	4500	300

	NIB	EXC.	V.G.	GOOD	FAIR	POOR

Model 170

Model was offered in 12-gauge only, with automatic ejectors. Boxlock action engraved, with fine full coverage scroll.

	NIB	EXC.	V.G.	GOOD	FAIR	POOR
—	6000	4900	3900	2500	300	

Model 127

Model was Merkel's finest side-by-side shotgun. Sidelock action featured full coverage fine line scroll engraving of the best quality.

	EXC.	V.G.	GOOD	FAIR	POOR
—	25000	19500	14500	6000	300

Model 47E

Same as above. Fitted with ejectors. Offered in 12-, 16- or 20-gauge. Supplied with fitted luggage case.

NIB	EXC.	V.G.	GOOD	FAIR	POOR
4000	3400	2300	1200	600	200

Model 147

Same as Model 8. Silver grayed receiver, with fine engraved hunting scenes, engraved border and screws. This model has been discontinued.

NIB	EXC.	V.G.	GOOD	FAIR	POOR
3700	3250	2300	1100	600	200

Model 147E

Same as above. Fitted with ejectors. Offered in 12-, 16-, 20- or 28-gauge. Supplied with fitted luggage case.

NIB	EXC.	V.G.	GOOD	FAIR	POOR
4750	3850	2700	1500	1000	300

Model 147EL

Similar to Model 147E, with fancy walnut stock. Supplied with fitted luggage case.

NIB	EXC.	V.G.	GOOD	FAIR	POOR
6000	4950	3400	2200	1000	3000

Model 122

Features same specifications as above models, but has false sideplates. Fitted with ejectors. Receiver is silver grayed, with fine engraved hunting scenes on false sideplates, engraved border and screws.

NIB	EXC.	V.G.	GOOD	FAIR	POOR
4000	3500	3000	1900	950	300

Model 47SL

Same as above, with scroll engraving in place of hunting scenes.

NIB	EXC.	V.G.	GOOD	FAIR	POOR
8200	6100	4400	3000	1750	300

Model 147SL

Features true Holland and Holland-style sidelocks, with cocking indicators. Gauge and barrel lengths as above. Stock fancy walnut. However, weight: 20-gauge 6.4 lbs.; 28-gauge about 6.1 lbs.

NIB	EXC.	V.G.	GOOD	FAIR	POOR
10000	7000	5500	3850	2250	300

Model 147SSL

Similar to Model 147SL. Fitted with removable side plates. Fancy walnut stock. Supplied with fitted luggage case.

NIB	EXC.	V.G.	GOOD	FAIR	POOR
8800	6500	5200	3000	2500	300

Models 247S/347S

Same as Model 147S, with different types of engraving.

Model 247S

Large scroll engraving.

NIB	EXC.	V.G.	GOOD	FAIR	POOR
7700	5800	4400	2500	2000	300

Model 347S

Medium scroll engraving.

NIB	EXC.	V.G.	GOOD	FAIR	POOR
7100	6100	4950	3850	2250	300

NIB	EXC.	V.G.	GOOD	FAIR	POOR

Model 447SL

Small scroll engraving. **NOTE:** Add $1,200 wood upgrade; $1,400 custom stock dimensions; $900 left-hand stocks.

NIB	EXC.	V.G.	GOOD	FAIR	POOR
9900	7300	6000	4400	2700	300

Model 280

Boxlock gun chambered for 28-gauge shell. Fitted with 28" barrels choked Improved Cylinder and Modified. Double triggers with ejectors. Straight-grip walnut stock. Scroll engraving, with case colored receiver. Weight about 5.2 lbs.

NIB	EXC.	V.G.	GOOD	FAIR	POOR
4000	3600	2650	1900	950	300

Model 280EL

Features Anson & Deely boxlock action, with engraved hunting scenes on a silver-grayed action. Double triggers. Fancy walnut, with straight-grip stock. Offered in 28-gauge, with 28" barrels. Fitted luggage case standard. Weight about 5.2 lbs. First imported in 2000.

NIB	EXC.	V.G.	GOOD	FAIR	POOR
6500	5500	3850	2500	1500	300

Model 280SL

Similar to Model 280EL, with English-style scroll engraving on H&H style sidelocks. Choice of pistol-/straight-grip fancy walnut stock. Fitted luggage case standard. First imported in 2000.

NIB	EXC.	V.G.	GOOD	FAIR	POOR
8250	7700	5500	3600	1700	300

Model 360

Boxlock model same as Model 280, but chambered for .410 bore. Straight-grip walnut stock. Scroll engraving on case colored receiver. Barrel is 28" choke Modified and Full. Weight about 5.2 lbs.

NIB	EXC.	V.G.	GOOD	FAIR	POOR
4200	3600	2650	1400	800	300

Model 360EL

Same as Model 280EL, but chambered for .410 shell. Fitted with 28" barrels. Fancy walnut. Fitted case. Weight about 5.5 lbs. First imported in 2000.

NIB	EXC.	V.G.	GOOD	FAIR	POOR
7000	5700	4100	2750	1300	300

Model 360SL

Same as Model 360EL, with English-style scroll engraving on H&H style sidelocks. Choice of pistol-/straight grip stock. First imported in 2000.

NIB	EXC.	V.G.	GOOD	FAIR	POOR
10500	8100	5900	3750	1600	300

Model 280/360 Two Barrel Set

Set consists of 28 gauge 28" barrel; .410 bore 28" barrel, with scroll engraving. Oil finish walnut stock. Double triggers. Straight grip stock.

NIB	EXC.	V.G.	GOOD	FAIR	POOR
6500	6000	5000	3750	1600	500

Model 280/360EL Two Barrel Set

Set consists of 28-gauge 28" barrel; .410 bore 28" barrel, with engraved hunting scenes. Fancy walnut stock. Double triggers. Straight-grip stock. First imported in 2000.

NIB	EXC.	V.G.	GOOD	FAIR	POOR
9500	8000	6000	3750	1600	500

Model 280/360SL Two Barrel Set

Same as above, with English-style scroll engraving. Choice of pistol-/straight-grip stock. First imported in 2000.

NIB	EXC.	V.G.	GOOD	FAIR	POOR
15500	11500	8000	5500	3500	500

Model 1620

A boxlock side-by-side gun chambered for 16-gauge shell. Fitted with 28" barrels; double triggers; barrel chokes Improved Cylinder and Modified; ejectors; straight-grip walnut stock, with oil finish; case colored receiver finish; light scroll engraving; fitted luggage case. Weight about 6.1 lbs. **NOTE:** Add $2,300 two-barrel set. Second set 20-gauge 28" barrels.

NIB	EXC.	V.G.	GOOD	FAIR	POOR
4200	3600	2500	1800	1000	300

Model 1620E

Similar to Model 1620, with fine engraved hunting scenes on silver-grayed receiver.

NIB	EXC.	V.G.	GOOD	FAIR	POOR
5000	4000	3000	2000	1000	300

	NIB	EXC.	V.G.	GOOD	FAIR	POOR

Model 1620EL

As above, with high-grade walnut straight-grip stock and deeply engraved hunting scenes. **NOTE:** Add $2,900 two-barrel set. Second set 20-gauge 28" barrels.

6000	5000	3850	2200	1100	300

Model 1620SL

Similar to 1620 models above, with grayed sidelocks with deeply engraved hunting scenes. High-grade walnut stock, with oil finish. Weight is 6.6 lbs. **NOTE:** Add $3,800 two-barrel set. Second set 20-gauge 28" barrels.

11000	8400	6100	3750	1800	500

Model 1622

Introduced in 2006. This 16-gauge boxlock side-by-side features full sideplates; case hardened receiver with cocking indicators; ejectors; single selective or double triggers; pistol-grip or English style stock. Fixed IC and Mod. chokes. **NOTE:** Add 50 percent for 2-barrel set. Second set 20-gauge 28" barrels.

4000	3200	2550	1700	1400	300

Model 1622E

Similar to 1622, with fine engraved hunting scenes on silver-grayed receiver.

7500	5700	4100	2750	1300	300

Model 1622EL

Similar to Model 1622E, with luxury grade wood. **NOTE:** Add 30 percent for 2-barrel set. Second set 20-gauge 28" barrel.

8800	6500	5200	3000	2500	300

OVER/UNDER SHOTGUNS

Model 102E

Was Merkel's standard over/under boxlock model. Offered in 12-gauge 28" barrels; 16-gauge 26" barrels. Both fitted with double triggers, semi-pistol grip and ejectors.

—	1800	1450	1100	650	400

Model 103E

Similar to standard, with more English scroll engraving coverage and better wood. Was offered in 12-, 16- and 20-gauge.

—	2450	1650	1350	950	600

Model 204E

Essentially a Model 203E, with finer engraving. Discontinued prior to 1939.

—	6600	4900	3300	2200	1750

Model 301E

Boxlock model with scalloped action. Chambered for 12-, 16-, 20-, 24-, 28- and 32-gauge. Engraving is an English scroll. Trigger guard is horn. Double triggers. Pistol-grip is standard. Produced prior to 1939.

—	4900	4000	2500	2000	1850

Model 302E

Similar to Model 301E. Fitted with sideplates. Full-coverage engraving features game scenes. Produced prior to WWII.

—	13250	11000	8250	4400	2000

Model 303 Luxus

Over/under Merkel is custom built to customer's specifications. Each gun is unique. Should be appraised by a knowledgeable individual who is familiar with quality European shotguns.

22000	18500	15000	—	—	—

Model 304E

Pre-war model was highest grade in Merkel's over/under shotgun line. Sidelock gun with full coverage scroll engraving of the highest quality. Fine line checkering and extra fancy wood make this gun difficult to appraise due to its rarity.

Model 400E

Higher grade over/under fitted with Kersten crossbolt, finer engraving and fancy wood. Merkel offered this grade in 12-, 16-, 20-, 24-, 28- and 32-gauge, with choice of barrel lengths. Produced

	NIB	EXC.	V.G.	GOOD	FAIR	POOR

prior to 1939.

	NIB	EXC.	V.G.	GOOD	FAIR	POOR
	—	1950	1450	1000	600	400

Model 401E

Similar to model above, with full coverage game scene engraving.

—	2750	2000	1350	800	600

Model 200E

Action on this model is a self-cocking Blitz, where hammers are attached to trigger plates. Locking mechanism is a Kersten double crossbolt lock, with release. Trigger may be single-selective or double. Manual safety is mounted on tang. Fitted with coil spring ejectors. Offered in 12- and 16-gauge with 28" solid rib barrels; 20-gauge with 26.75" barrels. Oil-finished stock offered with straight-/pistol-grip. Receiver case colored, with engraved border and screws. Weight: 12-gauge 7 lbs.; 16-gauge 6.8 lbs.; 20-gauge 6.4 lbs.

2900	2200	1650	1000	800	500

Model 201E

Same as Model 200E, with silver grayed receiver with fine engraved hunting scenes, engraved border and screws.

3700	3100	2500	1650	1000	750

Model 202E

Same basic specifications as Model 201E. Fitted with false side plates with cocking indicators.

8200	5500	3850	2500	1500	1000

Model 200ES

Features a Blitz action, with cocking indicators and Kersten double cross bolt lock, with release. Trigger is single-selective, with tang-mounted manual safety. Coil spring ejectors are standard. Offered in 12-gauge only, with 26.75" or 28" ventilated rib barrel. Walnut stock has skeet dimensions, with pistol-grip. Receiver silver grayed, with 112 coverage scroll engraving, engraved borders and screws. weighs about 7.3 lbs.

4400	3600	2750	2200	1500	1000

Model 200ET

Same as Model 200ES in trap configuration. Ventilated rib barrel length offered is 30".

4700	3850	3000	2250	1750	1000

Model 200SC (Sporting Clays)

Introduced in 1995. Offered in 12-gauge only, with 3" chambers and 30" barrels with ventilated rib. Fitted with a single-selective trigger adjustable for length of pull. Special walnut oil finished stock, with 26 lpi checkering. Pistol-grip and Pachmayr Sporting Clays recoil pad standard. Weight about 7.6 lbs. **NOTE:** Add $500 with Briley choke tubes.

7200	6000	3300	1500	900	450

Model 201ES

Same as Model 200SC, with full coverage scroll engraving.

4950	4050	3300	2500	2000	1000

Model 201ET

Same as Model 210ES. Fitted with 30" barrel and trap stock dimensions.

4950	4100	3300	2750	2000	1000

Model 203E

Has true Holland & Holland-style sidelocks, with cocking indicators. Sideplates are removable with cranked screw. Gauge selection and barrel are same as those listed above. Silver grayed receiver has English-style large scroll engraving. Model has been discontinued.

13500	10400	8250	5000	2500	1000

Model 303E

Same as Model 203E, with detachable sidelock plates with integral retracting hook. Model 303E has medium scroll work engraving and Holland & Holland-type ejectors.

18700	16500	13400	7500	5000	2500

Model 303EL

Features H&H-style sidelocks that are quick detachable without tools. Receiver is engraved with hunting scenes. Offered in 12-, 20- and 28-gauge. Double triggers. Fancy walnut stock, with pistol-/straight-grip. Weight about: 12-gauge 7 lbs.; 20-gauge 6.4 lbs.; 28-gauge 6.4 lbs. Fitted luggage case standard.

26000	18700	13000	7500	5000	2500

	NIB	EXC.	V.G.	GOOD	FAIR	POOR

Model 2000EL

Features Kersten crossbolt lock; scroll engraving on silver grayed receiver; modified Anson & Deely boxlock action. Offered in 12-, 20- or 28-gauge with ejectors, single-selective or double triggers, fancy wood and choice of pistol-/straight-grip stock. Weight about: 12-gauge 7 lbs.; 20-gauge 6.4 lbs.; 28-gauge 6.4 lbs.

7200	5100	3600	2200	1500	750

Model 2000EL Sporter

Similar to above model. Fitted with 30" barrels 12-gauge; 28" barrels 20- and 28-gauge.

7200	5200	3600	2200	1500	750

Model 2000CL

Introduced in 2005. Chambered for 12-, 20- or 28-gauge, with 28" barrels choked Improved Cylinder and Modified. Scroll engraved receiver, with case colors. Single selective trigger, with auto ejectors. High grade wood, with semi-pistol grip and straight-grip.

7700	5800	3750	2200	1500	750

Model 2000CL Sporter

As above, with 30" barrel 12-gauge with vent rib; 28" barrels with solid rib 20- and 28-gauge. Pistol-grip stock. Introduced in 2005. **NOTE:** Deduct $500 for 20- and 28-gauge.

8100	6100	3750	2200	1500	750

Model 2001EL

Similar to Model 2000, with finely engraved hunting scenes. Offered in 12-, 20-, 28-gauge.

9000	7500	4950	2900	2000	1000

Model 2001EL Sporter

Same as above, with 30" barrels 12-gauge; 28" barrels 20- and 28-gauge.

11000	7300	5300	3600	2000	1000

Model 2002EL

Features finely engraved hunting scenes, with arabesque style. Offered in 12-, 20-, 28-gauge.

11000	8800	6000	4400	2200	1200

Model 2016EL

16-gauge gun, with 28" barrels, single non-selective trigger and ejectors. Fixed chokes. Checkered walnut stock, with semi-pistol grip. Scroll engraving on case colored receiver. Weight about 6.6 lbs.

8750	7000	5000	3000	1500	750

Model 2016EL Two Barrel Set

As above, with extra set of 20-gauge 28" barrels with fixed chokes.

12000	10500	8000	5000	3000	1000

Model 2116EL

16-gauge model similar to above, with game scene engraving on case colored receiver.

9100	7700	5500	3200	2000	1000

Model 2116EL Two Barrel Set

As above, with extra set of 20-gauge 28" barrels with fixed chokes.

13000	9300	6950	4400	2900	2000

PRE-WAR SINGLE-SHOT AND BOLT-ACTION RIFLES

Merkel built special single-shot and bolt-action rifles. Produced prior to WWII. Seldom seen in United States. Buyer should exercise caution and seek expert assistance prior to sale.

Model 180

Top-lever single rifle, with double under lugs built on boxlock action. Stock is .750 with pistol-grip. Commonly referred to as a stalking rifle. Offered in a variety of European calibers. Rare Merkel.

—	3300	2400	1650	1000	500

Model 183

Top-lever model features Holland & Holland-type sidelock action, with sidelock on left side and removable sideplate on right side. Fitted with straight-grip stock, full-length forearm with sling swivels, fine line checkering and fancy wood. Rare rifle.

—	8300	5500	3850	2000	1200

	NIB	EXC.	V.G.	GOOD	FAIR	POOR

Model 190

Merkel's version of a Sporting rifle built on Mauser action. Offered in a variety of European calibers. Special order rifles that will be seen in a variety of configurations.

	6000	5000	3500	2000	1100	650

DOUBLE RIFLES, COMBINATION GUNS, DRILLINGS

Model 410E

Merkel's base boxlock model with ejectors. Produced prior to WWII.

	—	2500	1950	1350	750	500

Model 411E

Similar to above, with addition of a small coverage of scroll engraving.

	—	2750	2200	1650	1100	600

Model 300

Boxlock hammerless four barrel shotgun/rifle combination. Shotgun barrels were 12-, 16- or 20-gauge; while top rifle barrel was .22 rimfire with bottom rifle barrel .30-30 or .25-35. Probably any combination of rifle and shotgun could be used as this was a special order gun. Very rare.

Model 311E

Combination gun has additional English scroll engraving.

	—	8600	7200	5500	2250	1250

Model 312E

Fitted with sideplates and game scene engraving.

	—	10400	9000	7500	4000	2000

Model 313E

Model has sidelocks, with fine full coverage scroll engraving. Expert appraisal is recommended due to this model's rarity and unique features.

	18000	13000	11750	8800	4400	2000

Model 314E

Sidelock model is also rare and unique. Expert appraisal is recommended prior to sale. Extra barrels will frequently be seen with this model.

Model 128E

Side-by-side double rifle is a droplock design, with scroll and game scene engraving. Wood is Circassian walnut, with fine line checkering. Offered in a variety of European calibers.

Model 132E

Similar to Model 128E, with full coverage scroll engraving and fancy wood.

Model 140-1

Features Greener crossbolt scroll engraving, with case hardened receiver. Extractors and double triggers, with pistol-grip stock are standard. Offered in a wide variety of European and American calibers.

	6500	5200	4100	2900	2000	1000

Model 140-1.1

Same as above, with finely engraved hunting scenes.

	7400	6100	4400	2900	2000	1000

Model 140-2

Double rifle has an Anson & Deely boxlock action. Double triggers. Barrel length 23.6". Chambered for .375 H&H, .416 Rigby and .470 NE. Pistol-grip stock, with cheekpiece on oil finish walnut. Weight about 10.7 lbs. depending on caliber.

	11500	8250	6000	3750	2200	1500

Model 140-2.1

Similar to one above. Engraved with African game scenes.

	13400	9300	6600	3750	2200	1500

Model 150-1

Features an arabesque engraving on silver grayed receiver. Extractors, double triggers and pistol-grip are standard.

	8250	6600	5100	3000	2000	900

	NIB	EXC.	V.G.	GOOD	FAIR	POOR

Model 150-1.1

Same as above, with finely engraved hunting scenes.

NIB	EXC.	V.G.	GOOD	FAIR	POOR
9500	7700	6000	3500	2500	1000

Model 160S Luxus Double Rifle

Double rifle is part of Luxus series. Features highest quality sidelock action, wood and fittings. Offered in .222 Rem., 5.6x50R Magnum, .243, 6.5x57R, 7x57, 7x65, .3006, .30R Blaser, 8x57IRS, 8x57RS, .308 Win. and 9.3x74R. Weighs about 8 lbs. An expert appraisal should be sought prior to sale, due to unique nature of this model.

NIB	EXC.	V.G.	GOOD	FAIR	POOR
15000	12500	8500	5750	4300	1200

Model 160S-2.1

Same as above, with finely engraved hunting scenes. Chambered for .470 Nitro Express. Weight about 11 lbs.

NIB	EXC.	V.G.	GOOD	FAIR	POOR
28500	20750	16500	12000	7500	1500

Model 211E Rifle/Shotgun Combination

Over/under model features gray metal boxlock action, with hunting scenes. Top barrel available in 12-, 16- or 20-gauge; bottom barrel offered in .22 Hornet, 5.6R Magnum, 5.6R, .222 Rem., .243 Win., 6.5x55, 6.5x57R, 7x57R, 7x65R, .30-06, 8x57IRS, 9.3x74R and .375 H&H Magnum. Barrel has a solid rib. Trigger is single-selective. Select walnut stock is hand checkered. Weight about 7 lbs.

NIB	EXC.	V.G.	GOOD	FAIR	POOR
6600	4950	3850	2250	1500	700

Model 210E Rifle/Shotgun Combination

Same as above. Features scroll engraved case hardened receiver. Discontinued.

NIB	EXC.	V.G.	GOOD	FAIR	POOR
6900	5500	4400	2750	1200	700

Model 211E Rifle/Shotgun Combination

Similar to above, with finely engraved hunting scenes.

NIB	EXC.	V.G.	GOOD	FAIR	POOR
8300	6600	4900	3000	1500	750

Model 213E Rifle/Shotgun Combination

Combination gun features sidelocks, with English style large scroll engraving on silver grayed receiver. Fitted with double triggers and pistol-grip with cheekpiece.

NIB	EXC.	V.G.	GOOD	FAIR	POOR
13000	10000	8200	5500	1900	900

Model 313E Rifle/Shotgun Combination

Same as above, with finer scroll engraving and fancy wood.

NIB	EXC.	V.G.	GOOD	FAIR	POOR
19000	15000	8250	6500	2000	1000

Model 220E Over/Under Double Rifle

Boxlock design with Kersten double crossbolt, scroll engraved case hardened receiver, Blitz action, double triggers and pistol-grip stock with cheekpiece.

NIB	EXC.	V.G.	GOOD	FAIR	POOR
10000	6600	4950	3800	1700	825

Model 221E Over/Under Double Rifle

Similar to above, with game scene engraving on silver grayed receiver.

NIB	EXC.	V.G.	GOOD	FAIR	POOR
12500	9350	6300	4500	2300	900

Model 223E Over/Under Double Rifle

Fitted with sidelocks. Features English-style arabesque engraving in large scrolls on silver grayed receiver.

NIB	EXC.	V.G.	GOOD	FAIR	POOR
16000	14000	11000	8000	4200	1000

Model 240-1

Boxlock double rifle and shotgun. Chambered for 7x65R, .30R Blaser, 6.5x57R, 8x57IRS, 9.3x74R, .30-06 and .308 Win. Shotgun barrels are 20-gauge, with 23.6" barrels and double triggers. Ejectors. Scroll engraving. Walnut stock, with pistol-grip and cheekpiece. Weight about 10 lbs.

NIB	EXC.	V.G.	GOOD	FAIR	POOR
8000	6300	5000	4000	3000	1300

Model 240-1.1

As above, with hunting scene engraving on grayed receiver.

NIB	EXC.	V.G.	GOOD	FAIR	POOR
9100	7100	6000	5000	4000	1500

	NIB	EXC.	V.G.	GOOD	FAIR	POOR

Model 323E Over/Under Double Rifle

Similar to above, with finer engraving.

	NIB	EXC.	V.G.	GOOD	FAIR	POOR
	25000	19000	13500	9500	3200	1500

Model 95K Drilling

A three-barrel shotgun/rifle combination. Top two barrels are chambered for 12-, 16- or 20-gauge; bottom barrel available in rifle calibers from .22 Hornet to .375 H&H Magnum. Action is a boxlock design, with scroll engraving on borders and screws. Stock is select grade walnut, with raised comb, pistol-grip with cap, cheekpiece and plastic butt-plate. Weighs about 7.7 lbs. Discontinued

	NIB	EXC.	V.G.	GOOD	FAIR	POOR
	9400	7400	4700	3000	2000	1000

Model 96K

Similar to above, with scroll engraving on case hardened frame.

	NIB	EXC.	V.G.	GOOD	FAIR	POOR
	9800	7800	5000	3700	2200	1000

Model 96K—Engraved

Same as above, with finely engraved hunting scenes. Arabesque engraving on silver grayed receiver.

	NIB	EXC.	V.G.	GOOD	FAIR	POOR
	11000	8500	5500	4000	2700	1100

K-SERIES STALKING RIFLES

Model K-1 Jagd

Introduced in 2003. Single-shot break-open rifle. Chambered for .243, 270, 7x57R, .308 Win., .30-06, 7mm Rem. Magnum, .300 Win. Magnum and 9.3x74R cartridge. Fitted with 23.6" barrel. Hunting scene engraving. Weight about 5.4 lbs.

	NIB	EXC.	V.G.	GOOD	FAIR	POOR
	4200	2750	1900	1600	1100	600

POST-WAR BOLT-ACTION RIFLES

KR-1 Premium

Short-stroke bolt-action rifle. Chambered for .243, .308 or .30-06 and 7mm Rem. Magnum and .300 Win. Magnum calibers. Barrel length for standard calibers 20" or 22"; magnum calibers 22" or 24". Checkered walnut stock, with hog-back comb. Magazine capacity 3 rounds. Single set trigger. Interchangeable barrels. Arabesque engraving on bolt housing and trigger plate. Select walnut stock, with Bavarian cheekpiece. Weight about 6.4 lbs. depending on caliber and barrel length. Introduced in 2005. **NOTE:** Add $200 for magnum calibers.

	NIB	EXC.	V.G.	GOOD	FAIR	POOR
	3550	2900	2200	1650	900	450

KR-1 Weimar

As above, with rounded bolt housing. Hand chiselled engraving, with game scenes. Trigger and lockbolt head are gold titanium nitride plated. Select walnut stock, with rosewood forearm tip and Bavarian double fold cheekpiece. Introduced in 2005. **NOTE:** Add $200 for magnum calibers.

	NIB	EXC.	V.G.	GOOD	FAIR	POOR
	11000	8800	7100	5500	3000	600

RX Helix

This is a straight-pull bolt-action takedown rifle, with a universal-length action that accommodates calibers from .222 Remington to .300 Winchester Magnum. Two-piece stock is of No. 2-grade checkered walnut. Interchangeable barrels are available in many calibers. Introduced in 2013. Values shown are for standard model. Several higher-grade versions are available at prices up to $10,000.

	NIB	EXC.	V.G.	GOOD	FAIR	POOR
	3350	2800	2100	1600	800	300

Helix Explorer

The Explorer model has a synthetic stock and most features of RX Helix.

	NIB	EXC.	V.G.	GOOD	FAIR	POOR
	2550	2000	1500	1250	500	200

MERRILL, JAMES H.
Baltimore, Maryland

Merrill Rifle

Single-shot breech loading rifle. Chambered for .54-caliber. Utilizes percussion ignition system. Breech opens for loading by lifting and pulling back on a lever. Barrel 33" in length. Full-length walnut stock held on by two barrel bands. Mountings and patch box are brass; lock is case colored, with browned barrel. Lock marked "J.H. Merrill Balto./Pat. July 1858". There are military acceptance marks on stock. Approximately 775 of these rifles manufactured and purchased by government for use during Civil War. Made in 1864 and 1865.

	NIB	EXC.	V.G.	GOOD	FAIR	POOR
	—	—	7800	6350	2750	750

NIB	EXC.	V.G.	GOOD	FAIR	POOR

Merrill Carbine

Similar in appearance to rifle, except barrel length is 22"; stock only half-length with one barrel band. There are some variations that are quite subtle in appearance, but which have a considerable effect on values. We recommend that an independent appraisal be secured. Values given are for standard 1st and 2nd Types. Approximately 15,000 total manufactured. Most were used in Civil War.

1st Type

No eagle stamped on lock. Breech lever is flat.

—	—	3750	2750	1500	500

2nd Type

Eagle stamped on lock. Stock has no patch box. Breech lever has a round tip.

—	—	4250	3000	1750	600

MERRILL, LATROBE & THOMAS
S. Remington—Maker
Ilion, New York

Carbine

.58-caliber breech loading percussion carbine. Overall length 38"; barrel 21". Lock marked "S. Remington/ Ilion, N.Y."; barrel "Merrill, Latrobe & Thomas/Baltimore, Md./Patent Applied For". Approximately 170 made in 1855.

—	—	45000	35000	12500	700

MERRILL
Fullerton, California

Sportsman

Single-shot pistol manufactured in a variety of calibers. Either 9" or 12" octagonal barrel having a wide ventilated rib, adjustable sights and integral telescope mounts. Blued, with walnut grips. **NOTE:** Add $100 Interchangeable barrels; $25 wrist support.

—	700	575	325	175	125

MERRIMACK ARMS
See—Brown Manufacturing Co.

MERWIN & BRAY
Worcester, Massachusetts

Company marketed a number of firearms produced by various manufacturers under its own name.

Merwin & Bray Pocket Pistol

.32-caliber spur trigger single-shot pistol, with 3.5" barrel. Blued silver-plated, with walnut grips. Barrel marked "Merwin & Bray New York".

—	—	—	300	150	75

MERWIN HULBERT & CO.
New York, New York

Merwin Hulbert & Co., New York City. Founder Joseph Merwin had previously been involved in Merwin & Bray. Merwin Hulbert & Co. or its principals were also involved in Phoenix Rifle, Evans Rifle Company, American Cartridge Company and Hopkins & Allen of Norwich, CT. Most Merwin Hulbert revolvers will be marked with Hopkins & Allen name, in addition to Merwin Hulbert. They were made for a fairly brief period, with most production apparently taking place during 1870s & early 1880s.

There has been some confusion over a classification system for MH revolvers. System adopted here is based on distinctions listed in Art Phelps' book, The Story of Merwin Hulbert & Co. Firearms. We believe this is the first time Phelps system has been adapted to a list format.

LARGE-FRAME MERWIN HULBERT SIXGUNS

There has been a marked increase in interest in Merwin Hulbert & Co. over the past decade, with many coming to recognize them as one of the pre-eminent makers of large-frame revolvers used in the American West. Total production of large-frame revolvers has been estimated at a few thousand by some sources. However, frequency with which they are encountered suggests possibly greater production.

	NIB	EXC.	V.G.	GOOD	FAIR	POOR

MH used a unique system of opening, loading & unloading their revolvers which was supposed to allow selective ejection of spent shells, leaving remaining cartridges in place. A latch on bottom of frame is pushed toward rear of gun and barrel and cylinder are rotated to right (clockwise, as viewed from rear of revolver) 90 degrees. Barrel and cylinder are then pulled forward, far enough to allow empty brass to fall free. This system required exceptional quality machining and some modern authorities are on record as considering Merwin Hulbert to have the finest workmanship of all revolvers of that era.

All are .44-caliber 6-shot large-frame revolvers. Beyond that, to fully identify a large-frame Merwin Hulbert, you must specify the following:

1. MODEL DESIGNATION — First Model has an open top and scoop flutes, round barrel and two small screws above trigger guard. Second Model similar to first, except with only one screw above trigger guard. Third Model has a top-strap with standard flutes and a round barrel. Fourth Model is similar to third, except it has a ribbed barrel. Open-top 1st and 2nd Models seem to be more sought after. 4th Model is rare and will bring a premium from a serious Merwin collector.

2. FRONTIER ARMY or POCKET ARMY — Frontier Army models have a square butt and were made in 1st through 4th models. Pocket Army models have a bird's-head butt, with a pointed extension with lanyard hole and are found in 2nd or 3rd Model configuration. Generally, Frontier Army will bring more than Pocket Army.

3. SINGLE-ACTION or DOUBLE-ACTION — Topstrap models 3rd and 4th were manufactured in both single- and double-action. Single-action models tend to bring more.

4. BARREL LENGTH — Standard barrel length on Frontier Army 1st, 2nd & 3rd Models is 7", with 5.5" barrel common on 4th Model. Standard barrel length on Pocket Army was a more "pocket-sized" 3.5". However somewhat ironically, bird's-head butt models marked "Pocket Army" were also produced with full length 7" barrels. Generally, these longer barrels will bring a bit more than shorter ones.

5. CALIBER — Most common is .44-40 (designated "Winchester Calibre 1873"). Merwins were also chambered for .44 Merwin Hulbert (somewhat similar to S&W .44 American cartridge) and .44 Russian. Less common calibers may bring a small premium from serious Merwin collectors.

6. FOREIGN COPIES — Merwin Hulbert design was relatively widely copied during the period of use, particularly in Spain. It seems that much of this production may have gone to Mexico and some found their way to U.S. Although these Spanish copies may bear markings such as "System Merwin Hulbert" or other usage of words "Merwin Hulbert", they generally will not be found with Hopkins & Allen marking. Spanish firms making Merwin copies included Orbea Hermanos and Anitua y Charola. These Spanish copies may bring half or less of what an original Merwin will bring and it can sometimes take a fairly experienced eye to tell the difference.

7. ENGRAVING — Special order engraving was available and it was usually executed in a distinctive and colorful "punch dot" style, which has come to be associated with Merwins (although it is occasionally encountered on other makes of firearms). For a long time, this style was somewhat dismissed as a bit crude and lacking in artistry. However, a new appreciation of Merwin engraving has emerged and factory engraved pieces will bring a significant premium. Often, a panel scene depicts an animal, object or landmark. These panel scenes have an almost "folk art" quality to them and will enhance value further. Engraved Merwins are sometimes encountered with engraving filled with colored enamel, quite rare, and if original, this will bring a further premium.

8. FINISH — Vast majority were nickel plated. Original blued guns will bring a premium.

First Model Frontier Army, .44 Open Top
Two screws, square butt, 7" barrel.

	NIB	EXC.	V.G.	GOOD	FAIR	POOR
	—	—	5500	3000	1500	500

Second Model Frontier Army, .44 Open Top
One screw, square butt, 7" barrel.

	NIB	EXC.	V.G.	GOOD	FAIR	POOR
	—	—	4500	2750	1000	500

Second Model Pocket Army, .44 Open Top
Bird's-head butt. 3.5" barrel standard, 7" will bring a premium.

	NIB	EXC.	V.G.	GOOD	FAIR	POOR
	—	—	3500	2000	700	400

Third Model Frontier Army, Single-Action, .44 Topstrap
Square butt, 7" barrel.

	NIB	EXC.	V.G.	GOOD	FAIR	POOR
	—	—	3750	2250	800	450

	NIB	EXC.	V.G.	GOOD	FAIR	POOR

Third Model Frontier Army, Double-Action, .44 Topstrap

Square butt, 7" barrel.

NIB	EXC.	V.G.	GOOD	FAIR	POOR
—	—	3250	1750	700	400

Third Model Pocket Army, Single-Action, .44 Topstrap

Bird's-head butt. 3.5" barrel standard, 7" will bring a premium.

NIB	EXC.	V.G.	GOOD	FAIR	POOR
—	—	3250	1750	700	400

Third Model Pocket Army, Double-Action, .44 Topstrap

Bird's-head butt. 3.5" barrel standard, 7" will bring a premium.

NIB	EXC.	V.G.	GOOD	FAIR	POOR
—	—	3000	1600	650	400

Fourth Model Frontier Army, Single-Action, .44 Topstrap

Ribbed barrel, scarce. 5.5" barrel seems to be most common, also offered in 7" and 3.5".

NIB	EXC.	V.G.	GOOD	FAIR	POOR
—	—	5000	2750	800	550

Fourth Model Frontier Army, Double-Action, .44 Topstrap

Ribbed barrel. Barrel lengths as above.

NIB	EXC.	V.G.	GOOD	FAIR	POOR
—	—	4750	2500	750	550

SMALL-FRAME MERWIN HULBERT

POCKET REVOLVERS

.32 & .38 centerfire revolvers were manufactured with unique Merwin Hulbert twist-open system, like large frame revolvers. They were often advertised as chambered for .32 MH & Co. or .38 MH & Co. cartridges, but it appears as if these cartridges may have been essentially the same as .32 S&W and .38 S&W rounds. Of course, Merwin Hulbert revolvers were manufactured for original lower pressure black-powder loadings of these cartridges. Saw-handled grip frames were standard, although some were manufactured with distinctive Pocket Army type pointed "skullcrusher" bird's-head grip frames. These will generally bring a premium. Most common barrel length for most models is 3.5", with 5.5" barrels somewhat scarcer in most models and 2.75" barrels quite scarce and worth a premium. A number of police departments purchased small frame Merwin Hulbert revolvers in late 19th century. Department marked guns will bring a premium.

Terminology alert—note that .44-caliber "Pocket Army" model is a large-frame and listed in section above.

.22 Merwin Hulbert revolver is the only one not to use MH twist-open system. It is, instead, a tip-up revolver closely resembling S&W Model One.

First Pocket Model Single-Action

Spur-trigger, cylinder pin exposed at front of frame, round loading aperture in recoil shield (no loading gate), five-shot .38, scarce.

NIB	EXC.	V.G.	GOOD	FAIR	POOR
—	—	1250	800	300	175

Second Pocket Model Single-Action

Spur-trigger, cylinder pin exposed, sliding loading gate, five-shot .38.

NIB	EXC.	V.G.	GOOD	FAIR	POOR
—	—	1000	650	285	150

Third Pocket Model Single-Action Spur-Trigger

Enclosed cylinder pin, sliding loading gate, five-shot .38.

NIB	EXC.	V.G.	GOOD	FAIR	POOR
—	—	950	600	225	125

Third Pocket Model Single-Action w/Trigger Guard

Five-shot .38.

NIB	EXC.	V.G.	GOOD	FAIR	POOR
—	—	1000	675	285	150

Double-Action Pocket Model, Small Frame

.32-caliber five shot. Patent marked folding hammer spur will bring a small premium.

NIB	EXC.	V.G.	GOOD	FAIR	POOR
—	—	800	550	185	125

Double-Action Pocket Model, Medium Frame

Usually .38 five shot. Scarce .32 seven shot will bring a 25- to 50 percent premium. Patent marked folding hammer spur will bring a small premium.

NIB	EXC.	V.G.	GOOD	FAIR	POOR
—	—	900	900	225	150

	NIB	EXC.	V.G.	GOOD	FAIR	POOR

Tip-Up .22 Spur-Trigger

.22 rimfire, S&W patent infringement, looks similar to S&W Model. One Third Issue. Scarce. "Made by Merwin Hulbert & Co. for Smith & Wesson" marking will bring a small premium.

	NIB	EXC.	V.G.	GOOD	FAIR	POOR
	—	—	1000	650	275	175

MERWIN HULBERT RIFLES

Very similar in design to Hopkins & Allen single-shot breech loaders. Advertised in .22 and .32 rimfire, as well as .32 WCF, .38 WCF and .44 WCF. May have been offered in .32-40 and .38-55 chamberings. A 20-gauge shotgun barrel was offered separately for these rifles. Features included set trigger, rebounding hammer, pistol-grip stock and takedown. Seldom encountered, Merwin Hulbert name on these should bring a premium over standard Hopkins & Allen single-shot rifles. A small frame "Merwin Hulbert & Co's. Junior" rifle was also offered, chambered for .22 rimfire.

METROPOLITAN ARMS CO.
New York, New York

Established in February 1864, company manufactured copies of Colt Model 1851 and 1861 Navy Revolvers, as well as copies of Colt Model 1862 Police Revolver. Two of the firm's principle officers were Samuel and William Syms (formerly of Blunt & Syms) and it is believed that they were responsible for production. Curiously although, most Metropolitan pistols were produced during 1864 to 1866 period. Company itself was not dissolved until 1920.

1851 Navy Revolver

.36-caliber percussion revolver, with 7.5" octagonal barrel and 6-shot cylinder. Blued case hardened, with walnut grips. Barrel marked "Metropolitan Arms Co. New York". Approximately 6,000 made during 1860s. Those bearing H.E. Dimick markings are worth considerably more than standard marked examples.

Standard Navy Model

	NIB	EXC.	V.G.	GOOD	FAIR	POOR
	—	—	—	4100	1400	500

H.E. Dimick Navy Model

	NIB	EXC.	V.G.	GOOD	FAIR	POOR
	—	—	—	8000	3000	850

1861 Navy Revolver

.36-caliber percussion revolver, with 7.5" round barrel and 6-shot cylinder. Loading lever of rack-and-pinion type. Blued case hardened, with walnut grips. Barrel marked "Metropolitan Arms Co. New York". Approximately 50 made in 1864 and 1865.

	NIB	EXC.	V.G.	GOOD	FAIR	POOR
	—	—	—	8000	3300	950

Police Revolver

.36-caliber percussion revolver, with 4.5", 5.5" or 6.5" round barrels and fluted 5-shot cylinder. Blued case hardened, with walnut grips. Barrel normally marked "Metropolitan Arms Co. New York", although examples have been noted without any markings. Approximately 2,750 made between 1864 and 1866.

	NIB	EXC.	V.G.	GOOD	FAIR	POOR
	—	—	2400	1650	650	250

MIIDA
Marubeni America Corp.
Japan

Model 612

12-gauge boxlock over/under shotgun, with 26" or 28" ventilated rib barrels, single-selective trigger, automatic ejectors. Blued, with walnut stock. Imported between 1972 and 1974.

	NIB	EXC.	V.G.	GOOD	FAIR	POOR
	—	900	750	600	400	250

Model 612 Skeet

As above, with 27" Skeet choked barrels. Some engraving. Imported between 1972 and 1974.

	NIB	EXC.	V.G.	GOOD	FAIR	POOR
	—	900	750	600	400	250

Model 2100 Skeet

Similar to Model 612, with more engraving coverage.

	NIB	EXC.	V.G.	GOOD	FAIR	POOR
	—	950	800	650	450	300

Model 2200 Trap or Skeet

As above, with 30" trap or 27" skeet bored barrels. More finely engraved. Imported between 1972 and 1974.

	NIB	EXC.	V.G.	GOOD	FAIR	POOR
	—	1100	850	700	450	300

NIB	EXC.	V.G.	GOOD	FAIR	POOR

Model 2300 Trap or Skeet

More finely finished Model 2200. Imported from 1972 until 1974.

	EXC.	V.G.	GOOD	FAIR	POOR
—	1200	900	750	500	300

Model GRT Trap or GRS Skeet

12-gauge boxlock shotgun. Fitted with false sideplates, 27" skeet or 29" Full choked barrels, single-selective trigger, automatic ejector. Imported between 1972 and 1974.

	EXC.	V.G.	GOOD	FAIR	POOR
—	2250	1850	1250	800	500

MILLER ARMS
Sturgis, South Dakota

NOTE: There are a large number of extra costs options available for these rifles.

Standard Rifle

Single shot falling block rifle. Fitted with 26" round barrel. Chambered for centerfire cartridges up to .375-caliber. Stock is checkered XXX walnut, with pistol-grip. Quarter rib scope base. Weight depends on caliber.

NIB	EXC.	V.G.	GOOD	FAIR	POOR
4500	3500	2000	1300	700	350

Low Boy

Features 24" half round/half octagon barrel. All other features as above.

NIB	EXC.	V.G.	GOOD	FAIR	POOR
5000	4000	2250	1300	700	350

Model F

Similar to standard rifle, with addition of 26" octagon barrel, tang sight. Globe front sight. All calibers to .45-110.

NIB	EXC.	V.G.	GOOD	FAIR	POOR
6000	4750	3000	2200	1300	500

MILTECH
Los Altos, California

Company rebuilds and refinishes selected military firearms. All firearms are thoroughly inspected for safety and are considered safe to shoot. All firearms have their original receivers and markings. These rifles are not stamped with Miltech name, but do have a unique Miltech pine crate serial numbered to gun as standard. Company will verify it did the rebuild if asked. All guns come with manual, sling and other selected accessories depending on model.

German Mauser Model 98k

NIB	EXC.	V.G.	GOOD	FAIR	POOR
1495	1150	900	750	550	300

M1 Garand

NOTE: International Harvester and Winchester add $225.

NIB	EXC.	V.G.	GOOD	FAIR	POOR
1595	1200	850	700	500	300

M1D Garand

NIB	EXC.	V.G.	GOOD	FAIR	POOR
2950	2500	1900	1350	700	400

M1 Carbine

NOTE: Rockola and Winchester add $200-300.

NIB	EXC.	V.G.	GOOD	FAIR	POOR
1295	1050	800	575	375	200

Model 1941 Johnson

NIB	EXC.	V.G.	GOOD	FAIR	POOR
5000	4000	3000	2000	1000	500

Model 1903 Springfield

NIB	EXC.	V.G.	GOOD	FAIR	POOR
1495	1150	900	750	550	300

Model 1903A3 Springfield

NIB	EXC.	V.G.	GOOD	FAIR	POOR
1495	1150	900	750	550	300

Model 1903 Mark I Springfield

NIB	EXC.	V.G.	GOOD	FAIR	POOR
1550	1225	975	800	575	325

	NIB	EXC.	V.G.	GOOD	FAIR	POOR

Model 1917 U.S. Enfield

	NIB	EXC.	V.G.	GOOD	FAIR	POOR
	1495	1150	900	750	550	300

MINNEAPOLIS F. A. CO.
Minneapolis, Minnesota

Palm Pistol

.32-caliber radial cylinder pistol, with 1.75" barrel. Manufactured by Ames Manufacturing Company (see Ames entry). Nickel-plated, with hard rubber grips. Sideplates marked "Minneapolis Firearms Co." and "The Protector". Several thousand sold during 1890s.

		V.G.	GOOD	FAIR	POOR
—	—	2250	1850	950	300

MIROKU B. C.
Miroku, Japan

Firearms produced by this manufacturer have been imported and marketed by a variety of companies such as Charles Daly, Browning, Winchester and SKB.

MITCHELL ARMS, INC.
Santa Ana, California

Importer and distributor of foreign-made firearms. Company no longer in business. However, some Mitchell models were available under Brolin Arms through 1998. Brolin Arms was no longer in business as of 1999. Company also imported Yugoslavian-manufactured semi-automatic AK-47 rifles in 7.62x39mm, as well as 7.62x54mm.

RIFLES

Galil

.22 or .22 Magnum caliber copy of Galil rifle. Introduced in 1987.

500	400	300	150	125	100

MAS

.22 or .22 Magnum caliber copy of French MAS Bullpup Service Rifle. Introduced in 1987.

400	325	200	150	125	100

AK-22

.22 or .22 Magnum caliber copy of AK-47 rifle. Introduced in 1985.

400	300	250	125	100	75

M-16

.22 rimfire copy of Colt AR-15. Introduced in 1987.

325	250	150	125	100	75

PPSH-30/50

.22 or .22 Magnum caliber copy of PPSH Submachine gun.

375	325	225	150	75	60

HANDGUNS

Trophy II

Semi-automatic pistol chambered for .22 LR cartridge. Offered in 7.25" fluted or 5.5" bull barrel. Barrels are interchangeable. Trigger adjustable for weight and pull. Walnut grips, with thumb rest standard.

400	325	275	200	150	100

Citation II

Similar to Trophy II, with matte satin finish.

375	300	250	200	150	100

Sharpshooter II

Stainless steel target pistol, with 5.5" bull barrel to which barrel weights can be added. Fully adjustable rear sight. Checkered walnut grips standard.

325	275	225	200	150	100

	NIB	EXC.	V.G.	GOOD	FAIR	POOR

Olympic I.S.U.

Competition pistol features 6.75" barrel, with integral stabilizer. Rear sight adjustable as is trigger. Barrel weights are adjustable as well as removable.

	525	475	400	300	200	100

Victor II

.22-caliber pistol built from stainless steel. Has interchangeable barrels in 4.5" or 5.5" lengths. Barrels have full length ventilated ribs, checkered walnut grips with thumb rest. Gold plated trigger is adjustable.

	450	375	325	250	175	125

Victor II with Weaver Rib

	525	450	375	275	175	125

High Standard Collectors' Association Special Editions

Limited run of Mitchell's version of High Standard pistol, with special roll marking on slide "High Standard / Collectors Association / Special Edition" and a special serial number series with HSCA prefix. Manufactured by Pastucek Industries, Fort Worth, Texas.

Trophy II

5.5" barrel. See standard Mitchell guns for rest of description.

	420	325	—	—	—	—

Victor II

4.5" barrel. See standard Mitchell guns for rest of description.

	450	325	—	—	—	—

Citation II

7.25" barrel. See standard Mitchell guns for rest of description.

	400	300	—	—	—	—

Three Gun Set

Includes Trophy II, Olympic ISU and Victor II. Eleven sets manufactured.

	1400	1100	—	—	—	—

Six Gun Set

Includes 5.5" Trophy II, 6.75" Olympic II, 4.5" Victor II, Sharpshooter II, Citation II and 4.5" Sport King II. Nineteen sets manufactured.

	2450	1975	—	—	—	—

Skorpion

.32-caliber semi-automatic pistol, with 4.75" barrel. Either 20- or 30-shot magazine. Blued, with plastic grips. Imported from Yugoslavia in 1987 and 1988 only.

	—	600	500	425	350	175

Spectre

9mm caliber semi-automatic pistol, with 8" shrouded barrel. Either 30- or 50-shot magazine. Blued, with plastic grips. Also produced with 18" barrel and folding buttstock. Imported from Yugoslavia in 1987 and 1988.

	—	600	500	425	350	175

MITCHELL'S MAUSERS
Fountain Valley, California

Black Arrow

.50-caliber bolt-action rifle, with 5-round box magazine. Fitted with recoil compensator, iron sights, bipod.

	6000	5000	4000	2700	1600	500

Centurion

Double-action revolver, with 4" or 6" barrel. Chambered for .357 Magnum cartridge. Blued or stainless steel.

	695	550	400	300	200	100

Valkyrie

Chambered for .44 Magnum cartridge. Choice of 4" or 6" barrel. Blued or stainless steel.

	895	700	500	400	300	200

	NIB	EXC.	V.G.	GOOD	FAIR	POOR

Gold Series '03

Chambered for 9mm, .40 S&W or .45 ACP cartridge. Built on Model 1911 Government Model. Blued or stainless steel.

	NIB	EXC.	V.G.	GOOD	FAIR	POOR
	795	600	450	325	250	150

Escalade

Slide-action shotgun chambered for 12-gauge shell. Fitted with 18.5" barrel; 28" vent rib barrel; 22" barrel with Turkey choke. Turkish walnut stock. Blued.

	NIB	EXC.	V.G.	GOOD	FAIR	POOR
	395	300	250	200	150	100

Sabre

Semi-automatic 12-gauge shotgun. Choice of 22" vent rib barrel; 28" vent rib barrel. Blued.

	NIB	EXC.	V.G.	GOOD	FAIR	POOR
	495	400	350	300	250	150

Mauser M98 North American

Bolt-action rifle fitted with Mauser 98 action. Offered in most standard hunting calibers. **NOTE:** Magnum calibers add $2,000.

	NIB	EXC.	V.G.	GOOD	FAIR	POOR
	7000	6000	4500	2275	1500	400

Mauser M98 Varmint

As above chambered for .22-250 or .220 Swift.

	NIB	EXC.	V.G.	GOOD	FAIR	POOR
	6000	5000	3500	1775	1000	300

Mauser M98 African/Alaskan

Chambered for heavy calibers up to .500 Jeffery.

	NIB	EXC.	V.G.	GOOD	FAIR	POOR
	8000	7500	6500	2500	1500	500

MK ARMS, INC.
Irvine, California

Model 760

9mm caliber semi-automatic carbine, with 16" shrouded barrel, fixed sights and 14-, 24- or 36-shot magazine. Parkerized with folding stock. Introduced in 1983.

	NIB	EXC.	V.G.	GOOD	FAIR	POOR
	950	700	575	400	250	125

MKE
Ankara, Turkey

Kirrikale

7.65 or 9mm short semi-automatic pistol, with 4" barrel and 7-shot magazine. Unauthorized copy of Walther PP. Blued, with plastic grips.

	NIB	EXC.	V.G.	GOOD	FAIR	POOR
	450	375	275	225	150	100

MODESTO SANTOS CIA.
Eibar, Spain

Action, Corrientes, and M.S.

6.35mm or 7.65mm caliber semi-automatic pistol of low quality. Marked on slide "Pistolet Automatique Model 1920". Blued, with composition grips having monogram "M.S." cast in them. Manufactured between 1920 and 1935.

	NIB	EXC.	V.G.	GOOD	FAIR	POOR
	—	275	175	125	75	50

Action

6.35mm or 7.65mm semi-automatic pistol. Marked on slide "Pistolet Automatique Modele 1920". Often found bearing trade name "Corrientes" as well as maker's trademark "MS".

	NIB	EXC.	V.G.	GOOD	FAIR	POOR
	—	275	175	115	80	60

MONTENEGRAN-GASSER
See—Gasser, Leopold

MOORE'S PATENT FIREARMS CO.
Brooklyn, New York

In 1866, this company became known as National Arms Company.

No. 1 Derringer

.41-caliber spur trigger all metal pistol, with 2.5" barrel. Blued or silver-plated. Approximately 10,000 manufactured between 1860 and 1865. Also marketed as No. 1 Derringer by Colt Company after they purchased National Arms Company in 1870.

	NIB	EXC.	V.G.	GOOD	FAIR	POOR

1st Variation Marked "Patent Applied For

	—	—	3200	2500	1100	400

2nd Variation Marked "D. Moore Patented Feb. 19 1861

	—	—	2200	1500	700	250

Standard Model Marked "Moore's Pat F.A. Co.

	—	—	1200	850	350	150

National Arms Co. Production.

	—	—	1250	875	385	150

Iron Model

	—	—	1300	1100	550	250

Pocket Revolver

.32 teat fire caliber spur trigger revolver, with round 3.25" barrel and 6-shot cylinder. Blued or silver plated, with walnut grips. Approximately 30,000 manufactured between 1864 and 1870.

	—	—	800	550	275	100

Belt Revolver

.32 rimfire caliber revolver, with 4", 5" or 6" octagonal barrel and 7-shot cylinder. Barrel and cylinder blued. Brass frame sometimes silver-plated, with walnut grips. Barrel marked "D. Moore Patent Sept. 18, 1860". Several thousand manufactured between 1861 and 1863.

	—	—	1450	950	350	150

MORGAN & CLAPP
New Haven, Connecticut

Single-Shot Pocket Pistol

.22- or .23-caliber spur trigger single-shot pistol, with 3.5" octagonal barrel. Blued silver-plated frame, with walnut grips. Barrel marked "Morgan & Clapp New Haven". Active 1864 to 1867.

	—	—	1150	650	250	100

MORINI
Italy

C-80 Standard

.22-caliber single-shot pistol, with free floating 10" barrel, match sights. Adjustable frame and grips. Discontinued in 1989.

	—	1100	800	675	550	250

CM-80 Super Competition

As above, with trigger adjustable from 5 to 120 grams pressure, Plexiglass front sight, polished finish. Discontinued in 1989.

	—	1200	900	750	650	300

Model 84E Free Pistol

Introduced in 1995. Competition pistol features 11.4" barrel chambered for .22 LR. Single-shot. Adjustable sights with adjustable electronic trigger. Weight about 44 oz.

	1650	1150	900	700	500	200

MORRONE
Hope Valley, Rhode Island
See—Rhode Island Arms Company

MORSE
Greenville, South Carolina
State Armory

Morse Carbine

Overall length 40"; barrel length 2"; caliber .50 (other calibers are known to have been made on an experimental basis). Round barrel blued; frame brass; stock walnut or beechwood. Approximately 1,000 manufactured during Civil War.

	—	—	27000	23000	7500	1500

NIB	EXC.	V.G.	GOOD	FAIR	POOR

MOSSBERG, O. F. & SONS, INC.
North Haven, Connecticut

Founded by Oscar F. Mossberg in 1892 at Fitchburg, Massachusetts. Company for a time was located at Chicopee Falls, Massachusetts and since 1962 has been in North Haven, Connecticut. Oldest family-owned firearms manufacturer in America.

HANDGUNS

Brownie

.22-caliber four-barreled pocket pistol, with revolving firing pin. Pistol resembles a semi-automatic. Manufactured from 1906 to approximately 1940. Premium for in box with papers.

750	450	325	300	225	150

RIFLES

Model K

.22-caliber slide-action rifle, with 22" barrel, tubular magazine, internal hammer and takedown system. Blued, with walnut stock. Discontinued in 1931.

—	350	250	150	75	50

Model M

As above, with 24" octagonal barrel. Manufactured from 1928 and 1931.

—	350	250	150	75	50

Model L

.22-caliber Martini-style single-shot takedown rifle, with 24" barrel. Manufactured from 1927 to 1932.

—	600	475	350	175	100

Beginning in 1930, Mossberg company manufactured a variety of utilitarian single-shot and repeating bolt-action rifles. Later they introduced a similar line of semi-automatic rifles. As these arms were intended for extensive use and were low-priced, values for them may be categorized as listed.

Bolt-Action Rifles

Model10	Model 25	Model 340M
Model 14	Model 25A	Model 341
Model 140B	Model 26B	Model 342K
Model 140K	Model 26C	Model 346B
Model 142A	Model 30	Model 346K
Model 142K	Model 320B	Model 352K
Model 144	Model 320K	
Model 144LS	Model 321K	
Model 146B	Model 340B	
Model 20	Model 340K	

400	300	200	100	75	50

Semi-Automatic Rifles

Model 50	Model 152K
Model 51	Model 350K
Model 51M	Model 351C
Model 151K	Model 351K
Model 151M	Model 432
Model 152	

350	300	200	150	100	50

Targo Smoothbore Series

Early 1940s, Mossberg produced a series of bolt-action .22 rimfire rifles, with smoothbore barrels. Rifles were mainly designed for clay target game called Targo, in which shooters used .22 LR shot ammunition. Game never achieved much popularity. Rifled barrel section several inches long could be attached to muzzle, which allowed use of standard ammunition. Some models came with a smoothbore attachment that extended length of barrel. Other accessories included clay target launcher that attached to barrel, case designed for rifle and supply of small clay targets. There were several model variations: single shot (Model 26T), two repeater models with 7-round magazines (42T and 42TR) and fourth version with an extended 15-round clip (B42T). Most of these rifles were produced from 1940-1942 and again in late '40s, after WWII. Two models were introduced briefly in early 1960s, Model 320TR single shot and 340TR repeater.

NIB	EXC.	V.G.	GOOD	FAIR	POOR

NOTE: Add 50 percent for original case and all original accessories; 20 percent for Model 26T or B42T0 rarest models of this series.

500	425	350	250	200	100

Model 400 Palomino

.22-caliber lever-action rifle, with 22" barrel, open sights and tubular magazine. Also made with 18.5" barrel. Blued, with walnut stock. Manufactured from 1959 to 1964.

350	300	200	150	100	50

Model 702 Plinkster

Introduced in 2004. This .22-caliber semi-automatic rifle fitted with 18" barrel and adjustable sights. Detachable 10-round magazine. Blued finish. Choice of black synthetic, hardwood, synthetic thumb-hole, solid pink, pink camo or Mossy Oak New Break-up camo finish stock. Weight about 4 lbs. Also available as scope package (add 10 percent). Tiger maple or carbon fiber stock and chromed barrel and receiver. By 2008, a variety of color and stock options, including a modern synthetic version of Mossberg's old flip-down fore-end and thumb-hole stocks had been added to line. These will bring more or less than values listed, according to local demand.

175	145	110	75	50	25

Model 702 International Plinkster

Features 21" chrome barrel, with iron sights. Black synthetic stock. Weight about 4.5 lbs. **NOTE:** Add $75 for muzzle-brake.

195	160	125	90	65	40

Model 817 Varmint

Introduced in 2008. Offering by Mossberg International features 21" free-floating blued or brushed chrome barrel, hardwood or black synthetic stock, factory Weaver mounts, detachable box magazine and .17 HMR chambering.

175	150	125	100	75	50

Tactical .22

AR-styled rimfire auto-loading rifle, with 18" free-floating barrel. Matte blue finish. Matte black synthetic stock, with fixed or adjustable length of pull. Magazine capacity 10 or 25 rounds. Quad fore-end for unlimited mounting opportunities of optical or light systems. Peep rear and front post sight are standard.

235	200	160	120	100	80

Model 100 ATR (All-Terrain Rifle)

Introduced in 2005. Bolt-action rifle chambered for .270 or .30-06 calibers. Fitted with 22" barrel. No sights. Choice of black synthetic, synthetic walnut or camo stock. Matte blue or all-weather finish. Weight about 7 lbs.; .243, 308. Also available as 3X9 scope package. **NOTE:** Add 10 percent for scope; $40 for all-weather finish.

360	300	250	200	150	100

Model 100 ATR Night Train

Similar to above, with black synthetic stock, factory-mounted 4x16 scope, bipod and .308 Winchester chambering. Introduced 2008.

375	325	275	225	165	125

Model 100 ATR Super Bantam

Similar to Model 100 ATR. Chambered only in .243 and .308. No sights. Synthetic black stock adjustable for length of pull. Introduced in 2007.

360	300	250	200	150	100

Model 800

Bolt-action rifle manufactured in a variety of calibers, with 22" barrel and folding leaf rear sight. Blued, with walnut stock. Introduced in 1967.

400	325	200	150	100	75

Model 800D

As above, with comb stock, rosewood fore-end tip and pistol-grip cap. Manufactured from 1970 to 1973.

400	300	250	200	150	100

Model 800V

As above, with 24" heavy barrel not fitted with sights. Introduced in 1968.

400	300	225	150	100	75

	NIB	EXC.	V.G.	GOOD	FAIR	POOR

Model 800M

As above, with Mannlicher-style stock.

	NIB	EXC.	V.G.	GOOD	FAIR	POOR
	500	375	250	200	150	100

Model 800SM

As above, with 4X scope.

	NIB	EXC.	V.G.	GOOD	FAIR	POOR
	550	425	275	225	150	100

Model 801 Half-Pint Plinkster

Entry-level .22 LR single-shot rifle, with removable magazine plug to allow insertion of 10-round magazine. 16" barrel, hardwood stock, adjustable open sights. Overall weight 4 lbs. Introduced 2008.

	NIB	EXC.	V.G.	GOOD	FAIR	POOR
	150	125	100	75	50	25

Model 802 Plinkster

Bolt-action rifle chambered in .22 LR, with 18" steel barrel. Black synthetic stock with schnabel. Available with 4X scope package (add 10 percent). Introduced 2006.

	NIB	EXC.	V.G.	GOOD	FAIR	POOR
	150	125	100	75	50	25

Model 817 Plinkster

Similar to Model 802 Plinkster. Chambered in .17 HMR. Introduced in 2007.

	NIB	EXC.	V.G.	GOOD	FAIR	POOR
	175	150	125	100	75	50

Model 810

.270 to .338 Winchester Magnum caliber bolt-action rifle, with 22" or 24" barrel. Fitted with folding rear sight. Blued, with Monte Carlo-style stock. Introduced in 1970.

	NIB	EXC.	V.G.	GOOD	FAIR	POOR
	—	275	250	200	150	100

Model 472C

.30-30 or.35 Remington caliber lever-action rifle, with 20" barrel, open sights and tubular magazine. Blued, with walnut stock. Introduced in 1972.

	NIB	EXC.	V.G.	GOOD	FAIR	POOR
	—	250	195	150	100	75

Model 472P

As above, with pistol-grip stock. Not fitted with saddle ring.

	NIB	EXC.	V.G.	GOOD	FAIR	POOR
	—	250	195	150	100	75

Model 472 One in Five Thousand

As above, with etched receiver, brass buttplate, saddle ring and barrel band. Total 5,000 made in 1974.

	NIB	EXC.	V.G.	GOOD	FAIR	POOR
	—	400	350	300	200	150

Model 479 PCA

Similar to Model 472C in .30-30 caliber, with 20" barrel. Blued, with walnut stock.

	NIB	EXC.	V.G.	GOOD	FAIR	POOR
	—	250	195	150	100	75

Model 479 RR (Roy Rogers)

As above, with gold-plated trigger, barrel band and "Roy Rogers" signature. Total 5,000 made in 1983.

	NIB	EXC.	V.G.	GOOD	FAIR	POOR
	—	325	250	200	150	100

Model 464 Lever-Action Centerfire

Side-loading top-ejecting lever rifle, with button-rifled 20" barrel, blued finish and hardwood stock. Straight-/pistol-grip stock. Tang-mounted thumb safety. Chambered in .30-30.

	NIB	EXC.	V.G.	GOOD	FAIR	POOR
	—	400	350	300	200	150

Model 464 Lever-Action Rimfire

Rimfire version of above, with 18" barrel.

	NIB	EXC.	V.G.	GOOD	FAIR	POOR
	—	375	300	250	200	150

SSi-One Sporter

Introduced in 2000. Single-shot rifle chambered for .223, .243, 270 Win., .308 and .30-06 cartridges. Fitted with 24" barrel, without sights. Matte blue finish. Checkered walnut stock. Weight about 8 lbs. Interchangeable barrels including 12-gauge.

SSi-One Varmint

Similar to single-shot model above. Fitted with 24" bull barrel chambered for .22-250 cartridge. Walnut stock. Weight about 10 lbs. Introduced in 2000. Interchangeable barrels.

	NIB	EXC.	V.G.	GOOD	FAIR	POOR

SSi-One Slug

Single-shot model similar to other SSi-One guns. Fitted with 24" fully rifled 12-gauge barrel. Walnut stock. Weight about 8 lbs. Interchangeable barrels. Introduced in 2000.

SSi-One Turkey

Same as above, with 24" smoothbore barrel. Will handle 3.5" magnum 12-gauge shells. Weight about 7.5 lbs. Introduced in 2001.

Model 1500

.223 to .338 Winchester Magnum bolt-action rifle, with 22" or 24" barrel, 5- or 6-shot magazine and various sights. Blued, with hardwood or walnut stock. Manufactured by Howa in Japan. Also known as Smith & Wesson Model 1500. Offered in 1986 and 1987.

Mountaineer Grade I

—	350	250	225	150	125	

Mountaineer Grade II

—	325	275	250	175	125	

Varmint

24" heavy barrel.

—	350	300	275	200	150	

Model 1550

As above in .243, .270 or .30-06 caliber. Offered in 1986 and 1987.

—	325	275	250	175	125	

Model 1700 LS

Similar to above in same calibers, with 22" barrel not fitted for sights. Machine jeweled bolt and knurled bolt handle. Blued, with walnut stock. Schnabel fore-end. Offered in 1986 and 1987.

—	400	350	275	200	150	

Mossberg 4x4

Bolt-action centerfire rifle. Chambered in .25-06, .270, .30-06, 7mm Rem Magnum, .300 Win Magnum, .338 Win Magnum. Barrel length 22" (iron sight) or 24" (sightless). Detachable box magazine, two-position safety. Walnut, laminated or black synthetic stock, with lightening cutouts in butt and fore-end. Scope package also available. Introduced in 2007.

475	375	300	225	175	125	

Mossberg 4X4 Classic Stock Synthetic

Similar to above, with black synthetic stock. Marinecote metal surfaces.

—	450	350	275	200	125	

Mossberg 4X4 Scoped Combo

Similar to above, with matte blue finish and 3x9 scope. Various stock compositions, including laminate.

—	450	350	275	200	125	

Mossberg 4X4 Classic Walnut Stock

Similar to above, with checkered walnut stock.

—	500	450	350	225	150	

Model MMR Hunter

AR-15 style semi-automatic carbine in .223/5.56 NATO, with 20" free-floated barrel, start SE-1 pistol-grip, fixed A-2 stock, round aluminum handguard, flattop receiver. Available in black, Mossy Oak Brush or Mossy Oak Treestand camo. Available in several other variations including Tactical model

885	790	700	600	450	300	

Model MVP Flex

Bolt-action centerfire in .223/5.56 or .308/7.62 NATO. Feeds from any AR-15 or AR-10 magazine. Synthetic FLEX system stock. Barrel 18.5" or 20" with or without threaded muzzle and flash hider (on 18.5" model). Also available in Predator/Varmint variation with target-style laminated stock and Patrol Model with 16.25" barrel in .223, .308 or .300 Blackout. Deduct 10 percent for Predator/Varmint; 25 percent for Patrol model.

850	700	625	500	400	300	

NIB	EXC.	V.G.	GOOD	FAIR	POOR

SHOTGUNS

Mossberg manufactured a variety of shotguns that were sold at low to moderate prices. Values for these arms are approximately all the same.

Miscellaneous Bolt-Action Shotguns

Model 73	Model 190K	Model 395T
Model 173	Model 195D	Model 395S
Model 173Y	Model 195K	
Model 183D	Model 385K	
Model 183K	Model 385T	
Model 183T	Model 390K	
Model 185D	Model 390T	
Model 185K	Model 395K	
Model 190D		

NIB	EXC.	V.G.	GOOD	FAIR	POOR
—	150	125	90	65	35

Model 695

Introduced in 1969. Bolt-action shotgun chambered for 12-gauge shell. Barrel length 22" with rifled or plain bore. Finish matte blue. In 1997, offered with 22" plain ported barrel with rifled bore. Magazine capacity 3 rounds. Weight about 7.5 lbs.

NIB	EXC.	V.G.	GOOD	FAIR	POOR
275	225	175	150	125	100

Model 695 Camo

Introduced in 2000. Same as standard Model 695, with addition of Woodlands camo finish.

NIB	EXC.	V.G.	GOOD	FAIR	POOR
375	325	275	250	195	150

Model 200K

12-gauge slide-action shotgun, with 28" barrel and Mossberg select choke. Blued, with composition slide handle. Walnut stock. Manufactured from 1955 to 1959.

NIB	EXC.	V.G.	GOOD	FAIR	POOR
—	150	125	100	75	50

MODEL 500 SERIES

12-, 20-gauge or .410 bore slide-action shotgun. Manufactured in a variety of barrel lengths and styles as listed.

Model 500 Regal

NIB	EXC.	V.G.	GOOD	FAIR	POOR
—	250	200	150	100	75

Model 500 Field Grade

NIB	EXC.	V.G.	GOOD	FAIR	POOR
285	250	200	150	100	75

Model 500 Steel Shot

Chrome bore.

NIB	EXC.	V.G.	GOOD	FAIR	POOR
—	300	250	200	125	100

Model 500 Slugster

Crown grade, iron sights.

NIB	EXC.	V.G.	GOOD	FAIR	POOR
—	275	250	200	150	100

Model 500 Camper

18.5" barrel, camo case.

NIB	EXC.	V.G.	GOOD	FAIR	POOR
—	295	275	225	175	100

Model 500 Hi-Rib Trap

NIB	EXC.	V.G.	GOOD	FAIR	POOR
—	275	250	200	150	100

Model 500 Super Grade

NIB	EXC.	V.G.	GOOD	FAIR	POOR
—	300	275	225	175	100

Model 500 Pigeon Grade

NIB	EXC.	V.G.	GOOD	FAIR	POOR
—	375	300	250	200	125

Model 500 Pigeon Grade Trap

NIB	EXC.	V.G.	GOOD	FAIR	POOR
—	450	375	300	250	175

Model 500 Persuader

Riot gun, 18.5" barrel 12-gauge; 20" barrel 20-gauge (added 2008).

NIB	EXC.	V.G.	GOOD	FAIR	POOR
300	275	225	175	100	75

	NIB	EXC.	V.G.	GOOD	FAIR	POOR

Model 500 Mariner

Marinecote finish.

	400	325	225	200	150	125

Model 500 Cruiser

Pistol-grip only.

	375	300	250	200	125	100

Model 500 Muzzleloader Combo

	350	325	275	225	200	150

Model 500 Bantam

Introduced in 1996. Slightly smaller overall than full-size guns. Chambered for 20-gauge shell. Fitted with 22" shotgun barrel; 24" rifled vent rib barrel. Walnut stock. Weight about 6.9 lbs.

	275	225	200	150	125	100

Model 500 Super Bantam Field

Introduced in 2005. Features 20-gauge 3" chamber, with 22" ventilated rib barrel with choke tubes. Blued finish. Synthetic stock, with adjustable length of pull. Weight about 5.25 lbs.

	315	275	175	125	100	75

Model 500 Super Bantam Turkey

20-gauge 3" model has 22" vent rib ported barrel, with extra full choke. Synthetic camo stock. Adjustable stock for length of pull. Weight about 5.25 lbs. Introduced in 2005.

	375	325	250	175	150	100

Model 500 Super Bantam Slug

20-gauge model features full rifled 24" ported barrel, with adjustable sights. Synthetic stock, with blue or camo finish. Weight about 5.25 lbs. Introduced in 2005. In 2008, a version with an integrated scope base was added to this series.

	375	325	250	175	150	100

Model 500 Super Bantam Combo

Introduced in 2005. Features 22" vent rib barrel, with choke tubes; 24" fully rifled ported barrel. Camo finish, with adjustable length of pull synthetic stock. Weight about 5.25 lbs.

	400	325	275	200	150	125

Model 500 Bullpup

12 gauge slide-action Bullpup shotgun, with 18.5" or 20" shrouded barrel. Matte black finish, with composition stock. Introduced in 1986. Discontinued. Values shown are for 6-shot version. **NOTE:** Add 25 percent for 8-shot.

	600	500	375	250	150	100

Model 500 Slug Gun Viking Grade

Introduced in 1996. A 12-gauge with 24" rifled barrel; iron sights; green synthetic stock. **NOTE:** In 1997, Mossberg introduced ported barrels on some of its slug models. These ported barrels will be seen on rifled barrels only.

	300	275	225	175	100	75

Model 500 Grand Slam Turkey

12- or 20-gauge 3" gun. Introduced in 2004. Offered with 20" vent rib barrel; adjustable fiber optic sights; ported Extra Full choke tube. Available in Realtree Hardwood or Mossy Oak Break-Up camo pattern. Weight about: 7 lbs. 12-gauge; 6.75 lbs. 20-gauge.

	375	325	250	175	150	100

Model 500 Flyway Series

Introduced in 2005. A 12-gauge 3.5", with 28" vent rib barrel with fiber optic front sight. Choke tubes. Advantage camo synthetic stock. Weight about 7.5 lbs.

	400	325	225	200	150	125

Model 500 FLEX

Introduced in 2012, this variant of Model 500 series features FLEX TLS (Tool-less Locking System), which allows user a simple method of changing stocks, fore-ends and recoil pad. This system is offered in field and tactical models in 12- or 20-gauge. Values are for field model. **NOTE:** Deduct $75 to $100 for tactical.

	600	500	425	350	300	150

	NIB	EXC.	V.G.	GOOD	FAIR	POOR

Model 500 Duck Commander

Same features as FLEX series with Max-5 Realtree camo, premium Tru-Glo/Tru-Bead dual color front fiber optic sight, logo of Duck Commander TV show engraved on stock and American flag bandana. Introduced in 2014.

725	650	500	400	300	200

Model 500 Combo

500 series has a total of nine combination sets available to choose from. They are combination of shotgun barrels and rifled barrels for different hunting applications. Offered in both 12- and 20-gauge sets of same gauge only.

400	325	275	225	175	125

Model 500 USA

Introduced in 1997. Similar to military model. Has Parkerized finish, with heavy-duty sling swivels. Fitted with plain 20" barrel choked Cylinder. Stock black synthetic. Magazine capacity 6 rounds. Weight about 7.2 lbs.

250	200	175	150	125	100

Model 500 HS (Home Security)

Chambered for .410 shell. Fitted with 18.5" barrel. Magazine capacity 5 rounds. Synthetic stock and blue finish. **NOTE:** In 1999, Mossberg offered a .50 muzzle-loader 24" fully rifled barrel that will fit directly onto any six-shot Model 500.

350	325	275	225	200	150

Model 500 Rolling Thunder

Home defense/tactical model is a 3" 12-gauge. Featuring pistol-grip, 23" barrel with heat shield and recoil-reducing stabilizer and six-round capacity.

400	325	275	225	175	125

Model 500 Tactical Cruiser "Door Buster

Similar to above, with serrated muzzle. A TALO exclusive.

525	425	325	225	175	125

Model 500 Tactical

Model 500 Tactical 8-shot pump has 20" barrel and ghost ring sights. Black synthetic pistol-grip stock can be adjusted to provide a 10.75" to a 14-5/8" length of pull. Weight: 6.25 lbs. Capacity: 7+1. Matte blue finish.

480	440	400	370	320	280

Model 500 JIC (Just In Case)

Survival model is a 3" 12-gauge. Featuring pistol-grip, 18.5" barrel and weatherproof pack tube. Three different models available with different finishes and accessory packages. **NOTE:** Add 15 percent for nickel finish; 10 percent for JIC II with black finish in black nylon case.

375	325	250	175	150	100

Model 505 Youth

Offered in 20-gauge or .410 bore. Fitted with 20" vent rib barrel with choke tubes 20-gauge; fixed modified choke .410 bore. Wood stock, with recoil pad. Blued finish. Weight about 5.25 lbs.

315	275	175	125	100	75

Model 510 Mini Shotgun

Compact pump-action shotgun. Based on Model 500 action. Chambered in 3" 20-gauge and .410 bore. Features include 18.5" vent rib barrel with interchangeable (20-gauge) or fixed (.410 bore) choke, black synthetic stock, inserts to adjust length of pull from 10.5" to 11.5" and 4-shot capacity. Weight 5 lbs.

315	275	175	125	100	75

MODEL 535 SERIES

Model 535 ATS (All Terrain Shotgun) Field

Introduced in 2005. This 12-gauge 3.5" model features 28" vent rib barrel with choke tubes. Blued finish, with checkered wood stock with pistol-grip. Weight about 6.75 lbs.

375	325	250	175	150	100

Model 535 ATS Turkey

As above, with 22" vent rib barrel with extra full choke. Fiber optic front sight. Synthetic stock, with matte blue or camo finish. Weight about 6.5 lbs. Introduced in 2005. **NOTE:** Add $55 for camo finish.

375	325	250	175	150	100

	NIB	EXC.	V.G.	GOOD	FAIR	POOR

Model 535 ATS Waterfowl

Fitted with 28" vent rib barrel with choke tubes. Fiber optic front sight. Synthetic stock, with matte blue or camo finish. Weight about 6.75 lbs. Introduced in 2005. **NOTE:** Add $55 for camo finish.

375	325	250	175	150	100

Model 535 ATS Slugster

Fitted with fully rifled 24" vent rib barrel with adjustable sights. Choice of matte blue or camo finish. Synthetic stock. Weight about 7 lbs.

375	325	250	175	150	100

Model 535 ATS Combos

Set offered in several different configurations: Field/Deer, 28" and 24"; Turkey/Deer, 22" and 24"; Turkey/Slug/Waterfowl, 22" and 28". Weights from 6.5 to 7 lbs. depending on barrel length. Introduced in 2005. **NOTE:** Add $55 for camo finish.

475	400	350	225	150	175

MODEL 590 SERIES

Model 590 Special Purpose

Fitted with 20" shrouded barrel, bayonet lug, Parkerized or blued finish. Speed feed stock. Ghost ring sights. Introduced in 1987. Weight about 7.25 lbs.

325	275	200	175	125	100

Model 590 Mariner

Marinecote finish.

425	350	275	225	150	100

Model 590DA

12-gauge introduced in 2000. Features 6-round tubular magazine and 18.5" barrel. Choice of plain bead sight or ghost ring sights. Choke is fixed Modified. Weight about 7 lbs. A 14" barreled model also offered, but NFA rules apply. **NOTE:** Add $50 for ghost ring sights.

500	400	300	200	150	100

Model 590 Bullpup

Model 500 with 20" barrel and 9-shot magazine. Introduced in 1989. Discontinued.

600	500	400	250	200	125

Model 590A1 Blackwater

590A1 Blackwater pump is a 12-gauge with 3" chamber, 20" long heavy-walled barrel, measures 41" overall. Ghost ring/AR-style sights. Length of pull 13.875". Features synthetic Speedfeed stock and Parkerized finish. Thumb safety is atop receiver. Capacity 8+1 rounds, weight 7.25 lbs. Blackwater logo etched on receiver.

585	500	425	350	300	150

Model 590 Tri Rail

Tri-Rail Model 590 pump chambered for 3" 12-gauge loads. Features protective heat shield on its 20" barrel. Overall length 40.875". Has synthetic Speedfeed stock. Bead front sight. Tri-Rail fore-end, with removable side rails and integral bottom rail. Extended magazine gives gun an 8+1 capacity. Matte blue finish. Length of pull 13.8". Weight 7.25 lbs.

540	490	440	390	300	150

Model 590 A1

Model 590A1 features adjustable aluminum stock and ghost ring sights. Heavy-walled barrel 20" long. Length of pull can be adjusted between 10.5" and 14.25". Weight 7.5 lbs. Capacity 8+1. Parkerized finish.

480	420	325	250	200	125

MODEL 835 SERIES

Model 835 Ulti-Mag

12-gauge Magnum slide-action shotgun. Features 24" or 28" ventilated rib barrel fitted for choke tubes; 6-shot magazine; composition camo or walnut stock; barrel is ported. Introduced in 1988. In 1998, offered with Shadow Grass camo pattern on both stock and barrel. In 1999, offered with Woodland camo. Weight 7.3 to 7.7 lbs. In 2000, offered with Realtree Hardwoods camo finish.

425	350	275	225	150	100

	NIB	EXC.	V.G.	GOOD	FAIR	POOR

Model 835 Ulti-Mag Viking Grade

Introduced in 1996. Features 12-gauge 3.5" magnum chamber. Green synthetic stock. Modified choke tube. Furnished with 28" vent rib barrel.

300	250	200	175	125	100

Model 835 Ulti-Mag Crown Grade

Crown Grade features checkered walnut stock, with fluted comb. Chambered for 12-gauge with 3.5" chamber. Offered in 24" or 28" vent rib barrels, with blued or camo finish. Weight about 7.3 to 7.7 lbs.

375	300	225	200	150	100

Model 835 Ulti-Mag Crown Grade Combo Model

Same as above. Offered with 28" vent rib barrel; 24" rifled barrel. Iron sights.

425	325	250	225	175	150

Model 835 Ulti-Mag Grand Slam Turkey

Introduced in 2004. This 12-gauge 3.5" features 20" vent rib overbored barrel, with Extra Full ported choke tube. Magazine capacity 6 rounds 2.75" shells; 5 rounds 3"; 4 rounds 3.5" shells. Adjustable fiber optic sights. Available in Realtree Hardwoods camo or Mossy Oak Break-Up. Weight about 7.25 lbs.

400	325	275	225	175	125

Model 835 Ulti-Mag Thumbhole Turkey

New in 2006. Dedicated pump-action 12-gauge turkey. Features thumbhole stock and overbored barrel. Chambered for 3.5" shells. X-Factor ported choke tube. Barrel 20". Adjustable fiber-optic front and rear sights. Weight about 7.75 lbs. Available in Mossy Oak New Break-Up camo or Realtree Hardwoods Green camo.

475	400	325	250	200	125

Model 835 Ulti-Mag Tactical Turkey

Same as above, with extended pistol-grip stock that is adjustable for length of pull from 10.75" to 14.5".

475	400	325	250	200	125

Model 835 Wild Turkey Federation

As above, with Wild Turkey Federation medallion inlaid in stock. Introduced in 1989.

475	400	325	250	200	125

Model 835 American Field

12-gauge has checkered walnut stock, 28" ventilated rib barrel with Modified choke tube. Weight about 7.7 lbs.

300	275	225	200	150	100

Model 835 Ulti-Mag Duck Commander

Same features as 835 Ulti-Mag slide-action series, with addition of Max-5 Realtree camo, premium Tru-Glo/Tru-Bead dual color front fiber optic sight, logo of Duck Commander TV show engraved on stock and American flag bandana. Introduced in 2014.

625	550	400	325	250	150

MODEL 935 MAGNUM SERIES

935 Magnum series of guns introduced in 2004.

Model 935 Magnum Waterfowl Camo

12-gauge 3.5" semi-automatic. Available with 26" or 28" vent rib overbored barrel with fiber optic bead and choke tubes. Offered with Mossy Oak Break-Up or Advantage Max-4 camo pattern. Magazine capacity 5 rounds 3"; 4 rounds 3.5". Weight about 7.75 lbs.

600	500	400	250	200	125

Model 935 Magnum Slugster

Similar to above, with 24" fully rifled barrel, rifle sights, Realtree AP camo overall.

600	500	400	250	200	125

Model 935 Magnum Turkey/Deer Comb

Similar to above, with interchangeable 24" Turkey barrel, Mossy Oak New Break-up camo overall.

700	600	500	350	275	150

NIB	EXC.	V.G.	GOOD	FAIR	POOR

Model 935 Magnum Turkey Camo

12-gauge 3.5" model features 24" vent rib overbored barrel with adjustable fiber optic sights. Ultra Full choke tube. Offered in Mossy Oak Break-Up or Hardwoods HD-Green. Weight about 7.75 lbs.

600	500	400	250	200	125

Model 935 Magnum Turkey Pistol Grip

Similar to above, with full pistol-grip stock.

625	525	425	275	225	150

Model 935 Magnum Waterfowl Synthetic

12-gauge 3.5" gun features 26" or 28" vent rib overbored barrel with choke tubes. Fiber optic bead. Matte black finish, with black synthetic stock. Weight about 7.75 lbs.

550	450	350	250	150	125

Model 935 Magnum Turkey Synthetic

As above, with 24" vent rib overbored barrel with Ultra Full choke tube. Weight about 7.75 lbs.

550	450	350	250	150	125

Model 935 Magnum Waterfowl/Turkey Combo

Similar to above, with 24" Turkey; 28" Waterfowl barrels, Mossy Oak New Break-up finish overall.

800	650	500	400	250	150

Model 935 Grand Slam Turkey

12-gauge 3.5" model features 22" vent rib overbored barrel with Extra Full ported choke tube. Adjustable fiber optic sights. Offered in Realtree Hardwoods green or Mossy Oak Break-Up camo pattern. Camo sling included. Weight about 7.5 lbs.

650	550	450	275	225	150

Model 935 Magnum

Chambered for 12-gauge 3.5" Magnum. This semi-automatic model is offered in waterfowl or turkey versions, with several camo options and barrel lengths. **NOTE:** Add $100 for full camo coverage; $150 for Grand Slam model with ported barrel; $200 for pistol-grip stock.

600	515	425	350	250	150

Model 935 Duck Commander

Same features as 935 Magnum semi-automatic series, with addition of Max-5 Realtree camo, premium Tru-Glo/Tru-Bead dual color front fiber optic sight, logo of Duck Commander TV show engraved on stock and American flag bandana. Introduced in 2014.

825	750	600	450	300	200

MODEL 930 SERIES

12-gauge 3" chamber semi-automatic shotgun series. Introduced in 2005.

Model 930 Field

12-gauge 3" gun fitted with 26" or 28" vent rib barrels with choke tubes. Barrel is ported. Checkered walnut stock, with recoil pad. Magazine capacity 5 rounds. Blued finish. Weight about 7.75 lbs.

525	425	325	225	175	125

Model 930 Turkey

Fitted with synthetic stock and 24" vent rib ported barrel. Chokes are extra full extended tubes. Offered with matte blue or camo finish. Weight about 7.5 lbs. **NOTE:** Add $100 for camo finish.

500	400	300	200	150	100

Model 930 Turkey Pistol Grip

Similar to above, with full pistol-grip stock, matte black or Mossy Oak Obsession camo finish overall.

650	550	450	275	225	150

Model 930 Waterfowl

Fitted with 28" vent rib ported barrel with choke tubes. Choice of matte blue or camo finish. Weight about 7.75 lbs. **NOTE:** Add $100 for camo finish.

500	400	300	200	150	100

	NIB	EXC.	V.G.	GOOD	FAIR	POOR

Model 930 Slugster

Features 24" vent rib ported barrel, with plain or Monte Carlo synthetic stock. Matte blue or camo finish. Weight about 7.5 lbs. **NOTE:** Add $100 for camo finish.

525	425	325	225	175	125

Model 930 Tactical

3" 12-gauge has 18.5" barrel and cylinder bore. Synthetic stock, with matte black finish. **NOTE:** Add $75 for ventilated heat shield.

500	400	300	200	150	100

Model 930 Road Blocker

Similar to above, with muzzle-brake.

525	425	325	225	175	125

Model 930 SPX

Billed as "home security" model, 3" 12-gauge SPX has 7-round magazine tube, 18.5" barrel, Picatinny rail, ghost ring rear sight and fiber-optic front sight. **NOTE:** Deduct 10 percent for white dot sights.

500	400	300	225	150	125

Model 930 Home Security/Field Combo

Combo unit with 18.5" Cylinder bore barrel; 28" ported Field barrel; black synthetic stock; matte black finish.

600	500	400	300	200	150

MODEL 3000 SERIES

Model 3000

12- or 20-gauge slide-action shotgun. Manufactured in a variety of barrel lengths and styles. Blued, with walnut stock. Also known as Smith & Wesson Model 3000.

—	325	250	175	125	75

Model 3000 Waterfowl

As above, with matte finish. Fitted with sling swivels and accompanied by a camouflage sling. Produced in 1986.

—	350	275	200	150	100

Model 3000 Law Enforcement

As above, with 18.5" or 20" cylinder-bore barrel. Manufactured in 1986 and 1987.

—	375	275	200	150	100

MODEL 1000 SERIES

Model 1000

12- or 20-gauge semi-automatic shotgun. Manufactured in a variety of barrel lengths and styles. Receiver of an aluminum alloy and blued. Also known as Smith & Wesson Model 1000. Offered in 1986 and 1987.

—	300	250	200	150	100

Model 1000 Slug

As above, with 22" barrel fitted with rifle sights. Offered in 1986 and 1987.

—	325	250	200	125	100

Model 1000 Super Series

As above, with steel receiver. Self-regulating gas system that allows use of standard or Magnum shells.

—	375	300	250	150	100

Model 1000 Super Waterfowl

Matte finish.

—	375	300	250	150	100

Model 1000 Super Slug

Rifle sights.

—	375	300	250	150	100

	NIB	EXC.	V.G.	GOOD	FAIR	POOR

Model 1000 Super Trap

30" high rib barrel.

	—	395	325	275	175	125

Model 1000 Super Skeet

25" barrel.

	—	395	325	275	175	125

MODEL 9200 SERIES

Model has a variety of configurations. A 12-gauge semi-automatic, with walnut or camo synthetic stock. Barrel lengths from 22" to 28". Weights from 7 to 7.7 lbs.

Model 9200 Viking Grade

350	300	275	200	100	75

Model 9200 USST Crown Grade

400	350	300	200	100	75

Model 9200 Combos

475	425	350	250	150	100

Model 9200 Special Hunter

28" vent rib barrel, with synthetic stock.

475	425	350	250	150	100

Model 9200 Deer Combo

475	425	350	250	150	100

Model 9200 Turkey Camo

475	425	350	250	150	100

Model 9200 Crown Grade Bantam

395	350	300	250	125	75

Model 9200 Jungle Gun

12-gauge auto-loader fitted with plain 18.5" barrel with bead sight. Barrel choked Cylinder. Chambers are 2.75". Magazine capacity 5 rounds. Parkerized finish. Synthetic stock.

525	450	325	200	150	125

Model SA-20

Synthetic-stocked matte black 20-gauge autoloader. Chambered for 3" shells. Has 26" or 28" vent-rib barrel. Comes with five choke tubes. Weight about 6 lbs. Bantam model has 1" shorter length of pull and 24" barrel. Weighs about 5.6 lbs. Introduced in 2008.

400	350	300	200	100	75

Model SA-20 Tactical

Mossberg's SA-20 Tactical Autoloader in 20-gauge only. Easy-Load elevator facilitates fast one-handed reloading. Top-mounted Picatinny-style rail accommodates optical sights, while magazine tube rail allows mounting lights, lasers and other accessories. Ghost ring rear and fiber optic front sights. Gas-operated action. Capacity: 4+1. Cylinder-bore barrel 20" long. Available with conventional black synthetic or synthetic pistol-grip stock. Weight about 6 lbs.

480	440	400	370	320	280

Model 5500 MKI I

12-gauge semi-automatic shotgun. Supplied with 26" barrel 2.75" shells; 28" barrel 3" shells. Blued, with walnut stock. Introduced in 1989.

300	235	200	175	150	125

RESERVE SERIES

Introduced in 2005 and 2008. Over/under and side-by-side guns in 12-, 20-, 28-gauge and .410 bore. Made in Turkey.

Silver Reserve Field Over/Under

Offered in 12-gauge 28" vent rib barrels; 20-gauge 26" or 28" vent rib barrels; 28-gauge 26" vent rib barrels; .410 bore with 26" vent rib barrels. All gauges have choke tubes except .410 with fixed chokes. Steel silvered receiver, with scroll engraving and game scenes in gold. Checkered walnut stock, with recoil pad. Single trigger. Weight 6 lbs. to 7.7 lbs. depending on gauge. **NOTE:**

NIB	EXC.	V.G.	GOOD	FAIR	POOR

Add 20 percent for 28-gauge and .410 bore.

600	500	300	200	150	100

Silver Reserve Sporting Over/Under

As above in 12-gauge only, with 28" vent 10mm rib barrels with choke tubes and ported barrels. Weight about 7.7 lbs.

700	600	425	300	225	125

Silver Reserve Side-by-Side

New in 2008. Side-by-side version of Silver Reserve. Comes in 12-gauge 26" or 28" barrels; 20- and 28-gauge 26" barrels. Stock and fore-end is select black walnut, with satin finish. Receiver satin-finished silver, with scroll engraving. Barrels blued. Bores chrome-plated. All models come with five choke tubes. Weight: 6.4 to 6.5 lbs. 20- and 28-gauge; 7.2 lbs. 12-gauge.

850	750	600	450	250	150

Onyx Reserve Sporting Side-by-Side

Similar to Silver Reserve Sporting, with blued receiver.

800	700	575	400	225	150

MOUNTAIN ARMS
Ozark, Missouri

Wildcat

Similar to Rau Arms Wildcat (q.v.) and Garcia Bronco, with plastic stock inserts. Takedown model offered as well. Estimated 6,243 produced 1971-1978. First several thousand bore Rau Arms label.

225	175	125	100	65	35

MOUNTAIN RIFLES, INC.
Palmer, Alaska

Mountaineer

Bolt-action rifle. Introduced in 1997. Built on Remington action with Model 70 style bolt release. Factory muzzle-brake installed with open sights. Timney trigger standard. Stock fiberglass. Finish Parkerized. Chambered for many different calibers from .223 Rem. to .416 Rem., including Dakota and Weatherby cartridges. Weight starts about 6 lbs. depending on caliber. Several options that will affect price. Left-hand offered as an option.

2195	1750	1400	1100	750	300

Super Mountaineer

Similar to Mountaineer, but bolt is fluted and hollow. Barrel is match grade stainless steel, with muzzle-brake. Kevlar/Graphite stock. Wide variety of calibers. Weight starts about 4.25 lbs. depending on caliber.

2895	2350	1900	1500	1000	400

Pro Mountaineer

Built on Winchester Model 70 action. Premium match grade barrel, with muzzle-brake. Model 70 trigger. Stainless steel matte finish. Kevlar/Graphite stock. Wide variety of calibers. Weight starts about 6 lbs.

2895	2350	2350	1900	1500	400

Pro Safari

Built on MRI action with controlled feed. Premium match grade barrel. Timney trigger. Matte blue finish. Exhibition grade walnut stock, with custom bottom metal. Weight starts about 7 lbs. depending on caliber. Caliber from .223 to .458 Lott.

4495	3500	2300	1750	1200	500

Ultra Mountaineer

Built on MRI action, with premium match grade barrel and muzzle-brake. Timney trigger. Parkerized finish. Kevlar/Graphite stock. Calibers from .223 to .505 Gibbs. Weight begins at 5 lbs. depending on caliber. **NOTE:** Add $500 for Rigby-length calibers.

2995	2500	2200	1900	1500	400

MUGICA, JOSE
Eibar, Spain
See—Llama

Trade name found on Llama pistols that were manufactured by Gabilondo.

	NIB	EXC.	V.G.	GOOD	FAIR	POOR

MURFEESBORO ARMORY
Murfeesboro, Tennessee

Established in 1861 by William Ledbetter. Made copies of U.S. Model 1841 Rifle complete with patchbox and double strapped nose cap. Barrel bands pinned to stock. Between 270 and 390 made from October of 1861 through March of 1862. Overall length 48.75"; barrel length 33"; .54-caliber. Unmarked except for serial number on various parts including barrel.

—	—	27500	16500	6600	2000

MURPHY & O'CONNEL
New York, New York

Pocket Pistol
.41-caliber single-shot percussion pocket pistol, with 3" barrel, German silver mounts. Walnut stock. Manufactured during 1850s.

—	—	3500	2950	1100	450

MURRAY, J. P.
Columbus, Georgia

Percussion Rifle
.58-caliber percussion rifle, with 33" barrel, full stock and brass mounts. Also made with 23.5" to 24" barrel as a carbine. Lock marked "J.P. Murray/Columbus Ga.". Several hundred manufactured between 1862 and 1864.

—	—	50000	33000	14000	1500

MUSGRAVE
Republic of South Africa

RSA NR I Single-Shot Target Rifle
.308-caliber single-shot bolt-action rifle, with 26" barrel, match sights, adjustable trigger. Target-style stock made of walnut. Manufactured between 1971 and 1976.

—	550	425	300	225	125

Valiant NR6
.243, .270, .308, .30-06 and 7mm Remington Magnum caliber bolt-action sporting rifle, with 24" barrel, open sights. English-style stock. Imported from 1971 to 1976.

—	450	350	275	175	125

Premier NR5
As above, with 26" barrel. Pistol-grip Monte Carlo-style stock. Discontinued in 1976.

—	550	450	325	225	150

MUSKETEER RIFLES
Firearms International/Garcia
Washington, D.C.

Sporter
.243 to .300 Winchester Magnum caliber bolt-action rifle, with 24" barrel without sights. Monte Carlo-style stock. Imported between 1963 and 1972. **NOTE:** Add 20 percent for magnum chamberings.

—	500	375	275	195	120

Deluxe Sporter
As above, with adjustable trigger. More finely figured walnut stock.

—	550	400	300	200	125

Carbine
Sporter, with 20" barrel.

—	500	375	275	195	120

N

	NIB	EXC.	V.G.	GOOD	FAIR	POOR

NATIONAL ARMS CO.
Brooklyn, New York
See—Moore's Patent Firearms Co.

Successor to Moore's Patent Firearms Company in 1865. Purchased by Colt Company in 1870.

Large Frame Teat-Fire Revolver

.45 teat fire caliber revolver with 7.5" barrel and 6-shot cylinder. Blued or silver-plated with walnut grips. Barrel marked "National Arms Co. Brooklyn". Exact number of these revolvers made is unknown. Estimated to be fewer than 30.

—	—	24500	19000	6050	850

No. 2 Derringer

.41-caliber spur trigger pocket pistol with 2.5" barrel. Blued or silver-plated with walnut grips. Later manufactured by Colt Company as their No. 2 Derringer.

—	—	1750	1300	550	150

NAVY ARMS COMPANY
Martinsburg, West Virginia

Founded in 1957 by the late Val Forgett, Jr. Over the years, this company has imported many black powder and modern surplus firearms and replicas. Many of the models imported are classified as curios and relics. In 2012 Navy Arms, now operated by Val Forgett III, temporarily suspended the importation side of the business. Presently the company is working with Winchester and Turnbull Manufacturing Co. on marketing a series of Winchester Model 1873 rifles. Shown on these following pages are examples of the many firearms that have been imported by Navy Arms.

Winchester/Turnbull Model 1873 Rifle

Available exclusively from Navy Arms, this is a faithful reproduction of the "Gun That Won the West". Chambered in .45 Colt or .357 Magnum, with a Turnbull color case-hardened frame, deluxe checkered American walnut stock and fore-end, 20" or 24.250" octagonal barrel, semi-buckhorn rear and gold bead front sight. Introduced in 2014.

2250	1800	—	—	—	—

SHOTGUNS

Model 83

12- or 20-gauge Magnum over/under shotgun. Manufactured in a variety of barrel lengths and styles, with double triggers and extractors. Blued, engraved, with walnut stock. Introduced in 1985.

500	400	275	200	175	100

Model 93

As above, with automatic ejectors.

575	475	300	250	200	100

Model 95

As above, with single trigger and screw-in choke tubes.

600	500	350	250	200	100

Model 96 Sportsman

As above in 12-gauge only, with gold-plated receiver.

600	500	350	250	200	100

Model 100

12-, 20-, 28-gauge or .410 bore over/under boxlock shotgun, with 26" ventilated rib barrels, single trigger and extractors. Blued, chrome-plated, with walnut stock. Introduced in 1989. **NOTE:** Add 20 percent for .410.

450	350	200	150	100	75

Model 100 Side-by-Side

12- or 20-gauge Magnum boxlock double-barrel shotgun, with 27.5" barrels, double triggers and extractors. Blued, with walnut stock. Imported between 1985 and 1987.

—	475	350	250	200	100

	NIB	EXC.	V.G.	GOOD	FAIR	POOR

Model 150

As above, with automatic ejectors.

	NIB	EXC.	V.G.	GOOD	FAIR	POOR
	—	495	375	300	225	125

Model 105

12- or 20-gauge and .410 bore folding single barrel shotgun, with 26" or 28" blued barrel, chrome-plated engraved receiver and hardwood stock. Introduced in 1985.

NIB	EXC.	V.G.	GOOD	FAIR	POOR
125	80	75	65	50	35

Model 105 Deluxe

As above, with vent rib barrel. Checkered walnut stock.

NIB	EXC.	V.G.	GOOD	FAIR	POOR
150	100	85	75	60	45

REPLICA LONG GUNS

Harpers Ferry Flint Rifle

Copy of 1803 rifle in original .54-caliber. Features rust blued 35" barrel. Weight 8.5 lbs.

NIB	EXC.	V.G.	GOOD	FAIR	POOR
600	475	350	300	200	100

Harpers Ferry "Journey of Discovery" Rifle

Similar to Harpers Ferry Flint Rifle above, with oil finished walnut stock and brass fittings. Brass patch box engraved "Lewis and Clark's 'Journey of Discovery'; 1803 to 1806". Introduced in 2003.

NIB	EXC.	V.G.	GOOD	FAIR	POOR
775	600	475	275	175	100

Brown Bess Musket

Replica copy of second model used between 1760 and 1776. Bright finish on metal and one-piece walnut stock, with polished brass locks. Barrel length 42"; weight 9.5 lbs.

NIB	EXC.	V.G.	GOOD	FAIR	POOR
800	625	500	300	200	100

Brown Bess Carbine

Same as above. Fitted with 30" barrel. Weighs 7.75 lbs.

NIB	EXC.	V.G.	GOOD	FAIR	POOR
800	625	500	300	200	100

1777 Charleville Musket

Copy of French flintlock in .69-caliber. Fittings are steel, with brass front sight and flashpan. Barrel length 44.625"; weight about 8.75 lbs

NIB	EXC.	V.G.	GOOD	FAIR	POOR
900	700	550	400	300	150

1777 Standard Charleville Musket

Same as above, with polished steel barrel and select walnut stock.

NIB	EXC.	V.G.	GOOD	FAIR	POOR
900	700	550	400	300	150

1816 M.T. Wickham Musket

Furnished in .69-caliber, with steel ramrod and button head. Brass flashpan and walnut stock standard.

NIB	EXC.	V.G.	GOOD	FAIR	POOR
600	550	450	350	250	200

1808 Springfield Musket

A U.S. copy of 1763 Charleville musket, with 1808 Springfield markings. Barrel length 44"; weight 8.75 lbs.

NIB	EXC.	V.G.	GOOD	FAIR	POOR
950	800	600	400	200	100

Pennsylvania Long Rifle

Model offered in either percussion or flintlock ignition. Choice of .32- or .45-caliber. Has octagonal 40.5" rust blued barrel, polished lock, double set triggers and brass furniture on walnut stock. Weighs 7.5 lbs.

Percussion

NIB	EXC.	V.G.	GOOD	FAIR	POOR
450	375	250	200	150	100

Flintlock

NIB	EXC.	V.G.	GOOD	FAIR	POOR
475	400	275	225	150	100

	NIB	EXC.	V.G.	GOOD	FAIR	POOR

Kentucky Rifle

Offered in either percussion or flintlock ignition. Has blue steel barrel, case colored lockplate and polished brass patch box inletted into walnut stock. Available in .45- or 50-caliber. Barrel length 35"; weight 6 lbs. 14 oz.

Percussion

	NIB	EXC.	V.G.	GOOD	FAIR	POOR
	475	325	200	150	100	75

Flintlock

	NIB	EXC.	V.G.	GOOD	FAIR	POOR
	495	335	225	150	100	75

Mortimer Flintlock Rifle

Offered in .54-caliber, with rust blued barrel, walnut stock with cheekpiece and checkered straight-grip. Has external safety and sling swivels. Barrel length 36"; weight 9 lbs. Optional shotgun barrel. Made by Pedersoli. **NOTE:** Optional shotgun barrel add $240.

	NIB	EXC.	V.G.	GOOD	FAIR	POOR
	900	750	600	500	450	150

Tryon Creedmoor Rifle

.45-caliber model features heavy blued 33" octagonal barrel, hooded front sight, adjustable tang sight, double set triggers, sling swivels and walnut stock. Weighs about 9.5 lbs.

	NIB	EXC.	V.G.	GOOD	FAIR	POOR
	800	600	525	450	400	150

Standard Tryon Rifle

Same as above, without target sights.

	NIB	EXC.	V.G.	GOOD	FAIR	POOR
	700	500	350	300	250	200

Deluxe Tryon Rifle

Same as above, with polished and engraved lock and patch box.

	NIB	EXC.	V.G.	GOOD	FAIR	POOR
	750	525	375	325	250	200

Parker-Hale Whitworth Rifle

Replica of British sniper rifle. In .451-caliber. Used by Confederates during Civil War. Round 36" barrel. Features globe front sight and ladder rear sight. Walnut stock is hand checkered. Weighs 9 lbs. 10 oz. **NOTE:** Limited edition telescope add $150.

	NIB	EXC.	V.G.	GOOD	FAIR	POOR
	850	675	600	450	300	150

Parker-Hale Volunteer Rifle

.451-caliber rifle, with hand checkered walnut stock. Fitted with 32" barrel, with globe front sight and ladder rear sight. Weighs 9.5 lbs.

	NIB	EXC.	V.G.	GOOD	FAIR	POOR
	825	650	550	400	300	150

Parker-Hale 3 Band Volunteer Rifle

Same basic specifications as Whitworth rifle. Furnished with Alexander Henry rifling.

	NIB	EXC.	V.G.	GOOD	FAIR	POOR
	750	650	600	400	250	50

Rigby Target Rifle

1880s replica chambered for .451-caliber. Fitted with adjustable front sight and vernier tang sight. Lock, breech plug, trigger guard, buttplate and escutcheons are case colored. Barrel length 32"; weight 7 lbs. 12 oz.

	NIB	EXC.	V.G.	GOOD	FAIR	POOR
	700	500	450	300	200	100

1861 Springfield Rifle

.58-caliber replica. Fitted with 1855-style hammer. Barrel length 40"; weight 10 lbs. 4 oz.

	NIB	EXC.	V.G.	GOOD	FAIR	POOR
	550	425	350	300	200	100

Model 1873 Springfield Officer's Trapdoor

Features single set trigger, case colored breechblock, deluxe walnut stock, adjustable rear peep sight with Beech front sight. Chambered for .45-70 cartridge. Fitted with 26" round barrel. Weight about 8 lbs. Introduced in 2003.

	NIB	EXC.	V.G.	GOOD	FAIR	POOR
	900	750	495	350	300	200

1862 C.S. Richmond Rifle

Confederate rifle is .58-caliber. Faithful reproduction of those produced at Richmond Armory. Barrel length 40"; weighs 10 lbs. 4 oz.

	NIB	EXC.	V.G.	GOOD	FAIR	POOR
	550	425	350	300	200	100

	NIB	EXC.	V.G.	GOOD	FAIR	POOR

J.P. Murray Carbine

Confederate cavalry .58-caliber carbine. Has case colored lock and brass furniture on walnut stock. Barrel length 23.5"; weight 8 lbs. 5 oz.

	495	325	250	200	150	100

1863 Springfield Rifle

Exact replica of famous Springfield Musket. Barrel length 40", with 3 barrel bands. All metal parts are finished bright. Weighs 9.5 lbs.

	550	425	350	300	200	100

1841 Mississippi Rifle

Also known as "Yager" rifle; offered in either .54- or .58-caliber. Barrel length 33"; weighs 9.5 lbs.

	450	325	250	200	150	100

Zouave Rifle

Civil War replica is .58-caliber. Polished brass hardware and blued 33" barrel. Weighs 9 lbs.

	450	325	250	200	150	100

Parker-Hale 1861 Musketoon

Made by Gibbs Rifle Company using 130-year-old gauges for reference. This .577-caliber replica features 24" barrel, with folding ladder military sight. Stock is walnut and lock case colored. All furniture polished brass. Weighs 7.5 lbs.

	400	325	250	200	150	100

Navy Arms Musketoon

Same as above. Manufactured in Italy.

	400	325	250	200	150	100

Parker-Hale 1858 Two Band Musket

.577-caliber model based on 1858 Enfield naval pattern. Fitted with military sight graduated to 1,100 yards. Case colored lock. Walnut stock with brass fittings. Barrel length 33"; weighs 8.5 lbs.

	550	425	350	300	200	100

Navy Arms 1858 Two Band Musket

Same as above. Built in Italy.

	450	325	250	200	150	100

Parker-Hale Three Band Musket

Replica based on design produced between 1853 and 1863. Rear sight based on an 1853 model graduated to 900 yards. Fitted with case colored lock. Walnut stock with brass furniture. Barrel length 39"; weighs 9 lbs.

	600	475	400	300	200	100

Navy Arms Three Band Musket

Same as above. Produced in Italy.

	475	350	300	250	200	100

Navy Arms Revolving Carbine

Fitted with 20" barrel. Chambered for .357 Magnum, .44-40 or .45 Colt cartridge. Has revolving 6-shot cylinder. Straight-grip stock with brass buttplate and trigger guard. Action based on Remington Model 1874 revolver. Introduced in 1968. Discontinued in 1984.

	600	500	400	300	200	100

1859 Sharps Infantry Rifle

.54-caliber copy of three band Sharps. Barrel length 30". Case hardened receiver and patch box. Blued barrel and walnut stock. Weight about 8.5 lbs.

	1150	800	600	400	300	150

1859 Berdan Sharps Rifle

Similar to 1859 Sharps, with double-set triggers.

	1200	850	650	450	325	150

1873 Sharps No. 2 Creedmore

Chambered for .45-70 cartridge. Fitted with 30" round barrel. Polished nickel receiver. Target-grade rear tang sight and front globe sight, with inserts. Checkered walnut stock, with pistol-grip. Weight about 10 lbs. Introduced in 2002.

	1425	1000	750	550	375	200

	NIB	EXC.	V.G.	GOOD	FAIR	POOR

Sharps #2 Silhouette Rifle

Model identical to standard No. 2, with full octagon barrel. Weight about 10.5 lbs. Introduced in 2003.

	1325	1000	750	550	375	200

Sharps #2 Sporting Rifle

Same as No. 2 standard rifle, with case colored receiver. Introduced in 2003.

	1425	1000	750	550	375	200

1873 Sharps Quigley

Model chambered for .45-70 cartridge. Fitted with heavy 34" octagon barrel. Case hardened receiver with military patch box. Open sights. Weight about 13 lbs. Introduced in 2002.

	1490	1100	850	625	395	225

1874 Sharps Infantry Rifle

Model fitted with 30" round barrel. Chambered for .45-70 cartridge. Blued barrel, with case hardened receiver. Walnut stock, with 3 barrel bands. Weight about 8.5 lbs.

	1150	800	600	400	300	150

1874 Sharps Sniper Rifle

Same as 1874 Infantry rifle, with double-set triggers.

	1200	850	650	450	325	150

Sharps Cavalry Carbine

Breech-loading .54-caliber carbine, with 22" blued barrel. Military-style sights, walnut stocks and saddle bar with ring are standard. Weighs 7 lbs. 12 oz.

	1050	800	600	400	300	150

Sharps Cavalry Carbine Cartridge Model

Same as above. Chambered for .45-70 Government cartridge.

	1150	800	600	400	300	150

1874 Sharps Plains Rifle

Features case colored receiver, blued barrel and checkered walnut stock. Offered in .44-70 or .54-caliber percussion. Barrel length 28.5"; weight 8 lbs. 10 oz.

	1150	800	600	400	300	150

1874 Sharps Sporting Rifle

Similar to above. Features full pistol-grip, 32" medium weight octagonal barrel, double-set triggers and case colored frame. Weight about 10.75 lbs.

	1325	1000	750	550	375	200

1874 Sharps Buffalo Rifle

Chambered for .45-70 or .45-90 cartridge. Fitted with 28" heavy octagon barrel. Buttstock checkered. Weight about 12 lbs.

	1325	1000	750	550	375	200

1874 Sharps No. 3 Long Range Rifle

Built by Pedersoli. Fitted with 34" medium weight octagon barrel, globe target front sight and match grade rear tang sight. Double-set trigger. Case hardened frame. Walnut stock. Weight about 11 lbs.

	1800	1325	950	725	400	300

1873 Winchester Rifle

Replica features case colored receiver, blued octagon 24" barrel and walnut stocks. Offered in either .44-40 or .45 Long Colt. Weighs about 8 lbs. 4 oz.

	900	725	600	500	400	200

1873 Winchester Carbine

Same specifications as rifle. Fitted with 19" round barrel, blued receiver and saddle ring. Weighs 7 lbs. 4 oz.

	900	725	600	500	400	200

1873 Winchester Sporting Rifle

Features 24.25" octagonal barrel, case colored receiver and checkered pistol-grip. Offered in .44-40 or. 45 Long Colt. Weighs about 8 lbs. 14 oz.

	950	750	650	525	400	200

	NIB	EXC.	V.G.	GOOD	FAIR	POOR

1873 Sporting Long Range Rifle

Similar to Winchester Sporting Rifle. Chambered for .44-40 cartridge. Fitted with 30" octagon barrel. Long-range rear tang sight. Weight about 7.5 lbs. Introduced in 2002.

	NIB	EXC.	V.G.	GOOD	FAIR	POOR
	1075	850	750	625	500	250

1873 Border Model

Introduced in 2000. Features 20" blued octagon barrel, with buckhorn rear sight. Magazine capacity 10 rounds. Walnut checkered pistol-grip stock, with oil finish. Chambered for .357 Magnum, .44-40 or .45 Colt cartridge.

	NIB	EXC.	V.G.	GOOD	FAIR	POOR
	975	800	700	550	450	225

1866 "Yellowboy" Rifle

Features brass receiver, 24" octagon barrel and walnut stocks. Weighs 8.5 lbs.

	NIB	EXC.	V.G.	GOOD	FAIR	POOR
	850	675	525	450	300	150

1866 "Yellowboy" Carbine

Same as above. Fitted with 19" round barrel and saddle ring. Weighs 7 lbs. 4 oz.

	NIB	EXC.	V.G.	GOOD	FAIR	POOR
	850	675	525	450	300	150

1866 "Yellowboy" Short Rifle

Introduced in 2000. Features 20" barrel with buckhorn rear sight. Walnut stock with oil finish. Receiver is yellow brass. Chambered for .38 Special, .44-40 or .45 Colt cartridge. Magazine capacity 10 rounds.

	NIB	EXC.	V.G.	GOOD	FAIR	POOR
	850	675	525	450	300	150

Iron Frame Henry

Replica of famous and rare .44-40 Iron Frame Henry. Features case colored frame. Barrel length 24"; weighs 9 lbs.

	NIB	EXC.	V.G.	GOOD	FAIR	POOR
	925	750	650	500	400	200

Blued Iron Frame Henry

Same as above. Furnished with highly polished blued receiver.

	NIB	EXC.	V.G.	GOOD	FAIR	POOR
	925	750	650	500	400	200

Military Henry

Based on brass frame military version of Henry rifle. Furnished with sling swivels mounted on left side. Buttplate fitted with trap door. Caliber .44-40; barrel length 24"; weighs 9 lbs. 4 oz.

	NIB	EXC.	V.G.	GOOD	FAIR	POOR
	900	725	625	500	400	200

Henry Carbine

Brass frame carbine version. Features 22" barrel. Chambered for .44-40 cartridge. Weighs 8 lbs. 12 oz.

	NIB	EXC.	V.G.	GOOD	FAIR	POOR
	875	700	600	500	400	200

Henry Trapper

Replica not based on actual Henry. Fitted with unique 16.5" barrel. Brass frame model weighs 7 lbs. 7 oz. Chambered for .44-40 cartridge.

	NIB	EXC.	V.G.	GOOD	FAIR	POOR
	875	700	600	500	400	200

1892 Rifle

Lever-action rifle chambered for .357 Magnum, .44-40, .45 Colt or .32-20 cartridge. Octagon 24.25" barrel. Walnut stock, crescent butt and blued or case colored receiver. Weight about 6.25 lbs.

	NIB	EXC.	V.G.	GOOD	FAIR	POOR
	525	425	350	300	250	200

1892 Short Rifle

Same as above, with 20" octagon barrel. Weight about 6.25 lbs.

	NIB	EXC.	V.G.	GOOD	FAIR	POOR
	525	425	350	300	250	200

1892 Carbine

Similar to short rifle. Fitted with 20" round barrel. Saddle ring on left side of receiver. Weight about 5.75 lbs.

	NIB	EXC.	V.G.	GOOD	FAIR	POOR
	450	350	300	250	200	150

1892 Brass Frame Carbine

Same as above, with polished brass receiver.

	NIB	EXC.	V.G.	GOOD	FAIR	POOR
	450	350	300	250	200	150

NIB	EXC.	V.G.	GOOD	FAIR	POOR

1892 Brass Frame Rifle

Same as carbine, with polished brass receiver.

525	425	350	300	250	200

No. 2 Creedmoor Target Rifle

Reproduction of Remington No. 2 Creedmoor. Features case colored receiver, tapered 30" octagonal barrel, hooded front sight, Creedmoor tang sight and walnut stock, with checkered pistol-grip. Furnished in .45-70 Government. Weighs 9 lbs.

900	725	625	500	400	200

Rolling Block Buffalo Rifle

Replica of Remington Buffalo rifle. Fitted with 26" or 30" octagonal or half octagonal barrel, case colored receiver, blade front sight, notch rear sight, brass trigger guard and walnut stocks. Tang drilled and tapped for tang sight.

750	600	475	300	200	100

Half Octagon Barrel Model

750	600	475	300	200	100

"John Bodine" Rolling Block Rifle

Chambered for .45-70 cartridge. Fitted with 30" octagon barrel. Double-set triggers. Match-grade rear tang sight. Weight about 12 lbs. Introduced in 2002.

1550	1150	800	575	350	200

1885 High Wall

Chambered for .45-70 cartridge. Fitted with 30" medium heavy octagon barrel. Case colored receiver, target sights and walnut stocks. Also available with 28" round barrel. **NOTE:** Reduce price by $100 for Buckhorn sights; $60 for 28" barrel.

900	725	600	500	400	200

1873 Springfield Infantry Rifle

Copy of Trapdoor Springfield. Chambered for .45-70. Fitted with 32.5" barrel. Walnut stock and case hardened breechlock. Weight about 8.25 lbs.

975	800	600	500	400	200

1873 Springfield Cavalry Carbine

Same as above, with 22" barrel. Weight about 7 lbs.

875	700	600	500	400	200

Ithaca/Navy Hawken Rifle

Offered in either .50- or .54-caliber percussion. Features 31.5" rust blued octagon barrel. Percussion lockplate is case colored. Rest of hardware is blued, with exception of nose cap and escutcheons. Weighs about 9 lbs. 13 oz.

350	300	250	200	150	100

Hawken Rifle

Features case colored lock, 28" blued octagon barrel, adjustable sights, double-set triggers and hooked breech. Polished brass furniture and patch box are mounted on walnut stock. Weighs about 8.5 lbs.

300	200	175	125	95	60

Hawken Hunter Rifle

Offered in .50-, .54- or .58-caliber. Features blued hardware, adjustable sights, case colored lock and hooked breech. Walnut stock hand checkered, with cheekpiece. Rubber recoil pad standard. Barrel length 28".

295	190	150	100	75	60

Hawken Hunter Carbine

Same as above. Fitted with 22.5" barrel. Weighs about 6 lbs. 12 oz.

295	190	150	100	75	60

Kodiak MKIV Double Rifle

Built in Europe by Pedersoli. Chambered for .45-70 cartridge. Features walnut stock, with cheekpiece and hand checkering. Barrel length 24", with adjustable sights. Engraved sideplates are polished bright. Sling swivels standard. Weighs 10.2 lbs.

4500	3350	2500	1500	600	400

	NIB	EXC.	V.G.	GOOD	FAIR	POOR

Mortimer Flintlock or Percussion Shotgun

Replica of 12-gauge English Mortimer. Features waterproof pan, roller frizzen (flintlock only), external safety. All parts case colored. Barrel length 36"; weighs 7 lbs.

975	800	600	500	400	200

Fowler Shotgun

12-gauge side-by-side, with straight-grip stock. Features hooked breech and 28" blued barrels. Sideplates are engraved and case colored. Double triggers and checkered walnut stock standard. Weighs 7.25 lbs.

550	395	300	250	200	100

Navy Arms Steel Shot Magnum

Same as above in 10-gauge. Weighs 7 lbs. 9 oz.

575	400	295	125	100	75

T&T Shotgun

Turkey and trap have straight-grip stock and 28" barrel choked Full and Full. Locks are case colored and engraved. Checkered walnut stock. Weighs 7.5 lbs.

550	395	300	250	200	100

Japanese Tanegashima Matchlock

Model is .50-caliber, with 41" barrels. Weighs 8.5 lbs.

1150	800	600	400	300	150

HANDGUNS

Le Page Pistol

.44-caliber percussion pistol. Has 10.25" tapered octagon barrel, adjustable single-set trigger. Lock, trigger guard and buttcap engraved. Hand checkered walnut stocks. Weighs 36 oz.

450	375	300	250	200	100

Single Cased Set

580	530	475	400	300	150

Double Cased Set

995	875	750	600	400	200

Flintlock

Same as above, with flintlock ignition. Weighs 41 oz.

470	425	350	250	150	100

Smoothbore Flintlock Pistol

Same as above, with smooth bore.

470	425	350	250	150	100

Smoothbore Flintlock Pistol Single Cased Set

800	700	600	400	300	150

Smoothbore Flintlock Pistol Double Cased Set

1395	1275	1050	600	400	200

Kentucky Pistol

Percussion replica of a pistol developed in 1840s. Has 10.125" blued barrel, case colored lock, brass furniture and trigger guard, with walnut stock. Weighs 32 oz.

295	225	200	125	85	60

Single Cased Set

350	275	225	175	125	75

Double Cased Set

550	450	350	250	150	100

Flintlock Pistol

Same as above, with flintlock ignition.

225	175	150	100	75	60

Flintlock Pistol Single Cased Set

350	275	225	175	125	75

	NIB	EXC.	V.G.	GOOD	FAIR	POOR

Flintlock Pistol Double Cased Set

	NIB	EXC.	V.G.	GOOD	FAIR	POOR
	550	450	350	275	175	100

Harpers Ferry Pistol

Has .58-caliber rifled 10" barrel. Case hardened lock and walnut stock. Weight about 39 oz.

	NIB	EXC.	V.G.	GOOD	FAIR	POOR
	300	250	200	150	100	75

Pistol Single Cased Set

	NIB	EXC.	V.G.	GOOD	FAIR	POOR
	350	275	225	175	125	100

LE MAT PISTOLS

18th Georgia Le Mat Pistol

9-shot .44-caliber percussion revolver has 7.625" blued barrel and engraved cylinder. Engraved banner on left side of frame reads "DEO VINDICE". Hammer and trigger case colored. Stock checkered walnut. Comes with Le Mat mould and velvet draped French fitted case. Weighs 55 oz.

	NIB	EXC.	V.G.	GOOD	FAIR	POOR
	795	625	500	400	300	150

Beauregard Le Mat Pistol

Replica of Cavalry model. Comes cased.

	NIB	EXC.	V.G.	GOOD	FAIR	POOR
	1000	800	650	550	350	200

Navy Le Mat

Features knurled pin barrel release and spur barrel selector.

	NIB	EXC.	V.G.	GOOD	FAIR	POOR
	795	625	500	400	300	150

Army Le Mat

Features knurled pin barrel release and cross pin barrel selector.

	NIB	EXC.	V.G.	GOOD	FAIR	POOR
	795	625	500	400	300	150

Cavalry Le Mat

Features lanyard ring, spur trigger, lever type barrel release and cross pin barrel selector.

	NIB	EXC.	V.G.	GOOD	FAIR	POOR
	795	625	500	400	300	150

Starr Double-Action Model 1858 Army

Double-action revolver chambered for .44-caliber. Fitted with 6" barrel. Blued finish. Weight about 48 oz.

	NIB	EXC.	V.G.	GOOD	FAIR	POOR
	350	250	200	150	100	75

Starr Single-Action Model 1863 Army

Fitted with 8" barrel. Chambered for .44-caliber. Blued finish and walnut stock. Weight about 48 oz.

	NIB	EXC.	V.G.	GOOD	FAIR	POOR
	350	250	200	150	100	75

1862 New Model Police

Replica based on Colt .36-caliber pocket pistol of the same name. Features half fluted and re-dated cylinder. Case colored frame and loading gate. Polished brass trigger guard and backstrap. Barrel length 5.5"; weighs 26 oz.

	NIB	EXC.	V.G.	GOOD	FAIR	POOR
	300	250	175	150	100	75

1862 New Model Book-Style Cased Set

	NIB	EXC.	V.G.	GOOD	FAIR	POOR
	350	250	200	150	100	75

Paterson Revolver

Replica is five-shot .36-caliber. Cylinder is scroll engraved with stagecoach scene. Hidden trigger drops down when hammer is cocked. Barrel length 9"; weighs 43 oz.

	NIB	EXC.	V.G.	GOOD	FAIR	POOR
	475	425	350	250	150	100

Engraved Paterson Revolver

Features hand engraving with silver inlays.

	NIB	EXC.	V.G.	GOOD	FAIR	POOR
	575	475	350	250	200	100

1851 Navy

Colt replica offered in either .36- or .44-caliber. Naval battle scene engraved in cylinder. Octagon 7.5" barrel. Trigger guard and backstrap polished brass. Walnut grips are hand rubbed. Weighs 32 oz. **NOTE:** Optional shoulder stock add $100.

	NIB	EXC.	V.G.	GOOD	FAIR	POOR
	350	250	200	150	100	75

	NIB	EXC.	V.G.	GOOD	FAIR	POOR

Single Cased Set

	375	275	225	150	100	75

Double Cased Set

	550	450	375	275	200	100

1851 Navy Conversion

Replica of Colt 1851 Navy cartridge conversion. Offered in 38 Special or .38 Long Colt. Choice of 5.5" or 7.5" barrels. Weight about 40 oz.

	475	425	350	250	150	100

Augusta 1851 Navy Pistol

Available with either 5" or 7.5" barrel. Engraved with "A" coverage.

	350	250	200	150	100	75

Model 1851 Navy Frontiersman

Introduced in 2003. Features 5" .36-caliber barrel. Receiver, loading lever and hammer case colored. Barrel and cylinder charcoal blued. Fitted with German silver backstrap and walnut grips.

	350	250	200	150	100	75

Reb Model 1860 Pistol

Replica of Confederate Griswold and Gunnison revolver. Features blued round 7.5" barrel. Brass frame, trigger guard and backstrap. Offered in .36- or .44-caliber. Weighs 44 oz.

	165	150	125	90	75	35

Reb 1860 Sheriff's Model

Same as above. Fitted with 5" barrel. Weighs 40 oz.

	165	150	125	90	75	35

1847 Walker Dragoon

Replica of rare Colt .44-caliber revolver. Barrel and cylinder blued. Frame and loading lever case colored. Barrel length 9"; weighs 75 oz.

	400	325	275	250	200	100

Single Cased Set

	450	375	325	250	200	100

Single Deluxe Cased Set

	525	425	350	300	200	100

1860 Army Pistol

.44-caliber model features case colored frame and loading lever. Blued barrel, cylinder and backstrap. Trigger guard brass. Cylinder engraved with battle scene. Barrel length 8"; weighs 41 oz.

	350	250	200	150	100	75

Single Cased Set

	375	275	225	150	100	75

Double Cased Set

	550	450	375	275	200	100

1860 Army Conversion

Chambered for .38 Special or .38 Long Colt. Fitted with either 5.5" or 7.5" barrel. Blued finish. Walnut grips. Weight about 40 oz.

	475	425	350	250	150	100

1858 New Model Remington-Style Pistol

Replica has solid frame as did original. Frame and 8" barrel blued. Trigger guard brass. Walnut grips standard. Weighs 40 oz.

	350	250	200	150	100	75

Single Cased Set

	375	275	225	150	100	75

Double Cased Set

	550	450	375	275	200	100

NIB	EXC.	V.G.	GOOD	FAIR	POOR

Stainless Steel 1858 New Model Army
Same as above in stainless steel. Weighs 40 oz.

NIB	EXC.	V.G.	GOOD	FAIR	POOR
375	275	225	150	100	75

Single Cased Set

NIB	EXC.	V.G.	GOOD	FAIR	POOR
375	275	225	150	100	75

Double Cased Set

NIB	EXC.	V.G.	GOOD	FAIR	POOR
550	450	375	275	200	10

Brass Framed 1858 New Model Army
Version features highly polished brass frame. Barrel length 7.75".

NIB	EXC.	V.G.	GOOD	FAIR	POOR
165	150	125	90	75	35

Single Cased Set

NIB	EXC.	V.G.	GOOD	FAIR	POOR
250	200	150	100	75	60

Double Cased Set

NIB	EXC.	V.G.	GOOD	FAIR	POOR
395	325	300	250	200	100

1858 Target Model
Same as above. Features patridge front sight and adjustable rear sight. Barrel length 8".

NIB	EXC.	V.G.	GOOD	FAIR	POOR
300	225	175	125	75	50

Deluxe 1858 New Model Army
Replica built to exact dimensions as original. Barrel length 8", with adjustable front sight. Trigger guard silver plated. Action tuned for competition. Weighs 46 oz.

NIB	EXC.	V.G.	GOOD	FAIR	POOR
400	325	250	200	150	100

Spiller and Burr Pistol
.36-caliber pistol, with 7" blued octagon barrel. Frame brass, with walnut grips. Weighs 40 oz.

NIB	EXC.	V.G.	GOOD	FAIR	POOR
350	250	200	150	100	75

Single Cased Set

NIB	EXC.	V.G.	GOOD	FAIR	POOR
375	275	225	150	100	75

Double Cased Set

NIB	EXC.	V.G.	GOOD	FAIR	POOR
550	450	375	275	200	100

Rogers and Spencer
Features 7.5" blued barrel and frame. Offered in .44-caliber. Walnut grips. Weighs 48 oz.

NIB	EXC.	V.G.	GOOD	FAIR	POOR
375	275	225	150	100	75

"London Gray" Rogers and Spencer Pistol
Same as above, with burnished satin chrome finish.

NIB	EXC.	V.G.	GOOD	FAIR	POOR
375	275	225	150	100	75

Rogers and Spencer Target Model
Same as standard. Fitted with adjustable target sights.

NIB	EXC.	V.G.	GOOD	FAIR	POOR
375	275	225	150	100	75

1861 Navy Conversion
Replica of cartridge conversion 1861 Navy. Chambered for .38 Special or .38 Long Colt. Fitted with either 5.5" or 7.5" barrel. Weight about 40 oz.

NIB	EXC.	V.G.	GOOD	FAIR	POOR
475	425	350	250	150	100

1872 Colt Open Top
Features 5.5" or 7.5" barrel. Case hardened frame. Blued barrel and cylinder. Silver-plated brass trigger guard and backstrap. Walnut grips. Chambered for .38-caliber cartridge. Weight about 40 oz.

NIB	EXC.	V.G.	GOOD	FAIR	POOR
500	375	225	175	150	125

1873 Colt-Style Single-Action Army
Replica features case colored frame and hammer. Blued round barrel in 3", 4.75", 5.5" or 7.5" lengths. Trigger guard and cylinder blued. Offered in .44-40, .45 Long Colt, .357 Magnum and .32-20.

NIB	EXC.	V.G.	GOOD	FAIR	POOR
500	375	225	175	150	125

NIB	EXC.	V.G.	GOOD	FAIR	POOR

Model 1873 SAA Stainless Gunfighter
Introduced in 2003. Same as standard 1873. Features all stainless steel construction. Offered in .45 Colt and .357 Magnum caliber. Choice of 4.75", 5.5" or 7.5" barrel. Weight about 45 oz. depending on barrel length.

525	400	250	195	150	125

Economy Model 1873 S.A.A.
Same as above, with brass trigger guard and backstrap.

325	250	200	150	125	100

Nickel 1873 S.A.A.

525	400	250	195	150	125

1873 U.S. Cavalry Model
.45 Long Colt model features U.S. arsenal stampings, case colored frame and walnut grips. Barrel length 7.5"; weighs 45 oz.

500	375	225	175	150	125

1873 Pinched Frame Model
Replica of "pinched" frame 1873. "U" shape rear sight notch. Chambered for .45 Colt, with 7.5" barrel.

500	375	225	175	150	125

1873 Flat Top Target
Features windage adjustable rear sight on flat top frame. Spring loaded front sight. Barrel length 7.5". Offered in .45 Colt. Weight about 40 oz. Introduced in 1998.

500	375	225	175	150	125

Deputy Single-Action Army
Similar to Model 1873, with bird's-head grip. Barrel lengths 3", 3.5", 4" and 4.75". Chambered for .44-40 and .45 Colt.

400	325	250	200	150	100

Shootist Model S.A.A.
Reproduction of Colt 1873. Parts are interchangeable with originals. Blued barrel, cylinder, trigger guard and backstrap. Case hardened frame and hammer. Walnut grips. Offered in 4.75", 5.5" and 7.5" barrel lengths. Chambered for .357 Magnum, .44-40 or .45 Colt.

500	375	225	175	150	125

Scout Small Frame Revolver
Identical to Colt 1873 SAA, with smaller dimensions. Offered in .38 Special. Choice of 4.75" or 5.5" barrel. Weight about 30 oz. Introduced in 2003.

400	325	250	200	150	100

Deluxe 1873 Colt Revolver
Chambered for .32-20 cartridge. Features bright charcoal blue barrel, with case colored frame and hammer. Walnut grips. Fitted with 5.5" barrel. Limited production. Weight about 41 oz.

500	375	225	175	150	125

Bisley Model
Features famous Bisley grip. Barrel lengths 4.75", 5.5" and 7.5". Chambered for .44-40 or .45 Colt.

500	375	225	175	150	125

Bisley Flat Top Target
Similar to Bisley, with 7.5" barrel. Flat top frame, with adjustable front sight and windage adjustable rear sight. Chambered for .44-40 or .45 Colt. Weight about 40 oz.

525	400	250	195	150	125

1875 Remington-Style Revolver
Frame case colored. All other parts blued except brass trigger guard. Available in .44-40 or .45 Long Colt. Furnished with walnut grips. Barrel length 7.5"; weighs 41 oz.

500	375	225	175	150	125

	NIB	EXC.	V.G.	GOOD	FAIR	POOR

1890 Remington-Style Revolver

Modified version of 1875 model. Offered in .44-40 or .45 Long Colt. Web under barrel has been eliminated. Blued 5.5" steel barrel and frame. Lanyard loop on bottom of walnut grips. Weighs 39 oz.

NIB	EXC.	V.G.	GOOD	FAIR	POOR
500	375	225	175	150	125

TOP BREAK REVOLVERS

Model 1875 Schofield—Wells Fargo 5" barrel

NIB	EXC.	V.G.	GOOD	FAIR	POOR
750	650	525	450	350	125

Model 1875 Schofield—Cavalry 7" barrel

Reproduction of S&W Model 3 top break revolver in either .44-40 or .45 Long Colt. Cavalry model has 7" barrel; Wells Fargo model 5" barrel. Weight about 39 oz.

NIB	EXC.	V.G.	GOOD	FAIR	POOR
750	650	525	450	350	125

Model 1875 Schofield—Deluxe

Charcoal blue finish with gold inlays and "A" style hand engraving. Available in either Cavalry or Wells Fargo model. Special order only.

NIB	EXC.	V.G.	GOOD	FAIR	POOR
1000	800	675	550	425	200

Model 1875 Schofield—B Engraved

Available in Cavalry or Wells Fargo model. Grade "B" is style engraved, with 35 percent coverage. Special order only.

NIB	EXC.	V.G.	GOOD	FAIR	POOR
1100	900	775	650	525	250

Model 1875 Schofield—C Engraved

Available in Cavalry or Wells Fargo in "C" style engraving, with 50 percent coverage. Special order only.

NIB	EXC.	V.G.	GOOD	FAIR	POOR
1150	950	800	675	55	275

Model 1875 Schofield Founder's Model

Introduced in 2003 to honor Val Forgett, Sr. and Aldo Uberti. Features charcoal blued barrel and cylinder. Color case hardened receiver, backstrap, trigger guard and trigger. Grip white ivory polymer. Limited production. Special serial number prefix of "VF".

NIB	EXC.	V.G.	GOOD	FAIR	POOR
750	650	525	450	350	125

Model 1875 Schofield—Hideout

Short-barrel variation of Schofield. Fitted with 3.5" barrel. Chambered for .44-40 or .45 Colt cartridge. Weight about 38 oz.

NIB	EXC.	V.G.	GOOD	FAIR	POOR
750	650	525	450	350	125

New Model Russian

Built around single-action Smith & Wesson Model 3. Chambered for .44 Russian cartridge. Fitted with 6.5" barrel. Case colored spur trigger guard, latch and hammer. Blued frame, barrel and cylinder. Walnut grips. Weight about 40 oz. Introduced in 1999.

NIB	EXC.	V.G.	GOOD	FAIR	POOR
750	650	525	450	350	125

MILITARY SURPLUS ARMS

SKS Type 56 w/Scope Rail

Semi-automatic gas operated rifle. Chambered for 7.62x39 cartridge. Has 10-round clip. Fitted with scope rail on left side of receiver. Barrel length 20.5"; weight 8 lbs.

NIB	EXC.	V.G.	GOOD	FAIR	POOR
400	325	250	200	150	100

Standard SKS Type 56

Same as above, without scope rail.

NIB	EXC.	V.G.	GOOD	FAIR	POOR
400	325	250	200	150	100

Standard SKS Type 56 With Scope and Bipod

As above, with 2.75 power Type 89 scope and RPK style folding bipod.

NIB	EXC.	V.G.	GOOD	FAIR	POOR
400	325	250	200	150	100

SKS "Cowboy's Companion" Carbine

Barrel length version 16.5". Weighs 7 lbs. 8 oz.

NIB	EXC.	V.G.	GOOD	FAIR	POOR
400	325	250	200	150	100

	NIB	EXC.	V.G.	GOOD	FAIR	POOR

Military Version

Military version of "Cowboy's Companion". Fitted with short cruciform folding bayonet.

	NIB	EXC.	V.G.	GOOD	FAIR	POOR
	400	325	250	200	150	100

SKS "Hunter" Carbine

Checkered composite Monte Carlo stock, with full length pull. Comes with 5-round magazine.

	NIB	EXC.	V.G.	GOOD	FAIR	POOR
	400	325	250	200	150	100

TT-Olympia Pistol

Reproduction of Walther target pistol. Chambered for .22 LR. Barrel length 4.625"; weighs 27 oz.

	NIB	EXC.	V.G.	GOOD	FAIR	POOR
	275	200	150	125	100	50

TU-90 Pistol

Model based on Tokagypt pistol. Features wraparound grip, with thumb rest. Barrel length 4.5"; weighs 30 oz.

	NIB	EXC.	V.G.	GOOD	FAIR	POOR
	250	190	115	75	50	40

TU-KKW Training Rifle

Based on 98 Mauser. Chambered for .22 LR cartridge. Fitted with military sights, bayonet lug, cleaning rod and take down disc. Comes with detachable 5-round box magazine. Barrel length 26"; weighs 8 lbs.

	NIB	EXC.	V.G.	GOOD	FAIR	POOR
	325	275	200	150	100	60

TU-KKW Sniper Trainer

Same as above, with 2.75 power Type 89 scope. Quick detachable mounting system.

	NIB	EXC.	V.G.	GOOD	FAIR	POOR
	375	325	275	200	150	100

TU-33/40 Carbine

Based on WWII Mauser G 33/40 mountain carbine. Chambered for .22 LR or 7.62x39 cartridge. Barrel length 20.75"; weighs 7.5 lbs.

	NIB	EXC.	V.G.	GOOD	FAIR	POOR
	325	275	200	150	100	—

JW-15 Rifle

Bolt-action design based on BRNO Model 5 action. Chambered for .22 LR. Features adjustable sights, sling swivels, detachable 5-round magazine. Top of receiver dovetailed for easy scope mounting. Barrel 24" long; weighs 5 lbs. 12 oz.

	NIB	EXC.	V.G.	GOOD	FAIR	POOR
	100	80	70	60	50	35

Martini Target Rifle

.444 or .45-70 caliber single-shot Martini-action rifle, with 26" or 30" octagonal barrel, tang sight and walnut stock. Offered between 1972 and 1984.

	NIB	EXC.	V.G.	GOOD	FAIR	POOR
	—	625	500	400	300	150

Parker-Hale Sniper Rifle

See—Parker-Hale.

RPKS-74

5.56mm or 7.62x39mm caliber semi-automatic rifle, with 19" barrel. Patterned after Russian AK series rifles.

	NIB	EXC.	V.G.	GOOD	FAIR	POOR
	550	450	375	275	200	10

No. 5 Enfield Jungle Carbine

Replica chambered for .303 British cartridge. Fitted with cupped buttplate and flashider. Barrel length 20.5". Magazine capacity 10 rounds. Weight about 7 lbs.

	NIB	EXC.	V.G.	GOOD	FAIR	POOR
	375	325	275	200	150	100

No. 6 Enfield Jungle Carbine

Reproduction chambered for .303 British cartridge, with 20.5" barrel and flashider. Weight about 7 lbs. 10 round magazine.

	NIB	EXC.	V.G.	GOOD	FAIR	POOR
	375	325	275	200	150	100

Ishapore 2A No. 1 MK III Rifle

Refinished rifle with 25" barrel. Chambered for .308 Win. cartridge. Magazine capacity 12 rounds. Weight about 9.3 lbs.

	NIB	EXC.	V.G.	GOOD	FAIR	POOR
	350	250	200	150	100	75

	NIB	EXC.	V.G.	GOOD	FAIR	POOR

2A Tanker Carbine

Replica with short 20" barrel. Chambered for .308 Win. Magazine capacity 12 rounds. Weight about 8.7 lbs.

	375	325	275	200	150	100

MK III Tanker Carbine

Similar to above. Chambered for .303 British cartridge. Magazine capacity 10 rounds.

	375	325	275	200	150	100

Lithgow No. 1 MK III Rifle

Rifles in unissued condition. Barrel length 25". Chambered for .303 British cartridge. Magazine capacity 10 rounds. Weight about 9 lbs.

	400	325	250	200	150	100

No. 1 MK III Enfield Rifle

Standard MK III S.M.L.E. rifles that have been refinished. Barrel length 25.25". Magazine capacity 10 rounds of .303 British cartridge. Weight about 9 lbs.

	375	325	275	200	150	100

No. 4 Tanker Carbine

Cut-down version of No. 4 MK I Enfield. Barrel length 20.5". Chambered for .303 British cartridge. Magazine capacity 10 rounds. Weight about 8.2 lbs.

	350	250	200	150	100	75

No. 4 MK I Enfield Rifle

Reconditioned rifle. Barrel length 25". Magazine capacity 10 rounds of .303 British cartridge. Weight about 8.6 lbs.

	350	250	200	150	100	75

Savage No. 4 MK I Rifle

Chambered for .303 British cartridge, with 25" barrel. Stocks are unissued. Magazine capacity 10 rounds. Weight about 8.7 lbs.

	375	325	275	200	150	100

Luger

.22-caliber semi-automatic pistol, with 4", 6" or 8" barrel, fixed sights and 10-shot magazine. Blued, with walnut grips. Manufactured in U.S.A. - 1986 and 1987.

	—	325	275	225	175	125

Grand Prix Silhouette Pistol

.30-30, .44 Magnum, 7mm Special and .45-70 caliber single-shot pistol, with 13.75" barrel. Adjustable sights and aluminum heat-disbursing rib. Matte-blued, walnut grips and forearm. Manufactured in 1985.

	—	450	375	295	225	150

NEAL, W.
Bangor, Maine

Under Hammer Pistol

.31-caliber under hammer percussion pistol, with 5" to 8" barrels. Iron frame and walnut grip. Barrel marked "Wm. Neal/Bangor, Me.

	—	—	1350	1000	450	150

NEPPERHAN FIREARMS CO.
Yonkers, New York

Pocket Revolver

.31-caliber percussion revolver, with 3.5" to 6" barrels and 5-shot cylinder. Blued case hardened with walnut grips. Barrel marked "Nepperhan/Fire Arms Co" and on some additionally "Yonkers New York". Latter worth a slight premium over values listed. Approximately 5,000 made during 1860s.

	—	—	1400	1000	385	200

NESIKA BAY PRECISION, INC.
Sturgis, South Dakota

Hunting Rifles

Offered in a number of different calibers. Several stock options to choose from. All rifles fitted with adjustable trigger.

	4000	2900	2300	1500	750	400

NIB	EXC.	V.G.	GOOD	FAIR	POOR

Varmint Rifles

Offered in a variety of calibers, barrel lengths and weights. Single shot or repeater.

3500	2900	2300	1500	750	400

Urban Tactical Rifle

Chambered for .308 cartridge. Fitted with 20" fluted barrel. Detachable box magazine. Weight about 10 lbs. **NOTE:** .300 Win. Magnum add $100. Add 5-10 percent for Heavy Tactical version.

5800	4800	3500	2700	800	500

NEW ENGLAND FIREARMS CO.
Madison, North Carolina

Formerly located in Gardner, Massachusetts, New England Firearms (NEF), is part of the Freedom Group of gun companies headquartered in Madison, NC. Some models have been marketed under both the NEF brand and H&R 1871. After 2007, the NEF brand has been seen only on imported models.

Model R22

.22 Magnum or .32 H&R Magnum double-action revolver, with 2.5", 4" or 6" barrel. Either 6- or 9-shot cylinder. Blued or nickel-plated, with walnut grips. Introduced in 1988.

150	100	80	70	60	40

Excell

Introduced in 2005. Chambered for 12-gauge 3" shell. Fitted with 28" vent rib barrel, with choke tubes. Checkered black synthetic stock. Magazine capacity 5 rounds. Weight about 7 lbs.

450	375	295	225	150	100

Excell Waterfowl

As above, with Realtree Advantage Wetlands camo finish. Introduced in 2005.

475	400	325	250	175	125

Excell Turkey

Fitted with 22" barrel with choke tubes and fiber optic front sight. Realtree Advantage Hardwoods camo finish. Weight 7 lbs. Introduced in 2005.

475	400	325	250	175	125

Excell Combo

Model has black synthetic stock and two barrels: 28" vent rib with choke tubes and 24" rifled barrel. Weight about 7 lbs. depending on barrel length. Introduced in 2005.

500	425	345	260	185	135

Pardner

12-, 16-, 20-gauge or .410 bore single-shot shotgun, with 24", 26" or 28" barrel. Blued, with walnut stock. Introduced in 1987.

150	100	80	70	60	40

Pardner Youth

Similar to above. Offered only in 20-, 28-gauge and .410 bore. Fitted with 26" barrel. Weight between 5 and 6 lbs.

150	100	80	70	60	40

Special Purpose

Similar model offered only in 10-gauge. Available in several different configurations: 10-gauge with hardwood stock 28" barrel; camo model with 28" barrel and camo model with 32" barrel choked Modified; black matte finish model with 24" barrel with screw-in turkey Full choke. Weight about 9.5 lbs.

250	175	125	100	75	50

Pardner Pump Turkey

Chambered for 12-gauge 3" shell. Fitted with 22" barrel with turkey choke tube. Magazine capacity 5 rounds. Weight about 7.5 lbs. Introduced in 2005.

275	225	175	125	100	75

Pardner Pump Walnut Shotgun

12- or 20-gauge pump-action shotgun, with American walnut furniture, 26" or 28" vent rib barrel, 3" chamber and screw-in choke tube. Weight 7.5 lbs.

—	275	225	175	125	100

	NIB	EXC.	V.G.	GOOD	FAIR	POOR

Pardner Pump Synthetic Shotgun

Similar to above, with black synthetic buttstock and fore-end.

	—	225	175	150	100	75

Pardner Pump Field Shotgun

Similar to above, with Realtree APG HD camo finish.

	—	275	225	175	125	100

Pardner Pump Compact Field Shotgun

Similar to above, with 1.25" shorter length of pull and 21" barrel.

	—	225	175	150	100	75

Pardner Pump Compact Walnut Shotgun

Similar to Pardner Pump Walnut, with 1.25" shorter length of pull and 21" barrel. Weight 6.25 lbs.

	—	225	175	150	100	75

Pardner Pump Compact Synthetic Shotgun

Similar to above, with black synthetic buttstock and fore-end.

	—	225	175	150	100	75

Pardner Pump Combo

Introduced in 2005. Features two 12-gauge 3" barrels. One 28" with vent rib and choke tubes other 22" rifled slug barrel. Walnut stock. Weight about 7.5 lbs. depending on barrel length.

	275	225	175	125	100	75

Pardner Pump Protector

Similar to Pardner Pump, with matte black finish throughout. Synthetic buttstock and fore-end. Also available with carbon fiber dipped stock.

	—	225	175	150	100	75

Survivor

Based on single-shot break-action design. Rifle or shotgun fitted with synthetic stock, with integral storage compartments. Offered in .410/.45 Colt, 12- and 20-gauge, .223 Rem. and .357 Magnum. Barrel length 22". Weight about 6 lbs.

	200	175	150	125	100	75

Handi-Rifle (aka Handi-Gun)

.22 Hornet, .223, .243, .270, .280, .30-30, .44 Magnum or .45-70 caliber version of above. A 22" barrel fitted with open sights. Blued, with walnut stock. Introduced in 1989. In 2003, offered in stainless steel. In 2004, .22-250, .25-06 and .204 calibers added. In 2005, .500 S&W added.

	275	200	150	125	100	75

Tracker

Single-shot break-open shotgun. Offered in 12- and 20-gauge, with rifled or cylinder bore barrel both 24" long. Equipped with adjustable rifle sights. Weight about 6 lbs.

	150	125	100	75	60	50

Super Light Rifle

Single-shot rifle chambered for .22 Hornet or .223 Rem. Fitted with 20" light weight barrel. Choice of scope mount, no sights or adjustable rear sight and ramp front sight. Black polymer stock, with semi-beavertail fore-end. Weight about 5.5 lbs.

	175	125	100	75	60	50

Huntsman

Blackpowder gun, with break-open action. Hardwood pistol-grip stock. Fitted with 24" barrel. Chambered for .45- or .50-caliber slug. Recoil pad. Weight about 6.5 lbs. Introduced in 2002. In 2003, offered in stainless steel.

	175	125	100	75	60	50

Tracker II

Combination two-barrel set. Blackpowder and 12-gauge slug barrel. Case colored frame. Hardwood stock.

	275	225	175	125	100	—

Handi-Rifle Combo

Combination two-barrel set. .50 blackpowder and .243 Win. barrel. Hardwood stock. No iron sights.

	275	225	175	125	100	—

	NIB	EXC.	V.G.	GOOD	FAIR	POOR

Sportster

Single-shot .22-caliber short/LR or .22 WMR rifle, with 20" barrel. No iron sights. Black polymer Monte Carlo stock, with matte black metal finish. Scope mount rail. Weight about 5.5 lbs.

	175	125	100	75	60	50

Sportster Youth

As above, with standard stock. Weight about 5.25 lbs.

	175	125	100	75	60	50

Sportster .17 HMR

Single-shot chambered for .17 HMR cartridge. Fitted with 22" heavy varmint barrel. No iron sights. Black polymer Monte Carlo stock, with matte black metal finish. Weight about 7 lbs.

	175	125	100	75	60	50

Sportster .17 M2

As above chambered for .17 Mach2 cartridge. Introduced in 2005.

	175	125	100	75	60	50

Sportster SL

Semi-automatic rifle chambered for .22 LR cartridge. Fitted with 19" barrel. Walnut finished hardwood stock, with Monte Carlo and pistol-grip. Adjustable sights. 10 round magazine. Weight about 5.5 lbs. Introduced in 2004.

	150	125	100	75	60	50

Sportster Versa-Pack

Two-barrel set: 22" .410 barrel; other 20" .22-caliber barrel. Hardwood stock, with straight-grip. Iron sights. Weight about 5.5 lbs.

	250	175	125	100	75	50

Sidekick Muzzleloader

Introduced in 2004. Features break-open action, side lever release chambered for .50-caliber ball. Barrel length 24" or 26". American hardwood stock, with pistol-grip and recoil pad. Black matte finish or stainless steel. Adjustable fiber optic sights. Weight about 6.5 lbs. **NOTE:** Add $70 for stainless steel.

	200	165	125	100	75	50

NEW ULTRA LIGHT ARMS
Granville, West Virginia

Previously known as Ultra Light Arms, this manufacturer makes a variety of bolt-action rifles fitted with Douglas barrels of varying lengths, custom triggers and reinforced graphite stocks. Values listed are for base models. **NOTE:** Forbes Rifles, LLC makes a production-grade version of Model 24B rifle. See that listing.

Model 20 (Short Action)

Weight 4.5 lbs., with 22" barrel. Composte stock, with choice of colors or camo finish. Adjustable trigger. No sights. Offered in left-/right-hand.

	3100	2750	2500	1850	900	500

Model 20 RF Rimfire

Weight about 4.5 lbs., with 22" barrel. Stock synthetic, with choice of colors or camo finish. No sights. Adjustable trigger. Available as single-shot or repeater.

	1600	1300	1100	600	450	250

Model 20 Hunter's Pistol

Bolt-action repeating pistol designed with serious hunter in mind. Offered in various popular calibers, with 14" high-quality Douglas heavy barrel. Has 5-shot magazine. Matte blued, with reinforced graphite Kevlar stock. Introduced in 1987.

	1250	1000	800	625	500	300

Model 24 (Long Action)

Weight about 5.25 lbs., with 22" barrel.

	3100	2750	2500	1850	900	500

Model 28 Magnum

Weight about 5.75 lbs., with 24" barrel.

	3300	3050	2750	1950	900	500

	NIB	EXC.	V.G.	GOOD	FAIR	POOR

Model 40 Magnum

Weight about 7.5 lbs., with 26" barrel.

	NIB	EXC.	V.G.	GOOD	FAIR	POOR
	3300	3050	2750	1950	900	500

Model 90

Muzzle-loading rifle built with either .45- or .50-caliber barrel. Graphite stock. Williams sights. Barrel length 28". Adjustable trigger. Weight about 6 lbs.

	950	750	600	475	350	200

Model 290

Blackpowder model with 209 Primer ignition, .45- or .50-caliber, 24" button-rifled barrel, Timney trigger, Kevlar stock with recoil pad, sling swivels, scope mount.

	1200	1100	900	750	650	300

NEWBURY ARMS CO.
Catskill, New York
Albany, New York

Pocket Pistol

.25-caliber spur trigger pocket pistol, with 4" octagonal barrel. Blued, silver-plated with walnut grips.

	—	—	2400	2050	875	200

Pocket Revolver

.26-caliber double-action percussion revolver, with 5" barrel and C-shaped exposed trigger. Blued, with iron or brass frame and walnut grips. Barrel marked "Newbury Arms Co. Albany". Produced in limited numbers between 1855 and 1860.

	—	—	7800	6900	3000	750

NEWCOMB, H. G.
Natchez, Mississippi

Pocket Pistol

.41-caliber percussion pocket pistol, with 2.5" barrel, German silver mounts and walnut stock. Manufactured in 1850s.

	—	—	2400	1850	700	250

NEWTON ARMS CO.
Buffalo, New York

Also known as Buffalo Newton Rifle Company and Charles Newton Rifle Company. In operation from 1913 to 1932.

NOTE: Any rifles listed chambered for a Newton caliber, will bring a premium over standard calibers of about 25 percent.

Newton-Mauser Rifle

.256 Newton caliber bolt-action rifle, with 24" barrel and double-set triggers. Blued, with walnut stock. Manufactured circa 1914.

	—	—	1300	850	500	300

Standard Rifle First Type

.22, .256, .280, .30, .33 and .35 Newton as well as .30-06 caliber bolt-action rifle, with 24" barrel. Open or aperture sights and double-set triggers. Blued, with walnut stock. Manufactured between 1916 and 1918.

	—	2500	2150	1500	900	400

Standard Rifle Second Model

.256, .30, or .35 Newton as well as .30-06 caliber bolt-action rifle as above, with Enfield-style bolt handle. Manufactured after 1918.

	—	2500	2150	1500	900	400

Buffalo Newton Rifle

As above marked "Buffalo Newton Rifle Company".

	—	2000	1650	1000	600	300

NIB	EXC.	V.G.	GOOD	FAIR	POOR

NICHOLS & CHILDS
Conway, Massachusetts

Percussion Belt Revolver

.34-caliber percussion revolver, with 6" round barrel and 6-shot cylinder. Blued or browned, with walnut grips. Estimated fewer than 25 made in 1838.

NIB	EXC.	V.G.	GOOD	FAIR	POOR
—	—	1450	1175	4900	1250

Revolving Percussion Rifle

.36- or .40-caliber percussion rifle, with 22", 26" or 30" barrel and 5-, 6-, 7- or 9-shot cylinder. Blued or browned, with walnut stock and patch box. Believed approximately 150 made between 1838 and 1840.

NIB	EXC.	V.G.	GOOD	FAIR	POOR
—	—	25000	16500	6600	2000

NIGHTHAWK CUSTOM
Berryville, Arkansas

Custom Talon/Talon II

1911-style semi-automatic with 5" (Talon) or 4.25" (Talon II) barrel and fixed or adjustable sights. Several other barrel lengths/finishes available.

NIB	EXC.	V.G.	GOOD	FAIR	POOR
2400	1950	1550	1200	700	300

Custom Predator

1911-style semi-automatic with 4.25"or 5" barrel and fixed or adjustable sights. Several other barrel lengths/finishes available.

NIB	EXC.	V.G.	GOOD	FAIR	POOR
2800	2350	1850	1400	750	300

GRP

Global Response Pistol. 1911-style semi-automatic, with 4.25" or 5" barrel and fixed or adjustable sights. Several other barrel lengths/finishes available.

NIB	EXC.	V.G.	GOOD	FAIR	POOR
2400	1950	1550	1200	700	300

Heinie Signature Series

Competition, Government Recon or Officer Compact configurations, all chambered in 9mm. 5" barrel except for Compact which is 4.25". Heinie Slant Pro sights. Recon has accessory rail. Many custom features.

NIB	EXC.	V.G.	GOOD	FAIR	POOR
3100	2700	2100	1600	1000	350

Lady Hawk

Medium-frame 1911-style pistol in 9mm or .45 ACP with 4.25" match-grade barrel, titanium blue Perma Kote finish with hard chrome controls. Sights are Heinie Straight-Eight Slant Pro. Ultra thin chain link front and back strap for reduced grip circumference.

NIB	EXC.	V.G.	GOOD	FAIR	POOR
3100	2700	2100	1600	1000	350

Falcon

Full-size 1911 design with Coyote Tan, black or OD Green finish, dimpled grip, front and rear cocking serrations, Heinie Ledge rear sight. Chambered in 9mm, 10mm or .45 ACP

NIB	EXC.	V.G.	GOOD	FAIR	POOR
2800	2400	2000	1500	800	350

Bob Marvel Custom 1911

This model features Nighthawk/Marvel Everlast Recoil System, which allows a shooter to go at least 10,000 rounds before a spring change is necessary. Felt recoil and muzzle flip are also reduced. Other features include fully adjustable sights that have been recessed into the slide and dehorned, hand stippling on top of slide and a one-piece mainspring housing/magwell.

NIB	EXC.	V.G.	GOOD	FAIR	POOR
3500	2850	2150	1650	800	340

T3

Compact 1911-style pistol, with Officers-size frame and Commander-size slide and barrel. All steel frame and slide, horizontally slanted serrations on mainspring housing and rear of slide, blue or stainless finish. Other features include Heinie Slant-Pro Straight Eight night sights, custom lightweight aluminum trigger and extended mag well. Designed by renowned custom pistolsmith Bob Marvel.

NIB	EXC.	V.G.	GOOD	FAIR	POOR
2850	2500	2000	1450	800	300

NOBLE
Haydenville, Massachusetts

In business between 1946 and 1971. Company manufactured a variety of plain utilitarian firearms. In general, these arms are all worth approximately the same, that is, less than $200 in excellent condition.

	NIB	EXC.	V.G.	GOOD	FAIR	POOR

Noble firearms represent an attractive opportunity for beginning collectors, as most can be had very inexpensively.

RIFLES

Model 10

.22-caliber bolt-action single-shot rifle, with 24" barrel. Pistol-grip stock with no checkering. Open sights. Produced in late 1950s.

	NIB	EXC.	V.G.	GOOD	FAIR	POOR
	—	75	60	50	40	30

Model 20

.22-caliber bolt-action rifle. Fitted with 22" barrel. Open sights. Produced from late 1950s to early 1960s.

	NIB	EXC.	V.G.	GOOD	FAIR	POOR
	—	75	60	50	40	30

Model 33

.22-caliber slide-action rifle. Fitted with 24" barrel and tubular magazine. Tenite stock. Produced from late 1940s to early 1950s.

	NIB	EXC.	V.G.	GOOD	FAIR	POOR
	—	80	70	60	50	40

Model 33A

Same as above, with wood stock.

	NIB	EXC.	V.G.	GOOD	FAIR	POOR
	—	75	60	50	40	30

Model 222

Single-shot bolt-action rifle chambered for .22-caliber cartridge. Plain pistol-grip stock.

	NIB	EXC.	V.G.	GOOD	FAIR	POOR
	—	85	75	60	50	40

Model 235

Rather dopey but kinda cute .22-caliber slide-action rifle, with 24" barrel. Tubular magazine. Plain pistol-grip stock and grooved slide handle.

	NIB	EXC.	V.G.	GOOD	FAIR	POOR
	—	200	125	75	60	50

Model 275

.22-caliber lever-action rifle, with tubular magazine. Fitted with 24" barrel. Plain stock has semi-pistol grip.

	NIB	EXC.	V.G.	GOOD	FAIR	POOR
	—	175	100	80	60	50

SHOTGUNS

Model 40

Hammerless slide-action shotgun chambered for 12-gauge shell. Fitted with tubular magazine, 28" barrel with multi choke. Plain pistol stock, with grooved slide handle.

	NIB	EXC.	V.G.	GOOD	FAIR	POOR
	—	125	100	85	70	50

Model 50

Same as above, without multi choke.

	NIB	EXC.	V.G.	GOOD	FAIR	POOR
	—	115	90	80	65	50

Model 60

Hammerless slide-action shotgun in 12- or 16-gauge. Tubular magazine. Fitted with 28" barrel with adjustable choke. Plain pistol-grip stock, with grooved slide handle.

	NIB	EXC.	V.G.	GOOD	FAIR	POOR
	—	175	150	125	100	75

Model 65

Same as above, without adjustable choke.

	NIB	EXC.	V.G.	GOOD	FAIR	POOR
	—	150	125	100	75	60

Model 66CLP

Offered in 12- or 16-gauge. Slide-action shotgun fitted with 28" plain barrel and keyed lock fire control system.

	NIB	EXC.	V.G.	GOOD	FAIR	POOR
	—	160	140	110	85	70

Model 66RCLP

Similar to above, with 28" vent rib barrel. Checkered pistol-grip stock. Adjustable choke standard.

	NIB	EXC.	V.G.	GOOD	FAIR	POOR
	—	200	175	150	125	100

	NIB	EXC.	V.G.	GOOD	FAIR	POOR

Model 66RLP
Same as above, without adjustable choke.

	—	175	150	125	100	75

Model 66XL
Similar to above, with plain barrel. Checkering only on slide handle.

	—	150	125	100	75	60

Model 70CLP
Similar to Model 66 series. Offered in .410 bore, with 26" barrel and adjustable choke. Both buttstock and slide handle checkered.

	—	175	150	125	100	75

Model 70RCLP
This variation fitted with 26" ventilated rib barrel.

	—	200	175	150	125	100

Model 70RLP
Model has vent rib barrel. No adjustable choke.

	—	175	150	125	100	75

Model 70XL
This version has no adjustable choke. Fitted with 26" vent rib barrel. Stock checked.

	—	125	100	80	70	60

Model 602RCLP
Hammerless slide-action shotgun chambered for 20-gauge shell. Fitted with 28" vent barrel and adjustable choke. Checkered pistol-grip stock, with slide handle.

	—	225	200	175	125	100

Model 602CLP
Same as above, with plain barrel.

	—	175	150	125	100	75

Model 602RLP
Same as Model RCLP, without addition of adjustable choke device.

	—	200	175	150	125	100

Model 602XL
Same as above, with only slide handle checkered.

	—	150	125	100	75	60

Model 662
20-gauge slide-action shotgun. Has plain aluminum barrel, with checkered pistol-grip and slide handle. Receiver is made from aluminum. Produced in late 1960s.

	—	200	175	150	125	100

Model 80
Semi-automatic inertia-operated shotgun. Chambered for .410 shell. Fitted with 26" barrel, plain pistol stock with slotted forearm. Produced in early to mid 1960s.

	—	250	200	150	125	100

Model 166L
12-gauge slide-action shotgun, with key lock system. Fitted with 24" barrel bored for rifled slug. Lyman peep rear sight with post front sight. Checkered pistol and slide handle.

	—	250	200	150	125	100

Model 420
Box lock design side-by-side shotgun, with double triggers. Offered in 12-, 16-, 20-gauge and .410 bore. Barrel lengths 28" for all gauges; except .410 is 26". Lightly engraved frame. Checkered walnut stock and splinter forearm.

	—	300	250	200	150	100

Model 450E
Similar to Model 420, with addition of automatic ejectors and not offered in .410 bore. Checkered pistol-grip stock, with beavertail forearm. Produced in late 1960s.

	—	350	275	225	175	125

NORINCO
Peoples Republic of China
China North Industries Corp.

Norinco is a state-owned conglomerate in China. Exported firearms to United States from 1988 to 1995. Importation of Norinco firearms was banned in conjunction with 1994 Crime Bill and various trade sanctions against China, with the exception of several shotguns that were marketed between 1999 and 2002.

ATD .22

.22-caliber semi-automatic rifle, with 19.4" barrel and 11-shot magazine located in butt. Blued, with hardwood stock. Importation began in 1987.

NIB	EXC.	V.G.	GOOD	FAIR	POOR
200	150	125	100	75	50

EM-321

.22-caliber slide-action rifle, with 19.5" barrel and 10-shot tubular magazine. Blued, with hardwood stock. Introduced in 1989.

NIB	EXC.	V.G.	GOOD	FAIR	POOR
150	100	85	75	65	50

Model HL-12-203 Shotgun

12-gauge boxlock over/under shotgun, with 30" ventilated rib barrels fitted for choke tubes. Single trigger and automatic ejectors. Blued, with hardwood stock. Introduced in 1989.

NIB	EXC.	V.G.	GOOD	FAIR	POOR
400	325	275	225	175	125

Model HL-12-102 Shotgun

12-gauge slide-action shotgun, with 28" barrel and 3-shot magazine. Blued, with hardwood stock. Introduced in 1989.

NIB	EXC.	V.G.	GOOD	FAIR	POOR
275	225	200	175	125	100

Model 97 Hammer Pump

Similar in appearance to Winchester Model 1897 shotgun. Fitted with 20" barrel with cylinder choke. Hardwood stock.

NIB	EXC.	V.G.	GOOD	FAIR	POOR
375	275	200	150	100	75

Type 54-1 Tokarev

7.62x25mm caliber semi-automatic pistol, with 4.6" barrel, fixed sights and 8-shot magazine. Blued, with plastic grips. Imported in 1989.

NIB	EXC.	V.G.	GOOD	FAIR	POOR
—	300	250	200	100	80

1911 A1

Steel-framed clone of 1911 .45 A1 semi-automatic. Very popular with competition shooters as a platform for custom guns. No longer imported.

NIB	EXC.	V.G.	GOOD	FAIR	POOR
—	400	350	200	100	80

Model 213 Pistol

Copy of Browning P-35 semi-automatic pistol. Sold in 1988 only.

NIB	EXC.	V.G.	GOOD	FAIR	POOR
—	250	200	150	100	75

Type 59 Makarov

.380 or 9mm Makarov caliber double-action semi-automatic pistol, with 3.5" barrel and 8-shot magazine. Blued, with plastic grips.

NIB	EXC.	V.G.	GOOD	FAIR	POOR
—	275	250	225	175	125

SKS Rifle

7.62x39mm caliber semi-automatic rifle, with 20.5" barrel. Folding bayonet and either 10-shot fixed or 30-shot detachable magazine. Blued, with hardwood stock. Importation began in 1988.

NIB	EXC.	V.G.	GOOD	FAIR	POOR
—	400	300	225	150	100

Type 84S AK

Similar to AKS service rifle in 5.56mm caliber, with 16" barrel and 30-shot magazine.

NIB	EXC.	V.G.	GOOD	FAIR	POOR
900	800	700	550	350	200

Type 84S-1

As above, with under-folding metal stock.

NIB	EXC.	V.G.	GOOD	FAIR	POOR
1050	900	750	575	375	225

Type 84S-3

As above, with composition stock.

NIB	EXC.	V.G.	GOOD	FAIR	POOR
1000	850	700	600	400	225

	NIB	EXC.	V.G.	GOOD	FAIR	POOR

NORTH & COUCH
New York, New York

Animal Trap Gun

.28- or .30-caliber percussion pepperbox, with either 1.75" or 2.12" barrel group. Hammer made with or without spur. Marked "North & Couch, Middletown, Conn." or "North & Couch New York". Manufactured during 1860s.

Disk Hammer Model

NIB	EXC.	V.G.	GOOD	FAIR	POOR
—	—	2200	1850	700	300

Spur Hammer Model

NIB	EXC.	V.G.	GOOD	FAIR	POOR
—	—	3000	2750	900	350

NORTH AMERICAN ARMS
Provo, Utah

Mini-Revolver

.22 or .22 Magnum caliber spur trigger revolver, with 1" or 2.5" barrel and 5-shot cylinder. Stainless steel, with plastic or laminated rosewood grips. Introduced in 1975. Made in styles listed.

Standard Rimfire Version

NIB	EXC.	V.G.	GOOD	FAIR	POOR
225	175	150	—	125	100

2 Cylinder Magnum Convertible Version

NIB	EXC.	V.G.	GOOD	FAIR	POOR
275	200	175	—	145	125

Viper Belt Buckle Version

NIB	EXC.	V.G.	GOOD	FAIR	POOR
225	175	150	—	125	100

Magnum Version

NIB	EXC.	V.G.	GOOD	FAIR	POOR
250	200	175	—	150	100

Standard 3 Gun Set

NIB	EXC.	V.G.	GOOD	FAIR	POOR
725	575	400	—	300	225

Deluxe 3 Gun Set

NIB	EXC.	V.G.	GOOD	FAIR	POOR
800	650	475	—	375	275

Cased .22 Magnum

NIB	EXC.	V.G.	GOOD	FAIR	POOR
350	250	200	—	150	125

Companion

.22-caliber cap-and-ball mini revolver. Has 1.125" barrel. Overall length 4.6"; weight about 5 oz.

NIB	EXC.	V.G.	GOOD	FAIR	POOR
200	165	150	125	100	75

Super Companion

Same as above, with longer cylinder. Has 1.62" barrel. Weighs about 7 oz.

NIB	EXC.	V.G.	GOOD	FAIR	POOR
200	165	150	125	100	75

Black Widow

Five-shot fixed-sight revolver, with 2" or 4" barrel and oversize black rubber grips. Chambered for .22 LR or .22 Win. Magnum stainless steel. Weight about 8.8 oz. **NOTE:** Add $20 for adjustable sights.

NIB	EXC.	V.G.	GOOD	FAIR	POOR
280	225	175	125	100	75

Mini-Master

Similar to Black Widow, with 2" or 4" barrel. Choice of either .22 LR or .22 Win. Magnum stainless steel. Weight about 10.7 oz. **NOTE:** Add $20 for adjustable sights.

NIB	EXC.	V.G.	GOOD	FAIR	POOR
280	225	175	125	100	75

"The Earl" Single-Action Revolver

Single-action mini-revolver patterned after 1858-style Remington percussion revolver. Chambered in .22 Magnum, with .22 LR accessory cylinder. Features include 4" octagonal barrel, spur trigger, five-shot cylinder, faux loading lever that serves as cylinder pin release, wood grips, fixed notch rear sight and barleycorn front sight. Overall length 7.75". Weight 6.8 oz.

.22 Magnum only

NIB	EXC.	V.G.	GOOD	FAIR	POOR
290	225	175	125	100	75

	NIB	EXC.	V.G.	GOOD	FAIR	POOR

.22 convertible

	NIB	EXC.	V.G.	GOOD	FAIR	POOR
	325	275	200	150	125	100

Single-Action Revolver

Polished stainless steel single-action revolver. Chambered for .45 Win. Magnum and .450 Magnum Express cartridge. Has 7.5" barrel and 5-shot cylinder. Transfer bar safety and grips are walnut. Discontinued in 1988. Available with two cylinders. **NOTE:** Add $200 for extra cylinder.

—	1200	950	700	400	250	

Guardian

Semi-automatic double-action-only pocket pistol. Chambered in .32 ACP, .32 NAA or .25 NAA. Magazine capacity 6 rounds. Barrel length 2.2"; overall length 4.4"; weight empty 13.5 oz. Introduced in 1998. **NOTE:** Add 25 percent for Crimson Trace laser grips.

400	300	225	175	150	125	

Guardian .380

Similar to above. Chambered for .380 cartridge. Barrel length 2.5". Magazine capacity 6 rounds. Weight about 19 oz. **NOTE:** Add 25 percent for Crimson Trace laser grips.

450	350	250	195	175	150	

NORTH AMERICAN ARMS CORP.
Toronto, Canada

Brigadier

.45 ACP caliber semi-automatic pistol, with 5" barrel, 8-shot magazine and alloy frame. Weight 4.5 lbs. Produced in limited quantity between 1948 and 1951. Rarely if ever seen. **NOTE:** Value should be in excess of $5000 in Excellent or better condition.

NORTH AMERICAN SAFARI EXPRESS
Liege, Belgium
See—Francotte

Trade name used by Francotte on their double rifles imported and distributed by Armes De Chasse of Chads Ford, Pennsylvania.

NORTON ARMAMENT CORPORATION
Mt. Clemens, Michigan
See—Budischowsky

Firm manufactured Budischowsky Model TP-70 semi-automatic pistols prior to 1979. After that date, these arms were made by American Arms and Ammunition Company. Values below are for early Michigan production. **NOTE:** Deduct 15 percent for later Florida and Utah production.

—	500	375	250	125	100	

NORWICH PISTOL CO.
Norwich, Connecticut

Established in 1875 by New York retailer Maltby, Curtis & Company. This firm manufactured a wide variety of inexpensive spur trigger revolvers that were sold under these trade names: America, Bulldozer, Challenge, Chieftain, Crescent, Defiance, Hartford Arms, Maltby Henley, Metropolitan Police, Nonpariel, Norwich Arms, Parole, Patriot, Pinafore, Prairie King, Protector, Spy, True Blue, U.M.C. Winfield Arms. Company ceased operations in 1881. Value for any of its arms listed is approximate.

—	—	300	200	75	50	

NOSLER CUSTOM
Bend, Oregon

Nosler Custom Model 48 Sporter

Bolt-action centerfire rifle. Chambered in various calibers, 24" barrel, round top receiver, onyx gray composite stock. Introduced 2007. Price shown includes scope. Limited edition series has high grade walnut stock, double square bridge action, with integral scope bases. Only 500 made. **NOTE:** Add 50 percent for limited edition model.

2850	2600	2100	1350	800	500	

Nosler Model 48 Professional

Custom made on Nosler action, with glass-bedded Aramid Fiber reinforced composite stock. Match-grade, hand-lapped stainless steel barrel. Custom three-pound trigger, two-position

NIB	EXC.	V.G.	GOOD	FAIR	POOR

safety, choice of fixed or detachable magazine. Available in most popular calibers from .22-250 to 9.3x62mm.

2500	2100	1850	1200	600	350

Nosler Custom Rifle (Limited Edition)

Built on Nosler action, with integral scope bases, hand-lapped stainless steel barrel, glass bedded American walnut stock with 20 lpi checkering. Comes with choice of three VX-3 Leupold scopes with matching serial number and custom reticle designed for different chamberings. Limited to 500 rifles per series. Offered in .300 WSM, .280 Ackley Improved, .338 Win. Magnum.

4000	3750	3200	2600	—	—

Nosler Varmageddon

AR-15 style semi-automatic in .223 Rem. Features include 18" Noveske stainless barrel, with 1/2 x 28 muzzle threads, low profile gas block, Noveske backup iron sights, forged Vltor upper receiver. Comes with Leupold CDS VX3 4.5-14x50 scope and mounts, Harris bi-pod, soft case and two boxes of Nosler Varmageddon ammo. Made for Nosler by Noveske Rifleworks. New in 2013

2100	1850	1600	1400	—	—

NOWLIN MANUFACTURING COMPANY
Claremore, Oklahoma

Match Classic

This 1911 pistol has a wide range of features. Can be chambered in 9mm, .38 Super, 9x23, .40 S&W and .45 ACP. Has 5" barrel, adjustable trigger, checkered main spring housing, hardwood grips, front and rear cocking serrations. Price listed for basic pistols. Options will greatly affect price.

1600	1250	800	600	400	250

Compact Carry

Similar to Match Classic, with exception of 4" barrel on full-size frame. Again, options will greatly affect price.

1495	1100	700	500	300	200

Match Master

These hand-built pistols offered choice of S.T.I., Caspian Hi-Cap or Nowlin STD Government frames. Available in 9mm, 9x23, .38 Super, .40 S&W and .45 ACP. Many special features included in standard pistol. Many extra cost options are available. **NOTE:** Add $140 for hard chrome finish.

2400	1750	1200	800	600	300

	NIB	EXC.	V.G.	GOOD	FAIR	POOR

O.D.I.
Midland Park, New Jersey

Viking

.45-caliber double-action semi-automatic pistol, with 5" barrel and 7-shot magazine. Stainless steel, with teak grips. Manufactured in 1981 and 1982.

700	625	375	300	200	100

Viking Combat

As above, with 4.25" barrel.

700	625	375	300	200	100

O.K.
Unknown
See—Marlin

OBREGON
Mexico City, Mexico

This is a .45-caliber semi-automatic pistol, with 5" barrel. Similar to Colt M1911A1, with combination side and safety latch on left side of frame. Breech is locked by rotating barrel, instead of Browning swinging link. This unusual locking system results in a tubular front end appearance to pistol. Originally designed for Mexican military, it was not adopted as such and only about 1,000 pistols were produced and sold commercially. Pistol is 8.5" overall; weighs about 40 oz. Magazine holds seven cartridges. A rare pistol; independent appraisal suggested prior to sale.

—	3750	2300	1850	1550	800

O'CONNELL, DAVID
New York, New York

Pocket Pistol

.41-caliber percussion pocket pistol, with 2.5" barrel, German silver mounts and walnut stock. Manufactured during 1850s.

—	—	3650	3000	1025	300

O'DELL, STEPHEN
Natchez, Mississippi

Pocket Pistol

.34- to .44-caliber percussion pocket pistol, with 2" to 4" barrel, German silver mounts and walnut stock. Manufactured during 1850s.

—	—	6750	6000	2500	950

OHIO ORDNANCE INC.
Chardon, Ohio

Model 1918A3 Self-Loading Rifle

Semi-automatic version of famed Browning Automatic Rifle. Chambered for .30-06 cartridge and has a 20-round magazine. Introduced in this configuration in 1996. **NOTE:** Add $200 for .308 or 8mm caliber guns. Subtract 10 percent for bakelite stock.

3800	3300	2500	1850	1500	750

Colt Browning Water Cooled Gun

Introduced in 2001, this semi-automatic version of famous Browning Model 1928 belt-fed machine gun. Model features .30-06 or 7.65 Argentine caliber belt-fed gun, with tripod, wooden ammo box, water hose, water can and one 250 cloth belt. **NOTE:** Add $200 for .308 or 8mm caliber guns.

3700	3300	2500	1850	1500	750

1919A4

Semi-automatic version of air-cooled belt-fed .30-caliber 1919 machine gun. Chambered for .308/7.62 NATO.

3250	2800	2000	1250	1100	500

	NIB	EXC.	V.G.	GOOD	FAIR	POOR

OJANGUREN Y VIDOSA
Eibar, Spain

This typical Eibar company produced mediocre firearms from early 1920s. Forced out of business during Spanish Civil War.

Apache (Model 1920)

Typical Eibar Browning copy chambered for 6.35mm cartridge. Low quality associated with most Spanish arms of this era. Slide marked "Pistole Browning Automatica Cal. 6.35 Apache". Finish is blued and plastic grips have a head with a beret and word "Apache" molded into them.

—	250	175	125	75	50	

7.65mm

As above chambered for 7.65mm cartridge.

—	275	225	190	100	75	

Ojanguren

Trade name this company used to cover line of revolvers they produced in 1930s. Produced two in .32-caliber and two chambered for .38 Special cartridge. Similar in appearance and barrel lengths of 3" or 6". Finishes are blued, with plastic grips. One of the .38-caliber models "Legitimo Tanque" is a reasonably well-made gun that was popular with Spanish target shooters. These guns have little collector or practical value and are all priced alike.

—	175	125	100	75	50	

Tanque

Blowback-operated semi-automatic chambered for 6.35mm cartridge. Has a 1.5" barrel and is actually an original design, which was rarely found on Eibar guns of this period. Has an oddly shaped slide and barrel is retained by means of a screw in front of frame. It has a 6-shot magazine and slide marked "6.35 Tanque Patent". Plastic grips have a tank molded into them and word "Tanque", as well as letters "O&V".

—	175	125	100	75	50	

OLD WEST GUN CO.
Houston, Texas
See—Cimarron Arms

An importer of reproduction firearms primarily manufactured by Aldo Uberti of Italy. In 1987 this company purchased the inventory of Allen Firearms and subsequently changed their name to Cimarron Arms.

OLYMPIC ARMS, INC.
Olympia, Washington

PISTOLS

Black Widow

.45-caliber semi-automatic pistol, with 3.9" barrel and 6-shot magazine. Nickel-plated, with ivory Micarta grips with a spider engraved on them.

700	575	450	350	300	200

Enforcer

.45-caliber semi-automatic pistol, with 3.8" barrel and 6-shot magazine. Parkerized, anodized or nickel-plated, with rubber grips. Weight approximately 36 oz.

650	500	400	350	300	200

Match Master

As above, with 5" barrel and 7-shot magazine. Weight about 40 oz.

650	500	400	350	300	200

Match Master 6"

Same as above, with 6" barrel and slide. Weight approximately 44 oz.

675	550	400	350	300	200

	NIB	EXC.	V.G.	GOOD	FAIR	POOR

Cohort

Fitted with 4" bull barrel. Full size frame. Magazine capacity 7 rounds. Weight about 38 oz.

	675	550	400	350	300	200

Safari G.I.

Model built on Match Master frame, with 5" barrel and fixed sights. Finish is flat black Parkerized. Checkered walnut grips.

	600	450	400	350	300	200

Schuetzen Pistol Works Big Deuce

Model made in Olympic Arms specialty shop called, Schuetzen Pistol Works. Marked "Schuetzen Pistol Works" on slide and "Safari Arms" on frame. Introduced in 1995. Semi-automatic pistol chambered for .45 ACP cartridge. Fitted with 6" barrel, smooth walnut grips and a number of other custom features. Magazine capacity 7 rounds. Weight approximately 40 oz. Black slide, with stainless steel frame.

	950	800	700	500	275	150

Schuetzen Pistol Works Crest

Similar to above model with same markings. This version features .45 ACP pistol, with 4.5", 5" or 5.5" barrel. Checkered walnut grips. Offered in both right-/left-hand configurations. Stainless steel finish. Introduced in 1993. Weight about 39 oz. depending on barrel length. **NOTE:** Left-hand model will bring a small premium.

	800	650	550	400	275	150

Schuetzen Pistol Works Griffon

Similar to above specialty models. This version fitted with 5" barrel and smooth walnut grips. Magazine capacity 10 rounds. Stainless steel finish. Numerous custom features. Introduced in 1995.

	1300	1150	975	650	400	200

Schuetzen Pistol Works Carrier

Special built model along the lines of Detonics Score Master, with adjustable sights.

	700	600	500	400	250	150

Black-Tac

Semi-automatic .45 ACP pistol treated with "black-tac" process – advantages of hard chrome without its drawbacks such as embrittlement.

	800	650	500	400	275	150

Constable

Semi-automatic pistol chambered for .45 ACP, with 4" barrel, 5.75" sight radius, 7+1 capacity, weight 35 oz. Introduced 2006.

	950	800	700	500	275	150

Custom Street Deuce

Semi-automatic chambered for .45 ACP, with 5.2" bull barrel, 7" sight radius, 7+1 capacity, weight 38 oz. Many options. Introduced 2006.

	1300	1150	975	650	400	200

Custom Journeyman

Semi-automatic chambered for .45 ACP, with 4" bull barrel, 6" sight radius, 6+1 capacity, weight 35 oz. Many options. Introduced 2006.

	1100	800	675	500	300	150

Trail Boss

Semi-automatic pistol in Westerner line chambered for .45 ACP, with 6" barrel, 8" sight radius, 7+1 capacity, weight 43 oz. Introduced 2006.

	950	800	700	500	275	150

Westerner

Semi-automatic pistol chambered for .45 ACP, with 5" barrel, 7" sight radius, 7+1 capacity, weight 39 oz. Introduced 2006.

	950	800	700	500	275	150

Model OA-93-PT

Similar to OA-93-CAR, with F8R handguard, vertical grip, post-ban muzzle-brake and detachable stock.

	1100	800	675	500	300	150

	NIB	EXC.	V.G.	GOOD	FAIR	POOR

Wolverine

Polymer-frame vent rib replica of old "ray gun" .22 Whitney Wolverine semi-automatic pistol. Cool, baby!

	NIB	EXC.	V.G.	GOOD	FAIR	POOR
	300	265	250	200	150	100

RIFLES

SGW Ultra Match (PCR-1)

Match grade copy of AR-15, with 20" or 24" barrel. Not fitted with carrying handle. Weight about 10 lbs.

	NIB	EXC.	V.G.	GOOD	FAIR	POOR
	1250	1000	800	500	400	200

Model PCR-2

Similar to above, with 16" match grade barrel, post front and E2 rear sight. Weight approximately 8.2 lbs.

	NIB	EXC.	V.G.	GOOD	FAIR	POOR
	1300	1050	850	550	450	225

Model PCR-3

Same as above, with forged T-12 upper receiver.

	NIB	EXC.	V.G.	GOOD	FAIR	POOR
	1300	1050	850	550	450	225

Model PCR-4

This version fitted with 20" steel barrel. Post front sight and A-1 style rear sight. Weight approximately 8.5 lbs.

	NIB	EXC.	V.G.	GOOD	FAIR	POOR
	900	725	575	450	350	150

Model PCR-5

Similar to above, with 16" barrel. Weight about 7 lbs.

	NIB	EXC.	V.G.	GOOD	FAIR	POOR
	900	725	575	450	350	150

Model PCR-6

AR-15 style rifle chambered for 7.62x39 Russian caliber. Fitted with 16" barrel. Post front sight and A-1 style rear sight. Weight about 7 lbs.

	NIB	EXC.	V.G.	GOOD	FAIR	POOR
	900	725	575	450	350	150

Model PCR-7 "Eliminator"

Shortened version of PCR-4. Fitted with 16" barrel, A2 handguard, A2 stock and A2 pistol-grip. Weight about 7.6 lbs.

	NIB	EXC.	V.G.	GOOD	FAIR	POOR
	900	725	575	450	350	150

Model PCR-Service Match

.223-caliber rifle has 20" stainless steel match barrel. Fitted with post front sight and E-2 style rear sight. Weight about 8.7 lbs.

	NIB	EXC.	V.G.	GOOD	FAIR	POOR
	1100	800	675	500	300	150

Ultra CSR Tactical Rifle

Bolt-action rifle chambered for .308 Winchester cartridge. Barrel length 26". Magazine capacity 5 rounds. Tactical-style stock is black synthetic, with aluminum bedding block. Comes complete with scope rings and Harris bipod in a hardcase. Weight approximately 9.4 lbs.

	NIB	EXC.	V.G.	GOOD	FAIR	POOR
	1100	800	675	500	300	150

Model CAR-97

Chambered for .223 cartridge or optional 9mm, .40 S&W or .45 ACP pistol cartridges. Fitted with 16" barrel and non-collapsible CAR-style stock. Overall length 34"; weight about 7 lbs. **NOTE:** Add $50 for pistol cartridge conversion.

	NIB	EXC.	V.G.	GOOD	FAIR	POOR
	900	725	575	450	350	150

Model OA-96

Model has 6" barrel with pistol-grip only, no buttstock. The 30-round magazine is pinned and cannot be detached. Break-open-action allows loading with stripper clips. Overall length 15.75"; weight about 4.2 lbs. BATFE approved.

	NIB	EXC.	V.G.	GOOD	FAIR	POOR
	1100	800	675	500	300	150

Model OA-98

Similar to OA-93, with lightening holes on grip mount and magazine. Fitted with 6" barrel. No vertical grip. Weight about 3 lbs. No buttstock.

	NIB	EXC.	V.G.	GOOD	FAIR	POOR
	1100	800	675	500	300	150

	NIB	EXC.	V.G.	GOOD	FAIR	POOR	

UM-1P

Gas-operated .223 semi-automatic target rifle based on AR-15 chassis. Features include 24" stainless steel bull barrel, anodized finish, pistol-grip with bottom swell, Picatinny rail, Harris bipod and competition trigger.

	900	725	575	450	350	150	

UM-1

Similar to UM-1P, with 20" stainless steel bull barrel, standard pistol-grip, no bipod.

	900	725	575	450	350	150	

SM-1P

Tricked-out AR-15 in .223 with 20" stainless steel barrel, free-floating sleeve handguard, carry handle upper or Picatinny rail flattop, pneumatic recoil buffer, Bob Jones interchangeable sight system, competition trigger and Maxhard receivers.

	1300	1050	850	550	450	225	

SM-1

Similar to SM-1P, with standard receivers, trigger and sights. No pneumatic recoil buffer.

	1000	700	575	450	300	150	

ML-1

Similar to SM-1, with 16" barrel, flash hider, 6-position collapsible buttstock and free-floating aluminum tube handguard.

	1000	700	575	450	300	150	

ML-2

Similar to ML-1, with flat-top upper receiver. Picatinny rails, standard buttstock and bull barrel.

	1000	700	575	450	300	150	

Model K8

Similar to ML-2, with 20" barrel and extended aluminum tube handguard.

	1000	700	575	450	300	150	

Model K8-MAG

Similar to K8, with 24" bull barrel and chambered in .223 WSM, .243 WSM or .25 WSM.

	1000	700	575	450	300	150	

K3B

Features include 16" chrome-moly barrel with flash-hidefully adjustable rear sight, 6-position collapsible buttstock and carbine-length handguard.

	900	725	575	450	350	150	

K3B-M4

Similar to K3B, with M4S fiberite handguard with heatshield and 32.25" overall length.

	900	725	575	450	350	150	

K3B-CAR

Similar to K3B, with 30.5" overall length.

	900	725	575	450	350	150	

K3B-FAR

Similar to K3B, with Featherweight barrel and weight of 5.84 lbs.

	900	725	575	450	350	150	

K4B

Similar to K3B, with 20" barrel and rifle-length fiberite handguard.

	900	725	575	450	350	150	

K4B-A4

Similar to K4B, with ventilated FIRSH rifle-length handguard.

	950	775	600	475	375	175	

LTF

Features include 16" chrome-moly barrel, free-floating FIRSH handguard with Picatinny rails, ACE FX skeleton stock, ERGO pistol-grip and multiple-aperture flipup sight system.

	1100	800	675	500	350	150	

	NIB	EXC.	V.G.	GOOD	FAIR	POOR

LT-M4
Similar to LTF, with 16" stainless steel barrel.

	1100	800	675	500	350	150

K16
Similar to K8, with 16" bull chrome-moly barrel.

	800	625	475	400	300	125

GI-16
Basic AR-15-inspired semi-automatic rifle chambered in .223. 16" chrome-moly barrel, with flash-hider, 6-position collapsible buttstock, carbine-length handguard and rear sight adjustable for windage only.

	900	725	575	450	350	150

Plinker Plus
Similar to GI-16, with standard buttstock.

	800	625	475	400	250	100

Plinker Plus 20
Similar to Plinker Plus, with 20" barrel and rifle-length handguard.

	850	675	525	425	300	125

K7 Eliminator
Similar to K4B, with 16" barrel, extended handguard and sight radius of 20" barreled models.

	900	725	575	450	350	150

K30
Similar to GI-16 chambered in .30 Carbine. Includes mag well insert to accept military-spec magazines.

	900	725	575	450	350	150

K9/K10/K40/K45
Similar to K30 and chambered respectively for 9mm Parabellum, 10mm, .40 S&W and .45ACP. Models use converted surplus military magazines.

	900	725	575	450	350	150

K9-GL/K40-GL
Similar to K9 and K40. Accepts standard Glock pistol magazines.

	900	725	575	450	350	150

Model OA-93-CAR
Features include OA-93 FT recoil-reducing upper, 16" chrome-moly barrel, with Phantom flash hider and side-folding buttstock.

	1000	700	575	450	300	150

Model OA-93-PT
Similar to OA-93-CAR, with F8R handguard, vertical grip, post-ban muzzle-brake and detachable stock.

	1000	700	575	450	300	150

Olympic Arms Gamestalker
Sporting AR-style rifle chambered in .223, .243, .25 WSSM and .300 OSSM. Features include forged aluminum upper and lower; flat top receiver with Picatinny rail; gas block front sight; 22" stainless steel fluted barrel; free-floating slotted tube handguard; camo finish overall; ACE FX skeleton stock. Price: $1,359.

OMEGA
Springfield Armory
Geneseo, Illinois

Omega Pistol
High-grade target-type pistol patterned after Colt Model 1911 pistol, with marked improvements. Chambered for .38 Super, 10mm and .45 ACP cartridges. Barrel is 5" or 6" in length and has polygonal rifling. Barrels are furnished ported or plain and feature a lockup system that eliminates barrel link and bushing associated with normal Browning design. Pistol has a dual extractor system, adjustable sights and Pachmayr grips. Introduced in 1987.

	900	725	575	450	350	150

	NIB	EXC.	V.G.	GOOD	FAIR	POOR

Over/Under Shotgun

12-, 20-, 28-gauge and .410 bore boxlock over/under shotgun, with 26" or 28" ventilated rib barrels, single trigger and extractors. Blued, with walnut stock.

	NIB	EXC.	V.G.	GOOD	FAIR	POOR
	—	450	300	200	150	125

Side-by-Side Shotgun

20-, 28-gauge and .410 bore boxlock double-barrel shotgun, with 26" barrels, double triggers and extractors. Blued, with hardwood stock.

	—	350	250	150	100	75

Single Barreled Shotgun

12-, 20-gauge and .410 bore single barrel shotgun. Manufactured in a variety of barrel lengths and fitted with an extractor. Blued, with hardwood stock.

	—	125	85	65	50	35

OMEGA FIREARMS CO.
Flower Mound, Texas

Bolt-Action Rifle

A .25-06 to .358 Norma Magnum bolt-action rifle, with 22" or 24" barrel, octagonal bolt, adjustable trigger and rotary magazine. Blued, with two-piece walnut or laminated stock. Discontinued circa 1975.

	—	800	650	550	424	200

OPUS SPORTING ARMS, INC.
Long Beach, California

Opus One

A .243, .270 or .30-06 caliber bolt-action rifle, with 24" barrel, well figured walnut stock and ebony pistol-grip cap as well as fore-end tip. Built on Model 70 Winchester action. Manufactured in 1987 and 1988.

	—	2250	1600	1150	700	350

Opus Two

As above in 7mm Remington Magnum and .300 Winchester Magnum.

	—	2500	1750	1250	750	350

Opus Three

As above in .375 Holland & Holland and .458 Winchester Magnum.

	—	3000	2000	1500	900	500

ORBEA & CIA
Eibar, Spain

Pocket Pistol

6.35mm semi-automatic pistol, with 2.5" barrel. Blued, with plastic grips. Slide marked "Orbea y Cia Eibar Espana Pistola Automatica Cal. 6.35". Manufactured from approximately 1918 to 1936.

	—	250	175	125	75	50

ORTGIES, HEINRICH & CO.
Erfurt, Germany

Ortgies Pistol

6.35mm or 7.65mm semi-automatic pistol, with 2.75" or 3.25" barrel. Blued, with walnut grips. Slide marked "Ortgies & Co. Erfurt". After 1921, these pistols were manufactured by Deutsche Werke. **NOTE:** Deduct $100 for 6.35 mm.

	—	550	300	175	125	85

ORVIS
Sunderland, Vermont

Importer and retailer of sporting goods including foreign manufactured firearms. Orvis sells some of these side-by-side and over/under guns under its own name. Most are made by Beretta, Arrieta or other Italian manufacturers. Values approximate those of similar models made by gunmakers.

	NIB	EXC.	V.G.	GOOD	FAIR	POOR

OSBORN, S.
Canton, Connecticut

Under Hammer Pistol

.34-caliber under hammer percussion pistol, with 7" half octagonal barrel, brass mounts and walnut grip. Barrel marked "S. Osborn/Canton, Conn.

NIB	EXC.	V.G.	GOOD	FAIR	POOR
—	—	800	550	250	125

OSGOOD GUN WORKS
Norwich, Connecticut

Duplex Revolver

.22-caliber spur trigger revolver, with two super-imposed barrels; upper most of .22-caliber and lower .32-caliber. Cylinder with eight .22 chambers. Hammer fitted with movable firing pin so the pistol can be used either as revolver or single shot, with .32-caliber barrel. Blued or nickel-plated, with hard rubber grips. Barrel marked "Osgood Gun Works-Norwich Conn." and "Duplex". An unknown quantity manufactured during 1880s.

NIB	EXC.	V.G.	GOOD	FAIR	POOR
—	—	1600	875	350	100

OVERTON, JOHN
Nashville, Tennessee

Formerly armorer at Harpers Ferry Armory. He delivered 81 rifles copying U.S. Model 1841, with saber bayonet lug on right side of barrel. Unmarked externally but are serial numbered internally. Overall length ca. 48.75"; barrel length 33"; .54-caliber.

NIB	EXC.	V.G.	GOOD	FAIR	POOR
—	—	18500	14000	5500	2000

OWA
Osterreiche Werke Anstalt
Vienna, Austria

OWA Pocket Pistol

6.35mm semi-automatic pistol, with 2" barrel. "OWA" logo cast in grips. Blued, with plastic grips. Manufactured between 1920 and 1925.

NIB	EXC.	V.G.	GOOD	FAIR	POOR
—	400	325	200	150	1000

P

	NIB	EXC.	V.G.	GOOD	FAIR	POOR

P.38

GERMAN WWII SERVICE PISTOL

NOTE: For history, technical data, descriptions, photos and prices see: Standard Catalog of Military Firearms.

WALTHER COMMERCIAL

Commercial version of P.38 is identified by commercial proofmarks of a crown over N or an eagle over N. Production started around serial number 1000 and went through 26659. First of commercial pistols and a high-quality well made gun, with complete inscription on left slide. Few of these early pistols were equipped with checkered wooden grips. Quality decreased as war progressed. Many variations of these commercial models and values can range up to more than $30,000. Suggested these pistols be appraised and evaluated by an expert. For post-war Walther P.38 pistols, see Walther section.

Few of Walther Commercial Model variations are listed.

MOD HP

H Prefix w/rectangular firing pin

	NIB	EXC.	V.G.	GOOD	FAIR	POOR
	—	3200	2000	950	750	450

Early w/High Gloss Blue

	NIB	EXC.	V.G.	GOOD	FAIR	POOR
	—	3000	1750	750	600	400

.30 caliber, extremely rare

	NIB	EXC.	V.G.	GOOD	FAIR	POOR
	—	28000	—	—	—	—

Early w/High Gloss Blue & Alloy Frame

	NIB	EXC.	V.G.	GOOD	FAIR	POOR
	—	10000	6500	3500	2000	1000

Croatian Contract
100 built, 6 known

	NIB	EXC.	V.G.	GOOD	FAIR	POOR
	—	10000	—	—	—	—

Late w/Military Blue Finish
NOTE: Add $500 for "Eagle/359" on right side.

	NIB	EXC.	V.G.	GOOD	FAIR	POOR
	—	2000	1400	750	550	350

MOD P38—Late with Military Blue
1800 produced.

	NIB	EXC.	V.G.	GOOD	FAIR	POOR
	—	2700	1750	750	600	400

"ac45" Zero Series
1200 made.

	NIB	EXC.	V.G.	GOOD	FAIR	POOR
	—	2800	1750	750	600	400

WALTHER MILITARY

ZERO SERIES

First Issue

	NIB	EXC.	V.G.	GOOD	FAIR	POOR
	—	9500	8000	6000	3500	1500

Second Issue

	NIB	EXC.	V.G.	GOOD	FAIR	POOR
	—	8000	6750	5250	2000	1000

Third Issue

	NIB	EXC.	V.G.	GOOD	FAIR	POOR
	—	3500	2200	1250	800	500

480 CODE

	NIB	EXC.	V.G.	GOOD	FAIR	POOR
	—	7000	5000	3250	1750	1000

"AC" CODES
This variation follows 480 code.

	NIB	EXC.	V.G.	GOOD	FAIR	POOR

AC" CODES

"AC" (no date)

	—	9000	7500	5000	3000	2000

"AC" CODES

"AC40"

Added

	—	3800	2500	1750	1000	600

Standard

	—	3000	2000	1200	700	500

"AC41"

1st Variation

	—	2200	1100	700	500	350

2nd Variation

	—	2000	1000	700	450	300

3rd Variation

	—	1500	800	600	400	300

"AC42"

1st Variation

NOTE: Add $800 for "byf" Mauser code

	—	1300	550	400	350	275

2nd Variation

	—	1100	500	400	300	250

"AC43"

1st Variation

	—	900	450	300	250	200

2nd Variation

	—	900	450	300	250	200

Single Line Slide

	—	1200	550	450	350	250

"AC44"

NOTE: Add $300 for FN frame (Eagle/140).

	—	800	450	300	250	200

"AC45"

NOTE: Add $200 for pistols with Czech barrels; barrel code "fnh".

1st Variation

	—	800	450	300	250	200

2nd Variation

	—	950	500	325	300	250

3rd Variation

	—	750	400	300	250	200

MAUSER MILITARY

"byf42"

	—	2200	1200	700	500	300

"byf43"

	—	950	550	300	250	200

	NIB	EXC.	V.G.	GOOD	FAIR	POOR

"byf44"

NOTE: Add $100 for dual tone finish. A combination of blue and gray components.

	—	950	550	300	250	200

AC43/44—FN slide

	—	2200	1200	725	550	400

"SVW45"

German Proofed

	—	2900	2000	1300	550	400

French Proofed

	—	650	400	300	250	200

"SVW46"— French Proofed

	—	800	500	400	350	300

MAUSER "POLICE" P.38

"byf/43"

	—	2500	1700	1200	800	500

"byf/44"

	—	2500	1700	1200	800	500

"ac/43"

	—	5000	3500	2000	1250	800

"ac/44"

	—	5000	3500	2000	1250	800

"svw/45"

	—	6000	4500	2500	1600	1000

SPREEWERKE MILITARY

"cyq"

Eagle /211 on frame

2 known.

	—	5000	—	—	—	—

1st Variation

	—	1400	1000	750	600	500

Standard Variation

NOTE: If "A" or "B" prefix add $250.

	—	800	400	275	250	200

Zero Series

NOTE: Add $250 for AC43 or AC44 marked "FN" slide.

	—	1250	550	400	350	275

POST-WAR PISTOLS

Standard Slides

	—	400	250	200	175	150

Single Line Code (Rare)

	—	1000	550	350	250	200

Manurhin

	—	400	300	200	175	150

P.A.F.
Pretoria Small Arms Factory
Pretoria, South Africa

	NIB	EXC.	V.G.	GOOD	FAIR	POOR

P.A.F. Junior

.22- or .25-caliber semi-automatic pistol, with 2" barrel and 6-shot magazine. Blued, with plastic grips. Slide marked "Junior Verwaardig in Suid Afrika Made in South Africa". Manufactured during 1950s.

	—	350	250	125	100	70

PAGE-LEWIS ARMS CO.
Chicopee Falls, Massachusetts

Model A Target

.22-caliber single-shot lever-action rifle, with 20" barrel and open sights. Blued, with walnut stock. Manufactured from 1920 to 1926.

	—	300	225	175	125	100

Model B Sharpshooter

As above, with 24" barrel and longer fore-end.

	—	300	225	175	125	100

Model C Olympic

As above, with 24" barrel and improved sights.

	—	375	275	200	150	100

Challenge Model 49

Single-shot .22 LR boy's rifle. Manufactured cira 1925-1930. Stamped on top of barrel "Page Lewis Arms Co., Chicopee Falls, Mass USA/22 LR" Model 49. 22" long barrel, fixed front and rear sights.

	—	150	100	75	50	35

PALMER
Windsor, Vermont
E. G. Lamson & Co.

Palmer Bolt-Action Carbine

.50-caliber single-shot bolt-action carbine, with 20" round barrel, walnut half stock and full sidelock. Blued and case hardened. Receiver marked "Wm. Palmer / Patent / Dec.22, 1863" and lock "G.Lamson & Co./ Windsor, Vt." Approximately 1,000 made in 1865.

	—	3000	2250	1500	700	250

PARA USA (PARA-ORDNANCE)
Pineville, North Carolina

Previously known as Para-Ordnance of Scarborough, Ontario, Canada. In 2009, company relocated to Pineville, North Carolina. In January, 2012, assets of Para USA were purchased by Freedom Group, parent company of Remington, Marlin, Bushmaster and several other gun makers.

Para Elite Series

In 2013 Para USA introduced a new family of 1911-style pistols in a wide range of models. Caliber: .45 ACP, 9mm (Elite LS Hunter only). Capacity: 6, 7 or 8 rounds; 9 rounds (9mm LS Hunter). Barrel: 3", 4" or 5" (.45 models), 6" (9mm LS Hunter). Pro Model has Ed Brown mag well, HD extractor, checkered front strap and mainspring housing, Trijicon sights. Add $250 for Pro Model; $200 LS Hunter.

	850	785	650	500	—	—

Para 1911 100th Anniversary

Classic 1911 styling to commemorate the centennial of design. Caliber .45 ACP, military-style thumb and grip safeties, solid muzzle bushing and hammer. Three-dot sights. Weight 39 oz., 5" barrel, Covert Black finish. Smooth cocobolo grips. Comes with one 7- and one 8-round magazine.

	925	775	665	500	350	200

Model P14.45

Similar in appearance to Colt Government model. This .45 ACP semi-automatic pistol features 5" barrel, flared ejection port, combat style hammer, beveled magazine well and 13-round magazine capacity. Overall length 8.5"; weight 40 oz. for steel and stainless steel version; 31 oz. for alloy frame model. Finish black except for stainless steel model. **NOTE:** Add $50 for steel frame; $45 for stainless steel; $30 for duo-tone.

	700	550	500	400	300	200

	NIB	EXC.	V.G.	GOOD	FAIR	POOR

Model P14.45 Limited

Similar to above. Extra features such as full length recoil guide, beavertail grip safety, adjustable rear sight, competition hammer, lowered ejection port, front and rear slide serrations and trigger overtravel stop. Match grade barrel. Choice of black carbon steel or stainless steel finish. Weight about 40 oz.

	1200	900	725	575	400	200

Model P14.45 LDA/P14.45 LDA Stainless

Essentially same as P14.45, with double-action trigger. Offered in black carbon steel only. Weight about 40 oz. First introduced in 1999. **NOTE:** Add $50 for stainless steel.

	800	600	400	350	225	150

Model P16.40

Essentially same as Model 14.45, except chambered for .40 S&W cartridge. Magazine capacity 15 rounds. **NOTE:** Add $50 for steel frame; $45 for stainless steel; $30 for duo-tone.

	800	600	400	350	225	150

Model P16.40 Limited

Similar to above. Extra features such as full length recoil guide, beavertail grip safety, adjustable rear sight, competition hammer, lowered ejection port, front and rear slide serrations and trigger overtravel stop. Match grade barrel. Black carbon steel finish.

	1200	900	725	575	400	200

Model P16.40 LDA

Double-action version of P16.40 in black carbon steel only. First offered in 1999.

	800	600	400	350	225	150

Model P13.45

Introduced in 1994. This .45 ACP model features 4.25" barrel with 13-round magazine. Grip is .25" longer than 12.45 model. Offered in light alloy, carbon or stainless steel. Overall length 7.75"; height is 5.25"; weight about 36 oz. in steel version, 28 oz. in alloy version. **NOTE:** Add $50 for steel frame; $45 for stainless steel; $30 for duo-tone.

	600	450	350	300	200	100

Model P13.45/P12.45 Limited

Similar to above, with extra features such as full length recoil guide, beavertail grip safety, adjustable rear sight, competition hammer, lowered ejection port, front and rear slide serrations and trigger overtravel stop. Match grade barrel. Black carbon steel finish.

	800	600	400	350	225	150

Model P12.45 LDA/P12.45 LDA

Fitted with a 3.5" barrel and 12-round magazine capacity. Features double-action trigger. Finish is black. Weight about 34 oz. Introduced in 2000. **NOTE:** Add $50 for stainless steel.

	750	600	450	300	200	100

Model P12.45/P12.40

Similar to Model P14 but in a smaller package. Introduced in 1993. Has all the same features as Model P14. Magazine capacity 11 rounds. Available in alloy, steel or stainless steel. Weighs 24 oz. in alloy; 33 oz. in steel. P12.40 is same model chambered for .40 S&W cartridge. **NOTE:** Add $50 for steel frame; $45 for stainless steel; $30 for duo-tone.

	800	600	400	350	225	150

Model P10.45/P10.40/P10.9

Introduced in 1996. At the time, was smallest semi-automatic .45 ACP in production. Overall length 6.5"; height of 4.5". Magazine capacity 10 rounds. Barrel length 3.5". Offered in stainless steel, duo-tone or black alloy finish. Chambered for .40 S&W cartridge and 9mm cartridge. Weight about 31 oz. for stainless; 24 oz. for alloy. **NOTE:** Add $50 for steel frame; $45 for stainless steel; $30 for duo-tone.

	600	450	350	300	0	100

Model P10.45 Limited

Similar to above. Extra features such as full length recoil guide, beavertail grip safety, adjustable rear sight, competition hammer, lowered ejection port, front and rear slide serrations and trigger overtravel stop. Match grade barrel. Black carbon steel finish.

	650	500	400	300	200	100

	NIB	EXC.	V.G.	GOOD	FAIR	POOR

Model P18.9

Chambered for 9mm cartridge. Fitted with 5" barrel. Finish stainless steel. Rear sight adjustable; dovetail front sight. Magazine capacity 18 rounds (10 rounds for US and Canada). Weight about 40 oz.

775	625	500	350	200	125

Model P18.9 LDA

Double-action version of P18-9. Offered in black carbon steel only. Introduced in 1999.

775	625	500	350	200	125

Model C7.45 LDA (Para Companion)

.45 ACP pistol fitted with 3.5" barrel. Stainless steel slide and frame. Low profile fixed sights. Magazine capacity 7 rounds. Weight about 32 oz.

700	550	400	300	200	100

Model C6.45 LDA (Para Carry)

Similar to above, with 3" barrel and 6-round magazine. Weight about 30 oz.

750	575	550	375	200	100

Model Stealth Carry

Introduced in 2005. Chambered for .45 ACP cartridge. Fitted with 3" barrel with Novak adjustable sights. LDA trigger. Black slide and frame. Black polymer grips. Magazine capacity 6 rounds. Weight about 30 oz.

850	675	550	425	300	150

Model Para CCW

Introduced in 2003. This .45 ACP model features 4.25" barrel, with stainless steel receiver and frame. Magazine capacity 7 rounds. Fitted with LDA trigger system. Weight about 34 oz.

900	800	650	500	350	125

Model Para Companion Carry Option

Similar to CCW above. Fitted with 3.5" barrel. Weight about 32 oz. Introduced in 2003.

775	575	400	300	200	100

Model Tac-Four

.45 ACP model features LDA trigger system. Fitted with 4.25" barrel and stainless steel slide and frame. Early models shipped with two pre-ban 13-round magazines. Later models will ship with two 10-round magazines. Weight about 36 oz. Introduced in 2003.

900	800	650	500	350	125

Model Tac-Four LE

Same as above. Shipped with two 13-round magazines to certified law enforcement only, back in the ban days.

900	800	650	500	350	125

PARA PXT SERIES PISTOLS

In 2004, company introduced new extractor called Power Extractor (PXT). Company also added a number of new finishes and features for its PXT line. All Para pistols have integral ramp barrels that are of match grade quality. All pistols have full-length guide rod, match trigger, flared ejection port, extended slide lock safety, beavertail grip safety, cocobolo stocks with gold medallion and high-visibility low-mount dovetail three-dot sights.

Para introduced five finishes:

1. Sterling—All stainless steel, black slide with polished sides.
2. Stealth—Black slide, black frame with black fire controls.
3. Black Watch—Black slide, green frame with green fire controls on hi-cap models and black controls on single- stack models.
4. Regal—Black slide, black frame with stainless steel fire controls.
5. Spec Ops—Green slide, green frame with black fire controls.

SINGLE ACTION, SINGLE STACK MODELS

Model LTC

This .45 ACP pistol has a 4.25" ramped match barrel, with steel receiver and Regal finish. Fixed 3-dot sights. Cocobolo wood grips, with gold medallion. Magazine capacity 7 rounds. Weight about 37 oz.

775	575	400	300	200	100

	NIB	EXC.	V.G.	GOOD	FAIR	POOR

Model LTC Alloy

As above, with alloy frame. Weight about 28 oz.

	775	575	400	300	200	100

Model LTC Stainless

Same as Model LTC, with stainless steel frame and slide. Weight about 35 oz. Introduced in 2005.

	800	625	500	400	150	125

Hawg 9

Chambered for 9mm cartridge. Fitted with 3" ramped barrel. Alloy receiver and steel slide. Fixed 3-dot sights. Black polymer stocks with black slide, black frame and stainless steel fire controls. Weight about 24 oz.; 12-shot magazine. Introduced in 2005.

	800	625	500	400	150	125

Hawg 7

Caliber .45 ACP, single-action trigger, stainless steel slide, alloy frame with Griptor grooves, extended thumb and grip safeties, fiber optic front and 2-dot rear sights, 7-round magazine. Weight 32 oz., 3.5" barrel with Covert Black finish. Introduced in 2011.

	800	675	550	400	300	200

Model OPS

.45 ACP pistol fitted with 3.5" barrel. Has stainless steel frame and slide. Low mount fixed sights. Cocobolo grips. Magazine capacity 7 rounds. Weight about 32 oz. Introduced in 2005.

	850	675	550	425	300	150

Model 1911

.45 ACP model has 5" barrel, with steel receiver and Regal finish. Magazine capacity 7 rounds. Weight about 39 oz.

	775	575	400	300	200	100

1911 SSP

7+1 capacity .45 ACP 1911-style semi-automatic, with 5" barrel. Competition triggers and hammers. Fixed sights. Cocobolo grip panels. Weight 39 oz.

	925	800	675	500	400	175

GI Expert LTC

Caliber .45 ACP, single-action trigger, Commander-length stainless slide on alloy frame, extended grip safety, competition trigger, fiber optic front and 2-dot rear sights. Weight 28 oz., 4.25" barrel with Covert Black finish. Magazine capacity 8-rounds.

	750	635	500	400	300	200

1911 Wild Bunch

Designed for SASS Traditional and Modern "Wild Bunch" shooting matches. Class 1911 features. Caliber .45 ACP, traditional thumb and grip safeties, hammer, solid trigger, recoil system, 7-round magazine, plain sights and barrel without integral ramp. Weight 39 oz., 5" barrel with Covert Black finish. Introduced in 2011.

	685	585	475	400	300	200

HIGH CAPACITY, SINGLE ACTION MODELS

Warthog

Introduced in 2004. This .45 ACP pistol fitted with 3" barrel. Receiver is alloy. Black slide and frame with stainless steel fire controls. Overall length 6.5"; height 4.5". Magazine capacity 10 rounds. Weight about 24 oz. In 2005, chambered for 9mm cartridge.

	925	800	675	500	400	175

Stainless Warthog

Stainless .45 ACP with 10+1 capacity. Barrel 3", weight 31 oz. Fixed 3-dot sights and plastic grips. Introduced 2006.

	875	675	575	400	300	150

Stealth Warthog

Chambered for .45 ACP cartridge. Fitted with 3" ramped barrel. Black alloy slide with black frame and black fire controls. Tritium night sights. Extended slide lock, beavertail grip and firing pin. Weight about 24 oz. Introduced in 2004.

	850	675	550	425	300	150

	NIB	EXC.	V.G.	GOOD	FAIR	POOR

Slim Hawg

.45 ACP pistol with 6+1 capacity. Single-stack single-action 1911. Barrel 3", weight 30 oz. Stainless construction, checkered wood grips. Fixed 3-dot sights. Introduced 2006.

850	675	550	425	300	150

Lite Hawg 9

Double-stack 12+1 capacity single-action 9mm in non-reflective black finish. Barrel 3", weight 31.5 oz. Fixed 3-dot sights. Introduced 2006.

850	675	550	425	300	150

P12.45

.45 ACP model fitted with 3.5" barrel. Has stainless steel receiver and finish. Magazine capacity 10 or 12 rounds. Weight about 34 oz.

800	625	500	400	150	125

P13.45

.45 ACP pistol has 4.25" barrel, with stainless steel receiver and Spec Ops finish. Magazine capacity 10 or 13 rounds. Weight about 36 oz.

750	575	550	375	200	100

Midnight Blue P14-45

Double-stack 14+1 single-action .45 ACP in non-reflective black. 5" barrel, fixed 3-dot sights and black plastic grips. Introduced 2006.

750	575	550	375	200	100

Hi-Cap LTC

Introduced in 2005. Chambered for .45 ACP cartridge and fitted with 4.25" barrel with low mount fixed sights. Slide and frame are green, with black fire controls. Black polymer grips. Magazine capacity 14 rounds. Weight about 37 oz.

850	675	550	425	300	150

Stealth P14.45

.45 ACP model fitted with 5" barrel. Has steel receiver with Stealth finish. Magazine capacity 10 or 14 rounds. Weight about 40 oz.

850	675	550	425	300	150

P14.45

As above, with stainless steel receiver and finish.

925	800	675	500	400	175

14.45 Tactical

Based upon classic Para-Ordnance 14.45 high-capacity 1911 design in .45 ACP. Stainless steel slide and frame with 14-round double-stack magazine. Custom features include Ed Brown National Match barrel, bushing, slide stop and checkered mainspring housing; Dawson Precision mag well; ambidextrous thumb safeties; extended grip tang and accessory rail. Sights are adjustable rear and fiber optic front. Covert Black finish. Weight 42 oz., barrel length 5". PXT Tactical model same except for single-stack frame, 8-round magazine, 4.25" barrel and weight of 36 oz.

1350	1150	875	650	350	200

P18.45

Chambered for 9mm Parabellum cartridge. Fitted with 5" barrel. Receiver and finish stainless steel. Magazine is 10 or 18 rounds. Weight about 40 oz.

850	675	525	375	200	125

HIGH CAPACITY, SINGLE ACTION, LIMITED MODELS

S12.45 Limited

.45 ACP pistol has 3.5" barrel, with stainless steel receiver and Sterling finish. Magazine capacity 10 or 12 rounds. Weight about 34 oz. Introduced in 2005.

925	800	675	500	400	175

S13.45 Limited

.45 ACP pistol with 4.25" barrel. Stainless steel receiver and Sterling finish. Spurless hammer. Magazine capacity 10 or 13 rounds. Weight about 36 oz.

925	800	675	500	400	175

NIB	EXC.	V.G.	GOOD	FAIR	POOR

Stealth S14.45 Limited

.45 ACP pistol fitted with 5" barrel. Has steel receiver with Stealth finish. Magazine capacity 10 or 14 rounds. Weight about 40 oz.

925	800	675	500	400	175

S14.45 Limited

As above, with stainless steel receiver and Sterling finish.

1000	795	600	450	275	225

Long Slide Limited

Lengthened barrel and slide for competition or hunting. Caliber .435 ACP. Weight 41 oz., barrel length 6". Front and rear slide serrations, ambidextrous thumb safeties, extended grip safety, adjustable rear and fiber optic front sight, 14-round magazine and stainless finish. Introduced in 2011.

1200	1025	825	650	450	300

Stealth S16.40 Limited

Chambered for .40 S&W cartridge. Fitted with 5" barrel. Receiver steel with Stealth finish. Magazine capacity 10 or 16 rounds. Weight about 40 oz.

1100	950	750	500	400	175

S16.40 Limited

As above, with stainless steel receiver and Sterling finish.

925	800	675	500	400	175

18.9 Limited

Chambered for 9mm Parabellum. Features include stainless steel slide and frame with dual grasping grooves, 18-round magazine, adjustable rear and fiber optic front sight, ambidextrous thumb safeties, extended grip tang and competition trigger. Weight 40 oz., barrel length 5". Finish bright stainless.

1100	875	750	575	350	200

Todd Jarrett .40 USPSA P-16

Limited edition 16+1 (or 10+1) .40 S&W custom competition pistol, with adjustable rear sight and fiber optic front sight. 5" barrel, weight 40 oz. Covert non-reflective black or sterling finish.

1500	1250	900	675	450	200

Todd Jarrett .45 USPSA

Limited edition 8+1 .45 ACP caliber custom competition pistol, with adjustable rear sight and fiber optic front sight. 5" barrel, weight 39 oz. Covert non-reflective black or stainless finish.

1500	1250	900	675	450	200

LDA, DOUBLE ACTION, SINGLE STACK

CARRY OPTION

Companion II

Caliber .45 ACP, Light Double Action (LDA) trigger, Commander-length stainless slide on full-size stainless frame, extended grip safety, fiber optic front sight and 8-round magazine. Weight 35 oz., 4.25" barrel, with Covert Black finish. Introduced in 2011.

775	650	550	400	300	200

Carry Model

.45 ACP model has 3" barrel and stainless steel receiver and finish. Magazine capacity 6 rounds. Weight about 30 oz.

925	800	675	500	400	175

Stealth Carry

Similar to above, with Stealth finish and Novak adjustable sights.

925	800	675	500	400	175

CCO (Companion Carry Option)

.45 ACP model fitted with 3.5" barrel. Receiver and finish stainless steel. Magazine capacity 7 rounds. Weight about 32 oz.

850	700	575	400	300	125

	NIB	EXC.	V.G.	GOOD	FAIR	POOR

CCW

Similar to above, with 4.45" barrel. Weight about 34 oz.

	850	700	575	400	300	125

DOUBLE ACTION ONLY, SINGLE STACK MODELS

Black Watch Companion

.45 ACP pistol fitted with 3.5" barrel. Receiver stainless steel with black watch finish. Magazine capacity 7 rounds. Weight about 32 oz.

	850	675	525	375	200	125

TAC-S

Chambered for .45 ACP cartridge, with 4.45" barrel. Steel receiver and Spec Ops finish. Magazine capacity 7 rounds. Weight about 35 oz.

	750	575	550	375	200	100

Black Watch SSP

.45 ACP pistol has 5" barrel, with steel receiver and Black Watch finish. Fixed 3-dot sights. Match trigger. Cocobolo wood grip, with gold medallion. Magazine capacity 7 rounds. Weight about 39 oz.

	750	575	550	375	200	100

SSP

Similar to above, with stainless steel receiver and finish.

	800	625	500	400	150	125

LDA, DOUBLE ACTION, SINGLE STACK

LIMITED MODELS

Stealth Limited

.45 ACP pistol has 5" barrel, with adjustable sights. Receiver steel with Stealth finish. Magazine capacity 7 rounds. Weight about 40 oz.

	850	700	575	400	300	125

Limited

.45 ACP model has 5" barrel. Stainless steel receiver with Sterling finish. Magazine capacity 7 rounds. Weight about 40 oz. Adjustable sights.

	925	800	675	500	400	175

LDA, DOUBLE ACTION, HIGH CAPACITY

CARRY OPTION SERIES

Carry 12

.45 ACP pistol with 3.5" barrel. Fitted with night sights. Receiver and finish stainless steel. Magazine capacity is 10 or 12 rounds. Weight about 34 oz.

	850	700	575	400	300	125

Tac-Four

.45 ACP model fitted with 4.35" barrel. Stainless steel receiver with Spec Ops finish. Magazine capacity 10 or 13 rounds. Sights are 3-dot. Weight about 36 oz.

	850	700	575	400	300	125

Tac-Five

Light double-action 9mm with 18+1 capacity. 5" barrel, weight 37.5 oz., stainless finish, adjustable rear sight, plastic grips.

	850	700	575	400	300	125

LDA, DOUBLE ACTION, HIGH CAPACITY MODELS

Stealth Hi-Cap .45

.45 ACP pistol has 5" barrel, with steel receiver and Stealth finish. Spurless hammer. Sights are 3-dot. Magazine capacity 10 or 14 rounds. Weight about 40 oz.

	800	625	500	400	150	125

	NIB	EXC.	V.G.	GOOD	FAIR	POOR

Hi-Cap .45

Similar to above, with stainless steel receiver and finish.

	NIB	EXC.	V.G.	GOOD	FAIR	POOR
	800	625	500	400	150	125

Colonel

.45 ACP pistol fitted with 4.25" barrel, with low mount fixed sights. Slide and frame are green, with black fire controls. Black polymer grips. Magazine capacity 14 rounds. Weight about 37 oz. Introduced in 2005.

	800	625	500	400	150	125

Hi-Cap .40

Chambered for .40 S&W cartridge. Fitted with 5" barrel and 3-dot sights. Stainless steel receiver and finish. Magazine capacity 10 or 16 rounds. Weight about 40 oz.

	800	625	500	400	150	125

Stealth Hi-Cap 9

9mm pistol fitted with 5" barrel with 3-dot sights. Steel receiver with Stealth finish. Magazine capacity 10 or 18 rounds. Weight about 40 oz.

	800	625	500	400	150	125

Hi-Cap 9

Similar to above, with stainless steel receiver and finish.

	850	700	575	400	300	125

Covert Black Nite-Tac

Introduced in 2005. This .45 ACP pistol fitted with 5" barrel and covert black finish. Low mount fixed sights. Magazine capacity 14 rounds. Weight about 40 oz.

	850	700	575	400	300	125

Nite-Tac

As above, with stainless steel frame and slide. Introduced in 2005.

	800	625	500	400	150	125

Nite-Tac .40

.40 S&W 16+1 capacity double-action duty pistol, with fixed sights. 5" barrel, weight 40 oz., stainless finish.

	800	625	500	400	150	125

Nite-Tac 9

9mm 18+1 double-action duty pistol, with fixed sights. 5" barrel, weight 40 oz., stainless finish.

	800	625	500	400	150	125

LDA, DOUBLE ACTION, HIGH CAPACITY, LIMITED

Hi-Cap Limited .40

.40 S&W pistol has 5" barrel with 3-dot sights. Stainless steel receiver with Sterling finish. Magazine capacity 16 rounds. Weight about 40 oz.

	1000	875	725	575	400	200

Stealth Hi-Cap Limited 9

Chambered for 9mm cartridge. Fitted with 5" barrel with 3-dot sights. Receiver steel with Stealth finish. Magazine capacity 18 rounds. Weight about 40 oz.

	1000	875	725	575	400	200

Hi-Cap Limited 9

As above, with stainless steel receiver and Sterling finish.

	1200	975	825	650	450	225

Stealth Hi-Cap Ltd .45

.45 ACP pistol has 5" barrel with 3-dot sights and spurless hammer. Receiver steel with Stealth finish. Magazine capacity 10 or 14 rounds. Weight about 40 oz.

	1000	875	725	575	400	200

Hi-Cap Limited .45

Similar to above, with stainless steel receiver and Sterling finish.

	1100	975	825	650	450	225

	NIB	EXC.	V.G.	GOOD	FAIR	POOR

TTR RIFLE SERIES

Para's Tactical Target Rifle based on AR platform, with 16.5" barrel, 30-round magazine. Chambered in .223 Rem./5.56x45 NATO. Flat Top upper receiver, full-length Picatinny rail, short or long-rail forearm, adjustable buttstock. Delayed impingement gas system, front and rear flip-up sights. Accepts all M16 and AR-15 magazines. Manufactured 2009 - 2011.

1950	1700	1450	1100	900	400

PARDINI
Italy

Standard Target Pistol

.22-caliber semi-automatic pistol, with 4.7" barrel, adjustable rear sight and adjustable trigger. Blued, with two sizes of walnut grips. One suitable for use by ladies. Introduced in 1986.

1450	1200	975	800	600	350

Rapidfire Pistol

Similar to above in .22 short, with alloy bolt, 4.6" barrel and enclosed grip. Weight about 43 oz. Introduced in 1995.

1450	1200	975	800	600	350

Centerfire Pistol

Similar to standard model in .32 Smith & Wesson caliber. Introduced in 1986.

1450	1200	975	800	600	350

Free Pistol

.22-caliber single-shot pistol, with 9.8" barrel, adjustable sights and grip. Furnished with barrel weights. Weight about 35 oz. Introduced in 1995.

1550	1300	1050	900	700	450

PARKER-HALE LTD.
Birmingham, England

S&W Victory Conversion

.22-caliber double-action revolver, with 4" barrel and 6-shot cylinder. Blued, with walnut grips. Alteration of Smith & Wesson Victor model.

—	295	200	150	100	75

Model 1200

.22-250 to .300 Win. Magnum bolt-action rifle, with 24" barrel and open sights. Blued, with walnut stock.

700	550	450	400	350	250

Model 1100 Lightweight

As above, with 22" barrel and 4-shot magazine. Introduced in 1985.

600	475	400	300	250	200

Model 81 Classic

.22-250 to 7mm Rem. Magnum bolt-action rifle, with 24" barrel and open sights. Blued, with walnut stock. Introduced in 1985.

875	750	600	500	400	350

Model 81 African

As above in .375 H&H caliber. Introduced in 1986.

1750	1200	1100	700	500	350

Model 84 Target

Similar to Model 81 in .308-caliber, with adjustable rear sights and adjustable cheekpiece.

1300	1000	800	600	450	250

Model 85 Sniper

As above, with scope and bipod.

3250	2500	975	—	—	—

Model 640E Shotgun

12-, 16- or 20-gauge boxlock double-barrel shotgun. Manufactured in a variety of barrel lengths with double triggers and extractors. Blued, French case hardened with walnut stock. Introduced in 1986.

575	450	400	300	250	200

	NIB	EXC.	V.G.	GOOD	FAIR	POOR

Model 640A

As above, with pistol-grip, beavertail fore-end and single trigger. Introduced in 1986.

	675	550	500	400	300	200

Model 645E

As above, but more finely finished and engraved.

	700	550	500	400	300	200

Model 670E

Sidelock double-barrel shotgun made on special order. Introduced in 1986.

	3000	2500	1850	1200	750	400

Model 680E—XXV

As above, with case hardened lockplates and 25" barrels.

	3000	2500	1850	1200	750	400

BLACKPOWDER REPRODUCTIONS

1853 Enfield Rifle Musket

Three band version in .577-caliber. Barrel length 39". Rear sight graduated to 900 yards. Weight about 9 lbs.

	600	475	375	250	175	75

1858 Enfield Naval Pattern Rifle

Naval version with two bands in .577-caliber. Barrel length 33". Walnut stock with brass furniture. Rear sight adjustable to 1100 yards. Weight approximately 8.5 lbs.

	550	425	325	200	125	50

1861 Enfield Artillery Carbine Musketoon

Artillery version in .577-caliber, with 24" barrel. Walnut stock, with brass furniture. Rear sight adjustable to 600 yards. Weight about 7.5 lbs.

	550	425	325	200	125	50

Whitworth Military Target Rifle

Model in .451-caliber. Barrel length 36". Weight about 9.9 lbs.

	875	700	550	400	200	100

Whitworth Sniping Rifle

Same as above, with brass scope and mounts.

	1400	1050	800	550	300	150

Volunteer Percussion Target Rifle

Rifle in .451-caliber and fitted with 33" barrel. Two banded design, with walnut stock and brass furniture. Adjustable rear sight. Weight approximately 9.5 lbs.

	850	650	550	400	200	100

PARKER
Springfield, Massachusetts

4-Shot Pistol

.33-caliber percussion pistol, with 4" half-octagonal barrel and 4-shot sliding chamber. Marked "Albert Parker/Patent Secured/Springfield, Mass." Original finish unknown, with walnut grips. Prospective purchasers are advised to secure a qualified appraisal prior to acquisition.

	—	—	15000	13500	6000	2000

PARKER BROS.
Meriden, Connecticut

Perhaps best known of all American shotgun manufacturers. Established by Charles Parker shortly after the Civil War. This company has produced a wide variety of shotguns in a number of different styles over the years. In early 1930s, company was purchased by Remington Arms Company.

Parker shotguns are among the most collectible of American-made shotguns. Both beginner and veteran collectors should be aware that originality and condition are absolutely critical in establishing such high values for these shotguns. There are numerous upgraded and refinished guns that are represented

	NIB	EXC.	V.G.	GOOD	FAIR	POOR

as original. Beware that such misrepresentations exist, because refinished and upgraded Parker guns should sell for as much as 50 to 75 percent below the price of an original gun. Extreme caution should be exercised and we would recommend that an expert be consulted. Even the most advanced collectors may benefit from such consultations. Also, prices indicated for guns in excellent condition may fluctuate drastically, especially in high grade or small bore guns, due to their extreme rarity.

In addition, uncommon extras such as single triggers, ventilated ribs, beavertail forearms, straight-grip stocks and skeleton steel buttplates may add substantial value to an individual gun. Extra sets of factory barrels that were installed at the time of delivery will add an average of 30 percent premium. This premium will increase with grade and gauge; higher the grade and smaller the gauge, higher the premium.

Letters of authenticity are available. These letters are a must in order for any Parker gun to attain maximum value. Contact: Executive Secretary Parker Gun Collectors Association, P.O. Box 126502, Harrisburg, PA 17112. Letter is $40 for members of PCGA and $100 for non-members.

VH

12-, 16-, 20-, 28-gauge or .410 bore boxlock double-barrel shotgun. Manufactured in a variety of barrel lengths with double triggers and extractors. Blued, case hardened receiver with walnut stock. Only 2,297 guns had single triggers, only 3,983 guns had straight-grip stocks. Approximately 78,659 were made: 10-gauge—20, 12-gauge—51,901, 16-gauge—14,446, 20-gauge—10,406, 28-gauge—1,417, .410 bore—469. Also made with automatic ejectors and known as Model VHE. The E suffix was used on all models to denote automatic ejectors. **NOTE:** Add 40 percent VHE; 60 percent 20-gauge; 500 percent 28-gauge and .410 bore.

	NIB	EXC.	V.G.	GOOD	FAIR	POOR
	—	5000	4000	2950	2000	1000

PH

Similar to above, with a small amount of scroll engraving. Slightly better grade of walnut. Approximately 1,339 were made: 10-gauge—798, 12-gauge—839, 16-gauge—208, 20-gauge—204, 28-gauge—5, .410 bore—4. **NOTE:** Add 40 percent PHE (ejectors); 60 percent 20-gauge; extremely rare 28-gauge and .410 bore models, prices can command a 1000 percent premium.

	NIB	EXC.	V.G.	GOOD	FAIR	POOR
	—	5500	4250	3350	2100	1000

GH

Similar to above, with a modest amount of scroll and game scene engraving. Barrels marked "Parker Special Steel". Only about 430 G grades were built with straight-grip stocks. Approximately 4,291 were made: 8-gauge—11, 10-gauge—63, 12-gauge—2,501, 16-gauge—607, 20-gauge—990, 28-gauge—91, .410 bore—28. **NOTE:** Add 35 percent GHE (ejectors); 15 percent 16-gauge; 50 percent 20-gauge; 300 percent 28-gauge; 500 percent .410 bore.

	NIB	EXC.	V.G.	GOOD	FAIR	POOR
	—	7000	5500	4000	3000	1000

DH

As above, but more finely finished. Engraving coverage more profuse. Most modern D grade guns were fitted with Titanic barrels. Only about 280 were built with Parker single triggers; about 280 built with ventilated ribs. Approximately 9,346 were made: 8-gauge—10, 10-gauge—45, 12-gauge—6,330, 16-gauge—1,178, 20-gauge—1,536, 28-gauge—187, .410 bore—60. **NOTE:** Add 35 percent DHE (ejectors); 15 percent 16-gauge; 50 percent 20-gauge; 300 percent 28-gauge; 500 percent .410 bore.

	NIB	EXC.	V.G.	GOOD	FAIR	POOR
	—	8500	7000	5000	3500	1000

CH

As above, with more scroll and game scene engraving coverage. Marked with Acme steel barrels. Only about 93 C grades had straight-grip stocks. Approximately 697 were made: 8-gauge—2, 10-gauge—9, 12-gauge—410, 16-gauge—105, 20-gauge—149, 28-gauge—16, .410 bore—6. **NOTE:** Add 35 percent CHE (ejectors); 10 percent 16-gauge; 40 percent 20-gauge; 400 percent 28-gauge; 700 percent .410 bore.

	NIB	EXC.	V.G.	GOOD	FAIR	POOR
	—	16000	14000	9000	6500	1500

BH

As above, but offered in a variety of different styles of engraved decoration. Only about 66 guns had straight-grip stocks, 29 had beavertail fore-ends, 20 were built with vent ribs and 57 had single triggers. Approximately 512 were made: 10-gauge—2, 12-gauge—317, 16-gauge—71, 20-gauge—109, 28-gauge—13. **NOTE:** Prospective purchasers are advised to secure qualified appraisal prior to acquisition. Add 35 percent BHE (ejectors); 15 percent 16-gauge; 50 percent 20-gauge; 450 percent 28-gauge.

	NIB	EXC.	V.G.	GOOD	FAIR	POOR
	—	20000	17000	13000	10000	2500

	NIB	EXC.	V.G.	GOOD	FAIR	POOR

AH

As above, but highly engraved with finely figured walnut stocks. Most had Acme steel barrels. About 42 A grade guns were built with straight-grip stocks. Approximately 167 were made: 10-gauge—1, 12-gauge—92, 16-gauge—23, 20-gauge—44, 28-gauge—6, .410 bore—1. **NOTE:** Add 30 percent AHE (ejectors); 25 percent 16-gauge; 75 percent 20-gauge; 450 percent 28-gauge; 600 percent .410 bore.

	NIB	EXC.	V.G.	GOOD	FAIR	POOR
	—	35000	30000	20000	15000	2500

AAH

As above, with either Whitworth or Peerless barrels. Not made in .410 bore. Engraving is more extensive and of first quality. Only one AA grade has ventilated rib, ten were built with single trigger and 95 had straight-grip stocks. Approximately 238 were made: 10-gauge—2, 12-gauge—185, 16-gauge—19, 20-gauge—27, 28-gauge—5. **NOTE:** Due to rarity of this grade, prospective purchasers are advised to secure qualified appraisal prior to acquisition. Add 30 percent AAHE (ejectors); 35 percent 16-gauge; 75 percent 20-gauge; 250 percent 28-gauge.

	NIB	EXC.	V.G.	GOOD	FAIR	POOR
	—	55000	45000	37500	20000	3000

A-1 Special

As above, but made strictly on special order. Not manufactured in .410 bore. Two A-1 Specials were built with ventilated rib, 7 had single triggers, 3 had beavertail fore-ends and 24 were built with straight-grip stocks. Approximately 79 were made: 12-gauge—55, 16-gauge—6, 20-gauge—11, 28-gauge—7. **NOTE:** Add 35 percent 16-gauge; 75 percent 20-gauge; 400 percent 28-gauge.

	NIB	EXC.	V.G.	GOOD	FAIR	POOR
	—	100000	80000	65000	35000	5000

Single-Barrel Trap

12-gauge single-shot shotgun, with 30", 32" or 34" barrel. Automatic ejector and walnut stock. Produced in a variety of grades as listed. Prospective purchasers are advised to secure a qualified appraisal prior to acquisition.

S.C. Grade

	NIB	EXC.	V.G.	GOOD	FAIR	POOR
	—	8500	6500	4000	2000	1000

S.B. Grade

	NIB	EXC.	V.G.	GOOD	FAIR	POOR
	—	10000	7500	5500	2400	1600

S.A. Grade

	NIB	EXC.	V.G.	GOOD	FAIR	POOR
	—	14000	13000	10000	5000	2000

S.A.A. Grade

	NIB	EXC.	V.G.	GOOD	FAIR	POOR
	—	25000	20000	15000	10000	5000

S.A-1 Special Grade

	NIB	EXC.	V.G.	GOOD	FAIR	POOR
	—	30000	25000	18000	12000	5000

Under Lifter Hammer Gun

Side hammer double-barrel shotgun. Manufactured in a variety of gauges, with barrel release located in front of trigger guards. Damascus barrels, case hardened locks, blued furniture with walnut stocks. Manufactured during 1870s and later.

	NIB	EXC.	V.G.	GOOD	FAIR	POOR
		6000	3200	1500	800	600

Trojan

12-, 16- or 20-gauge boxlock double-barrel shotgun. Manufactured in a variety of barrel lengths, with double triggers and extractors. Only 27 Trojans were built with single triggers. Blued, case hardened receiver, with walnut stock. Approximately 33,000 were made: 12-gauge—21,977, 16-gauge—6,573, 20-gauge—5450. **NOTE:** Add 20 percent 16-gauge; 40 percent 20-gauge;

	NIB	EXC.	V.G.	GOOD	FAIR	POOR
	—	3800	3000	2000	1000	600

PARKER FIELD & SONS
London, England

Gas Seal Revolver

.42-caliber percussion revolver, with 6" barrel and 6-shot cylinder. Blued, case hardened with walnut grips. Manufactured during 1860s.

	NIB	EXC.	V.G.	GOOD	FAIR	POOR
	—	—	2500	1950	900	450

	NIB	EXC.	V.G.	GOOD	FAIR	POOR

PARKER GUN

Parker Gun, a division of Remington Arms Company, offers a current production of this classic shotgun. Made by Connecticut Shotgun Manufacturing Co., the AAHE Grade is offered only in 28-gauge. This made-to-order gun is priced from $49,000 and must be ordered directly from Remington, P.O. Box 700, Madison, NC 27025.

PARKER REPRODUCTIONS
Japan

Company had exact reproductions of Parker D, DHE, B and A-1 Special shotguns made in Japan. They are of the finest quality and workmanship. Styles of engraving and features of these shotguns correspond exactly to original Parker Arms. Following values are a starting point.

DHE Grade

Side-by-side shotgun offered in 12-, 20- and 28-gauge. Barrel lengths 26" or 28" with solid matte rib. Stocks are select walnut, with choice of pistol-/straight-grip. Choice splinter or beavertail forearms offered. Single-/double triggers available. Receiver case colored and scroll engraved with game scenes to match original Parker DHE grade. Weight: 12-gauge 6.75 lbs.; 20-gauge 6.5 lbs.; 28-gauge 5.3 lbs.

12 Gauge

NOTE: Add 30 percent 20-gauge; 40 percent 28-gauge.

NIB	EXC.	V.G.	GOOD	FAIR	POOR
4000	3000	2400	1800	1200	400

16/20 Combination

Introduced in 1993. Limited to 500 sets. Offered with 28" barrels only. This set features 16-gauge barrel on 20-gauge frame. Weighs 6.25 lbs.

NIB	EXC.	V.G.	GOOD	FAIR	POOR
11000	8900	7500	3500	2000	650

28 Gauge

NIB	EXC.	V.G.	GOOD	FAIR	POOR
6000	4250	3000	2000	1400	400

28 Gauge/.410 Bore Combination

NOTE: Add $990 for additional barrel; $170 for beavertail forearm. D Grade three-barrel sets are offered in 16/20/20 combinations for additional $2300.

NIB	EXC.	V.G.	GOOD	FAIR	POOR
15000	12000	9000	7500	3000	1000

DHE Grade Steel-Shot Special

Offered in 12-gauge only, with 28" barrels. Fitted with 3" chambers and special chrome lined barrels. Weighs 7 lbs.

NIB	EXC.	V.G.	GOOD	FAIR	POOR
6000	5000	3950	2200	1200	400

BHE Grade Limited Edition

Features engraving similar to original Parker BHE Grade. Fancy walnut stocks with fine line checkering was standard. Offered in 12-, 20- and 28-gauge. A 28-gauge/.410 bore combination was also offered. Only 100 shotguns in this grade produced in 1989.

NIB	EXC.	V.G.	GOOD	FAIR	POOR
8500	6500	5000	2250	900	450

2-Barrel Set

NIB	EXC.	V.G.	GOOD	FAIR	POOR
15000	11500	9500	4000	2000	750

A-1 Special

Introduced in 1988. Grade featured fine scroll engraving and presentation French walnut with custom checked pattern. Stock was hand carved with fleur-de-lis and features 32 lpi checkering. Grip cap was rosewood and gold or gold initial plate on straight-grip guns. Gold wire was used on breech end on barrels. Serial numbers were in gold relief as were the word "SAFE" and "L" and "R" on models with selective single trigger. Barrel flats and frame water table were jeweled. This grade offered in 12-, 20- and 28-gauge with a few early guns sold with 28-gauge/.410 bore combinations. Furnished with English-style oak-and-leather case with canvas and leather cover, engraved snap caps and engraved oil bottle.

12 or 20 Gauge

NIB	EXC.	V.G.	GOOD	FAIR	POOR
13000	11500	9000	6500	5000	700

28 Gauge

NIB	EXC.	V.G.	GOOD	FAIR	POOR
16000	14000	9500	7000	3500	600

A-1 Special Custom Engraved

A custom A-1 Special hand-engraved to each individual customer's specifications. Only limited number of these shotguns were built. Initial price in 1989 was $10,500. Sky's the limit on a gun of this sort.

	NIB	EXC.	V.G.	GOOD	FAIR	POOR

PEABODY
Providence, Rhode Island
Providence Tool Company

For historical information, photos and data on Peabody military rifles see Standard Catalog of Military Firearms.

Peabody Rifle and Carbine

.43 Spanish, .443, .45 Peabody, .45-70, .50 or .50-70 caliber single-shot rifle, with 33" or 20" (carbine) barrel. Either full-length or half stock. Receiver marked "Peabody's Patent July 22, 1862 / Manf'd by Providence Tool Co. Prov. R.I." Blued, with walnut stock. Produced in large quantities during 1860s and 1870s.

NIB	EXC.	V.G.	GOOD	FAIR	POOR
—	—	1950	900	300	100

Sporting Rifle

As above in sporting configuration. Either 26" or 28" barrels. Frame marked, "Peabody's Patent, July 22, 1862 / Manf'd by Providence Tool Co., Prov. R.I.". Blued, case hardened with walnut stock. Manufactured approximately 1866 to 1875.

NIB	EXC.	V.G.	GOOD	FAIR	POOR
—	—	5500	3000	1100	400

PEABODY-MARTINI SPORTING RIFLES

For historical information, photos and data on Peabody-Martini military rifles see Standard Catalog of Military Firearms.

Creedmoor

.40-90 or .44-100 caliber Martini-action single-shot rifle, with 32" round/octagonal barrel, butt-mounted vernier rear sight, combination wind gauge and spirit level front sight. Receiver marked, "Peabody & Martini Patents" and barrel "Manufactured by the Providence Tool Co. Providence R.I. U.S.A.". Blued, case hardened with walnut stock.

NIB	EXC.	V.G.	GOOD	FAIR	POOR
—	—	8250	3850	1650	550

Creedmoor Mid-Range

Similar to above in .40-70 or .40-90 caliber, with 28" round/octagonal barrel, vernier tang sight and wind gauge front sight. Blued, case hardened with walnut stock.

NIB	EXC.	V.G.	GOOD	FAIR	POOR
—	—	6600	3700	1400	400

What Cheer

Creedmoor without pistol-grip.

NIB	EXC.	V.G.	GOOD	FAIR	POOR
—	—	6600	3600	1350	400

What Cheer Mid-Range

Mid-Range Creedmoor without pistol-grip.

NIB	EXC.	V.G.	GOOD	FAIR	POOR
—	—	5500	3100	1100	300

Kill Deer

.45-70 caliber single-shot Martini-action rifle, with 28" or 30" round/octagonal barrels, adjustable tang rear sight and globe front sights. Blued, case hardened with walnut stock.

NIB	EXC.	V.G.	GOOD	FAIR	POOR
—	—	8250	4700	1650	500

PEAVY, A. J.
South Montville, Maine

Knife-Pistol

.22-caliber single-shot knife pistol. Constructed of steel and brass with folding trigger. Sideplates marked "A.J. Peavy Pat. Sept. 5, '65 & Mar. 27, '66". Produced between 1866 and 1870.

NIB	EXC.	V.G.	GOOD	FAIR	POOR
—	—	6000	4700	1900	500

PECARE & SMITH
New York, New York

Pepperbox

.28-caliber 4-/1-shot percussion pepperbox, with folding trigger and 4" barrel group. Barrel group enclosed within an iron casing. Blued, silver-plated frame with walnut grips. Barrel casing marked "Pecare & Smith". Manufactured during 1840s and early 1850s.

NIB	EXC.	V.G.	GOOD	FAIR	POOR
—	—	4800	3000	1300	350

	NIB	EXC.	V.G.	GOOD	FAIR	POOR

Ten-Shot Pepperbox (rare)

	—	—	9500	6600	2750	600

PEDERSEN, JOHN D.
Denver, Colorado & Jackson, Wyoming

Pedersen Rifle

	—	15000	7500	5000	2500	500

Pedersen Carbine

	—	17500	8500	6000	3000	—600

PEDERSEN CUSTOM GUNS
North Haven, Connecticut

Division of O.F. Mossberg Company. Operated between 1973 and 1975.

Model 4000 Shotgun

Mossberg Model 500 slide-action shotgun. In 12-, 20-gauge or .410 bore, with 26", 28" or 30" ventilated rib barrels. Blued, engraved with walnut stock. Manufactured in 1975.

	—	400	350	250	200	100

Model 4000 Trap

Chambered for 12-gauge only, with 30" Full choke barrel. Monte Carlo stock with factory recoil pad.

	—	500	400	300	200	100

Model 4500

As above, with reduced amount of engraving.

	—	425	325	225	175	100

Model 4500 Trap

Same as Model 4000 Trap, with less engraving.

	—	400	350	250	200	100

Model 1500

12-gauge Magnum over/under shotgun, with 26", 28" or 30" ventilated rib barrels, single-selective trigger and automatic ejectors. Blued, with walnut stock. Weight about 7.5 lbs. depending on barrel length. Manufactured between 1973 and 1975.

	—	900	775	550	300	200

Model 1500 Skeet

Similar to above, fitted with skeet-style stock, 27" barrels and skeet chokes.

	—	950	825	600	350	200

Model 1500 Trap

Model fitted with Monte Carlo-style stock. Choice of 30" or 32" barrels.

	—	950	825	600	350	200

Model 1000

As above in two grades of decoration. Manufactured between 1973 and 1975.

Grade I

	—	1750	1250	800	500	200

Grade II

	—	1500	1000	750	400	200

Model 1000 Magnum

Chambered for 12-gauge 3" shell. Fitted with 30" barrels.

Grade I

	—	1600	1200	800	500	200

Grade II

	—	1400	1100	750	400	200

	NIB	EXC.	V.G.	GOOD	FAIR	POOR

Model 1000 Skeet

Offered in 12-gauge only, with 26" or 28" barrels. Skeet-style stock and chokes.

Grade I

	—	1750	1250	800	400	200

Grade II

	—	1500	1000	750	400	200

Model 1000 Trap

Chambered for 12-gauge. Fitted with 30" or 32" barrels. Trap-style Monte Carlo stock.

Grade I

	—	1600	1200	800	500	200

Grade II

	—	1400	1100	750	400	200

Model 2000

12- or 20-gauge boxlock double-barrel shotgun, with 26", 28" or 30" barrels. Single-selective trigger and automatic ejectors. Produced in two grades of decoration. Manufactured in 1973 and 1974.

Grade I

	—	2000	1500	1000	600	200

Grade II

	—	1750	1250	800	400	200

Model 2500

12- or 20-gauge boxlock double-barrel shotgun, with 26" or 28" barrels. Double triggers and automatic ejectors. Blued, with walnut stock.

	—	400	300	250	150	200

Model 3000

Mossberg Model 810 bolt-action rifle. Manufactured in .270 to .338 Win. Magnum caliber, with 22" or 24" barrel with open sights. Produced in three grades.

Grade III—Plain

	—	450	400	350	150	200

Grade II

	—	525	425	350	150	200

Grade I

	—	800	650	500	200	200

Model 4700

Mossberg Model 472 lever-action in .30-30 or .35 Rem. caliber, with 24" barrel and 5-shot tubular magazine. Blued, with walnut stock.

	—	450	375	275	175	100

PEDERSOLI, DAVIDE

Brescia, Italy

Davide Pedersoli & Co. was founded in 1957 by the late Davide Pedersoli. In nearly half-century since, Pedersoli has established itself as a manufacturer of extremely high-quality replica and modern firearms. Pedersoli products are frequently marked with importer's or retailer's name (e.g., Dixie Gun Works or Cabela's) rather than Pedersoli brand, usually at widely varying discounts. Many muzzle-loading rifles and pistols are available in kit form at reduced prices. **NOTE:** Rapidly-fluctuating currency markets can result in values for newly-imported Pedersoli guns being 10-15 percent higher than values listed below.

HANDGUNS

Mang In Graz Pistol

Recreation of single-shot .38- or .44-caliber percussion pistol. Made circa 1850 by Martin Mang. **NOTE:** Add 10 percent for target; 20 percent for deluxe.

	1100	750	500	400	300	150

NIB	EXC.	V.G.	GOOD	FAIR	POOR

Kuchenreuter Pistol

Recreation of single-shot .38- or .44-caliber percussion pistol. Made circa 1854 by Bartholomaus Kuchenreuter of Steinweg, Germany. **NOTE:** Add 20 percent for deluxe.

1350	900	600	500	400	200

Mortimer Pistol

Recreation of single-shot .44 caliber pistol. First made circa 1810 by H. W Mortimer & Son of London. Smooth or rifled barrel. Percussion and flint versions available. **NOTE:** Add 10 percent for Match model; 20 percent for deluxe.

895	755	525	375	250	100

LePage Dueller

Recreation of single-shot .31-, .36- or .44-caliber dueling pistol. Made by Henry LePage circa 1840. Percussion and flint versions available. .**NOTE:** Add 20 percent for deluxe.

895	755	525	375	250	100

Charles Moore Dueling Pistol

Recreation of single-shot .36- or .44-caliber dueling pistol. Made by Charles Moore of London circa 1800. Percussion and flint versions available. **NOTE:** Add 10 percent for target model.

600	450	300	200	100	50

Carleton Underhammer Pistol

Recreation of saw-handled .36-caliber underhammer percussion pistol. circa 1850.

750	600	450	300	150	75

Remington Pattern Target Revolver

Replica of Remington "1858-style" .44-caliber percussion revolver.

450	350	250	100	75	50

Rogers & Spencer Target Percussion Target Revolver

Replica of .44-caliber Rogers and Spencer revolver, that didn't quite make it in time for Civil War.

425	325	250	100	75	50

Kentucky Pistol

Recreation of single-shot .45-, .50- and .54-caliber pistol of American colonial era. Flint and percussion versions available. **NOTE:** Add 50 percent for "Silver Star" models.

300	250	225	150	100	50

Bounty Pistol

Similar to Kentucky Pistol standard version, with 16" barrel. .45- or .50-caliber only.

300	250	225	150	100	50

Navy Moll Pistol

Similar to Kentucky pistol, with brass trim. Flint and percussion versions available. .45-caliber.

425	325	250	100	75	50

Harper's Ferry Pistol

Recreation of .58-caliber flintlock pistol procured for U. S. Navy in 1806.

425	325	250	100	75	50

Queen Anne Pistol

Recreation of English 17th-century cannon-barrel flintlock pistol. .50-caliber smoothbore barrel. Steel or brass construction.

375	295	225	75	50	25

An IX Pistol

Recreation of .69-caliber Napoleonic flintlock cavalry pistol of 1803. Brass trim.

500	400	300	200	100	50

An XIII Pistol

Simplified 1806 version of An IX pistol.

500	400	300	200	100	50

	NIB	EXC.	V.G.	GOOD	FAIR	POOR

Remington Rider Derringer

Recreation of Remington Rider single-shot .177 percussion parlor pistol. Available in white or with casehardened gold-toned or engraved/silvered finish. Pricing for basic model.

175	150	100	75	50	25

Derringer Liegi

Recreation of circa 1850 screw-barrel percussion pocket pistol, with folding trigger and bag grip. .44-caliber. **NOTE:** Add 10 percent for engraved model.

175	150	100	75	50	25

Zimmer Pistol

Recreation of circa 1850 single-shot percussion parlor pistol. .177-caliber; fluted grip with butt cap. Discontinued.

500	400	300	200	100	50

Saloon Pistol

Recreation of circa 1850 single-shot percussion parlor pistol. .36- or .177-caliber. Discontinued.

500	400	300	200	100	50

RIFLES

Swivel-Breech Rifle

Muzzle-loading over/under rotating percussion rifle in .45-, .50- or .54-caliber. Browned barrel, walnut stock. Discontinued.

700	625	500	350	175	100

Bristlen A. Morges Target Rifle

Recreation of 1850-vintage percussion target rifle made by Marc Bristlen of Morges, Switzerland. Schuetzen-style buttplate, double triggers, false muzzle. Shoots .35- or .45-caliber elongated conical. **NOTE:** Add 20 percent for deluxe model.

1350	900	600	500	400	200

Waadtlander Target Rifle

Similar to Bristel A. Morges target rifle. Rifled for .45-caliber round ball. **NOTE:** Add 20 percent for deluxe version.

1350	900	600	500	400	200

Swiss Rifle

Similar to Waadtlander Target Rifle in flintlock, with 29.5" barrel.

1350	900	600	500	400	200

Wurttemberg Mauser

Replica of 1857 Mauser military percussion rifle. Shoots .54 Minie ball. Designed for 100m target shooting.

1000	850	700	575	400	125

Gibbs Rifle

Recreation of 1865-vintage long-range percussion rifle made by George Gibbs of London. Shoots elongated .40- or .45-caliber conicals.

1350	900	600	500	400	200

Tryon Rifle

Recreation of noteworthy American percussion plains rifle circa 1850. .45-, .50- or .54-caliber. **NOTE:** Add 10 percent for Creedmore; 20 percent for deluxe target.

750	600	450	300	150	75

Mortimer Rifle

Recreation of arms made circa 1850 by H. W Mortimer & Son of London. Percussion and flint versions available. Various configurations including Whitworth, Vetterli and 12-gauge fowler.

1050	875	600	500	400	175

Indian Trade Musket

Recreation of 18th-century flintlock smoothbore fusil as typified by colonial and early 19th-century trading companies.

825	750	650	500	400	175

	NIB	EXC.	V.G.	GOOD	FAIR	POOR

Frontier Rifle

Recreation of typical American hunting rifle circa 1800-1840. .32-, .36-, .45-, .50- and .54-caliber versions available in flintlock and percussion. Various barrel lengths.

	NIB	EXC.	V.G.	GOOD	FAIR	POOR
	750	600	450	300	150	75

Kentucky Rifle

Recreation of Pennsylvania-style rifle circa 1800. .32-, .45- and .50-caliber percussion or flintlock. **NOTE:** Add 35 percent for "Silver Star" model.

	750	600	450	300	150	75

Alamo Rifle

Recreation of long rifle used in Mexican War of 1840s. Double triggers; .32-, .45- or .50-caliber.

	825	750	650	500	400	175

Cub

Scaled-down Pennsylvania-type rifle in .36-, .45- or .50-caliber. Percussion or flint. **NOTE:** Add 25 percent for flint.

	550	425	350	250	200	100

Country Hunter

Exceedingly simple half-stock .50-caliber percussion or flintlock rifle.

	500	425	350	250	200	100

Jager Rifle

Massive, decidedly Germanic .54-caliber percussion or flintlock rifle based on Teutonic hunting arms, circa 1750-1850.

	950	875	700	550	375	200

Leger 1763 Charleville Musket

Recreation of Revolution-era .69-caliber smoothbore flintlock musket.

	1050	875	600	500	400	175

Revolutionnaire 1777 Musket

Similar to Charleville musket in detail. Patterned after muskets used in French Revolution.

	1050	875	600	500	400	175

Corrige An IX

Similar to Revolutionnaire 1777 musket. Differing in details of frizzen, etc.

	1050	875	600	500	400	175

An IX Dragoon Musket

Similar to Corrige An IX musket, with 40.5" cavalry-length barrel.

	1050	875	600	500	400	175

Austrian 1798 Flintlock Musket

Similar to 1777 musket, with Austrian modifications in barrel bands, bayonet mount, etc.

	1050	875	600	500	400	175

Prussian 1809 Flintlock Musket

Similar to French 1777 musket in .75-caliber with "Potsdam" markings.

	1050	875	600	500	400	175

Brown Bess Flintlock Musket

Recreation of legendary .75-caliber smoothbore musket. Used by British troops before, during and after American Revolutionary War.

	950	875	700	550	375	200

Springfield 1795 Musket

Recreation of America's first indigenous military arm, .69-caliber smoothbore.

	950	875	700	550	375	200

Harper's Ferry 1816 Musket

Recreation of U.S. martial .69-caliber smoothbore flintlock musket.

	950	875	700	550	375	200

	NIB	EXC.	V.G.	GOOD	FAIR	POOR

Rocky Mountain Hawken

Faithful recreation of legendary plains rifle, .54-caliber.

NIB	EXC.	V.G.	GOOD	FAIR	POOR
850	695	550	400	250	125

Springfield 1861 Rifle

Recreation of .58-caliber percussion rifle. Used in American Civil War.

NIB	EXC.	V.G.	GOOD	FAIR	POOR
950	875	700	550	375	200

Kodiak Combination Gun

Percussion side-by-side rifle/shotgun combination, with 12-gauge smoothbore barrel and .50-, .54- and .58-caliber rifled barrel.

NIB	EXC.	V.G.	GOOD	FAIR	POOR
1100	850	600	425	300	200

Kodiak Double Rifle

Side-by-side double percussion rifle in .50-, .54-, .58- and .72-caliber. Sights regulated to 75 yards.

NIB	EXC.	V.G.	GOOD	FAIR	POOR
1200	950	700	475	325	200

Rolling Block Rifle

Replica of famous Remington rolling block single-shot rifle, circa 1867-1890. Various centerfire chamberings and configurations including Baby carbine. Prices shown are for standard version in .45-70.

NIB	EXC.	V.G.	GOOD	FAIR	POOR
950	875	700	550	375	200

1859 Sharps Cavalry Carbine

Replica of Sharps percussion carbine with 22" barrel, patchbox and elevator sight; .54-caliber. Available as Infantry Rifle with 30" barrel.

NIB	EXC.	V.G.	GOOD	FAIR	POOR
895	825	775	675	475	200

1862 Robinson Confederate Sharps

Similar to 1859 Sharps carbine, with different barrel band, receiver details and rear sight.

NIB	EXC.	V.G.	GOOD	FAIR	POOR
800	675	575	400	300	125

Sharps 1863 Sporting Rifle

Replica of Sharps sporting rifle, with 32" barrel, set trigger and sculpted fore-end; .45- or .54-caliber. .45-caliber version rifled for elongated conicals.

NIB	EXC.	V.G.	GOOD	FAIR	POOR
850	725	625	450	350	150

1874 Sharps

High-quality replica of first Sharps chambered for metallic cartridges. Chamberings include .45-70, .45-90, .45-110, .45-120, .50-70 and .50-90. Several variations available including Sporting Standard Sporting, Cavalry Rifle, Cavalry Carbine, Sporting Deluxe, Sporting Extra Deluxe, Silhouette Standard, Silhouette Deluxe, Boss, Business Rifle, Buffalo, Billy Dixon, Long Range, Quigley, Creedmore #2 and Competition Standard. Prices given are for Standard Sporting model.

NIB	EXC.	V.G.	GOOD	FAIR	POOR
1100	850	600	425	300	200

1873 Trapdoor Springfield

Replica of famous single-shot cartridge rifle chambered in .45-70. Several variations available including Standard Rifle, Standard Carbine, Officer's Model and Long Range Model. Prices given are for Standard Rifle. **NOTE:** Add 30 percent for deluxe models.

NIB	EXC.	V.G.	GOOD	FAIR	POOR
1100	850	600	425	300	200

Kodiak Mark IV Express Rifle

Side-by-side double rifle chambered for .45-70 cartridge.

NIB	EXC.	V.G.	GOOD	FAIR	POOR
4500	3750	3000	2000	900	300

Pedersoli Lightning Rifle

Updated replica of Model 1883 Colt Lightning Magazine Rifle. Pump action with magazine disconnector. Chambered for .44-40 and .45 Colt.

NIB	EXC.	V.G.	GOOD	FAIR	POOR
1100	850	600	425	300	200

	NIB	EXC.	V.G.	GOOD	FAIR	POOR

SHOTGUNS

Double Percussion Shotgun

Side-by-side muzzle-loading shotgun in 10-, 12- and 20-gauge. Interchangeable chokes. Camo models available. Prices given are for basic version in 12-gauge.

NIB	EXC.	V.G.	GOOD	FAIR	POOR
650	550	475	300	175	125

Coach Shotgun

Side-by-side 12-gauge percussion shotgun, with 20" barrels. Discontinued.

NIB	EXC.	V.G.	GOOD	FAIR	POOR
600	525	450	275	150	125

Mortimer Shotgun

Recreation of 12-gauge Fowlers. Made circa 1830-1850 by H. W Mortimer & Son of London. Percussion and flint versions available.

NIB	EXC.	V.G.	GOOD	FAIR	POOR
1100	850	600	425	300	200

MODERN MUZZLELOADERS

Denali

In-line .50-caliber muzzle-loader, with lever-operated break-open action. Walnut/blue or camo/blue finish. **NOTE:** Add 15 percent for camo.

NIB	EXC.	V.G.	GOOD	FAIR	POOR
380	350	275	200	100	50

Brutus 94

In-line .50-caliber muzzle-loader. Blued/composite, blued/synthetic or stainless/blued/walnut finish. **NOTE:** Add 15 percent for camo.

NIB	EXC.	V.G.	GOOD	FAIR	POOR
350	300	200	125	100	75

Brutus Ovation

In-line .50-caliber muzzle-loader, with interchangeable barrels. Developed in cooperation with Mid-Western Outdoor Specialties and so marked. One-piece stock. Blued/hardwood or blued/camo finish. **NOTE:** Add 15 percent for camo.

NIB	EXC.	V.G.	GOOD	FAIR	POOR
350	300	200	125	100	75

Rolling Block Percussion Rifle

.50-caliber muzzle-loading version of Remington rolling block rifle. Blued/hardwoods or blued/camo finish.

NIB	EXC.	V.G.	GOOD	FAIR	POOR
350	300	200	125	100	75

PERAZZI
Brescia, Italy

Company founded in 1957. During 1970s, Ithaca and Winchester imported and sold Perazzi shotguns. Perazzi has now taken over its own importation and distribution in United States, with creation of Perazzi USA, Inc. Many shooters consider Perazzi to be finest currently produced shotgun in the world. Perazzi has an extensive variety of models to choose from. In addition, each model may be available in different grades. These grades are based on type of finish, engraving and wood quality. Vast majority of Perazzi shotguns that are sold in this country are Standard Grade guns. According to Perazzi USA, these Standard Grade guns account for approximately 98 percent of North American sales. Therefore, it is unlikely that shooter or collector will encounter high-grade Perazzi guns. It should be pointed out that in some models no Extra Grade or Extra Gold Grade shotguns have ever been sold in United States. For benefit of reader, an approximate description of each grade follows. It is a general description because Perazzi customer may order practically any combination of finishes or engraving patterns he or she desires. Use this list as a general guide. It is suggested that anyone wanting to know more about Perazzi guns buy a copy of Karl Lippard's book, Perazzi Shotguns. He can be reached at P.O. Box 60719, Colorado Springs, CO.

OUT-OF-PRODUCTION SHOTGUNS

NOTE: Very high premiums on early SCO and higher grades.

COMP 1-SB TRAP (Standard Grade)

Single barrel trap gun in 12-gauge only, with 32" or 34" vent rib barrel.

NIB	EXC.	V.G.	GOOD	FAIR	POOR
—	2500	1750	1000	750	500

	NIB	EXC.	V.G.	GOOD	FAIR	POOR

COMP 1-TRAP (Standard Grade)

Over/under version of above model.

	NIB	EXC.	V.G.	GOOD	FAIR	POOR
	—	4800	4000	3000	2250	500

Light Game Model (Standard Grade)

Offered in 12-gauge, with 27.5" vent rib barrel. Trigger group not detachable. Produced between 1972 and 1974.

	—	6250	4750	3000	1400	500

MT-6 Model (Standard Grade)

Offered in 12-gauge, with tapered vent rib. Trigger group not removable. Discontinued in 1983.

	—	3800	3000	2000	1000	400

MX3

Model discontinued in 1988. Available in 12-gauge only for single barrel trap, over/under trap, combination trap, skeet and sporting configurations. **NOTE:** Add 50 percent for Combination Trap Guns.

Standard Grade

	—	3500	3000	2250	1750	400

SC3 Grade

	—	5000	4000	3000	2200	500

SCO Grade

	—	6500	5500	4000	2500	500

Gold Grade

	10000	8500	5900	2700	—	700

Grand American Special

Introduced in 1988. Features high ramped rib similar to MX3 model. Fore-end was grooved. Discontinued in 1991. Offered in single barrel trap, combination trap and over/under trap configurations.

Standard Grade

	—	5250	4250	3500	2000	700

SC3 Grade

	—	6500	5250	4500	3000	700

SCO Grade

	—	8000	6500	5500	3750	700

Gold Grade

	—	10000	7500	6000	4000	700

SCO Grade w/Sideplates

	—	13500	10000	7500	6000	700

Gold Grade w/Sideplates

	—	15000	12000	8500	6500	700

SHO Model

Over/under sidelock model available in 12-gauge only, in both Type 1 and Type 2 configurations. Type 1 does not have rebounding firing pins and worth approximately 50 percent less than; Type 2 models that are fitted with rebounding firing pins. No parts available in this country or at the factory for Type 1 guns. An expert appraisal recommended for this model due to its unique features.

SHO model features silver finish with fine scroll engraving, with game scenes to customer's specifications. Select walnut stock built to customer's dimensions, with fine line checkering. Custom built shotgun. Special order only. Sky's the limit.

DHO Model

Side-by-side shotgun offered in 12-gauge only. Has full sidelocks and silver receiver finish. Scroll and game scene engraving of same quality as SHO Model. Fancy walnut stock, with fine line checkering. An expert appraisal recommended for this model due to its unique

	NIB	EXC.	V.G.	GOOD	FAIR	POOR

features. Special order only. Sky's the limit.

DHO Extra Gold

Available in any gauge and barrel length combination. Only finest presentation walnut and checkering. Totally custom built shotgun. Special order only. Sky's the limit.

RECENT PRODUCTION SHOTGUNS

MX9

Introduced in 1993. Features removable inserts on rib to adjust point of impact; walnut stock with adjustable comb. Offered in 12-gauge with 32" or 34" barrel. Screw-in chokes in trap configuration and single barrels in Trap/Combo models. Competition version also offered with unique vent rib inserts to correct for point of impact. Trigger group removable. Available in several different grades of ornamentation.

Standard Grade

	NIB	EXC.	V.G.	GOOD	FAIR	POOR
—	6500	5000	3500	1800	700	

SC3 Grade

	NIB	EXC.	V.G.	GOOD	FAIR	POOR
—	11500	6000	5000	3000	700	

SCO Grade

	NIB	EXC.	V.G.	GOOD	FAIR	POOR
—	18000	8000	7000	3500	7000	

Standard Grade Trap Combo

	NIB	EXC.	V.G.	GOOD	FAIR	POOR
—	9500	6500	5000	3500	900	

MX10

Introduced in 1993. Single Barrel Trap models feature different method of rib height and pattern adjustment. Has adjustable stock. Available in 12-gauge, with 32" or 34" barrels. Trap/Combo models offered in 12-gauge, with 29.5" or 31.5" over/under barrels with 32" or 34" single barrel. Chokes are fixed. Competition models offered in 12- and 20-gauge with choice of 29.5" or 31.5" barrel for 12-gauge and 29.5" barrel for 20-gauge. Ventilated rib height adjustable as is comb position on stock. Trigger removable.

Standard Grade

	NIB	EXC.	V.G.	GOOD	FAIR	POOR
—	8250	7000	6000	4300	700	

SC3 Grade

	NIB	EXC.	V.G.	GOOD	FAIR	POOR
—	10000	8500	7000	5200	700	

SCO Grade

	NIB	EXC.	V.G.	GOOD	FAIR	POOR
—	13500	11000	8500	6750	700	

Standard Grade Combo Model

	NIB	EXC.	V.G.	GOOD	FAIR	POOR
—	15000	13000	10500	5000	700	

TM I Special Standard Grade

Basic single barrel Perazzi. Trap model offered in 12-gauge, with 32" or 34" barrel. Trigger adjustable.

	NIB	EXC.	V.G.	GOOD	FAIR	POOR
—	4000	2000	1250	850	700	

TMX Special

Similar to TM I Special, with select walnut.

Standard Grade

	NIB	EXC.	V.G.	GOOD	FAIR	POOR
—	5000	4200	2700	1900	700	

SCO Grade

	NIB	EXC.	V.G.	GOOD	FAIR	POOR
—	8000	6000	5000	2100	700	

MX8 Special

Features low contour vent rib, adjustable trigger and grooved fore-end. **NOTE:** Some SCO engraving patterns on early models have sold in $30,000 to $45,000 price range, depending on engraver. Get an expert appraisal. Beware of counterfeits.

Standard Grade

	NIB	EXC.	V.G.	GOOD	FAIR	POOR
—	5500	4000	3000	2000	700	

SC3 Grade

	NIB	EXC.	V.G.	GOOD	FAIR	POOR
—	7500	5500	3800	2500	700	

	NIB	EXC.	V.G.	GOOD	FAIR	POOR
SCO Grade						
	—	13000	10500	8000	5000	700
Standard Grade Trap Combo						
		7500	5000	3500	2000	700

MX8/20

First introduced in 1993. Features removable trigger group. Available in 20-gauge only. Choice of 27.5", 28.375", 29.5" flat ventilated rib barrels. Choice of fixed or screw-in chokes on sporting model. Stock custom made to customer's dimensions, with beavertail fore-end.

Standard Grade					
10000	8500	6500	4800	2000	—
SC3 Grade					
16000	14500	12000	7500	3000	—
SCO Grade					
30000	24000	17500	12000	5000	—

MX8/20-8/20C

Introduced in 1993. Offered in 20-gauge, with 26" or 27.625" vent rib barrels. Trigger group removable. Stock is high-grade walnut custom made to customers' specifications. Fore-end is round. MX8/20 supplied with fixed chokes; MX8/20C has 5 screw-in choke tubes. **NOTE:** Add $400 for MX8/20C values.

Standard Grade					
10500	9000	7000	5000	2250	—
SC3 Grade					
16500	13500	10000	8000	4000	—
SCO Grade					
32000	25000	20000	14000	7000	—

MX7 Standard Grade

Introduced in 1993. Over/under trap offered in 12-gauge, with 29.5" or 31.5" over/under barrels with either 32" or 34" single barrel. Has a non-renewable trigger group feathering fixed coil spring trigger mechanism. Trigger is selective and works in conjunction with safety catch. Vent rib is ramped on Combo Trap model. Walnut stock custom made to customer's dimensions.

—	4500	3200	2500	1750	700

MX7C Standard Grade

Introduced in 1993. Offered in 12-gauge, with non-renewable trigger group. Has coil spring mechanism, fully selective in conjunction with safety. Offered in 27.5", 29.5" or 31.5" flat vent rib barrels. Screw-in chokes are standard. Walnut stock custom made to customer's dimensions. Fore-end is beavertail.

—	5500	4000	3000	2000	700

DB81 Special

Offered in 12-gauge only. Features high ramped ventilated rib. Trigger adjustable, with internal selector. Barrel lengths 29.5" or 31.5". **NOTE:** Add $1,000 for two fore-ends and two triggers for Trap/Combo models.

Standard Grade					
—	8700	6500	5200	2500	700
SC3 Grade					
—	11000	8000	7000	3500	700
SCO Grade					
—	17500	12500	10000	6500	700

COMPETITION MODELS

Competition versions are over/under shotguns in trap, skeet, pigeon and sporting models. Stock dimensions based on particular model chosen. Trap models feature trap stock dimensions and forearm designed for that purpose. Other models have their own particular specifications. However, prices are based on a common style referred to by Perazzi as Competition. Thus, all models within this group are priced the same regardless of specific type.

	NIB	EXC.	V.G.	GOOD	FAIR	POOR

Mirage Special Standard Grade

Features adjustable trigger. Available in 12-gauge, with choice of 27.5", 28.375", 29.5" or 31.5" ventilated rib barrels.

	NIB	EXC.	V.G.	GOOD	FAIR	POOR
	—	5500	3750	2500	1100	700

Mirage Special Sporting Standard Grade

Similar to Mirage Special, with external trigger selection and screw-in chokes. Offered in 12-gauge only. Choice of 27.5", 28.375" or 29.5" vent rib barrels.

	NIB	EXC.	V.G.	GOOD	FAIR	POOR
	—	4500	3250	2500	1100	700

Mirage Special Sporting Classic Standard Grade

Features same basic specifications as Mirage Special Sporting. Addition of scroll border on receiver and trigger guard. Wood is slightly higher quality. Offered in 12-gauge only, with 27.5", 28.375" or 29.5" vent rib barrels.

	NIB	EXC.	V.G.	GOOD	FAIR	POOR
	—	4500	3250	2500	1100	700

Mirage MX8 Standard Grade

	NIB	EXC.	V.G.	GOOD	FAIR	POOR
	—	5800	4250	3000	1500	700

SCO Model

Similar to MX8. Offered only in 12-gauge. Barrel lengths from 27.5" to 31.5". Trigger adjustable instead of removable.

	NIB	EXC.	V.G.	GOOD	FAIR	POOR
	—	10500	6000	4500	3000	700

Mirage Special 4-Gauge Set

Similar to Mirage Special in appearance and specifications. Fitted with four barrel sets with 27.62" barrels in 12-, 20-, 28-gauge and .410 bore. **NOTE:** 28.37" barrels add $2,000; 29.5" barrels add $3,000.

Standard Grade

	NIB	EXC.	V.G.	GOOD	FAIR	POOR
	—	—	10000	7000	4500	700

SC3 Grade

	NIB	EXC.	V.G.	GOOD	FAIR	POOR
	—	21000	15000	10000	7500	700

SCO Grade

	NIB	EXC.	V.G.	GOOD	FAIR	POOR
	—	28000	19000	12500	8500	700

MX12/12C

Offered in 12-gauge only, with 26.75" or 27.5" vent rib barrels. Single-selective trigger nonrefillable. Walnut stock fitted with schnabel fore-end. Receiver has light-scroll engraved border. MX12 supplied with fixed chokes; MX12C fitted with 5 screw-in choke tubes. **NOTE:** Add $400 to MX12 prices to get MX12C values.

Standard Grade

	NIB	EXC.	V.G.	GOOD	FAIR	POOR
	11000	9000	6800	4500	2000	1000

SC3 Grade

	NIB	EXC.	V.G.	GOOD	FAIR	POOR
	18000	15000	12000	9000	5000	1200

SCO Grade

	NIB	EXC.	V.G.	GOOD	FAIR	POOR
	30000	26000	20000	15000	10000	3000

MX20/20C

Offered in 20-gauge. Features non-removable trigger group. Frame smaller than 12-gauge. Offered with 26" or 27.5" vent rib barrels. MX20 has fixed chokes; MX20C supplied with 5 screw-in choke tubes. **NOTE:** Add $400 to MX20 prices to get MX20C values.

Standard Grade

	NIB	EXC.	V.G.	GOOD	FAIR	POOR
	11500	9000	6800	4500	2000	1000

SC3 Grade

	NIB	EXC.	V.G.	GOOD	FAIR	POOR
	18500	15000	12000	9000	5000	1200

SCO Grade

	NIB	EXC.	V.G.	GOOD	FAIR	POOR
	32000	25000	20000	13500	7000	3000

NIB	EXC.	V.G.	GOOD	FAIR	POOR

MX28 and MX410

Introduced in 1993, these two models feature a non-removable trigger group and special small frame for each. MX28, .28-gauge weighs about 5.5 lbs.; MX410, .410 bore weighs slightly less. Both supplied with fixed chokes, flat ribs, custom made stocks and round foreends. Each model offered with choice of 26" or 27.5" barrels. Both MX28 and MX410 are priced the same.

Standard Grade

21000	16000	12000	9000	6000	1000

SCO Grade

42000	36000	29000	20000	10000	3000

MX-2000

In 12-, 20-, 28-gauge or .410 bore in several grades and styles. Standard features include fixed or removable trigger group, choke tubes or fixed chokes, fixed or adjustable ventilated rib and comb. Prices shown are for Game, Sporting, Pigeon, Skeet and Trap models. Add 50 percent for Gold grades, which have higher levels of engraving, gold inlays and wood.

8750	7750	6000	4200	3000	1000

PERRY & GODDARD
Renwick Arms Co.
New York, New York

Derringer

.44-caliber single-shot spur trigger pistol, with 2" octagonal barrel. Blued or silver-plated, with walnut or gutta-percha grips. Barrel may be swiveled so either end can serve as chamber and marked "Double Header/ E.S. Renwick". Produced in limited quantities during 1860s.

—	—	21000	9400	1500	500

PERRY PATENT FIREARMS CO.
Newark, New Jersey

Perry Single-Shot Pistol

.52-caliber breech-loading percussion pistol, with 6" round barrel. Blued, with walnut grips. Barrel marked "Perry Patent Firearms Co./Newark, N.J." Approximately 200 made between 1854 and 1856 in two styles.

1st Type

Long contoured trigger guard opening lever.

—	—	4950	1900	500	200

2nd Type

S curved shorter trigger guard. Automatic primer feed that protrudes from butt.

—	—	4700	1650	500	200

Perry Carbine

.54-caliber breech-loading percussion carbine, with 20.75" barrel and half-length walnut stock secured by one barrel band. Blued, with case hardened lock. Approximately 200 were made.

—	27500	13000	8250	3600	1000

PERUGINI & VISINI
Brescia, Italy

Arms by this maker were imported by W.L. Moore of Westlake Village, California.

Liberty Model

Side-by-side 12-, 20-, 28-gauge and .410 bore shotgun, with 28" barrels. Anson & Deeley action with double Purdy lock. Blued overall, with checkered walnut stock.

7500	6000	4500	2500	1250	750

Classic Model

12- or 20-gauge double-barrel shotgun, with Holland & Holland-style sidelock and double Purdy lock. Barrels are 28". Single trigger and automatic ejectors. Sidelocks and mounts engraved and blued. Well figured checkered walnut stock.

15000	11500	9500	4000	2000	1000

	NIB	EXC.	V.G.	GOOD	FAIR	POOR

Bolt-Action Rifle

Mauser-type bolt-action rifle. Available in a variety of chamberings, with 24" or 26" barrels. Sights not furnished. Well figured checkered walnut stock.

NIB	EXC.	V.G.	GOOD	FAIR	POOR
6500	4250	3000	1500	900	500

Deluxe Bolt-Action Rifle

As above, with first quality walnut stocks and case.

NIB	EXC.	V.G.	GOOD	FAIR	POOR
7500	5000	3500	1500	1000	600

Eagle Single-Shot

Anson & Deeley single-shot rifle. Fitted with either 24" or 26" barrels, open sights, automatic ejector and adjustable trigger. Stock of checkered walnut.

NIB	EXC.	V.G.	GOOD	FAIR	POOR
7500	4250	4000	1500	1000	600

Boxlock Express Rifle

Anson & Deeley action double-barrel rifle. Chambered for .444 Marlin or 9.3x74R cartridges. Barrel length 24". Fitted with express sights. Double triggers and automatic ejectors. Receiver case hardened. Barrels and mounts blued. Checkered walnut stock.

NIB	EXC.	V.G.	GOOD	FAIR	POOR
7000	5500	3750	2000	1500	500

Magnum Over/Under

Anson & Deeley action over/under rifle. Available in .375 H&H and .458 Win. Magnum. Barrels are 24" and fitted with express sights. Double triggers and automatic ejectors. Receiver and barrels blued. Stock checkered walnut.

NIB	EXC.	V.G.	GOOD	FAIR	POOR
7000	5500	3750	2000	1500	500

Super Express Rifle

H&H-style sidelock double-barrel rifle, with 24" barrel. Fitted with express sights. Available in a variety of chamberings. Receiver and sidelocks either case hardened or bright finish. Fully engraved. Checkered walnut stock.

NIB	EXC.	V.G.	GOOD	FAIR	POOR
20000	17500	13000	10000	6500	1000

Victoria Side-by-Side Rifle

Similar to Boxlock Express Rifle. Chambered for .30-06, 7x65R or 9.3x74R cartridges. Either 24" or 26" barrels were available. Double triggers and automatic ejectors. Blued, with minimal engraving. Stock checkered walnut.

NIB	EXC.	V.G.	GOOD	FAIR	POOR
6500	5250	4000	3000	1500	750

Selous Side-by-Side Rifle

First quality double-barrel express rifle, with 24" or 26" barrels. Fully detachable H&H-style sidelocks, double triggers and automatic ejectors. Fully engraved, with well figured checkered walnut stocks.

NIB	EXC.	V.G.	GOOD	FAIR	POOR
22500	17500	12500	6000	3000	1500

PETTINGILL C. S.

New Haven, Connecticut
Rogers, Spencer & Co.
Willowvale, New York

Pocket Revolver

Hammerless double-action .31-caliber percussion revolver, with 4" octagonal barrel. Frame of brass or iron. Blued barrel. Grips of oil finished walnut. First and Second Models marked "Pettingill's Patent 1856" as well as "T.K. Austin". Third Model marked "Pettengill Patent 1856" and "Raymond and Robitaille Patented 1858". Approximately 400 manufactured in late 1850s and early 1860s.

1st Model

Brass frame.

NIB	EXC.	V.G.	GOOD	FAIR	POOR
—	—	2750	2000	1100	400

2nd Model

Iron frame.

NIB	EXC.	V.G.	GOOD	FAIR	POOR
—	—	1650	1000	660	200

3rd Model

Iron frame and improved action.

NIB	EXC.	V.G.	GOOD	FAIR	POOR
—	—	1400	800	450	200

	NIB	EXC.	V.G.	GOOD	FAIR	POOR

Navy Revolver

As above in .34-caliber, with 4.5" barrel and 6-shot cylinder. Frame of iron, blued overall and grips of walnut. Model marked "Pettengill's Patent 1856" and "Raymond & Robitaille Patented 1858". Approximately 900 manufactured in late 1850s and early 1860s.

—	—	3500	1900	775	250	

Army Revolver

As above in .44-caliber. Fitted with 7.5" barrel. Frame of iron case hardened, octagonal barrel blued, grips of oil finished walnut. Early production models marked as Navy models, while later production examples marked "Petingill's Patent 1856, pat'd July 22, 1856 and July 27, 1858". Believed 3,400 made in 1860s. **NOTE:** Some examples will be found with government inspector's marks and worth approximately 25 percent more.

—	—	4950	2250	1650	500	

PFANNL, FRANCOIS
Krems, Austria

Erika

4.25mm semi-automatic pistol, with hinged barrel assembly. Barrel length 1.5" or 2.25". Grips marked "Erika". Approximately 3,500 made between 1912 and 1926.

—	3000	2500	1750	900	500	

PGM PRECISION
France

Model PGM

Highly sophisticated semi-automatic rifle. Designed and built on modular component system. Barrel change is fast. Available calibers .308 Win., .300 Savage, 7mm-08, .243 and .22-250. Match grade barrel length 23.4". Fully adjustable trigger and buttstock. Adjustable bipod. Five-round magazine standard. Weight about 13 lbs.

13500	9000	7000	3500	1750	1000

PHILLIPS & RODGERS INC.
Huntsville, Texas

Medusa Model 47

Introduced in 1996. Unique multi-caliber revolver. Designed to chamber, fire and extract almost any cartridge. Using 9mm, .357 or .38 cartridges—total of about 25 different calibers. Barrel length 2.5", 3", 4", 5" or 6". Rubber grips and interchangeable front sights. Finish is matte blue. Rarely if ever encountered. Discontinued.

1100	850	550	450	275	150

Ruger 50 Conversion

Conversion executed on a new revolver converts .44 Magnum Ruger into .50 Action Express. Stainless steel or blue, with 5-shot cylinder. Barrel length 6.5".

1000	800	550	450	275	150

PHOENIX
Lowell, Massachusetts

Pocket Pistol

Rare .25 ACP semi-automatic pistol, with 2.25" barrel and 6-round magazine. Receiver and slide blued. Grips are hard rubber. Manufactured during 1920s.

—	950	700	350	200	100	

PHOENIX ARMS
Ontario, California

HP22

Pocket-size semi-automatic pistol chambered for .22 LR cartridge. Barrel length 3". Magazine capacity 11 rounds. Offered in bright chrome or polished blue finish. Black checkered grips. Top of gun fitted with vent rib. Overall length 4.1"; weight about 20 oz.

175	125	90	65	40	25

HP25

Same as above. Chambered for .25 ACP cartridge. Magazine capacity 10 rounds.

175	125	90	65	40	25

	NIB	EXC.	V.G.	GOOD	FAIR	POOR

HP22/HP25 Target

Conversion kit to convert HP22/HP25 into target pistol. Kit includes extended vent rib barrel and convertible 10-round magazine. Finish either blue or nickel.

100	75	60	40	30	25

Raven

Small pocket-size semi-automatic pistol chambered for .25 ACP cartridge. Magazine capacity 6 rounds. Barrel length 2.4", with fixed sights. Offered in 3 finishes: bright chrome, satin nickel or polished blue. Grips either ivory, pink pearl or black. Overall length 4.8"; weight about 15 oz.

175	125	90	65	40	25

PHOENIX ARMS CO.
Liege, Belgium
See—Robar and de Kirkhave

PICKERT, FRIEDRICH
Arminius Waffenfabrik
Zella-Mehlis, Germany

Firm produced revolvers bearing trade name "Arminius". Revolvers manufactured by Pickert are of double-action type, with or without exposed hammers. Some models fitted with ejectors, while others have removable cylinders. Calibers and barrel lengths vary. After WWII, trade name was acquired by Hermann Wiehauch.

Arminius 7.65mm

Five-shot concealed hammer revolver in 7.65mm caliber. Arminius head on grips.

—	350	225	175	125	90

Arminius Single-Shot Target Pistol

Single-shot target pistol chambered for .22-caliber cartridge. Some built under name PICKERT. Arminius name seen on frame.

—	900	700	600	400	300

Pickert Revolver

Similar to Arminius revolver, with half-round half-octagon barrel. Chambered for 7.54mm cartridge.

—	275	225	175	150	100

PIEPER, HENRI & NICOLAS
Liege, Belgium

Originally founded by Henri Pieper in 1859. Company was reorganized in 1898, when his son Nicolas assumed control. Firm perhaps best known for a series of semi-automatic pistols that are listed below. Pieper also manufactured a bewildering variety of drillings, combination guns, cape guns, rook rifles, salon rifles and even volley guns. These guns must be evaluated on their own merits and their value strictly a function of what the market will bear.

Pieper Model 1907

6.35 or 7.65mm semi-automatic pistol. Featuring hinged barrel assembly 2.5" in length. Receiver and barrel blued. Grips hard rubber with firm's trademark cast in them. Model 1907 variation does not have hinged barrel assembly. Model 1908 also known as "Basculant"; Model 1918 as "Demontant".

—	250	150	125	100	75

Model 1908/Basculant

Tipping barrel pistol chambered for 6.35mm Auto cartridge. Similar in appearance to Model 1907, with several improvements. Front end of barrel retained by a pivot bolt. Recoil spring rod had a hook that engaged lug on slide.

—	275	175	150	125	100

Pieper Bayard Revolver

In competition with Nagant gas seal revolver, Henri Pieper developed a superior design. Revolvers of this type have 5" barrels and chambered for 8mm cartridges. First model had automatic ejection system; second utilized swing-out cylinder. Standard finish blued. Checkered hard rubber grips.

—	1000	750	500	250	100

	NIB	EXC.	V.G.	GOOD	FAIR	POOR

Legia

Patterned after that of Browning. Chambered for 6.35mm cartridge. Standard magazine holds 6 rounds; 10-round available.

	NIB	EXC.	V.G.	GOOD	FAIR	POOR
—	250	150	125	100	75	

Bayard

6.35, 7.65 or 9mm short semi-automatic pistol, with 2.5" barrel. Standard magazine capacity 6 rounds. Slide stamped "Anciens Etablissement Pieper Liege, Belgium".

	NIB	EXC.	V.G.	GOOD	FAIR	POOR
—	250	150	125	100	75	

PIETTA, F.LLI
Gussago, Italy

This is a manufacturer of current and replica firearms, best known for its single-action revolvers. These models are imported by Cimarron, Taylor's and Co., Heritage, Cabela's, Dixie Gun Works and Navy Arms. Refer to these importers under their individual listings.

PILSEN, ZBROVKA
Pilsen, Czechoslovakia

Pocket Pistol

Essentially a Model 1910 Browning semi-automatic pistol, without grip safety. Pistol was 7.65mm caliber and had 3.5" barrel, with 6-round magazine. Slide marked "Akciova Spolecnost drive Skodovny zavody Zbrovka Plzen". Standard finish blued. Grips hard rubber. Manufactured during 1920s.

	NIB	EXC.	V.G.	GOOD	FAIR	POOR
—	300	200	150	125	100	

PIOTTI
Brescia, Italy

Italian gun making firm located in Gardone Val Trompia in province of Brescia. Shotguns are hand crafted and limited to a few each year. Each gun made to individual specifications. Many consider them one of the best double shotguns made in the world today. Actions are either Anson & Deeley boxlock or Holland & Holland sidelock. Several features offered on these shotguns at no additional cost: type of stock and forearm, barrel length and chokes, rib, action shape and finish.

Other features are considered extra cost options and will affect value of gun. These are: single triggers, detachable sidelocks, automatic safety, recoil pads, upgraded wood, engraving and multi-gauge sets. With exception of a few grades, Piotti guns are available in 10-, 12-, 16-, 20-, and 28-gauge and .410 bore. Depending on gauge, barrel lengths are from 25" to 32".

Model Piuma (BSEE)

Firm's standard boxlock offering. Available in 12-gauge to .410 bore. Features ejectors and scalloped frame. Fine scroll and rosette engraving standard. **NOTE:** Around serial number 9000 or 1989, Piotti began building Model BSEE to same standards as King Model. Therefore, guns below serial number 9000 deduct about 40 percent from prices listed.

NIB	EXC.	V.G.	GOOD	FAIR	POOR
14250	10500	7500	6000	4000	700

Westlake Model

Piotti's second quality model. Features case colored receiver, with gold line work. Offered in 12-, 16- and 20-gauge. Discontinued in 1989.

NIB	EXC.	V.G.	GOOD	FAIR	POOR
13000	10500	8000	6000	3500	700

Over/Under Gun

Features King 2 engraving, which has light border scroll with 10 percent coverage. Custom engraving patterns available at extra charge.

NIB	EXC.	V.G.	GOOD	FAIR	POOR
44750	33500	25000	17500	10000	1000

Model King No. I

Features sidelock with fine line scroll engraving, with full coverage. Gold crown inlaid on top lever prior to 1989. H&H or Purdey-style engraving. Select walnut, with hand checkering standard. Chambered from 10-gauge to .410 bore.

NIB	EXC.	V.G.	GOOD	FAIR	POOR
33000	25000	18000	12500	8000	2700

Monte Carlo Model

Less expensive version of King Model. Had H&H or Purdey-style engraving. Discontinued in 1989. Upgraded and became part of King Model. This occurred around serial number 9000.

NIB	EXC.	V.G.	GOOD	FAIR	POOR
14000	10000	7000	6000	3500	700

	NIB	EXC.	V.G.	GOOD	FAIR	POOR

Model King Extra

Similar to King No. 1, with addition of a number of engraving styles from English to game scenes with gold inlays. Because of the wide variety of engraving patterns offered, it is advisable to secure a qualified appraisal before purchase.

Model Lunik

Fitted with Holland & Holland sidelocks. Engraving is Renaissance-style relief cut scroll engraving. Gold crown inlaid on top lever. Offered in gauges from 10-gauge to .410 bore.

	33000	25000	18000	12000	7000	1700

Model Monaco

Sidelock model features all the best Piotti has to offer. Extra attention paid to hand work and fitting. Only finest European hardwoods used. Available in 10-gauge to 410 bore. Offered with three different types of engraving designated No. 1, No. 2 and No. 4.

No. 1 or No. 2

	42000	35000	28000	19500	12000	2000

No. 3

	46000	40000	32000	22000	13000	2000

No. 4

	56000	45000	36000	28000	—	—

PLAINFIELD MACHINE CO.
Dunelien, New Jersey

Super Enforcer

Cut-down version of U.S. M1 Carbine, with 12" barrel and pistol-grip. Finish blued. Stocks walnut.

	—	600	475	375	225	100

M1 Carbine

Commercial reproduction of U.S. M1 Carbine. Finish blued. Walnut stock.

	—	400	350	225	150	100

M1 Paratrooper Carbine

As above, with telescoping wire buttstock and walnut fore-end.

	—	475	375	275	200	125

PLAINFIELD ORDNANCE CO.
Middlesex, New Jersey

Stainless steel .22-caliber semi-automatic pistol, with 10-shot magazine and 1" barrel. Also available in .25 ACP. Conversion kits were available.

Model 71

Conversion Kit

	—	50	40	30	25	20

.22 or .25 Caliber Pistol

	—	175	125	100	75	50

Model 72

As above, with alloy frame.

	—	175	125	100	75	50

PLANT'S MANUFACTURING CO.
New Haven, Connecticut

Army Model Revolver

Large single-action revolver. Chambered for .42-caliber cup-primed cartridge that loads from front of cylinder. Barrel length 6" and octagonal form with rib. Frame made of either brass or iron. Finish blued, with walnut or rosewood grips. Interchangeable percussion cylinders also made for these revolvers. If present, values would be increased approximately 30 percent. Revolver was marketed by Merwin & Bray. Approximately 1,500 of 1st and 2nd Models manufactured; 10,000 of 3rd Model in 1860s.

	NIB	EXC.	V.G.	GOOD	FAIR	POOR

1st Model Brass Frame

Marked "Plant's Mfg. Co. New Haven, Ct." on barrel, "M & B" on side of frame and "Patented July 12, 1859" on cylinder. Approximately 100 manufactured.

	NIB	EXC.	V.G.	GOOD	FAIR	POOR
	—	—	2750	1025	700	150

1st Model Iron Frame

As above, with iron frame. Approximately 500 made.

	NIB	EXC.	V.G.	GOOD	FAIR	POOR
	—	—	2750	1025	700	300

2nd Model Rounded Brass Frame

Distinguished by markings "Merwin & Bray, New York" on frame and patent date "July 21, 1863". Approximately 300 made.

	NIB	EXC.	V.G.	GOOD	FAIR	POOR
	—	—	3600	1400	700	300

2nd Model Iron Frame

As above, with iron frame.

	NIB	EXC.	V.G.	GOOD	FAIR	POOR
	—	—	2500	825	500	300

3rd Model

As above, with flat brass frame.

	NIB	EXC.	V.G.	GOOD	FAIR	POOR
	—	—	1900	1300	450	150

Pocket Revolver

Similar to Army model described above except chambered for .30-caliber cartridges. Barrel length 3.5", five-shot cylinder. Frame normally silver plated, barrel and cylinder blued and grips of rosewood or walnut. Model encountered with a variety of retailer's markings: Eagle Arms Co., New York, "Reynolds, Plant & Hotchkiss, New Haven, Ct.", and "Merwin & Bray Firearms Co., N.Y." Approximately 20,000 were made.

	NIB	EXC.	V.G.	GOOD	FAIR	POOR
	—	—	1100	600	250	100

POINTER
Hopkins & Allen
Norwich, Connecticut

Single-Shot Derringer

Unmarked Hopkins & Allen single-shot pistol stamped "Pointer" on barrel. Barrel length 2.75", caliber .22, frame of nickel-plated brass. Barrel swings sideways for loading. Bird's-head walnut grips. Believed about 2,500 made between 1870 and 1890.

	NIB	EXC.	V.G.	GOOD	FAIR	POOR
	—	—	450	375	250	100

POLY-TECHNOLOGIES, INC./POLY-TECH
China

SKS

Semi-automatic rifle. Chambered for 7.62x39mm cartridge, with 20.5" barrel and 10-shot fixed magazine. Based on Soviet Siminov carbine. Finish blued. Stock and hand guard made of Chinese hardwood.

	NIB	EXC.	V.G.	GOOD	FAIR	POOR
	425	375	200	150	100	50

AKS-762

Semi-automatic version of Chinese-type 56 Assault rifle. Chambered for 7.62x39mm cartridge, with 16.5" barrel. Furnished with 20-round magazine and Chinese bayonet. Finish blued. Stock is hardwood. **NOTE:** Add $250 folding stock model; 15 percent for milled receiver.

	NIB	EXC.	V.G.	GOOD	FAIR	POOR
	950	800	675	500	350	200

AK-47/S

Chambered for 7.62x39 cartridge. **NOTE:** Add $350 folding stock model; $15 with Soviet-style bayonet.

	NIB	EXC.	V.G.	GOOD	FAIR	POOR
	1350	1150	850	750	600	400

M-14/S

Reproduction of U.S. M14 rifle. Chambered for 7.62mm cartridge, with 22" barrel and 20-round magazine. Finish blued. Stock is hardwood.

	NIB	EXC.	V.G.	GOOD	FAIR	POOR
	1000	875	675	500	350	200

POND, LUCIUS, W.
Worchester, Massachusetts

Pocket Revolver

Single-action spur trigger .32-caliber revolver, with octagonal barrels of 4", 5" or 6" length. Barrel top strap and cylinder pivots upwards for loading. Made with either brass or iron frames. A screwdriver fitted in butt. Revolvers were an infringement of Rollin White's patent, they were discontinued. Some revolvers found with inscription "Manuf'd. for Smith & Wesson Pat'd. April 5, 1855". These examples worth approximately 20 percent more than values listed.

Brass Framed Revolver

—	—	1100	875	350	100

Iron Framed Revolver

—	—	1000	775	300	75

Separate Chamber Revolver

To avoid Rollin White patent, this revolver chambered for .22- or .32-caliber rimfire cartridges that fit into separate steel chamber inserts that can be removed from front of cylinder for loading. The .22-caliber version has 3.5" octagonal barrel with 7-round unfluted cylinder; .32-caliber version has 4", 5" or 6" octagonal barrel and 6-shot unfluted cylinder. Frames are silver-plated brass. Barrels and cylinders blued. Grips of walnut. Standard markings include "L.W. Pond, Worcester, Mass." and patent dates. Approximately 2,000 manufactured in .22-caliber; 5,000 in .32-caliber between 1863 and 1870.

.22 Caliber Version

—	—	1750	1400	550	150

.32 Caliber Version

—	—	1750	1400	550	150

PORTER, P. W.
New York, New York

Turret Revolver

Extremely rare 9-shot vertical cylinder .41-caliber percussion revolver, with 5.25" round barrel. Trigger guard is also a lever that turns cylinder and cocks hammer. Automatic primer system also fitted to this revolver. Manufactured during 1850s in an unknown quantity.

—	—	23500	19500	8800	100

Turret Rifle

9-shot vertical cylinder .44-caliber rifle, with either 26" or 28" octagonal barrel. Only markings are "Address P.W. Porter/New York". Four variations of this rifle known. The 22" barreled carbine would command 25 percent premium. Approximately 1,250 manufactured during 1850s.

1st Model with Canister Magazine

Fitted with a 30-shot round canister magazine over turret. Made in Tennessee and extremely rare. Most often canisters are not encountered and values reflect this. Approximately 25 made.

—	—	37500	30000	13500	2000

2nd Model (New York)

—	—	15000	12000	5125	1000

3rd Model (New York)

Model has screw-off cover over magazine.

—	—	13000	1050	5200	1000

4th Model (New York)

As above, without automatic primer magazine. Nipples are exposed.

—	—	10500	8800	4150	750

PRAHA ZBROJOVKA
Prague, Czechoslovakia

Established in 1918 by A. Novotny. Company ceased operations in 1926.

VZ2L

7.65mm semi-automatic pistol. Patterned after Model 1910 Browning, without grip safety. Barrel length 3.5", magazine capacity 6 rounds, grips of wood. Slide marked "Zbrojowka Praga Praha".

—	400	250	200	150	100

NIB	EXC.	V.G.	GOOD	FAIR	POOR

Praga 1921

6.35mm semi-automatic pistol, with slide of stamped steel cut with a finger groove at front. Folding trigger. Barrel 2" in length. Slide marked "Zbrojowka Praga Praha Patent Cal 6.35". Grips of molded plastic, with name "Praga" cast in them. A dangerous feature of this pistol is that it is striker-fired with no hammer. Intended to be carried fully loaded and cocked in the pocket with absolutely no safety of any kind. I do not recommend this. Folding trigger does not spring out until slide is drawn back slightly by using finger groove in front of it.

—	375	225	200	150	100

PRAIRIE GUN WORKS
Winnipeg, Manitoba, Canada

M-15

Lightweight mountain rifle chambered for .22-250, 6mm-284, .25-284, 6.5-284, 7mm-08, .308 Win. and most short calibers. Built on Remington 700 action, with 20" lightweight barrel. Stock is Kevlar and comes in either green, black or gray. Barrel length usually 20". Weight about 4.75 lbs.

2600	2200	1750	1200	800	500

M-18

Similar to above. Chambered for long action calibers. Fitted with barrel lengths from 22" to 24". Weight about 5.25 lbs.

2600	2200	1750	1200	800	500

PRANDELLI & GASPARINI
Brescia, Italy

Boxlock Side-by-Side Shotgun

Good quality double-barrel 12- or 20-gauge shotgun, with 26" or 28" barrels. Single-selective trigger, automatic ejectors and Anson & Deeley action. Blued, stock of select walnut.

—	2500	1750	1100	700	450

Sidelock Side-by-Side Shotgun

Similar to above, with full sidelocks.

—	3500	2650	1500	900	500

Boxlock Over/Under Shotgun

Over/under double-barrel 12- or 20-gauge shotgun, with 26" or 28" barrels, single triggers and automatic ejectors. Blued, with select walnut stock.

—	2750	1850	1200	900	350

Sidelock Over/Under Shotgun

As above, with full sidelocks.

—	3000	2500	1800	950	450

PRATT, GEORGE
Middletown, Connecticut

Trap Gun

Doubled-barreled stationary burglar alarm or animal trap gun. Chambered for .38-caliber centerfire. Barrel 4" in length. All components are made of cast iron, with galvanized finish. Barrels and action mounted on round base, which can turn 360 degrees. Patent date "Dec. 18, 1883" marked on gun. Many manufactured between 1880 and early 1890s.

—	—	1800	1200	500	150

PRATT, H.
Roxbury, Massachusetts

Under Hammer Pistol

.31-caliber percussion single-shot pistol, with 8.5" octagonal barrel. Frame marked "H. Pratt's/Patent". Manufactured during 1850s.

—	—	1700	1350	650	200

	NIB	EXC.	V.G.	GOOD	FAIR	POOR

PRECISION SMALL ARMS
Aspen, Colorado

PSA-25

Semi-automatic pistol chambered for .25 ACP. Barrel length 2.13". Magazine capacity 6 rounds. Frame and slide steel alloy. Weight 9.5 oz.; overall length 4.11". Grips black polymer. Standard finish black oxide. Modeled after Browning Baby. **NOTE:** Add $50 brushed chrome finish; $75 stainless steel.

525	400	300	225	150	75

Featherweight Model

Same as above, with aluminum frame. Chrome slide with gold-plated trigger.

1000	850	700	475	250	100

Diplomat Model

Black oxide, with gold highlights and ivory grips.

1000	850	700	500	400	200

Montreaux Model

Gold plated with ivory grips.

825	750	600	450	300	200

Renaissance Model

Same as above, with hand engraved steel frame and slide. Antique stain chrome finish.

2600	2100	1600	1200	700	300

Imperiale

Inlaid gold filigree over blue, with scrimshawed ivory grips.

3300	2750	2100	1500	850	350

PREMIER
Italy and Spain

Trade name used by various retailers on shotguns manufactured in Italy and Spain that were imported during late 1950s and early 1960s.

Regent Side-by-Side Shotgun

Double-barrel shotgun, with 26" to 30" barrels. Available in all standard gauges. Receiver blued, stock of walnut. Normally found with pistol-grip and beavertail fore-end.

—	450	250	200	150	100

Regent Magnum

As above chambered for 3.5" 10-gauge Magnum cartridge. Barrels 32" in length and choked Full and Full.

—	500	300	250	200	150

Brush King

Identical to Regent Model, except fitted with 22" Modified and Improved Cylinder barrels. Straight-grip English-style stock.

—	500	375	250	200	150

Ambassador Model

More ornate version of Regent Model.

—	600	450	300	250	175

Presentation Custom Grade

Custom-order shotgun, with game scenes and gold and silver inlays.

—	2500	1750	1250	850	400

PRESCOTT, E. A.
Worcester, Massachusetts

Percussion Pocket Revolver

.31-caliber percussion spur trigger revolver, with either 4" or 4.25" octagonal barrel and 6-shot cylinder. Frame brass. Grips walnut. Believed approximately 100 manufactured during 1860 and 1861.

—	—	3700	2500	1125	200

	NIB	EXC.	V.G.	GOOD	FAIR	POOR

Pocket Revolver

.22- or .32-caliber spur trigger revolver, with 3" or 4" barrel. .22-caliber version has 7-shot cylinder; .32 caliber version 6-shot cylinder. Standard markings "E.A. Prescott Worcester Mass. Pat. Oct. 2, 1860". Approximately 1,000 manufactured between 1862 and 1867.

—	—	1050	825	350	100	

Navy Revolver

Single-action revolver fitted with conventional trigger. Chambered for .38 rimfire cartridges, with 7.25" octagonal barrel. Unfluted cylinder holds 6 shots. Frame either silver-plated brass or blued iron; barrel and cylinder blued, with walnut grips. Barrel marked "E.A. Prescott, Worcester, Mass. Pat. Oct. 2, 1860". Believed several hundred manufactured between 1861 and 1863. Iron frame model will bring a small premium.

—	—	1850	1400	550	200	

Army Revolver

Similar in appearance to Navy model, with larger frame. Chambered for .44-caliber rimfire cartridge. Fitted with 9" octagon barrel, with extractor rod and loading gate on right side of frame. Very rare.

—	—	24500	19500	8800	600	

Belt Revolver

Although similar in appearance to early Smith & Wesson revolvers, Prescott has a solid frame. Available in either .22- or .32-caliber: .22-caliber has 3" barrel; .32-caliber 5.75" barrel. Markings are identical found on Pocket Revolver. Approximately 300 manufactured between 1861 and 1863.

—	—	1150	825	325	100	

PRETORIA
Pretoria, South Africa
See—P.A.F.

PRINZ
Germany

Grade 1 Bolt-Action Rifle

High quality bolt-action rifle. Chambered for .243, .30-06, .308, 7mm Rem. Magnum or .300 Win. Magnum cartridges. Barrel length 24", double-set triggers available. Finish blued. Stock oil-finished select walnut. Introduced in 1989.

1200	950	700	450	325	150	

Grade 2 Bolt-Action Rifle

As above, with rosewood fore-end tip. Pistol-grip cap.

1300	1075	750	475	350	175	

Tip Up Rifle

High quality single-shot rifle. Available in a variety of American cartridges. Barrel length 24". Not furnished with sights. Finish blued, stock of select walnut.

3000	2250	1700	1135	850	300	

Model 85 "Princess"

Combination 12-gauge shotgun and rifle, with 24" or 26" barrels, double triggers and automatic ejectors. Finish blued, stock of select walnut.

3500	2850	2100	1650	1000	300	

PROFESSIONAL ORDNANCE, INC.
Ontario, California

Company was purchased by Bushmaster.

Carbon-15 Pistol—Type 97

Introduced in 1996. Semi-automatic pistol built on carbon fiber upper and lower receiver. Chambered for 5.56 cartridge. Has 7.25" fluted stainless steel barrel. Ghost ring sights are standard. Magazine is AR-15 compatible. Quick detach compensator. Furnished with 10-round magazine. Weight about 46 oz. NOTE: Pistol has several options that will affect value.

925	700	550	425	300	150	

	NIB	EXC.	V.G.	GOOD	FAIR	POOR

Carbon-15 Rifle—Type 97

Similar to above. Fitted with 16" barrel, quick detachable buttstock, quick detach compensator, Weaver type mounting base. Overall length 35"; weight about 3.9 lbs.

	NIB	EXC.	V.G.	GOOD	FAIR	POOR
	950	725	600	500	350	150

Carbon-15 Rifle—Type 97S

Introduced in 2000. Rifle incorporated several new features. Fore-grip is double walled and insulated with a sheet of ultra-lightweight alumina silica ceramic fiber. Recoil buffer has been increased in size by 30 percent for less recoil. New ambidextrous safety has been added. New multi carry silent sling with Hogue grip standard. Weight about 4.3 lbs.

	NIB	EXC.	V.G.	GOOD	FAIR	POOR
	1285	950	700	550	375	150

Carbon-15 Pistol—Type 21

Introduced in 1999. Features light profile stainless steel 7.25" barrel. Ghost ring sights are standard. Optional recoil compensator. A 30-round magazine standard until supplies are exhausted. Weight about 40 oz.

	NIB	EXC.	V.G.	GOOD	FAIR	POOR
	925	700	550	425	300	150

Carbon-15 Rifle—Type 21

Fitted with 16" light profile stainless steel barrel. Quick detachable stock, weaver mounting base. Introduced in 1999. Weight about 3.9 lbs.

	NIB	EXC.	V.G.	GOOD	FAIR	POOR
	1150	900	650	500	325	125

PROTECTION
Unknown

Protection Pocket Revolver

.28-caliber percussion spur-trigger revolver, with 3.25" octagonal barrel and 6-shot cylinder roll engraved with police arrest scene. Frame brass. Grips walnut. Cylinder marked "Protection". Approximately 1,000 manufactured during late 1850s and early 1860s.

1st Model

Roll engraved cylinder.

	NIB	EXC.	V.G.	GOOD	FAIR	POOR
	—	—	1500	1150	450	100

2nd Model

Plain cylinder above serial no. 650.

	NIB	EXC.	V.G.	GOOD	FAIR	POOR
	—	—	1300	950	350	100

PTK INTERNATIONAL, INC.
Atlanta, Georgia
See—Poly-Technologies, Inc.

PULASKI ARMORY
Pulaski, Tennessee

Founded in 1861, this firm produced rifles for State of Tennessee. Overall length 48.5" to 49.5"; round barrels 32.5" to 33.25"; caliber .54. Resembles U.S. Model 1841 Rifles without patchbox. Had single screw sporting locks, with diamond-shaped ferrules. Usually marked on barrel "PULASKI T. C.S.A. 61". Production estimated about 300.

	NIB	EXC.	V.G.	GOOD	FAIR	POOR
	—	—	16500	10000	5000	1500

PUMA

Model 92 Rifle

Copy of Winchester lever-action rifle. Fitted with 24" octagon barrel. Chambered for .44 Magnum, .357 Magnum, .454 Casull or .45 Colt cartridge. Offered in a variety of finishes: stainless steel; blued; blued and brass; blued and case colored. Fitted with crescent butt and hardwood stock. **NOTE:** Add $50 for stainless steel.

	NIB	EXC.	V.G.	GOOD	FAIR	POOR
	550	425	350	275	200	100

Model 92 Carbine

This model is also available with a 20" round barrel chambered as above and also in .454 Casull and .480 Ruger. Fitted with a shotgun butt.

	NIB	EXC.	V.G.	GOOD	FAIR	POOR
	550	425	350	275	200	100

	NIB	EXC.	V.G.	GOOD	FAIR	POOR

NOTE: Add $50 for stainless steel.

Model available with 20" round barrel. Chambered as above and in .454 Casull and .480 Ruger. Fitted with shotgun butt. **NOTE:** Add $50 for stainless steel.

	NIB	EXC.	V.G.	GOOD	FAIR	POOR
	550	425	350	275	200	100

Model 92 Trapper

Introduced in 2004. Features 16" barrel, with large-loop lever and saddle ring. Available in all calibers noted above.

	NIB	EXC.	V.G.	GOOD	FAIR	POOR
	550	425	350	275	200	100

PPS22

New in 2009. A .22 LR version of Soviet PPSh sub-machine gun. Comes with one 50-round drum magazine.

	NIB	EXC.	V.G.	GOOD	FAIR	POOR
	575	475	350	275	200	100

PURDEY, J. & SONS LTD.
London, England

Perhaps the finest manufacturer of shotguns, double-barrel and bolt-action rifles in the world. Virtually all their products are made on special order and impossible to establish general values for their products. Prospective purchasers are advised to seek qualified guidance prior to acquisition of any arms made by this maker. Prices listed are for standard guns with no extras. Below, are approximate base prices for new custom shotguns and rifles based on the exchange rate between English pound and U.S. dollar as of September, 2014. Prices do not include VAT, which is approximately 20 percent. These guns are made to order to buyer's specifications and can be made in any gauge or caliber.

CURRENT PRODUCTION

Hammerless Ejector Side-by-Side Game Gun

Available in 12-, 16-, 20-, 28-gauge and .410 bore. Engraved sidelocks.

	NIB	EXC.	V.G.	GOOD	FAIR	POOR
	136,500	—	—	—	—	—

Hammerless Ejector Over/Under Gun

Offered in 12-, 16-, 20-, 28-gauge and .410 bore, with sidelocks.

	NIB	EXC.	V.G.	GOOD	FAIR	POOR
	149,750	—	—	—	—	—

Double-Barreled Rifle

Custom made side-by-side double rifle with sidelocks. **NOTE:** Up to .375 bore size: $190,000; .375 to .500 bore size: $190,000; .500 bore size and up: $201,650.

OLDER MANUFACTURED SHOTGUNS AND RIFLES

Best Quality Game Gun

NOTE: Add 50 percent for 20-gauge; 80 to 100 percent for 28-gauge or .410 bore.

	NIB	EXC.	V.G.	GOOD	FAIR	POOR
	40000	35000	27500	20000	8000	—

Best Quality Heavy Duck Gun

	NIB	EXC.	V.G.	GOOD	FAIR	POOR
	24000	20000	12500	7500	5000	—

Best Quality Over/Under

NOTE: Add 50 percent for 20-gauge; 100 percent for 28-gauge.

	NIB	EXC.	V.G.	GOOD	FAIR	POOR
	50000	42000	32000	25000	9000	—

Double Rifle

.300 H&H

	NIB	EXC.	V.G.	GOOD	FAIR	POOR
	—	55000	47500	40000	25000	—

.375 H&H

	NIB	EXC.	V.G.	GOOD	FAIR	POOR
	—	70000	60000	50000	35000	—

	NIB	EXC.	V.G.	GOOD	FAIR	POOR
.470 N.E.						
	—	90000	75000	65000	45000	—
.600 N.E.						
	—	100000	85000	70000	55000	—

PYRENEES
Hendaye, France

Founded in 1923, this company has produced a variety of models. Most popular of which was "Unique" series. Prior to 1939, a variety of trade names were marked on their products such as these: Superior, Capitan, Cesar, Chantecler, Chimere Renoir, Colonial, Prima, Rapid Maxima, Reina, Demon, Demon-marine, Ebac, Elite, Gallia, Ixor, Le Majestic, St. Hubert, Selecta, Sympathique, Touriste, Le Sanspariel, Le Tout Acier, Mars, Perfect, Triomphe Francais, Unis & Vindex. Following 1939, this company's products are simply stamped "Unique".

NOTE: During World War II production at this company was taken over by the Nazis. Consequently, the various models listed will be found with German inspection marks. These arms are worth approximately 25 percent more than the values listed.

Model 10 Unique

6.35mm semi-automatic pistol similar to Model 1906 Browning. Slide marked "Le Veritable Pistolet Francais Unique". Introduced in 1923.

—	295	195	165	100	75

Model 11

As above, with grip safety and loaded chamber indicator.

—	325	225	195	150	100

Model 12

As above, without loaded chamber indicator.

—	295	195	165	100	75

Model 13

As above, with 7-shot magazine.

—	295	195	165	100	75

Model 14

As above, with 9-shot magazine.

—	295	195	165	100	75

Model 15

As above in 7.65mm caliber. Introduced in 1923.

—	295	195	165	100	75

Model 16

As above, with 7-shot magazine.

—	295	195	165	100	75

Model 17

As above, with 9-shot magazine.

—	325	225	195	150	100

Model 18

7.65mm caliber semi-automatic pistol. Patterned after Model 1920 Browning, without grip safety.

—	295	195	165	100	75

Model 19

As above, with 7-shot magazine.

—	295	195	165	100	75

Model 20

As above, with 9-shot magazine.

—	325	225	195	150	100

	NIB	EXC.	V.G.	GOOD	FAIR	POOR

Model 21

As above chambered for 9mm short cartridge.

	NIB	EXC.	V.G.	GOOD	FAIR	POOR
	—	325	225	195	150	100

POST-WAR UNIQUE

Model BCF66

9mm short semi-automatic pistol, with 3.5" barrel, open top slide and external hammer. Slide marked "Armes Unique Hendaye BP France". Blued finish. Plastic grips.

	NIB	EXC.	V.G.	GOOD	FAIR	POOR
	—	295	195	165	100	75

Model C

Virtually identical to Model 17 listed above. Slide marked "7.65 Court 9 coups Unique". Blued finish. Plastic grips with trademark "PF" in a circle cast into them.

	NIB	EXC.	V.G.	GOOD	FAIR	POOR
	—	250	175	150	125	75

Model F

Identical to Model C, except chambered for 9mm Short cartridges. Magazine capacity 8 rounds.

	NIB	EXC.	V.G.	GOOD	FAIR	POOR
	—	295	195	165	100	75

Model D

.22-caliber semi-automatic pistol, with barrels ranging from 4" to 7.5" in length. The 7.5" barreled version fitted with muzzle-brake. Magazine capacity 10 rounds. Finish blued, plastic grips.

	NIB	EXC.	V.G.	GOOD	FAIR	POOR
	—	275	225	200	150	125

Model DES/VO

Identical to Model D, but chambered for .22 Short cartridges.

	NIB	EXC.	V.G.	GOOD	FAIR	POOR
	—	275	225	200	150	125

Model L

Similar to Model D, except chambered for .22, .32 ACP and 9mm Short cartridges. Available with steel or alloy frame.

	NIB	EXC.	V.G.	GOOD	FAIR	POOR
	—	295	195	165	100	75

Model DES 69

As above, with better quality sights, special trigger and improved grips.

	NIB	EXC.	V.G.	GOOD	FAIR	POOR
	—	325	225	195	150	100

Model 2000

	NIB	EXC.	V.G.	GOOD	FAIR	POOR
	1250	950	775	500	350	150

QUACKENBUSH

Herkimer, New York

Quackenbush Safety Cartridge Rifle

Single-shot takedown boy's rifle, chambered for .22 rimfire cartridges in either .22 Short or .22 Long. Barrel length 18". Weight about 4.5 lbs. All metal parts nickel-plated. Breech swings to side for loading. Stock of walnut. Manufactured between 1886 and about 1920. Approximately 50,000 produced. Quackenbush also made nickel-plated nutcrackers. Who'd'a thought?

| — | — | 800 | 650 | 300 | 150 |

Junior Safety Rifle

Same as above, with skeleton stock. Built between 1893 and 1920. About 7,000 guns manufactured. Weight about 4 lbs.

| — | — | 950 | 600 | 200 | 100 |

Bicycle Rifle

Chambered for .22 cartridge, this rifle fitted with 12" barrel. Skeleton wire pistol grip.

| — | — | 1300 | 750 | 350 | 150 |

QUINABAUG MFG. CO.

Southridge, Massachusetts

Under Hammer Pistol

.31 caliber percussion under hammer pistol, with barrels from 3" to 8" in length. Frame of blued iron, grips of walnut or maple. Top of frame marked "Quinabaug Rifle M'g Co. Southbridge, Mass." Barrels are normally marked "E. Hutchings & Co. Agents". Manufactured during 1850s.

| — | — | 1900 | 1400 | 600 | 200 |

R

	NIB	EXC.	V.G.	GOOD	FAIR	POOR

R. G. INDUSTRIES
Miami, Florida
Rohm Gmbh
Sontheim/Brenz, Germany

An importer of inexpensive handguns of dubious quality that ceased operations in 1986.

RG-25

A .25-caliber semi-automatic pistol. Available with either blued or chrome-plated finish.

—	75	65	50	25	0

RG-16

A double-barrel .22-caliber chrome-plated derringer.

—	75	65	50	20	0

RG-17

As above, except chambered for. 38 Special cartridge.

—	75	70	60	25	0

RG-14

A .22-caliber double-action revolver, with 4" barrel and 6-shot cylinder. Blued finish, plastic grips.

—	75	70	60	25	0

RG-30

A .22 LR or Magnum double-action revolver. Blued finish, plastic grips.

—	75	65	50	25	0

RG-40

A .38 Special double-action revolver, with swing-out cylinder. Blued finish, plastic grips.

—	75	70	60	25	0

RG-57

A .357 or .44 Magnum double-action revolver, with 6-shot cylinder. Blued finish, checkered wood grips.

—	75	70	60	25	0

RG-63

A .22-caliber double-action revolver resembling Colt Model 1873.

—	75	70	60	25	0

RG-66

A .22 or .22 Magnum single-action revolver patterned after Colt Model 1873.

—	90	70	50	25	0

RG-66T

As above, with adjustable sights.

—	90	70	50	25	0

RG-74

A .22-caliber double-action revolver, with swing-out cylinder.

—	75	65	55	25	0

RG-88

A .357 Magnum double-action revolver, with swing-out cylinder.

—	75	65	55	25	0

R.E.
Valencia, Spain

The initials "R.E." stand for "Republica Espana". This copy of the Spanish Army Model 1921, also known as the Astra 400, was produced between 1936 and 1939 during the Spanish Civil War by the

NIB	EXC.	V.G.	GOOD	FAIR	POOR

Republican forces. This variation can be identified by the "RE" monogram on the butt and the absence of any manufacturer's stampings.

NIB	EXC.	V.G.	GOOD	FAIR	POOR
—	475	325	250	175	100

RADOM
Radom, Poland

For history, technical data, descriptions, photos and prices see the Standard Catalog of Military Firearms.

VIS-35 Reissue

This is an exact copy of original VIS-35 pistol. Limited to 100 pistols, with fewer than that number imported into U.S. Importer, "Dalvar of USA" is stamped on barrel. **NOTE:** Deduct 50 percent for "non-eagle" version.

NIB	EXC.	V.G.	GOOD	FAIR	POOR
2300	2000	1500	1100	600	300

RANDALL FIREARMS CO.
Sun Valley, California

This company was in operation from 1983 to 1985. It was the first manufacturer to mass-produce 1911-type pistols in stainless steel. Also, the first to make a mirror-image left-hand variation. Many models were offered, most in .45 ACP or 9mm. Records show only two samples were chambered in .38 Super. Total production of Randall Firearms Co. was almost 10,000 pistols.

Model A111

Caliber .45 Auto; barrel length 5"; round-slide top, right-hand with fixed sights. Total production: 3,431. **NOTE:** Add a premium of $100 for Exc. thru Good prices for original box.

NIB	EXC.	V.G.	GOOD	FAIR	POOR
1050	950	650	400	350	200

Model A121

Caliber .45 Auto; barrel length 5"; flat-slide top, right-hand with fixed sights. Total production: 1,067. **NOTE:** Add a premium of $100 for Exc. thru Good prices for original box.

NIB	EXC.	V.G.	GOOD	FAIR	POOR
1150	1000	800	425	375	200

Model A131

Caliber .45 Auto; barrel length 5"; flat-slide top, right-hand with Millet sights. Total production: 2,083. **NOTE:** Add a premium of $100 for Exc. thru Good prices for original box.

NIB	EXC.	V.G.	GOOD	FAIR	POOR
1300	1050	875	550	400	200

Model A112

Caliber 9mm; barrel length 5"; round-slide top, right-hand with fixed sights. Total production: 301. **NOTE:** Add a premium of $100 for Exc. thru Good prices for original box.

NIB	EXC.	V.G.	GOOD	FAIR	POOR
1350	950	900	575	425	200

Model A122

Caliber 9mm; barrel length 5"; flat-slide top, right-hand with fixed sights. Total production: 18. **NOTE:** Add a premium of $100 for Exc. thru Good prices for original box.

NIB	EXC.	V.G.	GOOD	FAIR	POOR
1900	1600	1350	800	540	300

Model A211

Caliber .45 Auto; barrel length 4.25"; round-slide top, right-hand with fixed sights. Total production: 922. **NOTE:** Add a premium of $100 for Exc. thru Good prices for original box.

NIB	EXC.	V.G.	GOOD	FAIR	POOR
1150	1000	800	425	375	200

Model A231

Caliber .45 Auto; barrel length 4.25"; flat-slide top, right-hand with Millet sights. Total production: 574. **NOTE:** Add a premium of $100 for Exc. thru Good prices for original box.

NIB	EXC.	V.G.	GOOD	FAIR	POOR
1350	950	900	575	425	200

Model A212

Caliber 9mm; barrel length 4.25"; round-slide top, right-hand with fixed sights. Total production: 76. **NOTE:** Add a premium of $100 for Exc. thru Good prices for original box.

NIB	EXC.	V.G.	GOOD	FAIR	POOR
1450	1050	925	650	500	300

Model A232

Caliber 9mm; barrel length 4.25"; flat-slide top, right-hand with Millet sights. Total production: 5. **NOTE:** Add a premium of $100 for Exc. thru Good prices for original box.

NIB	EXC.	V.G.	GOOD	FAIR	POOR
2400	1900	1565	—	—	—

	NIB	EXC.	V.G.	GOOD	FAIR	POOR

Model A311

Caliber .45 Auto; barrel length 4.25"; round-slide top, right-hand with fixed sights. Total production: 361. **NOTE:** Add a premium of $100 for Exc. thru Good prices for original box.

	NIB	EXC.	V.G.	GOOD	FAIR	POOR
	1700	1375	1150	900	700	300

Model A331 Curtis LeMay

Caliber .45 Auto; barrel length 4.25"; flat-slide top, right-hand with Millet sights. Total production: 293.

	NIB	EXC.	V.G.	GOOD	FAIR	POOR
	1800	1475	1250	950	735	300

Model A312

Caliber 9mm; barrel length 4.25"; round-slide top, right-hand with fixed sights. Total production: 2. **NOTE:** Add a premium of $100 for Exc. thru Good prices for original box.

	NIB	EXC.	V.G.	GOOD	FAIR	POOR
	3750	3300	2575	—	—	—

Model A332

Caliber 9mm; barrel length 4.25"; flat-slide top, right-hand with Millet sights. Total production: 9. **NOTE:** Add a premium of $100 for Exc. thru Good prices for original box.

	NIB	EXC.	V.G.	GOOD	FAIR	POOR
	2250	1775	1450	1000	750	300

Model B111

Caliber .45 Auto; barrel length 5"; round-slide top, left-hand with fixed sights. Total production: 297. **NOTE:** Add a premium of $100 for Exc. thru Good prices for original box.

	NIB	EXC.	V.G.	GOOD	FAIR	POOR
	1900	1550	1200	975	700	300

Model B121

Caliber .45 Auto; barrel length 5"; flat-slide top, left-hand with fixed sights. Total production: 110. **NOTE:** Add a premium of $100 for Exc. thru Good prices for original box.

	NIB	EXC.	V.G.	GOOD	FAIR	POOR
	2250	1775	1450	1000	750	300

Model B122

Caliber 9mm; barrel length 5"; flat-slide top, left-hand with fixed sights. Total production: 2.

	NIB	EXC.	V.G.	GOOD	FAIR	POOR
	4000	3500	2675	—	—	—

Model B123

Caliber .38 Super; barrel length 5"; flat-slide top, left-hand with fixed sights. Total production: 2.

	NIB	EXC.	V.G.	GOOD	FAIR	POOR
	4000	3500	2675	—	—	—

Model B131

Caliber .45 Auto; barrel length 5"; flat-slide top, left-hand with Millet sights. Total production: 225. **NOTE:** Add a premium of $100 for Exc. thru Good prices for original box.

	NIB	EXC.	V.G.	GOOD	FAIR	POOR
	2075	1700	1400	875	700	300

Model B311

Caliber .45 Auto; barrel length 4.25"; round-slide top, left-hand with fixed sights. Total production: 52. **NOTE:** Add a premium of $100 for Exc. thru Good prices for original box.

	NIB	EXC.	V.G.	GOOD	FAIR	POOR
	2250	1775	1450	1000	750	300

Model B312

Caliber 9mm; barrel length 4.25"; round-slide top, left-hand with fixed sights. Total production: 9. **NOTE:** Add a premium of $100 for Exc. thru Good prices for original box.

	NIB	EXC.	V.G.	GOOD	FAIR	POOR
	3750	3300	2575	—	—	—

Model B331

Caliber .45 Auto; barrel length 4.25"; flat-slide top, left-hand with Millet sights. Total production: 45. **NOTE:** Add a premium of $100 for Exc. thru Good prices for original box.

	NIB	EXC.	V.G.	GOOD	FAIR	POOR
	2500	2050	1675	1100	600	300

Model C311

Caliber .45 Auto; barrel length 4.25"; round-slide top, right-hand with fixed sights. Total production: 1.

	NIB	EXC.	V.G.	GOOD	FAIR	POOR
	4250	—	—	—	—	—

Model C332

Caliber 9mm; barrel length 4.25"; flat-slide top, right-hand with Millet sights. Total production: 4.

	NIB	EXC.	V.G.	GOOD	FAIR	POOR
	1900	1550	1200	975	700	300

	NIB	EXC.	V.G.	GOOD	FAIR	POOR

Model B321 SET

	24500	—	—	—	—	—

Model A111/111 Matched Set

Serial numbers: RFOOOOOC, RFOO001C, RFOO010-C, RFOO024C.

	9200	—	—	—	—	—

Austrian Randall

Total production: 5. Due to the rarity, values for this model are very speculative. An expert appraisal is advised.

RANDALL MAGAZINES

.45 LeMay—Right-Hand

	100	90	80	80	—	—

.45 LeMay—Dogleg Right-Hand

	80	70	70	70	—	—

.45 LeMay—Left-Hand

	150	130	125	125	—	—

.45 LeMay—Dogleg Left-Hand

	140	130	120	120	—	—

.45 Service—Right-Hand

	60	45	40	40	—	—

.45 Service—Left-Hand

	125	115	100	100	—	—

9mm Service—Right-Hand

	125	115	100	100	—	—

9mm Service—Left-Hand

	200	175	150	150	—	—

RANGER ARMS, INC.
Gainesville, Texas

.22 Rifle

Bolt-action rifle produced in .22 LR. Checkered walnut Monte Carlo stock. Manufactured in early 1970s.

	—	200	150	100	75	50

Statesman

Bolt-action rifle produced in various centerfire calibers, with 22" barrel, no sights and checkered walnut stock. Standard finish blued. Manufactured in early 1970s.

	—	900	750	600	350	200

Statesman Magnum

As above, but chambered for Magnum calibers, with 24" barrel.

	—	950	800	650	375	200

Senator

As above, with a better finish.

	—	1000	850	700	525	250

Senator Magnum

As above, chambered for Magnum cartridges.

	—	1150	900	750	575	250

Governor

As above, with better walnut and finer lined checkering.

	—	1300	1050	800	600	300

	NIB	EXC.	V.G.	GOOD	FAIR	POOR

Governor Magnum

As above, chambered for Magnum cartridges.

	—	1540	1200	950	750	300

RAPTOR ARMS CO.
Shelton, Connecticut

Raptor Bolt-Action Rifle

Economy-class bolt rifle introduced in 1997. Chambered for .270, .30-06, .243, .25-06 and .308 calibers. Fitted with 22" barrel and black synthetic checkered stock. An upgrade model was available with wooden stock. Adjustable trigger. Weight about 7.5 lbs.

275	225	175	125	100	75

Peregrine Bolt-Action Rifle

Similar to above, with checkered hardwood stock. Special order.

275	225	175	125	100	75

RAST & GASSER
See—Gasser

RAU ARMS CORP.
El Dorado, Kansas

Wildcat

Single-shot pivoting-barrel .22 rimfire rifle. Skeletonized stock, with walnut or mahogany inset. Fore-end acts as extractor. Similar in overall look to FIE/Garcia Bronco in .22 only. Mfg. 1969-1970, with 2500-3000 produced. Later produced by Mountain Arms. See that listing.

Model 500

Blued, with walnut stock insert.

300	200	150	100	75	45

Model 600 Deluxe

Chrome finish, with mahogany stock insert.

325	225	175	125	95	50

RAVELL
Barcelona, Spain

Maxim Double Rifle

Holland & Holland-styled sidelock double-barrel rifle. Available in either .375 Holland & Holland or 9.3x74R, with 23" barrels having express sights. Double triggers and automatic ejectors. Sidelocks and mounts engraved. Stock of well figured walnut. Normally fitted with a recoil pad.

4500	3500	2750	1850	1250	850

RAVEN ARMS
Industry, California

P-25

A .25-caliber semi-automatic pistol, with 2.75" barrel and 6-round magazine. Available with blued, chrome or nickel-plated finish and walnut grips. Manufacture ceased in 1984.

	—	100	75	50	35	25

MP-25

As above, with die-cast frame and imitation ivory grips.

110	80	55	45	35	25

READ & WATSON
Danville, Virginia

During 1862 and 1863, Read & Watson produced approximately 900 altered Hall rifles for the State of Virginia. These arms were made from Hall rifles issued to the state prior to the Civil War. The original breech loading mechanisms were removed and a brass breech piece or receiver was secured in their place. New buttstocks were fitted and the original Hall furniture was reused. Carbines have

	NIB	EXC.	V.G.	GOOD	FAIR	POOR

an overall length of 42.125"; barrel length of 26"; in .52-caliber. Position and style of serial numbers varies.

	NIB	EXC.	V.G.	GOOD	FAIR	POOR
	—	—	18500	15500	7100	1000

RECORD-MATCH ANSCHUTZ
Zelia-Mehlis, Germany

Model 210 Free Pistol

Single-shot .22-caliber target pistol using Martini falling block action. Barrel length 11", set trigger and adjustable sights. Blued finish, with checkered walnut grips and fore-end. Manufactured during 1930s.

	NIB	EXC.	V.G.	GOOD	FAIR	POOR
	—	1500	1200	1000	825	400

Model 210A

As above, with a lightweight alloy frame.

	NIB	EXC.	V.G.	GOOD	FAIR	POOR
	—	1425	1125	975	775	350

Model 200 Free Pistol

As above, without a set trigger.

	NIB	EXC.	V.G.	GOOD	FAIR	POOR
	—	1125	1050	875	550	300

REEDER, GARY CUSTOM GUNS
Flagstaff, Arizona

This company offers complete guns as listed below. It also offers custom options built on customer guns as well. An extensive number of custom options is available on any of these models. Prices listed below reflect the standard for that particular model. Retail prices only are listed below due to lack of active secondary market for these limited edition guns. Reeder is a custom manufacturer, or re-stylist, working primarily with Ruger frames. Only a representative sampling of his works is presented here and the values are estimates only. Since many of Reeder's guns are made to custom specs, their value is largely a matter of finding the right buyer.

Arizona Ranger Classic

Built on a Ruger Vaquero frame. Chambered for .45 Long Colt cartridge. Fitted with choice of 4.5", 5.5", or 7.5" barrel. Blue or stainless steel finish. Special engraving, with Stag grips.

	NIB	EXC.	V.G.	GOOD	FAIR	POOR
	1400	1225	975	—	—	—

Badlands Classic

Built on a Ruger Vaquero frame. Chambered for .45 Long Colt cartridge, with an extra .45 ACP cylinder. Fitted with 4.5" barrel. Special engraving. Pearl grips.

	NIB	EXC.	V.G.	GOOD	FAIR	POOR
	1400	1225	975	—	—	—

Black Widow

Chambered for .44 Magnum cartridge. Fitted with 4.625" barrel, with black Chromex finish. Round butt, with black Cape Buffalo grips. Engraved with Black Widow on each side of cylinder. Built on a Ruger Super Blackhawk.

	NIB	EXC.	V.G.	GOOD	FAIR	POOR
	1300	1075	850	—	—	—

Black Widow II

Similar to Black Widow. Chambered for .45 Long Colt cartridge. Barrel length 4.5".

	NIB	EXC.	V.G.	GOOD	FAIR	POOR
	1350	1125	900	—	—	—

Cowboy Classic

Built on a Ruger Vaquero frame. Chambered for .45 Long Colt, with 6.75" barrel. Stainless steel or black Chromix finish. Ivory polymer or pearlite grips. Special engraving.

	NIB	EXC.	V.G.	GOOD	FAIR	POOR
	1350	1125	900	—	—	—

Cowtown Classic

Built on a Ruger Vaquero frame. Chambered for .45 Long Colt, with 7.5" barrel. Special engraving. Walnut grips.

	NIB	EXC.	V.G.	GOOD	FAIR	POOR
	1350	1125	900	—	—	—

Gamblers Classic

Built on a Ruger Vaquero frame. Chambered for .45 Long Colt, with 2.5" barrel. Stainless steel or black Chromix finish. Choice of black or white pearl grips. No ejector rod. Special engraving.

	NIB	EXC.	V.G.	GOOD	FAIR	POOR
	1350	1125	900	—	—	—

	NIB	EXC.	V.G.	GOOD	FAIR	POOR

Lone Star Classic

Built on a Ruger Vaquero frame. Chambered for .45 Long Colt cartridge, with 7.5" barrel. Stainless steel finish. Special engraving and walnut grips, with five notches.

	1350	1125	900	—	—	—

Long Rider Classic

Built on a Ruger Vaquero frame. Chambered for .45 Long Colt cartridge, with 4.5", 5.5" or 7.5" barrel. Special engraving with black Chromix finish. Gunfighter grip, with simulated pearl or ivory.

	1350	1125	900	—	—	—

Texas Ranger Classic

Built on a Ruger Vaquero frame. Chambered for .45 Long Colt cartridge, with 4.5", 5.5" or 7.5" barrel. Stainless steel finish. Special engraving. Simulated pearl gunfighter grips.

	1350	1125	900	—	—	—

Trail Rider Classic

Built on a Ruger Vaquero frame. Chambered for .45 Long Colt cartridge, with 7.5" barrel. Black Chromix finish. Special engraving. Simulated pearl grips.

	1350	1125	900	—	—	—

Tombstone Classic

Built on a Ruger Vaquero frame. Chambered for .45 Long Colt cartridge, with 3.5" barrel. Black Chromix finish. Special engraving. Simulated pearl or ivory bird's-head grips.

	1350	1125	900	—	—	—

Doc Holliday Classic

Built on a Ruger Vaquero frame. Chambered for .45 Long Colt cartridge, with 3.5" barrel. Stainless steel or black Chromix finish. Special engraving. Simulated pearl gambler grips.

	1350	1125	900	—	—	—

Night Rider

Built on a Ruger Vaquero frame. Chambered for .44-40 cartridge, with 7.5" barrel. Black Chromix finish. Special engraving. Stag grips.

	1350	1125	900	—	—	—

Ultimate Vaquero

Built on a Ruger Vaquero frame. Chambered for .45 Long Colt cartridge, with 4" barrel. Stainless steel or black Chromix finish. Special engraving. Simulated pearl gambler grips.

	1350	1125	900	—	—	—

Ultimate Bisley

Built on a Ruger Vaquero frame. Chambered for .45 Long Colt or .44 Magnum cartridge, with 4.5", 5.5", 6.5" or 7.5" barrel. Black Chromix finish. Special engraving. Simulated pearl or ivory Bisley grips.

	1350	1125	900	—	—	—

Long Colt Hunter

Built on a Ruger Blackhawk frame. Chambered for .45 Long Colt cartridge, with 5.5" or 7.5" barrel. Stainless steel finish. Adjustable rear sight, with gold bead front sight. Special engraving. Ebony grips.

	1350	1125	900	—	—	—

Long Colt Hunter II

Built on a Ruger Redhawk frame. Chambered for .45 Long Colt or .44 Magnum cartridge, with 5" barrel. Stainless steel finish. Special engraving. Wooden gunfighter grips.

	1350	1125	900	—	—	—

African Hunter

Built on a Ruger Bisley or Super Blackhawk frame. Chambered for .475 or .500 Linebaugh cartridge, with 6" barrel. Available with or without muzzle-brake. Adjustable rear sight and interchangeable front sights. Stainless steel or black Chromix finish. Special engraving. Ebony grips.

	1350	1125	900	—	—	—

NIB	EXC.	V.G.	GOOD	FAIR	POOR

Ultimate 41

Built on a Ruger Blackhawk frame. Chambered for .41 Magnum or .41 GNR cartridge, with 4.5", 5.5" or 7.5" barrel. Unfluted cylinder. Stainless steel finish. Adjustable rear sights. Special engraving. Ebony grips.

1500	1295	950	—	—	—

Coyote Classic

Built on a Ruger frame. Chambered for .22 Hornet, .22 K Hornet, .218 Bee, .218 Mashburn Bee, .17 Ackley Bee, .17 Ackley Hornet, .256 Winchester and .25-20, with 8" barrel. Adjustable rear sight drilled and tapped for scope mount. Black Chromix or stainless steel finish. Special engraving. Laminated cherry grips.

1350	1125	900	—	—	—

Classic Hunter

Built on a Ruger Vaquero frame. Chambered for .475 Linebaugh cartridge, with heavy 6" barrel. Black Chromix finish. Special engraving. Laminated ironwood, cherry or walnut gunfighter grips.

1500	1295	950	—	—	—

Alaskan Grizzly

Built on a Ruger Vaquero frame. Chambered for .475 or .500 Linebaugh cartridge, with customer's choice of barrel. Black Chromix or stainless steel finish. Special engraving. Horn or black laminated gunfighter grips.

1350	1125	900	—	—	—

Ultimate Back Up 2

Built on a Ruger Blackhawk or Super Blackhawk frame. Chambered for .475 or .500 Linebaugh cartridge, with 3.5" ported barrel. Stainless steel finish. Special engraving. Laminated wood or Buffalo horn grips.

1500	1295	950	—	—	—

Montana Hunter

Built on a Ruger Blackhawk or Super Blackhawk frame. Chambered for .45 Long Colt or .44 Magnum cartridge, with customer's choice of barrel. Stainless steel finish. Special engraving. Laminated gunfighter grips.

1350	1125	900	—	—	—

Alaskan Survivalist

Built on a Ruger Redhawk frame. Chambered for .45 Long Colt or .44 Magnum cartridge, with 3" barrel. Adjustable rear sight. Stainless steel finish. Special engraving. Ebony round butt grips.

1350	1125	900	—	—	—

American Hunter

Built on a Winchester Model 94 big bore frame. Chambered for .444 Marlin cartridge. Black Chromix finish. Ghost ring rear sight. Special engraving. Checkered walnut stock.

1350	1125	900	—	—	—

Alaskan Classic

Built on a Marlin Model 1895 frame. Chambered for .45-70 cartridge. Barrel length 16.5". Black Chromix finish. Ghost ring rear sight. Special engraving. Checkered walnut stock.

1500	1295	950	—	—	—

Buffalo Hunter

Built on a Marlin Model 1895 frame. Chambered for .475 GNR cartridge. Barrel length 18". Full length magazine tube. Black Chromix finish. Peep rear sight. Special engraving. Checkered walnut stock.

1500	1295	950	—	—	—

Kodiak Hunter

Built on a Contender frame. Chambered for .50 Action Express or .454 Casull cartridge. Barrel length 10". Black Chromix finish. Adjustable rear sight, with barrel band front sight. Special engraving. Walnut grips.

1350	1125	900	—	—	—

Ultimate Encore

Built on a Thompson/Center frame. Chambered for a variety of big bore cartridges. Fitted with 15" barrel, with muzzle-brake. Black Chromix finish. Ghost ring rear sight. Special engraving.

1350	1125	900	—	—	—

	NIB	EXC.	V.G.	GOOD	FAIR	POOR

Ultimate 44

Built on customer's Ruger Hunter. Model features: extra long five-shot cylinder; Bisley hammer and trigger; special grip frame, with laminated cherry grips; Magna-Ported barrel; sling swivels and action job. Game scene engraving.

NIB	EXC.	V.G.	GOOD	FAIR	POOR
1500	1295	950	—	—	—

Southern Comfort

Built on customer's Blackhawk or Super Blackhawk Ruger. Revolver features five-shot cylinder. Chambered for .454 Casull cartridge. Tear drop hammer, special set back trigger, special grip frame and light engraving. Barrel length to customer's choice.

NIB	EXC.	V.G.	GOOD	FAIR	POOR
1500	1295	950	—	—	—

Professional Hunter

Model features a number of special features, from extended frame to five-shot cylinder. Choice of calibers from .224 GNR to .500 Maximum. Fitted with 8" barrel, with heavy taper. Limited production.

NIB	EXC.	V.G.	GOOD	FAIR	POOR
2750	2295	1650	—	—	—

Ultimate 480

Model built on customer's Ruger Blackhawk or Super Blackhawk frame. Chambered for .480 cartridge. Cylinder has five rounds. Heavy barrel to customer's length. Special grip. Blued or stainless steel.

NIB	EXC.	V.G.	GOOD	FAIR	POOR
1400	1195	875	—	—	—

Ultimate 500

Model chambered for .500 S&W cartridge. Fitted with heavy five-shot cylinder. Barrel length of customer's choice. Black or ivory Micarta grips. Engraved games scenes and other special features.

NIB	EXC.	V.G.	GOOD	FAIR	POOR
2750	2295	1650	—	—	—

Classic 45

Model chambered for .45 Colt, .45 ACP or .45 Schofield cartridge, without full moon clips. Fitted with six-shot unfluted cylinder. Special set back trigger, Bisley hammer, Super Blackhawk or Blackhawk stainless steel frame and other special features.

NIB	EXC.	V.G.	GOOD	FAIR	POOR
1350	1125	900	—	—	—

Big 5 Classic

Single-shot rifle built on customer's Ruger No. 1 rifle. Chambered for .500 Jeffery cartridge. Fitted with heavy barrel to customer's length and muzzle-brake. Tuned action. Buttstock weight added. Game scene engraved.

NIB	EXC.	V.G.	GOOD	FAIR	POOR
2200	1725	1150	—	—	—

The BMF

Model features 4" barrel. Chambered for .500 Maximum cartridge and Magna-Ported. Bisley grip. Satin stainless steel finish, with black Micarta grips. Game scene engraved.

NIB	EXC.	V.G.	GOOD	FAIR	POOR
2750	2295	1650	—	—	—

Double Duce

Ruger Single Six revolver. Fitted with eight-shot cylinder and 8" barrel for .22 WMR cartridge. Longer grip frame, with red cherry grips. Game scene engraved.

NIB	EXC.	V.G.	GOOD	FAIR	POOR
1350	1125	900	—	—	—

Ultimate Black Widow

Model built on customer's Blackhawk, Bisley or Super Blackhawk Ruger. Chambered for .475 or .500 Linebaugh. Heavy duty five-shot cylinder. Barrel length to customer's choice. Bisley grip, with black Micarta grips. Black Chromix finish.

NIB	EXC.	V.G.	GOOD	FAIR	POOR
1350	1125	900	—	—	—

REFORM
August Schuler
Suhl, Germany

Reform Pistol

A 6.35 or .25 ACP four barreled double-action pistol. Constructed so that barrel unit rises upward when trigger is pulled. Superficially resembles a semi-automatic pistol. Blued, with hard rubber grips. Manufactured between 1906 and about 1913.

NIB	EXC.	V.G.	GOOD	FAIR	POOR
—	1750	1200	950	600	375

	NIB	EXC.	V.G.	GOOD	FAIR	POOR

REID, JAMES
New York, New York

Model 1 Revolver

Spur trigger .22-caliber revolver, with 3.5" octagonal barrel and 7-shot unfluted cylinder. Blued, with walnut grips. Barrel marked "J. Reid, New York". Approximately 500 manufactured between 1862 and 1865.

NIB	EXC.	V.G.	GOOD	FAIR	POOR
—	—	1175	950	375	100

Model 2 Revolver

As above in .32-caliber. Barrel marked "Address W.P. Irving, 20 Cliff Street. N.Y." or "James P. Fitch. N.Y." Approximately 1,300 manufactured between 1862 and 1865.

NIB	EXC.	V.G.	GOOD	FAIR	POOR
—	—	1175	950	385	100

Model 3 Revolver

Similar to above, with grip angle sharpened. Chambered for .32 rimfire cartridge, with 4.75" barrel. Cylinder chambers are threaded so that percussion nipples can be inserted. Barrel marked "J. Reid N.Y. City". Approximately 300 made between 1862 and 1865.

NIB	EXC.	V.G.	GOOD	FAIR	POOR
—	—	1550	1375	550	200

Model 4 Revolver

As above, with barrel lengths varying from 3.75" to 8". Approximately 1,600 manufactured between 1862 and 1865.

NIB	EXC.	V.G.	GOOD	FAIR	POOR
—	—	1550	1375	550	200

"My Friend" Knuckle Duster

A 7-shot .22-caliber revolver. Constructed entirely of metal, without a barrel. Frame of silver-plated brass or blued iron. Marked "My Friend Patd. Dec. 26, 1865". Grip is formed with a finger hole so that the pistol can be used as a set of brass knuckles.

Brass Frame

NIB	EXC.	V.G.	GOOD	FAIR	POOR
—	1550	1200	800	500	200

Iron Frame

NIB	EXC.	V.G.	GOOD	FAIR	POOR
—	2800	2250	800	500	250

.32 Caliber Knuckle Duster

As above in .32 caliber. Approximately 3,400 manufactured between 1869 and 1884.

Brass Frame

NIB	EXC.	V.G.	GOOD	FAIR	POOR
—	1800	1500	800	600	200

Iron Frame

NIB	EXC.	V.G.	GOOD	FAIR	POOR
—	2800	2250	1300	800	250

.41 Caliber Knuckle Duster

As above in .41 caliber. Marked "J. Reid's Derringer". Approximately 300 manufactured between 1875 and 1878.

NIB	EXC.	V.G.	GOOD	FAIR	POOR
—	18500	15000	9000	6500	1500

Model No. 1 Knuckle Duster

As above with 3" barrel. Approximately 350 made between 1875 and 1880.

NIB	EXC.	V.G.	GOOD	FAIR	POOR
—	3350	2750	1300	850	250

Model No. 2 Knuckle Duster

As above with 1.75" barrel. Approximately 150 made between 1875 and 1880.

NIB	EXC.	V.G.	GOOD	FAIR	POOR
—	3950	3000	1700	1250	500

Model No. 3 Derringer

A .41-caliber revolver, with 3" octagonal barrel and 5-shot fluted cylinder. Frame silver-plated and barrel as well as cylinder blued. Approximately 75 made between 1880 and 1884.

NIB	EXC.	V.G.	GOOD	FAIR	POOR
—	2900	2500	1200	950	350

Model No. 4 Derringer

As above, with brass frame and walnut grips. Marked "Reid's Extra". Approximately 200 made during 1883 and 1884.

NIB	EXC.	V.G.	GOOD	FAIR	POOR
—	1800	1500	1000	700	250

	NIB	EXC.	V.G.	GOOD	FAIR	POOR

New Model Knuckle Duster

Similar to Model 2, with 2" barrel and 5-shot cylinder. Barrel marked "Reid's New Model .32 My Friend". Approximately 150 made in 1884.

—	1800	1500	1050	650	250	

REISING ARMS CO.
Hartford, Connecticut

Standard Model

A .22-caliber semi-automatic pistol, with hinged 6.5" barrel and 10-round magazine. Standard finish blued, however, nickel-plated versions are known. Slide marked with company's name and patent dates. Bakelite grips impressed with a bear's head and motto "Reising, It's A Bear". Manufactured in both New York City and Hartford during 1920s. CAUTION: High-velocity ammunition should not be used in these pistols.

New York Manufacture

—	900	750	500	300	100	

Hartford Manufacture

—	450	350	275	175	100	

REMINGTON ARMS COMPANY, INC.
Madison, North Carolina

Founded in 1816 by Eliphalet Remington. Company has distinction of being oldest firearms manufacturing firm in United States. Since 1856, it has been known by four different names: between 1856 and 1888, E. Remington & Sons; 1888-1910, Remington Arms Company; 1910-1925, Remington Arms U.M.C. Company (Union Metallic Cartridge Company); and 1925 to present, Remington Arms Company.

1st Model Remington-Beals Revolver

A .31-caliber 5-shot percussion revolver, with 3" octagonal barrel. Cylinder turning mechanism is mounted on left outside frame. Blued case hardened, silver-plated, brass trigger guard and gutta-percha grips. Barrel marked, "F. Beal's Patent, June 24, '56 & May 26, '57"; frame "Remington's Ilion, N.Y.". Approximately 5,000 manufactured in 1857 and 1858.

—	4500	3000	2500	500	300	

2nd Model Remington-Beals Revolver

Spur trigger .31-caliber 5-shot percussion revolver, with 3" octagonal barrel. Blued case hardened, with squared gutta-percha grip. Barrel marked "Beals Patent 1856 & 57, Manufactured by Remingtons Ilion, N.Y.". Approximately 1,000 manufactured between 1858 and 1860.

—	6000	5000	4500	2500	1000	

3rd Model Remington-Beals Revolver

A .31-caliber 5-shot percussion revolver, with 4" octagonal barrel. Loading lever mounted beneath barrel. Blued case hardened, with gutta-percha grips. Barrel marked "Beals Pat. 1856, 57, 58" and also "Manufactured by Remingtons, Ilion, N.Y.". Approximately 1,500 manufactured in 1859 and 1860.

—	4500	4000	3350	1150	500	

Remington-Rider Revolver

Double-action .31-caliber percussion revolver, with 3" barrel and 5-shot cylinder. Most of these revolvers were blued but a few were nickel-plated case hardened, with gutta-percha grips. This model also encountered altered to .32 rimfire. Barrel marked "Manufactured by Remingtons, Ilion, N.Y., Riders Pt. Aug. 17, 1858, May 3, 1859". Approximately 20,000 manufactured between 1860 and 1873. **NOTE:** Cartridge variation worth approximately 20 percent less than original percussion version.

—	2500	1400	1100	675	300	

Remington-Beals Army Revolver

A .44-caliber percussion revolver, with 8" barrel and 6-shot cylinder. Blued case hardened, with walnut grips. Barrel marked "Beals Patent Sept. 14, 1858 Manufactured by Remington's Ilion, New York". Approximately 2,500 manufactured between 1860 and 1862. **NOTE:** Martially marked example extremely rare and would be worth approximately 35 percent additional.

—	6500	4750	2500	1500	500	

	NIB	EXC.	V.G.	GOOD	FAIR	POOR

Remington-Beals Navy Revolver

Similar in appearance to Remington-Beals Army Revolver in .36-caliber, with 7.5" octagonal barrel. First examples of this model were fitted with a loading lever that would not allow cylinder pin to be completely removed. These examples are worth approximately 80 percent more than standard model. Approximately 1,000 of these revolvers were purchased by the United States government and martially marked examples are worth approximately 40 percent more than values listed below. Manufactured from 1860 to 1862. Total production of approximately 15,000.

—	6500	4750	2500	1500	500	

1861 Army Revolver

A .44-caliber percussion revolver, with 8" octagonal barrel and 6-shot cylinder. Loading lever is cut with a slot so that cylinder pin can be drawn forward without lever being lowered. Blued case hardened, with walnut grips. Barrel marked "Patented Dec. 17, 1861 Manufactured by Remington's, Ilion, N.Y.". Some examples were converted to .46-caliber rimfire cartridge and would be worth approximately 25 percent more than original martially marked standard percussion model. Approximately 12,000 manufactured in 1862. This model also known as "Old Army Model".

—	7000	4750	2000	1000	500	

1861 Navy Revolver

As above in .36-caliber, with 7.25" octagonal barrel. Blued case hardened, with walnut grips. This model also found altered to .38 metallic cartridge. Cartridge examples are worth approximately 35 percent less than percussion versions. Approximately 8,000 manufactured in 1862. **NOTE:** Add 25 percent for martial.

—	6000	5000	2500	1500	500	

New Model Army Revolver

A .44-caliber 6-shot percussion revolver, with 8" octagonal barrel. Blued case hardened, with walnut grips. Barrel marked "Patented Sept. 14, 1858 E. Remington & Sons, Ilion, New York, U.S.A. New Model". Approximately 132,000 made between 1863 and 1873.

Standard Model—Military Version

—	7000	5750	3750	1800	400	

Civilian Model—No Government Inspector's Markings

—	6000	5000	3000	1000	400	

.44 or .46 Cartridge Conversion

—	4800	3000	1400	875	400	

New Model Navy Revolver

As above in .36-caliber, with 7.23" octagonal barrel. Approximately 22,000 made between 1863 and 1875.

Military Version

—	6200	5000	3200	1500	400	

Civilian Version

—	5200	4000	2400	1000	400	

.38 Cartridge Conversion—1873 to 1888

—	4200	2400	1000	450	300	

New Model Single-Action Belt Revolver

As above with 6.5" barrel. Blued or nickel-plated case hardened, with walnut grips. This model sometimes encountered altered to .38 cartridge. Cartridge examples are worth approximately 25 percent less than values listed below. Approximately 3,000 made between 1863 and 1873. **NOTE:** Blued models will command a premium.

—	4800	3000	1500	1000	500	

Remington-Rider Double-Action Belt Revolver

Double-action .36-caliber percussion revolver, with 6.5" octagonal barrel marked "Manufactured by Remington's, Ilion, N.Y. Rider's Pt. Aug. 17, 1858, May 3, 1859". Blued or nickel-plated case hardened, with walnut grips. This model also found converted to cartridge and such examples would be worth approximately 20 percent less than values listed below. Several hundred of this model were made with fluted cylinders and are worth a premium of about 25 percent. Approximately 5,000 made between 1863 and 1873.

—	4500	2750	1500	900	400	

NIB	EXC.	V.G.	GOOD	FAIR	POOR

New Model Police Revolver

A .36-caliber percussion revolver, with octagonal barrels ranging from 3.5" to 6.5" and 5-shot cylinder. Blued or nickel-plated case hardened, with walnut grips. This model also found converted to cartridge and such examples would be worth approximately 20 percent less than values listed below. Approximately 18,000 manufactured between 1863 and 1873. **NOTE:** Blued models will command a premium.

	4200	3000	2000	800	300

New Model Pocket Revolver

A .31-caliber spur trigger percussion revolver, with octagonal barrels ranging from 3" to 4.5" in length and 5-shot cylinder. Blued or nickel-plated case hardened, with walnut grips. Barrel marked "Patented Sept. 14, 1858, March 17, 1863 E. Remington & Sons, Ilion, New York U.S.A. New Model.". Approximately 25,000 manufactured between 1863 and 1873. **NOTE:** Add 15 percent for blued models.

1st Version
Brass frame and trigger.

	4200	3200	1800	1300	300

2nd Version
Iron frame, brass trigger.

		2750	1400	900	300

3rd Version
Iron frame, iron trigger.

		2400	1200	800	300

.32 Cartridge Conversion

		2200	1000	600	300

Remington-Rider Derringer

Small silver-plated brass single-shot .17-caliber percussion pistol, with 3" round barrel. Barrel marked "Rider's Pt. Sept. 13, 1859". Approximately 1,000 manufactured between 1860 and 1863. Beware of fakes.

		6900	3300	975	300

Zig-Zag Derringer

A 6-shot .22-caliber revolving barrel pocket pistol, with barrels 3.25" in length. Barrels are cut with zigzag grooves, which are part of the revolving mechanism. Trigger is formed as a ring that when moved forward and rearward turns the barrels and cocks the internal hammer. Barrel group marked "Elliot's Patent Aug. 17, 1858 May 29, 1860" as well as "Manufactured by Remington's Ilion, N.Y.". Approximately 1,000 manufactured in 1861 and 1862.

	5000	3600	1650	650	300

Remington-Elliot Derringer

A 5-shot .22-caliber or 4-shot .32-caliber pepperbox pistol, with a revolving firing pin. Blued or nickel-plated, with hard rubber grips. Barrel group marked "Manufactured by E. Remington & Sons, Ilion, N.Y. Elliot's Patents May 19, 1860 - Oct.1, 1861". Approximately 25,000 manufactured between 1863 and 1888.

5-shot .22 caliber

	5000	3600	1500	750	200

4-shot .32 caliber

	5000	3600	1500	750	200

Vest Pocket Pistol

A .22-caliber single-shot pistol, with 3.25" barrel. Blued or nickel-plated, with walnut grips. Barrel marked "Remington's Ilion, N.Y. Patent Oct. 1, 1861". Early examples have been noted without any barrel markings. Approximately 25,000 manufactured from 1865 to 1888. **NOTE:** Add 35 percent premium for blued models.

	3000	2000	1000	400	200

Large-Bore Vest Pocket Pistol

As above in .30-, .32- or .41-caliber, with barrel lengths of either 3.5" or 4". Blued or nickel-plated, with walnut or rosewood grips. Barrel markings as above, except for the addition of patent date, November 15, 1864. Smaller caliber versions are worth approximately 20 percent more than .41-caliber. Approximately 10,000 manufactured from 1865 to 1888. **NOTE:** Add 35 percent premium for blued models.

	3300	2200	1200	350	150

NIB	EXC.	V.G.	GOOD	FAIR	POOR

Remington-Elliot Single-Shot Derringer

A .41-caliber single-shot pistol, with 2.5" round barrel. Blued or nickel-plated, with walnut, ivory or pearl grips. Barrel marked "Remingtons, Ilion, N.Y. Elliot Pat. Aug. 27, 1867". Approximately 10,000 manufactured between 1867 and 1888. **NOTE:** Add 35 percent premium for blued models. For all variations of Remington Over/Under Derringer below, examine closely for broken or cracked barrel hinge and subtract from value accordingly.

NIB	EXC.	V.G.	GOOD	FAIR	POOR
—	3500	2500	1200	400	125

REMINGTON OVER/UNDER DERRINGERS

Double-barrel .41-caliber pocket pistol, with 3" round barrels that pivot upward for loading. There is a lock bar to release barrels on the right side of frame. Firing pin raises and lowers automatically to fire each respective barrel. It has a spur trigger and bird's-head grip. Finish either blued or nickel-plated and featured with walnut, rosewood or checkered hard rubber grips. Examples with factory pearl or ivory grips would be worth a small premium. Approximately 150,000 manufactured between 1866 and 1935.

Early Type I

Manufactured without an extractor, this type marked "E." Remington & Sons, Ilion, N.Y." on one side and "Elliot's Patent Dec. 12, 1865" on other side of barrel rib. Only a few hundred manufactured in 1866. **NOTE:** Add 25 percent premium for blued models.

NIB	EXC.	V.G.	GOOD	FAIR	POOR
—	5000	4500	3000	2000	1000

Type I Mid-Production

As above fitted with an extractor. Manufactured in late 1860s. **NOTE:** Add 25 percent premium for blued models.

NIB	EXC.	V.G.	GOOD	FAIR	POOR
—	3500	2750	1100	550	250

Type I Late Production

Fitted with an automatic extractor and marked on top of barrel rib. Manufactured from late 1860s to 1888. **NOTE:** Add 25 percent premium for blued models.

NIB	EXC.	V.G.	GOOD	FAIR	POOR
—	4500	3400	2200	1000	200

Type II

Marked "Remington Arms Co., Ilion, N.Y." on barrel rib. Manufactured between 1888 and 1911. **NOTE:** Add 25 percent premium for blued models.

NIB	EXC.	V.G.	GOOD	FAIR	POOR
—	2500	1900	1200	600	200

Type III

Marked "Remington Arms - U.M.C. Co., Ilion, N.Y." on barrel rib. Manufactured between 1912 and 1935. **NOTE:** For Type III models, blue or nickel prices are the same.

NIB	EXC.	V.G.	GOOD	FAIR	POOR
—	1750	1000	875	450	200

Remington-Rider Magazine Pistol

A 5-shot .32-caliber magazine pistol, with spur trigger and 3" octagonal barrel. Magazine located beneath barrel and can be loaded from front. Blued nickel-plated or case hardened, with walnut, pearl or ivory grips. Barrel marked "E. Remington & Sons, Ilion, N.Y. Riders Pat. Aug. 15, 1871". Approximately 10,000 manufactured between 1871 and 1888. **NOTE:** Add 50 percent premium for blued finish.

NIB	EXC.	V.G.	GOOD	FAIR	POOR
—	3000	1950	825	350	150

Model 1865 Navy Rolling Block Pistol

Spur trigger single-shot rolling block .50-caliber rimfire cartridge pistol, with 8.5" round barrel. Blued case hardened, with walnut grips and fore-end. Barrel marked "Remingtons, Ilion N.Y. U.S.A. Pat. May 3d Nov. 15th, 1864 April 17th, 1866". Examples bearing military inspection marks are worth approximately 25 percent more than values listed below. Examples are also found altered to centerfire cartridge and these are worth approximately 10 percent less than values listed below. Approximately 6,500 manufactured between 1866 and 1870.

NIB	EXC.	V.G.	GOOD	FAIR	POOR
—	6000	4500	3000	1000	400

Model 1867 Navy Rolling Block Pistol

A .50-caliber single-shot rolling block pistol, with 7" round barrel. Blued case hardened, with walnut grips and fore-end. Majority of these pistols were purchased by the United States government. Civilian examples without inspection marks are worth approximately 30 percent more than values listed.

NIB	EXC.	V.G.	GOOD	FAIR	POOR
—	6000	4500	3000	1000	400

NIB	EXC.	V.G.	GOOD	FAIR	POOR

Model 1871 Army Rolling Block Pistol

A .50-caliber rolling block single-shot pistol, with 8" round barrel. Blued case hardened, with walnut grips and fore-end. Distinguishing feature of this model is, it has a rearward extension at top of the grip and a squared butt. Approximately 6,000 manufactured between 1872 and 1888. Engraved ivory-stocked versions, as pictured below, will bring considerable premiums.

—	3500	2350	1800	875	400

Remington-Smoot No. 1 Revolver

A .30-caliber spur trigger revolver, with 2.75" octagonal barrel and 5-shot fluted cylinder. Blued or nickel-plated, with walnut or hard rubber grips. Barrel rib marked "E. Remington & Sons, Ilion, N.Y. Pat. W. S. Smoot Oct. 21, 1873". Examples dating from beginning of production are found with a revolving recoil shield. Such examples would command approximately 300 percent premium over values listed. **NOTE:** Add 50 percent premium for blued finish.

—	2000	1650	1100	675	250

Remington-Smoot No. 2 Revolver

As above in .32-caliber. Approximately 20,000 manufactured between 1878 and 1888. **NOTE:** Add 50 percent premium for blued finish.

—	1800	875	600	275	100

Remington-Smoot No. 3 Revolver

Two variations of this spur trigger .38-caliber revolver exist. One with rounded grip and no barrel rib; other with squared back, squared butt grip with barrel rib. Centerfire versions are also known and are worth approximately 10 percent more than values listed below. Blued or nickel-plated, with hard rubber grips. Approximately 25,000 manufactured between 1878 and 1888. **NOTE:** Add 50 percent premium for blued finish.

—	1700	650	550	325	100

New No. 4 Revolver

A .38- or .41-caliber spur trigger revolver, with 2.5" barrel and no ejector rod. Blued or nickel-plated, with hard rubber grips. Barrel marked "E. Remington & Sons, Ilion, N.Y.". Approximately 10,000 manufactured between 1877 and 1888. **NOTE:** Add 50 percent premium for blued finish.

—	1700	775	475	225	100

Remington Iroquois Revolver

A .22-caliber spur trigger revolver, with 2.25" barrel and 7-shot cylinder. Blued or nickel-plated, with hard rubber grips. Barrel marked "Remington, Ilion, N.Y." and "Iroquois". Some examples of this model will be found without Remington markings. Approximately 10,000 manufactured between 1878 and 1888. **NOTE:** Add 50 percent premium for blued finish.

—	2000	1100	825	385	150

Model 1875 Single-Action Revolver

A .44 Remington or .44-40 or .45-caliber single-action revolver, with 7.5" barrel. Blued or nickel-plated case hardened, with walnut grips. Some examples are found fitted with a lanyard ring at butt. Barrel marked "E. Remington & Sons Ilion, N.Y. U.S.A.". Approximately 25,000 manufactured between 1875 and 1889. **NOTE:** Add 40 percent for blued version.

—	14000	10000	6000	3000	1000

Model 1890 Single-Action Revolver

A .44-40 caliber single-action revolver, with 5.5" or 7.5" barrel and 6-shot cylinder. Blued or nickel-plated, with hard rubber grips bearing monogram "RA" at top. Barrel marked "Remington Arms Co., Ilion, N.Y.". Approximately 2,000 manufactured between 1891 and 1894. Beware of fakes. **NOTE:** Add 40 percent for blued version.

—	15000	10000	6000	3000	1000

Model 1891 Target Rolling Block Pistol

A .22, .25 Stevens or .32 S&W caliber single-shot rolling block pistol, with 10" half octagonal barrel fitted with target sights. Blued case hardened, with walnut grips and fore-end. Barrel marked "Remington Arms Co. Ilion, N.Y."; frame "Remingtons Ilion N.Y. U.S.A. Pat. May 3 Nov. 15, 1864 April 17, 1866 P S". An extremely rare pistol, with slightly more than 100 manufactured between 1892 and 1898. Prospective purchasers are advised to secure a qualified appraisal prior to acquisition.

—	4000	3700	2750	1200	500

NIB	EXC.	V.G.	GOOD	FAIR	POOR

Model 1901 Target Rolling Block

As above, with exception that the bridge block thumb piece has been moved out of the line of sight and rear sight is mounted on frame instead of barrel. Approximately 735 manufactured between 1901 and 1909.

	4000	3650	2750	1200	500

Mark III Signal Pistol

A 10-gauge spur trigger flare pistol, with 9" round barrel. Frame of brass and barrel of iron finished matte black, with walnut grips. Barrel marked "The Remington Arms - Union Metallic Cartridge Co., Inc. Mark III, Remington Bridgeport Works Bridgeport, Connecticut U.S.A.". Approximately 25,000 manufactured between 1915 and 1918.

		725	375	110	55

Model 51

A .32- or .380-caliber semi-automatic pistol, with 3.5" barrel and magazines capable of holding either 7 or 8 cartridges depending on caliber. Blued, with hard rubber grips having legend "Remington UMC" in a circle at top. Slide marked "The Remington Arms - Union Metallic Cartridge Co., Inc. Remington Ilion Wks. Ilion, N.Y. U.S.A. Pedersen's Patents Pending". Later versions carried a 1920 and 1921 patent date. Early examples have nine grooves on slide; later models have 15 grooves, with frame marked "Remington Trademark". Early variations are worth approximately 10 percent more than values listed below; .32-caliber examples are worth approximately 25 percent additional. Approximately 65,000 manufactured between 1918 and 1934.

	750	575	350	125	75

Model 53

Built in 1917 in .45 ACP for U.S. government test. Similar to Model 51, except for size and an external hammer. Tested by US Army and Navy. Overall length 8.25"; weight about 35 oz.; magazine capacity 7 rounds. Too rare to price.

1911R1 SERIES

Model 1911R1

Combines traditional 1911 features with modern touches. Caliber .45 ACP. Carbon steel slide and frame, traditionally styled trigger, hammer, recoil system, walnut grips, 7-round magazine, thumb and grip safeties. Dovetailed front and rear sights, with white dots, lowered and flared ejection port. Weight 38.5 oz., 5" barrel and Satin Black Oxide or stainless finish. Model 1911 Enhanced has match-grade barrel and bushing, front cocking serrations, extended thumb safety and beavertail tang, textured grips, adjustable rear and fiber optic front sights and lightweight trigger and hammer. Introduced 2010. **NOTE:** Add 30 percent for Enhanced model.

600	525	435	350	200	150

Model 1911R1 Centennial

Same features as 1911R1, with special Centennial engravings on slide, Centennial serial number range, dovetailed brass-bead front and black serrated rear sight. Custom grips with Remington medallions.

1100	925	800	600		

Model 1911R1 Centennial Limited Edition

Same features as above, plus uniquely engraved slide with gold banner, custom charcoal blued finish, 24-karat gold front sight, smooth exhibition grade walnut grips. Each Limited Edition model is hand assembled and comes in a custom wood presentation case. Introduced in 2011. Production scheduled for only 300 units.

2000	1900	1800			

Model 1911R1 Enhanced

Same features and dimensions as other 1911R1 models, with custom enhancements. In .45 ACP, with 8-round magazine. Adjustable rear sight, fiber optic front sight. Hardwood checkered grips. Front and rear slide serrations, with checkered mainspring housing. Aluminum anodized trigger. Match grade barrel and bushing. Carbon steel frame and slide, with satin black oxide finish. Custom carrying case. Introduced 2012; stainless version 2013.

875	775	675	550	400	350

Model 1911R1 Carry

Same general specifications as other 1911R1 models. Added features include: all sharp edges have been dehorned; Novak combat sights, with tritium front sight; Cocobolo checkered grips; Beavertail grip safety, with checkered memory bump; rear slide serrations, with checkered mainspring housing and front strap; aluminum anodized trigger; match grade barrel and bushing;

	NIB	EXC.	V.G.	GOOD	FAIR	POOR

carbon steel frame and slide, with satin black oxide finish. Custom carrying case. 8+1 capacity. Introduced 2013.

	NIB	EXC.	V.G.	GOOD	FAIR	POOR
	1150	1000	900	700	450	350

RIFLES

Model 1841 "Mississippi Rifle"

A .54-caliber percussion rifle, with 33" barrel and full stock secured by two barrel bands. Lock marked (Remington's Herkimer N.Y.) is case hardened. Barrel browned and furniture of brass. Stock fitted with brass patch box on right side. Approximately 20,000 manufactured between 1846 and 1855.

	NIB	EXC.	V.G.	GOOD	FAIR	POOR
	—	—	2000	1750	750	400

Model 1861 U.S. Rifle Musket

A .58-caliber percussion rifle, with 40" barrel and full length stock secured by three barrel bands. Lock marked "Remington's Ilion, N.Y.". Finished in white, with walnut stock. Approximately 40,000 manufactured between 1864 and 1866.

	NIB	EXC.	V.G.	GOOD	FAIR	POOR
		4500	3000	1250	500	200

Model 1863 Zouave Rifle

A .58-caliber percussion rifle, with 33" barrel and full length stock secured by two barrel bands. Lock case hardened and marked "Remington's Ilion N.Y.". Barrel blued and furniture of brass. Approximately 12,500 manufactured between 1862 and 1865.

	NIB	EXC.	V.G.	GOOD	FAIR	POOR
		6000	4000	2250	1500	500

Breech-Loading Carbine

A .46 or .50 rimfire single-shot rolling block carbine, with 20" barrel. Blued case hardened, with walnut stock. Tang marked "Remington's Ilion, N.Y. Pat. Dec. 23, 1863 May 3 & Nov. 16, 1864". The .50-caliber version worth approximately 15 percent more than .46-caliber. Approximately 15,000 .50-caliber variations were made, most of which were sold to France. Approximately 5,000 carbines were made in .46-caliber. Manufactured from 1864 to 1866.

	NIB	EXC.	V.G.	GOOD	FAIR	POOR
	—	—	3750	1500	500	200

Revolving Rifle

A .36- or. 44-caliber revolving rifle, with either 24" or 28" octagonal barrels and 6-shot cylinder. Trigger guard formed with scrolled finger extension at rear. Blued case hardened, with walnut stock. These rifles are also encountered converted to cartridge and would be worth approximately 20 percent less than percussion values listed below. Barrel marked "Patented Sept. 14, 1858 E. Remington & Sons, Ilion, New York, U.S.A. New Model". The .44-caliber model will bring a premium of about 15 percent and is rare. Approximately 1,000 manufactured between 1866 and 1879.

	NIB	EXC.	V.G.	GOOD	FAIR	POOR
	—	20000	11500	8000	5500	900

Remington-Beals Rifle

A .32- or .38-caliber sliding barrel single-shot rifle, with octagonal barrels of 24", 26" or 28" length. Barrel can be moved forward by lowering trigger guard/lever. This model found with either frames made of brass or iron, the latter being worth approximately 20 percent more than values listed below. Walnut stock. Barrel marked "Beals Patent June 28, 1864 Jan. 30, 1866 E. Remington & Sons, Ilion, New York.". Approximately 800 manufactured between 1866 and 1888. Few examples are known to have been factory engraved. Prospective purchasers are advised to secure a qualified appraisal prior to acquisition.

	NIB	EXC.	V.G.	GOOD	FAIR	POOR
	—	2500	1500	950	400	150

U.S. Navy Rolling Block Carbine

	NIB	EXC.	V.G.	GOOD	FAIR	POOR
	—	4000	3250	2750	1000	350

Model 1867 Navy Cadet Rifle

	NIB	EXC.	V.G.	GOOD	FAIR	POOR
	—	3500	2750	1400	700	350

Rolling Block Military Rifles

	NIB	EXC.	V.G.	GOOD	FAIR	POOR
	—	—	900	750	400	100

NO. 1 ROLLING BLOCK SPORTING RIFLE

Standard No. 1 Sporting Rifle

Single-shot rolling block rifle. Produced in a variety of calibers from .40-50 to .50-70 centerfire, as well as .32, .44 and .46 rimfire. Standard barrel lengths were either 28" or 30" and of octagonal form.

	NIB	EXC.	V.G.	GOOD	FAIR	POOR
	—	4000	3500	2500	1500	500

	NIB	EXC.	V.G.	GOOD	FAIR	POOR

Long-Range Creedmoor Rifle

A .44-90, .44-100 or .44-105 caliber rolling block rifle, with 34" half-octagonal barrel, long-range vernier tang sights and globe front sights. Blued case hardened, with walnut stock and checkered pistol-grip. Rifle was available with a number of optional features. A qualified appraisal should be secured if those features are in doubt. Produced from 1873 to 1890.

		10000	8500	5750	2500	500
	—					

Mid-Range Target Rifle

As above, except chambered for .40-70, .44-77, .45-70 or .50-70 caliber, with 28" or 30" half-octagonal barrels. Produced from 1875 to 1890.

		6000	2750	1750	300
—	—				

Short-Range Rifle

As above, chambered for cartridges between .38- and .44-caliber, with 26" or 30" round or octagonal barrels. Open rear sight, with Beach front sight. Walnut stock is checkered. Produced from 1875 to 1890.

		5000	2750	1675	250
—	—				

Black Hills Rifle

As above in .45-60 caliber, with 28" round barrel. Fitted with open sights and plain straight-grip stock. Produced from 1877 to 1882.

		5000	2750	1675	250
—	—				

Shotgun

As above in 16-gauge, with either 30" or 32" Damascus or fluid steel barrels. Produced from 1870 to 1892.

	2800	1650	1200	750	150
—					

Baby Carbine

As above, with 20" thin round barrel. Chambered for .44-40 cartridge and fitted with a saddle ring on the left side of frame. Blued case hardened, with walnut stock and carbine buttplate. Manufactured from 1892 to 1902.

	8000	4250	2250	900	200
—					

Model 1-1/2 Sporting Rifle

Lightweight variation of above, using 1.25" wide No. 1 rolling block action. Chambered for rimfire cartridges from .22 to .38 Extra Long, as well as centerfire cartridges from .32-20 to .44-40. Medium weight octagonal barrels from 24" to 28" in length, with open rear and blade-type front sight. Blued case hardened, with walnut stock. Several thousand manufactured between 1888 and 1897.

	2800	2000	950	400	100
—					

Model 2 Sporting Rifle

As above using No. 2 action. Chambered for various cartridges from .22- to .38-caliber, with 24" or 26" octagonal barrels. Blued case hardened, with walnut stock. Produced with a number of optional features that affect its value. Prospective purchasers are advised to secure a qualified appraisal prior to acquisition. Manufactured from 1873 to 1910.

	2400	1500	600	250	100
—					

No. 4 Rolling Block Rifle

Built on lightweight No. 4 action. Rifle was available in .22, .25 Stevens or .32-caliber, with either 22.5" or 24" octagonal barrel. Blued case hardened, with walnut stock. Takedown version was also made and these are worth approximately 10 percent more than values listed. Approximately 50,000 manufactured between 1890 and 1933.

	900	700	400	200	75
—					

No. 4 S Military Rifle

At the request of United States Boy Scouts in 1913, Remington Company designed a military style rifle having a 28" barrel and full length fore-end secured by one barrel band. A short upper hand guard was also fitted and a bayonet stud is found at the muzzle. In 1915, designation of this model was changed from "Boy Scout" to "Military Model". Approximately 15,000 manufactured between 1913 and 1923.

	2250	950	400	275

No. 5 Rolling Block Rifle

Built on No. 5 action, this rifle was designed for smokeless cartridges. Made in a variety of barrel lengths, calibers and in a carbine version. Blued case hardened, with walnut stock.

		2250	800	350	100
—	—				

	NIB	EXC.	V.G.	GOOD	FAIR	POOR

No. 5 Sporting or Target Rifle

Chambered for .30-30, .303 British, 7mm, .30 U.S., .32-40, .32 U.S. and .38-55 cartridges. Offered with 28" or 30" round barrels. Features a plain straight-grip stock, with half-length fore-end. Has open rear sights and was available with double-set triggers that would add approximately 10 percent to value. Manufactured between 1898 and 1905.

NIB	EXC.	V.G.	GOOD	FAIR	POOR
—	—	5750	2250	850	300

Model 1897

A 7x57mm and .30 U.S. caliber full stock rolling block rifle. Model 1902 is of identical form, except it was fitted with an automatic ejector. Manufactured from 1897 to 1902.

NIB	EXC.	V.G.	GOOD	FAIR	POOR
—	2800	1250	550	250	100

Carbine

As above fitted with 20" round barrel and half-length fore-end secured by one barrel band.

NIB	EXC.	V.G.	GOOD	FAIR	POOR
—	—	1750	750	350	100

No. 6 Rolling Block Rifle

Lightweight small rifle designed expressly to be used by young boys. Chambered for .22 rimfire cartridge, as well as .32 Short or Long. Also produced with smoothbore barrel to be used with shot cartridges. Round barrel 20" in length. Has a takedown action, with barrel held on by a knurled knob underneath the frame. It is a lightweight rolling block, with a thin operating knob on the breech. Finish is blued overall. Early models featured case-colored frame and these versions would be worth approximately 10 percent additional. Has a straight-grip walnut stock, with a small forearm. Over 250,000 manufactured between 1902 and 1903.

NIB	EXC.	V.G.	GOOD	FAIR	POOR
—	750	475	300	100	75

No. 7 Rolling Block Rifle

Readily identifiable by its accentuated checked pistol-grip. Available in .22 or .25-10 Stevens caliber, with 24", 26" or 28" half octagonal barrels. Fitted with a tang mounted aperture rear sight. Blued case hardened, with walnut stock. Approximately 1,000 manufactured between 1903 and 1911.

NIB	EXC.	V.G.	GOOD	FAIR	POOR
—	6500	5000	3000	2000	500

REMINGTON-HEPBURN RIFLES

Remington-Hepburn No. 3 Rifle

Lever activated falling block single-shot rifle designed by Lewis Hepburn. Available in a variety of calibers from .22 Winchester centerfire to .50-90 Sharps. Octagonal or round barrels 26", 28" or 30" length. Blued case hardened, with walnut stock. Available with a variety of optional features that affect value considerably. Prospective purchasers are advised to secure a qualified appraisal prior to acquisition. Approximately 10,000 manufactured between 1883 and 1907.

NIB	EXC.	V.G.	GOOD	FAIR	POOR
—	—	4000	2000	1200	300

Remington-Hepburn No. 3 Match Rifle

As above fitted with a high comb buttstock and nickel-plated Schuetzen buttplate. Manufactured in various calibers from .25-20 Stevens to .40-65, with 30" half octagonal barrels. Model was made in two versions: "A Quality" with plain stock, tang mounted rear sight and a Beach front sight; "B Quality" with checkered walnut stock having a cheek rest, checkered fore-end, vernier rear sight and combination wind gauge and spirit level front sight. Double set triggers were also available and these would add approximately 10 percent to values listed below. Approximately 1,000 manufactured between 1883 and 1907.

A Quality

NIB	EXC.	V.G.	GOOD	FAIR	POOR
—	—	7500	4750	1800	350

B Quality

NIB	EXC.	V.G.	GOOD	FAIR	POOR
—	—	8250	5000	1900	500

Remington-Hepburn No. 3 Long-Range Creedmoor Rifle

As above in .44-caliber, with 32" or 34" half-octagonal barrel. Long-range vernier rear sight, combination wind gauge and spirit level front sight. Deluxe checkered walnut stock and rubber shotgun buttplate. Produced with a number of optional features that affect value. Prospective purchasers are advised to secure a qualified appraisal prior to acquisition. Manufactured from 1880 to 1907.

NIB	EXC.	V.G.	GOOD	FAIR	POOR
—	—	7500	4750	1800	350

Remington-Hepburn No. 3 Mid-Range Creedmoor Rifle

As above chambered for .40-65 cartridge. Fitted with 28" barrel.

NIB	EXC.	V.G.	GOOD	FAIR	POOR
—	—	5000	2250	950	350

NIB	EXC.	V.G.	GOOD	FAIR	POOR

Remington-Hepburn No. 3 Long-Range Military Rifle

Rare variation that is chambered for .44-20 Remington cartridge. Has round 34" barrel and full-length forearm held on by two barrel bands. Blued case-colored finish. Stock is walnut. There are two basic versions: plain grade, has uncheckered straight-grip stock, with military-type sights; fancy grade, features high-grade checkered pistol-grip stock, with full-length checkered fore-end, vernier tang sight, wind gauge and spirit lever front sight. A few manufactured in the 1880s.

Plain Grade

—	6000	4500	2500	1200	400

Fancy Grade

—	9000	7500	3750	1500	600

Remington-Hepburn No. 3 Schuetzen Match Rifle

As above instead of side lever the action is raised or lowered by means of lever on the trigger guard. Chambered for various popular cartridges. Offered with 30" or 32" part-octagonal heavy barrel. Features vernier tang sight, with hooded front sight. Standard with double-set triggers and palm rest. Finish blued and case-colored, with high-grade checkered walnut stock and fore-end. Has ornate Swiss-type Schuetzen buttplate. Also known as "Walker-Hepburn Rifle". There were two versions available. One, standard breech-loader with Remington Walker-marked barrel; the other, a muzzle-loading variation fitted with a removable false muzzle. This version was supplied with brass bullet starter and other accessories. Prospective purchasers are advised to secure a qualified appraisal prior to acquisition.

Breechloading Version

—	—	27500	12500	3500	900

Muzzleloading Version

—	—	42500	17500	5000	1500

Remington-Hepburn No. 3 High-Power Rifle

Model No. 3 also available in a variety of smokeless cartridges: .30-30, .30-40, .32 Special, .32-40 and .38-55. Standard barrel lengths were 26", 28" or 30". Produced from 1900 to 1907.

—	4000	2500	1750	650	250

REMINGTON-KEENE MAGAZINE RIFLE

Bolt-action rifle chambered for .40, .43 and .45-70 centerfire cartridges, with 22", 24.5", 29.25" or 32.5" barrels. Readily identifiable by exposed hammer at end of the bolt. Blued case hardened hammer and furniture, with walnut stock. Receiver marked "E. Remington & Sons, Ilion, N.Y." together with patent dates 1874, 1876 and 1877. Magazine on this rifle was located beneath the barrel. Receiver fitted with a cut-off so that rifle could be used as a single-shot. Approximately 5,000 manufactured between 1880 and 1888 in variations listed.

Sporting Rifle
24.5" barrel.

—	3450	2000	750	350	150

Army Rifle
Barrel length 32.5". Full-length stock secured by two barrel bands.

—	—	—	3500	950	450

Navy Rifle
As above, with 29.25" barrel.

—	—	—	4500	1750	450

Carbine
As above, with 22" barrel. Half-length fore-end secured by one barrel band.

—	—	5750	3250	1250	350

Frontier Model (aka Indiana Scout Carbine)

As above, with 24" barrel. Half-length fore-end secured by one barrel band. Those purchased by United States Department of Interior for arming Indian Police are marked "U.S.I.D." on receiver.

—	—	5250	2500	850	

REMINGTON-LEE RIFLES

Remington-Lee Magazine Rifle

Designed by James Paris Lee. Rifles of this type were originally manufactured by Sharps Rifle Company in 1880. Remington Company began production of this model in 1881, after Sharps

	NIB	EXC.	V.G.	GOOD	FAIR	POOR

Company ceased operations. Approximately 100,000 Lee magazine rifles manufactured between 1880 and 1907. Their variations are listed.

Remington-Lee Model 1879 Sharps Mfg.

Barrel length 28", with full-length stock secured by two barrel bands. Barrel marked "Sharps Rifle Co. Bridgeport, Conn." and "Old Reliable" in rectangular cartouche. Approximately 300 made prior to 1881.

NIB	EXC.	V.G.	GOOD	FAIR	POOR
—	—	4750	3000	2000	600

Remington-Lee Model 1879 U.S. Navy Model

NIB	EXC.	V.G.	GOOD	FAIR	POOR
—	4000	2800	1600	750	250

Remington-Lee Model 1879 Sporting Rifle

Barrel length 28" or 30"; .45-70 or .45-90 caliber. Checkered pistol-grip stock, with sporting-style fore-end. Markings on receiver as above. Approximately 450 made.

NIB	EXC.	V.G.	GOOD	FAIR	POOR
—	—	2500	1750	700	250

Remington-Lee Model 1879 Military Rifle

Identical to Navy model, except chambered for .43 Spanish cartridge. Limited number were produced in .45-70 caliber. Spanish versions are worth approximately 25 percent less than values listed below. Approximately 1,000 were made. Majority of these rifles were made for export.

NIB	EXC.	V.G.	GOOD	FAIR	POOR
—	3200	2200	1250	500	150

Remington-Lee Model 1882 Army Contract

NIB	EXC.	V.G.	GOOD	FAIR	POOR
—	4000	2800	1250	750	300

Remington-Lee Model 1885 Navy Contract

NIB	EXC.	V.G.	GOOD	FAIR	POOR
—	4000	2800	1750	750	300

Remington-Lee Model 1882 & 1885 Military Rifles

Barrel length 32". Full-length stock secured by two barrel bands. Chambered for .42 Russian, .43 Spanish, .45 Gardner or .45-70 cartridges. Values for those rifles not in .45-70 caliber would be approximately 25 percent less than those listed. Approximately 10,000 Model 1882 rifles were made; 60,000 Model 1885 rifles. Two models can be differentiated by the cocking piece on the bolt of Model 1885 is larger. Majority of these rifles were made for foreign contracts and commercial sales.

NIB	EXC.	V.G.	GOOD	FAIR	POOR
—	—	1795	950	400	150

Remington-Lee Model 1882 & 1885 Sporting Rifle

As above chambered for .45-70 and .45-90 caliber, with 26" or 30" octagonal barrels and walnut sporting stocks. Approximately 200 were made.

NIB	EXC.	V.G.	GOOD	FAIR	POOR
—	—	2400	1750	750	200

Remington-Lee Model 1882 & 1885 Carbine

As above, with 24" barrel and half-length fore-end secured by one barrel band. Prospective purchasers are advised to secure a qualified appraisal prior to acquisition.

NIB	EXC.	V.G.	GOOD	FAIR	POOR
—	—	2400	1750	750	200

Remington-Lee Model 1899

Designed for use with smokeless and rimless cartridges. Marked on receiver "Remington Arms Co. Ilion, N.Y. Patented Aug. 26th 1884 Sept. 9th 1884 March 17th 1885 Jan 18th 1887". Produced from 1889 to 1907 in variations listed.

Military Rifle

NIB	EXC.	V.G.	GOOD	FAIR	POOR
—	3000	2000	1000	400	200

Military Carbine

NIB	EXC.	V.G.	GOOD	FAIR	POOR
—	3200	2200	1250	500	250

Remington-Lee Sporting Rifle

As above, with 24", 26" or 28" round or octagonal barrel. Half-length sporting stock, with checkered pistol-grip. Approximately 7,000 were manufactured.

NIB	EXC.	V.G.	GOOD	FAIR	POOR
—	—	1250	500	200	100

Remington Lebel Bolt-Action Rifle

NIB	EXC.	V.G.	GOOD	FAIR	POOR
—	—	750	450	150	100

Remington Mosin-Nagant Bolt-Action Rifle

NIB	EXC.	V.G.	GOOD	FAIR	POOR
—	—	600	300	100	75

	NIB	EXC.	V.G.	GOOD	FAIR	POOR

U.S. Model 1917 Magazine Rifle

NIB	EXC.	V.G.	GOOD	FAIR	POOR
—	—	1250	600	150	100

Remington-Whitmore Model 1874

Sidelock double-barrel shotgun, combination shotgun/rifle or double-barrel rifle, with 28" or 30" fluid steel barrels. Also available with Damascus barrels. Barrels released by pushing forward the top lever. Blued case hardened, with straight- or semi-pistol grip walnut stock. Barrels marked "A. E. Whitmore's Patent Aug. 8, 1871, April 16, 1872". Rib between barrels marked "E. Remington & Sons, Ilion, N.Y.". Several thousand manufactured between 1874 and 1882.

Shotgun

NIB	EXC.	V.G.	GOOD	FAIR	POOR
—	—	1750	850	450	100

Combination Gun (Rare)

NIB	EXC.	V.G.	GOOD	FAIR	POOR
—	—	4250	3200	1500	300

Double Rifle
Very rare.

NIB	EXC.	V.G.	GOOD	FAIR	POOR
—	—	9000	4250	1500	500

Model 1882 Shotgun

Sidelock double-barrel 10- or 12-gauge shotgun, with 28" or 30" fluid steel or Damascus barrels. Blued case hardened, with checkered pistol-grip stock and hard rubber buttplate. Barrels are marked "E. Remington & Sons, Ilion, N.Y." and lock marked "Remington Arms Co.". This model has a conventional top lever that moves to the side. Offered with optional engraving. Such models should be individually appraised. Approximately 7,500 manufactured between 1882 and 1889.

NIB	EXC.	V.G.	GOOD	FAIR	POOR
—	—	1250	750	300	100

Model 1883 through 1889 Shotgun

Sidelock 10-, 12- or 16-gauge double-barrel shotgun, with fluid steel or Damascus barrels 28" to 32" in length. Models 1883, 1885, 1887 and 1889 are all somewhat alike, varying only in form of their hammers and internal mechanisms. Blued case hardened, checkered pistol-grip stock with a grip cap. Available in a variety of styles including highly engraved models that should be individually appraised. Approximately 30,000 manufactured between 1883 and 1909.

NIB	EXC.	V.G.	GOOD	FAIR	POOR
—	—	1800	1100	800	200

Model 1893 (No. 9)

Single-barrel hammer gun in 10-, 12-, 16-, 20-, 24- and 28-gauge. Barrel lengths from 28" to 34". Case colored frame, with hard rubber buttplate.

NIB	EXC.	V.G.	GOOD	FAIR	POOR
—	—	—	600	250	100

Hammerless Shotgun Model 1894

Boxlock 10-, 12- or 16-gauge double shotgun, with fluid steel or Damascus barrels 26" to 32" in length. Blued case hardened, with pistol-grip stock. Available in a variety of styles. It is advised that highly engraved examples should be individually appraised. **NOTE:** Add 25 percent premium for fluid steel barrels.

NIB	EXC.	V.G.	GOOD	FAIR	POOR
—	1750	1250	750	300	100

Model 1900 Shotgun

As above in 12- and 16-gauge only. Same cautions apply to highly engraved examples.

NIB	EXC.	V.G.	GOOD	FAIR	POOR
—	1500	1000	600	250	100

Model 8 Rifle

A .25, .30, .32 or .35 Remington semi-automatic rifle. Featuring 22" barrel, with open sights. Barrel covered by a full- length tube that encloses the recoil spring. Blued, with walnut stock. Approximately 60,000 made between 1906 and 1936 in styles listed. **NOTE:** Add 35 percent for .25 Remington. Some collectors will pay and demand, prices substantially in excess of those listed below for Grades C, D and E

Standard Grade

NIB	EXC.	V.G.	GOOD	FAIR	POOR
1200	900	700	550	250	125

Model 8A
Checkered stock.

NIB	EXC.	V.G.	GOOD	FAIR	POOR
1400	1000	800	600	300	150

Model 8C

NIB	EXC.	V.G.	GOOD	FAIR	POOR
3000	2500	1500	900	500	300

	NIB	EXC.	V.G.	GOOD	FAIR	POOR

8D Peerless
Light engraving.

	NIB	EXC.	V.G.	GOOD	FAIR	POOR
	6000	5000	3500	1750	800	400

8E Expert

	7500	6000	4000	2250	1100	450

8F Premier
Heavily engraved.

	10000	8500	7500	3750	1600	700

Model 81 Woodsmaster

Improved variation of Model 8. Chambered for same calibers (but not .25 apparently) as well as .300 Savage cartridge. Produced from 1936 to 1950 in styles listed. **NOTE:** Add 300 percent for police model, with detachable 15-round magazine.

Standard Grade

	1100	900	750	500	250	125

Model 81A

	1200	1000	850	500	250	125

81D Peerless
Engraved.

	7500	6000	4000	2250	1100	450

81F Premier
Heavily engraved.

	10000	8500	7500	3750	1600	700

Model 12 or 12A

A .22-caliber slide-action rifle, with 22" round or octagonal barrel having open sights. Blued, with walnut stock. Manufactured from 1909 to 1936 in styles listed.

Model 12A

	1000	800	600	300	225	150

Model 12B
.22 Short Gallery Model.

	1500	1100	900	700	400	150

Model 12C
24" octagon barrel.

	1200	1000	750	500	300	175

12C N.R.A. Target
Limited production.

	1500	1300	1100	825	500	300

Model 12CS
.22 Remington Special.

	1300	1000	900	700	400	175

12D Peerless
Light engraving.

	6000	5000	3750	1800	1000	500

12E Expert

	8000	7500	4000	2250	1200	800

12F Premier
Heavily engraved.

	10000	9000	5250	3150	1500	800

Model 121 and/or 121A

A .22-caliber slide-action rifle, with 24" round barrel. Blued, with walnut stock. Manufactured from 1936 to 1954 in styles listed.

Standard Grade

	750	600	500	300	175	100

	NIB	EXC.	V.G.	GOOD	FAIR	POOR

121D Peerless
Engraved.

	NIB	EXC.	V.G.	GOOD	FAIR	POOR
	6500	5000	3750	1800	1000	500

121F Premier
Heavily engraved.

	NIB	EXC.	V.G.	GOOD	FAIR	POOR
	9000	7500	5250	3150	1500	800

Model 121S
.22 WRF.

	NIB	EXC.	V.G.	GOOD	FAIR	POOR
	1100	850	700	400	350	250

121SB—Smoothbore
There are four different variations of this smoothbore rifle. Seek expert advice before a sale.

	NIB	EXC.	V.G.	GOOD	FAIR	POOR
	1200	1000	800	650	400	300

Model 14 or 14A
A .25, .30, .32 or .35 Remington caliber slide-action rifle, with 22" round barrel and open sights. Blued, plain walnut stock. Manufactured from 1912 to 1936. **NOTE:** Add 85 percent for .25 Remington.

	NIB	EXC.	V.G.	GOOD	FAIR	POOR
	—	900	750	500	300	200

Model 14R
As above, with 18.5" barrel.

	NIB	EXC.	V.G.	GOOD	FAIR	POOR
	—	1500	800	500	300	200

Model 14-1/2
As above, except chambered for .38-40 or .44-40 cartridge, with 22.5" barrel. Carbine with 18.5" barrel, known as Model 14-1/2R, would be worth approximately 10 percent more than values listed. Manufactured from 1912 to 1922.

	NIB	EXC.	V.G.	GOOD	FAIR	POOR
	—	2000	1250	700	350	250

Model 16
A .22-caliber (Remington Automatic, not interchangeable with anything else) semi-automatic rifle, with 22" barrel and open sights. Blued, with walnut stock. Later production examples were known as Model 16A. Manufactured from 1914 to 1928.

	NIB	EXC.	V.G.	GOOD	FAIR	POOR
	1000	900	600	250	125	75

Model 141
A .30, .32 or .35 Remington caliber slide-action rifle, with 24" barrel having open sights. Blued, with plain walnut stock. Later production versions of this rifle were known as Model 141A. Manufactured from 1936 to 1950.

	NIB	EXC.	V.G.	GOOD	FAIR	POOR
	1500	1250	800	500	250	175

Model 25
A .25-20 or .32-20 caliber slide-action rifle, with 24" barrel having open sights. Blued, with walnut stock. Later production examples were known as Model 25A. Carbine version with an 18" barrel as Model 25R. Manufactured from 1923 to 1936. **NOTE:** Add 100 percent for rifles with 18" barrels.

	NIB	EXC.	V.G.	GOOD	FAIR	POOR
	—	1000	750	400	250	200

Model 24
Designed by John M. Browning. Semi-automatic rifle in .22-caliber, with 19" barrel and open sights. Blued, with walnut pistol-grip stock. Later production versions were known as Model 24A. Produced from 1922 to 1935.

	NIB	EXC.	V.G.	GOOD	FAIR	POOR
	1200	1000	600	400	200	100

Model 241 Speedmaster
A .22-caliber takedown semi-automatic rifle, with 24" barrel and open sights. Blued, with walnut stock. Later production versions were known as Model 241A. Approximately 56,000 made between 1935 and 1949 in styles listed.

	NIB	EXC.	V.G.	GOOD	FAIR	POOR
	1200	800	650	550	350	200

Model 241

	NIB	EXC.	V.G.	GOOD	FAIR	POOR
	750	550	400	250	200	150

241D Peerless
Engraved.

	NIB	EXC.	V.G.	GOOD	FAIR	POOR
	6500	5000	3750	1800	1000	500

	NIB	EXC.	V.G.	GOOD	FAIR	POOR

241E Expert

	8000	7500	4000	2250	1200	800

241F Premier

Heavily engraved.

	10000	9000	5250	3150	1500	800

Model 550A

A .22 Short, Long or LR caliber semi-automatic rifle, with 24" barrel and open sights. Blued, with walnut pistol-grip stock. Approximately 220,000 made between 1941 and 1971.

—	350	275	150	100	75

Model 550P

As above, with aperture rear sight.

—	375	300	175	125	100

Model 550-2G

As above, except fitted with shell deflector and screw eye for securing it to a shooting gallery counter.

500	400	375	225	135	75

Model 30A "Express"

Sporting rifle using U.S. Model 1917 Enfield bolt-action. Chambered for various Remington cartridges as well as 7x57mm and .30-06 cartridges. Barrel length 22". Checkered walnut stock. Carbine model fitted with 20" barrel was known as Model 30R. Manufactured from 1921 to 1940.

—	950	700	475	175	100

Model 30S

As above chambered for .257 Roberts, 7x57 and .30-06 cartridges. Barrel 24", with Lyman receiver sight. Select checkered walnut stock. Manufactured from 1930 to 1940.

—	1300	975	495	250	150

Model 41A "Targetmaster"

This is a bolt-action rimfire rifle chambered for .22-caliber Short, Long and LR. Barrel 27", with open rear sight and bead front sight. Pistol-grip stock is plain. Produced from 1936 to 1940.

—	300	200	150	100	50

Model 41AS

Same as above. Chambered for .22 Remington Special or .22 WRF cartridge.

—	275	175	125	100	75

Model 41P

Same as Model 41A, with addition of rear peep sight and hooded front sight.

—	325	225	175	125	50

Model 41SB

Same as Model 41A, except used with .22 shot cartridge. Barrel is smoothbore.

—	350	275	195	150	75

Miscellaneous Remington Bolt Action Rimfires, 1930-1970

From 1930 to 1970, Remington Company produced a variety of single-shot and repeating .22-caliber rifles. Values for these are much the same, consequently, they are listed for reference only.

Model 33	Model 510 X
Model 33 NRA	Model 511 A
Model 34	Model 511 P
Model 34 NRA	Model 511 X
Model 341 A	Model 512 A
Model 341 P	Model 512 P
Model 341 SB	Model 512 X
Model 510	Model 514
Model 510 P	Model 514 P
Model 510 SB	Model 514 BC

300	250	200	125	75	50

	NIB	EXC.	V.G.	GOOD	FAIR	POOR

Model 37

A .22-caliber bolt-action magazine target rifle, with heavy 28" barrel. Featuring target-sights and telescope bases. Blued, with walnut target style stock. Manufactured from 1937 to 1940.

	NIB	EXC.	V.G.	GOOD	FAIR	POOR
	1200	1000	600	400	300	250

Model 37-1940

As above, with improved lock, trigger pull and redesigned stock. Manufactured from 1940 to 1954.

	NIB	EXC.	V.G.	GOOD	FAIR	POOR
	1300	1100	750	500	300	200

Model 504

This .22-caliber bolt action rifle, was introduced in 2004. Barrel 20", with no sights. American walnut stock, with checkering and pistol-grip. Satin blue metal finish. Six round flush mounted detachable magazine. Receiver drilled and tapped for scope mounts. Weight about 6 lbs. Discontinued 2006.

	NIB	EXC.	V.G.	GOOD	FAIR	POOR
	650	550	400	300	200	100

Model 504 Custom

Introduced in 2005. Model features fancy walnut stock.

	NIB	EXC.	V.G.	GOOD	FAIR	POOR
	1000	850	625	400	225	125

Model 504-T LS HB

Introduced in 2005. Model features 20" heavy barrel, with blued finish. Chambered for .22 LR or .17 HMR cartridge. Brown laminate stock, with Monte Carlo comb. Weight about 8.5 lbs.

	NIB	EXC.	V.G.	GOOD	FAIR	POOR
	800	675	475	275	250	150

Model 541 S Custom

A .22-caliber bolt-action magazine rifle, with 24" barrel. Blued, with scroll engraved receiver. Checkered walnut stock having a rosewood pistol-grip cap and fore-end tip. Manufactured from 1972 to 1984.

	NIB	EXC.	V.G.	GOOD	FAIR	POOR
	700	600	500	375	200	125

Model 541T

As above, drilled and tapped for telescopic sights. Introduced in 1986.

	NIB	EXC.	V.G.	GOOD	FAIR	POOR
	375	275	200	175	125	75

Model 541T Heavy Barrel

This model same as standard 541-T, with exception of 24" heavy barrel. First introduced in 1993.

	NIB	EXC.	V.G.	GOOD	FAIR	POOR
	450	350	300	250	200	125

Model 547

High-quality magazine-fed .17 or .22 rimfire sporter, with walnut stock, crowned muzzle, tuned rigger and other goodies. Suspiciously similar to defunct Model 504. Dealer exclusive for 2007.

	NIB	EXC.	V.G.	GOOD	FAIR	POOR
	1000	775	600	400	275	200

Model 511 Scoremaster

A .22-caliber bolt-action magazine sporting rifle, with 22" barrel. Blued, with walnut stock. Six-round magazine.

	NIB	EXC.	V.G.	GOOD	FAIR	POOR
	375	325	250	175	125	75

Model 512

Bolt-action .22 rimfire repeater identical to 511, except with tubular magazine located beneath the barrel. Capacity is 15 LR, 17 Long and 22 Short cartridges. Manufactured from 1940 to 1962. All 500 series models (510, 511, 512, 513 and 521) feature a red cocking indicator at the rear of bolt.

	NIB	EXC.	V.G.	GOOD	FAIR	POOR
	400	350	275	200	150	100

Model 513 TR Matchmaster

A .22-caliber bolt-action magazine target rifle, with heavy 27" barrel and Redfield aperture rear sight. Blued, with target-style walnut stock. Manufactured from 1940 to 1969.

	NIB	EXC.	V.G.	GOOD	FAIR	POOR
	500	400	300	200	150	100

Model 513 S

As above, with Marble sights and checkered walnut sporting-style stock. Manufactured from 1941 to 1956.

	NIB	EXC.	V.G.	GOOD	FAIR	POOR
	—	750	625	475	375	225

	NIB	EXC.	V.G.	GOOD	FAIR	POOR

Model 514

Bolt-action single-shot .22 rimfire rifle manufactured from 1948 to 1971. Total of 770,932 were made, with standard barrels and sights. Another 5,617 were made with Routledge Bore barrels, which were meant for use only with .22 LR Shot loads and came with a shotgun-style bead front sight. These rifles have 24" smoothbore barrel, with bore diameter of .22" that opens up to .40 for the last 12". Routledge Bore Model 514 was never in Remington catalog and available only on special order. Design originated with Michigan trap shooter and gunsmith Fred Routledge in 1938. **NOTE:** Add $100 for Routledge barrel.

300	250	200	125	75	50

Model 521 TL Jr.

A .22-caliber bolt-action magazine target rifle, with heavy 25" barrel and Lyman sights. Blued, with target-style walnut stock. Manufactured from 1947 to 1969.

400	350	250	175	125	75

Model 760

Slide-action sporting rifle chambered for various popular centerfire cartridges from .222 up to .35 Remington cartridge, with 22" round barrel and open sights. Features detachable box magazine. Blued, with checkered walnut pistol-grip stock. Manufactured between 1952 and 1982. Examples of this rifle chambered for .222, .223, .244 and .257 Roberts are worth a premium of 100 to 200 percent over other calibers. This model was produced in styles listed.

Standard Model

—	500	395	275	195	150

Carbine
18.5" barrel.

—	525	395	275	195	150

760D Peerless
Engraved.

—	5000	3500	2250	1100	450

760F Premier
Game scene engraved.

—	9000	6000	4500	1700	550

760F Gold Inlaid

—	10000	7000	5250	2200	750

Bicentennial
1976 only.

—	550	495	295	200	150

ADL

—	525	395	275	195	150

BDL
Basketweave checkering.

—	525	395	275	195	150

Model 552A Speedmaster

A .22-caliber semi-automatic rifle, with 23" barrel and open sights. Blued, with pistol-grip walnut stock. Manufactured from 1959 to 1988.

300	250	225	150	75	50

Model 552 BDL

As above, with more fully figured stock and impressed checkering. Introduced in 1966.

425	300	225	150	100	75

Model 552 BDL Deluxe Speedmaster NRA Edition

Introduced in 2005. Features walnut stock, with checkering and high gloss finish. Blued receiver and barrel, with NRA logos etched on both sides of receiver.

520	400	300	195	125	95

	NIB	EXC.	V.G.	GOOD	FAIR	POOR

Model 572 Fieldmaster

A .22-caliber slide-action rifle, with 21" barrel and open sights. Blued, with walnut stock. Manufactured from 1955 to 1988.

	NIB	EXC.	V.G.	GOOD	FAIR	POOR
	350	300	225	150	75	50

Model 572 BDL

As above, with more fully figured walnut stock and impressed checkering. Introduced in 1966.

	NIB	EXC.	V.G.	GOOD	FAIR	POOR
	425	300	225	150	110	85

Model 572SB

Same as Model 572, with asmoothbore barrel. Chambered for .22 LR shot cartridge.

	NIB	EXC.	V.G.	GOOD	FAIR	POOR
	325	275	200	125	75	60

Model 572 BDL Smoothbore

Similar to Model 572, with unrifled barrel for use with shot cartridges. Introduced as a special production item in 2007.

	NIB	EXC.	V.G.	GOOD	FAIR	POOR
	425	300	225	150	110	85

Model 580

A .22-caliber single-shot bolt-action rifle, with 24" barrel, open sights and Monte Carlo-style stock. Blued. Manufactured from 1968 to 1978.

	NIB	EXC.	V.G.	GOOD	FAIR	POOR
	—	250	200	150	75	50

Model 580 BR

Same as above, with 1" shorter buttstock.

	NIB	EXC.	V.G.	GOOD	FAIR	POOR
	250	200	150	175	75	50

Model 580 SB

Same as Model 580, with smoothbore barrel for .22 LR shot cartridges.

	NIB	EXC.	V.G.	GOOD	FAIR	POOR
	300	250	175	125	75	50

Model 581

A .22-caliber bolt-action magazine rifle. Blued, with 24" barrel and walnut stock. Manufactured from 1967 to 1983.

	NIB	EXC.	V.G.	GOOD	FAIR	POOR
	300	250	175	125	75	50

Model 581 Left-Hand

Same as above. Built for left-handed shooter.

	NIB	EXC.	V.G.	GOOD	FAIR	POOR
	295	250	175	125	75	50

Model 581-S

As above, fitted with 5-round detachable magazine. Introduced in 1986.

	NIB	EXC.	V.G.	GOOD	FAIR	POOR
	300	250	175	125	75	50

Model 582

As above, fitted with tubular magazine in place of detachable box magazine. Manufactured from 1967 to 1983.

	NIB	EXC.	V.G.	GOOD	FAIR	POOR
	300	250	175	125	75	50

Model 591

A 5mm rimfire Magnum bolt-action rifle, with 24" barrel and Monte Carlo-style stock. Approximately 20,000 made between 1970 and 1973.

	NIB	EXC.	V.G.	GOOD	FAIR	POOR
	450	300	225	175	125	75

Model 592

As above, with tubular magazine. Approximately 7,000 were made.

	NIB	EXC.	V.G.	GOOD	FAIR	POOR
	450	300	225	175	125	75

Model 740

Semi-automatic rifle, with 22" barrel and detachable box magazine. Chambered in .244 Rem., .280 Rem., .308 or .30-06. Blued, with plain walnut stock. Also available with 18.5" barrel that would be worth approximately 10 percent more than values listed below. Manufactured from

	NIB	EXC.	V.G.	GOOD	FAIR	POOR

1955 to 1960. **NOTE:** Add 30 percent premium for .244 Remington.

	—	300	225	200	150	100

ADL

As above, with a checkered walnut stock with a pistol-grip.

	—	350	250	225	150	100

BDL

As above, with more finely figured walnut stock.

	—	400	275	250	150	100

Model 742

A 6mm Remington, .243, .280, .30-06 or .308-caliber semi-automatic rifle, with 22" barrel and 4-shot magazine. Also available with 18" barrel in calibers .308 and .30-06 that are worth approximately 10 percent more than values listed below. Blued, with checkered walnut stock. Manufactured from 1960 to 1980.

	—	350	275	250	150	100

BDL Standard Grade

As above, with Monte Carlo-style stock and basketweave checkering.

	—	375	275	225	175	125

742D Peerless

Engraved.

	—	5000	3500	2250	1100	450

742F Premier (Game Scene)

	—	9000	6000	4500	1700	550

742F Premier (Gold Inlaid)

	—	10000	7000	5250	2200	750

Bicentennial

Mfg. 1976 only.

	—	550	495	295	200	150

Model 76 Sportsman

A .30-06 slide-action rifle, with 22" barrel and 4-shot magazine. Blued, with walnut stock. Manufactured from 1985 to 1987.

	—	325	225	175	125	75

Model 7600

Variation of the above. Chambered for a variety of cartridges from 6mm Remington to .35 Whelen, with 22" barrel and detachable magazine. Also available with 18.5" barrel. Blued, with checkered walnut stock. In 1996, fine line engraving on receiver was offered as standard.

Standard Grade

615	450	325	225	150	100

7600D Peerless

Engraved.

	—	5000	3500	2250	1100	450

7600F Premier

Game scene engraved.

	—	9000	6000	4500	1700	550

Premier

Gold inlaid.

	—	10000	7000	5250	2200	750

Synthetic

Same as standard grade Model 7600, with black synthetic stock. A .30-06 carbine version is also available. Introduced in 1998.

510	375	275	200	150	100

Special Purpose

Same configuration as standard Model 7600. Equipped with a special finish on both the wood and metal that is non-reflective. First offered in 1993.

600	475	350	225	150	100

	NIB	EXC.	V.G.	GOOD	FAIR	POOR

7600P Patrol

Introduced in 2002, this rifle is chambered for .308 cartridge. Fitted with 16.5" barrel. Synthetic stock, with matte black finish. Parkerized finish on metal. Wilson Combat rear ghost ring sights, with AO front sight. Weight about 7 lbs.

600	475	350	225	150	100

Buckmasters ADF (American Deer Foundation)

Introduced in 1997. Built only for that year. Chambered for .30-06 cartridge and is a limited edition item. Fitted with 22" barrel and special fine line engraved receiver.

600	475	350	225	150	100

Model 7600 Custom Grade

Custom Shop model available in three levels of engraving, gold inlay, wood grade and finish, metal work finish, recoil pad/buttplate and dimensions. Each gun should be individually appraised prior to sale.

D Grade

—	5000	3500	2250	1100	450

F Grade

—	9000	6000	4500	1700	550

F Grade with Gold Inlay

—	10000	7000	5250	2200	750

Model Six

Centerfire slide-action rifle, with 22" barrel and 4-shot detachable magazine. Blued, with walnut stock. Manufactured from 1981 to 1987.

—	450	350	275	200	125

Model 7615 Tactical Pump Carbine

Pump-action rifle based on Model 7600 action and chambered in .223 Remington, with 16.5" barrel. Folding synthetic stock. Introduced in 2007.

600	475	350	225	150	100

Model 7615 Special Purpose Synthetic

Similar to Model 7615 Tactical, with fixed stock and Picatinny rail. Dealer exclusive for 2007.

625	500	375	250	175	125

Model 7615 Camo Hunter

Similar to Model 7615 Tactical, with fixed buttstock and entirely camo-finished except for action parts and trigger guard assembly. Introduced in 2007.

650	525	400	265	195	150

Model 7615 Ranch Carbine

Similar to Model 7615 Tactical, with fixed walnut buttstock and fore-end. 18.5" barrel. No iron sights. Drilled and tapped for scope mounts. Introduced in 2007.

625	500	375	250	175	125

Model 74 Sportsman

A .30-06 caliber semi-automatic rifle, with 22" barrel and 4-shot detachable magazine. Blued, with walnut stock. Manufactured from 1985 to 1987.

—	350	250	175	125	75

Model Four

As above, with select Monte Carlo-style stock. Manufactured from 1982 to 1987.

—	500	400	350	275	175

Model 7400

This is a semi-automatic rifle with a 22" barrel. It is chambered for the .243, .270, .280, .30-06, .308 and the .35 Whelen. Blued with a checkered walnut stock. Average weight is about 7.5 lbs. Introduced in 1982. In 1996 this model was offered with fine line engraving on the receiver as standard.

600	475	350	250	200	100

Synthetic

Similar to Model 7400, with black non-reflective synthetic stock. A .30-06 carbine also offered. Introduced in 1998.

550	400	300	200	150	100

	NIB	EXC.	V.G.	GOOD	FAIR	POOR

Weathermaster

Introduced in 2003. Semi-automatic model features weather-resistant black synthetic stock and matte nickel-plated receiver, barrel and magazine. Barrel length 22", with iron sights. Chambered for .30-06 or .270 Win. cartridges. Weight about 7.5 lbs.

650	525	400	300	200	100

Carbine

Same as above, with 18.5" barrel. Chambered for .30-06 cartridge.

550	400	300	200	150	100

Special Purpose

Same configuration as standard Model 7400. Equipped with special finish on both the wood and metal that is non-eflective. First offered in 1993.

450	350	300	250	200	100

Buckmasters ADF (American Deer Foundation)

Introduced in 1997. Built only in that year as a limited model. Chambered for .30-06 cartridge. Fitted with 22" barrel. Special fine line engraving and polished blue finish. American walnut stock, with Monte Carlo and cut checkering. Weight is 7.5 lbs.

600	500	400	300	200	100

Model 7400 Custom Grade

Custom Shop model available in three levels of engraving, gold inlay, wood grade and finish, metal work finish, recoil pad/buttplate and dimensions. Each gun should be individually appraised prior to sale.

F Grade

—	9000	6000	4500	1700	550

F Grade with Gold Inlay

—	10000	7000	5250	2200	750

Model 750 Woodsmaster

Wood-stocked version of Model 7400 semi-automatic. Rifle version has 22" barrel; carbine has 18.5" barrel. Introduced 2006.

650	550	400	275	175	100

Model 750 Synthetic

Similar to Model 750 Woodsmaster, with black synthetic stock and fore-end. Introduced in 2007.

625	550	400	300	225	125

Model R-15 VTR Predator Rifle

AR-style rifle chambered for .223 Remington or .204 Ruger. Supplied with one 5-shot magazine, but accepts AR-style higher-cap magazines. 22" fluted barrel; fixed stock. Finish: Advantage MAX-12 HD overall.

1100	900	695	500	250	125

Model R-15 VTR Predator Carbine

Similar to above, with 18" barrel.

1100	900	695	500	250	125

Model R-15CS VTR Predator Carbine

Similar to above, with collapsible buttstock.

1145	950	750	550	275	150

Model R-15 Hunter

Similar to R-15 in .30 Remington AR or .450 Bushmaster, 22" barrel, Realtree AP HD camo.

1200	975	750	550	275	150

Model R-15 VTR Byron South Edition

.223, 18" barrel, Advantage MAX-1 HD camo.

1200	975	750	550	275	150

Model R-15 VTR SS Varmint

As above, with 24" stainless steel barrel.

1200	975	750	550	275	150

	NIB	EXC.	V.G.	GOOD	FAIR	POOR

Model R-15 VTR Thumbhole

Similar to R-15 Hunter, with thumbhole stock.

NIB	EXC.	V.G.	GOOD	FAIR	POOR
1300	1075	850	595	295	150

Model R-25 Modular Repeating Rifle

Enhanced AR-style semi-automatic rifle. Chambered in .243, 7mm-08 and .308 Winchester. Features include 20" chrome-moly barrel, single-stage trigger, four-round magazine, aluminum alloy upper and lower Mossy Oak Treestand camo finish overall. Overall length 38.25"; weight 7.75 lbs.

NIB	EXC.	V.G.	GOOD	FAIR	POOR
1375	1100	850	650	275	150

REMINGTON'S "NYLON SERIES" .22 RIFLES

Model 10 Nylon

Bolt-action single shot. Approximately 10,700 (approx. 2000 smoothbore and only 200 of those with 24" barrel) produced from 1962-1964. Mohawk brown nylon stock, with white accents, chrome spoon style bolt handle, safety engages upon cocking, .22 short, long and long rifle. Model available in both rifled and smoothbore versions (smoothbore barrels are marked "smoothbore" and in barrel lengths of 19.5" and 24". **NOTE:** Add 100 percent+ for 24" versions; 100 percent+ for NIB.

10 (model)

NIB	EXC.	V.G.	GOOD	FAIR	POOR
—	700	600	500	300	200

10 (SB)

NIB	EXC.	V.G.	GOOD	FAIR	POOR
—	1000	800	700	500	450

Model 11 Nylon

Bolt-action repeater, 6- or 10-round metal box magazine. Approximately 22,500 produced from 1962-1964. Mohawk brown nylon stock, with white accents, chrome spoon style bolt handle, manual right side safety. .22 short, long or long rifle. Barrel lengths 19.5" and 24". **NOTE:** Add 100 percent for 24" version.

NIB	EXC.	V.G.	GOOD	FAIR	POOR
—	475	375	300	275	175

Model 12 Nylon

Bolt-action repeater, 14 round external tubular magazine under the barrel. Approximately 27,600 produced from 1962-1964. Mohawk brown nylon stock, with white accents, chrome spoon style bolt handle, manual right side safety. .22 short, long or long rifle. Barrel lengths 19.5" and 24". **NOTE:** Add 100 percent for 24" version.

NIB	EXC.	V.G.	GOOD	FAIR	POOR
—	475	375	300	275	175

Model 66 Nylon

Semi-automatic, 19.5" barrel, 14 round tubular magazine fed through buttplate. In excess of 1,000,000 produced from 1959-1987. Seven different variations of style and color were sold. Non-serialized prior to 1968 gun control act of 1968. An "A" prefix was added to serialization in 1977.

66 (MB) "Mohawk" Brown"

Blued metal parts, dark chocolate brown stock with white accents, .22 LR ONLY. 1959-1987. Approx. 678,000.

66 (SG) "Seneca" Green"

Blued metal parts, dark olive green stock (often confused with MB in artificial light) with white accents, .22 LR ONLY, 1959-1962. Approx. 45,000.

66 (AB) "Apache" Black"

Bright chrome plated metal parts, black stock with white accents, .22 LR ONLY. 1962-1983. Approx. 220,000.

66 (BD) "Black Diamond"

Blued metal parts, black stock with black diamonds in fore-end. Remainder of accents are white, .22 LR ONLY, 1978-1987. Approx. 56,000.

66 (GS) "Gallery Special"

Blued metal parts, dark brown stock with white accents. Barrel marked .22 SHORT. Distinguished by shell deflector over ejection port and loop on fore-end for counter chain. 1961-1981. Approx. 6500.

66 (AN) "150th Anniversary Rifle"

Blued metal parts, dark brown stock with white accents, .22 LR ONLY. Distinguished by 150th Anniversary stamping on left side of receiver cover. 1966 ONLY. Approx. 4000.

	NIB	EXC.	V.G.	GOOD	FAIR	POOR

66 (BI) "Bicentennial Rifle"

Blued metal parts, dark brown stock with white accents, .22 LR ONLY. Distinguished by eagle and 1776/1976 stamping on left side of receiver cover. 1976 ONLY. Approx. 10,000.

66 (MB)

	NIB	EXC.	V.G.	GOOD	FAIR	POOR
	400	350	300	150	125	100

66 (SG)

	NIB	EXC.	V.G.	GOOD	FAIR	POOR
	600	550	450	325	275	175

66 (AB)

	NIB	EXC.	V.G.	GOOD	FAIR	POOR
	600	500	425	350	250	125

66 (BD)

	NIB	EXC.	V.G.	GOOD	FAIR	POOR
	450	425	375	300	250	150

66 (GS)

	NIB	EXC.	V.G.	GOOD	FAIR	POOR
	1300	1200	950	700	450	300

66 (AN)

	NIB	EXC.	V.G.	GOOD	FAIR	POOR
	750	700	600	450	300	250

66 (BI)

	NIB	EXC.	V.G.	GOOD	FAIR	POOR
	700	600	500	325	275	200

Model 76 Nylon

Lever-action repeater. Only lever-action Remington ever produced. 19.5" barrel, 14 round tubular magazine, fed through buttplate. Produced from 1962-1964 in three different variations.

76 (MB) "Trailrider"

Blued metal parts, dark brown stocks with white accents. Approximately 25,300 produced.

	NIB	EXC.	V.G.	GOOD	FAIR	POOR
	—	1700	600	500	375	250

76 (AB) "Trailrider"

Bright chrome metal parts, black stock with white accents. Approximately 1600 produced.

	NIB	EXC.	V.G.	GOOD	FAIR	POOR
	—	2000	800	700	500	400

76 (not cataloged)

Blued metal parts, black stock with white accents. Production numbers do not exist.

	NIB	EXC.	V.G.	GOOD	FAIR	POOR
	—	1800	675	600	400	300

76 (MB)

	NIB	EXC.	V.G.	GOOD	FAIR	POOR
	—	1700	600	500	375	250

76 (AB)

	NIB	EXC.	V.G.	GOOD	FAIR	POOR
	—	2000	800	700	500	400

76 (Not cataloged)

	NIB	EXC.	V.G.	GOOD	FAIR	POOR
	—	1800	675	600	400	300

Model 77 Nylon

Known as 77 (MB): Semi-automatic, 19.5" barrel, 5 round plastic box magazine. Blued metal parts, dark brown stock with white accents. .22 LR ONLY. 1970-1971. Approx. 15,300 produced. This model was replaced by Model 10C in 1972. **NOTE:** Add 100 percent for NIB.

	NIB	EXC.	V.G.	GOOD	FAIR	POOR
	—	500	375	300	200	150

Model 10C Nylon

Known as 10C. Identical copy of 77 (MB), except box magazine capacity was increased to 10 rounds. 1972-1978. Approx. 128,000 produced. **NOTE:** Add 50 percent for NIB.

	NIB	EXC.	V.G.	GOOD	FAIR	POOR
	—	325	275	225	175	100

Model 77 Apache Nylon

Known as "APACHE 77". Semi-automatic, 19.5" barrel, 10 round plastic box magazine. Metal parts coated with black "teflon-like" finish, bright green stock with swirls of orange, brown and black (highly variable), not to be confused with the 66 (SG). Rifle was contracted as an "exclusive" run, marketed by K-Mart. Number manufactured is hazy, but estimates run from 54,000 to over 100,000. Produced from 1987-1989. **NOTE:** Add 100 percent for NIB.

	NIB	EXC.	V.G.	GOOD	FAIR	POOR
	—	350	250	200	140	120

	NIB	EXC.	V.G.	GOOD	FAIR	POOR

Model 522 Viper

Introduced in 1993. Model 522 Viper is a new Remington .22 rimfire caliber semi-automatic design. Black stock made from synthetic resin, while receiver is made from a synthetic as well. Features 20" barrel and 10-shot detachable clip. Weighs 4.6 lbs.

NIB	EXC.	V.G.	GOOD	FAIR	POOR
160	120	100	80	60	40

MODEL 597 SERIES

Model 597

Introduced in 1997. Automatic .22 LR rimfire rifle features carbon steel barrel, with alloy receiver. All metal has a non-reflective matte black finish. Stock is dark gray synthetic. Barrel length 20". Weight about 5.5 lbs.

NIB	EXC.	V.G.	GOOD	FAIR	POOR
225	150	100	70	50	25

Sporter

Introduced in 1998. This version of Model 597 has a blued finish, with hardwood stock and beavertail-style forearm. Magazine capacity 10 rounds.

NIB	EXC.	V.G.	GOOD	FAIR	POOR
225	150	100	70	50	25

Stainless Sporter

Same as Model 597SS. Fitted with hardwood stock. Introduced in 2000.

NIB	EXC.	V.G.	GOOD	FAIR	POOR
275	200	150	100	75	25

LSS

This version of Model 597 is similar to above, with addition of a laminated stock and stainless steel finish.

NIB	EXC.	V.G.	GOOD	FAIR	POOR
300	225	175	125	100	50

SS

This version is also chambered for .22 LR. Has a stainless steel barrel on an alloy receiver. Stock is gray synthetic, with beavertail style forearm. Magazine capacity 10 rounds. Weight about 5.5 lbs. Introduced in 1998.

NIB	EXC.	V.G.	GOOD	FAIR	POOR
240	175	125	100	75	25

HB

Introduced in 2001. Features 20" carbon steel heavy barrel. Chambered for .22 LR cartridge. Fitted with brown laminated stock. No sights. Weight about 6 lbs.

NIB	EXC.	V.G.	GOOD	FAIR	POOR
275	225	165	125	75	25

HB Magnum

Same as model above. Chambered for .22 Winchester Magnum cartridge. Introduced in 2001.

NIB	EXC.	V.G.	GOOD	FAIR	POOR
425	325	200	165	125	50

Magnum

This model features 20" carbon steel barrel, alloy receiver and black synthetic stock. Chambered for .22 Win. Magnum cartridge. Weight about 6 lbs.

NIB	EXC.	V.G.	GOOD	FAIR	POOR
350	250	200	150	100	50

Magnum LS

Chambered for .22 Magnum. Receiver and barrel blued, with gray laminated hardwood stock and beavertail- style forearm. Magazine capacity 10 rounds. Introduced in 1998. In 2003, this model was also offered chambered for .17 HMR cartridge.

NIB	EXC.	V.G.	GOOD	FAIR	POOR
375	275	195	145	100	50

Custom Target

This model available on special order from Custom Shop. Chambered for .22 LR cartridge. Has a 20" stainless steel heavy target barrel, without sights. Stock is green laminated-wood target style, with pistol-grip. Trigger is custom tuned. Weight about 7.5 lbs. Introduced in 1998.

NIB	EXC.	V.G.	GOOD	FAIR	POOR
600	475	400	275	200	150

Custom Target Magnum

Similar to model above. Chambered for .22 Win. Magnum. Weight about 8 lbs. Introduced in 1998. Special order item only.

NIB	EXC.	V.G.	GOOD	FAIR	POOR
750	600	500	375	250	175

NIB	EXC.	V.G.	GOOD	FAIR	POOR

LSS

Similar to Model 597, with laminated stock, stainless barrel and 3-9X scope. Dealer exclusive for 2007.

275	200	150	100	75	25

Synthetic Scope Combo

"Package rifle" similar to Model 597, with 3-9X scope included. Introduced in 2007.

300	225	175	125	100	50

TVP (Target/Varmint/Plinker)

Ultra-funky .22 LR autoloader built on Model 597 chassis. Features include bolt-guidance system, with twin tool-steel guide rails; laminated skeletonized wood stock; non-glare matte finish; 10-shot metal detachable magazine; last-shot hold-open bolt for added safety. Scope rail. Introduced in 2008.

530	465	395	275	175	125

Yellow Jacket

Similar to above, with yellow and black laminated stock.

500	395	225	150	100	75

Blaze Camo

Model 597, with synthetic stock molded in screamin' blaze orange and black.

275	225	165	125	75	25

Pink Camo

Similar to above, with pink – yes pink – and black camo-pattern stock.

275	225	165	125	75	25

FLX

Similar to Model 597 Blaze/Pink camo, with FLX Digital Camo stock.

275	225	165	125	75	25

AAC

Same features as other 597 models, except it has 16.5" barrel that will accept AAC flash hider, muzzle break or suppressor. Staggered-stack magazine holds 10 rounds. Weight 5.5 lbs.

195	165	140	115	100	75

VTR - Quad Rail

Semi-automatic rifle chambered in .22 LR. Styled to resemble AR. Features include matte blued finished; black synthetic stock; 16" barrel; Pardus A2-style collapsible pistol-grip stock; quad-rail free-floated tube; 10-round magazine.

400	360	325	275	210	150

VTR A-2 Fixed Stock

Similar to VTR - Quad Rail, with fixed A2-style stock. Standard handguard, with quad rail.

400	360	325	275	210	150

VTR Collapsible Stock

Similar to VTR A-2 Fixed Stock, with Pardus A2-style collapsible pistol-grip stock.

400	360	325	275	210	150

VTR A-TACS Camo

Semi-automatic rifle chambered in .22 LR. Styled to resemble AR. Features include ATACS camo finish overall; 16" barrel; Pardus A2-style collapsible pistol-grip stock; round handguard without rails; receiver-mounted optics rail; 10-round magazine.

525	465	425	350	275	185

Model Five

.22 rimfire bolt-action sporter. Calibers .22 LR, .22 WMR, .17 HMR; five-shot detachable magazine; barrel 22" blued, with iron sights; receiver blued for scope mounts; stock laminated walnut, with QD swivels. Introduced 2006. **NOTE:** Add 10 percent for .22 WMR.

300	250	175	125	75	25

	NIB	EXC.	V.G.	GOOD	FAIR	POOR

MODEL 40X SERIES

Target Rifle

A .22-caliber rimfire single-shot bolt-action rifle, with heavy 28" barrel. Fitted with Redfield Olympic sights or telescopic sight bases. Blued, with walnut target style stock having a hard rubber butt-plate. Manufactured from 1955 to 1964.

875	750	550	425	350	300

Sporter

As above, with 24" barrel, 5-shot magazine. Walnut sporting style stock. Fewer than 700 made between 1969 and 1980.

4500	3750	3000	2250	1000	500

Centerfire Target

Chambered for .222, .222 Magnum, .308 or .30-06 centerfire cartridges. Manufactured from 1961 to 1964.

—	700	500	400	300	200

40XB Rangemaster Centerfire

Model built in Custom Shop. Features stainless steel barrel, receiver and bolt. Receiver drilled, tapped and fitted with 27.25" heavy target barrel. Trigger fully adjustable. Choice of walnut or synthetic stock. Starting in 1998, this model was offered with a special laminated thumbhole stock. Offered in calibers from .222 to .300 Win. Magnum. Rifle is built to order. Made since 1964.

2100	1800	1325	1000	600	250

40XB BR

A bench rest Custom Shop version of above model. Rifle has 22" stainless heavy barrel. Chambered for .22 BR Remington. Adjustable trigger. Built to order.

1200	1000	850	600	450	200

40XB Tactical Rifle

First offered in 2003. Bolt-action rifle features Teflon coated stainless steel 27.25" barrel. Chambered for .308 Win. cartridge. Fitted with H.S. Precision tactical stock, with vertical pistol-grip. Remington 40-X trigger.

2400	2100	1600	1200	700	350

40XS Tactical

Bolt-action rifle chambered in .308 Winchester or .338 Lapua Magnum. Features include 416 stainless steel Model 40-X 24" 1:12 barreled action; black polymer coating; McMillan A3 series stock, with adjustable length of pull and comb; adjustable trigger and all-steel trigger guard; Harris bipod, with quick adjust swivel lock Leupold Mark IV 3.5-10x40mm long range M1 scope with Mil Dot reticle; Badger Ordnance all-steel Picatinny scope rail and rings. **NOTE:** Deduct 50 percent if without Leupold scope, Harris Bipod, Badger Ordnance Picatinny rail.

4000	3600	3000	2000	—	—

40XR KS Sporter

Rimfire model in .22 LR or .22 WMR. Sporter contoured 24" barrel, Kevlar stock, no sights. Magazine capacity 5+1. Made from 1994 to 2000.

1300	1000	850	600	450	350

40XR Custom Sporter

From Remington Custom Shop, high-grade version of 40X rimfire, with specifications made to order. In .22 LR or .22 WMR. Limited production.

4200	3750	3200	2400	1500	500

Model XR-100 Rangemaster

Introduced in 2005. Features 26" barrel. Chambered for .204 Ruger, .223 or .22-250 calibers. Black laminate stock, with thumbhole and vented forearm. Adjustable trigger. Blued finish. Weight about 9.12 lbs.

880	675	500	395	275	150

Model XC KS

Custom Shop position rifle, with 24" stainless steel heavy barrel. Chambered for .223 Rem. and .308 Win. cartridges. Kevlar stock, with palm rail. Weight about 11 lbs.

2650	2225	1850	1400	800	400

	NIB	EXC.	V.G.	GOOD	FAIR	POOR

Model 673 Guide Rifle

Introduced in 2003. Bolt-action rifle features 22" vent rib barrel. Chambered for 6.5 mm Rem. Magnum, .308, .300 RUM or.350 Rem. Magnum cartridge. Adjustable rear sight. Stock is dark and light tan laminate, with checkering. Magazine capacity three rounds. Weight about 7.5 lbs. Discontinued 2006. Slight premium for .300 RUM.

	650	525	400	300	200	150

Model 720A

A .257 Roberts, .270 or .30-06 bolt-action sporting rifle, with 22" barrel and 5-shot integral magazine. Blued, with checkered walnut stock. Approximately 2,500 manufactured in 1941. **NOTE:** Deduct 40 percent if .30-06 caliber.

	3000	2400	1875	1300	700	400

Model 721

A .264 Magnum, .270, .280 or .30-06 bolt-action rifle, with 24" barrel and 4-shot magazine. Blued, with plain walnut stock. Manufactured from 1948 to 1962.

Standard Version

	500	450	350	200	150	100

ADL

Checkered stock.

	550	475	375	250	200	125

BDL

High grade stock.

	600	500	400	300	250	150

Model 721A Magnum

.300 H&H or .264 Win.

	650	550	400	350	275	150

Model 722

Short-action variation of Model 721. Chambered for .222 Rem., .222 Rem. Magnum, .243 Win., .244 Rem., .257 Roberts, .300 Savage, .308 Winchester. BDL models featured high-grade select walnut stocks; ADL had checkered stocks. Made from 1948 to 1962. **NOTE:** Add 25 percent for BDL; 10 percent for ADL; 25 percent for .222 Rem. Magnum, .243, .257 or .308 chamberings.

	550	450	350	200	150	100

Model 725 ADL

Short-lived but well-made model. Offered in .222 Rem., .243 Win., .244 Rem., .270 Win., .280 Rem., and .30-06 Springfield. Four-round magazine capacity (5 in .222). Adjustable open rear sight, hooded ramp front. Checkered walnut stock, with Monte Carlo comb, sling swivels. Barrel length: 22" (24" .222). Weight about 7 lbs. Made from 1958 to 1961.

	—	800	525	275	225	150

Model 725 Kodiak

A .375 Holland & Holland Magnum or .458 Winchester Magnum bolt-action sporting rifle, with 26" barrel, muzzle-brake, open sights and 3-shot magazine. Blued, with checkered walnut stock. Manufactured in 1961. Very limited production.

	5000	4000	3000	2000	1000	300

Model 78 Sportsman

Centerfire bolt-action sporting rifle, with 22" barrel and 4-shot magazine. Blued, with walnut stock. Introduced in 1985. Calibers: .223, .243, .270, .308, .30-06.

	335	275	225	200	150	100

Model 600

Centerfire bolt-action sporting rifle, with 18.5" ventilated rib barrel and checkered walnut stock. Manufactured from 1964 to 1967. Calibers: .222 Rem., .223 Rem., 6mm Rem., .243, .308, .35 Rem. **NOTE:** Add 100 percent for .223 Rem.

	—	550	450	350	225	150

Model 600 Mohawk

As above, with plain barrel. Chambered only for .222 Remington, .243 Winchester or .308 Winchester cartridges. Manufactured from 1971 to 1979.

	—	450	375	225	175	125

NIB	EXC.	V.G.	GOOD	FAIR	POOR

Model 600 Magnum

As above, chambered for 6.5mm Rem. Magnum and .350 Rem. Magnum cartridges. Stock of laminated walnut and beechwood. Manufactured from 1965 to 1967.

—	1000	750	600	450	200

Model 660

Improved version of Model 600. Manufactured from 1968 to 1971.

—	550	425	350	250	200

Model 660 Magnum

As above, chambered for either 6.5mm Rem. Magnum or .350 Rem. Magnum cartridges. Fitted with laminated stock.

—	1000	750	600	450	200

MODEL 700 SERIES

Model 700 ADL

Centerfire bolt-action sporting rifle, with either 20", 22" or 24" barrel, open sights and 4-shot magazine. Blued, with checkered Monte Carlo-style walnut stock. Introduced in 1962. Model was available in most popular calibers from .222 Rem. to .300 Win. Magnum.

425	325	250	200	150	100

Model 700 ADL Synthetic

Model features black matte metal finish, with 22" or 24" barrel on Magnums. Synthetic stock is black, with checkering, recoil pad and sling swivel studs. Receiver drilled and tapped for scope. Offered in .243, .270, .30-06 and 7mm Rem. Magnum. In 1998, this model was available in .223 Rem. and .300 Win. Magnum.

350	300	250	200	150	100

Model 700 ADL Synthetic Youth

Introduced in 1998. This model has a shortened synthetic stock, with 13" lop. Offered in .243- and .308-calibers.

400	300	250	200	150	100

Model 700 BDL

Same as above, with hinged floorplate, cut checkering, black fore-end tip and pistol-grip cap. Offered in a wide variety of calibers from .17 Rem. to .338 Rem. Ultra Magnum. Weights between 7.25 lbs. to 7.62 lbs. depending on caliber and barrel length.

715	525	400	275	225	150

Model 700 BDL LH (Left-Hand)

Model also offered in selected calibers for left-hand shooters. They are: .270 Win., 7mm Rem. Magnum, .30-06 and .300 Rem. Ultra Magnum.

800	700	500	325	250	150

Model 700 BDL (DM)

Same as above but introduced in 1995, with detachable magazine.

715	525	400	300	225	150

Model 700 BDL LSS

This Model 700, introduced in 1996, with synthetic stock and stainless steel bolt, floor plate, trigger guard and sling swivels. Action and barrel are stainless steel as well. In 1997, .260 Rem. cartridge was also available.

600	475	400	350	300	200

Model 700 BDL SS DM—Magnum Rifle

Introduced in 1996. Model 700 version fitted with factory installed muzzle-brake on its Magnum calibers: 7mm Rem. Magnum, .300 Win. Magnum, .300 Wthby. Magnum, .338 Win. Magnum and .338 Rem. Ultra Magnum. Weight about 7.5 lbs. In 1997, 7mm STW cartridge was added to this model.

675	500	400	300	200	150

Model 700 BDL SS Short Action

Fitted with a stainless steel 24" barrel. Chambered for 7mm Rem. Ultra Magnum and .300 Rem. Ultra Magnum Black synthetic stock. No sights. Weight about 7.325 lbs. Introduced in 2003.

775	625	500	395	300	175

NIB	EXC.	V.G.	GOOD	FAIR	POOR

Model 700 BDL SS Camo Special Edition (RMEF)

A special edition rifle for the Rocky Mountain Elk Foundation. Fitted with a 24" barrel. Chambered for .300 Rem. Ultra Magnum cartridge. Camo stock, with stainless steel receiver and barrel. Weight about 7.5 lbs. Introduced in 2001. In 2002, 7mm Rem. Ultra Magnum chambering was added for one year only. In 2003, .300 Rem. Ultra Magnum was offered.

NIB	EXC.	V.G.	GOOD	FAIR	POOR
835	650	500	395	300	175

Model 700 50th Anniversary Edition

Introduced in 2012, this is a recreation of original M700 BDL of 1962. Satin finished walnut stock has a cheek piece, cut fleur-de-lis checkering, white-line spacers, black fore-end, grip caps and black recoil pad. Laser engraving on floorplate commemorates the 50th anniversary. Barrel length 24". Chambered for 7mm Remington Magnum, the cartridge that was introduced with the Model 700 BDL.

NIB	EXC.	V.G.	GOOD	FAIR	POOR
1250	1000	850	—	—	—

Model 700 EtronX

Introduced in 2000. Rifle features new technology that electronically discharges the round resulting in nearly instant ignition. LED located on top of grip that shows safe or fire and chamber status. Also, a low battery indicator and malfunction indicators as well. Fitted with 26" stainless steel fluted barrel. Stock is fiberglass and graphite reinforced with Kevlar. Chambers are .220 Swift, .22-250 Rem. and .243 Win. cartridges. Average weight about 8.88 lbs. Gun was a flopperoo, but is now considered an almost-prime collectible. Discontinued 2004.

NIB	EXC.	V.G.	GOOD	FAIR	POOR
1450	1300	1150	700	500	300

Model 700 Sendero

This Model 700 configuration chambered for .25-06, .270, 7mm Rem. Magnum, .300 Win. Magnum. Fitted with synthetic stock and 26" heavy barrel.

NIB	EXC.	V.G.	GOOD	FAIR	POOR
600	475	400	300	200	150

Model 700 Sendero SF

Introduced in 1996. Model features stainless steel fluted barrel. Synthetic stock, with full length bedding. Weighs about 8.5 lbs. Chambered for same calibers as standard Sendero above, except for .270. In 1997, 7mm STW cartridge was made available for this model. In 2003, 7mm Rem. Ultra Magnum and .300 Rem. Ultra Magnum were added calibers.

NIB	EXC.	V.G.	GOOD	FAIR	POOR
900	800	600	450	350	200

Model 700 Sendero SF-II

Similar to Sendero SF, with HS Precision synthetic stock. Chambered in .264 WM, 7mm RM, 7mm RUM, .300 WM and .300 RUM. Introduced 2006.

NIB	EXC.	V.G.	GOOD	FAIR	POOR
1150	985	835	700	500	300

Model 700 Sendero Composite

Introduced in 1999. Features a composite barrel of graphite fiber, with stainless steel liner. Stock is synthetic. Calibers available are .25-06, 7mm STW and .300 Win. Magnum. Barrel length 26". Weight just under 8 lbs.

NIB	EXC.	V.G.	GOOD	FAIR	POOR
1400	1250	975	700	475	300

Model 700 Mountain Rifle

As above, with tapered 22" blued lightweight barrel. Checkered walnut stock. Introduced in 1986.

NIB	EXC.	V.G.	GOOD	FAIR	POOR
425	325	250	200	150	100

Model 700 KS Mountain Rifle

As above, with lightweight Kevlar stock. Introduced in 1986.

NIB	EXC.	V.G.	GOOD	FAIR	POOR
750	700	600	500	400	300

Model 700 Mountain Rifle (DM)

Introduced in 1995. Same as standard Mountain Rifle, with detachable magazine. In 1998, available in .260 Rem. caliber.

NIB	EXC.	V.G.	GOOD	FAIR	POOR
780	575	425	300	250	175

Model 700 Safari Grade

As Model 700BDL. Chambered for 8mm Rem. Magnum, .375 Holland & Holland, 8mm Rem. Magnum, .416 Rem.Magnum or .458 Winchester Magnum cartridges. 24" barrel and 3-shot magazine. Blued, with finely figured walnut checkered stock. Model KS Safari Grade was fitted with Kevlar stock and would be worth approximately 20 percent more than values listed. Introduced in 1962.

NIB	EXC.	V.G.	GOOD	FAIR	POOR
1500	1300	1000	700	400	300

	NIB	EXC.	V.G.	GOOD	FAIR	POOR

Model 700 RS

As above chambered for .270 Winchester, .280 Remington or .30-06 cartridges. 22" barrel and 4-shot magazine. Blued, with DuPont Rynite stock. Manufactured during 1987 and 1988.

	NIB	EXC.	V.G.	GOOD	FAIR	POOR
	—	550	425	350	250	150

Model 700 FS

As above, with Kevlar stock.

	—	550	475	400	300	200

Model 700 BDL European

First available in 1993. Model features oil finish stock, with Monte Carlo comb and raised cheekpiece. Checkering is fine line. In addition, rifle has hinged floorplate, sling swivel studs, hooded ramp front sight and adjustable rear sight. Offered in these calibers: .243, .207, .280, 7mm-08, 7mm Magnum, .30-06 and .308.

	675	400	350	300	250	200

Model 700 BDL Stainless Synthetic

Offered in 1993. Features stainless steel receiver, barrel and bolt. Synthetic stock has straight comb, raised cheekpiece and hinged floor plate. Metal finished in a black matte non-reflective finish. Available in 14 calibers from .223 to .338 Win. Magnum. All barrel lengths regardless of caliber are 24".

	750	600	500	300	200	150

Model 700 BDL Stainless Synthetic (DM)

Same as above, with detachable magazine. Introduced in 1995.

	800	650	525	350	200	150

Model 700 CDL

Model introduced in 2004. Features classic-style checkered walnut stock, with black fore-end tip and grip cap. Hinged floor plate. Chambered for .243, .270, 7mm-08, 7mm Rem. Magnum, 7mm Rem. Ultra Magnum, .30-06, .300 Win. Magnum and .300 Rem. Ultra Magnum. Standard calibers are fitted with 24" barrel; magnum calibers have 26" barrel. Weight about 7.5 lbs. depending on caliber.

	740	550	400	295	200	125

Model 700 CDL SF (2009)

Similar to above, but chambered in .257 Roberts.

	740	550	400	295	200	125

Model 700 CDL Boone and Crockett

Similar to Model 700 CDL, with B&C laser-engraved barrel. Dealer exclusive for 2007.

	750	560	400	295	200	125

Model 700 CDL SF Ltd.

Similar to Model 700 CDL, with engraved floorplate and stainless fluted barrel. Chambered in .30-06 and .17 Remington Fireball. 2006 "Centennial" model commemorates centennial of .30-06 cartridge. Introduced in 2006 for one year only. Reintroduced in .260 Remington in 2008. .280 Remington added 2010.

	1100	900	675	450	275	150

Model 700 Mountain Rifle Stainless Synthetic

This model same as Mountain Rifle, with stainless steel receiver, bolt and barrel. Offered in .25-06 Rem., .270, .280 and .30-06. All calibers supplied with 22" barrel. In 1998, available in .260 Rem. caliber.

	830	600	450	300	225	150

Model 700 LSS Mountain Rifle

Introduced in 1999. Fitted with two-tone laminated stock, with black fore-end tip and cheekpiece. Stainless steel barrel and action. Offered in .260 Remington, 7mm-08 Rem., .270 Win., and .30-06. Barrel length 22". Weight about 6.5 lbs.

	830	625	450	300	200	100

Model 700 Titanium

Introduced in 2001. Features titanium receiver drilled and tapped for scope mounts. Fitted with 22" stainless steel barrel. Chambered for both long and short calibers. Synthetic stock. Weight about 5.25 lbs. In 2002, .308 Win. chambering was added.

	1270	950	700	500	300	175

NIB	EXC.	V.G.	GOOD	FAIR	POOR

Model 700 Varmint Special Synthetic

Stock on this model is reinforced with DuPont Kevlar fiberglass and graphite. Rifle offered with heavy barrel. All metal has fine matte black finish. Barrel rests on a machined aircraft-grade aluminum bedding stock. Receiver drilled and tapped for scope mounts. Offered in .22-250, .223 and .308 calibers. In 1993, .220 Swift was added to the line. This model was later dropped from the product line. In 2000, it was reintroduced in all calibers above, but the .220 Swift.

NIB	EXC.	V.G.	GOOD	FAIR	POOR
600	475	400	350	300	200

Model 700 VS SF (Varmint Synthetic Stainless Fluted)

Introduced in 1994. Features stainless steel barrel, receiver and action. Fitted with 26" heavy varmint barrel that has a spherical concave crown contour. Six flutes reduce barrel weight and help cooling. Synthetic stock made from fiberglass reinforced with graphite is standard. Stock is dark gray. Offered in .223, .220 Swift, .22-250 and .308 calibers. The .243 Win. cartridge added to this model in 1997. Weighs about 8.375 lbs. In 1998, barrel was fluted and ported.

NIB	EXC.	V.G.	GOOD	FAIR	POOR
800	650	500	400	300	150

Model 700 Varmint Special Wood

Same as above, but furnished with walnut stock. Offered in these calibers: .222, .22-250, .223, 6mm, .243, 7mm-08 and .308.

NIB	EXC.	V.G.	GOOD	FAIR	POOR
825	675	525	400	300	150

Model 700 Varmint Laminated Stock (VLS)

Same as above, but furnished with special laminated stock. Introduced in 1995. The 7mm-08 Rem. cartridge was added in 1997. In 1998, a beavertail fore-end was added, as well as .260 Rem. and 6mm Rem. calibers.

NIB	EXC.	V.G.	GOOD	FAIR	POOR
750	575	425	300	250	150

Model 700 VS Composite (Varmint Synthetic Composite)

This model fitted with a graphite fiber composite barrel. Chambered for .223 Rem., .22-250 or .308 cartridges. Stock is synthetic. Barrel lengths are 26". Weight is 7.9 lbs. Introduced in 1999.

NIB	EXC.	V.G.	GOOD	FAIR	POOR
1675	1250	950	600	425	300

Model 700 LV SF (Light Varmint)

Introduced in 2004. Features black synthetic stock, with 22" stainless steel fluted barrel. Chambered for .17 Rem, .221 Rem Fireball, .223 and .22-250. Weight about 6.75 lbs.

NIB	EXC.	V.G.	GOOD	FAIR	POOR
950	700	475	300	225	125

Model 700 VS SF II

Introduced in 2005. Features varmint synthetic stock, with stainless steel action and stainless fluted barrel. Chambered for .204 Ruger, .220 Swift, 223 and .22-250. Barrel length 26". Weight about 8.5 lbs.

NIB	EXC.	V.G.	GOOD	FAIR	POOR
1025	775	600	475	250	125

Model 700 VSF

Chambered for .17 Remington Fireball, .204 Ruger, .220 Swift, .223 or .22-250. Fitted with 26" blued fluted heavy barrel. Tan synthetic stock. Weight about 8.5 lbs. Introduced in 2005.

NIB	EXC.	V.G.	GOOD	FAIR	POOR
930	700	475	300	225	125

Model 700 LSS LH (Laminated Stock SS Left-Hand)

Introduced in 1998. Features stainless steel barreled action, with satin finish. Stock similar to BDL style, with Monte Carlo comb and cheekpiece, with hinged floor plate. Barrel is 24", with no sights. Offered in .270, .30-06, 7mm Rem. Magnum and .300 Win. Magnum.

NIB	EXC.	V.G.	GOOD	FAIR	POOR
700	550	400	300	250	150

Model 700 SPS

Introduced in 2005. Features an improved synthetic stock, RS recoil pad and hinged floorplate. Chambered for short, standard and long action calibers. Supplied with sling swivels studs. Matte blue finish. Weight about 7.5 lbs. depending on caliber and barrel length.

NIB	EXC.	V.G.	GOOD	FAIR	POOR
575	450	300	200	150	100

Model 700 SPS Synthetic Left hand

Similar to Model 700 SPS, but configured for left-handed shooters.

NIB	EXC.	V.G.	GOOD	FAIR	POOR
575	450	300	200	150	100

	NIB	EXC.	V.G.	GOOD	FAIR	POOR

Model 700 SPS Varmint

Varmint version of Model 700 SPS, with 26" heavy-contour barrel. Synthetic stock, with weight-reducing cuts in fore-end. Available in a variety of chamberings from .17 Remington Fireball to .308 Winchester. Introduced in 2007.

NIB	EXC.	V.G.	GOOD	FAIR	POOR
575	450	300	200	150	100

Model 700 SPS Dangerous Game

Similar to 700 SPS, but chambered in .375 H&H Magnum. A TALO exclusive.

NIB	EXC.	V.G.	GOOD	FAIR	POOR
675	550	400	275	200	150

Model 700 SPS Stainless

As above, with matte stainless steel barrel and action. No Ultra magnum calibers offered in this configuration. Introduced in 2005.

NIB	EXC.	V.G.	GOOD	FAIR	POOR
610	475	350	225	150	100

Model 700 SPS DM

Same as Model SPS, with detachable magazine. Matte blue finish. Introduced in 2005.

NIB	EXC.	V.G.	GOOD	FAIR	POOR
575	450	300	200	150	100

Model 700 SPS Youth

Offered in both long and short action calibers. Features barrel lengths of 20" and 22" depending on caliber. Weight about 7 lbs. Introduced in 2005.

NIB	EXC.	V.G.	GOOD	FAIR	POOR
525	425	275	175	125	100

Model 700 SPS Tactical

Similar to Model 700 Police, with 20" barrel and in calibers .223 and .308. Laser-engraved tactical barrel. Dealer exclusive for 2007.

NIB	EXC.	V.G.	GOOD	FAIR	POOR
800	675	500	375	250	175

Model 700 SPS Tactical AAC

Special Purpose Synthetic version of Model 700. 20" heavy-contour hammer-forged barrel, with threaded muzzle. Chambered in .308 Winchester. Hogue Overmolded Ghillie Green pillar-bedded stock, with semi-beavertail forearm, Super-Cell recoil pad. Remington X-Mark Pro externally adjustable trigger. Black oxide finish. Weight 7.5 pounds.

NIB	EXC.	V.G.	GOOD	FAIR	POOR
650	550	475	400	300	200

Model 700 VTR A-TACS Camo with Scope

Bolt action rifle chambered in .223 and .308 Win. Features include ATACS camo finish overall; triangular contour 22" barrel has an integral muzzle-brake; black overmold grips; 1:9 (.223-caliber) or 1:12 (.308) twist; factory-mounted scope.

NIB	EXC.	V.G.	GOOD	FAIR	POOR
875	750	625	550	380	225

Model 700 XCR

Introduced in 2005. Features stainless steel action and barrel, synthetic stock, rubber grip and forearm panels, hinged floorplate and RS recoil pad. Chambered for .270 Win., .280 Rem., 7mm Ultra Magnum, .30-06, .300 WSM and .300 Win. Magnum cartridges. Barrel lengths 24" and 26" depending on caliber. Weight around 7.5 lbs. depending on caliber. **NOTE:** Add $25 for magnum calibers.

NIB	EXC.	V.G.	GOOD	FAIR	POOR
865	650	500	375	295	125

Model 700 XCR (Rocky Mountain Elk Foundation)

As above, with camo stock, engraved floorplate and 7mm Rem. Magnum caliber. Introduced in 2005.

NIB	EXC.	V.G.	GOOD	FAIR	POOR
865	650	500	375	295	125

Model 700 XCR II RMEF Limited Edition

Reintroduction of Rocky Mountain Elk Foundation rifle in .257 Weatherby Magnum. Features include 26" barrel, with Black TriNyte finish and nickel floor plate. Realtree AP-HD stock, with Hogue Overmolded Grip Panels, X-Mark Pro externally adjustable trigger and SuperCell recoil pad. Introduced in 2013.

NIB	EXC.	V.G.	GOOD	FAIR	POOR
1075	950	800	—	—	—

Model 700 SPS Tactical II

Available in .223 Rem., .300 Black Out or .308 Win. Threaded muzzle, with 16.5" heavy barrel: 1/2 x 28 on .223 Rem., 5/8 x 24 on .300 Black Out and .308 Win. Hogue Chillie Green Overmolded stock and X-Mark Pro trigger. Introduced 2013.

NIB	EXC.	V.G.	GOOD	FAIR	POOR
700	600	500	450	—	—

	NIB	EXC.	V.G.	GOOD	FAIR	POOR

Remington R15 MOE

Semi-automatic .223 (AR-15 type), with AAC 51 Tooth Brakeout flash hider, Magpul Grip and trigger guard, competition two-stage trigger finished in Mossy Oak Brush camo. Available with: 16" barrel with collapsible stock and mid-length fore-end; 18" carbine with fixed stock and Dissipator fore-end; 18" barrel carbine with collapsible stock and Dissipator fore-end; 22" barrel rifle with fixed stock and Dissipator fore-end. Introduced 2013.

1200	1050	800	700	—	—

Remington 700 XCR II

Bolt-action rifle chambered in .25-06 Rem., .270 Win, .280 Rem., 7mm Rem. Magnum, 7mm Rem. Ultra Magnum, .300 WSM, .300 Win Magnum, .300 Rem. Ultra Magnum, .338 Win. Magnum, .338 Rem. Ultra Magnum, .375 H&H, .375 Rem. Ultra Magnum, .30-06 Springfield. Features include black TriNyte corrosion control system coating; coated stainless steel barrel and receiver; olive drab green Hogue overmolded synthetic stock; SuperCell recoil pad; X-Mark Pro Trigger System; 24" or 26" barrel depending on chambering.

825	735	600	500	350	200

Remington 700 XCR II - Bone Collector Edition

Similar to Remington 700 XCR II, with Realtree AP HD camo stock.

900	785	675	550	380	225

Model 700 Classic

Limited edition model was furnished with a straight comb, satin finished walnut stock, sling swivel studs and hinged magazine floorplate. Series began in 1981. Each year Remington offered Model 700 Classic in a special chambering, concluding the series in 2005. **NOTE:** Add 25 percent for .250 Savage, .257 Roberts, 6.5x55 or 7x57.

A list of chamberings by year.

1981—7MM Mauser	1994—6.5X55
1982—.257 Roberts	1995—.300 Win. Mag.
1983—.300 H&H Mag.	1996—.375 H&H Mag.
1984—.250-3000	1997—.280 Rem.
1985—.350 Rem. Mag.	1998—8mm Rem. Mag.
1986—.264 Win. Mag.	1999—.17 Remington
1987—.338 Win. Mag.	2000—.223 Remington
1988—.35 Whelen	2001—7mm-08
1989—.300 Wthby. Mag.	2002—.221 Rem.Fireball
1990—.25-06 Rem.	2003—.300 Savage
1991—7mm Wthby. Mag.	2004—8mm Mauser
1992—.220 Swift	2005—.308 Winchester
1993—.222 Rem.	

900	700	600	500	350	250

Model 700 Custom

Special order rifle available in either American, English or California walnut. Stock can be fitted to customer's own dimensions. Engraving available as is a large selection of calibers. Model 700 Custom rifles should be priced individually and an appraisal should be obtained.

"C" Grade

Introduced in 2003. Custom Shop bolt-action rifle. Fitted with fancy walnut Monte Carlo stock and rosewood fore-end tip and grip cap. Offered in all standard calibers. Barrel length 24" for all calibers, except Ultra Magnums which are 26".

2700	2200	1700	1200	600	250

AWR (Alaskan Wilderness Rifle)

Built in Custom Shop. Features blind magazine and stainless steel components on black matte synthetic stock. Fitted with 24" barrel. All metal parts finished in a black satin. Offered in .300 Weatherby Magnum, 7mm Rem. Magnum, .300 Win. Magnum, .338, and .375 calibers. In 1998, 7mm STW added as an additional caliber. Weighs about 6.75 lbs. Built to order.

1400	1100	850	700	350	200

APR (African Plains Rifle)

Custom Shop model features hinged floorplate, 26" barrel and blue metal finish. Stock is laminated Monte Carlo style, with cheekpiece. Fitted with black rubber recoil pad. Offered in same calibers as Model 700 AWR. Weighs about 7-3/4 lbs.

2400	2000	1500	1000	500	250

	NIB	EXC.	V.G.	GOOD	FAIR	POOR

ABG (African Big Game)

Custom Shop rifle fitted with laminated stock, matte finished receiver, barrel and 3-round detachable magazine. Chambered for .375 Rem. Ultra Magnum, .375 H&H, .416 Rem. Magnum and .458 Win. Magnum. Introduced in 2001. Many extra cost options are offered for Custom Shop firearms.

2750	2350	1800	1250	750	350

Model 700 Safari KS Stainless

New addition to Remington line in 1993. Safari KS Stainless has a special reinforced Kevlar stock in a non-reflective gray finish. Checkering is 18 lpi. Offered in these calibers: .375 H&H Magnum, .416 Rem. Magnum and the .458 Win. Magnum.

925	800	650	450	300	200

Model 700 Police

Chambered for .223 cartridge. Fitted with 26" heavy barrel (1-9" twist), black synthetic stock and Parkerized finish.

850	675	500	395	200	125

Model 700 Police DM

Same as above. Chambered for .308 Win. (1-12" twist) or .300 Win. Magnum (1-10" twist). Detachable magazine standard. **NOTE:** Add $20 for .300 Win. Magnum model.

850	675	500	395	200	125

Model 700 Police Lightweight Tactical

Chambered for .308 Win. cartridge. Fitted with 20" fluted barrel (1-12" twist). Stock is slim composite Kevlar, with dual front swivel studs. Parkerized finish. Detachable magazine. Weight about 7.5 lbs. Introduced in 1998.

700	550	400	300	200	125

Model 700 XCR Tactical Long Range Rifle

Chambered in .223 Rem., .300 Lapua and .338 WM. Crowned stainless varmint contour 26" barrel. Olive drab Bell & Carlson synthetic stock. Coated overall with TriNyte Corrosion Control finish. Introduced in 2007. **NOTE:** Add 50 percent for .338 Lapua.

925	800	675	500	300	150

Model 700 XCR Compact Tactical

Similar to above, with Black TriNyte PVD coating OD green stock; hinged floorplate magazine; dual front swivel studs and rear stud; free-floating 20" barrel with LTR-style fluting; 40-X externally adjustable trigger; tactical-style 1 in 9" (223-caliber) or 1 in 12" twist (308-caliber). Chambered in .223 and .308.

1400	1150	875	650	475	200

Model 700 Target Tactical Rifle

Bolt-action rifle chambered in .308 Winchester. Features include: 26" triangular counterbored barrel, with 1: 11-1/2 rifling; textured green Bell & Carlson varmint/tactical stock, with adjustable comb and length of pull; adjustable trigger; satin black oxide finish on exposed metal surfaces; hinged floorplate; SuperCell recoil pad; matte blue on exposed metal surfaces. Overall length 45.75". Weight 11.75 lbs.

1800	1550	1175	850	675	300

Model 700 VTR Varmint-Tactical Rifle

Bolt-action rifle chambered in .17 Remington Fireball, .204 Ruger, .22-250, .223 Remington, .243 Winchester and .308 Winchester. Features include: 22" triangular counterbored barrel; olive drab overmolded or Digital Tiger TSP Desert Camo stock ,with vented semi-beavertail fore-end; tactical-style dual swivel mounts for bipod; matte blue on exposed metal surfaces. Overall length 41.625". Weight 7.5 lbs.

750	625	500	375	200	125

Model 700 VTR Desert Recon

Similar to above, with Digital Desert Camo stock. Chambered for .223 and .308 Winchester only.

750	625	500	375	200	125

Model 700 XHR Extreme Hunting Rifle

Bolt-action rifle chambered in .243 Winchester, .25-06, .270 Winchester, 7mm-08, 7mm Remington Magnum, .300 Winchester Magnum, 7mm Remington Ultra Magnum, .30-06 and

	NIB	EXC.	V.G.	GOOD	FAIR	POOR

.300 Remington Ultra Magnum. Features include: 24", 25" or 26" triangular magnum-contour counterbored barrel; adjustable trigger; synthetic stock finished in Realtree AG HD camo; satin black oxide finish on exposed metal surfaces; hinged floorplate; SuperCell recoil pad. Overall length 41.625" to 46.5". Weight 7.25 lbs. to 7.625 lbs.

	850	675	500	395	200	125

Model 700 SPS Buckmasters Edition

Similar to Model 700 SPS, with engraved floorplate and camo stock. Also available in Youth model. Chambered in .243 only. Introduced in 2007.

	500	450	400	350	300	150

Model 700 Alaskan Ti

Lightweight (6.25 lbs.) version of Model 700, with titanium receiver, 24" fluted stainless barrel and Bell & Carlson synthetic stock. Chambered in a variety of long, short and super-short cartridges. Introduced in 2007.

	1600	1350	1050	775	500	200

Model 700 LSS 50th Anniversary of the .280 Remington

Similar to Model 700 LSS, in .280 Remington. Dealer exclusive for 2007.

	800	675	500	375	250	175

Model 700 VL SS Thumbhole

Similar to Model 700 VS Composite, with brown laminated thumbhole stock and stainless steel barrel. Introduced in 2007.

	900	750	500	300	200	125

Model 700 Tactical Weapons System

This set designed for law enforcement use. Features Model 700 Police chambered for .308 Win. cartridge, 24" barrel (1-12" twist), and detachable magazine. Furnished with Leupold VARI X III scope, with rings and base; Harris 1A2 bipod, sling, lens covers and case.

	2500	2000	1650	1150	800	500

Model 710

Introduced in 2001. Rifle chambered for .270 Win. or .30-06 cartridge. Fitted with 22" barrel and dark gray synthetic stock. Detachable box magazine. Supplied with pre-mounted Bushnell Sharpshooter 3-9x scope. Barrel finish ordnance gray steel, with matte finish. Weight about 7.12 lbs. In 2004, 7mm Rem. Magnum and .300 Win Magnum chamberings were added. In 2005, receiver was extruded solid steel. Calibers: .243, 7mm RM, .300 WM.

	375	285	225	195	150	100

Model 710 Youth

Similar to Model 710, with 20" barrel and 39.5" overall length. Chambered in .243 Win. Introduced 2006.

	375	285	225	195	150	100

Model 783

Bolt-action repeater in .270 Win., 7mm Rem. Magnum, .308 Win., .30-06. Cylindrical receiver, with barrel attached via external nut, injection molded synthetic stock, pillar bedded action, detachable box magazine, recoil pad and Crossfire trigger. New for 2013.

	400	365	330	300	250	200

Model 788

Centerfire bolt-action sporting rifle, with either 22" or 24" barrel and plain walnut stock. An 18" barrel carbine was also manufactured and worth approximately 10 percent more than values listed below. Manufactured from 1967 to 1983. **NOTE:** Add 30 percent premium for .44 Magnum; 25 percent for .30-30; 20 percent premium for 7mm-08 caliber; 40 percent premium for left-hand models in 6mm and .308.

	—	500	425	375	300	250

Model Seven

Centerfire bolt-action sporting rifle, with 18.5" barrel and 4- or 5-shot magazine. Blued, with checkered walnut stock. Chambered for .17 Rem., .222 Rem., .223 Rem., .243 Rem., 6mm Rem., .260 Rem., 7mm-08 Rem. and .308 Win. Introduced into Remington product line in 1982.

	600	475	325	275	200	100

Model Seven FS

As above, with Kevlar stock. Introduced in 1987.

	600	525	450	375	275	150

	NIB	EXC.	V.G.	GOOD	FAIR	POOR

Model Seven Synthetic

Updated Synthetic short-action series in .223 Remington, .243 Winchester, .260 Remington, 7mm-08 Remington and .308 Winchester. 20" satin blue carbon steel barrel and matte black stock. Externally adjustable X-Mark Pro trigger is standard. No sights furnished. Weight 6.5 lbs. Compact version has 18" barrel, chambered in .243 or 7mm-08 only.

585	500	425	365	300	200

Model Seven SS (Stainless Synthetic)

Introduced in 1994. Features stainless steel barrel, receiver and bolt with matte finish. Fitted with 20" barrel and hinged floorplate. Synthetic stock is textured black. Available in .243, 7mm-08 and .308. In 1997, .260 Rem. cartridge was also offered. Weight about 6.25 lbs.

625	450	350	300	200	150

Model Seven LSS

Model has stainless steel barrel and action. Fitted with satin finished laminated stock. Chambered for .22-250, .243, and 7mm-08 Rem. Weight about 6.5 lbs. Introduced in 2000.

625	500	375	300	200	100

Model Seven LS

Model offers a laminated stock, with carbon steel blued barrel. Offered in calibers: .22-250, .243, .260 Rem., 8mm-08 Rem. and .308 Win. Weight about 6.5 lbs. Introduced in 2000.

625	500	375	300	200	100

Model Seven MS

First introduced in 1993. Available through Remington Custom Shop. Rifle features 20" barrel, with Mannlicher stock made from select grain wood and laminated for strength. Available in most short-action calibers including .222 Rem., .223 Rem., .22-250, .243 Win., 6mm Rem., .250 Savage, .257 Roberts, .260 Rem., 7mm-08, .308 Win., .35 Rem., .350 Rem. Magnum. **NOTE:** Add 20 percent for .250 Savage, .257 Roberts, .35 Rem.

2400	2100	1500	900	600	400

Model Seven AWR

Alaskan Wilderness Model has black synthetic stock, stainless steel action, and 22" barrel with black matte Teflon finish. Weight 6.125 lbs. Detachable 3-shot magazine. Available from Remington Custom Shop from 2002 - 2008. Chambered only in 6.8 Rem. SPC, 7mm Rem. SAUM or .300 Rem. SAUM. Replaced by Model Seven AWR II in 2008. This model came with 20" or 22" stainless steel barrel, Bell & Carlson olive green fiberglass stock and hinged floorplate. Chamberings include .260 Rem., .270 WSM, 7mm-08, 7mm Rem. SAUM, .308 Win., .300 WSM, .300 Rem. SAUM and .350 Rem. Magnum. **NOTE:** Add 10 percent for AWR II

2400	1800	1500	500	350	250

Model Seven Youth

First offered in 1993. This variation is a youth version of standard Model 7. Buttstock is 1" shorter than standard. Available in 6mm, .243, and 7mm-08. In 1998, available in .260 Rem. caliber.

600	495	350	225	175	100

Model Seven CDL

Similar to Model Seven, with satin walnut, satin blue finish, sightless barrel and Limbsaver recoil pad. Introduced 2006.

775	625	550	400	275	150

Model Seven XCR Camo

Similar to Model Seven LSS, with camo stock, fluted barrel and weather-resistant coating. Chambered in .243, 7mm-08, .308, .270 WSM and .300 WSM. Introduced in 2007.

775	650	500	395	275	175

Model Seven 25th Anniversary Version

Similar to Model Seven in 7mm-08 only, with 25th anniversary medallion inset at pistol-grip cap area. High-sheen blued finish on receiver, bolt and 22" standard-contour barrel. X-Mark Pro Trigger and SuperCell recoil pad. Introduced 2008.

950	700	550	350	250	150

Model Seven Predator

Similar to Model Seven, with full coverage in Mossy Oak Brush camo; fluted magnum contour 22" barrel; synthetic stock as on Model Seven XCR; X-Mark Pro Trigger. Chambered in .17 Remington Fireball, .204, .223, .22-250 and .243.

800	650	500	395	275	175

	NIB	EXC.	V.G.	GOOD	FAIR	POOR

Model 770

Package rifle similar to Model 710, with redesigned bolt assembly and magazine catch. Chambered in .243, .270, 7mm-08, .308, .30-06 and .300 WM. Available in Youth model. Chambered in .243 only. Introduced in 2007. In 2008, a version with stainless steel barrel and receiver and full camo finish was introduced. A 3-9X Bushnell scope is included. **NOTE:** Add $75 for camo finish.

400	300	225	175	100	50

Model 770 Youth

Similar to Model 770, with shorter stock and barrel.

375	275	200	165	90	50

Model 715 Sportsman

Similar to Model 770. Dealer exclusive for 2007.

375	275	200	165	90	50

Model 798

Long-action sporting rifle built on reworked 98 Mauser action. Calibers: .243, .308, .30-06, .270, .300 WM, .375 H&H, .458 WM. Barrel 22" or 24" blued sightless. Stock brown laminated, with recoil pad. Claw extractor, 2-position safety, hinged floorplate. **NOTE:** Add 10 percent for Magnum chamberings; 30 percent for .375 and .458. Introduced 2006.

575	400	300	200	125	100

Model 798 Stainless Laminate

Similar to Model 798, with laminated stock and stainless barrel. Chambered in .243, .25-06, .270, .30-06, 7mm Magnum, .300 WM and .375 H&H Magnum. Introduced in 2007. **NOTE:** Add 25 percent for .375.

650	475	350	250	175	125

Model 798 SPS

Similar to Model 798, with blued barrel and black synthetic stock. Introduced 2008.

575	400	300	200	125	100

Model 798 Safari

Similar to Model 798. Chambered in .375 H&H or .458 Winchester Magnum. Introduced 2008.

850	700	575	400	325	250

Model 799

Similar to Model 798, but short-action without recoil pad. Calibers .22 Hornet, .222 Remington, .22-250, .223, 762X39. Introduced 2006.

525	400	300	200	125	100

Model 1816 Commemorative Flint Lock Rifle

Introduced in 1995. Features .50-caliber 39" octagonal barrel. Stock is hand finished extra fancy curly maple. Built for one year only. Special order only.

1825	1200	850	700	500	300

Remington No. 1 Rolling Block Mid-Range

Classic rifle reintroduced into Remington line in 1997. Features 30" half octagon, half-round barrel. Chambered for .45-70 Government cartridge. Designed for use with black powder and lead cast bullets. Receiver is case colored. All barrel, receiver and metalwork markings match original rifle. Rear tang-mounted vernier sight and front globe sight, with interchangeable inserts. Single set trigger is standard. Steel buttplate. Weight about 9.75 lbs.

2200	1900	1500	1200	700	400

Remington Mid-Range Sporter Rolling Block

Introduced in 1998. Features 30" round barrel, with pistol-grip sporter stock. Adjustable rear sight. Chambered for .30-30, .444 Marlin and .45-70 Government. A number of extra cost options are available, including barrels, sights, fancy wood, etc. Prices listed below are for standard model.

1800	1600	1350	900	600	350

Model SPR18 Single Shot Rifle

Break-action rifle, with silvertone receiver and fluted barrel. Calibers .223, .243, .270, .30-06, .308. Weight 6.75 lbs. Imported; introduced 2005.

260	225	175	150	100	75

	NIB	EXC.	V.G.	GOOD	FAIR	POOR

Model SPR22 Double Rifle

Top-lever operated break-action SXS double rifle in .30-06 and .45-70. Double triggers, tang safety. Barrels can be regulated via jackscrew. Imported; introduced 2005.

1000	850	700	600	450	300

Model SPR94 Combo Gun

Over/under rifle shotgun. Combinations .410/.22 rimfire, .410/.17HMR, .410/.22WMR, 12-gauge/.223, 12-gauge/.30-06, 12-gauge/.308. Double triggers, tang safety. Imported; introduced 2005.

850	700	600	450	300	200

Model 412

Compact single-shot chambered for .22 LR. 19.5" blued barrel, hardwood stock. Introduced 2006.

165	125	100	75	50	25

MODERN MUZZLELOADERS

Model 700 ML

Introduced in 1996. An in-line design and first built on a modern action. Chambered for .50- or .54-caliber bullet. Fitted with synthetic stock and rubber recoil pad. Barrel length 24". Weight about 7.75 lbs. Camo stock option added in 1997. Discontinued 2006.

350	250	200	150	100	75

Model 700 ML Custom

Introduced in 1997. Model similar to above featuring satin metal finish and gray laminated thumbhole stock, with roll-over cheekpiece. Discontinued.

550	425	350	275	200	100

Model 700 MLS

Same as above, with stainless steel barrel and action. Discontinued.

400	300	250	200	150	100

Model 700 MLS Custom

Similar to above model, with satin stainless steel finish and two-toned gray laminated thumbhole stock, with roll-over cheekpiece. Introduced in 1997. Discontinued.

600	475	375	325	225	125

Model 700 ML Youth

Similar to Model ML. Shortened stock, with 13" lop and rubber recoil pad. Discontinued.

370	300	250	200	150	100

Genesis Muzzleloaders

Fixed-breech hammer-fired muzzle-loaders manufactured in a variety of configurations. Imported. Manufactured from 2006 to 2008.

200	180	160	135	110	85

SHOTGUNS

Model 11

12-, 16- or 20-gauge semi-automatic shotgun, with barrels ranging in length from 26" to 32". Designed by John M. Browning. Produced under license from Fabrique Nationale. Blued, with checkered walnut stock. Approximately 300,000 made from 1911 to 1948. **NOTE:** Add 30 percent for solid or vent rib to listed values.

—	800	650	500	400	300

11B Special
Engraved.

—	1400	1100	600	500	400

11D Tournament

—	2200	1600	1000	600	450

11E Expert
Engraved.

—	4500	3250	2700	1500	300

	NIB	EXC.	V.G.	GOOD	FAIR	POOR

11F Premier

Heavily engraved.

	—	9000	7000	5000	3500	500

11R

20" barrel riot gun.

	—	1000	850	700	500	400

Model 10A

A 12-, 16- or 20-gauge slide-action shotgun, with barrels ranging from 26" to 32". Takedown blued, with plain walnut stock. Manufactured from 1907 to 1929.

	—	375	300	250	200	100

Model 17

A 20-gauge slide-action shotgun, with barrels ranging in length from 26" to 32". Takedown blued, with plain walnut stock. Approximately 48,000 made from 1917 to 1933. **NOTE:** Add 25 percent for vent rib.

	—	395	300	250	175	100

Model 29

As above, chambered for 12-gauge cartridges. Approximately 24,000 manufactured from 1929 to 1933. **NOTE:** Add 40 percent for 32" barrels; 25 percent for vent rib.

	—	450	350	300	200	175

Model 31

A 12-, 16- or 20-gauge slide-action shotgun, with barrels ranging in length from 26" to 32". Magazine capacity either 2 or 4 rounds. Takedown blued, with walnut stock. Approximately 160,000 made from 1931 to 1949. **NOTE:** Add 50 percent for 32" barrel; 40 percent for early models with checkered stocks; 25 percent for solid or vent rib; 25 percent for early banded barrels.

	—	450	325	275	200	125

MODEL 870 SERIES

Model 870 Wingmaster

A 12-, 16-, or 20-gauge slide-action shotgun, with 26", 28" or 30" barrels and 5-shot tubular magazine. Blued, with plain walnut stock. Manufactured from 1950 to 1963. **NOTE:** Add 10 percent for vent rib.

	—	350	225	200	150	100

Model 870 Field Wingmaster

As above, with checkered walnut stock and screw-in choke tubes. Introduced in 1964. In 1980, 16-gauge was dropped as an offering, but was later reinstated (see below).

	550	450	300	225	150	100

Model 870 Field Wingmaster 16 Gauge

In 2002, 16-gauge was reintroduced into the Wingmaster line. Offered with 26" or 28" vent rib barrel and choke tubes. Walnut stock, with blued finish. Weight about 7 lbs. Offered in 16-gauge in other configurations listed.

	600	475	375	250	200	100

Model 870 Wingmaster NRA Edition

A 12-gauge 3" gun, with 28" vent rib barrel and choke tubes. Walnut stock, with checkering. Blued receiver, with NRA logos on both sides. Introduced in 2005.

	550	450	300	225	150	100

Model 870 Wingmaster Jr.

Introduced in 2005. Features a 20-gauge gun, with 18.75" vent rib barrel and choke tubes. Checkered walnut stock, with recoil pad. Blued finish. Weight about 6 lbs.

	550	450	300	225	150	100

Model 870 Field Wingmaster Small Bores

Introduced in 1999. Now offered in both 28-gauge and .410 bore. Checkered walnut stock. High polish blue finish. Both guns are fitted with 25" barrels. 28-gauge has RemChokes while .410 comes with fixed Modified chokes. Weight about 6 lbs. Price listed is for .410 bore. **NOTE:** Add $50 for 28-gauge.

	600	475	395	300	275	200

NIB	EXC.	V.G.	GOOD	FAIR	POOR

Model 870 Magnum

As above chambered for 12- or 20-gauge. 3" Magnum shells. Introduced in 1964. Choke tubes introduced in 1987.

| 575 | 425 | 300 | 225 | 150 | 100 |

Model 870 Express

As above for 3", 12-gauge shells, with 28" ventilated rib and one choke tube. Parkerized, with matte finished stock. Introduced in 1987.

| 330 | 250 | 200 | 150 | 100 | 75 |

Model 870 Express Synthetic

| 330 | 250 | 200 | 150 | 100 | 75 |

Model 870 Express Synthetic Youth

| 300 | 250 | 200 | 150 | 100 | 75 |

Model 870 Express Jr. NWTF Edition

20-gauge model fitted with 18.75" vent rib barrel, with choke tubes. Synthetic stock has camo finish. Metal matte black. Weight about 6 lbs. Introduced in 2005.

| 320 | 250 | 200 | 150 | 100 | 75 |

Model 870 Express Super Magnum

Introduced in 1998. Similar to 870 Express, but chambered for 3.5" 12-gauge. Offered in walnut stock, with blued 28" barrel. Matte black synthetic, with 26" or 28" barrel or various camo finishes. Also available as a combo, with extra 20" rifled deer barrel. **NOTE:** Add $100 for camo; 20 percent for combo with deer barrel. Introduced in 1998.

| 425 | 330 | 225 | 175 | 125 | 100 |

Model 870 Express Super Magnum Fall Flight

Chambered for 12-gauge, with either 2.75", 3" or 3.5" shells. Fitted with 30" vent rib barrel andchoke tubes. Skyline Fall Flight camo finish. Weight about 7.75 lbs. Introduced in 2005.

| 475 | 375 | 275 | 225 | 175 | 150 |

Model 870 Express Synthetic Super Mag Turkey-Waterfowl Camo

Pump action shotgun. Chambered in 12-gauge, 2.75" to 3.5" shells. Features include full Mossy Oak Bottomland camo coverage; 26" barrel with HiViz fiber-optics sights; Wingmaster HD Waterfowl and Turkey Extra Full RemChokes; SuperCell recoil pad; drilled and tapped receiver.

| 515 | 440 | 375 | 315 | 200 | 150 |

Model 870 Super Mag Turkey-Predator Camo with Scope

Pump action shotgun chambered in 12-gauge, 2.75" to 3.5" shells. Features include 20" barrel; TruGlo red/green selectable illuminated sight mounted on pre-installed Weaver-style rail; black padded sling; Wingmaster HD Turkey/Predator RemChoke; full Mossy Oak Obsession camo coverage; ShurShot pistol-grip stock, with black overmolded grip panels; TruGlo 30mm Red/Green Dot Scope pre-mounted.

| 575 | 500 | 425 | 350 | 200 | 150 |

Model 870TA Trap

As above, with competition ventilated rib and checkered stock. Produced in 12-gauge only. Discontinued in 1986.

| 500 | 400 | 300 | 200 | 150 | 100 |

Model 870TB Trap

As above, with 28" or 30" Full choke, ventilated rib barrel and trap-style walnut stock. Manufactured from 1950 to 1981.

| — | 450 | 325 | 275 | 200 | 125 |

Model 870TC Trap

As above, with finely figured walnut stock and screw-in choke tubes.

| 575 | 475 | 400 | 350 | 250 | 150 |

Model 870 Express Deer Gun

Model fitted with 20" fully rifled barrel, iron sights, and Monte Carlo stock. Also offered with 20" IC rifle sighted barrel. Available in 12-gauge only.

| 370 | 275 | 200 | 150 | 125 | 100 |

NIB	EXC.	V.G.	GOOD	FAIR	POOR

Model 870 Express Deer/Turkey Combo

This 3" 12-gauge has a 21" barrel threaded for RemChokes for turkey hunting and 23" rifled slug barrel, with cantilever scope mount for deer hunting. Receiver and barrel are matte black; synthetic stock is Mossy Oak Break-Up camo.

625	500	425	350	250	150

Model 870 Express Left-Hand

Left-hand version of Express model fitted with 28" vent rib barrel. Checkered hardwood stock. Black matte finish.

360	275	200	150	100	75

Model 870 Express Synthetic Turkey Camo

12-gauge pump action shotgun chambered for 2.75" and 3" shells. Features include 21" vent rib bead-sighted barrel; standard Express finish on barrel and receiver; Turkey Extra Full RemChoke; synthetic stock with integrated sling swivel attachment.

445	385	325	275	200	150

Model 870 Express Super Magnum Turkey

This 12-gauge gun will handle 2.75", 3" or 3.5" shells. Fitted with 23" vent rib barrel, black synthetic stock and matte black metal finish. Weight about 7.25 lbs. Introduced in 1999.

390	290	200	150	100	75

Model 870 Express Synthetic Deer

Fitted with 20" fully rifled barrel, with adjustable rifle sights. Black synthetic stock, with Monte Carlo comb and matte black finish. Weight about 7 lbs. Introduced in 1999.

370	275	200	150	100	75

Model 870 Express Compact Deer

20-gauge; similar to Model 870 Express Synthetic Deer, with smaller dimensions.

425	300	200	150	100	75

Model 870 Express Compact Pink Camo

20-gauge; similar to Model 870 Express, with pink camo synthetic stock.

370	275	200	150	100	75

Model 870 Express Compact Synthetic

Similar to above, with matte black synthetic stock.

370	275	200	150	100	75

Model 870 Express Compact Camo

Similar to above, with camo buttstock and for-end.

395	295	215	150	100	75

Model 870 Express Compact Jr.

Similar to above, with shorter barrel and lop.

370	275	200	150	100	75

Model 870 Express Combos

Offered in both 12- and 20-gauge, with 26" vent rib modified barrel and 20" fully rifled deer barrel.

500	395	250	200	150	100

Model 870 Express Youth Gun

Available in 20-gauge only. This shotgun is built for children. Has 13" length of pull and 21" vent rib barrel. Sold with Modified RemChoke tube.

330	250	200	150	125	100

Model 870 Express Turkey

Furnished in 12-gauge, with 21" vent rib barrel. Extra-full RemChoke Turkey tube.

345	250	175	150	125	100

Model 870 Express Camo Turkey

Similar to Express Turkey, with complete coverage of camo stock. Metal is matte black.

400	300	225	150	100	75

	NIB	EXC.	V.G.	GOOD	FAIR	POOR

Model 870 20 Gauge Express Youth Camo Turkey

Similar to Model 870 Express Camo. In 20-gauge, with shortened stock (13" lop).

	400	300	225	150	100	75

Model 870 Express Small Game

Offered in 20-gauge or .410 bore. Model has a nonreflective metal and wood finish. The .410 bore furnished with 25" vent rib Full choke barrel; 20-gauge available with 26" or 28" vent rib barrel, with Modified RemChoke tube.

	225	200	175	150	125	100

Model 870 Express HD (Home Defense)

Introduced in 1995. Features 18" 12-gauge barrel, with cylinder barrel and front bead sight. Weight about 7.25 lb.

	345	250	175	150	125	100

Model 870 Classic Trap

Introduced in 2000. Features special fine line engraving, with gold inlays. Stock is select walnut, with Monte Carlo comb, 30" barrel, with contoured vent rib. Ventilated recoil pad, with white-line spacers. Choke tubes. Weight about 8 lbs.

	675	550	450	300	200	—

Model 870 Special Field

Remington pump-action shotgun available in either 12- or 20-gauge. Features English-style straight-grip stock, 21" vent rib barrel and slim shortened slide handle. Weight 12-gauge 7 lbs.; 20-gauge 6.25 lbs. Comes with a set of RemChoke tubes.

	650	550	375	250	150	100

Model 870 Rifle Deer Gun

New 20-gauge model introduced in 1994. Features fully rifled 20" barrel. Has a new scope rail design that is more rigid. Finish is blue and Monte Carlo stock is walnut. Equipped with recoil pad and checkering.

	450	400	350	300	200	100

Model 870 Brushmaster Deer Gun

12-gauge slide-action shotgun. Fitted with 20" RemChoke plain barrel and Monte Carlo stock. Available for either left- or right-hand shooters.

	350	300	250	200	150	100

Model 870 Express Youth Turkey Camo

Similar to model above. Chambered for 20-gauge shell. Finished with Realtree Camo. Weight about 6 lbs.

	400	300	225	150	125	100

Model 870 Youth Deer Gun

Chambered for 20-gauge shell. Fitted with 21" full choked barrel. Realtree Camo finish. Magazine capacity 4 rounds. Weight about 6 lbs.

	350	300	250	200	150	100

Model 870 Security

Offered in 12-gauge only. This personal protection shotgun has 18.5" Cylinder-choked plain barrel, with front bead sight.

	350	300	250	200	150	100

Model 870 SPS-Camo

Offered in 12-gauge only. Choice of 26" or 28" vent rib barrel, with RemChoke tubes. Wood and metal are finished in brown camo color. Introduced in 2001.

	600	425	325	225	175	125

Model 870 SPS Super Magnum Camo

Chambered for 12-gauge shells, with chambers that will handle both 3" Magnum, 3.5" Magnum, as well as all 2.75" shells. Barrel is 23", with ventilated rib and RemChokes. Finish is Mossy Oak camo. Weight about 7.25 lbs. Introduced in 1999.

	600	425	325	225	175	125

NIB	EXC.	V.G.	GOOD	FAIR	POOR

Model 870 SPS-BG Camo

First time available in 1993. Features 12-gauge 20" plain barrel, with IC and Turkey Super Full RemChoke tubes. Wood and metal are finished in brown camo color.

400	300	225	175	125	100

Model 870 SPS Fully Rifled Deer Gun

20-gauge model features 18.5" fully rifled heavy barrel, with no sights. Receiver has cantilever scope mount. Black synthetic stock. Black matte finish. Weight about 8 lbs. Magazine capacity 4 rounds. Introduced in 2004.

500	375	250	175	125	100

Model 870 SPS Super Slug Deer Gun

Features 23" fully rifled modified contour barrel which is equipped with a barrel mounted cantilever scope mount. Stock is black synthetic. Weight about 8 lbs. Introduced in 1999.

600	425	325	250	175	100

Model 870 SPS-T

12-gauge model comes standard with 21" vent rib barrel, RemChoke tubes in IC and Turkey Super Full, black synthetic stock and black matte finish.

575	475	400	350	250	150

Model 870 SPS-T Camo

Same as above, with exception of 21" vent rib barrel. IC and Turkey Super Full RemChoke tubes. Both wood and metal are finished in green camo color.

600	425	325	250	175	100

Model 870 SPS-T Youth Turkey Camo

Finished in Mossy Oak Break-Up. Chambered for 12-gauge shell. Fitted with 20" Super Full choke. Weight about 7.125 lbs. Introduced in 2001.

565	450	325	250	175	125

Model 870 SPS-T Super Magnum Camo

This 12-gauge model will handle 2.75", 3" and 3.5" shells. Fitted with 23" barrel and RemChokes. Finish Mossy Oak camo. Weight about 7.25 lbs. Introduced in 1999.

615	425	325	250	175	125

Model 870 SPS-T Camo NWTF 25th Anniversary

Fitted with 21" barrel that has special fiber optic sighting system. NWTF logo on left side of receiver. Introduced in 1998.

600	450	325	250	175	125

Model 870 SPS-T Super Mag

Similar to Model 870 SP-T Thumbhole, with pistol-grip stock and vent rib barrel.

630	450	350	275	200	150

Model 870 SPS-T/20

20-gauge turkey gun features 3" chamber, 23" vent rib barrel, R3 recoil pad and full coverage in Mossy Oak New Break-Up camo. Drilled and tapped for scope mount.

550	450	325	250	195	150

Model 870 SPS-T Camo

Chambered for 20-gauge 3" shell. Fitted with 20" barrel and full choke. Stock is Mossy Oak camo. Fiber optic front sight. Weight about 6 lbs. Introduced in 2003.

600	450	325	250	175	125

Model 870 SP-T Super Magnum Thumbhole

12-gauge 3.5" gun fitted with 23" barrel and choke tubes. Mossy Oak Obsession finish. Open sights, with fiber-optic front sight. Weight about 8 lbs. Introduced in 2005.

650	500	350	250	175	125

Model 870 Dale Earnhardt Limited Edition

12-gauge with 28" vent rib barrel and choke tubes. Checkered walnut stock. Receiver engraved with Earnhardt's likeness and gold signature. High polish blue finish. Weight about 8 lbs. Introduced in 2005.

650	500	350	250	175	125

	NIB	EXC.	V.G.	GOOD	FAIR	POOR

Model 870 Marine Magnum

This 12-gauge shotgun has a nickel finish on the inside and outside of receiver and barrel. Synthetic stock is checkered. The 18" barrel is bored cylinder. Fitted with 7-round magazine. Sling swivel studs are standard.

	560	325	275	225	175	125

Model 870 SPS

Offered in 12-gauge only. Synthetic stock and black matte finish. Barrel either 26" or 28", with ventilated rib and RemChoke tubes.

	325	275	225	175	125	100

Model 870 SPS-Deer

Available with 20" rifle and plain barrel. This 12-gauge shotgun has black synthetic stock and black matte finish. First introduced in 1993.

	550	450	325	250	195	150

Model 870 Police

This model comes in a wide variety (21) of 12-gauge configurations. Fitted with barrel from 14" (Class III), 18" or 20". Most with Parkerized finish, although some variations have blued finish. Wood, folding, Speedfeed or synthetic stock. Rifle or bead sights. Some configurations with ghost ring and tritium night sights. Some variations have 7- or 8-round magazine extensions, depending on barrel length.

	650	525	400	300	225	125

Model 870 Tac-2 SpecOps Stock

Tactical 3" 12-gauge. Available with Knoxx pistol-grip or folding stock. Barrel 18", with fixed Cylinder choke. Magazine capacity 6 shells. Weight is 7 lbs.

	615	425	325	250	175	125

Model 870 Tac-3 Speedfeed IV

Tactical 3" 12-gauge, with pistol-grip stock and 20" barrel. Extended 7-round magazine. Weight is 7.5 lbs.

	600	450	325	250	175	125

Model 870 Tac-3 Folder

As above, with Knoxx Spec-Ops folding stock. Weight is 7 lbs.

	600	450	325	250	175	125

Model 870 Express Tactical A-TACS Camo

Pump action shotgun chambered for 2.75" and 3" 12-gauge. Features include full A-TACS digitized camo; 18.5" barrel; extended ported Tactical RemChoke; SpeedFeed IV pistol-grip stock with SuperCell recoil pad; fully adjustable XS ghost ring sight rail with removable white bead front sight; 7-round capacity with factory-installed 2-shot extension; drilled and tapped receiver; sling swivel stud.

	600	525	450	375	275	185

Model 870 Custom Grade

Custom Shop model available in three levels of engraving, gold inlay, wood grade and finish, metal work finish, recoil pad/buttplate and dimensions.

D Grade

	3000	200	1100	—	—	—

F Grade

	6000	4000	2250	—	—	—

F Grade with Gold Inlay

	10000	7500	5000	—	—	—

Model 870 SP-T Thumbhole

Introduced in 2005. This 3.5" 12-gauge is designed specifically for turkey hunting. Full coverage in Mossy Oak Obsession camo and thumbhole stock. The 23" barrel features fiber-optic adjustable rifle sights and is drilled and tapped for scope mounting. Includes R3 recoil pad, sling, swivels and turkey super full choke tube.

	615	425	325	250	175	125

NIB	EXC.	V.G.	GOOD	FAIR	POOR

Model 870 Special Purpose Thumbhole

Laminated stock 12-gauge slug gun, with 3" chamber and 23" fully rifled cantilever barrel.

525	475	350	275	200	150

Model 870 XCS Marine Magnum

New in 2007, this weather-resistant 870 is a 3" 12-gauge, with full black TriNyte coverage, 18" fixed Cylinder barrel and 7 round capacity. Weight is 7.5 lbs.

675	495	400	300	200	125

Model 870 SPS MAX Gobbler

Dedicated turkey gun is a 3.5" 12-gauge. Featuring length-adjustable Knoxx SpecOps stock, 23" barrel, fiber-optic rifle sights, Super Full turkey choke tube and full coverage in Realtree APG camo. Drilled and tapped for Weaver style mount. Weight is 8 lbs.

650	550	425	350	225	150

Model 870 20 Gauge Lightweight Magnum

Fixed-choke, high-gloss 3" version of Model 870 Wingmaster, with impressed checkering. Introduced mid-1980s. Also chambers 2.75" shells. Discontinued.

550	450	325	250	195	150

Model 870 Wingmaster 100th Anniversary

Commemorative Edition 12-gauge celebrating 100 years of Remington pump shotguns (dating from introduction of Model 10 in 1908). Introduced in 2008. Offered only for one year. Gold-inlaid logos on both sides of receiver and "B" Grade American walnut stock, with high-gloss finish. Includes three choke tubes.

875	600	475	350	200	125

Model 870 American Classic

Part of Remington American Classic series honoring some of the great models of the 20th century. Inaugurating this line in 2014, is this special edition Model 870 pump action and a comparable Model 1100 semi-automatic. Features include a higher B-grade walnut stock, gold filled engraving and ventilated recoil pad, with white outline as was found on the originals.

1050	850	—	—	—	—

Model 870 with Claro Walnut

This 2008 upgrade to 870 Wingmaster. Features semi-fancy claro walnut stock and fore-end. Available in 3" 12- and 20-gauge, with 28" and 26" barrels, respectively. Three choke tubes included.

875	600	475	350	200	125

Model 870 Express Magnum ShurShot Cantilever

This 3" 12-gauge has a 23" fully rifled barrel, with cantilever scope mount. Matte black finish. Weight about 7.75 lbs.

550	450	325	250	195	150

Model 870 SPS ShurShot Synthetic Super Slug

Pump-action shotgun based on 870 platform. Chambers 12-gauge 2.75" and 3" shells interchangeably. Extra-heavy (1" dia.) 25.5" fully rifled barrel pinned to receiver. SuperCell recoil pad. Drilled and tapped for scope mounts, with Weaver rail included. Matte black metal surfaces, Mossy Oak Treestand ShurShot buttstock and fore-end. Overall length 47". Weight 7.875 lbs.

550	450	325	250	195	150

Model 870 Express Super Magnum Waterfowl

Introduced in 2008. This dedicated waterfowl gun is completely finished in Mossy Oak Duck Blind camo. The 3.5" 12-gauge has 28" barrel, HiViz single bead sight and weighs about 7.5 lbs. Includes one choke tube.

350	300	250	200	150	100

Model 870 Express Magnum ShurShot Turkey

Turkey-dedicated model has matte black finish, with ShurShot pistol-grip/thumbhole stock and fore-end finished in Mossy Oak Obsession camo. The 3" 12-gauge has 21" barrel. Includes a Turkey Extra Full choke tube. Weight about 7.5 lbs.

500	400	325	250	175	100

Model 870 SPS ShurShot Turkey

New in 2008. This 12-gauge chambered for shells up to 3.5". Features Remington's ShurShot pistol-grip/thumbhole stock. Fully covered in Realtree's APG HD camo. Has 23" non-vent rib

NIB	EXC.	V.G.	GOOD	FAIR	POOR

barrel outfitted with fiber-optic rifle-type sights and includes an extended Turkey RemChoke. Weight about 7.5 lbs.

625	495	400	300	200	125

Model 870 Express Tactical

Similar to Model 870, in 12-gauge only (2.75" and 3" interchangeably) with 18.5" barrel, Tactical RemChoke extended/ported choke tube, black synthetic buttstock and fore-end, extended magazine tube, gray powdercoat finish overall. 38.5" overall length. Weight 7.5 lbs.

575	465	325	250	195	150

Model 870 Express Tactical with Ghost Ring Sights

Similar to Model 870 Express Tactical, with top-mounted accessories rail and XS ghost ring rear sight.

625	495	400	300	200	125

Model 870 Tactical Desert Recon

Tactical version 870 features Digital Tiger desert camo on synthetic stock and fore-end. Olive-drab powder-coated barrel and receiver. Available with 18" (6-round mag. capacity) or 20" (7-round mag. capacity) barrel. Speedfeed I (shell holding) or Speedfeed IV (pistol-grip) stock. **NOTE:** Add 10 percent for Speedfeed IV stock.

625	495	400	300	200	125

Model 887 Nitro Mag Pump Shotgun

Pump-action shotgun based on Model 870. Chambers 3.5", 3" and 2.75" 12-gauge shells interchangeably. Black matte ArmorLokt rustproof coating throughout. SuperCell recoil pad. 28" barrel, with solid rib. Hi-Viz front sight, with interchangeable light tubes. Black synthetic stock, with contoured grip panels.

445	385	325	275	200	150

Model 887 Nitro Mag Waterfowl

Similar to above, with Advantage Max-4 camo overall.

450	400	350	300	200	100

Model 887 Bone Collector Edition

Pump action shotgun chambered in 12-gauge, 2.75" to 3.5" shells. Features include ArmorLokt rustproof coating; synthetic stock and fore-end; 26" barrel; full camo finish; integral swivel studs; SuperCell recoil pad; solid rib and HiViz front sight. Bone Collector logo.

560	475	400	335	250	150

Model 887 Nitro Mag Camo Combo

Pump action shotgun chambered in 12-gauge, 2.75" to 3.5" shells. Features include 22" turkey barrel, with HiViz fiber-optic rifle sights and 28" waterfowl, with HiViz sight; extended Waterfowl and Super Full Turkey RemChokes are included; SuperCell recoil pad; synthetic stock and fore-end, with specially contoured grip panels; full camo coverage.

625	535	460	385	325	200

Model 887 Nitro Mag Tactical

Pump action shotgun chambered in 12-gauge, 2.75" to 3.5" shells. Features include 18.5" barrel, with ported extended tactical RemChoke; 2-shot magazine extension; barrel clamp, with integral Picatinny rails; ArmorLokt coating; synthetic stock and fore-end, with specially contour grip panels.

450	400	350	275	200	150

Model 48 Sportsman

A 12-, 16- or 20-gauge semi-automatic shotgun, with 26", 28" or 32" barrels and 3-shot tubular magazine. Blued. with checkered walnut stock. Approximately 275,000 made from 1949 to 1959. **NOTE:** Add 20 percent for vent rib.

—	325	300	250	175	100

Model 11-48

As above, with addition of 28-gauge and .410 bore. Approximately 425,000 made from 1949 to 1968. **NOTE:** Add 225 percent premium for 28-gauge.

—	300	250	200	150	75

	NIB	EXC.	V.G.	GOOD	FAIR	POOR

Model 58 Sportsman

A 12-, 16- or 20-gauge semi-automatic shotgun, with 26", 28" or 30" barrels and 3-shot tubular magazine. Receiver is scroll engraved and blued. Checkered walnut stock. Approximately 270,000 made from 1956 to 1963.

	NIB	EXC.	V.G.	GOOD	FAIR	POOR
	—	300	250	200	150	75

Model 878 Automaster

As above in 12-gauge only. Approximately 60,000 made from 1959 to 1962.

	NIB	EXC.	V.G.	GOOD	FAIR	POOR
	—	350	250	175	125	75

MODEL 1100 SERIES

A 12-, 16-, 20- or 28-gauge or .410 bore semi-automatic shotgun, with barrels ranging in length from 26" to 30". Fitted with choke tubes after 1987. Blued, with checkered walnut stock. Manufactured beginning in 1963. **NOTE:** Smaller bore versions are worth approximately 20 percent more than values listed.

NIB	EXC.	V.G.	GOOD	FAIR	POOR
550	450	350	200	150	100

Model 1100 Classic Field

Introduced in 2003. This shotgun is chambered for 16-gauge shell. Fitted with choice of 26" or 28" vent rib barrel, with RemChoke tubes. Checkered walnut stock, with pistol-grip. High polish blue finish. Magazine capacity 4 rounds. Weight about 7 to 7.25 lbs. depending on barrel length.

NIB	EXC.	V.G.	GOOD	FAIR	POOR
800	600	450	300	200	100

Model 1100 Small Game

Available in 20-, 28-gauge or .410 bore. Fitted with 25" vent rib barrels. 28-gauge and .410 have fixed chokes, while 20-gauge has RemChoke tubes.

NIB	EXC.	V.G.	GOOD	FAIR	POOR
500	450	400	350	250	150

Model 1100 Youth Gun

Offered in 20-gauge only, with 21" vent rib 2.75" barrel. Stock has special 13" length of pull. Gun supplied with a set of RemChoke tubes.

NIB	EXC.	V.G.	GOOD	FAIR	POOR
600	400	350	300	200	150

Model 1100 Youth Synthetic

Fitted with 21" vent rib barrel, this 20-gauge gun has a 1" shorter length of pull than standard. Matte black finish. Black synthetic stock. Weight about 6.5 lbs. Introduced in 1999.

NIB	EXC.	V.G.	GOOD	FAIR	POOR
575	400	300	225	150	100

Model 1100 Youth Synthetic Camo

Same as model above, with Realtree camo finish and chambered for 20-gauge 3" Magnum shells. Weight about 6.75 lbs. Introduced in 1999.

NIB	EXC.	V.G.	GOOD	FAIR	POOR
695	475	325	225	175	100

Model 1100 Tournament Skeet

Offered in 20-, 28-gauge and .410 bore. The 28-gauge and .410 come with 25" Skeet choked vent rib barrels, while 20-gauge is supplied with 26" Skeet choked vent rib barrel.

NIB	EXC.	V.G.	GOOD	FAIR	POOR
800	650	500	400	250	150

Model 1100 Tournament Skeet, 12 Gauge

Introduced in 2003. Model fitted with 26" light contour vent rib barrel. Stock is semi-fancy walnut. Receiver is rolled-marked "tournament skeet". Supplied with extended choke tubes and gold-plated trigger. Weight about 7.75 lbs.

NIB	EXC.	V.G.	GOOD	FAIR	POOR
650	500	400	300	200	100

Model 1100 Classic Trap

Model features 30" low-profile vent rib barrel. Stock is semi-fancy walnut, with Monte Carlo comb and ventilated recoil pad. Receiver has fine line engraving, with gold inlays. Trigger is gold. Weight about 8.25 lbs.

NIB	EXC.	V.G.	GOOD	FAIR	POOR
850	725	600	475	350	200

Model 1100 Sporting 12

Introduced in 2000. This 12-gauge model features 28" low profile vent rib barrel. Stock is walnut, with cut checkering and Sporting Clays-style recoil pad. Gold trigger and fine line engraving on receiver. Weight about 8 lbs.

NIB	EXC.	V.G.	GOOD	FAIR	POOR
725	650	475	400	300	150

	NIB	EXC.	V.G.	GOOD	FAIR	POOR

Model 1100 Sporting 20

Model has high grade walnut stock, with glass finish and recoil pad. Fitted with 28" barrel, with target sights. Interchangeable chokes. Introduced in 1998.

700	625	425	400	300	150

Model 1100 Sporting 28

Introduced in 1996. this version chambered for 28-gauge shell. fitted with interchangeable chokes and 25" vent rib barrel. stock is walnut, with Tournament grade checkering and recoil pad.

825	700	575	475	350	200

Model 1100 Competition Master

Introduced in 2003. Model features 12-gauge gun chambered for 2.75" shell. Fitted with 22" vent rib barrel, with RemChokes and fiber optic front sight. Has gray synthetic stock, with matte black finish on receiver and barrel. Magazine extension has 8-round capacity. Receiver mounted ammo carrier for seven extra shells. Weight about 8 lbs. Designed for practical shooting competition.

725	600	425	400	300	150

Model 1100 Competition

Introduced in 2005. Model chambered for 12-gauge shells, with 2.75" chamber. Fitted with 30" target style barrel, with 10mm vent rib. Extended choke tubes. Receiver nickel plated. Stock is semi-fancy American walnut, with checkering and high gloss finish. Adjustable comb offered as option. Weight about 8 lbs. **NOTE:** Add $175 for adjustable comb model.

950	775	650	525	350	175

Model 1100 LT-20

20-gauge model features choice of 26" or 28" vent rib barrels, with RemChoke tubes. Blue finish and walnut Monte Carlo stock. Recoil pad and cut checkering are standard. Weight 6.75 to 7 lbs. depending on barrel length.

600	450	400	300	200	150

Model 1100 LT-20 "Limited"

20-gauge lightweight Model 1100 Field gun. Stock 1" shorter than standard and 23" barrel for youthful beginner shooters of smaller stature.

675	525	475	375	275	200

Model 1100 1 OF 3000

September 1980, Remington announced Model 1100 Limited Edition "One of Three Thousand". High grade gun, with positive cut checkered fancy American walnut wood, fitted rosewood grip cap, thin brown butt pad, 14K gold trimmed and etched with hunting scenes on receiver. All metal parts including receiver, barrel, bolt and magazine cap have a high-luster finish. Available only in 1980.

2000	1600	1000	800	400	250

Model 1100 Special Field

In 12-, 20-gauge or .410 bore. Shorter variation of standard 1100. Barrel length was originally 21" (1983-1993) and was changed to 23" from (1994 to 1999) when model was discontinued. Checkered walnut stock, with straight-grip. Ventilated rib on all models. **NOTE:** Add 20 percent for .410 bore.

600	500	400	350	300	150

Model 1100 TBMC Trap Gun

12-gauge, with 30" vent rib barrel in full or modified trap chokes. Featured a figured and checkered stock and fore-end. Had a rubber recoil pad. Monte Carlo style stock was optional. A left-hand version of this gun was also available. Due to a shortage of American walnut, in mid-year Remington began fitting some Model 1100 and Model 870 Field Grade shotguns with lightweight mahogany stocks and fore-ends.

725	650	475	400	300	150

Model 1100 LT-20 Deer Gun

Same as above, with 21" barrel, adjustable sights and improved cylinder choke. Satin finish with American walnut stock. Weight about 6.5 lbs.

525	450	400	300	200	150

Model 1100 LT-20 Synthetic

Same as above, with synthetic stock and recoil pad.

550	375	325	275	200	150

NIB	EXC.	V.G.	GOOD	FAIR	POOR

Model 1100 LT-20 Magnum

20-gauge Model 1100 chambered for 3" 20-gauge shell. Fitted with 28" vent rib barrel, with interchangeable chokes. Checkered walnut stock. Weight about 7 lbs.

NIB	EXC.	V.G.	GOOD	FAIR	POOR
575	395	400	300	200	150

Model 1100 LT-20 Synthetic Camo NWTF 25th Anniversary

Model fitted with 21" barrel, with special fiber optic sighting system. NWTF logo on left side of receiver. Introduced in 1998.

NIB	EXC.	V.G.	GOOD	FAIR	POOR
650	525	450	300	250	125

Model 1100 Synthetic

Introduced in 1995. Model furnished with black synthetic stock, with black matte metal finish. Available in both 12- and 20-gauge. Weight about 6.75 to 7 lbs. depending on barrel length. In 2003, this model was offered chambered for 16-gauge shell.

NIB	EXC.	V.G.	GOOD	FAIR	POOR
550	450	350	250	200	100

Model 1100 Synthetic Deer Gun

Same as above, with 21" fully rifled barrel with cantilever rail for scope mounting. Furnished with 2.75" chamber. Stock is black synthetic, with checkering and Monte Carlo-style cheekpiece. Recoil pad is standard.

NIB	EXC.	V.G.	GOOD	FAIR	POOR
525	450	400	300	200	150

Model 1100 Competition Synthetic

The 1100 Competition Synthetic is super-tuned for competitive shooters. Overbored 30" barrel, with lengthened forcing cones. Optimized for 2.75" target loads and light field loads. Receiver and all internal parts have nickel-Teflon finish. Synthetic stock has SuperCell recoil pad. 12-gauge only. Weight 8.25 lbs.

NIB	EXC.	V.G.	GOOD	FAIR	POOR
900	800	675	525	400	250

Model 1100 Custom Grade

Custom Shop model available in three levels of engraving, gold inlay, wood grade and finish, metal work finish, recoil pad/buttplate and dimensions. Each gun should be individually appraised prior to a sale.

D Grade

NIB	EXC.	V.G.	GOOD	FAIR	POOR
3000	200	1100	—	—	—

F Grade

NIB	EXC.	V.G.	GOOD	FAIR	POOR
6000	4000	2250	—	—	—

F Grade with Gold Inlay

NIB	EXC.	V.G.	GOOD	FAIR	POOR
10000	7500	5000	—	—	—

Model 1100 G3

Introduced in 2006. updated 1100 features Realwood high gloss semi-fancy stock and for-end. Available in 12- and 20-gauge, with 26" or 28" barrel. chambered for 3" shells. Includes five Pro Bore chokes for 12-gauge; five Remchokes for 20-gauge. R3 recoil pad and high-grade travel case. Left-handed version was added in 2008.

NIB	EXC.	V.G.	GOOD	FAIR	POOR
825	600	450	300	225	150

Model 1100 Tactical Speedfeed IV

All-black 2.75" 12-gauge has an 18" barrel, with fixed Improved Cylinder choke and Speedfeed IV stock. Extended 6-round magazine. Weight 7.5 lbs.

NIB	EXC.	V.G.	GOOD	FAIR	POOR
825	600	450	300	225	150

Model 1100 Tactical Standard Stock

Tactical 2.75" 12-gauge has 22" barrel threaded for RemChokes. Extended 8-round magazine.

NIB	EXC.	V.G.	GOOD	FAIR	POOR
825	600	450	300	225	150

Model 1100 Premier Sporting

Introduced in 2008. A dedicated sporting clays gun. Premier Sporting comes in 12-, 20-, 28-gauge and .410 bore, with 2.75" chamber (3" in .410). Polished nickel receiver, with fine-line embellishments and gold accents. Stock and fore-end are semi-fancy American walnut, with high-gloss finish. Full line of Briley choke tubes and Premier Sporting hard case are included. Weight about 8 lbs. in 12-gauge; 7 lbs. in 20-gauge; 6.5 lbs. in 28-gauge and .410 bore. **NOTE:** Add 5 percent for 28-gauge and .410 bore.

NIB	EXC.	V.G.	GOOD	FAIR	POOR
1150	1000	850	675	475	300

	NIB	EXC.	V.G.	GOOD	FAIR	POOR

Model 1100 50th Anniversary Limited Edition

Model 1100s most popular semi-automatic shotgun in the world. To commemorate 50 years of service to shooters, this Limited Edition model has machine-cut engraved receiver, with gold fill and high-grade walnut stock. White diamond grip cap and white line spacer recall the style of stock in 1963. In 12-gauge only, with 28" ventilated rib barrel. Introduced 2013, with limited production.

NIB	EXC.	V.G.	GOOD	FAIR	POOR
1800	1600	1400	—	—	—

Model 1100 American Classic

Part of Remington American Classic series honoring some of the great models of the 20th century. Inaugurating this line in 2014 is this special edition Model 1100 semi-automatic and comparable Model 870 pump action. Features include higher B-grade walnut stock, gold filled engraving and ventilated recoil pad with white outline, as was found on the originals.

NIB	EXC.	V.G.	GOOD	FAIR	POOR
1450	1200	—	—	—	—

MODEL 11-87 SERIES

Model 11-87 Premier

A 3" 12-gauge semi-automatic shotgun, with 26" to 32" ventilated rib barrels having screw-in choke tubes. Blued, with checkered walnut stock. Weight about 7.75 lbs. Introduced in 1987. In 1999, this model was offered in a left-hand version.

NIB	EXC.	V.G.	GOOD	FAIR	POOR
700	600	450	300	200	150

Model 11-87 Premier 20 Gauge

Introduced in 1999. Built on a small frame receiver. Will chamber both 2.75" and 3" shells. Available in both 26" and 28" vent rib barrels, with twin beads. Barrels are built for RemChokes. Stock is walnut, with gloss finish. Weight about 7 lbs.

NIB	EXC.	V.G.	GOOD	FAIR	POOR
675	575	425	300	225	125

Model 11-87 Dale Earnhardt Tribute

Introduced in 2003 to honor Dale Earnhardt. This 12-gauge is fitted with 28" vent rib barrel and walnut stock with checkering. Engraved on receiver is a likeness of Earnhardt, his signature and scroll work. Inlayed in gold. Serial numbers start with "DE3." Weight about 7.75 lbs.

NIB	EXC.	V.G.	GOOD	FAIR	POOR
675	575	425	300	225	125

Model 11-87 Upland Special

Model offered in 12- or 20-gauge, with 23" barrel and twin bead sights. Chambered for 3" shells. Stock is walnut, with straight-grip. Choke tubes standard. Weight about 7.25 for 1-gauge; 6.5 lbs. for 20-gauge. Introduced in 2000.

NIB	EXC.	V.G.	GOOD	FAIR	POOR
725	600	450	300	225	125

Model 11-87 Premier Cantilever Scope Mount Deer Gun

Semi-automatic model has a Monte Carlo stock and option of barrel-mounted scope (not included). Optional with fully rifled barrel 21" long, with 1-in-35" twist. Also available in 21" nonrifled barrel, with Rifled and IC RemChoke tubes. Available in 12-gauge only. Sling swivel studs and camo are standard.

NIB	EXC.	V.G.	GOOD	FAIR	POOR
800	675	400	300	200	150

Model 11-87 Premier Trap

Available in either right- or left-hand models and straight or Monte Carlo comb. 2.75" chamber, 30" vent rib overbored barrel and special Rem. Trap choke tubes. Model set up to handle 12-gauge target loads only.

NIB	EXC.	V.G.	GOOD	FAIR	POOR
525	475	425	300	200	150

Model 11-87 Premier SC (Sporting Clays)

Model features special target stock, with 3.16" length of pull longer than standard and .250" higher at heel. Butt pad is radiused at the heel and rounded at toe. Receiver top, barrel and rib have a fine matte finish on the blueing. Vent rib is a medium wide 8mm, with stainless steel mid bead and Bradley-style front bead sight. Gun supplied new with these RemChoke tubes: Skeet, Improved Skeet, Improved Cylinder, Modified and Full. Supplied from factory with a two-barrel custom fitted hard case.

NIB	EXC.	V.G.	GOOD	FAIR	POOR
750	600	450	350	200	150

Model 11-87 SC NP (Sporting Clays Nickel-Plated)

Same as above, with nickel-plated receiver.

NIB	EXC.	V.G.	GOOD	FAIR	POOR
800	650	500	400	300	200

	NIB	EXC.	V.G.	GOOD	FAIR	POOR

Model 11-87 SPS-BG Camo

12-gauge model fitted with rifle sighted 21" barrel, with brown camo finish on stock and metal parts. Introduced in 1993.

	NIB	EXC.	V.G.	GOOD	FAIR	POOR
	525	475	425	300	200	150

Model 11-87 SPS-T Camo

Same as above, but supplied with 21" vent rib barrel with IC and Turkey Super Full Rem. choke tubes. Camo finish is green. Introduced in 1993.

	NIB	EXC.	V.G.	GOOD	FAIR	POOR
	550	450	350	250	200	150

Model 11-87 SPS

This 12-gauge model furnished with 26" or 28" vent rib barrel, with IC Mod. and Full RemChoke tubes. Stock is black synthetic material and metal finished in black matte. In 1997, a camo version was introduced.

	NIB	EXC.	V.G.	GOOD	FAIR	POOR
	500	400	300	250	200	150

Model 11-87 SPS-Deer

Same as above, with 21" rifled sighted barrel. First introduced in 1993.

	NIB	EXC.	V.G.	GOOD	FAIR	POOR
	525	475	425	300	200	150

Model 11-87 Waterfowl

12-gauge gun fitted with 28" vent rib barrel with choke tubes and Hi-Viz sights. Camo pattern is Mossy Oak Shadow-grass. Weight about 8.25 lbs. Introduced in 2004.

	NIB	EXC.	V.G.	GOOD	FAIR	POOR
	925	700	600	500	350	175

Model 11-87 SPS-T

Same as above, with 21" vent rib barrel with IC and Turkey Super Full RemChoke tubes. In 1997, camo version was introduced.

	NIB	EXC.	V.G.	GOOD	FAIR	POOR
	525	475	425	300	200	150

Model 11-87 SPS-T Camo NWTF 25th Anniversary

Model has 21" barrel, with special fiber optic sighting system. NWTF logo on left side of receiver. Introduced in 1998.

	NIB	EXC.	V.G.	GOOD	FAIR	POOR
	700	595	425	300	200	150

Model 11-87 SP Super Magnum

Introduced in 2000. Chambered for 12-gauge 3.5" Magnum shell. Fitted with 26" or 28" vent rib barrel. Walnut stock, with flat finish. Recoil pad. Matte black finish. Weight about 8.25 lbs.

	NIB	EXC.	V.G.	GOOD	FAIR	POOR
	675	500	350	300	125	100

Model 11-87 SPS Super Magnum

Same as above, with black synthetic stock. Introduced in 2000. Weight about 8.25 lbs.

	NIB	EXC.	V.G.	GOOD	FAIR	POOR
	675	500	350	300	125	100

Model 11-87 SPS-T Super Magnum (NWTF Edition)

Introduced in 2005. Features 12-gauge 3.5" chamber, with 23" barrel with choke tubes and iron sights. Mossy Oak Obsession camo stock, with Monte Carlo comb. Weight about 8 lbs.

	NIB	EXC.	V.G.	GOOD	FAIR	POOR
	950	775	650	525	350	175

Model 11-87 Police

Offered chambered for 12-gauge shells. Features synthetic stock, 18" barrel with bead rifle or ghost ring sights and 7-shot magazine extension. **NOTE:** Add $20 for rifle sights; $60 for ghost ring sights.

	NIB	EXC.	V.G.	GOOD	FAIR	POOR
	675	500	350	300	125	100

Model 11-87 Custom Grade

Custom Shop model available in three levels of engraving, gold inlay, wood grade and finish, metal work finish, recoil pad/buttplate and dimensions.

D Grade

	NIB	EXC.	V.G.	GOOD	FAIR	POOR
	3000	200	1100	—	—	—

F Grade

	NIB	EXC.	V.G.	GOOD	FAIR	POOR
	6000	4000	2250	—	—	—

F Grade with Gold Inlay

	NIB	EXC.	V.G.	GOOD	FAIR	POOR
	10000	7500	5000	—	—	—

NIB	EXC.	V.G.	GOOD	FAIR	POOR

Model 11-87 Sportsman Synthetic

Introduced in 2005. Model features black synthetic stock, with choice of 12- or 20-gauge 3" chambers; 26" or 28" barrels with Mod. choke tube. Weight about 7.75 to 8.25 lbs. depending on gauge and barrel length.

675	500	350	300	125	100

Model 11-87 Sportsman Super Magnum

In 2008, Remington added this 3.5" version of 11-87 Sportsman. Has 28" barrel. Weighs 8.25 lbs.

750	625	550	400	300	200

Model 11-87 Sportsman Rifled

A 12-gauge 3" gun, with 21" rifled barrel with cantilever scope mount. Black synthetic stock, with black metal finish. Weight about 8.5 lbs. Introduced in 2005.

675	500	350	300	125	100

Model 11-87 Sportsman Youth

A 20-gauge 3" gun, with 21" vent rib barrel and choke tubes. Black synthetic stock. Length of pull 13". Weight about 6.5 lbs. Introduced in 2005.

600	450	400	300	200	150

Model 11-87 Sportsman Compact Synthetic

Similar to Model 11-87 black synthetic, with reduced overall dimensions.

700	595	500	350	225	150

Model 11-87 Sportsman Youth Camo

Same as above, with full coverage in Mossy Oak Break-Up camo.

750	625	550	400	300	175

Model 11-87 Sportsman NRA Edition

This 12-gauge 3" model fitted with 28" vent rib barrel, with choke tubes. Synthetic stock, with Mossy Oak New Break-Up camo. NRA logo on left side of matte black receiver. Introduced in 2005.

675	500	350	300	125	100

Model 11-87 SP Thumbhole

Laminated thumbhole stock 12-gauge slug gun, with 3" chamber and 21" fully rifled cantilever barrel.

700	595	500	350	225	150

Model 11-87 SPS-T Super Magnum

Similar to Model 11-87 SP Thumbhole, with pistol-grip stock and vent rib barrel.

750	625	550	400	300	200

Model 11-87 SP-T Thumbhole

This 12-gauge with 3.5" chamber is made specifically for turkey hunting. Camouflaged in Mossy Oak Obsession, with R3 recoil pad and thumbhole stock. The 23" barrel has fiber-optic adjustable rifle sights and drilled and tapped for scope mounting. Includes a turkey super full choke tube and sling/swivels. Introduced 2006.

750	625	550	400	300	200

Model 11-87 Sportsman Camo

New in 2007. Camo version of Sportsman comes in 12- and 20-gauge, with 26" or 28" barrel. Finished in Mossy Oak Break-Up camo.

750	625	550	400	300	200

Model 11-87 Sportsman Camo Rifled

Camo 12-gauge slug gun, with 21" barrel and cantilever scope mount.

750	625	550	400	300	200

Model 11-87 Sportsman Camo Youth

Youth model in 20-gauge, with shorter length of pull. Introduced in 2007. Weight about 6.5 lbs.

700	595	500	350	225	150

Model 11-87 Sportsman Field

Semi-automatic shotgun chambered in 12- and 20-gauge, 2.75" and 3" shells. Features include 26" (20-gauge) or 28" (12-gauge) barrel; vent rib; RemChokes (one supplied); sati-

NIB	EXC.	V.G.	GOOD	FAIR	POOR

finished walnut stock and fore-end with fleur-de-lis pattern; dual sights; nickel-plated bolt and trigger.

680	575	435	350	225	150

Model 11-87 Sportsman Super Mag Synthetic

Semi-automatic shotgun chambered in 12-gauge, 3.5" shells. Features include black matte synthetic stock and fore-end; rubber overmolded grip panels on stock and fore-end; black padded sling; HiViz sights featuring interchangeable light pipe; 28" vent-rib barrel; SuperCell recoil pad; RemChoke.

730	650	550	425	250	175

Model 11-87 Sportsman Super Mag Shurshot Turkey

Similar to 11-87 Sportsman Super Mag Synthetic, with ambidextrous ShurShot pistol-grip stock; full Realtree APG HD coverage; 23" barrel with fully adjustable TruGlo rifle sights. Wingmaster HD Turkey Choke included.

875	750	625	500	300	175

Model 11-87 SPS Super Magnum Waterfowl

This 3.5" 12-gauge is finished in Mossy Oak Duck Blind camo. Has 30" barrel and includes three chokes. Weight 8.25 lbs.

950	775	650	525	350	175

Model 11-87 Sportsman Super Mag ShurShot Turkey

New in 2008. Specialized turkey shotgun, with ShurShot stock is a 3.5" chamber 12-gauge with 23" non-vent-rib barrel. Comes with fiber-optic rifle-type sights and synthetic stock and fore-end. Gun is fully covered in Realtree APG HD camo. Weightabout 7.6 lbs.

800	695	550	450	300	175

Model 11-87 Sportsman Super Magnum Waterfowl

Full coverage in Mossy Oak Duck Blind camo. Shell-holding Speedfeed stock and three choke tubes.

850	725	595	475	325	195

Model 11-87 Sportsman ShurShot Cantilever

Dedicated slug gun in 3" 12-gauge features 23" fully rifled barrel, with cantilever scope mount. Is matte black, with synthetic stock and fore-end finished in Realtree Hardwoods HD camo. Weight about 8 lbs.

850	725	595	475	325	195

Model 11-96 Euro Lightweight

Introduced in 1996. Based on Model 11-87 action. Two vent rib barrel lengths are offered: 26" and 28" supplied with three RemChokes. Fine line engraving on receiver and checkered Claro walnut stocks are standard. Blued finish. Weight about 7 lbs. Made for one year only.

1000	875	625	500	325	200

Model SP-10

A 3.5" 10-gauge semi-automatic shotgun, with 26" or 30" ventilated rib barrels having screw-in choke tubes. Matte blued, with checkered walnut stock.

1500	1275	950	775	600	300

Model SP-10 Magnum Camo

Introduced in 1993. This 10-gauge semi-automatic is designed for the turkey or deer hunter. Available with either 26" or 30" vent rib barrel or 22" deer barrel. Additional barrel option is 23" vent rib barrel, with camo finish. All barrels are fitted with RemChoke tubes.

1550	1325	1000	825	625	325

Model SP-10 Magnum Camo NWTF 25th Anniversary

This model has a special fiber optic sighting system. "NWTF" logo is on left side of receiver. Barrel length 23". Introduced in 1998.

1550	1325	1000	825	625	325

Model SP-10 Synthetic

Model features black synthetic stock, with 26" barrel. Chambered for 10-gauge shells. Matte black metal finish. Choke tubes standard. Introduced in 2000. Weight about 10 lbs.

1300	1150	900	775	575	300

	NIB	EXC.	V.G.	GOOD	FAIR	POOR

Model SP-10 RC/VT

This 10-gauge gun introduced in 2005. Fitted with 26" vent rib barrel, with choke tubes. Mossy Oak Obsession finish. Weight about 10.75 lbs.

1300	1150	900	775	575	300

Model SP-10 Custom Grade

Custom Shop model available in three levels of engraving, gold inlay, wood grade and finish, metal work finish, recoil pad/buttplate and dimensions. Limited production or activity on used gun market. Price estimates for NIB models start at $2000 to $3000 and vary depending on quality of custom features.

Model SP-10 Magnum Waterfowl

New in 2007. This waterfowl-specific model is a synthetic-stock 3.5" 10-gauge, with Mossy Oak Duck Blind camo finish and 26" barrel. Includes three Briley ported choke tubes. Weight about 10.9 lbs.

1550	1325	1000	825	625	325

Model SP-10 Magnum Thumbhole Camo

Special turkey model features synthetic thumbhole stock and complete Mossy Oak Obsession camo finish. Barrel is 23". Briley ported turkey choke included. Weight is 10.9 lbs.

1650	1500	1200	900	675	350

Model 105CTi

New in 2006. Ultralight gas-operated 12-gauge autoloader, features advanced recoil reduction and bottom feed and ejection. Available with 26" or 28" barrel. Satin finish walnut stock. Chambered for 3" shells. Includes three Pro Bore chokes. Weighs about 7 lbs. Discontinued in 2009.

1175	950	800	600	475	275

Versa Max

Versa Max gas-operated semi-automatic shoots everything from 2.75" target loads to 3.5" Magnums. Synthetic stock in black and camo finishes is fully adjustable for length-of-pull, drop-of-comb and cast. 12-gauge only; 26" and 28" barrels; 7.7 lbs. Introduced in 2011. Also available with Wood-Tech stock finish, Realtree and Mossy Oak camo, Tactical model and special-finish "Zombie" models. Values shown are for standard synthetic stock model. **NOTE:** Add $250 for camo finishes or Tactical model; $175 for Wood-Tech or Zombie finishes

1200	1100	1000	850	600	300

Model 32

A 12-gauge over/under shotgun, with 26", 28" or 30" separated barrels and single-selective trigger. Approximately 15,000 made from 1932 to 1942. **NOTE:** Add 10 percent for solid or vent rib.

Standard Grade

—	2500	2250	1600	1250	1000

Skeet

—	2750	2250	1950	1500	1250

TC

—	2750	2500	2250	1750	1450

TC 32D Grade

3000	2000	1100	—	—	—

TC 32F Grade

6000	4000	2250	—	—	—

TC 32E Expert

10000	7500	5000	—	—	—

Model 3200

A 12-gauge over/under shotgun, with 26", 28" or 30" separated ventilated rib barrels, single-selective trigger and automatic ejector. Blued, with checkered walnut stock. Manufactured from 1972 to 1984.

Field Grade

—	800	725	600	450	300

	NIB	EXC.	V.G.	GOOD	FAIR	POOR

Magnum
3" chambers.

	—	1000	850	750	550	300

Skeet

	—	1200	995	800	600	300

4-Gauge Set

	—	5500	4750	3500	2450	1500

Trap

	—	1200	995	800	600	300

Special Trap
Deluxe wood.

	—	1350	1150	750	700	300

Competition Trap
Engraved.

	—	2750	2000	1350	950	300

Premier
Heavily engraved.

	—	5500	4750	3900	—	—

One of One Thousand
1,000 produced.

	—	3500	3000	2500	—	—

Model 300 Ideal

This 12-gauge over/under shotgun, was introduced in 2000. Offered with choice of 26", 28" or 30" barrels. Single-selective trigger and automatic ejectors. Metal finish is blue. Stock is walnut, with semi-gloss finish. Solid black recoil pad. Weight about 7.62 lbs. for 28" barrels. Dropped from production in 2001.

1650	1400	1150	700	575	300

Model 90-T Single-Barrel Trap

Offered in 12-gauge only. Single-barrel Trap shotgun fitted with either 32" or 34" overbored Full choke barrel.

3600	2500	1450	1100	600	300

Model 90-T Single-Barrel Trap (High Rib)

Same as described above, with exception of an adjustable high rib for shooters who prefer a more open target picture and higher head position.

3600	2500	1450	1100	600	300

Model 332

Reintroduction in 2002 of famous Remington Model 32. Features mechanical set trigger, automatic ejectors, with choice of vent rib barrel lengths in 26", 28" and 30". Checkered walnut stock. Black oxide metal finish. Chambered for 12-gauge, with 3" chambers. Weight about 7.75 lbs. depending on barrel length.

1250	900	750	600	400	250

Remington Peerless

Introduced in 1993. New Remington over/under shotgun offered in 12-gauge only. Available in 26", 28" and 30" vent rib barrel lengths and fitted with RemChoke tubes (IC, M, F). Sideplates are removable. Stock is American walnut. Production stopped in 1998.

1250	900	750	600	400	250

Model 396 Sporting

Introduced in 1996. Over/under shotgun designed for sporting clay shooting. Offered in 12-gauge only, with 30" barrels. Chokes are interchangeable RemChoke system. Fancy American stock, with satin finish. Scroll engraving on receiver and blue finish. Weight about 8 lbs.

2150	1700	1150	875	500	300

Model 396 Skeet

Same as above, with choice of 28" or 30" barrels.

2150	1700	1150	875	500	300

NIB	EXC.	V.G.	GOOD	FAIR	POOR

Model 396 Custom Grade

Custom Shop model available in three levels of engraving, gold inlay, wood grade and finish, metal work finish, recoil pad/buttplate, and dimensions. Each gun should be individually appraised prior to sale. Limited production or activity on used gun market. Price estimates for NIB models start at $2000 to $3000 and vary depending on quality of custom features.

PREMIER SERIES OVER/UNDERS

Introduced in 2006. Italian-made over/unders in Premier Series. Feature premium figured walnut stocks, Schnabel fore-ends, ProBore chokes, 3" chambers (2.75" in 28-gauge). Includes a hardside case.

STS Competition

This 12-gauge with 28", 30" or 32" overbored barrels has an engraved nickel-plated receiver and high-gloss finished stock. Weight about 7.8 lbs. **NOTE:** Add 15 percent for adjustable-stock model.

NIB	EXC.	V.G.	GOOD	FAIR	POOR
1500	1300	950	700	550	300

Field Grade

Available in 12-, 20- and 28-gauge, with satin finish and nickel receiver. Available with 26" or 28" barrels. Includes three flush chokes. Weight about 6.5 lbs. for 20- and 28-gauge; 7.5 lbs. for 12-gauge.

NIB	EXC.	V.G.	GOOD	FAIR	POOR
1400	1200	900	650	500	300

Upland Grade

As above, with oil finish stock and case colored receiver with gold game bird scene.

NIB	EXC.	V.G.	GOOD	FAIR	POOR
1450	1250	900	675	525	300

RGS

Special Conservation Gun of the Year in 2007 for Ruffed Grouse Society. A 20-gauge, with 26" barrels, satin oil finished stock and satin black oxide receiver. Includes five choke tubes. Weight is 6.5 lbs.

NIB	EXC.	V.G.	GOOD	FAIR	POOR
1650	1400	1150	700	575	300

Remington Parker AAHE Double

Built to order. Side-by-side double is exact in every respect to original Parker Brothers shotguns. Made from 1860s to 1937 and again until 1942 after Remington purchased the company. In 2006, Remington partnered with Connecticut Shotgun Mfg. Co., to build high-grade AAHE model. Offered in 28-gauge only, with many options including stock dimensions and engraving patterns. Prices start at $49,000.

BOLT-ACTION HANDGUNS

Model XP-100

A .221 Remington Fireball or .223 Remington caliber bolt-action single-shot pistol. Available with or without 14.5" ventilated rib barrel and adjustable sights. Blued, with nylon stock. Introduced in 1963. Discontinued.

NIB	EXC.	V.G.	GOOD	FAIR	POOR
800	600	375	300	225	175

Model XP-100 Silhouette

As above chambered for either 7mm Remington or .35 Remington cartridges. Fitted with 15" barrel drilled and tapped for a telescope. Discontinued.

NIB	EXC.	V.G.	GOOD	FAIR	POOR
725	525	325	250	200	125

Model XP-100 Custom

Custom-made version of above, with 15" barrel. Either nylon or walnut stock. Available in .223 Remington, .250 Savage, 6mm Benchrest, 7mm Benchrest, 7mm-08, or .35 Remington calibers. Introduced in 1986. Discontinued.

NIB	EXC.	V.G.	GOOD	FAIR	POOR
950	800	650	550	425	300

Model XP-100 Hunter

Model features laminated wood stock, 14.5" drilled and tapped barrel and no sights. Offered in these calibers: .223 Rem., 7mm BR Rem., 7mm-08 Rem., and .35 Rem. Discontinued.

NIB	EXC.	V.G.	GOOD	FAIR	POOR
800	675	375	300	250	175

Model XP-100R Repeater

Introduced in 1998. Model chambered for .22-250, .223, .260 and .35 Rem. cartridges. Fitted with 14.5" barrel that is drilled and tapped for sights. Receiver drilled and tapped for scope mounts. Fiberglass stock. Weight about 4.5 lbs. Manufactured 1998. Discontinued.

NIB	EXC.	V.G.	GOOD	FAIR	POOR
950	800	500	450	225	200

NIB	EXC.	V.G.	GOOD	FAIR	POOR

SPARTAN GUNWORKS BY REMINGTON

Line of imported firearms was introduced into Remington line in 2004 and discontinued in 2009.

Model SPR 210

Side-by-side gun, with single-selective trigger and auto ejectors. Box lock receiver is nickel. Fitted with 26" or 28" barrels, with choke tubes in 12- and 20-gauge. Fixed chokes in 28-gauge and .410 bore. Also offered with 20" barrel, with choke tubes and blued receiver. Checkered walnut stock, with recoil pad. Weight about 6.75 lbs. depending on gauge and barrel length. **NOTE:** Add $30 for 28-gauge and .410 bore.

NIB	EXC.	V.G.	GOOD	FAIR	POOR
475	400	350	225	175	100

Model SPR 220

Double trigger model, with 20" barrels and choke tubes. Extractors. Nickel or blued receiver. Walnut stock, with recoil pad. Weight about 6.25 lbs.

NIB	EXC.	V.G.	GOOD	FAIR	POOR
425	375	300	200	150	100

Model SPR 310

An over/under gun chambered for 12-, 20-, 28-gauge and .410 bore. Choice of 26" or 28" vent rib barrels, with choke tubes; or 26" barrels for 28-gauge and .410 bore. Single selective trigger and auto ejectors. Checkered walnut stock, with recoil pad. Weight about 7.5 lbs.

NIB	EXC.	V.G.	GOOD	FAIR	POOR
475	400	350	225	175	125

Model SPR 310S

This model chambered for 12- and 20-gauge 3" shell. Fitted with 29.5" (12-gauge) or 28.5" (20-gauge) ported barrels with choke tubes. Checked walnut stock, with recoil pad. Weight about 7.5 lbs.

NIB	EXC.	V.G.	GOOD	FAIR	POOR
700	600	475	350	275	200

Model SPR 100/Sporting

Single shot gun chambered for 12- and 20-gauge or .410 bore. Fitted with 29.5" (12-gauge), 28.5" (20-gauge) or 26" (.410) barrel. Single trigger, with ejectors or extractors. Youth model also offered with 24" barrel chambered for .410 bore. Checkered walnut stock, with recoil pad. Weight about 6.25 lbs. **NOTE:** Add $40 for Sporting models.

NIB	EXC.	V.G.	GOOD	FAIR	POOR
250	175	125	100	75	50

Model SPR 18

Single shot rifle chambered for .223, .243, .270 or .30-06 calibers. Nickel receiver. Fitted with 23.5" barrel, with iron sights. Checkered walnut stock, with recoil pad. Weight about 6.75 lbs.

NIB	EXC.	V.G.	GOOD	FAIR	POOR
275	200	150	125	95	75

Model SPR 22

Side-by-side double rifle chambered for .30-06 or .45-70 calibers. Fitted with 23.5" barrels. Blued receiver and checkered walnut stock, with recoil pad. Weight about 7.5 lbs.

NIB	EXC.	V.G.	GOOD	FAIR	POOR
1000	825	700	575	400	250

Model SPR 94

Model features an under/under rifle/shotgun combination. Chambered for .410/17HMR, .410/.22WMR, 12-/.223, 12-/.30-06 or 12-/.308. Fitted with 24" barrel, with iron sights. Checkered walnut stock, with recoil pad. Blued receiver. Weight about 8 lbs. depending on combination. **NOTE:** Add 30 percent for centerfire models.

NIB	EXC.	V.G.	GOOD	FAIR	POOR
375	300	225	150	100	75

REMINGTON CUSTOM SHOP

Remington Custom Shop builds a number of specialty rifles and shotguns as well as specific custom guns for its customers. Remington will build a wide number of special features from special wood type, finish and styling options to engraving. These special order features add considerably to the cost of a gun and will affect its price. Custom Shop can be reached at 315-895-3288 for current prices and availability.

REMINGTON 180TH ANNIVERSARY LIMITED EDITION RIFLES AND SHOTGUNS

Remington manufactured 180 each of these firearms to commemorate the founding of the company in 1816:

Model 700, Model 7600, Model 7400, Model 870, and Model 11-87.

These firearms featured fine line hand engraving, with gold embellishments. Rifles were chambered for .30-06 cartridge, with 22" barrels; shotguns were chambered for 12-gauge shell,

NIB	EXC.	V.G.	GOOD	FAIR	POOR

with 26" vent rib barrels with RemChokes. All guns had blue finishes, with high gloss semi-fancy walnut stocks. Any estimate about current values would be quite speculative. If sold in a five-gun set, each should have matching serial numbers. Suggested retail price for the five-gun set was $6,925 in 1996. Individual guns carried these suggested retail prices:

Model 700   180th Anniversary Commemorative—$1,372
Model 7400   180th Anniversary Commemorative—$1,372
Model 7600   180th Anniversary Commemorative—$1,332
Model 870   180th Anniversary Commemorative—$1,305
Model 11-87   180th Anniversary Commemorative—$1,465

RENETTE, GASTINNE
Paris, France

SHOTGUNS

Model 105

Anson & Deeley action 12- or 20-gauge double-barrel shotgun. Available in a variety of barrel lengths, with double triggers and automatic ejectors. Blued, case hardened with checkered walnut stock.

NIB	EXC.	V.G.	GOOD	FAIR	POOR
—	4000	3200	2500	1700	300

Model 98

As above, except more finely finished.

NIB	EXC.	V.G.	GOOD	FAIR	POOR
—	5200	4500	3500	2800	300

Model 202

A 12- or 20-gauge sidelock double-barrel shotgun. Made only on custom order. French case hardened. Blued, with checkered walnut stock.

NIB	EXC.	V.G.	GOOD	FAIR	POOR
—	9000	7000	5000	3450	300

Model 353

Custom manufactured double-barrel shotgun, with detachable sidelocks. Highly finished.

NIB	EXC.	V.G.	GOOD	FAIR	POOR
—	35000	30000	1700	8000	500

RIFLES

Type G Rifle

A .30-06, 9.3x74R, or .375 Holland & Holland double-barrel rifle, with 24" barrels, express sights, double triggers and automatic ejectors. Engraved. Blued, with checkered walnut stock.

NIB	EXC.	V.G.	GOOD	FAIR	POOR
—	5500	3700	3000	2000	650

Type R Deluxe

As above, engraved with hunting scenes and more finely figured walnut stock.

NIB	EXC.	V.G.	GOOD	FAIR	POOR
—	7000	5000	3400	2900	750

Type PT President

As above, inlaid in gold with extremely well figured walnut stock.

NIB	EXC.	V.G.	GOOD	FAIR	POOR
—	8000	6400	4000	3500	950

Mauser Bolt-Action

A custom-made bolt-action rifle built on a Mauser action. Choice of calibers and stock styles. Base price listed.

NIB	EXC.	V.G.	GOOD	FAIR	POOR
—	11000	9000	6500	3000	750

Deluxe Mauser Bolt-Action

Same as above, with fancy wood and other options.

NIB	EXC.	V.G.	GOOD	FAIR	POOR
—	20000	14000	9000	6500	1250

RENWICK ARMS CO.
See—Perry & Goddard

REPUBLIC ARMS, INC.
Chino, California

This company was in business from 1997 to 2001. The Republic Patriot pistol may still be available from Cobra Enterpises.

	NIB	EXC.	V.G.	GOOD	FAIR	POOR

RAP 440

Pistol chambered for .40 S&W or 9mm cartridges. It is double-action/single-action operation. Fitted with 3.75" barrel. Magazine capacity of 7 rounds. Grips are two-piece black plastic. Weight about 32 oz. Sights are three dot, with fixed ramp front and windage adjustable rear. Introduced in 1998. Imported by TSF of Fairfax, Virginia.

550	450	300	200	150	100

Republic Patriot

Double-action-only .45 ACP caliber pistol, with 3" barrel and fixed sights. Black polymer frame, with checkered grips and stainless steel slide. Magazine capacity 6 rounds. Weight about 20 oz. Introduced in 1997.

325	250	200	150	100	75

RETOLAZA HERMANOS
Eibar, Spain

Brompetier

Folding trigger 6.35mm or 7.65mm caliber double-action revolver, with 2.5" barrel. Safety mounted on left side of frame. Manufactured until 1915.

—	250	125	85	70	45

Gallus or Titan

A 6.35mm semi-automatic pistol. Normally marked "Gallus" or "Titan". Blued, with plastic grips.

—	275	150	100	75	50

Liberty, Military, Retolaza, or Paramount

A 6.35mm or 7.65mm semi-automatic pistol, with 3" barrel and 8-shot magazine. Slide marked with any of the trade names listed above.

—	275	150	100	75	50

Puppy

Folding trigger .22-caliber double-action revolver, with 5-shot cylinder. Trade name "Puppy" stamped on barrel.

—	175	125	75	50	25

Stosel

A 6.35mm semi-automatic pistol. Marked on slide "Automatic Pistol Stosel No. 1 Patent". Blued, with plastic grips.

—	275	150	100	75	50

Titanic

A 6.35mm semi-automatic pistol, with 2.5" barrel. Slide marked "1913 Model Automatic Pistol Titanic Eibar". Blued, with plastic grips.

—	275	150	100	75	50

REUNIES
Liege, Belgium

Dictator

A 6.35mm semi-automatic pistol, with 1.5" barrel and 5-shot magazine. Name "Dictator" together with company's details stamped on slide. Pistol features bolt of tubular form, front end of which is hollow and encloses the barrel breech. Manufactured from 1909 to approximately 1925.

—	275	150	100	75	50

Texas Ranger or Cowboy Ranger

Patterned after Colt Model 1873 revolver. Pistol is .38 Special caliber. Barrel is 5.5" and marked with company's details, either the legend "Cowboy Ranger" or "Texas Ranger". Manufactured from 1922 to 1931.

—	350	200	100	75	50

REUTH, F.
Hartford, Connecticut

Animal Trap Gun

Cast iron .28- to .50-caliber percussion trap gun. Either single- or double-barrels 3.5" or 5" in length. Firearm fires a barbed arrow and is triggered by a cord attached to an animal trap or bait. Barrels marked "F. Reuth's Patent, May 12, 1857". Several hundred made between

	NIB	EXC.	V.G.	GOOD	FAIR	POOR

1858 and 1862. **NOTE:** Single-barrel model is more common than double-barrel and is worth approximately 20 percent less.

	NIB	EXC.	V.G.	GOOD	FAIR	POOR
	—	—	2000	1650	550	150

REXIO DE ARMAS (COMANCHE)
Argentina

RS 22

A 9-shot revolver chambered for .22 LR cartridge. Choice of blued or stainless steel frame. Fixed or adjustable sights. Barrel lengths are 4" or 6". Fitted with rubber grips. **NOTE:** Add $30 for stainless steel.

235	175	150	125	75	50

RS 22M

Same as above, but chambered for .22 Win. Magnum cartridge. **NOTE:** Add $30 for stainless steel.

235	175	150	125	75	50

RJ 22

This revolver chambered for .22 LR cartridge. Fitted with 3", 4" or 6" barrel. Checkered walnut or synthetic grips. Adjustable rear sight. Blued finish.

175	125	95	75	50	25

RJ 38

Same as above, but chambered for .38 Special cartridge.

175	125	95	75	50	25

RS 357

Same as above, but chambered for .357 Magnum cartridge. Offered with 3", 4" or 6" barrels. **NOTE:** Add $30 for stainless steel.

235	175	125	95	75	50

Outfitter Single-Shot

Break down single pistol. Chambered for .45 Colt/.410 .22 LR or .22 Win. Magnum. Blued 10" barrel, with synthetic grip. Weight about 43 oz.

200	150	—	—	—	—

Outfitter Single-Shot Compact

Same as above, with 6" barrel in .22 Win. Magnum or .45 Colt/.410.

200	150	125	95	75	50

RHEINMETALL
Sommerda, Germany

Dreyse 6.35mm Model 1907

A 6.35mm semi-automatic pistol, with 2" barrel. Manual safety and 6-shot magazine. Weight about 14 oz. Slide marked "Dreyse". Blued, with hard rubber grips having trademark "RFM" molded in them. Patent for this design was issued in 1909 to Louis Schmeisser.

—	400	250	200	150	100

Dreyse 7.65mm Model 1907

As above, but chambered for 7.65mm cartridge. Barrel is 3.6", with 7-shot magazine. Weight about 25 oz. Blued, with horn grips.

—	300	200	150	125	75

Dreyse 9mm

As above, but chambered for 9mm cartridge. Barrel is 5", with 8-shot magazine. Weight about 37 oz. Slide marked "Rheinische Mettallwaaren Und Maschinenfabrik, Sommerda". Blued, with hard rubber grips. Manufactured prior to 1916 and in small numbers.

—	4500	3750	2500	1500	750

Rheinmetall 32

A 7.65mm semi-automatic pistol, with 3.65" barrel and 8-shot magazine. Slide marked "Rheinmetall ABT. Sommerda". Blued, with walnut grips. Overall length 6.5"; weight about 23.5 oz. Production of this pistol began in 1920.

—	350	225	175	125	90

	NIB	EXC.	V.G.	GOOD	FAIR	POOR

Rheinmetall 9mm

This is a 9mm version of Rheinmetall. Built in 1935 to compete with 9mm Parabellum German military pistols of that time. It was unsuccessful.

	—	Too Rare To Price	—	—	—	—

Dreyse Light Rifle or Carbine

Model 1907 in caliber 7.65 Browning. Fitted with a fixed stock and 6-round magazine.

—	1850	1400	1150	700	300

RHODE ISLAND ARMS CO.
Hope Valley, Rhode Island

Morrone

A 12- or 20-gauge over/under boxlock shotgun, with 26" or 28" barrels, single trigger and automatic ejectors. Blued with either straight- or pistol-grip walnut checkered stock. 450 made in 12-gauge; 50 in 20-gauge. Manufactured from 1949 to 1953.

—	1700	1200	850	600	350

RICHLAND ARMS CO.
Blissfield, Michigan

This company, which ceased operation in 1986, imported a variety of Spanish-made shotguns.

Model 41 Ultra Over/Under

A 20-, 28-gauge or .410 bore double-barrel shotgun, with 26" or 28" ventilated rib barrels, single non-selective trigger and automatic ejectors. French case hardened receiver and checkered walnut stock.

—	300	250	200	150	100

Model 747 Over/Under

As above in 20-gauge only, with single-selective trigger.

—	425	350	300	250	175

Model 757 Over/Under

Greener-style boxlock 12-gauge double-barrel shotgun, with 26" or 28" ventilated rib barrels, double triggers and automatic ejectors. Finished as Model 747.

—	300	250	200	175	125

Model 787 Over/Under

As above, fitted with screw-in choke tubes.

—	450	375	325	275	200

Model 808 Over/Under

A 12-gauge double-barrel shotgun, with 26", 28" or 30" ventilated rib barrels, single trigger and automatic ejectors. Blued, with checkered walnut stock. Manufactured in Italy from 1963 to 1968.

—	425	350	300	250	175

Model 80 LS

A 12-, 20-gauge or .410 bore single-barrel shotgun, with 26" or 28" barrels. Blued, with checkered walnut stock.

—	175	125	100	80	60

Model 200

Anson & Deeley-style 12-, 16-, 20-, 28-gauge or .410 bore double-barrel shotgun, with 22", 26" or 28" barrels, double triggers and automatic ejectors. Blued, with checkered walnut stock.

—	350	300	250	200	125

Model 202

As above, with an extra set of interchangeable barrels. Imported from 1963 to 1985.

—	325	275	225	175	100

Model 711 Magnum

As above, chambered for 3" shells and fitted with 30" or 32" barrels.

—	350	300	250	200	150

	NIB	EXC.	V.G.	GOOD	FAIR	POOR

Model 707 Deluxe

As above, more finely finished and fitted with well figured walnut stocks.

	NIB	EXC.	V.G.	GOOD	FAIR	POOR
	—	350	300	250	200	150

RICHMOND ARMORY
Richmond, Virginia

Carbine

This weapon was manufactured for use by Confederate States of America and is extremely collectible. This muzzle-loading carbine is chambered for .58-caliber percussion and has a 25" round barrel and full-length stock that is held on by two barrel bands. It was manufactured from parts that were captured at Harper's Ferry Armory in 1861. Locks are marked "Richmond, VA" and dated from 1861 to 1865. There are sling swivels in front of trigger guard and on the front barrel band; a third swivel is on the underside of buttstock. Quantity manufactured is not known. Made between 1861 and 1865.

	NIB	EXC.	V.G.	GOOD	FAIR	POOR
	—	—	28500	22000	8250	1000

Musketoon

Weapon is similar to the carbine, except barrel is 30" in length and front sight is also the bayonet lug. There is no sling swivel on buttstock. Manufactured between 1861 and 1865.

	NIB	EXC.	V.G.	GOOD	FAIR	POOR
	—	—	24000	19000	7700	1000

Rifled Musket

This model also similar to the Carbine, with 40" barrel and full-length stock held on by three barrel bands. Front sling swivel is on the middle barrel band instead of front band. Manufactured between 1861 and 1865.

	NIB	EXC.	V.G.	GOOD	FAIR	POOR
	—	—	30000	22000	8250	1000

RIEDL RIFLE CO.
Westminster, California

Single-Shot Rifle

Company produced custom order dropping block single-shot rifles in a variety of calibers and barrel lengths. Rifles were normally fitted only with telescopic or target sight bases. Blued, with checkered walnut stock. Premium for African or Magnum chamberings.

	NIB	EXC.	V.G.	GOOD	FAIR	POOR
	—	1750	1500	1250	750	400

RIFLESMITH INC.
Sheridan, Montana
See—Axtell Rifle Co.

RIGBY, JOHN & CO., LTD.
London, England

This company was established in the 18th century in U.K. and has produced a wide variety of firearms over the years. It traces its roots back to 1735 in Dublin, where the company was known for its percussion dueling pistols. A branch was opened in London in 1865, where some of the world's finest double rifles were made for more than 130 years, many of them made to order. In 1997 a group of investors moved the company to Paso Robles, California where production continues on a limited number of Rigby models. Current prices start at $32,000 for double rifles and $40,000 for shotguns.

RIFLES

Magazine Rifle

Utilizing a Mauser action, this rifle is available in a number of calibers, barrel lengths and with either 3- or 5-shot magazine. Checkered walnut stock.

	NIB	EXC.	V.G.	GOOD	FAIR	POOR
	—	12500	10000	7000	4000	1000

African Express Magazine Rifle

Utilizing a square bridge Mauser action, this rifle is chambered for .375 Holland & Holland, .404 Gibbs, .416 Rigby, .458 Winchester Magnum and .505 Gibbs cartridges. Barrel lengths vary from 20" to 24" and 4-shot magazine is standard.

	NIB	EXC.	V.G.	GOOD	FAIR	POOR
	—	25000	20000	15000	10000	2000

Single-Shot Rifle

Utilizing a Farquharson falling block action, this rifle is chambered for a variety of cartridges. Has a 24" barrel. Receiver finely engraved and blued. Stock of well figured walnut.

	NIB	EXC.	V.G.	GOOD	FAIR	POOR
	—	8000	7000	5500	2500	600

	NIB	EXC.	V.G.	GOOD	FAIR	POOR

Second Quality Boxlock Double Rifle

Double-barrel rifle chambered for cartridges from .275 Magnum to .577 Nitro Express, with 24" to 28" barrel. Fitted with express sights. Double triggers and automatic ejectors. Blued, with light engraving. Checkered walnut stock.

	NIB	EXC.	V.G.	GOOD	FAIR	POOR
	—	20000	17000	11000	5500	900

Best Quality Boxlock Double Rifle

As above, but more finely engraved. Better quality walnut stocks.

	NIB	EXC.	V.G.	GOOD	FAIR	POOR
	—	30000	22500	15000	7500	1000

Best Quality Sidelock Double Rifle

As above, but fitted with full sidelocks. Best bouquet engraving. Finely figured walnut stocks.

	NIB	EXC.	V.G.	GOOD	FAIR	POOR
	—	50000	42500	33000	15000	1500

SHOTGUNS

Sidelock Double

Offered in all gauges, with choice of barrel lengths, chokes, stock dimensions, grip and fore-end styles. Double triggers and automatic ejectors. Prices shown are for Sandringham Grade. Regal Grade has higher grade wood and engraving. Made in London prior to 1998. **NOTE:** Add 20 percent for Regal Grade; 30 percent for 20-gauge; 40 percent for 28-gauge or .410 bore.

NIB	EXC.	V.G.	GOOD	FAIR	POOR
9000	7500	6000	4500	3000	1000

Boxlock Double

Same features and options as above, except boxlock action. Prices shown are for Chatsworth Grade. Sackville Grade has higher grade wood and engraving. Made in London prior to 1998. **NOTE:** Add 30 percent for Sackville Grade; 20 percent for 20-gauge; 30 percent for 28-gauge or .410 bore.

NIB	EXC.	V.G.	GOOD	FAIR	POOR
4500	3700	2800	2000	1500	500

RIGDON, ANSLEY & CO.
Augusta, Georgia

1851 Colt Navy Type

A .36-caliber percussion revolver, with 7.5" barrel and 6-shot cylinder. Blued, with walnut grips. Initial production examples marked "Augusta, GA. C.S.A." and later models "C.S.A." Approximately 1,000 manufactured in 1864 and 1865.

Early Production Model

NIB	EXC.	V.G.	GOOD	FAIR	POOR
—	—	70000	61000	27500	2000

Standard Production Model

NIB	EXC.	V.G.	GOOD	FAIR	POOR
—	—	63500	4950	1925	1500

RIPOMANTI, GUY
St. Etienne, France

Side-by-Side Shotgun

A high-grade shotgun offered on a strictly made-to-order basis. There is a boxlock model that begins at $8,500 and a sidelock that is priced from $22,500. These prices rise depending on the options and embellishments desired. These guns are rarely seen on the used-gun market.

Side-by-Side Double Rifles

Extremely high-grade and basically made to order. They are rarely encountered on today's market. They have been imported since 1988. They range in price from $11,000 up.

Over/Under Double Rifle

A boxlock action over/under chambered for the 9.3x74R cartridge. The barrels are 23.5" in length and have express sights. There are double triggers and automatic ejectors. This model is highly engraved and features a high-grade, hand-checkered walnut stock.

NIB	EXC.	V.G.	GOOD	FAIR	POOR
12500	9750	7750	5000	4000	900

RIVERSIDE ARMS CO.
Chicopee Falls, Massachusetts
See—Stevens, J. Arms Co.

	NIB	EXC.	V.G.	GOOD	FAIR	POOR

Double-Barrel Shotguns

Brand name used by J. Stevens Arms Co. on many good quality double-barrel shotguns. Value depends on model, gauge and condition. From $100 to $1,600. See also Stevens.

RIZZINI, BATTISTA
Bresica, Italy

NOTE: There are a number of extra cost options for Rizzini guns that can greatly affect price. Extra barrels and upgraded wood are such options.

SHOTGUNS

Aurum Light

Over/under model features choice of 24.5" to 27.5" vent rib barrel. Figured oil finish walnut stock, with hand checkering and pistol-grip. Game scene engraved receiver. Auto ejectors and single-selective trigger. Weight about 6 lbs.

NIB	EXC.	V.G.	GOOD	FAIR	POOR
2250	1650	1250	975	700	500

Artemis Classic

Model features engraved sideplates with game scenes. Offered in 12-, 16-, 20-, 28-gauge as well as .410 bore. Barrel lengths from 24" to 27.5". Auto ejectors and single-selective trigger. Figured walnut stock, with hand checkering and pistol-grip. Weight about 6 lbs.

NIB	EXC.	V.G.	GOOD	FAIR	POOR
3200	2700	2300	1900	1000	500

Artemis Deluxe

Similar to standard Artemis, with the addition of gold inlaid game scenes and fancy walnut stock. Cased.

NIB	EXC.	V.G.	GOOD	FAIR	POOR
5000	4200	3500	2500	1250	600

Artemis EL

Model features sideplates, with hand engraved English scroll and game scenes. Extra fancy walnut stock. Cased.

NIB	EXC.	V.G.	GOOD	FAIR	POOR
18000	13500	10000	8000	6000	900

Upland EL

NIB	EXC.	V.G.	GOOD	FAIR	POOR
4000	3500	3000	2500	1250	600

S780 Emel

Boxlock model offered in 12-, 16-, 20-, 28-gauge or .410 bore. Barrel lengths from 24" to 27.5". Hand engraved receiver with game scenes. Auto ejectors and single-selective trigger. Fancy walnut stock, with hand checkering. Leather case. Weight: 12-gauge about 6.8 lbs.; smaller gauges about 6 lbs.

NIB	EXC.	V.G.	GOOD	FAIR	POOR
13500	11000	8750	7000	4250	900

S782 Emel Field Classic

Model similar to S792, with the addition of hand engraved gold inlaid game scenes.

NIB	EXC.	V.G.	GOOD	FAIR	POOR
15000	13000	10000	8750	5700	900

S790 Emel Field

Model similar to S780, with the exception of thistle-leaf style engraving pattern.

NIB	EXC.	V.G.	GOOD	FAIR	POOR
10500	8000	6500	5000	4250	900

S792 Emel Field

Model features sideplates engraved with English scroll and game scenes. Extra select walnut stock. Available in 12-, 16-, 20-, 28-gauge and .410 bore. Barrel lengths from 24" to 27.5".

NIB	EXC.	V.G.	GOOD	FAIR	POOR
11000	9750	8000	6750	5000	900

Premier Sporting

Model offered in 12- or 20-gauge. Choice of barrel lengths from 27.5" to 31.5". Blued boxlock action, with auto ejectors and single-selective trigger. Select walnut stock, with hand checkering and oil finish. Pistol-grip stock and beavertail fore-end. Weight about 7.5 lbs.

NIB	EXC.	V.G.	GOOD	FAIR	POOR
3000	2750	2100	1600	900	500

Sporting EL

NIB	EXC.	V.G.	GOOD	FAIR	POOR
3750	2800	2200	1750	975	600

	NIB	EXC.	V.G.	GOOD	FAIR	POOR

S790 EL Sporting

Model offered in 12-gauge only. Choice of barrels from 27.5" to 31.5". Boxlock action with chrome plate. Auto ejectors and single-selective trigger. Fancy walnut pistol-grip stock. Weight about 7.5 lbs.

NIB	EXC.	V.G.	GOOD	FAIR	POOR
7500	6250	5000	3750	2900	800

Rizzini Omnium

This model represents entry level of Rizzini over/unders, but it has features not found on comparably priced guns. These include jeweled monoblocs, braised ribs, precisely regulated trigger and choice of blued or coin finish. Other features are interchangeable choke tubes, checkered walnut stock with Schnabel fore-end, ventilated rib, automatic ejectors and scroll engraving. In 12- or 20-gauge, with frame sizes appropriate to gauge. **NOTE:** Add $200 for Omnium Light model, with coin finish.

NIB	EXC.	V.G.	GOOD	FAIR	POOR
2250	1875	1550	1000	750	300

EXPRESS RIFLES

Express 90 L

Over/under rifle chambered for 7x65R, 8x57JRS, 9.3x74R, .30-06, .308 Win., and .444 Marlin. Barrel length is 16". Boxlock action with case colored receiver. Auto ejectors and single trigger. Pistol-grip walnut stock with Bavarian cheekpiece. Hand checkered and oil finish stock. Weight about 8 lbs.

NIB	EXC.	V.G.	GOOD	FAIR	POOR
4750	4250	3500	2500	1750	800

Express 92 EL

Same calibers as above model. Sideplates engraved with English scroll and game scenes. Extra select walnut stock, with pistol-grip and round cheekpiece.

NIB	EXC.	V.G.	GOOD	FAIR	POOR
11000	9500	8000	5500	2500	900

RIZZINI, FRATELLI
Brescia, Italy

Early guns were manufactured with Antonio Zoli. As a result, these were off-the-shelf guns of lower prices. These early guns were imported by Abercombie and Fitch of New York. Some of these guns will be stamped with the A&F address on the barrel. These side-by-side guns have a boxlock action.

NOTE: At the present time this Italian gun company builds about 24 shotguns a year. Each gun is highly individualized for the customer. The company produces only two models. These are listed to give the reader some idea of the value of one of these models. None of these models includes the cost of engraving and multi barrel set and multi gauge sets are extra.

Rizzini models with serial numbers above #1709 have their own patented action and the prices listed reflect that action. Guns listed have a H&H style action and should deduct approximately 30 percent from the prices listed.

Lusso Grade

12 gauge

NIB	EXC.	V.G.	GOOD	FAIR	POOR
3200	2850	2200	1600	900	400

20 gauge

NIB	EXC.	V.G.	GOOD	FAIR	POOR
3700	3250	2800	2200	1500	550

28 gauge and .410 bore

NIB	EXC.	V.G.	GOOD	FAIR	POOR
4000	3600	3000	2500	1700	600

Extra Lusso Grade—Scalloped receiver

12 gauge

NIB	EXC.	V.G.	GOOD	FAIR	POOR
4800	4150	3250	2700	1500	700

20 gauge

NIB	EXC.	V.G.	GOOD	FAIR	POOR
5450	4600	3500	2900	1650	700

28 gauge

NIB	EXC.	V.G.	GOOD	FAIR	POOR
5850	4900	3750	3250	1900	700

.410 bore

NIB	EXC.	V.G.	GOOD	FAIR	POOR
6250	5250	3900	3500	2350	750

NIB	EXC.	V.G.	GOOD	FAIR	POOR

Model R-1

Available in 12-gauge to .410 bore. Choice of barrels from 25" to 30", single-/double trigger, pistol-/straight-grip, rib, barrel length and chokes are standard items on this model. Features Holland & Holland sidelock action.

12, 16, or 20 gauge

NIB	EXC.	V.G.	GOOD	FAIR	POOR
85000	72000	57500	40000	—	—

28 gauge or .410 bore

NIB	EXC.	V.G.	GOOD	FAIR	POOR
90000	76000	62000	45000	—	—

Model R-2

Model has a boxlock action and removable inspection plate on the bottom of frame. Stock and forearm fitted with Turkish Circassian walnut. Offered in 12-gauge to .410 bore.

NIB	EXC.	V.G.	GOOD	FAIR	POOR
17000	14000	1000	7500	5000	700

NOTE: Engraving extras for above models will add $8,700 for English scroll pattern and $22,000 for Fracassi style engraving. Other types of engraving are offered. Extra set of barrels in same gauge add 15 percent.

ROBAR AND DE KIRKHAVE
Liege, Belgium

Model 1909-1910

A 6.35mm or 7.65mm caliber semi-automatic pistol, with 3" barrel. Barrel located under the recoil spring housing. Slide marked "Pistolet Automatique Jieffeco Depose Brevete SGDG". Blued, with plastic grips. Manufactured from 1910 to 1914. Copy of Browning Model 1900.

NIB	EXC.	V.G.	GOOD	FAIR	POOR
—	500	400	300	200	100

Model 1911

Semi-automatic pistol in caliber 6.35mm. Same as Model 1909-1910. Slide serrations have been added at the muzzle.

NIB	EXC.	V.G.	GOOD	FAIR	POOR
—	500	400	300	200	100

Model 1912

Semi-automatic pistol in caliber 7.65mm. Similar to Model 1909-1910. Slide serrations have been added at the muzzle.

NIB	EXC.	V.G.	GOOD	FAIR	POOR
—	500	400	300	200	100

Melior Model 1907

Semi-automatic pistol in calibers 6.35mm and 7.65mm. Barrel located under the recoil spring housing.

NIB	EXC.	V.G.	GOOD	FAIR	POOR
—	500	400	300	200	100

Melior Model 1913-1914

Semi-automatic pistol in caliber 6.35mm and 7.65mm. Same as Model 1907, with slide serrations at the muzzle.

NIB	EXC.	V.G.	GOOD	FAIR	POOR
—	500	400	300	200	100

Melior Pocket Model

Semi-automatic pistol in 6.35mm caliber. Nearly identical to Jieffeco's made by the same company, Robar. Manufactured in 1920s and imported into U.S. by Phoenix Arms Company, Mass. Phoenix name appears on the pistol. Model resembles the FN Browning Model 1910.

NIB	EXC.	V.G.	GOOD	FAIR	POOR
—	350	250	175	125	75

Melior Vest Pocket Model

Semi-automatic pistol in caliber 6.35mm, with open-top slide. Blue finish, with black checkered rubber grips. Robar logo "ROC" on each grip.

NIB	EXC.	V.G.	GOOD	FAIR	POOR
—	300	250	200	150	100

Melior Model .22 Long Rifle

Semi-automatic pistol chambered for .22 LR cartridge. Very similar in appearance to the Pocket Model, with no squeeze grip safety.

NIB	EXC.	V.G.	GOOD	FAIR	POOR
—	500	400	300	200	100

	NIB	EXC.	V.G.	GOOD	FAIR	POOR

Melior Model .22 Target

Semi-automatic in .22 LR caliber. Barrel is detachable so that various lengths may be used. Knurled nut at front of the slide allows for barrel changes.

	NIB	EXC.	V.G.	GOOD	FAIR	POOR
	—	500	400	300	200	100

New Model Jieffeco (7.65mm)

In the 1920s, Robar and de Kirkhave introduced a New Model, Jieffeco. Similar to FN Browning Model 1910. At this time, the right to import Jieffeco into the U.S. was arranged with Davis Warner Arms Corp., New York, whose company name was used on the pistol. Model is a semi-automatic pistol in caliber 7.65mm. On the slide is "Pistolet Automatique Jieffeco Repose".

	—	350	250	175	125	75

New Model Jieffeco (6.35mm)

Similar to 7.65mm model, this compact variation is chambered in 6.35mm or .25 ACP. On the slide is "Pistolet Automatique Jieffeco Made in Liege, Belgium. Davis Warmer Arms Corporation, New York".

	—	350	250	175	125	75

Mercury

As above in .22-caliber. Imported by Tradewinds of Tacoma, Washington. Slide marked "Mercury Made in Belgium". Blue or nickel-plated. Manufactured from 1946 to 1958.

	—	200	150	125	100	75

ROBAR COMPANIES
Phoenix, Arizona

This company has been building precision rifles, shotguns and pistols since 1983.

Robar Patriot Tactical Shotgun

Built on a Remington Model 870. Features 18" barrel, express sights, seamless extended magazine tube, sidesaddle shell carrier, Wolff springs, etc.. Roguard/NP3 finish.

765	600	500	400	300	100

Robar Spec Ops Tactical Shotgun

Similar to model above. Fitted with tactical ghost ring night sights, safety and sling.

990	800	700	600	400	100

Robar Elite Tactical Shotgun

Model features a number of special options: Robar choke with forcing cone; modified bolt; Pachmayr pad; etc.

1700	1350	1000	875	600	300

Robar MK I Tactical Rifle

Model is built on Remington Model 700 action, with 24" heavy factory barrel. Chambered for .308 or .223 cartridge. Fitted with gray Choate Ultimate sniper stock, Robar bipod and adjustable trigger. Roguard/MP3 finish.

3400	2900	2250	1600	900	300

Robar MK II Tactical Rifle

As above but chambered for .308 cartridge only. Special trigger job and special hand finish of internal parts and chamber.

3400	2900	2250	1600	900	300

Robar SR60 Precision Rifle

Model is fully accurized Remington Model 700 action, with bench rest quality barrel and chamber. Custom stock, with hand bedding and pillars. Choice: .308 with 20" or 24" barrel; .223 with 24" barrel.

3900	3500	2900	2200	1400	500

ROBBINS & LAWRENCE
Windsor, Vermont

Pepperbox

A .28- or .31-caliber percussion 5 barrel pistol, with barrel groups measuring 3.5" or 4.5" in length. Ring trigger, blued iron frame with simple scroll engraving. Browned barrels are marked "Robbins & Lawrence Co. Windsor, VT. Patent. 1849". Barrel groups for this pistol were made in

	NIB	EXC.	V.G.	GOOD	FAIR	POOR

two types: fluted in both calibers; ribbed in .31-caliber only. Approximately 7,000 made between 1851 and 1854.

NIB	EXC.	V.G.	GOOD	FAIR	POOR
—	—	2700	2200	650	200

ROBERTS DEFENSE
Oshkosh, Wisconsin

This manufacturer of 1911-type semi-automatic pistols started production in 2013. All models are chambered in .45 ACP and are hand fitted throughout the entire assembly process.

Operator Series

Offered in full- or Commander-size, with forged steel frame and true Picatinny rail. Dark Ops model has black nitride frame and slide. Desert Ops model has Flat Dark Earth Ceracote frame and black nitride slide.

NIB	EXC.	V.G.	GOOD	FAIR	POOR
1400	1200	975	700	350	200

Recon Series

In full-size, Commander or Officer frame sizes, with 5", 4.25" or 3.5" barrel lengths. Models have a lightweight alloy frame, black finish and fiber optic front sights.

NIB	EXC.	V.G.	GOOD	FAIR	POOR
1275	1050	900	550	300	200

Super Grade Custom Series

These models come in all three frame sizes. Choice of all stainless or stainless frame, with black nitride slide. Grips are checkered wood. All components are of match grade quality.

NIB	EXC.	V.G.	GOOD	FAIR	POOR
1325	1120	925	500	300	200

ROBERTSON
Philadelphia, Pennsylvania

Pocket Pistol

A .41-caliber single-shot percussion derringer. Barrels ranging in length from 3" to 4.5". Barrel marked "Robertson, Phila.

NIB	EXC.	V.G.	GOOD	FAIR	POOR
—	—	2000	1650	500	200

ROBINSON, ORVIL
See—Adirondack Arms Company

ROBINSON, S.C.
Richmond, Virginia

From December of 1862 through March 1 of 1863, S.C. Robinson produced copies of the Sharps carbine. These arms had an overall length of 38.5", with .52-caliber barrels 21.5" long. Lockplates were marked "S.C. ROBINSON/ARMS MANUFACTORY/RICHMOND VA/1862" along with the serial number. Barrels were marked forward of the rear sight "S.C. ROBINSON/ARMS MANUFACTORY", as well as "RICHMOND VA/1862" to rear of the sight. Total number made estimated to be slightly more than 1,900.

In March of 1863, Robinson factory was taken over by Confederate States Government. Carbines produced after that date are only stamped with the serial number on their lockplates and "RICHMOND VA" on their barrels. Total number made in excess of 3,400.

Robinson Sharps

NIB	EXC.	V.G.	GOOD	FAIR	POOR
—	—	37000	30000	9300	1500

Confederate Sharps

NIB	EXC.	V.G.	GOOD	FAIR	POOR
—	—	32000	27500	8250	1500

ROBINSON ARMAMENT CO.
Salt Lake City, Utah

Super VEPR

Semi-automatic rifle made in Russia. Chambered for .308, .223 or 7.62x39mm cartridge. Uses an RPK-type receiver. Chrome lined 21.65" barrel. Walnut thumbhole stock. Black oxide finish. Weight about 8.5 lbs.

NIB	EXC.	V.G.	GOOD	FAIR	POOR
1200	800	675	500	400	200

M-96 Expeditonary Rifle

Chambered for .223 or 7.62x39mm cartridge. Can use either AK or AR magazines. Quick-change barrel. Adjustable gas operating system. Can interchange calibers without tools. Built in U.S.A.

NIB	EXC.	V.G.	GOOD	FAIR	POOR
1750	1400	1100	800	575	300

	NIB	EXC.	V.G.	GOOD	FAIR	POOR

M-96 Carbine

As above, with shorter barrel.

	1750	1400	1100	800	575	300

M-96 Top Fed

Model has same specifications as the rifle, but magazine is fitted to top of the receiver.

	1900	1550	1175	900	625	350

ROCK ISLAND ARMORY
(TRADE NAME OF ARMSCOR)
Pahrump, Nevada

Arms Corp. of the Philippines manufactures firearms under both Armscor and Rock Island brand names. For Armscor models, see that listing.

M1911-A1 FSP

Full-size 1911-pattern pistol in 9mm, .38 Super or .45 ACP. Blue, Duracoat, stainless or two-tone finish, front and rear slide serrations, rubber grips, standard or night sights. In standard or high-capacity variations. FS Match Model has fiber optic front sight, bobbed hammer, checkered walnut grips. Also available in compact version (CSP), with 3.5" barrel. **NOTE:** Add $200 for FS Match; $100 for Meprolight night sights.

	425	375	325	300	250	225

TCM

1911-style series chambered for .22 TCM cartridge. Centerfire round based on necked-down 9mm case, with .223 bullet. In standard, mid-size or target variations. Introduced 2013.

	750	675	600	500	—	—

M2011-A1

High capacity or single-stack configurations in .45 ACP or high-capacity 9mm. Features include fiber optic front and adjustable white-dot rear sights, combat hammer, extended grip and thumb safeties and tactical accessory rail.

	600	525	450	400	300	225

MAPP

Single-/double-action design based on CZ-75 series. In 9mm with 16-shot magazine, 3.5" or 4" barrel, Picatinny rail, adjustable rear sight, ambidextrous safety.

	450	400	350	300	250	225

ROCK RIVER ARMS, INC.
Colona, Illinois

This manufacturer of AR-style rifles and carbines, also made a series of 1911-pattern pistols for several years. In 2012, the decision was made to concentrate on the AR product line. All 1911 models listed in the following pages are discontinued.

PISTOLS

Elite Commando

Built on a National Match frame, with 4" National Match slide with double serrations and lowered ejection port (5" barrel optional). Front strap is 30 lpi. Night sights standard. Aluminum trigger and many more customs features. Checkered cocobolo grips. Guaranteed 2.5" groups at 50 yards. Chambered for .45 ACP cartridge.

	1725	1300	950	775	500	300

Standard Match

Many of the same features as above model, without night sights. Also chambered for .45 ACP cartridge.

	1025	750	600	450	300	200

National Match Hardball

Similar features as above models, with adjustable rear Bomar sight with dovetail front sight. Chambered for .45 ACP cartridge.

	1500	1100	825	675	500	300

NIB	EXC.	V.G.	GOOD	FAIR	POOR

Bullseye Wadcutter

Model features Rock River slide scope mount. Guaranteed to shoot 1.5" groups at 50 yards. Chambered for .45 ACP.

1650	1250	925	750	525	325

Basic Limited Match

Similar to Bullseye Wadcutter, with Bomar adjustable rear sight and dovetail front sights. Chambered for .45 ACP.

1700	1300	950	750	525	325

Limited Match

Match pistol comes standard with many custom features. Guaranteed to shoot 1.5" groups at 50 yards. Chambered for .45 ACP.

2050	1550	1150	800	575	350

Hi-Cap Basic Limited

Model gives the customer a choice of STI, SVI, Para-Ordnance or Entreprise frames. Many special features. Chambered for .45 ACP. **NOTE:** Add $200 for Para-Ordnance or Entreprise frames.

1895	1500	1200	800	575	300

Ultimate Match Achiever

An IPSC-style pistol, with scope and three port muzzle compensator. Many special features. Chambered for .38 Super cartridge.

2250	1750	1150	800	575	350

Match Master Steel

A Bianchi-style pistol, with scope and three port muzzle-brake. Chambered for .38 Super Cartridge.

2350	1850	1200	850	600	375

Basic Carry

Introduced in 2005. This .45 ACP model features a 5" match barrel, checkered front strap, lowered and flared ejection port, Novak rear sight, dehorned for carry and rosewood grips. Many other special features.

1525	1150	825	675	500	300

Pro Carry

Similar to Basic Carry, with 4.25", 5" or 6" barrel. Choice of Heinie or Novak tritium sights and polished finish; guaranteed to shoot 2.5" group at 50 yards with select ammunition. Other options available.

1795	1400	1100	675	500	250

Tactical Pistol

This .45 ACP pistol fitted with a 5" slide with front serrations and match grade barrel. Heine or Novak rear sight, checkered front strap, tactical mag catch and safety. Dehorned for carry. Rosewood grips. Introduced in 2005. **NOTE:** Add $200 for Black "T" finish.

1925	1450	1200	800	575	300

Limited Police Competition 9mm

9mm model features 5" slide with double serrations. Three position rear sight with dovetail front sight. Checkered front strap. Deluxe blued finish. Deluxe grips. Many other special features. Introduced in 2005. **NOTE:** Add $200 for Black "T" finish.

2310	1750	1150	800	575	350

Unlimited Police Competition 9mm

Similar to above, with additional special features such as 6" slide. Introduced in 2005. **NOTE:** Add $200 for Black "T" finish.

2310	1750	1150	800	575	350

RIFLES

CAR A2

These are AR-15-style rifles. Chambered for .223 cartridge. Fitted with 16" barrel with CAR handguards. Two stage trigger. Choice of A2 or non-collapsible buttstock. Choice of black or green furniture. Weight about 7 lbs. **NOTE:** Add $25 for non-collapsible buttstock.

925	750	600	500	375	200

	NIB	EXC.	V.G.	GOOD	FAIR	POOR

CAR A2M

Same as above, with mid-length handguard. **NOTE:** Add $25 for non-collapsible buttstock.

	925	750	600	500	375	200

CAR A4

Similar to models above, with flattop receiver and CAR handguard. **NOTE:** Add $25 for non-collapsible buttstock.

	925	750	600	500	375	200

CAR A4M

Flattop receiver with mid-length handguard. **NOTE:** Add $25 for non-collapsible buttstock.

	925	750	600	500	375	200

Standard A2

AR-15-style rifle fitted with 20" barrel. Chambered for .223 cartridge. Two stage trigger. Fixed stock and full-length hand guard. Weight about 8.2 lbs.

	925	750	600	500	375	200

National Match A2

Model features .22 Wylde chamber, with 20" Wilson air-gauged match stainless steel barrel. A2 receiver. Two stage trigger. Free float high temp thermo mold handguard. Match sights. Weight about 9.7 lbs.

	1265	950	800	650	500	300

Standard A4 Flattop

Same as Standard A2, with flattop receiver.

	925	750	600	500	375	200

Varmint Rifle

Flattop model fitted with 24" stainless steel barrel, without sights. Chambered for .223 cartridge. Fixed stock. Two-stage trigger. Weight about 9.5 lbs.

	1050	875	600	475	375	200

Varmint EOP (Elevated Optical Platform)

Chambered for .223, with Wylde chamber. Fitted with Wilson air-gauged bull stainless steel barrel. Choice of 16", 18", 20" and 24" barrel lengths. Free float aluminum handguard. National Match two stage trigger. Weight about: 8.2 lbs with 16" barrel; 10 lbs with 24" barrel. **NOTE:** Add $10 for each barrel length over 16".

	1050	875	600	475	375	200

Advanced Hunter

Chambered for 5.56/.223 Remington. Carbine-style adjustable stock, 18" cryogenically treated stainless steel barrel with tactical muzzle-brake. Half-quad free-floating mid-length hand guard, winter designed trigger guard, two-stage trigger. Numerous options. Introduced in 2011.

	1100	1000	850	700	400	250

NM A2-DCM Legal

Fitted with 20" stainless steel barrel. National Match sleeve and specially selected upper and lower to ensure tight fit. Special high temp handguards. Two-stage trigger. National Match sights. Weight about 9 lbs.

	1200	1000	825	600	450	200

Government Model

Chambered for .223 cartridge. Fitted with 16" Wilson chrome barrel with A2 flash hider. National Match two stage trigger. A4 upper receiver. Flip-up rear sight. EOTech M951 light system. Surefire M73 Quad Rail handguard, and 6 position tactical CAR stock. Weight about 8.2 lbs.

	2310	1750	1150	800	575	350

Tactical CAR A4

.223-caliber rifle has 16" Wilson chrome barrel, with A2 flash hider. A4 upper receiver, with detachable carry handle. Two stage National Match trigger. R-4 handguard. Six position tactical CAR stock. Weight about 7.5 lbs.

	950	800	650	500	350	200

Elite CAR A4

As above, with mid-length handguard. Weight about 7.7 lbs.

	950	800	650	500	350	200

	NIB	EXC.	V.G.	GOOD	FAIR	POOR

Tactical CAR UTE (Universal Tactical Entry) 2

.223-caliber rifle has 16" Wilson chrome barrel, with A2 flash hider. R-2 handguard. Upper receiver is a UTE2, with standard A4 rail height. Two stage trigger and 6 position CAR tactical stock. Weight about 7.5 lbs.

950	800	650	500	350	200

Elite CAR UTE 2

As above, with mid-length handguard. Weight about 7.7 lbs.

950	800	650	500	350	200

Entry Tactical

.223 model features 16" Wilson chrome barrel, with R-4 profile. A4 upper receiver, with detachable carry handle. National Match two stage trigger. Six position tactical CAR stock. R-4 handguard. Weight about 7.5 lbs.

950	800	650	500	350	200

TASC Rifle

Rifle features 16" Wilson chrome barrel, with A2 flash hider. A2 upper receiver, with windage and elevation rear sight. R-4 handguard. A2 buttstock. Weight about 7.5 lbs.

925	750	600	500	375	200

LAR-15 X-1 Rifle

Featuring .223 Wylde chamber, a hybrid chamber designed to better accept both 5.56 NATO and .223 Remington ammo. Forged upper and lower receivers, 18" fluted stainless barrel with Rock River Beast or Hunter muzzle-brake and low profile gas block are other features. Buttstock is RRA A2 or CAR, with Hogue Rubber pistol-grip and RRA's TRO-XL extended length free float rail handguard. The X-1 Rifle is available in other variations and chamberings, including 6.5 SPCII, .458 Socom and 7.62 NATO.

X-1 .223 Wylde

1250	1000	700	550	350	200

X-1 6.8 SPCII or .458 Socom

1050	800	600	400	300	150

X-1 7.62 NATO

1500	1300	1050	800	450	200

ROGERS & SPENCER
Utica, New York

Army Revolver

.44-caliber 6-shot percussion revolver, with 7.5" octagonal barrel. Barrel marked "Rogers & Spencer/Utica, N.Y." Blued case hardened hammer, with walnut grips bearing inspector's mark "RPB". Approximately 5,800 made between 1863 and 1865.

—	—	3500	2500	1000	550

ROGUE RIFLE COMPANY
Prospect, Oregon
See—Chipmunk Rifles

ROGUE RIVER RIFLEWORKS
Paso Robles, California

Boxlock Double Rifle

These rifles are custom fitted and available in any barrel length or caliber from .22 Hornet to .577 NE. Anson & Deeley boxlocks. Choice of finish, fore-end, engraving, wood and various other options. Each rifle should be appraised individually before a sale. Prices listed are for basic rifle with no extras.

17500	15000	12000	9500	5000	900

Sidelock Double Rifle

These rifles are custom fitted and available in any barrel length or caliber from .22 Hornet to .577 NE. Holland & Holland pattern sidelocks. Choice of finish, fore-end, engraving, wood and various other options. Each rifle should be appraised individually before a sale. Prices listed are for basic rifle with no extras.

50000	42500	30000	17000	7500	900

NIB	EXC.	V.G.	GOOD	FAIR	POOR

ROHM GMBH
Sonthein/Brenz, Germany

This firm produced a variety of revolvers marked with various trade names that were imported into the United States prior to 1968. Essentially, they are of three types: 1) solid-frame, gateloading models; 2) solid-frame, swingout-cylinder revolvers; and 3) solid-frame, swingout-cylinder revolvers. They are of low quality and little collector interest.

ROHRBAUGH
Bayport, New York

R9/R9S

Introduced in 2004. A very small 9mm pistol. Offered with or without sights. Magazine capacity 6 rounds. Barrel length 2.9"; height 3.7"; length 5.2"; slide width .812"; weight about 12.8 oz. Values shown are for basic model.

1200	950	775	600	400	200

380/380S

—	950	775	600	400	200

ROMERWERKE
Suhl, Germany

Romer

A .22-caliber semi-automatic pistol, with 2.5" or 6.5" barrel and 7-shot magazine. Barrels are interchangeable and marked "Kal. .22 Long Rifle"; slide marked "Romerwerke Suhl". Blued, with plastic grips. Manufactured between 1924 and 1926.

—	625	500	450	325	225

RONGE, J. B.
Liege, Belgium

Bulldog

A .32-, .380- or .45-caliber double-action revolver, with 3" barrel. Unmarked except for monogram "RF" on grips. Various trade names have been noted on these revolvers and are believed to have been applied by retailers. Manufactured from 1880 to 1910.

—	250	150	100	75	50

ROSS RIFLE CO.
Quebec, Canada

Designed by Sir Charles Ross, this controversial straight-pull action rifle was made in a wide range of commercial and military variations from 1903 to 1917. In recent years, some models have become quite collectible. Models listed are a sampling of the many different variations. **NOTE:** Some models should not be fired before they are checked by a gunsmith familiar with the Ross design.

Mark I

Barrel length 28"; .303-caliber. "Harris Controlled Platform Magazine" can be depressed by external lever to facilitate loading.

—	1800	1500	1000	600	400

Mark I Carbine

As above, with 22" barrel.

—	1600	1200	800	500	300

Mark II

As above, with modified rear sight.

—	2000	1600	1100	650	400

Mark III (Military)

Introduced in 1910, with improved lockwork and stripper clip guides. **NOTE:** Mark III and Model 1910 (M10) rifles can be very dangerous to fire if bolt has been taken apart and incorrectly reassembled. DO NOT FIRE one of these rifles without having it examined by a gunsmith who is totally familiar with the Ross design.

—	1900	1550	1050	600	400

	NIB	EXC.	V.G.	GOOD	FAIR	POOR

Mark III/M-10 Sporter Rifle

.280 Ross or .303-caliber straight-pull sporting rifle, with 24" barrel and open sights. Blued, with checkered walnut stock. **NOTE:** Mark III and Model 1910 (M10) rifles can be very dangerous to fire if bolt has been taken apart and incorrectly reassembled. DO NOT FIRE one of these rifles without having it examined by a gunsmith who is totally familiar with the Ross design.

.280 Ross Caliber

—	2000	1600	1100	600	400

.303 British Caliber

—	1600	1250	850	400	300

ROSSI, AMADEO
São Leopoldo, Brazil

Rossi handguns are manufactured under license by Taurus.

SHOTGUNS

Overland Shotgun

An exposed hammer sidelock 12- and 20-gauge or .410 bore double-barrel shotgun, with 26" or 28" barrels and double triggers. Manual extractors. Blued, with walnut stock. Discontinued in 1988.

250	225	200	150	100	75

Squire Shotgun

A 12- and 20-gauge or .410 bore double-barrel shotgun, with 20", 26" or 28" barrels, double triggers and manual ejectors. Blued, with walnut stock.

350	300	250	200	150	100

Field Grade Shotgun

Single-shot tip-open gun, with oil-finish hardwood stock, low profile hammer and pistol-grip. No checkering. Offered in 12- and 20-gauge or .410 bore. Barrel length 28"; weight about; 5.25 lbs. for 12- and 20-gauge; 4 lbs. for .410 bore.

115	75	50	25	—	10

Youth Model Shotgun

Same as above, with shorter length of pull and 22" barrel. Offered in 20-gauge and .410 bore only. Weight: 20-gauge about 5 lbs.; 3.75 lbs. for .410 bore.

115	75	50	25	—	10

Matched Pair Combo Guns

Model matches single-barrel shotgun, with .22 LR barrel. Offered in 12-/.22, 20-/.22 and .410/.22. Adjustable sights on rifle barrel. Blued finish.

165	125	100	65	50	25

Stainless Matched Pair Combo Guns

Similar to above, with stainless barrel/receiver. Introduced 2008.

200	165	125	100	75	50

Trifecta

Similar to Matched Pair, with black synthetic stock and blued barrel; includes easily interchangeable .243 Winchester or .44 Magnum, .22 Long Rifle and 20-gauge barrels.

300	250	200	150	100	75

Turkey Gun

Introduced in 2008. A specialized version of Roosi's 12-gauge single-shot shotgun. Features a 3.5" chamber, fiber optic sights, drilled and tapped barrel, included scope mount base and a removable Briley Extended Turkey Choke.

200	165	125	100	75	50

Rossi Circuit Judge

Revolving shotgun chambered in .410 bore (2.5" or 3") .45 Colt. Based on Taurus Judge handgun. Features include 18.5" barrel; fiber optic front sight; 5-round cylinder; hardwood Monte Carlo stock.

600	—	—	—	—	—

	NIB	EXC.	V.G.	GOOD	FAIR	POOR

RIFLES

Model 62

Copy of Winchester Model 62 rifle. Either 16.5" or 23" round or octagonal barrels. Blued or stainless steel, with walnut stock. Imported from 1988 to 1998.

	200	165	125	100	75	50

Model 59

As above, in .22 Magnum caliber.

	250	200	150	110	85	60

Model 92

Copy of Winchester Model 1892. Chambered for .357 Magnum, .44 Magnum, .45 Colt or .44-40. Either 16" or 20" barrel. Blued, with walnut stock. Engraved version of this model worth approximately 20 percent more than the values listed. **NOTE:** Add $75 for stainless steel version introduced in 1997.

	475	350	295	225	175	100

Model 92 Rifle

Introduced in 1997. Model fitted with 24" half octagon barrel and brass blade front sight. Magazine capacity 13 rounds of .45 Colt. Weight about 6.8 lbs.

	500	375	325	250	200	125

Rossi Rio Grande

Variation of Model 92. Chambered for .45-70 plus .410-bore shotshell. Side ejection and hammer extension allow a scope to be mounted easily. Scope-mounting rail is atop the receiver. Barrel is 20", with adjustable rear open sight, bead front. Hardwood stock with recoil pad. Cross bolt safety.

	500	400	350	275	200	100

Model 92 Large Loop

Model has 16" barrel. Chambered for .44 Magnum or .45 Colt cartridge. Weight about 5.5 lbs. Finish is blue. Introduced in 1997.

	475	350	295	225	175	100

Model 65

Similar to Model 92. Chambered for either .44 Special or .44 Magnum cartridge. Barrel length 20". Blued, with walnut stock. Introduced in 1989.

	500	375	325	250	200	125

Single-Shot Rifle

Offered in a variety of configurations. Chambered for .22 LR, .22 Magnum, .357 Magnum, .44 Magnum, .45 Colt, .223 Rem. and .243-calibers. Fitted with 23" barrel, with wood stock and choice of matte blue or stainless steel finish. Weight varies from 4.75 lbs. to 6.25 lbs. depending on caliber. **NOTE:** Add $30 for stainless steel; $10 for .357 and .44; $30 for .223 or .243.

	225	175	125	100	75	50

Single Shot Rifle—Heavy Barrel

Chambered for .223, .243 and .22-250. Rifle fitted with 23" heavy barrel, with plain wood stock. Matte blue finish. Weight about 7 lbs. introduced in 2005.

	230	175	125	100	75	50

Muzzleloading Rifle

Rifle has .50-caliber bore. Fitted with 23" barrel. Hardwood stock, with recoil pad. Weight about 6.3 lbs. Introduced in 2003. Blue or stainless steel. **NOTE:** Add $35 for matte stainless steel finish.

	165	130	100	75	50	25

Muzzleloader Matched Pair

A .50-caliber muzzle-loader, with an extra 20-gauge or .243 or .270 barrel. All matched pairs come with blued finish. Price listed for 20-gauge barrel. **NOTE:** Add $40 for .243; $150 for .270.

	250	200	150	100	75	50

Rossi Blued Synthetic Matched Pair

Single-shot combo outfit consisting of interchangeable rifle and shotgun barrels. Synthetic stock, blued barrel and receiver. Combinations include 12- or 20-gauge/.22LR, .22 WMR, .17 HMR,

	NIB	EXC.	V.G.	GOOD	FAIR	POOR

.223, .243, .270, .308, .30-06 and .410 bore/.22 LR or .410 bore/.17 HMR. Youth and full-size versions available.

	250	200	150	100	75	50

Rossi Stainless Synthetic Matched Pair

Single-shot combo outfit consisting of interchangeable rifle and shotgun barrels. Synthetic stock, stainless barrel and receiver. Combinations include 12- or 20-gauge/.22LR, .22 WMR, .17 HMR, .223, .243, .270, .308, .30-06 and .410 bore/.22 LR or .410 bore/.17 HMR. Youth and full-size versions available.

	275	225	165	115	90	50

Rossi Wizard

Single-shot rifle chambered in 23 different rimfire/centerfire/shotshell/muzzle-loading configurations. Features include drop-barrel action; quick toolless barrel interchangeability; fiber optic front sight; adjustable rear sight, with barrel-mounted optics rail; hardwood or camo Monte Carlo stock.

	225	200	175	150	110	80

Rossi Ranch Hand

Based upon Rossi's R92 lever-action rifle. Calibers: .38/.357, .44 Magnum or .45 Colt. Barrel length 12"; overall length 24"; weight 4.9 lbs. (empty). Large loop lever 6-round tubular magazine, shortened hardwood buttstock. Open buckhorn rear sight, bead front. Blue or case-hardened carbon steel receiver, with saddle ring.

	450	400	325	250	200	100

HANDGUNS

Model 51

A .22-caliber double-action revolver, with 6" barrel, adjustable sights and 6-shot cylinder. Blued, with walnut grips. Imported prior to 1986.

	—	150	100	75	50	40

Model 511 Sportsman

As above, with 4" barrel. Made of stainless steel, with walnut grips. Introduced in 1986.

	225	200	150	125	100	75

Model 461

A 6-round revolver chambered for .357 Magnum cartridge. Fitted with 2" barrel. Rubber grips and blued finish. Weight about 26 oz.

	300	225	195	150	125	75

Model 462

Same as above, with stainless steel finish.

	350	275	225	165	140	90

Model 68S

This new version was introduced in 1993. Features a shrouded ejector rod and fixed sights. Chambered for .38 Special cartridge. Offered with either 2" or 3" barrel. Grips wood or rubber. Finish is blue or nickel. Weighs about 23 oz.

	175	150	125	100	75	60

Model 69

As above in .32 Smith & Wesson caliber, with 3" barrel and 6-shot cylinder. Imported prior to 1986.

	—	125	100	75	50	40

Model 70

As above in .22-caliber, with 3" barrel and 6-shot cylinder. Imported prior to 1986.

	—	125	100	75	50	40

Model 84

Stainless steel .38 Special caliber double-action revolver, with ribbed 3" or 4" barrel. Blued, with walnut grips. Imported in 1985 and 1986.

	—	175	150	125	100	75

	NIB	EXC.	V.G.	GOOD	FAIR	POOR

Model 851

As above, with either 3" or 4" ventilated rib barrel and adjustable sights.

	200	175	150	125	100	75

Model 68

A .38 Special double-action revolver, with 2" or 3" barrel and 5-shot cylinder. Blued or nickel-plated, with walnut grips.

	225	175	150	125	100	75

Model 31

A .38 Special caliber double-action revolver, with 4" barrel and 5-shot cylinder. Blued or nickel-plated, with walnut grips. Imported prior to 1986.

	225	175	150	125	100	75

Model 677

This model first introduced in 1997. Chambered for .357 Magnum cartridge. Matte blue finish, with 2" barrel and black rubber grips. Weight about 26 oz.

	300	250	200	150	125	100

Model 88S

Introduced in 1993. This improved model has the same features of Model 68, with addition of a stainless finish. Chambered for .38 Special cartridge. Fitted with either 2" or 3" barrel. Available with either wood or rubber grips. Cylinder holds 5 cartridges. Weighs about 22 oz.

	325	275	225	165	140	100

Model 351

This revolver chambered for .38 Special +P cartridge. Fitted with 2" barrel and rubber grips. 5 round cylinder. Blued finish. Weight about 24 oz.

	300	250	200	150	125	100

Model 352

Same as above, with stainless steel finish.

	325	275	225	165	140	100

Model 951

A .38 Special caliber double-action revolver, with 3" or 4" ventilated rib barrel and 6-shot cylinder. Blued, with walnut grips. Introduced in 1985.

	300	250	200	150	125	100

Model 971

As above in .357 Magnum caliber, with solid ribbed 4" barrel and enclosed ejector rod. Adjustable sights. Blued, with walnut grips. Introduced in 1988.

	300	250	200	150	125	100

Model 971 Comp

Introduced in 1993. Similar to Model 971, with the addition of a compensator on 3.25" barrel. Overall length 9"; weight 32 oz. Chambered for .357 Magnum cartridge.

	335	265	200	150	125	100

Model 971 Comp Stainless

As above but constructed of stainless steel, with checkered black rubber grips. Introduced in 1989.

	350	275	225	150	125	100

Model 972

Revolver; 6-shot polished stainless double-action .357 Magnum. Adjustable rear sight and red insert on front sight. 6" barrel, rubber grip, 35 oz. Uses Taurus security system. Introduced 2006.

	375	295	250	150	125	100

Model 877

Introduced in 1996. This 6-shot revolver is chambered for .357 Magnum cartridge. Fitted with 2" heavy barrel. Stainless steel, with black rubber grips. Weight about 26 oz.

	350	275	225	150	125	100

	NIB	EXC.	V.G.	GOOD	FAIR	POOR

Model 89
As above in .32 Smith & Wesson caliber, with 3" barrel.

	325	275	225	165	140	100

Model 971 VRC (vented rib compensator)
Introduced in 1996. This variation features a choice of 2.5", 4" or 6" vent rib barrel, with integral compensator. Stainless steel, with black rubber grips. Weight from 30- to 39 oz. depending on barrel length.

	375	295	250	150	125	100

Model 988 Cyclops
Introduced in 1997. Chambered for .357 Magnum cartridge. Fitted with four recessed compensator ports on each side of muzzle. Offered in 6" or 8" barrel lengths. This six-shot double-action revolver weighs about: 44 oz. for 6" model; 51 oz. for 8" model. Stainless steel finish.

	525	475	350	275	200	150

Model 720
Double-action revolver chambered for .44 Special. Features five-round cylinder and 3" barrel. Overall length 8"; weight about 27.5 oz. Finish stainless steel.

	525	475	350	275	200	150

ROTH-SAUER
See—Sauer, J. P. & Son

ROTTWEIL
Rottweil, West Germany

Model 650
A 12-gauge over/under shotgun, with 28" ventilated rib barrels, screw-in choke tubes, single-selective trigger and automatic ejectors. Receiver engraved and case hardened. Checkered stock of well figured walnut. Imported prior to 1987.

	—	900	700	550	425	150

Model 72
A 12-gauge over/under shotgun, with 28" ventilated rib barrels, screw-in choke tubes, single-selective trigger and automatic ejectors. Blued, with well figured checkered walnut stock. Imported prior to 1988.

	—	2200	1550	975	650	350

Model 72 American Skeet
As above, with 26.75" ventilated rib barrel, single-selective trigger and automatic ejectors. Receiver also engraved. Imported prior to 1988.

	—	2200	1550	975	650	350

Model 72 Adjustable American Trap
As above, with 34" ventilated rib barrel adjustable to point of impact. Imported prior to 1987.

	—	2200	1550	975	650	350

Model 72 American Trap
As above, without the barrel being adjustable to point of impact.

	—	2100	1450	875	550	300

Model 72 International Skeet
As above, with 26.75" ventilated rib barrels choked Skeet. Imported prior to 1988.

	—	2100	1450	875	550	300

Model 72 International Trap
As above, with 30" high ventilated rib barrels that are choked Improved, Modified and Full. Imported prior to 1988.

	—	2100	1450	875	550	300

	NIB	EXC.	V.G.	GOOD	FAIR	POOR

ROYAL AMERICAN SHOTGUNS
Woodland Hills, California

Model 100

A 12- or 20-gauge over/under shotgun, with 26", 28" or 30" ventilated rib barrels, double triggers and extractors. Blued, with walnut stock. Imported from 1985 to 1987.

	NIB	EXC.	V.G.	GOOD	FAIR	POOR
	—	550	375	250	175	150

Model 100AE

As above, with single trigger and automatic ejectors.

	NIB	EXC.	V.G.	GOOD	FAIR	POOR
	—	650	475	275	200	175

Model 600

A 12-, 20-, 28-gauge or .410 bore double-barrel shotgun, with 25", 26", 28" or 30" ventilated rib barrels, double triggers and extractors. Blued, with walnut stock. Imported from 1985 to 1987.

	NIB	EXC.	V.G.	GOOD	FAIR	POOR
	—	600	425	300	200	175

Model 800

A 2gauge or .410 bore detachable sidelock double-barrel shotgun, with 24", 26" or 28" barrels, double triggers and automatic ejectors. Blued French case hardened, with English-style walnut stock. Imported from 1985 to 1987.

	NIB	EXC.	V.G.	GOOD	FAIR	POOR
	—	1550	1200	900	675	400

RUBY ARMS COMPANY
Guernica, Spain

Ruby

A 6.35mm or 7.35mm caliber semi-automatic pistol, with 3.5" barrel and 6-shot magazine. Slide marked "Ruby". Blued, with plastic grips.

	NIB	EXC.	V.G.	GOOD	FAIR	POOR
	—	275	175	125	75	50

RUGER
See—Sturm, Ruger Co.

RUPERTUS, JACOB
Philadelphia, Pennsylvania

Navy Revolver

This model equally as rare as Army model. Chambered for .36-caliber percussion. Otherwise, quite similar in appearance to Army model. Approximately 12 manufactured in 1859. Both of these revolvers were manufactured for test purposes and were not well-received by the military, so further production was not accomplished.

	NIB	EXC.	V.G.	GOOD	FAIR	POOR
	—	—	15000	11750	5500	1250

Pocket Model Revolver

Smaller version of Army and Navy model. Chambered for .25-caliber percussion. It has no loading lever but has a 3.125" octagonal barrel. Approximately 12 manufactured in 1859.

	NIB	EXC.	V.G.	GOOD	FAIR	POOR
	—	—	11000	8250	3600	950

Double-Barrel Pocket Pistol

A .22-caliber double-barrel pistol, with 3" round barrels and a spur trigger. Hammer fitted with a sliding firing pin. Blued, with walnut grips.

	NIB	EXC.	V.G.	GOOD	FAIR	POOR
	—	—	2400	1900	850	200

Army Revolver

An extremely rare revolver. Chambered for .44-caliber percussion. Has a 7.25" octagon barrel, with an integral loading lever that pivots to the side instead of downward. Hammer is mounted on the side and there is a pellet priming device located on the backstrap. There is only one nipple on the breech that lines up with top of the cylinder. Cylinder is unfluted and holds 6-shots. Finish is blued, with walnut grips; frame marked "Patented April 19, 1859". There were less than 12 manufactured in 1859. It would behoove one to secure a qualified independent appraisal if a transaction were contemplated.

	NIB	EXC.	V.G.	GOOD	FAIR	POOR
	—	—	28500	12000	5500	1500

Single-Shot Pocket Pistol

A .22, .32, .38 or .41 rimfire single-shot pistol, with half-octagonal barrels ranging in length from 3" to 5". Barrel marked "Rupertus Pat'd. Pistol Mfg. Co. Philadelphia". Blued, with walnut

	NIB	EXC.	V.G.	GOOD	FAIR	POOR

grips. Approximately 3,000 made from 1870 to 1885. **NOTE:** The .41-caliber variety is worth approximately 200 percent more than the values listed.

NIB	EXC.	V.G.	GOOD	FAIR	POOR
—	—	900	650	225	75

Spur Trigger Revolver

A .22-caliber revolver, with 2.75" barrel and unfluted 7-shot cylinder. Top strap marked "Empire Pat., Nov. 21, 71". Blued or nickel-plated, with walnut grips. Also made in .32 and .32 rimfire, with 5-shot semi-fluted cylinder. A larger model in .41 rimfire with 5-shot semi-fluted cylinder was made with top strap marked "Empire 41". Made during 1870s and 1880s. **NOTE:** Add 20 percent for .41-caliber.

NIB	EXC.	V.G.	GOOD	FAIR	POOR
—	—	450	250	175	100

RWS
Dynamit Nobel
Nurenberg, Germany

Model 820 S

A .22-caliber target rifle, with 24" heavy barrel and adjustable aperture sights. Trigger is fully adjustable. Three-position adjustable match stock, with stippled pistol-grip and fore-end. Discontinued in 1986.

NIB	EXC.	V.G.	GOOD	FAIR	POOR
1650	1275	975	625	450	250

Model 820 SF

As above, with a heavier barrel. Discontinued in 1986.

NIB	EXC.	V.G.	GOOD	FAIR	POOR
1700	1350	1000	550	400	250

Model 820 K

Offhand "Running Boar" model of above, with lighter barrel. Furnished without sights. Discontinued in 1986.

NIB	EXC.	V.G.	GOOD	FAIR	POOR
1700	1350	1000	550	400	250

S

	NIB	EXC.	V.G.	GOOD	FAIR	POOR

S.A.E.
Miami, Florida

S.A.E. was an importer of Spanish shotguns, some of very fine quality. Most notable of these is the S.A.E. line of Sarasqueta shotguns from Eibar, Spain. Not all S.A.E. shotguns are marked with the maker's name.

Model 210S

A 12-, 20-gauge or .410 bore double-barrel shotgun, with 26" or 28" barrels. Double triggers and manual extractors. Blued French case hardened, with checkered walnut stock. Imported in 1988.

	NIB	EXC.	V.G.	GOOD	FAIR	POOR
	—	475	395	300	225	150

Model 340X

Holland & Holland-style sidelock 10- or 20-gauge double-barrel shotgun, with 26" barrels. Double triggers and automatic ejectors. Blued case hardened, with checkered English style walnut stock. Imported in 1988.

	NIB	EXC.	V.G.	GOOD	FAIR	POOR
	—	850	675	500	400	200

Model 209E

As above, except also chambered for .410 bore cartridges and more finely engraved. Imported in 1988.

	NIB	EXC.	V.G.	GOOD	FAIR	POOR
	—	1100	850	700	550	250

Model 70

A 12- or 20-gauge over/under shotgun, with 26" ventilated rib barrels, screw-in choke tubes, single trigger and automatic ejectors. Modestly engraved receiver is either blued or French case hardened. Stock of finely figured walnut. Imported in 1988.

	NIB	EXC.	V.G.	GOOD	FAIR	POOR
	—	500	375	250	200	100

Model 66C

12-gauge over/under shotgun, with 26" or 30" ventilated rib barrels choked for skeet or trap, single trigger and automatic ejectors. Boxlock action fitted with false sideplates, which are engraved and gold inlaid. Blued, with checkered Monte Carlo-style stock and beavertail forearm. Imported in 1988.

	NIB	EXC.	V.G.	GOOD	FAIR	POOR
	—	1100	850	700	575	300

S.E.A.M.
Eibar, Spain

This retailer sold a number of pistols produced, by the firm of Urizar, prior to 1935.

Praga

A 7.65-caliber semi-automatic pistol marked "Praga Cal 7.65" on the slide. Blued, with plastic grips impressed with trademark S.E.A.M.

	NIB	EXC.	V.G.	GOOD	FAIR	POOR
	—	275	175	125	90	65

S.E.A.M.

A 6.35mm semi-automatic pistol, with 2" barrel. Slide marked "Fabrica de Armas SEAM". Blued, with black plastic grips having trademark "SEAM" cast into them.

	NIB	EXC.	V.G.	GOOD	FAIR	POOR
	—	250	175	125	90	65

Silesia

As above in 7.65mm caliber, with 3" barrel. Slide stamped with "Silesia".

	NIB	EXC.	V.G.	GOOD	FAIR	POOR
	—	250	175	125	90	65

S.W.D., INC.
Atlanta, Georgia

Cobray M-11

A 9mm semi-automatic pistol, with 32-round magazine. Parkerized finish.

	NIB	EXC.	V.G.	GOOD	FAIR	POOR
	—	550	495	400	275	100

NIB	EXC.	V.G.	GOOD	FAIR	POOR

M-11 Carbine

As above, with 16.25" barrel enclosed in a shroud. Fitted with a telescoping wire stock.

—	800	650	550	275	100

Terminator

A 12- or 20-gauge single-shot shotgun, with 18" cylinder bored barrel. Parkerized finish. Said to be exceptionally rare, but attracts little interest.

—	150	80	70	60	50

SABATTI

See—European American Armory Corp.

SACKET, D. D.
Westfield, Massachusetts

Under Hammer Pistol

A .34 or .36 single-shot percussion pistol, with half octagonal 3" or 4" barrel marked "D. D. Sacket/Westfield/Cast Steel". Manufactured during 1850s.

—	—	1550	1200	550	165

SAFARI ARMS
Phoenix, Arizona

In operation from 1978 to 1987. Company was purchased by Olympic Arms of Olympia, Washington, in 1987. The models listed are currently produced by that company under different trade names.

Enforcer

A .45-caliber semi-automatic pistol, with 3.9" barrel and 5-shot magazine. Patterned after Colt Model 1911. Blued, Armaloy, electroless nickel-plate or Parkerized finish, with checkered walnut or neoprene grips.

700	600	500	400	350	150

Match Master

As above, with 5" barrel.

700	600	500	400	350	150

Black Widow

As above, with ivory Micarta grips etched with a black widow.

700	600	500	400	350	150

Model 81

As above, without grip etching. Also offered in .38-caliber.

800	700	600	500	400	200

Model 81L

As above, with 6" barrel.

850	750	650	550	450	200

Ultimate Unlimited

Bolt-action single-shot pistol, with 15" barrel. Chambered for a variety of cartridges. Blued, with laminated stock.

850	750	650	550	450	200

Survivor I Conversion Unit

Conversion unit lifted to Model 1911 frame that alters that pistol to a bolt-action carbine. Barrel length 16.25", caliber .223, folding stock.

300	275	250	200	150	100

Counter Sniper Rifle

A .308-caliber bolt-action target rifle, with heavy 26" barrel and 20-round detachable magazine. Matte blued, with colored composite stock.

1200	1050	850	650	450	200

SAIGA
Izhevsk, Russia

A series of AK type rifles and shotguns manufactured in Russia by Izhmash.

	NIB	EXC.	V.G.	GOOD	FAIR	POOR

RIFLES

Model IZ-114, AZ-132

Kalashnikov-type semi-automatic rifle chambered in .223 Rem. (IZ-114) or 7.62x39mm (IZ-132). Black synthetic or wood stock and forearm, 16" or 20.5" barrel. Imported by several companies including EAA, U.S. Sporting Goods and others.

325	300	275	225	200	150

Model AZ-139

Same as above, except in .308 Win. and 22" barrel.

500	425	350	300	250	150

Model 100

Hunting style semi-automatic rifle, with synthetic stock in .223, 7.62x39, .308 or .30-06. Magazine capacity 3 or 10 rounds.

685	600	500	350	250	150

SHOTGUNS

Model 109

Semi-automatic shotgun based on AK-47 design. In 12- or 20-gauge or .410 bore. Black synthetic stock and forearm, 5- or 10-shot magazine. **NOTE:** Add $75 for .410 bore.

550	475	425	300	250	150

SAKO
Riihimaki, Finland

NOTE: Arms produced by this company prior to 1972 are worth approximately 25 percent more than arms of the same type produced thereafter. Prices for fair and poor condition reflect worth of the action. In 2000, Beretta Holding Co. purchased Sako and distributes product line through Beretta U.S.A.

Standard Sporter

Bolt-action magazine rifle produced in a wide variety of calibers, with varying barrel lengths, etc. Blued, with checkered walnut stocks.

—	750	650	450	400	300

Deluxe Model

As above, with engraved floorplate and checkered Monte Carlo-style stock. Featuring a rosewood pistol-grip cap and fore-end tip.

—	900	750	600	450	400

Finnbear

As above, with a long action available in a variety of large bore calibers. Fitted with 20" or 23.5" barrel. Blued, with a checkered stock. For .458 Winchester Magnum (only 20 produced), values double. **NOTE:** Add 15 percent for other Magnum chamberings or Deluxe version; 20 percent for Mannlicher Carbine version.

—	1000	850	650	400	300

Forester

As above, with a shorter action suitable for use with intermediate cartridges. **NOTE:** Add 20 percent for Mannlicher Carbine version.

—	1000	850	650	400	300

Vixen

As above, with a short action. **NOTE:** Add 20 percent for Mannlicher Carbine version.

—	1000	850	650	400	300

FN Action

Manufactured from 1950 to 1957. This model utilized a Fabrique Nationale manufactured receiver. Chambered for .270 Winchester and .30-06 cartridges. Otherwise, as above.

—	800	600	475	400	300

FN Magnum Action

As above, with a long action for .300 and .375 Holland & Holland.

—	900	700	550	400	300

	NIB	EXC.	V.G.	GOOD	FAIR	POOR

Anniversary Model

A 7mm Remington Magnum bolt-action rifle, with 24" barrel. Blued, checkered walnut stock. A total of 1,000 were manufactured. As with any commemorative firearm, this model should be NIB to realize its full resale potential.

2500	850	750	450	400	300

Finnwolf

A 4-shot lever-action rifle produced in .243- and .308-calibers. Blued, checkered walnut stock. Manufactured from 1962 to 1974.

—	1400	1200	750	450	300

Finnfire

Bolt-action rifle is chambered for .22 LR cartridge. Fitted with a 22" barrel and choice of iron sights or no sights. European walnut stock. A 5-shot detachable magazine is standard. Weight about 5.25 lbs.

1150	950	700	575	400	300

Finnfire Heavy Barrel

Same as above, with a heavy barrel.

1150	950	700	575	400	300

Finnfire Hunter

Introduced in 2000. This bolt-action model is chambered for .22 LR cartridge. Fitted with a 22" barrel and Sako 75 style select walnut stock. Weight about 5.75 lbs.

1150	950	700	575	400	300

Finnfire Sporter

This model chambered for .22 LR cartridge and built on P94S action. Has a walnut stock, with adjustable cheekpiece and buttplate spacer system that allows for length of pull and buttplate angle adjustment. Trigger is adjustable. Introduced in 1999.

1150	950	700	575	400	300

Sako Quad Combo

Introduced in 2005. This bolt-action rifle features four interchangeable barrels in four different rimfire calibers. Black synthetic stock. Detachable 5-round magazine. Included barrels are: .22 Long Rifle; .22 WMR; .17 HMR; .17 Mach 2. All 22" in length. Blued finish. Weight about 5.75 lbs. **NOTE:** NIB price for rifles with only one barrel is $948. Extra barrels are $260 each.

1450	1300	1075	800	500	300

Hunter

This model offered in three action lengths: short; medium; long. Short action calibers available are: .17 Rem., .222, .223 in 21.25" barrel. Medium action calibers are: .22-250, .243, .308 and 7mm-08 in 21.75" barrel. Long action calibers are: .25-06, .270 Win., .280 Rem., .30-06 for 22" barrel length. In 24" barrel the long action calibers are: 7mm Rem. Magnum, .300 Win. and .300 Wby. Magnum, .338 and .375 Win. Magnum and .416 Rem. Magnum. In 1996, .270 Wthby Magnum, 7mm Wthby Magnum and .340 Wthby were added to the long action calibers. Available in left-handed version for all but short action calibers. Adjustable trigger is standard. Checkered European walnut stock. Weight for short action 6.25 lbs.; medium action 6.5 lbs.; long action 7.75 to 8.25 depending on caliber.

Medium Action

1200	1050	875	600	500	300

Short Action

NOTE: Add 10 percent to Medium Action prices for .222 Rem. and .223 Rem.; 20 percent to Medium Action prices for .17 Rem.

Long Action

NOTE: Add 10 percent for long action calibers in .300 and .338 Win. Magnum; 20 percent for .375 H&H Magnum; 25 percent for .416 Rem. Magnum.

1400	1175	1000	750	600	300

Carbine

As above, with 18.5" barrel. Produced with either medium or long-length action.

1200	1050	875	600	500	300

Long Range Hunting Rifle

Similar to the long action Hunter. Fitted with 26" fluted barrel. Chambered for .25-06, .270 Win., 7mm Rem. Magnum and .300 Win. Magnum. Introduced in 1996. **NOTE:** Add 10 percent to

	NIB	EXC.	V.G.	GOOD	FAIR	POOR

medium action prices for .222 Rem. and .223 Rem.; 20 percent to medium action prices for .17 Rem.

1500	1300	1050	875	650	300

Laminated Model

This model features a laminated checkered hardwood stock made up of 36 layers. Solid recoil pad is standard as are quick detachable sling swivels. Available in both medium and long action calibers. Medium action calibers are: .22-250, .243, .308 and 7mm-08 with 21.75" barrel; weight of 6.5 lbs. Long action calibers are: .25-06, .270, .280, .30-06 with 22" barrel; weight of 7.75 lbs. Offered with 24" barrels are: 7mm Rem. Magnum, .300, .338 Win. Magnum and .375 H weight is 7.75 lbs.

Medium Action

NOTE: Add 10 percent to prices for .222 Rem. and .223 Rem.; 20 percent for .17 Rem.

1200	1050	875	600	500	300

Long Action

NOTE: Add 10 percent for long action calibers in .300 and .338 Win. Magnum; 20 percent for .375 H&H Magnum; 25 percent for .416 Rem. Magnum.

1400	1175	1000	750	600	300

FiberClass

This model features a black plain fiberglass stock. Offered in long action calibers only. The .25-06, .270, .280 and .30-06 are fitted with 22" barrels and weigh 7.25 lbs. The 7mm Rem. Magnum, .300 Win. Magnum, .338 Win. Magnum and .375 H&H are fitted with 24" barrel and weigh 7.25 lbs. The .416 Rem. Magnum has a 24" barrel and weighs 8 lbs. NOTE: Add 10 percent for long action calibers in .300 and .338 Win. Magnum; 20 percent for .375 H&H Magnum; 25 percent for .416 Rem. Magnum.

1050	800	600	500	400	400

FiberClass Carbine

As above, with a fiberglass stock.

1050	800	600	500	400	400

Carbine

Model features a Mannlicher-style stock, with a two-piece forearm. Has a checkered walnut stock, with oil finish. Offered in both medium and short actions, all with 18.5" barrels. In medium action .243 and .308 are available and weigh 6 lbs. Long action calibers are .270 and .30-06 weighing 7.25 lbs.; .338 Win. Magnum and .375 H&H weighing 7.75 lbs. NOTE: Add 10 percent for long action calibers in .338 Win. Magnum; 20 percent for .375 H&H Magnum.

Medium Action

1200	1050	875	600	500	300

Long Action

NOTE: Add 10 percent for long action calibers in .338 Win. Magnum; 20 percent for .375 H&H Magnum.

1200	1050	875	600	500	300

Varmint-Heavy Barrel

Checkered walnut stock on this model features an extra wide beavertail forearm, with oil finish. Offered in both short and medium action. All are fitted with a 23" heavy barrel weighing 8.5 lbs. Short action calibers are: .17 Rem., .222 and .223. Medium action calibers are: .22-250, .243, .308 and 7mm-08.

Short Action

NOTE: Add 10 percent for .222 and .223 Rem.; 20 percent for .17 Rem.

1200	1050	875	600	500	300

Medium Action

1200	1050	875	600	500	300

PPC Bench Rest/Varmint

Similar to Varmint but single-shot. Fitted with 23.75" barrel. Weighs 8.75 lbs. Available in short action special calibers .22 PPC and 6mm PPC.

1350	1150	975	650	500	300

Classic Grade

Hand-checkered select walnut stock, with matte lacquer finish is featured on this grade. Offered in medium and long action. Long action rifles are offered in left-hand model. Medium action

NIB	EXC.	V.G.	GOOD	FAIR	POOR

caliber is .243 Win., with 21.75" barrel and weight of 6 lbs. Long action calibers are: .270, .30-06 and 7mm Rem. Magnum. with 24" barrels and weight about 7.5 lbs.

NIB	EXC.	V.G.	GOOD	FAIR	POOR
1200	1050	875	600	500	300

Deluxe Grade

This model features a high grade European walnut stock, with hand cut basket weave checkering. Fore-end tip and grip are fitted with rosewood. English-style recoil pad is standard. Long action models are offered in left-hand configuration. Like the Hunter model short, medium and long actions are available in the same calibers, barrel lengths and weights..

Medium Action

NIB	EXC.	V.G.	GOOD	FAIR	POOR
1400	1175	1000	750	600	300

Short Action

NOTE: Add 10 percent for .222 and .223 Rem.; 20 percent for .17 Rem.

Long Action

NOTE: Add 10 percent for long action calibers in .300 and .338 Win. Magnum; 20 percent for .375 H&H Magnum; 25 percent for .416 Rem. Magnum; $100 for left-hand models.

NIB	EXC.	V.G.	GOOD	FAIR	POOR
1400	1175	1000	750	600	300

Super Grade/Super Deluxe

Similar to Deluxe Grade. Offered with fancy walnut stock and oak-leaf carving. Floor plate and trigger guard are engraved. Pistol-grip cap has inlaid silver plate. Offered in same actions and calibers as Hunter and Deluxe Grades.

Medium Action

NIB	EXC.	V.G.	GOOD	FAIR	POOR
2500	1750	1200	750	625	300

Short Action

NOTE: Add 10 percent for .222 and .223 Rem.

Long Action

NOTE: Add 10 percent for long action calibers in .300 and .338 Win. Magnum; 20 percent for .375 H&H Magnum; 25 percent for .416 Rem. Magnum.

NIB	EXC.	V.G.	GOOD	FAIR	POOR
2500	1750	1200	750	625	300

Safari Grade

As above chambered for .300 Winchester Magnum, .338 Winchester Magnum or .375 Holland & Holland cartridges.

NIB	EXC.	V.G.	GOOD	FAIR	POOR
3250	2500	1900	1100	800	400

MODEL 75 SERIES

Introduced in March 1997. Based on a new design by Sako. Each of the five different action sizes is manufactured for a specific range of calibers. Its action, barrel and stocks are all redesigned components. Offered in a variety of configurations and calibers. Sako actions are offered separately in carbon steel, white and stainless steel.

Model 75 Hunter

This model available in five different action sizes for calibers from .17 Rem. to .416 Rem. Magnum. Weight varies from 6.37 lbs. to 9 lbs. Barrel lengths from 22" to 24.37". Choice of checkered walnut stock or black synthetic stock. All Hunter models are sold without sights as standard, but open sights are an option. Magazine is detachable except for .300 Rem. Ultra Magnum and .416 Rem. Magnum. Single set trigger is an option. In 2003, a left-hand model was offered in .270 Win and .30-06. In 2004, .270 WSM and .300 WSM calibers were added. **NOTE:** Add $30 for long action calibers from .270 to .416.

NIB	EXC.	V.G.	GOOD	FAIR	POOR
1425	1050	700	500	400	300

Model 75 Stainless Synthetic

Same as above but available with synthetic stock and stainless steel barrel and action. Offered in calibers from .22-250 to .375 H&H. **NOTE:** Add $30 for long action calibers.

NIB	EXC.	V.G.	GOOD	FAIR	POOR
1500	1100	750	600	400	300

Model 75 Deluxe

Model features all the elements of the Hunter model, with the addition of special checkering on select walnut stock with special black finish. All models have a hinged floor plate. In 2004, .270 WSM and .300 WSM calibers were added. Weight about 7.75 lbs. **NOTE:** Add $100 for long action calibers.

NIB	EXC.	V.G.	GOOD	FAIR	POOR
1600	1050	800	700	500	400

	NIB	EXC.	V.G.	GOOD	FAIR	POOR

Model 75 Big Game Deluxe

Similar to M75 Deluxe, except chambered for .416 Rem. Magnum cartridge. Fitted with iron sights.

	1600	1050	800	700	500	400

Model 75 Varmint

This model chambered for .17 Rem., .222 Rem., .223 and .22-250, all with 24" heavy barrels. In 1999, Sako added the .22 PPC and 6mm PPC calibers. Other calibers are .260 Remington, .308 and .204 Ruger. Weighs about 8.4 lbs. Walnut stock.

	1250	950	750	600	450	400

Model 75 Varmint Set Trigger

As above, with single-set trigger. Introduced in 2005.

	1550	1100	875	700	500	400

Model 75 Varmint Stainless

Introduced in 1999. This model similar to Varmint 75, with stainless steel barrel. Magazine is detachable but can be loaded through the ejection port. Trigger is adjustable. Offered in all calibers as the standard Model 75 Varmint. Weights vary from about 8 lbs. to 8.6 lbs. Stock is laminated.

	1200	1050	875	600	500	300

Model 75 Varmint Stainless Set Trigger

As above, with stainless steel barrel and receiver. Laminated stock. Weight about 9 lbs. Introduced in 2005.

	1400	1175	1000	750	600	300

Model 75 Finnlight

Introduced in 2001. This bolt-action rifle features short, medium and long action calibers. Stainless steel barrel lengths from 20.25" to 22.5" depending on caliber. Barrels are fluted. Synthetic stock. Weight about 6.5 lbs. depending on caliber. In 2003, offered in .300 WSM caliber.

	1300	1075	900	650	500	300

Model 75 Grey Wolf

Bolt action rifle chambered for a wide variety of calibers from .223 to 7mm WSM. Stainless steel barrel is either 22.5" or 24.3" depending on caliber, without sights. Gray stock is laminated and checkered. Rubber recoil pad. Detachable magazine. Weight about 7.75 lbs. depending on caliber. Introduced in 2005.

	1400	1175	1000	750	600	300

Model 75 Custom Deluxe

Introduced in 2003. Features an oil-finished premium-grade walnut stock, with a special fine-line checkering pattern. Factory recoil pad. Chambered for .270 Win or .30-06 cartridges.

	3250	2500	1900	1100	800	400

Model 75 Custom Single Shot

Introduced in 2004. This single-shot model chambered for .308 cartridge. Fitted with 23.625" heavy fluted stainless steel barrel, without sights. Checkered laminated stock, with beavertail forearm. Weight about 9 lbs.

	3250	2500	1900	1100	550	400

Model 75 Super Deluxe

A special order rifle. Advise obtaining an expert opinion before a sale. Prices listed are for the base rifle.

	2500	2100	1600	1275	600	400

Model 78

A .22 or .22 Hornet bolt-action rifle, with 22" barrel. Blued, with checkered walnut stock. Discontinued in 1986.

	—	850	675	500	375	250

Model 2700 Finnsport

A .270 to .300 Winchester Magnum bolt-action rifle, with 22" barrel. Blued, checkered walnut stock. Discontinued in 1985.

	—	900	750	600	475	200

NIB	EXC.	V.G.	GOOD	FAIR	POOR

Safari 80th Anniversary Model

A limited edition rifle. Built on the Sako 75 Magnum long action. Chambered for .375 H&H cartridge. Match grade heavy barrel. Select grade walnut stock, with straight comb and ebony fore-end tip. Quarter rib. Equipped with Swarovski PV-1 1.25x24 scope. Engraved floor plate. Supplied with hand-made leather case, with cleaning accessories. Limited to 80 rifles worldwide. Serial numbers 200101 to 200180.

NIB	EXC.	V.G.	GOOD	FAIR	POOR
15950	12500	8500	—	—	—

Sako 85 Hunter

Bolt-action centerfire rifle chambered in short and long calibers ranging from .223 Remington to .375 H&H Magnum. Controlled round feeding. Checkered walnut stock. Satin blued sightless 22.4375", 22.875" or 24.375" barrel. Introduced in 2007. **NOTE:** Add 30 percent premium for .375.

NIB	EXC.	V.G.	GOOD	FAIR	POOR
1100	900	775	600	475	300

Sako 85 Stainless Synthetic

Similar to Sako 85 Hunter, with stainless steel receiver and barrel. Introduced 2007.

NIB	EXC.	V.G.	GOOD	FAIR	POOR
1200	1000	875	650	525	350

Sako 85 Finnlight

Similar to Sako 85 Stainless Synthetic, with recoil pad and ultra-lightweight synthetic stock. Chambered in long and short cartridges ranging from .243 to .300 Win Magnum. Introduced 2007.

NIB	EXC.	V.G.	GOOD	FAIR	POOR
1550	1100	875	700	500	400

Sako 85 Varmint

Similar to Sako 85 Hunter, with recoil pad and 7.5 oz. set trigger. Chambered in .204 Ruger, .243, .22-250 or .308. Introduced 2007.

NIB	EXC.	V.G.	GOOD	FAIR	POOR
1300	1075	900	650	500	300

Sako 85 Laminated SS Varmint

Similar to Sako 85 Varmint, with laminated stock and stainless steel barrel. Introduced 2007.

NIB	EXC.	V.G.	GOOD	FAIR	POOR
1400	1175	1000	750	600	300

Sako A7 American Bolt-Action Rifle

Bolt-action rifle chambered in .22-250, .243 Win., .25-06, .260 Rem., .270 Win., .270 WSM, .300 WSM, .30-06, .300 WM, .308 Win., .338 Federal, .7mm Rem. Magnum, 7mm-08. Features include blued or stainless barrel (22.4375" standard, 24.375" magnum) and receiver, black composite stock with sling swivels and recoil pad, two-position safety, adjustable trigger, detachable 3+1 box magazine. Weight 6 lbs., 3 oz. to 6 lbs., 13 oz.

NIB	EXC.	V.G.	GOOD	FAIR	POOR
850	725	575	400	300	200

Sako A-7 Tecomate

Chambered in .270 WSM (23" barrel) or .300 WSM (24.25") barrel. Magazine capacity 4 rounds. Features a new Bell & Carlson Medalist composite stock. Integral aluminum bedding system, CNC produced from aircraft quality 6061-T6 aluminum. Flat bottom receiver. Stainless action. Introduced in 2011.

NIB	EXC.	V.G.	GOOD	FAIR	POOR
1200	1025	850	600	300	100

Sako Classic Deluxe

High grade version of Model 85. Oil-finished walnut stock, with palm swell and cheekpiece, pronounced pistol-grip, rosewood pistol and fore-end tip. Barrel band for sling swivel. Free-floating barrel. All metal parts are highly polished and blued. Medium or long action depending upon caliber. Adjustable trigger. Open sights are available. Five cartridges available to include .270 Winchester, 7x64, .30-06, .370 Sako Magnum and .375 H&H. Introduced in 2011.

NIB	EXC.	V.G.	GOOD	FAIR	POOR
3450	3100	2600	2000	1600	500

Sako 85 Bavarian

Available in full length (shown) or carbine style. Offered in most standard calibers, plus 6.5x55 Swedish. Comes with set trigger and adjustable express sights. Stock is oil finished high-grade checkered walnut, with rosewood grip and fore-end caps. Carbine has full-length Mannlicher-style stock, with Bavarian-style comb and cheekpiece. **NOTE:** Add 15 percent for Carbine model.

NIB	EXC.	V.G.	GOOD	FAIR	POOR
1950	1750	1400	1000	750	250

Sako 85 Kodiak

Weatherproof design has stainless steel barrel and action. Gray laminated stock reinforced with two crossbolts. Free-floating bull barrel in 21", 22.5" or 24.3" lengths. Offered in calibers from .22-250 to .375 H&H.

NIB	EXC.	V.G.	GOOD	FAIR	POOR
1750	1525	1200	800	450	200

	NIB	EXC.	V.G.	GOOD	FAIR	POOR

Sako Black Bear Series

Model 85 variation available in short and medium actions only. Short action chambered in .308 Win. or .338 Federal; medium action in .30-06, 8x57 JS, 9.3x62 and 9.3x66 (.370) Sako. Controlled feeding, detachable magazine, single-stage adjustable trigger. Black injection molded stock, with Soft Touch areas around pistol-grip and fore-end. Open sights are available. Scope can be mounted to integral Sako mounting system on receiver. Bull barrel, free-floating and hammer forged. Brown Bear model has similar features, but with brown laminated hardwood stock. Chambered in .338 Win. Magnum or .375 H&H. Introduced in 2011.

1600	1350	1100	950	600	300

TRG-S

Model features a unique cold-forged receiver. Stock is special reinforced polyurethane Monte Carlo, without checkering. Recoil pad has spacer for adjustable length of pull. Trigger is adjustable. Detachable magazine holds 5 rounds. Offered in a variety of calibers from .243 to .375 H&H. Non-Magnum calibers fitted with 22" barrel, weighs 7.75 lbs.; Magnum calibers fitted with 24" barrel, weighs 7.75 lbs. In 1996, .270 Withby Magnum, 7mm Withby Magnum, .340 Withby Magnum, as well as 6.5x55S were added.

1000	850	675	500	350	250

TRG-21

Receiver similar to TRG-S, with polyurethane stock featuring a unique design. Chambered for .308 cartridge. Trigger is adjustable for length and two-stage pull; also for horizontal or vertical pitch. Has several options that would affect price; muzzle-brake, one-piece scope mount, bipod, quick detachable sling swivels and military nylon sling. Offered in .308 Win. only. Fitted with 25.75" barrel; weighs 10.5 lbs.

2500	2000	1500	1000	600	400

TRG-22

Similar to TRG-21. Meets exact specifications to comply with Finish military requirements. Chambered for .308 cartridge. Introduced in 2000. Offered in both green and black finish. Weight about 10.25 lbs. **NOTE:** Add $2,250 for folding stock version.

3000	2400	1850	1250	800	500

TRG-41

Exactly the same as TRG-21, except chambered for .338 Lapua Magnum cartridge.

4350	3500	2500	—	—	—

TRG-42

Similar to TRG-41. Meets exact specifications to comply with Finish military requirements. Chambered for .338 Lapua or .300 Win. Magnum cartridge. Introduced in 2000. Weight about 11.25 lbs.

4000	3000	2000	—	—	—

SAM, INC.
Special Service Arms Mfg., Inc.
Reston, Virginia

Model 88 Crossfire

Semi-automatic combination 12-gauge/.308-caliber shotgun/rifle, with 7-shot shotgun magazine and 20-shot rifle magazine. Barrel length 20". Matte black finish, with composition stock. This weapon can be fired in either mode by means of a selector switch mounted on receiver.

1900	1500	1175	800	550	300

SAMCO GLOBAL ARMS, INC.
Miami, Florida

This firm imports a variety of military surplus firearms, that under current law, are marked with the importer's name.

SARASQUETA, FELIX
Eibar, Spain

Merke

A 12-gauge over/under double-barrel shotgun, with 22" or 27" ribbed and separated barrels, nonselective trigger and manual extractors. Blued, checkered walnut stock. Imported in 1986 only.

—	500	375	200	150	100

	NIB	EXC.	V.G.	GOOD	FAIR	POOR

SARASQUETA, J. J.
Eibar, Spain

Model 107E

A 12-, 16- or 20-gauge boxlock double-barrel shotgun, with a variety of barrel lengths, double triggers and automatic ejectors. Blued, with checkered walnut stock. Discontinued in 1984.

	—	425	300	275	225	100

Model 119E

As above, with a more finely figured walnut stock.

	—	525	400	375	325	150

Model 130E

As above, but engraved.

	—	950	700	600	450	250

Model 131E

As above, with considerably more engraving.

	—	1350	900	800	650	350

Model 1882 E LUXE

As above, with a single-selective trigger and gold inlays. Silver inlaid version is sold for approximately 10 percent less.

	—	1750	1250	900	650	350

SARASQUETA, VICTOR
Eibar, Spain

Model 3

A 12-, 16- or 20-gauge boxlock or sidelock double-barrel shotgun. Available in a variety of barrel lengths, with double triggers and automatic ejectors. Blued, with checkered straight stock. Sidelock version is worth approximately 20 percent more than values listed. Basic Model 3 was offered in a variety of grades featuring different amounts of engraving and better quality wood. These shotguns are listed under the model designations of 4 to 12E.

	—	650	500	450	350	300

Model 4

	—	1200	1000	875	600	300

Model 4E (Auto-ejectors)

	—	1600	1400	1100	800	400

Model 203

	—	700	600	525	425	325

Model 203E

	—	900	750	625	475	375

Model 6E

	—	1400	1250	875	525	425

Model 7E

	—	1500	1350	1000	750	475

Model 10E

	—	2600	2100	1650	950	750

Model 11E

	—	3000	2600	2000	1150	850

Model 12E

	—	3200	2850	2200	1300	1000

SARDIUS
Israel

SD-9

A 9mm double-action semi-automatic pistol, with 3" barrel and 6-shot magazine. Matte black finish, with composition grips. Imported since 1988.

425	300	250	200	150	100

	NIB	EXC.	V.G.	GOOD	FAIR	POOR

SARSILMAZ
Mercan/Istanbul, Turkey

Professional

CZ-75-style compensated semi-automatic in white chrome finish chambered for 9mm. Single-action with adjustable trigger, laser engraving. 16 or 18 round capacity. 42.3 oz.; 5.1" barrel. MSRP: $437.

K2

CZ-75-style double-action semi-automatic in white chrome or blued. Chambered for 9mm. 16 or 18 round capacity. 35.3 oz.; 4.6" barrel. Plastic grips.

—	300	225	175	125	50	

Kama Sport

CZ-75-style semi-automatic 9mm in white chrome or blued. Double-action with 3.9" compensated barrel, laser engraving. 15+1 or 17+1 capacity. 35.4 oz. Plastic grips.

—	325	250	195	135	50	

Kama

CZ-75-style semi-automatic 9mm in white chrome or blued. Double-action with 4.3" compensated barrel, laser engraving. 15+1 or 17+1 capacity. 35.4 oz.; 7.7". Plastic grips.

—	300	225	175	125	50	

Kilinc 2000 Mega

CZ-75-style semi-automatic 9mm in white chrome or blued. Double-action with 4.7" barrel. 16 or 18 capacity. 35 oz. Plastic grips. Fixed sights.

—	300	225	175	125	50	

Kilinc 2000 Light

CZ-75-style semi-automatic 9mm in white chrome, blued or camo. Double-action with 4.7" barrel, laser engraving. 15+1 or 17+1 capacity. 35.4 oz. Plastic grips.

—	300	225	175	125	50	

Hancer 2000/2000 Light

CZ-75-style semi-automatic 9mm in white chrome or blued. Double-action with 3.9" barrel, laser engraving. 13+1 capacity. 33.5 oz. (25.4 oz. Light model). Plastic grips.

—	300	225	175	125	50	

Bernardelli

CZ-75-style double-action semi-automatic in 9mm. Black/white or blued finish. The 15+1 model has a 4.7" barrel, 27 oz., Plastic grips. The 13+1 model has a 3.9" barrel; 26.7 oz. Plastic grips, fixed sights.

—	300	225	175	125	50	

SAUER & SON, J. P.
Suhl and Eckernfoerde, Germany

Oldest firearms manufacturing firm in Germany. Founded in 1751 in Suhl. During this period the company produced high quality handguns and long guns. In 1938, it introduced a new double-action semi-automatic pistol, Sauer 38H. Pistol had the first decocking lever ever used on a mass produced pistol. In 1951, company relocated to Eckernfoerde where it continued to produce high quality firearms. **NOTE:** Model 90 Supreme and Model 202 have been imported by SIGARMS Inc.

Bolt-Action Rifle

Mauser action sporting rifle. Chambered for a variety of cartridges, with either 22" or 24" barrel featuring a raised rib. Double-set triggers, express sights. Blued, with checkered walnut stock. Manufactured prior to WWII.

—	1250	900	6500	400	300	

Model 200

Bolt-action rifle chambered for a variety of cartridges. Short or medium length actions, 24" barrels, set trigger, 4-round magazine. Blued, checkered walnut stock. Discontinued 1987. Extra barrels add $235.

1350	1050	700	500	425	350	

Model 200 Lightweight

As above, with an alloy receiver. Discontinued in 1987.

—	1100	900	550	325	250	

NIB	EXC.	V.G.	GOOD	FAIR	POOR

Model 200 Lux

As above, with finely figured walnut stock, rosewood pistol-grip cap and fore-end tip. Gold-plated trigger and a machine jewelled bolt. Imported prior to 1988.

—	1200	950	700	475	400

Model 200 Carbon Fiber

Model 200 fitted with a carbon composition stock. Imported in 1987 and 1988.

—	1300	1100	800	500	400

Model 202 Supreme

Bolt-action rifle with a barrel change feature. Fitted with adjustable two-stage trigger, quick-change fluted barrel, black rubber recoil pad and removable box magazine. Stock is select American claro walnut, with high gloss finish and rosewood fore-end and grip cap. Buttstock has a Monte Carlo comb and cheekpiece. Offered in .243, .270, .308 and .30-06. Barrel length for these calibers is 23.6". Weight about 7.7 lbs. Supreme Magnum series available in 7mm Magnum, .300 Win. Magnum and .375 H&H Magnum. Barrel length for these Magnum calibers is 26". Weight about 8.4 lbs.

2700	2000	1350	1000	750	400

Model 202 Takedown

This model is a true takedown. Introduced in 2003. Chambered for .300 Win. Magnum and .375 H&H. Other calibers will be offered in the future. Fancy Turkish walnut stock, with Monte Carlo and rosewood fore-end tip. Base price listed.

5700	4400	2900	2000	1200	400

Model S202 Wolverine

Similar to Model 202 Supreme above, with 25.6" barrel, beavertail fore-end and adjustable cheekpiece. Chambered in various varmint calibers.

—	2300	1950	1500	1050	400

Model S202 Highland

Similar to Model 202 Supreme above, with 20" barrel, schnabel fore-end and easily-detachable buttstock. Chambered in .308 Winchester and various European cartridges.

—	2500	1950	1500	1050	400

Model S202 Forest

Carbine-style version of Model 202 Highland above. Intended specifically for drive hunts. Has standard fore-end and 25.6" barrel. Chambered in various varmint calibers.

—	2500	1950	1500	1050	400

Model S202 Hardwood

Similar to Model 202 Highland above. Oddly enough, with a synthetic stock with orange inserts. Chambered in .308 Winchester and various European cartridges.

—	2300	1950	1500	1050	400

Model S202 Match

Target version of Model 202, with 26.8" match barrel, wide fore-end. Chambered in .300 Winchester Magnum and 6.5x55 Swedish.

—	2500	1950	1500	1050	400

Model S202 Outback

Similar to Model 202 Hardwood above, with lightweight construction and plain black synthetic stock

—	2500	1950	1500	1050	400

Model S202 Team Sauer

Classically-styled sporter version of Model 202, with heavy medium or magnum-weight barrel. Walnut Monte Carlo stock. Chambered in various European and American long-action cartridges from 6.5x55 Swedish up to .300 Winchester Magnum.

—	1950	1600	1250	800	400

Model 90

Bolt-action rifle produced in a number of calibers and in all action lengths, with 23" or 26" barrels. Detachable magazine. Blued, with checkered walnut stock.

—	1300	1100	675	500	300

	NIB	EXC.	V.G.	GOOD	FAIR	POOR

Model 90 Stutzen

As above, with a full-length Mannlicher-style stock. Imported prior to 1990.

	—	1350	1150	725	550	350

Model 90 Safari

Model 90 made for use with .458 Winchester Magnum cartridge. Fitted with a 24" barrel. Imported from 1986 to 1988. **NOTE:** Model 90 Series of bolt-action rifles was available in a deluxe version that differed with grade of workmanship and materials utilized. This deluxe series would be worth approximately 60 percent additional.

	—	2300	2000	1250	900	400

Model 90 Supreme

Similar to above, with gold-plated trigger, machine jewelled bolt and finely figured checkered walnut stock. Introduced in 1987.

	—	2500	2200	1425	1000	400

SSG-3000

See entry in SIG-Sauer section.

SG 550 Sniper

NOTE: For other current Sauer rifles see SIGARMS.

5500	4750	3875	2700	2000	500

SHOTGUN/RIFLE COMBINATIONS

Luftwaffe M30 Survival Drilling

Double-barrel 12-gauge by 9.3x74R combination shotgun/rifle, with 28" barrels. Blued, with checkered walnut stock and marked with Nazi inspection. Stampings on stock and barrel breech. Normally furnished with an aluminum case. **NOTE:** Add 50 percent to prices for case.

20000	15000	9500	6000	3250	1500

Model 3000 Drilling

Model was chambered for a variety of gauges and calibers. Built upon a boxlock action, with a Greener crossbolt. Action is lightly engraved. Blued, checkered walnut stock.

5500	3700	2750	2000	1500	1250

Model 54 Combo

Combination rifle/shotgun. Chambered for a variety of gauges and calibers, with an action as above. Discontinued in 1986.

	—	3000	2250	1750	1400	1200

SHOTGUNS

Model 60

A 12-, 16- or 20-gauge double-barrel boxlock shotgun. Produced in a variety of barrel lengths, with double triggers and manual extractors. Blued, with checkered walnut stock. Produced prior to WWII.

	—	1300	950	725	550	400

Royal Model

A 12- or 20-gauge boxlock double-barrel shotgun, with 26", 28" or 30" barrels. Single-selective triggers, with automatic ejectors. Frame is scalloped. Blued, with checkered walnut stock. Manufactured from 1955 to 1977.

	—	1500	1250	1000	750	500

Grade I Artemis

A 12-gauge sidelock double-barrel shotgun, with 28" barrels, single-selective trigger and automatic ejector. Engraved, blued with checkered walnut stock. Manufactured from 1966 to 1977.

	—	5000	4250	3500	2500	2000

Grade II Artemis

As above, but more finely finished.

	—	6500	5750	4750	3500	3000

	NIB	EXC.	V.G.	GOOD	FAIR	POOR

Model 66

A 12-gauge sidelock double-barrel shotgun, with 26", 28" or 30" barrel. Single-selective trigger and automatic ejectors. Blued, checkered walnut stock. Produced in three different grades that have different degrees of engraving. Produced from 1966 to 1975.

Grade I

	NIB	EXC.	V.G.	GOOD	FAIR	POOR
	—	2000	1800	1500	1150	800

Grade II

	NIB	EXC.	V.G.	GOOD	FAIR	POOR
	—	3000	2800	2500	2150	1800

Grade III

	NIB	EXC.	V.G.	GOOD	FAIR	POOR
	—	3750	3500	2850	2500	2000

PISTOLS

Written and compiled by our very good friend Jim Cate.

Bär Pistol

Invented by Burkard Behr and made by Sauer. This was Sauer's first modern small pistol. It has stacked barrels (over/under configuration) that allow the shooter to fire two shots, rotate the barrel and then fire two more shots before loading. It was first patented in Germany in 1897 and in the USA in 1899. It shoots the 7mm Bär cartridge only. (DO NOT ATTEMPT TO FIRE THE .25 ACP/6.35mm CARTRIDGE IN THIS PISTOL.) It was made from 1897 to 1911 or 1912. Some pistols have Bakelite grips; some have diamond-pattern checkered wood grips. A case extractor rod screws into the bottom of the frame. No trigger guard. **NOTE:** Add $150 for original box and instructions.

	NIB	EXC.	V.G.	GOOD	FAIR	POOR
	—	1250	800	450	275	—

Roth-Sauer Model

Very first automatic pistol produced by J.P. Sauer & Son. Designed by Karl Krinka for George Roth. Available only in 7.65 Roth-Sauer caliber. A locked breech design, beautifully finished and extremely well made. Later this design was modified and became the Roth-Steyr military pistol, which was adopted by Austria in 1907. A difficult-to-find pistol.

	NIB	EXC.	V.G.	GOOD	FAIR	POOR
	—	2500	1800	900	500	300

SAUER MODEL 1913 FIRST SERIES

First Series, which incorporates an extra safety button on the left side of frame near trigger and rear sight is simply a milled recess in the cocking knob itself. Serial number range runs from 1 to approximately 4750. First series is found only in 7.65mm caliber. All were for commercial sales as far as can be determined. Some were tested by various militaries, no doubt.

A. European variation—all slide legends are in the German language.

B. English Export variation—slide legends are marked, J.P. Sauer & Son, Suhl - Prussia, "Sauer's Patent" Pat'd May 20 1912.

Both were sold in thick paper cartons or boxes, with the color being a reddish purple with gold colored letters, etc. Examples of the very early European variation are found with the English language brochure or manual as well as an extra magazine, cleaning brush and grease container. These were shipped to England or the U.S. prior to Sauer producing the English Export variation. **NOTE:** Original box with accessories and manual: Add $500 if complete and in very good to excellent condition.

A. European variation:

	NIB	EXC.	V.G.	GOOD	FAIR	POOR
	—	1500	900	650	400	250

B. English Export variation

	NIB	EXC.	V.G.	GOOD	FAIR	POOR
	—	1800	1200	800	500	300

SAUER MODEL 1913 SECOND SERIES

Extra safety button eliminated. Rear sight acts as cocking knob retainer.

Commercial variation

Normal European/German slide markings are normally found; however it has been called to my attention that there are English Export pistols in this SECOND SERIES. They have the English markings on the slide which are similar to those found on the FIRST SERIES of the Model 1913. This is applicable to both the 7.65mm and 6.35mm Model 1913/19 pistols. These are exceptional scarce pistols and should command at least a 50 percent premium, perhaps more due to their rarity. This commercial variation had factory manuals printed in English, Spanish and German

	NIB	EXC.	V.G.	GOOD	FAIR	POOR

which came with the cardboard boxed pistols. **NOTE:** With the original Sauer box, accessories and manual: Add $300 if in very good to excellent condition.

Caliber 7.65mm variation

	NIB	EXC.	V.G.	GOOD	FAIR	POOR
	—	450	375	300	250	100

Caliber 7.65 variation with all words in English (i.e Son, Prussia, etc.)

	NIB	EXC.	V.G.	GOOD	FAIR	POOR
	—	800	575	450	300	200

Police Variations

These will be standard German Commercial configuration, but nearly always having Zusatzsicherung (additional safety) added to pistol. Safety is found between regular safety lever and top of left grip. Police used both calibers 7.65mm and 6.35mm, but 7.65 was predominant. After early part of 1930s, 6.35 was not available to police departments. Thus, 6.35mm police marked Sauer is rather scarce in relation to 7.65mm caliber. Few in 7.65mm are dated 1920 on left side of frame and were used by auxiliary policemen in Bavaria. Normal police property markings are on front or rear grip straps. Most were originally issued with at least two magazines and police accepted holster. Mags were usually numbered and holsters are found with and without pistol numbers. **NOTE:** Add 10 percent for one correctly numbered magazine; 20 percent if found with both correctly numbered magazines; 30 percent if found with correct holster and magazines.

Caliber 6.35mm police marked without Zusatzsicherung

	NIB	EXC.	V.G.	GOOD	FAIR	POOR
	—	500	350	275	200	75

Caliber 6.35mm police marked with Zusatzsicherung

	NIB	EXC.	V.G.	GOOD	FAIR	POOR
	—	550	375	275	200	75

Caliber 7.65mm police marked without Zusatzsicherung

	NIB	EXC.	V.G.	GOOD	FAIR	POOR
	—	575	325	275	175	125

Caliber 7.65mm police marked with Zusatzsicherung

	NIB	EXC.	V.G.	GOOD	FAIR	POOR
	—	575	400	275	175	125

R.F.V. (Reich Finanz Verwaltung)

This Sauer variation is rarely found in any condition. R.F.V. markings and property number could be 1 to 4 digits. This variation is found in both calibers. Used by the Reich's Customs and Finance department personnel.

Caliber 6.35mm R.F.V. marked pistols

	NIB	EXC.	V.G.	GOOD	FAIR	POOR
	—	1000	750	500	350	250

Caliber 7.65mm R.F.V. marked pistols

	NIB	EXC.	V.G.	GOOD	FAIR	POOR
	—	750	600	400	300	200

Imperial Military Variations

Normal German commercial variations of the time period. Either Imperial Eagle acceptance marking applied on front of trigger guard and having small Imperial Army inspector's acceptance marking (crown over a scriptic letter) on right side of frame close to Nitro proof; or just Imperial Army inspector's marking alone. Usually pistols are found in 40000 to 85000 range. However, quantity actually of Imperial Military accepted is quite low even though thousands were privately purchased by officer corps. There are examples in 6.35mm which are Imperial Military accepted, but these are very scarce. **NOTE:** Add 30 percent for 6.35mm.

Caliber 7.65mm Imperial Military accepted pistols

	NIB	EXC.	V.G.	GOOD	FAIR	POOR
	—	1100	650	350	275	150

Paramilitary marked Sauer pistols of the 1925-35 period

Very few Model 1913 pistols would have been marked by paramilitary groups or organizations of this period. Usually this marking is no more than a series of numbers above another series of numbers, such as 23 over 12. These are found usually on the left side of frame next to left grip. Most of these numbers are indicative of property numbers assigned to a particular pistol belonging to a particular SA Group, Stahlhelm or right-wing organization such as Red Front (early communist). Any pistol of this type should be examined by an expert to determine if it is an original example.

	NIB	EXC.	V.G.	GOOD	FAIR	POOR
	—	550	450	300	200	100

Norwegian police usage, post World War II

After the war was over, many surplus German weapons were put back into use by the government of Norway. Germans had occupied this country and large numbers of weapons remained when the fighting ended. This included a large number of surplus Sauer pistols being utilized by the police (POLITI) forces. Most of the Sauers that were used by the Politi, which have been imported into the U.S. have been Model 1913; however, there were a number of Model 1930 pistols which reached our country as well. All examples, regardless of model, have the word POLITI stamped on the slide as well as a rampant lion on a shield under a crown marking.

	NIB	EXC.	V.G.	GOOD	FAIR	POOR

Following this is the property number. This number is also stamped into the left side of the frame. Most saw much usage during the post-war period. All are in 7.65mm caliber.

	NIB	EXC.	V.G.	GOOD	FAIR	POOR
	—	350	300	200	150	100

Model 1913/19 in 6.35mm

This particular pistol must be divided into three (3) sub-variations. This variation appears to be in a serial number range of its own. First sub-variation appears to run from 1 to 40000. It is highly doubtful if this quantity was manufactured. Second sub-variation incorporates a Zusatzsicherung or Additional Safety which can be seen between the normal safety lever and top of the left grip. It locked the trigger bar when in use. This second range appears to run from approximately serial number 40000 to 51000 which probably was continuous in the number produced. Lastly, third sub-variation examples were manufactured during or after 1926. Trigger guard has a different shape; slide has a greater area of vertical milled finger grooves; added Additional safety (Zusatzsicherung) now acts as the hold open device as well. These are found up to approximately 57000. Then a few examples of the first sub-variation are found from 57000 up to about 62500. This was, no doubt, usage of remaining parts. **NOTE:** Any commercial pistol could be special ordered with a factory nickel finish, special grip material (pearl, wood, etc.) as well as different types of engraving. It would be in your best interest to have these pistols examined by an expert.

Caliber 6.35mm first sub-variation

	NIB	EXC.	V.G.	GOOD	FAIR	POOR
	—	450	375	250	150	75

Caliber 6.35mm second sub-variation

	NIB	EXC.	V.G.	GOOD	FAIR	POOR
	—	475	375	250	150	75

Caliber 6.35mm third sub-variation

	NIB	EXC.	V.G.	GOOD	FAIR	POOR
	—	650	500	500	200	100

Caliber 6.35mm English export variation

	NIB	EXC.	V.G.	GOOD	FAIR	POOR
	—	1000	700	500	300	200

1926 Export Model

This variation's name comes from actual Sauer factory records found in the Suhl Archive. An interim pistol produced during 1926 to early 1929 period. Found only in 7.65mm caliber. This was an advancement of the normal 1913 design, which included changes in: (1) safety lever's design that became a slide hold open device as well; (2) shape of the frame was altered in that the trigger guard became more streamlined and the rear of frame was shortened and serrations were added to the slide as well as cocking knob. These are found in 162000 to 169000 range in relatively small clusters. Two to four thousand are presumed to have been manufactured. A scarce Sauer pistol! To date, none have been seen in nickel.

NIB	EXC.	V.G.	GOOD	FAIR	POOR
1075	825	700	500	300	150

W.T.M.-Westentaschen Model—Vest Pocket Model

Several variations of vest pocket pistols were manufactured. First was called Model 1920 by the Sauer firm. We usually refer to it as Model 1924. Pistol, as well as all other W.T.M. examples, were designed to carry in your pocket. Quite small in size and found only in 6.35mm or .25 ACP caliber. Later in 1928, an updated version became available and was referred to as Model 1928. These differed in internal parts design and slide configuration. Bottom of grip marked "Cal.6.35.28.". Last version appeared in 1933 and still utilized same grips, but trigger and other small parts differed. All three were available in blue or nickel finish, engraving and fancy grip material. Very few Model 1933 had stainless steel (NIROSTA marked) barrels.

Model 1920

Serrations on front and rear of slide.

NIB	EXC.	V.G.	GOOD	FAIR	POOR
800	600	500	300	200	75

Model 1928

"Cal. 6.35.28" on black Bakelite grips.

NIB	EXC.	V.G.	GOOD	FAIR	POOR
800	600	500	350	200	75

Model 1933

Different type of trigger. Found in 253000 to early 254000 serial number range. **NOTE:** Add $200 factory nickel; $250 factory engraving; $250 exotic grip material; $500 factory paper box with cleaning brush, extra magazine and brochure; $750 in original factory imitation leather covered metal presentation case with accessories; $500 NIROSTA marked stainless barrel.

NIB	EXC.	V.G.	GOOD	FAIR	POOR
1050	850	600	400	275	150

MODEL 1930 VARIATIONS

Dutch Models

These different types of Dutch pistols will have JOH MUNTS - AMSTERDAM on left side of slide. Grips are usually mottled gray color. Sauer manufactured different pistols for Dutch police, Navy,

	NIB	EXC.	V.G.	GOOD	FAIR	POOR

Army, Department of Finance, S.M.N. (Steam Ships Netherlands) and possibly other agencies.
NOTE: Accessories: cleaning rod, brush, aluminum oil bottle and manuals, add accordingly.

Dutch Police

First variation manufactured w/o adjustable front sight and lanyard loop.

	NIB	EXC.	V.G.	GOOD	FAIR	POOR
	—	700	500	350	250	125

Amsterdam Police

Manufactured w/o adjustable sight, but having lanyard loop.

	NIB	EXC.	V.G.	GOOD	FAIR	POOR
	1500	1300	1050	800	450	200

Navy

Made w/o adjustable sight. Anchor & Crown marked on rear grip strap.

	NIB	EXC.	V.G.	GOOD	FAIR	POOR
	1500	1300	1050	800	450	200

S.M.N.

Found with and w/o adjustable front sights, no lanyard loop. S.M.N. marked horizontally near bottom of rear grip strap.

	NIB	EXC.	V.G.	GOOD	FAIR	POOR
	1500	1300	1050	800	450	200

Department of Finance

Found with and w/o adjustable front sight, no lanyard loop. DF over date-1933 on rear grip strap.

	NIB	EXC.	V.G.	GOOD	FAIR	POOR
	—	850	700	385	250	150

1930 Commercial Model

These pistols were for sale in Germany and other countries through normal commercial outlets. Very few are factory nickeled, engraved or both; some are with NIROSTA marked barrels and a very few were made in Duralumin or Dural. Standard caliber was 7.65mm, but a very limited number were made in .22 LR (.22 Long). Standard grip material is black Bakelite. Most of the regular pistols were purchased by military officers, some went to paramilitary groups such as the SA. **NOTE:** Add $100 for any variation listed with nickel finish; $500 for engraving; $600 for both nickel and engraving; $750 for nickel, engraving and with a fancy grip material (pearl or ebony, etc.).

Standard Commercial

	NIB	EXC.	V.G.	GOOD	FAIR	POOR
	1500	1300	1050	800	450	200

Standard Commercial with NIROSTA marked barrel, 7.65mm

	NIB	EXC.	V.G.	GOOD	FAIR	POOR
	1500	1300	1050	800	450	200

Standard Commercial in .22 LR (.22 Long)

	NIB	EXC.	V.G.	GOOD	FAIR	POOR
	—	2500	1800	1200	500	300

Duralumin (Dural) Variation, 7.65mm

	NIB	EXC.	V.G.	GOOD	FAIR	POOR
	—	3500	2750	2000	1200	450

BEHORDEN MODEL

Behorden (Authority) Model is different from Model 1930. It has a trigger safety and a loaded indicator provided.

Behorden Commercial

These are normally found with a high polished blued finish. Were available with a nickel finish, engraving, or both, as well as fancy grip material and NIROSTA marked barrel. Regular caliber is 7.65mm, but a very few are know in .22 LR that are probably prototype pistols. **NOTE:** Add $100 for nickel finish; $250 for engraving; $350 for both; $500 with nickel, engraving and a fancy grip material; $500 for NIROSTA marked stainless barrel; 300 percent for .22-caliber.

	NIB	EXC.	V.G.	GOOD	FAIR	POOR
	—	675	550	400	350	200

Late Behorden Commercial

These are actually Model 1930 pistols found in 220000 to 223000 serial number range. They do not have trigger safety and/or indicator pin.

	NIB	EXC.	V.G.	GOOD	FAIR	POOR
	—	600	450	300	200	125

Duralumin Model (Dural)

Frame and slide are made of Duralumin material. These are rare pistols! **NOTE:** Add $250 for stainless barrel.

Blue Anodized Variation

Found with and w/o NIROSTA marked barrels.

	NIB	EXC.	V.G.	GOOD	FAIR	POOR
	—	4000	3500	2500	1500	850

	NIB	EXC.	V.G.	GOOD	FAIR	POOR

Nonanodized Variation
Found with and w/o NIROSTA marked barrels.

	NIB	EXC.	V.G.	GOOD	FAIR	POOR
	—	4000	3500	2500	1500	850

Presentation Examples of Anodized and Nonanodized Variations
Please consult an expert for pricing.

Police Models
Examples will be found with police acceptance on the left side of trigger guard. In a few cases on the front or rear grip straps. Black Bakelite grips are standard.

Sunburst K Police Acceptance
Non-adjustable front sight (a round blade).

	NIB	EXC.	V.G.	GOOD	FAIR	POOR
	—	800	650	400	275	200

Sunburst K Police Acceptance
Adjustable front sight.

	NIB	EXC.	V.G.	GOOD	FAIR	POOR
	—	800	625	450	300	225

Diamond in Sunburst Police Acceptance
All known are with the adjustable front sight.

	NIB	EXC.	V.G.	GOOD	FAIR	POOR
	—	1250	900	550	300	225

Grip Strap Marked Variations
(Having abbreviations of a city and property number of the pistol on grip strap.) Very few of these are known. Examples are S.Mg. 52, Sch. 78, etc.

	NIB	EXC.	V.G.	GOOD	FAIR	POOR
	—	750	550	375	250	150

MODEL 36/37
These very few pistols are all prototype Sauer pistols which preceded Model 38. They are in 210,000 range. Please consult an expert to determine value! EXTREMELY RARE.

MODEL 38 AND 38-H (H MODEL) VARIATIONS
Model 38
This pistol started at 260000. Crown N Nitro proofed, has cocking/decocking lever, loaded indicator pin and is double-action. High polish blue in 7.65m/m (standard production pistol); found without thumbsafety on slide; with pinned mag release. VERY RARE.

One Line Slide Legend Variation (pinned magazine release button - no screw)
Crown N proofs. Approximately 250 produced. Extremely rare!

	NIB	EXC.	V.G.	GOOD	FAIR	POOR
	—	3800	3000	2000	600	300

Two Line Slide Legend Variation (pinned magazine release button - no screw)
C/N proofs, blued, with pinned magazine release (about 850 produced) VERY RARE. **NOTE:** Add $250 factory nickel; $350 factory chrome; $1000 engraving; $500 NIROSTA marked barrel.

	NIB	EXC.	V.G.	GOOD	FAIR	POOR
	—	2600	2000	1500	500	275

Two Line Slide Legend Variation (magazine release button)
C/N proofs, blued, magazine release button retained by a screw. RARE. **NOTE:** Add $250 factory nickel; $350 factory chrome; $1000 engraving; $500 NIROSTA marked barrel.

	NIB	EXC.	V.G.	GOOD	FAIR	POOR
	—	2500	1500	900	500	275

SA der NSDAP Gruppe Thuringen Marked Variation
Blued, C/N proofs, with magazine release button held by a screw. VERY RARE.

	NIB	EXC.	V.G.	GOOD	FAIR	POOR
	—	5500	4500	2500	650	275

Model 38 pistols converted to H Models by Sauer factory
Currently fewer than 30 known examples in collections. Thumbsafety levers were added. Unique milling on left side of slide determines these pistols in 262xxx, 263xxx and 264xxx ranges. Includes SA der NSDAP Gruppe Thringen marked pistols.

	NIB	EXC.	V.G.	GOOD	FAIR	POOR
	—	3500	2000	1000	450	—

Model 38-H or H Model
This model has a thumbsafety on the slide, CROWN N NITRO proof, high polish blued finish, a cocking/decocking lever, double-action. Found in 7.65m/m caliber as the standard production

NIB	EXC.	V.G.	GOOD	FAIR	POOR

pistol. This model is found only with two line slide legend or logo. Type 1, variation 2.

Standard Commercial Variation

NOTE: Add $100 for factory nickel (factory chromed has not been identified); $1000 for factory engraving; $250 for exotic grip material; $500 for NIROSTA marked stainless barrel.

NIB	EXC.	V.G.	GOOD	FAIR	POOR
—	1200	900	600	300	175

SA der NSDAP Gruppe Thuringia Variation

Same as Standard above. Having SA markings on slide, with blued finish. VERY RARE.
NOTE: Add $1200 for SA marked Akah holster in excellent condition.

NIB	EXC.	V.G.	GOOD	FAIR	POOR
—	4500	3500	2500	900	400

L.M. Model

(Leicht Model-lightweight model); frame and slide made of DURAL (Duralumin), in the 264800 range, with thumb safety and regular black Bakelite grips. EXTREMELY RARE.

NIB	EXC.	V.G.	GOOD	FAIR	POOR
—	6500	5000	3000	1500	850

Flash Light Model

Only four known examples of this variation. Battery flash light attached by four screws to pistol. Carried by SS night patrol at the Reich's chancellory in Berlin. No specific markings, but known serial numbers are 266814, 266842, 266845.

NIB	EXC.	V.G.	GOOD	FAIR	POOR
—	Too Rare To Price	—	—	—	—

Police Accepted Variation

Found with Police Eagle C acceptance on left trigger guard and having Crown N proofs. RARE.

NIB	EXC.	V.G.	GOOD	FAIR	POOR
—	3000	2500	1850	500	175

TYPE TWO MODEL 38-H (H MODEL)

There are no Model 38 pistols in Type Two description, only H Model with thumbsafety. These begin at serial number 269100 and have Eagle N Nitro proofs, with blued high polish finish and black Bakelite grips. Normal caliber is 7.65mm.

H Model - Type Two

Standard Commercial

NOTE: Add $1500 boxed examples complete with factory manual, clean ring rod, all accessories, extra magazine, etc.; $250 factory nickel; $350 factory chrome; $1000 factory engraving.

NIB	EXC.	V.G.	GOOD	FAIR	POOR
1850	1200	850	600	300	200

.22 Caliber Variation

Slide and magazines marked CAL. .22 LANG. (Some with steel frame and slides; some with Dural frames and slides.) Found in 269900 range. Very Rare.

NIB	EXC.	V.G.	GOOD	FAIR	POOR
—	6000	4500	3000	1000	600

Jager Model

Special order pistol in .22-caliber. Similar in appearance to Walther's 1936 Jagerschafts pistol. Very rare.

NIB	EXC.	V.G.	GOOD	FAIR	POOR
—	6250	5000	3000	1000	400

Police Eagle C and Eagle F Acceptance Variations

First Eagle N (post January 1940) police accepted pistols. Found in 270000 to 276000 ranges. **NOTE:** Add 50 percent for E/F.

NIB	EXC.	V.G.	GOOD	FAIR	POOR
—	1250	800	600	325	200

German Military Variation

First official military accepted range of 2,000 pistols. In a range found between 271000 to 273000. Two Eagle 37 military acceptance marks found on trigger guard.

NIB	EXC.	V.G.	GOOD	FAIR	POOR
—	3850	2500	1300	700	300

Second Military Variation

Pistols found with high polish finish. Have only one Eagle 37 acceptance mark. Letter H found on all small parts.

NIB	EXC.	V.G.	GOOD	FAIR	POOR
—	1650	1450	800	400	200

Police Eagle C Acceptance

This variation includes remainder of high polish blued police accepted pistols. **NOTE:** Add $50 matching magazine; $200 both matching mags and correct police holster; $300 both matching mags and correct matching numbered police accepted and dated holster.

NIB	EXC.	V.G.	GOOD	FAIR	POOR
—	950	600	450	275	175

NIB	EXC.	V.G.	GOOD	FAIR	POOR

TYPE THREE 38-H MODEL (H MODEL)

Terminology used because the change of exterior finish of Sauer pistols. Due to urgency of the war, order was received not to polish exterior surfaces of pistols, as had been done previously. Also a change in formulation of grip's material. Later in this range there will be found stamped parts, zinc triggers and magazine bottoms, etc. used to increase pistol's production. Type Three has a full slide legend.

H Model - Type Three

Military Accepted
One Eagle 37 Waffenamt mark.

—	850	650	400	275	150

Commercial
Only Eagle N Nitro proof marks. **NOTE:** See Type Two Commercial. Prices apply here also.

1650	800	500	400	250	150

Police Accepted with the Police Eagle C Acceptance
NOTE: See Type Two Police. Prices apply here also.

—	850	650	350	250	150

TYPE FOUR 38-H MODEL (H MODEL)

Continuation of pistol as described in Type Three, except J.P. Sauer & Sohn, Suhl legend is dropped from slide and only CAL. 7.65 is found on left side. Word PATENT may or may not appear on right side. Many are found with a zinc trigger.

H Model - Type Four

Military Accepted

—	850	650	400	275	150

Commercial
Having only Eagle N Nitro proofs. **NOTE:** See Type Two Commercial info. Prices apply here also.

1650	800	600	400	250	150

Police Accepted with the Police Eagle C Acceptance
NOTE: See Type Two Price info. Prices apply here also.

—	850	650	450	300	150

Eigentum NSDAP SA Gruppe Alpenland Slide Marked Pistols
Unique pistols found in 456000 and 457000 serial number ranges. Have thumb safety levers on slides.

—	4000	3000	2000	600	400

NSDAP SA Gruppe Alpenland Slide Marked Pistols
Unique pistols found in 465000 serial number range. Have thumb safety levers on slide.

—	4000	3000	2000	600	400

Himmler Presentation Pistols
These desirable pistols have high polish finish with DEM SCHARFSCHUTZEN - H. HIMMLER on left side of slide (with no other markings) and J.P. SAUER & SON over CAL. 7.65 on right side (opposite of normal). Pistols came in imitation leather cover metal cases, with cloth interiors having a cleaning brush, extra magazine and cartridges. Very rare pistols! Extremely rare if cased! Only 12 are known presently.

40000	38500	25000	18000	5000	1500

Model 38

To speed up production even more thumb safety (Handsicherung-Hammer safety) was eliminated. Side continues to be marked only with CAL. 7,65. Frame's serial number changes from right side to left side at 472000, with overlaps up to 489000.

Military Accepted
One Eagle 37 Waffenamt mark.

—	700	500	400	250	175

Commercial
Only the Eagle N Nitro proofs. **NOTE:** See Type Two Commercial info, prices apply here also.

1400	600	475	350	250	175

	NIB	EXC.	V.G.	GOOD	FAIR	POOR

Police Accepted with Police Eagle C Acceptance

	—	700	500	400	300	200

Police Accepted with Police Eagle F Acceptance

	—	1250	800	600	325	200

TYPE FIVE MODEL 38 & H MODEL PISTOLS

Two different basic variations of Type Five Sauer pistols. Either may or may not have thumb safety lever on slide. Main criteria is whether frame is factory numbered as per normal and follows chronological sequence of those pistols in preceding model. After frames were used which were already numbered and finished upon arrival of U.S. Army, last variation came about. Neither variation has any Nitro proof marks. **NOTE:** There are some pistols which have post-war Russian Crown N Nitro proofs. Russians assembled or refurbished a very few pistols after U.S. Army left Suhl after the war. Several have been found with newly made barrels in 7.65mm, with C/N proof. Hard to find Sauer!

First Variation

Factory numbered sequential frames starting on or near serial number 506800. Slides and breech blocks may or may not match.

	—	550	450	300	225	100

Second Variation

Started with serial number 1; made from mostly rejected parts, generally have notched trigger guards, may or may not be blued, no Nitro proofs, slides may or may not have factory legends, etc. Approximately 300 assembled. Definitely rare Sauer pistols.

	—	900	650	450	300	150

SAVAGE & NORTH
Middletown, Connecticut

Figure 8 Revolver

A .36 caliber percussion revolver with a 7" octagonal barrel and 6-shot cylinder. The barrel marked "E. Savage, Middletown. CT./H.S. North. Patented June 17, 1856." The four models of this revolver are: (1) With a rounded brass frame, and the mouths of the chamber fitting into the end of the barrel breech; (2) with a rounded iron frame and a modified loading lever that is marked "H.S. North, Patented April 6, 1858" ; (3) with a flat-sided brass frame having a round recoil shield; (4) with an iron frame. Approximately 400 of these revolvers were manufactured between 1856 and 1859.

First Model

	—	—	16500	7250	1500	500

Second Model

	—	—	9900	3850	850	400

Third Model

	—	—	9900	3850	850	400

Fourth Model

	—	—	11000	4400	1000	450

SAVAGE ARMS CORPORATION
Utica, New York
Westfield, Massachusetts

Model 1895

A .303 Savage caliber lever-action rifle with a 26" or 30" barrel and 5-shot rotary magazine. Identifiable by the hole in the breechbolt. The barrel marked "Savage Repeating Arms Co. Utica, N.Y. U.S.A. Pat. Feb. 7, 1893, July 25, 1893. CAL. .303". Blued with a walnut stock. Approximately 8,000 were manufactured between 1895 and 1899. **NOTE:** For carbine version add 100 percent.

	—	6000	5000	3750	2000	900

Model 1899-A 22" Barrel Short Rifle

Chambered for .303, .30-30, .25-35, .32-40, .38-55. Serial number range from 10000 to 220000. Produced from 1899 to 1922. Same cocking indicator as the 1899-A rifle. **NOTE:** Add 50 percent for .25-35, .32-40, and .38-55 calibers.

	—	1600	100	600	300	100

NIB	EXC.	V.G.	GOOD	FAIR	POOR

Model 1899-A 26" Round Barrel Rifle

A .25-35, .30-30, .303 Savage, .32-40 or .38-55, .300 Savage caliber lever-action rifle with 26" barrel marked "Savage Arms Company, Utica, N.Y. Pat. Feb. 7, 1893, July 25.'93, Oct.3.'99 .CAL.30." Manufactured between 1899 and 1926/27. Blued with a walnut stock. Serial number range 10000 to 300000. Block cocking indicator on bolt to s/n 90000 then changed to pin indicator on tang. **NOTE:** Add 50 percent for .25-35, .32-40, and .38-55 calibers.

—	1500	1000	600	250	100

Model 1899-B 26" Octagon Barrel Rifle

In calibers .303, .30-30, .25-35, .32-40, .38-55. Manufactured between 1899 and 1915. Serial number range 10000 to 175000. Same cocking indicator as 1899-A rifle. **NOTE:** Add 50 percent for .25-35, .32-40, and .38-55 calibers.

—	1900	1300	800	350	150

Model 1899-C 26" Half Octagon Barrel Rifle

In calibers .303, .30-30, .25-35, .32-40, .38-55. Manufactured between 1899 and 1915. Serial number range 10000 to 175000. Same cocking indicator as 1899-A rifle. **NOTE:** Add 50 percent for .25-35, .32-40, and .38-55 calibers.

—	2300	1700	1100	400	150

Model 1899-D Military Musket

Chambered for .303 Savage only, with 28" barrel. Fitted with full military stocks. Produced from 1899 to 1915. Several hundred produced for Canadian Home Guard during WWI. These will have rack number on buttplate.

7500	6500	5000	3700	1000	400

Model 1899-F Saddle Ring Carbine

Fitted with 20" barrel only in calibers .303, .30-30, .25-35, .32-40, .38-55. Built from 1899 to 1919 in serial number range 19000 to 200000. Same cocking indicator as 1899-A rifle. Earliest style with barrel band is rarest variation. **NOTE:** Add 100 percent for .25-35, .32-40 and .38-55 calibers; 200 percent for barrel band carbine.

—	2400	1600	1000	700	350

Model 1899-CD Deluxe Rifle

In calibers .303, .30-30, .25-35, .32-40, .38-55. Serial number range 50000 to 175000. Built from 1905 to 1917. Same cocking indicator as the 1899-A rifle. The standard Deluxe 1899 rifle with 26" round, octagon, or half octagon barrel with pistol grip stock and checkering. Takedown barrel or short 22" barrel. **NOTE:** Add 30 percent for .25-35, .32-40, and .38-55 calibers.

—	3000	2200	1600	600	250

Model 1899-H Featherweight Rifle

Chambered for .303, .30-30, .25-35, and .22 HP Savage in 20" barrel. Serial number range 50000 to 220000. Built from 1905 to 1919. The revolutionary .22 HP cartridge was introduced in this model in 1912. Most 1899-Hs are found with takedown barrels. **NOTE:** Add 50 percent for .25-35, add 25 percent for .22HP.

—	1900	1400	700	300	100

Model 1899 .250-3000 Savage Rifle

This deluxe Model 1899 was developed to introduce the Charles Newton designed .250-3000 Savage cartridge. Fitted with a 22" featherweight takedown barrel, pistol grip, checkered perch belly stock, unique checkered trigger. Built from 1914 to 1921 in the 146500 to 237500 serial number range.

—	1800	1500	800	350	100

Model 99-B 26"/24" Standard Weight Takedown

Chambered for .303, .30-30, and .300 Savage. Serial number range 200000 to 344000. Produced from 1920 to 1934. In 1926 a new 24" barrel with ramp front sight was introduced.

—	1200	900	500	300	100

Model 99-C 22" Standard Weight Short Rifle

Chambered for .303, .30-30, and .300 Savage. Serial number range 238000 to 290000. Built from 1922 to 1926. This model looks like a shortened 26" rifle but with a heavily crowned muzzle.

—	1100	800	500	200	100

Model 99-D 22" Standard Weight Takedown Rifle

Chambered for .303, .30-30, and .300 Savage. Serial number range 238000 to 290000. Built from 1922 to 1926. Same heavily crowned muzzle as 99-C.

—	1200	900	500	200	100

NIB	EXC.	V.G.	GOOD	FAIR	POOR

Model 99-E Lightweight Rifle

Chambered for .22 HP, .30-30, .303, .250-3000, and .300 Savage. Manufactured between 1922 and 1934. Serial number range 238000 to 344000. In 1926 new ramp front sight introduced. **NOTE:** Add 25 percent for .22 Hi Power and .250-3000 calibers.

—	1450	950	600	300	100

Model 99-F Lightweight Takedown Rifle

As above, but in lightweight takedown barrels in 20", 22", and 24". Chambered for .22 HP, .30-30, .303, .250-3000, and .300 Savage.These barrels were tapered lightweight barrels. Manufactured between 1920 and 1940. Serial number range 200000 to 398000. In 1926 new ramp front sight introduced. Early versions look similar to Model 1899-H featherweight. In 1938 checkered stocks offered this option is rare. **NOTE:** Add 50 percent for .22 HP, and .250-3000. Add 75 percent for 1938 checkered stocks.

—	1700	1200	700	300	100

Model 99-G Deluxe Takedown Pistol Grip Rifle

Calibers and barrel lengths as above, with a pistol grip checkered stock. Manufactured between 1922 and 1941. Serial number range 238000 to 407000. No takedown Model 99s made after 1941. **NOTE:** Add 50 percent for .22 Hi Power and 25 percent for .250-3000.

—	1950	1400	800	300	100

Model 99-H Carbine/Barrel Band Carbine

Fitted with 20" or 22" barrels and chambered for .30-30, .303, .250-3000, and .300 Savage. serial number range 220000 to 400000. Built between 1923 and 1940. Distinctive plain stocks with no flat pads on side of buttstock. Curved carbine style butt-plate. In 1931 barrel band added to fore-end, then commonly called the "barrel band carbine." In 1935 flat pads added to buttstock sides. Also front ramp sight added. **NOTE:** Add 50 percent for 1935 barrel band carbine. Add 25 percent for .250-3000, and .300 Savage.

—	1200	800	500	200	100

Combination Cased Set .300 Savage/.410 Barrel

Fitted with 22" or 24" barrels with .410 barrels and .300 Savage in Model 99-F, 99-G, or 99-K configuration. In black fitted case. Serial number range 240000 to 350000. built from 1922 to 1934. Be aware that the barrel address on the .410 barrel matches that on the rifle barrel and that the .410 barrel takes up correctly on the receiver, and that the case fits the .410 barrel and receiver.

—	4000	2500	1500	800	300

Model 99-A 24" Featherweight Rifle

Fitted with a 24" barrel with new 1926 ramp front sight. Chambered for .303, .30-30, or .300 Savage. Serial number range 290000 to 370000. Built from 1926 to 1937. Buttplate is older 1899 crescent style.

—	900	700	5500	250	75

Model 99-K Deluxe Engraved Rifle

The premier Savage Model 99 with an engraved receiver. Fitted with a checkered pistol grip stock of select American walnut and a takedown frame. Hand honed and hand fitted. Chambered for .22 HP, .30-30, .303, .250-3000 and .300 Savage. Fitted with 22" or 24" barrels. Serial number range 285000 to 398000. Manufactured between 1926 and 1940. **NOTE:** Add 30 percent for .22 caliber Hi Power. Some of these models found with cased set with .410 barrel. Add $700 for V.G. case and barrels.

3500	3000	2500	1400	600	200

Model 99-R Heavy Stocked Rifle

This model features a heavy pistol grip checkered stock with rounded forend tip. Fitted with a 22" or 24" barrel and chambered for .250-3000, .303, .300 Savage, .308, .243, and .358 calibers. Serial number range 340000 to 1060000. Manufactured between 1932 and 1960. **NOTE:** Add 50 percent for .358 and 100 percent for rare uncataloged .30-30. Approximately 10 made for A.F. Stoeger of N.Y.C. for N.Y. State Police in 1935 in serial number range 348600. Most of these are found with Redfield No. 102 side peep sight and 1/4" rack number stamped in stock below pistol grip.

—	1300	800	550	200	100

Model 99-RS Special Sights

As above, with a Lyman aperture rear tang sight. In 1940 this was changed to a Redfield micrometer tang sight. This was the first model fitted with Savage quick release sling swivels. No .30-30 calibers made in this model. Manufactured between 1932 and 1942. **NOTE:** Add 50 percent for .358.

—	1500	1000	600	350	200

NIB	EXC.	V.G.	GOOD	FAIR	POOR

Model 99-EG Standard Weight Rifle

Produced with plain uncheckered pistol grip stock until 1940. Available in .22 Hi Power, .250 Savage, .30-30, .303 Savage. .300 Savage, .308, .243, and .358. Serial number range 350000 to 1060000. Manufactured between 1935 and 1960. **NOTE:** For pre-1940 uncheckered stocks add 20 percent. Add 100 percent for rifles chambered for .22 Hi Power and .358.

—	900	650	400	200	75

Model 99-T Deluxe Featherweight Rifle

This is the classic short barrel deluxe Model 99 with semi-beavertail fore-end and distinct long checkering pattern. Fitted with 20" or 22" barrels and chambered for .250-3000, .30-30, .303, .22 HP or .300 Savage. Serial number range 350000 to 400000. Manufactured between 1935 and 1940. **NOTE:** Add 100 percent for .22 Hi Power caliber, 20 percent for .250-3000.

2000	1750	1200	800	450	200

Model 99-F Featherweight Rifle

First Savage made with model designation visible on outside. Located at rear on right side of barrel. True featherweight with slender 22" barrel, lightweight stocks with butt end hollowed out. Chambered for .250-3000, .300 Savage, .308, .243, .284 and .358 calibers. Built from 1955 to 1973. **NOTE:** Add 75 percent for .284 and .358 calibers; 50 percent for .250 Savage.

1200	1000	800	500	250	75

Model 99-DL Deluxe Monte Carlo Rifle

Deluxe version of Model 99EG. Available in .243, .250 Savage, .300 Savage, .284, .358 and .308 calibers. Monte Carlo-style stock. Manufactured between 1960 and 1973. **NOTE:** Add 75 percent for .358 and .284 calibers.

900	800	550	350	200	100

Model 99-E Economy Rifle

Ugly duckling of Savage line. Model 99-E lacked many standard features such as left side cartridge counter, tang sight holes, walnut stocks and capped pistol grip. Fitted with 20", 22" or 24" barrels and chambered for .250-3000, .300 Savage, .243 and .308 calibers. Built from 1960 to 1984. **NOTE:** Model 99-E was last original rotary magazine. Model 99 when production discontinued in 1984.

850	750	575	375	150	50

Model 99-C Clip Magazine Rifle

Recent production model in .22-250, .243, .284 Winchester, 7mm-08 or .308 caliber, with 22" barrel and open sights. Blued, with walnut stock. Model features clip magazine and is first modification in Model 99 in 66 years. Introduced in 1965. Dropped from production and reintroduced in 1995 in .243 and .308 calibers. Approximate weight 7.75 lbs. **NOTE:** Add 50 percent for .22-250, .284 and 7mm-08.

850	550	400	250	150	50

Model 99-DE Citation Grade Rifle

Premier Savage with engraved receiver. Nickel-like finish and impressed checkering on select walnut stocks. Marked 99-M. Offered in .243, .284 and .308 calibers, with 22" barrel only. Manufactured between 1965 and 1970. **NOTE:** Add 30 percent for .284 caliber.

1750	1600	1200	700	400	200

Model 99-PE Presentation Grade Rifle

Presentation grade Model 99, with engraved receiver and hand-checkered finely figured walnut stock. Mountain lion on right side of receiver and elk on left side. Chambered for .243, .284 and .308 caliber, with 22" barrel. Manufactured between 1965 and 1970. **NOTE:** Add 30 percent for .284 caliber.

2500	2000	1500	800	500	300

Model 1895 Anniversary Edition

A .308 caliber reproduction of the Model 1895 with a 24" octagonal barrel, engraved receiver and walnut stock with a schnabel fore-end. Brass crescent buttplate, brass medallion inlaid in stock. There were 9,999 manufactured in 1970.

950	775	600	450	300	200

Model 99-A Saddle Gun

A variation of the original Model 99A with a 20" or 22" barrel. Chambered for the .243, .250 Savage, .300 Savage, .308, and .375. Serial number range in new "A" series on left side. Manufactured between 1971 and 1982. **NOTE:** Add 25 percent for .375 caliber.

1200	800	500	400	300	200

	NIB	EXC.	V.G.	GOOD	FAIR	POOR

Model 99-.358 and 99-.375 Brush Guns

Similar to the Model 99-A straight grip saddle gun, but in .358 and .375 Win. (1980) calibers. Has plain grooved fore-end, rubber recoil pad. Serial number range in the "A" series on left side. Built from 1977 to 1980. **NOTE:** Add 25 percent for .358 Win. caliber.

1200	800	500	400	300	200

Model 99-CD Deluxe Clip Model

The North American classic rifle with distinct stocks of checkered walnut with long grooved fore-end, deep shaped pistol grip, and Monte Carlo stock with cheekpiece. Fitted with 22" barrel and chambered for .250-3000, .308, or .243. Serial number range in new "A" series on left side. Built from 1975 to 1980.

1100	850	600	400	300	200

Model 99-CE (Centennial Edition)

Introduced in 1995 this limited edition rifle is chambered for the .300 Savage cartridge. Limited to 1,000 rifles with serial numbers from AS0001 to AS1000. Engraved receiver with gold inlays. Select American walnut stock with Monte Carlo comb.

1600	1300	900	750	500	250

Model 1903

A .22 caliber slide-action rifle with a 24" octagon barrel having open sights. Blued with a walnut stock. Manufactured between 1903 and 1922. Late model rifles have updated slide handle and pistol-grip stock in same style as Model 1914.

600	500	400	250	150	100

Model 1903 Gallery Model

Same general specifications as Model 1903 except for a mechanical counter attached to record shots fired.

700	600	500	350	150	100

Model 1903 Factory Engraved Models

NOTE: These models are seldom seen. Secure a qualified appraisal prior to a sale. Add premiums as shown.

Grade EF

Grade "B" checkering, fancy English walnut stock, Savage 22B front sights, and 21B rear sight. **NOTE:** Add 50 percent.

Expert Grade

Fancy American walnut stock, Grade "A" engraving, Grade "B" checkering, and standard sights. **NOTE:** Add 150 percent.

Grade GH

Plain American walnut stock, Grade "A" checkering, 22B front sight, and 21B rear sight. **NOTE:** Add 50 percent.

Gold Medal Grade

Plain American walnut stock, animal ornamentation on receiver, Grade "A" checkering, and standard sights. **NOTE:** Add 60 percent.

Model 1909

As above, with a 20" barrel. Manufactured between 1909 and 1915.

700	600	500	350	150	100

Model 1911

Produced from 1911 to 1915 in .22 short only. Bolt-action repeater. American walnut stock. Shotgun steel buttplate, bead front sight with adjustable open rear sight. Tubular magazine is loaded through buttstock and has capacity of 20 rounds. Weight is approximately 4 lbs.

—	475	425	225	125	100

Model 1912

A .22 caliber semi-automatic rifle with a 20" barrel, open sights and in takedown form. Magazine capacity is 7 rounds. Blued with a walnut stock. Manufactured between 1912 and 1916. Weight is about 4.5 lbs.

650	550	450	300	125	90

Model 6

Similar to the above, with a 24" barrel and tubular magazine. The walnut stock checkered prior to 1938 and plain after 1965.

—	350	300	200	125	50

	NIB	EXC.	V.G.	GOOD	FAIR	POOR

Model 7

As above, with a detachable magazine. Manufactured between 1938 and 1954.

	—	350	300	200	125	50

Model 1914

As above, with a 24" octagonal barrel. Manufactured between 1914 and 1926.

	—	350	300	200	125	50

Model 25

A .22 caliber slide-action rifle with a 24" octagonal barrel, open sights and tubular magazine. Blued with a plain walnut stock. Manufactured between 1925 and 1929.

	—	450	350	250	200	125

Model 29

Similar to above but with a 22" octagonal barrel, later changed to round on post-war rifles, and a checkered walnut stock, later changed to plain on post-war rifles. Manufactured between 1929 and 1967.

	—	450	325	200	150	100

Model 170

A .30-30 or .35 Remington caliber slide-action rifle with a 22" barrel and 3-shot tubular magazine. Blued with a walnut stock. Manufactured between 1970 and 1981.

	—	550	400	250	175	100

Model 1904

A .22 caliber single-shot bolt-action rifle with an 18" barrel and walnut stock. Manufactured between 1904 and 1931. After 1915 this model became known as the Model 04.

	—	200	150	100	75	50

Model 1905

As above, with a 24" barrel. Manufactured between 1905 and 1919.

	—	200	150	100	75	50

Model 1905 Style "B

Same as the Model 1905 target but with shotgun buttplate.

	—	375	300	200	150	50

Model 1905 Special Target Rifle

This model is the same as the Model 1905 Target Rifle except for hand checkered fancy American walnut stock.

	—	450	325	250	150	100

Model 19 NRA

A .22 caliber bolt-action rifle with a 25" barrel, detachable magazine and full-length military-style stock. Approximately 50,000 were manufactured total between 1919 and 1937.

	—	395	250	175	100	75

Model 19L

As above, with a Lyman receiver sight. Manufactured between 1933 and 1942.

	—	425	275	225	200	150

Model 19M

As above, with a 28" barrel fitted with telescope sight bases. Manufactured between 1933 and 1942.

	—	395	250	175	100	75

Model 19H

The Model 19 chambered for .22 Hornet. Manufactured between 1933 and 1942.

	—	600	475	350	300	200

Model 3

A .22 caliber single-shot bolt-action rifle with a 24" barrel, open sights and walnut stock. Manufactured between 1933 and 1952.

	—	200	150	100	75	50

	NIB	EXC.	V.G.	GOOD	FAIR	POOR

Model 4

Similar to the above, with a 24" barrel and 5-shot magazine. Produced from 1932 to 1964.

	—	200	150	100	75	50

Model 4M

As above, in .22 Magnum. Produced from 1960 to 1964.

	—	225	175	110	75	50

Model 5

The Model 4 with a tubular magazine. Manufactured between 1933 and 1964.

	—	200	150	100	75	50

Model 1920

A .250-3000 or .300 Savage caliber bolt-action rifle with a 22" or 24" barrel, open sights and 5-shot magazine. Blued, with a walnut stock and schnabel fore-end. Manufactured between 1920 and 1929. An improved version of this rifle was introduced in 1926 that was heavier and had a Lyman #54 peep sight.

	—	1000	600	465	300	200

Model 1922

This model is a variation of the Model 19 NRA with a sporting-style stock and schnabel fore-end. Fitted with a 23" round barrel it was chambered for the .22 caliber cartridge. This model superceded the Model 23 and looks like a Model 23 sporter. Introduced in 1922 and discontinued in 1923. Very rare.

	—	750	600	475	300	200

Model 23A

This bolt-action .22 LR rifle was introduced in 1923 and features a 5-round detachable box magazine and 23" barrel with open sights. The large loading port on the left side of the receiver permitted easy single-shot loading. The stock was plain with pistol grip and a schnabel fore-end. A varnish wood finish was applied to this model. Production stopped in 1933.

	—	350	275	150	125	100

Model 23AA

This was an improved version of the Model 23A introduced in 1933. It features better speed lock, redesigned stock with oil finish. The receiver was tapped for No. 15 Savage extension peep sight. The rifle weighs approximately 6 lbs. Production ceased in 1942.

	395	295	200	150	125	

Model 23B

Similar to the Model 23A except chambered for the .25-20 cartridge. Barrel length was 25" and forearm was a full 1.5" wide beavertail. Receiver was tapped for peep sight and magazine capacity was 4 rounds. Production on the Model 23B was from 1923 to 1940.

	—	375	325	250	200	100

Model 23C

The same configuration as the Model 23B with the exception of the caliber .32-20. Manufactured from 1923 to 1946.

	—	375	325	250	200	100

Model 23D

The same configuration as the Model 23B but chambered for the .22 Hornet cartridge. Manufactured from 1932 to 1948.

	—	375	325	250	200	100

Model 40 (Old Model)

Similar to the above but in .250-3000, .300 Savage, .30-30, and .30-06 caliber. Manufactured between 1928 and 1940.

	—	425	350	295	250	175

Model 45 Super

Similar to old Model 40, with a Lyman receiver sight and checkered walnut stock. Manufactured between 1928 and 1940.

	—	400	350	300	200	150

	NIB	EXC.	V.G.	GOOD	FAIR	POOR

Model 35

A .22 caliber bolt-action rifle with a 22" barrel, open sights and 5-shot magazine. Blued with a Monte Carlo-style hardwood stock.

	—	175	150	125	75	50

Model 46

As above with a tubular magazine. Manufactured between 1969 and 1973.

	—	175	150	125	75	50

Model 340

A .22 Hornet, .222 Remington, .223, or .30-30 caliber bolt-action rifle with a 22" or 24" barrel, open sights and 4- or 5-shot magazine. Blued, with a plain walnut stock. Manufactured between 1950 and 1985.

	—	375	325	250	200	100

Model 342

As above, but in .22 Hornet caliber. Manufactured between 1950 and 1955.

	—	375	325	250	200	100

MODEL 110 SERIES

Model 110 Sporter

A bolt-action rifle manufactured in a variety of calibers with a 22" barrel, open sights and 4-shot magazine. Blued with a walnut stock. Manufactured between 1958 and 1963.

400	325	250	175	125	100

Model 110-M

Similar to the above, in 7mm Magnum to .338 Winchester Magnum. Manufactured between 1963 and 1969.

400	325	275	200	150	125

Model 110-D

Similar to the Model 110 in .22-250 to .338 Winchester Magnum caliber with a detachable magazine. Manufactured between 1966 and 1988.

400	300	250	200	150	100

Model 110-P Premier Grade

As above, with a finely figured walnut stock, rosewood fore-end tip and pistol grip cap. Manufactured between 1964 and 1970.

650	575	450	325	250	200

Model 110-PE

As above, with an engraved receiver, magazine floorplate and trigger guard. Manufactured between 1968 and 1970.

900	800	700	500	400	300

Model 110-F

DuPont Rynite stock and sights. Discontinued.

450	400	350	300	250	200

Model 110-FX

As above without sights. Discontinued.

400	350	300	250	200	150

Model 110-FP

Composite stock and 24" heavy barrel. In 2003 the Savage AccuTrigger was added to this model. Discontinued.

600	450	325	225	150	150

Model 110-G

Checkered hardwood stock and sights. Discontinued.

425	325	275	225	175	125

Model 110-GX

As above without sights. Discontinued.

400	300	250	200	150	100

NIB	EXC.	V.G.	GOOD	FAIR	POOR

Model 110-CY

A compact version of the Model 110 series. Shorter length of pull on walnut stock and 22" barrel. Overall length is 42-1/2". Weight is about 6-1/2 lbs. Chambered in .223, .243, .270, .300 Savage, and .308 calibers. Discontinued.

NIB	EXC.	V.G.	GOOD	FAIR	POOR
400	300	250	200	150	100

Model 110-FP Tactical

Offered in calibers from .223 Rem. to .300 Win. Mag this bolt-action rifle has a 24" heavy barrel with recessed muzzle. The synthetic stock is black as are all other surfaces. Available in both right- and left-hand versions. Weight is approximately 8.5 lbs. Discontinued.

NIB	EXC.	V.G.	GOOD	FAIR	POOR
600	450	325	225	150	150

Model 110-FP Duty

Introduced in 2002 this model is chambered for the .308 cartridge and features a 24" free-floating barrel with open sights. Black synthetic stock. Third swivel stud for bipod. Matte blue finish. Magazine capacity is 4 rounds. Weight is about 8.5 lbs. Discontinued.

NIB	EXC.	V.G.	GOOD	FAIR	POOR
600	450	300	250	200	100

Model 110-FP-LE1

Similar to the Model 110FP-Duty (.308) but with a 20" barrel. No sights. Weight is about 8.25 lbs. Introduced in 2002. Discontinued.

NIB	EXC.	V.G.	GOOD	FAIR	POOR
500	375	275	225	175	100

Model 110-FP-LE2

Same as the model above but fitted with a 26" barrel. Weight is about 8.75 lbs. Introduced in 2002. Discontinued.

NIB	EXC.	V.G.	GOOD	FAIR	POOR
500	375	275	225	175	100

Model 110-Fiftieth Anniversary

Short-action rifle commemorating the 50th anniversary of the Model 10. Chambered in .300 Savage with 22-inch barrel. 1000 numbered rifles, high-luster blued barrel and action, unique checkering pattern on select walnut stock, high-grade hinged floorplate, Scroll pattern on receiver, 24-karat gold plated double barrel bands, 24-karat gold plated AccuTrigger, embossed recoil pad.

NIB	EXC.	V.G.	GOOD	FAIR	POOR
1000	750	600	475	300	200

Savage Axis Series

Comes in long or short action, offered in eight cartridge choices from .223 Remington to .30-06 Springfield. Stainless action, natural color. Detachable box magazine. Right-hand action only. Synthetic stock with camo or black matte finish. Drilled and tapped for scope mounts. Also available with 3-9x40 mounted scope. Previously called "The Edge". **NOTE:** Add 15 percent for camo stock, 20 percent for scope.

NIB	EXC.	V.G.	GOOD	FAIR	POOR
300	265	225	200	150	100

110 BA Law Enforcement Rifle

Bolt action rifle chambered .300 Win. Mag. And .338 Lapua Mag. Features include aluminum stock that features Savage's innovative three-dimensional bedding system; interchangeable buttstocks and pistol grips; three-sided accessory rail; 5-round detachable magazine; high-efficiency muzzle-brake; Magpul PRS adjustable stock; 26-inch carbon steel barrel.

NIB	EXC.	V.G.	GOOD	FAIR	POOR
1900	1650	1400	1100	700	300

MODEL 111 SERIES

Model 111 Classic Hunter Series

All models under this series are fitted with a classic American designed straight comb stock with pistol grip. Chambered in 13 different calibers from .223 Rem. to the .338 Win. Mag. Weights vary with caliber and stock type but range from 6-3/8 to 7 lbs. Models are fitted with a detachable or internal magazine. All Hunter series rifles are drilled and tapped for scope mounts.

Model 111G

Top loading with walnut stock with recoil pad. chambered for the .25-06, .270, .30-06, 7mm Rem. Mag., or the .300 Win. Mag. Fitted with 22" or 24" barrel depending on caliber with iron sights. Weight is about 7 lbs.

NIB	EXC.	V.G.	GOOD	FAIR	POOR
495	375	275	200	150	100

	NIB	EXC.	V.G.	GOOD	FAIR	POOR

Model 111GCNS

This is a long action model as above with 22" or 24" barrel depending on caliber with no sights. Introduced in 2005.

	515	400	325	250	175	100

Model 111GC

Detachable magazine with walnut stock and recoil pad. Discontinued.

	450	350	300	250	200	150

Model 111GL

Same as the Model 111G model but with left hand action.

	485	350	250	200	150	100

Model 111F

Top loading with graphite stock. Chambered for the .25-06, .270, .30-06, 7mm Rem. Mag., .300 Win. Mag., and the .338 Win. Mag. cartridges. Fitted with either a 22" or 24" barrel depending on caliber with iron sights. Black synthetic stock. Weight is about 6.75 lbs. depending on caliber.

	485	350	250	200	150	100

Model 111FL

As above but with left hand action.

	485	350	250	200	150	100

Model 111FC

Detachable magazine with graphite stock. Discontinued.

	450	350	300	250	200	150

Model 111FCNS

Introduced in 2005 this model is chambered for the .25-06, .270, .30-06, 7mm Rem. Mag., .300 Win. Mag., and the .338 Win. Mag calibers. Fitted with 22" or 24" barrel with no sights. Black synthetic stock. Weight is about 6.75 lbs. depending on caliber.

	505	375	275	—	—	—

Model 111FXP3

Top loading with graphite stock and 3x9 scope, rings, and bases, and sling.

	515	400	350	300	200	150

Model 111FCXP3

Same as above but detachable magazine.

	515	400	350	300	200	150

Model 111FAK

Blued steel barrel, composite stock, muzzlebrake. Discontinued.

	450	350	300	250	200	150

MODEL 112 SERIES

Model 112BT / 112BT-S (Long Action)

Introduced for the first time in 1994 this model is a competition grade rifle. Chambered for the .223 Rem. and the .308 Win. it features a 26" heavy stainless steel barrel fitted to an alloy steel receiver. In 1995 the .300 Win. Magnum was added to the line referred to as the Model 112BT-S. The barrel finish is black. The stock is laminated with ambidextrous palm swell and adjustable cheek rest. Weight is about 11 lbs.

	1025	850	700	500	300	250

Model 112 Series Varmint Rifles

This series of varmint rifles features 26" barrels. Offered with either composite or laminated wood stocks all Model 112s are top loading and all are drilled and tapped for scope mounting. Available in .223, .22-250, and .220 Swift the BV configuration weighs about 10-1/2 lbs. while the FV configuration weighs about 9 lbs.

Model 112BVSS (Long Action)

This model has a laminated wood stock with high comb and ambidextrous palm swell. It is fitted with a stainless steel barrel, bolt and trigger guard. In 1996 the .300 Win. Mag., 7mm Rem. Mag., .308 Win., .30-06, and .25-06 was added to this model.

	720	550	400	275	200	150

	NIB	EXC.	V.G.	GOOD	FAIR	POOR

Model 112BVSS-S

Same as above but single-shot.

	600	450	325	225	150	150

Model 112FVSS

This version also is fitted with a stainless steel barrel and a composite stock This version was fitted with a stainless steel "fluted" barrel in 1995. Several new calibers were added as well: 300 Win. Mag., 7mm Rem. Mag., .25-06 Rem. In 2003 the Savage AccuTrigger was added to this model.

	475	400	350	300	200	150

Model 112FVSS-S

This is a single-shot version of the above model.

	475	400	350	300	200	150

Model 112FV

This is similar to the model above but with a blued barrel.

	375	300	250	200	150	100

Model 112BT—Competition Grade

This model was introduced in 1996. It is a competition rifle. It features a 26" blackened stainless steel barrel and custom target style laminated stock with adjustable cheek rest. Chambered for .223 or .308 cartridges. Weight is approximately 11 lbs. The barrel is pillar bedded.

	950	850	700	500	300	250

MODEL 114 SERIES

Model 114C—Classic

This model, introduced in 2000, features a select grade oil finished walnut stock with cut checkering. No sights. Chambered for .270 and .30-06 with 22" barrel, and 7mm Mag. and .300 Win. Mag with 24" barrel.

	615	450	325	225	—	—

Model 114CE—Classic European

Introduced in 1996 this rifle is chambered for the .270 Win., .30-06, 7mm Rem. Mag., and .300 Win. Mag. Barrel lengths are 22" or 24" depending on caliber. It has an oil-finished stock with skip line checkering and cheekpiece. The fore-end tip is a schnabel type. Rubber recoil pad and pistol grip cap are standard. High luster blue finish. Approximate weight is 7.12 lbs. Discontinued.

	550	475	400	350	300	150

Model 114CU

This model has a select grade walnut oil finished stock. The finish is a high polish blue and the bolt has a laser etched Savage logo. A detachable magazine is standard. The receiver is drilled and tapped for a scope mount. Offered in .270, .30-06, 7mm Rem. Mag., and .300 Win. Mag. Weights are about 7-1/8 lbs. Discontinued.

	500	425	325	250	200	150

Model 114U—Ultra

Introduced in 1999 this model features a high gloss walnut stock with custom checkering. Blued finish is high luster with a laser-etched Savage logo on the bolt body. Chambered for the .270 Win., .30-06, 7mm-08 Rem., and .300 Win. Mag cartridges. Barrel length is 22" and 24" depending on caliber. Weight is about 7 lbs.

	500	425	325	250	200	150

MODEL 116 SERIES

This series of rifles feature graphite stocks and stainless steel barreled actions. An adjustable muzzlebrake is also included. All rifles in the 116 series are drilled and tapped for scope mounts.

Model 116FCSAK (Long Action)

Features a detachable box magazine. The 22" barrel is fluted. Offered in .270, .30-06, 7mm Rem. Mag., .300 Win. Mag., and .338 Win. Mag. Weighs about 6-1/2 lbs.

	660	500	375	250	175	175

Model 116FSAK (Long Action)

Same as model above but with on-off choice for muzzlebrake given to shooter. AccuTrigger added in 2004.

	600	450	325	225	175	175

	NIB	EXC.	V.G.	GOOD	FAIR	POOR

Model 116BSS

Introduced in 2001 this model features a laminated stock. It is chambered for the .270 Win., .30-06, 7mm Rem. Mag., .300 Win. Mag., and the .300 Rem. Ultra Mag. cartridges. Fitted with either a 24" or 26" stainless steel barrel depending on caliber. No sights. Weight is about 7.5 lbs. depending on caliber. Discontinued.

625	500	365	225	175	175

Model 116FSS (Long Action)

This is the standard configuration for the 116 series. This model features a top-loading action with 22" or 24" barrel depending on caliber. There is no muzzlebrake fitted to this model. Weight is approximately 6-3/4 lbs. Offered in 7 calibers from .223 to .338 Win. Mag. AccuTrigger added in 2004.

550	475	375	300	200	150

Model 116FCS

Same as above but with stainless steel removable box magazine.

550	475	375	300	200	150

Model 116FSK—Kodiak (Long Action)

This model features a top loading action with a 22" barrel with muzzlebrake. Weight is approximately 7.25 lbs.

575	495	385	300	200	150

Model 116SE—Safari Express

Introduced in 1994 this rifle features select grade walnut stock with ebony tip and deluxe checkering. Barrel and action are stainless steel with adjustable muzzlebrake. Offered in .300 Win. Mag., .338 Win. Mag., and .458 calibers. In 1995 the .425 Express cartridge was added. In 2000 this model had a stainless steel action and barrel. Weight is approximately 8-1/2 lbs. Discontinued.

1100	950	775	600	475	300

Model 116US

Introduced in 1995 this model features a stainless steel action and barrel with a high gloss American walnut stock with ebony tip and custom checkering. Offered in .270 Win., .30-06, 7mm Rem. Mag., and .300 Win. Mag. Barrel is 22" on the two smaller calibers and 24" on the magnum calibers. Discontinued.

600	500	400	300	250	200

MODEL 12 SERIES VARMINT

Introduced in 1998 this series features a short action heavy barrel line of rifles designed for long-range shooting.

Model 12BVSS

This model features a 26" fluted stainless steel barrel with recessed crown and a brown laminated stock with beavertail fore-end. Chambered for .223, .22-250, and .308. Magazine capacity is 4 rounds. Weight is approximately 9.5 lbs. Introduced in 1998. In 2003 the Savage AccuTrigger was added to this model.

720	550	400	275	200	100

Model 12BVSS-S

Same as above but in a single-shot version chambered for .223 and .22-250. Weight is 9 lbs. In 2003 the Savage AccuTrigger was added to this model.

720	550	400	275	200	150

Model 12BVSS-SXP

Introduced in 2003 this single-shot model is chambered for the .223 Rem. or .22-250 Rem. cartridge. Fitted with a 26" stainless steel fluted barrel. Savage AccuTrigger. Stock is a target-style heavy prone laminate. Weight is about 12 lbs.

675	525	400	275	200	150

Model 12BTCSS

Similar to Model 12BVSS but with laminated thumbhole Monte Carlo stock with short action and detachable box magazine.

725	550	400	275	200	100

NIB	EXC.	V.G.	GOOD	FAIR	POOR

Model 12FVSS

This model has a 26" stainless steel fluted barrel and a synthetic stock. Offered in .223, .22-250, and .308 calibers. Weight is about 9 lbs. Introduced in 1998. A left-hand version is also offered. In 2003 the Savage AccuTrigger was added to this model.

600	500	375	250	200	100

Model 12FVSS-S

Same as above but in a single-shot configuration chambered for .223 or .22-250. Weight is about 9 lbs. In 2003 the Savage AccuTrigger was added to this model. Discontinued.

550	450	325	225	175	100

Model 12FV (Short Action)

This model is similar to the other 12 Series rifles but with blued actions and 26" barrels that are nonfluted. Synthetic stock. Chambered for .223 or .22-250. Weight is about 9 lbs. Introduced in 1998. In 2003 the Savage AccuTrigger was added to this model.

575	495	385	300	200	150

Model 12FLV

As above but with left hand action. Introduced in 2005.

575	495	385	300	200	150

Model 12VSS—Varminter (Short Action)

Introduced in 2000 this model features a Choate adjustable black synthetic stock. A heavy fluted stainless steel barrel. Box magazine holds 4 rounds. Chambered for .223 or .22-250 cartridges. Weight is approximately 15 lbs. In 2003 the Savage AccuTrigger was added to this model.

700	525	375	275	200	100

Model 12 Varminter Low Profile

Introduced in 2004 this model is chambered for the .223 Rem. or .22-250 cartridge and fitted with a 26" heavy fluted stainless steel barrel with no sights. Low-profile laminated stock with extra wide beavertail forearm. Adjustable trigger. Available as a repeater or single shot. Weight is about 10 lbs.

600	500	375	250	200	100

Model 12 LRPV Long Range Precision Varminter

Similar to Model 12 FVSS but with 30" stainless bull barrel and various accurizing refinements. Chambered in .204 Ruger, .223 Remington and .22-250. Introduced in 2007. Available in single shot and 4+1 repeating versions.

850	700	575	425	300	150

Model 12 Varminter Low Profile

Available in single shot and 4+1 repeating versions. Chambered in .22 Hornet, .204, .223, .22-250 and .243. Laminated stock, fluted 26-inch barrel. Left hand version available.

950	800	650	500	350	175

12 FCV Varmint Rifle

The new model 12 FCV varmint rifle includes the AccuStock with beavertail fore-end, AccuTrigger, detachable box magazine and a heavy fluted barrel.

675	600	525	450	300	150

Model 12 F-Class Target Rifle

International-class target rifle chambered in .6.5x284 Norma. Ventilated fore-end, laminated "under-hold" target stock, oversize bolt knob, AccuTrigger, 30" stainless barrel. Also available in Model 12F/TR version with conventional buttstock and elevated cheekpiece. Introduced in 2007.

1200	1000	750	600	475	200

Model 12 Long Range Precision

Target series rifle with target style AccuTrigger, HS Precision fiberglass matte black stock. Fluted barrel 26" long. Detachable magazine with 4-round capacity. Weight is 11 pounds, overall length 46.25". Chambered in .243 winchester, .260 Remington or 6.5 Creedmoor.

925	825	700	550	400	250

Model 12 Palma

Target rifle designed for Palma Trophy Match competition in .308 Win. caliber. Single shot with 30" stainless steel heavy barrel, laminated adjustable stock and Savage AccuTrigger.

1800	1525	1250	900	500	250

	NIB	EXC.	V.G.	GOOD	FAIR	POOR

MODEL 40 VARMINT HUNTER

Model 40 Varmint Hunter

This model, introduced in 2004, is chambered for the .22 Hornet or .223 Rem. cartridge. Fitted with a 24" heavy barrel with no sights. Laminated stock with wide beavertail forearm. Blued. Single shot. Weight is about 7.75 lbs. **NOTE:** Add $30 for .223 Rem. model.

400	300	250	200	150	100

MODEL 10 SERIES

Model 10FP—Tactical (Short Action)

This is a short action model chambered for the .223 or .308 calibers. Fitted with a 24" barrel. Black synthetic stock. Drilled and tapped for scope mount. Weight is approximately 8 lbs. Introduced in 1998. In 2003 the Savage AccuTrigger was added to this model. Premium for Choate or McMillan stock.

545	450	325	225	150	100

Model 10FLP

Same as above but in left-hand. In 2003 the Savage AccuTrigger was added to this model.

550	450	325	225	150	100

Model 10FM—Sierra

This model features a 20" barrel chambered for .223, .243, or .308 calibers. In 2002 the .300 WSM caliber was added. Black synthetic stock. Magazine capacity is 4 rounds. Weight is approximately 6 lbs. Introduced in 1998. Discontinued.

500	400	300	150	125	100

Model 10FCM—Sierra

Introduced in 2005 this model features a 20" light barrel with detachable magazine. Chambered for the .243, 7mm-08 Rem., .308, .270, and .300 WSM calibers. Black synthetic stock. Weight is about 6.25 lbs.

550	450	325	225	150	100

Model 10FCM—Scout Rifle

Chambered for the 7mm-08 Rem. or .308 Win. cartridge this model is fitted with a 20" barrel, removable ghost ring rear sight, one-piece scope mount, and other special features. Weight is about 6.2 lbs. Introduced in 1999. Discontinued in 2005 but reintroduced in 2007.

545	450	325	225	150	100

Model 10GY Youth

This model is similar to the Model 10FM but features a shortened hardwood stock. It is fitted with a 22" barrel and has open sights. It is chambered for .223, .243, or .308 calibers. Weight is about 6.25 lbs. Introduced in 1998.

450	325	225	165	125	100

Model 10 Predator Hunter

Similar to Model 110FCM but with overall camo finish, 22" medium-contour barrel, and AccuTrigger. Chambered in .204 Ruger, .22-250 and .223. Introduced in 2007. **NOTE:** The Savage Predator line of rifles now includes a version with the new AccuStock Savage launched in 2009. This version has the AccuStock, AccuTrigger, detachable box magazine and a medium-contour fluted barrel. The stock is finished in Realtree Advantage Max 1 and the metal is matte black. MSRP is $945.

600	475	350	275	200	100

Model 10XP Predator

Package rifle with factory-mounted scope, entirely covered in camo finish. 22-inch barrel, chambered in .204, .223 and .22-250. Introduced in 2008.

650	500	395	300	225	125

Model 10XP Predator Hunter Bolt-Action Rifle Package

Bolt-action rifle similar to Model 10 but chambered in .223, .204, .22-250 or .243 Win. Includes 4-12x40 scope, 22" barrel, Accu-Trigger, choice of Realtree Snow or Mossy Oak Brush camo overall.

725	575	425	325	250	150

NIB	EXC.	V.G.	GOOD	FAIR	POOR

LAW ENFORCEMENT SERIES

Model 10FP-LE1

Chambered for the .308 Win. cartridge and fitted with a 20" heavy barrel with no sights. Black synthetic stock. AccuTrigger. Weight is about 8.25 lbs. Introduced in 2003.

550	450	325	225	150	100

Model 10FP-LE1A

As above but chambered for the .223 Rem. cartridge as well as the .308. Black synthetic Choate adjustable stock with accessory rail. Weight is about 10.75 lbs. Introduced in 2003.

650	500	395	300	225	125

Model 10FP-LE2B

This bolt-action model is chambered for the .308 Win. cartridge and fitted with a McMillan fiberglass tactical stock. Barrel is 26" with no sights. AccuTrigger. Matte blue finish. Weight is about 10 lbs. Introduced in 2003.

800	675	525	400	300	175

Model 10FP-LE2

Introduced in 2003 this model features a 26" barrel chambered for the .308 Win. cartridge and fitted with a black synthetic stock. AccuTrigger. Weight is about 8.75 lbs.

650	500	395	300	225	125

Model 10FP-LE2A

This model is chambered for the .223 or .308 cartridge and fitted with a 26" heavy barrel with no sights. Black synthetic Choate adjustable stock with accessory rail. Weight is about 11.25 lbs. Introduced in 2003.

725	575	425	325	250	150

Model 10FPXP-LEA

This item is a package of both rifle and scope with accessories. Features Model 10FP, with 26" barrel and black synthetic stock. Leupold 3.5-10x40 black matte scope, with Mil Dot scope covers and one-piece base. Harris bipod and heavy duty aluminum case. Weighs about 10.5 lbs. Introduced in 2003.

1950	1450	1100	700	450	300

Model 10FPXP-LE

As above, with Choate adjustable stock and accessory rail. Weighs about 11.25 lbs. Introduced in 2003.

1805	1350	1000	600	350	200

Model 10FCP-HS Precision

Similar to Model 110FP-LE1 but with one-piece HS Precision synthetic target stock and detachable box magazine. Introduced in 2007.

650	500	395	300	225	125

Model 10FCP Choate

Similar to Model 10FP-LE1 but with Choate synthetic stock. Introduced in 2007.

675	535	395	300	225	125

Model 10FCP McMillan

Similar to Model 10FP-LE1 but with synthetic McMillan precision stock. Introduced in 2007.

1100	900	725	575	400	200

Model 10FPXP-HS Precision

Similar to Model 10FPXP-LEA but with HS Precision Tactical Stock. Introduced 2006.

1725	1500	1250	800	600	300

Model 10FP-HS

Similar to Model 10FP-LE1 but with HS Precision Tactical stock. Introduced 2006.

950	800	625	475	300	200

Model 10 Precision Carbine

Similar to Model 10 but with 20" medium contour barrel, synthetic camo Accu-Stock. Chambered in .223/.308.

800	675	525	400	300	175

	NIB	EXC.	V.G.	GOOD	FAIR	POOR

Model 10FLCP

Similar to Model 10 FCP but in left-hand configuration, with standard stock or Accu-Stock.

	NIB	EXC.	V.G.	GOOD	FAIR	POOR
	800	675	525	400	300	175

Model 10 BAS Law Enforcement Bolt-Action Rifle

Bolt-action repeater based on Model 10 action but with 24" fluted heavy barrel with muzzle brake, M4-style collapsible buttstock, pistolgrip with palm swell, all-aluminum Accustock, picatinny rail for mounting optics. Chambered in .308 Winchester.

	NIB	EXC.	V.G.	GOOD	FAIR	POOR
	1600	1350	1000	750	500	300

Model 10 BAT-S

Similar to above but with multi-adjustable buttstock.

	NIB	EXC.	V.G.	GOOD	FAIR	POOR
	1700	1400	1075	800	550	325

MODEL 10 SERIES MUZZLELOADER

Model 10ML-II

This model is fitted with a .50 caliber 24" barrel with adjustable sights. Synthetic stock. Blued finish. Weight is about 7.75 lbs.

	NIB	EXC.	V.G.	GOOD	FAIR	POOR
	530	375	300	200	150	100

Model 10MLSS-II

As above in stainless steel.

	NIB	EXC.	V.G.	GOOD	FAIR	POOR
	590	375	325	200	150	100

Model 10ML-II Camo

This model, introduced in 2002, has a camo stock finish with blued barrel and action.

	NIB	EXC.	V.G.	GOOD	FAIR	POOR
	570	425	300	200	150	100

Model 10MLSS-II Camo

This model has a camo stock finish with stainless steel barrel and action. Introduced in 2002.

	NIB	EXC.	V.G.	GOOD	FAIR	POOR
	625	475	350	200	150	100

Model 10MLBSS-II

This model features a brown laminate stock with stainless steel action and barrel. Weight is 8.75 lbs. Introduced in 2002.

	NIB	EXC.	V.G.	GOOD	FAIR	POOR
	665	500	375	200	150	100

Model 10ML-IIXP

Introduced in 2002 this model has a blued action and barrel with a synthetic stock. Fitted with a 3-9x40mm scope. Weight is 9.25 lbs.

	NIB	EXC.	V.G.	GOOD	FAIR	POOR
	570	425	300	200	150	100

Model 10MLSS-IIXP

Same as above but with stainless steel barrel and action.

	NIB	EXC.	V.G.	GOOD	FAIR	POOR
	625	475	350	200	150	100

MODEL 11 SERIES

Model 11F

This model features a short action chambered for the .223, .22-250, .243, or .308 calibers. Barrel lengths are 22" with open sights. Black synthetic stock. Weight is approximately 6.75 lbs. Introduced in 1998.

	NIB	EXC.	V.G.	GOOD	FAIR	POOR
	485	350	250	175	125	100

Model 11FCNS

Introduced in 2005 this model is chambered for the .22-250, .243, 7mm-08, .308, .270 WSM, .7mm WSN, and the .300 WSM cartridges. Barrel length is 22" or 24" depending on caliber without sights. Detachable box magazine. Black synthetic stock. Weight is about 6.5 lbs. depending on caliber.

	NIB	EXC.	V.G.	GOOD	FAIR	POOR
	500	375	250	175	125	100

Model 11 Lightweight Hunter

Chambered for five standard cartridges plus 6.5 Creedmoor. Lightweight at 5-1/2 pounds with a satin-finished American walnut wood stock. AccuTrigger, detachable box magazine, matte blue barrel and action with spiral fluted bolt. Barrel length is 20-inches.

	NIB	EXC.	V.G.	GOOD	FAIR	POOR
	750	650	500	400	250	150

	NIB	EXC.	V.G.	GOOD	FAIR	POOR

Model 11G

Chambered for .223, .243, .22-250, or .308 calibers and fitted with a 22" barrel. Wood stock has fancy checkering pattern, black recoil pad, and a gold medallion. Fitted with open sights. Weight is about 6.75 lbs. Introduced in 1998.

500	375	250	175	125	100

Model 11BTH

Laminated, thumbhole-stock version of the Model 11 chambered in .204, .223, .22-250 and .22 Hornet. 22-inch blued barrel.

625	475	350	200	150	100

Model 11GCNS

This model, introduced in 2005, is chambered for the .22-250, .243, 7mm-08, .308, .270 WSM, 7mm WSM, and the .300 WSM cartridges. Fitted with a 22" or 24" barrel depending on caliber without sights. Checkered walnut stock. Detachable box magazine. Weight is about 6.75 lbs. depending on caliber.

525	400	300	200	150	100

Model 11FYCAK

Short-action youth model chambered in .243, 7mm-08, and .308. Barrel: 22-inch blued with muzzlebrake, no sights. Stock: Black composite. Weight 6.5 lbs.; 41.5-inch overall length. Introduced 2006.

515	400	300	200	125	100

Model 111FYCAK

Similar to Model 11FYCAK but long-action chambered for .25-06, .270 and .30-06. Introduced 2006.

515	400	300	200	125	100

Model 11BTH

Laminated, thumbhole-stock version of the Model 11 chambered in .204, .223, .22-250 and .22 Hornet. 22-inch blued barrel.

625	475	350	200	150	100

Model 111FHNS

Similar to Model 111FCNS but with hinged floorplate. Introduced 2006.

515	400	300	200	125	100

Model 11FCXP3

Similar to Model 111FCXP3 but in short-action. Introduced 2006.

515	400	300	200	125	100

Model 11FYCXP3

Similar to Model 11FCXP3 but in youth version chambered in .243 Win.

450	325	250	175	150	100

MODEL 14 SERIES

Model 14 Classic

Short-action chambered for .22-250, .243, .270 WSM, 7mm-08, .300 WSM and .308. Barrel: 22-inch or 24-inch polished blue without sights. Stock: Select lacquered walnut with contrasting forend. Introduced 2006. Also available in American Classic version with optional left hand action.

600	500	400	300	200	100

Model 14 Left Hand

Similar to above but in left hand and chambered in .250 Savage and .300 Savage only. Suggested retail price: $779.

Model 114 Classic

Similar to Model 14 Classic but long-action chambered for .270, 7mm RM and .300 WM. Introduced 2006. Also available in American Classic version with optional left hand action.

625	475	350	200	150	100

Model 14 Euro Classic

Similar to Model 14 Classic but with iron sights. Introduced 2006.

625	475	350	200	150	100

	NIB	EXC.	V.G.	GOOD	FAIR	POOR

Model 114 Euro Classic

Similar to Model 114 Classic but with iron sights. Introduced 2006.

	625	475	350	200	150	100

Model 14 / 114 American Classic Stainless

Traditional design has an oil-finished American walnut stock featuring wrap-around checkering, a back fore-end tip and no Monte-Carlo. Available in short and long-action versions. Short action is chambered for .243 or .308 Win., long action in .270 Winchester, .30-06 and 7mm Rem. Magnum, all with a 22-inch barrel. Introduced in 2011.

	825	750	650	500	350	150

MODEL 16 SERIES

Model 16FSS

This is a short action with a top-loading design and a magazine capacity of 4 rounds. Chambered for the .223, .243, or .308 calibers. Fitted with a 22" stainless steel barrel. Black synthetic stock. Introduced in 1998.

	550	425	325	250	200	100

Model 16FLSS

Same as above but with left-hand action.

	550	425	325	250	200	100

Model 16FCSAK

Introduced in 2005 this model is chambered for the .243, 7mm-08 Rem., .308, .270 WSM, 7mm WSM, and the .300 WSM cartridges. Fitted with a 22" or 24" barrel depending on caliber. Detachable box magazine. Black synthetic stock. Weights are between 7.75 and 7.25 lbs. depending on caliber.

	660	500	400	300	200	100

Model 16FCSS

This model is chambered for the .22-250, .243, 7mm-08 Rem., .308, .270 WSM, 7mm WSM, and the .300 WSM cartridges. Fitted with a 22" or 24" depending on caliber. Detachable box magazine. Black synthetic stock. Weight is about 6.5 lbs. depending on caliber. Introduced in 2005.

	570	425	375	250	175	125

Model 16BSS

Introduced in 2002 this model features a shot action chambered for the 7mm RSUM, .300 RSUM, and the .300 WSM cartridges. Fitted with a 24" stainless steel barrel drilled and tapped for scope mounts. Laminated stock with cut checkering. Weight is about 7.75 lbs. Discontinued.

	640	475	400	300	200	100

Model 16FHSAK

Similar to Model 116FHSAK but short-action only. Introduced 2006.

	600	475	350	200	150	100

Model 16FHSS

Similar to Model 16FSS but with hinged floorplate. Introduced 2006.

	600	475	350	200	150	100

Long Range Precision Varminter

Single-shot bolt action chambered in .204 Ruger, .223 or .22-250. Features include AccuTrigger and oversized bolt handle. Composite stock, sightless stainless steel fluted barrel. Weight: 11.25 lbs. Introduced 2006. about 6.5 lbs. depending on caliber. Introduced in 2005.

	900	750	600	450	300	200

Model 112 Varmint, Low Profile

Long-action bolt rifle chambered for .25-06 (4) and .300 WM (3). Stock: Brown laminated with recoil pad. Barrel: 26-inch sightless stainless steel bull. Weight: 11.25 lbs.

	600	475	350	200	150	100

Model 25 Lightweight Varminter

Short-action rifle chambered in .204 and .223. Medium-contour fluted barrel with recessed target crown, free-floating sleeved barrel, dual pillar bedding, three locking lugs, 60-degree bolt lift, AccuTrigger adjustable from 2.5 to 3.25 lbs., detachable box magazine. Weight 8.25 lbs.

	575	450	325	250	150	100

	NIB	EXC.	V.G.	GOOD	FAIR	POOR

Model 25 Lightweight Varminter Thumbhole

Similar to above but with thumbhole stock.

	NIB	EXC.	V.G.	GOOD	FAIR	POOR
	650	525	400	325	275	125

Model 25 Classic Sporter

Short-action rifle chambered in .204 and .223. Free-floating sleeved barrel, Dual pillar bedding, three locking lugs, 60-degree bolt lift, AccuTrigger adjustable from 2.5 to 3.25 lbs., Detachable box magazine. Satin lacquer American walnut stock with contrasting forend tip and wraparound checkering.

	600	475	350	200	150	100

Model 25 Walking Varminter

Chambered for .204 Ruger, .22 Hornet, .222 Remington, .223 Remington and 5.7x28mm. Features a 22-inch barrel sleeved for rigidity. Triple pillar bedding and Weaver scope bases. Has a three-lug bolt with a 60-degree throw to allow mounting of a large diameter. AccuTrigger is standard, center feed detachable magazine and synthetic stock.

	475	425	350	250	200	150

Savage Edge Bolt Action Rifle

Entry-level bolt-action repeating rifle chambered in .223, .22-250, .243 Win., 7mm-08, .308 Win., .25-06, .270 Win., and .30-06. Features include 22-inch matte black barrel, synthetic black stock, 4-round capacity; detachable box magazine, drilled and tapped for scope mounts. Also available in camo finish (Edge Camo); XP variation (with 3x9 scope); and Camo XP (with camo finish and scope). In 2011 the name of this model was changed to the Axis. **NOTE:** Add 15 percent for camo stock, 20 percent for scope.

	300	265	225	200	150	100

RIMFIRE RIFLES

NOTE: As of 2006, virtually all Savage rimfire rifles (with the exception of the 30G and semi-autos) were equipped with AccuTrigger as a standard feature.

Model 60

A .22 caliber semi-automatic rifle with a 20" barrel, open sights, and tubular magazine. Blued with a Monte Carlo-style walnut stock. Manufactured between 1969 and 1972.

	—	100	80	70	50	35

Model 64G

Introduced in 1996 this semi-automatic .22 long rifle has a 20.25" barrel and 10-shot detachable magazine. The finish is blue and the stock has a Monte Carlo with checkered pistol grip. Bead front sight with adjustable open rear sight is standard. Weight is about 5.5 lbs.

	160	125	90	60	50	40

Model 64GXP

As above but with unmounted 4x15mm scope.

	170	125	100	80	60	50

Model 64BTV

Similar to Model 64 but with laminated thumbhole stock.

	170	125	100	80	60	50

Model 64F

Introduced in 1997 this model features a black synthetic stock with blue finish. Chambered for .22 LR and fitted with a 20.25" barrel. Weight is approximately 5.5 lbs.

	140	120	90	65	50	25

Model 64FSS

Similar to the model above but with stainless steel action and barrel. Introduced in 2002.

	200	150	110	75	50	25

Model 64FV

Introduced in 1998 this model features a heavy 21" target barrel with no sights. A black synthetic stock is standard. Chambered for the .22 LR cartridge. Weight is about 6 lbs. Discontinued.

	150	125	90	65	50	25

Model 64FVXP

Similar to Model 64FV but with scope package. Introduced 2006.

	190	150	110	75	50	25

Model 64FVSS

Similar to the Model FV but with stainless steel action and barrel. Introduced in 2002. Discontinued.

NIB	EXC.	V.G.	GOOD	FAIR	POOR
225	175	125	100	75	50

Model 64FXP

This is a package model that offers a .22 LR gun with 20.25" barrel with detachable 10-round magazine. It comes with a 4x15mm scope as well as open sights. Introduced in 1998. Weight is about 5.25 lbs.

NIB	EXC.	V.G.	GOOD	FAIR	POOR
150	125	90	65	50	25

Model 88

As above, with a hardwood stock. Manufactured between 1969 and 1972.

NIB	EXC.	V.G.	GOOD	FAIR	POOR
—	100	80	70	50	35

Model 90 Carbine

As above, with a 16.5" barrel and carbine-style stock. The fore-end is secured to the barrel by a barrel band. Discontinued.

NIB	EXC.	V.G.	GOOD	FAIR	POOR
—	100	80	70	50	35

Model 93G

Introduced in 1996 this model is a bolt-action repeating rifle chambered for the .22 WMR cartridge. It is fitted with a 20.75" barrel with 5-shot magazine. It has a walnut-stained hardwood stock with cut checkering. Open sights standard. Weight is about 5.75 lbs. In 2001 this model was offered in a left-hand version (Model 93GL).

NIB	EXC.	V.G.	GOOD	FAIR	POOR
195	150	100	75	60	50

Model 93FS

This .22 WMR model features a stainless steel finish with a 20.75" barrel and black synthetic stock. Five-round magazine. Front bead sight and sporting rear sight. Introduced in 1997. Weight is about 5.5 lbs. Discontinued.

NIB	EXC.	V.G.	GOOD	FAIR	POOR
195	150	100	75	60	50

Model 93 Classic

Similar to Model 93G but with sporter-weight barrel and oil-finished premium walnut stock. AccuTrigger. Introduced in 2007.

NIB	EXC.	V.G.	GOOD	FAIR	POOR
475	375	325	200	150	100

Model 93 Classic Thumbhole

Similar to above but with thumbhole stock.

NIB	EXC.	V.G.	GOOD	FAIR	POOR
515	400	300	200	125	100

Model 93XP

.22 WMR package gun with 22-inch barrel and factory-mounted 3x9 scope. Finished overall with Mossy Oak Brush stock.

NIB	EXC.	V.G.	GOOD	FAIR	POOR
400	325	250	150	100	75

Model 93FVSS

This model features a 21" heavy barrel chambered for the .22 WMR cartridge, recessed target muzzle and stainless steel barreled action. Equipped with black synthetic stock. Magazine capacity is 5 rounds. Weight is about 6 lbs. Introduced in 1998.

NIB	EXC.	V.G.	GOOD	FAIR	POOR
275	200	150	100	70	50

Model 93BTVS

Similar to Model 93FVSS but with laminated thumbhole stock. Introduced in 2007.

NIB	EXC.	V.G.	GOOD	FAIR	POOR
400	325	250	150	100	75

Model 93F

Similar to the above model but with blued finish and a synthetic stock with open sights. Weight is approximately 5 lbs. Introduced in 1998.

NIB	EXC.	V.G.	GOOD	FAIR	POOR
185	125	95	65	50	25

Model 93R17-F

This bolt-action rifle is chambered for the .17 HMR cartridge and fitted with a 20.75" barrel with no sights. Black synthetic stock. Magazine capacity is 5 rounds. Blued finish. Weight is about 5 lbs. Introduced in 2003.

NIB	EXC.	V.G.	GOOD	FAIR	POOR
225	175	125	100	75	50

NIB	EXC.	V.G.	GOOD	FAIR	POOR

Model 93R17-BVSS

Similar to the above model but with 21" stainless steel barrel with no sights and laminated hardwood stock. Weight is about 6 lbs. Introduced in 2003.

| 325 | 250 | 190 | 125 | 75 | 50 |

Model 93R17-FSS

This .17 HMR caliber rifle has a 20.75" stainless steel barrel with no sights and black synthetic stock. Weight is about 5 lbs. Introduced in 2003.

| 250 | 180 | 130 | 100 | 75 | 50 |

Model 93R17-Camo

As above but with Realtree Hardwoods camo stock. Weight is about 5 lbs. Introduced in 2003.

| 250 | 180 | 130 | 100 | 75 | 50 |

Model 93R17-FVSS

As above but with 21" stainless steel heavy barrel. Weight is about 6 lbs. Introduced in 2003.

| 275 | 210 | 150 | 125 | 75 | 50 |

Model 93R17-GV

This .17 HMR model has a walnut finished hardwood checkered stock and 21" heavy barrel with no sights. Blued finish. Weight is about 6 lbs. Introduced in 2003. A left-hand model is also available.

| 230 | 175 | 125 | 100 | 75 | 50 |

Model 93R17-GVXP

Similar to Model 93R17-GV but with scope package. Introduced 2006.

| 250 | 180 | 130 | 100 | 75 | 50 |

Model 93R17-FXP

Similar to Model 93R17-F but with scope package. Introduced 2006.

| 250 | 180 | 130 | 100 | 75 | 50 |

Model 93FVSS-XP

Similar to Model 93FVSS but with scope package. Introduced 2006.

| 300 | 225 | 150 | 125 | 75 | 50 |

Model 93FSS

Similar to discontinued Model 93FS but with no sights and AccuTrigger. Introduced 2006.

| 275 | 210 | 150 | 125 | 75 | 50 |

Model 93FV

Similar to Model 93F but with AccuTrigger. Introduced 2006.

| 250 | 180 | 130 | 100 | 75 | 50 |

Model 93R17-BTVS

Similar to Model 93R17-BVSS but with laminated thumbhole stock. Introduced 2006.

| 350 | 295 | 245 | 195 | 150 | 100 |

Model 93R17BLTVS

Similar to above but in left hand. Suggested retail price: $441.

Model 93R17-BV

Similar to Model 93R17-GV but with brown laminated stock with wide beavertail forend. Introduced 2006.

| 350 | 295 | 245 | 195 | 150 | 100 |

Model 93R17 Classic

Similar to Model 93R17 but with sporter-weight barrel and oil-finished premium walnut stock. AccuTrigger. Introduced in 2007.

| 450 | 345 | 295 | 200 | 135 | 100 |

Model Mark II BRJ

Similar to Mark II, Model 93 but features spiral fluting pattern on a heavy barrel, blued finish and Royal Jacaranda wood laminate stock. In .22 LR, .22 WMR or .17 HMR.

| 400 | 350 | 300 | 250 | 200 | 100 |

	NIB	EXC.	V.G.	GOOD	FAIR	POOR

Model Mark II TRR-SR

Similar to Mark II, Model 93 but features heavy barrel, matte finish and a tactical-style wood stock.

	NIB	EXC.	V.G.	GOOD	FAIR	POOR
	475	425	350	300	250	150

Model CUB-G (Mini-Youth)

Introduced in 2003 this single-shot bolt-action rifle is chambered for the .22 caliber cartridge. Barrel length is 16" and the walnut-stained hardwood stock is proportionally scaled down. Weight is about 3.3 lbs. In 2005 this model was offered in .17 HM2.

	NIB	EXC.	V.G.	GOOD	FAIR	POOR
	155	125	100	75	50	25

Model CUB-T

Similar to Model CUB-G, with laminated thumbhole stock. Introduced in 2007.

	NIB	EXC.	V.G.	GOOD	FAIR	POOR
	235	195	145	100	75	50

Model B Mag

Bolt-action rimfire chambered for .17 Win. Super Magnum (.17 WSM) cartridge. New compact action design, with rear locking lugs and cock-on-close bolt. AccuTrigger is user-adjustable without special tools. Features include: center-feed rotating 8-round magazine, black synthetic stock, matte black finish, 22" carbon steel barrel. New in 2013.

	NIB	EXC.	V.G.	GOOD	FAIR	POOR
	315	275	225	—	—	—

Model 30G "Stevens Favorite"

Based on Stevens Favorite model. Lever-action single-shot .22 caliber rifle. Fitted with 21" half octagonal barrel. Walnut stock with schnabel fore-end. Blued finish. Weight about 4.25 lbs. Introduced in 1999. Additional calibers added are .22 WMR and .22 Hornet. **NOTE:** Add $35 for .22WMR; $60 for .22 Hornet.

	NIB	EXC.	V.G.	GOOD	FAIR	POOR
	325	275	225	150	100	50

Model 30G "Favorite" Takedown

Introduced in 2004 this model has a takedown feature. Offered in .17 HMR and .22 LR. The .17 HMR is fitted with a 21" full octagon barrel with sights and scope base included. The .22 LR model is fitted with a 21" half octagon barrel with sights. **NOTE:** Add $65 for .17 HMR model.

	NIB	EXC.	V.G.	GOOD	FAIR	POOR
	325	275	225	150	100	50

MARK I & II SERIES

Introduced in 1996 this series of .22 caliber rifles feature both single-shot and repeating models. They are available in both right- and left-hand models.

Mark I-G

This is a bolt-action single-shot rifle chambered for the .22 Short, Long, or Long Rifle cartridges. It is fitted with a 20.75" barrel and has a cut checkered walnut finished stock. Bead front sight and open adjustable rear sight. Offered in both right- and left-hand models. Weight is about 5.5 lbs.

	NIB	EXC.	V.G.	GOOD	FAIR	POOR
	150	100	80	70	60	50

Model Mark I-FVT

Similar to Model Mark I-G but with synthetic stock, rear peep sight and hooded front sight. Introduced 2006.

	NIB	EXC.	V.G.	GOOD	FAIR	POOR
	200	150	100	80	70	60	—

Mark I-GY (Youth Model)

Same as above but fitted with a 19" barrel and shorter buttstock. Weight is about 5 lbs.

	NIB	EXC.	V.G.	GOOD	FAIR	POOR
	150	100	80	70	60	50

Mark I-GSB Smoothbore

This version of the Mark I is a smoothbore model made for .22 caliber shot cartridges. Barrel length is 20.75" and weight is about 5.5 lbs.

	NIB	EXC.	V.G.	GOOD	FAIR	POOR
	150	100	80	70	60	50

Mark II-G

This model is a bolt-action repeater with 10-shot magazine. It is chambered for the .22 LR cartridge. Checkered walnut finished stock. Open sights. Barrel length is 20.75". Offered in both right- and left-hand versions. Weight is approximately 5.5 lbs.

	NIB	EXC.	V.G.	GOOD	FAIR	POOR
	170	125	90	70	60	50

	NIB	EXC.	V.G.	GOOD	FAIR	POOR

Mark II-GY (Youth Model)

Same as above but with 19" barrel and shorter stock.

	170	125	90	70	60	50

Mark II-GXP

Same as the Mark II-G model but includes an unmounted 4x15mm scope. Discontinued.

	130	100	80	70	60	50

Mark II-FSS

This is a stainless steel .22 caliber rifle with 20.75" barrel and 10-round magazine. Receiver is dovetailed for scope mounting. Stock is black synthetic. Weight is about 5 lbs.

	210	150	110	75	65	45

Mark II-LV

This .22 caliber is fitted with a 21" heavy barrel. It has a laminated hardwood stock with cut checkering. Blue finish and 10-round magazine. Weight is approximately 6.5 lbs. Introduced in 1997. Discontinued.

	200	150	110	75	65	45

Mark II-F

This model has the standard Mark II barreled action with a black synthetic stock. Detachable 10-round magazine is standard. Weight is about 5 lbs. Introduced in 1998. .17 Hornady Mach 2 added in 2006.

	150	110	80	70	65	45

Mark II-FXP

Similar to the Mark II-F but with a 4x15mm scope. Weight is approximately 5.25 lbs. First offered in 1998.

	155	110	80	70	65	45

Model Mark II Camo

Similar to Model Mark II-F but with forest camo synthetic stock. Introduced 2006.

	200	165	135	100	75	50

Mark II-FV

Introduced in 1998 this model features a 21" heavy barrel with blue alloy steel receiver. Stock is black synthetic. Magazine capacity is 5-round detachable magazine. Weight is about 6 lbs. .17 Hornady Mach 2 added in 2006.

	215	150	110	80	60	45

Model Mark II-FVXP

Similar to Model Mark II-FV but with scope package. Introduced 2006.

	250	195	150	125	75	50

Model Mark II-FVT

Similar to Model Mark II-FV but with rear peep sight and hooded front sight. Introduced 2006.

	315	250	195	145	100	75

Model Mark II-BV

This model features a 21-inch stainless steel bull barrel without sights and a brown laminate stock. Chambered in .22 LR. Introduced 2006.

	300	225	175	150	100	75

Model Mark II BTV

Similar to above but with laminated thumbhole vent stock, Accu-Trigger, blued receiver and bull barrel.

	375	325	250	150	125	100

Mark II BVTS

Similar to above but with stainless barrel/receiver; available in right- or left-hand (BTVLS) configuration. Suggested retail price: $393 (standard); $441 (left hand).

	395	350	265	165	140	125

	NIB	EXC.	V.G.	GOOD	FAIR	POOR

Model Mark II Classic

Similar to Mark II-FV but with sporter-weight barrel and oil-finished premium walnut stock. AccuTrigger. Introduced in 2007. Add $50 for thumbhole stock.

	NIB	EXC.	V.G.	GOOD	FAIR	POOR
	395	350	295	225	150	100

MODEL 900 SERIES

First offered in 1996. Series consists of .22 caliber rimfire target rifles in various configurations. All available in both right-/left-hand versions.

Model 900B—Biathlon

Rifle features hardwood stock, with 5-round magazine, carrying and shooting rails, butt hook and hand stop. Barrel length 21" and comes with snow cover. Receiver sight are peep variety and front sight has 7 aperture inserts as standard. Weight about 8.25 lbs.

475	400	350	300	2175	125

Model 900 TR—Target

Model has one-piece hardwood stock, with shooting rail and hand stop. Rear sight is adjustable peep and front sight has 7 aperture inserts. Barrel length 25". Five-shot magazine standard. Weight about 8 lbs.

400	325	275	225	150	100

Model 900S—Silhouette

Version features 21" heavy barrel, with recessed target style crown. Fitted with one-piece silhouette-style stock, with high comb and satin walnut finish. Receiver drilled and tapped for scope mount. Weight about 8 lbs.

400	325	275	225	150	100

Model 24

External hammer combination rifle/shotgun, with 24" barrels. Blued, with walnut stock. Manufactured from 1950 to 1965 in a variety of styles. Standard chambering was .22 by .410.

550	500	400	325	250	150

Model 24S

Similar to above, except has side-mounted operating lever. Available with 20-gauge lower barrel.

450	375	325	250	200	150

Model 24MS

Similar to above, except rifle barrel chambered for .22 WMR.

600	525	425	350	275	175

Model 24DL

Satin chrome with checkered stock.

—	450	375	325	175	125

Model 24 Field—Lightweight Version

—	450	375	275	150	100

Model 24C

Nickel finish.

—	450	375	275	150	100

Model 24VS

.357 Magnum or .357 Maximum/20 gauge, nickel finish.

675	575	450	400	300	200

Model 24F

DuPont Rynite stock.

500	400	325	250	150	100

Model 2400

Combination 12 gauge by .222 or .308 caliber over/under rifle/shotgun, with 23.5" barrels and Monte Carlo-style stock. Made by Valmet. Imported between 1975 and 1980.

—	700	575	450	350	275

	NIB	EXC.	V.G.	GOOD	FAIR	POOR

Model 389

Over/under design with 12-gauge 3" magnum shotgun barrel over rifle barrel. Chambered for .222 Rem. or .308 Winchester. Double triggers, hammerless action, checkered walnut stock. Made in 1988 and 1989.

	NIB	EXC.	V.G.	GOOD	FAIR	POOR
	800	700	600	450	350	200

Model 42

Over/under design with .22 Long Rifle or WMR rifle barrel over .410 shotgun barrel. Separated barrels with black synthetic stock and sling swivels. Opens with lever in front of trigger guard. New in 2013

	NIB	EXC.	V.G.	GOOD	FAIR	POOR
	400	350	300	—	—	—

SAVAGE SHOTGUNS

Model 411 Upland Sporter

SEE—Stevens.

Model 420

A 12, 16, or 20 gauge boxlock over/under shotgun with 26", 28", or 30" barrels, double triggers and extractors. Manufactured between 1937 and 1943.

	NIB	EXC.	V.G.	GOOD	FAIR	POOR
	—	500	400	300	200	150

Model 420 with Single Trigger

	NIB	EXC.	V.G.	GOOD	FAIR	POOR
	—	500	400	300	200	150

Model 430

As above, with a checkered walnut stock and solid barrel rib. Produced from 1937 to 1943.

	NIB	EXC.	V.G.	GOOD	FAIR	POOR
	—	550	450	350	200	150

Model 430 with Single Trigger

	NIB	EXC.	V.G.	GOOD	FAIR	POOR
	—	600	450	300	200	150

Model 320

This is a side-by-side model.

	NIB	EXC.	V.G.	GOOD	FAIR	POOR
	—	800	650	500	400	300

Model 412

.410 bore adapter.

	NIB	EXC.	V.G.	GOOD	FAIR	POOR
	—	80	60	50	40	30

Model 412F

.410 bore adapter.

	NIB	EXC.	V.G.	GOOD	FAIR	POOR
	—	50	45	40	35	25

Model 220

A 12, 16, 20 or .410 bore boxlock single barrel shotgun with 26" to 32" barrels. Blued with a walnut stock. Manufactured between 1938 and 1965.

	NIB	EXC.	V.G.	GOOD	FAIR	POOR
	—	100	80	70	50	35

Model 210F

Introduced in 1996 this bolt-action shotgun has a 24" rifled barrel for slugs. It is chambered for the 3" 12 gauge shell. No sights. Magazine holds 2 rounds. Weight is about 7.5 lbs.

	NIB	EXC.	V.G.	GOOD	FAIR	POOR
	575	500	425	350	200	125

Model 210F Slug Warrior Camo

As above but with camo stock.

	NIB	EXC.	V.G.	GOOD	FAIR	POOR
	595	525	450	375	225	150

Model 210FT

Introduced in 1997 this is a 12 gauge bolt-action shotgun with a camouflage finish. Chambered for 3" shells and fitted with a 24" barrel. 2-round magazine. Approximate weight is 7.5 lbs. Drilled and tapped for scope mounting.

	NIB	EXC.	V.G.	GOOD	FAIR	POOR
	575	500	425	350	200	125

	NIB	EXC.	V.G.	GOOD	FAIR	POOR

Model 720

A 12 or 16 gauge semi-automatic shotgun with 26" to 32" barrels. Blued with a walnut stock. Manufactured between 1930 and 1949.

	NIB	EXC.	V.G.	GOOD	FAIR	POOR
	—	450	375	275	225	100

Model 726 Upland Sporter

As above, with a 2-shot magazine. Manufactured between 1931 and 1949.

	NIB	EXC.	V.G.	GOOD	FAIR	POOR
	—	450	375	275	225	100

Model 740C Skeet

The Model 726 with a 24.5" barrel featuring a Cutts compensator and skeet-style stock. Manufactured between 1936 and 1949.

	NIB	EXC.	V.G.	GOOD	FAIR	POOR
	—	450	375	275	225	100

Model 745

The Model 720 in 12 gauge with an alloy receiver and 28" barrel. Manufactured between 1940 and 1949.

	NIB	EXC.	V.G.	GOOD	FAIR	POOR
	—	450	375	275	225	100

Model 755

A 12 or 16 gauge semi-automatic shotgun with 26" to 30" barrels. Blued with a walnut stock. Also available with Savage Super Choke. Manufactured between 1949 and 1958.

	NIB	EXC.	V.G.	GOOD	FAIR	POOR
	—	295	225	175	125	75

Model 775

As above, with an alloy receiver. Manufactured between 1950 and 1966.

	NIB	EXC.	V.G.	GOOD	FAIR	POOR
	—	295	225	175	125	75

Model 750

A 12 gauge semi-automatic shotgun with a 26" or 28" barrel. The Model 750SC fitted with the Savage Super Choke and the Model 750AC with a Poly Choke. Blued with a walnut stock. Manufactured between 1960 and 1967.

	NIB	EXC.	V.G.	GOOD	FAIR	POOR
	—	295	225	175	125	75

Model FA-1

This is Savage Fox semi-automatic shotgun imported from Japan in 1981 and 1982. Marked KTG. Offered in 12 gauge only with 28" or 30" vent rib barrels. Walnut stock with cut checkering. Magazine capacity is 4 rounds. Weight is about 7.5 lbs.

	NIB	EXC.	V.G.	GOOD	FAIR	POOR
	—	350	300	250	200	150

Model FP-1

Similar to the above model but with 3" chambers and a 5-round magazine capacity.

	NIB	EXC.	V.G.	GOOD	FAIR	POOR
	—	350	300	250	200	150

Model 21

This is a slide-action shotgun built between 1920 and 1928. Chambered for 12 gauge with 26", 28", 30", or 32" barrel. Walnut pistol grip stock and slide handle. Takedown. Almost identical to the famous Winchester Model 12. Offered in a number of different configurations including standard grade, Trap grade, Tournament grade, and Riot Model. About 13,000 were built.

	NIB	EXC.	V.G.	GOOD	FAIR	POOR
	—	450	375	275	225	100

Model 28

This slide-action shotgun is an improved version of the Model 21. It was manufactured from 1928 to 1934. There are several variations of this gun including the Model 28-A, a standard grade; the Model 28-B, a standard grade with raised matted rib; a Model 28-C, a Riot gun; a Model 28-D, a Trap grade; and in 1931 a Model 28-3, an improved version with checkering and roll marked game scenes on the receiver.

	NIB	EXC.	V.G.	GOOD	FAIR	POOR
	—	450	375	275	225	100

Model 30

A 12, 16, 20 or .410 bore slide-action shotgun with 26" to 30" ventilated rib barrels. Blued with a walnut stock. Manufactured between 1958 and 1978.

	NIB	EXC.	V.G.	GOOD	FAIR	POOR
	—	300	195	150	100	75

	NIB	EXC.	V.G.	GOOD	FAIR	POOR

Model 242

A .410 bore boxlock double-barrel over/under shotgun with 26" barrels, single trigger, extractors and exposed hammer. Manufactured between 1977 and 1981.

	—	550	475	350	225	125

Model 550

A 12 or 20 gauge boxlock side-by-side double-barrel shotgun with 26", 28", or 30" barrels, single triggers and automatic ejectors. Blued with a hardwood stock. Manufactured between 1971 and 1973. Barrels were built by Valmet.

	500	400	300	200	150	

Model 440

An Italian made 12 or 20 gauge boxlock over/under shotgun with 26", 28", or 30" ventilated rib barrels, single-selective trigger and extractors. Blued with a walnut stock. Manufactured between 1968 and 1972.

	—	600	500	400	300	200

Model 440A

	—	600	500	400	300	200

Model 440B-T

	—	800	650	500	350	250

Model 444 Deluxe

As above, with a more finely figured stock and automatic ejectors. Imported between 1969 and 1972.

	—	550	475	400	300	225

Model 444

	—	600	500	400	300	200

Model 444B

	—	700	550	400	300	250

Model 440T

A 12 gauge Model 440 with 30" barrels and a trap-style stock. Imported between 1969 and 1972.

	—	600	500	400	300	200

Model 330

A Valmet manufactured 12 or 20 gauge over/under shotgun with 26", 28", or 30" barrels, single-selective trigger and extractors. Blued with a walnut stock. Imported between 1970 and 1978.

	—	800	650	500	350	250

Model 333

As above, with a ventilated rib and automatic ejectors. Imported between 1973 and 1980.

	—	700	550	400	300	200

Model 333T

As above, with a 30" barrel and trap-style stock. Imported between 1972 and 1980.

	—	800	650	500	350	250

Model 312 Field Over/Under

	—	800	600	450	300	200

Model 312 Trap

	—	700	600	550	350	200

Model 312 Sporting Clay

	—	800	600	450	300	200

Model 320 Field

	—	800	600	450	300	200

	NIB	EXC.	V.G.	GOOD	FAIR	POOR	

(SAVAGE) FOX B MODELS

The Fox Model B was introduced about 1939 by Savage for the hunter who wanted better fit and finish than offered by the Stevens brand Model 530. It was made in many variations until 1988.

Fox Model B—Utica, NY

1000	800	600	450	400	350

Fox Model B—Chicopee Falls, Mass. (later Westfield, Mass.)

800	750	500	400	350	300

Fox Model B—Single Trigger

900	800	600	500	400	300

Fox Model BDL

1000	800	700	600	400	350

Fox Model BDE

1000	800	700	600	400	350

Fox Model BST

800	700	600	500	400	300

Fox Model BSE

1000	750	650	550	450	350

Fox Model BE

1000	800	600	450	400	350

Milano

This Italian-made over/under is available in 12, 20 and 28 gauges and .410-bore on frames scaled to match, all with 28" barrels and 3" chambers. Single selective trigger. Three choke tubes (fixed IC and Mod. on .410-bore). Automatic ejectors.

1000	825	675	475	300	150

PISTOLS

Elbert Searle was granted a patent on an automatic pistol which utilized the bullet's torque to twist barrel into a locking position with slide. Patent also featured a double-row staggered magazine which increased capacity over ordinary pistols. Patent was sold to Savage and first Savage automatic pistol Model 1907 was produced. **NOTE:** Savage automatic pistols with original cardboard box will bring between $50 and $100 premium. Instruction pamphlet, cleaning brush or other advertising material is present, price will escalate.

Model 1907

A .32 or .380 semi-automatic pistol with a 3.75" or 4.25" barrel depending upon caliber and a 9- or 10-shot magazine. Blued with hard rubber rectangular grips. This model is often incorrectly termed the Model 1905 or Model 1910. **NOTE:** The .380 caliber model is worth approximately 30 percent more than the values listed.

—	525	350	250	150	100

Model 1907 Portugese Contract

Similar to the commercial guns but with a lanyard ring same as the French contract model. Original Portugese pistols will have the Portugese Crest on the grips. Only about 1,150 of these pistols were produced. Very rare. Proceed with caution.

—	1700	1250	950	600	300

Model 1915 Hammerless

Similar to Model 1907, except fitted with grip safety and internal hammer. Approximately 6,500 pistols produced in .32 caliber and 3,900 in .380 caliber. Manufactured between 1915 and 1917. Rarest of regular-production Savage automatic pistols.

.32 Caliber

—	800	600	500	400	200

.380 Caliber

—	1200	900	600	500	300

	NIB	EXC.	V.G.	GOOD	FAIR	POOR

Model 1917

As above, with external hammer and without grip safety. Form of grip frame widened in kind of trapezoidal shape. Manufactured between 1917 and 1928. **NOTE:** Add $100 for .380.

	—	450	375	300	250	200

Model 6.35mm

A small number of .25 caliber Savage pistols were manufactured between 1915 and 1919. Perhaps less than 25 were built. There are two major variations of this pistol. First, is the wide or 10-serrations grip, and second the 27-serrations grip variation. This change occured around 1917. Magazine capacity was 6 to 7 rounds. Very rare.

	—	8000	7000	4000	2500	1000

Model 1907 Test Pistol

Manufactured in 1907 in .45 ACP this pistol was tested in the U.S. Army trials. About 290 pistols were produced for these trials. Double-stack magazine held 8 rounds.

	—	13500	11000	9500	6000	4000

Model 1910 Test Pistol

This was a modified Model 1907 with a heavier slide that was not concave like the Model 1907. There was a total of nine Model 1910s built. Too Rare To Price

	—	—	—	—	—	—

Model 1911 Test Pistol

This example was completely modified with a longer and thinner grip. Checkered wood grips were attached by friction instead of screws, the slide release was modified, a full grip safety was added, and a heavier serrated hammer (cocking lever) was added. Four of these pistols were built. Serial #1 has never been located. Too rare to price.

Model 101

.22 caliber single-shot pistol resembling a revolver with a 5.5" barrel. Blued with hardwood grips. This pistol was made in Chicopee Falls or Westfield, Mass. Manufactured between 1960 and 1968.

	—	225	175	125	100	75

500 HANDGUN SERIES

Introduced in 1998 this line of short action handguns feature a left-hand bolt and a right-hand ejection. All are fitted with an internal box magazine, composite stock and 14" barrel.

Model 501F—Sport Striker

This handgun is fitted with a left-hand bolt and 10" free floating barrel. Detachable clip holds 10 rounds of .22 LR cartridges. Drilled and tapped for scope mount. Weight is about 4 lbs. Introduced in 2000.

350	295	250	175	150	100	

Model 501FXP

Introduced in 2002 this model is similar to the one above but fitted with a 1.25-4x28mm scope with soft case.

375	325	265	195	165	110	

Model 502F—Sport Striker

Same as 501F but chambered for .22 WMR cartridge. Magazine capacity is 5 rounds. Introduced in 2000.

375	325	265	195	165	110	

Model 503F—Sport Striker

Same as the Model 502F-Sport Striker but chambered for the .17 HMR cartridge. Blued finish. Weight is about 4 lbs. Introduced in 2003.

375	325	265	195	165	110	

Model 503FSS—Sport Striker

As above but with stainless steel action and barrel.

395	350	290	210	180	125	

Model 510F Striker

Blued barrel action and chambered for .22-250, .243, or .308 calibers. Weight is approximately 5 lbs.

475	400	350	295	175	150	

	NIB	EXC.	V.G.	GOOD	FAIR	POOR

Model 516FSS

Similar to the model above but with stainless steel barreled action.

	495	425	365	310	195	150

Model 516FSAK

Features a stainless steel barreled action with adjustable muzzlebrake.

	525	450	395	345	225	165

Model 516FSAK Camo

As above but with Realtree Hardwood camo stock. Chambered for the .300 WSM cartridge. Weight is about 5.5 lbs. Introduced in 2002.

	600	525	450	300	235	75

Model 516BSS

Fitted with a laminated thumbhole stock, left-hand bolt for right-hand ejection, 14" barrel. This model is chambered for the .223, .243, 7mm-08 Rem., .260 Rem., and .308 Win. calibers. Magazine capacity is 2 rounds. Weight is about 5 lbs. Introduced in 1999.

	600	525	450	300	235	75

Model 516BSAK

Similar to the model above but chambered for the .223 or .22-250 cartridges. The 14" barrel is fitted with an adjustable muzzlebrake. Introduced in 1999.

	600	525	450	300	235	75

SAVAGE REVOLVING FIREARMS CO.
Middletown, Connecticut

Navy Revolver

A .36 caliber double-action percussion revolver with a 7" octagonal barrel and 6-shot cylinder. The frame marked "Savage R.F.A. Co./H.S. North Patented June 17, 1856/Jan. 18, 1859, May 15, 1860." Approximately 20,000 were manufactured between 1861 and 1865, of which about 12,000 were purchased by the U.S. Government.

	—	—	4250	1750	700	500

SCATTERGUN TECHNOLOGIES
Formerly—Nashville, Tennessee
Berryville, Arkansas

NOTE: In 1999 Scattergun Technologies was purchased by Wilson Combat and became a division of Wilson Combat.

TR-870

This model is based on the Remington Model 870 slide-action shotgun. It is offered in a wide variety of configurations with different features. The standard model is fitted with an 18" barrel and chambered for the 12 gauge shell. The stock is composite with recoil pad. Tactical fore-end has flashlight built in. Ghost Ring rear sight. Front sight has tritium insert. Six-round shell carrier on left side of receiver. Introduced in 1991. Weight for standard model is approximately 9 lbs. Prices listed are for the standard model.

	1000	800	650	550	300	200

WILSON COMBAT CURRENT PRODUCTION MODELS

NOTE: Add $100 to all models with Armor-Tuff finish

Standard Model

Based on the Remington 12 gauge 3" 870 Magnum this model is fitted with an 18" barrel with cylinder bore. Adjustable Ghost Ring rear sight with tritium front sight. Seven-round extended magazine. Side saddle shell carrier. Synthetic stock. Tactical sling is standard. Parkerized finish. Fitted with a SURE-FIRE tactical light.

	1150	850	625	500	400	300

Border Patrol Model

Similar to the standard model but without the tactical light. A 14" barrel is offered on this model but all NFA rules apply to the purchase of a short barrel shotgun.

	875	650	475	300	200	150

	NIB	EXC.	V.G.	GOOD	FAIR	POOR

Professional Model

This model features all of the standard model components but it is fitted with a 14" barrel. Magazine capacity is 6 rounds. All NFA rules apply to purchase of short barrel shotgun.

	1175	875	650	500	400	300

Entry Model

This model has all the features of the standard model but is fitted with a 12.5" barrel. Magazine capacity is 5 rounds. All NFA rules apply to the purchase of a short barrel shotgun.

	950	700	600	500	400	300

K-9 Model

This model is built on a Remington 12 gauge 3" 11-87 Magnum semi-automatic. Fitted with Ghost Ring rear sights and tritium front sight. Extended magazine holds 7 rounds. Barrel is 18". Synthetic stock with side saddle shell carrier. Parkerized finish.

	1075	800	700	600	500	350

SWAT Model

Similar to the K-9 model but fitted with a tactical light and 14" barrel. All NFA rules apply to the purchase of a short barrel shotgun.

	1350	1000	800	650	550	400

SCCY INDUSTRIES
South Daytona, Florida

SCCY CPX

Hammer-fired double-action-only compact 9mm pistol, with black polymer frame, stainless steel slide and barrel. Black or matte stainless finish. Available with or without thumb safety. Introduced 2012.

	280	250	230	185	150	100

SCHALK, G. S.
Pottsville, Pennsylvania

Rifle Musket

A .58 caliber percussion rifle with a 40" round barrel and full length stock secured by three barrel bands. The barrel marked "G. Schalk Poftsville 1861." Finished in white with a walnut stock. Approximately 100 were manufactured.

	—	—	6900	3300	750	500

SCHALL & CO.
New Haven, Connecticut

Manufactured the Fiala repeating pistol for Fiala. Later, after Fiala's bankruptcy, Schall provided parts, repair service, and produced repeating pistols with the Schall name. Marketed by Schall between about 1930 and 1935.

Repeating Pistol

A .22 caliber pistol with 10-shot magazine. Tapered 6.5" barrel with fixed sights and blued finish. Rear sight is much simpler than those on the Fiala. Grips are wood with ribs running lengthwise. Typically marked "schall & co./new haven, conn usa" but guns exist with no markings. Note that the original Fiala pistols had 7.5" barrels, but not so the Schalls (a fact revealed to us by our friend Jack in Florida).

	—	500	425	325	190	170

SCHMIDT, HERBERT
Ostheim, West Germany

Model 11, Liberty 11, and Eig Model E-8

A .22 caliber double-action revolver with a 2.5" barrel and 6-shot cylinder. Blued with plastic grips.

	—	125	80	60	40	25

Model 11 Target

As above, with a 5.5" barrel and adjustable sights.

	—	150	120	75	45	30

	NIB	EXC.	V.G.	GOOD	FAIR	POOR

Frontier Model or Texas Scout

.22 caliber revolver with a 5" barrel and 6-shot cylinder. Blued with plastic grips.

	NIB	EXC.	V.G.	GOOD	FAIR	POOR
	—	125	80	60	40	25

SCHMIDT & COMPANY, E.
Houston, Texas

Pocket Pistol

A .45 caliber percussion single-shot pistol with a 2.5" barrel, German silver mounts and walnut stock. The barrel marked "E. Schmidt & Co. Houston." Manufactured between 1866 and 1870.

	EXC.	V.G.	GOOD	FAIR	POOR
—	—	9000	4400	1000	350

SCHNEIDER & CO.
Memphis, Tennessee

Pocket Pistol

A .41 caliber single-shot percussion pocket pistol with a 3.5" octagonal barrel, iron or German silver mounts and a walnut stock. The lock marked "Schneider & Co./Memphis, Tenn." Manufactured 1859 and 1860.

	EXC.	V.G.	GOOD	FAIR	POOR
—	—	4500	1850	650	300

SCHNEIDER & GLASSICK
Memphis, Tennessee

Pocket Pistols

A .41 caliber percussion pocket pistol with a 2.5" barrel, German silver mounts and walnut stock. The barrel marked "Schneider & Glassick, Memphis, Tenn." Manufactured 1860 to 1862.

	EXC.	V.G.	GOOD	FAIR	POOR
—	—	7000	5250	2500	800

SCHOUBOE
See—Dansk Rekylriffel Syndikat

SCHUERMAN ARMS, LTD.
Scottsdale, Arizona

Model SA40

Introduced in 2004 this bolt-action rifle is chambered for a wide variety of calibers from short action to long magnum. Offered in both right-hand and left-hand models. Barrel lengths from 20" to 26" in stainless steel. No sights. Stock is laminated fiberglass sporter style. Retail prices atart at $5440. **NOTE:** There are a number of extra costs options that may be ordered with this model. These options will affect price.

SCHULER, AUGUST
Suhl, Germany

Reform

A 6.35mm caliber four-barreled pocket pistol with 2.5" barrels. The barrel unit rises as the trigger is pulled. Blued with walnut or hard rubber grips. Manufactured between 1907 and 1914.

	EXC.	V.G.	GOOD	FAIR	POOR
—	850	750	650	450	300

SCHULTZ & LARSEN
Ofterup, Denmark

Model 47 Match Rifle

A .22 caliber single-shot bolt-action rifle with a 28" barrel, adjustable sights and adjustable trigger. Blued with an ISU-style stock.

	EXC.	V.G.	GOOD	FAIR	POOR
—	800	650	550	400	250

Model 61 Match Rifle

As above, but fitted with a palm rest.

	EXC.	V.G.	GOOD	FAIR	POOR
—	1000	850	750	600	300

Model 62 Match Rifle

Similar to the above, but manufactured for centerfire cartridges.

	EXC.	V.G.	GOOD	FAIR	POOR
—	1250	900	750	650	350

	NIB	EXC.	V.G.	GOOD	FAIR	POOR

Model 54 Free Rifle

Similar to the above, with a 27" barrel and ISU stock.

—	950	800	700	550	300

Model 68 DL

A .22-250 to .458 Winchester Magnum bolt-action rifle with a 24" barrel, adjustable trigger and well figured walnut stock.

—	850	700	600	450	200

SCHWARZLOSE, ANDREAS
Berlin, Germany

Military Model 1898 (Standart)

A semi-automatic pistol with a 6.5" barrel, rotary locked bolt, 7-shot magazine and adjustable rear sight. Chambered for the 7.63x25mm Borchardt cartridge. Weight is about 28 oz. Blued with walnut grips. The pistol was neither a commercial or military success, and fewer than 500 were made. (CAUTION: Although the 7.63x25mm Mauser cartridge will chamber, it's too powerful for this firearm).

—	24000	20000	12000	5500	3000

SEARS, ROEBUCK & CO. BRAND
Chicago, Illinois

Double-Barrel Shotguns

Between 1892 and 1988 the world's largest mail order house carried a huge inventory of sporting doubleguns including any foreign and domestic brands whose makers did not object to Sears' famous price discounts. To increase sales volume, however, Sears also created its own brands which they supported with innovative design, extravagant advertising claims, unbeatable pricing and excellent quality control. These doubles, like many other firearms products handled by Sears, were listed in its very detailed semiannual catalog from about 1892, when the company first offered doubleguns, until about 1988 when social and political pressures made the company stop handling firearms.

Sears marketing people gave birth to and successfully exploited many house and private brands which we no longer associate with Sears at all. In fact, many of these brands clearly rollmarked on guns are now unfamiliar to many collectors. Frequently seen and important in the market segment which many might describe as affordable doubles are some of the most often seen Sears trade names or brands. Listed in chronological order: T. Barker, S.R. & Co., Triumph, Thomas Barker, Sam Holt, Chicago Long Range Wonder, American Bar Lock, Meriden Fire Arms Co., Norwich, A. J. Arbrey Gun Co., New England, Gladiator, Berkshire, Ranger, Eastern Arms Co., J.C. Higgins, Sears, and Ted Williams. These guns were of good quality but sold at bargain prices which gave them tremendous appeal. They were made for Sears to Sears' specifications by a number of American firms and a few foreign ones as well, all of which produced excellent shotguns under their own names. Among the best-known American companies were J. Stevens, Savage Arms, A.H. Fox, High Standard, N.R. Davis, Crescent Firearms, Ithaca, A. Fyrberg, Colton Mfg. Co., Marlin, Hunter Gun Co., Baker Gun Co., and probably a few others. Among the foreign makers were AYA, H. Pieper, Janssen, SKB, Rossi, CBC, and A. Zoli.

Sears customers were not aware of this but they did trust Sears name and bought many millions of these shotguns over the nearly 100 years that Sears was in the business. Today these guns are becoming recognized as interesting and valuable collectibles in their own special niche. Their values range from $100 to $3,500 or more depending on make, model, decoration, if any, and relative rarity.

SEAVER, E.R.
New York, New York

Pocket Pistol

A .41 caliber percussion pocket pistol with a 2.5" barrel, German silver mounts and a walnut stock.

—	—	2300	1825	975	400

SECURITY INDUSTRIES
Little Ferry, New Jersey

Model PSS

A .38 Special double-action revolver with a 2" barrel, fixed sights and 5-shot cylinder. Stainless steel with walnut grips. Manufactured between 1973 and 1978.

—	250	150	125	100	75

	NIB	EXC.	V.G.	GOOD	FAIR	POOR

Model PM357

As above, with a 2.5" barrel and in .357 Magnum caliber. Manufactured between 1975 and 1978.

NIB	EXC.	V.G.	GOOD	FAIR	POOR
—	300	200	175	150	100

Model PPM357

As above, with a 2" barrel and a hammer without a finger spur. Manufactured between 1975 and 1978.

NIB	EXC.	V.G.	GOOD	FAIR	POOR
—	300	200	175	150	100

SEDCO INDUSTRIES, INC.
Lake Elsinore, California

This company was in business from 1988 to 1990.

Model SP22

A .22 caliber semi-automatic pistol with a 2.5" barrel. Blackened or nickel-plated with plastic grips. Introduced in 1989.

NIB	EXC.	V.G.	GOOD	FAIR	POOR
125	90	65	50	35	25

SEDGELY, R. F., INC.
Philadelphia, Pennsylvania

R.F. Sedgely produced specialized bolt-action rifles using Model 1903 Springfield action. As these arms were for the most part custom order pieces, it is impossible to provide standardized values. It should be noted that his prime engraver was Rudolph J. Kornbrath. Sedgely also made a .22-caliber hammerless pistol.

SEECAMP, L. W. CO., INC.
Milford, Connecticut

LWS .25 ACP Model

A .25 caliber semi-automatic pistol with a 2" barrel, fixed sights and 7-shot magazine. Stainless steel with plastic grips. Approximately 5,000 were manufactured between 1982 and 1985.

NIB	EXC.	V.G.	GOOD	FAIR	POOR
500	400	300	200	150	100

LWS .32 ACP Model

A .32 caliber double-action semi-automatic pistol with a 2" barrel and 6-shot magazine. Matte or polished stainless steel with plastic grips.

NIB	EXC.	V.G.	GOOD	FAIR	POOR
525	450	400	350	200	150

Matched Pair

A matched set of the above, with identical serial numbers. A total of 200 sets were made prior to 1968.

NIB	EXC.	V.G.	GOOD	FAIR	POOR
—	900	800	700	500	350

LWS .380 Model

Same as the .32 caliber but chambered for the .380 cartridge. Essentially the same weight and dimensions as the .32 caliber pistol. Introduced in 1999.

NIB	EXC.	V.G.	GOOD	FAIR	POOR
900	650	500	400	300	100

SEMMERLING
Waco, Texas
See—American Derringer Corporation

SERBU FIREARMS
Tampa, Florida

BFG-50 Rifle

This is .50 caliber single-shot bolt-action rifle fitted with a 29.5" barrel. Also offered with 36" barrel. Parkerized finish. Weight is about 22 lbs.

NIB	EXC.	V.G.	GOOD	FAIR	POOR
2195	1600	1275	1000	700	350

BFG-50 Carbine

As above but fitted with a 22" barrel. Weight is about 17 lbs.

NIB	EXC.	V.G.	GOOD	FAIR	POOR
2195	1600	1275	1000	700	350

NIB	EXC.	V.G.	GOOD	FAIR	POOR

BFG-50A

This model is a gas operated semi-automatic takedown rifle with a 25" barrel. Parkerized finish. Magazine capacity is 10 rounds. Weight is about 25 lbs.

6700	5200	400	2750	1700	500

SHARPS ARMS CO., C.
Big Timber, Montana

This company was founded in 1975 in Richland, Washington, and moved to Big Timber, Montana, in 1980. It also produced custom-built rifles included the Model 1877 Sharps and others to individual customer specifications. The models listed are standard production models without extras.

Model 1874 Sharps Hartford Sporting Rifle

Chambered for a number of popular blackpowder calibers and fitted with either a 26", 28", or 30" tapered octagon barrel, double set triggers. American walnut stock with Hartford semi cresent steel butt. Silver nose cap. Case colored receiver with blued barrel. Optional sights. Weight depending on barrel length is about 10 lbs.

2300	1775	1350	1200	800	500

Model 1874 Bridgeport Sporting Rifle

As above, with Bridgeport checkered steel butt. Schnabel-style fore-end.

2300	1775	1350	1200	1000	500

Model 1875 Carbine—Hunters Rifle

Offered in a variety of calibers from .38-55 to .50-70. Fitted with a choice of tapered round military-style barrels. Lengths 22", 24" or 26". Full buckhorn and silver blade sights. Semi-cresent military-style butt, with slender fore-end. Case colored receiver and blued barrel. Double set triggers.

2300	1775	1350	1200	1000	500

Model 1874 Boss Gun

This model features engraved receiver, XXX fancy walnut, 34" #1 heavy tapered octagon barrel, long range tang sight, buckhorn rear sight, globe with post front sight, and Hartford nose cap. Calibers offered from .38-55 to .50-100. Weight is about 13.5 lbs. with 34" #1 barrel. **NOTE:** For Grade II add $750, for Grade III add $1,500.

4395	3250	2250	1500	1000	500

Model 1875 Target & Sporting Rifle

Offered in a variety of calibers this rifle is fitted with a 30" heavy tapered round barrel. American walnut stock with pistol grip. Case colored receiver with blued barrel. Single trigger. Price listed is without sights.

1500	1300	1075	900	775	400

Model 1875 Classic Rifle

This model features a receiver with octagon top and with tapered octagon barrel lengths from 26" to 30". American walnut stock with straight grip and crescent butt. Single trigger. German steel nose cap. Case colored receiver with blued barrel. Weight is about 9.5 lbs. with 30" barrel. Priced without sights.

1500	1300	1075	900	775	400

Model 1885 High Wall Sporting Rifle

Offered with choice of .26", 28", or 30" tapered octagon barrel. Calibers are from .22 to .45-120. Single trigger. American walnut stock with straight grip and oil finish. Checkered steel butt plate. Schnabel forend. Priced without sights. Weight is about 9.25 lbs. with 30" barrel.

2200	1750	1450	1195	750	400

Model 1885 High Wall Classic Rifle

As above but with crescent butt. Stock with cheek rest and silver inlay in forend.

2200	1750	1450	1195	750	400

SHARPS RIFLE MANUFACTURING COMPANY
Hartford, Connecticut

The first Sharps rifles to be manufactured were made by A.S. Nippes of Mill Creek, Pennsylvania. Later they were made by Robbins & Lawrence of Windsor, Vermont. It was not until 1855 that Sharps established his own factory in Hartford, Connecticut. After his death in 1874, the company was reorganized as the Sharps Rifle Company and remained in Hartford until 1876 when it moved to Bridgeport, Connecticut. It effectively ceased operations in 1880. The following descriptions are just a brief guide and are by no means exhaustive.

	NIB	EXC.	V.G.	GOOD	FAIR	POOR

Model 1849

A breechloading .44 caliber percussion rifle with a 30" barrel having a wooden cleaning rod mounted beneath it. The breech is activated by the trigger guard lever, and there is an automatic disk-type capping device on the right side of the receiver. The finish is blued and case colored. The stock is walnut with a brass patch box, buttplate, and forend cap. It is marked "Sharps Patent 1848." There were approximately 200 manufactured in 1849 and 1850 by the A.S. Nippes Company.

	NIB	EXC.	V.G.	GOOD	FAIR	POOR
	—	—	23000	18000	7500	1500

Model 1850

As above, with a Maynard priming mechanism mounted on the breech. Marked "Sharps Patent 1848" on the breech and the barrel "Manufactured by A.S. Nippes Mill Creek, Pa." The priming device marked "Maynard Patent 1845." There were approximately 200 manufactured in 1850. This model is also known as the 2nd Model Sharps.

	NIB	EXC.	V.G.	GOOD	FAIR	POOR
	—	—	21000	15000	6000	1200

Model 1851 Carbine

A single-shot breechloading percussion rifle in .36, .44, or .52 caliber with a 21.75" barrel and Maynard tape priming device. Blued and case hardened with a walnut stock and forearm held on by a single barrel band. The buttplate and barrel band are brass, and the military versions feature a brass patch box. The tang marked "C. Sharps Patent 1848," the barrel "Robbins & Lawrence," and the priming device "Edward Maynard Patentee 1845." Approximately 1,800 carbines and 180 rifles were manufactured by Robbins & Lawrence in Windsor, Vermont, in 1851. **NOTE:** Those bearing U.S. inspection marks are worth approximately 75 percent more than the values listed.

	NIB	EXC.	V.G.	GOOD	FAIR	POOR
	—	—	12000	9500	4250	1000

Model 1852

Similar to the above, but with Sharps' Patent Pellet Primer. The barrel marked "Sharps Rifle Manufg. Co. Hartford, Conn." Blued, case hardened, brass furniture and a walnut stock. Manufactured in carbine, rifle, sporting rifle and shotgun form. Approximately 4,600 carbines and 600 rifles were made between 1853 and 1855.

Military Carbine

	NIB	EXC.	V.G.	GOOD	FAIR	POOR
	—	—	9000	6750	3000	750

Military Rifle

	NIB	EXC.	V.G.	GOOD	FAIR	POOR
	—	—	12500	9750	4000	1000

Sporting Rifle

	NIB	EXC.	V.G.	GOOD	FAIR	POOR
	—	—	6500	4250	1750	500

Shotgun

	NIB	EXC.	V.G.	GOOD	FAIR	POOR
	—	—	4700	3250	1250	500

Model 1853

As above, but without the spring retainer for the lever hinge being mounted in the forestock. Approximately 10,500 carbines and 3,000 rifles were made between 1854 and 1858.

Military Carbine

	NIB	EXC.	V.G.	GOOD	FAIR	POOR
	—	—	8500	6250	2750	750

Military Rifle

	NIB	EXC.	V.G.	GOOD	FAIR	POOR
	—	—	12000	9500	4000	1000

Sporting Rifle

	NIB	EXC.	V.G.	GOOD	FAIR	POOR
	—	—	4500	2750	1250	450

Shotgun

	NIB	EXC.	V.G.	GOOD	FAIR	POOR
	—	—	4300	2500	1000	450

Model 1855

As above, in .52 caliber and fitted with a Maynard tape primer that is marked "Edward Maynard Patentee 1845." Approximately 700 were made between 1855 and 1856.

	NIB	EXC.	V.G.	GOOD	FAIR	POOR
	—	—	14500	10500	4250	1000

Model 1855 U.S. Navy Rifle

As above, with a 28" barrel, full-length stock and bearing U.S. Navy inspection marks. Approximately 260 were made in 1855.

	NIB	EXC.	V.G.	GOOD	FAIR	POOR
	—	—	13000	10500	4000	1000

	NIB	EXC.	V.G.	GOOD	FAIR	POOR

Model 1855 British Carbine

The Model 1855 with British inspection marks. Approximately 6,800 were made between 1855 and 1857.

	NIB	EXC.	V.G.	GOOD	FAIR	POOR
	—	—	8750	6250	3000	850

SHARPS STRAIGHT BREECH MODELS

Model 1859 Carbine

Similar to the above models, but with the breech opening cut on an almost vertical angle.

22" Barrel, Brass Mountings

	—	—	7700	6250	2500	500

Iron Mountings

	—	—	—	3250	1500	500

Model 1863 Carbine

	—	—	5000	3250	1500	500

Model 1863 Rifle

Without bayonet lug.

	—	—	4500	3750	1500	500

Model 1865 Rifle

Without bayonet lug.

	—	—	4200	3250	1000	500

Model 1865 Carbine

	—	—	4500	3750	1750	500

Model 1859 Rifle

30" Barrel

	—	—	5500	4250	2000	800

36" Barrel

	—	—	5500	4250	2000	800

Sporting Rifle

As above, with octagonal barrels, set triggers and finely figured walnut stocks. The Model 1853 Sporting rifle was built as a special order. About 32 were produced. The Model 1863 Sporting Rifle was also built on special order. About 16 were produced. No two of this model are alike. All reside in museums or collections.

Coffee-Mill Model

Some Sharps' carbines were fitted with coffee-mill style grinding devices set into their buttstocks. CAUTION: These arms are exceptionally rare and extreme caution should be exercised prior to purchase. Fakes exist.

	—	—	65000	42500	15000	5000

Metallic Cartridge Conversions

In 1867 approximately 32,000 Model 1859, 1863 and 1865 Sharps were altered to .52-70 rimfire and centerfire caliber.

	—	—	5500	4250	2000	600

Model 1869

A .40-50 to .50-70 caliber model produced in a military form with 26", 28", or 30" barrels; as a carbine with 21" or 24" barrels and in a sporting version with various barrel lengths and a fore-end stock fitted with a pewter tip. Approximately 650 were made.

Carbine

.50-70, saddle ring on frame.

	—	—	5500	4250	1750	500

Military Rifle

.50-70, 30" barrel with three barrel bands.

	—	—	6500	5250	2000	800

	NIB	EXC.	V.G.	GOOD	FAIR	POOR

Sporting Rifle
26" barrel, .44-77 and .50-70.

	NIB	EXC.	V.G.	GOOD	FAIR	POOR
	—	—	8000	6500	3000	950

Model 1870 Springfield Altered
Chambered for .50-70 caliber and fitted with a 35.5" barrel with two barrel bands, walnut stock, case hardened lock and breechlock. Buttplate stamped "US." Also built for Army trials with 22" barrel converted to centerfire.

First Type
Most common, straight breech.

	NIB	EXC.	V.G.	GOOD	FAIR	POOR
	—	—	5000	3750	1750	500

Second Type
Model 1874 action, serial #1 to 300.

	NIB	EXC.	V.G.	GOOD	FAIR	POOR
	—	—	8000	6000	2750	750

Carbine
22" barrel converted to centerfire.

	NIB	EXC.	V.G.	GOOD	FAIR	POOR
	—	—	10500	8250	5000	1250

Model 1874
This model was manufactured in a variety of calibers, barrel lengths, and stock styles. The barrel markings are of three forms: initially, "Sharps Rifle Manufg. Co. Hartford, Conn." ; then, "Sharps Rifle Co. Hartford, Conn." ; and finally "Sharps Rifle Co. Bridgeport, Conn." As of 1876 "Old Reliable" was stamped on the barrels. This marking is usually found on Bridgeport-marked rifles only. The major styles of this model are listed.

Military Carbine
.50-70, 21" barrel (460 made).

	NIB	EXC.	V.G.	GOOD	FAIR	POOR
	—	—	7950	5500	2750	750

Military Rifle
In .45-70 and .50-70 centerfire caliber with a 30" barrel and full-length fore-end secured by three barrel bands. Approximately 1,800 made.

	NIB	EXC.	V.G.	GOOD	FAIR	POOR
	—	—	7500	5000	2250	750

Hunter's Rifle
In .40, .44, .45-70, and .50-70 caliber with 26", 28", or 30" round barrels having open sights. Approximately 600 were manufactured.

	NIB	EXC.	V.G.	GOOD	FAIR	POOR
	—	—	8000	6250	2750	800

Business Rifle
In .40-70 and .45-75 Sharps caliber with a 26", 28", or 30" round barrel, adjustable sights and double-set triggers. Approximately 1,600 manufactured.

	NIB	EXC.	V.G.	GOOD	FAIR	POOR
	—	—	7750	6000	3250	1000

Sporting Rifle
Offered in a variety of calibers, barrel lengths, barrel weights, barrel styles and stock styles. Approximately 6,000 were manufactured.

	NIB	EXC.	V.G.	GOOD	FAIR	POOR
	—	—	15000	8500	4000	1500

Creedmoor Rifle
With a checkered pistol grip stock, vernier sights, combination wind gauge and spirit level front sight, set trigger and shotgun style butt. Approximately 150 were made.

	NIB	EXC.	V.G.	GOOD	FAIR	POOR
	—	—	24000	17500	8500	2000

Mid-Range Rifle
Similar to the above, with a crescent buttplate. Approximately 180 were made.

	NIB	EXC.	V.G.	GOOD	FAIR	POOR
	—	—	22500	15000	6500	1500

Long-Range Rifle
As above with a 34" octagonal barrel. Approximately 425 were manufactured.

	NIB	EXC.	V.G.	GOOD	FAIR	POOR
	—	—	23000	16500	6000	1500

Schuetzen Rifle
Similar to the above, with a checkered pistol grip stock and fore-end, a large Schuetzen style buttplate, double-set triggers and a vernier tang sight. Approximately 70 were manufactured.

	NIB	EXC.	V.G.	GOOD	FAIR	POOR
	—	—	22500	15000	6500	2000

	NIB	EXC.	V.G.	GOOD	FAIR	POOR

Model 1877

Similar to the Model 1874, and in .45-70 caliber with a 34" or 36" barrel which is marked "Sharps Rifle Co. Bridgeport, Conn. Old Reliable." Approximately 100 were manufactured in 1877 and 1878.

	NIB	EXC.	V.G.	GOOD	FAIR	POOR
	—	—	30000	10000	5000	2000

MODEL 1878 SHARPS-BORCHARDT

An internal hammer breechloading rifle manufactured from 1878 to approximately 1880. frame marked "Borchardt Patent Sharps Rifle Co. Bridgeport Conn. U.S.A.". **NOTE:** Be advised that the actions on Borchardt Sporting Rifles are worth a minimum of $750. Military actions are not as difficult to locate as Sporting actions. For the sake of continuity, rifles in poor condition but with usable actions are priced at the minimum of $750.

Carbine

Approximately 385 were made in .45-70 caliber, with 24" barrel. Fore-end secured by one barrel band.

	NIB	EXC.	V.G.	GOOD	FAIR	POOR
	—	—	4700	3750	1500	750

Military Rifle

Approximately 12,000 were made in .45-70 caliber, with 32.25" barrels. full stocks secured by two barrel bands.

	NIB	EXC.	V.G.	GOOD	FAIR	POOR
	—	—	3000	1250	900	750

Sporting Rifle

Approximately 1,600 were made in .45-70 caliber, with 30" round or octagonal barrels.

	NIB	EXC.	V.G.	GOOD	FAIR	POOR
	—	—	6000	2500	800	750

Hunter's Rifle

Approximately 60 were made in .40-caliber, with 26" barrels. Plain walnut stocks.

	NIB	EXC.	V.G.	GOOD	FAIR	POOR
	—	—	4500	1750	1000	750

Business Rifle

Approximately 90 were made with 28" barrels in .40-caliber.

	NIB	EXC.	V.G.	GOOD	FAIR	POOR
	—	—	4500	2000	1000	750

Officer's Rifle

Approximately 50 were made in .45-70 caliber, with 32" barrels and checkered walnut stocks.

	NIB	EXC.	V.G.	GOOD	FAIR	POOR
	—	—	7500	3750	1500	750

Express Rifle

Approximately 30 were made in .45-70 caliber, with 26" barrels, set triggers and checkered walnut stocks.

	NIB	EXC.	V.G.	GOOD	FAIR	POOR
	—	—	12500	6000	2000	800

Short-Range Rifle

Approximately 155 were made in .40-caliber, with 26" barrels. Venier rear sights, wind gauge front sight and checkered walnut stock.

	NIB	EXC.	V.G.	GOOD	FAIR	POOR
	—	—	7500	3750	1000	800

Mid-Range Rifle

Similar to above, with 30" barrel. Approximately 250 were manufactured.

	NIB	EXC.	V.G.	GOOD	FAIR	POOR
	—	10000	7000	4000	2000	900

Long-Range Rifle

Similar to above, with different sights. Approximately 230 were manufactured.

	NIB	EXC.	V.G.	GOOD	FAIR	POOR
	—	—	16000	6500	2500	900

C. Sharps & Company and Sharps & Hankins Company Breechloading, Single-Shot Pistol

A .31-, .34- or .36-caliber breechloading percussion pistol, with 5" or 6.5" round barrels. Blued case hardened, with walnut stock.

	NIB	EXC.	V.G.	GOOD	FAIR	POOR
	—	—	7000	5000	2000	600

Pistol-Grip Rifle

A .31- or .38-caliber breechloading percussion rifle resembling above. Manufactured in a variety of barrel lengths. Blued case hardened, with walnut stock having German silver mounts.

	NIB	EXC.	V.G.	GOOD	FAIR	POOR
	—	—	6800	4750	2500	750

	NIB	EXC.	V.G.	GOOD	FAIR	POOR

Percussion Revolver

A .25-caliber percussion revolver, with 3" octagonal barrel and 6-shot cylinder. Blued, with walnut grips. barrel marked "C. Sharps & Co., Phila. Pa.". Approximately 2,000 manufactured between 1857 and 1858.

	NIB	EXC.	V.G.	GOOD	FAIR	POOR
	—	—	4250	3000	1250	500

4-Shot Pepperbox Pistols

Between 1859 and 1874, these companies manufactured 4 barrel cartridge pocket pistols in a variety of calibers, barrel lengths and finishes. Barrels slide forward for loading. The major models are listed.

Model 1

Manufactured by C. Sharps & Co., in .22 rimfire caliber.

	NIB	EXC.	V.G.	GOOD	FAIR	POOR
	—	—	800	600	250	100

Model 2

As above, in .30 rimfire caliber.

	NIB	EXC.	V.G.	GOOD	FAIR	POOR
	—	—	800	600	250	100

Model 3

Manufactured by Sharps & Hankins. Marked "Address Sharps & Hankins Philadelphia Penn." on the frame. Caliber. 32 short rimfire.

	NIB	EXC.	V.G.	GOOD	FAIR	POOR
	—	—	950	750	300	150

Model 4

Similar to above in .32 Long rimfire, with rounded bird's-head grip.

	NIB	EXC.	V.G.	GOOD	FAIR	POOR
	—	—	950	750	300	150

Model 1861 Navy Rifle

A .52 Sharps & Hankins caliber breechloading single-shot rifle, with 32.75" barrel. Full stock secured by three barrel bands. Blued case hardened, with walnut stock. Approximately 700 made in 1861 and 1862.

	NIB	EXC.	V.G.	GOOD	FAIR	POOR
	—	—	5000	300	2000	700

Model 1862 Navy Carbine

A .24 -caliber breechloading carbine, with 24" leather covered barrel. Case hardened with walnut stock. Frame marked "Sharps & Hankins Philada.". Approximately 8,000 manufactured between 1861 and 1862.

	NIB	EXC.	V.G.	GOOD	FAIR	POOR
	—	—	5000	3500	2000	700

Short Cavalry Carbine

Similar to above, with 19" blued barrel. Approximately 500 were manufactured.

	NIB	EXC.	V.G.	GOOD	FAIR	POOR
	—	—	5000	3500	2000	700

Army Model

Similar to above, with 24" barrel that does not have a leather covering. Approximately 500 were purchased by the Army.

	NIB	EXC.	V.G.	GOOD	FAIR	POOR
	—	—	4750	3000	1750	700

SHATTUCK, C. S.
Hatfield, Massachusetts

Double-Barrel Shotguns

In addition to single-barrel shotguns, Shattuck made about 1,000 hammerless doubles.

	NIB	EXC.	V.G.	GOOD	FAIR	POOR
	—	1000	500	400	300	200

Boom

A .22 caliber spur trigger revolver with a 2" octagonal barrel and 6-shot cylinder. Nickel-plated with rosewood or walnut grips. The barrel marked "Boom" and "Pat. Nov. 4. 1879." Manufactured during the 1880s.

	NIB	EXC.	V.G.	GOOD	FAIR	POOR
	—	—	400	150	100	75

Pocket Revolver

A .32 caliber spur trigger revolver with a 3.5" octagonal barrel and 5-shot cylinder. Nickel-plated with hard rubber grips. The barrel marked "C. S. Shattuck Hatfield, Mass. Pat. Nov. 4, 1879." Manufactured during the 1880s.

	NIB	EXC.	V.G.	GOOD	FAIR	POOR
	—	—	500	200	150	100

	NIB	EXC.	V.G.	GOOD	FAIR	POOR

SHAW & LEDOYT
Stafford, Connecticut

Under Hammer Pistol

A .31 caliber under hammer percussion pistol with a 2.5" to 3.5" half-octagonal barrel. Blued with a brass mounted walnut grip. The frame marked "Shaw & LeDoyt/Stafford. Conn." Manufactured during the 1850s.

			V.G.	GOOD	FAIR	POOR
	—	—	1750	1300	550	150

SHAWK & MCLANAHAN
St. Louis, Missouri

Navy Revolver

A .36 caliber percussion revolver with an 8" round barrel and 6-shot cylinder. Blued with a brass frame and walnut grips. Marked "Shawk & McLanahan, St. Louis, Carondelet, Mo." Produced in limited quantities prior to 1860.

			V.G.	GOOD	FAIR	POOR
	—	15000	12000	5500	2000	

SHERIDAN PRODUCTS, INC.
Racine, Wisconsin

Knockabout/Model D

A .22 caliber single-shot pistol with a 5" barrel having fixed sights. Blued with plastic grips. Manufactured between 1953 and 1960.

		EXC.	V.G.	GOOD	FAIR	POOR
	—	350	225	175	100	50

SHILEN RIFLES, INC.
Ennis, Texas

Model DGA Bench Rest Rifle

A centerfire single-shot bolt-action rifle with a 26" barrel and either fiberglass or walnut stock.

		EXC.	V.G.	GOOD	FAIR	POOR
	—	1750	1400	1100	850	500

Model DGA Sporter

A .17 Remington to .308 Winchester caliber bolt-action sporting rifle with a 24" barrel furnished without sights. Blued with a walnut stock.

		EXC.	V.G.	GOOD	FAIR	POOR
	—	1750	1400	1100	850	500

Model DGA Varminter

As above, in varmint calibers with a 25" barrel.

		EXC.	V.G.	GOOD	FAIR	POOR
	—	1750	1400	1100	850	500

Model DGA Silhouette Rifle

As above, in .308 Winchester only.

		EXC.	V.G.	GOOD	FAIR	POOR
	—	1750	1400	1100	850	500

SHILOH RIFLE MFG. CO., INC.
Big Timber, Montana

Established in Farmingdale, New York, in 1976, this company moved to Big Timber, Montana, in 1983 with the name Shiloh Products. It changed its name to Shiloh Rifle Manufacturing Co. in that same year. In 1985 the company began marketing its products factory direct. In 1991 Robert, Phyllis, and Kirk Bryan purchased the company. Those interested in the Sharps reproduction rifles manufactured by this company are advised to contact them in Big Timber. **NOTE:** The company will build a rifle to customers' specifications. It is therefore possible that many of these rifles have special-order features that are not reflected in the base model price. Since Shiloh is in effect a custom (or at least semi-custom) manufacturer, the rifles listed here are representative but not inclusive.

Model 1863 Military Rifle

A .54 caliber percussion rifle with a 30" barrel, single- or double-set triggers and full-length walnut stock secured by three barrel bands.

NIB	EXC.	V.G.	GOOD	FAIR	POOR
1900	1650	1100	900	700	500

Model 1863 Sporting Rifle

As above, with a 30" octagonal barrel, sporting sights and a half-length stock.

NIB	EXC.	V.G.	GOOD	FAIR	POOR
1800	1550	1050	850	600	450

	NIB	EXC.	V.G.	GOOD	FAIR	POOR

Model 1863 Military Carbine
The Model 1863 with a 22" round barrel and carbine stock secured by one barrel band.

	1900	1650	1100	900	700	500

Model 1862 Confederate Robinson
As above, with a 21.5" barrel, brass buttplate and barrel band.

	1900	1650	1100	900	700	500

Model 1874 Creedmore Target Rifle
This model is furnished with a 32" 1/2 round, 1/2 octagon barrel. Extra-fancy wood stock with pistol grip, no cheek rest, and shotgun butt. Single trigger. No sights.

	2700	2250	1700	1300	800	500

Model 1874 Buffalo Rifle (Quigley)
Offered in .45-70 or .45-110 with 34" heavy octagon barrel. Mid-range tang sight with globe front sight. Semi buckhorn rear sight. Double-set triggers. Military buttstock with patch box. No cheek rest and straight-grip stock.

	3300	2750	2100	1700	1200	500

Model 1874 Long Range Express Rifle
Manufactured in a variety of calibers with a 34" octagonal barrel, double-set triggers, vernier rear sight and globe front sight.

	2200	1750	1450	1195	750	400

Model 1874 Montana Roughrider Rifle
As above, with either octagonal or half-octagonal barrels ranging in lengths from 24" to 34".

	2200	1750	1450	1195	750	400

Saddle Rifle
As above, with a 26" barrel and shotgun butt.

	2200	1750	1450	1195	750	400

No. 1 Sporter Deluxe Rifle
Similar to the above, with a 30" octagonal barrel.

	2200	1750	1450	1195	750	400

No. 3 Standard Sporter
As above, with a military-style stock.

	2200	1750	1450	1195	750	400

The Business Rifle
As above, with a heavy 28" barrel.

	2200	1750	1450	1195	750	400

Model 1874 Military Rifle
The Model 1874 with a 30" round barrel, military sights and full-length stocks secured by three barrel bands.

	2200	1750	1450	1195	750	400

Model 1874 Carbine
Similar to the above, with a 24" round barrel.

	2000	1550	1150	750	500	300

The Jaeger
The Model 1874 with a 26" half-octagonal barrel, open sights and pistol-grip stock with a shotgun butt.

	2200	1750	1450	1195	750	400

Hartford Model
A reproduction of the Sharps Hartford Model.

	2200	1750	1450	1195	750	400

Model 1874 Military Carbine
Similar to the Military Rifle, but with a 22" round barrel.

	2200	1750	1450	1195	750	400

	NIB	EXC.	V.G.	GOOD	FAIR	POOR

SIG-HAMMERLI
Lenzburg, Switzerland

Model P240 Target Pistol

A .32 Smith & Wesson Long Wadcutter or .38 Midrange caliber semi-automatic pistol with a 5.9" barrel, adjustable rear sight, adjustable trigger and 5-shot magazine. Blued, with adjustable walnut grips. Imported prior 1987.

	NIB	EXC.	V.G.	GOOD	FAIR	POOR
	—	1300	1150	950	750	600

.22 Conversion Unit

A barrel, slide, and magazine used to convert the above to .22 caliber.

	—	500	450	400	300	200

Model P208S

This is a semi-automatic target pistol chambered for the .22 LR cartridge. The barrel length is 5.9" long with adjustable sights. Sight radius is 8.2". Trigger has adjustable pull weight, travel, slack weight, and creep. Grips are stippled walnut with adjustable palm shelf. Weight is approximately 37 oz. empty.

1900	1600	1300	1100	750	500

Model P280

This model is a semi-automatic pistol chambered for the .22 LR cartridge or the .32 S&W Long Wadcutter. Single-action-only. Barrel length is 4.6" with a sight radius of 8.7". Adjustable sights. Trigger is adjustable for pull weight, take-up, let-off, and creep. Stippled walnut grip with adjustable palm shelf. Weight is 35 oz. for the .22 caliber and 42 oz. for the .32 caliber. Magazine capacity is six .22 caliber rounds and five .32 caliber rounds.

1200	10000	800	650	500	300

Model P160/162

This .22 LR single-shot pistol is designed for international free pistol competition. Barrel length is 11.3" with a sight radius of 14.6". Trigger is fully adjustable as are the sights. Stippled walnut grips with adjustable palm shelf and rake angle. The Model 160 has a mechanical trigger while the Model 162 is fitted with an electric trigger.

2300	2000	1700	1250	800	400

Trailside PL 22

Introduced in 1999 this semi-automatic pistol is chambered for the .22 LR cartridge. Barrel length is 4.5" or 6" with fixed sights. Synthetic grips. Two-tone finish. Magazine capacity is 10 rounds. Weight is about 28 oz. with 4.5" barrel and 30 oz. with 6" barrel. **NOTE:** Add $90 for 6" barrel.

575	500	375	295	200	100

Trailside PL 22 Target

Similar to the PL 22 with the addition of adjustable sights and walnut grips. Introduced in 1999. **NOTE:** Add $25 for 6" barrel.

595	525	400	325	225	125

Trailside Competition

Introduced in 2004 this .22 caliber model features a 6" barrel with adjustable sights and adjustable competition grip, counterweights, and two-tone finish. Magazine capacity is 10 rounds. Weight is about 36 oz.

800	675	500	425	300	150

SIG
Neuhausen, Switzerland

P 210

Pistol introduced in 1947. Standard issue sidearm of Swiss military from 1949 to 1975. Also issued to Danish Army as Model M49. Chambered in 9mm Parabellum, 7.65 (.30 Luger) and .22 Long Rifle, with 8-round magazine. A .22 conversion kit also available for centerfire models. Short-recoil operated single-action pistol, with frame-mounted manual safety and 4.75" barrel. Several variations of original P210 were imported into U.S. from 1950s until about 1987, with limited importation of a few more models until 2007. Upgraded and improved version introduced in 2011 as P210 Legend. See listing under SIG Sauer. **NOTE:** Add premium of 40 to 50 percent for .22 LR conversion kit.

P210 Danish Army Model M49

3000	2500	2000	1500	800	400

	NIB	EXC.	V.G.	GOOD	FAIR	POOR

P 210-1

Fixed sights, walnut grips, polished finish. Imported until 1986.

	2600	2200	1700	1100	500	350

P 210-2

Fixed sights, plastic or wood grips, matte finish. Imported 1987 to 2002. **NOTE:** Add 50 percent premium for West German Police model, with loaded chamber indicator.

	2000	1600	1000	750	400	300

P 210-5

Adjustable sights, extended frame and barrel (5"), wood or rubber grips, matte finish, adjustable trigger. Push-button magazine release. Limited importation from 1997 to 2007.

	2250	1850	1650	1000	600	400

P 210-6

As above, with 4.75" barrel.

	2250	1850	1650	1000	600	400

P210-7

In .22 LR caliber. Fewer than 500 made.

	3500	2900	2400	1600	1000	400

P210-8

Special order target model, with adjustable sights, wood grips, heavy frame. Available from 2001 to 2003 only. Limited importation.

	3800	3200	2650	1800	1000	400

SIGARMS/SIG-SAUER
Eckernforde, Germany
Neuhausen, Switzerland
Exeter, New Hampshire

In 1985, SIG established a U.S. presence by opening SIG Arms in Exeter, New Hampshire. Name was changed to Sig-Sauer in 2007. Most current SIG firearms are manufactured in U.S., but some are imported from Switzerland or Germany. Since 2000, SIG has been owned by Luke and Ortmeier Group, which also owns Blaser, Mauser and J.P. Sauer.

PISTOLS

P210

Model reintroduced into U.S. in 2001. Based on Swiss military version first built in 1949. Designed primarily as a target pistol and furnished in four different variations. All variations chambered for 9mm cartridge. **NOTE:** Older P210 models imported before 1968 without importer stamps and pistols built during late 1940s and early 1950s, may bring a premium to collectors. Be aware that extra barrels, conversion kits and other special order features will add additional value.

P210 Legend

Updated variation of P210. Features include side-mounted magazine release, improved and extended beavertail, black Nitron finish and choice of fixed or adjustable sights. Available only in 9mm. Introduced in 2011. Made in Germany. **NOTE:** Add $200 for adjustable sights.

	2000	1850	1500	1100	700	400

P220

High-quality double-action semi-automatic pistol chambered for .38 Super, .45 ACP and 9mm Parabellum. Has 4.41" barrel and fixed sights. Features de-cocking lever that was found originally on Sauer Model 38H. Two versions of this pistol—one with bottom magazine release (commonly referred to as European model); other with release on side (commonly referred to as American model), as on Model 1911 Colt. Frame is lightweight alloy, matte-finished and available in either blue, nickel, or K-Kote finish. Black plastic grips. The .45 ACP magazine capacity 7 rounds, weighs 25.7 oz.; .38 Super magazine capacity 9 rounds, weighs 26.5 oz.; 9mm magazine holds 9 rounds, overall weight 26.5 oz. Manufactured from 1976 and still in production. The 9mm and .38 Super versions are no longer in production. Prices listed are for guns with standard blue finish. **NOTE:** Add $40 K-Kote finish; $40 nickel slide; $100 Stainless steel. In 2004 a blued version with tactical rail was offered.

	825	600	400	300	200	150

	NIB	EXC.	V.G.	GOOD	FAIR	POOR

P220 .22

As above chambered for .22 LR cartridge.

	NIB	EXC.	V.G.	GOOD	FAIR	POOR
	500	400	300	200	150	100

P220 ST

As above chambered for .45 ACP cartridge. Features stainless steel frame and slide, with tactical rail. Also includes a SIGARMS tactical knife and aluminum carrying case. Weight about 39 oz.

	NIB	EXC.	V.G.	GOOD	FAIR	POOR
	875	700	550	425	300	150

P220 Sport

Introduced in 1999, this .45 ACP pistol is similar to P220. Addition of 5.5" barrel, with stainless steel compensator. Frame and slide are stainless steel. Magazine capacity 7 rounds. Weight about 44 oz.

	NIB	EXC.	V.G.	GOOD	FAIR	POOR
	1400	1250	1000	775	500	300

P220R SAO

An 8+1 or 10+1 capacity single-action semi-automatic chambered for .45 ACP. Polymer grip and Nitron finish, 4.4" barrel, weight 30.4 oz., 5-lb. trigger. Picatinny rail. Introduced 2006.

	NIB	EXC.	V.G.	GOOD	FAIR	POOR
	750	600	475	350	200	150

P220R DAK

Semi-automatic with 8+1 or 10+1 capacity chambered for .45 ACP. Polymer grip and Nitron finish, 4.4" barrel, weight 30.4 oz., 7.5-lb. trigger. Picatinny rail. Introduced 2006.

	NIB	EXC.	V.G.	GOOD	FAIR	POOR
	875	700	600	475	350	200

P220 SAS

An 8+1 capacity double-action semi-automatic chambered for .45 ACP. Fixed sights, wood grips, 4.4" barrel, weight 30.4 oz., 6.5-lb. trigger. Introduced 2006.

	NIB	EXC.	V.G.	GOOD	FAIR	POOR
	1000	875	725	600	400	200

P220 Carry SAS

An 8+1 capacity double-action semi-automatic chambered for .45 ACP. Fixed sights, wood grips, 3.9" barrel, weight 30.4 oz., 6.5-lb. trigger. Introduced 2006.

	NIB	EXC.	V.G.	GOOD	FAIR	POOR
	900	795	700	550	400	200

P220 Carry

An 8+1 or 10+1 capacity single-/double-action semi-automatic chambered for .45 ACP. Fixed sights, polymer grips, 3.9" barrel, weight 30.4 oz. Introduced 2006.

	NIB	EXC.	V.G.	GOOD	FAIR	POOR
	875	725	600	450	350	200

P220R Equinox

An 8+1 or 10+1 capacity single-/double-action semi-automatic chambered for .45 ACP. Fixed sights, wood grips, 4.4" barrel, weight 30.4 oz. Introduced 2006.

	NIB	EXC.	V.G.	GOOD	FAIR	POOR
	1200	1050	750	600	450	300

P220R Carry Equinox

An 8+1 or 10+1 capacity single-/double-action semi-automatic chambered for .45 ACP. Fixed sights, wood grips, 3.9" barrel, weight 30.4 oz. Introduced 2006.

	NIB	EXC.	V.G.	GOOD	FAIR	POOR
	875	700	575	450	350	200

P220 Langdon Edition

.45 ACP pistol introduced in 2004. Features 4.4" barrel, Nill wood grips, fiber optic sight, competition rear sight, front serrations, short trigger and other special features. Two-tone finish. Magazine capacity 8 rounds. Weight about 41 oz. Manufactured 500.

	NIB	EXC.	V.G.	GOOD	FAIR	POOR
	1300	1050	800	600	450	250

P220 Combat

Similar to P220, with sand-colored alloy slide and steel frame. Threaded barrel for suppressor. Capacity 8+1 or 10+1. Designed for SOCOM sidearm trials. Introduced in 2007.

	NIB	EXC.	V.G.	GOOD	FAIR	POOR
	1100	950	750	600	400	200

P220 Match

Similar to P220, with 5"barrel. Adjustable sights. Introduced 2007.

	NIB	EXC.	V.G.	GOOD	FAIR	POOR
	950	800	675	500	300	150

	NIB	EXC.	V.G.	GOOD	FAIR	POOR

P220 Super Match

Super-accurized version of P220 Match, with single-action-only trigger, beavertail safety and custom wood grips. Limited edition.

NIB	EXC.	V.G.	GOOD	FAIR	POOR
1200	975	850	600	400	200

P220 Compact

Similar to P220, with 3.9" barrel and 6+1 capacity. Single-action-only or single-/double-action. Various finishes, grip and sight options.

NIB	EXC.	V.G.	GOOD	FAIR	POOR
950	800	675	500	375	200

P220 Elite

Similar to P220, with SIG's new Short Reset Trigger or SRT. Beavertail safety, front cocking serrations, front strap checkering, SIGLITE\xa8 Night Sights and custom wood grips. Introduced in 2008. Also available in single action-only model.

NIB	EXC.	V.G.	GOOD	FAIR	POOR
950	800	675	500	375	200

P220 Elite Stainless

Similar to above in stainless. Introduced 2008.

NIB	EXC.	V.G.	GOOD	FAIR	POOR
1250	1100	875	650	450	200

P220 Carry Elite Stainless

Compact version of above, with 3.9" barrel; chambered in .45 ACP; 8-round capacity. Introduced 2008.

NIB	EXC.	V.G.	GOOD	FAIR	POOR
1250	1100	875	650	450	200

P220 Platinum Elite

Fine-tuned enhanced version of P220 Elite, with front cocking serrations, front strap checkering, SIGLITE Adjustable Combat Night Sights and custom aluminum grips.

NIB	EXC.	V.G.	GOOD	FAIR	POOR
1000	825	700	550	400	200

P220 Extreme

Two-tone black Nitron/stainless finish, with front slide serrations, Siglite night sights, Hogue G10 grips

NIB	EXC.	V.G.	GOOD	FAIR	POOR
1000	850	750	600	450	350

P224

Sub-compact variation of P220/229 series, with double-stack magazine, steel slide, alloy frame, black wood grips and Siglite night sights. In 9mm, .357 Sig or .40 S&W. Available with DA/SA or DAK trigger. Introduced in 2012

NIB	EXC.	V.G.	GOOD	FAIR	POOR
1000	875	675	500	400	250

P225

Similar to Model P220, except chambered for 9mm cartridge. More compact pistol, with 3.86" barrel. Has 8-shot detachable magazine and adjustable sights. Finish is matte blue. K-Kote or electroless nickel plate, with black plastic grips. Overall length 7.1"; height 5.2"; weighs 26.1 oz. No longer in production. **NOTE:** Add $70 K-Kote finish; $70 nickel slide.

NIB	EXC.	V.G.	GOOD	FAIR	POOR
625	575	500	400	200	150

P225 Limited

This 9mm 3.9" model features Novak low-carry rear sight, three magazines, SIG-Sauer range bag. Introduced in 2004. Weight about 26 oz.

NIB	EXC.	V.G.	GOOD	FAIR	POOR
800	625	500	395	275	150

P226

Model is full size high-capacity pistol, with 4.41" barrel chambered for 9mm or .40 S&W cartridge. In 1996 this model also available chambered for .357 SIG cartridge. Available with 15- or 20-round detachable magazine and high-contrast sights. Either blued, electroless nickel plated or polymer finish known as K-Kote. Overall length 7.7"; height 5.5"; weighs 26.5 oz. This model introduced in 1983. Add $50 for K-Kote finish; $50 for nickel slide. In 2003 this pistol available with integral rail system on frame. In 2004 this pistol offered with optional Crimson Trace laser grips. **NOTE:** Add $125 for Crimson Trace laser grips.

NIB	EXC.	V.G.	GOOD	FAIR	POOR
825	600	550	450	300	200

P226BR .22

Similar to above in .22 LR. **NOTE:** Add $125 for Crimson Trace laser grips.

NIB	EXC.	V.G.	GOOD	FAIR	POOR
550	475	350	250	175	100

	NIB	EXC.	V.G.	GOOD	FAIR	POOR

P226 Navy Seal

Special limited edition 9mm pistol fitted with 4.4" barrel. Special serial numbers from "nsw0001" and above. Black finish.

	1400	900	750	550	400	300

P226 ST

Similar to P226, with stainless steel frame and slide. Offered in 9mm, .40 S&W and .357 SIG. Barrel length 4.4". Magazine capacity 10 rounds. Weight about 39 oz. Features include reverse two-tone finish, 3-dot sights and Hogue rubber grips. Very limited production in 2004 and 2005.

	1000	850	700	575	400	200

P226 Sport Stock

Introduced in 2002, this 9mm pistol features heavy match barrel and adjustable rear sight. Hand tuned. Specifications same as P226 ST. Available by special order only.

	1600	1450	1200	950	700	300

P226 Sport

Introduced in 2001, this model similar to other SIG Sport models. Chambered for 9mm Luger cartridge. Stainless steel slide and frame. Adjustable target sights and competition barrel weight.

	1350	1175	1000	850	700	300

JP226 Jubilee Pistol

Variation is a special limited edition of P226. Each gun carries a special serial number prefixed JP. Grips are hand carved select European walnut. Slide and frame covered with solid gold wire inlays. Trigger, hammer, decocking lever, slide catch lever and magazine catch are all gold plated. Each pistol comes in custom fitted hard case of full leather. No longer imported into U.S. Fewer than 250 imported between 1991 and 1992.

	1795	1500	1200	900	700	400

P226R DAK

Introduced in 2005. Features double-action only DAK trigger system, with double strike capability. Chambered for 9mm, .357 SIG or .40 S&W cartridge. Barrel 4.4". Fixed sights. Magazine capacity 10, 12 or 15 rounds depending on caliber. Weight about 32 oz. for 9mm; 34 oz. for .357 SIG or .40 S&W models.

	900	775	600	450	300	200

P226 X-Five

Single-action model chambered for 9mm or .40 S&W cartridge. Fitted with 5" barrel. Adjustable rear sight and trigger pull. Slide has front cocking serrations. Checkered wood Null grips. Magazine capacity 19 rounds for 9mm; 14 rounds for .40 S&W. Stainless steel finish. Weight about 47 oz.

	1700	1525	1275	900	550	300

P226 Tactical

9mm pistol has 4.98" extended threaded barrel. Fixed sights. Alloy frame. Magazine capacity 15 rounds. Weight about 32 oz. Black finish. Ellett Brothers exclusive. Introduced in 2005.

	900	795	600	450	300	150

P226 SAS

Double-action semi-automatic, with 12+1 capacity chambered for .40 S&W. Fixed sights, wood grips, 4.4" barrel, weight 34 oz., 6.5-lb. trigger. Introduced 2006.

	875	750	600	475	300	150

P226R Equinox

An 10+1 or 12+1 capacity single-/double-action semi-automatic chambered for .40 S&W. Fixed sights, wood grips, 4.4" barrel, weight 34 oz. Introduced 2006.

	1175	1025	875	700	550	350

P226 SCT

All black Nitron finished P226. Featuring front cocking serrations, SIGLITE rear night sight, TRUGLO tritium fiber optic front sight. Comes with four newly designed 20-round magazines for 9mm; or four 15-round magazines for .40S&W.

	950	825	700	575	400	200

P226 Elite

Introduced 2008. Similar to P226, with redesigned short-reset trigger and improved ergonomics. Chambered in 9mm, .40 S&W and .357 SIG. Model P226 Enhanced Elite has

NIB	EXC.	V.G.	GOOD	FAIR	POOR

same features as P226 Elite, with addition of ergonomic one-piece reduced-reach polymer grips.

| 1050 | 900 | 825 | 675 | 450 | 250 |

P226 Elite Stainless

Similar to above in stainless steel.

| 1100 | 1000 | 900 | 750 | 475 | 275 |

P226 Platinum Elite

Fine-tuned enhanced version of P226 Elite, with front cocking serrations, front strap checkering, SIGLITE Adjustable Combat Night Sights and custom aluminum grips.

| 1250 | 1175 | 950 | 775 | 500 | 300 |

Mosquito

Model essentially a P226 reduced to 90 percent of its original size. Double-/single-action trigger fitted with 3.98" barrel. Chambered for .22 Long Rifle cartridge. Polymer frame with Picatinny rail. Fixed sights. Magazine capacity 10 rounds. Weight about 24.5 oz. Black finish. Introduced in 2005.

| 325 | 300 | 250 | 200 | 150 | 100 |

P226 SAO

Single-action only variation of Model P226. Made in Germany. Introduced 2013.

| 1100 | 1000 | 850 | 600 | 450 | 350 |

P226 MK25 Navy Model

A 9mm semi-automatic model, with choice of black Nitron or Flat Dark Earth finish, Picatinny rail and night sights. Added touch of an anchor engraved on the slide.

| 1000 | 900 | 750 | 500 | 400 | 250 |

P227

A .45 ACP chambered semi-automatic, with a slender double-stack 10-round magazine. P227 comes in several variations, with either 3.9" or 4.4" barrel. Edges are dehorned and models available with or without a Picatinny rail. Siglite night sights are standard. **NOTE:** Add $100 for Equinox model, with wood grips.

| 950 | 850 | 725 | 450 | 375 | 200 |

P228

Compact version of P226 fitted with 3.86" barrel. Chambered for 9mm cartridge. Available in blue, K-Kote or nickel finish, with black grips. Overall length 7.1"; height 5.4"; weighs 26.1 oz. Made from 1990 to 1997, reintroduced 2004 to 2006. **NOTE:** Add $50 K-Kote finish; $50 nickel slide.

| 725 | 600 | 475 | 350 | 200 | 150 |

P228 (New Model)

Reintroduced in 2013. Black Nitron or stainless two-tone finish. Standard single-/double-action operation, Siglite night sights, two 15-round magazines.

| 1000 | 850 | 700 | 500 | 400 | 350 |

P229

Similar to P228 except chambered for .40 S&W cartridge. Has blackened stainless steel slide and lightweight aluminum alloy frame. Slide slightly larger to accommodate more powerful cartridge. In 1996, 9mm chamber also offered. Overall length 7.1"; height 5.4". Introduced in 1992, pistol weighs 27.54 oz. and magazine capacity of 12 rounds. In 1994, company introduced a new caliber for this model; .357 SIG developed by Federal. Magazine capacity 12 rounds.

| 800 | 675 | 550 | 400 | 250 | 150 |

P229 Nickel

Same as standard P229. with full nickel finish over stainless steel slide and alloy frame. Weight about 27.5 oz. Introduced in 1998.

| 850 | 525 | 600 | 450 | 275 | 175 |

P229 Stainless

Introduced in 2005. Same features as standard P229 except for stainless steel slide and frame. Weight about 41 oz. Magazine capacity 12 rounds.

| 900 | 775 | 600 | 475 | 300 | 150 |

	NIB	EXC.	V.G.	GOOD	FAIR	POOR

P229 Sport

Chambered for .357 SIG cartridge. Fitted with 4.8" barrel, with muzzle compensator. Adjustable target sights. Both frame and slide are stainless steel. Magazine capacity 10 rounds. Weight approximately 41 oz. Introduced in 1998.

NIB	EXC.	V.G.	GOOD	FAIR	POOR
1500	1350	1175	950	600	400

P229 Limited

.40 S&W pistol features 3.9" barrel with fixed sights. Stainless steel slide with Nitron finish. Scroll engraving on top of slide, high polished 24 kt gold accents on trigger, hammer, magazine catch and grip screws. Hardwood grips.

NIB	EXC.	V.G.	GOOD	FAIR	POOR
950	825	675	500	350	200

P229 Combo

Chambered for .40 S&W cartridge and fitted with 3.9" barrel. Fixed sights. Black Nitron finish. Spare barrel chambered for .357 SIG included. Magazine capacity 10 rounds. Weight about 30 oz. Introduced in 2004.

NIB	EXC.	V.G.	GOOD	FAIR	POOR
900	775	625	450	300	175

P229 Elite

P229 Elite features ergonomic beavertail grip, front cocking serrations, front strap checkering, SIGLITE Night Sights, custom wood grips and new Short Reset Trigger or SRT. Available in 9mm and .40 S&W. P229 Enhanced Elite has same features as P229 Elite, with addition of ergonomic one-piece reduced-reach polymer grips.

NIB	EXC.	V.G.	GOOD	FAIR	POOR
1100	900	825	675	450	250

P229 Platinum Elite

Fine-tuned enhanced version of P229 Elite, with front cocking serrations, front strap checkering, SIGLITE Adjustable Combat Night Sights and custom aluminum grips.

NIB	EXC.	V.G.	GOOD	FAIR	POOR
1100	900	800	695	475	300

1911 C3

1911-style 6+1 autoloader in .45 ACP. 4-2/4" barrel, alloy frame. Introduced in 2008.

NIB	EXC.	V.G.	GOOD	FAIR	POOR
900	775	600	475	300	150

1911 Platinum Elite

1911-style 8+1 autoloader in .45 ACP. 5"barrel, Nitron frame, aluminum grips. Introduced in 2008.

NIB	EXC.	V.G.	GOOD	FAIR	POOR
1100	950	800	675	500	300

1911 Platinum Elite Carry

Compact version of above, with 4.5" barrel. Introduced in 2008.

NIB	EXC.	V.G.	GOOD	FAIR	POOR
1250	1025	875	750	575	350

1911-22

Same dimensions as standard 1911 pistol. Caliber .22 LR, alloy frame and slide, 10-round magazine, blowback operated, extended thumb safety, extended beavertail grip safety, magazine disconnect safety, skeletonized hammer and trigger. Weighs 18 ounces, Nitron finish.

NIB	EXC.	V.G.	GOOD	FAIR	POOR
340	285	235	200	165	100

1911 Scorpion

Caliber .45 ACP, stainless steel slide and frame, 8-round magazine, extended thumb safety, extended beavertail grip safety, skeletonized hammer and flat trigger, checkered front strap and mainspring housing, Low-Mount night sights and accessory rail. Frame and slide has Cerkote desert tan finish, grips are Hogue G10 Magwell with Piranha texture.

NIB	EXC.	V.G.	GOOD	FAIR	POOR
975	850	700	500	300	150

Model GSR

.45 ACP pistol introduced in 2004. Fitted with 5" barrel. Single-action only. Offered with white stainless steel frame and slide or blued frame and slide. Also offered with black Nitron finish. Tac rail standard. Hand fitted. Magazine capacity 8 rounds. Weight about 39 oz.

NIB	EXC.	V.G.	GOOD	FAIR	POOR
775	650	500	375	250	150

REVOLUTION SERIES

Revolution

All-stainless frames and slides in four configurations. Novak Night Sights, Rose- or Diamond Wood custom grips. Stainless or Nitron finish. 8+1 capacity, 45 ACP, single-action, 5" barrel, 40.3

	NIB	EXC.	V.G.	GOOD	FAIR	POOR

oz. Introduced 2006.

	900	775	600	475	300	150

Revolution Custom STX

Single-action .45 ACP stainless semi-auto with 8+1 capacity. Adjustable combat night sights and custom wood grip panels, 5" barrel, 40.6 oz. Introduced 2006.

	1100	950	800	675	500	300

Revolution TTT

Stainless semi-auto with 8+1 capacity. Single-action .45 ACP. Adjustable combat night sights and custom wood grip panels, 5" barrel, 40.3 oz. Introduced 2006.

	1000	850	675	575	425	300

Revolution XO

Single-action .45 ACP stainless semi-auto with 8+1 capacity. Polymer grip panels. 8.65" LOA, 5" barrel, 40.3 oz. Introduced 2006.

	900	775	600	475	300	150

Revolution Target

Single-action .45 ACP stainless semi-auto with 8+1 capacity. Adjustable target night sights. Custom wood grip panels, 5" barrel, 40.3 oz. Stainless or Nitron finish. Introduced 2006.

	950	825	650	495	325	150

Revolution Carry

Single-action .45 ACP stainless semi-auto with 8+1 capacity. Fixed sights. Custom wood grip panels, 4" barrel, 35.4 oz. Stainless or Nitron finish. Introduced 2006.

	900	775	600	475	300	150

Revolution Compact

Stainless semi-auto single-action .45 ACP with 6+1 capacity. Fixed sights. Custom wood grip panels, 4" barrel, 30.3 oz. Stainless or Nitron finish. Introduced 2006.

	950	825	650	495	325	150

Revolution Compact SAS

Dehorned version of Revolution Compact.

	950	825	650	495	325	150

Revolution Compact C3

Similar to Revolution Compact but with black anodized alloy frame and stainless or Nitron-finished slide.

	950	825	650	495	325	150

Revolution Custom Compact RCS

Stainless semi-auto single-action .45 ACP with 6+1 capacity. Fixed sights. Custom wood grip panels, 4" barrel, 30.3 oz. Stainless or Nitron finish. Introduced 2006.

	950	825	650	495	325	150

P229R DAK

Introduced in 2005 this model features double action only DAK trigger system with double strike capability. Chambered for the 9mm, .357 SIG, or .40 S&W cartridge with a 4.4" barrel. Fixed sights. Magazine capacity is 10, 12, or 15 rounds depending on caliber. Weight is about 32 oz. for 9mm and 34 oz. for .357 SIG or .40 S&W models.

	850	525	600	450	275	175

P229 SCT

All black, Nitron finished P229 featuring front cocking serrations, a SIGLITE rear night sight, a TRUGLO tritium fiber optic front sight and comes with four newly designed 17-round magazines for the 9mm version or four 14-round magazines for the .40S&W version.

	1100	950	800	675	500	300

P238

A compact .380 single-action with 1911-style controls, but no grip safety. Offered in many grip and finish variations. Ambidextrous safety available. **NOTE:** Add $100 for rosewood grips or Hogue rubber grips, $50 for ambidextrous safety.

	635	550	450	400	300	200

	NIB	EXC.	V.G.	GOOD	FAIR	POOR

P938

A slightly larger version of the P238 and chambered in 9mm. Other features are similar to the P238. Available with several grip and finish options.

	700	620	515	450	350	225

P239

Introduced in 1996 this pistol is chambered for the 9mm, .40 S&W, or .357 SIG cartridge. It is double/single-action or double-action-only. The barrel is 3.6" long and the overall length is 6.6". Weight is 25 oz. It is fitted with a single column magazine with 7 rounds for the .357 SIG and 8 rounds for the 9mm. **NOTE:** All of the above SIG pistols from the P220 to the P239 are available with "SIGLITE" night sights. Add $80 for these optional sights.

	725	600	475	350	200	150

P239 Limited

This .40 S&W model features a rainbow titanium slide. Trigger, hammer, grip screws, and control levers also rainbow titanuim. Magazine capacity is 7 rounds. Weight is about 27 oz. Introduced in 2004.

	725	600	475	350	200	150

P230

This is a semi-automatic, compact, pocket-type pistol chambered for .22 LR, .32 ACP, .380 ACP, and 9mm Ultra. It has a 3.62" barrel and either a 10-, 8-, or 7-round magazine, depending on the caliber chambered. The pistol weighs between 16.2 oz. and 20.8 oz. The finish is blued or stainless, with black plastic grips; and it was manufactured from 1976. In 1996 a two-tone finish was offered. No longer in production. **NOTE:** For stainless steel finish add $85 and for stainless steel slide add $35.

	450	375	300	250	200	150

P232

An improved model of the P230. Incorporates numerous changes to improve function and reliability. Basic features, operation, and dimensions remain the same as the P230.

	450	375	300	250	200	150

P232 (1998 Model)

In 1998 this model has as standard features night sights and Hogue grips with an all stainless steel finish. Chambered for .380 ACP, the pistol has a 7-round magazine capacity. Weight is about 21 oz.

	500	375	300	250	200	150

P232 Limited

This .380 pistol features a black finish, night sights, and satin nickel accents. Hogue rubber grips with finger grooves. Magazine capacity is 7 rounds. Weight is about 28 oz. Introduced in 2004.

	575	450	375	250	200	100

P245 Compact

Introduced in 1999 this model is chambered for the .45 ACP cartridge. It is fitted with a 3.9" barrel. Magazine capacity is 6 rounds. Overall length is 7.3". Weight is about 28 oz. Available finishes are blue and K-Kote. SIGLITE night sights are also available.

	775	650	500	375	250	150

P245 Custom Shop

Introduced in 2004 this .45 ACP pistol is limited to 75 guns. It features a Teflon-impregnated nickel slide, frame, trigger, hammer, etc. Hand-tuned action. Target crowned barrel. Novak low-carry sights, limited edition markings. Weight is about 27 oz.

	2100	1700	1450	1000	600	350

P250 Compact

Introduced in 2008. A 9mm semiauto pistol of so-called "modular design" that enables the shooter to quickly remove the functional mechanism and place it into the polymer grip of his choice. This allows an immediate change in caliber and size; (subcompact, compact and full). And after any change the pistol delivers both outstanding accuracy and reliable functionality. Its modularity not only provides incredible ease of maintenance, but also provides a solution for accommodating different hand sizes— there are 6 different ergonomic combinations for each size, accomplished by changes in grip circumference and trigger style. Matte or duotone finish.

	650	525	450	375	300	150

NIB	EXC.	V.G.	GOOD	FAIR	POOR

P290

New micro-compact pistol for concealed carry. Caliber 9mm Parabellum, is double-action only with stainless steel slide, polymer frame, 6-round magazine, three-dot sights and removable grip panels. Weight is 20.5 ounces, barrel length 2.9-inches. Finish is Nitron or two-tone stainless. Available with detachable laser sight. **NOTE:** Add $70 for laser sight.

650	550	465	400	325	150

P320

Double-action-only semi-automatic available in 9mm or .40 S&W. Barrel length 4.7". Double-stack magazine capacity is 14 rounds (.40); 17 rounds (9mm). Other features include Siglite night sights, interchangeable grip panels and black Nitron finish.

600	525	450	350	300	200

SIG PRO SERIES

SP2340

Introduced in 1998 this model is chambered for the .357 SIG or .40 S&W cartridge. It is built on a polymer frame with accessory rails on the dust cover. Barrel length is 3.9". Standard finish is blue. Weight is about 28 oz. Comes with two sets of interchangeable grips and two 10-round magazines. Available in single-action/double-action or double-action-only.

650	525	450	375	300	150

SP2009

Similar to the SP2340 but chambered for the 9mm cartridge. Weight is about 25 oz. Magazine capacity is 10 rounds.

500	425	350	225	175	100

SP2022

Chambered for the 9mm, .357 SIG, or .40 S&W cartridges and fitted with a 3.85" barrel with fixed sights. Polymer frame. Black finish. Weight is about 27 to 30 oz. depending on caliber. Magazine capacity is 10 or 12 rounds depending on caliber.

575	450	325	250	200	150

SHOTGUNS

Model SA3 Hunter

Introduced in 1997 this over/under shotgun is chambered for the 20 gauge shell and fitted with 26" or 28" barrels. It has single-selective trigger and automatic ejectors. The stock is figured walnut with pistol grip. The receiver is polished steel with engraved game scenes. Weight is approximately 6.8 lbs.

1200	1050	750	600	400	300

Model SA3 Sporting

This 12 gauge over/under gun was introduced in 1998 and features a 28" or 29.5" barrel with wide 11mm rib and front and mid-target sights. Both barrels and action are blued. Walnut stock with pistol grip and recoil pad. Weight is about 7.3 lbs.

1675	1250	1000	700	500	400

Model SA5 Sporting

Introduced in 1998 this 12 gauge is fitted with a choice of 28" or 29.5" barrels. Single-selective trigger and automatic ejectors are standard. Barrels are fitted with a 10mm rib. Receiver is polished steel with engraved clay target on each side. Weight is about 7.6 lbs.

2500	2000	1500	1100	750	500

AURORA SERIES

These shotguns were first imported and introduced into the SIG product line in 2000. They are made in Italy by B. Rizzini. All the guns in this series are over/under guns.

Aurora TR Field Shotguns

All of the TR field guns are offered in 12, 20, and 28 gauge as well as .410 bore. All have single triggers and ejectors. Barrel lengths are 26" or 28". Weights vary from 7 lbs. for the 12 gauge to 6 lbs. for the .410. Select walnut stock with oil finish. Cut checkering of 20 lpi. Choke tubes on the 12 and 20 gauge models and fixed chokes on the 28 and .410 models.

TR 20U

This model features a boxlock action with case hardened frame. No engraving. Straight-grip stock.

2000	1750	1475	1200	900	400

	NIB	EXC.	V.G.	GOOD	FAIR	POOR

TR 20

This model features a boxlock action with nickel finish and no engraving. Pistol grip.

	1850	1500	1325	1000	750	300

TR 30

This model features a case hardened action with side plates. No engraving. Pistol grip.

	2225	1850	1550	1375	1000	400

TR 40 Silver

Model features a silver action, side plates with gold inlaid game scenes. Pistol-grip.

	2575	2100	1550	1200	950	450

TR 40 Gold

This features a case hardened action with side plates and gold inlaid game scenes. Pistol grip.

	2675	2000	1450	1100	800	500

New Englander

Introduced in 2000 jointly by SIG and L.L. Bean this over/under gun is chambered in 12 and 20 gauge with choice of 26" or 28" barrels. Single-selective trigger, auto ejectors, choke tubes all standard. L.L. Bean logo inlaid in gold on receiver. Select turkish walnut stock with oil finish. Prince of Wales-style pistol grip and rubber recoil pad.

	1995	1500	1200	900	700	350

TT 25 Competition

This model is offered in both 12 and 20 gauge with a choice of 28" to 32" barrels for the 12 gauge and 28" or 30" barrels for the 20 gauge. Choke tubes. Single-selective auto ejectors are standard. Wide competition vent rib. Pistol grip on select walnut stock with 20 lpi checkering. Weight for 12 gauge is about 7.25 lbs. while the 20 gauge weighs about 6.75 lbs.

	1995	1500	1200	900	700	350

TT45

Similar to the TT25 but with the addition of a case hardened receiver and side plates with engraving and gold inlay game scenes.

	3275	2795	2200	1775	1300	450

RIFLES

SIG AMT

This is a semi-automatic rifle chambered for .308 cartridge. Fitted with a 19" barrel and wooden buttstock and forearm. Folding bipod standard. Box magazine capacity is 5, 10, or 20 rounds. Weight is about 10 lbs. Built from 1960 to 1974.

	4500	3800	3100	2500	1500	1000

SIG PE-57

Similar to the above but chambered for the 7.5x55 Swiss cartridge.

	4500	3800	3000	2500	1500	1000

SIG 550

This semi-automatic rifle is chambered for .223 cartridge and fitted with a 18" barrel.

	9000	7000	5500	3000	1800	1000

SIG 551

Same as above but fitted with a 16" barrel.

	10500	9500	7500	4000	2000	1000

SSG 2000

This is a high-grade, bolt-action, sniping-type rifle chambered for .223, 7.5mm Swiss, .300 Weatherby Magnum, and .308 Winchester. It has a 24" barrel and was furnished without sights. It has a 4-round box magazine. The finish is matte blue with a thumbhole-style stippled walnut stock with an adjustable cheekpiece. This model was discontinued in 1986.

	8000	6000	3500	2700	1500	—

SSG 3000

Chambered for the .308 Win. cartridge this model is fitted with a 23.4" barrel and ambidextrous McMillian Tactical stock. Magazine capacity is 5 rounds. Overall length is 46.5", and approximate

	NIB	EXC.	V.G.	GOOD	FAIR	POOR

weight is 12 lbs. This model comes in three different packages.

Level I

Base model with no bipod or scope, but with carrying case.

	NIB	EXC.	V.G.	GOOD	FAIR	POOR
	2550	2000	1600	1350	950	600

Level II

At this level a Leupold Vari-X III 3.5-10x40mm Deplex scope and Harris bipod with carrying case.

	NIB	EXC.	V.G.	GOOD	FAIR	POOR
	3500	2750	2300	1700	1200	600

Level III

Rifle is supplied with a Leupold Mark 4 M1-10x40mm Mil-Dot Scope with Harris bipod and carrying case.

	NIB	EXC.	V.G.	GOOD	FAIR	POOR
	4500	3500	2700	2400	1500	700

Conversion Kit—.22 LR

In 2001 a .22 caliber conversion was offered for the SSG 3000 rifle. The kit includes a heavy contured barrel, bolt, and 5-round magazine.

	NIB	EXC.	V.G.	GOOD	FAIR	POOR
	750	—	—	—	—	—

Model SHR 970

Introduced in 1998 this bolt-action rifle is chambered for the .25-06 Rem., .270, .280 Rem., .30-06, or .308 cartridges. It has a 22" barrel and the receiver is drilled and tapped for scope mounts. Detachable box magazine. Stock is black synthetic or walnut. Barrels are interchangeable. Weight is about 7.2 lbs. **NOTE:** Add $30 for walnut stock.

	NIB	EXC.	V.G.	GOOD	FAIR	POOR
	725	650	575	400	300	200

Model SHR 970 Magnum

Same as above but chambered for 7mm Rem. Mag or .300 Win. Mag. Barrel length is 24". Weight is about 7.4 lbs. **NOTE:** Add $30 for walnut stock.

	NIB	EXC.	V.G.	GOOD	FAIR	POOR
	775	725	625	450	350	250

Model SHR 970 Tactical

This model was introduced in 2000 and features a McMillan stock, non-reflective metal coating, heavy fluted contoured barrel, integral muzzlebrake. The rifle is chambered for .308 Win. or .300 Win. Mag cartridges. Receiver is drilled and tapped for scope mount and the stock has a fitted rubber recoil pad.

	NIB	EXC.	V.G.	GOOD	FAIR	POOR
	1400	1200	1000	775	600	400

Model 202 Standard

This bolt-action rifle features a choice of synthetic or Turkish walnut stock. Bolt is jeweled. Detachable 3-round box magazine. Offered in standard calibers from .22-250 to .30-06 and magnum calibers from 7mm Rem. Mag. to .375 H&H Mag. Barrel length is 24" for standard calibers and 26" for magnum calibers. Weight is about 7.5 lbs. depending on caliber.

	NIB	EXC.	V.G.	GOOD	FAIR	POOR
	1650	1200	975	750	600	400

Model 202 Lightweight

This model features a black synthetic stock fluted barrel chambered for the .22-250, .243, .25-06, .270, or .30-05 calibers. Barrel length is 24". Magazine capacity is 3 rounds. Alloy receiver and quick change barrel system are standard. Weight is about 6.5 lbs. Introduced in 2001.

	NIB	EXC.	V.G.	GOOD	FAIR	POOR
	1600	1150	925	700	550	350

Model 202 Varmint

This model is chambered for the .22-250, .243, or .25-06 cartridge. Fitted with a 26" fluted bull barrel. Stock is Turkish walnut with adjustable cheekpiece. Three-round detachable box magazine. Quick change barrel system. Weight is approximately 9.5 lbs.

	NIB	EXC.	V.G.	GOOD	FAIR	POOR
	1600	1150	925	700	550	350

Model 202 Supreme

This bolt-action model is chambered for .243, .25-06, 6.5x55 Swedish, .270 Win., .308 Win., or .30-06. It is fitted with a 24" barrel with choice of synthetic or walnut stock. Magazine capacity is 3 rounds. Weight is approximately 7.7 lbs. No sights. **NOTE:** Add $50 for walnut stock.

	NIB	EXC.	V.G.	GOOD	FAIR	POOR
	1800	1650	1400	1100	800	400

Model 202 Supreme Magnum

As above but chambered for 7mm Rem. Mag, .300 Win. Mag, .300 Wby Mag., or .375 H&H Mag. Magazine capacity is 3 rounds. Choice of synthetic or walnut stock. Weight is about 8.4 lbs.

	NIB	EXC.	V.G.	GOOD	FAIR	POOR

NOTE: Add $50 for walnut stock.

	1875	1725	1475	1150	850	450

SIG 556

Generally similar to the SIG 556 but made in the USA. Chambered in 5.56 NATO. Collapsible stock, 16" mil-spec barrel, picatinny rail and all the trendy tactical goodies. Introduced 2006.

	1200	1000	850	750	500	400

SIG 556 SWAT

The SIG556 SWAT features a 16-inch military grade cold hammer forged barrel, chambered in 5.56mm NATO, with a twist rate of 1 in 7". High performance flash suppressor, vented tactical quad rail forearm machined from aircraft grade aluminum alloy and hard coat anodized for durability, quad rail with four picatinny rails, picatinny equipped receiver. The rifle comes standard with the flip-up combat front and rear sight system. The trigger housing is machined from an aircraft grade aluminum alloy forging with a hard-coat anodized finish designed to survive extreme conditions. The rifle comes equipped with a smooth two-stage trigger, ambidextrous safety and is designed to accept standard AR magazines.

	1500	1300	1100	950	875	600

SIG 556 HOLO

Similar to above but with holographic sight and without quad rail and other features.

	1550	1350	1100	900	800	400

SIG 556 DMR

A sniper version of the SIG 556 SWAT with bipod and other accurizing features.

	1650	1500	1350	1000	850	500

SIG516 Gas Piston Rifle

AR-style rifle chambered in 5.56 NATO. Features include 14.5", 16", 18" or 20" chrome-lined barrel; free-floating aluminum quad rail fore-end with four M1913 Picatinny rails; threaded muzzle with standard (0.5x28TPI) pattern; aluminum upper and lower receiver is machined; black anodized finish; 30-round magazine; flattop upper; various configurations available.

	1100	950	800	650	500	300

SIG716 Tactical Patrol Rifle

AR-10 type rifle chambered in 7.62 NATO/.308 Winchester. Features include gas-piston operation with 3 round-position (4-position optional) gas valve; 16", 18" or 20" chrome-lined barrel with threaded muzzle and nitride finish; free-floating aluminum quad rail fore-end with four M1913 Picatinny rails; telescoping buttstock; lower receiver is machined from a 7075-T6 Aircraft grade aluminum forging; upper receiver machined from 7075-T6 aircraft grade aluminum with integral M1913 Picatinny rail.

	1900	1750	1500	1250	900	450

Sauer SSG 3000

Imported by SIG-Sauer from 2000 to 2012. A 5-round bolt-action sniper rifle chambered in .308 Winchester. Heavy-contoured hammer forged barrel fitted with flash suppressor/muzzle-brake to provide greater accuracy, with reduced muzzle signature. Both barrel and receiver feature black oxide finish to eliminate glare. Short, smooth 60 degree bolt throw allows for rapid operation. Like safety release bolt action is quiet. Massive six-lug lockup system used to give SSG 3000 greater strength and accuracy. Pistol grip and fully adjustable stock give shooter a custom fit. Trigger adjustable for trigger position, trigger take up, let-off point and trigger pull weight. Receiver on SSG 3000 features dovetail that will accept a wide range of sighting systems, including factory available M1913 rail. Price include Leupold Vari-X III 3.5-10x40 scope.

	4000	3550	2700	2000	1200	600

SIG 50

Bolt-action tactical rifle chambered for .50 BMG cartridge. Designed for ultra long-range tactical applications. Match-grade trigger set for 3-1/2 lbs. Stock has adjustable cheekpiece, pistol grip and length of pull. Barrel is 29" heavy fluted with muzzle-brake. Full length machined rails allow mounting of accessories. Fluted bolt, heavy duty steel bipod, Duracoat coating. Weight 23.5 pounds. Introduced in 2011.

	8300	7400	6350	—	—	—

SIG M400

Direct impingement gas operating system, with 16" barrel, M4-type buttstock, 30-shot magazine. Available in several variations.

	900	800	700	600	450	350

NIB	EXC.	V.G.	GOOD	FAIR	POOR

SILMA
Italy

STANDARD MODELS

Model 70 EJ

This over/under gun is chambered for the 12 or 20 gauge shell with 28" vent rib barrels with choke tubes. Single-selective trigger and auto ejectors. Checkered walnut stock. Weight for 12 gauge is about 7.6 lbs. and for the 20 gauge about 6.9 lbs. Silver engraved receiver.

12 Gauge

950	800	675	495	300	200

20 Gauge

875	725	600	400	265	150

DELUXE MODELS

Model 70 EJ

This model is chambered for the 12, 20, 28, or .410 shell and fitted with 28" vent rib barrels. Checkered select walnut stock with deluxe engraved receiver. Weights are 7.6 lbs. for 12 gauge and 6.9 lbs. for smaller gauges.

12 Gauge

1050	750	600	475	350	200

20 Gauge

950	700	550	425	300	175

28 and .410 Gauge

1075	800	650	525	400	250

Superlight

This model is offered in 12 or 20 gauge with 28" barrels with choke tubes. Checkered select walnut stock. Receiver is made from alloy steel. Weight for 12 gauge is about 6.7 lbs. and about 6.3 lbs. for the 20 gauge.

1100	825	675	550	425	275

Clays Model

This model is designed for sporting clays and is chambered for the 12 gauge 3" shell. Fitted with a 28" barrel with choke tubes and wide ventilated rib. Checkered select walnut stock.

1300	975	775	625	500	400

SIMPLEX
Unknown

Simplex

A German design based on the Bergmann-Mars pistol. An 8mm caliber semi-automatic pistol with a 2.6" barrel and a front mounted 5-round magazine. Blued with hard rubber grips having the trade name "Simplex" cast in them. Manufactured from approximately 1901 to around 1906. Early samples may have come from Germany and later pistols are thought to have been produced in Belgium.

—	1650	1050	550	400	200

SIMPSON, R. J.
New York, New York

Pocket Pistol

A .41 caliber single-shot percussion pocket pistol with a 2.5" barrel, German silver mounts and walnut stock. Manufactured during the 1850s and 1860s.

—	—	2400	1750	700	300

SIMSON & COMPANY
Suhl, Germany

See—Luger

NOTE: Models listed and pictured are taken from a mid-1930s Simson catalog. Because the company was Jewish-owned the Nazis took control in the mid-1930s changing the name to "Berlin Suhler Waffen". Prices are estimates.

	NIB	EXC.	V.G.	GOOD	FAIR	POOR

SHOTGUNS

Model 235

Side-by-side shotgun chambered for 12 or 16 gauge with Anson & Deely action. Scalloped frame with scroll engraving. Walnut stock with pistol grip. Double triggers.

	NIB	EXC.	V.G.	GOOD	FAIR	POOR
	—	900	700	550	400	350

Model 73

Similar to the above model but with more scroll engraving coverage.

	—	950	750	600	400	350

Model 74

This model features deep cut game scene engraving. Select walnut stock with fine-line checkering.

	—	1100	800	600	450	350

Model 74E

Same as above but with automatic ejectors.

	—	1200	850	650	450	350

Model 76

This side-by-side model is fitted with game scene engraved side plates and offered in 12 or 16 gauge.

	—	1400	1100	800	550	400

Model 76E

As above but with automatic ejectors.

	—	1500	1200	850	550	400

PISTOLS

Model 1922

A 6.35mm semi-automatic pistol with a 2" barrel and 6-shot magazine. The slide marked "Selbstlade Pistole Simson DRP" and "Waffenfabrik Simson & Co Suhl." Blued, with black plastic grips.

	—	600	475	400	300	100

Model 1927

Similar to the above, with a slimmer frame stamped with the trademark of three overlapping triangles having the letter "S" enclosed.

	—	600	475	400	300	100

SIRKIS INDUSTRIES, LTD.
Ramat-Gan, Israel

SD9

A 9mm double-action semi-automatic pistol with a 3" barrel, fixed sights and 7-shot magazine. Blued with plastic grips. Also known as the Sardius.

	—	325	275	225	175	100

Model 35 Match Rifle

A .22 caliber single-shot bolt-action rifle with a 26" free floating barrel, adjustable rear sight and adjustable trigger. Blued with a walnut stock.

	—	600	550	500	400	200

Model 36 Sniper's Rifle

A 7.62x54mm caliber semi-automatic rifle with a 22" barrel. Matte blued with a composition stock.

	—	675	600	550	450	200

SKB ARMS COMPANY
Omaha, Nebraska

This respected Japanese manufacturer began making shotguns for U.S. market in 1960s. Made various models for Browning, Weatherby and other American brands. In 1970s, SKB began marketing many models under its own name. End of 2009, SKB factory closed its doors. Final inventory was purchased by G. U. Inc. of Omaha, Nebraska. As of mid 2013, G.U. Inc. began importing several shotgun

	NIB	EXC.	V.G.	GOOD	FAIR	POOR

models from Turkey under the SKB brand. Approximately 1967 to 1977, Ithaca imported a series of over/under and side-by-side shotguns from SKB. These models were virtually identical to other SKB-made guns and had the same model numbers. Values shown in this section also apply to Ithaca guns.

SIDE-BY-SIDE GUNS

Model 100

A boxlock 12 or 20 gauge double-barrel shotgun with 25" to 30" barrels, single-selective trigger and automatic ejectors. Blued with a walnut stock. Imported prior to 1981. Discontinued.

NIB	EXC.	V.G.	GOOD	FAIR	POOR
1200	1000	900	800	550	400

Model 150

As above, with some engraving, a beavertail forearm and a figured walnut stock. Imported from 1972 to 1974.

NIB	EXC.	V.G.	GOOD	FAIR	POOR
1250	1000	900	800	550	400

Model 200

As above, with a French case hardened and scalloped receiver. Discontinued.

NIB	EXC.	V.G.	GOOD	FAIR	POOR
1300	1150	900	675	500	400

Model 200E

As above, with an English-style stock. Imported prior to 1989.

NIB	EXC.	V.G.	GOOD	FAIR	POOR
1350	1200	850	650	450	350

Model 280

Same as the Model 200 but fitted with a straight grip stock. Discontinued.

NIB	EXC.	V.G.	GOOD	FAIR	POOR
1400	1200	850	650	450	350

Model 300

As above, with more engraving and a figured walnut stock. Discontinued.

NIB	EXC.	V.G.	GOOD	FAIR	POOR
1450	1250	900	700	475	350

Model 385

Similar to the Model 300 but chambered for the 12, 20 or 28 gauge shell. Scroll engraved frame with semi-fancy walnut. Pistol-grip or straight-grip stock. Limited quantities imported. Weight is approximately 7 lbs. depending on barrel length and gauge. Discontinued.

NIB	EXC.	V.G.	GOOD	FAIR	POOR
1800	1600	1475	1100	700	400

Model 385 2 Barrel Set

Same as above but with a 20 and 28 gauge set of barrels in either 26" or 28". Discontinued.

NIB	EXC.	V.G.	GOOD	FAIR	POOR
2600	2500	2250	1300	900	500

Model 385 Sporting Clays

This model is chambered for 12, 20, or 28 gauge and fitted with a 28" barrel. Pistol-grip stock. Weight is about 7 lbs. depending on gauge. Discontinued. **NOTE:** For extra set of 20 or 28 gauge barrels add $900.

NIB	EXC.	V.G.	GOOD	FAIR	POOR
1850	1750	1475	1100	700	400

Model 400E

As above, with engraved false sideplates and an English-style stock. Imported prior to 1990.

NIB	EXC.	V.G.	GOOD	FAIR	POOR
1750	1600	1400	900	700	400

Model 480E

As above, with a French case hardened receiver and more finely figured walnut stocks. Discontinued.

NIB	EXC.	V.G.	GOOD	FAIR	POOR
1800	1650	1475	1100	700	400

Model 485

This model features an engraved sideplate boxlock action chambered for 12, 20, or 28 gauge with 26" or 28" barrels. Choke tubes. Weight is approximately 7.7 lbs. Discontinued.

NIB	EXC.	V.G.	GOOD	FAIR	POOR
2750	2100	1500	900	650	300

Model 485 2 Barrel Set

Same as above but with an extra set of barrels in 20/28 gauge combinations with 26" barrels. Choice of pistol-grip or straight-grip stock. Discontinued.

NIB	EXC.	V.G.	GOOD	FAIR	POOR
3900	3000	1850	1500	1200	500

NIB	EXC.	V.G.	GOOD	FAIR	POOR

OVER/UNDER GUNS

MODEL 85TSS SERIES

This series, introduced in 2004, features a low-profile boxlock action fitted with an inertia trigger (12 and 20 gauge), mechanical on 28 and .410 bore. Single-selective trigger with manual safety. Silver nitride finish. Barrels have automatic ejectors, ventilated rib and choke tubes. Pigeon porting is optional. Stocks are American walnut with matte finish and fitted with Pachmayr recoil pad. Adjustable comb stock is optional.

Model 85TSS Sporting Clays

Chambered for the 12, 20, 28 gauge, and .410 bore, this model features a choice of 28", 30", or 32" barrels on the 12 gauge guns and 28" or 30" barrels on the small bore guns. Choke tubes. Choice of fixed or adjustable comb. Choice of multiple barrel sets. Weight on 12 gauge guns is about 8.5 lbs. depending on barrel length and 7.5 lbs. on the smaller bore guns. **NOTE:** Add $175 for adjustable comb, $1,200 for two- barrel sets and $2,800 for three-barrel 20, 28 and .410 set.

1875	1600	1425	1075	800	450

Model 85TSS Trap

This 12 gauge 3" trap model is fitted with a choice of 30" or 32" backbored barrels with adjustable 12mm rib. Choice of fixed or adjustable comb with or without Monte Carlo. Weight is about 8.75 lbs. **NOTE:** Add $175 for adjustable comb.

1875	1600	1425	1075	800	450

Model 85TSS Trap Unsingle

This model is a single barrel trap gun with choice of 32" or 34" adjustable rib barrel with choice of standard comb or Monte Carlo with or without adjustable comb. Weight is about 9 lbs. **NOTE:** Add $175 for adjustable comb.

2100	1900	1625	1250	1000	500

Model 85TSS Trap Unsingle Combo

This model features a 32" or 34" single barrel and 30" or 32" over/under barrels. Barrel rib is adjustable. Choice of Monte Carlo or standard stock with or without adjustable comb. **NOTE:** Add $175 for adjustable comb.

3175	2500	2250	1875	1300	600

Model 85TSS Skeet

This model is offered in 12, 20, and 28 gauge as well as .410 bore. The 12 gauge model is offered with a choice of 28", 30" or 32" backbored barrels with 9.5mm rib. Small gauges are offered with a choice of 28" or 30" backbored barrels with 8.5mm rib. Weight for 12 gauge gun is about 8.35 lbs. and 7.5 lbs. for smaller gauges. Choice of fixed or adjustable comb. **NOTE:** Add $175 for adjustable comb. Add $2,800 for three-barrel set.

2100	1900	1625	1250	1000	500

Model 500

A 12, 20, 28 gauge or .410 bore over/under shotgun with 26", 28" or 30" ventilated rib barrels. Blued with a walnut stock. Imported from 1966 to 1979.

850	700	575	400	325	200

Model 505 Field

The 505 Series is also produced in sporting clays, trap and skeet configurations, which are valued at approximately 10 percent additional.

1270	950	700	500	350	250

Model 505 3-Gauge Skeet Set

As above, with 3 sets of barrels.

2500	1800	1400	975	650	650

Model 585

Similar to the Model 505 but offered in 12, 20, and 28 gauge and .410 bore as well. Barrel lengths are 26" or 28". Weight is about 7.25 lbs. for small bores and 8 lbs. for 12 gauge guns.

1550	1200	950	650	400	300

	NIB	EXC.	V.G.	GOOD	FAIR	POOR

Model 585 Gold Package

Has all of the features of the 585 series with the addition of a gold-plated trigger, gold-plated game scenes, and schnabel fore-end. Choice of blued or silver receiver.

	NIB	EXC.	V.G.	GOOD	FAIR	POOR
	1600	1250	975	675	425	300

Model 585 Skeet

Offered in 12-, 20- or 28-gauge and .410 bore, with 28" barrels. Skeet stock and beavertail forearm. Black recoil pad. Weight 12 gauge about 8 lbs.

	NIB	EXC.	V.G.	GOOD	FAIR	POOR
	1600	1250	975	675	425	300

Model 585—3 Barrel Skeet Set

Fitted with 20, 28 gauge and .410 bore barrels. Skeet choked.

	NIB	EXC.	V.G.	GOOD	FAIR	POOR
	2500	2250	1875	1300	600	400

Model 585—3 Barrel Skeet Set Gold Package

Same as above but with engraving and choice of silver or blued receiver.

	NIB	EXC.	V.G.	GOOD	FAIR	POOR
	2600	2350	1875	675	600	400

Model 585 Youth/Ladies

This model is similar to the 585 but with a shortened length of pull to 13.5". Weight of 20 gauge model is approximately 6.6 lbs. Weight of 12 gauge is about 7.5 lbs.

	NIB	EXC.	V.G.	GOOD	FAIR	POOR
	1525	1300	975	700	350	200

Model 585 Youth Gold Package

Same as above but with gold trigger, gold-plated game scenes, and schnabel forend. Choice of silver or blued receiver.

	NIB	EXC.	V.G.	GOOD	FAIR	POOR
	1625	1375	1025	750	400	200

Model 585 Upland

Similar to the 585 series except for straight-grip stock. Offered in 12, 20, and 28 gauge all with 26" barrels. Weight for 12 gauge is about 7.75 lbs. and for 20 and 28 gauge about 6.75 lbs.

	NIB	EXC.	V.G.	GOOD	FAIR	POOR
	1525	1300	975	700	350	200

Model 585 Upland Gold Package

This model has the additional gold package features of gold trigger, gold game scenes, and schnabel fore-end. Choice of silver or blued receiver.

	NIB	EXC.	V.G.	GOOD	FAIR	POOR
	1600	1375	1025	750	350	225

Model 600

Similar to Model 585, with silver-plated receiver.

	NIB	EXC.	V.G.	GOOD	FAIR	POOR
	1000	875	650	500	350	200

Model 600 Magnum

As above, chambered for 3", 12 gauge cartridges. Imported from 1969 to 1972.

	NIB	EXC.	V.G.	GOOD	FAIR	POOR
	—	900	675	525	375	200

Model 600 Trap Gun

As above, with 30" or 32" barrels trap choked, with a high comb walnut stock.

	NIB	EXC.	V.G.	GOOD	FAIR	POOR
	1000	875	650	500	350	200

Model 600 Skeet Gun

As above, chambered for 12, 20, 28 or .410 bore cartridges with 26" or 28" barrels that are skeet choked.

	NIB	EXC.	V.G.	GOOD	FAIR	POOR
	1000	875	650	500	350	200

Model 600 Skeet Combo Set

As above, with an extra set of three interchangeable barrels. Furnished with a carrying case.

	NIB	EXC.	V.G.	GOOD	FAIR	POOR
	2900	2550	2100	1650	1200	600

Model 605

Similar to Model 600, with an engraved and French case hardened receiver. **NOTE:** The 605 Series is also available in trap or skeet configurations. The values are similar.

	NIB	EXC.	V.G.	GOOD	FAIR	POOR
	1250	950	700	500	400	400

NIB	EXC.	V.G.	GOOD	FAIR	POOR

Model 605 3-Gauge Skeet Set

As above, with three extra sets of barrels.

| 2900 | 2550 | 2100 | 1650 | 1200 | 600 |

Model 680E

Similar to the Model 600, with an engraved receiver and English-style stock. Imported from 1973 to 1976.

| 1400 | 1100 | 850 | 600 | 500 | 250 |

Model 685

This over/under shotgun is offered in 12, 20, and 28 gauge as well as .410 bore. Barrel lengths are 26" or 28" with choke tubes. The engraved receiver has a silver finish with gold inlays. The walnut stock is semi-fancy.

| 1400 | 1100 | 850 | 600 | 500 | 250 |

Model 700 Trap Gun

Similar to the Model 600 Trap, with a wider rib, additional engraving and a figured walnut stock. Imported from 1969 to 1975.

| 1600 | 1250 | 975 | 675 | 425 | 300 |

Model 700 Skeet Gun

As above, with skeet chokes.

| 1700 | 1350 | 1050 | 775 | 500 | 350 |

Model 785

Offered in 12, 20, and 28 gauge as well as .410 bore this over/under features 26" or 28" barrels with choke tubes, single trigger, ejectors, and checkered walnut stock. The silver receiver is scroll engraved. Weight is about 8 lbs. for 12 gauge and 7.25 lbs. for small bores.

| 1800 | 1500 | 900 | 750 | 500 | 300 |

Model 785—2 Barrel Set

These two barrel sets are in combination 12/20, 20/28, and 28/.410 bore with 26" and 28" barrels.

| 2900 | 2650 | 2200 | 1775 | 1200 | 600 |

Model 785 Sporting Clays

Chambered for 12, 20, and 28 gauge with barrels lengths from 28" to 32" in 12 gauge and 28" in 20 and 28 gauge. Recoil pad standard. **NOTE:** For Sporting Clays set add $900.

| 2250 | 1750 | 1150 | 1400 | 900 | 500 |

Model 785 Skeet

Offered in 12, 20, 28, and .410 bore with 28" barrels. Recoil pad standard.

| 2250 | 1750 | 1150 | 1400 | 900 | 500 |

Model 785 3-Gauge Skeet Set

This model furnished with 12, 20, and 28 gauge barrel all 28" in length. Weight is about 7.3 lbs. regardless of gauge.

| 4400 | 3250 | 2500 | 1700 | 1200 | 600 |

Model 785 Trap

Offered in 12 gauge with or without Monte Carlo stock. Barrel length either 30" or 32". Ventilated recoil pad standard.

| 2250 | 1750 | 1150 | 1400 | 900 | 500 |

Model 785 Trap Combo

Features a 30" or 32" over/under barrels with a single 32" or 34" barrel. Choice of standard stock or Monte Carlo.

| 3050 | 2250 | 1250 | 100 | 700 | 375 |

Model 800 Trap Gun

As above, but with trap chokes and more engraving. Imported from 1969 to 1975.

| 2000 | 1000 | 850 | 650 | 550 | 250 |

Model 800 Skeet Gun

As above, in 12 or 20 gauge with 26" or 28" skeet choked barrels. Imported from 1969 to 1975.

| 2000 | 1000 | 850 | 650 | 550 | 250 |

	NIB	EXC.	V.G.	GOOD	FAIR	POOR

Model 880 Crown Grade

A false sidelock 12, 20, 28 or .410 bore boxlock double-barrel shotgun with a single-selective trigger and automatic ejectors. The engraved sideplates and receiver are French case hardened, and the figured walnut stock is checkered. Imported prior to 1981.

1900	1700	1350	1100	900	450

Model 885

A false sidelock 12, 20, 28 or .410 bore boxlock shotgun. Similar to the Model 800.

1600	1250	1050	900	700	300

Model 5600

This over/under gun is offered in 12 gauge only in either trap or skeet configurations.

875	775	650	500	400	200

Model 5700

Similar to the above but with light scroll engraving on the receiver and figured walnut stock.

900	800	675	525	425	200

Model 5800

Similar to Model 5600, with more engraving coverage on receiver. Fancy walnut stock.

950	800	700	550	450	175

GC 7

This over/under series was last produced by SKB. Three versions offered: Game Bird, Clays and Trap. Game Bird and Clay guns made in 12, 20, 28 gauge and .410 bore, with Trap only in 12 gauge. All models made on a low-profile boxlock action, with Greener-type crossbolt, automatic ejectors and single selective trigger. Barrels are 26" to 34", with lengthened forcing cones and Briley choke tubes. Each series made in three grades, with escalating levels of engraving and wood quality. Prices shown for Grade I. **NOTE:** Add 20 to 30 percent for Grade II; 40 to 50 percent for Grade III. Multi-barrel sets can bring up to 100 percent premium.

Game Bird

1500	1200	900	750	500	400

Clays and Trap

1600	1300	1000	800	600	400

Model 7300

12 or 20 gauge slide-action shotgun. Blued, with walnut stock. Imported prior to 1981.

—	300	250	200	150	100

Model 7900

As above, but skeet choked.

400	300	250	200	150	100

Model 300

A 12 or 20 gauge semi-automatic shotgun with 26", 28", or 30" barrels. Blued with a walnut stock. Imported from 1968 to 1972. **NOTE:** Ventilated rib barrel add 20 percent.

—	450	395	350	300	200

Model 1300

A redesigned version of the Model 300 with a ventilated rib barrel and screw-in choke tubes. Imported since 1988.

450	400	350	300	200	150

Model XL 900 MR

A 12 gauge, semi-automatic shotgun with 26" to 30" ventilated- rib barrels, and etched alloy receiver and checkered walnut stock. Imported prior to 1981.

—	475	425	375	325	200

Model 1900

As above, but also chambered for 20-gauge shells. Available with 22", 26" or 28" ventilated rib barrels and screw-in choke tubes. Blued, with walnut stock.

500	425	375	300	250	175

	NIB	EXC.	V.G.	GOOD	FAIR	POOR

Model 3000

Similar to the above, with a modified receiver design. Imported prior to 1990.

	NIB	EXC.	V.G.	GOOD	FAIR	POOR
	—	475	400	350	250	150

POST 2013 PRODUCTION

Model 200 Field

Side-by-side model made in 20-, 28-gauge and .410 bore, with an oil-finished hand checkered Turkish walnut stock, Prince of Wales pistol-grip and beavertail fore-end. Sculpted and hand-engraved box lock receiver has bison bone charcoal case hardening. Other features include single-selective trigger, automatic ejectors, bright blue finish and five interchangeable choke tubes. Imported from Turkey. **NOTE:** Add $150 for 28-gauge or .410 bore.

NIB	EXC.	V.G.	GOOD	FAIR	POOR
1750	1500	1225	900	450	200

Model 200 Sporting

Same general features as 200 Field grade. Also available in 12-gauge. Barrel lengths are 28" or 30" in all gauges and have a raised ventilated rib. **NOTE:** Add $100 for 28-gauge or .410 bore models.

NIB	EXC.	V.G.	GOOD	FAIR	POOR
2100	1825	1500	1100	500	250

Model 250 Field

Same features as 200 Field, except has engraved decorative sideplates.

NIB	EXC.	V.G.	GOOD	FAIR	POOR
2200	1850	1700	1300	550	300

Model 590

Over/under model in 12- or 20-gauge, with features similar to Model 200 side-by-side series. Imported from Turkey.

NIB	EXC.	V.G.	GOOD	FAIR	POOR
1100	900	750	600	300	200

Model 90 TSS

Over/under model in 12- or 20-gauge, with features designed for trap, skeet or sporting clays. These features include a stock with adjustable comb and length of pull, and a high ventilated rib. Skeet has fixed stock. Imported from Turkey. **NOTE:** Deduct $250 for skeet model.

NIB	EXC.	V.G.	GOOD	FAIR	POOR
1500	1300	1050	800	450	200

Model 7000 SL

A true side-lock model featuring Holland & Holland 7-pin removable sidelocks, with safety sears. Premium grade Turkish walnut stock, with extensive fine-line hand checkering on grip, butt and fore-end. Special order only. Made in Turkey.

NIB	EXC.	V.G.	GOOD	FAIR	POOR
5800	5200	4500	—	—	—

Century III

Single-barrel trap gun in 12-gauge, with 30" or 32" ventilated rib barrel, fixed or adjustable Grade II walnut stock, lengthened forcing cone, competition choke tube system, laser engraving. Made in Turkey. **NOTE:** Add $150 for adjustable stock.

NIB	EXC.	V.G.	GOOD	FAIR	POOR
1000	850	700	500	350	200

Model IS300

This semi-automatic in 12-gauge only operates on an inertia-recoil action. Available with a synthetic, camo or oil-finished walnut stock, back-bored barrels and competition choke tube system. Made in Turkey. **NOTE:** Deduct $75 for synthetic stock.

NIB	EXC.	V.G.	GOOD	FAIR	POOR
600	500	400	300	200	100

SLOTTER & CO.
Philadelphia, Pennsylvania

Pocket Pistol

A .41 caliber percussion pocket pistol with a 2.5" to 3.5" barrel, German silver mounts and walnut stock. Marked "Slotter & Co. Phila." Manufactured during 1860s.

NIB	EXC.	V.G.	GOOD	FAIR	POOR
—	—	3000	2200	950	250

SMITH, L. C.
Syracuse, New York
Hunter Arms Company
Fulton, New York

	NIB	EXC.	V.G.	GOOD	FAIR	POOR

One of the finest American-made double-barrel shotguns and very collectible in today's market. It was manufactured between 1880 and 1888 in Syracuse, New York; and between 1890 and 1945 in Fulton, New York, by the Hunter Arms Company. In 1945 Marlin Firearms Company acquired Hunter Arms, and the L.C. Smith was made until 1951. In 1968 the L.C. Smith was resurrected for five years, and production ceased in 1973. Marlin brought the L.C. Smith brand to market with models imported from Italy from 2004 to 2010. The values given are approximate for standard production models; and we strongly feel that competent, individual appraisals should be secured, especially on the rarer and higher grade models, if a transaction is contemplated.

The values given are for fluid steel, hammerless guns only. Damascus-barreled guns have become collectible if they are in very good or better condition, and values are approximately the same as for the fluid steel models. Damascus guns in less than good condition are worth considerable less.

Early Hammerless Shotguns

The models listed were manufactured between 1890 and 1913. They are chambered for 10, 12, 16, and 20 gauge and were produced with various barrel lengths and choke combinations. They feature full sidelock actions. The difference in the models and their values is based on the degree of ornamentation and the quality of materials and workmanship utilized in their construction. The general values furnished are for 10, 12 or 16 gauge guns only.

NOTE: 20 gauge add 50 percent. A premium for 25 percent for 10 gauge and 16 gauge guns should be added. Single-selective trigger add $250. Automatic ejectors add 30 percent.

00 Grade
60,000 manufactured.

NIB	EXC.	V.G.	GOOD	FAIR	POOR
—	2050	1800	1300	650	400

0 Grade
30,000 manufactured.

NIB	EXC.	V.G.	GOOD	FAIR	POOR
—	2150	1900	1400	700	450

No. 1 Grade
10,000 manufactured.

NIB	EXC.	V.G.	GOOD	FAIR	POOR
—	3150	2600	1950	800	550

No. 2 Grade
13,000 manufactured.

NIB	EXC.	V.G.	GOOD	FAIR	POOR
—	3500	2900	1625	900	700

No. 3 Grade
4,000 manufactured.

NIB	EXC.	V.G.	GOOD	FAIR	POOR
—	4250	3400	2275	1000	750

Pigeon Grade
1,200 manufactured.

NIB	EXC.	V.G.	GOOD	FAIR	POOR
—	6500	5200	4000	1800	1000

No. 4 Grade
500 manufactured.

NIB	EXC.	V.G.	GOOD	FAIR	POOR
—	8800	7300	5800	3000	2000

A-1 Grade
700 manufactured, all damascus, no 20-gauge.

NIB	EXC.	V.G.	GOOD	FAIR	POOR
—	6500	4250	2750	1750	1000

No. 5 Grade
500 manufactured.

NIB	EXC.	V.G.	GOOD	FAIR	POOR
—	9750	8100	5800	3250	2000

Monogram Grade
100 manufactured.

NIB	EXC.	V.G.	GOOD	FAIR	POOR
—	13000	9750	6900	3750	2500

A-2 Grade
200 manufactured.

NIB	EXC.	V.G.	GOOD	FAIR	POOR
—	17500	11500	8550	4500	3750

A-3 Grade
20 manufactured. Too rare to generalize a value.

	NIB	EXC.	V.G.	GOOD	FAIR	POOR

Later Production Hammerless Shotguns

These were manufactured at Fulton, New York, between 1914 and 1951. They are side-by-side double-barrel shotguns chambered for 12, 16, and 20 gauge, as well as the .410. They are offered with various barrel lengths and choke combinations. They feature a full sidelock action and are available with double or single triggers, extractors, and automatic ejectors. The finishes are blued and case colored, with checkered walnut stocks that are of either straight, semi-pistolgrip, or pistolgrip configurations. The various models differ as to the degree of ornamentation and the quality of materials and workmanship utilized in their construction. These are highly collectible American shotguns. Because these guns were manufactured as late as 1951, mint original specimens and even unfired new in the box guns will be offered for sale occasionally. These guns are worth considerably more than excellent condition guns and more than ever an individual, expert authentication and appraisal is recommended if a transaction is anticipated.

NOTE: The values supplied are for 12 gauge models only. For 16 gauge add 25 percent premium. For 20 gauge add 50 percent premium. For .410 bore add 200 percent premium (field grade), 300 percent to 400 percent for higher grades. Single-selective triggers add $250 premium. For automatic ejectors add 30 percent premium.

Field Grade

	NIB	EXC.	V.G.	GOOD	FAIR	POOR
—	1800	1500	1125	700	350	

Specialty Grade

	NIB	EXC.	V.G.	GOOD	FAIR	POOR
—	3400	3150	2150	1200	400	

Skeet Special Grade

	NIB	EXC.	V.G.	GOOD	FAIR	POOR
—	3400	3150	2225	1300	500	

Premier Skeet Grade

	NIB	EXC.	V.G.	GOOD	FAIR	POOR
—	3700	3150	2250	1350	500	

Eagle Grade

	NIB	EXC.	V.G.	GOOD	FAIR	POOR
—	5350	4350	3150	1700	500	

Crown Grade

With this grade, automatic ejectors became standard equipment. The .410 bore is extremely rare in this model and nonexistent in higher grades. There were only six manufactured, and they cannot be generally evaluated.

	NIB	EXC.	V.G.	GOOD	FAIR	POOR
—	7000	5350	4400	2950	500	

Ideal Grade

With this grade, automatic ejectors became standard equipment. The .410 is extremely rare in this model and nonexistent in higher grades; there were only six manufactured, and they cannot be generally evaluated.

	NIB	EXC.	V.G.	GOOD	FAIR	POOR
—	2350	1950	1700	900	500	

Trap Grade

With this grade, automatic ejectors became standard equipment. The .410 is extremely rare in this model and nonexistent in higher grades; there were only six manufactured, and they cannot be generally evaluated.

	NIB	EXC.	V.G.	GOOD	FAIR	POOR
—	2800	2350	1900	1100	500	

Monogram Grade

There were two higher grades offered: the Premier Grade and the Deluxe Grade. They are extremely rare, and there have not been enough transactions to generally evaluate them. This version is offered standard with automatic ejectors and a single-selective trigger.

	NIB	EXC.	V.G.	GOOD	FAIR	POOR
—	15000	12000	8750	600	500	

HUNTER ARMS BOXLOCKS

These shotguns are inexpensive, high quality boxlocks built with quality equal to the Field Grade L.C. Smith. The receiver, forend iron, trigger guard and triggers are all machined from forgings. Durability of these guns has proven to be excellent.

Fulton Model

A utility side-by-side boxlock shotgun chambered for 12, 16, 20 gauge and .410 bore. It was offered with various barrel length and choke combinations. It has double triggers and extractors with a non-selective single trigger option. Values given are for 12 gauge only. **NOTE:** For 20 gauge add 50 percent premium. For .410 bore add 250 percent premium. For 16 gauge add 25 percent. For single trigger add $150.

	NIB	EXC.	V.G.	GOOD	FAIR	POOR
—	1150	925	600	425	150	

	NIB	EXC.	V.G.	GOOD	FAIR	POOR

Fulton Special

A slightly higher grade version of the Fulton Model featuring modest engraving and pointed checkering. **NOTE:** For 20 gauge add 50 percent premium. For 16 gauge add 25 percent. For single trigger add $200.

	EXC.	V.G.	GOOD	FAIR	POOR
—	1400	1050	750	500	200

Hunter Special

Similar to the Fulton Model but features the L.C. Smith rotary locking bolt. **NOTE:** For 20 gauge add 75 percent premium. For .410 bore add 300 percent premium. for 16 gauge add 25 percent.

	EXC.	V.G.	GOOD	FAIR	POOR
—	1100	950	750	500	200

Single Barrel Trap Guns

High quality, break-open, single-shot trap guns chambered for 12 gauge only. They feature 32" or 34" vent rib barrels that are full-choked. They have boxlock actions and are standard with automatic ejectors. The finish is blued and case colored, and they have a checkered walnut stock with a recoil pad. The various models differ in the amount of ornamentation and the quality of the materials and workmanship utilized in their construction. There was a total of approximately 2,650 manufactured between 1917 and 1951. Although these firearms are actually rarer and just as high in quality as their side-by-side counterparts, they are simply not as collectible as the side-by-side variations.

NOTE: There were only two Premier Grade and three Deluxe Grade trap guns manufactured. This rarity makes it unrealistic to give an estimate of values. Beware of fakes.

Olympic Grade

	EXC.	V.G.	GOOD	FAIR	POOR
—	2050	1775	1300	900	500

Specialty Grade

	EXC.	V.G.	GOOD	FAIR	POOR
—	2600	1950	1400	1000	800

Crown Grade

	EXC.	V.G.	GOOD	FAIR	POOR
—	4250	3700	2800	1850	500

Monogram Grade

	EXC.	V.G.	GOOD	FAIR	POOR
—	7650	6500	4350	2800	500

1968 Model

A side-by-side double-barrel shotgun chambered for 12 gauge with a 28" vent rib barrel, choked Full and Modified. It features a sidelock action with double triggers and extractors. The finish is blued and case colored, with a checkered walnut stock. This shotgun was offered by Marlin between 1968 and 1973.These are less desirable than earlier models because of manufacturing expedients used. Investment cast receiver rather than machined forgings were used. Cyanide case-hardening replaced bone charcoal hardening and aluminum vent ribs were used. A thin brown polymer layer was used to create the fit between the lock plates and buttstock which is a departure from traditional fitting.

NIB	EXC.	V.G.	GOOD	FAIR	POOR
1750	1475	1100	850	450	300

1968 Deluxe Model

Similar to the 1968 model but features a Simmons floating rib and a beavertail-type forearm. It was manufactured by Marlin between 1971 and 1973.

NIB	EXC.	V.G.	GOOD	FAIR	POOR
2200	1800	1350	1100	700	400

L.C. SMITH 2005-2009 (MARLIN)

Model LC12-DB

Introduced in 2005. Italian-made side-by-side gun chambered for 12-gauge 3" shell. Single trigger, selective ejectors and 3 choke tubes. Barrel length 28". Checkered walnut stock, with pistol-grip. Beavertail forearm. Recoil pad. Weight about 6.25 lbs.

NIB	EXC.	V.G.	GOOD	FAIR	POOR
1500	1250	950	800	675	300

Model LC20-DB

As above but chambered for 20-gauge 3" shell. Fitted with 26" barrel. Weight about 6 lbs. Introduced in 2005.

NIB	EXC.	V.G.	GOOD	FAIR	POOR
1500	1250	950	800	675	300

Model LC12-OU

A 12-gauge 3" over/under gun, with 28" vent rib barrels. Checkered walnut stock, with pistol-grip. Choke tubes. Weight about 7.25 lbs. Introduced in 2005.

NIB	EXC.	V.G.	GOOD	FAIR	POOR
1000	875	725	600	400	300

	NIB	EXC.	V.G.	GOOD	FAIR	POOR

Model LC20-OU

As above in 20-gauge, with 3" chamber. Barrel length 26". Weight about 6.75 lbs. Introduced in 2005.

	NIB	EXC.	V.G.	GOOD	FAIR	POOR
	1000	875	725	600	400	300

Model LC28/LC410-DB

The 28-gauge and .410 bore models were introduced in 2007. Both have 2.75" chambers and 26" barrels. Selective automatic ejectors. Case-colored receiver, with gold game birds. Three choke tubes. Weight about 6.5 lbs.

	NIB	EXC.	V.G.	GOOD	FAIR	POOR
	1100	975	825	675	450	350

SMITH, OTIS
Rockfall, Connecticut

This company manufactured a line of single-action, spur-trigger revolvers that are chambered for .22, .32, .38, and .41 rimfire cartridges. The pistols have varying barrel lengths. The cylinder access pin is retained by a button on the left side of the frame. The cylinder usually holds five shots. The finishes are either blued or nickel-plated, with bird's-head grips. The quality was considered to be mediocre.

Model 1883 Shell-Ejector

A single-action, break-open, self ejecting revolver with a ribbed 3.5" barrel chambered for .32 centerfire. It has a 5-shot fluted cylinder and a spur trigger. It was quite well made. The finish is nickel-plated, with black plastic grips.

	NIB	EXC.	V.G.	GOOD	FAIR	POOR
	—	—	500	275	100	75

Model 1892

A double-action, concealed-hammer revolver chambered for the .38 centerfire cartridge. It has a 4" barrel and, for the first time, a conventional trigger and trigger guard. It is gateloaded and has a solid frame. It is nickel-plated with black plastic grips and also appeared under the Maltby, Henley & Company banner marked "Spencer Safety Hammerless" or "Parker Safety Hammerless." The Otis Smith Company ceased operations in 1898.

	NIB	EXC.	V.G.	GOOD	FAIR	POOR
	—	—	500	275	100	75

SMITH & WESSON
Springfield, Massachusetts

SMITH & WESSON ANTIQUE HANDGUNS

NOTE: A surprising number of pistols are still found in their original boxes, even for older models. This can add 100 percent to the value of the pistol.

Model 1, 1st Issue Revolver

This was the first metallic-cartridge arm produced by Smith & Wesson. It is a small revolver that weighs approximately 10 oz. and is chambered for the .22 Short rimfire cartridge. The octagonal barrel is 3.25" long. It holds 7 cartridges. The barrel and nonfluted cylinder pivot upward upon release of the under the frame. This model has a square butt with rosewood grips. The oval brass frame is silver-plated. The barrel and cylinder are blued. The barrel is stamped with the company name and address; the patent dates also appear. The sides of the frame are rounded on the 1st issue. Other characteristics which distinguish the more valuable 1st issue from later issues include a perfectly round side plate and a hinged hammer spur. Smith & Wesson manufactured approximately 11,000 of these revolvers between 1857 and 1860. Since this was the first of its kind, it is not difficult to understand the need for the number of variations within this model designation. Many small improvements were made on the way to the next model. These variations are as follows:

1st Type

Serial range 1 to low 200s, revolving recoil shield, bayonet type catch on frame. **NOTE:** Rarity makes valuation speculative.

	NIB	EXC.	V.G.	GOOD	FAIR	POOR
	—	—	15000	10000	8000	1000

2nd Type

Serial range low 200s to 1130, improved recoil plate.

	NIB	EXC.	V.G.	GOOD	FAIR	POOR
	—	—	10000	6000	2500	500

3rd Type

Serial range 1130 to low 3000s, bayonet catch dropped for spring-loaded side catch.

	NIB	EXC.	V.G.	GOOD	FAIR	POOR
	—	7500	5500	4000	2500	500

	NIB	EXC.	V.G.	GOOD	FAIR	POOR

4th Type
Serial range low 3000s to low 4200s, recoil shield made much smaller.

NIB	EXC.	V.G.	GOOD	FAIR	POOR
—	3000	2250	1800	1250	300

5th Type
Serial range low 4200s to low 5500s, has 5-groove rifling instead of 3.

NIB	EXC.	V.G.	GOOD	FAIR	POOR
—	3000	2250	1800	1250	300

6th Type
Serial range low 5500s to end of production 11670. A cylinder ratchet replaced the revolving recoil shield.

NIB	EXC.	V.G.	GOOD	FAIR	POOR
—	2000	1600	1400	1000	250

Model 1, 2nd Issue
Similar in appearance to the 1st Issue this 2nd Issue variation has several notable differences that make identification rather simple. The sides of the frame on the 2nd Issue are flat not rounded as on the 1st Issue. The sideplate is irregular in shape—not round like on the 1st Issue. The barrel was 3-3/16" in length. The barrel is stamped "Smith & Wesson" while the cylinder is marked with the three patent dates: April 3, 1858, July 5 1859, and December 18, 1860. There have been 2nd Issue noted with full silver or nickel-plating. Smith & Wesson manufactured approximately 115,000 of these revolvers between 1860 and 1868. The serial numbers started around 1100 where the 1st Issue left off and continued to 126400. There were approximately 4,400 revolvers marked "2D Quality" on the barrels. These revolvers were slightly defective and were sold at a lesser price. They will bring an approximate 100 percent premium on today's market.

NIB	EXC.	V.G.	GOOD	FAIR	POOR
—	900	750	600	250	100

Model 1, 3rd Issue
This is a redesigned version of its forerunners. Another .22 Short rimfire, 7-shot revolver, this model has a fluted cylinder and round barrel with a raised rib. This variation was manufactured totally from wrought iron. The three patent dates are stamped on top of the ribbed barrel as is "Smith & Wesson." It features bird's-head type grips of rosewood and is either fully blued nickel-plated, or two-toned with the frame nickel and the barrel and cylinder blued. There are two barrel lengths offered: 3.25" and 2-11/16". The shorter barrel was introduced in 1872. Serial numbering began with #1 and continued to 131163. They were manufactured between 1868 and 1882. The Model 1 3rd Issue was the last of the tip-up style produced by Smith & Wesson.

Shorter Barreled Version
Rare.

NIB	EXC.	V.G.	GOOD	FAIR	POOR
—	1500	1350	800	400	100

Longer Barreled Version

NIB	EXC.	V.G.	GOOD	FAIR	POOR
—	750	500	275	200	100

Model 1-1/2 1st Issue (1-1/2 Old Model)
This model was the first of the .32-caliber Rimfire Short revolvers that S&W produced. It is a larger version of the Model 1 but is physically similar in appearance. The Model 1-1/2 was offered with a 3.5" octagonal barrel and has a 5-shot nonfluted cylinder and a square butt with rosewood grips. In 1866 a 4" barrel version was produced for a short time. It is estimated that about 200 were sold. The finish is blued or nickel-plated. The serial numbering on this model ran from serial number 1 to 26300; and, interestingly to note, S&W had most of the parts for this revolver manufactured on contract by King & Smith of Middletown, Connecticut. Smith & Wesson merely assembled and finished them. They were produced between 1865 and 1868. **NOTE:** Add a 50 percent premium for the 4" barrel variation.

NIB	EXC.	V.G.	GOOD	FAIR	POOR
—	795	650	400	200	100

Model 1-1/2 2nd Issue (1-1/2 New Model)
The factory referred to this model as the New Model 1-1/2 and it is an improved version of the 1st Issue. It is somewhat similar in appearance with a few notable exceptions. The barrel is 2.5" or 3.5" in length, round with a raised rib. The grip is of the bird's-head configuration, and the 5-shot cylinder is fluted and chambered for the .32 Long rimfire cartridge. The cylinder stop is located in the top frame instead of the bottom. The finish and grip material are the same as the 1st Issue. There were approximately 100,700 manufactured between 1868 and 1875.

3.5" Barrel

NIB	EXC.	V.G.	GOOD	FAIR	POOR
900	800	650	375	175	100

2.5" Barrel
Rare. Watch for fakes.

NIB	EXC.	V.G.	GOOD	FAIR	POOR
2500	1500	1100	600	350	100

	NIB	EXC.	V.G.	GOOD	FAIR	POOR

Model 1-1/2 Transitional Model

Approximately 650 of these were produced by fitting 1st Issue cylinders and barrels to 2nd Issue frames. They also have 1st Model octagon barrels with 2nd Model bird's-head grips. These revolvers fall into the serial number range 27200-28800.

—	—	3000	1500	800	300	

Model 2 Army or Old Model

Similar in appearance to the Model 1 2nd Issue, this revolver was extremely successful from a commercial standpoint. It was released just in time for the commencement of hostilities in the Civil War. Smith & Wesson had, in this revolver, the only weapon able to fire self-contained cartridges and be easily carried as a backup by soldiers going off to war. This resulted in a backlog of more than three years before the company finally stopped taking orders. This model is chambered for .32 Long rimfire cartridge and has a 6-shot nonfluted cylinder and 4", 5", or 6" barrel lengths. It has a square butt with rosewood grips and is either blued or nickel-plated. There were approximately 77,155 manufactured between 1861 and 1874. Rare.

5" or 6" Barrel

Standard barrel.

—	2450	1500	950	450	300	

4" Barrel

Rare, use caution. **NOTE:** A slight premium for early two-pin model. For rare 8" model add 800 percent.

—	—	6000	3650	1500	500	

.32 Single-Action (so-called "1-1/2 Frame" Centerfire)

This model represented the first .32 S&W centerfire caliber top-break revolver that automatically ejected the spent cartridges upon opening. It is similar in appearance to the Model 1-1/2 2nd Issue. This model has a 5-shot fluted cylinder and a bird's-head grip of wood or checkered hard rubber and was offered with barrel lengths of 3", 3.5", 6", 8", and 10". The 8" and 10" barrel are rare and were not offered until 1887. This model pivots downward on opening and features a rebounding hammer that made the weapon much safer to fully load. There were approximately 97,599 manufactured between 1878 and 1892.

Early Model w/o Strain Screw—Under #6500

—	1200	600	300	175	75	

Later Model with Strain Screw

—	1000	450	300	150	75	

8" or 10" Barrel

Very rare; use caution.

—	—	4500	2500	800	400	

.38 Single-Action 1st Model (Baby Russian)

This model is sometimes called the "Baby Russian." It is a top break, automatic-ejecting revolver chambered for the .38 S&W centerfire cartridge. Offered with either a 3.25" or 4" round barrel with a raised rib, has a 5-shot fluted cylinder, and finished in blue or nickel plating. A 5" barrel was added as an option a short time later. The butt is rounded, with wood or checkered hard rubber grips inlaid with the S&W medallion. It has a spur trigger. Approximately 25,548 were manufactured in 1876 and 1877, of which 16,046 were nickel and 6,502 were blued.

—	2000	1200	900	350	150	

.38 Single-Action 2nd Model

With the exception of an improved and shortened extractor assembly and the availability of additional barrel lengths of 3.25", 4", 5", 6", 8", and 10" with the 8" and 10" barrel lengths being the most rare, this model is quite similar in appearance to the 1st Model. There were approximately 108,225 manufactured between 1877 and 1891.

8" and 10" Barrel

Very rare, use caution.

—	—	4000	2250	950	500	

3.25", 4", 5", and 6" Barrel Lengths

Small premium for 5" or 6" lengths.

—	700	350	225	175	75	

.38 Single-Action 3rd Model

This model differs from the first two models because it is fitted with a trigger guard. It is chambered for the .38 S&W centerfire cartridge, has a 5-shot fluted cylinder, and is a top break design with automatic ejection upon opening. The barrel lengths are 3.25", 4", and 6". The finish

	NIB	EXC.	V.G.	GOOD	FAIR	POOR

is blued or nickel-plated. The butt is rounded, with checkered hard rubber grips featuring S&W medallions. There were approximately 26,850 manufactured between 1891 and 1911.

	—	2000	1300	1000	600	200

.38 Single-Action Mexican Model

This extremely rare model is quite similar in appearance to the 3rd Model Single-Action. The notable differences are the flat hammer sides with no outward flaring of the spur. The spur trigger assembly was not made integrally with the frame but is a separate part added to it. One must exercise extreme caution as S&W offered a kit that would convert the trigger guard assembly of the Third Model to the spur trigger of the Mexican Model. This, coupled with the fact that both models fall within the same serial range, can present a real identification problem. Another feature of the Mexican Model is the absence of a half cock. The exact number of Mexican Models manufactured between 1891 and 1911 is unknown but it is estimated that the number is small.

	—	3950	3650	1500	950	400

.32 Double-Action 1st Model

This is one of the rarest of all S&W revolvers. There were only 30 manufactured. It also has a straight-sided sideplate that weakened the revolver frame. Perhaps this was the reason that so few were made. This model was the first break-open, double-action, automatic-ejecting .32 that S&W produced. It features a 3" round barrel with raised rib, a 5-shot fluted cylinder, and round butt with plain, uncheckered, black hard rubber grips. The finish is blued or nickel-plated. All 30 of these revolvers were manufactured in 1880. **NOTE:** Rarity makes valuation speculative.

	—	—	12000	7500	4000	1000

.32 Double-Action 2nd Model

This revolver is chambered for the .32 S&W cartridge and has a 3" round barrel with a raised rib. The 5-shot cylinder is fluted, and the finish is blued or nickel-plated. It is a top break design with a round butt. The grips are either checkered or floral-embossed hard rubber with the S&W monogram. This model has an oval sideplate, eliminating the weakness of the 1st Model. There were approximately 22,142 manufactured between 1880 and 1882.

	—	700	350	225	175	75

.32 Double-Action 3rd Model

This model incorporates internal improvements that are not evident in appearance. The most notable identifiable difference between this model and its predecessors is the surface of the cylinder. The flutes are longer; there is only one set of stops instead of two; and the free groove is no longer present. There were approximately 21,232 manufactured in 1882 and 1883.

	—	625	350	225	175	75

.32 Double-Action 4th Model

This model is quite similar in appearance to the 3rd Model except that the trigger guard is oval in shape instead of the squared back of the previous models. There were also internal improvements. There were approximately 239,600 manufactured between 1883 and 1909. **NOTE:** Add a 50 percent premium for revolvers built before 1898.

	—	575	300	200	125	65

.32 Double-Action 5th Model

The only difference between this model and its predecessors is that this model has the front sight machined as an integral part of the barrel rib. On the other models, the sight was pinned in place. There were approximately 44,641 manufactured between 1909 and 1919.

	—	500	375	250	125	100

SAFETY HAMMERLESS

This model was a departure from what was commonly being produced at this time. Some attribute the Safety Hammerless design to D.B. Wesson's hearing that a child had been injured by cocking and firing one of the company's pistols. This story has never been proven. Nevertheless, the concealed hammer and grip safety make this an ideal pocket pistol for those needing concealability in a handgun. This is a small revolver chambered for .32 S&W and .38 S&W cartridges. It has a 5-shot fluted cylinder and is offered with a 2", 3", and 3.5" round barrel with a raised rib. The butt is rounded and has checkered hard rubber grips with the S&W logo. The finish is blue or nickel plated. The revolver is a top break, automatic-ejecting design; and the 1st Model has the latch for opening located in the rear center of the top strap instead of at the sides. The latch is checkered for a positive grip. This model is commonly referred to as the "Lemon Squeezer" because the grip safety must be squeezed as it is fired.

.32 Safety Hammerless (aka .32 New Departure or .32 Lemon Squeezer) 1st Model

Push button latch serial number 1- 91417, built 1888-1902. **NOTE:** Add a 50 percent premium for revolvers built before 1898.

	—	475	275	165	100	50

	NIB	EXC.	V.G.	GOOD	FAIR	POOR

.32 Safety Hammerless 2nd Model

T-bar latch, pinned front sight, serial number 91418-169999, built 1902 to 1909.

	—	450	275	165	100	50

.32 Safety Hammerless 3rd Model

T-bar latch, integral forged front sight, serial number 170000-242981, built 1909 to 1937. **NOTE:** For 2" barrel, Bicycle Model add 200 percent.

	—	450	325	265	150	50

.38 Double-Action 1st Model

This model is similar in appearance to the .32 1st Model, having a straight cut side-plate, but is chambered for the .38 S&W cartridge. The grips are checkered, and there were 4,000 manufactured in 1880.

	—	1200	650	400	250	75

.38 Double-Action 2nd Model

This is similar in appearance to the .32 2nd Model but is chambered for the .38 S&W cartridge. There were approximately 115,000 manufactured between 1880 and 1884.

	550	375	225	200	100

.38 Double-Action 3rd Model

Essentially the same in appearance as the .32 Model but chambered for the .38 S&W cartridge, it is also offered with a 3.25", 4", 5", 6", 8", and 10" barrel. There were numerous internal changes in this model similar to the .32 Double-Action 3rd Model. There were approximately 203,700 manufactured between 1884 and 1895.

8" and 10" Barrel

Rare, use caution.

	—	—	2500	1500	800	200

Standard Barrel

	—	550	450	325	200	75

.38 Double-Action 4th Model

This is the .38 S&W version of the 4th Model and is identical in outward appearance to the 3rd Model. The relocation of the sear was the main design change in this model. There were approximately 216,300 manufactured between 1895 and 1909. **NOTE:** Add a 20 percent premium for revolvers built before 1898.

	—	495	230	225	150	75

.38 Double-Action 5th Model

This model is the same as the .32 except that it is chambered for the .38 S&W cartridge. There were approximately 15,000 manufactured between 1909 and 1911.

	—	525	385	225	150	75

.38 Double-Action Perfected

A unique top-break with both a barrel latch similar to the other top-breaks and a thumbpiece similar to the hand ejectors; also the only top-break where the trigger guard is integral to the frame rather than a separate piece. Produced from 1909 to 1911 in their own serial number range. About 59,400 were built.

	—	600	525	295	165	85

.38 Safety Hammerless 1st Model

Z-bar latch, serial number range 1 to 5250, made 1887 only. **NOTE:** Also offered with a 6" barrel. RARE! Add 50 percent.

	—	900	600	425	250	100

.38 Safety Hammerless 2nd Model

Push button latch protrudes above frame, serial number 5251-42483, built 1887-1890.

	—	500	350	250	175	100

.38 Safety Hammerless 3rd Model

Push button latch flush with frame, serial number 42484-116002, 1890-1898.

	—	475	355	225	165	100

.38 Safety Hammerless Army Test Revolver

There were approximately 100 sold to U.S. government in 1890. They have 3rd Model features but are in 2nd Model serial number range, 41333-41470. Fitted with 6" barrels and marked "US".

	NIB	EXC.	V.G.	GOOD	FAIR	POOR

CAUTION: Be wary of fakes. **NOTE:** Rarity makes valuation speculative.

	NIB	EXC.	V.G.	GOOD	FAIR	POOR
	—	—	10000	7500	4000	—

.38 Safety Hammerless 4th Model

This model was produced in .38 S&W only, and the only difference in the 4th Model and the 3rd Model is the adoption of the standard T-bar type of barrel latch as found on most of the top break revolvers. ".38 S&W Cartridge" was also added to the left side of the barrel. There were approximately 104,000 manufactured between 1898 and 1907; serial number range 116003 to 220000.

	NIB	EXC.	V.G.	GOOD	FAIR	POOR
	—	450	335	275	110	50

.38 Safety Hammerless 5th Model

This is the last of the "Lemon Squeezers," and the only appreciable difference between this model and the 4th Model is that the front sight blade on the 5th Model is an integral part of the barrel and not a separate blade pinned onto the barrel. There were approximately 41,500 manufactured between 1907 and 1940; serial number range 220001 to 261493. **NOTE:** 2" barrel version add 50 percent.

	NIB	EXC.	V.G.	GOOD	FAIR	POOR
	—	500	395	275	110	50

Model 3 American 1st Model

This model represented a number of firsts for the Smith & Wesson Company. It was the first of the top break, automatic ejection revolvers. It was also the first Smith & Wesson in a large caliber (it is chambered for the .44 S&W American cartridge as well as the .44 Henry rimfire on rare occasions). It was also known as the 1st Model American. This large revolver is offered with an 8" round barrel with a raised rib as standard. Barrel lengths of 6" and 7" were also available. It has a 6-shot fluted cylinder and a square butt with walnut grips. It is blued or nickel-plated. It is interesting to note that this model appeared three years before Colt's Single-Action Army and perhaps, more than any other model, was associated with the historic American West. There were only 8,000 manufactured between 1870 and 1872.

Standard Production Model

NOTE: Add 25 percent for "oil hole" variation found on approximately the first 1,500 guns. Add 50 percent for unusual barrel lengths other than standard 8". Original "Nashville Police" marked guns worth a substantial premium.

	NIB	EXC.	V.G.	GOOD	FAIR	POOR
	—	—	7000	3500	1500	500

Transition Model

Serial number range 6466-6744. Shorter cylinder (1.423"), improved barrel catch.

	NIB	EXC.	V.G.	GOOD	FAIR	POOR
	—	—	6000	3000	1500	500

U.S. Army Order

Serial number range 125-2199. One thousand (1,000) produced with "U.S." stamped on top of barrel; "OWA," on left grip.

	NIB	EXC.	V.G.	GOOD	FAIR	POOR
	—	—	17500	7500	3000	500

.44 Rimfire Henry Model

Only 200 produced throughout serial range. **NOTE:** Rarity makes valuation speculative.

	NIB	EXC.	V.G.	GOOD	FAIR	POOR
	—	—	12000	6000	3000	500

Model 3 American 2nd Model

An improved version of the 1st Model. The most notable difference is the larger diameter trigger pivot pin and the frame protrusions above the trigger to accommodate it. The front sight blade on this model is made of steel instead of nickel silver. Several internal improvements were also incorporated into this model. This model is commonly known as the American 2nd Model. The 8" barrel length was standard on this model. There were approximately 20,735 manufactured, including 3,014 chambered for .44 rimfire Henry, between 1872 and 1874. **NOTE:** There have been 5.5", 6", 6.5", and 7" barrels noted; but they are extremely scarce and would bring a 40 percent premium over the standard 8" model. Use caution when purchasing these short barrel revolvers.

.44 Henry Rimfire

	NIB	EXC.	V.G.	GOOD	FAIR	POOR
	—	—	6500	3250	1500	500

Standard 8" Model, .44 American Centerfire

	NIB	EXC.	V.G.	GOOD	FAIR	POOR
	—	6750	5000	3000	1250	500

Model 3 Russian 1st Model

This model is quite similar in appearance to the American 1st and 2nd Model revolvers. S&W made several internal changes to this model to satisfy the Russian government. The markings on this revolver are distinct; and the caliber for which it is chambered, .44 S&W Russian, is different. There

NIB	EXC.	V.G.	GOOD	FAIR	POOR

were approximately 20,000 Russian-Contract revolvers. The serial number range is 1-20000. They are marked in Russian Cyrillic letters. The Russian double-headed eagle is stamped on the rear portion of the barrel with inspector's marks underneath it. All of the contract guns have 8" barrels and lanyard swivels on the butt. These are rarely encountered, as most were shipped to Russia. The commercial run of this model numbered approximately 4,655. The barrels are stamped in English and include the words "Russian Model." Some are found with 6" and 7" barrels, as well as the standard 8". There were also 500 revolvers that were rejected from the Russian contract series and sold on the commercial market. Some of these are marked in English; some, Cyrillic. Some have the Cyrillic markings ground off and the English restamped. This model was manufactured from 1871 to 1874.

Russian Contract Model, Cyrillic Barrel Address

NIB	EXC.	V.G.	GOOD	FAIR	POOR
—	—	7000	3500	2000	500

Commercial Model

NIB	EXC.	V.G.	GOOD	FAIR	POOR
—	—	5000	2750	1250	500

Rejected Russian Contract Model

NIB	EXC.	V.G.	GOOD	FAIR	POOR
—	—	5000	2750	1250	500

Model 3 Russian 2nd Model

This revolver was known as the "Old Model Russian." This is a complicated model to understand as there are many variations within the model designation. The serial numbering is quite complex as well, and values vary greatly due to relatively minor model differences. Before purchasing this model, it would be advisable to secure competent appraisal as well as to read reference materials solely devoted to this firearm. This model is chambered for the .44 S&W Russian, as well as the .44 Henry rimfire cartridge. It has a 7" barrel and a round butt featuring a projection on the frame that fits into the thumb web. The grips are walnut, and the finish is blue or nickel-plated. The trigger guard has a reverse curved spur on the bottom. There were approximately 85,200 manufactured between 1873 and 1878.

Commercial Model
6,200 made, .44 S&W Russian, English markings.

NIB	EXC.	V.G.	GOOD	FAIR	POOR
—	—	3250	1500	850	400

.44 Rimfire Henry Model
500 made.

NIB	EXC.	V.G.	GOOD	FAIR	POOR
—	—	4750	2250	1000	500

Russian Contract Model
70,000 made; rare, as most were shipped to Russia. Cyrillic markings; lanyard swivel on butt.

NIB	EXC.	V.G.	GOOD	FAIR	POOR
—	—	3500	1750	950	500

1st Model Turkish Contract
.44 rimfire Henry, special rimfire frames, serial-numbered in own serial number range 1-1000.

NIB	EXC.	V.G.	GOOD	FAIR	POOR
—	—	6000	3750	1750	500

2nd Model Turkish Contract
Made from altered centerfire frames from the regular commercial serial number range. 1,000 made. Use caution with this model.

NIB	EXC.	V.G.	GOOD	FAIR	POOR
—	—	4500	2250	1000	500

Japanese Govt. Contract
Five thousand made between the 1-9000 serial number range. The Japanese naval insignia, an anchor over two wavy lines, found on the butt. The barrel is Japanese proofed, and the words "Jan.19, 75 REISSUE July 25, 1871" are stamped on the barrel, as well.

NIB	EXC.	V.G.	GOOD	FAIR	POOR
—	—	3500	1700	950	500

Model 3 Russian 3rd Model

This revolver is also known as the "New Model Russian." The factory referred to this model as the Model of 1874 or the Cavalry Model. It is chambered for the .44 S&W Russian and the .44 Henry rimfire cartridge. The barrel is 6.5", and the round butt is the same humped-back affair as the 2nd Model. The grips are walnut; and the finish is blue or nickel-plated. The most notable differences in appearance between this model and the 2nd Model are the shorter extractor housing under the barrel and the integral front sight blade instead of the pinned-on one found on the previous models. This is another model that bears careful research before attempting to evaluate. Minor variances can greatly affect values. Secure detailed reference materials and qualified appraisal. There were approximately 60,638 manufactured between 1874 and 1878.

Commercial Model
.44 S&W Russian, marked "Russian Model" in English, 13,500 made.

NIB	EXC.	V.G.	GOOD	FAIR	POOR
—	—	9000	5000	2500	500

	NIB	EXC.	V.G.	GOOD	FAIR	POOR

.44 Henry Rimfire Model

	NIB	EXC.	V.G.	GOOD	FAIR	POOR
	—	—	4500	2700	900	500

Turkish Model

Five thousand made from altered centerfire frames. Made to fire .44 Henry rimfire. "W" inspector's mark on butt. Fakes have been noted; be aware.

	NIB	EXC.	V.G.	GOOD	FAIR	POOR
	—	—	4500	2700	900	500

Japanese Contract Model

One thousand made; has Japanese naval insignia, an anchor over two wavy lines, stamped on the butt.

	NIB	EXC.	V.G.	GOOD	FAIR	POOR
	—	—	3100	1950	850	500

Russian Contract Model

Barrel markings are in Russian Cyrillic. Approximately 41,100 were produced.

	NIB	EXC.	V.G.	GOOD	FAIR	POOR
	—	—	3100	1950	850	500

Model 3 Russian 3rd Model (Loewe & Tula Copies)

The German firm of Ludwig Loewe produced a copy of this model that is nearly identical to the S&W. This German revolver was made under Russian contract, as well as for commercial sales. The contract model has different Cyrillic markings than the S&W and the letters "HK" as inspector's marks. The commercial model has the markings in English. The Russian arsenal at Tula also produced a copy of this revolver with a different Cyrillic dated stamping on the barrel.

Loewe

	NIB	EXC.	V.G.	GOOD	FAIR	POOR
	—	—	2900	1750	700	400

Tula

	NIB	EXC.	V.G.	GOOD	FAIR	POOR
	—	—	3350	2000	800	400

Model 3 Schofield 1st Model

US" Contract

3,000 issued.

	NIB	EXC.	V.G.	GOOD	FAIR	POOR
	—	12500	7500	4250	2250	500

Civilian Model

No "US" markings, 35 made, Very Rare. **NOTE:** Use caution. UNABLE TO PRICE. At least double the military model values. Expert appraisal needed.

Model 3 Schofield 2nd Model

No "US" markings, 35 made, Very Rare.

"US" Contract

4,000 issued.

	NIB	EXC.	V.G.	GOOD	FAIR	POOR
	—	10500	6500	4000	2250	500

Civilian Model

646 made.

	NIB	EXC.	V.G.	GOOD	FAIR	POOR
	—	12000	7000	4000	2000	500

Model 3 Schofield—Surplus Models

After the government dropped the Schofield as an issue cavalry sidearm, the remaining U.S. inventory of these revolvers was sold off as military surplus. Many were sold to National Guard units; and the remainder were sold either to Bannerman's or to Schuyler, Hartley & Graham, two large gun dealers who then resold the guns to supply the growing need for guns on the Western frontier. Schuyler, Hartley & Graham sold a number of guns to the Wells Fargo Express Co. These weapons were nickel-plated and had the barrels shortened to 5", as were many others sold during this period. Beware of fakes when contemplating purchase of the Wells Fargo revolvers.

Wells Fargo & Co. Model

	NIB	EXC.	V.G.	GOOD	FAIR	POOR
	—	—	8000	4000	2000	500

Surplus Cut Barrel—Not Wells Fargo

	NIB	EXC.	V.G.	GOOD	FAIR	POOR
	—	—	3500	2000	1200	500

New Model No. 3 Single-Action

Always interested in perfecting the Model 3 revolver D.B. Wesson redesigned and improved the old Model 3 in the hopes of attracting more sales. The Russian contracts were almost filled so the company decided to devote the effort necessary to improve on this design. In 1877 this project was undertaken. The extractor housing was shortened; the cylinder retention system was improved; and the shape of the grip was changed to a more streamlined and attractive configuration. This New Model has a 3.5", 4", 5", 6", 6.5", 7", 7.5", or 8" barrel length with

NIB	EXC.	V.G.	GOOD	FAIR	POOR

a 6-shot fluted cylinder. The 6.5" barrel and .44 S&W Russian chambering is the most often encountered variation of this model, but the factory considered the 3-1/2" and 8" barrels as standard and these were kept in stock as well. The New Model No. 3 was also chambered for .32 S&W, .32-44 S&W, .320 S&W Rev. Rifle, .38 S&W, .38-40, .38-44 S&W, .41 S&W, .44 Henry rimfire, .44 S&W American, .44-40, .45 S&W Schofield, .450 Rev., .45 Webley, .455 MkI and .455 MkII. They are either blued or nickel-plated and have checkered hard rubber grips with the S&W logo molded into them, or walnut grips. There are many sub-variations within this model designation, and the potential collector should secure detailed reference material that deals with this model. There were approximately 35,796 of these revolvers manufactured between 1878 and 1912. Nearly 40 percent were exported to fill contracts with Japan, Australia, Argentina, England, Spain, and Cuba. There were some sent to Asia, as well. The proofmarks of these countries will establish their provenance but will not add appreciably to standard values.

Standard Model
6.5" barrel, .44 S&W Russian.

—	5000	3700	2000	1000	500

Japanese Naval Contract
Largest foreign purchaser of this model. More than 1,500 produced, with anchor insignia stamped on the frame.

—		3700	2000	1000	500

Japanese Artillery Contract
This variation numbered in 25000 serial range. They are blued, with 7" barrel and lanyard swivel on the butt. Japanese characters are stamped on the extractor housing.

—		5000	2500	1250	500

Maryland Militia Model
Variation is nickel-plated, has 6.5" barrel and chambered for .44 S&W Russian cartridge. Butt stamped "U.S." and inspector's marks "HN" and "DAL" under date 1878 appear on the revolver. There were 280 manufactured between serial numbers 7126 and 7405. **NOTE:** Rarity makes valuation speculative.

—		10000	6000	3000	500

Argentine Model
Essentially not a factory contract but a sale through Schuyler, Hartley and Graham. They are stamped "Ejercito/Argentino" in front of the trigger guard. Order amounted to some 2,000 revolvers between serial numbers 50 and 3400.

—	—	7000	3500	1750	500

Australian Contract
This variation is nickel-plated and chambered for .44 S&W Russian cartridge. Marked with Australian Colonial Police Broad Arrow on the butt. There were 250 manufactured with 7" barrels and detachable shoulder stocks. Stock has Broad Arrow stamped on lower tang. There were also 30 manufactured with 6.5" barrels, without the stocks. They all are numbered in 12000-13000 serial range.

Revolver with Stock and Holsters
NOTE: Deduct 40 percent for no stock.

—		8000	4750	2750	500

Turkish Model
Essentially the New Model No. 3 chambered for .44 rimfire Henry cartridge. Stamped with letters "P", "U" and "AFC" on various parts of the revolver. Barrels are all 6.5"; finish blued, with walnut grips. Lanyard swivels are found on the butt. There were 5,461 manufactured. Serial numbered in their own range starting at 1 through 5461, between 1879 and 1883.

—		7000	3500	1750	500

New Model No. 3 Target Single-Action
This revolver is similar in appearance to the standard New Model No. 3, but was the company's first production target model. It has a 6.5" round barrel with a raised rib and 6-shot fluted cylinder and is finished in blue or nickel-plated. The grips are either walnut or checkered hard rubber with the S&W logo molded into them. This model is chambered in either .32 S&W or.38 S&W. The company referred to these models as either the .32-44 Target or the .38-44 Target depending on the caliber. The designation of .44 referred to the frame size, i.e. a .32 caliber built on a .44 caliber frame. This model was offered with a detachable shoulder stock as an option. These stocks are extremely scarce on today's market. There were approximately 4,333 manufactured between 1887 and 1910. **NOTE:** Shoulder stock add 50 percent.

—	—	3100	1350	850	400

	NIB	EXC.	V.G.	GOOD	FAIR	POOR

New Model No. 3 Frontier Single-Action

This is another model similar in appearance to the standard New Model No. 3. It has a 4", 5", or 6.5" barrel and is chambered for the .44-40 Winchester Centerfire cartridge. Because the original New Model No. 3 cylinder was 1-7/16" in length this would not accommodate the longer .44-40 cartridge. The cylinder on the No. 3 Frontier was changed to 1-9/16" in length. Later the company converted 786 revolvers to .44 S&W Russian and sold them to Japan. This model is either blued or nickel-plated and has checkered grips of walnut or hard rubber. They are serial numbered in their own range from 1 through 2072 and were manufactured from 1885 until 1908. This model was designed to compete with the Colt Single-Action Army but was not successful.

.44-40—Commercial Model

—	—	5000	2500	1250	500	

Japanese Purchase Converted to .44 S&W Russian

—	—	4000	2000	1000	500	

New Model No. 3—.38 Winchester

This variation was the last of the New Model No. 3s to be introduced. It was offered in .38-40 Winchester as a separate model from 1900 until 1907. The finish is blue or nickel-plate, and the grips are checkered hard rubber or walnut. Barrel lengths of 4" or 6.5" were offered. This model was not at all popular, as only 74 were manufactured in their own serial range 1 through 74. Today's collectors are extremely interested in this extremely rare model. **NOTE:** Rarity makes valuation speculative.

—	—	14000	8000	4000	500	

.44 Double-Action 1st Model

This model is a top break revolver that automatically ejects the spent cartridge cases upon opening. The barrel latch is located at the top and rear of the cylinder; the pivot, in front and at the bottom. This model was also known as "The D.A. Frontier" or "The New Model Navy." The revolver is chambered for the .44 S&W Russian and was built on a modified Model 3 frame. It is also found on rare occasions chambered for the .38-40 and the .44-40 Winchester. The barrel lengths are 4", 5", 6", and 6.5", round with a raised rib. A 3-1/2" barrel was produced on this model by special request. Collectors should be aware that the barrel for this model and the New Model No. 3 were interchangeable and the factory did in fact use barrels from either model. The serial number on the rear of the barrel should match the number on the butt, cylinder and barrel latch. The cylinder holds 6 shots and is fluted. It has double sets of stop notches and long free grooves between the stops. It is serial numbered in its own range, beginning at 1. There were approximately 54,000 manufactured between 1881 and 1913.

Standard .44 S&W Russian

—	—	2000	1300	700	400	

Model .44 Double-Action Wesson Favorite

The Favorite is basically a lightened version of the 1st Model D.A. .44. The barrel is thinner and is offered in 5" length only. There are lightening cuts in the frame between the trigger guard and the cylinder; the cylinder diameter was smaller, and there is a groove milled along the barrel rib. The Favorite is chambered for the .44 S&W Russian cartridge and has a 6-shot fluted cylinder with the same double-cylinder stop notches and free grooves as the 1st Model Double-Action .44. The company name and address, as well as the patent dates, are stamped into the edge of the cylinder instead of on the barrel rib. It is serial-numbered in the same range, between 9000 and 10100. The revolver was most often nickel-plated but was also offered blued. The grips are walnut or checkered hard rubber with the S&W logo molded in. There were approximately 1,000 manufactured in 1882 and 1883. Use caution when purchasing a blued model. **NOTE:** Rarity makes valuation speculative. Blued finish add 25 percent.

—	—	9000	5000	2500	500	

Model .44 Double-Action Frontier

Chambered for the .44-40 cartridge. This is a separate model from the .44 Double-Action 1st Model. It has a longer 19/16" cylinder like the later .44 double-action 1st Model's. Produced from 1886 to 1916 with their own serial number range. Approximately 15,340 built.

—	—	1850	1200	750	400	

Model .38 Winchester Double-Action

Similar to the .44 Double-Action 1st Model except for the chamber. Fitted with long cylinder. Approximately 276 produced in their own serial number range from 1900 to 1910.

—	—	5500	3000	1250	500	

	NIB	EXC.	V.G.	GOOD	FAIR	POOR

1st Model Single-Shot

This unusual pistol combines the frame of the .38 Single-Action 3rd Model with a single-shot barrel. This model is a top break and functions exactly as the revolver models do. The barrel length is 6", 8", or 10"; and the pistol is chambered for .22 LR, .32 S&W, and .38 S&W. The finish is blue or nickel plated, with a square butt. The grips are checkered hard rubber extension types for a proper target hold. This pistol is considered quite rare on today's market, as only 1,251 were manufactured between 1893 and 1905.

.22 L.R.

—	2000	1500	1000	600	400	

.32 S&W

—	2200	1750	1275	700	500	

.38 S&W

—	2500	1900	1400	750	500	

2nd Model Single-Shot

The 2nd Model single-shot has a frame with the recoil shield removed, is chambered for the .22 LR only, and is offered with the 10" barrel. The finish is blue or nickel plated, and the grips are checkered hard rubber extension types. There were approximately 4,617 manufactured between 1905 and 1909.

1500	1100	650	350	175	

3rd Model Single-Shot

The basic difference between this model and the 2nd Model is that this pistol could be fired double-action as well as single-action, and the frame came from the double-action perfected model. There were 6,949 manufactured between 1909 and 1923.

—	2000	1400	1200	600	300

Straight Line Single-Shot

Unique pistol that very much resembles a semi-automatic. Barrel is 10" in length and pivots to left for loading. Chambered for .22 LR cartridge and finished in blue, with walnut grips inlaid with S&W medallions. Hammer is straight-line in function and does not pivot. There were 1,870 manufactured between 1925 and 1936.

—	3200	2500	1500	750	400

.32 Hand Ejector Model of 1896 or .32 Hand Ejector 1st Model

This model was the first time S&W made a revolver with a swing-out cylinder. Interestingly, there is no cylinder latch; but the action opens by pulling forward on the exposed portion of the cylinder pin. This frees the spring tension and allows the cylinder to swing free. Another novel feature of this model is the cylinder stop location, which is located in the top of the frame over the cylinder. This model is chambered for the .32 S&W Long cartridge, has a 6-shot fluted cylinder, and is offered with 3.25", 4.25", and 6" long barrels. It is available with either a round or square butt, has checkered hard rubber grips, and is blued or nickel-plated. Factory installed target sights were available by special order. The company name, address, and patent dates are stamped on the cylinder instead of on the barrel. There were approximately 19,712 manufactured between 1896 and 1903.

900	650	425	350	200	150

Hand Ejector Model of 1903

Quite different from its predecessor. Cylinder locks front and back; cylinder stop located in bottom of frame and familiar sliding cylinder latch found on left side of frame. Barrel lengths 3.25", 4.25" and 6". The 6-shot cylinder is fluted. Revolver chambered for .32 S&W Long. Offered either blued or nickel-plated. Round butt grips are checkered hard rubber. Approximately 19,425 manufactured in 1903 and 1904; serial number range 1 to 19425.

—	1500	1100	800	400	250

.32 Hand Ejector Model of 1903 1st Change

Model differs internally from model of 1903. Serial number range 19426 to 51126 is really the only way to differentiate the two. Approximately 31,700 manufactured between 1904 and 1906.

—	1750	1300	800	500	300

.32 Hand Ejector Model of 1903 2nd Change

Produced from 1906 to 1909 in serial number range 51127 to 95500. A total of 44,373 manufactured.

.32 Hand Ejector Model of 1903 3rd Change

Produced from 1909 to 1910 in serial number range 95501 to 96125. A total of 624 manufactured.

	NIB	EXC.	V.G.	GOOD	FAIR	POOR

.32 Hand Ejector Model of 1903 4th Change

Produced in 1910 in serial number range 96126 to 102500. A total of 6,374 manufactured.

.32 Hand Ejector Model of 1903 5th Change

Produced from 1910 to 1917 in serial number range 102500 to 263000. A total of 160,500 manufactured.

.32 Hand Ejector Third Model

Produced from 1911 to 1942 in serial number range 263001 to 536684. A total of 273,683 were manufactured.

	—	650	500	375	250	150

K-32 Hand Ejector First Model

This is one of the rarest pre-war K-frame revolvers. Chambered for the .32 S&W Long cartridge, less than 100 were made between 1936 and 1941. After WWII this model was part of the K-22/K-32/K-38 Masterpiece series of 6-inch barreled, target-sighted revolvers. Due to the rarity of this model, an expert appraisal is essential.

	—	18000	13500	9000	3500	800

.22 Ladysmith 1st Model

Designed primarily as a defensive weapon for women. Small size and caliber made it ideal for that purpose. 1st Model Ladysmith chambered for .22 Long cartridge. Has 7-shot fluted cylinder. Barrel lengths 3" and 3.5". Weighs 9-5/8 oz. Either blued or nickel-plated. Round butt with checkered hard rubber grips. Checkered cylinder-latch button on left side of frame. Approximately 4,575 manufactured between 1902 and 1906.

	—	2500	1700	1100	650	450

.22 Ladysmith 2nd Model

Essentially quite similar in appearance to 1st Model. Difference being in pull-forward cylinder latch located under barrel replacing button on left side of frame. New method allowed lockup front and back for greater action strength. Barrel length 2.25" was dropped; caliber and finishes the same. Approximately 9,374 manufactured between 1906 and 1910; serial number range 4576 to 13950.

	—	2300	1500	900	500	300

.22 Ladysmith 3rd Model

Quite different in appearance to 2nd Model. Features square butt and smooth walnut grips, with inlaid S&W medallions. Barrel lengths remained the same, with addition of 2.25" and 6" variation. Under barrel cylinder lockup was not changed, nor caliber and finishes. Approximately 12,200 manufactured between 1910 and 1921; serial number range 13951 to 26154. **NOTE:** Add 50 percent premium for 2.25" and 6" barrel lengths.

	—	2300	1500	900	500	300

K-22 Outdoorsman/Masterpiece

Pre-war version of the K-22 K-frame, 6" barreled revolver chambered for the .22 Short, Long and Long Rifle. Walnut grips, adjustable rear sight, ribbed barrel. Manufactured from 1931 to 1940. In 1940 the name was changed to K-22 Masterpiece and an improved adjustable rear sight was added. The S&W short action was another improvement. Only about 1,000 K-22 Masterpieces were manufactured in 1940. **NOTE:** Add 100 percent premium for 1940 manufacture in 682,420 - 696,952 serial number range.

2500	2000	1600	1000	500	300	

.38 Hand Ejector Military & Police 1st Model or Model of 1899

Early swing-out cylinder revolver. No front lockup for action. Release is on left side of frame. Chambered for .38 S&W Special and .32 Winchester centerfire cartridge (.32-20). Has 6-shot fluted cylinder. Offered with 4", 5", 6", 6.5" or 8" barrel in .38 caliber; 4", 5" and 6.5" in .32-20 caliber. Finish is blued or nickel-plated; grips checkered walnut or hard rubber. Manufactured between 1899 and 1902: 20,975 in .38 caliber serial number range 1 to 20975; 5,311 in .32-20 caliber serial number range 1 to 5311.

	—	1750	1300	800	500	300

Commercial Model

	—	1500	1200	800	450	350

U.S. Navy Model

Produced 1,000 in 1900. .38 S&W, 6" barrel, blued with checkered walnut grips. "U.S.N." stamped on butt. Serial number range 5000 to 6000.

	—	3500	2600	1500	750	400

	NIB	EXC.	V.G.	GOOD	FAIR	POOR

U.S. Army Model

Produced 1,000 in 1901. Same as Navy Model except marked "U.S.Army/Model 1899" on butt. "K.S.M." and "J.T.T." on grips. Serial number range 13001 to 14000.

	—	3500	2600	1500	750	400

.38 Hand Ejector M&P 2nd Model or Model of 1902

The 2nd Model is similar in appearance to the 1st Model. The major difference is the addition of the front lockup under the barrel, and the ejector rod was increased in diameter. Barrel lengths for the .38 S&W were 4", 5", 6" or 6.5" while the .32-20 was available in 4", 5" or 6.5" barrel lengths. Both calibers were offered in round butt only configuration. There were approximately 12,827 manufactured in .38 S&W in 1902 and 1903; serial number range 20976 to 33803. In the .32-20 caliber 4,499 were produced; serial number range 5312 to 9811. **NOTE:** Add 250 percent for U.S. Navy Model.

	—	1200	900	500	250	100

.38 Hand Ejector M&P 2nd Model, 1st Change

Built between 1903 and 1905 this variation represents the change to the square butt, which made for better shooting control and standardized frame shape. Both the .38 S&W and the .32-20 were available in 4", 5", or 6-1/2" barrel lengths. The company manufactured 28,645 .38 calibers; serial number range 33804 to 62449 and produced 8,313 .32-20s; serial number range 9812 to 18125.

	—	1100	800	400	250	100

.38 Hand Ejector Model of 1905

This model was a continuation of the .38 M&P Hand Ejector series. Built from 1905 to 1906 it was available in 4", 5", 6", and 6-1/2" barrels for both the .38 and .32-20 calibers. Finished in either blue or nickel with round or square butt the .38 caliber model serial number range was from 62450 to 73250 or about 10,800 produced. The .32-20 caliber serial number range spans 18126 to 22426 or 4,300 produced. **NOTE:** Prices for the following four variations will be the same as those noted above.

	—	1200	950	650	400	150

.38 Hand Ejector Model of 1905, 1st Change

Produced from 1906 to 1908 this model is similar to the original model of 1905 with regard to barrel lengths, finish and butt styles. The 1st change in .38 caliber was produced in serial number range 73251 to 120000 with 46,749 sold. In .32-20 caliber the serial-number range was 22427 to 33500 with 11,073 sold.

.38 Hand Ejector Model of 1905, 2nd Change

Produced from 1908 to 1909 only internal changes were made to this model. The best approach to differentiate this model is by serial number. The .38 caliber serial number range was from 120001 to 146899 with 26,898 produced. In the .32-20 caliber the serial number range is between 33501 and 45200 with 11,699 produced.

.38 Hand Ejector Model of 1905, 3rd Change

Produced from 1909 to 1915 the 3rd Change variation was available in only 4" or 6" barrel lengths for both the .38 and .32-20 models. The .38 caliber serial number range was between 146900 to 241703 with 94,803 sold.

.38 Hand Ejector Model of 1905, 4th Change

This last variation was also the longest production run. Produced from 1915 to 1942 the .38 caliber model was available in 2", 4", 5", or 6", barrel lengths while the .32-20 caliber was offered in 4", 5", or 6" barrel lengths. The .38 caliber serial number range was from 241704 to 1000000. The .32-20 caliber model was produced from 1915 to 1940 in serial number range from 65701 to 144684.

.22-32 Hand Ejector

This is a very interesting model from the collector's point of view. Phillip B. Bekeart, a San Francisco firearms dealer requested that S&W manufacture a .22 caliber target-grade revolver on the heavier .32 frame. He believed in his idea so passionately that he immediately ordered 1,000 of the guns for himself. This initial order is found within the serial number range 1 to 3000 and are known to collectors as the authentic Bekearts. The remainder of the extensive production run are simply .22-32 Hand Ejectors. This model is chambered for .22 LR cartridge and has a 6-shot fluted cylinder with 6" barrel. The finish is blue, with square butt and checkered extension-type walnut grips. There were only 292 revolvers of his initial order delivered to Mr. Bekeart, but the first 1,000 pistols are considered to be True Bekearts. The production number of each respective pistol is stamped into the base of the extended wooden grips. S&W went on to manufacture several hundred thousand of these revolvers between 1911 and 1953.

Bekeart Model

Serial number range 138226 to 139275 in the .32 Hand Ejector series, production number stamped on butt. Professional appraisal should be secured.

	—	1500	1400	900	700	250

	NIB	EXC.	V.G.	GOOD	FAIR	POOR

Standard Model

	—	600	400	250	200	125

.22-32 Kit Gun (Pre WWII)

Model has same features as Standard Model, except for a smaller grip frame and 4" barrel.

3500	3000	2400	1600	600	250

.44 Hand Ejector 1st Model

Model also known by collectors as ".44 Triple Lock" or "The New Century". Triple Lock nickname came from a separate locking device located on extractor rod shroud that is used in addition to usual two locks. Chambered for .44 S&W Special cartridge or .44 S&W Russian. On a limited basis it is also chambered in .44-40, .45 Colt, .455 Mark II and .38-40. Fluted cylinder holds 6 shots. Barrel offered in standard lengths of 5" or 6.5". Limited quantity of 4" barrels produced. Finish is blued or nickel-plated; grips checkered walnut with gold S&W medallion on later models. Approximately 15,375 manufactured between 1908 and 1915. **NOTE:** Add premium of 100 percent for factory target sights.

.44 S&W Special

	—	2800	2000	1500	800	500

Other Calibers (Rare)

	—	4200	3600	2200	1200	600

.44 Hand Ejector 2nd Model

Quite similar in appearance to 1st Model. Major difference is elimination of third or triple lock device and heavy ejector rod shroud. Other changes are internal and not readily apparent. Standard in .44 S&W Special chambering, but offered rarely in .38-40, .44-40 and .45 Colt. Specimens have been noted with adjustable sights in 6.5" barrel lengths. Standard barrel lengths 4", 5" and 6.5". Approximately 17,510 manufactured between 1915 and 1937 in serial number range 15376 to 60000. **NOTE:** Add premium of 50 percent for factory target sights.

.44 S&W Special

	—	2500	1900	1200	600	300

.38-40, .44-40 or .45 Colt

Very few factory models were made in these calibers. Values shown are speculative. Use caution and consult an expert appraiser.

	—	5000	4000	2800	1000	500

.44 Hand Ejector 3rd Model or Model of 1926

This model is similar in appearance to the 2nd Model but brought back the heavy ejector rod shroud of the 1st Model without the triple lock device. Barrel lengths were 4", 5", and 6-1/2". The .44 Hand Ejector Model was manufactured between 1926 and 1949.

.44 S&W Special

	—	3500	2400	2000	1000	500

.44-40 or .45 Colt

Very few factory models were made in these calibers. Values shown are speculative. Use caution and consult an expert appraiser.

	—	5500	4500	3000	1000	500

.44 Hand Ejector 4th Model (Target Model)

The 4th Model featured a ribbed barrel, micrometer adjustable sight, and short throw hammer. Never a popular seller this model had only 5,050 pistol produced between 1950 and 1966.

	—	3000	2400	2000	1000	500

.45 Hand Ejector U.S. Service Model of 1917

WWI was on the horizon, and it seemed certain that the United States would become involved. The S&W people began to work with the Springfield Armory to develop a hand ejector model that would fire the .45-caliber Government cartridge. This was accomplished in 1916 by the use of half-moon clips. The new revolver is quite similar to the .44 Hand Ejector in appearance. It has a 5.5" barrel, blued finish with smooth walnut grips, and a lanyard ring on the butt. The designation "U.S.Army Model 1917" is stamped on the butt. After the war broke out, the government was not satisfied with S&W's production and actually took control of the company for the duration of the war. This was the first time that the company was not controlled by a Wesson. The factory records indicate that there were 163,476 Model 1917s manufactured between 1917 and 1919, the WWI years. After the war, the sale of these revolvers continued on a commercial and contract basis until 1949, when this model was finally dropped from the S&W product line.

Military Model

	—	1500	1200	1000	400	200

	NIB	EXC.	V.G.	GOOD	FAIR	POOR

Brazilian Contract

25,000 produced for the Brazilian government in 1938. The Brazilian crest is stamped on the sideplate.

	—	1100	800	500	250	125

Commercial Model

High gloss blue and checkered walnut grips.

	—	2000	1500	1000	475	300

.455 Mark II Hand Ejector 1st Model

This model was designed the same as the .44 Hand Ejector 1st Model with no caliber stamping on the barrel. It has a barrel length of 6.4". Of the 5,000 revolvers produced and sold only 100 were commercial guns, the rest were military. Produced between 1914 and 1915. The commercial model is worth a premium.

	—	1400	1150	700	400	200

.455 Mark II Hand Ejector 2nd Model

Similar to the first model without an extractor shroud. Barrel length was also 6.5". Serial number range was 5000 to 74755. Manufactured from 1915 to 1917.

	—	1300	1050	600	350	175

S&W .35 Automatic Pistol

Production of the .35 Automatic was S&W's first attempt at an auto-loading pistol. As was always the case, the company strived for maximum safety and dependability. This model has a 3.5" barrel and a 7-shot detachable magazine and is chambered in .35 S&W Automatic, a one-time-only cartridge that eventually proved to be the major downfall of this pistol from a commercial standpoint. There were two separate safety devices—a revolving cam on the backstrap and a grip safety on the front strap that had to be fully depressed simultaneously while squeezing the trigger. The finish is blue or nickel-plated; and the grips are walnut, with the S&W inlaid medallions. The magazine release slides from side to side and is checkered, expensive to manufacture, and destined to be modified. There were approximately 8,350 manufactured.

	—	750	450	300	200	150

S&W .32 Automatic Pistol

In 1921 it became apparent to the powers that controlled S&W that the .35-caliber automatic was never going to be a commercial success. Harold Wesson, the new president, began to redesign the pistol to accept the .32 ACP, a commercially accepted cartridge, and to streamline the appearance to be more competitive with the other pistols on the market, notably Colt's. This new pistol used as many parts from the older model as possible for economy's sake. The pivoting barrel was discontinued, as was the cam-type safety in the rear grip strap. A magazine disconnector and a reduced-strength recoil spring to ease cocking were employed. The barrel length was kept at 3.5", and the 7-shot magazine was retained. The finish is blued only, and the grips are smooth walnut. There were only 957 of these manufactured between 1924 and 1936. They are eagerly sought by collectors.

	—	2500	1750	1100	700	500

SMITH & WESSON MODERN HANDGUNS

With development of Hand Ejector Models and swing-out cylinders, Smith & Wesson opened the door to a number of new advancements in the revolver field. New system allowed for a solid frame, making weapon much stronger than old top break design. Company also developed different basic frame sizes and gave them letter designations. I frame, which later developed into slightly larger J frame, was used for .22-32 and small concealable .38 revolvers. Medium K frame used for .38 duty-/target-type weapons. N frame was heavy-duty frame used for larger .357, .44 and .45 caliber revolvers. Hand ejector went through many evolutionary changes over the years. Beginning in 1959, all S&W models were given numerical designations — Model 10, Model 14, etc. Models are cataloged here by their numerical designations, brief description given and current values offered. Important to note that S&W revolvers we see marketed by company today have undergone many changes in reaching its present configuration. Early models featured five screws in their construction, not counting grip screw. Four screws fastening sideplate and another through front of trigger guard that retained cylinder stop plunger. First change involved elimination of top sideplate screw and five-screw Smith & Wesson became four-screw. Later the frame was changed to eliminate cylinder stop plunger screw and three-screw was created. Some models offered with flat cylinder latch that was serrated instead of familiar checkering. In 1978, method of attaching barrel to frame was changed and familiar pin was eliminated. At the same time, recessed cylinder commonly found on magnum models was also eliminated. All these factors have a definite affect on value and collect ability of a particular S&W handgun.

NOTE: Pre-model number designations are listed in parentheses after model number. Premium up to 100 percent can apply to some of these handguns if accompanied by original box, and if both

NIB	EXC.	V.G.	GOOD	FAIR	POOR

gun and box are in excellent or better condition. See Performance Center pages at end of Smith & Wesson section for many special and limited editions of these handguns.

Model 10 (.38 Military & Police)

This model has been in production in one configuration or another since 1899. It was always the mainstay of the S&W line and was originally known as the .38 Military and Police Model. The Model 10 is built on the K, or medium frame, and was always meant as a duty gun. It was offered with a 2", 3", 4", 5", or 6" barrel. Currently only the 4" and 6" are available. A round or square butt is offered. It is chambered for the .38 Special and is offered in blue or nickel-plate, with checkered walnut grips. The model designation is stamped on the yoke on all S&W revolvers. This model, with many other modern S&W pistols, underwent several engineering changes. These changes may affect the value of the pistol and an expert should be consulted. The dates of these changes are as follows:

10-None-1957	10-1-1959	10-2-1961
10-3-1961	10-4-1962	10-5-1962
10-6-1962		

NIB	EXC.	V.G.	GOOD	FAIR	POOR
500	300	200	150	125	90

Victory Model

Manufactured during WWII. This is a Model 10 with sandblasted and parkerized finish, lanyard swivel and smooth walnut grips. Serial number has a V prefix. Model available in only 2" and 4" barrel lengths. Victory Model discontinued April 27, 1945, with serial number VS811119. **NOTE:** Top strap marked Navy will bring 75 percent premium. Navy variation with both top strap and side plate marked will bring 100 percent premium. Navy variation marked "N.Y.M.I." will bring 125 percent premium. Revolvers marked "U.S.G.C." or "U.S.M.C." will bring premium of unknown amount. Exercise caution.

NIB	EXC.	V.G.	GOOD	FAIR	POOR
750	625	500	400	300	200

Model 11 (.38/200 British)

First produced in 1947, S&W received many contracts for this service pistol. Nicknamed .38/200 British Service Revolver. Company sold many of these models throughout 1950s and 1960s. Several rare variations of this model will greatly affect its value. Consult an expert if special markings and barrel lengths are encountered.

NIB	EXC.	V.G.	GOOD	FAIR	POOR
1200	900	600	500	400	300

Model 12 (.38 Military & Police Airweight)

The Model 12 was introduced in 1952, starting serial number C223999, and is merely a Model 10 with a lightweight alloy frame and cylinder. In 1954 the alloy cylinder was replaced with one of steel that added an additional 4 ounces in weight. Discontinued in 1986. **NOTE:** Aluminum cylinder model add 40 percent.

NIB	EXC.	V.G.	GOOD	FAIR	POOR
—	700	500	250	125	100

USAF M-13 (Aircrewman)

This model was manufactured in the early 1950s for the U.S. Air Force on the Model 12 K-frame. The revolvers were chambered in .38 Special and have an alloy frame and cylinder. They were to be carried by pilots and other flight-crew members for emergency use. The Air Force ultimately rejected the model because of problems encountered with the alloy cylinder and most were destroyed. Because of this, the Aircrewman is one of the rarest modern-day Smith & Wesson revolvers. Serial numbers are in the C247000 to C406000 range and it is not known how many still exist. The genuine model is seldom seen for sale. Numerous fakes have been documented, so it is strongly suggested that a knowledgeable S&W expert be consulted for an appraisal. A few "Baby" Aircrewman 5-shot revolvers were made on the S&W J-frame and it is believed that fewer than 15 of these guns still exist. Because of the rarity of these two models and the few actual transactions that have occurred in recent years, it is not possible to list meaningful values.

Model 13 (.357 Military & Police)

This is simply the Model 10 M&P chambered for the .357 Magnum and fitted with a heavy barrel. It was introduced in 1974.

NIB	EXC.	V.G.	GOOD	FAIR	POOR
525	425	350	275	175	125

Model 14 (K-38 Masterpiece)

Model also known as "K-38". In 1957 "Model 14" stamped on yoke. Offered in 6" barrel with adjustable sights. In 1961 single-action version with faster lock time was offered. Discontinued in 1981. **NOTE:** Single-action model add 25 percent.

NIB	EXC.	V.G.	GOOD	FAIR	POOR
700	625	500	400	300	200

Model 15 (K-38 Combat Masterpiece)

Also known as "Combat Masterpiece". Produced at request of law enforcement officers who wanted "K-38" fitted with 4" barrel. Production in 1950. Discontinued in 1987.

NIB	EXC.	V.G.	GOOD	FAIR	POOR
750	675	550	450	300	200

	NIB	EXC.	V.G.	GOOD	FAIR	POOR

Model 16 (K-32 Masterpiece)

Also known as the "K-32" until 1957, this model is identical in appearance to the Model 14 except that it is chambered for .32 S&W. The Model 16 did not enjoy the commercial popularity of the Model 14 and was dropped from the line in 1973. Only 3,630 K-32s/Model 16s were sold between 1947 and 1973. Reintroduced in 1990 in .32 Magnum and discontinued in 1993. **NOTE:** Add 25 percent for 1946 - 1957 production (no Model 16 marking).

2750	2200	1800	1200	400	200

Model 16 (.32 Magnum)

Reintroduced in 1990 in .32 Magnum and discontinued in 1993.

1250	800	450	200	150	100

K-32 Combat Masterpiece

S&W produced a limited number of 4" barreled K-32 revolvers. They were never given a number designation, as they were discontinued before 1957 when the numbering system began.

2600	2000	1500	900	350	300

Model 17 (K-22)

Numerical designation S&W placed on "K-22" in 1957. Target model .22 rimfire revolver has always been popular since its introduction in 1946. Offered in 4", 6" and 8-3/8" barrel lengths, with all target options. The 8-3/8" barrel dropped from product line in 1993. Finish is blued, with checkered walnut grips.

800	700	650	500	375	275

Model 17 Plus

Introduced in 1996 this new version of the old Model 17 has a 10-round cylinder for its .22 LR cartridges. It features a 6" full lug barrel with Patridge front sight and adjustable rear sight. The hammer is semi-target style and the trigger is a smooth combat style. Finish is matte black and the grips are Hogue black rubber. Drilled and tapped for scope mounts. Weight is about 42 oz. Discontinued.

650	475	300	175	125	100

Model 617 Plus

Identical to the Model 17 but furnished with stainless steel frame and cylinder.

575	400	250	200	150	100

Model 647

Introduced in 2003 this revolver is chambered for the .17 HMR cartridge. Fitted with a 8.375" barrel with full lug. Six-round cylinder capacity. Stainless steel finish. Adjustable rear sight. Hogue rubber grips. Fitted with a target trigger and hammer. Drilled and tapped for scope. Weight is about 52.5 oz. Discontinued.

775	525	375	225	175	100

Model 648

Identical to the Model 617 but chambered for the .22 Magnum rimfire cartridge.

675	500	375	225	175	100

Model 648 (New Model)

Introduced in 2003. Medium frame revolver chambered for .22 WMR cartridge. Fitted with 6" full lug barrel. Pinned Patridge front sight and adjustable rear sight. New extractor system. Drilled and tapped for scope mount. Stainless steel finish. Weight 45 oz.

NOTE: On "K Frame" Target Models:

1. Factory eliminated upper corner screw from side plate in 1955. The 5-screw became a 4-screw. Change occurred around serial number K260000.

2. Model number designations were stamped on yoke in 1957.

700	525	395	250	200	125

Model 18 (K-22 Combat Masterpiece)

This is the model designation for the 4"-barrel "Combat Masterpiece" chambered for the .22 rimfire.

—	675	475	300	200	125

Model 19 (.357 Combat Magnum)

Introduced in 1954 at the urging of Bill Jordan, a competition shooter with U.S. Border Patrol. He went on to become a respected gun writer. Built on "K-Frame" and was first medium frame revolver chambered for powerful .357 Magnum cartridge. Since its inception, Model 19 has been one of S&W's most popular revolvers. First revolver to be introduced as a three-screw model.

	NIB	EXC.	V.G.	GOOD	FAIR	POOR

Originally offered with 4" heavy barrel with extractor shroud; 6" became available in 1963. Finish is blued or nickel plated. Grips are checkered walnut. Goncalo Alves target stocks first appeared in 1959. In 1968 a 2.5" round butt version was introduced. Model 19 has been basis for two commemorative's—Texas Ranger/with Bowie Knife and Oregon State Police/with Belt Buckle. No longer in production.

Model 19 (.357 combat Magnum)

Combat Magnum (Pre-Model 19, 1954-1958)
NOTE: Add 50 percent for nickel finish.

NIB	EXC.	V.G.	GOOD	FAIR	POOR
1800	1500	1100	850	500	300

Model 19 (.357 Combat Magnum)

Model 19, 19-1
NOTE: Add 40 percent for nickel finish.

NIB	EXC.	V.G.	GOOD	FAIR	POOR
1200	950	750	500	300	200

Model 19-2, 19-3

NIB	EXC.	V.G.	GOOD	FAIR	POOR
650	550	450	375	300	200

Oregon State Police Cased with Buckle

NIB	EXC.	V.G.	GOOD	FAIR	POOR
900	—	—	—	—	—

Texas Ranger Cased with Knife

NIB	EXC.	V.G.	GOOD	FAIR	POOR
700	—	—	—	—	—

Model 20 (.38/.44 Heavy Duty)

Known as the ".38/.44 Heavy Duty" before the change to numerical designations this model was brought out in 1930 in response to requests from law enforcement personnel for a more powerful sidearm. This model, along with the .38-44 S&W Special cartridge, was an attempt to solve the problem. The revolver was manufactured with a standard 5" long barrel but has been noted rarely as short as 3.5" and as long as 8-3/8". It was built on the large N-frame and is blued or nickel-plated, with checkered walnut grips. Eventually the popularity of the .357 Magnum made the Model 20 superfluous, and it was discontinued in 1966. Post-war production for this model was about 20,000 revolvers. **NOTE:** Pre-war add 50 percent.

NIB	EXC.	V.G.	GOOD	FAIR	POOR
1250	1000	850	600	450	200

Model 21 (1950 Military)

This model was known as the "1950 Military" and the "4th Model .44 Hand Ejector" before the Model 21 designation was applied in 1957. The Model 21 was chambered for the .44 Special cartridge and equipped with fixed sights. The Model 21 was built on the N frame and is quite rare, as only 1,200 were manufactured in 16 years of production. It was discontinued in 1966.

NIB	EXC.	V.G.	GOOD	FAIR	POOR
2800	2500	1800	950	650	500

Model 21 Thunder Ranch

This limited edition variation is a 4" barreled .44 Special with a gold-plated logo of the legendary Arizona shooting school on the frame.

NIB	EXC.	V.G.	GOOD	FAIR	POOR
800	650	500	400	300	200

Model 696

Introduced in 1997 this model features a 3" underlug barrel. chambered for the .44 Special and fitted on an L-frame, capacity is 5 rounds. Grips are Hogue black rubber. Finish is stainless steel. Weight is approximately 48 oz.

NIB	EXC.	V.G.	GOOD	FAIR	POOR
850	725	600	450	300	—

Model 22 (1950 .45 Military)

This model was known as the "1950 .45 Military" before 1957. It was actually introduced in 1951 and is similar in appearance to the Model 21 except that it is chambered for the .45 Auto Rim or .45 ACP cartridge. Half-moon clips are used with the latter. There were 3,976 manufactured between 1951 and 1966. Beginning serial number for this model was S85,000.

NIB	EXC.	V.G.	GOOD	FAIR	POOR
1850	1550	1350	950	650	500

Model 23 (.38-44 Outdoorsman)

The .38-44 Outdoorsman was the model name of this N-frame revolver before the 1957 designation change. This is simply the Model 20 with adjustable sights. It was introduced in 1931 as a heavy-duty sporting handgun with hunters in mind. S&W produced 4,761 of these pre-war revolvers. It features a 6.5" barrel and blued finish and was the first S&W to have the new checkered walnut "Magna" grips. After 1949 this revolver was thoroughly modernized and had the later ribbed barrel. There were a total of 8,365 manufactured before the model was

	NIB	EXC.	V.G.	GOOD	FAIR	POOR

discontinued in 1966. 6,039 were of the modernized configuration. **NOTE:** Add 50 percent for pre-war production.

	1700	1500	1200	600	250	200

Model 22 – Thunder Ranch .45 ACP

Limited edition six-shot single/double-action chambered for .45 ACP. Blued with 4" tapered barrel, 37.5 oz. Cocobolo grips engraved with Thunder Ranch insignia. Fixed sights. Serial numbers begin with TRR0000.

	—	850	675	500	250	200

Model 24 (.44 Target Model of 1950)

This model was introduced as the .44 Target Model of 1950. It is simply the N-frame Model 21 with adjustable target sights. This revolver was quite popular with the long-range handgunning devotees and their leader, Elmer Keith. The introduction of the .44 Magnum in 1956 began the death knell of the Model 24, and it was finally discontinued in 1966. S&W produced a total of 5,050 Model 24s. It was reintroduced in 1983 and 1984—and then was dropped again. **NOTE:** Add 25 percent for 4" barrel, 40 percent for 5". Deduct 60 percent for 1983-84 model.

	2500	2000	1600	1000	650	500

Model 25 (.45 Target Model of 1950)

Prior to the model designation change in 1957 this model was also known as the .45 Target Model of 1955, this was an improved version of the 1950 Target .45. The Model 25 features a heavier barrel 4", 6.5", or 8" in length with blued or nickel-plated finish. All target options were offered. The Model 25 is chambered for the .45 ACP or .45 Auto-rim cartridges. This model was later chambered for .45 Colt as the Model 25-5. **NOTE:** Add 100 percent premium for .45 Colt.

	1750	1550	1350	950	650	500

Model 25-3 125th Anniversary with Case

	1300	—	—	—	—	—

Model 25-2

This is the discontinued modern version of the Model 25 chambered in .45 ACP. The 6.5" barrel is shortened to 6" and is available in a presentation case.

	900	775	650	400	300	150

Model 25 Mountain Gun

Introduced in 2004 this .45 Colt N-frame round butt model features a 4" tapered barrel with black blade front sight and adjustable rear sight. Cocobolo wood grips. Blued finish. Weight is about 40 oz.

	750	625	500	425	300	150

Model 625-2

This is the stainless steel version of the Model 25-2. It is fitted with a 5" barrel and has Pachmayr SK/GR gripper stocks as standard. Designed for pin shooting. Weight is about 45 oz.

	750	625	500	425	300	150

Model 625 IDPA

As above but fitted with a 4" barrel, adjustable rear sight, patridge front sight, and Hogue grips. Introduced in 2002. Weight is about 43 oz.

	1000	850	700	575	400	200

Model 625 JM (Jerry Miculek)

Introduced in 2005 this model is chambered for the .45 ACP cartridge and fitted with a 4" full lug barrel with adjustable rear sight and Patridge front sight. Capacity is 6 rounds. Wood grips. Weight is about 43 oz.

	750	625	500	425	300	150

Model 625 Mountain Gun

Offered first time in 1996. Chambered for .45 Colt cartridge. Fitted with 4" tapered barrel, with ramp front sight and adjustable rear sight. Frame is drilled and tapped for scope mount.

	650	500	400	300	200	125

Model 610

Introduced in 1998 this revolver is chambered for the 10mm cartridge. It is fitted with a 6.5" full-lug barrel and an unfluted cylinder. Hogue grips are standard. Adjustable rear sight. Interchangeable front sight. Weight is approximately 52 oz.

	750	625	500	425	300	150

NIB	EXC.	V.G.	GOOD	FAIR	POOR

Model 26 (1950 .45 Target)

This is the numerical designation of the 1950 .45 Target Model. This large N-frame revolver is basically the same as the Model 25 but has a lighter, thinner barrel. This caused its unpopularity among competitive shooters who wanted a heavier revolver. This brought about the Model 25 and the demise of the Model 26 in 1961 after only 2,768 were manufactured. The Model 26 also has two additional variations and are marked 26-1 and 26-2.

NIB	EXC.	V.G.	GOOD	FAIR	POOR
3500	2500	1800	1000	500	200

Factory Registered .357 Magnum

In the early 1930s, a gun writer named Phillip B. Sharpe became interested in the development of high performance loads to be used in the then-popular .38-44 S&W revolvers. He repeatedly urged the company to produce a revolver especially made to handle these high pressure loads. In 1934 S&W asked Winchester to produce a new cartridge that would create the ballistics that Sharpe was seeking. This new cartridge was made longer than the standard .38 Special case so that it could not inadvertently be fired in an older gun. The company never felt that this would be a commercially popular venture and from the onset visualized the ".357 Magnum" as a strictly deluxe hand-built item. They were to be individually numbered, in addition to the serial number, and registered to the new owner. The new Magnum was to be the most expensive revolver in the line. The gun went on the market in 1935, and the first one was presented to FBI Director J. Edgar Hoover. The gun was to become a tremendous success. S&W could only produce 120 per month, and this did not come close to filling orders. In 1938 the practice of numbering and registering each revolver was discontinued after 5,500 were produced. The ".357 Magnum," as it was designated, continued as one of the company's most popular items.

The Factory Registered Model was built on the N-frame. It could be custom ordered with any barrel length from 3.5" up to 8-3/8". The finish is blue, and the grips are checkered walnut. This model was virtually hand-built and test targeted. A certificate of registration was furnished with each revolver. The registration number was stamped on the yoke of the revolver with the prefix "Reg." This practice ceased in 1938 after 5,500 were produced.

NOTE: For top dollar, all accessories and registration letter must be present.

NIB	EXC.	V.G.	GOOD	FAIR	POOR
13500	10000	8500	5000	2000	500

Pre-war .357 Magnum

Same as Factory Registered Model, without certificate and individual numbering. Approximately 1,150 manufactured between 1938 and 1941. Production ceased for WWII weapons production.

NIB	EXC.	V.G.	GOOD	FAIR	POOR
8000	6500	5000	3500	1500	500

Model 27 (.357 Magnum)

In 1948 after end of WWII, production of this revolver commenced. New rebound slide operated hammer block and short throw hammer were utilized. Barrel lengths offered were 3.5", 5", 6", 6.5" and 8-3/8". In 1957, model designation was changed to Model 27; in 1975 target trigger, hammer and Goncalo Alves target grips were made standard. Some additional variations may be of interest to the collector. Around serial number SI71584, the three-screw side plate model was first produced. In 1960, designation -1 was added to model indicating change to a left-hand thread to extractor rod. In 1962, cylinder stop was changed which disposed the need for a plunger spring hole in front of trigger guard. Change was indicated by a -2 behind model number. **NOTE:** Add $1,000 premium for pre-1957 production; $100 for early 4-screw model; add 25 percent for 2.5 or 5" barrel

NIB	EXC.	V.G.	GOOD	FAIR	POOR
800	700	600	450	350	300

Model 627

This is special edition stainless steel version of the Model 27 and is offered with a 5-1/2" barrel. Manufactured in 1989 only. Approximately 4,500 produced.

NIB	EXC.	V.G.	GOOD	FAIR	POOR
650	450	350	300	200	150

Model 627 Pro Series

Introduced in 2008. This is an eight-shot .357 revolver with stainless steel frame, adjustable sights, 4-inch barrel and various accurizing refinements.

NIB	EXC.	V.G.	GOOD	FAIR	POOR
—	900	675	495	300	150

Model 28 (Highway Patrolman)

Model 28 revolver was extremely popular among law enforcement officers. Many police agencies were interested in purchasing such a weapon—except for cost. In 1954, S&W produced a new model, called at the time, "Highway Patrolman". Model had all desirable performance features of deluxe Model 27, but lacked cosmetic features that drove up price. Finish is matte blue; rib sandblasted instead of checkered or serrated; grips are standard checkered walnut. Barrel lengths are 4" and 6.5". On late models, 6.5" barrel reduced to 6", as on all S&Ws. Model designation changed to Model 28 in 1957. S&W discontinued Model 28 in 1986. **NOTE:** Add 25

	NIB	EXC.	V.G.	GOOD	FAIR	POOR

percent premium for pre-Model 28. For top dollar, all accessories and registration letter must be present.

	700	625	500	400	325	250

Model 29 (.44 Magnum)

Early 1950s handgun writers, under leadership of Elmer Keith, were in the habit of loading .44 Special cartridge to high performance levels and firing them in existing .44 Hand Ejectors. They urged S&W to produce a revolver strong enough to consistently fire these heavy loads. In 1954, Remington at the request of S&W, produced the .44 Magnum cartridge. Cases with .357 Magnum were longer so that they would not fit in chambers of older guns. First .44 Magnum became available for sale in early 1956. First 500 were made with 6.5" barrel; 4" became available later that year. In 1957, model designation was changed to 29 and 8-3/8" barrel was introduced. Model 29 available in blue or nickel-plate. Came standard with all target options. Offered in a fitted wood case. Model 29 is considered by many knowledgeable people to be the finest revolver S&W has ever produced. Older Model 29 revolvers are in a different collector category than most modern S&W revolvers. Early four-screw models can be worth 100 percent premium in excellent condition. These early models were produced from 1956 to 1958. Approximately 6,500 were sold. One must regard these revolvers on a separate basis and have them individually appraised for proper valuation. In 1993, 4" barrel dropped from production.

	2500	2000	1400	1000	400	250

Early 5-Inch Barrel Model 29

This is the rarest of the Model 29s. A total of 500 were manufactured in 1958. Collectors are cautioned to exercise care before purchasing one of these rare Model 29 variations.

	4000	3200	2500	1500	500	300

Model 629

This revolver is simply a stainless steel version of the Model 29 chambered for the .44 Magnum. In 2002 this model was offered with HiViz sights.

	700	550	400	300	200	125

Model 629 Classic

This model has additional features that the standard Model 629 does not have such as: Chamfered cylinder, full lug barrel, interchangeable front sights, Hogue combat grips, and a drilled and tapped frame to accept scope mounts.

	700	550	400	300	200	125

Model 629 Classic DX

Has all of the features of the Model 629 Classic, introduced in 1991, plus two sets of grips and five interchangeable front sights. Available in 6.5" or 8-3/8" barrel. A 5" barrel option was offered in 1992 but dropped in 1993.

	750	600	500	400	300	200

Model 629 Mountain Gun

This limited edition 6-shot revolver, introduced in 1993, features a 4" barrel chambered for the .44 Magnum. Built on the large N frame this pistol is made from stainless steel and is drilled and tapped for scope mounts. It is equipped with a Hogue round butt rubber monogrip. Standard sights are a pinned black ramp front sight and an adjustable black rear blade. Weight is approximately 40 oz. Model was re-introduced in 1999.

	675	450	400	350	300	150

Model 629 Backpacker

This 1994 variation of the Model 629 is built on the N-frame with round butt. Cylinders are fluted and chamfered. Barrel length is 3" with adjustable rear sight. The finish is stainless steel and Hogue rubber grips are standard. Weight is approximately 40 oz.

	750	600	500	400	300	200

Model 629 Classic Powerport

Introduced in 1996 this model offers a integral compensator with a 6.5" full lug barrel. The Patridge front sight is pinned and the rear sight is fully adjustable. The frame is drilled and tapped for scope mounts. Synthetic Hogue combat-style grips are standard. Weight is approximately 52 oz.

	700	550	400	300	200	125

Fiftieth Anniversary Model 29

A commemorative edition of the classic .44 Magnum. Carbon steel with polished blue finish. Double-action 6-shot. LOA 12", 6.5" barrel, 48.5 oz. Cocobolo wood grips with 24kt gold anniversary logo.

	1500	1000	550	350	200	150

NIB	EXC.	V.G.	GOOD	FAIR	POOR

NIGHT GUARD SERIES REVOLVERS

Model 310 Night Guard

Large-frame snubnose revolver chambered in 10mm/.40 S&W (interchangeable). Six-shot cylinder, 2.75" barrel, fixed tritium sights, synthetic grips. Scandium frame, stainless steel cylinder, matte black finish throughout. Weight 28 oz.

900	775	600	475	300	150

Model 357 Night Guard

Don't let the model name fool you. Large-frame snubnose revolver chambered in .41 Magnum. Six-shot cylinder, 2.75" barrel, fixed tritium sights, synthetic grips. Scandium frame, stainless steel cylinder, matte black finish throughout. Weight 29.7 oz.

900	775	600	475	300	150

Model 325 Night Guard

A 2-1/2" snubbie chambered for .45 ACP. Tritium sights, scandium alloy frame, matte black finish overll. Neoprene grips. Introduced 2008.

900	775	600	475	300	150

Model 327 Night Guard

Large-frame snubnose revolver chambered in .357 Magnum/.38 Special +P (interchangeable). Six-shot cylinder, 2.5" barrel, fixed tritium sights, synthetic grips. Scandium frame, stainless steel cylinder, matte black finish throughout. Weight 27.6 oz.

900	775	600	475	300	150

Model 329 Night Guard

Large-frame snubnose revolver chambered in .44 Magnum/.44 Special (interchangeable). Six-shot cylinder, 2.5" barrel, fixed tritium sights, synthetic grips. Scandium frame, stainless steel cylinder, matte black finish throughout. Weight 29.3 oz.

900	775	600	475	300	150

Model 386 Night Guard

Medium-frame snubnose revolver chambered in .357 Magnum/.38 Special +P (interchangeable). Seven-shot cylinder, 2.5" barrel, fixed tritium sights, synthetic grips. Scandium frame, stainless steel cylinder, matte black finish throughout. Weight 24.5 oz.

850	725	550	425	300	150

Model 396 Night Guard

Medium-frame snubnose revolver chambered in .44 Special. Five-shot cylinder, 2.5" barrel, fixed tritium sights, synthetic grips. Scandium frame, stainless steel cylinder, matte black finish throughout. Weight 24.2 oz.

850	725	550	425	300	150

Model 315 Night Guard

Medium-frame snubnose revolver chambered in .38 Special +P. Six-shot cylinder, 2.5" barrel, fixed tritium sights, synthetic grips. Scandium frame, stainless steel cylinder, matte black finish throughout. Weight 24.0 oz.

850	725	550	425	300	150

Model 30 (The .32 Hand Ejector)

This model was built on the small I frame and based on the .32 Hand Ejector Model of 1903. This older model was dropped from production in 1942. It was re-introduced in 1949 in a more modern version but still referred to as the .32 Hand Ejector. In 1957 the model designation was changed to Model 30. In 1960 this frame size was dropped, and the J frame, which had been in use since 1950, became standard for the Model 30. S&W stamped -1 behind the model number to designate this important change in frame size. The Model 30 is chambered for the .32 S&W long cartridge. It has a 6-shot cylinder and 2", 3", 4", and 6" barrel lengths. It has fixed sights and is either blued or nickel-plated. The butt is round, with checkered walnut grips. It was discontinued in 1976.

—	425	300	200	150	100

Model 31 (.32 Regulation Police)

This model is the same as the Model 30 with a square butt. It was known as the .32 Regulation Police before 1957. Discontinued.

—	425	300	200	150	100

	NIB	EXC.	V.G.	GOOD	FAIR	POOR

Model 31 (.32 Regulation Police Target)

The Target model of the Regulation Police is rare. Only 196 of these special variations were produced in 1957. All specifications are the same as the Model 31 except for the addition of adjustable sights.

	NIB	EXC.	V.G.	GOOD	FAIR	POOR
	—	1500	925	750	525	300

Model 32 (.38/.32 Terrier)

This model, known as the Terrier prior to 1957, was introduced in 1936. It is essentially a .38 Regulation Police chambered for .38 S&W and with a 2" barrel and round butt. Like the Model 30 and 31 this revolver was originally built on the I-frame, which was changed to the J frame in 1960. The -1 behind the model number signifies this change. It is offered in blue or nickel-plate and has a 5-shot cylinder, fixed sights, and checkered walnut grips. This model was discontinued in 1974. **NOTE:** A limited production version with alloy frame and steel cylinder was produced as the Model 032. Add 30 percent for this model.

	NIB	EXC.	V.G.	GOOD	FAIR	POOR
	—	425	300	200	150	100

Model 33 (.38 Regulation Police)

This model is simply the .38 Regulation Police with a square butt and 4" barrel chambered for the .38 S&W. The factory referred to this model as the .38-.32 revolver. It, too, was built on the small I frame and later changed to the J frame in 1960. The Model 33 was discontinued in 1974.

	NIB	EXC.	V.G.	GOOD	FAIR	POOR
	—	425	300	200	150	100

Model 34 (.22/.32 Kit Gun)

Introduced in 1936 as the .22-32 Kit Gun, it has a 2" or 4" barrel, either round or square butt, and adjustable sights. This model underwent several modifications before it reached its present form. S&W modernized this revolver in 1953 with the addition of a coil mainspring and micro-click sights. The Model 34 is built on this improved version. The revolver is a .32 Hand Ejector chambered for the .22 rimfire. It is built on the I frame until 1960 when the changeover to the improved J frame occurred. The -1 behind the model number indicates this variation. The Model 34 is offered blued or nickel-plate.

	NIB	EXC.	V.G.	GOOD	FAIR	POOR
	550	425	300	250	175	100

1946-1952 Production

	NIB	EXC.	V.G.	GOOD	FAIR	POOR
	1200	1000	850	600	300	200

1953-1991 Production

	NIB	EXC.	V.G.	GOOD	FAIR	POOR
	700	550	450	350	250	200

Model 35 (.22/.32 Target)

This is a square-butt, 6"-barreled version of the .22/32 Hand Ejector. It was known prior to 1957 as the .22/32 Target. It underwent the same changes as the Model 34 but was discontinued in 1973.

	NIB	EXC.	V.G.	GOOD	FAIR	POOR
	1000	800	600	400	275	100

AIRLITE SERIES (TITANIUM CYLINDER—ALUMINUM

ALLOY FRAME)

Model 317 AirLite

This 8-round revolver was introduced in 1997 and is chambered for the .22 LR cartridge. It is fitted with a 2" barrel, serrated ramp front sight, fixed rear sight, and Dymondwood boot grips. It is produced from carbon and stainless steel and also aluminum alloy on a J frame. Its weight is about 9.9 oz.

	NIB	EXC.	V.G.	GOOD	FAIR	POOR
	550	400	375	295	175	100

Model 317 AirLite Kit Gun

This version of the Model 317 was introduced in 1998 and is fitted with a 3" barrel with adjustable rear sight. Choice of Dymondwood grips or Uncle Mike's Combat grips. Weight is about 12 oz. In 2001 this model was offered with HiViz green dot front sight.

	NIB	EXC.	V.G.	GOOD	FAIR	POOR
	700	550	425	300	200	150

Model 317 AirLite Ladysmith

This model features a 2" barrel and Dymondwood grips. Display case is standard. Weight is about 10 oz.

	NIB	EXC.	V.G.	GOOD	FAIR	POOR
	700	550	425	300	200	150

Model 331 AirLite

This model is chambered for the .32 H&R Magnum cartridge on a J frame. Barrel length is 1-7/8". Exposed hammer offers single or double-action. The frame is aluminum, as is the

NIB	EXC.	V.G.	GOOD	FAIR	POOR

barrel shroud and yoke. The cylinder is titanium. The barrel has a stainless steel liner. Matte finish. Because the revolver is made from aluminum and titanium it has a two-tone appearance because of the two different materials. Choice of wood or rubber boot grips. Capacity is 6 rounds. Weight is about 12 oz. with rubber grip and 11.2 oz. with wood grip. Introduced in 1999.

700	550	425	300	200	150

Model 332 AirLite

This model is similar to the Model 331 above but with a concealed hammer, double-action configuration. Weight is 12 oz. with rubber grips and 11.3 oz. with wood grips.

700	550	425	300	200	150

Model 337 AirLite

This model has an aluminum frame, exposed hammer, titanium cylinder. Front sight is black and pinned. Smooth trigger. Cylinder capacity is five rounds. Chambered for .38 Special +P ammo. Barrel length is 1-7/8". Wood or rubber grips. Weight with wood grips is about 11.2 oz., with rubber grips about 12 oz. Introduced in 1999.

600	450	325	250	175	100

Model 342 AirLite

Similar to Model 340, with double-action-only concealed hammer. Weight 11.3 oz. with wood grips; 12 oz. with rubber grips. Introduced in 1999.

700	550	425	300	200	150

Model 325PD

Introduced in 2004 this 6-round large frame revolver is chambered for the .45 ACP cartridge. Fitted with a 2.75" barrel. Wooden grips and HiViz sights. Black oxide finish. Weight is about 21.5 oz.

900	775	600	450	300	150

Model 337 Kit Gun

Similar to the Model 337 but fitted with a 3" barrel. Adjustable rear sight. Weight is about 13.5 oz. In 2001 this model was offered with HiViz green dot front sight.

650	475	325	250	175	100

Model 337 PD

Similar to the Model 337 but with a matte black finish over the aluminum frame and Hogue Bantam grips. Weight is 10.7 oz. Introduced in 2000.

600	450	325	250	175	100

Model 340

Introduced in 2001 this hammerless model features a Scandium alloy frame and is fitted with a 1.875" barrel. Chambered for the .357 Magnum cartridge with a 5-round cylinder. Matte stainless gray finish. Pinned black front sight. Hogue Bantam grips standard. Weight is about 12 oz.

700	550	425	300	200	150

Model 340 PD

Same as the Model 340 but with a gray/black finish. Also introduced in 2001.

750	500	375	275	200	150

Model 342 PD

Similar to the Model 337 but with matte black finish over the aluminum frame and Hogue Bantam grips. Weight is about 10.8 oz. Introduced in 2000.

700	550	425	300	200	150

Model 351PD

This 7-shot revolver is chambered for the .22 Magnum cartridge and fitted with a 1.875" barrel. Black oxide finish. Rubber grips. HiViz sights. Weight is about 10.6 oz.

625	475	350	225	175	75

Model 360

This J frame model features a Scandium alloy frame with exposed hammer and 5-shot cylinder. Fixed sights on a 1.875" barrel. Matte stainless grey finish. Weight is about 12 oz. Introduced in 2001.

700	550	425	300	200	150

	NIB	EXC.	V.G.	GOOD	FAIR	POOR

Model 360 Kit Gun

This version of the M360 is fitted with a 3.125" barrel with HiViz green dot front sight and adjustable rear sight. Weight is about 14.5 oz. Introduced in 2001.

| | 700 | 550 | 425 | 300 | 200 | 150 |

Model 386

Introduced in 2001 this L frame model features a 6-shot cylinder chambered for the .357 Magnum cartridge. Fitted with a 3.125" barrel with HiViz green dot front sight and adjustable rear sight. Scandium alloy frame with matte stainless gray finish. Weight is about 18.5 oz. Hogue Batam grips.

| | 800 | 675 | 500 | 400 | 300 | 200 |

Model 386 PD

Same as above but with gray/black finish and 2.5" barrel with red ramp front sight and adjustable rear sight. Weight is about 17.5 oz.

| | 800 | 675 | 500 | 400 | 300 | 200 |

Model 386 Sc/S

Single-/double-action L-frame revolver in .38/.357 Magnum. 7-shot cylinder, 2.5" barrel, Patridge front sight, adjustable rear, scandium/alloy frame, matte black finish, rubber grips. Introduced 2007.

| | 750 | 600 | 475 | 350 | 250 | 175 |

Model 386 XL Hunter

Single/double action L-frame revolver chambered in .357 Magnum. Features include 6-inch full-lug barrel, 7-round cylinder, Hi-Viz fiber optic front sight, adjustable rear sight, candium frame, stainless steel cylinder, black matte finish, synthetic grips.

| | 750 | 625 | 550 | 465 | 350 | 150 |

Model 396 Mountain Lite

This L frame revolver is chambered for the .44 Special cartridge. It is fitted with a five round titanium cylinder and aluminum alloy frame. Barrel length is 3" and has a green HiViz front sight and an adjustable rear sight. Introduced in 2000. Weight is approximately 19 oz.

| | 750 | 600 | 475 | 350 | 250 | 175 |

Model 242

This medium frame revolver is chambered for the .38 Special +P cartridge. Semi-concealed hammer and 2.5" barrel. Pinned black ramp front sight. Black rubber boot grips. Seven-round cylinder. Matte alloy and titanium finish. Weight is about 19 oz. Introduced in 1999. This model is no longer in production.

| | 550 | 450 | 300 | 225 | 175 | 75 |

Model 296

Also a medium frame revolver chambered for the .44 Special cartridge. Fitted with a 2.5" barrel. Concealed hammer. Cylinder capacity is 5 rounds. Weight is about 19 oz. Introduced in 1999.

| | 700 | 550 | 425 | 300 | 200 | 150 |

Model 586

Six or seven shot double action revolver (L frame) chambered for the .357 Magnum cartridge. It will also chamber and fire .38 Special cartridges. The 686 has been available with 2-1/2-; 3-; 4-; 5- 6- and 8-3/8-inch barrel lengths. Blued frame and cylinder, adjustable sights, walnut Magna or rubber grips.

| | 550 | 425 | 300 | 200 | 150 | 100 |

Model 686

Six or seven shot double action revolver (L frame) chambered for the .357 Magnum cartridge. It will also chamber and fire .38 Special cartridges. The 686 has been available with 2-1/2-; 3-; 4-; 5- 6- and 8-3/8-inch barrel lengths. Stainless steel frame and cylinder, adjustable sights, walnut Magna or rubber grips. Introduced in 1980.The Performance Center also made a limited number of 686s in .38 Super for competitive shooters. Add 50% for Super.

| | 700 | 550 | 425 | 300 | 200 | 150 |

Model 329PD

Chambered for the .44 Magnum cartridge and fitted with a 4" barrel, this large frame revolver has a Scandium frame with matte black finish. Orange dot front sight and adjustable rear sight. Cylinder capacity is six rounds. Wood or rubber grips. Weight is approximately 26.5 oz. Introduced in 2003.

| | 800 | 675 | 500 | 400 | 300 | 200 |

	NIB	EXC.	V.G.	GOOD	FAIR	POOR

Model 610 (2007 Reintroduction)

This N frame model is chambered for the 10mm cartridge and fitted with a variety of barrel lengths. Adjustable rear sight. Six-round non-fluted cylinder. Hogue rubber combat grips. Stainless steel finish. Weight is about 50 oz. for 4-inch model. Reintroduced in 2007.

750	600	475	350	250	175

Model 36 (.38 Chief's Special)

This model, known as the Chief's Special, was introduced in 1950. It was built on the J frame and is chambered for the .38 Special cartridge. It holds 5 shots, has a 2" or 3" barrel, and was initially offered in a round butt. In 1952 a square-butt version was released. It is finished in blue or nickel-plate and has checkered walnut grips. A 3" heavy barrel was first produced in 1967 and became standard in 1975. The 2" barrel was dropped from production in 1993.

575	375	275	200	150	100

Model 36LS (.38 Ladysmith)

This model is similar to the Model 36 with the exception that it is only offered with a 2" barrel, comes with rosewood grips and a soft carrying case. Weighs 20 oz.

625	450	300	200	150	100

Model 36 (Chief's Special Target)

Since 1955 a limited number of Chief's Specials with adjustable sights have been manufactured. They have been offered with 2" or 3" barrels, round or square butts, and either blue or nickel-plated. Between 1957 and 1965, these target models were stamped Model 36 on the yoke. The revolvers manufactured between 1965 and the model discontinuance in 1975 were marked Model 50. This is a very collectible revolver. A total of 2,313 of these special target models were sold in various model designations. Some are more rare than others.

—	775	575	300	200	125

Model 37

Introduced in 1952 as the Chief's Special Airweight, this revolver initially had an alloy frame and cylinder. In 1954, following many complaints regarding damaged revolvers, the cylinders were made of steel. Barrel lengths, finishes, and grip options on the Airweight are the same as on the standard Chief Special. In 1957 the Model 37 designation was adopted. These early alloy frame and cylinder revolvers were designed to shoot only standard velocity .38 Special cartridges. The use of high velocity ammunition was not recommended by the factory. **NOTE:** All 1998 and later production models were rated for +P ammunition.

575	375	275	200	150	100

Model 637

Same as the model above but with aluminum frame and stainless steel finish. **NOTE:** Current production models are now rated for +P ammunition.

575	375	275	200	150	100

Model 637 Carry Combo

As above but supplied with Kydex carry holster. Introduced in 2004.

575	375	275	200	150	100

Model 637 Power Port Pro Series

Aluminum J-frame 5-shot revolver with stainless steel cylinder chambered for .38 Special (5 shots). 2-1/8-inch ported black stainless barrel. Introduced 2008. Dealer sets pricing.

575	375	275	200	150	100

Model 637CT

Same as Model 6377 but with Crimson Trace lasergrips.

650	575	375	275	200	100

Model 38 (Airweight Bodyguard)

This model was introduced in 1955 as the Airweight Bodyguard. This was a departure from S&W's usual procedure in that the alloy-framed version came first. The Model 38 is chambered for .38 Special and is available with a 2" barrel standard. Although a 3" barrel was offered, it is rarely encountered. The frame of the Bodyguard is extended to conceal and shroud the hammer but at the same time allow the hammer to be cocked by the thumb. This makes this model an ideal pocket revolver, as it can be drawn without catching on clothing. It is available either blue or nickel-plated, with checkered walnut grips. **NOTE:** All 1998 and later production models were rated for +P ammunition.

525	350	225	175	125	100

NIB	EXC.	V.G.	GOOD	FAIR	POOR

Model 638

Same as the model above but with aluminum frame and stainless steel finish. **NOTE:** Current production models are now rated for +P ammunition.

475	375	300	225	175	125

Model 49 (Bodyguard)

This model was introduced in 1959 and is identical in configuration to the Model 38 except that the frame is made of steel.

—	575	450	300	250	200

Model 649 (Bodyguard Stainless)

This stainless steel version of the Model 49 was introduced in 1985. It is also available in .357 Magnum. As of 1998 this model was also offered in a .38 Special-only version.

500	350	225	200	175	125

Model 40 (aka Model 42) Centennial

This model was introduced in 1952 as Smith & Wesson's 100th anniversary and appropriately called the "Centennial Model." It is of the Safety Hammerless design. This model was built on the J frame and features a fully concealed hammer and a grip safety. The Model 40 is chambered for the .38 Special cartridge. It is offered with a 2" barrel in either blue or nickel plate. The grips are checkered walnut. The Centennial was discontinued in 1974.

625	550	375	225	150	100

Model 42—Airweight Centennial

This model is identical in configuration to the Model 40 except that it was furnished with an aluminum alloy frame. It was also discontinued in 1974.Editors **NOTE:** The first 37 Model 42s were manufactured with aluminum alloy cylinders. They weigh 11-1/4 ounces compared to 13 ounces for the standard model. The balance of Model 42 production was with steel cylinders. Add 300 percent for this extremely rare variation.

450	400	325	200	150	100

Model 640 Centennial

A stainless steel version of the Model 40 furnished with a 2" or 3" barrel. Both the frame and cylinder are stainless steel. The 3" barrel was no longer offered as of 1993. As of 1998 this model was also offered in a .38 Special-only version.

500	375	250	200	150	100

Model 640 Centennial .357 Magnum

Introduced in 1995 this version of the Model 640 is chambered for the .357 cartridge and fitted with a 2-1/8" barrel. The gun is stainless steel with a fixed notch rear sight and pinned black ramp front sight. It is 6-3/4" in length and weighs 25 oz.

525	400	250	200	150	100

Model 642 Centennial Airweight

Identical to the Model 640 with the exception of a stainless steel cylinder and aluminum alloy frame. Furnished with a 2" or 2.5" barrel. Discontinued in 1992. Replaced by the Model 442 which was introduced in 1993. This model was reintroduced in 1996. **NOTE:** Current production models are now rated for +P ammunition.

450	300	250	200	150	100

Model 642CT (Crimson Trace)

As above but fitted with Crimson Trace laser grips. Weight is about 15 oz. Introduced in 2004.

650	575	375	275	200	100

Model 642LS Ladysmith

Similar to Model 642 but fitted with smooth combat wood grips and a softside carry case. **NOTE:** Current production models are now rated for +P ammunition.

575	450	325	275	175	100

Model 642 PowerPort Pro Series

Similar to Model 642 buit with gray aluminum frame and black stainless ported barrel. Dealer sets pricing. Introduced 2008.

575	450	325	275	175	100

	NIB	EXC.	V.G.	GOOD	FAIR	POOR

Model 631

This revolver is chambered for the .32 Magnum cartridge and is fitted with a 2" (fixed sights) or 4" (adjustable sights) barrel. Stainless steel finish. Weight with 23" barrel is 22 oz. Produced in 1990.

NIB	EXC.	V.G.	GOOD	FAIR	POOR
650	575	375	275	200	100

Model 631 Lady Smith

Similar to the above model but with rosewood grips and laser etched. Fitted with 2" barrel.

NIB	EXC.	V.G.	GOOD	FAIR	POOR
650	575	375	275	200	100

Model 632 Centennial

This model is similar to the other Centennial models but is chambered for the .32 H&R Magnum cartridge. It comes standard with a 2" barrel, stainless steel cylinder and aluminum alloy frame. Dropped from the product line in 1993.

NIB	EXC.	V.G.	GOOD	FAIR	POOR
650	575	375	275	200	100

Model 632 PowerPort Pro Series

J-frame revolver chambered in .327 Federal Magnum. Six-shot cylinder, 3" full-lug ported barrel with full-length extractor. Pinned, serrated front sight, adjustable rear. Synthetic grips. Stainless steel frame and cylinder.

NIB	EXC.	V.G.	GOOD	FAIR	POOR
775	650	495	350	250	175

Models 637 CT/638 CT/642 CT

Similar to Models 637, 638 and 642 but with Crimson Trace Laser Grips. Suggested retail price $920.

Model 042 Centennial Airweight

This model was produced in 1992 but is not catalogued. It is chambered for .38 Special and fitted with a 2" barrel. The frame is alloy. Marked "MOD 042." No grip safety. Blued finish. Weight is about 16 oz. Supposedly a reworked Model 642 "blemish gun" distributed through a national wholesaler.

NIB	EXC.	V.G.	GOOD	FAIR	POOR
650	575	375	275	200	100

Model 442 Centennial Lightweight

This 5-shot revolver is chambered for the .38 Special and is equipped with a 2" barrel, aluminum alloy frame, and carbon steel cylinder. It has a fully concealed hammer and weighs 15.8 oz. The front ramp sight is serrated and the rear sight is a fixed square notch. Rubber combat grips from Michael's of Oregon are standard. Finish is either blue/black or satin nickel. Introduced in 1993. **NOTE:** Current production models are now rated for +P ammunition.

NIB	EXC.	V.G.	GOOD	FAIR	POOR
400	300	250	200	150	100

Model 442/642/640/632 Pro Series

Double action only J-frame with concealed hammers chambered in .38 Special +P (442 & 642), .357 Magnum (640) or .327 Federal (632). Features include 5-round cylinder, matte stainless steel frame, fixed sights or dovetail night sights (632, 640), synthetic grips, cylinder cut for moon clips (442, 642, 640). Suggested retail price $640 (standard) to $916 (night sights).

Model 438

J-frame double-action-only revolver chambered in .38 Special +P. Five-shot cylinder, 1.87" barrel, fixed front and rear sights, synthetic grips. Aluminum alloy frame, stainless steel cylinder. Matte black finish throughout.

NIB	EXC.	V.G.	GOOD	FAIR	POOR
575	450	325	275	175	100

Model 940

Styled like the other Centennial models, this model is chambered for the 9mm Parabellum cartridge. It has a stainless steel cylinder and frame and is furnished with a 2" or 3" barrel. The 3" barrel version was dropped from production in 1993.

NIB	EXC.	V.G.	GOOD	FAIR	POOR
700	550	425	300	200	150

Model 43 (.22/.32 Kit Gun Airweight)

This model was built on the J frame, is chambered for .22 rimfire, has a 3.5" barrel, and is offered in a round or square butt, with checkered walnut grips. It has adjustable sights and is either blued or nickel-plated. The frame is made of aluminum alloy. Except for this, it is identical to the Model 34 or .22/.32 Kit Gun. This model has a rare 2" barrel configuration as well as a .22 WRM model. The Model 43 was introduced in 1954 and was discontinued in 1974.

NIB	EXC.	V.G.	GOOD	FAIR	POOR
650	575	375	275	200	100

Model 51 (.22/.32 Kit Gun Magnum)

This model is simply the Model 34 chambered for the .22 Winchester Magnum rimfire. It was first introduced in 1960 beginning with serial number 52637. Available in both round and square

	NIB	EXC.	V.G.	GOOD	FAIR	POOR

butt with the round butt variation having a total production of only 600. The Model 51 was discontinued in 1974.

	—	675	400	250	200	125

Model 651

This stainless steel version of the Model 51 .22 Magnum Kit Gun was manufactured between 1983 and 1987.

	—	675	400	250	200	125

Model 73

Produced in about 1973 this revolver was built on a special "C" size frame. Cylinder holds 6 rounds and is chambered for the .38 Special cartridge. Fitted with a 2" barrel. A total of 5,000 were built. All but 20 were destroyed. An extremely rare S&W revolver. Marked, "MOD 73" on yoke.

8500	—	—	—	—	—

Model 45 (Post Office)

This model is a special purpose K-frame Military & Police Model chambered for the .22 rimfire. It was designed as a training revolver for police departments and the U.S. Postal Service. This model was manufactured in limited quantities between 1948 and 1957. In 1963 production abruptly began and ended again. There were 500 of these revolvers released on a commercial basis, but they are rarely encountered.

1250	800	650	450	300	100

Model 48 (K-22 Masterpiece Magnum)

Introduced in 1959 and is identical to the Model 17 or K-22 except that it is chambered for the .22 WRM cartridge. Offered in 4", 6", and 8-3/8" barrel lengths, it has a blued finish. Discontinued in 1986.

700	500	275	225	150	100

Model 53 (Magnum Jet)

Introduced in 1961 and chambered for the .22 Jet, a Remington cartridge. The barrel lengths were 4", 6", and 8-3/8" and the finish is blued. Sights were adjustable and the revolver was furnished with cylinder inserts that would allow .22 rimfire cartridges to be fired. The frame had two firing pins. Approximately 15,000 were produced before it was discontinued in 1974. Price includes guns with individual chambered inserts. **NOTE:** Add $150 for auxiliary .22 LR cylinder.

1500	750	450	350	250	200

Model 57

This revolver was introduced in 1964 and is chambered for the .41 Magnum cartridge. It is built on the N frame. Offered in 4", 6", and 8-3/8" barrel lengths, it has a blued frame and adjustable sights. Model designations are: 57-1 1982; 57-2 1988; 57-3 1990; 57-4 1993.

600	400	275	225	200	150

Model 657

This is a stainless steel version of the Model 57 and was introduced in 1980. Still in production. In 2001 this model was reintroduced again with a 7.5" barrel with pinned front sight and adjustable rear sight. Hogue rubber combat grips. Weight is about 52 oz.

670	525	425	295	200	150

Model 56 (KXT-38 USAF)

Introduced in 1962, this is a 2" heavy barrel built on the K frame. Chambered for .38 Special. Marked "U.S." on backstrap. Total of 15,205 were produced by the time it was discontinued in 1964. Most were reportedly destroyed by the Air Force.

5500	4250	3000	2000	1250	800

Model 58

This model is chambered for the .41 Magnum and is fitted with fixed sights. Offered in blued or nickel finish and with 4" barrel. Checkered walnut grips are standard. Introduced in 1964.

1100	650	450	300	225	125

Model 547

Introduced in 1980 and chambered for the 9mm cartridge and offered with either 3" or 4" barrel. Finish is blued. Discontinued.

650	475	375	275	200	125

NIB	EXC.	V.G.	GOOD	FAIR	POOR

Model 460 XVR

Introduced in 2005 this model is chambered for the .460 S&W magnum, which has the highest muzzle velocity of any production handgun. Fitted with a 8-3/8" barrel with interchangeable compensators. Frame size is extra large. Capacity is 5 rounds. Adjustable sights with Hi-Viz front sight. Finger groove grips. Satin stainless finish. Weight is about 72.5 oz. **NOTE:** Add $135 for 4" barrel model.

1000	875	750	600	400	300

Model 460V

X-frame double-action trigger and 5" barrel in .460 S&W Magnum caliber. Also accepts .454 Casull and .45 Colt. Sorbothane recoil-reducing grip, interchangeable muzzle compensator. 5-shot, stainless with satin finish. 62.5 oz. Introduced 2006.

1000	875	750	600	400	300

Model 500

Introduced in 2003 this revolver is chambered for the .500 S&W Magnum cartridge. Fitted with a 8.375" barrel with compensator and built on the X frame. Cylinder holds five rounds. Stainless steel frame and barrel. Interchangeable front blade sight and adjustable rear sight. K-frame size Hogue grips. Weight is about 72.5 oz. In 2004 this model was offered with a 4" barrel with compensator. Weight is about 56 oz. 6.5-inch model introduced 2008. **NOTE:** Add $135 for 4" barrel model.

1000	875	750	600	400	300

Model 60

Introduced in 1965 this model is similar to the Model 36 but in stainless steel. Offered in 2" barrel with fixed sights, walnut grips, and smooth trigger. Some 2" Model 60s were produced with adjustable sights add 50 percent. The 3" barrel version comes with a full underlug, adjustable sights, serrated trigger, and rubber grips. The 2" version weighs about 20 oz. while the 3" version weighs approximately 25 oz. In 1996 this model was offered chambered for the .357 Magnum cartridge. This new version is fitted with a 2-1/8" barrel. The 2-1/8" barrel weighs about 23 oz. This model was also offered in a .38 Special-only version.

2" Barrel

450	350	300	200	125	100

3" Barrel

475	375	350	250	150	100

5" Barrel

Introduced in 2005.

550	475	375	295	200	125

Model 60LS (LadySmith)

Chambered for the .38 Special with 2" barrel and stainless steel frame and cylinder. This slightly smaller version of the Model 60 is made for small hands. A new version offered in 1996 is chambered for the .357 Magnum cartridge.

450	350	300	200	125	100

Model 60 with Hi-Viz Sight

Similar to Model 60 but with light-gathering Hi-Viz red dot front sight and adjustable rear sight. Introduced 2007.

525	400	300	225	175	100

Model 60 Pro Series

Similar to Model 60 but in .38/.357 with night front sights, "high-hold" enforcing walnut grips, 3-inch battel and matte stainless finish. Introduced 2008.

650	475	375	275	200	125

Model 63

This model, introduced in 1977, is simply the Model 34 made of stainless steel.

500	375	250	225	200	150

Model 64 (Military & Police Stainless)

This model is the stainless steel version of the Model 10 M&P. It was introduced in 1970. The Model 64-1 variation was introduced in 1972 and is the heavy barrel version.

500	325	275	225	175	125

	NIB	EXC.	V.G.	GOOD	FAIR	POOR

Model 65 (.357 Military & Police Heavy Barrel Stainless)

This is the stainless steel version of the Model 13 M&P .357 Magnum. It was introduced in 1974.

	425	300	275	225	175	125

Model 66 (.357 Combat Magnum Stainless)

Released in 1970, this is the stainless steel version of the Model 19 or Combat Magnum. It is chambered for the .357 Magnum, has adjustable sights, a square butt with checkered walnut grips, and was initially offered with a 4" barrel. In 1974 a 2.5" barrel, round butt version was made available. It was available in a 6" barrel, as well as all target options until discontinued in 1993. Reintroduced in 2014.

	575	400	250	200	150	125

Model 67 (.38 Combat Masterpiece Stainless)

Introduced in 1972 this is a stainless steel version of the Model 15 with a 4" barrel. It is chambered for the .38 Special cartridge. Model designation changes are as follows: {None} 1972 to 1977; {-1} 1977 to 1988; {-2} 1988 to 1993; {-3} 1993 to present.

	500	300	250	200	150	100

Model 69

Built on the L frame, this is a five-shot .44 Magnum, with 4.25" barrel and stainless finish. Sights are Smith & Wesson's classic white-outline adjustable rear and red-ramp front. Grips are synthetic, with finger grooves. Introduced in 2014.

	725	625	500	385	275	200

Model 650

Introduced in 1983 this stainless steel model is built on a J frame with a 3" heavy barrel chambered for the .22 WRM. It has a round butt and fixed sights. Discontinued in 1988.

	600	450	250	175	125	100

Model 651

This J-frame model was introduced in 1983 and chambered for the .22 WRM and fitted with a 4" barrel. Stainless steel finish and adjustable sights. Designation changes are: {None} 1983 to 1988; {-1} 1988 to 1990; {-2} 1988 to 1990.

	575	400	250	200	150	100

Model 686 Powerport

Introduced in 1995 this version of the Model 686 features a 6" full lug barrel with integral compensator. The frame is drilled and tapped for scope mounts. Hogue grips are furnished as standard.

	650	550	450	400	300	200

Model 686 Plus Mountain Gun

This model is fitted with a 4" tapered barrel and chambered for the .357 Magnum cartridge. It has adjustable rear sights. Hogue rubber grips are standard. Stainless steel finish. Weight is about 44 oz.

	650	475	450	400	300	200

Model 686 Magnum Plus

Offered for the first time in 1996 this model features a 7-shot cylinder. It is available with 2.5", 4", or 6" barrel lengths. It is fitted with a red ramp front sight and a fully adjustable rear sight. The frame is drilled and tapped for scope mounts. Hogue synthetic grips are standard. The stainless steel is satin finished. Weight is between 35 oz. and 45 oz. depending on barrel length.

	625	500	450	400	300	200

Model 686—5" Barrel

This .357 Magnum stainless steel model is fitted with a 5" barrel with HiViz front sight and adjustable rear sight. Cylinder holds 7 rounds. Cocobolo wood grips. Weight is about 41 oz. Introduced in 2004.

	575	475	395	300	200	100

Model 686 Plus

Single-/double-action L-frame revolver in .38/.357 Magnum. 7-shot cylinder, 3" barrel, Patridge front sight, adjustable rear, stainless finish, rubber grips. Introduced 2007.

	600	550	450	400	300	200

	NIB	EXC.	V.G.	GOOD	FAIR	POOR

Model 686 Plus Pro Series

Single-/double-action L-frame revolver chambered in .357 Magnum. Features include 5-inch barrel with tapered underlug, 7-round cylinder, satin stainless steel frame and cylinder, synthetic grips, interchangeable and adjustable sights. From the S&W Performance Center.

750	650	500	400	300	200

Model 929

Built on the N frame, this is an 8-shot 9mm revolver, used by Smith & Wesson competitive shooter Jerry Miculek. Barrel length 6.5". Adjustable rear and Patridge front sight. From the S&W Performance Center.

975	800	650	500	400	250

Model M986

From the S&W Performance Center, this 9mm is built on the L frame, with seven-shot cylinder. Designed for use with moon clips. Barrel length 5". Sights are adjustable rear and Patridge style front.

975	800	650	500	400	250

Model M&P R8

An 8-shot .357/.38 Special revolver built on Smith & Wesson's N frame. Has a 5" barrel and Scandium alloy frame. Weight 36 oz. Sights are adjustable V-notch rear and interchangeable-dot front. Other features include an accessory rail and synthetic grips, with finger grooves. From the S&W Performance Center.

1125	975	800	600	350	250

Model 619

This model is chambered for the .357 Magnum cartridge and fitted with a 4" two-piece semi-lug barrel with fixed sights. Stainless steel frame and barrel. Capacity is 7 rounds. Medium frame. Weight is about 37.5 oz. Rubber grips. Introduced in 2005.

575	475	395	300	200	100

Model 620

Similar to the model above but with a 4" barrel with adjustable rear sight and red ramp front sight. Weight is about 37.9 oz. Introduced in 2005.

600	550	450	400	300	200

Model 3 Schofield

A reintroduction of the famous Schofield revolver. This is a single-action top-break model chambered for the .45 S&W cartridge. Barrel length is 7". Frame and barrel are blue while hammer and trigger are case hardened. Sights are a fixed rear notch and half moon post front. Walnut grips. Weight is 40 oz. Reintroduced in 2000. In 2002 this model was offered in a 7" nickel version as well as a 5" blue and 5" nickel configuration.

1750	1400	1050	800	500	300

HERITAGE SERIES REVOLVERS

These revolvers are built by the S&W Performance Center and produced for Lew Horton Distributing Co. Each model is similar in appearance to the original but has modern internal features. These handguns are produced in limited runs of from 100 units to 350 units.

Model 1917

Chambered for the .45 ACP cartridge and fitted with a 5.5" heavy tapered barrel. High-profile front blade sight with fixed rear sight. Checkered service grips with lanyard ring. Offered in blue, case-colored, or military finish. Shipped in a S&W collectible box. **NOTE:** Add $60 for case color finish.

900	775	600	450	300	150

Model 15

This revolver is chambered for the .38 S&W Special. Fitted with a 4" barrel. Grips are S&W checkered target. Adjustable rear sight. Offered in nickel or color case hardened.

800	675	550	400	250	125

Model 15 McGivern

Similar to the above model but fitted with 5" barrel and checkered diamond grips. Engraved sideplate of McGivern's speed record. Blue finish.

900	775	600	450	300	150

	NIB	EXC.	V.G.	GOOD	FAIR	POOR

Model 17

Chambered for the .22 caliber cartridge and fitted with a 6" barrel with patridge front sight and adjustable rear sight. Four screw sideplate. Diamond checkered S&W walnut grips. Blue or case colored finish. **NOTE:** Add $30 for case colored finish.

800	675	550	400	250	125

Model 24

This model is chambered for the .44 Special cartridge and fitted with a 6.5" tapered barrel. McGivern gold-bead front sight with adjustable rear sight. Four-screw sideplate, chamfered charge holes, checkered diamond grips. **NOTE:** Add $60 for case colored finish.

900	775	600	450	300	150

Model 25

Similar to the Model 24 but chambered for the .45 Colt cartridge. Blue or case colored finish. **NOTE:** Add $30 for case colored finish.

900	775	600	450	300	150

Model 29

Similar to the Model 24 and Model 25 but chambered for the .44 Magnum cartridge. Oversized wood grips. Blue or nickel finish. Was to be produced in 2002 only. Serial numbers to begin with "DBW2005.

900	775	600	450	300	150

CLASSIC SERIES

Model 14 Classic

Recreation of the vintage Model 14 revolver chambered in .38 Special +P. Six-shot cylinder, 6" barrel with pinned Patridge front sight and micro-adjustable rear. Carbon steel frame and cylinder with blued finish. Weight 34.5 oz.

800	675	525	400	275	150

Model 14 Classic (nickel)

Same as above but with nickel finish. Discontinued.

900	775	600	500	375	200

Model 15 Classic

Identical to Model 14 Classic, except with 4" barrel.

800	675	525	400	275	150

Model 17 Masterpiece Classic

Recreation of the K-22 Masterpiece in .22 LR with blue finish, 6" barrel, adjustable rear sight and wood grips.

850	725	550	400	275	150

Model 36 Classic

Replica of vintage Model 36 Chief's Special in .38 Special. Five-shot cylinder. Carbon steel frame, 1-7/8" or 3" barrel, fixed sights. Blued, case colored, or nickel finish with Altamont wood grips. Introduced 2007.

600	500	400	250	150	100

Model 21 Classic

Replica of vintage Model 21 N-frame revolver in .44 Special. Six-shot cylinder. Carbon steel frame, 4" barrel, fixed sights. Blued, case colored, or nickel finish with Altamont wood grips. Introduced 2007.

900	750	525	400	275	150

Model 22 Classic

Replica of vintage Model 22 N-frame revolver in .45 ACP. Six-shot cylinder. Carbon steel frame, 4" barrel, fixed sights. Blued, case colored, or nickel finish with Altamont wood grips. Introduced 2007.

900	750	525	400	275	150

Model 22 of 1917 Classic

Similar to Model 22 Classic but without ejector rod shroud and with lanyard ring on butt. Replica of U.S. Army WWI-era revolver. Introduced 2007.

900	700	525	400	275	150

	NIB	EXC.	V.G.	GOOD	FAIR	POOR

Model 24 Classic
In .44 Special with 6.5" barrel, wood grips with square butt and adjustable rear sight.

	850	725	550	400	275	150

Model 25 Classic
Identical to Model 24 Classic, except chambered for .45 Colt.

	850	725	550	400	275	150

Model 27 Classic
Reintroduction of vintage Model 27. Available in blue or bright nickel finish. 6.5" barrel, walnut grips. Introduced 2008. **NOTE:** Add 25 percent for 75th Anniversary Model.

	900	700	525	400	275	150

Model 29 Classic
Replica of original (1956) Model 29 N-frame revolver in .44 Magnum. Six-shot cylinder. Carbon steel frame, 6.5" barrel, fixed sights. Blued or nickel finish with or without engraving. Altamont wood grips. Introduced 2007.

	900	775	600	500	375	200

Model 10 Classic
Single/double action K frame revolver chambered in .38 Special. Features include bright blue steel frame and cylinder, checkered wood grips, 4" barrel, adjustable patridge-style sights.

	600	500	450	375	275	150

Model 40/42 Centennial Classic
This recreation of the 5-shot J-frame model, is designed for double-action only operation with a fully concealed hammer and grip safety. The Model 40 has a steel frame and weighs 19 oz. Model 42 has an alloy frame and weighs 13 oz.

	650	550	450	375	300	200

Model 48 Classic
Single/double action K frame revolver chambered in .22 Magnum Rimfire (.22 WMR). Features include bright blue steel frame and cylinder, checkered wood grips, 4" or 6" barrel, adjustable patridge-style sights.

	750	625	500	400	275	150

MILITARY & POLICE (M&P) SERIES
M&P340
Double-action-only revolver built on Centennial (hammerless J) frame. .357 Magnum/.38 Special; five-shot cylinder; 1.87" barrel with fixed night sights. Matte black finish on scandium/alloy frame. Introduced 2007.

	700	575	400	250	150	100

M&P340CT
Similar to above but with Crimson Trace lasergrips. Introduced 2007.

	825	700	600	500	350	175

M&P360
Double-action-only revolver built on Chief's Special (hammered J) frame. .357 Magnum/.38 Special; five-shot cylinder; 1.87" barrel with fixed night sights. Matte black finish on scandium/alloy frame. Introduced 2007.

	700	575	400	250	150	100

M&PR8
Double-action-only revolver built on large (N) frame. .357 Magnum/.38 Special; eight-shot cylinder; 5" barrel with adjustable Patridge sights with interchangeable inserts. Matte black finish on scandium/alloy frame. Introduced 2007.

	1100	850	600	500	375	200

Governor
Built on the Smith & Wesson L frame, this six-shot revolver can fire .410 shotshells, .45 Colt and .45 ACP (with moon clips) ammunition. Scandium alloy frame, stainless steel cylinder, Tritium night sight, internal security lock and Hogue synthetic grips. Barrel length is 2.75-inches, weight 29.6 ounces, overall length 8.5-inches with matte black finish. Available with Crimson Trace Laser grips. Introduced in 2011. **NOTE:** Add $200 for Crimson Trace Laser grips.

	650	525	425	365	250	150

	NIB	EXC.	V.G.	GOOD	FAIR	POOR

SEMI-AUTOMATIC PISTOLS

NOTE: Pistols with Smith and Wesson factory-installed night sights add $100 to NIB and Exc. prices; S&W factory engraving add $1,000 for Class C (1/3 coverage); $1,250 for Class B (2/3 coverage); $1,500 for Class A (full coverage). See Performance Center section at end of Smith & Wesson section for special and limited edition version of many of these models.

Model 39

This was the first double-action semi-automatic pistol produced in the United States. It was introduced in 1957. It had an alloy frame and was chambered for the 9mm Parabellum or .30 Luger. The barrel was 4" and the finish was either blued or nickel with checkered walnut grips. The rear sight was adjustable. Magazine capacity is 8 rounds. Discontinued in 1982. The .30 Luger model is very rare and was mostly sold in Europe. **NOTE:** Add 150 percent for .30 Luger.

600	450	250	200	150	100

Model 39 Steel Frame

A total of 927 steel frame Model 39s were produced. A rare pistol; use caution.

1750	1200	700	550	400	250

Model 59

Introduced in 1971 this pistol is similar to the Model 39 but with a wide grip to hold a double column magazine of 14 rounds. Furnished with black checkered plastic grips. Discontinued in 1982.

575	500	350	200	150	100

Model 439

Introduced in 1979 this is an improved version of the Model 39. Furnished with adjustable rear sight. Discontinued in 1988.

600	450	350	325	250	100

Model 639

This is a stainless steel version of the Model 439. Introduced in 1984 and discontinued in 1988.

600	450	350	325	250	100

Model 459

This improved-sight version of the 15-shot Model 59 9mm pistol was introduced in 1979 and discontinued in 1987.

600	450	350	325	250	100

Model 659

This stainless steel version of the Model 459 9mm pistol features an ambidextrous safety and all other options of the Model 459. Introduced in 1982 and discontinued in 1988.

550	425	350	300	250	150

Model 539

This is yet another version of the Model 439 9mm pistol. It incorporates all the features of the Model 439 with a steel frame instead of aluminum alloy. This model was introduced in 1980 and discontinued in 1983.

525	400	350	300	250	200

Model 559

This variation of the Model 459 9mm pistol has a steel frame instead of aluminum alloy. It is identical in all other respects.

475	400	350	300	250	200

Model 469

The Model 469 was brought out in answer to the need for a more concealable high-capacity pistol. It is essentially a "Mini" version of the Model 459. It is chambered for the 9mm Parabellum and has a 12-round detachable magazine with a finger-grip extension and a shortened frame. The barrel is 3.5" long; the hammer is bobbed and does not protrude; the safety is ambidextrous. The finish is matte blue, with black plastic grips. The Model 469 was introduced in 1983 and discontinued in 1988.

450	375	325	275	200	150

Model 669

This is a stainless steel version of the Model 469 9mm pistol. All of the features of the 469 are incorporated. The Model 669 was manufactured from 1986 to 1988.

475	425	350	300	250	200

	NIB	EXC.	V.G.	GOOD	FAIR	POOR

Model 645

The Model 645 is a large-framed, stainless steel double-action pistol chambered for the .45 ACP cartridge. It has a 5" barrel, adjustable sights, and a detachable 8-shot magazine. It is offered with fixed or adjustable sights and an ambidextrous safety. The grips are molded black nylon. S&W manufactured this pistol between 1985 and 1988.

600	450	375	325	250	150

Model 745—IPSC

This model is similar in outward appearance to the Model 645 but is quite a different pistol. The Model 745 is a single-action semi-automatic chambered for the .45 ACP cartridge. The frame is made of stainless steel, and the slide of blued carbon steel. The barrel is 5", and the detachable magazine holds eight rounds. The sights are fully adjustable target types. The grips are checkered walnut. Introduced in 1986 and discontinued in 1990.

775	600	500	400	350	250

TARGET PISTOLS

Model 41

NOTE: For full set of steel and aluminum barrel weights add up to $500 depending on condition. For .22 Short conversion kit add $750 depending on condition. For military marked pistols add 400 percent.

1100	850	600	500	325	150

Model 41 (New Model)

This model was restyled in 1994 featuring recontoured hardwood stocks, a Millet adjustable rear sight, and a drilled and tapped barrel for scope mounting.

775	600	500	400	350	250

Model 41-1

This model was introduced in 1960 and is chambered for the .22 Short rimfire only. It was developed for the International Rapid Fire competition. In appearance it is quite similar to the Model 41 except that the slide is made of aluminum alloy, as well as the frame, in order to lighten it to function with the .22 Short cartridge. This model was not a commercial success like the Model 41, so it was discontinued after fewer than 1,000 were manufactured.

1200	900	725	500	375	225

Model 41 Fiftieth Anniversary Edition

Similar to original Model 41 but machine-engraved with Class A+ coverage, gold plated borders, and glass-topped presentation case. Introduced 2008. Serial Number Range: FYA0001 - FYA0500.

1600	1400	1200	900	600	400

Model 46

This was a lower-cost version of the Model 41. It was developed for the Air Force in 1959. Its appearance was essentially the same as the Model 41 with a 7" barrel. Later a 5" barrel was introduced, and finally in 1964 a heavy 5.5" barrel was produced. This economy target pistol never had the popularity that the more expensive Model 41 had, and it was discontinued in 1968 after approximately 4,000 pistols were manufactured.

1100	900	800	650	400	200

Model 61 Escort

In 1970 the Model 61 was introduced as the only true pocket automatic that S&W produced. It was chambered for the .22 LR cartridge with a 2-1/2" barrel and 5-round magazine. It was offered in either blued or nickel finish with black checkered plastic grips. It was dropped from the product line in 1974.

300	225	200	150	100	75

Model 52A

Introduced in 1961 in the .38 AMU caliber for the Army marksmanship training. Army rejected the pistol and the 87 units built were released to the public. The letter "A" is stamped behind the model designation. A rare find; only 87 were produced. Use caution.

3000	2500	2000	1500	750	500

Model 52 (.38 Master)

Introduced in 1961 as a target pistol chambered for the .38 Special mid-range wad cutter cartridge. It is similar in appearance to the Model 39 but is single-action-only by virtue

	NIB	EXC.	V.G.	GOOD	FAIR	POOR

of a set screw. Fitted with a 5" barrel and a 5-round magazine. It has a blued finish with checkered walnut grips. About 3,500 of these pistols were produced in this configuration until discontinued in 1963.

	NIB	EXC.	V.G.	GOOD	FAIR	POOR
	975	750	550	450	300	200

Model 52-1

In 1963 this variation featured a true single-action design and were produced until 1971.

	NIB	EXC.	V.G.	GOOD	FAIR	POOR
	850	725	450	350	300	200

Model 52-2

Introduced in 1971 with a coil spring-style extractor. Model was discontinued in 1993.

	NIB	EXC.	V.G.	GOOD	FAIR	POOR
	750	600	475	400	300	200

Model 2214 (The Sportsman)

This semi-automatic pistol is chambered for the .22 LR and designed for casual use. It is fitted with a 3" barrel and has a magazine capacity of 8 rounds. The slide is blued carbon steel and the frame is alloy. Introduced in 1990, discontinued 1997.

	NIB	EXC.	V.G.	GOOD	FAIR	POOR
	250	200	150	125	100	50

Model 2206

This .22 LR pistol is offered with either a 4-1/2" or 6" barrel. Magazine capacity is 12 rounds. Adjustable rear sight. Stainless steel frame and slide.

	NIB	EXC.	V.G.	GOOD	FAIR	POOR
	300	250	175	125	100	50

Model 2206 TGT (Target)

Introduced in 1995 this version of the Model 2206 features a selected 6" barrel, bead blasted sighting plane and polished flat side surfaces. A Patridge front sight and Millet adjustable rear sight are standard. In addition the model has a serrated trigger with adjustable trigger stop and a 10-round magazine.

	NIB	EXC.	V.G.	GOOD	FAIR	POOR
	350	300	250	200	150	100

Model 422 Field

Introduced in 1987 this .22 LR pistol has a 4-1/2" barrel or 6" barrel with an alloy frame and steel slide. The magazine capacity is 10 rounds. This model has fixed sights and black plastic grips. Finish is matte blue.

	NIB	EXC.	V.G.	GOOD	FAIR	POOR
	350	275	225	125	100	50

Model 422 Target

Same as the Field model but fitted with adjustable sights and checkered walnut grips.

	NIB	EXC.	V.G.	GOOD	FAIR	POOR
	350	275	225	125	100	50

Model 622 Field

This is a stainless steel version of the Model 422 Field.

	NIB	EXC.	V.G.	GOOD	FAIR	POOR
	400	300	225	150	125	75

Model 622 Target

This is the stainless steel version of the Model 422 Target.

	NIB	EXC.	V.G.	GOOD	FAIR	POOR
	400	300	225	150	125	75

Model 622VR

Redesigned in 1996 this .22 caliber model features a 6" ventilated rib barrel. It is fitted with a matte black trigger and a new trigger guard. The front sight is a serrated ramp style with an adjustable rear sight. Weight is approximately 23 oz. Grips are black polymer.

	NIB	EXC.	V.G.	GOOD	FAIR	POOR
	375	275	200	150	100	75

Model 22A Sport

Introduced in 1997 this model features a choice of 4", 5.5", or 7" barrel. It is chambered for the .22 LR cartridge. Magazine capacity is 10 rounds. Rear sight is adjustable. Grips are either two-piece polymer or two-piece Soft Touch. Frame and slide are aluminum alloy and stainless steel. Finish is blue. Weight is approximately 28 oz. for 4" model and 32 oz. for 5.5" model. Weight of 7" model is about 33 oz. Prices quoted are for 4" model. In 2001 this model was furnished with a Hi-Viz green dot front sight. In 2008 a full-camo version was introduced (add $40).

	NIB	EXC.	V.G.	GOOD	FAIR	POOR
	290	200	150	100	75	50

	NIB	EXC.	V.G.	GOOD	FAIR	POOR

Model 22S Sport

This model, also introduced in 1997, is similar to the above model but with 5.5" and 7" barrel on stainless steel frames. Weight is about 41 oz. and 42 oz. respectively. In 2001 this model was furnished with a Hi-Viz green dot front sight.

	NIB	EXC.	V.G.	GOOD	FAIR	POOR
	300	225	175	150	100	50

Model 22A Target

This .22 caliber target pistol has a 10-round magazine, adjustable rear sight, and target grips with thumb rest. The barrel is 5.5" bull barrel. Finish is blue. Weight is about 39 oz. Introduced in 1997.

	NIB	EXC.	V.G.	GOOD	FAIR	POOR
	290	200	150	100	75	45

Model 22S Target

Same as above but with stainless steel frame and slide. Weight is approximately 48 oz.

	NIB	EXC.	V.G.	GOOD	FAIR	POOR
	300	225	175	150	100	50

Model 22A Camo

Introduced in 2004 this .22 LR model features a Mossy Oak Break-Up finish. Weight is about 39 oz.

	NIB	EXC.	V.G.	GOOD	FAIR	POOR
	325	250	175	150	100	50

Model 3904

In 1989 S&W redesigned the entire line of 9mm semi-automatic handguns. The 3904 is chambered for the 9mm Parabellum and has an 8-shot detachable magazine and 4" barrel with a fixed bushing. The frame is alloy, and the trigger guard is squared for two-hand hold. The magazine well is beveled, and the grips are one-piece wrap-around made of delrin. The three-dot sighting system is employed. This model has been discontinued.

	NIB	EXC.	V.G.	GOOD	FAIR	POOR
	450	400	325	300	275	225

Model 3906

This is the stainless steel version of the Model 3904. The features are the same. It was introduced in 1989. This model has been discontinued.

	NIB	EXC.	V.G.	GOOD	FAIR	POOR
	450	400	325	300	275	225

Model 3914

Offered as a slightly smaller alternative to the Model 3904, this 9mm pistol has a 3-1/2" barrel, 8-round magazine, and blued carbon steel slide and alloy frame.

	NIB	EXC.	V.G.	GOOD	FAIR	POOR
	525	450	400	350	300	250

Model 3913

This version is similar to the Model 3914 but features a stainless steel slide and alloy frame.

	NIB	EXC.	V.G.	GOOD	FAIR	POOR
	525	450	400	350	300	250

Model 3914LS

This is a redesigned Model 3914 that has a more modern appearance. The LS refers to LadySmith and is chambered for the 9mm cartridge. All other features are the same as the Model 3914 including the blued carbon slide and alloy frame.

	NIB	EXC.	V.G.	GOOD	FAIR	POOR
	525	450	400	350	300	200

Model 3913LS

This model is identical to the Model 3914LS with the exception of the stainless steel slide.

	NIB	EXC.	V.G.	GOOD	FAIR	POOR
	525	450	400	350	300	200

Model 3954

Similar to the Model 3914 but offered in double-action-only. Discontinued in 1993.

	NIB	EXC.	V.G.	GOOD	FAIR	POOR
	525	450	400	350	300	200

Model 915

Introduced in 1993 this model is chambered for the 9mm cartridge and features a 4" barrel, matte blue finish, fixed rear sight, and wraparound rubber grips. Overall length is 7.5" and weight is about 28 oz.

	NIB	EXC.	V.G.	GOOD	FAIR	POOR
	400	350	250	200	150	100

Model 5904

This is a full high capacity, 15-shot version of the Model 3904. It was introduced in 1989 and features a slide mounted decocking lever and 4" barrel. This version has a blued carbon steel

	NIB	EXC.	V.G.	GOOD	FAIR	POOR

slide and alloy frame. This model is no longer in production.

	525	450	375	325	275	200

Model 5903

The same caliber and features as the Model 5904 and Model 5906, but furnished with a stainless steel slide and alloy frame.

	525	450	400	350	300	250

Model 5906

This is a stainless steel version of the Model 5904. Both the slide and frame are stainless steel.

	525	450	375	275	200	—

Model 5906 Special Edition

A double-action semi-automatic pistol chambered for the 9mm with a 15-round magazine. The frame and slide have a special machine finish while the grips are one-piece wrap-around Xenoy. The front sight is a white dot post and the rear sight is a Novak L-Mount Carry with two white dots. This model has a manual safety/decocking lever and firing pin safety. Introduced in 1993.

	575	450	350	300	250	150

Model 5926

S&W offers a 9mm pistol similar to the 5906 but with a frame mounted decocking lever. Both the slide and frame are stainless steel. Discontinued in 1993.

	525	450	375	300	250	150

Model 5946

This 9mm pistol offers the same features as the Model 5926, but in a double-action-only mode. The hammer configuration on this model is semi-bobbed instead of serrated.

	525	450	400	350	300	250

Model 5967

This is a 9mm model with a M5906 frame and a 3914 slide. It has a stainless steel frame and blued slide. Novak Lo-Mount fixed sights. Introduced in 1990 and sold through Lew Horton.

	600	475	400	350	300	250

Model 6904

This is the concealable, shortened version of the Model 5904. It has a 12-shot magazine, fixed sights, bobbed hammer, and a 3.5" barrel.

	525	450	400	350	300	250

Model 6906

This version has a stainless steel slide and alloy frame but otherwise is similar to the Model 6904.

	525	450	400	350	300	200

Model 6946

This is a double-action version of the Model 6906.

	525	450	400	350	300	200

Model 4003

This pistol is chambered for the .40 S&W cartridge and is fitted with a 4" barrel, 11-round magazine, serrated hammer with a stainless steel slide and alloy frame.

	575	500	400	350	300	200

Model 4004

Identical to the Model 4003 except for a blue carbon steel slide and alloy frame. Discontinued in 1993.

	575	500	400	350	300	200

Model 4006

This model is identical to the Model 4003 except that both the slide and frame are made from stainless steel. This adds 8 oz. to the weight of the pistol.

	575	500	400	350	300	200

Model 4026

Similar to the Model 4006 this version has a frame-mounted decocking lever.

	575	500	400	350	300	200

	NIB	EXC.	V.G.	GOOD	FAIR	POOR

Model 4046

Similar to the Model 4006 but with a double-action-only configuration.

	575	500	400	350	300	250

Model 4013

A compact version of the 4000 series, this .40 caliber model features a 3-1/2" barrel, eight-round magazine, and stainless steel slide and alloy frame.

	575	500	400	350	300	200

Model 4014

Identical to the Model 4013 except for a blued carbon steel slide and alloy frame.

	575	500	400	350	300	200

Model 4053

Identical to the Model 4013, stainless steel slide and alloy frame, except offered in a double-action-only configuration.

	575	500	400	350	300	200

Model 4054

This model is the same as the Model 4053 except for a blued carbon steel slide and alloy frame. Dropped from S&W product line in 1992.

	575	500	400	300	250	200

Model 411

This model was introduced in 1993 as a no frills model and features an alloy frame, 4" barrel, matte blue finish, fixed sights, and wrap-around rubber grips. Chambered for .40 S&W cartridge with 11-round magazine capacity. Overall length is 7.5" and weight is approximately 29 oz.

	400	350	300	250	200	150

Model 1006

This is a full-size 10mm pistol with a 5" barrel, nine-round magazine, and choice of fixed or adjustable sights. Both the slide and frame are stainless steel.

	675	550	400	350	300	200

Model 4056 TSW

This is a double-action-only pistol chambered for the .40 S&W cartridge. Fitted with a 3.5" barrel with white dot sights. Curved backstrap. Stainless steel and alloy frame. Stainless steel finish. Magazine capacity is nine rounds. Introduced in 1997. Weight is approximately 36 oz.

	700	575	400	325	250	150

Model 1066

This is a slightly smaller version of the Model 1006 and is furnished with a 4-1/4" barrel. Discontinued in 1993.

	675	550	400	350	300	200

Model 1076

Identical to the Model 1066 with the exception of the frame mounted decocking lever.

	675	550	400	350	300	200

Model 1086

Similar to the Model 1066 but offered in double-action-only. This model was discontinued in 1993.

	650	525	375	300	250	200

Model 1026

Similar to the Model 1006 with a 5" barrel this model has a frame mounted decocking lever.

	675	550	400	350	300	200

Model 4506

This is the newly designed double-action .45 ACP pistol. It is all stainless steel and has a 5" barrel, 8-shot detachable magazine, and wrap-around black Delrin grips. This model is no longer in production.

	550	475	400	350	300	250

	NIB	EXC.	V.G.	GOOD	FAIR	POOR

Model 4505

This version is identical to the Model 4506 with the exception of a blued slide and frame.

	550	475	400	350	300	250

Model 4516

Offered in a .45 caliber this 4500 series is a compact version of the full size .45 caliber S&W autos. Furnished with a 3-3/4" barrel and a 7-round magazine this model has a stainless slide and frame. Discontinued in 1991. This model was reintroduced in 1994.

	550	475	425	375	300	250

Model 4536

A compact version and similar to the Model 4616 this pistol is offered with a decock lever on the frame.

	550	475	400	350	300	250

Model 4546

A full size version of the Model 4506 but offered in double-action-only.

	550	475	400	350	300	250

Model 4040PD

When introduced in 2003 this was the first Scandium frame S&W pistol. Chambered for the .40 S&W cartridge and fitted with a 3.5' barrel. White dot front sight with Novak Lo Mount rear sight. Matte black finish. Magazine capacity is seven rounds. Soft rubber grips. Weight is about 25.6 oz.

	700	575	400	325	250	150

Model SW1911

Introduced in 2003 this is a full size pistol chambered for the .45 ACP and 9mm Parabelluum cartridges. Fitted with a 5" barrel with white dot front sight and Novak Lo-Mount rear sight. Stainless steel frame and slide. Checkered black rubber grips. Magazine capacity is 8 rounds (9 in 9mm). Weight is about 39 oz. In 2005 this model was also offered with wood grips and black oxide finish.

	965	750	600	500	375	200

Model SW1911 Adjustable

As above but fitted with adjustable sights. Introduced in 2004.

	850	700	600	500	375	200

Model SW1911Sc

This .45 ACP model is fitted with a Commander size slide and Scandium frame. Fixed sights. Checkered wood grips. Black oxide finish. Weight is about 28 oz. Introduced in 2004.

	900	750	650	550	400	250

Model 1911 PD

This .45 ACP model is offered with either a 4.25" barrel or 5" barrel with Novak low mount sights. Wood grips. The frame is alloy with black finish. Magazine capacity is 8 rounds. Weight is about 28 oz. for 4.25" model and 29.5 oz. for the 5" model.

	850	700	600	500	375	200

Model SW1911 E Series

Full-size 1911-style pistol. Caliber .45 ACP, stainless steel frame and slide with "fish scale" scalloped slide serrations front and rear. Other features include checkered front strap and mainspring housing, oversized extractor, enlarged ejection port, titanium firing pin and laminated textured wood grips. Available with Crimson Trace Laser grips. Introduced in 2011. **NOTE:** Add 20 percent for Crimson Trace Laser grips. Add 30 percent for integral accessory rail.

	800	685	575	450	300	150

Model SW1911 DK (Doug Koenig)

Introduced in 2005 this .45 ACP model is fitted with a 5" stainless steel barrel. Adjustable rear sight with black blade front sight. Frame is stainless steel with black carbon steel slide. Wood grips. Magazine capacity is 8 rounds. Weight is about 41 oz.

	850	700	600	500	375	200

Model SW1911 Pro Series

Similar to Model SW1911, with Novak fiber optic sights, skeletonized trigger and various tactical/performance enhancements. Introduced 2008. Available in .45 ACP or 9mm.

	1100	950	800	600	375	250

	NIB	EXC.	V.G.	GOOD	FAIR	POOR

Model SW1911 Pro Sub-Compact

Chopped 1911-style semi-automatic pistol. Chambered for .45 ACP. 7+1 capacity, 3" barrel. Wood grips, scandium frame with stainless steel slide, matte black finish throughout. Overall length 6.9"; weight 26.5 oz.

NIB	EXC.	V.G.	GOOD	FAIR	POOR
950	800	600	400	300	250

TSW SERIES (Tactical Smith & Wesson)

This series is an upgrade of the older Smith & Wesson pistol series, many of which have been discontinued. These pistols come with either a traditional double-action trigger or a double-action-only trigger. All TSW pistols have an equipment rail for mounting lights or lasers. All are marked "TACTICAL S&W" on the slide.

3913/3953 TSW

Chambered for 9mm cartridge and fitted with a 3.5" barrel. White dot front sight and Novak Lo-Mount rear sight. Aluminum alloy frame. Magazine capacity is 7 rounds. Weight is about 25 oz. Stainless steel finish. The 3913 is traditional double-action while the 3953 is double-action-only.

NIB	EXC.	V.G.	GOOD	FAIR	POOR
650	525	475	400	325	125

4013/4053 TSW

This pistol is chambered for the .40 S&W cartridge and fitted with a 3.5" barrel. White dot front sight and Novak Lo-Mount rear sight. Aluminum alloy frame and stainless steel slide. Magazine capacity is 9 rounds. Weight is about 27 oz. The 4013 is traditional double-action while the 4053 is double-action-only.

NIB	EXC.	V.G.	GOOD	FAIR	POOR
650	525	475	400	325	125

4513/4553 TSW

This model is chambered for the .45 ACP cartridge and fitted with a 3.75" barrel. White dot front sight and Novak Lo-Mount rear sight. Aluminum alloy frame with stainless steel slide. Magazine capacity is 7 rounds. Weight is about 29 oz. The 4513 is traditional double-action while the 4553 is double-action-only. **NOTE:** The double-action-only model 4553 is $50 less.

NIB	EXC.	V.G.	GOOD	FAIR	POOR
650	525	475	400	325	125

5903/5906/5943/5946 TSW

These pistols are chambered for the 9mm cartridge and fitted with a 4" barrel. Fixed sights standard (5903, 5906, 5943, 5946) adjustable sights (5906) optional as well as night sights (5906). Offered in traditional double-action (5903, 5906) as well as double-action-only (5943, 5946). Magazine capacity is 10 rounds and weight is about 38 oz. Stainless steel finish. **NOTE:** Add $100 for night sights, add $50 for adjustable sights.

NIB	EXC.	V.G.	GOOD	FAIR	POOR
650	525	475	400	325	125

4003/4006/4043/4046 TSW

This model comes in the same configurations as the 5903 group except these pistols are chambered for the .40 S&W cartridge. Magazine capacity is 10 rounds. Weight is about 28 oz. **NOTE:** Add $100 for night sights, add $50 for adjustable sights.

NIB	EXC.	V.G.	GOOD	FAIR	POOR
650	525	475	400	325	125

4563/4566/4583/4586 TSW

Similar to the above model but chambered for the .45 ACP cartridge and fitted with a 4.25" barrel. Same configurations as above. Weight is about 31 oz. **NOTE:** Add $100 for night sights, add $50 for adjustable sights.

NIB	EXC.	V.G.	GOOD	FAIR	POOR
650	525	475	400	325	125

CHIEF'S SPECIAL SERIES

CS9

Chambered for 9mm cartridge. Fitted with 3" barrel. Has stainless steel slide and aluminum alloy frame. Also available in blued finish. Hogue wraparound grips are standard. Fixed sights. Magazine capacity 7 rounds. Weight about 21 oz.

NIB	EXC.	V.G.	GOOD	FAIR	POOR
550	395	315	250	200	125

CS45

Similar to the model above but chambered for the .45 ACP cartridge. Barrel length is 3.25". Magazine capacity is six rounds. Weight is about 24 oz.

NIB	EXC.	V.G.	GOOD	FAIR	POOR
575	400	315	250	200	125

	NIB	EXC.	V.G.	GOOD	FAIR	POOR

CS40

This Chief's Special model is chambered for the .40 S&W cartridge. Barrel length is 3.25". Magazine capacity is seven rounds. Weight is about 24 oz.

	550	395	315	250	200	125

CS40 Two-Tone

Same as above, with alloy frame and black slide. Limited edition. Introduced in 2000.

	575	400	315	250	200	125

SIGMA SERIES

SW40F

This new pistol was introduced in 1994 and was a departure from the traditional S&W pistol. The pistol features a stainless steel barrel, carbon steel slide, and polymer frame. Offered in .40 S&W and 9mm calibers with 15-round and 17-round capacities.

	450	400	350	300	250	200

Compact SW9C

Same as above but with barrel and slide 1/2" shorter than full size Sigma. Offered in both .40 S&W and 9mm.

	450	400	350	300	250	200

SW9M

Introduced in 1996 this pistol is chambered for the 9mm cartridge. It is fitted with a 3.25" barrel and has a magazine capacity of seven rounds. The frame is polymer and the slide carbon steel. Height is 4.5" and overall length is 6.25". Weight is 18 oz.

	450	400	350	300	250	200

SW9V

Chambered for the 9mm cartridge this model is fitted with a 4" barrel and 10-round magazine. It has a traditional double action. White dot sights are standard. Grips are integral to the frame. Stainless steel slide. Satin stainless finish with choice of gray or black frame. Weight is about 25 oz. Introduced in 1997.

	450	400	350	300	250	200

SW9P

Same as the Model SW9V with the addition of a ported barrel. Introduced in 2001.

	450	400	350	300	250	200

SW9G

Same as the standard SW9 but with a black Melonite stainless steel slide and NATO green polymer frame. Introduced in 2001.

	450	400	350	300	250	200

SW40V

Same as above but chambered for .40 S&W cartridge. Weight is 25 oz. Introduced in 1997.

	450	400	350	300	250	200

SW40P

Same as the Model SW40V but with the addition of a ported barrel. Introduced in 2001.

	450	400	350	300	250	200

SW40G

Same as the standard SW40 pistol but with a black Melonite stainless steel slide and NATO green polymer frame. Introduced in 2001.

	450	400	350	300	250	200

SW380

Introduced in 1995 this model is chambered for the .380 ACP cartridge. Barrel length is 3" with overall length 5.8". Empty weight is 14 oz. with a magazine capacity of 6 rounds.

	325	275	200	150	100	75

ENHANCED SIGMA SERIES

Introduced in 1999 this series features a shorter trigger pull, slide stop guard, redesigned extractor and ejector. The ejection port is also lower. These pistols are also fitted with an accessory groove. Checkering pattern is more aggressive.

NIB	EXC.	V.G.	GOOD	FAIR	POOR

SW9E

Chambered for the 9mm cartridge this model has a 4" barrel with Tritium sights. Stainless steel slide with black Melonite finish. Magazine capacity is 10 rounds. Weight is about 25 oz.

NIB	EXC.	V.G.	GOOD	FAIR	POOR
375	300	225	175	150	75

SW40E

Similar to the above model but chambered for the .40 S&W cartridge. Weight is about 24 oz.

NIB	EXC.	V.G.	GOOD	FAIR	POOR
375	300	225	175	150	75

SW9VE

This model is chambered for the 9mm cartridge and fitted with a 4" barrel. Fixed sights and stainless steel slide. Weight is about 25 oz.

NIB	EXC.	V.G.	GOOD	FAIR	POOR
375	300	225	175	150	75

SW40VE

Similar to the model above but chambered for the .40 S&W cartridge. Weight is about 24 oz.

NIB	EXC.	V.G.	GOOD	FAIR	POOR
375	300	225	175	150	75

SW99

This model features a polymer frame designed and manufactured in Germany by Walther. The slide and barrel are manufactured by S&W in the U.S. Chambered for either the 9mm or .40 S&W cartridge this model is fitted with a 4" barrel on the 9mm model and a 4.125" barrel on the .40 S&W model. Adjustable rear sights. Decocking slide-mounted lever. Barrel and slide are stainless steel with black Melonite finish. Trigger is traditional double-action. Magazine capacity is 10 rounds. Weight is about 25 oz. Introduced in 1999.

NIB	EXC.	V.G.	GOOD	FAIR	POOR
400	350	300	225	150	75

SW99 Compact

Introduced in 2003 this model is similar to the full size SW99 but with a 3.5" barrel and shorter grip frame. Chambered for both the 9mm or .40 S&W cartridge. Stainless steel barrel and slide with polymer frame. Magazine capacity is 10 rounds for 9mm and eight rounds for the .40 S&W. Weight is about 23 oz.

NIB	EXC.	V.G.	GOOD	FAIR	POOR
400	350	300	225	150	75

SW99 .45 ACP

Same as the SW99 but chambered for the .45 ACP cartridge. Magazine is nine rounds. Weight is about 26 oz. Introduced in 2003.

NIB	EXC.	V.G.	GOOD	FAIR	POOR
500	400	325	250	150	100

SW990L Compact

Introduced in 2005 this model is chambered for the 9mm or .40 S&W cartridge. Barrel length is 3.5". Adjustable rear sight with dot front sight. Polymer frame with stainless steel slide with Melonite finish. Plastic grips. Magazine capacity is 10 rounds for the 9mm and 8 rounds for the .40 S&W model. Weight is about 23 oz.

NIB	EXC.	V.G.	GOOD	FAIR	POOR
475	400	300	225	150	100

SW990L Full Size

Similar to the above model but chambered for the 9mm, .40 S&W and .45 ACP cartridges. Barrel lengths are 4" for the 9mm; 4.125" for the .40 S&W; and 4.25" for the .45 ACP. Magazine capacity is 16 rounds for the 9mm and 12 rounds for the .40 S&W model. Weight is about 25 oz. Introduced in 2005. **NOTE:** Add $40 for .45 ACP model.

NIB	EXC.	V.G.	GOOD	FAIR	POOR
500	400	325	250	150	100

410

This model was first introduced in 1996. It features an alloy frame with carbon steel slide. It is chambered for the .40 S&W cartridge. Barrel length is 4". The magazine capacity is 10 rounds and the overall length is 7.5". Weight is approximately 29 oz.

NIB	EXC.	V.G.	GOOD	FAIR	POOR
450	400	325	250	150	100

410 Two-Tone

Same as the Model 410 but with alloy finish frame and black slide. Limited edition.

NIB	EXC.	V.G.	GOOD	FAIR	POOR
475	400	325	250	150	100

410S

Introduced in 2003 this is a stainless steel version of the Model 410. Weight is about 28 oz.

NIB	EXC.	V.G.	GOOD	FAIR	POOR
475	400	300	250	150	100

	NIB	EXC.	V.G.	GOOD	FAIR	POOR

457

Introduced in 1996 this .45 ACP model features a 3.75" barrel with rounded trigger guard and double-action. It is fitted with a single side decocker. Magazine capacity is seven rounds. Overall length is 7.25" and weight is about 29 oz. The frame is alloy and the slide a carbon steel. Finish is matte black.

500	400	325	250	150	100

457S

Same as above but in stainless steel. Weight is about 29 oz. Introduced in 2003.

500	400	325	250	150	100

908

Introduced in 1996 this is an economy compact pistol. It is chambered for the 9mm cartridge and is fitted with a 3.5" barrel. The action is traditional double-action. Fixed rear sight. Magazine capacity is eight rounds. Overall length is 6-7/8" and weight is about 26 oz.

450	400	325	225	150	100

908S

Same as the Model 908 but in stainless steel. Weight is about 24 oz. Introduced in 2003.

475	425	350	250	150	100

908S Carry Combo

Introduced in 2004 this model is the same as above with the addition of a Kydex carry holster.

500	400	325	250	150	100

909

Introduced in 1995 this pistol is chambered for the 9mm cartridge. It has a blue carbon steel slide, aluminum alloy frame, and is double-action. It has a single column magazine and curved backstrap.

405	350	250	150	100	75

910

Also introduced in 1995. Same as above model but with double-column magazine and straight backstrap.

400	300	200	150	100	75

910S

Introduced in 2003 this is a stainless steel version of the Model 910. Weight is about 28 oz.

400	325	250	150	100	75

MILITARY & POLICE (M&P) SERIES

Model M&P9m

Full-size Military and Police semi-automatic chambered in 9mm. Capacity 17+1, 4.25" barrel, 6.5 lb. trigger, weight 24.25 oz. Picatinny rail and polymer frame. Optional tritium low-light sights. Introduced 2006.

500	425	300	225	150	75

Model M&P9-JG

Similar to above, with interchangeable palmswell grip panels, including two pink ones. Dealer sets pricing. Introduced 2008.

475	425	300	225	150	75

Model M&P9 Pro Series

Similar to M&P9 and M&P40, with green fiber optic sights and interchangeable palmswell grip panels. Black Melonite finish. Introduced 2008.

600	475	350	250	150	75

Model M&P9L

Similar to M&P9, with 5" barrel. Introduced 2008.

575	425	300	225	150	75

M&P 40

Full-size semi-automatic chambered in .40 S&W. First of new Military and Police series. Capacity 15+1, 4.25" barrel, .5 lb. trigger, weight 24.25 oz. Polymer frame and Picatinny rail. Optional tritium low-light sights. Introduced 2006.

475	425	300	225	150	75

	NIB	EXC.	V.G.	GOOD	FAIR	POOR

M&P .357 SIG

Full-size Military and Police semi-automatic chambered in .357 Magnum. Capacity 15+1, 4.25" barrel, 6.5 lb. trigger, weight 24.25 oz. Polymer frame and Picatinny rail. Optional tritium low-light sights. Introduced 2006.

	NIB	EXC.	V.G.	GOOD	FAIR	POOR
	575	425	300	225	150	75

M&P45

Semi-automatic similar to M&P40 in .45 ACP. Black or Dark Earth Brown finish. Introduced 2007.

	NIB	EXC.	V.G.	GOOD	FAIR	POOR
	575	425	300	225	150	75

M&P45 with Thumb Safety

Similar to above, with ambidextrous thumb safety. Introduced 2008.

	NIB	EXC.	V.G.	GOOD	FAIR	POOR
	585	435	310	235	160	75

M&P9c

Semi-automatic compact model similar to M&P9, with 3.5" barrel, short grip frame and 10+1 or 12+1 capacity. Black Melonite finish. Introduced 2007.

	NIB	EXC.	V.G.	GOOD	FAIR	POOR
	475	425	300	225	150	75

M&P40c

Semi-automatic compact model similar to M&P9c in .40 S&W. Black Melonite finish. Introduced 2007.

	NIB	EXC.	V.G.	GOOD	FAIR	POOR
	475	425	300	225	150	75

M&P357c

Semi-automatic compact model similar to M&P40c in .357 SIG. Black Melonite finish. Introduced 2007.

	NIB	EXC.	V.G.	GOOD	FAIR	POOR
	575	425	300	225	150	75

Model M&P Shield

Subcompact version of M&P series in 9mm or .40 S&W. Barrel is 3.1", weight 19 oz. Available in two grip lengths, with one additional round in longer magazine. Capacity: 7 or 8 rounds 9mm; 6 or 7 rounds .40 S&W. Introduced in 2012

	NIB	EXC.	V.G.	GOOD	FAIR	POOR
	400	350	300	250	200	175

SW9VE Allied Forces

Similar to SW9VE, with black Melonite slide. Adopted by Afghanistan internal security and border forces. Introduced 2007. Add 75 percent for "Disaster Ready Kit" (case and emergency supplies).

	NIB	EXC.	V.G.	GOOD	FAIR	POOR
	575	425	300	225	150	75

SW40VE Allied Forces

Similar to SW9VE Allied Forces in .40 S&W. Introduced 2007. Add 75 percent for "Disaster Ready Kit" (case and emergency supplies).

	NIB	EXC.	V.G.	GOOD	FAIR	POOR
	575	425	300	225	150	75

S&W M&P VTAC

Caliber 9mm Parabellum/.40 S&W. Magazine capacity: 19 (9mm); 17 (.40). Stainless steel slide, polymer frame with Flat Dark Earth finish. Striker fired double-action-only ambidextrous slide release and reversible magazine catch. Weight 24 oz., 4.25" barrel with VTAC Warrior night sights.

	NIB	EXC.	V.G.	GOOD	FAIR	POOR
	665	550	475	400	300	150

M&P22

Rimfire version of M&P pistol. Striker-fired with aluminum alloy slide and polymer frame. Magazine capacity 10 or 12 rounds. Ambidextrous thumb safety and slide release. Reversible magazine catch. Weight 24 ounces, barrel length 4.1". Introduced in 2011.

	NIB	EXC.	V.G.	GOOD	FAIR	POOR
	375	325	275	225	150	100

SMITH & WESSON COMMEMORATIVES
(REFERENCE ONLY)

Smith & Wesson has, over the years, built many special edition handguns. These guns have been to commemorate some important national or regional event or group. The company has also built a large number of special edition handguns for certain distributors such as Lew Horton which is listed. There are well over 200 special production guns not reflected in this pricing guide. Not even Smith & Wesson has all of the information on these guns and with many the number is so small that a market price would not be possible to establish. Listed are a number of Smith &

NIB	EXC.	V.G.	GOOD	FAIR	POOR

Wesson Commemoratives that we do have information on. Due to the difficulty in determining value only the original retail price is listed. Remember to receive full value for these guns they must be NIB, unfired with unturned cylinders.

Model 14 Texas Ranger Comm.

Introduced in 1973. Supplied with 4" barrel and cased. Edition limited to 10,000. 8,000 of these had knives. Serial numbers TR 1 to TR 10000.Original Retail Introductory Price: $250.00

Model 25-3 S&W 125th Anniversary Comm.

Introduced in 1977. Limited edition of 10,000. Serial numbers SW0000 to SW10000. Deluxe models marked 25-4.Original Retail Introductory Price: $350.00

Model 26-4 Georgia State Police Comm.

Introduced in 1988/1989 and supplied with a 5" barrel. Total production of 802 guns. Known Serial numbers BBY00354 to BBY0434.Original Retail Introductory Price: $405.00

Model 27 .357 50th Anniversary Comm.

Introduced in 1985 and supplied with a 5" barrel and cased. Limited edition to 2,500 guns. Serial numbers REG0001 to REG2500.Original Retail Introductory Price: N/A

Model 29-3 Elmer Keith Comm.

Introduced in 1986 and supplied with a 4" barrel. Gun etched in gold. Limited edition of 2,500 guns. Serial numbers EMK0000 to EMK0100 for Deluxe models and EMK 010 to EMK2500 for standard model.Original Retail Introductory Price: $850.00

Model 544 Texas Wagon Train 150 Anniversary Comm.

Introduced in 1986 and limited to 7801 guns. Serial numbers TWT0000 to TWT7800.Original Issue Introductory Price: N/A

Model 586 Mass. State Police Comm.

Introduced in 1986 and fitted with a 6" barrel. Limited to 631 guns. Serial numbers with ABT-AUC prefix.Original Retail Introductory Price: N/A

Model 629-1 Alaska 1988 Iditarod Comm.

Introduced in 1987 and limited to 545 guns. Serial numbers from AKI0001 to AKI0545.Original Retail Introductory Price: N/A

Model 745 IPSC Comm.

Introduced in 1986 and limited to 5362 guns. Serial numbers DVC0000 to DVC5362.Original Retail Introductory Price: N/A

Model 4516-1 U.S. Marshall Comm.

Introduced in 1990 and limited to 500 guns. Serial numbers USM0000 to USM0499.Original Retail Introductory Price: $599.95

Model SW1911 PD Gunsite Commemorative

Honors Lt. Col. Jeff Cooper's Gunsite Training Academy. Scandium alloy, single-action .45 ACP with 4.25" barrel and 8+1 capacity. Fixed sights. 28 oz. Introduced 2006.

950	700	600	500	350	175

Model SW1911 – Rolling Thunder Commemorative

Limited edition commemorates American POW-MIAs. Rolling Thunder and POW-MIA logos in imitation bonded ivory grips. Chambered for .45 ACP. Blued, 8+1 capacity, 5" barrel, 38.5 oz. Introduced 2006.

950	700	600	500	350	175

SMITH & WESSON PERFORMANCE CENTER HANDGUNS (REFERENCE ONLY)

Role of Smith & Wesson's Performance Center has changed since it was established in 1990. What was once a specialized tune-up and competition one-off production department, has now become a separate facility in providing specialized and limited handguns to the public, often with distributors participation. Change came about 1991, when Performance Center initiated its own limited edition designs. These editions are generally limited between 300 and 600 pistols for each model. Performance Center, in fact, has its own distinct product line. Performance Center pistols are made in its own shop using its own designers. One of these distributors that has played a major role in offering these special guns to the public is Lew Horton Distribution Company.

.40 S&W Tactical

Limited edition semi-automatic handgun offered exclusively by Lew Horton through Performance Center. Special pistol fitted with 5" match-grade barrel, hand fit spherical barrel bushing, custom tuned action, special trigger job, oversized frame and slide rails, wrap-around straight backstrap grip. Replaceable front and Novak rear sights. Special serial numbers. Offered in 1992. Limited to 200 units. Suggested Retail Introductory Price: $1,500.

.40 S&W Compensated

Similar to the .40 S&W Tactical but furnished with a 4.625" barrel and single chamber compensator. This is also a Lew Horton/Performance pistol. A production of 250 units. Offered in 1992. Suggested Retail Introductory Price: $1,700

.40 S&W Performance Action Pistol

Offered in limited quantities in 1990, this Performance Center .40 S&W semi-automatic pistol was used by the Smith & Wesson shooting team. The frame and barrel are stainless steel with blued carbon steel slide, two port compensator, two fitted and numbered 13-round magazines, 5.25" match grade barrel extended frame beavertail, square combat trigger guard, oversize magazine release button, spherical barrel bushing, wrap-around straight backstrap grip, extended magazine funnel, and BoMar adjustable rear sight. The action is tuned for accuracy and precision. Suggested Retail Introductory Price: N/A

Model 681 Quadport

A Lew Horton revolver limited to 300 guns with special serial numbers. This 7-shot revolver has a 3" barrel underlug quadport barrel. The action is tuned, cylinders are chamfered and the trigger has an overtravel stop. Sights are fixed combat type. Suggested Retail Introductory Price: $675

Model 686 Competitor

Introduced by Lew Horton and the Performance Center for 1993 this limited edition revolver features a match grade barrel and unique under barrel weight system. The action has been custom tuned and the receiver is drilled and tapped for scope mounts. Charge holes are chambered, ejector rod housing is enclosed, and the grip is an extended competition type. Special serial numbers. Suggested Retail Introductory Price: $1,100

Model 686 Hunter

Similar to the Model 686 Competitor. This is also a limited edition Lew Horton revolver chambered for the .357 Magnum and features the under barrel weight system, internal scope mount, and custom tuned action. Special serial numbers. Suggest Retail Introductory Price: $1,154

Model 686 Carry Comp 4

Offered in limited quantities by Lew Horton and the Performance Center in 1992 this new design features the unique single chamber integral barrel compensator. Front is windage adjustable and the action is custom tuned. Chambered for the .357 Magnum cartridge. Special serial numbers. Suggested Retail Introductory price: $1,000

Model 686 Carry Comp 3

The 1993 Lew Horton limited edition version of the Model 686 Carry Comp 4" model with a 3" barrel. The same features apply to both models. Suggested Retail Introductory Price: $1,000

Model 686 Plus

This Lew Horton model features a 7-round cylinder with chamfered charge holes for use with full moon clips for both .38 Special and .357 Magnum cartridges. Fitted with a tapered 6" barrel with countersunk muzzle. Gold bead front sight and adjustable rear sight. Altamont wood grips are standard. Stainless steel finish. Weight is approximately 44 oz. Suggested Retail Introductory Price: $930

Model 686 - .38 Super

Introduced in 2003 this six-round revolver is chambered for the .38 Super cartridge and fitted with a 4" barrel with tapered lug. Interchangeable red ramp front sight and adjustable rear sight. Stainless steel with glass bead finish. Cocobolo grips. Weight is about 37 oz. Distributed by Bangers. Suggested Retail Introductory Price: N/A

Model 629 Hunter

Introduced in 1992 by Lew Horton and the Performance Center this limited edition revolver features a new design that utilizes a 6" under barrel weight system, special integral barrel compensator. The action has been custom tuned and the receiver has an integral scope mount. Chambered for the .44 Magnum. Special finger groove grips are standard. Special serial numbers. Suggested Retail Introductory Price: $1,234

Model 629 Hunter II

Another Lew Horton/Performance Center limited edition revolver that features 2x Nikon scope with steel see-through rings. The barrel is Mag-Na-Ported and incorporates the Performance Center's under barrel weight arrangement. The action is custom tuned and the revolver is supplied with a ballistic nylon range carry bag. Special serial numbers. Suggested Retail Introductory Price: $1,234

Model 629 Comped Hunter

Offered through RSR this model features a 6" barrel with 4-port detachable compensator. The cylinder is unfluted. Sights are adjustable, fitted with Altamount wood grips. Tuned action. Stainless steel. Weight is approximately 59 oz. Suggested Retail Introductory Price: $1,100

Model 629 12" Hunter/7.5" Hunter

Introduced in 2000 this Lou Horton revolver is fitted with a 12" barrel with Patridge front sight and Wilson silhouette adjustable rear sight. Hogue Combat grips. Finish is glassbead stainless steel. Comes with a Waller 21" gun rug. Weight is about 65 oz. A 7.5-inch version was introduced in 2008. Suggested Retail Introductory Price: $1,025

Model 629 Magnum Hunter Trail Boss

Exclusive to RSR this limited edition model is chambered for the .44 Magnum cartridge and is fitted with a 3" barrel. Stainless steel finish. Suggested Retail Introductory Price: $733

Model 629 Compensated Hunter

Chambered for the .44 Magnum cartridge and fitted with a 7.5" barrel with compensator. Barrel also has removable stainless steel scope mount. Open sights fitted with adjustable orange ramp front and adjustable rear sight. Rosewood grips. Six-round cylinder. Weight is 52 oz. Talo exclusive. Introduced in 2001. Suggested Retail Introductory Price: $1190

Model 629 Stealth Hunter

Fitted with a 7.5" ported barrel and chambered for the .44 magnum cartridge. Six-round cylinder. The finish is black-T and NATO green. Red ramp Millett front sight and adjustable rear sight. Hogue rubber combat grips standard. Furnished with lockable aluminum case. Weight is about 56 oz. Introduced in 2001. Camfour Distributor exclusive. Suggested Retail Introductory Price: $1,025

Model 629 Extreme

Chambered for the .44 Magnum cartridge and fitted with a 12" barrel with sling swivel. Bomar sights. Rubber grips. Suggested Retail Introductory Price: $1,025

Model 629 Carry Comp

Introduced in 1992 by Lew Horton and the Performance Center this limited edition revolver is chambered for the .44 Magnum cartridge. It features an integral ported 3" barrel, fluted cylinder, radiused charge holes, dovetail front and fixed groove rear sight. Fitted with a rubber combat grip. The action is custom by the Performance Center. Special serial numbers. Suggested Retail Introductory Price: $1,000

Model 629 Carry Comp II

A limited edition 1993 offering by Lew Horton and the Performance Center similar to the 1992 Model 629 Carry Comp with the exception that this 1993 model has a special unfluted cylinder and fully adjustable rear sight. Special serial numbers. Suggested Retail Introductory Price: $1,000

Model 629 Comped Hunter

Chambered for the .44 Magnum cartridge and built with a 7.5" barrel with a tapered full length lug and compensator. Front sight is drift adjustable orange ramp. Adjustable rear sight. Stainless steel with glass bead finish. Removable scope mount. Rosewood grips. Weight is about 52 oz. Introduced in 2003. Suggested Retail Introductory Price: $1,100

Model 610

Introduced in 1998 by Lew Horton this model features a 3" full lug barrel chambered for the 10mm cartridge. Nonfluted cylinder, red ramp front sight and white outline rear sight. Rosewood grips. Limited to 300 revolvers. Suggested Retail Introductory Price: $740

Model 640 Carry Comp

Introduced in 1991 by Lew Horton and the Performance Center this revolver is chambered for the .38 S&W Special, but with a strengthened action to handle +P loads. Fitted with a heavy 2.625" barrel with unique integral barrel compensator. The front sight is replaceable and adjustable for windage. The rear sight is a fixed groove. Custom trigger job and custom tuned action are also part of the package. Special serial numbers. Suggested Retail Introductory Price: $750

Model 640 .357 Quadport

Introduced in 1996. Similar to the model above but chambered for the .357 Magnum cartridge and quadported. Limited to 190 revolvers. Special serial numbers. Suggested Retail Introductory Price: $675

Model 460 Airweight

Chambered for the .38 Special cartridge, this model is fitted with a 2" Mag-Na-Ported barrel and a five-shot cylinder. Fixed sights. Eagle Secret Service grips. Weight is about 16 oz. Limited to 450 revolvers. Introduced in 1994. Suggested Retail Introductory Price: $580

Model 625 Light Hunter

This is a large frame revolver chambered for the .45 Colt. It is fitted with a 6" Mag-Na-Ported barrel with integral Weaver-style base. It has a stainless steel finish and black Hogue rubber grips. Drift adjustable Millet front and fully adjustable rear sight. Offered in limited quantities. Introduced in 1997 by RSR. Suggested Retail Introductory Price: $580

Model 625

Introduced in 1998 this model is chambered for the .45 ACP or .45 Colt cartridge. Fitted with a 3" full lug barrel, fluted cylinder, and rosewood grips. Limited to 150 revolvers in each chambering. Suggested Retail Introductory Price: $755

Model 625 V-Comp

Chambered for the .44 Magnum cartridge this model is fitted with a 4" barrel and removable three-port compensator. Front sight is a red ramp with black adjustable rear sight. Hogue wood combat grips. Furnished with aluminum case. Weight is about 43 oz. Finish is stainless steel. Distributed by RSR. Introduced in 1999. Suggested Retail Introductory Price: $1,000

Model 625—5.25

Introduced in 2001 this model features a special Jerry Miculek Hogue laminated combat grip. Chambered for the .45 ACP cartridge and fitted with a 5.25" barrel. Stainless steel finish. Interchangeable gold bead front sight and adjustable rear sight. Weight is about 42 oz. Camfour exclusive. Suggested Retail Introductory Price: N/A

Model 627—8 Shot

Chambered for the .357 Magnum cartridge this revolver has an 8-round capacity. Drilled and tapped with adjustable sights on a 5" tapered and contoured barrel. Tuned action. Hogue wood grips. Satin stainless steel finish. Weight is approximately 44 oz. A Lew Horton exclusive. Introduced in 1997. Suggested Retail Introductory Price: $1,160

Model 627 Defensive—8 Shot

Chambered for the .357 Magnum this model is fitted with an eight-round unfluted cylinder recessed for full moon clips. Barrel length is 2-5/8". Adjustable rear sight and drift adjustable front sight. Wooden eagle boot grips. Weight is about 38 oz. Introduced in 1999. Furnished with aluminum case. Suggested Retail Introductory Price: $1,025

Model 651

This is a limited edition revolver by RSR chambered for the .22 WMR cartridge. Fitted with a 2" barrel and boot grips. Stainless steel finish. Suggested Retail Introductory Price: $492

"Shorty-Forty" .40 S&W

Introduced in 1992 and available exclusively from Lew Horton, this limited edition Performance Center pistol features a light alloy frame, oversize slide rails, and spherical barrel bushing. A match grade barrel is joined to a custom tuned action. Special serial numbers. Suggested Retail Introductory Price: $950

Model 647 Varminter

Introduced in 2003 this model is chambered for the .17 HMR cartridge and fitted with a 12" fluted barrel with a removable black Patridge front sight. Adjustable rear sight. Integral scope mount on barrel. Six-round cylinder. Stainless steel finish. Weight is about 54 oz. Suggested Retail Introductory Price: $1,100

Model 500 Magnum Hunter

Introduced in 2003 this revolver is chambered for the .500 S&W cartridge and fitted with a 10.5" barrel with compensator. Sling swivel studs and sling are standard. Orange dovetail ramp front sight and adjustable rear sight. Stainless steel with glass bead finish. Hogue rubber grips. Weight is approximately 82 oz. Suggested Retail Introductory Price: $1390

Model 460XVR

Built for serious handgun hunters. Chambered for the .460 S&W Magnum. Stainless steel cylinder, frame and barrel, 5-round capacity, adjustable rear and removable Partridge front sight. Other features include sling swivels, dual accessory rails and synthetic grips. Weight is a hefty

79.2 ounces, 12-inch fluted barrel with compensator. Re-introduced in 2011 by the Performance Center. Suggested Retail Introductory Price: $1,619.

"Shorty Forty" Mark III

Offered in 1995 this Lew Horton exclusive features low-mount adjustable sights, hand-fitted titanium barrel bushing, checkered front strap. The action as been hand honed and the pistol is sold with two magazines; one 11 rounds and the other nine rounds. Suggested Retail Introductory Price: $1,000

Shorty .45

Introduced by Lew Horton in 1996 this .45 ACP pistol has a hand-fitted titanium barrel bushing, oversize frame and slide rails, match grade barrel, checkered front strap, hand honed double-action, and special serial numbers. Suggested Retail Introductory Price: $1,095

Shorty Nine

This Lew Horton exclusive is limited to 100 units. It features a hand-fitted titanium barrel bushing, oversize slide rails, action job, low mount adjustable sights, checkered front strap, match grade barrel, and two tone finish. Furnished with two 12-round magazines. Suggested Retail Introductory Price: $1,000

9 Recon

This is an RSR exclusive and introduced in 1999. Chambered for the 9mm cartridge this model is fitted with a 3.5" barrel. Rear sight is Novak Lo-Mount. Hogue wraparound rubber grips. The slide is black carbon steel with an alloy frame. Magazine capacity is 12 rounds. Weight is about 27 oz. Suggested Retail Introductory Price: $1,178

Performance Center .45 Limited

This Lew Horton model is a full-size single-action pistol. Handfitted titanium barrel bushing, fitted slide lock, match grade barrel, adjustable sights, oversize magazine well, tuned action, and checkered front strap. Suggested Retail Introductory Price: $1,400

45 Recon

Another RSR pistol chambered for .45 ACP cartridge. An enhanced version of "Shorty 45". The 4.25" barrel is ported, with Novak Lo-Mount sights. Hogue wraparound rubber grips. Stainless steel slide and barrel, with aluminum frame. Weight about 28 oz. Magazine capacity 7 rounds. Matte black finish. Furnished with aluminum case. Suggested Retail Introductory Price: $1,221

Shorty .356 TSW

This new cartridge is also available in another Lew Horton/Performance Center limited edition pistol with a 4" barrel. It features a steel frame and hand-fitted slide, with spherical barrel bushing. The double-action is custom tuned by the Performance Center. Magazine holds 12 rounds. Similar in appearance to the "Shorty-Forty." Offered in 1993. Special serial numbers. Suggested Retail Introductory Price: $1,000

Model .356 TSW "Limited" Series

This is a Lew Horton gun. This model is chambered for the new .356 TSW caliber (TSW stands for Team Smith & Wesson). This is a new caliber, actually a 9mm x 21.5mm cartridge, with ballistics of around 1,235 fps with a 147-grain bullet. Designed as a low-end .357 competition pistol. Built for the competitive shooter (IPSC) it features a 15-round magazine and distinctive profile and markings. The single-action trigger is adjustable for reach while the slide, frame, and barrel are custom fitted. The gun comes with a spherical barrel bushing and adjustable BoMar sights. The frame grip is checked 20 line to the inch, the magazine well is extended as is the magazine release. The magazine is fitted with a pad. Suggested Retail Introductory Price: $1,350

Model 5906 Performance Center

Introduced in 1998. This 9mm pistol features front slide serrations, ambidextrous decocker, titanium coated barrel bushing, match grade barrel and Novak Lo-Mount sights. Sold with one 15-round magazine and one 10-round magazine. Stainless steel finish. Suggested Retail Introductory Price: $1,200

Model 845 of 1998

This .45 ACP caliber model has a 5" match grade barrel with hand lapped rails on frame and slide. Patridge front sight and adjustable Bomar rear sight. Single-action trigger is tuned and the slide has front serrations. Magazine capacity is 8 rounds. Stainless steel finish. Limited to 150 pistols. Suggested Retail Introductory Price: $1,500

Model .45 CQB Combat

Introduced in 1998 this Lew Horton model features a 4" match grade barrel. Novak Lo-Mount sights. Double-action trigger with ambidextrous decocker. Available in both a matte black and stainless steel finish. Matte black model has alloy frame and weighs about 30 oz. Stainless steel version has stainless frame and weighs about 38 oz. Suggested Retail Introductory Price: $1,200

Model 945

This is a single-action-only pistol chambered for the .45 ACP cartridge. Fitted with a 5" match grade barrel and Bomar adjustable rear sight. Grips are checkered black/silver wood laminate with matte stainless steel slide and frame. Magazine capacity is 8 rounds. Empty weight is approximately 44 oz. Introduced in 1998. Suggested Retail Introductory Price: $1,600

Model 945 Black Model

This Performance Center Model features a 3.25" barrel with black stainless steel slide. Frame is aluminum. Novak Lo-Mount sights. Hogue checkered wood laminate grips. Furnished with two 6-round magazines and a locking aluminum gun case. Weight is about 24 oz. Exclusive with RSR. Suggested Retail Introductory Price: $1,550

Model 945-40

This PC model is fitted with a 3.75" barrel chambered for the .40 S&W cartridge. Novak Lo-Mount sights and Hogue checkered wood laminate grips are standard. Furnished with two 7-round magazines and a locking aluminum case. Clear glassbead finish. Exclusive with Sports South. Suggested Retail Introductory Price: $1,275

Model 945 Micro

Similar to the Model 945 Black Model but with stainless steel finish. Exclusive with Camfour Distributor. Suggested Retail Introductory Price: $1,300

Model SW945

This .45 ACP pistol is fitted with a 5" barrel with Wilson Combat adjustable rear sight. Scalloped slide serrations both front and rear. Checkered wood grips. Many special features. Weight is about 40.5 oz. Suggested Retail Introductory Price: $2,085

Model SW1911

Chambered for the .45 ACP cartridge and fitted with a 5" barrel with adjustable rear sight. Checkered wood grips. Many special features. Scalloped slide serrations front and rear. Black Melonite finish. Magazine capacity is 8 rounds. Weight is about 41 oz. Also offered in a stainless steel version for $160 less. Suggested Retail Price: $2,270

Model SW1911 DK

This model is chambered for the .38 Super cartridge and fitted with a 5" barrel with adjustable rear sight. Smooth wood grips with DK logo. Stainless steel finish with scalloped serrations at rear of slide. Many special features. Magazine capacity is 10 rounds. Weight is about 41.5 oz. Introduced in 2005. Suggested Retail Price: $2,320

SW1911 Tactical Rail

One of Tactical Rail Series for SWAT Teams and tactical applications. Picatinny rail and fixed sights. Blued or stainless, single-action .45 ACP with 5" barrel and 8+1 capacity. 39 oz. Introduced 2006. MSRP: $1,057

Model 66 .357 Magnum F-Comp

A Performance Center revolver designed as a carry gun. Furnished with a 3" ported barrel and full underlug. The thumbpiece has been cut down to accommodate all speed loaders and the charge holes are countersunk. The K-frame action has been custom tuned and the rear sight is a fully adjustable black blade while the front sight features a Tritium dot night sight. Furnished with a round butt combat-style rubber grip. This revolver has a stainless steel finish. Weight is about 35 oz. This is a Lew Horton special limited edition, 300 units. **NOTE:** In 2003 this revolver was produced for all S&W stocking dealers. Suggested Retail Introductory Price: $800

Model 66

An RSR exclusive this model is chambered for the .357 Magnum cartridge and fitted with a 3" barrel. Red ramp front sight. Stainless steel finish. Limited edition. Suggested Retail Introductory Price: $490

Model 681 Quad Port

Chambered for the .357 Magnum cartridge and fitted with a 3" barrel with Quad porting. Fixed rear sight. Seven-round cylinder with moon clips. Two sets of grips are standard: Hogue Bantam and checkered wood laminate. Stainless steel finish. Weight is about 35 oz. Camfour exclusive. A 4" barrel version is also available. Suggested Retail Introductory Price: $850

Model 25

This PC model is a reintroduction of the original Model 25. Chambered for the .45 Colt cartridge and fitted with a tapered 6" barrel with pinned gold bead patridge front sight. Four screw frame.

	NIB	EXC.	V.G.	GOOD	FAIR	POOR

Furnished with locking aluminum case. Weight is about 42 oz. Sports South exclusive.

	900	750	650	550	375	—

Model 657

This Lew Horton/Performance Center revolver is fitted with a 3" full lug barrel chambered for the .41 Magnum cartridge. Fluted cylinder with red ramp front sight and white outline rear. Rosewood grips. Limited to 150 revolvers in 1998. Suggested Retail Introductory Price: $720

Model 657 Classic

Offered in limited quantities of 350 units this Lew Horton/Performance Center revolver features an unfluted cylinder and 6.5" barrel on a drilled and tapped N frame. Chambered for the .41 Magnum cartridge this handgun is fitted with adjustable rear sight. Special serial numbers. Suggested Retail Introductory Price: $550

Model 657 Defensive

Introduced in 1999 by Lou Horton, this .41 Magnum revolver is fitted with a 2-5/8" barrel with drift adjustable Millet front sight and fully adjustable rear sight. Stainless steel finish with 6-shot nonfluted cylinder. Hogue combat grips. Weight is about 40 oz. Furnished with aluminum case. Suggested Retail Introductory Price: $1,025

Model 657 Hunter

Introduced in 1995 this is an RSR Wholesale Guns exclusive. Fitted with an integral weaver base, Mag-Na-Ported 6" barrel with Millet red ramp front sight and adjustable rear sight. This model has a stainless steel finish, special serial numbers, chamfered charge holes, and adjustable trigger stop. Limited to 500 guns. Suggested Retail Introductory Price: $1,000

Model 19 .357 Magnum K-Comp

This is the same gun as the F-Comp but furnished with a black matte finish and is sold through stocking dealers on a unlimited basis. Suggested Retail Introductory Price: $800

Model 60 Carry Comp

Introduced in the summer of 1993 this J-frame revolver is fitted with a 3" full underlug barrel with integral compensator. The charge holes are radiused for quick loading and the action is tuned by the Performance Center. The pistol is rated for +P ammunition. The grips are fancy wood contoured for speed loaders. This Lew Horton revolver is limited to 300 guns and has special serial numbers. Suggested Retail Introductory Price: $795

Paxton Quigley Model 640

This is a Performance Center offering restricted to 300 revolvers. Built around the Model 640 this limited edition handgun has a 2" compensated barrel, windage adjustable front sight, specially tuned action, and a tapestry soft gun case. Each gun has a distinct serial number range. Suggested Retail Introductory Price: $720

Model 640 Centennial Powerport

Introduced in 1996 this model is a Lew Horton exclusive. It is fitted with a 2-1/8" barrel with integral compensator. The front sight is a black blade with Tritium insert and the rear is a fixed notch. The cylinder holds five .357 or .38 rounds. Stainless steel with Pachmayr decelerator compact grips. Overall length is 6.75" and weight is about 25 oz. Limited to 300 units. Suggested Retail Introductory Price: $675

Model 327 Carry

Introduced in 2004 this 8-shot model is chambered for the .357 Magnum cartridge. Barrel length is 2" with dovetail .260 orange ramp. Scandium alloy frame with stainless steel barrel, titanium cylinder and shroud. Black oxide finish except for gray cylinder. Cocobolo wood grips. Weight is about 21 oz. Suggested Retail Price: $1,226

Model 940 Centennial .356

Offered exclusively from Lew Horton this J-frame revolver is chambered for the new .356 cartridge and has a 2" compensated barrel. It will also fire the 9mm cartridge. This gun features a tuned action, radius hammer and trigger and special serial numbers. Suggested Retail Introductory Price: $760

Model 13 .357

This is a Lew Horton exclusive that features a 3" barrel with 4 Mag-Na-Ports, a bobbed hammer for double-action-only, chambered charge holes, beveled cylinder, contoured grip and thumb latch for speed loader clearance, overtravel trigger stop, and FBI grips. Limited to 300 guns. Suggested Retail Introductory Price: $730

Model 845 Single-Action

Offered by Lew Horton this pistol is chambered for the .45 ACP and is designed for the competitive shooter. Adjustable reach trigger precision fitted slide, frame and barrel are some of the special features. The barrel bushing is spherical and the front sight is dovetailed. The magazine well is extended as is the magazine release and safety. Both front and rear sight are adjustable. Suggested Retail Introductory Price: $1,470

Model 952

Chambered for the 9mm cartridge, this semi-automatic pistol has 5" barrel. Stainless steel frame and slide. Adjustable rear sight. Checkered wood grips. Magazine capacity is nine rounds. Weight is about 41 oz. Suggested Retail Introductory Price: $2,030

Model 1911

This .45 ACP PC model features a 5" barrel, micro-click adjustable black rear sight and dovetail black front sight. Checkered wine laminate grips. Stainless steel frame and slide with black oxide finish. Magazine capacity is 8 rounds. Weight is about 41 oz. Introduced in 2004. Suggested Retail Price: $2,270

SMITH & WESSON LONG ARMS

.320 Revolving Rifle Model

Model is rare and unique—prize to a S&W collector. Revolving Rifle chambered for .320 S&W Revolving Rifle cartridge. Has a 6-shot fluted cylinder and offered with 16", 18" and 20" barrel. Only 76 rifles are nickel-plated and remainder of production are blued. Butt is rounded, with red hard rubber checkered grips and forearm of the same material. Detachable shoulder stock, with black hard rubber buttplate featuring S&W logo. Rifle furnished in a leather carrying case with accessories. As fine a firearm as this was, it was a commercial failure for S&W; they finally came to the realization the public did not want a revolving rifle. They manufactured only 977 of them between 1879 and 1887. **NOTE:** Values are for complete unit. Deduct 40 percent without stock. Add 10 percent for 16" or 20" barrels.

—	12000	9000	6000	2000	1500

Model A Rifle

A bolt-action with 23.75" barrel, chambered for .22-250, .243, .270, .308, .30-06, 7mm Magnum, and .300 Winchester Magnum. It has a folding rear sight and a checkered Monte Carlo stock with contrasting rosewood fore-end tip and pistol grip cap. It was manufactured for S&W by Husqvarna of Sweden. From 1969 to 1972.

400	325	275	200	150	100

Model B

As above, with a schnabel fore-end and 20.75" barrel.

425	350	295	200	150	100

Model C

As above, with a cheekpiece.

425	350	295	225	175	125

Model D

As above, with a Mannlicher-style stock.

700	600	400	350	250	150

Model 1500 Series

A bolt-action series of hunting rifles made for Smith & Wesson by Howa of Japan in 1983 and 1984. Calibers included .222 Rem., .223 Rem., .22-250 Rem., .243 Win., .25-06 Rem., .270 Win., 7mm Rem. Mag., .308 Win., .30-06 and .300 Win. Mag.. Offered in several variations with blue or stainless receiver, plain or checkered wood stock (Deluxe model). Barrel lengths are 22-inches except 24-inches for magnum calibers. A heavy barrel varmint version was available. The Model 1700 Classic Hunter was similar, except for a removable magazine and schnabel fore-end. **NOTE:** Add 10 percent for Deluxe or Varmint model, 15 percent for Model 1700.

450	400	350	300	250	150

I-Bolt Rifle

This bolt-action hunting rifle was made in the U.S.A. by Smith & Wesson from 2008 to 2009 in .25-06, .270 Win., .30-06, 7mm Rem. Mag. and .300 Win. Mag.. Offered with wood, synthetic or camo stock, and blue or stainless finish. Integral Picatinny rail. **NOTE:** Add 10 percent for camo stock.

475	425	365	300	250	150

M&P15 Military and Police Tactical Rifle

Gas-operated semi-auto built along lines of AR-15. Caliber: 5.56mm NATO. Magazine capacity: 30. Barrel: 16-inch 1:9. Stock: Six-position telescoping composite. Weight: 6.74 lbs. unloaded.

NIB	EXC.	V.G.	GOOD	FAIR	POOR

Sights: Adjustable front and rear. Variants: M&P15A & M&P15T (no carry handle; folding battle sight). Introduced 2006.

1200	950	800	675	450	200

M&P 15 PC

Generally similar to the M&P rifle but with accurized tubular floated barrel, 2-stage match trigger, 20" matte stainless barrel. No sights. Introduced 2007.

1750	1300	950	800	550	250

M&P 15 Sport

A more economical addition to the M&P rifle line. Chambered for the 5.56 NATO with a black anodized upper and lower receiver of 7075 T6 aluminum. Polymer hand guard, 16-inch 4140 steel barrel. Adjustable sights, single-stage trigger, chrome-lined gas key and bolt carrier. Flash suppressor compensator. Introduced in 2011.

665	550	475	400	300	150

M&P 15PC Camo

AR-style semi-auto rifle chambered for .223 Remington/5.56 NATO. A2 configuration, 10-round magazine. No sights but integral front and rear optics rails. Two-stage trigger, aluminum lower, stainless 20" barrel with 1:8 twist. Finished in Realtree Advantage Max-1 camo. Overall length 38.5" , weight 8.2 lbs.

1500	1075	875	750	500	275

M&P 15VTAC Viking Tactics

AR-style semi-auto rifle chambered in .223 Remington/5.56 NATO. Six-position CAR stock. 16" barrel. Surefire flash-hider and G2 light with VTAC light mount; VTAC/JP handguard; JP single-stage match trigger and speed hammer; three adjustable picatinny rails; VTAC padded two-point adjustable sling. Overall length 35" extended, 32" collapsed; weight 6.5 lbs. 30-round magazine.

1750	1300	950	800	550	250

M&P 15 Piston Rifle

Similar to AR-derived M&P15, with gas piston. Chambered in 5.56 NATO. Features include adjustable gas port, optional Troy quad mount handguard, chromed bore/gas key/bolt carrier/chamber, 6-position telescoping or MagPul MOE stock, flattop or folding MBUS sights, aluminum receiver, alloy upper and lower, black anodized finish, 30-round magazine, 16" barrel with birdcage. Suggested retail price $1531 (standard handguard), $1692 (Troy quad mount handguard).

M&P 15 300 Whisper

Chambered for .300 Whisper cartridge. Comes with or without suppressor. Stock and fore-end in Realtree APG camo.

950	850	700	500	400	300

M&P 15R

This variation chambered for Russian 5.45x39mm cartridge. Made from 2008 to 2011.

900	800	750	500	300	200

M&P 15-22

.22 LR rimfire verson of AR-derived M&P tactical autoloader. Features include blowback action, 15.5" or 16" barrel, 6-position telescoping or fixed stock, quad mount Picatinny rails, plain barrel or compensator, alloy upper and lower, matte black finish, 10- or 25-round magazine.

450	400	350	250	200	175

M&P 10

AR-style rifle chambered for 7.62 NATO/.308 Winchester, with 18" barrel. Features include ambidextrous safety and magazine catch, and a gas block with integral Picatinny accessory rail.

1375	1125	950	700	400	250

Model 916

A series of slide-action shotguns made in the U.S.A. by Smith & Wesson from 1972 to 1981. Made in 12, 16 and 20 gauge in various barrel lengths with fixed chokes. Ventilated rib or plain barrel. Offered in both solid-frame and takedown versions. **NOTE:** Add 10 percent for ventilated rib, 10 percent for takedown model.

200	180	150	120	100	75

Model 3000

Slide-action shotgun made in Japan by Howa for Smith & Wesson and imported from 1982 to about 1989. In 12 or 20 gauge with a 3-inch chamber, checkered wood stock and fore-end, and

NIB	EXC.	V.G.	GOOD	FAIR	POOR

fixed chokes or choke tubes. Standard barrel lengths of 26, 28 or 30-inches. Also offered in 18 or 20-inches in police model, and 22-inches in a slug gun with rifle sights. **NOTE:** Add 10 percent for choke tubes.

350	320	280	225	180	100

Model 1000

A series of gas-operated semi-auto shotguns patterned after the Remington Model 1100. Offered in 12 or 20 gauge with barrel length from 22 to 30-inches and with fixed chokes or interchangeable tubes. Checkered walnut stock and fore-end, engraved aluminum receiver. Available in several variations including waterfowl, trap and skeet models. **NOTE:** Add 25 percent for waterfowl model, 50 percent for trap gun.

400	350	285	220	150	100

Model 1012/1020

This series of gas-operated semi-autos were imported by S&W from Turkey from 2007 to 2009. Available in 12 gauge (1012) or 20 gauge (1020) with barrel lengths from 24 to 30-inches, and five choke tubes. Stock is adjustable for length and drop. Satin finished walnut or black synthetic stock, or total camo coverage. **NOTE:** Add 20 percent for camo coverage, 30 percent for 3.5-inch 12 ga. model.

500	425	385	325	250	200

Elite Gold & Silver Series

Elite Gold model is a side-by-side in 20 gauge only with quality double-gun features. Grade III checkered walnut stock with English-style straight grip or pistol grip, and a choice of single or double triggers. Automatic ejectors, color case hardened frame, fixed chokes of IC/M or M/F with barrel lengths of 26 or 28-inches. Weight is approx. 6.5 lbs. Elite Silver is over/under in 12 gauge only with features similar to Elite Gold except the over/under has five choke tubes, single trigger and recoil pad. Weight is approx. 7.5 lbs. Both of these models were imported from Turkey from 2007 to 2010.

1800	1500	1100	800	500	250

SMITH AMERICAN ARMS COMPANY
Springfield, Massachusetts

Smith Carbine

A .50 caliber breechloading percussion carbine with a 21.75" round barrel having an octagonal breech. Blued, case hardened with a walnut stock. The barrel marked "Address/Poultney & Trimble/Baltimore, USA" and the frame "Smith's Patent/June 23, 1857" as well as "American Arms Co./Chicopee Falls." Approximately 30,000 were manufactured, most of which were purchased by the United States government. The sales agents were Poultney & Trimble of Baltimore, Maryland.

—	—	2750	1200	500	200

SNAKE CHARMER
Sporting Arms Manufacturing, Inc.
Little Field, Texas

Snake Charmer

A .410 bore single-shot shotgun, with 18.5" barrel. Stainless steel, with composition stock.

200	125	100	75	50	25

SNEIDER, CHARLES E.
Baltimore, Maryland

Two-Cylinder Revolver

A .22 caliber spur trigger revolver with a 2.75" octagonal barrel and twin seven-shot cylinders that can be pivoted. The barrel marked "E. Sneider Pat. March 1862." Produced in limited quantities during the 1860s.

—	—	14000	11000	5500	1250

SODIA, FRANZ
Ferlach, Austria

A wide variety of double-barrel shotguns, drillings, and combination shotgun/rifles are made by this maker.

NIB	EXC.	V.G.	GOOD	FAIR	POOR

SOKOLOVSKY CORP. SPORT ARMS
Sunnyvale, California

.45 Automaster

A .45 caliber stainless steel semi-automatic pistol with a 6" barrel fitted with Millet adjustable sights and six-shot magazine. Approximately 50 of these pistols have been made since 1984.

4850	3800	2750	2000	1500	500

SPALDING & FISHER
Worcester, Massachusetts

Double Barreled Pistol

A .36 caliber percussion double-barrel pocket pistol with 5.5" barrels, blued iron frame and walnut grips. The top of the barrels marked "Spalding & Fisher." Produced during the 1850s.

—	—	1350	925	400	100

SPANG & WALLACE
Philadelphia, Pennsylvania

Pocket Pistol

A .36 caliber percussion pocket pistol with a 2.5" to 6" barrel, German silver furniture and checkered walnut stock. The barrel marked "Spang & Wallace/Phila." Manufactured during late 1840s and early 1850s.

—	—	2850	1500	750	200

SPENCER
Boston, Massachusetts

Spencer Carbine

This was one of the most popular firearms used by Union forces during the Civil War. It is chambered for a metallic rimfire cartridge known as the "No. 56." It is actually a .52 caliber and was made with a copper case. The barrel is 22" in length. The finish is blued, with a carbine-length walnut stock held on by one barrel band. There is a sling swivel at the butt. There were approximately 50,000 manufactured between 1863 and 1865.

—	—	7500	5000	2500	500

Military Rifle—Navy Model

This model is similar to the carbine, with a 30" round barrel and a full-length walnut stock held on by three barrel bands. It features an iron fore-end tip and sling swivels. The Civil War production consisted of two models. A Navy model was manufactured between 1862 and 1864 (there were approximately 1,000 of these so marked).

—	—	10000	7500	5000	1000

Military Rifle—Army Model

There were approximately 11,450 produced for the Army during the Civil War. They are similar to the Navy model except that the front sight doubles as a bayonet lug. They were manufactured in 1863 and 1864.

—	—	8000	6000	2500	600

Springfield Armory Post-war Alteration

After the conclusion of the Civil War, approximately 11,000 carbines were refurbished and rechambered for .50 caliber rimfire. The barrels were sleeved, and a device known as the "Stabler cut-off" was added to convert the arm to single-shot function. Often they were refinished and restocked. The inspector's marks "ESA" will be found in an oval cartouche on the left side of the stock. These alterations took place in 1867 and 1868.

—	—	5250	3950	1700	500

Model 1865 Contract

This model was manufactured by the Burnside Rifle Company in 1865. They are similar to the Civil War-type carbine and are marked "By Burnside Rifle Co./Model 1865." There were approximately 34,000 manufactured. Old records show that 30,500 were purchased by the United States government, and 19,000 of these had the Stabler cut-off device.

—	—	5300	3250	1250	500

NIB	EXC.	V.G.	GOOD	FAIR	POOR

SPENCER ARMS CO.
Windsor, Connecticut

Slide-Action Shotgun

From 1882 to 1889 they manufactured the first successful slide action repeating shotgun. Designed by Christopher M. Spencer who also designed the Civil War era Spencer military carbines. The shotgun came in both solid and takedown models in both 12 and 10 gauge. In 1890 Francis Bannerman & Sons of New York bought the patents and machinery and moved the operation to Brooklyn, New York. They produced what is known as the Spencer Bannerman models from 1890 to 1907. The later Bannerman models are worth 50 percent less than the Spencer models.

—	—	1000	600	200	125

NOTE: The takedown model is worth 20 percent premium and 10 gauge models are worth a 10 percent premium.

SPENCER REVOLVER
Maltby, Henley & Company
New York, New York

Safety Hammerless Revolver

A .32 caliber hammerless double-action revolver with a 3" barrel. The frame and barrel made of brass, the cylinder of steel and the grips are of walnut. The barrel is marked "Spencer Safety Hammerless Pat. Jan. 24, 1888 & Oct. 29, 1889." Manufactured by the Norwich Pistol Company circa 1890.

—	—	500	225	150	100

SPHINX
Sphinx Engineering SA
Porrentru, Switzerland
Imported by Sile Distributors Inc.

AT-380

Semi-automatic pistol is a small .380-caliber in double-action-only. Magazine capacity 11 rounds. Offered in stainless steel, blued or two-tone finish. Barrel 3.27"; overall length 6.03". Sights are fixed and grips are black checkered plastic. Weight 25 oz.

600	550	400	300	200	100

AT-2000 SERIES PISTOLS

A series number applied to several different variations of the same basic design. Based on CZ 75 pistol. The AT-2000 is a semi-automatic pistol offered in 9mm and .40 S&W. Barrel lengths are different depending on variation, but AT-2000 can be converted from double-action to double only in just a matter of minutes.

AT-2000S/SDA

Model chambered for 9mm or .40 S&W cartridge. Barrel length 4.53". Overall length 8.12". Magazine capacity 15 rounds for 9mm; 13 rounds for .40 S&W. Available in double-action (S) or double-action-only (SDA). Offered with two-tone or all blued finish. Weighs 35 oz.

1500	1150	875	675	600	300

AT-2000P/PDA

A slightly smaller of the AT-2000S. Magazine capacity 13 rounds for 9mm; 11 rounds for .40 S&W. Features are the same except barrel length is 3.66". Overall length 7.25"; weight is 31 oz.

1500	1150	875	675	600	300

AT-2000PS

This version, sometimes referred to as Police Special, features the shorter barrel of the AT-2000P model on the larger AT-2000S frame. Barrel length 3.66". Magazine capacity 15 rounds for 9mm and 13 rounds for .40 S&W.

1500	1150	875	675	600	300

AT-2000H/HDA

Smallest version of AT-2000 series. Magazine capacity 10 rounds for 9mm; 8 rounds for .40 S&W. Barrel length 3.34". Overall length 6.78"; weight 26 oz.

1500	1150	875	675	600	300

	NIB	EXC.	V.G.	GOOD	FAIR	POOR

AT-2000C

This is the competitor model. Features a competition slide, dual port compensator, match barrel and Sphinx scope mount. Offered in double-/single-action. Available in 9mm, 9x21 and .40 S&W.

NIB	EXC.	V.G.	GOOD	FAIR	POOR
2200	1600	1200	800	600	400

AT-2000CS

Same as above model. Fitted with BoMar adjustable sights.

NIB	EXC.	V.G.	GOOD	FAIR	POOR
2250	1650	1250	850	650	425

AT-2000GM

Grand Master model. Features are similar to AT-2000C. Offered in single-action-only.

NIB	EXC.	V.G.	GOOD	FAIR	POOR
3000	2550	2100	1750	1250	500

AT-2000GMS

Same as above. Fitted with BoMar adjustable sights.

NIB	EXC.	V.G.	GOOD	FAIR	POOR
3050	2600	2150	1800	1300	525

3000

16+1 autoloader chambered in 9mm or .45 ACP. Stainless steel frame and slide, manual safety, single/double/decocking action. Weight 40.56 oz. Also available in compact version.

NIB	EXC.	V.G.	GOOD	FAIR	POOR
2000	1650	1150	500	300	200

SPIES, A. W.
New York, New York

Pocket Pistol

A .41 caliber percussion pocket pistol with a 2.5" barrel, German silver furniture and a checkered walnut stock. Produced during the 1850s.

NIB	EXC.	V.G.	GOOD	FAIR	POOR
—	—	1950	1775	900	300

SPILLER & BURR
Atlanta, Georgia

Navy Revolver

A .36-caliber percussion revolver, with 6" or 6.5" octagonal barrel and 6-shot cylinder. Barrel and cylinder blued. Frame of brass, with walnut grips. Some pistols are marked "Spiller & Burr" while others are simply marked "C.S.". Approximately 1,450 made between 1862 and 1865. .

NIB	EXC.	V.G.	GOOD	FAIR	POOR
—	—	45000	22500	15500	1500

SPITFIRE
JSL (Hereford) Ltd.
Hereford, England

This semi-automatic pistol is a design based on the CZ 75. This is a hand-built pistol designed by John Slough and built from a solid block of steel. The stainless steel frame and slide are cut with spark erosion and diamond grinding. Barrels are built and bored in the same factory. This is primarily a competition pistol. Manufactured 1992-1994.

Standard Model (G1)

Chambered for the 9x21, 9mm Parabellum, or .40 S&W cartridges this pistol uses the locked breech concept. The trigger system is single and double-action and it is fitted with an ambidextrous safety. The barrel is 3.7" and the overall length is 7.1". Magazine capacity of the 9mm is 15 rounds. Sights are fixed. Empty weight is 35 oz. Finish is stainless steel. Comes supplied with presentation box, two magazines, and allen key.Discontinued.

NIB	EXC.	V.G.	GOOD	FAIR	POOR
1300	900	700	500	300	200

Master Model

This is similar to the Standard Model but without sights. It is fitted with a stainless steel bridge mount to take an Aimpoint sight. Also has a dual port compensator. Supplied with presentation box and two magazines. Discontinued.

NIB	EXC.	V.G.	GOOD	FAIR	POOR
2100	1750	1250	800	400	200

Squadron Model

This model has a Standard Model frame, adjustable rear sight slide, adjustable rear sight slide with compensator, Master Model slide and barrel with stainless steel bridge mount and Aimpoint

NIB	EXC.	V.G.	GOOD	FAIR	POOR

sight, four magazines, screwdriver, allen key, oil bottle, spare springs, cleaning kit, and fitted leather case. Discontinued.

6000	4800	2100	900	450	200

Sterling Model (G2)

This model is chambered for the 9x21, 9mm Parabellum, or .40 S&W cartridges. Its features are the same as the Standard Model with the exception that it has adjustable sights. Discontinued.

1400	1000	800	600	300	200

Super Sterling (G7)

Also chambered for the 9x21, 9mm Parabellum, and .40 S&W this model features a single port compensator, 4.3" barrel, and overall length of 8.25". Weight is approximately 36 oz. Discontinued.

1600	1200	900	700	350	200

Competition Model (G3)

Chambered for 9x21, 9mm Parabellum, or .40 S&W cartridge this model features a tapered slide rib, adjustable rear sight, dual pod compensator, match hammer, adjustable trigger stop with presentation box. Barrel is 5.27" with compensator and weight is 40 oz. Discontinued.

1800	1400	1000	800	400	200

Battle of Britain Commemorative

This is a limited edition of 1,056 Spitfires in 9mm Parabellum. Each one represents one of the Spitfire aircraft. The stainless steel slide has the inscription "Battle of Britain-50th Anniversary," the grips are checkered walnut, log book of history of that particular aircraft, and a wooden presentation box with engraved plaque. Discontinued.

1950	1400	1000	800	400	200

Westlake Britarms

This is a .22 LR Match pistol. Barrel length is 5.77", sight base is 8.42", magazine capacity is 5 rounds. Weight is approximately 47 oz. Trigger is adjustable for length, front and rear trigger stops, adjustable palm rest on contoured wood grips, take-down barrel design with removable weight. Limited importation.

1850	1400	1000	800	400	200

SPRINGFIELD ARMORY

Springfield Armory was our country's first federal armory, beginning in 1777 in Springfield, Massachusetts, at a site chosen by George Washington. For almost two centuries, it was the primary facility for the manufacturer of firearms for the armed forces of the United States, until its closing in 1968. For information on the many models made at Springfield Armory, please refer to Standard Catalog of Military Firearms, now in its 7th Edition, published by Gun Digest Books, a division of F&W Media. Current manufacturer and importer of modern rifles and handguns, Springfield Armory, Inc. of Geneseo, Illinois, is not associated with the historic military armory of the same name.

SPRINGFIELD ARMORY INC.

Geneseo, Illinois

RIFLES

M1 Garand Rifle

A .270 (discontinued), .308 or .30-06 caliber semi-automatic rifle with a 24" barrel and 8-shot magazine. Patterned directly after the U.S. M1 Rifle.

—	1000	825	550	400	300

Iwo Jima M1 Garand

Similar to standard M1 Model but shipped in reproduction WWII-era crate with signed decorative lithograph. Introduced 2006.

1600	1300	1000	800	400	200

M1A Basic Rifle

Chambered for .308 Win. and fitted with a painted black fiberglass stock. Barrel length is 22" without flash suppressor. Front sights are military square post and rear military aperture (battle sights). Magazine capacity is 5, 10, or 20 box. Rifle weighs 9 lbs.

1250	1000	850	650	400	250

	NIB	EXC.	V.G.	GOOD	FAIR	POOR

D-Day M1 Garand Limited Edition

Introduced in 2005 this model is chambered for the .30-06 cartridge and fitted with a 24" barrel. Military style sights. Two-stage military trigger. Limited to 1,944 rifles, each with a military-style wooden crate. Each side of the buttstock has stamped memorials to D-Day.

	NIB	EXC.	V.G.	GOOD	FAIR	POOR
	1600	1200	925	675	425	250

M1A Standard Rifle

This model is chambered for the .308 Win. or .243 cartridge. Also fitted with a 22" barrel but with adjustable rear sight. Fitted with a walnut stock with fiberglass hand guard, it comes equipped with a 20-round box magazine. Weighs 9 lbs.

	NIB	EXC.	V.G.	GOOD	FAIR	POOR
	1500	1100	850	650	400	250

M1A-A1 Bush Rifle

Chambered for .308 or .243 cartridge with choice of walnut stock, black fiberglass, or folding stock (no longer produced). Fitted with 18.25" barrel. Rifle weighs 8.75 lbs. **NOTE:** Add $250 for folding stock.

	NIB	EXC.	V.G.	GOOD	FAIR	POOR
	1400	1100	850	650	400	250

M1A Scout Squad Rifle

This .308 model is fitted with an 18" barrel and a choice of fiberglass or walnut stock. Military sights. Supplied with 10-round magazine. Weight with fiberglass stock is about 9 lbs., with walnut stock about 9.3 pounds.

	NIB	EXC.	V.G.	GOOD	FAIR	POOR
	1800	1100	750	550	300	175

M1A National Match

Chambered for .308 as standard or choice of .243 cartridge. Fitted with a medium weight National Match 22" glass bedded barrel and walnut stock. Special rear sight adjustable to half minute of angle clicks. Weighs 10.06 lbs.

	NIB	EXC.	V.G.	GOOD	FAIR	POOR
	2050	1400	1000	700	500	250

M1A Super Match

This is Springfield's best match grade rifle. Chambered for .308 as standard and also .243 cartridge. Fitted with special oversize heavy walnut stock, heavy Douglas match glass bedded barrel, and special rear lugged receiver. Special rear adjustable sight. Weighs 10.125 lbs. **NOTE:** For walnut stock and Douglas barrel add $165. For black McMillan stock and Douglas stainless steel barrel add $600. For Marine Corp. camo stock and Douglas stainless steel barrel add $600. For adjustable walnut stock and Douglas barrel add $535. For adjustable walnut stock and Krieger barrel add $900.

	NIB	EXC.	V.G.	GOOD	FAIR	POOR
	2500	1850	1350	900	600	300

M1A Model 25 Carlos Hathcock

Introduced in 2001 this model features a match trigger, stainless steel heavy match barrel, McMillan synthetic stock with adjustable cheek pad, Harris Bi-pod, and other special featirtes. Chambered for the .308 cartridge. Weight is about 12.75 lbs. A special logo bears his signature.

	NIB	EXC.	V.G.	GOOD	FAIR	POOR
	4650	3450	2500	1750	800	400

M21 Law Enforcement/Tactical Rifle

Similar to the Super Match with the addition of a special stock with rubber recoil pad and height adjustable cheekpiece. Available as a special order only. Weighs 11.875 lbs.

	NIB	EXC.	V.G.	GOOD	FAIR	POOR
	3000	2600	2000	1500	650	350

M1A SOCOM 16

This M1A1 rifle features a 16.25" barrel with muzzlebrake. Black fiberglass stock with steel buttplate. Forward scout-style scope mount. Front sight post has tritium insert. Weight is about 9 lbs. Introduced in 2004.

	NIB	EXC.	V.G.	GOOD	FAIR	POOR
	1575	1250	875	650	400	250

M1A SOCOM II

Introduced in 2005 this model features a full length top rail and short bottom rail for accessories. Weight is about 11 lbs.

	NIB	EXC.	V.G.	GOOD	FAIR	POOR
	1700	1450	950	700	450	300

M1A SOCOM Urban Rifle

Similar to the SOCOM but with black and white camo stock. Introduced in 2005.

	NIB	EXC.	V.G.	GOOD	FAIR	POOR
	1725	1475	950	700	450	300

	NIB	EXC.	V.G.	GOOD	FAIR	POOR

IDF Mauser Rifle Model 66SP

This is a bolt-action rifle chambered for the .308 Win. cartridge. Adjustable trigger for pull and travel. Barrel length is 27". Specially designed stock has broad fore-end and a thumb hole pistol grip. Cheekpiece is adjustable as is the recoil pad. Supplied with case. This rifle is military issue. Fewer than 100 imported into the U.S.

	NIB	EXC.	V.G.	GOOD	FAIR	POOR
	2200	1750	950	700	450	300

SAR-48

This is the pre-ban version of the SAR-4800.

	NIB	EXC.	V.G.	GOOD	FAIR	POOR
	1400	1200	850	600	500	250

SAR-4800

This is a semi-automatic gas operated rifle, similar in appearance to the FN-FAL/LAR rifle, chambered for the .308 Win. cartridge. It is fitted with a 21" barrel and has a fully adjustable rear sight. Weight is approximately 9.5 lbs. No longer imported.

	NIB	EXC.	V.G.	GOOD	FAIR	POOR
	1600	1200	800	600	400	250

SAR-8

This semi-automatic rifle is similar in appearance to the HK-91. It is chambered for the .308 Win. and is of the recoil operated delayed roller-lock design. Barrel length is 18" and the rear sight is fully adjustable. Weight is about 8.7 lbs. No longer imported.

	NIB	EXC.	V.G.	GOOD	FAIR	POOR
	950	750	600	400	300	200

SAR-8 Tactical

Similar to the above model but fitted with a heavy barrel. Introduced in 1996. No longer imported. Fewer than 100 imported into U.S.

	NIB	EXC.	V.G.	GOOD	FAIR	POOR
	1450	1100	750	600	400	300

M6 Scout

A .22, .22 Magnum, or .22 Hornet and .410 bore over-and-under combination shotgun rifle with an 18" barrel. Black anodized finish with a synthetic stock. Discontinued. The US-made version commands a premium over the Czech-made. Add 30 percent for Hornet. Values shown are for US-made version.

	NIB	EXC.	V.G.	GOOD	FAIR	POOR
	600	450	295	200	100	50

M6 Scout—Stainless Steel

Same as above but in stainless steel. First introduced in 1996. Discontinued.

	NIB	EXC.	V.G.	GOOD	FAIR	POOR
	625	475	325	225	150	75

PISTOLS

M6 Scout Pistol

As above but with 10" barrel and no folding stock. Parkerized or stainless steel finish. Weight is about 28 oz. Introduced in 2002. Discontinued. **NOTE:** Add $30 for stainless steel.

	NIB	EXC.	V.G.	GOOD	FAIR	POOR
	575	425	295	200	100	50

Model 1911-A1

A 9mm, .38 Super or .45 caliber copy of the Colt Model 1911-A1 semi-automatic pistol. Blued or Parkerized. Introduced in 1985.

	NIB	EXC.	V.G.	GOOD	FAIR	POOR
	625	425	375	350	300	250

Model 1911-A1 Service Model

Introduced in 2003 this .45 ACP pistol has a 5" barrel with Bo-Mar adjustable three-dot rear sight. This model also has a number of special features such as extended mag well, titanium firing pin, and beavertail grip safety. Stainless steel magazine capacity is seven rounds. Black stainless steel finish. Weight is about 35 oz.

	NIB	EXC.	V.G.	GOOD	FAIR	POOR
	925	750	600	500	400	200

Model 1911-A1 Service Mil-Spec

Chambered for the .45 ACP cartridge and fitted with a 5" barrel. Fixed sights. Matte stainless steel finish. Black plastic grips. Weight is about 36 oz. Introduced in 2003.

	NIB	EXC.	V.G.	GOOD	FAIR	POOR
	610	475	375	350	300	250

NIB	EXC.	V.G.	GOOD	FAIR	POOR

Model 1911-A1 Service Model Lightweight

This .45 ACP pistol has a 5" barrel with lightweight alloy frame and bi-tone finish. Novak Lo-Mount sights. A large number of special features. Checkered cocobolo grips. Magazine capacity is seven rounds. Weight is about 30 oz. Introduced in 2003.

875	700	600	500	400	200

Model 1911-A1 Stainless

Similar to the standard Model 1911 but chambered for the .45 ACP cartridge and offered in stainless steel. Equipped with three-dot sights, beveled magazine well, and checkered walnut grips. Weighs about 39.2 oz. **NOTE:** For Bomar sights add $50.

900	750	625	400	350	200

Model 1911-A1 Factory Comp

Chambered for the .45 ACP or the .38 Super this pistol is fitted with a three chamber compensator. The rear sight is adjustable, an extended thumb safety and Videcki speed trigger are standard features. Also checkered walnut grips, beveled magazine well and Commander hammer are standard. Weighs 40 oz. **NOTE:** Factory Comp pistols chambered for .38 Super may bring a small premium.

1050	925	750	600	500	300

Model 1911-A1 Factory Comp High Capacity

Same as above but with 13-round magazine.

1050	925	750	600	500	300

Model 1911-A2 S.A.S.S.

This is a single-shot pistol built on the Model 1911 frame. Available in two barrel lengths; 10.75" and 14.9". Offered in .22 LR, .223, 7mm-08, 7mmBR, .357 Magnum, .308 and .44 Magnum calibers. This conversion kit is available for those wishing to use it on their own Model 1911 pistol frames.

500	400	325	275	200	100

Model 1911-A1 Defender

Chambered for the .45 ACP cartridge this pistol is fitted with a tapered cone dual port compensator. It also is fitted with reversed recoil plug, full length recoil spring guide, fully adjustable rear sight, serrated front strap, rubberized grips, and Commander-style hammer. Eight-round magazine capacity. The finish is bi-tone. Weighs 40.16 oz.

875	700	600	500	400	200

Model 1911-A1 Loaded Defender Lightweight

As above but with loaded features: precision fit frames, slides and barrels, flat serrated mainspring housing, lowered and flared ejection port, Delta lightweight hammer, loaded chamber indicator, titanium firing pin, carry bevel treatment, ambidextrous thumb safety, high hand beavertail grip safety, dovetail front sight, Novak or adjustable rear sight, and adjustable speed trigger.

950	775	675	550	450	250

Model 1911-A1 Compact

Available in blue or bi-tone this .45 ACP is fitted with a 4.5" barrel and compact compensator. It is equipped with Commander-style hammer and three-dot sights. Walnut grips are standard. Comes with 7-round magazine. Weighs 37.2 oz. **NOTE:** For stainless steel add $40.

900	750	625	400	350	200

Lightweight Compact Comp

Fitted with a 4-1/2" barrel and single port compensator. Magazine hold 8 rounds of .45 ACP. Frame is alloy and weight is 30 oz.

900	750	625	400	350	200

Model 1911-A1 Compact Mil-Spec

This model is the same as the standard blued steel Compact model but with a Parkerized finish.

850	700	575	350	300	200

Model 1911-A1 Long Slide

This model features a 6" barrel, 3-dot fixed sights, checkered wooden grips, and an 8-round magazine capacity. Finish is stainless steel. Weight is about 38 oz. Introduced in 1997.

950	775	675	550	450	250

	NIB	EXC.	V.G.	GOOD	FAIR	POOR

Model 1911-A1 Loaded Long Slide

As above but with loaded features: precision fit frames, slides and barrels, flat serrated mainspring housing, lowered and flared ejection port, Delta lightweight hammer, loaded chamber indicator, titanium firing pin, carry bevel treatment, ambidextrous thumb safety, high hand beavertail grip safety, dovetail front sight, Novak or adjustable rear sight, and adjustable speed trigger.

NIB	EXC.	V.G.	GOOD	FAIR	POOR
1100	950	775	600	475	350

Model 1911-A1 Champion

This .45 ACP pistol has a shortened slide, barrel, and reduced size frame. The Champion is fitted with 4" barrel, 8-round magazine, Commander hammer, checkered walnut grips, and special 3-dot sights. Weighs 33.4 oz.

NIB	EXC.	V.G.	GOOD	FAIR	POOR
795	650	500	400	295	150

Model 1911-A1 Champion Mil-Spec

Same as above but with a Parkerized finish.

NIB	EXC.	V.G.	GOOD	FAIR	POOR
700	600	400	350	225	125

Model 1911-A1 Stainless Champion

Same as above but offered in stainless steel. Weighs about 33.4 oz.

NIB	EXC.	V.G.	GOOD	FAIR	POOR
850	700	575	350	300	200

Model 1911-A1 Loaded Champion Stainless

As above but with loaded features: precision fit frames, slides and barrels, flat serrated mainspring housing, lowered and flared ejection port, Delta lightweight hammer, loaded chamber indicator, titanium firing pin, carry bevel treatment, ambidextrous thumb safety, high hand beavertail grip safety, dovetail front sight, Novak or adjustable rear sight, and adjustable speed trigger.

NIB	EXC.	V.G.	GOOD	FAIR	POOR
1000	875	700	575	500	300

Champion Compact

Includes same features as Champion but with a shortened grip frame length and a 7-round magazine. Weighs 32 oz.

NIB	EXC.	V.G.	GOOD	FAIR	POOR
850	700	575	350	300	200

Model 1911 Loaded Champion Lightweight

This model has a lightweight aluminum frame with Novak night sights. Checkered rubber grips. Finish is OD green and Black Armory Kote. Weight is about 28 oz. Introduced in 2004.

NIB	EXC.	V.G.	GOOD	FAIR	POOR
850	700	575	350	300	200

Ultra Compact 1911-A1

This model features a 3-1/2" barrel with a 7-1/8" overall length. It has a stainless steel frame, beveled mag well, speed trigger, match grade barrel, and walnut grips. Weighs 31 oz.

NIB	EXC.	V.G.	GOOD	FAIR	POOR
850	700	575	350	300	200

Ultra Compact Lightweight MD-1

Same as above but in .380 caliber with alloy frame. Weighs 24 oz.

NIB	EXC.	V.G.	GOOD	FAIR	POOR
700	600	400	350	225	125

Ultra Compact 1911-A1 Mil-Spec

Same as the Ultra Compact Model but with a Parkerized or blued finish.

NIB	EXC.	V.G.	GOOD	FAIR	POOR
750	650	450	350	225	125

V10 Ultra Compact 1911-A1

Same as the Ultra Compact 1911-A1 but fitted with a compensator built into the barrel and slide.

NIB	EXC.	V.G.	GOOD	FAIR	POOR
900	750	625	400	350	200

V10 Ultra Compact 1911-A1 Mil-Spec

Same as above but with Parkerized finish.

NIB	EXC.	V.G.	GOOD	FAIR	POOR
850	700	575	350	300	200

Model 1911-A1 High Capacity

This model is chambered in .45 ACP (10-round magazine) or 9mm caliber (16-round magazine). Standard features include Commander hammer, walnut grips, and beveled magazine well. Blued finish. Weighs 42 oz. In 1997 this model was offered in stainless steel and Parkerized finish. **NOTE:** For stainless steel add $40, for Parkerized finish deduct $25.

NIB	EXC.	V.G.	GOOD	FAIR	POOR
650	525	400	300	200	100

	NIB	EXC.	V.G.	GOOD	FAIR	POOR

Compact High Capacity

Same as above but with an 11-round magazine.

	650	525	400	300	200	150

Ultra Compact High Capacity

This .45 ACP model is offered in three different 3.5" barrel variations: stainless steel, Parkerized, and ported. Standard magazine capacity is 10 rounds. Weight is about 31 oz. **NOTE:** Add $60 for stainless steel and $100 for ported models.

	700	600	400	350	225	125

Micro Compact—Parkerized

Chambered for the .45 ACP cartridge and fitted with a 3" bull barrel. Aluminum frame with steel slide. Novak night sights. Cocobolo grips. Offered with Parkerized finish. Weight is about 24 oz. Magazine capacity is six rounds. Introduced in 2002.

	850	700	575	350	300	200

Micro Compact—Stainless

As above but with stainless steel frame and slide and Novak tritium night sights. Weight is about 24 oz. Introduced in 2003.

	900	750	625	400	350	200

Micro Compact—O.D. Green

As above but with Armory Kote green finish. Pearce grips. Introduced in 2003.

	900	750	625	400	350	200

Micro Compact—Black Stainless

As above but with black stainless steel finish and Slimline cocobolo grips. Weight is about 32 oz. Introduced in 2003.

	900	750	625	400	350	200

Micro Compact Lightweight

This model is similar to the other Micro models but is fitted with an aluminum frame and Novak night sights. Cocobolo wood grips. Bi-Tone finish. Equipped with XML Mini Light. Introduced in 2004. Weight is about 24 oz.

	900	750	625	400	350	200

Loaded Micro Compact Lightweight

As above but with loaded features: precision fit frames, slides and barrels, flat serrated mainspring housing, lowered and flared ejection port, Delta lightweight hammer, loaded chamber indicator, titanium firing pin, carry bevel treatment, ambidextrous thumb safety, high hand beavertail grip safety, dovetail front sight, Novak or adjustable rear sight, and adjustable speed trigger. Introduced in 2005.

	1000	975	775	600	475	300

Model 1911-A1 Mil-Spec Operator

Chambered for the .45 ACP and fitted with a 5" barrel. This model features a Picatinny rail system on the frame. Fixed sights. Magazine capacity is 7 rounds. Parkerized finish.

	900	750	625	400	350	200

Model 1911-A1 Loaded Operator

Introduced in 2002 this model features a integral Picatinny rail on the frame. Chambered for the .45 ACP cartridge and fitted with a 5" barrel. Novak night sights. Parkerized finish. Magazine capacity is 7 rounds.

	1150	950	700	500	375	250

Combat Commander

A copy of the Colt Model 1911-A1 Combat Commander chambered for .45 ACP only. Introduced in 1988.

	600	500	400	350	225	125

Trophy Match

This model has special features such as fully adjustable target sights, match grade 5" barrel, and special wide trigger. Weight is approximately 36 oz. Available in blue, stainless steel, or bi-tone finish. In 1997 this model was offered chambered for the 9mm cartridge. Values would be the same for both .45 ACP and the 9mm models. **NOTE:** For stainless steel add $40.

	1000	975	775	600	475	300

	NIB	EXC.	V.G.	GOOD	FAIR	POOR

Loaded Leatham Trophy Match

Introduced in 2005 this .40 S&W pistol is fitted with a 5" barrel with fully adjustable target sights. Black Polymer grips. Dawson magazine well, tuned trigger, match barrel and bushing, checkered front strap and other special features. Black finish. Weight is about 39 oz.

1200	1075	900	700	575	300

1911 GI SERIES

Full Size

Chambered for the .45 ACP cartridge and fitted with a 5" barrel. Old style fixed sights. Standard checkered brown plastic grips. Lanyard loop on mainspring housing. Stainless steel frame and slide. Magazine capacity is 7 rounds. Weight is about 36 oz. Introduced in 2004. This model is also offered with Parkerized finish or OD green finish. Also offered in stainless steel. **NOTE:** Deduct $45 for Parkerized or OD finish. Add $30 for stainless steel.

560	450	375	325	250	125

Full Size High-Capacity

As above but with 10-round magazine. Weight is about 38 oz. Introduced in 2005.

600	500	425	375	295	175

Champion

This model is a scaled-down version of the full-size model above. Fitted with a 4" fully supported barrel and low-profile military sights. This model also has double diamond walnut grips. Black finish. Weight is about 34 oz. Introduced in 2004. Also offered with Parkerized finish.

600	500	425	375	295	175

Champion Lightweight

Introduced in 2005 this .45 ACP model is fitted with a 4" barrel with fully supported ramp. Low profile military sights. Checkered walnut grips. Weight is about 28 oz.

600	500	425	375	295	175

Micro-Compact

As above but fitted with a 3" fully supported and ramped barrel. Magazine capacity is 6 rounds. Weight is about 32 oz. Introduced in 2004.

600	500	425	375	295	175

P9 SERIES

This is a double-action 9mm, .45 ACP, or .40 S&W pistol based on the Czech CZ 75 design. It incorporates several design features including: stainless steel trigger, sear safety mechanism, extended sear safety lever, redesigned back strap, lengthened beavertail grip area, and a new high strength slide stop. This model discontinued in 1993.

Model P9 Standard

This is the standard pistol fitted with a 4.7" barrel, low profile target sights, and a ribbed slide. The 9mm has a 16-round magazine, the .45 ACP has a 10-round magazine, and the .40 S&W holds 12 rounds. Offered in either blue or stainless finish. Weighs about 35 oz.

600	500	425	375	295	175

Model P9 Factory Comp.

This is a competition pistol fitted with triple port compensator, extended magazine release, adjustable rear sight, slim competition wood grips, and bi-tone finish. Weighs 34 oz. Dropped from the Springfield product line in 1993.

700	600	400	350	225	125

Model P9 Ultra (IPSC Approved)

This competition pistol features a longer slide and barrel, 5". Special target sights, rubberized competition grips. Pistol is engraved with IPSC logo. Available in bi-tone finish only. Weighs 34.5 oz. Dropped from production in 1993.

775	575	425	350	250	200

Super Tuned Champion

Introduced in 1997 this model features a 4" barrel chambered for the .45 ACP cartridge, Novak fixed Lo-Mount sights. Tuned and polished extractor and ejector. Polished feed ramp and barrel throat. Magazine capacity is 7 rounds. Choice of blued or Parkerized finish. Weight is approximately 36 oz.

850	700	575	350	300	200

NIB	EXC.	V.G.	GOOD	FAIR	POOR

Super Tuned V10

Similar to the model above but with 3.5" barrel. Finish is bi-tone or stainless steel. Weight is about 33 oz. Introduced in 1997. Add $100 for stainless steel.

1000	895	700	600	400	250

Super Tuned Standard

This model features a 5" barrel with stainless steel finish. Weight is about 39 oz. Has all other super tune features. Introduced in 1997.

1000	895	700	600	400	250

Range Officer

A 1911 pistol ready to compete out of the box. Caliber: .45 ACP and 9mm. Five-inch barrel with blue finish, forged steel slide and frame, 7-round magazine. Other features include adjustable rear sight, match grade barrel and bushing, checkered mainspring housing, lightweight Delta hammer, extended thumb safety and beavertail grip tang. Weight is 40 ounces.

800	675	550	450	350	200

Tactical Response Pistol (TRP)

This .45 ACP pistol is fitted with a 5" barrel and choice of stainless steel or black Armory Kote finish. Fully checkered front strap and mainspring housing. Novak Lo-Mount sights. Magazine capacity 8 rounds. Weight is about 37 oz.

1360	1150	850	600	400	250

TRP Champion

Same as above but with a 3.9" barrel and black Armory Kote finish. Weight is about 33 oz.

1175	950	800	600	400	200

TRP Pro

This model is fitted with a 5" barrel and many special features including Novak Lo-Mount tritium sights. Magazine capacity is 7 rounds. Meets specifications for FBI SWAT team. Weight is 36 oz.

2000	1750	1200	900	675	300

TRP Operator

This model has all the features of the TRP series with the addition of an integral light rail on the frame. Fitted with a 5" barrel. Adjustable night sights. Introduced in 2002. **NOTE:** Add $60 for night sights. Add $100 for OD green frame and slide.

1350	1025	800	600	400	250

Lightweight Operator

Blued, semi-auto .45 ACP with 5" bull barrel. Fixed sights, 5-6-lb. trigger pull, Cocobolo grips, 31 oz. Picatinny rail. Introduced 2006.

850	700	575	350	300	200

Lightweight Champion Operator

Similar to above but with 4" bull barrel. Introduced 2006.

850	700	575	350	300	200

Enhanced Micro Pistol (EMP)

Tiny little 1911-style semi-automatic chambered in 9mm Parabellum or .40 S&W. Short-/single-action design, 7-shot capacity, 3" bull barrel, fixed sights. Stainless frame that is .125" shorter than the company\qs Compact models. Premium for night sights and other refinements.

1175	950	800	600	400	200

XD PISTOLS

These pistols are fitted with a polymer frame, grip safety, chamber indicator and raised firing pin indicator. Offered in black finish as well as O.D. green.

XD 4"

Chambered for the 9mm, .40 S&W, .357 SIG, or .45 GAP cartridges. Barrel length is 4". Magazine capacity for 9mm is 15 rounds; for .40 S&W 12 rounds, for the .357 SIG 12 rounds, and for the .45 GAP 9 rounds. Weight is about 23 oz. **NOTE:** Add $60 for night sights. Add $100 for OD green frame and slide.

550	450	350	250	175	125

	NIB	EXC.	V.G.	GOOD	FAIR	POOR

XD 4" Bi-Tone

Offered in 9mm or .40 S&W this 4" pistol has a black polymer frame and stainless steel slide. Magazine capacity is 10 rounds. Weight is about 26 oz. Introduced in 2003.

	NIB	EXC.	V.G.	GOOD	FAIR	POOR
	585	495	375	275	200	150

XD V-10 Ported 4"

Similar to XD but with 4" ported barrel chambered for the 9mm, .40 S&W or .357 SIG. Black finish. Weight is about 26 oz.

	NIB	EXC.	V.G.	GOOD	FAIR	POOR
	550	450	350	250	175	125

XD 5" Tactical

This model is fitted with a 5" barrel and chambered for the 9mm, .40 S&W or .357 SIG cartridges. Magazine capacity is 10 rounds. Weight is about 26 oz. Offered in black or O.D. green finish. In 2005 the .45 GAP cartridge was also offered for this model. Magazine capacity for 9mm is 15 rounds; for .40 S&W 12 rounds, for the .357 SIG 12 rounds, and for the .45 GAP 9 rounds. Weight is about 31 oz.

	NIB	EXC.	V.G.	GOOD	FAIR	POOR
	600	450	350	250	200	150

XD 5" Tactical Pro

Introduced in 2003 this model features a Robar NP3 finish, fiber optic front sight and fixed rear sight. The frame is built with an oversized beavertail frame extension of a higher grip. Chambered for the 9mm, .357 SIG., 40 S&W, or the .45 GAP cartridge. Magazine capacity for 9mm is 15 rounds; for .40 S&W 12 rounds, for the .357 SIG 12 rounds, and for the .45 GAP 9 rounds. Weight is about 31 oz.

	NIB	EXC.	V.G.	GOOD	FAIR	POOR
	875	750	600	500	375	250

XD 5" Bi-Tone Tactical

Introduced in 2005 this model is chambered for the .45 GAP cartridge and fitted with a 5" barrel. Black polymer frame and stainless steel slide. Magazine capacity is 9 rounds. Weight is about 31 oz.

	NIB	EXC.	V.G.	GOOD	FAIR	POOR
	600	500	400	300	200	125

XD Sub-Compact

Introduced in 2003 this polymer pistol is chambered for the 9mm or .40 S&W cartridge and fitted with a 3" barrel. Fitted with light rail on the dust cover. Grip safety and safe action trigger. Magazine capacity is 10 rounds. Weight is about 20 oz. Fixed sights. **NOTE:** For night sights add $60. Add $70 for XML Mini light.

	NIB	EXC.	V.G.	GOOD	FAIR	POOR
	550	450	350	250	175	125

XD 45 ACP

Polymer semi-auto in black, green or bi-tone holds 13+1 .45 ACP. Imported from Croatia. Fixed sights. Service model: 4" barrel, 30 oz. Tactical model: 5" barrel, 32 oz. Picatinny rail. Introduced 2006.

	NIB	EXC.	V.G.	GOOD	FAIR	POOR
	585	495	375	275	200	150

LEATHAM LEGEND SERIES

This series was introduced in 2003 and will be identified with a unique series markings, serial number, and certificate of authenticity. Two sets of grips will come with each pistol: one cocobolo with lazer engraved signature of Rob Leatham and the other a black micarta double diamond slimline grips. A custom aluminum case is standard for this series.

TGO 1

This is a full custom pistol from the Springfield Custom Shop with Nowlin Match Grade throated barrel and bushing, Robar bi-tone finish, Bomar low-mount adjustable sights, and a number of other custom features. Chambered for the .45 ACP cartridge. Weight is about 38 oz. Four magazines are standard.

	NIB	EXC.	V.G.	GOOD	FAIR	POOR
	2400	1875	1500	—	—	—

TGO 2

Similar to the TGO 1, but hand-built by the Springfield Armory.

	NIB	EXC.	V.G.	GOOD	FAIR	POOR
	1900	1500	1200	—	—	—

TGO 3

This model is an enhanced high-end production model with a lightweight aluminum slide. Bi-tone finish. Weight is about 30 oz.

	NIB	EXC.	V.G.	GOOD	FAIR	POOR
	1295	1025	800	—	—	—

	NIB	EXC.	V.G.	GOOD	FAIR	POOR

XD(M)

Enhanced variation of XD series with interchangeable backstraps, improved magazine release and disassembly design. Offered in 9mm, .40 S&W or .45 ACP, with 4.5" barrel. Three-dot sights with night sights available. Black or two-tone polymer frame, Ultra Safety Assurance trigger, striker fired, grip safety, ambidextrous magazine releases, accessory rail, loaded chamber and cocked striker indicators. Weight about 27 oz. with empty magazine. Also available in competition model (9mm only) with 5.25" barrel with lightening cut on top of slide

650	525	400	300	200	100

XDM-3.8

Sub-compact model chambered in 9mm Parabellum (19+1) and .40 S&W (16+1). Features include 3.8" steel full-ramp barrel; dovetail front and rear 3-dot sights (tritium and fiber-optics sights available); polymer frame; stainless steel slide with slip-resistant slide serrations; loaded chamber indicator; grip safety. Black, bi-tone or stainless steel finish. Overall length 7", weight 27.5 oz. (9mm).

650	525	400	300	200	100

XD-S

Designed for concealed carry, this member of the XD polymer-frame series is a single-stack 9mm or .45 ACP, with 3.3" or 4" barrel. Sights are fiber optic front and dovetail rear. Magazine capacity 7 rounds for 9mm; 5 rounds for .45 ACP.

500	435	350	300	250	200

SPRINGFIELD CUSTOM SHOP

This specialty shop was formed to build custom pistols to the customer's own specifications. When these one-of-a-kind pistols are encountered it is advisable for the shooter or collector to get an independent appraisal. The Springfield Custom also offers standard custom and Racegun packages that are readily available and in stock. These pistols are commercially available.

Custom Carry

Chambered for the following cartridges: .45 ACP, 9mm Parabellum, .38 Super, 10mm, .40 S&W, 9mm x 21. Pistol is fitted with fixed 3-dot sights, speed trigger, Match barrel and bushing, extended thumb safety, beveled magazine well, Commander hammer, polished feed ramp and throated barrel, tuned extractor, lowered and flared ejection port, fitted slide to frame, full length spring guide rod, and walnut grips. Supplied with two magazines and plastic carrying case.

1600	1450	1075	800	500	300

Basic Competition Model

Chambered for the .45 ACP this model features a variety of special options for the competition shooter. Special BoMar sights, match trigger, custom slide to frame fit, polished feed-ramp and throated barrel are just some of the features of this pistol.

1800	1600	1275	1050	650	400

N.R.A. PPC

Designed to comply with NRA rules for PPC competition this pistol is chambered for the .45 ACP cartridge with a match grade barrel and chamber. It has a polished feedramp, throated barrel, recoil buffer system, walnut grips, and fully adjustable sights. It is sold with a custom carrying case.

1600	1450	1075	800	500	300

Trophy Master Expert Limited Class

Chambered for .45 ACP Adjustable BoMar rear sight, match barrel, polished ramp and throated barrel, extended ambidextrous thumb safety, beveled and polished magazine well, full length recoil spring guide, match trigger, Commander hammer, lowered and flared ejection port, tuned extractor, fitted slide to frame, extended slide release, flat mainspring housing, Pachmayr wraparound grips, two magazines with slam pads and plastic carrying case.

2100	1750	1300	950	600	400

Expert Pistol

Similar to the above model but progressive triple port compensator.

2200	1850	1400	1000	650	400

Bureau Model 1911-A1

Introduced in 1998 this model features a 5" match barrel, a speed trigger, lowered and flared ejection port, beavertail grip safety, Lo-Mount Novak night sights, front strap checkering, Black T finish and special serial numbers with FBI prefix. Bureau Model markings on slide.

2100	1750	1300	950	600	400

	NIB	EXC.	V.G.	GOOD	FAIR	POOR

Springfield Formula "Squirtgun"

Chambered for .45 ACP, .38 Super, 9mmx19, 9mmx21, and 9mmx23. Fitted with a high capacity 20-round frame, customer specifications sights, hard chrome frame and slide, triple chambered tapered cone compensator, full recoil spring guide and reverse plug, shock butt, lowered and flared ejection port, fitted trigger, Commander hammer, polished feed ramp and throated barrel, flat checkered mainspring housing, extended ambidextrous thumb safety, tuned extractor, checkered front strap, bottom of trigger guard checkered, rear of slide serrated, cocking sensations on front of slide, built in beveled magazine well, and checkered wood grips.

3500	2950	2500	2000	1400	700

Bullseye Wadcutter

Chambered for .45 ACP, .38 Super, 10mm, and .40 S&W. Slide is fitted with BoMar rib. Standard features include full length recoil spring guide rod, speed trigger, Commander hammer, lowered and flared ejection port, tuned extractor, fitted slide to frame, beveled magazine well, checkered front strap, checkered main spring housing, removable grip cope mount, match barrel and bushing, polished feed ramp and throated barrel, walnut grips, and two magazines with slam pads.

1800	1600	1275	1050	650	400

Trophy Master Distinguished Pistol

This model is chambered for the following cartridges: .45 ACP, .38 Super, 10mm, .40 S&W, 9mmx21. Special BoMar adjustable rear sight with hidden rear leaf, triple port compensator on match barrel, full length recoil spring guide rod and recoil spring retainer, shock butt, lowered and flared ejection port, fitted speed trigger, Commander hammer, polished feed ramp and throated barrel, flat checkered magazine well and mainspring housing matched to beveled magazine well, extended ambidextrous thumb safety, tuned extractor, checkered front strap, flattened and checkered trigger guard, serrated slide top and compensator, cocking sensations on front of slide, checkered walnut grips, two magazines with slam pads, and carrying case.

2450	1900	1350	1000	650	500

Distinguished Limited Class

Similar to the above model but built to comply with USPSA "Limited Class" competition rules. This model has no compensator.

2695	2000	1500	1000	650	500

CMC Formula "Squirtgun"

Chambered for .45 ACP, .38 Super, 9mmx19, 9mmx21, 9mmx23. This pistol has a 20-round magazine and a modular frame. All other features the same as the Trophy Master.

2750	2000	1200	800	400	200

National Match Model

As above, with a National Match barrel and bushing, adjustable sights and checkered walnut grips. Introduced in 1988.

1535	1150	850	600	400	300

Competition Grade

As above, hand-tuned, Match Grade trigger, low-profile combat sights, an ambidextrous safety, and a Commander-type hammer. Furnished with Pachmayr grips. Introduced in 1988.

1600	1200	900	650	400	350

A Model Master Grade Competition Pistol

Similar to the Custom Carry Gun, with a National Match barrel and bushing. Introduced in 1988.

1700	1500	1250	850	400	350

Model B-1 Master Grade Competition Pistol

Specially designed for USPSA/IPSC competition. Introduced in 1988.

2000	1750	1250	850	400	350

High Capacity Full-House Race Gun

Built with all available race gun options. Offered in .45 ACP, 9x25 Dillon, .38 Super, and custom calibers on request.

3085	2300	1700	1200	700	400

Night Light Standard

Introduced in 1996 as a limited edition from Springfield distributor Lew Horton this full size Model 1911A1 pistol is chambered for the .45 ACP. It has a lightweight frame and slide with Millett night sights with Hogue rubber wraparound grips. Fitted with extended beavertail safety. Weight 29 oz.

620	500	400	300	200	100

NIB	EXC.	V.G.	GOOD	FAIR	POOR

Night Light Compact

This model was also introduced by Lew Horton in 1996 and is similar to the above model but fitted with a 4.25" barrel and lightweight frame and slide. Weight is 27 oz.

| 620 | 500 | 400 | 300 | 200 | 100 |

Night Compact

Same as above but with a steel frame and slide.

| 620 | 500 | 400 | 300 | 200 | 100 |

Omega

A .38 Super, 10mm Norma, or .45 caliber semi-automatic pistol with a 5" or 6" polygon rifled barrel, ported or unported, adjustable sights and Pachmayr grips. Patterned somewhat after the Colt Model 1911. Introduced in 1987. **NOTE:** Caliber Conversion Units add $400.

| 650 | 500 | 350 | 250 | 200 | 125 |

XD Custom Pro

This pistol is built in the Custom Shop and is available in service and tactical sizes. Tactical calibers offered are: 9mm, .40 S&W, and .45 GAP. In Tactical sizes the following calibers are offered: 9mm, .40 S&W, .357 SIG, and .45 GAP. Among some of the special features are: high hand frame relief, overtravel stop, low-mount Bomar sights. Extended magazine release. National Match barrel and special finish.

| 1500 | 1100 | 825 | 675 | 500 | 300 |

XD Carry Pro

This model is offered in subcombact, service and tactical sizes. In subcompact size the following calibers are offered: 9mm and .40 S&W. Many special features as listed above.

| 750 | 550 | 400 | 300 | 200 | 100 |

SPRINGFIELD ARMS COMPANY
Springfield, Massachusetts

Belt Model

A .31 caliber percussion revolver with 4", 5", or 6" round barrels, centrally mounted hammer, and an etched 6-shot cylinder. Made with or without a loading lever. Early production versions of this revolver are marked "Jaquith's Patent 1838" on the frame and later production were marked "Springfield Arms" on the top strap. Approximately 150 were made.

| — | — | 2600 | 1925 | 875 | 200 |

Warner Model

As above, but is marked "Warner's Patent Jan. 1851." Approximately 150 of these were made.

| — | — | 3200 | 2750 | 1325 | 250 |

Double Trigger Model

As above, with two triggers, one which locks the cylinder. Approximately 100 were made in 1851.

| — | — | 2750 | 2200 | 875 | 200 |

Pocket Model Revolver

A .28 caliber percussion revolver with 2.5" round barrel, centrally mounted hammer, no loading lever and etched 6-shot cylinder. Marked "Warner's Patent Jan. 1851" and "Springfield Arms Company." Blued, case hardened with walnut grips. Early production examples of this revolver do not have a groove on the cylinder and have a rounded frame. Approximately 525 were made in 1851.

| — | — | 1750 | 1250 | 585 | 150 |

Ring Trigger Model

As above, but fitted with a ring trigger that revolved the cylinder. Approximately 150 were made in 1851.

| — | — | 1725 | 1275 | 550 | 200 |

Double Trigger Model

As above, with two triggers set within a conventional trigger guard. Forward trigger revolves the cylinder. Approximately 350 made in 1851.

| — | — | 1625 | 1275 | 550 | 200 |

	NIB	EXC.	V.G.	GOOD	FAIR	POOR

Late Model Revolver

As above, except that the cylinder is automatically turned when the hammer is cocked. The top strap marked "Warner's Patent/James Warner, Springfield, Mass." Approximately 500 were made in 1851.

NIB	EXC.	V.G.	GOOD	FAIR	POOR
—	—	1300	875	325	100

Dragoon

A .40 caliber percussion revolver with either a 6" or 7.5" round barrel, some fitted with loading levers, others without. The top strap marked "Springfield Arms Company." Blued with walnut grips. Approximately 110 revolvers were manufactured in 1851.

NIB	EXC.	V.G.	GOOD	FAIR	POOR
—	—	10000	8800	3850	950

Navy Model

A .36 caliber percussion revolver with a 6" round barrel, centrally mounted hammer, and 6-shot etched cylinder. The top strap marked "Springfield Arms Company." Blued, case hardened with walnut grips. This model was manufactured in two variations, one with a single trigger and the other with a double trigger, the forward one of which locks the cylinder. Both variations had loading levers. Approximately 250 of these pistols were made in 1851.

NIB	EXC.	V.G.	GOOD	FAIR	POOR
—	—	6000	4250	1650	500

Double-Barrel Shotguns

The Springfield Arms Co. was bought by Stevens who used the Springfield brand name on many good quality single and double-barrel shotguns. Values range from $100 to $1,600 depending on model, gauge, and condition. See also Stevens.

SQUIBBMAN

SEE—Squires Bingham Mfg. Co., Inc.

SQUIRES BINGHAM MFG. CO., INC.

Rizal, Philippine Islands

Firearms produced by this company are marketed under the trademark Squibbman.

Model 100D

A .38 Special caliber double-action swingout cylinder revolver with a 3", 4", or 6" ventilated rib barrel, adjustable sights, matte black finish and walnut grips.

NIB	EXC.	V.G.	GOOD	FAIR	POOR
—	175	100	80	60	40

Model 100DC

As above, without the ventilated rib.

NIB	EXC.	V.G.	GOOD	FAIR	POOR
—	200	100	80	60	40

Model 100

As above, with a tapered barrel and uncheckered walnut grips.

NIB	EXC.	V.G.	GOOD	FAIR	POOR
—	200	100	80	60	40

Thunder Chief

As above, but in .22 or .22 Magnum caliber with a heavier ventilated rib barrel, shrouded ejector, and ebony grips.

NIB	EXC.	V.G.	GOOD	FAIR	POOR
—	225	125	100	80	60

SSK INDUSTRIES

Bloomingdale, Ohio

SSK-Contender

A custom-made pistol available in 74 different calibers from .178 Bee to .588 JDJ and built on a Thompson/Center action.

NIB	EXC.	V.G.	GOOD	FAIR	POOR
1250	1050	875	600	550	300

SSK-XP100

A custom-made pistol utilizing a Remington XP100 action. Available in a variety of calibers and sight configurations.

NIB	EXC.	V.G.	GOOD	FAIR	POOR
1400	1225	900	625	575	400

.50 Caliber XP100

As above, with an integral muzzlebrake and reinforced composition stock.

NIB	EXC.	V.G.	GOOD	FAIR	POOR
1750	1500	1250	1000	750	450

	NIB	EXC.	V.G.	GOOD	FAIR	POOR

STAFFORD, T. J.
New Haven, Connecticut

Pocket Pistol

A .22 caliber single-shot spur trigger pistol with a 3.5" octagonal barrel marked "T.J. Stafford New Haven Ct.," silver-plated brass frame and walnut or rosewood grips.

	NIB	EXC.	V.G.	GOOD	FAIR	POOR
	—	—	775	600	250	100

Large Frame Model

As above, but in .38 rimfire caliber with a 6" barrel.

	NIB	EXC.	V.G.	GOOD	FAIR	POOR
	—	—	1050	850	400	200

STAG ARMS
New Britain, Connecticut

NOTE: All Stag rifles are available in left hand configuration. Prices are approximately $25 - $40 higher than right handed models listed here.

Stag-15 Model 1 Pre-Ban

Basic M-4 Carbine pattern. Cal. 5.56mm/.223. 16-inch M-4 barrel with flash hider and bayonet lug. A2 upper receiver with adjustable rear sight. Six-position collapsible buttstock.

NIB	EXC.	V.G.	GOOD	FAIR	POOR
950	800	675	500	350	200

Stag-15 Model 2 Pre-Ban

As above but with a flat top upper receiver. Includes MI ERS flip type rear sight assembly.

NIB	EXC.	V.G.	GOOD	FAIR	POOR
950	800	675	500	350	200

Stag-15 Model 2 T

As above but with a A.R.M.S. sight system and Samson MRFS-C four sided hand guard.

NIB	EXC.	V.G.	GOOD	FAIR	POOR
1050	900	775	600	400	250

Stag-15 Model 3 Pre-Ban

M-4 type carbine featuring a flat top receiver and gas block with picatinny rails. Six position collapsible buttstock.

NIB	EXC.	V.G.	GOOD	FAIR	POOR
950	800	675	500	350	200

Stag-15 Model 4 Pre-Ban

An A-2 type rifle featuring a 20-inch barrel. Flash hider and bayonet lug.

NIB	EXC.	V.G.	GOOD	FAIR	POOR
950	800	675	500	350	200

Stag 6.8 Model 5 Pre-Ban

Cal. 6.8 SPC. 16-inch barrel. Flat top receiver with picatinny rail. Six position collapsible buttstock. 25-round magazine.

NIB	EXC.	V.G.	GOOD	FAIR	POOR
1050	900	775	600	400	250

Stag-15 Model 6 Pre-Ban Super Varminter

24" heavy barrel. No flash hider. Flat top receiver with picatinny rail. Two stage trigger. Free float round hand guard. A2 type fixed stock.

NIB	EXC.	V.G.	GOOD	FAIR	POOR
1050	900	775	600	400	250

Stag-8T

AR/M4-style in .223 Rem./5.56 NATO, with 16" chrome-lined barrel. Adjustable gas piston action, synthetic pistol grip, Diamondhead VRS-T aluminum handguard and flip-up front and rear sights.

NIB	EXC.	V.G.	GOOD	FAIR	POOR
1000	900	800	500	400	300

STALCAP, ALEXANDER T.F.M.
Nashville, Tennessee

First in business during the 1850s, Stalcap received a contract in 1862, to modify sporting arms for military use. Overall length 50-7/8" to 51-3/4"; octagonal barrels 35-1/4" - 36" turned round at muzzle for socket bayonets; .54 caliber. Rifles assembled with sporting locks, new stocks and brass furniture. At least 102 rifles were delivered in 1862. These arms are unmarked.

	NIB	EXC.	V.G.	GOOD	FAIR	POOR
	—	—	6500	4250	2000	1000

	NIB	EXC.	V.G.	GOOD	FAIR	POOR	

STANDARD ARMS CO.
Wilmington, Delaware

Model G

Chambered for .25 Remington, .30 Remington and .35 Remington, with 22" barrel. Open sights. Integral box magazine and closable gas port that allowed the rifle to be used as a slide action. Blued, with walnut stock. Produced in limited quantities, circa 1910. A notorious jamamatic. Bronze alloy buttplate and fore-end.

—	750	600	450	250	150		

Model M

Manually-operated pump-only version of Model G.

—	900	725	550	300	150		

STAR, BONIFACIO ECHEVERRIA
Eibar, Spain
SEE—Echeverria

STARR, EBAN T.
New York, New York

Single-Shot Derringer

A .41 caliber single-shot pistol with a pivoted 2.75" round barrel. The hammer mounted on the right side of the frame and the trigger formed in the shape of a button located at the front of the frame. The frame marked "Starr's Pat's May 10, 1864." The brass frame silver-plated, the barrel blued or silver-plated with checkered walnut grips. Manufactured from 1864 to 1869.

—		2300	1850	825	200		

Four Barreled Pepperbox

A .32 caliber 4 barreled pocket pistol with 2.75" to 3.25" barrels. The frame marked "Starr's Pat's May 10, 1864." Brass frames, silver-plated. The barrel is blued with plain walnut grips. This pistol was produced in six variations.

First Model

Fluted breech and a barrel release mounted on the right side of the frame.

—	—	3900	2750	875	200		

Second Model

Flat breech.

—	—	2500	1925	650	200		

Third Model

Rounded breech with a visible firing-pin retaining spring.

—	—	2350	1650	550	150		

Fourth Model

Rounded breech without visible springs.

—	—	2100	1650	550	150		

Fifth Model

A larger, more angular grip.

—	—	1950	1400	450	150		

Sixth Model

The frame length of this variation is of increased size.

—	—	2100	1650	550	150		

STARR ARMS COMPANY
New York, New York

1858 Navy Revolver

A .36 caliber double-action percussion revolver with a 6" barrel and 6-shot cylinder. Blued, case hardened with walnut grips. The frame marked "Starr Arms Co. New York." Approximately 3,000 were made between 1858 and 1860.

Standard Model

—	—	4100	3250	1100	350		

	NIB	EXC.	V.G.	GOOD	FAIR	POOR

Martially Marked (JT)

	NIB	EXC.	V.G.	GOOD	FAIR	POOR
	—	—	5100	4250	1750	700

1858 Army Revolver

A .44 caliber double-action percussion revolver with a 6" barrel and 6-shot cylinder. Blued, case hardened with walnut grips. The frame marked "Starr Arms Co. New York." Approximately 23,000 were manufactured.

	—	6200	4300	2500	1100	300

1863 Army Revolver

Similar to the above, but single-action and with an 8" round barrel. Approximately 32,000 were manufactured between 1863 and 1865.

	—	6750	4700	3250	1500	350

Percussion Carbine

A .54 caliber breechloading percussion carbine with a 21" round barrel secured by one barrel band. Blued, case hardened with a walnut stock. The lock marked "Starr Arms Co./Yonkers, N.Y."

	—	—	3500	2750	1250	400

Cartridge Carbine

Similar to the above, but in .52 rimfire caliber. Approximately 5,000 were manufactured.

	—	—	3750	2500	1000	350

STEEL CITY ARMS, INC.
Pittsburgh, Pennsylvania

Double Deuce

A .22 caliber stainless steel double-action semi-automatic pistol with a 2.5" barrel, 7-shot magazine and plain rosewood grips. Introduced in 1984.

	—	300	250	200	150	100

STENDA WAFFENFABRIK
Suhl, Germany

Pocket Pistol

A 7.65mm semi-automatic pistol similar to the "Beholla," the "Leonhardt," and the "Menta." Stenda took over the production of the Beholla pistol design at the close of WWI. The only major difference in the Stenda design was the elimination of the Beholla's worst feature, the pin that went through the slide and retained the barrel. It was replaced by a sliding catch that anchored it in place and unlocked the slide so that the barrel could be removed without the need of a vise and drift pin. The Stenda pistol can be identified by the fact that there are no holes through the slide and there is a catch on the frame above the trigger. The finish blued, with plastic grips; and the slide is marked "Waffenfabrik Stendawerke Suhl." Approximately 25,000 manufactured before production ceased in 1926.

	—	450	275	225	165	100

STERLING ARMAMENT LTD.
London, England

Parapistol MK 7 C4

A 9mm semi-automatic pistol with a 4" barrel, and detachable magazines of 10-round capacity. Black wrinkled paint finish with plastic grips.

600	475	400	300	200	100

Parapistol MK 7 C8

As above, with a 7.8" barrel.

625	500	400	300	200	100

Sterling MK 6

A semi-automatic copy of the Sterling submachine gun with a 16.1" barrel, folding metal stock and side mounted magazine. Finished as above.

1500	950	750	500	300	200

Sterling AR 180

A copy of the Armalite Model AR18, 5.56mm rifle. Finished with either black wrinkled paint or, more rarely, blued.

1100	750	600	500	350	200

	NIB	EXC.	V.G.	GOOD	FAIR	POOR

STERLING ARMS CORPORATION
Gasport, New York

Model 283 Target 300

This pistol is similar in appearance to Hi-Standard semi-automatic pistols. Chambered for the .22 LR cartridge it was offered with 4", 4-1/2", or 8" barrels. Rear sight is adjustable and magazine holds 10 rounds. Grips are black plastic. Weight is approximately 36 oz.

300	250	175	100	75	60

Model 284 Target 300L

Similar to the above model except for 4-1/2" or 6" tapered barrel with barrel band.

325	275	175	100	75	60

Model 285 Husky

Similar to the Model 283 with the exception of fixed sights. Offered with 4-1/2" barrel only.

300	250	175	100	75	60

Model 286 Trapper

Similar to the Model 284 except for fixed sights.

300	250	175	100	75	60

Model 287 PPL .380

This is a pocket-size semi-automatic pistol chambered for the .380 ACP cartridge. Fitted with a 1" barrel it has a 5-1/4" length overall. Magazine holds 6 rounds. Weight is approximately 22 oz.

225	175	125	75	50	25

Model PPL .22

This is a small pocket pistol similar to the Model 287 but chambered for the .22 LR cartridge. Barrel is 1" long. Pistol weighs about 24 oz.

275	225	150	75	60	50

Model 300

Similar to the Model 287 but chambered for the .25 ACP cartridge. It has a 2-1/4" barrel with a 6-round magazine. Length is 5" overall and the weight is about 14 oz.

250	225	150	75	50	40

Model 300S

This is the stainless steel version of the Model 300.

265	235	165	75	50	40

Model 302

Identical to the Model 300 except that it is chambered for the .22 LR cartridge.

250	225	150	75	50	40

Model 302S

Same as above but in stainless steel.

265	235	165	75	60	50

Model 400

This is a double-action semi-automatic pistol chambered for the .380 ACP cartridge with a 3-1/2" barrel. Magazine holds 7 rounds. Pistol is 6-1/2" overall and the weight is approximately 24 oz.

300	275	200	125	100	75

Model 400S

This is the stainless steel version of the Model 400.

325	300	2255	125	100	75

Model 402

Similar to the Model 400 except chambered for the .22 LR cartridge.

250	225	150	75	60	40

Model X-Caliber

A single-shot .22 LR, .22 WMR, .357 Magnum, or .44 Magnum pistol with interchangeable barrels from 8" and 10". Adjustable rear sight. Finger groove grips. Deduct 50 percent for rimfire.

450	400	300	225	150	100

NIB	EXC.	V.G.	GOOD	FAIR	POOR

STEVENS ARMS CO., J.
Chicopee Falls, Massachusetts

In 1864, this firm began doing business as J. Stevens & Company. In 1888, it was incorporated as J. Stevens Arms & Tool Company. It operated as such until 1920, when it was taken over by Savage Arms Company. It has operated as an independent division in this organization since. This company produced a great many firearms—most that were of an affordable nature. They are widely collected, and one interested in them would take advantage of the literature available on the subject.

Vest Pocket Pistol

This is a single-shot pocket pistol chambered for the .22 and the .30 rimfire cartridges. The .22 caliber version is rarely encountered and would be worth approximately 25 percent more than the values illustrated. It has a 2.75" part-octagonal barrel that pivots upward for loading. It has an external hammer and a spur-type trigger. The frame is nickel-plated or blued, with a blued barrel. The odd shaped flared grips are made of rosewood. The first models were marked "Vest Pocket Pistol" only. Later models have the barrels marked "J. Stevens & Co. Chicopee Falls, Mass." There were approximately 1,000 manufactured between 1864 and 1876.

—	5000	3450	2300	1300	1000

Pocket Pistol

This is a more conventional-appearing, single-shot pocket pistol chambered for either the .22 or the .30 rimfire cartridges. It has a 3.5" part-octagonal barrel that pivots upward for loading. It features a plated brass frame with either a blued or nickel-plated barrel and rosewood, two-piece grips. The barrel is marked "J. Stevens & Co. Chicopee Falls, Mass." There were approximately 15,000 manufactured between 1864 and 1886.

—	700	500	250	125	100

Gem Pocket Pistol

This is a single-shot, derringer-type pocket pistol chambered for either the .22 or .30 rimfire cartridges. It has a 3" part-octagonal barrel that pivots to the side for loading. It has a nickel-plated brass frame with either a blued or plated barrel. It has bird's-head grips made of walnut or rosewood. The barrel is marked "Gem." The Stevens name or address does not appear on this firearm. There were approximately 4,000 manufactured between 1872 and 1890.

—	1100	900	600	425	300

.22 or .41 Caliber Derringer

This is a single-shot pocket pistol chambered for the .22 or .41 caliber rimfire cartridge. It has a 4" part-octagonal barrel that pivots upward for loading. It has a spur trigger and an external hammer. The frame is plated brass with a blued barrel. It has walnut bird's-head grips. This firearm is completely unmarked except for a serial number. There were approximately 100 manufactured in 1875.

.22 Caliber

—	6500	6000	5000	3000	1500

.41 Caliber

—	6200	5600	4000	2500	1400

No. 41 Pistol

This is a single-shot pocket pistol chambered for the .22 and .30 Short cartridges. It has a 3.5" part-octagonal barrel that pivots upward for loading. It features an external hammer and a spur-type trigger. It has an iron frame with the firing pin mounted in the recoil shield. It is either blued or nickel-plated, with square-butt walnut grips. There were approximately 90,000 manufactured between 1896 and 1916.

—	500	425	300	250	135

Single-Shot Pistol

This is a single-shot pistol chambered for the .22 or .30 rimfire cartridges. It has a 3.5" part-octagonal barrel that pivots upward for loading. It is quite similar in appearance to the original pocket pistol. It has a plated brass frame and either a blued or nickel-plated barrel with walnut, square-butt grips. The barrel is marked "J. Stevens A&T Co." There were approximately 10,000 manufactured between 1886 and 1896.

—	550	400	300	200	150

Tip Up Rifles

This series of rifles was produced by Stevens beginning in the 1870s through 1895. There are a number of variations, but they are all quite similar in appearance. They feature a distinctive sloped frame made of iron and nickel-plated. Most frames are similar in size, but there is a slightly lighter frame used on the "Ladies Model" rifles. These Tip Up rifles are chambered for various calibers from the .22 rimfire to the .44 centerfire cartridges. They are offered with barrel lengths of 24", 26", 28", or 30". The actions are nickel-plated, as well as the trigger guards and the buttplates. The barrels are blued, and the two-piece stocks are of walnut. They are offered with various buttplates and sights. A shotgun version is also offered. There are a number of variations that differ only slightly, and the model numbers are not marked on the rifles. We suggest securing a qualified appraisal if in doubt. The major variations and their values are as follows:

Ladies Model—.22 or .25 Rimfire Only, 24" or 26" Barrel

NIB	EXC.	V.G.	GOOD	FAIR	POOR
—	3750	3200	2400	1500	700

Tip Up Rifle—Without Fore-end

NIB	EXC.	V.G.	GOOD	FAIR	POOR
—	750	650	500	250	200

Tip Up Rifle—With Fore-end, Swiss-Type Buttplate

NIB	EXC.	V.G.	GOOD	FAIR	POOR
—	1250	1000	600	400	250

Tip Up Shotgun—All Gauges, 30" or 32" Barrel

NIB	EXC.	V.G.	GOOD	FAIR	POOR
—	600	500	300	150	100

Ideal Single-Shot Rifle

This excellent rifle was manufactured by Stevens between 1896 and 1933. It is a single-shot, falling-block type action that is activated by a trigger guard-action lever. It was produced in many popular calibers from .22 rimfire up to .30-40. It was also manufactured in a number of special Stevens calibers. It was offered with various length barrels in many different grades, from plain Spartan starter rifles up to some extremely high-grade Schuetzen-type target rifles with all available options. In 1901 Harry Pope of Hartford, Connecticut, went to work for Stevens and brought his highly respected barrel to the Stevens Company. He remained an employee for only two years, and the firearms produced during this period have the name "Stevens-Pope" stamped on the top of the barrel in addition to the other factory markings. Rifles marked in this manner and authenticated would be worth an approximate 50 percent premium if they are in very good to excellent condition. Due to numerous variations and options offered, we strongly recommend securing a qualified appraisal, especially on the higher-grade Ideal series rifles, before a purchase.

No. 44

This version is chambered for various calibers and is offered with a 24" or 26" barrel. It has an open rear sight with a Rocky Mountain-type front sight. The finish is blued and case colored, with a walnut stock. There were approximately 100,000 manufactured between 1896 and 1933.

NIB	EXC.	V.G.	GOOD	FAIR	POOR
—	1300	1080	700	400	225

No. 44-1/2

This rifle is similar in appearance to the No. 44 but features an improved action. It has barrel lengths up to 34" and will be found with the Stevens-Pope barrel. It was manufactured between 1903 and 1916.

NIB	EXC.	V.G.	GOOD	FAIR	POOR
—	2175	1950	1500	1000	725

No. 044-1/2

This version is also known as the English Model rifle and is similar to the No. 44-1/2 except that it has a shotgun butt and a tapered barrel. There were a number of options offered that would affect the value. It was manufactured between 1903 and 1916.

NIB	EXC.	V.G.	GOOD	FAIR	POOR
—	2175	1950	1500	1000	725

No. 45

This version is also known as the Range Rifle. It is chambered for various calibers from the .22 rimfire to .44-40. Its identifying features are the Beach sights with an additional vernier tang sight and a Swiss-type buttstock. It is offered with a 26" or 28" part-octagonal barrel. It was manufactured between 1896 and 1916. Values listed are for the standard version. **NOTE:** Deduct 25 percent for .44 action.

NIB	EXC.	V.G.	GOOD	FAIR	POOR
—	2375	2150	1600	1100	825

No. 46

Same as the No. 45 but with a fancy wood stock. Manufactured from 1896 to 1902. Built in No. 44 action-only.

NIB	EXC.	V.G.	GOOD	FAIR	POOR
—	2700	2375	1900	1500	1100

No. 47

This version is similar to the No. 45, with a pistol grip buttstock. **NOTE:** Deduct 25 percent for .44 action.

NIB	EXC.	V.G.	GOOD	FAIR	POOR
—	5400	4750	3600	3000	1200

	NIB	EXC.	V.G.	GOOD	FAIR	POOR

No. 48

Same as the No. 47 but with a fancy wood checkered stock. Manufactured from 1896 to 1902. Built in a No. 44 action-only. This is a very rare model.

	—	6000	5100	4200	3000	2000

No. 49

This model is also known as the "Walnut Hill Rifle." It is a high grade target rifle chambered for many calibers between the .22 rimfire and the .44-40. It is offered with a 28" or 30" part-octagonal barrel that is medium- or heavy-weight. It was furnished with a globe front sight and a vernier tang sight. It is blued with a case-colored frame and has a high-grade, checkered, varnished walnut stock that has a high comb and features a pistol grip, cheekpiece, Swiss-type buttplate, and a loop-type trigger guard lever that resembles that of a lever-action rifle. The receiver is engraved, and there were a number of options available that would increase the value when present. We recommend an appraisal when in doubt. This rifle was manufactured between 1896 and 1916.

	—	8000	7500	4500	3000	2000

Model 50

This version is identical to the Model 49 but was offered with a higher-grade walnut stock. This is a very rare model.

	—	9200	8600	5200	3500	2400

Model 51

This version is known as the "Schuetzen Rifle" and is quite similar to the No. 49 except that it features double-set triggers, a higher-grade walnut stock, a wooden insert in the trigger guard action lever, and a heavy, Schuetzen-type buttplate. There were many options available on this model, and we recommend securing an appraisal when in doubt. It was manufactured between 1896 and 1916.

	—	15000	13000	8250	5000	2500

No. 52

This version is also known as the "Schuetzen Junior". It is similar to the No. 51 except that it features more engraving and a higher-grade walnut stock. It was manufactured between 1897 and 1916.

	—	15000	13000	8250	5000	2500

No. 53

This model is the same as the No. 51 except for the addition of a fancy wood stock and palm rest. Produced from 1896 to 1902 and offered only with a No. 44 action. This is a rare rifle.

	—	13000	10000	8000	5000	2500

No. 54

Similar to No. 52, except it has double-set triggers, a palm rest and a heavy Swiss-style buttplate. Offered with 30" or 32" part-octagonal heavy barrel. This was Stevens' top-of-the-line rifle. Offered with many options. An appraisal should be secured if in doubt. It was manufactured between 1897 and 1916. **NOTE:** Prices are based on a No. 44-1/2 action. A No. 44 action will bring 20 percent less than the prices listed.

	—	19500	17500	12500	9000	5500

No. 55

This version is one of the Stevens' Ideal Ladies Models. It is chambered for the smaller rimfire calibers between .22 Short and .32 Long rimfire. It features a 24" or 26" part-octagonal barrel with a vernier tang sight. The finish is blued and case-colored, with a checkered pistol grip walnut stock that features a Swiss-type buttplate. This is a lighter weight rifle that was manufactured between 1897 and 1916.

	—	7000	5500	3750	2200	1100

No. 56

This Ladies' Model rifle is similar to the No. 55 except that it is chambered for centerfire cartridges and has a higher-grade walnut stock. It was made on the improved No. 44-1/2 action. It was manufactured between 1906 and 1916.

	—	7500	6000	4250	2400	1200

No. 404

This version is chambered for the .22 rimfire cartridge only. It features a 28" round barrel with a globe front sight and a Lyman No. 42 receiver sight. The finish is blued and case-colored. It has a walnut straight-grip stock with a semi-beavertail fore-end. It features a shotgun-type buttplate. It was manufactured between 1910 and 1916.

	—	1300	1075	875	750	600

	NIB	EXC.	V.G.	GOOD	FAIR	POOR

No. 414

This version is also known as the Armory Model and is chambered for the .22 LR cartridge only. It was built on a No. 44 action and features a 26" round barrel. It has a Rocky Mountain front sight with a Lyman receiver sight at the rear. The finish is blued and case-colored, with a straight-grip walnut stock and fore-end held on by a single barrel band. It was manufactured between 1912 and 1932.

	NIB	EXC.	V.G.	GOOD	FAIR	POOR
	—	1000	750	550	300	275

No. 417 Walnut Hill Model

This is a heavy single-shot, lever action target rifle chambered for the .22 LR, .22 Short, or .22 Hornet cartridges. Weight is approximately 10.5 lbs. Produced from 1932 to 1940.

	NIB	EXC.	V.G.	GOOD	FAIR	POOR
	—	1625	1300	850	600	400

No. 417 1/2 Walnut Hill Model

This model is a sporting version of the Model 417. Weight is about 8.5 lbs. Manufactured from 1932 to 1940.

	NIB	EXC.	V.G.	GOOD	FAIR	POOR
	—	1725	1400	950	700	450

No. 418 Walnut Hill Jr.

This is a light single-shot lever action target rifle chambered for .22 LR or .22 Short. Weight is about 6.5 lbs. Manufactured from 1932 to 1940.

	NIB	EXC.	V.G.	GOOD	FAIR	POOR
	—	975	800	550	300	200

No. 418 1/2 Walnut Hill Jr.

Similar to the Model 418 but chambered for .25 rimfire or .22 WRF cartridges. It is also fitted with sporting sights. Manufactured from 1932 to 1940.

	NIB	EXC.	V.G.	GOOD	FAIR	POOR
	—	975	800	550	300	200

BOY'S RIFLES

Stevens Company produced an extensive line of smaller, single-shot rifles chambered for small calibers and intended primarily for use by young shooters. These firearms have become quite collectible and are considered a field of specialty by many modern collectors. **NOTE:** There are many variations that were available with a number of options that would affect their value. We supply information and values for the major variations but would recommend securing a qualified appraisal if in doubt.

"FAVORITE" RIFLES

This series of rifles is chambered for the .22, .25, and .32 rimfire. It has a 22" part-octagonal barrel and is blued, with a case-colored frame. It has a takedown-type action with an interchangeable barrel feature. It was available with optional sights, as well as buttplates. There were approximately 1,000,000 manufactured between 1893 and 1939. The variations are listed.

1st Model Favorite

This version is chambered for the .22 or .25 rimfire cartridge. It has a removable sideplate on the right side of the receiver not found on any other variation. There were approximately 1,000 manufactured between 1893 and 1894.

	NIB	EXC.	V.G.	GOOD	FAIR	POOR
	—	1300	875	700	500	350

No. 17

This is the standard, plain version with open sights.

	NIB	EXC.	V.G.	GOOD	FAIR	POOR
	—	600	435	325	175	125

No. 20

This version is chambered for the .22 or .32 rimfire shot cartridges and has a smoothbore barrel and no rear sight.

	NIB	EXC.	V.G.	GOOD	FAIR	POOR
	—	650	475	350	175	125

No. 21

This version is known as the Bicycle rifle and features a 20" barrel with open sights standard. It was furnished with a canvas carrying case that would be worth approximately a 30 percent premium. It was manufactured between 1898 and 1903.

	NIB	EXC.	V.G.	GOOD	FAIR	POOR
	—	800	625	375	170	110

	NIB	EXC.	V.G.	GOOD	FAIR	POOR

No. 21 Ladies Model

This version bears the same model number as the Bicycle rifle but has a 24" barrel and a high grade, checkered walnut stock with a Swiss buttplate. It features a vernier tang sight. It was manufactured between 1910 and 1916.

	NIB	EXC.	V.G.	GOOD	FAIR	POOR
	—	7000	5500	3750	2200	1100

No. 16

This version is known as the "Crack Shot." It is chambered for .22 or .32 rimfire cartridges with a 20" round barrel. It has a rolling-block-type action with a thumb lever on the side. It is a utility-type rifle with open sights, a blued and case-colored finish, and a plain two-piece walnut stock with a rubber buttplate. The barrel is marked "Crack Shot" along with the standard Stevens' barrel address markings. It was manufactured between 1900 and 1913.

	NIB	EXC.	V.G.	GOOD	FAIR	POOR
	—	600	500	350	225	100

No. 16-1/2

This version is similar to the No. 16 except that it is chambered for the .32 rimfire shot cartridge with a smoothbore barrel. It was manufactured between 1900 and 1913.

	NIB	EXC.	V.G.	GOOD	FAIR	POOR
	—	625	525	375	250	125

No. 23—Sure Shot

This version is chambered for the .22 rimfire cartridge. It has a 20" round barrel that pivots to the right for loading. There is a barrel release on the frame. This version is blued and case-colored, with a plain walnut buttstock and no fore-end. It was manufactured between 1894 and 1897.

	NIB	EXC.	V.G.	GOOD	FAIR	POOR
	—	2700	2375	1500	1000	600

No. 15

This version also known as "Maynard Junior". Chambered for .22 rimfire cartridge and has an 18" part-octagonal barrel. Action is similar to Civil War Maynard rifle, with a trigger guard-activating lever. Finish is all blued, with board-type buttstock and no forearm. Barrel marked "Stevens Maynard, J. R." in addition to the standard Stevens' barrel address. Manufactured between 1902 and 1912.

	NIB	EXC.	V.G.	GOOD	FAIR	POOR
	—	600	500	350	225	100

No. 15-1/2

This is a smoothbore version of the No. 15.

	NIB	EXC.	V.G.	GOOD	FAIR	POOR
	—	625	525	375	250	125

No. 14

Also known as "Little Scout". It is a utility takedown rifle that is blued, with a one-piece board-type stock. Features a rolling-block-type action. Manufactured between 1906 and 1910.

	NIB	EXC.	V.G.	GOOD	FAIR	POOR
	—	550	425	300	225	100

No. 14-1/2

This version is similar to the No. 14 except that it has a two-piece stock. It is also marked "Little Scout." It was manufactured between 1911 and 1941.

	NIB	EXC.	V.G.	GOOD	FAIR	POOR
	—	500	375	200	150	100

No. 65

This version is known as the "Little Krag". It is a single-shot bolt-action rifle chambered for the .22 rimfire cartridge. It has a one-piece stock and a 20" round barrel that was marked "Little Krag". This version is quite scarce. It was manufactured between 1903 and 1910.

	NIB	EXC.	V.G.	GOOD	FAIR	POOR
	—	600	500	350	200	100

No. 12

This version is also known as the "Marksman". It is chambered for the .22, .25, and the .32 rimfire cartridges. It has a 22" barrel that pivots upward for loading. It is activated by an S-shaped trigger guard lever. It was manufactured between 1911 and 1930.

	NIB	EXC.	V.G.	GOOD	FAIR	POOR
	—	550	425	300	225	100

No. 26

This version is also known as the "Crack Shot". It has a rolling block-type action and is chambered for .22 or the .32 rimfire cartridges. It is offered with an 18" or 20" round barrel. It is blued and has a two-piece stock. It was manufactured between 1912 and 1939.

	NIB	EXC.	V.G.	GOOD	FAIR	POOR
	—	550	425	300	225	100

	NIB	EXC.	V.G.	GOOD	FAIR	POOR

No. 26-1/2

This is the smoothbore version of the No. 26.

	—	550	500	350	250	100

No. 11—Junior

Single-shot rolling block rifle chambered for .22 rimfire cartridge. Has a 20" blued barrel and board-type stock without a buttplate. Last model offered in Boy's Rifle series. Manufactured between 1924 and 1931.

	—	550	425	300	225	100

Model 71

This was a reintroduced version of the "Stevens Favorite." It is chambered for the .22 LR cartridge and has a 22" octagonal barrel. The finish is blued and case-colored, with a plain walnut stock that has an inlaid medallion and a crescent buttplate. There were 10,000 manufactured in 1971.

	400	300	175	125	100	75

Model 72

This is a reintroduced version of the "Crack Shot" that features a single-shot, falling block action. It is chambered for the .22 rimfire cartridge and has a 22" octagon barrel with open sights. It is blued and case-colored, with a straight walnut stock. It was introduced in 1972.

	400	300	175	125	100	75

Model 70

This is a slide-action rifle chambered for the .22 rimfire cartridge. It is also known as the "Visible Loading Rifle." It features a 20" round barrel with a 3/4-length, tubular magazine. The finish is blued and case-colored, and it has a walnut stock. It features open sights but was available with other options. It was offered as the No. 70-1/2, 71, 71-1/2, 72, and 72-1/2. These different model numbers denote various sight combinations. Otherwise, they are identical. They were manufactured between 1907 and 1932.

	—	450	350	225	100	75

No. 80

This is a slide-action repeating rifle chambered for the .22 rimfire cartridge. It has a 24" round barrel with a tubular magazine. It features open sights and is blued, with a walnut stock. It was manufactured between 1906 and 1910.

	—	500	350	225	175	100

High Power Rifle

This is a series of lever-action hunting rifles chambered for the .25, .300, .32, and the .35 Remington centerfire cartridges. It features a 22" round barrel with a tubular magazine. The finish is blued, with a walnut stock. It is available in four variations: the No. 425, No. 430, No. 435, and the No. 440. These designations denote increased ornamentation and high quality materials and workmanship used in construction. There were approximately 26,000 manufactured between 1910 and 1917.

No. 425

	—	1150	900	600	300	200

No. 430

	—	1300	1000	650	400	300

No. 435

	—	1750	1400	1000	600	400

No. 440

	—	3350	3000	2400	1600	850

SPORTING PISTOLS

Beginning in 1869 the Stevens Company produced a series of single-shot, break-open target and sporting pistols that pivot upward for loading. They are chambered for the .22 and the .25 rimfire cartridges, as well as various centerfire cartridges from the .32 Short Colt to the .44 Russian. These pistols were made with various barrel lengths and have either a spur trigger or conventional trigger with a guard. They are all single-actions with exposed hammers. The finishes are nickel-plated frames with blued barrels and walnut grips. These variations and their values are listed.

Six-inch Pocket Rifle

This version is chambered for the .22 rimfire cartridge and has a 6" part-octagonal barrel with open sights. The barrel is marked "J. Stevens & Co. Chicopee Falls, Mass." There were approximately 1,000 manufactured between 1869 and 1886.

—	750	500	400	350	200

No. 36

This version is known as the Stevens-Lord pistol. It is chambered for various rimfire and centerfire calibers up to .44 Russian. It is offered with a 10" or 12" part-octagonal barrel and features a firing pin in the frame with a bushing. It has a conventional trigger with a spurred trigger guard. It features the standard Stevens barrel address. It was named after Frank Lord, a target shooter well-known at this time. There were approximately 3,500 manufactured from 1880 to 1911.

—	1750	1400	1000	650	400

First Issue Stevens-Conlin

This version is chambered for the .22 or .32 rimfire cartridges. It has a 10" or 12" part-octagonal barrel. It features a plated brass frame with a blued barrel and checkered walnut grips with a weighted buttcap. This version has a spur trigger either with or without a trigger guard. It was named after James Conlin, the owner of a shooting gallery located in New York City. There were approximately 500 manufactured between 1880 and 1884.

—	2700	2300	1700	900	500

Second Issue Stevens-Conlin No. 38

Similar to First Issue, with conventional trigger, spurred trigger guard and fully adjustable rear sight. Approximately 6,000 manufactured between 1884 and 1903.

—	1850	1625	1200	800	450

No. 37

This version is also known as the Stevens-Gould and was named after a 19th century firearms writer. It resembles the No. 38 without the spur on the trigger guard. There were approximately 1,000 manufactured between 1889 and 1903.

—	2600	2200	1300	850	450

No. 35

This version chambered for .22 rimfire, .22 Stevens-Pope and .25 Stevens cartridges. Offered with 6", 8", 10" or 12.25" part-octagonal barrel. Firing pin has no bushing. Features an iron frame that is either blued or plated with a blued barrel. Plain walnut grips with a weighted buttcap. It featured open sights. Approximately 43,000 manufactured between 1923 and 1942. **NOTE:** Longer barrels worth a premium.

—	450	325	275	175	100

No. 35 Target

This version is similar to the No. 35 but has a better quality trigger guard and sights. There were approximately 35,000 manufactured between 1907 and 1916.

—	500	400	325	200	100

No. 35 Off-Hand/Auto-Shot Shot Gun

The Stevens No. 35 is a .410 bore pistol manufactured by the J. Stevens Arms Co., Chicopee Falls, Massachusetts. It was available with an 8" or 12.25" smoothbore barrel, for 2.5" shells only, in two variations: the Off-Hand Shot Gun (1923 to 1929) and the Auto-Shot (1929 to 1934). Total production is unknown because the .410 and .22 rimfire variations of the No. 35 share the same serial number range. Researcher Ken Cope estimates total Auto-Shot production was approximately 2,000, and Off-Hand production at 20,000 to 25,000. Production was halted after the government ruled the .410 Stevens to be a "firearm" in the "any other weapon" category under the NFA in 1934, when its retail price was about $12. The Stevens does not possess the same collector appeal as other .410 smoothbore pistols, because (1) its relatively light weight makes it an uncomfortable shooter, and (2) the gun is not well made. **NOTE:** 8" barrel commands a 25 to 50 percent premium.

No. 35 Off-Hand Shot Gun

Serial range from 1 to 43357.

—	400	250	200	100	75

No. 35 Auto-Shot

—	450	300	200	125	100

	NIB	EXC.	V.G.	GOOD	FAIR	POOR

No. 43

This version also called the Diamond. Produced in two distinct variations called the First Issue and Second Issue. First Issue has a brass frame; Second Issue an iron frame and no firing pin bushing. Otherwise they are quite similar and would be valued the same. They are chambered for .22 rimfire cartridge and offered with either 6" or 10" part-octagonal barrel. Frames are either nickel-plated or blued, with blued barrels and square-butt walnut grips. Approximately 95,000 manufactured between 1886 and 1916. **NOTE:** Add 25 percent premium for 10" barrels.

—	600	400	250	150	75

No. 10 Target Pistol

This version was a departure from its predecessors. Very much resembles a semi-automatic pistol, but in reality a single-shot. Chambered for .22 rimfire cartridge. Has an 8" round barrel that pivots upward for loading. It has a blued steel frame, with checkered rubber grips. Instead of the usual exposed hammer, this version has a knurled cocking piece that extends through the rear of the frame. Approximately 7,000 manufactured between 1919 and 1933.

—	400	300	200	150	100

POCKET RIFLES

This series of pistols is similar to the target and sporting pistols except that these were produced with detachable shoulder stocks that bear the same serial number as the pistol with which they were sold. They are sometimes referred to as Bicycle rifles. The collector interest in these weapons is quite high; but it would behoove one to be familiar with the provisions of the Gun Control Act of 1968 when dealing in or collecting this variation—as when the stock is attached, they can fall into the category of a short-barreled rifle. Some are considered to be curios and relics, and others have been totally declassified; but some models may still be restricted. We strongly recommend securing a qualified, individual appraisal on these highly collectible firearms if a transaction is contemplated.**NOTE:** The values supplied include the matching shoulder stock. If the stock number does not match the pistol, the values would be approximately 25 percent less; and with no stock at all, 50 percent should be deducted.

Old Model Pocket Rifle

This version is chambered for the .22 rimfire cartridge and has an 8" or 10" part-octagonal barrel. It has a spur trigger and an external hammer on which the firing pin is mounted. The extractor is spring-loaded. It has a plated brass frame, blued barrel, and either walnut or rosewood grips. The shoulder stock is either nickel-plated or black. The barrel is marked "J. Stevens & Co. Chicopee Falls, Mass." There were approximately 4,000 manufactured between 1869 and 1886.

—	900	700	550	325	200

Reliable Pocket Rifle

This version is chambered for the .22 rimfire cartridge and in appearance is quite similar to the Old Model. The basic difference is that the extractor operates as a part of the pivoting barrel mechanism instead of being spring-loaded. The barrel is marked "J. Stevens A&T Co." There were approximately 4,000 manufactured between 1886 and 1896.

—	800	625	500	400	300

No. 42 Reliable Pocket Rifle

This version is similar to the first issue Reliable except that it has an iron frame with the firing pin mounted in it without a bushing. The shoulder stock is shaped differently. There were approximately 8,000 manufactured between 1896 and 1916.

—	700	575	475	350	250

First Issue New Model Pocket Rifle

This version is the first of the medium-frame models with a frame width of 1". All of its predecessors have a 5/8" wide frame. This model is chambered for the .22 and .32 rimfire cartridges and is offered with barrel lengths of 10", 12", 15", or 18" that are part-octagonal in configuration. The external hammer has the firing pin mounted on it. It has a plated brass frame, blued barrel, and either walnut or rosewood grips. The shoulder stock is nickel-plated and fitted differently than the small-frame models in that there is a dovetail in the butt and the top leg is secured by a knurled screw. The barrel is marked "J. Stevens & Co. Chicopee Falls, Mass." There were approximately 8,000 manufactured between 1872 and 1875.

—	1100	1000	650	500	400

Second Issue New Model Pocket Rifle

This version is similar to the First Issue except that the firing pin is mounted in the frame with a bushing. There were approximately 15,000 manufactured between 1875 and 1896.

—	975	850	600	500	350

	NIB	EXC.	V.G.	GOOD	FAIR	POOR

Vernier Model

This version is similar to the Second Issue except that it features a vernier tang sight located on the back strap. There were approximately 1,500 manufactured between 1884 and 1896.

	—	1200	900	650	525	300

No. 40

This version is similar to its medium-frame predecessors except that it has a longer grip frame and a conventional trigger with trigger guard. There were approximately 15,000 manufactured between 1896 and 1916.

	—	975	850	650	400	300

No. 40-1/2

This version is similar to the No. 40, with a vernier tang sight mounted on the back strap. There were approximately 2,500 manufactured between 1896 and 1915.

	—	1100	975	700	550	400

No. 34 (Hunter's Pet)

This is the first of the heavy-frame pocket rifles that featured a 1.25" wide frame. This version is also known as the "Hunter's Pet." It is chambered for many popular cartridges from the .22 rimfire to the .44-40 centerfire. It is offered with a part-octagonal 18", 20", 22", or 24" barrel. It has a nickel-plated iron frame and blued barrel. The detachable stock is nickel-plated, and the grips are walnut. There were few produced with a brass frame; and if located, these would be worth twice the value indicated. The firing pin is mounted in the frame with the bushing, and it features a spur trigger. There were approximately 4,000 manufactured between 1872 and 1900.

	—	1250	1050	700	450	350

No. 34-1/2

This version is similar to the No. 34 except that it features a vernier tang sight mounted on the back strap. There were approximately 1,200 manufactured between 1884 and 1900.

	—	1425	1250	900	650	450

BOLT-ACTION UTILITY RIFLES

Stevens Company produced a number of inexpensive, utilitarian, bolt-action rifles. These were both single-shot and repeaters. They have been popular over the years as starter rifles for young shooters. Their values are quite similar and are listed for reference purposes only.

Model 053—Single-Shot
Model 066—Tube Mag.
Model 084—5-Shot Mag.
Model 15—Single-Shot
Model 419—Single-Shot
Model 49—Single-Shot
Model 51—Single-Shot
Model 53—Single-Shot
Model 66—Tube Mag.

Model 056—5-Shot Magazine
Model 083—Single-Shot
Model 086—Tube Magazine
Model 15Y—Single-Shot
Model 48—Single-Shot
Model 50—Single-Shot
Model 52—Single-Shot
Model 56—5-Shot Magazine

	—	—	200	100	70	50

Model 416

A target rifle chambered for .22 LR cartridge. Has 24" heavy barrel, with aperture sights. Features 5-round detachable magazine. Blued, with a target-type walnut stock.

	—	450	350	200	150	100

Model 322

This is a bolt-action sporting rifle chambered for the .22 Hornet cartridge. It has a 20" barrel with open sights and a detachable box magazine. The finish is blued, with a plain walnut stock.

	—	175	125	100	75	50

Model 322-S

This version features an aperture rear sight.

	—	225	125	100	75	50

	NIB	EXC.	V.G.	GOOD	FAIR	POOR

Model 89

This is a single-shot, Martini-type, falling-block rifle chambered for the .22 LR cartridge. It has an 18.5" barrel and a trigger guard loop-lever activator. The finish is blued, with a straight walnut stock. It was introduced in 1976 and is no longer manufactured.

—	125	80	70	60	40

Model 87M

Designed to look like the M1 Garand this rifle was chambered for the .22 rimfire cartridge.

—	600	500	375	225	150

Model 987

This is a blowback-operated semi-automatic rifle chambered for the .22 LR cartridge. It has a 20" barrel with a 15-round tubular magazine. The finish is blued, with a hardwood stock.

—	150	100	75	50	25

ECONOMY LINE (SAVAGE, 2006)

Model 200

Long- or short-action bolt rifle chambered in .223, .22-250, .243, 7MM-08, .308, .25-06, .270, .30-06, 7mm RM, or .300 WM. Gray checkered synthetic stock and 22-inch (short-action) or 24-inch (long-action) blued sightless barrel. Introduced 2006.

325	275	225	175	125	100

Model 200XP Long or Short Action Package Rifle

Similar to above, with 4x12 scope.

375	300	250	200	150	125

Model 200XP Camo

Similar to above, with camo stock.

400	325	275	225	175	150

Cadet Mini-Youth

Similar to Savage Cub .22 rimfire. Introduced 2006.

200	150	125	100	75	50

Model 315 Youth

Similar to Cadet Mini-Youth, with sightless barrel. Introduced 2006.

200	150	125	100	75	50

Model 310

Five-shot bolt-action repeater chambered for .17 HMR. Detachable box magazine, synthetic stock, blued 20.75" sightless barrel. Introduced 2006.

200	150	125	100	75	50

Model 310 Heavy Barrel

Similar to Stevens Model 310, with 21" bull barrel. Introduced 2006.

225	175	150	115	75	50

Model 300

Clip-fed bolt-action repeater chambered for .22 rimfire. Gray synthetic stock and 20.75" blued barrel. Also available with scope package (add 10 percent). Introduced 2006.

200	150	125	100	75	50

Model 305

Similar to Model 310. Chambered in .22 WMR. Introduced 2006.

225	175	150	115	75	50

MISCELLANEOUS SINGLE-SHOT SHOTGUNS

This company manufactured a number of single barrel break-open, single-shot shotguns. They were produced chambered for various gauges with various-length barrels and chokes. They are quite similar in appearance and were designed as inexpensive utility-grade weapons. There is

	NIB	EXC.	V.G.	GOOD	FAIR	POOR

little or no collector interest in them at this time and their values are similar. They are listed for reference purposes only.

Model 89	Model 97	Model 108	Model 170
Model 90	Model 100	Model 110	Model 180
Model 93	Model 102	Model 120	Model 944
Model 94	Model 104	Model 125	Model 958
Model 94A	Model 105	Model 140	Model 970
Model 94C	Model 106	Model 160	
Model 95	Model 107	Model 165	

NIB	EXC.	V.G.	GOOD	FAIR	POOR
—	150	100	75	50	25

Model 182

This is a single-shot, break-open shotgun chambered for 12 gauge. It is offered with a 30" or 32" trap choked barrels and features a hammerless action with an automatic ejector and a lightly engraved receiver. The finish is blued, with a checkered trap-grade stock.

NIB	EXC.	V.G.	GOOD	FAIR	POOR
—	175	125	100	75	50

Model 185

This version features a half-octagonal barrel with an automatic ejector and a checkered walnut stock. **NOTE:** Damascus barrel deduct 25 percent.

NIB	EXC.	V.G.	GOOD	FAIR	POOR
—	175	125	100	75	50

Model 190

This is a 12-gauge hammerless gun with an automatic ejector. It is lightly engraved with a half-octagonal barrel. **NOTE:** Damascus barrel deduct 25 percent.

NIB	EXC.	V.G.	GOOD	FAIR	POOR
—	175	125	100	75	50

Model 195

This is another deluxe version that features engraving, a half-octagonal barrel, and a high-grade, checkered walnut stock. **NOTE:** Damascus barrel deduct 25 percent.

NIB	EXC.	V.G.	GOOD	FAIR	POOR
—	350	250	200	150	100

Model 240

This over/under model features a boxlock frame with exposed hammers.

NIB	EXC.	V.G.	GOOD	FAIR	POOR
—	400	300	250	200	150

Model .22/.410

Over/under .22/.410 combo gun, with Tenite stock. Manufactured 1939-1950.

NIB	EXC.	V.G.	GOOD	FAIR	POOR
—	350	300	250	175	100

DOUBLE-BARREL SHOTGUNS

STEVENS BRAND

The firm of J. Stevens and its successors, produced a number of utility-grade side-by-side double-barrel shotguns between 1877 and 1988. They are chambered for 10-, 12-, 16- or 20-gauge and .410 bore. Stevens shotguns in 10-gauge and .410 bore will normally bring a premium as do guns with single triggers and ejectors. They have various length barrels and choke combinations. They feature double triggers and extractors except where noted. A complete list of Stevens brand models including the three in-house brands: Riverside, Springfield and Super Value, are listed.

Model 1877—Hammer Boxlock

NIB	EXC.	V.G.	GOOD	FAIR	POOR
—	575	450	350	250	200

Model 250—Hammer Sidelock

NIB	EXC.	V.G.	GOOD	FAIR	POOR
—	575	450	350	250	200

Model 225—Hammer Boxlock

NIB	EXC.	V.G.	GOOD	FAIR	POOR
—	575	450	350	250	200

Model 260—Hammer Sidelock

NIB	EXC.	V.G.	GOOD	FAIR	POOR
—	575	450	350	250	200

Model 270—Hammer Sidelock

NIB	EXC.	V.G.	GOOD	FAIR	POOR
—	575	450	350	250	200

	NIB	EXC.	V.G.	GOOD	FAIR	POOR

Model 280—Hammer Sidelock

		EXC.	V.G.	GOOD	FAIR	POOR
	—	575	450	350	250	200

Model 325—Hammerless Boxlock

	—	450	400	350	250	200

Model 350—Hammerless Boxlock

	—	450	400	350	250	200

Model 360—Hammerless Boxlock

	—	450	400	350	250	200

Model 370—Hammerless Boxlock

	—	450	400	350	250	200

Model 380—Hammerless Boxlock

	—	575	450	350	250	200

Model 235—Hammer Boxlock

	—	450	400	350	250	200

Model 335 (Early)—Hammerless Boxlock

	—	450	400	350	250	200

Model 335 (Late)—Hammerless Boxlock

	—	450	400	350	250	200

Model 255—Hammer Sidelock

	—	450	400	350	250	200

Model 265—Hammer Sidelock

	—	450	400	350	250	200

Model 355—Hammerless Boxlock

	—	800	575	450	350	250

Model 365—Hammerless Boxlock

	—	925	625	500	400	300

Model 375 (London Proofs)—Hammerless Boxlock

	—	1500	950	700	450	350

Model 375 (U.S.)—Hammerless Boxlock

	—	1100	700	575	400	300

Model 385 (London Proofs)—Hammerless Boxlock

	—	1650	1050	700	450	350

Model 385 (U.S.)—Hammerless Boxlock

	—	1200	850	575	450	300

Model 345—Hammerless Boxlock

	—	575	450	350	250	200

Model 330—Hammerless Boxlock

	—	450	400	350	250	200

Model 515—Hammerless Boxlock

	—	625	525	450	350	300

Model 515—Single Trigger Hammerless Boxlock

	—	750	575	450	350	300

Model 500—Skeet Hammerless Boxlock

	—	1250	925	800	700	400

Model 530—Hammerless Boxlock

	—	450	400	350	250	200

	NIB	EXC.	V.G.	GOOD	FAIR	POOR

Model 530M—Tenite Hammerless Boxlock

	—	450	400	350	250	200

Model 530M—Tenite Single Trigger Hammerless Boxlock

	—	750	575	450	350	300

Model 530A—Hammerless Boxlock

	—	450	400	350	250	200

Model 530A—Single Trigger Hammerless Boxlock

	—	525	450	350	300	250

Model 311—Tenite Hammerless Boxlock

	—	450	400	350	250	200

Model 331—Single Trigger Hammerless Boxlock

	—	525	400	300	250	200

Model 311—Tenite Single Trigger Hammerless Boxlock

	—	575	500	450	350	300

Model 311A—Hammerless Boxlock

	—	525	450	350	250	200

Model 311C—Hammerless Boxlock

	—	400	350	250	200	150

Model 311D—Hammerless Boxlock

	—	450	400	350	250	200

Model 311E—Hammerless Boxlock

	—	600	450	400	300	250

Model 311F—Hammerless Boxlock

	—	450	400	350	250	200

Model 311H—Hammerless Boxlock

	—	450	400	350	250	200

Model 311H—Vent Rib Hammerless Boxlock

	—	500	450	350	300	250

Model 311J/R—Hammerless Boxlock

	—	400	350	250	200	150

Model 311J/R—Solid Rib Hammerless Boxlock

	—	400	350	250	200	150

Model 311H—Waterfowler Hammerless Boxlock

	—	700	575	450	350	250

Model 240—.410 Over/Under Hammer Tenite

RIVERSIDE BRAND

Model 215—Hammer Boxlock

	—	750	525	400	250	200

Model 315 (Early)—Hammerless Boxlock

	—	575	450	350	250	200

Model 315 (Late)—Hammerless Boxlock

	—	575	450	350	250	200

SUPER VALUE BRAND

Model 511—Hammerless Boxlock

	—	525	400	300	200	150

	NIB	EXC.	V.G.	GOOD	FAIR	POOR

Model 511—Sunken Rib Hammerless Boxlock

NIB	EXC.	V.G.	GOOD	FAIR	POOR
—	575	450	350	200	150

SPRINGFIELD BRAND

Model 215—Hammer Boxlock

NIB	EXC.	V.G.	GOOD	FAIR	POOR
—	575	450	350	250	150

Model 311—Hammerless Boxlock

NIB	EXC.	V.G.	GOOD	FAIR	POOR
—	575	450	350	250	150

Model 315—Hammerless Boxlock

NIB	EXC.	V.G.	GOOD	FAIR	POOR
—	575	450	350	250	200

Model 3150—Hammerless Boxlock

NIB	EXC.	V.G.	GOOD	FAIR	POOR
—	700	575	400	250	200

Model 3151—Hammerless Boxlock

NIB	EXC.	V.G.	GOOD	FAIR	POOR
—	850	700	450	350	250

Model 3151—Single Trigger Hammerless Boxlock

NIB	EXC.	V.G.	GOOD	FAIR	POOR
—	950	800	575	450	300

Model 311—Single Trigger Hammerless Boxlock

NIB	EXC.	V.G.	GOOD	FAIR	POOR
—	800	700	575	450	300

Model 5151—Hammerless Boxlock

NIB	EXC.	V.G.	GOOD	FAIR	POOR
—	575	450	350	250	200

Model 5151—Single Trigger Hammerless Boxlock

NIB	EXC.	V.G.	GOOD	FAIR	POOR
—	700	525	400	300	200

Model 311—New Style Hammerless Boxlock

NIB	EXC.	V.G.	GOOD	FAIR	POOR
—	575	450	350	250	150

Model 311—New Style Tenite Hammerless Boxlock

NIB	EXC.	V.G.	GOOD	FAIR	POOR
—	575	450	350	250	150

Model 511—Sunken Rib Hammerless Boxlock

NIB	EXC.	V.G.	GOOD	FAIR	POOR
—	575	450	350	250	150

Model 511—Hammerless Boxlock

NIB	EXC.	V.G.	GOOD	FAIR	POOR
—	525	400	300	200	150

Model 511A—Hammerless Boxlock

NIB	EXC.	V.G.	GOOD	FAIR	POOR
—	525	400	300	200	150

STEVENS/SAVAGE SHOTGUNS

Model 411 Upland Sporter

Introduced in 2003. Side-by-side shotgun chambered for 12- or 20-gauge and .410 bore. The 12-gauge fitted with 28" barrels; 20-gauge and .410 have 26" barrels. Single trigger with ejectors. False sideplates are laser engraved. European walnut stock, with pistol-grip and splinter fore-end. Weight about 6.75 to 6.5 lbs. depending on gauge. **NOTE:** Add 50 percent for 20-gauge and .410 bore models.

NIB	EXC.	V.G.	GOOD	FAIR	POOR
550	425	350	300	200	125

STEVENS DATE CODE

Collectors will find a date code stamped on every double-barrel shotgun in the Stevens brands produced between March 1949 and December 1968. Usually, it is behind the hinge pin or ahead of the trigger guard on the bottom of the frame. It will appear as a small circle containing a number and letter. The letters correspond to the years shown in the following table. Significance of the numbers is not known.

	NIB	EXC.	V.G.	GOOD	FAIR	POOR

DATE CODES

A-1949	B-1950	C-1951	D-1952
E-1953	F-1954	G-1955	H-1956
I-1957	J-1958	K-1959	L-1960
M-1961	N-1962	P-1963	R-1964
S-1965	T-1966	U-1967	V-1968
W-1969	X-1970		

BOLT-ACTION SHOTGUNS

The Stevens Company produced a number of bolt-action shotguns that are either single-shot or repeaters. They are chambered for the 20 gauge or .410 and blued with walnut stocks. The values for these utility-grade shotguns are similar.

Model 237—Single-Shot   Model 39—Tube Magazine
Model 258—Clip Fed   Model 58—Clip Fed
Model 37—Single-Shot   Model 59—Tube Magazine
Model 38—Clip Fed

—	125	100	75	50	35

SLIDE-ACTION UTILITY-GRADE SHOTGUNS

J. Stevens Arms Company also produced a series of utility-grade slide-action shotguns. They are chambered for various gauges, barrel lengths and chokes. Finishes are blued, with walnut stocks. Values are similar and listed for reference purposes.

Model 67   Model 77-AC   Model 520   Model 621
Model 67-VR   Model 77-M   Model 522   Model 820
Model 77   Model 77-SC   Model 620

—	225	150	125	100	75

Model 620 U.S. Marked Trench Gun

NOTE: Add $150 for bayonet.

—	3000	2500	1650	1200	750

Model 124

A manually-operated bolt-action shotgun chambered for 12-gauge. Has 28" barrel, with various chokes, blued and brown plastic Tenite stock. An odd duck: looks like a semi-automatic and is often mistaken for such.

—	225	175	75	65	50

Model 67

Slide-action shotgun chambered for 12- or 20 gauge and .410 bore. Has 3" chambers. Offered with various barrel lengths and choke tubes, with 5-shot tube magazine. Features a blued steel receiver, with a walnut stock. Discontinued in 1989.

	250	175	150	100	75

Model 675

Slide-action shotgun chambered for 12-gauge, with 24" vent rib barrel and iron sights. Finish is blued, with a hardwood stock and recoil pad. Manufactured in 1987 and 1988.

—	275	240	200	150	100

Model 69-RXL

A matte-finished riot version of Model 67 series slide-action shotgun. Has 18.25" cylinder-bore barrel and furnished with a recoil pad. Discontinued in 1989.

—	250	175	150	100	75

Model 350 Pump Shotgun

Pump-action shotgun chambered for 2.75" and 3" 12-gauge. Features include all-steel barrel and receiver; bottom-load and -eject design; black synthetic stock; 5+1 capacity. Price: $267 (Field Model w/ 28" barrel, screw-in choke); $241 (Security Model w/ 18" barrel, fixed choke); $307 (Combo Model with Field and Security barrels); $254 (Security Model with 18.25" barrel w/ ghost ring rear sight).

	NIB	EXC.	V.G.	GOOD	FAIR	POOR

STEYR
Steyr, Austria

STEYR & MANNLICHER PISTOLS

By Joseph Schroeder: Not all Mannlicher pistols made by Steyr. Many pistols made by Steyr were not designed by Mannlicher. However, since by far greatest number of Mannlicher's pistols were made by Steyr we believe it will be appropriate to include all of Ferdinand Ritter von Mannlicher's pistols along with other Steyr designs under this heading.

Schoenberger

Considered by many to be the first "commercial" semi-automatic pistol. Only about two dozen were made in 1892. Steyr-made 8mm Schoenberger was based on patents granted to Laumann in 1890-91. Had a magazine in front of trigger guard. Too rare to price.

Mannlicher Model 1894

Mannlicher's first "successful" self-loading pistol. Model 1894 had a blow-forward action and double-action lockwork. Earliest examples were made in Austria, probably by Steyr, in 7.6mm. Greatest number made by SIG in 1896-97 for Swiss army tests. These 100 pistols had shorter barrel, smaller frame and in 6.5mm. Prices are for Swiss examples. **NOTE:** Add 20 percent for 7.6mm pistols.

—	13200	9900	6600	5500	3000

Mannlicher Model 1896/03

Most confusing of Mannlicher's pistols. Earliest examples, which have fixed magazine and ribbed barrel, may have been made by Steyr and are very rare. Later versions, with removable box magazine, have been called "Model 1896/03" and "Model 1901", and made as both pistol and pistol-carbine, possibly in Switzerland. Chambered for 7.65mm Mannlicher cartridge, which is really a 7.65mm Borchardt. Prices listed are for standard later model pistol or pistol-carbine (12" barrel, tangent sight); double prices for early pistol or late model pistol with detachable holster stock.

—	8250	5500	3850	2750	1500

Mannlicher Model 1899

Earliest version of Mannlicher's final semi-automatic pistol design. Only about 250 made by Dreyse in Soemmerda, Germany. Chambered for tapered case 7.63mm Mannlicher cartridge. Distinguished by large safety lever on left side, takedown screw under barrel and Dreyse markings.

—	9400	7150	4950	3850	2000

Mannlicher Model 1901

Marked "WAFFENFABRIK Steyr" on left side and "SYSTEM MANNLICHER" on right. Model 1901 is distinguished by its checkered grips, rear sight located on rear of barrel, 8-round fixed magazine. Serial numbers to little over 1000.

—	3300	2450	1750	900	700

Mannlicher Model 1905

Improved version of Model 1901. Longer grip holding 10 rounds, grooved wooden grips, rear sight on rear of breechblock and "MODEL 1905" added to right side. Later production moved all markings to left side so Argentine crest could be placed on right side. Prices listed for original commercial Model 1905, NOT a re-blued Argentine contract with crest ground off. Subtract 60 percent for reworked examples.

—	2425	1875	1350	800	400

Argentine Contract

—	2750	2250	1650	900	500

Roth Steyr Model 1907

Based on patents granted to Karel Krnka and Georg Roth. The 8mm Model 1907 had rotating barrel locking system and was first self-loading pistol adopted by Austro-Hungarian Army. **NOTE:** Add 20 percent for early Steyr examples without large pin visible on right side of frame, or for those made in Budapest instead of Steyr. Slight premium for correct stripper clips.

—	1250	750	600	350	250

Steyr Model 1908 Pocket Pistol

Based on Belgian patents of Nicholas Pieper. These .25 and .32 caliber pocket pistols featured tipping barrels built by Steyr under license from Pieper in Liege. Production suspended during WWI, but may have resumed after war ended. Prices for either caliber.

—	385	275	165	100	75

	NIB	EXC.	V.G.	GOOD	FAIR	POOR

Steyr Hahn Model 1911 Commercially Marked

NOTE: Military versions of this model see Standard Catalog of Military Firearms.

	NIB	EXC.	V.G.	GOOD	FAIR	POOR
	—	2200	1650	1220	875	450

Steyr Model SP

Steyr's first post WWII pistol. Model SP was a beautifully made .32 ACP. Being double-action-only and more expensive than most of its contemporaries, was not competitive and discontinued in early 1960s. Fewer than 1,000 made. Slide marked "STEYR-DAIMLER-PUCH A.G. MOD.SP KAL. 7.65mm".

	—	950	825	550	385	200

Steyr Model GB

GB introduced in mid-1970s as a 9mm Parabellum military pistol. Large in size, with 18-round magazine capacity. Other features included polygon rifling and gas trap around barrel to delay breech opening. Initially produced as Rogak P-18 by L.E.S. of Morton Grove, Illinois. Discontinued due in part to quality control problems. Just over 2,000 made. Later production by Steyr as GB was to much higher standards, but GB never achieved much popularity and discontinued in 1988.

Rogak P-18

	—	425	350	250	175	125

Steyr GB

	—	800	675	525	400	200

RIFLES

Following Steyr/Mannlicher guns were imported by GSI Inc. Trussville, Alabama. **NOTE:** Earlier models see Mannlicher Schoenauer.

SPORTER SERIES

Series includes rifles that are lightweight and have reduced overall length. All Sporter models have interchangeable 5-round rotary magazine. Stock is oil-finished walnut in either Mannlicher full stock design or half stock version. In both stock configurations an oval European cheekpiece is standard. Rifles offered in four different action lengths: SL (super light), L (light), M (medium) or S (magnum). Also available either single-/double set triggers.

Model M72 L/M

.243, .270, 7x57mm, 7x64mm, .308 or .30-06 caliber bolt-action rifle, with 23" fluted barrel and single-/double set triggers. Blued, checkered walnut stock. Manufactured from 1972 to 1980.

	—	1325	1025	750	550	450

Model SL

Model features super light action. Offered with 20" barrel in full stock version or 23-1/6" barrel in half stock version. Rubber buttpad standard. Model does not have fore-end tip on its half stock variation. Offered in following calibers: .222 Rem., .222 Rem. Magnum, .223 and 5.6x50 Magnum. Weighs about 6.2 lbs. with full stock; 6.3 lbs. with half stock.

2000	1650	1000	750	500	300

Model SL Carbine

As above, with 20" fluted barrel. Mannlicher-style stock.

1950	1750	1050	800	550	350

Varmint Model

Model features heavy 26" barrel. Chambered for .222 Rem., .223, 5.6x57, .243 Win., .308 Win. and .22-250. Fore-end of stock is ventilated. Grip enlarged and textured. Choice of single-/double set triggers. Recoil pad standard. Weighs about 8 lbs.

1950	1750	1050	800	550	350

Model L

Rifle has light action. Offered in same stock configuration and barrel lengths as Model SL. Calibers are: 5.6x57, .243 Win., .308, .22-250 and 6mm Rem. Weighs about 6.3 lbs. with full stock; 6.4 lbs. with half stock.

1850	1650	1000	750	500	300

Luxus Series

Luxury model offers choice of full or half stock variations in select walnut, with fine line checkering. Pistol grip is steeply angled. Luxus rifles fitted with swept back European cheekpiece. Single set trigger standard. Box magazine holds 3 rounds. Optional engraving and

NIB	EXC.	V.G.	GOOD	FAIR	POOR

stock carving may be encountered on these models, that will dramatically affect price. Luxus rifles available with light, medium or magnum length actions.

Luxus Model L

Same dimensions and barrel lengths as Sporter version. Calibers are: 5.6x57, .243 Win., .308, .22-250 and 6mm Rem.

NIB	EXC.	V.G.	GOOD	FAIR	POOR
2400	2000	1100	800	600	350

Luxus Model M

Same dimensions and barrel lengths as Sporter Model M. Available in these calibers: 6.5x57, .270 Win., 7x64, .30-06, 9.3x 626.5x55, 7.5 Swiss, 7x57 and 8x57JS.

NIB	EXC.	V.G.	GOOD	FAIR	POOR
2400	2000	1100	800	600	350

Luxus Model S

Same as Sporter Model S. Offered in following calibers: 6.5x68, 7mm Rem. Magnum, .300 Win. Magnum and 8x68S.

NIB	EXC.	V.G.	GOOD	FAIR	POOR
2400	2000	1100	800	600	350

Model M

Model features medium action. Has same barrel and stock configurations as other two models listed above. Exception, has no buttpad and does have fore-end tip on its half stock variation. Available in these calibers: 6.5x57, .270 Win., 7x64, .30-06, 9.3x62, 6.5x55, 7.5 Swiss, 7x57 and 8x57JS. Weighs about 6.8 lbs. with full stock; 7 lbs. with half stock.

NIB	EXC.	V.G.	GOOD	FAIR	POOR
2500	2100	1200	900	600	300

Professional Model M

Model fitted with medium weight action. Features black synthetic checkered stock. Comes fitted with ventilated rubber recoil pad. Offered with 20" or 23.6" barrel. Available with single-/double set trigger. Available in these calibers: 6.5x57, .270 Win., 7x64, .30-06, 9.3x62, 6.5x55, 7.5 Swiss, 7x57 and 8x57JS. Weighs about 7.25 lbs.

NIB	EXC.	V.G.	GOOD	FAIR	POOR
1500	1200	950	700	600	300

Model S/T

Similar to above in heavy barreled version. Offered in these calibers: 9.3x64, .375 H&H and .458 Win. Magnum. Optional buttstock magazine available. Weighs about 9 lbs.

NIB	EXC.	V.G.	GOOD	FAIR	POOR
2100	1900	1400	1100	800	500

Tropical Rifle

As above, with 26" heavy barrel. Chambered for .375 Holland & Holland and .458 Winchester Magnum. Not imported after 1985.

NIB	EXC.	V.G.	GOOD	FAIR	POOR
—	2000	1750	1100	650	450

Model MIII Professional

Introduced in 1995. Economy version of Model M Professional. Fitted with 23.5" barrel, black synthetic stock and choice of single-/double set triggers. Offered in .25-06, .270 Win., .30-06 and 7x64 calibers. Weight about 7 lb. 5 oz. **NOTE:** Checkered walnut stock add $100.

NIB	EXC.	V.G.	GOOD	FAIR	POOR
1000	800	600	400	300	200

STEYR SBS (SAFE BOLT SYSTEM)

Series introduced in 1997. Features a newly designed bolt. Offered in two distinct models: SBS Forester and SBS ProHunter.

SBS ProHunter

Model has 23.6" barrel, 4-round magazine and single adjustable trigger. Offered in .243 Win., .25-06, .270 Win., 7mm-08, .308 Win., .30-06, 7mm Rem. Magnum, .300 Win. Magnum and several European calibers. Weight about 7.5 lbs. Furnished with black synthetic stock, recoil pad and buttspacers. Introduced in 1999. **NOTE:** Add $150-$300 for custom metric calibers; $30 for 7mm Magnum and .300 Win. Magnum calibers.

NIB	EXC.	V.G.	GOOD	FAIR	POOR
750	650	575	400	300	150

SBS ProHunter Stainless Steel

Same as ProHunter model, with stainless steel action and barrel. Introduced in 2000. **NOTE:** Add $150-$300 for custom metric calibers; $30 for 7mm Magnum and .300 Win. Magnum calibers.

NIB	EXC.	V.G.	GOOD	FAIR	POOR
900	750	675	500	400	250

SBS ProHunter Camo

Same as standard ProHunter, with camo synthetic stock. **NOTE:** Add $150-$300 for custom metric calibers; $30 for 7mm Magnum and .300 Win. Magnum calibers.

NIB	EXC.	V.G.	GOOD	FAIR	POOR
1000	850	700	575	400	200

NIB	EXC.	V.G.	GOOD	FAIR	POOR

SBS ProHunter Camo Stainless Steel

Same as above, with stainless steel action and barrel. **NOTE:** Add $150-$300 for custom metric calibers; $30 for 7mm Magnum and .300 Win. Magnum calibers.

1050	900	750	600	475	250

SBS ProHunter Mountain Rifle

Chambered for .243, .25-06, .270 and 7mm-08 calibers. Fitted with 20" barrel and no sights. Receiver engraved "Mountain Rifle". Synthetic stock with recoil pad standard. Weight is 7.25 lbs. Introduced in 1999.

1000	850	700	575	400	200

SBS Pro-Hunter Mountain Stainless Steel

Same as ProHunter Mountain, with stainless steel action and barrel. Introduced in 2000.

1050	900	750	600	425	200

SBS ProHunter Mountain Camo

Same as ProHunter, with camo synthetic stock. Introduced in 2000.

1150	1000	850	700	475	250

SBS ProHunter Mountain Camo Stainless Steel

Same as above, with stainless steel action and barrel. Introduced in 2000.

1150	1000	850	700	475	250

SBS ProHunter (Youth/Ladies)

Fitted with walnut stock and buttspacers (to create shorter length of pull). Extra thick recoil pad. Chambered for .243, 7mm-08 and .308. Weight about 7.25 lbs. Introduced in 1999.

1000	850	700	575	400	200

SBS ProHunter Compact

Same as above, with black synthetic stock. Offered with stainless steel action and barrel. **NOTE:** Add $80 for stainless steel.

1000	850	700	575	400	200

SBS ProHunter 376 Steyr

Chambered for .376 Steyr cartridge. Fitted with 20" barrel and iron sights. Synthetic stock, with special thick pad. Weight about 8 lbs. Introduced in 1999.

1200	950	800	675	400	200

SBS Forester

Same as Pro Hunter model. Furnished with walnut stock and recoil pad. **NOTE:** Add $150-$300 for custom metric calibers; $30 for 7mm Rem. Magnum and .300 Win. Magnum.

850	725	625	500	400	200

SBS Classic American

Features 23.6" barrel, single adjustable trigger, stain finish walnut stock with recoil pad. Offered in calibers from .243 to .300 Win. Magnum. Weight about 7.2 lbs. Introduced in 2000. **NOTE:** Add $150-$300 for custom metric calibers; $30 for 7mm Magnum and .300 Win. Magnum calibers.

1500	1100	850	650	500	300

SBS Classic Mannlicher

Offered in same calibers as above, except for 7mm Rem. Magnum and .300 Win. Magnum. Fitted with 25.6" barrel. Walnut stock is full Mannlicher style, with recoil pad. Fitted with open sights. Weight about 7.2 lbs. Introduced in 2000.

2300	2000	1600	1000	675	400

SBS Forester Mountain Rifle

Walnut stock with 20" barrel and no sights. Chambered for a variety of calibers including .243, .25-06, .270, 7mm-08, .308, .30-06 and 6.5x55. Receiver engraved "Mountain Rifle". Introduced in 1999.

850	725	625	500	400	200

Mannlicher SBS European—Half Stock

Fitted with 23.6" barrel and iron sights. Chambered for wide variety of American and European calibers from .243 to 9.3x62. European style figured walnut stock. Adjustable trigger. Recoil pad. Weight about 7.5 lbs.

2795	2200	1750	1200	700	400

	NIB	EXC.	V.G.	GOOD	FAIR	POOR

Mannlicher SBS European—Half Stock Carbine

Same as above, with 20" barrel.

NIB	EXC.	V.G.	GOOD	FAIR	POOR
2795	2200	1750	1200	700	400

Mannlicher SBS European—Full Stock

Same as above, with full European stock covering 20" barrel.

NIB	EXC.	V.G.	GOOD	FAIR	POOR
2895	2300	1800	1250	750	450

Mannlicher SBS Magnum European—Half Stock

Chambered for 7mm Rem. Magnum, .300 Win. Magnum, 6.5x68 and 8x68S calibers. Fitted with 25.6" barrel and iron sights. Walnut stock. Weight about 7.75 lbs.

NIB	EXC.	V.G.	GOOD	FAIR	POOR
2895	2300	1800	1250	750	450

Steyr Scout—Jeff Cooper Package

Developed by Col. Jeff Cooper. Chambered for .308 Win. cartridge. Fitted with 19" fluted barrel. Stock is gray synthetic, with removable buttspacers and folding bi-pod. Magazine capacity 5 rounds, with optional 10-round magazines available. Weight about 7 lbs. with scope; 6.3 lbs. with no scope. Adjustable single trigger. Factory-installed Leupold M8 2.5x28mm scope. Introduced in 1998.

NIB	EXC.	V.G.	GOOD	FAIR	POOR
2600	2000	1600	1100	650	400

Steyr Scout Package

Similar to Jeff Cooper Package, without Jeff Cooper logo. Stock black synthetic. Offered in .223 Rem., .243 Win., 7mm-08 as well as .308 and .375 Steyr calibers.

NIB	EXC.	V.G.	GOOD	FAIR	POOR
2100	1800	1550	1000	700	400

Scout

Same as above but rifle only.

NIB	EXC.	V.G.	GOOD	FAIR	POOR
2100	1800	1550	1000	700	400

Steyr Scout Tactical

Model has 19.25" fluted barrel. Chambered for .223 or .308 Win. cartridge. Integral bipod. Emergency ghost ring sights. **NOTE:** Add $100 for stainless steel.

NIB	EXC.	V.G.	GOOD	FAIR	POOR
2050	1500	1000	800	750	425

PRECISION/TACTICAL RIFLES

Model SSG-PI

Model features black synthetic stock, originally designed as military sniper rifle. Fitted with cocking indicator, single-/double set trigger, 5-round rotary magazine or 10-round magazine. Receiver milled to NATO specifications for Steyr ring mounts. Barrel length 26". Weighs about 9 lbs. Offered in .308 Win. **NOTE:** Originally called SSG 69.

NIB	EXC.	V.G.	GOOD	FAIR	POOR
1700	1300	1000	800	600	400

SSG-PII Police Rifle

Version of SSG, with heavier 26" barrel. Larger knob-style bolt handle. Weighs about 10 lbs. 11 oz.

NIB	EXC.	V.G.	GOOD	FAIR	POOR
1700	1300	1000	800	600	400

SSK-PIIK Police Kurz

Similar to above, with 20" heavy barrel. Weight about 10 lbs.

NIB	EXC.	V.G.	GOOD	FAIR	POOR
1700	1300	1000	800	600	400

SSG-PII & PIIK McMillan

Fitted with McMillan A-3 stock, adjustable cheekpiece and removable buttspacers. Special forearm rail.

NIB	EXC.	V.G.	GOOD	FAIR	POOR
2300	1750	1350	950	750	500

SSG-PIV

Similar to PIIK, with 16.75" heavy barrel and removable flash hider. Barrel is threaded. Weight about 9 lbs. 11 oz.

NIB	EXC.	V.G.	GOOD	FAIR	POOR
2500	2000	1500	1000	750	500

Match

NIB	EXC.	V.G.	GOOD	FAIR	POOR
3000	2500	2000	1500	800	500

	NIB	EXC.	V.G.	GOOD	FAIR	POOR

SSG 08

Bolt-action chambered in .308 Win., .300 Win. Magnum and .338 Lapua Magnum. Barrel length 20" to 23.6", with muzzle-brake. Fully adjustable aluminum folding stock and pistol grip, Versa-Pod and optics rail.

NIB	EXC.	V.G.	GOOD	FAIR	POOR
5000	4000	3200	2500	2000	500

Match UIT

Designed as an international target rifle. Features special shaped pistol grip, adjustable trigger for length of pull and pressure. Enlarged bolt handle and non-glare barrel. Chambered for .308 Win. cartridge.

NIB	EXC.	V.G.	GOOD	FAIR	POOR
3900	3500	3000	2000	1500	1000

JAGD Match

Introduced in 1995. Features choice of 20" or 23.5" barrel with sights. Stock is laminated. Full stock version offered on 20" barrel; half stock offered on 23.5" barrel. Available in a variety of configurations, with calibers from .222 Rem. to .458 Win. Magnum.

NIB	EXC.	V.G.	GOOD	FAIR	POOR
1750	1250	900	500	350	200

SBS TACTICAL SERIES

SBS Tactical

Fitted with black synthetic stock, 20" barrel with no sights. Chambered for .308 cartridge. Removable buttspacers. Black bolt body. Receiver engraved "SBS Tactical". Introduced in 1999. Weight about 7.25 lbs. **NOTE:** Add $100 for stainless steel (introduced 2000).

NIB	EXC.	V.G.	GOOD	FAIR	POOR
1150	950	700	550	300	200

SBS Tactical Heavy Barrel

Model also has black synthetic stock. Fitted with 26" heavy barrel and no sights. Black bolt body. Receiver engraved "SBS Tactical HB". Weight about 8 lbs. Introduced in 1999. Offered with 20" barrel called "HBC". Both barrel lengths chambered for .308 cartridge.

NIB	EXC.	V.G.	GOOD	FAIR	POOR
1250	1050	800	650	300	200

SBS Tactical Heavy Barrel Carbine

Features 20" heavy barrel, no sights, matte blue finish. Chambered for .308 caliber. Introduced in 2000.

NIB	EXC.	V.G.	GOOD	FAIR	POOR
1150	950	700	550	300	200

SBS Tactical McMillan

Fitted with 26" barrel chambered for .308 cartridge. Has McMillan A-3 stock. Oversize bolt handle. Weight about 9.8 lbs. Introduced in 1999.

NIB	EXC.	V.G.	GOOD	FAIR	POOR
1600	1250	950	750	60	400

SBS CISM Rifle

Chambered for .308 cartridge and fitted with 19.7" heavy barrel. Stock is laminated wood, with black lacquer finish. Stock has forearm rail, with handstop adjustable buttplate and cheekpiece. Trigger is adjustable. Weight about 10.25 lbs. Introduced in 1999.

NIB	EXC.	V.G.	GOOD	FAIR	POOR
3295	2500	1950	1600	1200	700

SBS Tactical Elite Heavy Barrel

Introduced in 2000. Features 26" heavy barrel, no sights, matte blue finish, Zytel stock with adjustable cheekpiece and buttplate. Full length Picatinny mounting rail. Magazine capacity 5 or 10 rounds. Chambered for .308 cartridge. **NOTE:** Add $100 for stainless steel; $1,000 for ZF optics.

NIB	EXC.	V.G.	GOOD	FAIR	POOR
2400	1750	1400	1000	700	400

SBS Tactical Elite Heavy Barrel Carbine

Same as Tactical Elite Heavy Barrel. Fitted with 20" heavy barrel. Introduced in 2000.

NIB	EXC.	V.G.	GOOD	FAIR	POOR
2400	1750	—	—	—	—

Steyr AUG

5.56mm semi-automatic Bullpup rifle, with 20" barrel incorporating Swarovski 1.5x telescopic sight. Green carbon composite stock. Weight about 8.5 lbs. Recommend independent local appraisals.

NIB	EXC.	V.G.	GOOD	FAIR	POOR
3700	3100	2500	1600	1300	650

	NIB	EXC.	V.G.	GOOD	FAIR	POOR

Steyr AUG—Police Model

Same as above, with black stock and 16" barrel.

	3700	3100	2500	1600	1300	650

Steyr AUG Special Receiver

Receiver only. Special flattop with Stanag mounting.

	3700	3100	2500	1600	1300	650

Steyr USR

Post-ban version of AUG. Fitted with Swarovski 1.5x scope and gray synthetic stock.

	3700	3100	2500	1600	1300	650

Steyr Zephyr

.22 caliber rimfire bolt-action carbine. Has 5-round detachable magazine, dovetailed receiver for scope rings. Fitted with full stock. Made from 1953 to 1968.

	—	1800	1475	1150	800	400

PISTOLS

Model SPP

Introduced in 1993, this is a 9mm semi-automatic pistol. Made from synthetic materials and operates on a delayed blowback rotating barrel system. Magazine capacity either 15 or 30 rounds. Barrel length 5.9"; overall length 12.75"; weight about 42 oz. Due to its appearance and design, this pistol was banned from importation into U.S. shortly after its introduction. Because of this circumstance price of this pistol may fluctuate widely.

	1000	900	750	600	500	400

Model M

Chambered for .40 S&W, 9mm or .357 SIG cartridge. Semi-automatic pistol has polymer frame and 3 user selectable safety systems. Loaded chambered indicator. Triangle/Trapezoid sights. Limited access lock with key. Weight about 28 oz. Magazine capacity 10 rounds. Introduced in 1999.

	500	400	325	275	235	200

Model M-A1

Updated version of Model M, with redesigned grip frame and Picatinny rail. Striker-fired DA-only pistol in 9mm, .357 SIG and .40 S&W. Magazine capacity: 15 for 9mm, 12 for .40 and .357 SIG. 3.5" or 4" barrel (S-A1).

	500	400	325	275	235	200

STEYR HAHN

See—Steyr

STEYR MANNLICHER

See—Steyr

STI INTERNATIONAL

Georgetown, Texas

LS9 & LS40

Single stack pistol chambered for the 9mm or .40 S&W cartridge. Fitted with a 3.4" barrel and short grip. Heine Low Mount sights. Rosewood grips. Matte blue finish. Magazine capacity is 7 rounds for 9mm and 6 rounds for .40 S&W. Weight is about 28 oz.

	850	675	550	400	300	200

BLS9 & BLS40

Same as above but with full length grip. Magazine capacity is 9 rounds for 9mm and 8 rounds for .40 S&W.

	825	650	525	375	275	200

Ranger

Chambered for the .45 ACP cartridge and fitted with a 3.9" barrel with short grip. Fixed STI sights. Blued frame with stainless steel slide. Weight is about 29 oz.

	950	775	600	500	400	200

	NIB	EXC.	V.G.	GOOD	FAIR	POOR

Ranger II

Chambered for .45 ACP cartridge and fitted with 4.15" ramped bull barrel. Slide is flat top, with rear serrations and chamfered fore-end. Ambidextrous safety and high rise grip safety. Adjustable rear sight. Blued lower frame. Weight about 39 oz.

	925	800	675	525	400	200

Trojan

Chambered for the .45 ACP, .40 Super, .40 S&W, and 9mm cartridge. Fitted with a 5" barrel. Rosewood grips. Matte blue finish. Eight-round magazine capacity. Weight is about 36 oz. **NOTE:** For .40 Super with .45 ACP conversion add $275. For Trojan with 6" slide add $250.

	1150	925	750	600	500	300

Tactical 4.15

Chambered for the 9mm, .40 S&W, or the 45 ACP cartridge. Fully supported ramped 4.15" bull barrel. Frame has tactical rail. Slide has rear serrations. Fixed rear sight. Aluminum magazine well. Black polycoat finish. Weight is about 34.5 oz.

	1750	1475	1150	900	650	350

Tactical

As above but with 5" barrel. Flat blue finish. Weight is about 39 oz.

	1750	1475	1150	900	650	350

Trubor

Chambered for the 9mm major, 9x23, or .38 Super cartridges. Steel frame. Fully supported and ramped one piece with bull barrel with integral compensator. Slide has front and rear serrations. Sights are C-More or OK Red Dot reflix. Blued finish. Weight is about 42.5 oz. with scope.

	2500	2100	1600	1200	900	500

Lawman

This .45 ACP pistol has a 5" ramped barrel with match grade bushing. Aluminum trigger. Series 70 grip safety. Novak 3 dot sights. Checkered walnut grips. Polymer finish with brown slide over tan frame. Weight is about 36 oz.

	1200	975	825	675	500	250

Xcaliber Single Stack

Chambered for the .450 SMC cartridge and fitted with a 6" slide. Adjustable rear sight. Weight is about 38 oz. Blue finish. Single stack magazine. Discontinued.

	1475	1275	1050	775	500	350

Xcaliber Double Stack

Same as the Xcaliber Single Stack except that this model has a double stack magazine. Discontinued.

	1800	1600	1175	900	600	400

Executive

Chambered for the .40 S&W cartridge. Fitted with a 5" ramped bull barrel. Adjustable rear sight. Gray synthetic grip and hard chrome slide. Weight is about 39 oz. Double stack magazine.

	2350	2000	1650	1100	725	400

VIP

Chambered for the .45 ACP cartridge and fitted with a 3.9" ramped bull barrel. Stainless steel flat top slide. Fixed rear sight. Ten-round magazine capacity. Weight is about 25 oz.

	1400	1100	800	650	400	250

Edge

Chambered for the 9mm, 10mm, .40 S&W, and .45 ACP cartridge with 5" ramped bull barrel. Dual stack magazine. Bomar style sights. Blue finish. Weight is about 39 oz.

	1800	1400	1000	700	500	300

Eagle

Chambered for customer's choice of caliber and fitted with 5" ramped bull barrel. Fixed sights. Blued frame and stainless steel slide. Weight is about 30 oz.

	1700	1200	900	600	400	250

Duty One

Chambered for the 9mm, .40 S&W, or .45 ACP cartridges. Five-inch bull barrel is fully supported and ramped. Steel frame with single stack magazine with front strap checkering and tactical

NIB	EXC.	V.G.	GOOD	FAIR	POOR

rail. Grips are rosewood. Slide has front and rear serrations. Adjustable sights. Finish is flat blue. Weight is about 38 oz.

| 1100 | 900 | 750 | 500 | 400 | 250 |

Duty CT

1911-style steel frame single-stack with integral tactical rail and rosewood grips. 5" slide/barrel, fixed 2-dot tritium rear sight. 36.6 oz. Also available in 4.15" commander size. Blued.

| 1100 | 900 | 750 | 500 | 400 | 250 |

Competitor

Chambered for the .38 Super cartridge and fitted with a 5.5" ramped bull barrel with compensator. Fitted with a C-More scope. Stainless steel slide. Weight is about 44 oz. with scope and mount. Discontinued.

| 2350 | 2000 | 1650 | 1100 | 725 | 400 |

Grandmaster

Custom built to customer's specifications in 9mm major, 9x23, and .38 Super.

| 2800 | 2500 | 2000 | 1500 | 850 | 500 |

Rangemaster

Fitted with a 5" fully supported and ramped bull barrel and chambered for the 9mm or .45 ACP cartridge, this pistol has a full length dust cover, checkered front strap and mainspring housing and square trigger guard. Front and rear slide serrations. Adjustable sights. Rose grips. Polished blue finish. Weight is about 38 oz.

| 1500 | 1350 | 1100 | 800 | 500 | 250 |

Rangemaster II

Single-stack blued variation of Rangemaster. Chambered for 9mm, .40 S&W, .45 ACP. 5" slide/barrel, 37 oz. Introduced 2006.

| 1300 | 1125 | 900 | 600 | 400 | 200 |

Targetmaster

As above but with 6" barrel.

| 1650 | 1250 | 900 | 650 | 400 | 250 |

Stinger

Chambered for the 9mm or .38 Super cartridge. Fitted with a 3.9" barrel with compensator. Sights are OKO or C-More on STI mount. Blued finish. Weight is about 38 oz.

| 2775 | 2275 | 1850 | 1450 | 900 | 500 |

Hawk 4.3

This pistol is modeled on the 1911 design and is equipped with a 4.3" barrel with steel slide. The frame of the pistol is made from polymer and features and increased magazine capacity while retaining the 1911 grip thickness. Chambered for .38 Super, .45 ACP, .40 S&W, 10mm, and 9x25 calibers. Built primarily for competition shooting. Discontinued.

| 1700 | 1200 | 900 | 600 | 400 | 250 |

Night Hawk 4.3

Chambered for .45 ACP only with 4.3" bull barrel and a host of special features such a narrow tactical safety, front and rear slide serrations, and extended dust cover. Tritium sights optional. Blued finish. Weight is 33 oz. Discontinued.

| 1925 | 1600 | 1300 | 1050 | 750 | 400 |

Falcon 3.9

Similar to the above model but fitted with a 3.9" barrel. Weight is approximately 30 oz. with steel frame and 25 oz. with aluminum frame. Discontinued.

| 1925 | 1600 | 1300 | 1050 | 750 | 400 |

Sparrow 5.0

Chambered for the .22 LR cartridge only and fitted with a 5" bull barrel with fixed sights. Weight is approximately 30 oz. Discontinued.

| 925 | 800 | 675 | 525 | 400 | 200 |

Edge 5.1

Chambered for .40 S&W only with 5" bull barrel and many special features. BoMar front and rear sights. Weight is 39 oz.

| 1800 | 1400 | 1000 | 700 | 500 | 300 |

NIB	EXC.	V.G.	GOOD	FAIR	POOR

Eagle 5.1

Similar to the Model 2011 Hawk but furnished with a 5" barrel. Comes standard with BoMar adjustable sights.

NIB	EXC.	V.G.	GOOD	FAIR	POOR
1925	1600	1300	1050	750	400

Eagle 5.5

Similar to above model but furnished with a 5-1/2" barrel with compensator.

NIB	EXC.	V.G.	GOOD	FAIR	POOR
2395	1950	1600	1200	850	500

Eagle 6.0

Chambered for 9mm, .38 Super, .40 S&W, or .45 ACP cartridges. Fitted with a 6" bull barrel. Many special features. BoMar front and rear sights. Blued finish. Weight is about 42 oz.

NIB	EXC.	V.G.	GOOD	FAIR	POOR
1925	1600	1300	1050	750	400

Hunter 6.0

Chambered for the 10mm cartridge only and fitted with a 6" bull barrel. Heavy extended frame. Many special features. Leupold 2x scope. Blued finish. Weight with scope 51 oz.

NIB	EXC.	V.G.	GOOD	FAIR	POOR
2350	1900	1600	1200	850	500

Special Edition

Chambered for the 9mm, .40 S&W or .45 ACP cartridge and fitted with a fully supported and ramped 5" bull barrel. Hi-Rise grip. Sights are Dawson fiber optic with adjustable rear. Slide has Saber Tooth serrations and custom engraving. Finish is 24 karat gold on all steel parts except barrel. Weight is about 38 oz.

NIB	EXC.	V.G.	GOOD	FAIR	POOR
2900	2500	1975	1600	1200	500

I.P.S.C. 30th Anniversary

Similar to the Special Edition but with hard chrome upper with color inlays and blued lower.

NIB	EXC.	V.G.	GOOD	FAIR	POOR
2775	2400	1700	1400	950	450

TruSight

Semi-auto pistol chambered for 9mm, .40 S&W, .45 ACP; double-stack magazine. Steel frame, 4.15" slide/barrel. Dawson fiber optic front sight, adjustable rear sight. 36.1 oz. Blued with multiple options. IPSC, USPSA approved. Introduced 2006.

NIB	EXC.	V.G.	GOOD	FAIR	POOR
1800	1575	1200	900	600	350

Legacy

Chambered for .45 ACP single-stack. 5" slide/barrel, LOA 8.5", 38 oz. with adjustable rear sight. Cocobola smooth grips. IDPA, USPSA approved. Introduced 2006.

NIB	EXC.	V.G.	GOOD	FAIR	POOR
1500	1300	1050	750	600	300

GP6

Polymer-framed single/double action pistol with ambidextrous safeties and fized three-dot sight system. Chambered in 9mm Parabellum.

NIB	EXC.	V.G.	GOOD	FAIR	POOR
650	500	375	250	175	75

Sentinel Premier

Top-of-the-line ISPC and IDPA competition 1911, with Dawson Precision/STI "Perfect Impact" style white outline tritium adjustable sights and STI Tritium competition front; forged steel government length standard-width frame; and many other refinements. Sentinel Premier comes standard with case, owner's manual and one Wilson Combat Elite Tactical magazine.

NIB	EXC.	V.G.	GOOD	FAIR	POOR
1700	1500	1300	1000	800	450

Limited Edition 20th Anniversary

1911-style semi-auto pistol chambered in 9x19, .38 Super, .40 S&W, and .45 ACP to commemorate 20th anniversary. Features include ambidextrous thumb safeties and knuckle relief high-rise beavertail grip safety; gold TiN (or Titanium Nitride) coating; full length steel bar stock slide with custom serrations specific to this model; 5-inch fully ramped and supported bull barrel; STI adjustable rear sight and a Dawson fiber optic front sight. STI will only build 200 of these pistols and the serial numbers reflect this (1 of 200, 2 of 200, etc.)

NIB	EXC.	V.G.	GOOD	FAIR	POOR
3200	2900	2600	—	—	—

Duty One

1911-style semi-auto pistol chambered in .45 ACP. Features include government size frame with integral tactical rail and 30 lpi checkered front strap; milled tactical rail on the dust cover of the frame; ambidextrous thumb safeties; high rise beavertail grip safety; lowered and flared ejection port; fixed rear sight; front and rear cocking serrations; 5-inch fully supported STI International

NIB	EXC.	V.G.	GOOD	FAIR	POOR

ramped bull barrel.

1300	1100	850	700	300	200

Apeiro

1911-style semi-auto pistol chambered in 9x19, .40 S&W, and .45 ACP. Features include Schuemann "Island" barrel; patented modular steel frame with polymer grip; high capacity double-stack magazine; stainless steel ambidextrous thumb safeties and knuckle relief high-rise beavertail grip safety; unique sabertooth rear cocking serrations; 5-inch fully ramped, fully supported "island" bull barrel, with the sight milled in to allow faster recovery to point of aim; custom engraving on the polished sides of the (blued) stainless steel slide; stainless steel magwell; STI adjustable rear sight and Dawson fiber optic front sight; blued frame.

2200	1850	1500	1200	800	400

Eclipse

Compact 1911-style semi-auto pistol chambered in 9x19, .40 S&W, and .45 ACP. Features include slide with rear cocking serrations, over-sized ejection port; 2-dot tritium night sights recessed into the slide; high-capacity polymer grip; single sided blued thumb safety;bobbed, high-rise, blued, knuckle relief beavertail grip safety; 3-inch barrel. Also comes with alloy frame as Escort model.

1625	1400	1185	900	600	300

Texican Single Action Revolver

SAA-styled revolver chambered in .38 Special and .45 Colt. Features include 4.75- or 6.5-inch (.45) or 5.25-inch barrel (.38). Features include competition sights, springs, triggers and hammers; color case hardening and blued finish standard.

1100	935	775	600	300	200

FPI 2260 Rifle

Chambered for the .22 Long Rifle cartridge. Aluminum receiver with adjustable trigger and quick magazine release. Integral scope mount.

1000	850	675	500	300	150

Sporting Competition Rifle

AR-style semi-auto rifle chambered in 5.56 NATO. Features include 16-inch 410 stainless 1:8 barrel; mid-length gas system; Nordic Tactical Compensator and JP Trigger group; custom STI Valkyrie hand guard and gas block; flat-top design with Picatinny rail; anodized finish with black Teflon coating. Also available in Tactical configuration.

1175	1000	825	650	350	250

STOCK, FRANZ
Berlin, Germany

Stock

A .22, 6.35mm or 7.65mm semi-automatic pistol with an open topped slide. The frame marked "Franz Stock Berlin." Blued with black composition grips impressed with the name "Stock" at the top. Manufactured from 1918 to the early 1930s.

—	525	400	300	250	150

STOCKING & CO.
Worcester, Massachusetts

Pepperbox

A .28 or .316 barreled percussion pepperbox revolver with barrel lengths from 4" to 6". The hammer is fitted with a long cocking piece at the rear and the trigger guard may or may not be made with a spur at the rear. Blued with walnut grips. The barrel group marked "Stocking & Co., Worcester." Manufactured between 1846 and 1854.

—	—	1950	1650	600	200

Single-Shot Pistol

A .36 caliber single-shot percussion pistol of the same pattern as the pepperbox with a 4" half octagonal barrel. Marked as above. Manufactured from 1849 to 1852.

—	—	1200	850	350	100

STOEGER, A. F./STOEGER INDUSTRIES

First guns shown, pistols, were imported many years ago to South Hackensack, New Jersey. All the rest have been imported by Stoeger Industries in: Accokeek, Maryland

	NIB	EXC.	V.G.	GOOD	FAIR	POOR

HANDGUNS

.22 Luger

A .22 caliber simplified copy of the German Model P.08 semi-automatic pistol with a 4.5" or 5.5" barrel and an aluminum frame. The word "Luger" is roll engraved on the right side of the frame. Blued with checkered brown plastic grips. Made by Erma.

	NIB	EXC.	V.G.	GOOD	FAIR	POOR
	—	350	275	200	150	100

Target Luger

As above, with adjustable target sights. Made by Erma.

	NIB	EXC.	V.G.	GOOD	FAIR	POOR
	—	375	295	225	175	125

Luger Carbine

As above, with an 11" barrel, walnut fore-end and checkered walnut grips. Furnished with a red velvet lined black leatherette case. Manufactured during the 1970s. Made by Erma.

	NIB	EXC.	V.G.	GOOD	FAIR	POOR
	—	1100	775	500	350	150

American Eagle Luger

This is identical to the German design. It is chambered for the 9mm with a 7-round magazine and fitted with a 4" barrel. Checkered walnut grips. Stainless steel. Weight is about 32 oz.

	NIB	EXC.	V.G.	GOOD	FAIR	POOR
	1100	975	650	450	300	100

American Eagle Navy Model

Same as above but with a 6" barrel.

	NIB	EXC.	V.G.	GOOD	FAIR	POOR
	1200	1075	700	450	300	100

Cougar

Double-action semi-automatic offered in 9mm. .40 S&W or .45 ACP. Manufactured in Turkey and based on the Beretta model of the same name. Traditional DA/SA design with ambidextrous safety/decocking lever, white dot sights and Picatinny rail (.45 only). Also made in compact variation.

	NIB	EXC.	V.G.	GOOD	FAIR	POOR
	425	375	325	275	200	150

Pro Series 95

Target pistol in .22 LR with 5.5" or 7.25" barrel, adjustable trigger and sights. Imported by Stoeger in 1995 and 1996. **NOTE:** Add $75 for bull barrel.

	NIB	EXC.	V.G.	GOOD	FAIR	POOR
	450	400	350	300	250	150

SHOTGUNS

Model 2000

This is a semi-automatic shotgun chambered for the 12 gauge shell. Fitted with 26", 28", or 30" vent rib barrel. Single trigger with screw-in chokes. Weight is about 7 lbs. Introduced in 2001.

	NIB	EXC.	V.G.	GOOD	FAIR	POOR
	500	400	300	200	150	75

Model 2000 Deluxe

Same as above but with high grade walnut stock and etched receiver with gold trigger.

	NIB	EXC.	V.G.	GOOD	FAIR	POOR
	625	500	400	300	250	125

Model 2000 Camo

As above but with Advantage Timber HD camo stock.

	NIB	EXC.	V.G.	GOOD	FAIR	POOR
	500	400	300	200	150	75

Model 2000 Slug

This model is chambered for the 12 gauge shell with 3" chamber. Barrel length is 24". The gun is fitted with a black synthetic stock. Smooth bore barrel. Adjustable rifle-type sights. Optional field-style barrels in 24", 26", or 28". Weight is approximately 6.7 lbs. Introduced in 2003.

	NIB	EXC.	V.G.	GOOD	FAIR	POOR
	450	350	250	175	125	50

Model 2000 Synthetic

As above with choice of 24", 26" or 28" vent rib barrel. Black synthetic stock. Weight about 6.8 lbs. Introduced in 2003.

	NIB	EXC.	V.G.	GOOD	FAIR	POOR
	500	400	300	200	150	75

Model 3000

Semi-automatic chambered for 2.75" and 3" loads. Minimum recommended load 3-dram, 1-1/8 oz. Magazine capacity: 4+1. Inertia-driven action based on Benelli operating system. Barrel: 26"

	NIB	EXC.	V.G.	GOOD	FAIR	POOR

or 28" with 3 choke tubes. Finish: black synthetic or camo (Realtree APG or Max-4). Introduced in 2013. **NOTE:** Add $75 for camo finish.

	475	400	350	285	235	200

Model 3500

12-gauge auto-loader comes with either 24", 26" or 28" barrel. Fitted with ventilated stepped rib and fiber-optic front sight. Inertia operation. Weight 7.5 lbs. Alloy receiver drilled and tapped. Includes Weaver-style scope base. All M3500s come supplied with five choke tubes (Extra-full turkey, Full, Modified, Improved Cylinder and Cylinder). Shim kit provides drop and cast adjustment. Threaded steel recoil reducer (included) can be installed in buttstock to help manage felt recoil from heavy Magnum loads. Available in three different finishes: matte black synthetic, Realtree APG or Realtree Max-4. **NOTE:** Add 20 percent for total camo coverage.

	535	450	385	325	250	200

Coach Gun

This is a side-by-side gun chambered for the 12 or 20 gauge shell as well as the .410 shell. Fitted with 20" barrels with double triggers. Improved Cylinder and Modified fixed chokes. Weight is about 7 lbs. **NOTE:** Add $50 for nickel finish.

	400	275	225	175	125	75

Silverado Coach Gun

Offered in 12 and 20 gauge as well as .410 bore with straight- or pistol-grip stock and matte nickel finish. Straight-stock version is offered in 12 and 20 gauge only. Weight is about 6.5 lbs.

	450	320	250	175	125	75

Coach Gun Supreme

This model is similar to the above but offered with blue, stainless, or nickel receiver. Introduced in 2004. **NOTE:** Add $10 for stainless and $30 for nickel.

	450	320	250	175	125	75

Uplander

This side-by-side shotgun is chambered for the 12, 16, 20, 28, and .410 bores. with choice of 26" or 28" barrels. Fixed chokes. Double triggers. Weight is about 7.25 lbs.

	375	275	175	125	100	75

Uplander Special

As above but with straight grip and oil finish stock. Offered in 12, 20, or 28 gauge. Weight is about 7.3 lbs.

	395	300	200	150	100	75

Uplander Supreme

Same as above but with select wood and screw-in chokes.

	425	350	250	175	125	100

Uplander English

This variation is fitted with a straight-grip stock and chambered for the 20 gauge or .410 bore. Fitted with 24" barrels. Weight is about 7 lbs. Also available with a short stock.

	395	300	200	150	100	75

Uplander Youth

Offered in 20 gauge or .410 bore this model features a 13" LOP with 22" barrels choked Improved Modified and Modified. Weight is about 6.75 lbs.

	375	275	175	125	100	75

Condor

This over/under shotgun is chambered 12, 16 and 20 gauges and .410 bore. Available with 26" and 28" barrels in all gauges and 26" barrel in .410 bore. Single trigger. Blued finish. The 16-gauge is chambered for 2.75" shells. All others have 3" chambers. Weights run from 6 lbs. to 7.4 lbs. depending on bore.

	375	275	175	125	100	75

Condor Special

Similar to the standard Condor model but with matte stainless receiver and rubbed oil finish stock. Introduced in 2003.

	475	375	295	200	125	100

	NIB	EXC.	V.G.	GOOD	FAIR	POOR

Condor Combo

This model, introduced in 2004, features a two-barrel set of 12 and 20 gauge. Barrel length on the 12 gauge is 28" and 26" on the 20 gauge. Choke tubes. Offered in 3 grades: Field, Special, and Supreme. Introduced in 2004.

Field

NIB	EXC.	V.G.	GOOD	FAIR	POOR
500	400	300	200	100	75

Special

NIB	EXC.	V.G.	GOOD	FAIR	POOR
650	500	400	275	175	125

Supreme

NIB	EXC.	V.G.	GOOD	FAIR	POOR
775	650	500	300	200	150

Condor Supreme Deluxe

Similar to the above model but with cut checkering and high polish blue. Offered in 12 and 20 gauge with 26" or 28" barrels as well as 24" barrels for the 20 gauge. Automatic ejectors.

NIB	EXC.	V.G.	GOOD	FAIR	POOR
500	400	300	200	100	75

Condor Competition

These 3" 12 and 20 gauge over/unders feature 30" barrels, AA Grade wood and adjustable combs. Three choke tubes. Weight is about 7.3 lbs. in 20 gauge and 7.8 lbs. in 12 gauge.

NIB	EXC.	V.G.	GOOD	FAIR	POOR
650	500	400	275	175	125

Condor Competition Combo

As above with 12 gauge and 20 gauge barrels.

NIB	EXC.	V.G.	GOOD	FAIR	POOR
775	650	500	300	200	150

Condor Outback

New in 2007, the Outback comes in 12 and 20 gauge chambered for 3" shells. The finish is either A Grade satin walnut stock with blued barrels and receiver or matte black walnut stock with polished barrels and receiver. Barrels are 20" with rifle sights. Includes two choke tubes. Add $40 for black/nickel finish.

NIB	EXC.	V.G.	GOOD	FAIR	POOR
375	275	175	125	100	75

Single Barrel Classic Youth

Available in 20 gauge or .410 bore with a 13" length of pull and 22" vent rib barrel. Straight-grip stock. Weight is about 5 lbs.

NIB	EXC.	V.G.	GOOD	FAIR	POOR
125	100	75	50	25	10

Single Barrel Classic

As above but with standard length of pull and available in 12, 20 or .410 bore. Barrel length on 12 gauge is 26" or 28"; on 20 gauge length is 26". On .410 bore barrel length is 24". Open pistol grip. Weight is about 5.5 lbs.

NIB	EXC.	V.G.	GOOD	FAIR	POOR
125	100	75	50	25	10

Single Barrel Special

As above but with stainless steel frame. Offered in 12, 20, or .410 bore. Weight is about 5.5 lbs.

NIB	EXC.	V.G.	GOOD	FAIR	POOR
125	100	75	50	25	10

P-350

This pump-action 12 gauge shotgun was introduced in 2005. All versions are chambered for 3.5" shells. Available with 24", 26" or 28" barrel in matte black synthetic or Advantage Timber camo finish; available with 26" or 28" barrel in Max-4 camo finish. Comes with 5 choke tubes. Weight is about 6.8 lbs. Also available is a Defense model with 18.5" barrel and fixed cylinder bore. Add 15 percent for camo models.

NIB	EXC.	V.G.	GOOD	FAIR	POOR
275	225	175	125	100	50

P-350 Camo

This pump-action 12 gauge is chambered for 3.5" shells. It has a 24", 26" or 28" barrel and a matte black, Max-4, Timber or APG finish. There are also some pistol-grip stock offerings with 24" barrels. Includes five choke tubes. Weight is about 6.8 lbs. Add $20 for pistol-grip stock. Add $75 for camo finish.

NIB	EXC.	V.G.	GOOD	FAIR	POOR
350	275	225	150	125	75

P-350 Defense

Same as above in a matte black finish with 18.5", fixed cylinder choke barrel. Add $20 for pistol-grip stock.

NIB	EXC.	V.G.	GOOD	FAIR	POOR
300	225	175	125	100	50

	NIB	EXC.	V.G.	GOOD	FAIR	POOR

STREET SWEEPER
Atlanta, Georgia

Street Sweeper

A 12-gauge semi-automatic double-action shotgun, with 18" barrel and 12-shot rotary drum magazine. Matte black finish. Introduced in 1989. **NOTE:** This firearm is now on the restricted list as a Class III weapon and subject to NFA rules. This model requires registration with BATFE to avoid federal penalties. Make sure the shotgun is transferable prior to sale.

2195	—	—	—	—	—

STURDIVANT, LEWIS G.
Talladega, Alabama

Received contract from the state of Alabama for 2,000 "Mississippi" or "Enfield" rifles. Two hundred and eighty were received on this contract. These arms resemble U.S. Model 1841 Rifles without patchboxes. Overall length 48.5"; barrel length 33"; .577 caliber. Unmarked.

STURM, RUGER & CO.
Southport, Connecticut

SEMI-AUTOMATIC RIMFIRE PISTOLS

Standard Model "Red Eagle Grips"

A blowback semi-automatic, with a fixed exposed 4.75" barrel. Receiver is tubular, with a round bolt. There is a 9-shot detachable magazine. Sights are fixed. Finish is blued. Black hard rubber grips on this first model feature a red Ruger eagle or hawk medallion on the left side. There were approximately 25,600 manufactured before Alexander Sturm's death in 1951, but this model may be seen as high as the 35000 serial number range. Because variations of this model exist, an expert opinion should be sought before a final price is established. **NOTE:** Factory verified plated pistols will bring between $2,500 and $5,000 depending on condition. Approximately 890 pistols were shipped in a wooden "salt cod" box. Add a premium of $3000 if NIB, $1000 to $2000 if good to excellent condition.

750	550	450	325	250	150

Standard Model

This model is identical to Red Eagle, except that after Sturm's death the grip medallions were changed from red to black. Pistol was produced from 1952-1982 in 4.75" and 6" barrels. There are a great many variations of this pistol, but a book dealing with this pistol alone should be consulted as the differences in variations are subtle and valuation of these variations is definitely a matter for individual appraisal.

450	400	300	250	200	100

Standard Model—Marked "Hecho en Mexico"

Early in 1957, Ruger shipped 250 sets of parts to Armanex in Mexico. Armanex fabricated barrels for the sets of parts and then finished and assembled 250 pistols—200 with a 4.75" barrel and 50 with 6.5" barrel. Due to the rarity of these pistols, an expert examination and appraisal is recommended.

1750	1500	1200	850	600	400

Mark I Target Model

The success of the Ruger Standard Model led quite naturally to a demand for a more accurate target model. In 1951 a pistol that utilized the same frame and receiver with a 6-7/8", target-type barrel and adjustable sights was introduced. Early target models number 15000 to 16999 and 25000 to 25300 have Red Eagle grips. In 1952 a 5-1/4" tapered barrel model was introduced, but was soon discontinued. In 1963 the popular 5-1/2" bull barrel model was introduced. These models enjoyed well deserved success and were manufactured from 1951-1982.

Red Eagle 6-7/8" barrel

750	675	500	350	250	150

Black or Silver Eagle 6-7/8" barrel

NOTE: Add 35 percent for original hinged box; $75-$100 with factory supplied muzzle-brake; 50 percent for other Mark I Target models under serial number 72500 in original hinged box.

450	400	300	250	200	125

5-1/4" Tapered Barrel Model

NOTE: Add 50 percent if in original 5.25" marked hinged box.

875	750	600	400	300	200

	NIB	EXC.	V.G.	GOOD	FAIR	POOR

5-1/2" Bull Barrel Model

NIB	EXC.	V.G.	GOOD	FAIR	POOR
450	400	300	250	200	125

Rollmarked with U.S. on Top of Frame

These pistols will have either .0625" or .125" high serial numbers. **NOTE:** Add 25 percent if pistol has .125" high serial numbers.

NIB	EXC.	V.G.	GOOD	FAIR	POOR
—	875	700	550	400	300

Stainless Steel 1 of 5,000

This model is a special commemorative version of the first standard with the "Red Eagle" grips. It is made of stainless steel and is rollmarked with Bill Ruger's signature on it. The pistol is encased in a wood "salt cod" case.

NIB	EXC.	V.G.	GOOD	FAIR	POOR
395	350	300	225	175	125

MARK II .22 CALIBER PISTOL SPECIFICATIONS

Supplied in .22 LR, with various barrel weights and lengths. Magazine capacity 10 rounds. Trigger is grooved, with curved finger surface. High speed hammer provides fast lock time. Grips are sharply checkered and made of black gloss delrin material. Stainless steel models have a brushed satin finish. **NOTE:** Beginning in 2004, all Ruger adjustable sight .22 pistols were drilled and tapped for an included Weaver-type scope base adapter.

STANDARD MODEL MARK II

Generally an improved version of first Ruger pistol. There is a hold-open device and magazine holds 10 rounds. Introduced in 1982.

NIB	EXC.	V.G.	GOOD	FAIR	POOR
350	250	150	125	100	75

Model MK450

Introduced in 1999 to commemorate the 50th anniversary of the first Ruger rimfire pistol. Fitted with a 4.75" barrel with fixed sights. Chambered for the .22 LR cartridge. The pistols grips have a red Ruger medallion and Ruger crest on the barrel. Furnished in a red case. Weight is about 35 oz. Production limited to one year.

NIB	EXC.	V.G.	GOOD	FAIR	POOR
385	350	250	175	125	75

Model MK6

Same as above but with 6" barrel. Weight 37 oz.

NIB	EXC.	V.G.	GOOD	FAIR	POOR
350	275	225	125	100	75

Model KMK4

This model is the same as the Mark II Standard except that it is made of stainless steel.

NIB	EXC.	V.G.	GOOD	FAIR	POOR
375	300	200	150	125	100

Model KMK6

Same as above, with 6" barrel. Weight about 37 oz. **NOTE:** In 1997, Ruger produced 650 of Model MK6 with special features for "Friends of the NRA" auction of the same year. These guns have high polish blueing, faux ivory grip panels, gold inlaid National Rifle Association inscription and gold inlaid number of "1 of 650" to "650 of 650".

NIB	EXC.	V.G.	GOOD	FAIR	POOR
375	300	200	150	125	100

Target Model

Model incorporates the same improvements as Mark II Standard. Offered with 5.5" bull, 6.875" tapered and 10" heavy barrel. A 5.25" tapered barrel was added in 1990, but discontinued in 1994. Blued finish. This model has adjustable target sights. Introduced in 1982. **NOTE:** In 1989, approximately 2,000 5.5" bull barrel Mark II pistols, with blue barreled receivers and stainless steel grip frames were produced by Ruger on order from a Ruger distributor. They exist in the 215-25xxx to 215-43xxx serial number range.

NIB	EXC.	V.G.	GOOD	FAIR	POOR
400	350	300	225	175	125

Stainless Steel Target Model

Model same as blued version, but made of stainless steel.

NIB	EXC.	V.G.	GOOD	FAIR	POOR
450	400	350	300	250	200

Government Model

Similar to blue Mark II Target, with 6.875" bull barrel. The civilian version of a training pistol that the military is purchasing from Ruger. Only difference is this model does not have the U.S. markings. **NOTE:** Add a premium of 150 to 175 percent for models with "U.S." marking. An expert examination and appraisal is suggested.

NIB	EXC.	V.G.	GOOD	FAIR	POOR
450	325	225	200	150	100

NIB	EXC.	V.G.	GOOD	FAIR	POOR

Stainless Steel Government Model

Stainless steel version of Government Model. **NOTE:** Same with U.S. markings. These are found in serial number range of 210-00001 to 210-18600. Only a couple dozen are in civilian hands.

475	350	250	225	175	125

Competition Model KMK678GC

Competition model features a stainless steel frame, with checkered laminated hardwood thumb rest grips, heavy 6.875" bull barrel factory drilled and tapped for scope mount, Partridge type front sight undercut to prevent glare and adjustable rear sight. Weighs 45 oz. **NOTE:** In 1997, Ruger produced 204 of these pistols in blue instead of stainless steel for one of their distributors. They are very scarce. In 1995, Ruger produced a similar blued pistol (1,000 total: 500 each with or without scope rings) with 5.5" slab side barrels. These are not marked "Competition Target Model" like the previously described variation.

400	325	275	200	125	100

Bull Barrel Model MK4B

Introduced in 1996 this bull barrel variation has a blued finish with a 4" barrel. Grips are checkered composition. Weight is about 38 oz.

400	325	275	200	125	100

RUGER 22/45 MODEL

This .22 LR caliber pistol has the same grip angle and magazine latch as the Model 1911 .45 ACP. The semi-automatic action is stainless steel and the grip frame is made from Zytel, a fiberglass reinforced lightweight composite material. Front sight is Patridge-type. This model is available in several different configurations. A 4" tapered barrel and standard model sights, a 5.25" tapered barrel with target sights, or a 5.5" bull barrel with target sights. The 5.25" barrel was discontinued in 1994.

KP4

This model features a 4.75" standard weight barrel with fixed sights. Pistol weighs 28 oz.

300	275	250	200	125	75

KP514

Furnished with a target tapered barrel 5.25" in length. Comes with adjustable sights. Pistol weighs 38 oz. Model now discontinued.

300	200	175	150	100	75

KP512

Model equipped with 5.5" bull barrel, with adjustable sights. Weighs 42 oz. **NOTE:** In 1995, Ruger produced 500 22/45s with stainless steel 6.875" Government type barreled receivers for one of their distributors. They appear around the 220-59xxx serial number range. In 1997, another Ruger distributor succeeded in contracting Ruger to make a similar 22/45 only in blue, with 6.875" slab side bull barrels. Approximately 1,000 were produced, with serial numbers extending to 220-87xxx serial number range.

300	200	175	150	100	75

P4

A limited number, about 1,000, of this variation were produced in 1995 with a 4" bull barrel on a P frame. It was introduced into the product line as a production pistol in 1997. Weight is approximately 31 oz.

350	200	150	100	75	50

22/45 Threaded Barrel

Variation of Model 22/45 with muzzle threaded to accept various accessories. Muzzle is capped to protect threads, receiver and barrel drilled and tapped to accept accessory rails. Weight is 32 ounces; 4.5-inch barrel with blue finish.

375	325	285	200	135	100

P512

This variation of the stainless steel version has a blued receiver with P-style frame.

350	250	150	100	75	60

22/45 Lite

Lightened version of standard 22/45 model, with 4.4" barrel. Weight 23 oz. Introduced in 2012.

425	375	300	225	150	100

NIB	EXC.	V.G.	GOOD	FAIR	POOR

MARK III .22 CALIBER PISTOL SPECIFICATIONS

Mark III series was introduced in 2004. Series features a newly designed magazine release button located on left side of the frame. Mark III pistols also have a visible loaded chamber indicator, an internal lock, magazine disconnect, re-contoured sights and ejection port.

Standard Pistol

Introduced in 2005 this .22 caliber pistol is fitted with a 4.75" or 6" barrel. Fixed rear sight. Blued finish. Magazine capacity is 10 rounds. Black checkered grips. Weight is about 35 oz. depending on barrel length.

300	250	185	150	100	75

Hunter

This .22-caliber pistol fitted with 6.88" target crowned fluted stainless steel barrel. Adjustable rear sight, with Hi-Viz front sight. Checkered Cocobolo grips. Drilled and tapped for scope mount. Supplied with green case, scope base adapter and 6 interchangeable LitePipes for front sight. Weight about 41 oz. Introduced in 2005. **NOTE:** Add 50 percent for Crimson Trace laser-grips (limited edition for 2008).

575	500	400	325	225	125

Competition

This .22-caliber model features 6.88" flat sided heavy barrel, with adjustable rear sight and Patridge front sight. Stainless steel finish. Checkered wood grips. Weight about 45 oz. Introduced in 2005.

535	425	350	275	175	100

Mark III 22/45 Standard Pistol

This .22 caliber pistol has a grip frame similar to the Colt 1911 pistol. The 4" bull barrel is flat sided. Blued steel frame. Fixed sights. Magazine capacity is 10 rounds. Grips are checkered black polymer. Weight is about 29 oz.

300	225	175	125	100	75

Mark III 22/45 Stainless

Similar to above, with stainless barrel, aluminum upper receiver, Zytel polymer frame.

425	375	325	250	175	125

Mark III 512 Pistol

This .22 LR pistol has a 5.5" bull barrel and adjustable rear sight. Steel frame is blued. Checkered black synthetic grips. Weaver-style scope base adapter included. Magazine capacity is 10 rounds. Weight is about 41 oz.

350	300	225	175	125	100

Mark III 22/45 Hunter

Similar to 22/45 .22 pistol but with Mark III-style improvements. 6-7/8" or 4-1/2" fluted barrel, HiViz front sight with six interchangeable inserts. Blued or stainless finish. Pricing is for stainless model. Introduced in 2007.

465	395	300	225	150	100

Mark III 22/45RP Pistol

Semi-automatic pistol chambered in .22 LR. Features include polymer frame with grip panels that recreate feel of 1911; 1911-style controls including magazine button, manual safety and bolt stop locations as classic 1911 pistol; slim polymer grip frame with serrated front strap and checkered back strap; blued alloy steel 5.5" bull barrel with fixed front sight and micro-adjustable rear sight; adjustable sights drilled/tapped for Weaver mounts. Weighs 31 oz. Offered in several variations including 22/45 Lite with weight of 23 oz., 4.4" stainless steel threaded barrel. Introduced in 2013.

425	375	300	265	235	200

Charger

Introduced in 2008 and discontinued in 2012. A 10" barrel pistol version of 10/22 .22 LR rifle. Black matte finish, black laminated stock (other colors available), bipod and Weaver-style mounts. Includes one 10-round magazine.

375	300	225	175	125	100

OLD MODEL SINGLE-ACTION REVOLVERS (PRE-TRANSFER BAR)

Single Six Revolver

This is a .22 rimfire, 6-shot, single-action revolver. It was first offered with a 5-1/2" barrel length and a fixed sight. In 1959 additional barrel lengths were offered for this model in

	NIB	EXC.	V.G.	GOOD	FAIR	POOR

4-5/8", 6-1/2", and 9-1/2". It is based in appearance on the Colt Single-Action Army, but internally it is a new design that features coil springs instead of the old-style, flat leaf springs. It also features a floating firing pin and is generally a stronger action than what was previously available. The early model had a flat loading gate and was made this way from 1953-1957, when the contoured gate became standard. Early models had checkered hard rubber grips changed to smooth varnished walnut by 1962. Black eagle grip medallions were used from the beginning of production to 1971 when a silver eagle grip medallion replaced it. No "Red Eagle" single-sixes were ever produced. This model was manufactured from 1953-1972.

Flat Gate Model

60,000 produced.

NOTE 1: Be aware that revolvers serial numbered under 2000 will bring a premium of 25 percent to 125 percent depending on condition, low serial number, and color of cylinder frame—bright reddish purple the most desirable.

NOTE 2: Values cited below are for unconverted examples and for converted examples with original parts present.

900	700	500	450	225	150

Contoured Gate Model

Introduced 1957. There were 258 5.5" barrel factory engraved pistols in this model. Add a 25 percent premium for 3-screw models. **NOTE:** Be aware that 4-5/8" and 9.5" barrel lengths will bring a premium. Add $3,500 to $6,000 for factory engraved and cased models.

700	600	500	350	200	125

SINGLE SIX ENGRAVED SERIES

Between 1954 and 1958, 250 Single Sixes were engraved by the factory. They are known as RSSE models, for Ruger Single Six Engraved. These are extremely rare and among the most collectible of all Ruger firearms. A total of 22 revolvers were sent to Spain for engraving and 238 were engraved by Charles Jerred in the U.S. (See the article "Fancy Rugers" elsewhere in this book for some history and photographs of these beautiful sixguns.) Due to the rarity of these models and the fact that most are in the hands of collectors, values shown here are quite speculative. Whether buying or selling, an appraisal by a knowledgeable Ruger expert would be required.

Spanish Engraved (serial no. 7 and 8; and 5100 to 5119)

22500	20000	16000	—	—	—

All Blue Jerred Engraved

18000	15000	12000	—	—	—

Standard Jerred Engraved

10000	8500	6500	—	—	—

Single Six Convertible

This model is similar to the Single Six but is furnished with an extra .22 rimfire Magnum cylinder. **NOTE:** Barrel lengths in 4-5/8" and 9.5" will bring a premium.

650	550	450	375	225	150

Single Six .22 Magnum Model

This model is similar to the Single Six except that it is chambered for the .22 rimfire Magnum and the frame was so marked. It was offered in the 6.5" barrel length only and was manufactured for three years. An extra long rifle cylinder was added later in production. The serial numbers are in the 300000-340000 range.

600	500	400	350	200	125

Lightweight Single Six

Model similar to Single Six, with aluminum alloy frame and 4-5/8" barrel. Variation produced between 1956 and 1958. In serial number range 200000-212000. Approximately first 6,500 produced with alloy cylinders and steel chamber inserts. **NOTE:** Stamped after serial number or on bottom of frame. Varieties of "S" marked lightweights exist. Individual evaluation and appraisal recommended. These are factory seconds and are verifiable. **NOTE:** Original Lightweight Single-Six boxes add 25 to 40 percent.

Silver Anodized Frame with Aluminum Cylinder Model with Martin Hardcoat Finish

1500	1100	900	750	500	300

	NIB	EXC.	V.G.	GOOD	FAIR	POOR

Black Anodized Aluminum Frame and Cylinder Model

	NIB	EXC.	V.G.	GOOD	FAIR	POOR
	1100	950	700	600	350	250

Black Anodized Frame with Blue Steel Cylinder Model

	950	800	600	500	300	200

Silver Anodized Aluminum Frame with Blue Steel Cylinder and "S" Marking

Only a few hundred pistols, in this variation, were produced by the factory with an "S" suffix.

	1600	1200	900	750	500	300

Super Single Six

Introduced in 1964. Single Six with adjustable sights. Prices listed for pistols with 5.5" and 6.5" barrels. **NOTE:** Listed models are factory verifiable.

	600	500	400	350	200	125

4-5/8" Barrel

200 built.

	1750	1500	1200	900	500	250

Nickel-Plated Model

Approximately 100 built.

	2350	1900	1600	1200	600	300

Bearcat (Old Model)

Scaled-down version of single-action. Chambered for .22 rimfire. Has 4" barrel and unfluted roll engraved cylinder. Frame is alloy and has a brass colored anodized alloy trigger guard. Finish is blue and grips are plastic impregnated wood until 1963, thereafter, walnut with eagle medallions were used. Manufactured from 1958-1970. **NOTE:** Add $150 to $200 premium for a serial number under 30000; $350 for black anodized trigger guard; 20 percent for alphabet prefix serial number.

	450	350	300	265	225	175

Super Bearcat (Old Model)

This model is similar to the with a steel frame and, on later models, a blued steel trigger guard and grip frame. The early examples still used brass. This model was manufactured from 1971 to 1974.

	575	500	395	275	225	175

Flattop—.357 Magnum

The success of the Single Six led to the production of a larger version chambered for the .357 Magnum cartridge. This model is a single-action, with a 6-shot fluted cylinder and a flat top strap with adjustable "Micro sight." The barrel length is 4-5/8", 6.5", and 10". The finish is blue with checkered hard rubber grips on the early examples and smooth walnut on later ones. There were approximately 42,600 manufactured between 1955 and 1962.

4-5/8" Barrel

	1200	1000	600	350	250	200

6-1/2" Barrel

	1000	850	600	450	350	250

10" Barrel

	2800	2500	1000	850	750	600

Blackhawk Flattop .44 Magnum

In 1956 the .44 Magnum was introduced, and Ruger jumped on the bandwagon. This is similar in appearance to the .357 but has a slightly heavier frame and a larger cylinder. It was available in a 6.5", 7.5", and 10" barrel. It was manufactured from 1956-1963. There were approximately 29,700 manufactured.

6-1/2" Barrel

	1250	800	600	450	350	250

7-1/2" Barrel

	1325	950	700	600	450	300

10" Barrel

	3000	2000	1200	800	700	400

NIB	EXC.	V.G.	GOOD	FAIR	POOR

Blackhawk

This model is similar to the "Flattop," but the rear sight is protected by two raised protrusions—one on each side. It was available chambered for the .30 Carbine, .357 Magnum, .41 Magnum, or the .45 Colt cartridge. Barrel lengths are 4-5/8" or 6.5" in .357 Magnum and .41 Magnum. .45 Colt version has 4-5/8" and 7.5" barrel lengths. The .30 Carbine is furnished with a 7.5" barrel only. The finish is blue, and the grips are walnut with Ruger medallions. This model was produced from 1962 to 1972. Note that the "Old Style" Blackhawk (i.e., pre-transfer bar) is a popular platform for custom revolvers, so prices may exceed those shown depending on circumstances. **NOTE:** Add 20 percent for .41 Mag. and 50 percent for .45 Colt and 35 percent for .30 Carbine. Original verified factory brass grip frame will add at least $800 to above prices. It was available chambered for the .357 Magnum or .41 Magnum (4-5/8" or 6-1/2" barrel), or .45 Colt (4-5/8" or 7-1/2" barrel). The .41 Magnum with factory installed brass frame will bring $1000 to $2500 depending on condition.

NIB	EXC.	V.G.	GOOD	FAIR	POOR
700	500	350	200	150	125

Blackhawk Convertible

This model is the same as the Blackhawk with an extra cylinder to change or convert calibers. The .357 Magnum has a 9mm cylinder, and the .45 Colt has a .45 ACP cylinder. **NOTE:** The 4-5/8" barrel will bring a slight premium. Nonprefix serial numbered .357/9mm Blackhawks will bring a premium.

.357/9mm

NIB	EXC.	V.G.	GOOD	FAIR	POOR
750	650	450	300	200	150

.45 L.C./.45 ACP

NIB	EXC.	V.G.	GOOD	FAIR	POOR
1250	1100	800	600	400	200

Super Blackhawk Old Model

The formidable recoil of the .44 Magnum cartridge was difficult to handle in a revolver with a small grip such as found on the Blackhawk, so it was decided to produce a larger-framed revolver with increased size in the grip. The rear of the trigger guard was squared off, and the cylinder was left unfluted to increase mass. This model was offered with a 7.5" barrel; 600 6.5" barrel Super Blackhawks were produced by factory error. This model is blued and has smooth walnut grips with medallions. The first of these revolvers were offered in a fitted wood case and are rare today. The Super Blackhawk was made from 1959-1972. **NOTE:** For pistols with verified factory installed brass grip frame each example should be appraised. For pistols with brass grip frames add $250 to the prices listed.

NIB	EXC.	V.G.	GOOD	FAIR	POOR
800	600	400	300	200	150

Early Model in Wood Presentation Case

NIB	EXC.	V.G.	GOOD	FAIR	POOR
1200	1000	750	475	400	300

In Fitted White Cardboard Case

NIB	EXC.	V.G.	GOOD	FAIR	POOR
1800	1600	1000	950	875	675

Long Grip Frame in Wood Case

300 guns built.

NIB	EXC.	V.G.	GOOD	FAIR	POOR
2000	1800	1150	1050	800	675

Factory Verified 6-1/2" Barrel

Approximately 600 guns built in the 23000-25000 serial number range.

NIB	EXC.	V.G.	GOOD	FAIR	POOR
1500	1300	950	700	450	375

Hawkeye Single-Shot

The shooting public wanted a small-caliber, high-velocity handgun. The Smith & Wesson Model 53, chambered for the .22 Jet, appeared in 1961; and the cartridge created extraction problems for a revolver. Ruger solved the problem with the introduction of the Hawkeye—a single-shot that looked like a six shooter. In place of the cylinder was a breech block that cammed to the side for loading. This pistol was excellent from an engineering and performance standpoint but was not a commercial success. The Hawkeye is chambered for the .256 Magnum, a bottleneck cartridge, and has an 8.5" barrel and adjustable sights. The finish is blued with walnut, medallion grips. The barrel Is tapped at the factory for a 1" scope base. This pistol is quite rare as only 3,300 were produced in 1963 and 1964.

NIB	EXC.	V.G.	GOOD	FAIR	POOR
2500	1900	1400	850	600	500

EDITOR'S COMMENT: All the above single-action Ruger pistols, fitted with factory optional grips, will bring a premium regardless of model. This premium applies to pistols manufactured from 1954 to 1962 only. For optional grips premium is: Ivory $800; Stag $400.

NIB	EXC.	V.G.	GOOD	FAIR	POOR

NEW MODEL SINGLE-ACTION REVOLVERS

Ruger firm in 1973, completely modified their single-action lockwork to accommodate a hammer block or transfer bar. This hammer block or transfer bar prevented accidental discharge, should a revolver be dropped. In doing so, the company circumvented a great deal of potential legal problems and made collectibles out of previous models.

Super Single Six Convertible (New Model)

This model is similar in appearance to the old model, but has the new hammer block safety system. Frame has two pins instead of three screws and opening the loading gate frees the cylinder stop for loading. Barrel lengths are 4.625", 5.5", 6.5" and 9.5". Sights are adjustable and finish is blued. Grips are walnut, with a medallion. An interchangeable .22 Magnum cylinder is supplied. Introduced in 1973 and currently in production.

NIB	EXC.	V.G.	GOOD	FAIR	POOR
450	350	250	200	175	125

Stainless Steel Single Six Convertible

Same as standard blued model, but made from stainless steel. Offered with 4.625", 6.5" and 9.5" barrel. **NOTE:** Add 40 percent premium for pre-warning pistols (1973-1976) with 4.625" or 9.5" barrel; 100 percent premium, at least, to NIB prices for pistols with 4.625" barrels with "made in the 200th year of American Liberty" rollmark on the barrel.

NIB	EXC.	V.G.	GOOD	FAIR	POOR
475	400	300	250	225	175

New Model Single Six (.22 LR only) "Star" Model

This model was produced in blue and stainless for one year only in 4-5/8", 5-1/2", 6-1/2", and 9-1/2" barrel lengths. Very low production on this model.

Blue Variation 5.5" or 6.5" Barrel

NIB	EXC.	V.G.	GOOD	FAIR	POOR
450	400	350	300	275	200

9.5" Barrel—Rare

NIB	EXC.	V.G.	GOOD	FAIR	POOR
550	500	450	400	350	250

4.62" Barrel—Very Rare

NIB	EXC.	V.G.	GOOD	FAIR	POOR
800	750	450	400	350	250

Stainless Variation 5.5" or 6.5" Barrel

NIB	EXC.	V.G.	GOOD	FAIR	POOR
450	350	275	225	175	150

9.5" Barrel

NIB	EXC.	V.G.	GOOD	FAIR	POOR
600	500	400	300	225	175

4.62" Barrel—Rare

NIB	EXC.	V.G.	GOOD	FAIR	POOR
650	550	500	400	300	200

Fixed Sight New Model Single Six

First made as drift adjustable rear sight (500 each in 4-5/8", 5-1/2", and 6-1/2" blue) and now a catalogued item as a pinched frame style fixed rear sight. Barrel lengths are offered in 5-1/2" and 6-1/2" lengths. Finish is blued or glossy stainless steel. Rear sight is fixed. Weights are between 32 and 38 oz. depending on barrel length and cylinder.

Blued Finish

NIB	EXC.	V.G.	GOOD	FAIR	POOR
325	295	250	165	125	100

Stainless Steel

NIB	EXC.	V.G.	GOOD	FAIR	POOR
395	300	250	200	150	125

Colorado Centennial Single Six

This model had a stainless steel grip frame, and the balance is blued. It has walnut grips with medallion insert. The barrel is 6-1/2", and the revolver is furnished with a walnut case with a centennial medal insert. There were 15,000 manufactured in 1975.

NIB	EXC.	V.G.	GOOD	FAIR	POOR
500	400	300	200	125	100

Model "SSM" Single Six

This is the Single Six chambered for the .32 H&R Magnum cartridge. The first 800 pistols were marked with "SSM" on the cylinder frame and will bring a slight premium. Sold from 1984 to 1997. Adjustable sights.

NIB	EXC.	V.G.	GOOD	FAIR	POOR
700	525	375	225	150	125

New Model Single Six .32 H&R

Introduced in 2000. Revolver chambered for .32 H&R Magnum cartridge. Fitted with 4.625" barrel. Offered in blue or stainless steel. Short (1/4" shorter) simulated ivory grips. Vaquero-style

	NIB	EXC.	V.G.	GOOD	FAIR	POOR

frame with fixed sights. Values shown are for stainless. Deduct 25 percent for blued.

	525	400	300	225	175	125

New Model Single Six 50th Anniversary Model

Introduced in 2003 this model features a 4.625" barrel with blued finish. Top of barrel is rollmarked "50 years of single six 1953-2003" . Comes standard with both .22 LR and .22 WMR cylinders. Cocobolo grips with red Ruger medallion. Packaged in a red plastic case with special "50 Year" label. Offered only in 2003.

425	350	300	225	175	125

New Model Super Single Six

Chambered for the .22 LR and a separate cylinder for the .22 WMR cartridge. Barrel lengths are 4.625", 5.5", 6.5", and 9.5". Rosewood grips and adjustable or fixed sights. Blued finish except for optional stainless steel on 5.5" or 6.5" revolvers. Weight is about 35 oz. depending on barrel length. **NOTE:** For stainless steel models add $80.

375	325	275	225	175	125

New Model Super Single Six, .17 HMR

As above but with 6.5" barrel and chambered for the .17 HMR cartridge. Weight is about 35 oz. Introduced in 2003.

400	350	275	225	175	125

New Model Single Six Hunter Convertible

This model is chambered for the .17 HMR/.17 Mach 2. Fitted with a 7.5" barrel with adjustable rear sight. Stainless steel finish with black laminate grips. The integral barrel rib machined for scope rings. Weight is about 45 oz. Introduced in 2005.

675	500	500	300	250	175

Single-Ten

10-shot version of Single-Six, with 5.5" barrel and walnut Gunfighter grips. Other features include satin stainless finish and Williams adjustable fiber optic sights. Introduced in late 2011. A 9-shot variation with 6.5" barrel introduced in 2013 as Single-Nine.

525	450	385	300	220	150

Single-Nine

Identical to Single Ten, except chambered for .22 Winchester Magnum Rimfire. Has 9-round cylinder.

525	450	385	300	220	150

Buckeye Special

This model was built in 1989 and 1990. It is chambered for the .38-40 or 10mm and .32-20 or .32 H&R cartridges.

750	600	400	275	200	125

New Model Blackhawk

Similar in appearance to old model Blackhawk. Offered in same calibers and barrel lengths. Has transfer bar safety device. Introduced in 1973. Chambered in .30 Carbine, .357 Magnum, .41 Magnum and .45 Colt. Various barrel lengths.

500	425	300	200	150	125

New Model Blackhawk Flattop

The .44 Special Blackhawk became a reality in 2010. Made only in Flattop design, with blue finish and 4.625" or 5.5" barrel.

500	425	300	200	150	120

New Model Blackhawk Bisley

Based on Colt Bisley frame, with adjustable sights and longer grip frame. Chambered in .44 Magnum or .45 Colt, with 7.5" barrel, blue finish, alloy frame and hardwood grips.

700	600	475	375	300	250

50th Anniversary New Model Blackhawk NVB34-50

Introduced in 2005. Features smaller original size XR-3 grip, smaller main frame with checkered hard rubber grips. Adjustable rear sight. Special commemorative gold roll mark on top of barrel. Chambered for .357 Magnum and fitted with 4.625" barrel. Weight about 45 oz. All Blackhawk revolvers now feature this new/old smaller main frame.

575	425	300	200	150	125

	NIB	EXC.	V.G.	GOOD	FAIR	POOR

Stainless Steel Blackhawk (New Model)

New Model Blackhawk made from stainless steel. To date offered in .357, .44, .45 L.C. and .327 Federal calibers.

NIB	EXC.	V.G.	GOOD	FAIR	POOR
600	500	420	300	200	150

Blackhawk Convertible (New Model)

This model is the same as the Blackhawk with interchangeable conversion cylinders—.357 Magnum/9mm and .45 Colt/.45 ACP. Prices listed are for blued model.

NIB	EXC.	V.G.	GOOD	FAIR	POOR
465	350	250	175	150	125

.45 ACP & .45 Long Colt Convertible (1998)

NIB	EXC.	V.G.	GOOD	FAIR	POOR
550	450	350	275	225	150

Stainless Model .357/9mm

300 guns built.

NIB	EXC.	V.G.	GOOD	FAIR	POOR
925	700	600	500	375	250

Fiftieth Anniversary .44 Magnum Flattop New Model Blackhawk

Six-shot, single-action .44 Magnum (also accepts .44 Special) with 6.5" barrel and adjustable rear sight, 47 oz. Recreation of original .44 Falt-Top Blackhawk. Blued with checkered rubber grips. Gold, color-filled rollmark on top of barrel. Introduced 2006.

NIB	EXC.	V.G.	GOOD	FAIR	POOR
750	625	525	400	350	300

Model SRM Blackhawk .357 Maximum

This is the New Model Blackhawk with a 7.5" or 10.5" barrel. It was chambered for the .357 Maximum and was intended for silhouette shooting. This model experienced problems with gas erosion in the forcing cone and under the top strap and was removed from production in 1984 after approximately 9200 were manufactured.

NIB	EXC.	V.G.	GOOD	FAIR	POOR
—	675	575	400	275	250

Super Blackhawk (New Model)

This model is similar in appearance to the Old Model but has the transfer bar safety device. It was manufactured from 1973 to the present and commenced at serial number 81-00001.

NIB	EXC.	V.G.	GOOD	FAIR	POOR
600	550	450	325	250	175

Super Blackhawk Stainless Steel

This model is the same as the blued version but is made of stainless steel. In 1998 this model was offered in 4-5/8" or 7-1/2" barrels with hunter grip frame and laminated grip panels. **NOTE:** Add $50 to prices for hunter grip frame and laminated grip panels.

NIB	EXC.	V.G.	GOOD	FAIR	POOR
650	600	500	350	250	175

Super Blackhawk Hunter

Introduced in 2002 this .44 or .41 Magnum model features a 7.5" barrel with integral full-length solid rib for scope mounts. Stainless steel. Adjustable rear sight. Scope rings included. Weight is about 52 oz.

NIB	EXC.	V.G.	GOOD	FAIR	POOR
800	700	500	350	250	175

50th Anniversary Matched Set .357 and .44 Magnum

Matched pair of Ruger New Blackhawks, one in .44 and the other in .357, commemorating 50th anniversary of Ruger Blackhawk revolver. Gold-filled rollmarked 6-1/2" and 4-5/8" barrels, respectively. Includes presentation case. Production limited. Introduced 2007.

NIB	EXC.	V.G.	GOOD	FAIR	POOR
1350	1150	900	775	600	400

Bisley Model

This model has the modified features found on the famous old Colt Bisley Target model—the flat top frame, fixed or adjustable sights, and the longer grip frame that has become the Bisley trademark. The Bisley is available chambered for .22 LR, .32 H&R Magnum, .357 Magnum, .41 Magnum, .44 Magnum, and .45 Long Colt. The barrel lengths are 6.5" and 7.5"; cylinders are either fluted or unfluted and roll engraved. The finish is a satin blue, and the grips are smooth Goncalo Alves with medallions. The Bisley was introduced in 1986. **NOTE:** Approximately 750 stainless grip frame .22 caliber Bisleys were made. These will demand a premium. Add $100 for stainless and $125 for convertible stainlesss.

.22 LR and .32 H&R Magnum

NOTE: Add $100 for .32 Magnum Bisley.

NIB	EXC.	V.G.	GOOD	FAIR	POOR
425	375	225	200	150	125

NIB	EXC.	V.G.	GOOD	FAIR	POOR

.357 Magnum, .41 Magnum, .44 Magnum, .45 Colt

600	500	375	300	200	125

Shootists Bisley

Produced in 1994 for the Shootist organization in memory of Tom Ruger. Chambered for the .22 cartridge these revolvers were limited to 52 total produced. They were stainless steel and were fitted with 4-5/8" barrels. The barrels were marked, "IN MEMORY OF OUR FRIEND TOM RUGER THE SHOOTIST 1994" . Some of these revolvers, but not all, have the name of the owner engraved on the backstrap. **NOTE:** Due to this model's rarity, values are speculative.

2500	2000	1200	1000	—	—

Old Army Percussion Revolver

A .45-caliber percussion revolver, with 5" or 7.5" barrel. Has 6-shot cylinder, with blued finish and walnut grips. Beginning in 1994, this model offered with fixed sights. Weight about 46 oz. All models now discontinued. **NOTE:** Add $450 for pistols with original factory installed brass grip frame; 20 percent for 5.5" model.

575	475	375	250	175	150

Old Army Stainless Steel

This model is the same as the blued version except that it is made of stainless steel. Add 200 percent for stainless 200th Year model.

650	525	400	275	225	150

Ruger Vaquero

This single-action pistol was introduced in 1993 and was voted handgun of the year by the shooting industry. It is a fixed sight version of the New Model Blackhawk. It is available in stainless steel or blued with case-colored frame. Offered in three different barrel lengths: 4.62", 5.5", and 7.5". Chambered for the .45 Long Colt. In 1994 the .44-40 and .44 Magnum calibers were added to the Vaquero line. Capacity is 6 rounds. Weighs between 39 and 41 oz. depending on barrel length. Discontinued; superseded by New Vaquero. **NOTE:** Vaqueros with 4-5/8" barrel chambered for .44 Magnum in both blue and stainless are uncatalogued, add 25 percent.

500	425	325	200	150	100

Ruger Bisley Vaquero

Introduced in 1997 this model features a 5.5" barrel chambered for .44 Magnum or .45 Long Colt. Grips are smooth rosewood. Finish is blued with case colored frame. Blade front sight and notch rear. Weight is about 40 oz. Discontinued.

600	500	425	325	225	150

Ruger Vaquero Bird's-head

Introduced in 2001 this model features a bird's-head grip. Chambered for the .45 Long Colt cartridge and fitted with a 5.5" barrel. Offered in stainless steel and blued finish. Weight is about 40 oz. Discontinued.**NOTE:** In 2002 this model was offered with 3.75" barrel and black Micarta grips. In 2003 this model was offered chambered for the .357 Magnum cartridge. Simulated ivory grips are also offered.

650	550	400	300	175	125

"Cowboy Pair"

Matched pair of engraved and consecutively serial-numbered New Vaquero revolvers in .45 Colt. Includes lined wood collector case. Production limited to 500 sets. Introduced 2007.

3500	3000	2500	1350	1000	600

Ruger New Vaquero

Introduced in 2005 this model features a slimmer pre-1962 XR-3 style grip frame with color case finish. The cylinder frame is mid-size. The cylinder is beveled. The ejector rod head is crescent shaped. Chambered for the .357 Mag or .45 Colt. Barrel lengths are 4.625", 5.5", and 7.5" (not in .357). Choice of case colored finish or stainless steel. Black checkered grips. Weight is about 37 oz depending on barrel length.

575	475	400	300	200	100

Ruger New Model Bisley Vaquero

Similar to New Vaquero but with Bisley-style hammer and grip frame. Chambered in .357 and .45 Colt. Features include a 5.5" barrel, simulated ivory grips, fixed sights, six-shot cylinder. Overall length 11.12" . Weight: 45 oz. Add 15 percent for stainless steel finish.

565	425	325	225	165	150

New Ruger Bearcat (Super Bearcat)

This old favorite was reintroduced in 1994. This new version is furnished with a .22 LR cylinder and a .22 WMR cylinder. Barrel length is 4" with fixed sights. Grips are walnut. Offered with blued

	NIB	EXC.	V.G.	GOOD	FAIR	POOR

finish. **NOTE:** There was a factory recall on the magnum cylinders. Bearcats with both cylinders are very rare.

Blue

	NIB	EXC.	V.G.	GOOD	FAIR	POOR
	425	325	250	175	125	100

Stainless Steel

	NIB	EXC.	V.G.	GOOD	FAIR	POOR
	450	350	275	200	150	125

Convertible (Recalled)

	NIB	EXC.	V.G.	GOOD	FAIR	POOR
	1100	1000	900	650	400	200

New Model Super Bearcat

Reintroduced in 2002 this .22 caliber model features a stainless steel or blued finish, 4" barrel with fixed sights and rosewood grips. Weight is about 24 oz. **NOTE:** Add $50 for stainless steel version.

	NIB	EXC.	V.G.	GOOD	FAIR	POOR
	425	325	250	175	125	100

Fiftieth Anniversary New Bearcat

Gussied-up version of the New Bearcat (.22 LR only) commemorating the 50th anniversary of the original Bearcat. Blued finish with gold-filled anniversary script, gold-colored trigger guard and special box with anniversary booklet. Manufactured in 2008 only.

	NIB	EXC.	V.G.	GOOD	FAIR	POOR
	700	600	500	—	—	—

DOUBLE-ACTION REVOLVERS

Security Six

This revolver, also known as the Model 117, is chambered for the .357 Magnum cartridge and has a 2.75", 4", or 6" barrel. It features adjustable sights, with blue or stainless finish and a square butt, with checkered walnut grips. It was manufactured between 1970 and 1985. Early guns with fixed sights and square butt were also marked "Security-Six" . The model was later termed "Service-Six" and was so marked. The prices listed are only for the adjustable sight and square butt "Security-Six" models. **NOTE:** Fixed sight guns marked Security-Six and round butt Security-Sixes with adjustable sights are worth a premium.

	NIB	EXC.	V.G.	GOOD	FAIR	POOR
	450	400	350	295	200	150

Speed Six

This model is known as the Model 207, chambered for .357 Magnum; Model 208, chambered for .38 Special; and Model 209, chambered for 9mm. It has a 2.75" or 4" barrel, fixed sights, and a round butt with checkered walnut grips and was blued. There are some with factory bobbed hammers. This model was introduced in 1973. Discontinued. Add 200 percent for military (lanyard ring) and .38 S&W (not .38 Special) marked models.

	NIB	EXC.	V.G.	GOOD	FAIR	POOR
	400	350	300	250	200	150

Models 737, 738, 739

These are the designations for the stainless steel versions of the Speed-Six. They are the same revolver except for the material used in the manufacture. **NOTE:** Add $150 for 739.

	NIB	EXC.	V.G.	GOOD	FAIR	POOR
	500	425	350	300	225	125

GP-100

Model chambered for .327 Federal or .357 Magnum/.38 Special. Available with fixed or adjustable sights. Barrel lengths of 3", 4" or 6" and a frame designed for constant use of heavy Magnum loads. Rear sight has a white outline and front sight features interchangeable colored inserts. Finish is blued. Grips are a new design made of rubber, with smooth Goncalo Alves inserts. Introduced in 1986.

	NIB	EXC.	V.G.	GOOD	FAIR	POOR
	550	400	325	250	150	100

GP-100 Stainless

Same as GP-100, except material used is stainless steel.

	NIB	EXC.	V.G.	GOOD	FAIR	POOR
	600	450	375	300	200	150

GP-100 Match Champion

This .357 Magnum model has a slab-sided, half-lug 4.2" barrel. Novak Lo-Mount rear and green fiber-optic front sights. Stainless finish and Hogue hardwood grips, with stippled sides. Introduced in 2014.

	NIB	EXC.	V.G.	GOOD	FAIR	POOR
	725	600	450	300	225	150

	NIB	EXC.	V.G.	GOOD	FAIR	POOR

SP-101

This model is similar in appearance to the GP-100 but has a smaller frame and is chambered for the .22 LR (6-shot), .38 Special (5-shot), .357 Magnum (5-shot), and 9mm (5-shot). The grips are all black synthetic, and the sights are adjustable for windage. Barrel lengths are 2" or 3", and construction is of stainless steel. This model was introduced in 1989. 6" barrel is available for .22 caliber. .327 Federal Magnum chambering added 2008. Add $100 for Crimson Trace lasergrips (limited edition for 2008).

525	425	300	200	150	125

SP-101 Spurless-Hammer

Introduced in 1993. Features an SP-101 without an exposed hammer spur. Available in two calibers: .38 Special and .357 Magnum, with 2.25" barrel. This double-action revolver has fixed sights and holds 5 rounds. Weight about 26 oz.

550	450	325	225	150	125

Redhawk

Large frame double-action revolver was chambered for .357 and .41 Magnums until 1992 and for .44 Magnum until it was discontinued in 2009. Barrel lengths are 5.5" and 7.5". Finish is blued and grips are smooth walnut. Redhawk was introduced in 1979. **NOTE:** Add 100 percent for .357; 50 percent for .41.

650	500	425	350	250	150

Redhawk Stainless Steel

Same as blued version, except constructed of stainless steel. Chambered for .357 Magnum until 1985; .41 Magnum until 1992; and currently for .44 Magnum. In 1998, this model was offered chambered for .45 Long Colt cartridge, in barrel lengths of 4", 5.5" and 7.5". This model was temporarily discontinued in 2013, but back in production in 2014. **NOTE:** Add 100 percent for .357; 50 percent for .41.

800	675	525	400	300	200

Redhawk 4-Inch .45 Colt (2008)

Similar to original stainless Redhawk but in .45 Colt only and with a 4" barrel. Hogue molded grips.

800	700	600	450	300	200

Super Redhawk

This is a more massive version of the Redhawk. It weighs 53 oz. and is offered with a 7.5" or 9.5" barrel. It is made of stainless steel with either brushed or dull grey finish, and the barrel rib is milled to accept the Ruger scope-ring system. The grips are the combination rubber and Goncalo Alves-type found on the GP-100. This revolver was introduced in 1987. In 1999 this model was offered chambered for the .454 Casull cartridge with 7.5" or 9.5" barrel. In 2001 this model was offered in .480 Ruger caliber in 7.5" or 9.5" barrel. Also available jn .44 Magnum. **NOTE:** Add $200 for .454 Casull or .480 Ruger caliber. Revolvers chambered for the .454 Casull also accept .45 Long Colt cartridges.

740	550	400	275	200	150

Super Redhawk Alaskan

This revolver is chambered for the .454 Casull and the .45 Colt interchangeable or the .480 Ruger cartridge. Barrel length is 2.5" with adjustable rear sight. Cylinder capacity is 6 rounds. Stainless steel finish. Hogue Tamer rubber grips. Weight is about 42 oz. Introduced in 2005. .44 Magnum chambering added 2007.

850	700	500	375	250	200

Police Service-Six

This model is also known as the Model 107, chambered for .357 Magnum; the Model 108, chambered for the .38 Special; and the 109, chambered for the 9mm. The barrel is 2.75" or 4". A few 6" barrel Service-Sixes were also produced and these are worth a premium. It has fixed sights and a square butt, with checkered walnut grips. The finish is blued. The 9mm was discontinued in 1984; the other two calibers, in 1988. Add 60 percent for 9mm.

425	350	300	200	150	100

Model 707 and 708

This is the designation for the stainless versions of the Police Service-Six. It was not produced in 9mm, and only the 4" barrel was offered. This model was discontinued in 1988.

450	375	300	200	150	100

LCR Lightweight Compact Revolver

Polymer-frame compact revolver chambered in .22 LR, .38 Special and .357 Magnum. Features include five-shot stainless steel cylinder finished in Advanced Target Gray, 1.875" stainless steel

NIB	EXC.	V.G.	GOOD	FAIR	POOR

barrel, fixed sights, Hogue or Crimson Trace grips, matte black frame. Overall length 6.5". Weight 13 oz. **NOTE:** Add $75 for .357 Magnum chambering; $200 for Crimson Trace Lasergrips.

NIB	EXC.	V.G.	GOOD	FAIR	POOR
425	350	250	200	150	100

SEMI-AUTOMATIC CENTERFIRE HANDGUNS

P-85

This model was Ruger's entry into the wonder-nine market. While it was announced in 1985, it was 1987 before it went into production. P-85 was the first of a series of "P" model Ruger pistols, which remained in production through 2013. It was also the first Ruger firearm manufactured at the Prescott, Arizona plant. This was a very successful, moderately priced double-action, high-capacity 9mm pistol, at a time when law enforcement and much of the civilian market was embracing this type of pistol. Original model had a matte black finish, black synthetic grips and an alloy frame and steel slide. Other features were 4.5" barrel, fixed three-dot sights and ambidextrous safety. **NOTE:** As of 2013, all P-series pistols had been discontinued.

NIB	EXC.	V.G.	GOOD	FAIR	POOR
400	360	300	275	200	150

KP85

This model is the same as matte black version, except receiver assembly is made of stainless steel.

NIB	EXC.	V.G.	GOOD	FAIR	POOR
425	375	325	295	200	150

KP89X

Introduced in 1993 this pistol features a stainless steel convertible safety model which comes with both 9mm and .30 Luger barrels. The barrels are interchangeable without the use of tools. Magazine capacity is 15 rounds. Less than 6,000 produced.

NIB	EXC.	V.G.	GOOD	FAIR	POOR
500	400	345	245	200	150

P89

Introduced in 1991. This semi-automatic pistol is chambered for 9mm cartridge. Has a blued finish and 15-round magazine. Safety is a manual ambidextrous lever type. Barrel is 4.5". Empty weight about 36 oz.

NIB	EXC.	V.G.	GOOD	FAIR	POOR
425	350	300	225	150	100

KP89

Same configuration as P89, but furnished with a stainless steel finish. Introduced in 1991.

NIB	EXC.	V.G.	GOOD	FAIR	POOR
450	375	325	250	150	100

P89DC

This model features a blued finish and is chambered for the 9mm Parabellum cartridge but is fitted with a decock-only lever (no manual safety). After decocking the gun can be fired by a double-action pull of the trigger.

NIB	EXC.	V.G.	GOOD	FAIR	POOR
425	375	350	250	200	150

KP89DC

Stainless steel version of P89DC, with decock only.

NIB	EXC.	V.G.	GOOD	FAIR	POOR
450	375	325	250	150	100

KP89DAO

Chambered for 9mm cartridge. This model is the stainless steel double-action-only version of above model.

NIB	EXC.	V.G.	GOOD	FAIR	POOR
450	375	325	250	150	100

KP90

Chambered for .45 ACP cartridge. This model is in stainless steel. Magazine holds 7 rounds. Fitted with a manual safety. Introduced in 1991.

NIB	EXC.	V.G.	GOOD	FAIR	POOR
500	450	375	285	225	150

KP90DC

Stainless steel version of KP90, with a decock-only system. Chambered for .45 ACP cartridge.

NIB	EXC.	V.G.	GOOD	FAIR	POOR
500	450	375	285	225	150

P90

Same as above model, with blued finish. Introduced in 1998.

NIB	EXC.	V.G.	GOOD	FAIR	POOR
475	425	350	275	225	150

	NIB	EXC.	V.G.	GOOD	FAIR	POOR

KP91DC

This model features a stainless steel finish and is chambered for the .40 S&W cartridge. Magazine capacity is 11 rounds. It has a decock-only system. Introduced in 1992. Discontinued.

475	375	325	295	200	150

KP91DAO

Chambered for the .40 S&W with stainless steel finish it features a double-action-only system. Discontinued.

475	375	325	295	200	150

P93D

This is a blued version with ambidextrous decocker and 3.9" barrel. Introduced in 1998.

400	300	250	200	150	100

KP93DC

Introduced in 1993 as a compact model. Stainless steel and chambered for 9mm cartridge. Magazine capacity 15 rounds. Available in decock-only configuration. Barrel length 3.9". Weight about 24 oz. empty.

475	425	350	275	225	150

KP93DAO

Double-action-only version of KP93 compact series.

475	425	350	275	225	150

KP94

Introduced in 1994 this model is smaller than the full-size P series pistols and the compact P93 pistols. Offered in 9mm or .40 S&W calibers this pistol has an aluminum alloy frame and stainless steel slide. Barrel length is 4-1/4" and magazine capacity for the 9mm is 15 rounds and for the .40 11 rounds. Weight is approximately 33 oz. It is offered in double-action-only as well as traditional double-action. A decock-only model is available also.

415	350	300	250	200	150

KP94DC

This is similar to the model above but in decock only.

415	350	300	250	200	150

P94

This is a blued version of the KP94. Introduced in 1998.

400	300	250	200	150	100

KP94DAO

Same as the KP94 model but in double-action-only.

400	350	300	250	200	150

KP944

Chambered for .40 S&W cartridge. This model has a stainless steel tapered slide, 11-round magazine and manual safety. Models made after September, 1994 have a 10-round magazine.

450	400	350	275	225	150

KP944DC

Same as above, with a decock-only system.

450	400	350	275	225	150

KP944DAO

Same as model above, with double-action-only model of fire.

450	400	350	275	225	150

P95

Introduced in 1996. This 9mm pistol features 3.9" barrel, polymer frame and stainless steel slide. Decocker only. Fixed 3-dot sights are standard. Overall length 7.3". Empty weight about 29 oz. In 2001, model was offered with a manual safety and blued finish.

450	350	300	225	150	100

KP95DC

Same as matte black version of P95, only this is in stainless steel. Has a decock-only lever.

450	350	300	225	150	100

	NIB	EXC.	V.G.	GOOD	FAIR	POOR

P95DAO

Same as above but in double-action-only.

| | 450 | 350 | 300 | 225 | 150 | 100 |

KP95DAO

Same as the model above but in double-action-only. In 2001 this model was offered with a manual safety and blued finish.

| | 450 | 350 | 300 | 225 | 150 | 100 |

KP97D

Introduced in 1999 this decock-only model is chambered for the .45 ACP cartridge. It has a stainless steel slide. Magazine capacity is 7 rounds. Fixed sights. Weight is about 27 oz.

| | 450 | 350 | 300 | 225 | 150 | 100 |

KP97DAO

Same specifications as the model above but in double-action-only. Introduced in 1999.

| | 450 | 350 | 300 | 225 | 150 | 100 |

KP345

Introduced in 2004 this .45 ACP model features a 4.2" stainless steel barrel and stainless steel slide. Fixed sights. Internal lock, loaded chamber indicator, magazine disconnect, and a new cam block design to reduce recoil. Black polymer checkered grips. Magazine capacity is 8 rounds. Weight is about 29 oz. Available with ambidextrous safety or decocker.

| | 550 | 425 | 300 | 250 | 175 | 125 |

KP345PR

Similar to the model above but fitted with a Picatinny-style rail under the forward portion of the frame. Introduced in 2004.

| | 550 | 425 | 300 | 250 | 175 | 125 |

SR9 / SR40

Introduced in 2008. Ruger's first striker-fired semi-automatic pistol. Chambered in 9mm Parabellum or .40 S&W. Double-action only with 4.14" barrel, 17+1 capacity. Available in three finish configurations: stainless steel slide with matte black frame; blackened stainless slide with matte black frame; blackened stainless slide with matte black frame. Also available in compact version with 3.5" barrel (SR9c, SR40c). **NOTE:** Ruger recalled all early-production SR9 pistols with a "330" serial number prefix because of a potential safety issue. SR40 has a 15-round magazine.

| | 450 | 350 | 300 | 225 | 150 | 100 |

SR45

Slightly larger variation of SR40. Chambered for .45 ACP, with 10-round magazine, 4.5" barrel.

| | 475 | 425 | 375 | 300 | 250 | 200 |

SR22

Polymer-frame semi-automatic in .22 Long Rifle. Barrel length 3.5", overall length 6.4". Weight unloaded 17.5 oz. Features include Picatinny accessory rail, interchangeable grips and adjustable sights. Thumb safety/decocking lever and magazine release are all ambidextrous. **NOTE:** Add $25 for threaded barrel or silver anodized finish.

| | 350 | 300 | 275 | 225 | 150 | 100 |

LCP (Lightweight Compact Pistol)

Introduced in 2008. Ruger's first true pocket pistol. Chambered in .380 (6+1 capacity), with 2.75" barrel. Double action only. Glass-filled nylon frame, with steel barrel. Black matte finish.

| | 325 | 285 | 235 | 185 | 125 | 100 |

LCP Crimson Trace

Similar to above, with CT laser grips.

| | 475 | 425 | 350 | 275 | 225 | 150 |

LC9

Subcompact 9mm pistol designed for concealed carry. Magazine capacity 7 rounds, barrel length 3.12", weight 17.1 oz. Steel slide, glass-filled nylon receiver, double-action-only trigger, hammer-fired operation. Three-dot sights, loaded-chamber indicator, manual safety, magazine disconnect and slide stop. **NOTE:** Add $100 for Crimson Trace LG-431 laser sight.

| | 385 | 335 | 285 | 200 | 150 | 100 |

	NIB	EXC.	V.G.	GOOD	FAIR	POOR

LC380

Variation of LC9. Chambered for .380 ACP cartridge. Dimensions identical to LC9. New 2013.

	NIB	EXC.	V.G.	GOOD	FAIR	POOR
	350	300	250	200	150	125

SR1911

Caliber .45 ACP, stainless steel slide and frame, 8-round magazine, extended thumb safety, grip tang and magazine release, Novak Lo-Mount 3-dot sights, checkered mainspring housing and hardwood grips. Standard 1911 dimensions and controls. Introduced in 2011. A Commander-size model with 4.25" barrel introduced in 2013.

	NIB	EXC.	V.G.	GOOD	FAIR	POOR
	725	600	500	400	350	200

SEMI-AUTOMATIC RIFLES

10/22 Standard Carbine With Walnut Stock

This model has an 18.5" barrel and is chambered for the .22 LR. It has a 10-shot, detachable rotary magazine and a folding rear sight. The stock is smooth walnut, with a barrel band and carbine-style buttplate. This rifle enjoys a fine reputation for accuracy and dependability and is considered an excellent value. It was introduced in 1964. **NOTE:** Birch stock deduct $20.

	NIB	EXC.	V.G.	GOOD	FAIR	POOR
	275	225	125	100	75	50

10/22 Standard Carbine Stainless Steel

Same as above but with stainless steel barrel and receiver.

	NIB	EXC.	V.G.	GOOD	FAIR	POOR
	300	250	150	125	100	75

10/22 Magnum

Introduced in 1999. Chambered for .22 Magnum cartridge. Barrel length 18.5". Folding rear sight and gold bead front sight. Hardwood stock. Weight about 5.5 lbs. Discontinued.

	NIB	EXC.	V.G.	GOOD	FAIR	POOR
	950	800	700	500	350	200

10/22 Sporter (Finger Groove Old Model)

Similar to Standard Carbine, except it has a Monte Carlo stock, finger-groove fore-end and no barrel band. Manufactured between 1966 and 1971. **NOTE:** Add 300 percent for factory hand checkering.

	NIB	EXC.	V.G.	GOOD	FAIR	POOR
	650	575	450	350	250	200

10/22 Deluxe Sporter

Same as the Sporter, with checkered stock and better buttplate. Introduced in 1971.

	NIB	EXC.	V.G.	GOOD	FAIR	POOR
	325	250	150	125	100	75

10/22 International Carbine

This model is similar to the Standard Carbine, with a full-length, Mannlicher-style stock. It was manufactured between 1966 and 1971 and is fairly rare on today's market. **NOTE:** Factory hand checkering add 50 percent.

	NIB	EXC.	V.G.	GOOD	FAIR	POOR
	—	1100	625	450	300	250

10/22 International Carbine (New Model)

This 1994 model is a reintroduction of the older version. It is offered in either a blued or stainless steel finish. Barrel length is 18-1/2". Magazine capacity is 10 rounds. The hardwood stock had no checkering when this model was first introduced. Shortly after introduced the factory began checkering these stocks. Weight is about 5.2 lbs. Discontinued.

	NIB	EXC.	V.G.	GOOD	FAIR	POOR
	465	300	225	—	—	—

Model 10/22T

Introduced in 1996 this model is a target version of the 10/22 line. It has a laminated American hardwood stock with blued heavy barrel with hammer-forged spiral finish. Rifle comes standard without sights. Barrel length is 20". Weight is approximately 7.25 lbs.

	NIB	EXC.	V.G.	GOOD	FAIR	POOR
	450	350	275	200	150	100

Model 10/22TNZ

This target model features a 20" stainless steel barrel and receiver with laminated thumbhole stock. No sights. Weight is about 7 lbs. Introduced in 2001.

	NIB	EXC.	V.G.	GOOD	FAIR	POOR
	500	375	275	200	150	100

Model 10/22 Canadian Centennial

In 1966 and 1967 approximately 4,500 10/22 Sporters were built for the Canadian Centennial. The first 2,000 were sold with a Remington Model 742 in .308 caliber with matching serial

	NIB	EXC.	V.G.	GOOD	FAIR	POOR

numbers. The Ruger Sporter may be checkered or uncheckered. The two-gun set was either boxed separately or together.

Two Gun Set

	NIB	EXC.	V.G.	GOOD	FAIR	POOR
	700	—	—	—	—	—

10/22 Only

	NIB	EXC.	V.G.	GOOD	FAIR	POOR
	450	—	—	—	—	—

10/22 Laminated Stock Carbine

Produced in varying quantities since 1986 these models are becoming quite collectible. The stocks range in color from dark green to gray and various shades of brown. Because there are so many different variations each should be individually appraised. Prices listed are for blued carbine models. **NOTE:** In stainless steel add approximately $40 to NIB price.

NIB	EXC.	V.G.	GOOD	FAIR	POOR
250	200	175	150	125	100

10/22 Laminated Stock Sporter Model

This model has a tree bark laminated stock.

NIB	EXC.	V.G.	GOOD	FAIR	POOR
325	275	225	175	150	100

10/22 Laminated Stock International

This stainless steel model was an exclusive Wal-Mart product. A few of these models in blue were also produced.

Blue

NIB	EXC.	V.G.	GOOD	FAIR	POOR
400	325	250	200	150	100

Stainless Steel

NIB	EXC.	V.G.	GOOD	FAIR	POOR
350	275	225	175	125	100

10/22 All Weather

This model is fitted with a stainless steel barrel and action and synthetic stock. Introduced in 1997. In 2001 this model was offered with blued finish. **NOTE:** Deduct $40 for blued model.

NIB	EXC.	V.G.	GOOD	FAIR	POOR
300	225	175	125	100	70

Model 10/22 Carbine 40th Anniversary

Model is blued with hardwood stock. Equipped with a 40th anniversary clear magazine, with red rotor and original scope base adapter. A nickel-silver medallion is inlaid on right side of the buttstock.

NIB	EXC.	V.G.	GOOD	FAIR	POOR
280	225	175	125	100	75

10/22 50th Anniversary

In 2013 and early 2014, Ruger staged a contest for 10/22 fans to design a 50th Anniversary Model. The winning entry became a production model in mid 2014. It has an 18.5" stainless barrel, black composite stock with adjustable comb and length of pull, ghost ring adjustable sights and grooved fore-end. MRSP at its 2014 introduction was $379

NIB	EXC.	V.G.	GOOD	FAIR	POOR
300	275	—	—	—	—

10/22 Compact Rifle 10/22 CRR

Similar to 10/22 standard rifle, with 16.25" blued barrel, shorter hardwood stock, fiber optic sights and 34.5" overall length. Introduced 2006.

NIB	EXC.	V.G.	GOOD	FAIR	POOR
275	225	175	125	100	75

K10/22T Ruger 10/22 Target Stainless

Similar to 10/22 Target but with stainless steel barrel and laminated stock.

NIB	EXC.	V.G.	GOOD	FAIR	POOR
495	425	350	275	200	150

10/22-T

Similar to 100/22 Target Stainless but with blued steel barrel and blued receiver. Introduced in 2007.

NIB	EXC.	V.G.	GOOD	FAIR	POOR
450	350	275	200	150	100

10/22RPFCARH (Lipsey's Distributor's Special)

Similar to 10/22 but covered throughout with RealTree Hardwoods HD camo finish. Introduced 2008.

NIB	EXC.	V.G.	GOOD	FAIR	POOR
275	225	175	125	100	75

	NIB	EXC.	V.G.	GOOD	FAIR	POOR

10/22VLEH Target Tactical Rifle

Semi-automatic rimfire rifle chambered in .22 LR. Features include precision-rifled cold hammer-forged spiral-finished 16-1/8" crowned match barrel; Hogue® OverMolded® stock; 10/22T target trigger; precision-adjustable bipod for steady shooting from bench; 10-round rotary magazine. Weight: 6-7/8 lbs.

485	400	350	300	225	150

10/22 Takedown

Takedown model. Barrel and fore-end separate from rest of rifle. Features same as other 10/22 models. Comes with nylon carry bag. **NOTE:** Add $20 for threaded 16.6" barrel and flash suppressor.

365	320	280	235	225	200

Model 10/17

Introduced in 2004. Chambered for .17 HMR cartridge. Fitted with 20" barrel. Magazine capacity 9 rounds. Weight about 6.5 lbs. Discontinued.

600	475	300	200	150	100

SR-22 Rifle

AR-style semi-automatic rifle chambered in .22 LR, based on 0/22 action. Features include all-aluminum chassis replicating the AR-platform dimensions between the sighting plane, buttstock height and grip; Picatinny rail optic mount includes a six-position telescoping M4-style buttstock (on a Mil-Spec diameter tube); Hogue Monogrip pistol-grip; buttstocks and grips interchangeable with any AR-style compatible option; round mid-length hand-guard mounted on a standard-thread AR-style barrel nut; precision-rifled cold hammer forged 16.125" alloy steel barrel capped with an SR-556/Mini-14 flash suppressor.

535	460	385	325	250	150

Model 44 Carbine

This model is a short, 18.5" barreled, gas-operated carbine chambered for the .44 Magnum cartridge. It has a 4-shot, nondetachable magazine, a folding rear sight, and a plain walnut stock. This is a handy deer hunting carbine manufactured between 1961 and 1985.

550	450	350	300	200	150

Deerstalker Model

The same as the Model 44 Carbine with "Deerstalker" stamped on it. This model was manufactured in 1961 and 1962 only.

950	800	600	400	300	200

Model 44 RS

This is the Model 44 with sling swivels and an aperture sight. **NOTE:** "Liberty" -marked 44RS carbines are extremely rare and will bring a premium.

—	600	550	350	200	150

Model 44 Sporter (Finger Groove Old Model)

This version has a Monte Carlo stock, finger groove fore-end, and no barrel band. It was manufactured until 1971. **NOTE:** Factory hand checkered models will bring at least a 75 percent premium.

—	750	600	400	250	200

Model 44 International Carbine

This version features a full-length, Mannlicher-style stock. It was discontinued in 1971 and is quite collectible. **NOTE:** Factory hand checkered models will bring at least a 50 percent premium.

—	800	600	425	350	275

Model 44 25th Anniversary Model

This version is lightly engraved, has a medallion in the stock and was only made in 1985, the last year of production.

550	400	350	300	250	200

Model 99/44 Deerfield Carbine

While chambered in .44 Magnum, this model not related to .44 Carbine, but a variation of Mini-14 and was in production from 2000 to 2006. Fitted with an 18.5" barrel, this gas operated rifle has a hardwood stock and 4-round magazine capacity. Adjustable rear sight. Blued finish. Weight about 6.2 lbs. This rifle will not cycle .44 Special ammo. Discontinued.

700	525	400	275	200	150

	NIB	EXC.	V.G.	GOOD	FAIR	POOR

Mini-14

This is a paramilitary-style carbine chambered for the .223 Remington and on a limited basis for the .222 cartridge. It has an 18.5" barrel and is gas-operated. The detachable magazines originally offered held 5, 10 or 20 rounds. The high-capacity magazines are now discontinued, and prices of them are what the market will bear. The Mini-14 has a military-style stock and aperture sight. It was introduced in 1975. 20-round magazine added 2009.

600	500	400	275	200	150

Mini-14 Stainless Steel

The same as the Mini-14 except constructed of stainless steel.

650	550	450	300	200	150

Mini-14 Target Rifle

Acccurized version of the Mini-14 but with matte stainless barrel and reciver, black laminated thumbhole stock, adjustable harmonic dampener. No sights. Also available with non-thumbhole synthetic stock. Introduced in 2007.

1025	900	775	600	400	250

Mini-14 Ranch Rifle

This model is similar to the standard Mini-14, with a folding rear sight and the receiver milled to accept the Ruger scope-ring system. The rings are supplied with the rifle. 6.8 Remington chambering also available. **NOTE:** Models chambered in .222 caliber will bring a premium.

625	500	450	350	250	175

Mini-14 Stainless All-Weather Ranch Rifle

Introduced in 1999 this model has all the features of the stainless steel Ranch Rifle with the addition of a black polymer stock. Weight is about 6.5 lbs.

810	600	450	300	200	150

NRA Mini-14

Ruger NRA Mini-14 Rifle with two 20-round magazines, gold-tone medallion in grip cap, and special serial number sequence (NRA8XXXXX). Produced in 2008 only. Also available with 5-round magazines.

1000	700	575	—	—	—

Mini-14 ATI Stock

Tactical version of Mini-14 but with six-position collapsible stock or folding stock, grooved pistol grip, multiple picatinny optics/accessories rails. Suggested retail price: $872.

675	550	425	300	200	150

Mini-14 Tactical Rifle

Similar to Mini-14 but with 16-12" barrel with flash hider, black synthetic stock, adjustable sights.

700	525	400	275	200	150

SR-556

AR-style semi-automatic rifle chambered in 5.56 NATO. Feature include two-stage piston; quad rail hand-guard; Troy Industries sights; black synthetic fixed or telescoping buttstock; 16.12" 1:9 steel barrel with birdcage; 10- or 30-round detachable box magazine; black matte finish overall. The 6.8 PPC was added in 2010, but discontinued after one year.

1750	1400	1250	900	600	250

SR-762

Same basic AR-style design of SR-556, but modified to handle 7.62 NATO (.308 Win.) cartridge.

1900	1550	1300	900	500	250

Mini-Thirty

This model brought out by Ruger in 1987. Similar in appearance to standard Mini-14. Supplied with Ruger scope rings. Chambered in 7.63x39; 6.8mm chambering added in 2007.

550	450	300	250	200	150

Mini-Thirty Stainless with Synthetic Stock

700	550	450	300	200	150

GB Model

This model has a factory-installed folding stock, flash suppressor, and bayonet lug. It was designed and sold by Ruger to law enforcement agencies. A number have come on the civilian market through surplus sales and police trade-ins. With the assault rifle hysteria, prices of this model have fluctuated wildly in some areas. Now that Ruger has discontinued the folding stock and the high-capacity

NIB	EXC.	V.G.	GOOD	FAIR	POOR

magazines, this could become even less predictable. Note that this is a semi-automatic and totally different than the full-auto version of this weapon available only through Class 3 dealers.

	1350	1100	650	400	300

PC4/PC9 Carbine

Semi-automatic carbine chambered for 9mm (PC9) or .40 S&W (PC4) cartridges. Fitted with 16.25" barrel and black synthetic stock. Post front sight with adjustable rear sight. A receiver sight is also offered. Detachable magazine has 10-round capacity. Weight about 6.4 lbs. Introduced in 1998. Discontinued. **NOTE:** Add $30 for receiver sight.

625	450	325	225	150	100

SINGLE-SHOT RIFLES

Ruger has announced a change in the available calibers for No. 1 series of single-shot rifles. Beginning in 2014, each variation will be chambered in only one caliber, and that caliber will be changed every year. In 2014, Light Sporter was made only in .280 Remington, Varminter in .220 Swift, International in .257 Roberts, Medium Sporter in 9.3x62 and Tropical in .450/400 Nitro Express 3". It is unknown how this limiting of caliber choices will affect values of Ruger No. 1s in the future.

No. 1 Light Sporter (1-A)

Features open sights, barrel band on lightweight barrel and Alexander Henry-style forearm. Offered with 22" barrel in many popular calibers. Weighs 7.25 lbs.

1050	900	750	550	350	200

No, 1 Light Standard (1-AB)

Similar to Light Sporter 1-A, with 22" sightless blued barrel.

900	800	650	450	300	200

No. 1 Standard (1-B)

Furnished with no sights, medium barrel, semi-beavertail forearm and quarter rib with 1" Ruger scope rings. Weighs 8 lbs. Introduced in 1966. Chambered in most popular calibers at various times. **NOTE:** Add 25 to 50 percent premium for rare calibers like .257 Roberts, 6.5 Rem. Magnum, 7x57 Mauser.

965	725	550	375	250	200

No. 1 Standard Stainless (1-B-BBZ)

In production from 2000 to 2010. Chambered in most popular calibers from .204 Ruger to .458 Winchester. Gray laminate stock. Barrel lengths from 22" to 26".

995	750	550	375	250	200

No. 1 Tropical (1-H)

Fitted with open sights. Barrel band on heavy barrel, with Alexander Henry-style forearm. Weighs 9 lbs. **NOTE:** In 2001, offered with stainless steel finish and black laminated stock in .375 H&H. In 2003, .458 Lott and .405 Win. cartridges were added. In 2008, .450/.400 Nitro Express added. In 2009, .416 Ruger added. Few 24" heavy barrel 1-H rifles chambered for .45-70 Government cartridge up to 1976. These bring substantial premium and should be appraised individually. **NOTE:** Add 100 percent for .404 Jeffery caliber; 250 percent for .45-70.

1050	900	750	550	350	200

No. 1 International (1-RSI)

This No. 1 rifle features a lightweight barrel, with full length forearm and open sights. Weighs 7.25 lbs.

1100	950	800	600	400	250

No. 1 Medium Sporter (1-S)

Medium Sporter equipped with open sights, barrel band on medium weight barrel and Alexander Henry-style forearm. Weighs 8 lbs. In 2001, offered in stainless steel and black laminated stock in .45-70 caliber. Chambered in a wide range of calibers including .218 Bee to .480 Ruger. In 2009, .300 H&H, .338 Ruger Compact Magnum, .375 Ruger, .460 S&W Magnum, .480Ruger/.475 Linebaugh added. **NOTE:** A 50th Anniversary No. 1 Medium Sporter Model in .45-70 with engraving and high grade walnut stock offered in 1999. Add 100 percent premium for this model.

1000	850	700	500	300	200

No. 1 Special Varminter (1-V)

Model furnished with no sights, heavy barrel, target scope blocks with 1" Ruger scope rings and semi-beavertail forearm. Weighs about 9 lbs.

1100	950	800	600	400	250

	NIB	EXC.	V.G.	GOOD	FAIR	POOR

No. 1 Stainless Varminter (1-V-BBZ)

Introduced in 2000. Features a laminated wood stock and stainless steel finish. Chambered for .22-250. Fitted with a 24" barrel. Weight about 9 lbs.

	995	750	550	375	250	200

No. 3 Carbine

This model is a less elaborate, inexpensive version of the No.1. Action is the same except the lever is less ornate in appearance and lacks the locking bar. Unchecked stock is of a military carbine style, with a barrel band. Similar in appearance to Model 44 and 10/22. This serviceable rifle was chambered for .45-70 when it was released in 1972. Later chamberings added .22 Hornet, .30-40 Krag, .223, .44 Magnum and .375 Winchester. Barrel is 22" long. There is a folding rear sight. Discontinued in 1987. **NOTE:** Add 25 percent premium for .44 Magnum or .375 Winchester.

	—	625	500	300	200	125

BOLT-ACTION RIFLES

Ruger introduced Model 77R in 1968. It filled the need for a good quality, reasonably priced, bolt-action hunting rifle. It has been a commercial success. There are certain variations of this rifle that collectors actively seek. One should avail oneself of the specialized literature on this model and secure individual appraisals on rare variations, as the differences are slight and beyond the scope of this book.

Model 77-R/RS

This model was introduced in 1968. It is offered with a 22", 24", or 26" barrel. The Model 77 is chambered for most calibers from .22-250 through .458 Win. Mag. The action is of a modified Mauser-type, finished in blue with a checkered walnut stock and red rubber buttplate. The rifle is available milled for Ruger scope rings or in the round-top style that allows the mounting of any popular scope ring system. This model is designated 77R when supplied with rings only; and 77RS, when supplied with rings and sights. This model was replaced by the Model 77 MK II.

	500	400	350	300	250	200

Model 77-RS

NOTE: Add $400 for 6.5 Rem., .284, .350 Rem.

	550	450	400	300	250	200

Model 77 Flat Bolt

This is an example of the slight variations that make this model collectible. This is essentially the same rifle with the knob on the bolt handle flattened. They were only produced in the configuration until 1972. Watch for fakes, and read specialized material. Calibers such as the 6.5 Rem. Mag., .284, and .350 Rem. Mag. will bring a premium especially in the RS model. Nonprefixed rifles exists in calibers and configurations other than those advertised by Ruger. These should be individually appraised. **NOTE:** Add $400 for 6.5 Rem., .284, .350 Rem.

	—	650	500	400	350	275

Model 77 RL & RLS

This variation is similar to the standard model except that it features an ultralight 20" barrel and black forearm tip. This model was also available in an 18.5" carbine version with sights designated the RLS. This model was also in an 18.5" carbine version with sights designated the RLS. They were chambered for the .22-250, .243, .257, .270, .250-3000, .308, and .30-06. Weight is only 6 lbs.

	550	450	375	325	275	225

Model 77V Varmint

This variation is similar to the standard Model 77 except that it has a 24" heavy barrel that is drilled and tapped for target-scope bases and has a wider beavertail forearm. It is chambered for the .22-250, .243, 6mm, .25-06, .280, and .308. This model was also chambered for the .220 Swift in a 26" heavyweight barrel.

	500	400	350	300	250	200

Model 77 RSI

This version of the Model 77 has a full-length, Mannlicher-style stock and was chambered for the .22-250, .250-3000, .243, .270, 7mm-08, .308 and the .30-06.

	700	600	500	300	275	200

Model 77 RS African

This is a heavier-barreled version, with a steel trigger guard and floorplate. Earlier versions were stocked with fine-quality Circassian walnut. This rifle is chambered for the .458 Winchester Magnum. **NOTE:** Fewer than 50 rifles chambered for the .416 Taylor cartridge were produced up

NIB	EXC.	V.G.	GOOD	FAIR	POOR

to 1976. Selling prices range from $3,000 to $5,000 and should be individually appraised. **NOTE:** Add $100 for early models with Circassian walnut stocks.

700	550	400	350	300	250

Model 77/17

Introduced in 2003. Chambered for .17 HMR cartridge and fitted with 22" barrel with no sights. Walnut stock, with blued finish. Magazine capacity 9 rounds. Weight about 6 lbs.

700	600	475	375	250	150

Model 77/17 Synthetic

As above but with black synthetic stock and blued finish.

625	475	350	250	175	125

Model 77/17 Varmint

As above but with black laminate stock and 24" stainless steel heavy barrel with no sights. Weight is about 7 lbs.

685	500	375	265	195	145

Model 77/17RM2

Introduced in 2005. Chambered for .17 Mach 2 caliber and fitted with 20" barrel with no sights. Walnut stock, with checkering. Blued finish. Weight about 6.5 lbs. Discontinued.

625	475	350	250	175	125

Model 77/17RM2 Stainless Steel

As above, with stainless steel finish and black laminate stock. Weight about 7.25 lbs. Introduced in 2005. Discontinued.

745	625	500	400	275	150

Model 77/22

A high quality, .22 rimfire (LR and WMR) rifle designed for the serious shooter. Has a 20" barrel and 10-shot detachable rotary magazine. Made of steel and stock with checkered walnut. Available with sights, scope rings or both as an extra-cost ($20) option. Introduced in 1984. Early guns without 77/22 rollmark on the receiver will bring a premium.

700	600	475	375	250	150

Model 77/22 Synthetic Stock

This version is quite similar to the standard 77/22, with a black-matte-finished synthetic stock.

625	450	350	250	200	150

Model 77/22 Stainless Steel/Synthetic Stock

This model same as blued version, except made of stainless steel.

750	650	500	400	275	150

Model 77/22 Varmint

Introduced in 1993 this model features a stainless steel finish, laminated wood stock, heavy 20" varmint barrel with no sights. Scope rings are included as standard. Chambered for the .22 LR or Win. Mag. Rimfire.

650	525	425	300	250	150

Model 77/22M

This model is simply the 77/22 chambered for .22 Magnum cartridge. Finish is blue. Magazine capacity 9 rounds.

700	600	475	375	250	150

Model 77/22M Stainless Steel

Same as blued 77/22M only constructed of stainless steel.

750	650	500	400	275	150

Model 77/22—.22 Hornet

Introduced in 1994. This version of 77/22 series is chambered for .22 Hornet cartridge. Furnished with or without sights. Barrel is 20". Has a 6-round detachable rotary magazine. Stock is checkered walnut, with sling swivels. Weight about 6 lbs. Also available chambered for .17 Hornet.

725	625	500	375	250	150

	NIB	EXC.	V.G.	GOOD	FAIR	POOR

Model K77/22VHZ

Introduced in 1995 this .22 Hornet variation features a stainless steel heavyweight barrel and laminated American hardwood stock. Offered without sights.

	685	525	425	300	250	150

Model 77R MKII

Introduced in 1992 this model is the basic Model 77 rifle. Features blued metal parts and no sights. Available in 15 different calibers from .223 to .338 Win. Mag. in barrel lengths from 22" to 24" depending on caliber. Comes from factory with scope bases and rings. Rifle weighs approximately 7 lbs.

	715	525	375	250	200	150

Model 77RP MKII

This model was also introduced in 1992 and differs from the Model 77R with the addition of stainless steel barrel and receiver and synthetic stock. Available in 10 calibers. In 1998 the .25-06 caliber was added to this model.

	715	525	375	250	200	150

Model 77RS MKII

This is a blued version of the basic rifle with the addition of open sights. Available in 9 calibers from .243 Win. to .458 Win. Mag.

	760	600	450	350	250	175

Model 77RSP MKII

Stainless version of the basic rifle, with the addition of a synthetic stock and open sights. Available in 6 calibers: .243, .270, 7MM Rem. Magnum, .30-06, .300 Win. Magnum, .338 Win. Magnum. Introduced in 1993.

	500	400	350	300	250	175

Model 77RSI MKII

Also introduced in 1993 this model features a blued barrel and full-length walnut stock. Offered in four calibers, all with 18" barrel. The calibers are: .243, .270, .30-06, and .308.

	820	600	450	350	250	175

Model 77RL MKII

This model features a short action in six calibers from .223 to .308, all with 20" barrel. Rifle weighs about 6 lbs. Introduced in 1992.

	770	575	425	300	200	150

Model 77LR MKII

This model is a left-handed rifle furnished in long action calibers: .270, 7mm Rem. Mag., .30-06, .300 Win. Mag. Introduced in 1992.

	770	575	425	300	200	150

Model 77RLP MKII

Introduced in 1999 this model is similar to the RL model above, but with an all-weather synthetic stock. Weight is about 6.5 lbs.

	715	525	400	275	200	150

Model 77VT MKII

This rifle was introduced in 1993 and is a target rifle. Furnished with no sights, heavy laminated wood stock with beavertail fore-end, and adjustable trigger. Barrel, bolt, and action are stainless steel. Weighs approximately 9.75 lbs. Furnished in eight calibers from .223 to .308.

	820	650	475	350	250	175

Model 77RBZ MKII

This model features a stainless steel barrel and action fitted with laminated hardwood stock. No sights. Weight is approximately 7.25 lbs. Offered in a wide variety of calibers from .223 to .338 Win. Mag. Introduced in 1997.

	600	500	400	300	225	175

Model 77RSBZ MKII

Same as above but fitted with open sights. Introduced in 1997.

	800	650	475	350	250	125

NIB	EXC.	V.G.	GOOD	FAIR	POOR

Model 77CR MKII Compact Rifle

Introduced in 2001. Features 16.5" barrel, with 4-round magazine. Chambered for .223 Rem., .243 Win., .260 Rem. and .308 Win. cartridges. Blued model fitted with walnut stock; stainless steel model with black laminated stock. Weight about 5.75 lbs. **NOTE:** Add $50 for stainless steel model (M77CRBBZ).

650	550	400	275	200	150

Model 77 Express MKII

Introduced in 1992 the Ruger Express Mark II rifle features a select Circassian walnut straight comb checkered stock. The checkering is 22 lpi and the buttstock is fitted with a rubber recoil pad. The pistol grip is fitted with a metal grip cap. The barrel length is 22" and features a blade front sight, V-notch rear express sights, and the receiver is machined for scope mounts, which are included. Available in these calibers: .270, .30-06, 7mm Rem. Mag., .300 Win. Mag., .338 Win. Mag. Rifle weighs about 7.5 lbs.

1200	850	650	550	400	200

Model 77 Magnum MKII RSM

Similar in all respects to Model 77 Express MKII, except offered in these calibers: .375 H&H, .416 Rigby and .458 Lott. Weight about: 9.25 lbs. for .375; 10.25 lbs. for.416 and .458 Lott.

1975	1500	1100	750	525	350

M77 MKII Frontier Rifle

Bolt-action rifle based on M77 MKII chassis. Configured for "scout" -style scope mount system. Chambered in .243, .308, 7mm-08, .300 WSM, .325 WSM. 338 Federal. Gray laminated stock, 16.5" blued or stainless barrel (add 15 percent for stainless). Introduced 2005; stainless barrel and action model introduced 2006 (add 10 percent). .338 Federal and .358 Winchester added 2008. Discontinued 2008.

600	500	400	300	225	175

Guide Gun

Compact variation of Model 77 Mark II, with 20" barrel, muzzle-brake, barrel band, express-style sights and integral scope mounts. Green Mountain laminated hardwood stock, with adjustable length of pull. Introduced in 2013.

1075	950	800	650	500	300

Gunsite Scout

Based on Ruger M77 rifle design. 16.5" barrel and forward mounted Picatinny rail for intermediate eye relief scopes. Chambered in .308 Win., with 10-round detachable magazine, integral scope mounts with rings and flash suppressor. Adjustable ghost ring rear sight and ramp front. Black/gray laminated stock, with checkering and soft rubber recoil pad with spacers.

850	750	600	450	300	200

Model 77/44RS

Bolt-action chambered for .44 Magnum cartridge. Features 18.5" barrel, with open sights. Stock is American walnut, with rubber buttpad and checkering on forearm and pistol-grip. Detachable rotary magazine has 4 round capacity. Weight about 6 lbs. Introduced in mid-1997. Discontinued in 2004, reintroduced in 2009, with synthetic or Next GI Vista camo stock. **NOTE:** Deduct $100 for older model with wood stock.

750	650	500	400	275	150

Model 77/44RSP

Introduced in 1999 this model has a matte stainless steel barrel and action and a black synthetic stock. Chambered for .44 Magnum cartridge. Weight is about 6 lbs.

575	465	375	250	175	125

Model 77/357

Rotary magazine rifle similar to 77/44RS, except chambered for .357 Magnum/.38 Special rounds.

700	600	450	385	250	200

HAWKEYE SERIES

Few exceptions Hawkeye Series introduced in 2007. Replaced Ruger's M77 Mark II line. In 2010, Hawkeye series began being offered in left-hand versions.

HM77R Hawkeye

Slimmed-down version of the M77. American walnut stock, blued barrel, Mauser-style controlled feed extractor, soft red rubber recoil pad, stainless steel bolt, new LC6 trigger, engraved solid steel floorplate. Chambered in.2506, 7mm-08, 7mm Magnum, .308, .30-06, .300 Win Mag, .338

	NIB	EXC.	V.G.	GOOD	FAIR	POOR

Win Mag. Left-hand and laminate-stock versions available. Introduced in 2007. In 2008 a left-hand version (HM77LR) was introduced at no extra charge.

| | 650 | 550 | 400 | 225 | 175 | 125 |

M77 Hawkeye Ultra-Light

Similar to Hawkeye but with lightweight 20" blued barrel; chambered in .223, .243 Winchester, .257 Roberts, .270 Winchester, .308 Winchester and .30-06.

| | 700 | 600 | 450 | 300 | 225 | 175 |

M77 Hawkeye All-Weather Ultra-Light

Similar to above but with black synthetic stock and matte stainless barrel and receiver; chambered in .204, .223, .243 Winchester, .270 Winchester and .30-06.

| | 600 | 500 | 400 | 300 | 225 | 175 |

M77 Hawkeye Compact

Similar to M77 Hawkeye Ultra-Light but with 16.5" barrel and smaller overall dimensions; chambered in .223, .243 Winchester, .260 Remington, 7mm-08, .308 Winchester, 6.8 SPC, and 7.62x39.

| | 700 | 600 | 500 | 400 | 300 | 175 |

M77 Hawkeye Laminate Compact

Similar to above but with black laminate stock and matte stainless barrel and receiver.

| | 650 | 525 | 425 | 300 | 250 | 150 |

M77 Hawkeye All-Weather

All-weather version of HM77R Hawkeye, with synthetic stock and stainless barrel. Same chamberings as HM77R, with .338 Federal and .358 Winchester as well. Introduced in 2007. Left hand version introduced in 2008.

| | 700 | 550 | 425 | 300 | 225 | 150 |

M77PRCM Hawkeye Compact Magnum

Similar to Hawkeye, with .500" shorter synthetic stock, stainless steel barrel and receiver. Chambered for .416 Ruger, .375 Ruger, .300 Ruger Compact Magnum, .338 Ruger Compact Magnum. Introduced 2008.

| | 775 | 675 | 550 | 450 | 325 | 195 |

M77RCM Hawkeye Compact Magnum

Similar to above, with blued barrel and walnut stock. Introduced 2008.

| | 800 | 700 | 575 | 475 | 350 | 200 |

M77 Hawkeye Alaskan

Similar to M77 All-Weather, with iron sights, Diamond black finish, stainless or matte blued barrel/receiver and Hogue stock. Chambered in .375 Ruger or .416 Ruger. Introduced in 2007. Left hand model introduced 2008.

| | 1000 | 850 | 700 | 500 | 300 | 200 |

M77 Hawkeye African

Similar to M77 All-Weather, with checkered walnut stock and express-style sights. Chambered in .223 Rem., 9.3x62, .300 Win. Magnum, .338 Win. Magnum and .375 Ruger. Introduced in 2007. Left-hand version introduced in 2008.

| | 1050 | 875 | 750 | 550 | 300 | 200 |

M77 Hawkeye Tactical

Similar to M77 Hawkeye but with 20" matte blue heavy barrel, overmolded Hogue synthetic stock; chambered in .223, .243 Winchester and .308 Winchester.

| | 875 | 750 | 625 | 500 | 300 | 200 |

M77 Hawkeye Predator

Similar to M77 Hawkeye, with 24" matte stainless barrel. Green-toned Green Mountain laminate stock. Chambered in .204, .223 and .22-250.

| | 850 | 650 | 525 | 425 | 300 | 200 |

M77 Hawkeye International

Similar to Hawkeye but with 18.5" barrel and full-length Mannlicher-style stock; chambered in .243, .270 and .308 Winchester and .30-06.

| | 825 | 725 | 600 | 475 | 350 | 225 |

	NIB	EXC.	V.G.	GOOD	FAIR	POOR

American Rifle

Budget-price bolt-action in .22-250, .243, .270 Win., 7mm-08, .308, .30-06. Features 4-shot rotary magazine, black composite stock and matte black finish. Include tang safety, adjustable trigger and free-floating hammer-forged barrel. Introduced in 2012.

400	350	300	250	225	200

American Rimfire Rifle

In 2014, a rimfire version of American Rifle was introduced. Similar features as the centerfire model. Available in a full-size version, with 22" barrel; compact model, with 18" barrel.

280	235	200	175	150	125

MUZZLELOADERS

Model 77/50RS

This model is an in-line percussion rifle chambered for .50-caliber. Fitted with a 22" barrel and open sights. Stock is birch, with rubber buttplate and no checkering. Blued finish. Weight about 6.5 lbs. Introduced in mid-1997. Discontinued.

425	325	225	175	125	100

Model 77/50RSO

Similar to model above, with straight-grip checkered walnut stock and curved buttplate. Introduced in 1998.

475	350	250	200	125	100

Model 77/50RSBBZ

Introduced in 1998. Features all the specifications of Model 77/50RS, with addition of black/gray laminated stock and stainless steel finish.

500	375	275	225	125	100

Model 77/50RSP

This model has a stainless steel barrel and action. Fitted with a black synthetic stock and pistol-grip. Weight about 6.5 lbs. Introduced in 1999.

575	400	300	200	125	100

LEVER-ACTION RIFLES

Model 96/17

Introduced in 2003. Chambered for .17 HMR cartridge. Fitted with an 18.5" barrel. Magazine capacity 9 rounds. Hardwood stock and open sights. Weight about 5.25 lbs. Discontinued.

450	350	250	200	150	125

Model 96/22

Introduced into the Ruger line in 1996. Chambered for .22 LR. Stock is American hardwood. Barrel length 18.5". Magazine capacity 10 rounds. Open sights are standard. Weight about 5.25 lbs. Discontinued.

400	300	200	175	150	125

Model 96/22M

Same as above but chambered for .22 WMR cartridge. Magazine capacity 9 rounds. Discontinued.

500	425	350	285	200	125

Model 96/44

Same as .22-caliber, except chambered for .44 Magnum cartridge. Magazine capacity 4 rounds. Weight about 5.875 lbs. Discontinued.

550	450	350	285	200	125

SHOTGUNS

Red Label Early Production

The Red Label over/under shotgun was introduced in 1977, only in 20-gauge, with a 12-gauge version added in 1982 and 28-gauge in 1995. Original Red Label had a blue finish on both receiver and barrels, and fixed chokes with 26" or 28" barrels, ventilated rib and bead front sight. Interchangeable choke tubes were offered as a option in 1988 and became standard in 1990. Stainless receiver with a blued barrel became optional in 1985 and then became standard starting

NIB	EXC.	V.G.	GOOD	FAIR	POOR

in 1989. General features include single selective mechanical trigger, selectie automatic ejectors and checkered American walnut stock, with pistol-grip or English-type straight-grip. Streamlined box-lock action has no exposed pins or screws. Weights ranged from 7 to 8 lbs. Red label was in production through 2011. After a hiatus of a couple years and a few minor changes, it returned to the Ruger catalog in 2014.

1500	1200	950	750	400	250

Red Label 2014 Model

After a two-year absence from the Ruger catalog, Red Label returned in 2014 in a slightly redesigned form. It looks much like the original but has a few changes, mostly on the inside. Some of these changes have lowered production costs a bit, meaning suggested retail price is about $500 less than the previous model. New model's receiver is a one-piece casting, compared to two pieces welded together on the old version. Locking lugs do not protrude through receiver as on the earlier model, and the gun's balance point is a bit further back for an improved handling feel. One noticeable change is the lack of side ribs between barrels, which were on the original but were removable by the user. Another way to tell the new model from the old, is the top lever now has a stainless finish. The new Red Label was introduced at the 2014 SHOT Show only in 12-gauge, but a 20-gauge is expected in the near future.

1200	1000	800	600	—	—

Red Label Sporting Clays

Introduced in 1994. Offered in 20-gauge, with 3" chambers and 30" barrels. Walnut stock has checkering and pistol-grip. Weight about 7 lbs.

1600	1300	1050	800	400	200

Red Label All-Weather

Offered in 12-gauge only, with 26", 28" or 30" barrels. Fitted with black synthetic stock and pistol-grip. Weight about 7.5 lbs. Introduced in 1999.

1300	875	650	400	300	250

Hand Engraved Red Label Series

This series of hand-engraved Red Labels was first catalogued in 1996, with three different engraving coverages. A total of 375 were produced by several prominent engravers, between 1997 and 2000.

Grade 1

2400	2000	1500	1200	—	—

Grade 2 (1/3 coverage)

2600	2200	1700	1400	—	—

Grade 3 (2/3 coverage)

3000	2500	2000	1700	—	—

Engraved Red Label

This model features a scroll engraved receiver, with a gold inlaid game bird appropriate to gauge. 12-gauge pheasant; 20-gauge grouse; 28-gauge woodcock. Walnut stock. Other specifications same as standard Red Label shotguns. Introduced in 2000 and made until 2011. Premium for 28-gauge.

1800	1500	1200	900	500	300

Engraved Red Label All-Weather

Introduced in 2000. Features scroll engraved receiver, with gold inlaid duck. Offered in 12-gauge only, with 26", 28" or 30" barrel.

1675	1325	1075	750	500	300

Woodside Over/Under

Introduced in 1995. Features a Circassian walnut stock, with either pistol-grip or straight-grip. Available in 12- or 20-gauge, with barrel lengths of 26", 28" or 30". Screw-in chokes are standard. **NOTE:** Woodside shotgun was also available in three different engraving patterns. Discontinued 2002.

1500	1300	950	650	300	250

Trap Model

Introduced in 2000. A 12-gauge single-barrel trap gun, with 34" barrel choked Full and Modified. Fitted with a mechanical trigger and auto ejector. Stock is select walnut, with adjustable cheekpiece and buttplate. Receiver is engraved. Weight about 9 lbs.

3800	3000	2500	1800	900	500

	NIB	EXC.	V.G.	GOOD	FAIR	POOR

Gold Label Side-by-Side

Introduced in 2002. Chambered for 12-gauge 3" shell. Offered with 28" barrels and choke tubes. Choice of pistol-/straight-grip checkered walnut stock. Ejectors and single trigger. Weight about 6.33 lbs. Discontinued 2008.

NIB	EXC.	V.G.	GOOD	FAIR	POOR
3500	3000	2300	1600	900	450

SUNDANCE INDUSTRIES, INC.
North Hollywood, California

This company was in business from 1989 to 2002.

Model D-22M

A .22 or .22 Magnum caliber double-barrel over/under pocket pistol, with 2.5" barrels and aluminum alloy frame. Blackened finish or chrome-plated, with either simulated pearl or black grips. Introduced in 1989.

NIB	EXC.	V.G.	GOOD	FAIR	POOR
—	225	175	125	100	75

Model BOA

Introduced in 1991. Semi-automatic pistol chambered for .25 ACP cartridge. Fitted with 2.5" barrel, with fixed sights. Grip safety. Choice of black or chrome finish. Magazine capacity 7 rounds. Weight about 16 oz.

NIB	EXC.	V.G.	GOOD	FAIR	POOR
125	100	80	70	50	25

Model A-25

Similar to BOA, without grip safety.

NIB	EXC.	V.G.	GOOD	FAIR	POOR
125	100	80	70	50	25

Model Laser 25

Similar to Model BOA, with grip safety. Equipped with a laser sight. Laser activated by squeezing grip safety. Weight with laser 18 oz. Introduced in 1995.

NIB	EXC.	V.G.	GOOD	FAIR	POOR
220	175	125	100	75	50

Sundance Point Blank

An over/under derringer chambered for .22 LR cartridge. Fitted with3" barrel and double-action trigger. Enclosed hammer. Matte black finish. Weight about 8 oz. Introduced in 1994.

NIB	EXC.	V.G.	GOOD	FAIR	POOR
95	80	70	50	25	10

SUPER SIX LTD.
Fort Atkinson, Wisconsin

Bison Bull

Massive single-action .45-70 revolver, with blued carbon steel (Bison Bull) or engraved molybdenum bronze (Golden Bison Bull) frame. Adjustable sights, 10.5" barrel, 17.5" overall length, weight 6 lbs. Introduced 2006. Value shown for blued version. **NOTE:** Add 350 percent for engraved version.

NIB	EXC.	V.G.	GOOD	FAIR	POOR
1200	1050	900	775	600	500

SUTHERLAND, S.
Richmond, Virginia

Pocket Pistol

A .41-caliber percussion single-shot pistol, with round barrels of 2.5" to 4" in length. German silver mounts and walnut stock. Lock normally marked "S. Sutherland" or "S. Sutherland/Richmond". Manufactured during 1850s.

NIB	EXC.	V.G.	GOOD	FAIR	POOR
—	—	2950	2200	800	300

SYMS, J. G.
New York, New York

Pocket Pistol

A .41-caliber single-shot percussion pistol, with 1.5" to 3.5" barrels. German silver mounts and walnut stock. Lock normally marked "Syms/New York" . Manufactured during 1850s.

NIB	EXC.	V.G.	GOOD	FAIR	POOR
—	—	2600	2150	825	300

T

	NIB	EXC.	V.G.	GOOD	FAIR	POOR

TACONIC FIREARMS LTD.
Cambridge, New York

M98 Ultimate Hunter

Bolt-action rifle based on M98 Mauser action. Available in calibers from .22-250 to .358 Win. Stainless steel and barrel length 22". Titanium grip cap. Stock is XXX English walnut, with cheekpiece and oil finish. Ebony fore-end tip. Scope bases are integral to receiver. Prices listed are for standard rifle. There is an extensive list of options which will greatly affect price. For example, an optional quarter rib will add $1000 to the base price of gun. Value speculative.

6000 — 10000

TALLASSEE
Tallassee, Alabama

Carbine

A .58-caliber single-shot percussion carbine, with 25" round barrel and full-length stock secured by two barrel bands. Fitted with sling swivels. Barrel and lock finished in bright brass furniture and walnut stock. Lock marked "C.S./Tallassee/ Ala." Approximately 500 of these carbines manufactured in 1864. Very Rare.

—	—	100000	70000	40000	10000

TANFOGLIO
Valtrompia, Italy

Products of this company, which was established in the late 1940s, have been imported into the United States by various companies including Eig Corporation, F.I.E. of Hialeah, Florida, and Excam.

Sata

A .22 or 6.35mm caliber semi-automatic pistol, with 3" barrel. Slide marked "Pistola SATA Made in Italy"; grips "SATA". Blued, with black plastic grips.

—	250	175	125	90	75

Titan

A 6.35mm caliber semi-automatic pistol, with 2.5" barrel and external hammer. Slide marked "Titan 6.35"; on U.S. imported examples "EIG". Blued, with plastic grips.

—	250	175	125	90	75

Super Titan

Similar in design to above, with larger frame. In .380 ACP. Walnut grips.

—	265	195	150	125	95

TA 90 or TZ-75

A 9mm caliber semi-automatic pistol, with 4.75" barrel and 15-shot magazine. Blued or chrome-plated, with walnut or rubber grips. Those imported by Excam were known as Model TA 90, while those imported by F.I.E. are known as Model TZ-75.

450	400	350	300	250	200

TA 90B

As above, with a 3.5" barrel, 12-shot magazine and Neoprene grips. Introduced in 1986.

450	400	350	300	250	200

TA 90 SS

As above, with a ported 5" barrel, adjustable sights and two-tone finish. Introduced in 1989.

650	600	500	450	400	300

TA 41 AE

As above, in .41 Action Express caliber. Introduced in 1989.

500	450	400	350	300	250

TA 41 SS

As above, with ported 5" barrel, adjustable sights and two-tone finish. Introduced in 1989.

650	600	500	450	400	300

	NIB	EXC.	V.G.	GOOD	FAIR	POOR

TA 76

A .22-caliber single-action revolver, with 4.75" barrel and 6-shot cylinder. Blued or chrome-plated, with brass back strap and trigger guard. Walnut grips.

	NIB	EXC.	V.G.	GOOD	FAIR	POOR
	100	90	80	65	50	25

TA 76M Combo

As above, with 6" or 9" barrel. Interchangeable .22 Magnum caliber cylinder.

	NIB	EXC.	V.G.	GOOD	FAIR	POOR
	110	100	90	75	60	35

TA 38SB

A .38 Special caliber over/under double-barrel pocket pistol, with 3" barrels and hammer block safety. Blued, with checkered nylon grips. Discontinued in 1985.

	NIB	EXC.	V.G.	GOOD	FAIR	POOR
	—	100	90	80	60	40

TANNER, ANDRE
Switzerland

Model 300 Free Rifle

A 7.5mm Swiss or .308-caliber single-shot rifle. Varying length barrels having adjustable target sights and adjustable trigger. Walnut stock fitted with palm rest and adjustable cheekpiece. Blued.

NIB	EXC.	V.G.	GOOD	FAIR	POOR
4750	3750	3000	2500	1500	750

Model 300S

As above, with 10-shot magazine. Not fitted with a palm rest. Discontinued in 1988.

NIB	EXC.	V.G.	GOOD	FAIR	POOR
4500	3500	2750	2250	1250	750

Model 50F

As above in .22-caliber, with thumbhole stock. Discontinued in 1988.

NIB	EXC.	V.G.	GOOD	FAIR	POOR
3750	3000	2500	1750	900	500

TARPLEY J. & F. AND E. T. GARRETT & CO.
Greensboro, North Carolina

Carbine

A .52-caliber breechloading single-shot percussion carbine, with 22" round barrel and plain walnut buttstock. Blued, with case hardened frame. Tang marked "J H Tarpley's./Pat Feb 14./1863". Over 400 of these carbines manufactured.

NIB	EXC.	V.G.	GOOD	FAIR	POOR
—	—	80000	65000	30000	10000

TAURUS INTERNATIONAL MFG. CO.
Porto Alegre, Brazil

PISTOLS

PT-92C

This 9mm model is a large capacity semi-automatic pistol, with 4.25" barrel. Drift adjustable 3-dot combat rear sight. Magazine holds 13 rounds in a double column. Choice of blued, stain nickel or stainless steel finish. Brazilian hardwood grips are standard. Weighs 31 oz.

NIB	EXC.	V.G.	GOOD	FAIR	POOR
450	325	275	220	160	100

PT-92

Slightly larger and heavier version of PT-92C. Has 5" barrel, with drift adjustable 3-dot combat rear sight. Magazine capacity 15 rounds. Model is 1" longer overall than above model. Weighs 34 oz. Also available in blued, nickel and stainless steel. **NOTE:** Add $20 for stainless steel; $50 for blue with gold finish; $60 for stainless steel with gold accents; $250 for blued or stainless steel .22 LR conversion kit.

NIB	EXC.	V.G.	GOOD	FAIR	POOR
400	300	225	150	100	75

PT-99

Similar in appearance and specifications to PT-92. This version has additional feature of fully adjustable 3-dot rear sight. **NOTE:** Add $20 for stainless steel finish.

NIB	EXC.	V.G.	GOOD	FAIR	POOR
425	325	250	150	100	75

NIB	EXC.	V.G.	GOOD	FAIR	POOR

PT-92AF

A 9mm caliber double-action semi-automatic pistol, with 4.92" barrel, exposed hammer and 15-shot magazine. Blued or nickel-plated, with plain walnut grips.

400	350	300	250	200	150

PT-100

Similar to other full-size Taurus semi-automatics, except chambered for .40 S&W cartridge. Supplied with 5" barrel, with drift adjustable rear sight. Magazine capacity 11 rounds. Also available in blued, nickel or stainless steel. Weighs 34 oz. **NOTE:** Add $50 for Special Edition, blued steel with gold fixtures and rosewood grips; $110 for blued steel with gold fixtures and pearl grips.

500	400	300	200	150	100

PT-101

Same as model above, but furnished with fully adjustable rear 3-dot combat sight.

450	350	300	250	150	100

Deluxe Shooter's Pak

Offered by Taurus as a special package. Consists of pistol, with extra magazine in a fitted custom hard case. Available for these models: PT-92, PT-99, PT-100, and PT-101. **NOTE:** Add approximately 10 percent to prices of these models for this special feature.

PT-138

Introduced in 1998. This polymer frame pistol chambered for .380 cartridge. Fitted with 4" barrel in either blue or stainless steel. Weight about 16 oz. Magazine capacity 10 rounds.

Blue

350	250	200	175	125	100

Stainless Steel

375	275	225	175	125	100

PT-908

Semi-automatic double-action pistol chambered for 9mm Parabellum cartridge. Fitted with 3.8" barrel, with drift adjustable rear 3-dot combat sight. Magazine capacity 8 rounds in a single column. Available in blued, satin nickel or stainless steel. Stocks are black rubber. Weighs 30 oz. Introduced in 1993.

375	325	275	225	150	100

PT-911

Model introduced in 1997. Chambered for 9mm cartridge. Fitted with 4" barrel. Magazine capacity 10 rounds. Choice of blue or stainless steel. Weight about 28 oz. Black rubber grips are standard. **NOTE:** Add $20 for stainless steel.

450	350	275	225	175	125

PT-111

Chambered for 9mm cartridge. Fitted with 3.25" barrel. Magazine is 10 rounds. Weight about 19 oz. **NOTE:** Add $15 for matte stainless steel finish; $80 for night sights.

375	300	250	175	125	100

PT-140

Chambered for .40 S&W cartridge. Fitted with 3.25" barrel. Magazine capacity 10 rounds. Weight about 19 oz. **NOTE:** Add $15 for matte stainless steel finish; $80 for night sights.

350	300	265	180	125	100

PT-140 Millennium

Chambered for .40 S&W cartridge. Fitted with 3.25" barrel. Features polymer frame and either blue or stainless steel slide. Fixed sights. Magazine capacity 10 rounds. Weight about 19 oz. **NOTE:** Add $75 for night sights.

Blue

345	315	225	150	100	75

Stainless Steel

375	325	250	175	100	75

PT-145 Millennium

Similar to PT-140. Chambered for .45 ACP cartridge. Barrel length 3.27". Weight about 23 oz. Magazine capacity 10 rounds. **NOTE:** Add $75 for night sights.

Blue

345	315	225	150	100	75

	NIB	EXC.	V.G.	GOOD	FAIR	POOR

Stainless Steel

	NIB	EXC.	V.G.	GOOD	FAIR	POOR
	375	325	250	175	100	75

Millennium Pro

Introduced in 2003. This pistol is third generation series in Millennium line. Features captured dual spring and guide assembly, re-engineered magazine release and internal firing pin lock. Larger 3-dot sighting system, positive slide serrations, internal magazine base extension and enlarged external safety with positive click are other improvements.

365	300	200	150	100	75

Model 609TI-PRO

Similar to Millennium Pro, with titanium slide. Chambered in 9mm Parabellum. Features include 13+1 capacity, 3.25" barrel, checkered polymer grips, Heinie Straight-8 sights. Overall length 6.125"; weight 19.7 oz.

500	450	325	225	175	125

PT-400/400SS

Chambered for .400 CorBon cartridge. Fitted with 4.25" ported barrel, with fixed sights. Magazine capacity 8 rounds. Offered in blue or stainless steel. Rubber grips. Weight about 30 oz.

Blue

375	300	200	150	100	75

Stainless Steel

420	325	225	150	100	75

PT-132

Chambered for .32 ACP cartridge. Fitted with 3.25" barrel. Magazine capacity 10 rounds. Weight about 20 oz. **NOTE:** Add $15 for matte stainless steel finish.

325	275	200	150	100	75

PT-58

Introduced in 1988. Chambered for .380 ACP cartridge. Fitted with 4" barrel, with drift adjustable rear sight. Conventional double-action design. Available in blued, satin nickel or stainless steel. Fitted with Brazilian hardwood grips. Weighs 30 oz.

300	250	200	150	100	75

PT-145

Chambered for .45 ACP cartridge. Fitted with 3.25" barrel. Magazine capacity 10 rounds. Weight about 23 oz. **NOTE:** Add $15 for matte stainless steel finish; $80 for night sights.

325	275	250	200	150	100

PT-45

Introduced in 1994. Semi-automatic double-action pistol. Chambered for .45 ACP cartridge. Barrel is 3.75" in length. Magazine capacity 8 rounds. Offered in blued or stainless steel, with grips of Brazilian hardwood. Fixed sights are standard. Overall length 7.1"; weight about 30 oz.

Blue

350	275	200	150	100	75

Stainless Steel

400	325	250	200	150	100

PT-745B/SS

Chambered for .45 ACP cartridge. Fitted with 3.25" barrel. Fixed sights. Polymer grips. Blue or stainless steel. Magazine capacity 6 rounds. Weight about 21 oz. Introduced in 2004. **NOTE:** Add $15 for stainless steel.

375	315	275	225	125	175

PT-640B/SS

Similar to above model. Chambered for .40 S&W cartridge. Magazine capacity 10 rounds. Weight about 24 oz. Introduced in in 2004. **NOTE:** Add $15 for stainless steel.

375	315	275	225	125	175

PT-24/7-45B

This .45 ACP pistol fitted with 4.25" barrel and fixed sights. Ribbed grips. Blued receiver. Magazine capacity 12 rounds. Weight about 27 oz. Introduced in 2004. **NOTE:** Add $15 for stainless steel slide.

400	300	285	225	150	100

	NIB	EXC.	V.G.	GOOD	FAIR	POOR

PT-24/7 G2

Double-/single-action semi-automatic pistol. Chambered in 9mm Parabellum (15+1), .40 S&W (13+1), and .45 ACP (10+1). Features include blued or stainless finish; "Strike Two" capability; new trigger safety; low-profile adjustable rear sights for windage and elevation; ambidextrous magazine release; 4.2" barrel; Picatinny rail; polymer frame; polymer grip with metallic inserts and three interchangeable backstraps. Also offered in compact model, with shorter grip frame and 3.5" barrel.

425	350	300	250	175	125

PT-24/7-PRO Standard

4" barrel; stainless, duotone or blued finish.

400	300	285	225	150	100

PT-24/7-PRO Compact

3.2" barrel; stainless, titanium or blued finish.

400	300	285	225	150	100

PT-24/7-PRO Long Slide

5.2" barrel; matte stainless, blued or stainless finish.

400	300	285	225	150	100

PT-24/7-9B

As above, but chambered for 9mm cartridge. Magazine capacity 17 rounds. Weight about 27 oz. Introduced in 2005. **NOTE:** Add $15 for stainless steel slide.

400	300	285	225	150	100

PT-24/7-40B

As above, but chambered for .40 S&W cartridge. Magazine capacity 15 rounds. Weight about 27 oz. Introduced in 2005. **NOTE:** Add $15 for stainless steel slide.

400	300	285	225	150	100

PT-24/7LS-9SS-17

Full-size stainless semi-automatic chambered for 9mm. Long grip, long slide. Capacity 17+1. Single-/double-action. 5" barrel. Weight 27.2 oz. Fixed 2-dot rear sight. Also in short grip 10+1 capacity. Introduced 2006. Price is for stainless.

425	345	295	245	175	125

PT-24/79SSC-17

Compact stainless semi-automatic chambered for 9mm. Short grip, short slide. Capacity 15+1. Single-/double-action. 5" barrel. Weight 27.2 oz. Fixed 2-dot rear sight. Also in short grip 10+1 capacity. Introduced 2006. Price is for stainless.

400	300	285	225	150	100

PT-24/7PLS-9SSPTi-17

Full-size semi-automatic chambered for 9mm. Capacity 17+1 or 10+1. Single-/double-action. Titanium slide, 4" barrel. Weight 27.2 oz. Introduced 2006.

400	300	285	225	150	100

PT-24/7 OSS

Introduced in 2007. Available in .45 ACP, .40 S&W and 9mm Parabellum. 12+1 capacity (.45), single-/double-action. Ambidextrous decock and safety, match grade barrel, polymer frame with steel upper. Claimed to exceed all requirements set by United States Special Operations Command. Developed to compete in SOCOM pistol trials. **NOTE:** Add 5 percent for stainless.

425	345	295	245	175	125

PT-24/7PLS-9SSCTi-17

Compact semi-automatic chambered for 9mm. Capacity 17+1. Single-/double-action. Titanium slide, 3.3" barrel. Weight 25.4 oz. Introduced 2006.

425	345	295	245	175	125

PT-24/7PLS

Similar to above, with 5" barrel. Chambered in 9mm Parabellum, .38 Super and .40 S&W.

425	345	295	245	175	125

2045 Large Frame Pistol

Similar to Taurus Model 24/7, but chambered in .45 ACP only. Features include polymer frame, blued or matte stainless steel slide, 4.2" barrel, ambidextrous "memory pads" to promote safe

	NIB	EXC.	V.G.	GOOD	FAIR	POOR

finger position during loading, ambi three-position safety/decocker. Picatinny rail system, fixed sights. Overall length 7.34". Weight 31.5 oz.

	450	375	325	250	175	125

809-B 9mm

Introduced in 2008. Basically a Model 24/7 OSS, with an exposed hammer. 17+1 capacity, black Tenifer finish.

	550	425	350	275	200	150

800 Series Compact

Compact double-/single-action semi-automatic pistol chambered in 9mm (12+1), .357 SIG (10+1) and .40 cal. (10+1). Features include 3.5" barrel; external hammer; loaded chamber indicator; polymer frame; blued or stainless slide.

	485	410	350	275	200	150

PT191140B

1911-style .40-caliber semi-automatic. Blued steel. 5" barrel, 8+1 capacity. Weight 32 oz. Fixed Heinie two-dot straight-eight sight. Blue or stainless. Introduced 2006. **NOTE:** Add 10 percent for stainless.

	675	550	425	300	200	125

PT1911

Blued or stainless 1911-style single action in .45 ACP. 8+1 capacity. LOA 8.5". Weight 32 oz. 5" barrel, fixed Heinie two-dot straight-eight sight. Numerous options. Introduced 2006. **NOTE:** Add 10 percent for alloy frame and Picatinny rail versions (added 2007); 10 percent for stainless.

	675	550	425	300	200	125

Model 1911B-9

Similar to above, but chambered in 9mm Parabellum (9+1).

	675	550	425	300	200	125

Model 1911B-38

Similar to above, but chambered in .38 Super.

	675	550	425	300	200	125

Model 1911HC

Similar to Taurus Model 1911, with 12+1 capacity; .45 ACP only.

	725	600	475	375	250	150

PT-745GB

Blued semi-automatic in .45 GAP, with 7+1 capacity. 3.25" barrel, fixed sights, weight 22 oz., polymer grip plates. Introduced 2006.

	375	300	225	175	125	100

PT745B/SS-LS

Blued or stainless semi-automatic in .45 ACP. 4.25" barrel, weight 23.3 oz. 7+1 capacity, polymer grip plates. Introduced 2006.

	375	300	225	175	125	100

PT917B20

9mm blued or stainless semi-automatic, with 20+1 capacity. Fixed sights, 4" barrel, weight 31.8 oz. Introduced 2006.

	375	300	225	175	125	100

PT609Ti-13

This 9mm semi-automatic has titanium finish plus 13+1 capacity, 3.25" barrel. Fixed sights, weight 19.2 oz. Introduced 2006.

	500	425	300	225	150	100

PT138BP12 Millennium Pro

Blued or stainless SA/DA semi-automatic in .380 ACP, with 12+1 capacity. Fixed sights, 3.25" barrel, weight 18.7 oz. Introduced 2006. Also available in .32 ACP and .40 S&W.

	400	300	285	225	150	100

	NIB	EXC.	V.G.	GOOD	FAIR	POOR

PT-38B/SS

Chambered for .38 Super cartridge. Fitted with 4.25" barrel, with fixed sights. Grips are checkered rubber. Blued or stainless steel. Magazine capacity 10 rounds. Weight about 30 oz. Introduced in 2004. **NOTE:** Add $15 for stainless steel.

425	345	295	245	175	125

PT-38SSSPRL

Introduced in 2005. Chambered for .38 Super cartridge. Fitted with 4.25" barrel. Magazine capacity 10 rounds. Finish is stainless steel and gold. Weight about 30 oz. **NOTE:** Deduct $60 for stainless steel only.

475	400	300	225	150	100

738 TCP Compact Pistol

Lightweight DAO semi-automatic pistol. Chambered for .380 ACP. Features include 3.35" barrel; polymer frame; blued (738B), stainless (738SS) or titanium (738Ti) slide; concealed hammer; low-profile fixed sight; ambi safety; loaded chamber indicator. Capacity 6+1 (standard magazine) or 8+1 (extended magazine). Overall length 5.195". Weight 9 oz. (titanium slide) to 10.2 oz.

300	275	250	225	150	100

709 "Slim"

Semi-automatic pistol chambered in 9mm Parabellum. Features include streamlined profile, 3.25" barrel, 7+1 capacity, fixed sights, checkered polymer grips, choice of blued (709B) or stainless (709SS) slide. Single-/double-action. Overall length 6.25". Weight 10 oz.

400	300	285	225	150	100

638 Pro Compact

Caliber .380 ACP, steel slide, polymer frame, 15-round magazine. Barrel length 3.2". Single-action trigger has integral safety. Other features include ambidextrous thumb safety, accessory rail, adjustable rear sight and loaded chamber and cocked striker indicators. Taurus Security System. Weight 28 oz. Blue or matte stainless finish.

410	350	300	250	200	150

DT Hybrid

Caliber 9mm Parabellum/.40 S&W, steel slide, polymer/steel frame, 3.2" barrel. Magazine capacity 13 rounds, 11 for .40. Single-action trigger has Strike Two capability. Integral trigger safety, manual safety and Taurus Security System. Ambidextrous magazine release, adjustable rear sight and loaded-chamber indicator. Weight 24 oz. Finish blue or matte stainless.

465	400	350	285	200	150

917

Lightweight compact semi-automatic chambered in 9mm Parabellum. Matte blue or stainless finish, 17+1 or 20+1 capacity. Introduced 2007.

400	300	285	225	150	100

PT-945C

Introduced in 1995. This .45 ACP double-action pistol features 4" barrel, with 8-round magazine. Grips are black rubber. Sights are drift adjustable 3-dot combat style. Weight about 30 oz. Offered in blue or stainless steel, with or without ported barrel.

Blue

NOTE: Add $45 for blued finish with gold accents and ported barrel; $35 for ported barrel and blue finish; $40 for ported barrel.

450	350	250	200	150	100

Stainless Steel

NOTE: Add $40 for ported barrel with stainless steel finish or Stainless steel finish with gold accents.

475	400	300	250	150	100

PT-945S

Same as above, but chambered for .45 Super cartridge. Introduced in 1998.

Blue

450	350	250	200	150	100

Stainless Steel

475	375	275	225	150	100

	NIB	EXC.	V.G.	GOOD	FAIR	POOR

PT-940

Similar to the PT-945 except chambered for the .40 S&W cartridge. Fitted with a 4" barrel. Magazine capacity is 10 rounds. Choice of blue or stainless steel. Black rubber grips. Weight is approximately 28 oz. Introduced in 1997. **NOTE:** Add $20 for stainless steel.

	425	315	265	200	125	75

PT-938

Chambered for .380 ACP cartridge. Fitted with 3" barrel. Black rubber grips. Choice of blue or stainless steel. Weight about 27 oz. Introduced in 1997.

	365	300	245	175	80	50

922 Sport

Introduced in 2003. Semi-automatic .22-caliber pistol features lightweight polymer frame. Single-/double-action trigger. Barrel length 6". Magazine capacity 10 rounds. Adjustable sights. Weight about 25 oz. **NOTE:** Add $15 for matte stainless steel finish.

	310	250	175	150	100	75

PT-22

Semi-automatic double-action-only pistol. Features 2.75" barrel, with fixed sights and manual safety. Chambered for .22 LR cartridge. Magazine capacity 8 rounds. Stocks are Brazilian hardwood. Finish available in either blue, blue with gold trim, nickel or two-tone. Weighs 12.3 oz. **NOTE:** Add $50 for Special Edition, blued steel with gold fixtures and rosewood grips; $110 for blued steel with gold fixtures and pearl grips.

	250	175	250	75	60	50

PT-922

.22-caliber pistol has 6" barrel, with fiber optic adjustable sights. Polymer grips. 10-round magazine. Blued finish. Weight about 29 oz. Introduced in 2004.

	365	300	245	175	80	50

PT-25

Similar in appearance to PT-22. Chambered for .25 ACP cartridge. Magazine capacity 9 rounds. Fitted with 2.75" barrel. Offered in blue, blue with gold trim, two-tone finish or nickel. **NOTE:** Add $50 for Special Edition, blued steel with gold fixtures and rosewood grips; $110 for blued steel with gold fixtures and pearl grips.

	250	175	125	75	60	50

22PLY/25PLY Small Polymer Frame Pistols

Similar to Taurus Models PT-22 and PT-25, with lightweight polymer frame. Features include .22 LR (22PLY, 9+1) or .25 ACP (25PLY, 8+1) chambering, 2.33" tip-up barrel, matte black finish, extended magazine with finger lip, manual safety. Overall length 4.8". Weight 10.8 oz.

	225	200	175	—	—	—

REVOLVERS

Model 17MB2/MSS2

This 8-shot revolver chambered for .17 HMR cartridge. Fitted with 1.75" barrel, with fixed sights. Blued or stainless steel. Hard rubber grips. Weight about 22 oz. Introduced in 2004. **NOTE:** Add $45 for stainless steel.

	360	280	225	175	150	100

Model 73

A .32 Smith & Wesson Long double-action swing-out cylinder revolver, with 3" barrel and 6-shot cylinder. Blued or nickel plated, with walnut grips.

	250	195	150	125	100	75

Model 80

Full-size 6-round .38 Special. with 3" or 4" heavy tapered barrel. Supplied with fixed sights. Offered with blued or stainless steel (offered new in 1993) finish. Brazilian hardwood grips are standard. Weighs 30 oz. **NOTE:** Add $45 for stainless steel

	285	195	135	110	85	700

Model 82

Nearly identical to Model 80. Model 82 has 3" or 4" heavy solid rib barrel in place of heavy tapered barrel. Weighs 34 oz. **NOTE:** Add $40 for stainless steel.

	285	195	135	110	85	70

	NIB	EXC.	V.G.	GOOD	FAIR	POOR

Model 82B4

Chambered for .38 Special +P cartridge. Fitted with 4" heavy solid rib barrel. Cylinder holds 6 rounds. Rubber grips. Fixed sights. Blue finish. Weight about 37 oz.

	295	250	200	125	100	75

Model 82SS4

Same as above, with stainless steel finish. Weight about 37 oz.

	315	265	185	125	100	75

Model 827B4

Chambered for .38 Special +P cartridge. Fitted with 4" heavy barrel, with solid rib. Cylinder is 7 shots. Rubber grips. Blued finish. Weight about 37 oz. Fixed sights.

	300	250	200	150	100	75

Model 827SS4

Same as above, with stainless steel finish. Weight about 35 oz.

	350	300	250	175	125	75

Model 83

Similar to Model 82, except for fully adjustable rear sight and Patridge-type front sight. Offered with 4" barrel only, with blued or stainless steel (new for 1993) finish. Weighs 34 oz.

	300	250	200	150	100	75

Model 86

Similar to Model 83, with exception of 6" barrel, target hammer, adjustable trigger and blue-only finish. Weighs 34 oz.

	325	275	225	175	125	75

Model 85

Double-action revolver chambered for .38 Special. Available in either 2" or 3" heavy solid rib barrel fitted with ejector shroud. Sights are fixed. Blued finish and stainless steel (new for 1993) are offered, with Brazilian hardwood grips. Weighs 21 oz. with 2" barrel. Beginning in 1996, model was furnished with Uncle Mike's Boot Grips. **NOTE:** Add $50 for Special Edition, blued steel with gold fixtures and rosewood grips; $110 for blued steel with gold fixtures and pearl grips.

	300	225	175	125	100	75

Model 85 Stainless

As above in stainless steel. Beginning in 1996, furnished with Uncle Mike's Boot Grips.

	350	275	225	200	150	100

Model 85CH

Same as above, but offered in 2" or 3" barrel with shrouded hammer. Double-action-only. **NOTE:** Add $50 for stainless steel; $25 for ported barrel on 2" models.

	300	225	175	125	100	75

Model 85 UL

Double-action revolver built on small aluminum frame. Chambered for .38 Special cartridge. Fitted with 2" barrel. Choice of blue or stainless steel finish. Weight about 17 oz. Introduced in 1997. **NOTE:** Add $50 for Special Edition, blued steel with gold fixtures and rosewood grips; $110 for blued steel with gold fixtures and pearl grips; $30.00 for stainless steel.

	325	250	195	150	125	100

Model 85 Hy-Lite Magnesium

Similar to Model 85. Weighs only 13.8 oz. Gray alloy frame and Hy-Lite sights. Introduced 2007.

	375	300	250	200	175	125

Model 85 Ultra-Lite Gray

Similar to Model 85, with lightweight magnesium frame. Fixed or fiber-optic front sight. Introduced 2007.

	375	300	250	200	175	125

Similar to Model 85, with titanium cylinder and barrel shroud. Introduced 2007.

Model 85 Ultra-Lite Titanium

	475	400	275	200	175	125

	NIB	EXC.	V.G.	GOOD	FAIR	POOR

Model 85 View

Variant of Model 85 series of 5-shot .38-Special revolvers. Sideplate on right side of frame made of clear Lexan polycarbon thermoplastic, showing inner working's of the revolver's mechanism. Rest of frame is aluminum, with silver or pink finish. Cylinder and barrel are of titanium. Introduced in 2014.

500	425	385	—	—	—

Model 850

Chambered for .38 Special cartridge. Fitted with 2" barrel, with fixed sights. Hammerless with 5-round cylinder. Rubber grips. Weight about 23 oz. Choice of blue or stainless steel. **NOTE:** Add $50 for stainless steel.

375	300	250	200	175	125

Model 850 Ultra-Lite Blue

Similar to Model 850, with lightweight alloy frame. Introduced 2007.

375	300	250	200	175	125

Model 850 Ultra-Lite Stainless Steel

Similar to Model 850 Ultra-Lite Blue, with stainless finish. Introduced 2007.

375	300	250	200	175	125

Model 605

Similar to Model 650, with ultra-lightweight frame. Blue or stainless finish. Weight 23 oz. Introduced 2007.

375	300	250	200	175	125

Taurus Polymer Protector

Single-/double-action revolver chambered in .38 Special +P. Features include 5-round cylinder; polymer frame; faux wood rubber-feel grips; fixed sights; shrouded hammer with cocking spur; blued finish; 2.5" barrel. Weight 18.2 oz.

380	320	275	230	200	150

Model 650

Same as Model 850, but chambered for .357 Magnum cartridge. **NOTE:** Add $50 for stainless steel.

375	300	250	200	175	125

Taurus 405 Revolver

Chambered for .40 S&W, with steel cylinder, alloy frame, 5-round capacity, 2" barrel. Taurus Security System and Ribber (ribbed) grips. Weight 29 oz. Blue or matte stainless finish. Available in .44 Special as Model 445, with weight of 22 oz. **NOTE:** Add 15 percent for stainless finish.

385	325	275	235	200	150

Model 851 and 651 Revolvers

Small-frame SA/DA revolvers similar to Taurus Model 85, with Centennial-style concealed-hammer frame. Chambered in .38 Special +P (Model 851) or .357 Magnum (Model 651). Features include five-shot cylinder; 2" barrel; fixed sights; blue, matte blue, titanium or stainless finish; Taurus security lock. Overall length 6.5". Weight 15.5 oz. (titanium) to 25 oz. (blued and stainless).

400	300	285	225	150	100

Model 94

Double-action revolver chambered for .22 LR cartridge. Swing-out cylinder holds 9 rounds. Available with heavy solid rib, 3" or 4" barrel. In 1996, a 5" barrel option was added in both blue and stainless steel. Ramp front sight with fully adjustable rear sight. Offered in blued or stainless steel, with Brazilian hardwood grips. Weighs 25 oz. with 4" barrel.

Blue

350	275	225	200	150	100

Stainless Steel

375	300	250	225	175	125

Model 94 UL

Introduced in 1997. Built on small aluminum frame, with 2" barrel. Chambered for .22 LR cartridge. Choice of blue or stainless steel. Weight about 14 oz.

400	300	285	225	150	100

	NIB	EXC.	V.G.	GOOD	FAIR	POOR

Model 941

Similar in appearance to Model 94. This version chambered for .22 WMR. Available with choice of 3" or 4" heavy solid rib barrel. In 1996, a 5" barrel option was added that holds 8 rounds. Ramp front sight, with fully adjustable rear sight. Available in blued or stainless steel. Brazilian hardwood grips. Weighs 27.5 oz.

Blue

	NIB	EXC.	V.G.	GOOD	FAIR	POOR
	350	250	175	125	100	75

Stainless Steel

	NIB	EXC.	V.G.	GOOD	FAIR	POOR
	375	275	200	150	100	75

Model 941 UL

Same as standard Model 941, with aluminum frame and 2" barrel. Weight about 18 oz. Introduced in 1997.

	NIB	EXC.	V.G.	GOOD	FAIR	POOR
	400	300	285	225	150	100

Model 96

Full-size .22 LR revolver, with 6" heavy solid rib barrel. Fully adjustable rear sight, with target hammer and adjustable target trigger. Cylinder holds 6 rounds. Available in blued only, with Brazilian hardwood grips. Weighs 34 oz.

	NIB	EXC.	V.G.	GOOD	FAIR	POOR
	300	250	200	150	125	100

Model 741

Double-action revolver chambered for .32 H&R Magnum cartridge. Features 3" or 4" heavy solid rib barrel, with fully adjustable rear sight. Swing-out cylinder holds 6 rounds. Available in either blued or stainless steel model (stainless steel model introduced in 1993), with Brazilian hardwood grips. Weighs 30 oz. **NOTE:** Add $40 for stainless steel.

	NIB	EXC.	V.G.	GOOD	FAIR	POOR
	200	175	150	125	100	75

Model 761

Similar to Model 741. This version has 6" barrel, target hammer and adjustable target trigger. Available blued only. Weighs 34 oz.

	NIB	EXC.	V.G.	GOOD	FAIR	POOR
	350	250	175	125	100	75

Model 65

Double-action revolver chambered for .357 Magnum cartridge. Offered with 2.5" or 4" heavy solid rib barrel, with ejector shroud. Fitted with fixed sights. Brazilian hardwood grips. Available blued or stainless steel. The 2.5" barrel is a new addition to Model 65 for 1993. Weighs 34 oz. with 4" barrel. **NOTE:** Add $40 for stainless steel.

	NIB	EXC.	V.G.	GOOD	FAIR	POOR
	325	225	150	125	100	75

Model 605

Introduced in 1995. Revolver chambered for .357 Magnum cartridge. Fitted with 2.25" or 3" heavy barrel. Offered in blue or stainless steel. Weighs 25 oz.

Blue

	NIB	EXC.	V.G.	GOOD	FAIR	POOR
	325	225	150	125	100	75

Stainless Steel

	NIB	EXC.	V.G.	GOOD	FAIR	POOR
	375	275	200	150	100	75

Model 605 Custom (B2C)

Same as above. Offered with 2.25" compensated barrel.

Blue

	NIB	EXC.	V.G.	GOOD	FAIR	POOR
	400	300	285	225	150	100

Stainless Steel

	NIB	EXC.	V.G.	GOOD	FAIR	POOR
	450	350	300	250	150	100

Model 605CHB2/SS2

Chambered for .357 Magnum cartridge. Fitted with 2.25" solid rib barrel and 5-shot cylinder. Model offered with concealed hammer. Weight about 24 oz.

Blue

	NIB	EXC.	V.G.	GOOD	FAIR	POOR
	350	250	175	125	100	75

Stainless Steel

	NIB	EXC.	V.G.	GOOD	FAIR	POOR
	375	275	200	150	100	75

	NIB	EXC.	V.G.	GOOD	FAIR	POOR

Model 605CHB2C/SS2C

Same as above, with concealed hammer and ported barrels.

Blue

350	250	175	125	100	75

Stainless Steel

375	275	200	150	100	75

Model 66

Similar to Model 65. Offered with a choice of 2.5", 4" or 6" barrel, with fully adjustable rear sight. Either blued or stainless steel. Weighs 35 oz. with 4" barrel. The 2.5" barrel was introduced in 1993.

225	200	175	150	125	100

Model 66CP

Similar to Model 66. Features compensated heavy solid rib 4" or 6" ejector shroud barrel. Introduced in 1993. Weighs 35 oz.

250	225	200	150	125	100

Model 66B4/SS4

Chambered for .357 Magnum cartridge, with 4" solid rib barrel and 7-shot cylinder. Adjustable sights. Rubber grips. Weight about 38 oz.

Blue

350	275	225	150	125	100

Stainless Steel

400	325	275	225	150	100

Model 607

Introduced in 1995. This .357 Magnum model features choice of 4" or 6.5" integral compensated barrel in either blue or stainless steel. The 6.5" barrel fitted with a vent rib.

Blue

325	275	225	200	150	100

Stainless Steel

400	350	300	200	150	100

Model 606

Introduced in 1997. This 6-round model chambered for .357 Magnum cartridge. Fitted with 2" solid rib barrel, with ramp front sight and notched rear sight. Available in double-action, single- or double-action-only. Offered in blue or stainless steel. Rubber grips are standard. Weight about 29 oz. A number of variations offered on this model. **NOTE:** Add $50 for stainless steel.

375	275	200	150	100	75

Model 608

Introduced in 1996. Revolver chambered for .357 Magnum cartridge. Cylinder bored for 8 rounds. Offered in 4" and 6.5" barrel lengths, with integral compensator. Front sight serrated ramp, with red insert and rear is adjustable. Offered in both blued and stainless steel versions. Weight about 51.5 oz. with 6.5" barrel.

Blue

425	325	250	200	150	100

Stainless Steel

450	350	300	200	150	100

Model 689

Chambered for .357 Magnum cartridge. Features heavy vent rib barrel in either 4" or 6" lengths. Fully adjustable rear sight is standard. Offered in blued or stainless steel. Weighs 37 oz. In 1998, this model fitted with 7-round cylinder.

375	275	200	150	100	75

Model 617

Chambered for .357 Magnum cartridge with 7-round cylinder. Fitted with 2" barrel. Choice of blue or stainless steel finish. Some variations offered a ported barrel. Introduced in 1998.

Blue

400	325	275	225	175	125

NIB	EXC.	V.G.	GOOD	FAIR	POOR

Stainless Steel

400	325	275	225	175	125

Ported Barrel

425	325	250	200	150	100

Model 617 CHB2/SS2

Chambered for .357 Magnum cartridge. Features concealed hammer, 2" solid rib barrel and fixed sights.

Blue

350	275	225	175	125	100

Stainless Steel

425	325	250	200	150	100

Model 627 Tracker

Chambered for .357 Magnum cartridge. Has 7-round cylinder. The 4" barrel is ported, with heavy underlug. Adjustable rear sight. Matte stainless steel finish. Introduced in 2000.

450	325	275	225	175	125

Model 669

Chambered for .357 Magnum cartridge. Features 4" or 6" heavy solid rib barrel, with full shroud. Fully adjustable rear sight. Available with blued or stainless steel finish. Brazilian hardwood grips are standard. Weighs 37 oz. with 4" barrel. **NOTE:** Add $60 for stainless steel.

375	275	200	150	100	75

Model 669CP

Variation of Model 669 was introduced in 1993. Features 4" or 6" compensated barrel. Fully adjustable rear sights are standard. Offered with either blue or stainless steel finish. Weighs 37 oz. In 1998, this model fitted with 7-round cylinder. **NOTE:** Add $60 for stainless steel.

425	325	250	200	150	100

Model 415

Chambered for .41 Magnum cartridge. Fitted with 2.5" ported barrel. Fixed sights. Rubber grips. Matte stainless steel finish. Weight about 30 oz.

450	350	300	200	150	100

Model 431

Chambered for .44 Special cartridge. This double-action revolver furnished with 3" or 4" heavy solid rib barrel, with ejector shroud. Cylinder capacity 5 rounds. Fixed sights are standard. Choice of blued or stainless steel finish. Weighs 35 oz. **NOTE:** Add $60 for stainless steel.

450	350	300	200	150	100

Model 817 (Ultra-Lite)

Chambered for .357 Magnum cartridge. Fitted with 7-shot cylinder and 2" solid rib barrel. Features an alloy frame. Stainless steel or blued finish. Some models are ported. Weight about 21 oz. **NOTE:** Add $20 for ported barrels.

Blue

350	275	225	175	125	100

Stainless Steel

390	325	275	225	175	100

Model 441

Similar to Model 431. Furnished with additional choice of 6" barrel as well as 3" or 4". Comes standard with fully adjustable rear sight. Cylinder capacity 5 rounds. Blued or stainless steel finish. Weighs 40.25 oz. with 6" barrel. **NOTE:** Add $60 for stainless steel.

395	300	240	150	125	100

Model 444 Multi

Model features 4" barrel, with adjustable sights. Chambered for .44 Magnum cartridge. Cylinder holds 6 rounds. Frame is alloy, with titanium cylinder. Grips have cushion inset. Weight about 28 oz. Introduced in 2004.

575	475	375	300	275	200

	NIB	EXC.	V.G.	GOOD	FAIR	POOR

Model 905I-B1/SS1

Introduced in 2003. Revolver chambered for 9mm pistol cartridge. Barrel length 2". Cylinder capacity 5 rounds. Weight about 21 oz. Blue or stainless steel finish. **NOTE:** Add $45 for matte stainless steel finish.

	NIB	EXC.	V.G.	GOOD	FAIR	POOR
	385	325	250	175	100	75

Model 951SH2

Chambered for 9mm cartridge. Fitted with 2" barrel, with adjustable sights. Cylinder holds 5 rounds. Titanium frame and finish. Rubber grips. Weight about 16 oz.

	NIB	EXC.	V.G.	GOOD	FAIR	POOR
	475	350	265	200	150	100

Model 907SH2

9mm revolver has 7-shot cylinder, 2" barrel, with fixed sights and rubber grips. Titanium frame and finish. Weight about 17 oz. Introduced in 2004.

	NIB	EXC.	V.G.	GOOD	FAIR	POOR
	475	350	265	200	150	100

Model 907B2/SS2

Chambered for 9mm cartridge. Fitted with 2" barrel, with fixed sights. Rubber grips. Ultra light alloy frame in blue or stainless steel. Weight about 18.5 oz. Introduced in 2004. **NOTE:** Add $45 for stainless steel.

	NIB	EXC.	V.G.	GOOD	FAIR	POOR
	390	300	250	200	150	100

RAGING BULL SERIES

Model 218 Raging Bee

Introduced in 2002. Chambered for .218 Bee cartridge. Fitted with 10" vent rib barrel, with adjustable sights. Cylinder holds 8 rounds. Matte stainless steel finish.

	NIB	EXC.	V.G.	GOOD	FAIR	POOR
	900	775	600	475	350	200

Model 22H Raging Hornet

Chambered for .22 Hornet cartridge. Has 10" barrel, with base mount and adjustable sights. Matte stainless steel finish. Cylinder holds 8 rounds. Rubber grips.

	NIB	EXC.	V.G.	GOOD	FAIR	POOR
	750	675	550	400	300	200

Model 30C Raging Thirty

Chambered for .30 Carbine cartridge. Fitted with 10" vent rib barrel, with adjustable sights. Cylinder holds 8 rounds. Supplied with full moon clips. Matte stainless steel finish. Introduced in 2002.

	NIB	EXC.	V.G.	GOOD	FAIR	POOR
	750	675	550	400	300	200

Model 416 Raging Bull

Model has 6.5" vent rib ported barrel, with adjustable sights. Chambered for .41 Magnum cartridge. Matte stainless steel finish. Introduced in 2002. Cylinder holds 6 rounds.

	NIB	EXC.	V.G.	GOOD	FAIR	POOR
	625	500	400	300	225	100

Model 454 Raging Bull

Chambered for .454 Casull. Built on a large frame, with 5-round capacity. Barrel lengths 5", 6.5" or 8.375". Barrels fitted with ventilated rib and integral compensator. Sights are adjustable. Finish blue or stainless steel. Black rubber or walnut grips. Weight is 53 oz. with 6.5" barrel.

Blue

	NIB	EXC.	V.G.	GOOD	FAIR	POOR
	700	650	575	450	325	175

Stainless Steel

	NIB	EXC.	V.G.	GOOD	FAIR	POOR
	750	675	550	400	300	200

Black Stainless Steel

	NIB	EXC.	V.G.	GOOD	FAIR	POOR
	750	675	550	400	300	200

Model 500 Magnum Raging Bull

Introduced in 2004. Chambered for .500 Magnum cartridge. Ventilated barrel length 10", with adjustable sights. Cushion inset grips. Stainless steel finish. Weight about 72 oz.

	NIB	EXC.	V.G.	GOOD	FAIR	POOR
	900	775	600	475	350	200

Model 500MSS2 Raging Bull

Stainless .500 S&W Magnum, with 5-shot capacity, 2.25" barrel, soft rubber grips. Weight 68 oz. Adjustable rear sight, single-/double-action. Introduced in 2006.

	NIB	EXC.	V.G.	GOOD	FAIR	POOR
	900	775	600	475	350	200

NIB	EXC.	V.G.	GOOD	FAIR	POOR

Model 44/444

Introduced in 1994. Heavy frame revolver chambered for .44 Magnum cartridge. Offered with choice of three barrel lengths: 4" with solid rib; 6.5" with vent rib; 8.375" with vent rib. All Model 44s have a built in compensator. Front sight is a serrated ramp, with adjustable rear sight. Offered in either blued or stainless finish. Weight 53 oz. for 6.5" barrel.

Blue

—	425	300	200	150	100

Stainless Steel

600	475	375	250	200	125

TRACKER SERIES

Model 17

Introduced in 2002. Features 6.5" or 12" vent rib barrel. Chambered for .17 HMR cartridge. Adjustable sights. Matte stainless steel finish. Cylinder holds 7 rounds. Weight about 41 oz. for 6.5"; 50 oz. for 12".

375	300	225	175	125	100

Model 970

Chambered for .22 LR cartridge. Fitted with 6.5" vent rib heavy barrel, with adjustable sights. Matte stainless steel finish. Rubber grips. Cylinder holds 7 rounds. Introduced in 2002.

300	200	165	125	100	75

Model 971

Same as Model 970, but chambered for .22 Magnum cartridge. Introduced in 2002.

300	200	165	125	100	75

Tracker .22/.22 Mag.

Same as Model 971, except chambered for .22 LR, with interchangeable .22 WMR cylinder. Both cylinders hold 9 rounds. Weight: 38 to 44 oz., with 4.5" or 6" barrel. Blue or matte stainless finish. **NOTE:** Add 10 percent for stainless.

465	400	350	285	200	150

Model 425 Tracker

Chambered for .41 Magnum cartridge. Features 4" heavy underlug ported barrel. Adjustable rear sight. Cylinder chambered for 5 rounds. Matte stainless steel finish. Introduced in 2000.

425	325	250	200	150	100

Model 44 Tracker

.44 Magnum revolver has 4" barrel, with adjustable sights and Ribber (ribbed) grips. Five-shot cylinder. Stainless steel finish. Weight about 34 oz. Introduced in 2004.

425	325	250	200	150	100

Tracker .45

Similar to other Tracker models, but chambered in .45 ACP (via full-moon clips), with 5-shot cylinder. 4" barrel, with Picatinny rail. Stainless steel frame and cylinder. Introduced 2007.

450	350	275	225	175	125

Model 445

Small frame revolver chambered for .44 Special cartridge. Fitted with 2" barrel, with ramp front sight and notched rear sight. Cylinder holds 5 rounds. Black rubber grips. Offered in blue or stainless steel. Weight about 28 oz. Factory barrel porting, add $20, is optional. Introduced in 1997. **NOTE:** Add $50 for stainless steel.

425	325	250	200	150	100

Model 450

Chambered for .45 Long Colt cartridge. Features 2" heavy solid rib barrel, with 5-shot cylinder and fixed sights. Ported barrel. Rubber grips. Stainless steel finish. Weight about 28 oz. **NOTE:** Add $30 for Ultra Lite model.

450	350	275	225	175	125

Model 455

Introduced in 2002. Chambered for .45 ACP cartridge. Offered with choice of 2", 4" or 6.5" barrel. Barrels of 4" and 6.5" have adjustable sights. Matte stainless steel finish. Rubber grips. Supplied with full moon clips.

450	350	275	225	175	125

	NIB	EXC.	V.G.	GOOD	FAIR	POOR

Model 460

Chambered for .45 Long Colt cartridge. Fitted with either 4" or 6.5" vent rib barrel, with adjustable sights. Matte stainless steel finish. Introduced in 2002.

450	350	275	225	175	125

Model 45

Chambered for .45 Long Colt. Fitted with choice of 6.5" or 8.375" heavy vent rib barrels. Cylinder holds 6 rounds. Rubber grips, ported barrels and adjustable sights are standard. Weight about 53 oz. with 6.5" barrel.

Blue

450	350	275	225	175	125

Stainless Steel

—	375	300	225	200	125

Model 627

Chambered for .357 Magnum cartridge. Fitted with 4" ported or 6.5" vent rib ported barrel, with adjustable sights. Rubber grips. Matte stainless steel finish. Introduced in 2002. **NOTE:** Add $200 for titanium model.

425	350	275	225	150	100

Tracker 10mm 10TSS4

Matte stainless 10mm, with 4" barrel and fixed sights. Five-shot, rubber grip. Weight 34.8 oz. Introduced 2006.

500	400	295	250	175	125

Tracker 10SS8

10mm 6-shot matte stainless, with either 6.5" (54.5 oz.) or 8.375" (59.5 oz.) barrel. Fixed sights, rubber grips. Introduced 2006.

500	400	295	250	175	125

Tracker 4510TKR

Shoots 2.5" .410 bore shells or .45 Colt. Holds 5 shots. Stainless or blued, 2.25" or 6.5" barrel, rubber grip. Single-/double-action, 9.1" LOA. Weight 32 oz. Introduced 2006.

500	400	295	250	175	125

Tracker 590 5mm

Double-action 9-shot stainless steel revolver. Chambered in 5mm Remington Magnum Rimfire. Introduced 2008. Discontinued 2011.

400	350	300	225	200	150

JUDGE SERIES

Judge

Stainless steel- or lightweight alloy-frame version of Tracker Model 4410. Chambered in 3" .410/.45 Colt (4510TKR-3MAG) or 2.5" .410/.45 Colt (4510TKR-3UL) with 3" (3" Magnum) or 2.5" barrel (2.5"). Introduced 2007.

525	425	300	265	195	150

Model 4510TKR-SSR

Similar to Judge, with ported barrel and tactical rail.

600	525	425	300	265	175

Judge Public Defender Polymer

Single-/double-action revolver chambered in .45 Colt/.410 (2-1/2). Features include 5-round cylinder; polymer frame; Ribber rubber-feel grips; fiber-optic front sight; adjustable rear sight; blued or stainless cylinder; shrouded hammer with cocking spur; blued finish; 2.5" barrel. Weight 27 oz.

550	450	375	300	250	150

Judge Public Defender Ultra-Lite

Single-/double-action revolver chambered in .45 Colt/.410 (2-1/2). Features include 5-round cylinder; lightweight aluminum frame; Ribber rubber-feel grips; fiber-optic front sight; adjustable rear sight; blued or stainless cylinder; shrouded hammer with cocking spur; blued finish; 2.5" barrel. Weight 20.7 oz.

600	500	425	325	250	150

	NIB	EXC.	V.G.	GOOD	FAIR	POOR

Raging Judge Magnum

Single-/double-action revolver chambered for .454 Casull, .45 Colt, 2.5" and 3" .410. Features include 3" or 6" barrel; fixed sights with fiber-optic front; blued or stainless steel finish; vent rib for scope mounting (6" only); cushioned Raging Bull grips.

825	700	550	400	350	200

Raging Judge Magnum Ultra-Lite

Single-/double-action revolver chambered for .454 Casull, .45 Colt, 2.5" and 3" .410. Features include 3" or 6" barrel; aluminum alloy frame; fixed sights with fiber-optic front; blued or stainless steel finish; cushioned Raging Bull grips. Weight: 41.4 oz. (3" barrel).

875	725	575	425	350	200

SILHOUETTE SERIES

Model 17-12

Chambered for .17 HMR cartridge. Fitted with 12" vent rib silhouette barrel. Adjustable sights. Cylinder holds 7 rounds. Matte stainless steel finish. Introduced in 2002.

700	600	475	350	200	150

Model 66

Chambered for .357 Magnum cartridge. Fitted with 12" barrel, with adjustable sights. Choice of blue or stainless steel finish. Rubber grips. Introduced in 2002. **NOTE:** Add $60 for stainless steel.

525	425	300	265	195	150

Model 980

Chambered for .22 LR cartridge. Fitted with 12" target barrel, with adjustable sights. Cylinder holds 7 rounds. Matted stainless steel finish. Rubber grips. Introduced in 2002.

375	350	300	250	200	150

Model 981

Same as Model 980, but chambered for .22 Magnum cartridge.

375	350	300	250	200	150

Model 217

Chambered for .218 Bee cartridge. Fitted with 12" vent rib barrel, with adjustable sights. Cylinder holds 7 rounds. Matte stainless steel finish. Introduced in 2002.

900	775	600	475	350	200

TITANIUM SERIES

Introduced in 1999. This series of revolvers features titanium barrels, with stainless steel bore liners, titanium frames and cylinders. Hammers, triggers, latches, ejector rod and other small parts are made from case hardened chrome moly steel. All Taurus Titanium revolvers have factory porting and rated for +P ammunition. Rubber grips are standard. Three different finishes are offered: Bright Spectrum blue, Matte Spectrum blue and Matte Spectrum gold.

Model 85Ti

Chambered for .38 Special. Fitted with 2" barrel, with 5-shot cylinder. Fixed sights.

525	425	300	200	150	100

Model 731Ti

Chambered for .32 H&R Magnum. Fitted with 2" barrel, with 6-shot cylinder. Fixed sights.

525	425	300	200	150	100

Model 617Ti

Chambered for .357 Magnum. Fitted with 2" barrel and 7-shot cylinder. Fixed sights. Weight about 20 oz.

600	525	425	300	265	175

Model 627Ti

Features 7-round cylinder chambered for .357 Magnum cartridge. Fitted with ported 4" barrel, with adjustable sights. Gray finish. Weight about 28 oz. depending on barrel length.

700	600	475	350	200	150

	NIB	EXC.	V.G.	GOOD	FAIR	POOR

Model 415Ti

Chambered for .41 Magnum. Fitted with 2.5" barrel, with 5-shot cylinder. Fixed sights. Weight about 21 oz.

	600	475	350	250	150	125

Model 425Ti

Chambered for .41 Magnum cartridge and has 5-round cylinder. Ported 4" barrel, with adjustable rear sight. Gray finish. Introduced in 2000.

	600	475	350	250	150	125

Model 450Ti

Chambered for .45 Long Colt. Fitted with 2" barrel, with 5-shot cylinder. Fixed sights. Weight about 19 oz.

	600	475	350	250	150	125

Model 445Ti

Chambered for .44 Special. Fitted with 2" barrel, with 5-shot cylinder. Fixed sights. Weight about 20 oz.

	600	475	350	250	150	125

Model UL/Ti

Chambered for .38 Special. Has Titanium cylinder and alloy frame. Fitted with 2" unported barrel. Cylinder is 5 shot. Fixed sights.

	525	425	300	200	150	100

GAUCHO SERIES

S/A-45, B/S/SM

Chambered for .45 Colt cartridge. Fitted with 5.5" barrel, with fixed sights. Checkered wood grips. Blued or stainless steel finish. Weight about 37 oz. Introduced in 2004. Discontinued. **NOTE:** Add $15 for stainless steel.

	400	325	275	225	175	125

S/A-45, S/S/CH

Chambered for .45 Colt cartridge. Fitted with 5.5" barrel, with fixed sights. Choice of Sundance stainless steel finish or case hardened blued finish. Weight about 37 oz. Introduced in 2004.

	400	325	275	225	175	125

S/A-357-B, S/SM, S/S, CHSA

Single-action 6-shot chambered for .357/.38-caliber. Barrel lengths 4.75" (36.2 oz.), 5.5" (36.7 oz.), 7.5" (37.7 oz.). Fixed sights. Blued matte stainless, polished stainless or blued/case hardened receiver. Introduced 2006. **NOTE:** Add $15 for stainless steel.

	400	325	275	225	175	125

S/A-44-40-B, S/SM, S/S, CHSA

Single-action 6-shot chambered for .44-40 caliber. Barrel lengths 4.75" (36.2 oz.), 5.5" (36.7 oz.), 7.5" (37.7 oz.). Fixed sights. Blued matte stainless, polished stainless or blued/case hardened receiver. Introduced 2006.

	450	375	300	225	175	125

S/A-45-B12, S/SM12, S/S12, CHSA12

Single-action Buntline-style 6-shot revolver chambered for .45 Colt. Barrel length 12" (41.5 oz.). Fixed sights. Blued matte stainless, polished stainless or blued/case hardened receiver. Introduced 2006. Discontinued. **NOTE:** Add $15 for stainless steel.

	450	375	300	250	195	100

RIFLES

Model 62

Introduced in 2000. Replica of Winchester Model 62 .22-caliber rifle. Fitted with 23" barrel and adjustable rear sight. Magazine capacity 13 rounds. Weight about 5 lbs. Hardwood stock. **NOTE:** In 2003, this model offered in both .22 WMR and .17 HMR calibers. Add 15 percent for stainless.

	350	300	225	175	125	75

	NIB	EXC.	V.G.	GOOD	FAIR	POOR

Model 62 Carbine

Same as above, with 16.5" barrel. Magazine capacity 12 rounds. Weight about 4.5 lbs. Introduced in 2000. **NOTE:** In 2003, this model offered in .22 WMR and .17 HMR calibers. Add 10 percent for stainless.

350	300	225	175	125	75

Model 62 Upstart

Similar to Model 62 above, with shorter buttstock. Introduced in 2002.

350	300	225	175	125	75

Model 72

Same as Model 62, but chambered for .22 Magnum cartridge. **NOTE:** Add $15 for stainless steel.

350	300	225	175	125	75

Model 72 Carbine

Same as Model 62 Carbine, but chambered for .22 Magnum cartridge. **NOTE:** Add $15 for stainless steel.

350	300	225	175	125	75

Model 63

Copy of Winchester Model 63 in takedown. Chambered for .22 LR cartridge. Fitted with 23" round barrel, with adjustable rear sight. Offered in blue or stainless steel. Introduced in 2002. In 2003, this model reportedly also offered chambered for .17 HMR and .22 WMR. Discontinued.

300	245	200	150	100	75

Model 62LAR Lever Rifle

Lever-action rifle chambered in .22 LR. 23" blued barrel, walnut-finish hardwood stock. Introduced 2006.

300	250	200	150	125	100

Model 62LAR-SS

Similar to Model 62LAR in stainless steel. Introduced 2006.

350	300	225	175	150	125

Thunderbolt

Slide-action rifle a knockoff of Colt Lightning rifle. Chambered for .45 Colt cartridge as well as .38/.357 Magnum. Fitted with 26" barrel, with adjustable sights. Blued or stainless steel finish. Stocks are hardwood. Weight about 8.125 lbs. Introduced in 2004. **NOTE:** Add $50 for stainless steel or bright "Sundance" stainless finish.

550	450	325	250	175	150

CT9G2

Semi-automatic carbine, with hybrid aluminum/polymer construction. Reinforced steel frame. Lower receiver made with high-strength polymer reinforced with steel. Upper receiver has flat top Picatinny rail. Two-position safety lever. Adjustable rear sight, fixed front. Ambidextrous slide catch. Available in 9mm, .40 S&W, .45 ACP. Taurus Security System installed. Introduced in 2011.

700	600	500	—	—	—

TAYLOR, L.B.
Chicopee, Massachusetts

Pocket Pistol

A .32-caliber spur trigger single-shot pocket pistol, with 3.5" octagonal barrel marked "L. B. Taylor & Co. Chicopee Mass.". Silver-plated brass frame, blued barrel and walnut grips. Manufactured during late 1860s and early 1870s.

—	—	1150	875	385	100

TAYLOR'S & CO., INC.
Winchester, Virginia

HANDGUNS

Napoleon Le Page Pistol (Model 551)

Percussion French-style duelling pistol. Chambered for .45-caliber. Fitted with 10" octagon barrel. Walnut stock, silver plated buttcap and trigger guard. Double-set triggers. Made by Uberti.

450	375	300	250	200	100

	NIB	EXC.	V.G.	GOOD	FAIR	POOR

Kentucky Pistol (Model 550)

Chambered for .45-caliber ball. Fitted with 10" barrel. Bird's-head grip, with brass ramrod thimbles and case hardened sidelock. Made by Uberti.

NIB	EXC.	V.G.	GOOD	FAIR	POOR
295	225	200	125	85	60

Colt Model 1847 Walker (Model 500A)

Fitted with 9" round barrel. Chambered for .44-caliber. Has 6-round engraved cylinder. Steel frame and backstrap. Brass trigger guard. One-piece walnut grips. Made by Uberti.

NIB	EXC.	V.G.	GOOD	FAIR	POOR
400	325	275	250	200	100

Colt Model 1851 Navy

Offered with either brass or steel frame. Brass backstrap and trigger guard. Chambered for .36-caliber. Fitted with 7.5" barrel. Cylinder holds 6 rounds. One-piece walnut grip. Brass frame model made by Armi San Marco; steel frame model made by F.lli Pietta.

Brass Frame (Model 210)

NIB	EXC.	V.G.	GOOD	FAIR	POOR
295	225	200	125	85	60

Steel Frame (Model 245)

NIB	EXC.	V.G.	GOOD	FAIR	POOR
350	250	200	150	100	75

Remington Model 1858

A .44-caliber either brass or steel frame. Brass trigger guard model, with 8" octagon barrel. Cylinder holds 6 rounds. Two-piece walnut grips. Brass frame made by F.lli Pietta; steel frame made by Armi San Marco.

Brass Frame (Model 410)

NIB	EXC.	V.G.	GOOD	FAIR	POOR
295	225	200	125	85	60

Steel Frame (Model 430)

NIB	EXC.	V.G.	GOOD	FAIR	POOR
350	250	200	150	100	75

Colt Model 1848 Baby Dragoon (Models 470, 471, 472)

Chambered for .31-caliber. Fitted with 5-round cylinder. Barrel length 4". Choice of blued or white steel frame. Brass backstrap and trigger guard. One-piece walnut grip. Made by Uberti.

NIB	EXC.	V.G.	GOOD	FAIR	POOR
350	250	200	150	100	75

Starr Model 1858 (Model 510, 511)

Offered in either double- or single-action. Chambered for .44-caliber. Fitted with 6" round barrel. Made by F.lli Pietta.

NIB	EXC.	V.G.	GOOD	FAIR	POOR
350	250	200	150	100	75

Colt Model 1860 Army

Features 8" round barrel except for Sheriff's model which is 5.5". Choice of brass or steel frame. Brass backstrap and trigger guard. Chambered for .44-caliber. One-piece walnut grip. Brass frame model made by Armi San Marco; steel frame by Uberti. **NOTE:** Half-fluted cylinder model also offered.

Brass Frame (Model 300)

NIB	EXC.	V.G.	GOOD	FAIR	POOR
295	225	200	125	85	60

Steel Frame (Model 310, 312, 315)

NIB	EXC.	V.G.	GOOD	FAIR	POOR
350	250	200	150	100	75

Colt Dragoon (Models 485A, 490A, 495A)

Offered in 1st, 2nd and 3rd models each. Fitted with 7.5" barrel. Chambered for .44-caliber. Steel frame, brass backstrap and trigger guard. The 2nd and 3rd models have square cylinder stop. Loading lever inverted on 3rd model. All have one-piece walnut grip. Made by Uberti. **NOTE:** Add $15 for 3rd model.

NIB	EXC.	V.G.	GOOD	FAIR	POOR
350	250	200	150	100	75

Colt Model 1861 Navy (Model 210)

Chambered for .36-caliber. Fitted with 7.5" round barrel. Cylinder 6 rounds. Brass frame, backstrap and trigger guard. One-piece walnut grip. Made by Uberti.

NIB	EXC.	V.G.	GOOD	FAIR	POOR
295	225	200	125	85	60

Colt Model 1862 Police (Model 315B)

Fitted with 6.5" round barrel. Chambered for .36-caliber. Case hardened frame, with brass backstrap and trigger guard. Made by Uberti.

NIB	EXC.	V.G.	GOOD	FAIR	POOR
350	250	200	150	100	75

	NIB	EXC.	V.G.	GOOD	FAIR	POOR

Colt Model 1862 Pocket (Model 315C)

Similar to above model, but fitted with 6.5" octagonal barrel. Made by Uberti.

	NIB	EXC.	V.G.	GOOD	FAIR	POOR
	350	250	200	150	100	75

Remington Model 1863 Pocket (Model 435)

Chambered for .31-caliber ball. Fitted with 3.5" barrel. Cylinder is 5 rounds. Frame, backstrap and trigger guard are brass. Walnut grip. Made by Armi San Marco.

	NIB	EXC.	V.G.	GOOD	FAIR	POOR
	295	225	200	125	85	60

Colt Model 1873 Cattleman (Models 700, 701, 702)

Famous replica made in several different configurations. Offered in barrel lengths of 4.75", 5.5" and 7.5". Calibers are: .45 Colt, .44-40, .44 Special, .38-40, .357 Magnum and .45 ACP. Frame case hardened, with steel backstrap. One-piece walnut grip. Made by Uberti. **NOTE:** Add $80 for dual cylinder; $80 for nickel finish.

	NIB	EXC.	V.G.	GOOD	FAIR	POOR
	500	375	225	175	150	125

Colt Model 1873 Bird's-head (Models 703A, 703B, 703C)

Same as above. Offered with bird's-head grip.

	NIB	EXC.	V.G.	GOOD	FAIR	POOR
	500	375	225	175	150	125

Colt Model 1873 "Outfitter"

Chambered for .45 Colt or .357 Magnum cartridge. Fitted with 4.75", 5.5" or 7.5" barrel. Stainless steel finish. Walnut grips.

	NIB	EXC.	V.G.	GOOD	FAIR	POOR
	500	375	225	175	150	125

HARTFORD ARMORY MODELS

Introduced to Taylor product line in 2004. This company produces revolvers made entirely in U.S. Each gun comes with a lifetime warranty. All Hartford Armory revolvers come in a numbered wooden case, with brass snap caps and brass plaque.

Remington Model 1875

Offered in these calibers: .38/.357, .44-40, .44 Special/Magnum or .45 Colt. Barrel lengths 5.75" or 7.5". Walnut grips. Armory dark blue finish.

	NIB	EXC.	V.G.	GOOD	FAIR	POOR
	900	800	700	600	450	300

Remington Model 1890

Offered in .38/.357, .44-40, .44 Special/Magnum or .45 Colt. Choice of 5.5" or 7.5" barrel. Armory dark blue finish. Walnut grips.

	NIB	EXC.	V.G.	GOOD	FAIR	POOR
	900	800	700	600	450	300

RIFLES

Kentucky Rifle

Offered in either flintlock or percussion. Rifle is .40-caliber. Fitted with 3.5" barrel. One-piece stock, with brass fixtures.

Flintlock (Model 183)

	NIB	EXC.	V.G.	GOOD	FAIR	POOR
	495	335	225	150	100	75

Percussion (Model 182)

	NIB	EXC.	V.G.	GOOD	FAIR	POOR
	475	325	200	150	100	75

Model 1842 U.S. Percussion Musket (Model 125)

Offered as a smoothbore or rifled musket, with 42" .69-caliber barrel. Finish is in white. One-piece walnut stock.

Smoothbore

	NIB	EXC.	V.G.	GOOD	FAIR	POOR
	450	325	250	200	150	100

Rifled with Rear Sight (Model 126)

	NIB	EXC.	V.G.	GOOD	FAIR	POOR
	450	325	250	200	150	100

Model 1855 U.S. Percussion Musket (Model 116)

Model has .58-caliber 40" barrel, with rear sight. One-piece walnut stock. White satin finish.

	NIB	EXC.	V.G.	GOOD	FAIR	POOR
	500	375	225	175	150	125

	NIB	EXC.	V.G.	GOOD	FAIR	POOR

Model 1853 3-Band Enfield Musket (Model 120)

Rifled musket has 39" .58-caliber barrel. Blued finish. One-piece walnut stock. Brass buttplate, nosecap and trigger guard.

| 475 | 350 | 300 | 250 | 200 | 100 |

Model 1858 2-Band Enfield Musket (Model 121)

Similar to above, with .58-caliber 33" barrel.

| 475 | 350 | 300 | 250 | 200 | 100 |

Model 1861 Springfield Musket (Model 110)

Model has 40" .58-caliber barrel, with one-piece walnut stock. White satin finish.

| 550 | 425 | 350 | 300 | 200 | 100 |

Model 1862 C.S. Richmond Musket (Model 115)

Fitted with 40" .58-caliber barrel, with three barrel bands. Brass buttplate and nosecap. White satin finish. One-piece walnut stock.

| 550 | 425 | 350 | 300 | 200 | 100 |

Model 1863 Remington Zouave (Model 140)

Fitted with 33" barrel. Chambered for .58-caliber ball. One-piece walnut stock. Blued finish, brass buttplate, nosecap, trigger guard, patchbox and barrel bands.

| 450 | 325 | 250 | 200 | 150 | 100 |

Henry Rifle

Lever-action rifle chambered for .44-40 or .45 Colt cartridge. Fitted with 24.25" octagon barrel. Walnut stock. Open sights.

Brass Frame (Model 198)

| 875 | 700 | 600 | 500 | 400 | 200 |

Iron Frame (Model 199)

| 925 | 750 | 650 | 500 | 400 | 200 |

Winchester Model 1866 (Model 201)

Chambered for .44-40 or .45 Colt cartridge. Fitted with 24.25" octagon barrel. Brass frame. Open sights. Made by Uberti.

| 830 | 650 | 575 | 400 | 300 | 175 |

Winchester Model 1866 Yellowboy Carbine (Model 202)

Same as above, with 19" round barrel and additional .38 Special caliber. Made by Uberti.

| 850 | 675 | 525 | 450 | 300 | 150 |

Winchester Model 1873 (Model 200)

Lever action model chambered for .44-40 or .45 Colt cartridge. Fitted with 24.25" octagon barrel. Made by Uberti.

| 900 | 725 | 600 | 500 | 400 | 200 |

Winchester Model 1873 Carbine (Model 200B)

Chambered for .45 Long Colt cartridge. Fitted with 19" barrel. Magazine capacity 10 rounds. Walnut stock. Case colored frame.

| 900 | 725 | 600 | 500 | 400 | 200 |

Winchester Model 1873 Sporting Rifle (Model 200C)

Chambered for .45 Long Colt cartridge. Fitted with 30" octagon barrel. Checkered walnut stock, with pistol-grip. Case colored frame. Blued barrel.

| 900 | 725 | 600 | 500 | 400 | 200 |

Winchester Model 1885 High Wall (Model 203)

Offered with 30" or 32" barrels. Chambered for .45-70 cartridge. Walnut stock.

| 900 | 725 | 600 | 500 | 400 | 200 |

Winchester Model 1885 Low Wall Sporting Rifle (Model 204)

Single-shot rifle chambered for .22 LR, .32-20 or .38-40 cartridge. Checkered walnut stock.

| 900 | 725 | 600 | 500 | 400 | 200 |

	NIB	EXC.	V.G.	GOOD	FAIR	POOR

Winchester Model 92

Introduced in 2004. Lever-action rifle chambered for .32-20, .32 H&R Magnum, .357 Magnum, .38 Special, .38-40, .44-40, .44 S&W or .45 Colt. Barrel length 20" or 24" octagon. Takedown feature. Hardwood stock, with blued barrel finish and case colored frame.

	725	625	450	300	250	200

Sharps Model 1859 Infantry (Model 151)

Rifle fitted with 30" round barrel. Chambered for .54-caliber cartridge. One-piece walnut, with 3 barrel bands. Adjustable rear sight.

	1150	800	600	400	300	150

Sharps Model 1859 Berdan Military (Model 152)

.54-caliber rifle fitted with 30" round barrel. One-piece walnut stock, with 3 barrel bands. Adjustable rear sight. Fitted with double-set triggers.

	1150	800	600	400	300	150

Sharps Model 1859 Cavalry (Model 153)

Model has 22" round barrel, with adjustable rear sight. Chambered for .54-caliber. Walnut stock fitted with patch box.

	1150	800	600	400	300	150

Sharps Model 1863 Cavalry (Model 154)

Similar to Model 1859 Cavalry, without patch box.

	1150	800	600	400	300	150

Sharps Model 1863 Sporting Rifle (Model 131)

.54-caliber model offered with either 30" or 32" octagon barrel. Single- or double-set triggers. Walnut stock. **NOTE:** Add $20 for double-set trigger.

	1150	800	600	400	300	150

Sharps Model 1874 Sporting Rifle (Model 138)

Offered with a variety of features. Available in .45-70 with choice of: 30" or 32" octagon barrel; single trigger or double-set triggers. Also available with Hartford-style pewter fore-end tip. In this configuration, available in .45-70, .40-65, .45-90 or .45-120 calibers. Checkered stock, with patch optional. **NOTE:** Add $125 for Hartford-style fore-end tip; $250 for checkered stock with patch box.

	895	700	545	400	315	175

Sharps Model 1874 Deluxe Sporting Rifle (Model 155)

This .45-70 caliber model features hand checkered walnut stock, with oil finish. Receiver is in white, with standard scroll engraving. **NOTE:** Add $800 for Deluxe Model 1874 with gold inlay.

	1800	1350	1050	775	595	200

Sharps Model 1874 Infantry Rifle (Model 157)

This .45-70 caliber model features 30" round barrel, with 3 barrel bands. One-piece walnut stock. Adjustable rear sight. Single trigger. Patch box in stock.

	1325	1000	750	550	375	200

Sharps Model 1874 Berdan Rifle (Model 158)

Similar to above, with double-set trigger.

	1325	1000	750	550	375	200

Sharps Model 1874 Cavalry (Model 159)

This .45-70 caliber model fitted with 22" round barrel. Adjustable rear sight.

	1150	800	600	400	300	150

Spencer Model 1865 Carbine (Model 160)

Lever-action model chambered in a choice of calibers: .56-50, .44 Russian or .45 Schofield. Fitted with 20" round barrel. Walnut stock. Case hardened receiver. Blued barrel. Made by Armi Sport.

	1200	1050	875	750	500	400

Spencer Model 1865 Rifle

As above, with 30" barrel and three barrel bands. Chambered for .56-50 cartridge.

	1200	1050	875	750	500	400

	NIB	EXC.	V.G.	GOOD	FAIR	POOR

TERRIER ONE

Terrier One

A .32-caliber double-action swing-out cylinder revolver, with 2.25" barrel and 5-shot cylinder. Nickel-plated, with checkered walnut grips. Manufactured from 1984 to 1987.

NIB	EXC.	V.G.	GOOD	FAIR	POOR
—	100	75	50	30	25

TERRY, J. C.
New York City, New York

Pocket Pistol

A .22-caliber spur trigger single-shot pocket pistol, with 3.75" round barrel. Back strap marked "J.C. Terry/Patent Pending". Silver-plated brass frame, blued barrel and rosewood or walnut grips. Manufactured in late 1860s.

NIB	EXC.	V.G.	GOOD	FAIR	POOR
—	—	1300	950	475	100

TEXAS CONTRACT RIFLES

Three contractors produced rifles for the State of Texas during 1862 and 1863. One of these patterns has a sporting back-action lock, Enfield barrel bands, an overall length of 47.375", heavy 32" long barrel of .58-caliber. Total deliveries by all contractors amounted to 1,464 rifles. Quality of these arms was decidedly inferior and often complained about.

TEXAS GUNFIGHTERS
Ponte Zanano, Italy

Shootist Single-Action

A .45 Long Colt caliber single-action revolver, with 4.75" barrel. Nickel-plated, with one-piece walnut grips. Made by Aldo Uberti. Introduced in 1988.

NIB	EXC.	V.G.	GOOD	FAIR	POOR
400	350	250	200	150	75

1-of-100 Edition

As above, with one-piece mother-of-pearl grips. Fitted in a case, with an additional set of walnut grips. 100 were made in 1988.

NIB	EXC.	V.G.	GOOD	FAIR	POOR
450	375	295	225	175	100

TEXAS LONGHORN ARMS, INC.
Richmond, Texas

Jezebel

A .22 or .22 Magnum single-shot pistol, with 6" barrel. Stainless steel, with walnut stock and fore-end. Introduced in 1987.

NIB	EXC.	V.G.	GOOD	FAIR	POOR
750	675	600	550	500	350

Texas Border Special

A .44 Special or .45 Colt caliber single-action revolver, with 3.5" barrel and Pope-style rifling. Blued case hardened, with one-piece walnut grips.

NIB	EXC.	V.G.	GOOD	FAIR	POOR
1500	1250	1000	800	600	300

Mason Commemorative

As above in .45 Colt, with 4.75" barrel and Mason's insignia. Gold inlaid. Introduced in 1987.

NIB	EXC.	V.G.	GOOD	FAIR	POOR
1500	1250	1000	800	600	300

South Texas Army

As above, with 4.75" barrel. Chambered for .357 Magnum cartridge. Fitted with conventional one-piece walnut grips.

NIB	EXC.	V.G.	GOOD	FAIR	POOR
1500	1250	1000	800	600	300

West Texas Target

As above, with 7.5" barrel and flat top frame. In .32-20 caliber in addition to calibers noted above.

NIB	EXC.	V.G.	GOOD	FAIR	POOR
1500	1250	1000	800	600	300

Grover's Improved Number Five

Similar to above in .44 Magnum, with 5.5" barrel. Serial Numbered K1 to K1200. Introduced in 1988.

NIB	EXC.	V.G.	GOOD	FAIR	POOR
2300	1350	800	—	—	—

	NIB	EXC.	V.G.	GOOD	FAIR	POOR

Texas Sesquicentennial Commemorative

As above, engraved in style of Louis D. Nimschke. One-piece ivory grips and fitted case.

	2500	2000	1500	900	750	400

THAMES ARMS CO.
Norwich, Connecticut

A .22-, .32-, or .38-caliber double-action top break revolver, with varying length barrels. Normally marked "Automatic Revolver", which refers to cartridge ejector. Nickel-plated, with walnut grips.

—	500	200	100	75	50

THIEME & EDELER
Eibar, Spain

Pocket Pistol

A 7.65mm caliber semi-automatic pistol, with 3" barrel marked "T E". Blued, with black plastic grips. Manufactured prior to 1936.

250	150	100	75	50

THOMPSON
See—Auto Ordnance Corp.

THOMPSON/CENTER ARMS
Springfield, Massachusetts

Thompson/Center Arms Co. was founded in Rochester, New York in 1965 by K.W. Thompson and Warren Center. Company's first gun was a break-open, single-shot pistol, known as Contender. More than 400,000 were produced between 1967 and 2000, when the original model was discontinued. In 2007, Thompson/Center became a division of Smith & Wesson and production was moved to Springfield, Massachusetts.

CONTENDER

Standard version was offered with 10" octagon barrel. Later with 10" Bull barrel, 10" vent rib barrel, 14" Super models, 14" Super with vent rib, 16" Super models and 16" Super models with vent rib. Stainless steel finish was available on all models except 10" octagon barrel. Action on these handguns is a single-shot break open design. Unless otherwise stated, barrels are blued. Competitor grip is walnut, with rubber insert mounted on back of grip. Finger groove grip is also available made from walnut, with finger notching and thumb rest. Fore-end is American black walnut in various length and designs depending on barrel size. Stainless steel models have rubber grips, with finger grooves. Standard sights are standard Patridge rear, with ramp front. An adjustable rear sight was offered as an option. Barrels with vent ribs were furnished with fixed rear sight and bead front sight. **NOTE:** Early frames with no engraving, called flatsides, and those with eagle engraving bring between $2,000 and $2,500 on collector market.

NOTE: Barrel interchangeability is acceptable for blued barrels and frames, with stainless steel barrels and frames. DO NOT interchange Alloy II barrels and frames with either blued or stainless steel components.

10" Octagon Barrel Model

This was the first Contender design. Offered in .22 LR only. Supplied with adjustable rear sight and mounting holes for scope. Grips are Competitor or rubber. Weighs about 44 oz.

375	300	250	200	150	100

10" Bull Barrel Model

Comes standard with adjustable rear sight, mounting holes for scope mounts and Competitor grips for blued models; rubber grips on stainless models. Available in blued or stainless steel. Offered in these calibers as complete pistols: .22 LR, .22 LR Match, .22 Win. Magnum (blued only), .22 Hornet, .223, 7mm T.C.U. (blued only), .30-30, .32-20 (blued only), .357 Magnum, .357 Rem. Max (blued only), .44 Magnum, .45 Colt, .410 bore. In 1994, Thompson/Center introduced .300 Whisper cartridge to its Contender product line. Weighs about 50 oz.

375	300	250	200	150	100

10" Vent Rib Model

Features a raised vent rib and chambered for .45 Long Colt/.410 bore. Rear sight is fixed and front sight a bead. Detachable choke screws into the muzzle for use with .410 shell. Furnished with Competitor grips or rubber grips.

370	320	270	220	150	100

	NIB	EXC.	V.G.	GOOD	FAIR	POOR

Super 14" Model

Features a 14" bull barrel. Furnished with adjustable rear sight and ramp front sight. Drilled and tapped for scope mounts. Competitor or rubber grips are offered. Available in blued or stainless steel finish. Furnished in these calibers in a complete pistol only: .22 LR, .22 LR Match, .17 Rem. (blued only), .22 Hornet, .222 Rem. (blued only), .223 Rem., 7mm T.C.U. (blued only), 7-30 Waters, .30-30, .357 Rem. Max (blued only), .35 Rem., .375 Win. (blued only), .44 Magnum (blued only). Weighs about 56 oz.

400	360	300	250	200	150

Super 14" Vent Rib Model

Similar to 10" vent rib model. Chambered for .45 Long Colt/.410 bore. Furnished with 14" vent rib barrel.

475	385	325	275	215	150

Super 16" Model

Fitted with 16.25" tapered barrel and two position adjustable rear sight. Drilled and tapped for scope mount. Furnished with Competitor grips or rubber grips. Choice of blued or stainless steel finish. Available in these calibers as complete pistols only: .22 LR, .22 Hornet, .223 Rem., 7-30 Waters, .30-30, .35 Rem., .45-70 Government. Weighs about 56 oz.

370	320	275	215	150	100

Super 16" Vent Rib Model

Chambered for .45 Long Colt/.410 bore. Offered for the first time in 1993. All other features same as other Contender .45/.410 bore pistols.

390	350	300	250	175	125

Contender Hunter Model

Model is designed for handgun hunting. Offered in two barrel lengths: 12" and 14". Barrels fitted with compensator and 2.5 power scope. There are no iron sights fitted. Nylon carrying sling and soft leather carrying case are standard. Offered in these calibers: 7-30 Waters, .30-30 Win., .35 Rem., .45-70 Government, .44 Magnum, .223 Rem. and .375 Win. Fitted with Competitor grips. Offered in blued or stainless steel finish. Weighs about 64 oz.

575	500	400	300	200	100

G2 CONTENDER SERIES

Introduced in 2003. A second generation Contender that features: a slightly different look; simplified internal design that allows re-cocking the hammer, without having to break open the action; differently shaped grips that give more clearance between grip and finger guard. These G2 firearms will accept previously manufactured Contender barrels and fore-ends, but not grips.

G2 Contender

Offered with both 12" and 14" barrels. Chambered for .22 Hornet, .357 Magnum, .44 Magnum, .45 Colt/.410 in 12" barrels. In 14" barrel chambered for .17 HMR, .22 LR, .22 Hornet, .223 Rem., 7-30 Waters, .30-30, .44 Magnum, .45 Colt/.410 and .45-70. Adjustable sights. Drilled and tapped for scope mounts. Walnut grips. Weight for 12" barreled guns about 3.5 lbs.; 14" barreled guns about 3.75 lbs. In 2004, the .204 Ruger and .375 JDJ calibers were added.

560	450	375	300	250	175

G2 Contender Rifle

Rifle fitted with 23" barrel, with no sights. Chambered for .17 HMR, .22 LR, .223 Rem., .30-30 and .45-70. Walnut stock, with blued finish. Weight about 5.4 lbs. In 2004, .375 JDJ and .204 Ruger calibers were added.

600	500	400	325	275	200

G2 Contender Shotgun

Chambered for .410 bore shell. Fitted with 24" ventilated rib barrel. Walnut stock. Weight about 5.4 lbs. Introduced in 2004.

600	500	400	325	275	200

CONTENDER CARBINE MODEL

Model is built from same design as Contender Model. Features completely interchangeable barrels. Chambered for 12 different cartridges from .22 LR to .35 Rem. A .410 bore shotgun barrel is also offered. Standard model has 21" barrel stocked with walnut; stainless steel models a composite stock in fitted walnut is also available. All are drilled and tapped for scope mounts. Available in blued or stainless steel.

	NIB	EXC.	V.G.	GOOD	FAIR	POOR

Standard 21" Carbine

Fitted with 21" plain barrel and walnut stocks. Offered in these calibers as a complete gun only: .22 LR, .22 LR Match (blued only), .17 Rem. (blued only), .22 Hornet, .223 Rem., 7-30 Waters, .30-30, .35 Rem. (blued only), .375 Win. (blued only). Weighs 5 lbs. 3 oz.

	NIB	EXC.	V.G.	GOOD	FAIR	POOR
	500	400	350	300	250	200

21" Carbine .410 Bore

Same as above, with vent rib barrel and screw-in choke.

	NIB	EXC.	V.G.	GOOD	FAIR	POOR
	475	375	300	250	200	100

16" Youth Model Carbine

Special walnut buttstock, with 12" length of pull and 16.25" barrel. Short buttstock can be replaced with standard buttstock. Blued or stainless steel finish. Complete guns offered in same calibers as 21" Carbine, with exception of .375 Win. and addition of .45 Long Colt/.410 bore with vent rib barrel.

	NIB	EXC.	V.G.	GOOD	FAIR	POOR
	475	375	300	250	200	100

ENCORE SERIES

Encore Pistol

Introduced in 1996. Single-shot pistol will feature barrels chambered for .30-06, .308 Win., 7mm-08 Rem., .223 Rem., .22-250 Rem., .44 Magnum and 7mmBR. Offered with 10.625", 15" or 24" barrels. This new handgun is designed for use with higher pressure cartridges. Barrels will not interchange with Contender. Weight with 10.625" barrel 56 oz.; 15" barrel about 4 lbs.; 24" barrel about 6.75 lbs. **NOTE:** Add $60 for stainless steel frame and barrels.

	NIB	EXC.	V.G.	GOOD	FAIR	POOR
	550	450	375	300	250	175

HotShot Youth Rifle

Single-shot dropping-barrel rifle chambered in .22 LR. Features include crowned 19" steel barrel, exposed hammer, synthetic fore-end and buttstock, peep sight (receiver drilled and tapped for optics), three stock pattern options (black, Realtree AP and pink AP). Overall weight 3 lbs., 11.5" length of pull.

	NIB	EXC.	V.G.	GOOD	FAIR	POOR
	195	165	125	100	75	50

Encore Rifle

Similar to Encore pistol, with longer barrels and walnut stock and forearm. A wide variety of calibers offered from .22-250 to .300 Win. Magnum. Barrel lengths from 24" to 26". Heavy barrels are offered in 7mm Rem. Magnum, .300 Win. Magnum and .22-250. These are offered with no sights. Weight about 6 lbs. 12 oz. for 7mm-08 with 24" barrel. Introduced in 1997. In 1998, .260 Rem., .280 Rem. and .45-70 Government cartridges were added. In 1999, stainless steel frame and barrels were offered as well as blued. In 2003, .375 H&H Magnum with 26" barrel without sights was offered. In 2004, .280 Rem., .204 Ruger and .405 Win. were added. **NOTE:** Add about $60 for stainless steel frame and barrels.

	NIB	EXC.	V.G.	GOOD	FAIR	POOR
	650	550	425	300	225	175

Encore Katahdin Carbine

Fitted with heavy 18" barrel, with integral muzzle-brake. Offered in .444 Marlin, .450 Marlin and .45-70 Government calibers. Blued finish, with composite stock and adjustable fiber optic sights. Weight about 6.75 lbs. Introduced in 2002.

	NIB	EXC.	V.G.	GOOD	FAIR	POOR
	650	550	425	300	225	175

Encore Katahdin Turkey Gun

A 12-gauge 3" chamber gun, with 20" barrel and screw-in Turkey chokes. Open sights. Realtree Hardwoods HD camo composite stock. Weight about 6 lbs. Introduced in 2005.

	NIB	EXC.	V.G.	GOOD	FAIR	POOR
	750	575	450	325	225	200

Encore Shotgun 20 Gauge

Introduced in 1998. Fitted with 26" 20-gauge vent rib barrel. Walnut stock and fore-end. Choke tubes are standard.

	NIB	EXC.	V.G.	GOOD	FAIR	POOR
	650	550	425	300	225	175

Encore Camo Shotgun 12 Gauge

Features 24" smoothbore barrel, with screw-in turkey choke, camo stock and metal pattern. Blued frame, with composite stock. Introduced in 2002.

	NIB	EXC.	V.G.	GOOD	FAIR	POOR
	750	575	450	325	225	200

	NIB	EXC.	V.G.	GOOD	FAIR	POOR

Encore Shotgun 12 Gauge

Features 3" chamber and 26" ventilated rib barrel, with bead front sight. Blued, with walnut stock. Weight about 6.6 lbs. Introduced in 2004.

	750	575	450	325	225	200

Encore Rifled Shotgun 20 Gauge

Introduced in 2000. Features 26" rifled shotgun barrel chambered for 20-gauge shell. Adjustable rear sight. Walnut stock and blued finish.

	650	550	425	300	225	175

Encore Rifled Shotgun 12 Gauge

Introduced in 2002. Fitted with 24" rifled barrel, with adjustable fiber optic sights. Blued, with walnut stock.

	650	550	425	300	225	175

Encore Turkey Gun

Introduced in 2005. Chambered for 20-gauge shell, with 3" chamber. Barrel 26", with open sights and screw-in Turkey chokes. Realtree Hardwoods HD camo composite stock.

	650	550	425	300	225	175

PRO HUNTER SERIES

Pro Hunter

Similar to Encore rifle, with plain or fluted barrel. Various finish and stock options. Barrels interchange with standard Encore barrels. Muzzle-loading and pistol versions available. Introduced 2007.

	650	500	400	275	200	100

Pro Hunter Predator Rifle

Contender-style break-action single shot rifle. Chambered in .204 Ruger, .223 Remington, .22-250 and .308 Winchester. Features include 28" deep-fluted interchangeable barrel, composite buttstock and fore-end with non-slip inserts in cheekpiece, pistol-grip and fore-end. Max 1 camo finish overall. Overall length 42.5". Weight 7.75 lbs.

	750	650	500	400	300	250

Pro Hunter Turkey Gun

Contender-style break-action single shot shotgun. Chambered in 12- or 20-gauge and 3" shells. Features include 24" barrel, with interchangeable choke tubes (Extra Full supplied), composite buttstock and fore-end with non-slip inserts in cheekpiece, pistol-grip and fore-end. Adjustable fiber optic sights, Sims recoil pad, AP camo finish overall. Overall length 40.5". Weight 6.5 lbs.

	750	650	525	400	250	150

Pro Hunter Katahdin

Chambered in .45-70, .460 S&Ws or .500 S&W. This break-action single-shot has 20" interchangeable fluted barrel, Flex-Tech stock with textured and grooved grip surfaces and an adjustable rear and fiber optic front sights.

	700	600	485	—	—	—

ICON SERIES

Icon

Bolt-action centerfire rifle chambered in .22-250, .243, .308 and .30 Thompson-Center. Barrel length 22" (iron sight) or 24" (sightless). Detachable box magazine, Introduced in 2007.

	900	800	675	525	300	200

Icon Classic Long Action Rifle

Similar to Icon, with long-action design and chambered for .270, .30-06, .300 Winchester Magnum and 7mm Remington Magnum.

	1000	850	700	600	400	200

Icon Weathershield Medium Action Rifle

Similar to Icon, with stainless steel barrel and receiver. Black synthetic or Realtree AP Camo stock.

	1000	850	700	600	400	200

	NIB	EXC.	V.G.	GOOD	FAIR	POOR

VENTURE SERIES

Venture Medium Action Rifle

Bolt action rifle chambered in .204, .22-250, .223, .243, 7mm-08, .308 and 30TC. Features include 24" crowned medium weight barrel, classic styled composite stock with inlaid traction grip panels, adjustable 3.5 to 5 lb. trigger along with drilled and tapped receiver (bases included). 3+1 detachable nylon box magazine. Overall length 43.5". Weight 7 lbs.

NIB	EXC.	V.G.	GOOD	FAIR	POOR
500	400	325	250	175	100

Venture Predator PDX Rifle

Bolt action rifle chambered in .204, .22-250, .223, .243, .308. Similar to Venture Medium action, with heavy deep-fluted 22" barrel and Max-1 camo finish overall. Overall length 41.5". Weight 8 lbs.

NIB	EXC.	V.G.	GOOD	FAIR	POOR
600	500	425	350	275	200

Venture Weather Shield

Advanced Weather Shield finish for durability. Classic styled composite stock, with Hogue Overmolded Grip panels. Classic styled composite stock. T/C large bolt design for smooth operation. 60 degree bolt lift. Receiver drilled and tapped, with bases included. Magazine capacity, 3+1. Available in short and long-action models for most standard, magnum and WSM cartridges.

NIB	EXC.	V.G.	GOOD	FAIR	POOR
525	450	380	325	225	150

Dimension

Bolt-action rifle available in 10 calibers from .204 Ruger to .300 Win. Magnum. Barrel lengths 22" or 24". Synthetic stock has competition cheekpiece. Other features are an aluminum receiver, free-floated barrel and choice of right- or left-hand action. Introduced in 2012.

NIB	EXC.	V.G.	GOOD	FAIR	POOR
600	525	450	400	350	200

OTHER RIFLES

Model R55

Semi-automatic rifle chambered for .17 Mach 2 cartridge. Fitted with 20" match grade barrel, with adjustable sights. Black composite or laminated hardwood stock. Receiver blued or stainless steel. Magazine capacity 5 rounds. Weight about 5.5 lbs. Introduced in 2005. **NOTE:** Add $65 for black composite stock.

NIB	EXC.	V.G.	GOOD	FAIR	POOR
550	450	375	300	250	175

TCR 87 Hunter Model

Single-shot top lever rifle. Chambered for cartridges from .22 LR to .308 Win. Fitted with 23" barrel. Finish blue, with walnut stock. Discontinued as a regular production rifle in 1993.

NIB	EXC.	V.G.	GOOD	FAIR	POOR
650	550	425	300	225	175

T/C 22 LR Classic

Introduced in 2000. A semi-automatic rifle chambered for .22 LR cartridge. Fitted with 22" match grade barrel. Walnut stock, with Monte Carlo comb. Adjustable rear sight. Magazine capacity 8 rounds. Weight about 5.5 lbs.

NIB	EXC.	V.G.	GOOD	FAIR	POOR
450	350	275	225	175	100

.22 Classic Benchmark

An updated version of Classic, with 18" heavy barrel and no sights. Wood laminated target stock. Magazine capacity 10 rounds. Weight about 6.8 lbs. Introduced in 2003.

NIB	EXC.	V.G.	GOOD	FAIR	POOR
475	375	300	250	200	100

Silver Lynx

This .22-caliber semi-automatic rifle introduced in 2004. Fitted with a 20" stainless steel barrel. Black composite stock, with Monte Carlo comb. Magazine capacity 5 rounds. Weight about 5.5 lbs.

NIB	EXC.	V.G.	GOOD	FAIR	POOR
400	300	225	150	100	75

BLACKPOWDER FIREARMS

System 1

Introduced in 1997. This concept features complete muzzle-loading system, with interchangeable barrels. Offered with .32-, .50-, .54-, .58-caliber and 12-gauge shotgun barrels, with walnut stock and blued finish. Or stainless steel, with synthetic stock. Barrel lengths are 26". Weight about 7.5 lbs. Sights are adjustable. **NOTE:** Add $30 for synthetic stock and stainless steel.

NIB	EXC.	V.G.	GOOD	FAIR	POOR
350	300	225	175	125	75

NIB	EXC.	V.G.	GOOD	FAIR	POOR

Thunder Hawk

Introduced in 1993. Features .50-caliber caplock in-line ignition, with 21" round barrel. Rear sight is adjustable, with ramp front sight. Stock is plain American black walnut, with rubber recoil pad. Trigger is adjustable. In 1994, available in stainless steel. Weighs 6.75 lbs.

225	200	175	150	100	75

Thunder Hawk Shadow

Introduced in 1996. Features in-line ignition in .50- or .54-caliber, with 24" round barrel. Comes standard with black checkered composite stock. Weight about 7 lbs. In 1997, offered with camouflage stock and blued finish.

300	250	200	150	100	75

Grey Hawk

Stainless steel composite stock rifle is a .50-caliber cap-lock, with 24" round barrel. Utilizes a hooked breech system. Lock is a heavy-duty coil spring, with floral engraving pattern. Adjustable rear sight and bead front sight are standard. Weighs about 7 lbs.

225	200	175	150	100	75

Hawken Caplock Rifle

Available in .45-, .50-, and .54-caliber. Rifle has 28" octagonal barrel and hooked breech system. Triggers are fully adjustable and can function as double set or single stage. Adjustable sights, with bead front sight are standard. Trim is solid brass. Stock select American walnut, with cheekpiece. Weighs about 8.5 lbs.

300	250	200	150	100	75

Hawken Flintlock Rifle

Offered in .50-caliber, with 28" octagonal barrel. All other features same as above.

310	260	200	150	100	75

Hawken Custom/Elite

Introduced in 1994. Model is .50-caliber traditional cap-lock rifle, with double set triggers and crescent butt. Select American walnut stock, with no patch box. Finish is high luster blue.

400	350	275	175	100	75

Omega 45/Omega 50

Muzzle-loader chambered for .45- or .50-caliber. Fitted with 28" round barrel. Adjustable sights. Composite or laminated stock. Weight about 7 lbs. Introduced in 2002. **NOTE:** Add $50 for stainless steel; $60 for Realtree camo stock.

535	425	325	250	150	75

Omega Pivoting Breech Rifle

Introduced in 2004. Rifle has 28" stainless steel fluted barrel bored for .50-caliber slug. Laminated wood thumbhole stock. Fiber optic sights. Weight about 7 lbs.

400	350	275	175	100	75

Renegade Caplock Rifle

Offered in .50- or .54-caliber, with 26" octagonal barrel. Adjustable triggers can function as double set or single stage. Adjustable sights, with blued trim. Walnut stock. Offered in either right- or left-hand models. Weighs about 8 lbs.

460	350	250	150	100	75

Renegade Flintlock

Available in .50-caliber and right hand only. Other features same as Caplock model.

460	350	250	150	100	755

Big Boar Rifle

Hooked breech model features .58-caliber, with 26" octagonal barrel. Single trigger and adjustable sights are standard. Trim is blued steel. American walnut stock, with rubber pad. Weighs about 7.75 lbs.

550	400	300	250	200	100

High Plains Sporter

A .50-caliber caplock, with 24" round barrel. Lock is case-colored. Choice of adjustable open sights or tang sight. Trim is blued. Stock is walnut, with rubber recoil pad, pistol-grip and sling swivel studs. Weighs about 7 lbs.

275	250	200	150	100	75

	NIB	EXC.	V.G.	GOOD	FAIR	POOR

Tree Hawk

Available in either caplock: .50-caliber or 12-gauge. .50 caliber carbine has 21" barrel and offered in camo colors; 12 gauge shotgun fitted with 27" barrel and also comes in camo colors. Weight about 6.75 lbs.

Rifle

275	250	200	150	100	75

Shotgun

275	250	200	150	100	75

White Mountain Carbine

Available in either .45-, .50- or .54-caliber caplock or .50 flintlock. Fitted with 20.5" octagon barrel. Lock is case-colored and trim blued. Stock is walnut, with rubber recoil pad. Weighs about 6.5 lbs. Discontinued.

400	350	275	175	100	75

Black Mountain Magnum

Introduced in 1999. Features 26" round barrel, with choice of walnut or composite stock. Chambered for .50-, .54-caliber or 12-gauge, with 27" round barrel. All models are caplock. Blued finish. Discontinued.

400	350	275	175	100	75

Pennsylvania Hunter

Offered in .50-caliber caplock or flintlock. Fitted with octagon/round barrel in either 31.5" or 21.5". Fully adjustable sights, walnut stock and blued trim are standard. Rifle weighs about 7.5 lbs.; carbine about 6.5 lbs. Discontinued.

Rifle

400	325	250	200	150	100

Carbine

400	325	250	200	150	100

Pennsylvania Match Rifle

Similar to Pennsylvania Hunter Rifle, except equipped with tang peep sight and globe front sight. Discontinued.

—	450	375	300	250	175

New Englander Rifle

Offered in either .50- or .54-caliber caplock, with walnut stock and 26" round barrel. Adjustable sights. Weighs about 7 lbs. 15 oz. A 12" barrel is optional. Discontinued. **NOTE:** Add $150 for interchangeable shotgun barrel.

350	275	200	150	100	75

New Englander Shotgun

Same as above, with 27" barrel in 12-gauge, with screw in full choke. Weighs about 6 lbs. 8 oz. Discontinued.

350	275	200	150	100	75

New Englander Composite

Offered with composite stock. The .50- or .54-caliber rifle has 24" barrel and 12-gauge shotgun has 27" barrel. Discontinued.

Rifle

350	275	200	150	100	75

Shotgun

350	275	200	150	100	75

Scout Carbine

Muzzle-loading carbine of .50- or .54-caliber, with in-line ignition system. Offered with either walnut or composite stock (first offered in 1993). Fitted with 21" round barrel. Adjustable rear sight and fixed blade front sight. Brass barrel band and trigger guard on walnut stock; blued barrel band and trigger guard on composite stock. Weighs about 7 lbs. 4 oz. Discontinued.

Walnut Stock

325	275	200	150	100	75

Composite Stock

250	225	175	150	100	75

	NIB	EXC.	V.G.	GOOD	FAIR	POOR

Scout Rifle

Similar to Scout Carbine, with 24" stepped half-round, half-octagonal barrel. Weight about 8 lbs. Discontinued.

Walnut Stock

	NIB	EXC.	V.G.	GOOD	FAIR	POOR
	425	350	275	225	150	100

Composite Stock

	NIB	EXC.	V.G.	GOOD	FAIR	POOR
	400	325	250	200	150	100

Scout Pistol

Same design as Scout carbine. Single-action pistol available in .45-, .50- or .54-caliber. Fitted with 12" barrel, adjustable rear sight and blued finish with brass trigger guard. Black walnut grips. Weighs 4 lbs. 6 oz. Discontinued.

	NIB	EXC.	V.G.	GOOD	FAIR	POOR
	250	225	200	175	100	75

Fire Hawk Deluxe

Introduced in 1996. An in-line muzzle-loader. Offered in either .50- or .54-caliber, with blued or stainless steel barrel. Semi-fancy checkered walnut stock has a cheekpiece. Round barrel is 24" long. Adjustable rear leaf sight, with ramp style front bead. Weight about 7 lbs.

	NIB	EXC.	V.G.	GOOD	FAIR	POOR
	400	325	250	200	125	100

Fire Hawk

Similar to Deluxe Fire Hawk, with standard American walnut stock or composition stock.

	NIB	EXC.	V.G.	GOOD	FAIR	POOR
	300	250	200	150	100	75

Thumbhole Stock

	NIB	EXC.	V.G.	GOOD	FAIR	POOR
	325	275	225	175	100	75

Camo Stock

	NIB	EXC.	V.G.	GOOD	FAIR	POOR
	325	275	225	175	100	75

Bantam

	NIB	EXC.	V.G.	GOOD	FAIR	POOR
	275	225	175	125	100	75

.32 & .58 caliber models

	NIB	EXC.	V.G.	GOOD	FAIR	POOR
	300	250	200	150	100	75

Fire Storm

Offered as a percussion or flintlock. Fitted with 26" barrel chambered for .50-caliber. Black composite stock. Adjustable fiber optics rear sight. Weight about 7 lbs. Introduced in 2000.

	NIB	EXC.	V.G.	GOOD	FAIR	POOR
	375	300	225	150	100	75

Black Diamond

An in-line muzzle-loading rifle, with removable breech plug. Fitted with 22.5" .50-caliber barrel. Stock is Rynite. Choice of blue or stainless steel. Introduced in 1998. Discontinued. **NOTE:** Add $50 for stainless steel.

	NIB	EXC.	V.G.	GOOD	FAIR	POOR
	325	275	225	175	100	75

Black Diamond XR

This .45- or .50-caliber muzzle-loader is fitted with 26" round barrel. Offered with blued finish, camo or stainless steel. Weight about 6.75 lbs. Introduced in 2002. Discontinued.

	NIB	EXC.	V.G.	GOOD	FAIR	POOR
	375	300	225	150	100	75

Triumph

.50-caliber toggle-breech inline muzzle-loader, with only four moving parts. Blued/synthetic, Weathershield/synthetic or Weathershield/stainless finish. Introduced 2007.

	NIB	EXC.	V.G.	GOOD	FAIR	POOR
	425	350	275	225	150	100

Impact Muzzleloading Rifle

.50-caliber single shot rifle. Features include 209 primer ignition, sliding hood to expose removable breechplug, synthetic stock adjustable from 12.5" to 13.5", 26" blued 1:28 rifled barrel, adjustable fiber optic sights, aluminum ramrod, camo composite stock, QLA muzzle system. Weight 6.5 lbs. **NOTE:** Add $20 for camo stock.

	NIB	EXC.	V.G.	GOOD	FAIR	POOR
	200	175	140	100	80	50

NorthWest Explorer Muzzleloading Rifle

.50-caliber single shot rifle. Features include dropping block action, #11 percussion cap ignition, 28" blued or Weathershield 1:48 rifled barrel, adjustable fiber optic sights, aluminum ramrod,

	NIB	EXC.	V.G.	GOOD	FAIR	POOR

black or camo composite stock with recoil pad, QLA muzzle system. Weight 7 lbs. **NOTE:** Add $60 for Realtree Hardwoods camo stock.

280	235	200	175	125	75

G2 Contender Muzzleloader

A 209x45 24" muzzle-loader barrel. Will interchange with G2 Contender rifle barrels. Weight about 5.5 lbs.

600	500	400	325	275	200

G2 Contender Muzzeloader .50 caliber

In .50-caliber, with 24" barrel. Weight about 6.5 lbs. Introduced in 2005.

600	500	400	325	275	200

Encore 209x50 Mag Rifle

Muzzle-loading rifle chambered for .50-caliber. Fitted with 26" barrel. Designed to handle Magnum loads of up to 150 grains of FFG black powder. Blued or stainless steel finish. Introduced in 1998. **NOTE:** Add $75 for stainless steel; $140 for Realtree camo stock

650	500	400	275	200	100

Encore 209x50 Mag Carbine

Similar to above model. Fitted with 20" ported barrel. Realtree camo stock. Weight about 6.75 lbs. Introduced in 2004.

650	500	400	275	200	100

Encore 209x50 Pistol

Model features 15" barrel chambered for .50-caliber. Walnut stock and blued finish. Weight about 16 oz. Introduced in 2000.

550	450	375	300	250	175

THUNDER FIVE
MIL Inc.
Piney Flats, Tennessee

Thunder-Five

Five shot double-action revolver, with 2" rifled barrel, matte finish, ambidextrous hammer block safety, Pachmayr grips, chambered in .45 Long Colt/.410 shotgun.

575	425	345	250	200	150

TIKKA
Tikkakoski, Finland

RIFLES

Whitetail Hunter

Rifle features hand checkered walnut stock, with matte lacquer finish. Furnished without sights, but receiver is grooved. Magazine is detachable box type. Three action lengths are offered: short, medium and long. In short action calibers choices are: .17 Rem., .223, .22-250, .243, and .308 with 22.4" barrels and weight of 7 lbs.; medium action: .270 and .30-06 with 22.4" barrels and weight of 7.3 lbs.; long action: 7mm Rem. Magnum, .300 and .338 Win. Magnum with 24.4" barrel and weight of 7.5 lbs.

725	600	500	400	200	150

Whitetail Hunter Deluxe

Similar to standard model above, but furnished with cheekpiece, select walnut stock, rosewood pistol-grip cap and fore-end tip. Metal surfaces are a highly polished blue. Same calibers as offered above.

875	700	600	400	200	150

Whitetail/Battue Rifle

Rifle was originally designed for the French market. Barrel is 20.5" long and fitted with a raised quarter rib. Walnut is checkered, with rubber recoil pad standard. A black fiberglass stock is offered as an option. In a medium action only caliber is .308. In a long action the calibers are: .270, .30-06, 7mm Rem. Magnum, .300 and .338 Win. Magnum. All models weigh about 7 lbs. In 2000, this was offered in a left-hand model. **NOTE:** Add $50 for stainless steel finish; $20 for Magnum calibers; $60 for left hand model.

650	500	400	275	200	100

	NIB	EXC.	V.G.	GOOD	FAIR	POOR

Varmint/Continental Rifle

Model features 23.5" heavy barrel, without sights. Checkered walnut stock has a wide fore-end. Offered in .17 Rem., .223, .22-250, .243 and .308. Weighs about 8.5 lbs.

	725	600	500	400	200	150

Long Range Hunting

Same as above in .25-06, .270, .7mm Magnum and .300 Win. Magnum. Fitted with 26" heavy barrel.

	725	600	500	400	200	150

Sporter

Introduced in 1998. Features a select walnut stock, adjustable cheekpiece, adjustable buttplate, adjustable trigger. Comes without open sights. Detachable 5-round magazine. Chambered for .223, .22-250 and .308 calibers.

	950	825	675	500	395	200

T3 Hunter

Introduced in 2003. This bolt-action rifle features a hand-forged barrel and adjustable trigger. Offered in standard and Magnum calibers from .223 to .338 Win. Magnum. Walnut stock with recoil pad. Detachable magazine holds three rounds for all calibers except .223 (four). No sights. Barrel lengths are 22.5" and 24.25" for standard and Magnum calibers respectively. Weight about 6.75 lbs.

	750	625	500	400	200	150

T3 Lite

As above, with a black synthetic stock and blued finish. Introduced in 2003.

	675	550	425	325	150	100

T3 Lite Stainless

As above, with stainless steel barrel and synthetic stock.

	725	600	500	400	200	150

T3 Big Boar

Bolt action rifle chambered for .308, .30-06 or .300 WSM cartridges. Fitted with 19" barrel with no sights. Black synthetic stock, with recoil pad. Blued finish. Magazine capacity 3 rounds. Weight about 6 lbs. Introduced in 2005.

	725	600	500	400	200	150

T3 Super Varmint

Bolt-action model chambered for .223 Rem., .22-250 Rem. or .308 cartridge. Stainless steel receiver and barrel, with Picatinny rail on receiver. Barrel length 23.3". Black synthetic stock has adjustable comb. Adjustable trigger. Detachable magazine. Introduced in 2005.

	1575	1350	1100	750	575	300

T3 Varmint

Chambered for .223, .22-250 and .308 cartridges. Fitted with 23.3" barrel with no sights. Synthetic stock, with blued finish. Adjustable trigger. Rubber recoil pad. **NOTE:** Add $70 for stainless steel version.

	850	725	575	400	295	150

T3 Tactical

Introduced in 2004. Rifle chambered for .223 or .308 cartridge. Fitted with 20" barrel with muzzle-brake. Black synthetic varmint-style stock, with adjustable cheekpiece. Detachable magazine capacity 5 rounds. Picatinny rail on receiver top.

	1500	1350	1050	850	575	350

Tikka Target

Bolt-action rifle chambered for .223, .22-250, 7mm-08 Rem., .308 Win. and 6.5x55 Swedish Mauser cartridge. Fitted with 23.25" barrel. Adjustable walnut target stock. Trigger is adjustable for weight. No sights. Weight about 9 lbs.

	950	825	675	500	395	200

SHOTGUNS/DOUBLE RIFLES
(FORMERLY VALMET)

Tikka, Valmet and Sako have been merged into one company, SAKO Ltd. These firearms are now manufactured in Italy under the brand name Tikka. Parts are interchangeable between the Valmet guns, made in Finland and Tikka guns made in Italy.

	NIB	EXC.	V.G.	GOOD	FAIR	POOR

412S Shotgun

Over/under shotgun available in 12-gauge only, with 26" or 28" barrels. Stock is checkered European walnut. Weighs about 7.25 lbs.

	NIB	EXC.	V.G.	GOOD	FAIR	POOR
	950	800	650	500	300	200

412S Shotgun/Rifle

Same as above, with 12-gauge barrel and choice of .222 or .308 barrel. Barrel length 24". Weighs 8 lbs.

	1000	850	700	500	300	200

412S Double Rifle

Same as above, with 24" over/under rifle barrel in 9.3x74R. Weighs about 8.5 lbs.

	1150	950	750	500	300	200

412S Sporting Clays

Introduced in 1993. Offered in 12-gauge, with 28" barrels and choke tubes.

	1000	850	700	500	300	200

512S Field Grade

Introduced in 2000. Over/under gun chambered for 12-gauge 3" shell. Fitted with either 26" or 28" choke tube barrels. **NOTE:** Add $650 per set for shotgun/rifle barrel sets.

	1125	850	750	500	300	200

512S Sporting Clays

This 12-gauge 3" model is fitted with 30" barrel and choke tubes.

	1175	900	750	500	300	200

TIMBER WOLF

See—Action Arms Ltd.

TIPPING & LAWDEN

Birmingham, England

Thomas Revolver

A .320, .380 or .450 double-action revolver, with 4.5" barrel and 5-shot cylinder. Utilizing a cartridge extraction system, designed by J. Thomas of Birmingham. in which the barrel and cylinder may be moved forward. Manufactured from 1870 to 1877.

	—	—	1400	950	400	175

TIPPMAN ARMS

Fort Wayne, Indiana

Model 1917

A .22-caliber semi-automatic one-half scale reproduction of Browning Model 1917 water-cooled machine gun. Barrel length 10". A tripod was sold with this model. Manufactured in 1986 and 1987.

	5750	5250	—	—	—	—

Model 1919 A-4

A .22-caliber semi-automatic one-half scale reproduction of Browning Model 1919 A-4 machine gun. Barrel length 11". Furnished with a tripod. Manufactured in 1986 and 1987.

	3000	2750	—	—	—	—

Model .50 HB

A .22 Magnum caliber semi-automatic one-half scale reproduction of Browning .50-caliber machine gun. Barrel length 18.25". Furnished with a tripod. Manufactured in 1986 and 1987.

	6000	5500	—	—	—	—

TISAS (TRABZON GUN INDUSTRY CORP.)

Trabzon, Turkey

Fatih 13

Beretta-style autopistol clone chambered in .32 ACP. Introduced 1994.

	300	225	150	125	75	50

Kanuni 16

Single-/double-action autopistol chambered in 9mm Parabellum, with 15- or 17-shot capacity. Black, chrome or chrome/gold finish. Introduced 1999.

	325	225	150	125	75	50

	NIB	EXC.	V.G.	GOOD	FAIR	POOR

Kanuni S

Lightweight version of Kanuni 16. Black, chrome or chrome/black finish. Introduced 2000.

	325	225	150	125	75	50

Zigana M16

Single-/double-action autopistol chambered in 9mm Parabellum, with 15- or 17-shot capacity and 5" barrel. Introduced 2000.

	395	300	225	195	150	75

Zigana K

Compact version of Zigana M16, with 4" barrel. Introduced 2002.

	395	300	225	195	150	75

Zigana T

Longer (5.5") barrel version of Zigana M16. Introduced 2002.

	395	300	225	195	150	75

Zigana Sport

Compensated version of Zigana K, with 4.5" barrel. Introduced 2005.

	395	300	225	195	150	75

Zigana C45

Similar to Zigana M16. Chambered in .45 ACP, with 4.75" barrel. Introduced 2005.

	395	300	225	195	150	75

Zigana F

Meltdown" version of Zigana M16, with radiused edges and improved ergonomics. Introduced 2007.

	395	300	225	195	150	75

TOBIN ARMS MANUFACTURING CO.
Norwich, Connecticut and Windsor, Ontario, Canada

Tobin Arms Manufacturing Co. operated from about 1905 to 1925 making an exposed hammer double and two hammerless models in four grades. The "Simplex" was cleverly designed (based on a patent by C.M. Wollam) side plated double-barrel internal hammer shotgun which resembled the Hopkins and Allen guns of that time. Some may have been private branded. Most of the Tobin doubles were made in Norwich, Conn. and are so marked. After 1909, operations were transferred to Windsor, Ont., Canada. Some guns will be found with that address. Tobin guns are not often seen by collectors and are highly prized because of their relative rarity and they were considered good guns by top dealers such as C.J. Godfrey Co. of New York City and Iver Johnson Sporting Goods of Boston. Values depend on condition and range from $200 in poor condition to $1000 and up for engraved versions in good to very good condition.

NOTE: Tobin also manufactured a .22 rimfire single-shot rifle apparently during the period 1910-1925. These are rather scarce and their value is estimated to be in the $500 - $700 range, depending on condition.

A rough timeline of Tobin Arms Manufacturing Company follows:

1903: founded by Frank M. Tobin in Norwich, CT.

1904-1909: manufactured hammer and hammerless sidelock shotguns (12ga. and 16ga.) in Norwich, Connecticut, USA

1909: purchased by a group of Canadian Investors and moved to Woodstock, ON, CAN

1910-1923/25: manufactured shotguns and rifles (entire product list unknown)

1923/25: purchased by sporting goods distributor G.B.Crandall

1923/25-1951: G.B.Crandall continued production until 1951 (possibly under the name GB Crandall)

Thanks to Jack of Florida for furnishing us with this information!

TODD, GEORGE H.
Montgomery, Alabama

Rifled Musket

A .58-caliber single-shot percussion rifle, with 40" barrel and full length stock secured by three barrel bands. Barrel and lock finished in bright brass furniture and walnut stock. Lock marked "George H. Todd/ Montgomery, Ala." TOO RARE TO PRICE.

	NIB	EXC.	V.G.	GOOD	FAIR	POOR

TOMISKA, ALOIS
Pilsen, Czechoslovakia

Little Tom

A 6.35mm or 7.65mm caliber semi-automatic pistol, with 2.5" barrel. Slide marked "Alois Tomiska Plzen Patent Little Tom". Grips inlaid with a medallion bearing the monogram "AT". Blued, with checkered walnut grips. Manufactured from 1908 to 1918. Subsequently produced by Wiener Waffenfabrik.

—	550	425	350	250	125

TORKELSON ARMS CO.
Harfield, Warren, and Worcester, Massachusetts

Double-Barrel Shotguns

Reinhard T. Torkelson's company made double-barrel boxlock side-by-side hammerless shotguns, in four models at several locations between 1885 and 1910. He worked with Iver Johnson at Fitchburg, Mass. and also built guns carrying Lovell (Boston) name. His "New Worcester" marked guns are quite common. They were sold by Sears and other large and well known houses.

—	600	300	200	150	100

TRADEWINDS
Tacoma, Washington

Model H-170

A 12-gauge semi-automatic shotgun, with 26" or 28" ventilated rib barrel and 5-shot tubular magazine. Blued anodized alloy receiver and walnut stock.

—	300	250	225	150	100

Model 260-A

A .22-caliber semi-automatic rifle, with 22.5" barrel, open sights and 5-shot magazine. Blued, with a walnut stock.

—	200	175	125	100	75

Model 311-A

A .22-caliber bolt-action rifle, with 22.5" barrel, open sights and 5-shot magazine. Blued, with walnut a stock.

—	175	150	100	75	50

Model 5000 "Husky"

A centerfire bolt-action rifle, with 24" barrel, adjustable sights and 4-shot magazine. Blued, with a walnut stock.

—	350	300	275	200	100

TRADITIONS
Old Saybrook, Connecticut

OVER/UNDER SHOTGUNS

These shotguns are built by the Italian firm of Fausti Stefano and Emil Rizzini.

Hunter

Introduced in 2001. Features choice of 12- or 20-gauge chambers, with 26" or 28" vent rib barrels with fixed chokes. Single-selective trigger. Extractors. Checkered walnut stock. Blued frame and barrels. Black rubber recoil pad. Weight about 7.25 lbs. for 12-gauge; 6.75 lbs. for 20-gauge.

650	525	400	300	225	150

Field I

Model offered in 12-, 20-, 28-gauge and .410 bore. Barrel lengths 26". Fixed chokes. Single-selective trigger and extractors. Coin finish engraved receiver. Checkered walnut stock. Black rubber recoil pad. Weight similar to Hunter model, with .410 bore weighing about 6.5 lbs.

575	450	375	275	200	125

Field II

Similar to Field I, with additional choice of 16-gauge with 28" barrels. Also features screw-in chokes and automatic ejectors.

750	625	500	375	250	125

	NIB	EXC.	V.G.	GOOD	FAIR	POOR

Field II Combo

Model features 20-gauge and .410 bore two barrel set. Both barrels are 26", with fixed chokes. Checkered walnut stock. Weight about 6 lbs. Introduced in 2004.

1400	1200	950	800	500	300

Field III Gold

Similar to the other Field series of guns, but offered in 12-gauge only with 26" or 28" barrels. Select oil finish walnut stock. Engraved receiver, with gold pheasants and woodcock.

1100	950	800	675	500	250

Upland II

Offered in both 12- and 20-gauge, with 26" barrels in 12-gauge and 24" or 26" barrels in 20-gauge. Straight-grip walnut stock. Engraved blued receiver. Schnabel fore-end. Choke tubes. Single-selective trigger and auto ejectors. Weight for 12-gauge gun about 7.25 lbs.; 20-gauge about 6.25 lbs.

800	650	500	350	275	150

Upland III

Introduced in 2001. Features a 12-gauge gun, with 26" vent rib barrels. High grade checkered walnut stock, with hand engraved receiver with gold. Schnabel fore-end. Single-selective trigger and auto ejectors standard. Screw-in chokes. Black rubber recoil pad. Weight about 7.25 lbs.

1400	1200	950	800	500	300

Sporting Clay II

This 12-gauge gas operated model has either 28" or 30" vent rib ported barrels. Screw-in extended choke tubes. Checkered walnut stock, with blued receiver and barrels. Weight about 8 lbs.

900	775	650	475	300	150

Sporting Clay III

Model features choice of 12- or 20-gauge, with 28" or 30" vent rib barrels. High grade checkered walnut stock. Choke tubes. Weight about 8.5 lbs. for 12-gauge; 8.25 lbs. for 20-gauge. **NOTE:** Add $200 for 20-gauge gun.

1400	1200	950	800	500	300

Waterfowl II

Introduced in 2001. This 12-gauge model fitted with 28" vent rib barrels and 3.5" chambers. Finish on stock and barrels is Advantage Wetlands camo. Blued engraved receiver. Recoil pad. Single-selective trigger, with auto ejectors. Weight about 7.25 lbs.

800	650	500	350	275	150

Turkey II

Offered in 12-gauge, with choice of 24" or 26" vent rib barrels. Mossy Oak Break-Up finish camo, with blued receiver. X-Full choke. Single-selective trigger and auto ejectors. Weight about 7 lbs.

800	650	500	350	275	150

Mag Hunter II

This 12-gauge features 28" barrels, with 3.5" chambers. Engraved blued receiver with walnut stock or blued receiver with Realtree Max-4 finish. Rubber recoil pad. Single selective trigger, with auto ejectors. Screw-in chokes. Weight about 7 lbs. **NOTE:** Add 10 percent for camo model.

900	765	650	500	350	175

Real 16

16-gauge gun fitted with 26" vent rib barrels. Checkered walnut stock. Choke tubes. Single trigger, with auto ejectors. Receiver is game scene engraved. Weight about 6.75 lbs. Introduced in 2004.

1100	950	800	675	500	250

Real 16 Gold

As above, with gold-filled birds on receiver.

1400	1200	950	800	500	300

Gold Wing II Silver

Chambered for 12-gauge 3" shell. Fitted with 28" vent rib barrels, with choke tubes. Single trigger and auto ejectors. Receiver engraved with game scenes. High grade walnut stock, with oil finish. Weight about 7.5 lbs.

1500	1300	1100	850	675	300

	NIB	EXC.	V.G.	GOOD	FAIR	POOR

Gold Wing III

As above, with case colored receiver with gold inlays.

| | 2000 | 1750 | 1400 | 1050 | 800 | 400 |

Gold Wing III Silver

As above, with silver receiver with gold inlays.

| | 2100 | 1850 | 1500 | 1150 | 875 | 450 |

Gold Wing SL III

As above, with case colored side plates and gold inlays.

| | 2200 | 1950 | 1575 | 1225 | 950 | 450 |

Gold Wing SL III Silver

As above, with silver side plates and gold inlays.

| | 2300 | 2050 | 1675 | 1300 | 1000 | 500 |

SIDE-BY-SIDE SHOTGUNS

These side-by-side guns are imported from the Italian firm of Fausti Stanfano.

Elite I DT

Model offered in 12-, 20-, 28-gauge and .410 bore. All gauges fitted with 26" barrels, with fixed chokes. Double triggers and extractors. Walnut stock. Weight about 6 lbs. **NOTE:** Add $60 for 28-gauge and .410 bore models.

| | 750 | 600 | 400 | 300 | 200 | 100 |

Elite I ST

Same as above, with single-selective trigger.

| | 900 | 750 | 550 | 425 | 300 | 150 |

Elite Hunter

Introduced in 2001. Features either 12- or 20-gauge gun, with 26" barrels with screw-in chokes. Walnut stock, with beavertail fore-end. Single non-selective trigger. Weight about 6.5 lbs.

| | 950 | 800 | 600 | 475 | 350 | 200 |

Elite Field III ST

Introduced in 2001. Model offered in either 28-gauge or .410 bore, with 26" barrels. High grade walnut stock, with straight-grip. Fixed chokes. Engraved receiver with gold. Weight about 6.25 lbs.

| | 2000 | 1750 | 1400 | 1050 | 800 | 400 |

Uplander II Silver

Chambererd for 12-gauge with 28" barrels or 20-gauge with 26" barrels. Choke tubes. Silver receiver, with light scroll engraving. Checkered stock, with high grade walnut. Straight-grip. Single trigger and auto ejectors. Weight about 6.75 lbs.

| | 2100 | 1850 | 1500 | 1150 | 875 | 450 |

Uplander III Silver

As above, with more extensive engraving with gold inlays.

| | 2700 | 2350 | 1950 | 1600 | 900 | 500 |

Uplander V Silver

As above, with sideplates, extensive engraving and gold inlays.

| | 3000 | 2650 | 2200 | 1800 | 1100 | 600 |

SEMI-AUTOMATIC SHOTGUNS

ALS Field

Introduced in 2001. Model offered in both 12- and 20-gauge, with 24", 26" or 28" vent rib barrel. Walnut stock, with black pad. Blued receiver and barrels. Screw-in chokes. Weight about 6.25 lbs.

| | 450 | 350 | 225 | 175 | 125 | 100 |

ALS Hunter

Same as above, with synthetic stock with 26" or 28" barrels.

| | 450 | 350 | 225 | 175 | 125 | 100 |

NIB	EXC.	V.G.	GOOD	FAIR	POOR

ALS Waterfowl

This 12-gauge has Advantage Wetlands camo. Fitted with 28" barrel, with screw-in chokes. Weight about 6.5 lbs.

500	400	300	225	175	100

ALS Turkey

Same as above, with 21" barrel and Mossy Oak Break-up camo. Weight about 6 lbs.

500	400	300	225	175	100

TRANTER, WILLIAM
Birmingham, England

William Tranter produced a variety of revolvers on his own. A number of other makers produced revolvers based upon his designs. Consequently, "Tranter's Patent" is to be found on revolvers made by such firms as Deane, Adams and Deane, etc.

Model 1872

A .38-caliber double-action revolver, with 6" octagonal barrel and 6-shot cylinder. Blued, with walnut grips.

—	—	2200	975	400	200

Model 1878

A .450-caliber double-action revolver, with 6" octagonal barrel. Blued, with walnut grip. Manufactured from 1878 to 1887.

—	—	2750	1350	500	250

TRIPLETT & SCOTT/MERIDEN MANUFACTURING COMPANY
Meriden, Connecticut

Repeating Carbine

A .50-caliber carbine, with either 22" or 30" round barrel and 7-shot magazine located in the butt. Model loaded by turning barrel until it comes in line with the magazine. Blued case hardened, with walnut stock. Approximately 5,000 made in 1864 and 1865. **NOTE:** Add 20 percent for even scarcer 22" barrel version.

—	—	3500	1500	500	200

TRISTAR SPORTING ARMS
N. Kansas City, Missouri

In 2000, Tristar bought American Arms. American Arms no longer exists, but some of its models will appear under Tristar name. For American Arms firearms built prior to sale, see that section.

SILVER SERIES

Series of over/under guns that were produced by Spanish company Zabala.

Silver Sporting

Offered in 12-gauge, with 28" or 30" barrels. Single-selective trigger, auto ejectors, choke tubes, ported barrels with target rib. Checkered walnut stock, with pistol-grip and recoil pad.

800	675	525	400	200	125

Specialty Magnums

A 12-gauge Magnum chambered for 3.5" shell. Fitted with 28" barrel. Choke tubes. Checkered black walnut stock, with pistol-grip. In 2003, a camo finish was offered for this model. **NOTE:** Add $85 for camo finish.

645	500	400	300	200	100

Silver Hunter

Offered in both 12- and 20-gauge, with 26" or 28" vent rib barrels. Single-selective trigger, choke tubes, engraved receiver with silver finish. Checkered walnut stock, with pistol-grip.

625	500	400	300	200	100

Silver II

As above, with fixed chokes for 16-, 28-gauge and .410 bore models.

670	525	425	325	225	125

Silver Classic

Model offered in 12- and 20-gauge, with 28" vent rib barrels and choke tubes. Frame is case colored and scroll engraved. Single-selective trigger and ejectors. Weight about 6.75 lbs.

800	650	500	400	300	175

	NIB	EXC.	V.G.	GOOD	FAIR	POOR

BASQUE SERIES

Series of side-by-side shotguns. Introduced in 2003. They were produced in Spain by Zabala.

Brittany Sporting

Offered in 12- and 20-gauge, with 28" barrels, 3" chambers and choke tubes. Action is boxlock, with sideplates scroll engraved with case coloring. Semi-fancy checkered walnut stock, with oil finish and pistol-grip. Semi-beavertail fore-end. Single-selective trigger and ejectors. Weight about 6.75 lbs.

NIB	EXC.	V.G.	GOOD	FAIR	POOR
850	750	600	400	300	150

Brittany

Model features boxlock action, with case-colored frame with scroll engraving. Straight-grip walnut stock, with semi-beavertail fore-end. Offered in 12-, 16-, 20-, 28-gauge and .410 bore, with 3" chambers and choke tubes. Weight 6.2 - 7.4 lbs. depending on gauge.

NIB	EXC.	V.G.	GOOD	FAIR	POOR
900	800	650	450	300	200

Brittany Classic

Enhanced Brittany model. Features fancy walnut wood and rounded pistol-grip, cut checkering, engraved case colored frame and auto selective ejectors. Available in 12-, 16-, 20-, 28-gauge and .410 bore, all with 3" chambers and 27" barrels. Weight about 6.7 lbs. in 12-gauge and slightly less in sub-gauges.

NIB	EXC.	V.G.	GOOD	FAIR	POOR
1050	875	700	575	400	200

York

Side-by-side, with blued engraved receiver and 3" chambers. Comes in 12- and 20-gauge, with 26" or 28" barrels. Walnut pistol-grip stock and rubber recoil pad.

NIB	EXC.	V.G.	GOOD	FAIR	POOR
625	500	400	300	200	100

Hunter Lite

Over/under with silver alloy engraved frame, 3" chambers, extractors, choke tubes and walnut pistol-grip stock and forearm. Weight: 20-gauge with 26" barrels 5.4 lbs.; 12-gauge with 28" barrels 6 lbs.

NIB	EXC.	V.G.	GOOD	FAIR	POOR
450	325	225	175	100	75

Hunter

Similar to Hunter Lite, with blued steel frame.

NIB	EXC.	V.G.	GOOD	FAIR	POOR
450	325	225	175	100	75

Field Hunter

Based on Hunter, this model includes selective auto ejectors and five choke tubes.

NIB	EXC.	V.G.	GOOD	FAIR	POOR
575	450	325	250	150	100

Gentry/Gentry Coach

Model offered in 12-, 16-, 20-, 28-gauge and .410 bore in Gentry and 12- and 20-gauge in Gentry Coach. Barrel lengths are 28" for Gentry (26" for 28-gauge and .410 bore) and 20" for Gentry Coach. Boxlock action, with engraved antique silver finish. Walnut stock, with pistol-grip. Choke tubes. Single-selective trigger. Weight about 6.5 lbs. depending on gauge.

NIB	EXC.	V.G.	GOOD	FAIR	POOR
750	625	500	400	250	100

Derby Classic

Model features sidelock frame and action that is engraved and case colored. Offered in 12-gauge, with fixed chokes in modified and full. Fitted with 28" barrel. Double trigger and automatic ejectors. Weight about 7.75 lbs.

NIB	EXC.	V.G.	GOOD	FAIR	POOR
1200	1000	800	650	450	200

TSA SERIES

These gas-operated semi-automatics are available in 12- and 20-gauge, with barrels from 24" to 26" depending on model.

TSA Field

Walnut fore-end and pistol-grip stock, 3" chamber, 3 choke tubes and magazine-cut-off feature. Weight about 5.7 lbs. in 20-gauge; 6.5 lbs. in 12-gauge depending on barrel length. 20-gauge available in youth model.

NIB	EXC.	V.G.	GOOD	FAIR	POOR
375	325	275	175	125	75

	NIB	EXC.	V.G.	GOOD	FAIR	POOR

TSA Synthetic and Synthetic Mag

Same features as TSA Field Model, with non-glare black synthetic stock and fore-end. Also available with complete Realtree Max-4 coverage. Mag model has 3.5" chamber.

NIB	EXC.	V.G.	GOOD	FAIR	POOR
375	325	275	175	125	75

300 SERIES

Tristar 300 series over/under guns were imported from Turkey.

Model 333

This over/under gun available in 12- or 20-gauge, with 26", 28" or 30" barrels in 12-gauge. Hand engraved frame. Fitted with 3" chambers and choke tubes. Single-selective triggers and auto ejectors. Fancy Turkish walnut stock. Weighs about 7.75 lbs. for 12-gauge; 7.5 lbs. for 20-gauge.

NIB	EXC.	V.G.	GOOD	FAIR	POOR
650	600	425	325	225	150

Model 333SC

Similar to above model, with addition of 11mm sporting rib, recoil pad, forcing cones, and ported barrels. Extended choke tubes.

NIB	EXC.	V.G.	GOOD	FAIR	POOR
700	650	475	375	250	175

Model 333SCL

Same features as Model 333SC, with special stock.

NIB	EXC.	V.G.	GOOD	FAIR	POOR
700	650	475	375	250	175

Model 333L

Same features as Model 333, with a special stock designed for women. Length of pull shorter, with special Monte Carlo comb.

NIB	EXC.	V.G.	GOOD	FAIR	POOR
650	600	425	325	225	150

Model 330

This over/under model has a standard Turkish walnut stock, with etched engraved frame. Offered in 12- and 20-gauge. Single trigger, with extractors and fixed chokes.

NIB	EXC.	V.G.	GOOD	FAIR	POOR
450	325	225	175	100	75

Model 330D

Same as model above, with addition of selective auto ejectors.

NIB	EXC.	V.G.	GOOD	FAIR	POOR
500	400	300	225	175	100

Model 300

Model features an underlug action lock, with double triggers and extractors. Frame is etched. Offered in 12-gauge only, with 26" or 28" barrels with fixed chokes.

NIB	EXC.	V.G.	GOOD	FAIR	POOR
450	325	225	175	100	75

Model 311

This is a side-by-side gun in 12- or 20-gauge, with 26" or 28" barrels with choke tubes. Standard Turkish walnut. Blued frame.

NIB	EXC.	V.G.	GOOD	FAIR	POOR
500	400	300	225	175	100

Model 311R

Same as above, with 20" barrel choked Cylinder and Cylinder.

NIB	EXC.	V.G.	GOOD	FAIR	POOR
500	400	300	225	175	100

EMILIO RIZZINI (Old Nova Series)

Gun line no longer imported. Tristar Nova series were imported from Italy.

TR-L

Offered in 12- or 20-gauge, with choice of 28" or 30" vent rib barrels. Choke tubes standard. Standard grade walnut, with pistol-grip. Action is silver finish boxlock, with auto ejectors and single-selective trigger. Weight about 7.5 lbs. Stock dimensions are made for a smaller shooter. Introduced in 1998.

NIB	EXC.	V.G.	GOOD	FAIR	POOR
1000	850	700	575	400	200

TR-SC

Similar to Nova L. Offered in 12-gauge only, with standard stock dimensions. Semi-fancy walnut stock, with pistol-grip. Black sporting clays-style recoil pad. Weight between 7.5 and 8 lbs. depending on barrel length. Introduced in 1998.

NIB	EXC.	V.G.	GOOD	FAIR	POOR
1000	850	700	575	400	200

	NIB	EXC.	V.G.	GOOD	FAIR	POOR

TR-I

Offered in 12- and 20-gauge, with 26" or 28" barrels with fixed chokes. Walnut stock, with hand checkering and pistol-grip. Beavertail fore-end. Boxlock action is blue, with single-selective trigger and extractors. Weight about 7.5 lbs. Introduced in 1998.

	650	600	425	325	225	150

TR-II (Nova II)

Same as above, but fitted with automatic ejectors.

	700	650	475	375	250	175

TR-Mag

Similar to the Nova I. Chambered for 10- and 12-gauge with 3.5" shell. Choice of 24" or 28" vent rib barrels, with choke tubes. Non-reflective non-glare blue finish. Introduced in 1998. **NOTE:** Add $175 for 12-gauge with ejectors; $350 for 10-gauge gun.

	750	650	475	375	250	175

TTR-Royal

Model offered in 12-, 20- or 28-gauge, with 28" ported choke tube barrels, straight-grip semi-fancy walnut stock and auto ejectors. Silver receiver, with gold engraving.

	1300	1250	1100	875	600	300

TR-Class SL

Top-of-the-line model, with sculptured frame and engraved side plates. Offered in 12-gauge only.

	1775	1500	1250	1000	750	500

411 SERIES

Shotguns are made in Italy by R.F.M. Luciano Rota.

Model 411

Side-by-side double is imported from Italy and introduced in 1998. Chambered for 12- or 20-gauge and .410 bore, with choice of 26" or 28" barrels with choke tubes or fixed chokes. Boxlock action, with engraving and case coloring. Double triggers and extractors. Standard walnut stock, with pistol-grip and splinter forearm. Weight between 6 and 6.5 lbs.

	850	675	500	375	250	150

Model 411R

Offered in 12- or 20-gauge, with 20" barrel. Fixed cylinder chokes. Extractors. Weight about 6.5 lbs. for 12-gauge; 6 lbs. for 20-gauge.

	750	650	475	375	250	175

Model 411D

Similar to Model 411, with engraved case, colored finish on receiver, auto ejectors, single trigger and straight-grip stock. Weight for 28-gauge about 6.25 lbs.; 12 gauge about 7 lbs.

	1050	875	700	575	400	200

Model 411F

Same as Model 411D, with silver engraved receiver.

	1600	1400	1050	800	600	400

PHANTOM SERIES

Shotguns were made in Turkey by Eqsilah. Discontinued in favor of new redesigned gun found under Diana Series.

Phantom Field

Gas operated semi-automatic shotgun. Chambered for 12-gauge and 2.75" or 3" shell. Fitted with 24", 26" or 28" barrel. Checkered walnut stock, with pistol-grip. Screw-in chokes. Five-round magazine. **NOTE:** Add $75 for Magnum models.

	425	325	275	200	150	100

Phantom Synthetic

Same as above, with synthetic stock. **NOTE:** Add $75 for Magnum models.

	395	300	225	195	150	75

	NIB	EXC.	V.G.	GOOD	FAIR	POOR

Phantom HP

Same features as Phantom Field, except with synthetic stock, 19" barrel and swivel studs.

NIB	EXC.	V.G.	GOOD	FAIR	POOR
395	300	225	195	150	75

BREDA SERIES

Semi-automatic shotguns are made in Italy by Breda. Guns first imported by Tristar in 2003.

Ermes

Chambered for 12-gauge 3" shell. Fitted with either 26" or 28" vent rib barrel. Inertia operated recoil system. Checkered walnut stock, with pistol-grip. Choice of black, nickel, gold or silver alloy receiver finish. Receiver engraved with hunting scenes. Adjustable stock spacers. Weight about 7.75 lbs.

Gold

NIB	EXC.	V.G.	GOOD	FAIR	POOR
1935	1500	1250	1075	800	400

Silver

NIB	EXC.	V.G.	GOOD	FAIR	POOR
1725	1350	1100	900	650	300

Nickel

NIB	EXC.	V.G.	GOOD	FAIR	POOR
1650	1200	1050	750	500	300

Black

NIB	EXC.	V.G.	GOOD	FAIR	POOR
1260	975	750	600	500	250

Astra 20

A 20-gauge model, with 26" vent rib barrel. Black receiver. Walnut with pistol-grip and solid rubber recoil pad. Furnished with five choke tubes. Weight about 6 lbs.

NIB	EXC.	V.G.	GOOD	FAIR	POOR
1140	900	750	600	465	200

Mira Sporting

Semi-automatic shotgun is gas operated. Chambered for 12-gauge shell, with 3" chamber. Fitted with 30" vent rib barrel, with 10mm wide rib. Checkered walnut stock, with pistol-grip. Weight about 7 lbs.

NIB	EXC.	V.G.	GOOD	FAIR	POOR
875	700	550	400	300	200

Mira Camo

As above, with 28" barrel and camo finish.

NIB	EXC.	V.G.	GOOD	FAIR	POOR
875	700	550	400	300	200

CD DIANA SERIES

Shotguns were made in Turkey by Eqsilah. This line replaced Phantom Series. First imported by Tristar in 2003.

CD Diana Field

Gas operated semi-automatic shotgun. Chambered for 12-gauge 3" shell. Fitted with 26", 28" or 30" vent rib barrel. Checkered walnut stock, with pistol-grip. Choke tubes. Magazine cutoff. Weight about 7 lbs. depending on barrel length.

NIB	EXC.	V.G.	GOOD	FAIR	POOR
425	325	275	200	150	100

CD Diana Synthetic

As above, with black synthetic stock. Also offered with 3.5" chamber. Weight about 6.75 lbs.
NOTE: Add $90 for 3.5" Magnum model.

NIB	EXC.	V.G.	GOOD	FAIR	POOR
400	300	250	200	150	100

CD Diana Slug

12-gauge gun fitted with 24" rifled slug barrel, with open adjustable sights. Black synthetic stock. Weight about 6.75 lbs.

NIB	EXC.	V.G.	GOOD	FAIR	POOR
425	325	275	200	150	100

CD Diana Camo Mag

Similar to models above, with camo stock and barrel. Choice of 24" or 28" barrel, with 3.5" chamber. Weight about 6.75 lbs.

NIB	EXC.	V.G.	GOOD	FAIR	POOR
575	450	350	225	175	100

	NIB	EXC.	V.G.	GOOD	FAIR	POOR

Pee Wee

Single-shot bolt-action rifle chambered for .22 LR cartridges. Stock is walnut and about 1/2 the size of an adult rifle. Weight about 2.75 lbs. Open sights. Finish is blue.

NIB	EXC.	V.G.	GOOD	FAIR	POOR
200	150	100	75	50	25

HANDGUNS

Model C-100

Compact model based on CZ75 design. DA/SA operation. Chambered in 9mm or .40 S&W, with 11- and 15-round magazine capacities, respectively. Blue or chrome finish, with 3.9" barrel, checkered polymer grips and fixed sights. Introduced in 2013.

NIB	EXC.	V.G.	GOOD	FAIR	POOR
400	360	320	285	—	—

Model L-120

Full-size model based on CZ75 design in 9mm only. Similar features to those found on C-100, except with 4.7" barrel, 17 round magazine capacity. Available in chrome finish.

NIB	EXC.	V.G.	GOOD	FAIR	POOR
400	360	320	285	—	—

TROCAOLA (TAC)
Eibar, Spain

Break-Top Revolvers

This maker produced a variety of .32-, .38- and .44-caliber top break revolvers between approximately 1900 and 1936. These pistols can be identified by the monogram "TAC" stamped on left side of the frame. **NOTE:** Add 50 percent premium for .44 models.

NIB	EXC.	V.G.	GOOD	FAIR	POOR
—	275	175	125	100	75

TRYON, EDWARD K. & COMPANY
Philadelphia, Pennsylvania

Pocket Pistol

A .41-caliber single-shot percussion pocket pistol, with 2" or 4" barrel, German silver mounts and walnut stock. Lock marked "Tryon/Philada". Manufactured during the 1860s and 1870s.

NIB	EXC.	V.G.	GOOD	FAIR	POOR
—	—	2550	1900	750	200

TUCKER SHERARD & COMPANY
Lancaster, Texas

Dragoon

A .44-caliber percussion revolver, with 7.75" round barrel. Fitted with loading lever and 6-shot cylinder. Barrel marked "Clark, Sherard & Co., Lancaster, Texas". Cylinder etched in two panels, with crossed cannons and legend "Texas Arms". Approximately 400 revolvers of this type were made between 1862 and 1867. Prospective purchasers are advised to secure a qualified appraisal prior to acquisition.

NIB	EXC.	V.G.	GOOD	FAIR	POOR
—	—	60000	55000	22000	13000

TUFTS & COLLEY
New York, New York

Pocket Pistol

A .44-caliber single-shot percussion pocket pistol, with 3.5" barrel, German silver mounts and walnut stock. Lock marked "Tufts & Colley"; barrel "Deringer/Pattn.". Manufactured during 1860s.

NIB	EXC.	V.G.	GOOD	FAIR	POOR
—	—	2450	1900	825	200

TURBIAUX, JACQUES
Paris, France
See—Ames

TURNER, THOMAS
Redding, England

	NIB	EXC.	V.G.	GOOD	FAIR	POOR

Pepperbox

A .476 double-action percussion pepperbox having 6 barrels. Blued case hardened, with walnut grips. Left side of frame engraved in an oval "Thomas Turner, Redding".

NIB	EXC.	V.G.	GOOD	FAIR	POOR
—	—	5500	1900	975	400

TYLER ORDNANCE WORKS
Tyler, Texas

This company produced 56 Austrian rifles, 508 Enfield rifles, 423 Hill rifles and 1,009 Texas rifles during the Civil War. **NOTE:** These rifles are very rare.

Tyler Texas Rifle

A .57-caliber single-shot rifle, with 27" barrel and full stock secured by two barrel bands. Lock marked "Texas Rifle/Tyler/Cal. .57".

NIB	EXC.	V.G.	GOOD	FAIR	POOR
—	—	62500	44000	16500	12000

Hill Rifle

A .54-caliber single-shot percussion rifle, with 27" barrel and full stock secured by two brass barrel bands. Iron trigger guard and buttplate. Lock marked "Hill Rifle/Tyler/Tex/ Cal. .54".

NIB	EXC.	V.G.	GOOD	FAIR	POOR
—	—	58000	40000	15000	12000

U

	NIB	EXC.	V.G.	GOOD	FAIR	POOR

U.S. ARMS CO.
Riverhead, New York
See—United Sporting Arms, Inc.

U.S. M1 CARBINE
Various Manufacturers

For history, technical data, descriptions, photos and prices, see Standard Catalog of Military Firearms under United States Rifles. Prices listed are for rifles in original, unaltered condition. **NOTE:** Rifles that have been refinished or restored deduct about 50 percent.

Inland

NIB	EXC.	V.G.	GOOD	FAIR	POOR
2000	1800	1200	600	425	350

Underwood

NIB	EXC.	V.G.	GOOD	FAIR	POOR
2000	1800	1250	550	400	275

S.G. Saginaw

NIB	EXC.	V.G.	GOOD	FAIR	POOR
2000	1800	1400	700	450	375

IBM

NIB	EXC.	V.G.	GOOD	FAIR	POOR
2200	1900	1500	1000	500	250

Quality Hardware

NIB	EXC.	V.G.	GOOD	FAIR	POOR
2000	1700	1100	525	375	250

National Postal Meter

NIB	EXC.	V.G.	GOOD	FAIR	POOR
2100	1800	1100	575	375	250

Standard Products

NIB	EXC.	V.G.	GOOD	FAIR	POOR
2150	1900	1200	600	425	250

Rockola

NIB	EXC.	V.G.	GOOD	FAIR	POOR
2400	2000	1400	750	475	350

SG Grand Rapids

NIB	EXC.	V.G.	GOOD	FAIR	POOR
2400	2000	1400	600	425	350

Winchester

NIB	EXC.	V.G.	GOOD	FAIR	POOR
2500	2200	1700	1100	600	375

Irwin Pedersen

NIB	EXC.	V.G.	GOOD	FAIR	POOR
4200	3500	2500	1300	800	500

M1 Carbine Cutaway

NIB	EXC.	V.G.	GOOD	FAIR	POOR
—	2500	1500	900	600	500

M1 Carbine Sniper with infra red conversion

NIB	EXC.	V.G.	GOOD	FAIR	POOR
—	1450	1000	800	400	300

U.S. M1 A1 Paratrooper Model

NIB	EXC.	V.G.	GOOD	FAIR	POOR
—	4500	3500	2500	1250	750

U.S. ORDNANCE
Reno, Nevada

Models listed are machined to military specifications and semi-automatic only.

M-60

7.62mm belt-fed semi-automatic weapon. Modeled after famous machine gun used in Vietnam. Fitted with 22" barrel. Weight about 24 lbs.

NIB	EXC.	V.G.	GOOD	FAIR	POOR
10000	8900	7000	5500	4000	2500

	NIB	EXC.	V.G.	GOOD	FAIR	POOR

M-60E3

Shorter more lightweight version of standard M-60. Fitted with 17" barrel. Weight about 18 lbs.

NIB	EXC.	V.G.	GOOD	FAIR	POOR
8900	7000	5500	4000	3000	1750

Browning Model 1919

Belt-fed model chambered for 7.62mm/.30-06 cartridges. Fitted with 23" barrel. Weight about 30 lbs. Prices listed are for gun only. **NOTE:** Add $125 for A6 stock, bipod and carry handle; $450 for A4 tripod.

2800	2400	1900	1500	1200	900

Vickers

Chambered for .303 cartridge and belt-fed. Weight about 40 lbs. Prices listed are for gun only. **NOTE:** Add $500 for Tripod.

4800	4000	3000	2200	1700	900

U.S. REPEATING ARMS CO.

See—Winchester

UBERTI, ALDO/UBERTI USA

Ponte Zanano, Italy

Company manufactures high-grade reproductions of famous Western-style American firearms. Their products have been imported over the years by a number of different companies. They produce both blackpowder guns and cartridge firearms that are included in this section. This Italian manufacturer builds high quality firearms of the American West. Featured are Colt, Winchester and Remington. Each importer stamps its name on the firearm in addition to Uberti address. In 2000, Beretta Holding Company purchased Uberti.

Paterson Revolver

Exact copy of famous and rare Colt pistol. Offered in .36-caliber, with engraved 5-shot cylinder. Barrel is 7.5" long and octagonal forward of lug. Frame and backstrap are case hardened steel. Grips are one-piece walnut. Overall length 11.5"; weight about 2.5 lbs.

400	300	200	125	100	75

Walker Colt Revolver

Faithful reproduction of famous and highly sought-after Colts. Caliber is .44 and round barrel is 9" long. Frame case hardened steel. Trigger guard brass. 6-shot cylinder engraved with fighting dragoon scene. Grip one-piece walnut. Overall length 15.75"; weight a hefty 70 oz.

500	400	300	200	125	100

Colt Whitneyville Dragoon

Transition Walker, reduced version of Model 1847 Walker. Fitted with 7.5" barrel. Chambered for .44-caliber.

475	375	200	125	100	75

Colt 1st Model Dragoon Revolver

Shorter version of Walker and evolved directly from that original design. A 6-shot .44-caliber, with 7.5" barrel. Frame color case hardened steel. Backstrap and trigger guard brass. Grips one-piece walnut. Overall length 13.5"; weight about 63 oz.

400	300	250	125	100	75

Colt 2nd Model Dragoon Revolver

Differs from 1st model in that cylinder bolt slot is square instead of oval.

400	300	250	125	100	75

Colt 3rd Model Dragoon Revolver

Model varies from 2nd model as follows:

a: Loading lever taper is inverted.

b: Loading lever latch hook is different shape.

c: Loading lever latch.

d: Backstrap steel and trigger guard brass oval.

e: Frame is cut for shoulder stock.

350	225	175	125	100	75

NIB	EXC.	V.G.	GOOD	FAIR	POOR

Colt Model 1849 Wells Fargo

No loading lever. Chambered for .31-caliber cartridge. Barrel is octagonal. Frame case colored and hardened steel. Backstrap and trigger guard brass. Cylinder engraved and holds 5 rounds. Grip one-piece walnut. Overall length 9.5"; weight 34 oz.

325	200	150	125	100	75

Pocket Revolver

Same as Wells Fargo, with addition of loading lever.

325	200	150	125	100	75

Colt Model 1848 Baby Dragoon

Similar is appearance to Model 1849, with 4" tapered octagonal barrel and square back trigger guard. No loading lever. Weight about 23 oz.

325	200	150	125	100	75

Model 1851 Navy Colt

Chambered for .36-caliber, with engraved 6-shot cylinder. Tapered octagonal barrel 7.5". Frame case colored steel. Backstrap and oval trigger guard brass. Grips one-piece walnut. Overall length 13"; weight about 44 oz.

400	300	250	125	100	75

Model 1861 Navy Colt

Sometimes referred to as "New Navy". Similar in appearance to Model 1851. Offered in two variations: military version has steel backstrap, trigger guard and cut for shoulder stock; civilian version has brass backstrap, trigger guard and not cut for shoulder stock.

Military Model

400	300	250	125	100	75

Civilian Model

400	300	250	125	100	75

Colt Model 1860 Army

Chambered for .44-caliber ball. Fitted with round tapered 8" barrel. Revolver has 6-shot engraved cylinder. Grips one-piece walnut. Overall length 13.75"; weight about 42 oz.

Military

Steel backstrap, brass trigger guard and cut for shoulder stock.

400	300	250	125	100	75

Fluted Cylinder Military

400	300	250	125	100	75

Civilian

Brass backstrap and trigger guard. Not cut for shoulder stock.

400	300	250	125	100	75

Colt Model 1862 Police Revolvers

Chambered for .36-caliber. Fitted with round tapered barrel in 4.5", 5.5" or 6.5" and 5-shot fluted cylinder. Frame color case hardened steel. Backstrap and trigger guard brass. Grips one-piece walnut. Weight about 25 oz.

400	300	250	125	100	75

Colt Model 1862 Pocket Navy Revolver

Similar to Model 1862 Police. Fitted with 5-shot engraved non-fluted cylinder. Barrel lengths 4.5", 5.5" and 6.5". Weight about 27 oz.

400	300	250	125	100	75

Colt Model 1868 Army Thuer Conversion

450	325	225	175	150	100

Remington Model 1858 New Army .44 Caliber

Chambered for .44-caliber and fitted with tapered octagonal 8" barrel. Cylinder holds 6-shots. Frame blued steel. Trigger guard brass. Grips two-piece walnut. Overall length 13.75"; weight about 42 oz.

300	200	150	125	100	75

Remington Model 1858 New Army .36 Caliber

Similar to above. Fitted with 7.375" tapered octagonal barrel. Weight about 40 oz.

400	300	250	125	100	75

NIB	EXC.	V.G.	GOOD	FAIR	POOR

Remington Model 1858 New Army .44 Caliber Target

Version fitted with fully adjustable rear sight and ramp front sight.

425	325	275	150	125	75

Remington Model 1858 New Army .44 Caliber Stainless Steel

All parts stainless steel.

425	325	275	150	125	75

Remington Model 1858 New Army .44 Cal. SS Target

Same as Target Model. All parts stainless steel.

450	325	250	200	125	75

Remington Model 1858 Target Revolving Carbine

Chambered for .44-caliber and fitted with 18" octagon barrel. Frame blued steel. Trigger guard brass. Stock select walnut. Overall length 35"; weight about 4.4 lbs.

425	300	200	150	100	75

1875 Remington "Outlaw"

Replica of original Remington cartridge pistol. Chambered for .357 Magnum, .44-40, .45 ACP, .45 ACP/.45 L.C. conversion and .45 Colt. Frame case colored steel. Trigger guard brass. Offered with 7.5" round barrel either blued or nickel-plated. Two-piece walnut grips. Overall length 13.75"; weight about 44 oz.

450	325	250	200	125	75

Remington Model 1875 Frontier

Introduced in 2005. Features 5.5" barrel chambered for .45 Colt cartridge. Case colored frame with blued barrel, backstrap and trigger guard. Two-piece walnut grips. Weight about 40 oz.

500	375	250	175	150	100

Remington Model 1890 Police

A 5.5"-barreled replica of original Remington Pistol. Chambered for .357 Magnum, .44-40, .45 ACP, .45 ACP/.45 L.C. conversion and .45 Colt. Frame case colored steel. Trigger guard brass. Available either blued or nickel-plate. Grips two-piece walnut and fitted with grip ring. Overall length 11.75"; weight about 41 oz.

500	375	250	175	150	100

Model 1871 Rolling Block Pistol

Single-shot target pistol chambered for .22 LR, .22 Magnum, .22 Hornet, .222 Rem., 223 Rem., .45 Long Colt or .357 Magnum. Has blued 9.5" half-octagonal half-round barrel. Case colored receiver. Walnut grip and forearm. Trigger guard brass. Overall length 14"; weight about 44 oz.

500	375	250	175	150	100

Model 1871 Rolling Block Carbine

Similar to pistol, with 22.5" half-octagonal half-round barrel. Full-length walnut stock. Trigger guard and buttplate brass. Overall length 35.5"; weight about 4.8 lbs.

650	525	400	275	200	125

Henry Rifle

Brass-framed reproduction of famous Winchester/Henry Rifle. Chambered for .44-40 or .45 Colt cartridge and basically only departure from being a true and faithful copy. Octagonal barrel 24.25" on rifle model; 22.25" on carbine model. Also two Trapper models offered: 18.5" barrel and 16.5" version. High-quality rifle and amazingly close to original in configuration. Three grades of engraving available. Weights are rifle 9.2 lbs.; carbine 9 lbs.; 18.5" trapper 7.9 lbs.; 16.5" trapper 7.4 lbs. Finish can be steel, standard blued or charcoal blue. **NOTE:** Add $350 Grade A; $450 Grade B; $600 Grade C.

900	700	550	450	350	200

Winchester Model 1866

Faithful replica of Winchester 1866. Chambered for .22 LR, .22 Magnum, .38 Special, .44-40 and .45 Long Colt. Rifle version has brass frame and 24.25" tapered octagon barrel. Frame finish brass, with walnut stock. Weight about 8 lbs.

800	650	550	450	350	200

1866 Yellowboy Carbine

Similar to standard rifle. Offered with 19" round tapered barrel.

700	600	500	450	350	200

	NIB	EXC.	V.G.	GOOD	FAIR	POOR

Winchester Model 1873 Carbine

Reproduction of Winchester 1873. Chambered for .357 Magnum, .45 Long Colt and .44-40. Case colored steel receiver and 19" round tapered barrel. Lever also case colored. Stock and forearm walnut. Overall length 38.25"; weight about 7.4 lbs.

NIB	EXC.	V.G.	GOOD	FAIR	POOR
900	700	500	450	350	200

Winchester Model 1873 Rifle

Similar to Carbine, with 24.25" octagonal barrel. Overall length 43.25"; weight about 8.2 lbs. **NOTE:** Extra barrel lengths from 20" to 30" in .45 L.C. and .44-40 also offered at extra cost.

NIB	EXC.	V.G.	GOOD	FAIR	POOR
950	750	600	450	350	200

Winchester 1873 Short Sporting Rifle

As above fitted with 20" octagon barrel.

NIB	EXC.	V.G.	GOOD	FAIR	POOR
950	800	600	450	350	200

Winchester 1873 Half-Octagon Rifle

Same as above, with 24.25" half octagon barrel. Stock has checkered pistol-grip.

NIB	EXC.	V.G.	GOOD	FAIR	POOR
1000	800	600	450	350	200

Winchester 1873 Musket

Chambered for .44-40 or .45 Long Colt cartridge. Fitted with 30" barrel, full stock and three barrel bands. Magazine capacity 14 rounds. Weight about 9 lbs.

NIB	EXC.	V.G.	GOOD	FAIR	POOR
1000	800	600	450	350	200

Model 1885 High Wall Single-Shot Carbine

Chambered for .38-55, .30-30, .44-40, .45 Colt, .40-65 or .45-70, with 28" barrel. Walnut stock.

NIB	EXC.	V.G.	GOOD	FAIR	POOR
825	600	450	350	250	200

Model 1885 High Wall Single-Shot Rifle

Same as above, with 30" barrel.

NIB	EXC.	V.G.	GOOD	FAIR	POOR
900	675	500	400	300	200

Model 1885 High Wall Single-Shot Rifle Pistol Grip

Fitted with 30" or 32" barrel and checkered pistol-grip stock. Same calibers as above.

NIB	EXC.	V.G.	GOOD	FAIR	POOR
1000	800	600	450	350	200

Winchester 1885 Low Wall Sporting Rifle

Version of Low Wall Winchester. Chambered for .22 Hornet, .30-30, .44 Magnum or .45 Colt cartridges. Fitted with 30" octagon barrel. Walnut stock with pistol-grip. Weight about 7.5 lbs. Introduced in 2004.

NIB	EXC.	V.G.	GOOD	FAIR	POOR
950	800	600	450	350	200

Winchester 1885 Low Wall Schuetzen

As above chambered for .45 Colt cartridge. Fitted with palm rest and Swiss butt. Weight about 7.75 lbs. Introduced in 2004.

NIB	EXC.	V.G.	GOOD	FAIR	POOR
1200	950	800	600	450	350

Hawken Santa Fe

Based on famous original rifle. Reproduction bored for .54-caliber and fitted with 32" octagon barrel. Double set trigger and case hardened lock plate standard. Stock ferrule and wedge plates are German silver. Stock is walnut with cheekpiece. Overall length 50"; weight about 9.5 lbs. Available in kit form.

NIB	EXC.	V.G.	GOOD	FAIR	POOR
350	300	250	200	150	100

Cattleman

Single-action revolver patterned closely after Colt Single-Action Army. Chambered in various popular calibers: .357 Magnum, .44-40, .44 Special, .45 ACP, .45 L.C./.45 ACP convertible and .45 Colt. Offered with barrel lengths of 4.75", 5.5" and 7.5". Also with either modern or black powder-type frame. Brass or steel backstraps. Finish blued, with walnut grips. Sheriff's Model with 3" barrel and no ejector rod chambered for .44-40 and .45 Colt also available and valued the same. Weight about 38 oz. for 5.5" barrel gun.

NIB	EXC.	V.G.	GOOD	FAIR	POOR
400	275	225	150	100	75

Cattleman Flattop Target Model

Similar to standard Cattleman, with adjustable rear sight.

NIB	EXC.	V.G.	GOOD	FAIR	POOR
435	350	275	225	175	125

	NIB	EXC.	V.G.	GOOD	FAIR	POOR

Cattleman Gunfighter NM

Chambered for .45 Colt cartridge. Fitted with 4.75", 5.5" or 7.5" barrel. Black checkered grip, with matte blued finish. Weight about 37 oz. Introduced in 2005.

400	275	225	150	100	75

Cattleman Cody NM

As above, with nickel finish and ivory-style grips.

500	375	250	175	150	100

Cattleman Frisco NM

As above, with charcoal blued barrel and case colored frame. Pearl grips.

500	375	250	175	150	100

Cattleman El Patron CMS

Designed for Cowboy Mounted Shooter (CMS) competition. Caliber .357 Magnum or .45 Colt. Steel cylinder, frame and barrel, 6-round capacity, single action trigger, low profile hammer, fixed sights and wood grips. Weight 36.8 oz. Barrel 3.5" or 4", with blue/case hardened or stainless finish. **NOTE:** Add 25 percent for stainless finish.

525	425	350	300	225	150

Bisley

Chambered for .32-20, .38 Special, .357 Magnum, .38-40, .44-40 and .44 Special. Fitted with 4.75", 5.5" or 7.5" barrel. Case hardened frame with two-piece walnut grips.

435	350	275	225	175	125

Flattop

As above, with adjustable rear sight.

435	350	275	225	175	125

Buntline Carbine

Version has 18" barrel. Fitted with permanently mounted shoulder stock, with brass buttplate and sling swivel. Chambered for .44-40, .45 Long Colt, .357 Magnum and .44 Magnum. Offered with fixed or adjustable sights.

450	400	350	300	250	200

Buckhorn Buntline

Version chambered for .44 Magnum. Has 18" round barrel and cut for attaching shoulder stock. Steel backstrap and trigger guard. Overall length 23"; weight about 57 oz. **NOTE:** Detachable shoulder stock add 25 percent.

400	325	300	250	200	100

Buckhorn Target

Same as above. Fitted with adjustable rear sight and ramp front sight. Has flat upper frame.

450	350	300	250	200	100

Phantom

Similar to Buckhorn. Chambered for .44 and .357 Magnum. Round 10.5" barrel. Frame blued, with blued steel backstrap. One-piece walnut grips, with anatomic profile. Adjustable sight. Weight about 53 oz.

400	275	225	150	100	75

New Thunderer Model

Designed and imported exclusively by Cimarron Arms, for single-action shooting competition. Fitted with bird's-head grip with hard rubber. Chambered for .357 Magnum, .44 Special, .44 WCF and .45 Colt. Offered in barrel lengths of 3.5" and 4.75". Finish in nickel or blued, with case colored frame.

450	350	300	250	200	100

1873 Stallion

Scaled-down version chambered for .22 LR/.22 Magnum. Blued, with case colored frame. Features one-piece walnut grips.

350	295	250	200	150	100

Tornado

Five-shot revolver chambered for .454 Casull. Fitted with 4.75", 5.5" or 7.5" with ported barrel. Sandblasted nickel finish. Weight about 47 oz.

1000	900	750	600	500	400

	NIB	EXC.	V.G.	GOOD	FAIR	POOR

No. 3 Schofield Revolver

Patterned after original S&W revolver. Chambered for .44-40 or .45 Colt cartridge. Fitted with 3.5", 5" or 7" barrel. Weight with 7" barrel about 40 oz.

	NIB	EXC.	V.G.	GOOD	FAIR	POOR
	800	700	600	475	325	200

No. 3 New Model Russian

Chambered for .44 Russian cartridge. Fitted with 6" or 7" barrel.

	NIB	EXC.	V.G.	GOOD	FAIR	POOR
	900	800	700	575	400	300

Inspector Model

Double-action revolver built on same general lines as Colt Detective. Cylinder holds 6 cartridges. Chambered for .38 Special. Offered in barrel lengths with fixed sights: 2", 2.125", 2.5", 3", 4", 6". Also offered in 4" or 6" barrel lengths with adjustable sights. Grips are walnut. Finish blued or chrome. With 3" barrel weight about 24 oz.

	NIB	EXC.	V.G.	GOOD	FAIR	POOR
	275	200	150	125	100	75

UHLINGER, WILLIAM P.
Philadelphia, Pennsylvania

Pocket Revolver

.32-caliber spur trigger revolver, with 2.75" or 3" octagonal barrel and unfluted 6-shot cylinder. Blued, with rosewood or walnut grips. Manufactured during late 1860s and early 1870s. Uhlinger-manufactured pistols will often be found with retailer's names on them, such as D.D. Cone, Washington, D.C.; J.P. Lower; W.L. Grant.

Long Cylinder (1-3/16")

	NIB	EXC.	V.G.	GOOD	FAIR	POOR
	—	—	800	600	250	100

Short Cylinder (1")

	NIB	EXC.	V.G.	GOOD	FAIR	POOR
	—	—	650	425	175	75

.32 Rimfire Model (5", 6", or 7" Barrel)

	NIB	EXC.	V.G.	GOOD	FAIR	POOR
	—	—	800	600	250	100

ULTIMATE
See—Camex-Blaser USA, Inc.

ULTRA LIGHT ARMS
See—New Ultra Light Arms

UMAREX USA
Fort Smith, Arkansas

Umarex Colt Tactical Rimfire M4 Ops Carbine

Blowback semi-automatic rifle styled to resemble Colt M16. Chambered in .22 LR. Features include 16.2" barrel; front sight adjustable for elevation; adjustable rear sight; alloy lower; adjustable telestock; flattop receiver with removable carry handle; 10- or 30-round detachable magazine.

	NIB	EXC.	V.G.	GOOD	FAIR	POOR
	500	425	365	300	225	150

Umarex Colt Tactical Rimfire M4 Carbine

Blowback semi-automatic rifle styled to resemble Colt M4. Chambered in .22 LR. Features include 16.2" barrel; front sight adjustable for elevation; adjustable rear sight; alloy lower; adjustable telestock; flattop receiver with optics rail; 10- or 30-round detachable magazine.

	NIB	EXC.	V.G.	GOOD	FAIR	POOR
	550	465	400	335	250	165

Umarex Colt Tactical Rimfire M16 Rifle

Blowback semi-automatic rifle styled to resemble Colt M16. Chambered in .22 LR. Features include 21.2" barrel; front sight adjustable for elevation; adjustable rear sight; alloy lower; fixed stock; flattop receiver; removable carry handle; 10- or 30-round detachable magazine.

	NIB	EXC.	V.G.	GOOD	FAIR	POOR
	500	425	365	300	225	150

Umarex Colt Tactical Rimfire M16 SPR Rifle

Blowback semi-automatic rifle styled to resemble Colt M16 SPR. Chambered in .22 LR. Features include 21.2" barrel; front sight adjustable for elevation; adjustable rear sight; alloy lower; fixed stock; flattop receiver with optics rail; removable carry handle; 10- or 30-round detachable magazine.

	NIB	EXC.	V.G.	GOOD	FAIR	POOR
	575	485	425	360	275	185

	NIB	EXC.	V.G.	GOOD	FAIR	POOR

Umarex H&K 416-22

Blowback semi-automatic rifle styled to resemble H&K 416. Chambered in .22 LR. Features include metal upper and lower receivers; RIS - rail interface system; retractable stock; pistol-grip with storage compartment; on-rail sights; rear sight adjustable for wind and elevation; 16.1" barrel; 10- or 20-round magazine. Also available in pistol version with 9" barrel.

	575	485	425	360	275	185

Umarex H&K MP5 A5

Blowback semi-automatic rifle styled to resemble H&K MP5. Chambered in .22 LR. Features include metal receiver; compensator; bolt catch; NAVY pistol-grip; on-rail sights; rear sight adjustable for wind and elevation; 16.1" barrel; 10- or 25-round magazine. Also available in pistol version with 9" barrel and SD-type fore-end.

	450	375	300	250	200	150

UNCETA
See—Astra-Unceta SA

UNION
Unknown

Pocket Pistol

.22 caliber spur trigger single-shot pistol, with 2.75" barrel marked "Union". Nickel-plated with walnut grips.

	—	—	650	400	100	75

UNION FIRE ARMS COMPANY
Toledo, Ohio

Company was incorporated in 1902 and used names of Union Fire Arms, Union Arms Company, Illinois Arms Company (made for Sears) and Bee Be Arms Company. In 1917, company was either bought up or absorbed by Ithaca Gun Company.

NOTE: Union Fire Arms Company (or Union Firearms Company, as it is sometimes known) slide action shotguns are not commonly seen. Though not widely collected, they seem to attract considerable interest as oddities, much as Spencer/Bannerman slide action shotguns do. Values given below are approximate; as always, true value lies in eyes of buyer, not seller.

Double Barrel Shotguns

Union's predecessor, Colton Manufacturing Co. (1894-1902), made a double for Sears. Cleverly designed with coil mainspring striker locks set into sideplates. Union double in 12- and 16-gauge, with steel or Damascus barrels derived from it, but was a traditional hammerless sidelock side-by-side well-made gun (1902-1913) and also sold by Sears. Values depend on grade and condition. Union also offered, about 1905, an unusual boxlock hammer gun Model 25 in 12-gauge only. Employs external hammers, but they are mounted within frame and spurs protrude in front of topsnap opener. These guns are hard to find and values range from $300 to $1,200 depending on condition. Produced with steel twist or Damascus barrels only in plain grade.

	—	1300	525	4050	300	200

Model 24

Slide action Model 25 Peerless, was a fancy version of Model 24 and Model 25A, which was a trap model. Manufactured from 1902 to 1913 in 12- or 16-gauge, with 24", 26", 28" or 32" steel or Damascus barrels. Gun had unique double trigger. Front trigger cocked and decocked an internal firing pin and back trigger fired the gun. Gun is marked on left side of frame and pump release is on right side. Model had one serious drawback, the slide that extracted a spent shell extended back over comb of stock. This often hit shooter's thumb knuckle and caused injury. In 1907, Union redesigned their slide by reducing its length and shielding it behind a steel plate that covered rear half of opening. These are Model 24, 25 and 25A improved versions. Approximately 17,000 of all models combined were made.

	—	—	750	300	200	100

Model 50

Manufactured 1911 to 1913. Basically redesign of Model 24. Main distinguishing feature of Model 50 was the frame sloped down to meet comb of stock. Double trigger system was replaced by single trigger. Came in 12- or 16-gauge, with 26", 28", 30" or 32" Krupp steel barrel. Fewer than 3,000 made.

	—	—	850	400	300	200

	NIB	EXC.	V.G.	GOOD	FAIR	POOR

Model 22

Essentially a no frills Model 23. Same barrel length and steel options. Plain walnut stock and no engraving. Fewer than 10,000 Model 22 and 23s made.

	—	—	300	100	75	50

Model 23

Manufactured between 1902 and 1913. Hammerless double with-/without automatic ejectors. Some engraving, came in both single-/double-trigger models. This was their top grade gun. Came in 12- and 16-gauge, with 28", 30" or 32" steel twist or Damascus barrels.

	—	—	450	150	125	100

Diamond Grade

Manufactured between 1905 and 1910. Unique octagonal breech in 12-gauge only with 30" steel laminated or Damascus barrel. Premium grade single-shot. Few were made.

	—	—	450	200	100	50

Model 18

Manufactured 1906 to 1913. Came in 12- or 16-gauge with 30", 32", 34" or 36" steel barrel. Plain single-shot. Very few made.

	—	—	200	75	50	25

Reifngraber

.32 or .38 S&W caliber gas operated semi-automatic pistol, with 3" barrel. Blued, with walnut grips. Approximately 100 were manufactured.

	—	—	2250	1100	500	350

Automatic Revolver

.32 S&W caliber similar to Webley Fosbery semi-automatic revolver, with 3" barrel. Blued, with either walnut or hard rubber grips. Cylinder has zigzag grooves.

	—	—	3250	1250	500	250

UNIQUE
Hendaye, France
See—Pyrenees

UNITED SPORTING ARMS, INC.
Tucson, Arizona

Blued Guns (Seville, etc.)

	N/A	500	450	350	—	—

Blue Silhouette (10.5" barrels)

NOTE: Add $100 stainless; $250 stainless long-frame models (calibers .357 Maximum/Super Magnum and .357 USA/Super Magnum).

	N/A	600	550	500	—	—

Silver Sevilles

	N/A	550	475	400	—	—

Stainless Steel Guns

	N/A	600	525	450	—	—

Tombstone Commemorative

	1000	750	625	525	—	—

Quik-Kit Stainless Steel

NOTE: Quik-Kit guns with extra barrel and cylinder add $200 for each barrel and cylinder. Deduct 10 percent if United Sporting Arms, Hauppauge, N.Y. Deduct 20 percent if United Sporting Arms, Post Falls, ID. Add 20 percent if El Dorado Arms (either N.Y. or N.C.). Add 10 percent for 1.5" barrel Sheriff's Model. Add 20 percent for 10.5" barrel. Add 20 percent for bird's-head grip frame. Add 20 percent if brass grip frame.

	1500	1250	800	—	—	—

Quik-Kit Blued

	1200	1000	650	—	—	—

NIB	EXC.	V.G.	GOOD	FAIR	POOR

UNITED STATES ARMS
Otis A. Smith Company
Rockfall, Connecticut

Single-Action Revolver

.44 rimfire and centerfire single-action revolver, with 7" barrel and integral ejector. Hammer nose fitted with two firing pins so rimfire or centerfire cartridges can be used interchangeably. Barrel marked "United States Arms Company - New York"; top strap "No. 44". Blued, with either hard rubber or rosewood grips. Manufactured in limited quantities. Circa 1870 to 1875.

NIB	EXC.	V.G.	GOOD	FAIR	POOR
—	—	4750	3250	1250	500

UNITED STATES FIRE ARMS MFG.
(Formerly United States Patent Firearms Mfg. Co.)
Hartford, Connecticut

This company produced a wide variety of high quality replica handguns and rifles from 1992 until 2012.

Single-Action Army Revolver

Offered in wide variety of calibers including .22 rimfire, .32 WCF, .38 S&W, .357 Magnum, .38-40, .41 Colt, .44 Russian, .44-40, .45 Colt and .45 ACP. Barrel lengths 4.75", 5.5", 7.5" with or without ejector. Modern cross pin frame available for additional $10. Prices listed for standard grips and finish, Armory bone case finish and Dome blue finish.

NIB	EXC.	V.G.	GOOD	FAIR	POOR
975	900	800	675	525	300

Single-Action Army Revolver Pre-War

As above, with pre-war "P" frame.

NIB	EXC.	V.G.	GOOD	FAIR	POOR
1395	1150	950	700	550	300

Shooting Master

Large-frame model in .357 Magnum with 7.5" barrel, U.S. hard rubber grips, blue finish and enlarged trigger guard. Adjustable rear sight, 6-round cylinder. Introduced in 2011. Also available in .327 Federal, with 8-shot cylinder (Sparrowhawk model).

NIB	EXC.	V.G.	GOOD	FAIR	POOR
1300	1100	950	800	525	250

Flattop Target Model

Offered with same calibers as Single-Action Army above. Barrel lengths 4.75", 5.5" and 7.5". Grips two-piece hard rubber. Prices listed for standard finish. Introduced in 1997.

NIB	EXC.	V.G.	GOOD	FAIR	POOR
1665	1450	1200	900	675	400

Rodeo

Single-action revolver offered in .45 Colt, .44-40, .44 Special, .32-20, .38-40 and .38 Special calibers. Choice of 4.75" or 5.50" barrel. Satin blue finish, with bone case hammer. "US" hard rubber grips standard.

NIB	EXC.	V.G.	GOOD	FAIR	POOR
625	550	450	350	250	175

Rodeo II

Similar to Rodeo, with matte nickel finish and Burlwood grips.

NIB	EXC.	V.G.	GOOD	FAIR	POOR
575	475	350	275	225	200

Buntline

Features all blued finish, with 16" barrel. Chambered for .45 Colt cartridge.

NIB	EXC.	V.G.	GOOD	FAIR	POOR
2300	1750	1475	1100	700	450

Buntline Special

Fitted with 16" barrel. Chambered for .45 Colt cartridge. Supplied with nickel stock. Limited edition. Cased.

NIB	EXC.	V.G.	GOOD	FAIR	POOR
2895	2250	1750	1475	1100	700

China Camp Cowboy Action Gun

Chambered for .45 Colt cartridge, but other calibers available from .32 WCF to .44 WCF. Barrel lengths 4.75", 5.5" and 7.5". Special action job. Two-piece hard rubber grips standard. Finish is silver steel.

NIB	EXC.	V.G.	GOOD	FAIR	POOR
1395	1150	950	700	550	300

Henry Nettleton Revolver

Exact reproduction of U.S. Government inspector model, produced in Springfield Armory. Offered in 5.5" and 7.5" models. Introduced in 1997. Discontinued.

NIB	EXC.	V.G.	GOOD	FAIR	POOR
1575	1450	1200	900	600	350

	NIB	EXC.	V.G.	GOOD	FAIR	POOR

.22 Plinker

Chambered for .22 cartridge. Fitted with choice of barrel lengths: 4.75", 5.5" or 7.5". Extra .22 WMR cylinder included.

	975	875	725	550	300	150

.22 Target

As above, with adjustable rear sight and replaceable front sight blade.

	1665	1450	1200	900	675	400

Gunslinger

Offered in .45 Colt, .44 Special, .44 WCF, .38 Special, .38 WCF or .32 WCF. Choice of 4.75", .5.5" or 7.5" barrel. Cross pin frame. Hard rubber grips. Aged bluing finish. Black style frame optional. **NOTE:** Add $135 for black powder frame.

	1145	1025	800	625	500	250

Custer Battlefield Gun

Replica of 1873 revolver used during height of Indian Wars, including Custer's Last Stand. Limited edition with cartouche of Ordnance Sub-inspector Orville W. Ainsworth; serial range 200 - 14,343. Six shot 7.5" barrel. Antique Patina aged blue. One-piece walnut stock.

	1625	1450	1200	900	675	400

Hunter

Revolver chambered for .17 HMR cartridge. Fitted with 7.5" barrel, with adjustable rear sight and replaceable front sight blade. Finish matte blue. Discontinued.

	975	875	725	550	300	150

Sheriff's Model

Chambered for wide variety of calibers from .45 Colt to .32 WCF. Choice of 2.5", 3", 3.5" or 4" barrel. No ejector. **NOTE:** Add $250 for nickel finish.

	975	875	725	550	300	150

Omni-Potent Bird's-Head Model

Chambered for .45 Colt, .45 ACP, .44 Special, .44 WCF, .38 Special, .38 WCF or .32 WCF cartridges. Offered with bird's-head grips. Available with 3.5", 4" or 4.75" barrel lengths.

	1625	1450	1200	900	675	400

Omni-Potent Snubnose

As above, with 2", 3" or 4" barrel without ejector.

	1475	1300	1050	800	575	400

Omni-Potent Target

Choice of 4.75", 5.5" or 7.5" barrel, with adjustable rear sight and replaceable front blade sight.

	1395	1150	950	700	550	300

Bisley Model

Based on famous Bisley model. Reproduction features barrel lengths of 4.75", 5.5", 7.5" and 10". The .45 Colt caliber is standard, but .32 WCF, .38 S&W, .44 S&W, .41 Colt, .38 WCF, .44 WCF are optional. Introduced in 1997. **NOTE:** Add $60 for 10" models.

	1575	1450	1200	900	600	350

Target

As above, with adjustable rear sight and replaceable blade front sight.

	1625	1450	1200	900	675	400

Pony Express

Features 5.50" engraved barrel and frame, with special finish. Ivory grips etched with pony express rider. Custom gun.

	3895	3500	2950	2200	1500	700

Sears 1902 Colt

Replica of Sears 1902 Colt SAA. Fitted with 5.50" barrel, pearl grips, full coverage engraving with gold line work on cylinder and barrel. Custom gun.

	8995	7500	6000	500	4000	1000

	NIB	EXC.	V.G.	GOOD	FAIR	POOR

Model 1910

Stylized version of early Colt Model 1910 .45 ACP pistol.

	NIB	EXC.	V.G.	GOOD	FAIR	POOR
	1895	1700	1550	1200	900	500

Model 1911 Army or Navy

Faithful version of early Colt Model 1911 military model.

	NIB	EXC.	V.G.	GOOD	FAIR	POOR
	1700	1500	1100	900	500	350

Ace .22 LR

Recreation of 1911-style Colt Ace .22 LR, with 10+1 capacity. Walnut grips. Introduced 2006.

	NIB	EXC.	V.G.	GOOD	FAIR	POOR
	1850	1650	1100	900	500	350

Super .38

1911-style semi-automatic. Blued finish; chambered for .38 Super Automatic with 9+1 capacity. Walnut grips. Introduced 2006.

	NIB	EXC.	V.G.	GOOD	FAIR	POOR
	1800	1600	1200	900	500	350

RIFLES

Cowboy Action Lightning

Copy of Colt Lightning rifle. Chambered for .44-40, .45 Colt or .38 WCF cartridge. Fitted with 26" round barrel. Walnut stock with crescent butt. Magazine capacity 15 rounds. Introduced fall of 2003. Discontinued.

	NIB	EXC.	V.G.	GOOD	FAIR	POOR
	1625	1450	1200	900	675	400

Cowboy Action Carbine

As above, with 20" round barrel. Magazine capacity 12 rounds. Discontinued.

	NIB	EXC.	V.G.	GOOD	FAIR	POOR
	1625	1450	1200	900	675	400

Lightning Magazine Rifle

Premium version of Cowboy Action Lightning. Features choice of 26" round-/half-round or octagon barrel. Checkered American walnut forearm, with non-checkered stock with oil finish. Many extra cost options are offered for this model. Discontinued. **NOTE:** Add $200 for half round barrel. Fancy wood, pistol-grip, finish and engraving offered for this rifle.

	NIB	EXC.	V.G.	GOOD	FAIR	POOR
	1625	1450	1200	900	675	400

Lightning Magazine Carbine

As above, with 20" round barrel. Discontinued.

	NIB	EXC.	V.G.	GOOD	FAIR	POOR
	1625	1450	1200	900	675	400

Lightning Baby Carbine

Fitted with 20" special round tapered barrel. Lightweight carbine forearm with border line. Discontinued.

	NIB	EXC.	V.G.	GOOD	FAIR	POOR
	1995	1825	1600	1250	950	650

UNITED STATES REVOLVER ASSOCIATION

See—Harrington & Richardson Arms Co.

UNITED STATES SMALL ARMS CO.

Chicago, Illinois

Huntsman Model Knife Pistol

Made from approximately 1918-1930. Too Rare To Price.

UNIVERSAL FIREARMS

Hialeah, Florida/Jacksonville, Arkansas

Universal merged with Iver-Johnson in 1985 and relocated to Arkansas in 1986. Universal operated out of Florida from late 1950s to 1985.

Model 7312

12-gauge over/under shotgun. Separated 30" ventilated rib barrels, single-selective trigger and automatic ejectors. Case hardened receiver engraved. Blued, with walnut stock. Imported from Italy.

	NIB	EXC.	V.G.	GOOD	FAIR	POOR
	—	1250	900	450	300	175

	NIB	EXC.	V.G.	GOOD	FAIR	POOR

Model 7412

As above, with extractors. Imported from Italy.

	—	1000	750	400	250	150

Model 7712

As above, with 26" or 28" barrels, nonselective single trigger and extractors. Imported from Italy.

	—	550	400	350	250	100

Model 7812

As above, with more detailed engraving and automatic ejectors. Imported from Italy.

	—	700	550	450	350	150

Model 7912

As above, with gold wash frame and single-selective trigger. Imported from Italy.

	—	1350	1000	750	600	300

Model 7112

12-gauge double-barrel boxlock shotgun, with 26" or 28" barrels, double triggers and extractors. Blued case hardened, with walnut stock. Imported from Italy.

	—	450	300	250	200	100

Double Wing

10-, 12-, 20-gauge or .410 bore boxlock double-barrel shotgun, with 26", 28" or 30" barrels, double triggers and extractors. Blued, with walnut stock. Imported from Italy. Premium for 10-gauge and .410 bore.

	—	450	300	250	200	100

Model 7212

12-gauge single-barrel trap shotgun, with 30" ventilated rib, ported barrel and automatic ejector. Engraved case hardened receiver and walnut stock. Imported from Italy.

	—	1200	850	650	450	300

Model 1000 Military Carbine

Copy of U.S. M1 Carbine, with 18" barrel. Blued, with birchwood stock.

	—	400	250	200	100	75

Model 1003

As above, with 16", 18" or 20" barrel.

	—	350	200	150	100	75

Model 1010

As above but nickel-plated.

	—	375	225	175	125	100

Model 1015

As above but gold-plated.

	—	400	250	200	150	125

Model 1005 Deluxe

As above, with polished blue finish and Monte Carlo-style stock.

	—	375	225	150	100	75

Model 1006 Stainless

As Model 1000 in stainless steel.

	—	450	300	225	125	100

Model 1020 Teflon

As above, with black or gray Dupont Teflon-S finish.

	—	375	225	175	125	100

Model 1256 Ferret

Model 1000 in .256 Winchester Magnum caliber.

	—	350	200	175	125	100

	NIB	EXC.	V.G.	GOOD	FAIR	POOR

Model 3000 Enforcer

Pistol version of Model 1000, with 11.25" barrel and 15- or 30-shot magazines. Prices for blued models. **NOTE:** Add 20 percent Nickel finish; 40 percent Gold-plated; 30 percent Stainless steel; 20 percent Teflon-S.

	NIB	EXC.	V.G.	GOOD	FAIR	POOR
	—	375	225	200	150	100

Model 5000 Paratrooper

Model 1000, with 16" or 18" barrel and folding stock. This model in stainless steel known as Model 5006.

	NIB	EXC.	V.G.	GOOD	FAIR	POOR
	—	400	250	200	125	100

1981 Commemorative Carbine

Limited production version of Model 1000 cased with accessories. Produced in 1981.

	NIB	EXC.	V.G.	GOOD	FAIR	POOR
	500	350	250	200	100	75

Model 2200 Leatherneck

.22 caliber version of U.S. M1 Carbine, with 18" barrel and blowback action. Blued, with birchwood stock.

	NIB	EXC.	V.G.	GOOD	FAIR	POOR
	—	300	175	150	100	75

URIZAR, TOMAS
Eibar, Spain

Celta, J. Cesar, Premier, Puma, and Union

6.35mm semi-automatic pistol, with 3" barrel. Slide marked with trade names listed above. Blued, with black plastic grips cast with a wild man carrying a club.

	NIB	EXC.	V.G.	GOOD	FAIR	POOR
	—	250	150	125	90	75

Dek-Du

5.5mm folding trigger double-action revolver, with 12-shot cylinder. Later versions made in 6.35mm. Manufactured from 1905 to 1912.

	NIB	EXC.	V.G.	GOOD	FAIR	POOR
	—	225	125	100	75	50

Express

6.35mm semi-automatic pistol, with 2" barrel. Slide marked "The Best Automatic Pistol Express". Blued, with walnut grips. A 7.65mm variety exists with 4" barrel.

	NIB	EXC.	V.G.	GOOD	FAIR	POOR
	—	225	125	100	75	50

Imperial

6.35mm caliber semi-automatic pistol, with 2.5" barrel. Model actually made by Aldazabal. Manufactured circa 1914.

	NIB	EXC.	V.G.	GOOD	FAIR	POOR
	—	225	125	100	75	50

Le Secours or Phoenix

7.65mm semi-automatic pistol marked with either trade names listed above.

	NIB	EXC.	V.G.	GOOD	FAIR	POOR
	—	225	125	100	75	50

Princeps

6.35mm or 7.65mm semi-automatic pistol. Marked on slide "Made in Spain Princeps Patent".

	NIB	EXC.	V.G.	GOOD	FAIR	POOR
	—	225	125	100	75	50

Venus

7.65mm semi-automatic pistol, with grips having trade name "Venus" cast in them.

	NIB	EXC.	V.G.	GOOD	FAIR	POOR
	—	225	125	100	75	50

USELTON ARMS INC.
Goodlettsville, Tennessee

NOTE: Values shown for basic models. Sky's the limit.

Compact Classic

Chambered for .45 ACP cartridge, with 5" barrel. Checkered rosewood grips. Low-profile sights. Black and gray finish. Magazine capacity 7 rounds. Weight about 32 oz.

	NIB	EXC.	V.G.	GOOD	FAIR	POOR
	1995	1700	1500	1100	800	500

	NIB	EXC.	V.G.	GOOD	FAIR	POOR

Ultra Compact Classic

1911-style semi-automatic in .45 caliber, with fixed sights. Barrel 4.25", weight 34 oz., trigger pull 3-4 lb., 7+1 capacity. Rosewood or imitation ivory grips. Introduced 2006.

1995	1700	1500	1100	800	500

Compact Classic Companion

Chambered for .357 Sig or .40 S&W cartridge. Fitted with 5" barrel. Low-profile sights. Black or polymer ivory grips. Stainless or gray finish. Magazine capacity 7 rounds. Weight about 32 oz.

2250	1900	1700	1250	900	600

Carry Classic

Chambered for .45 ACP cartridge. Fitted with 4.25" barrel with low-profile sights. Rosewood or polymer ivory grips. Gray and black finish. Magazine capacity 7 rounds. Weight about 34 oz.

1995	1700	1500	1100	800	500

Ultra Carry

.45 ACP model features Damascus slide and titanium frame. Fitted with 3" barrel with low-profile sights. Magazine capacity 7 rounds. Weight about 27 oz. **NOTE:** Also offered in titanium and stainless for $2350; stainless and black for $1850.

3250	2900	2500	2000	1500	800

Tactical 1911

Chambered for .45 ACP cartridge. Fitted with 5" barrel with Caspian adjustable sights. Rubber grips and moly coat finish. Magazine capacity 8 rounds. Weight about 40 oz.

2200	1975	1600	1200	1000	500

Classic National Match

.45 ACP pistol has 5" barrel, with Caspian adjustable sights. Black aluma grips and finish. Magazine capacity 8 rounds. Weight about 40 oz. **NOTE:** Add $300 for compensator.

2200	1975	1600	1200	1000	500

UZI ISRAELI MILITARY INDUSTRIES

See—Vector Arms, Inc.

Uzi Carbine Model A

Chambered for 9mm cartridge. Fitted with 16" barrel with 25-round magazine. Gray Parkerized finish. Built from 1980 to 1983.

1600	1450	1200	800	600	450

Uzi Carbine Model B

9mm, .41 Action Express or .45-caliber semi-automatic carbine, with 16.1" barrel. Magazines 20-, 25- or 32-shot box. A 50-shot drum magazine available in 9mm caliber. Black Parkerized finish. Plastic grips and folding stock. Strongly suggested that buyer or seller seek qualified local appraisal. First produced in 1983. Model no longer imported as of 1989.

1500	1350	1100	750	550	400

Uzi Mini-Carbine

As above in 9mm or .45-caliber, with 19.75" barrel. No longer imported.

2250	1600	1150	800	600	400

Uzi Pistol

As above in 9mm or .45 ACP, with 4.5" barrel, pistol-grip, no rear stock and 20-shot magazine. No longer imported.

850	700	550	450	350	250

UZI EAGLE PISTOLS

As of 1999, these pistols no longer imported into U.S.

Full Size Model

Introduced in 1997. Double-action pistol chambered for 9mm and .40 S&W cartridge. Barrel length 4.4"; overall length 8.1". Tritium night sights standard.

550	425	350	275	200	150

NIB	EXC.	V.G.	GOOD	FAIR	POOR

Short Slide Model

Introduced in 1997. Double-action pistol chambered for 9mm, .40 S&W and .45 ACP cartridge. Barrel length 3.7"; overall length 7.5". Tritium night sights standard.

600	475	400	325	250	200

Compact Model

Introduced in 1997. Double-action pistol chambered for 9mm, .40 S&W and .45 ACP cartridge. Barrel length 3.5"; overall length 7.2". Tritium night sights standard. Magazine capacity: 8 rounds .45 ACP; 10 rounds other calibers. Double-action-only an option for this model.

600	475	400	325	250	200

Polymer Compact Model

Introduced in 1997. Double-action pistol chambered for 9mm and .40 S&W cartridge. Barrel length 3.5"; overall length 7.2". Tritium night sights standard.

550	425	350	275	200	150

V

NIB	EXC.	V.G.	GOOD	FAIR	POOR

VALKYRIE ARMS, LTD.
Olympia, Washington

Valkyrie Arms filed for bankruptcy in early 2008.

Browning 1919 A4 .30 Caliber

Semi-automatic version of famous Browning machine gun. Chambered for .30-06 or .308 cartridge. Comes equipped with tripod, pintle, T&E, belly linker and 200 links. An A6 configuration available. Introduced in1996.

NIB	EXC.	V.G.	GOOD	FAIR	POOR
2850	2000	1500	1100	750	600

U.S. M3-A1

Re-creation of famous "grease gun" in semi-automatic. Barrel length 16.5". Supplied with three 30-round magazines. **NOTE:** Dummy suppressor add $50; real suppressor add $300 plus transfer tax of $200. All NFA rules and state laws must be followed for suppressors.

NIB	EXC.	V.G.	GOOD	FAIR	POOR
1500	1250	1000	750	500	300

DeLisle Carbine

Copy of famous World War II commando carbine used by British forces. Chambered for .45 ACP. Integral suppressor. All NFA rules must be followed. Only 167 original WWII carbines were produced. **NOTE:** Dummy suppressor deduct $300.

NIB	EXC.	V.G.	GOOD	FAIR	POOR
1575	1250	1000	750	500	300

VALMET, INC.
Jyvaskyla, Finland

M-62S

Semi-automatic copy of Finnish M-62 service rifle in 7.62x39 caliber. Patterned after Russian AK47. Fitted with walnut or tubular steel stock. Manufactured after 1962.

NIB	EXC.	V.G.	GOOD	FAIR	POOR
—	3000	2800	2300	900	750

M-71S

As above in 5.56mm caliber. Available with composition stock.

NIB	EXC.	V.G.	GOOD	FAIR	POOR
—	1350	1000	850	650	450

Model 76s

As above in 5.56mm, 7.62x39mm or 7.62x51mm. Either 16.75" or 20.5" barrel.

5.56mm

NIB	EXC.	V.G.	GOOD	FAIR	POOR
—	1750	1500	1250	750	600

7.62x39mm

NIB	EXC.	V.G.	GOOD	FAIR	POOR
—	3000	2750	2500	2000	1250

Model 78

As above in 7.62x51mm, 7.62x39 or .223, with 24.5" barrel, wood stock and integral bipod.

NIB	EXC.	V.G.	GOOD	FAIR	POOR
—	2150	1700	1300	850	600

Model 212 Lion

12-gauge over/under shotgun, with 26", 28" or 30" barrels, single-selective trigger and extractors. Blued, with walnut stock. Manufactured from 1947 to 1968. Amazingly similar to Savage Model 330 over/under. Values shown for standard field grade.

NIB	EXC.	V.G.	GOOD	FAIR	POOR
—	750	625	500	400	300

Model 412 Combination Gun

12-gauge .30-06 over/under combination gun. Built on frame of 12-gauge Lion shotgun. Discontinued.

NIB	EXC.	V.G.	GOOD	FAIR	POOR
—	1900	1475	1200	1050	700

NIB	EXC.	V.G.	GOOD	FAIR	POOR

VALTRO
Italy

1998 A1

Model 1911 clone chambered for .45 ACP and fitted with match grade 5" barrel. Many special features include checkered front strap, beavertail grip safety, deluxe wood grips, serrated slide front and back, beveled magazine well. Weight about 40 oz. Introduced in 1998.

2250	1950	1600	1275	800	500

Tactical 98 Shotgun

Chambered for 12-gauge and fitted with 18.5" or 20" ported barrel. Choice of pistol-grip or standard stock. Extended magazine with 5- or 7-rounds. Ghost ring sights.

—	900	750	675	500	325

PM5

Slide-action shotgun chambered for 12-gauge 3" shell. Barrel length 20" choked Cylinder. Box-fed magazine. Value shown for pre-ban model.

—	—

VARNER SPORTING ARMS, INC.
Marietta, Georgia

Company made several over/under shotguns and rifle/shotgun combinations for Savage Company. These are no longer being imported into this country. Rifles listed are all patterned after Stevens Favorite model.

Hunter

.22-caliber single-shot rifle, with 21.5" half-octagonal takedown barrel fitted with an aperture rear sight. Blued, with well-figured walnut stocks. Introduced in 1988.

375	300	250	200	150	100

Hunter Deluxe

As above, with case hardened receiver and more finely figured stock.

500	400	350	250	175	125

Presentation Grade

As above, with target hammer and trigger. Hand checkered stock.

575	475	425	350	250	200

No. 1 Grade
Engraved.

650	550	500	450	350	200

No. 2 Grade

775	650	600	500	400	200

No. 3 Grade

1100	850	700	550	350	200

VECTOR ARMS, INC.
North Salt Lake, Utah

Mini Uzi

Smaller version of full size Uzi. Chambered for 9mm cartridge only. Fitted with 18" barrel.

Pre-Ban

—	2000	1700	1400	1050	700

Post-Ban

—	1500	1250	1050	700	500

Uzi

Semi-automatic pre-ban Uzi carbine, with 18" barrel. Chambered for 9mm cartridge. Receiver built by Group Industries of Louisville, Kentucky, prior to May 1986. Receiver fixed parts manufacturing and receiver assembly by Vector Arms. Only 97 of these semi-automatic receivers manufactured.

NIB	EXC.	V.G.	GOOD	FAIR	POOR

NOTE: Add $200 for .45 ACP or .22-caliber conversion kit.

Pre-Ban

	NIB	EXC.	V.G.	GOOD	FAIR	POOR
	—	1500	1250	1050	700	500

Post-Ban

	NIB	EXC.	V.G.	GOOD	FAIR	POOR
	—	1200	1050	800	675	500

VEKTOR
Pretoria, South Africa

Company made a variety of handguns and rifles for U.S. market until 2001. Now only manufactures firearms for South African military and law enforcement.

HANDGUNS

Model Z88

Semi-automatic pistol chambered for 9mm cartridge. Has 5" barrel and fixed sights. Weight about 35 oz. Blue finish. Magazine capacity 15 rounds or 10 in U.S. Clone of Beretta 92.

NIB	EXC.	V.G.	GOOD	FAIR	POOR
600	475	350	250	175	100

Model SP1 Service Pistol

Model chambered for 9mm cartridge and fitted with 4.625" barrel. Fixed sights. Weight 35 oz. Blue finish. Magazine capacity 15 rounds or 10 in U.S. **NOTE:** Add $30 for anodized or nickel finish.

NIB	EXC.	V.G.	GOOD	FAIR	POOR
600	475	350	250	175	100

Model SP1 Sport

Similar to SP1. Features 5" barrel, with three-chamber compensator. Blue finish. Weight about 38 oz.

NIB	EXC.	V.G.	GOOD	FAIR	POOR
725	575	450	350	275	175

Model SP1 Tuned Sport

Model has three-chamber compensator on 5" barrel. Adjustable straight trigger and LPA 3-dot sighting system. Nickel finish. Weight about 38 oz.

NIB	EXC.	V.G.	GOOD	FAIR	POOR
1200	950	800	575	400	300

Model SP1 Target

9mm model fitted with 6" barrel with adjustable straight trigger. LPA 3 dot sighting system. Weight about 40.5 oz. Two-tone finish.

NIB	EXC.	V.G.	GOOD	FAIR	POOR
1200	950	800	575	400	300

Model SP1 Compact (General's Model)

Compact version of 9mm pistol fitted with 4" barrel. Fixed sights. Blue finish. Magazine capacity 15 rounds or 10 in U.S. Weight about 31.5 oz.

NIB	EXC.	V.G.	GOOD	FAIR	POOR
650	525	400	300	200	75

Model SP2

Full size service pistol chambered for .40 S&W cartridge. Fitted with 4.625" barrel. Fixed sights. Magazine capacity 11 rounds or 10 in U.S. Blued finish. Weight about 35 oz.

NIB	EXC.	V.G.	GOOD	FAIR	POOR
650	525	400	300	200	75

Model SP2 Compact (General's Model)

Compact .40 S&W pistol, with 4" barrel. Magazine capacity 11 rounds or 10 in U.S. Weight about 31.5 oz. Blue finish. Fixed sights.

NIB	EXC.	V.G.	GOOD	FAIR	POOR
650	525	400	300	200	75

Model SP2 Competition

Model chambered for .40 S&W cartridge and fitted with 5.875" barrel. Features enlarged safety levers and magazine catch. Frame has been thickened for scope mount. Beavertail grip and straight trigger. Weight about 42 oz.

NIB	EXC.	V.G.	GOOD	FAIR	POOR
1000	750	600	450	325	200

Model SP1 Ultra Sport

Model designed for IPSC open-class competition. Barrel length 6", with 3" chamber compensator. Chambered for 9mm cartridge. Optical scope mount, with Weaver rails. Magazine

NIB	EXC.	V.G.	GOOD	FAIR	POOR

capacity 19 rounds or 10 in U.S. Weight about 41.5 oz. Priced with Lynx scope.

NIB	EXC.	V.G.	GOOD	FAIR	POOR
2150	1800	1575	1200	800	500

Model SP2 Ultra Sport

Same as above chambered for .40 S&W cartridge. Magazine capacity 14 rounds or 10 in U.S.

NIB	EXC.	V.G.	GOOD	FAIR	POOR
2150	1800	1575	1200	800	500

Model SP2 Conversion Kit

Made for SP2, this is a 9mm conversion kit that consists of 9mm barrel, recoil spring and 9mm magazine.

NIB	EXC.	V.G.	GOOD	FAIR	POOR
200	150	100	75	50	25

Model CP-1 Compact

Chambered for 9mm cartridge and fitted with 4" barrel. Polymer frame and fixed sights. Weight about 25 oz. Magazine capacity 13 rounds standard, 12 rounds compact or 10 rounds in U.S. Offered with black or nickel slide. **NOTE:** This model was recalled in 2000 due to safety concerns.

NIB	EXC.	V.G.	GOOD	FAIR	POOR
475	375	250	150	100	50

RIFLES

Vektor H5 Pump-Action Rifle

Pump-action rifle chambered for .233 cartridge. Fitted with thumbhole stock and 22" barrel. Magazine capacity 5 rounds.

NIB	EXC.	V.G.	GOOD	FAIR	POOR
850	725	600	475	300	200

Vektor 98

Built on Mauser action and chambered for a variety of calibers from .243 to .375 H&H. Fitted with one-piece walnut stock, with hand checkering. Magazine capacity 5 rounds. Open sights on Magnum calibers only.

NIB	EXC.	V.G.	GOOD	FAIR	POOR
1200	950	800	575	400	300

Vektor Lyttelton

Rifle features numerous special features. Fitted with classic walnut stock and wraparound checkering. Fixed sights. Calibers offered from .243 to .375 H&H.

NIB	EXC.	V.G.	GOOD	FAIR	POOR
1595	1400	1100	800	575	300

VENUS WAFFENWERKE
Zella Mehlis, Germany

Venus

6.35mm, 7.65mm or 9mm semi-automatic pistol, with 3.5" barrel. Slide marked "Original Venus Patent" and grips bear monogram "OW". Designed by Oskar Will. Blued, plastic grips. Manufactured from 1912 to 1914.

NIB	EXC.	V.G.	GOOD	FAIR	POOR
—	700	550	400	250	100

VERNEY-CARRON
St. Etienne, France

Concours

12-gauge over/under boxlock shotgun, with 26" or 28" ventilated rib barrels, single-selective triggers, automatic ejectors and profuse engraving. Blued French case hardened, with checkered walnut stock. First imported in 1978.

NIB	EXC.	V.G.	GOOD	FAIR	POOR
—	1450	900	700	600	300

Skeet Model

As above, with 28" Skeet-choked barrel and pistol-grip stock.

NIB	EXC.	V.G.	GOOD	FAIR	POOR
—	1600	1050	700	600	300

Snake Charmer II

.410 single-barrel break-action shotgun, with stainless steel barrel and receiver. Black ABS stock. Overall length 29".

NIB	EXC.	V.G.	GOOD	FAIR	POOR
—	175	150	100	75	50

NIB	EXC.	V.G.	GOOD	FAIR	POOR

VERONA
Italy
HUNTING SHOTGUNS

Model SX401/S

12- or 20-gauge 3" semi-automatic model. Offered with 26" or 28" vent rib barrel, with choke tubes. Checkered Turkish walnut stock. Weight about 6.75 lbs.

NIB	EXC.	V.G.	GOOD	FAIR	POOR
800	600	475	350	150	100

Model SX405/S/L

As above, with black composite stock. Weight about 6.5 lbs.

NIB	EXC.	V.G.	GOOD	FAIR	POOR
700	600	550	300	100	75

Model SX405W/H/SW/SH

12-gauge 3" Magnum semi-automatic gun. Choice of 26" or 28" vent rib barrel, with wetland or hardwood camo pattern. Weight about 6.5 lbs.

NIB	EXC.	V.G.	GOOD	FAIR	POOR
800	600	475	350	150	100

LX501

Over/under shotgun chambered for 12-, 20-, 28-gauge and .410 bore. Single-selective trigger. Ejectors. Blued steel receiver. Walnut stock, with machine checkering. Offered with 28" vent rib barrels. Screw-in chokes for 12- and 20-gauge. Fixed chokes for 28-gauge and .410 bore. Chambers are 3" for all gauges except 28-gauge. Weight between 6.25 lbs. and 6.75 lbs. depending on gauge. **NOTE:** Add $30 for 28-gauge and .410 bore.

NIB	EXC.	V.G.	GOOD	FAIR	POOR
1000	875	600	400	300	225

LX692G

Model also offered in 12-, 20-, 28-gauge and .410 bore, with 28" vent rib barrels. Receiver fitted with sideplate. Gold inlaid hunting scenes on three sides. Matte finish walnut stock, with schnabel forearm, hand-cut checkering. Weight between 7.25 lbs. and 7.75 lbs. depending on gauge. **NOTE:** Add $40 for 28-gauge; $25 for .410 bore.

NIB	EXC.	V.G.	GOOD	FAIR	POOR
1250	1100	875	725	500	300

LX692G-20/28

Same as above. Features 20-gauge gun, with extra set of 28-gauge barrels. Choke tubes standard. Weight about 7.5 lbs. with 20-gauge barrels.

NIB	EXC.	V.G.	GOOD	FAIR	POOR
2000	1800	1500	1200	900	500

Model LX1001 Express Combo

Over/under gun features two sets of barrels; one for 20-gauge 2.75"; other either .223, .243, .270, .308 or .30-06. The 20-gauge barrels are 28" vent rib and rifle barrels are 22". Checkered walnut stock, with oil finish. Engraved receiver.

NIB	EXC.	V.G.	GOOD	FAIR	POOR
2580	2300	1975	1600	900	600

LX702G

Model offered in both 12- and 20-gauge, with 28" barrel chambered for 3" shells. Features case colored receiver, with side plates. Receiver engraved on three sides with gold inlaid upland bird hunting scenes. Full-figured Turkish walnut, with hand checkering and oil finish. Single-selective trigger, black recoil pad, ejectors and schnabel forearm. Weight: 12-gauge about 7 lbs.; 20-gauge about 6 lbs.

NIB	EXC.	V.G.	GOOD	FAIR	POOR
1375	1200	950	700	500	350

SIDE-BY-SIDE SHOTGUNS

Model SS662GL

Side-by-side offered in 20- or 28-gauge, with 28" barrels choked Modified and Full. Double triggers. Engraved receiver. Checkered walnut stock, with straight-grip. Weight about 6 lbs. Made by Bernardelli. **NOTE:** Add 20 percent for 28-gauge.

NIB	EXC.	V.G.	GOOD	FAIR	POOR
2200	2000	1750	1400	1000	500

Model SS772GL

As above, with slightly more engraving. **NOTE:** Add 20 percent for 28-gauge.

NIB	EXC.	V.G.	GOOD	FAIR	POOR
2450	2200	1850	1550	1175	550

	NIB	EXC.	V.G.	GOOD	FAIR	POOR

SPORTING/COMPETITION SHOTGUNS

LX680

Chambered for 12- or 20-gauge shells, with 2.75" chambers. Single-selective trigger, ejectors, lightly engraved steel receiver. Walnut stock, with beavertail firearm and hand-cut checkering. Ventilated recoil pad standard. Fitted with 28" barrels, with ventilated rib between barrels. Choke tubes. Weight about 6.5 lbs. depending on gauge.

1075	900	700	525	375	250

LX692GS

Similar to above, with sideplates and gold inlaid hunting scenes.

1425	1300	1050	750	500	350

LX680C S&T

Over/under model features choice of 28" or 30" 11mm vent rib barrels on 12-gauge frame. Single-selective trigger, ejectors. Matte finish Turkish walnut stock, with hand-cut checkering, beavertail forearm, wider comb. Lightly engraved steel receiver. Ventilated rib between barrels. Choke tubes. Weight about 7.75 lbs. depending on barrel length. 28" barrel model designated as Skeet/Sporting and 30" model designated Trap.

1175	1000	800	600	425	275

LX692GC S&T

Same as above, with sideplates and gold inlaid game scenes.

1550	1400	1150	850	600	350

LX702GC S&T

Model features case colored receiver and sideplates, with gold inlaid birds. Offered in 12-gauge only. Choice of 28" or 30" barrels. Weight about 7.5 lbs.

1625	1475	1175	800	600	350

Model SX801/L

Semi-automatic 12-gauge 2.75" shotgun. Fitted with choice of 28" or 30" vent rib ported barrels, with choke tubes and Hi-Viz sights. Walnut stock, with choice of Monte Carlo comb or adjustable comb. Weight about 6.75 lbs.

865	700	575	400	275	200

Model SX801G/GL

As above, with higher grade walnut stock.

1060	900	725	600	450	200

Model LX980CS

12-gauge 2.75" over/under gun. Fitted with 30" ported barrels, with extended choke tubes. Removable trigger assembly. Black receiver. Checkered select walnut stock. Weight about 7.5 lbs.

3525	3200	2500	2000	1550	600

Model LX980GCS/GCT

As above, with choice of 30" or 32" ported barrels. Select walnut stock has adjustable comb. Weight about 7.5 lbs.

3775	3400	2800	2250	1700	650

VICKERS, LTD.
Crayford/Kent, England

Jubilee

.22-caliber single-shot Martini-action rifle, with 28" barrel, adjustable sights and pistol-grip walnut stock. Blued. Manufactured prior to WWII.

—	1000	700	550	375	200

Empire

As above, with 27" or 30" barrel and straight stock.

—	1000	700	550	375	200

NIB	EXC.	V.G.	GOOD	FAIR	POOR

VICTOR EJECTOR

See—Crescent F. A. Co.

VICTORY ARMS CO., LTD.

Northhampton, England

Model MC5

9mm, .38 Super, .41 Action Express, 10mm or .45-caliber semi-automatic pistol, with 4.25", 5.75" or 7.5" barrel, 10-, 12- or 17-shot magazine, decocking lever and Millett sights. Interchangeable barrels were available. Introduced in 1989.

500	400	300	250	200	150

VIRGINIAN

See—Interarms

VOERE

Kufstein, Austria

In 1987 this company was purchased by Mauser-Werke. Voere actions are used in rifles made and sold by KDF, Inc. (Kleinguenther), of Seguin, Texas. Values for older-production rifles are listed.

Model 1007

Bolt-action rifle chambered for .22 LR cartridge and fitted with 18" barrel. Open sights. Beechwood stock. Introduced in 1984. Discontinued in 1991.

450	375	300	200	150	75

Model 1013

Bolt-action rifle chambered for .22 WMR cartridge and fitted with 18" barrel. Magazine capacity 8 rounds. Open sight with adjustable rear. Military-style stock is oil finished. Double set triggers.

650	575	500	375	250	125

Model 2107

.22 LR bolt-action rifle has a 19.5" barrel, with Monte Carlo stock. Eight-round magazine. Weight about 6 lbs.

650	575	500	375	250	125

Model 2107 Deluxe

Bolt-action rifle chambered for .22 LR cartridge. Checkered stock, with raised cheekpiece. Discontinued in 1988.

650	575	500	375	250	125

Model 2114S

Semi-automatic rifle chambered for .22 LR cartridge and fitted with 18" barrel. Magazine capacity 15 rounds. Open sight. Stock is beechwood. Single-stage trigger. No longer in production.

450	375	300	200	150	75

Model 2115

Similar to above, with checkered stock. Weight about 5.75 lbs. Discontinued in 1995.

500	425	350	250	200	100

Model 2150

Bolt-action centerfire rifle chambered for calibers from .22-250 to .338 Win. Magnum. Fitted with 22" barrels (24" on Magnums). Open sights with adjustable rear sight. Checkered walnut stock, with oil finish. Built on M98 Mauser action. Weight about 8 lbs. depending on caliber. Discontinued in 1995.

—	1500	1200	850	550	300

Model 2155

Similar to Model 2150, with no sights and double-set triggers. Discontinued in 1995.

—	1650	1350	1000	700	225

Model 2165

Similar to above, with open sights, walnut stock with Bavarian cheekpiece and schnabel forearm. Rosewood grip cap. Discontinued.

—	1650	1350	1000	700	225

	NIB	EXC.	V.G.	GOOD	FAIR	POOR

Model 2185

Semi-automatic centerfire rifle chambered for 7x64, .308 and .30-06 cartridges. Fitted with 20" barrel and open sights, with adjustable rear sight. Checkered walnut stock. Available with full stock as well. **NOTE:** Add $100 for Mannlicher stock.

	NIB	EXC.	V.G.	GOOD	FAIR	POOR
	—	1500	1200	950	850	400

Model 2185 Match

Same as Model 2185 except for 5-round magazine, hooded front sight, laminated stock with adjustable cheekpiece. Discontinued in 1994.

	NIB	EXC.	V.G.	GOOD	FAIR	POOR
	4000	3400	2750	1150	650	400

Model Titan

Centerfire bolt-action rifle chambered in calibers from .243 to .375 H&H. Fitted with 24" or 26" barrels depending on caliber. No sights. Checkered Monte Carlo walnut stock, with oil finish. Discontinued in 1988.

	NIB	EXC.	V.G.	GOOD	FAIR	POOR
	—	1200	1000	775	500	350

Model Titan Menor

Bolt-action rifle chambered for .222 Rem. and .223 Rem. Fitted with 23.5" barrel and 3-round magazine. No sights. Checkered Monte Carlo walnut stock, with rosewood grip cap. Introduced in 1986; dropped in 1988.

	NIB	EXC.	V.G.	GOOD	FAIR	POOR
	—	1000	800	600	400	250

Model VEC-91 Series

Bolt-action rifle that fires caseless 5.7mm ammo. Adjustable rear sight on 20" barrel. Checkered walnut stock with cheekpiece. Electronic trigger. Limited importation into U.S. from 1991 to approximately 2008. Seldom seen for sale on used gun market, in part due to expensive caseless ammunition.

	NIB	EXC.	V.G.	GOOD	FAIR	POOR
	2000	1600	1450	1000	—	—

VOLCANIC ARMS COMPANY
New Haven, Connecticut
See—Winchester Repeating Arms Co.

VOLQUARTSEN CUSTOM
Carroll, Iowa

Company started in 1973 and began specializing in Ruger 10/22 aftermarket conversions. In 1997 the company began producing its own receivers. **NOTE:** Volquartsen offers beaucoup options on a wide variety of rifles. Values shown below are for more-or-less base models.

SEMI-AUTO RIFLES

Rifles are based on Ruger 10/22 design. Chambered for .22 LR or .22 WMR cartridge.

Standard

Fitted with 18.5" stainless steel barrel. Hogue rubber stock or brown laminated stock. No sights. Integral Weaver rail.

	NIB	EXC.	V.G.	GOOD	FAIR	POOR
	1350	1200	950	700	550	300

Lightweight

Model has 16.5" carbon-fiber barrel. Choice of rubber or laminated stock. Integral Weaver rail.

	NIB	EXC.	V.G.	GOOD	FAIR	POOR
	1370	1220	975	725	550	300

Deluxe

Model has 20" stainless steel fluted and compensated barrel. Choice of laminated or rubber stock.

	NIB	EXC.	V.G.	GOOD	FAIR	POOR
	1360	1200	950	700	550	300

SIGNATURE SERIES

Fitted with 20" stainless steel fluted and compensated barrel. Engraved receiver, trigger guard and rings. Comes with Nikon 3.3x10 Titanium scope. Fancy walnut stock.

	NIB	EXC.	V.G.	GOOD	FAIR	POOR
	3000	2650	2200	1600	1200	500

VG-1

Model has 20" stainless steel fluted and compensated barrel. Fitted with green McMillan fiberglass stock. Finish is black epoxy powder coating. Offered in .22 WMR only.

	NIB	EXC.	V.G.	GOOD	FAIR	POOR
	1900	1700	1400	1150	900	500

	NIB	EXC.	V.G.	GOOD	FAIR	POOR

VX-2500

Model features 20" stainless steel fluted and compensated barrel. Fitted with VX-2500 stock, with aluminum forearm. Designed for benchrest shooting.

	2000	1750	1500	1200	900	500

VX-5000

Fitted with 18" carbon-fiber lightweight barrel, with compensator. Comes standard with VX-5000 stock, with aluminum fore-end.

	2200	1950	1700	1400	1000	600

PISTOLS

Pistols based on Ruger MK II design.

Black Cheetah Pistol

Special order only.

Compact

Fitted with 3.5" bull barrel and Hogue Monogrip. Adjustable rear sight and target front sight. Stainless steel finish. Weight about 42 oz.

	1000	850	700	525	400	300

Deluxe

Model fitted with 5" to 10" special heavy barrel depending on customer's requirements. Adjustable rear sight and target front sight. Target grips. Stainless steel finish.

	1250	1000	900	700	575	450

Masters

Masters features 6.5" barrel, with aluminum alloy-finned underlug. Top rib has front blade sight with an adjustable rear sight. Rib is cut to accommodate optics. Integral compensator. Weight about 56 oz.

	1600	1350	1200	900	650	500

Olympic

Olympic designed for NRA or UIT competitive shooting. Has a 7.5" match barrel, with unique gas chamber for recoil-free shooting. Target front sight and adjustable rear sight. Weight about 36 oz.

	1750	1450	1300	1000	650	500

Stingray

Fitted with 7.5" match-grade barrel, with radial flutes. Compensator standard. Supplied with either Ultra Dot red dot optic or TL rear optic. Weight about 56 oz.

	1600	1350	1200	900	650	500

Terminator

Model fitted with 7.5" match barrel, with integral compensator. Choice of Weaver-style or .375" tip-off scope mounting system. **NOTE:** Add $150 for Ultra Dot optics.

	1600	1350	1200	900	650	500

Ultra-Lite Match

	1600	1350	1200	900	650	500

V-6

V-6 has 6" vent rib triangular-shaped match barrel, with full-length underlug. Adjustable rear sight and target front sight. Rubber target grips. Weight about 36 oz.

	1350	1200	950	700	550	300

V-2000

Fitted with 6" match barrel. Alloy-finned underlug. Rubber target grips. Adjustable rear sight with target front sight. Weight about 37 oz.

	1350	1200	950	700	550	300

V-Magic II

Model has 8" fluted match barrel, with integral compensator. Rubber target grips and Ultra Dot red dot optic. No open sights. Weight about 46 oz.

	1350	1200	950	700	550	300

VOLUNTEER ENTERPRISES
Knoxville, Tennessee
See—Commando Arms

VOUZELAUD
Paris, France

Model 315 E

12-, 16-, or 20-gauge boxlock shotgun, with 20" barrels, double triggers and straight-gripped stock. Blued case hardened. Imported prior to 1988.

| — | 7500 | 6000 | 4000 | 2000 | 900 |

Model 315 EL

As above, with more engraving. Available in 28-gauge or .410 bore, which are worth approximately $1,000 more than values listed.

| — | 10000 | 8000 | 5000 | 2500 | 1100 |

Model 315 EGL

As above, with French case hardened receiver. Discontinued in 1987.

| — | 15000 | 12000 | 8500 | 4000 | 1500 |

Model 315 EGL-S

As above, with engraved hunting scenes. Discontinued in 1987.

| — | 5500 | 4500 | 3500 | 2000 | 1000 |

	NIB	EXC.	V.G.	GOOD	FAIR	POOR

WALCH, JOHN
New York, New York

Navy Revolver

A .36-caliber superimposed load percussion revolver, with 6" octagonal barrel and 6-shot cylinder. Fitted with 12 nipples, two hammers and two triggers. Barrel marked "Walch Firearms Co. NY." and "Patented Feb. 8, 1859." Blued, with walnut grips.

NIB	EXC.	V.G.	GOOD	FAIR	POOR
—	—	13000	9000	4000	950

Pocket Revolver

A spur trigger .31-caliber 10-shot percussion revolver, with either brass or iron frame and walnut grips. Iron frame version is worth approximately 50 percent more than brass variety.

NIB	EXC.	V.G.	GOOD	FAIR	POOR
—	—	5000	2750	1000	300

WALDMAN
Germany

Waldman

A 7.65mm semi-automatic pistol, with 3.5" barrel and 8-shot magazine. Slide marked "1913 Model Automatic Pistol" and some examples are marked "American Automatic Pistol". Blued, with checkered walnut grips inlaid with a brass insert marked "Waldman.

NIB	EXC.	V.G.	GOOD	FAIR	POOR
—	300	225	200	150	100

WALLIS & BIRCH
Philadelphia, Pennsylvania

Pocket Pistol

A .41-caliber single-shot percussion pocket pistol, with 2.5" or 3" barrel, German silver furniture and walnut stock. Barrel is marked "Wallis & Birch Phila.". Produced during 1850s.

NIB	EXC.	V.G.	GOOD	FAIR	POOR
—	—	4050	2250	800	250

WALTHER, CARL
Zella Mehilis and Ulm/Donau, Germany

Model 1

A 6.35mm semi-automatic pistol. Barrel lengths of 2" to 6". Blued, with checkered hard rubber grips. Walther logo on each grip. Introduced in 1908.

NIB	EXC.	V.G.	GOOD	FAIR	POOR
—	1000	700	400	200	200

Model 2

A 6.35mm semi-automatic pistol, with a knurled bushing at the muzzle that retains the mainspring. There are two variations: a fixed rear sight; a pop-up rear sight. Blued, with checkered hard rubber grips. Walther logo on each grip. Introduced in 1909.

Fixed Sights

NIB	EXC.	V.G.	GOOD	FAIR	POOR
—	800	600	300	200	150

Pop Up Sights

NIB	EXC.	V.G.	GOOD	FAIR	POOR
—	1800	1000	600	400	300

Model 3

7.65mm semi-automatic pistol having smooth barrel bushing. Blued, with checkered hard rubber grips. Walther logo on each grip. Introduced in 1910.

NIB	EXC.	V.G.	GOOD	FAIR	POOR
4000	3000	2000	1000	400	200

Model 4

A 7.65mm semi-automatic pistol larger than preceding models. Many variations of this model produced. Blued, with checkered hard rubber grips. Walther logo on each grip. Introduced 1910.

NIB	EXC.	V.G.	GOOD	FAIR	POOR
700	600	500	400	275	150

Model 5

A 6.35mm semi-automatic pistol that is almost identical to Model 2. Fixed sights. Blued, with checkered hard rubber grips. Walther logo on each grip.

NIB	EXC.	V.G.	GOOD	FAIR	POOR
600	500	400	300	200	150

	NIB	EXC.	V.G.	GOOD	FAIR	POOR

Model 6

9mm semi-automatic pistol. Largest of Walther numbered pistols. Approximately 1,500 manufactured. Blued, with checkered hard rubber grips. Walther logo on each grip. Sometimes seen with plain checkered wood grips. Introduced 1915.

	9000	7500	5000	3000	1500	700

Model 7

A 6.35mm semi-automatic pistol in the same style as Model 4. Blued, with checkered hard rubber grips. Walther logo on each side. Introduced in 1917.

	800	700	500	300	200	150

Model 8

A 6.35mm semi-automatic pistol. Finish is either blue, silver or gold. Most were unengraved, but three types of engraving coverage were available from the factory: slide only, slide and frame and complete coverage overall. Grips are checkered hard rubber, with WC logo on one grip and 6.35mm on opposite side. Ivory grips are seen with many of the engraved models. Introduced in 1920 and produced until 1944. **NOTE:** Add $500 for factory case.

Blue, Silver or Gold Finish

	—	750	600	300	200	150

Engraved Slide

	—	1000	700	500	300	200

Engraved Slide and Frame

	—	2500	2000	1100	450	300

Engraved, Complete Coverage

	—	4000	3500	1400	500	300

Model 9

A 6.35mm semi-automatic pistol. Smaller than Model 8. Built as Model 1, with exposed barrel. Same finishes and engraving as Model 8. Introduced 1921 and produced until 1944. All values the same as Model 8.

Sport Model 1926/ Walther Hammerless Target 22/ Walther Standard Sport/ Walther 1932 Olympia/ Sport Model Target/ Special Stoeger Model

All of these .22 LR caliber semi-automatic pistols are the same target pistol. Introduced by Walther in 1926. A well-made pistol, with a barrel length between 6" to 16". Has one-piece checkered wrap-around wood grips. There was also a .22 Short version of Olympia model produced for rapid fire Olympic shooting. There was also a torpedo-shape target weight available for shooters. **NOTE:** Add $200 for target weight; $500 for case.

	—	1000	850	550	350	250

Walther 1936 Olympia

This semi-automatic target pistol in .22-caliber resembled the earlier 1932 Olympia, but with many improvements. There were four standard models produced with many variations of each one. These variations included many barrel lengths. Both round and octagon barrels. There were duraluminum slides, frames and triggers. Various weight configurations to as many as four separate weights to one gun. One-piece wrap-around checkered wood grips in different configurations for the individual shooter. Produced until 1944. **NOTE:** Prices are for Standard Model. Add $100 for Pentathlon or Hunter; $200 for Rapid Fire; $250 for weights. The four models were:

1. Funfklamph Pentathlon
2. Jagerschafts—Hunter
3. Sport or Standard Model
4. Schnellfeur—Rapid Fire

	—	1500	1300	750	475	250

Model MP

A 9mm semi-automatic pistol that was the forerunner of Model AP and P.38 series. Found in variations that resemble a large Model PP or P.38. Blued finish, with one-piece wrap-around checkered wood grips.

	—	35000	30000	25000	20000	15000

Model AP

A 9mm semi-automatic pistol that was the forerunner of Model P.38. A hammerless pistol in various barrel lengths. Sometimes with duraluminum frames and some with stocks. Blued finish,

NIB	EXC.	V.G.	GOOD	FAIR	POOR

with one-piece wraparound checkered wood grips. **NOTE:** Add $4000 with stock.

	28000	25000	20000	15000	10000

Model PP

Semi-automatic pistol in .22-, .25-, .32- and .380-caliber. Introduced in 1928. First successful commercial double-action pistol. Manufactured in finishes of blue, silver and gold, with three different types of engraving. Grips generally two-piece black or white plastic, with Walther banner on each grip. Grips in wood or ivory are seen, but usually on engraved guns. Many variations of Model PP and numerous NSDAP markings seen on pre-1946 models that were produced during Nazi regime. All reflect various prices.

.22 Caliber

1200	800	600	350	250	150

.25 Caliber

8000	6500	5000	3000	1500	700

.32 Caliber, High Polished Finish

1000	850	650	325	225	175

.32 Caliber, Milled Finish

800	700	500	250	200	125

.380 Caliber

2000	1600	1300	800	475	350

.32 Caliber, with Duraluminum Frame

1000	900	700	550	400	200

.32 Caliber, with Bottom Magazine Release

1500	1400	1000	600	400	200

.32 Caliber, with Verchromt Finish

3000	2800	2500	1200	700	400

.32 Caliber, Allemagne Marked

950	850	700	550	325	250

.32 Caliber, A. F. Stoeger Contract

2700	2500	1750	1050	700	400

.32 Caliber, with Waffenampt Proofs, High Polished Finish

1700	1500	1200	600	275	150

.32 Caliber, with Waffenampt Proofs, Milled Finish

900	700	500	325	250	150

.32 Caliber, in Blue Finish and Full Coverage Engraving

NOTE: Add $500 for ivory grips; $700 for leather presentation cases; $1000 for .380-caliber.

	5000	4000	3000	1200	700

.32 Caliber, in Silver Finish and Full Coverage Engraving

NOTE: Add $500 for ivory grips; $700 for leather presentation cases; $1000 for .380-caliber.

	5500	4500	3000	1200	700

.32 Caliber, in Gold Finish and Full Coverage Engraving

NOTE: Add $500 for ivory grips; $700 for leather presentation cases; $1000 for .380-caliber.

	5800	5000	3500	1500	700

.32 Caliber, Police Eagle/C Proofed, High Polished Finish

1600	1200	800	375	250	150

.32 Caliber, Police Eagle/C and Police Eagle/F Proofed, Milled Finish

1000	900	600	375	275	150

.32 Caliber, NSKK Marked on the Slide

NOTE: Add $1,000 with proper NSKK DRGM AKAH holster.

3500	3000	2700	850	550	300

	NIB	EXC.	V.G.	GOOD	FAIR	POOR

.32 Caliber, NSDAP Gruppe Markings
NOTE: Add $1,000 with proper SA DRGM AKAH holster.

NIB	EXC.	V.G.	GOOD	FAIR	POOR
2700	2500	2000	1000	500	300

.32 Caliber, PDM Marked with Bottom Magazine Release

NIB	EXC.	V.G.	GOOD	FAIR	POOR
2400	2000	1500	1100	475	300

.32 Caliber, RJ Marked

NIB	EXC.	V.G.	GOOD	FAIR	POOR
1400	900	700	475	400	150

.32 Caliber, RFV Marked, High Polished or Milled Finish

NIB	EXC.	V.G.	GOOD	FAIR	POOR
1400	900	700	475	400	150

.32 Caliber, RBD Munster Marked

NIB	EXC.	V.G.	GOOD	FAIR	POOR
2500	2200	1750	1200	650	400

.32 Caliber, RpLt Marked

NIB	EXC.	V.G.	GOOD	FAIR	POOR
1650	1500	1200	700	375	200

.32 Caliber, Statens Vattenfallsverk Marked

NIB	EXC.	V.G.	GOOD	FAIR	POOR
1650	1500	1200	700	375	200

.32 Caliber, AC Marked

NIB	EXC.	V.G.	GOOD	FAIR	POOR
800	700	500	300	250	150

.32 Caliber, Duraluminum Frame

NIB	EXC.	V.G.	GOOD	FAIR	POOR
1000	900	700	500	400	150

.380 Caliber, Bottom Magazine Release and Waffenampt Proofs

NIB	EXC.	V.G.	GOOD	FAIR	POOR
2400	2000	1500	700	500	300

Model PPK

Semi-automatic pistol in .22-, .25-, .32- and .380-caliber. Introduced six months after Model PP in 1929. A more compact version of Model PP, with one less round in magazine. One-piece wraparound checkered plastic grips in brown, black and white. Walther banner on each side of grips. Model PPK will be found with same types of finishes as Model PP, as well as the same styles of engraving. Grips in wood or ivory are seen with some of the engraved models. As with the Model PP, there are many variations of Model PPK and numerous NSDAP markings seen on the pre-1946 models that were produced during the Nazi regime. All reflect various prices.

.22 Caliber

NIB	EXC.	V.G.	GOOD	FAIR	POOR
1900	1700	1500	750	325	175

.25 Caliber

NIB	EXC.	V.G.	GOOD	FAIR	POOR
8500	6000	4000	1850	1000	500

.32 Caliber, High Polished Finish

NIB	EXC.	V.G.	GOOD	FAIR	POOR
1400	950	750	450	250	150

.32 Caliber, Milled Finish

NIB	EXC.	V.G.	GOOD	FAIR	POOR
1300	900	700	400	250	150

.380 Caliber

NIB	EXC.	V.G.	GOOD	FAIR	POOR
4250	3000	2500	1600	750	375

.32 Caliber, with Duraluminum Frame

NIB	EXC.	V.G.	GOOD	FAIR	POOR
2000	1500	1300	600	400	200

.32 Caliber, Marked Mod. PP on Slide

NIB	EXC.	V.G.	GOOD	FAIR	POOR
6000	5000	4000	2500	1500	1000

.32 Caliber, with Panagraphed Slide

NIB	EXC.	V.G.	GOOD	FAIR	POOR
2000	1200	750	450	300	200

.32 Caliber, with Verchromt Finish

NIB	EXC.	V.G.	GOOD	FAIR	POOR
3800	2800	2500	1200	700	350

.32 Caliber, in Blue Finish and Full Coverage Engraving
NOTE: Add $1,000 for ivory grips; $1,000 for leather presentation cases; $1,000 for .380-caliber.

NIB	EXC.	V.G.	GOOD	FAIR	POOR
—	5000	3500	2500	1200	700

	NIB	EXC.	V.G.	GOOD	FAIR	POOR

.32 Caliber, in Silver Finish and Full Coverage Engraving
NOTE: Add $1,000 for ivory grips; $1,000 for leather presentation cases; $1,000 for .380-caliber.

	—	6000	4000	3000	1500	700

.32 Caliber, in Gold Finish and Full Coverage Engraving
NOTE: Add $1,000 for ivory grips; $1,000 for leather presentation cases; $1,000 for .380-caliber.

	—	6500	5500	3500	1500	700

.32 Caliber, Czechoslovakian Contract

	2000	1850	1500	1000	550	300

.32 Caliber, Allemagne Marked

	1150	1000	800	600	400	250

.32 Caliber, with Waffenampt Proofs and a High Polished Finish

	2400	1900	1600	900	400	250

.32 Caliber, with Waffenampt Proofs and a Milled Finish

	1700	1500	1300	750	300	175

.32 Caliber, Police Eagle/C Proofed, High Polished Finish

	1500	1200	1000	500	300	175

.32 Caliber, Police Eagle/C Proofed. Milled Finish

	1100	900	700	375	275	175

.32 Caliber, Police Eagle/F Proofed, Duraluminum Frame, Milled Finish

	1600	1300	1000	550	350	225

.22 Caliber, Late War, Black Grips

	2400	1800	1500	600	450	300

.32 Caliber, Party Leader Grips, Brown

	8000	6000	5500	3000	2250	2000

.32 Caliber, Party Leader Grips, Black
NOTE: Add $1,500 with proper Party Leader DRGM AKAH holster.

	8000	6000	5500	3200	2550	2500

.32 Caliber, RZM Marked

	3000	2400	1700	800	400	300

.32 Caliber, PDM Marked with Duraluminum Frame and Bottom Magazine Release

	3500	3200	2800	1300	750	450

.32 Caliber, RFV Marked

	3000	2500	2000	1150	650	400

.32 Caliber, DRP Marked

	2800	2400	1800	1200	450	275

.32 Caliber, Statens Vattenfallsverk

	1700	1500	1200	700	450	300

WALTHER POST-WORLD WAR II

Manufactured by the firm of Manufacture de Machines du Haut Rhin at Mulhouse, France under license by Walther.

Model PP—Some with Duraluminum Frames

.22 Caliber

	850	750	600	400	275	175

.32 Caliber

	600	500	375	350	275	175

.380 Caliber

	850	750	600	400	275	175

	NIB	EXC.	V.G.	GOOD	FAIR	POOR

Model PP—All Three Calibers Finished In Blue, Silver and Gold with Full Coverage Engraving

Model P— All Three Calibers Finished In Blue, Silver and Gold with Full Coverage Engraving

Blue

	NIB	EXC.	V.G.	GOOD	FAIR	POOR
	—	1900	1500	900	600	300

Model PP—All Three Calibers Finished In Blue, Silver and Gold with Full Coverage Engraving

Silver

	NIB	EXC.	V.G.	GOOD	FAIR	POOR
	—	1900	1500	900	600	300

Gold

	NIB	EXC.	V.G.	GOOD	FAIR	POOR
	—	1900	1500	900	600	300

Model PP Mark II

These Walthers were manufactured under license by Walther and produced by the Manurhin Company. They were sold exclusively by Interarms, Alexandria, Virginia. Mark IIs were the same pistols as those above and have the same types of finish and engraving as well as the same value.

Model PP Manurhin

Manurhin Company manufactured with Manurhin logo and inscription. Usually "licensed by Walther" somewhere on the pistol. Same pistols as those above. Bearing the same types of finish and engraving and having the same values.

Model PP Sport, Manurhin

.22-caliber. Same gun as Model PP, with different barrel lengths running from 5.75" to 7.75". It is basically a target .22, with adjustable rear sights for elevation and windage. Front sight is also adjustable. There is a barrel bushing at the muzzle that attaches the front sight to the barrel. Grips are contoured checkered plastic and are either squared at the bottom of the grips or are in the shape of an inverted bird's-head.

	NIB	EXC.	V.G.	GOOD	FAIR	POOR
	—	900	600	450	375	275

Model PP Sport C, Manurhin

.22-caliber. Same gun as Model PP Sport, but in single-action with a spur hammer. Has front and rear adjustable sights and squared target grips in checkered black, brown and plastic. Blued and silver finish.

	NIB	EXC.	V.G.	GOOD	FAIR	POOR
	—	900	600	450	375	275

Model PP Sport, Walther

A .22-caliber Sport was manufactured by Manurhin, but sold by Walther with Walther logo and inscription. Same gun as Model PP Sport, Manurhin. Only sold for a period of two years.

	NIB	EXC.	V.G.	GOOD	FAIR	POOR
	—	900	600	450	375	275

Model PP 50th Anniversary Commemorative Model

In .22- or .380-caliber. Blued, with gold inlays and hand-carved grips with oak leaves and acorns. Walther banner carved into each side of grips. Wood presentation case.

	NIB	EXC.	V.G.	GOOD	FAIR	POOR
	1500	1000	750	500	300	

Model PPK—Some with Duraluminum Frames

.22 Caliber

	NIB	EXC.	V.G.	GOOD	FAIR	POOR
	—	750	600	400	275	175

.32 Caliber

	NIB	EXC.	V.G.	GOOD	FAIR	POOR
	—	550	400	350	275	175

.380 Caliber

	NIB	EXC.	V.G.	GOOD	FAIR	POOR
	—	750	600	400	275	175

Model PPK—All Three Calibers Finished In Blue, Silver and Gold With Full Coverage Engraving

Blue

	NIB	EXC.	V.G.	GOOD	FAIR	POOR
	—	1900	1500	750	450	300

Silver

	NIB	EXC.	V.G.	GOOD	FAIR	POOR
	—	1900	1500	750	450	300

	NIB	EXC.	V.G.	GOOD	FAIR	POOR

Gold

	NIB	EXC.	V.G.	GOOD	FAIR	POOR
	—	1900	1500	750	450	300

Model PPK Mark II

These Walthers were manufactured under license by Walther and produced by the Manurhin Company. They were sold exclusively by Interarms, Alexandria, Virginia. Mark IIs were the same pistols as those above and have the same types of finish and engraving as well as the same value.

Model PPK Manurhin

Manurhin Company manufactured with Manurhin logo and inscription. Usually "Licensed by Walther" somewhere on the pistol. Same pistols as above. Bearing the same types of finish and engraving and having the same value.

Model PPK 50th Anniversary Commemorative Model

In .22- or .380-caliber. Blued, with gold inlays and hand-carved grips with oak leaves and acorns. Walther banner carved into each side of grips. Wood presentation case.

	NIB	EXC.	V.G.	GOOD	FAIR	POOR
	—	2100	1800	1250	1000	500

Model PPK American

In 1986, Model PPK was licensed by the Walther Company to be manufactured in the United States. Finish is stainless steel. Caliber is .380.

	NIB	EXC.	V.G.	GOOD	FAIR	POOR
	—	500	375	300	200	150

Model PPK/S

This Walther originally manufactured in Germany in .22-, .32- and .380-caliber. For sale in U.S. market after introduction of United States Gun Control Act of 1968. Basically a Model PP, with cut-off muzzle and slide. Has two-piece black checkered plastic grips as seen on Model PP. Finished in blue, nickel, dull gold and verchromt. Prices shown for .380 model. For .32 deduct 15 percent; .22 add 15 percent.

	NIB	EXC.	V.G.	GOOD	FAIR	POOR
	600	525	450	400	350	250

Model PPK/S American

Manufactured in United States. Same as German Model PPK/S. Caliber .380. Pistol finished in blue or stainless steel.

	NIB	EXC.	V.G.	GOOD	FAIR	POOR
	—	500	375	300	200	150

Model TP

A Walther-manufactured semi-automatic pistol in .22- and .25-calibers. Patterned after the earlier Model 9. Finish is blue. Silver black plastic checkered grips, with Walther banner medallions in each grip.

	NIB	EXC.	V.G.	GOOD	FAIR	POOR
	—	900	700	500	375	250

Model TPH

A Walther-manufactured semi-automatic pistol in .22- and .25-calibers. A double-action pistol, with duraluminum frame. Finished in blue or silver. Two-piece black checkered plastic grips. Full coverage engraving available. **NOTE:** Add $300 for engraved model.

	NIB	EXC.	V.G.	GOOD	FAIR	POOR
	—	650	500	450	350	250

Model TPH American

This semi-automatic produced in both .22- and .25-calibers. Licensed by Walther and manufactured in the United States. Produced in stainless steel. Has two-piece black plastic checkered grips. It is a double-action pistol.

	NIB	EXC.	V.G.	GOOD	FAIR	POOR
	—	400	300	200	150	100

Model PP Super

A .380 and 9x18 caliber double-action semi-automatic manufactured by Walther. Similar in design to Model PP, with P.38 type of mechanism. Finish is blue. Grips are wraparound black checkered plastic or a type of molded wood colored plastic.

	NIB	EXC.	V.G.	GOOD	FAIR	POOR
	—	750	450	350	250	150

Model P.38

Following WWII, P.38 was reintroduced in a variety of calibers, with 5" barrel and alloy or steel frame.

.22 Caliber

	NIB	EXC.	V.G.	GOOD	FAIR	POOR
	1200	850	650	500	350	200

Other Calibers

	NIB	EXC.	V.G.	GOOD	FAIR	POOR
	750	600	500	400	300	200

	NIB	EXC.	V.G.	GOOD	FAIR	POOR

Steel-Framed (Introduced 1987)

Factory-engraved versions of P.38 pistol were blued, chrome, silver or gold-plated. We suggest that a qualified appraisal be secured when contemplating purchase.

	NIB	EXC.	V.G.	GOOD	FAIR	POOR
	1400	1250	1000	750	500	400

Model P.38K

As above, with 2.8" barrel. Front sight is mounted on the slide. Imported between 1974 and 1980.

	NIB	EXC.	V.G.	GOOD	FAIR	POOR
	—	900	650	450	300	200

Model P.38 II

	NIB	EXC.	V.G.	GOOD	FAIR	POOR
	—	800	550	350	250	200

Model P.38 IV

Redesigned version of above, with 4.5" barrel and 8-shot magazine. Fitted with a decocking lever and adjustable sights. Imported prior to 1983.

	NIB	EXC.	V.G.	GOOD	FAIR	POOR
	—	900	650	450	300	200

CURRENTLY IMPORTED WALTHER HANDGUNS— WALTHER USA

In 1999, Carl Walther Gmbh of Germany and Smith & Wesson entered into a joint agreement to import and distribute Walther-branded firearms and accessories into U.S. beginning August 1, 1999. In 2012, Walther established Walther Arms, Inc. in Fort Smith, Arkansas to import and sell all Walther products in USA beginning in 2013.

Model PP Limited Edition

Introduced in 2000. A limited edition of 100 pistols chambered in .380 ACP and 50 pistols chambered in .32 ACP. Finish is a high-polish blue. Slide marked "LAST EDITION 1929-1999." Supplied with a special case with certificate and video of the history of Walther.

	NIB	EXC.	V.G.	GOOD	FAIR	POOR
	1350	1100	900	700	500	300

Model PPK/E—Walther USA

Introduced in 2000. Pistol chambered for .380 or .32 ACP cartridges. Later in that year .22 LR. Has a double-action trigger. Produced in Hungary by Walther. Barrel length 3.4". Magazine capacity is seven rounds for .380 and eight rounds for .32 ACP and .22 LR. Blued finish and plastic grips.

	NIB	EXC.	V.G.	GOOD	FAIR	POOR
	400	325	250	195	125	75

Model PPK

Chambered for .380 ACP or .32 ACP cartridge. Fitted with 3.35" barrel. Offered in blue or stainless steel. Black plastic grips. Fixed red-dot sights. Magazine capacity: 6 rounds for .380 ACP; 7 rounds for .32 ACP. Weight about 21 oz.

	NIB	EXC.	V.G.	GOOD	FAIR	POOR
	550	425	300	250	175	75

Model PPK/S

Same as PPK, with .25" longer grip. Magazine capacity: 7 rounds .380 ACP; 8 rounds .32 ACP. Weight about 23 oz. Offered in blue, stainless steel and two-tone finish. **NOTE:** In 2013, .22 LR version reintroduced with magazine capacity of 10 rounds. Deduct 15 percent for this chambering.

	NIB	EXC.	V.G.	GOOD	FAIR	POOR
	550	425	300	250	175	75

Model PPS

Striker-fired compact DAO semi-auto pistol. Chambered in .40 S&W (6 rounds) or 9mm Parabellum (7 rounds). Features include polymer frame and grip, decocker button, loaded chamber indicator, 3.2" stainless steel barrel, integral Weaver-style accessory rail, black Tenifer finish overall.

	NIB	EXC.	V.G.	GOOD	FAIR	POOR
	625	535	450	350	250	150

Seventy-fifth Anniversary PPK

Blued, with wood grips. Machine engraving. Available in .380 ACP with 6+1 capacity. Special SN beginning with 0000PPK. Shipped with glass-top display case. Single-/double-action 3.3" barrel. Weight 20.8 oz. Windage-adjustable rear sight. Introduced 2006.

	NIB	EXC.	V.G.	GOOD	FAIR	POOR
	800	700	600	400	—	—

Model P5

A 9mm semi-automatic pistol, with double-action firing mechanism. One of the first Walthers to have a decocker lever. Finish is a combination of black matte and high polish. Has black plastic checkered grips.

	NIB	EXC.	V.G.	GOOD	FAIR	POOR
	1350	1000	750	500	300	200

	NIB	EXC.	V.G.	GOOD	FAIR	POOR

Model P5, Compact

A shorter version of standard Model P5.

	1450	1100	850	600	375	250

Model P5 One Hundred Year Commemorative

Blued, with gold inlays and hand-carved grips with oak leaves and acorns. Walther banner carved into each side of grips.

	2750	1950	1600	1000	750	400

Model P88

A 9mm semi-automatic in double-action, with ambidextrous decocking lever. Fifteen-shot magazine and two-piece black checkered plastic grips. Combination of high polish and black matte finish.

	1700	1525	1275	975	700	400

Model P88 Compact

A shorter version of standard Model P88.

	1600	1425	1135	850	600	400

Model P99

Introduced in 1997. A single-/double-action design, with 4" barrel and polymer frame. Chambered for 9mm or .40 S&W cartridge. Magazine capacity of 10 rounds (16 rounds in 9mm; 12 rounds in .40 S&W for law enforcement). Front sight is interchangeable. Rear sight is windage adjustable. Total length 7". Weight about 25 oz. Finish is blue tenifer.

	800	700	550	450	300	200

Model P99 Compact AS/QA

Model chambered for 9mm cartridge, with double-action trigger and 9mm or .40 S&W cartridges. Quick action striker fired. Barrel length 3.5", with fixed sights. Magazine capacity: 10 rounds for 9mm; 8 rounds for .40 S&W. Weight about 19 oz.

	675	575	400	325	200	175

Model P990

Double-action-only version of P99.

	675	550	400	325	200	175

Model P99 QPQ

Similar to P99, with silver tenifer finish.

	750	625	475	375	275	250

Model P990 QPQ

Double-action-only version of P99 QPQ.

	750	625	475	375	275	250

Model P99 QA

Similar to P99, with constant short trigger pull. Trigger pull approximately 6.5 lbs. Offered in both 9mm and .40 S&W calibers. Introduced in 2000.

	675	575	400	325	200	175

Model P99 Military

Similar to P99, with military finish.

	675	575	400	325	200	175

Model P99 La Chasse DU

Model features laser engraving on blue tenifer slide.

	750	625	475	375	275	250

Model P99 La Chasse

Model features hand engraving on gray tenifer slide.

	1675	1350	1100	750	500	300

Model P99 Commemorative

Limited edition P99 that features a high polish blue slide, with a special serial number and marking" COMMEMORATIVE FOR THE YEAR 2000". Offered in both 9mm and .40 S&W calibers. Each handgun comes with a special certificate and video of the history of Walther.

	750	625	475	375	275	250

	NIB	EXC.	V.G.	GOOD	FAIR	POOR

Walther PPQ

Caliber: 9mm Parabellum or .40 S&W. Steel slide polymer frame, with interchangeable backstraps. Magazine capacity: 15/12 (9mm); 17/14 (.40). Other features include front slide serrations, Quick Defense Trigger with integral safety, ambidextrous slide and magazine release, adjustable rear sight and loaded-chamber indicator. Weight 24.5 oz., barrel length 4". Finish matte black.

NIB	EXC.	V.G.	GOOD	FAIR	POOR
625	525	450	380	325	200

Model PPX

Polymer frame hammer-fired DA-only pistol, in 9mm or .40 S&W. Features include loaded-chamber viewpoint, ambidextrous slide stop, reversible mag release, two drop safeties and firing pin block. Black or stainless finish. New 2013. **NOTE:** Add $50 for stainless.

NIB	EXC.	V.G.	GOOD	FAIR	POOR
400	350	300	275	250	200

Model P22 Standard

Introduced in 2002. This .22-caliber pistol chambered for LR cartridge. Barrel length 3.4". Polymer frame, with double-action trigger. Adjustable rear sight. Magazine capacity 10 rounds. Weight about 20 oz. **NOTE:** In 2003, model offered with military black slide and green frame or silver slide with black frame. Carbon fiber-framed model also available at about same price as standard models. Barrels are interchangeable on both P22 pistols.

NIB	EXC.	V.G.	GOOD	FAIR	POOR
400	325	250	200	150	75

Model P22 Target

Similar to standard P22 model, with 5" barrel with barrel weight. Weight about 21 oz.

NIB	EXC.	V.G.	GOOD	FAIR	POOR
425	350	275	225	175	75

Model FP

A .22 LR caliber single-shot target pistol that fires electrically. Has micro-adjustable electric firing system, with micrometer sights. Contoured wooden grips that are adjustable. Barrel is 11.7". Finish is blued.

NIB	EXC.	V.G.	GOOD	FAIR	POOR
—	2000	1600	1000	500	400

Model GSP

Semi-automatic target pistol in .22 LR and .32-calibers. Pistol has 4.5" barrel, 5-shot magazine and contoured wood target grips. Blued finish. Sold with attache extra barrel case and accessories.

NIB	EXC.	V.G.	GOOD	FAIR	POOR
—	1600	1200	750	650	300

Model GSP-C

Almost same pistol as Model GSP, but in .32-caliber S&W wadcutter.

NIB	EXC.	V.G.	GOOD	FAIR	POOR
—	1500	1100	750	650	300

Model OSP

A .22 Short semi-automatic target pistol. Similar to Model GSP. Pistol is made for rapid fire target shooting. Blued finish, with contoured wood grips.

NIB	EXC.	V.G.	GOOD	FAIR	POOR
—	1800	1200	750	650	300

Free Pistol

.22-caliber single-shot target pistol, with 11.7" barrel, micrometer sights, adjustable grips and electronic trigger. Blued.

NIB	EXC.	V.G.	GOOD	FAIR	POOR
1900	1600	1200	900	700	550

Model R99

This 6-shot revolver chambered for .357 Magnum cartridge. Barrel length 3". Weight about 28 oz. Offered in blue or stainless steel. Introduced in 1999. Said to be a close ringer for S&W M19, but with different grips.

NIB	EXC.	V.G.	GOOD	FAIR	POOR
1500	1300	1100	950	700	500

Model SP22-M1

.22 LR autoloader, with aluminum frame and 4" barrel.

NIB	EXC.	V.G.	GOOD	FAIR	POOR
400	325	350	150	100	75

Model SP22-M2

Similar to above, with 6" barrel.

NIB	EXC.	V.G.	GOOD	FAIR	POOR
400	325	250	150	100	75

	NIB	EXC.	V.G.	GOOD	FAIR	POOR

Model SP22-M3

Similar to above, with match-grade barrel and adjustable trigger.

	475	400	325	200	150	100

Model SP22-M4

Similar to above, with wooden free-style grip assembly.

	750	675	550	400	250	150

RIFLES

Model B

A .30-06 caliber bolt-action rifle, with 22" barrel, 4-shot magazine and single-/double-set triggers. Double-set triggers are worth approximately 20 percent more than values listed. Blued, with walnut stock.

	—	775	700	450	250	175

Olympic Single-Shot

A .22-caliber bolt-action rifle, with 26" barrel, adjustable target sights and walnut stock. Fitted with palm rest and adjustable buttplate. Blued.

	—	1150	950	800	500	400

Model V

A .22-caliber single-shot bolt-action rifle, with 26" barrel and adjustable sights. Blued, with plain walnut stock. Manufactured before WWII.

	—	550	450	300	200	150

Model V Champion

As above, with checkered walnut stock.

	—	600	500	350	250	200

Model KKM International Match

A .22-caliber single-shot bolt-action rifle, with 28" barrel and adjustable sights. Blued, with walnut stock. Fitted for palm rest and adjustable buttplate. Manufactured after WWII.

	—	1550	1275	850	450	350

Model KKM-S

As above, with adjustable cheekpiece.

	—	1625	1350	850	500	400

Model KKW

As above, with military-style stock.

	—	1250	975	600	250	175

Model KKJ Sporter

A .22-caliber bolt action rifle, with 22.5" barrel and 5-shot magazine. Blued, with checkered walnut stock. Model was available with double-set triggers and their presence would add approximately 20 percent to values listed. Manufactured after WWII.

	—	900	800	550	350	300

Model KKJ-MA

As above, in .22 Magnum rimfire.

	—	850	750	550	350	300

Model KKJ-HO

As above, in .22 Hornet.

	—	950	850	650	450	350

Model SSV Varmint

A .22-caliber bolt-action single-shot rifle, with 25.5" barrel not fitted with sights. Monte Carlo-style stock. Blued. Manufactured after WWII.

	—	700	600	475	375	300

Model UIT BV Universal

As above, with adjustable target sights. Walnut stock fitted with a palm rest and adjustable buttplate.

	1750	1500	1250	900	650	500

	NIB	EXC.	V.G.	GOOD	FAIR	POOR

Model UIT Match

As above, with stippled pistol-grip and fore-end. Also available with an electronic trigger that would add approximately $50 to values listed.

	1350	1100	800	600	450	400

GX 1

As above, with adjustable Free Rifle stock.

	2250	2000	1750	1250	850	700

Prone Model 400

Target rifle in .22-caliber, with prone position stock.

	800	700	600	450	350	300

Model KK/MS Silhouette

A .22-caliber bolt-action rifle, with 25.5" front-weighted barrel furnished without sights. Thumbhole stock, with adjustable buttplate. Introduced in 1984.

	1300	1100	850	700	550	400

Running Boar Model 500

As above, with 23.5" barrel.

	1550	1350	950	750	600	450

Model WA-2000

A .300 Winchester Magnum or .308-caliber bolt-action sporting rifle. Produced on custom order. Imported prior to 1989.

	30000	25000	20000	—	—	—

Model G22

A .22-caliber rifle, with 20" barrel and adjustable sights. Features a cocking indicator, integrated lock, slide safety and multi function rail. Black or green finish. Weight about 6 lbs. This model also sold as a package.

	450	350	225	175	125	100

Package A1 with Walther rifle scope

	500	400	275	225	175	150

Package A2 with laser

	500	400	275	225	175	150

Package A3 with Walther rifle scope & laser

	500	400	275	225	175	150

Package A4 with Walther PS22 red-dot sight

	500	400	275	225	175	150

SHOTGUNS

Model SF

A 12- or 16-gauge boxlock double-barrel shotgun. Fitted with double triggers and extractors. Blued, with checkered walnut stock fitted with sling swivels.

	—	1150	900	750	600	450

Model SFD

As above, with stock having a cheekpiece.

	—	1150	900	750	600	450

WALTHER MANURHIN
Mulhouse, France

Manurhin-manufactured Walther pistols are listed in Walther section under their respective model headings.

WARNANT, L. AND J.
Ognee, Belgium

Revolver

Modeled after pistols manufactured by Smith & Wesson. Warnants produced a variety of revolvers in .32-, .38- or .45-caliber, between 1870 and 1890.

	—	—	250	175	100	50

	NIB	EXC.	V.G.	GOOD	FAIR	POOR

Semi-Automatic Pistol

A 6.35mm semi-automatic pistol, with 2.5" barrel and 5-shot magazine. Slide marked "L&J Warnant Bte 6.35mm". Blued, with black plastic grips bearing monogram "L&JW". Manufactured after 1908.

	—	350	200	150	100	75

1912 Model

A 7.65mm caliber semi-automatic pistol, with 3" barrel and 7-shot magazine. Slide marked "L&J Warnant Brevetes Pist Auto 7.65mm". Manufactured prior to 1915.

	—	350	200	150	100	75

WARNER, CHAS.
Windsor Locks, Connecticut

Pocket Revolver

A .31-caliber percussion revolver, with 3" round barrel and 6-shot unfluted cylinder. Cylinder marked "Charles Warner. Windsor Locks, Conn.". Blued, with walnut grips. Approximately 600 made between 1857 and 1860.

	—	—	1625	1300	500	100

WARNER, JAMES
Springfield, Massachusetts

Revolving Carbines

A variety of revolving carbines were made by this maker. Nearly all of which are .40-caliber, with octagonal barrels measuring 20" to 24" in length. Most commonly encountered variations are listed.

Manually Revolved Grooved Cylinder

Model fitted with two triggers, one of which is a release so that the cylinder can be manually turned. Not fitted with a loading lever. Top strap marked "James Warner/Springfield, Mass.". Approximately 75 made in 1849.

	—	—	7500	4700	2200	500

Retractable Cylinder Model

This version has a cylinder that fits over the breech and it must be retracted before it can be manually rotated. Cylinder release is a button located in front of the trigger. It is marked "James Warner/Springfield Mass" and with an eagle over the letters "U.S.". Cylinder is etched and there is no loading lever. Has a walnut stock, with patch box and no forearm. Approximately 25 were manufactured in 1849.

	—	—	9500	6900	3000	800

Automatic Revolving Cylinder

Cylinder is automatically turned when hammer is cocked. Fitted with loading lever. Marked "Warner's Patent/Jan. 1851" and "Springfield Arms Co.". Approximately 200 made during 1850s.

	—	—	7500	4700	1900	500

Belt Revolver

A .31-caliber double-action percussion revolver, with 4" or 5" round barrel and 6-shot etched cylinder. Blued, with walnut grips. No markings appear on this model except for the serial number. Manufactured in 1851.

	—	—	2100	1650	675	100

Pocket Revolver

A .28-caliber percussion revolver, with 3" octagonal barrel and 6-shot cylinder. Barrel marked "James Warner, Springfield, Mass., USA". Blued, with walnut grips. Approximately 500 were made.

	—	—	1050	725	275	100

Second Model

As above, with either 3" or 4" barrel marked "Warner's Patent 1857".

	—	—	1100	750	325	100

Third Model

As above, in .31-caliber.

	—	—	1000	650	300	100

	NIB	EXC.	V.G.	GOOD	FAIR	POOR

Single-Shot Derringer

A .41-caliber rimfire single-shot pocket pistol, with 2.75" round barrel, brass frame and walnut grips. As this model is unmarked, it can only be identified by the large breechblock which lifts upward and to the left for loading.

—	—	22500	19000	7250	1000

Pocket Revolver

A .30-caliber rimfire revolver, with 3" barrel and 5-shot cylinder. Barrel marked "Warner's Patent 1857". Blued or nickel-plated, with walnut grips. Approximately 1,000 made during late 1860s.

—	—	975	600	165	75

WARNER ARMS CORPORATION
Brooklyn, New York and Norwich, Connecticut

Established in 1912, this firm marketed revolvers, rifles, semi-automatic pistols and shotguns made for them by other companies (including N.R. Davis & Sons, Ithaca Gun Company and so forth). In 1917, the company was purchased by N.R. Davis & Company. See also Davis-Warner. The arms marketed by Warner prior to 1917 are listed.

SHOTGUNS

Single Trigger Hammerless Utica Special Double-Barrel

In 12-gauge, with 28", 30" or 32" barrels.

Double Trigger Hammerless Double-Barrel

In 12- or 16-gauge, with 28", 30" or 32" barrels.

Grade X, SF, XT, SFT, XD and XDF Hammer Guns

In 12-, 16- or 20-gauge, with 28", 30" or 32" barrels.

Field Grade Hammer Gun

In 12- or 16-gauge, with 28" or 30" barrels.

Boxlock Hammerless

In 12- or 16-gauge, with 28", 30" or 32" barrels.

RIFLES

Number 522

A .22-caliber single-shot rifle, with 18" barrel.

Number 532

A .32-caliber single-shot rifle, with 18" barrel.

REVOLVERS

Double-Action

.32- and .38-caliber, with 4" or 5" barrels.

Double-Action Hammerless

.32- and .38-caliber, with 4" or 5" barrels.

SEMI-AUTOMATIC PISTOLS

"Faultless" : Warner-Schwarzlose Model C, .32 ACP

—	—	500	300	200	100

WEATHERBY
Paso Robles, California

Company was founded by Roy Weatherby in 1945 in South Gate, California. His original rifles were custom guns made to order on Mauser actions. In 1956, he contracted with both Sako and Schultz & Larsen to manufacture complete rifles, while he continued to make custom guns in California. In 1958, Weatherby introduced his Mark V action, which was designed to handle high pressures of his proprietary cartridges. Mark V action was made in U.S. with rifles assembled and finished in Weatherby shop in South Gate. Mark V featured a very modern stock design with glossy finish, high comb for scope use and contrasting grip and fore-end caps. Beginning in 1959, rifles were made in what was then West Germany. In 1972, production was moved to Japan, where rifles were made until 1995. Since that year, Weatherby rifles have all been made in U.S. Barreled action for Mark V is made by ATEK in Brainerd, Minnesota and action for Vanguard is made by Howa in Japan. Both Mark V and Vanguard are assembled in Paso Robles, California, Weatherby shop. For many years, Weatherby shotguns were made in Japan or Italy. Current models are made in Turkey.

Mark V

A deluxe bolt-action repeating rifle. Chambered for various popular standard calibers, as well as the full line of Weatherby cartridges from .240 Weatherby Magnum to .300 Weatherby Magnum. Furnished with either 24" or 26" barrel, without sights. Has either 3- or 5-round magazine, depending on caliber. Has a deluxe high-polish blued finish, with select skip-line checkered walnut stock with rosewood forearm tip and pistol-grip cap. Rifle available with a left-hand action.

| 1200 | 1050 | 800 | 600 | 500 | 250 |

Mark V Deluxe

Stepped-up version of classic Mark V. Features include deluxe Claro walnut Monte Carlo stock, with rosewood for-end, 26" or 28" high-polish blued sightless barrel. Chambered in .257, .270, 7mm, .300, .30-378, .340, .378, .416 and .460 Weatherby Magnum. Also available in short-action model in .22-250, .243 Win., .240 Weatherby, .25-06, .270 Win., 7mm-08, .280 Rem., .308 Win., .30-06. **NOTE:** Add 25 percent for .30-378 Weatherby Magnum.

| 2400 | 2000 | 1300 | 1075 | 800 | 350 |

Mark V Sporter

Introduced in 1993. Model identical to Mark V Deluxe, without custom features. Metal is a low luster finish. Stock is Claro walnut, with high gloss finish. Monte Carlo comb, with raised cheekpiece and black 1" recoil pad are standard features on this model. Available in Weatherby calibers from .257 through .340 plus .270 Win., .30-06, 7mm Rem. Magnum, .300 Win. Magnum, .338 Win. Magnum. Weighs 8 to 8.5 lbs. depending on caliber.

| 1100 | 950 | 800 | 650 | 500 | 300 |

Mark V .375 Weatherby Magnum

This version was manufactured in Germany only. Chambered for currently obsolete .375 Weatherby Magnum cartridge. This version has become very collectible.

| 5000 | 3500 | 3000 | 2500 | 2000 | 1500 |

Mark V .378 Weatherby Magnum

This version chambered for .378 Weatherby Magnum cartridge. Furnished with 26" barrel only. **NOTE:** Add 50 percent for German guns in this caliber.

| 2300 | 1825 | 1550 | 1200 | 850 | 500 |

Mark V .416 Weatherby Magnum

This is an extremely powerful rifle suitable for hunting the biggest game. Introduced in 1989.

| 2400 | 1825 | 1550 | 1200 | 850 | 500 |

Mark V .460 Weatherby Magnum

This is said to be the most powerful commercial rifle available in the world, with the possible exception of some of the recently-reintroduced British nitro chamberings. Available with 24" or 26" heavy barrel, with an integral recoil-reducing muzzle-brake. Has a custom reinforced stock. **NOTE:** Add 100 percent for German guns in this caliber.

| 2500 | 2200 | 1850 | 1500 | 1000 | 600 |

Mark V Dangerous Game Rifle

Model introduced in 2001. Features synthetic stock, with Monte Carlo and 24" or 26" barrel, with barrel band and hooded front sight depending on caliber. Chambered for .378-, .416- and .460-Weatherby Magnum. Adjustable trigger. Weight between 8.74 and 9.5 lbs. depending on caliber. In 2003, .458 Lott was offered for this model.

| 2500 | 2200 | 1850 | 1500 | 1000 | 600 |

Mark V Euromark

Model features hand-checkered oil-finished Claro walnut stock, with ebony fore-end tip and pistol-grip cap. Has satin blued finish. Introduced in 1986.

| 1500 | 1300 | 1050 | 800 | 575 | 350 |

Mark V Fluted Stainless

Introduced late in 1996. Features a fluted stainless steel barrel. Chambered for .257 Weatherby Magnum to .300 Weatherby Magnum calibers as well as 7mm Rem. Magnum and .300 Win.

	NIB	EXC.	V.G.	GOOD	FAIR	POOR

Magnum. Stock is synthetic, with raised comb and checkered stock. Weight varies depending on caliber.

	NIB	EXC.	V.G.	GOOD	FAIR	POOR
	1200	1050	800	600	500	250

Mark V Fluted Synthetic

Similar to above model, with blued carbon steel action and barrel with synthetic stock. Introduced late in 1996.

	NIB	EXC.	V.G.	GOOD	FAIR	POOR
	1000	850	650	450	400	200

Mark V SLS

Model features stainless steel barreled action, with laminated wood stock fitted with a 1" black recoil pad. Rifle chambered for .257 through .340 Weatherby Magnum calibers as well as 7mm Rem. Magnum, .300 and .338 Win. Magnum and .375 H&H Magnum. Weight about 8.25 lbs. depending on caliber. Introduced in late 1996.

	NIB	EXC.	V.G.	GOOD	FAIR	POOR
	1200	1050	800	600	500	250

Mark V Varmint

This version chambered for .22-250 and .224 Weatherby cartridge. Offered with 24" or 26" heavy barrel. **NOTE:** Add 50 percent for German built.

	NIB	EXC.	V.G.	GOOD	FAIR	POOR
	975	800	750	550	450	400

Mark V Lazermark

This version had a laser-carved pattern on the stock and forearm in place of usual checkering. Introduced in 1985.

	NIB	EXC.	V.G.	GOOD	FAIR	POOR
	2000	1750	1500	1100	600	300

Mark V Fibermark Composite

This version has a matte blue finish. Furnished with a synthetic black wrinkle-finished stock. Chambered for calibers from .22-250 to .375 H&H. Barrel lengths from 24" to 26" depending on caliber.

	NIB	EXC.	V.G.	GOOD	FAIR	POOR
	1250	1000	800	550	400	250

Mark V Ultramark

Custom-finished version, with a glass-bedded action and special high-polish blue. Action is hand-honed. Walnut stock features basket weave checkering. Introduced in 1989.

	NIB	EXC.	V.G.	GOOD	FAIR	POOR
	2400	2000	1650	1200	800	500

Mark V Accumark

Introduced in 1995. Rifle features Mark V Magnum action. Trigger is preset at factory for 3.5 lbs. of pull. Fully adjustable for sear engagement at let-off weight. Action metal is black oxide coated, with bead blast matte finish. Stainless steel barrel 26" in length, with low luster brushed finish. Weight about 8 lbs. Offered in all Weatherby calibers from .240 to .340 Wby. Magnum, plus 7mm Rem. Magnum, 7mm STW and .300 Win. Magnum.

	NIB	EXC.	V.G.	GOOD	FAIR	POOR
	1700	1100	950	800	500	300

Mark V Accumark RC

Upgraded model with Range Certified (RC) guarantee to deliver sub-MOA 3-shot groups with Weatherby ammo. Chambered in all Weatherby Magnums up to .340, plus .270 Win., 7mm Rem., .308 Win., .30-06, .300 Win. Magnum and .338 Lapua. Button rifled free floated barrel, with target crown, T-6 bedding block, tuned/adjustable trigger.

	NIB	EXC.	V.G.	GOOD	FAIR	POOR
	2100	1500	1250	1000	600	400

35th Anniversary Commemorative Mark V

Specially embellished rifle commemorated 35th anniversary of the company. There were 1,000 produced in 1980. As with all commemoratives, it must be NIB with all furnished materials to be worth top dollar.

	NIB	EXC.	V.G.	GOOD	FAIR	POOR
	1500	1300	1000	750	500	350

40th Anniversary Commemorative Mark V

Similar to 35th Anniversary model. Only 200 manufactured in 1985

	NIB	EXC.	V.G.	GOOD	FAIR	POOR
	1500	1300	1000	750	500	350

50th Anniversary Commemorative Mark V

Chambered only in .300 Weatherby Magnum, with high-grade walnut Monte Carlo stock. Limited manufacture in 1995.

	NIB	EXC.	V.G.	GOOD	FAIR	POOR
	2000	1500	1200	750	500	350

	NIB	EXC.	V.G.	GOOD	FAIR	POOR

1984 Olympic Commemorative Mark V

This specially embellished Mark V rifle has gold-plated accents. Exhibition-grade walnut stock, with a star inlay. There were 1,000 manufactured in 1984. This is a commemorative rifle and must be NIB to bring premium value.

NIB	EXC.	V.G.	GOOD	FAIR	POOR
1600	1300	1050	750	500	350

Safari Grade Mark V

Custom-order version available chambered from .300 Weatherby Magnum through .460 Weatherby Magnum. Available with a number of custom options. Ordered with an 8- to 10-month delivery delay.

NIB	EXC.	V.G.	GOOD	FAIR	POOR
6000	5000	3700	3000	1200	600

Crown Grade Mark V

Weatherby's best-grade rifle. Available on a custom-order basis only. Features an engraved receiver and barrel, with exhibition-grade hand-checkered walnut stock. Also furnished with an engraved scope mount.

NIB	EXC.	V.G.	GOOD	FAIR	POOR
8000	7000	5500	4000	1500	500

Mark V Super Varmint Master (SVM)

Introduced in 2000. Features 26" stainless steel barrel. Stock is laminated, with Monte Carlo comb. Fully adjustable trigger. Chambered for .220 Swift, .223 Rem., .22-250, .243 Win., 7mm-08, and .308 Win. Also offered in a single-shot configuration. Weight about 8.5 lbs.

NIB	EXC.	V.G.	GOOD	FAIR	POOR
1675	1400	1200	900	600	350

Mark V Special Varmint Rifle (SVR)

Introduced in 2003. Features 22" Krieger heavy barrel, Monte Carlo composite stock, black recoil pad and matte black finish. Adjustable trigger is standard. Available in .223 Rem. and .22-250. Weight about 7.25 lbs.

NIB	EXC.	V.G.	GOOD	FAIR	POOR
1100	1000	800	700	500	300

MARK V LIGHTWEIGHT RIFLES

Mark V Synthetic Lightweight

Chambered in calibers from .22-250 to .308 Win.. Fitted with 24" barrel. Synthetic stock, with Monte Carlo comb. Magazine capacity 5 rounds. Weight about 6.5 lbs. A carbine version is offered, with 20" barrel in .243, 7mm-08 and .308. Weight about 6 lbs.

NIB	EXC.	V.G.	GOOD	FAIR	POOR
900	750	600	475	350	250

Mark V Stainless Lightweight

Similar to model above, with stainless steel barrel and action. Weight about 6.5 lbs. Carbine version also available.

NIB	EXC.	V.G.	GOOD	FAIR	POOR
1100	950	800	650	525	300

Mark V Sporter Lightweight

Chambered for calibers ranging from .22-250 to .308 Win.. Fitted with 24" barrel. Stock is Claro walnut, with Monte Carlo comb. Weight about 6.75 lbs.

NIB	EXC.	V.G.	GOOD	FAIR	POOR
1050	900	750	600	475	250

Mark V Accumark Lightweight

Chambered for calibers from .22-250 to .300 Wby.. Fitted with 24" barrel. Magazine capacity 5 rounds. Special laminated synthetic stock. Weight about 7 lbs. Introduced in 1998.

NIB	EXC.	V.G.	GOOD	FAIR	POOR
1250	1000	900	800	650	400

Mark V Ultra Lightweight

Similar to above model, with lightened components. Calibers begin with .243 and go to .300 Wby.. Fitted with 24" or 26" barrel depending on caliber. Weight about 5.75 lbs. Introduced in 1998. In 2000, model offered in a left-hand version. In 2001, model available chambered for .338-06 A-Square cartridge.

NIB	EXC.	V.G.	GOOD	FAIR	POOR
1450	1200	950	700	450	300

Mark V Deluxe Lightweight

This model in its lightweight configuration offered in calibers from .22-25- to .30-06. These calibers are fitted to a 24" barrel. Fitted with hand select walnut Monte Carlo stock, with rosewood fore-end tip and pistol-grip cap. Fine line checkering. Weight about 6.75 lbs. Introduced in 1999.

NIB	EXC.	V.G.	GOOD	FAIR	POOR
1650	1250	1000	800	600	400

	NIB	EXC.	V.G.	GOOD	FAIR	POOR

Mark V SPM (Super Predator Master)

Introduced in 2001. Features 24" blackened stainless steel fluted barrel. Chambered for .223 Rem., .22-250 Rem., .243 Win., 7mm-08 Rem. and .308 Win. cartridges. Fully adjustable trigger. Synthetic stock. Weight about 6.5 lbs. Right-hand only.

	1600	1300	1050	750	500	350

Mark V SBGM (Super Big Game Master)

Model features 24" blackened stainless steel barrel Krieger fluted barrel (26" for Magnum calibers). Fully adjustable trigger. Tan composite stock, with raised comb Monte Carlo. Pachmayr Decelerator recoil pad. Offered in a wide variety of calibers from .240 Weatherby Magnum to .300 Weatherby Magnum. Weight about 5.75 lbs.; 6.75 lbs. for Magnum rifles. Introduced in 2002. **NOTE:** Add $60 for Magnum calibers.

	1650	1250	1000	800	600	400

THREAT RESPONSE RIFLE SERIES

These rifles are based on Mark V action.

TRR

Chambered for .223 or .308 Win. cartridge. Fitted with 22" heavy-contour black Krieger barrel. Black composite stock, with raised comb Monte Carlo. Flat-bottom forearm. Fully adjustable trigger. Recoil pad. Introduced in 2002.

	1250	1000	900	800	650	400

TRR Magnum

As above chambered for .300 Win. Magnum, .300 Wby. Magnum, .30-378 Wby. Magnum or .338-378 Wby. Magnum. Barrel length 26". **NOTE:** Add $150 for .30-378 and .338-378 calibers.

	1450	1200	950	700	450	300

TRR Magnum Custom

Model has all the features of TRR Magnum, with addition of a fully adjustable stock. DO NOT use this model until company performs a safety upgrade to the bolt. Rifle can accidentally discharge without the bolt being fully engaged. Affected rifles bear serial numbers from one of these series on the receiver: 00001 through 03810; V00001 through V80966; VX00001 through VX44065; VS00001 through VS23699; VL00001 through VL46984; W00001 through W0099; NV0001 through NV0099. For more information contact Weatherby at 800-227-2018. **NOTE:** Add $150 for .30-378 or .338-378 calibers.

	2500	2200	1900	1600	1250	500

TRR RC (Range Certified)

Model features laminated stock, with three-position buttstock, 26" Krieger barrel with Accubrake and fully adjustable hand-tuned trigger. Offered in .300 Win. Magnum, .300 Weatherby Magnum, .30-378 Weatherby, .338 Lapua and .338/378 Weatherby.

	3500	3000	2400	1700	800	350

VANGUARD

Vanguard (early production)

This was Weatherby's Japanese-manufactured economy rifle. Chambered for various popular standard American cartridges from .22-50 to .300 Win. Magnum cartridge. A bolt-action repeater, with 24" barrel furnished without sights. Has either 3- or 5-shot magazine; finish is polished blue, with select checkered walnut stock with a rosewood fore-end tip and pistol-grip cap. Discontinued in 1988.

	—	1100	925	750	600	350

Vanguard VGS

This satin-finish version was discontinued in 1988.

	—	1000	825	650	500	300

Vanguard VGL

Lightweight carbine version has 20" barrel. Discontinued in 1988.

	—	900	725	550	400	250

Fiberguard

This version has matte-blued finish, with green fiberglass stock. Discontinued in 1988.

	—	750	575	400	300	200

	NIB	EXC.	V.G.	GOOD	FAIR	POOR

Vanguard Classic I

This version chambered for various popular standard calibers. Has 24" barrel and either 3- or 5-shot magazine. Satin blue finish and select checkered oil-finished walnut stock. Introduced in 1989.

	700	600	500	400	300	200

Vanguard Classic II

A more deluxe version, with higher-grade walnut stock.

	725	625	525	425	325	225

Vanguard VGX Deluxe

This version has high-gloss Monte Carlo-type stock and high-polished blued finish. Introduced in 1989.

	800	700	600	500	400	300

Vanguard Weatherguard

This version has wrinkle-finished black synthetic stock. Introduced in 1989. In 2003, offered in stainless steel. **NOTE:** Add $120 for stainless steel.

	650	500	400	300	225	175

Vanguard Synthetic

This model features upgraded composite stock, with Monte Carlo comb, a ring/base scope mounting system and 24" barrel. Calibers from .223 Rem. to .338 Win. Magnum, including .257 Weatherby. Weight about 7.75 lbs. Introduced in 2004.

	400	350	300	250	175	100

Vanguard Stainless

Similar to Vanguard Synthetic, with stainless steel barrel and receiver.

	575	500	450	350	275	125

Vanguard Sporter

Similar to model above, with figured walnut stock, rosewood fore-end tip and fine line checkering. Chambered for calibers from .270 to .338 Win. Magnum. Barrel length 24". Weight about 8 lbs. Introduced in 2004. Also available with detachable magazine.

	550	450	350	250	175	100

Vanguard Sporter SS

Similar to Vanguard Sporter, with stainless steel barrel and receiver.

	675	575	475	375	275	125

Vanguard Varmint Special

Chambered in .223, .22-250 or .308. Blued #3 contour heavy crowned 22" barrel. Adjustable trigger. Synthetic tan composite stock, with black spiderweb pattern. Introduced 2006.

	575	475	375	275	195	125

Vanguard Synthetic Package

Introduced in 2004. Features 24" barrel, with adjustable trigger. Chambered for a variety of calibers from .223 Rem. to .338 Win. Magnum. Supplied with Bushnell Banner 3-9x40 scope, sling, and hard case. Weight about 7.75 lbs.

	650	550	350	275	225	150

Vanguard Sub-MOA Matte or Stainless

Introduced in 2005. Features a guarantee to shoot .99" at 100 yards. Calibers from .223 Rem. to .338 Win. Magnum. Barrel length 24", with Monte Carlo Fiberguard stock. Adjustable trigger. Weight about 7.75 lbs. Also available in stainless steel. **NOTE:** Add $120 for stainless steel.

	800	700	600	500	300	200

Vanguard Sub-MOA Varmint

Similar to Vanguard Varmint Special, with ventilated beavertail fore-end. Chambered in .204, .223, .22-250 and .308. Introduced 2006.

	925	800	650	500	300	200

Vanguard Compact

Chambered for ..223, 22-250, .243 or .308. Fitted with 20" barrel and scaled-down hardwood stock, with shorter length of pull. Also included is a full size composite stock. Weight about 6.75 lbs. Introduced in 2005.

	550	450	350	250	175	100

	NIB	EXC.	V.G.	GOOD	FAIR	POOR

Vanguard Youth Compact

Similar to above, with synthetic stock. Introduced 2008.

NIB	EXC.	V.G.	GOOD	FAIR	POOR
550	450	350	250	175	100

Vanguard Deluxe

Similar to Vanguard, but features 24" polished blued barrel, glossy select Monte Carlo walnut stock, with rosewood fore-end and adjustable trigger. Chambered in .270, .30-06, .257 Weatherby Magnum and .300 Weatherby Magnum. Introduced 2006.

NIB	EXC.	V.G.	GOOD	FAIR	POOR
750	650	550	450	325	225

VANGUARD SERIES 2

Vanguard Series 2 Back Country

All Vanguard Series 2 rifles guaranteed to shoot 3-shot group of less than 1" at 100 yds. when used with specified Weatherby factory or premium ammunition. Available in .240, .257 and .300 Weatherby Magnum, plus .270 Win., .30-06, .300 Win. Magnum. Features include match-grade adjustable trigger, fluted 24" barrel, pillar-bedded Monte Carlo composite stock, with spiderweb accents, Pachmayr Decelerator recoil pad, CeraKote Tactical Grey finish. Average weight of 6.75 lbs.

NIB	EXC.	V.G.	GOOD	FAIR	POOR
1250	1100	950	800	500	350

Vanguard Series 2 Sporter

Vanguard model has classic Weatherby look, with Monte Carlo A-grade turkish walnut stock with raised comb, rosewood fore-end and fine-line diamond point checkering. Other features similar to Back Country model. Chambered in most popular caliber from .223 to .338 Win. Magnum, including .257 and .300 Weatherby Magnums. Deluxe model has higher grade wood, with high gloss finish. Add $300 for his model.

NIB	EXC.	V.G.	GOOD	FAIR	POOR
750	650	525	400	300	250

Vanguard Series 2 Synthetic

Available in a wide range of calibers from .223 to .338 Win. Magnum, including .240, .257 and .300 Weatherby Magnums. Composite Griptonite stock. Barrel is 24" No. 2 contour. Weight from 7.25 to 7.5 lbs. Blue or stainless finish. Add $100 for stainless. Also offered in youth model with 20" barrel. Deduct 10 percent for this model.

NIB	EXC.	V.G.	GOOD	FAIR	POOR
600	525	450	375	300	250

Vanguard Series 2 Varmint Special

Similar to Synthetic model in .223, .22-250 and .308 Win., with semi-heavy No. 3 contour 20" barrel. Weight about 8.75 lbs.

NIB	EXC.	V.G.	GOOD	FAIR	POOR
750	650	525	400	300	250

Weathermark

Introduced in 1993. Features checkered composite stock, with matte blue metal finish. Available in Weatherby calibers from .257 through .340 and .270 Win., 7mm Rem. Magnum, .30-06, .300 and .338 Win. Magnum. Weighs 7.5 lbs.

NIB	EXC.	V.G.	GOOD	FAIR	POOR
550	450	350	250	175	100

Weathermark Alaskan

Similar to Weathermark, with checkered composite stock. Barreled action is electroless nickel, with non-glare finish. Muzzle-brake optional. Available in same calibers as Weathermark. Weighs 7.7 lbs.

NIB	EXC.	V.G.	GOOD	FAIR	POOR
750	650	550	450	325	225

WBY-X

This series of colorful and stylized bolt-actions built on Vanguard Series 2 design. Moderately priced but offer most of the features of other Weatherby rifles. All variations feature composite stocks, with camo finishes. Most models are offered in popular calibers from .223 Rem. to .300 Win. Magnum. Introduced in 2014.

NIB	EXC.	V.G.	GOOD	FAIR	POOR
650	600	500	350	250	200

Mark XXII

Semi-automatic rifle chambered for .22 LR cartridge. Two versions—one with detachable magazine; other with tubular magazine. Has 24" barrel, with adjustable sights. Select checkered walnut stock, with rosewood forearm tip and pistol-grip cap. Model originally produced in Italy and later manufactured in Japan. Introduced in 1965. Discontinued in 1989. **NOTE:** Premium for Italian guns.

NIB	EXC.	V.G.	GOOD	FAIR	POOR
550	450	350	275	225	200

	NIB	EXC.	V.G.	GOOD	FAIR	POOR

Mark XXII Bolt Action

Based on Anschutz design. Available in .22 Long Rifle or .17 HMR. Classic Mark V-style high-gloss walnut Monte Carlo stock, with precision cut checkering, rosewood fore-end tip and grip cap. Target-grade barrel is 23", weight 6.5 lbs. Fully adjustable single-stage trigger. Introduced in 2007. **NOTE:** Add 10 percent for .17 HMR.

NIB	EXC.	V.G.	GOOD	FAIR	POOR
800	685	560	450	400	300

CUSTOM RIFLES

NOTE: Weatherby custom rifles offered with many different options that will affect price. Consult an expert prior to sale.

Vanguard Sage Country Custom

Introduced in 2008. Similar to Vanguard Synthetic, with injection-molded Desert Camo stock. Available in a variety of chamberings from .223 to .338 Winchester Magnum.

NIB	EXC.	V.G.	GOOD	FAIR	POOR
600	500	400	300	225	175

Vanguard Back Country Custom

Introduced in 2008. Lightweight version of Vanguard Synthetic, with fluted barrel, textured stock and overall weight of 6.75 lbs. Available in a variety of chamberings from .257 Weatherby Magnum to .300 Weatherby Magnum.

NIB	EXC.	V.G.	GOOD	FAIR	POOR
950	850	725	625	425	200

Classic Custom

Model features oil-finished French walnut stock, with 20 lpi checkering, ebony fore-end tip, metal grip cap and skeletonized steel buttplate. All metal work is matte blue. Calibers are all Weatherby from .257 Wby. Magnum to .340 Wby. Magnum.

NIB	EXC.	V.G.	GOOD	FAIR	POOR
5100	4600	3500	2250	900	500

Safari Grade Custom

Model features oil-finish French walnut stock, with Monte Carlo comb with fleur-de-lis checkering. Ebony fore-end tip and pistol-grip cap. Damascened bolt and follower, with checkered bolt handle. Quarter rib. Engraved floorplate "Safari Custom." Calibers from .257 Wby. Magnum to .460 Wby. Magnum.

NIB	EXC.	V.G.	GOOD	FAIR	POOR
5300	4800	3700	2450	1050	550

Crown Custom

Model features hand-carved walnut stock, with buttstock inlay, damascened bolt and follower with checkered bolt handle. Engraved barrel, receiver and trigger guard. Floorplate engraved with gold inlays.

NIB	EXC.	V.G.	GOOD	FAIR	POOR
7500	6250	5000	3000	1500	750

Royal Custom

Introduced in 2002. Features Monte Carlo hand-checkered stock of fancy Claro walnut, with high-gloss finish. Engraved receiver, bolt sleeve and floorplate. Barrel length 26". Available in a wide variety of calibers.

NIB	EXC.	V.G.	GOOD	FAIR	POOR
5300	4800	3700	2450	1050	550

Outfitter Custom

Model features Bell & Carlson synthetic stock, with custom camo and Pachmayr pad. Lightweight stainless steel fluted barrel. Titanium nitride finish on all metalwork.

NIB	EXC.	V.G.	GOOD	FAIR	POOR
2250	1700	1400	1100	700	400

Outfitter Krieger Custom

Model features Bell & Carlson synthetic stock, with custom camo and Pachmayr pad. Custom Krieger stainless steel fluted barrel. Titanium nitride finish on all metalwork.

NIB	EXC.	V.G.	GOOD	FAIR	POOR
3500	3000	2500	2000	1300	600

Chris Kyle Limited Edition

From the Weatherby Custom Shop, this special limited edition rifle is in honor of Navy Seal Sniper Chris Kyle, who died in 2013. A portion of the proceeds from the sale of this rifle are donated to the Kyle family. Chambered in .300 Win. Magnum. Rifle has a hand-laminated composite stock, with raised comb and Kryptek Highlander camo pattern. Other features include a fully adjustable trigger, fluted and free-floated stainless steel barrel, Pachmayr Decelerator pad and Chris Kyle frog logo on the floorplate

NIB	EXC.	V.G.	GOOD	FAIR	POOR
3000	2700	—	—	—	—

NIB	EXC.	V.G.	GOOD	FAIR	POOR

SEMI-AUTO & PUMP SHOTGUNS

PA-08 PUMP-ACTION SERIES

Weatherby introduced this line of pump-action shotguns in 2008. All models come in 12-gauge, with 3" chambers and have chrome-lined barrels. Knoxx stock models reduced recoil and are adjustable in length.

PA-08 Upland

This model has a walnut stock and fore-end, with low-lustre finish. Matte black metal work. Available with 28" or 26" barrel. Includes three choke tubes.

325	275	225	175	125	75

PA-08 Knoxx Strutter X

Strutter models feature synthetic stock and 24" vent rib barrel. Three choke tubes included. Add 15 percent for Apparition Excel camo pattern.

425	375	325	250	175	100

PA-08 Knoxx HD

Home defense model features 18" non-vent-rib barrel and cylinder choke.

425	375	325	250	175	100

PA-08 Field/Slug Combo

Field and Slug-gun Combo pump features both a 28" field barrel for hunting birds and 24" rifled slug barrel for deer. Field barrel is chrome lined and has a ventilated rib. Integral choke system features Briley thread pattern and comes with improved cylinder, Modified and full-choked tubes. The 8-groove Slug barrel has a Weaver-compatible cantilevered scope mount base. Matte black finish. Weight about 6.75 lbs. Introduced in 2011.

430	380	340	300	270	220

PA-459 Turkey Camo

Pump gun features Mothwing Camo's Spring Mimicry pattern on stock and fore-end. The 12-gauge gun has 19" barrel, 13.5" length of pull and overall length of 40". Weight about 6.5 lbs. Integral Picatinny rail allows mounting optical sights or other accessories. Rail has a clamp-style LPA ghost ring rear sight adjustable for windage and elevation.

450	390	360	320	290	250

Centurion

Gas-operated semi-automatic shotgun chambered for 12-gauge. Offered with various barrel lengths and chokes. Has a checkered walnut stock. Manufactured between 1972 and 1981.

450	400	300	250	200	150

Centurion Deluxe

This version is slightly engraved. Features vent ribbed barrel and higher-grade wood.

500	400	325	275	225	175

Model 82

Gas-operated semi-automatic shotgun chambered for 12-gauge, with 2.75" or 3" chambers. Has various barrel lengths, with vent ribs and screw-in choke tubes. Features an alloy receiver and deluxe checkered walnut stock. Also available as the Buckmaster, with 22" open-choked barrel. Introduced in 1983.

500	450	400	350	300	250

Model SAS Field

Introduced in 1999. Gas-operated semi-automatic model features a high-grade Claro walnut stock, with black pistol-grip cap. Fine-line checkering. Chambered for 12- or 20-gauge. Fitted with 26", 28" or 30" vent rib barrels in 12-gauge; 26" or 28" vent rib barrels in 20-gauge. Weight about: 7.5 lbs. for 12-gauge; 7 lbs. for 20-gauge, depending on barrel lengths., Fitted with Briley choke tubes.

700	550	450	325	250	200

Model SAS Camo

Model offered with either Shadowgrass or Superflauge camo stocks. Available in 12-gauge only, with 3" chambers. Shadowgrass offered with 26" or 28" barrels; Superflauge with 24" or 26" barrels. Weight about 7.5 lbs.

Shadow Grass

750	600	500	375	300	225

	NIB	EXC.	V.G.	GOOD	FAIR	POOR

Superflauge

	750	600	500	375	300	225

Model SAS Slug Gun

Model features 22" rifled barrel chambered for 3" 12-gauge shell. Barrel has cantilever base for scope mounts. Walnut stock has raised Monte Carlo comb. Sling swivel studs. Weight about 7.25 lbs. Introduced in 2003.

	750	600	500	375	300	225

Model SAS Sporting Clays

This 12-gauge gun fitted with 28" or 30" vent rib ported barrel. Walnut stock, with pistol-grip. Choke tubes standard. Weight about 7.5 lbs. Introduced in 2002.

	800	650	550	425	350	250

Model SAS Synthetic

Model features black synthetic stock chambered for 12- or 20-gauge barrels as above. Introduced in 2000.

	525	450	375	300	250	175

SA-08 Upland

This semi-automatic was new in 2008. Features walnut stock, with oil finish. Available in 12- and 20-gauge, with 3" chambers and 28" or 26" barrels. Three choke tubes included.

	650	550	450	250	175	150

SA-08 Youth

As above in 20-gauge, with 26" barrel only and shorter 12.5" length of pull.

	550	425	300	250	175	150

SA-08 Entré Rios

Entré Rios autoloader has a scaled-down frame for 28-gauge. Features include a select cut-checkered walnut stock and high-gloss finish on barrel and receiver. Comes equipped with Skeet Improved cylinder and Modified choke tubes. Weight 5.25 lbs. Available with 26" or 28" barrel.

	600	500	425	365	310	200

SA-459 TR

Gas-operated autoloader features a bolt with an oversized hourglass design that's easily located in the dark. Comes equipped with a new TR accessory rail for mounting tactical lights or laser sights. Also has a fully adjustable LPA-style ghost ring sight. Pistol-grip buttstock has rubber-textured grip. Available in 12- or 20-gauge. Barrel length 18.5"; weight 7 lbs.

	625	550	400	325	250	150

OLDER MODEL PUMP SHOTGUNS

Patrician

Slide-action shotgun chambered for 12-gauge. Offered with various barrel lengths and choke combinations. Has a vent rib barrel, blued finish and checkered walnut stock. Manufactured between 1972 and 1981.

	400	350	325	300	250	175

Patrician Deluxe

Slightly engraved version, with fancier-grade walnut.

	450	425	400	350	275	200

Model 92

Slide-action shotgun chambered for 12-gauge, with 2.75" or 3" chambers. Offered with 26", 28" or 30" ventilated rib barrels, with screw-in choke tubes. Features a short twin-rail slide action and engraved alloy receiver. Finish is blued, with deluxe checkered walnut stock. A Buckmaster model with 22" open-choke barrel and rifle sights is also available.

	350	300	250	200	175	125

SIDE-BY-SIDE GUNS

These shotguns are built in Spain.

Athena SBS

Introduced in 2002. Features a case colored boxlock receiver, with false sideplates with scroll engraving. Offered in 12- or 20-gauge, with 26" or 28" barrels. Choke tubes. Turkish walnut

	NIB	EXC.	V.G.	GOOD	FAIR	POOR

stock, with straight-grip and recoil pad. Checkering is 22 lpi. Single trigger and ejectors. Weight about 7 lbs.

	1550	1200	1000	750	500	400

Athena D'Italia

Introduced in 2005. Chambered for the 12-, 20- or 28-gauge. Fitted with 28" barrels for 12-gauge; 26" barrels for 20- and 28-gauge. Receiver has silver sideplates, with scroll engraving. Checkered walnut stock, with straight-grip. Weight about 7 lbs. **NOTE:** Add $135 for 28-gauge.

	2840	2100	1600	1100	750	500

Athena D'Italia PG

Introduced in 2006. Model offered in same configurations as D'Italia. Identical in action and frame to D'Italia, with rounded pistol-grip stock and single gold trigger. Laser-cut checkering at 20 lpi. Introduced 2006. Pricing is for 12- and 20-gauge. **NOTE:** Add $200 for 28-gauge.

	3200	2500	2000	1500	1050	500

Athena D'Italia Deluxe

Renaissance floral engraving, with Bolino style game scene. AAA Fancy Turkish walnut, with 24 lpi hand checkering adorn this straight-grip stocked model. Available in 12-, 20- and 28-gauge, with 26" or 28" barrels with fixed IC and Mod. chokes. Single trigger. Introduced 2006.

	7000	6000	4750	3000	2200	600

Orion SBS

A lower cost alternative to Athena. Turkish walnut stock, with pistol-grips and 18 lpi checkering. Case colored boxlock receiver. Offered in 12-, 20-, 28-gauge and .410 bore. Choke tubes except for .410 bore. Choice of 26" or 28" barrels. Weight about 7 lbs. Introduced in 2002.

	1750	1100	900	650	475	300

OVER/UNDER GUNS

Regency Field Grade

This is an over/under double-barrel shotgun chambered for 12- or 20-gauge. Has various length vent ribbed barrels and boxlock action, with engraved false sideplates. Features a single-selective trigger and automatic ejectors. Finish is blued, with checkered walnut stock. Imported from Italy between 1972 and 1980. Also offered as a trap grade with same value.

	1500	1200	1000	700	400	300

Olympian

Similar to Regency, with less engraving. Not imported after 1980. Skeet and trap as well as a field-grade model were available. Values were similar.

	1000	800	650	500	350	225

Orion Upland

This 12- or 20-gauge model features a Claro walnut stock, with rounded pistol-grip and slim forearm. Plain blued receiver. Choice of 26" or 28" vent rib barrel, with 3" chambers. Multi-choke system. Introduced in 1999.

	1200	1000	800	600	450	300

Orion Grade I

An over/under double-barrel shotgun chambered for 12- or 20-gauge, with 3" chambers. Offered with 26" or 28" vent rib barrels, with screw-in chokes. Has a single-selective trigger and automatic ejectors. Boxlock action features no engraving. Finish is blued, with checkered walnut stock. Introduced in 1989.

	1200	1000	800	650	450	300

Orion Grade II Skeet

Model supplied with Claro walnut checkered stock, with full pistol-grip and rosewood grip cap. Receiver matte blue, with scroll engraving. Barrel has matte vent rib, with side vents and mid-point head with white bead front sight. Special ventilated recoil pad. Offered in 12- and 20 gauge, with 26" barrels. Fixed Skeet chokes are standard. Weight for: 12 gauge 7.5 lbs.; 20-gauge 7.25 lbs.

	950	800	700	600	400	200

Orion Grade II Sporting Clays

Similar to Classic model, with full pistol-grip and rosewood grip cap. Receiver is silver gray, with scroll engraving. Claro walnut stock is checkered, with high-gloss finish. Offered in 12-gauge, with 28" to 30" vent rib barrels. Supplied with five screw-in choke tubes.

	1300	1050	800	600	400	200

	NIB	EXC.	V.G.	GOOD	FAIR	POOR

Orion Grade II Double Trap

Model features an integral multi-choke tube. Monte Carlo stock has a rosewood pistol-grip cap, with diamond shaped inlay. Receiver is blue, with scroll engraving. Available with 30" or 32" vent rib barrels. Weighs 8 lbs.

950	800	700	550	400	200

Orion Grade II Single Trap

Similar to Double Trap. Furnished with single 32" barrel. Weighs 8 lbs.

950	800	700	550	400	200

Orion Grade II

This version is lightly engraved. Has a high-gloss finish. Otherwise, similar to Grade I.

1200	1050	925	800	600	250

Orion Grade II Classic Field

Introduced in 1993. Features rounded pistol-grip and slim forearm design. Walnut stock is oil finished. Receiver is blued, with game scene engraving. Solid recoil pad is standard. Available in 12-, 20- and 28-gauge, with vent rib barrel lengths from 26" to 30" depending on gauge. Screw-in choke tubes standard. Weighs 6.5 lbs. to 8 lbs. depending on gauge.

950	800	700	550	400	200

Orion Grade II Classic Sporting Clays

Introduced in 1993. Has rounded pistol-grip, with slender forearm and oil-finished stock. Receiver is blued, with scroll engraving. A stepped competition matte vent rib, with additional side vents is supplied. Recoil pad has a special radius heel. Offered in 12-gauge with 28" barrel. Furnished with five screw-in choke tubes. Weighs 7.5 lbs.

1000	850	750	600	400	200

Orion Super Sporting Clays (SSC)

Introduced in 1999. This 12-gauge model features walnut stock, with sporter-style pistol-grip and cast off. Barrel lengths are 28", 30" or 32", with 3" chambers and 12mm grooved rib. Barrels are also ported and backbored. Comes with five choke tubes. Weight about 8 lbs.

1750	1400	1150	925	750	350

Orion Grade III

This version has a game scene-engraved coin-finished receiver and higher-grade walnut. Introduced in 1989.

1400	1100	850	650	500	300

Orion Grade III Classic Field

New for 1993. Features a rounded pistol-grip and slim forearm with oil finish, Claro walnut, with fine line checkering. Receiver is silver gray, with scroll engraving and gold game bird overlays. Available in 12-gauge with 28" vent rib barrels; 20-gauge with 26" vent rib barrels. Screw-in choke tubes standard.

1600	1400	1000	750	500	300

Orion Grade III Classic English Field

Model features English-style straight-grip stock. Choice of 12-gauge with 28" barrel; 20-gauge with 26" or 28" barrels. Receiver is engraved and stock is oil-finished hand-checkered. Weight about: 12 gauge 7 lbs.; 20-gauge 6.5 lbs. Introduced in 1996.

1450	1200	925	800	600	250

Orion D'Italia

Engraved silver-finish metalwork and fineline 20 lpi checkering. Turkish walnut stock, with high-gloss finish. Available in 12-gauge with 28" barrel; 20-gauge with 26" barrel.

1750	1500	1200	900	750	400

Athena Grade III Classic Field

Offered in 12- or 20-gauge. Features hand select Claro walnut stock, with oil finish. Pistol-grip is rounded. Silver-gray sideplates feature a rose and scroll engraving pattern with gold overlaid hunting scenes. Available with 26" or 28" vent rib barrels, with multi-choke system. Weight about: 7.5 lbs. 12-gauge; 7 lbs. 20-gauge. Introduced in 1999. In 2001, a 28-gauge version was offered with 26" or 28" barrels.

1700	1500	1250	900	600	350

Athena Grade IV

An over/under double-barrel shotgun chambered for 12-, 20-, 28-gauge and .410 bore. It has 3" chambers. Offered with various barrel lengths, with vent ribs and screw-in choke tubes.

NIB	EXC.	V.G.	GOOD	FAIR	POOR

Has a boxlock action, with Greener crossbolt single-selective trigger and automatic ejectors. Engraved false sideplates and satin nickel-plated action. Barrels are blued, with select checkered walnut stock. Introduced in 1989.

2100	1700	1500	1100	750	450

Athena Grade V Classic Field

Introduced in 1993. Features rounded pistol-grip, with slender forearm. High-grade Claro walnut stock is oil finished, with fine line checkering. Receiver has a side plate that is silver/gray, with rose and scroll engraving. Vent rib barrels also have side vents. An Old English recoil pad is supplied. Offered in 12-gauge with 26", 28" or 30" barrels; 20-gauge with 26" and 28" barrels. Choke tubes are standard. Weatherby Athena Master skeet tube set: 12-gauge 28" skeet shotgun, plus two each 20-, 28-gauge and .410 bore fitted full-length Briley tubes with integral extractors. Packed in custom fitted aluminum case (not shown). **NOTE:** Add 50 percent for Master Skeet Set.

2800	2400	1800	1400	900	500

Competition Model Athena

This is either a trap or skeet version, with stock dimensions designed for either skeet or trap and competition-type ribs.

1650	1400	1150	1000	750	600

HANDGUNS

Mark V – CFP (Compact Firing Platform)

Bolt-action handgun, with 5+1 capacity. 16" barrel, adjustable trigger, composite stock. Available in .223, .22-250, .243 and 7mm-08. 5.25 lb. Introduced 2006.

1300	1050	800	600	400	200

Mark V Accumark CFP

Model similar to Accumark rifle. Features synthetic stock of Kevlar and fiberglass. Stock has a matte black gel-coat finish. Offered in .223 Rem., .22-250, .243 Win., 7mm-08 and .308 Win. calibers. Fluted barrel length is 15". Weight about 5 lbs. Introduced in 2000.

1050	800	600	400	225	150

WEAVER ARMS
Escondido, California

Nighthawk Assault Pistol

A 9mm semi-automatic pistol with a 10" or 12" barrel, alloy receiver and ambidextrous safety. Blackened with plastic grips. Introduced in 1987.

550	450	400	350	300	150

Nighthawk Carbine

As above, with a 16.1" barrel, retractable shoulder stock, 25-, 32-, 40-, or 50-shot magazine. Introduced in 1984.

600	500	450	350	300	150

WEBLEY & SCOTT, LTD.
Birmingham, England

Established in 1860, this firm has produced a wide variety of firearms over the years and has been known as Webley & Scott, Ltd. since 1906. **NOTE:** For all Webley .455 revolvers deduct 35 percent if converted to .45 ACP/.45 Auto Rim.

Model 1872 Royal Irish Constabulary

A .450 double-action revolver with a 3.25" barrel, 5-shot cylinder and rotating ejector. This model was also offered with 2.5" and 3.5" barrels. Blued with checkered walnut grips.

—	1000	750	475	250	150

Model 1880 Metropolitan Police

As above, with a 2.5" barrel and 6-shot cylinder.

—	1000	750	475	250	150

Model 1878 Webley-Pryse

Chambered for the .455 and .476 Eley cartridge. **NOTE:** Add 200 percent premium for revolvers chambered for .577. Deduct 50 percent for revolvers chambered for cartridges below .442.

—	2100	1500	950	550	300

	NIB	EXC.	V.G.	GOOD	FAIR	POOR

New Model 1883 R.I.C.

Similar to the Model 1880, but in .455 caliber with a 4.5" barrel. Also made with a 2.5" barrel.

	—	900	750	425	250	100

Model 1884 R.I.C. Naval

As above, with a brass frame and oxidized finish. Barrel length 2.75" and of octagonal form.

	—	2250	1650	1225	600	500

British Bulldog

Similar to the new Model 1883 R.I.C. blued, checkered walnut grips. Those engraved on the back strap "W.R.A. Co." were sold through the Winchester Repeating Arms Company's New York sales agency and are worth a considerable premium over the values listed. Manufactured from 1878 to 1914. **NOTE:** Add a premium for U.S. dealer markings, see model description.

	—	900	550	325	200	150

Pug

Similar to the British Bulldog but somewhat smaller. Interesting in that it has a manual safety. Chambered in .450, .442, and possibly others as well.

	—	800	500	325	200	150

Model 1878 Army Express Revolver

A .455 caliber double-action revolver with a 6" barrel and integral ejector. Blued with one-piece walnut grips. **NOTE:** Add 100 percent premium for single-action version. Add 25 percent for .45 Long (.45 Colt) markings.

	2100	1500	850	500	350	

Webley Kaufmann Model 1880

A top break, hinged-frame double-action revolver chambered for the .450 centerfire cartridge, with a 5.75" barrel and a curved bird's-head butt. Blued, with walnut grips.

	—	2300	1000	800	600	300

Webley-Green Model

A double-action, top break revolver chambered for the .455 cartridge, with a 6" ribbed barrel and a 6-shot cylinder. The cylinder flutes on this model are angular and not rounded in shape. Blued, with checkered walnut, squared butt grips with a lanyard ring on the butt. Introduced in 1882 and manufactured until 1896. Also known as the "WG" model.

	—	1900	1350	700	500	200

Mark I

A .442, .455, or .476 double-action top break revolver with a 4" barrel and 6-shot cylinder. Blued with checkered walnut grips. Manufactured from 1887 to 1894.

	950	550	375	250	150	

Mark II

As above, with a larger hammer spur and improved barrel catch. Manufactured from 1894 to 1897.

	925	550	350	225	100	

Mark III

As above, with internal improvements. Introduced in 1897.

	—	975	600	325	200	75

Mark IV

As above, with a .455 caliber 3", 4", 5", or 6" barrel. This model was also available in .22 caliber with 6" barrel, .32 caliber with 3" barrel, and .38 caliber with 3", 4", or 5" barrel.

	—	900	575	375	200	75

Mark IV Target

Chambered for the .22 caliber cartridge and fitted with a 6" barrel with target sights.

	—	1450	1000	800	500	300

Mark V

Similar to Mark IV, with a 4" or 6" barrel. Manufactured from 1913 to 1915.

	—	1000	695	395	250	150

	NIB	EXC.	V.G.	GOOD	FAIR	POOR

Mark VI

Similar to Mark V in design but with a smaller frame, 4" or 6" barrel and modified grip. Chambered for .38/200 (.38 S&W). Pricing is for commercial version. Subtract 40 percent for WAR FINISH-marked examples.

	NIB	EXC.	V.G.	GOOD	FAIR	POOR
	—	800	600	375	225	150

Mark VI .22 Rimfire

A standard-size Mark V chambered for the .22 rimfire cartridge used as a training pistol. Manufactured in 1918 and quite scarce.

	NIB	EXC.	V.G.	GOOD	FAIR	POOR
	—	850	650	450	350	200

WEBLEY SEMI-AUTOMATIC PISTOLS

Webley-Fosbery Automatic Revolver

Recoil forces the top half of this unusual pistol back to cock the hammer, while a stud in the frame cams the cylinder around to bring a fresh chamber into position. Early examples under serial number 75 or so appear to be hand-made as no two seem to be identical; these bring a 100 percent premium over late-model pistols. Other low-number guns, under serial number 300 or so, also differ in appearance from the later production and bring a 25 percent premium. Early production was all in .455 Webley with a 6-round cylinder; a .38 ACP version with an 8-round cylinder was introduced about 1903 but is much scarcer than the .455.

.455 Caliber

	NIB	EXC.	V.G.	GOOD	FAIR	POOR
	—	9000	4500	3000	2000	1250

.38 Caliber

	NIB	EXC.	V.G.	GOOD	FAIR	POOR
	—	10000	7250	4500	3000	2000

Model 1904

Made experimentally in both .38 ACP and .455 calibers. Highest serial numbered 1904 known in 30s. Very few seem to have survived. A later Webley experimental Model 1906 made in .45 for the U.S. Army trial, but apparently never submitted. Either model is too rare to price.

Model 1905

Webley's first commercial semi-automatic pistol was this compact .32 caliber. The earliest Model 1905s have a diagonal flat machined on the slide and a hammer-mounted safety; these bring about a 50 percent premium. The Model 1905 was replaced by the Model 1908 after about perhaps 20,000 were made.

	NIB	EXC.	V.G.	GOOD	FAIR	POOR
	—	1200	1000	750	400	250

Model 1907

The 1907 is a .25 caliber pistol with an outside hammer and was one of Webley's most popular handguns; it remained in production until WWII and over 50,000 were made.

	NIB	EXC.	V.G.	GOOD	FAIR	POOR
	—	800	600	400	200	100

Model 1908

The Model 1908 is a slight redesign of the Model 1905. Webley's most popular self-loading pistol, it remained in production until WWII. Examples bearing a crown and the letters "MP" were made for the Metropolitan Police and bring a slight premium.

	NIB	EXC.	V.G.	GOOD	FAIR	POOR
	—	650	550	350	175	125

Model 1909

The Model 1909 is a modified and enlarged version of the Model 1908, chambered for the 9mm Browning Long cartridge. It was never popular, and manufacture ended in 1914 with just under 1,700 made. Its most unusual feature was the slide release on top of the slide.

	NIB	EXC.	V.G.	GOOD	FAIR	POOR
	—	1475	850	500	300	200

Model 1910 .380

The Model 1910 .380 was simply a Model 1908 modified to accept the .380 cartridge. Never very popular, under 2,000 were sold.

	NIB	EXC.	V.G.	GOOD	FAIR	POOR
	—	1500	875	525	—	—

Model 1910 .38 ACP

This was Webley's first locked-breech pistol, based closely on the experimental Model 1906 design and chambered for the .38 ACP cartridge. There are two models, both with internal hammers, but one with a grip safety and the later without. Total production for both was under 1,000, so both are rare.

	NIB	EXC.	V.G.	GOOD	FAIR	POOR
	—	2250	1500	900	500	350

	NIB	EXC.	V.G.	GOOD	FAIR	POOR

Model 1911

The Model 1911 is a single-shot .22 caliber training version of the Model 1908, and developed specifically for the Metropolitan Police. It features a "blow open" action that ejects the fired cartridge but remains open for reloading, and the bottom of the frame is slotted for attaching a shoulder stock. Stocks are quite rare, and will probably add more than 100 percent to the value of the pistol.

—	1750	1400	1100	800	300

Model 1912

A perceived need for a hammerless version of the Model 1907 .25 caliber led to the introduction of the Model 1912. It actually does have an internal hammer, but the recoil spring is two coils in the slide instead of the large V-spring under the right grip frame found in all other Webley semi-automatic pistols. Not as popular as the Model 1907, production totaled almost 15,000 vs. over 50,000 for the hammer model.

—	1200	1000	750	400	200

Model 1913

The Model 1913 was the result of years of development in conjunction with the British government and was finally adopted in 1913 as the Model 1913 MK1N for Royal Navy issue. It has the same breech-locking system as the Model 1910, but has an external hammer and is chambered for the .455 Webley Self-Loading cartridge. About 1,000 Model 1913s were sold commercially and serial-numbered along with the smaller-caliber pistols. In 1915 a variation of the Model 1913 with butt slotted for a shoulder stock, an adjustable rear sight, and a hammer safety adopted for use by the Royal Horse Artillery. Shoulder stocks are very rare, and will double values listed for the RHA model. All militaries were numbered in their own series; about 10,000 made in both variations.

—	1950	1200	800	500	300

(RHA model)

—	5000	4000	3000	1000	600

Model 1922

The Model 1922 was a redesign of the Model 1909 in hopes of military adoption. The grip safety was replaced by a manual safety mounted on the slide, the grip angle was changed, and a lanyard ring added to the butt. Unfortunately for Webley its only official use was by the Union Defense Force of South Africa (1,000 pistols). South African guns are marked with a large "U" with an arrow in it and bring a 20 percent premium.

—	3000	2500	2000	1000	600

WEIHRAUCH, HANS HERMANN
Melrichstadt, West Germany

Model HW 60M

A .22 caliber single-shot bolt action rifle with a 26.75" barrel and adjustable sights. Blued with a walnut stock.

800	650	550	400	350	250

Model HW 66

A .22 Hornet or .222 Remington bolt action rifle with a stainless steel 26" barrel and single- or double-set triggers. Blued with a walnut stock.

700	550	500	350	300	200

Model HW-3

A double-action, solid-frame, swing-out cylinder revolver chambered for .22 LR or .32 Smith & Wesson long cartridges with a barrel length of 2.75", and a cylinder holding either seven or eight cartridges. Blued, with walnut grips. In America, this revolver was known as the Dickson Bulldog. In Europe it was known as the Gecado.

—	100	75	50	35	25

Model HW-5

As above, with a 4" barrel. Sold in the United States under the trade name "Omega."

—	100	75	50	35	25

Model HW-7

As above, in .22 caliber with a 6" barrel and 8-shot cylinder. Sold in the United States as the "Herter's Guide Model." Also available with target sights and thumbrest grips as the Model HW-7S.

—	100	75	50	35	25

	NIB	EXC.	V.G.	GOOD	FAIR	POOR

Model HW-9

These pistols all carry the Arminius trademark, a bearded head wearing a winged helmet. The model number will be found on the cylinder crane; the caliber, on the barrel; and the words "Made in Germany" on the frame.

	NIB	EXC.	V.G.	GOOD	FAIR	POOR
	—	100	75	50	35	25

WEISBURGER, A.
Memphis, Tennessee

Pocket Pistol

A .41 caliber percussion single-shot pocket pistol with 2.5" barrel, German silver furniture and a walnut stock. Manufactured during the 1850s.

	NIB	EXC.	V.G.	GOOD	FAIR	POOR
	—	—	6500	5100	3250	1800

WESSON, EDWIN
Hartford, Connecticut

Dragoon

A .45 caliber percussion revolver with a 7" round barrel and 6-shot unfluted cylinder. The barrel blued, the frame case hardened and the walnut grips fitted with a brass buttcap. Manufactured in 1848 and 1849.

	NIB	EXC.	V.G.	GOOD	FAIR	POOR
	—	—	13500	9500	5000	1750

WESSON, FRANK
Worcester & Springfield, Massachusetts

Manual Extractor Model

A .22 caliber spur trigger single-shot pistol with a 4" octagonal barrel and thin brass frame. The barrel release is located in the front of the trigger. No markings. Approximately 200 were made in 1856 and 1857.

	NIB	EXC.	V.G.	GOOD	FAIR	POOR
	—	—	1400	950	400	100

First Model Small Frame

As above, with a 3", 3.5", or 6" half-octagonal barrel. Blued with rosewood or walnut grips. The barrel marked "Frank Wesson Worcester Mass/Pat'd Oct. 25, 1859 & Nov. 11, 1862." Serial numbered from 1 to 2500.

	NIB	EXC.	V.G.	GOOD	FAIR	POOR
	—	—	900	575	225	75

Second Type

As above, with a flat sighted frame and a circular sideplate.

	NIB	EXC.	V.G.	GOOD	FAIR	POOR
	—	—	900	575	225	75

First Model Medium Frame

As above, in .30 or .32 rimfire with a 4" half-octagonal barrel and an iron frame. Approximately 1,000 were made between 1859 and 1862.

	NIB	EXC.	V.G.	GOOD	FAIR	POOR
	—	—	950	600	225	75

Medium Frame Second Model

As above, with a longer spur trigger and a slightly wider frame at the barrel hinge. Manufactured from 1862 to 1870.

	NIB	EXC.	V.G.	GOOD	FAIR	POOR
	—	—	950	600	225	75

Small Frame Pocket Rifle

A .22 caliber spur trigger single-shot pistol with a 6" half octagonal barrel and narrow brass frame. This model is adopted for use with a detachable skeleton shoulder stock. The barrel marked "Frank Wesson Worcester, Mass." Manufactured from 1865 to 1875 with approximately 5,000 made. **NOTE:** Matching shoulder stock add 100 percent. Prices are for pistols only.

	NIB	EXC.	V.G.	GOOD	FAIR	POOR
	—	—	1500	925	350	100

Medium Frame Pocket Rifle

As above in .22, .30 or .32 rimfire, with 10" or 12" half octagonal barrel. Approximately 1,000 made from 1862 to 1870. **NOTE:** Add 100 percent for matching shoulder stock. Prices are for pistols only.

	NIB	EXC.	V.G.	GOOD	FAIR	POOR
	—	—	1000	650	200	75

NIB	EXC.	V.G.	GOOD	FAIR	POOR

Model 1870 Small Frame Pocket Rifle

As above, in .22 caliber with a 10", 12", 15", or 18" or 20" half octagonal barrel that rotates to the side for loading. This model was made with either a brass or iron frame. It has a half cocked notch on the hammer. **NOTE:** Matching shoulder stock add 100 percent. Prices are for pistol only.

NIB	EXC.	V.G.	GOOD	FAIR	POOR
—	—	1000	650	200	75

1870 Medium Frame Pocket Rifle First Type

As above, but with a slightly larger frame chambered for .32 rimfire. Approximately 5,000 were made from 1870 to 1893. **NOTE:** Matching shoulder stock add 100 percent. Prices are for pistols only.

NIB	EXC.	V.G.	GOOD	FAIR	POOR
—	—	1000	650	200	75

1870 Medium Frame Pocket Rifle Second Type

As above, with an iron frame and a push-button half cocked safety. **NOTE:** Matching shoulder stock add 100 percent. Prices are for pistols only

NIB	EXC.	V.G.	GOOD	FAIR	POOR
—	—	900	475	175	75

1870 Medium Frame Pocket Rifle Third Type

As above, with three screws on the left side of the frame. **NOTE:** Matching shoulder stock add 100 percent. Prices are for pistols only.

NIB	EXC.	V.G.	GOOD	FAIR	POOR
—	—	900	475	175	75

1870 Large Frame Pocket Rifle First Type

As above, in .32, .38, .42, or .44 rimfire with an octagonal barrel from 15" to 24" in length. The barrel marked "Frank Wesson Worcester, Mass Patented May 31, 1870." Fewer than 250 of these rifles were made between 1870 and 1880. **NOTE:** Matching shoulder stock add 100 percent. Prices are for pistols only.

NIB	EXC.	V.G.	GOOD	FAIR	POOR
—	—	2750	1500	550	200

1870 Large Frame Pocket Rifle Second Type

As above, with a sliding extractor. **NOTE:** Matching shoulder stock add 100 percent. Prices are for pistols only.

NIB	EXC.	V.G.	GOOD	FAIR	POOR
—	—	2750	1500	550	200

Small Frame Superposed Pistol

A .22 caliber spur trigger over/under pocket pistol with 2" or 2.5" octagonal barrels that revolve. Approximately 3,500 were made between 1868 and 1880. On occasion. this pistol is found with a sliding knife blade mounted on the side of the barrels. The presence of this feature would add approximately 25 percent to the values listed.

NIB	EXC.	V.G.	GOOD	FAIR	POOR
—	—	3000	1750	850	250

Medium Frame Superposed Pistol

As above, in .32 rimfire with 2.5" or 3.5" barrels. As with the smaller version, this pistol is occasionally found with a sliding knife blade mounted on the barrels that would add 25 percent to the values listed. Manufactured from 1868 to 1880.

First Type Marked "Patent Applied For

NIB	EXC.	V.G.	GOOD	FAIR	POOR
—	—	2500	1250	400	100

Second Type Marked "Patent December 15, 1868

NIB	EXC.	V.G.	GOOD	FAIR	POOR
—	—	2450	1200	400	100

Third Type Full-Length Fluted Barrels

NIB	EXC.	V.G.	GOOD	FAIR	POOR
—	—	2750	1500	450	150

Large Frame Superposed Pistol

As above, in .41 rimfire with a 3" octagonal barrel fitted with a sliding knife blade. Approximately 2,000 were made from 1868 to 1880.

NIB	EXC.	V.G.	GOOD	FAIR	POOR
—	—	4200	2750	1250	400

No. 1 Long Range Rifle

A .44-100 or .45-100 caliber single-shot dropping block rifle with a 34" octagonal barrel. Blued with a checkered walnut stock. The barrel marked "F. Wesson Mfr. Worcester, Mass. Long Range Rifle Creedmoor." Manufactured in 1876.

NIB	EXC.	V.G.	GOOD	FAIR	POOR
—	—	12500	4500	2000	500

No. 2 Mid-Range or Hunting Rifle

Similar to the above, with the firing pin located in a bolster on the right side of the receiver. The trigger guard has a rear finger loop. Standard barrel length 28", 32", and 34" and marked "F.

	NIB	EXC.	V.G.	GOOD	FAIR	POOR

Wesson Maker Worcester, Mass." The 32" and 34" barrels are occasionally marked "Long Range Rifle Creedmoor." Approximately 100 were made.

	NIB	EXC.	V.G.	GOOD	FAIR	POOR
	—	—	7250	3750	1750	500

No. 2 Sporting Rifle

A .38-100, .40-100, or .45-100 caliber single-shot dropping-barrel-action rifle with barrels ranging from 28" to 34" in length. Approximately 25 were made.

	NIB	EXC.	V.G.	GOOD	FAIR	POOR
	—	—	8250	3750	1750	500

Military Carbine

Fitted with a 24" barrel with sling swivels and chambered for the .44 caliber rimfire cartridge. Approximately 4,500 were manufactured. **NOTE:** Add 100 percent for martially marked examples.

	NIB	EXC.	V.G.	GOOD	FAIR	POOR
	—	—	6000	2500	1100	500

WESSON & LEAVITT
Chicopee Falls, Massachusetts

Revolving Rifle

A .40 caliber percussion revolving rifle with a 16" to 24" round barrel and 6-shot cylinder. Blued with a walnut stock. Approximately 25 were made in 1849.

	NIB	EXC.	V.G.	GOOD	FAIR	POOR
	—	—	13000	7500	3500	950

Dragoon

A .40 caliber percussion revolver with a 6.25" or 7" round barrel and 6-shot cylinder. These pistols are marked "Mass. Arms Co./Chicopee Falls." Approximately 30 were made with the 6.25" barrel and 750 with the 7" barrel. Manufactured in 1850 and 1851.

	NIB	EXC.	V.G.	GOOD	FAIR	POOR
	—	—	9000	4750	2000	500

WESSON FIREARMS, DAN
Norwich, New York

Also See—Wesson Firearms Co., Inc., separate listing.

In 1996 the assets of the Wesson Firearms Co. was purchased by the New York International Corp. Full production of new models occurred in 1997. These firearms are laser marked on the barrel or frame with: "NYI" in an oval and below "DAN WESSON FIREARMS" on the next line "NORWICH, NEW YORK USA." In April, 2005 Dan Wesson Firearms was acquired by CZ-USA. Production continues at the Norwich, New York, facility.

NEW GENERATION SMALL-FRAME SERIES

NOTE: The "7" prefix denotes stainless steel frame and barrel. For models listed add between 4 percent and 9 percent depending on barrel length and for stainless steel.

Model 22/722

This is a 6-shot revolver chambered for .22 caliber cartridge. Interchangeable barrel lengths are 2.5", 4", 5.6", 8", and 10". Adjustable rear sight and interchangeable front sight. Hogue finger groove rubber grips. Weight is 36 oz. for 2.5" barrel and 58 oz. for 10" barrel.

	NIB	EXC.	V.G.	GOOD	FAIR	POOR
	485	375	300	250	200	145

Model 22M/722M

Same as above but chambered for .22 Win. Mag. cartridge.

	NIB	EXC.	V.G.	GOOD	FAIR	POOR
	525	400	300	225	175	145

Model 32/732

Same as above. Chambered for .32 H&R cartridge.

	NIB	EXC.	V.G.	GOOD	FAIR	POOR
	550	425	325	250	195	165

Model 3220/73220

Same as above but chambered for the .32-20 cartridge.

	NIB	EXC.	V.G.	GOOD	FAIR	POOR
	550	425	325	250	195	165

Model 15/715

Same as above but chambered for the .38 Special and .357 Magnum cartridges.

	NIB	EXC.	V.G.	GOOD	FAIR	POOR
	525	400	300	225	175	145

Model 715 (Current Production)

Made from 100 percent stainless steel and chambered in .357 Magnum. Traditional double-action with dual cylinder lockup, six-round capacity, fully adjustable rear sight, transfer bar ignition and

	NIB	EXC.	V.G.	GOOD	FAIR	POOR

interchangeable barrel with ventilated rib. Includes barrel wrench kit. Weight 46 ounces, 6-inch barrel, bright stainless finish. Reintroduced in 2011.

	NIB	EXC.	V.G.	GOOD	FAIR	POOR
	975	850	700	500	350	200

NEW GENERATION LARGE-FRAME SERIES

NOTE: The "7" prefix denotes stainless steel frame and barrel. For models listed add between 4 percent and 9 percent depending on barrel length and for stainless steel.

Model 41/741

This is a large-frame revolver with 6-shot cylinder. Interchangeable barrels in 4", 6", 8", and 10". Adjustable rear sight with interchangeable front sight. Hogue finger grip rubber grips standard. Weight is from 49 oz. for 4" barrel to 69 oz. for 10" barrels.

	575	475	350	225	175	125

Model 44/744

Same as above but chambered for .44 Magnum cartridge.

	575	475	350	225	175	125

Model 45/745

Same as above but chambered for .45 Colt cartridge.

	600	500	375	250	200	125

Model 360/7360

Same as above but chambered for .357 Magnum cartridge.

	575	475	350	225	175	125

Model 460/7460

Same as above but chambered for the .45 ACP, .45 Auto Rim, .45 Super, .45 Win. Mag, or .460 Rowland.

	750	625	500	400	300	200

NEW GENERATION SUPERMAG-FRAME SERIES

NOTE: The "7" prefix denotes stainless steel frame and barrel. For models listed add between 4 percent and 9 percent depending on barrel length and for stainless steel.

Model 40/740

This is a 6-shot revolver chambered for .the .357 Magnum, .357 Super Magnum/Maximum cartridges with interchangeable barrels in 4", 6", 8", or 10" lengths. Adjustable rear sight and interchangeable front sights. Hogue finger groove rubber grips standard. Weight range from 51 oz. for 4" barrel to 76 oz. for 10" barrel.

	1300	1125	850	675	400	250

Model 414/7414

Same as above but chambered for .414 Super Magnum cartridge.

	1300	1125	850	675	400	250

Model 445/7445

Same as above but chambered for .445 Super Mag. cartridge.

	1500	1325	1050	875	550	350

NEW GENERATION COMPENSATED SERIES

NOTE: The "7" prefix denotes stainless steel frame and barrel. For models listed add between 4 percent and 9 percent depending on barrel length and for stainless steel.

Model 15/715

This is a 6-shot revolver that is chambered for the .357 Magnum cartridge and offered with interchangeable barrels in 4", 6", or 10" lengths. Barrels have an integral compensator. Adjustable rear sight and interchangeable front sight. Hogue finger groove rubber grips.

	575	450	325	250	175	100

Model 41/741

Same as above but chambered for .41 Magnum cartridge.

	675	550	425	350	250	125

Model 44/744

Same as above but chambered for .44 Magnum cartridge.

	675	550	425	350	250	125

	NIB	EXC.	V.G.	GOOD	FAIR	POOR

Model 45/745

Same as above but chambered for .45 Colt cartridge.

NIB	EXC.	V.G.	GOOD	FAIR	POOR
675	550	425	350	250	125

Model 360/7360

Same as above but chambered for .357 Magnum on large frame.

NIB	EXC.	V.G.	GOOD	FAIR	POOR
675	550	425	350	250	125

Model 445/7445 (Alaskan Guide)

Chambered for the .445 SuperMag cartridge. Fitted with a 4" heavy ported barrel. Special matte black coating over stainless steel. Introduced in 2002.

NIB	EXC.	V.G.	GOOD	FAIR	POOR
1000	800	675	500	375	250

Model 460/7460

Same as above but chambered for the .45 ACP, .45 Auto Rim, .45 Super, .45 Win. Mag., or the .460 Rowland cartridgs.

NIB	EXC.	V.G.	GOOD	FAIR	POOR
825	650	500	375	200	125

STANDARD SILHOUETTE SERIES

NOTE: All Standard Silhouette series revolvers are stainless steel.

Model 722 VH10

This is a 6-shot revolver chambered for the .22 caliber cartridge. Interchangeable barrel system. Choice of fluted or non-fluted cylinders. Patridge front sight and adjustable rear sight. Hogue finger groove rubber grips standard. Lightweight slotted 8" shroud.

NIB	EXC.	V.G.	GOOD	FAIR	POOR
825	650	500	375	200	125

Model 7360 V8S

Same as above but chambered for the .357 Magnum cartridge.

NIB	EXC.	V.G.	GOOD	FAIR	POOR
825	650	500	375	200	125

Model 741 V8S

Same as above but chambered for the .41 Magnum cartridge with 8" slotted shroud.

NIB	EXC.	V.G.	GOOD	FAIR	POOR
825	650	500	375	200	125

Model 741 V10S

Same as above but with 10" slotted shroud.

NIB	EXC.	V.G.	GOOD	FAIR	POOR
925	750	600	475	300	175

Model 744 V8S

Chambered for .44 Magnum cartridge and fitted with an 8" slotted shroud.

NIB	EXC.	V.G.	GOOD	FAIR	POOR
825	650	500	375	200	125

Model 744 V10S

Same as above but fitted with a 10" slotted shroud.

NIB	EXC.	V.G.	GOOD	FAIR	POOR
925	750	600	475	300	175

Model 740 V8S

Chambered for the .357 Super Mag. and fitted with an 8" slotted shroud.

NIB	EXC.	V.G.	GOOD	FAIR	POOR
925	750	600	475	300	175

Model 7414 V8S

Chambered for the .414 Super Mag and fitted with an 8" slotted shroud.

NIB	EXC.	V.G.	GOOD	FAIR	POOR
925	750	600	475	300	175

Model 7445 V8S

Chambered for the .445 Super Mag. and fitted with an 8" slotted shroud.

NIB	EXC.	V.G.	GOOD	FAIR	POOR
925	750	600	475	300	175

Dan Wesson VH8

.445 SuperMag revolver designed for barrel interchangeability. Also fires standard .44-caliber rounds. Stainless, 6-shot; 8" barrel, 4.1 lb. Single/double action. Introduced 2006.

NIB	EXC.	V.G.	GOOD	FAIR	POOR
1100	950	775	600	450	275

	NIB	EXC.	V.G.	GOOD	FAIR	POOR

SUPER RAM SILHOUETTE SERIES

NOTE: All Super Ram Silhouette series revolvers are stainless steel.

Model 722 VH10 SRS1

This model is chambered for the .22 caliber cartridge and is fitted with a 10" slotted shroud barrel. Interchangeable barrel system. Adjustable Bomar rear sight. Bomar SRS-1 hood front sight. Fluted or non-fluted cylinders. Hogue finger groove rubber grips.

925	750	600	475	300	175

Model 7360 V8S SRS1

Same as above but chambered for .357 Magnum cartridge. Fitted with an 8" slotted shroud.

1100	950	775	600	450	275

Model 741 V8S SRS1

Same as above but chambered for .41 Magnum cartridge and fitted with an 8" slotted shroud.

1100	950	775	600	450	275

Model 741 V10S SRS1

Same as above but fitted with a 10" slotted shroud.

1100	950	775	600	450	275

Model 744 V8S SRS1

Same as above but chambered for the .44 Magnum cartridge and fitted with an 8" slotted shroud.

1100	950	775	600	450	275

Model 744 V10S SRS1

Same as above but fitted with a 10" slotted shroud.

1100	950	775	600	450	275

Model 740 V8S SRS1

Same as above but chambered for .357 Super Mag. and fitted with an 8" slotted shroud.

1200	1050	875	700	550	300

Model 7414 V8S SRS1

Same as above but chambered for .414 Super Mag. and fitted with an 8" slotted shroud.

1200	1050	875	700	550	300

Model 7445 V8S SS1

Same as above but chambered for .445 Super Mag. and fitted with an 8" slotted shroud.

1200	1050	875	700	550	300

PISTOL PACK SERIES

This series consists of a Dan Wesson revolver of the customer's choice with adjustable rear sight and four barrel assemblies in the small-frame calibers (2.5", 4", 6", and 8"); the large frame and supermag frame have three barrel assemblies (4", 6", and 8"). Also included is a cleaning kit, wrench kit, extra exotic wood grips, instruction manual and fitted hard case. Choice of blue or stainless steel finish ("7" prefix).

Model 22/722

Chambered for .22 LR.

1200	1050	875	700	550	300

Model 32/732

Chambered for .32 H&R Magnum.

1200	1050	875	700	550	300

Model 3220/73220

Chambered for the .32-20.

1200	1050	875	700	550	300

Model 15/715

Chambered for the .357 Magnum.

1200	1050	875	700	550	300

Model 41/741

Chambered for the .41 Magnum.

1450	1250	1050	850	650	350

	NIB	EXC.	V.G.	GOOD	FAIR	POOR

Model 44/744
Chambered for the .44 Magnum.

	1450	1250	1050	850	650	350

Model 45/745
Chambered for the .45 Colt.

	1450	1250	1050	850	650	350

Model 460/7460
Chambered for the .45 ACP, .45 Auto Rim, .45 Super, .45 Win. Mag, .460 Rowland.

	1450	1250	1050	850	650	350

Model 40/740
Chambered for the .357 Maximum.

	1650	1300	1150	950	750	450

Model 414/7414
Chambered for the .414 Super Mag.

	1650	1300	1150	950	750	450

Model 445/7445
Chambered for the .445 Super Mag.

	1650	1300	—	—	—	—

HUNTER PACK SERIES
The Hunter Pack comes with a Dan Wesson revolver of the customer's choice with adjustable rear sight and two 8" barrel assemblies, one with open sights and one drilled and tapped with Burris or Weaver mount installed. Extra set of exotic wood grips, wrench kit, cleaning kit, and manual. Offered in blue or stainless steel ("7" prefix).

Model 22/722
Chambered for .22 LR.

	1200	950	—	—	—	—

Model 32/732
Chambered for .32 H&R Magnum.

	1200	950	—	—	—	—

Model 3220/73220
Chambered for .32-20.

	1200	1050	875	700	550	300

Model 15/715
Chambered for .357 Mag.

	1200	1050	875	700	550	300

Model 41/741
Chambered for the .41 Mag.

	1450	1250	1050	850	650	350

Model 44/744
Chambered for the .44 Mag.

	1450	1250	1050	850	650	350

Model 45/745
Chambered for the .45 Colt.

	1450	1250	1050	850	650	350

Model 460/7460
Chambered for the .45 ACP, .45 Auto Rim, .45 Super, .45 Win. Mag., .460 Rowland.

	1450	1250	1050	850	650	350

Model 40/740
Chambered for the .357 Maximum.

	1650	1300	1150	950	750	450

	NIB	EXC.	V.G.	GOOD	FAIR	POOR

Model 414/7414

Chambered for the .414 Super Mag.

1650	1300	1150	950	750	450

Model 445/7445

Chambered for the .445 Super Mag.

1650	1300	1150	950	750	450

PISTOLS

Pointman Major

This is a semi-auto pistol chambered for the .45 ACP cartridge. Many special features including interchangeable front sight, Jarvis match barrel, adjustable rear sight, beveled magazine well, and others. Stainless steel slide and frame. Rosewood checkered grips. Slide serrations both front and rear. A high sighting rib with interchangeable sights. Introduced in 2000.

1200	1050	800	625	500	300

Pointman Seven

Has many of the same features as the Pointman Major with blued slide and frame and no sighting rib.

1100	950	700	525	400	300

Pointman Minor

Same as above except blued slide and frame and no match barrel.

1100	950	700	525	400	300

Pointman Seven Stainless

Same as above with stainless steel frame and slide.

1200	1050	800	625	500	300

Pointman Guardian

This model is fitted with a 4.25" barrel and match trigger group. Adjustable rear sight, plus many other special features. Blued frame and slide with sighting rib.

1200	1050	800	625	500	300

Pointman Guardian Duce

Same as above but with blued steel slide and stainless steel frame.

825	675	525	400	300	175

Pointman Major Australian

Introduced in 2002 this model features a fully adjustable Bomar-style target sight. Unique slide top configuration that features a rounded radius with lengthwise sight serrations. Slide has Southern Cross engraved on right side. Chambered for the .45 ACP cartridge only.

1200	1050	800	625	500	300

Pointman Hi-Cap

This .45 ACP pistol is fitted with a 5" barrel and blued carbon alloy wide-body frame with a 10-round magazine. Fixed rear target sight. Extended thumb safety as well as other special features.

1100	950	700	525	400	300

Pointman Dave Pruitt Signature Series

This pistol is fitted with a 5" match-grade barrel with a rounded top slide with bead blast matte finish. Chevron-style cocking serrations. Fixed rear sight with tactical/target ramp front sight. Many special features.

1100	950	700	525	400	300

RZ-10

10mm single-action semi-auto with 8+1 capacity. 5" barrel, 2.4 lb. Fixed sights. Introduced 2006.

1100	950	700	525	400	300

RZ-45 Heritage

Same as the discontinued RZ-10 except in .45 ACP. The RZ refers to "Razorback" which is based on the serrated Clark-style target rib machined onto the top of the slide. Introduced in 2010.

1100	950	700	525	400	200

	NIB	EXC.	V.G.	GOOD	FAIR	POOR

Guardian

Designed for concealed carry with Bobtail frame. Caliber is .45 ACP with steel slide, alloy frame, Novak Lo-Mount night sights, extended thumb and grip safeties, 8-round magazine and stippled Shadow grips. Weight 28.8 ounces, 4.3-inch barrel and black Duty finish.

NIB	EXC.	V.G.	GOOD	FAIR	POOR
1300	1100	850	600	450	300

Valor

Full-size 1911-style .45 ACP with black ceramic coated or matte stainless finish. Slimline G10 grips, Heinie Ledge Straight-Eight Night Sights.

NIB	EXC.	V.G.	GOOD	FAIR	POOR
1675	1350	1050	800	500	400

Pointman Nine

Full-size 1911-style in 9mm with 9+1 capacity. Front and rear slide serrations, adjustable rear sight, fiber optic front.

NIB	EXC.	V.G.	GOOD	FAIR	POOR
1300	1100	850	600	450	300

PATRIOT SERIES

Patriot Marksman

Introduced in 2002 this .45 ACP pistol has a 5" match grade barrel. Fixed sights. Many special features such as a beveled mag well, lowered and flared ejection port. Checkered wood grips. Magazine capacity is 8 rounds. Weight is about 38 oz.

NIB	EXC.	V.G.	GOOD	FAIR	POOR
795	650	525	400	300	175

Patriot Expert

As above but fitted with a Bomar target-style adjustable rear sight.

NIB	EXC.	V.G.	GOOD	FAIR	POOR
900	750	625	500	400	225

RIFLES

Coyote Target

Chambered for the .22 LR or .22 Magnum cartridge and fitted with an 18.375" heavy bull barrel. Receiver is drilled and tapped for scope mount. Hardwood stock with high comb and flat-bottom fore-end. Magazine capacity is 6 or 10 rounds. **NOTE:** It is unknown whether the Dan Wesson Coyote rifles were ever actually produced; we suspect not. The values shown are based on 2002 suggested retail prices.

NIB	EXC.	V.G.	GOOD	FAIR	POOR
275	—	—	—	—	—

Coyote Classic

This model is also chambered for the .22 LR or .22 Magnum cartridge. Fitted with a 22.75" barrel with open sights. Drilled and tapped for scope mount. Checkered hardwood stock. Magazine capacity is 6 or 10 rounds. Introduced in 2002.

NIB	EXC.	V.G.	GOOD	FAIR	POOR
235	—	—	—	—	—

WESSON FIREARMS CO., INC.
Palmer, Massachusetts

The company was founded in 1968 by Daniel B. Wesson, the great-grandson of D.B. Wesson, co-founder of Smith & Wesson. This line of handguns is unique for its barrel/shroud interchangeability. Dan Wesson revolvers have established themselves as champion metallic silhouette competition guns. The company offers a comprehensive line of handguns for almost every use. The company will also custom build a handgun to customer specifications. Dan Wesson Arms was restructured on January 4, 1991, and identified as Wesson Firearms Company, Inc. Wesson handguns made after this date will be stamped with this new corporate name. In 1995 the company declared bankruptcy. (See WESSON FIREARMS, DAN)

Model 11

A .357 Magnum caliber double-action swing-out cylinder revolver with interchangeable 2.5", 4", or 6" barrels and a 6-shot cylinder. Blued with walnut grips. Manufactured in 1970 and 1971. **NOTE:** Extra barrels add 25 percent per barrel.

NIB	EXC.	V.G.	GOOD	FAIR	POOR
300	275	150	125	100	75

Model 12

As above, with adjustable target sights.

NIB	EXC.	V.G.	GOOD	FAIR	POOR
350	27	200	175	125	100

	NIB	EXC.	V.G.	GOOD	FAIR	POOR

Model 14

As above, with a recessed barrel locking nut and furnished with a spanner wrench. Manufactured from 1971 to 1975.

	350	250	175	150	100	75

Model 15

As above, with adjustable target sights.

	375	275	200	175	125	100

Model 8

As above, in .38 Special caliber.

	325	225	150	125	100	75

Model 9

As the Model 15, with adjustable sights and in .38 Special caliber. Manufactured from 1971 to 1975.

	350	275	200	175	125	100

.22 CALIBER REVOLVERS

Model 22

This is a double-action target revolver chambered for the .22 LR cartridge. It is available in 2", 4", 6", and 8" barrel length with a choice of standard rib shroud, ventilated rib shroud, or ventilated heavy rib shroud. All variations feature an adjustable rear sight, red ramp interchangeable front sight and target grips. Offered in bright blue or stainless steel finish. For revolvers with standard barrel assembly weights are: 2"—36 oz., 4"—40 oz., 6"—44 oz., and 8"—49 oz.

Model 722

Same as above but with stainless steel finish.

Model 22M

Same as above but chambered for .22 Magnum with blued finish.

Model 722M

Same as above but chambered for .22 Magnum with stainless steel finish. **NOTE:** Add 10 percent to prices for stainless steel finish.

Standard Rib Shroud

	375	300	200	150	100	75

Ventilated Rib Shroud

	400	325	225	150	100	75

Ventilated Heavy Rib Shroud

	425	330	240	200	125	100

P22 Pistol Pac

This model is also a target revolver similar to the Model 22 and its variations. Chambered for the .22 LR or .22 Magnum, it is also offered with three types of barrel shrouds: standard, ventilated, or ventilated heavy. It is available in blued or stainless steel finish. The principal feature of the Pistol Pac is the three barrel assemblies in 2.5", 4", 6", and 8" with extra grips, four additional front sights, and a fitted carrying case. **NOTE:** Add 10 percent to prices for stainless steel finish.

Standard Rib Shroud

	750	550	400	350	300	150

Ventilated Rib Shroud

	800	600	500	450	350	150

Ventilated Heavy Rib Shroud

	800	600	500	450	350	150

HP22 Hunter Pac

This model is chambered for the .22 Magnum cartridge. The set includes a ventilated heavy 8" shroud, a ventilated 8" shroud only with Burris scope mounts and Burris scope in either 1.5x4X variable or fixed 2X, a barrel changing tool, and fitted carrying case. Finish is blued or stainless steel. **NOTE:** Hunter Pacs are a special order item and should be evaluated at the time of sale.

NIB	EXC.	V.G.	GOOD	FAIR	POOR

.32 CALIBER REVOLVERS

Model 32

This model is a target revolver chambered for the .32 H&R Magnum cartridge. It is offered in 2", 4", 6", or 8" barrel lengths with choice of rib shrouds. All variations are fitted with adjustable rear sight, red ramp interchangeable front sight, and target grips. Available in blued or stainless steel finish. Weights depend on barrel length and shroud type but are between 35 oz. and 53 oz.

Model 732

Same as above but with stainless steel finish.

Model 322

Same as above but chambered for .32-20 cartridge with blued finish.

Model 7322

Same as above but chambered for .32-20 cartridge with stainless steel finish. **NOTE:** Add 10 percent to prices for stainless steel finish.

Standard Rib Shroud

NIB	EXC.	V.G.	GOOD	FAIR	POOR
475	325	200	150	100	75

Ventilated Rib Shroud

NIB	EXC.	V.G.	GOOD	FAIR	POOR
500	350	225	150	100	75

Ventilated Heavy Rib Shroud

NIB	EXC.	V.G.	GOOD	FAIR	POOR
525	375	250	150	100	75

P32 Pistol Pac

This set offers the same calibers, barrel shrouds, and finishes as the above models but in a set consisting of 2", 4", 6", and 8" barrels with extra grips, four additional sights, and fitted case. **NOTE:** Add 10 percent to prices for stainless steel finish.

Standard Rib Shroud

NIB	EXC.	V.G.	GOOD	FAIR	POOR
1200	1000	650	500	400	300

Ventilated Rib Shroud

NIB	EXC.	V.G.	GOOD	FAIR	POOR
1200	1000	650	500	400	300

Ventilated Heavy Rib Shroud

NIB	EXC.	V.G.	GOOD	FAIR	POOR
1200	1000	650	500	400	300

329HP32 Hunter Pac

This model is chambered for the .32 H&R Magnum or .32-20 cartridge. The set includes a ventilated heavy 8" shroud, a ventilated 8" shroud only with Burris scope mounts and Burris scope in either 1.5x4X variable or fixed 2X, a barrel-changing tool, and fitted carrying case. Finish is blued or stainless steel.**NOTE:** Hunter Pacs are a special order item and should be evaluated at the time of sale.

.357 MAGNUM AND .38 CALIBER REVOLVERS

Model 14

This is a double-action service revolver chambered for the .357 Magnum cartridge. Available with 2", 4", or 6" barrel with service shroud. It has fixed sights, service grip, and is offered in blued or stainless steel finish.

Model 714

Same as above but with stainless steel finish.

Model 8

Same as above but chambered for .38 Special cartridge with blued finish.

Model 708

Same as above but chambered for .38 Special with stainless steel finish. **NOTE:** Add 10 percent to prices for stainless steel finish.

NIB	EXC.	V.G.	GOOD	FAIR	POOR
400	350	250	125	100	75

P14/8 Pistol Pac

This set consists of a 2", 4", and 6" barrel with service shroud and fixed sights. It has an extra grip and fitted carrying case. The P14 is chambered for the .357 Mag. and the P8 is chambered for the .38 Special.

NIB	EXC.	V.G.	GOOD	FAIR	POOR
800	700	600	500	400	300

NIB	EXC.	V.G.	GOOD	FAIR	POOR

Model 15

This model is designed as a double-action target revolver chambered for the .357 Magnum cartridge. It is available with 2", 4", 6", 8", and 10" barrel lengths with standard rib shroud. It features adjustable rear sight, red ramp interchangeable front sight, and target grips. Offered with blued finish. Weights according to barrel length are: 2"-32 oz., 4"-36 oz., 6"-40 oz., 8"-44 oz., 10"-50 oz.

Model 715

Same as above but with stainless steel finish.

Model 9

Same as above but chambered for .38 Special cartridge with blued finish.

Model 709

Same as above but with stainless steel finish. **NOTE:** Add 10 percent to prices for stainless steel finish.

Standard Rib Shroud

NIB	EXC.	V.G.	GOOD	FAIR	POOR
800	700	600	500	400	300

Ventilated Rib Shroud

NIB	EXC.	V.G.	GOOD	FAIR	POOR
800	700	600	500	400	300

Ventilated Heavy Rib Shroud

NIB	EXC.	V.G.	GOOD	FAIR	POOR
800	700	600	500	400	300

330HP15 Hunter Pac

This model is chambered for the .357 Magnum cartridge. The set includes a ventilated heavy 8" shroud, a ventilated 8" shroud only with Burris scope mounts and Burris scope in either 1.5x4X variable or fixed 2X, a barrel changing tool, and fitted carrying case. Finish is blued or stainless steel. **NOTE:** Hunter Pacs are a special order item and should be evaluated at the time of sale.

331Model 40/Supermag

This model is a target revolver chambered for the .357 Maximum cartridge. It has an adjustable rear sight, red ramp interchangeable front sight, ventilated rib shroud, and target grip. Barrel lengths are 4", 6", 8", or 10". A ventilated slotted shroud is available in 8" only. For 1993 a compensated barrel assembly, "CBA," was added to the product line as a complete gun. Finish is blued. Weighs approximately 64 oz. with ventilated rib shroud barrel. Add 20 percent for Model 740 in stainless steel. **NOTE:** Add 10 percent to prices for stainless steel finish. For .357 Supermag with compensated barrel assembly add $30.

Ventilated Rib Shroud

NIB	EXC.	V.G.	GOOD	FAIR	POOR
1100	950	750	600	450	300

Ventilated Slotted Shroud—8" barrel only

NIB	EXC.	V.G.	GOOD	FAIR	POOR
1100	950	750	600	450	300

Ventilated Heavy Rib Shroud

NIB	EXC.	V.G.	GOOD	FAIR	POOR
1100	950	750	600	450	300

332HP40 Hunter Pac

This model is chambered for the .357 Supermag cartridge. The set includes a ventilated heavy 8" shroud, a ventilated 8" shroud only with Burris scope mounts and Burris scope in either 1.5x4X variable or fixed 2X, a barrel changing tool, and fitted carrying case. Finish is blued or stainless steel. **NOTE:** Hunter Pacs are a special order item and should be evaluated at the time of sale.

Model 375

This model, also known as the .375 Supermag, is chambered for the .357 Maximum cartridge, based on the .375 Winchester cartridge. Offered in 6", 8", 10" barrels in ventilated, ventilated heavy, or ventilated slotted rib barrels. Sights are interchangeable and adjustable. Available in bright blue finish only. Weighs approximately 64 oz. with ventilated rib shroud barrel.

Ventilated Rib Shroud

NIB	EXC.	V.G.	GOOD	FAIR	POOR
1100	950	750	600	450	300

Ventilated Heavy Rib Shroud

NIB	EXC.	V.G.	GOOD	FAIR	POOR
1100	950	750	600	450	300

Ventilated Slotted Shroud—8" barrel only

NIB	EXC.	V.G.	GOOD	FAIR	POOR
1100	950	750	600	450	300

P15/9 Pistol Pac

This model is a set with 2", 4", 6", and 8" barrels with standard rib shroud. Chambered for the .357 or .38 Special with standard rib shroud, four additional sights, and extra grip, and carrying

NIB	EXC.	V.G.	GOOD	FAIR	POOR

case. The P15 is chambered for the .357 Mag. while the P9 is chambered for the .38 Special. **NOTE:** Add 10 percent to prices for stainless steel finish.

Standard Rib Shroud

| 800 | 700 | 600 | 500 | 400 | 300 |

Ventilated Rib Shroud

| 800 | 700 | 600 | 500 | 400 | 300 |

Ventilated Heavy Rib Shroud

| 800 | 700 | 600 | 500 | 400 | 300 |

354HP375 Hunter Pac

This model is chambered for the .375 Supermag cartridge. The set includes a ventilated heavy 8" shroud, a ventilated 8" shroud only with Burris scope mounts and Burris scope in either 1.5x4X variable or fixed 2X, a barrel changing tool, and fitted carrying case. Finish is blued or stainless steel. **NOTE:** Hunter Pacs are a special order item and should be evaluated at the time of sale.

.41, .44 MAGNUM, AND .45 LONG COLT REVOLVERS

Model 44

This model is a target double-action revolver chambered for the .44 Magnum. It has 4", 6", 8", or 10" barrels with ventilated rib shrouds. Other features include: adjustable rear sight, red ramp interchangeable front sight, and target grips. Finish is bright blue. Weights with 4" barrel—40 oz., 6"—56 oz., 8"—64 oz., and 10"—69 oz.

Model 744

Same as above but with stainless steel finish.

301Model 41

Same as above but chambered for .41 Magnum with blued finish.

302Model 741

Same as above but with stainless steel finish.

Model 45

Same as above but chambered for .45 Long Colt with bright blue finish.

Model 745

Same as above but with stainless steel finish. **NOTE:** Add 10 percent to prices for stainless steel finish.

Ventilated Rib Shroud

| 1000 | 850 | 550 | 450 | 300 | 200 |

Ventilated Heavy Rib Shroud

| 1000 | 850 | 550 | 450 | 300 | 200 |

P44/P41/P45 Pistol Pac

This set features a 6" and 8" barrel assembly with ventilated rib shroud, an extra grip, two additional front sights, and a fitted carrying case. Chambered for .41 Magnum, .44 Magnum, or .45 Long Colt. **NOTE:** Add 10 percent to prices for stainless steel finish.

Ventilated Rib Shroud

| 1000 | 850 | 550 | 450 | 300 | 200 |

Ventilated Heavy Rib Shroud

| 1000 | 850 | 550 | 450 | 300 | 200 |

357HP41/44 Hunter Pac

This model is chambered for either the .41 or .44 Magnum cartridge. The set includes a ventilated heavy 8" shroud, a ventilated 8" shroud only with Burris scope mounts and Burris scope in either 1.5x4X variable or fixed 2X, a barrel changing tool, and fitted carrying case. Finish is blued or stainless steel. **NOTE:** Hunter Pacs are a special order item and should be evaluated at the time of sale.

359Model 445

This double-action target revolver is chambered for the .445 Supermag cartridge. Barrel lengths offered are 8" with ventilated slotted rib shroud, 8" ventilated heavy slotted rib shroud, or 10" ventilated slotted rib shroud. Barrel lengths are also available in 4", 6", 8", and 10" with choice of ventilated rib or ventilated heavy rib shrouds. Introduced in 1993 is a compensated barrel assembly available as a complete gun. This is designated the "CBA." Fitted with adjustable rear

	NIB	EXC.	V.G.	GOOD	FAIR	POOR

sights, red ramp interchangeable front sight, and target grips. Finish is bright blue. Typical weight with 8" ventilated rib shroud barrel is about 62 oz.

Model 7445

Same as above but with stainless steel finish. **NOTE:** Add 10 percent to prices for stainless steel finish. For .44 Magnum and .445 Supermag with compensated barrel assembly add $30.

Ventilated Rib Shroud

1100	950	750	600	450	300

Ventilated Heavy Rib Shroud

1100	950	750	600	450	300

Model 7445 Alaskan Guide Special

This limited edition model (only 500 were produced) is chambered for the .445 Supermag cartridge. It features a 4" ventilated heavy compensated shroud barrel assembly, synthetic grips, and a matte black titanium nitride finish. Overall barrel length is 5.5" and the revolver weighs 56 oz.

950	700	600	350	200	100

HP455 Hunter Pac

This model is chambered for the .445 Supermag cartridge. The set includes a ventilated heavy 8" shroud, a ventilated 8" shroud only with Burris scope mounts and Burris scope in either 1.5x4X variable or fixed 2X, a barrel changing tool, and fitted carrying case. Finish is blued or stainless steel. **NOTE:** Hunter Pacs are a special order item and should be evaluated at the time of sale.

FIXED BARREL HANDGUNS

Model 38P

This model is a 5-shot double-action revolver designed for the .38 Special cartridge. Barrel is 2.5" with fixed sights. Choice of wood or rubber grips. Finish is blued. Weighs 24.6 oz.

350	225	150	125	100	75

Wesson Firearms Silhouette .22

This model is a 6-shot .22 LR single-action-only revolver with a 10" barrel. Fitted with compact-style grips, narrow notch rear sight with choice of ventilated or ventilated heavy rib shroud. Finish is blued or stainless steel. Weighs 55 oz. with ventilated rib shroud and 62 oz. with ventilated heavy rib shroud. **NOTE:** Add 10 percent to prices for stainless steel finish.

Ventilated Rib Shroud

495	325	275	200	150	100

Ventilated Heavy Rib Shroud

495	350	285	200	150	100

Model 738P

Same as above but with stainless steel finish.

525	350	285	200	150	100

Model 45/745 Pin Gun

This model uses a .44 Magnum frame with 5" barrel with two-stage compensator. Choice of ventilated or ventilated heavy rib shroud configuration. Chambered for .45 ACP with or without half moon clips. Finish is blued or stainless steel. Weighs 54 oz. **NOTE:** Add 10 percent to prices for stainless steel finish.

Ventilated Rib Shroud

1100	950	750	600	450	300

Ventilated Heavy Rib Shroud

1100	950	750	600	450	300

Model 14/714 Fixed Barrel Service

Same features as the .357 Magnum Model 14 without the interchangeable barrels. Barrel length are either 2.5" or 4" with fixed sights. Offered in either blued or stainless steel. Weighs 30 oz. with 2.5" barrel and 34 oz. with 4" barrel. **NOTE:** Add 10 percent to prices for stainless steel finish.

275	235	150	125	100	75

	NIB	EXC.	V.G.	GOOD	FAIR	POOR

Model 15/715 Fixed Barrel Target

Same as the .357 Magnum Model 15 with target sights and grips. Fixed barrel lengths are either 3" or 5". Available in blued or stainless steel. Weighs 37 oz. with 3" barrel and 42 oz. with 5" barrel. **NOTE:** Add 10 percent to prices for stainless steel finish.

300	250	160	125	100	75

WESTERN ARMS

See—Bacon Arms Co.

WESTERN ARMS CORPORATION

See—Ithaca Gun Co.

WESTERN FIELD
Montgomery Ward

"Western Field" is the trade name used by Montgomery Ward & Company on arms that they retail. See Firearms Trade Names List at the end of this book.

WESTLEY RICHARDS & CO., LTD.
Birmingham, England

A wide variety of firearms have been produced by this company since its founding. Presently, it produces boxlock and sidelock double-barrel shotguns of both side-by-side and over/under form, bolt-action rifles and double-barrel rifles. Prospective purchasers are advised to secure individual appraisals prior to acquisition.

B Model SxS Boxlock, Pre-WWII

NOTE: Add 50 percent for 20 gauge, 80 percent for 28 gauge.

5000	4250	3500	2800	—	—

Best Quality Sidelock, Current Model

30000	26500	22500	17500	—	—

Magazine Rifle

12500	10000	8500	7250	—	—

Boxlock Double Rifle

39000	33000	26500	22000	—	—

Best Quality Over/Under Shotgun, Current Model

55000	47500	40000	32000	—	—

WHITE, ROLLIN
Lowell, Massachusetts

Pocket Pistol

A .32 or .38 rimfire spur trigger single-shot pistol with a 3" or 5" octagonal barrel. Brass or iron frames with walnut grips. The .38 caliber version with the 5" barrel was not produced in large quantities and therefore is worth approximately 25 percent more than the values listed. The barrels are marked "Rollin White Arms Co., Lowell, Mass."

—	—	900	750	350	150

Pocket Revolver

A .22 caliber spur trigger revolver with a 3.25" octagonal barrel and 7-shot cylinder. The brass frame silver-plated, barrel blued and grips of walnut. This revolver was marked in a variety of ways including "Rollin White Arms Co., Lowell, Mass.," "Lowell Arms Co., Lowell, Mass.," or "Made for Smith & Wesson by Rollin White Arms Co., Lowell, Mass." Approximately 10,000 were made during the late 1860s.

—	—	775	600	250	75

WHITNEY ARMS COMPANY
ELI WHITNEY, SR./P. & E.W. BLAKE/ELI WHITNEY, JR.

As the United States' first major commercial arms maker, Eli Whitney's New Haven plant, which began production in 1798 and continued under family control for the next 90 years, was one of the more important American arms manufactories of the 19th century. Its products, accordingly, are eminently collectible. Moreover, during its 90 years of operation, the Whitney clan produced a number of unusual arms, some exact copies of regulation U.S. martial longarms, others variations and derivatives of U.S. and foreign longarms, a variety of percussion revolvers, and finally a variety of single-shot and repeating

	NIB	EXC.	V.G.	GOOD	FAIR	POOR

breechloading rifles in an attempt to capture a portion of the burgeoning market in these cartridge arms during the post-Civil War period. Contrary to the prevailing myth, Eli Whitney, Sr., who also invented the cotton gin, did NOT perfect a system of interchangeability of parts in the arms industry. His contributions in this line were more as a propagandist for the concept that was brought to fruition by others, notably Simeon North and John Hall.

Eli Whitney, Sr. Armory Muskets, 1798-1824. 1798 U.S. Contract Muskets, Types I-IV

On 14 January 1798, Eli Whitney, Sr., having convinced the U.S. War Department that he could mass-produce interchangeable parts muskets, was awarded a contract for 10,000 muskets following the "Charlesville" (French M1766) pattern, then also being copied at the newly opened Springfield Armory and most of the U.S. musket contractors. Whitney's 1798 contract muskets measure between 58-7/8" and 57-3/4" in overall length, with the longer arms delivered earlier. The .69-caliber smoothbore barrels measure approximately 44", though most are shy of that length by anywhere from 1/16" to a maximum of 1-1/4". Lockplates are flat with a beveled edge and are marked "U.STATES" in a curve on the pointed tail and with a perched eagle with down folded wings over "NEW HAVEN" forward of the cock. Four differences in the material and manner of attachment of the pan distinguish the subtypes. The first deliver of 500 muskets in September of 1801 had an integral, faceted iron pan (Type I); the second delivery of 500 muskets in June of 1802 also had faceted iron pans, but were detachable (Type II). The 1,000 muskets delivered in September of 1802 and March of 1803 had faceted, detachable pans, but these were made of brass instead of iron (Type III). The final 8,000 muskets, delivered between 1803 and 1809, had detachable brass pans with a rounded bottom that Whitney copied from the French M1777 musket (Type IV) and a rounded cock, also copied from the French M1777 musket. Generally speaking, due to the limited production of Types I - III, they should command a higher price; prices are given for the more common Type IV 1798 contract musket. It should be noted however, that about 1804 Whitney delivered 112 Type IV muskets to Connecticut's "1st Company of Governor's Foot Guards." Although similar to the Type IV musket, these 112 arms are distinguished by the absence of the "U.STATES" on the tail of the lock and the addition of the name "CONNECTICUT" to the left side plate. Such an arm should demand a considerable premium over the usual Type IV musket.

—	—	7500	4500	2000	500

Whitney Connecticut, New York, and U.S. 1812 Contract Muskets

In 1808, Whitney received a contract from the state of New York for 2,000 muskets. In 1810, he received a second contract from the same source for an additional 2,000 muskets, all of which were eventually delivered by mid-1813. In the interim, in 1809, the state of Connecticut contracted with Whitney to deliver 700 muskets per year over the next three years. With the outbreak of the War of 1812, in July of 1812, a contract was let to Eli Whitney for 15,000 muskets (later extended by another 3,000 muskets), conforming to the pattern he had made for the state of New York, but with 42"-long barrels. All of these contract muskets shared most of the same features. Overall length was 58". The .69-caliber smoothbore barrel was nominally 42", though the two state contracts did not rigidly enforce that dimension. The lockplate of these muskets bore the inscription "NEW HAVEN" within a curving scroll forward of the cock. Like the Type III 1798 U.S. contract muskets, the lockplates incorporated a detachable round-bottomed brass pan and a round faced cock. The stock was distinguished by having a low, virtually nonexistent comb similar to that of the 1816 musket pattern. The New York state contract muskets are distinguished by having the state ownership mark "SNY" on the axis of the barrel near the breech. (It should be noted that the first 1,000 muskets delivered under the U.S. 1812 contract were also delivered to New York, but these have the mark across the breech at right angles to the axis of the barrel.) The Connecticut contract muskets are distinguishable by having the state-ownership mark "S.C." (for "state of Connecticut" on the barrel and the top of the comb of the stock. On Connecticut muskets in better condition, the Connecticut coat of arms (a shield with three clusters of grape vines) should also be visible struck into the wood on the left side of the musket opposite the lock. Verifiable Connecticut and New York contract muskets should bring a premium over the U.S. contract muskets.

—	—	6000	3250	1500	500

Whitney (and P. & E.W. Blake) U.S. M1816/1822 Contract Muskets

The U.S. M1816/1822 muskets manufactured at Whitney's Armory were identical to those produced at the U.S. Armories at Springfield and Harpers Ferry. The overall length was 57-3/4". The 42"-long, .69-caliber smoothbore barrels were finished with a browning solution until 1831; after that date the metal was left in the polished "bright." The stock and the lock reflect Whitney's earlier attempts impart his design elements into the U.S. patterns. The stock had the low comb of his M1812 musket and the lock incorporated the rounded cock and round bottomed brass pan that he had championed from the French M1777 musket. The lock markings varied during the period that the arm was produced, though all were marked on the pointed tail with the vertical stamp: "NEW HAVEN" arced around the date (1825-1830), or in three vertical lines: "NEW / HAVEN / (date: 1831-1842)." Those made between 1825 and 1830 under the direct supervision of Whitney's nephews bore the two line mark "U.S. / P. & E.W. BLAKE" forward of the cock; those made from 1830 to 1837 bear the "U.S" over "E. WHITNEY" with a crossed arrow and olive branch between; after 1837 the crossed arrow and olive branch motif was eliminated in favor of the simple two lines. In addition to the Whitney Armory's federal contracts, Whitney executed at least one contract with the state of South Carolina in the mid-1830s for an estimated 800 to 2,000 muskets. Basically identical in

NIB	EXC.	V.G.	GOOD	FAIR	POOR

configuration to the federal contract muskets, the South Carolina muskets were distinguished by the substitution of "S.C." for "U.S." over the "E. WHITNEY" stamp of the lockplate. They also bear the state ownership mark "So. CAROLINA" on the top of the barrel. Due to their relative rarity and Confederate usage (especially if altered to percussion by means of a brazed bolster), the South Carolina contract arms should bring a considerable premium.

—	—	6500	3500	1500	500

Whitney Armory U.S. M1816/M1822 Muskets, Flintlock or Altered to Percussion and Adapted with "Sea Fencible" Heavy Buttplates

A number of the Whitney U.S. M1816/M1822 muskets were delivered to the Commonwealth of Massachusetts under the terms of the 1808 Militia Act. Many of these were subsequently altered to percussion at the Watertown Arsenal near Boston for the state after 1850. At some time in their career both some of the flintlock arms and those that had been altered to percussion were adapted to a heavy brass buttplate with a peculiar knob at its heel. In the process the buttstock was usually narrowed to conform to the width of the new buttplate. Because many of the muskets encountered with this buttplate bore the inspection mark of Samuel Fuller ("SF/V" within a lozenge), these arms were initially considered to have been made for the Massachusetts "Sea Fencible" organizations formed during and after the War of 1812. That appellation, however, has been dismissed, although the exact purpose of the new buttplate and the date of its application are not known. These butt-plates are usually (but not necessarily) found on Whitney contract muskets and invariably are marked with the Massachusetts state ownership mark "MS" on the barrel as well as rack numbers on the tang of the buttplate itself. Despite the unknown purpose of these arms, they command a considerable premium over standard flintlock or altered to percussion Whitney muskets.

—	—	6500	3500	1250	400

Whitney Armory U.S. M1816/M1822 Muskets, Altered to Percussion

From 1850 through 1856, many of the contract muskets in store at the U.S. arsenals were altered from flintlock to percussion by means of the "Belgian" or "cone-in barrel" method. The system of alteration involved the removal of the flintlock battery from the lock, filing in the screw holes from those parts, substituting a percussion hammer for the cock, plugging the vent, removing the breech plug so as to "upset" the upper, right-hand side top of the barrel, drilling and threading the "upset" section for a cone, reinserting the breech plug, and screwing in a new percussion cone. The percussioned musket was effective but the barrel was considerably weakened by the process, and while some were rifled during the American Civil War, most saw service in that conflict as smoothbores. As a general rule, the muskets so altered generally command about one-third the price of the arm in original flintlock. Exceptions are those with state ownership marks (eg. "OHIO" in the stock), with regimental marks, or with the so-called "Sea Fencible" buttplate.

Whitney Armory Muskets, 1825-1842

Eli Whitney died in 1825. Although he had a son destined to take over the family business, Eli Whitney, Jr. was only 5 years old when his father passed away and could not assume legal possession until he turned 21 in 1842. In the interim, the company was administered by the senior Whitney's trustees, Henry Edwards and James Goodrich, while the plant itself was run by Whitney's nephews, Philo and Eli Whitney Blake. During their control of the factory, three contracts were fulfilled for the U.S. government, one awarded in August of 1822 for 15,000 muskets (delivered between 1826 and 1830), a second awarded in March of 1830 for 8,750 muskets (delivered between 1831 and 1836) and a final contract in January of 1840 for 3,000 muskets (delivered between 1840 and 1842). An additional 6,750 were delivered under annual allotments granted by the War Department between 1835 and 1839 over and above the contracts for distribution to the states under the 1808 Militia Act. Although the 1840 contract had originally called for U.S. M1840 muskets, in April of that year, the contract was altered so that Whitney's plant could continue to deliver what it had delivered consistently from 1824, the U.S. M1816/1822 flintlock musket.

Eli Whitney, Jr. Armory Rifles and Rifle-Muskets, 1842-1865

Upon reaching the age of 21 in 1842, Eli Whitney, Jr. assumed command of his late father's gun making empire. Although he realized that the armory required updating to meet the improved tolerances adopted by the U.S. War Department, he also realized that a profit might be made in turning out arms of lesser standards for independent sale to the militia or the states. As a result, the younger Whitney's product line included not only several of the regulation U.S. longarms, but also a number of "good and serviceable" militia arms, including:

Whitney U.S. M1841 Contract Rifle (unaltered)

Between 1842 and 1855 Eli Whitney, Jr. received five contracts from the U.S. War Department to manufacture the newly adopted U.S. M1841 percussion rifle: 7,500 on October of 1842 (delivered between 1844 and 1847), 7,500 in March of 1844, subsequently extended to 10,000 in January of 1849 (delivered between 1849 and 1853) 5,000 (previously contracted for by Edward K. Tryon) in October of 1848 (delivered contiguous with the 1848 contract for 10,000), 5,000 in 1853 (delivered between 1853 and 1855), and 100 in 1855 (delivered that year). All except the final 1,100 delivered in 1855 conformed to the model made at Harpers Ferry, and of those 1,100,

	NIB	EXC.	V.G.	GOOD	FAIR	POOR

the only difference of 500 of them was the ramrod. This rifle was 49" in length, overall, having a 33" long browned barrel with .54 caliber rifled (7 groove) bore. The barrel bears the stamp of inspection at the breech, usually "U S /(inspectors' initials) / P," while the left flat (after mid-1848 for Whitney rifles) should also bear the stamping "STEEL" to indicate that the barrel had been rolled from "cast steel." Furniture is brass, the buttplate bearing the stamped letters, "U S." The lockplate is flat with a beveled edge and bears the horizontal two line inscription "E. WHITNEY" / "U S" forward of the hammer and the vertical, two line inscription "N. HAVEN" / (date) on the tail. (The date also appears on the breech plug tang). As originally made, the M1841 rifle was not adapted for a bayonet, though several modifications were made to the rifle between 1855 and 1862 to affect that adaptation.

		7500	4750	1750	500
—	—				

Whitney U.S. M1841/1855 Contract Rifle, Adapted to Saber Bayonet and Long Range Sights

Before the final 600 rifles (of the 2,600 made in 1855) left the factory, the U.S. War Department contracted with Whitney to bring them up to the standards of the modified U.S. M1841 rifle then being produced or adapted at the Harpers Ferry Armory. The adaptation was two fold. First, a long range rear "ladder" style rear sight, having a 2-1/4" base was soldered to the top of the barrel; then a 1/2" long bayonet lug with 1" guide was brazed to the right side of the barrel, 2-1/2" from the muzzle. To permit disassembly, the old front band was removed and replaced with a shortened version. A new ramrod (also applied to 500 rifles without this adaptation), having an integral iron head cupped for the newly adopted "Minie ball" replaced the flat brass headed ramrod to complete the process; the rifle remained in .54 caliber with 7 grooves. Neither was the front sight modified. Bayonets were furnished by the Ames Manufacturing Company on a separate contract. Rifles so adapted at the Whitney Armory are among the rarer variants of the U.S. M1841 line and prices reflect that rarity.

		7500	4750	1750	650
—	—				

Whitney U.S. M1841 Contract Rifles, Adapted to Saber Bayonets and Long Range Rear Sights (Colt 1862 Adaptation)

A large number of unaltered U.S. M1841 rifles remained on hand in U.S. Arsenals when the Civil War broke out, primarily those of Whitney's and Robbins & Lawrence's manufacture. To upgrade these rifles, revolver maker, Samuel Colt arranged to purchase 10,500 and adapt them to bayonets and long-range sights. The sight that he affixed consisted of the two leaf rear sight he had been using on his revolving rifles, with one leaf flopping forward and one flopping backward from the 100 yard block. The saber bayonet lug he attached consisted of a blued clamping ring with integral 1/2"-long lug attached that could fastened to the barrel so that the lug projected from the right side. These lugs were numbered both to the bayonet and the rifle's barrel, the number appearing on the lower surface of the barrel just behind the location of the clamping ring. Colt also bored the rifles up to .58 caliber, leaving some with 7 grooves but rerifling others with 3 wide grooves. An estimated half of the 10,200 rifles so modified by Colt were of Whitney's earlier production. Due to the Colt association, rifles so modified usually command slightly higher prices than other Civil War adaptations for saber or socket bayonets.

		7500	4750	1750	650
—	—				

Whitney South Carolina Contract M1841 Rifle

To meet the perceived needs of South Carolina during the anti-slavery debates following the Mexican War Annexation, Whitney produced a variant of the U.S. M1841 rifle for that state, delivering only 274 in 1849. The marking of this rifle differed only in having the letters "S C" on the plate beneath the "E. WHITNEY" stamp. Because South Carolina had previously contracted for 1,000 variant M1841 rifles from William Glaze & Co. in 1853 which accepted a socket bayonet, Whitney provided the 274 1849 dated rifles with that provision also, although the lug was located under the barrel instead of atop it. Because the socket bayonet dominated the forward 3" of the barrel, the front sight was relocated to the top of the upper strap of the front band. Rifles from this contract are exceedingly rare.

		10000	6500	3250	950
—	—				

Whitney "Good & Serviceable" M1841 Derivatives

From parts or entire rifles rejected for his federal contracts for U.S. M1841 rifles, between 1848 and 1860, Eli Whitney, Jr. assembled a number of rifles similar in overall characteristics to the federal contract rifles but differing both in quantity and in a number of minor details. At least four variations were produced between 1855 and 1862 and sold to various states or independent militia companies. Distinguishing characteristics of these four are:

Type I. M1841 rifle adapted to saber bayonet but not to long range sights. A 1/2" long saber bayonet lug (either with or without the 1" guide) brazed to the right side of the barrel; long front band replaced with short double strapped band left over from 1855 contract. Some of this type (without 1" guide) are known with "OHIO" state ownership marks and are thought to be from among the 420 purchased by the state in 1861 from Schuyler, Hartley, & Graham. Examples are

	NIB	EXC.	V.G.	GOOD	FAIR	POOR

known with the lockplate dated 1855 and without any date or "US" stamp below "E. WHITNEY."

Type II. M1841 rifle adapted to saber bayonet and Sharps long range sight.

These rifles also bear the 1/2" brazed saber bayonet lug (with the 1" guide) and the short front band, but they also have a Sharps M1853 "ladder" rear sight added in lieu of the standard notched iron block. Moreover, rifles in this configuration lack the brass patchbox lid and its underlying cavity for implements and greased patches.

Type III. M1841 rifle adapted to socket bayonet and Sharps long range sight.

These late-production (1859-1860) derivatives of the M1841 rifle are adapted to the Sharps long-range sight used on the Type II. rifles but have a patch box. Unlike standard production, however, it is covered with an iron lid and hingle. The trigger guard strap is also iron. Lock plates delete both the date from the tail and the "US" under "E. WHITNEY." An iron stud is added below the barrel near the muzzle for a socket bayonet, necessitating the relocation of the brass blade front sight to the upper strap of the forward band. Probably fewer than 100 of this configuration were made, making it the most desirable of the derivative M1841 rifles.

Type IV. M1841 rifle unadapted using modified parts.

Rifles of this configuration use the same markings as the type III rifles but delete entirely the patch box and its lid (like the type II rifles). The trigger guard strap is iron and the lock screws seem to be the same as Whitney used for his Whitney short Enfield derivative rifles. It is suspected that these rifles were purchased from New York dealers and sold to Georgia during the secession crisis of 1860-1861, thereby enhancing their collector's value, though in general Whitney M1841 derivative rifles are equal in pricing:

—	—	6500	3250	1250	500

Whitney M1842 Rifled Musket Derivative

Using rejected U.S. M1842 barrels sold at auction by the Springfield Armory, Whitney assembled approximately 2,000 .69 caliber rifled muskets that he exchanged with the state of New Hampshire in 1858 for a number of old flintlock muskets owned by that state. These rifled muskets exhibit a number of anomalies from the U.S. M1842 musket, although overall length (57-3/4") and the barrel length (42") remain the same as that musket, the bores are rifles with 7 narrow grooves, and in addition to the dates and inspection marks placed at Springfield usually bear the state ownership mark "NEW HAMPSHIRE" on the top of the barrel. In finishing these rifled muskets, Whitney utilized a number of parts from other gun makers, including Sharps M1853 "ladder" style carbine rear sights, bands from the Robbins & Lawrence P1853 Enfield rifle-musket contract, and internal lock parts remaining from his M1841 rifles. Parts that are unique to these muskets include the iron nosecap and the flat lockplate. The lockplates are unmarked, but the barrels usually show a letter/number code common to Whitney's production during this period. Despite a production of approximately 2,000 muskets, the survival rate for this type of arm is quite low.

—	—	6500	3250	1250	400

Whitney P1853 "Long Enfield" Rifle-Musket Derivative

Having secured a number of bands and other furniture from the Robbins & Lawrence contract for P1853 Enfield rifle-muskets, about 1859 Whitney developed a derivative of that arm that combined those bands with a 40"-barrel .58 caliber, rifled with 7 grooves that basically resembled the configuration of the U.S. M1855 rifle-musket, a copy of which Whitney was also making. The 56"-long rifle-musket that resulted was sold to state militia companies and two states, Maryland purchasing 2,000 and Georgia contracting for 1,700 (of which 1,225 were delivered). Although several of the components of the furniture were from the Robbins & Lawrence contract, the nosecap was pewter (Enfield style), and the iron buttplate and brass trigger guard bow/iron strap were of a style peculiar to Whitney' Enfield series. The rear sight resembled the ladder pattern of the U.S. M1855 rifle musket. The unique flat, unbeveled lockplate simply bears the one line stamp, "E. WHITNEY" forward of the hammer.

—	—	6500	3250	1250	600

Whitney P1853 "Short Enfield" Rifle Derivative

Total production of these rifles is estimated to have been between 800 and 1,000, with approximately half of the number going to southern states. Prices should not vary between the four types; however, confirmed Confederate usage will increase the value significantly.

Type IV. Identical to Type III but with a new single leaf rear sight on a 1-1/4" long base.

—	—	8500	4250	2000	600

Whitney M1855 Rifle Derivative

At the same time that Whitney advertised his Enfield derivative series of rifle-muskets and rifles, he also indicated the availability of a short rifle with saber bayonet. This rifle combined rejected barrels made at Harpers Ferry in 1858 for the U.S. M1855 rifles with rejected, unmilled Maynard tape primer lockplates that had been shaved of their top "hump," marked forward of the hammer with the single line stamp, "E. WHITNEY." The buttplate and the trigger guard also conform to that of the U.S. M1855 rifle, but the bands are brass, remaining from Whitney's M1841/1855 rifle contract. Early in production these rifles used round brass lock screw washers following the M1855 pattern; later production used the winged brass lock screw washers that Whitney inherited from

NIB	EXC.	V.G.	GOOD	FAIR	POOR

the Robbins & Lawrence P1853 rifle-musket contract and which he used on his Enfield series derivatives. At least two patterns of saber bayonet were used on this rifle.

—	—	7000	3500	1250	500

Whitney M1855 Rifle-Musket Derivative

In 1861, Whitney accepted a U.S. contract to produce 40,000 U.S. "M1855" rifle-muskets. What Whitney had in mind under this contract and what the War Department demanded were two different arms. Whitney's product was similar to the U.S. M1855 rifle-musket but differed in a number of respects. The 40" barrel was .58 caliber but was rifled with 7 rather than 3 grooves and was adapted to the English P1853 socket bayonet he had been using on his Enfield derivative rifle-muskets. The initial rear sight, while similar to the U.S. M1855 type, was slightly shorter, having a 2-5/16" base. (On later production, Whitney substituted a shorter, 1-1/4"-long base with a single, pierced leaf sight.) The nosecap, moreover, was made of pewter and followed the Enfield pattern rather than being malleable iron of the U.S. M1855 pattern. On later production, Whitney also substituted brass winged lock screw washers from his Enfield derivative series. The lockplates for these arms were drawn from complete Maynard locks made at the federal armories in 1858 and 1859 but later rejected for flaws. Upon these plates Whitney stamped "E. WHITNEY / N. HAVEN," as on his early Connecticut contract M1861 derivative rifle-muskets. Except for the letter/number code, the barrels are unmarked. Examples are known whose stocks bear indications of issue to the 8th Connecticut Infantry during the Civil War, suggesting Whitney may have sold the few made to Connecticut under his first state contract. Arms with these regimental marks should command a premium over unmarked arms.

—	—	7000	3500	1250	500

Whitney M1861 Connecticut Contract Rifle-Musket Derivative

In 1861 and 1862, Eli Whitney, Jr. entered into two contracts with his home state of Connecticut for respectively 6,000 and 8,000 rifle-muskets generally conforming to the U.S. M1861 rifle musket. A number of exceptions to the U.S. model, however, were permitted. On the first contract, the 40" barrels were in .58 caliber but were made with 7 groove rifling instead of 3 groove; on the second contract, the arms were made with 3-groove rifling. Nosecaps for both contracts were of the U.S. M1855/1861 pattern but were cast in pewter instead of malleable iron. An exception was also permitted in the rear sights, which initially were the same 1-1/4" long base with pierced single leaf that Whitney had used on his Type IV short Enfield derivative rifles, though later the base was changed to conform to the pattern adopted for the U.S. M1861 rifle-musket but still retaining the single leaf. Lockplates were M1861-style, marked forward of the hammer "E. WHITNEY / N. HAVEN" on early production and with an eagle surmounting a panoply of flags and trophies over "WHITNEYVILLE" on later production. The barrels bore the typical Whitney letter/number code and were adapted to the Enfield pattern socket bayonets rather than the U.S. M1855 socket bayonets. Later production occasionally bears the inspection letters "G.W.Q."

—	—	6000	2750	1150	400

Whitney "High Humpback" Lockplate M1861 Rifle-Musket Derivative

With the completion of his Connecticut contracts, Whitney combined the excess parts from its production with some of the unmilled and unshaved lockplates that he still had on hand from his M1855 Rifle Derivatives. The 56"-long rifle-muskets that resulted have 40" barrels in .58 caliber with 3-groove rifling and a rear sight that conforms to the U.S. M1861 pattern that Whitney began making in 1863. The flat, beveled unmilled lockplates bear the two line stamp "E. WHITNEY / N. HAVEN" that Whitney had used on his M1855 rifle-musket derivative and on the early M1861 Connecticut contract rifle-muskets, but showing considerable wear, to the extent that the second line is often incomplete or missing entirely. Photograph evidence indicates that the 21st Connecticut Infantry received some of these rifle-muskets. They are often mistaken as a southern purchase, which artificially raises the asking prices.

—	—	7000	3250	1250	500

Whitney "Manton" M1861 Rifle-Musket Derivative

In order to dispose of some of his inferior arms from the second Connecticut state contract, Whitney assembled at least 1,300 bearing a fictitious Old English lock stamp "Manton" forward of the hammer and the date "1862" on its tail. In most respects this arm resembled the U.S. M1861 rifle musket, complete with 3-groove rifling in its .58-caliber, 40" barrel with typical Whitney letter/number code near the muzzle (and often also marked "G.W.Q. on its left flat). Nosecaps, in typical Whitney style, were case from pewter instead of being formed from malleable iron. The rear sight closely follows the M1861 pattern but lacks the step on its side walls since it utilized a simple pierced leaf instead of the compound double leaf of the M1861 rifle-musket. These arms were disposed of in the New York City market after the 1863 Draft Riot and issued to the New York National Guard.

—	—	8250	4250	2000	600

Whitney "Direct Vent" M1861 Rifle-Musket Derivatives

In his continued efforts to dispose of surplus and rejected parts from his Connecticut and federal contracts, Whitney devised in 1863 a rifle-musket generally conforming to the M1861 rifle-musket except in two notable features. The bolster, instead of projecting considerably away from the barrel and having a clean-out screw was relatively short and flat faced. The process of making

	NIB	EXC.	V.G.	GOOD	FAIR	POOR

this bolster eliminated one production sequence, since it was not possible to drill the hole for the cone directly to the barrel. To accommodate the new cone position, the lockplates were made flat, without the bevel, and inletted flush with the stock. Lockplates bear the eagle surmounting the panoply of flags and trophies over "WHITNEYVILLE" stamp forward of the hammer, and are known with "1863" on the tail or without any date. The rear sight is the same as used on the "Manton" rifle-musket derivative. Arms with barrels than 40", 39", and 30" exist, all in .58 caliber with 3-groove rifling; however, the shortest of these may be post-war modifications for cadet use. Quantities made are not known, but surviving examples suggest limited production, probably to use faulty parts from the 1863 federal contract.

—	—	7000	3250	1250	400

Whitney U.S. M1861 Contract Rifle-Musket

In October of 1863, Whitney secured a contract with the U.S. War Department to produce 15,000 U.S. M1861 rifle-muskets. The arms manufactured under this contract conform in all respects to the Springfield Model adopted in 1861. The 40" barrel is in .58 caliber and rifled with 3 grooves; its rear sight conforms to the two-leaf model with stepped side walls. Nosecap is M1861 style and made of malleable iron. Socket bayonets furnished with them conform to the U.S. M1855/ M1861 pattern. Marks include "US" on buttplate and standard inspection marks on barrel and stock. Lockplate marked with eagle surmounting letters "US" forward of the hammer and "WHITNEYVILLE" on the forward projection of the plate; date, "1863" or "1864" stamped on tail of the plate.

—	—	7000	3250	1250	400

Whitney U.S. Navy Contract Rifle

In July of 1861, Whitney entered a contact with the U.S. Navy to produce 10,000 rifles of the "Plymouth Pattern." So called after the U.S. Navy warship whereupon the first Harpers Ferry trial rifles had been developed, the new Navy rifle borrowed many of its characteristics from the French M1846 "carbine a tige." Overall length was 50" with a 34"-long barrel bearing a saber bayonet lug with guide extending nearly to the muzzle on its right side. The bore was .69 caliber, rifled with three broad lands and grooves. The rear sight copied the French M1846 and M1859 styles, i.e. it has an elevating ladder but no sidewalls. On early production the sights are serially numbered to the rifle's serial number (appearing on the breech plug tang). Barrels bear the standard U.S. inspection marks on the left quarter flat and the production date ("1863" or "1864") on the top of the barrel near the breech. Two lock markings have been encountered. The earlier production uses flat beveled plate marked with the date "1863" on its tail and an eagle surmounting a panoply of flags and trophies over the name "WHITNEYVILLE." In later (after serial no. 3,000) the lock's tail is marked "1864" and the stamping forward of the hammer matches that on the U.S. M1861 Whitney contract rifle-muskets, i.e. a small eagle over "U S" and "WHITNEYVILLE" in the forward projection of the plate. Inspector's initials (F.C.W.) appear on the barrel and in a cartouche on the stock.

—	—	8250	4250	1750	600

The Whitney Arms Company, 1865-1888

With the close of the American Civil War, Eli Whitney, Jr. again turned his eyes to the manufacture of inexpensive arms from parts remaining on hand from his Civil War contracts. Extra barrels were turned into inexpensive muzzleloading shotguns, and a few breechloading designs were toyed with. Following Remington's example, Whitney soon realized that a substantial profit could be made in the production of single-shot martial arms for foreign governments. The result was a series of breechloading arms that copied many salient features of the Remington line, including a direct copy after the expiration of the Remington patent for the "rolling block" mechanism. Not until the late 1870s did Whitney acquire the rights to several patents that led to the production of a lever-action repeating rifle. During the post-war period, revolver production, which had begun with evasions of Colt's patents in the decade prior to the Civil War, mushroomed with the production of small spur-trigger rimfire cartridge revolvers. Despite the variety of arms produced, by 1883 Whitney was considering the sale of his company. Business reverses over the next five years necessitated the sale of the firm to Winchester in 1888. Primarily interested securing in the patent rights for Whitney's lever-action series of rifles, Winchester closed the plant and moved its machinery to New Haven. After 90 years of production, the Whitneyville Armory ceased to exist.

Single Barreled Percussion Shotgun

This firearm was manufactured by Whitney out of surplus .58 caliber rifle barrels that were opened up and converted to smoothbore .60-caliber shotgun barrels. They are offered in lengths of 28" to 36" and are marked "Whitney Arms Co., Whitneyville, Conn. Homogeneous Wrought Steel." The finish is blued, with varnished walnut stocks that are crudely checkered. There were approximately 2,000 manufactured between 1866 and 1869. These guns are rarely encountered on today's market.

—	—	1300	950	400	150

	NIB	EXC.	V.G.	GOOD	FAIR	POOR

Double-Barreled Percussion Shotgun

The specifications for this version are similar to that of the single barrel except that there are two side-by-side barrels with double locks and hammers and double triggers. They are slightly more common than the single barreled version.

	NIB	EXC.	V.G.	GOOD	FAIR	POOR
	—	—	1300	950	400	150

Swing-Breech Carbine

This is a single-shot breechloading carbine chambered for the .46-caliber rimfire cartridge. It has a 22" round barrel with a button-released breechblock that swings to the side for loading. The finish is blued, with a walnut stock. There were fewer than 50 manufactured in 1866.

	NIB	EXC.	V.G.	GOOD	FAIR	POOR
	—	—	6000	3250	1750	600

Whitney-Cochran Carbine

This is a single-shot breechloading carbine chambered for the .44 rimfire cartridge. It has a 28" round barrel with a lever-activated breechblock that raises upward for loading. It was manufactured under license from J.W. Cochran. The finish is blued, with a walnut stock. There is a saddle ring on the left side of the frame. It is marked "Whitney Arms Co. - Whitneyville, Conn." This gun was produced for the 1867 Government Carbine Trials. There were fewer than 50 manufactured in 1866 and 1867.

	NIB	EXC.	V.G.	GOOD	FAIR	POOR
	—	—	7000	3500	1500	600

Excelsior

This is a single-shot rifle chambered for the .38, .44, or .50 rimfire cartridges. It is found with various-length octagonal or round barrels. The finish is blued, with a walnut stock and forearm held on by one barrel band. The breechblock pivots downward for loading. There is a center-mounted hammer. It is marked "Whitney Arms Co. Whitneyville Conn." The shorter barreled carbine versions have a saddle ring on the frame. There were approximately 200 manufactured between 1866 and 1870.

	NIB	EXC.	V.G.	GOOD	FAIR	POOR
	—	—	6700	2750	1150	400

Whitney-Howard Lever Action ("Thunderbolt)

This is a single-shot breechloader that is chambered for the .44 rimfire cartridge. It has also been noted as a shotgun chambered for 20 gauge smoothbore with barrels from 30" to 40" in length. The rifle version has barrel lengths from 22" to 28". The breechblock is opened by means of a combination lever and trigger guard. There is also a carbine version with barrel lengths of 18.5" or 19". There were approximately 2,000 manufactured totally between 1866 and 1870.

Shotgun

	NIB	EXC.	V.G.	GOOD	FAIR	POOR
	—	—	1400	650	300	100

Rifle

	NIB	EXC.	V.G.	GOOD	FAIR	POOR
	—	—	1600	900	450	150

Carbine

	NIB	EXC.	V.G.	GOOD	FAIR	POOR
	—	—	2000	1250	500	200

Whitney Phoenix

There is little known about the origin of this model. It is built on a patent issued to Whitney in 1874. There are a number of variations that are all marked "Phoenix, Patent May 24, 74." The Whitney name is not marked on any of the versions. They are all single-shot breechloaders with a breechblock that lifts to the right side and upward for loading. The barrels are all blued, with either case colored or blued receivers and walnut stocks. There were approximately 25,000 total manufactured between 1867 and 1881. The models and values are listed.

Gallery Rifle

This version is chambered for the .22 rimfire caliber and has a 24" half-octagonal barrel. Its production was quite limited.

	NIB	EXC.	V.G.	GOOD	FAIR	POOR
	—	—	3250	1500	600	200

Shotgun

This is a smoothbore version chambered for 10, 12, 14, 16, or 22 gauge. It has smoothbore barrels between 26" and 32" in length. There were approximately 5,000 manufactured.

	NIB	EXC.	V.G.	GOOD	FAIR	POOR
	—	—	1100	600	250	100

Military Rifle

This version is chambered for the .433, .45, or .50 caliber centerfire cartridges. It has a 35" round barrel with a full-length, two-piece walnut stock held on by three barrel bands. There are approximately 15,000 manufactured. Many were sent to Central or South America.

	NIB	EXC.	V.G.	GOOD	FAIR	POOR
	—	—	5750	3000	1250	400

	NIB	EXC.	V.G.	GOOD	FAIR	POOR

Schuetzen Rifle

This is a target-shooting version chambered for the .38, .40, or .44 centerfire cartridges. It has either a 30" or 32" octagonal barrel with a Schuetzen-type walnut stock and forearm that features hand checkering. It has a nickel-plated, Swiss-style buttplate and adjustable sights with a spirit level. This model has been noted with double-set triggers. There were few manufactured.

NIB	EXC.	V.G.	GOOD	FAIR	POOR
—	—	6000	3250	1250	400

Civilian Carbine

This version is chambered for the .44 caliber centerfire and has a 24" round barrel. The finish is blued, with a case colored frame and a walnut stock and forearm held on by one barrel band. It has military-type sights, buttplate, and a saddle ring mounted on the frame. There were approximately 500 manufactured.

NIB	EXC.	V.G.	GOOD	FAIR	POOR
—	—	4800	2500	850	400

Military Carbine

This version is chambered for the .433, .45, or .50 centerfire cartridges. It has a 20.5" round barrel and was manufactured for Central and South America. It is very rarely encountered on today's market.

NIB	EXC.	V.G.	GOOD	FAIR	POOR
—	—	5000	2750	1000	400

Whitney-Laidley Model I Rolling Block

Whitney acquired manufacturing rights for this model from the inventors T. Laidley and C.A. Emery, who had received the patent in 1866. Whitney immediately started to modify the action to become competitive with the Remington Rolling Block. There were approximately 50,000 manufactured total between 1871 and 1881. There are a number of variations of this model.

Military Carbine

There were approximately 5,000 manufactured chambered for the .433, .45, or .50 centerfire cartridges. It has a 20.5" round barrel with military-type sights and a saddle ring on the receiver. The finish is blued, with a case colored frame and a walnut stock. Most of them were shipped to Central or South America.

NIB	EXC.	V.G.	GOOD	FAIR	POOR
—	—	3500	1750	700	250

Civilian Carbine

This version is chambered for .44 rimfire or centerfire and .46 rimfire. It has either an 18.5" or 19.5" barrel. It is blued, with a case colored frame. The stock is walnut. A nickel-plated version is also available. There were approximately 1,000 of this version manufactured.

NIB	EXC.	V.G.	GOOD	FAIR	POOR
—	—	2800	1750	700	250

Military Rifle

This version is chambered the same as the Military Carbine but has either a 32.5" or 35" round barrel with a full-length two-piece stock held on by three barrel bands. The finish is blued, with a case colored receiver and a walnut stock. There were approximately 30,000 manufactured. Most were shipped to Central or South America.

NIB	EXC.	V.G.	GOOD	FAIR	POOR
—	—	3950	2000	800	300

Gallery Rifle

This is a .22 caliber sporting-rifle version with a 24" octagonal barrel. The finish is similar to the Military Rifle. There were approximately 500 manufactured.

NIB	EXC.	V.G.	GOOD	FAIR	POOR
—	—	3400	1750	700	250

Sporting Rifle

This version is chambered for .38, .40, .44, .45, or .50 centerfire, as well as .32, .38, or .44 rimfire. It features barrel lengths from 24" to 30" in either round or octagonal configurations. The finish is similar to the Military Rifle, and there were approximately 5,000 manufactured.

NIB	EXC.	V.G.	GOOD	FAIR	POOR
—	—	3950	2000	750	300

Creedmoor No. 1 Rifle

This version is chambered for the .44 caliber cartridge and has a 32" or 34" barrel that is either round or octagonal in configuration. It has a blued finish with case colored frame and a hand checkered, select walnut stock and forearm. It features vernier adjustable sights with a spirit level. It is marked "Whitney Creedmoor." There were fewer than 100 manufactured.

NIB	EXC.	V.G.	GOOD	FAIR	POOR
—	—	11500	6250	2750	850

Creedmoor No. 2 Rifle

This version is similar to the No. 1 Rifle except that it is chambered for the .40 caliber cartridge with either a 30" or 32" barrel.

NIB	EXC.	V.G.	GOOD	FAIR	POOR
—	—	9500	4250	1750	500

	NIB	EXC.	V.G.	GOOD	FAIR	POOR

Whitney-Remington Model 2 Rolling Block

When Remington's patent for the Rolling Block action expired, Whitney was quick to reproduce the action, labeling it his "New Improved System." It is essentially quite similar to Remington's Rolling Block and is easily recognized when compared with the Model 1 because it has only two parts — the hammer and the breechblock. The frame is also rounded. The tang on this model is marked "Whitney Arms Company, New Haven Ct USA." There were approximately 50,000 total manufactured between 1881 and 1888. There are a number of variations are listed.

Shotgun

This is a smoothbore version chambered for 12, 14, 16, or 20 gauge. It is offered with barrel lengths between 26" and 30". Twenty inch barrels have also been noted.

—	—	1300	650	250	100

Military Carbine

This version is chambered for the .433 and .45 centerfire cartridges. It has a 20.5" barrel and is blued, with a case colored receiver and walnut stock. There were approximately 5,000 manufactured. Most were sent to South or Central America.

—	—	3400	1750	700	300

Civilian Carbine

This version is chambered for the .44 rimfire or centerfire cartridge with an 18.5" round barrel. The finish is similar to the Military Carbine. There were approximately 2,000 manufactured.

—	—	3100	1600	600	250

Military Rifle

This version is chambered for the .433, .45, or .50 centerfire cartridge. It has a 32.5" or 35" barrel. It is finished similarly to the Military Carbine. There were approximately 39,000 manufactured.

—	—	3950	2000	750	300

No. 1 Sporting Rifle

This version is chambered for various popular sporting cartridges and is offered with barrel lengths from 26" to 30", either round or octagonal in configuration. The finish is blued, with a case colored receiver and a varnished walnut stock. There were many options available that could radically affect the value, and a qualified appraisal would be advisable. There were approximately 3,000 manufactured.

—	—	4850	2500	1000	400

No. 2 Sporting Rifle

This is a smaller version of the No. 1 Rifle, chambered for the .22 rimfire, .32, .38, and .44-40 centerfire cartridges. Again, a qualified appraisal would be helpful, as many options can affect the value.

—	—	3400	1750	700	250

Whitney-Burgess-Morse Rifle

This is a lever action repeating rifle chambered for the .45-70 Government cartridge. There are three variations. All have a magazine tube mounted beneath the barrel with blued finishes and walnut stocks. The barrels are marked "G. W. Morse Patented Oct. 28th 1856." The tang is marked "A. Burgess Patented Jan. 7th, 1873, Patented Oct 19th 1873." There were approximately 3,000 total manufactured between 1878 and 1882. The variations are listed.

Sporting Rifle

This version has a 28" octagonal or round barrel. The magazine tube holds 9 rounds. There are a number of options available that can increase the value drastically; and we recommend competent, individual appraisal. Value given is for a standard model.

—	—	6500	3250	1250	400

Military Rifle

This version has a 33" round barrel with a full-length forearm held on by two barrel bands. It features military sights and has an 11-round tubular magazine. It has a bayonet lug and sling swivels. This variation is also found chambered for the .43 Spanish and .42 Russian cartridges. There were approximately 1,000 manufactured.

—	—	8000	4250	2000	700

Carbine

This version has a 22" round barrel with a full-length forearm held on by one barrel band. It has a 7-round tubular magazine and a saddle ring attached to the frame. There were approximately 500 manufactured.

—	—	9000	4750	2250	750

	NIB	EXC.	V.G.	GOOD	FAIR	POOR

Whitney-Kennedy Rifle

This is a lever action repeating rifle that was manufactured in two sizes. It has a magazine tube mounted under the barrel and a blued finish with a case colored lever. The stock is walnut. The barrel is marked "Whitney Arms Co New Haven, Conn. U.S.A." Occasionally, the word "Kennedy" is marked after the Whitney name. There are two major variations. One features a standard-type action lever; and the other, the same "S" -shaped lever that is found on the Burgess model. This version would be worth approximately 10 percent additional. As with many of the rifles of this era, there were many options available that will affect the values. We strongly recommend securing a qualified appraisal for all but the standard models if a transaction is contemplated. There were approximately 15,000 manufactured between 1879 and 1886. The variations of the Whitney-Kennedy and their values are listed.

Small Frame Sporting Rifle

This version is chambered for the .32-20, .38-40, and the .40-40 cartridges. It has a 24" barrel that is either round or octagonal in configuration. Examples will be noted with either a full-length or half-length tubular magazine.

—	—	5000	2750	1200	500	

Large Frame Sporting Rifle

This version is chambered for the .40-60, .45-60, .45-75, and the .50-90 cartridges. The .50-caliber version is uncommon and will bring a 20 percent premium. The barrel lengths offered are 26" or 28".

—	—	6000	3000	1350	500	

Military Rifle

This is a large-frame model, chambered for the .40-.60, .44-.40, and the .45-60 cartridges. It has a 32.25" round barrel and either an 11- or 16-round tubular magazine. It has a full-length walnut forend held on by two barrel bands and features a bayonet lug and sling swivels. There were approximately 1,000 manufactured. Most were shipped to Central or South America.

—	—	6400	3750	1750	550	

Military Carbine

This is built on either the small-frame or large-frame action and is chambered for the .38-40, .44-40, .40-60, or .45-60 cartridges. It has either a 20" or 22" round barrel and a 9- or 12-round tubular magazine, depending on the caliber. It has a short forend held on by a single barrel band. There were approximately 1,000 manufactured. Most were sent to Central or South America.

—	—	6400	3750	1750	550	

Hooded Cylinder Pocket Revolver

This is an unusual revolver that is chambered for .28 caliber percussion. It has a manually rotated, 6-shot hooded cylinder that has etched decorations. The octagonal barrel is offered in lengths of 3" to 6". There is a button at the back of the frame that unlocks the cylinder so that it can be rotated. The finish is blued, with a brass frame and two-piece rounded walnut grips. It is marked "E. Whitney N. Haven Ct." There were approximately 200 manufactured between 1850 and 1853.

—	—	5750	3250	1500	600	

Two Trigger Pocket Revolver

This is a conventional-appearing pocket revolver with a manually rotated cylinder. There is a second trigger located in front of the conventional trigger guard that releases the cylinder so that it can be turned. It is chambered for .32 caliber percussion and has an octagonal barrel from 3" to 6" in length. It has a 5-shot unfluted cylinder that is etched and a brass frame. The remainder is blued, with squared walnut two-piece grips. An iron-frame version is also available, but only 50 were produced. It would bring approximately 60 percent additional. There were approximately 650 total manufactured between 1852 and 1854.

—	—	2750	2000	850	300	

Whitney-Beals Patent Revolver

This was an unusual, ring-trigger pocket pistol that was made in three basic variations.

First Model

This version is chambered for .31-caliber percussion and has barrels of octagonal configuration from 2" to 6" in length. It has a brass frame and a 6-shot cylinder. It is marked "F. Beals/New Haven, Ct." There were only 50 manufactured.

—	—	5000	3500	1500	450	

.31 Caliber Model

This version has an iron frame and a 7-shot cylinder. The octagonal barrels are from 2" to 6" in length. It is marked "Address E. Whitney/Whitneyville, Ct." There were approximately 2,300 manufactured.

—	—	2500	1500	600	200	

	NIB	EXC.	V.G.	GOOD	FAIR	POOR

.28 Caliber Model

Except for the caliber, this model is similar to the .31 Caliber Model. There were approximately 850 manufactured.

	NIB	EXC.	V.G.	GOOD	FAIR	POOR
	—	—	2750	1750	700	300

Whitney 1851 Navy

This is a faithful copy of the 1851 Colt Revolver. It is virtually identical. There is a possibility that surplus Colt parts were utilized in the construction of this revolver. There were approximately 400 manufactured in 1857 and 1858.

	NIB	EXC.	V.G.	GOOD	FAIR	POOR
	—	—	9000	4250	1750	650

WHITNEY NAVY REVOLVER

This is a single-action revolver chambered for .36 caliber percussion. It has a standard octagonal barrel length of 7.5". It has an iron frame and a 6-shot unfluted cylinder that is roll engraved. The finish is blued, with a case colored loading lever and two-piece walnut grips. The barrel is marked either "E. Whitney/N. Haven" or "Eagle Co." There are a number of minor variations on this revolver, and we strongly urge competent appraisal if contemplating a transaction. There were 33,000 total manufactured between 1858 and 1862.

First Model

Nearly the entire production of the First Model is marked "Eagle Co." The reason for this marking is unknown. There are four distinct variations of this model.

First Variation

This model has no integral loading-lever assembly and has a thin top strap. There were only 100 manufactured.

	NIB	EXC.	V.G.	GOOD	FAIR	POOR
	—	—	5400	3750	1500	550

Second Variation

This version is similar to the First Variation, with an integral loading lever. There were approximately 200 manufactured.

	NIB	EXC.	V.G.	GOOD	FAIR	POOR
	—	—	5000	3000	1200	400

Third Variation

This is similar to the Second, with a three-screw frame instead of four screws. The loading lever is also modified. There were approximately 500 manufactured.

	NIB	EXC.	V.G.	GOOD	FAIR	POOR
	—	—	4800	2500	1000	300

Fourth Variation

This version has a rounded frame and a safety notch between the nipples on the rear of the cylinder. There have been examples noted marked "E. Whitney/N. Haven." There were approximately 700 manufactured.

	NIB	EXC.	V.G.	GOOD	FAIR	POOR
	—	—	4800	2500	1000	300

Second Model

First Variation

This version features a more robust frame with a brass trigger guard. The barrel is marked "E. Whitney/N. Haven." The cylinder pin is secured by a wing nut, and there is an integral loading lever. There were approximately 1,200 manufactured.

	NIB	EXC.	V.G.	GOOD	FAIR	POOR
	—	—	3750	2000	900	300

Second Variation

This version has six improved safety notches on the rear of the cylinder. There were approximately 10,000 manufactured.

	NIB	EXC.	V.G.	GOOD	FAIR	POOR
	—	—	3200	1750	750	250

Third Variation

This version has an improved, Colt-type loading-lever latch. There were approximately 2,000 manufactured.

	NIB	EXC.	V.G.	GOOD	FAIR	POOR
	—	—	3200	1750	750	250

Fourth Variation

This is similar to the Third except the cylinder is marked "Whitneyville." There were approximately 10,000 manufactured.

	NIB	EXC.	V.G.	GOOD	FAIR	POOR
	—	—	3200	1750	750	250

Fifth Variation

This version has a larger trigger guard. There were approximately 4,000 manufactured.

	NIB	EXC.	V.G.	GOOD	FAIR	POOR
	—	—	3200	1750	750	250

	NIB	EXC.	V.G.	GOOD	FAIR	POOR

Sixth Variation

This version has the larger trigger guard and five-groove rifling instead of the usual seven-groove. There were approximately 2,500 manufactured.

NIB	EXC.	V.G.	GOOD	FAIR	POOR
—	—	3200	1750	750	250

WHITNEY POCKET REVOLVER

This is a single-action revolver chambered for .31 caliber percussion. It has octagonal barrels between 3" and 6" in length. It has a 5-shot unfluted cylinder that is roll engraved and marked "Whitneyville." The frame is iron with a blued finish and a case colored integral loading lever. The grips are two-piece walnut. The development of this model, as far as models and variations go, is identical to that which we described in the Navy Model designation. The values are different, and we list them for reference. Again, we recommend securing qualified appraisal if a transaction is contemplated. There were approximately 32,500 manufactured from 1858 to 1862.

First Model

First Variation

NIB	EXC.	V.G.	GOOD	FAIR	POOR
—	—	3750	2000	900	300

Second Variation

NIB	EXC.	V.G.	GOOD	FAIR	POOR
—	—	2200	1250	500	200

Third Variation

NIB	EXC.	V.G.	GOOD	FAIR	POOR
—	—	1900	1000	400	150

Fourth Variation

NIB	EXC.	V.G.	GOOD	FAIR	POOR
—	—	1900	1000	400	150

Fifth Variation

NIB	EXC.	V.G.	GOOD	FAIR	POOR
—	—	1900	1000	400	150

Second Model

First Variation

NIB	EXC.	V.G.	GOOD	FAIR	POOR
—	—	1700	900	400	100

Second Variation

NIB	EXC.	V.G.	GOOD	FAIR	POOR
—	—	1700	900	400	100

Third Variation

NIB	EXC.	V.G.	GOOD	FAIR	POOR
—	—	1700	900	400	100

Fourth Variation

NIB	EXC.	V.G.	GOOD	FAIR	POOR
—	—	1700	1000	425	125

New Model Pocket Revolver

This is a single-action, spur-triggered pocket revolver chambered for .28-caliber percussion. It has a 3.5" octagonal barrel and a 6-shot roll engraved cylinder. It features an iron frame with a blued finish and two-piece walnut grips. The barrel is marked "E. Whitney/N. Haven." There were approximately 2,000 manufactured between 1860 and 1867.

NIB	EXC.	V.G.	GOOD	FAIR	POOR
—	—	2000	1250	500	200

Rimfire Pocket Revolver

This is a spur-trigger, single-action, solid-frame pocket revolver that was produced in three frame sizes, depending on the caliber. It is chambered for the .22, .32, and .38 rimfire cartridges. The frame is brass, and it is found in a variety of finishes- nickel-plated or blued, or a combination thereof. The bird's-head grips are rosewood or hard rubber; ivory or pearl grips are sometimes encountered and will bring a slight premium in value. The barrels are octagonal and from 1.5" to 5" in length. The barrels are marked "Whitneyville Armory Ct. USA." They have also been noted with the trade names "Monitor," "Defender," or "Eagle." They were commonly referred to as the Model No. 1, No. 1.5, Model 2, or Model 2.5. The values for all are quite similar. There were approximately 30,000 manufactured of all types between 1871 and 1879.

NIB	EXC.	V.G.	GOOD	FAIR	POOR
—	—	750	500	200	75

WHITNEY FIREARMS COMPANY
Hartford, Connecticut

Wolverine

A .22 caliber semi-automatic pistol with a 4.75" barrel. Blued or nickel-plated with plastic grips and an aluminum alloy frame. This pistol is readily distinguishable by its streamlined form. Approximately 13,000 examples were made with the blue finish and 900 with a nickel-plated finish. Some slides are marked "Wolverine Whitney Firearms Inc., New Haven, Conn USA." Others

	NIB	EXC.	V.G.	GOOD	FAIR	POOR

are marked "Whitney" only. The Wolverine-marked pistols are considered more rare. Pistol were produced in two locations: New Haven, Connecticut and Hartford, Connecticut. Manufactured from 1955 to 1962. Now being reproduced by Olympic Arms. Pricing is for original version.

Blue Finish

Blued pistols most often have brown or black grips.

750	550	400	350	250	200

Nickel-Plated

Nickeled pistols most often have white plastic grips.

2000	1800	1500	1250	800	500

WHITWORTH

See—Interarms

WICHITA ARMS, INC.

Wichita, Kansas

Classic Rifle

A single-shot bolt-action rifle produced in a variety of calibers with a 21" octagonal barrel. Offered with Canjar adjustable triggers. Blued with a checkered walnut stock.

3000	2500	2250	1850	1250	1000

Varmint Rifle

As above, with a round barrel.

2000	1750	1500	1250	1000	800

Silhouette Rifle

As above, with a 24" heavy barrel, gray composition stock and 2-oz. Canjar trigger.

2200	1900	1700	1000	850	650

Wichita International Pistol

A single-shot pivoted barrel target pistol produced in a variety of calibers from .22 to .357 Magnum with a 10.5" or 14" barrel fitted with either adjustable sights or telescopic sight mounts. Stainless steel with walnut forestock and grips.

800	650	400	350	300	200

Wichita Classic Pistol

A bolt action single-shot pistol chambered for a variety of calibers up to .308, with a left-hand action and 11.25" barrel. Blued with a walnut stock.

3000	2500	2250	1850	1250	1000

Wichita Classic Engraved

As above, but embellished.

5000	4250	3500	2500	2000	1500

Wichita Silhouette Pistol

As above, in 7mm HMSA or .308 with a 15" barrel. The walnut stock is made so that the pistol grip is located beneath the forward end of the bolt.

1100	950	750	600	500	400

Wichita MK40

As above, with a 13" barrel, multi-range sights and either a composition or walnut stock. Standard finish is blued, however, this model was also made in stainless steel.

1100	950	750	600	500	400

WICKLIFFE RIFLES

Triple S Development
Wickliffe, Ohio/Austinburg, Ohio

NOTE: The Wickliffe Rifle Company has been reorganized as a maker of custom single-shot rifles. Values below are for the original Wickliffe guns.

Model 76

A single-shot falling-block rifle produced in a variety of calibers from .22 Hornet to .45-70 with a 22" lightweight or 26" heavyweight barrel. Blued with a walnut stock. Introduced in 1976. Discontinued.

—	1200	1000	750	550	300

	NIB	EXC.	V.G.	GOOD	FAIR	POOR

Model 76 Deluxe

As above, with a nickel-silver pistol grip cap, machine jeweled breechblock and more finely figured walnut stock. Introduced in 1976.

—	1450	1250	900	700	450

Traditionalist

The Model 76 in .30-06 or .45-70 caliber with a 24" barrel having open sights and a checkered walnut buttstock. Introduced in 1979.

—	1200	1000	750	550	300

Stinger

Similar to the Model 76, but chambered for .22 Hornet or .223 Remington with a 22" barrel fitted with a Burris 6X power telescope. Blued with a checkered Monte Carlo-style stock. Introduced in 1979.

—	1200	1000	750	550	300

Stinger Deluxe

As above, with a superior grade of finish and more finely figured walnut stock.

—	1250	1050	800	575	300

WIENER WAFFENFABRIK
Vienna, Austria

Little Tom

A 6.35mm or 7.65mm double-action semi-automatic pistol with a 2.5" barrel. The slide marked "Wiener Waffenfabrik Patent Little Tom," and the caliber. Blued with either walnut or plastic grips inlaid with a medallion bearing the company's trademark. Approximately 10,000 were made from 1919 to 1925.

—	500	450	400	250	175

WILDEY FIREARMS CO., INC.
Cheshire, Connecticut
Newburg, New York
Warren, Connecticut

Wildey Auto Pistol

Gas-operated, rotary-bolt, double-action semi-automatic pistol. Chambered for .357 Peterbuilt, .45 Winchester Magnum or .475 Wildey Magnum cartridges, with 5", 6", 7", 8" or 10" ventilated rib barrels. Gas-operated action is adjustable and features a single-shot cutoff. Rotary bolt has three heavy locking lugs. Constructed of stainless steel, with adjustable sights and wood grips. Values of this rarely encountered pistol are based not only on condition, but caliber—as well as serial-number range. Earlier-numbered guns being worth a good deal more than later production models. All Wildey models are no longer in production.

Cheshire, Connecticut, Address

Produced in .45 Winchester Magnum only. Serial numbered from No. 1 through 2489. **NOTE:** Serial numbers above 200 would be worth approximately $200 less respectively in each category of condition.

Serial No. 1 through 200

2000	1500	1200	950	750	500

Survivor Model

This model was manufactured in Brookfield, Connecticut. **NOTE:** Add $100 for 12" barrel; $500 for 14" barrel; $1,100 for 18" Silhouette model.

1500	1000	750	550	450	300

Hunter Model

As above, with matte stainless steel finish.

1775	1250	900	700	600	450

Pin Gun

Gas-operated auto-loading pistol for competition shooting in polished or matte stainless, with muzzle-brake. Variety of calibers and barrel lengths (7", 8", 10", 12", 14"). Weight 4.09 lb. (8" barrel).

2000	1500	1200	950	750	500

	NIB	EXC.	V.G.	GOOD	FAIR	POOR

Wildey Carbine

Model features 18" barrel, with forearm. Calibers from .44 Auto Magnum to .475 Wildey Magnum. Choice of polished or matte stainless steel. **NOTE:** Add $ 225 for matte stainless finish.

| 2500 | 2000 | 1550 | 1000 | 750 | 500 |

Presentation Model

As above, but engraved and fitted with hand-checkered walnut grips.

| 3000 | 2500 | 1950 | 1400 | 900 | 600 |

JAWS Viper

Jordanian Arms & Weapons System manufactured in Jordan. Semi-automatic chambered for 9mm, .40 S&W, 45 ACP. Barrels: 4.4" and 5". 10-round magazine. Stainless finish with rubberized grip. .

| — | 725 | 500 | 375 | 250 | 150 |

WILKINSON ARMS CO.
Covina, California

Diane

A .25-caliber semi-automatic pistol, with 2.25" barrel and 6-shot magazine. Blued, with plastic grips.

| — | 400 | 325 | 200 | 150 | 100 |

Terry Carbine

A 9mm caliber semi-automatic carbine, with 16.25" barrel, adjustable sights and 30-shot magazine. Matte blued, with either black composition or maple stock.

| — | 675 | 450 | 325 | 200 | 125 |

WILLIAMSON
New York, New York

Derringer

A .41-caliber single-shot pocket pistol, with 2.5" sliding barrel. Blued, with silver-plated furniture and checkered walnut grip. Barrel marked "Williamson's Pat. Oct. 2, 1866 New York". Fitted with an auxiliary percussion cap chamber adaptor. Manufactured from 1866 to approximately 1870.

| — | — | — | 1250 | 500 | 100 |

WILSON, J. P.
Ilion, New York

Percussion Alarm Gun

This unusual little device is chambered for .22-caliber percussion. Consists of approximately a 1" rectangular brass block, with a chamber bored into it that accepts a blackpowder charge. There is no provision for a projectile. There is a spring retained arm on top, which works as a hammer. As the device is activated by a door or a window, the hammer snaps closed, striking a percussion cap that causes the charge to fire, thereby creating an alarm notifying that the perimeter has been breached. It is marked "J. P. Wilson/Patented Feb. 8, 1859/Ilion, NY".

| — | — | 1200 | 850 | 350 | 100 |

WILSON COMBAT
Berryville, Arkansas

Wilson began making custom 1911-style pistols using Colt slides and frames in 1977. Company produces a wide range of quality components for 1911 pistols, such as slides, triggers, safeties, barrels, etc. Models listed are for complete factory-built-and-assembled guns. These factory-built pistols are sold with a lifetime warranty, even to subsequent buyers. Pistols listed are divided into two categories. Semi-custom pistols are off-the-shelf guns available through participating dealers. Custom pistols are special order guns. Models listed below are representative, not inclusive.

POLYMER FRAME PISTOLS

Tactical Carry (KZ-45)

Chambered for .45 ACP cartridge. Fitted with 5" stainless steel match barrel. This model has numerous special features such as night sights and front and rear slide serrations. Frame is stainless steel and reinforced polymer. Magazine capacity 10 rounds. Finish is black polymer. Weight about 31 oz. Introduced in 1999. Discontinued.

| 1050 | 900 | 750 | 600 | 500 | 300 |

	NIB	EXC.	V.G.	GOOD	FAIR	POOR

KZ 9mm

Polymer-frame 1911 chambered for 9mm. Full size is 16+1 capacity, with 5" barrel; weight 33 oz. Compact size is 14+1 capacity, with 4.1" barrel; weight 31 oz. Introduced 2006. Discontinued.

1500	1350	1200	900	750	300

Spec-Ops 9

An upgraded model based on the discontinued KZ-9. Like the KZ-9, it has a polymer frame and 16 round magazine. Chambering is 9mm only. Barrel is 4.5"; weight unloaded 29.6 oz.

1950	1500	1200	900	450	200

ADP 9mm

Polymer frame. Capacity 11 rounds; weight 19.5 oz.; overall length 6.3"; barrel 3.75". Introduced 2006.

675	525	400	300	200	125

SEMI-CUSTOM PISTOLS

Model 1996A2

Introduced in 1996. Offered in a number of different configurations. These configurations affect price. Base pistol chambered for .45 ACP cartridge. Has snag-free sights and blue finish. Barrel length 5"; magazine capacity 8 rounds; weight about 38 oz. There are numerous special features on the standard pistol. **NOTE:** Add $70 for tritium night sights; $125 for Wilson adjustable sights; $275 for nights sights, ambi safety, hard chrome frame; $325 for Wilson adjustable sights, ambi safety, hard chrome frame.

1450	1150	1000	800	625	300

Protector

Model fitted to a 5" slide, with match barrel adjustable sights and numerous other special features. Weight about 38 oz. Black polymer finish on slide and frame. Introduced in 1996. **NOTE:** Add $100 for stainless steel.

1795	1450	1150	900	650	400

Protector Compact

Same as above, with 4.25" match-grade barrel. Weight about 34 oz. Introduced in 1996.

1795	1450	1150	900	650	400

Sentinel Ultra Compact

This .45 ACP pistol fitted with 3.6" heavy tapered cone handfitted barrel, night sights, high-ride beavertail and numerous special features. Magazine capacity 6 rounds. Weight about 29 oz. Finish is a black polymer.

2100	1675	1300	950	700	450

Tactical

This .45 ACP pistol fitted with 5" tapered cone handfitted barrel. Cocking serrations on front and rear of slide. High-ride beavertail safety and other special features. Night sights are standard. Cocobolo grips. Weight about 38 oz. Finish is black polymer. Magazine capacity 8 rounds. Introduced in 1999.

1825	1450	1100	900	700	400

Classic

This model has a 5" barrel, adjustable sights, hard chrome finish on frame and other special features. Weight about 38 oz. Introduced in 1996. **NOTE:** Add $100 for stainless steel.

1895	1500	1200	900	700	400

Service Grade Target

Chambered for .45 ACP cartridge. Features 5" stainless steel match handfitted barrel, with full length guide rod. Front and rear cocking serrations. Magazine well is beveled and grips are cocobolo. Numerous other special features. Weight about 38 oz. Finish is black polymer. Magazine capacity 8 rounds.

1825	1450	1150	850	650	350

Custom Carry Revolver

Built on a Smith & Wesson .357 Magnum Model 66. Features 2.5" barrel, with adjustable night sights. Cylinder is chambered and grip is black nylon, with smooth finish. Stainless steel finish. Weight about 30 oz.

1175	950	800	650	500	300

	NIB	EXC.	V.G.	GOOD	FAIR	POOR

.22 Classic Rimfire Pistol

Chambered for .22-caliber rimfire cartridge. Fitted with a 5" barrel. Hard chrome frame and black anodized slide. Weight less than standard .45-caliber pistol. Introduced in 1996.

1125	975	800	625	500	250

CUSTOM-BUILT PISTOLS

Wilson Custom pistols bear the Wilson Combat or Wilson Custom label on right side of frame on the dust cover. Full custom guns are typically built on a Colt, Springfield Armory, Norinco, STI, Strayer Voight or Wilson Combat gun.

Combat Classic Super Grade (Tactical Super Grade)

Fitted with a 5" match-grade handfit stainless steel barrel. Adjustable sights, high ride beavertail safety, contoured magazine well and polymer slide with hard chrome frame. Weight about 45 oz. In 9mm, .38 Super, .40 S&W, 10mm and .45 ACP.

3595	2850	2300	1900	1500	600

Tactical Super Grade Compact

Similar to above model, with 4.1" match grade barrel. Magazine capacity 7 rounds. Weight about 40 oz. Introduced in 2003. Available in 9mm, .38 Super, .45 ACP.

4475	3900	3200	2500	1850	650

Wilson X-TAC

Caliber .45 ACP, steel frame and slide, 8 round magazine, special XTAC-pattern slide serrations and texturing on front strap and mainspring housing, stainless match-grade barrel and bushing, extended thumb safety, beavertail tang, G10 grips and contoured mag well. Weight 38.1 oz., 5" barrel with black Parkerized finish.

2000	1700	1450	1150	750	300

CQB Light-Rail Lightweight

Calibers: 9mm Parabellum, .38 Super, .45 ACP. Compact size with 4" barrel, steel slide, alloy round butt frame. Weight 27.34 oz. Comes with two 8-round and one 7-round magazine, fiber optic front sight, integral accessory rail, G10 grips, extended thumb safety, beavertail tang, checkered front strap and mainspring housing. Several other sizes and variations available in CQB series.

2300	1976	1650	1300	850	300

Ultralight Carry Series

Full-size 1911 with aluminum frame, steel slide. Chambered in 9mm Parabellum, .38 Super or .45 ACP. Stainless fluted 5" barrel. Comes with one 7- and two 8-round magazines. Other features include countersunk slide stop, integral accessory rail, contoured mag well, G10 grips, extended thumb safety, beavertail tang, checkered front strap and mainspring housing. Weight 26.5 oz. Several Armor-Tuff finish options including black, O.D., silver, tan or two-tone. Compact model has 4" barrel (all calibers), Sentinel 3.6" barrel (9mm only).

3400	3000	2500	2000	1200	400

Stealth Defense System

Built with a 4.25" slide with match-grade stainless steel barrel. Features night sights, checkered front strap and mainspring housing with numerous special features. Black polymer finish. Weight about 34 oz. Offered in 9mm, .38 Super, .40 S&W, .45 ACP.

2895	2250	1700	1300	900	400

Defensive Combat Pistol

This .45 ACP pistol built with a 5" match-grade stainless steel barrel, night sights and numerous special features. Finish is black polymer. Weight 38 oz.

2395	1850	1250	1000	600	300

Classic Master Grade

This .45 ACP pistol fitted with a 5" stainless steel handfitted match-grade barrel. Numerous special features such as ultralight hammer, ambidextrous safety, etc. Finish is stainless steel frame and black polymer slide. Weight about 38 oz. Magazine capacity 8 rounds.

2895	2250	1700	1300	900	400

Tactical Elite

Similar to other Wilson pistols, with the addition of special tactical heavy tapered cone barrel.

2895	2250	1700	1300	900	400

NIB	EXC.	V.G.	GOOD	FAIR	POOR

Defensive Combat Pistol Deluxe

This model has a 5" match-grade stainless steel barrel and numerous special features. Fitted with adjustable sights. Weight about 38 oz. Finish is black polymer.

2595	2000	1350	1050	700	300

Professional Model Pistol

Introduced in 2004. This .45 ACP pistol features 4.1" stainless steel match barrel, tactical combat sights with tritium inserts. Many custom features. Magazine capacity 8 rounds. Offered in gray/black, green/black, or all-black finish. Weight about 35 oz.

1215	1650	1375	1100	750	450

Competition Pistols

Wilson Combat offers custom-built pistols to customer's specifications. An expert appraisal is recommended prior to sale.

TACTICAL RIFLES

UT-15 Urban Tactical

Semi-automatic rifle fitted with 16.25" fluted barrel with tactical muzzle-brake. Flattop receiver. Aluminum handguard. Chambered for .223 cartridge. Parkerized finish. Accepts all M-16/AR-15 magazines. Weight about 6.5 lbs. **NOTE:** Add $100 for Armor-Tuff finish.

1900	1700	1450	1100	900	500

Tactical Hunter LW 6.8

Chambered for Remington 6.8 SPC, with 15-round magazine. Stainless lightweight match-grade 16" or 18" barrel. Forged upper and lower receivers. Enhanced bolt and carrier with NP3 coating. Wilson Combat Quadrail, Accu-Tac flash hider. Armor Tuff polymer finish in black, gray or tan. Collapsible stock.

2000	1700	1450	1150	750	300

TPR-15 Tactical Precision Rifle

Model fitted with a match-grade 18" fluted barrel. Free-floating aluminum handguard. Chambered for .223 cartridge. Weight about 6.5 lbs. Parkerized finish. **NOTE:** Add $100 for Armor-Tuff finish.

2500	2300	1950	1300	1100	600

M-4T Tactical Carbine

Features 16.25" M-4 style heavy barrel, with muzzle-brake. Flattop receiver. Chambered for .223 cartridge. Parkerized finish. Weight about 6.5 lbs. **NOTE:** Add $100 for Armor-Tuff finish.

1900	1700	1450	1100	900	500

TL-15 Tactical Lightweight

Introduced in 2002. This flattop model features match-grade 16.25" lightweight barrel, with muzzle-brake. Aluminum handguard and fixed buttstock. Chambered for .223 cartridge. Black Mil-Spec finish. **NOTE:** Add $100 for Armor-Tuff finish.

1900	1700	1450	1100	900	500

Super Sniper

Fitted with 20" stainless steel match grade barrel, with a 1 in 8 twist. Flat top receiver. Offered in Parkerized or Armor-Tuff finish. **NOTE:** Add $100 for Armor-Tuff finish.

2350	2100	1800	1500	1150	600

WINCHESTER REPEATING ARMS
New Haven, Connecticut

Prices given here are for, the most part, standard guns without optional features that were so often furnished by the factory. These optional or extra-cost features are too numerous to list and can affect price of shotgun or rifle to an enormous degree. In some cases, these options are one of a kind. Collectors and those interested in Winchester firearms have the benefit of some original factory records. These records are now stored in Cody Firearms Museum, Buffalo Bill Historical Center, P.O. Box 1000, Cody, Wyoming (307) 587-4771. For a $25 fee, museum will provide factory letters containing original specifications of certain Winchester models using original factory records. **CAUTION:** Buyers should confirm by Cody letter any special-order feature on any Winchester within the Cody record range before paying a premium for a scarce feature.

Hunt Repeating Rifle

Walter Hunt described his repeating rifle as the Volition Repeater. Hunt was granted U.S. patent number 6663 in August 1849 for his repeating rifle that was to pave the way for future

	NIB	EXC.	V.G.	GOOD	FAIR	POOR

generations of Winchester repeating rifles. Hunt's rifle design was unique and innovative as was his patent number 5701 for a conical lead bullet that was to be fired in his rifle. This ingenious bullet had a hole in its base filled with powder and closed by a disc with an opening in the middle to expel the ignition from an independent priming source that used priming pellets made of fulminate of mercury. The rifle actually worked but only the patent model was built; it is now in the Cody Firearms Museum.

Jennings

Second in the evolutionary line of Winchester rifles is the Jennings. Made by Robbins & Lawrence of Windsor, Vermont, this rifle incorporated the original concept of the Hunt design with the additional improvements utilized by Lewis Jennings. The Jennings rifle is important not only as a link in the chain of repeating-rifle development but also because it introduced Benjamin Henry Tyler to the concept of the tubular magazine lever-action repeating rifle. The Jennings rifle was built in three separate and distinct models. While total production of the three types was contracted for 5,000 guns, it is probable that only about 1,000 were actually produced.

First Model

The First Model Jennings was built in a .54 caliber, breech-loading, single-shot configuration with a ring trigger, oval trigger guard, and 26" barrel. A ramrod was fixed to the underside of the barrel as well. This variation was made from 1850 to 1851.

—	—	35000	25000	7000	1500	

Second Model

The Second Model Jennings was produced adopting the improvements made by Horace Smith. This Second Model is a breech-loading repeating rifle with an under barrel magazine tube and a 26" barrel. The frame is sculpted, unlike the First Model. The ring trigger is still present, but the trigger guard was removed as part of the design change. The caliber remained a .54, and the rifle was fitted with a 25" barrel. The Second Model was produced in 1851 and 1852.

—	—	30000	20000	5000	1200	

Third Model

The Third Model represents an attempt by investors to use the remaining parts and close out production. The .54 caliber Third Model was a muzzleloading rifle with a ramrod mounted under the barrel and a 26-1/2" barrel. The frame was the same as that used on the First Model, but the trigger was more of the conventional type. The trigger guard had a bow in the middle giving this model a distinctive appearance. This variation was produced in 1852 and marks the end of the early conceptual period in repeating rifle development.

—	—	23500	9500	4500	1500	

Smith & Wesson Volcanic Firearms

An interesting connection in the evolution of the lever-action repeating firearm is found in the production of a small group of pistols and rifles built in Norwich, Connecticut, by Horace Smith and Daniel Wesson under the firm name of Smith & Wesson. The company built two types of Volcanic pistols. One was a large-frame model with an 8" barrel and chambered in .41 caliber. About 500 of these large frames were produced. The other pistol was a small-frame version with a 4" barrel chambered in .31 caliber. Slightly more of these small-frame pistols were built, about 700, than the large-frame version. In both variations the barrel, magazine, and frame were blued. Smith & Wesson also produced a lever-action repeating rifle. These rifles are exceedingly rare with fewer than 10 having been built. They were chambered for the .528 caliber and were fitted with 23" barrels. Because of the small number of rifles built, no value is offered.

4" Pistol

—	—	—	11000	4000	1000	

8" Pistol

—	—	—	13000	6000	1500	

Volcanic Firearms (Volcanic Repeating Arms Company)

With the incorporation of the Volcanic Repeating Arms Company, a new and important individual was introduced who would have an impact on the American arms industry for the next 100 years: Oliver F. Winchester. This new company introduced the Volcanic pistol using the improvements made by Horace Smith and Daniel Wesson. Volcanic firearms are marked on the barrel, "THE VOLCANIC REPEATING ARMS CO. PATENT NEW HAVEN, CONN. FEB. 14, 1854." The Volcanic was offered as a .38 caliber breechloading tubular magazine repeater with blued barrel and bronze frame. These pistols were available in three barrel lengths.

6" Barrel

—	—	—	7000	3500	1500	

8" Barrel

—	—	—	7000	3500	1500	

	NIB	EXC.	V.G.	GOOD	FAIR	POOR

16" Barrel

NOTE: A few Volcanic pistols were produced with detachable shoulder stocks. These are considered quite rare. For original guns with this option, the prices listed should be increased by 25 percent.

	NIB	EXC.	V.G.	GOOD	FAIR	POOR
	—	—	—	14000	5500	2500

Volcanic Firearms (New Haven Arms Company)

In 1857 the New Haven Arms Company was formed to continue the production of the former Volcanic Repeating Arms Company. Volcanic firearms continued to be built but were now marked on the barrel, "NEW HAVEN, CONN. PATENT FEB. 14, 1854." The Volcanic pistols produced by the New Haven Arms Company were built in .30 caliber and used the same basic frame as the original Volcanic. These pistols were produced in 3-1/2" and 6" barrel lengths.

3-1/2" Barrel

	EXC.	V.G.	GOOD	FAIR	POOR
—	—	6500	5000	2500	1500

6" Barrel

	EXC.	V.G.	GOOD	FAIR	POOR
—	—	7500	5750	3000	1500

Lever Action Carbine

New Haven Arms introduced, for the first time, a Volcanic rifle that featured a full-length slotted magazine tube with a spring-activated thumbpiece follower that moved along the entire length of the magazine tube. These rifles were chambered for .38 caliber cartridge and were offered in three barrel lengths: 16", 20", and 24".

16" Barrel

	EXC.	V.G.	GOOD	FAIR	POOR
—	40000	26000	16000	6000	2000

20" Barrel

	EXC.	V.G.	GOOD	FAIR	POOR
—	45000	23000	19000	8000	3000

24" Barrel

	EXC.	V.G.	GOOD	FAIR	POOR
—	55000	37000	22500	10000	3000

Henry Rifle

With development of B. Tyler Henry's improvements in metallic rimfire cartridge and his additional improvements in Volcanic frame, direct predecessor to Winchester lever-action repeater was born. New cartridge was .44 caliber rimfire. Henry rifle featured 24" octagon barrel with tubular magazine holding 15 shells. Rifle had no forearm. Furnished with walnut buttstock with two styles of buttplates: early rounded heel crescent shape seen on guns produced from 1860 to 1862; later sharper heel crescent butt found on guns built from 1863 to 1866. Early models produced from 1860 to 1861 were fitted with an iron frame; later models built from 1861 to 1866 were fitted with brass frames. About 14,000 Henry rifles were made during entire production period; only about 300 were iron frame rifles.

Iron Frame Rifle

	EXC.	V.G.	GOOD	FAIR	POOR
—	—	120000	65000	30000	13000

Brass Frame Rifle

	EXC.	V.G.	GOOD	FAIR	POOR
—	—	53000	37500	17500	9000

Martially Inspected Henry Rifles

Beginning in 1863, Federal Government ordered 1,730 Henry Rifles for use in Civil War. Most of these government-inspected rifles fall into serial number range 3000 to 4000, while balance are close to this serial-number range. They are marked "C.G.C." for Charles G. Chapman, government inspector. These Henry rifles were used under actual combat conditions and for that reason it is doubtful there are any rifles that would fall into excellent condition category. Therefore, no price is given. **NOTE:** There are many counterfeit examples of these rifles. It is strongly advised that an expert in this field be consulted prior to sale.

	EXC.	V.G.	GOOD	FAIR	POOR
—	—	85000	40000	20000	9000

Winchester's Improvement Carbine

Overall length 43-1/2"; barrel length 24"; caliber .44 rimfire. Walnut stock with a brass buttplate; the receiver and magazine cover/fore-end of brass; the barrel and magazine tube blued. The magazine loading port is exposed by sliding the fore-end forward. This design was protected by O.F. Winchester's British Patent Number 3285 issued December 19, 1865. Unmarked except for internally located serial numbers. Approximately 700 manufactured in December of 1865 and early 1866, the majority of which were sold to Maximilian of Mexico. Prospective purchasers are strongly advised to secure an expert appraisal prior to acquisition.

	EXC.	V.G.	GOOD	FAIR	POOR
—	35000	27500	19500	13000	9000

	NIB	EXC.	V.G.	GOOD	FAIR	POOR

Model 1866

In 1866, New Haven Arms Company changed its name to Winchester Repeating Arms Company. First firearm to be built under Winchester name was Model 1866. This first Winchester was a much-improved version of Henry. New magazine tube, developed by Nelson King Winchester's plant superintendent, was a vast improvement over slotted magazine tube used on Henry and its predecessor. Old tube allowed dirt to enter through slots and was weakened because of it. King's patent, assigned to Winchester, featured a solid tube that was much stronger and reliable. His patent also dealt with an improved loading system for the rifle. Rifle now featured loading port on right side of receiver with spring-loaded cover. Frame continued to be made from brass. Model 1866 was chambered for .44 caliber Flat Rimfire or .44 caliber Pointed Rimfire. Both cartridges could be used interchangeably.

Barrel on Model 1866 marked with two different markings. First, which is seen on early guns up to serial number 23000 reads, "HENRY'S PATENT-OCT. 16, 1860 KING'S PATENT-MARCH 29, 1866". Second marking reads, "WINCHESTER'S-REPEATING-ARMS.NEW HAVEN, CT. KING'S-IMPROVEMENT-PATENTED MARCH 29, 1866 OCTOBER 16, 1860". There are three basic variations of Model 1866:
1. Sporting Rifle round or octagon barrel. Approximately 28,000 produced.
2. Carbine round barrel. Approximately 127,000 produced.
3. Musket round barrel. Approximately 14,000 produced.

Rifle and musket held 17 cartridges; carbine capacity of 13 cartridges. Unlike Henry, Model 1866s were fitted with walnut forearm. Model 1866 discontinued in 1898 with approximately 170,000 guns produced. Model 1866 sold in various special order configurations such as: barrels longer or shorter than standard, including engraved guns. Prices listed represent only standard-model 1866s. Guns with special-order features, an independent appraisal from an expert is highly recommended.

First Model Rifle

First style has both Henry and King patent dates stamped on barrel. Flat-loading port cover and two-screw upper tang. Perhaps most distinctive feature of First Model is rapid drop at top rear of receiver near hammer. Often referred to as "Henry Drop", a reference to same receiver drop found on Henry rifle. First Models will be seen up through 15000 serial number range.

	NIB	EXC.	V.G.	GOOD	FAIR	POOR
	—	85000	45000	20000	13000	4000

First Model Carbine

	NIB	EXC.	V.G.	GOOD	FAIR	POOR
	—	40000	26000	17000	11000	3000

Second Model Rifle

The second style differs from the first most noticeably in its single screw upper tang and a flare at the front of the receiver to meet the forearm. The Second Model also has a more gradual drop at the rear of the receiver than the First Model. The Second Style Model 1866 appears through serial number 25000.

	NIB	EXC.	V.G.	GOOD	FAIR	POOR
	—	25000	19000	10500	7500	4000

Second Model Carbine

	NIB	EXC.	V.G.	GOOD	FAIR	POOR
	—	25000	16000	9500	6750	3500

Third Model Rifle

Third style's most noticeable characteristic is more moderately curved receiver shape at rear of frame. Serial number now stamped in block numerals behind trigger, thus allowing numbers to be seen for first time without removing stock. Barrel marking stamped with Winchester address. Third Model found between serial numbers 25000 and 149000. For the first time, musket version was produced in this serial-number range.

	NIB	EXC.	V.G.	GOOD	FAIR	POOR
	—	22000	15000	8000	5000	3000

Model 1866

Third Model Carbine

	NIB	EXC.	V.G.	GOOD	FAIR	POOR
	—	25000	17000	9500	5500	3500

Third Model Musket

	NIB	EXC.	V.G.	GOOD	FAIR	POOR
	—	25000	17000	9500	5500	3500

Model 1873

Third Model Musket

	NIB	EXC.	V.G.	GOOD	FAIR	POOR
	—	12000	10000	8000	4500	2500

Model 1866

Fourth Model Rifle

Fourth style has even less pronounced drop at top rear of frame. Serial number stamped in script on lower tang under lever. Fourth Model seen between serial number 149000 and

	NIB	EXC.	V.G.	GOOD	FAIR	POOR

170100. Late guns having iron buttplate instead of brass.

	—	25000	17000	9500	5500	3500

Fourth Model Carbine

	—	18000	13000	11000	3500	2500

Fourth Model Musket

	—	14500	11000	8000	3500	2500

Model 1866 Iron Frame Rifle Musket

Overall length 54-1/2"; barrel length 33-1/4"; caliber .45 centerfire. Walnut stock with case hardened furniture, barrel burnished bright, the receiver case hardened. The finger lever catch mounted within a large bolster at the rear of the lever. Unmarked except for serial numbers that appear externally on the receiver and often the buttplate tang. Approximately 25 made during the early autumn of 1866.26Value speculative.

Model 1866 Iron Frame Swiss Sharpshooters Rifle

As above, but in .41 Swiss caliber and fitted with a Scheutzen style stock supplied by the firm of Weber Ruesch in Zurich. Marked Weber Ruesch, Zurich on the barrel and serial numbered externally. Approximately 400 to 450 manufactured in 1866 and 1867.

Model 1867 Iron Frame Carbine

Overall length 39-1/4"; barrel length 20"; caliber .44 rimfire. Walnut stock with case hardened furniture; the barrel and magazine tube blued; the receiver case hardened. The finger lever catch mounted within the rear curl of the lever. Unmarked except for serial numbers that appear externally on the receiver and often the buttplate tang. Approximately 20 manufactured. Prospective purchasers are strongly advised to secure an expert appraisal prior to acquisition.

Model 1868 Iron Frame Rifle Musket

Overall length 49-1/2" (.455 cal.), 50-1/2" or 53" (.45 and .47 cal.); barrel length 29-1/2" (.455 cal.) and 30-1/4" or 33" (.45 and .47 cal.); calibers .45, .455, and .47 centerfire. Walnut stock with case hardened or burnished bright (.45 and .47 cal.) furniture; the barrel burnished bright; the receiver case hardened or burnished bright (.45 and .47 cal.). The finger lever catch mounted on the lower receiver tang. The rear of the finger lever machined with a long flat extension on its upper surface. Unmarked except for serial number. Approximately 30 examples made in .45 and .455 caliber and 250 in .47 caliber.

Model 1868 Iron Frame Carbine

Overall length 40"; barrel length 20"; caliber .44 centerfire. Walnut stock with case hardened furniture; barrel and magazine tube blued; the receiver case hardened. The finger lever catch as above. Unmarked except for serial numbers (receiver and buttplate tang). Approximately 25 manufactured.

Model 1873

This Winchester rifle was one of the most popular lever-actions the company ever produced. This is the "gun that won the West" and with good reason. It was chambered for the more powerful centerfire cartridge, the .44-40. Compared to the .44 Henry, this cartridge was twice as good. With the introduction of the single-action Colt pistol in 1878, chambered for the same cartridge, the individual had the convenience of a pistol for protection and the accuracy of the Winchester for food and protection. The .44-40 was the standard cartridge for the Model 1873. Three additional cartridges were offered but were not as popular as the .44. The .38-40 was first offered in 1879 and the .32-20 was introduced in 1882. In 1884 the Model 1873 was offered in .22 caliber rimfire with a few special order guns built in .22 extra long rimfire. Approximately 19,552 .22 caliber Model 1873s were produced.

Early model 1873s were fitted with an iron receiver until 1884, when a steel receiver was introduced. The Model 1873 was offered in three styles:

1. Sporting Rifle, 24" round, octagon, or half-octagon barrel. Equipped standard with a crescent iron buttplate, straight-grip stock and capped forearm.
2. Carbine, 20" round barrel. Furnished standard with a rounded iron buttplate, straight-grip stock, and carbine style fore-end fastened to the barrel with a single barrel band.
3. Musket, 30" round barrel. Standard musket is furnished with a nearly full-length forearm fastened to the barrel with three barrel bands. The buttstock has a rounded buttplate.

The upper tang was marked with the model designation and the serial number was stamped on the lower tang. Caliber stampings on the Model 1873 are found on the bottom of the frame and on the breech end of the barrel. Winchester discontinued the Model 1873 in 1919, after producing about 720,000 guns.The Winchester Model 1873 was offered with a large number of extra-cost options that greatly affect the value of the gun. For example, Winchester built two sets of special Model 1873s: the 1-of-100 and the 1-of-1000. Winchester sold only eight 1-of-100 Model 1873s, and 136 of the 1-of-1000 guns that were built. In 1991 a few of these special guns were sold at auction and brought prices exceeding $75,000. The prices listed here are for standard guns only. For Model 1873 with special

NIB	EXC.	V.G.	GOOD	FAIR	POOR

features, it is best to secure an expert appraisal. Model 1873s with case colored receivers will bring a premium.

The Winchester Model 1873 was offered with a large number of extra-cost options that greatly affect the value of the gun. For example, Winchester built two sets of special Model 1873's: the 1-of-100 and the 1-of-1000. Winchester sold only eight 1-of-100 Model 1873s, and 136 of the 1-of-1000 guns that were built. In 1991 a few of those special guns were sold at auction and brought prices exceeding $75,000. The prices listed here are for standard guns only. For Model 1873 with special features, it is best to secure an expert appraisal. Model 1873s with case colored receivers will bring a premium.

First Model Rifle

The primary difference between the various styles of the Model 1873 is found in the appearance and construction of the dust cover. The First Model has a dust cover held in place with grooved guides on either side. A checkered oval finger grip is found on top of the dust cover. The latch that holds the lever firmly in place is anchored into the lower tang with visible threads. On later First Models, these threads are not visible. First Models appear from serial number 1 to about 31000.

NIB	EXC.	V.G.	GOOD	FAIR	POOR
—	18000	15000	6000	3000	1400

First Model Carbine

NIB	EXC.	V.G.	GOOD	FAIR	POOR
—	22000	18000	7500	4000	2500

First Model Musket

NIB	EXC.	V.G.	GOOD	FAIR	POOR
—	14000	12000	5000	2500	1000

Second Model Rifle

The dust cover on the Second Model operates on one central guide secured to the receiver with two screws. The checkered oval finger grip is still used, but on later Second Models this is changed to a serrated finger grip on the rear of the dust cover. Second Models are found in the 31000 to 90000 serial number range.

NIB	EXC.	V.G.	GOOD	FAIR	POOR
—	10000	8000	4000	2000	1250

Second Model Carbine

NIB	EXC.	V.G.	GOOD	FAIR	POOR
—	15000	13000	7000	3000	1000

Second Model Musket

NIB	EXC.	V.G.	GOOD	FAIR	POOR
—	5000	4000	2000	1250	900

Third Model Rifle

The central guide rail is still present on the Third Model, but it is now integrally machined as part of the receiver. The serrated rear edges of the dust cover are still present on the Third Model.

NIB	EXC.	V.G.	GOOD	FAIR	POOR
—	6000	4000	2000	1000	750

Third Model Carbine

NIB	EXC.	V.G.	GOOD	FAIR	POOR
—	12500	8000	5000	2000	800

Model 1873 .22 Rimfire Rifle

Winchester's first .22 caliber rifle and the first .22 caliber repeating rifle made in America was introduced in 1884 and discontinued in 1904. Its drawback was the small caliber. The general preference during this period of time was for the larger-caliber rifles. Winchester sold a little more than 19,000 .22 caliber Model 1873s.

NIB	EXC.	V.G.	GOOD	FAIR	POOR
—	8000	6500	3000	1700	750

Model 1876

Winchester's Model 1876, sometimes referred to as the Centennial Model, was the company's response to the public's demand for a repeater rifle capable of handling larger and more potent calibers. Many single-shot rifles were available at this time to shoot more powerful cartridges, and Winchester redesigned the earlier Model 1873 to answer this need. The principal changes made to the Model 1873 were a larger and stronger receiver to handle more powerful cartridges. Both the carbine and the musket had their forearms extended to cover the full length of the magazine tube. The carbine barrel was increased in length from 20" to 22", and the musket barrel length was increased from 30 to 32". The Model 1876 was the first Winchester to be offered with a pistol-grip stock on its special Sporting Rifle. The Model 1876 was available in these calibers: .45-77 W.C.F., .50-95 Express, .45-60 W.C.F., .40-60 W.C.F. The Model 1876 was offered in four different styles:

1. Sporting Rifle, 28" round, octagon, or half-octagon barrel. This rifle was fitted with a straight-grip stock with a crescent iron buttplate. A special sporting rifle was offered with a pistol-grip stock.
2. Express Rifle, 26" round, octagon, or half-octagon barrel. The same sporting rifle stock was used.

3. Carbine, 22" round barrel with full-length forearm secured by one barrel band and straight grip stock.
4. Musket, 32" round barrel with full-length forearm secured by one barrel band and straight grip stock. Stamped on the barrel is the Winchester address with King's patent date. The caliber marking is stamped on bottom of the receiver near the magazine tube and the breech end of the barrel. Winchester also furnished the Model 1876 in 1-of-100 and 1-of-1000 special guns. Only eight 1-of-100 1876s were built and 54 1-of-1000 76s were built. As with their Model 1873 counterparts, these rare guns often sell in the $75,000 range or more. Approximately 64,000 Model 1876s were built by Winchester between 1876 and 1897. As with other Winchesters, the prices given are for standard guns.

First Model Rifle

As with the Model 1873, the primary difference in model types lies in the dust cover. The First Model has no dust cover and is seen between serial number 1 and 3000.

NIB	EXC.	V.G.	GOOD	FAIR	POOR
—	17500	12000	6000	2750	1000

First Model Carbine

NIB	EXC.	V.G.	GOOD	FAIR	POOR
—	12000	9500	6500	2500	1000

First Model Musket

NIB	EXC.	V.G.	GOOD	FAIR	POOR
—	20000	19000	10000	5000	1500

Second Model Rifle

The Second Model has a dust cover with guide rail attached to the receiver with two screws. On the early Second Model an oval finger guide is stamped on top of the dust cover while later models have a serrated finger guide along the rear edge of the dust cover. Second Models range from serial numbers 3000 to 30000.

NIB	EXC.	V.G.	GOOD	FAIR	POOR
—	11000	7500	4000	2000	1000

Second Model Carbine

NIB	EXC.	V.G.	GOOD	FAIR	POOR
—	11000	7500	4000	2000	1000

Second Model Musket

NIB	EXC.	V.G.	GOOD	FAIR	POOR
—	20000	15000	8000	1750	1000

Second Model Northwest Mounted Police Carbine

The folding rear sight is graduated in meters instead of yards.

NIB	EXC.	V.G.	GOOD	FAIR	POOR
—	15000	9000	4500	2000	1250

Third Model Rifle

The dust cover guide rail on Third Model 76s is integrally machined as part of the receiver with a serrated rear edge on the dust cover. Third Model will be seen from serial numbers 30000 to 64000.

NIB	EXC.	V.G.	GOOD	FAIR	POOR
—	9000	5500	3250	1500	750

Third Model Carbine

NIB	EXC.	V.G.	GOOD	FAIR	POOR
—	12500	8000	3000	2000	1250

Third Model Musket

NIB	EXC.	V.G.	GOOD	FAIR	POOR
—	14000	10000	7500	4000	1000

Winchester Hotchkiss Bolt-Action Rifle

This model is also known as the Hotchkiss Magazine Gun or the Model 1883. This rifle was designed by Benjamin Hotchkiss in 1876, and Winchester acquired the manufacturing rights to the rifle in 1877. In 1879 the first guns were delivered for sale. The Hotchkiss rifle was a bolt-action firearm designed for military and sporting use. It was the first bolt-action rifle made by Winchester. The rifle was furnished in .45-70 Government, and although the 1884 Winchester catalog lists a .40-65 Hotchkiss as being available, no evidence exists that such a chamber was ever actually furnished. The Model 1883 was available in three different styles:

1. Sporting Rifle, 26" round, octagon, or half-octagon barrel fitted with a rifle-type stock that included a modified pistol grip or straight-grip stock.
2. Carbine, 24" round or 22-1/2" round barrel with military-style straight-grip stock.
3. Musket, 32" or 28" round barrel with almost full-length military-style straight-grip stock. Winchester produced the Model 1883 until 1899, having built about 85,000 guns.

First Model Sporting Rifle

This model has the safety and a turn button magazine cut-off located above the trigger guard on the right side. The Sporting Rifle is furnished with a 26" round or octagon barrel while the carbine has a 24" round barrel with a saddle ring on the left side of the stock. The musket has a 32" round barrel with two barrel bands, a steel forearm tip, and bayonet attachment under the barrel. The serial number range for the First Model is between 1 and about 6419.

NIB	EXC.	V.G.	GOOD	FAIR	POOR
—	2000	1650	1250	800	400

	NIB	EXC.	V.G.	GOOD	FAIR	POOR

First Model Carbine

	NIB	EXC.	V.G.	GOOD	FAIR	POOR
	—	5500	2500	1500	900	500

First Model Musket

	NIB	EXC.	V.G.	GOOD	FAIR	POOR
	—	2000	1650	1250	800	400

Second Model Sporting Rifle

On this model the safety is located on the top left side of the receiver, and the magazine cutoff is located on the top right side of the receiver to the rear of the bolt handle. The sporting rifle remains unchanged from the First Model with the above exceptions. The carbine has a 22-1/2" round barrel with a nickeled forearm cap. The musket now has a 28" barrel. Serial number range for the Second Model runs from 6420 to 22521.

Second Model Carbine

	NIB	EXC.	V.G.	GOOD	FAIR	POOR
	—	1750	1400	900	600	300

Second Model Musket

	NIB	EXC.	V.G.	GOOD	FAIR	POOR
	—	4500	2250	1000	750	500

Third Model Sporting Rifle

The Third Model is easily identified by the two-piece stock separated by the receiver. The specifications for the sporting rifle remain the same as before, while the carbine is now fitted with a 20" barrel with saddle ring and bar on the left side of the frame. The musket remains unchanged from the Second Model with the exception of the two-piece stock. Serial numbers of the Third Model range from 22552 to 84555.

	NIB	EXC.	V.G.	GOOD	FAIR	POOR
	—	1650	1250	800	500	300

Third Model Carbine

	NIB	EXC.	V.G.	GOOD	FAIR	POOR
	—	1650	1250	800	500	300

Third Model Musket

	NIB	EXC.	V.G.	GOOD	FAIR	POOR
	—	1650	1250	800	500	300

Model 1885 (Single-Shot)

The Model 1885 marks an important development between Winchester and John M. Browning. The Single-shot rifle was the first of many Browning patents that Winchester would purchase and provided the company with the opportunity to diversify its firearms line. The Model 1885 was the first single-shot rifle built by Winchester. The company offered more calibers in this model than any other. A total of 45 centerfire calibers were offered from the .22 extra long to the 50-110 express, as well as 14 rimfire caliber from .22 B.B. cap to the .44 flat Henry. Numerous barrel lengths, shapes and weights were available as were stock configurations, sights, and finishes. These rifles were also available in solid frame and takedown styles. One could almost argue that each of the 139,725 Model 1885s built are unique. Many collectors of Winchester Single-Shot specialize in nothing else. For this reason it is difficult to provide pricing that will cover most of the Model 1885s that the collector will encounter. However the prices given here are for standard guns in standard configurations.

The Model 1885 was offered in two basic frame types:

A. The High Wall was the first frame type produced and is so called because the frame covers the breech and hammer except for the hammer spur.
B. The breech and hammer are visible on the Low Wall frame with its low sides. This frame type was first introduced around the 5000 serial number range.

Both the High Wall and the Low Wall were available in two type frame profiles; the Thickside and the Thinside. The Thickside frame has flat sides that do not widen out to meet the stock. The Thickside is more common on the low wall rifle and rare on the High Walls. The Thinside frame has shallow milled sides that widen out to meet the stock. Thinside frames are common on High Wall guns and rare on Low Wall rifles.

1. The standard High Wall rifle was available with octagon or round barrel with length determined by caliber. The buttstock and forearm were plain walnut with crescent buttplate and blued frame.
2. The standard Low Wall featured a round or octagon barrel with length determined by caliber and plain walnut stock and forearm with crescent buttplate.
3. The High Wall musket most often had a 26" round barrel chambered for the .22 caliber cartridge. Larger calibers were available as were different barrel lengths. The High Wall Musket featured an almost full length forearm fastened to the barrel with a single barrel band and rounded buttplate.
4. The Low Wall musket is most often referred to as the Winder Musket named after the distinguished marksman, Colonel C.B. Winder. This model features a Lyman receiver sight and was made in .22 caliber.
5. The High Wall Schuetzen rifle was designed for serious target shooting and was available with numerous extras including a 30" octagon barrel and medium weight without rear sight seat; fancy walnut checkered pistol grip Schuetzen-style buttplate; checkered forearm; double set

	NIB	EXC.	V.G.	GOOD	FAIR	POOR

triggers; spur finger lever, and adjustable palm rest.

6. The Low Wall carbine was available in 15", 16", 18", and 20" round barrels. The carbine featured a saddle ring on the left side of the frame and a rounded buttplate.

7. The Model 1885 was also available in a High Wall shotgun in 20 gauge with 26" round barrel and straight grip stock with shotgun style rubber buttplate. The Model 1885 was manufactured between 1885 and 1920 with a total production of about 140,000 guns.

CALIBER NOTE: As stated above it is difficult to provide pricing on specific rifles, especially calibers, because of the wide range of variables. However, the collector may find it useful to know that the most common rimfire calibers were the .22 Short, .22 WCF, and .22 Long, in that order, with the .22 Long Rifle a distant fourth. The most common centerfire chambers were the .32 WCF and the .32-40. Other popular centerfire calibers were the .38-55, .25-20, .44 WCF, .32 Long WCF, and the .45-70. There were a number of chamberings that are extremely rare (one of each built). It is strongly recommended that research is done prior to a sale.

Standard High Wall Rifle

NIB	EXC.	V.G.	GOOD	FAIR	POOR
—	5000	3500	2200	1500	950

Standard Low Wall Rifle

NIB	EXC.	V.G.	GOOD	FAIR	POOR
—	1800	1500	1400	1200	900

High Wall Musket

NIB	EXC.	V.G.	GOOD	FAIR	POOR
—	1600	1300	1000	700	425

Low Wall Musket (Winder Musket)

NIB	EXC.	V.G.	GOOD	FAIR	POOR
—	1400	1200	800	500	300

High Wall Schuetzen Rifle

NIB	EXC.	V.G.	GOOD	FAIR	POOR
—	10000	7000	3000	1850	1000

Low Wall Carbine

NIB	EXC.	V.G.	GOOD	FAIR	POOR
—	7500	5000	3500	2750	1500

High Wall Shotgun

NIB	EXC.	V.G.	GOOD	FAIR	POOR
—	4500	3000	2250	1250	850

Model 1886

Based on a John Browning patent, the Model 1886 was one of the finest and strongest lever-actions ever utilized in a Winchester rifle. Winchester introduced the Model 1886 in order to take advantage of the more powerful centerfire cartridges of the time.

Model 1886 Rifles and carbines were furnished with black, walnut stocks, case hardened frames, and blued barrels and magazine tubes. In 1901 Winchester discontinued the use of case hardened frames on all its rifles and used blued frames instead. For this reason, case hardened Model 1886 rifles will bring a premium. Winchester provided a large selection of extra cost options on the Model 1886, and for rifles with these options, a separate evaluation should be made by a reliable source. The Model 1886 was produced from 1886 to 1935 with about 160,000 in production.

The rifle was available in 10 different chambers:

.45-70 U.S. Government	.50-110 Express
.45-90 W.C.F.	.40-70 W.C.F.
.40-82 W.C.F.	.38-70 W.C.F.
.40-65 W.C.F.	.50-100-450
.38-56 W.C.F.	.33 W.C.F.

The most popular caliber was the .45-70 Government. Prices of the Model 1886 are influenced by caliber, with the larger calibers bringing a premium. The 1886 was available in several different configurations.

1. Sporting Rifle, 26", round, octagon and half-octagon barrel, full or half magazine and straight-grip stockwith plain forearm.

2. Fancy Sporting Rifle, 26" round or octagon barrel, half or full magazine and fancy checkered walnut pistol-grip with checkered forearm.

3. Takedown Rifle, 24" round barrel, full or half magazine with straight-grip stock fitted with shotgun rubber buttplate and plain forearm.

4. Extra Lightweight Takedown Rifle, 22" round barrel, full or half magazine with straight-grip stock fitted with shotgun rubber buttplate and plain forearm.

5. Extra Lightweight Rifle, 22" round barrel, full or half magazine with straight-grip stock fitted with a shotgun rubber buttplate and plain forearm.

6. Carbine, 22" round barrel, full or half magazine with straight-grip stock and plain forearm.

	NIB	EXC.	V.G.	GOOD	FAIR	POOR

7. Musket, 30" round barrel, musket-style forearm with one barrel band. Military-style sights. About 350 Model 1886 Muskets were produced.

NOTE: For .50 Express add a premium of 20 percent. Case colored Model 1886s will bring a premium of 20 percent.

Sporting Rifle

	NIB	EXC.	V.G.	GOOD	FAIR	POOR
	—	15000	15000	7500	5000	2500

Fancy Sporting Rifle

	NIB	EXC.	V.G.	GOOD	FAIR	POOR
	—	25000	14500	8000	6000	3000

Takedown Rifle—Standard

	NIB	EXC.	V.G.	GOOD	FAIR	POOR
	—	12500	900	4200	2000	700

Extra Lightweight Takedown Rifle—.33 caliber

	NIB	EXC.	V.G.	GOOD	FAIR	POOR
	—	9000	5000	2000	750	400

Extra Lightweight Takedown Rifle—Other Calibers

	NIB	EXC.	V.G.	GOOD	FAIR	POOR
	—	8750	6000	1800	1250	500

Extra Lightweight Rifle—.33 caliber

	NIB	EXC.	V.G.	GOOD	FAIR	POOR
	—	6000	4000	1800	1000	500

Extra Lightweight Rifle—Other Calibers

	NIB	EXC.	V.G.	GOOD	FAIR	POOR
	—	7000	5500	3000	950	500

Carbine

Model 1886 carbine barrels are 22". A few were Trappers with 20" barrels. Add 50 percent if Trapper.

	NIB	EXC.	V.G.	GOOD	FAIR	POOR
	—	19000	11000	7500	4500	2000

Musket

	NIB	EXC.	V.G.	GOOD	FAIR	POOR
	—	19000	15000	9000	3500	1500

Model 71

When Winchester dropped the Model 1886 from its line in 1935, the company replaced its large-bore lever-action rifle with the Model 71 chambered for the .348 caliber. The Model 71 is similar in appearance to the Model 1886 with some internal parts strengthened to handle the powerful .348 cartridge. The rifle was available in three basic configurations:

1. Standard Rifle, 24" round barrel, 3/4 magazine, plain walnut pistol-grip stock and semi-beavertail forearm.
2. Standard Rifle (Carbine), 20" round barrel, 3/4 magazine, plain walnut pistol-grip stock and semi-beavertail forearm.
3. Deluxe Rifle, 24" round barrel, 3/4 magazine, checkered walnut pistol-grip stock and checkered semi-beavertail forearm. The frames and barrels were blued on all models of this rifle.
4. Deluxe Rifle (Carbine), 20" round barrel, 3/4 magazine, checkered walnut pistol-grip stock and checkered semi-beavertail forearm. The frames and barrels were blued on all models of this rifle.

The Model 71 was produced from 1935 to 1957, with about 47,000 built.

NOTE: For pre-war Model 71s add a premium of 20 percent. The pre-war Model 71 has a longer tang than its post-war equivalent. For a bolt peep sight add 10 percent.

Standard Rifle

	NIB	EXC.	V.G.	GOOD	FAIR	POOR
	—	1500	1200	800	400	300

Standard Rifle (Carbine)

	NIB	EXC.	V.G.	GOOD	FAIR	POOR
	—	3250	2000	1600	1200	650

Deluxe Rifle

	NIB	EXC.	V.G.	GOOD	FAIR	POOR
	—	3500	3050	800	525	425

Deluxe Rifle (Carbine)

	NIB	EXC.	V.G.	GOOD	FAIR	POOR
	—	4100	3500	2000	1250	700

Model 1892

The Model 1892 was an updated successor to the Model 1873 using a scaled down version of the Model 1886 action. The rifle was chambered for the popular smaller cartridges of the day, namely the .25-20, .32-20, .38-40, .44-40, and the rare .218 Bee. The rifle was available in several different configurations.

1. Sporting Rifle, solid frame or takedown (worth an extra premium of about 20 percent), 24" round, octagon, or half-octagon barrel with 1/2, 3/3 or full magazines. plain straight-grip walnut stock with capped forearm.

	NIB	EXC.	V.G.	GOOD	FAIR	POOR

2. Fancy Sporting Rifle, solid frame or takedown (worth an extra premium of about 20 percent), 24" round, octagon, or half-octagon barrel with 1/2, 3/3 or full magazines. Checkered walnut pistol-grip walnut stock with checkered capped forearm.
3. Carbine, 20" round barrel, full or half magazine, plain walnut straight-grip stock with one barrel band forearm. Carbines were offered only with solid frames.
4. Trapper's Carbine, 18", 16", 15", or 14" round barrel with the same dimensions of standard carbine. Federal law prohibits the possession of rifles with barrel lengths shorter then 16". The Model 1892 Trapper's Carbine can be exempted from this law as a curio and relic with federal permit providing the trapper is an original trapper and left the factory with the short trapper barrel.
5. Musket, 30" round barrel with full magazine. Almost full length forearm held by two barrel bands. Buttstock is plain walnut with straight grip.

The Model 1892 was built between 1892 and 1932 with slightly more than 1 million sold. The Model 1892 carbine continued to be offered for sale until 1941.

NOTE: Antique Winchester Model 1892s (pre-1898 manufacture) will bring a premium of 10 percent.

Sporting Rifle

—	5000	3500	1250	700	350

Fancy Sporting Rifle

—	12000	7500	4000	2500	1000

Carbine

—	3500	2500	1700	1200	600

Trapper's Carbine

NOTE: Add 20 percent for 15" barrel; 50 percent for carbines chambered for .25-20 cartridge.

—	12000	8500	4000	2500	1250

Musket

—	—	9500	4500	2500	1500

Based on a John M. Browning patent, the Model 1894 was the most successful centerfire rifle Winchester ever produced. This model is still in production, and the values given here reflect those rifles produced before 1964, or around serial number 2550000. The Model 1894 was the first Winchester developed especially for the smokeless powder and was chambered for these cartridges: .32-40, .38-55, .25-35 Winchester, 30-30 Winchester, and the .32 Winchester Special. The rifle was available in several different configurations.

1. Sporting Rifle, 26" round, octagon or half-octagon barrel, in slid frame or takedown. Full, 2/3, or 1/2 magazines were available. Plain walnut straight or pistol-grip stock with crescent buttplate and plain capped forearm.
2. Fancy Sporting Rifle, 26" round, octagon or half-octagon barrel, in slid frame or takedown. Full, 2/3, or 1/2 magazines were available. Fancy walnut checkered straight or pistol-grip stock with crescent buttplate and checkered fancy capped forearm.
3. Extra Lightweight Rifle, 22" or 26" round barrel with half magazine. plain walnut straight-grip stock with shotgun buttplate and plain capped forearm.
4. Carbine, 20" round barrel, plain walnut straight-grip stock with carbine style buttplate. Forearm was plain walnut uncapped with one barrel band. Carbines were available with solid frame only. Carbines made prior to 1925 were fitted with a saddle ring on the left side of the receiver and worth a premium over carbines without a saddle ring.
5. Trappers Carbine, 18", 16", 15", or 14". Buttstock, forearm, and saddle ring specifications same as standard carbine. All Model 1894s were furnished with blued frames and barrels, although case hardened frames were available as an extra-cost option. Case colored Model 1894s are rare and worth a considerable premium, perhaps as much as 1,000 percent. Guns with extra-cost options should be evaluated by an expert to determine proper value. Between 1894 and 1963, approximately 2,550,000 Model 1984s were sold.

NOTE: Antique Winchester Model 1894s (pre-1898 manufacture) will bring a premium of 10 percent. First year production guns, October 1894 to December 1894, documented by the Cody Museum will command a 100 percent premium.

NOTE: Values are for guns with saddle rings. For carbines without saddle rings deduct 35 percent. Add 25 percent for carbines chambered for .25-35 or .38-55 cartridge.

Model 1894

First Model Sporting Rifle

Very early model that incorporates a screw entering the receiver over the loading port from the outside. Rare.

—	7000	4000	2000	1250	500

	NIB	EXC.	V.G.	GOOD	FAIR	POOR

Sporting Rifle

	NIB	EXC.	V.G.	GOOD	FAIR	POOR
	—	4000	3000	1500	850	450

NOTE: Takedown versions are worth approximately 20 percent more.

Fancy Sporting Rifle

	NIB	EXC.	V.G.	GOOD	FAIR	POOR
	—	12000	7500	3500	2000	900

NOTE: Takedown versions are worth approximately 20 percent more. Fancy Sporting Rifles were also engraved at the customer's request. Check factory where possible and proceed with caution. Factory engraved Model 1894s are extremely valuable.

Extra Lightweight Rifle

	NIB	EXC.	V.G.	GOOD	FAIR	POOR
	—	5000	3500	1500	1000	450

Carbine

	NIB	EXC.	V.G.	GOOD	FAIR	POOR
	—	3000	2000	600	400	200

Trapper's Carbine

	NIB	EXC.	V.G.	GOOD	FAIR	POOR
	—	6500	4250	2500	1500	700

NOTE: Add 30 percent for carbines chambered for .25-35 or .38-55 calibers.

Model 53

This model was in fact a slightly more modern version of the Model 1892 offered in these calibers: .25-20, .32-20, and the .44-40. It was available in only one style: the Sporting Rifle, 22" round barrel, half magazine, straight- or pistol-grip plain walnut stock with shotgun butt. It was available in solid frame or takedown with blued frame and barrel. The Model 53 was produced from 1924 to 1932 with about 25,000 built. **NOTE:** Add 10 percent for takedown model. Add 40 percent for rifles chambered for .44-40 cartridge. A few of these rifles were fitted with stainless steel barrel in the early 1930s. If the black paint on these barrels is in good condition, they will bring a substantial premium.

	NIB	EXC.	V.G.	GOOD	FAIR	POOR
	—	3000	2000	1000	500	300

Sporting Rifle

	NIB	EXC.	V.G.	GOOD	FAIR	POOR
	—	3000	2000	1000	500	300

Model 55

This model was a continuation of the Model 1894 except in a simplified version. Available in the same calibers as the Model 1894, this rifle could be ordered only with a 24" round barrel, plain walnut straight-grip stock with plain fore-end and shotgun butt. Frame and barrel were blued with solid or takedown features. This model was produced between 1924 and 1932 with about 21,000 sold. Serial numbers for the Model 55 were numbered separately until about serial number 4500; then the guns were numbered in the Model 1894 sequence. **NOTE:** .25-35 caliber will bring about a 60 percent premium. Add 10 percent for models with solid frames.

	NIB	EXC.	V.G.	GOOD	FAIR	POOR
	—	1500	1000	650	450	200

Standard Rifle

	NIB	EXC.	V.G.	GOOD	FAIR	POOR
	—	1500	1000	650	450	200

Model 64

An improved version of the Model 55, this gun featured a larger magazine, pistol-grip stock, and forged front sight ramp. The trigger pull was also improved. Frame and barrel were blued. Chambered for the .25-35 Win., .30-30 Win., .32 Win. Special, and the .219 zipper added in 1938 (and discontinued in the Model 64 in 1941). Serial number of the Model 64 was concurrent with the Model 1894. Built between 1933 and 1957, approximately 67,000 were sold. This model was reintroduced in 1972 and discontinued in 1973. The values listed are for the early version only.

	NIB	EXC.	V.G.	GOOD	FAIR	POOR
	—	1200	900	500	300	200

Standard Rifle

20" barrel. **NOTE:** Deluxe model add 50 percent to prices. Rifles chambered for .219 Zipper and .25-35 cartridges add 100 percent. Add 10 percent for bolt peep sight. Model 64s in .219 Zipper left factory with bolt peep sights as original equipment.

	NIB	EXC.	V.G.	GOOD	FAIR	POOR
	—	1200	900	500	300	200

Carbine

	NIB	EXC.	V.G.	GOOD	FAIR	POOR
	—	1550	1000	650	500	250

Model 65

Continuation of Model 53. Offered in three calibers: .25-20, .32-20 and .218 Bee. Had several improvements over Model 53, namely magazine capacity increased to seven cartridges, forged ramp for front sight and lighter trigger pull. Model 65 available only in solid blued frame with blued barrel and pistol grip with plain walnut stock. About 5,700 of these rifles built between 1933 and 1947. **NOTE:** Add 10 percent for bolt peep sight. Model 65s in .218 Bee left factory with bolt peep sights as original equipment.

NIB	EXC.	V.G.	GOOD	FAIR	POOR
—	5000	4000	2000	1000	500

Model 1895

The Model 1895 was the first nondetachable box magazine rifle offered by Winchester. Built on a John M. Browning patent, this rifle was introduced by Winchester to meet the demand for a rifle that could handle the new high-power, smokeless hunting cartridges of the period. The Model 1895 was available in these calibers: .30-40 Krag, .38-72 Winchester, .40-72 Winchester, .303 British, .35 Winchester, .405 Government, 7.62 Russian, .30-03, and .30-06. The rifle gained fame as a favorite hunting rifle of Theodore Roosevelt. Because of its box magazine, the Model 1895 has a distinctive look like no other Winchester lever-action rifle. The rifle was available in several different configurations:

1. Sporting Rifle, 28" or 24" (depending on caliber) round barrel, plain walnut straight-grip stock with plain walnut fore-end. The first 5,000 rifles were manufactured with flat-sided receivers, and the balance of production were built with the receiver sides contoured. After serial-number 60000, a takedown version was available.
2. Fancy Sporting Rifle, 28" round barrel, fancy walnut checkered straight-grip stock and fancy walnut checkered forearm. Rifles with serial numbers below 5000 had flat sided frames.
3. Carbine, 22" round barrel, plain walnut straight-grip stock with military-style hand guard forend. Some carbines are furnished with saddle rings on left side of receiver.
4. Musket:
A. Standard Musket, 28" round, plain walnut straight-grip stock with musket style fore-end with two barrel bands.
B. U.S. Army N.R.A. Musket, 30" round barrel, Model 1901 Krag-Jorgensen rear sight. Stock similar to the standard musket. This musket could be used for "Any Military Arm" matches under the rules of the National Rifle Association.
C. N.R.A. Musket, Models 1903 and 1906, 24" round barrel with special buttplate. Also eligible for all matches under "Any Military Arm" sponsored by the NRA. This musket was fitted with the same stock as listed above.
D. U.S. Army Musket, 28" round barrel chambered for the .30-40 Krag. Came equipped with or without knife bayonet. These muskets were furnished to the U.S. Army for use during the Spanish-American War and are "US" marked on the receiver.
E. Russian Musket, similar to standard musket but fitted with clip guides in the top of the receiver and with bayonet. Approximately 294,000 Model 1895 Muskets were sold to the Imperial Russian Government between 1915 and 1916. The first 15,000 Russian Muskets had 8" knife bayonets, and the rest were fitted with 16" bayonets.

The Model 1895 was produced from 1895 to 1931 with about 426,000 sold.

NOTE: Add a 10 percent premium for rifles built before 1898.

Sporting Rifle

NIB	EXC.	V.G.	GOOD	FAIR	POOR
—	5000	3000	1200	700	300

NOTE: Flat-side rifles will bring a premium of 100 percent. Takedown rifles will add an additional 15 percent.

Fancy Sporting Rifles

NIB	EXC.	V.G.	GOOD	FAIR	POOR
—	7000	5000	1500	1100	500

NOTE: Flat-side rifles will bring a premium of 100 percent. Takedown rifles will add an additional 15 percent.

Carbine

NIB	EXC.	V.G.	GOOD	FAIR	POOR
—	5500	3250	1550	900	300

Standard Musket

NIB	EXC.	V.G.	GOOD	FAIR	POOR
—	3200	1800	1000	600	300

U.S. Army N.R.A. Musket

NIB	EXC.	V.G.	GOOD	FAIR	POOR
—	4500	2000	1200	800	400

N.R.A. Musket, Model 1903 and 1906

NIB	EXC.	V.G.	GOOD	FAIR	POOR
—	5500	2500	1200	800	400

U.S. Army Musket

NIB	EXC.	V.G.	GOOD	FAIR	POOR
—	5000	3000	1500	850	450

	NIB	EXC.	V.G.	GOOD	FAIR	POOR

Russian Musket

	—	4000	2500	1000	500	250

Breechloading Double-Barrel Shotgun

Winchester imported an English-made shotgun sold under the Winchester name between 1879 and 1884. The gun was available in 10 and 12 gauge with 30" or 32" Damascus barrels. It was sold in five separate grades referred to as "classes." The lowest grade was the "D" and the best grade was called the "Match Grade." These were marked on the sidelocks. The center rib was stamped "Winchester Repeating Arms Co., New Haven, Connecticut, U.S.A." Prices shown for "D" grade. Add 10 percent for "C" grade; 20 percent for "B" grade; and 30 percent for "A" grade. About 10,000 of these guns were imported by Winchester.

Class A, B, C, and D

	—	2500	2250	1250	850	500

Match Gun

	—	5000	4000	1800	850	500

Model 1887 Shotgun

Winchester enjoyed a great deal of success with its imported English shotgun, and the company decided to manufacture a shotgun of its own. In 1885 it purchased the patent for a lever-action shotgun designed by John M. Browning. By 1887 Winchester had delivered the first model 1887 in 12 gauge and shortly after offered the gun in 10 gauge. Both gauges were offered with 30" or 32" Full choked barrels, with the 30" standard on the 12 gauge and 32" standard on the 10 gauge. A Riot Gun was offered in 1898 both in 10, and 12 gauge with 20" barrels choked cylinder. Both variations of the Model 1887 were offered with plain walnut pistol-grip stocks with plain fore-end. The frame was case hardened and the barrel blued. Between 1887 and 1901 Winchester sold approximately 65,000 Model 1887 shotguns.

Standard Shotgun

	—	2750	1500	850	500	300

Riot Shotgun

	—	3000	2000	950	600	400

Model 1901 Shotgun

This model is a redesign of the Model 1887 shotgun and was offered in 10 gauge only with a 32" barrel choked Full, Modified, or Cylinder. The barrel was reinforced to withstand the new smokeless powder loads and the frame was blued instead of case hardened. The stock was plain walnut with a modified pistol and plain forearm. The Model 1901 was built between 1901 and 1920 with about 65,000 guns sold.

	—	1500	1000	600	400	250

Model 1893

This was the first slide-action repeating shotgun built by Winchester. It featured an exposed hammer and side ejection. Based on a John M. Browning patent, this model was not altogether satisfactory. The action proved to be too weak to handle smokeless loads, even though the gun was designed for black powder. The gun was offered in 12 gauge with 30" or 32" barrels choked Full. Other chokes were available on special order and will command a premium. The stock was plain walnut with a modified pistol grip, grooved slide handle, and hard rubber buttplate. The receiver and barrel were blued. Winchester produced the Model 1893 between 1893 and 1897, selling about 31000 guns.

	—	1000	700	600	325	250

Model 1897

The Model 1897 replaced the Model 1893, and while similar to the Model 1893, the new model had several improvements such as a stronger frame, chamber made longer to handle 2.75" shells, frame top was covered to force complete side ejection, the stock was made longer and with less drop. The Model 1897 was available in 12 or 16 gauge with the 12 gauge offered either in solid or takedown styles and the 16 gauge available in takedown only. The Model 1897 was available with barrel lengths of 20", 26", 28", 30" and 32" and in practically all choke options from full to cylinder. The shotgun could be ordered in several different configurations:
1. Standard Gun, 12 or 16 gauge, 30" barrel in 12 gauge and 28" barrel in 16 gauge, with plain walnut modified pistol-grip stock and grooved slide handle. Steel buttplate standard.
2. Trap Gun 12 or 16 gauge, 30" barrel in 12 gauge and 28" barrel in 16 gauge, fancy walnut stock with oil finish checkered pistol-grip or straight-grip stock with checkered slide handle. Marked "TRAP" on bottom of frame.
3. Pigeon Gun, 12 or 16 gauge, 28" barrel on both 12 and 16 gauge, straight- or pistol-grip stock same as Trap gun, receiver hand engraved.
4. Tournament Gun, 12 gauge only with 30" barrel, select walnut checkered straight-grip stock and checkered slide handle, top of receiver is matted to reduce glare.

	NIB	EXC.	V.G.	GOOD	FAIR	POOR

5. Brush Gun, 12 or 16 gauge, 26" barrel, Cylinder choke, has a slightly shorter magazine tube than standard gun, plain walnut modified pistol-grip stock with grooved slide handle.
6. Brush Gun, Takedown, same as above with takedown feature and standard length magazine tube.
7. Riot Gun, 12 gauge, 20" barrel bored to shoot buckshot, plain walnut modified pistol-grip stock with grooved slide handle. Solid frame or takedown.
8. Trench Gun, same as Riot Gun but fitted with barrel hand guard and bayonet.

The Winchester Model 1897 was a great seller for Winchester. During its 60-year production span, 1,025,000 guns were sold.

NOTE: Add 100 percent for 16 gauge guns in excellent, very good and good condition.

Standard Gun

	NIB	EXC.	V.G.	GOOD	FAIR	POOR
	—	1300	850	650	300	200

Trap Gun

	NIB	EXC.	V.G.	GOOD	FAIR	POOR
	—	1500	1200	800	500	400

Pigeon Gun/High Grade

	NIB	EXC.	V.G.	GOOD	FAIR	POOR
	—	8000	6000	5000	4000	500

Tournament Gun

	NIB	EXC.	V.G.	GOOD	FAIR	POOR
	—	2000	1700	900	750	400

Brush Gun

	NIB	EXC.	V.G.	GOOD	FAIR	POOR
	—	950	750	600	500	400

Riot Gun

	NIB	EXC.	V.G.	GOOD	FAIR	POOR
	—	1600	1050	750	450	300

Trench Gun

NOTE: Add 100 percent for 16-gauge guns in excellent, very good and good condition; 100 percent for military markings.

	NIB	EXC.	V.G.	GOOD	FAIR	POOR
	—	3500	2900	2250	1500	600

Winchester-Lee Straight Pull Rifle

U.S. Navy Musket

	NIB	EXC.	V.G.	GOOD	FAIR	POOR
	—	2500	2000	1500	700	500

Commercial Musket

	NIB	EXC.	V.G.	GOOD	FAIR	POOR
	—	2500	2000	1500	700	500

Sporting Rifle

	NIB	EXC.	V.G.	GOOD	FAIR	POOR
	—	2500	2000	1500	700	500

Model 1890

The Model 1890 was the first slide-action rifle ever produced by Winchester. Designed by John and Matthew Browning, this rifle was chambered for the .22 Short, Long, and Winchester Rimfire cartridges (the WRF cartridge was developed by Winchester specifically for the Model 1890) not on an interchangeable basis. In 1919 the .22 LR cartridge was offered as well. The rifle was a slide-action top ejecting rifle with an 18" under barrel magazine tube. All Model 1890s were furnished standard with plain walnut straight stocks with crescent buttplate and 12 groove slide handle. This rifle was one of the company's best selling small caliber firearms and was in worldwide use. The Model 1890 came in three separate and distinct variations that greatly affect its value:

1. First Model, solid frame, 24" octagon barrel, case hardened frame, and fixed rear sight. Approximately 15,552 of these First Model guns were produced, and their distinctive feature is concealed locking lugs and solid frame. Serial numbered on the lower tang only. Built from 1890 to 1892.
2. Second Model, takedown, 24" octagon barrel, case hardened frame, and adjustable rear sight. Serial numbered from 15553 to 112970 (on lower tang only) these Second Model guns feature the same concealed locking lugs but with the added takedown feature. A Deluxe version was offered with fancy walnut checkered straight- or pistol-grip stock and grooved slide handle.
2A. Second Model (blued frame variation), same as above but with blued frame. Serial numbered from 112971 to 325250 (on lower tang until 232328, then also on bottom front end of receiver) these blued frame Second Models are much more numerous than the case hardened variety. A Deluxe version was offered with fancy walnut checkered straight- or pistol-grip stock and grooved slide handle.
3. Third Model, takedown, 24" octagon barrel, blued frame, adjustable rear sight. Serial numbered from 325251 to as high as 853000 (numbered on both the lower tang and bottom front of receiver) the distinctive feature of the Third Model is the locking cut made on the front top of the receiver to allow the breech bolt to lock externally. A Deluxe version was offered with fancy walnut checkered stock, straight or pistol grip with grooved slide handle.

	NIB	EXC.	V.G.	GOOD	FAIR	POOR

Winchester offered many extra-cost options for this rifle that will greatly affect the value. Secure an expert appraisal before proceeding. The Model 1890 was produced from 1890 to 1932 with approximately 775,000 guns sold.

NOTE: For Third Models chambered for .22 LR add 25 percent premium.

First Model—Standard Grade

	NIB	EXC.	V.G.	GOOD	FAIR	POOR
	—	9000	5000	2500	1250	750

Second Model—Case Hardened FrameStandard

	NIB	EXC.	V.G.	GOOD	FAIR	POOR
	—	6000	3500	2000	1000	500

Deluxe

	NIB	EXC.	V.G.	GOOD	FAIR	POOR
	—	10000	7000	3500	2000	1000

Second Model—Blued FrameStandard

	NIB	EXC.	V.G.	GOOD	FAIR	POOR
	—	2500	1700	1500	750	250

Deluxe

	NIB	EXC.	V.G.	GOOD	FAIR	POOR
	—	7500	5500	3000	1500	750

CALIBER NOTE: As stated above it is difficult to provide pricing on specific rifles, especially calibers, because of the wide range of variables. However, the collector may find it useful to know that the most common rimfire calibers were the .22 Short, .22 WCF, and .22 Long, in that order, with the .22 Long Rifle a distant fourth. The most common centerfire chambers were the .32 WCF and the .32-40. Other popular centerfire calibers were the .38-55, .25-20, .44 WCF, .32 Long WCF, and the .45-70. There were a number of chamberings that are extremely rare (one of each built). It is strongly recommended that research is done prior to a sale.

Third Model Standard

	NIB	EXC.	V.G.	GOOD	FAIR	POOR
	—	2000	1400	900	450	250

Deluxe

	NIB	EXC.	V.G.	GOOD	FAIR	POOR
	—	6500	4000	2000	1000	750

Model 1906

In 1906 Winchester decided to offer a lower-cost version of the Model 1890. The Model 1906 used the same receiver but was fitted with a 20" round barrel and plain gumwood straight-grip stock. When the Model 1906 was first introduced, it sold for two-thirds of the price of the Model 1890. For the first two years the gun was chambered for the .22 Short cartridge only. In 1908 the rifle was modified to shoot .22 Short, Long, and LR cartridges interchangeably. This modification ensured the Model 1906's success, and between 1906 and 1932 about 800,000 were sold.

All Model 1906s were of the takedown variety. The Model 1906 is available in three important variations:

1. 22 Short Only, 20" round barrel, straight-grip gumwood stock and smooth slide handle. These were built from serial number 1 to around 113000. 2.Standard Model 1906, 20" round barrel, straight-grip gumwood stock with 12 groove slide handle. Serial numbered from 113000 to 852000. 3.Model 1906 Expert, 20" round barrel, pistol-grip gumwood stock with fluted smooth slide handle. Expert was available from 1918 to 1924 and was offered in three different finishes regular blued finish, half nickel (receiver, guard, and bolt), and full nickel (receiver, guard, bolt, and barrel nickeled).

Model 1906 .22 Short Only

	NIB	EXC.	V.G.	GOOD	FAIR	POOR
	—	2500	1750	750	500	200

Standard Model 1906

	NIB	EXC.	V.G.	GOOD	FAIR	POOR
	2000	1500	750	400	400	200

Model 1906 Expert

	NIB	EXC.	V.G.	GOOD	FAIR	POOR
	—	2500	1850	950	500	300

NOTE: Prices are for half-nickel Experts. Add 10 percent for blued guns and 100 percent for full nickel.

Model 61

Winchester developed the Model 61 in an attempt to keep pace with its competitors' hammerless .22 rifles. The Model 61 featured a 24" round or octagonal barrel and could be ordered by the customer in a variety of configurations. Collector interest in this rifle is high because of the fairly large number of variations. The Model 61 is often considered a companion to the Winchester Model 12 and Model 42 shotguns. The following is a list of chamber and barrel variations found in this model:

1. 24" round barrel, .22 Short, Long, LR
2. 24" octagonal barrel, .22 Short only add 150 percent.

NIB	EXC.	V.G.	GOOD	FAIR	POOR

3. 24" octagonal barrel, .22 LR only add 150 percent.
4. 24" octagonal barrel, .22 W.R.F. only add 100 percent.
5. 24" round barrel, .22 LR Shot only add 200 percent.
5A. 24" round barrel, shot only Routledge bore add 200 percent.
6. 24" round barrel, .22 W.R.F. only add 125 percent.
7. 24" round barrel, .22 LR only add 50 percent.
8. 24" round barrel, .22 Winchester Magnum add 50 percent.
9. 24" round barrel, .22 Short only add 100 percent.

The Model 61 was fitted with a plain walnut pistol-grip stock with grooved slide handle. All Model 61s were of the take down variety. Pre-war models will have a short slide handle. Manufactured between 1932 and 1963, approximately 342,000 guns were sold.

Pre-war

NOTE: Single caliber models will command a premium of 50 percent depending on caliber. Octagon barrel models will command a premium of 75 percent. .22 LR shot only models will bring a premium of 250 percent.

NIB	EXC.	V.G.	GOOD	FAIR	POOR
3000	2200	1600	800	400	200

Post-war

NIB	EXC.	V.G.	GOOD	FAIR	POOR
2000	1400	1200	600	300	250

Magnum

NOTE: This variation (Model 61 Magnum) was produced from 1960 to 1963.

NIB	EXC.	V.G.	GOOD	FAIR	POOR
2800	2400	1600	775	600	400

Model 62 and 62A

When the Model 1890 and Model 1906 were dropped from the Winchester product line in 1932, the company introduced the Model 62 to take their place. An updated version of the earlier slide-action .22 rifles, the Model 62 was fitted with a 23" round barrel and was capable of shooting .22 Short, Long and LR cartridges interchangeably. Winchester offered a Gallery version of the Model 62 that was chambered for .22 Short only. Some of these Gallery guns have "Winchester" stamped on the left side of the receiver. Winchester Model 62 Gallery rifles have a triangular loading port on the loading tube that the standard models did not have. A change in the breech bolt mechanism brought about a change in the name designation from Model 62 to Model 62A. This occurred around serial number 98000. The letter "A" now appears behind the serial number. This model stayed in production until 1958 and collectors will concede a premium for guns built prior to WWII with small slide handles. The stock was of plain walnut with straight grip and grooved slide handle. Both the receiver and barrel were blued. All Model 62 and 62As were takedown. Approximately 409,000 guns were sold.

Pre-war

NOTE: Barrels marked with Model 62 are worth more than barrels marked with Model 62A by approximately 15 percent. Gallery models will bring a premium of 300 percent.

NIB	EXC.	V.G.	GOOD	FAIR	POOR
2200	1500	850	400	250	150

Post-war

NIB	EXC.	V.G.	GOOD	FAIR	POOR
1100	850	600	500	225	125

Model 62 Gallery

.22 Short only with triangular loading port & "winchester" stamped on side of receiver. **NOTE:** A Model 62 with "winchester" stamped on the side of the receiver is more desirable than one without the stamping. Deduct 10 percent for Gallery rifles without this stamping.

NIB	EXC.	V.G.	GOOD	FAIR	POOR
3200	2000	1000	650	400	200

Model 1903

The first semi-automatic rifle produced by Winchester was designed by T.C. Johnson. This rifle was offered in a takedown version only and was available in a 20" round barrel chambered for the .22 Winchester Automatic Rimfire. This ammunition is no longer produced and when found is very expensive. The tubular magazine is located in the buttstock and holds 10 cartridges. The rifle was available in two different configurations:

1. Standard Rifle, 20" round barrel, plain walnut straight-grip stock with plain fore-end. Steel crescent butt was standard.
2. Deluxe Rifle, 20" round barrel, fancy checkered walnut pistol-grip stock with checkered forearm. Manufactured from 1903 to 1932, about 126,000 were sold.

Standard

NIB	EXC.	V.G.	GOOD	FAIR	POOR
—	850	550	325	200	100

Deluxe

NIB	EXC.	V.G.	GOOD	FAIR	POOR
—	1800	1100	700	500	250

NOTE: The first 5,000 guns were built without safeties, and the first 15,000 guns were furnished with bronze firing pins instead of steel. These early Model 1903s will bring a premium of 30 percent.

	NIB	EXC.	V.G.	GOOD	FAIR	POOR

Model 63

The Model 63 took the place of the Model 1903 in 1933 in an attempt by Winchester to solve the problem of having to use a special .22 caliber cartridge in the gun to operate the blowback system. It is a very high quality semi-automatic rifle. Many collectors and shooters considered it the best rimfire semi-automatic rifle ever produced.The Model 63 was chambered for the .22 LR cartridge and was available in a 20" barrel for the first four years or until about serial number 9800. Thereafter, the model was offered with a 23" round barrel for the remainder of the production period. The gun was fitted with a plain walnut pistol-grip stock and forearm. The tubular magazine was located in the buttstock that came with a steel buttplate. The last 10,000 Model 63s were sold with a grooved receiver top to make the addition of a scope easier. Manufactured between 1933 and 1958, about 175,000 guns were sold. **NOTE:** Grooved top receivers command a premium of 20 percent.

20" Barrel

	NIB	EXC.	V.G.	GOOD	FAIR	POOR
	2750	1400	800	500	400	250

23" Barrel

	NIB	EXC.	V.G.	GOOD	FAIR	POOR
	2200	1600	900	600	400	200

Model 1905

The Model 1905 was a larger version of the Model 1903, developed by T.C. Johnson to handle the more powerful centerfire cartridges. It was chambered for the .32 Winchester Self-Loading and .35 Self-Loading cartridges, loading by means of a detachable box magazine. Available in takedown only, this model was offered in two different styles:
1. Sporting Rifle, 22" round barrel, plain walnut straight grip (changed to pistol grip in 1908) stock with plain fore-end.
2. Fancy Sporting Rifle, 22" round barrel, fancy walnut checkered pistol-grip stock with checkered fore-end. This model was the first Winchester semi-automatic rifle to fire centerfire cartridges. Produced from 1905 to 1920 with about 30,000 rifles sold.

Sporting

	NIB	EXC.	V.G.	GOOD	FAIR	POOR
	—	700	550	350	175	125

Fancy Sporting

	NIB	EXC.	V.G.	GOOD	FAIR	POOR
	—	900	750	500	200	150

Model 1907

The Model 1907 was an improved version of the Model 1905 and chambered for the new .351 Winchester Self-Loading cartridge. Outward appearance was the same as Model 1905 except for 20" round barrel. This rifle was available in three different styles:
1. Sporting Rifle, 20" round barrel, plain walnut pistol-grip stock with plain fore-end. Discontinued in 1937.
2. Fancy Sporting Rifle, 20" round barrel, fancy walnut checkered pistol-grip stock and checkered fore-end.
3. Police Rifle, 20" round barrel, plain walnut pistol-grip stock and beavertail fore-end. This version was fitted with a leather sling and with or without knife bayonet. First introduced in 1937. Winchester discontinued this model in 1957 after having sold about 59,000 guns.
NOTE: Post-WWII Model 1907s command a premium over the values shown below.

Sporting

	NIB	EXC.	V.G.	GOOD	FAIR	POOR
	—	750	500	350	175	125

Fancy Sporting

	NIB	EXC.	V.G.	GOOD	FAIR	POOR
	—	850	650	450	200	150

Police

	NIB	EXC.	V.G.	GOOD	FAIR	POOR
	—	950	750	575	300	250

Model 1910

This model was similar to the Model 1907 but the action was made stronger to handle the new Winchester .401 Self-Loading cartridge. The specifications for this model are the same as the Model 1907. Built between 1907 and 1936, only about 21,000 of these guns were sold.

Sporting

	NIB	EXC.	V.G.	GOOD	FAIR	POOR
	—	900	750	550	400	200

Fancy Sporting

	NIB	EXC.	V.G.	GOOD	FAIR	POOR
	—	1000	800	600	450	250

Model 55 (Rimfire Rifle)

Not to be confused with the lever-action model, this .22 caliber rifle was a semi-automatic (auto-ejecting, actually) single-shot with a 22" round barrel. Fitted with a plain walnut pistol-grip one-piece stock and fore-end. The safety goes on when each cartridge is inserted into the chamber.

NIB	EXC.	V.G.	GOOD	FAIR	POOR

This model was not serial numbered and was produced from 1957 to 1961 with about 45,000 guns sold.

NIB	EXC.	V.G.	GOOD	FAIR	POOR
—	400	350	225	150	75

Model 74

This was a semi-automatic chambered for either the .22 Short or the .22 LR. The rifle has a tubular magazine in the buttstock and a 24" round barrel. The bolt on this rifle was designed to be easily removed for cleaning or repair. The stock was plain walnut pistol-grip with semi-beavertail fore-end. A Gallery Special was offered that was chambered for the .22 Short and fitted with a steel shell deflector. This gallery model was also available with chrome trimmings at extra cost.

Sporting

NIB	EXC.	V.G.	GOOD	FAIR	POOR
—	400	300	225	150	100

Gallery Special—.22 Short Only

NOTE: For Gallery models with chrome trimmings, add a premium of 50 percent.

NIB	EXC.	V.G.	GOOD	FAIR	POOR
—	800	600	325	225	150

Model 77

This rifle was built on the blow-back design for semi-automatic rifles and is chambered for the .22 LR. It features a 22" round barrel and either a detachable box magazine or under barrel tubular magazine. The rifle has a trigger guard made of nylon. It has a plain walnut pistol-grip stock with semi-beavertail fore-end and composition buttplate. Built between 1955 and 1963, Winchester sold about 217,000 of these rifles. **NOTE:** Models with tubular magazines will bring a premium of 10 percent to 20 percent.

NIB	EXC.	V.G.	GOOD	FAIR	POOR
—	500	375	250	175	75

Model 100

This rifle is a gas operated semi-automatic and chambered for the .243, .308, and .284 caliber cartridges. The Model 100 was the first commercial Winchester self-loading, centerfire rifle made since the Winchester Model 1905, the Model 1907, and the Model 1910. These models were produced until 1936/37. Winchester did produce the M1 Carbine during WWII. It was available in a rifle version with a 22" round barrel and a carbine version with a 19" barrel. Both were furnished with a detachable box magazine. The stock was a one-piece design with pistol grip and was offered in either hand-cut checkering or pressed basket weave checkering. Rifles were introduced in 1960 and the carbine in 1967. The Model 100 was last produced in 1973 with about 263,000 guns sold.

Rifle

NOTE: Pre-1964 models 15 percent premium. Prices given are for .308 caliber; for .243 add 15 percent, for .284 add 20 percent.

NIB	EXC.	V.G.	GOOD	FAIR	POOR
—	600	475	350	250	200

Carbine

Only about 53,000 carbines were made, about one for every five rifles.

NIB	EXC.	V.G.	GOOD	FAIR	POOR
—	675	525	400	325	225

NOTE: Add 25 percent premium for .243, and 100 percent for .284.

Model 88

The Model 88 was a modern short-stroke lever-action chambered for the .243, .308, 284 and .358 calibers. It was available in a rifle version with 22" round barrel and a carbine version with 19" round barrel. The carbine model was not chambered for the .358 cartridge. Both were furnished with a detachable box magazine. The stock was a one-piece design with pistol grip and was offered with hand-cut checkering or pressed basket weave checkering after 1964. The rifle was introduced in 1955 and the carbine was first offered in 1968. Both versions were discontinued in 1973 with about 283,000 sold.

Rifle

NOTE: Pre-1964 models add 25 percent premium. Prices above are for .308 caliber; for .243 add 15 percent, .284 add 75 percent, and for 358 add 100 percent. This model was offered with no front or rear sights (Gopher Special) for a few years prior to 1962. Add 100 percent for this variant. Beware of fakes.

NIB	EXC.	V.G.	GOOD	FAIR	POOR
—	900	750	500	300	250

Carbine

Only 28,000 carbines were built, about 1 for every 10 rifles. Rarely encountered. **NOTE:** Add 25 percent for .243, add 100 percent for .284 calibers. The carbine was not offered in .358 caliber.

NIB	EXC.	V.G.	GOOD	FAIR	POOR
—	1300	1150	900	650	300

NIB	EXC.	V.G.	GOOD	FAIR	POOR

Model 99 or Thumb Trigger

This rifle was a modification of the Model 1902 without a traditional trigger. The rifle was fired by depressing the trigger with the thumb, which was part of the sear and extractor located behind the bolt. The rifle was chambered for the .22 Short and Long until 1914 when it was also chambered for the .22 Extra Long. All cartridges could be shot interchangeably. The stock was the same as the Model 1902, Gumwood stained walnut, without the trigger or trigger guard. This model was not serial numbered. Built between 1904 and 1923. Winchester sold about 76,000 rifles.

—	2400	2000	1000	700	500

Model 1900

This single-shot bolt-action .22 caliber rifle was based on a John M. Browning design. The rifle was furnished with an 18" round barrel and chambered for the .22 Short and Long interchangeably. The stock was a one-piece plain gumwood straight grip without a buttplate. The rifle was not serial numbered. It was produced from 1899 to 1902 with about 105,000 sold.

—	2000	1000	450	300	200

Model 1902

Also a single-shot, this model was of the same general design as the Model 1900 with several improvements: a special shaped metal trigger guard was added, a shorter trigger pull, a steel buttplate, a rear peep sight, and the barrel was made heavier at the muzzle. The rifle was chambered for the .22 Short and Long cartridges until 1914 when the .22 Extra Long was added. In 1927 the .22 Extra Long was dropped in favor of the more popular .22 LR. All of these cartridges were interchangeable. The stock was a one-piece plain gumwood with straight grip (the metal trigger guard added a pistol grip feel) and steel buttplate, which was changed to composition in 1907. This model was not serial numbered. About 640,000 Model 1902s were sold between 1902 and 1931 when it was discontinued.

—	1000	750	400	225	125

Model 1904

This model was a slightly more expensive version of the Model 1902. It featured a 21" round barrel, a one-piece plain gumwood straight-grip stock (the metal trigger guard gave the rifle a pistol grip feel) with a small lip on the fore-end. Rifle was chambered for the .22 Short and Long until 1914 when the .22 Extra Long was added. The .22 LR cartridge was added in place of the Extra Long in 1927. This model was not serial numbered. Produced between 1904 and 1931, about 303,000 rifles were sold.

—	900	675	350	200	100

Model D Military Rifle

Overall length 46-3/8"; barrel length 26"; caliber 7.62mm. Walnut stock with blued barrel, receiver, magazine housing and furniture. Receiver ring over barrel breech stamped with serial number and Winchester proofmark. A total of 500 Model D Rifles were shipped to Russia for trial in March of 1917. Value Speculative.

Imperial Bolt-Action Magazine Rifle (Model 51)

Designed by T.C. Johnson, approximately 25 of these rifles were made during 1919 and 1920 in two different styles and three calibers. The takedown variation has an overall length of 42-1/4", barrel length 22" and was made in .27, .30-06 and .35 Newton calibers. The solid frame version is identical in form, dimensions and calibers. Sight configurations and markings vary. Value Speculative.

Model 43

Introduced in 1949, this rifle was chambered for the .218 Bee, .22 Hornet, .25-20 Winchester, and the .32-20 Winchester. The rifle was a bolt-action with detachable box magazine, fitted with a 24" round barrel and front sight ramp forged integrally with barrel. This model was not drilled and tapped for scope blocks except for a few late rifles. This model was available in two styles:

1. Standard Rifle, 24" round barrel, plain walnut pistol-grip stock and fore-end. One inch sling swivels are standard.
2. Special Rifle, 24" round barrel, select walnut checkered pistol-grip stock and checkered fore-end. Furnished with either open sporting rear sight or Lyman 57A micrometer receiver sight.

The Model 43 was produced from 1949 to 1957 with about 63,000 sold.

NOTE: For rifles chambered for .25-20 and .32-20 add a 50 percent premium. For rifles with non-factory drilled and tapped scope holes deduct 40 percent.

Standard

—	800	700	550	300	200

Special or Deluxe

—	1500	1200	800	450	175

	NIB	EXC.	V.G.	GOOD	FAIR	POOR

Model 47

This model was a single-shot bolt-action rifle chambered for the .22 Short, Long, and LR interchangeably. The rifle was furnished with a 25" round barrel, plain walnut pistol-grip stock and fore-end. The bolt, bolt handle, and trigger are chrome plated. This model has a special bolt with a post on the underside. This moves into the safety position when the bolt is closed.This model was not serial numbered. Produced between 1948 and 1954, Winchester sold about 43,000 guns. **NOTE:** Add 10 percent premium for Model 47 with factory peep sight.

	NIB	EXC.	V.G.	GOOD	FAIR	POOR
	—	450	350	250	200	150

Target Rifle

Fitted with a 28" round standard weight or heavyweight barrel, plain walnut modified pistol-grip stock with correct bolt.

	NIB	EXC.	V.G.	GOOD	FAIR	POOR
	—	750	600	450	250	150

Model 52

One of the finest small-caliber bolt-action rifles ever built, the Model 52 was Winchester's answer to the increased demand for a military-style target rifle following WWI. The Model 52 was a well-made quality-built bolt-action rifle. The rifle was chambered for the .22 LR cartridge. Designed by T.C. Johnson, this rifle was built in several different configurations over its production life:

1. Model 52 with finger groove in fore-end and one barrel band. Produced from 1920 to 1929.
2. Model 52 Target Rifle, same as above but without finger groove in fore-end and has first speed lock. Made from 1929 to 1932.
3. Model 52A Target Rifle, same as above with addition of reinforced receiver and locking lug. Made from 1932 to 1935.
4. Model 52B Target Rifle, same as above with addition of adjustable sling swivel and single-shot adapter. Made from 1935 to 1947.
5. Model 52C Target Rifle, same as above with addition of an easily adjustable vibration-free trigger mechanism. Made from 1947 to 1961.
6. Model 52D Target Rifle, this is a single-shot rifle with free-floating barrel and new design stock with adjustable hand-stop channel.
7. Model 52 Bull Gun, same as target rifle but fitted with extra heavyweight barrel. Made from 1939 to 1960. The Bull Barrel measures 1.125" at the receiver juncture while the heavyweight measures 1". Both barrels measure .875" at the muzzle.
8. Model 52 International Match, a free-style stock with thumb hole and adjustable buttstock and fore-end introduced in 1969. International Prone model with no thumb hole or adjustable buttplate and fore-end was introduced in 1975. Both discontinued in 1980.
9. Model 52 Sporter, 24" round barrel, select walnut checkered pistol-grip stock with cheekpiece and fore-end with black plastic tip. Pistol grip was furnished with hard-rubber grip cap. The Model 52 Sporter was introduced in 1934 and discontinued in 1958. It went through the same improvements as the Target Rifle, thus the designation Model 52A Sporter, etc.

Standard

	NIB	EXC.	V.G.	GOOD	FAIR	POOR
	—	1250	1000	750	250	300

Target

	NIB	EXC.	V.G.	GOOD	FAIR	POOR
	—	1750	1500	1150	900	350

Target—Speed Lock

	NIB	EXC.	V.G.	GOOD	FAIR	POOR
	—	1700	1400	1050	900	350

Model 52A Target Heavy Barrel—Rare

	NIB	EXC.	V.G.	GOOD	FAIR	POOR
	—	1700	1400	1050	900	350

Model 52B Target Heavy & Standard Barrel

	NIB	EXC.	V.G.	GOOD	FAIR	POOR
	—	1500	1300	950	700	300

Model 52B Target Bull Barrel

	NIB	EXC.	V.G.	GOOD	FAIR	POOR
	—	1700	1400	1050	900	350

Model 52C Target

	NIB	EXC.	V.G.	GOOD	FAIR	POOR
	—	1700	1400	1050	800	500

Model 52D Target

	NIB	EXC.	V.G.	GOOD	FAIR	POOR
	—	1800	1500	1300	1050	500

Model 52B Bull Gun

	NIB	EXC.	V.G.	GOOD	FAIR	POOR
	—	1800	1500	1300	1050	500

Model 52C Bull Gun

	NIB	EXC.	V.G.	GOOD	FAIR	POOR
	—	1800	1500	1300	1050	500

	NIB	EXC.	V.G.	GOOD	FAIR	POOR

International Match
Approximately 300 manufactured.

Free Style

	NIB	EXC.	V.G.	GOOD	FAIR	POOR
—	3550	2900	2050	1200	600	

Prone
NOTE: Post-WWII Model 1907s command a premium over the values shown below.

	NIB	EXC.	V.G.	GOOD	FAIR	POOR
—	1600	1350	1150	800	600	

Model 52C Sporter

NIB	EXC.	V.G.	GOOD	FAIR	POOR
5000	4100	3400	2300	1800	900

Model 52B Sporter

NIB	EXC.	V.G.	GOOD	FAIR	POOR
4000	3600	2750	2000	1500	500

Model 52B Sporter

NIB	EXC.	V.G.	GOOD	FAIR	POOR
4500	3900	3200	2400	1850	600

Model 54

The Model 54 was to centerfire cartridges what the Model 52 was to rimfire cartridges. The Model 54 was also a quality-made bolt-action rifle with a nondetachable box magazine and was chambered for a variety of calibers: .270, .30-06, .30-30, 7mm, 7.65, 9.mm, .250-3000, .22 Hornet, .220 Swift, and .257 Roberts. This was Winchester's first bolt-action rifle built for heavy, high velocity ammunition. The rifle was available in several different styles:

1. Standard Rifle, 24" or 20" round barrel (except .220 Swift which was 26"), plain walnut checkered pistol-grip stock and fore-end.
2. Carbine, 20" round barrel, plain walnut pistol-grip stock with finger groove on each side of fore-end.
3. Sniper's Rifle, 26" round heavyweight barrel, plain walnut pistol-grip stock and fore-end.
4. N.R.A. Rifle, 24" round barrel, select walnut checkered pistol-grip stock and fore-end.
5. Super Grade Rifle, 24" round barrel, select walnut checkered pistol-grip stock with cheekpiece and checkered fore-end with black plastic tip. Pistol grip was capped with hard rubber cap. Super Grade was equipped with 1" detachable sling swivels.
6. Target Rifle, 24" round heavyweight barrel, plain walnut checkered pistol-grip stock and fore-end.
7. National Match Rifle, 24" round barrel, plain walnut special target stock and fore-end.

The Model 54 was introduced in 1925 and was discontinued in 1936 with about 50,000 guns sold. **NOTE:** The rare calibers are the 7mm, 7.65mm and the 9mm, which bring considerable premiums (in some cases as much as 250 percent) over standard calibers. Popular calibers such as .22 Hornet, .220 Swift, .30-30, and .257 Roberts will also bring a premium. Proceed with caution on Model 54s with rare caliber markings.

Standard

	NIB	EXC.	V.G.	GOOD	FAIR	POOR
—	1300	1100	800	600	425	

Carbine

	NIB	EXC.	V.G.	GOOD	FAIR	POOR
—	1400	1200	900	700	475	

Sniper's Rifle

	NIB	EXC.	V.G.	GOOD	FAIR	POOR
—	1800	1500	1200	1000	550	

N.R.A.

	NIB	EXC.	V.G.	GOOD	FAIR	POOR
—	1800	1500	1200	1000	550	

Super Grade

	NIB	EXC.	V.G.	GOOD	FAIR	POOR
—	2400	1950	1600	1350	600	

Target

	NIB	EXC.	V.G.	GOOD	FAIR	POOR
—	1800	1500	1200	1000	550	

National Match

	NIB	EXC.	V.G.	GOOD	FAIR	POOR
—	1800	1500	1200	1000	550	

Model 56

This model was designed to be a medium-priced bolt-action rimfire rifle. It featured a detachable box magazine and was chambered for the .22 Short or .22 LR cartridges. The rifle was offered in two styles:
1. Sporting Rifle, 22" round barrel, plain walnut pistol-grip stock and fore-end.

	NIB	EXC.	V.G.	GOOD	FAIR	POOR

2. Fancy Sporting Rifle, 22" round barrel, fancy walnut checkered pistol-grip stock and fore-end. Both styles had a fore-end with a distinctive lip on the fore-end tip. The rifle was introduced in 1926 and was discontinued in 1929 with about 8,500 rifles sold. **NOTE:** Add a 50 percent premium for rifles chambered for .22 Short only.

Sporting

—	1500	1000	750	525	400

Fancy Sporting

Very rare, use caution.

—	3000	2000	1500	900	750

Model 57

The Model 57 was close in appearance to the Model 56 with the addition of a heavier stock, target sights, and swivel bows attached to the stock. The rifle was chambered for the .22 Short or .22 LR and featured a 22" round barrel with detachable box magazine. The stock was plain walnut with pistol grip and plain fore-end. The rifle was introduced in 1927 and dropped from the Winchester line in 1936 having sold only about 19,000 guns. **NOTE:** Add 20 percent premium for web sling.

—	950	700	450	325	250

Model 58

This model was an attempt by the company to market a low-priced .22 caliber rimfire rifle in place of its Models 1902 and 1904. This was a single-shot bolt-action, cocked by pulling the firing pin head to the rear. It had an 18" round barrel and was chambered for the .22 Short, Long, and LR interchangeably. The stock was a one-piece plain wood with straight grip. This model was not serial-numbered. The Model 58 was introduced in 1928 and discontinued in 1931. About 39,000 were sold.

—	800	700	450	300	200

Model 59

The Model 59 was essentially a Model 58 with the addition of a pistol-grip stock and a 23" round barrel. Introduced in 1930, it was dropped from the product line in the same year with a total sales of about 9,000 guns.

—	1000	800	550	400	200

Model 60 and 60A

This rifle used the same action as that of the Model 59. When the rifle was first introduced in 1931, it was furnished with a 23" round barrel which was changed to 27" in 1933. Several other mechanical improvements were included with this model; perhaps the most noticeable were the chrome-plated bolt, bolt handle, and trigger. The stock was plain wood with pistol grip. In 1933 the Model 60A was added, which was the same rifle but in a target configuration. The front sight was a square top military blade with a Lyman 55W receiver sight. The Model 60 was discontinued in 1934 with about 166,000 rifles sold. The Model 60A was dropped in 1939 with only about 6,100 rifles sold.

Model 60

—	375	250	200	150	100

Model 60A

—	500	425	300	200	100

Model 67

Winchester again upgraded and improved the Model 60 with an expansion of the styles offered to the shooting public. The standard chamber for the rifle was .22 Short, Long, and LR interchangeably with the W.R.F. only added in 1935:

1. Sporting Rifle, 27" round barrel, stock similar to the Model 60.
2. Smoothbore Rifle, 27" barrel, chambered for the .22 long shot or .22 LR shot.
3. Junior Rifle, 20" round barrel and shorter stock.
4. Rifle with miniature target boring, 24" round barrel, chambered for .22 LR shot.

Model 67s were not serial numbered for domestic sales but were numbered for foreign sales. Introduced in 1934 the gun was dropped from the line in 1963 having sold about 384,000. Many of these models were fitted at the factory with telescopes and the bases were mounted on the rifle and the scope was packed separately.

Sporting

—	450	350	250	175	100

	NIB	EXC.	V.G.	GOOD	FAIR	POOR

Smoothbore

	—	800	600	400	250	200

Junior

	—	500	350	275	200	125

Miniature Target Rifle

This model is marked "for shot only" and has beads instead of standard iron rifle sights.

	—	1200	900	700	400	300

Model 677

This model looked the same as the Model 67 but was manufactured without iron sights and therefore will have no sight cuts in the barrel. The rifle was furnished with either 2-3/4 power scopes or 5 power scopes. This model was not serial numbered. Introduced in 1937 and discontinued in 1939. **NOTE:** Add 100 percent premium for rifles chambered for .22 WRF.

	—	2400	1800	1100	600	300

Model 68

Another takeoff on the Model 67, this model differed only in the sight equipment offered. Winchester fitted this rifle with a peep sight. First sold in 1934 the Model 68 was dropped in 1946 with sales of about 101,000. **NOTE:** Rifles with factory scopes and no sights add 50 percent. For rifles with factory scopes and no sights chambered for .22 WRF add 400 percent.

With Scope

	—	900	775	450	300	200

Without Scope

	—	300	225	150	100	75

Model 69 and 69A

This model was designed by Winchester to answer the demand for a medium-priced hunting and target .22 rimfire bolt-action rifle. The rifle had a detachable box magazine, and many were offered with factory-installed telescopes in 2-3/4 and 5 power. The stock was plain walnut with pistol grip and plain fore-end. This model was not serial numbered. The 69A version was introduced in 1937 and featured an improved cocking mechanism. Introduced in 1935 as the Model 69, this gun was dropped in 1963 with sales of about 355,000 guns. **NOTE:** Add 25 percent for Target Model. Add 35 percent for grooved receiver.

		475	400	350	200	100

Model 697

The Model 697 was similar in appearance to the Model 69 except it was equipped exclusively for a telescope. Winchester offered either a 2-3/4 or 5-power scope with the bases attached at the factory and the scope packed separately. Built between 1937 and 1941 with small sales, this model was not serial numbered. **NOTE:** For factory scopes with no sights add 50 percent.

	—	2000	1200	800	600	400

Model 70

Considered by many as the finest bolt-action rifle ever built in the United States, the pre-1964 Model 70 is highly sought after by shooters and collectors alike. Its smooth, strong action has no peer. It is often referred to as "The Riflemen's Rifle." The Model 70 is an updated and improved version of the Model 54 and features a hinged floorplate, new speed locks, new safety design that does not interfere with telescope, manually releasable bolt stop, more attractive buttstock and fore-end, and forged steel trigger guard. Like many Winchesters, the Model 70 was available with several extra-cost options that should be evaluated by an expert. The values listed are given for pre-1964 Model 70s with serial numbers from 1 to 581471. This rifle was available in several different styles:

1. Standard Grade, 24" round barrel (except 26" round barrel for .220 Swift and .300 H&H Magnum—25" round barrel for .375 H&H Magnum after 1937), plain walnut checkered pistol stock and fore-end. Built from 1936 to 1963.
2. Standard Grade Carbine, 20" round barrel, chambered for .22 Hornet, .250-3000, .257 Roberts, .270, 7mm, and .30-06, same stock as Standard Grade. Built from 1936 to 1946.
3. Super Grade Rifle, same barrel and calibers as Standard Grade, select walnut checkered and capped pistol-grip stock with cheekpiece and checkered fore-end with plastic tip. Built from 1936 to 1960.
4. Featherweight, 22" round barrel chambered for .243, .264, .270, .308, .30-06, and .358. Fitted with aluminum trigger guard, aluminum buttplate, and aluminum floor plate. Later versions with plastic buttplate. Built from 1952 to 1963.

	NIB	EXC.	V.G.	GOOD	FAIR	POOR

5. Featherweight Super Grade, same as above except not chambered for the .358 cartridge, but fitted with Super Grade stock. Built from 1952 to 1963.
6. National Match, same as Standard Grade but fitted with target type stock and telescope bases. Chambered for .30-06 only. Discontinued in 1960.
7. Target, 24" round medium-weight barrel with same stock as National Match in .243 and .30-06 calibers. Discontinued in 1963.
8. Varmint, 26" round barrel with heavier varmint stock, chambered for .243 and the rare .220 Swift. Built from 1956 to 1963.
9. Westerner, 26" round barrel with Standard Grade stock, chambered for .264 Winchester Magnum. Built from 1960 to 1963. Fitted with a solid rubber pad for early production guns and a vented pad for later guns.
10. Alaskan, 25" round barrel, with Standard Grade stock, chambered for .338 Winchester Magnum and .375 H&H Magnum. Built from 1960 to 1963. Fitted with a solid rubber pad marked Winchester for early production guns and a vented pad both marked Winchester for later guns.
11. Bull Gun, 28" round barrel, same stock as National Match, chambered for .30-06 and .300 H&H Magnum. Built from 1936 to 1963. The standard calibers offered for the Model 70 are these, in order of rarity: .300 Savage, .35 Rem., .458 Win Magnum, 7mm, .358 Win., .250-3000 Savage, .300 Win Magnum, .338 Win. Magnum, .375 H&H Magnum, .257 Roberts, .220 Swift, .22 Hornet, .264 Win. Magnum, .300 H&H Magnum, .308 Win., .243 Win., .270 W.C.F., .30-06.

Prices for the Model 70 are, in many cases, based on the caliber of the rifle; the more rare the caliber, the more premium the gun will command. Many pre-1964 Model 70s are still available in new condition in the original box with all papers. Add 25 to 50 percent if the box is serial numbered to the gun. Use caution prior to purchase of NIB guns due to fake boxes and papers.

PRICING NOTE: The asterisk (*) signifies the value of the rifle with respect to a usable action. Model 70 unaltered receivers bring $500 regardless of the condition of the barrel and stock. If the receiver is unusable then the rifle is worth the value of its usable parts, i.e. less than $500.

For Model 70s with "X" or "D" prefix add a collector premium of 10 percent. These letters indicate that there were two rifles mistakenly stamped with the same serial number.

Standard Rifle .30-06 Springfield (1937-1963)

Pre-War

	NIB	EXC.	V.G.	GOOD	FAIR	POOR
—	2200	1600	1100	500*	500*	

Post-War

	NIB	EXC.	V.G.	GOOD	FAIR	POOR
—	1450	1200	800	500*	500*	

.270 Win. (1937-1963)

Pre-War

	NIB	EXC.	V.G.	GOOD	FAIR	POOR
—	2200	1900	1000	500*	500*	

Post-War

	NIB	EXC.	V.G.	GOOD	FAIR	POOR
—	1550	1400	900	500*	500*	

.243. Win. (1955-1963)

NOTE: Post-WWII Model 1907s command a premium over the values shown below.

	NIB	EXC.	V.G.	GOOD	FAIR	POOR
—	2750	2200	1100	500*	500*	

.300 H&H Magnum (1937-1963)

Pre-War

	NIB	EXC.	V.G.	GOOD	FAIR	POOR
—	3100	2500	1700	1000	500*	

Post-War

	NIB	EXC.	V.G.	GOOD	FAIR	POOR
—	2650	2000	1400	850	500*	

.264 Win. Magnum (1959-1963)

	NIB	EXC.	V.G.	GOOD	FAIR	POOR
—	2500	2000	1400	850	500*	

.22 Hornet (1937-1958)

Pre-War

	NIB	EXC.	V.G.	GOOD	FAIR	POOR
—	3000	2400	2000	1000	500*	

Post-War

	NIB	EXC.	V.G.	GOOD	FAIR	POOR
—	2750	2000	1500	750	500*	

.220 Swift (1937-1963)

Pre-War

	NIB	EXC.	V.G.	GOOD	FAIR	POOR
—	3000	2400	1750	900	500*	

	NIB	EXC.	V.G.	GOOD	FAIR	POOR

Post-War

| | — | 2500 | 1750 | 1200 | 650 | 500* |

.257 Roberts (1937-1959)

Pre-War

| | — | 3200 | 2500 | 1500 | 950 | 500* |

Post-War

| | — | 2900 | 2100 | 1400 | 750 | 500* |

.375 H&H Magnum (1937-1963)

Pre-War

| | — | 4300 | 3700 | 2200 | 1350 | 500* |

Post-War

| | — | 3200 | 2500 | 1800 | 1000 | 500* |

.338 Win. Magnum (1959-1963)

| | — | 3150 | 2550 | 1550 | 900 | 500* |

.300 Win. Magnum (1962-1963)

| | — | 2650 | 2250 | 1200 | 750 | 500* |

.250-3000 Savage (1937-1949)

| | — | 4750 | 3500 | 2500 | 1200 | 500* |

7mm (1937-1949)

| | — | 5900 | 4800 | 2700 | 1700 | 700 |

.35 Rem. (1944-1947)

| | — | 8900 | 6050 | 3700 | 2000 | 950 |

.300 Savage (1944-1950s?)

| | — | 9400 | 8300 | 3800 | 2000 | 950 |

.458 Win. Magnum African

Built in Supergrade only, 1956-1963.

| | — | 7400 | 5350 | 4200 | 2750 | 1350 |

Featherweight

NOTE: Add 100 percent for .358 Win. For .264 and .270 calibers add 25 percent.

| | — | 2200 | 1450 | 1075 | 700 | 450 |

Featherweight Super Grade

| | — | 5400 | 4300 | 3200 | 1650 | 1000 |

Standard Grade Carbine

NOTE: For Supergrade rifles add 100 percent.

| | — | 2900 | 2000 | 1400 | 950 | 650 |

National Match

| | — | 3400 | 2550 | 1850 | 950 | 600 |

Target

| | — | 2450 | 2100 | 1150 | 750 | 550 |

Varmint

NOTE: Add 40 percent premium for .220 Swift.

| | — | 2350 | 1950 | 950 | 600 | 375* |

Bull Gun

| | — | 3900 | 3200 | 2450 | 850 | 600 |

Model 72

This model is a bolt-action rifle with tubular magazine. It is chambered for the .22 Short, Long and LR cartridges interchangeably. Early rifles were available with 2.75 or 5 power telescopes, but the majority were furnished with either open sights or peep sights. This rifle was available in two different configurations:

NIB	EXC.	V.G.	GOOD	FAIR	POOR

1. Sporting Rifle, 25" round barrel, chambered for the .22 Short, Long, and LR cartridges, one-piece plain walnut pistol-grip stock and fore-end.
2. Gallery Special, 25" round barrel, chambered for .22 Short only, stock same as Sporting Rifle. This model was not serial numbered. It was built between 1938 and 1959 with about 161,000 rifles sold.

NOTE: Gallery Special will command a premium of 100 percent. For rifles with factory scopes and no sights add 200 percent depending on condition. Add 25 percent premium for peep sights. Add 20 percent for Model 72A with grooved receiver.

—	425	350	275	200	125

Model 75

Available in two styles:

1. Sporting Rifle, 24" round barrel, chambered for .22 LR, select walnut checkered pistol-grip stock and fore-end. This rifle was furnished with either open rear sights or a Lyman 57E receiver sight.
2. Target Rifle, 28" round barrel, chambered for .22 LR, plain walnut pistol-grip stock and fore-end. The Target Rifle was furnished with either a Winchester 8-power telescope or a variety of target sights.

This model was discontinued in 1958 with about 89,000 sold.

Sporter

—	1500	1000	800	500	350

Target

—	900	700	600	500	200

Model SXR Super X Rifle

Gas-operated semi-automatic patterned after Browning BAR ShortTrac and LongTrac. Calibers: .30-06 (4), .300WM (3), .270 WSM (3), .300 WSM (3). Barrel: 22" (.30-06), 24". Weight: 7.25 lbs. Stock: Two-piece checkered walnut. Introduced 2006.

600	500	400	325	250	125

SHOTGUNS

Model 12

This model was designed by T.C. Johnson and was the first slide-action hammerless shotgun built by Winchester. The Model 12 enjoyed great success in its 68-year history, and over two million were sold. This was a high quality, well-made shotgun that is still in use in the hunting and shooting fields across the country. All Model 12s were of the takedown variety. The Model 12 was dropped from regular product line in 1963, but a special model was produced in the Custom Shop until 1979. In 1972 Winchester resurrected the Model 12 in its regular production line in 12 gauge only and ventilated rib. This reintroduced Model 12 was dropped in 1980. The prices listed are for guns made prior to 1964 or for guns with serial numbers below 1968307. This shotgun was offered in several different styles:

1. Standard Grade, 12, 16, 20, and 28 gauge, with plain, solid rib, or vent rib round barrels of standard lengths (26", 28", 30", 32"), plain walnut pistol-grip stock with grooved slide handle. Built from 1912 to 1963.
2. Featherweight, same as above with lightweight alloy trigger guard. Built between 1959 and 1962.
3. Riot Gun, in 12 gauge only with 20" round choked cylinder, stock same as Standard Grade. Built between 1918 and 1963.
4. Trench Gun, chambered for 12 gauge only with 20" round barrel with ventilated hand guard over barrel, fitted with bayonet lug. All metal surfaces are "Parkerized," and these shotguns should be U.S. marked as a military firearm. Introduced in 1918 and built for U.S. Armed Forces on special order.
5. Skeet Grade, chambered for 12, 16, 20, and 28 gauge with 26" round barrel with solid or ventilated rib, select walnut checkered pistol stock and special checkered extension slide handle (longer than standard). Built from 1933 to 1963.
6. Trap Grade, chambered for 12 gauge only with 30" round barrel with solid rib or ventilated rib, select walnut pistol or straight-grip stock, checkered extension slide handle. Built from 1914 to 1963.
7. Heavy Duck Gun, chambered in 12 gauge only with 30" or 32" round barrel with plain, solid, or ventilated rib, plain walnut pistol-grip stock fitted with Winchester solid red rubber recoil pad, plain grooved slide handle. Built from 1935 to 1963.
8. Pigeon Grade, chambered for 12, 16, 20, and 28 gauges with standard barrel lengths and choice of ribs. This was a special order shotgun and will be seen in many different variations, most of these guns were factory engraved. Built 1914 to 1963.

The Model 12 shotgun will be seen in many different combinations of gauges, barrel lengths, ribs and stocks, all of which determine value. The more rare a particular combination, the higher the price. The buyer is urged to be extremely cautious before purchasing the more rare

	NIB	EXC.	V.G.	GOOD	FAIR	POOR

combinations, such as a 28 gauge. The best advice is to seek assistance from an expert and get as many opinions as possible. The prices listed are for guns in standard configurations. **NOTE:** The following applies to all models. For 16 gauge add 10 percent. For 20 gauge add 50 percent. For 28 gauge add 600 percent. For guns with solid rib add 20 percent. For guns with Winchester Special ventilated rib add 30 percent. For guns with milled rib add 40 percent. Add 20 percent for 32" barrels on any Model 12 model. Add 30 percent premium for original box and papers.

Standard Grade—12 gauge

	NIB	EXC.	V.G.	GOOD	FAIR	POOR
	—	850	700	600	500	200

Featherweight

	NIB	EXC.	V.G.	GOOD	FAIR	POOR
	—	800	700	600	575	200

Riot Gun

	NIB	EXC.	V.G.	GOOD	FAIR	POOR
	—	2400	1700	900	700	250

Trench Gun

	NIB	EXC.	V.G.	GOOD	FAIR	POOR
	—	7500	6000	4000	1500	1000

Skeet Grade

	NIB	EXC.	V.G.	GOOD	FAIR	POOR
	—	2200	1700	900	600	350

Trap Grade

	NIB	EXC.	V.G.	GOOD	FAIR	POOR
	—	2000	1500	800	550	400

Heavy Duck Gun

NOTE: Heavy Duck Guns with solid ribs add 25 percent premium.

	NIB	EXC.	V.G.	GOOD	FAIR	POOR
	—	1150	900	350	425	300

Pigeon Grade

	NIB	EXC.	V.G.	GOOD	FAIR	POOR
	—	3750	2300	1600	750	500

Model 25

This model is similar in appearance to the Model 12 but does not have the takedown feature. All guns were solid frame. The Model 25 was furnished in 12 gauge with 26" or 28" plain round barrel, plain walnut pistol-grip stock with grooved slide handle. This was an attempt by Winchester to introduce a less expensive version of the Model 12. Introduced in 1949 it was dropped from the product line in 1954 having sold about 88,000 guns.

	NIB	EXC.	V.G.	GOOD	FAIR	POOR
	—	700	550	400	250	100

Model 20

In order to utilize the expanded production facilities left over from WWI, Winchester introduced a series of three different models of single-shot shotguns; the Model 20 was the first of the three. This model has a visible hammer and a top lever frame. It was the first Winchester to have this type of breakdown action. It was chambered for the .410, 2.5" shell. The barrel is 26" round choked full, plain walnut pistol-grip stock with hard rubber buttplate. The fore-end has a small lip on the front end. The Model 20 was dropped from the product line in 1924 having sold about 24,000 guns.

	NIB	EXC.	V.G.	GOOD	FAIR	POOR
	—	750	500	350	200	150

Model 36

The Model 36 was the second of the single-shot shotguns to be introduced in 1920. This model features a bolt-action that is cocked by pulling the firing pin head to the rear. It is fitted with an 18" round barrel, chambered for the 9mm Long Shot, 9mm Short Shot and 9mm Ball interchangeably, plain gumwood straight-grip stock with special metal pistol grip trigger guard. Winchester referred to this model as the "Garden Gun" for use against birds and pests around the house and barn. This model was not serial numbered. It was dropped from the product line in 1927 having sold about 20,000 guns.

	NIB	EXC.	V.G.	GOOD	FAIR	POOR
	—	1000	775	475	300	225

Model 41

This was the third of the low-priced single-shot shotguns to be announced in 1920. Like the Model 36, the Model 41 was a bolt-action arrangement but of much stronger construction and design. It features a 24" round barrel, chambered for the .410 2-1/2" shell, plain walnut pistol-grip stock and fore-end. Straight-grip stock was furnished at no extra charge. This model was not serial numbered. It was discontinued in 1934 having sold about 22,000 guns.

	NIB	EXC.	V.G.	GOOD	FAIR	POOR
	—	600	500	350	300	200

MODEL 21

The Model 21 was Winchester's finest effort with regard to quality, reliability, and strength. Developed in the late 1920s the introduction of this fine side-by-side shotgun was delayed by the

	NIB	EXC.	V.G.	GOOD	FAIR	POOR

company's financial troubles. When Winchester was purchased by the Olin family, the Model 21 was assured the attention it richly deserved due to John M. Olin's love for the gun. Despite the Model 21 being offered as a production gun it was, in fact, a hand-built custom-made shotgun. Almost each Model 21 built has a personality of its own because each shotgun is slightly different with regard to chokes, barrel lengths, stock dimensions, and embellishments. The gun was introduced in 1931. From 1931 to 1959 the Model 21 was considered a production line gun and about 30,000 were sold. In 1960, when the Custom Shop was opened, the Model 21 was built there using the same procedures. Sales during the Custom Shop era were about 1,000 guns. Winchester changed the name of some of the Model 21 styles but the production methods stayed the same. In 1981 Winchester sold its firearms division to U.S. Repeating Arms Company including the right to build the Model 21. Again the production procedures stayed the same as did many of the former employees. U.S. Repeating Arms expanded and changed some of the style designations for the Model 21. Production was discontinued in about 1991. No sales figures are available for this time period. Collectors and shooters will be given the price breakdown for all three eras of production separately.

NOTE: Fewer than 50 .410 Model 21s were built between 1931 and 1959 in all grades. The number of 28 gauge Model 21s built is unknown but the number is probably no greater than the .410 bore.

Model 21—1931 to 1959

The Model 21 was available in several different styles and configurations:

1. Standard Grade, chambered in 12, 16, and 20 gauge with barrel length from 26", 28", 30", and 32" with matted rib or ventilated rib, select walnut checkered pistol- or straight-grip stock with checkered beavertail fore-end. Built from 1931 to 1959.
2. Tournament Grade, same as above with special dimension stock. Marked "TOURNAMENT" on bottom of trigger plate. Built from 1933 to 1934. 3.Trap Grade, same as above with slightly better-grade wood and stock made to customers' dimensions. Marked "TRAP" on trigger plate. Built from 1932 to 1959.
4. Skeet Grade, same as above with the addition of the 28 gauge, stock furnished with checkered butt. Marked "SKEET" on trigger plate. Built from 1936 to 1959.
5. Duck Gun, chambered for 12 gauge 3" magnum shells, 30" or 32" barrels, Standard Grade stock except for shorter length of pull. Marked "DUCK" on trigger plate. Built from 1940 to 1952.
6. Magnum Gun, chambered for 3" 12 or 20 gauge, same stock as Duck Gun. Not marked on trigger plate. Built from 1953 to 1959.
7. Custom Built/Deluxe Grade, chambered for 12, 16, 20, 28, and .410, barrel lengths from 26" to 32", stock built to customers specifications using fancy walnut. Marked "CUSTOM BUILT" on top of rib or "DELUXE" on trigger plate. These grades are frequently but not always engraved. Built from 1933 to 1959.

NOTE: Some early Model 21s were furnished with double triggers, extractors, and splinter fore-ends. This combination reduces the price of the gun regardless of grade. Deduct about 25 percent.

Standard Grade - 12 gauge

—	6000	5000	3750	2400	2000

Standard Grade - 16 gauge

—	8500	6700	5650	4700	4200

Standard Grade - 20 gauge

—	9500	7500	6500	5100	4700

Tournament Grade - 12 gauge

—	6500	5200	4150	3500	3300

Tournament Grade - 16 gauge

—	8500	7200	6000	5000	4500

Tournament Grade - 20 gauge

—	10000	8200	7200	6000	4800

Trap Grade - 12 gauge

—	6800	5300	4250	3800	3600

Trap Grade - 16 gauge

—	8500	7300	6100	5300	4900

Trap Grade - 20 gauge

—	9000	7500	6550	5800	5300

	NIB	EXC.	V.G.	GOOD	FAIR	POOR

Skeet Grade - 12 gauge

	NIB	EXC.	V.G.	GOOD	FAIR	POOR
	—	6500	5000	3950	3400	3200

Skeet Grade - 16 gauge

	NIB	EXC.	V.G.	GOOD	FAIR	POOR
	—	8200	7200	6000	4900	4400

Skeet Grade - 20 gauge

	NIB	EXC.	V.G.	GOOD	FAIR	POOR
	—	9500	7800	6600	5000	4500

Duck/Magnum Gun

NOTE: Add 30 percent for 20 gauge Magnum. Factory ventilated ribs command a premium of about $1,800 on 12 gauge guns and $2,500 on 20 and 16 gauge guns. Models 21s with factory furnished extra barrels will bring an additional premium of about $2,500. Refinished and restored Model 21s are in a somewhat unique category of American-made collectible shotguns. A gun that has been professionally refinished by a master craftsman will approximate 90 percent of the value of factory original guns.

	NIB	EXC.	V.G.	GOOD	FAIR	POOR
	—	6500	5100	4450	4000	3800

Custom Built/Deluxe Grade

The prices paid for guns of this grade are determined by gauge, barrel and choke combinations, rib type, stock specifications and engraving. Expert appraisal is recommended.

It is best to secure a factory letter from the Cody Firearms Museum. With respect to such a letter, it is important to note that these records are incomplete and may be inaccurate in a few cases. Records for Model 21s built during the 1930s may be missing. Special-order guns may have incomplete records. In such cases, a written appraisal from an authoritative collector or dealer may be helpful.

12 gauge

	NIB	EXC.	V.G.	GOOD	FAIR	POOR
	—	8000	7000	5750	4500	4000

16 gauge

	NIB	EXC.	V.G.	GOOD	FAIR	POOR
	—	9000	8000	6750	5500	4500

20 gauge

	NIB	EXC.	V.G.	GOOD	FAIR	POOR
	—	10500	8500	7250	6000	5000

.410 Bore

	NIB	EXC.	V.G.	GOOD	FAIR	POOR
	—	50000	40000	31000	26000	22000

Custom Shop Model 21s—1960 to 1981

When Winchester moved the production of the Model 21 into the Custom Shop, the number of styles was greatly reduced. There were now three distinct styles:

1. Custom Grade, chambered in 12, 16, 20, 28 gauge and .410 bore in barrel lengths from 26" to 32". Matted rib, fancy walnut checkered pistol- or straight-grip stock with checkered fore-end. Guns with pistol grips furnished with steel grip cap. A small amount of scroll engraving was provided on the frame of this grade.
2. Pigeon Grade, same chambers and barrel lengths as above with the addition of choice of matted or ventilated rib, leather-covered recoil pad, style "A" carving on stock and fore-end, and gold engraved pistol grip cap. The frame was engraved with the 21-6 engraving pattern.
3. Grand American Grade, same chambers and barrel lengths as Pigeon Grade with the addition of "B" carving on the stock and fore-end, 21-6 engraving with gold inlays, extra set of interchangeable barrels with extra fore-end. All of this was enclosed in a leather trunk case.

EDITOR'S COMMENT: According to Ned Schwing's excellent book, "Winchester's Finest, The Model 21", there were only eight 28 gauge and five .410-bore models made during the Custom Shop production era from 1960 to 1981. Any price estimates would be highly speculative.

Custom Grade—12 Gauge

NOTE: Add $4,000 for 16 gauge. Add $5,000 for 20 gauge.

	NIB	EXC.	V.G.	GOOD	FAIR	POOR
	—	10000	8500	7300	6000	5200

Pigeon Grade—12 Gauge

NOTE: Add $6,000 for 16 gauge. Add $5,000 for 20 gauge.

	NIB	EXC.	V.G.	GOOD	FAIR	POOR
	—	19000	16500	12500	10000	8000

Grand American—12 Gauge

NOTE: Add $15,000 for 16 gauge (extremely rare). Add $5,000 for 20 gauge.

	NIB	EXC.	V.G.	GOOD	FAIR	POOR
	—	32000	25000	17500	14000	13000

NIB	EXC.	V.G.	GOOD	FAIR	POOR

ENGRAVED MODEL 21S

Winchester catalogued a number of special-order engraving patterns which ranged from a small amount of scroll (#1) to full-coverage game scene and scroll (#6). In addition, there were a few guns engraved on special order to the customer's request. Engraved guns are extremely rare, and the value added will vary with the rarity of the gauge and the date of manufacture. The following table represents the value added for various standard engraving patterns on 12 gauge guns for the "Custom Shop" (1960-1982) and "Pre-Custom Shop" (1932-1959) periods. However, it is advisable to seek the opinion of an authorive collector or dealer prior to a sale.

Engraving Pattern	Pre-Custom Shop	Custom Shop
#1	30 percent	20 percent
#2	40 percent	30 percent
#3	60 percent	45 percent
#4	70 percent	50 percent
#5	90 percent	70 percent
#6	100 percent	80 percent

Custom Shop Model 21s—1982 to 1993

When U.S. Repeating Arms Company took over the production of the Model 21, the Pigeon Grade was dropped from the line. The Grand American Grade was retained with all the features of its predecessor but with the addition of a small-bore set featuring a 28 gauge and .410 bore set of barrels. Two new grades were introduced in 1983: the Standard Custom Grade and the Special Custom Built. In addition to these grades, the factory would undertake to build for its customers whatever was desired. Due to the unique nature of these guns, it is advised that an expert appraisal be sought to establish a value. While the changeover from Winchester to U.S. Repeating Arms was a transfer of business assets and the craftsmen and personnel remained the same, collectors are reluctant to assign the same values to U.S. Repeating Arms Model 21s as those produced by Winchester. No official production figures are available for U.S.R.A. Model 21s, but the number is most likely small; perhaps around 200 guns.

Standard Custom Built

9000	7000	6000	5000	4500	4000

Grand American

19000	14000	10500	8500	6000	5000

Grand American Small Gauge Set—28 or .410 bore

62500	46500	37500	27000	22000	20000

CURRENT MODEL 21 PRODUCTION

In 1995, Connecticut Shotgun Mfg. Co. purchased the assets of the Winchester Model 21 Custom Shop. Beginning in 2002, Winchester licensed CSMC to build Model 21s on a custom-order basis in a wide variety of grades and models, made to the buyer's specifications. For more information, see the listing for Connecticut Shotgun Mfg. Co. in this edition.

Model 24

The Model 24 was Winchester's attempt to develop a medium-priced double-barrel shotgun. Like the Model 21, it was a top lever breakdown model that was available in 12, 16, and 20 gauge in various barrel lengths from 26" to 30". Offered in a Standard model only with double triggers, raised matted rib, plain walnut pistol- or straight-grip stock with semi-beavertail fore-end, the Model 24 was introduced in 1939 and was discontinued in 1957 with about 116,000 guns sold. **NOTE:** Add 10 percent for 16 gauge. Add 25 percent for 20 gauge.

—	750	500	400	250	200

Model 37

This model was developed to keep pace with Winchester's competitors in the low-price single-barrel exposed-hammer shotgun market. The shotgun was available in 12, 16, 20, 28 gauge and .410 bore with barrel lengths from 26" to 30". The stock was plain walnut with pistol grip and semi-beavertail fore-end. This model was not serial numbered. Introduced in 1936 it stayed in the company line until 1963, having sold slightly over 1,000,000 guns. **NOTE:** Add 15 percent premium for so-called "red letter" (red-filled "W" on bottom of receiver).

12 gauge

—	400	350	300	250	100

16 gauge

—	450	400	350	300	75

20 gauge

—	600	525	500	425	100

28 gauge

—	2000	1600	1150	850	450

	NIB	EXC.	V.G.	GOOD	FAIR	POOR

.410 bore

NOTE: 12 and 16 gauge guns add 50 percent premium for 32" barrels. Use caution for 28 gauge guns. Many fakes are seen for sale.

	NIB	EXC.	V.G.	GOOD	FAIR	POOR
	—	1000	850	500	300	100

Youth Model

26" Modified choke barrel, Win. red factory pad. 20 gauge only.

	NIB	EXC.	V.G.	GOOD	FAIR	POOR
	—	600	550	450	350	125

Model 42

Commentary and values by Bud Bugni.

First slide-action shotgun ever developed exclusively for .410 bore. Invented by William Roemer, Model 42 was in effect, at least in outward appearance, a miniature Model 12. This shotgun was quality-built, fast-handling, racy looking shotgun that many refer to as "Everybody's Sweetheart". Model 42 was first American .410 bore chambered for new 3" shell as well as 2.5" shell. Model 42 offered in several different configurations throughout its production. These configurations will greatly influence value:

1. Standard Grade: 26" or 28" plain or solid rib barrel, plain walnut pistol-grip stock with grooved slide handle. Fitted with composition buttplate. Straight grip offered on Standard Grade on special order basis, but is extremely rare. Built from 1933 to 1963.
2. Skeet Grade: 26" or 28" plain, solid rib or ventilated rib barrel. Select walnut checkered pistol or straight-grip stock with checkered extension slide handle. Skeet Grade offered in Full, Modified, Improved Cylinder, Cylinder as well as Skeet chokes. Built from 1933 to 1963.
3. Trap Grade: 26" or 28" plain or solid rib barrel. Fancy walnut special checkered pistol or straight-grip stock with special checkered extension slide handle. Trap Grade checkering pattern has one closed diamond on each side of pistol grip or, in case of straight grip, diamond is located on underside of grip. Extension slide handle has two uncut diamonds on each side. Most were stamped "TRAP" on bottom of receiver under serial number. Built from 1934 to 1939.
4. Deluxe Grade: continuation of Trap Grade. Available with ventilated rib in 1954. Some early models stamped "DELUXE" on bottom of receiver. This stamping is seldom seen and probably discontinued around 1949. Built from 1940 to 1963. 5.Pigeon Grade: same as above Deluxe Grade, but engraved with pigeon on lower magazine tube. Very few of this grade were built by Winchester and majority were done in late 1940s. Authentic Pigeon Grade 42s appear to have been built between 1945 and 1949. Some estimate less than 50 were produced. This is a rare Model 42. Seek an expert opinion before sale.

As of late, I have heard horror stories from sincere, honest, decent folks who have purchased misrepresented guns from either unscrupulous sellers or sellers who simply do not know their products. In some cases there are no return privileges, or buyer was unable to authenticate his purchase in a timely manner. This often has resulted in a heavy financial loss and that's a dish served cold. Contributors are listed in Standard Catalog of Firearms. These knowledgeable and dedicated people are eager to assist readers, or refer them to sources who can.—Bud Bugni

NOTE: Engraved Model 42s will occasionally be seen. Collectors are urged to seek expert advice on these rare and expensive guns. Model 42 produced from 1933 to 1963. About 164,000 were sold. Factory service and repair for this model were discontinued in February of 1972.

EXTRA BARRELS: Winchester offered extra interchangeable barrels for its Model 42s at customer's request beginning in 1934. These extra sets of barrels are a rare option. Both barrels should have same barrel markings and matching serial numbers before originality can be considered. Values are difficult to determine, but as a general rule add 60 percent to price of a Model 42 if it has factory-original extra barrel.

EDITOR'S COMMENT: Contrary to traditional views, Winchester did install factory ventilated ribs on its Model 42. Former employees and factory drawings substantiate this fact. However, subject of what is a factory rib and what is not has been covered in great detail in an excellent book on Model 42. Seek expert advice before selling or purchasing any Model 42 with ventilated rib.

NOTE: Pigeon Grade Model 42s with documentation on expert authentication add 100 percent. Must be individually appraised. Proceed with caution.

Cutts Compensator Guns: Approximately 66 original Cutts Compensator guns were produced in the Winchester factory, making this one of the rarest options on Model 42. New information reveals that Cutts Compensators were available on Model 42 as early as 1950. This offering appeared in Winchester retail price list dated December 15, 1950. Considering this, since ventilated ribs were not offered on M42 until 1954, one may see an original "Cutts Gun" with plain or solid rib barrel minus a choke mark. NOTE: Add 25 percent for original Cutts guns; deduct 50 percent for non-original Cutts guns.

Standard Grade

NOTE: Standard Grade guns with solid ribs add 50 percent; pre-war guns add 25 percent.

	NIB	EXC.	V.G.	GOOD	FAIR	POOR
	3000	1950	1150	900	700	400

NIB	EXC.	V.G.	GOOD	FAIR	POOR

Skeet Grade—Solid Rib
NOTE: Add 25 percent guns chambered for 2.5" shells; pre-war guns 30 percent; Skeet Grade guns with no rib deduct 25 percent.

6500	5000	4250	3500	1950	1250

Skeet Grade—Ventilated Rib
NOTE: Add 25 percent chambered for 2.5" shells.

7500	6000	4750	3500	2200	1250

Trap Grade - Plain or Solid Rib

—	12500	10500	9500	5500	3000

Deluxe Grade—Solid Rib

12000	9500	8500	6000	3500	1250

Deluxe Grade—Ventilated Rib

14000	12000	10950	7500	4800	2400

Model 1911

This was Winchester's first self-loading shotgun and was developed by T.C. Johnson in order to keep pace with the Remington Auto-Loading Shotgun Model 11, which was developed by John M. Browning with help from T.C. Johnson. Because of the delays involved in developing a brand new design, the Model 1911 was introduced on October 7, 1911. The shotgun was a recoil operated mechanism, had a tubular magazine and had the takedown feature. The shotgun was available in two styles:

1.   Plain Model 1911, 26" or 28" barrel, 12 gauge, choked full, modified, or cylinder, plain birch laminated pistol-grip stock and fore-end with hard rubber buttplate.
2. Fancy Model 1911, same as above with fancy birch laminated stock.

Because of the hurry in getting the model ready for production, the shotgun demonstrated design weakness and never proved satisfactory. It was discontinued in 1925 with about 83,000 guns sold.

Plain

—	650	375	300	250	200

Fancy

—	800	500	400	300	250

Model 40

This model represents Winchester's second attempt to build a self-loading long recoil-operated repeating shotgun. This shotgun was a hammerless tubular magazine gun without the hump at the rear of the receiver. Available in 12 gauge only with barrel lengths from 28" to 30". The Standard Grade had plain walnut checkered pistol-grip stock and fore-end. The Skeet Grade was fitted with select walnut checkered pistol-grip stock and checkered fore-end. The Model 40 suffered from the same design problems as the Model 11, and sales were small. Introduced in 1940 and discontinued in 1941, Winchester sold about 12,000 guns.

Standard Grade

—	650	500	400	275	200

Skeet Grade

—	950	600	500	300	250

Model 50

The Model 50 was the company's third attempt to produce a satisfactory self-loading repeating shotgun. Winchester went to the short recoil system, utilizing a floating chamber design. This model was available in several different styles:

1. Standard Grade, 12 or 20 gauge with plain or ventilated rib in lengths from 26" to 30", plain walnut checkered pistol-grip stock and fore-end.
2. Skeet Grade, 12 or 20 gauge with 26" ventilated rib barrel. Walnut checkered pistol-grip stock and fore-end.
3. Trap Grade, 12 gauge with 30" ventilated rib barrel, walnut checkered Monte Carlo stock and fore-end.
4. Pigeon Grade, 12 or 20 gauge with barrel lengths to customers' specifications. Fancy walnut checkered stock and fore-end. Made on special orders only.
5. Featherweight, a lighter version of all the above except Trap Grade.

This model begins with serial number 1000. This model was successful and was built between 1954 and 1961. Winchester sold about 200,000 guns.

NOTE: Add 10 percent for 20 gauge. Add 20 percent for vent rib on standard grade guns.

Standard Grade

—	550	400	300	200	150

	NIB	EXC.	V.G.	GOOD	FAIR	POOR

Skeet Grade

| | — | 600 | 500 | 350 | 250 | 200 |

Trap Grade

| | — | 600 | 500 | 350 | 250 | 200 |

Pigeon Grade

| | — | 1800 | 1200 | 750 | 450 | 250 |

Featherweight

| | — | 600 | 500 | 350 | 250 | 200 |

Model 59

The fourth and final pre-1964 Winchester self-loading shotgun, featured a steel and fiberglass barrel with aluminum alloy receiver. The gun was available in 12 gauge only with barrel lengths from 26" to 30" with a variety of chokes. In 1961 Winchester introduced the "Versalite" choke tube, which gave the shooter a choice of Full, Modified, or Improved Cylinder chokes in the same barrel. This model was available in two different styles:

1. Standard Grade, plain walnut checkered pistol-grip stock and fore-end.
2. Pigeon Grade, select walnut checkered pistol-grip and fore-end.

Winchester sold about 82,000 of these guns between 1960 and 1965.

NOTE: This shotgun was also made in 10 gauge (very rare), 20 gauge and 14 gauge. If any of these very low production or prototype guns are encountered, use extreme caution and seek an expert appraisal.

NOTE: Add 40 percent premium for barrels with three Versalite chokes and wrench. Add 20 percent premium for original box and papers.

Standard Grade

| | — | 650 | 550 | 450 | 350 | 250 |

Pigeon Grade

| | — | 2500 | 2000 | 1200 | 600 | 300 |

POST-1963 RIFLES

Model 121

This is a single-shot, bolt-action rifle chambered for the .22 rimfire cartridge. It has a 20.75" barrel with open sights. The finish is blued, with a plain walnut stock. It was manufactured between 1967 and 1973. A youth model with a shorter stock was designated the 121Y and is valued the same.

| | — | 225 | 150 | 100 | 60 | 40 |

Model 131

This is a bolt-action repeater chambered for the .22 rimfire cartridge. It has a 20.75" barrel with open sights and a 7-round, detachable magazine. The finish is blued, with a plain walnut stock. It was manufactured between 1967 and 1973. A tubular magazine version was designated the Model 141 and is valued the same.

| | — | 250 | 175 | 100 | 60 | 40 |

Model 310

This is a single-shot, bolt-action rifle chambered for the .22 rimfire cartridge. It features a 22" barrel with open sights. The finish is blued, with a checkered walnut stock. It was manufactured between 1972 and 1975.

| | — | 250 | 150 | 125 | 100 | 75 |

Model 320

This is a bolt-action repeating rifle that is similar in configuration to the Model 310 single-shot. It has a 5-round, detachable box magazine. It was manufactured between 1972 and 1974.

| | — | 400 | 300 | 250 | 175 | 125 |

Model 250

This is a lever-action repeating rifle with a hammerless action. It is chambered for the .22 rimfire cartridge and has a 20.5" barrel with open sights and a tubular magazine. The finish is blued, with a checkered pistol-grip stock. It was manufactured between 1963 and 1973.

| | — | 200 | 125 | 80 | 60 | 40 |

	NIB	EXC.	V.G.	GOOD	FAIR	POOR

Model 250 Deluxe

This version is similar to the Model 250 and is furnished with select walnut and sling swivels. It was manufactured between 1965 and 1971.

	NIB	EXC.	V.G.	GOOD	FAIR	POOR
	—	275	195	125	100	75

Model 255

This version is simply the Model 250 chambered for the .22 WMR cartridge. It was manufactured between 1964 and 1970.

	NIB	EXC.	V.G.	GOOD	FAIR	POOR
	—	225	150	100	70	50

Model 255 Deluxe

This version was offered with select walnut and sling swivels. It was manufactured between 1965 and 1973.

	NIB	EXC.	V.G.	GOOD	FAIR	POOR
	—	375	250	175	125	75

Model 490

This is a blowback-operated, semi-automatic rifle chambered for the .22 LR cartridge. It has a 22" barrel with open sights and a 5-round, detachable magazine. The finish is blued, with a checkered stock. It was manufactured between 1975 and 1980.

	NIB	EXC.	V.G.	GOOD	FAIR	POOR
	—	350	225	165	100	75

Model 270

This is a slide-action rifle chambered for the .22 rimfire cartridge. It has a 20.5" barrel and a tubular magazine. The finish is blued, with a checkered walnut stock. It was manufactured between 1963 and 1973.

	NIB	EXC.	V.G.	GOOD	FAIR	POOR
	—	350	225	165	100	75

Model 63 (1997)

Introduced in 1997 this is a re-creation of the famous Model 63 .22 caliber auto. Fitted with a 23" barrel and 10-round tubular magazine. The receiver top is grooved for scope mounting.

Grade I

NIB	EXC.	V.G.	GOOD	FAIR	POOR
800	525	—	—	—	—

High Grade

Engraved receiver with gold accents and select walnut stock.

NIB	EXC.	V.G.	GOOD	FAIR	POOR
1050	850	700	575	400	300

Wildcat

Bolt-action repeater styled after Mosin-Nagant military sporter. Caliber: .22 LR. Magazine: 5- and 10-round detachable. Stock: checkered walnut with schnabel. Barrel: 21-inch blued. Weight: 4.5 lbs. Imported. Introduced 2006. Sporter and Target/Varmint versions available. Add 5 percent for Target/Varmint.

NIB	EXC.	V.G.	GOOD	FAIR	POOR
240	175	150	125	95	50

Model 94

This is the post-1964 lever-action carbine chambered for the .30-30, 7-30 Waters, and the .44 Magnum cartridges. It is offered with a 20" or 24" barrel and has a 6- or 7-round, tubular magazine depending on barrel length. The round barrel is offered with open sights. The forearm is held on by a single barrel band. The finish is blued, with a straight-grip walnut stock. In 1982 it was modified to angle ejection to simplify scope mounting. It was introduced as a continuation of the Model 94 line in 1964. In 2003 a top-tang safety was installed and the .480 Ruger caliber was added. The Model 94 series was discontinued in 2006. Premium for unusual chamberings such as 7-30 Waters, etc.

NIB	EXC.	V.G.	GOOD	FAIR	POOR
800	600	425	300	200	100

Model 94 Traditional—CW

As above but with checkered walnut stock. Chambered for the .30-30, .44 Mag., and the .480 Ruger cartridge. **NOTE:** For .44 Mag. add $20. For the .480 Ruger add $70.

NIB	EXC.	V.G.	GOOD	FAIR	POOR
850	575	450	325	225	125

Model 94 Ranger

Chambered for .30-30 cartridge and fitted with a 20" barrel. Weight is about 6.25 lbs. In 2003 a top-tang safety was installed.

	NIB	EXC.	V.G.	GOOD	FAIR	POOR
	—	450	300	225	150	100

	NIB	EXC.	V.G.	GOOD	FAIR	POOR

Model 94 Ranger Compact

Introduced in 1998 this model features a 16" barrel with 12.5" lop. Chambered for .30-30 or .357 Magnum. Furnished with black recoil pad. Post-style front sight with adjustable rear sight. Hardwood stock. Weight is approximately 5.87 lbs

	NIB	EXC.	V.G.	GOOD	FAIR	POOR
	—	475	325	250	150	100

Model 94 Black Shadow

This model features a black synthetic stock with nonglare finish and black recoil pad. Offered in .30-30, .44 Magnum, or .444 Marlin. Fitted with a 20" barrel. Weight is about 6.5 lbs. Introduced in 1998.

NIB	EXC.	V.G.	GOOD	FAIR	POOR
600	475	375	250	225	175

Model 94 Deluxe

Checkered stock.

NIB	EXC.	V.G.	GOOD	FAIR	POOR
850	675	550	400	300	200

Model 94 Win-Tuff

Laminated stock.

NIB	EXC.	V.G.	GOOD	FAIR	POOR
500	400	275	225	165	125

Model 94 XTR

Select, checkered walnut stock, discontinued 1988.

NIB	EXC.	V.G.	GOOD	FAIR	POOR
—	700	450	350	250	175

Model 94 XTR Deluxe

Fancy checkering.

NIB	EXC.	V.G.	GOOD	FAIR	POOR
—	725	475	375	275	200

Model 94 Trapper

16" barrel. Chambered for the .30-30, .357 Mag., .44 Mag, or .45 Colt cartridge. In 2003 a top-tang safety was installed.

NIB	EXC.	V.G.	GOOD	FAIR	POOR
750	575	450	350	250	150

Model 94 Antique Carbine

Gold-plated saddle ring.

NIB	EXC.	V.G.	GOOD	FAIR	POOR
—	800	600	475	350	200

Model 94 Wrangler

.32 Win. Special.

NIB	EXC.	V.G.	GOOD	FAIR	POOR
—	900	725	525	400	250

Model 94 Wrangler II

Loop lever.

NIB	EXC.	V.G.	GOOD	FAIR	POOR
700	525	425	300	150	—

Model 94 Legacy 20-inch

This Model 94 is fitted with a 20" barrel and chambered for the .30-30 Win. but it is fitted with a half pistol-grip stock. Both walnut buttstock and forearm are cut checkered. Weight is 6.5 lbs. In 2003 a top-tang safety was installed.

NIB	EXC.	V.G.	GOOD	FAIR	POOR
900	750	600	475	300	200

Model 94 Legacy 24-inch

Introduced in 2005 this model features a 24" round barrel with full length magazine. Checkered walnut stock with semi-pistol grip. Chambered for the .30-30, .357 Mag., .44 Rem. Mag. or the .45 Colt cartridge. Drilled and tapped for scope mount. Blued finish. Weight is about 6.75 lbs.

NIB	EXC.	V.G.	GOOD	FAIR	POOR
900	750	600	475	300	200

Model 94 Legacy 26-inch

Similar to the model above but offered in both round and octagon barrel and blue or case colored receiver. Marbles' tang sight. Chambered for the .30-30 or .38-55 calibers. Weight is about 7 lbs. Introduced in 2005. Premium for .38-55. **NOTE:** Add $55 for case colored receiver. Add $100 for octagon barrel.

NIB	EXC.	V.G.	GOOD	FAIR	POOR
1100	875	750	575	400	300

Model 94 XTR Big Bore

This version is chambered for the .307, .356, or the .375 Win. cartridges. It features the angle-ejection and is blued with a walnut, Monte Carlo-type stock and recoil pad. The round barrel is

NIB	EXC.	V.G.	GOOD	FAIR	POOR

20" in length. It has a 6-round, tubular magazine. It was introduced in 1978. Deduct 12.5 percent for .375.

NIB	EXC.	V.G.	GOOD	FAIR	POOR
1050	900	775	575	400	300

Model 94 Centennial Limited Editions

Introduced in 1994 these models celebrate the 100-year anniversary of the Winchester Model 1894. Offered in three grades, these models are of limited production. The Grade I is limited to 12,000 rifles while the High Grade is limited to 3,000 rifles. Only 94 of the Custom Limited model were produced. Each Limited model has different grades of select walnut and engraving coverage. All are chambered for the .30-30 Winchester cartridge.

Grade I

1200	1000	900	700	575	400

High Grade

1900	1300	1075	900	750	600

Custom High Grade

4750	3900	2500	1000	750	450

Model 94 Heritage—Limited 1 of 1000

Introduced in 2002 and limited to 1,000 rifles. Fitted with half round/half octagon 26" barrel. Engraved with #3 pattern with gold plate. Fancy walnut stock. Chambered for the .38-55 cartridge.

5000	4000	3000	1750	1200	600

Model 94 Heritage—Custom 1 of 100

Similar to the above model but with finer wood and engraved with #2 pattern with gold. Limited to 100 rifles. Introduced in 2002.

7500	—	—	—	—	—

Model 94 Trails End

This model is chambered for the .357 Mag., .44 Mag., and .45 Colt. Offered with standard-size loop lever or Wrangler-style loop. Introduced in 1997. Add $500 to NIB for .25-35 Win.

1375	1050	825	600	450	300

Model 94 Trails End Octagon

As above but with 20" octagon barrel and choice of blued or case colored receiver. Crescent butt. Weight is about 6.75 lbs. Introduced in 2004. **NOTE:** Add $60 for case colored receiver.

1395	1100	850	600	450	300

Model 94 Trails End Hunter

Offered in .25-35 Win, .30-30 Win, or .38-55 Win and fitted with a 20" round or octagon barrel. Plain walnut stock. Blued finish on round barrel model and case colored finish on octagon model. Weight is about 6.5 lbs. Introduced in 2005. **NOTE:** Add $290 for octagon barrel model.

1375	1050	825	600	450	300

Model 94 Timber Carbine

Introduced in 1999 this model is chambered for the .444 Marlin cartridge. Barrel is 17.75" long and ported. Hooded front sight. Magazine capacity is 5 rounds. Weight is about 6 lbs. Finish is blue. Walnut stock. In 2004 this rifle was chambered for the .450 Marlin cartridge.

1000	850	700	600	400	300

Model 94 Timber Scout

This model, introduced in 2005, features an 18" barrel chambered for the .30-30 Win. or .44 Rem. Mag. cartridges with a quick detachable scope mount attached to the barrel for long eye relief. Plain walnut stock with pistol grip. Blued finish. Weight is about 6 lbs. Scope not included.

900	750	600	475	300	200

Model 94 Pack Rifle

This lever-action model features an 18" barrel chambered for the .30-30 or .44 Magnum. It has a walnut stock with pistol grip and no checkering. Magazine is 3/4-style and has a 4-round capacity for the .30-30, and five rounds for the .44 Mag. Open sights. Weight is about 6.25 lbs. Introduced in 2000.

900	750	600	475	300	200

Winchester Model 1894 Custom Grade

Lever-action rifle chambered in .30-30. Features include 24" half-round, half octagon deeply blued barrel; buckhorn rear sight with Marbles gold bead front sight; Grade IV/V walnut stock and

NIB	EXC.	V.G.	GOOD	FAIR	POOR

fore-end with a rich, high gloss finish; deep scroll engraving on both sides of the blued receiver. Commemorates the 200th anniversary of Oliver F. Winchester's birth. An early Winchester Repeating Arms crest graces the left side of the receiver, with the right side bearing the words, "Two Hundred Years, Oliver F. Winchester", and the dates, "1810 - 2010", in gold. The barrel is deeply polished, with the signature of Oliver F. Winchester in gold on the top of the bolt. Sold individually in limited quantities and in 500 sets with the High Grade.

1800	1550	1300	—	—	—

Winchester Model 1894 High Grade

Lever-action rifle chambered in .30-30. Features include 24" half-round, half octagon deeply blued barrel; buckhorn rear sight with Marbles gold bead front sight; silver nitride receiver; Grade II/III high gloss walnut stock and fore-end with a rich, high gloss finish; delicate scroll work, with Oliver F. Winchester's signature in gold on top of the bolt. The left side of receiver bears an early Winchester Repeating Arms crest; on right side are the words, "Two Hundred Years, Oliver F. Winchester", and the dates, "1810 - 2010". Sold individually in limited quantities and in 500 sets with the Custom Grade.

1300	1100	900	—	—	—

Model 71

A true reproduction of the original. Drilled and tapped for a receiver sight. Barrel is 24", polished blue and round. Oil finished American walnut stock for fore-end cap, no checkering. Marble gold bead front sight, buckhorn rear sight. Chambered for original caliber only, .348 WCF. Introduced in 2011.

1300	1100	—	—	—	—

Model 94 Short Rifle

New for 2011, the latest incarnation of the famous Model 94 Carbine with 20" round barrel and straight grip walnut stock. Rifle-styled fore-end has black grip cap and full-length magazine. Receiver drilled and tapped for scope mounts with hammer extension included. Marble gold bead front sight, semi-buckhorn rear. Overall length 38" and weight is 6.75 lbs. Chambered in .30-30 Winchester only.

1000	875	750	—	—	—

Model 94 Sporter

Reminiscent of the original Model 1894 Rifle, this new for 2011 model has a 24" half-round, half-octagon blued barrel and a satin oil-finished American walnut stock with steel crescent buttplate and double-line bordering checkering pattern. Blue receiver drilled and tapped for optical sights. Gold bead front sight, buckhorn sight at rear. Hammer extension included. Available in .30-30 or .38-55 Winchester.

1175	1000	850	—	—	—

Model 1886 Short Rifle

Reintroduction of a version of the famed Model 1886 with Grade I American walnut stock. Blue steel fore-end cap and crescent buttplate. Barrel is 24" with full-length tubular magazine that holds six cartridges. Chambered in .45-70 Government. Elegant satin finish on all wood, no checkering. Deep blue receiver, barrel and lever. Top tang safety, adjustable rear buckhorn sight with fine gold Marble front sight.

1125	975	825	—	—	—

Model 1892 Carbine

New version of the rifle made famous by actor John Wayne. Chambered for .357 Magnum, .44 Remington Magnum or .45 Colt. American walnut stock with straight grip. 21" round barrel, receiver and lever are deeply polished and blued. Full-length magazine. Front and rear iron sights.

950	800	700	—	—	—

MODEL 9400 SERIES

Model 9410

Introduced in 2001 this model features a .410 shotgun in a lever-action configuration. Barrel length is 24" and is smoothbore with cylinder choke or Invector chokes. Chambered is 2.5". Magazine capacity is nine rounds. Tru-glo front sight. Weight is about 6.75 lbs. In 2003 a top-tang safety was installed.

1450	1100	900	750	600	400

Model 9410 Semi-Fancy

As above but with semi-fancy walnut stock with checkering. Introduced in 2004.

1600	1200	975	825	650	400

	NIB	EXC.	V.G.	GOOD	FAIR	POOR

Model 9410 Packer

Introduced in 2002 this model features a 20" barrel with 3/4 magazine and pistol-grip stock. Weight is about 6.5 lbs.

NIB	EXC.	V.G.	GOOD	FAIR	POOR
1000	850	700	600	400	300

Model 9410 Packer Compact

Introduced in 2003 this model features a reduced length of pull to 12-1/2". Fitted with Invector chokes. Weight is about 6.25 lbs.

NIB	EXC.	V.G.	GOOD	FAIR	POOR
1000	850	700	600	400	300

Model 9410 Ranger

This version is the same as the standard or traditional Model 9410 but hardwood stock without checkering. Weight is about 6.75 lbs. Fitted with top-tang safety. Introduced in 2003.

NIB	EXC.	V.G.	GOOD	FAIR	POOR
900	750	575	450	300	250

Model 9422

Introduced in 1972 this model is chambered for the .22 rimfire and .22 Magnum rimfire cartridges. It was fitted with a 20.5" barrel, front ramp sight with hood, and adjustable semi-buckhorn rear sight. Tubular magazine holds 21 Shorts, 17 Longs, and 15 LR cartridges. The Magnum version holds 11 cartridges. Weight is about 6.25 lbs. Two-piece American walnut stock with no checkering. Between 1972 and 1992 approximately 750,000 Model 9422s were produced.

NIB	EXC.	V.G.	GOOD	FAIR	POOR
850	675	525	375	225	125

Model 9422 XTR

This is a deluxe lever-action rifle chambered for the .22 rimfire cartridge. It is a takedown rifle with a 20.5", round barrel and a tubular magazine. The finish is blued with a checkered, high-gloss, straight-grip walnut stock. It was introduced in 1978. A .22 Magnum version is also available and would be worth approximately $100 additional.

NIB	EXC.	V.G.	GOOD	FAIR	POOR
1000	850	700	600	400	300

Model 9422 XTR Classic

This version is similar to the standard Model 9422 XTR except that it features a 22.5" barrel and a satin-finished, plain, pistol-grip walnut stock. It was manufactured between 1985 and 1987.

NIB	EXC.	V.G.	GOOD	FAIR	POOR
1100	925	750	650	450	325

Model 9422 WinTuff

This model features an uncheckered laminated wood stock that is brown in color. Chambered for both the .22 Rimfire and the .22 Winchester Magnum Rimfire. Weighs 6.25 lbs. Other features are the same as the standard Model 9422.

NIB	EXC.	V.G.	GOOD	FAIR	POOR
850	675	525	375	225	125

Model 9422 WinCam

This model is chambered only for the .22 Winchester Magnum Rimfire. The laminated stock is a green color. Weighs 6.25 lbs.

NIB	EXC.	V.G.	GOOD	FAIR	POOR
850	675	525	375	225	125

Model 9422 Trapper

Introduced in 1996 this model features a 16.5" barrel. It has an overall length of 33". Weight is 5.5 lbs.

NIB	EXC.	V.G.	GOOD	FAIR	POOR
850	675	525	375	225	125

Model 9422 High Grade

This variation of the Model 9422 series features a specially engraved receiver and fancy wood stock. Barrel length is 20.5". Weight is about 6 lbs.

NIB	EXC.	V.G.	GOOD	FAIR	POOR
1000	850	700	600	400	300

Model 9422 25th Anniversary Rifle

Introduced in 1997 this model features 20.5" barrel. Limited quantities.

Grade I

Engraved receiver.

NIB	EXC.	V.G.	GOOD	FAIR	POOR
1000	850	700	600	400	300

High Grade

Engraved receiver with silver border.

NIB	EXC.	V.G.	GOOD	FAIR	POOR
1450	1100	900	750	600	400

NIB	EXC.	V.G.	GOOD	FAIR	POOR

Model 9422 Legacy

This model has a semi-pistol-grip stock of checkered walnut. Will shoot .22 caliber LR, L, or S cartridges. Fitted with a 16" barrel. Weight is about 6 lbs. Introduced in 1998.

850	675	525	375	225	125

Model 9422 Large Loop & Walnut

Introduced in 1998 this model features a walnut stock with large loop lever. Large loop offered on .22 LR, L, or S model. Standard lever on .22 WMR version. Fitted with 16" barrel. Weight is about 6 lbs.

900	750	575	450	300	250

Model 9422 High Grade Series II

This model features a high-grade walnut stock with cut checkering. Receiver engraved with dogs and squirrels. Fitted with 16" barrel. Weight is about 6 lbs. Introduced in 1998.

1450	1100	900	750	600	400

Model 9417 Traditional

Introduced in 2003 this model is chambered for the .17 HMR cartridge and fitted with a 20.5" barrel. Adjustable sights. Checkered walnut stock with straight grip. Weight is about 6 lbs.

1200	975	850	675	400	300

Model 9417 Legacy

Similar to the model above but fitted with a 22.5" barrel and checkered walnut with pistol grip. Weight is about 6 lbs. Introduced in 2003.

1200	975	850	675	400	300

MODEL 9422 TRIBUTE SERIES

As of 2005 the Model 9422 production will end. These final production Model 9422s will be limited to a total production of 9,422 rifles. Each rifle will have the Winchester Horse and Rider on one side and the Model 9422 tribute logo on the other side.

Traditional Tribute

This model features a 20.5" barrel with high grade checkered walnuty stock. Blued receiver with high-relief silver inlay on both sides of the receiver.

1400	1200	975	825	650	300

Legacy Tribute

Similar to the model above but with semi-pistol grip and 22.5" barrel.

1500	1300	1075	925	650	300

Custom Traditional Tribute

This model is fitted with a 20.5" barrel, high grade checkereed walnut stock. High-relief scroll engraved receiver with gold logos on both sides. Limited to 222 rifles.

2600	2200	1650	1200	800	500

Special Edition Traditional Tribute

This model has a 20.5" barrel with checkered walnut straight grip stock and engraved blued receiver. Engraved logos on both sides of receiver.

1200	975	850	675	400	300

Special Edition Legacy Tribute

This 22.5" barrel model has a checkered semi-pistol grip stock Blued receiver with engraved logos on both sides.

1200	975	850	675	400	300

Model 64 (Post-'64)

This is a post-1964 version of the lever-action Model 64. It is chambered for the .30-30 cartridge and has a 24" round barrel with open sights and a 5-round, 2/3-length tubular magazine. The finish is blued with a plain walnut pistol-grip stock. It was manufactured between 1972 and 1974.

—	800	650	550	375	250

Model 1885 Low Wall

Introduced in fall of 1999 this single-shot model is chambered for the .22 LR or .17 Mach II cartridge. It is fitted with a 24.5" half octagon barrel with leaf rear sight. Drilled and tapped for a tang sight. Crescent steel buttplate. Walnut stock. Weight is about 8 lbs. Limited to 2,400 rifles.

	NIB	EXC.	V.G.	GOOD	FAIR	POOR

Grade I

NIB	EXC.	V.G.	GOOD	FAIR	POOR
1050	900	750	600	500	300

High Grade

NIB	EXC.	V.G.	GOOD	FAIR	POOR
1300	1050	875	750	600	400

Model 1885 High Wall Hunter

Single-shot; patterned after original Model 1885 designed by John Browning. Calibers: .223, .22-250, .270 WSM, 7mm WSM, .300 WSM, .325 WSM. Stock: Checkered walnut. Barrel: 28-inch blued, sightless octagon with Pachmayr pad. Weight: 8-1/2 lbs.

NIB	EXC.	V.G.	GOOD	FAIR	POOR
1100	925	750	650	450	325

Model 1885 .30-06 Centennial High Wall Hunter

Similar to Model 1885 High Wall Hunter but with premium wood and gold inlay on receiver. Commemorates centennial of .30-06 cartridge. Introduced 2006.

NIB	EXC.	V.G.	GOOD	FAIR	POOR
1300	1125	875	750	550	325

Model 1885 Low Wall Classic

This single-shot rifle is chambered for the .17 HMR cartridge and fitted with a 24" octagon barrel. Checkered walnut stock with straight grip and schnabel fore-end. Adjustable sights. Weight is about 8 lbs. Introduced in 2003. In 2005 the .17 Mach 2 caliber was offered in this model.

NIB	EXC.	V.G.	GOOD	FAIR	POOR
1100	925	750	650	450	325

Model 1885 Low Wall 17 Mach 2

Similar to Model 1885 High Wall but with low-profile receiver, crescent buttplate, and 24-inch barrel. Chambered for 17 Mach 2 rimfire cartridge. Introduced 2006.

NIB	EXC.	V.G.	GOOD	FAIR	POOR
1050	900	750	600	500	300

Model 1892

Introduced in mid-1997 this model is chambered for the .357 Magnum, .44-40 and .45 Colt cartridges. It features a straight grip, full magazine, and crescent buttplate.

Grade I

2,500 rifles with engraved receiver.

NIB	EXC.	V.G.	GOOD	FAIR	POOR
900	800	700	550	450	325

High Grade

1,000 rifles with gold accents.

NIB	EXC.	V.G.	GOOD	FAIR	POOR
1500	1300	1075	925	650	300

Model 1892 Short Rifle

This model is fitted with a 20" barrel and chambered for the .45 Colt, .357 Magnum, .44 Magnum and .44-40 cartridges. Walnut stock and blued barrel and receiver. Weight is about 6.25 lbs. Introduced in 1999.

NIB	EXC.	V.G.	GOOD	FAIR	POOR
1200	975	850	675	400	300

Model 1892 Carbine

Similar to 1892 Short Rifle with satin-finished stock, full-length 10-shot magazine with barrel band. Introduced in 2011. Also available with large-loop lever.

NIB	EXC.	V.G.	GOOD	FAIR	POOR
1000	850	700	500	350	200

John Wayne Model 1892 High Grade

Features silver-nickel receiver with engraved portrait of actor on the receiver. Banners on sides of receiver have silver-nickel engraving: "John Wayne-American 1907-2007" and "Courage, Strength, Grit". In .44-40 caliber with 18.5" barrel, large-loop lever, adjustable rear sight, blue hammer and trigger. Custom Grade has checkered stock, gold engraving, blue receiver. Limited editions with 4,000 High Grade and 1,000 Custom Grade. Manufactured 2007-2009. **NOTE:** Add $1000 for Custom Grade.

NIB	EXC.	V.G.	GOOD	FAIR	POOR
1750	1650	1550	—	—	—

Model 1886

Introduced to the Winchester line in 1997 this was a non-cataloged item. This model features a 26" octagon barrel, semi-pistol grip, and crescent buttplate.

Grade I

2,500 rifles blued receiver.

NIB	EXC.	V.G.	GOOD	FAIR	POOR
1050	900	750	600	500	300

	NIB	EXC.	V.G.	GOOD	FAIR	POOR

High Grade
1,000 rifles with gold accents on receiver.

	NIB	EXC.	V.G.	GOOD	FAIR	POOR
	1500	1300	1075	925	650	300

Model 1886 Take Down Classic
Introduced in 1999 this model is chambered for the .45-70 cartridge and features a 26" barrel with takedown feature. Walnut stock with pistol grip and crescent butt. Magazine capacity is 8 rounds. Weight is about 9.25 lbs.

	NIB	EXC.	V.G.	GOOD	FAIR	POOR
	1300	1125	875	750	550	325

Model 1886 Extra Light
This model is similar to the Model 1886 Classic but fitted with a 22" round tapered barrel and half magazine. Chambered for the .45-70 cartridge. Shotgun butt. Weight is about 7.25 lbs. Limited edition. Introduced in 2000.

Grade I (3,500)

	NIB	EXC.	V.G.	GOOD	FAIR	POOR
	1100	925	750	650	450	325

High Grade (1,000)

	NIB	EXC.	V.G.	GOOD	FAIR	POOR
	1500	1300	1075	925	650	300

Model 1895 Limited Edition
Introduced in 1995 this reproduction of the famous Model 1895 is offered in .30-06 caliber with 24" barrel. Magazine capacity is 4 rounds. Weight is approximately 8 lbs. Available in two grades, each limited to 4,000 rifles. Reintroduced in 2010 in .30-40 Krag caliber.

Grade I

	NIB	EXC.	V.G.	GOOD	FAIR	POOR
	1050	900	750	600	500	300

High Grade

	NIB	EXC.	V.G.	GOOD	FAIR	POOR
	1500	1300	1075	925	650	300

Model 1895—Limited Edition for the year 2000
Same as above but chambered for the .405 Win. cartridge. Introduced in 2000.

Grade I

	NIB	EXC.	V.G.	GOOD	FAIR	POOR
	1100	925	750	650	450	325

High Grade

	NIB	EXC.	V.G.	GOOD	FAIR	POOR
	1500	1300	1075	925	650	300

Model 1895 Saddle Ring Carbine
Patterned after original Model 1895 carbine. Features include blued 22-inch barrel, ladder style rear sight; D&T for Lyman side mount; saddle ring on left side of receiver; rollmarked -inch.30 Gov't 06.-inch Chambered in .30-06 only; commemorates centennial of .30-06 cartridge. Introduced 2006.

	NIB	EXC.	V.G.	GOOD	FAIR	POOR
	1200	975	850	675	400	300

Model 1895 Theodore Roosevelt Safari Centennial High Grade
Lever-action rifle patterned after original Winchester Model 1895. Chambered in .405 Winchester; commemorates Theodore Roosevelt's 1909 African Safari. 24" blued round barrel, 4-round box magazine, checkered walnut fore-end and buttstock with inlaid "TR" medallion, engraved and silvered receiver. Weight: 8 lbs.

	NIB	EXC.	V.G.	GOOD	FAIR	POOR
	1600	1375	1075	925	650	300

Custom Grade
Similar to above but with jeweled hammer, fancier wood and engraving, gold-filled highlights and numerous accessories. Production limited to 1000 sets.

	NIB	EXC.	V.G.	GOOD	FAIR	POOR
	3000	2500	1950	1575	1200	700

Model 52B Sporting Rifle
A 1993 limited-edition rifle (6,000 guns) that is a faithful reproduction of the famous Winchester Model 52 Sporter. Equipped with a 24" barrel, adjustable trigger, and "B" style cheekpiece. This model was reissued in 1997 and limited to 3,000 rifles.

	NIB	EXC.	V.G.	GOOD	FAIR	POOR
	750	600	475	350	225	150

POST-1964 MODEL 70

These post-Model 70 rifles were fitted with redesigned actions and bolt with free-floating barrels and new style stocks with impressed checkering. In 1994, U.S. Repeating Arms reintroduced the pre-1964 Model 70 action on many of its Model 70 rifles. At the present time this new action

	NIB	EXC.	V.G.	GOOD	FAIR	POOR

does not affect values but may do so in the future depending on shooter reaction. In October of 2007, Winchester Repeating Arms announced that the pre-'64-style Model 70 would once again be produced – this time at the FN plant in Columbia, So. Carolina.

Model 70—Standard Grade

This is a bolt-action sporting rifle chambered for various popular calibers such as the .22-250, .222 Rem., .243 Win., .270 Win., .30-06, and .308 Win. It features a 22" barrel with open sights and a 5-round, integral box magazine. The finish is blued with a Monte Carlo-type stock furnished with sling swivels. It was manufactured between 1964 and 1971.

	NIB	EXC.	V.G.	GOOD	FAIR	POOR
	—	600	475	325	175	110

Model 70 Varmint

Chambered for the .22-25, .222 Rem., and .243 Win. cartridges this rifle is fitted with a 24" heavyweight barrel with no sights. Magazine capacity is 5 rounds. Weight is about 9.75 lbs. Built from 1964 to 1971.

	NIB	EXC.	V.G.	GOOD	FAIR	POOR
	—	600	450	300	150	100

Model 70 Westerner

This model is chambered for the .264 Win. Magnum and .300 Win. Magnum cartridges. Open sights, 24" barrel. Ventilated recoil pad. Weight is about 7.25 lbs. Built from 1964 to 1971.

	NIB	EXC.	V.G.	GOOD	FAIR	POOR
	—	650	475	325	175	110

Model 70 African

Chambered for the .458 Win. Magnum cartridge this rifle is fitted with a 22" barrel with open sights. Magazine capacity is 3 rounds. Weight is about 8.5 lbs. Built from 1964 to 1971.

	NIB	EXC.	V.G.	GOOD	FAIR	POOR
	—	925	750	485	275	175

Model 70 Magnum

Chambered for the 7mm Rem. Mag., .300 Win. Mag., and .375 H&H cartridges. Barrel length is 24". Weight is about 7.75 lbs. Built from 1964 to 1971.

	NIB	EXC.	V.G.	GOOD	FAIR	POOR
	—	750	585	375	225	175

Model 70 Deluxe

Built from 1964 to 1971, this rifle features a Monte Carlo stock with hand checkering and ebony fore-end tip. Offered in .243, .270, .30-06, .300 Win. Mag. Fitted with 22" barrel except magnums, which have 24" barrel. Weight is about 7.5 lbs.

	NIB	EXC.	V.G.	GOOD	FAIR	POOR
	—	750	575	350	175	125

Model 70 Mannlicher

This is a full-length, Mannlicher-type stocked version of the Model 70 bolt-action rifle that is chambered for the .243, .270, .308, and the .30-06 cartridges. It was introduced in 1969. It features a 19" barrel with open sights. The finish is blued. It was discontinued in 1972. Only 2,401 were produced. Excellent quality.

	NIB	EXC.	V.G.	GOOD	FAIR	POOR
	—	975	825	625	425	310

Model 70 Target Rifle

This version is chambered for the .308 or the .30-06 cartridges. It was offered with a 24" heavy barrel without sights. It is furnished with bases for a target scope. The finish is blued with a heavy walnut target stock with a palm rest. Weight is approximately 10.25 lbs.

	NIB	EXC.	V.G.	GOOD	FAIR	POOR
	—	875	775	575	375	260

Model 70 International Match Army

This version is chambered for the .308 cartridge and has a 24" heavy barrel furnished without sights. It has an adjustable trigger and is blued, with a target-type heavy stock that had an accessory rail and an adjustable butt.

	NIB	EXC.	V.G.	GOOD	FAIR	POOR
	—	950	850	600	400	300

Model 70A

This is a utility version of the bolt-action post-1964 Model 70. It was furnished without a hinged floorplate. The finish is blued, with a walnut stock. It was manufactured between 1972 and 1978.

	NIB	EXC.	V.G.	GOOD	FAIR	POOR
	—	500	400	350	300	125

Model 670

Economy-grade version of the Model 70. Hardwood stock, iron sights, non-hinged floorplate, 22" blued barrel. Manufactured from 1967 to 1973.

	NIB	EXC.	V.G.	GOOD	FAIR	POOR
	—	450	400	300	250	100

NIB	EXC.	V.G.	GOOD	FAIR	POOR

Model 70 XTR Featherweight

This gun was built after the takeover by the U.S.R.A. Company. It is a bolt-action sporting rifle chambered for various calibers from .22-250 up to the .30-06 cartridges. It has a 22" barrel that is furnished without sights and features either a short- or medium-length action. It has a 5-round, integral magazine. The finish is blued, with a checkered walnut stock. It was introduced in 1981.

	725	625	450	325	265
—					

Model 70 Fiftieth Anniversary Model

This is a commemorative version of the post-1964 Model 70 bolt-action rifle. It is chambered for the .300 Win. Mag. and is offered with a 24" barrel. It is engraved and high-gloss blued with a deluxe, checkered walnut stock. There were 500 manufactured in 1987. In order to realize collector potential, it must be NIB with all supplied materials.

1500	1400	1200	900	500	300

Model 70 XTR Super Express

This is a heavy-duty version of the post-1964 Model 70 chambered for the .375 H&H and the .458 Win. Mag. cartridges. It is offered with a 22" or 24" heavy barrel and a 3-round, integral box magazine. This version has extra recoil lugs mounted in the stock and is blued with a select, straight-grain walnut stock and a recoil pad standard.

1100	925	750	650	450	325

Model 70 XTR Varmint

This version is chambered for the .22-250, .223, and the .243 cartridges. It has a 24" heavy barrel and is furnished without sights. It has a 5-round magazine and is blued with a heavy walnut stock. It was introduced in 1972.

650	550	400	250	200	100

Model 70 Winlight

This version is offered in various calibers between .270 and the .338 Win. Mag. It features a matte-blue finish and a fiberglass stock. It is offered with a 22" or a 24" barrel and a 3- or 4-round magazine. It was introduced in 1986.

700	550	400	250	200	100

Ranger (Model 70)

This is a utility-grade, bolt-action rifle chambered for the .270 Win., .30-06, and the 7mm Rem. Mag. cartridges. It is offered with a 22" or a 24" barrel with open sights and has a 3- or 4-round box magazine. The finish is blued with a plain hardwood stock.

450	300	275	225	150	100

Model 70 Featherweight

Bolt-action rifle chambered in .22-250, .243, 7mm-08, .308, .270 WSM, 7mm WSM, .300 WSM, .325 WSM, .25-06, .270, .30-06, 7mm Remington Magnum, .300 Winchester Magnum, .338 Winchester Magnum. 22" blued barrel (24" in magnum chamberings), satin-finished checkered Grade I walnut stock, controlled round feeding. Capacity 5 rounds (short action) or 3 rounds (long action). Weight: 6-1/2 to 7-1/4 lbs. Pachmayr Decelerator pad. No sights but drilled and tapped for scope mounts. Values shown are for long action. Deduct 15 percent for short action. **NOTE:** In 2003 a left-hand model was offered. Add $35. For stainless steel model add $60.

850	650	450	375	225	125

Model 70 Featherweight Classic All-Terrain

Introduced in 1996, this model features a weather-resistant stainless steel barrel and action with fiberglass/graphite black synthetic stock. Offered in .270 Win., .30-06, 7mm Rem. Mag., .330 Win. Mag. Weight is about 7.25 lbs. Also offered with the BOSS system. **NOTE:** Add $100 for BOSS.

950	650	450	325	225	125

Model 70 Featherweight Super Short

Introduced in 2003 this rifle features a shorter receiver to handle the .223 WSSM and .243 WSSM cartridges. Fitted with a 22" barrel and a checkered walnut stock with solid recoil pad. Weight is about 6 lbs.

770	600	500	400	300	200

Model 70 Classic Laredo

First offered in 1996, this model features a heavy 26" barrel with pre-1964 action on a gray synthetic stock. Chambered for the 7mm Rem. Mag and the .300 Win. Mag. The forearm is a beavertail. Finish is matte blue. In 1997 this model was offered chambered for the 7mm STW

NIB	EXC.	V.G.	GOOD	FAIR	POOR

cartridge. In 1998 this model was offered with fluted barrel. **NOTE:** Add $100 for BOSS. Add $125 for fluted barrel.

NIB	EXC.	V.G.	GOOD	FAIR	POOR
750	650	550	500	400	300

Model 70 Classic Compact

Introduced in 1998, this model is a scaled-down version of the Featherweight. It has a length of pull of 12.5" and a 20" barrel. Chambered for .243, .308, and 7mm-08 calibers. Checkered walnut stock. Weight is about 6.5 lbs.

NIB	EXC.	V.G.	GOOD	FAIR	POOR
750	650	550	500	400	300

Model 70 Classic Sporter LT

Introduced in 1999, this model is chambered for a wide variety of calibers from .25-06 to .338 Win. Mag. Fitted with a 24" or 26" barrel depending on caliber and no sights. Walnut stock with butt pad. Blued finish. Also offered in left-hand models from .270 to .338 Win. Mag. Weight is about 8 lbs. **NOTE:** Add $30 for left-hand models.

NIB	EXC.	V.G.	GOOD	FAIR	POOR
750	650	550	500	400	300

Model 70 Classic Safari Express

This model is chambered for the .375 H&H Magnum, .416 Rem. Magnum and .458 Win. Magnum. Fitted with a 24" barrel and magazine capacity is 4 rounds. Walnut stock with open sights. Left-hand model offered in .375 H&H. Weight is about 8.5 lbs. Introduced in 1999. **NOTE:** Add $30 for .375 H&H left-hand model.

NIB	EXC.	V.G.	GOOD	FAIR	POOR
1350	1100	900	650	500	300

Model 70 Super Grade

Another U.S.R.A. rifle that features a select walnut stock, claw-controlled round feed, a single reinforced cross bolt, 24" barrel shipped with bases and rings. The buttstock has a straight comb with classic cheekpiece and deep-cut checkering. Available in .270, .30-06, 7mm Rem. Magnum, .300 Win. Magnum, .338 Win. Magnum, .270 WSM, .300 WSM. Rifle weighs approximately 7.75 lbs.

NIB	EXC.	V.G.	GOOD	FAIR	POOR
1500	1300	1075	925	650	300

Model 70 RMEF Super Grade

As above but with stainless steel action and barrel. Chambered for the .300 Win. Mag. cartridge. Fitted with a 26" barrel. Checkered walnut stock with solid recoil pad. Weight is about 8 lbs. Introduced in 2003. Special RMEF (Rock Mountain Elk Foundation) emblem on grip cap. Limited production.

NIB	EXC.	V.G.	GOOD	FAIR	POOR
1600	1400	1175	975	650	300

Model 70 RMEF Super Grade III

This model is chambered for the .325 WSM or .300 WSM calibers and fitted with a 24" stainless steel barrel without sights. Super Grade walnut checkered stock with shadow line cheek piece. Weight is about 7.75 lbs. RMEF grip cap medallion. Introduced in 2005.

NIB	EXC.	V.G.	GOOD	FAIR	POOR
1200	950	875	650	500	300

Model 70 Classic Super Grade III

Similar to the model above but chambered for a variety of short action calibers including WSM calibers. Fitted with a 24" barrel with no sights except for .300 Win. Magnum and .338 Win. Magnum which have 26" barrels. Weight is about 7.75 to 8 lbs. depending on caliber. Introduced in 2005.

NIB	EXC.	V.G.	GOOD	FAIR	POOR
1400	1100	875	650	500	300

Model 70 Super Express

A U.S.R.A. version of the post-1964 XTR Super Express. Specifications are the same as the earlier model. Rifle weighs 8.5 lbs. Introduced in 1993.

NIB	EXC.	V.G.	GOOD	FAIR	POOR
1500	1200	1075	975	650	300

Model 70 Heavy Varmint

Introduced by U.S.R.A. in 1993, this rifle features a fiberglass/graphite stock with heavy 26" stainless steel barrel. Offered in .223, .22-250, .243, and .308. In 1997, this model was offered chambered for the .222 Rem. cartridge. Rifle weighs about 10.75 lbs.

NIB	EXC.	V.G.	GOOD	FAIR	POOR
750	575	500	425	375	200

Model 70 Heavy Varmint—Fluted Barrel

Introduced in 1997, this model is similar to the above Varmint with the addition of a fluted barrel. Calibers are also the same as the above model.

NIB	EXC.	V.G.	GOOD	FAIR	POOR
825	625	500	475	350	250

	NIB	EXC.	V.G.	GOOD	FAIR	POOR

Model 70 Stainless

All-metal parts are stainless steel, including the barrel, with synthetic stock. Available with 24" barrel and chambered for .270, .30-06, 7mm Rem. Mag., .300 Win. Mag., and .338 Win. Mag. Weighs about 7.5 lbs. Currently in production. In 2001 this model was offered chambered for the .300 Winchester Short Magnum (WSM) cartridge.

850	650	450	375	225	125

Model 70 Classic Laminated Stainless

Introduced in 1998 this model features a laminated stock and stainless steel barrel and action. Offered in .270, .30-06, 7mm Rem. Mag., .300 Win. Mag., and .338 Win. Mag. Pre-1964 action. Bolt is jeweled and bolt handle is knurled. Barrel lengths are 24" and 26", depending on caliber. Weight is about 8 lbs. In 2001, this model was offered chambered for the .300 Winchester Short Magnum (WSM) cartridge.

850	650	450	375	225	125

Model 70 Classic Camo Stainless

This model features a Sporter-style stock with 24" or 26" barrel and Mossy Oak Treestand camo on the stock. Chambered for .270 Win., .30-06, 7mm Rem. Mag., and .300 Win Mag. Magazine capacity is 5 rounds. Weight is about 7.5 lbs. Introduced in 1998.

850	650	450	375	225	125

Model 70 SM

This rifle features a synthetic stock with black matte finish. Barrel length is 24". Available in 10 calibers from .223 Rem. to .375 H&H Mag. Depending on caliber, rifle weighs between 7 and 8 lbs.

850	650	450	375	225	125

Model 70 DBM-S

Similar to Model 70 SM but fitted with detachable box magazine. The metal parts are blued and the stock is synthetic. Offered in eight calibers from .223 Rem. to .338 Win. Mag. Furnished with scope bases and rings are open sights. Rifle weighs about 7.25 lbs., depending on caliber. Introduced in 1993.

650	550	450	375	225	125

Model 70 Varmint

Similar to the Model 70 Heavy Varmint but furnished with a traditional walnut stock and 26" medium-heavy barrel. Offered in .223 Rem., .22-250, .243, and .308. Weighs 9 lbs.

700	600	450	325	225	150

Model 70 DBM

DBM stands for detachable box magazine. Fitted with a straight-comb walnut stock. Jeweled bolt with blued receiver. Shipped with scope bases and rings or open sights. Rifle offered in eight calibers from .223 Rem. to .300 Win. Mag. Rifle weighs about 7.35 lbs., depending on caliber. Introduced in 1993.

700	600	450	325	225	150

Model 70 Sporter

U.S.R.A.'s basic Model 70 offering. Straight-comb walnut stock with checkering, jeweled bolt and blued receiver and barrel are standard. Available in 12 calibers from .223 Rem. to .338 Win. Mag. including .270 Weatherby Mag. and .300 Weatherby Mag. Barrel length is 24" and is available with either scope bases and rings or open sights. Rifle weighs about 7.5 lbs.

700	600	450	325	225	150

Model 70 WinTuff

Similar to the Sporter except fitted with a laminated hardwood straight-comb stock with cheekpiece. Offered in 24" barrel lengths with a choice of 6 calibers from .270 Win. to .338 Win. Mag. Furnished with scope bases and rings. Rifle weighs about 7.65 lbs., depending on caliber.

700	600	450	325	225	150

Model 70 Lightweight

Similar to the Model 70 Winlight. Offered with straight-comb checkered walnut stock with knurled bolt and blued receiver and barrel. The barrel is 22" without sights. Offered in 5 calibers: .223, .243, .270, .308, and .30-06. Rifle weighs about 7 lbs., depending on caliber.

700	600	450	325	225	150

	NIB	EXC.	V.G.	GOOD	FAIR	POOR

Model 70 Black Shadow

Chambered for the .270, .30-06, 7mm Rem. Mag., and .300 Win. Mag. and fitted with a 22" or 24" barrel, depending on caliber. Finish is matte black with composite stock. Push-feed action. Weight Is 7.25 lbs. Introduced In 1998.

	NIB	EXC.	V.G.	GOOD	FAIR	POOR
	550	450	375	325	225	150

Model 70 Ultimate Shadow

Introduced in 2003 this bolt-action model features a new black synthetic stock design with improved gripping surfaces and soft recoil pad. This model has a blued action and barrel. Chambered for the .300 WSM, .270 WSM, or the 7mm WSM cartridges. Fitted with a 24" barrel. Weight is about 6.75 lbs. Also offered with stainless action and barrel. **NOTE:** For stainless steel model add $45.

	NIB	EXC.	V.G.	GOOD	FAIR	POOR
	800	700	425	350	275	125

Model 70 Ultimate Shadow Camo

As above but with Mossy Oak New Break-Up camo. Introduced in 2004.

	900	800	525	450	375	150

Model 70 Super Shadow Super Short

Similar to the above model but chambered for the .223 WSM or .243 WSM cartridge. Fitted with a 22" barrel and blind magazine. Weight is about 6 lbs. Introduced in 2003.

	700	600	450	325	225	150

Model 70 Super Shadow

Similar to the Ultimate Shadow but fitted with a controlled round push feed bolt. Chambered for the .300 WSM, .270 WSM, or the 7mm WSM cartridge. Fitted with a 22" barrel, composite stock and blind magaziine. Weight is about 6.75 lbs. Introduced in 2003. New calibers: .243, .308, .270, .30-06, .300WM.

	700	600	450	325	225	150

Model 70 Stealth

This is a varmint model with 26" heavy barrel chambered for .223 Rem., .22-250, or .308 Win. It has a push-feed bolt-action. Black synthetic stock. Matte black finish. Weight is approximately 10.85 lbs. In 2004 the .223 WSSM, .243 WSSM and the .25 WSSM calibers were added.

	850	650	450	375	225	125

Model 70 Coyote

This model, introduced in 2000, has a push-feed bolt-action and is chambered for the .223 Rem, .22-250, and .243 Win. calibers. Fitted with a medium-heavy 24" stainless steel barrel with laminated stock and large fore-end. Weight is about 9 lbs. In 2002 the rifle was offered in .270 WSM, 7mm WSM, and .300 WSM. In 2005 the .325 WSM was added to this model. Discontinued 2006.

	750	650	450	375	225	125

Model 70 Coyote Lite

Introduced in 2005 this model features a lightweight composite stock with skeletonized aluminum block bedding. Recoil pad. Fluted 24" medium-heavy barrel with no sights. Offered in .223 Rem and all WSSM and WSM calibers. New calibers: .22-250, .243, .308. **NOTE:** Add $40 for stainless steel.

	850	650	450	375	225	125

Model 70 Ladies/Youth Ranger

A scaled-down version of the Ranger. Length of pull is 1" shorter than standard. Rifle weighs 6.5 lbs. Chambered in .243 and .308. In 1997 this model was offered chambered for the .223 Rem. and the 7mm-08 Rem. cartridges.

	450	300	275	225	150	100

Model 70 Shadow Elite Stainless

Bolt-action rifle. Calibers: .22-250, .243, .308, .270, .30-06, .300 WM, .338 WM, .375 H&H, .270 WSM, 7mm WSM, .300 WSM, .325 WSM. Barrel: Stainless steel, 24-inch or 26-inch (.300, .338 WM). Stock: Overmolded composite. Weight: 6-1/2 – 7-3/4 lbs. Magazine capacity: 3 or 5 (.22-250, .243, .308, .270, .30-06). Introduced 2006.

	800	700	425	350	275	125

Model 70 Shadow Elite Camo Stainless

Similar to Shadow Elite Stainless but with Mossy Oak New Break Up camo synthetic stock.

	850	750	475	350	275	125

	NIB	EXC.	V.G.	GOOD	FAIR	POOR

Model 70 Pro Shadow Blued

Bolt-action rifle. Calibers: .22-250, .243, .308, .270, .30-06, 7mm RM, .300 WM, .270 WSM, 7mm WSM, .300 WSM, .325 WSM. Barrel: Blued steel, 22-inch (standard) or 24-inch (magnum). Stock: Overmolded composite. Weight: 6-1/2 – 7 lbs. Magazine capacity: 3 (magnum) or 5 (standard). Introduced 2006.

650	550	375	250	175	125

Model 70 Pro Shadow Stainless

Similar to Pro Shadow blued but with stainless steel barrel and .338 WM and .375 H&H chamberings.

700	600	450	325	225	150

Model 70 Laminated Coyote Outback Stainless

Similar to Model 70 Coyote Lite but with skeletonized laminated stock and stainless steel only. Calibers: .22-250, .243, .308, .270, .30-06, 7mm RM, .300 WM, .270 WSM, 7mm WSM, .300 WSM, .325 WSM. Weight: 7-3/4 lbs. Introduced 2006.

750	650	450	375	225	125

Model 70 Laminated Coyote Gray or Brown Stainless

Similar to Model 70 Laminated Coyote Outback but with non-fluted barrel and choice of brown or gray laminated stock.

700	600	450	325	225	150

POST-2007 MODEL 70

In 2006, Winchester closed its factory in New Haven, CT and discontinued production of Model 70 and Model 94 rifles. Late in 2007, it was announced that production of Model 70 would resume at FN plant in Columbia, SC. FN (Fabrique Nationale of Belgium) is parent company of Winchester. Following models are produced at South Carolina plant.

Model 70 Featherweight Deluxe

Pre-64 action, three-position safety, jeweled bolt, knurled bolt handle, walnut stock with slight schnabel, cut checkering, Pachmayr Decelerator recoil pad., 22" or 24" barrel depending on caliber. Chambered for variety of cartridges from .243 to .325 Winchester Short Magnum. Weight 6.5 to 7 lbs. Introduced in 2008. **NOTE:** Add $50 for magnum calibers.

800	650	525	450	375	325

Model 70 Sporter Deluxe

Similar to above, with non-schnabel fore-end and cheekpiece. **NOTE:** Add $50 for magnum calibers.

800	650	525	450	375	325

New Model 70 Super Grade Special Limited Edition

Very fancy version of Model 70 featuring post-'64 action, ultra-premium walnut, gold-filled engraving, black fore-end cap, steel grip cap and shadowline cheekpiece. Only 250 produced in 2008. Chambered in .300 Win. Magnum only.

2400	2000	1650	1300	900	500

Model 70 Extreme Weather SS

Post-'64 style action with 22", 24" or 26" barrel depending on chambering. Three-position safety, fluted stainless barrel and Bell and Carlson composite stock. Chambered for variety of cartridges from .243 to .325 Win. Short Magnum.

1000	750	550	425	275	175

Model 70 FW Compact

Featherweight Compact made for smaller-framed shooters. Light mountain type rifle weighing 6.5 lbs. with 20" barrel. Pre-'64 Controlled Round Feed and three-position safety. M.O.A. adjustable trigger system. Jeweled bolt body with knurled bolt handle. Walnut stock with fancy checkering pattern. Chambered for .22-250 Rem., .243 Win., 7mm-08 Rem. or .308 Win. Introduced in 2011.

765	650	550	450	350	200

Model 70 Safari Express

Designed for dangerous game. Calibers include .375 H&H, .416 Rem. Magnum or .458 Win. Magnum. Express sights, 24" barrel, satin finished and checkered walnut stock. Other features include reinforced crossbolts, dual recoil lugs and Pachmayr Decelerator recoil pad. Weight: 9 lbs.

1200	1000	800	650	500	350

	NIB	EXC.	V.G.	GOOD	FAIR	POOR

Model 70 75th Anniversary Super Grade

Commemorate 75th Anniversary of rifle, Winchester introduced in 2012 this special edition in .30-06 caliber. Grade IV/V Full Fancy walnut stock. One-piece bottom metal has engraving with scroll pattern of 75th Model 70 emblem. Other features include pre-64 style controlled-round feed with claw extractor and Pachmayr Decelerator recoil pad.

NIB	EXC.	V.G.	GOOD	FAIR	POOR
1800	1700	1600	—	—	—

Model 70 Alaskan

Reintroduction of classic pre-64 Model in .30-06, .300 Win. Magnum, .338 Win. Magnum or .375 H&H. Checkered Monte Carlo walnut stock and fore-end. Barrel is 25" with folding rear and gold bead front sights. Has pre-'64 controlled-round feed and claw extractor. Also available with gray laminate stock and stainless steel barrel. **NOTE:** Add $200 for laminate/stainless model.

NIB	EXC.	V.G.	GOOD	FAIR	POOR
1100	900	750	600	500	400

Model 70 Jack O-Connor Tribute

Limited edition rifle honoring Jack O'Connor, dean of outdoor writers of 20th century who had a long association with Model 70. Chambered in his favorite caliber, .270 Win., with 22" hammer-forged barrel. Pre-64 style action with controlled-round feed, claw extractor, AA-grade French walnut stock with shadowline cheekpiece and ebony fore-end tip. Other features include engraved pistol-grip cap and floorplate. O'Connor's signature in nickel on trigger guard. Rifle was offered in two grades with higher-grade version having AAA-grade French walnut stock and checkered metal buttplate. Introduced in 2012 with limited production only in that year. **NOTE:** Add $500 for higher-grade model.

NIB	EXC.	V.G.	GOOD	FAIR	POOR
2000	1900	1650	—	—	—

WINCHESTER CUSTOM GUN SHOP

NOTE: There were a number of special order options offered by Custom shop that greatly affect price, such as special-order engraving, stock carving, wood, sights, etc. Strongly suggested that an independent appraisal be secured prior to sale.

Model 94 Custom Limited Edition New Generation

This lever-action rifle is stocked with fancy checkered walnut with pistol grip and long nose fore-end. Custom engraved with gold inlaid moose on right side and gold inlaid buck and doe on the left side. Fitted with tang safety. Barrel is 20" and chambered for the .30-30 cartridge. Introduced in 2003. Weight is about 6.25 lbs.

NIB	EXC.	V.G.	GOOD	FAIR	POOR
3000	2500	2100	—	—	—

Model 70 Featherweight Ultra Grade

Limited to 1,000 rifles, this model is profusely engraved with game scene and gold line inlaid. Serial number inlaid in gold. Offered in .270 caliber with very fine-figured walnut stock with fine line checkering. Mahogany fitted case. Strongly suggest a qualified appraisal before sale.

NIB	EXC.	V.G.	GOOD	FAIR	POOR
4000	3500	—	—	—	—

Model 70 Custom Featherweight

Introduced in 2003 this rifle is chambered for the .270, 7mm Win. Mag., or the .30-06. Fitted with a 22" barrel. Semi-fancy walnut stock with schnabel fore-end. Offered in blued or stainless steel finish in either right- or left-hand models. Weight is about 7.25 lbs.

NIB	EXC.	V.G.	GOOD	FAIR	POOR
3500	—	—	—	—	—

Model 70 Custom Carbon

This rifle features a stainless steel action with Shilen barrel wrapped in graphite epoxy. Fitted with a black composite stock. Chambered for the .270 WSM, 7mm WSM, .300 WSM, .25-06 Rem., or the .338 Win. Mag. cartridge. Fitted with a 24" barrel on all calibers but the .338 (26"). Weight is about 6.5 lbs. on the WSM calibers and 7 lbs. of the others. Magazine capacity is three rounds. Introduced in 2003.

NIB	EXC.	V.G.	GOOD	FAIR	POOR
3200	—	—	—	—	—

Model 70 Custom Sharpshooter

A U.S.R.A. Custom Shop gun. This model is fitted with a stainless steel Schneider barrel with hand-honed action and hand fitted. The stock is a custom McMillan A-2 glass bedded stock. Offered in .223 Rem., .22-250 Rem., .308 Win. and .300 Win. Mag. Comes from the factory with a hard case. Currently in production.

NIB	EXC.	V.G.	GOOD	FAIR	POOR
2500	—	—	—	—	—

NIB	EXC.	V.G.	GOOD	FAIR	POOR

Model 70 Custom Classic Sharpshooter II

Same as above but introduced in 1996 with an H-S heavy target stock, a pre-1964 action stainless steel H-S barrel. Weight is about 11 lbs. Offered in .22-250, .308, .30-06, and .300 Win. Mag.

2250	—	—	—	—	—

Model 70 Custom Sporting Sharpshooter

Essentially a take-off on the Custom Sharpshooter but configured for hunting. Fitted with a McMillan sporter-style gray stock and Schneider stainless steel barrel. Offered in .270 Win., .300 Win., and 7mm STW. Introduced in 1993.

2000	—	—	—	—	—

Model 70 Custom Classic Sporting Sharpshooter II

Introduced in 1996 this is an updated version of the model above. It features a pre-1964 action with H-S special fiberglass stock and stainless steel barrel. Available in 7mm STW, .300 Win. Mag. Weight is about 8.5 lbs.

2500	—	—	—	—	—

Model 70 Custom Grade

This custom built Model 70 is hand finished, polished, and fitted in the Custom Shop. Internal parts are hand honed while the barrel is lead lapped. The customer can order individual items to his or her own taste, including engraving, special stock dimensions and carvings, etc. Each Custom Grade Model 70 should be priced on an individual basis.

Model 70 Custom Express

Also built in the Custom Shop this model features figured walnut, hand-honed internal parts, bolt and follower are engine turned. A special 3-leaf rear sight is furnished also. Offered in .375 H&H Mag., .375 JRS, .416 Rem. Mag., .458 Win. Mag., and .470 Capstick.

3000	—	—	—	—	—

Model 70 Custom African Express

Introduced in 1999 this model is chambered for the .340 Wby., .358 STA, .375 H&H, .416 Rem. Mag., and the .458 Win. Mag. Fitted with a 24" barrel and a magazine capacity of 4 rounds. Express sights. Weight is about 9.75 lbs. Ebony pistol grip cap, and select walnut stock.

3850	—	—	—	—	—

Model 70 Custom Safari Express

This model has a figured walnut stock with the bolt and follower engine turned. Express sights. Chambered in .340 Wby., .358 STA, .375 H&H, .416 Rem. Mag., and .458 Win. Mag. Barrel length is 24". Weight is about 9.5 lbs. Introduced in 1999.

2500	—	—	—	—	—

Model 70 Custom "Ultra Light" Mannlicher

This model features a full-length stock of figured walnut with smooth tapered barrel and blued action. Chambered for .260 Rem., .308 Win., and 7mm-08. Fitted with a 19" barrel with optional open sights. Weight is about 6.75 lbs. Introduced in 1999.

2500	—	—	—	—	—

Model 70 Ultimate Classic

This model features a number of special options as standard. Included is a pre-1964 action, choice of round, round fluted, 1/2 octagon 1/2 round barrel, full tapered octagon barrel, blued or stainless steel barrel actions, fancy American walnut stock, special Custom Shop serial numbers and proof stamp, inletted swivel bases, red recoil pad, fine cut checkering, and a hard case. Offered in a wide variety of calibers from .25-06 to .338 Win. Mag. Weight is about 7.5 to 7.75 lbs. depending on caliber. Also available in stainless steel. **NOTE:** In 1997 this model was introduced in a left-hand version.

2450	—	—	—	—	—

Model 70 Custom Short Action

This custom shop model is fitted with a 22" match-grade barrel Controlled feed. Chambered for short-action calibers from .243 to .358. Semi-fancy walnut stock. Hand-cut checkering. Supplied with hard case. Weight is about 7.5 lbs. Introduced in 2000. In 2003 this model was offered in a left-hand version.

2700	—	—	—	—	—

Model 70 Custom Extreme Weather

This custom shop model is fitted with a round or fluted 24" match-grade barrel. Both barrel and action are stainless steel. McMillan fiberglass stock with cheekpiece. Chambered in calibers

	NIB	EXC.	V.G.	GOOD	FAIR	POOR

from .25-06 to .338 Win. Mag. Weight is about 7.5 lbs. Introduced in 2000. Lightweight Extreme Weather II model introduced 2006 (6-1/4 – 7 lbs.). MSRP: $2800.

1950	—	—	—	—	—

Model 70 Custom Take Down

Introduced in 1998 this composite stock rifle has a special take down feature. Chambered for .375 H&H, .416 Rem. Mag., .300 Win Mag., 7mm STW. Magazine capacity is 3 rounds. Barrel length is 26". Weight is between 8.5 and 9 lbs. Offered in fluted barrel in .300 Win. Mag. and 7mm STW.

3300	—	—	—	—	—

Model 70 Custom 100th Anniversary .30-06

Semi-fancy walnut Featherweight stock with single steel crossbolt, one-piece engraved floorplate, high-lustre blued and engraved 22-inch barrel. Commemorates centennial of .30-06 cartridge. Introduced 2006; only 100 manufactured.

2700	—	—	—	—	—

Model 70 Custom Special "70 Years of the Model 70

Calibers: .270, .30-06 Springfield, .300 WM. Barrel: 24-inch or 26-inch (.300 WM) blued sightless. Engraved floorplate and barrel. Stock: semi-fancy checkered walnut. Introduced 2006, only 70 manufactured per caliber.

2800	—	—	—	—	—

Model 70 Custom Maple

Calibers: .284, .270, .308, .30-06. Barrel: 24-inch blued. Weight: 7-3/4 lbs. Stocked in fiddleback maple with pre-'64 pattern checkering. Quantities "very limited." Introduced 2006.

4400	—	—	—	—	—

Model 70 Custom Continental Hunter

Calibers: .284, .270, .308, .30-06. Barrel: 22-inch blued or stainless Krieger. Stock: glossy claro walnut, round knob pistol grip, schnabel fore-end.

5300	—	—	—	—	—

Model 70 Custom Stainless Laminate

Calibers: .270 WSM, 7mm WSM, .300 WSM, .325 WSM. Barrel: 24-inch stainless sporter. Stock: black/gray or brown Featherweight laminated with schnabel and Pachmayr pad.

2300	—	—	—	—	—

Model 94 Custom Limited Edition

This is essentially a special order Model 94 with choice of engraving and stock carving. Chambered for the .44-40 and fitted with a 24" octagonal barrel. Fancy walnut stock. Limited to 75 rifles. Weight is about 7.75 lbs. Suggest an appraisal prior to a sale.

2300	—	—	—	—	—

Model 9410 Custom

Introduced in 2005 this .410 shotgun is fitted with a 24" round barrel and full length magazine. Case colored receiver with semi-fancy checkered walnut stock. Weight is about 7 lbs.

2300	—	—	—	—	—

POST-1964 SHOTGUNS

MODEL 12 "Y" SERIES

Model 12 Field Grade

This is a later version of the slide-action Model 12, chambered for 12 gauge only. It was offered with a 26", 28", or 30" vent rib barrel with various chokes. The finish is blued with a jeweled bolt and a hand-checkered, select walnut stock. This version is easily recognizable as it has the letter Y serial number prefix. It was manufactured between 1972 and 1976.

—	950	800	650	485	300

Model 12 Super Pigeon Grade

This is a deluxe version that features extensive engraving and fancy checkering. It was offered with a turned action and select, fancy-grade walnut. It was a limited-production item produced between 1964 and 1972. It was briefly reintroduced in 1984 and discontinued again in 1985.

—	3000	2400	1850	1400	950

	NIB	EXC.	V.G.	GOOD	FAIR	POOR

Model 12 Skeet

This version is similar to the Field Grade but is offered with a 26", vent rib, skeet-bored barrel. The finish is blued, with a skeet-type stock and recoil pad. It was manufactured between 1972 and 1975.

	NIB	EXC.	V.G.	GOOD	FAIR	POOR
	—	950	850	750	450	300

Model 12 Trap Grade

This version features a 30" vent rib barrel with a Full choke. It is blued with a trap-type, standard, or Monte Carlo stock with a recoil pad. It was manufactured between 1972 and 1980.

	—	935	830	725	425	215

Model 12 (Limited Edition)

Available in 20 gauge only. Furnished with a 26" vent rib barrel choked Improved Cylinder. The walnut stock is checkered with pistol grip. Introduced in 1993 and available in three different grades.

Grade I
4,000 guns.

	1000	800	650	450	200	100

Grade IV
1,000 guns, gold highlights.

	1400	1100	850	500	200	100

Model 42 (Limited Edition)

A reproduction of the famous Winchester Model 42 .410 bore slide-action shotgun. Furnished with a 26" ventilated rib barrel choked Full. The receiver is engraved with gold border. Introduced in 1993 and limited to 850 guns.

	1800	1400	1000	500	300	150

Model 1200

This is a slide-action shotgun chambered for 12, 16, or 20 gauge. It was offered with a 26", 28", or 30", vent rib barrel with various chokes. It has an alloy receiver and is blued, with a checkered walnut stock and recoil pad. It was manufactured between 1964 and 1981. This model was offered with the plastic Hydrocoil stock, and this would add approximately 35 percent to the values given.

	—	300	250	200	150	100

Ducks Unlimited Model

Available through Ducks Unlimited chapters. An independent appraisal is suggested.

MODEL 1300 SERIES

Discontinued in 2006.

Model 1300 XTR

Chambered for 12 and 20 gauge with 3" chambers. It is a takedown gun that is offered with various-length vent rib barrels with screw-in choke tubes. It has an alloy frame and is blued with a walnut stock. It was introduced in 1978.

	475	350	275	200	150	100

Model 1300 Waterfowl

This version is chambered for 12 gauge, 3" only. It has a 30" vent rib barrel with screw-in choke tubes. It is matte-blued, with a satin-finished walnut stock and a recoil pad. It was introduced in 1984. A laminated WinTuff stock was made available in 1988 and would add $10 to the value.

	400	300	250	200	150	100

Model 1300 New Shadow Grass

Introduced in 2004 this 12 gauge 3" gun is fitted with either a 26" or 28" vent rib barrel with choke tubes. Composite stock has New Shadow Grass camo pattern. Weight is about 7 lbs.

	470	370	250	200	150	100

Model 1300 WinCam Turkey Gun

This version is similar to the Model 1300 Turkey Gun, with a green, laminated hardwood stock. It was introduced in 1987. A WinTuff version is also available and would add $20 to the values given.

	475	350	275	200	150	100

Model 1300 Stainless Security

This version is chambered for 12 or 20 gauge and is constructed of stainless steel. It has an 18" cylinder-bore barrel and a 7- or 8-shot tubular magazine. It is available with a pistol-grip stock,

NIB	EXC.	V.G.	GOOD	FAIR	POOR

which would add approximately 50 percent to the values given.

475	350	275	200	150	100

Model 1300 Turkey

This slide-action model features a 22" vent rib barrel chambered for 3" 12 gauge shells. Supplied with choke tubes. Gun weighs 7.25 lbs.

475	350	275	200	150	100

Model 1300 Realtree Turkey

Introduced in 1994, this model features a synthetic stock camouflaged with Realtree. The receiver and 22" barrel are matte finish.

475	350	275	200	150	100

Model 1300 Mossy Oak Break-Up Turkey

Same as above but with Mossy Oak Break-Up camo stock and gun. Introduced in 2000.

475	350	275	200	150	100

Model 1300 Black Shadow Turkey

This model was also introduced in 1994 and features a black composite stock with a nonglare finish on the barrel, receiver, bolt, and magazine. Barrel has vent rib and is 22" in length.

475	350	275	200	150	100

Model 1300 National Wild Turkey Federation Series III

Engraved receiver, camo stock, open sights on a 22" plain barrel, and all metal and wood parts are nonglare. Comes with a quick detachable sling. Offered in 12 gauge only. Gun weighs 7.25 lbs.

575	420	350	250	150	100

Model 1300 National Wild Turkey Federation Series IV

Introduced in 1993, this model is similar to the Series II with the addition of a 22" vent rib barrel. Stock is black laminated. Comes with quick detachable sling. Gun weight 7 lbs.

600	520	350	250	150	100

Model 1300 NWTF Short Turkey

This 12 gauge gun is fitted with an 18" barrel with extended choke tubes. Fiber Optic sights. Mossy Oak camo stock. NWTF medallion on pistol grip cap. Weight is about 6.5 lbs. Introduced in 2005.

475	350	275	200	150	100

Model 1300 Whitetails Unlimited Slug Hunter

This slide-action model features a full-length rifle barrel chambered for 3" 12 gauge shells. Barrel is choked Cylinder. Fitted with a checkered walnut stock with engraved receiver. Receiver is drilled and tapped for bases and rings, which are included. Comes equipped with camo sling. Weighs 7.25 lbs.

475	350	275	200	150	100

Model 1300 Slug Hunter

Similar to the Whitetails Unlimited model, but without the engraved receiver.

475	350	275	200	150	100

Model 1300 Buck and Tom

Introduced in 2002 for both deer and turkey. Camo stock. Fitted with a 22" barrel with choke tubes for both deer and turkey. Receiver drilled and tapped for scope mount. Weight is about 6.75 lbs.

525	400	325	250	175	125

Model 1300 Universal Hunter

Introduced in 2002, this model features a camo stock with 26" vent rib barrel. Choke tubes. Weight is about 7 lbs.

550	425	375	275	225	125

Model 1300 Black Shadow Deer

Introduced in 1994, this 12 gauge Model 1300 features a black composite stock with nonglare finish on the bolt, barrel, receiver, and magazine. Barrel is 22" with ramp front sight and adjustable rear sight. In 2000 this model was offered with a rifled barrel for shooting sabot slugs. **NOTE:** Add $25 for rifled barrel.

475	350	275	200	150	100

	NIB	EXC.	V.G.	GOOD	FAIR	POOR

Model 1300 Black Shadow Field

Same as above but fitted with a 26" or 28" vent rib barrel chambered for 3" Mag. shells. Weight is about 7 lbs.

	NIB	EXC.	V.G.	GOOD	FAIR	POOR
	475	350	275	200	150	100

Model 1300 Sporting/Field

This 12 gauge gun has a 28" vent rib barrel with five choke tubes. Checkered walnut stock. Black recoil pad. Weight is about 7.5 lbs. Introduced in 2002.

	475	350	275	200	150	100

Model 1300 Sporting/Field Compact

As above but with 24" barrel and 1" shorter length of pull. Introduced in 2002.

	475	350	275	200	150	100

Model 1300 Walnut Field

This 12 gauge 3" gun is fitted with either 26" or 28" vent rib barrels with choke tubes. Checkered walnut stock with recoil pad. Weight is about 7.25 lbs. Introduced in 2004.

	475	350	275	200	150	100

Model 1300 Slug Hunter Sabot (Smoothbore)

Similar to the Slug Hunter but furnished with a smoothbore barrel with a special extended screw-in choke tube that is rifled.

	425	300	225	150	125	100

Model 1300 Upland Special

This 12 gauge slide-action shotgun is fitted with a 24" vent rib barrel and straight-grip walnut stock. Weight is about 7 lbs. Introduced in 1999. In 2000 this model was offered in 20 gauge with 24" vent rib barrel.

	600	500	400	300	200	100

Model 1300 Upland Special Field

This model, introduced in 2004, features a choice of 12 or 20 gauge 3" guns with 24" vent rib barrel with choke tube. Checkered walnut stock with straight grip. Weight is about 6.75 lbs.

	600	500	400	300	200	100

Model 1300 Ranger

This slide-action shotgun is a lower-cost version of the Model 1300. Furnished with a hardwood stock and available in 12 or 20 gauge with 26" or 28" vent rib barrel. WinChokes are included.

	300	225	190	165	125	100

Model 1300 Ranger Ladies/Youth-Compact

Available in 20 gauge only this model has a 1" shorter than standard length of pull and a 22" vent rib barrel. Choke tubes are included. Gun weighs 6.75 lbs.

	300	225	190	165	125	100

Model 1300 Ranger Deer Slug

Comes in two principal configurations: a 12 gauge 22" smooth barrel with Cylinder choke; and a 12 gauge 22" rifled barrel. Both are chambered for 3" shells and weigh 6.75 lbs.

	300	200	175	150	125	100

Model 1300 Ranger Deer Combo

The Model 1300 Ranger Deer Combos are available in three different configurations. One: 12 gauge 22" smooth barrel and 28" vent rib barrel with WinChokes. Two: 12 gauge 22" rifled barrel with 28" vent rib barrel with WinChokes. Three: 20 gauge 22" smooth barrel with 28" vent rib barrel with WinChokes.

12 Gauge Combo

	375	275	225	190	165	100

20 Gauge Combo

	375	275	225	190	165	100

Model 1300 Defender Combo

This personal defense slide-action shotgun features an 18" Cylinder choked barrel and a 28" vent rib barrel with modified WinChoke and an accessory pistol grip. A hardwood stock comes fitted to the gun.

	425	300	225	150	125	100

NIB	EXC.	V.G.	GOOD	FAIR	POOR

Model 1300 Defender 5-Shot

Same as above but furnished with a hardwood stock only and 18" barrel.

NIB	EXC.	V.G.	GOOD	FAIR	POOR
425	300	225	150	125	100

Model 1300 Camp Defender

Introduced in 1999 this 12 gauge model features a 22" barrel and walnut stock. Magazine capacity is five rounds. Barrel fitted with rifle sights. Weight is about 7 lbs. Comes with Cylinder choke tube.

NIB	EXC.	V.G.	GOOD	FAIR	POOR
425	300	225	150	125	100

Model 1300 Defender 8-Shot

Same as above but furnished with an 18" barrel with extended magazine tube.

NIB	EXC.	V.G.	GOOD	FAIR	POOR
425	300	225	150	125	100

Model 1300 Defender Synthetic Stock

Same as above but fitted with a black synthetic full stock. Available in either 12 or 20 gauge.

NIB	EXC.	V.G.	GOOD	FAIR	POOR
425	300	225	150	125	100

Model 1300 Defender Pistol Grip

Same as above but fitted with a black synthetic pistol grip and extended magazine tube.

NIB	EXC.	V.G.	GOOD	FAIR	POOR
425	300	225	150	125	100

Model 1300 Lady Defender

Chambered for the 20 gauge shell, this model features an 18" barrel with 8-round capacity. Pistol-grip stock. Introduced in 1997.

NIB	EXC.	V.G.	GOOD	FAIR	POOR
425	300	225	150	125	100

Model 1300 Stainless Marine

This 12 gauge slide-action shotgun comes with a black synthetic full stock with all metal parts chrome plated. Barrel is 18" and magazine tube holds 7 rounds. Gun weighs 6.75 lbs.

NIB	EXC.	V.G.	GOOD	FAIR	POOR
600	500	400	300	200	100

Model 1300 Stainless Marine with Pistol Grip

Same as above with black synthetic pistol grip in place of full buttstock. Gun weighs 5.75 lbs.

NIB	EXC.	V.G.	GOOD	FAIR	POOR
600	500	400	300	200	100

SPEED PUMP SERIES

This family of inertia-assisted slide-action shotguns was introduced in 2008 to take the place of the discontinued Model 1300. The 3" 12 gauge is available with a 26" or 28" barrel. Three choke tubes included. Weight is 7 to 7.25 lbs.

Speed Pump Walnut Field

High-gloss walnut with traditional checkering.

NIB	EXC.	V.G.	GOOD	FAIR	POOR
375	325	275	200	150	100

Speed Pump Black Shadow Field

Synthetic stock and fore-end with matte black metal.

NIB	EXC.	V.G.	GOOD	FAIR	POOR
375	325	275	200	150	100

Speed Pump Defender

This home-security 12 gauge has an 18" , cylinder choke barrel and 5-round magazine tube. Weight is about 6.5 lbs.

NIB	EXC.	V.G.	GOOD	FAIR	POOR
375	325	275	200	150	100

Model SXP Series

The Super X Pump is successor to Speed Pump series and features the same inertia-assisted action. Comes in 12 gauge only, with 3" chamber, 26" or 28" back-bored barrel with Invector choke tubes. Weight is approx. 6.8 lbs. Field grade model has Black Shadow composite stock. Waterfowl variation (shown) has full coverage Mossy Oak Duck Blind camo. Also available with 18", straight cylinder barrel as Defender model. Prices are for Black Shadow field model. **NOTE:** Add 20 percent for Waterfowl model, deduct 20 percent for Defender.

NIB	EXC.	V.G.	GOOD	FAIR	POOR
400	360	325	275	225	150

NIB	EXC.	V.G.	GOOD	FAIR	POOR

Model 9410

A variation of the Model 94 lever-action rifle chambered for the .410-bore shotgun. Available in several versions. SEE: Model 9400 Series in the lever-action rifle section.

Model 1500 XTR

This is a gas-operated, semi-automatic shotgun chambered for 12 or 20 gauge, with a 28" vent rib barrel with screw-in chokes. The finish is blued, with a walnut stock. It was manufactured between 1978 and 1982.

NIB	EXC.	V.G.	GOOD	FAIR	POOR
550	425	325	225	175	150

Super X Model 1

This is a self-compensating, gas-operated, semi-automatic shotgun chambered for 12 gauge. It was offered with a 26", 28", or 30" vent rib barrel with various chokes. It features all-steel construction and is blued, with a checkered walnut stock. It was manufactured between 1974 and 1981.

NIB	EXC.	V.G.	GOOD	FAIR	POOR
—	800	675	525	400	250

Super X Model 1 Custom Competition

This is a custom-order trap or skeet gun that features the self compensating, gas-operated action. It is available in 12 gauge only from the Custom Shop. It is offered with a heavy degree of engraving on the receiver and a fancy, checkered walnut stock. Gold inlays are available and would add approximately 50 percent to the values given. This model was introduced in 1987.

NIB	EXC.	V.G.	GOOD	FAIR	POOR
1450	1100	925	775	650	500

Super X2 3.5" Magnum

Introduced in 1999, this model is a gas-operated design chambered for 3.5" 12 gauge shells. Fitted with a black synthetic stock and choice of 24", 26" or 28" vent rib barrels. Invector chokes. Magazine capacity is five rounds. Weight is about 7.5 lbs. depending on barrel length. Matte black finish.

NIB	EXC.	V.G.	GOOD	FAIR	POOR
950	875	700	525	450	300

Super X2 Turkey

Similar to the X2 Magnum but with 24" vent rib barrel with truglo sights. Extra-Full choke. Weight is about 7.25 lbs. Black synthetic stock. Introduced in 1999.

NIB	EXC.	V.G.	GOOD	FAIR	POOR
950	875	700	525	450	300

Super X2 Turkey Mossy Oak Break-Up

Same as above but with Mossy Oak Break-Up camo on stock and gun. Introduced in 2000.

NIB	EXC.	V.G.	GOOD	FAIR	POOR
1025	900	700	525	450	350

Super X2 NWTF Turkey

Introduced in 2005 this 3.5" 12 gauge gun is fitted with a 24" vent rib barrel with extra full extended choke tubes. Three dot TRUGLO sights. Mossy Oak camo stock. A brass NWTF medallion on the pistol grip cap. Weight is about 7.5 lbs.

NIB	EXC.	V.G.	GOOD	FAIR	POOR
1235	950	1025	900	700	450

Super X2 Universal Hunter

Similar to the Super X2 Turkey but with a 26" barrel with Extra-Full choke tube. Weight is about 7.75 lbs. Introduced in 2002.

NIB	EXC.	V.G.	GOOD	FAIR	POOR
1025	900	700	525	450	350

Super X2 Camo Waterfowl

Chambered for 12 gauge 3.5" shells and fitted with a 28" vent rib barrel, this model features a Mossy Oak camo finish. Weight is about 8 lbs. Introduced in 1999. In 2004 a New Shadow Grass camo pattern was added.

NIB	EXC.	V.G.	GOOD	FAIR	POOR
1025	900	700	525	450	350

Super X2 Magnum Greenhead

Introduced in 2002, this model is chambered for the 12 gauge 3.5" shell and has a composite stock that is green in color. Fitted with 28" barrel. Weight is about 8 lbs.

NIB	EXC.	V.G.	GOOD	FAIR	POOR
1025	900	700	525	450	350

Super X2 Magnum Field

This model is chambered for the 12 gauge 3" shell and is offered with either a walnut stock or black synthetic stock. Choice of 26" or 28" vent rib barrel with Invector chokes. Weight is about 7.25 lbs. Introduced in 1999.

NIB	EXC.	V.G.	GOOD	FAIR	POOR
950	875	700	525	450	300

NIB	EXC.	V.G.	GOOD	FAIR	POOR

Super X2 Light Field

Checkered walnut stock with choice of 26" or 28" vent rib barrel with choke tubes are featured on this 12 gauge gun. Weight is about 6.5 lbs. Introduced in 2005.

Super X2 Cantilever Deer

This 12 gauge model has a 22" fully rifled barrel with fold-down rear sight and scope mount. Black composite stock. Weight is about 7.25 lbs. Introduced in 2002.

950	875	700	525	450	300

Super X2 Practical

Introduced in 2002, this model is designed for competition shooting. Fitted with a 22" barrel with ghost ring sight and 8-round magazine. Black composite stock. Weight is about 8 lbs.

1025	900	700	525	450	350

Super X2 Sporting Clays

Introduced in 2001, this model features a 12 gauge gun with choice of 28" or 30" barrels with high post rib. Barrels are back bore with Invector chokes. Adjustable comb. Weight is about 8 lbs.

1200	950	750	575	500	350

Super X2 Sporting Clays Signature II

This 3" 12 gauge gun is fitted with a 30" barrel with choke tubes. The hardwood stock is painted black metallic. The receiver is a red anodized alloy. Weight is about 8.25 lbs. Introduced in 2005.

1025	900	700	525	450	350

Super X2 Signature Red Sporting

This 12 gauge 3" shell model features a hardwood stock with red Dura-Touch coating. Fitted with a 30" vent rib barrel with five choke tubes. Weight is about 8 lbs. Introduced in 2003.

950	875	700	525	450	300

SUPER X3 SERIES

Introduced in 2006, The Super X3 12 gauge features weight and recoil reducing features and a .742" back-bored barrel. It is available in a variety of configurations weighing under 7 lbs. in the 3" Field model and about 7.5 lbs. in composite, camo and 3.5" models. All models except Cantilever Deer included three choke tubes.

Super X3 Field

Walnut stock and 26" or 28" barrel.

1200	950	750	575	500	350

Super X3 Composite

Matte black stock and fore-end. Available in 26" or 28" barrel and 3" or 3.5" chamber. **NOTE:** Add $100 for 3.5" model.

1200	950	750	575	500	350

Super X3 Camo

Composite camo stock with 3.5" chamber. Available in various camo patterns with 26" and 28" barrel.

1200	950	750	575	500	350

Super X3 Cantilever Deer

Slug gun with 22" barrel with cantilever scope mount and 3" chamber.

950	875	700	525	450	300

Super X3 "Flanigun" Exhibition/Sporting

With a red receiver and fore-end cap, this is a duplicate of the gun used by exhibition shooter Patrick Flanigan but with a shorter magazine tube. It has a 3" chamber and 28" barrel.

1200	950	750	575	500	350

Super X3 Classic Field

Introduced in 2008, the Classic Field is similar to the Super X3 Field but with traditional sharp checkering on pistol grip and fore-end. Barrel length is 26" or 28".

950	875	700	525	450	300

NIB	EXC.	V.G.	GOOD	FAIR	POOR

Super X3 Turkey

New in 2008, this dedicated turkey model has a 3.5" chamber, 24" barrel, extra-full choke tube and complete coverage in Mossy Oak New Breakup camo. Price includes a TruGlo red-dot scope. Weight is 7.5 lbs.

1200	950	750	575	500	350

Model 1400

This is a gas-operated, semi-automatic shotgun chambered for 12, 16 or 20 gauge. It was offered with a 26", 28" or 30" vent rib barrel with various chokes. The finish is blued, with a checkered walnut stock. It was manufactured between 1964 and 1981. The Hydrocoil plastic stock was available on this model and would add approximately 35 percent to the values given.

450	350	300	250	200	125

New Model 1400

This is a gas-operated, semi-automatic shotgun chambered for 12 or 20 gauge. It is offered with a 22" or 28" vent rib barrel with screw-in chokes. The finish is blued, with a checkered walnut stock. It was introduced in 1989.

450	350	300	250	200	125

Model 1400 Ranger

This is a utility-grade, gas-operated, semi-automatic shotgun chambered for 12 or 20 gauge. It is offered with a 28" vent rib barrel with screw-in chokes, as well as a 24" slug barrel with rifle sights. The finish is blued, with a checkered stock. A combination two-barrel set that includes the deer barrel would be worth approximately 20 percent additional. This model was introduced in 1983.

400	300	250	200	150	100

Model 1400 Quail Unlimited

This 12 gauge semi-automatic shotgun model was introduced in 1993. It features compact engraved receiver with 26" vent rib barrel supplied with WinChoke tubes. Stock is checkered walnut. Gun weighs 7.25 lbs.

400	300	250	200	150	100

Model 1400 Ranger Deer Combo

This model features a 12 gauge 22" smooth barrel and a 28" vent rib barrel with three WinChokes.

400	300	250	200	150	100

Model 37A

Introduced in 1973. It is single-shot shotgun with exposed hammer. Offered in 12, 16, 20, and 28 gauge as well as .410 bore. All guns choked Full except youth model choked Modified. Walnut finish on hardwood stock. Pistol-grip cap with white spacer. Weight is about 6 lbs. About 395,000 were produced until 1980.

—	350	250	225	175	115

Model 22

Introduced in 1975 this side-by-side shotgun was manufactured by Laurona in Spain to Winchester's specifications for the European market. It had an oil-finished stock with checkered pistol grip semi-beavertail forearm and hand engraved receiver. The finish is black chrome. The gun was fitted with double triggers, matted rib and offered in 12 gauge only with 28" barrels. It weighs 6-3/4 lbs. Rare.

1250	950	700	550	400	200

Model 91

This over/under shotgun was built for Winchester by Laurona for its European markets. Offered in 12 gauge only with 28" barrels the barrels were fitted with a ventilated rib. The gun was offered with single or double triggers with hand-checkered walnut stock with oil finish and hand-engraved receiver. The finish was black chrome. Gun weighs 7-1/2 lbs. Rare.

1100	800	600	500	400	200

Supreme Field

Introduced in 2000, this over/under gun is chambered for the 12 gauge 3" shell and fitted with 28" vent rib barrels with Invector chokes. Walnut stock with pistol grip and blued engraved receiver. Weight is about 7.5 lbs.

1025	900	700	525	450	350

	NIB	EXC.	V.G.	GOOD	FAIR	POOR

Supreme Sporting

Similar to the above model but fitted with a choice of 28" or 30" barrels chambered for 12 gauge 2.75" shells. Barrels are ported. Adjustable trigger. Polished silver receiver with blued barrels. Weight is about 7.5 lbs. Introduced in 2000.

NIB	EXC.	V.G.	GOOD	FAIR	POOR
1200	950	750	575	500	350

Supreme Elegance

Introduced in 2003 this over/under model is chambered for the 12 gauge 3" shell. Choice of 26" or 28" vent rib barrels with three choke tubes. Grayed receiver with scroll and bird scenes. Weight is about 7 lbs. depending on barrel length.

NIB	EXC.	V.G.	GOOD	FAIR	POOR
1400	1100	850	500	200	100

MODEL 23 SERIES

Model 23 XTR

This is a side-by-side, double-barrel shotgun chambered for 12 or 20 gauge. It is offered with 25.5", 26", 28" or 30" barrels with 3" chambers and various choke combinations. It is a boxlock gun that features a single trigger and automatic ejectors. It is scroll-engraved with a coin-finished receiver, blued barrels and a checkered, select walnut stock. It was introduced in 1978. This model is available in a number of configurations that differ in the amount of ornamentation and the quality of materials and workmanship utilized in their construction. These models and their values are listed. Discontinued.

NIB	EXC.	V.G.	GOOD	FAIR	POOR
2000	1800	1400	1050	850	500

Pigeon Grade

With WinChokes.

NIB	EXC.	V.G.	GOOD	FAIR	POOR
—	2300	1950	1600	1300	5000

Pigeon Grade Lightweight

Straight stock.

NIB	EXC.	V.G.	GOOD	FAIR	POOR
—	2450	2100	1750	1400	500

Model 23 Golden Quail

This series was available in 28 gauge and .410, as well as 12 or 20 gauge. It features 25.5" barrels that are choked improved cylinder/modified. It features a straight-grip, English-style stock with a recoil pad. This series was discontinued in 1987. **NOTE:** Add 20 percent for 20 gauge, 50 percent for 28 gauge or .410 bore.

NIB	EXC.	V.G.	GOOD	FAIR	POOR
3000	2700	2400	2000	1200	500

Model 23 Light Duck

This version is chambered for 20 gauge and was offered with a 28" Full and Full-choked barrel. There were 500 manufactured in 1985.

NIB	EXC.	V.G.	GOOD	FAIR	POOR
3100	2900	2600	1800	800	500

Model 23 Heavy Duck

This version is chambered for 12 gauge with 30" Full and Full-choked barrels. There were 500 manufactured in 1984.

NIB	EXC.	V.G.	GOOD	FAIR	POOR
3200	3000	2600	1800	800	500

Model 21

This is a high-quality, side-by-side, double-barrel shotgun that features a boxlock action and is chambered for 12, 16, 20, and 28 gauges, as well as .410. See previous Model 21 entry.

MODEL 101 SERIES

Model 101 Field Grade

This is an over/under, double-barrel shotgun chambered for 12, 20 and 28 gauge, as well as .410. It was offered with 26", 28" or 30" vent rib barrels with various choke combinations. Since 1983 screw-in chokes have been standard and models so furnished would be worth approximately $50 additional. This is a boxlock gun with a single-selective trigger and automatic ejectors. The receiver is engraved; the finish, blued with a checkered walnut stock. It was manufactured between 1963 and 1987. **NOTE:** 28 gauge add 40 percent; .410 add 50 percent.

NIB	EXC.	V.G.	GOOD	FAIR	POOR
1500	1350	1200	1050	850	500

Waterfowl Model

This version of the Model 101 is chambered for 12 gauge with 3" chambers. It has 30" or 32" vent rib barrels and a matte finish.

NIB	EXC.	V.G.	GOOD	FAIR	POOR
—	1900	1675	1400	800	400

	NIB	EXC.	V.G.	GOOD	FAIR	POOR

Model 101 Magnum

This version is similar to the Field Grade, chambered for 12 or 20 gauge with 3" Magnum chambers. It was offered with 30" barrels with various chokes. The stock is furnished with a recoil pad. It was manufactured between 1966 and 1981.

Model 101 Skeet Grade

This version was offered with 26" skeet-bored barrels with a competition rib and a skeet-type walnut stock. It was manufactured between 1966 and 1984.

	—	1500	1250	1050	850	500

Model 101 Three-Gauge Skeet Set

This combination set was offered with three barrels, chambered for 20 and 28 gauge, as well as .410. It was furnished with a fitted case and manufactured between 1974 and 1984.

	—	3500	2600	1800	800	500

Model 101 Trap Grade

This version is chambered for 12 gauge only and was offered with 30" or 32" competition ribbed barrels, choked for trap shooting. It is furnished with a competition-type stock. It was manufactured between 1966 and 1984.

	—	1400	1100	925	700	500

Model 101 Pigeon Grade

This is a more deluxe-engraved version of the Model 101, chambered for 12, 20, or 28 gauge, as well as .410. It features a coin-finished receiver with a fancy checkered walnut stock. It was introduced in 1974.

	—	3000	2600	1800	1275	750

Model 101 Super Pigeon Grade

This is a deluxe version of the Model 101, chambered for 12 gauge. It is heavily engraved with several gold inlays. The receiver is blued, and it features a high-grade walnut stock with fleur-de-lis checkering. It was imported between 1985 and 1987.

	—	5500	4200	3500	2800	1000

Model 101 Diamond Grade

This is a competition model, chambered for all four gauges. It was offered in either a trap or skeet configuration with screw-in chokes, an engraved matte-finished receiver, and a select checkered walnut stock. The skeet model features recoil-reducing muzzle vents.

	—	2000	1625	1250	900	680

Model 101 Pigeon Grade Trap

This deluxe dedicated trap gun was introduced in 2008. It features a Grade III/IV walnut stock with a high-gloss finish and a raised comb. Barrels are 30" or 32" . Three choke tubes included. Weight is 7.5 to 7.75 lbs. **NOTE:** Add 5 percent for adjustable comb stock.

1750	1500	1300	975	600	400

Model 501 Grand European

This is an over/under, double-barrel shotgun chambered for 12 or 20 gauge. It was available in trap or skeet configurations and was offered with a 27", 30", or 32" vent rib barrel. It is heavily engraved and matte-finished, with a select checkered walnut stock. It was manufactured between 1981 and 1986.

	—	2700	2100	1700	1300	500

Model 501 Presentation Grade

This is a deluxe version chambered in 12 gauge only. It is ornately engraved and gold-inlaid. The stock is made out of presentation-grade walnut. It was furnished with a fitted case. It was manufactured between 1984 and 1987.

	—	3400	2750	2200	1600	500

Select Model 101 Field

This Belgian-made version of Winchesters popular Model 101 was introduced in 2007. It features Grade II/III walnut, 26" or 28" barrels and deep-relief engraving on the blued receiver that mimics the original 101. Classic white line spacer and vented recoil pad. Three choke tubes. Weight is about 7.2 lbs. Introduced in 2007.

1600	1400	1150	900	650	400

	NIB	EXC.	V.G.	GOOD	FAIR	POOR

Select Model 101 Sporting

Similar to Field model plus competition features such as a wider rib, adjustable trigger, white mid-bead and five extended Signature choke tubes. Ported barrels are 28", 30" or 32".

NIB	EXC.	V.G.	GOOD	FAIR	POOR
1675	1475	1225	1050	775	450

Combination Gun

This is an over/under rifle/shotgun combination chambered for 12 gauge over .222, .223, .30-06, and the 9.3x74R cartridges. It features 25" barrels. The shotgun tube has a screw-in choke. It is engraved in the fashion of the Model 501 Grand European and features a select checkered walnut stock. It was manufactured between 1983 and 1985.

NIB	EXC.	V.G.	GOOD	FAIR	POOR
—	3000	2500	1600	1200	700

Express Rifle

This is an over/under, double-barreled rifle chambered for the .257 Roberts, .270, 7.7x65R, .30-06, and the 9.3x74R cartridges. It features 23.5" barrels with a solid rib and express sights. It is engraved with game scenes and has a satin-finished receiver. The stock is checkered select walnut. It was manufactured in 1984 and 1985.

NIB	EXC.	V.G.	GOOD	FAIR	POOR
—	3500	3000	2100	1700	900

Model 96 Xpert

This is a utility-grade, over/under, double-barrel shotgun that is mechanically similar to the Model 101. Chambered for 12 or 20 gauge and offered with various barrel lengths and choke combinations. It has a boxlock action with single-selective trigger and automatic ejectors. The plain receiver is blued, with a checkered walnut stock. Manufactured between 1976 and 1982. A competition-grade model for trap or skeet was also available and would be worth approximately the same amount.

NIB	EXC.	V.G.	GOOD	FAIR	POOR
—	1025	900	700	525	350

Model 1001 Field

A new addition to the U.S.R.A. product line for 1993. This over/under shotgun was available in 12 gauge only, with a 28" ventilated rib barrel furnished with WinPlus choke tubes. A walnut checkered pistol stock is standard. The finish is blued with scroll engraving on the receiver. The receiver top has a matte finish. The gun weighs 7 lbs. subject to a 1995 recall.

NIB	EXC.	V.G.	GOOD	FAIR	POOR
1000	850	700	500	350	200

Model 1001 Sporting Clays I & II

This model features different stock dimensions, a fuller pistol grip, a radiused recoil pad, and a wider vent rib fitted on a 28" barrel (Sporting Clays I model, the Sporting Clays II features a 30" barrel). Comes complete with choke tubes. The frame has a silver nitrate finish and special engraving featuring a flying clay target. Introduced in 1993. Gun weighs 7.75 lbs. Subject to a 1995 recall.

NIB	EXC.	V.G.	GOOD	FAIR	POOR
1100	950	800	600	350	200

SELECT OVER/UNDER SERIES

This series of over/under shotguns was introduced into the Winchester line in 2004. The series features a low-profile receiver with unique engraving, lightweight barrels and contoured walnut stocks with distinctive checkering patterns.

Select Midnight

High-gloss bluing on receiver and barrels with gold accent game bird pattern on both sides and bottom of the receiver. Satin finished Grade II/III walnut. Oval checkering pattern. Choke tubes. Introduced 2006. Available in 26" and 28" barrels.

NIB	EXC.	V.G.	GOOD	FAIR	POOR
1600	1400	1150	900	650	400

Select White Field

An engraved silver nitride receiver is featured on both versions of the White Field. The Traditional model has traditional checkering and the Extreme model features the Select Series' unique oval checkering pattern. Both versions have choke tubes and are available in 26" and 28" barrels. Introduced 2006.

NIB	EXC.	V.G.	GOOD	FAIR	POOR
1300	1200	1100	900	650	400

Select Energy Sporting

Chambered for the 12 gauge 2.75" shell and offered with a choice of 28", 30", or 32" vent rib barrels with choke tubes and porting. Truglo front sight. Adjustable trigger shoe. Walnut stock with recoil pad. Weight is about 7.62 lbs. Adjustable comb available. **NOTE:** Add $150 for adjustable comb.

NIB	EXC.	V.G.	GOOD	FAIR	POOR
1600	1400	1150	900	650	400

Select Energy Trap

This 12 gauge model is fitted with a choice of 30" or 32" back-bored ported barrels. Wide vent rib. Choke tubes. Walnut stock with Monte Carlo comb. Weight is about 7.8 lbs. Adjustable comb

	NIB	EXC.	V.G.	GOOD	FAIR	POOR

available. **NOTE:** Add $150 for adjustable comb.

	1600	1400	1150	900	650	400

Select Elegance (Supreme)

This 12 gauge gun features full coverage engraving with game scenes. Choice of 26" or 28" vent rib barrels with choke tubes. Walnut stock with unique checkering pattern. Weight is about 7 lbs.

	1800	1400	1150	900	650	400

Select Field

This 12 gauge 3" gun is fitted with a choice of 26" or 28" vent ribs barrels with choke tubes. Engraved receiver with oval checkering pattern. Weight is about 7 lbs.

	1400	1200	950	700	450	300

Select Traditional Elegance

Similar to the Select Elegance but with traditional checkering pattern.

	1400	1200	950	700	450	300

Select Deluxe Field

New in 2007, this Belgian-made 3" 12 gauge features an engraved steel receiver with silver nitride finish and Grade II walnut. Barrels are 26", 28" or 30". Three chokes included. Weight is about 7.25 lbs.

	1600	1400	1150	900	650	400

Select Platinum Field

This 3" 12 gauge was introduced in 2007. It is Belgian-made and comes with 28" or 30" barrels, Grade II/III walnut and deep relief engraving. Includes three Signature extended choke tubes and hard case.

	2050	1800	1575	1200	900	500

Select Platinum Sporting

Similar to the Platinum Field with 28", 30" or 32" ported barrels, wide rib, adjustable trigger shoe and five Signature extended choke tubes and hard case.

	2200	1950	1725	1375	1075	500

WINCHESTER COMMEMORATIVE RIFLES

Beginning in the early 1960s, Winchester produced a number of special Model 1894 rifles and carbines that commemorated certain historic events, places or individuals. In some cases they are slightly embellished and in others are quite ornate. If a Winchester commemorative rifle has been cocked leaving a line on the hammer or the lever, many collectors will show little or no interest in its acquisition. If they have been fired, they will realize little premium over a standard, Post-1964 Model 94. A number of commemorative's have been ordered by outside concerns and are technically not factory issues. Most have less collectibility than the factory-issued models. There are a number of concerns that specialize in marketing the total range of Winchester commemorative rifles. Listed are the factory-issue commemorative's with their current value, issue price and the number manufactured.

	NIB	ISSUE	AMT. MFG.		NIB	ISSUE	AMT. MFG.
1964 Wyoming Diamond Jubilee—Carbine				**1968 Buffalo Bill—Rifle**			
	1200	100	1,500		700	130	—
1966 Centennial—Rifle				**1968 Buffalo Bill "1 or 300"—Rifle**			
	700	125	102,309		3500	1000	300
1966 Centennial—Carbine				**1969 Theodore Roosevelt—Rifle**			
	700	125	102,309		700	135	—
1966 Nebraska Centennial—Rifle				**1969 Theodore Roosevelt—Carbine**			
	1200	100	2,500		700	135	52,386
1967 Canadian Centennial—Rifle				**1969 Golden Spike Carbine**			
	650	125	—		700	120	69,996
1967 Canadian Centennial—Carbine				**1970 Cowboy Commemorative Carbine**			
	650	125	90,301		750	125	27,549
1967 Alaskan Purchase Centennial—Carbine				**1970 Cowboy Carbine "1 of 300**			
	1250	125	1,500		3500	1000	300
1968 Illinois Sesquicentennial—Carbine				**1970 Northwest Territories (Canadian)**			
	600	110	37,648		1000	150	2,500
1968 Buffalo Bill—Carbine							
	700	130	112,923				

	NIB	ISSUE	AMT. MFG.

1970 Northwest Territories Deluxe (Canadian)

NIB	ISSUE	AMT. MFG.
1300	250	500

1970 Lone Star—Rifle

NIB	ISSUE	AMT. MFG.
700	140	—

1970 Lone Star—Carbine

NIB	ISSUE	AMT. MFG.
700	140	38,385

1971 NRA Centennial—Rifle

NIB	ISSUE	AMT. MFG.
700	150	21,000

1971 NRA Centennial—Musket

NIB	ISSUE	AMT. MFG.
700	150	23,400

1971 Yellow Boy

NIB	ISSUE	AMT. MFG.
1300	250	4,900

1971 Royal Canadian Mounted Police (Canadian)

NIB	ISSUE	AMT. MFG.
900	190	9,500

1971 Mounted Police (Canadian)

NIB	ISSUE	AMT. MFG.
1000	190	5,100

1971 Mounted Police, Presentation

NIB	ISSUE	AMT. MFG.
10000	—	10

1974 Texas Ranger—Carbine

NIB	ISSUE	AMT. MFG.
800	135	4,850

1974 Texas Ranger Presentation Model

NIB	ISSUE	AMT. MFG.
3500	1000	150

1974 Apache (Canadian)

NIB	ISSUE	AMT. MFG.
900	150	8,600

1974 Commanche (Canadian)

NIB	ISSUE	AMT. MFG.
900	230	11,500

1974 Klondike Gold Rush (Canadian)

NIB	ISSUE	AMT. MFG.
900	240	10,200

1975 Klondike Gold Rush—Dawson City Issue (Canadian)

NIB	ISSUE	AMT. MFG.
8500	—	25

1976 Sioux (Canadian)

NIB	ISSUE	AMT. MFG.
900	280	10,000

1976 Little Bighorn (Canadian)

NIB	ISSUE	AMT. MFG.
1000	300	11,000

1976 U.S. Bicentennial Carbine

NIB	ISSUE	AMT. MFG.
800	325	19,999

1977 Wells Fargo

NIB	ISSUE	AMT. MFG.
800	350	19,999

1977 Legendary Lawman

NIB	ISSUE	AMT. MFG.
800	375	19,999

1977 Limited Edition I

NIB	ISSUE	AMT. MFG.
1600	1500	1,500

1977 Cheyenne—.22 Cal. (Canadian)

NIB	ISSUE	AMT. MFG.
1100	320	5,000

1977 Cheyenne—.44-40 Cal. (Canadian)

NIB	ISSUE	AMT. MFG.
900	300	11,225

1977 Cherokee—.22 Cal. (Canadian)

NIB	ISSUE	AMT. MFG.
1100	385	3,950

1977 Cherokee—.30-30 Cal. (Canadian)

NIB	ISSUE	AMT. MFG.
900	385	9,000

1978 "One of One Thousand" (European)

NIB	ISSUE	AMT. MFG.
8250	5000	250

1978 Antler Game Carbine

NIB	ISSUE	AMT. MFG.
800	375	19,999

1979 Limited Edition II

NIB	ISSUE	AMT. MFG.
1600	1500	1,500

1979 Legendary Frontiersman Rifle

NIB	ISSUE	AMT. MFG.
800	425	19,999

1979 Matched Set of 1,000

NIB	ISSUE	AMT. MFG.
2800	3000	1,000

1979 Bat Masterson (Canadian)

NIB	ISSUE	AMT. MFG.
900	650	8,000

1980 Alberta Diamond Jubilee (Canadian)

NIB	ISSUE	AMT. MFG.
1000	650	2,700

1980 Alberta Diamond Jubilee Deluxe (Canadian)

NIB	ISSUE	AMT. MFG.
1800	1900	300

1980 Saskatchewan Diamond Jubilee (Canadian)

NIB	ISSUE	AMT. MFG.
1000	695	2,700

1980 Saskatchewan Diamond Jubilee Deluxe (Canadian)

NIB	ISSUE	AMT. MFG.
1800	1995	300

1980 Oliver Winchester

NIB	ISSUE	AMT. MFG.
900	375	19,999

1981 U.S. Border Patrol

NIB	ISSUE	AMT. MFG.
1000	1195	1,000

1981 U.S. Border Patrol—Member's Model

NIB	ISSUE	AMT. MFG.
1000	695	800

1981 Calgary Stampede (Canadian)

NIB	ISSUE	AMT. MFG.
1800	2200	1,000

1981 Canadian Pacific Centennial (Canadian)

NIB	ISSUE	AMT. MFG.
900	800	2,000

1981 Canadian Pacific Centennial Presentation (Canadian)

NIB	ISSUE	AMT. MFG.
1800	2200	300

1981 Canadian Pacific Employee's Model (Canadian)

NIB	ISSUE	AMT. MFG.
900	800	2,000

1981 John Wayne (Canadian)

NIB	ISSUE	AMT. MFG.
1600	600	1,000

1981 John Wayne

NIB	ISSUE	AMT. MFG.
1600	600	49,000

1981 Duke

NIB	ISSUE	AMT. MFG.
3750	2250	1,000

1981 John Wayne "1 of 300" Set

NIB	ISSUE	AMT. MFG.
7500	10000	300

1982 Great Western Artist I

NIB	ISSUE	AMT. MFG.
1550	2200	999

1982 Great Western Artist II

NIB	ISSUE	AMT. MFG.
1500	2200	999

1982 Annie Oakley

NIB	ISSUE	AMT. MFG.
1300	699	6,000

1983 Chief Crazy Horse

NIB	ISSUE	AMT. MFG.
800	600	19,999

1983 American Bald Eagle

NIB	ISSUE	AMT. MFG.
800	895	2,800

	NIB	ISSUE	AMT. MFG.
1983 American Bald Eagle—Deluxe	4000	2995	200
1983 Oklahoma Diamond Jubilee	1750	2250	1,001
1984 Winchester—Colt Commemorative Set	2750	3995	3,250
1985 Boy Scout 75th Anniversary .22 Cal.	1100	615	15,000
1985 Boy Scout 75th Anniversary—Eagle Scout	6000	2140	1,000
Texas Sesquicentennial Model—Rifle .38-55 Cal.	2750	2995	1,500
Texas Sesquicentennial Model—Carbine .38-55 Cal.	1000	695	15,000
Texas Sesquicentennial Model Set with Bowie Knife	6500	7995	150
1986 Model 94 Ducks Unlimited	900	—	2,800
1986 Statue of Liberty	9000	6500	100
1986 120th Anniversary Model—Carbine .44-40 Cal.	950	995	1,000
1986 European 1 of 1,000 Second Series (European)	1000	6000	150
1987 U.S. Constitution 200th Anniversary .44-40	15000	12000	17
1990 Wyoming Centennial—30-30	1600	895	500
1991 Winchester 125th Anniversary	6500	4995	61
1992 Arapaho—30-30	1600	895	500
1992 Ontario Conservation—30-30	1600	1195	400
1992 Kentucky Bicentennial—30-30	1600	995	500
1993 Nez Perce—30-30	1600	995	600
1995 Florida Sesquicentennial Carbine	1600	1195	360
1996 Wild Bill Hickok Carbine	1600	1195	350
2008 John Wayne 1892 .44-40	2000	2000	N/A

WINDSOR
Windsor, Vermont
Robbins & Lawrence
Hartford, Connecticut

Windsor Rifle-Musket

A .577-caliber single-shot percussion rifle, with 39" round barrel secured by three barrel bands. Lock marked "Windsor". Rifles of this pattern were contracted for/by the British Government. Lock and barrel finished in white, brass furniture and walnut stock. Approximately 16,000 made from 1855 to 1858.

NIB	EXC.	V.G.	GOOD	FAIR	POOR
—	—	3750	3000	950	300

WINSLOW ARMS CO.
Camden, South Carolina

Bolt Action Rifle

High-grade semi-custom sporting rifle built upon a number of actions. Offered in all popular calibers from .17 Remington to .458 Winchester Magnum, with 24" barrel and 3-shot magazine. Larger Magnum models have 26" barrel and 2-shot magazine. Two basic stocks are offered—Conventional Bushmaster, which features a standard pistol-grip and beavertail forearm; Plainsmaster, which has a full curled hooked pistol-grip and wide flat beavertail forearm. Both have Monte Carlo-style stocks, with recoil pads and sling swivels. Offered in a choice of popular woods, with rosewood fore-end tips and pistol-grip caps. Eight different grades of this rifle are available. Following lists the values applicable for each.

Commander Grade

Figured walnut stock. Rosewood forearm tip and grip cap. White line recoil pad. FN Supreme action.

	EXC.	V.G.	GOOD	FAIR	POOR
—	1450	1050	925	700	550

Regal Grade

All features of Commander Grade plus ivory and ebony inlay on stock, French-style checkering, jeweled bolt.

	EXC.	V.G.	GOOD	FAIR	POOR
—	2200	1800	1225	900	600

	NIB	EXC.	V.G.	GOOD	FAIR	POOR

Regent Grade
As above, with addition of hand-carved checkering.

		2375	1850	1250	900	600
	—					

Regimental Grade
As above, with addition of basket weave carving, two ivory stock inlays and large ivory and ebony inlay on both sides of butt stock with animal silhouette.

	—	3000	2200	1500	1200	650

Crown Grade
As above, with more elaborate ivory inlays on stock.

	—	3700	2550	1800	1500	650

Royal Grade
As above, with addition of even more elaborate stock carving and ivory and ebony inlay.

		4500	3250	2000	1600	650

Imperial Grade
As above, with addition of engraved barrel from receiver to 11" forward. Engraved receiver ring, bolt handle and trigger guard. Engraved scope mounts and rings.

		5000	3750	2500	2000	700

Emperor Grade
As above, with addition of gold raised relief animals, engraved receiver and forward part of barrel with muzzle tip engraved as well. Highest Winslow grade.

		6250	5000	4000	3000	700

WISEMAN, BILL & CO.
Bryan, Texas

Rifle
Custom order bolt-action rifle utilizing a Sako action, McMillan stainless steel barrel and laminated stock. The action components Teflon coated. Made in four styles: Hunter, Hunter Deluxe, Maverick and Varminter.

	—	2500	2150	1750	1500	600

Silhouette Pistol
Custom made single-shot pistol produced in a variety of calibers, with 14" fluted stainless steel barrel and laminated pistol-grip stock. Furnished without sights. Introduced in 1989.

	—	1750	1450	1100	800	600

WITNESS
See — European American Armory

WOLF SPORTING PISTOLS
Importer — Handgunner Gunshop
Topton, Pennsylvania

Wolf SV Target
Chambered for 9x19, 9x21, 9x23, .38 Super, .40 S&W or .45 ACP. Barrel 4.5" long. Weight 44 oz. Many special features. Built in Austria. Price listed for basic pistol. A number of special order items are offered. Check with importer before a sale. First imported in 1998.

2000	1600	1250	1000	750	600

Wolf SV Match
Chambered for 9x19, 9x21, 9x23, .38 Super, .40 S&W or .45 ACP. Barrel 5.5" long. Weight 44 oz. Many special features. Built in Austria. Price listed for basic pistol. A number of special order items are offered. Check with importer before a sale. First imported in 1998.

2000	1600	1250	1000	750	600

WOODWARD, JAMES & SONS
London, England
Prior to WWII, this company produced a variety of boxlock and sidelock shotguns that are regarded as some of the best made. Prospective purchasers should secure a qualified appraisal prior to acquisition.

WURFFLEIN, ANDREW & WILLIAM
Philadelphia, Pennsylvania

Pocket Pistol
A .41-caliber percussion single-shot pocket pistol, with either 2.5" or 3" barrel, German silver furniture and checkered walnut stock. Lock marked "A. Wurfflein / Phila." Manufactured during

	NIB	EXC.	V.G.	GOOD	FAIR	POOR

1850s and 1860s.

	NIB	EXC.	V.G.	GOOD	FAIR	POOR
	—	—	2600	1750	700	200

Single-Shot Target Pistol

A .22-caliber single-shot pistol, with half-octagonal barrels measuring from 8" to 16" in length. Barrel pivots downward for loading and marked "W. Wurfflein Philad'a Pa. U.S.A. Patented June 24th, 1884". Blued, with walnut grips. Also available with detachable shoulder stock, which if present, would add approximately 35 percent to values listed. Manufactured from 1884 to 1890.

	—	—	2600	1750	700	200

Single-Shot Rifle

Single-shot rifle produced in a variety of calibers, with octagonal barrel lengths of 24" to 28". Available with a wide variety of optional features.

	—	—	2400	1250	350	150

Mid-range Model

As above, with 28" or 30" half-octagonal barrel.

	—	—	4250	3000	950	400

Model No. 25

Highest grade rifle manufactured by Wurfflein.

	—	—	4500	3500	1250	600

X

	NIB	EXC.	V.G.	GOOD	FAIR	POOR

XL
HOPKINS & ALLEN
Norwich, Connecticut

Derringer

.41-caliber spur trigger single-shot pistol, with 2.75" octagonal barrel. Either iron or brass frame. Blued nickel-plated, with rosewood grips. Barrel marked "XL Derringer". Manufactured during 1870s.

	—	1650	1295	950	500	150

Vest Pocket Derringer

As above in .22-caliber, with 2.25" round barrel. Normally full nickel-plated. Barrel marked "XL Vest Pocket". Manufactured from 1870s to 1890s.

	—	—	1350	750	325	125

XPERT
HOPKINS & ALLEN
Norwich, Connecticut

Xpert Derringer

.22- or .30-caliber spur trigger single-shot pistol, with round barrels 2.25" to 6" in length. Nickel-plated finish, with rosewood grips. Breechblock pivots to left side for loading. Barrel marked "Xpert-Pat. Sep. 23. 1878". Manufactured during 1870s.

	—	—	875	700	400	125

Xpert Pocket Rifle

Similar to derringer, with same size frame fitted with 7.5" barrel. Chambered for .22 cartridge, as well as .30-caliber rimfire. Supplied with wire stock. Values for gun with stock. Produced from about 1870 to 1890s.

	—	—	1475	1150	500	150

Z

	NIB	EXC.	V.G.	GOOD	FAIR	POOR

ZANOTTI, FABIO
Brescia, Italy

Model 625

12-gauge to .410 bore boxlock double-barrel shotgun, with automatic ejectors and single-selective trigger. Blued, with checkered walnut stock.

6500	5200	4700	3500	2500	500

Model 626

As above, engraved with either scroll work or hunting scenes.

7000	5700	5200	4000	2800	500

Giacinto

External hammer boxlock shotgun produced in a variety of gauges, with double triggers.

6500	5200	4700	3500	2500	500

Maxim

Similar to Model 625 fitted with detachable sidelocks.

7000	5700	5200	4000	2800	500

Edward

As above, but more intricately engraved.

12000	9000	6500	4500	3000	1500

Cassiano I

As above, with exhibition grade engraving.

13000	9000	7000	6000	4000	2000

Cassiano II

As above, with gold inlays.

14500	12000	9500	7000	5000	2500

Cassiano Executive

Strictly custom-made shotgun produced to client's specifications.

45000	—	—	—	—	—

Z-B RIFLE CO.
Brno, Czechoslovakia

Model ZKW-465 Varmint Rifle

Mauser bolt-action rifle chambered for .22 Hornet cartridge. Has 23" barrel, with three-leaf folding rear sight. Offered standard with double-set triggers. Finish blued, with select walnut checkered stock.

—	1600	1150	975	800	500

ZEHNER, E. WAFFENFABRIK
Suhl, Germany

Zehna

6.35mm semi-automatic pistol, with 2.5" barrel and 5-shot magazine. Slide marked "Zehna DRPA", and caliber on later production models. Blued, with black plastic grips bearing monogram "EZ". Approximately 20,000 made from 1921 to 1927.

—	395	300	250	175	100

ZEPHYR
Eibar, Spain
Importer—Stoegers

Woodlander II

12- or 20-gauge boxlock shotgun, with varying barrel lengths, double triggers and extractors. Blued, with walnut stock.

600	450	400	300	200	100

	NIB	EXC.	V.G.	GOOD	FAIR	POOR

Uplander

12-, 16-, 20-, 28-gauge or .410 bore sidelock double-barrel shotgun, with varying barrel lengths, double triggers and automatic ejectors. Blued, with walnut stock.

	850	700	500	400	300	150

Upland King

As above in 12- or 16-gauge, with ventilated-rib barrels.

	1150	800	700	600	400	250

Vandalia

12-gauge single-barrel trap gun, with 32" full choked barrel. Blued, with walnut stock.

	750	600	550	450	300	150

Sterlingworth II

Identical to Woodlander, with sidelocks.

	850	700	550	450	300	150

Victor Special

12-gauge boxlock double-barrel shotgun, with 25", 28" or 30" barrels, double triggers and extractors. Blued, with walnut stock.

	525	400	300	250	175	100

Thunderbird

10-gauge Magnum boxlock double-barrel shotgun, with 32" full choked barrels, double triggers and automatic ejectors. Blued, with walnut stock.

	950	700	600	500	400	200

Honker

10-gauge Magnum single-barrel shotgun, with 36" full choked and ventilated rib barrel. Blued, with walnut stock.

	600	450	400	300	200	100

ZM WEAPONS
Bernardton, Massachusetts

LR-300 Sport Rifle

Highly modified AR-15 chambered for .223 cartridge. Fitted with 16.25" barrel and true folding stock. Ghost ring rear sight and adjustable post front sight, with tritium insert is standard. Weight about 7.2 lbs. Introduced in 1997.

	—	1600	1200	950	775	500

ZOLI, ANTONIO
Brescia, Italy

Silver Hawk

12- or 20-gauge boxlock double-barrel shotgun. Produced in a variety of barrel lengths and chokes, with double trigger. Engraved, blued with walnut stock.

	—	1025	900	850	600	450

Ariete M2

12-gauge boxlock double-barrel shotgun, with 26" or 28" barrels, non-selective single trigger and automatic ejectors. Engraved, blued with walnut stock.

	—	1150	1000	850	700	350

Empire

As above in 12- or 20-gauge, with 27" or 28" barrels. Engraved, French case hardened blued with walnut stock.

	—	2300	1950	1400	1250	400

Volcano Record

12-gauge sidelock double-barrel shotgun, with 28" barrels. Available in a variety of chokes, single-selective trigger and automatic ejectors. Engraved, French case hardened blued with walnut stock.

	—	7000	6000	5000	4000	500

	NIB	EXC.	V.G.	GOOD	FAIR	POOR

Volcano Record ELM

Model strictly custom-ordered shotgun produced to purchaser's specifications. Value speculative.

	—	16000	13500	10500	8500	500

Silver Snipe

12- or 20-gauge over/under shotgun. Produced with varying lengths, ventilated rib barrels, single trigger and extractors. Engraved, blued with walnut stock.

	—	600	450	400	325	275

Golden Snipe

As above more finely finished. Fitted with automatic ejectors.

	—	650	500	450	350	300

Delfino

As above in 12- or 20-gauge Magnum, with 26" or 28" ventilated rib barrels, non-selective single trigger and automatic ejectors. Engraved, blued with walnut stock.

	—	575	425	325	275	250

Ritmo Hunting Gun

As above in 12-gauge Magnum, with 26" or 28" separated ventilated rib barrels, single-selective trigger and automatic ejectors. Engraved, blued with walnut stock.

	—	650	500	450	400	350

Condor Model

As above in 12-gauge, with 28" skeet bored barrels. Wide competition rib, single-selective trigger and automatic ejectors. Engraved, French case hardened blued with walnut stock.

	—	1100	800	650	500	400

Angel Model

As above in field grade version.

	—	1100	800	600	500	400

Ritmo Pigeon Grade IV

As above, with 28" separated ventilated rib barrels, single-selective trigger, automatic ejectors and extensively engraved. French case hardened, blued with finely figured walnut stock.

	—	2250	1600	1200	800	600

Model 208 Target

As above, with 28" or 30" trap or skeet bored barrels. Fitted with a wide ventilated rib.

	—	1200	850	700	600	500

Model 308 Target

As above, but more finely finished.

	—	1500	1100	850	700	500

Combinato

.222 or .243 and 12- or 20-gauge over/under combination rifle/shotgun, with engraved boxlock-action, double triggers and folding rear sight. French case hardened, blued with walnut stock.

	—	2500	1700	1250	950	500

Safari Deluxe

As above, with false sidelocks engraved with scrolls or hunting scenes.

	—	5000	4000	2850	1500	650

ZOLI USA, ANGELO
Brescia, Italy

Slide-Action Shotgun

12-gauge Magnum slide-action shotgun. Produced with a variety of barrel lengths, with detachable choke tubes. Blued, with walnut stock.

400	300	250	200	150	100

	NIB	EXC.	V.G.	GOOD	FAIR	POOR

Diano I

12-, 20-gauge or .410 bore single-shot folding barrel shotgun. Produced in a variety of barrel lengths. Blued, with walnut stock.

	175	100	90	80	60	40

Diano II

As above, with bottom lever instead of top release lever.

	175	100	90	80	60	40

Apache

12-gauge Magnum lever-action shotgun, with 20" barrel. Fitted with detachable choke tubes. Blued, with walnut stock.

	500	400	350	300	250	150

Quail Special

.410 Magnum bore double-barrel shotgun, with 28" barrels and single trigger. Blued, with walnut stock.

	325	200	150	125	100	75

Falcon II

As above, with 26" or 28" barrels and double triggers.

	325	200	150	125	100	75

Pheasant

12-gauge Magnum double-barrel shotgun, with 28" barrels, single trigger and automatic ejectors. Blued, with walnut stock.

	450	350	300	250	200	150

Classic

As above, with 26" to 30" barrels fitted with detachable choke tubes, single-selective trigger and automatic ejectors. Blued, with walnut stock.

	850	700	600	500	300	200

Snipe

.410 bore over/under shotgun, with 26" or 28" barrels and single trigger.

	400	300	200	175	150	100

Dove

Similar to above.

	400	300	200	175	150	100

Texas

12-, 20-gauge or .410 bore over/under shotgun, with 26" or 28" barrels, double triggers and bottom barrel release lever.

	350	250	200	150	100	75

Field Special

12- or 20-gauge Magnum double-barrel shotgun. Produced in a variety of barrel lengths. Single trigger and extractors. Blued, with walnut stock.

	550	400	300	250	200	100

Pigeon Model

As above, but more finely finished.

	550	400	300	250	200	100

Standard Model

Similar to above in 12- and 20-gauge only.

	500	400	300	250	200	100

Special Model

As above, with detachable choke tubes and single-selective trigger.

	600	450	300	250	200	100

NIB	EXC.	V.G.	GOOD	FAIR	POOR

Deluxe Model

As above, but engraved with better quality walnut.

| 800 | 600 | 500 | 400 | 300 | 150 |

Presentation Model

As above, with false sidelocks and finely figured walnut stock.

| 950 | 700 | 600 | 450 | 350 | 200 |

St. George's Target

12-gauge over/under shotgun trap or skeet bore, with various barrel lengths, single-selective trigger and automatic ejectors. Blued, with walnut stock.

| 1200 | 900 | 700 | 600 | 550 | 250 |

St. George Competition

12-gauge single-barrel gun, with extra set of over/under barrels.

| 1950 | 1600 | 1200 | 950 | 500 | 300 |

Express Rifle

.30-06, 7x65Rmm or 9.3x74Rmm over/under double-barrel rifle, with single triggers and automatic ejectors. Blued, with walnut stock.

| 4250 | 3500 | 2500 | 1750 | 1200 | 600 |

Express EM

As above, but more finely finished.

| 5500 | 4000 | 3000 | 1500 | 1000 | 750 |

Savana E

As above, with double triggers.

| 6500 | 5250 | 4500 | 3500 | 2750 | 1500 |

Savana Deluxe

As above, engraved with hunting scenes.

| 8000 | 7000 | 6000 | 4750 | 3500 | 2000 |

AZ 1900C

.243, .270, 6.5x55mm, .308 or .30-06 bolt-action rifle, with 24" barrel and open sights. Blued, with walnut stock.

| 850 | 700 | 500 | 400 | 300 | 150 |

AZ 1900M

Same as above, with Bell & Carlson composite stock.

| 750 | 600 | 450 | 350 | 275 | 200 |

AZ 1900 Deluxe

As above, but more finely finished.

| 1100 | 800 | 650 | 500 | 400 | 200 |

AZ 1900 Super Deluxe

As above, engraved with finely figured walnut stock.

| 1500 | 1000 | 800 | 600 | 450 | 250 |

Patricia Model

As above in .410 Magnum bore, with 28" ventilated rib barrels, various chokes, single-selective trigger and automatic ejectors. Engraved, blued with finely figured walnut stock.

| 1500 | 1100 | 950 | 750 | 650 | 400 |

Condor

.30-06 or .308 and 12-gauge over/under combination shotgun rifle, with double triggers, extractors and sling swivels. Blued, with walnut stock.

| 1500 | 1050 | 850 | 700 | 500 | 300 |

Airone

As above, with false sidelocks.

| 1650 | 1250 | 1000 | 800 | 600 | 300 |

	NIB	EXC.	V.G.	GOOD	FAIR	POOR

Leopard Express

.30-06, .308, 7x65Rmm or .375 Holland & Holland over/under double-barrel rifle, with 24" barrels. Express sights, double triggers and extractors. Blued, with walnut stock.

	1750	1400	1000	800	600	300

ZULAICA, M.
Eibar, Spain

Zulaica

Solid-frame .22-caliber revolver, with 6-shot cylinder that has zigzag grooves on its exterior surface. Fired by an external hammer. Frame is hollow, with a rod inside of it that connects to breechblock. Serrated cocking piece connected to this rod that is found at top rear of frame. When fired, cartridge case blows from cylinder and activates breechblock similar to a semi-automatic pistol.

	—	1000	800	600	350	250

ROYAL

Royal was applied to a number of pistols produced by this company as listed.

Royal

6.35mm or 7.65mm semi-automatic pistol. Normally marked on slide "Automatic Pistol 6.35 Royal" or "Automatic Pistol 7.65 Royal".

	—	300	175	100	75	50

7.65mm

As above in 7.65mm caliber, with 5.5" barrel and 12-shot magazine.

	—	325	200	125	100	75

6.35mm

Rather poor copy of Mauser Model C/96 semi-automatic pistol, with fixed lockwork.

	—	900	700	500	300	150

Vincitor

6.35mm or 7.65mm caliber semi-automatic pistol. Patterned after Model 1906 Browning. Slide marked "SA Royal Vincitor". Blued, with plastic grips.

	—	300	175	100	75	50